lonely

West Africa

Mary Fitzpatrick
Andrew Burke
Greg Campbell
Bethune Carmichael
Matt Fletcher
Frances Linzee Gordon
Anthony Ham
Amy Karafin
Kim Wildman
Isabelle Young

LONELY PLANET PUBLICATIONS
Melbourne • Oakland • London • Paris

WEST AFRICA

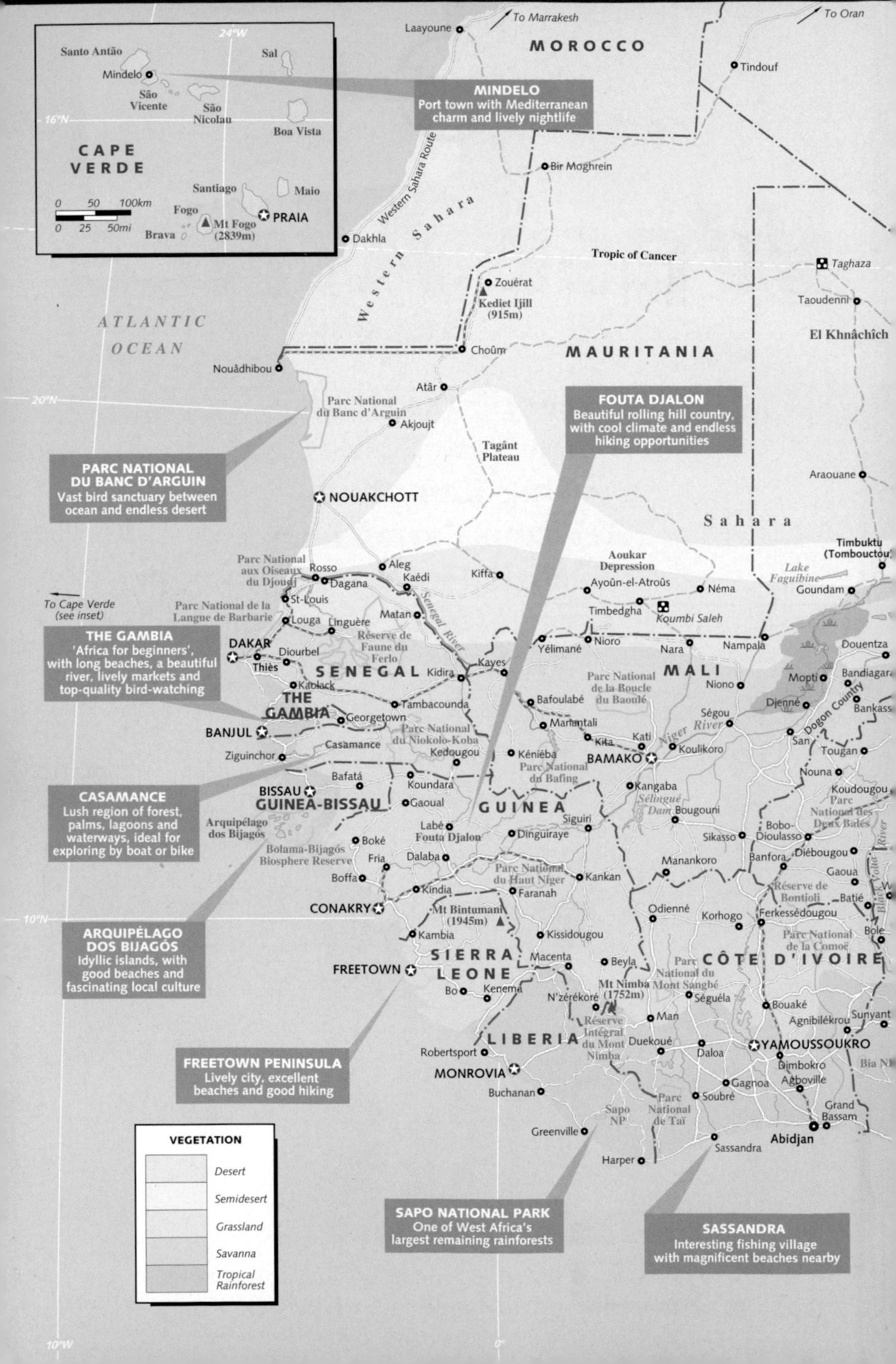

Santo Antão
Sal
Mindelo
São Vicente
São Nicolau
Boa Vista
CAPE VERDE
Santiago
Maio
Fogo
Brava
Mt Fogo (2839m)
PRAIA
0 50 100km
0 25 50mi
24°W
16°N
To Marrakesh
To Oran
Laayoune
MOROCCO
Tindouf
MINDELO
Port town with Mediterranean charm and lively nightlife
Bir Moghrein
Western Sahara Route
Western Sahara
Dakhla
Tropic of Cancer
Taghaza
Zouérat
Kediet Ijill (915m)
Taoudenni
El Khnâchîch
ATLANTIC OCEAN
Nouâdhibou
Choûm
MAURITANIA
Atâr
20°N
Parc National du Banc d'Arguin
Akjoujt
FOUTA DJALON
Beautiful rolling hill country, with cool climate and endless hiking opportunities
Tagânt Plateau
PARC NATIONAL DU BANC D'ARGUIN
Vast bird sanctuary between ocean and endless desert
NOUAKCHOTT
Araouane
Sahara
Timbuktu (Tombouctou)
Parc National aux Oiseaux du Djoudj
Rosso
Aleg
Aoukar Depression
Lake Faguibine
Dagana
Kaédi
Kiffa
Ayoûn-el-Atroûs
Néma
Goundam
To Cape Verde (see inset)
St-Louis
Senegal River
Parc National de la Langue de Barbarie
Louga
Linguère
Matam
Timbedgha
Koumbi Saleh
THE GAMBIA
'Africa for beginners', with long beaches, a beautiful river, lively markets and top-quality bird-watching
DAKAR
Thiès
Diourbel
Réserve de Faune du Ferlo
Yélimané
Nioro
Nara
Nampala
Douentza
SENEGAL
Kidira
Kayes
MALI
Parc National de la Boucle du Baoulé
Mopti
Bandiagara
Kaolack
Niono
Dogon Country
Djenné
Bankass
THE GAMBIA
Georgetown
Tambacounda
Bafoulabé
Ségou
BANJUL
Parc National du Niokolo-Koba
Manantali
Niger River
Kita
Kati
San
Casamance
Kedougou
Koulikoro
Tougan
Ziguinchor
Kéniéba
BAMAKO
Parc National du Bafing
Nouna
Bafatá
Koundara
Kangaba
BISSAU
Sélingué Dam
Koudougou
GUINEA-BISSAU
Gaoual
GUINEA
Parc National des Deux Balés
CASAMANCE
Lush region of forest, palms, lagoons and waterways, ideal for exploring by boat or bike
Arquipélago dos Bijagós
Labé
Fouta Djalon
Siguiri
Bougouni
Bobo-Dioulasso
Boké
Dinguiraye
Sikasso
Bolama-Bijagós Biosphere Reserve
Fria
Dalaba
Manankoro
Banfora
Diébougou
Boffa
Kankan
Parc National du Haut Niger
Gaoua
Réserve de Bontioli
Kindia
Faranah
Batié
CONAKRY
Mt Bintumani (1945m)
Odienné
Korhogo
Ferkessédougou
Black Volta River
10°N
Parc National de la Comoé
Bole
ARQUIPÉLAGO DOS BIJAGÓS
Idyllic islands, with good beaches and fascinating local culture
Kambia
Kissidougou
SIERRA LEONE
Macenta
Beyla
Parc National du Mont Sanghé
CÔTE D'IVOIRE
FREETOWN
Bo
Kenema
N'zérékoré
Mt Nimba (1752m)
Séguéla
Bouaké
Réserve Intégral du Mont Nimba
Man
Agnibilékrou
Sunyani
LIBERIA
Duekoué
Daloa
YAMOUSSOUKRO
FREETOWN PENINSULA
Lively city, excellent beaches and good hiking
Robertsport
Dimbokro
MONROVIA
Gagnoa
Agboville
Buchanan
Soubré
Parc National de Taï
Sapo NP
Grand Bassam
Greenville
Abidjan
Sassandra
Harper
VEGETATION
Desert
Semidesert
Grassland
Savanna
Tropical Rainforest
SAPO NATIONAL PARK
One of West Africa's largest remaining rainforests
SASSANDRA
Interesting fishing village with magnificent beaches nearby
10°W
0°

WEST AFRICA

MALI
The jewel in the crown of West Africa: intriguing traditional architecture, Niger River, energetic market towns, fascinating cultures, top-quality hiking
GOROM-GOROM
Vibrant Thursday market
AGADEZ
Remote Sahara oasis and gateway to the Aïr Massif and the Ténéré Desert beyond
NORTHERN CAMEROON
Striking, rocky terrain, picturesque villages, intriguing cultures and good hiking
ABOMEY & OUIDAH
Ancient, intriguing civilisations with a slaving history and captivating voodoo culture
THE NIGER DELTA
Palm-fringed beaches, mangrove waterways and tranquil villages
KUMASI
Heartland of the Ashanti, famed for their gold, kente cloth and stools
LOMÉ
Cosmopolitan city with great beaches, and the nearby hills of Kpalimé bedecked with butterflies
To Oran
To Algiers
To Algiers
To Tripoli
0 250 500km
0 150 300mi
ALGERIA
LIBYA
MALI
NIGER
CHAD
BURKINA FASO
NIGERIA
BENIN
TOGO
GHANA
CAMEROON
EQUATORIAL GUINEA
GABON
CONGO
Adrar
In Salah
Reggane
Route du Tanezrouft
Route du Hoggar
Hoggar Mountains
Tamanrasset
Tropic of Cancer
Madama
Djado
Djado Plateau
Bordj-Mokhtar
Tessalit
Mt Gréboun (1944m)
Réserve Naturelle Nationale de l'Aïr et du Ténéré
Aïr Massif
Séguédine
In Guezzam
Assamakka
Iferouâne
Aïr Mountains
To Abéché
Arlit
Assodé
Mt Takolokouzet (1295m)
Ténéré Desert
Bilma
Anéfis
Sahara
Timia
Mt Bagzane (2022m)
Bilma Desert
Adrar des Ifôghas
Niger River
Gourma-Rharous
Bourem
In-Gall
Agadez
Gao
Tillia
Le Main de Fatma
Ansongo
Ménaka
Réserve d'Ansongo-Ménaka
Aderbissinat
Tanout
Tahoua
Gorom-Gorom
Djibo
Dori
Téra
Tillabéri
Birni N'Konni
Madaoua
Gouré
Nguigmi
Ouahigouya
NIAMEY
Tessaoua
Zinder
Maradi
Diffa
To Abéché
Dogondoutchi
Kaya
Yako
Dosso
Sokoto
Katsina
Gashua
Lake Chad
OUAGADOUGOU
Koupéla
Fada N'Gourma
Parc National du W
Hadejia-Nguru Wetlands
N'DJAMÉNA
Parc National de Tambi Kaboré
Parc National d'Arli
Gaya
Malanville
Gusau
Kano
Maiduguri
Potsikum
Parc National de la Pendjari
Kandi
Kamuku WR
Mandara Mountains
Mokolo
Parc National Waza
Maroua
Pô
Bolgatanga
Bawku
Dapaong
Tanguiéta
Jos Plateau
Biu
Parc National de la Kéran
Natitingou
Kontagora
Kaduna
Bauchi
Mole NP
Kandé
Nikki
Jos
White Volta
Djougou
Yankari NP
Tamale
Parakou
ABUJA
Sokodé
Mambila Mountains
Lake Lagdo
Parc National de Bouba Ndjida
Parc National de Fazao-Malfakassa
Salaga
Ilorin
Lake Volta
Savalou
Savé
Lokoja
Makurdi
Benue River
Parc National de la Bénoué
Atakpamé
Oshogbo
Chappal Wadi (2418m)
Techiman
Digya NP
Abomey
Ibadan
N'Gaoundéré
Kpalimé
Mt Agou (986m)
PORTO NOVO
Akure
Ogoja
Gembu
Kumasi
Ho
Ouidah
Cotonou
Lagos
Enugu
Cross River NP
Bamenda Mountains
Tibati
To Bangui
Kakum NP
Koforidua
LOMÉ
Benin City
Onitsha
Bamenda
Mt Oku (3011m)
Lake Mbakaou
Keta
Mamfe
ACCRA
Bight of Benin
Warri
Owerri
Foumban
Cape Coast
Aba
Calabar
Korup National Park
Port Harcourt
Nkongsamba
Sanaga River
Bertoua
Gulf of Guinea
Niger Delta
Kumba
Mt Cameroon (4095m)
Buea
Douala
YAOUNDÉ
Kenzou
Bight of Biafra
Abong Mbang
MALABO
Edéa
Mbalmayo
Réserve de Boumba-Bek
Parc National de la Lobéké
Réserve du Dja
Kribi
Campo
Parc National de Campo-Ma'an
Réserve de Nki
Moloundou
LIBREVILLE
10°E
20°E

West Africa
5th edition – October 2002
First published – September 1988

Published by
Lonely Planet Publications Pty Ltd ABN 36 005 607 983
90 Maribyrnong St, Footscray, Victoria 3011, Australia

Lonely Planet Offices
Australia Locked Bag 1, Footscray, Victoria 3011
USA 150 Linden St, Oakland, CA 94607
UK 10a Spring Place, London NW5 3BH
France 1 rue du Dahomey, 75011 Paris

Photographs
Many of the images in this guide are available for licensing from Lonely Planet Images.
w www.lonelyplanetimages.com

Front cover photograph
Local people dancing on a beach at sunset, Senegal
(Barbara Maurer/Tony Stone Library)

ISBN 1 74059 249 2

Printed by The Bookmaker International Ltd
Printed in China

Contents – Text

BURKINA FASO 173

CAMEROON 216

CAPE VERDE 274

CÔTE D'IVOIRE 300

Contents – Maps

LIBERIA

MALI

MAURITANIA

NIGER

NIGERIA

SENEGAL

SIERRA LEONE

TOGO

The Authors

Mary Fitzpatrick

After completing graduate studies in Washington, DC, her home town, Mary set off for several years working in Europe. Her fascination with languages and cultures soon led her further south to Africa, where she lived for six years, working first on development projects in Mozambique, and later as a freelance writer in Liberia and Sierra Leone. In between, Mary has travelled in over 70 countries, including much of West Africa. Elsewhere, her journeys have taken her on foot through remote Malagasy villages, by dhow to palm-fringed East African islands, and on bicycle through Tibet and south-western China. She speaks several languages and dabbles in many more. Mary has authored or co-authored numerous other Africa titles for Lonely Planet including *Read This First: Africa*, *Tanzania*, *Mozambique*, *Madagascar*, *East Africa*, *Southern Africa* and *Africa on a shoestring*. Mary updated the introductory chapters for this book. She also updated the Liberia chapter and wrote the Cameroon chapter.

Andrew Burke

Andrew was raised in Sydney, Australia, and first set foot in Africa as an impressionable 19-year-old. The 'Dark Continent' made quite an impression and during the next decade he funded several return visits. He also spent time as a journalist in Asia, the Middle East, North America and Europe. Andrew worked on newspapers, including the *Australian Financial Review* in Sydney, and the *Financial Times* and *Independent on Sunday* in London, before embarking on a full-time career in travel writing. Andrew has also worked on Lonely Planet's *South Africa, Lesotho & Swaziland*, *West Africa* and *The Gambia & Senegal* guides. He is based in Hong Kong. Andrew updated The Gambia and Senegal chapters.

Greg Campbell

Having cut his teeth as a war correspondent and author in Bosnia, Kosovo and Sierra Leone, Greg Campbell was ready for the challenge of tackling Nigeria in peacetime. A freelance writer living in Colorado, his work has appeared in the *Christian Science Monitor*, the *San Francisco Chronicle*, *In These Times* and a number of regional newspapers. He is the author of two books, *The Road to Kosovo; A Balkan Diary* (1999), and the forthcoming *Blood Diamonds; Tracing the Deadly Path of the World's Most Precious Stones* (2002), both published by Westview Press. If he didn't write so much, he would really enjoy rock climbing and snowboarding. He lives with his five-year-old son Turner in Longmont, Colorado. Greg updated the Nigeria and Sierra Leone chapters.

Bethune Carmichael

Born in Scotland, Bethune's first great journey was to Australia at the age of 11. While that trip continues, it's regularly interspersed with outings to Africa, the Middle East, Asia and Europe. After earning a masters in environmental science, Bethune edited for

Radio Japan in Tokyo. Back in Australia he gained a post-grad degree in publishing before joining Lonely Planet, where he has been an editor for eight years. He has coordinated the editing of numerous Lonely Planet guides to Europe, Africa and the Middle East, and helped establish the company's *Guide to Aboriginal Australia*. Bethune updated the Côte d'Ivoire chapter.

Matthew Fletcher

As a child Matt spent his holidays in rainy English seaside resorts developing a skill for passing on random, fictitious facts to innocent tourists. He now travels worldwide doing much the same. It was a trip to Mozambique that inspired a career in travel writing and Matt has contributed to Lonely Planet's *Walking in Spain*, *Walking in Australia*, *Morocco*, *Kenya*, *East Africa* and *Tonga* guides, and has yet to be rumbled. For Lonely Planet's *Unpacked* and *Unpacked Again* he got stranded in a Madagascan swamp and had a dingo steal his breakfast. A travel writer of the old school, he's never forgotten his father's sagely advice – always have enough money in your pocket for a pint. Matt updated the Mali chapter for this book.

Frances Linzee Gordon

Frances' first 'travel article' was written under duress following a school scholarship to Venice at the age of 17. Still travelling and still under duress, she now writes guidebooks and travel articles for her sins. She is the author of Lonely Planet's *Ethiopia, Eritrea & Djibouti*, co-author of *Morocco* and a contributor to various other titles. She is currently studying part-time for an MA in African and Middle Eastern history at SOAS in London and will soon present a travel documentary on Ethiopia. Frances has a passion for all forms of dangerous sports, learning languages and, above all, pickled onions. Frances updated the Cape Verde chapter.

Anthony Ham

Anthony worked as a refugee lawyer for three years, during which time he completed a masters degree in Middle Eastern politics. After tiring of daily battles with a mean-spirited Australian government, he set out to see the world and restore his faith in humanity. Sitting on the running boards of a train in Thailand, he decided to become a writer and ever since has been travelling throughout the Arab world and Africa. On his travels for Lonely Planet, Anthony has eaten rat in Côte d'Ivoire, been arrested in Iran and found himself constantly overwhelmed by the many kindnesses from anything-but-ordinary people. Whenever circumstances permit, he heads for the Sahara. Anthony has worked on Lonely Planet's *Middle East*, *Africa*, *Iran*, *India*, *North India*, *Libya* and *Jordan*. Anthony updated the Burkina Faso, Mauritania and Niger chapters.

Amy Karafin

Amy Karafin grew up on the USA's Jersey shore, where she developed a keen curiosity about the horizon, and has spent the last

six years alternating living in New York and travelling in Asia and West Africa. Before visiting Guinea and Guinea-Bissau, she edited guidebooks for the competition in a big grey building in midtown Manhattan. Eventually she tired of sending writers out on exciting trips and realised that a Peugeot taxi through a dry forest, no matter how crowded, would beat the subway. She now lives in Dakar, where she's writing and translating, dancing *sabar*, and deriving lessons in humanity from everyday Africans. Amy updated the Guinea and Guinea-Bissau chapters for this edition.

Kim Wildman

Kim grew up in Toowoomba, Queensland, with parents who unwittingly instilled in her the desire to travel at young age by extending the immediate family to include 11 exchange students. After graduating from Queensland College of Art, having studied photography, Kim packed her backpack and headed to the USA and Bermuda. But it was her next adventure to Southern Africa that inspired her to combine her three loves: photography, writing and travel. Kim has a BA in journalism and has worked on Lonely Planet's *Romania & Moldova*, *South Africa, Lesotho & Swaziland*, *Eastern Europe* and *Europe on a shoestring* and she co-authored *Athens*. Kim updated the Benin and Togo chapters.

Isabelle Young

Having run out of things to do with a comma, Isabelle jumped at the chance to take a break from LP's editorial department to do what she loves best: checking out hotel bathrooms. Various trips through Africa, the Middle East, India and Australia have given her extensive experience in this field, as well as an incurable urge to see more. A chance encounter with a handsome Australian at a Ouagadougou swimming pool in 1991 eventually led her to a life among the gum trees and a job as editor in LP's Melbourne office. As well as editing a few books over the years, Isabelle coordinated and wrote the 1st edition of Lonely Planet's *Healthy Travel* series. Isabelle updated the Ghana chapter for this book.

FROM THE AUTHORS

Mary Fitzpatrick Thanks first and foremost to my husband, Rick, for his enthusiasm, support and endless patience, and for the many hours helping with background research.

In Cameroon, I owe a large debt of gratitude to Janine van Sant and the other Peace Corps volunteers who spent part of their New Year's holiday providing me with all sorts of useful tips and information. In particular I'd like to mention Jason Astle for making eastern Cameroon much more manageable, as well as Peter Byers, Heather Grimm, Adam Roise, Elizabeth Richardson, Christopher & Sarah Casarez, Jaime Bonk, Brian Haase, Melodie Griffis, Amanda Roy, Jenny Bussey, Dan Howell, Teresa Liechtfield,

Traci Baumgardner, Anna Russo & family, Vincent Baxter, Matthew Rippey, Melissa, Jason Steele and Lisa Bender.

I'd like to also express my appreciation to Judith Hall and Patrick Stubbs for their generous assistance with Korup National Park; Dr Leonard Usongo; Laurie Clark & Paul Blackmore; Mr Hamadou Paul; Greg & Annette Beyer and Steve & Lorrie Wittig and families.

Last but not least for Cameroon, a big thanks to Antonio Antiochia and Carla Mudgett for spending so much time helping me track down missing bits and pieces of information in Yaoundé, for so patiently fielding my many last-minute questions, and for their hospitality.

In Liberia, I'd like to thank the staff at SCNL and Reg Hoyt for the assistance with Sapo National Park.

Finally, many thanks to my co-authors on this book for taking the time to forward me so much regional information, above and beyond the call of duty.

Andrew Burke My thanks go to the countless people who informed, directed, transported, travelled, ate, drank or just chatted with me during my research in Gambia and Senegal.

But my first thank you goes to Anne Hyland in Hong Kong, a very special woman whose love and support endure great distances and extended separations and provide a steadying anchor in an often unpredictable existence. Thanks again for being there when I get home.

In Gambia, I'm especially grateful to Geri Mitchell and Maurice Phillips, whose hospitality, endless ideas, introductions and answers, and indefatigable energy for their adopted country were an inspiration; Ousainou Jagne of Timbooktoo for imparting some of his encyclopaedic knowledge of West African books and media to me; and Astrid Bojang for the fastest email replies in West Africa. Up river, thanks to Lawrence and James at Makasutu for living their dream and sharing it (and a lot of beer) with me; and Lamin Raul Bamba for expert guiding around Georgetown.

In Senegal, the great advice, lodgings and good company of Sonia Marcus, Anna Auster and Toubab the bunny were invaluable, and enjoyable, during repeated visits to Dakar. Elsewhere, Peace Corps volunteers were invariably generous with their time and knowledge: a big thanks to Natalie Cash and Chubby, the wiliest dog in West Africa, for the lowdown on Kolda and the long ride to Dakar; Jamie Lovett for her help from remote Dar Salam; Randy Chester and Shannon Gordon in Tambacounda; Eduard Valor in St-Louis; and Abigail, Betsy, Fred and particularly Vonnie Moler in Kedougou – good luck wherever you guys end up. In Casamance, thanks to the Chiche clan of Veronique and Philip in Ziguinchor and Pierre and Marie at Cap Skiring; and, on Île de Carabane, to Dennis Baker, Claire and Alphonse for news, views and an excellent meal.

Thanks too to overlanders Robert Hasse and Tim Urban; colleague Nick Ray; cyclist Holger Schulze; Nicole Fonck-Deruiseau in St-Louis; Ingemo Lindroos and Marcus Floman; Sarah Holtz in Dakar; 'chimp man' Michel Waller; Rassine Sy and family in Mbaké; and my wonderful family in Australia. At LP Melbourne the editors and cartographers demonstrated the height of professionalism during a difficult time: thanks to Julia, Pablo, Hilary, Kerryn, and to Kim and Vince – enjoy your new careers.

Finally a big thank you to the people of The Gambia and Senegal – may you have even more to smile about in the future.

Greg Campbell Of all the people who deserve my thanks for helping me during my travels – and there are many – none deserve it more than my parents, who endured brain-rattling emails of near-death experiences with aplomb and support. I hope I can be as understanding when my son, Turner, reaches the age of exploration and travel. In Sierra Leone, special thanks go to Margaret Novicki of the United Nations Mission in Sierra Leone and Nigerian Maj Mohammed Yerima for getting me into and out of places that most travellers would never wish to be. Thanks also to RUF Maj T-Ray and RUF Maj Gabrille Kallon for their protection and guidance in Kailahun and Makeni, respectively. In Freetown, thanks to Jango, Robert, Clifford and the staff of the Solar Hotel and Jay's Guest House. In Nigeria, special praise needs to be lavished on Patterson Ogon of the Ijaw Council for Human Rights without whom my visit would literally have been impossible. Thanks as well to Greg Avery, who embodies all that anyone could ever ask for in a travelling companion, Freida and Tomas of the German embassy for the lift from Yankari National Park and the close encounter with stampeding elephants, Josephine Jackson for the tour of Calabar and the endless list of drivers, hotel clerks, moneychangers, gimcrack salesmen, okada drivers, dash-demanders, crooked cops and area boys who make any visit to Nigeria as colourful and satisfying as can be expected. Finally, I owe a great deal of humble thanks to Tiffany Schauer, for keeping me sane and in love, no matter what corner of the world I find myself in.

I would like to dedicate my portion of this book to the memories of those who died during the 27 January 2002 ammunition warehouse explosion in Lagos.

Bethune Carmichael Many thanks to Liliane Koulaté and Monsieur Bakayoko, at the Man Office Ivoirien du Tourism, for their insightful guidance. Thanks also to Madam Denba of the Abidjan Office Ivoirien du Tourism and guide John Nagnama in Korhogo. In Edinburgh, many thanks to Zoe Carmichael, Mahli Storm and Yvonne Kirkus for their hospitality, and to Jamie Coates for his technical support. In Paris thanks to Mathieu Farge. In Australia, thanks to Kim Hutchins and Justin Flynn.

Matthew Fletcher A big thanks to fellow travellers Clare, Kate and Anna. Special thanks to Violet Diallo at the British embassy whose enthusiasm for Mali is infectious. Also thanks to Helen

O'Leary, Andries Siebrits, Joan Dobler, Tim Dodman, Rod East, Ian Redmond and Anne Mounicot for streams of background information. Tim, Eddie and the US marines provided some top clubbing tips and Sean, Nicky, Bill, Cath, Dan and Willy Wonker gave valuable insight into bars.

Many beers are still owed to US PCVs, especially Greg Silverman, Laura Coatta, Lesley Keith, Erin McNamee, Blaire and Abbey. Thanks to Zanna and Katie Mckay, Mohamed, Marie and Willy Wonker for great food and times.

Thanks to Ali Tembeli, Karen Crabb and especially Boubacar Ouologuem for an unforgettable Dogon trek, and to Assou in Mopti for sorting everything out.

Kate and Cheik helped in Sibi and John 'Mac' McKinney helped in Dogon and beyond. Also thanks to Dave and Michelle Knight and Gareth Taylor for luxuary in Sadiola and to the Catholic mission in Gao for their hospitality.

Lastly thanks to Bando, Ag, Blob and Ceri for taking care of business back home.

Frances Linzee Gordon Thanks in particular to Maria da Luz Martins, Djamila Silva and Cristolita Spenser of TACV, Praia; Maria Das Dores Santos at Arca Verde; Vera Barboa of Santo Antão Tourism Office; Guilherme Cardosa, Chief of Immigration services, Praia; Isabel Duarte, Promex, Praia; Franklin Aguiar, Commercial Director at CS Lines for information, a tour of Praia and an evening's introduction to Cape Verde's fabulous music scene; and to Firmino João Brito, Chef de Turno, Immigration for his clemency. Grateful thanks also to Dr Wayne Dooling and Dr David Appleyard of SOAS, London, for showing such patience and tolerance while I missed class after class of my MA.

Anthony Ham As always I found myself overwhelmed with assistance by so many people along the way. In Burkina Faso I am particularly indebted to the staff at the Hôtel Belle Vue, Les Pavillons Vert and Bagdad Café for their unfailing patience. I am also grateful to Dolores in Dori and Gorom-Gorom, and to Yatinga in Bobo for teaching so much about the dignity of his people. A big thank you again to Miles Roddis for his invaluable insights before setting out and for making the chapter such an easy one to update. In Niger, special thanks to Moussa Touboulou in Agadez for the unfailing warmth of his welcome and allowing me to better understand Tuareg culture; to Céline and Akly Joulia-Boileau in Agadez for their efforts to build community and protect heritage; the members of the Trust for African Rock Art whom I met in Agadez; Youssef in Agadez for his friendship; Saminou in Maradi for telling me the painful truth about his town; Ann and Holly for enlivening slow Agadez days; and Ikhawasse for his hospitality in Niamey. In Mauritania, thanks to Mouloud for his silent but attentive company on the journey through Adrar; Jean Vidal for being such a wise and cheeky travel companion; and Dave

Greenhaigh and friend of the Mine Action Group for making those long days of waiting in Nouakchott that much easier to bear.

Thank you to Lauren who, as always, ensured such a soulful time in Sarajevo en route to Africa. Back home, a massive thank you to my family and friends for their patience, understanding and warmth despite my long absences, especially Jan, Ron, Lisa, Greg, my very special niece Alexandra, and Damien. And finally a special dedication to Greta, my other niece who was born while I was in Ouagadougou – may your world be as big as your smile.

Amy Karafin Special thanks to Vergas Kwashie, for teaching me about kindness, love and Africa; Barry and Betsy Karafin for the solid upbringing as well as for their endurance and extensive logistical support; Mohamed Kouyaté and family, especially Oumou, Fatim, Kandia, Djougou, and Aisha; Papa, Hadja, Kadijah, Mama, Mariama, and everyone at Carrefour Chinois; Robert Disney and Matthew Olins for the recommendations and advice; Moustapha Diallo at Guinea's Office National du Tourisme; Benoît Millimono and Dr Nanténin Friki Camara at the University of Faranah; David Brugière at the Parc National de Haut Niger for all the translations and a fascinating talk about the forest; Reiner Kappner at the Hotel Camayenne; Will and Charlie Bethel; Mario Martins Cá; Gigi Goodhart; Victor Teixeira; Maurício Insumbo at the Parque Natural dos Tarrafes do Rio Cacheu; and João Sousa Cordeiro and Justino Biai at the UICN, for their friendly assistance, in addition to the bird books.

Kim Wildman There were many people in Togo who generously donated their time and knowledge. Those to whom I am especially grateful include Gloria Kouloba and Bagna Momo, Deborah and Bruce Edwards, Adrian Cruikshank, Kate Jenkins and Joe Bardsley for showing me the highs and lows of Lomé's night life, Ian, Tom and Ben Sayer, Marie Franklin, Andrew MacManus, Lucy License, David and Audrey Barnes, Jeni Sayer and all the staff and students from the British School of Lomé.

In Benin I'm indebted to Trevor Salmon and Guy Catherine for all their help and guidance. Also to Grania Lorghnan, Caroline Irby and Thomas Conlon for sharing their views of Cotonou with me.

Last and far from least, my biggest thanks goes to Michael Rimmer who endured my presence for so long and who never failed to answer all my questions (even after I left the region).

Isabelle Young First, a big thank you to all the Ghanaians we met while we were researching this chapter, who were unfailingly friendly and helpful and who made travelling in their country such a privilege and pleasure. Also in Ghana, thanks to Cynthia Evans and her colleagues at the Peace Corps in Accra; to Gala Wagner for her invaluable insights and for answering my endless questions; to Melanie Walling in Domama for being so unfazed by our presence; to Robert Agbozo at the British Council in Accra and Nina Chachu in Kumasi; to Charles Kwaku Buabin at the tourist board in Kumasi for fitting more than humanly possible into a day tour; to Andrew Murphy and his colleagues at the NCRC for their time and effort; to John Pobee Dawson at the Panafest offices in Cape Coast; and to Tenko Computer for sorting us out in Bimbilla. At LP, thanks to Miles Roddis, author of the last edition, for his help during the planning stages and for giving me such beautifully crafted text to work with; to Mary Fitzpatrick for being an exemplary coordinating author; to Virginia Maxwell for sending me to Ghana in the first place; and to Kim Hutchins, Hilary Rogers and the WAF editing team for making the process run so smoothly.

Finally, I'm enormously grateful to my long-suffering travelling companion David Petherbridge, who helped with much of the research and even found time to take some pretty decent pictures along the way.

This Book

The first two editions of West Africa were written and researched by Alex Newton. Alex was joined by David Else for the 3rd edition while the 4th edition was updated by David Else, Alex Newton, Jeff Williams, Mary Fitzpatrick and Miles Roddis. For this, the 5th edition, Mary Fitzpatrick was the coordinating author and updated Liberia and the introductory chapters. She also wrote Cameroon, the new addition to this book. Kim Wildman updated Benin and Togo, Anthony Ham updated Burkina Faso, Mauritania and Niger while Frances Linzee Gordon was responsible for updating Cape Verde. Bethune Carmichael updated Côte d'Ivoire, Andrew Burke had his hands full updating The Gambia and Senegal, Isabelle Young updated Ghana and Amy Karafin updated Guinea and Guinea-Bissau. Finally, Matthew Fletcher updated Mali and Greg Campbell braved it in Nigeria and Sierra Leone.

From the Publisher

West Africa 5 had, what seemed like, a cast of hundreds. Justin Flynn had the unenviable task of coordinating the project and had terrific help from a willing and able team of editors including Julia Taylor, Hilary Rogers, Isabelle Young, Evan Jones, Jenny Mullaly, Kerryn Burgess, Bethune Carmichael, Liz Filleul and Thalia Kalkipsakis. Thanks to Celia Wood, Virginia Maxwell, Adrienne Costanzo, Brigitte Ellemor, Bridget Blair, Kim Hutchins and Mary Neighbour for artwork checking. The cartography and design was expertly handled by Hunor Csutoros, with assistance from Amanda Sierp, Csanád Csutoros, Jody Whiteoak, Lachlan Ross, Pablo Gastar and Sarah Sloane.

Thanks to Simon Bracken for the cover design, Emma Koch for the Language chapter, and Hunor for the climate charts, map legend and decorative borders.

Special thanks to Kim Hutchins, Bridget Blair and Vince Patton for overseeing the project, and to Jocelyn Harewood for the index.

THANKS
Many thanks to the travellers who used the last edition and wrote to us with helpful hints, advice and interesting anecdotes. Your names appear on page 874 of this book.

Foreword

ABOUT LONELY PLANET GUIDEBOOKS

The story begins with a classic travel adventure: Tony and Maureen Wheeler's 1972 journey across Europe and Asia to Australia. There was no useful information about the overland trail then, so Tony and Maureen published the first Lonely Planet guidebook to meet a growing need.

From a kitchen table, Lonely Planet has grown to become the largest independent travel publisher in the world, with offices in Melbourne (Australia), Oakland (USA), London (UK) and Paris (France).

Today Lonely Planet guidebooks cover the globe. There is an ever-growing list of books and information in a variety of media. Some things haven't changed. The main aim is still to make it possible for adventurous travellers to get out there – to explore and better understand the world.

At Lonely Planet we believe travellers can make a positive contribution to the countries they visit – if they respect their host communities and spend their money wisely. Since 1986 a percentage of the income from each book has been donated to aid projects and human rights campaigns, and, more recently, to wildlife conservation.

Although inclusion in a guidebook usually implies a recommendation we cannot list every good place. Exclusion does not necessarily imply criticism. In fact there are a number of reasons why we might exclude a place – sometimes it is simply inappropriate to encourage an influx of travellers.

UPDATES & READER FEEDBACK

Things change – prices go up, schedules change, good places go bad and bad places go bankrupt. Nothing stays the same. So, if you find things better or worse, recently opened or long-since closed, please tell us and help make the next edition even more accurate and useful.

Lonely Planet thoroughly updates each guidebook as often as possible – usually every two years, although for some destinations the gap can be longer. Between editions, up-to-date information is available in our free, quarterly *Planet Talk* newsletter and monthly email bulletin *Comet*. The *Upgrades* section of our website (w www.lonelyplanet.com) is also regularly updated by Lonely Planet authors, and the site's *Scoop* section covers news and current affairs relevant to travellers. Lastly, the *Thorn Tree* bulletin board and *Postcards* section carry unverified, but fascinating, reports from travellers.

Tell us about it! We genuinely value your feedback. A well-travelled team at Lonely Planet reads and acknowledges every email and letter we receive and ensures that every morsel of information finds its way to the relevant authors, editors and cartographers.

Everyone who writes to us will find their name listed in the next edition of the appropriate guidebook, and will receive the latest issue of *Comet* or *Planet Talk*. The very best contributions will be rewarded with a free guidebook.

We may edit, reproduce and incorporate your comments in Lonely Planet products such as guidebooks, websites and digital products, so let us know if you don't want your comments reproduced or your name acknowledged.

How to contact Lonely Planet:

Online: e talk2us@lonelyplanet.com.au, w www.lonelyplanet.com
Australia: Locked Bag 1, Footscray, Victoria 3011
UK: 10a Spring Place, London NW5 3BH
USA: 150 Linden St, Oakland, CA 94607

Introduction

Call it mystique or adventure, whatever, West Africa has a power of attraction which, despite its often rugged conditions, continues to entice travellers.

One of the region's attractions is its diversity of activities and sights. Travel here could find you camel trekking on the edge of the Sahara, hiking on shaded forest trails, relaxing on the beach or meandering along idyllic palm-lined creeks. You will see elaborate mud-brick mosques in Mali, gleaming high-rise office buildings in Côte d'Ivoire, colonial-era forts and castles in Ghana and humble thatched huts in villages throughout the region.

Another drawcard is the vitality that surrounds you wherever you go – the vibrancy of the streets, the pulsating rhythms of nightclubs, crowded and colourful markets. There are natural attractions as well, from tranquil lagoons to great rivers such as the Niger and the Gambia, dense rainforest and windswept sand dunes, savanna plains and lushly vegetated hills. Within these natural environments is an impressive range of animals, including stunning and prolific birdlife. You will see elephants gathered around watering holes in northern Cameroon, flocks of pelicans and flamingos in river deltas or along the coast in Mauritania,

WEST AFRICA

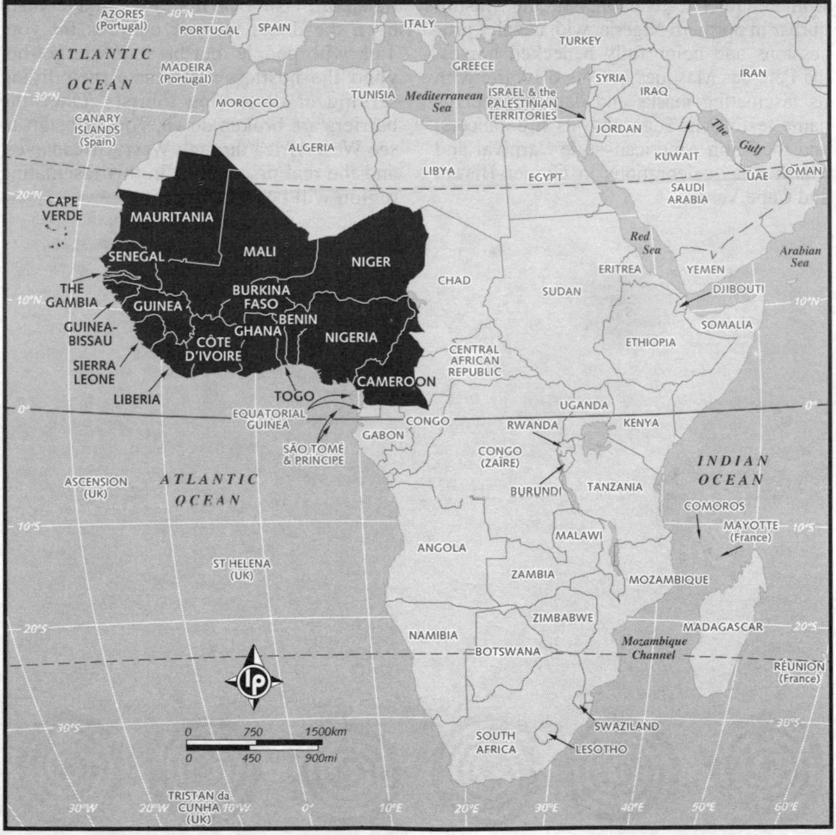
AZORES (Portugal)
PORTUGAL
SPAIN
ITALY
TURKEY
ATLANTIC OCEAN
MADEIRA (Portugal)
GREECE
SYRIA
IRAN
TUNISIA
Mediterranean Sea
ISRAEL & the PALESTINIAN TERRITORIES
IRAQ
MOROCCO
CANARY ISLANDS (Spain)
JORDAN
The Gulf
ALGERIA
KUWAIT
LIBYA
EGYPT
UAE
OMAN
SAUDI ARABIA
CAPE VERDE
MAURITANIA
MALI
NIGER
SENEGAL
Red Sea
Arabian Sea
ERITREA
YEMEN
CHAD
SUDAN
DJIBOUTI
THE GAMBIA
GUINEA
BURKINA FASO
BENIN
GUINEA-BISSAU
GHANA
NIGERIA
SOMALIA
CÔTE D'IVOIRE
ETHIOPIA
SIERRA LEONE
CENTRAL AFRICAN REPUBLIC
CAMEROON
LIBERIA
TOGO
UGANDA
EQUATORIAL GUINEA
CONGO
RWANDA
KENYA
GABON
SÃO TOMÉ & PRINCIPE
CONGO (ZAÏRE)
INDIAN OCEAN
ASCENSION (UK)
ATLANTIC OCEAN
BURUNDI
TANZANIA
COMOROS
MAYOTTE (France)
MALAWI
ANGOLA
ST HELENA (UK)
ZAMBIA
MOZAMBIQUE
ZIMBABWE
NAMIBIA
MADAGASCAR
Mozambique Channel
BOTSWANA
RÉUNION (France)
SWAZILAND
SOUTH AFRICA
LESOTHO
0 750 1500km
0 450 900mi
TRISTAN da CUNHA (UK)
40°N
30°N
20°N
10°N
0°
10°S
20°S
30°S
30°W
20°W
10°W
0°
10°E
20°E
30°E
40°E
50°E
60°E

and bushbucks, waterbucks, hippos and more.

West Africa's main attractions, however, are its people and cultures, of which you'll find an astounding richness and variety. Near Timbuktu and on the edge of the Sahara, you'll see nomadic Tuareg with their camels and flowing indigo robes. In southern Mali and many other areas, you'll encounter nomadic Fula with their cattle and characteristic circular, peaked hats, while in the urban areas of Guinea and Senegal women of various ethnic groups are elegantly dressed in the elaborately embroidered grand boubou.

If you time things right, you'll also be able to experience the region's cultures at some of its many festivals. One of the most famous festivals is the Cure Salée in Niger, especially that of the Wodaabé, when young herders paint their faces in order to attract women. Other festivals include the Muslim durbar in northern Nigeria, with cavalry processions and colourfully bedecked horses; the Fête des Masques in Côte d'Ivoire, with its fascinating masks and dancing; the Igname festival in Togo with its fire dancers; and the Latin American–style Carnival and Mardi Gras celebrations in Guinea-Bissau and Cape Verde.

Whatever it is that lures you to West Africa, be prepared to rough it. Travel is often uncomfortable: bumping over hot and dusty roads through dry Sahelian landscapes, slogging through mud during the rains along the coast, being squashed into half a seat (if you're lucky) in an overcrowded bush taxi, or being stranded for hours in an airport waiting for a hopelessly delayed connection. While there are ample five-star facilities in major cities for those with the finances, travelling at the budget level will most likely mean at least some nights spent in very basic conditions.

Even when it is uncomfortable, though, travel in West Africa is never dull. The key to getting under the surface and understanding what the region is really about is to leave your preconceptions behind. Get to know West Africans – travel on public transport, visit local markets – and let them open the doors to their cultures for you. Talk with people, but be sure you get beyond the hustlers who make their living serving or disserving tourists. Once the barriers are broken down, you will start to see West Africa through West African eyes, and the real discoveries in this fascinating region will begin to appear.

Facts about West Africa

HISTORY

West Africa's national boundaries are a result of recent phenomena imposed on the region by European colonial powers within the last two centuries. Before this, the region was home to a fascinating array of states and kingdoms. Although the names of some of these – the Empires of Ghana and Mali, for example – are memorialised in present-day place names, many have been largely forgotten by Westerners. Yet, they are of great importance in understanding the area's peoples and cultures, particularly as West Africa's modern political borders bear little relation to the territories of its many ethno-linguistic groups.

This section provides an overview of the history of the region, focusing on the period before European influence significantly penetrated the interior. For accounts of the colonial and postcolonial periods in each country, see the individual country chapters.

Early History

In comparison with East and Southern Africa, relatively little archaeological evidence documenting early hominid species has been found in West Africa. However, fossils found elsewhere on the African continent suggest that early members of the genus *Homo* were present in the region from at least one million years ago. The earliest definitive evidence of human life in West Africa – tools and other artefacts found in Senegal, Guinea, Mali, Mauritania and elsewhere – dates back to 200,000 BC. These tools are attributed to *Homo erectus*, the predecessor of *Homo sapiens* (modern man).

More recent archaeological clues indicate that somewhere between 6000 and 10,000 years ago, agricultural development began in the regions now occupied by the Sahara desert, which was then interspersed with waterways and was much wetter than it is now. From around 5000 BC, global climatic changes caused the savanna to begin to dry out, making agriculture more difficult and forcing the early farmers to move. These climatic changes also caused the vegetation south of the savanna to become less dense, and this area – today known as the Sahel – was occupied instead.

Evidence discovered in the Sahel shows that by 4000 to 3000 BC, people had domesticated cattle and were also cultivating and harvesting indigenous plants, including millet (a cereal crop), yam (root tubers) and rice. Remains of pottery, stone hoes and digging tools dating from around the same period provide further evidence of a sedentary, non-nomadic lifestyle. Other tools, including hand-scythes used for cutting grasses, have also been found.

Early Societies

Agriculture led to the development of organised societies, as communities had to develop systems of cooperation or control. Additionally, farming could support larger numbers of people, so populations started to expand. The earliest evidence of organised society in West Africa dates from around 1500 BC, in present-day Mauritania, where remains of stone villages and domestic animals have been found. Similar remains have been found in what is now northern Nigeria. It is likely that settlements of this type were established across the Sahel, which was more vegetated at that time than it is today.

Of the early societies that inhabited the Sahel during this period, two dominant groups emerged: the first along the Niger River, and the second around Lake Chad – both areas well suited to agriculture. These groups built large stone villages and even towns, and were in contact with other African peoples, particularly those living on the southern shores of the Mediterranean. Ancient rock paintings discovered in the Sahara indicate that horse-drawn chariots were used to cover great distances – the precursors to today's trans-Sahara overlanders.

The Iron Age

The earliest evidence of iron-working in West Africa is found in central Nigeria and dates from around 450 BC. Knowledge of iron-working was probably introduced to the region either from Egypt via the Nile Valley and Lake Chad, or across the Sahara from North Africa. However, some authorities believe that the use of iron actually developed in West Africa, and that the knowledge went the other way, to Egypt.

Iron-working had major ramifications across the region, as iron tools were much more efficient than those made from stone or bronze. It was now possible for people to clear forest, which until then had hindered farming (especially cereal production), and expand or migrate into new territories. This process was usually gradual, as weaker tribes were slowly absorbed by intermarriage with more powerful groups.

The First Cities

Jenné-Jeno (in present-day Mali), established around 300 BC, is believed to have been one of the earliest urban settlements in West Africa. It is likely that several similar settlements were established elsewhere around this time and during the following few centuries, and by around AD 500, towns and villages were dotted across the region.

As the 1st millennium progressed, trade increased significantly between the regions south and north of the Sahara. Goods transported across the desert included salt, gold, silver and ivory; there was also trade in slaves. Some of the early settlements on the edge of the desert were well placed to take advantage of the trade (and eventually control it), so they increased in size, wealth and power. Large villages became towns or city-states, and a few even developed into powerful confederations and empires.

African Migrations

The migrations of African peoples in the precolonial era were not sudden mass movements, but gradual expansions over hundreds, or even thousands, of years. They consisted of many short moves – from valley to valley, or from one cultivation area to the next – with dominant peoples slowly absorbing and assimilating other groups in the process. The most successful migratory group in Africa were the Bantu people. Originally from the area that is now Nigeria and Cameroon, the Bantu began to slowly make their way eastward and southward through the forests of Central Africa, beginning about 2000 BC for reasons that are not yet fully understood. The introduction of iron accelerated this process, with the Bantu spreading through the Congo basin to reach the East African plateau around 100 BC. Over the next thousand years they moved down the continent as far as present-day Zimbabwe and South Africa. Today, the vast majority of indigenous peoples in Africa south of the equator are of Bantu origin. The only West African countries with significant Bantu populations are Nigeria and Cameroon.

Early Empires

Empire of Ghana The Empire of Ghana (which has no geographic connection with the present-day country) was the first major state of its kind established in West Africa. Its early origins are unclear, but according to some theories it may have developed as early as the 4th century AD as the small kingdom of Wagadu. More certain is that by the 5th century it was an established centre of the Soninké people, and that it flourished from the 8th to 11th centuries. The capital was Kumbi Saleh, in present-day Mauritania, about 200km north of modern Bamako (Mali). Power was based on the control of trans-Saharan trade, and at its height the empire covered much of present-day Mali and parts of eastern Senegal.

Islam was introduced by traders from the north, and was adopted by local merchants and some members of the political elite, but the Empire of Ghana did not fully embrace the new religion. The empire was destroyed in the late 11th century by the better-armed Muslim Berbers of the Almoravid empire from Mauritania and Morocco. At around the same time, the Tukulor (or Tekrur) empire was established by the Tukulor people in what is now northern Senegal. It also based its power on control of the trans-Saharan trade, and flourished during the 9th and 10th centuries.

Empire of Mali In the middle of the 13th century Sundiata Keita, leader of the Malinké people, founded the Empire of Mali in the region between the present-day countries of Senegal and Niger. By the beginning of the 14th century the empire had expanded further to control almost all trans-Saharan trade. It brought great wealth to the rulers of Mali, who embraced Islam with enthusiasm.

When Emperor Mansa Musa went on a pilgrimage to Mecca in the early 14th century, he took an entourage of 60,000 people. In Egypt, he presented so many people with lavish gifts of gold that the metal's value slumped for several years.

During this period the trans-Saharan trade reached its peak, and the wealth created meant Mali's main cities became major centres of finance and culture. Most notable was Timbuktu, where two Islamic universities were founded, and Arab architects were employed to design new mosques, some of which can still be seen today.

Empire of Songhaï While Mali was at the height of its powers, the Songhaï people had established their own city-state to the east around Gao (in present-day Mali). This city-state became powerful and well organised, and by the middle of the 15th century had eclipsed the Empire of Mali and incorporated Timbuktu and Djenné. A hallmark of the Empire of Songhaï was the creation of a professional army and a civil service with provincial governors. The state even subsidised Muslim scholars, judges and doctors. By the 16th century, Timbuktu was an important commercial city, with about 100,000 inhabitants. This golden period ended with an invasion by Berber armies from Morocco in the late 16th century.

Later States & Empires To the west of Mali, on the coast near the site of present-day Dakar in Senegal, the Wolof people established the Empire of Jolof (also spelt Yollof). Meanwhile, to the east of Mali the Hausa people created several powerful city-states, such as Katsina, Kano and Zinder (still important trading towns today), but they never amalgamated into a single empire. East of here, on the shores of Lake Chad, yet another empire, that of Kanem-Borno, was founded in the early 14th century and at its height covered a vast area including some parts of present-day Niger, Nigeria, Chad and Cameroon. It remained a powerful force in the region until the 19th century.

To the south of the Sahel empires, mostly in the period between the 13th and 16th centuries, several smaller states were established in forested areas and where gold was produced. These states prospered from trade with their larger northern neighbours. They included the kingdoms of Benin (in present-day Nigeria), Dahomey (Benin), Mossi (Burkina Faso) and Akan-Ashanti (Ghana).

European Interest

Around this time, European interest in West Africa began to increase. The trans-Saharan trade carried gold from the coastal regions via the Mediterranean to the courts and treasuries of countries such as England, France, Spain and Portugal, and as early as the 13th century the financial stability of several major European powers depended largely on the supply of West African gold. There were frequent reports of the wealthy empires south of the Sahara, although no European had yet visited the region.

Prince Henry of Portugal (Henry the Navigator, 1394–1460) encouraged explorers to sail down the coast of West Africa, which soon became known as Guinea. His intention was to bypass the Arab and Muslim domination of the trans-Saharan gold trade and reach the source by sea. By the early 15th century, Portuguese ships had reached the Canary Islands and the coast of what is now Western Sahara. In 1443 ships reached the mouth of the Senegal River, and a year later another ship rounded a peninsula on the coast of Senegal, which was named Cabo Verde or Green Cape (it is now called Cap Vert, the site of Dakar, and is not to be confused with the Cape Verde islands). In a series of later voyages the Portuguese pushed further south: Sierra Leone in 1462, Fernando Po (now Bioko in Equatorial Guinea) in 1472 and Cape Cross (Namibia) in 1485.

As the Portuguese made contact with local chiefs and started to trade for gold and ivory, the great empires of the Sahel lost their monopoly and started to decline. The coastal states, however, benefited from contact with the new arrivals and continued to prosper.

In 1482 the Portuguese built a fortified trading post at Elmina, on the coast of today's Ghana, which was the earliest European structure in sub-Saharan Africa. But trade never fulfilled the hopes of the earlier pioneers. Elmina became a staging point for the increasing number of ships sailing between Portugal and the Far East, where commodities were proving more profitable than those from Africa.

By 1500, Portuguese ships had also sailed some distance upstream along the Senegal and Gambia Rivers, using these waterways as vital routes into the interior. It has even been suggested that the Gambia River's name derives from the Portuguese word *cambio,* meaning 'exchange' or 'trade'. But West Africa had few other large rivers that allowed access to the interior, and most trade remained based on the coast.

The Rise of Islam

In the interior, events took a different course, and were profoundly influenced by the rise of Islam. Islam, which was founded in Arabia by the Prophet Mohammed around the year AD 620, first reached the Sahel around AD 900, brought by traders from present-day Morocco and Algeria. It gained a footing and soon became the religion of the rulers and the wealthy in West Africa; ordinary people generally did not adopt it, preferring to retain their traditional beliefs. However, rulers skilfully combined aspects of Islam and traditional religion in the administration of the state, and this fusing of beliefs remains a feature of West African life today.

Islam's position as the dominant religion in the Sahel was solidified in the 17th and 18th centuries. During this time, various factors, including the decline of the old empires, the increased power of the coastal states, the rise in European influence, the corresponding rise in trade and slavery, and the introduction of guns, led to a period of instability across much of West Africa, particularly in the Sahel, and Islam filled the vacuum. The power of the leaders grew in religious as well as political and economic matters; their followers enthusiastically spread the faith, and Islamic jihads (holy wars) were declared on groups of non-believers. In time, several Muslim states were established. These included Futa Toro (in northern Senegal), Futa Djalon (Guinea), Masina (Mali) and the Sokoto state of Hausaland (Niger and Nigeria).

Sufism, a type of Islam that emphasises mystical and spiritual attributes, became particularly popular. A central aspect of Sufism is the influence of religious teachers, many of whom are ascribed divine powers and the ability to communicate with Allah. (Orthodox Islam is more egalitarian and does not allow for intermediaries of this nature.) Commentators have suggested that this master–follower relationship found favour in West Africa because it mirrored the hierarchical social structures already in place.

European Expansion

While Islam was becoming firmly established, Europeans began to penetrate the interior. One explorer was Mungo Park, a Scottish doctor who travelled from the Gambia River to reach the Niger River in present-day Mali. Later explorers included Scotsman Hugh Clapperton, who reached Kano in northern Nigeria, and the British brothers Richard and John Lander, who finally established that the Niger River flowed into the Atlantic. Meanwhile, other explorers were trying to reach the fabled city of Timbuktu; Frenchman René Caillié was finally successful in 1828.

As European influence grew in the first half of the 19th century, jihads were fought less against 'infidel' Africans and more against Europeans – particularly against the French, who were pushing deeper into this part of the region. The most notable leader of the time was Omar Tall (also spelt Umar Taal), who led a major campaign against the French from around 1850 until he was killed in 1864. After his death, the jihads continued as the 'Marabout Wars', as they were called, in Senegal until the 1880s.

Early Colonialism

In the second half of the 19th century, the trans-Atlantic slave trade came to an end (although it continued in some parts of Africa for many decades more). This was partly the result of a liberalisation of attitudes brought on by the Enlightenment, but also due to the Industrial Revolution that led to a demand for stable, compliant colonies supplying raw materials and providing a market for finished goods.

In West Africa, the main European powers had established pockets of territory on the coast. These included the French enclave of Dakar (which would later become the capital of Senegal), and the British ports of Freetown (Sierra Leone) and Lagos (Nigeria). Portugal was no longer a major force, but had retained some territory – notably, Bissau, capital of today's Guinea-Bissau. There had been several military expeditions to the interior, with the French active primarily in the Sahel regions and the British penetrating the region mostly from the south coast. Various minor treaties were made with local chiefs, but there was still little in the way of formally claimed territory.

Slave Trade

Slavery had existed in West Africa for many centuries, and expanded in significant part with the rise of Islam, which prohibits the enslavement of Muslims. However, the Portuguese also contributed greatly to the trade, taking slaves to work on the large sugar plantations that had been established in Portuguese settlements on the other side of the Atlantic (including in present-day Brazil) between 1575 and 1600.

By the 17th and 18th centuries, other European nations (particularly England, Spain, France and Holland) had established colonies in the Americas, and were growing sugar, tobacco, cotton and other crops. Huge profits could be made from these commodities, and the demand for slaves to work the plantations was insatiable.

In most cases, European traders encouraged Africans on the coast to attack neighbouring tribes and take captives. These were brought to the coastal slaving stations and exchanged for European goods such as cloth and guns, enabling more neighbours to be invaded and more slaves to be captured. A triangular trans-Atlantic trade route developed – the slaves were loaded onto ships and transported to the Americas; the raw materials they produced were transported to Europe; and finished goods were transported from Europe to Africa once again to be exchanged for slaves and to keep the whole system moving. The demand for slaves was maintained because conditions in the plantations were so bad that life expectancy after arriving in the Americas was often no more than a few years.

Exact figures are impossible to come by, but it is estimated that from the end of the 15th century until around 1870 (when the slave trade was abolished) as many as 20 million Africans were captured. Between 25% and 50% of this number died, mostly while being transported. Accounts written at the time describe hundreds of slaves packed tightly between decks so low there was only room to lay down. Food or water was often not provided and the faeces or vomit from those above fell through the planking onto those lying below. It is not surprising that only around 10 million (according to some estimates) actually arrived in the Americas. These figures are hotly debated by historians, and sometimes obscure the main issue, which is that whatever the actual numbers, the slave trade was undeniably cruel and inhuman.

By the 1870s, political events in Europe had led to increasing competition among France, Britain, Belgium, the recently formed state of Germany and other nations. This battle for dominance was played out in large part in Africa, in a sudden rush of land-grabbing that became known as the Scramble for Africa.

The Scramble for Africa

The European land-grabbing frenzy was triggered in 1879 by King Leopold of Belgium's claim to the Congo, now known as Congo (Zaïre). France responded by establishing territory in the neighbouring area, which became known as French Congo (present-day Congo) and Gabon. Meanwhile, the British were increasing their influence and showing interest in territories in East Africa, as part of a plan to control the headwaters of the Nile, and in turn the strategic Suez Canal, the route to India. Germany's leader, Bismarck, claimed various bits of Africa, including Togo and Cameroon.

All the European powers wanted to strengthen their positions and occupy territories as soon as possible. In 1881 France invaded Tunis, and in 1882 Britain invaded Egypt. The following year, Britain staked a claim to much of East Africa, and to territories in West Africa – such as Gambia, Sierra Leone, the Gold Coast (Ghana) and Nigeria. At the same time, France claimed much of the Sahel belt eastward from its territory in Senegal. France also claimed much of the Sahara itself, to link up with its possessions in North Africa, which had become French territory earlier in the century.

The various claims of the European powers were settled at the Berlin Conference of 1884–85, when most of the continent of Africa was split neatly into colonies. Britain got a few West African coastal territories plus most of East and Southern Africa, Belgium got the Congo, Germany kept Togo and Cameroon (and added the area that is present-day Tanzania and Namibia to its far-flung empire), while Portugal kept

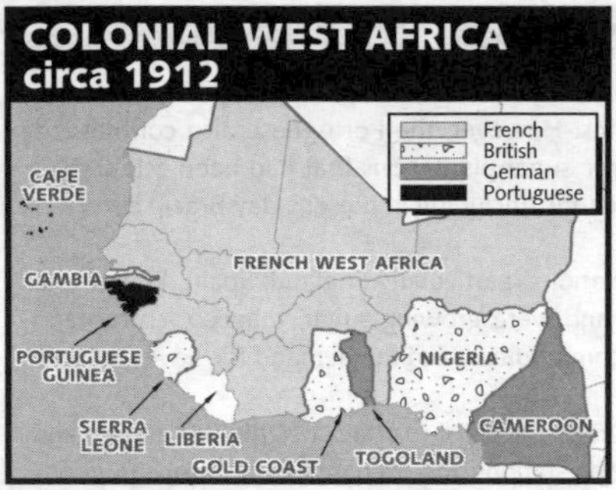
COLONIAL WEST AFRICA
circa 1912
French
British
German
Portuguese
CAPE VERDE
FRENCH WEST AFRICA
GAMBIA
PORTUGUESE GUINEA
NIGERIA
SIERRA LEONE
LIBERIA
CAMEROON
GOLD COAST
TOGOLAND

Guinea-Bissau, the islands of Cape Verde, Equatorial Guinea and the territories in the south that would become the modern states of Mozambique and Angola. France was awarded most of West and Central Africa – a vast area covering almost one-third of the entire continent that became known as Afrique Occidentale Française (French West Africa) or the French Soudan (to distinguish it from Anglo-Egyptian Sudan, now the modern state of Sudan).

20th Century

Following the Berlin Conference, the European powers consolidated their presence in the new colonies. Although there was plenty of anti-European feeling among Africans, local resistance was generally sporadic. When uprisings did occur, most were easily put down by well-armed European soldiers.

Despite lip service to the idea of introducing 'civilisation' to the 'heathen natives', the main aim of the European governments was to exploit the colonies for raw materials. In some areas, gem and gold mining was developed, but generally West Africa had little in the way of bulk minerals such as coal. Consequently, labour-intensive plantations were established, and cash crops such as coffee, cocoa, rubber, cotton and groundnuts (peanuts) soon came to dominate the economies of the fledgling colonies, and to be a major source of employment – not always voluntary – for local people.

After WWI, Germany lost its African possessions, and the administration of Togo and Cameroon was entrusted to Britain and France, with the divisive effects still evident today. Generally speaking, through the first half of the 20th century France controlled its colonies in West Africa with a firm hand, although a policy of 'assimilation' allowed Africans to become French citizens if they virtually abandoned their African identity. Britain was slightly more liberal in its approach towards its colonies, although there was no equivalent assimilation policy, while Portugal ruled its empire in Africa with a rod of iron.

Independence

After WWII, a rising tide of nationalism developed in the colonies, with increasingly loud cries for independence. Although these were at first fiercely resisted by France and (to a lesser extent) Britain, the colonial rulers eventually capitulated. In 1957 Ghana became the first country in West Africa to gain independence, followed by Guinea in 1958. In 1960 independence was granted to Benin, Côte d'Ivoire, Nigeria, Togo, Senegal and several other countries. Most other countries in the region became independent in the following few years, ending in 1965 with Gambia.

Once again, the former powers had different approaches to the new independent states: France encouraged its former colonies to remain closely tied in a trade-based 'community', and most did (Guinea was a notable exception). Britain reduced its power and influence in the region, while Portugal grimly hung on to its colonies for another decade or more. France maintained battalions of its own army in several former colonies, while Britain's provision of military assistance was more behind the scenes.

During the rest of the 1960s and into the 1970s, optimism started to fade. Colonialism had created fragile economies based on cash crops prone to huge price fluctuations, and ethnic tensions were created by artificial boundaries and divide-and-rule policies. Border disputes, separatist uprisings and civil wars became common events, and continued into the 1980s. Elected leaders were unable or unwilling to combat their nation's economic and social problems, and military takeovers and coups d'état became more frequent. Corruption, embezzlement and mismanagement by presidents and other politicians also became common problems in West Africa, and life for ordinary people became increasingly difficult.

During the Cold War period, anticommunist dictators were propped up with finance and arms from the West (with the backing of transnational corporations that stood to gain from the region's raw materials), while leaders who declared themselves Marxist were similarly supported by the Soviet bloc. Rebels, separatists and opposition figures often found it easy to get backing from whichever side was not behind that country's leader, and for many years Africa (along with other parts of the developing world) became the superpowers' battleground and the site of many unpleasant 'dirty wars', all too easily forgotten today.

The 1990s and the end of the east–west split led to dramatic changes throughout West Africa as the popular demand for democracy gained strength and multiparty elections were held in several countries (see Government & Politics later in this chapter, and in the individual country chapters). However, these developments were overshadowed by the resumption of brutal rebel warfare in Sierra Leone, resulting in murders, maimings and thousands of refugees and internally displaced people. (See History in the Sierra Leone chapter for more details.)

Now, in the early years of the new millennium, West Africa's future remains as enigmatic as ever. While there are several bright spots where democracy seems to have taken root (Ghana, for example), there are just as many places where multiparty politics exists in name only, and where corrupt and dictatorial regimes continue to squander national resources. What is clear from West Africa's long history is that there will be no fast changes, and that anything positive and lasting will come from within. Nonetheless, this is no excuse for the former colonial powers and other Western nations to sit by without recognising the stakes and acknowledging their debts to the region.

GEOGRAPHY

West Africa can be divided into three geographical areas that form horizontal bands across the region: a northern band of desert, a southern band of woodland and forest, and a semidesert zone in between known as the Sahel (see the boxed text 'The Sahel', later).

West Africa has few mountains. Much of the region is flat or gently undulating plateau, broken by a few highland areas. These include the range along the border between Nigeria and Cameroon (the highest point, Chappal Wadi, is 2418m); the Jos Plateau and Shebsi Mountains in Nigeria; the hills around Mt Bintumani (1945m) in Sierra Leone; the rocky Aïr Massif in Niger; the hill country around Mt Nimba (1752m), in the border area between Guinea, Côte d'Ivoire and Liberia; and the hills of the Fouta Djalon in western Guinea, which extend into southeastern Senegal. The peaks of the volcanic Cape Verde islands are also notable: the highest is Mt Fogo (2839m). Mt Cameroon (4095m), in the country of the same name, is the highest point in West Africa.

Although West Africa's highland areas are limited, they create headwaters for several rivers. The largest river in the region is the Niger River, which rises in the Fouta Djalon highlands of Guinea and flows in a great curve (known as the Niger Bend or Boucle du Niger) through Mali northeast to Mopti, where it spreads out to form a maze of swamps and channels called the Niger Inland Delta. The top of the bend touches the edge of the Sahara near Timbuktu, and the river then flows southeast through Niger and Nigeria to enter the Atlantic at the vast Niger Delta west of Port Harcourt.

Other major rivers of the region include the Senegal River, in the north of the country of the same name, which forms the border with Mauritania; the Gambia River, again giving its name to the country it flows through; the Casamance River in southern Senegal; the Volta River in Ghana and Burkina Faso; and the Benue River (a major tributary of the Niger) in Nigeria and Cameroon.

While some of West Africa's boundaries may be loosely defined, the region's irrefutable western and southern limit is the Atlantic Ocean. Many major cities – Dakar, Banjul, Bissau, Conakry, Freetown, Monrovia, Abidjan, Accra, Lomé, Cotonou, Porto Novo, Lagos and Douala – are strung along the coast like beads in a chain, in some areas forming an almost constant linear urban sprawl, cut only by national frontiers.

CLIMATE

In the northern parts of West Africa temperature patterns are hot from April to September, and cool (or not so hot) in the winter from October to March, although places on the coast (eg, Nouakchott in Mauritania) will be relatively cooler than those deep in the interior (eg, Gao in Mali).

The Sahel

The Sahel is the part of West Africa between the Sahara desert in the north and the forested zone of the south – a vast horizontal band stretching from the Atlantic coast into the countries of Chad and Sudan. The Sahel is usually described simply as 'semidesert'. However, within its boundaries are many different subregions. In the north, near the true desert, the Sahel is dry and sparsely vegetated; in the south, nearer the forests, the Sahel gets more rainfall and contains areas of light woodland. Additional factors such as mountains and rivers can also influence the vegetation pattern within the Sahel. Other definitions used for this area include semidesert savanna, Guinea savanna, Sudanese savanna, dry savanna or dry woodland savanna.

The countries covered in this book that are considered to be all or partly in the Sahel are Senegal, Gambia, Guinea, Mali, Burkina Faso, Niger and Nigeria. However, the boundaries are not fixed, and much of northern Mali and Niger is true desert, while southern Nigeria and southeastern Guinea are in the forest zone. (It's also important to note that the 'forest zone' term is used in areas where the *natural* vegetation is forest, despite the fact that much of this area has been cleared for farmland.) In the same way, the northern parts of the coastal countries of Côte d'Ivoire, Ghana, Togo, Benin and Cameroon are relatively dry, and so are sometimes described as having a Sahelian climate or vegetation.

The term 'Sahel' (or 'Sahelian') is also used to describe characteristic aspects of the region. For example, 'Sahelian architecture' refers to the mud-brick and render style used to such stunning effect on the great mosques found in Mali and Niger. In the same way, you'll come across 'Sahelian music' or 'Sahelian food'.

In the southern parts of the region temperatures are high from October to February, at their peak from March to May, then lower from May to September, although, again, much depends on the distance from the ocean.

While minimum temperatures are fairly constant throughout the year in the coastal countries, in the northern parts of West Africa minimums are much lower in January than they are in May or August. Deep in the desert, water bags have been known to freeze briefly on winter nights.

The West African climate is dominated more by rainfall than by temperature, and the dry and wet seasons are among the most important climatic factors to consider when planning your trip. Generally, the dry season in the southern coastal countries is November to April, while in the Sahel countries it's October to May. The rainy season in the coastal countries is May to October. The wettest areas are Guinea, Sierra Leone and Liberia, where annual rainfall often exceeds 4000mm. In the Sahel countries, the rainy season is from June to September. In all areas, rainy periods get shorter, and rainfall levels decrease, as you move further north and away from the ocean. Humidity is another important climatic factor. Most people find dry heat, such as that found in the Sahel, easier to handle than the wet heat of the coast.

For specific details, see the climate charts in the country chapters.

ECOLOGY & ENVIRONMENT

Major environmental issues in West Africa include deforestation, soil erosion, air and water degradation, uncontrolled logging, urban encroachment and habitat and wildlife destruction.

Deforestation is one of the most visible environmental problems, with West Africa's remaining forest areas representing only a fraction of the original forest cover. Some forest area is lost to increased population growth and a corresponding increase in the clearing of natural forest for farmland. Bushfires are started by local farmers to promote new growth for livestock, to control pests such as the tsetse fly and to flush out wild animals, which can then be hunted. On a larger and more significant scale, rainforests in some countries are being commercially logged, frequently with no effective regulation. Potential earnings in lucrative global timber markets do much to encourage the tolerance of destructive logging practices.

The Harmattan

Harmattan (from a Hausa word meaning 'north wind') refers to the cool, dry winds that originate in the Sahara and blow throughout much of West Africa during the November to March dry season. The winds gain force from about mid-December onwards, and bring with them dust from the Sahara. Even when the wind stops blowing, conditions remain hazy until the first May rains. It is no problem at all to travel during this period – in fact, in many countries in the region, the months from November to January are considered to be the best for travel. However, on bad days, visibility can be reduced to around 1km, which may result in aircraft delays, and photographers can expect 'overcast' pictures.

The results of deforestation can be devastating. Many bird and animal species lose vital habitats, and local human populations lose their lifeblood. Soil erosion, the eventual reduction of cultivable areas, reduced water catchment areas, and decreased availability of traditional building materials, foodstuffs and medicines are among the many other negative effects.

Fortunately, deforestation – along with other environmental issues in West Africa – has gained increasing international attention. In Cameroon, for example, a new national park was recently declared, therefore protecting an important rainforest area. In Liberia – home to about 40% of the last remaining 'Upper Guinean' rainforest that originally stretched from Sierra Leone eastward to Ghana – several international environmental organisations have pledged resources to help improve forestry and environmental management, with particular focus on the forest areas protected by Sapo National Park.

Also, throughout the region the lesson has come to the forefront that sustainable protection and conservation of West Africa's forests will only come when local people are involved, and not separated from their traditional sources of livelihood. In several forestry projects in Gambia and Ghana, for example, natural woodland areas are not simply fenced off, but rather used in a sustainable way for the benefit of local communities, with the emphasis on sustainable resource management. Dead wood can be used for timber, fruits and edible leaves can be collected, and grasses can be harvested for thatch. These products can be used or sold, but all activities take place without destroying the growing trees. In this way, local people view the forest as a source of produce, income or employment, and have a real incentive to protect it in the long term.

Community-Based Conservation

These projects are just a few examples of how environmental schemes can never really be successful without the willing inclusion of local people. 'Community-based conservation' is now a critical concept, as organisations recognise the importance of including local inhabitants in environmental planning. The sometimes altruistic environmental sentiments often expressed in the West (that forests or other natural areas should be conserved simply because they look nice) is a luxury that the people of Africa can ill afford.

For many years, conservationists regarded human populations as a negative factor, and in many instances local inhabitants were excluded from national parks or other protected wildlife areas because it was assumed that they damaged natural resources. But now it has been realised that if there are tangible benefits for local inhabitants (such as increased income from tourists who come to visit wilderness areas), then natural environments have a much better chance of evading complete destruction.

Global Links

In discussions of environmental issues in West Africa and elsewhere on the continent, there is often a tendency to emphasise local factors contributing to these problems (eg, wood-burning creates deforestation; overgrazing causes soil erosion) while ignoring the bigger picture. It's important to keep things in perspective – to look also into our own backyards, and to remember the links between environmental issues and both national and global economic and political situations.

An example of the connection between regional environmental conservation efforts and global politics is seen in the ongoing discussion of poverty alleviation. Many international bodies favour alleviating poverty through large-scale economic development initiated by loans, on the assumption that this will eventually provide income for citizens. However, such economic development often brings with it severe environmental damage; heavy industry creates air and water pollution, and inevitably requires the use of natural resources. Large-scale farming also causes pollution and soil erosion, and frequently leads to the displacement of people from their land. This results in increased poverty levels, a drift towards urban centres, disintegration of communities and traditional values, and further environmental degradation in rural areas. Furthermore, if the West is any example, the success of large-scale economic development would arguably worsen the overall picture by putting excessive pressure on the world's resources.

Currently, the developed world uses a far greater proportion of the earth's resources than the developing world, and does so at an unsustainable rate. An urban citizen of Britain, Australia or the USA, for example, consumes more than 50 times more of the earth's resources than a rural inhabitant of Niger or Guinea-Bissau. If the 'poor' countries 'caught up' with the 'rich' countries, it is easy to imagine the pressure placed on the earth's resources. Thus, while focusing on the one hand on assisting economic development in Africa, it is just as critical that efforts be made to reduce Western consumption, and to ensure that resources on all sides are used sustainably.

FLORA & FAUNA

Vegetation

The vegetation zones of West Africa are linear, and correspond to the three main bands outlined under Geography earlier in this chapter.

Forest & Woodland Much of the coastal area is situated between 5° and 10° north of the equator, where rainfall is heavy. The natural vegetation created by this climate is dense rain-fed lowland forest (or just 'rainforest') where trees can reach heights of 45m. The upper branches form a continuous canopy, often blocking light from the forest floor, which hinders growth of smaller plants, although vines and other epiphytes flourish. In woodland areas the trees tend to be lower and more spread out so that their upper branches do not form a continuous canopy, which allows other plants to grow in between.

Because vast areas of this natural vegetation have been cleared for logging and agriculture, very little of the original West African forest remains, except in parts of Liberia, Sierra Leone, southwestern Côte d'Ivoire and southern and eastern Cameroon. Smaller areas of woodland exist in several

The Baobab Tree: A Symbol of Africa

Along with the flat-topped acacia, the baobab tree *(Adansonia digitata)* is an instantly recognisable symbol of Africa. Its thick, sturdy trunk and stunted root-like branches are featured on countless postcards and brochures. Baobabs grow in most parts of West Africa, and in many other areas of the continent, usually in savanna zones where rainfall is limited. Many cultures have their own version of a story that involves the tree displeasing a deity who plucked it in anger and thrust it back into the ground upside down – hence the root-like branches.

Despite the misdemeanours of its ancestor, today's baobab is held in high regard by local people. Its wizened appearance, combined with an ability to survive great droughts and live for many hundreds of years, means the baobab is often revered and believed to have magical powers. Old trees often develop cavities, which are sometimes used to inter a revered griot (praise singer). Smaller holes are used by birds and animals.

The baobab also has many practical uses. The hollow trunk sometimes holds rainwater, making it a useful reservoir in times of drought. The tree's large pods (sometimes called 'monkey bread') contain seeds encased in a sherbet-like substance that can be eaten or made into a drink. The pods themselves are used to make cups or bowls (often for drinking palm wine), and any not suitable for this purpose are used as fuel. They burn slowly and are especially good for smoking fish. The leaves of the baobab can be eaten when chopped, boiled and made into a sauce; they can also be dried and ground into a paste to use as a poultice for skin infections and joint complaints. Even the flowers are used, for decoration at ceremonies.

countries, including Benin, Ghana, Guinea, Nigeria and Togo.

Savanna & Semidesert In the northern parts of the coastal countries the climate is drier. The forest and woodland give way to a vegetation zone defined as 'savanna and semidesert'. Here, the landscape consists primarily of well-dispersed trees, the most common being various species of acacia, and low scrub bush, although ribbons of dense gallery forest occur along river courses. Gallery forest is similar to rainforest but is fed by ground water rather than rain, so many of the vines characteristic of rainforest are absent. This zone is usually called the Sahel, and covers most of Senegal, southern Mali, southern Niger, Burkina Faso and northern Nigeria.

Desert North of the Sahel is the true desert, where rainfall and vegetation growth is minimal. Of the countries in this book, the desert covers northern Mali and Niger, plus most of Mauritania.

Mammals

Although West Africa takes a distant second to East and Southern Africa when it comes to wildlife viewing, it is still home to an impressive variety of animals. The region's national parks and wildlife reserves contain most of the classic African mammal species, including elephants, lions and leopards – although these are rarely seen. There are also significant wildlife populations, including elephants, in rainforest areas, although animals are generally hidden by the dense vegetation. Buffaloes also exist in West Africa, but are the forest type – smaller and redder than the East African version. Observing larger mammals is not always straightforward because of the dense vegetation and the animals' skittishness. Also, poaching has considerably reduced populations in the region over the past several decades.

Mammals more readily seen include several beautiful antelope species, such as bushbucks, reedbucks, waterbucks, kobs, roans, elands, oribis, sitatungas and various gazelles and duikers. The Sahel-dwelling dama gazelle is the largest gazelle species in Africa, but this animal is now close to extinction as its grazing lands have been taken over by cattle and reduced by desertification. Wild pig species include giant hogs and bush pigs (the West African species is browner than those in East Africa and is often called the red river hog), which inhabit forest areas, and warthogs, frequently seen in drier savanna areas.

Possibly the best-known and most easily observed mammals of West Africa are monkeys. These include several types of colobus and green or vervet monkeys. Other primates include mangabeys, baboons, galagos (bushbabies), as well as chimpanzees and the rare and endangered drill.

In the rivers, including the upper reaches of the Niger and Gambia Rivers, hippos can sometimes be seen, but hunting and the restriction of natural grazing grounds mean that their numbers are low. Some hippos have adapted to live in salt water and exist in coastal areas; a few forest areas of West Africa, including in Liberia, are home to very small populations of pygmy hippos, which are less aquatic than their larger cousins.

Other marine mammals found in the region include dolphins, especially where the region's main rivers meet the ocean, and manatees (sea cows) – giant seal-like relatives of the elephant that inhabit mangrove and delta areas along the coast.

Birds

West Africa is renowned for its birdlife, with more than 1000 species recorded to date. Many are endemic, while others are passage migrants that fly down the Atlantic coast to and from their wintering grounds.

Wild Wildlife

West Africa's wildlife is just that – wild. Respect the powers of nature, and keep a healthy distance between you and any elephant, lion, rhino or other wild animal that you may be lucky enough to encounter. Never get between a mother and her calves or cubs, and if you want good photos, invest in a telephoto lens instead of approaching an animal at close range. On safaris, heed the advice of your guide, and respect park regulations, especially those that require you to stay in a vehicle. Exercise care when boating or swimming (which shouldn't be done in most African wilderness areas anyway), and be particularly aware of the dangers posed by crocodiles and hippos.

Still others are nomads that fly from one part of Africa to another, taking advantage of seasonal plenty before moving on. Among those you're likely to see are flamingos, storks and pelicans around waterways; beautiful gannets and fish-eating cormorants in coastal areas; turacos, including the striking violet turaco; and African grey and red-billed hornbills. For tips on some good bird-watching areas, see the boxed text 'Where to Look for West Africa's Birds', below.

Reptiles & Amphibians

West Africa's most notable reptile is the Nile crocodile, which was once abundant all over

Where to Look for West Africa's Birds

You'll encounter birds almost everywhere in your travels, although weather and temperature can affect the numbers you will see. Good places to concentrate your efforts are parks and reserves set up to protect wildlife and wildlife habitats. A few countries also have reserves specifically for birds.

One of West Africa's best bird-watching destinations is tiny **Gambia**, with more than 560 species recorded and several easily accessed bird-watching sites. Abuko Nature Reserve is closest to the capital (Banjul) and hosts a surprising diversity of birds, especially of forest species. Tanji Bird Reserve, on the Atlantic coast, protects a patchwork of habitat on the flyway for migrating birds. Although it covers only 600 hectares, close to 300 species have been recorded here. Kiang West National Park, one of the country's largest protected areas, is also a good place for birding (see also Birds under Flora & Fauna in The Gambia chapter).

Senegal also offers some excellent birding, particularly in the Parc National de la Langue de Barbarie and Parc National aux Oiseaux du Djoudj. Both are famous for vast pelican and flamingo flocks, and Djoudj is a Unesco world heritage site, where almost 400 bird species have been recorded. In Parc National du Niokolo-Koba, also a world heritage site, about 350 bird species have been recorded. There are several other good sites in the northern Casamance near Kafountine (see Bird-Watching under Kafountine in the Senegal chapter).

The rainforests of **Côte d'Ivoire's** Parc National d'Assagny are home to a large variety of birds, and in Parc National de la Marahoué, nearly 300 species have been recorded. Parc National de la Comoë also supports an abundance of birds.

Mali is often underestimated for bird-watching, but has some good sites. See the boxed text 'Mali's Birds' under Flora & Fauna in the Mali chapter.

In **Burkina Faso**, Ranch de Nazinga and Lake Tengréla are both worth a look.

In **Ghana**, Kakum Nature Park and Owabi Wildlife Sanctuary both host diverse birdlife, as does the coastal wetlands around the Volta estuary. In Mole National Park more than 300 species have been recorded.

Public access to **Mauritania's** remote Parc National du Banc d'Arguin may be restricted during the breeding season, but it is one of the best sanctuaries in West Africa, and a crossroads for birds migrating between Europe and Southern Africa. See Parc National du Banc d'Arguin in the Mauritania chapter for more details.

It's unlikely you'll be able to reach **Sierra Leone's** Tiwai Island Wildlife Sanctuary until the country's political situation settles down. However, before the fighting, more than 120 bird species had been identified there, including hornbills, kingfishers and the rare white-breasted guinea fowl. Around Mt Bintumani, to the north, the endangered rufous fishing-owl has been sighted, while various habitats in Outamba-Kilimi National Park have traditionally supported many species, including kingfishers, hornbills, herons, hawks and the spectacular great blue turaco.

Nigeria offers some fine birding: Yankari National Park has a stunning array of about 600 species. Other good places to start include Kamuku Wildlife Reserve west of Kaduna and the Hadejia-Nguru Wetlands, which is about 200km northeast of Kano and is an important resting place for migratory birds and endemic species.

In **Cameroon**, rewarding birding destinations include Mt Cameroon, which has several endemics, and the lushly vegetated Korup National Park, which has more than 300 species.

David Andrew

the region. These days its numbers have been drastically reduced by hunting and habitat destruction, and few remain, although you may see them along the larger rivers such as the Gambia, Senegal and Niger. Two lesser-known species, the dwarf crocodile and slender-nosed crocodile, also occur. In several countries, including Mali and Côte d'Ivoire, crocodiles are regarded as sacred.

Along the coast of West Africa, and on some of the offshore islands, turtles can be seen. The females come to the beaches to lay eggs in the sand, sometimes laying several hundred at a time, but the species is in decline, as nesting areas are damaged or inhabited by humans. Additionally, adults are hunted or suffer from the effects of water pollution – specifically from floating plastic bags, which they mistake for food and try to eat.

Other reptiles to watch out for – but which shouldn't inspire paranoia – are snakes. West Africa has a complement of both venomous and harmless snakes, but most fear humans and you'd be 'lucky' to even see one. The largest snake is the nonvenomous python, which grows to more than 5m in length. It kills by coiling around and suffocating its prey, although fortunately it doesn't usually fancy humans. The venomous puff adder reaches about 1m in length and, like all reptiles, enjoys sunning itself. It isn't aggressive but, being very slow, it is sometimes stepped on by unwary people before it has had time to wake up and move out of the way. When stepped on, it bites. Take care when hiking in bush areas, especially in the early morning when this snake is at its most lethargic; high boots and trousers are good protection.

Lizards are ubiquitous in West Africa from the desert to the rainforest, and from the bathroom ceiling to the kitchen sink. The largest of these is the monitor (often up to 2m in length), which spends a lot of time lying around rivers and water holes, perhaps dreaming of being a crocodile. You're more likely to see agama – lizards about 20cm long with purple bodies and orange heads, energetically doing press-ups on walls and boulders. And in any house or small hotel you'll inevitably see geckos running around on the walls or hiding behind pictures, with their sucker-like feet and near-transparent skin. They can appear alarming, but you'll soon get used to these harmless creatures – they help to keep the flies away too.

Other insect-eaters include frogs, which inhabit riverside reeds and mangroves, and toads, which are happier out of water than their froggy relatives.

Insects

The forest areas of West Africa are particularly rich in insect life, and the list of species is mind-boggling (many more are yet to be recorded). Entomologists will have their own agendas but the casual traveller won't fail to notice huge centipedes and millipedes, colourful spiders and columns of viciously biting safari ants. You may not see termites, but you can't fail to see termite mounds: solid towers of soil and sand up to 3m high where each grain has been painstakingly glued together with the termites' adhesive saliva. The forests are also particularly rich in butterflies.

Other than malaria-carrying mosquitoes, insects to be wary of include scorpions, which often hide under stones or logs and can sting if disturbed or threatened. They can also crawl into shoes or under sleeping bags during the night, so give everything a shake if you're sleeping in the bush.

National Parks

For many travellers, the main problem in West Africa isn't the lack of animals – it's the lack of easy access to national parks where animals can be seen. Many parks are in remote areas where access by public transport is not always possible, and walking in the park itself is usually forbidden. Walking safaris, as found in East and Southern Africa, are virtually unknown in West Africa.

Having said that, several parks can be visited on a locally organised tour, or simply by hiring a taxi. Details are given in the individual country chapters.

Generally, national parks do not receive many visitors, and tourist facilities are limited or nonexistent. For some people, this is an attraction – they find it more satisfying to stalk and observe the animals rather than jostle for space with other visitors.

Some parks are open year-round, but many are open only in the dry season from November to the end of May. In December, some park tracks may still be waterlogged, and dense vegetation makes spotting animals difficult. Later in the year, animals are easier to see as the ground cover withers, but the parks get hot and dusty. Just before the rains break is an excellent time for viewing, but conditions can be uncomfortably hot. Whenever you visit, bring along a pair of binoculars.

GOVERNMENT & POLITICS

The end of the Cold War had a profound impact on African political systems. Previously, dictators argued that democracy wasn't necessarily the best system for Africa. In truth, this was a facade for tyranny, but as long as a dictator remained loyal to either the West or the Eastern bloc, they were supplied with arms and bilateral 'aid' money to prevent any chance of a switch to the other side. The fact that the dictators squandered the money, raped their countries and brutally oppressed their subjects was conveniently overlooked.

Towards the end of the 1980s and into the 1990s, as the people of Eastern Europe threw out their dictators, Africans began looking at their own leaders and wondering what right they had to stay in power for so long without periodic public approval. At the same time, support to Africa from the Soviet bloc dwindled, so the Western nations had less need to prop up their own allies. Suddenly, the dictators' positions started to look decidedly shaky as pro-democracy and multiparty movements sprang up in many parts of Africa.

These moves towards democracy were supported by the USA, through the World Bank, and by the French, with both countries demanding further political reform in return for financial assistance. Critics hold that the sudden interest in African democracy, although more laudable than the old-style support for dictators, is based firmly on economic motives – a stable country makes more money – rather than on a desire for basic freedoms or human rights.

One of West Africa's most autocratic governments was in Benin, but at a major political gathering in 1990, delegates demanded and received long-time president Mathieu Kérékou's resignation (although he retained control of the army), along with a new constitution and the promise of free, multiparty elections. A new government was elected in 1991, but became increasingly autocratic, and four years later Kérékou was voted back into power. Although many observers remain sceptical – particularly in the wake of the disputed 2001 elections – events of the past decade are nevertheless generally seen as progress towards establishment of a democratic system.

Similar events occurred in Mali during 1991, when President Moussa Traoré (in power since 1968) was ousted. The new leadership is now supporting a multiparty system and open elections.

In Ghana, Jerry Rawlings, who thrust his way to power by army coup, twice had his legitimacy confirmed by elections acknowledged as free and fair. In late 2000, to the surprise of everyone, Rawlings stepped down, and opposition party leader John Kufuor was elected to the presidency in a peaceful polling.

And yet the overall picture remains far from rosy. In Niger, although there has been an impressively smooth transition from military to democratic rule, the foundation is still fragile and many observers remain only cautiously optimistic. And even in apparently stable countries, coups are still a real possibility, as illustrated by Gambia's 1994 military takeover, the coup in Guinea-Bissau in 1998, and recent events in Côte d'Ivoire, once viewed as a model of stability in the region. Less dramatic but just as much of a dark spot are those countries where multiparty politics exists, but in name only, with all power effectively in the hands of the ruling party. A good example is Cameroon, where President Paul Biya has clung to power since 1982 through a combination of political shrewdness, repression of opposition and arbitrary suspensions of the constitution. Genuine democracy is still far from being guaranteed across the region.

ECONOMY

Facts & Figures

Several West African countries – including Guinea-Bissau, Cape Verde, Mali and Benin – have recorded impressive, positive GNP growth rates in recent years. Despite this and several other bright spots in the picture, and despite the region's great natural wealth, local economies are weak, and West Africans have among the lowest per-capita income levels in the world.

According to recent per-capita GNP statistics from the World Bank, Sierra Leone – the poorest West African country – is also the poorest country in the world, with a per-capita GNP of US$130. Burkina Faso, Guinea-Bissau, Liberia, Mali and Niger all have per-capita GNPs of US$250 or less, putting them among the poorest 10 countries in the world. Even oil-rich Nigeria has just US$260, while most other West African countries, including Benin, Gambia, Ghana and Mauritania, have between US$300 and US$500. The high rollers are Cameroon, Senegal and Côte d'Ivoire, which all have between US$500 and US$700, and Cape Verde, which has around US$930. In contrast, most Western industrialised nations have per-capita GNPs of US$20,000 to US$30,000 and more. In crude terms, the average Western citizen is up to 100 times richer than their West African counterpart.

The per-capita GNP figure is admittedly a blunt instrument, as it is concerned only with economic values. Because of this, the United Nations devised the Human Development Index (HDI), which measures the overall achievements of a country according to factors such as life expectancy and education standards, as well as income. However, even when examined in light of these criteria, the picture is similarly grim, with Sierra Leone still coming out at the bottom, and Niger ranking 161st out of 162 countries surveyed, closely followed by Burkina Faso at 159 and Mali at 153. Most other countries in West Africa are also ranked low, with Senegal at 145, Côte d'Ivoire at 144, Mauritania at 139, Nigeria at 136, Cameroon at 125 and Ghana at 119; Cape Verde is the highest, at 91. Liberia does not appear on these rankings because of lack of data.

In human terms, these figures indicate how daily life is an economic struggle for most inhabitants of the region. Life expectancy is around 50 years in many parts of West Africa and is even lower in some countries (38 years in Sierra Leone and 44 years in Guinea-Bissau and Niger). Between 100 and 200 children in every 1000 die before the age of five, although annual population growth rates are around 3% – among the highest in the world. Unemployment and underemployment are also very high. Because people have insufficient money to buy food and can only grow cereal crops, nutritional intakes are low. As a result, a large proportion of the population, especially children, is susceptible to disease, yet there are few medical services.

International Debt

On the macroeconomic level, one of the main factors affecting this situation is international debt, which for much of the past decade has suffocated many West African economies. The current crisis began in the 1970s when the rise in oil prices led to an increase in commercial lending, often with little concern for safeguards or collateral. At the same time, Western governments and international bodies such as the World Bank and the IMF encouraged developing countries to take on loans. In some cases, loans were components of so-called development projects. Many were linked to the production of cash crops or minerals for export, or for sales of imported goods (such as armaments), from which the lending countries would benefit. Although there were undoubtedly improvements in some areas, particularly in infrastructure, much of the money was wasted – spent by dictators on their military, presidential palaces and other impressive buildings, inefficient nationalised industries or grandiose schemes such as dams and motorways. Billions of dollars were also simply embezzled, and little, if any, reached ordinary people in the form of lasting social and other benefits.

Meanwhile, prices for commodities (such as cotton grown in Mali or groundnuts in Senegal) dropped. As the countries of West Africa earned less from their exports, it became increasingly difficult for them to meet interest payments. Increases in the cost of importing Western manufactured goods created severe trade imbalances.

The Debt Crisis

The situation peaked in the early 1980s, when the term 'debt crisis' was coined. It was a crisis for the West African nations and other developing countries who could no longer afford to pay interest, but even more of a crisis for the major banks who stood to lose their money.

To avert an impending crash, several Western governments bailed out the banks, while the IMF and other lenders introduced 'structural adjustment' or restrictions on the spending allowed by the debtor countries. In West Africa, this may have helped to control corruption and inefficiency, but for ordinary people things got worse – their wages went down, the price of food went up and services such as schools and hospitals were cut. Opponents of the World Bank, the IMF and other large development organisations pointed out that, quite apart from human and environmental costs, loans were failing on the economic front too, with most countries worse off economically in the 1990s than they were at independence. Because so much money was being required to service the debt (ie, pay off the interest, rather than the loan itself), less money was available to spend on useful things such as schools and hospitals. While government corruption and inefficiency undoubtedly exacerbated the situation, the greater concern was the amount of money being absorbed by the outstanding debts.

The Solution?

During the 1990s, there were increasingly loud calls from various charitable, human rights, church and welfare organisations for Western banks and lender nations to write off the loans to developing countries. They made the argument that the lender nations were never going to get the original money back anyway, and that annual interest repayments were only stifling poor nations' economies and harming the populations. Furthermore, in many cases, the interest paid by the debtor countries over the years exceeded the amount of the original debt. To put the figures into perspective, one UN statistic noted that provision of universal access to basic social services, and the alleviation of income poverty would cost roughly US$80 billion – less than the combined net worth of the world's seven richest people.

Thanks to this increased attention, relief finally began to come, although only in small trickles. The IMF and World Bank launched an initiative focused on debt reduction for designated Heavily Indebted Poor Countries (HIPC), including many in West Africa. However, much of this debt relief is tied to adoption of World Bank and IMF conditions that are widely viewed as unduly restrictive, or that in the end leave the indebted country about where it was prior to the debt relief. Also, while a few Western nations have agreed to write off some loans, others remain resolute that the money must be repaid.

From a travellers' perspective, informing yourself of the issues is a critical first step. When you are travelling independently in West Africa, you will probably gain many insights into daily life in the region on the microeconomic level. You'll also gain a greater understanding of the often rampant corruption, at the expense of the citizens, in some of the countries in which you travel. Armed with this knowledge, you can then examine the actions of your government and institutions back home from a more critical and informed perspective. The next step is moving towards involvement in some sort of real and lasting solution to West Africa's debt crisis and to improvement of its fragile economic situation. Although it is easy to look at some of the numbers and get discouraged, it's worth keeping in mind that West Africa, like Africa as a whole, is not an area of cohesion, mass movements or sweeping generalities. Its history is one of hundreds of independent tribal groups, dozens of different states, different languages, different traditions. Just as historical change in the region prior to colonial involvement happened step by step and group by group, so too will economic change. The biggest successes you're likely to see while in West Africa – even if you stay for a longer period – are within one small village, or in one relatively limited region. But these, taken together, will ultimately work to affect the big picture. Hopefully sooner rather than later, if we all play our part and share the responsibility, this shocking situation will improve.

EDUCATION

Generally speaking, all the countries in West Africa have state educational systems that follow patterns established by their colonial powers, with primary, secondary and tertiary stages. In Islamic countries, Koranic schools operate in parallel to the state educational system.

In most countries primary education is theoretically available for all children, whereas only those who pass relevant examinations can go to secondary school and university. In reality, which children go to school and how far up the ladder they progress is determined by their family income rather than by academic performance:

Female Genital Mutilation in West Africa

Female genital mutilation (FGM), often euphemistically termed 'female circumcision' or 'genital alteration', is widespread throughout West Africa. The term covers a wide range of procedures, from a small, mainly symbolic, cut, to the total removal of the external genitalia (known as infibulation). In West Africa, the procedure usually involves removal of the entire clitoris. The World Health Organisation's estimates range from about 30% to 59% of women altered in Côte d'Ivoire to about 90% of women altered in Sierra Leone.

Although outsiders often believe that FGM is associated with Islam, in fact it predates the religion (there are historical records of infibulation dating back 6000 years). The procedure is usually performed by midwives on girls and young women. They sometimes use modern surgical instruments but usually it's done with a razor blade or a piece of glass. If the procedure is done in a traditional setting the girl will not be anaesthetised, although nowadays many families take their daughters to clinics to have the procedure performed by a trained doctor. Complications, especially in the traditional setting, include infection of the wound, leading to death, or scarring which makes childbirth and urination difficult.

In West Africa, genital alteration is seen as important for maintaining traditional society. An unaltered woman would dishonour her family and lower its position in society, as well as ruining her own chances for marriage – an altered woman is thought to be a moral woman, and more likely a virgin. Many believe that if left, the clitoris can make a woman infertile or damage, even kill, her unborn children.

Although FGM is deeply ingrained in West African societies, there are moves to make it illegal. Five countries have banned the procedure, although there are doubts about how well this is working. Practitioners are afraid of being arrested, but find it hard to go against tradition. In other countries, women's groups are trying to raise awareness about the dangers.

some children may not be able to afford school fees or extra items such as uniforms and books (especially if they want to go beyond primary school). Also, children from poor families may be kept away from school to work in the fields or to provide income from other employment.

Across the region, these problems are compounded by restrictions on the government revenue available for education. Although many West African countries spend a relatively high proportion of public cash on education (higher, in percentage terms, than some Western countries) the actual amount per child is still very low.

The end result is simply not enough schools to cater for everyone. The distribution of schools is also a problem, especially in rural areas. Many schools have to operate two 'shifts', with one lot of children coming in the morning and another in the afternoon. Even so, classes may hold more than 100 pupils, sitting three or four to a desk and sharing books and pens. At the same time, teachers are grossly underpaid and often undertrained, and many become understandably demoralised, causing standards to slip.

In most cases, fewer than 25% of West African children receive a secondary education, and the rates are much lower in some countries (eg, 7% in Niger and 14% in Guinea), according to World Bank statistics. As a result, literacy rates across West Africa are low – ranging from a high of about 75% in Cameroon to a low of 15% in Niger, with most countries in the region falling between about 35% and 45% (according to UNDP statistics).

ARTS

West Africa has a rich artistic heritage and tradition, including sculpture (in wood, bronze and other materials), masks, striking textiles, jewellery, basketwork and leatherwork. See the special section 'Arts & Craftwork', as well as the Arts headings in the individual country chapters, for a guide to the diversity of styles and techniques that you will find in the region.

The Books section in the Regional Facts for the Visitor chapter lists some recommendations for further reading on West African arts. When you are on the road, visiting museums can further enrich your understanding.

Literature

West Africa has a rich heritage of traditional storytelling, and modern-day writers are no less prolific. Listed here is a brief selection of classic works by African authors of international renown. All are pan-African, or universal, in their scope, and all are highly recommended, wherever you travel in the region. Many of these titles are published as part of the Heinemann African Writers series. For more titles by regional authors see the individual country chapters; for books about West Africa, see Books in the Regional Facts for the Visitor chapter.

For a good introduction to the literature of the region, the most useful anthology is the *Traveller's Literary Companion – Africa* edited by Oona Strathern, which contains more than 250 prose and poetry extracts from all over Africa, and has an introduction to the literature of each country, plus a list of 'literary landmarks' – features that appear in novels written about the country. Poetry anthologies include *The Heinemann Book of African Poetry in English* edited by Adewale Maja-Pearce, and *The Penguin Book of Modern African Poetry* edited by Moore and Beier.

West African literature is dominated by Nigerian writers. These include Wole Soyinka, who won the Nobel Prize for Literature in 1986 – the first author from Africa to achieve this accolade. His most well-known works include the plays *A Dance of the Forest*, *The Man Died*, *Opera Wonyosi* and *A Play of Giants*. He has also written poetry (including *Idane & Other Poems*), novels (including *The Interpreters*), and the fantastical childhood memoir *Ake*. Soyinka's works are noted as expressions of his social vision and strong beliefs, and are praised for their complex writing style.

Amos Tutuola is another Nigerian writer; his *The Palm-Wine Drinkard* was published in the early 1950s. This work is often regarded as the first great African novel, a link between traditional storytelling and the modern novel. Dylan Thomas, poet and critic, described it as 'brief, thonged, grisly and bewitching'. It's about an insatiable drunkard who seeks his palm-wine tapster in the world of the dead.

Chinua Achebe, also of Nigeria, is also well known. His *Things Fall Apart* (1958) is a classic; it has sold more than eight million copies in 30 languages, more than any other African work. Set in the mid-19th century, this novel studies the collision between precolonial Ibo society and European missionaries. A more recent work is *Anthills of the Savannah*, a satirical study of political disorder and corruption. It was a finalist for the 1987 Booker Prize.

Another Nigerian author is Ben Okri, whose novel *The Famished Road* won the Booker Prize in 1991. When critics grumbled that to appreciate the book's style and symbolism the reader had to 'understand Africa', Okri recalled reading Victorian novelists such as Dickens as a schoolboy in Nigeria. He continues to fuse modern style with traditional mythological themes in his later novels *Songs of Enchantment* and *Astonishing the Gods*.

Buchi Emecheta, also from Nigeria, is one of Africa's most successful female authors. Her novels include *Slave Girl*, *Rape of Shavi* and *Kehinde*, and focus with humour and irrepressible irony on the struggles of African women to overcome their second-class treatment by society.

Another well-known Nigerian writer is Ken Saro-Wiwa, although in other countries he is more famous for his politics than for his writings (see the boxed text 'Ken Saro-Wiwa' in the Facts about Nigeria section of the Nigeria chapter). His last novel was *Pita Dumbroks Prison*. He was hanged in 1995.

Cameroon's best-known literary figure is the late Mongo Beti, who is also one of the most famous writers from the continent. *The Poor Christ of Bomba* is Beti's cynical recounting of the failure of a missionary to convert the people of a small village. Other works by Beti include *Mission to Kala* and *Remember Ruben*.

One of Gambia's best-known novelists is William Conton, whose 1960s classic *The African* is a semiautobiographical tale of an African student in Britain who later returns to his homeland and becomes president.

Ghana's foremost writer is Ayi Kwei Armah – not a well-known name outside the country, although *The Beautiful Ones Are Not Yet Born*, published in 1969, is a classic tale of corruption and disillusionment in post-independence Africa. Ama Ata Aidoo, one of Ghana's (and West Africa's) few

[Continued on page 48]

PEOPLES OF THE REGION

More than anything else, it is West Africa's people and the richness of their cultural traditions that lure travellers to the region and form the highlight of any visit. The diversity you will encounter is astounding, with several hundred different groups, each with their own customs and language.

Following are brief profiles of some of the larger or more well-known groups, highlighting a few of the more intriguing aspects of their cultures. The descriptions are ordered roughly geographically, moving from west to east across the region.

Fula

The Fula (also called Fulani, Peul or Foulbé in French-speaking countries) are tall, lightly built people who have been settling across the West African savanna for centuries. They are estimated to number more than 12 million, and are found from Senegal to as far east as Cameroon and beyond. The Tukulor (Toucouleur) and the Wolof of Senegal, as well as the Fulbe Jeeri of Mauritania, are all of Fula origin.

Although the Fula were originally nomadic cattle herders, many are now settled farmers, while others continue to follow their herds seasonally in search of pasture, living in grass huts resembling large beehives. Those Fula with no cattle of their own often work as herdsmen, looking after other peoples' cattle. Cattle occupy a central position in society, with Fula often putting the welfare of their cattle above their own. Islam also plays a central role. Town-dwelling Fula (referred to as Fulani Gida in some areas) adopted Islam as early as the 12th century and were major catalysts in its spread.

The nomadic Fula, or Wodaabé, are known for their public initiation ceremony in which young boys are lashed with long rods to the accelerating rhythm of drums, as part of their passage into manhood. Although there are many onlookers, including potential brides, the boys must show no fear, though their ordeal leaves them scarred. At the annual Gerewol festival, where the young Wodaabé meet prospective marriage partners, men pay great attention to their appearance, adorning themselves with shining jewellery, feathers, sunglasses and elaborate make-up – anything to create an impression, and to look their best for the women.

Wolof

The Wolof heartland is in Senegal, where these people comprise about 36% of the population, and are active in the Muslim brotherhoods.

Wolof society is hierarchical, with hereditary castes determining traditional occupations and status. Today, though, traditional family status is now only important for marriage and traditional occupations such as blacksmiths and griots (praise singers).

Although Islam has been an influence in Wolof areas since the 11th century, many traditional beliefs persist. For example, the main street

Inset: Huge gold earrings are worn by wealthy Fula women (Illustration by Sarah Jolly)

of a Wolof village is always crooked, as a straight one is believed to invite bad spirits. There is also a belief in a snake monster so terrible that to look upon it causes death. In order to guard against witches and other forms of evil, many Wolof wear leather-bound amulets containing written verses of the Koran.

The Wolof, who are of Fula origin, tend to be tall, and striking in their traditional flowing robes of white, dark blue or black. The women wear a series of loose, layered gowns, each a little shorter than the one underneath. Men wear long gowns over loose, white pantaloons that overhang the knee.

Tuareg

The Tuareg are nomadic, camel-owning Berber-speakers who traditionally roamed across the Sahel from Mauritania to western Sudan. In recent times, they have had to abandon their traditional way of life, primarily because of droughts, and many have moved southwards to settle near cities.

The Tuareg follow a rigid status system. The veils or *taguelmoust* that extend from a Tuareg man's turban are both a source of protection against the desert winds and sand in the desert, and a social requirement, as it is considered improper for a Tuareg man to show his face to a man of higher status. You are unlikely to see a Tuareg man remove his shawl to expose the lower half of his face in company, and when Tuareg men drink tea, they are supposed to pass the glass under their taguelmoust so as not to reveal the mouth.

The taguelmoust is also the symbol of a Tuareg's identity, and the way it is wrapped changes from tribe to tribe. It is typically 5m long and made of blue or black cotton. If you have the opportunity to meet a Tuareg chief or elders, you may be required to wear a taguelmoust.

The Tuareg are sometimes called the 'blue people' because the indigo of their clothing rubs off on their skin – an effect that they admire. Tuareg women weave artificial strands into their plaits and attach cowrie shells. They also can be recognised by their large pieces of silver jewellery; silver is generally preferred to gold.

The *croix d'Agadez* is one of the best-known Tuareg symbols, together with intricately decorated dagger handles. The crosses are in silver filigree, and the Tuareg believe they are powerful talismans offering protection against 'the evil eye'. Some have phallus designs and are used as fertility symbols for both sexes, while others are for good luck and protection. The designs of the crosses vary slightly, depend-

ing on which desert town they were made in. Tuareg men use the crosses as a form of currency to buy cattle; between trades the crosses are worn by Tuareg wives as a sign of wealth.

Dogon

The Dogon, who live in the area around Mali's Falaise de Bandiagara (Bandiagara Escarpment), are among the region's most intriguing people, and are also known for their masks. There are various types, including the famous *iminana*, which can be up to 10m high, the bird-like *kanaga*, which protects against vengeance (of a killed animal), and the house-like *sirige*, which represents the house of the *hogon*, who is responsible for passing on Dogon traditions to younger generations. For more on the Dogon, see the special section 'Dogon Arts & Culture' in the Mali chapter.

Bambara

The Bambara (also known as Bamana) are the largest ethnic group in Mali, comprising about 33% of the population. Although they are Muslim, many have retained traditional beliefs and customs. One of the most important of these is an occupational caste system, which includes farmers, leather-workers, poets and blacksmiths. As in many other West African societies, blacksmiths hold an esteemed position among the Bambara. Not only do they make hoes for producing food, but also door locks that protect women and children, and guns that arm the village. All of these are furnished with spiritual power as well as utility. Door locks often have a water-lizard symbol to protect the house from thieves, or a long-eared creature similar to a bat that is said to hear every sound, and protects the household.

The Bambara are known for their artwork, especially woodcarvings and masks. Each of the occupational groups or castes has its own initiation rituals, for which particular masks are required, and it is only the blacksmiths who inherit the capacity to tap into the spiritual power, *nyama*, that enables them to transform wood and iron into masks and other religious objects. Because nyama is inherited, blacksmiths must marry within their own occupational group.

Perhaps the best-known image of the Bambara is the *chiwara*, a stylised antelope with long arched neck and horns. According to legend, the Creator sent an antelope to teach the Bambara how to cultivate grain.

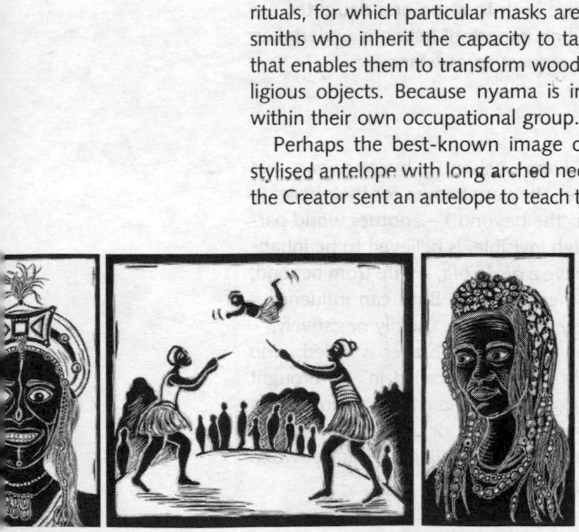

Malinké

The Malinké (in some areas synonymous with, or closely related to, the Mandinka or Mandingo) are part of the larger Mande group, which also includes the Bambara and the Soninké, and is believed to have originated as early as 4000 years ago. It was at this

time that various agricultural peoples of the southern Sahara merged with indigenous hunter-gatherers of the Niger River basin. Today, the Malinké are found in southern Mali as well as northern Guinea, Côte d'Ivoire, Senegal and Gambia. They are famed hunters and warriors and were prominent converts to Islam from around the 11th century. In the mid-13th century, the Malinké founded the powerful Empire of Mali. Thanks to their central position, they were able to control almost all trans-Saharan commerce – from the gold trade on the coast to the commodities trade coming south across the desert from the Mediterranean states.

Originally the Malinké were divided into 12 clans, each with its own king and highly stratified castes. The heads of these 12 clans formed a royal council, which elected a single leader, known as a *mansa*. The traditional hunter societies of the Malinké, with their secret initiation rites, still thrive today.

Dan

The Dan (also known as the Yacouba) inhabit the mountainous area around Man in Côte d'Ivoire. Masks are an important part of Dan culture. Each village has several great masks that represent its collective memory and which are glorified during times of happiness and abundance. Masks are regarded as divinities and as repositories of knowledge. They dictate the community values that give the clan cohesiveness and help to preserve its customs. For example, harvest-time yields, or whether a woman will give birth to a son or a daughter, are believed to depend on masks, and no important action is undertaken without first addressing a mask to request its assistance.

Baoulé

The Baoulé, who separated from Ghana's Ashanti in bygone years, live in eastern and central Côte d'Ivoire. They are known for their belief in the *blolo* (meaning 'elsewhere' or 'the beyond') – another world parallel to our own. The blolo, although invisible, is believed to be inhabited by people. A man may even have a *blolo bla*, a wife from beyond, and a woman a *blolo bian*, or other husband. Both can influence a partner's wellbeing, marital stability and sex life, usually negatively.

To counteract problems such as these, a soothsayer is called, who usually recommends that the blolo partner be 'called in' or 'brought down' to prevent further havoc. This can be done either by moulding a cone of fine kaolin clay mixed with secret herbs, or by fashioning a clay or wooden statue of the blolo partner, thus controlling the parallel-world partner and limiting further damage.

Senoufo

The Senoufo, who live in Côte d'Ivoire, Burkina Faso and Mali, are renowned as skilled farmers. Animals are held in high regard in Senoufo culture, and when someone dies, it is believed that they are transformed into the clan's animal totem.

As a result, many Senoufo dances are associated with animals. One of these is the dance of the leopard men, which is performed in Natiokabadara, near Korhogo, as well as in other Senoufo areas when young boys return from their Poro (part of the secret Lô association) initiation-training sessions. In this and other dances, masks – often of animal heads – are instrumental in making contact with the gods and driving away bad spirits.

Blacksmiths also hold a special position in Senoufo society, as is the case with many other groups in the region. Their relationship with iron (which is from the earth) and with fire, invests them with special power, and their caste presides over funerals. When someone dies, the corpse is carried through the village in a procession, while men in grotesque masks chase away the soul. It is the blacksmiths – believed to be immune to evil spirits – who dig the grave and place the corpse inside, after which they present a last meal to the deceased, and then feast and celebrate.

Lobi

The Lobi live in southwestern Burkina Faso, as well as in northern Côte d'Ivoire and Ghana, in distinctive mud-brick compounds resembling small fortresses. They follow ancestor-based beliefs and their traditions are very well preserved.

The Lobi don't use masks. Most of their woodcarvings are of human figures, typically 35cm to 65cm high, which represent deities and ancestors. The woodcarvings are used for ancestral shrines, and traditionally were found in every home. The Lobi also carve staffs and three-legged stools with human or animal heads, as well as combs with human figures or geometric decorations. Lobi carvings are distinguished by their rigid appearance, with arms generally positioned straight down, along the sides of the body. They are also notable for their realistic and detailed renderings of certain body parts, particularly the navel, eyes and hair.

Bobo

The Bobo, who escaped subjugation by the Mossi, live in western Burkina Faso around Bobo-Dioulasso. They are renowned for their mask traditions, involving many different types of masks, including the famous butterfly and helmet masks.

The large, horizontal butterfly masks are typically about 1.5m wide and painted red, black and white. They are worn during funeral rites, and when invoking the deity known as 'Do' in planting-time ceremonies asking for rain and for a good harvest. The form of a butterfly is used because butterflies appear in great swarms immediately after the first rains and are thus associated with the planting season. The dancer twists his head so rapidly that the mask almost appears to be spinning. Other animals used for Bobo masks include owls, buffaloes, antelopes, crocodiles and scorpions. The masks are usually tall, and have bold-coloured patterns similar to those adorning the butterfly masks.

Mossi

The Mossi, who are concentrated in the central plateau area in and around Ouagadougou, are the largest ethnic group in Burkina Faso. In the 14th century, they established powerful kingdoms in this area after leaving their original homeland around the Niger River and moving westward. The Mossi are known for their rigid social hierarchies and elaborate rituals, and they still exert considerable political influence in Burkina Faso today. Historically, they resisted invasion by the Muslim Empire of Mali, and today many continue to follow traditional beliefs.

Artistically, the Mossi are best known for their tall wooden antelope masks, often more than 2m high and painted red and white. Male and female antelope masks are distinguished from each other by their top sections. Female masks feature a human female figure, while male masks consist of a nonhuman plank-like structure. At the bottom of these masks is a small, oval face bisected by a serrated vertical strip, with triangular eyeholes on either side. The masks were originally worn primarily at funerals.

Ashanti

Inhabiting the heart of the now thinning forest of southern Ghana are the Ashanti, whose kingdom was famed for its gold, its royalty and its traditional state organisation. One of the famous war leaders against the British was Yaa Asantewaa, queen mother of Ejisu, who in 1900 shamed the Ashanti army into entering battle by leading them herself.

As the political role of the state declined under colonial rule, a new source of wealth emerged. Cocoa underpinned the prosperity of town and village life, and traditional crafts such as stool carving, kente cloth weaving and goldsmithing continued to embellish the ritual and ceremony of traditional life. Today, it is the aesthetic of traditional life and its chiefly ceremony that give Ashanti culture its appeal to the traveller. Some of the best-known African artefacts and symbols in Europe and North America are Ashanti, including kente cloth, carved stools and Adinkra symbols. For more on this group, see the special section 'Ashanti Arts & Culture' in the Ghana chapter.

Ewe

The Ewe people of Ghana and Togo are known for hard work, tidy villages, their love of education, their spirituality, and the power of their traditional shrines and priests. There has, however, been recent condemnation of the traditional institution of Trokosi, in which young girls are given as virtual slave-wives to priests in order to appease the spirits. The supreme deities of the Ewe are Mawu-Lisa, the female-male moon-sun twins.

The Ewe are also known for their subtly coloured kente cloth and for their *vu gbe* (talking drums). The tonality of the Ewe spoken language and the rhythm of particular phrases and proverbs are combined in drumming to produce messages that range from commonplace ones that everyone understands to a specialised repertoire known only to the master drummers. Drum language is used for communication, especially in times of crisis. It is also an integral part of religious song and dance. Ewe dances are widely appreciated for their fast and intricate movements, especially of the shoulders and feet.

Songhaï

The Songhaï live predominantly in Niger (where they are the fourth-largest grouping) and in northern Mali, between Timbuktu and Gao. Historically, the Songhaï trace their roots back to the 7th or 8th century when Aliman Za (or Dia) arrived at the upper Niger River from Mandinka (Malinké) lands further west and forced out the local fisherpeople. Other theories claim that it was the Tuareg that founded the original Songhaï state, while yet another hypothesis states that the ancestors of the Songhaï were the original inhabitants of the Upper Niger. The truth is probably a mixture of all three theories, and in any case, it's generally agreed that the Songhaï are of Nilo-Saharan stock. Some Songhaï make a distinction between the Songhaï of Gao (supposedly of pure blood) and those of Timbuktu (who have mixed with Tuareg and Moors).

Songhaï villages are divided into neighbourhoods, each of which elects a head. These heads then come together to elect a village chief, who typically is of noble descent. Most Songhaï consider themselves Muslim, although their religious practices are often mixed with strong traditional elements, including ancestor worship and witchcraft. Large communities often have both a mosque as well as a troupe that specialises in mediums for spirit intervention.

Songhaï are traditionally farmers, who often have strong bonds with their Tuareg neighbours. There is even an affectionate term in the Songhaï language that refers to the nomadic Tuareg as 'our Tuareg'.

Hausa

Hausaland extends over much of northern Nigeria (where the Hausa make up the largest ethnic group) and into Niger, and Hausa culture is closely intertwined with Islam. You may see Quranic script together with symbols of modern technology, such as bicycles and aeroplanes, in the mud-relief patterns on house walls in the old quarters of Nigerian towns such as Kano and Zaria. Traditionally, Hausa women rarely step from behind the walls of their compounds. Many trade home-processed foods, crafts and other goods from home, while children are sent to run errands between compounds.

The emirs of the Hausa states are known for the pomp with which they live and travel. Their bodyguards traditionally wear chain mail, carry spears and ride strikingly caparisoned horses, while attendants on foot wear red turbans, and brilliant red and green robes. These days, however, it's more likely that you'll see an emir riding slowly through town in a large, American car, with the horn sounding.

Many rural Hausa farm grains, cotton and groundnuts, and sacks of groundnuts stacked in pyramids are one of the distinctive sights of many Hausa markets.

Hausaland is one of the few places where cloth is dyed with natural indigo, and if you travel in this region, you'll probably see the drying cloths, patterned in shades of blue on blue, and contrasting with the surrounding mud-red urban landscape.

Yoruba

Yorubaland extends from southwestern Nigeria to neighbouring Benin. Most Yoruba traditionally prefer to live in towns, migrating seasonally to their more-distant farmlands. The urban culture of the Yoruba has facilitated the development of trade and elaborate arts, including the famous Benin bronzes. The old quarters of Yoruba cities contain large household compounds of extended families. Every town has an *oba* (crowned chief). The traditional head of all Yorubas is the *Alafin*, who

lives at Oyo, in Nigeria, while the *oni* (chief priest) lives at Ife. Formality, ceremony and hierarchy govern Yoruba social relations, and ostentation in dress and jewellery is a social requirement for women at traditional functions.

Igbo

The Igbo (also known as Ibo) occupy a large, densely settled farming area in southeastern Nigeria. They form Nigeria's third-largest ethnic group, are predominantly Christian, and have a reputation for hard work, ambition and a love of education.

Traditional-minded Igbo will not eat the new season's yam until Ikeji, the annual new yam festival, when thanks are given to the gods for a productive year. The most important Ikeji festival takes place in September at Arochukwu. Judges select the best village presentation of dance, parade and music.

An Igbo receives his destiny or *chi* directly from Chukwu, the benign god of creation. At death, a person returns his chi and joins the world of ancestors and spirits. From this spirit world, the deceased watches over the living descendants, perhaps returning one day with a different chi. A traditionalist's daily preoccupation is to please and appease the *alusa* – the lesser spirits who can blight a person's life if offended and bestow rewards if pleased. According to tradition, those who died a bad death – for instance in childbirth or through suicide – were denied proper burial and entry into the realm of the ancestors. Instead, they were thrown into the forest where they became harmful wandering ghosts.

David Else, Katie Abu & Matt Fletcher

All illustrations by Sarah Jolly

[Continued from page 38]

well-known female writers, wrote *Changes: A Love Story*, a contemporary novel about a modern Ghanaian woman's life in Accra.

The African Child (also called *The Dark Child)* by Camara Laye of Guinea was first published in 1954, and is one of the most widely printed novels by an African. Laye was born in Guinea in 1924, studied in France and returned to write this largely autobiographical work, in which he describes his childhood among the Malinké tribe, surrounded by ritual magic and superstition, and his emergence into manhood and independence.

God's Bits of Wood by Sembène Ousmane (Senegal), is one of the few Francophone novels that is well known and readily available in English, and is probably the most widely acclaimed book by any Senegalese author. Another Senegalese writer is Mariama Bâ, whose novel *So Long a Letter* won the Noma Award for publishing in Africa. The late Leopold Senghor, former Senegalese president and a literary figure of international note, is the author of several collections of poetry and writings, including *Shadow Songs* and *Nocturnes*. See also Literature under Arts in the Senegal chapter.

Film

A small but significant West African film industry has existed in the region since the heady days of newly won independence in the 1960s. At that time, some countries in the region nurtured cultural links with the Soviet Union, and several directors trained in Moscow, returning home to make films – often with state support or funding – based on overtly Marxist themes.

Common themes explored by the first wave of postcolonial film makers included the exploitation of the masses by colonialists, neocolonialists and, later, corrupt and inefficient independent governments. Another theme was the clash between tradition and modernity. Films frequently portrayed African values – usually in a rural setting – suffering from Western cultural influence in the shape of industrialisation and urban deprivation.

The 1970s was the zenith of African film making, and many films from this era still inspire the new generation of directors working today. However, through the 1980s and 1990s and into the 21st century, directors have found it increasingly hard to arrange other essential aspects of film making, such as finance, production facilities and – most crucially – distribution. The lack of a good distribution network for African films makes it difficult for travellers to see them, even though most of the continent's directors (outside South Africa) are from West Africa, particularly the Francophone countries. Every town has at least one cinema, but the films on show are invariably American action or Indian drama, rather than anything from, or relevant to, the region. A notable exception is the biennial Fespaco film festival held in Burkina Faso (for more details see the boxed text 'Fespaco' under Ouagadougou in the Burkina Faso chapter).

There are a few major names and films to look out for. From Senegal, a leading figure is Ousmane Sembène, whose works include *Borom Sarret* (1963), the first commercial film to be made in post- independence Africa. Sembène's later films include *Xala* and *Camp Thiaroye*. Other Senegalese directors and films include Ahmed Diallo's *Boxumaleen*, Mansour Wade's *Picc Mi*, Amadou Seck's *Saaraba* and Djibril Diop's *Le Franc*.

Mali's leading director is Souleymane Cissé, whose 1970s films include *Baara* and *Cinq Jours d'Une Vie*. Later films include *Yeelen*, a prizewinner at the 1987 Cannes festival, and *Waati*, which was made in South Africa. Other Malian film makers include Alkady Kaba (who made *Wamba*), Sega Coulibaly, Adama Drabo and Abdoulaye Ascofare. Cheik Omar Sissoko, who made *Finzan* and *Gimba*, was the winner of the Etalon de Yennega, Africa's 'Oscar', at the 1995 Fespaco.

Film makers from Burkina Faso include Djim Mamadou Kola, whose career stretches from *Le Sang de Paris* (1971) to *Etrangers* (1993), Gaston Kaboré (who made *Wend Kuuni* and *Zan Boko*), and Idrissa Ouedraogo, the only West African film maker to find genuine commercial success in the West; his films include *Yaaba* and *Samba Traoré*, and most recently *Kini* and *Adams*.

SOCIETY & CONDUCT

One of the highlights of travel in West Africa is meeting the people, and learning about

Minding Your Manners

If you are invited to share a meal with locals, there are a few customs to observe. You'll probably sit with your hosts on the floor, and it's sometimes polite to take off your shoes. It may be impolite, however, to show the soles of your feet, so make sure you observe what your hosts do.

The food is served in one or two large dishes, and is normally eaten by hand. Beginners will just pick out manageable portions with their fingers, but experts dig deep, forming a ball of rice and sauce with the fingers. Everybody washes their hands before and after eating. As an honoured guest you might be passed choice morsels by your hosts, and it's usually polite to finish eating while there's still food in the bowl to show you have had enough.

While eating with your hand is a bit of an art and takes some practice, it should soon start to feel natural. At the outset, you probably won't offend anybody by asking for a spoon. The most important thing, however you eat, is to use only the right hand (as the left hand is traditionally used for more personal, less delicious, matters).

their customs and traditions. Although Africans are generally very easy-going towards foreigners, there are a few things that are frowned upon throughout the region. These include public nudity, open displays of anger, open displays of affection among people of the same or opposite sex, and vocal criticism of the government or country.

Social Structures

Many West African people organise their society along hierarchical lines, with status determined by birth. At the top are traditional noble and warrior families, followed by farmers, traders and persons of lower caste, such as blacksmiths, leather-workers, woodcarvers, weavers and musicians; slaves were once at the bottom of the social hierarchy. Although this status no longer officially exists, many descendants of former slaves still work as tenant farmers for the descendants of their former masters. However, modernity is increasingly eroding traditional hierarchies. The government official who shows contempt for a rural chief may actually be a member of a lower caste who went away to the city and acquired an education and an office job.

Ceremonies are very important in traditional societies, as they reinforce social structures. Much of West Africa's cultural life revolves around events such as baptisms or naming ceremonies, circumcisions, weddings and funerals. At baptisms, guests bring gifts for both the mother and father – a small amount of money is perfectly acceptable. There will be a ceremony followed by a meal, typically a slaughtered sheep or goat. At weddings there is likely to be an official ceremony followed by more festivities at the family's home. Most events involve traditional music and dancing, when men and women may dance separately. If there's modern music, younger people of both sexes may dance together. Either way, if you want to join in, observe what's going on around you and act accordingly.

Village festivals (*fêtes* in French) may be held to honour dead ancestors, local traditional deities and to celebrate the end of the harvest. Some festivals include singing and dancing; some favour parades, sports or wrestling matches. In some areas you may see puppets used to tell stories, or to elaborate performances with masks, which play an important part in traditional life.

For more information on specific festivals, see Public Holidays & Special Events in the Regional Facts for the Visitor chapter.

Greetings

Great importance is placed on greetings in West Africa. Muslims will almost certainly start with the traditional Islamic greetings, '*Salaam aleikum*' and '*Aleikum asalaam*' ('Peace be unto you', 'And peace be unto you'). This is followed by several more questions, such as 'How are you doing?', 'How is the family?', 'How are the people of your village?'. The reply is usually '*Al humdul'allah*' (meaning 'Thanks be to God'). In cities, the traditional greetings may give way to shorter versions in French or English, but they're never forgotten.

Although it's not necessary for foreigners to go through the whole routine, it's important to use greetings whenever possible. Even for something simple such as exchanging money or asking directions, always start with 'Good day, how are you? Can you help me

Marriage

In many parts of West Africa, marriage is an expensive affair. Gifts from the groom to the bride's family can easily cost several hundred dollars – and this in a region where annual incomes of US$200 are typical. Many men cannot afford to get married before their late 20s or 30s.

Despite the financial constraints, in traditional society (among Muslims and some non-Muslim people), men who can afford more than one wife usually marry two, three or even four women (the Quran allows up to four). You will be told (by men) that women are not averse to polygamy, and that the wives become like sisters, helping each other with domestic and child-rearing duties. In reality, however, most first wives definitely don't like their husbands marrying again. On the other hand, there's not much women can do, as leaving a marriage simply because a husband takes another wife can bring shame to the woman and her family. She might be cast out of the family home or even physically beaten as punishment by her own father or brothers. A particularly incisive account of the clash between modern and traditional views on polygamy is given in *So Long a Letter* by Senegalese author Miriama Bâ.

please?'. Launching straight into business is considered rude.

Learning some greetings in the local language will smooth the way considerably. Even a few words make a big difference (see the Language chapter near the back of the book for phrases).

Deference

In traditional societies, older people (especially men) are treated with deference. Teachers, doctors and other professionals (usually men) often receive similar treatment. When you meet people holding positions of authority, such as police officers, immigration officials or village chiefs (usually men), it is important to be polite. Officials are usually courteous but can make things awkward for you, and this is when manners, patience and cooperation on your side are essential to get you through. Undermining an official's authority or insulting an ego will get you nowhere, and will usually only serve to waste time, tie you up in red tape and inspire closer scrutiny of future travellers.

At the other end of the spectrum, children rate very low on the social scale. They are expected to do as they're told without complaint, and to defer to adults in all situations. Unfortunately for half the region's population, the status of women is only slightly higher. In traditional rural areas, women are expected to dress and behave with modesty, especially in the presence of chiefs or other esteemed persons.

When visiting rural settlements, it is a good idea to request to see the chief to announce your arrival and request permission before wandering through a village. You will rarely be refused.

Another consideration is eye contact, which is usually avoided, especially between men and women in the Sahel. If a West African doesn't look you in the eye during a conversation, remember that they're being polite, not cold.

Dress

West Africans place great importance on appearance, and generally dress conservatively, especially in the Sahel and inland areas, so it's not surprising that clothes worn by travellers (eg, singlets, shorts or tight trousers) are often considered offensive. In Africa, the only people wearing shorts or tatty clothes are children, labourers and the poor, which is why bare-legged

Shaking Hands

Handshaking is often an important part of greetings. At social gatherings, when both arriving and departing, it is customary for men to go around the room, greeting and shaking hands with other men, and sometimes also with older women. Use a soft – rather than overly firm – handshake.

Some Muslim men prefer not to shake hands with women, and West African women don't usually shake hands with their male counterparts, so it might be considered odd if you do. However, Western women in traditional situations often find they hold the privileged position of 'honorary man' and any extraneous handshaking will generally not cause offence.

Les Modes d'Afrique

Great emphasis is placed on dress in West Africa. In the big cities, you'll see everything from the latest Parisian fashions to the most traditional outfits. For most people, the traditional outfit is the grand boubou. For men, this is an elaborately embroidered robe-like garment reaching the ground, with deep vents down each side; baggy trousers and a shirt are worn underneath. This outfit is invariably worn on important occasions, but is also sometimes worn in everyday situations. Women's boubous are similar, but may have even more embroidery, and are often worn with a matching headscarf. For everyday wear, women often wear a loose top and a *pagne* (length of colourful printed cotton cloth worn around the waist for a skirt).

travellers often get treated with contempt. In general, the more professional you look, the better you will be received and treated.

For women, in addition to respecting local sensibilities, dressing modestly also helps minimise hassles. Whether you're male or female, from a practical point of view, keeping reasonably covered with loose-fitting clothes helps prevent sunburn.

Begging

In Africa, there is no government welfare cheque for the unemployed, crippled, homeless, sick or old; the only social security system is the extended family. People with no family are forced to beg, although the extended family support system is very effective, and there are remarkably few beggars, considering the region's overall economic poverty.

Because helping the needy is part of traditional African culture, and one of the pillars of Islam by which Muslims reach paradise, you will see even relatively poor people giving to beggars. If you want to give, even a very small coin is appreciated. If you don't have any change, just say 'next time' or something similar, and at least greet the person and acknowledge their presence. Of course, sometimes it's hard to differentiate between hustlers and those in dire need, with no family support, such as the blind, crippled, old, or unmarried mothers. If in doubt, consider giving money to the beggars local people give money to – they are the best judges of who is deserving and who is not. If you're considering a larger donation, it's best to channel this through one of the many aid organisations working in the region.

Gifts & Tips

'Do you have something for me?' or '*Donnez-moi un cadeau*' becomes a familiar refrain everywhere you go, usually from children, but also from youths and adults. Part of this expectation comes from a belief that anyone to whom God has been good (and all foreigners are thought to be rich – which, relatively, they are) should be willing to spread some wealth around. People may ask for your hat, shoes or camera, or simply for money, all within a couple of minutes of meeting you. But generally, this is just a 'worth a try' situation, and your polite refusal will rarely offend.

Even if your refusal to give a gift is accepted, you may be asked by your new-found friend for your address, so that you can become pen friends or correspondents. Don't be surprised if the letters you get a few months later include copious greetings, reports on the health of family members – and a request for some money. Once again, it's a 'worth a try' situation. In any case, cash sent later in an envelope nearly always gets 'lost' at the post office. Your best option is to politely refuse to give out your address in the first place.

When a gift is given in return for a service it becomes more like a tip (although in Francophone countries both words translate as *cadeau*). Simply being pointed in the right direction is not a significant service, whereas being helped for 10 minutes to find a hotel probably is. When deciding how much to give, enough for a drink (tea, coffee or soft drink) is usually sufficient. If you're not prepared to offer a tip, don't ask for significant favours. Do remember, however, that some people will help you out of genuine kindness and will not be expecting anything in return.

Things sometimes work the other way. West Africans are frequently very friendly towards foreigners, and after just a few minutes of talking they may offer you food or a bed for the night. You may want to repay such kindness with a gift such as tea, perfume or kola nuts, but money is usually the easiest thing to give and is always very much appreciated. When deciding how much money to give, consider what you would have paid for a similar meal or hotel room were it not for your hosts' kindness. Experiencing local hospitality will definitely enhance your travelling experience. However, using it merely as a way to save money is not acceptable. Be aware that in tourist areas you'll encounter local men who make a living by talking to foreigners, then providing 'friendly' services – anything from information and postcards to hard drugs and sex – for money. Steer clear – these hustlers should be avoided.

Bribery

A gift or tip becomes a completely different matter when you have to pay to get something done. In this case it's effectively a bribe (also called a cadeau in Francophone countries or a 'dash' in English-speaking countries). For example, a border customs official may go through your belongings, then ask: 'Don't you have something extra?' implying that if you don't give them a gift the search could go on for hours.

The best way to deal with this is to feign ignorance, smile a lot, be patient and simply bluff your way through. Creative approaches can also work well in diffusing the situation; for example, good-humouredly saying that you were actually just wondering what they might have for you, or greeting a gendarme as an old friend (thus leaving him wondering where he met you last), inquiring about his family, or exchanging a few words in the local language.

Occasionally requests may become threats, such as denying entrance to the country. This is usually just a bluff, although it can last several minutes – just keep smiling and being patient. You might ask to see a senior officer, but threats, or shows of anger and annoyance, won't get you anywhere. If you're asked to wait around, being conversant with the results of the latest local soccer match – always a good conversation starter – is another good trick. Be personable and calm, and give the official plenty of room to back down and save face. In virtually all cases, you'll soon be allowed to continue.

If your documents are not in order, you're more vulnerable. It helps to know the regulations, however, because officials often trump up fictitious ones simply to create a bribe situation.

There are occasionally cases where playing the system is unavoidable and where offering a small dash or cadeau may be your only option. If you hear talk about 'special fees' being required to get what you want, it's a good hint that the official is after a bribe. However, with patience, good humour and basic interpersonal skills it's almost always possible to avoid these instances. Never simply offer to pay. And, if you really have no choice but to pay, remember that the 'fee' is always negotiable.

Kola Nuts

Kola nuts are yellow or purple nuts, about half the size of a golf ball, which are sold in streets and markets everywhere in West Africa. They are known for their mildly hallucinogenic effects. West Africans traditionally give kola nuts as gifts, and they are also a good option for travellers to carry and give to people in exchange for their kindness (or if you want to endear yourself to your fellow passengers in a bush taxi). The nuts last longer if you keep them moist but will become mouldy in a day or two if kept in a plastic bag. Despite the nuts' popularity among West Africans, most foreigners find them too bitter to chew and anyone looking for a high is usually disappointed.

RELIGION

The religions of West Africa fall into three main categories: Islam, Christianity and traditional beliefs. Accurate figures are difficult to come by, but in general, roughly half of all West Africans are Muslim, particularly those living in the desert and Sahel countries. Christianity is more widespread in the southern coastal countries than in the northern Sahel countries. (Also see Religion in the individual country chapters.)

Islam

Origins of Islam Between AD 610 and AD 620 in the city of Mecca, Saudi Arabia, the Prophet Mohammed called on the people to turn away from pagan worship and submit to Allah, the one true god. His teachings appealed to the poorer levels of society and angered the wealthy merchant class. In AD 622 Mohammed and his followers were forced to

Tips for the Traveller in Islamic Areas

When you visit a mosque, take off your shoes; women should cover their heads and shoulders with scarves. In some mosques, women are not allowed to enter if prayers are in progress or if the imam (prayer leader) is present; in others, there may be separate entrances for men and women.

If you have hired a guide or taxi driver for the day, remember that he'll want to say his prayers at the right times, so look out for signs that he wants a few moments off, particularly around noon, late afternoon and sunset. Travellers on buses and bush taxis should also be prepared for prayer stops at these times.

Despite the Islamic proscription against alcohol, some Muslims may enjoy a quiet drink. Even so, it's impolite to drink alcohol in their presence unless they show approval.

During Islamic holidays, shops and offices may close. Even if the offices are officially open, during the Ramadan period of fasting, people become soporific (especially when Ramadan falls in the hot season) and very little gets done.

flee to Medina. This migration, the Hejira, marks the beginning of the Islamic calendar, year 1 AH (anno Hegirae). By AD 630 (8 AH) Mohammed had gained a larger following and returned to Mecca. He died in AD 632, but within two decades most of Arabia was converted to Islam. Over the following centuries, Islam spread through North and West Africa, down the coast of East Africa, into several parts of Southern and Eastern Europe and eastward across Asia.

In its journey from Arabia to West Africa, Islam adapted to local conditions by evolving features that would not be recognised by purists in Cairo or Mecca. Most notable of these are the marabouts – holy men who act as a cross between priest, doctor and adviser for local people. In some countries, especially Senegal, marabouts wield considerable political power.

The Five Pillars of Islam The five pillars of Islam (the basic tenets that guide Muslims in their daily lives) are as follows:

- *shahada* (the profession of faith): 'There is no god but Allah, and Mohammed is his Prophet' is the fundamental tenet of Islam.
- *salat* (prayer): Muslims must face Mecca and pray at dawn, noon, mid-afternoon, sunset and nightfall.
- *zakat* (alms): Muslims must give a portion of their income to the poor and needy.
- *sawm* (fasting): Ramadan commemorates Mohammed's first revelation, and is the month when all Muslims fast from dawn to dusk.
- *hajj* (pilgrimage, usually written *hadj* in West Africa): It is the duty of every Muslim who is fit and can afford it to make the pilgrimage to Mecca at least once in a lifetime. This can involve a lifetime of saving money, and it's not unusual for families to save up and send one member. Before the advent of air travel, the pilgrimage often involved an overland journey of a year or more. In West Africa, those who complete the pilgrimage receive the honorific title of Hadj for men, and Hadjia for women. If you meet someone with this prefix, you may appreciate the honour this bestows on them in the community.

For information on Islamic holidays, including a table of dates, see Public Holidays & Special Events in the Regional Facts for the Visitor chapter.

Traditional Religions

Before the arrival of Islam and Christianity, every race, tribe or clan in West Africa practised its own traditional religion. While many people in the Sahel converted to Islam, and those in the south converted to Christianity, traditional religions remained strong in many parts of the region. Today, traditional beliefs frequently exist alongside established aspects of Islam or Christianity, and firm lines between one set of values and another are impossible to draw. When discussing traditional beliefs, terms such as 'juju', 'voodoo' and 'witchcraft' are frequently employed. In certain contexts these may be correct, but they cannot be applied to all traditional African religions.

There are hundreds of traditional religions in West Africa, with considerable areas of overlap, but no great temples or written scriptures. Beliefs and traditions can be complex and difficult to understand, but several common factors can be outlined. The description here provides an overview only, and is necessarily very simplified.

Almost all traditional religions are animist, meaning they are based on the attribution of life or consciousness to natural objects or phenomena. Thus a certain tree, mountain, river or stone may be sacred because it represents, is home to, or simply *is* a spirit or deity. The number of deities of each religion varies, as does the phenomena that represents them. The Ewe of Togo and Ghana, for example, have more than 600 deities, including one that represents the disease smallpox.

Several traditional religions accept the existence of a supreme being or creator, as well as the spirits and deities, although this figure is considered too exalted to be concerned with humans. Communication is possible only through the lesser deities or through the intercession of ancestors. Thus, in many African religions, ancestors play a particularly strong role. Their principal function is to protect the tribe or family, and they may on occasion show their pleasure or displeasure. Many traditional religions hold that the ancestors are the real owners of the land, and while it can be enjoyed and used during the lifetime of their descendants, it cannot be sold. Displeasure may be shown in the form of bad weather or a bad harvest, or when a living member of the family becomes sick.

Communication with ancestors or deities may take the form of prayer, offerings (possibly with the assistance of a holy man, or occasionally a holy woman) or sacrifice. Requests may include good health, bountiful harvests and numerous children. Many village celebrations are held to ask for help from (or in honour of) ancestors and deities. The Dogon people from the Bandiagara Escarpment in Mali, for instance, have celebrations before planting to ensure good crops and after harvest to give thanks. Totems, fetishes and charms are also important aspects of traditional religions (for more details, see Totems, Fetishes & Charms in the special section 'Arts & Craftwork').

PEOPLE & LANGUAGES

There is a huge number of tribes or ethnic groups in West Africa, which makes travel in the region so fascinating. For example, Guinea-Bissau, a country of less than one million people, has at least 20 ethnic groups; and there are about 280 ethnic groups among Cameroon's approximately 15 million inhabitants.

When colonial-era borders were drawn, this diversity was ignored. As a result, most West African countries today incorporate many groups, all with vastly different languages, religions and cultures. Also, in many cases, national borders divide ethnic groups. The Hausa, for example, are found in Niger and Nigeria, and the Malinké (and the closely related Mandinka) are found in Guinea, Côte d'Ivoire, Mali, Senegal and Gambia.

In some countries, the population may be fairly evenly divided among groups, but in other countries a single group may predominate either numerically or through disproportionate control of the political system. In Mali, for example, the largest group, the Bambara, represents only 23% of the total population but controls most aspects of the government and economy.

For more information on the people of West Africa, refer to the 'Peoples of the Region' special section, as well as the Population & People sections of the individual country chapters.

Official Languages

Of the 17 countries in West Africa, French is the official language in eight (Benin, Burkina Faso, Côte d'Ivoire, Guinea, Mali, Niger, Senegal and Togo); English in five (Gambia, Ghana, Liberia, Nigeria and Sierra Leone); and Portuguese in two (Cape Verde and Guinea-Bissau). Cameroon is bilingual (French and English), and Arabic is the official language of Mauritania. It might seem like a regrettable legacy of the colonial period that the official languages are non-African, but these languages do play a useful, 'neutral' role. For a government to choose one local language for the official language would be politically disastrous, and only some of the people would be able to speak it anyway.

For travellers in West Africa, it makes things much easier to be able to speak at least a few words of the official language in each country. Assuming most readers of this book have at least a basic grounding in English, communication in the English-speaking countries of Gambia, Ghana, Liberia, Nigeria and Sierra Leone will be straightforward. In Francophone countries, although

Mandingo vs Mandinka

One result of the European language influence in West Africa is that the same African word or sound may be spelt differently according to the nationality of the original colonial recorder. Travelling through the region, you'll soon realise that many groups of people have more than one name. For example, the Jola people in Gambia (a former British colony) spread over the border into Senegal (a former French colony), where they are known as the Diola. The Fula people, who are spread across much of northern West Africa, were identified by the French as 'Peul' and by the English as 'Fulani', the former being the singular and the latter the plural used by these people to identify themselves. Their language is known as Fula or Pulaar.

Name differences may also arise when groups are divided into subgroups, as sometimes the name of a relatively minor clan is given to the whole group. Similarly, spellings of names can vary, either according to the language of the country's original colonial power, or as linguistic studies become more phonetically precise. For example, Peul can be spelt Peulh; Tamashek (the language of the Tuareg) is generally spelt Tamachek by French speakers; and the Toucouleur of northern Senegal are now often called the Tukulor.

Also, the definitions of ethnic groups don't always correlate with those of language groups. Usually an ethnic group is defined as a people sharing the same language – a common tongue is the most fundamental aspect that links the people of the group together – but linguists and anthropologists can give language groups confusingly wide or narrow margins, sometimes incorporating several subgroups (or sub-subgroups) which are determined by languages that may be mutually unintelligible, even though they share a common root. Thus the Malinké people of Senegal and Guinea and the Mandinka people of Gambia are sometimes regarded as the same ethnic group with different names determined only by geography. Linguists, however, point out that their languages differ in some respects and therefore the two peoples should be categorised separately – even though their languages are both part of the wider Manding language group. To add even further to the confusion, both the Malinké and the Mandinka are sometimes called the Mandingo.

some English is spoken in tourist areas, once you get off the beaten track a handful of French words will smooth the way considerably. The same applies in the Portuguese-speaking countries, although French is commonly spoken in tourist areas of Guinea-Bissau. In Mauritania, although Arabic is the official language, French is widely spoken.

Indigenous Languages

West African languages are classified by linguists and anthropologists in a complex and constantly shifting system of groups and subgroups. The following outline is necessarily very simplified.

The major language family in Africa is the Niger-Congo family and includes six subordinate groups, all of which are found in West Africa: West Atlantic, Mande, Kwa, Voltaic (Gur), Adamawa-Eastern and Benue-Congo.

The West Atlantic group of languages, found primarily along the western coastal regions of Senegal, Gambia, Guinea-Bissau and Sierra Leone, includes Wolof, Jola, Bijago, Temne and Fula (also called Fulani or Pulaar). Fula has also spread inland through northern Senegal, northwestern and northern Guinea and central Mali, with speakers as far west as Niger, Nigeria and northern Cameroon.

The distinct Mande group is found in southern Mali and much of Guinea, with significant pockets in Senegal, Gambia, Burkina Faso, Sierra Leone, Liberia and Côte d'Ivoire. Languages in this group are mostly tonal, and include Malinké (and the closely related Mandinka), Bambara, Bozo, Mende, Dan, Kpelle and Susu.

The Kwa group of languages is spread along the southern Atlantic coast from Liberia through the southern parts of Côte d'Ivoire, Ghana, Togo and Benin to Nigeria, and includes Ashanti, Ewe, Fon, Yoruba, Ibo, Bassa and Krahn.

The Voltaic (Gur) group of languages lies to the north of the Kwa group and covers the northern parts of Côte d'Ivoire, Ghana, Togo and Benin, and much of Burkina Faso. Languages in this group include Mossi and Bassari.

The Adamawa-Eastern group consists of more than 100 languages, including many of those spoken throughout much of northern Cameroon. Languages of this group are

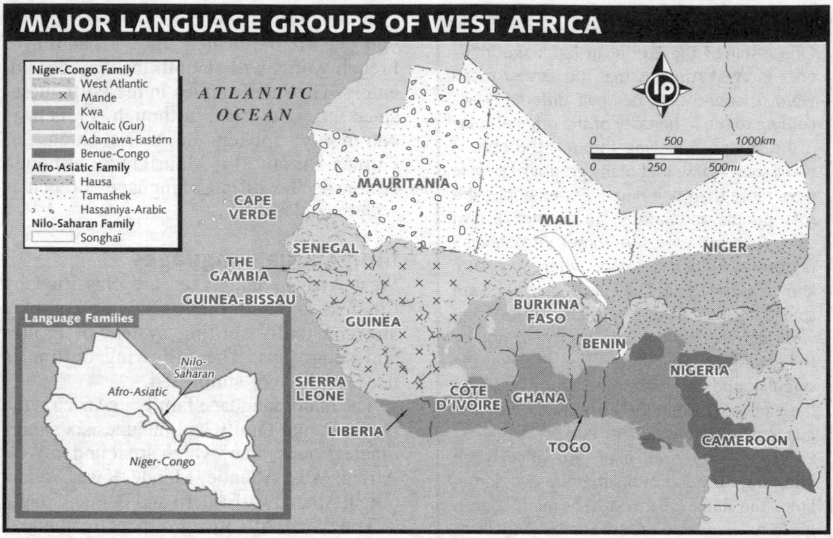

Niger-Congo Family
West Atlantic
Mande
Kwa
Voltaic (Gur)
Adamawa-Eastern
Benue-Congo
Afro-Asiatic Family
Hausa
Tamashek
Hassaniya-Arabic
Nilo-Saharan Family
Songhaï
ATLANTIC OCEAN
0 500 1000km
0 250 500mi
MAURITANIA
CAPE VERDE
MALI
NIGER
SENEGAL
THE GAMBIA
GUINEA-BISSAU
GUINEA
BURKINA FASO
BENIN
NIGERIA
SIERRA LEONE
CÔTE D'IVOIRE
GHANA
LIBERIA
TOGO
CAMEROON
Language Families
Nilo-Saharan
Afro-Asiatic
Niger-Congo

MAJOR LANGUAGE GROUPS OF WEST AFRICA

also widespread in the Central African Republic, and in Congo (Zaïre).

In central Nigeria and in Cameroon, you will find languages belonging to the large Benue-Congo group, which also includes the Bantu subgroup and encompasses many of the languages spoken throughout East and Southern Africa. Cameroon and eastern Nigeria represent the westernmost extent of Bantu languages in West Africa.

Many languages spoken in the northern part of West Africa belong to the Afro-Asiatic (or Hamito-Semitic) family, which includes Arabic, as well as languages belonging to the Chadic group. The major Chadic language is Hausa, spoken in Niger and Nigeria and used as a lingua franca throughout much of West Africa. Other Afro-Asiatic languages are Tamashek (also spelt Tamachek), spoken by the Tuareg people; and Hassaniya, an Arabic-Berber dialect spoken in Mauritania. Songhaï, spoken along the Niger River in Mali and Niger, is considered to be distinct and is a member of the Nilo-Saharan family.

Most West Africans are multilingual and this, combined with the use of common languages, means the many different languages used in the region do not pose a communication problem. However, many political issues can be more clearly understood when viewed in terms of ethnicity, with language usually the chief identifying marker of each ethnic group. A major feature of Nigerian politics and culture, for example, is the delicate balance between the Igbo, Yoruba and Hausa people, with their different histories, cultures and religions.

Creole Languages

West African creole languages – formed by the combination of African and European languages – include Crioulo, which is a mixture of Portuguese and various local languages, and is spoken in Guinea-Bissau and Cape Verde; Krio, a mixture of English and African languages from all over the region introduced by freed slaves, and spoken in Sierra Leone; and pidgin English, spoken in parts of Cameroon.

ARTS & CRAFTWORK

West Africa is known for its rich artistic heritage. Most tribal groups have a long history of skilled artisanship, and throughout the region you will be confronted with a variety of fascinating traditional sculpture (in wood, bronze and other materials), masks, striking textiles, jewellery, basketwork and leatherwork.

Masks

In West Africa there is a staggering range of shapes and styles of masks, from the tiny 'passport' mask of the Dan to the snake-like Dogon *iminana* mask, which can tower up to 10m in height.

Masks, which are usually created by professional artisans, can be made of wood, brass, tin, leather, cloth, glass beads, natural fibres and even (in the case of the Ashanti) gold. They are also made in a number of forms, including face masks, helmet masks (which cover the whole head), headdresses (which are secured to the top of the head), the massive *nimba* masks of the Baga tribe in Guinea (which are carried on the dancer's shoulders) and the famous ivory hip masks from the Kingdom of Benin (present-day Nigeria), which are worn around the waist.

PATRICK SYDER

Inset: A silversmith in Djenné, Mali, sitting by his collection of jewellery (Photo by Ariadne van Zandbergen)

Right: Dogon masked dancer performing a harvest ceremony, Mali

The mask is only part of a complex costume that often covers the dancer's entire body. Made of plant fibre or cloth, often with elaborate appliqué, the costume is usually completed with a mane of raffia surrounding the mask. Most masks are associated with dance, although some are used as prestige symbols and are worn as amulets.

When masks and costumes are worn for a dance, which is accompanied by percussive music and song, they come alive, and convey their meaning to the audience. Masked dances fulfil a variety of functions. They are used in initiation and coming-of-age ceremonies; in burial rituals, when dancing and celebrations assist the spirit of the dead to forsake the earth and reside with ancestors; and in fertility rituals, which are associated with agriculture and the appeasement of spirits to ensure a successful harvest; or with matters relating to childbirth. Masks also fulfil the function of entertainment, with community-based dances and theatrical plays being created for social education and enjoyment.

West African masks are usually classified as anthropomorphic (resembling the human form) and zoomorphic (the representation of deities in the form of animals). Anthropomorphic masks are often carefully carved and can be very realistic. Many tribal groups use masks representing beautiful maidens, whose features reflect the aesthetic ideal of the people. The zoomorphic masks mostly represent dangerous and powerful nature spirits, and can be an abstract and terrifying combination of gaping jaws, popping eyes and massive horns. Some masks combine human and animal features. These convey the links between humans and animals, in particular the ability to gain and control the powers of animals and the spirits they represent.

Christianity, Islam and the 20th century have had a major impact on the animist masked dances of West Africa. Many dances are no longer performed, and sometimes those that are have transformed from sacred rituals to forms of entertainment. Masking traditions were never static and many have transmuted over time. It is still possible to see masked dances in West Africa, although they may be specially arranged 'tourist' performances. Getting to see the real thing is often a matter of being in the right place at the right time.

Textiles

West Africa is famous for the beauty, vitality, colour and range of its textiles. Wool, cotton, nylon, rayon and silk are woven on a variety of looms; this work is usually done by men. Most cloth is woven in narrow strips that are then sewn together. As many West Africans now wear Western clothes, the skills required to produce the finer textiles are disappearing. The colourful cloth, in two or three pieces, worn by women all throughout West Africa, is usually imported or locally produced 'Dutch wax', a factory-made material using stencils and a batik process (whereby the parts of the fabric not to be dyed are covered by wax).

Kente Cloth

Probably the best-known West African fabric is the colourful kente cloth from Ghana, made by the Ashanti people. Clothing is one of the most visual and important marks of distinction in Ashanti society. The basic garment for men is a long rectangular piece of *ntoma* (cloth) passed over the left shoulder and brought around the body like a toga. The most impressive material used for such garments is silk, which is woven in narrow, brightly coloured strips with complex patterns and rich hues. Kente cloth is worn only in the southern half of Ghana and is generally reserved for prestigious events.

The earliest kente cloth was cotton, but from the 18th century Ashanti weavers began incorporating designs using unravelled, imported Dutch silk. Today, only the more-expensive kente cloth contains silk (or imported rayon). The weaving is done exclusively by men, usually outdoors.

The Ewe also weave kente cloth, but their designs are somewhat different and include motifs of geometric figures. Every design has a meaning; some designs are reserved exclusively for royal families.

Adinkra Cloth

Just as impressive as kente cloth, *adinkra* cloth is also from Ghana. It is a colourful cotton material with black geometric designs or stylised figures stamped on it. The word 'adinkra' means 'farewell', and Ghanaians consider this fabric most appropriate for funerals.

Originally the printing was done on cotton pieces laid on the ground. Today, the cotton fabric is cut in long pieces, spread on a raised padded board and held in place by nails. The symbolic designs are cut on calabash stamps, and the dye is made from the bark of a local tree called *badie*. The printer dips the calabash into the hot dye and presses it onto the fabric. Each colour has a special significance: vermilion (red) symbolises the earth, blue symbolises love, and yellow symbolises success and wealth.

Bogolan Cloth

From the Sahel region of Mali comes *bogolan* cloth (called *bokolanfini* in Bambara, and often simply referred to as 'mud cloth'). This textile can

DENNIS WISKEN/SIDEWALK GALLERY

Right: Bogolan cloth

be found in markets throughout much of West Africa. The cloth is woven in plain cotton strips, sewn together and dyed yellow using a solution made from the leaves of a local tree. It is then covered in designs using various types of mud from different sources: mud from sandstone outcrops is used for reds and oranges; mud from riverbeds is used for blacks and greys. The cloth is left to dry in the sun, and the mud designs are then removed, leaving their imprint – the effect is very striking.

Designs are traditionally geometric and abstract, but bogolan cloth made specifically for tourists is more representational, showing animals, markets or village scenes. Some designs are very complex and involve many hours of work by the artists, who are all women. Bogolan cloth is usually used for wall hangings and bedcovers, and is also sometimes used for making waistcoats, caps and bags.

Indigo Cloth

Another classic West African fabric is the indigo-dyed cotton worn primarily by the Tuareg as robes and headdresses. The indigo colour comes from the *indigofera* plant and the indigo vine; the plant is crushed and fermented, and then mixed with an alkaline solution producing the dye. The dyed cloth is often beaten with a mallet to produce a sheen. Other West African tribes noted for their use of indigo include the Hausa, Baoulé, Yoruba and Soninké.

The Yoruba produce an indigo-dyed cloth, *aderi*, which has designs that are applied using the tie-dye technique or by painting motifs with a dye-resistant starch. The Dogon also produce an indigo cloth, which has characteristic geometric patterns.

Other Textiles

The Fula have a caste of weavers, called Maboub, who produce blankets known as *khasa*. These blankets are usually made from camel's hair, although the term is sometimes used to describe cotton blankets as well. The Maboub also make rare and expensive wedding blankets. These large and elaborately detailed textiles are traditionally displayed around the marriage bed.

The Fon and the Fanti are known for their appliqué banners and flags. Shapes of people and animals are cut from colourful material and are carefully sewn onto a cloth panel.

The Hausa are known for their embroidery, which was once hand-stitched onto their robes and caps. Although now machine-stitched, the designs remain unchanged. In keeping with Islam, Hausa designs are nonfigurative.

Jewellery

Jewellery is important to both men and women in West Africa, and you'll see a fascinating variety of designs.

Beads are more than simple adornment; they are often used as objects representing spiritual values, and can play a major role in community rituals such as birth, circumcision, marriage and death. Since the arrival of Europeans, beads have tended to be made of glass; local jewellers copied the highly decorative millefiori trading beads from Venice, which featured flowers, stripes and mosaic designs. Discarded

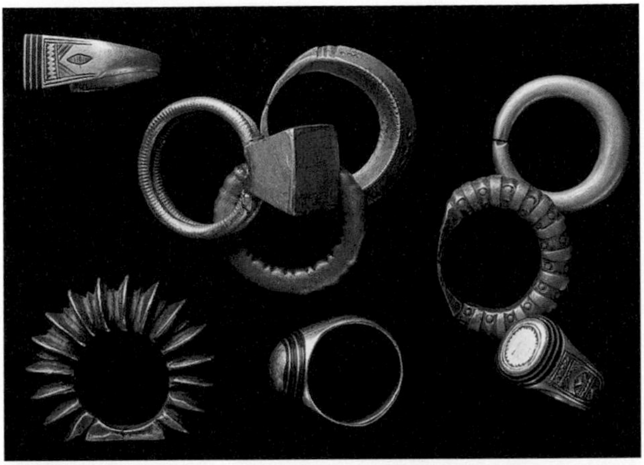

DENNIS WISKEN/SIDEWALK GALLERY

bottles and medicine jars were pulverised into a fine powder to be remade into glass beads. Many glass beads are tiny and are sold by weight, hence their name 'pound beads'. Today, the Krobo in Ghana still melt powdered glass in terracotta moulds, while the Nupe in central Nigeria wind molten glass on long iron rods to make beads and bracelets. Referred to as *bakim-mutum* by bead traders throughout West Africa, beads are commonly worn by village chiefs and elders as a sign of power and wealth.

In Mali you'll see large amber beads worn by Fula women. The Dogon also treasure amber, and use it in their necklaces, bracelets and pendants. They also use beads made of stone and terracotta incised with geometric patterns.

A variety of other materials are used in Africa for making beads, including coral, shells, copal, amazonite, silver, gold and brass. Women sometimes have to make do with cheaper elements. Among the Bella, for instance, plastic and imitation amber beads are sometimes used, and coins may be used instead of silver.

Rings in West Africa are sometimes stunning. In Burkina Faso, look out for Bobo bronze rings, which often have intricate designs, including a tick bird, a warrior on horseback or a chameleon. In Mali, older Dogon men wear large bronze rings as a sign of status. All over the region you'll find beautiful dark-green malachite jewellery, which usually comes from Congo (Zaïre). Cowrie shells are often used to decorate jewellery; for a long time these shells were used as money in many areas of Africa.

In most areas of the region, the preferred metal for jewellery is gold, but in and near the Sahara, the Tuareg and Moors prefer silver. In West Africa, both metals are usually sold by weight, with the artwork included in the price. The Ashanti are famous for their goldwork in jewellery, ornaments and staffs. The Tuareg are renowned for their intricate silverwork in jewellery and in the decoration of the handles of their daggers. Tuareg men and women often wear silver crosses as pendants around their necks. These come in various designs, characterised by protective symbolism. Some incorporate circle and phallus

Top right: Tuareg toe rings – traditional jewellery from Niger

DENNIS WISKEN/SIDEWALK GALLERY

designs, or fertility symbols; those representing a camel's eye or jackal tracks are symbolic of power and cunning.

Totems, Fetishes & Charms

An important feature of traditional religions is the totem, which is an object (usually representing an animal) that serves as an emblem for a particular tribe, and is usually connected with the original ancestor of that group. It is taboo for a member of the clan whose totem is, for example, a snake, to harm any snake, as this would be harming the ancestor. Other common totems include lions, crocodiles and birds.

Fetishes are another important feature in animism. These are objects (sometimes called charms) believed to embody a spirit, and can take many forms. For example, bird skulls and other animal parts may be used as charms by a learned elder for helping people communicate with their ancestors. The elders (usually men) that are responsible for these sacred objects are sometimes called fetish-priests.

The most common charms found throughout West Africa are the small leather or metal amulets, often containing a sacred object, that are worn by people around the neck, arm or waist. These are called gris-gris and are usually worn to ward off evil or bring good luck. Many

Left: Tuareg amulet, the most common charm found in West Africa

West African Muslims also wear gris-gris, called *t'awiz* in other Islamic countries; there is often a small verse from the Koran inside.

Figurative Sculpture

African sculpture is considered one of the most dynamic and influential art forms. Once relegated to curio cabinets and dusty museum storerooms, and labelled as crude, barbaric and primitive, African carving finally gained credibility in the early 20th century when Picasso, Matisse and others found inspiration in its radical approach to the human form.

Most West African sculpture is carved in wood, but some superb bronze and iron figures are also produced, and some funerary figures are created in terracotta and mud. The strange and uncompromising forms found in West African sculpture are not the unique creations of an inspired artist – the sculptures have always been made to fulfil specific functions within the tribe.

In West Africa, sculpture is mostly used in connection with ancestor or spirit worship. Many tribal groups believe that the spirits of the dead can have a major impact, both positive and negative, on a person's life. Ancestral figures are carved and placed in shrines and altars where they receive libations and sacrificial blood. Some tribes carve figures that are cared for by women to ensure fertility and in the hope that the child will inherit the fine looks represented in the sculpture. The famous *akuaba* 'doll' of the Ashanti is the best-known example of this. Prestige objects are also carved, such as figurative staffs of office, commemorative statues and other regalia used by kings, chiefs, traditional healers and diviners as emblems of power.

West African sculpture is usually created by a professional artist, who is usually male and has learned his craft through an apprenticeship. Mostly a family- or caste-specific occupation, the forms and skills are passed down from generation to generation, resulting in highly refined styles. Some tribes, however, have no professional carvers, and the work is carved by any member of the group.

The process is not unchanging – occasionally a virtuoso carver will introduce new elements that may then be incorporated by other artists. In many cases a carver will be commissioned to create a work. After payment has been arranged, the carver selects the wood required, which can involve lengthy rituals. The carver blocks out the form using an adze, completing the finer details with a knife and, traditionally, sanding the carving with a species of rough leaf.

Across the many tribal-specific styles produced in West Africa, some common characteristics can be identified. The figure is usually symmetrical and faces forward; the features are impassive and the arms are held to the side with the legs slightly bent at the knees.

Certain features may be exaggerated, and the head is almost always large in proportion to the body. The surface of the carving is often blackened and there may be crusty deposits of sacrificial material. Sometimes the carving is highly polished or painted with ochre or imported enamel paint. The carving will often have tribal marks carved or burnt into the face and torso, even though such fashions may no longer be practised.

Bronze Casting

West Africa is famous for its traditions of casting brass and bronze using the *cire perdue* (lost wax) technique. Bronze and brass are different compounds, but it is not usually possible to distinguish between them without scientific analysis (the terms are used interchangeably here). The casting process involves creating a sculpture out of wax; the sculpture is then dipped in a solution of silt and mud. When the sculpture is dry, clay is built around the form to create a strong mould. The mould is then heated and the wax is melted out. Molten bronze is then poured into the empty mould and, when cool, the mould is broken away to reveal the bronze sculpture. Each cast is therefore unique. This process is thought to have produced the 1000-year-old beautifully intricate bronzes of the Ibo-Ikwu, which can be seen today in the National Museum in Lagos. Today, latex is often used instead of wax, which creates an even finer detail.

West Africa's best-known castings were created for the Kingdom of Benin in present-day Nigeria. Plaques, statues and masks were produced to decorate the palaces and compounds of the kings and chiefs. The Yoruba cast ritual staffs called *edan*. These comprise male and female figures in bronze, surmounting an iron tip and joined together by a chain.

Figurative weights for weighing gold were cast by the Ashanti, and often symbolised the colourful proverbs for which the Ashanti are known. Crab claws, groundnuts, locusts and even chicken feet were cast using a similar technique.

DENNIS WISKEN/SIDEWALK GALLERY

Left: Intricate detail on a pair of Benin-style bronze heads

Regional Facts for the Visitor

HIGHLIGHTS

The following is a selection of places in West Africa that most visitors find interesting, rewarding or enjoyable. Throughout the region, however, it's the atmosphere of the places and the cultures and activities of their people that are often more interesting than tangible tourist 'sights'. In Bamako (Mali), for example, you could rush around the city's official attractions (such as the mosque and museum) in half a day, but if you spend time strolling through the markets and along the river bank, sitting in a pavement café watching the world go by, or just talking to locals, you'll get much more out of your visit.

In the Adrar region of **Mauritania**, you'll see the ancient Saharan caravan towns of Chinguetti and Ouadâne, the verdant Terjît oasis and spectacular desert scenery. Along the coast is the remote Parc National du Banc d'Arguin, one of the world's major bird-breeding grounds.

Cape Verde's striking scenery alone makes it well worth a visit, and it offers West Africa's best diving as well as some good hiking.

On the coast, **Gambia** is a natural gateway and introduction to the region. It's compact and easily reached from Europe, with long beaches, a beautiful river, lively markets and good bird-watching.

Senegal has a host of attractions, including the lively markets of Dakar and the fascinating colonial centres of Île de Gorée and St-Louis. Casamance, a lush region of forest, palms, lagoons and waterways, gets the most votes. It has a network of cheap *campements* (lodges), and is ideal for exploring by bicycle. However, check the security situation before you travel here. The Siné-Saloum Delta is similarly beautiful and more readily experienced by boat or on foot.

In **Mali**, the area around Mopti is arguably the jewel in the crown of West Africa; from here the cities of Djenné and Timbuktu, and the fascinating Dogon Country can be reached. This area boasts intriguing traditional architecture and culture, a rich history, the beautiful Niger River, bustling market towns, and good hiking.

In **Burkina Faso** don't miss Gorom-Gorom's swirling Thursday market – it's an ethnic kaleidoscope where Sahel meets savanna. Parc National d'Arli, in the south of the country, is rich in birdlife and offers good opportunities for spotting leopards, crocodiles and antelopes.

Niger has a beautiful desert landscape, with a thin, green fertile band along the Niger River, where you will find the top-quality Parc National du W, the only place in the Sahel where giraffes can be seen. To the north is the *banco* (mud-brick) city of Agadez, with its distinctive mosque, the stark and dramatic Aïr Massif and the rolling dunes of the Ténéré Desert.

Back on the coast, **Guinea-Bissau** is often overlooked, but the islands of the Arquipélago dos Bijagós are idyllic, with good beaches and fascinating local culture. Next door is **Guinea**, where the highlight is undoubtedly the Fouta Djalon, an area of beautiful rolling hills, with a cool climate and good hiking.

Both **Sierra Leone** and **Liberia** have suffered severely from the effects of war, but when things return to normal, travellers will enjoy the highlights of the Freetown peninsula in Sierra Leone, which has excellent beaches and good hiking, or to Sapo National Park in Liberia, which encompasses one of West Africa's last remaining rainforests. If this national park proves to be unreachable, the beaches along the coast between Monrovia and Buchanan are consolation enough.

Côte d'Ivoire has many highlights. In the west, Parc National de Taï offers controlled ecotourism in the country's largest rainforest, while along the coast are some beautiful beaches at Grand Béréby and Monogaga. Man is a good base for getting to know the Dan (also known as Yacouba) people and their rich culture of dances and masks, while from Korhogo you can visit the artisan villages of the Senoufo.

Laid-back **Ghana** is another high point of the region. Around Kumasi you will find the heartland of the rich Ashanti culture. Along the coast west of Accra are picturesque fishing villages, beaches and a string of historic, but sobering, slaving forts, including Cape Coast Castle with its fascinating museum.

World Heritage Sites

Sites in West Africa considered to be of global significance by Unesco include the following:

Benin	• Royal palaces of Abomey
Cameroon	• Dja Reserve
Cape Verde	• Cidade Velha
Côte d'Ivoire	• Parc National de Taï • Parc National de la Comoë
Ghana	• Coastal forts and castles • Ashanti traditional buildings in Kumasi
Guinea	• Nimba Mountains (also extending into Côte d'Ivoire)
Mali	• Djenné (old town) • Timbuktu • Falaise de Bandiagara (Dogon Country)
Mauritania	• Parc National du Banc d'Arguin • The ksour (fortified areas, or old quarters) of Ouadâne, Chinguetti, Tichit and Oualâta
Niger	• Réserve Naturelle Nationale de l'Aïr et du Ténéré • Parc National du W
Senegal	• Île de Gorée • St-Louis • Parc National aux Oiseaux du Djoudj • Parc National du Niokolo-Koba

Benin has remarkably diverse attractions, including the stilt villages near Ganvié, the voodoo and old slaving centre of Ouidah, and Parc National de la Pendjari.

Togo is known for cosmopolitan Lomé, and the nearby 'butterfly hills' of Kpalimé are also popular destinations.

Nigeria is the giant of West Africa and crowded, crime-ridden Lagos is a nightmare. However, the historic cities of Kano and Zaria are a refreshing contrast, or you can escape the bustle by retreating to Yankari National Park, or by exploring the cool Jos Plateau.

Cameroon offers a bit of everything: striking mountain scenery and ancient tribal kingdoms around Bamenda, picturesque villages perched on rocky cliffs near Maroua, relaxing beaches near Kribi, good museums in Yaoundé and Foumban, dense rainforests, and Mt Cameroon (4095m), the region's highest peak.

SUGGESTED ITINERARIES

Distances in West Africa are large and transport infrastructure is, for the most part, undeveloped, so allow plenty of time for travel. If time is limited, it's best to concentrate on visiting just one or two areas and explore them in depth, rather than trying to fit in too many places and spending most of your visit in transit.

With two weeks (the minimum for doing the region any justice), you could fly to/from Dakar (Senegal) or Banjul (Gambia) and do a circular tour of Senegal and Gambia, or you could fly to/from Accra and do a tour of Ghana, or to/from Douala or Yaoundé and do a short tour of Cameroon. You could also fly into Accra and then head straight to Togo and Benin, spending your two weeks in these countries. Alternatively, fly into Dakar, or Conakry (Guinea), and combine a taste of those countries with a visit to Cape Verde. With three weeks you could go further afield, perhaps combining Senegal and Mali, or Ghana and Côte d'Ivoire, or Ghana, Togo and Benin. Mali or Niger alone could easily occupy you for at least three weeks, as could a combination of Ghana and Burkina Faso, or (more rushed) Ghana, Burkina Faso and part of Côte d'Ivoire.

A popular route is to fly into Dakar, travel through Senegal, Mali and Burkina Faso then to Ghana and fly out of Accra. You could do this route in four weeks, but five or six weeks would be better, and two months would allow time to visit other countries, too. For example, from Senegal, you could go north into Mauritania, or loop down through Guinea-Bissau and Guinea before reaching Mali or Côte d'Ivoire.

In a three- to six-month grand tour, you could start in Dakar or Gambia, head south and east through Guinea-Bissau, Guinea, Côte d'Ivoire and Ghana, then east into Togo, Benin, Nigeria and on to Cameroon, or north into the Sahel regions of Burkina Faso or Niger and then back west, following the Niger River through Mali, and returning to the start via Mauritania.

PLANNING

When to Go

The best time to visit West Africa is the drier and generally cooler period from November to February (see Climate in the Facts about West Africa chapter). Any time up to April (in the southern coastal countries) or May (in the Sahel countries) is also dry; from then on it gets progressively hotter. From May/June to September/October is the rainy season, which is not optimal for travelling, although in the Sahel rain only falls for a few hours per day, keeping temperatures down and the skies clear of dust.

If you do travel in West Africa during the rains, the biggest challenge will probably be getting around. Most major roads in the region are tar or all-weather dirt, but minor roads often become impassable, especially if you're travelling by public transport. Many wildlife reserves are also closed from June to November, as tracks can become too muddy to negotiate. On the positive side, you'll have things to yourself, and the scenery in many areas will be lush and green.

In addition to the rains, other factors to consider when planning your trip are tourist seasons and festivals. Although West Africa is not a major tourist destination compared with other parts of the continent, there are some areas where tourists congregate at certain times of the year. For example, hotels along the coasts of Senegal and Gambia are packed with European sunbathers on package tours from December to March (and to a lesser extent, in November and April). The Dogon Country area of Mali is also crowded at this time, especially in December and January.

Experiencing regional festivals can be a highlight of travel in the region, and it's worth considering timing your trip to coincide with some of the major ones. In the Sahel countries, especially note when Ramadan and major Islamic holidays will take place. For an overview, see Public Holidays & Special Events later in this chapter.

What Kind of Trip

Important considerations here are what type of transport you will use, whether to travel solo or with others, and whether to travel independently or as part of an organised tour.

While some people tour West Africa in their own vehicle, the majority of travellers use buses, bush taxis and trains. This is a lot slower than with a private vehicle, and you probably won't reach as many places, but it's inexpensive and a great way to experience local life.

Independent solo travel is one of the best ways to meet and get to know local people. Getting around by public transport is straightforward and inexpensive, and locals are always ready to help. Travelling independently as a couple, or with a friend or two, may cut you off a bit from locals (as you'll talk to each other on the bus, rather than to the people sitting next to you) but it's a good way of cutting costs. For example, you can share hotel rooms, and in national parks or wilderness areas the cost of hiring guides or boats can be shared. With a small group, you can also consider hiring a car or perhaps a boat (eg, for a trip down the Niger River in Mali) for a few days in order to reach areas that are more problematic or time-consuming by public transport.

Organised tours can be arranged locally or at home, and can last anywhere from a few days to several months. Tours have the advantage of eliminating time-consuming logistics (such as sorting out food and accommodation), and are a good option if you have more money than time or don't wish to travel alone. Organised tours (or hired cars) are also the only way to visit some national parks. However, they will almost always be more expensive than doing things yourself. To make things more affordable, solo travellers can try to team up with others, while small groups can arrange 'private tours' and have some room for price negotiation. For more information, see Organised Tours in the Getting There & Away chapter.

Maps

For regional coverage, the regularly updated Michelin map *Africa: North and West* (sheet No 953, formerly No 153, scale 1:4,000,000) is one of the best and most detailed, and something of a classic. It's lent its name to the 153 Club whose members have driven across the Sahara and around West Africa, and – together with this guidebook, of course – is something no overland driver should be without. Even so, expect a few discrepancies between the map and reality, especially regarding road information, as old tracks get upgraded and once-smooth highways become potholed disasters. Also, the map excludes the southernmost portion of Cameroon.

Other maps include the Bartholemew *Africa West* (1:3,500,000), which lacks the route accuracy of the Michelin but has the advantage of contour shading, and the similar map put out by RV Reise-und Verkehrsverlag in Germany (which also excludes southern Cameroon). For wider travels, Bartholemew's *Africa: Continental Travel Map* shows all the main routes and towns, with contour shading, and makes a good souvenir for afterwards.

Maps of individual countries are described in more detail in the relevant chapters, but worth noting is the Institut Géographique National (IGN) *Pays et Villes du Monde* series, which includes Benin, Burkina Faso, Cameroon, Côte d'Ivoire, Guinea, Guinea-Bissau, Mali, Niger, Senegal and Togo. IGN also produces *Carte de l'Afrique* sheets, which were surveyed in the 1960s and don't seem to have been updated since, as well as a dated map encompassing several national parks in the region (Arli, Pendjari, W, Comoë and Kéran). For the former British colonies, including Nigeria and Gambia, the *Traveller's Map* series produced by Macmillan is best. Macmillan also puts out a good map of Cameroon. *International Travel Maps* cover several West African countries including Cameroon, Gambia, Ghana, Senegal and Sierra Leone.

What to Bring

It pays to travel light in West Africa. With a small, light bag, you'll be unencumbered in crowds, you can avoid having your belongings loaded onto bus roof racks (where it may be damaged or tampered with) and you're less likely to have hassles with luggage fees on bush taxis. Ideally, try to bring only what fits into a backpack small enough to pass as hand luggage on the plane.

Unless you'll be on an organised tour where you won't have to handle your own luggage, backpacks are by far the most practical type of luggage. A smaller daypack is useful for when your main bag is left at a hotel. Whatever you bring, it's a good idea to put your clothes and other gear in plastic bags inside your pack to protect them from moisture and dust.

Clothes Throughout the region, clothing should be lightweight and modest. Items to consider bringing include a few shirts, trousers and/or a skirt, shorts, underwear, socks, a strong pair of shoes and flip-flops (thongs) or sandals for showers and beaches. Women should have at least one pair of slacks or a skirt or other wrap, and both men and women should have shirts with sleeves. A hat is essential, as are sunglasses, and a lightweight sweatshirt is useful from December to February in the Sahel and in areas at altitude. During the rains, you'll need a waterproof jacket. Anything else you find yourself without can easily be bought along the way, either new, second-hand, or tailor-made.

Given the emphasis that West Africans place on dress, especially in the cities, consider taking a set of smart clothes for special occasions such as visa applications, crossing troublesome borders, or if you're invited to somebody's house. Military-style gear isn't recommended, as you may be taken for a soldier.

Equipment Essentials include a basic medical kit (see the boxed text 'Medical Kit Check List' later in this chapter), a sturdy water bottle, water purifier and filter (if you will be in rural areas), torch and spare batteries, and a mosquito net; free-standing nets are heavier than regular ones, but often more practical.

Optional items include camera and film, binoculars, universal washbasin plug, travel alarm clock, Swiss Army–style knife, a length of cord for drying clothes or securing a mozzie net, sewing kit and small calculator (for working out exchange rates). A padlock can be useful to secure your pack from opportunistic thieves, and for when hotel locks are dodgy. Earplugs can be handy as cheap hotels are often noisy. If you'll be doing any boat travel, a waterproof bag to protect the contents of your backpack is useful, as is a smaller one for your daypack.

Other things include a wash kit and towel. If you wear contact lenses, bring all the cleaning and soaking solutions you will need, as well as a pair of prescription glasses as a back up, or for when the air is too dusty to wear your contact lenses.

Camp sites are limited, and cater mainly to travellers with their own vehicles, so it's hardly worth carrying around a tent and camping gear. A lightweight sleeping bag is useful in the cooler months, particularly if you're sleeping on roofs, as is often an option. A sleeping sheet is especially useful for cheap hotels where bedding is either not provided or is less than appealing.

RESPONSIBLE TOURISM

Tourism is one of the largest industries in the world, and the effects of tourists on destinations can be both substantial and positive. For example, in areas with wildlife or interesting natural features such as waterfalls and forests, if at least a portion of tourist revenues goes to local inhabitants they will have an incentive to protect the areas further, while at the same time being able to maintain their traditional lifestyles. Other positive effects of tourism can include job creation, and support for local craft industries. Even in protected areas that may not be of great interest to tourists, or may be difficult to reach, the essential incentive to protect the area will still be present if local people can gain some benefit (eg, from employment or indirectly through wood harvesting or limited hunting) rather than being completely excluded. This can be seen in some protected areas in Gambia. At Kiang West National Park, for example, the continuation of certain activities, such as cattle grazing and (more controversially) rice cultivation, is permitted in the park. At Niumi National Park, also in Gambia, community groups have been established to give local people a formal voice in the park management structure – ideally so they can benefit from the sustainable use of natural resources. On the Gambian coast, areas of ecological importance are being earmarked as tourist attractions in their natural state. Local people stand to benefit from the income this will attract, which in turn will hopefully ensure the area's long-term survival. Another example illustrating how the link between tourism and conservation can be positively exploited is seen in Parc National de Taï (Côte d'Ivoire), which protects one of West Africa's largest stands of rainforest. Thanks to the efforts of a village tourism project, forest clearing and poaching have decreased significantly in recent years. (See the boxed text 'Conservation & Ecotourism: The Taï Example' in the Côte d'Ivoire chapter.)

Tourism can also have very negative effects, though, particularly when destinations cannot cope with the number of tourists they attract, leading to damage to natural ecologies and human environments. In an effort to counter these effects, some companies

Guidelines for Responsible Tourism

In regions such as West Africa where the global inequities of wealth distribution are so apparent, it's particularly important to ensure that your travel enjoyment is not at the expense of locals and their environment. The UK-based organisation, Tourism Concern (☎ 020-7753 3330, fax 7753 3331, W www.tourismconcern.org.uk), Stapleton House, 277–281 Holloway Rd, London N7 8HN, has established a set of guidelines for travellers interested in minimising the negative impact they have on the environment and people of countries they visit. These include:

- Save precious natural resources. Try not to waste water. Switch off lights and air-conditioning when you go out. Avoid places that clearly consume limited resources such as water and electricity at the expense of local residents.
- Support local enterprise. Use locally owned hotels and restaurants and support trade and craft workers by buying locally made souvenirs. But help safeguard the environment by avoiding souvenirs made from local wildlife, particularly endangered species.
- Ask before taking close-up photographs of people. If you don't speak the language, a gesture will be understood and appreciated.
- Please don't give money, sweets, pens etc to children. It encourages begging. A donation to a recognised project – a health centre or school – is more constructive.
- Respect for local etiquette earns you respect. Politeness is a virtue in all parts of the world, but remember that people have different ideas about what's polite. In many places, revealing clothes are insensitive to local feelings. Similarly, public displays of affection are often culturally inappropriate.
- Learn something about the history and current affairs of the country. It helps you understand the idiosyncrasies of its people, and helps prevent misunderstandings and frustrations.
- Be patient, friendly and sensitive. Remember that you are a guest.

offer 'ecofriendly' or 'ecotourism' holidays. Originally, these terms designated tourism that focused on respect for local cultures and conservation of human and natural environments. Now, though, they have become overused and are often meaningless. When planning your trip, don't be fooled by travel companies claiming to be 'ecofriendly' just because they do things outdoors. Activities such as desert driving, hiking, boating, wildlife viewing or sightseeing trips to remote and fragile areas can be more environmentally or culturally harmful than conventional hotel holidays in specially developed resorts. Environmentalists point out that, although tourism relies on natural resources such as healthy wildlife populations or rich cultural traditions, it often does little to sustain them. If you want to support tour companies with a good environmental record, look beyond vague 'ecofriendly' claims and ask what they are really doing to protect or support the environment and the people who live there.

Visitors to Africa are often asked by environmental organisations to consider the amount of money they pay during their holiday, and to ensure that as much as possible stays within the 'host' country to the benefit of local people. Overland truck passengers and independent backpackers can contribute just as much to local economies as high-rolling tourists who come to a country on a short all-inclusive trip paid for overseas.

Another important dimension of responsible tourism is the manner and attitude that visitors assume towards locals. Respect is of the utmost importance, both in personal dealings as well as in your overall behaviour and your style of dress. One aspect of respect relates to indiscriminate gift-giving, which has the effect of undermining societal structures. There are many missions and aid agencies in West Africa doing good work. Channelling your donations and gifts through them is the best way to ensure that they will reach the people who need them most.

TOURIST OFFICES

With just a handful of exceptions, West Africa is not geared for tourism, and there are few tourist offices abroad. Some countries run small tourist offices at their embassies, which may be helpful for getting brochures or general travel information.

Once in West Africa, some countries have Ministry of Tourism information offices, but apart from offering a few old brochures they're unlikely to be of much assistance, especially for budget travellers. Notable exceptions – where a town or city may have a genuinely useful tourist office – are listed in individual country chapters. You'll usually have more success inquiring with staff at tour companies or hotels.

VISAS & DOCUMENTS

Passport

Before travelling in West Africa, make sure you have enough empty pages in your passport. You will need about two pages per country – one for the visa and another for the border stamps, plus extra pages for countries where you may have to report to police along the way. Many officials prefer passports that expire at least six months after your trip ends.

Visas

This section contains general information about visas – for country-specific visa information, see the Facts for the Visitor sections of the individual country chapters.

The general rule for West Africa is to get your visas before leaving home. They are rarely issued at land borders and only occasionally at airports. Also, if you're flying from outside Africa, many airlines won't let you on board without a visa anyway.

Visa agencies are worth considering if you need visas to several countries before you leave home, or if there's no relevant embassy in your home country. For longer trips or more flexibility, it's possible to get most of your visas in the region as you go along, although this requires some advance planning.

Visa fees average between US$20 and US$50, with prices often varying depending on where you apply. Multiple-entry visas usually cost more than single-entry visas. Check the visa's validity length and its start date when deciding where to make your application. When applying for a visa, you may have to show proof that you intend to leave the country (eg, an air ticket) or that you have enough funds to support yourself during your visit.

Most visa applications require between two and four passport photos, either black and white or colour. Inexpensive photo shops are found throughout the region, and rural areas invariably have a village photographer who can do the job for you.

Travel Insurance

A travel insurance policy to cover theft and loss is recommended, and some sort of medical insurance is essential. Always check the small print when shopping around. Some policies specifically exclude 'dangerous activities', which can include scuba diving, motorcycling and even trekking, and a locally acquired motorcycle licence may not be valid under some policies. Also, some policies offer lower and higher medical-expense options, with the higher ones chiefly for countries such as the USA, which have extremely high medical costs.

Hospitals in Africa are not free, and the good ones are not cheap. If your policy requires you to pay on the spot and claim later, make sure you keep all documentation. Some policies ask you to call collect (reverse charges) to a centre in your home country where an immediate assessment of your problem is made.

Check in particular that the policy covers an emergency flight home, as emergency air evacuations can be extremely expensive.

Other Documents

You may need other documents, including: proof of your vaccinations, especially yellow fever (required in most countries – see Health later for more details) and a student or youth card (occasionally good for various discounts).

If you intend to hire a car, you will need your driving license and an International Driving Permit (IDP). IDPs are easy and inexpensive to get in your home country – they are usually issued by major motoring associations, such as the AA in Britain – and are useful if you're driving in countries where your own licence may not be recognised (officially or unofficially). They have the added advantage of being written in several languages, with a photo and many stamps, and so look more impressive when presented to car-rental clerks or policemen at road blocks.

Copies

Photocopies of all your important documents, plus tickets and credit cards, will help speed up replacement if the originals are lost or stolen. Keep these, and a list of your travellers-cheque numbers, separate from other valuables, and leave copies with someone at home so they can be faxed to you if necessary.

EMBASSIES & CONSULATES

It's important to realise what your own embassy – the embassy of the country of which you are a citizen – can and can't do to help if you get into trouble.

Generally speaking, embassy staff won't be much help in emergencies if the trouble is remotely your own fault. Remember that you are bound by the laws of the country you are in. Your embassy will not be sympathetic if you end up in jail after committing a crime locally, even if such actions are legal in your own country.

In genuine emergencies you might get some assistance, but only if other channels have been exhausted. For example, if you need to get home urgently, a free ticket home is exceedingly unlikely – the embassy would expect you to have insurance. If you have all your money and documents stolen, it might assist with getting a new passport, but a loan for onward travel will be out of the question.

Some embassies used to keep letters for travellers or have a small reading room with home newspapers and magazines, but few provide these services any more.

See the Facts for the Visitor sections of the individual country chapters for addresses and contact details of embassies and consulates. Note that in some parts of Africa, countries are represented by an 'honorary consul' who is not a full-time diplomat but rather is usually an expatriate with limited duties.

MONEY

Details on currencies and places to exchange money are given in the Facts for the Visitor sections of the country chapters. Throughout the regional chapters and in countries where inflation is high, prices are quoted in US dollars.

The principal currency of the region is the West African CFA (Communauté Financière Africaine) franc, which is used in Benin, Burkina Faso, Côte d'Ivoire, Guinea-Bissau, Mali, Niger, Senegal and Togo, and is now valued at €0.15 per CFA100. It can also be used (or easily exchanged for local currency) in some other West African countries, such as Gambia, Guinea and Ghana.

Prior to 1 January 2002, the CFA was fixed against (and supported by) the French franc (FF) at a rate of 100:1, effectively making it a 'hard' currency. For travellers, one result of this arrangement was that some banks would change FF cash into CFA without charging a fee or commission. As this book went to press, it was unclear whether banks would be as willing to waive commissions for euro transactions as for those involving French francs. However, at hotels and foreign-exchange (forex) bureaus, expect rates of €650 or lower, and plan on paying commissions when changing euro (or any other denomination) travellers cheques into CFA.

Cameroon, as well as neighbouring Central African countries, use the Central African CFA franc, which is linked to the euro at the same rate as the West African CFA franc, and with the West African CFA at a rate of one to one. However, you can't make payments with Central African CFA in the West African CFA zone or vice versa.

The political leaders of Gambia, Ghana, Guinea, Nigeria and Sierra Leone – the majority of West Africa's non-CFA block – have confirmed their intent to move towards their own common currency, to be known as the 'eco'. The goal is for the eco to merge with the CFA by 2004, creating a single currency throughout most of West Africa, although it is unlikely that this timeline will be met. In the meantime, countries outside the CFA zone each have their own individual currencies.

Exchanging Money

In CFA-zone countries, the best currency to travel with is the euro, in a mixture of cash and travellers cheques, and it's essential to take some euros in cash. Other major international currencies such as the US dollar and the UK pound can be changed in capital cities and tourist areas, but at less-favourable rates. In the non-CFA countries, the best currency to travel with is US dollars (in a mix of cash and travellers cheques), with euros, UK pounds and other major currencies accepted in larger cities.

The main places to change money are banks and – in some countries – forex bureaus. Where they exist, forex bureaus are often more efficient than banks, usually offer slightly higher rates and are open longer hours, though many don't accept travellers cheques. Charges and commissions vary, with some banks and forex bureaus charging a flat fee, and others a percentage commission; some charge both a fee and a commission. The bank or forex bureau with the higher commission, though, may also offer a higher exchange rate – so you could still be better off.

At the time of writing, it was possible to get both West and Central African CFA francs at the forex bureau in Paris' Charles de Gaulle airport. If this service continues and if you're waiting for a connecting flight in Paris, it's worth getting some CFA to tide you over for your first day or two in West Africa, especially if you're heading to a country such as Cameroon, where commissions for currency exchanges are high.

Towards the end of your trip, ensure that you're not left with large amounts of local currency. Apart from export restrictions, exchanging CFA francs in countries outside the region is difficult or impossible, except for France. In most countries within the CFA zone, it's relatively easy to change remaining CFA into euros, but difficult to change CFA to dollars. On leaving non-CFA countries, it's usually not possible to reconvert local currency into foreign currency, except in Gambia where it's relatively straightforward, although rates are low.

Also note that if you're travelling between the West African and Central African CFA zones, it's easy to change CFA notes of one zone for those of the other at banks, but more difficult to change coins.

Cash & Travellers Cheques Cash is far more convenient than travellers cheques but cannot be replaced if lost or stolen. Travellers cheques are refundable if lost or stolen, although in some West African countries (ie, Cameroon, Côte d'Ivoire and Guinea-Bissau), they are either difficult to exchange, attract high exchange commissions, or both, and throughout the region, banks in smaller towns will often not accept them. The best strategy is to take a mixture of cash and travellers cheques. Well-known brands of travellers cheques are better as they're more likely to be recognised by bank staff. American Express (AmEx), followed by Thomas Cook/MasterCard, are the most widely accepted, and some banks will take only one or the other.

For both cash and travellers cheques, take a mixture of high and low denominations. If you're about to leave the region, or a certain country, this will enable you to change enough currency for just a few days without having lots of spare cash to get rid of. Also, a supply of small denomination cash notes (eg, US$1 and US$5 and the euro equivalent) can come in handy for cases when change is unavailable.

In addition to your main travel funds, carry some cash with you – perhaps about US$300 – set aside specifically as a contingency fund for emergencies. At least part of this should be in euros if you will be travelling in Francophone West Africa.

Note that the USA changed the design of the US$100 bill in the mid-1990s and old-style US$100 notes are not accepted at places that don't have a light machine for checking watermarks.

ATMs Automated teller machines (ATMs) exist in a few capitals and large cities in West Africa and, in theory, accept credit and debit cards from banks with reciprocal agreements. While in a few countries you'll often meet with success, there are enough problems – including finding a machine inoperable, or losing your card – that it's best to regard them only as an emergency standby. The main exception to this is Côte d'Ivoire, where you'll need to rely on ATMs. See Money in the Côte d'Ivoire chapter for details.

Credit Cards You can occasionally use a credit card or charge card to pay for some items, but these are usually limited to top-end hotels and restaurants, car-rental companies and occasionally air tickets; an extra commission is often attached, usually ranging from 3% to 15%. You can also use your card to withdraw cash at some banks in the region, especially in countries that use CFA. However, as with ATMs and, except as noted otherwise in the country chapters, it's best not to count on this as computer breakdowns and other problems can leave you stranded. Where credit-card advances are possible, the process is sometimes straightforward with minimal hassle, but usually it is time consuming – sometimes taking up to a day or more. It can also be expensive if extra commissions are charged, and the maximum withdrawal amount is often restricted. Visa is the most widely accepted, followed by MasterCard.

An advantage of debit cards is there's no bill to pay (assuming you have the money in your account), so are more suited for longer travels. However, they are not accepted by many car-rental agencies and by some banks and ATMs, which means they are not very practical in much of West Africa. Also, the risk may be higher if the card is stolen.

International Transfers These transfers can save you from carrying around large amounts of notes and cheques if you are travelling for a long time, and can be useful for topping up your funds. However, the process is generally expensive and time consuming in West Africa, and is generally best used only as a last resort. Transfers usually take at least three to four days, and sometimes several weeks to clear, and occasionally there are hassles such as the local bank denying receiving your money after it has actually arrived. If you do need to transfer money, ask your forwarding bank to send you separate confirmation with full details, including the routing or transfer number, account and branch numbers, and address and telephone contacts. With this, you can then go to the recipient bank with proof that your money has been sent.

Most countries will only give you cash in local currency. Check the regulations in advance to avoid winding up with large sums of unconvertible currency.

Western Union Money Transfer has representatives in many West African countries,

Don't Forget the Purchase Receipt!

Wherever you are in the region, most banks require you to show your original purchase receipts in order to change travellers cheques, so it's essential to bring these. Carry them with you (separately from your cheques), but also leave a copy at home, as well as elsewhere in your luggage in case the original receipts or the cheques themselves are stolen.

and is a good starting point, although its local partners are not always particularly efficient.

Currency Regulations Except in CFA-zone countries, the import and export of local currency is either prohibited or severely restricted – typically limited to the equivalent of about US$10 – although enforcement of this regulation is fairly lax. As part of their fiscal control, some countries use currency declaration forms. More commonly, control consists simply of questioning as to how much currency you have. You'll then be asked to turn any extra over to the underpaid and ever-hopeful airport agents. Occasionally you may be asked to open your wallet or show the contents of your pockets. Recently in Abidjan airport, we watched during the boarding of one international flight as several unsuspecting travellers were asked by uniformed officials how much currency they had with them in total (not just local currency). Several who displayed wallets containing several hundred dollars cash were then asked to go into a small side office away from the watching eyes of other passengers, where they were prevailed upon to relinquish some of the money for a fictitious currency regulation violation. To avoid a scenario like this, it's worth doing a bit of advance planning before getting to the airport. Divide your money and store it in several places so it's not all in one lump, and try to look as savvy as possible when going through customs checks. Responding creatively to questions is also helpful – for example, explaining that you relied on credit card for the majority of your expenses (be prepared to show a card), or (if it's true) explaining that you're just in transit and thus don't have much money with you.

Black Market In some countries, artificially low fixed exchange rates create a demand for unofficial hard currency, so you can get more local money by changing on the so-called 'black market'. In CFA-zone countries, this is not a consideration because local currency is easily converted and the rate is pegged to the euro. In many other countries, banks and forex bureaus offer floating rates, so any black market has also disappeared, although you may be offered from 5% to 10% more than bank rates by shady characters on the street, who often hang out around markets or outside banks and post offices. Unofficial moneychangers are also tolerated by the authorities in many border areas, where there are rarely banks.

Although you may have no choice at a border crossing, the general rule throughout West Africa is to never change money on the street. The chances of getting ripped off are high, and even if the moneychanger is honest, you don't know who's watching from the other side of the street. Even at borders, be alert, as changers are notorious for pulling all sorts of stunts with bad rates and folded notes.

Try to anticipate your needs and change enough in advance to cover yourself on weekends and during nonbanking hours. If you do get stuck outside banking hours, you can try changing money at top-end hotels or tour companies, although rates are likely to be poor. Airport exchange bureaus also are often open longer hours and on weekends. Another option, and much better than changing on the street, is to ask discreetly at a shop selling imported items. 'The banks are closed, do you know anyone who can help me...?' is a better approach than 'Do you want to change money?'.

In countries with a real black market, where you can get considerably more for your money, don't forget that this is morally questionable and against the law. What's more, dealers often work with corrupt policemen and can trap you in a set-up where you may be 'arrested', shaken down and eventually lose all your money.

Security

To keep your money, passport and air ticket safe from pickpockets, secure a pouch under your clothes. Ideally, your money should be divided into several smaller stashes and stored in various places on your body. If your hotel seems trustworthy, you can leave some of it in the hotel safe, preferably in some sort of lockable pouch or at least in a signature-sealed envelope so that any tampering will be evident. When walking about town, keep a small amount of cash – including ready change and small bills – separate from your other money and handy, so that you don't need to pull out large wads of bills for paying taxi fares or making purchases. This may also be useful as a decoy to give to any assailant if you happen to be robbed, while the remainder of your valuables remain safely hidden.

Costs

Compared with many other parts of the developing world, travel in West Africa is expensive and travellers who have been in South America, India or even parts of Europe are often shocked when they come here. Very generally speaking, prices of things in West Africa are around 50% to 75% of what they are in Europe, Australasia or North America, and imported items may be twice what they cost in the West. Exceptions to the generally high prices include locally produced items such as food and locally brewed beer, and local transport.

Accommodation costs start from about US$5 a night for a bed in a very basic local resthouse, to US$10 to US$15 for something a bit more comfortable, US$30 to US$70 for mid-range hotels, and up to US$100 or US$200 and sometimes more for top-end establishments.

Food can be very cheap if you eat from markets and street stalls. In local restaurants, plan on meals costing between US$2 and US$7. In capital cities or resort areas, meals at places catering primarily to foreigners can easily cost US$15.

Local transport is inexpensive; most people travel by bush taxi, bus or train, for which you should expect to pay about US$1 to US$2 per 100km throughout the region. Car rental, however, averages about US$100 per day and sometimes more, plus petrol. When estimating your costs, you should also include items such as visa fees and national park admission charges, plus the cost of organised tours or activities such as hiking, where local guides have to be hired. Taking all these into account, shoestring travellers could get by on about US$15 per day (or even less), if you really work at it. For a bit more comfort, US$25 to US$40 per day is a reasonable budget. With US$50 per day or more at your disposal, you could stay in decent hotels, eat well and travel quite comfortably (if good transport is available!).

Tipping & Bargaining

There are few clear rules on tipping in West Africa. In general, only the wealthy (ie, well-to-do locals and nearly all foreign visitors) are expected to tip. Anyone staying in a fancy hotel would be expected to tip porters and other staff, but there would not be the same expectation from a backpacker in a cheap hotel.

Everyone – locals and foreigners – is expected to tip around 10% at the better restaurants, although service is sometimes included in the bill. At the more basic restaurants and eating houses no tips are expected from anyone. There's a grey area between these two classes of restaurants, where tipping is rarely expected from locals, but may be expected of foreigners. Even wealthier West Africans will sometimes tip at smaller restaurants – not so much because it's expected, but as a show of status.

Locals seldom tip in privately hired taxis, but some drivers expect well-heeled travellers to tip about 10%, especially if you have hired the vehicle for a lengthy trip. In shared taxis around cities tipping is almost unheard of. If you rent a car with driver, a tip is always expected, usually about 10% of the total rental cost, and more if it is a multiday rental or if your driver has been exceptionally good.

POST & COMMUNICATIONS

Post and telephone services are moderately reliable in most West African capitals and cities. In rural areas, though, service can range from slow to nonexistent. For details on rates and prices see the Facts for the Visitor sections of the individual country chapters.

Post

Letters sent from a major capital take about a week to 10 days to reach most parts of Europe, and about two weeks to reach North America or Australasia – although it's sometimes much longer. For more speed and certainty, a few countries have 'express' services, but the main alternative option is a courier service. DHL, for example, has offices in most West African capitals.

The most common way to receive mail is the poste restante service, where letters are held for your collection at a post office. Although some smaller post offices may offer this service, it's more reliable to use the main post office in a capital or large city.

Letters should be addressed clearly to you, with your family name in capitals and underlined, at Poste Restante, General Post Office (English-speaking countries) or PTT

The Fine Art of Bargaining

In many West African countries, bargaining over prices is a way of life. Visitors often have difficulty with this idea, as they are used to things having a fixed value, whereas in West Africa commodities are considered worth whatever their seller can get for them. It really is no different to the concept of an auction and should be treated as one more intriguing aspect of travel in the region.

Basics

In markets selling basic items such as fruit and vegetables traders will sometimes put their asking price high when they see you, a wealthy foreigner. If you pay this – whether out of ignorance or guilt about how much you have compared with most local people – you may be considered foolish, but you'll also be doing fellow travellers a disservice by creating the impression that all foreigners are willing to pay any price named. You may also harm the local economy: by paying high prices you put some items out of the local people's reach. And who can blame the traders – why sell something to a local when foreigners will pay twice as much? So, in cases such as this, you may need to bargain over the price.

Having said that, many traders will quote you the same price that locals pay, particularly away from cities or tourist areas, so it's important not to go around expecting everybody to charge high prices. It's also important to keep things in perspective and not haggle over a few cents. After the first few days in a country (when you'll inevitably pay over the odds a few times) you'll soon get to learn the standard prices for basic items, though prices can change depending on where you buy. For example, a soft drink in a city may be one-third the price you'll pay in a remote rural area, where transport costs have to be paid. Conversely, fruit and vegetables are cheaper in the areas where they're actually grown.

Souvenirs

At craft and curio stalls, where items are specifically for tourists, it's a completely different story, and bargaining is very much expected. The trader's aim is to identify the highest price you're willing to pay. Your aim is to find the price below which the vendor will not sell. People have all sorts of formulae for working out what this should be, but there are no hard-and-fast rules. Some traders may initially ask a price four (or more) times higher than what they're prepared to accept, although it's usually lower than this. Decide what you want to pay or what others have told you they've paid; your first offer should be about half this. At this stage, the vendor may laugh or feign outrage, while you plead abject poverty. The trader's price then starts to drop from the original quote to a more realistic level. When it does, you begin making better offers until you arrive at a mutually agreeable price.

And that's the crux – *mutually agreeable*. Travellers often moan about how they were 'overcharged' by souvenir traders. But, when things have no fixed price, nobody really gets overcharged. If you don't like the price, then don't pay it.

The best results when bargaining usually come from a friendly and spirited exchange, and there's never any point in losing your temper. If the effort seems a waste of time, politely take your leave. Sometimes traders will call you back if they think their stubbornness may be counterproductive. Very few will pass up the chance of making a sale, however thin the profit.

If traders won't come down to a price you feel is fair (or if you can't afford the asking price), it either means they really aren't making a profit, or that if you don't pay their prices, they know somebody else will.

(Francophone countries), then the town and country where you want to collect the mail.

To collect your mail, you generally need to show your passport or other identification. Letters sometimes take a few weeks to work through the system, so have them sent to a place where you're going to be for a while, or will be passing through more than once. Some poste restante services levy a nominal charge when you collect mail, and many limit the length of time they will hold letters (usually one month).

Some hotels and tour companies operate mail-holding services, and AmEx customers can have mail sent to company branches.

Telephone & Fax

Most cities and large towns have public telephone offices at the post office where you can make international calls and send faxes. There are also private telecommunications centres in major towns and cities throughout the region.

Telephone and fax connections to places outside West Africa are reasonably good, as the transmission is via satellite, though it's generally much easier and less expensive to call in the other direction – from the USA, Europe or Australasia to West Africa. However, calls between African countries are often relayed on land lines or through Europe, which means the reception is frequently bad – assuming you can get a call through in the first place. For calls to other countries within the African continent, there's also often a wait – from a few minutes up to several hours, depending on your location and the time of day – between the time you place your call with an operator and the time you actually get through.

Costs for international calls and faxes to Europe, the USA or Australasia start at about US$3 to US$4 per minute, with a few countries offering slightly reduced rates at night and on weekends. In many West African countries you can buy phonecards at post offices or telephone offices, or at shops near cardphones. These usually make international calls slightly cheaper, but the cards are generally only sold during regular business hours so you'll need to plan ahead. At some airports and top-end hotels in the major capitals, telephones may accept credit cards, but at high rates.

Dial-direct or 'home-direct' numbers are available from a few West African countries. With these, you can dial directly to an operator in your home country, who you can then request to reverse the charges, or to charge the call to a phone-company charge card or to your home number. These home-direct numbers are usually toll free, but if you are using a public phone booth you may need a coin or local phonecard to be connected. Check with your home phone company for access numbers and a listing of the countries where they have home-direct numbers.

Country codes for dialling West African countries are given in the facts box at the start of each country chapter.

Mobile (cell) phones are common in most West African cities, where they can be easily and relatively inexpensively rented or purchased. They are also becoming increasingly popular with hotels and businesses since land lines are often unreliable. Coverage, however, is still quite limited, and nonexistent in most rural areas.

Telegram

This archaic method of communication is often overlooked, and has been largely superseded by email, but if all you want to do is to send home an 'All OK' message, and no email is available, it can be cheaper than using a telephone or fax. A 10-word minimum (including address) is sometimes imposed but the charge is rarely more than US$3. Inquire at main post offices.

Email & Internet Access

There are Internet cafés in all capital cities and in a few larger towns as well, but not in smaller towns or rural or remote areas. Internet cafés in capital cities are often open evenings and weekends, as well as regular business hours. Costs are generally inexpensive, except in places where it's a long-distance call to access the server. Speeds range from fast to extremely slow, and can be quite erratic.

In a few places where there's no Internet access, you may find a telecommunications shop where you can send and receive email messages. Also, a fair number of tour companies and mid-range and top-end hotels have email facilities and will allow clients to send and receive messages, usually at a minimal cost.

DIGITAL RESOURCES

The World Wide Web is a rich resource for travellers. You can research your trip, hunt down bargain air fares, book hotels, check on weather conditions or chat with locals and other travellers about the best places to

French Keyboards

Many Internet cafés in Francophone West Africa have 'French' keyboards, which can slow you down when typing if you are not used to them. Happily, though, some are loaded with English-language settings. To 'Anglicise' a keyboard, look for a 'Fr' icon on the bottom right of the screen, and scroll up to click on 'En'.

Amy Karafin

visit (or avoid). Some websites that may be of interest to travellers to West Africa are listed in this section.

The Lonely Planet website (W www.lonelyplanet.com) is a good place to start looking. Here you'll find succinct summaries on travelling to most places on earth, postcards from other travellers and the Thorn Tree bulletin board, where you can ask questions before you go or dispense advice when you get back. You can also find travel news and updates to many of our most popular guidebooks, and the subWWWay section links you to the most-useful travel resources elsewhere on the Web.

Websites worth taking a look at for background information on West Africa include the following:

African Birdclub This site contains interesting reading and links for those going to West Africa for bird-watching.
W www.africanbirdclub.org

AllAfrica.com This is one of the most comprehensive news sites, with news from all over the continent.
W www.allafrica.com

BBC World Service – The Story of Africa The BBC site has historical information about West Africa and elsewhere on the continent, and links to research sites on West African kingdoms and more.
W www.bbc.co.uk/worldservice/africa/features/storyofafrica

Ecowas This is the official site of the Economic Community of West African States (Ecowas), with detailed economic and other information.
W www.ecowas.int

Index on Africa This is a comprehensive site put together by the Norwegian Council for Africa, with a reading list, good links, country-by-country cultural information, a language database and more.
W www.afrika.no

IRINNews This site has updated information on refugee issues and on regional trouble spots put out by the UN Humanitarian Information network.
W www.irinnews.org

University of Pennsylvania African Studies This is an excellent and comprehensive site with individual country pages and many links.
W www.sas.upenn.edu/African_Studies/Home_Page/Country.html

For other sources of African news, you could try the following websites: Africa Daily (W www.africadaily.com); AfricaOnline (W www.africaonline.com); BBC World Service (W news.bbc.co.uk); and PanaPress (W www.panapress.com).

In addition, Lonely Planet's homepage (W www.lonelyplanet.com) has links to sites on various West African countries. For country-specific websites, see the individual country chapters.

BOOKS

This section primarily lists publications focusing on all or part of West Africa. For information on local and country-specific literature, see Literature under Arts in the Facts about West Africa chapter, and the Arts and Books sections of individual country chapters.

If you're planning to take your own vehicle to or around West Africa, a selection of handbooks is listed under Taking Your Own Vehicle in the Land section of the Getting There & Away chapter.

Note that bookshops and libraries search for publications by title or author, so publisher details have not been included unless particularly relevant. Also note that we have only listed titles available in English; there are many more publications in French.

The nearest you'll get to a pocket library is *Africa* by Phyllis Martin & Patrick O'Meara, with scholarly but accessible essays on a wide range of subjects including history, religion, colonialism, sociology, art, music, popular culture, law, literature, politics, economics and the development crisis.

Lonely Planet

For more in-depth coverage, Lonely Planet has a travel guide to *The Gambia & Senegal*, and all the countries in the region are also included in *Africa on a shoestring*, which covers the continent in brief for budget travellers.

For onward travel, the *East Africa* guide includes Kenya, Tanzania, Uganda, Rwanda and Burundi, while *Southern Africa* includes Mozambique, Malawi, Zambia, Zimbabwe, Botswana, Namibia, South Africa and other countries.

Also look out for *Mali Blues: Travelling to an African Beat* by Lieve Joris, published in Lonely Planet's travel-literature series. It's a collection of four stories set in Mali, Mauritania and Senegal, in which the writer captures the rhythms of everyday life in the region, and tells the uplifting and tragic stories of its people.

For Francophone Africa, Lonely Planet's *French phrasebook* is highly recommended, as is Lonely Planet's *Portuguese phrasebook* for travel in Guinea-Bissau and Cape Verde.

If it's your first time in Africa, check out Lonely Planet's *Read This First: Africa*.

Travel

Travels in West Africa by Mary Kingsley was written in the late 19th century and, despite the title, is mostly confined to Cameroon and Gabon. It captures the spirit of the age, as the author describes encounters with wild places and wild people, all the while gathering fish specimens and facing every calamity with flamboyance, good humour and typically Victorian fortitude.

The Fearful Void by Geoffrey Moorhouse is a classic account of the author's 1970s attempt to cross the Sahara west to east, going via Chinguetti in Mauritania and Timbuktu in Mali. It examines the basis of fear, 'an extremity of human existence'.

Impossible Journey: Two Against the Sahara by Michael Asher is an enthralling account of the first successful west-to-east camel crossing of the Sahara, starting in Mauritania and passing through Mali and Niger before ending at the Nile. Asher's wife, who joined him on the trip a short time after their meeting and marriage, took the stunning photos.

Desert Travels by desert expert Chris Scott is a lighthearted and readable account of various journeys by motorbike in the Sahara and West Africa, as the author graduates from empty-tanked apprentice to expert dune-cruiser and desert connoisseur.

Anatomy of Restlessness by Bruce Chatwin is a collection of writings, which includes discussion of Chatwin's most recurring theme – the clash between nomads and settled civilisations – and a section on his 1970 visit to Timbuktu. This theme is also explored in his famous book *The Songlines*, which includes brief descriptions of Mauritania's nomadic Namadi people.

Chatwin's bewitching *Photographs & Notebooks* contains an intriguingly eclectic collection of pictures and observations from his travels, mainly in Mauritania, Mali and Benin.

For a more unusual kind of travel book, try *The Ends of the Earth* by Robert Kaplan. The author visits areas frequently seen as cultural, political and ecological devastation zones, including West Africa, analysing what he sees (Liberian refugee camps, the breakdown of society in Sierra Leone, the massive growth of urban poverty along the coastal strip from Lomé to Abidjan) in terms of the present and the future – about which he cannot help but be darkly pessimistic.

The Resource Guide to Travel in Sub-Saharan Africa has an extensive, critical review of all guidebooks, maps, travelogues and specialist manuals to the region, plus information on travel magazines, bookshops, publishers, libraries, tourist organisations, special-interest societies and conservation projects. Volume 1 covers East and West Africa.

Fiction

The Viceroy of Ouidah by Bruce Chatwin tells the story (partly based on fact) of a Brazilian trader stranded on the Slave Coast in the 17th century. But it's much more than this; with unique style and characteristic insight Chatwin also writes about history, imagination, human wanderlust and the spirit of Africa.

A Good Man in Africa by William Boyd is a humorous novel about a junior diplomat's struggles to maintain composure, all the time dealing with diplomats, presidents, girlfriends and the weather. *Brazzaville Beach*, set in West Africa, is far more mature, and discusses a range of themes, including the behavioural development of chimpanzees, human academic vanity and depressing African civil wars.

The Music in My Head by Mark Hudson is an engaging and darkly amusing novel about the power, influence and day-to-day realities of modern African music, set in a mythical city, instantly recognisable as Dakar. The urban atmosphere is perfectly captured, and extra twists include an unreliable, Nabokovian narrator.

Field Guides

At some national parks, locally produced booklets are occasionally available detailing local birds and other animals. If you have a deeper interest, a good regional field guide is recommended. For mammals, the classic volume for many years has been *Mammals of Africa* published by Collins, but it's now a bit dated. The more recently published *Kingdon Field Guide to African Mammals* by Jonathan Kingdon is highly regarded by naturalists. The author is a leading authority, and the book covers more than 1000 species, and discusses ecology, evolutionary relationships and conservation status as well as notes on identification and distribution, with colour pictures and maps.

For birds, try *A Field Guide to the Birds of West Africa* by W Serle & GJ Morel or *A Guide to the Birds of Western Africa* by Nik Borrow & Ron Demey. The more detailed but much heavier *Birds of Africa* by EK Urban, CH Fry & S Keith is a six-volume set with excellent illustrations. If you're heading to Cape Verde, try *A Birder's Guide to the Cape Verde Islands* by Dave Sargeant or *Birds of the Cape Verde Islands* by Cornelius J Hazevoet. Other specialised titles include *Forest Birds in Côte d'Ivoire* by ME Hartshore, PD Taylor & IS Francis; *The Birds of Ghana: An Annotated Checklist* by LG Grimes; and *The Birds of Nigeria: An Annotated Checklist* by JH Elgood.

History & Politics

A History of Africa by JD Fage, and *A Short History of Africa* by JD Fage & Roland Oliver are both comprehensive and concise paperbacks, covering the entire continent.

Africa Since 1800 by Roland Oliver & Anthony Atmore, covers the precolonial period up to 1875, followed by partition and colonial rule, independence and the post-independence decades. Other books by the same authors include *Africa in the Iron Age* and *The African Middle Ages 1400-1800*.

African Civilization Revisited: From Antiquity to Modern Times and *A History of West Africa 1000-1800* are just two of the many books by Basil Davidson, a leading and influential writer on African history.

West Africa Since 1800 by JB Webster & AA Boahen provides good in-depth treatment of the region in recent times.

The Africans by David Lamb is a portrait of early 1980s Africa, rich in political and social detail. The author visited 46 countries, revelling in midnight flights to witness little-known coups in obscure countries, but some critics suggest this rapid approach prevented in-depth understanding.

Africa: Dispatches From a Fragile Continent by Blaine Harden provides provocative and pessimistic reading on several topics, including the failure of African political leadership (the 'Big Man' syndrome).

In *Masters of Illusion – The World Bank and the Poverty of Nations*, Catherine Caufield discusses the influence that the global-development lending agency has had on poor countries around the world. The book's observations – that the social and environmental effects of projects are inadequately analysed – are shocking, while the conclusions – that despite loans totalling billions of US dollars the people of the developing world are worse off now than before – calls the whole institution into question.

Ecology & Environment

Africa in Crisis by Lloyd Timberlake emphasises that ecological issues cannot be regarded in isolation, and focuses on the political and environmental factors contributing to drought and famine in Africa, particularly the roles of international aid organisations and African leaders.

Squandering Eden by Mort Rosenblum & Doug Williamson is highly readable and proposes that broad-based stable development is dependent totally on workable relationships between African landholders and their environment.

African Silences by Peter Matthiessen is a deeply gripping, beautifully written book about the author's journeys through parts of West and Central Africa, and includes descriptions of research trips to estimate elephant populations in the region.

Arts

African Art by Frank Willett is a superb, well-illustrated and wide-ranging introductory paperback, while *African Art in Cultural Perspective* by William Bascom focuses on West and Central African sculpture. The large-format, full-colour and fantastically detailed *Africa Adorned* by Angela Fisher has an excellent section on West African jewellery and how it relates to cultural and social structures.

More specialist titles include *A Short History of African Art* by Gillon Werner; *African Traditional Architecture* by Susan Denyer; *African Textiles* by John Picton & John Mack, the best book on the subject, with numerous photographs; *Africa Through the Eyes of Women Artists* by Betty La Duke; *African Hairstyles* by Esi Sagay; and *Beads From the West African Trade* by Picard African Imports. *Beads* by Janet Coles & Robert Budwig has a section on Africa and is beautifully illustrated. *The Royal Arts of Africa: The Majesty of Form* by Suzanne Blier has several relevant chapters, including one on Cameroonian art (some excellent examples of which you can see in the Musée d'Art Camerounais in Yaoundé).

African Arts is a superb quarterly published by the African Studies Center (UCLA, Los Angeles, CA 90024), with good photography and well-researched articles.

NEWSPAPERS & MAGAZINES

There are no daily or weekly newspapers that cover the whole of West Africa, but several countries have national papers with good regional coverage. These are listed in the individual country chapters. Magazines covering the region, produced in English and available in most English-speaking countries (in Africa and elsewhere), include:

African Business It provides economic reports, finance and company news.

Africa Today This magazine has good political and economic news, plus business, sport and tourism.

Business in Africa This bimonthly concentrates on business and tourism, with a leaning towards West African and South African subjects.

Focus on Africa Published quarterly by the BBC, it has excellent news stories, accessible reports and a concise rundown of recent political events.

New African With a reputation for accurate and balanced reporting, this magazine has a mix of politics, financial and economic analysis, features on social and cultural affairs, sport, art, health and recreation.

West Africa This is a long-standing and respected weekly concentrating on political and economic news.

The most widely available French-language periodical is *Jeune Afrique*, a popular weekly magazine covering regional and world events.

RADIO & TV

All countries in the region have state-run and commercial radio stations, a few of which are listed in the country chapters.

International radio stations include Voice of America (for information on broadcast frequencies see its website on **W** www.voa.gov) and, better, the BBC World Service, especially its excellent Focus on Africa programme, which is widely listened to in many parts of West Africa. Both programmes can be picked up on various short-wave frequencies (listed in the BBC *Focus on Africa* magazine and on the website **W** www.bbc.co.uk) and are also relayed on FM by several local radio stations.

Many top-end and mid-range hotels have satellite dishes to receive international TV such as CNN and BBC World, as well as French channels.

PHOTOGRAPHY & VIDEO

You'll find plenty of subjects in West Africa for photography (with a video or 'normal' camera), but if this is a primary reason for your visit try to avoid the harmattan season, which is at its height in many areas of the region from late December to February (see Climate in the Facts about West Africa chapter for more details).

Film & Equipment

Film in West Africa is expensive (from US$6/14 for 24/36 exposures) because it is imported. Outside capital cities only standard print film (not slide or large format) is available. Even if the expiry date is still good, film may have been damaged by the heat. It's best to bring all you need with you.

The sunlight in West Africa is frequently very intense, so most people find 100ASA perfectly adequate, with possibly 200ASA or 400ASA for long-lens shots or visits to coastal areas in the rainy season.

Useful photographic accessories might include a small flash, a cable or remote shutter release, filters and a cleaning kit. Also, remember to take spare batteries.

Finally, some airports have x-ray machines for checking baggage that may not be safe for film. Even so-called film-safe models affect high-speed film (1000ASA and higher), especially if the film goes through several checks during your trip, so you may want to use a protective lead bag – they're fairly inexpensive. Alternatively, carry your film in your pocket or small plastic container, and have it checked manually by customs officials.

Photography Hints

Timing

The best times to take photographs on sunny days are the first two hours after sunrise and the last two before sunset. This takes advantage of the colour-enhancing rays cast by a low sun. Filters (eg, ultraviolet, polarising or 'skylight') can also help produce good results; ask for advice in a good camera shop.

Exposure

When photographing animals or people, take light readings on the subject and not the brilliant African background or your shots will turn out underexposed.

Camera Care

Factors that can spoil your camera or film include heat, humidity, very fine sand, saltwater and sunlight. Take appropriate precautions.

Wildlife Photography

For wildlife shots, a good lightweight 35mm SLR automatic camera with a lens between 210mm and 300mm should do the trick. Videos with zoom facility may be able to get closer. If your subject is nothing but a speck in the distance, try to resist wasting film, but keep the camera ready.

Restrictions

Avoid taking pictures of bridges, dams, airports, military equipment, government buildings and anything else that could be considered strategic. You may be arrested or have your film and camera confiscated. Some countries – usually those with precarious military governments – are particularly sensitive. If in doubt, ask first.

Photographing People

Always ask permission before photographing people, and respect their wishes. While some West Africans may enjoy being photographed, others do not. They may be superstitious about your camera, suspicious of your motives, or simply interested in whatever economic advantage they can gain from your desire to photograph them, and demand a fee for any shots taken. Other locals maintain their pride and never want to be photographed, money or not.

Given that cameras are a relative luxury throughout most of the region, some people may agree to be photographed in exchange for receiving a copy. If you don't carry a Polaroid camera, take their address and make it clear that you'll post the photo. Your promise will be taken seriously. Never say you'll send a photo and then don't. If you know you won't be able to come through on a promise, just say that so many people ask you for photos that it's impossible to send one to everyone.

Video photographers should follow the same rules, as most locals find them even more annoying and offensive than still cameras. The bottom line is, always ask permission first, whether you have a still camera or a video camera.

Sacred Sites

Some local people may be offended if you take pictures of their place of worship or a natural feature with traditional religious significance. In some instances, dress may be important. In mosques, for instance, wearing long trousers and removing your shoes may make it more likely that your hosts won't object.

For more details, look for Lonely Planet's *Travel Photography: A Guide to Taking Better Pictures* by Richard I'Anson. It's full of helpful tips for photography while on the road.

For video cameras, you may find tapes in capitals and other large towns, but qualities and formats vary. While travelling, you can recharge batteries in hotels as you go along, so take the necessary charger, plugs and transformer for the country you are visiting.

TIME

Burkina Faso, Côte d'Ivoire, Gambia, Ghana, Guinea, Guinea-Bissau, Liberia, Mali, Mauritania, Senegal, Sierra Leone and Togo are at GMT/UTC. Cape Verde is one hour behind. Benin, Cameroon, Niger and Nigeria are one hour ahead. None of the West African countries in this book observe daylight saving.

When it's noon in the following West African countries, not taking account of daylight saving, the time elsewhere is:

	Benin, Cameroon Niger & Nigeria	Cape Verde	other countries
London	11am	1pm	noon
New York	6am	8am	7am
Paris	noon	2pm	1pm
Sydney	9pm	11pm	10pm

ELECTRICITY

Electricity supply in West Africa is 220V. Liberia uses 110V as well. Plugs are usually the European two-round-pin variety. In former British colonies you may also find plugs with three square pins, as used in Britain.

WEIGHTS & MEASURES

The metric system is used in West Africa. To convert between metric and imperial units see the conversion chart at the back of this book.

LAUNDRY

Outside of top-end hotels, laundry is usually washed by hand, often with brushes or on cement or rocks, which will cause your clothes to wear quickly if you spend much time in the region. Also, everything is always impeccably pressed (included in the price). Most places charge per piece. Rates are higher at top-end and mid-range hotels, sometimes several dollars per piece. At budget hotels, it may be as low as US$0.10 or US$0.20 per piece, and rates are sometimes negotiable. In the rainy season, keep in mind that it may take longer than usual to get your clothes back, as drying time depends on the sun. Dry-cleaning services are limited to major cities.

TOILETS

There are two main types of toilet: Western sit-down style, with a toilet bowl and seat; and African squat style, with a hole in the ground. Standards for both vary tremendously, from pristine to unusable.

In rural areas, squat toilets are built over a deep hole in the ground. These are called 'long drops', and the waste matter just fades away naturally, as long as the hole isn't filled with too much other rubbish (such as paper or synthetic materials, including tampons).

Some Western toilets are not plumbed in, but just balanced over a long drop, although the lack of running water usually makes such cross-cultural mechanisms a disaster. A noncontact hole in the ground is better than a filthy bowl to hover over any day.

HEALTH

Travel health depends on your predeparture preparations, your daily health care while travelling and how you handle any medical problem that does develop. While the potential dangers can seem quite frightening, in reality few travellers experience anything more than an upset stomach.

Predeparture Planning

Immunisations Plan ahead for getting your vaccinations: some of them require more than one injection, while some vaccinations should not be given together. Note that some vaccinations should not be given to pregnant women or to people with allergies – discuss with your doctor.

It is recommended you seek medical advice at least six weeks before travel. Be aware that there is often a greater risk of disease with children and during pregnancy.

Discuss your requirements with your doctor, but vaccinations you should consider for this trip include the following (for more details about the diseases themselves, see the individual disease entries later in this section). Carry proof of your vaccinations, especially yellow fever, as this is needed to enter many countries in the region.

Diphtheria & Tetanus Vaccinations for these two diseases are usually combined and are recommended for everyone. After an initial course of three injections (usually given in childhood), boosters are necessary every 10 years.

Polio Everyone should keep up to date with this vaccination, which is normally given during childhood. A booster every 10 years maintains immunity.

Hepatitis A The vaccine (eg, Avaxim, Havrix 1440 or VAQTA) for hepatitis A provides long-term immunity (possibly more than 10 years) after an initial injection and a booster at six to 12 months. Alternatively, an injection of gamma globulin can provide short-term protection against hepatitis A – two to six months, depending on the dose given. It is not a vaccine, but is ready-made antibody collected from blood donations. It is reasonably effective and, unlike the vaccine, it is protective immediately, but because it is a blood product, there are current concerns about its long-term safety. Hepatitis A vaccine is also available in a combined form, Twinrix, with hepatitis B vaccine. Three injections over a six-month period are required, the first two providing substantial protection against hepatitis A.

Typhoid Vaccination against typhoid may be required if you are travelling for more than a couple of weeks in West Africa. It is available either as an injection or as capsules to be taken orally.

Cholera The current injectable vaccine against cholera is poorly protective and has many side effects, so it is not generally recommended for travellers. However, in some situations it may be necessary to have a certificate as travellers are very occasionally asked by immigration officials to present one, even though all countries and the World Health Organisation (WHO) have dropped cholera immunisation as a health requirement for entry.

Meningococcal Meningitis Vaccination is recommended for travellers to certain parts of West Africa (as well as some other parts of the world). A single injection gives good protection against the major epidemic forms of the disease for three years. Protection may be less effective in children under two years.

Hepatitis B Travellers who should consider vaccination against hepatitis B include those on a long trip, as well as those visiting countries (including many in West Africa) where there are high levels of hepatitis B infection, where blood transfusions may not be adequately screened or where sexual contact or needle sharing is a possibility. Vaccination involves three injections, with a booster at 12 months. More-rapid courses are available if necessary.

Yellow Fever This disease is endemic in West Africa and vaccination is recommended. Also, a yellow fever vaccine is now the only vaccine that is a legal requirement for entry into certain countries (including many in West Africa), though in some cases it is only be enforced if you are coming from an infected area.

Rabies Vaccination should be considered by those who will spend a month or longer in a country where rabies is common (including countries in West Africa), especially if they are cycling, handling animals, caving or travelling to remote areas, and for children (who may not report a bite). Pretravel rabies vaccination involves having three injections over 21 to 28 days. If someone who has been vaccinated is bitten or scratched by an animal, they will require two booster injections of vaccine; those not vaccinated require more.

Tuberculosis The risk of TB to travellers is usually very low, unless you will be living with or closely associated with local people in high-risk areas such as West Africa and some other parts of the world. Vaccination against TB (BCG) is recommended for children and young adults living in these areas for three months or more.

Malaria Medication Antimalarial drugs do not prevent you from being infected but kill the malaria parasites during a stage in their development and significantly reduce the risk of becoming very ill or dying. Expert advice on medication should be sought, as there are many factors to consider, including the area to be visited, the risk of exposure to malaria-carrying mosquitoes, the side effects of medication, your medical history and whether you are a child or an adult or pregnant. Travellers to isolated area in high-risk countries (including most countries in West Africa) may like to carry a treatment dose of medication for use if symptoms occur.

Health Insurance Make sure that you have adequate health insurance. See Travel Insurance under Visas & Documents earlier in this chapter for details.

Travel Health Guides Lonely Planet's *Healthy Travel Africa* is a handy pocket size and packed with useful information including pretrip planning, emergency first aid, immunisation and disease information, and what to do if you get sick on the road. *Travel with Children* from Lonely Planet also includes advice on travel health for younger children.

There are also a number of excellent travel health sites on the Internet. From the Lonely Planet home page there are links at W www.lonelyplanet.com/weblinks/wlheal.htm to the WHO and the US Centers for Disease Control & Prevention.

Other Preparations Make sure you're healthy before you start travelling. If you are going on a long trip make sure your teeth are OK. If you wear glasses take a spare pair and your prescription. If you wear contact lenses, also consider taking a spare pair, and bring along your prescription glasses as well as in some areas it is too dusty for contact lenses.

If you require a particular medication take an adequate supply, as it may not be

Medical Kit Check List

Following is a list of items you should consider including in your medical kit – consult your pharmacist for brands available in your country.

- ☐ **Aspirin or paracetamol (acetaminophen in the USA)** – for pain or fever
- ☐ **Antihistamine** – for allergies, eg, hay fever; to ease the itch from insect bites or stings; and to prevent motion sickness
- ☐ **Cold and flu tablets, throat lozenges and nasal decongestant**
- ☐ **Multivitamins** – consider for long trips, when dietary vitamin intake may be inadequate
- ☐ **Antibiotics** – consider including these if you're travelling well off the beaten track; see your doctor, as they must be prescribed, and carry the prescription with you
- ☐ **Loperamide or diphenoxylate** – 'blockers' for diarrhoea
- ☐ **Prochlorperazine or metaclopramide** – for nausea and vomiting
- ☐ **Rehydration mixture** – to prevent dehydration, which may occur, for example, during bouts of diarrhoea; particularly important when travelling with children
- ☐ **Insect repellent, sunscreen, lip balm and eye drops**
- ☐ **Calamine lotion, sting relief spray or aloe vera** – to ease irritation from sunburn and insect bites or stings
- ☐ **Antifungal cream or powder** – for fungal skin infections and thrush
- ☐ **Antiseptic (such as povidone-iodine)** – for cuts and grazes
- ☐ **Bandages, Band-Aids (plasters) and other wound dressings**
- ☐ **Water purification tablets or iodine**
- ☐ **Scissors, tweezers and a thermometer** – note that mercury thermometers are prohibited by airlines
- ☐ **Syringes and needles** – for injections in a country with medical hygiene problems. Ask your doctor for a note explaining why you have them.

available locally. Take part of the packaging showing the generic name rather than the brand, which will make getting replacements easier. It's a good idea to have a legible prescription or letter from your doctor to show that you legally use the medication to avoid any problems.

Basic Rules

Food There is an old adage which says: 'If you can cook it, boil it or peel it you can eat it...otherwise forget it'. Vegetables and fruit should be washed with purified water or peeled where possible. Beware of ice cream that is sold in the street or anywhere it might have been melted and refrozen; if there's any doubt (eg, a power cut in the last day or two), steer well clear. Shellfish such as mussels, oysters and clams should be avoided as well as undercooked meat, particularly in the form of mince. Steaming does not make shellfish safe for eating.

In West Africa, local-style food is usually safer than Western-style food because it's cooked much longer (sometimes all day) and the ingredients are invariably fresh. On the other hand, food in a smarter restaurant may have been lingering in a refrigerator in a city that has power-cuts.

Water The number one rule is *be careful of the water* and especially ice. If you don't know for certain that the water is safe, assume the worst. Reputable brands of bottled water or soft drinks are generally fine, although in some places bottles may be refilled with tap water. Only use water from containers with a serrated seal – not tops or corks. Take care with fruit juice, particularly if water may have been added. Milk should be treated with suspicion as it is often unpasteurised, though boiled milk is fine if it is kept hygienically. Tea or coffee should also be OK, since the water should have been boiled.

Water Purification The simplest way of purifying water is to boil it thoroughly. Vigorous boiling should be satisfactory; however, at high altitude (which excludes most of West Africa) water boils at a lower temperature, so germs are less likely to be killed. You should boil it for longer in these environments.

Consider purchasing a water filter for a long trip. There are two main kinds of filter. Total filters take out all parasites, bacteria and viruses and make water safe to drink. They are often expensive, but they can be more cost effective than buying bottled water. Simple filters (which can even be a nylon mesh bag) take out dirt and larger foreign bodies from the water so that chemical solutions work much more effectively; if water is dirty, chemical solutions may not work at all. It's very important when buying a filter to read the specifications, so that you know exactly what it removes from the water and what it doesn't. Simple filtering will not remove all dangerous organisms, so if you cannot boil water it should be treated chemically. Chlorine tablets will kill many pathogens, but not some parasites like giardia and amoebic cysts. Iodine is more effective in purifying water and is available in tablet form. Follow the directions carefully and remember that too much iodine can be harmful.

Medical Problems & Treatment

Self-diagnosis and treatment can be risky, so you should always seek medical help. In West Africa, most capitals and large towns have at least one hospital, as well as private clinics and surgeries, although these are not always well-stocked or well-staffed. The best care in the region is probably available in Abidjan (Côte d'Ivoire), where there are several Western-style clinics and hospitals. However, even here, for serious matters you'll probably need to return home. Throughout the region, if you fall sick and have a choice, try to find a private or mission-run hospital or clinic. Where available, medical facilities are listed in the Information sections of large cities in individual country chapters. Alternatively, an embassy, consulate or good hotel can usually recommend a local doctor or clinic, or a place to go for advice.

Pharmacies in major cities are generally well stocked for commonly used items, and usually don't require prescriptions; always check expiry dates. In smaller towns and rural areas, selection is limited, although you can often find antimalarials and paracetamol (though for both, and for any medication, it's best to bring what you think you will need from home).

Although we do give drug dosages in this section, they are for emergency use only. Correct diagnosis is vital. In this section we have used the generic names for medications – check with a pharmacist for brands available locally.

Note that antibiotics should ideally be administered only under medical supervision. Take only the recommended dose at the prescribed intervals and use the whole course, even if the illness seems to be cured earlier. Stop immediately if there are any serious reactions and don't use the antibiotic at all if you are unsure that you have the correct one. Some people are allergic to commonly prescribed antibiotics such as penicillin; carry this information (eg, on a bracelet) when travelling.

Environmental Hazards

Heat Exhaustion Dehydration and salt deficiency can cause heat exhaustion. Take time to acclimatise to high temperatures, drink sufficient liquids and do not do anything too physically demanding. Salt deficiency is characterised by fatigue, lethargy, headaches, giddiness and muscle cramps; salt tablets may help, but adding extra salt to your food is better.

Anhidrotic heat exhaustion is a rare form of heat exhaustion that is caused by an

Nutrition

If your food is poor, if you're on the road and missing meals or if you simply lose your appetite, you can soon start to lose weight and place your health at risk.

Make sure your diet is well balanced. Cooked eggs, beans and nuts are all safe ways to get protein. Fruit you can peel (eg, bananas, oranges or mandarins) is usually safe and a good source of vitamins. Note, however, that melons can harbour bacteria in their flesh and are best avoided. Try to eat plenty of grains (including rice) and bread. Remember that although food is generally safer if it is cooked well, overcooked food loses much of its nutritional value. If your diet isn't well balanced or if your food intake is insufficient, it's a good idea to take vitamin supplements.

Especially in West Africa's hot climate, make sure you drink enough – don't rely on feeling thirsty to indicate when you should drink. Not needing to urinate or small amounts of very dark yellow urine is a danger sign. Always carry a water bottle with you on long trips. Excessive sweating can lead to loss of salt and therefore muscle cramping. Salt tablets are not a good idea as a preventative, but in places where salt is not used much, adding salt to food can help.

inability to sweat. It tends to affect people who have been in a hot climate for some time, rather than newcomers. It can progress to heatstroke. Treatment involves removal to a cooler climate.

Heatstroke This serious, occasionally fatal, condition can occur if the body's heat-regulating mechanism breaks down and the body temperature rises to dangerous levels. Long, continuous periods of exposure to high temperatures and insufficient fluids can leave you vulnerable to heatstroke.

The symptoms are feeling unwell, not sweating very much (or at all) and a high body temperature (39°C to 41°C or 102°F to 106°F). Where sweating has ceased, the skin becomes flushed and red. Severe, throbbing headaches and lack of coordination will also occur, and the sufferer may be confused or aggressive. Eventually the victim will become delirious or convulse. Hospitalisation is essential, but in the interim get victims out of the sun, remove their clothing, cover them with a wet sheet or towel and then fan continually. Give fluids if they are conscious.

Jet Lag This condition is experienced when a person travels by air across more than three time zones (each time zone usually represents a one-hour time difference). It occurs because many of the functions of the human body (such as temperature, pulse rate and emptying of the bladder and bowels) are regulated by internal 24-hour cycles. When we travel long distances rapidly, our bodies take time to adjust to the 'new time' of our destination, and we may experience fatigue, disorientation, insomnia, anxiety, impaired concentration and loss of appetite. These effects will usually be gone within three days of arrival, but to minimise the impact of jet lag:

- Rest for a couple of days prior to departure.
- Try to select flight schedules that minimise sleep deprivation; arriving late in the day means you can go to sleep soon after you arrive. For very long flights, try to organise a stopover.
- Avoid excessive eating (which bloats the stomach) and alcohol (which causes dehydration) during the flight. Instead, drink plenty of non-carbonated, nonalcoholic drinks such as fruit juice or water.
- Avoid smoking.
- Make yourself comfortable by wearing loose-fitting clothes and perhaps bringing an eye mask and ear plugs to help you sleep.
- Try to sleep at the appropriate time for the time zone you are travelling to.

Motion Sickness Eating lightly before and during a trip will reduce the chances of motion sickness. If you are prone to motion sickness try to find a place that minimises movement – near the wing on aircraft, close to midships on boats, near the centre on buses. Fresh air usually helps; reading and cigarette smoke don't. Commercial motion-sickness preparations, which can cause drowsiness, have to be taken before the trip commences. Ginger (available in capsule form) and peppermint (including mint-flavoured sweets) are natural preventatives.

Prickly Heat This is an itchy rash caused by excessive perspiration trapped under the skin. It usually strikes people who have just arrived in a hot climate. Keeping cool, bathing often, drying the skin and using a mild talcum or prickly heat powder or resorting to air-conditioning may help.

Sunburn You can get sunburnt quickly in West Africa, even through cloud. Use sunscreen, a hat, and barrier cream for your nose and lips. Calamine lotion or a commercial aftersun preparation are good for mild sunburn. Wear good quality sunglasses, particularly if you are near water or sand.

Infectious Diseases

Bilharzia Also known as schistosomiasis, this disease is transmitted by minute worms. They infect certain varieties of freshwater snails found in rivers, streams, lakes and particularly behind dams. The worms multiply and are eventually discharged into the water.

The worm enters through the skin and attaches itself to your intestines or bladder. The first symptom may be a general feeling of being unwell, or a tingling and sometimes a light rash around the area where it entered. Weeks later a high fever may develop. Once the disease is established abdominal pain and blood in the urine are other signs. The infection often causes no symptoms until the disease is well established (several months to years after exposure) and damage to internal organs irreversible.

Avoiding swimming or bathing in fresh water where bilharzia is present is the main method of preventing the disease. Even deep water can be infected. If you do get wet, dry off quickly and dry your clothes as well.

A blood test is the most reliable way to diagnose the disease, but the test will not show positive until a number of weeks after exposure.

Diarrhoea Simple things such as a change of water, food or climate can all cause a mild bout of diarrhoea, but a few rushed toilet trips with no other symptoms is not indicative of a major problem.

Dehydration is the main danger with any diarrhoea, particularly in children or the elderly as dehydration can occur quite quickly. Under all circumstances *fluid replacement* (at least equal to the volume being lost) is the most important thing to remember. Weak black tea with a little sugar, soda water, or soft drinks allowed to go flat and diluted 50% with clean water are all good. With severe diarrhoea a rehydrating solution is preferable to replace minerals and salts lost.

Commercially available oral rehydration salts (ORS) are very useful; add them to boiled or bottled water. In an emergency you can make up a solution of six teaspoons of sugar and a half teaspoon of salt to 1L of boiled or bottled water. You need to drink at least the same volume of fluid that you are losing in bowel movements and vomiting. Urine is the best guide to the adequacy of replacement – if you have small amounts of concentrated urine, you need to drink more. Keep drinking small amounts often. Stick to a bland diet as you recover.

Gut-paralysing drugs such as loperamide or diphenoxylate can be used to bring relief from the symptoms, although they do not actually cure the problem. Only use these drugs if you do not have access to toilets, for example, if you *must* travel. Note that these drugs are not recommended for children under 12 years.

In certain situations antibiotics may be required: diarrhoea with blood or mucus (dysentery), any diarrhoea with fever, profuse watery diarrhoea, persistent diarrhoea not improving after 48 hours and severe diarrhoea. These suggest a more serious cause of diarrhoea and in these situations gut-paralysing drugs should be avoided.

In these situations, a stool test may be necessary to diagnose what bug is causing your diarrhoea, so you should seek medical help urgently. Where this is not possible the recommended drugs for bacterial diarrhoea (the most likely cause of severe diarrhoea in travellers) are norfloxacin 400mg twice daily for three days or ciprofloxacin 500mg twice daily for five days. These are not recommended for children or pregnant women. The drug of choice for children would be co-trimoxazole with dosage dependent on weight. A five-day course is given. Ampicillin or amoxycillin may be given in pregnancy, but medical care is necessary.

Two other causes of persistent diarrhoea in travellers are giardiasis and amoebic dysentery.

Giardiasis is caused by a common parasite, *Giardia lamblia*. Symptoms include stomach cramps, nausea, a bloated stomach, watery, foul-smelling diarrhoea and frequent gas. Giardiasis can appear several weeks after you have been exposed to the parasite. The symptoms may disappear for a few days and then return; this can go on for several weeks.

Amoebic dysentery, caused by the protozoan *Entamoeba histolytica*, is characterised by a gradual onset of low-grade diarrhoea, often with blood and mucus. Cramping abdominal pain and vomiting are less likely than in other types of diarrhoea, and fever may not be present. It will persist until treated and can recur and cause other health problems.

You should seek medical advice if you think you have giardiasis or amoebic dysentery, but where this is not possible, tinidazole or metronidazole are the recommended drugs. Treatment is a 2g single dose of tinidazole or 250mg of metronidazole three times daily for five to 10 days.

Fungal Infections These infections occur more commonly in hot weather and are usually found on the scalp, between the toes (athlete's foot) or fingers, in the groin and on the body (ringworm). You get ringworm (which is a fungal infection, not a worm) from infected animals or other people. Moisture encourages these infections.

To prevent fungal infections wear loose, comfortable clothes, avoid artificial fibres, wash frequently and dry yourself carefully.

If you get an infection, wash the infected area at least daily with a disinfectant or medicated soap and water, rinse and dry well. Apply an antifungal cream or powder like tolnaftate. Try to expose the area to air or sunlight as much as possible and wash all towels and underwear in hot water, change them often and let them dry in the sun.

Hepatitis This is a general term for inflammation of the liver. It is a common disease worldwide. There are several different viruses that cause hepatitis, and they differ in the way that they are transmitted. The symptoms are similar in all forms of the illness, and include fever, chills, headache, fatigue, feelings of weakness and aches and pains, followed by loss of appetite, nausea, vomiting, abdominal pain, dark urine, light-coloured faeces, jaundiced (yellow) skin and yellowing of the whites of the eyes. People who have had hepatitis should avoid alcohol for some time after the illness, as the liver needs time to recover.

Hepatitis A is transmitted by contaminated food or drinking water. You should seek medical advice, but there is not much you can do apart from resting, drinking lots of fluids, eating lightly and avoiding fatty foods. Hepatitis E is transmitted in the same way as hepatitis A; it can be particularly serious in pregnant women.

There are almost 300 million chronic carriers of **hepatitis B** in the world. It is spread through contact with infected blood, blood products or body fluids, for example, through sexual contact, unsterilised needles and blood transfusions, or contact with blood via small breaks in the skin. Other risk situations include shaving and tattoo or body piercing with contaminated equipment. The symptoms of hepatitis B may be more severe than type A and the disease can lead to long-term problems such as chronic liver damage, liver cancer or a long-term carrier state. Hepatitis C and D are spread in the same way as hepatitis B and can also lead to long-term complications.

There are vaccines against hepatitis A and B, but there are currently no vaccines against the other types of hepatitis. Following the basic rules about food and water (hepatitis A and E) and avoiding risk situations (hepatitis B, C and D) are important preventative measures.

HIV & AIDS Infection with the human immunodeficiency virus (HIV) may lead to acquired immune deficiency syndrome (AIDS), which is a fatal disease. Any exposure to blood, blood products or body fluids may put the individual at risk. The disease is often transmitted through sexual contact or dirty needles – vaccinations, acupuncture, tattooing and body piercing can be potentially as dangerous as intravenous drug use. HIV/AIDS can also be spread through infected blood transfusions; some developing countries, including those in West Africa, cannot afford to screen blood used for transfusions. If you do need an injection, ask to see the syringe unwrapped in front of you, or take a needle and syringe pack with you. However, fear of HIV infection should never preclude treatment for serious medical conditions.

Intestinal Worms These parasites are most common in rural, tropical areas, including much of West Africa. The different worms have different ways of infecting people. Some may be ingested on food such as undercooked meat (eg, tapeworms) and some enter through your skin (eg, hookworms). Infestations may not show up for some time, and although they are generally not serious, if left untreated some can cause severe health problems later.

Meningococcal Meningitis This serious disease can be fatal. There are recurring epidemics in much of the world, including much of sub-Saharan Africa.

A fever, severe headache, sensitivity to light and neck stiffness, which prevents forward bending of the head are the first symptoms. There may also be purple patches on the skin. Death can occur within a few hours, so urgent medical treatment is essential. Treatment is in the form of large doses of penicillin given intravenously, or through chloramphenicol injections.

Sexually Transmitted Infections (STIs) HIV/AIDS and hepatitis B can be transmitted through sexual contact – see the relevant entries earlier for more details. Other STIs include gonorrhoea, herpes and syphilis; sores, blisters or rashes around the genitals and discharges or pain when urinating are common symptoms. In some STIs, such as wart virus or chlamydia, symptoms may be less marked or not observed at all, especially in women. Chlamydia infection can cause infertility in men and women before any symptoms have been noticed. Syphilis symptoms eventually disappear completely but the disease continues and can cause severe problems in later years. While abstinence from sexual contact is the only 100% effective prevention, using condoms is also effective. The treatment of gonorrhoea and syphilis is with antibiotics. The different sexually transmitted diseases each require specific antibiotics.

Typhoid A dangerous gut infection, typhoid fever is caused by contaminated water and food. Medical help must be sought.

In its early stages sufferers may feel they have a severe cold or flu on the way, as early symptoms are a headache, body aches and a fever that rises a little each day until it is around 40°C (104°F) or more. The victim's pulse is often slow relative to the degree of fever present – unlike a normal fever where the pulse increases. There may also be vomiting, abdominal pain, diarrhoea or constipation.

In the second week the high fever and slow pulse continue and a few pink spots may appear on the body; trembling, delirium, weakness, weight loss and dehydration may occur. Complications such as pneumonia, perforated bowel or meningitis may occur.

Insect-Borne Diseases

Filariasis, leishmaniasis, Lyme disease, sleeping sickness, typhus and yellow fever are all insect-borne diseases, but they do not pose a great risk to travellers. For more information on them see Less Common Diseases later in this chapter.

Malaria This serious and potentially fatal disease is spread by mosquito bites. If you are travelling in endemic areas such as West Africa, it is extremely important to avoid mosquito bites and to take tablets to prevent this disease. Symptoms range from fever, chills and sweating, headache, diarrhoea and abdominal pains to a vague feeling of ill-health. Seek medical help immediately if malaria is suspected. Without treatment malaria can rapidly become more serious and can be fatal.

If medical care is not available, malaria tablets can be used for treatment. You need to use a malaria tablet that is different from the one you were taking when you contracted malaria in the first place. The standard treatment dose of mefloquine is two 250mg tablets and a further two six hours later. For Fansidar, it's a single dose of three tablets. If you were previously taking mefloquine and cannot get Fansidar, other alternatives are Malarone (atovaquone-proguanil; four tablets once daily for three days), halofantrine (three doses of two 250mg tablets every six hours) or quinine sulphate (600mg every six hours). There is a greater risk of side effects with these dosages than with normal use if used with mefloquine, so medical advice is preferable. Be aware also that halofantrine is no longer recommended by WHO as emergency standby treatment, because of side effects, and should only be used if no other drugs are available.

Travellers are advised to prevent mosquito bites at all times. The main messages are:

- Wear light-coloured clothing.
- Wear long trousers and long-sleeved shirts.
- Use mosquito repellents that contain the compound DEET on exposed areas of skin (prolonged overuse of DEET may be harmful, especially to children, but its use is considered far more preferable to being bitten by disease-transmitting mosquitoes).
- Avoid perfumes or aftershave.
- Use a mosquito net impregnated with mosquito repellent (permethrin) – it may be worth taking your own.
- Impregnating clothes with permethrin effectively deters mosquitoes and other insects.

Dengue Fever This viral disease is transmitted by mosquitoes and is fast becoming one of the top public-health problems in the tropical world. Unlike the malaria mosquito, the *Aedes aegypti* mosquito, which transmits the dengue virus, is most active during the day, and is found mainly in urban areas, in and around human dwellings.

Signs and symptoms of dengue fever include a sudden onset of high fever, headache, joint and muscle pains (hence its old name, 'breakbone fever') and nausea and vomiting. A rash of small red spots sometimes appears three to four days after the onset of fever. In the early phase of illness, dengue may be mistaken for other

Malaria – Deadly but Preventable

According to UN and WHO statistics, malaria is the world's most deadly tropical parasitic disease, killing one child every 30 seconds and killing more people than any other communicable disease except tuberculosis. Malaria deaths are estimated to be between 1.5 and 2.7 million per year, more than 90% of which occur in sub-Saharan Africa where many rural dwellers lack access to treatment or to preventative measures. African children under five years of age suffer an average of six bouts of the illness each year, with close to 3000 children under five years of age dying of malaria each day – a death toll that far exceeds the mortality rate from AIDS. Malaria causes severe anaemia and is also a major factor contributing to maternal deaths in sub-Saharan Africa. Pregnant mothers who have malaria and are HIV positive are also more likely to pass on their HIV status to their unborn child.

In economic terms, costs resulting from efforts to control the disease and to lost work days are estimated to total from 1% to 5% of the gross domestic product of Africa, and direct and indirect costs of the disease in sub-Saharan Africa exceed US$2 billion per year. Looked at from another perspective, the economic growth rates of African nations have been reduced by an estimated 40% as a result of malaria and malaria-related consequences.

Despite these grim statistics, malaria is preventable, treatable and curable. Just the single measure of sleeping under mosquito nets, for example, has been shown to reduce child deaths by 30% in several African countries. Also, while only a limited number of drugs exist for malaria treatment, studies have shown that their proper targeting and use can significantly reduce malaria disease and death. The main long-term hope is for a breakthrough in vaccine development. Various sample vaccines are currently under trial, and some optimistic estimates predict emergence of an effective vaccine within the next decade.

If you're travelling in West Africa, what does all this mean? First, take prophylaxis, and take precautions to avoid mosquito bites. Sleep under a net and pull on a long-sleeved shirt, trousers and socks in the evenings. Secondly, if you do start feeling fever, chills and other symptoms of malaria, go immediately to the nearest health clinic – every town has one – and get a malaria test. It usually doesn't cost more than US$1 and you'll have the results within a few minutes. Finally, back home, do what you can to lobby your government and local corporations to increase their support for malaria research and vaccine development, and their commitment to fighting the disease. While the human and economic toll is most visible in Africa, in the end, it affects us all.

infectious diseases, including malaria and influenza. Minor bleeding such as nose bleeds may occur in the course of the illness, but this does not necessarily mean that you have progressed to the potentially fatal dengue haemorrhagic fever (DHF). This is a severe illness, characterised by heavy bleeding, which is thought to be a result of a second infection due to a different strain (there are four major strains) and usually affects residents of the country rather than travellers. Recovery, even from simple dengue fever, may be prolonged, with tiredness lasting for several weeks.

You should seek medical attention as soon as possible if you think you may be infected. A blood test can exclude malaria and indicate the possibility of dengue fever. There is no specific treatment for dengue. Aspirin should be avoided, as it increases the risk of haemorrhaging. There is no vaccine against dengue fever. The best prevention is to avoid mosquito bites at all times by covering up, using insect repellents containing the compound DEET and mosquito nets – see Malaria earlier for more advice on avoiding mosquito bites.

Cuts, Bites & Stings

See Less Common Diseases later for details of rabies, which is passed through animal bites.

Cuts & Scratches Wash well and treat cuts with an antiseptic such as povidone-iodine. Where possible avoid bandages and Band-Aids, which can keep wounds wet. Coral cuts are notoriously slow to heal and if they are not adequately cleaned, small pieces of coral can become embedded in the wound.

Bedbugs & Lice Bedbugs live in various places, but particularly in dirty mattresses and bedding, evidenced by spots of blood on bedclothes or on the wall. Bedbugs leave itchy bites in neat rows. Calamine lotion or a sting-relief spray may help.

All lice cause itching and discomfort. They make themselves at home in your hair (head lice), your clothing (body lice) or in your pubic hair (crabs). You catch lice through direct contact with infected people or by sharing combs, clothing and the like. Powder or shampoo treatment will kill the lice and infected clothing should then be washed in very hot, soapy water and left in the sun to dry.

Bites & Stings Bee and wasp stings are usually painful rather than dangerous. However, in people who are allergic to them severe breathing difficulties may occur and require urgent medical care. Calamine lotion or a sting-relief spray will give relief and ice packs will reduce the pain and swelling. There are some spiders with dangerous bites but antivenins are usually available. Scorpion stings are notoriously painful. Scorpions often shelter under stones, or in shoes or clothing; shake out your clothes and check before dressing.

Leeches & Ticks Leeches may be present in damp rainforest conditions; they attach themselves to your skin to suck your blood. Trekkers often get them on their legs or in their boots. Salt or a lighted cigarette end will make them fall off. Do not pull them off, as the bite is then more likely to become infected. Clean and apply pressure if the point of attachment is bleeding. An insect repellent may keep them away.

You should always check all over your body if you have been walking through a potentially tick-infested area as ticks can cause skin infections and other more serious diseases. If a tick is found attached, press down around the tick's head with tweezers, grab the head and gently pull upwards. Avoid pulling the rear of the body as this may squeeze the tick's gut contents through the attached mouth parts into the skin, increasing the risk of infection and disease. Smearing chemicals on the tick will not make it let go and is not recommended.

Snakes Travellers in West Africa rarely see a snake, let alone get bitten by one. However, to minimise your chances of being bitten always wear boots, socks and long trousers when walking through undergrowth where snakes may be present. Don't put your hands into holes and crevices, and be careful when collecting firewood.

If you are unlucky enough to get bitten, remember that snake bites do not cause instantaneous death and in some areas, antivenins may be available. Immediately wrap the bitten limb tightly, as you would for a sprained ankle, and then attach a splint to immobilise it. Keep the victim still and seek medical help. Tourniquets and sucking out the poison are now comprehensively discredited.

Women's Health

Gynaecological Problems Antibiotic use, synthetic underwear, sweating and contraceptive pills can lead to fungal vaginal infections, especially when travelling in hot climates. Fungal infections are characterised by a rash, itch and discharge and can be treated with a vinegar or lemon-juice douche, or with yogurt. Nystatin, miconazole or clotrimazole pessaries or vaginal cream are the usual treatment. Maintaining good personal hygiene and wearing loose-fitting clothes and cotton underwear may help prevent these infections.

STDs are a major cause of vaginal problems. Symptoms include a smelly discharge, painful intercourse and sometimes a burning sensation when urinating. Medical attention should be sought and male sexual partners must also be treated. For more details see Sexually Transmitted Diseases earlier. Besides abstinence, the best thing is to practise safer sex using condoms.

Pregnancy It is not advisable to travel to some places while pregnant as some vaccinations normally used to prevent serious diseases are not advisable during pregnancy (eg, yellow fever). In addition, some diseases are much more serious for the mother (and may increase the risk of a stillborn child) in pregnancy (eg, malaria).

Most miscarriages occur during the first three months of pregnancy. Miscarriage is not uncommon and can occasionally lead to severe bleeding. The last three months should also be spent within reasonable distance of good medical care. A baby born as early as 24 weeks stands a chance of survival, but only in a good modern hospital. Pregnant women should avoid all unnecessary medication, although vaccinations and malarial prophylactics should still be taken where needed. Additional care should be taken to prevent illness and particular attention should be paid to diet and nutrition. Alcohol and nicotine, for example, should be avoided.

Less Common Diseases

The following diseases pose a small risk to travellers, and so are only mentioned in passing. Seek medical advice if you think you may have any of these diseases.

Cholera This is the worst of the watery diarrhoeas and medical help should be sought. Outbreaks of cholera are generally widely reported, so you can usually avoid problem areas. *Fluid replacement is the most vital treatment* – the risk of dehydration is severe as you may lose up to 20L a day. If there is a delay in getting to hospital, then begin taking tetracycline. The adult dose is 250mg four times daily. It is not recommended for children under nine years nor for pregnant women. Tetracycline may help shorten the illness, but adequate fluids are required to save lives.

Filariasis This is a mosquito-transmitted parasitic infection found in many parts of Africa and elsewhere. Possible symptoms include fever, pain and swelling of the lymph glands; inflammation of lymph drainage areas; swelling of a limb or the scrotum; skin rashes; and blindness. Treatment is available to eliminate the parasites from the body, but some of the damage already caused may not be reversible. Medical advice should be obtained promptly.

Leishmaniasis This is a group of parasitic diseases transmitted by sandflies, which are found in many parts of Africa (and elsewhere). Cutaneous leishmaniasis affects the skin tissue causing ulceration and disfigurement, and visceral leishmaniasis affects the internal organs. Seek medical advice, as laboratory testing is required for diagnosis and correct treatment. Avoiding sandfly bites is the best precaution. Bites are usually painless, itchy and yet another reason to cover up and apply insect repellent.

Rabies This fatal viral infection is found in many countries. Many animals can be infected (such as dogs, cats, bats and monkeys) and it is their saliva that is infectious. Any bite, scratch or even lick from an animal should be cleaned immediately and thoroughly. Scrub with soap and running water, and then apply alcohol or iodine solution. Medical help should be sought promptly to receive a course of injections to prevent the onset of symptoms and death.

Sleeping Sickness In parts of tropical Africa tsetse flies can carry trypanosomiasis, or sleeping sickness. The tsetse fly is about twice the size of a housefly and recognisable by the scissorlike way it folds its wings when at rest. Only a small proportion of tsetse flies carry the disease, but it is a serious disease that can be fatal without treatment. No protection is available except avoiding the tsetse fly bites. The flies are attracted to large moving objects such as safari buses, to perfume and aftershave and to colours such as dark blue. Swelling at the site of the bite, five or more days later, is the first sign of infection; this is followed within two to three weeks by fever.

Tetanus This disease is caused by a germ that lives in soil and in the faeces of horses and other animals. It enters the body via breaks in the skin. The first symptom may be discomfort in swallowing, or stiffening of the jaw and neck; this is followed by painful convulsions of the jaw and whole body. The disease can be fatal. It can be prevented by vaccination.

Tuberculosis (TB) TB is a bacterial infection usually transmitted from person to person by coughing but which may be transmitted through consumption of unpasteurised milk. Milk that has been boiled is safe to drink, and the souring of milk to make yogurt or cheese also kills the bacilli. Travellers are usually not at great risk as close household contact with the infected person is usually required before the disease is passed on. You may need to have a TB test before you travel as this can help diagnose the disease later if you become ill.

Typhus This disease is spread by ticks, mites or lice. It begins with fever, chills, headache and muscle pains followed a few days later by a body rash. There is often a large painful sore at the site of the bite and nearby lymph nodes are swollen and painful. Typhus can be treated under medical supervision. Seek local advice on areas where ticks pose a danger and always check your skin carefully for ticks after walking in a danger area such as a tropical forest. An insect repellent can help, and walkers in tick-infested areas should consider having their boots and trousers impregnated with benzyl benzoate and dibutylphthalate.

Yellow Fever This viral disease is endemic in many African countries and is transmitted by mosquitoes. The initial symptoms are fever, headache, abdominal pain and vomiting. Seek medical care urgently and drink lots of fluids.

WOMEN TRAVELLERS

When travelling in West Africa – solo or with other women – you're unlikely to encounter any more difficulties than you would elsewhere in the world. Many of the female authors of this book have travelled for extended periods – including solo – and lived in West Africa without incident and most did their research for this book travelling alone. In fact, more often than not, you'll meet only warmth and hospitality, and find that you receive kindness and special treatment that you wouldn't be shown if you were a male traveller. That said, you'll inevitably attract some attention. Here are a few tips:

- Dress modestly. This is the most successful strategy for minimising unwanted attention. Wear trousers or a long skirt, and a conservative top with a sleeve. Tucking your hair under a cap or tying it back, especially if it is blonde, also sometimes helps.
- Use common sense, trust your instincts and take the usual precautions when out and about. For example, if possible, avoid going out alone in the evenings, particularly on foot. Avoid isolated areas, roadways and beaches during both day and evening hours, and be cautious on beaches, many of which can become isolated very quickly. Throughout the region, hitching alone is not recommended. While you're likely to hear some horror stories (often of dubious accuracy) from expats who may be appalled at the idea of solo female travel, it's worth remembering that the incidence of real harm or rape is extremely rare.
- Don't worry about being rude, and don't feel the need to explain yourself. If you try to start explaining why you don't want to meet for a drink/go to a nightclub/get married on the spot, it may be interpreted as flirting. The more you try to explain, the more you'll see your hopeful suitor's eyes light up with that pleased, knowing look – 'ah, she's just playing hard to get, but really, she wants me...'.
- Ignore hissing, calls of *chérie*, or whatever – if you respond, it may be interpreted as a lead on.
- Don't worry about it all too much, and definitely don't let concerns ruin your trip. Remember that some sections of the region, such as parts of the Sahel, are wonderfully hassle free. On the other side of the issue, meeting local women can enrich your trip tremendously, although this can take some effort, particularly due to language barriers. Good places to try include tourist offices, government departments or even your hotel, where at least some of the staff are likely to be formally educated young to middle-aged women. In rural areas, starting points include women teachers at a local school, or staff at a health centre.

Tampons & Sanitary Pads

Tampons (usually imported from Europe) are available from pharmacies or large supermarkets in capitals throughout West Africa, and occasionally in larger towns. Elsewhere, the only choice is likely to be sanitary pads.

'C'est Madame? Ou bien, Mademoiselle?'

Women travelling on their own through Francophone West Africa will undoubtedly hear these words ad nauseam (roughly translated, the phrase means 'are you married or not'?). Sometimes, for example, when you're filling out forms or registering at a hotel, it's not ill-intentioned. But all too often, it's a leering soldier or border official who's a little too eager for company. Although there's not much you can do to prevent the question, having at least a fictitious husband – ideally one who will be arriving imminently at that very place – can help in avoiding further advances. If you are travelling with a male companion, a good way to avoid unwanted interest is to introduce him as your husband. If you're questioned as to why your husband/children aren't with you, just explain that you'll be meeting them later.

GAY & LESBIAN TRAVELLERS

All the countries covered in this book are conservative in their attitudes towards gays and lesbians, and gay sexual relationships are culturally taboo and rare to the point of nonexistence (although homosexual activity does occur, especially among younger men). In most places, open displays of affection are generally frowned upon, whatever your orientation, and show insensitivity to local feelings.

A USA-based tour company offering specialist tours for gay men and women, including to West Africa, is David Tours (☎ 949-723 0699, fax 723 0666, W www.davidtours.com), 310 Dahlia Place, Suite A, Corona del Mar, CA 92625-2821.

DISABLED TRAVELLERS

West Africa has few facilities for the disabled. This, combined with weak infrastructure throughout the region, can make travel difficult, although it's not impossible. Few hotels have lifts (and those that do are generally expensive), streets may be either badly potholed or else unpaved, footpaths are few and far between, and ramps and other things to ease access are often nonexistent. While accommodation at many budget hotels is on the ground floor, bathroom access can be difficult, and doors are not always wide enough for wheelchairs. Fortunately, these facts are counterbalanced by the fact that West Africans are usually very accommodating and willing to offer whatever assistance they can, as long as they understand what you need.

As for transport, most taxis in the region are small sedans, and buses are not wheelchair equipped. Minibuses and larger 4WD vehicles can usually be arranged through car-rental agencies in major towns and cities, although this will be pricey.

In general, travel and access will probably be easiest in places with relatively good tourism infrastructure, such as some of the coastal areas of Senegal and Gambia, or parts of Côte d'Ivoire near Abidjan. As far as we are aware, there are no facilities in the region specifically aimed at blind travellers.

Organisations that disseminate information on world travel for the mobility impaired include Mobility International USA (☎ 541-343 1284), PO Box 10767, Eugene, OR 97440, and Access-able Travel Source (☎ 303-232 2979, fax 239 8486, W www.access-able.com), PO Box 1796, Wheatridge, CO, USA. In the UK, a useful organisation is Radar (☎ 020-7250 3222, 250), City Rd, London EC1V 8AS. In Australia, you could try the National Information Communication Awareness Network (W www.nican.com.au).

SENIOR TRAVELLERS

In general, capital cities and larger towns will have the best selection of accommodation and dining options, as well as direct international air access. Some things to take into account, whatever your age, include:

- Transport – Road journeys can be rough, long and taxing even for the most physically fit travellers. To minimise rigours in this area, consider hiring a vehicle, although this will be expensive. Also remember that if the road is bad enough, the journey will be rough no matter what sort of vehicle you have.
- Luggage – Unless you are on an organised tour, or will be met at your destinations by friends with vehicles, backpacks are the most practical option.
- Weather – West Africa's weather can drain your energy. Most people find the dry heat of the Sahel easier to take than the humidity along the coast, and the cooler months (November to February) the most comfortable time to travel.

TRAVEL WITH CHILDREN

In West African countries with a mainstream tourism industry some package-tour hotels cater for families with children, and in large cities top-end hotels usually have rooms with three or four beds for only slightly more than a double. Alternatively, arranging an extra bed or mattress so that children can share a standard adult double is generally easy and inexpensive.

West Africans are very friendly, helpful and protective towards children, although there are very few child-oriented facilities in the region. In nontourist hotels there are generally no discounts for children. Likewise, on public transport, if you want a seat it has to be paid for. Most young local children travel for free on buses, but spend the whole journey on their parent's lap.

Regional highlights that appeal to adults (markets, mosques, mud-brick architecture, endless desert wilderness) often don't have such an attraction for children. Additionally, distances can be long, especially on

Baby Basics

We received the following letter from a Canadian family who travelled for six weeks in Senegal, Guinea and Guinea-Bissau with a one-year-old, and sent the following tips:

'In West Africa, travelling with a baby was not too difficult, even though life is different. People constantly wanted to touch him, and even though this bothered us on occasion, it was not serious. Most of the time we enjoyed the contact. We learned to travel light, and went with one 50L backpack and a baby carrier which also carried another 10L of luggage. Clothes could be washed every day, and dried while wearing them.

- We used small chlorine pills to clean water that was not bottled – apparently iodine may be harmful to children.
- In every capital we found nappies at grocery stores selling imported items. Sometimes the quality was poor so we secured them with strong sticky tape.
- Baby cereal and powdered milk were available in most towns, even small villages, and prices were similar to those at home.

In Senegal our baby got a rash caused by the heat and humidity. This was not dangerous, and with soothing powder it was gone in two days.'

Gino Bergeron, Julie Morin & 'little Thomas'

public transport. It's a good idea to have a supply of distractions, as well as some food, as what's available en route often is not suitable.

In addition to the length and discomfort involved in many road journeys, possible concerns include the scarcity of decent medical facilities, especially outside major cities, and the difficulty of finding clean, decent bathrooms outside of mid-range and top-end hotels. Canned baby foods, disposable nappies, wipes and similar items are available in some capital cities, but not elsewhere, although they are expensive. It's advisable to avoid feeding your children street food. Powdered milk and sometimes also baby cereal (usually with sugar in it) are relatively widely available, even in smaller towns.

On the plus side, we've heard from people who have travelled with children in West Africa and found the experience very enriching. Because foreign children are an unusual sight, they're a great conversation starter.

For malaria protection, bring mosquito nets along for your children and ensure that they sleep under them. Also bring along long-sleeved shirts and trousers for dawn and dusk.

For more information and hints on travelling with children, Lonely Planet's *Travel with Children* by Cathy Lanigan is highly recommended.

DANGERS & ANNOYANCES

It is difficult to make generalisations about the personal-safety situation in West Africa. While there may be considerable risk in some areas, other places are completely safe. The danger of robbery with violence is much more prevalent in cities and towns than in rural or wilderness areas, where it's relatively rare. Most cities have their dangerous streets and beaches, but towns can differ; there's more of a danger in those frequented by wealthy foreigners than in places off the usual tourist track.

The Sahel countries are among the safer places in the world, although Dakar has become much worse in recent years and many people have had bags snatched and pockets picked, sometimes violently (see the boxed text 'Dangers in Dakar' in the Senegal chapter). In cities such as Banjul (Gambia) and Bamako (Mali), attacks are not unknown, but generally the accompanying violence is limited. Travellers have, on occasion, been pushed to the ground and had daypacks or cameras stolen, but they haven't been knifed or otherwise injured. (In these cities, it's rare to hear of thieves carrying guns.)

In some of the southern cities, the picture is different. The worst place by far is Lagos (Nigeria), followed by Abidjan (Côte d'Ivoire). In countries recovering from civil war (such as Sierra Leone and Liberia) another danger is that of harassment and

Scams – Things to Look Out For

The main annoyance you'll come across in West Africa are the various hustlers, touts and con men who prey on tourists. Although they are not necessarily dangerous, awareness and suitable precautions are advisable. A few examples of the dazzling array of scams and con tricks that the hustlers of West Africa have perfected are presented here. Some are imaginative and amusing; others are serious and a cause for concern.

Dud Cassettes

Street sellers walk around with boxes of cassettes by local musicians. You browse, you choose, you pay. And then when you get back to your hotel and open the box it's got a cheap blank tape inside. Or the tape itself is missing, or the music is by a completely different artist. Tapes sealed in cellophane are normally fine, and of reasonable quality, but look at, or try to listen to, tapes before buying them.

Phone Numbers

You give your address to a local kid who says he wants to write you letters. He asks for your phone number too, and you think 'no harm in that'. Until the folks back home start getting collect calls in the middle of the night.

Remember Me?

A popular trick in the tourist areas is for local lads to approach you in the street pretending to be a hotel employee or 'son of the owner'. There's been a mix-up at the shop. Can you lend him some money? You can take it off the hotel bill later. He'll know your name and room number, and even give you a receipt. But, surprise, surprise, back at the hotel they've never heard of him, and the money is never seen again. The way to avoid the trap is to be polite but firm: you don't remember anyone, and you'd like to be alone.

Sock Sellers

A youth approaches you in the street with socks for sale. Even though you don't want them he follows you for a while. His buddy approaches from the other side and also tries to persuade you to buy the socks. He bends down to show you how well the socks would go with your outfit. You are irritated and distracted, and while you bend down to fend him off, whoosh, the other guy comes in from the blind side and goes straight for the pocket with your wallet in. The solution? Be firm, walk purposefully, stay cool, and never buy socks in the street.

A Nice Welcome

You may be invited to stay in someone's house, in exchange for a meal and drinks, but your new friend's appetite for food and beer may make this an expensive deal. More seriously, while you are dining, someone else will be back at the house of your 'friend' going through your bag. This scam is only likely to be tried in tourist areas (we heard about it in St-Louis in Senegal), but remember in remote or rural areas, you'll often come across genuine hospitality.

Police & Thieves

If you're unwise enough to sample local narcotics, don't be surprised if dealers are in cahoots with the local police, who then come to your hotel or stop you in the street and find you 'in possession'. Large bribes will be required to avoid arrest or imprisonment. Don't buy drugs, especially from strangers.

Spiked Drinks

It doesn't happen frequently, but often enough that you need to watch out: don't accept drinks from newly found acquaintances on buses or trains, or you may find yourself soon asleep, while your 'acquaintance' runs off with your wallet.

violence by rebel groups or former combatants, especially in rural areas. More specific details are given in the individual country chapters.

Safety Tips

The warnings in the previous section are not designed to put you off travelling in West Africa, but are intended to make you more aware of the dangers. Some simple precautions will hopefully ensure you have a trouble-free trip. Remember, many thousands of travellers enjoy travel throughout this region, and have no problems. The recommendations listed here are particularly relevant to cities, although some may apply to other places as well.

- Carry as little as possible. Thieves will be less interested if you're not carrying a daypack, camera and personal stereo. Consider leaving them in your room. Even passports, travellers cheques and credit cards can sometimes be left behind, if the hotel has a reliable safe or security box. If your hotel isn't too secure, though, then you will have to carry your valuables with you. You have to work out which is the safest option on a case by case basis. (Note that in many countries it's required to carry your passport at all times – although you're very unlikely to be stopped in the street by police and asked for it).
- Be discreet. Don't wear jewellery or watches. Use a separate wallet for day-to-day purchases, and keep the bulk of your cash out of sight, hidden in a pouch under loose-fitting clothing. For more advice, see Security under Money earlier in this chapter.
- Try not to look lost. Walk purposefully and confidently, and don't obviously refer to this guidebook or a map. Photocopy or tear out the pages you need, or duck into a shop or café to have a look at the map and get your bearings.
- Avoid back streets and risky areas at night. Take a taxi. A dollar or two for the fare might save you a lot of pain and trouble.
- Avoid getting in taxis – especially at night and especially if you're female – with two or more men inside, even (or especially) if the driver says they are his 'friends'.
- Consider hiring somebody locally to accompany you when walking around a risky area. It's usually not too difficult to find someone who wouldn't mind earning a few dollars for warding off potential molesters – ask at your hotel for a reliable recommendation.

PUBLIC HOLIDAYS & SPECIAL EVENTS

A highlight of any trip to West Africa is witnessing one of the many ceremonies that are an integral part of traditional culture in the region. Events such as naming ceremonies, weddings and circumcisions take place everywhere, and if you're lucky, you may be invited to take part. You'll also see village festivals, where people celebrate the end of a harvest, give thanks to a deity or honour their ancestors. All these ceremonies usually involve singing, dancing (often masked), music and other festivities, and are fascinating to watch, and some of the larger ones attract people from across the region.

In addition to these ceremonies, there are many public holidays – either government or religious – when businesses are closed. Public holidays vary from country to country, but some – including Christmas and New Year's Day – are observed throughout the region. Government holidays are often marked with parades, dancing and other events, while the Christian religious holidays invariably centre around beautiful church services and singing. On Tabaski, Eid al-Fitr and the other Islamic holidays, you'll probably see entire families – from the youngest children up to the elders and grandparents – dressed in their finest clothes, strolling in the streets or visiting the mosque.

See Public Holidays & Special Events in the Facts for the Visitor sections of the individual country chapters for country-specific listings. Some regional highlights are described, following.

Islamic Holidays

Important Islamic holidays, when much of West Africa's commercial life comes to a stop, include the following:

Considerations

Lest you get too paranoid, remember this. Considering the wealth of most tourists, and the unimaginable levels of poverty suffered by most West Africans, the incidence of robbery or theft in most countries in the region is incredibly low. Even a shoestring traveller's daily budget of US$15 a day is more than the average local labourer makes in a month.

When you sit in a bus station sipping a couple of soft drinks, which cost a dollar, and you see an old man selling fans made carefully from palm leaves for about one-quarter of this price, or a teenage youth trying to earn the same amount by offering to clean your shoes, it reminds you with a jolt that the vast majority of local people are decent and hard-working, and are seeking only the chance to make an honest living.

Tabaski (also called Eid al-Kebir) commemorates Abraham's readiness to sacrifice his son on God's command, and the last-minute substitution of a ram. It also coincides with the end of the pilgrimage to Mecca, and is the most-important Muslim event, marked in most countries by great feasts with roast sheep and a two-day public holiday.

Eid al-Fitr is the second major Islamic holiday, and marks the end of Ramadan, the annual fasting month when Muslims do not eat or drink during daylight hours, but break their fast after sundown. Throughout Ramadan, offices usually grind to a halt in the afternoon.

Eid al-Moulid celebrates the birthday of the Prophet Mohammed. It occurs about three months after Tabaski.

Since the Islamic calendar is based on 12 lunar months totalling 354 or 355 days, these holidays are always about 11 days earlier than the previous year. The exact dates depend on the moon and are announced for certain only about a day in advance. Estimated dates for these events are:

event	2002	2003	2004	2005
Ramadan begins	6 Nov	26 Oct	15 Oct	4 Oct
Eid al-Fitr	5 Dec	25 Nov	13 Nov	3 Nov
Tabaski	22 Feb	11 Feb	1 Feb	20 Jan
Eid al-Moulid	24 May	13 May	1 May	21 Apr

Festivals & Cultural Events

There are many fascinating festivals that take place throughout the year in various countries of the region. Following is a selection of some of the more-important and spectacular ones. The individual country chapters have more details on the major events. Many of the dates listed here are approximate – check locally before setting off.

January

Paris-Dakar Motor Rally
(1-22 January) This is Africa's biggest auto race; the route changes slightly every year, but usually finishes with a mad dash along the beach from St-Louis to Dakar in Senegal.

February

Fêtes des Masques
(throughout February) A time of spectacular festivals with masked dancing, held in the Man region (Côte d'Ivoire).

Argungu Fishing & Cultural Festival
(mid- to late February) This three-day festival held on the banks of the Sokoto River (Nigeria) includes spectacular displays of fishing, duck hunting and swimming, as well as diving competitions and canoe racing.

Fespaco
(last week of February, sometimes early March every odd year) This famous film festival is held in Ouagadougou (Burkina Faso).

Carnival
(February) Carnival is a Latin-style street festival in Bissau (Guinea-Bissau), with masks, parties and parades, marking the time leading up to the beginning of Lent.

Mardi Gras
This is a time of major celebration in Cape Verde (similar to Carnival in Guinea-Bissau), with street parades during the days leading up to Lent, and finishing on Mardi Gras (the Tuesday before Ash Wednesday, 40 days before Easter).

April

Independence Day
(4 April) This is Senegal's biggest public celebration; coincides with the West African International Marathon in Dakar.

Fête du Dipri
Held in Gomon (Côte d'Ivoire) in April (sometimes March), you'll see masked dancing, healing ceremonies and sacrifices.

May

Aboakyer (Deer Hunt)
(first weekend in May) The main event during this famous festival, held in Winneba (Ghana), is a competitive antelope hunt between two groups of men.

July

Bakatue Festival
(first Tuesday of July) This colourful harvest thanksgiving feast features music and dancing, held in Elmina (Ghana).

Tabaski Price Hikes

Two weeks before Tabaski, sheep prices rise steeply, as every family is expected to provide one during the celebrations. Those who cannot afford a sheep are socially embarrassed and most will do anything to scrape up the money. One-third of the slaughtered animal is supposed to be given to the poor, one-third to friends, and one-third is left for the family. If you can manage to get an invitation to a Tabaski meal (it usually takes place after prayers at the mosque), you'll be participating in Muslim West Africa's most important and festive day of the year.

August

Oshun Festival
(last Friday in August) Music, dancing and ritual sacrifices are the hallmarks of this famous Yoruba festival in Oshogbo (Nigeria).

September

Igname (Yam) Festival
(beginning of September) Fire dances are a highlight of this festival in Bassar (Togo).

Fetu Afahye Festival
(first Saturday in September) This colourful carnival is held in Cape Coast (Ghana).

Biennal
(starts around the second week of September in even years) This is a national sport and cultural festival, held in Bamako (Mali).

La Cure Salée
(usually the first half of September) La Cure Salée is an annual celebration that is famous all over Africa, by the Fula herders, near In-Gall (Niger). The most famous is that of the nomadic Woodaabé, who during their week-long Gerewol festival paint their faces and make themselves beautiful, and then line up in long rows for the single women to inspect. This is followed by camel races, ritualistic combat and long hours of dancing into the night.

November

Fête de l'Abissa
(early November, sometimes late October) A week-long traditional carnival, held at Grand Bassam (Côte d'Ivoire), and nearby at Gbregbo (near Bingerville) where the dead are honoured and evil spirits publicly exorcised.

December

Igue/Ewere Festival
(usually in the first half of December) A colourful seven-day festival with traditional dances, a mock battle and a procession to the palace to reaffirm loyalty to the oba. Held in Benin City (Nigeria).

Cattle Crossing
A vibrant annual festival of Fula cattle herders in Diafarabé (Mali); the date is not fixed until November.

ACTIVITIES

Cycling

In several parts of West Africa (in particular tourist areas such as the Gambian coast), bicycles can be hired by the hour, day or week, and can be a good way to tour a town or area. Your choice may range from a new, imported mountain bike (*vélo tout terrain* or VTT in French) to ancient, single gear, steel roadsters. Away from tourist areas, it's almost always possible to find locals willing to rent their bicycles for the day; good places to inquire include the market or your hotel. Costs range from US$1 to US$10 per day, depending on the bicycle and the area.

Paris-Dakar Rally

The Paris-Dakar Motor Rally, also known simply as 'Le Dakar', is considered to be one of the world's longest, hardest and most-dangerous driving events. It was the brainchild of French racing-driver Thierry Sabine and was first held in 1979, although adventurous motorists have been crossing the Sahara since the 1920s. The race is held annually in January, usually starting in Paris and finishing in Dakar (except the year it went all the way to Cape Town). The race always crosses the Sahara Desert, although the exact route changes every year. (For details, check the Paris-Dakar Rally website **W** www.dakar.com.) The route distance is around 10,000km and takes 20 days to complete, with speeds of well over 150km/h being achieved on open stretches of sand.

The pace, heat and terrain are so tough that of the 400 or so vehicles that start each year, less than half (and sometimes only around one-quarter) of this number cross the finish line. Categories include motorbikes, cars and trucks, and among the big names are international auto manufacturers such as Citroën and Yamaha who spend millions of US dollars on drivers, machines and support teams to ensure top rankings. Of equal interest are the 'privateers' – individuals or amateur teams who compete on shoestring budgets and keep the spirit of the original adventurers alive.

Some commentators have questioned the morality of a million-dollar orgy of Western consumerism blasting its way through the poverty-stricken Sahel. The sponsorship money the rally generates, for example, equals 50% of Mauritania's total aid budget, and each rally stage burns 10% of Mali's total annual fuel consumption. In fact, so much petrol is needed by the competitors that 'host' countries run short, some aid and relief operations report being unable to move their trucks for weeks. Competitors get killed most years, but when innocent villagers (who account for 75% of the overall numbers of deaths) get run over by speeding cars with a value many times the lifetime earnings of an entire town in, say, Mali or Senegal, the contrast is brought even more sharply into focus.

For information on cycling in West Africa and on bringing your own bicycle to the region, see Bicycle in the Getting Around chapter.

Fishing
There is reportedly some excellent deep-sea sport fishing off the West African coast, including off Côte d'Ivoire, Gambia, Mauritania, Senegal and Sierra Leone. Expect costs to start at well over US$100 a day per person. Good places to start your inquiries are top-end hotels and local boat clubs.

Football (Soccer)
Soccer is Africa's most popular sport. If you want to play, the universities and municipal stadiums are by far the best places to find a good-quality game, but outside every town is a patch of ground where informal matches are played most evenings (in coastal areas, the beach is used). The ball may be just a round bundle of rags, and each goal a couple of sticks, not necessarily opposite each other. You may have to deal with puddles, ditches and the odd goat or donkey wandering across the pitch, but the game itself will be taken seriously. Play is fast and furious, with the ball played low. Foreigners are usually warmly welcomed and joining in a game is one of the best ways to meet people. If you bring along your own football (deflated for travelling) you'll be a big hit.

Soccer in West Africa

All West African countries have football leagues and tournaments in which teams from different towns and cities compete on a national or regional basis. However, it's the international competitions that cause the greatest excitement among football fans. Africa's main international competitions include the African Champions League and the CAF Cup, both held annually. (CAF, Confédération Africaine de Football, is Africa's football governing body.)

The event with the highest profile, and the one which most captures the enthusiasm of Africans throughout the continent is the African Cup of Nations, held every two years in January. In the preliminary rounds, 34 national teams compete, with the 16 best teams then gathered together in one place for the final rounds.

At the 2002 African Cup of Nations held in Mali, West African national sides included defending champion Cameroon, Senegal, Nigeria, Mali, Ghana, Liberia, Togo, Burkina Faso and Côte d'Ivoire. In a suspenseful final that went into overtime and ended in a penalty shoot-out, Cameroon beat Senegal to become the first team since 1967 to win successive titles. It also joined Ghana and Egypt as the only four-time winners in the cup's history.

For the latest results and more details on all the African international competitions, fans can check out the CAF website (w www.cafonline.com).

Hiking
West Africa has many interesting possibilities for hiking, but the set-up in this region is very different from that in East or Southern Africa. There are few high mountains or wilderness areas with good walking conditions, so much of the hiking is in populated areas, where paths pass through fields and villages. If you have the time and inclination, and don't mind roughing things, hiking can be a great way to interact with the local inhabitants; on foot you can meet on more equal terms rather than stare at each other through the windows of a bush taxi. As there's very little formal organisation, expect to arrange everything yourself in most areas, plan on being self-sufficient (bring a good water filter/purifier), and be prepared to adapt your plans as you go.

In some places, because of the distances involved (or just to take a break from walking), it may also be necessary to use donkeys, hitching or public transport to get around. Among the better hiking destinations are northern and northwestern Cameroon, Cape Verde, Guinea (the hilly Fouta Djalon area) and Mali (along the famous Bandiagara Escarpment). See these and the other country chapters for more details.

Rock Climbing
West Africa has little in the way of climbing. While expats living in, say, Guinea or Ghana may find some outcrops suitable for one-pitch routes or 'bouldering', as a visitor it's generally not worth lugging rock-climbing equipment around West Africa. The main exception is the area of Hombori (Mali), where some spectacular rock formations

stand high above the desert floor and attract a small but growing number of serious rock climbers from Europe (see Hombori in the Mali chapter for details). Another area with some rock-climbing potential is the Bandiagara Escarpment, also in Mali. The famous French climber Christine Destiville established some routes here (and featured prominently in a TV film about climbing in Dogon Country) some years ago, and groups from Europe occasionally follow her footsteps (and handholds). Northern Cameroon also has some possibilities.

Swimming & Water Sports

All along the coast of West Africa, you have a choice of beaches where swimming is a major attraction. Some beaches are very touristy, whereas others may be inhabited by local fishing communities or completely deserted. Wherever you go, note that in many areas of the region, the beaches can slope steeply and the waves create a vicious undertow. Never plunge into the ocean without first seeking reliable local advice.

A safer, if less adventurous, option may be to use a swimming pool. Most large cities have a public swimming pool *(piscine)*, and major hotels often have pools that nonguests can use for a small fee. In a few places – for example, Dakar, Douala and Lomé – you can find 25m pools suitable for swimming laps.

For sailing, there are clubs in various cities along the coast, but they rarely have boats available for hire. Your other option is to hire a small sailing boat at a tourist area, such as Gambia's Atlantic Coast or Senegal's Petite Côte. Day trips on large crewed yachts are available in Dakar, Banjul, Freetown and occasionally Abidjan.

Sailboards are available for rent in Senegal (Dakar and the Casamance beach area), the Atlantic Coast resorts (Gambia), Freetown (Sierra Leone), Abidjan and Sassandra (Côte d'Ivoire), and Lomé and Lake Togo (Togo). Dakar is also a base for scuba diving and kayaking.

ACCOMMODATION

In all the countries covered in this book, there's almost always some sort of accommodation available in most mid-sized and larger towns, although quality varies widely. At the luxury end of the scale, West Africa has very few top-class hotels outside the capitals, and offers little in the way of exclusive wildlife lodges or tented camps as found in East or Southern Africa. Independent travellers on tighter budgets are fairly well catered for, although there are almost no backpacker lodges.

Throughout the region, price generally reflects standards (though not always). Hotels at the top end of the range – when you can find them – usually have clean, air-con rooms with private bathrooms. In the mid-range, rooms probably have fans instead of air-con, and usually have a bathroom, but there may not always be hot water. Near the budget end of the scale, hotel rooms are not always clean (they are sometimes downright filthy), bathrooms are usually shared and often in an appalling state, and a broken window may provide fresh air. Many hotels – of whatever quality – double as brothels.

There are missions throughout the region, though rooms are usually reserved for mission or aid workers and open to others only on a space-available basis. Where mission accommodation is available, it's invariably clean, safe and good value at the budget level.

Most towns and villages in Francophone countries have a campement. This could be loosely translated as 'inn', 'lodge', 'hostel' or even 'motel', but it is not a camp site (ie, a place for tents), although some campements also provide areas where you can pitch a tent. Traditionally, campements offered simple accommodation, less elaborate than hotels. However, while some campements remain cheap and simple, others are very good quality, with prices on a par with mid-range hotels. You'll find the occasional *auberge* (small hotel) too – again with a wide range of quality.

In many parts of West Africa, particularly in the Sahel during the hot season, people often sleep outside their hut or on the flat roof of their house, as it's much cooler. In some hotels this is also possible, and carrying a mattress onto the roof – where you'll have some breezes and views of the stars – is usually allowed if you ask. In trekking areas such as Mali's Dogon Country, it has become established practice for visitors to sleep on the roof of the campements in each village.

Maisons de passage (houses for travellers) tend to be on the basic side. Often near markets or bus stations, they provide a bed for travellers and little else. They invariably double as brothels.

Some hotels charge for a bed only, with all meals extra. If breakfast is included it's usually on a par with the standard of accommodation: a full buffet in the more-expensive places, coffee and bread further down the scale. In many countries, a government tourist tax is also charged.

There are not many dedicated camp sites in West Africa, and those that do exist cater mainly for overlanders in their own vehicle. However, some hotels and campements allow camping, or provide an area where tents can be pitched. Grassy sites are rare – you often have to force pegs through hard-packed gravel.

FOOD

West Africa has some wonderful dishes, and the combination of influences – including local, French and even Lebanese – has resulted in some delicious cuisine. The key is knowing where to find it, trying not to let the rather generous amounts of oil used in cooking bother you and learning to appreciate the atmosphere surrounding you as much as the food. The quality of food tends to vary considerably from country to country. Culinary highlights of the region, include Côte d'Ivoire and Cameroon, although you'll find delectable dishes in many other places as well. In desert countries such as Mauritania or Niger, ingredients are limited. In general, the countries with the best range of food tend to be those along the coast, where rainfall is plentiful and the crops are varied.

Street Food

A feature of West African travel is the availability of 'street food' – ideal if you're on the move or prefer to eat little and often. Street food rarely involves plates or knives; it's served on a stick, wrapped in paper or in a plastic bag. It tends to be very cheap, and is often delicious – especially the grilled fish.

On street corners and around bus stations, especially in the morning, you'll see small booths selling pieces of bread with fillings or toppings of butter, chocolate spread, mayonnaise or sardines. In the Francophone countries, the bread is cut from fresh French-style loaves or baguettes, but in the Anglophone countries the bread is often a less-delicious soft, white loaf. Price depends on the size of the piece of bread you want, and the type of filling. It's quite usual to ask for, say, a CFA75 chunk, with CFA75 of mayonnaise, giving you a sandwich for CFA150 (US$0.20).

One of the region's finest institutions (found mainly in the French-speaking countries) are the coffee stalls where clients sit on small benches around a table and drink glasses of Nescafé mixed with sweetened condensed milk, served with French-style bread, butter or mayonnaise – all for around US$0.50. Some also offer tea (made with a Lipton teabag), or even Milo, and a more enterprising 'caféman' might fry up eggs or serve sardines. Many coffee stalls are only open in the morning.

In the Sahel countries, usually around markets, you'll see women with large brown bowls covered with a wicker lid selling yogurt, that is sometimes mixed with pounded millet and sugar. This sells for around US$0.15 a portion – you can eat it on the spot, or take it away in a plastic bag. A variation is where the millet is boiled before being mixed with the yogurt to make more of a porridge.

In the evenings you can buy *brochettes* (small pieces of beef, sheep or goat meat skewered and grilled over a fire) or lumps of roast meat sold by guys who walk around pushing a tin oven on wheels. Around markets and bus stations, women serve deep-fried chips of cassava or some other root crop.

In Francophone countries, grilled and roast meat, usually mixed with onions and spices, is sold in shacks (basically an oven with a few walls around it). These are called *dibieteries* in some places, and you can eat on the spot (a rough bench might be provided) or take away. To feed one or two, ask for about CFA1000 worth (about US$2).

Another popular stand-by in the larger cities are Lebanese-style *chawarmas,* thin slices of lamb grilled on a spit, served with salad (optional) in Lebanese-style bread (pita) with a sauce made from chickpeas. These cost about US$1. Thanks to the region's significant Lebanese population, in many countries, particularly in capital cities, you can also usually find other delicious Lebanese specialities.

Sit-Down Meals

For something more substantial than street food, West African meals typically consist of a staple served with a sauce, with the great variety of ingredients making the sauce interesting. Dishes can be simple or very complex according to the skill of the cook, the availability of ingredients and the budget of the customers.

Some travellers have been lucky enough to stay with local people, where a great way to repay their hospitality is to pay for a special meal for the entire family. This way you'll also be able to see how meals are put together. For the full picture, visit the market with the lady of the house (it's always the women who do the cooking in domestic situations) and see the various ingredients being bought.

Staples One of the most common staples, especially in the Sahel, is rice. Millet is also common, although this grain is usually pounded into flour before it is cooked. In most rural areas this is done by hand with a large wooden mortar and pestle, sometimes for several hours. The millet flour is steamed and then moistened with water until it thickens into a stiff 'porridge' that can be eaten with the fingers. Sorghum is a similar grain crop, and is prepared in much the same way, although it's not used as much as millet.

In the countries nearer the coast, staples may be root crops such as yam or cassava (also called manioc), that are pounded or grated before being cooked. They're served as a near-solid glob, called *fufu* or *foufou* (sometimes also *foutou*) – kind of like mashed potatoes mixed with gelatine and very sticky. You grab a portion (with your right hand) form a ball, dip it in the sauce and eat. In the coastal countries, plantain (green banana) is also common – either fried, cooked solid or pounded into a fufu.

Sauces These are made from whatever is available. In some Sahel countries, groundnuts (peanuts) are common, and a thick brown groundnut sauce is often served, either on its own or with meat or vegetables mixed in with the nuts. Sometimes deep-orange palm oil is also added. Sauces are also made with vegetables or the leaves of staple food plants such as cassava. Okra is popular, particularly in coastal countries – the result is a slimy green concoction. Other vegetables used in meals include potatoes (*pommes de terre* in French), sweet potatoes *(patates)*, onions *(oignons)*, green beans *(haricots verte)* and tomatoes *(tomates)*. For flavour-

Vegetarian?

Vegetarianism as such is rarely understood in West Africa, and vegetarian restaurants are rare, although you can often find vegetarian dishes at Asian and Indian restaurants in capital cities. The main challenge is likely to be keeping some variety and nutritional balance in your diet, and getting enough protein, especially if you don't eat eggs and dairy products.

If you do eat eggs and dairy products, pizzas and omelettes make a change from the ubiquitous bean-and-vegetable dishes. Expensive imported cheese is usually available in capital cities. Otherwise, cheese is seldom available except for the ultra-processed triangular varieties, which are often sold in larger supermarkets.

Some street food is another option, although it's often greasy. The selection here includes cassava, yam and plantain chips, bread with mayonnaise, egg or chocolate spread, and fried dough balls. Alternatively, head for the markets and do your own catering. There are always plenty of fresh fruit and vegetables (usually sold in piles of four or five pieces), as well as nuts, including dollops of ground peanuts (local-style peanut butter) arranged on banana leaves. Bread and tins of margarine are readily available. Banana and ground-peanut sandwiches made with fresh bread are a nutritious option.

Keep in mind that even the most simple vegetable sauce may sometimes have a small bit of meat or animal fat in it, and chicken is usually not regarded as 'real' meat. Another factor to consider if you are invited to someone's home for dinner is the fact that meat – a luxury for most local residents – is often reserved for special occasions or honoured guests (such as yourself). This means that the beast in the cooking pot bubbling away on the fire may well have been slaughtered in your honour, so give some thought as to how you might deal with this situation in advance.

ing, chillis may be used, or *jaxatu* (pronounced ja-ka-too) – similar to a green or yellow tomato but extremely bitter.

Stock cubes or sachets of flavouring are ubiquitous across the region (Maggi is the most common trade name) and are often thrown into the pot as well. Where it can be afforded, or on special occasions, meat or fish is added to the sauce; sometimes succulent slices, sometimes heads, tails and bones. See the individual country chapters for more details on regional specialities.

Where to Eat

The best place to eat, if you're lucky enough to be invited, is at somebody's house. Most days, though, you'll be heading for a restaurant. The smallest, most simple eating houses usually have one or two meals available each day. It's usual to ask what they have, and base your choice – if any – on that. Meals will usually be straightforward – bowls of rice or another staple served with a simple sauce.

In slightly smarter places your choice may also include fried chicken or fish served with hot chips *(frites)*. Cooked vegetables, such as green beans, may also be available. Up a grade from here, mainly in cities, you'll find mid-range restaurants catering to well-off locals and foreigners. They may serve only 'international' dishes, such as steaks or pizzas, and these meals are usually expensive, particularly if some of the ingredients have been imported from Europe. Ironically, local specialities, such as fish and rice, may cost the same in this kind of place.

In many cities and tourist towns, 'fast food' is available. This refers less to the time it takes to serve, and more to the type of meal served – pizzas, burgers, hot dogs and Lebanese pita-bread sandwiches.

Fruit

Availability depends on the season, but the choice is always good and increases as you head south from the Sahel into the coastal countries. Fruits you're likely to see include oranges, mandarins and grapefruits (all often with green skin despite being ready to eat), bananas (many different colours and sizes), mangoes (also many varieties), papayas (pawpaws), pineapples, guavas and passionfruit.

DRINKS

Nonalcoholic Drinks

International and local brands of soft drinks are sold virtually everywhere. A tiny shop in a remote village may sell little food, but the chances are they'll have a few dusty bottles of Coca-Cola or Pepsi for sale. (Coke is called 'Coca' in Francophone countries.) Bottled mineral water is widely available in cities, towns and tourist areas.

Home-made soft drinks include ginger 'beer' and *bisap*, a purple mixture made from water and hibiscus leaves. These drinks are usually sold in plastic bags by children on the street. Although they are refreshing, the water may not be clean, so they're usually best avoided.

As with beers, prices for soft drinks vary from dirt cheap at the side of the road to extortionate at posh restaurants. As a guide, the price of a soft drink is nearly always about half the price of a beer at the same place.

In the Sahel countries, tea comes in two sorts. There's the type made with a tea bag (its local name is 'Lipton tea' even if the brand is actually something else), and there's the type of tea drunk by the local population – made with green leaves (often imported from China) and served with loads of sugar in small glasses. Mint is sometimes added, or the tea may be made from mint leaves alone. Half the fun of drinking local-style tea is the ritual that goes with it, taking at least an hour. Traditionally, the tea is brewed three times and poured from a small pot high above the glass.

Coffee is almost exclusively instant coffee (Nescafé is the usual brand), although *where* you drink it will determine the flavour. At the coffee stalls mentioned under Street Food earlier, it's mixed with sweetened condensed milk, and in some areas the water may be infused with a local leaf called *kinkiliba*, which gives it a woody tang – unusual but not unpleasant when you get over the shock. If you drink coffee at a smarter restaurant it will come as a cup of warm water, with the coffee in a sachet in the saucer – you add milk (usually powdered) and sugar as required.

Alcoholic Drinks

You can often find imported beers from Europe and the USA, but about 45 brands of beer are brewed in West Africa, with Nigeria alone producing about 30. Some beers are

European brands, brewed locally, others are specific to the region. The quality is often very good. Brands to look out for include: Club (Ghana, Nigeria and Liberia), Flag (Côte d'Ivoire and Senegal), Star (Sierra Leone, Ghana and Nigeria), Harp and Gulder (Nigeria and Ghana). Guinness is found in several countries, too. Expect to pay from about US$0.50 for a beer in a local bar, up to several dollars in a top-end hotel. Cold beers are often available, though in many places you'll need to specifically request this.

In the Sahel a rough, brown and gritty 'beer' made from millet is common, but West Africa's most-popular home brew is palm wine. The tree is tapped and the sap comes out already mildly fermented. Sometimes yeast is added and the brew is allowed to ferment overnight, which makes it much stronger. In Nigeria, it is even bottled in factories.

SHOPPING

A major feature of travel in West Africa is the vast range of artistic and craftwork items found across the region. These include masks, statues and other woodcarvings, hand-made textiles with a fantastic variety of colours and patterns, glass beads and jewellery made from gold and silver, as well as a fascinating assortment of pots, urns, stools, weapons, musical instruments and more.

Whether you're a serious collector or just looking for a souvenir from your trip, you'll find plenty to choose from, and prices are always more reasonable than they are at

Markets

The markets in West Africa are large, vibrant, colourful and always fascinating. The best are those in Abidjan, Dakar, Bamako, Banjul, Kano, Lomé, Niamey and Ouagadougou, but the markets in smaller places are also well worth a visit.

There are two main types of market. The most common are those where local people come to buy and sell everyday things such as fruit, vegetables and other items such as clothes and farm tools. In larger places, you'll also see stalls selling radios, cassette players and other electrical goods, imported shoes, hardware and car parts. The second type of market is aimed more at tourists, where you can buy art and craft items. In some places the main market and the tourist-oriented craft market are combined and these can be the most interesting to visit.

Bargaining

When it comes to buying souvenirs, bargaining is usually the name of the game. Many items do not have a fixed value, and prices have to be negotiated (see the boxed text 'The Fine Art of Bargaining' earlier in this chapter), but this is not always the case. With cloth sold by the metre, for example, you can expect little or no lowering of the price. The same is true of gold and silver; if the trader tells you the price and you come back with an offer one-third that amount, don't be surprised if they are genuinely insulted and refuse to talk further. In these cases, try to get a feel for prices beforehand. Ask knowledgeable locals or check out a fixed-price shop or hotel gift shop; prices in the market are typically half those in the stores. If you don't enjoy bargaining, stick to the fixed-price shops.

Hassles

Most travellers love to visit markets, but a few find them intimidating or annoying experiences. It can be hard dealing with eager traders when they grab you by the arm and not-so-gently pull you over to their stall 'just to see' *(pour voir seulement)*. Although traders in city or tourist markets are often very pushy, in local markets tourists are treated just like any other person there. If you want to sample a big traditional market, go early when the stalls are just opening and the vendors are still in low gear. It's usually cooler then as well.

As for persistent traders, if you really don't want anything they're offering, say 'No thanks' and move on. Once you move into another trader's pitch they'll usually back off. If they keep pulling you and you find it offensive, let them know in no uncertain terms – if your actions are clear, they'll stop.

In a few markets, the hassle can verge on danger, as pickpockets work the crowds or gangs of youths posing as merchants can surround tourists and snatch bags and cameras. For tips on safety, see Dangers & Annoyances earlier in this chapter.

home. Of course, many of the items you'll see in shops and markets are made expressly for the tourist trade, although these are often copies of traditional items. Even contemporary pieces of art are usually based on traditional designs.

Making items for sale is not new either: among the oldest 'tourist' art in sub-Saharan Africa was that produced by the Sapi people of Sierra Leone in the 15th century – they sold ivory salt pots and trumpets to the Portuguese traders.

See the special section 'Arts & Craftwork' for more details of the types of art and craftwork available. As well as these, other items commonly seen in West Africa are baskets and pottery with intricate designs, which are almost always produced by women. Leatherwork, with colourful incised patterns, mostly made from goat-hide, are created by men in the Sahel region.

Cassettes of local music are also a good buy – for more details see the special section 'The Music of West Africa', as well as the Shopping sections of individual town entries.

Antiques

Older wooden sculptures, particularly masks, headdresses and stools, from all over West and Central Africa are often sold in tourist markets. Some of the dusty pieces are genuine (which raises questions about the wisdom of promoting their sale and purchase). Others are replicas made specifically for sale – although they usually still have a nice 'worn' look, which you may find more preferable to the gloss of many new items.

Note that items that are authentic and valuable cannot be exported under the laws of most West African countries. Since very little art purchased by nonexperts fits this description, it's more a matter of being hassled by customs than doing something illegal. Nevertheless, in some countries such as Mali, Nigeria and Ghana, for genuine antiques you must get an export permit – usually from the museum in the capital. If the piece looks old, it might be worth letting the museum check it before you purchase, to avoid difficulties later.

Bringing Items Home

When you buy a new woodcarving you may find it has cracked by the time you get home. New wood must be dried slowly. Wrapping the carvings in plastic bags with a small water tray enclosed is one technique. If you see tiny bore marks with white powder everywhere, it means the powder-post beetle (frequently confused with termites) is having a fiesta. There are three remedies – zap the beasts in a microwave oven, stick the piece in the freezer for a week, or drench it with lighter fluid. You could also try fumigating items. Be warned that if you have wooden objects with insect damage, the items may be seized by customs and you will have to pay to have them fumigated.

If you buy textiles, note that some dyes, including indigo, may not be colour-fast. Soaking cloth in vinegar or very salty water may stop the dye running, but this method should only be used on cloth of one colour. Adinkra cloth is not meant to be washed.

MUSIC OF WEST AFRICA

Music is a major feature of West African culture, and some of the African continent's most famous musicians come from this region. Music is everywhere – loud with a pounding beat from the market cassette stalls, pure and sweet straight from a singer's mouth, scratchy and distorted on a bush-taxi radio, in the background at restaurants and in your face at bars and nightclubs. For many travellers, experiencing West African music, with its haunting rhythms and melodies, is the highlight of their trip.

African music can be divided into two categories: traditional music and pop music. Traditional music is predominant in rural areas, whereas pop music is largely an urban phenomenon. This division is not clear cut, though, because African pop draws inspiration from the styles and rhythms of traditional music.

Traditional Music

For the majority of West Africans, traditional music is the heart of their culture. Traditional music can be more difficult for foreigners to appreciate than the modern styles. To the uninitiated it may sound random, or simply monotonous. However, if you listen carefully you begin to follow and pick out the structure of the piece. If you are listening to a drum ensemble, try to focus on the sound (or rhythm) produced by just one of the drums – you'll begin to notice how it fits in with the others, and the entire pattern will become clearer. It's important to remember that typically African music is polyphonic and polyrhythmic, which means that there are many rhythms occurring simultaneously, without one dominating the other. This allows the listener to pick out certain melodies or rhythms and concentrate on them, which is what the dancers do.

An essential feature of traditional music is that it serves a social purpose. Not only does each social occasion have its own type of music, but, in addition, there are different kinds of music for women's groups, hunters, warriors etc.

In much of West Africa music was traditionally the province of one social group, the griots. The term 'griot' (pronounced gree-oh) is of French origin and means minstrel, musician or praise singer. Griot is a useful general term, but each linguistic group has its own word – *jali* in Mandinka, *gewel* in Wolof and *gawlo* in Fula (Pulaar).

Many West African societies were, and still are, highly stratified, with nobility at the top and descendants of slaves at the bottom. Artisans (blacksmiths, weavers, leather-workers etc) are a rank above the lowest. Griots were traditionally part of the artisan class, and they fulfil many important social functions.

Historically, griots had a close relationship with the royal courts, where they acted as translators and diplomats, but it was their role as oral historians that made them so important. In West Africa, the younger generation traditionally learns about the history of its society

Inset: *Djembe* drums in a range of sizes for sale in St-Louis, Senegal (Photo by Frances Linzee Gordon)

through word of mouth. The role of griots in this is crucial; they are the retainers of their culture's history, which they reveal through narratives recited or expressed in songs. For example, all griots know the epic of *Sundiata*, which describes the exploits of the warrior who founded the Empire of Mali in the 13th century AD. This song is well known throughout West Africa, and is just one of a large repertoire of narratives, including anticolonial songs, praise songs to famous warriors, and love songs.

Griots are also genealogists, and at weddings, naming ceremonies and other important events they are called upon to recount the names and deeds of the host's ancestors. Like other artisans, they are thought to possess spiritual powers, and this, coupled with their knowledge of the past, leads people to fear them.

Traditional Instruments

A distinctive aspect of traditional music is the instruments used. Traditional musicians generally use instruments made from local materials such as gourds, leather, cow horns and shells.

Drums A quick visit to almost any museum in West Africa will give you a good idea of the variety of drums used by musicians. These include the kettle, cylindrical and frame (similar to a tambourine) drums, as well as goblet- and hourglass-shaped ones. Drums are usually covered with cowhide or goatskin, although some use gazelle or snake skin. The immense variety of shapes and sizes reflects the diversity of natural materials available in West Africa. Another reason is that drums not only serve as musical instruments, but also as tools of communication. The drums used for long-distance messages are often made from the trunks of trees and can easily weigh several hundred kilograms. Drums also announce the arrival of important people.

The *tama* drum of the Wolof has become familiar in the West through its use in the music style known as *mbalax*, popularised by Senegal's Youssou N'Dour. The tama is a small, single-faced drum with strips of leather fixed to the skin and base, which, when squeezed under the musician's arm, change the tension of the surface of the skin and, therefore, its pitch. This variable pitch quality gives rise to the name 'talking drum', and good players can obtain a wide range of notes.

Another type of talking drum is used extensively in *juju* music (see Juju Music later for an explanation of this style). The player strikes the skin with a hooked stick, squeezing and releasing the tension of the skin to obtain the desired pitch.

The *djembe* is a popular drum used from Ghana to Senegal. It's shaped like a medieval chalice and is usually covered with goatskin (sometimes with the hair still attached), fastened by leather cord.

Drums are not usually played alone, but are often part of an ensemble. The Ewe people of Ghana are well known for their skill in drumming, and their drum ensembles can include up to 10 musicians. Tubular iron bells, gourd or calabash rattles and a large variety of upright drums make up the group and the rhythms are irresistible. You can also hear drum ensembles in Burkina Faso, Gambia, Guinea-Bissau, Nigeria and Senegal.

Stringed Instruments There is a huge variety of stringed instruments in West Africa, from a one-string plucked lute *(moolo)* or bowed fiddle *(riti-riti)* to the 21-string kora. The kora is historically the instrument of the griots, and is arguably one of the most sophisticated instruments in sub-Saharan Africa. It is a cross between a harp and a lute, with its strings divided into two rows, one of 11 strings, the other of 10. These are supported over a long neck (usually made of rosewood) by a wooden bridge, with a notch for each string, which is often ornately carved. Studs fasten the hide to the gourd and are often arranged in interesting patterns, which sometimes feature the player's name. The instrument is held upright in the lap of the seated player, who plucks the two rows of strings with the thumb and index finger of each hand. Kora players are often very highly skilled musicians who start learning their craft in early childhood. They are found throughout the Sahel, especially in Gambia, Guinea, Mali and Senegal.

Kora players can be heard at naming day or wedding ceremonies, which take place in cities, towns and villages throughout the region. Urban performances are more difficult to come by, although in tourist areas such as Gambia's Atlantic Coast resorts, hotels and restaurants often put on kora performances – look out for the talented Bajaly Suso, who often plays here. You could also try asking around at the local markets in the region; people should be able to point you in the right direction.

There is a wide range of kora music available internationally, with a greater range within West Africa. For an excellent example of kora music performed in the traditional style, look for the recordings by Jali Nyama Suso, a Gambian who wrote the country's national anthem. He appears on the double-set *A Search for the Roots of the Blues* as well as *Songs from The Gambia*. Other good kora players include Guinean Jali Musa Jawara (younger brother of pop star Mory Kanté), whose recording *Soubindoor* is worth finding, and Gambians Dembo Konté and Kausa Kouyate, who collaborated on the excellent *Simbomba*. In a different style is the kora music of Lamine Konté, from the Casamance region of Senegal, whose best work appears on *The Kora of Senegal Vols 1 & 2*. Delicately structured and with a Cuban feel, his music is well worth finding.

Another excellent kora player is Toumani Diabaté, a Malian whose classic recording Djelika features some the country's best musicians.

The *xalam* (pronounced khalam), as it's known in Wolof, is another important instrument of the griots. It's also known as *ngoni* in Bambara, *hoddu* in Fula and *konting* in Mandinka. It has three to five strings, which are plucked. The body of the xalam is carved out of a tree trunk to form a 'boat' shape, with goatskin (traditionally, the hide of a male gazelle) stretched over the opening and fastened to the sides by wooden pegs. A smooth piece of narrow wood serves as the neck, with the strings (originally thin strips of leather, but now fishing line is usually used) attached to it by leather collars. Interestingly, this instrument is regarded by musicologists as the ancestor of the banjo. Two of West Africa's most revered musicians (both now dead), Mali's Banzoumana Sissoko and Guinea's Kouyate Sory Kandia, were ngoni players.

Wind Instruments The most common wind instrument is the flute. Fula shepherds are reputed to play the most beautiful flute music, using an instrument made from a length of reed. You'll also see flutes made from millet stalks, bamboo and gourds. Other wind instruments include animal-tusk horns and trumpets made from gourds, metal, shells or wood. They are found all over West Africa and take a slightly different form in each area.

Xylophones The *balafon* is a type of wooden xylophone with between 15 and 19 rectangular keys made out of a hardwood. These are usually suspended over a row of gourds, which amplify the sound. The player (sometimes two) is usually seated and strikes the keys with two wooden mallets. The balafon is the name given to the instrument played by griots, and other types of xylophones have different names depending on the particular language group in the region. Souleymane Traoré, a Malian balafon player, has two very good recordings: *Hommage à Lamissa Bangaly* and *Confirmation*.

ARIADNE VAN ZANDBERGEN

Right: A musician playing a *balafon* beside a Wassu stone circle, an ancient Gambian burial site dating from AD 500 to 1000

Pop Music

African pop music can be said to have begun at the end of the 19th century with the beginning of the colonial era. Africans were then exposed for the first time to Western music (via phonographs and church choirs) and Western instruments (through regimental orchestras), and also through the music and instruments brought by sailors to Africa's busy ports. African musicians incorporated this wide variety of new sounds and influences into their own compositions, and it wasn't long before the music evolved into unique and popular African styles. These in turn have gone on to strongly influence and shape a number of Western musical styles. A brief description of the major African pop forms follows.

Highlife

During colonial times, Ghana was the richest country in the region and, not surprisingly, was where the influence of European music was felt

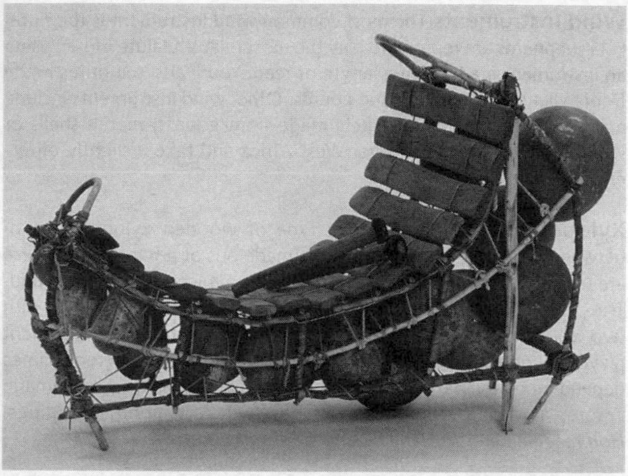

DENNIS WISKEN/SIDEWALK GALLERY

the most. What emerged was a Westernised style called 'highlife'. The Western influence was very noticeable in the dance bands that played to the African elites in the cities, less so in the bands that played in the hinterland. The new bands combined acoustic guitars with rattles, drums and other traditional instruments.

During WWII, Allied troops stationed in West Africa spread more new musical ideas, especially the then-popular 'swing' music. After the war, bands had a wide repertoire of sounds, including calypso. They began touring West Africa, igniting the highlife fire everywhere, and continuing to assimilate foreign musical styles. Black music from across the Atlantic had a big impact, especially jazz and soul.

Sahel Pop Music

Riding the crest of the world-music wave is the sound of West Africa's Sahel countries – Mali, Senegal and Gambia – with Guinean music following closely behind. From these countries come many of today's leading singers and musicians. The roots of their music offers an interesting insight into the development of their styles.

In the 1960s and '70s Cuban music was a major influence on the musical styles of the region. At the same time, many West African nations embarked on 'Authenticité' campaigns, which sought to encourage musicians to keep traditional African roots in their modern music. As a result, many musicians used the stories and melodies from the past in their new compositions. Ensembles and groups of musicians, called 'orchestras', were established with the aim of reinventing and revitalising traditional songs. Their influence on the West African music scene was enormous, and is the origin of today's distinct Sahel pop style.

There were many superb recordings made during this era. While some original cassettes are available in the region, many are now available on CD internationally, and can be found in good record stores worldwide. From Senegal, look out for the legendary Orchestra

Left: A traditional wooden xylophone, called a *balafon*, from Burkina Faso.

Baobab and its popular CD *Pirate's Choice*, a landmark export of African pop. The Royal Band and Canari de Kaolack are also popular. A six-volume set of CDs entitled *Dakar Sounds* showcases the major stars of the Senegalese scene.

From Mali, Salif Keita's (proclaimed by many as the 'Golden Voice of Africa') original band – the Rail Band of Bamako – is excellent, as is Keita's follow-up combination, Les Ambassadeurs. The Regional Orchestras of Mali series, through the Baerenreiter-Musicaphon label, are an absolute must for fans of this style.

Guinean music of the period was dominated by the government-controlled Syliphone label, which released recordings by Bembeya Jazz National, Keletigui et ses Tambourinis, Camayenne Sofa, and the all-female police group Les Amazones de Guinée, among a host of others.

Economic downturns in the 1980s led to the disbandment of most of these groups, but their music paved the way for the next wave of West African artists.

From Senegal, Youssou N'Dour's mbalax style is well known throughout the world; N'Dour has toured with Peter Gabriel. His music is a fusion of frenetic rhythms from the tama drum with funky bass and guitar lines creating an irresistible combination to dance to; aficionados should seek out N'Dour's earlier recordings with Etoile de Dakar. As popular as N'Dour is Baaba Maal, whose music incorporates traditional instruments alongside electric guitars.

From Mali, the hugely popular Oumou Sangaré's lyrics reflect the importance of love and freedom of choice in marriage. If you like the style look out for recordings by Sali Sidibé. Other good Malian women singers include Tata Bambo Kouyaté, Ami Koita and Kagbe Sidibé. Koita is a Malian female role model.

Blues lovers should check out Ali Farka Touré, who produces a mix of Arabic-influenced Malian sound with some American blues thrown in for good measure.

Guinean artists include Mory Kanté, whose 'kora funk' style is very popular in Europe and is similar to that of Salif Keita, and Sékou Diabaté, aka Diamond Fingers, the wonderful guitarist who played with Bembeya Jazz.

Afro-Beat

Afro-beat is a fusion of African melodies and rhythms with jazz and soul, popular particularly in Nigeria, and 'invented' in the 1960s by Fela Anikulapo Kuti (often known simply as Fela). Fela's songs dealt with corruption and police brutality, among other issues, and focused attention on the way Nigeria was being governed. As a result, Fela was imprisoned on several occasions on trumped-up charges.

Fela, who died in 1997, was probably Africa's best-known and most respected musician. Some of his best recordings are *Lady*, *Army Arrangement*, *Zombie*, and *Confusion*.

Similar in style is Sonny Okosun, who had a massive hit in 1978 with *Fire in Soweto*. His reggae-based music, while not as political as Fela's, retains many elements of highlife. Try to get hold of *The Ultimate Collection*, released in 2000, or the 1984 recording, *Liberation*.

Juju Music

In the 1920s in Lagos, traditional Yoruba talking drums (see Traditional Instruments earlier) were incorporated with the popular 'palm-wine' guitar style to form a new music known as juju. Juju music is characterised by sophisticated guitar work and tight vocal harmonies, backed by traditional drums and percussion. It is one of the best-loved styles in Nigeria.

The early exponents of juju found some commercial success through the release of their music on 78rpm records, although it wasn't until the introduction of amplification after WWII that juju really began to take off. Juju took over from highlife in Lagos during and after Nigeria's civil war (1967–70). Many of the highlife musicians were Igbo, who left Lagos for their eastern homeland to escape discrimination.

Leading musicians include King Sunny Ade, Ebenezer Obey and Shina Peters. Sunny Ade was influenced by Afro-beat and is probably the most famous juju musician. Check out his album *Synchro System*, which is excellent. Shina Peters is a juju star, and is particularly popular with the younger crowd. He modernised juju music by adding the funkiness of Yoruban drumming, Western-style guitars and multiple talking drums.

Congo Music

While fads in pop music come and go, there is one style that is universally popular – the music of Congo (Zaïre). This is the only music that is truly pan-African, popular from Senegal to Zimbabwe. The reason for this is that the Congolese artists produce some of the best dance music in the world – a heady mix of swirling guitars, punchy brass sections, bubbling bass and tight vocals.

It all began just after WWII, when radio stations began popularising the early Cuban rumba stars. 'Congo-bars' began to appear, offering dance music as well as refreshments. This early music featured acoustic guitars and empty bottles for percussion, but, with the arrival of the electric guitar and amplification, it eventually evolved into electric ensembles featuring a lead guitarist with a brass section and backing vocalists. Large orchestras emerged, many elaborating on traditional rumba patterns or modernising traditional songs.

In 1953 the popular Congolese band African Jazz, featuring Dr Nico, was established. This was followed three years later by the famous OK Jazz led by Franco, one of Africa's all-time most influential musicians (and still one of its most popular, despite his death in 1989). While musicians are constantly adding new ideas and arrangements to their songs, their music still retains the basic rumba framework. So if it sounds Latin, it's probably Congolese.

Another big star is Tabu Ley (aka Rochereau). Other leading musicians and groups include Kanda Bongo Man, Sam Mangwana, Papa Wemba, Langa Langa Stars, Bella Bella, Pierre Moutouri and Pamelo Mounka (both from neighbouring Congo) and Akédéngue (from Gabon). Leading female artists include M'Bilia Bel, Yshala Muana, M'Pongo Love and Abeti, all from Congo (Zaïre), and Nayanka Bell (from Côte d'Ivoire).

ARIADNE VAN ZANDBERGEN

Cuban Influence

The influence of Cuban music was pervasive in many West African countries. In the 1960s and '70s the pop music of Guinea, Mali, Côte d'Ivoire, and in particular, Senegal, was strongly influenced by Latin styles. The large orchestras of this period featured brass sections with brilliant soloists, and their music was based on Latin styles such as the rumba. Some groups of the time sung in Spanish. The salsa style was very popular in Senegal, with Africando (look out for the excellent CDs *Trovador* and *Tierra Tradicional*) and Le Super Cayor being the main exponents. Unlike the Congolese form, salsa music moves away from a reliance on electric guitars, and utilises flutes, violins, and a big-band-type brass section, and this style has enjoyed a revival in recent times.

Right: A band playing traditional instruments at the Roots Festival in Banjul, Gambia. The festival is a week-long celebration held every two years.

Makossa Music

Cameroon's distinctive *makossa* music has become increasingly popular in recent years throughout much of West Africa. It's a fusion of high-life and soul, and is strongly influenced by Congo music, with great use of the electric guitar.

The biggest star is still Manu Dibango, whose hit *Soul Makossa* in the mid-1970s put makossa music on the African musical map. His jazz-influenced music is more for listening to than for dancing. Francis Bebey and Isadore Tamwo are also extremely popular, while Sam Fan Thomas is Cameroon's king of *makassi*, a lighter sound than makossa but just as catchy. Bebey in particular experimented with a huge variety of musical styles, from classical guitar to traditional sanza to vocalisations of many different pygmy tribes to makossa to pop. Other makossa stars include Sam Fan Thomas, Sammy Njondji, Moni Bilé, Toto Guillaume and Ekambi Brillant.

Cape Verdean Music

Although not as popular as other music styles in West Africa, Cape Verdean music is nevertheless worth mentioning because of its distinctive, fast-paced Latin style. The dominant role of the guitar and electric piano without traditional African instruments set it apart. The leading musicians include Cesária Évora, Tam Tam 2000, Bana and Paulino Vieira. Évora appears on stage, barefoot, in support of disadvantaged women in Cape Verde, and sings about the plight of her country.

The Music Scene

The music industry in West Africa is huge and employs a significant section of the workforce. It's easy to find locally recorded cassettes (and imported CDs in large cities) of West and Central African music. Every town market has a small cassette shop, and in many places young men with boxes full of cassettes wander the streets. It's a good idea to go into a store and ask to hear something by the local recording stars. There is no better way to get to know the different styles and you may end up buying a cassette of next year's international success story.

Unfortunately, cassettes in West Africa are often of poor quality, as cheap tapes are used and the recordings themselves have often been pirated. It is possible (for a higher price) to obtain the original cassette, which will have a better sound than copies, but these are often in short supply and it can be difficult to tell an original-release cassette from a pirated copy (one indication is that a cassette cover of a copy is usually poorly overprinted). If you buy at a shop, you can listen to the tape first. Original cassettes cost US$3 to US$4, while cheap copies are around US$2.

To see a West African band, you normally need to be in one of the capital cities, although in some countries venues are surprisingly limited. The best cities in West Africa for hearing live-music performances are Lagos, Accra, Dakar, Abidjan, and Bamako. At weekends in Accra and elsewhere in Ghana, you can find live bands at many of the nightclubs. Other cities where you can find live bands include Conakry, Douala, Praia, Bissau and Niamey.

More details on local stars and names to look out for are given in the country chapters. If you want to buy West African music back home, check the World Music or African Music sections of large music shops. Specialist world music shops in Britain include Stern's (☎ 020-7387 5550, fax 7388 2756), 74–75 Warren St, London W1T 5PF,

ARIADNE VAN ZANDBERGEN

which also runs a worldwide mail-order service. In the USA, Africassette Music (☎ 313-881 4108, fax 881 0260, ⓔ rsteiger@africassette.com, ⓦ www.africassette.com), PO Box 24941, Detroit, MI 48224, also has a mail-order service. Both places also offer a wide selection of books on African music. In Australia, contact Blue Moon (☎ 03-9415 1157, fax 9415 1220), 54 Johnston St, Fitzroy, Vic 3065.

Graeme Counsel, Alex Newton & David Else

Right: A drummer performs on the streets of Île de Gorée, Senegal.

Getting There & Away

This chapter tells you how to reach West Africa from other parts of the world. Details on transport to and from specific countries are given in the Getting There & Away sections in individual country chapters.

AIR

Airports & Airlines

International airports in West Africa of most use to tourists (ie, those with the most frequent and more reasonably priced connections) are Abidjan (Côte d'Ivoire), Accra (Ghana), Bamako (Mali), Dakar (Senegal), Lagos (Nigeria) and Douala (Cameroon). There are also regular charter flights from some European countries to Banjul (Gambia). Flights to other places in the region are less convenient, more expensive, or both.

Where you fly to in the region depends on where you want to visit, but don't automatically aim for the airport nearest your intended starting point. Even if you want to start your travels in, for example, Mali, you may still find it cheaper and easier to fly to Banjul first, from where you can travel overland or take a regional flight.

Warning

The information in this chapter is particularly vulnerable to change. International air fares are volatile, schedules change, special deals come and go, and rules are amended. Airlines and governments seem to take a perverse pleasure in making fare structures and regulations as complicated as possible. In addition, the travel industry is highly competitive and agents' prices vary considerably.

Fares quoted in this book are approximate and based on the rates advertised by travel agents at the time of going to press. Airlines and travel agents mentioned in this chapter do not necessarily constitute a recommendation.

You should get quotes and advice from as many airlines and travel agents as possible – and make sure you understand how fares and tickets work – before you part with your hard-earned cash. The details given in this chapter should be regarded as pointers and are not a substitute for your own careful, up-to-date research.

European airlines regularly serving West African cities include Air France (Abidjan, Bamako, Conakry, Cotonou, Dakar, Douala, Lagos, Nouakchott, Niamey, Ouagadougou and Yaoundé), British Airways (Accra and Lagos), TAP Air Portugal (Bissau and Sal, Cape Verde), KLM-Royal Dutch Airlines (Abidjan, Accra, Lagos and Kano, Nigeria), Lufthansa Airlines (Accra and Lagos) and Iberia (Sal, Cape Verde). Swiss, the successor airline to Swissair is also worth contacting. For inexpensive fares to the Sahel countries, a good place to start is the increasingly popular Point Afrique (W www.point-afrique.com), which connects Paris and Marseilles with Atâr (Mauritania), Ouagadougou (Burkina Faso), Niamey (Niger) and various other destinations, and offers charter packages and good flight deals. Other airlines serving specific countries are detailed in the Getting There & Away sections of the individual country chapters.

Several African airlines also fly regularly between Europe and West Africa; a few also serve North America. The main one for years, Air Afrique, had just suspended its international flights shortly before this book went to press, although rumours are that it may resume at least partial operations in the near future. Ghana Airways, Nigeria Airways and Cameroon Airlines all have routes connecting Europe (London or Paris) and West Africa. Other African airlines serving the West African region include EgyptAir, Royal Air Maroc, Ethiopian Airlines and Kenya Airways. Although the routes offered by these airlines can be longer than those of European carriers, their prices are often cheaper.

Whichever airline you decide to take, it may be worth checking out the possibility of an open-jaw ticket (ie, flying into one country and out of another), as this often works out to be cheaper than booking a standard return in and out of one city, plus a connecting regional flight to get you back to your starting point.

Buying Tickets

To buy a ticket, it's usually not worth contacting airlines directly as their prices aren't the cheapest. Discounted tickets are released to selected travel agents and specialist discount agencies, and these are usually the best deals. Travel agents can also provide you with a wider choice than the airlines themselves. One exception to this is booking on the Internet. Many airlines offer some excellent fares on their websites. While there aren't too many deals to West Africa, there are some, and there are many bargain trans-Atlantic fares – useful if you will be flying to West Africa from North America. Many travel agencies also have websites, and there is an increasing number of online agents operating only on the Internet. Keep in mind, however, that while online ticket sales work well for simple one-way or return trips, the fare generators that post these tickets are no substitute for a travel agent who knows all about special deals, and can offer advice on related issues such as travel insurance and airline quality. Whichever route you choose, start as soon as you can: some cheap tickets must be bought months in advance, and some popular flights sell out early.

To find a suitable travel agent, look at the advertisements in weekend newspapers or travel magazines, or on the Internet. When comparing costs, you'll find that the cheapest flights are advertised by obscure 'bucket shops'. Many such firms are honest, but there are a few who will take your money and disappear. If you feel suspicious, pay only a small deposit. And once you have the ticket, ring the airline to confirm that you are actually booked on the flight before paying the balance. If they insist on cash in advance, go somewhere else. Some agents may tell you that the cheap flights in the ad are fully booked, 'but we have another one that costs a bit more...'. Or the agent may claim to have the last two seats available for the whole month, which they will hold for two hours only. These are all old tricks. Don't panic – keep ringing around.

Paying by credit card generally offers protection, as most card issuers provide refunds if you can prove you didn't get what you paid for. Similar protection can be obtained by buying a ticket from a bonded agent, such as one covered by the ATOL scheme in the UK, AATA in the USA, or AFTA in Australia. Well-known discount agents such as STA Travel, with offices worldwide are also reliable. It's generally not advisable to send money (even cheques) through the post unless the agent is very well established.

Once you have a list of five or six agents, start phoning around. Tell them where you want to fly, and they will offer you a choice of airline, route and fare. The fare is normally determined by the quality of the airline, the popularity of the route, the duration of the journey, the time of year, the length of any stopovers, the departure and arrival times, and any restrictions on the ticket. Not all scheduled flights are direct. For example, if you fly from London to Bissau on TAP Air Portugal, you have to change at Lisbon.

Charter flights are generally direct and cheaper than scheduled flights, so they are well worth considering. Some charter flights come as part of a package that includes accommodation and other services, but most charter companies sell 'flight only' tickets, which can be good deals.

Several airlines offer 'youth' or 'student' tickets, with sometimes significant discounts for people under 26 (sometimes 23) or in full-time education. Regulations vary, and not all agents will tell you about these offers. If you think you might be eligible, contact a specialist student travel agency – there's usually at least one in university towns and cities.

Once you have your ticket, keep a note of the number, flight numbers, dates, times and other details, and keep the information somewhere separate from your money and valuables. The easiest thing to do is to take a few photocopies – carry one with you and leave another at home. If the ticket is lost or stolen, this will help you get a replacement.

It's sensible to buy travel insurance early. If you get it the week before you fly, you may find, for example, that you're not covered for delays to your flight caused by industrial action. For more details see Travel Insurance under Visas & Documents in the Regional Facts for the Visitor chapter.

Travellers with Special Needs

If you have special needs of any sort – you've broken a leg, you're vegetarian, travelling in a wheelchair, taking the baby, terrified of flying – you should let the airline know as soon as possible so that they can make arrangements. Remind them when you reconfirm your booking (at least 72 hours before departure) and again when

Internet Air Fares

A few hours surfing the Web can help give you an idea of what you can expect in the way of good fares as well as be a useful source of information on routes and timetables. Remember that most online flight reservation services need credit-card details and, as many are US-based, they may only deliver to North American addresses.

Following are a few sites that may be useful. For additional websites, see the discount travel agency listings throughout this chapter's Air section, and the tour operator listings under Organised Tours, both elsewhere in this chapter.

Airlines

Air France W www.airfrance.com
Air Mauritanie W www.airmauritanie.mr
Cameroon Airlines W www.iccnet.cm/camair
Kenya Airways W www.kenya-airways.com
KLM-Royal Dutch Airlines W www.klm.com
Point Afrique W www.point-afrique.com
Royal Air Maroc W www.royalairmaroc.com
South African Airways W www.flysaa.com
TACV Cabo Verde Airlines W www.caboverde.com
TAP Air Portugal W www.tap-airportugal.pt

Online Ticket Sellers

Travel.com.au W www.travel.com.au
This site handles bookings for travel out of and around Australia.
OneTravel.com W www.onetravel.com
This site has cheap flights and good flexibility.
Microsoft Expedia W expedia.msn.com/daily/home/default.hts
Primarily for the US, this site offers lots of travel deals.
Sidestep W www.sidestep.com
This site is helpful primarily for trans-Atlantic flights, but it has some fares for West Africa as well.
Travelocity W www.travelocity.com
This site is good – once you're past the frustrating log-in procedure.

you check in at the airport. It may also be worth ringing around the airlines before you make your booking to find out how they can handle your particular needs.

Most international airports in Europe, North America and Australasia will provide escorts where needed, and there should be ramps, lifts, accessible toilets and reachable phones; airports in West Africa don't have these facilities. Deaf travellers can ask for airport and in-flight announcements to be written down for them.

Guide dogs for the blind will often have to travel in a specially pressurised baggage compartment with other animals, away from their owner; though smaller guide dogs may be admitted to the cabin. All guide dogs will be subject to the same quarantine laws (six months in isolation etc) as any other animal when entering or returning to countries currently free of rabies such as Britain or Australia.

Children under two travel for 10% of the standard fare (or free, on some airlines), as long as they don't occupy a seat. They don't get a baggage allowance either. 'Skycots' should be provided by the airline if requested in advance; these will take a child weighing up to about 10kg. Children between two and 12 can usually occupy a seat for half to two-thirds of the full fare, and do get a baggage allowance. Pushchairs can often be taken as hand luggage.

The UK

Numerous airlines fly between Britain and West Africa. Air France has a good network, flying via Paris and serving many cities in West Africa. Other airlines linking Britain and West Africa include Air Afrique (though at the time of writing, its international flights had been suspended), British Airways, Cameroon Airlines, Ethiopian Airlines (via Addis Ababa), Ghana Airways, KLM-Royal Dutch Airlines, Nigeria Airways, TAP Air Portugal and Royal Air Maroc.

Scheduled return flights from London to Dakar start at about UK£450, while London to Accra costs from UK£450 to UK£590 and London to Lagos about UK£490. With luck, you may occasionally find specials to any of these places from around UK£385. Low-season return fares between London and Abidjan or Bamako are around UK£420 to UK£560. During popular periods (such as the dry season for countries that are popular tourist destinations, or at busy holiday times such as Christmas or the end of Ramadan), prices may rise by another UK£70 to UK£100.

Cheaper fares are available to Banjul on charter flights catering for package tourists. Flights go mostly from London, but there are also departures from regional airports. The leading charter flight and tour operator is The Gambia Experience (see Organised Tours later in this chapter). You can buy flight tickets directly from the operators or from many high street travel agents. Flight-only fares start around UK£310 to UK£350, but some agents offer special deals that include accommodation – often in reasonable hotels – for only a little extra. Even if you don't stay in the hotel all the time, it can still be worth taking this offer; the airport transfers and first- or last-night bed can be very useful. Last-minute flight-only stand-bys can drop to as low as UK£240 or less – ideal if your dates are flexible, although there aren't too many of these. One-way flights may be cheaper, and some good deals are available if you're flexible.

There are many travel agents competing for your business. London is usually the best place to buy a ticket, although there are specialist travel agents outside the capital who are often just as cheap and can be easier to deal with. It's worth checking the ads in weekend newspapers or travel magazines, or in *Time Out*, but the following places are a starting point for discounted tickets. (Some of the agencies listed under Organised Tours, later in this chapter, also sell tickets.)

Africa Travel Centre (☎ 020-7387 1211, W www.africatravel.co.uk) 21 Leigh St, London WC1H 9QX
African Travel Specialists (☎ 0870-345 5454, e atsinquiry@aol.com) 229 Old Kent Rd, London SE1 5LU
Flightbookers (☎ 020-7757 2000, W www.ebookers.com) 177–178 Tottenham Court Rd, London W1P 9LF
STA Travel (☎ 020-7361 6161, 7581 4132, W www.statravel.co.uk) 86 Old Brompton Rd, London SW7 3LQ; with offices also in Manchester, Bristol and elsewhere
Trailfinders (☎ 020-7938 3939, W www.trailfinders.com) 194 Kensington High St, London W8 7RG

If you arrived in West Africa on a one-way ticket or overland, you might need to get a one-way flight home. For cheap flights direct to Britain, there are regular charter flights from Banjul to London and other cities, from around UK£350 – probably the cheapest way to get from West Africa to Europe. The main holiday company operating these flights is The Gambia Experience (see later in this chapter, and also in the Getting There & Away section in The Gambia chapter).

Continental Europe

You can fly from any European capital to any city in West Africa, but some routes are more popular and frequent (and usually cheaper) than others. Paris is a good hub. Return fares on scheduled flights from France to several West African capitals start from between €730 and €864 (about €665 to Lomé), going up to as high as €753 during popular periods such as holiday times, although you can occasionally find charters to Senegal for as little as €465, especially in the less popular periods.

It's also worth looking at flights from other cities. From Madrid, for example, you can get a return flight on Iberia airlines to Dakar for about €665. Another interesting option is to fly to Las Palmas in the Canary Islands, from where you can get flights on Air Mauritanie to Nouakchott and Nouâdhibou. SN Brussels Airlines is scheduled to begin flights from Brussels to Dakar, Conakry, Banjul and Monrovia in the near future. Travel agents and tour operators to try in **France** include:

OTU Voyages (☎ 01 44 41 38 50, W www.otu.fr) 39 ave Georges-Bernanos, 5e, Paris; with branches across the country
Voyageurs du Monde (☎ 01 42 86 16 00) 55 rue Ste-Anne, 2e, Paris

Travel agents and tour operators to try in **Belgium** include:

Acotra World (☎ 02-512 86 07) rue du Marché aux Herbes 110, 1000 Bruxelles
Connections (☎ 02-550 01 00, fax 512 94 47, W www.connections.be) rue du Midi 19–21, 1000 Bruxelles; branches in Gand and Liège
Eole (☎ 02-227 57 80, fax 219 90 73) chaussée de Haecht 43, 1210 Bruxelles
Joker Tourisme (☎ 02-426 00 03, W www.joker.be) Verdilaan 23, 1083 Ganshoren
Nouvelles Frontières (☎ 02-547 44 44) blvd Lemonnier 2, 1000 Bruxelles

Travel agents and tour operators to try in **Germany** include:

STA Travel (☎ 030-311 0950) Goethestrasse 73, 10625 Berlin; with branches in major cities

Travel agents and tour operators to try in **Italy** include:

CTS Viaggi (☎ 06-462 0431) 16 Via Genova, Rome

Travel agents and tour operators to try in **Switzerland** include:

SSR (☎ 022-818 02 02, W www.ssr.ch) 8 rue de la Rive, Geneva; with branches throughout the country
Nouvelles Frontières (☎ 022-906 80 80) 10 rue Chante Poulet, Geneva

If you didn't come on a return ticket, you can buy flights to any major European airport from most West African capital cities. The best places to try are Dakar and Abidjan, followed by Accra and possibly Bamako. Fares average from about US$500. Cheap charter flights to France from Lomé (Togo) are also available. Lagos has a good choice, but it's not worth going there just for a flight home.

North America

Ghana Airways has direct flights from New York to Accra for around US$1150 return, and Nigeria Airways flies direct between New York and Lagos for about US$1050 return. At the time of writing, Air Afrique had tentative plans to resume direct flights from New York to Dakar, to be priced around US$1100. Royal Air Maroc flies from New York to Abidjan, Bamako, Conakry, Dakar and Nouakchott, all via Casablanca. Return prices range from around US$1100 (Dakar) to US$1350. South African Airways has weekly flights from New York to Sal in Cape Verde (four times weekly) for about US$1000 return.

Most travellers go via Europe – usually London or Paris. Fares on these tickets (from the east coast) start at about US$1000, with most starting closer to US$1300. If you can find a good deal on the transatlantic leg of the trip, it can be cheaper to buy one ticket to London, and then a separate, discounted ticket onwards from there. From Canada, there are no direct flights to West Africa. You'll need to go via New York, or via London or another European capital.

In addition to the Internet, good places to start your search include the weekend editions of major newspapers such as the *New York Times* on the east coast, the *Los Angeles Times* or *San Francisco Examiner-Chronicle* on the west coast, the *Globe & Mail*, *Toronto Star* and *Vancouver Sun* in Canada, or in travel magazines for travel agents' advertisements. STA Travel (☎ 800-781 4040, W www.statravel.com) has offices in major cities nationwide. In Canada, try Travel CUTS (☎ 800-667 2887, W www.travelcuts.com). Several other discount agencies are listed following, although in the USA you won't find the good deals to West Africa that are available in London. Some of the companies listed under Organised Tours later in this chapter also sell flights.

Atlantic Fellowship (☎ 202-232 6990, 800-235 5220, W www.atlanticfellowship.com) 2204 Kalorama Rd, NW, Washington, DC 20008. Some West Africa fares, mostly to Accra and Lagos, and many discounted trans-Atlantic fares if you're flying to West Africa from North America.
Flytime Tours & Travel (☎ 212-760 3737, fax 594 1082, e flytimetravel@usa.net) 350 Fifth Ave, Suite 920, New York, NY 10118
MTS Travel (☎ 1-800-642 8315, 717-733-4131, fax 733 1909, W www.mtstravel.com) 124 East Main St, 4th Fl, Ephrata, PA. Primarily discounts for nonprofit organisations, but other consolidator fares also available.
Pan Express Travel (☎ 415-989 8282) 760 Market St, San Francisco, CA 94102
Tickets for Less (☎ 1-888-563 2731, e tflrates@att.net, W www.ticketsforless.com) 1801 JFK Blvd, Philadelphia, PA 19103
Travac Tours (☎ 1-800-872 8800, 212-563 3303, W www.thetravelsite.com) 989 Ave of the Americas, 16th Fl, New York, NY 10018
Uni Travel (☎ 314-569 2501, e online@unitravel.com, W www.unitravel.com) PO Box 12485, St Louis, MO 63132

Australasia

There are direct flights on Qantas and South African Airways from Perth and Sydney to Johannesburg, from where you can connect to several West African destinations, including Accra (Ghana), Abidjan (Côte d'Ivoire), Douala (Cameroon) and Lagos (Nigeria). Plan on paying from A$2280/NZ$3260 for the full routing.

Perhaps more exotic is a routing on EgyptAir, via Cairo, to Accra, Abidjan or Lagos (from A$2200). Prices for round-the-world tickets are usually more flexible; plan on paying from A$2900/NZ$3300.

It's also possible to fly via Europe. Airlines to try for reasonably priced fares include Qantas, Malaysia Airlines, Air New

Air Travel Glossary

Alliances
Many of the world's leading airlines are now intimately involved with each other, sharing everything from reservations systems and aircraft to check-in facilities and frequent-flyer schemes. Opponents say that alliances restrict competition. Whatever the arguments, there is no doubt that big alliances are the way of the future.

Courier Fares
Businesses often need to send urgent documents or freight securely and quickly. Courier companies hire people to accompany the package through customs and, in return, offer a discount ticket which is sometimes a bargain. However, you may have to surrender all your baggage allowance and take only carry-on luggage. Courier fares into West Africa are not very common. For any that do exist, London is the best place to look.

Fares
Airlines traditionally offer 1st class (coded F), business class (coded J) and economy class (coded Y) tickets. These days there are so many promotional and discounted fares available that few passengers pay full fare.

Lost Tickets
If you lose your airline ticket, an airline will usually treat it like a travellers cheque and, after inquiries, issue you with another one. Legally, however, an airline is entitled to treat it like cash and if you lose it then it's gone forever. Take very good care of your tickets.

Onward Tickets
An entry requirement for many countries is that you have a ticket out of the country. If you're unsure of your next move, the easiest solution is to buy the cheapest onward ticket to a neighbouring country or a ticket from a reliable airline which can later be refunded if you do not use it.

Open-Jaw Tickets
These are return tickets where you fly out to one place but return from another. If available, this can save you backtracking to your arrival point.

Overbooking
Since every flight has some passengers who fail to show up, airlines often book more passengers than they have seats. Usually excess passengers make up for the no-shows, but occasionally somebody gets 'bumped' onto the next available flight. Guess who it is most likely to be? The passengers who check in late. If you do get 'bumped', you are normally offered some form of compensation.

Reconfirmation
Some airlines require you to reconfirm your flight at least 72 hours prior to departure. Check your travel documents to see if this is the case.

Restrictions
Discounted tickets often have various restrictions on them – such as needing to be paid for in advance and incurring a penalty to be altered or cancelled. Others are restrictions on the minimum and maximum period you must be away.

Round-the-World Tickets
RTW tickets give you a limited period (usually a year) in which to circumnavigate the globe. You can go anywhere the carrying airlines go, as long as you stay within the set mileage/number of stops and, with some tickets, don't backtrack. The number of stopovers or total number of separate flights is decided before you set off and they usually cost a bit more than a basic return flight.

Ticketless
Travel Airlines are gradually waking up to the realisation that paper tickets are unnecessary encumbrances. On simple one-way or return trips, reservations details can be held on computer and the passenger merely shows ID to claim their seat.

Transferred Tickets
Airline tickets cannot be transferred from one person to another. Travellers sometimes try to sell the return half of their ticket, but officials can ask you to prove that you are the person named on the ticket. On an international flight, tickets are compared with passports.

Zealand, British Airways and Singapore Airlines.

In Australia, a good place to start your search for inexpensive deals is STA Travel (☎ 03-9349 2411, W www.statravel.com.au), with its main office at 222 Faraday St, Carlton, Victoria 3053, and offices in major cities and on many university campuses. Call 1300 360 960 Australiawide for the location of the nearest branch. Flight Centre is also good (☎ 131 600 Australiawide, W www.flightcentre.com.au), with its central office at 82 Elizabeth St, Sydney, and branches throughout Australia.

In New Zealand, Flight Centre (☎ 09-309 6171) has its central office in Auckland at National Bank Towers (corner of Queen and Darby Sts) and branches throughout the country. STA Travel (☎ 09-309 0458, W www.statravel.co.nz) has its main office at 10 High St, Auckland, with branches in Auckland, Hamilton, Palmerston North, Wellington, Christchurch and Dunedin.

For more options check the ads in travel magazines and weekend newspapers, including the Saturday issues of the *Sydney Morning Herald* or the *Age* in Australia, and the *New Zealand Herald* in New Zealand.

Africa

Many travellers on long trans-Africa trips fly some sections, either because time is short or simply because land routes are virtually impassable. One section frequently hopped is the Western Sahara (because it can be tricky for travellers without vehicles) by flying between Dakar (Senegal) or Nouakchott (Mauritania) and Casablanca (Morocco).

For travellers going to/from East or Southern Africa, the main hubs are Nairobi (Kenya), Addis Ababa (Ethiopia), and Johannesburg (South Africa), all of which have direct connections to West Africa – generally Accra or Abidjan, and sometimes to Lagos. Harare (Zimbabwe) is worth checking as well.

Airlines to try include South African Airways (which has connections from Johannesburg to Abidjan, Accra and Lagos), Ethiopian Airlines, Ghana Airways, Cameroon Airlines, Kenya Airways (with flights from Nairobi to Abidjan, Lagos and Douala) and possibly Air Afrique, if this airline resumes operations.

Expect to pay anywhere from US$500 upwards between Nairobi and Abidjan via Addis Ababa, about US$450 for a return excursion fare between Johannesburg and Accra, and about US$500 one way between Johannesburg and Lagos. Depending on which airline you use, you may need to follow a somewhat circuitous route (eg, Johannesburg to Abidjan via Addis Ababa on Ethiopian Airlines). Also keep in mind that flying across Africa – and particularly between East and West Africa – can be slow and subject to delays and cancellations. If you have connecting flights, allow yourself plenty of time.

STA (☎ 021-418 4689, W www.statravel.co.za) has several branches in South Africa, including one at 31 Riebeeck St, Cape Town, and is a good place to start for arranging discounted fairs. In Nairobi, try Flight Centres (☎ 02-210024, e fcswwat@arcc.or.ke) 2nd floor, Lakhamshi House, Biashara St, or Let's Go Travel (☎ 02-340331, W www.letsgosafari.com) on Standard St, near Koinange St.

The best connections from North Africa are on Royal Air Maroc, which has flights from Casablanca to Abidjan, Bamako, Conakry, Dakar and Nouakchott. The best deals are into Dakar, with return fares from Casablanca for around US$500.

LAND

Border Crossings

If you're travelling independently overland to West Africa – whether hitching, cycling, driving your own car or going by public transport – you can approach the region from three main directions: from the north, across the Sahara; from the south and southeast, through the countries bordering southern and eastern Cameroon; or from the east, through Chad.

If you're coming from the north, the main border crossing point into West Africa is just north of Nouâdhibou, via Morocco and the Western Sahara. There are also crossings at Bordj-Mokhtar and at Assamakka, where the trans-Saharan routes through Algeria enter Mali and Niger, respectively. For more information, see Crossing the Sahara later in this chapter.

If you come into West Africa from the south or southeast, the main border crossing points are at Garoua-Boulaï or at Kenzou (both for those travelling to/from the Central African Republic); at Kousséri, Bongor or Léré (for Chad); Moloundou, in Cameroon's far southeastern corner (for Congo); Kye Ossi (for Gabon); and Ebebiyin or Campo (for Equatorial Guinea). See the main Getting There & Away section in the Cameroon chapter for more details. Once in Cameroon, the most popular border crossing into Nigeria is at Ekok (Mfum on the Nigerian side), between Mamfe (Cameroon) and Ikom (Nigeria). If you're travelling in northern Cameroon there are several more crossing points – the one between Mora and Maiduguri is one of the busiest.

Your final option is to come into West Africa from the east. In addition to the route from N'djaména (Chad) to Kousséri (Cameroon), from where you can then continue to Nigeria, or else head south into Cameroon, it's also possible to take the 'long way around', crossing the border on the northern side of Lake Chad, on the route to Nguigmi (Niger). More details on the various border crossings are given in the Getting There & Away sections of the relevant country chapters.

Taking Your Own Vehicle

Driving your own car or motorbike to West Africa (and then around the region and possibly onwards to East or Southern Africa) is a vast subject beyond the scope of this book. Some recommended manuals covering this subject are listed following. These cover matters such as equipment, carnets, insurance, recommended routes, driving techniques, maintenance, repairs, navigation and survival. However, they are usually thin on practical information about places to eat and sleep (mainly because most overlanders use their vehicle as a mobile hotel) and on general background information about the country, including history, economy etc.

Adventure Motorcycling Handbook by Chris Scott. This book covers all parts of the world where tar roads end. It contains stacks of good information on the Sahara and West Africa, all combined with humour and personal insights.

Africa by Road by Bob Swain & Paula Snyder. This is recommended once you're across the desert. Half the book is no-nonsense advice on everything from paperwork and supplies to driving techniques, while the other half is a complete country-by-country rundown.

Sahara Handbook, The by Simon Glen. The longstanding classic manual if you're coming to West Africa overland in your own vehicle. Although it concentrates on the Algerian trans-desert routes (rather than the generally used Western Sahara route), it also includes coverage of the northern Sahel, and much of the general information is relevant.

Sahara Overland (published by Trailblazer) is a recommended, detailed and relatively recent book by desert specialist Chris Scott. It comprehensively covers all aspects of the Sahara for travellers on two or four wheels, with information on established and newer routes (including those in Mauritania, Mali, Niger and Libya), and more than 100 maps. Scott's highly recommended website (**W** www.sahara-overland.com) has updates of the book, as well as letters from travellers and extensive related information.

Shipping a Vehicle If you want to travel around West Africa using your own car or motorbike, but don't fancy the Sahara crossing, another option is to ship it. The usual way of doing this is to load the car onto a ship in Europe and take it off again at either Dakar or Banjul (although Abidjan and Tema, in Ghana, are other options).

Costs range from US$500 to US$1000 depending on the size of the vehicle and the final destination, but apart from cost your biggest problem is likely to be security – many drivers report theft of items from the inside and outside (such as lights and mirrors) of their car. Vehicles are usually left unlocked for the crossing and when in storage at the destination port, so chain or lock all equipment into fixed boxes inside the vehicle. Getting a vehicle out of port is frequently a nightmare, requiring visits to several different offices where stamps must be obtained and mysterious fees paid at every turn. You could consider using an official handling agent or an unofficial 'fixer' to take your vehicle through all this.

Crossing the Sahara

Three main routes cross the Sahara to West Africa: Route du Hoggar (through Algeria and Niger); Route du Tanezrouft (through Algeria and Mali); and the Western Sahara Route (through Morocco and Western Sahara into Mauritania). For most of the past decade, the Tanezrouft and Hoggar routes have been virtually unused by travellers due to the security situation in the region. The

Hoggar route has begun to open up again, although the Western Sahara route remains the most popular overland way to West Africa, with most drivers and nearly all independent travellers (hitching or on public transport) still using it. The Hoggar and Tanezrouft routes are mentioned only briefly following, and you'll need to get a thorough update on the security situation before setting off. The Tanezrouft route is considered dangerous and cannot be recommended. The Western Sahara route is described in somewhat more detail. Anybody planning to travel in the Sahara should check out the excellent website put together by Chris Scott (W www.sahara-overland.com), as well as get some of the books recommended in the preceding Taking Your Own Vehicle section. Be sure to bring sufficient food, water and warm clothes for the journey.

Route du Hoggar The Route du Hoggar through Algeria and Niger is tar, except for the 600km section between Tamanrasset ('Tam') and Arlit, although the tar is in poor condition on many sections. The fabulous Hoggar Mountains and Aïr Massif are well worth extra diversions, and the route passes several magnificent outcrops of wind-eroded rocks, while Agadez, at the end of the route, is one of the most interesting desert towns in West Africa. The Route du Hoggar was passable as this book went to print, with access via Tunisia, as the border between Morocco and Algeria is closed. The crossing is relatively trouble-free, although it generally involves hitching a ride in trucks or with travellers in their own vehicles between Tamanrasset and Arlit, from where there are buses to Agadez. Few travellers make the journey in reverse, due in large part to the difficulty of getting an Algerian visa in Niger. Travel in southern Algeria is increasingly popular, and northern Niger has also stabilised somewhat. However, the situation remains fragile, and you should thoroughly check out security issues and the route's current status before proceeding. While banditry still occurs, the stories are usually widely publicised in Agadez and, to a lesser extent, Tamanrasset, so keep an ear to the ground. Also, check in with the police before setting out, and where possible, avoid travelling at night (also on the stretch from Agadez towards Niamey via Tahoua).

Route du Tanezrouft The Route du Tanezrouft runs through Algeria and Mali, via Adrar and the border at Bordj-Mokhtar, ending in Gao. It is technically easier than the Route du Hoggar. However, the dirt section is more than 1300km long and has a reputation for being monotonous, although some travellers find that the sheer size and remoteness of the desert is better appreciated here. This consideration is more than outweighed by the significantly increased risk factor. Help, should you need it, is likely to be a long time coming. At present, this route is not safe for travellers.

Western Sahara Route Travel through Morocco is straightforward (see Lonely Planet's *Morocco* guide). About 500km south of Agadir you enter the disputed territory of Western Sahara, where the main road continues along the coast to Dakhla, from where it's another 460km to Nouâdhibou in Mauritania. In Dakhla, there are a few cheap hotels and a camp site (which also has some rooms) where all the overlanders stay. This is also the best place to find other travellers to team up with, or to look for a lift. If you're hitching, there's a thriving trade in second-hand cars being driven from Europe (especially France) to sell in West Africa, and these drivers are sometimes happy to pick up travellers, although sharing costs is expected. Use some care when finding a lift; hitchers are not allowed in Mauritanian vehicles, and there have been occasional scams where hitchers with local drivers have been abandoned in the desert unless they pay a large 'fee'.

Until recently, all travel south of Dakhla needed to be done in a military convoy. Now, the convoy has been disbanded and it is possible to continue independently, though it's still advisable for vehicles (especially 2WDs) to go in a group. In addition to hitching, there is reportedly regular public transport leaving Dakhla most mornings and heading south to the customs post of Guerguarat near the Mauritanian border. The final stretch to the border is unpaved and littered with landmines, so stay to the well-beaten track. After Mauritanian border formalities it's approximately 100km further to Nouâdhibou. There are searches for alcohol at the Mauritanian border, and heavy fines if you are caught with it, as well as plenty of hustlers.

From Nouâdhibou, most vehicles continue south down the coast to Nouakchott, through Parc National du Banc d'Arguin, including a 160km stretch along the beach at low tide. Some cars, most bikes and hitchers go east on the train to Choûm, and then take the road via Atâr and Akjout to Nouakchott. For more details on these options, see the Getting Around section in the Mauritania chapter, and refer to the website mentioned earlier in this section.

The Western Sahara route is possible year-round, although few people do it in the hot season. It's now legal for travellers to go south to north, although most traffic continues to be from north to south.

SEA

For most people, reaching West Africa by sea is not a viable consideration. The days of working your passage on commercial boats are long gone, although a few lucky travellers do manage to hitch rides on private yachts sailing from Spain, Morocco or the Canary Islands to Senegal, Gambia and beyond. Alternatively, several cargo shipping companies run from Europe to West Africa, with comfortable officer-style cabins available to the public; at the time of writing, there were no options from the USA. One of the main lines is Grimaldi, which has boats from Tilbury (London), Antwerp and elsewhere in Europe to Abidjan, Dakar, Douala, Lomé, Cotonou, Tema (Ghana), Freetown, Conakry and Lagos (though not all stops on all sailings), and one route from Antwerp to Brazil via Dakar.

Prices vary depending on the quality of the ship and on the cabin (inside cabins are cheaper), but expect to pay from US$1000 per person one way between Europe and Dakar in a double cabin. A typical voyage from London takes about eight days to Dakar and 13 days to Abidjan. To book this line, or others sailing to West Africa, contact Strand Voyages (☎ 020-7836 6363, fax 7497 0078), Charing Cross Shopping Concourse, Strand, London WC2N 4HZ, in the UK, or Freighter World Cruises (☎ 800-531 7774, 626-449 3106, fax 449 9573, e freighters@freighterworld.com, w www.freighterworld.com), 180 South Lake Ave, No 335, Pasadena, CA 91101, in the USA. Freighter World Cruises also publishes *Freighter Space Advisory*. Other contacts include Associated Oceanic Agencies Ltd (☎ 020-7930 5683, fax 7839 1961), 103 Jermyn St, London SW1Y 6EE, UK, and Freighter Travel Club of America at 3524 Harts Lake Loop, Roy, WA 98580, USA, which publishes *Freighter Travel News*. For further information, refer to *Travel by Cargo Ship*, a handy book by Hugo Verlomme.

ORGANISED TOURS

Two main sorts of tour are available. On an overland tour, you go from Europe to West Africa by land, visiting several countries along the way. Most are anywhere between two and six months long. On an inclusive tour you fly to your destination and spend two to three weeks in a single country. Between these two types is the option of joining an overland tour for a short section (usually three to five weeks), flying out and back at either end.

Where relevant, details of tours organised by local companies are listed in the Getting Around sections of the individual country chapters.

Overland Tours

For these trips, you travel in an 'overland truck' with about 15 to 28 other people, a couple of drivers/leaders, plus tents and other equipment. Food is bought along the way and the group cooks and eats together. Most of the hassles (such as border crossings) are taken care of by the leader. Disadvantages include a fairly fixed itinerary and the possibility of spending a long time with other people in relatively close confines. Having said that, overland truck tours are extremely popular.

The overland-tour market is dominated by British companies, although passengers come from many parts of the world. Most tours start in London and travel to West Africa via Europe and Morocco. Tours can be 'slow' or 'fast', depending on the number of places visited along the way. For those with limited time, most overland companies arrange shorter trips – for example London to Banjul or Dakar. For those with more time, there's also the option to do the West Africa trip as part of a longer trans-Africa trip to/from Nairobi or Harare. Most overland companies can arrange your flights to join and leave the tour. Alternatively, some of the specialist travel agents listed in the Air section earlier can also arrange tours.

Following is a list of some UK-based overland tour companies offering trips in West Africa.

African Trails (☎ 020-8742 7724, fax 8742 8621, W www.africantrails.co.uk) 12 Ivy St, Manchester M40 9LN

Dragoman (☎ 01728-861133, fax 861127, W www.dragoman.co.uk) Camp Green, Kenton Rd, Debenham, Stowmarket IP14 6LA

Encounter (☎ 020-7370 6845, fax 01728-861127, W www.encounter.co.uk) Camp Green, Kenton Rd, Debenham, Stowmarket IP14 6LA

Exodus Overland (☎ 020-8673 0859, fax 8673 0779) 9 Weir Rd, London SW12 0LT

Guerba (☎ 01373-858956, fax 838351, W www.guerba.com) Wessex House, 40 Station Rd, Westbury BA13 3JN

Nomadic Expeditions (☎ 0870-220 1718, fax 220 1719, W www.nomadic.co.uk) 22B Barkham Ride, Finchampstead, Wokingham, Berkshire RG40 4EU

Oasis Overland (☎ 01258-471155, fax 471166, W www.oasisoverland.com) 5 Nicholsons Cottages, Hinton St Mary, Dorset, DT10 1NF

Truck Africa (☎ 020-7731 6142, fax 7371 7445, W www.truckafrica.com) 37 Ranelagh Gardens Mansions, London SW6 3UQ

In North America and Australasia overland tour companies are represented by specialist travel agencies (see listings under Air, earlier in this chapter, and under Inclusive Tours). Also, you can start hunting for details on the Internet or in the advertisements in travel magazines and weekend papers.

Inclusive Tours

This type of tour includes your international flight, transport around the country, food, accommodation, excursions, local guide and so on. They are usually around two to three weeks long, and ideal if you want to visit West Africa, but lack the time or inclination for long-distance overland trucks or to organise things yourself.

The number of inclusive tour companies operating in West Africa is much smaller than in East or Southern Africa, but there's still a fair selection. Some of the overland companies listed earlier also run shorter inclusive tours, and this can be one of the best ways to reach the more unusual destinations such as Niger, which are not usually covered by the inclusive tour companies.

As with flights and overland tours, a good place to begin looking is the advertisements in the weekend newspapers and travel magazines. Several companies are also listed following, although this list is not exhaustive. In the **UK** try:

Afrikan Heritage (☎ 020-7328 4376) 60B Rowley Way, London NW8 0SJ. Gambian-run tours based in Gambia.

Dragoman (see listing under Overland Tours)

Exodus Overland (see listing under Overland Tours)

Explore Worldwide (☎ 01252-760200, e info@explore.co.uk) 1 Frederick St, Aldershot GU11 1LQ. Well-established company offering a wide range of adventurous and active tours and treks, including Mali.

Gambia Experience, The (☎ 02380-730888, fax 731122, e reservations@gambia.co.uk, W www.gambia.co.uk) Kingfisher House, Rownhams Lane, North Baddesley, Hampshire SO52 9LP. Leading operator of package holidays to Gambia, with some options in Senegal, plus a selection of specialist birding, fishing and cultural tours; sells excellent-value charter flights.

Guerba (see listing under Overland Tours)

Insight Travel (☎ 01995-606095, fax 602124, e insight@provider.co.uk) 6 Norton Rd, Preston, Lancashire PR3 1JY. This small agency, run by a former VSO field director in Ghana, offers trips based in Kumasi, with the opportunity of living with a Ghanaian family; activities offered include bird-watching, touring Ashanti craft villages, and lessons in dance, music or weaving.

Karamba Experience (☎/fax 01603-872402, e karamba@gn.apc.org, W www.karamba.co.uk) Ollands Lodge, Heydon, Norwich NR11 6RB. Holidays in Senegal, concentrating on learning to play drums and other African instruments, as well as time for the beach and other excursions.

Limosa Holidays (☎ 01263-578143, fax 579251) Suffield House, Northrepps, Norfolk NR7 0LZ. Specialist birding trips, including Gambia.

Naturetrek (☎ 01962-733051, fax 736426, e info@naturetrek.co.uk, W www.naturetrek.co.uk) Brighton Airesford, Hampshire SO24 9RB. Bird and wildlife specialists offering tours in Mali and Gambia.

Travelbag Adventures (☎ 01420-541007, fax 541022, e mail@travelbag-adventures.com, W www.travelbag-adventures.com) 15 Turk St, Alton GU34 1AG. Small group adventurous holidays all over the world, including Mali and Burkina Faso.

Wildwings (☎ 0117-965 8333, fax 937 5681, W www.wildwings.co.uk) 577–579 Fishponds Rd, Bristol BS16 3AF. Birding and wildlife specialists; expeditions and tours worldwide, including Senegal and Gambia.

In **France** try:

Explorator (☎ 01 53 45 85 85) 16 rue de la Banque, 75002 Paris. Destinations include the Sahara region, Senegal, Gambia and Mali.
Nouvelles Frontières (☎ 01 41 41 58 58) 87 blvd de Grenelle, 75015 Paris; with branches in France and French-speaking countries. Wide range of mainstream holidays and adventurous tours all over West Africa and beyond.
Terres d'Aventure (☎ 01 53 73 77 77) 6 rue Saint-Victor, 75005 Paris. Various adventurous trips in West Africa and the Sahara region, including Senegal and Mauritania.
Voyageurs en Afrique (☎ 01 42 86 16 60) 55 rue Sainte-Anne, 75002 Paris. Tours in Senegal, plus hotel booking and car rentals for independent travellers.

In the **USA** there are only a few companies that actually operate inclusive tours in West Africa. Most act as agents or reps for other companies based in Europe or Africa, or can provide you with a trip tailor-made to your own requirements. Companies include:

Adventure Center (☎ 510-654 1879, 800-227 8747, e tripinfo@adventurecenter.com, w www.adventurecenter.com) 1311 63rd St, Emeryville, CA 91608
Africa Desk (☎ 800-284 8796, 860-354 9341, e info@africadesk.com, w www.africadesk.com) Tours to many countries in the region.
Born Free Safaris (☎ 800-372 3274, 818-981 7185, fax 818-753 1460, w www.bornfreesafaris.com) 12509 Oxnard St, Suite H, North Hollywood, CA 91606
Cross Cultural Adventurers (☎ 703-237 0100, fax 237 2558, e piotrk@erols.com) Box 3285, Arlington, VA 22203. Customised tours to Mali, with extensions also possible in Senegal and Burkina Faso.
ITC (☎ 800-257 4981, e itcafrica@juno.com) 4134 Atlantic Ave, Suite 205, Long Beach, CA 90807. Customised tours to many West African countries.
Mountain Travel-Sobek (☎ 800-227 2384, fax 510-525 7710, w www.mtsobek.com) 6420 Fairmount Ave, El Cerrito CA 94530. Two to three week tours in Mali, Burkina Faso, Ghana, Togo and Benin.
Museum for African Art (☎ 212-966 1313, w www.africanart.org) 593 Broadway, New York, NY 10012. Offers cultural tours.
Spector Travel (☎ 617-338 0111, 800-879 2374, w www.spectortravel.com) 2 Park Plaza, Boston, MA 02116. This place is an Africa specialist, with tours to Mali, Gambia, Senegal, Cameroon and elsewhere in the region.
Turtle Tours (☎ 888-299 1439, 602-488 3688, fax 488 3406, e turtletours@earthlink.net, w www.turtletours.com) Box 1147, Carefree, AZ 85377. Tours for individuals and small groups in Mauritania, Mali, Niger, Cameroon and other countries in the region.
Wilderness Travel (☎ 800-368 2794, 510-558 2488, fax 558 2489, e info@wildernesstravel.com, w www.wildernesstravel.com) 1102 Ninth St, Berkeley, CA 94710. Trips to Niger, Mali and several other destinations throughout West Africa.

In **Canada** the situation is similar to that in the USA, with most companies acting as agents or representatives for other companies based in Europe or Africa. Possible starting points include the following:

Adventure Centre & Trek Holidays (☎ 416-922 7584, 800-276 3347) 25 Bellair St, Toronto, Ontario M5R 3L3
Connections Travel (☎ 604-738 9499) Suite 210, 1847 West Broadway, Vancouver BC V6J 1Y6
Fresh Tracks (☎ 800-627 7492, 604-737 7880, w www.freshtracks.com) 1847 West 4th Ave, Vancouver, BC V6J 1M4

In **Australasia** many of the tour companies listed earlier are represented by specialist travel agents, including the following:

Adventure World (☎ 02-8913 0755, fax 9956 7707, w adventureworld.com.au) 73 Walker St, North Sydney, NSW
Africa Travel Company (☎ 02-9264 7661, fax 9261 2907, e atc@wat.com.au) Level 1, 69 Liverpool St, Sydney, NSW 2000
Africa Travel Centre (☎ 09-520 2000, fax 520 2001) 21 Remuera Rd, Newmarket, Auckland
Intrepid Travel (☎ 1300 360 667, fax 03-9419 5878, w www.intrepidtravel.com.au) 11 Spring St, Fitzroy, Victoria

Getting Around West Africa

This chapter outlines the various ways of travelling around West Africa. For more details see the Getting There & Away and Getting Around sections of the individual country chapters.

AIR

West Africa is an enormous area, and if your time is limited, a few flights around the region can considerably widen your options. For those who are on tight schedules, flying can save hours or days, even within a country.

Some airlines and airports are very good, some are bad and some are definitely worth avoiding. Don't be surprised if you have to wait half a day at check-in (bring a good book), or if during the flight the cabin crew try to keep the door from coming off. Other horror stories involve airport clerks issuing more boarding passes than seats, and some unlucky passengers being dumped on the runway. Usually, however, there's not much choice, with only two or three airlines operating between most major cities. Regional airlines that enjoy comparatively good reputations include Air Mauritanie, Cameroon Airlines and Liberia's Weasua Air Transport (which wins our award for West Africa's most reliable airline). By contrast, Air Guinée, Ghana Airways and several others are notorious for cancellations and delays – although the reputation of these airlines seems very much route dependent, and all sometimes offer surprisingly decent service. Ghana Airways' international routes, for

Checking In

In many West African cities, check-in procedures are as much of an adventure as the flight itself. Conakry wins our vote as the airport with the most disorganised and chaotic check-in procedures, but every traveller probably has their own 'favourites'. Lagos is another notorious one. The fun starts from the moment you enter the airport. Underpaid security personnel, in an effort to subsidise their meagre incomes, often view the baggage check procedures as a chance to elicit bribes from tourists. After searching your bag, they will ask what you might have for them or, alternatively, try to convince you that you've violated some regulation. Be compliant with requests to open your baggage, be friendly and respectful, smile a lot, and you should soon be on your way. Also remember that, in some cases, officials may search your bag out of genuine curiosity.

After getting past the initial baggage check, you'll need to join the fray by the check-in counter. While some places have lines, most do not – just a sweaty mass of people, all waving their tickets and talking loudly to an invariably rather beleaguered-looking check-in clerk. Although everyone with a confirmed ticket usually gets on the flight, confirmed passengers are 'bumped' just frequently enough to cause many people, locals and foreigners alike, to panic wildly and lose all sense and civility when it seems there may not be enough seats to go around. The West African answer to this situation is the 'fixer' – enterprising locals who make their living by getting people smoothly checked in and through other formalities such as customs and airport tax. Sometimes they practically see you into your seat – all for fees ranging from a dollar or two up to about US$10. If you don't have a confirmed booking, the fee may be more, as some of the money has to go to the boarding pass clerk.

Without the services of a fixer, the best strategy for avoiding the chaotic scene is to arrive early at the airport – ideally at the start of the official reporting time or earlier. This way, you also have a better chance of getting a confirmed seat if too many 'confirmed' tickets have been sold.

Once you have your boarding pass in hand, there's usually a second luggage inspection as you pass from the check-in terminal to the waiting area. Then it's just a matter of waiting. Have a good book with you, or a pen and paper for catching up on correspondence, and perhaps a few pieces of fruit. Don't schedule any other critical plans for the day (especially connecting flights), and try to calm any frustration you may feel by remembering that by West African standards you're one of a privileged few who have the financial resources to even contemplate flying – and that your journey would be several days to several weeks longer via bush taxi, and much more uncomfortable.

example are generally much more reliable than some of their intra-African connections.

Because of the long distances, fares within West Africa are not cheap. Flying from Dakar (Senegal) to Abidjan (Côte d'Ivoire), for example, is equivalent to flying halfway across the USA. Some sample one-way fares are: Dakar to Bamako in Mali (about 500km) US$125; Banjul (Gambia) to Accra in Ghana (about 1000km) US$330; and Abidjan to Douala (about 1500km) US$370. Return fares are usually double the one-way fares, though less expensive excursion fares are often available, and sometimes youth or student fares.

It's often better to buy tickets in West Africa through a travel agency, rather than from the airline. They can explain the choice available, without you having to visit several airline offices, and the price is usually the same. They may also be able to help you with refunds if anything goes wrong. Usually, tickets issued by one airline are not acceptable ('endorsable') on another airline.

Once you've bought your ticket, reconfirm your reservation at least several times, especially if the airline you're flying with has a less-than-stellar reputation for reliability. After the flight, if you checked luggage, hold on to your baggage claim ticket until you've exited the baggage claim area at your destination, as you'll often be required to show it.

BUS & BUSH TAXI

The most common forms of public transport in West Africa are bus (*car* in Francophone countries) and bush taxi *(taxi brousse)*. Buses may be run by state-owned or private companies. Bush taxis are always private, although the driver is rarely the owner of the vehicle. Vehicles are usually located at bus and bush taxi parks, called *gare routière* or sometimes *autogare* in Francophone countries, 'garage', 'lorry park' or 'motor park' in English-speaking countries and *paragem* in Portuguese-speaking countries. The gare routière or motor park is usually in the centre of town, near the market. Most large cities have several gares routières, one for each main direction or destination.

In some countries buses are common and bush taxis are hard to find; in other countries it's the reverse. Either way, travel generally costs between US$1 and US$2 per 100km, although fares depend on the quality of the vehicle and the route. On routes between countries (eg, between Ouagadougou in Burkina Faso and Abidjan in Côte d'Ivoire) costs can be more because drivers have to pay additional fees (official and unofficial) to cross the border. You can save a bit of money by taking one vehicle to the border and then another on the other side, but this can considerably prolong the trip.

Bus

Long-distance buses (sometimes called a 'big bus', *grand car*, to distinguish it from a minibus) vary in size – from 35 to 70 seats – and services vary considerably between countries and areas. On the main routes buses are often good quality, with a reliable service and fixed departure times (although arrival times may be more fluid).

On quiet roads in rural areas, buses may be old and decrepit, and may have frequent breakdowns and regular stops to let passengers on or off. These buses have no timetable, and usually go when full or when the driver feels like it. They are also usually very overcrowded (in comparison with some of the better lines on major routes, where the one-person-per-seat rule is usually respected). Generally, bus fares are cheaper than bush taxi fares for a comparable route.

You may arrange a long ride by bus (or bush taxi), and find yourself transferring to another vehicle somewhere along the way. There is no need to pay more – your driver pays your fare directly to the driver of the next vehicle – but unfortunately it can mean long waits while the arrangements are made.

On some main-route buses, you can reserve in advance, which is often advisable. In some countries you book a place but not a specific seat. Just before the bus leaves, names get called out in the order that tickets were bought, and you get on and choose the seat you want – rather like answering the register at school. Seats to the front tend to be better ventilated and more comfortable. If you suffer from motion sickness, try to get a seat towards the front or in the middle. Whichever end of the bus you sit in, it's worth trying to get a seat on the side that will be away from direct sunlight for most of the journey.

Touts at the Gare Routière

At most gares routières, bush taxis leave on a fill-up-and-go basis, but problems can arise when you get more than one vehicle covering the same route. This is when a tout (called a *coti-man* in some countries) can earn money by persuading you to take 'his' car. Most will tell you anything to get you on board: 'this one is very fast', 'this minibus is leaving *now*', 'this bus is a good cheap price' etc. Another trick involves putting your baggage on the roof rack as a 'deposit' against you taking another car (which means you shouldn't give up your luggage until you're sure you'll stay with that vehicle).

Don't think that you're being targeted because you're a wealthy foreigner – the touts hassle everybody. In the end, it's always somewhat of a gamble, but the vehicle that has the most passengers will usually be the one to depart first.

Bush Taxi

A bush taxi is effectively a small bus. Almost without exception, bush taxis leave when full of passengers, not according to a timetable. As soon as one car leaves, the next one starts to fill. Depending on the popularity of the route, the car may take half an hour or several days to fill. Either way, drivers jealously guard their car's place in the queue.

Early customers can choose where to sit. Latecomers get no choice and are assigned to the least comfortable seats – usually at the back, where the seating is cramped and stuffy. If you have a choice, the best seats are those in the front, near the window. Some travellers prefer the very front, though you're first in line there if there's a collision. Better is the row behind the driver, near a window (ideally one that works – most don't), and preferably on the side with more shade during the journey.

If a bush taxi looks like it's going to get uncomfortably full you can buy two seats for yourself – it's simply double the price. Likewise, if you want to charter the whole car, take the price of one seat and multiply it by the number available. Occasionally you may also need to add a bit more for luggage, although in our experience this is rarely requested for charters.

If a group of passengers has been waiting a long time, and there are only two or three seats to fill, they may club together and pay extra so as to get moving. If you do this, don't expect a discount because you're saving the driver the hassle of looking for other passengers – time is not money in Africa. If you pick up someone along the way, however, the fare they pay goes to the passengers who bought the seats, not to the driver.

The best time by far to catch bush taxis is early morning; after that, you may have difficulty finding vehicles on many routes. Sometimes, however, departures are determined by market days, in which case afternoon may be best.

There are three main types of bush taxi in West Africa, as follows.

Peugeot Taxi Peugeot 504s, assembled in Nigeria or imported from Europe, are used all over West Africa and are also called *cinq-cent-quatre*, Peugeot taxi, *sept-place* and *brake*. With three rows of seats, they are built to take the driver plus seven passengers. In some countries this limit is observed. In others it's flagrantly flaunted. All 504s in Mali, for example, take the driver plus nine passengers. In Guinea you might be jammed in with at least a dozen adults, plus children and bags, with more luggage and a couple of extra passengers riding on the roof. That these cars do hundreds of thousands of kilometres on some of the worst roads in the world is a credit to the manufacturer and the ingenuity of local mechanics.

While some drivers are safe and considerate, others verge on insanity. Some cars are relatively new (there are quite a few Peugeot 505s, the later model, around these days) and well maintained, with comfortable seats. Others are very old, reduced to nothing more than chassis, body and engine: there's more weld than original metal, tyres are bald, most upholstery is missing, and little extras like windows, door handles and even exhaust pipes have long since disappeared.

Minibus Some routes are served by minibuses *(minicars)* – usually seating about 12 to 20 passengers. In some countries these are just large bush taxis, while in others they fill a category between bus and bush taxi. They are typically about 25% cheaper than 504s, and sometimes more

Luggage Fees

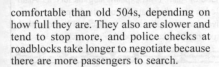

In many countries, transport fares are fixed by the government, so the only way the bush taxi drivers can earn a bit extra is to charge for luggage. Local people accept this, so travellers should too, unless of course the amount is unreasonable. The fee for a medium-sized rucksack is usually around 10% of the fare. Small bags will be less, and are often not charged at all – a good reason to travel light. If you think you're being overcharged, ask other passengers, out of earshot of the driver. Once you know the proper rate, bargaining will be easy and the price should soon fall.

comfortable than old 504s, depending on how full they are. They also are slower and tend to stop more, and police checks at roadblocks take longer to negotiate because there are more passengers to search.

Pick-Up With wooden seats down the sides, covered pick-ups *(bâchés)* are definitely 2nd class, but are sometimes the only kind of bush taxi available. They officially take around 16 passengers but are invariably stuffed with people and baggage, plus a few chickens, and your feet may be higher than your waist from resting on a sack of millet. Up on the roof go more bags, bunches of bananas, extra passengers and goats (also live). Bâché rides are often very slow, and police checks at roadblocks are interminable as drivers or passengers frequently lack vital papers. The ride is guaranteed to be unpleasant unless you adopt an African attitude, which means each time your head hits the roof as the vehicle descends into yet another big pothole, you roar with laughter. There's nothing like local humour to change an otherwise miserable trip into a tolerable, even enjoyable, experience.

TRUCK & HITCHING

In many countries, as you venture further into rural areas, the frequency of buses or bush taxis drops dramatically – sometimes to nothing. Then the only way around is to ride on local trucks, which is what the locals do. A 'fare' is payable to the driver, so in cases like this the line between hitching and public transport is blurred – but if it's the only way to get around, you don't have any choice anyway. Usually you'll be riding on top of the cargo – it may be cotton or rice in sacks, which are quite comfortable, but it might be logs or oil drums, which aren't.

If you want to hitch because there's no public transport leaving imminently from the gare routière, you'll normally have to go well beyond the town limits, as bush taxi drivers may take umbrage at other vehicles 'stealing' their customers. Even so, you'll probably still have to pay for your lift – but at least you'll get moving more quickly.

Hitching in the Western sense (ie, because you don't want to get the bus, or more specifically because you don't want to pay) is also possible, but may take a long time. The only people giving free lifts are likely to be foreign expatriates, volunteer aid-workers, or the occasional well-off local (very few West Africans own a car).

Most people with space in their car are likely to want payment – usually on a par with what a bus would have cost. The most common vehicles for lifts of this sort are driven by locals working for international agencies, government bodies or aid and relief organisations; all over West Africa you'll see smart Land Cruisers with words and badges on the doors (eg, Unesco, Ministry of Energy or 'Save the Sahel'), never more than a few years old, always going too fast, and always full of people. But if you've been waiting all day and one of these stops for you, you'll probably get in, however distasteful it might be.

This said, as in any other part of the world, hitching or accepting lifts is never entirely safe, and we don't recommend it. Travellers who decide to hitch should understand that they are taking a small but potentially serious risk. If you're planning to travel this way, take advice from other hitchers (locals or travellers) first. Hitching in pairs is obviously safer, and hitching through less salubrious suburbs, especially at night, is asking for trouble. Throughout most of the region, women should avoid hitching alone.

TRAIN

There are railways in Mauritania, Senegal, Mali, Côte d'Ivoire, Ghana, Burkina Faso, Togo, Benin, Nigeria and Cameroon. Most train services run only within the country of operation, but there are also international

Road Safety

Road safety (together with malaria) is probably your biggest safety risk when travelling in West Africa. Bush taxi drivers, in particular, often race along at hair-raising speeds and overtake blind to reach their destination before another car can get in front of them in the queue for the return journey. In addition, drivers can be sleepy from an 18-hour day, and drunk driving is often a problem. Travelling early in the morning is one step you can take to minimise the risks, as drivers are usually fresher and roads less travelled. Avoid night travel at all costs. If you are in a vehicle and feel unsafe, if it's a heavily travelled route, you can take your chances and get out at a major station en route to switch to another car (though don't expect any refunds, and the second vehicle may not be much better). You can also complain about the dangerous driving, although this usually doesn't have any effect and, unless things are really out of control, you'll seldom get support from the other passengers. Saying that you're feeling sick seems to get better results. Drivers are often quite considerate to ill or infirm passengers and, in any case, seem to care more about keeping vomit off their seats than about dying under the wheels of an oncoming lorry. You might also be able to rally other passengers to your side this way as well. Most locals take a stoic approach to the situation, with many viewing accidents as a matter of the will of God or Allah. (This explains slogans such as 'Allah Akhbar' painted on many vehicles – probably painted in the belief that a bit of extra help from above might see the vehicle through the day's runs.) Drivers, in particular, seem to discredit the idea that accidents are in any way related to vehicle speed or condition, or to wild driving practices.

services, notably between Dakar and Bamako, and between Ouagadougou and Abidjan.

Some trains are relatively comfortable, with 1st-class coaches, which may be air-conditioned. Some also have sleeping compartments, with two or four bunks. Other services are 2nd or 3rd class only, and conditions can be uncomfortable, with no lights, no toilets and no glass in the windows (no fun on long night journeys). Some trains have a restaurant on board, but you can usually buy things to eat and drink at every station along the way.

CAR & MOTORCYCLE

Some general points about driving your own vehicle to and around West Africa (or shipping it) are covered in the Land section of the Getting There & Away chapter. Your other option is to rent a car or motorbike. Whether you rent or bring you own vehicle, and especially the latter, there are a few things to remember.

The most important thing to be aware of is that throughout West Africa traffic drives on the right – as in continental Europe and the USA – even in countries that have a British colonial heritage (such as Gambia). Your next major consideration is the location of the principal routes. Some dirt roads can be used year-round, while others are impassable in the rains, and you can't necessarily tell this from road maps. Some tar roads become so badly potholed that a dirt road would be much better. Conditions can change from year to year, so the best way to keep up to date is to talk to other drivers, although you should also try to use the most recent maps you can.

The quality, availability and price of fuel (petrol and diesel – called *essence* and *gasoil*, respectively, in the Francophone countries, *gasolina* and *diesel*, or sometimes *gasóleo*, in Lusophone countries) varies depending on where you are in the region, and also between rural and urban areas. Where taxation, subsidies or currency rates make petrol cheaper in one country than its neighbour, you'll inevitably find traders who have carried large drums across the border and sell 'black market' fuel at the roadside. However, watch out for fuel sold in plastic bags or small containers along the roadside. While sometimes it's fine, it's often diluted with water or kerosene.

To drive a car or motorbike in West Africa you will need a driving licence and, ideally, an International Driving Permit (see Other Documents under Visas & Documents in the Regional Facts for the Visitor chapter for more details). If you're hiring a car, the rental agency will provide all your insurance papers – make sure they are up to date.

If you're bringing your own vehicle you'll need to arrange a *carnet* – a document for the car to prevent you importing or exporting it illegally. This is covered in more detail in the specialist manuals listed under Taking Your Own Vehicle in the Land section of the Getting There & Away chapter. For some more tips on driving in the region in general, see the boxed text, 'Car Hire, Chickens & Other Hazards of the Road', later in this chapter.

Rental

There are car rental agencies in most capital cities and tourist areas. Most international companies (Hertz, Avis, etc) are represented, plus smaller independent operators, but renting is invariably expensive – you can easily spend in one day what you'd pay for a week's rental in Europe or the USA. If the small operators charge less, it's usually because the vehicles are older and sometimes not well maintained. But sometimes it's simply because their costs are lower and they can do a better deal, so if you have the time, check around for bargains. You will need to put down a large deposit (credit cards are usually good for this).

It's very unlikely you'll be allowed to take a rental car across a border, but if you are (for example from Gambia into Senegal) make sure the paperwork is valid. If you're uncertain about driving, most companies provide a chauffeur at very little extra cost, and with many, a chauffeur is mandatory. In many cases it's cheaper to go with a chauffeur as you will pay less for insurance. It's also prudent, as getting stuck on your own is no fun.

In tourist areas, such as Gambia and Senegal, it is also possible to hire mopeds and motorbikes. In most other countries there is no formal rental available, but if you want to hire a motorbike (and know how to ride one) you can usually arrange something by asking around at an auto parts shop or repair yard, or by asking at the reception of your hotel. You can often be put in touch with someone who doesn't mind earning some extra cash by renting out their wheels for a day or two. Remember, though, that matters such as insurance will be easily overlooked, which is fine until you have an accident and find yourself liable for all bills. Also, if you do this, be sure to check out the motorbike in

Travel Distances (km)

	Abidjan (Côte d'Ivoire)	Accra (Ghana)	Bamako (Mali)	Banjul (The Gambia)	Bissau (Guinea-Bissau)	Conakry (Guinea)	Cotonou (Benin)	Dakar (Senegal)	Freetown (Sierra Leone)	Lagos (Nigeria)	Lomé (Togo)	Monrovia (Liberia)	Niamey (Niger)	Nouakchott (Mauritania)	Ouagadougou (Burkina Faso)	Praia (Cape Verde)	Yaoundé (Cameroon)
Abidjan (Côte d'Ivoire)	---																
Accra (Ghana)	560	---															
Bamako (Mali)	1160	1710	---														
Banjul (The Gambia)	2490	3210	1340	---													
Bissau (Guinea-Bissau)	2180	2900	1460	310	---												
Conakry (Guinea)	1700	2260	920	1230	980	---											
Cotonou (Benin)	910	360	2020	3360	3110	2610	---										
Dakar (Senegal)	2790	3350	1420	300	585	1530	3360	---									
Freetown (Sierra Leone)	1590	2090	1210	1440	1190	320	2440	1740	---								
Lagos (Nigeria)	1030	480	2140	3480	3230	2730	120	3560	2560	---							
Lomé (Togo)	760	200	1870	3220	2970	2460	160	3290	2290	280	---						
Monrovia (Liberia)	1020	1620	1040	1860	1610	710	1870	2160	570	1990	1720	---					
Niamey (Niger)	1570	1390	1410	2750	2880	2320	1040	2740	2900	1160	1190	2330	---				
Nouakchott (Mauritania)	2800	3360	1650	870	1180	2100	3670	570	2320	3790	3560	2730	3050	---			
Ouagadougou (Burkina Faso)	1070	970	900	2240	2360	1820	1120	2240	2400	1240	1240	1830	500	2550	---		
Praia (Cape Verde)	3140	3860	2420	1270	960	1880	4070	680	2150	4190	3930	2570	3830	1250	3330	---	
Yaoundé (Cameroon)	2650	2100	3760	4410	4160	4350	1740	4670	4120	1620	1620	3610	2090	5240	2860	5120	---

Car Hire, Chickens & Other Hazards of the Road

If you have never driven in a developing country before, hiring a self-drive car is not something to be undertaken lightly. Road conditions outside the capital are often bad and, apart from potholes and the inevitable chickens, dangers include people – especially children – and cows, goats and other larger animals moving unexpectedly into your path. Keep in mind that many locals have not driven themselves, and are thus not aware of necessary braking distances and similar concepts. Smaller roads are not tarred, so you need to be able to drive comfortably on dirt (and sometimes also on sand). One of the biggest hazards is overtaking blind or on curves. Moderate your speed accordingly, and when going around curves or blind spots yourself, be prepared to react to oncoming vehicles in your lane. If you see some branches in the road, it's usually a sign that there is a problem or a stopped vehicle in the road ahead, so you'll need to slow down.

There are very few signposts, so you should take a map and be able to read it. Also, outside capital cities, phones are few and far between, should you need to contact your rental company in case of a breakdown, and cellular telephone networks often don't reach rural areas.

Throughout the region, driving at night is unsafe; try to avoid doing so under all circumstances. If you do need to drive in the dark, be particularly alert for vehicles stopped in the roadway with no lights or hazard warnings. Basic mechanical knowledge – at the very least being able to change a wheel – is very useful. It's almost always best to take a chauffeur along. In addition to having mechanical knowledge, and (usually) knowledge of the route, they often can be helpful as translators.

advance to see that it's in acceptable mechanical condition.

Taxi Hire As an alternative to hiring a car, consider using a taxi by the day. It will probably cost you less (anywhere from about US$20 to US$50 per day), and if the car breaks down it will be the driver's problem. You can either hire a city taxi or a bush taxi (although in most places, you'll find that city taxis won't have the necessary paperwork for long-distance routes), or alternatively, ask around at your hotel and arrange something privately. Whatever vehicle you go with, make sure it's mechanically sound before agreeing to anything. Even if you know nothing about cars, just looking at the bodywork or listening to the engine will give you an idea. Also, don't forget to check the tyres. If they're completely bald, or badly out of alignment, it's probably better to look for another vehicle. If you're going on a longer trip, it's also worth checking that there's a spare (and the tools to change it). Hiring a car for a short test run in town is a good way to check out both vehicle and driver before finalising arrangements for a longer trip.

The price you pay will have to be worth the driver taking it out of public service for the day. If you want a deal including petrol, he'll reduce the speed to a slow trot and complain every time you take a detour. A fixed daily rate for the car, while you pay extra for fuel, is easier to arrange. Finding a car with a working petrol gauge may be tricky, but you can work on the theory that the tank will be empty when you start, and if you allow for 10km per litre on reasonable roads (more on bad roads) you should be OK.

BICYCLE

While cycling isn't exactly common in West Africa, there is a small but steady number of travellers who visit the region on bicycle. As long as you have sufficient time, and a willingness to rough things, cycling is an excellent way to get to know West Africa, as you'll often stay in small towns and villages, interact more with the local people without vehicle windows and other barriers between you, and eat West African food more frequently. Because of the distances involved, you'll need to plan your food and water needs in advance, and pay careful attention to choosing a route in order to avoid long stretches of semidesert, areas with no villages and heavily travelled roads. In general, cycling is best well away from urban areas, and in the early morning and late afternoon hours. When calculating your daily distances, plan on taking a break during the hottest midday period, and don't count on covering as much territory each day as you might in a northern European climate. Countries that are particularly good for cycling include southern Senegal (the security situation permitting), Gambia, southern Ghana, Togo and Benin; in all, distances between major points of interest are fairly manageable.

Mountain bikes are most suitable for cycling in West Africa, and will give you the greatest flexibility in setting your route. While heavy, single-speed bicycles can be rented in many towns (and occasionally mountain bikes), they are not good for anything other than short local rides, so you should plan on bringing your own bicycle into the country if you will be riding extended distances. To rent a bike locally, ask staff at hotels, or inquire at bicycle repair stands (every town market has one).

Apart from water, your main concern is likely to be motorists. Cyclists are regarded as 2nd-class citizens in West Africa, even more than they are in Western countries, so make sure you know what's coming up behind you and be prepared to take evasive action onto the verge, as local cyclists are often forced to do. A small rear-view mirror is well worth considering, especially if you'll be cycling in urban areas or on heavily travelled roads.

Other factors to consider are the intense heat, the long distances and places to stay. Throughout the region, the best time to cycle is in the cooler, dry period from mid-October to February. Even so, you'll need to work out a way to carry at least 4L of water, and you'll definitely need to carry a water filter and purifier. If you get tired, or simply want to cut out the boring bits, bikes can easily be carried on bush taxis, though you'll likely want to carry some rags to wrap around the gearing for protection. You'll need to pay a luggage fee for this, but it shouldn't be more than one-third to one-half the price of the journey. Wherever you go, be prepared to be met with great local curiosity (as well as much goodwill). As in most places in the world, don't leave your bike unattended for any lengthy period of time unless it's locked, and try to secure the main removable pieces. Taking your bike into your hotel room, should you decide to take a break from camping, is generally no problem (and is a good idea). If you're camping near settlements in rural areas, ask the village headman each night where you can stay. Even if you don't have a tent, he'll find you somewhere to sleep.

You'll need to carry sufficient spares, and be proficient at repairs. In particular, punctures will be frequent. Take at least four spare inner tubes, some tyre repair material and a spare tyre. Consider the number of tube patches you might need, square it, and pack those too. Some people don't like them, but we've found inner-tube protectors indispensable for minimising punctures. A highly recommended contact is the US-based International Bicycle Fund (☎/fax 206-628 9314, e ibike@ibike.org, w www.ibike.org/bikeafrica), a low-budget, socially conscious organisation that arranges tours in several West African countries and provides information.

Transporting your Bicycle

If you're planning to bring your bike with you on the plane to West Africa, some airlines ask that you partially dismantle it and put the pieces in a large bag or box. Bike boxes are available at some airports. Otherwise, you can arrange one in advance with your local bicycle shop. To fit it in the box, you'll usually need to take off (or turn) the handlebars, pedals and seat, and will need to deflate the tyres. Some airlines don't charge, while others (including many charter airlines) may levy an extra fee – usually about US$50 – because bike boxes are not standard size. Some airlines are willing to take your bike 'as is' – you can just wheel it to the check-in desk – although here, too, you'll still need to partially deflate the tyres, and usually also tie the handlebars into the frame. Check with the airline in advance about what their regulations are. If you don't want to be bothered with transport, and have plenty of time, you can also cycle to West Africa from Europe, coming down through Morocco and Mauritania.

BOAT

At several points along the West African coast you can travel by boat, either on a large passenger vessel or by local canoe. Some of the local canoe trips are definitely of the informal variety, and many are dangerous.

On most major rivers in the region, passenger boats serve towns and villages along the way, and can be an excellent way to see the country. One of the most popular boat trips for travellers is along the Niger River in Mali, but other riverboat options exist, for example along the Gambia and Senegal Rivers. For all, bring sufficient water and food, although you'll often be able to buy snacks and fruit along the way. Also bring something to protect yourself from the sun, as few boats have any shade, and something to waterproof your gear. Avoid getting on boats that are overloaded, or setting off when the weather is bad, especially on sea routes in coastal areas.

LOCAL TRANSPORT

Bus & Minibus

Many capitals have well developed city bus and minibus networks connecting the city centre and suburbs. In most other cities, it's minibuses only.

Shared Taxi

Many cities have shared taxis, which will stop and pick up more passengers even if they already have somebody inside. Some run on fixed routes, and are effectively a bus, only quicker and more comfortable. Others go wherever the first passenger wants to go, and other people will only be picked up if they're going in the same direction. They normally shout the name of the suburb they're heading for as the taxi goes past. In some places, it's common for the waiting passengers to call out the name of their destination or point in the desired direction as the taxi passes by. Once you've got the hang of the shared taxi system it's quick, safe and inexpensive, and an excellent way to get around cities – and also a good way to experience local life. It's also one of West Africa's great bargains, as fares seldom exceed US$0.30. It's always worth checking the fare before you get in the car, though, as they are not always fixed, and meters don't apply to shared trips. If you're the first person in the taxi, make it clear that you're expecting the driver to pick up others and that you don't want a private hire (*déplacement*, *depo*, 'charter' or 'town trip') all to yourself.

Private Taxi

Only in the bigger cities, such as Dakar, Abidjan and Ouagadougou, do taxis have meters *(compteurs)*. Otherwise, bargaining is required or you'll be given the legally fixed rate. In any case, determine the fare before getting into the taxi. The fare from most airports into town is fixed, but some drivers (in Dakar, for example) will try to charge at least double these. The price always includes luggage unless you have a particularly bulky item. Also, fares invariably go up at night, and sometimes also in rainy weather.

Motorcycle Taxi

In some countries, motorcycle taxis ('moto-taxis' or 'motos') are used. While they're often cheaper than shared taxis and handy for zipping around, safety can be an issue. If you have a choice, it's usually better to pay slightly more and go with a regular shared taxi.

ORGANISED TOURS

Compared with most areas of the world, West Africa has few tour operators. Tour companies are usually based in the capital cities, and typically offer excursions for groups (rather than individuals) from one-day to one-week trips, or longer. On most tours, the larger the group, the lower the cost per person. Information on local tour operators is given in the individual country chapters. Overland tours are discussed in the Getting There & Away chapter.

Benin

Benin, the birthplace of voodoo and seat of one of West Africa's most powerful kingdoms, once had a historical renown that extended far beyond the country's borders. Having emerged from its more recent Marxist past, Benin is now a vibrant country, and has embraced democracy and capitalism with characteristic fervour.

For travellers, Benin still possesses much of the mystique that captivated earlier European imagination. The fishing villages built on stilts are among the most famous images of Benin and are a must-see even if they are a little touristy these days. In the rural areas, life goes on as it has for centuries, and voodoo is still practised. In Ouidah, the old slave-trading centre on the coast, and Abomey, the centre of the kingdom of Dahomey, one of Africa's former great empires, you may even witness a voodoo ceremony.

The national parks in the north – Pendjari and W – are some of the better places in West Africa to see animals.

Benin at a Glance

Capital: Porto Novo
Population: 6.5 million
Area: 112,622 sq km
Head of State: President Mathieu Kérékou
Official language: French
Main local languages: Fon, Bariba, Dendi
Currency: West African CFA franc
Exchange rate: US$1 = CFA694
Time: GMT/UTC +1
Country telephone code: ☎ 229
Best time to go: January & February

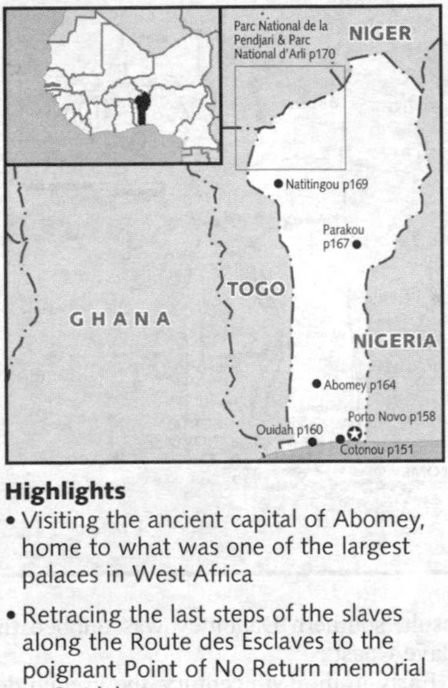
Parc National de la Pendjari & Parc National d'Arli p170
NIGER
Natitingou p169
Parakou p167
TOGO
GHANA
NIGERIA
Abomey p164
Porto Novo p158
Ouidah p160
Cotonou p151

Highlights

- Visiting the ancient capital of Abomey, home to what was one of the largest palaces in West Africa
- Retracing the last steps of the slaves along the Route des Esclaves to the poignant Point of No Return memorial in Ouidah
- Becoming entranced by Benin's rich voodoo centres of Ouidah and Abomey
- Exploring Ganvié, an extraordinary – though touristy – stilt village in the middle of Lake Nokoué
- Spying elephants, hippos, buffaloes, crocodiles and lions at Parc National de la Pendjari, one of the better wildlife parks in the region
- Taking respite from the Beninese heat and relaxing along the long, palm-fringed beaches at Grand Popo

Facts about Benin

HISTORY

More than 350 years ago, the area now known as Benin was split into numerous principalities. One of the chiefs quarrelled with his brother for the right to succession and, around 1625, settled in Abomey. He then conquered the neighbouring kingdom of the Dan, which became known as Dahomey (meaning 'in Dan's belly'). Each king pledged to leave his successor more land than he inherited, a pledge kept by waging war with his neighbours, particularly the powerful Yoruba of Nigeria. At the same time, the Portuguese, and later other Europeans, established trading posts along the coast, notably at Porto Novo and Ouidah.

The kingdom of Dahomey soon became rich by selling slaves to these traders and received luxury items and guns in return, thus enabling it to wage war against neighbouring kingdoms. For more than a century, an average of 10,000 slaves per year were shipped to the Americas (primarily Brazil and the Caribbean, in particular Haiti), taking their practice of voodoo with them. As a

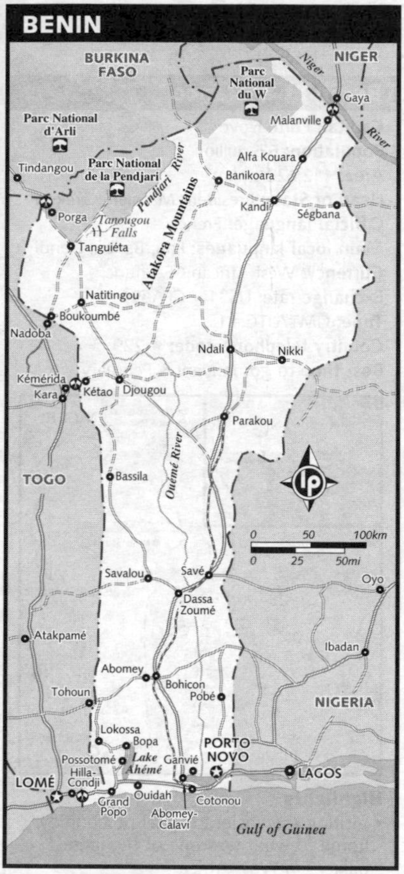
BENIN
BURKINA FASO
NIGER
Parc National du W
Niger River
Gaya
Malanville
Parc National d'Arli
Alfa Kouara
Tindangou
Parc National de la Pendjari
Pendjari River
Banikoara
Kandi
Ségbana
Porga
Tanougou Falls
Atakora Mountains
Tanguiéta
Natitingou
Boukoumbé
Nadoba
Ndali
Nikki
Kémérida
Kara
Kétao
Djougou
Parakou
Ouémé River
TOGO
Bassila
0 50 100km
0 25 50mi
Savalou
Savé
Oyo
Dassa Zoumé
Atakpamé
Ibadan
Abomey
Bohicon
Tohoun
Pobé
NIGERIA
Lokossa
Bopa
PORTO NOVO
Possotomé
Lake Ahémé
Ganvié
LAGOS
LOMÉ
Hilla-Condji
Ouidah
Grand Popo
Abomey-Calavi
Cotonou
Gulf of Guinea

result, southern Dahomey was dubbed the Slave Coast.

Early in the 19th century, the French defeated the kingdom of Dahomey, making it a colony and part of French West Africa. During the 70-year colonial period great progress was made in education, and hence many Dahomeyans were employed as government advisers throughout French West Africa.

Independence

When Dahomey became independent in 1960, Hubert Maga became the country's first president. Almost immediately, other former French colonies started deporting the Dahomeyans. Back in Dahomey without work, the Dahomeyans were the root of a highly unstable political situation. Three years after independence, after seeing how easily some disgruntled soldiers in Togo staged a coup, the military did the same in Dahomey.

During the next nine years, Dahomey had four more successful military coups, nine more changes of government and five changes of constitution: what the Dahomeyans called in jest *le folklore*.

The Revolution

In 1972, a group of officers led by Lieutenant Colonel Mathieu Kérékou seized power in a coup that initiated almost two decades of military dictatorship. The country then took a sharp turn to the left as it embraced Marxism. To emphasise the break from the past, Kérékou renamed the country to Benin. As part of this revolution, the government required schools to teach Marxism, and it set up collective farms and ordered students to work on them. It assigned areas of cultivation and production goals to every district and village, formed state enterprises, created a single central trade union and inculcated a more militant spirit in the army.

However, the revolution was always more rhetorical than real. The economy fell into a shambles: inflation and unemployment rose and salaries remained unpaid for months. People quickly lost interest in the Marxist-Leninist ideology and in one year alone, there were six attempted coups. Then in the late 1980s, workers and students went on strike.

In December 1989, the French recommended to Kérékou that the government hold a national conference and adopt constitutional changes. Kérékou followed their advice, renouncing Marxism-Leninism and calling for the drafting of a new constitution. Dissidents used the occasion to blame the government for leading the country into total bankruptcy, and for corruption and human rights abuses. The 488 delegates then engineered a coup, leaving Kérékou as merely head of the army. A new cabinet was formed with Nicéphore Soglo (a former dissident) as prime minister.

Benin Today

The first free multiparty elections were held in March 1991 and Soglo swept Kérékou from power. However, in the wake of popular discontent over austere economic measures (partly caused by the 1994 devaluation of the CFA) and increasing autocracy by the Soglo government, Kérékou was voted back into power in March 1996.

Five years later, in the March 2001 presidential elections, it was a case of history repeating itself as the two long-standing rivals, Kérékou and Soglo, faced each other again. However, Soglo and fellow opposition candidate Adrien Houngbédji of the PRD withdrew from the race alleging electoral fraud, paving the way for a landslide victory for the incumbent president.

Kérékou has since embarked on his second and final five-year term in office, although observers remain sceptical about the extent to which he has distanced himself from his dictatorial and communist ways.

GEOGRAPHY

Situated between Nigeria and Togo, Benin measures roughly 700km long and 120km across in the south, widening to about 300km in the north. Most of the coastal plain is a sand bar that obstructs the seaward flow of several rivers. As a result, there are lagoons a few kilometres inland all along the coast. Further inland a densely forested plateau replaces the coastal plains. In the far northwest the Atakora mountains reach 457m in height.

CLIMATE

In southern Benin, there are two rainy seasons: April to mid-July and mid-September to late October. The rains in the north fall from June to early October. Parts of the Atakora region occasionally receive heavy rainfall. In the north temperatures can reach 46°C, while the coastal south is cooler, with temperatures ranging from 18°C to 35°C. Harmattan winds blow from the north from December to March. The hottest time of the year is February to April.

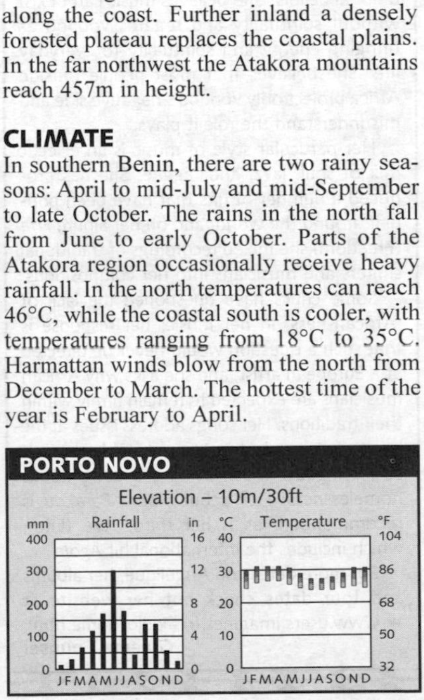
PORTO NOVO
Elevation – 10m/30ft
Rainfall
Temperature
mm
in
°C
°F
400
300
200
100
0
16
12
8
4
0
40
30
20
10
0
104
86
68
50
32
JFMAMJJASOND
JFMAMJJASOND

ECOLOGY & ENVIRONMENT

Deforestation and desertification are the major environmental problems with much of the rainforests in southern Benin having disappeared. In the north, droughts continue to severely affect marginal agriculture, while poaching is threatening the small remaining wildlife populations.

FLORA & FAUNA

Significant vestiges of wildlife are found in Parc National de la Pendjari and Parc National du W, including herds of elephants. The southern part of Benin is heavily burnt out as the human population scrambles for remaining areas to cultivate.

GOVERNMENT & POLITICS

The Marxist-inspired constitution, the Loi Fondamentale of 1977, was rescinded in 1988 and a new constitution was ratified two years later. The latter vested legislative authority in the hands of an 83-member national assembly and executive power in the president, who is elected by universal suffrage for five-year terms with a maximum of two terms, and in the council of ministers, including a prime minister whom the president appoints.

The constitution also created a true multiparty system. The main political parties today are the Front d'action pour le Rénouveau et le Développement (FARD), which is the ruling party, the Parti de la Renaissance du Bénin (PRB) and the Parti du Renouveau Démocratique (PRD).

ECONOMY

Benin's economy is primarily dependant on subsistence farming, which accounts for 38% of gross domestic product (GDP). Yams, maize, cassava and corn are the principal food crops. The country's main exports are cotton, palm oil, crude oil and cocoa beans, with cotton accounting for more than 75% of export earnings. Imports, however, exceed exports by about US$170 million.

Improved political stability and economic management enabled Benin to maintain an average of 5% in real growth output from 1996 to 1999; however, this was offset by rapid population growth. Benin also remains vulnerable to the political turmoil in Nigeria because of its critical dependency on its neighbour for fuel. While economic growth during 2000 was hampered by high fuel costs, the expansion of Cotonou's port and increased cotton production should lead to renewed growth beyond 2001.

POPULATION & PEOPLE

More than 50% of Benin's people belong to one of five ethnic groups: Fon, Yoruba, Bariba, Betamaribé and Fula.

The Fon (and the related Adja) comprise 40% of the population of Benin. Migrating from southwestern Nigeria in the 13th century to southern parts of Benin, they established a kingdom in what is known today as the village of Allada.

The Yoruba (called Nagot locally), who also migrated from Nigeria, occupy the southern and mideastern zones of Benin and are the second-largest ethnic group, comprising 12% of the population.

The Bariba, who comprise 9% of the population, live mostly in the Borgou region. According to legend, they migrated from the Bussa and Ife areas of Nigeria. Their most famous kingdom in Benin was centred at Nikki, and because of distance and earlier slave raids they have remained relatively aloof towards southern Benin.

The Betamaribé (often incorrectly referred to as the Somba) comprise 8% of the population and live in the northwest, around the Atakora mountains. Having lived for hundreds of years in relative seclusion from modern influences they have managed to keep much of their traditional culture intact (for details see the boxed text 'The Somba' later this chapter).

The Fula (also called Fulari or Peul) live primarily in the north and comprise 6% of the population.

Despite the underlying tensions between the southern and northern regions, the various groups live in relative harmony and have intermarried.

ARTS

Art & Craftwork

Benin's cultural history is rich, and traditional Beninese art has brought international attention to the legendary kingdom of Dahomey.

Traditionally, art served a spiritual purpose, but under the Fon kings, artisans and sculptors were called upon to create works that evoked heroism and enhanced the image of the rulers. Until the 19th century, artists and brass/silver casters were forbidden to work outside the palace walls. They became the historians of the era, creating richly coloured applique banners that depicted the events of past and reigning kings. Modern banners, depicting animals, hunting scenes and deities, are usually on black material with figures cut out of imported coloured cloth and sewn on.

Don't miss the bas-reliefs at the Royal Palace Museum in Abomey. These are polychrome bas-reliefs in clay that were used to decorate the palace, temples and chiefs' houses. The palace has been restored by the Getty Conservation Institute and has been designated a Unesco world heritage site.

Sculpture produced for the voodoo cults is considerably less refined than that supplied to the king. Figures called *bochio* are carved from the trunk of a tree and placed at the entrance of a village to discourage malevolent

Angélique Kidjo

Angélique Kidjo was born in Ouidah, which is known for its strong links to voodoo and traditional beliefs. She believes music can't exist without spirituality and regards voodoo as bringing energy and spirituality to everyday life. She believes that most people outside Africa project only voodoo's negative side and misunderstand the role it plays.

Her particular style of music is an eclectic mix of soul, jazz, and reggae. She has produced a number of hits that have been popular around the world, and on her album *Fifa* (Freedom) she mixed recordings of traditional singers and musicians into her compositions.

Some critics have questioned the lack of 'African-ness' in her music; her response is that such a question would never be directed at a European artist, and she asks why African musicians are expected to remain firmly within their traditions. Her songs address issues at the heart of many of Africa's social problems, such as *Houngbati* (Push Them), a song about homelessness. Her debut album *Parakou* is recommended, as is her third, *Aye* (Life), which includes the international hit *Agolo*.

For more details on Angélique, her albums and tour dates check out her website at **w** www.users.imaginet.fr/~kidjo/home.html.

Graeme Counsel

spirits. Some voodoo wood figures are combined with a variety of materials, such as bottles, padlocks and bones, to imbue them with power. Moulded figures of unfired clay represent Legba (a Fon god) and receive daily libations for the protection of the home.

Music

Angélique Kidjo, now a major international star, is Benin's most famous recording artist (see the boxed text 'Angélique Kidjo' for details). Other well known Beninese artists include Gnonnes Pedro, Nel Olivier and Yelouassi Adolphe, and the bands Orchestre Poly-Rythmo and Disc Afrique.

Dance

Throughout Benin there's a great variety of traditional dances and songs. These dances and ceremonies may be of a religious or cultural nature, or may concern the vital forces of the universe. They may also give praise or be a simple manifestation of joy, sorrow or communion with the spirits of the dead.

SOCIETY & CONDUCT

Within the narrow borders of Benin is an array of different ethnic groups, which adds to the diversity and interest of the country. Most of the groups are patrilineal and many still observe polygamy. This practice, however, is becoming increasingly rare among urban and educated Beninese. Marriages were and are still arranged by families and divorce is rare.

Most families support themselves through agriculture. Women control the local food distribution system, including the transport of produce to the market and the subsequent barter and sale.

The best way to observe traditional Beninese life is to attend a festival in a remote village. Dress conservatively and show respect for religious establishments and customs.

RELIGION

While 30% of the population is Christian and 20% is Muslim, 50% retain traditional beliefs. For information on these beliefs, see the boxed text 'Voodoo in Benin'.

LANGUAGE

French is the official language in Benin. Fon is the main indigenous language in the southern parts, while Bariba and Dendi are spoken in the north. Villagers on the border between Nigeria and Benin speak Yoruba, which is often referred to as Nagot. See the Language chapter for useful phrases in French, Fon and Yoruba.

Voodoo in Benin

The traditional religion of Benin conforms to the general pattern found in West Africa. There is a supreme being, and a host of lesser gods or spirits that are ethnically specific to their followers and to the part of the spiritual world inhabited by a person's ancestors. Traditional priests, variously known as fetish priests and priestesses or *juju* men, are consulted for their power to communicate with particular spirits and seek intercession with them. This communication is achieved through spirit possession and through ritual that often involves a gift or 'sacrifice' of palm wine, gin or food such as eggs, chickens or goats. The grace of the spirits is essential for protection and prosperity, and some spirits can be harnessed for malicious and selfish ends.

Fon and Ewe slaves exported through the Dahomey kingdom took these *loa* (spirits) and practices with them, establishing in Haiti and Cuba the religion now known as *vodou* (as it is currently spelt in these countries). Originally 'vodun' meant 'the hidden' or 'mystery'. Vodou developed independently, acquiring new spirits and incorporating features of Roman Catholicism that echoed aspects of its own beliefs. This 'vodou' version of African-derived religion has been both demonised and distorted by Hollywood.

The label 'vodou' also stuck in modern Benin where the Marxist government of Kérékou outlawed it as being inimical to a rational and socialist work ethic. Since a democratic government was installed here in 1989, traditional religious practice has been permitted. Vodun was formally recognised as a religion by the government of Benin in February 1996. Many, irrespective of their religion, also revere and seek protection and favours from the spirits to which they are tied by birth.

Katie Abu

Facts for the Visitor

SUGGESTED ITINERARIES

Cotonou, though heavily polluted, is a fascinating example of urban Africa and worth a week's stay. Add several more days to explore nearby tranquil Porto Novo, the capital, and Ganvié, the lacustrine stilt village. Those interested in voodoo will want to visit Ouidah and walk the Routes des Esclaves, a poignant reminder of a darker past. Grand Popo, further west, is for beach lovers. Lake Ahémé north of Grand Popo is surrounded by peaceful fishing villages. In Abomey you can see the royal palace of the Dahomey kingdom and explore the area on a *zemidjan* (moto-taxi), uncovering voodoo relics and disintegrating palace walls. Parakou, further north, is a good stopping point for a day, and handy for Natitingou and Parc National de la Pendjari. You could easily spend a week here, climbing, exploring the castlelike houses, looking for wildlife and cooling off in waterfalls.

PLANNING

Many roads in the south are impassable during the rainy season (April to mid-July and mid-September to the end of October). Parc National de la Pendjari may be inaccessible during the northern rainy season from June to October.

The best map by far is the 1:600,000 *Republique du Benin Carte Générale*, produced by the Institut Geographique National. It provides good country detail and includes insert city maps of Porto Novo and Cotonou.

VISAS & DOCUMENTS

Visas

Visas are required for all travellers except nationals of the Economic Community of West African States (Ecowas). If flying into Cotonou you will require a visa before arrival. A visa valid for 15/30 days costs UK£30/45 from the Beninese consulate in London; a single-entry visa (valid for 90 days) costs US$20 from the embassy in Washington, DC.

If crossing overland, it's far easier (and usually cheaper) to get a visa at the border, with the possible exception of the Niger-Benin border. Single-entry visas will cost CFA10,000 and are readily available at the borders. Crossing from Togo and Nigeria these are valid for 48 hours; from Burkina Faso and Niger they are valid for one week. Extensions are easy to obtain in Cotonou.

Visa Extensions You can get extensions of up to 30 days without problems in three to four days at the Direction Immigration/Emigration (☎ 31 42 13) in Cotonou. A 30-day extension costs CFA12,000; applications are accepted only from 8am to 11.30am Monday to Friday and then can be collected only between 3pm and 5.30pm. You'll need one passport photo.

Visas for Onward Travel In Benin you can get visas for the following neighbouring West African countries:

Burkina Faso, Côte d'Ivoire & Togo Three-month visas (CFA20,000) and transit visas (CFA6000) for these countries are issued by the French consulate in 24 to 48 hours. Two photos are required. Applications are accepted only from 8am to 11am Monday to Friday, and then can be collected only between 1.30pm and 5pm.

Ghana Visas take two days to issue and cost CFA12,000/30,000 for single/multiple entry. Four photos are required.

Niger Visas valid for up to three months cost CFA25,000 and can be collected within 24 hours. Two photos are required.

Nigeria The Nigerian embassy issues visas for its residents only, although it may consider your case if you have a letter from your embassy.

Other Documents

Officially an international vaccination certificate for yellow fever is required, although it is rarely checked at border crossings or at the airport.

EMBASSIES & CONSULATES

Beninese Embassies & Consulates

In West Africa, Benin has embassies in Côte d'Ivoire, Ghana, Nigeria and Niger – but not in Togo or Burkina Faso.

Elsewhere, Beninese embassies and consulates include the following:

Belgium (☎ 02-354 94 71) 5 Av de l'Observatoire, Brussels 1180
Canada (☎ 613-233 4429, fax 233 8952, ⓔ ambaben2@on.aira.com) 58 Glebe Ave, Ottawa, ON K1S 2C3
France (☎ 01 45 00 98 82, fax 01 45 01 82 02, ⓔ ambassade@ambassade-benin.org, Ⓦ www.ambassade-benin.org) 87 Av Victor Hugo, Paris 75116
Germany (☎ 0228-34 40 31, 34 40 32) Rüdigerstrasse 10 Postsech, 53178 Bonn
UK (☎ 020-8954 8800, fax 8954 8844) Dolphin House, 16 The Broadway, Stanmore, Middlesex HA7 4DW
USA (☎ 202-232 6656, fax 265 1996) 2124 Kalorama Rd, NW, Washington, DC 20008

Embassies & Consulates in Benin

Embassies and consulates in Contonou include the following:

France (☎ 30 02 25) Route de l'Aéroport, near the presidential palace
Consulate: (☎ 31 26 38, 31 26 80) Rue 651A
Germany (☎ 31 29 68) Patte d'Oie
Ghana (☎ 30 07 46) Route de l'Aéroport
Niger (☎ 31 40 30) Rue 651A; open 8am to noon and 3pm to 6pm Monday to Friday
Nigeria (☎ 30 11 42) Blvd de la Marina; open 10am to 2pm Monday to Friday
USA (☎ 30 06 50, fax 30 14 39) Patte d'Oie

CUSTOMS

All currency should be declared on arrival, as you are only allowed to export what you have declared. Exiting Benin you are permitted to take out 200 cigarettes and one bottle of wine or spirits.

MONEY

The unit of currency in Benin is the CFA franc.

country	unit		CFA
euro zone	€1	=	CFA656
UK	UK£1	=	CFA1024
USA	US$1	=	CFA694

Banks accept travellers cheques in most major currencies, although these can only be reliably changed in Cotonou. Cash advances against credit cards (Visa only) are also possible at the major banks in Cotonou. The best banks for changing money are Financial Bank, Bank of Africa and Ecobank.

POST & COMMUNICATIONS

Postcards and letters cost CFA200 per 10g to France, CFA350 elsewhere in Europe, and CFA450 to North America and Australasia.

International telephone calls and faxes can be made at telecom offices and private telephone agencies throughout Benin. The cost per minute is about CFA1350 to France, CFA1850 elsewhere in Europe, CFA1400 to North America, and CFA2640 to Australasia.

There are no internal area codes.

Cotonou has a few Internet centres. Access, which can at times be slow, costs around CFA500 per hour.

DIGITAL RESOURCES

A good place to start your cyber tour is at Ⓦ www.cotonou.com, which has general country information as well as accommodation, travel and news links. For local and regional news try Ⓦ www.beninpost.com.

PHOTOGRAPHY & VIDEO

A photo permit is not required, but be careful when taking shots of museums, fetish temples and cultural and religious ceremonies. You could upset a lot of people and end up being cursed. Rules are not clear-cut, so it's best to ask first. For general information see Photography & Video in the Regional Facts for the Visitor chapter.

NEWSPAPERS & MAGAZINES

Cotonou's dailies, which include *Le Nation* and *Le Soleil*, don't really fulfil their role as 'newspapers', but you may be able to glean local football results and seesawing political accusations from them. Some of the weekly papers are more readable. Foreign newspapers and magazines can occasionally be found at newspaper stands.

RADIO & TV

The state-run radio broadcasts in English, French and local languages. TV, including ATVS and the state-run ORTB, is usually poorly presented, and programmes sometimes change halfway through.

HEALTH

Malaria is a risk year-round in Benin, so you should take appropriate precautions. It's best to only drink water that has been treated. For general health information, see Health in the Regional Facts for the Visitor chapter.

WOMEN TRAVELLERS

Travelling in Benin presents few problems for women. Beyond the usual 'Where is your husband?' curiosity, the greatest annoyance is unwanted attention, especially from officials. The best tack in these situations is to say you are waiting for your husband.

As with anywhere else in the world use common sense – don't wander around alone at night, especially along the beaches or along Rue des Cheminots in Cotonou.

While it is not necessary to cover yourself from head to toe, it is advisable to dress in a modest fashion. If in doubt, look at what the local women are wearing and follow suit. For more information and advice, see Women Travellers in the Regional Facts for the Visitor chapter.

DANGERS & ANNOYANCES

Benin is a relatively secure country with only limited incidents of crime, which tourists can often avoid simply by being cautious.

Muggings are not uncommon along Cotonou's shoreline; the beach near the Benin Hotel is particularly bad, even during the day. Never walk on the beach alone, and even when walking with someone, don't carry or wear any valuables.

Cotonou's beaches are also plagued by pollution and dangerous currents – seek local advice before swimming.

BUSINESS HOURS

Business hours are 8am to 12.30pm and 3pm to 7pm Monday to Friday and 8am to 12.30pm Saturday. Government offices are open 7.30am to 12.30pm and 3.30pm to 6.30pm Monday to Friday.

Banking hours are generally 8am to 12.30pm and 3pm to 5pm Monday to Friday.

PUBLIC HOLIDAYS & SPECIAL EVENTS

Public holidays include:

New Year's Day 1 January
Vodoun 10 January
Martyr's Day 16 January
Liberation Day 28 February
Labour Day 1 May
Independence 1 August
Armed Forces Day 26 October
Republic Day 4 December
Harvest Day 31 December

Benin also celebrates the usual Christian and Muslim holidays. See Public Holidays & Special Events in the Regional Facts for the Visitor chapter for a table of dates of Islamic holidays.

Apart from the colourful annual Muslim celebrations in the northern towns, including Parakou and Kandi, the other main event is the annual Voodoo Festival, which is held in Ouidah (see the boxed text 'The Voodoo Festival' for details).

Every four years or so there is the seasonal 'whipping ceremony' in Boukombé, which seems to go on until the young men are satisfied that they have literally beaten each other black and blue. There are also many voodoo celebrations in Ouidah and Abomey; visiting these is usually a matter of luck.

ACTIVITIES

The beaches around Cotonou, with the exception of Jonquet Plage, are fairly ordinary. For better swimming, head for the beaches at Grand Popo and the Bouches du Roy. Many of the large hotels have swimming pools that nonguests can use.

If you get the chance, make sure you rent a bicycle (but don't expect 18-speed mountain bikes) and cycle around Porto Novo or Abomey.

The Voodoo Festival

Benin's most vibrant and colourful celebration is the annual Voodoo Festival held on 10 January. While celebrations take place all over the country, those in Ouidah, the historic centre of voodoo, are the best.

Since 1997, one year after the government officially decreed voodoo a religion, thousands of believers have flocked to Ouidah each year to reclaim and rejoice in their faith.

The main festivities take place on the beach near the Point of No Return monument at the end of Route des Esclaves. The celebrations, which are marked by much singing, dancing and beating of drums, only officially begin after the supreme chief of voodoo slaughters a goat to honour the spirits.

While the festival is certainly eye-opening, those expecting to see a scene reminiscent of *The Night of the Living Dead* will be sadly disappointed.

There are few organised hikes but there is nothing to prevent you walking from village to village on the fringes of Lake Nokoué, taking pirogue rides for some stretches.

ACCOMMODATION

Basic singles/doubles with a fan and a shared bathroom cost about CFA5000/6000, while comfortable air-conditioned rooms with a private bathroom are around CFA10,000. Tariffs should include the tourist tax of CFA500, and be listed prominently at the hotel entrance.

FOOD & DRINKS

The food in Benin is similar to that in Togo, and is unquestionably among the best in West Africa.

The local beer, La Béninoise, is a passable drop. The adventurous could try palm wine, *tchapallo* (a millet-based local brew) or *sodabe* (a good alternative fuel for NASA's fleet of spacecraft).

Getting There & Away

AIR

The main airport is on the western fringe of Cotonou, in Cocotiers. The departure tax is CFA3000. Departing from Cotonou is far less of a hassle than departing from some other West African countries.

Europe & the USA

There are four direct flights weekly between Paris and Cotonou on Air France. A standard return economy fare is about US$582/790 in the low/high season. If the flight schedules to Cotonou are inconvenient or if you're having problems getting a visa to Benin, consider flying to Lomé (Togo) and taking a taxi from there to Cotonou (three hours).

Between the USA and Cotonou, you'll have to take Air France from New York to Abidjan or Ouadadougou, transferring from there to Cotonou. Tickets cost around US$1279 return.

Africa

Air Burkina flies twice weekly from Cotonou to Lomé (US$32/35 one way/return) and thrice weekly to Ouagadougou in Burkina Faso (US$186/205). Air Gabon has regular flights from Cotonou to Abidjan (US$107/117).

Inter Aviation Service flies twice weekly from Johannesburg to Cotonou via Libreville (US$422 return). If you are heading to East Africa via Lagos, you may find it cheaper to fly from Cotonou to Lagos (Ghana Airways, US$32 one way) and transfer there rather than go overland to Lagos. This way you'll avoid having to get a Nigerian visa and escape the hassles of Lagos. You'll also be tucked safely away in the transit lounge, avoiding the chaos of the airport itself.

LAND

Border Crossings

There are four main border crossings into Benin: at Hilla-Condji (from Togo) in the southwest, at Kraké (on the Nigerian border) in the southeast, at Malanville (from Niger) in the northeast, and between Porga and Tindangou (in Burkina Faso) in the northwest. The Hilla-Condji crossing from Togo is relatively trouble-free, unlike the other three. The northern borders of Benin are open from 7am to 7.30pm, so keep that in mind when leaving Cotonou. The borders at Togo and Nigeria on the coastal route are open 24 hours.

Another good crossing point from Togo into Benin is at Kétao, east of Kara. This border closes at 6pm.

Burkina Faso

There's at least one bush taxi a day from Natitingou to Tanguiéta. Transport is scarce along the dirt road between Tanguiéta and the border (CFA2500, 65km), except on market day (Monday). STIF runs a weekly direct bus service from Cotonou to Ouagadougou (CFA14,000, 30 hours) on Wednesday.

Niger

Getting a bush taxi from Cotonou to Parakou (CFA6500, eight hours) is easy. From Parakou you can catch another bush taxi to the Niger border at Malanville (CFA4500, five hours). More convenient and less time consuming is Africalines' daily bus service from Cotonou to Malanville (CFA11,000, around 12 hours), which departs at 7am.

From Malanville a zemidjan can take you across the Niger River to Gaya (CFA1000) in Niger. It is also possible to catch a bush taxi that will take you across the border and direct to Dosso (CFA3000, 2½ hours), halfway between Niamey and Gaya.

The Cotonou to Malanville road is tarred, so you can travel the entire 1062km to/from Niamey quite smoothly.

Nigeria

In Cotonou, bush taxis and minibuses leave for Lagos frequently throughout the day from the Gare de l'Ancien Pont (CFA3000, three hours). Going to/from Lagos, you could save money by taking a taxi just to the border and changing there, as Nigerian taxis are cheaper than those in Benin. If you do this, you will need to change money at the border or carry naira with you.

In your own vehicle, the driving time between Lagos and Cotonou is three hours. Avoid arriving or leaving Lagos at rush hour (the 'go slow' between 6am and 10am and again between 3pm and 7pm) – it's a mess.

Togo

Cotonou and Lomé are connected by frequent bush taxis (CFA3000, three hours). In Cotonou, bush taxis leave for Lomé at all hours of the day and into the early evening from the Gare de Jonquet. There is also a daily STIF bus service from Cotonou to Lomé (CFA3000, three hours).

Getting Around

BUSH TAXI, MINIBUS & BUS

Minibuses and bush taxis are the principal means of transport between towns. A bush taxi from Cotonou costs CFA600 to Ouidah, CFA2000 to Abomey, CFA3000 to Lagos or Lomé and CFA6500 to Parakou, while minibuses generally cost about 25% less and take much longer. There is usually a negotiable surcharge for luggage.

Africalines operates four separate air-conditioned bus services from Cotonou going to Savalou (CFA3500, five hours), Parakou (CFA6500, seven hours), Natitingou (CFA8500, 10 hours) and Malanville (CFA11,000, around 12 hours), each departing daily at 7am. Returning services depart daily at 1pm from Savalou, 4pm from Parakou, 7am from Natitingou and 10am from Malanville.

It is best to book ahead for a seat as initially only passengers with tickets are allowed to enter, then it is a bun fight as the remaining would-be passengers scramble to get on and get a seat. The buses are, as usual in Africa, overloaded with passengers and luggage, but they are still far more comfortable, and in some cases cheaper, than bush taxis. Have the right amount of money for your destination if you are purchasing your ticket aboard, as the conductors don't always give change (even if they have it).

TRAIN

Benin's one railway line links Cotonou with Parakou via Bohicon (the stop for Abomey). There's a daily morning train in either direction; another with couchettes (sleeper cars) departs every other night in both directions. There is no dining car on the sleeper train, so be prepared. Bedding (a sheet) is provided, but you'll need to bring warm clothing.

Second-class seats on the train are significantly cheaper than taking a bush taxi but the carriages tend to be crowded with humanity and produce. First class is about as comfortable as you'll find on any train in West Africa.

Tickets in 1st class/2nd class/sleeper from Cotonou to Bohicon (about four hours) cost CFA1400/1100/3100 for a sleeper, and from Cotonou to Parakou (about 10 to 12 hours) costs CFA5600/4000/7000. Food is available at stations along the way.

CAR & MOTORCYCLE

Petrol costs about CFA350 per litre, but in recent years the price has fluctuated a bit because of instability in Nigeria, on which Benin depends for petrol. In Nigeria petrol is cheaper, so much of it is carried illegally across the border into Benin and sold on the black market at prices slightly below the official rate. Just look for the guys along the roads with 1L to 5L bottles.

All the major car rental companies have deserted their offices in Benin, so if you want private transport it is best to organise a private taxi through one of the major hotels in Cotonou, though this can prove quite costly.

LOCAL TRANSPORT

In all towns, you'll find zemidjans (roughly pronounced 'zemi-john'). While they are by far the fastest and most convenient way of getting around the cities, they are not as safe as regular taxis. You'll recognise them by the driver's yellow and green shirt (green and purple in some regional centres). Hail them just as you would a taxi. Be sure to discuss the price beforehand; otherwise, when you arrive at your destination the driver may demand an obscene fare. The typical fare is CFA150 to CFA250, depending on the length of the trip.

Cotonou

pop 761,900

Although Porto Novo is the official capital, Cotonou, Benin's most populous city, is the capital in everything but name. Cotonou means 'mouth of the river of death' in Fon – a reference to the role the Dahomeyan kingdom played in the exportation of slaves. In 1868, Cotonou was ceded to the French, but this was challenged in 1892 by the Dahomeyan King Behanzin, leading to the Franco-Dahomeyan campaigns of 1892, and ending in the defeat of the king and the formation of the French protectorate of Dahomey.

Today Cotonou is a large, chaotic city, but not without its charms. In addition to some fairly good beaches only a few kilometres from the centre of town, there are several good nightclubs, international hotels, craft centres and an abundance of good eateries. However, if you are not overwhelmed by the daily screech of thousands of zemidjans and the resultant pollution then you are the most hardened of travellers!

Orientation

The heart of town is the intersection of Av Clozel and Av Steinmetz. Going northeast along Av Clozel, one of the city's two main thoroughfares, you pass over the Pont Ancien into the Akpakpa sector; the road eventually turns into the highway to Porto Novo and Lagos. The new bridge is further to the north; the wide Blvd St Michel (which becomes Av du Nouveau Pont), the other main road, passes over it into Akpakpa, eventually connecting up with Av Clozel.

Maps A good city map is the 1:15,000 *Cotonou* produced by the Institut Géographique National de Bénin, which lists the city's hotels, cinemas, banks and markets; it costs CFA3500 and is available from most bookshops.

Information

Tourist Offices The Direction du Tourisme et de l'Hôtellerie (☎ 32 68 24, fax 32 68 23, ⓔ tourisme@elodia.intnet.bj), inconveniently located 2.5km from the centre just off Place de l'Étoile Rouge, can provide a few brochures in French and English, but is of limited use.

Money Financial Bank, Bank of Africa and Ecobank are the best places to change cash and travellers cheques. Financial Bank also gives advances on Visa cards quickly and easily (but applies exorbitant fees). All are generally open 8am to 12.30pm and 3pm to 5pm Monday to Friday.

There's a thriving black market for the Nigerian naira and CFA around the Jonquet district. The rate for the CFA is essentially the same as the bank rate; the difference is you can get money any day and virtually at any hour.

Post & Communications Cotonou's main post office, just off Av Clozel, is open 7am to 7pm Monday to Friday and 8am to 11.30pm Saturday. The poste restante here is excellent.

You can make overseas telephone calls (and send faxes) from the telecom (OPT) building, on Av Clozel; it's open 7.30am to midnight Monday to Saturday and 9am to 1pm Sunday.

The most reliable and cheapest Internet café is Soriex Information (☎ 31 43 19, fax 31 27 72), opposite Librairie Nôtre-Dame, on Av Clozel; it's open 8am to 10pm Monday to Friday and 9am to 8pm Saturday (CFA500 per hour). Access is also available at Sogimex Internet café and at Satellite Business Centre, one block south of Église St Michel.

Travel Agencies Two of the best agencies are Agence Africaine de Tourisme (☎ 31 54 14, fax 31 54 99) and Top Tours & Safaris (☎/fax 31 10 87). Both offer a wide range of information and tours, including pirogue fishing and trips by boat from Cotonou to Ganvié. Another good company is Concorde Voyages & Tourism (☎ 31 34 13, fax 31 32 24).

Bookshops Librairie Nôtre-Dame (☎ 31 40 94), next to the cathedral, has an excellent selection of cultural and historical books on Benin (in French) as well as a good selection of postcards. It also sells maps of Cotonou (CFA3500) and road maps of Benin (CFA7000).

Cultural Centres Centre Culturel Français (☎ 30 08 56, fax 30 11 51, W www.refer.org/benin_ct/tur/ccf/cotonou.htm) is next to the French embassy on Route de l'Aéroport. Movies are often screened at the American Cultural Center (☎ 30 03 12), just off Blvd de la Marina.

Medical Services Polyclinique les Cocotiers (☎ 30 14 20) is a private and efficient clinic at the Carrefour de Cadjehoun, across from the PTT Cadjehoun.

The best-stocked pharmacy is Pharmacie Camp Ghezo (☎ 31 55 52), just around the corner from the US embassy. For a *pharmacie de garde* (all-night pharmacy), try Pharmacie Jonquet (☎ 31 20 80) on Rue des Cheminots in the Jonquet district.

Dangers & Annoyances Muggings are not uncommon on Cotonou's shoreline; the beachfront between Bénin Hôtel and Hôtel de la Plage is very bad, even during the day. Take care in the Jonquet and Ganhie business districts from late afternoon onwards.

Grand Marché du Dantokpa

A must-see in Cotonou is the huge Grand Marché du Dantokpa that borders the lagoon and Blvd St Michel. This lively market sells everything from food items, radios, wax cloth, baskets, religious paraphernalia and pottery to bat wings and monkey testicles. The wax cloth selection is impressive.

One of the more amusing things you may find here is a love fetish, *le fetiche d'amour*. Rub it into your hands, whisper a girl's or boy's name to it seven times, touch the person and he or she is yours. The price is determined in a ceremony where a fetisher, to the sound of chanting and gongs, hurls into the air a piece of rope with bits of animals hanging off it.

Beaches

The closest good beach is the one to the east of the city centre, behind Hôtel Accor Aledjo and extending east to Hôtel El Dorado (4km east of the centre). It gets crowded at weekends. The best beaches, however, are further west of Cotonou – at Ouidah (41km) and Grand Popo (80km).

Places to Stay – Budget

Pension le Souvenir *(☎ 39 11 05, 38 Rue des Cheminots)* Singles/doubles CFA5500/6500. Pension le Souvenir is the most acceptable of the real cheapies, but it is often full. Rooms with fan are austere but clean and the bathroom is shared.

Pension des Familles *(☎ 31 51 25, Av Proche)* Rooms CFA3500-6500. This faded pink pension has adequate rooms with fan.

Pension de l'Amitié *(☎ 31 42 01)* Rooms CFA4500-5000. Just around the corner from Pension des Familles, this place offers spartan but quiet, clean and airy rooms with fan and shared bathroom.

Hôtel Babo *(☎ 31 46 07, Rue Agbeto Amadoré)* Rooms CFA6000-10,000. This long-standing hotel, five blocks south of Église St Michel, gets mixed reviews, but is a good budget option. Request a room on the top level as they are more spacious and airy.

Hôtel Pacific *(☎ 33 01 45)* Singles/doubles with fan CFA7000/10,000, doubles with air-con CFA15,500. Hôtel Pacific is a decent alternative on the other side of the Pont Ancien, but some rooms are small and gloomy. If you walk across the bridge at night be alert, as robberies have occurred there.

Hôtel le Crillon *(☎ 31 51 58)* Rooms with fan CFA6500-7500. The Crillon, in the city centre, is not a bad choice. The bathrooms are amazingly clean and the service is friendly.

Hôtel Concorde *(☎ 31 13 45, fax 31 13 68, Av Steinmetz)* Rooms with fan/air-con from CFA6800/18,000. Not far from the Vickinfel, this place offers good clean rooms with bathrooms, but it is often booked out.

Places to Stay – Mid-Range

Hôtel de France *(☎ 32 19 49, Av du Roi Guezo)* Rooms without/with air-con CFA8000/10,000. The 25-room Hôtel de France is north of Blvd St Michel, which is a bit off the beaten path, but all the taxi drivers know it. It's well maintained and has spacious, clean rooms with fans and carpets.

Hôtel de l'Union *(☎ 31 27 49, Blvd St*

COTONOU

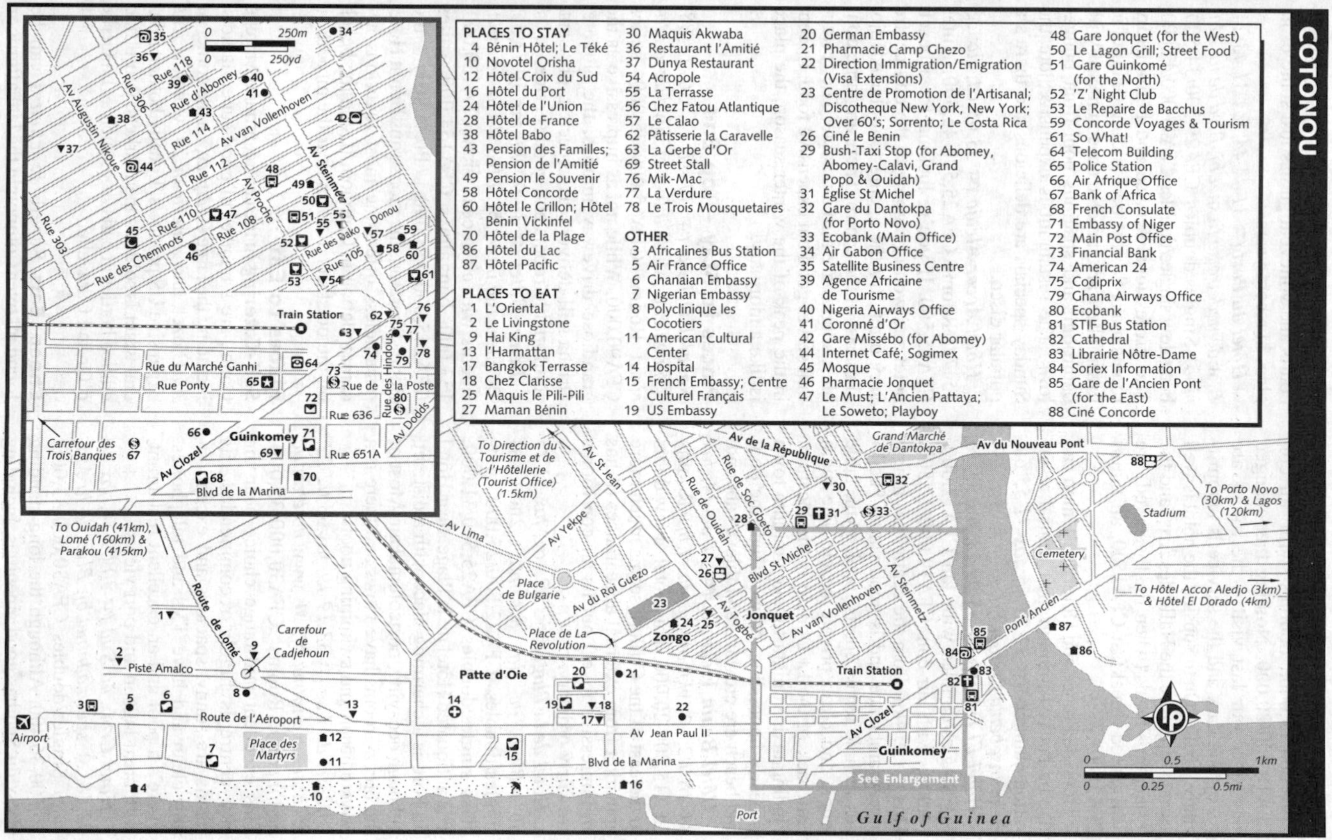

Train Station
Rue 118
Rue 306
Rue d'Abomey
Av Augustin Nikoue
Rue 114
Av van Vollenhoven
Av Steinmetz
Rue 112
Av Proche
Rue 110
Rue 108
Rue 303
Rue des Cheminots
Rue des Dako
Donou
Rue 105
Rue du Marché Ganhi
Rue Ponty
Rue de la Poste
Rue des Hindous
Rue 636
Av Dodds
Carrefour des Trois Banques
Guinkomey
Rue 651A
Av Clozel
Blvd de la Marina
0 250m
0 250yd
To Direction du Tourisme et de l'Hôtellerie (Tourist Office) (1.5km)
Av St Jean
Av de la République
Grand Marché de Dantokpa
Av du Nouveau Pont
To Porto Novo (30km) & Lagos (120km)
Stadium
Cemetery
To Hôtel Accor Aledjo (3km) & Hôtel El Dorado (4km)
To Ouidah (41km), Lomé (160km) & Parakou (415km)
Av Lima
Av Yekpe
Rue de Ouidah
Rue de Soc Gbeto
Blvd St Michel
Place de Bulgarie
Av du Roi Guezo
Av Togbé
Jonquet
Av van Vollenhoven
Av Steinmetz
Pont Ancien
Route de Lomé
Carrefour de Cadjehoun
Place de La Revolution
Zongo
Piste Amalco
Patte d'Oie
Train Station
Route de l'Aéroport
Airport
Av Jean Paul II
Av Clozel
Place des Martyrs
Blvd de la Marina
Guinkomey
See Enlargement
Port
Gulf of Guinea
0 0.5 1km
0 0.25 0.5mi

PLACES TO STAY
4 Bénin Hôtel; Le Téké
10 Novotel Orisha
12 Hôtel Croix du Sud
16 Hôtel du Port
24 Hôtel de l'Union
28 Hôtel de France
38 Hôtel Babo
43 Pension des Familles; Pension de l'Amitié
49 Pension le Souvenir
58 Hôtel Concorde
60 Hôtel le Crillon; Hôtel Benin Vickinfel
70 Hôtel de la Plage
86 Hôtel du Lac
87 Hôtel Pacific

PLACES TO EAT
1 L'Oriental
2 Le Livingstone
9 Hai King
13 l'Harmattan
17 Bangkok Terrasse
18 Chez Clarisse
25 Maquis le Pili-Pili
27 Maman Bénin
30 Maquis Akwaba
36 Restaurant l'Amitié
37 Dunya Restaurant
54 Acropole
55 La Terrasse
56 Chez Fatou Atlantique
57 Le Calao
62 Pâtisserie la Caravelle
63 La Gerbe d'Or
69 Street Stall
76 Mik-Mac
77 La Verdure
78 Le Trois Mousquetaires

OTHER
3 Africalines Bus Station
5 Air France Office
6 Ghanaian Embassy
7 Nigerian Embassy
8 Polyclinique les Cocotiers
11 American Cultural Center
14 Hospital
15 French Embassy; Centre Culturel Français
19 US Embassy
20 German Embassy
21 Pharmacie Camp Ghezo
22 Direction Immigration/Emigration (Visa Extensions)
23 Centre de Promotion de l'Artisanal; Discotheque New York, New York; Over 60's; Sorrento; Le Costa Rica
26 Ciné le Benin
29 Bush-Taxi Stop (for Abomey, Abomey-Calavi, Grand Popo & Ouidah)
31 Église St Michel
32 Gare du Dantokpa (for Porto Novo)
33 Ecobank (Main Office)
34 Air Gabon Office
35 Satellite Business Centre
39 Agence Africaine de Tourisme
40 Nigeria Airways Office
41 Coronné d'Or
42 Gare Missébo (for Abomey)
44 Internet Café; Sogimex
45 Mosque
46 Pharmacie Jonquet
47 Le Must; L'Ancien Pattaya; Le Soweto; Playboy
48 Gare Jonquet (for the West)
50 Le Lagon Grill; Street Food
51 Gare Guinkomé (for the North)
52 'Z' Night Club
53 Le Repaire de Bacchus
59 Concorde Voyages & Tourism
61 So What!
64 Telecom Building
65 Police Station
66 Air Afrique Office
67 Bank of Africa
68 French Consulate
71 Embassy of Niger
72 Main Post Office
73 Financial Bank
74 American 24
75 Codiprix
79 Ghana Airways Office
80 Ecobank
81 STIF Bus Station
82 Cathedral
83 Librairie Nôtre-Dame
84 Soriex Information
85 Gare de l'Ancien Pont (for the East)
88 Ciné Concorde

Michel) Singles without/with air-con CFA9000/15,000, doubles with air-con CFA18,000-20,000. Nothing has changed here since our last visit – the rooms are pokey and dark and the service is unremittingly woeful. On the upside the hotel is well located, opposite the Halle des Arts, and the restaurant's meals (when finally served) are well priced (breakfast CFA1500, all mains CFA2500).

Hôtel de France and Hôtel de l'Union can also be booked through their central reservation numbers *(☎ 31 27 66, fax 31 55 60, ⓔ hounseben@firstnet.bj)*.

Hôtel El Dorado *(☎ 33 09 23, fax 33 18 13)* Singles/doubles with fan CFA12,000/14,000, with air-con CFA19,000/22,500. This place, 4km from the centre, has a nice breezy ambience and is good value. Facilities include tennis courts, pool, gym, table tennis and clean private beach. The main drawback of the El Dorado is the location. Finding taxis at night to take you into town is nearly impossible. At weekends the pool and beach are crowded and thieves abound.

Hôtel Benin Vickinfel *(☎ 31 38 14, fax 31 18 02, ⓔ vkfhotel@intnet.bj)* Rooms CFA15,000-20,000. This hotel, a few doors to the east of the Crillon, seems much more upmarket from external appearances (it has an impressive foyer) but its air-con rooms are fairly ordinary.

Hôtel de la Plage *(☎ 31 25 61, fax 31 25 60, Blvd de la Marina)* 2nd-class singles/doubles CFA22,500/25,000, 1st-class singles/doubles CFA25,500/31,000. The antiquated Hôtel de la Plage, near Hôtel du Port, is a charming place with a distinct, although decaying, postcolonial air. Most of the breezy rooms have views and there is a private beach and swimming pool.

Hôtel du Lac *(☎ 33 19 19, fax 33 02 22, ⓔ hotelac@intnet.bj, ⓦ www.hoteldulacbenin.com)* Rooms CFA30,000-35,000. This excellent mid-range choice near the city centre is highly recommended. Its rooms are sunny, spacious and exceptionally clean and have TVs and telephones. There's a pool and an excellent restaurant, with great lagoon and port views.

Hôtel Croix du Sud *(☎ 30 09 54, fax 30 02 18, ⓔ sgeeh@intnet.bj, Blvd de la Marina)* Singles/doubles CFA30,000-33,000/35,500-36,400. Although the long-standing Croix du Sud has good amenities, including an Internet café, nightclub, pool, tennis courts and volleyball, it has lost some of its gloss in recent years.

Hôtel du Port *(☎ 31 44 44, fax 31 43 26, ⓔ w.demedeiros@firsnet.bj, Blvd de la Marina)* Singles/doubles CFA29,500/34,500, bungalow singles/doubles CFA37,000/42,000. The professional service and high-quality rooms make this the best mid-range hotel in town. There are carpeted air-con rooms with bathroom, and spacious pool-front bungalows. The restaurant is expensive, but the Sunday specials are delicious and there's a popular disco.

Hôtel Accor Aledjo *(☎ 33 05 61, fax 33 15 74)* Rooms CFA25,500-45,500, suites CFA85,500. If you're looking for a beach hotel and won't be going to the city centre very often, try the ageing four-star Aledjo, 3km east of the centre. There are large doubles; singles are also available. The restaurant serves good but expensive food. Except in the peak of the winter season, the place is like a mortuary.

Places to Stay – Top End

Novotel Orisha *(☎ 30 41 77, 30 41 88, ⓔ novatel.orisha@intnet.bj, Blvd de la Marina)* Rooms CFA65,000-75,000, suites CFA90,000. While not as impressive as the grandiose driveway implies, the Novotel Orisha still delivers, as expected, pleasant, comfortable rooms and good service.

Bénin Hôtel *(☎ 30 01 00, fax 30 11 55, ⓔ busness@intnet.bj, Blvd de la Marina)* Rooms with city/ocean view CFA120,000/133,000, bungalows CFA154,000, suites CFA245,000-355,000. Previously the Bénin-Sheraton, the monstrous Bénin Hôtel nonetheless offers the most luxurious accommodation in Cotonou. It's on the beach on the outskirts of town near the airport.

Places to Eat

Self-Catering In the centre, around Marché Ganhi, are a number of good supermarkets, including the large ***Codiprix***, on the corner of Av Clozel, and ***American 24***, which stocks expensive US products. Locally bottled mineral water is sold at supermarkets; you'll find chilled bottles at patisseries such as La Gerbe d'Or and Caravelle.

Cheap Eats Superb ***brochettes*** can be found all over Cotonou in the late afternoon and at night – just look for the smoking grills piled with meat on sticks. They sell for around CFA400 to CFA500. The ***stalls*** in front of Le Lagon Grill on Av Steinmetz, north of Hôtel Concorde, are perennial favourites.

There are also ***omelette men*** who set up shop around dusk and work throughout the night. They are everywhere, and you can usually spot their long tables with hot chocolate, coffee and tea containers spread across the top. You can get an entire breakfast here for around CFA400. The ***stall*** diagonally across from Hôtel de la Plage is consistently good.

Also good value are the ***sandwich ladies***, off Av Clozel, about 100m north of La Gerbe d'Or patisserie, who allow you to create your own sandwich with avocado, spaghetti, beef, eggs, pasta and loads more for around CFA400.

African About 100m southwest of Hôtel Babo, ***Restaurant l'Amitié*** serves up Senegalese food from CFA1000. Excellent fish and rice dishes dominate the menu. It's a great lunch-time place and ranks among Cotonou's best.

Chez Fatou Atlantique *(☎ 31 49 24, Av Steinmetz)* Meals from CFA1200. This place has been a popular hangout for years and serves tasty, reasonably priced Beninese and Nigerian dishes.

Maman Bénin *(☎ 32 33 38)* Meals from CFA1500. The long-standing Maman Bénin, behind Ciné le Bénin, has a large selection of West African dishes scooped from steaming pots. Upstairs is an air-con section serving similar meals for twice the price.

Dunya Restaurant *(☎ 31 23 75, Av Proche)* Meals around CFA3000. This place, one street south of Blvd St Michel, has a great setting and good food. Meals begin with a complimentary plate of crudites and the main meal includes a choice of rice, couscous or spaghetti.

Maquis le Pili-Pili *(☎ 31 50 48)* Meals CFA2500-4000. A couple of blocks behind Hôtel de l'Union, Pili-Pili, one of Cotonou's best places to sample Beninese dishes, is a slightly upmarket restaurant with a great ambience.

Maquis Akwaba *(☎ 32 18 51, Av Steinmetz)* Meals CFA2500-4000. This is another great African restaurant just off Blvd St Michel. Its impressive menu has dishes from all over the region, including Senegal, Nigeria, Cameroon and Côte d'Ivoire. You can also make special requests.

Asian Just off Carrefour de Cadjehoun, not far from the airport is ***Hai King*** *(☎ 30 60 08, Route de Lomé)*. Meals sell for around CFA3000. It's a friendly place with good food and snappy service and you can choose to sit downstairs in the air-conditioned restaurant or upstairs on the more-popular covered terrace.

Bangkok Terrasse *(Route de l'Aéroport)* Meals CFA2500-4500. The interior of this attractive eatery is charming but the portions are small.

European For relatively moderate prices, it's hard to beat the small but lively ***Le Calao*** *(☎ 31 24 66, Av Steinmetz)* in the heart of town. Meals cost CFA2000 to CFA3000 and it's popular with expats for its lengthy European menu and draught beer.

Chez Clarisse *(☎ 30 60 14)* Mains CFA1500-3500. This small French restaurant, not far from Bangkok Terrasse, rates highly with readers. If you are feeling ambitious try the *cuisses de grenouille sautées* (frog's legs) or the *brouchetted escargots* (snails) for CFA3500 each.

l'Harmattan *(☎ 30 08 91, Route de l'Aéroport)* Meals CFA2500-4000. This restaurant has been around for years and has a long-standing reputation among expats. It's not far from the statue at Place des Martyrs and is in a large straw hut.

La Terrasse *(☎ 31 52 08, Rue Guinkomey)* Mains around CFA4000. La Terrasse, in the city centre, is an upmarket restaurant with specialities such as Spanish rice dishes, couscous, *raclette*, which is similar to rice and couscous, and fondue.

Sorrento *(☎ 31 57 79, Blvd St Michel)* Mains CFA2500-4500. This is the only authentic Italian restaurant in Cotonou. It has decent pizza and other Italian and French dishes. It's within the Halle des Arts complex (at the back) on Blvd St Michel, and is open for lunch and dinner.

Le Costa Rica *(☎ 30 20 09, Blvd St Michel)* Meals CFA2400-4500. The recently relocated Le Costa Rica (it's now within the Centre de Promotion de l'Artisanal) is another favourite haunt of expats.

It is a good place for pizza, grilled steak and delectable seafood dishes and has great draught beer on tap.

Le Livingstone *(☎ 30 27 58, Piste Amalco)* Meals CFA2500-5500. Le Livingstone is a lively restaurant/bar close to the airport. Its menu includes pasta and pizza as well as meat and fish dishes.

La Verdure *(☎ 31 31 75)* Mains CFA3200-13,000. Tucked away just off Av Clozel is this great little seafood restaurant. From early afternoon onwards its bar is worked openly by local prostitutes; nonetheless the atmosphere is friendly and welcoming.

Le Trois Mousquetaires *(☎ 31 38 62)* Mains CFA6000-10,000. Near the cement works and just off Av Clozel is this superb, upmarket French restaurant with a menu that is both inventive and delicious. If you can afford one night of culinary pleasure this is the place to come.

Lebanese Directly across from Pâtisserie la Caravelle ***Mik-Mac*** *(☎ 31 39 79, Av Clozel)* has quick service and takeaways, though the portions are small. Meals cost around CFA1500.

L'Oriental *(☎ 30 18 27)* Buffet CFA5000. L'Oriental, at Quartier Haie Vive, has among the best and largest buffets in Cotonou; it's available on Wednesday and Sunday nights.

Cafés & Patisseries The most popular place for fresh bread, croissants and other pastries is ***La Gerbe d'Or*** *(☎ 31 42 58, Av Clozel)*. On the lower level you can buy bread, pastries, yogurt, milk and ice cream. On the second level is the restaurant/ice-cream parlour (closed Monday), which has a full menu plus sandwiches, hamburgers and chips.

Pâtisserie la Caravelle *(☎ 31 26 56, 2 Av Clozel)* Further along Av Clozel at the intersection of Av Steinmetz you will find this quaint coffee shop, which also has a terrace restaurant upstairs that overlooks the city centre.

Acrople *(☎ 31 01 33, Rue Goa)* Acrople is a good place for continental food, yummy pastries and burgers.

Entertainment

Bars If you can't find a place to drink in Cotonou you have lost either your sense of smell or your sight. There are *buvettes* (small bars) all over Cotonou. The liveliest bars in town are along the Jonquet strip; they fill up after dusk.

Le Calao *(☎ 31 24 66, Av Steinmetz)* This place has a popular bar with good beer on tap. It's very animated in the evenings. Nearby is the outdoor ***Le Lagon Grill***.

Other popular stalwarts are ***Le Costa Rica***, ***La Verdure*** and ***Le Livingstone*** (see Places to Eat).

Le Repaire de Bacchus *(☎ 95 22 55, Av Proche)* If your palate is craving something more refined, this upmarket wine bar is the place to come. Here you can sample excellent, but expensive, French wines (around CFA4500 per glass – a bottle is better value at around CFA15,000). If your budget won't stretch that far, stick to the local beers or come during 'happy hour' (6pm to 7pm daily).

Nightclubs There are a number of good nightclubs in Cotonou, regardless of the type of crowd and music you're in search of. The Jonquet strip is full of them, and they're wild and wicked.

The live and uncensored ***Le 2001*** is small, smoky and crowded, but it's good for dancing and has friendly owners. Other decadent places in the area are ***Le Must***, ***L'Ancien Pattaya***, ***Le Soweto*** and ***Playboy***. They are equally animated and all have good, upbeat music. Not far away back on Av Proche is the ***'Z' Night Club*** (open 24 hours), which is also a lot of fun.

In the Halle des Arts is the plush ***Discotheque New York, New York***, which is a haven for prostitutes with fetishes for mirrors. Close by is ***Over 60's***, which refers to the music played, not the age group of the clientele.

Le Téké at Benin Hôtel is a lot of fun on holidays and special occasions, when there's a crowd; otherwise it's usually pretty dead.

Music There are a number of places where you can go to hear a wide variety of live music.

Le Repaire de Bacchus (see Bars) runs a jazz club featuring local performers every Thursday starting at 9pm.

So What! *(☎ 01 14 64, Av Steinmetz)* Admission CFA3500. So What!, off the southern end of Av Steinmetz, is the most popular jazz club in town and has a variety of traditional Beninese musical performers and contemporary jazz artists.

Cinemas Good cinemas are ***Ciné le Bénin*** *(☎ 32 12 50)* near the Halle des Arts and ***Ciné Concorde*** *(☎ 33 39 72)* in Akpakpa, near the new bridge. Both show newish films from France and the USA (dubbed in French). Tickets are around CFA5000. You can also see films at the American and French cultural centres; they monthly pamphlets with upcoming programme details.

Shopping

If you're not looking for anything in particular and just want to browse, ***Centre de Promotion de l'Artisanal***, just west of the Halle des Arts on Blvd St Michel, is a good place to do this. The shops here offer a wide variety of woodcarvings, bronze sculptures, batiks, leather goods, jewellery and the famous Beninese applique banners.

Coronné d'Or *(☎ 31 58 64, Av Steinmetz)* Open 9am-1pm & 3pm-8pm Mon-Sat. This place, a block south of Nigeria Airways, has an impressive selection of bronzework, wall hangings, wood sculptures and jewellery.

Hôtel du Port Boutique *(☎ 31 44 44, Blvd de la Marina)* Open 10am-noon & 3pm-7pm daily. This nice boutique sells beautiful bathrobes, handbags, jewellery and other art and craft from Togo, Côte d'Ivoire and Congo (Zaïre).

For recordings of Beninese music, the best place is along the road just behind Marché Ganhi. Angélique Kidjo's recordings (including *Fifa*) cost about CFA2000. Other cassettes cost from CFA1000 to CFA1200.

Getting There & Away

Air The international airport is on the western fringe of town. For information on flights to/from Cotonou see the Getting There & Away section at the beginning of this chapter.

For flight information, ticket sales and reconfirmations, the following airlines have offices in Cotonou:

Air France (☎ 30 18 15) Route de l'Aéroport
Air Gabon (☎ 31 20 67) Av Steinmetz
Cameroon Airlines (☎ 31 52 17) Av Steinmetz
Ghana Airways (☎ 31 42 83) Av Steinmetz
Nigeria Airways (☎ 31 52 31) Av du Gouverneur Ballot

Bush Taxi, Minibus & Bus Cotonou has a rather confusing number of stations for minibuses, buses and bush taxis. It's best to catch a taxi or a zemidjan and ask the driver to take you to the right one.

Gare Jonquet on Rue des Cheminots, a couple of blocks west of Av Steinmetz, services western destinations such as Lomé (CFA3000, three hours) and Ouidah (CFA600, one hour). Gare Guinkomé has services to the northern centres including Parakou (CFA6500, eight hours). Gare de l'Ancien Pont, on the corner of Av Clozel and Rue des Libanais, services eastern destinations such as Lagos.

Bush taxis for Porto Novo (CFA500, 45 minutes) leave from Gare du Dantokpa at the new bridge; those to Abomey (CFA2000, two hours) leave from Gare Missébo, at the eastern end of Av van Vollenhoven. However, for Abomey, Abomey-Calavi (for Ganvié), Grand Popo and Ouidah it's far better to wait at the unofficial bush-taxi stop about 100m southwest of Église St Michel on Blvd St Michel.

Buses from the STIF station, just south of the cathedral, go regularly to Lomé (CFA3000, three hours) and Ouagadougou (CFA14,000, 30 hours).

Africalines (☎ 39 85 85, fax 30 85 89) on Route de l'Aéroport has daily bus services to Bohicon (CFA1500, three hours), Dassa (CFA3000, four hours), Savé (CFA3800, five hours), Parakou (CFA6500, seven hours), Natitingou (CFA8500, 10 hours), Kandi (CFA9400, around 10 hours) and Malanville (CFA11,000, around 12 hours).

Train The train station is in the heart of town one block north of Av Clozel and several blocks west of Av Steinmetz. See the main Getting Around section earlier in this chapter for more details of train services.

Getting Around

To/From the Airport A private taxi from the city centre to the airport costs around CFA2000, although drivers will demand double this amount *from* the airport. You can cut costs, if you don't have much to carry, by walking from the airport down Route de l'Aéroport to Place des Martyrs (20 minutes) and catching a shared taxi (CFA150 to CFA250) from there to the city centre.

Taxi A zemidjan will whiz you around town for CFA100 to CFA200 depending on the distance. Fares in regular taxis are CFA150 for a shared taxi (double that for fairly long trips) and CFA600 for a taxi to yourself. By the hour, taxis cost about CFA2000; rates double after 9pm.

AROUND COTONOU

Ganvié

The main attraction near Cotonou is Ganvié, where the 27,000 inhabitants live in bamboo huts on stilts several kilometres out on Lake Nokoué. Unfortunately, it has been so overrun by tourists that many children find it profitable to beg and will allow you to photograph them if you pay. You'll only be contributing to the problem if you agree.

However, Ganvié also provokes mixed feelings of fascination, pathos and respect. While it is possible to hire a pirogue to explore other less-visited villages on the lagoon, visiting Ganvié is still worthwhile, especially if you have a knowledgeable guide.

In the 18th century the Tofinu fled here from the warring Fon kingdoms in the north, where the land could no longer support the growing population. The swampy area around Lake Nokoué provided excellent protection against the Fon kingdoms because a religious custom banned their warriors from venturing into the water.

All the houses, restaurants, boutiques, hotels and even the post office in Ganvié are on wooden stilts about 2m above water level. The people live almost exclusively from fishing. As much breeders of fish as they are fishermen, the men plant branches on the muddy lagoon bottom. When the leaves begin to decompose, the fish congregate there to feed. After several days, the men return to catch the fish in a net. Most of the pirogues are operated by women, who do the selling of produce at market. Loaded with spices, fruits and fish, these pirogues are a colourful sight.

The best time to see Ganvié or other villages on the lagoon is early in the morning when it is still fairly cool. Unfortunately, the pirogue rental place doesn't open until 8am. Alternatively, try the late afternoon when the sun has lost its force.

Taking close-up photographs is nearly impossible because the people, especially the women, object to having their pictures taken. Please respect their wishes.

Places to Stay & Eat Regardless of where you stay in Ganvié, sleeping here can be expensive because you must pay twice for the pirogue (the second time to pick you up): about CFA3500 extra per person. However, you may be able to negotiate or hitch a pirogue ride with someone who is going to the morning market at the launching point in Abomey-Calavi.

Auberge Carrefour Ganvié Chez 'M' *(☎ 49 00 17)* Rooms CFA5000. This quaint bungalow-hotel has very nice rooms all with comfortable double beds, mosquito nets, decent bathrooms and flush toilets.

Chez Raphael *(☎ 49 01 75)* Rooms CFA5000. The striking bright pink Chez Raphael is hard to miss. The rooms here are more spacious, though the bathroom is shared.

Both hotels have ***restaurants*** that serve decent, well-priced meals.

Auberge du Lac *(☎ 36 03 44)* Rooms CFA6000. Alternatively there's this place in Abomey-Calavi less than 100m from the launching point. It has a small number of decent rooms. Be aware, though, that the rooms are also rented by the hour.

Getting There & Away From Cotonou catch a bush taxi to Abomey-Calavi (not to be confused with Abomey) on the western side of the lagoon (CFA300, 25 minutes). Taxis leave from the Gare du Dantokpa, or just hail one along Blvd St Michel. Most drivers will let you off right at the embarkation point, but if not, just walk down the hill (800m) to the pirogue moorings.

Africalines has a daily bus service that stops at Abomey-Calavi (CFA300). It departs Cotonou at 7am, but because of frequent stops it takes the better part of an hour to make this short trip.

At the official counter, you can get either a motorised boat or a pirogue across the lagoon to Ganvié. By motorised boat, the return journey takes about 1½ hours and will cost CFA7050 for one person (CFA5050 each for two to four people, CFA4050 each for five to nine people and CFA3050 each for 10 or more people). By pirogue, the cost is CFA6050 for one person (CFA5050 each for two to four people, CFA3050 for five to nine people and CFA2550 for 10 or more people) and the return trip takes 2½ hours. The pirogue is more serene, and you'll be able to talk to people passing by and hear the fishermen singing.

The South

PORTO NOVO

pop 225,400

Porto Novo, 30km to the east of Cotonou, looks more like an overgrown village than the official capital of Benin. But it is a far nicer place to stay than Cotonou.

Dating back to the 16th century, Porto Novo was named by the Portuguese after a town in Portugal to which they believed it bore a certain resemblance. The town has numerous buildings dating from early colonial times and has apparently seen better days. The Portuguese and wealthy Yoruba families once lived here and you can see a few of their homes, now dilapidated, in the old quarter to the east of the market.

Around 3km north of the city centre is Ouando, which has a fairly active market and some lively nightspots. Porto Novo is also a good place to look for pirogues to take you to some of the less-visited villages on Lake Nokoué.

In mid-January Porto Novo celebrates the city's Afro-Brazilian heritage with its own version of **Carnival**. This feast of food, music and dance is not to be missed. Contact Musée da Silva for more information.

Musée Éthnographique de Porto Novo

Opened in 1966, but revamped with funding from President Mitterrand (former president of France) after his visit in 1983, what was once a colonial-style structure housing orphans is now an interesting museum *(☎ 21 25 54; admission CFA1000; open 9am-noon & 3pm-6pm daily)*. Retracing the history of the Porto Novo kings, it has a grand collection of old Yoruba masks, some dating back to the 17th century. Other items on display are fetishes, carved drums and costumes. It's two of blocks northwest of Place Jean Bayal.

Palais Royal du Roi Toffa

Now officially called **Musée Honmé** *(☎ 21 35 66, fax 21 25 25, Rua Toffa; admission CFA1000; open 9am-6pm daily)*, but better known as the Palais Royal, this walled compound was the residence of King Toffa, who signed the first treaty with the French in 1883, conferring much territory to them. The kingdom of Porto Novo was one of the longest lasting in sub-Saharan Africa. It ended with the 25th king in 1976, when the five dynasties in Porto Novo had a disagreement and let the kingdom die.

Far from luxurious by Western standards, but nevertheless fascinating, the Palais Royal gives you a good idea of how African royalty lived. It was built in the late 17th century and has since been remodelled numerous times.

Musée da Silva

This new museum *(☎ 21 50 71, fax 21 26 99, ⓔ silvamus@leland.bj, Av Liotard; admission CFA1000; open 9am-6pm daily)* commemorates the Afro-Brazilian influence on the architecture, art and culture of Porto Novo. The museum's large complex consists of a traditional Afro-Brazilian house, dating to 1870, a small library, a hotel (see Places to Stay) and an open-air ***cinema*** *(admission CFA500; open Mon-Fri)* that screens French movies.

Mosque

Don't miss the unique mosque north of the market in the town centre. Originally a Brazilian-style church, built in the late 19th century, it has been converted into a mosque and painted in seemingly 20 different hues, making it perhaps the most colourful building in West Africa.

Grand Marché d'Adjara

This market, 10km north of Porto Novo on a back road to Nigeria, is held every fourth day, and is one of the most interesting in Benin. You'll find drums and other musical instruments, unique blue and white tie-dyed cloth, some of the best pottery in Benin, baskets and the usual fare. Pirogues are used to transport goods from nearby Nigeria.

Pirogue Rides

For a pirogue ride to some lagoon villages rarely visited by foreigners, the best place to inquire is next to the lagoon, about 50m east of the bridge. There's no fixed price as the pirogue men are rarely approached by foreigners. A trip in a pirogue to the nearest villages takes about four hours (one way). For a return trip the men ask around CFA20,000/30,000 for a pirogue/motorised boat, but you should be able to bargain.

Places to Stay

For a town as significant as Porto Novo there are surprisingly few accommodation options, but new places are always popping up.

Hôtel Malibu *(☎ 21 34 04, Blvd Lagunaire)* Rooms CFA3500-7000. Basically you are getting what you pay for here – gloomy rooms with grimy bathrooms. The attached restaurant serves inexpensive meals for around CFA1200.

Hôtel La Détente *(☎ 21 44 69, Blvd Lagunaire)* Rooms CFA5000. This is the best of the cheap options and the most central hotel. It has a large *paillote* (outdoor covered terrace) out the back – perfect for drinks, reading and viewing the lagoon – and a bar and restaurant. The rooms, while old fashioned, are clean with fans, shower and shared toilet.

For other budget accommodation check out the ***Catholic Mission*** on the road to Ouando, 1.5km from the centre, but note that your best 'Catholic' behaviour is expected at all times.

Musée da Silva *(☎ 21 50 71, fax 21 26 99, ⓔ silvamus@leland.bj, Av Liotard)* Rooms CFA12,500-18,500. The Musée da Silva has five large, airy rooms, each with private bathroom and air-con. Be sure to ask for a room on the inside of the complex as the outside ones overlook a busy street and can be quite noisy.

Hôtel Beaurivage *(☎ 21 23 99, Blvd Lagunaire)* Singles/doubles CFA15,500/18,500. The 19-room Beaurivage, overlooking the lagoon on the western end of town, has a lively ambience. The rooms, all with air-con, are comfortable and clean.

Hôtel Dona *(☎ 22 30 52, fax 21 25 25, Rue Catchi)* Singles/doubles/triples CFA16,500/18,500/21,500. The Dona, 1km north of the centre, is the most expensive hotel in town. It has pleasant air-con rooms.

Places to Eat

Comme Chez Soi *(Rue Obalédé)* Meals CFA350-500. For cheap African food, it's hard to beat this place, on the western side of Rond-Point Ataké.

Maquis Katchi Ambiance *(Rue Catchi)* Meals CFA350-500. This eatery is at the intersection of Route d'Ouando. If you are feeling adventurous try the local speciality, *agouti* (grasscutter – a large rodent).

Restaurant Mahi Meals CFA300-600. Locals swear by this restaurant, just south of Place Kokoyé; hearty meals include mutton, *njame* (yam) and sauce.

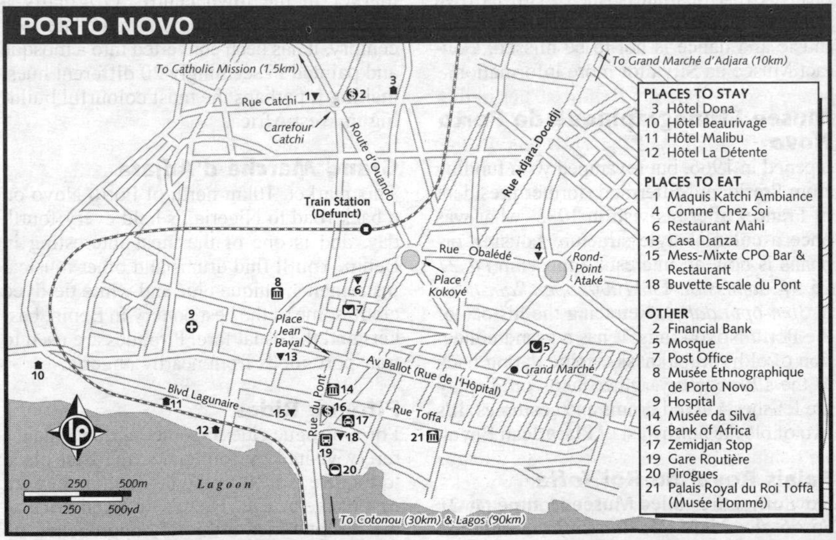
PORTO NOVO
To Catholic Mission (1.5km)
To Grand Marché d'Adjara (10km)
Rue Catchi
Carrefour Catchi
Route d'Ouando
Rue Adjara-Docadji
Train Station (Defunct)
Rue Obalédé
Place Kokoyé
Rond-Point Ataké
Place Jean Bayal
Av Ballot (Rue de l'Hôpital)
Grand Marché
Blvd Lagunaire
Rue du Pont
Rue Toffa
Lagoon
To Cotonou (30km) & Lagos (90km)
0 250 500m
0 250 500yd
PLACES TO STAY
3 Hôtel Dona
10 Hôtel Beaurivage
11 Hôtel Malibu
12 Hôtel La Détente
PLACES TO EAT
1 Maquis Katchi Ambiance
4 Comme Chez Soi
6 Restaurant Mahi
13 Casa Danza
15 Mess-Mixte CPO Bar & Restaurant
18 Buvette Escale du Pont
OTHER
2 Financial Bank
5 Mosque
7 Post Office
8 Musée Éthnographique de Porto Novo
9 Hospital
14 Musée da Silva
16 Bank of Africa
17 Zemidjan Stop
19 Gare Routière
20 Pirogues
21 Palais Royal du Roi Toffa (Musée Hommé)

Buvette Escale du Pont, adjacent to the *gare routière* (bus station), has cheap drinks and a good African menu, as does ***Mess-Mixte CPO Bar & Restaurant***, which is on Blvd Lagunaire.

Casa Danza *(☎ 21 33 70)* Mains CFA1100-3000. This tranquil eatery has a good choice of more-expensive Western-style food as well as some Beninese dishes. It's a block south of the Musée Éthnographique de Porto Novo on the same street.

Alternatives are the restaurants at hotels ***Dona*** and ***Beaurivage***, which are much more expensive.

Getting There & Away

Plenty of minibuses and bush taxis leave for Cotonou (CFA500, 45 minutes) from the gare routière, just north of the bridge. To Abomey from Porto Novo is CFA1900.

There are also frequent taxis from Porto Novo to Lagos in Nigeria (CFA2700).

Getting Around

If you are up to it (and experiences in Cotonou may well have scared you off) the best way to see Porto Novo is by zemidjan. A full town tour with the driver waiting should cost no more than CFA5000 for the day.

OUIDAH

pop 87,200

About 42km west of Cotonou is Ouidah, the voodoo centre of Benin and the second most popular tourist site in the country. (For more information about voodoo, see the boxed text 'Voodoo in Benin' earlier in this chapter). Until a wharf was built at Cotonou in 1908, Ouidah had the only port in the country. Its heyday was from 1800 to 1900, when slaves from Benin and eastern Togo were shipped from Ouidah to the USA, Brazil and Haiti, where the practice of voodoo remains strong. Good preliminary reading is Bruce Chatwin's excellent *The Viceroy of Ouidah* that tells part of the story of early Portuguese settlement – and creates a suitable mood for your visit.

A walk to the beach can be interesting and culturally enlightening; it's 4km south of town. You'll pass a big lagoon with people fishing and a small Ganvié-like village. There are voodoo ceremonies every weekend during the dry season and the annual Voodoo Festival is celebrated here in January (see the boxed text 'The Voodoo Festival' earlier in this chapter).

Musée d'Histoire d'Ouidah

This museum *(☎ 34 10 21; admission CFA1000; open 9am-noon & 3pm-6pm daily)*, two blocks east of the market, is part of an old Portuguese fort (Fortaleza São João Batista) built in 1721. The exhibits focus on the slave trade and the resulting links between Benin and Brazil and the Caribbean. There are also artefacts from voodoo culture and rooms presenting Benin's influences on its descendants in Haiti, Brazil and Cuba. You'll be shown skulls, ghost clothes, Portuguese gifts to the kings of Dahomey, old maps, engravings, photos showing the influence of Dahomeyan slaves on Brazilian culture, and traces of Brazilian architecture that the repatriated slaves brought back with them to Africa.

Route des Esclaves

The 4km Route des Esclaves, now the main road to the beach, starts near the Musée d'Histoire d'Ouidah. Lining its path are fascinating fetishes as well as monumental statues of old African symbols. This is the route that the slaves took to the coast to board the ships. Numerous historical and supernatural legends are associated with this road, giving it significance even today to the residents of Ouidah.

You'll pass through three villages en route to the beach. The third village was the actual holding point for slaves, as the fort was only for taking head counts. There is an interesting **memorial** here, known as 'The Point of No Return', in honour of those departed slaves. Walk through this grand arch, with its bas-relief depicting slaves in chains, to the water. Imagine the slaves climbing into lighters to go out to the 'slavers', turning to hear the waves crashing on the beach and then descending into dark holds on their way to the Americas.

If you don't want to walk, you can always find a zemidjan for about CFA1000.

Casa do Brazil

In 1992 the Casa do Brazil (sometimes referred to as La Maison de Brazil) was turned into a museum *(admission CFA1000; open 7am-7pm daily)*. It displays works depicting voodoo culture and the black diaspora, and has a good collection of black-and-white pictures of voodoo rituals – don't miss it. The house itself is the former residence of the Brazilian governor and was later occupied by a Portuguese family until they were ousted in the early 1960s.

The entrance fee includes a guide. Casa do Brazil is a 15-minute walk from the centre, near the civil prison. Plenty of zemidjans pass by.

Temple des Serpents

Snakes are especially important in Ouidah because traditionally they were fetishes and the principal object of worship. This explains why there's a sacred python temple *(admission CFA1000)* here. It's in the centre of town, half a block from the cathedral, but has become something of a tourist trap and appears less sacred because of this. The tour cost includes an explanation of the temple and some of the voodoo traditions. Don't expect much. Inside the temple the guide will lead you into a room, lift up some boards, and *voila* – harmless, sleeping snakes.

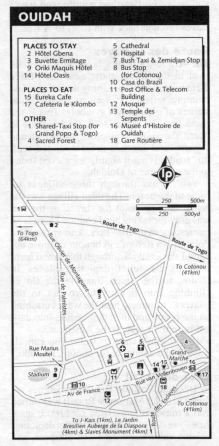

OUIDAH
PLACES TO STAY
2 Hôtel Gbena
3 Buvette Ermitage
9 Oriki Maquis Hôtel
14 Hôtel Oasis
PLACES TO EAT
15 Eureka Cafe
17 Cafeteria le Kilombo
OTHER
1 Shared-Taxi Stop (for Grand Popo & Togo)
4 Sacred Forest
5 Cathedral
6 Hospital
7 Bush Taxi & Zemidjan Stop
8 Bus Stop (for Cotonou)
10 Casa do Brazil
11 Post Office & Telecom Building
12 Mosque
13 Temple des Serpents
16 Museé d'Histoire de Ouidah
18 Gare Routière
0 250 500m
0 250 500yd
Route de Togo
Route de Togo
To Togo (64km)
To Cotonou (41km)
Rue Olivier de Montaguere
Rue de Palmistes
Rue Marius Moutel
Stadium
Grand Marché
Rue van Vollenhoven
Av de France
Route des Esclaves
To Cotonou (41km)
To J-Kais (1km), Le Jardin Bresilien Auberge de la Diaspora (4km) & Slaves Monument (4km)

Sacred Forest

This park consists of a small array of African deities representing fascinating legends and myths in the form of sculptures and woodcarvings. The deities are placed on the spiritual site where King Kpassé, founder of Ouidah, turned into a tree to hide from his adversaries. The tree, a rare and huge *iroki* tree, is alive today. Be sure to bow before Legba (the trickster in the voodoo pantheon and the 'guardian of the house') when you enter the park. The caretaker/guide will expect a tip for his informative tour.

Places to Stay & Eat

Buvette Ermitage *(☎ 34 13 89)* Rooms CFA4000. Buvette Ermitage, a block east of Rue Olivier, is the cheapest place in town. It has a very African feel and a pleasant terrace bar, but its rooms – which have fans and shared bathroom – are gloomy and noisy.

Oriki Maquis Hôtel *(☎ 34 10 04, Rue Marius Moutel)* Rooms CFA6000. A better possibility is the quiet, friendly Oriki, about 1km south of the crossroads on Route de Togo. The comfortable rooms have fans and are very good value. There is also a good ***restaurant/bar*** attached.

Le Jardin Bresilien Auberge de la Diaspora *(☎ 34 11 10, Route des Esclaves)* Singles/doubles CFA5500-6500/7000-8500. On the beach near the 'Point of No Return' memorial, this tranquil place is an excellent choice. There are three categories of rooms all simply furnished, with private bathrooms and fans. Its pleasant ***restaurant*** serves breakfast from CFA1200 and main meals from CFA3000.

There are two upmarket hotels in Ouidah.

Hôtel Oasis *(☎/fax 34 10 91, Rue van Vollenhoven)* Rooms CFA11,000-19,000. The Oasis is good value for money. It's in the heart of town not far from the fort. It has spacious, clean rooms with air-con and small but decent bathrooms. The attached ***restaurant*** serves a good range of meals from around CFA1500.

JANE SWEENEY

ARIADNE VAN ZANDBERGEN

DAN HERRICK

ARIADNE VAN ZANDBERGEN

ERIC L WHEATER

ERIC L WHEATER

West Africa's people and the richness of their cultural traditions are a highlight of any visit to the region; travellers will encounter an astounding diversity of customs and language. There are several hundred different tribal groups; Cameroon alone has about 280 ethnic groups among its 15 million inhabitants.

DAVID WALL

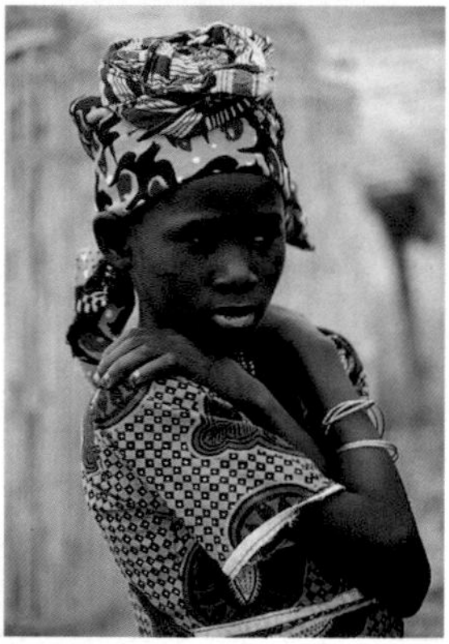

DAVID WALL

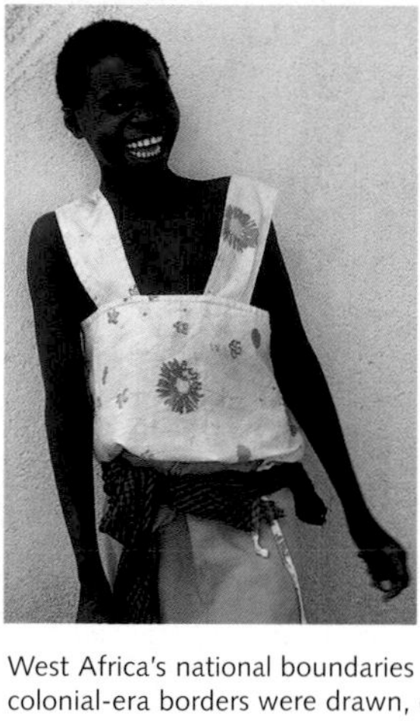

ERIC L WHEATER

KIM WILDMAN

West Africa's national boundaries were imposed on the region within the last two centuries; when colonial-era borders were drawn, cultural and tribal diversity was completely ignored. As a result, most West African countries today incorporate many groups, all with vastly different languages, religions and cultures. In many cases, national borders divide ethnic groups.

Hôtel Gbena *(☎ 34 12 15, Route de Togo)* Rooms CFA16,000. This is the other top-end place. It's on the bypass road 2km north of the town centre. Even though the gloomy rooms are clean, with air-con and bathrooms, at these rates they're expensive. The ***restaurant*** serves Western-style food; the menu du jour costs CFA3000.

The best places to eat are ***Hôtel Oasis*** and ***Oriki Maquis Hôtel***. Another good option is ***J-Kais*** *(☎ 34 12 78, Route des Esclaves)* where meals cost CFA3000 to CFA3500. This lively place specialises in pizza but also serves a good and filling menu du jour for CFA5000. Otherwise try the open-air ***Cafeteria de Kilombo***, across from the Musée d'Histoire d'Ouidah, or the amiable ***Eureka Cafe***, on Rue van Vollenhoven; meals cost from CFA400 at both.

Entertainment

The terrace bar at ***Buvette Ermitage*** is definitely the place to go for a drink at night.

The bar-dancing joint ***J-Kais*** *(Route des Esclaves)* on the beach road is a popular place for a drink. On Friday and Saturday evenings it also runs a popular disco (CFA1000).

Getting There & Away

The gare routière is permanently empty, so bush taxis – and occasional buses – to Cotonou leave from the area south of the hospital (CFA600, one hour). For Grand Popo and Togo, wait along the main road north of town.

GRAND POPO

About 80km west of Cotonou and 20km east of the Togo border, Grand Popo is one of the best getaway spots in Benin for travellers to spend a few idle days on the sand. It's set on a reasonably nice beach, although swimming is restricted because of strong currents. Travelling here via the coastal highway from either Cotonou or Lomé, you may see white flags flying from poles in small villages along the way; they identify voodoo practitioners.

On the main road you'll find **Villa Karo** *(☎ 43 03 58, ⓔ karo@internet.bj, ⓦ www.villa-karo.org)*, a Finnish-African cultural centre which runs a small **museum** *(admission by donation; open 11am-1pm Mon, Wed & Fri)*. There's also a **library** (books in French, Finnish and English) and on Friday evenings the centre operates a free open-air **cinema**.

Places to Stay & Eat

L'Auberge de Grand Popo *(☎ 43 00 47, fax 43 04 61, central reservations ☎/fax 31 38 62, ⓔ voyageur@intnet.bj)* Camping CFA1500 per person, tent hire CFA5000, singles/doubles with garden view CFA10,500/13,000, singles/doubles with ocean view CFA17,000/19,500, single/double bungalows CFA19,000/23,000. The long-standing and highly recommended L'Auberge de Grand Popo is right on the beach. It has rooms in a restored colonial building and in quaint garden bungalows. The menu in its pleasant terrace ***restaurant*** is quite impressive, but the meals are not cheap (CFA3800 to CFA4000).

Awalé Plage *(☎/fax 43 01 17, ⓔ awaleplage@yahoo.com)* Camping CFA1500 per person, tent hire CFA3000, single/double bungalows CFA12,000/16,000. This lively place, on the main highway just before the Grand Popo turn-off, has been given the thumbs up by LP readers. There is an excellent beach bar, the ***restaurant*** is good (meals from CFA3000 and breakfast from CFA1500), and you can hire boogie boards for CFA1000 all day. Each month the hotel hosts a full moon beach party with entertainment provided by local musicians.

Farafina, a friendly restaurant-bar near Villa Karo, serves good meals from around CFA2500. Even better are the informal ***seafood meals*** that the locals cook if you make arrangements beforehand.

Getting There & Away

From Cotonou, take a bush taxi from Autogare Jonquet (CFA1300, two hours) and have it drop you off at the Grand Popo junction on the main coastal highway, 20km east of the Togo border. The beach and hotel are 3.5km off the main road and are easily accessible via zemidjan (CFA200).

LAKE AHÉMÉ & AROUND

If you're looking for a place that's off the beaten track, head for the northern shores of Lake Ahémé, 40km southeast of Lokossa. There are fishing villages all around the lake, the main ones being Possotomé and Bopa, and the setting is very pleasant.

Possotomé, which is connected by road to Lokossa, is famous for its thermal springs, the country's primary source of mineral water. Here you can visit the factory that has been set up near the source for bottling the water. From the village you can rent a pirogue for a trip to the nearby fishing villages, including **Bopa**, a fascinating village on the western side of the lake. Voodoo practitioners here are possibly the most avid in Benin. Ask around to see if you can meet a local fetisher.

Lokossa, midway between Grand Popo and Abomey, is a convenient spot to find taxis east to Possotomé and Bopa and north to Abomey. If you stop here, check out the lively **market** (it operates every five days).

Places to Stay & Eat

Village Club Ahémé *(☎/fax 43 00 29, ⓔ village.aheme@intnet.bj)* Rooms CFA15,500-18,900, bungalows CFA22,500-35,400. This 20-room hotel on the water's edge near the thermal springs at Possotomé has seen better days. The ***restaurant*** is surprisingly good, but meals are expensive (breakfast costs CFA2400 and full meals cost CFA5000 to CFA6000). It is also possible to organise a boat ride over the lake from here for CFA2950.

Getting There & Away

From the coastal highway take the turn-off north to Lokossa. About 20km south of Lokossa you'll come to the Marché de Comé intersection. Take the dirt road heading east just after the co-op store for 17km to the lake and Possotomé. The fork to the left heads towards the hotel and Bopa. The former is about 500m down that road, on your right. If you want a bush taxi to either village, have look around the Marché de Comé intersection.

ABOMEY

pop 114,600

If you have time to visit only one town outside Cotonou, Abomey, 144km northwest of Cotonou, would be a good choice. Abomey is in Fon country and was the capital of the great kingdom of Dahomey. The main attractions are the restored royal palace and the excellent museum inside, which covers the history of the kingdom. The town itself is large and scruffy, but nonetheless exudes charm. Throughout Abomey you'll find traces of its glorious past.

Orientation & Information

There are few main roads in Abomey – dirt streets radiate from the central market passing *banco* (mud brick) houses and historic palaces. Use the water tower as a point of reference. Only the museum has information on the town's history; the rest is easy to discover yourself. Aux Délices de France, on the western side of the market, is the place to change money.

Musée Historique d'Abomey

Before the arrival of the French, Abomey's royal palace was one of the most impressive structures in West Africa. The first palace was constructed in 1645 by the third king of Dahomey. Each successive king built his own palace, so by the 19th century the palace compound was enormous, with a 4km perimeter and a 10m-high wall enclosing an area of 44 hectares and a court of 10,000 people.

The inner complex consists of a maze of courtyards, ceremonial rooms, burial chambers and a harem accommodating some 800 women. Following the defeat by the French in the late 19th century, Béhanzin, the 10th king, burned the palace as he fled advancing French forces.

Musée Historique d'Abomey *(☎ 50 03 14, ⓦ www.epa-prema.net/abomey/; admission CFA1500; open 8.30am-6pm Tues-Sun & 8.30am-5pm Sat & Mon)*, which dates from 1818, consists only of the places of Ghézo and Glélé, which survived the fire.

On the exterior of the palace are the **bas-reliefs** that depict the history of the Dahomey kingdom. Although many of the reliefs were destroyed in the fire, some have been saved and restored. These reliefs were a major factor in Unesco's decision to classify the palace as a world historic site.

Inside the museum a guide will show you rooms containing some 1050 relics of the kings including voodoo artefacts, skulls and Portuguese items (ranging from pistols to sets of china). Central to the collection are the elaborately carved **thrones** of the Dahomey kings. Ghézo's throne is particularly large and is mounted on four skulls (real) of vanquished enemies.

Also on display are the magnificent **applique banners** of the royal family. These wall hangings depict some of the country's bloody history, particularly the battles. One of them shows a scene of Glélé using a dismembered leg to pound his enemy's head.

The admission fee includes a guide (who expects a tip as well). The museum tour takes about an hour, at the end of which your guide takes you to the **Centre des Artisans** next door, where you'll see applique banners being made.

Places to Stay

Hôtel la Lutta *(☎ 04 61 77)* Doubles CFA4500. This cheap crumbling hotel is lost among a maze of sandy streets 300m southwest of the market – take a zemidjan. Mr 'La Lutta' (Adjolohoun Jean-Constant) is a never-ending source of information on Abomey and the Dahomey kingdoms (though he speaks little English) – the 'trail' described in this section is his suggestion. The food here is delicious; the *plat du jour* (meal of the day) costs CFA2800.

Chez Monique *(☎ 50 01 68)* Camping CFA2000 per person, doubles without/with shower CFA5000/7000. This pleasant place is about 500m northwest of the northern roundabout along the road to Cotonou. The breezy garden restaurant has a delightful tropical ambience. The rooms have insect screens and fans and the shared bathrooms are clean. The meals are very good but not cheap; the menu du jour costs CFA3500.

The Dahomey Trail

Most visitors to Abomey go to the museum and then move on – and learn little about the incredible civilisation that once flourished there. Abomey was once one of the most important sites in West Africa, as important as Kano and Benin City in Nigeria and the Dogon country in Mali. There are many other sights nearby. Negotiate a price for a zemidjan for half a day (about CFA2500 per person) and then ask the driver to follow this trail – inquire at Hôtel la Lutta for drivers who are familiar with the stops and places where you can take photographs. This trail is one of many variations offered by the drivers. It leads to unrestored palaces, fetish temples and other Dahomeyan relics in the countryside.

First stop is **Temple Zéwa**, a voodoo temple where two women were covered in oil and left to be eaten by red ants. Zéwa was the last to die. Each voodoo temple is dedicated to a different divinity (death, smallpox etc), and the practice of voodoo is still very active here.

Palais Ghézo is now a crumbling ruin with little left of the once impressive mud ramparts. Better restored is **Palais Agonglo**, which now houses a weaving centre; you can get access to the main courtyard with its bas-reliefs after paying a tip to the site supervisor. Restoration is still going on here.

Temple Sémassou is dedicated to the wife of Dahomey King Aglongo and gynaecological deformations. Sémassou is said to have given birth to a fetish instead of a child; the fetish was buried here and the temple built above it. Nearby is a large white fetish sans penis. It is believed that a female tourist broke off the oversized erect penis and kept it as a souvenir. Previously local women would straddle it to ensure their future productivity.

The next palace is the largest, **Palais Glélé**. Little is left, but the remaining mud walls show you how grand this palace once was. Head to **Palais Béhanzin** at Djimé – entry costs about CFA1000. The caretakers in the village will escort you around. Afterwards, go to the **Béhanzin statue**. It is said that he stands here without a roof over his head as punishment for allowing the defeat of the kingdom of Dahomey by the French.

The next stop is an absolute gem. The village of **Dozoéme** exists as it has for centuries, with its *forgerons* (blacksmiths) fashioning implements in their crude forges as they once did exclusively for the Dahomey kings. They now produce farm implements and kitchenware. They are amusing to talk to and they laugh at a foreigner's interest in their trade. They expect payment for photos (CFA500).

Head to **Palais Akaba**, once the most important of the palaces. Little is left of the ramparts, but the sheer size is overwhelming. The name Dahomey originated here: Two brothers, Dan and Akaba, fought for the right to succession. Dan was killed and the name 'Dahomey' comes from combining Dan and *homey* (in his belly).

Before returning to the museum to tie all the threads together, stop off at Agbodo to see the remains of the **moat** that once surrounded Abomey. It has largely filled in with debris over time but was once 60m deep and 15m wide and stretched for many kilometres around the town.

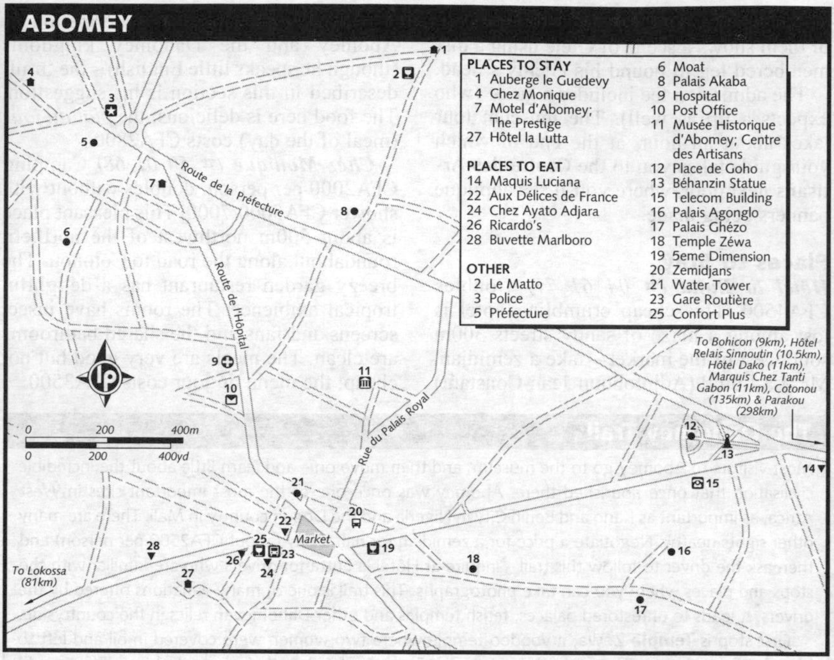
ABOMEY
PLACES TO STAY
1 Auberge le Guedevy
4 Chez Monique
7 Motel d'Abomey; The Prestige
27 Hôtel la Lutta
PLACES TO EAT
14 Maquis Luciana
22 Aux Délices de France
24 Chez Ayato Adjara
26 Ricardo's
28 Buvette Marlboro
OTHER
2 Le Matto
3 Police
5 Préfecture
6 Moat
8 Palais Akaba
9 Hospital
10 Post Office
11 Musée Historique d'Abomey; Centre des Artisans
12 Place de Goho
13 Béhanzin Statue
15 Telecom Building
16 Palais Agonglo
17 Palais Ghézo
18 Temple Zéwa
19 5eme Dimension
20 Zemidjans
21 Water Tower
23 Gare Routière
25 Confort Plus
Route de la Préfecture
Route de l'Hôpital
Rue du Palais Royal
Market
To Bohicon (9km), Hôtel Relais Sinnoutin (10.5km), Hôtel Dako (11km), Marquis Chez Tanti Gabon (11km), Cotonou (135km) & Parakou (298km)
To Lokossa (81km)
0 200 400m
0 200 400yd

Auberge le Guedevy *(☎ 50 03 04, fax 50 08 42)* Singles with fan CFA6500, singles/doubles with air-con CFA8500/10,500, bungalows with air-con CFA15,500-20,500. This place, about 2km north of the town centre, is a modern two-storey hotel that has a good restaurant with a European and African menu and a wide selection of cold drinks.

Motel d'Abomey *(☎ 50 00 75, fax 50 00 93, Rue de l'Hôpital)* Singles/doubles CFA10,000/12,000, bungalows CFA18,000-20,000. Near the northern roundabout this is the largest and best hotel in Abomey. Rooms are comfortable, with carpet and air-con. It also has 'African-style' bungalows with TVs and spacious bathrooms. Its classy restaurant serves expensive European food.

Some travellers prefer to stay in Bohicon, 9km to the east.

Hôtel Relais Sinnoutin *(☎ 51 10 88)* Rooms with fan/air-con CFA4500/8000. The best-value choice is the Relais Sinnoutin, 1.5km south of Bohicon on the Cotonou to Parakou highway. It's pleasant and well managed, and the restaurant serves Western-style and African food (mains CFA1800 to CFA1800). Rooms are spotless.

Hôtel Dako *(☎ 51 01 38, fax 51 02 38)* Standard rooms CFA12,000, large rooms CFA16,000-25,000. The rooms at the Dako, 500m south of the Relais Sinnoutin, have air-con but are cramped and overpriced for the quality. The larger rooms with balconies are more comfortable. There is also a pool (CFA1500 for nonguests). The expensive restaurant serves bland European dishes.

Places to Eat

Marquis Chez Tanti Gabon Meals CFA800-1500. This place, just across the street from Hôtel Dako in Bohicon, serves wonderful filling meals of African sauces with couscous, rice and pounded yam for lunch (before 2.30pm) and in the evening.

In Abomey, look around the market area for cheap street food. At the stall called ***Chez Ayato Adjara*** you can get a delicious meal for CFA400 to CFA1000. The speciality here is the delicious *pâte de maïs* (made from mashed maize) with either meat and cheese sauce or *gombo* (okra) sauce. Other good budget choices include ***Ricardo's***, which is also one of the better bars, and ***Buvette Marlboro***, which serves inexpensive lunches for around CFA600; both are on the road to Lokossa.

Maquis Luciana *(☎ 50 19 94)* Meals CFA1200-2000. The tranquil Maquis Luciana is an excellent little restaurant-cum-bar 100m off the main road to Bohicon. A large plate of fish or chicken with rice or couscous costs around CFA2000.

If you're self-catering, ***Aux Délices de France*** stocks lots of French goodies.

Entertainment

The Prestige *(Rue de l'Hôpital)* In Abomey, try the Prestige at Motel d'Abomey – it's one of the fanciest places in town.

5eme Dimension Admission CFA2500. A more animated crowd will be found at this air-conditioned place, not far east of the market. Entry includes a drink, and from then on drinks are CFA1000.

Good watering holes include ***Confort Plus***, across from the gare routière, and ***Le Matto***, opposite Chez Monique.

Getting There & Away

Plenty of bush taxis depart from Cotonou (CFA2000, three hours), sometimes with a connection at Bohicon (9km east of Abomey).

Bush taxis and zemidjans go between Abomey and Bohicon (around CFA200) during the day and in the early evening. Vehicles continuing to Parakou leave frequently from the gare routière in Abomey and stop off in Bohicon. In Bohicon, to hail a taxi headed north towards Parakou, just stand along the main road and wave.

Africalines' daily service departs Cotonou at 7am for Bohicon (CFA1500, three hours), from where you can catch a taxi to Abomey.

Alternatively, you could take the train. From Cotonou, the train takes 2½ hours to get to Bohicon. The Cotonou to Parakou morning train, stopping at Bohicon, leaves in either direction at 8am. The evening train from Cotonou leaves at 7pm on Tuesday, Thursday and Saturday; from Parakou it leaves at 6pm on Wednesday, Friday and Sunday. The fare from Cotonou to Bohicon is CFA1400/1100 for 1st/2nd class.

DASSA ZOUMÉ

pop 21,900

Dassa Zoumé, 200km north of Cotonou on the main north-south highway, is situated roughly halfway between Cotonou and Parakou. What makes the 'city of 41 hills' so interesting are the awesome rock formations around which the houses have been built. Dassa is also renowned for its annual pilgrimage (La Grotte) for Catholics throughout West Africa. They come to pay homage to the Virgin Mary, who is said to have appeared here once. These days it has evolved into more of a social than a religious gathering.

For cheap lodging, ask around the gare routière.

Auberge de Dassa *(☎/fax 53 00 98, central reservations ☎/fax 31 38 62, ⓔ voyageur@intnet.bj)* Camping CFA1500 per person, singles/doubles with fan CFA10,000/11,500, with air-con CFA14,000/16,500. This is the most expensive and nicest place in town. It is opposite the *rond-point* (roundabout) on the major highway and has an excellent ***restaurant*** that serves great steaks and desserts.

For details of how to get to Dassa Zoumé, see the Savé Getting There & Away section following.

SAVÉ

pop 35,200

Savé, 160km south of Parakou, is the home of many Yoruba people who migrated from Nigeria. If you enjoy rock climbing, stop here as there are accessible rock formations. Many of these rocks have a great deal of history behind them and are considered sacred, hence their name La Montagne Sacrée. Centuries ago, to counter attacks from their enemies from the south, the inhabitants would flee to the rocks and strategically placed boulders, then roll them down the hills as the enemy approached. There are also areas in these hills where village elders would go to pray to the deities.

The town's nicest hotel is ***Les Trois Mammelles***, with large spacious rooms with comfortable beds, and balconies overlooking the hills and much of Savé. The CFA6500 price is entirely negotiable. There's a popular open-air ***bar*** where you can enjoy the view of Savé over a cold beer.

Getting There & Away

Bush taxis from Cotonou to Dassa (CFA3000, four hours) and Savé (CFA3500, five hours) depart from under the new bridge next to the Grand Marché du Dantokpa.

Africalines runs a daily service from Cotonou departing at 7am that stops at both Dassa (CFA3000) and Savé (CFA3800).

You can also get to Dassa and Savé by train. The day train from Cotonou arrives at Bohicon between 10.30am and noon. It arrives at Dassa approximately one hour later (CFA2900/2500 for 1st/2nd class), and at Savé roughly two hours later (CFA2700/3700).

The North

PARAKOU

pop 198,000

Parakou, once a major slave-market town, is a bustling metropolis at the northern end of the train line. While there's not much to see, it is a convenient place to stop for the night if you're heading on to the wildlife parks or further north.

The centre of town is the area around the cinema at the intersection of Route de l'Aéroport, Rue des Cheminots and Route de Transa. There are three banks here; the Grand Marché is three blocks away to the southeast.

Places to Stay

Hôtel les Canaries *(☎ 61 11 69, Route de l'Hôtel Canaries)* Singles/doubles with fan & shared bathroom CFA4500/5000, with private bathroom CFA5500/7000, with air-con CFA8500/10,500. This long-standing hotel, about 400m east of the train station, has two courtyards with rooms opening onto them. The restaurant serves reasonably inexpensive meals (a large plate of spaghetti costs CFA1500), but it closes fairly early.

Auberge de Parakou *(☎ 61 03 05, central reservations ☎/fax 31 38 62, e voyageur@intnet.bj, Route de l'Hôtel Canaries)* Singles/doubles with fan CFA10,000/12,500, with air-con CFA14,000/16,500. This delightful auberge has large, spotlessly clean rooms with good-sized bathrooms complete with a bathtub. Its excellent French restaurant serves delicious meals.

Hôtel OCBN *(☎ 61 10 06)* Singles/doubles/triples CFA9500/16,000/22,500. The declining OCBN, in a quiet area just east of the train station and surrounded by trees and shrubs, has uninspiring but clean rooms with air-con; breakfast is CFA1500.

Hôtel la Princess *(☎ 61 01 32, fax 61 04 16)* Small rooms CFA11,900-17,900, deluxe rooms CFA17,900-21,900, single/double bungalows CFA25,000/27,000. This is the liveliest hotel in town and has a wide range of rooms. The deluxe rooms are spacious, carpeted bungalows with telephones and satellite TV. Opposite is a popular nightclub.

Hôtel Central *(☎ 61 01 24, fax 61 38 51)* Rooms CFA16,000-25,000. The Central is a charming old relic with a pleasant pool. The air-con rooms are quite cosy. The restaurant serves both European and African meals, and the menu du jour costs CFA5000.

Hôtel les Routiers *(☎ 61 04 01, fax 61 22 68, Route de Transa)* Singles/doubles from CFA22,000/25,000, suite CFA40,000. This establishment, 500m north of the heart of town, has long been the most popular top-end hotel in Parakou. You can't help but relax in the garden setting with its clean pool. There's also an excellent tennis court and a good, but expensive, French restaurant (the plat du jour is CFA7000 and large beers are CFA1000).

Places to Eat

An excellent place for ***street food*** is at the intersection about 200m northeast of Hôtel les Canaries, along the road running in front of the hotel.

Chez Mamou *(Route de Transa)* is a small buvette serving good cheap street food such as rice, couscous, salad and chicken. It's north of the town centre opposite ***Le Miel*** bakery. The bakery is a good place for vegetarian sandwiches, ham and cheese sandwiches, ice cream and, in the mornings, croissants and coffee.

La Face Douane Meals from CFA500. For inexpensive African food, head for this unmarked place, next to Hôtel OCBN. It is extremely popular at seemingly all hours of the day and serves pâté with sauce (CFA500).

Les Palmiers Meals from CFA1500. Many locals speak highly of this eatery at the back of Hôtel les Canaries, but the meals and service gets mixed reviews from readers.

Les Marmites du Roi *(☎ 61 08 78)* Meals CFA2500-3500. Les Marmites du Roi, one street south of Route de l'Hôtel Canaries,

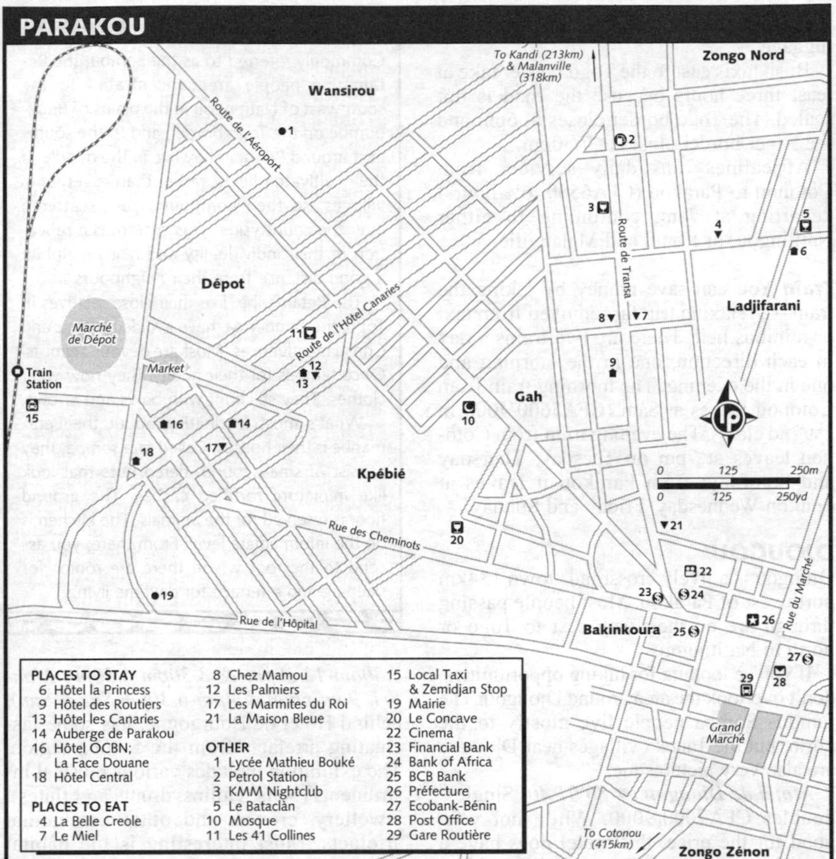
PARAKOU
Wansirou
Route de l'Aéroport
To Kandi (213km) & Malanville (318km)
Zongo Nord
Dépot
Route de l'Hôtel Canaries
Marché de Dépot
Market
Train Station
Gah
Route de Transa
Ladjifarani
Kpébié
Rue des Cheminots
Rue de l'Hôpital
Bakinkoura
Rue du Marché
Grand Marché
To Cotonou (415km)
Zongo Zénon
0 125 250m
0 125 250yd
PLACES TO STAY
6 Hôtel la Princess
9 Hôtel des Routiers
13 Hôtel les Canaries
14 Auberge de Parakou
16 Hôtel OCBN; La Face Douane
18 Hôtel Central
PLACES TO EAT
4 La Belle Creole
7 Le Miel
8 Chez Mamou
12 Les Palmiers
17 Les Marmites du Roi
21 La Maison Bleue
OTHER
1 Lycée Mathieu Bouké
2 Petrol Station
3 KMM Nightclub
5 Le Bataclàn
10 Mosque
11 Les 41 Collines
15 Local Taxi & Zemidjan Stop
19 Mairie
20 Le Concave
22 Cinema
23 Financial Bank
24 Bank of Africa
25 BCB Bank
26 Préfecture
27 Ecobank-Bénin
28 Post Office
29 Gare Routière

also has great African selections and excellent salads. You dine outdoors under paillotes.

La Belle Creole (☎ *61 10 25*) Mains CFA2500-4500. The popular La Belle Creole, on the northern side of town near Hôtel la Princess, serves excellent French fare but prices are on the high side.

La Maison Bleue Mains CFA2500-5000. This outstanding restaurant, near the Bank of Africa, has a wide range of tasty African and Western dishes.

Entertainment

Le Bataclàn, opposite Hôtel la Princess, is the hippest nightclub in Parakou. Locals can be found dancing into the wee hours here on Thursday (CFA1500), Friday (CFA2500) and Saturday (CFA4000).

A cheaper alternative is *KMM (Route de Transa)*, two blocks north of Hôtel des Routiers.

Le Concave, off Rue des Cheminots, is also a lot of fun. It's more casual and much less expensive than KMM, but finding a zemidjan in the wee hours of the morning is more difficult.

If you're just after a drink, buvettes abound – a local favourite is *Les 41 Collines* across from Hôtel les Canaries.

Getting There & Away

Bush Taxi, Minibus & Bus From the gare routière just north of the Grand Marché, bush taxis and minibuses go regularly to Cotonou (CFA6500, eight hours), Kandi (CFA3000, 3½ hours) and Malanville

(CFA4500, five hours). You'll pay extra for luggage.

Bush taxis east to the Togo border take at least three hours because the road is not sealed. The Togo border closes at 6pm and the Niger border closes at 7.30pm.

Africalines runs daily services from Cotonou to Parakou (CFA6500, 6½ hours) departing at 7am, continuing to either Natitingou, or Kandi and Malanville.

Train You can save money by taking the train – a relaxing trip far removed from taxi or minibus hell. There are two trains a day in each direction, one in the morning and one in the evening. The morning train from Cotonou leaves at 8am (CFA5600/4000 in 1st/2nd class). The evening train from Cotonou leaves at 7pm on Tuesday, Thursday and Saturday; from Parakou it leaves at 6pm on Wednesday, Friday and Sunday.

DJOUGOU

Djougou is a lively crossroads town 134km northwest of Parakou. Most people passing through are on their way east to Togo or north to Natitingou.

If you're looking for hiking opportunities, don't overlook the area around Djougou. The famous Somba people live mostly to the north, but the Tanéka villages near Djougou are also very picturesque.

Motel de Djougou *(☎ 80 01 40)* Singles/doubles CFA7000/9000. While not very good for the price, this motel does have a good bar-restaurant. The rooms have fans and showers.

For cheap food, try the area around the gare routière and adjoining market.

If travelling to Kara, there are connections to the border. It's easy to find vehicles going north to Natitingou. Any vehicle heading from Parakou to Natitingou should stop in Djougou.

NATITINGOU

pop 105,000

About 200km northwest of Parakou and pleasantly located at an altitude of 440m in the Atakora mountains, Natitingou is the starting point for excursions to Somba country to the east and south, as well as to Parc National de la Pendjari to the north.

Musée d'Arts et de Traditions Populaires de Natitingou *(admission CFA1000; open 8.30am-12.30pm & 3.30pm-6.30pm Mon-Fri, 9am-noon & 4pm-6.30pm Sat & Sun)*, behind Hôtel de Bourgogne, has some fascinating artefacts from the Somba region. The exhibition includes various musical instruments (bells, violins, drums and flutes), jewellery, crowns and other ceremonial artefacts. Most interesting is the habitat room, which has models of the different types of *tata somba* (Somba houses; see the boxed text 'The Somba' for details).

You could also check out **Kota Falls**, 15km southeast of Natitingou. It's off the main highway, on a well-maintained dirt road. It's a nice place to have a picnic, and for at least half the year during the rainy season, you can swim in the pool at the bottom of the falls.

Places to Stay & Eat

Auberge le Vieux Cavalier *(☎ 82 13 24)* Singles/doubles CFA6000/8000. This auberge is a good budget choice. Its simple air-con rooms are clean and the meals in the ***restaurant*** are inexpensive (CFA800 for a large plate of spaghetti).

Auberge Tanékas *(☎ 82 15 52)* Singles/doubles with fan CFA6500/8000, with air-

The Somba

Commonly referred to as the Somba, the Betamaribé people are concentrated to the southwest of Natitingou in the plains of Boukoumbé on the Togo border, and to the southeast around Perma. They live in the middle of their cultivated fields, rather than together in villages, so their compounds are scattered over the countryside. This custom is a reflection of their individuality and helps maintain a good distance from their neighbours.

The Betamaribé, like their close relatives in Togo, the Tamberma, have avoided Islamic and Christian influences. Most are devout animists. Once famous for their nudity, they now wear clothes. They still hunt with bows and arrows.

What's most fascinating about the Betamaribé is their houses. Called *tata somba*, they consist of small, round, tiered huts that look like miniature fortified castles. The ground floor is reserved for the animals. The kitchen is on the intermediate level. From there, you ascend to the roof where there are rooms for sleeping and a terrace for daytime living.

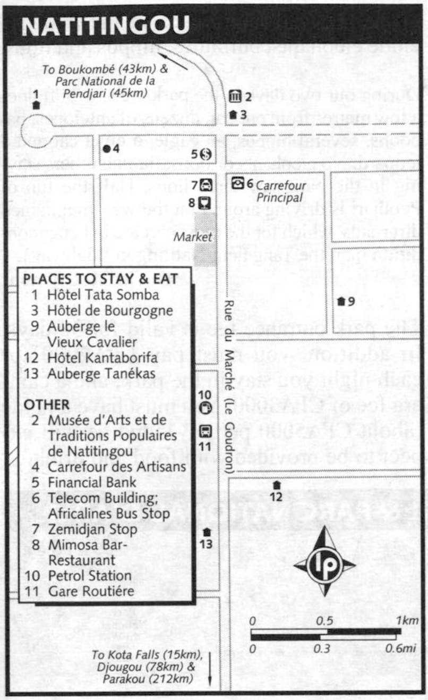
NATITINGOU
To Boukombé (43km) & Parc National de la Pendjari (45km)
Carrefour Principal
Market
Rue du Marché (Le Goudron)
PLACES TO STAY & EAT
1 Hôtel Tata Somba
3 Hôtel de Bourgogne
9 Auberge le Vieux Cavalier
12 Hôtel Kantaborifa
13 Auberge Tanékas
OTHER
2 Musée d'Arts et de Traditions Populaires de Natitingou
4 Carrefour des Artisans
5 Financial Bank
6 Telecom Building; Africalines Bus Stop
7 Zemidjan Stop
8 Mimosa Bar-Restaurant
10 Petrol Station
11 Gare Routiére
0 0.5 1km
0 0.3 0.6mi
To Kota Falls (15km), Djougou (78km) & Parakou (212km)

con 10,000/12,000. Auberge Tanékas, on the southern outskirts of town about 1.5km from the centre, has nice, spacious rooms. The hotel's ***restaurant*** is also quite popular and offers chicken, steak, omelettes and African specialities; the menu du jour costs CFA3000 and main dishes range from CFA1500 to CFA3000.

Hôtel Kantaborifa *(☎ 82 17 66)* Singles/doubles with fan CFA6500/8000, with air-con CFA10,500/12,000. This hotel is just off the main road about 500m northeast of Auberge Tanékas. It has quiet, clean rooms, and a ***restaurant***.

Hôtel de Bourgogne *(☎/fax 82 22 40)* Singles/doubles/triples with fan CFA9000/11,500/13,000, with air-con 13,000/15,500/17,500. This two-storey hotel, on the main road at the northern end of town, is a pleasant place with a good ***restaurant***.

Hôtel Tata Somba *(☎ 82 11 24, fax 82 15 84)* Singles/doubles CFA24,000/30,000. Hôtel Tata Somba, Natitingou's top hotel, is liveliest when the national park is open. It has a pool, a classy ***restaurant*** and a reproduction of a tata somba. Rates are 25% cheaper from 1 June to 30 September. You can also book rooms for the lodges at Parc National de la Pendjari here.

There are opportunities for drinking cheap beer and trying ***street food***, or just hanging out in Natitingou. A good place is the friendly ***Mimosa Bar-Restaurant***, just off the main road near the market.

Getting There & Away

From the gare routière on the main road, bush taxis and minibuses go to Parakou (CFA4000, five hours), although it is often quicker to get a connection in Djougou. There are also daily minibuses to Cotonou (CFA8500, 10 hours) and bush taxis to the Togo and Burkina Faso borders.

More comfortable is the daily Africalines bus from Natitingou to Cotonou (CFA8500, 10 hours), leaving at 7am from outside the OPT building.

BOUKOUMBÉ

On the border with Togo, 43km southwest of Natitingou, Boukoumbé is definitely a place worth visiting if you're in the Natitingou area. About 15km before town you'll pass near **Mt Kousso-Kovangou**, the highest mountain in Benin. About 3km further along this road you'll pass the Belvédère de Koussou-Kovangou, an observation point that offers fantastic views of the area.

The Boukoumbé **market** is the town's major attraction and not to be missed. The market here is as much a social event for people from near and far around the region to get together and drink *chouk* (sorghum beer) and party as it is for selling produce. Every four years or so, there is a **whipping ceremony**, in which the young men of the area beat each other black and blue. Boukoumbé is one of the few areas in Benin where you can buy traditional smoking pipes, which are truly rare souvenirs.

Some way off the road that runs by the Catholic mission is ***Auberge Villageoise de Tourisme***, a nice hotel with three decent rooms for around CFA6000 each, and a ***restaurant***.

Chez Pascaline, in the Zongo area, is the best place to eat in Boukoumbé, with fantastic and inexpensive wild-game meat, salads, rice and beans. This is also a good place to inquire about lodging with locals and the possibility of visiting nearby tatas. ***Street food*** can be found in the market area.

There is at least one taxi every day from Natitingou to Boukoumbé (CFA2000, two hours).

PARC NATIONAL DE LA PENDJARI

This 275,000-hectare national park *(admission CFA5000)*, 45km north of Natitingou, adjoins the Parc National d'Arli in Burkina Faso and is bordered to the west, north and east by the Pendjari River. It's much more developed for tourism than the Benin side of Parc National du W, so it receives the most visitors. It's open only from 15 December to 15 May, the best viewing time being near the end of the dry season when the animals start to hover around the water holes.

Animals you might see in the park include elephants, buffaloes, hippos and lions.

During our two days in the park we saw buffaloes a few metres from our car, dozens of antelopes, baboons, several hippos, an eagle, a civet cat and a leopard. No elephants or lions, though others staying in the park saw three lions. Half the fun of Pendjari is driving around on the well-maintained dirt roads, which for the most part are in better condition than the Tanguiéta-Natitingou 'highway'.

David McClymont

The park entrance fee is valid for 30 days. In addition, you must pay CFA2000 for each night you stay in the park, and a camera fee of CFA3000. You must have a guide (about CFA5000 per day), and he will expect to be provided with food and drink.

PARC NATIONAL DE LA PENDJARI & PARC NATIONAL D'ARLI

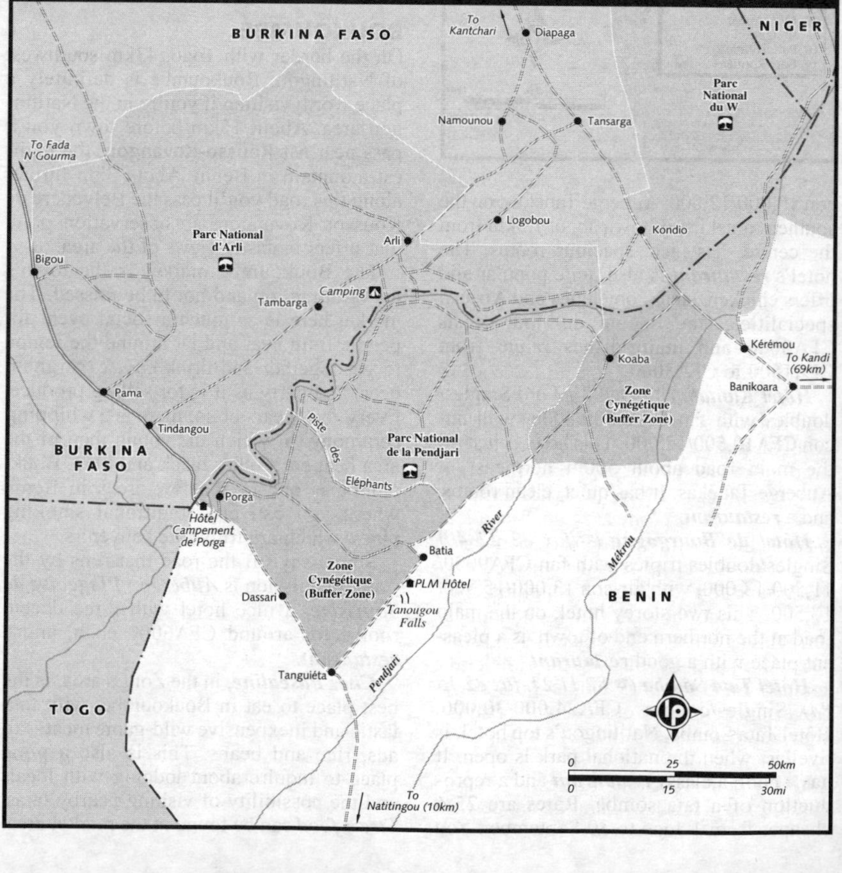
BURKINA FASO
To Kantchari
Diapaga
NIGER
Parc National du W
Namounou
Tansarga
To Fada N'Gourma
Logobou
Kondio
Parc National d'Arli
Arli
Bigou
Camping
Tambarga
Kérémou
To Kandi (69km)
Koaba
Banikoara
Zone Cynégétique (Buffer Zone)
Pama
Piste des Eléphants
Tindangou
Parc National de la Pendjari
BURKINA FASO
Porga
Hôtel Campement de Porga
River
Mékrou
Batia
Zone Cynégétique (Buffer Zone)
PLM Hôtel
Dassari
Tanougou Falls
BENIN
Tanguiéta
Pendjari
TOGO
0
25
50km
0
15
30mi
To Natitingou (10km)

Places to Stay & Eat

Many visitors stay in Natitingou and make excursions from there, but you'll have a better chance of seeing animals if you stay at the park itself. Due to the presence of lions, there are only certain areas, including Mare Yangouali and Pont d'Arli, where ***camping*** is permitted. Park wardens show you where.

In Tanguiéta, at the southern tip of the park, there are two very rustic ***campements*** – one of these is beside the river. There's also the well-run ***Hotel Baobab***, which has a good ***restaurant***.

Campement Relais de Tanougou at the Tanougou Falls is well located for an early-morning walk and swim. The circular bungalows have a bathroom behind a dividing wall. A bungalow costs CFA9000 for a single or double from December to May; meals are CFA3500. Prices are 25% cheaper during low season. Book with Hôtel Tata Somba (☎ 82 11 24) in Natitingou.

Most people keep going north to Porga. There, at the entrance to the park, is ***Hôtel Campement de Porga***. It's a larger place with a restaurant; basic rooms with fan/air-con cost CFA15,000/22,000. Nile perch and meat in season are restaurant specialities; breakfast is CFA2500. Again, book with Hôtel Tata Somba in Natitingou.

Getting There & Away

The main entrances to Pendjari are roughly 100km north of Natitingou. To get to the park from Natitingou, take the dirt road heading north for 45km to the fork in the road at Tanguiéta. From there most visitors head northwest for 59km to Porga near the Burkina Faso border. This village is the main entrance to the park and there's a campement near the gate. Alternatively, head about 40km northeast from Tanguiéta to Batia, the other park entrance. Many people prefer the latter because the route is shorter and in equally good condition. You can't walk into the park (hiking is not permitted), so go to one of the hotels in Natitingou and hitch a lift. Sharing the Hôtel Tata Somba's Land Rover is another possibility. Travel agencies in Cotonou will organise trips, but they are expensive.

KANDI & AROUND

Kandi, 213km north of Parakou on the way to Niger, is worth a stop for its **market**. The Bariba and Peul (Fula) people give the town a distinctive northern character, as do the voluptuous mango trees.

Some 40km north of Kandi on the road to Malanville near the small village of **Alfa Koura** is an interesting ecotourism project, run by the Centre Nationale de Gestion des Reserves de Faune, where you can **view elephants**. Readers have reported seeing up to 50 elephants in one day bathing and drinking in the water hole. The site is open from 7am to 6.30pm daily, from November to April. Visitors pay by the month (CFA5000), with an additional charge for cameras (CFA500) and videos (CFA1000); however, it is possible to negotiate a day price.

Places to Stay & Eat

The cheapest rooms in Kandi (CFA3000) are at ***Baobab 2000*** at the northern end of town. There are no fans and only bucket showers; rooms are small.

Auberge de Kandi *(☎ 63 02 43, central reservations ☎/fax 31 38 62, ⓔ voyageur@intnet.bj)* Camping CFA1500 per person, singles/doubles with fan CFA7000/9500. This auberge offers a good range of accommodation options.

Auberge la Recontre *(☎/fax 63 01 76)* Rooms with fan/air-con from CFA8000/14,000. Recommended by travellers, this place has a small paillote restaurant serving African and European food.

Gargoterie de Kandi behind the market has meals from CFA300. Another good option is ***La Masion Blanc*** (meals from CFA400), opposite Auberge la Recontre.

Good buvettes include ***Chalet du Lac*** and ***Coins du Soir***.

Getting There & Away

From Parakou, bush taxis head north to Kandi (CFA3000, 3½ hours). To get to the elephant viewing platform from Kandi catch a ride with one of the bush taxis heading to Malanville (CFA1500, 1½ hours).

MALANVILLE

This town is in the far north at the Niger border, on the main highway between Cotonou and Niamey. The ride from Parakou is scenic. Look for women selling red-skinned cheese on the way. Market day is Sunday, which is the best time to visit because of the rich mix of people you'll see.

Rose des Sables *(☎ 67 01 25)* Doubles CFA5000. Rose des Sables, 2km south of town, has adequate rooms with fans.

For ***food***, try near the gare routière.

A bush taxi between Malanville and Parakou takes five hours (CFA4500). A bus or minibus takes seven hours (CFA3000).

Africalines has a daily bus from Cotonou to Malanville (CFA11,000, 12 hours).

From Malanville, a zemidjan to Gaya in Niger (where you can get taxis to Niamey) is about CFA1000.

PARC NATIONAL DU W

The Benin section of Parc National du W (pronounced doo-blay-vay) is about twice as large as Pendjari. It straddles three countries: Benin, Burkina Faso and Niger. The one across the border is more accessible and has the best viewing trails (see the Niger chapter for details). Pendjari, W and d'Arli form, in effect, one big park and are surrounded by buffer zones managed for hunting (*zones cynégétiques*). You may see elephants, buffaloes, hippos, crocodiles and several species of antelopes.

To get to du W, go northeast from Batia for 100km to the intersection with the dirt road connecting Kondio (Burkina Faso) and Kérémou. Kérémou is the major entry point to the park on the Benin side. You will need your own 4WD transport.

Burkina Faso

Burkina Faso, previously known as Haute Volta (Upper Volta), is too often merely on a traveller's route to somewhere else. However, it is well worth visiting for its own sake; it's a place to slow down, step down a gear and unwind for a week or two. One of the world's poorest countries, Burkina Faso nonetheless hosts Africa's most important film festival, and the entire place runs with an efficiency that is the envy of many of its neighbours. Many would argue that the agreeably laid-back Burkinabé, as the population is called, are the country's best asset.

The capital, Ouagadougou (pronounced waga-**doo**-goo) or simply Ouaga, has little to detain you for more than a few days. But the countryside, with its gradation from desert and purest Sahel in the north through to the savanna of the central plateau and the rainforest lushness of the extreme southwest, is well worth exploring. The people are as varied as the terrain.

Burkina Faso at a Glance

Capital: Ouagadougou
Population: 11.6 million
Area: 274,122 sq km
Head of State: President Blaise Compaoré
Official language: French
Main local language: Moré
Currency: West African franc
Exchange rate: US$1 = CFA694
Time: GMT/UTC
Country telephone code: ☎ 226
Best time to go: November to February

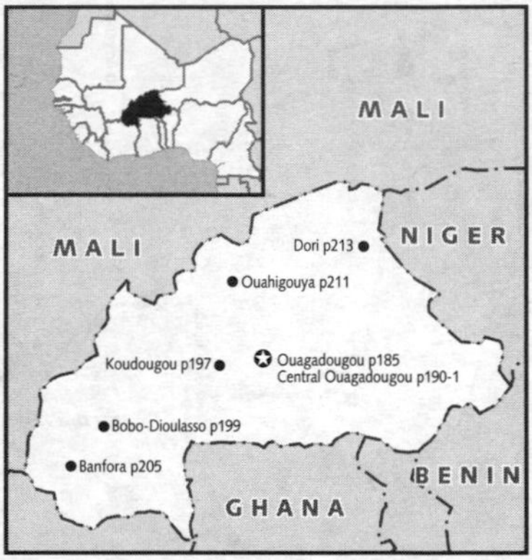
MALI
MALI
NIGER
Dori p213
Ouahigouya p211
Koudougou p197
Ouagadougou p185
Central Ouagadougou p190-1
Bobo-Dioulasso p199
Banfora p205
GHANA
BENIN

Highlights

- Kicking back in the languid charm of Bobo-Dioulasso, with its old quarter and distinctive Grande Mosquée
- Strolling through Ouagadougou by day and then dancing the night away
- Exploring the other-worldly landscapes of the Sindou Peaks near Banfora
- Marvelling at the intricate decoration of Bani's seven mosques
- Wandering amid the colour of Gorom-Gorom's Thursday market
- Searching for wildlife at Parc National d'Arli and Ranch de Nazinga

Facts about Burkina Faso

HISTORY

The earliest known inhabitants of present-day Burkina Faso were the Bobo, the Lobi and the Gourounsi, who were in the area by the 13th century. By the 14th century, Mossi peoples had begun to move westward from settlements near the Niger River.

The first Mossi kingdom was founded more than 500 years ago in Ouagadougou. Three more Mossi states were subsequently founded in other parts of what is today Burkina Faso, all paying homage to Ouagadougou, the strongest. The government of each of the states was highly organised, with ministers, courts and a cavalry known for its devastating attacks against the Muslim empires in Mali. They also fostered a rigid social hierarchy in which other ethnic groups within their domains were relegated to the lowest level. Only a few groups in the southwest, including the Bobo, Lobi and Senoufo, escaped subjugation.

During the Scramble for Africa in the second half of the 19th century, the French, expanding their territory in the continent's western bulge, broke up the traditional Mossi states, rather than reaching an accommodation with the traditional rulers.

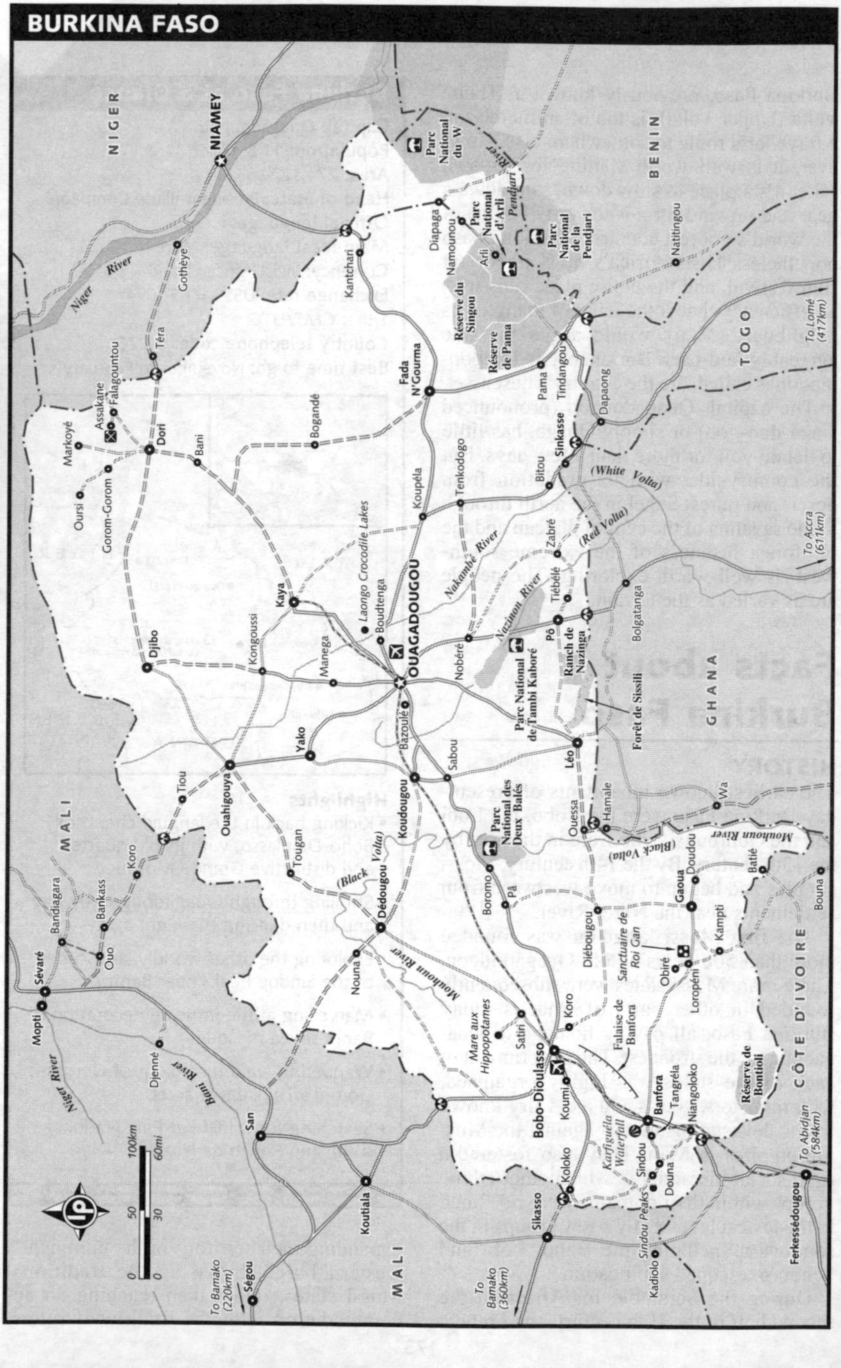
BURKINA FASO
NIGER
NIAMEY
Niger River
MALI
BENIN
TOGO
GHANA
CÔTE D'IVOIRE
OUAGADOUGOU
Bobo-Dioulasso
Parc National du W
Parc National d'Arli
Parc National de la Pendjari
Réserve du Singou
Réserve de Pama
Pendjari River
Parc National de Tambi Kaboré
Ranch de Nazinga
Forêt de Sissili
Parc National des Deux Balés
Réserve de Bontioli
Mare aux Hippopotames
Sanctuaire de Roi Gan
Falaise de Banfora
Karfiguéla Waterfall
Sindou Peaks
Laongo Crocodile Lakes
(White Volta)
(Red Volta)
(Black Volta)
Nakambé River
Nazinon River
Mouhoun River
Bani River
Gothèye
Téra
Falagountou
Assakane
Markoyé
Dori
Bani
Oursi
Gorom-Gorom
Bogandé
Kantchari
Diapaga
Namounou
Arli
Fada N'Gourma
Pama
Tindangou
Dapaong
Sinkasse
Bitou
Tenkodogo
Koupéla
Natitingou
Kaya
Boudtenga
Kongoussi
Djibo
Manega
Zabré
Tiébélé
Pô
Bolgatanga
Nobéré
Bazoulé
Yako
Sabou
Léo
Ouahigouya
Tiou
Koudougou
Hamale
Ouessa
Wa
Tougan
Dédougou
Boromo
Pa
Diébougou
Gaoua
Doudou
Batié
Bouna
Kampti
Loropéni
Obiré
Nouna
Koro
Satiri
Koumi
Banfora
Tangréla
Niangoloko
Sindou
Douna
Koloko
Kadiolo
Sikasso
Ferkessédougou
To Abidjan (584km)
To Accra (611km)
To Lomé (417km)
To Bamako (360km)
To Bamako (220km)
Ségou
Koutiala
San
Djenné
Mopti
Sévaré
Bandiagara
Bankass
Ouo
0 50 100km
0 30 60mi

Exploiting the latter's internal rivalries, the French had established their sway over the region by the early 20th century.

At first, in the 19th century the former Mossi states were assimilated into the vast Colonie du Haut Sénégal-Niger. Then, in 1919, the area was hived off for administrative convenience as a separate colony, the Upper Volta. In 1932, for purely commercial reasons, the French sliced it up, grafting more than half onto Côte d'Ivoire and the remainder onto Mali and Niger. This made it easier for the colonial government in Côte d'Ivoire to recruit the Mossi, forcing them to work there on French-owned plantations and on the railway between Abidjan and Ouagadougou. After WWII, Upper Volta once again became a separate entity, but the disparity continued; during its 60 years of colonial rule in West Africa, France focused its attention on Côte d'Ivoire and did little to develop Upper Volta.

Independence

During the 1950s, Upper Volta's most prominent African political leaders were Ouezzin Coulibaly, of the pan-West African political party the Rassemblement Démocratique Africain (RDA), and Maurice Yaméogo, one of the founders of the Union Démocratique Voltaïque (UDV), an opposing political party. During the late colonial period, these parties stood in uneasy conflict with the Mossi king who was openly pro-French in his leanings. When Coulibaly died in 1958, Yaméogo negotiated the amalgamation of the two parties and became president following independence in 1960.

Yaméogo became increasingly autocratic, banning all political parties except the UDV-RDA, and governing poorly with disastrous economic consequences. In 1966, after mass popular demonstrations, the military staged its first coup, led by Lieutenant-Colonel Sangoulé Lamizana, and jailed Yaméogo for embezzlement on a grand scale.

In 1970, the military stepped down, allowing a civilian government to take over under a constitution approved by referendum. This lasted for four years, until the army, led again by Lamizana, staged another coup. This time the military rulers suspended the constitution and banned all political activity by getting rid of the opposition, which was driven by one of the most powerful trade unions in Africa. Following a nationwide strike in 1975, the unions, by now the de facto opposition, forced the government to raise wages and, in 1978, got the new constitution and general elections that they had been pressing for.

Over the next five years there were three more coups. The last and most notable was in November 1982 when Captain Thomas Sankara, an ambitious young left-wing military star, staged a bloody putsch and seized power.

The Sankara Era

When in 1984 Sankara renamed the country Burkina Faso, meaning 'Land of the Incorruptible' or, more prosaically, the 'Country of Honest Men', he deliberately coined the phrase from each of the country's two major languages: the Moré word for 'pure' or 'incorruptible' and the Dioula term for 'homeland', and set about restructuring the economy to promote self-reliance in rural areas.

The approach of Sankara and his People's Salvation Council was unconventional. Modest Renault 5s, for example, were the official cars of the president and his ministers. In 1985, Sankara dismissed most of his cabinet and sent members to work on agricultural cooperatives. It was mainly show; a month later, they were back at their desks. Sankara then imposed a 25% cut in government salaries and ordered all rents for 1985 to be handed to the government instead of to landlords.

Blitz campaigns were his style. In one 15-day marathon, the government vaccinated about 60% of children against measles, meningitis and yellow fever. Unicef called it 'one of the major successes of the year in Africa'. Sankara called on every village to build a medical dispensary. The government then sent representatives from each village for training as front-line paramedics. Between 1983 and 1986, more than 350 communities built schools with their own labour and the education of school-age children increased by one-third to 22%.

Under Sankara the economy improved and there was little government corruption. Financial books were kept in good order, debt financing was kept to a minimum, budgetary commitments were adhered to and Burkina Faso was one of few countries in

Africa to enjoy per capita GNP growth during the 1980s. Most importantly at that time, people developed a genuine pride in their country.

Sankara was charismatic and the masses loved him for his blunt honesty. In December 1985, he engaged the country in a five-day war with Mali, which merely enhanced his popularity. But, while he had widespread popular support, Sankara alienated powerful interests such as the trade unions, landlords and other urban elites as well as many Western countries – particularly the USA and France. He did not live to see the realisation of his policies. In late 1987, a group of junior officers seized power. Sankara was taken outside Ouagadougou and shot. But Thom Sank, as Sankara is still known throughout the country, lives on in peoples' memories. Every 15 October, the anniversary of his assassination, the regime mounts a stilted celebration, while the 'Sankaristes' pay their own more spontaneous, genuine homage. His simple grave has become a place of discreet pilgrimage.

Burkina Faso Today

The new junta was headed by Captain Blaise Compaoré, Sankara's former friend and co-revolutionary, and son-in-law of the late Houphouët-Boigny, Côte d'Ivoire's long-standing leader. Compaoré attempted unsuccessfully to discredit Sankara with a 'rectification' campaign, designed to correct the 'deviations' of the previous government.

In late 1991, Compaoré achieved a modicum of legitimacy when, as sole candidate and on a low turnout, he was elected president. This legitimacy was compromised, however, when Clément Ouédraogo, the leading opposition figure, was assassinated a couple of weeks later. In May 1992, the government party, Organisation pour la Démocratie Populaire (ODP), won 78 of the 107 seats in the national assembly amid widespread accusations of fraud. In a surprise move the following month, a number of opposition MPs were invited to join the government.

In the legislative elections of 1997, the ODP, restyled as the Congrès pour la Démocratie et le Progrès (CDP), received a suspect 95% of votes cast by those who bothered to turn out. Presidential elections were held in November 1998 and it surprised no-one that Compaoré won 87.5% of the vote. Throughout 2000 and 2001, Compaoré was accused of involvement in the trade in illegal diamonds.

The country remains one of the more stable in the region, although rumblings of discontent continue. This friction spilled over into street demonstrations in April 2000, with demands for greater democratic pluralism, observance of human rights and independence of the judiciary and electoral commission, suggesting that many challenges lie ahead.

GEOGRAPHY

Landlocked Burkina Faso has a variety of landscapes. The harsh desert and semidesert of the north resembles the terrain of its neighbours, Mali and Niger. The country's dominant feature, however, is the vast central laterite plateau, where hardy trees and bushes thrive. It then gives way to woodland and savanna further south. In the southwest, around Banfora, the rainfall is heavier and there are forests as well as irrigated sugar-cane and rice fields.

The French named the country Upper Volta after its three major rivers – the Black, White and Red Voltas, known today as the Mouhoun, Nakambé and Nazinon rivers. All flow south into the world's largest artificial lake, Lake Volta, in Ghana.

CLIMATE

The main rains fall between June and October, when it becomes very humid in the south. From December to February the weather is marginally cooler, with daily maximums only occasionally exceeding 35°C. During this period, the dry heat is more bearable, although the dusty harmattan winds produce hazy skies. The hot season, when the mercury can rise well above 40°C in the capital, is from March to early June.

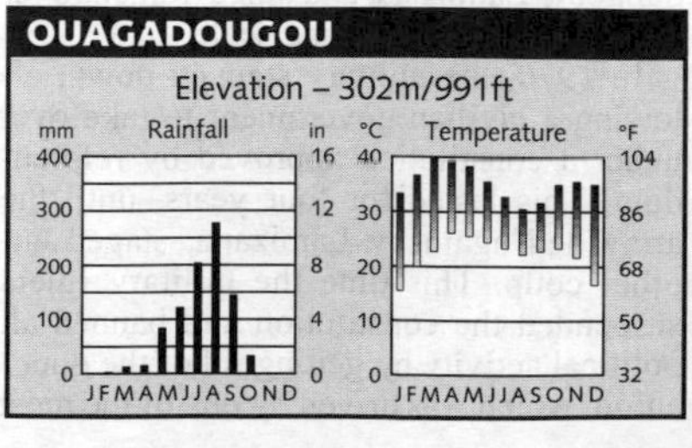
OUAGADOUGOU
Elevation – 302m/991ft
mm
Rainfall
in
400
300
200
100
0
16
12
8
4
0
JFMAMJJASOND
°C
Temperature
°F
40
30
20
10
0
104
86
68
50
32
JFMAMJJASOND

ECOLOGY & ENVIRONMENT

Burkina Faso suffers acutely from two related forms of environmental damage: deforestation and soil erosion. Some sources attribute a GNP loss as high as 9% annually to such degradation.

Nowadays, Ouagadougou is surrounded by a 70km stretch of land virtually devoid of trees. This is because firewood accounts for more than 90% of the country's energy consumption, not to mention commercial logging, slash-and-burn agriculture and animal grazing.

But all is not gloomy. Small-scale projects supported by nongovernmental organisations have been successful at addressing these issues. For example, farmers have been encouraged to return to traditional methods of cultivation, in particular the building of *diguettes* or stone lines laid along field contours which slow water run-off, maximise water penetration and reduce erosion. A highly successful World Health Organization (WHO) river blindness (onchocerciasis) eradication programme has also led to the repopulation and recultivation of large fertile areas.

Further, in 2001 a government-sponsored, small-scale irrigation project was launched in the village of Yakiya, 80km east of Ouagadougou, in an attempt to enable farmers to cultivate year-round rather than the current three to four months. Steering farmers away from a reliance on unpredictable rains and towards the use of groundwater resources, the ambitious project may be extended to half of the country's 8000 villages, and could enable Burkina Faso to be able to meet up to half of its total food needs.

FLORA & FAUNA

The drier northern part of the country is the domain of trees such as the acacia (including the gum arabic tree *Acacia senegal*, whose sticky resin is used in chewing gum) and the baobab. The word 'baobab' is a corruption of the Arabic *abu habeb* (seed bearer), and the tree looks as though it's been tipped upside down, its profusion of spindly branches resembling networks of roots. (For more information, see the boxed text 'The Baobab Tree' in the Flora & Fauna section in the Facts about West Africa chapter.)

Further south, tamarind and mango trees predominate while, in pockets of the south and southeast, the vegetation, which is similar to that of neighbouring Benin, becomes more lush. Here, especially at Parc National d'Arli, is the best chance of spotting large animals, including elephants, hippos, warthogs, baboons, monkeys, lions, leopards, crocodiles and various kinds of antelope.

GOVERNMENT & POLITICS

The head of government is the president. The country also has an elected 111-seat national assembly and an appointed upper house, the Chambre des Représentants. According to the constitution, legislative elections follow a five-year cycle, and the presidential term lasts seven years. The last elections to the national assembly were held in 1997, and presidential elections were staged in November 1998. Behind the scenes, traditional leaders still exert considerable influence.

ECONOMY

Burkina Faso has scarcely any exploitable natural resources and remains one of the world's five poorest countries. In 1998, Burkina Faso ranked 159th out of 162 countries on the UNDP's Human Development Index, based on a range of indicators from income to life expectancy and literacy. Agriculture, the mainstay of Burkina Faso's economy, remains a buoyant sector, employing some 90% of the work force. At the macro level, Burkina Faso is successfully implementing reforms dictated by the IMF and World Bank, and in 1996 the country was rewarded when France and other creditors agreed to write off much of Burkina Faso's foreign debt.

While this may have eased the pressure for governments, the poorest people still face a daily struggle for survival.

POPULATION & PEOPLE

With 11.6 million people, Burkina Faso, occupying an area about half the size of France, has some 60 ethnic groups. The largest of these is the Mossi, who make up almost half the population and are primarily concentrated in the central plateau area, including Ouagadougou. The Bobo live in the west around Bobo-Dioulasso, while the southwest around Gaoua is home to the Lobi. East of the Lobi, and transcending the border with Ghana, are the Gourounsi. In the Sahel areas of the north are the Hausa, the Fulani (also known as Peul-Fulani or Fula), the Bella and the Tuareg peoples, many of which are still seminomadic; the Gourmantché predominate in the east around Fada N'Gourma.

ARTS

Arts & Craftwork

While each ethnic group in Burkina Faso has its own artistic style, the work of the Mossi, the Bobo and the Lobi are the most famous; in the museums of Ouagadougou and Bobo-Dioulasso, you'll see examples of all three. The tall antelope masks of the Mossi and the butterfly masks of the Bobo are perhaps the best known. The Lobi are well known for their figurative sculptures.

See also the special section 'Arts & Craftwork'.

Music

Music, both modern and traditional, plays a dominant role in the daily life of the Burkinabé. Like its film industry, Burkina Faso's musicians are well-known throughout West Africa and the influences are from across the continent and Europe. In most large towns, music stores seemingly line every street and blare out the latest African hits well into the night. It is not unusual to come across backyard jam sessions, usually in late afternoon, by budding musicians who are often pretty heavy on the drums. In Ouagadougou and Bobo-Dioulasso, outdoor venues (usually cafés or bars) offer live music with both traditional troupes and modern ensembles on show. And music is the mainstay of many traditional festivals and ceremonies across the country.

Established local stars include Black So Man, Nick Domby, Youssou Camporé, Georges Ouédraogo, Nakelse Emmanuel and Amity Méria, a female vocalist. The group Farafina, originally from Bobo, continues to make waves, but nowadays it spends most of its time in Europe. Among the up-and-coming artists are Jean-Claude Bamogo, Roger Waongo and, for traditional music, Zougn Nazaganda.

See also the special section 'Music of West Africa'.

SOCIETY & CONDUCT

The Burkinabé are pretty laid-back, and if you breach local etiquette, most will be too polite to say anything. To avoid offence, however, dress as neatly as you can and avoid public displays of affection. Also avoid ostentatious displays of flesh; shorts are rarely worn, but three-quarter length pants are generally fine for both men and women. The imperative to dress modestly is particularly relevant in Muslim areas in the north.

RELIGION

The majority of the population observes traditional beliefs, based mainly on the worship of ancestors and spirits. About 25% of people, mostly those living in the north, follow Islam, and around 10% are Christian.

LANGUAGE

The official language is French. Of some 60 local languages, the most significant is Moré, the language of the Mossi and others living on the central plateau, which is spoken by more than half the population. Dioula is the lingua franca, the language of the market, even though within Burkina Faso it's nobody's mother tongue. It's closely related to Bambara, the major language of neighbouring Mali. Other significant local languages include Fula, Gourmantché and Gourounsi.

See the Language chapter for a list of useful phrases in French, Moré, Dioula and Fula.

Facts for the Visitor

SUGGESTED ITINERARIES

If you have a week at your disposal, you should plan on visiting Ouagadougou, which is a friendly, relaxed capital city with an active nightlife (two days), charming Bobo-Dioulasso (two to three days) and, if your schedule allows, the Thursday market of Gorom-Gorom and the mosques of Bani (two days).

With two weeks to spare, plan on spending more time in the southwest, especially in Bobo-Dioulasso, around Banfora in the country's 'green' belt; allow at least three extra days. Gaoua, further to the east and in the heart of Lobi country, is also worth a few days.

An alternative for lovers of wildlife who are visiting between December and May is to make a three- to four-day return trip to visit Parc National d'Arli or its less abundant neighbour, Ranch de Nazinga.

PLANNING

Try to avoid the rainy season between June and October, when humidity is high and the roads can become temporarily impassable.

Burkina Faso (1:1,000,000), a map published by the French-based Institut Géographique National, is the most widely available. It's available at the Institut Gèographique du Burkina (IGB; ☎ 32 48 23, fax 32 48 27) on Av de l'Indépendance or in many European bookshops.

VISAS & DOCUMENTS

Visas

Everyone except Economic Community of West African States (Ecowas) nationals needs a visa. You can buy a tourist visa at Ouagadougou airport for CFA10,000 and two photos, although you may have to return to pick up your passport and visa later the same day. Most land border posts also issue visas on arrival.

Burkinabé embassies can issue multiple-entry visas that are valid for three months. They require two photos and may ask for proof of yellow fever vaccination. In countries where Burkina Faso is not represented, French embassies normally issue visas on its behalf. Typical costs are US$25 in the USA, UK£20 in Britain, €15 to €35 in Europe and CFA16,400 from French embassies in West Africa. Burkinabé embassies in Africa can charge as much as US$40 for a visa.

Visas for Onward Travel Benin and Niger don't have embassies in Burkina Faso and the French consulate doesn't issue visas on their behalf. For Niger, it is possible to obtain a visa on arrival at the border but some Nigerien immigration officials will make you pay for your lack of planning and you'll have to extend your visa in any event as soon as you arrive in Niamey; it's better to get your visa elsewhere before you arrive.

If you just want to slip over the border to Benin to explore Parc National de la Pendjari, you can get a 48-hour visa at the border post. Visas cost CFA10,000.

Côte d'Ivoire Single-entry visas valid for up to 30 days cost CFA10,000; the multiple-entry variety costs CFA20,000 and are valid for one to three months. You'll need two photos. You can usually collect your visa the next day.

Ghana The Ghanaian embassy issues one-month visas within 24 hours for CFA12,000; you'll need an unjustifiable four photos (make sure they're identical).

Mali One-month visas cost CFA20,000 and are issued the same day.

Togo The French consulate issues visas for Togo, but they're only valid for 48 hours; once in Togo, you'll need to extend your visa. You'll need CFA16,400 and two photos. Visas are generally issued on the same day.

Other Documents

Proof of yellow fever vaccination is mandatory and is often checked at airports and most land borders. Several travellers have reported being asked for proof of inoculation against meningitis when arriving at land borders, especially between Mali and Burkina Faso. This isn't a standard requirement, but it be demanded if there's a local epidemic on either or both sides of the border.

EMBASSIES & CONSULATES

Burkinabé Embassies

In West Africa, Burkina Faso has embassies in Côte d'Ivoire, Ghana, Mali and Nigeria. For more details, see the Facts for the Visitor section of the relevant country chapter.

Burkinabé embassies outside Africa include the following:

Belgium (☎ 02-345 66 09) 16 Place Guy-d'Arezzo, Brussels 1180
France (☎ 01 43 59 90 63) 159 Blvd Haussmann, 75008 Paris
Germany (☎ 030-301 05 990) Karolingerplatz 10, 14052 Berlin
USA (☎ 202-332 5577) 2340 Massachusetts Ave, NW, Washington, DC 20008

In the UK, there is an honorary consul (☎ 020-7738 1800, fax 7738 2820) at 5 Cinnamon Row, Plantation Wharf, London SW11 3TW.

Embassies & Consulates in Burkina Faso

Embassies and consulates in Ouagadougou include the following:

Côte d'Ivoire (☎ 31 82 28) Corner of Av Raoul Follereau and Blvd du Faso; open 7.30am to noon and 3pm to 5pm Monday to Friday

France (☎ 30 67 74) Av de l'Indépendance, 100m west of Palais Présidentiel; open 8.30am to noon
Germany (☎ 30 67 31) Rue Joseph Badoua
Ghana (☎ 30 76 35) Av d'Oubritenga, opposite the Unesco office; open 8am to 2pm Monday to Friday
Mali (☎ 38 19 22) 2569 Av Bassawarga, just south of Av de la Résistance; open 7.30am to 4pm Monday to Friday
Nigeria (☎ 30 66 67) Av d'Oubritenga, 1km northeast of Place des Nations Unies
USA (☎ 30 67 23) Av Raoul Follereau

You can contact the British honorary consul through Ouagadougou's Hôtel Yibi (☎ 30 73 23, fax 30 59 00).

The Canadian embassy (☎ 31 18 94) on Av Agostino Neto represents Australia in consular matters.

CUSTOMS

There's no restriction on the import or export of CFA or foreign currencies. If you want to take out an artefact that's manifestly old and valuable, play it safe and get an export certificate from the Directeur du Patrimoine National in Ouagadougou. Inquire at the tourist office.

MONEY

The unit of currency in Burkina Faso is the West African CFA franc.

country	unit		CFA
euro zone	€1	=	CFA656
UK	UK£1	=	CFA1024
USA	US$1	=	CFA694

Banks that change money with a minimum of fuss include Banque Internationale du Burkina (BIB), with a branch at the Aéroport International d'Ouagadougou, Ecobank (conveniently open 8.30am to 5.30pm Monday to Friday and 9am to 1pm Saturday) and Banque Internationale pour le Commerce, l'Industrie et l'Agriculture du Burkina (Biciab). All change US dollar and euro travellers cheques, as well as cash.

Most banks will charge a 1% or 2% commission on travellers cheques, although the rate varies from branch to branch; banks sometimes refuse to accept certain brands of travellers cheques, but again there's no across-the-board policy. For travellers cheques, always be ready to show your proof of purchase.

Biciab's ATMs throughout the country issue easy cash advances against Visa (but not MasterCard), as long as you have a personal identification number (PIN).

Outside of Ouagadougou and Bobo-Dioulasso, you'll struggle to change anything other than euros.

If you're arriving from Ghana, you'll find Burkina Faso to be considerably more expensive.

POST & COMMUNICATIONS

The post offices in Ouagadougou and Bobo-Dioulasso offer travellers a poste restante service.

You can make international phone calls at Onatel offices from 7am to 10pm daily. A three-minute call costs CFA2500 (CFA750 for each additional minute) to Europe or the USA and CFA3960 (CFA1260 for each additional minute) to Australia.

There is reasonably priced Internet access (and pretty fast connections) in Ouagadougou, Bobo-Dioulasso and Ouahigouya.

There are no telephone area codes in Burkina Faso.

DIGITAL RESOURCES

A good website to start with is the Ouagadougou city hall site (W www.mairie-ouaga.bf), which has interesting tidbits on the capital.

PHOTOGRAPHY & VIDEO

You no longer need a photo or video permit for most of the country. Your photographic freedom, however, is far from absolute. The official off-limits list is formidable, and includes airports, bridges, reservoirs, banks, any military installations, police stations or government buildings (including the Palais Présidentiel) and post offices, train stations and bus and bush-taxi *(taxis brousse)* stations, TV/radio stations, petrol stations, grain warehouses, water towers, industrial installations and poor people. For more general information and advice, see the Photography & Video section in the Regional Facts for the Visitor chapter.

In the north, officials in Gorom-Gorom try to extract CFA5000 for a photo permit.

HEALTH

You'll need a yellow fever vaccination certificate to enter the country. Malaria exists year-round throughout the country, so you should take appropriate precautions.

Meningitis outbreaks, although rarely widespread, occur in the Sahel areas, especially during the dry season: At least 1000 Burkinabé die of malaria every year. Bilharzia (schistosomiasis) exists in many lakes and ponds, so you should avoid paddling or swimming in these. HIV/AIDS is also a serious problem in Burkina Faso, with the most recent statistics available citing more than 350,000 people as being HIV-positive (6.4% of the adult population).

For more information on these and other health matters, see the Health section in the Regional Facts for the Visitor chapter.

WOMEN TRAVELLERS

Burkinabé are, in general, a laid-back, friendly and polite people, and women travellers are unlikely to experience any more hassle here than in other countries in the region. For more information and advice, see Women Travellers in the Regional Facts for the Visitor chapter.

DANGERS & ANNOYANCES

Burkina Faso remains one of the safer countries in West Africa, but crime isn't unknown, particularly around big markets, cinemas and *gares routières* (bus stations), where it's usually confined to petty theft and pickpocketing. Crime is usually only a problem in Ouagadougou and Bobo-Dioulasso. There has been a small but growing number of reports of muggings in Ouagadougou, sometimes even with knives.

BUSINESS HOURS

Business hours are from 7.30am to noon and 3pm to 5.30pm Monday to Friday and 9am to 1pm Saturday. Government offices close on weekends.

Banks open from 7am to 11am and 3.30pm to 5pm Monday to Friday. Ecobank is a welcome exception (see Money earlier in the chapter).

PUBLIC HOLIDAYS & SPECIAL EVENTS

Public holidays include:

New Year's Day 1 January
Women's Day 8 March
Good Friday & Easter Monday March/April
Labour Day 1 May
Ascension Day 4–5 August
Anniversary of Sankara's overthrow 15 October
All Saints Day 1 November
Christmas Day 25 December

Burkina Faso also celebrates Islamic holidays, which change each year. See Public Holidays & Special Events in the Regional Facts for the Visitor chapter for estimated dates of Islamic holidays.

Fespaco is the biennial festival of African cinema, which takes place in Ouagadougou in odd-numbered years during February or March. In even-numbered years, Ouagadougou hosts the Salon International de l'Artisanat de Ouagadougou, which attracts artisans and vendors from all over the continent. This event alternates with Bobo's Semaine Nationale de la Culture, a week of music, dance and theatre held every even year during March or April. Each October, Ouagadougou plays host to the annual Festival des Arts Africains.

Anywhere, anytime, there are traditional festivities or *fêtes*, especially in the Bobo-Dioulasso area.

ACCOMMODATION

It's fairly easy to find basic accommodation with fan and shared bathroom for between CFA3500 and CFA5000. In Ouagadougou and Bobo, you can be lodged comfortably with air-con for between CFA12,000 and CFA15,000.

Within Ouagadougou and Bobo-Dioulasso you have to pay a *taxe de séjour* at each place you stay, also known as a *taxe communale*. It's a once-off payment, irrespective of the number of nights you stay at a hotel, and is calculated at CFA500 per person per hotel star rating.

FOOD

Food in Burkina Faso lacks the variety of some other West African countries. As is usual in the region, sauces are the mainstay. There's *riz sauce* (boiled rice with a sauce to pour over), *riz gras* (gooey rice cooked in animal fat, usually tomato flavoured), *sauce de poisson* (a fish-based sauce), *boeuf sauce aubergine* (sauce with beef and eggplant), *mouton sauce tomate* (sauce with mutton and tomatoes), *ragoût d'igname* (a yam-based stew), *riz sauce arachide*, also known as *riz sauce carachide* (rice with peanut

BURKINA FASO

sauce) and *sauce gombo* (a sticky okra-based stew).

Sauces are always served with a starch, usually rice or the Burkinabé staple, *tô*, a millet- or sorghum-based *pâte* (a pounded dough-like substance). Stewed *agouti* (grass-cutter, a large rodent) is a prized delicacy, as is *capitaine* (Nile perch). Lunch is the main meal; at night, grilled dishes are popular.

As throughout West Africa, grilled dishes of chicken and fish are available on seemingly every street corner and are often the cheapest foods on offer. Apart from the ubiquitos *brochettes* (grilled meat cooked on a stick, often with a peanut sauce), the more popular dishes include *poulet yassa* (grilled chicken in onion and lemon sauce) and *kedjenou* (slowly simmered chicken or fish with peppers and tomatoes).

DRINKS

Bottled Lafi spring water (CFA400 for a 1.5L bottle) is safe, as are the plastic sachets of Yilembe mineral water. Soft drinks are often known as *sucreries*.

Castel, Flag, Brakina and So.b.bra (just that; pronounced *so-bay-bra*) are popular and palatable lager-type beers.

Getting There & Away

AIR

Burkina Faso's main international airport is Aéroport International d'Ouagadougou. The national carrier is Air Burkina; other airlines servicing Burkina Faso are Ghana Airways and Air France.

There's an international departure tax of CFA8000 that is normally included in the price of your ticket.

Europe & the USA

Air France has four flights a week between Ouagadougou and Paris. An undiscounted return ticket costs around CFA394,500 (return tickets are cheaper than one way). From Paris, a one-way flight to Ouagadougou costs from €400, more during the peak months of July and August. Discounted tickets are difficult to come by.

Point Afrique (W www.point-afrique.com) has one flight a week from Paris/Marseilles to Ouagadougou. Return fares start from €410, plus taxes.

For travel to/from the USA, you have to transfer in Paris, Dakar or Abidjan.

Africa

There's a daily flight from Ouagadougou to Abidjan on Air Burkina (around CFA80,000 one way). Air Burkina flies to Bamako (Mali; CFA95,000) and Lomé (Togo; CFA125,000), as well as Cotonou (Benin) and Niamey (Niger). Some Air Burkina flights to Abidjan (Côte d'Ivoire) and Bamako go via Bobo-Dioulasso. Ghana Airways flies to Accra (Ghana) twice weekly (CFA186,400/272,600 for one way/return).

For travel to/from East and Southern Africa, you need to pick up a connection in Abidjan or Dakar.

LAND

Border Crossings

The main border crossings are at Niangoloko for Côte d'Ivoire; Tanguiéta for Benin; 15km south of Pô for Ghana; Sinkasse for Togo; east of Kantchari for Niger; and west of Tiou for Mali. Borders tend to be closed by 5.30pm or 6.30pm at the latest. Remember that there is a time change of one hour going from Burkina Faso into Benin or Niger (both ahead of Burkina Faso).

Benin

A Sotrao bus runs every Sunday from Ouagadougou to Tanguiéta (Benin; CFA5000). There's a twice-daily STMB bus (CFA2500, four hours, 225km) and daily minibuses (CFA3500) between Ouagadougou and Fada N'Gourma. Onward transport to the border (CFA3500) is scarce and fills up slowly.

Ask around the Total petrol station immediately north of Zaka on Av Yennenga in Ouagadougou, from where minibuses occasionally leave for Natitingou.

Côte d'Ivoire

Bus & Bush Taxi Large buses, mostly packed with migrant Burkinabé workers, leave Ouagadougou and Bobo-Dioulasso daily for Bouaké (CFA15,000, 925km from Ouagadougou), Yamoussoukro (CFA15,000) and Abidjan (CFA16,000). The full 1175km trip takes at least 24 hours – more if your bus stops overnight at the border. Central Transport International (CTI; ☎ 31 65 09) on Av

Niandé Ouédraogo is among those with a daily 6pm bus to Abidjan.

From Bobo-Dioulasso, Sans Frontière have two buses a day to Abidjan (CFA12,000, 17 to 19 hours) via Ferkessédougou (CFA6000) and Niangoloko (CFA1500), while Sotrakof also has a daily departure for the same prices.

A transborder bush taxi between Bobo-Dioulasso and Ferkessédougou is CFA7500.

Train The train connects Ouagadougou and Abidjan, leaving the Burkinabé capital on Tuesday, Thursday and Saturday at 8.30am, and arriving on the Atlantic coast more than 24 hours later. The cost for the full journey is CFA21,200/26,100 in 2nd/1st class; 2nd class can be very overcrowded. Food and drinks can be purchased from vendors at stops en route, but you'd be well advised to bring some of your own supplies to tide you over during the incomprehensible stops in the middle of nowhere. Chalkboard at stations along the way announce the *arrivée probable* (expected time of arrival) of l'Express.

Ghana

A Ghanaian VanefSTC (☎ 30 87 50) bus makes the 24-hour journey from Ouagadougou via Tamale (CFA7000, 363km) and Kumasi (CFA8000, 720km) to Accra (CFA10,000, 1000km) on Monday, Wednesday and Friday. You must report two hours before the 8.30am departure time and tickets must be purchased at least a day in advance.

STMB has two daily buses from Ouagadougou to Pô (CFA2500, 144km), 15km from the border, from where there's infrequent transport to the border (CFA1250) and on to Bolgatanga in Ghana (CFA1000). A bush taxi from Ouagadougou to Pô costs CFA3000. If you're coming the other way, there are usually bush taxis waiting on the Burkinabé side of the border ready to take you to Ouagadougou.

The other frequently used border crossing is at Hamale in the southwest of Burkina Faso. Coming from Ghana, you'll probably have to stay at Hamale's cheap hotel and catch the 8am bus to Bobo-Dioulasso the next morning.

Mali

From Bobo, Sans Frontière and Sotrakof each has a daily departure to Bamako (CFA8000, 15 hours) via Ségou (CFA6000, 10 to 12 hours). If you're heading from Bobo-Dioulasso to Mopti, Peugeot taxis (CFA8000, 12 to 15 hours) leave from Bobo's Gare de Mopti from about 7am or in the early evening; Sunday seems to be the best day. Sans Frontière also has an occasional bus from Bobo-Dioulasso to Mopti.

If you're heading for Dogon country, the road from Ouahigouya to the border is in good condition, but deteriorates on the Malian side. The most comfortable option is to take the daily (10am) Sogebaf bus to Koro (CFA2500, two to four hours). From there you'll need to connect by bush taxi to Bankass and then Mopti; on Saturday, market day in Koro, you stand a better chance of finding onward transport.

Niger

Niamey (CFA7500, 12 hours, 500km) is not well served from Ouagadougou. Sotrao has a Wednesday bus and the Niger-registered SNTV runs on Friday from Sotrao's office; buy your ticket at least a day in advance. Sans Frontière, CTI and STMB are among those with a daily (7am) service to Kantchari (CFA5000), from where there's intermittent transport across the frontier.

Minibuses to the Nigerien border (CFA5000) leave from Ouagadougou's main gare routière, but they're not frequent. It's CFA2000 from the border to Niamey.

Minibuses from Ouagadougou to Niamey (CFA9500, 11 to 14 hours) leave from the petrol stations immediately north of the Zaka in Ouagadougou.

Togo

At the time of writing, there were no buses connecting Burkina Faso and Togo; the most direct route by bus was to Accra in Ghana, and then changing there.

There are direct bush taxis from Ouagadougou's gare routière to Lomé (CFA15,000, 965km), but it's cheaper and less tiring to travel in stages. Take a minibus first to Bitou (40km from the border, CFA4500), then on to Dapaong (CFA2500).

Minibuses to the Togolese border often leave in the morning from the Total Petrol Station near Zaka in Ouagadougou. Alternatively, take any transport heading east and change in Koupéla. Expect heavy searches at the border, which closes at 6.30pm.

Getting Around

AIR
Air Burkina has at least three flights a week between Ouagadougou and Bobo-Dioulasso (CFA28,485).

BUS
Buses are the most reliable and comfortable way to get around. There are numerous companies from which to choose. Major transport companies, such as STMB, Sotrao, Sogebaf and Sans Frontière, have large buses with guaranteed seating and fixed departure times; most leave from their own offices.

BUSH TAXI & MINIBUS
Minibuses and bush taxis, mostly ageing Peugeot 504s, cover major towns, and also outlying communities that large buses don't serve. Most leave from the gares routières, and morning is the best time to find them. Minibuses are usually 33% cheaper than Peugeot taxis, but can take an age to fill up.

TRAIN
There are two train routes in Burkina Faso, but both are infinitely slower than road transport. Things have improved since the French-run Sitarail took over the service. The Abidjan-bound Express (still a manner of speaking only) leaves Ouagadougou on Tuesday, Thursday and Saturday at 8.30am and heads to Côte d'Ivoire via Koudougou (CFA1500/1900 for 2nd/1st class, two hours), Bobo-Dioulasso (CFA5800/7100, up to seven hours) and Banfora (CFA7400/9100, nine hours).

There's also a Saturday train between Ouagadougou and Kaya, leaving Ouagadougou at 8.20am and returning from Kaya at 2.30pm the same day (CFA2000/3000 for 2nd/ 1st class). Cancellations, even changes of day, are frequent.

CAR & MOTORCYCLE
Sealed roads are driveable year-round. During the rainy season, you may find your progress impeded by rain barriers, which are lifted once temporary flooding further down the road has abated.

A litre of petrol costs CFA380, super (premium) is CFA410 and *gasoil* (diesel) is CFA325.

ORGANISED TOURS
Because the wildlife parks and reserves are inaccessible by public transport, your only options are to hire a 4WD or take an organised tour. For details, see the relevant sections later in this chapter.

Ouagadougou

Ouagadougou became the capital of the Mossi empire in 1441 and, 250 years later, was chosen as the permanent residence of the Moro-Naba, the Mossi king. The town grew up around the imperial palace, and was extended during colonisation. The completion of the railway from Abidjan in 1954 resulted in the city expanding rapidly. The expansion process has been fuelled more recently by the country's rural exodus.

There's not a great deal to turn your head in Ouagadougou, but the city has a relaxed atmosphere and you'll find the people open and accessible. It's a relatively compact city that is easy to get around on foot.

Ouagadougou is one of the cultural centres of West Africa. Apart from its lively nightlife, it is the undisputed capital of African film, hosting the biennial Fespaco, Africa's premier film festival.

Orientation
Ouagadougou is built on a fairly regular grid pattern and the streets are well signed. Take your bearings from the unmistakable globe at the centre of the busy Place des Nations Unies, from which the city's five main boulevards lead. The human heart of town is the nearby Grand Marché, or central market, completed in 1989.

Along Av Yennenga is a concentration of budget hotels and inexpensive places to eat. Av de la Résistance du 17 Mai and Av Kwame Nkrumah, parallel but quite different in character, have several of Ouagadougou's swankier restaurants and upmarket clubs.

North of the railway line, especially around Marché Sankariaré and Av de la Liberté, are some of the city's best bargain hotels.

Information
Tourist Information Look for the ONTB (Office Nationale du Tourisme Burkinabé) sign stuck to the entrance door of the dusty

BURKINA FASO

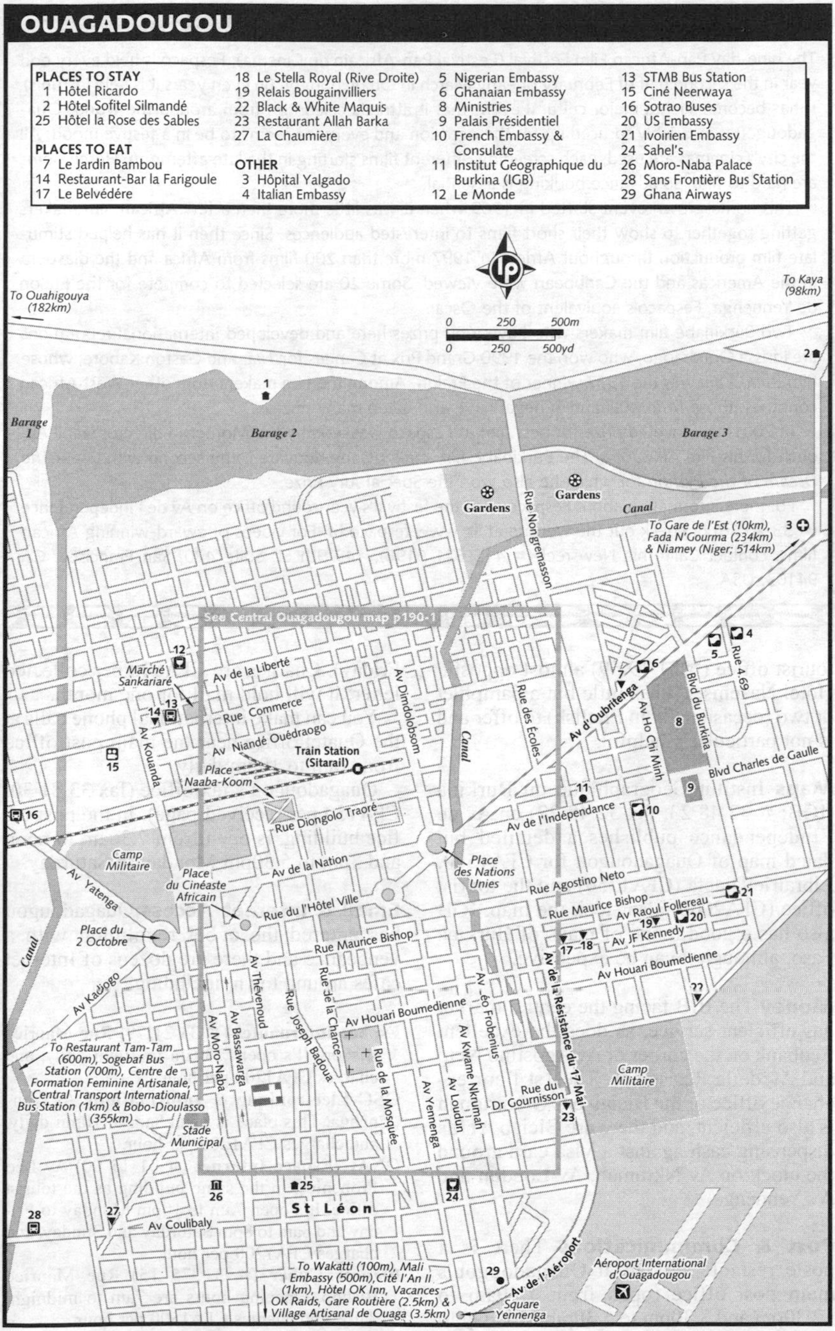
OUAGADOUGOU
PLACES TO STAY
1 Hôtel Ricardo
2 Hôtel Sofitel Silmandé
25 Hôtel la Rose des Sables
PLACES TO EAT
7 Le Jardin Bambou
14 Restaurant-Bar la Farigoule
17 Le Belvédère
18 Le Stella Royal (Rive Droite)
19 Relais Bougainvilliers
22 Black & White Maquis
23 Restaurant Allah Barka
27 La Chaumière
OTHER
3 Hôpital Yalgado
4 Italian Embassy
5 Nigerian Embassy
6 Ghanaian Embassy
8 Ministries
9 Palais Présidentiel
10 French Embassy & Consulate
11 Institut Géographique du Burkina (IGB)
12 Le Monde
13 STMB Bus Station
15 Ciné Neerwaya
16 Sotrao Buses
20 US Embassy
21 Ivoirien Embassy
24 Sahel's
26 Moro-Naba Palace
28 Sans Frontière Bus Station
29 Ghana Airways
To Ouahigouya (182km)
To Kaya (98km)
0 250 500m
0 250 500yd
Barage 1
Barage 2
Barage 3
Gardens
Gardens
Canal
Rue Nongremasson
To Gare de l'Est (10km), Fada N'Gourma (234km) & Niamey (Niger; 514km)
See Central Ouagadougou map p190-1
Marché Sankariaré
Av de la Liberté
Rue Commerce
Av Niandé Ouédraogo
Train Station (Sitarail)
Av Dimdolobsom
Canal
Rue des Ecoles
Av d'Oubritenga
Av Ho Chi Minh
Blvd du Burkina
Rue 4.69
Blvd Charles de Gaulle
Av Kouanda
Place Naaba-Koom
Rue Diongolo Traoré
Av de l'Indépendance
Camp Militaire
Place du Cinéaste Africain
Av de la Nation
Place des Nations Unies
Rue Agostino Neto
Av Yatenga
Rue du l'Hôtel Ville
Rue Maurice Bishop
Av Raoul Follereau
Place du 2 Octobre
Rue Maurice Bishop
Av JF Kennedy
Canal
Av Kadiogo
Av Thevenoud
Rue Joseph Badoua
Rue de la Chance
Av Léo Frobenius
Av de la Résistance du 17 Mai
Av Houari Boumedienne
Av Houari Boumedienne
Av Bassawarga
Av Moro-Naba
Rue de la Mosquée
Av Kwame Nkrumah
Av Loudun
Av Yennenga
Rue du Dr Gournisson
Camp Militaire
To Restaurant Tam-Tam (600m), Sogebaf Bus Station (700m), Centre de Formation Feminine Artisanale, Central Transport International Bus Station (1km) & Bobo-Dioulasso (355km)
Stade Municipal
St Léon
Av Coulibaly
Av de l'Aéroport
Aéroport International d'Ouagadougou
To Wakatti (100m), Mali Embassy (500m), Cité l'An II (1km), Hòtel OK Inn, Vacances OK Raids, Gare Routière (2.5km) & Village Artisanal de Ouaga (3.5km)
Square Yennenga

BURKINA FASO

Fespaco

The nine-day Pan-African Film Festival (Festival Pan-Africain du Cinema), Fespaco is held every odd year in the second half of February or early March in Ouagadougou (in even years it is held in Tunis). It has become such a major cultural event that it attracts celebrities from around the world. Ouagadougou is invariably spruced up for the occasion and everyone seems to be in a festive mood. All the city's cinemas are used, each screening different films starting in the late afternoon. Hotel rooms are hard to find, so advance booking is essential.

This home-grown event started in 1969 when it was little more than a few African film makers getting together to show their short films to interested audiences. Since then it has helped stimulate film production throughout Africa. In 1997 more than 200 films from Africa and the diaspora in the Americas and the Caribbean were viewed. Some 20 are selected to compete for the Étalon de Yennenga, Fespaco's equivalent of the Oscar.

Two Burkinabé film makers who have won prizes here and developed international reputations are Idrissa Ouedraogo, who won the 1990 Grand Prix at Cannes for *Tilä;* and Gaston Kaboré, whose film *Buud Yam* was the 1997 winner of the Étalon. Among the film makers from other West African countries, those from Mali and Senegal have also taken many prizes.

In 2001, the coveted prize for best film at Fespaco was won by the Moroccan director Nabil Ayouch for his film *Ali Zaoua*. The Burkinabé film maker Dany Kouyate came second with *Sya – The Dream of the Python* for which he also won the Special Jury Prize.

For more information about Fespaco, visit the festival's year-round office on Av de l'independence (☎ 33 20 66) or check out the website at W www.fespaco.bf. For videos of award-winning African films, contact California Newsreel (☎ 415-621 6196), 149 9th St, Suite 420, San Francisco, CA 94103, USA.

BURKINA FASO

tourist office (☎ 31 19 59) almost opposite Hôtel Nazemsé. It has little but a pamphlet or two (occasionally in English) to offer and is not particularly helpful.

Maps Institut Géographique du Burkina (IGB; ☎ 32 48 23, fax 32 48 27) on Av de l'Indépendance publishes a detailed but dated map of Ouagadougou for CFA1500. Librairie Diacfa (CFA1750) and the tourist office (CFA2000) also stock the map. IGB also has a good range of maps of Burkina Faso, although it can be expensive.

Money The BIB facing the central market has efficient service, as does the excellent Ecobank on the corner of Av Agostino Neto and Av de la Résistance. The 1st floor exchange office of the Biciab on Av Nkrumah is also efficient, and there are Biciab ATMs dispensing cash against a Visa card around the clock on Av Nkrumah, Av Loudun and Av Yennenga.

Post & Communications There is a poste restante service at Ouagadougou's main post office (open from 7.30am to 12.30pm and 3.30pm to 5.30pm Monday to Friday). Charges are CFA500 per collected letter; it will hold mail for one month.

You can make international phone calls at the Onatel office near the main post office from 7am to 10pm daily.

Ouagadougou's fax office (fax 33 81 30; CFA750 per received page), in the post office building, is open from 7.30am to noon and 3pm to 5.30pm Monday to Saturday.

Email & Internet Access Ouagadougou has entered the cyber revolution with a vengeance and there are dozens of Internet cafés around town, including:

Éspace Internautes (☎ 33 21 79) Rue Maurice Bishop. It's open 7.30am to 10pm daily, and charges CFA1200 per hour.

GSC Electronique & Informatique Av Yennenga. This place is open 8am to 10pm daily, and charges CFA1200 per hour.

ONAC Éspace Internet (☎ 31 13 00) Av Léo Frobenius, in the same building as the tourist office. It's open 7am to 10pm Monday to Friday and 8am to 8pm Saturday and Sunday, and charges CFA1200 per hour.

Planete Cyber (☎ 31 75 15) Rue Maurice Bishop. Opening hours are 7am to midnight daily, and charges CFA1500 per hour.

Travel Agencies & Tour Operators Several agencies offer individualised or programmed tours around Burkina Faso. Those that stand out for reliability and the range of tours are L'Agence Tourisme (☎ 31 84 43, fax 31 84 44) at Hôtel les Palmiers on Rue Joseph Badoua; Kenedia Travel (☎ 31 59 69, fax 31 59 70) on Av Nkrumah, Vacances OK Raids (☎ 38 27 49, fax 30 48 11, ⓔ okraid@mail.cenatrin.bf) at Hôtel OK Inn, and Safaris du Sourou (☎ 31 24 08, fax 31 24 10), at Hôtel Relax on Av de la Nation. For budget travellers, both the Auberge les Manguiers and Le Pavillon Vert (see Places to Stay – Budget) can also organise tours at a reasonable price.

For purchasing air tickets, the most professional and experienced agency is the IATA-registered Armelle Voyages (☎ 31 17 60) on Av Léo Frobenius.

Bookshops Librairie Diacfa, facing the Grand Marché on Rue du l'Hôtel Ville, carries a wide range of magazines and newspapers, including a few in English. It also stocks stationery items.

Radio For FM radio and news, tune to the following stations:

BBC Afrique	99.1
Horizon FM	104.4
Radio France Internationale	94.0
Radio Nationale	88.5
Radio Pulsar	94.8

BBC Afrique, the BBC French-language service for Africa, has some evening programming in English.

Medical Services In the event of an emergency, you'd be better off seeking a recommendation through your embassy or a top-end hotel. For minor illnesses or injuries, head to Hôpital Yalgado (☎ 31 16 55). Pharmacie Nouvelle on Rue Maurice Bishop is well stocked.

Dangers & Annoyances Most resident expats walk around Ouagadougou at night without qualms although it is, of course, prudent to watch your back, particularly on Av Yennenga and the southern stretches of Rue Joseph Badoua. There have recently been a few reports of muggings (some even in daylight and, occasionally, at knifepoint) of bag-carrying travellers, so carry as little as you need, never carry a bag after dark and walk with people you know. Always take a taxi after 10pm. It is worth remembering, however, that the overwhelming number of visitors experience no problems.

Should you have a problem in Ouagadougou, contact the police at the *commissariat central* (☎ 30 62 71).

Things to See & Do

Musée National *(☎ 33 06 37, Av de la Nation; admission CFA1000; open 9am-noon & 3.30pm-6pm Mon-Sat)* was still awaiting a move to its new premises at the time of research, and most items were still in crates. In the meantime, a small but interesting exhibition of masks were on temporary display on the ground floor of the Maison du Peuple. Highlights of the modest collection will be its ancestral statues, especially those from Lobi country, and the masks and traditional costumes.

Musée de la Musique *(☎ 31 09 27, Av d'Oubritenga; admission CFA1000; open 9am-noon & 3.30pm-6pm Tues-Sun)* is a good place to spend an hour if you have an interest in traditional music. The uncluttered displays include *tambours* (drums), flutes, xylophones and *luth* (harps) from around the country. Among the highlights are the impressive *Lan* or *castagnettes de pieds* (foot castanets). There are informative labels in French throughout, and a guide will show you around (a tip is appreciated) but it's only worthwhile if you speak French; otherwise he'll simply point and say 'drum'.

The **cathedral** is another heavy, stolid structure built to impress but not to charm. The **Maison du Peuple** claims to be inspired by Burkina Faso's traditional architecture but it's a million miles from the grace and understatement of traditional Burkinabé housing.

In an act of officially perpetrated vandalism, Sankara had the old **Grand Marché** razed and in its place erected the present ponderous concrete monstrosity. But beneath the angular, unadorned roof, the traders have again made it their own. It's a maze of crowded alleys; keep your bearings or you'll spend ages trying to get out.

Nonguests can go **swimming** in hotel pools at Hôtel Nazemsé, Hôtel de l'Indépendance, Hôtel Palm Beach, Hôtel Ricardo (all

CFA1500), Hôtel Relax (CFA2000) and Hôtel Sofitel Silmandé (CFA2500). There is also a pool at Restaurant la Colombe (CFA700). There are **tennis courts** at the Silmandé that nonguests can use; there's a **billiard table** at the Indépendance.

Places to Stay – Budget

Fondation Charles Dufour *(☎ 30 38 89, Rue de la Chance)* Floor mattress CFA1500, dorm bed CFA2500, singles/doubles with shared bathroom CFA4000/5000. This is a great place for price and ambience. Profits from this simple hotel and membership fees for the foundation (CFA10,000) go to support some 20 orphans whom Adama Yameogo feeds, lodges and educates. Even if you're not staying here, you might like to drop by and become a member. The tidy, well-maintained rooms come with mosquito net (though shared facilities are rather grimy). Filling meals cost CFA1500, or you can cook for yourself.

Centre d'Accueil des Soeurs Lauriers *(☎ 30 64 90)* Beds CFA4000. This place, within the cathedral compound, is a safe and hassle-free place for women travelling alone. Accommodation is in spotless rooms with mosquito net, shower and fan. Copious meals cost CFA1500.

Hôtel la Rose des Sables *(☎ 31 30 14)* Singles/doubles with fan CFA6000/8000, doubles with air-con CFA18,800. La Rose des Sables, south of the cathedral, is decent value and has a pleasant garden. Good meals cost from CFA2000.

Along Av Yennenga are several cheap but seedy hotels that are not recommended for women travelling alone.

Pension Guigsème *(Av Yennenga)* Singles/doubles with shared bathroom CFA3000/4000. This place is the cheapest of the cheap. The folk are friendly, the rooms basic and the shower area recalls the black hole of Calcutta.

Hôtel de la Paix *(☎ 33 52 93, Av Yennenga)* Singles/doubles with fan CFA5300/6800, rooms with bathroom & air-con CFA10,300. The generally clean rooms here are pretty good value, although they can get fiercely hot in summer and some of the air-conditioners appear to date from the colonial era. It's a friendly place and is located in a lively area.

Hôtel Idéal *(☎ 30 65 02, Av Yennenga)* Doubles with fan & shower CFA7500. The rooms here are a little overpriced and the toilets are shared, but the staff are friendly.

Hôtel Yennenga *(☎ 30 73 37, Av Yennenga)* Singles/doubles with fan & shower

Moro-Naba Ceremony

Such is the influence of the Moro-Naba of Ouagadougou, the emperor of the Mossi and the most powerful traditional chief in Burkina Faso, that the government will always consult him before making any major decision. The portly present Moro-Naba, the 37th, is, typically for his dynasty, an imposing figure.

The Moro-Naba ceremony, *la cérémonie du Nabayius Gou*, takes place around 7.15am every Friday. It's a very formal ritual that lasts only about 15 minutes. Prominent Mossis arrive by taxi, car and moped (also known as mobylettes), greet each other and sit on the ground according to rank: in the first row sit the Moro-Naba's spokesman and his chief ministers and, behind them, other dignitaries sit in descending order of seniority. The Moro-Naba appears, dressed in red, the symbol for war, accompanied by his saddled and elaborately decorated horse. There's a cannon shot, his most senior subjects approach to give obeisance and His Majesty retires, while his horse is unsaddled and beats the bounds of his palace at a brisk trot.

The Moro-Naba reappears, dressed all in white, a sign of peace, and his servants invite his subjects to the palace for a drink; millet beer for the animists and a Kola nut concoction for the Muslims. It's much more than an excuse for an early morning tipple as, within the palace, the Moro-Naba gives audience and hands down his verdict on local disputes and petty crimes. The preceding ritual serves to reinforce the Mossi social order.

The story behind the ceremony? As so often in Africa, there are several conflicting versions. The predominant one recounts how the Ouahigouya Mossi had stolen the Ouagadougou people's main fetish. As the king made ready for war, his ministers persuaded him to desist and undertook to recover the fetish.

CFA6200/7200, with toilet CFA7380/8380, with air-con CFA11,510/13,510. The decent rooms at the Hôtel Yennenga aren't a bad budget option.

Hôtel Delwendé *(☎ 30 87 57, Rue Maurice Bishop)* Singles/doubles with fan CFA7000/9000, with air-con CFA11,000/12,500. Above the unprepossessing entrance of the Delwendé are decent rooms with fan or affordable air-con. All rooms have showers. The long 2nd-floor balcony is a great place for drinks and watching the street life in the market area.

On the northern side of town are three highly recommended hotels.

Le Pavillon Vert *(☎/fax 31 06 11, Av de la Liberté)* Singles/doubles with fan & shared bathroom CFA5000/5500, with private bathroom CFA9000/10,000, with air-con CFA15,000/16,000. This is a favourite haunt of both French expats and travellers. It's a friendly, tranquil haven with *paillotes* (straw huts) and a good, though relatively pricey, open-air restaurant. The rooms with air-con are very spacious.

Auberge les Manguiers *(☎ 30 03 70, fax 30 03 75, Off Av de la Liberté)* Doubles with fan/air-con CFA14,500/18,500. Auberge les Manguiers is intimate and has pleasant rooms and a shady courtyard. The cooking here is similarly good and the welcome just as warm; there's even a minilibrary for guests.

Hôtel le Dapoore *(☎ 31 33 31, Rue du Commerce)* Doubles with fan from CFA7500, with air-con from CFA12,500. South of Av de la Liberté is the good-value Dapoore. Most of the rooms are quite spacious and clean, although some are quite run-down. All rooms have a bathroom.

Places to Stay – Mid-Range

Hôtel Belle Vue *(☎ 30 84 98, fax 30 00 37, Av Nkrumah)* Singles/doubles with bathroom CFA16,500/17,360. At this friendly and well-run place the small rooms, all with TV, air-con, mosquito net and phone, are particularly good value.

Hôtel Continental *(☎/fax 30 86 36, Av Loudun)* Rooms CFA10,000-16,000. Spacious, carpeted and sparsely furnished rooms at the Continental have the same facilities as the Hôtel Belle Vue although it's not quite as well maintained.

Hôtel Central *(☎ 33 34 17, Av de l'Hôtel Ville)* Singles/doubles with air-con CFA11,000/13,000, larger singles/doubles with phone & TV CFA24,000/28,500. Facing the market, Hôtel Central has a good but overpriced restaurant; the more-expensive rooms are quieter.

Hôtel les Palmiers *(31 84 43, fax 31 84 44, Rue Joseph Badoua)* Doubles/triples with bathroom CFA26,500/38,500. This French-run place has a delightful ambience, a sparklingly clean swimming pool and is superb value. The rooms have a touch of class and, not surprisingly, are often full, so book ahead.

Hôtel Yibi *(☎ 30 73 70, fax 30 59 00, Cnr Av Nkrumah & Rue du Dr Gournisson)* Singles/doubles CFA28,000/31,000 with air-con and TV. Hôtel Yibi deservedly pulls in the tour groups; it has very comfortable rooms.

Hôtel OK Inn *(☎ 37 00 20, fax 37 00 23, ⓔ hotelok-inn@cenatrin.bf, Off Blvd Circulaire)* Singles/doubles CFA27,500/32,000, bungalows CFA39,600. The French-owned Hôtel OK Inn is outstanding. The rooms are superb, there's a clean, short pool and a quality restaurant. Although on the southern outskirts of town, it offers a free shuttle into town five times a day.

Hôtel Ricardo *(☎ 31 17 17, fax 33 60 48)* Singles/doubles with air-con & TV CFA27,900/31,600. The colonial-style Ricardo is a bit out on a limb, but the staff are welcoming and it remains a justified favourite of overland tour groups. It has a lovely ambience, there's a small aviary in the garden and you may find yourself sharing the pool with a pair of ducks from the reservoir over the wall. It has a good restaurant, specialising in pizza, paella and grills. Although it's relatively remote, reception can have a metered taxi for you within five minutes.

Places to Stay – Top End

All rooms in this category come with air-con, TV and bathroom.

Hôtel de l'Indépendance *(☎ 30 60 60, fax 30 67 67, ⓔ hotelinde@cenatrin.bf, Av de la Resistance)* Doubles from CFA35,000. The Hôtel de l'Indépendance, 1km northeast of the Grand Marché, has comfortable rooms with satellite TV. There's a 50m pool, access to Ouagadougou's major tennis club and a billiard table.

Hôtel Palm Beach *(☎ 31 09 91, fax 36 68 39, Av Nkrumah)* Singles/doubles from

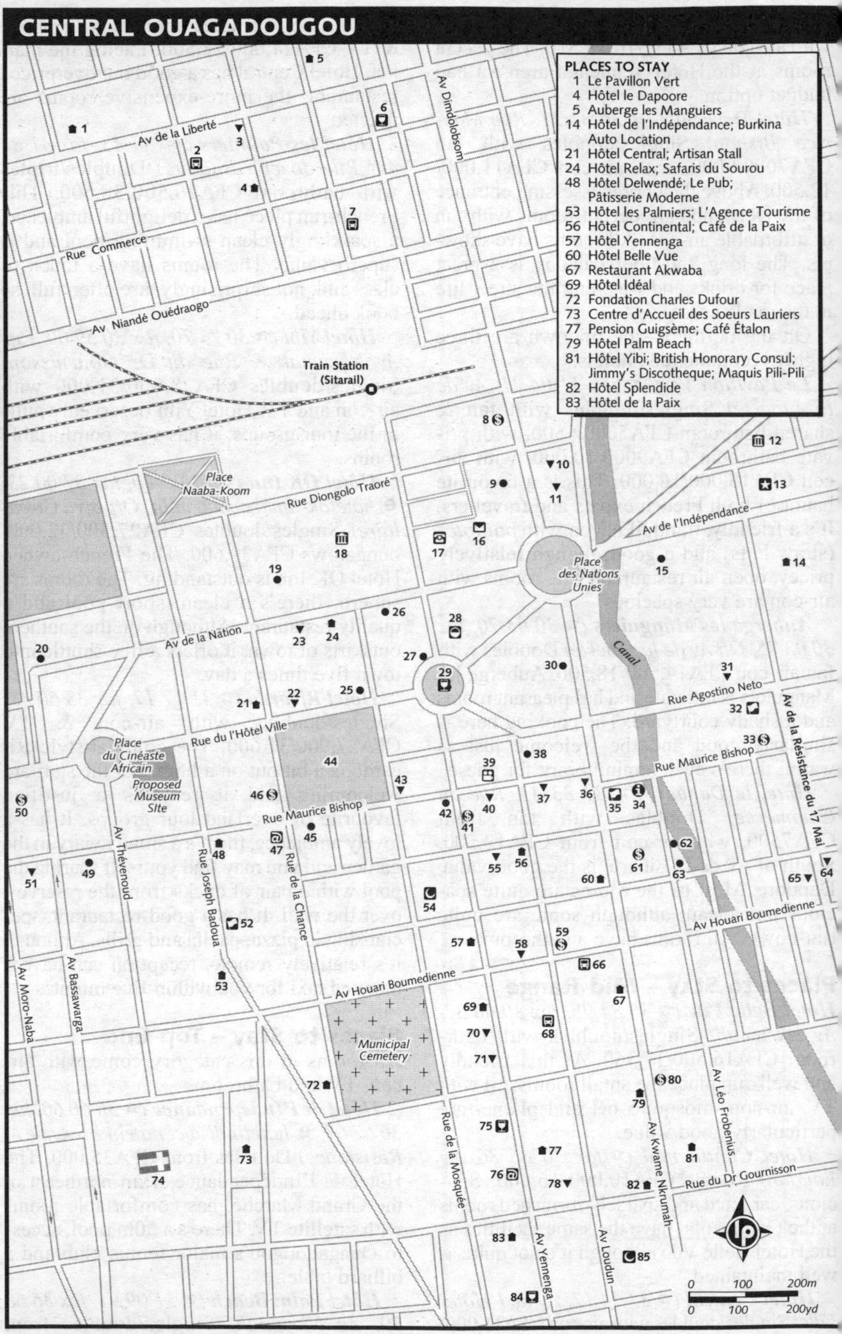
CENTRAL OUAGADOUGOU
PLACES TO STAY
1 Le Pavillon Vert
4 Hôtel le Dapoore
5 Auberge les Manguiers
14 Hôtel de l'Indépendance; Burkina Auto Location
21 Hôtel Central; Artisan Stall
24 Hôtel Relax; Safaris du Sourou
48 Hôtel Delwendé; Le Pub; Pâtisserie Moderne
53 Hôtel les Palmiers; L'Agence Tourisme
56 Hôtel Continental; Café de la Paix
57 Hôtel Yennenga
60 Hôtel Belle Vue
67 Restaurant Akwaba
69 Hôtel Idéal
72 Fondation Charles Dufour
73 Centre d'Accueil des Soeurs Lauriers
77 Pension Guigsème; Café Étalon
79 Hôtel Palm Beach
81 Hôtel Yibi; British Honorary Consul; Jimmy's Discotheque; Maquis Pili-Pili
82 Hôtel Splendide
83 Hôtel de la Paix
Av de la Liberté
Av Dimdolobsom
Rue Commerce
Av Niandé Ouédraogo
Train Station (Sitarail)
Place Naaba-Koom
Rue Diongolo Traoré
Av de l'Indépendance
Place des Nations Unies
Canal
Av de la Nation
Rue du l'Hôtel Ville
Place du Cinéaste Africain
Proposed Museum SIte
Rue Maurice Bishop
Rue Agostino Neto
Av de la Résistance du 17 Mai
Av Thévenoud
Rue Joseph Badoua
Rue de la Chance
Av Houari Boumedienne
Av Moro-Naba
Av Bassawarga
Municipal Cemetery
Rue de la Mosquée
Av Yennenga
Av Loudun
Av Kwame Nkrumah
Av Léo Frobenius
Rue du Dr Gournisson
0 100 200m
0 100 200yd

PLACES TO EAT
3 Maquis les Complices
10 Restaurant Les Tables de la Fortune
11 Le Verdoyant
22 Restaurant l'Eau Vive
23 Bagdad Café
31 La Colombe
36 Le Coq Bleu; Air Algérie
37 Le Vert Galant; Planete Cyber; Pharmacie Nouvelle
40 Sindabad's; Ciné Burkina
43 La Gourmandise
51 La Forêt
55 La Sorbetière
58 Restaurant da Chine; Pacific Auto Location; Palladium
64 Le Tambarze
65 Pâtisserie de Koulouba
70 Chez Awa; Restaurant Café Riale
71 Café Chez Salif
78 Nabonswende

OTHER
2 Sogebaf Bus Station
6 Bar Matata Plus; Le Casino
7 Central Transport International (CTI) Bus Station
8 BIB
9 Centre National d'Artisanat et d'Art
12 Musée de la Musique
13 Sûreté
15 Fespaco Office
16 Post Office
17 Onatel
18 Musée National; Maison du Peuple
19 Air France; Sortilèges
20 Air Burkina
25 Librairie Diacfa
26 Alimentation Cobodim
27 Nuances
28 Bush Taxis for Niger, Benin & Togo; Total Petrol Station
29 Zaka; Zaka Boutique
30 Palais du Justice
32 Canadian Embassy; Danish Embassy
33 Ecobank
34 ONTB (Tourist Office); ONAC Éspace Internet
35 Netherlands Embassy
38 Commissariat Central
39 Ciné Oubri
41 Biciab ATM
42 Scimas Supermarché
44 Grand Marché
45 Pharmacie Diawara
46 BIB Bank
47 Éspace Internautes
49 Ranch de Nazinga Office
50 BCEAO Bank (Central Bank)
52 German Embassy
54 Grande Mosquée
59 Biciab ATM
61 Biciab
62 Hôtel Nazemsé
63 Armelle Voyages
66 VanefSTC Ticket Office (Buses for Ghana)
68 Rayi's Transport
74 Cathedral
75 African Queen
76 GSC Electronique & Informatique
80 Ecobank; Kenedia Travel
84 Ludo Bar
85 Mosque

CFA34,520/37,180. The rooms at the Palm Beach are very attractive and comfortable, and there's a good pool. Prices are negotiable for longer stays.

Hôtel Splendide *(☎ 31 72 78, fax 31 72 91, ⓔ sph@fasonet.bf, Av Nkrumah)* Singles/doubles CFA45,000/48,500. Popular with business travellers, the Splendide has a decidedly upmarket feel. The buffet/continental breakfast costs CFA3500/5000.

Hôtel Relax *(☎ 31 32 33, fax 30 89 08, Av de la Nation)* Singles/doubles CFA34,500/38,000. The Relax is one block north of the Grand Marché and isn't bad value. The hotel has a pool.

Hôtel Sofitel Silmandé *(☎ 35 60 01, fax 30 09 71)* Doubles CFA75,000. Ouagadougou's smartest is the Hôtel Sofitel Silmandé. It has a long pool, a nightclub, a couple of restaurants, boutiques, taxi service, tennis courts and views overlooking the reservoir. Breakfast costs CFA7000.

Places to Eat

Budget There's a good choice of inexpensive street stalls and modest restaurants around Av Yennenga and Av Loudun. Perhaps the best value for money is ***Chez Awa*** *(☎ 31 25 75, Av Yennenga)*, where the folk are friendly and the portions generous. Nearby is ***Restaurant Café Riale*** *(☎ 31 44 30, Av Yennenga)*, the place to go for a great if expensive *sauce yassa* (grilled chicken in onion and lemon sauce; CFA2000), but the plain ***Café Chez Salif*** is cheaper; spaghetti with sauce, meat and chunky vegetables, for example, will set you back no more than CFA350. ***Café de la Paix*** *(☎ 30 86 36, Av Loudun)*, opposite Ciné Burkina, has a more varied selection but what's on the menu and what's available often don't correspond. ***Nabonswende*** sells yogurt and tasty spiced meat sandwiches.

Cité l'An II *(☎ 30 52 12, Av Bassawarga)* Mains from CFA600. Open noon-midnight daily. South of the centre, this popular and spacious open-air place is dimly lit at night but the grilled dishes are superb.

Restaurant-Bar la Farigoule *(☎ 31 70 49, Off Av Kouanda)* Mains from CFA1000. Open 6.30pm-midnight daily. This vast place near the STMB bus station is another venue with a variety of grills.

Restaurant Allah Barka (where the Senegalese *poulet yassa* is particularly good) and

Le Tambarze, both on Av de la Resistance du 17 Mai, and *Café Étalon* (Av Yennenga) are all rustic but pleasant with meals from CFA500. These places open from noon until around midnight.

Black & White Maquis *(Av Boumedienne)* Mains from CFA500. Open noon-11pm daily. This place is laid-back and agreeable.

Sindabad's *(Av Loudun)* Sandwiches CFA750, mains CFA1500-3500, pizzas from CFA3750. This place in the centre of town is excellent value. It's good for a snack such as a hamburger (CFA1250 to CFA2500 for a whopper among whoppers), sandwiches and more substantial Lebanese and other international selections.

There are also a number of cheap outdoor restaurants along or just off Av de la Liberté. Probably the pick of these is ***Maquis les Complices***, where the specialties include grilled dishes; an enormous plate of riz sauce is great value at just CFA400.

African An upmarket outdoor restaurant in a pleasant shady garden, ***La Forêt*** *(☎ 30 72 96, Av Bassawarga)* has mains from CFA2800 and is open from noon to 3pm and 6pm to 10.30pm daily. It offers a few selections each day, all well prepared.

La Colombe *(☎ 31 04 45, Off Rue Agostino Neto)* Mains from around CFA2500. This is another good place in a relaxing outdoor setting. Among its African specialities are poulet yassa and *kedjenou* (slowly simmered chicken or fish with peppers and tomatoes; both CFA2500) and *tieb bon djen* (strips of fried meat). Nonguests can use the swimming pool here for CFA700.

Restaurant Akwaba *(☎ 31 23 76, Av Nkrumah)* Mains with accompaniments around CFA4000. Open 11.30am-3pm & 6.30pm-11pm daily. For African food with top-class service and decor, this restaurant, with its mainly Ivoirian menu, is excellent and is deservedly popular with expats and locals alike. The service is good although the decor is marred by the spectacularly kitsch ceiling fans. The *brochette de capitaine* (grilled Nile perch; CFA3500) with *alloco* (fried plantains; CFA700) makes a remarkably satisfying meal.

Asian The food at ***Le Jardin Bambou*** *(☎ 31 35 14, Av d'Oubritenga)*, a Chinese-Vietnamese restaurant, is nothing special, but it's relatively affordable and the service is attentive. Mains cost from CFA1500, and it's open noon to 3pm and 6pm to 11pm daily. There's an air-con dining area and you can eat at the outside tables.

Restaurant da Chine *(☎ 31 18 60, Av Houari Boumedienne)* Mains from CFA2800. Open 11am-3pm & 7pm-11pm Tues-Sun. This place is more upmarket and centrally located than Le Jardin Bambou, and is pricier but also a step up in quality. The food and service are both good, although the waiters hover a bit when things are quiet.

Austrian Specialising in Austrian dishes, ***Restaurant Tam-Tam*** *(☎ 34 40 03, Av Kadiogo)* is open 11am to midnight Wednesday to Monday. It's a good place to eat before setting out on your bus ride from one of the nearby gares routières.

French Don't miss ***Restaurant l'Eau Vive*** *(☎ 30 63 03, fax 31 50 23, Av de l'Hôtel Ville)*, an Ouagadougou institution run by an order of nuns. Mains cost from CFA2500 and set menus from CFA4000; it's open noon to 2.15pm and 7.30pm to 10pm Monday to Saturday. At lunchtime, the air-con dining room provides a haven from the clamour of the market area right outside the front door. In the evening, you can dine in the tranquil mature garden. The food is mainly French, with a few African selections. Profits go to support the order's charitable works.

Restaurant Les Tables de la Fortune *(☎ 30 70 83, Av Dimdolobsom)* Mains from CFA3500. Open noon-3pm & 6pm-11pm Wed-Mon. Formerly known as La Fontaine Bleue, this French-owned restaurant has an attractive outdoor setting and serves delectable if pricey French and African cuisine. Go steady on the drinks, which are particularly expensive.

La Chaumière *(☎ 31 18 25, Av Coulibaly)* Mains from CFA3500. Open noon-3pm & 7pm-11pm Fri-Wed. This long-standing eatery, 1.5km southwest of the centre, is a local favourite and has Alsatian and Belgian specialities.

Le Pub *(☎ 31 25 25, Rue Maurice Bishop)* 2-course meals less than CFA5000. This small, friendly and central place near Hôtel Delwendé has tasty fare, and the French owner has a great selection of jazz CDs.

DAVID WALL

DAVID WALL

DAVID ELSE

PAUL DYMOND

FRANCES LINZEE GORDON

Scenes of daily life in West Africa: Ganvié stilt village, Lake Nokoué, Benin (top); pipers at the Palais Royale, Foumban, Cameroon (middle left); copying from the Koran onto a wooden 'slate', Mali (middle right); fetching water in Chinguetti, Mauritania (bottom left); painting the fishing boat, Porto Novo, Cape Verde (bottom right)

ARIADNE VAN ZANDBERGEN

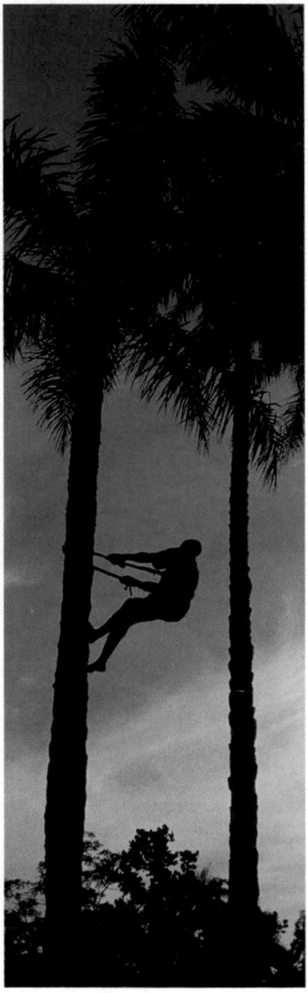

ANDREW BURKE

JANE SWEENEY

PETER PTSCHELINZEW

FRANCES LINZEE GORDON

All in a day's work: collecting fish for the market from offshore pirogues in Tanji, Gambia (top); hard at work in the Kofar Mata dye pits in Kano, Nigeria (middle); grinding millet in Timbuktu, Mali (middle right); collecting sap for palm wine at Makasutu Culture Forest, Gambia (left); waiting for a bite in St-Louis, Senegal (bottom right)

Le Stella Royal *(Rive Droite; ☎ 31 22 99, 206 Av Raoul Follereau)* Mains less than CFA5000. Open 11am-2.30pm & 6pm-10.30pm daily. Still known by many taxi drivers by its old name of Rive Droite, Le Stella Royal serves an imaginative range of predominantly French and African dishes.

Le Coq Bleu *(☎ 30 01 93, Cnr Rue Maurice Bishop & Av Kwame Nkurmah)* Mains from CFA3500. Open noon-2.30pm & 7pm-11pm Tues-Sun. This recommended place is the fanciest for quality French cooking. It may be more expensive than the competition but it offers excellent value for money. The blue decor is tasteful and soothing but the schmaltzy background music will have you scraping off the wallpaper. It also has a well-stocked bar.

And let's not forget the best of the hotel restaurants. ***Auberge les Manguiers*** and ***Le Pavillon Vert*** in particular offer good food in pleasant surroundings, although drinks can be expensive at the latter. The cuisine at the ***Hôtel OK Inn***, a favourite haunt of French expatriates, is impressive although expensive; for a weekend blowout, nothing beats the Sunday lunch buffet and barbecue.

Italian Just north of Place des Nations Unies, ***Le Verdoyant*** *(☎ 31 54 07, Av Dimdolobsom)* has mains from CFA2500 and pizzas from CFA3000. Open noon to 11pm Thursday to Tuesday, this popular and centrally located place has pleasant outdoor dining, and good service that diminishes a little when business is brisk. The lasagne (CFA2800) here is as good as you'll get anywhere.

Le Belvédère *(☎ 33 64 21, Av Raoul Follereau)* Mains from CFA2800. Open 6.30pm-11pm Wed-Mon. It doesn't try all that hard but Le Belvédère has an outdoor garden and an air-con dining room, serves good Italian and Lebanese food and bakes about the best pizza in town. It also does takeaway.

Relais Bougainvilliers *(☎ 31 48 81, Av JF Kennedy)* Mains from CFA2800. Open noon-3pm & 6pm-10.30pm daily. Around the corner, this place serves reasonable Italian selections either in the garden or in the air-con dining room.

Le Vert Galant *(☎ 30 69 80, Rue Maurice Bishop)* Mains from CFA3200. Open noon-2pm & 7pm-10.30pm Tues-Sat, 7pm-10.30pm Mon. This excellent French-run place has a wide-ranging menu (with French and Italian dishes), a pleasant dining area and bar, and attentive but unintrusive service. The spaghetti carbonara (CFA3300) is especially good. The starters and desserts are excellent but pricey. It's a popular place in the evenings.

Bagdad Café *(Av de la Nation)* This outdoor restaurant recently came under new management so it is difficult to predict its future direction. In its previous manifestation, it had a delightful ambience, good food and service, hip music and draught beer so hopefully it won't change too much.

Patisseries Ouagadougou has some good patisseries, or pastry shops. Hours are usually 6am to noon and 3pm to 7pm.

La Gourmandise facing the market's southeastern corner, is popular. It's on the 2nd floor and is great for watching the crowds. It stays open until midnight and serves beer and sandwiches. ***Pâtisserie Moderne***, starker and without the view, is also well situated (near Hôtel Delwendé).

La Sorbetière *(☎ 31 60 37, Av Babangida)* is a popular breakfast spot for wealthier Burkinabé. But the really discriminating locals patronise the cool, spacious ***Pâtisserie de Koulouba*** *(Av de la Résistance)*, which has a range of sandwiches and the widest selection of pastries.

Self-Catering Ouagadougou's largest and most popular supermarket among expats is ***Scimas Supermarché*** *(☎ 30 62 80, Cnr Av Yennenga & Rue Maurice Bishop)* open 8am to noon and 3pm to 6pm Saturday to Thursday. This is the place to go if you're craving a Magnum ice cream, Special K breakfast cereal, stuffed olives and plenty of less exotic produce. It also has a good wine selection.

Alimentation Cobodim *(☎ 30 63 50, Av de la Nation)* Open 8.30am-noon & 3.30pm-8.30pm Sat-Thur. Also centrally located and quite well stocked, Alimentation Cobodim is another good choice.

Entertainment

Bars At the time of research, ***Zaka*** *(☎ 31 53 12)* was Ouagadougou's premier live performance venue. It has drinks from CFA500 and is open from noon to 1am. There is nightly traditional and modern live music from 8.30pm (sometimes there's a small cover charge but usually it's free) and, less frequently, theatre. You can also dine (meals around CFA3000) at this popular and pleasant open-air watering hole in the heart of town. It's warmly recommended.

For late-night drinking, the liveliest area is along Av Yennenga. ***Ludo Bar*** *(☎ 30 65 11)*, with its large drinking area at the back, and the nearby ***African Queen***, are good, earthy and cheap.

Nightclubs There are two main fun areas: in the heart of town around Av Loudun and Av Nkrumah; and to the north, near Av de la Liberté.

Jimmy's Discotheque *(☎ 31 33 64, Av Nkrumah)* Admission CFA2500. If you're downtown, head to Jimmy's Discotheque which is a perennial favourite with Ouagadougou's youth. Jimmy's has air-con and, with drinks and admission both at CFA2500, is strictly for the well heeled. Nearby, ***New Jack*** *(☎ 31 53 16)* is a similarly flash joint with much the same prices.

Sahel's *(Av Loudun)* Admission free. Another lively place is Sahel's, which has drumming and live reggae music most nights.

Maquis Pili-Pili *(☎ 31 33 64, Av Nkrumah)* Admission free. This place has live blues music on weekends and also serves food.

Palladium *(Av Yennenga)* Admission CFA500. Closer to the centre, the Palladium features live music and has a large dance floor as well as food, including good brochettes and other snacks.

Bar Matata Plus *(Off Av de la Liberté)* Admission free. North of the railway at Bar Matata Plus, dancing to a live band starts at around 9pm. If you weary of the Matata, drift to its near-neighbour, ***Le Casino*** *(☎ 30 83 61)*.

Le Monde *(Off Av de la Liberté)* Admission CFA500, drinks from CFA1000. According to club cognoscenti, this long-standing club is still pretty cool.

Wakatti *(☎ 36 19 96, Av Bassawarga)* Admission CFA300. Last but not least, don't overlook the Wakatti, worth the trip south along Av Bassawarga.

Cinemas Built for Fespaco in the late 1960s, ***Ciné Burkina*** has a wide screen and good seats. It regularly shows African-produced films as well as recent international releases and a diet of kung fu and Bollywood potboilers.

Ciné Neerwaya *(☎ 31 72 72, Off Av Kouanda)* one block west of Av Kouanda is a pleasant alternative.

Shopping

Burkina Faso is an excellent place to look for masks and woodcarvings.

The ***Grande Marché*** merits a visit. There are some good craft stalls upstairs. In addition to local handicrafts, you'll find cloth and ready-made garments from the cotton mill in Koudougou and blankets from Dori. Steel yourself: the merchants here are – atypically for Burkinabé – at best importune and at times bordering on the aggressive.

Nuances *(☎ 31 72 74, fax 30 28 21, Av Yennenga)* This boutique is among the best in Burkina Faso, and has a terrific selection of artwork, jewellery, sculptures and other pieces from around Burkina Faso and much of Africa. Prices are fixed but very reasonable. The small courtyard often showcases exhibitions by local artists.

Zaka Boutique *(☎ 31 53 12)* Open 9am-11pm daily. This sophisticated boutique at the Zaka venue specialises in classy textiles, homeware and jewellery; some of the price tags are surprisingly reasonable.

Sortilèges *(☎ 31 60 80, Av de la Nation)* This place, next to Air France, is outstanding, though prices are expensive. It specialise in woodcarvings, especially masks and statues, but it also stocks some jewellery.

The small ***artisan stall*** under the balcony of Hôtel Central has a surprisingly wide range of masks and woodcarvings on sale at reasonable (and negotiable) prices.

Centre National d'Artisanat et d'Art *(☎ 30 68 35, Av Dimdolobsom)* Open 8am-noon & 3pm-6pm Mon-Fri. Profits here go directly to the artisan. The quality of the products is mixed, but take time to look over the bronze statues, wooden sculptures and colourful batiks. Apprentices and artisans here will gladly take you around their workshops and show you their craft. Follow your ears to the courtyard, where blacksmiths hammer and shape inventive and witty items from scrap iron.

Village Artisanal de Ouaga *(☎ 37 14 83, fax 37 14 59, ⓔ village.artisanal@cenatrin*

.bf, Blvd Circulaire) Open 8am-noon & 3pm-6pm Mon-Fri. The selection here is even wider than at the Centre National, and you can wander into the 'village' to see the artisans at work.

Centre de Formation Feminine Artisanale Open 7.30am-noon & 3.30pm-5.30pm Mon-Fri, 8am-noon Sat. Embroidered tablecloths and napkins, and woven rugs, are the speciality of this women's cooperative. It is in Gounghin, off the road to Bobo-Dioulasso on the western outskirts of town.

Getting There & Away

Air For details of international flights to/from Ouagadougou, see the Getting There & Away section earlier in this chapter. Air Burkina flights between Ouagadougou and Abidjan or Bamako make a stop in Bobo-Dioulasso five times a week.

The following airlines have offices in Ouagadougou:

Air Algérie (☎ 31 23 01, fax 30 58 82) Av Nkrumah
Air Burkina (☎ 30 76 76, 31 53 25) Av de la Nation
Air France (☎ 30 63 65, 30 63 66, 33 40 61) Av de la Nation
Ghana Airways (☎ 30 41 46) Av Nkrumah

Bus Most buses leave from the bus companies' depots rather than from the gare routière.

STMB (☎ 31 44 72) is, for the moment at least, the most reliable operator. It covers the following destinations:

destination	fare (CFA)	duration (hours)	frequency
Bobo	5000	5	5 daily
Dori	4000	5	2 daily
Fada N'Gourma	2500	4	4 daily
Ouahigouya	2500	2	4 daily
Pô	2500	2	2 daily

In addition to its five daily services without air-con to Bobo-Dioulasso (355km), STMB has two air-con services with more luxurious buses. The morning air-con bus leaves at 10am (CFA6500); the 2pm service (CFA8000) includes free soft drinks and snacks.

Sogebaf (☎ 34 42 55) has two main depots. Buses for Bobo-Dioulasso and Ouahigouya leave from the depot southwest of the town centre on Av Kadiogo; all other destinations are served from the depot just south of Av de la Liberté. Its departures include:

destination	fare (CFA)	duration (hours)	frequency
Bobo	5000	5	11 daily
Dori	4000	5	2 daily
Gorom-Gorom	5000	7	1 weekly (Wed)
Kaya	1500	3	2 daily
Ouahigouya	2500	2	8 daily

Sotrao, once the pride of Burkina Faso's fleet, has deteriorated rapidly and it services an ever-shrinking list of destinations. Don't be surprised if the list shrinks further by the time you read this. Most departures take place between 7am and 9am. Listed are the main destinations and fares from Ouagadougou; returns are the same day, unless shown otherwise:

destination	fare (CFA)	duration (hours)	frequency
Dédougou	3250	4	Mon, Wed, Sat (returns next day)
Djibo	2500	2½	Wed, Sat
Gaoua	5000	6	Mon, Wed, Sat (returns next day)
Kaya	1500	3	Mon, Wed, Sat
Kongoussi/ Djibo	2200	1½	Wed, Sat
Namounou	4750	8	Mon, Wed, Sat
Nouna	3500	4½	Mon, Wed, Sat (returns next day)
Pô	2500	2	daily
Tiébelé	1750	2½	Tues, Wed, Sat, Sun
Tougan	2500	4	Thur (returns Fri)

The best company for Koudougou (CFA1250, two hours) is Rayi's Transport (☎ 33 27 13) on Av Loudun. It has eight daily departures.

For details of services to Benin, Côte d'Ivoire, Ghana, Mali, Niger and Togo, see the Getting There & Away section earlier in this chapter.

Bush Taxi & Minibus Most bush taxis and minibuses leave in the early morning from the gare routière, 4km south of the centre. To get there, a shared taxi costs CFA250.

Train For details of train journeys from Ouagadougou, see Train in the Getting Around section earlier in this chapter.

Getting Around

To/From the Airport The 2km taxi journey from l'Aéroport International d'Ouagadougou to the centre costs about CFA1000 (50% more to Hôtel Sofitel Silmandé in the north). A shared taxi from nearby Av Nkrumah should cost CFA200. It's also possible to walk; Av Yennenga, with its many hotels, is only 1km away.

Taxi Green shared taxis, mostly beaten-up old Renaults, cost CFA200 for a ride within town. The basic rate for a private taxi (orange or green), which you commission just for yourself, is CFA500 and more for longer journeys. If you bargain hard, one by the hour will set you back CFA2500, or about CFA15,000 for a full day. Rates double after 10pm. Also handy if you're tired of bargaining are the yellow 'Taxi Urbain' (there are only a few), which have meters; you're most likely to find them along Rue Maurice Bishop.

Taxis are not too difficult to find during the day. At night, you'll find them, among other places, around Zaka (see Entertainment, earlier), at the taxi rank on Av d'Oubritenga just northeast of Place des Nations Unies, and outside the Hôtel de l'Indépendance.

Car Because insurance costs escalate if you drive yourself, it's cheaper to hire a car with a driver.

Vacances OK Raids (☎ 38 27 49, fax 30 48 11, 🆆 okraid@mail.cenatrin.bf) at Hôtel OK Inn is reliable and significantly cheaper than the competition. Typical costs including driver are CFA20,000 per day for a small car (CFA35,000 if you take the car out of town) and CFA65,000 for a 4WD. Unusually, there's no charge per kilometre.

Standard rates elsewhere start from CFA25,000/50,000 for a 2WD/4WD plus petrol and CFA150 to CFA250 per kilometre. Places worth trying include the long-established Burkina Auto Location (☎ 30 60 61, fax 30 67 67), based at the Hôtel de l'Indépendance, and Pacific Auto Location (☎ 24 07 52, 🆆 sadikous@yahoo.fr) on Av Houari Boumedienne. The latter is run by Sadikou Sampebgo, an accredited guide who charges CFA25,000/50,000 for a 2WD/4WD including driver and his guiding services; petrol is extra.

Bicycle & Moped The going rate to hire bicycles is CFA1500 to CFA2000 a day, and for mopeds it is CFA4000 to CFA5000; ask around your hotel. You can leave both bikes and mopeds safely for CFA50 at one of the myriad two-wheeler parks around town.

AROUND OUAGADOUGOU

Koudougou

pop 51,926

Koudougou is a dusty little city 97km to the west of Ouagadougou. Burkina Faso's third-largest settlement, it owes its commercial importance to the Faso Fani cotton mill, 3km out of town. With its wide, shaded avenues, Koudougou is a tranquil if unexciting place to stroll around after visiting the market, which has a vitality out of proportion to its size. The distinctively Sahelian style **Grande Mosquée** in the centre of town is worth a look.

Koudougou is a good base for exploring the nearby picturesque villages such as **Goundi** (8km) or **Sabou** and its crocodile lake (25km).

Places to Stay For a cheap, central option try ***Auberge Boulkiemdé*** *(☎ 44 11 51)*, but you do get what you pay for. Singles/doubles with fan and shower are CFA4000/8000. Some rooms are grotty to the point of being uninhabitable. There's a small restaurant and an external *piste* (dancing floor) – a mixed blessing if you're early to bed.

Hôtel Espérance *(☎ 44 05 59, Route de Dédougou)* Doubles with fan & shower CFA4000. The Espérance is much better value than Auberge Boulkiemdé and is worth the 1km walk from the centre. The folk are friendly and it's lovely and quiet.

Hôtel Photo Luxe *(☎ 44 00 87, fax 44 11 81, Route de Ouagadougou)* Doubles with fan & shower CFA6200, singles with air-con CFA8600, singles/doubles with bathroom & air-con CFA9700/10,900. The Photo Luxe, at the eastern entrance to town, is running downhill, but it has spotless rooms, a restaurant, a couple of bars and, at the weekend, the town's best nightspot. It's a bit out of town, but transport to Ouagadougou passes by the front door.

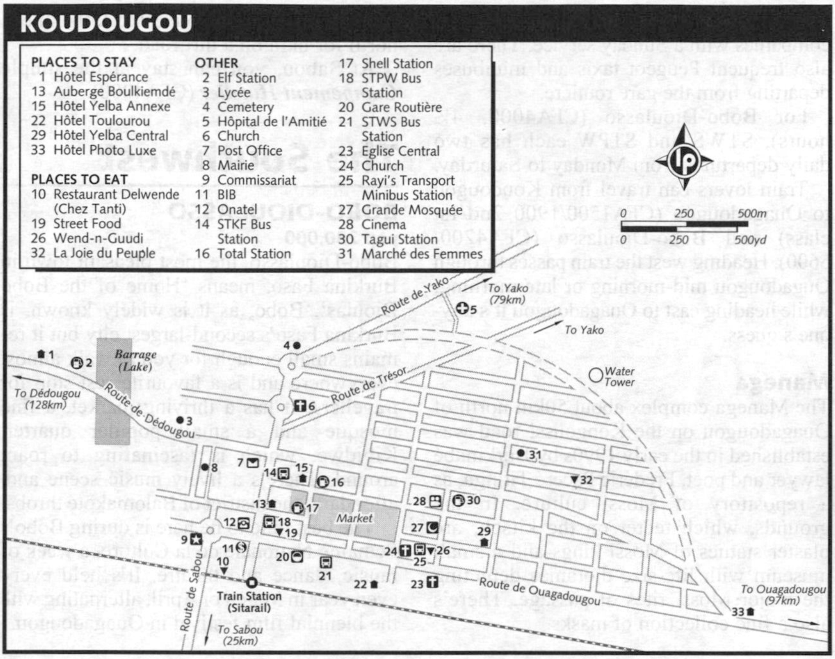
KOUDOUGOU
PLACES TO STAY
1 Hôtel Espérance
13 Auberge Boulkiemdé
15 Hôtel Yelba Annexe
22 Hôtel Toulourou
29 Hôtel Yelba Central
33 Hôtel Photo Luxe
PLACES TO EAT
10 Restaurant Delwende (Chez Tanti)
19 Street Food
26 Wend-n-Guudi
32 La Joie du Peuple
OTHER
2 Elf Station
3 Lycée
4 Cemetery
5 Hôpital de l'Amitié
6 Church
7 Post Office
8 Mairie
9 Commissariat
11 BIB
12 Onatel
14 STKF Bus Station
16 Total Station
17 Shell Station
18 STPW Bus Station
20 Gare Routière
21 STWS Bus Station
23 Eglise Central
24 Church
25 Rayi's Transport Minibus Station
27 Grande Mosquée
28 Cinema
30 Tagui Station
31 Marché des Femmes
0 250 500m
0 250 500yd
Route de Yako
To Yako (79km)
To Yako
Water Tower
Barrage (Lake)
To Dédougou (128km)
Route de Dédougou
Route de Trésor
Market
Route de Sabou
Train Station (Sitarail)
To Sabou (25km)
Route de Ouagadougou
To Ouagadougou (97km)

Hôtel Yelba Annexe *(☎ 44 09 39)* Singles/doubles with fan & bathroom CFA5750/7500. This centrally located hotel overlooks the market and the tidy rooms are far nicer than the exterior suggests.

Hôtel Yelba Central *(☎ 44 09 89)* Singles/doubles with a fan & shared bathroom CFA3000/6000, doubles with a fan & shower CFA8000, doubles with air-con & bathroom CFA12,000. This is another good choice and a little quieter than its near namesake. The rooms are good, the staff friendly and there are meals if you order in advance.

Hôtel Toulourou *(☎ 44 01 70)* Singles with air-con & shared/private bathroom CFA9400/12,500, doubles CFA16,800/18,800. Hôtel Toulourou, three blocks east of the train station, was built by Maurice Yaméogo, local boy made good and Burkina Faso's first president. With its attractive, air-con restaurant and shaded garden, it has weathered the years well. Guests can hire a hotel car to visit Sabou (CFA25,000 self-drive, CFA30,000 with driver).

Places to Eat & Drink The choice of places is limited. In addition to restaurants and bars at the major hotels, there are a few modest places.

Try ***Wend-n-Guudi***, one block south of the Grande Mosquée, for African food. The food is unexciting, but cheap.

You can also get good brochettes and guinea fowl on the street opposite the station road or inexpensive food in pleasant, simple surroundings at ***Restaurant Delwende*** *(Chez Tanti; ☎ 44 05 26)* nearer the station.

La Joie du Peuple Meals from CFA500. Open 11am-late. This restaurant-bar is best for African food, day or night. A spacious open-air place with funky paintings on the walls and recorded music, it has three or four African sauces to choose from. At night, it's also the best place for drinks and dancing.

Of the hotels, the restaurant at ***Hôtel Photo Luxe*** (see Places to Stay) is probably the best in town, though that's not saying much.

Getting There & Away Rayi's Transport (☎ 44 08 32), STWS (☎ 44 03 04), STPW (☎ 44 02 25) and STKF (☎ 44 17 06) all have at least seven buses a day from Monday to Saturday to/from Ouagadougou (CFA1250, two hours). Rayi's and STKF are the only companies with a Sunday service. There are also frequent Peugeot taxis and minibuses departing from the gare routière.

For Bobo-Dioulasso (CFA4000, 4½ hours), STWS and STPW each has two daily departures from Monday to Saturday.

Train lovers can travel from Koudougou to Ouagadougou (CFA1500/1900 2nd/1st class) and Bobo-Dioulasso (CFA4200/5600). Heading west the train passes through Ougadougou mid-morning or late morning, while heading east to Ouagadougou it's anyone's guess.

Manega

The Manega complex about 50km north of Ouagadougou on the Kongoussi road was established in the early 1990s by Burkinabé lawyer and poet, Frédéric Pacéré Titinga, as a repository of Mossi culture. In the grounds, which teeter on the kitsch, are plaster statues of Mossi kings and a small museum with life-size dioramas depicting the major Mossi rites of passage. There's also a fine collection of masks.

Laongo

At Laongo there's a rich outcrop of granite, varying from grey to pink. Here, the Ministry of Culture had the inspired idea of inviting Burkinabé and international sculptors to meet, relate and carve the rock. The results of this and subsequent workshops are chiselled in the pell-mell of rocks and boulders.

To get here, take the Fada N'Gourma road to the village of Boudtenga (32km), then head northeast on a dirt road to the village of Laongo.

Crocodile Lakes

If crocodiles give you frisson, there are a couple of sacred lakes within reach of Ouagadougou. The ritual's the same at each; you arrive, you're assailed by kids from whom you buy a live chicken at a sacrificial price, it's fed to a croc which lumbers out of the water and photos are taken of you, them and, grinning the widest, the croc.

Sabou, about 90km west on the Bobo-Dioulasso road and 25km from Koudougou, is on the tour bus circuit and is all the more hideous because of this fact. **Bazoulé** is less of a tourist trap but is catching up fast. Take the Bobo-Dioulasso road to the village of Tanghin Dassouri (about 30km), then head north for 6km on a dirt road.

At Sabou, you can stay at the simple ***Campement Hotelier*** (CFA4000).

The Southwest

BOBO-DIOULASSO

pop 230,000

Bobo-Dioulasso, the most pleasant town in Burkina Faso, means 'Home of the Bobo Dioulas'. Bobo, as it is widely known, is Burkina Faso's second-largest city but it remains small enough for you to walk almost everywhere and is a favourite rest stop for travellers. It has a thriving market, a fine mosque and a small popular quarter, Kibidwe, which is fascinating to roam around. There's a lively music scene and, after dark, the district of Balomakoté throbs.

The best time to be here is during Bobo's Semaine Nationale de la Culture, a week of music, dance and theatre. It's held every even year in March or April, alternating with the biennial film festival in Ouagadougou.

Orientation

The heart of town is the market, the Grand Marché. From the train station, Av de la Nation leads southeast to Place de la Nation, while Av de la Liberté heads northeast to Place du Paysan. The town's commercial core is the triangular area defined by these two roundabouts and the train station. The area south and east of the market houses many of the hotels, restaurants and banks.

Information

There is a poste restante counter at the post office.

Librairie Socifa, on Rue Joffre, stocks a good selection of international newspapers, including a few in English, as well as postcards, books and stationery.

Money Biciab, Ecobank and BIB change money, including travellers cheques in euros and US dollars (for which you'll need proof of purchase). Banks in Mali and Côte d'Ivoire are more challenging, so if you're going to either country, change money here.

The Biciab branch on the corner of Av Ponty and Av Ouédraogo has an ATM where you can extract CFAs from your Visa card.

BURKINA FASO

BOBO-DIOULASSO

PLACES TO STAY
3 Hôtel Méridien
9 Hôtel Hamdalaye
11 Ran Hôtel
23 L'Auberge
34 Hôtel Relax
36 Hôtel Teria
37 Hôtel l'Entente & Restaurant
45 Hôtel Renaissance
52 Hôtel Watinoma
58 Hôtel 421
59 Casafrica

PLACES TO EAT
15 Restaurant la Casa
19 La Sorbetière
27 Restaurant l'Express
29 Nouvelle Boule Verte
30 Restaurant l'Entente
38 Café des Amis
39 Restaurant Togolais; Street Vendors
40 Boulangerie Pastisserie la Bonne Miche
43 Restaurant Delwinde
44 L'Eau Vive
51 Restaurant Dan Kan
55 Bar-Restaurant Les Bambou

OTHER
1 Central Transport International
2 Sans Frontière Bus Station
4 Sogebaf Bus Station
5 STBF Bus Station
6 STMB Bus Station
7 Gare de Mopti
8 Ciné Sanyon
10 Grande Mosquée de Gérédougou
12 Cathedral
13 Librairie Socifa
14 Sotrakof Bus Station
16 Moped (Mobylette) Rentals
17 Grande Mosquée
18 Soweto Bar
20 Ecobank
21 Sogitel Cyber Café
22 Handicraft Shops
24 Restaurant Aux Delices
25 Le Makoumba Plus
26 Handicraft Shops
28 Biciab (ATM)
31 Handicraft Shops
32 Booby Supermarket
33 BIB
35 Oxygene; Café Bristel
41 Rakieta Bus Station
42 Intelec Cyber Café
46 Onatel
47 Sûreté
48 Post Office
49 Tropic Voyages Excursions
50 AST Travel Agency
53 Air Burkina
54 Momba So
56 Café le Colsa
57 Hôpital Sourou Sanou
60 Brakina Brewery
61 Gendarmerie
62 Musée Provincial du Houët
63 Haut Commisariat
64 Concorde

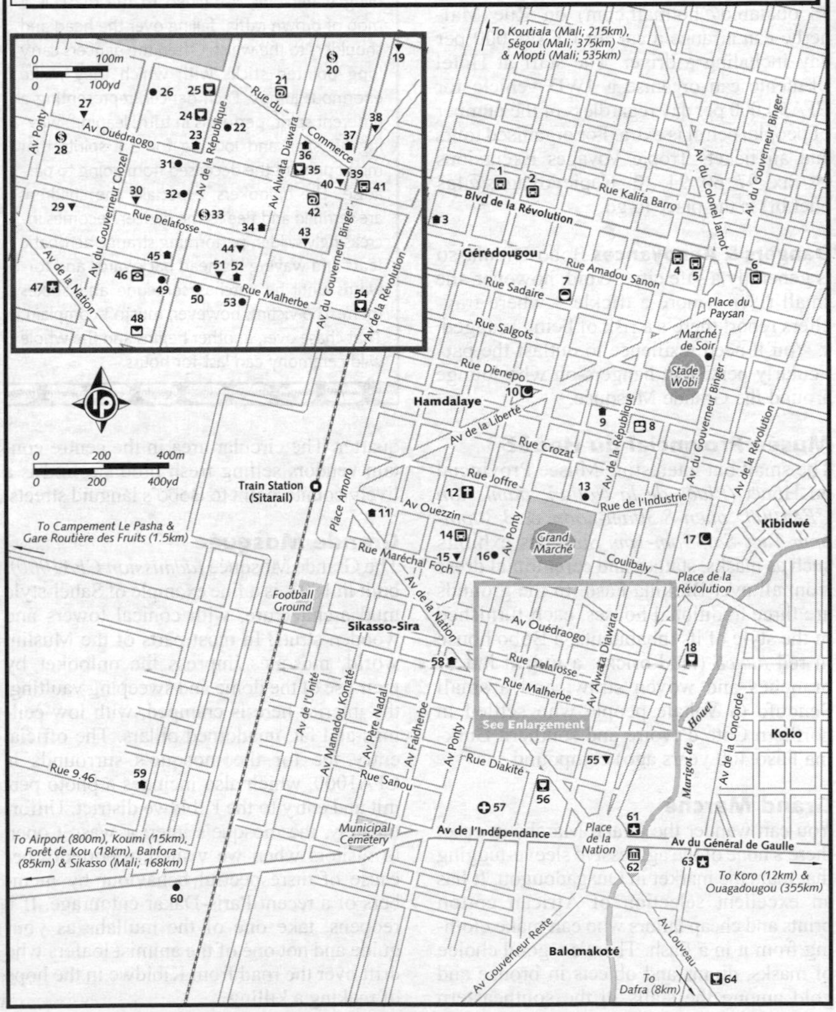

To Koutiala (Mali; 215km), Ségou (Mali; 375km) & Mopti (Mali; 535km)
Av Ponty
Av Ouédraogo
Rue du Commerce
Av Alwata Diawara
Av de la République
Av du Gouverneur Clozel
Rue Delafosse
Av de la Nation
Rue Malherbe
Av du Gouverneur Binger
Av de la Révolution
0 100m
0 100yd
Blvd de la Révolution
Rue Kalifa Barro
Av du Colonel Jamot
Gérédougou
Rue Amadou Sanon
Rue Sadaire
Rue Salgots
Rue Dienepo
Place du Paysan
Marché de Soir
Stade Wobi
Hamdalaye
Av de la Liberté
Rue Crozat
Rue Joffre
Rue de l'Industrie
Av Ouezzin
Train Station (Sitarail)
Place Amoro
Grand Marché
Coulibaly
Kibidwé
Place de la Révolution
Rue Maréchal Foch
To Campement Le Pasha & Gare Routière des Fruits (1.5km)
Football Ground
Sikasso-Sira
See Enlargement
Av de l'Unité
Av Mamadou Konaté
Av Père Nadal
Av Faidherbe
Marigot de Houet
Av de la Concorde
Koko
Rue 9.46
Rue Sanou
Rue Diakité
0 200 400m
0 200 400yd
To Airport (800m), Koumi (15km), Forêt de Kou (18km), Banfora (85km) & Sikasso (Mali; 168km)
Municipal Cemetery
Av de l'Indépendance
Place de la Nation
Av du Général de Gaulle
To Koro (12km) & Ouagadougou (355km)
Av Gouverneur Reste
Balomakoté
Av Louveau
To Dafra (8km)

Email & Internet Access Expect numerous Internet cafés to open around town in the coming years. In the meantime, try Intelec Cyber Café (☎ 97 25 20) on Av Ouédraogo, open 7am to 8pm Monday to Saturday, noon to 8pm on Sundays; it charges CFA3000 per hour. Also worth trying is the Sogitel Cyber Café (☎ 97 35 04) on Rue du Commerce, open 7am to midnight daily; connections here are slower, but it only charges CFA2000 per hour.

Travel Agencies AST (☎ 97 32 14, ⓔ ouatablo@hotmail.com) on Rue Malherbe can arrange a car for CFA25,000 per day including a driver. The staff at Hôtel l'Entente can organise a 4WD vehicle for CFA50,000 per day regardless of the number of people; petrol is extra. For organised tours and air tickets Tropic Voyages Excursions (☎/fax 97 60 94, ⓔ tropicvoyages@fasonet.bf) is the place to go.

Dangers & Annoyances Bobo-Dioulasso is generally a safe city. Avoid, however, the small river – more a trickle – where travellers report there's a risk of being mugged.

You'll need resilience to outlast the particularly persistent hangers-on who lounge around the Grande Mosquée.

Fêtes des Masques

In the Bobo-Dioulasso region, whenever there's a major funeral – such as that of a village chief, which takes place six months or so after his death – it's accompanied by a late night *fête des masques* (festival of masks) which features Bobo helmet masks, as well as other types of masks.

Masked men dance to an orchestra of flute-like instruments and narrow drums beaten with curved canes. Sometimes they're dressed in bulky black-and-brown raffia outfits, resembling scarecrows. Attached to the mask is a mop of brown raffia, falling over the head and shoulders to the waist. Often the dancers carry long pointed sticks with which they make enormous jumps. Each dancer, representing a different spirit, performs in turn, leaping, waving his stick and looking for evil spirits that might prevent the deceased from going to paradise. The onlookers, especially the children, are terrified and flee as the dancer becomes increasingly wilder, performing strange acrobatic feats and waving his head backwards and forwards until he catches someone and strikes them. The victim, however, mustn't complain. That chase over, another begins and the whole wild ceremony can last for hours.

Musée Provincial du Houët

The small but interesting Musée Provincial du Houët *(Place de la Nation; admission CFA1000; open 8.30am-noon & 3.30pm-6pm Tues-Sat, 9am-1pm Sun)* has exhibits such as masks, statues and ceremonial dress from all over Burkina Faso. In the grounds are three traditional houses, each furnished in the style of its inhabitants: a Bobo house in red *banco* (mud-brick); a Fulani hut of branches and woven straw; and a small Senoufo (a Voltaic people who settled in northern Côte d'Ivoire and southern Burkina Faso 400 years ago) compound.

Grand Marché

You can wander the Grand Marché at ease; there's none of the aggressive sleeve-tugging that mars the market in Ouagadougou. It has an excellent selection of African cotton prints and cheap tailors who can make clothing from it in a flash. There's a good choice of masks, drums and objects in bronze and gold among the stalls in the southeastern quarter. The circular area in the centre contain vendors selling fresh produce, and is a lively counterpoint to Bobo's languid streets.

Grande Mosquée

The Grande Mosquée *(admission CFA1000)*, built in 1893, is a fine example of Sahel-style mud architecture, with conical towers and wooden struts. In most parts of the Muslim world, mosques impress the onlooker by their use of the dome and sweeping vaulting; the interior here is cramped, with low ceilings and fat, unadorned pillars. The official entry fee for the mosque's surrounds is CFA1000, which also includes a photo permit and entry to the Kibidwe district. Unfortunately, the mosque's interior wasn't open to visitors when we visited, reportedly because of disrespectful behaviour by members of a recent Paris-Dakar entourage. If it reopens, take one of the mullahs as your guide and not one of the animist loafers who drift over the road from Kibidwe in the hope of making a killing.

Kibidwe

Just across the street to the east of the mosque is Kibidwe, the oldest part of town. You won't get around alone, so give in gracefully, make a contribution 'for the elders' and let yourself be guided; the best of the youths know their neighbourhood well, though their English is minimal. You'll see blacksmiths, potters, weavers, and **Sya**, the house of the ancestors and traditionally the oldest building in Bobo.

Activities

Nonguests can use the hotel **swimming pools** at L'Auberge, Ran Hôtel and Hôtel Relax (all CFA1500).

Places to Stay – Budget

Two places on the west side of town are highly recommended (a shared taxi from the centre to either costs CFA200, more after 8pm).

Casafrica *(☎ 98 01 57)* Camping CFA2000 per person, singles/doubles with mosquito net & fan CFA4500/5500, with bathroom CFA5000/6000. The hyper-friendly and highly recommended Casafrica can be found in a green and peaceful compound southwest of the town centre. Large beers cost CFA450, and Casafrica also has good meals.

Campement le Pacha *(☎ 98 09 84)* Camping CFA2000 per person, singles/doubles with mosquito net & fan CFA5500/6500, with air-con CFA10,000/11,000. The Franco-Swiss owned Campement le Pacha is 3km west of the centre near the gare routière. All rooms have shared facilities. There is a great garden restaurant.

Hôtel Renaissance *(☎ 98 23 31, Av de le République)* Rooms with fan from CFA4000, with fan, bathroom, balcony & mosquito net CFA6000, with air-con CFA12,000. Located close to the market, the Renaissance has some excellent budget rooms. The cheapest rooms are quite cramped but those for CFA6000 are superb value.

Hôtel Méridien *(☎ 98 03 42, Av de l'Unité)* Rooms with fan CFA4000-7000, singles/doubles with bathroom, air-con & mosquito net CFA8500/10,300. This place is friendly, reasonable value and, while handy for most bus depots, is a fair way from the town centre. The roof terrace is bleak but breezy and has a decent view over the city.

Hôtel Hamdalaye *(☎ 98 22 87, Rue Dienepo)* Rooms with fan CFA6200, with fan & bathroom CFA7350, with air-con & bathroom CFA11,500. In a good location close to transport and the town centre, the Hamdalaye is good value and has tidy, spacious rooms, although the mosquitos here can be a problem.

Hôtel l'Entente *(☎ 97 12 05, Rue du Commerce)* Rooms with fan/air-con CFA6500/15,400. This travellers' favourite has a pleasant bar-restaurant set in a garden, a relaxed ambience, friendly staff and large rooms.

Hôtel Teria *(☎ 97 19 72, Av Alwata Diawara)* Singles/doubles with fan & shower CFA6500/8000, with air-con CFA12,500/15,000. The Teria is quite a comfortable choice in a good, central location, although not all the rooms have a mosquito net. There's a reasonable restaurant here.

Places to Stay – Mid-Range & Top End

Hôtel Watinoma *(☎ 97 20 82, Rue Malherbe)* Singles/doubles CFA14,500/17,000. The Watinoma is quite a good, if unspectacular, mid-range option. The rooms have bathroom, TV and air-con; the restaurant is recommended.

Hôtel 421 *(☎ 97 20 11, Av de la Nation)* Singles/doubles with fan CFA10,000/12,500, with air-con & TV CFA15,000/17,500. Rates here are negotiable and are not bad mid-range value.

Hôtel Relax *(☎ 97 22 27, Av Alwata Diawara)* Small doubles from CFA14,500, singles/doubles with air-con & TV CFA27,000/30,000. The Relax has a pool and is good value within its category.

L'Auberge *(☎ 97 17 67, fax 97 21 37, Av Ouédraogo)* Singles/doubles CFA26,000/28,000. This friendly and recommended place has a pool, a couple of billiard tables, a good restaurant and a pavement terrace. The very attractive rooms have TV and air-con.

Ran Hôtel *(☎ 97 09 00, Av de la Nation)* Singles/doubles CFA25,070/31,860. The rather soulless Ran near the train station also has a pool. At weekends the nightclub next door can be noisy.

Places to Eat

Budget There are ***street vendors*** that sell juicy whole grilled chickens for CFA1500, notably outside the Restaurant Togolais. The relaxing ***Café des Amis***, two blocks east of the market, is good for light snacks. Also good for cheap, sit-down meals is ***Restaurant l'Express*** on Av Ouédraogo.

African As well as the places listed here, many of the hotel restaurants also offer African dishes.

Bar-Restaurant Les Bambou *(☎ 98 29 31, Av du Gouverneur Binger)* Meals from CFA800-3000. Open 6am-2.30pm & 6pm-midnight Mon-Sat, 6pm-midnight Sun. Les Bambou is a great place to spend an evening, and has tasty and reasonably priced food. It has a lovely garden dining area and live music most nights (see Entertainment following).

Restaurant Dan Kan *(Rue Malherbe)* Meals CFA2000. Not far from the Onatel office, the Dan Kan is good value and offers a wide range of salads and African dishes.

Restaurant Togolais *(Rue du Commerce)* Meals around CFA500. This earthy option serves good inexpensive food, even if there's not much that is specifically Togolese on offer.

Restaurant Delwinde *(Rue Delafosse)* This restaurant is known to locals as Chez Tanti Abi and has an unusually extensive and equally reasonable menu.

French You can eat under the stars at ***L'Eau Vive*** *(☎ 97 20 86, Rue Delafosse)* with mains from CFA2500 to CFA4500. It's open from noon to 2.30pm and 7.30pm to 10.30pm Monday to Saturday. L'Eau Vive is sister to the restaurant of the same name in Ouagadougou. Also run by nuns, the cooking is imaginative and the menu is varied. Main dishes all come with potatoes or vegetables.

Restaurant la Casa *(☎ 97 06 22, Off Rue Maréchal Foch)* Mains from CFA2500. Open noon-3pm & 7pm-10.30pm. Two blocks west of the market at the end of a shady arbour, La Casa is green and peaceful. All dishes are served with rice, chips or vegetables.

Nouvelle Boule Verte *(☎ 97 01 10, Rue Delafosse)* Mains CFA1500-2500. Open noon-2.30pm & 6pm-10.30pm daily. The friendly Nouvelle Boule Verte, three blocks south of the market, is friendly and serves good food (mainly French plus a few African dishes) at mid-range prices. Highlights on the menu include minestrone (CFA1500), brochette de capitaine (CFA2500) and espresso coffee (CFA450). It has what is possibly Bobo's cleanest toilet and washbasin with soap and towel.

Restaurant l'Entente *(☎ 97 03 96, Rue Delafosse)* Mains from CFA1200. Open 7.30am-11pm. Not to be confused with the restaurant of Hôtel l'Entente, this place is a good place to start the day with breakfast (from CFA1500). For lunch or dinner, the menu includes a wide range of entrees and mains, although don't expect everything to be available. Service is friendly and prices are reasonable.

You can eat well at several hotel restaurants, in particular those of ***L'Auberge*** (which includes a set three-course menu, changed daily, for CFA5500), ***Hôtel L'Entente***, ***Hôtel Watinoma*** and ***Hôtel 421***, where the restaurant menu, inspired by the owner's stays in France and China, is varied and inventive.

Cafés & Patisseries Near Place de la Révolution is the outstanding ***La Sorbetière*** *(Av du Gouverneur Binger)*. The pastries here are varied and delicious, and it also has sandwiches and large portions of pizza. It makes real espresso coffee and its own ice cream (CFA250 a scoop). Try the coconut and you'll melt.

Boulangerie Pâtisserie la Bonne Miche *(☎ 97 23 94, Av Ouédraogo)* A little bit cheaper and less spick-and-span, this patisserie two blocks southeast of the market has excellent bread and a range of pastries.

Self-catering Ideal for stocking up for long bus or train rides, ***Booby Supermarket*** *(☎ 97 01 54, Av de la République)* has a good range of grocery items.

Entertainment

Bobo-Dioulasso only really comes to life at the weekend; on weekdays, you're likely to be the only clients. One exception is the popular quarter of Balomakoté, which is rich in traditional music and is the area from where the internationally acclaimed group Farafina emerged. (Don't be misled by the hustlers who offer to take you to hear them play; they're far away, living it up in Europe.) Here, you'll enjoy great music in small, unpretentious ***buvettes*** (small cafés that double up as drinking places serving cheap meals) where you can drink *chopolo*, the local millet-based beer.

Bars The current 'in' spot in Bobo-Dioulasso is ***Bar-Restaurant Les Bambou*** *(☎ 98 29 31, Av du Gouverneur Binger)*, although fashions change fast. The cover charge is up to CFA600, and beers cost around CFA700. This terrific outdoor venue has traditional live music (especially Djembé music) at 8.30pm from Wednesday to Saturday.

Restaurant Aux Delices *(Av de la République)* is always packed in the evenings and the outdoor tables are a good place for a beer.

Café Bristel has little on offer in terms of food, but is popular with travellers and is a good place for a beer while watching the world go by on a warm afternoon.

Café le Colsa This is a tranquil open-air bar two blocks northwest of the Place de la Nation, which, like all bars, is best at night.

Soweto Bar, two blocks south of Place de la Révolution, is often crowded and is slightly seedy.

The garden of ***Hôtel L'Entente*** is laid-back, and the streetside terrace of ***L'Auberge*** is great for a drink and watching life pass by.

Nightclubs A popular place is ***Momba So***, where you can also eat well. Other top places for dancing include ***Oxygene***, and ***Le Makoumba Plus***, near the market, is also worth checking out.

Alternatively, head south from the centre to the friendly, outdoor bar-restaurant ***Concorde***. A shared taxi costs CFA150 and, to return, the owner will dragoon his son, a taxi driver by profession.

Cinemas The modern ***Ciné Sanyon*** is an excellent air-con cinema that shows good films, including runs and reruns of Burkinabé productions that have won international acclaim.

Shopping

Bobo-Dioulasso is an excellent place to pick up wooden masks and other carvings, especially Lobi and Bobo items. As well as the southwest quarter of the market, there are excellent ***handicraft shops*** along Av du Gouverneur Clozel, Av Ouédraogo opposite L'Auberge, and Av de la République.

For clothing, the Grand Marché is your best bet; for a tailor-made shirt expect to pay CFA1500 for cloth and CFA1500 for labour.

Getting There & Away

Air Air Burkina (☎ 97 13 48) has three flights per week to/from Ouagadougou (CFA28,485/56,670 for one way/return), three to Abidjan (CFA63,700/127,400) and one to Bamako (CFA52,400/101,600). The office is on Rue Malherbe.

Bus STMB (☎ 97 08 78) runs between Bobo-Dioulasso and Ouagadougou five times a day (five hours, CFA5000). It's worth paying an extra CFA1500 to take the 10am air-con service, and there's another at 2pm for CFA8000. Sans Frontière (☎ 97 04 79) has three buses every day to Ouagadougou (CFA5000), STBF (☎ 97 23 13) makes the trip four times a day and Sogebaf (☎ 97 02 54) buses leave almost hourly.

Rakieta (☎ 97 18 91) is a good local company that serves a variety of destinations in the southwest. In addition to its Ouagadougou service (CFA5000, two daily), Rakieta buses also service Banfora (CFA1000, 1½ hours, 10 daily), Gaoua (CFA3500, around five hours, three daily) and Oradora (CFA1000, 1½ hours, six daily).

For details on transport to Côte d'Ivoire and Mali, see the Getting There & Away section earlier in the chapter.

Bush Taxi & Minibus Nearly all bush taxis and minibuses leave from the gare routière (also known as the Autogare des Fruits) about 3km west of the city centre. To get there, head west along Rue Malherbe. Fares start from CFA5500 to Ouagadougou and CFA1500 to Banfora.

Train The Sitarail (☎ 97 10 91) train from Ouagadougou to Abidjan passes through Bobo-Dioulasso on Tuesday, Thursday and Saturday afternoon. The return, heading for Ouagadougou, is scheduled to arrive in Bobo about 3am. It's invariably late. Fares (1st/2nd class) are CFA4900/3200 to Ferkessédougou, CFA10,000/6600 to Bouaké and CFA16,700/11,100 to Abidjan.

Getting Around

To/From the Airport Expect to pay CFA250/1000 for a shared/private taxi between the airport and the city centre.

Taxi Taxis are plentiful and most trips within town cost between CFA150 and CFA250. Prices increase after 10pm and luggage costs extra. A shared taxi from the market to the gare routière costs CFA200 and a private one costs CFA500.

Bicycle & Moped To rent a bicycle for the day, ask at your hotel or around the market. A reasonable price is CFA1500 to CFA2000 per day.

For a moped, expect to pay CFA4000 to CFA5000 a day and CFA6000 for a motorbike. You'll find some for hire outside the old Air Afrique office, opposite the Grand Marché on Av Ponty. During the rainy season, visiting the surrounding villages by bicycle or moped can be a sticky experience.

AROUND BOBO-DIOULASSO

The traditional houses in the villages around Bobo-Dioulasso are characterised by their tall conical roofs and narrow storehouses linked by earth walls that give the compounds the look of squat medieval castles.

La Guinguette & Koumi

La Guinguette *(admission CFA1000)* is a crystal-clear bathing area, 18km from Bobo-Dioulasso in a lush forest, Forêt de Kou. Although it's popular at weekends, you'll probably have the place to yourself during the week. Camping is possible, but it's safer to ask the locals for a place to sleep in the village.

On the way, pause at the village of **Koumi** which has some fine ochre two-storey adobe houses, typical of the area.

From Bobo, take the Sikasso road to Koumi (15km). Just after the village, turn right and then take a left fork along a narrow, rough dirt track. After passing two villages, take a sharp right alongside the forest and follow the track to the river.

Koro

The village of Koro *(admission CFA1000)* is 14km east of Bobo, just off the main Ouagadougou road. Perched on the hillside, its houses, hewn into the natural rock, are unique in the area and there are fine panoramic views over the countryside from the top of the village.

Mare aux Poissons Sacrés

This sacred fish pond is some 8km southeast of Bobo, in the village of Dafra. The surrounding hills and the pond, at the base of a cliff and a 20- to 30-minute walk from the nearest parking spot, are memorable; the fish less so. Chickens, which you can buy on the spot, are sacrificed and thrown to the over-gorged *poissons sacrés* (sacred fish). It's all rather gruesome, with chicken feathers everywhere. Don't wear gold jewellery or anything red; both are prohibited at this sacred spot. A few louche characters prowl the place and there have been muggings, so go in a group.

From Place de la Nation in Bobo, head southeast on Av Louveau. After about 8km, ask for the turn-off to the right for Dafra. A taxi there and back from Bobo-Dioulasso should cost about CFA5000.

Mare aux Hippopotames

Some 66km northeast of Bobo, access to this lake isn't easy and the hippo population doesn't compare with that of Tengréla Lake (see Around Banfora). The local fishermen will take you in a pirogue to see them, but they're tough bargainers. A fact to ponder as you glide across the lake: more people are killed in Africa every year by hippos than by any other animal. The lake has bilharzia, so don't dive in.

Getting here is very difficult without a vehicle as there's no public transport beyond Satiri, which leaves you with a 22km walk. If you have wheels, head for Satiri, 44km northeast of Bobo-Dioulasso on the dirt road to Dédougou. From there, take a rough dirt road northwest which, after about 15km, forks off to the left (south) towards the lake. From July to September this road is often impassable.

BANFORA

Banfora is situated on the Ouagadougou-Abidjan train line and is a stopping point for buses between Bobo-Dioulasso and Côte d'Ivoire. Apart from its market, there's little of interest in town. That said, it's an ideal base for visiting the lush, green surrounding countryside, one of the more beautiful areas

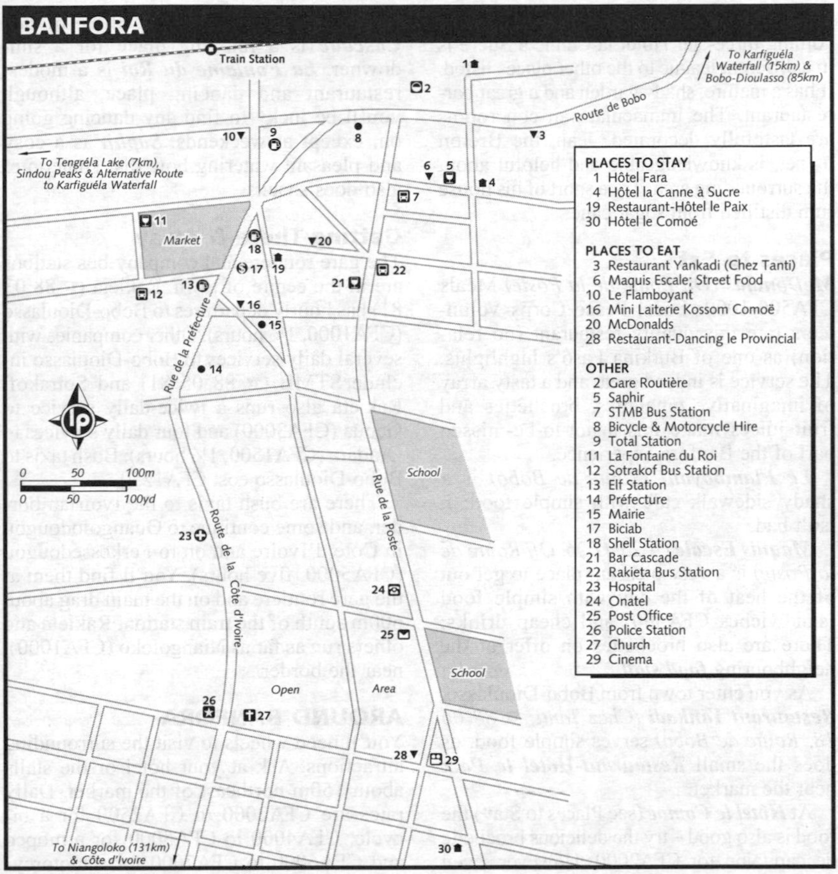
BANFORA
Train Station
To Karfiguéla Waterfall (15km) & Bobo-Dioulasso (85km)
Route de Bobo
To Tengréla Lake (7km), Sindou Peaks & Alternative Route to Karfiguéla Waterfall
Market
Rue de la Préfecture
School
Rue de la Poste
Route de la Côte d'Ivoire
Open Area
School
To Niangoloko (131km) & Côte d'Ivoire
0 50 100m
0 50 100yd
PLACES TO STAY
1 Hôtel Fara
4 Hôtel la Canne à Sucre
19 Restaurant-Hôtel le Paix
30 Hôtel le Comoé
PLACES TO EAT
3 Restaurant Yankadi (Chez Tanti)
6 Maquis Escale; Street Food
10 Le Flamboyant
16 Mini Laiterie Kossom Comoë
20 McDonalds
28 Restaurant-Dancing le Provincial
OTHER
2 Gare Routière
5 Saphir
7 STMB Bus Station
8 Bicycle & Motorcycle Hire
9 Total Station
11 La Fontaine du Roi
12 Sotrakof Bus Station
13 Elf Station
14 Préfecture
15 Mairie
17 Biciab
18 Shell Station
21 Bar Cascade
22 Rakieta Bus Station
23 Hospital
24 Onatel
25 Post Office
26 Police Station
27 Church
29 Cinema

in Burkina Faso and is ideal for a tour on two wheels with a host of attractions to explore.

For changing money, the Biciab facing the market only accepts euros in cash.

When we visited, many places around town advertised 'Internet' on the signs outside but this was an aspiration only – in reality, most were yet to take delivery of their first computer.

Places to Stay

Hôtel le Comoé *(☎ 88 01 51, Rue de la Poste)* Singles/doubles with fan CFA6000/7500, with air-con & bathroom CFA12,000/14,000. This sleepy hotel, with its pleasant courtyard and good restaurant, has a lovely languid air and is justifiably popular with travellers. It's a 15-minute walk or CFA200 taxi ride from the train or bus stations; ignore the cruel sign near the gare routière which claims it is only 250m to the hotel. Most rooms have mosquito nets.

Hôtel Fara *(☎ 88 01 17, Off Route de Bobo)* Singles/doubles with fan & doubles with air-con CFA9205. Set around a lifeless compound, the rooms with fan at this central hotel are dank and uninspiring, but those with air-con are surprisingly good value.

Restaurant-Hôtel le Paix *(☎ 88 00 16, Off Route de la Préfecture)* Room with fan & mosquito net CFA6000. The rooms here are simple, but it's very handy for the market, and breakfast is included. The shared bathrooms are very clean.

Hôtel la Canne à Sucre *(☎ 88 01 07, Off Route de la Poste)* Rooms with air-con &

bathroom CFA18,900. The excellent, welcoming three-star Hôtel la Canne à Sucre is in a different league to the other places listed. It has a mature, shady garden and a great bar-restaurant. The immaculate air-con rooms are tastefully decorated. Jean, the Breton owner, is knowledgeable and helpful about the surrounding area. Try a snort of his house rum distilled from sugar cane.

Places to Eat

McDonalds *(Off Route de la Poste)* Meals CFA500-1000. Local Peace Corps Volunteers rate this quality restaurant (no relation) as one of Burkina Faso's highlights. The service is indeed great and a tasty array of imaginative omelettes, brochettes and fruit juices make this a not-to-be-missed part of the Banfora experience.

Le Flamboyant *(Route de Bobo)* is a shady sidewalk café with simple food; it isn't bad.

Maquis Escale *(☎ 25 47 26, Off Route de la Poste)* is a very pleasant place to get out of the heat of the day with simple food (sandwiches CFA500) and cheap drinks. There are also brochettes on offer at the neighbouring ***food stall***.

As you enter town from Bobo-Dioulasso, ***Restaurant Yankadi*** *(Chez Tanti; ☎ 88 06 18, Route de Bobo)* serves simple food, as does the small ***Restaurant-Hôtel le Paix*** near the market.

At ***Hôtel le Comoé*** (see Places to Stay) the food is also good – try the delicious brochette de capitaine for CFA2000. However, even the simplest of dishes takes an eternity to arrive. If you're hungry or in a hurry, make for the nearby ***Restaurant-Dancing le Provincial*** *(Off Route de la Poste)* which has cold drinks, brochettes and a pleasant ambience.

The restaurant at ***Hôtel la Canne à Sucre*** (see Places to Stay) is far and away the best in town. The menu is extensive and varied and, with main dishes between CFA2500 and CFA3500, it's excellent value. The dining area is charming.

Mini Laiterie Kossom Comoë *(Off Rue de la Préfecture)* is a dairy, established with Canadian assistance, with fresh, safe yogurts for CFA150.

Entertainment

As well as the three hotels, there are a number of small ***buvettes*** in Banfora, which are all good for a drink. The paillote of ***Bar Cascade*** is a relaxing place for a sundowner. ***La Fontaine du Roi*** is a modest restaurant and dancing place, although you'll be lucky to find any dancing going on, except at weekends. ***Saphir*** is a cosy and pleasant watering hole that sometimes also does snacks.

Getting There & Away

The gare routière and company bus stations are in the centre of town. Rakieta (☎ 88 03 81) has hourly departures to Bobo-Dioulasso (CFA1000, 1½ hours). Other companies with several daily services to Bobo-Dioulasso include STMB (☎ 88 05 81) and Sotrakof. Rakieta also runs a twice-daily service to Gaoua (CFA3000) and four daily services to Oradara (CFA1500, 1½ hours). Bush taxis to Bobo-Dioulasso cost CFA1250.

There are bush taxis to the Ivoirian border, and some continue to Ouangolodougou in Côte d'Ivoire and on to Ferkessédougou (CFA5000, five hours). You'll find them at the gare routière and on the main drag about 600m south of the train station. Rakieta and others run as far as Niangoloko (CFA1000), near the border.

AROUND BANFORA

You'll need wheels to visit the surrounding attractions. Ask at your hotel or the stalls about 150m northeast of the market. Daily rates are CFA2000 to CFA2500 for a bicycle, CFA4000 to CFA5000 for a moped and CFA6000 to CFA7000 for a motorcycle, which is advisable if you're making the longer journey to the Sindou Peaks.

Tengréla Lake

This 100 hectare lake *(Lac de Tengréla; admission CFA2000)*, less than 10km west of Banfora on a good dirt road, makes a pleasant bicycle ride and is easy to find. You'll see fisherfolk, a variety of birdlife and, if you're lucky, hippos. The admission price includes a pirogue trip.

You can spend the night in one of the simple paillotes at ***Farafina Buvette***, owned by Suleimane, exuberant, dreadlocked and drum-crazy. The buvette, which serves capitaine or carp fresh from the lake, also makes a pleasant drinks or lunch stop, and you'll probably be treated to a throbbing recital from the owner's percussion school.

To get to the lake, take the dirt road that forks right at the Total petrol station in Banfora, then after about 6km turn left for the village of Tengréla. The lake is a further 1km beyond the village.

Karfiguéla Waterfall

Some 15km northwest of Banfora, these waterfalls *(Cascades de Karfiguéla; admission CFA1000)* are at their best during and just after the rainy season – when, unfortunately, the dirt tracks leading to the falls can be impassable. But, whatever the season, it's worth the journey. From below, you approach the falls through a magnificent avenue of mango trees; the chaotic jumble of rocks over which the water splays is a sight in itself.

You can camp beside the pool at the base of the falls; bring your own food and water.

From the waterfalls, you can walk or ride to the **Dômes de Fabedougou** (CFA500) by following the main irrigation pipe eastwards (take the stairs to the right of the falls). They're an escarpment-type formation and are good for rock climbing.

Getting There & Away Take the road to Sindou and then turn right at a sign near the Karfiguéla falls turn-off. When you reach the T-junction at the main irrigation canal that leads from the head of the falls, follow it to the left (upstream).

Alternatively, save yourself the possible frustration and take a guide (CFA4000 per day) and ride pillion on a hired moped. Never pay the guide until you return to Banfora: We have received reports of travellers being abandoned by taxi drivers or guides.

Sindou Peaks

The Sindou rock formations *(Pics de Sindou; admission CFA1000)* are a narrow, craggy chain that extends northeast from the dirt road, which you follow from Banfora for about 50km.

The tortuous cones of these structures, sculpted and blasted by the elements, were left behind when the surrounding softer rocks eroded away.

This area is ideal for a short, steep stroll, a day hike or even a couple of days' trekking, for which you'll need to bring all your own food, gear and water. There's plenty of flat ground at the base of the fingers and chimneys where you can stretch out a sleeping bag.

You can stay overnight for CFA1000 at the basic but friendly ***Auberge Soutarala*** in the Sindou, 2km beyond the peaks, where drinks are cool and food is filling. Turn left at the miniroundabout as you enter the village, and down a lane beside the dispensary.

GAOUA

Gaoua is a good base for exploring Lobi country. There's a vital Sunday market and, if you like your music traditional and untainted, it has some great *boîtes*, or informal nightclubs, with live music. There's no lack of choice and the ***Cabaret Pastis*** has been particularly recommended. There's also the small **Musée de Poni** *(☎ 87 01 69; admission CFA1000)* devoted to Lobi culture.

Places to Stay & Eat

For cheap accommodation try ***L'Hôtel de Poni*** *(☎ 87 02 00)*, which faces the main

> **Lobi Traditions**
>
> Lobi traditions are some of the best preserved in Africa. The *dyoro* initiation rites that take place every seven years, for example, are still widely observed. For three to six months, young men undergo severe physical tests of their manhood, and learn the clan's oral history and the do's and don'ts of their culture.
>
> Lobi art, in particular the wooden carvings (that play an essential role in protecting the family), is highly regarded by collectors. What's most fascinating for travellers, however, is the architecture of rural Lobi homes. The compounds are rectangular and – rare for constructions of mud – sometimes multistorey. Each structure, with high mud-brick walls and scarcely a slit for windows, is like a miniature fortress. Unlike most Africans, who live in villages, the Lobi (like the Somba and the Tamberma in northern Benin and Togo), live in their fields; a family compound may be several hundred metres from its nearest neighbours.
>
> In rural areas the Lobi don't warm easily to foreigners. Don't take photos without express permission, for instance, or even offer sweets to children. In towns such as Gaoua, however, the Lobi can be very friendly, and if you're invited to have some *chopolo*, the local millet beer, by all means accept.

square and charges CFA4000 for a room, or ***Hôtel 125***, where the prices are similar. ***Hôtel Hala*** *(☎ 87 01 21)*, just outside town, offers the best accommodation (rooms from CFA10,000) by far, and serves excellent Lebanese fare. For cheap food, your best bet is ***La Porte Ouverte***.

Getting There & Away

From Ouagadougou, Sotrao buses (CFA5000, six hours) leave on Monday, Wednesday and Saturday and return the next day. Rakieta buses run between Bobo-Dioulasso and Gaoua (CFA3500) three times daily. Rakieta (☎ 87 02 18) has a twice daily service to Banfora (CFA3000).

Bush taxis run from Gaoua to Ouagadougou, Bobo-Dioulasso and Banfora and, more frequently, to Diébougou, from where there's transport to/from Bobo-Dioulasso.

BURKINA FASO

AROUND GAOUA

Loropéni

Loropéni, 39km west of Gaoua on the road to Banfora, is the site of some **ancient ruins** whose origins remain unknown. The local Gan people call the complex *la maison de refuge*. The structures themselves are far from overwhelming; their interest lies in their being among the very few stone remains in West Africa. A further 8km northwest of Loropéni is the village of **Obiré** which houses the Sanctuaire de Roi Gan, the remains of a sanctuary of the Gan kings, including 12 statues representing the long-dead monarchs.

To get to Loropéni, head west from Gaoua on the Banfora road for 3.5km. At the top of a small hill, take a track to the right for about 500m.

BOROMO

Boromo is halfway between Ouagadougou and Bobo. Although the main section of the **Parc National des Deux Balés** is quite far away, there are several areas within 10km of Boromo where elephant sightings are common.

The only place to stay in Boromo itself is ***Relais Touristique*** *(☎ 44 06 84)*, with clean singles/doubles with fan for CFA3500/4500 (CFA5500/7000 with air-con). It's also the only place for food apart from the stalls at the bus stop. On the road to the national park is the new ***Campement Le Kaicedra*** *(☎ 21 26 91; in Ouagadougou 30 70 83)*, 7km from Boromo. Accommodation is in nice bungalows (CFA18,000 a double) right by the river where elephants often come to drink. The staff can arrange guides and will even pick you up from the bus station in Boromo if you ask nicely.

South & Southeast

FADA N'GOURMA

Fada N'Gourma, or Fada as it is often referred to, is 219km east of Ouagadougou. It's a sprawling, shady town and is the major settlement between the capital and Niamey in Niger. It's also the turn-off point for Parc National de la Pendjari and Natitingou, both in Benin. Its heart is the market and the tiny gare routière nearby, both on the main drag.

Fada N'Gourma is also renowned for its locally produced honey, *le miel de Gourma*, which is dark and tangy and is readily available at many roadside stalls.

Places to Stay & Eat

Le Campement Singles/doubles CFA2000/3000. This is the cheapest place to stay – if it's still open. It's just across the main highway from the gare routière.

Auberge Yemmamma *(☎ 77 00 39)* Singles/doubles with fan & bathroom CFA5000/5500, with air-con CFA6000/7000. This is the best hotel in town. It has paillotes with comfortable chairs and a popular outdoor bar-restaurant where meals start at CFA1500.

There are usually several ***vendors*** selling inexpensive local food around the gare routière. At the southeast corner of the market is a small ***food stall*** where you can get coffee, good yogurt and minced-meat sandwiches (CFA400). ***Restaurant de la Paix*** next to the Auberge Yemmamma has an attractive shaded eating area and offers standard fare for about CFA1500.

Getting There & Away

STMB (☎ 77 06 94) has four daily buses between Fada N'Gourma and Ouagadougou (CFA2500, four hours). Transport for Niger and, especially, Benin is scarce and fills up slowly. For the Parc National d'Arli, most travellers continue east to Kantchari before heading south.

PARC NATIONAL D'ARLI

In the southeast on the border with Benin, Parc National d'Arli *(admission CFA5000 per person, plus CFA1000 for obligatory guide; usually open 15 Dec to 15 May)* is Burkina Faso's major national park, and adjoins Benin's Parc National de la Pendjari (see that chapter for more details). Here, you have by far the best chance of spotting a variety of animals. The park is situated on a flood-prone lowland plain, bordered to the southeast by the Pendjari River. It's part of the same ecosystem as Benin's Parc National de la Pendjari, just across the river.

Animal species common to both parks include hippos, elephants, warthogs, baboons, monkeys, lions, leopards, crocodiles and various kinds of antelope. Bird species are also very varied. With your own vehicle, you can also see the Burkina Faso side of **Parc National du W** (usually open from 15 December to 15 May) to the east of Arli on the Nigérien border; the entrance is via Diapaga. This park straddles Burkina Faso, Niger and Benin; see the Niger chapter for more details.

If you have wheels, it's also possible to cross the Beninese border to visit Parc National de la Pendjari and the Benin section of Parc National du W. At the frontier, you can buy a 48-hour visa for CFA8000.

Places to Stay & Eat

Les Pavillons Safari d'Arli *(L'Agence Tourisme; ☎ 31 84 43, fax 31 84 44)* Rooms with fan & bathroom CFA16,500, with air-con CFA18,000. This complex has an attractive lodge, thatched-roof bungalows and an air-con bar-restaurant overlooking a clean pool. The fixed menu is CFA5000. At Les Pavillons, you can arrange to hire a 4WD. Camping near the lodge is also possible.

Getting There & Away

Without your own transport, Parc National d'Arli is extremely difficult to reach as public transport will only take you so far – and not far enough. You can hire a 4WD or you can take an organised tour (see Information under Ouagadougou for more details). L'Agence Tourisme is probably the best; its prices may seem expensive, but the company is highly professional, and once you tot up park charges, lodging, the hire of a compulsory guide and tracker, and car rental, it's scarcely cheaper to go it alone.

For the main (eastern) entrance, take the highway from Ouagadougou to Niamey as far as Kantchari (389km), then head south on a dirt road to Diapaga (56km), Namounou (25km) and Arli (48km). The nonstop driving time is about seven hours.

Sotrao buses leave Ouagadougou for Namounou on Monday, Wednesday and Saturday. From Namounou, however, traffic is very scarce.

RANCH DE NAZINGA

South of Ouagadougou near Pô and the Ghanaian border, Ranch de Nazinga *(Réserve de Nazinga; ☎ 30 84 43, 41 36 18, e ranch.nazinga@ceatrin.bf; admission CFA1000 per vehicle & CFA8500 per person, plus CFA2000 per outing for guide)* was established with Canadian assistance. The park's custodians are seeking to restock the area by raising the number of species of deer and antelope and releasing them into the wild.

Many deer and antelope, have been shot and most of the ranch's elephants have migrated westwards to the contiguous **Forêt de Sissili**, which is richer in animals. In the Nazinga reserve, there's a chance of seeing antelopes, monkeys, warthogs, crocodiles and a variety of bird species. A guide is compulsory and, unlike many national parks, you can walk around, but do so with caution. There's a camera/video tax of CFA1000/2500. If you reserve in advance, it's possible to hire a 4WD within the reserve for CFA15,000 per half day. ***Accommodation*** is available in two-bed bungalows for CFA12,500.

For information on the project and the reserve itself, visit the Ranch de Nazinga office in Ouagadougou (Rue Maurice Bishop). Nana Inoussa (☎ 25 17 75), a guide who can arrange a 4WD for CFA45,000 per day if you arrange it before setting out from Ouagadougou, is recommended by readers.

Places to Stay & Eat

Three-room ***chalets*** with bucket showers are CFA5000 and must be reserved in advance through Ouagadougou's tourist office (☎ 31 19 59). At the same site, basic ***huts***, which cost CFA500 per person, have bare rooms without mattresses, screens or locking doors. Meals are expensive and poor quality so it's best to bring your own food.

Getting There & Away

Driving time from Ouagadougou to Ranch de Nazinga is three hours; a 4WD is essential. Take the sealed road south to Pô (176km), then a dirt road west towards Léo. After 15km you'll come to a sign pointing south to Nazinga, some 40km further.

TIÉBÉLÉ

Tiébélé, 40km east of Pô via a dirt track, is in the heart of Gourounsi country and is famous for its fortress-like, windowless traditional houses. The houses are decorated by women, who work with guinea-fowl feathers, in geometrical patterns of red, black and white. From Tiébélé, you can go another 10km to the border village of **Boungou**, famous for its potters.

The North

Heading northwest from the capital, the road is sealed as far as Ouahigouya and is good quality as far as the border with Mali. Travelling northeast, the road is sealed to Kaya, but from there it's shake, rattle and roll on a rough track all the way to Gorom-Gorom.

OUAHIGOUYA

Ouahigouya (pronounced waee-**gee**-ya), 182km northwest of Ouagadougou by sealed road, is the country's fourth-largest city. It's a quiet place, except on Saturday night. Much of the activity during the day, such as it is, takes place around the market and on the long main drag. At night, the lively areas are around Ouahigouya's two cinemas.

During the Eid al-Fitr holiday, which marks the end of the fasting month of Ramadan, there's a famous pilgrimage to the mosque in **Ramatoulaye**, 25km east of town, between Baghélogo and Rambo.

The two banks in town, Biciab and BIB, change euros in cash but don't seem to have heard of US dollars. The Biciab branch has an ATM that gives cash advances on Visa. For Internet access, try Éspace Internautes (☎ 55 43 89) on Av de Mopti, which is open 7.30am to 9pm daily and charges CFA2000 per hour.

Maison du Naba Kango

A short walk northeast from Ouahigouya's market, Maison du Naba Kango dates back to the days of the Yatengo kingdom, a precolonial rival of the principal Mossi kingdom, centred in Ouagadougou. The compound, a traditional mud construction, contains houses for the Naba's 30 or so wives, several granaries, a small, plain reception room for guests and a fetish house, forbidden even to the Naba's children. To be granted an audience with the naba, king of the predominantly Mossi Yatengo province and second only in importance to his Ouagadougou counterpart, you must bring a present; money is most appreciated. If he's unavailable, one of his young sons, *les princes*, may show you around for a tip.

Places to Stay

Pension de Recueil *(☎ 55 00 09)* Singles/doubles with fan CFA3300/4800. This place, better known as Paul's Bar, is a great budget choice. If you arrive at night, look for the red light (appropriate, given some of the more transient clientele) over the doorway. The clean, simple rooms have shared facilities. You can have a drink in the relaxing, shady courtyard and a simple meal in the adjacent bar-restaurant. Paul is friendliness itself and if you ask him, he'll show you the nearby compound where his wife brews chapalo.

Plan International *(Av de Mopti)* has mattresses with mosquito nets – this is simple but friendly budget accommodation in the centre of town.

Hôtel Dunia *(☎ 55 05 95, Rue de Paris)* Doubles with air-con from CFA15,000. The Dunia is run by a friendly Syrian couple; staying here is like stepping into someone's home. There's a sitting room with satellite TV, a small pool (often empty) and a shady area in front, pleasant for a meal or drink. Madame's cooking is homely, plentiful and quite the best in town; meals cost CFA2500, and you'll need to order in advance.

Hôtel de l'Amitié *(☎ 55 05 21)* Singles/doubles CFA5000/6500, and with bathroom & air-con CFA10,000/12,000. This government-owned property, 1km northwest of the centre, and is also good value for money, though it's much more impersonal than Hôtel Dunia. It has a good restaurant where all main dishes are less than CFA2500.

Hôtel Colibri *(☎ 55 05 72, 55 07 87)* Doubles with fan/air-con & bathroom

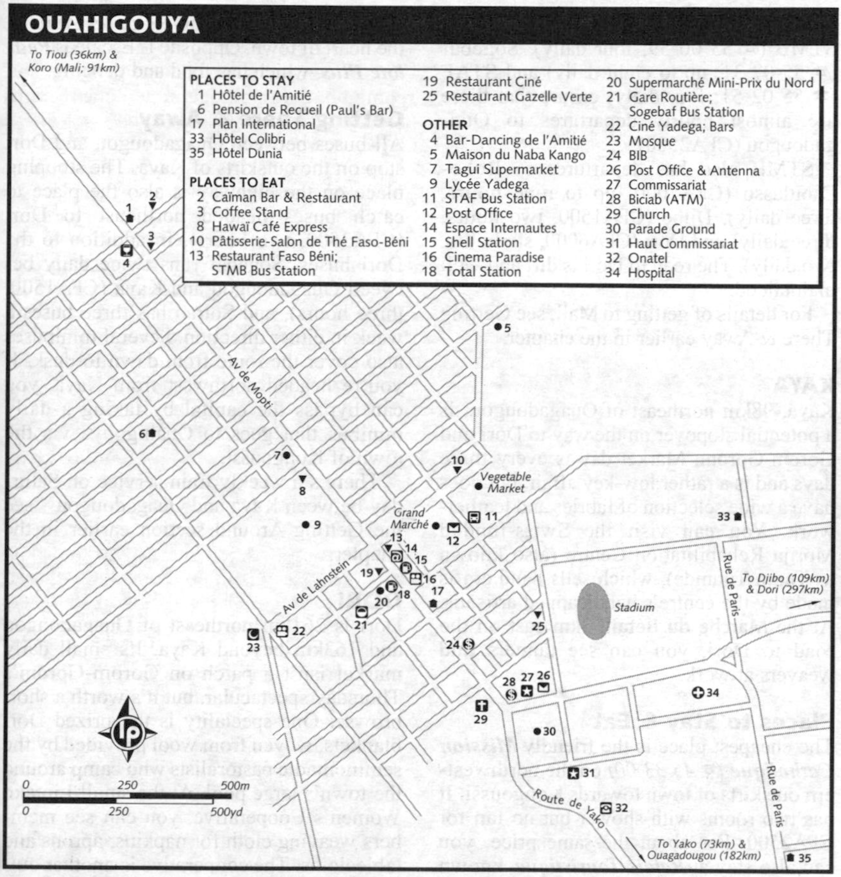
OUAHIGOUYA
To Tiou (36km) & Koro (Mali; 91km)
PLACES TO STAY
1 Hôtel de l'Amitié
6 Pension de Recueil (Paul's Bar)
17 Plan International
33 Hôtel Colibri
35 Hôtel Dunia
PLACES TO EAT
2 Caïman Bar & Restaurant
3 Coffee Stand
8 Hawaï Café Express
10 Pâtisserie-Salon de Thé Faso-Béni
13 Restaurant Faso Béni; STMB Bus Station
19 Restaurant Ciné
25 Restaurant Gazelle Verte
OTHER
4 Bar-Dancing de l'Amitié
5 Maison du Naba Kango
7 Tagui Supermarket
9 Lycée Yadega
11 STAF Bus Station
12 Post Office
14 Éspace Internautes
15 Shell Station
16 Cinema Paradise
18 Total Station
20 Supermarché Mini-Prix du Nord
21 Gare Routière; Sogebaf Bus Station
22 Ciné Yadega; Bars
23 Mosque
24 BIB
26 Post Office & Antenna
27 Commissariat
28 Biciab (ATM)
29 Church
30 Parade Ground
31 Haut Commissariat
32 Onatel
34 Hospital
Av de Mopti
Vegetable Market
Grand Marché
Av de Lahnstein
Stadium
Rue de Paris
To Djibo (109km) & Dori (297km)
Route de Yako
To Yako (73km) & Ouagadougou (182km)
0 250 500m
0 250 500yd

CFA4920/8925. Staff at the Colibri are charming. It's about 1km east of the centre, but the warmth of the welcome compensates for the distance. Rooms are arranged around a maturing compound.

Places to Eat & Drink

For inexpensive food, the tiny and central ***Restaurant Ciné*** has standard fare such as riz sauce for CFA350 and a small steak for CFA450.

For breakfast or a snack, ***Pâtisserie-Salon de Thé Faso-Beni*** (☎ *55 01 61*) opposite the vegetable market offers cold drinks, pastries and ice cream, expressed from a genuine Italian machine.

Restaurant Faso Béni (☎ *55 01 61*) next to the STMB bus station is a typical African chop bar where you can eat simply and plentifully.

Slightly more upmarket, ***Restaurant Gazelle Verte***, near the stadium, is relatively new and well worth a visit.

Craving an espresso coffee? Head for ***Hawaï Café Express*** that, in addition to coffee, serves good snacks.

In the evening, you can get grilled chicken and brochettes at ***Caïman Bar & Restaurant***, just behind Hôtel de l'Amitié. On Saturday evening, it's a good place to hang out until the nearby ***Bar-Dancing de l'Amitié*** *(admission CFA400)* livens up, typically around midnight.

Self-caterers could try ***Supermarché Mini-Prix du Nord*** (☎ *55 01 54*) near the gare routière or the ***vegetable market***.

Getting There & Away

STMB (☎ 55 00 59; four daily), Sogebaf (☎ 55 07 31; up to eight daily) and STAF (☎ 55 02 51; four daily) ensure that there are almost hourly departures to Ouagadougou (CFA2500).

STMB also has departures to Bobo-Dioulasso (CFA7000, up to nine hours, three daily), Djibo (CFA1500, two hours, three daily) and Dori (CFA6000, six hours, two daily). The road to Dori is dirt and well maintained.

For details of getting to Mali, see Getting There & Away earlier in the chapter.

KAYA

Kaya, 98km northeast of Ouagadougou, is a potential stopover on the way to Dori and Gorom-Gorom. Market day is every three days and is a rather low-key affair, but does have a wide selection of fabrics and leatherwork. You can visit the Swiss-funded Morija Rehabilitation Centre (also known as Tuum Tuumde), which sells handicrafts made by the centre's handicapped artisans. At the **Marché du Bétail**, 3km east on the road to Dori, you can see tanners and weavers at work.

Places to Stay & Eat

The cheapest place is the friendly ***Mission Catholique*** *(☎ 45 33 00)* on the northwestern outskirts of town towards Kongoussi. It has two rooms with shower but no fan for CFA2500. For about the same price, you can also stay at ***Relais Touristique***, known to locals simply as 'L'Auberge', on the road to Dori. The rooms without fan or mosquito nets are nothing special, but there's a good breeze from the nearby lake. Even if you don't stay here, it's a great place for a drink or meal as its terrace offers a scenic view of the lake. Decent cheap food includes brochettes (CFA200) and tasty french fries (CFA400).

There are two newish and more expensive hotels; ***Hôtel Kaziende*** *(☎ 45 35 35)* on the city's southern edge near the police station, and more expensive is ***Hôtel Zinoogo*** *(☎ 45 32 54)*, where singles/doubles with fan cost from CFA5000/6500 and air-con rooms cost CFA11,000/15,000. It has satellite TV and one of the city's top restaurants.

Other good places to eat include ***L'Escale*** on the road south to Ouagadougou, ***Mon Chou***, heading east, and ***Resto les Amis*** in the heart of town. Opposite L'Escale is ***Paillote Plus***, which has food and dancing.

Getting There & Away

All buses between Ouagadougou and Dori stop on the outskirts of Kaya. The stopping place on the highway is also the place to catch buses headed northeast to Dori (CFA2500, two hours). In addition to the Dori buses, Sogebaf runs twice daily between Ouagadougou and Kaya (CFA1500, three hours), and Sotrao has three buses a week in either direction. Several minibuses also cover the route from dawn to dusk. If you're headed northwest from Kaya, you can bypass the capital by taking a daily minibus that goes to Ouahigouya via the town of Kongoussi.

There's a weekly train service on Saturday between Kaya and Ouagadougou – see the Getting Around section earlier in the chapter.

DORI

Dori is 261km northeast of Ouagadougou and 163km beyond Kaya. Its small daily market isn't a patch on Gorom-Gorom's Thursday spectacular, but it's worth a short browse. One speciality is the prized Dori blankets, woven from wool provided by the seminomadic pastoralists who camp around the town's large pool. At the small Liptako Women's Cooperative, you can see members weaving cloth for napkins, aprons and tablecloths. The cooperative is another outlet for Dori blankets.

Dori may have few attractions of its own, but it nonetheless has its fair share of touts hanging on to Gorom-Gorom's coat tails. Most are friendly enough but they can be persistent.

Places to Stay

Hérbergement de Dori *(Hérbergement Sahel; ☎ 66 03 41)* Rooms with fan & shower CFA3300, with air-con up to CFA10,650. If you're after quiet accommodation, this place, east of the centre, is good, although it's a fair walk from the gares routières. The filthy shared toilets are not a place to linger.

Auberge Populaire Rooms from CFA3500. This place, on the northern side of town on the road to Gorom-Gorom, also

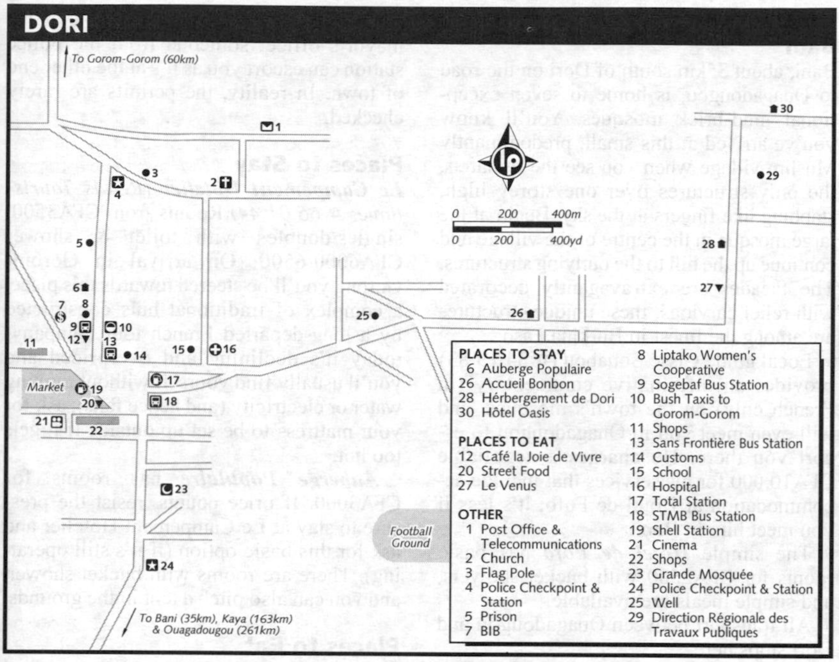
DORI
To Gorom-Gorom (60km)
To Bani (35km), Kaya (163km) & Ouagadougou (261km)
Market
Football Ground
0 200 400m
0 200 400yd
PLACES TO STAY
6 Auberge Populaire
26 Accueil Bonbon
28 Hérbergement de Dori
30 Hôtel Oasis
PLACES TO EAT
12 Café la Joie de Vivre
20 Street Food
27 Le Venus
OTHER
1 Post Office & Telecommunications
2 Church
3 Flag Pole
4 Police Checkpoint & Station
5 Prison
7 BIB
8 Liptako Women's Cooperative
9 Sogebaf Bus Station
10 Bush Taxis to Gorom-Gorom
11 Shops
13 Sans Frontière Bus Station
14 Customs
15 School
16 Hospital
17 Total Station
18 STMB Bus Station
19 Shell Station
21 Cinema
22 Shops
23 Grande Mosquée
24 Police Checkpoint & Station
25 Well
29 Direction Régionale des Travaux Publiques

known as Chez Tanti Véronique, has no-frills rooms with shared facilities. Not all the rooms have secure locks. Its large adjacent bar can be a lively place to spend the evening or an irritating sleep inhibitor, depending upon your mood and the hour.

Accueil Bonbon *(☎ 66 00 93)* Rooms with fan/air-con CFA8000/12,000. About 1.5km east of the main intersection, this place is a decent mid-range option; there's a restaurant here.

Hôtel Oasis *(☎ 66 03 41)* Small singles/doubles CFA9000/11,000, large rooms CFA16,000/18,000. Standards are beginning to slide, but the Oasis still represents good value. All cabins have air-con and bathroom. The smaller cabins are called, with some exaggeration, bungalows, while the larger ones, styled in an even greater flight of fancy as minivillas, include a spacious sitting area.

Places to Eat

You can eat simply at ***Café la Joie de Vivre***, which has riz gras for CFA200 and spaghetti for CFA300. ***Hôtel Oasis*** has a small restaurant serving cold drinks and meals that are simple, nourishing and inexpensive, but not of the quality you'd expect from a hotel of this category.

There is plenty of ***street food*** at the main intersection. If you're staying at the eastern end of town, the outdoor ***Le Venus*** serves filling, simple meals for CFA500.

Getting There & Away

Both STMB (☎ 66 03 32) and Sans Frontière operate a twice-daily service between Dori and Ouagadougou (CFA4000, five hours). Sogebaf has three buses a week from Ouagadougou to Gorom-Gorom that make a stop in Dori. There is also an intermittent service all the way to Markoyé (CFA2500).

For Gorom-Gorom, bush taxis (CFA2000, two hours) are plentiful on market day; most pull out by 8am. Seats in the cabin cost the same as those in the back so it's worth turning up as early as 6.30am because it is literally a case of first in, best dressed – if you're crammed into the back, you'll be coated in red dust long before you reach Gorom-Gorom. Locals often only pay CFA1000, so it's worth bargaining.

AROUND DORI

Bani

Bani, about 35km south of Dori on the road to Ouagadougou, is home to seven exceptional mud-brick mosques. You'll know you've arrived at this small, predominantly Muslim village when you see the minarets, the only structures over one storey high, stabbing like fingers at the sky. Begin at the large mosque in the centre of the village and continue up the hill to the outlying structures. The facades are extravagantly decorated with relief carvings; these unique structures are among the finest in Burkina Faso.

Local guide Cissé Souabou (☎ 34 19 83) provides an informative commentary (in French only) on the town's mosques, and will even meet you in Ouagadougou to escort you there. He charges a negotiable CFA10,000 for his services that include accommodation at Hôtel de Fofo; it's less if you meet him in Bani.

The simple ***Hôtel de Fofo*** has basic rooms for CFA2500 with bucket showers, and simple meals are available.

All transport between Ouagadougou and Dori stops here.

GOROM-GOROM

Gorom's main attraction is its market, held on Thursday, which gets into full swing about 11am.

Upon entering the town, you have to register at the commissariat and pay a 'tourist tax' of CFA1000. If you plan on using your camera, you also have to pay a steep CFA5000 for a photo permit (which covers the whole northern region) payable at the mayor's office; someone from the police station can escort you as it's at the other end of town. In reality, the permits are rarely checked.

Places to Stay

Le Campement Hôtelier *(Relais Touristique;* ☎ *66 01 44)* Rooms from CFA3500, singles/doubles with toilet & shower CFA6000/6500. On arrival in Gorom-Gorom, you'll be steered towards this place, a complex of traditional huts constructed by a long-departed French tour company; today it's declining and overpriced and you'll usually find yourself without running water or electricity (and hence fans); ask for your mattress to be set up outside if it gets too hot.

Auberge Populaire has rooms for CFA3000. If price counts, resist the pressure to stay at Le Campement Hôtelier and ask for this basic option (if it's still operating). There are rooms with bucket shower, and you can also pitch a tent in the grounds.

Places to Eat

There are few alternatives to the overpriced food at ***Le Campement Hôtelier*** *(☎ 66 01 44)*, which charges more than CFA2000 for rice and a quarter of the scrawniest chicken ever to scratch the dust. The best of these is the friendly ***Restaurant Inssa*** beside the Shell petrol station. There are also a couple of undistinguished ***Togolese chop houses*** in the market, a small ***café*** beside the gare routière and another by the Salle de Video.

Gorom-Gorom Market

Gorom-Gorom's Thursday market is the most colourful in all Burkina Faso. Its charm lies in the fact that it is an authentic local market drawing traders from all around the surrounding countryside. As such, its focus is entirely local, and tourists are simply part of the menagerie. The animal market, where camels, goats, sheep, donkeys and cattle are all traded, is just beyond the nearby town pond.

You'll see a variety of Sahel and Sahara ethnic groups: the Tuareg proudly on their camels and their former slaves, the Bella, who've taken over many of their erstwhile masters' skills in leatherwork, and Fulani herders and Songhaï farmers, each in their traditional dress.

The Tuareg men are easily identified by their long, flowing robes *(boubous)*, indigo turbans and elaborate silver swords. The Bella, both men and women, favour black or grey gowns with wide belts of richly decorated leather. Most elaborately dressed of all are the Fulani women. You can recognise them by the vivid, multicoloured dresses and complex hairstyles, usually braided and decorated with silver threads, tiny chains and colourful beads. These women carry their wealth with them in the form of beads, bracelets, heavy earrings or necklaces, many of solid silver with dangling Maria Theresa dollars.

Couscous goes for CFA400 and rice costs around CFA200.

Getting There & Away

The road between Dori and Gorom-Gorom is in poor condition. Sogebaf, CTI and ZSR buses (CFA7000, seven hours) leave Ouagadougou on Monday, Wednesday and Saturday, returning the next day. On market day, they depart from Gorom-Gorom soon after 2pm. If you leave Ouagadougou on the Wednesday and want to return to the capital the next day after visiting the market, these buses are your only option. Bush taxis head back to Dori (CFA2000, two hours) around 7pm after the market's all said and done.

AROUND GOROM-GOROM

You can hire a 4WD with driver from the hangers-on at Le Campement and visit some of the nearby Tuareg villages.

Further afield, Markoyé and Oursi can be visited as a day trip. **Markoyé**, 40km northeast of Gorom-Gorom on a sandy track towards the Nigerien border, has a vibrant camel and cattle market every Monday. It's the only day when you can be guaranteed a ride. A minibus leaves Gorom-Gorom at 7.30am, returning at 6pm.

Oursi, some 35km northeast of Gorom-Gorom, has some spectacular sand dunes, **Les Dunes d'Oursi**. If you can tear yourself from your bed, set off at 4am to catch the sunrise gilding their crests.

Cameroon

Cameroon has it all: rainforests and relaxing beaches in the south; rocky outcrops, terraced hillsides and hobbit-like villages in the north; West Africa's highest peak; and Parc National de Waza, with rewarding wildlife viewing. The country sits at the crossroads of West and Central Africa, and is one of the most culturally diverse on the continent, with a rich tapestry of indigenous cultures. Topping everything off are vibrant artistic and musical traditions, a network of ancient tribal kingdoms, and wonderful Cameroonian hospitality.

Cameroon at a Glance

Capital: Yaoundé
Population: 15 million
Area: 475,442 sq km
Head of State: President Paul Biya
Official languages: French, English
Main local languages: Fulfulde, Ewondo, Douala, plus many more
Currency: Central African CFA franc
Exchange rate: US$1 = CFA694
Time: GMT/UTC +1
Country telephone code: ☎ 237
Best time to go: November to February

Maroua p262
CHAD
Garoua p260
NIGERIA
Ring Road Area p252
N'Gaoundéré p258
CENTRAL AFRICAN REPUBLIC
Bamenda p250
Foumban p256
Mt Cameroon Area p245
Bafoussam p255
Douala pp240-41
Limbe p242
Yaoundé p233
Central Yaoundé p235
Kribi p270

Highlights

- Climbing Mt Cameroon, West Africa's highest peak
- Hiking among ancient tribal kingdoms and striking mountain scenery in the Ring Road area near Bamenda
- Exploring the mountains and picturesque villages around Maroua
- Spending time with Cameroonians, learning some Pidgin English and dining on grilled fish on the beaches around Limbe or Kribi
- Browsing at Foumban's market and visiting the Royal Palace and museum
- Watching wildlife at Parc National de Waza

Facts about Cameroon

HISTORY

Early History

As far back as 8000 BC, the area that is now Cameroon was a meeting point of cultures. In the south, the original inhabitants were various ethno-linguistic groups of short stature, collectively known as 'Pygmies'. Beginning about 2000 years ago, they were gradually displaced by Bantu peoples moving southeast from present-day Nigeria and the Sahel region, although large communities still remain.

In Cameroon's extreme north, near Kousséri and Lake Chad, the most significant early culture was that of the Sao people, who migrated from the Nile Valley. They are known for the pottery and bronze-work they left behind, before being absorbed by the powerful state of Kanem-Borno around the 8th or 9th century.

In the early 15th century, another important migration occurred when the Fulani (pastoral nomads from Senegal) began to move eastwards. By the late 16th century, they dominated much of northcentral Cameroon, adding further to the area's cultural heterogeneity.

The First Europeans & the Colonial Era

In 1472, Portuguese explorers sailed up the Wouri River, naming it Rio dos Camarões (River of Prawns), thus giving the country

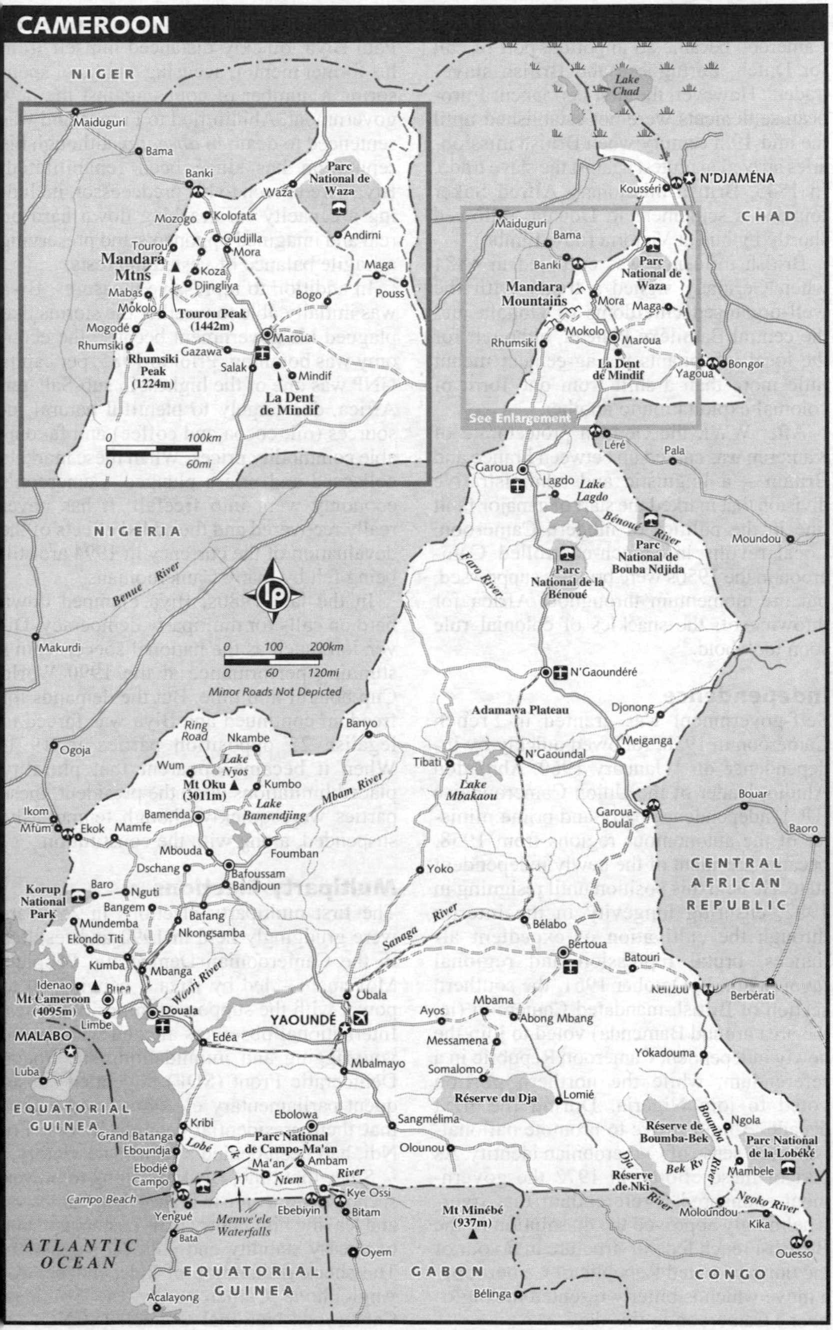
CAMEROON
NIGER
Lake Chad
N'DJAMÉNA
Kousséri
CHAD
Maiduguri
Bama
Banki
Parc National de Waza
Mandara Mountains
Mora
Maga
Mokolo
Rhumsiki
Maroua
La Dent de Mindif
Yagoua
Bongor
See Enlargement
Maiduguri
Bama
Banki
Waza
Parc National de Waza
Mozogo
Kolofata
Andirni
Tourou
Oudjilla
Mora
Mandara Mtns
Koza
Maga
Djingliya
Bogo
Pouss
Mabas
Mokolo
Tourou Peak (1442m)
Mogodé
Maroua
Rhumsiki
Gazawa
Salak
Mindif
Rhumsiki Peak (1224m)
La Dent de Mindif
0 100km
0 60mi
Léré
Pala
Garoua
Lagdo
Lake Lagdo
Bénoué River
Moundou
Parc National de Bouba Ndjida
Parc National de la Bénoué
Faro River
NIGERIA
Benue River
Makurdi
0 100 200km
0 60 120mi
Minor Roads Not Depicted
N'Gaoundéré
Adamawa Plateau
Djonong
Meiganga
Ring Road
Nkambe
Banyo
Ogoja
Lake Nyos
Tibati
N'Gaoundal
Wum
Mt Oku (3011m)
Kumbo
Mbam River
Lake Mbakaou
Bouar
Ikom
Bamenda
Lake Bamendjing
Mfum
Ekok
Mamfe
Garoua-Boulaï
Baoro
Foumban
Mbouda
Dschang
Bafoussam
Yoko
CENTRAL AFRICAN REPUBLIC
Korup National Park
Baro
Nguti
Bandjoun
Bangem
Bafang
Mundemba
Sanaga River
Bélabo
Nkongsamba
Ekondo Titi
Bertoua
Kumba
Mbanga
Batouri
Idenao
Buea
Wouri River
Kenzou
Berbérati
Mt Cameroon (4095m)
Obala
Douala
Limbe
YAOUNDÉ
Mbama
Ayos
Abong Mbang
MALABO
Edéa
Messamena
Yokadouma
Luba
Mbalmayo
Somalomo
Réserve du Dja
Lomié
EQUATORIAL GUINEA
Kribi
Ebolowa
Sangmélima
Ngola
Réserve de Boumba-Bek
Boumba River
Parc National de la Lobéké
Grand Batanga
Parc National de Campo-Ma'an
Eboundja
Lobé
Ck
Olounou
Ebodjé
Ma'an
Ambam
Dja River
Bek Rv
Réserve de Nki
Mambele
Campo
Ntem
River
Campo Beach
Kye Ossi
Ebebiyin
Bitam
Ngoko River
Moloundou
Kika
Yengué
Memve'ele Waterfalls
Mt Minébé (937m)
Bata
ATLANTIC OCEAN
Oyem
Ouesso
EQUATORIAL GUINEA
GABON
CONGO
Acalayong
Bélinga

CAMEROON

its name. Over the next two centuries, coastal Cameroon became an important port of call for Dutch, Portuguese and British slave-traders. However, the first permanent European settlements were not established until the mid-19th century when British missionaries arrived in protest against the slave trade. In 1845, British missionary Alfred Saker founded a settlement in Douala, followed shortly by one at Victoria (now Limbe).

British influence was curtailed in 1884 when Germany signed a treaty with the well-organised chiefdoms of Douala and the central Bamiléké Plateau, although for the local inhabitants the agreement meant little more than a shift from one form of colonial exploitation to another.

After WWI, the German protectorate of Kamerun was carved up between France and Britain – a linguistic and administrative division that marked the start of a major fault line in the politics of modern Cameroon. Local revolts in French-controlled Cameroon in the 1950s were brutally suppressed, but the momentum throughout Africa for throwing off the shackles of colonial rule soon took hold.

Independence

Self-government was granted in French Cameroon in 1958, followed quickly by independence on 1 January 1960. Ahmadou Ahidjo, leader of the Union Camerounaise (UC) independence party and prime minister of the autonomous regions from 1958, became president of the newly independent state. He held this position until resigning in 1982, ensuring longevity in the interim through the cultivation of expedient alliances, brutal repression and regional favouritism. In October 1961, the southern section of British-mandated Cameroon (ie, the area around Bamenda) voted to join the newly independent Cameroon Republic in a referendum, while the northern portion voted to join Nigeria. During the next decade, Ahidjo strove to promote nationalism and a sense of Cameroonian identity. As part of these efforts, in 1972 the government sponsored a referendum that overwhelmingly approved the dissolution of the British-French federal structure in favour of the unitary United Republic of Cameroon – a move which is bitterly resented in Anglophone Cameroon to this day.

In 1982, Ahidjo's hand-picked successor, Paul Biya, quickly distanced himself from his former mentor, accusing Ahidjo of sponsoring a number of coups against the new government. Ahidjo fled to France and was sentenced to death *in absentia*, although his reputation has since been rehabilitated. Biya owed much to his predecessor, including a capacity for cracking down hard on real and imagined opponents and preserving a fragile balance of vested interests.

In addition to repressive measures, Biya was initially able to weather the storms that plagued his government because the economy was booming. Prior to 1985, per capita GNP was one of the highest in sub-Saharan Africa, due largely to plentiful natural resources (oil, cocoa and coffee) and favourable commodity prices. When these markets collapsed and prices plunged, Cameroon's economy went into freefall. It has never really recovered and the added effects of the devaluation of the currency in 1994 are still being felt by many Cameroonians.

In the late 1980s, Biya clamped down hard on calls for multiparty democracy. Diversions such as the national soccer team's stunning performance at the 1990 World Cup bought him time. But the demands for freedom continued and Biya was forced to legalise 25 opposition parties in 1991. When it became apparent that plurality placed limitations upon the president, these parties were quickly, though temporarily, suspended, along with the constitution.

Multiparty Elections

The first multiparty elections in 25 years were grudgingly held in 1992 and resulted in the Cameroonian Democratic People's Movement – led by Biya – hanging on to power with the support of minority parties. International observers alleged widespread vote-rigging and intimidation. The Social Democratic Front (SDF) boycotted subsequent parliamentary elections amid claims that their presidential candidate, John Fru Ndi, had been denied a legitimate victory.

Since that time, Biya has clung to power, spending more time in France than Cameroon and leaving his country in its customary state of uneasy stability and political stagnation. The shock declaration of independence for Anglophone Cameroon by the Southern Cameroons National Council (SCNC) on

Buea radio on 30 December 1999 reflected growing discontent and sparked a further flurry of arrests.

In 1998 and again in 1999 the international anticorruption organisation, Transparency International, gave Cameroon the dubious distinction of being the world's most corrupt country. This affects every aspect of daily life, from dealings with petty government officials to the rampant destruction of the country's endangered rainforests by governmental logging interests.

Periodic states of emergency, ongoing repression and unrest in Anglophone areas continue to characterise the rule of Biya, who was elected to his 'second' seven-year term (the constitutional limit) in October 1997. Whether Biya (only Cameroon's second president in 40 years) will seek to further extend his term of office is anybody's guess. A more pressing concern in the eyes of most observers is that the fraud that marked the previous elections be avoided.

GEOGRAPHY

Much of southern Cameroon is a low-lying coastal plain covered by patches of equatorial rainforests extending eastwards towards the Central African Republic. In the centre, forming a barrier between north and south, is the sparsely populated savanna area of the Adamawa Plateau. North of here is a rolling, semi-arid landscape punctuated by rocky escarpments. It is fringed to the west by the barren, but beautiful, Mandara Mountains, and drained by rivers flowing into Lake Chad Basin. A chain of volcanic mountains, including the active Mt Cameroon, runs from the coast along the Nigerian border.

CLIMATE

The north has a single wet season from April/May to September/October. The hottest months here are March to May, when temperatures can soar to 40°C, although it's a dry (and therefore generally bearable) heat. The south has a humid, equatorial climate, with rain scattered throughout the year and almost continual high humidity. The main wet season here is June to October, when secondary roads often become impassable. From March to June are the light rains. Throughout Cameroon, November to February are the driest months, though dust from harmattan winds greatly restricts visibility.

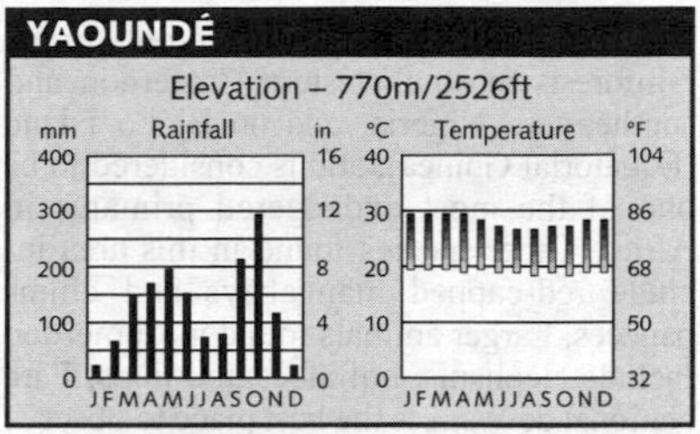
YAOUNDÉ
Elevation – 770m/2526ft
mm
Rainfall
in
°C
Temperature
°F
400
300
200
100
0
16
12
8
4
0
40
30
20
10
0
104
86
68
50
32
JFMAMJJASOND
JFMAMJJASOND

ECOLOGY & ENVIRONMENT

Dense forests cover about 22 million hectares in southern and eastern Cameroon, forming one of Africa's largest forest areas. However, despite improved government regulation of commercial logging, timber exploitation continues and many areas are in danger of depletion.

Among the bright spots in the picture are the efforts of Worldwide Fund for Nature (WWF), in collaboration with several government ministries, to expand Cameroon's network of protected areas. In addition to benefiting the forest, these efforts are also addressed at lessening the impact of commercial logging on the Baka (Pygmy) and other communities that depend on the forests for their livelihood, and in halting widespread poaching. The most notable progress in recent years has come in the southeast, where Lobéké – formerly a forest reserve – was recently awarded national park status, with Boumba-Bek and Nki forest reserves soon to follow. In the south, the Réserve de Campo was recently gazetted as a national park – in large part to ensure adequate environmental and community protection for areas through which the Chad-Cameroon oil pipeline will be passing.

The WWF office (☎ 221 6267, fax 221 4240), in the Bastos area of Yaoundé, has an informative website (W www.wwfcameroon.org) with detailed information about the southeastern reserves and other environmental hot spots in Cameroon.

FLORA & FAUNA

Many of Cameroon's protected areas are exceptionally biodiverse, with high levels of plant and animal endemism. In the Mt Cameroon area alone, for example, about 50 endemic plants have been identified, as well as several endemic bird species. Mt Cameroon and southern forest areas are also home to the drill, which is found only in the rainforests of southwestern Cameroon and southeastern Nigeria, and on Bioko Island (Equatorial Guinea), and is considered to be one of the most endangered primates in Africa. Other species found in this area include red-capped mangabeys and chimpanzees. Larger animals found in Cameroon include elephants, buffaloes and lions; Parc National de Waza is the best place to observe these. Forest elephants and buffaloes are found in many rainforest areas (along with gorillas and more), but are rarely seen due to dense vegetation. Bénoué and Bouba Ndjida parks near Garoua also host populations of large animals, including a population of West African black rhinos, but wildlife concentrations are not as high as in Waza.

Waza is the main wildlife-viewing park and the only one readily accessible to visitors. Korup National Park is the most accessible of Cameroon's protected rainforest areas.

GOVERNMENT & POLITICS

Cameroon has a multiparty system dominated by President Paul Biya and his RDPC (Rassemblement Démocratique du Peuple Camerounais), which holds the majority in the 180-member national assembly. However, there is little popular support for the government. The main opposition party is the predominantly Anglophone Social Democratic Front (SDF) led by John Fru Ndi, although its influence has weakened in recent years. Presidential elections are scheduled for 2004.

Administratively, the country is divided into 10 provinces and their names don't necessarily coincide with their geographical locations. Provinces (and their capitals) are: Littoral (Douala); South-West (Buea); North-West (Bamenda); West (Bafoussam); Central (Yaoundé); Adamawa (N'Gaoundéré); North (Garoua); Extreme North (Maroua); East (Bertoua); South (Ebolowa).

ECONOMY

At about US$645, Cameroon has one of West Africa's higher annual per capita income levels, although an estimated 48% of its people still live below the poverty line. Agriculture, primarily small-scale and subsistence farming, is the mainstay of the economy, employing approximately 80% of the population. Other important sectors include forestry and mining, although the country's mineral reserves are largely unexploited. Oil production – an important source of foreign revenue for the past two decades – is expected to decline in coming years unless new discoveries are made. Macroeconomic indicators (including an inflation rate of about 2% and annual economic growth of about 5%) are relatively good, and these, as well as progress with privatisation efforts, have caused observers to be cautiously optimistic about the country's economy. However, corruption is rampant at all levels, and daily life continues to be a struggle for most people.

POPULATION & PEOPLE

Cameroon has about 15 million inhabitants within its 475,442 sq km area. Population density is greatest in the south and southwest. Among the country's approximately 280 ethno-linguistic groups are the economically dominant Bamiléké (around Bafoussam, and in Douala and Yaoundé), the Fulani (Foulbé or Fula) in the north and northwest, and Tikar communities northeast of Foumban. In the south and east are various so-called 'Pygmy' tribes, primarily Baka. For more details on the Fulani, see the Peoples of the Region special section.

ARTS

Arts & Craftwork

The areas around Bali and Bamessing (both near Bamenda), and Foumban, are rich in high-quality clay, and some of Cameroon's finest ceramic work originates here. The northwestern highlands (Grassfields) area is also known for its woodcarvings, including masks. These masks often are representations of animals, and it is believed that the wearer of the mask can transform himself and take on the animal's characteristics and powers. Stylised representations of spiders, which symbolise wisdom, are common on carvings from the Grassfields area, especially on items belonging to the chief.

Cameroon also has some highly detailed bronze- and brass-work (including figurative art and pipes), particularly in Tikar areas north and east of Foumban. Carved wooden stools are generally round, except around Douala, where you'll see rectangular stools similar to those found elsewhere along the West African coast.

CAMEROON

'Pygmies'

The term 'Pygmies' has long been used by outsiders to refer to a diverse group of people – many of whom are short in stature – living in the forested areas of Cameroon and Central Africa. Traditionally, these people have lived by hunting and gathering wild forest resources that they either use themselves or trade in exchange for cultivated foods. Although 'Pygmy' is used generically, the 'Pygmies' do not view themselves as one culture (nor do they identify themselves as Pygmies). Rather, they belong to various distinct ethno-linguistic groups. In Cameroon, the most numerous are the Baka. Other groups include the Kola, the Medzan, the Aka and the Bofi.

Since early in the 1st millennium, these peoples and their traditional way of life have been under threat – first by Bantu groups who forced them to consolidate and withdraw as the Bantu migrated southeastwards through traditional Pygmy areas; later by colonial masters, who forced the Pygmies into more easily 'managed' roadside settlements where they were often exploited; and, more recently by forces such as multinational logging companies, mining, and government policies to encourage a more sedentary lifestyle. Now, while most Pygmies remain at least partially nomadic, many live in interdependent relationships with neighbouring Bantu farming peoples, although their exploitation continues.

Most Pygmies follow traditional religions, which typically centre around a powerful forest spirit, with the forest viewed as mother, father and guardian. Among the Baka, this forest god is known as Jengi. Jengi is also the name given to celebrations marking the rite of passage of young Baka men into adulthood.

Music

Cameroon has a rich musical heritage. The legendary Manu Dibango is probably the biggest name, and the one who brought international fame to Cameroonian *makossa*, a fusion of highlife and soul. The music of the versatile Francis Bebey incorporates everything from thumb piano to electric bass and draws on a range of styles. Other renowned makossa musicians include Sam Fan Thomas and Moni Bilé. Traditional musical instruments include drums, the zither, the xylophone, and the occasional *kora* (lute).

Literature

In addition to Mongo Beti (see Literature under Arts in the Facts about West Africa chapter), well-known literary figures include Kenjo Jumban, whose novel *The White Man of God* deals with the country's colonial experience, and Ferdinand Oyono, who's *Houseboy* and *The Old Man and the Medal* also deal with colonial themes. *The Crown of Thorns* by the prolific Linus Asong is well worth reading for insights into tribal society in northwestern Cameroon.

SOCIETY & CONDUCT

Dress throughout the country tends to be conservative, particularly in northern Cameroon. In general, the more professional you look, the better and more respectfully you will be treated.

Cameroonians are very hospitable, but especially in rural areas, they may be concerned about being exploited (which has happened all too often in the past) and may be therefore be suspicious of your motives. When travelling in places that don't receive many tourists, it's always best to announce your presence to the local chief (known as the *fon* in western Cameroon, and *lamido* in parts of the north). You'll also need to get the chief's permission to enter tribal lands, including various mountains and crater lakes. In many cases, a small gift is expected – a bottle of whisky or some money (about CFA2000) is usually appropriate.

It's never worth challenging an official's authority or showing anger – for example, at roadside police checkpoints. Patience, composure and a sense of humour will see you through most situations.

RELIGION

Estimates of the number of Christians range from about 15% to about 50%, with the actual figure probably somewhere in between. Throughout Cameroon, traditional animist religions are strong, with an adherence of between 25% and 40% of the population. Islam, followed by 20% to 25% of the population, is the predominant religion in the north among the Fulani people, although there are also sizeable numbers of fiercely non-Muslim animists (known collectively as Kirdi) in this region. Many groups in the rainforests of the south and east follow traditional religions.

LANGUAGE

French and English are the official languages, but English is rarely heard, except in the Anglophone northwest and southwest. There are about 280 indigenous languages (check **W** www.ethnologue.com/show_country.asp?name=Cameroon for a summary). Pidgin English is used as something of a lingua franca in many areas. In the north, Fulfulde fills this role. See the Language chapter for some useful French words and phrases.

Facts for the Visitor

SUGGESTED ITINERARIES

Travel in Cameroon is slow, especially off main routes, including in the Ring Road area and in the far north around Maroua; allow plenty of time and keep your schedule flexible.

With just a week starting from Douala, go to Limbe for a night or two to get your bearings, then – if you have an adventurous bent – head either to Mt Cameroon or to Korup National Park for a few days exploring, finishing again in Douala. Alternatively, if your interest is more in culture and history, go from Douala to Foumban (via Bafoussam). After a night there, head to the Ring Road area, ideally including a day in Bafut and a day hiking in the area between Bambui and Ndop. Finish in Douala or Yaoundé. (Better for this itinerary would be about 10 days.)

With two weeks, spend the first week exploring the Ring Road area and visiting Foumban. Then head to Yaoundé, from where you can fly north to Maroua and explore the surrounding area. With three weeks or more, you would have time to go from Yaoundé to N'Gaoundéré by train, and from there make your way north by road to Maroua, either flying or returning by road and train to Yaoundé or Douala.

With a month or more you'll have time to expand this itinerary, perhaps starting with a night or two in Limbe, followed by a climb of Mt Cameroon or a visit to Korup, before making your way up to Bamenda and the Ring Road area. During the dry season, you could then go from Kumbo on the Ring Road direct to Foumban; otherwise head to Foumban via Bafoussam. From here, make your way to Yaoundé to rest up for a day or two before heading north by train to N'Gaoundéré and beyond. Spend the remainder of the time exploring northern Cameroon.

PLANNING

The best months to visit are November to February, although you'll have harmattan haze during much of this time. The worst months are between July and October, when it's raining almost everywhere, and many roads are impassable.

Macmillan's *Road Map of Cameroon* (1998) is the best map, with city plans of Douala and Yaoundé on the reverse. It's occasionally available in Cameroon. Other maps include those of the Institut Géographique National and the International Travellers' Map series. Dated topographical maps are sold for CFA3000 at the Institut National de Cartographie (open 8.30am to 3pm Monday to Friday). It's on Av Monseigneur Vogt in Yaoundé, diagonally opposite BEAC (Banque des États de l'Afrique Central). Its maps covering the Mt Cameroon area are out of stock.

VISAS & DOCUMENTS

Visas

Visas are required by everyone and can be obtained in all neighbouring countries. A one month multiple-entry visa costs around US$50 and requires two photos. Issuing time ranges from 24 hours to one week.

Officially, you're required to get a visa before entering Cameroon if arriving from a country with a Cameroonian embassy. However, at the time of research, visas were being issued without hassle at the airports in Douala and Yaoundé for CFA30,000.

Visa Extensions You can obtain visa extensions in Yaoundé (one photo plus CFA15,000). With sufficient reason, they are also sometimes issued in regional capitals, though expect hassles.

Visas for Onward Travel In Cameroon, you can get visas for the following neighbouring countries:

Central African Republic (CAR) One month single-entry visas cost CFA25,000 plus two photos, and are processed within 24 hours.

CAMEROON

Chad One month single-entry visas cost CFA30,000 plus two photos and are usually issued the same day if you apply early.

Congo Three month single-entry visas cost CFA35,000 to CFA60,000 depending on nationality, plus two photos and a CFA1000 administration fee, and generally take two days to process.

Equatorial Guinea One month single-entry visas cost CFA36,000 for most nationalities, plus two photos. Applications are processed the same day for Americans, otherwise within three to four days. At the consulate in Douala visas are sometimes issued within 24 hours.

Gabon One-month visas for Gabon cost CFA40,000, require two photos and take two to three days to issue.

Nigeria Visas are generally issued only for residents of Cameroon, or – on an exceptional basis – for those with a letter from their own embassy. Cost varies depending on nationality, averaging about CFA35,000; two photos are also needed.

Vaccination Certificates

A yellow fever vaccination certificate is required to enter the country, and you'll need to carry it with you while travelling.

Making Things Official

Foreigners are required to carry their passports with them in Cameroon and you'll frequently be asked to show this at roadside checkpoints. Although police, in a search for bribes, may tell you otherwise, it's also permissible to carry an officially certified photocopy. This is preferable, as if your documents are stolen or an official decides to keep them, you'll still have the original.

Photocopy the title and visa pages of your passport, including the page showing your arrival date in Cameroon. Then go to the local Ministry of Finance (Minefi) office (found in most major towns), where you'll need to buy a *timbre* (stamp) for CFA500. Take the photocopy and stamp to the local police commissioner's office between 8am and 2pm Monday to Friday, together with your passport, and request that it be 'legalised'. Other than the cost of the stamp, there's no charge.

EMBASSIES & CONSULATES

Cameroon Embassies & Consulates

In West Africa, Cameroon has embassies in Côte d'Ivoire, Nigeria and Senegal. See the Facts for the Visitor sections of the relevant country chapters. Elsewhere, embassies and consulates include the following:

Australia (☎ 02-9876 4544, W www.cameroonconsul.com) 65 Bingara Rd, Beecroft, NSW
Belgium (☎ 02-345 1870) Av Brughmann 131–133, Brussels
Canada (☎ 613-236 1522) 170 Clemow Ave, Ottawa, Ontario
Central African Republic (☎ 611687) Av de la France, Bangui
Chad (☎ 512894) Rue des Poids Lourds, N'Djaména
Congo (☎ 833404) Rue Général Bayardelle, Brazzaville
Equatorial Guinea (☎ 2263) 19, Calle Rey Boncoro, Malabo
France (☎ 01 46 51 89 00, 01 47 43 98 33, fax 01 40 71 63 31) 73, Rue d'Auteuil 75016 Paris
Gabon (☎ 732910, 732800) Blvd Léon Mba, Libreville
Germany (☎ 0228-356 038) Rheinallee 76, Bonn
Italy (☎ 06-4429 1285, 3558 2234) via Syracusa 4/6, Rome
Netherlands (☎ 70-346 9715, W www.cameroon-embassy.nl) Amalistraat 14, The Hague
Switzerland (☎ 022-736 2022) 6, Rue Dunant, Geneva
UK (☎ 020-7727 0771) 84 Holland Park, London
USA (☎ 202-265 8790) 2349 Massachusetts Ave, NW, Washington, DC

Cameroon also has embassies in Egypt and Ethiopia.

Embassies & Consulates in Cameroon

The following embassies and consulates are in Yaoundé, except as noted. Australians can contact the Canadian embassy in an emergency.

Canada (☎ 223 2311) Immeuble Stamatiades, Av de l'Indépendance, Centre Ville
Central African Republic (☎ 220 5155) Rue 1863, off Rue 1810, Bastos; open 8.30am to 3.30pm Monday to Friday
Chad (☎ 221 0624) Rue Joseph Mballa Eloumden, Bastos; open 7.30am to noon and 1pm to 3pm Monday to Friday
Congo (☎ 221 2458) Rue 1815, Bastos; open 8am to 3pm Monday to Friday
Côte d'Ivoire (☎ 221 7459) Rue 1805, off Blvd de l'URSS, Bastos

CAMEROON

Equatorial Guinea (☎ 221 0804) Rue 1805, off Blvd de l'URSS, Bastos; open 9am to noon Monday to Friday
Consulate: (☎ 342 2729, 342 9609) Blvd de la République, Douala; open 9am to 3pm Monday to Friday
France (☎ 223 6399) Rue Joseph Atemengué, near Place de la Réunification
Consulate: (☎ 342 6250) Av des Cocotiers, Bonanjo, Douala
Gabon (☎ 220 2966) Rue 1816, off Rue 1810, Bastos; open 8.30am to 3.30pm Monday to Friday
Germany (☎ 221 0056) Av de Gaulle, Centre Ville
Liberia (☎ 221 5457, 220 9781) Blvd de l'URSS, Bastos
Nigeria (☎ 222 3455, 223 4523) off Av Monseigneur Vogt, near Marché du Mfoundi, Centre Ville; consulates in Douala and Buea
UK (☎ 222 0796) Av Churchill, Centre Ville; consulate in Douala (Blvd de la Liberté); open 9am to noon Monday to Friday
USA (☎ 223 0512) Rue de Nachtigal, south of Place de l'Indépendance, Centre Ville

CUSTOMS

There are no limits on importing currency or on exporting CFA to other Central African CFA countries (Chad, CAR, Congo, Equatorial Guinea and Gabon). When departing the Central African CFA zone, you are permitted to export a maximum of CFA25,000.

MONEY

Currency

The unit of currency is the Central African CFA franc.

Exchange Rates

country	unit		CFA
euro zone	€1	=	CFA656
UK	UK£1	=	CFA1024
USA	US$1	=	CFA694

Exchanging Money

The best currency to travel with is euros, followed a distant second by US dollars; other currencies attract high commissions and poor exchange rates, and even with the dollar, you're unlikely to get the official rates shown in the table above.

Banks for changing money include Amity, Banque Internationale du Cameroun pour l'Epargne et le Crédit (Bicec), Sociéte Générale de Banque au Cameroun (SGBC), Crédit Lyonnais, Commercial Bank of Cameroon (CBC – Douala branch only) and Standard Chartered Bank – though branches of these in smaller towns often don't do foreign exchange.

Banks are sometimes willing to change West African CFA notes to/from Central African CFA notes, but the only place to do this reliably, and to exchange CFA coins, is at the airport in Douala. Look for the small jewellery boutique between the arrivals and departures areas.

Cash Euros and dollars in cash can be exchanged at banks in most major towns, with commissions starting at about 2%. Other currencies are generally accepted only in Douala and Yaoundé, and at unfavourable rates. It's straightforward to change any remaining CFA to euros at the airport in Douala, or at banks in Douala and Yaoundé as long as the amount isn't too large. It's difficult, however, to obtain dollars. Banks in smaller towns often don't offer reverse exchanges.

Travellers Cheques Only major brands of travellers cheques can be changed at banks in Cameroon's larger towns, but they all charge high commissions and throughout the country you *must* have your original purchase receipt. The process is fairly efficient in Douala and Yaoundé; elsewhere expect delays. Banks in smaller towns usually don't accept cheques at all. Because of the high commissions, the difficulty of changing cheques in many areas of the country, and the relative uselessness of credit cards (see the following section), you'll need to carry sufficient cash to tide you over between major cities.

The most useful banks for changing travellers cheques (and their commissions at the time of research) are CBC (Douala branch only, CFA9000 flat fee), Crédit Lyonnais (4%, minimum CFA12,870), Bicec (5% plus 18.7% of the initial 5%), Amity (CFA14,800 flat fee) and Standard Chartered Bank (CFA26,000 flat fee).

ATMs & Credit Cards SGBC bank has ATMs in Douala and Yaoundé that accept Visa and Plus cards, and give CFA cash.

Credit cards are accepted only at a few mid-range and top-end hotels (many of which charge a 6% to 10% commission), and should not be relied upon. No banks provide cash advances.

International Transfers Given the high commissions charged for travellers cheques in Cameroon, international transfers are worth considering if you'll be on the road a long time, although they usually take at least three to four days. Western Union has branches in most major towns.

Black Market & Moneychangers The black market doesn't have much of a presence, but you'll probably be approached by moneychangers on the street. Rather than changing with them outside banking hours, it's much better to ask at shops selling imported goods whether they know anyone who can help you out. Rates are best for larger-denomination notes.

Security

Pickpocketing and bag snatchings are common, especially in markets, train stations, shared taxis and other crowded areas, and robberies, including at knife point, are a problem in Douala and Yaoundé, especially at night. Take the same precautions you would anywhere. Avoid carrying valuables with you on the street, don't carry a bag, take taxis at night and listen to local advice. For more tips, see Security under Money in the Regional Facts for the Visitor chapter.

Costs

At the budget level, dorm beds usually cost CFA2500 or less. Otherwise, plan on at least CFA5000 to CFA7000 per night for lodging, more in the cities, and about CFA3000 for food if you stick to street food and simple chop houses or 'off-licenses' (see Food later in this chapter). You'll need to work to keep total daily expenses, including public transport, much below CFA15,000. For more comfort, you'll probably pay from about CFA12,000 for a mid-range room, and from CFA5000 for a meal. There aren't many top-end choices, but where they exist, plan on CFA40,000 to CFA100,000 or more for a room and from CFA8000 for a meal.

Tipping & Bargaining

Bargaining is the name of the game in Cameroon, especially for anything tourist-related. For some tips, see the boxed text 'The Fine Art of Bargaining' in the Regional Facts for the Visitor chapter. However, in areas that don't receive many tourists, don't automatically assume that the price you're being quoted is too high. For example, taxi drivers in Cameroon don't seem to overcharge as much as they do elsewhere.

Sometimes you may be quoted a price as 'one, one hundred' or '*trois, trois cents*' etc, which is the Cameroonian way of saying 'CFA100 each' or 'CFA300 each'.

POST & COMMUNICATIONS

Post

Yaoundé and Douala have reliable poste restante services at their central post offices, with letters held for about two weeks (CFA200 per each letter collected). International post is fairly reliable for letters, less so for packages.

Telephone & Fax

International calls to Europe and North America cost from around CFA4000 per minute. The cheapest place to make these is at IntelCam offices (located at post offices). Connections are relatively good from Douala and Yaoundé, but less reliable elsewhere. Some Internet cafés offer inexpensive international dialling, but it's not reliable. There are privately owned *cabines téléphoniques* (telephone booths, also called *téléboutiques*) in most towns, and at some you can arrange to receive incoming calls (no reverse-charge) for a small fee. At many it's also possible to make outgoing international calls, though it's more expensive than at Intelcam and can be time consuming.

Within Cameroon, local calls cost about CFA100; domestic calls and calls to mobile (cell) telephones are charged by impulse and are much more expensive. There are no local telephone area codes. Telephone numbers countrywide were recently changed from six to seven digits. For old numbers: add a 2 before any beginning with 2, 30 or 31; and add 3 before any beginning with 32, 33 and up to 49. For mobile phone numbers, add 7 before those beginning with 6 or 7, and add 9 before those beginning with 8 or 9.

Cameroon's mobile phone network is reasonably good and gradually expanding. It costs CFA50,000 to CFA100,000 (including CFA10,000 call credit) to purchase a phone. The two carriers, MTN and Mobilis, have boutiques throughout the country for re-charging the cards.

Email & Internet Access

Except for eastern and northern Cameroon, there are Internet cafés in most major cities, with reasonably good connections. Costs average CFA1000 to CFA1500 per hour. It won't be too much longer before northern Cameroon is connected as well.

DIGITAL RESOURCES

Websites worth checking before starting your travels include:

WWF This is the informative site of its Cameroon office.
W www.wwfcameroon.org

African music If you're interested in Cameroonian and African music, this is a good place to start.
W www.africasounds.com

Ministry of Tourism This is the official site of the Ministry of Tourism, but it's in French.
W www.camnet.cm/mintour/tourisme/

NEWSPAPERS & MAGAZINES

Cameroon Tribune is the government-owned bilingual daily. The thrice-weekly *Le Messager* (French) is the main independent newspaper.

RADIO & TV

Most programming is government-run and in French, through Cameroon Radio-Television Corporation (CRTV). TVs at top-end hotels often have CNN or French news stations.

PHOTOGRAPHY & VIDEO

Many Cameroonians do not like having their picture taken, sometimes because of taboos associated with traditional beliefs. Always ask permission, and respect the answer. Don't photograph anything connected with the military, train stations, post offices, bridges or government buildings, and don't take out your camera in the presence of *gendarmes*, police or other officials.

HEALTH

Have a yellow fever vaccination before arriving in Cameroon. Malaria is endemic throughout most of Cameroon, so take the appropriate precautions. For more information, see Health in the Regional Facts for the Visitor chapter.

Yaoundé and Douala have reasonably good medical facilities, and there are a few decent clinics elsewhere, including in Bamenda and Kumbo. In general, though, there are no medical facilities outside major towns. Especially if you'll be in the east or in remote areas, get all the recommended vaccinations before arriving and bring a first-aid kit.

WOMEN TRAVELLERS

Women can expect few problems in the north. In the south, especially in Francophone coastal areas, you may encounter hissing or comments, but rarely anything threatening. For more information, see Women Travellers in the Regional Facts for the Visitor chapter. Tampons are available in Douala, Yaoundé and occasionally in larger towns.

DANGERS & ANNOYANCES

The security situation in Cameroon ebbs and flows, but some areas always require caution. Walking around Douala, Yaoundé, N'Gaoundéré or Bafoussam at night is unwise – take a taxi. By day you're unlikely to encounter many problems, although you should be wary of theft around bus stations and outside banks.

Several areas in the far north, including the roads from Kousséri to Maroua and from Kousséri to the Nigerian border, have experienced an increase in banditry. Most problems tend to happen at night, and before the Christmas and Tabaski holidays. In some areas, minibuses travel in a military convoy of sorts, although this is just as likely to be because the gendarmes accompanying the convoy earn about CFA3000 per vehicle, rather than from any actual security risk. In any case, night road travel here (and throughout the country) should be avoided. In the event that you do encounter a problem with road bandits, take solace in the fact that they generally won't harm you as long as there is no resistance – just hand over your valuables, which is what they're after.

The most tedious aspect of travel is the presence of interminable police checkpoints. Although most attention is focused on locals, always keep your passport (or certified copy – see the boxed text, 'Making it Official', earlier in this chapter) and vaccination certificate *(carte jaune)* handy, and be prepared to be told that your visa has expired. Unless it has, a calm refusal to play the game will generally see you back on the road without handing over any money. Note that visas are valid from the date you enter Cameroon, though officers seeking bribes may cite the date the visa was issued and count from there.

BUSINESS HOURS

Government offices are officially open from 7.30am to 3.30pm Monday to Friday. Businesses are open from 7.30am or 8am until 6pm or 6.30pm Monday to Friday, generally with a one- to two-hour break sometime between noon and 3pm. Most are also open from 8am to 1pm (sometimes later) on Saturday. Banks are open from 7.30am or 8am to 3.30pm Monday to Friday.

PUBLIC HOLIDAYS & SPECIAL EVENTS

Public holidays include:

New Year's Day 1 January
Youth Day 11 February
Easter March/April
Labour Day 1 May
National Day 20 May
Assumption Day 15 August
Christmas Day 25 December

There are also variable Islamic holidays (see Public Holidays & Special Events in the Regional Facts for the Visitor chapter).

ACTIVITIES

The main activities are hiking and trekking. Apart from Mt Cameroon, the best places for these are the Ring Road area near Bamenda and the Mandara Mountains near Maroua. There's nothing organised; in both areas you'll need to be self-sufficient. Although camping is possible in these areas, it's generally not worth carrying a tent unless you'll be spending significant time off the beaten track. You should, however, carry a good water filter/purifier.

ACCOMMODATION

With just a few exceptions, camping is unwise due to the very real possibility of theft. Most budget accommodation is in small, very basic *auberges* (hotels) or in missions. Only a handful of missions take travellers these days, but those that do are invariably good value. In budget hotels, expect a no-frills room with a narrow double bed, cold-water shower and sometimes a private bathroom. With luck, there will also be either a fan or air-con. Most larger towns have at least one mid-range option, generally rather faded but more than adequate and reasonably comfortable, almost always with private bathroom and usually with hot water and air-con. International standard top-end accommodation is available only in Yaoundé and Douala.

Breakfast is not included in room prices listed in this chapter, unless noted. It's usually CFA1000 to CFA2000 extra. An extra bed costs about CFA2000 at budget and mid-range places. Many hotels quote prices per room (with one double bed), rather than per person. A 'double' often means a room with two double beds.

FOOD

Cameroon has delicious cuisine. Sauces are accompanied by *riz* (rice) or a thick mashed potato-like substance that is either *couscous*, *pâte* (pronounced paht) or *fufu*, and made from rice, corn, manioc, plantains or bananas, depending on where you are. Popular accompaniments include *ndole* (a slightly bitter leaf sauce, often with fish, shrimp or meat) and *njama-njama*, made from the huckleberry leaf. Manioc leaves, a common ingredient, usually translates as *feuille* on menus.

Street food, usually *brochettes* or *soya* (grilled meat, usually on a skewer, and often with peanut sauce or another garnish), is excellent and inexpensive – from CFA50 a serving – as is the grilled fish (from about CFA1000).

For sit-down meals, there are chop houses and 'off-licences' – small places, often with just a table and bench, that serve food several nights per week costing from CFA500 to CFA1000 per meal.

Major towns will have at least one restaurant where you can get Western-style cuisine.

DRINKS

There are many varieties of local and imported beer; it costs from CFA350 or CFA400 in a local place to more than CFA1500 in pricier hotels. You can usually get it cold (no extra charge) if you ask. Local and international brands of soft drinks (sodas) are also widely available. Mineral water (often referred to as 'Tangui', a major brand) is sold in all major towns from CFA400 per 1.5L. Palm wine and local brews (*'white mimbo'* in some areas) are generally fairly lethal, if not from the alcohol content, then from the unpurified water that they may have been diluted with.

ENTERTAINMENT

Almost every town has several bars and nightclubs. Nightclubs get going after 11pm; it's best to go with locals, and not bring any valuables.

The best places for experiencing Cameroon's vibrant music and dance traditions are at local festivals (such as Bafut's end-of-year festival) and holidays (eg, Youth Day).

SPECTATOR SPORTS

Cameroon's Indomitable Lions successfully defended their title in the 2002 African Nations Cup, with the entire country watching their progress and a national holiday declared to celebrate the victory. Anywhere in the country it's possible to find local soccer matches to watch or join.

SHOPPING

Cameroon has excellent crafts, in particular masks and woodcarvings (west and northwest), and leatherwork and silver (northern Cameroon). Watch for the palm-sized 'passport masks' of the Bamoun people around Foumban; they shouldn't cost more than CFA1000, despite what vendors quote you.

There are also some good batiks and colourful textiles, especially in the north. Many larger towns have a *centre artisanal* or Prescraft centre, which are the best places to shop; central markets often don't sell crafts.

The best craft shopping is in Douala and Foumban, followed by Maroua and Yaoundé. It pays to bargain hard.

CAMEROON

Getting There & Away

AIR

Douala is Cameroon's air hub, with daily flights to Europe and connections to all neighbouring countries except (temporarily) Equatorial Guinea. Intercontinental carriers include Cameroon Airlines (Camair, the national airline), Air France and Swiss. See Getting There & Away in the Douala section for regional airline listings. There are also international airports at Yaoundé (with connections several times weekly to Europe), and Garoua (currently no intercontinental flights, though).

Departure tax for international flights is CFA10,000, payable in CFA, euros or US dollars.

Europe & North America

Return fares between Cameroon and Europe go for as low as CFA350,000, but are usually CFA550,000 or more. Camair and Air France have daily flights between Paris and Douala, and several times weekly between Paris and Yaoundé. Swiss has flights twice weekly between Zürich and Douala, and weekly to/from Yaoundé. Another option is Air Gabon, with flights connecting Douala with London and Rome via Libreville. All connections to/from North America are via Europe.

Africa

Camair flights connect Douala and Yaoundé three or four times weekly with N'Djaména (Chad), Lagos (Nigeria) and Abidjan (Côte d'Ivoire), and once or twice weekly with Cotonou (Benin), Ouagadougou (Burkina Faso), Dakar (Senegal), Bamako (Mali), Conakry (Guinea), Bangui (CAR), Nairobi (Kenya) and Johannesburg (South Africa). Camair also sometimes flies between Douala and Addis Ababa (Ethiopia).

Other regional connections to/from Douala include five times weekly with Libreville on Air Gabon; weekly with Brazzaville (Congo) on Lina Congo; and once or twice weekly with Lagos on Nigeria Airways. Flights to/from Malabo (Equatorial Guinea) were suspended at the time of writing, though were likely to resume by the time you read this. Kenya Airways flies twice weekly between Douala (weekly via Yaoundé) and Nairobi, sometimes via Abidjan.

Some regional fares are: Douala-Abidjan on Camair (CFA244,000 one way), Douala-Brazzaville on Lina Congo (CFA212,000 one way) and Douala-Nairobi on Kenya Airways (CFA450,000 one way).

LAND

Border Crossings

The main border crossings are Ekok and Banki (northwest of Mora) for Nigeria; Kousséri in the far north (for Chad); Garoua-Boulaï and Kenzou (for CAR); Kye Ossi (for Gabon); and Ebebiyin or Campo (for Equatorial Guinea). There's a crossing at Ouesso for Congo (Brazzaville), and several other crossings for Chad, although these are well off the beaten track and rarely used by travellers.

Central African Republic

The standard route is via Garoua-Boulaï. There's at least one bus daily from N'Gaoundéré to Garoua-Boulaï (CFA4000, 10 hours). From the south, there's a daily bus from Yaoundé to Bertoua, and then minibuses from there to Garoua-Boulaï. Semiregular buses and trucks go from Garoua-Boulaï to Bangui (about CFA12,000, two days), with an overnight in Bouar.

An alternate, equally rough route is to go to Batouri (either with the bus from Yaoundé or with the train as far as Bélabo and then with the bus). Once in Batouri, there's usually one vehicle daily at dawn to Kenzou. At the border, you'll need to walk across and catch a vehicle on the other side to Berbérati.

Chad

Minibuses run (sometimes with an armed escort) from Maroua to Kousséri (CFA4000, 3½ hours), from where motorcycle taxis (CFA750) take you across the bridge to the Chad border town of Nguelé or the remaining 7km into N'Djaména (CFA300). The border closes at 5.30pm. Few travellers pass this way, as there have been a spate of security incidents along the road between Mora and Kousséri, although things seem to have settled down recently. Get an update before setting off. You can also cross into southern Chad to the towns of Bongor or Léré through a combination of taxis brousses (bush taxis), and in the case of Bongor, a pirogue (dugout canoe) across the Logone River.

Congo

The overland route to Congo is strictly for the adventurous – a long, rough journey through dense rainforest on rutted dirt tracks, although the road is now somewhat better than it used to be. Alliance Voyages has a daily bus in the dry season from Yokadouma to Moloundou (CFA5000, eight hours, 215km). From Moloundou, you'll need to hitch a lift east to Kika, a logging town on the Ngoko River. Pirogues carry you across the border/river, and taxis brousses then take you to Ouesso in Congo (CFA5000, five hours). From Ouesso, there are sporadic barges to Brazzaville (about two weeks – yep, two weeks!).

Gabon & Equatorial Guinea

Regular taxis brousses and minibuses go from Yaoundé to Ebolowa (CFA2500, three hours, 168km), where you'll have to change for Ambam, three hours (90km) to the south.

In Ambam the road splits, the easterly route heading for Bitam, Oyem and Libreville (Gabon) and the westerly route heading for Ebebiyin and Bata (Equatorial Guinea). For both, you'll need to cross the Ntem River by ferry (at Kye Ossi for Gabon, and about 12km southeast of Ambam for Equatorial Guinea). From the border there are taxis brousses to Ebebiyin (2km) or Bitam (30km). In both cases, get your Cameroon exit stamp in Ambam, and, for Gabon, an entry stamp in Bitam – failure to get the latter can be expensive.

You can also enter Equatorial Guinea via the coast. There are buses daily between Kribi and Campo (CFA1500, three to four hours, 90km). Once in Campo, hire a moto-taxi (CFA500) to Campo Beach on the Ntem River, where you can get your passport stamped and find a pirogue for the five-minute crossing into Equatorial Guinea (CFA500). It's best to overnight in Campo and start early the next morning for Campo Beach, as there's no accommodation on either side of the border. Once across the river, there's generally one pick-up daily to Bata, usually departing in the morning, although it's sometimes much later. Transport to/from Bata is generally better on Monday, Wednesday and Friday. You can also take the pirogue further upstream on the Ntem to Yengué, and get transport to Bata from there.

Both Equatorial Guinea and Gabon use Central African CFA, so there's no need to change currency.

Nigeria

The most popular crossing is at Ekok, 60km west of Mamfe. There's frequent transport in the dry season between Mamfe and Ekok (CFA1500). Once over the border, catch a shared taxi from Mfum (the Nigerian border village) to Ikom (24km, CFA600) and Calabar (CFA2000, 2½ hours). The road is in decent condition during the dry season, though you'll probably be hassled the entire way through for bribes. The border closes at 7pm; if you're stuck, there are several basic places to stay in Ekok.

There's another crossing in the extreme north, from Maroua to Maiduguri via Banki. Take a minibus from Maroua to Banki (CFA1500, 1½ hours) via Mora; expect multiple immigration and customs checkpoints. From Banki there are shared taxis to Maiduguri (CFA1500, 1½ hours).

SEA

Equatorial Guinea, Gabon & São Tomé

There are no regular ferry services from Cameroon to either Libreville (Gabon) or São Tomé. For Malabo, however, there are occasional passenger boats leaving from Limbe; expect to pay somewhere between CFA5000 and CFA10,000. See Getting There & Away in the Limbe section for more details.

Nigeria

Frequent boats connect Limbe and Idenao (45km northwest of Limbe) with Oron (in Nigeria, south of Calabar). Most are cargo boats ferrying smuggled goods, although there are also some fairly reliable passenger speedboats. Expect to pay from CFA20,000 to CFA35,000 on a speedboat (about four hours). The security situation in the area isn't good as you'll need to pass through the disputed Bakassi Peninsula area, and we heard that travellers weren't permitted in Oron at the time of research, so get an update before heading this way.

In any case, don't take the cargo boats (although these are much cheaper), as many will deposit you in the middle of the night in the middle of nowhere to avoid customs controls, not to mention problems with overloading and sinkings.

ORGANISED TOURS

Several tour operators listed under Organised Tours in the regional Getting There & Away chapter also handle Cameroon.

Getting Around

AIR

Camair flights connect Yaoundé and Douala daily, and both these cities from three to six times weekly with N'Gaoundéré, Garoua, Maroua and Bertoua. There are frequent delays and schedule changes, and sometimes cancellations, especially during the harmattan when visibility in N'Gaoundéré and Maroua may prohibit landing. But on the whole, service is reasonably good and much better than it used to be. Sample one-way fares include: Yaoundé to N'Gaoundéré (CFA46,100), Douala to N'Gaoundéré (CFA60,200) and Douala to Garoua (CFA80,000). Domestic departure tax is CFA500.

BUS

Agency *(agence de voyages)* buses run between Yaoundé and Douala and to most larger towns, although there's no bus service across the Adamawa Plateau between Yaoundé and N'Gaoundéré. On busy routes, buses are often large and reasonably comfortable; otherwise expect minivans or 30-seater 'Coastal' buses. The various agencies come and go, but main ones at the moment (with a sampling of routes) include Central Voyages (Douala to Yaoundé, Douala to Kribi), the accident-prone Guaranti Express (also spelled Guarantee; Limbe to Bamenda, Douala to Yaoundé, Bamenda to Yaoundé), Binam (Bafoussam to Yaoundé, Bafoussam to Foumban), Woïla Voyages (N'Gaoundéré to Garoua and Maroua) and Alliance Voyages (Yaoundé to Bertoua, and several other eastern Cameroon destinations).

Each agency has its own office in the towns it serves, and arrivals and departures are from this office, rather than from the main motor park or *gare routière*. When you're ready to travel, the best thing to do is ask staff at your hotel which agency is best for your destination and get a taxi to take you to that agency – all drivers know the agency offices. For main routes such as Douala to Yaoundé, agency buses often adhere to a schedule, and leave approximately when they say they will. Also, they generally abide by the one person-per-seat rule. It's a good idea to arrive at the agency office at least one hour prior to the anticipated departure to get a decent seat. On

Road Hazards

Road accidents are probably the biggest safety risk if you're travelling around Cameroon by public transport. Speeds are high, and drivers are often tired from long hours at the wheel. Passing on blind curves is common, as are vehicles stopped in the roadway. We had several taxi drivers explain that they weren't going fast at all as the odometer registers up to about 220km/h on most cars, and they had not yet exceeded that...

Avoid night travel, try to avoid vehicles that are loaded so high on top that their balance is off, and try to stick with reputable agencies. If all else fails and you're still terrified, you can always do as one Cameroonian we met does – get some valium at the local pharmacy, sleep through the journey, and hope for the best. For some more tips see the boxed text 'Road Safety' in the regional Getting Around chapter.

routes without many vehicles, try to book a seat the night before.

In addition to the agencies, there are nonagency vehicles – usually minivans or small Peugeots – that service the same routes, as well as off-the-beaten-track destinations that the agencies don't reach. These vehicles are known as *clandos*, and usually charge about the same price as the agencies but tend to be more overcrowded and leave when full. If you have a choice, it's better to go with an agency as vehicles tend to be in marginally better condition, you'll probably have fewer delays and hassles at police checkpoints, and – in the far north where armed banditry can be a problem – they're considered a bit safer.

On some shorter routes, there are also taxis brousses – basically the same as clandos, but a bit more 'official'. Taxis brousses and clandos use the main and invariably chaotic gare routière for departures/arrivals. In many towns, there will be several gares routières, so you'll need to find the one for the direction in which you're travelling. Whenever you get there, it's likely you'll have a wait, although transport is almost always best and quickest in the early morning.

If you're transiting through a city (eg, from Limbe to Kribi via Douala), you'll need to catch local transport to get you from the agency office or gare routière of your incoming bus to the agency office for your connecting bus. If you know your way around, shared taxis are cheapest, but generally, and especially if your luggage is unwieldy, it's better to charter a taxi. For more details, see under Local Transport later in this section.

Major routes are sealed, including Douala–Yaoundé–Bafoussam–Bamenda, Douala–Limbe, Bafoussam–Foumban, and N'Gaoundéré–Kousséri. Otherwise, much of the country's road network is unpaved, and secondary routes are quite often impassable during the rains.

TRAIN

Cameroon's rail system (Camrail) operates three main lines: Yaoundé to N'Gaoundéré, Yaoundé to Douala and Douala to Kumba. The Yaoundé-N'Gaoundéré line is in reasonable condition and is used frequently by travellers. It's also the only realistic option other than flying, as road travel between these cities takes several days.

Trains go daily in each direction, departing Yaoundé at 6.10pm, and N'Gaoundéré at 6.20pm. Arrivals are about 8.30am the next morning if all goes according to schedule, which it often doesn't, so plan on 12 to 30 hours journey time. An advantage of getting delayed is that you'll get to see the scenery en route.

For seating, there's a choice of 1st class *couchettes* (sleeping compartments) for CFA17,500/18,000 per person in a four-/two-bed cabin; 1st-class airline-style seats (CFA12,000); and crowded 2nd-class benches (CFA9000). The couchettes are the only recommendable option, in part because you'll be in an enclosed cabin. Seats in 1st and 2nd class are in open wagons, with no way to secure your bag. Couchettes should be booked 48 hours before departure, although you may have luck getting one the day before departure. Confirm this when booking, but currently it's possible to reserve a couchette without making payment until the morning of departure. This is good, as if the train is delayed you still have flexibility to change your plans. You'll need to purchase the ticket no later than about 9am on the morning of departure, as thereafter all unpurchased seats are put back up for sale.

Even in couchettes, be alert for thieves; don't leave the window open at night or store anything on the overhead racks. The train has a restaurant car where you can buy meals, soft drinks and beer.

The line between Yaoundé and Douala is seldom used as buses are faster and more regular. Trains depart daily from Douala at 7.15am and 1.30pm, and from Yaoundé at 7.40am and 1.30pm, (CFA5000/2800 1st/2nd class, four to six hours). Food is available in both directions on the second departure only. If you're travelling between Douala and N'Gaoundéré, you'll need to change trains at Yaoundé.

There's also a line between Douala and Kumba departing four times daily in each direction (2½ hours).

CAR & MOTORCYCLE

Car hire can be arranged in major towns. Several agencies are listed in the Douala and Yaoundé sections, with rates from about CFA60,000 per day. Otherwise, car hire can be arranged through hotels or tour operators, or privately, in which case rates (with driver) average from CFA25,000 per day plus petrol. It's best not to hire yellow cabs for longer journeys as most lack the necessary paperwork to carry passengers outside the town limits. Petrol averages CFA450 per litre.

LOCAL TRANSPORT

Shared taxis are the main form of local transport for getting around within a town (except in the north). Stand on the roadside in the direction you want to go and call out your destination when a shared taxi passes. If the driver is going your way, he'll toot the horn. Once you get the hang of it, it's a great system. The fare is a bargain CFA100 (CFA150 in larger cities), slightly more at night or for more-distant destinations.

While the vast majority of shared-taxi rides are without incident, there have been a few cases of robberies in Douala and Yaoundé and it pays to keep your wits about you. If you're female, avoid getting in a vehicle with only men as passengers, especially at night. Also, if someone other than the driver asks your destination, don't get in – just wait for another vehicle. If you get bad vibes after you've gotten into a taxi, it's cheap enough that you can just pay, get out and wait for another vehicle.

To charter a taxi for yourself (*taxi course* or *depo*), the base rate for town rides is CFA1000 (or from CFA2000 per hour, within the central area). If there aren't already other passengers in the taxi, make it clear to the driver whether you want a depo, or not. Note that at most motor parks, taxis waiting for incoming buses are for hire only, so if you take them, you'll pay charter prices.

Motorcycle taxis ('moto-taxis' or 'motos') are the main way of getting around in northern Cameroon. They charge CFA100 within town, more at night or for anything away from the central area. Just hail the driver and tell him your destination. In some areas (eg, around Maroua), motos are also used for longer journeys when there is no vehicle transport. This is fun for the first few kilometres, but gets uncomfortable for the long haul.

ORGANISED TOURS

The main area for organised tours is in the north, around Maroua. See that section for listings of tour operators. The travel agencies listed in the Douala and Yaoundé sections also organise trips elsewhere in the country.

Yaoundé

pop 1.1 million

Yaoundé is set in a lushly vegetated area at about 750m altitude and is unique among West African capitals for its hilly environment. It's not as lively as Douala, but most travellers prefer it here, and it's a good place to rest from the road and take care of necessities. The climate is relatively cool, but it still can get sticky and sudden downpours are common.

Orientation

Yaoundé's streets have no obvious pattern, and it can take some time to get oriented. The focal point of the lower-lying Centre Ville is Place Ahmadou Ahidjo. From here, Blvd du 20 Mai runs northwest to the landmark Hilton hotel and the administrative district (Quartier du Lac). North from here, the road winds uphill to Carrefour Nlongkak, a major intersection. About 1.5km further up is Carrefour Bastos and the upscale Bastos residential quarter where many embassies are located, as well as some good restaurants. Overlooking town to the northwest, about 5km from the centre, is

YAOUNDÉ

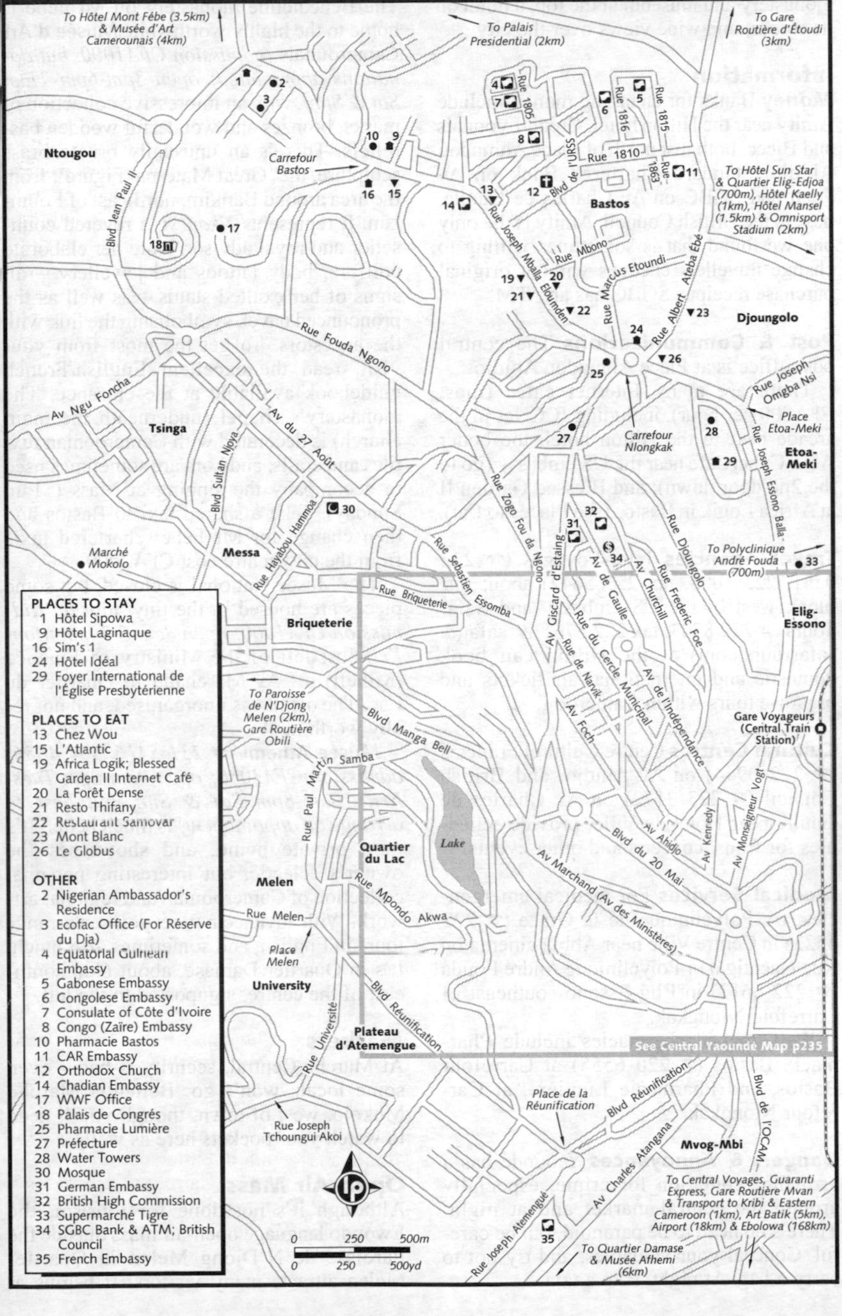
To Hôtel Mont Fébe (3.5km) & Musée d'Art Camerounais (4km)
To Palais Presidential (2km)
To Gare Routière d'Étoudi (3km)
Ntougou
Carrefour Bastos
Bastos
Rue 1805
Rue 1816
Rue 1815
Rue 1810
Rue 1863
Blvd de l'URSS
To Hôtel Sun Star & Quartier Elig-Edjoa (700m), Hôtel Kaelly (1km), Hôtel Mansel (1.5km) & Omnisport Stadium (2km)
Blvd Jean Paul II
Rue Joseph Mballa Eloumden
Rue Mbono
Rue Marcus Etoundi
Rue Albert Ateba Ebe
Djoungolo
Rue Fouda Ngono
Carrefour Nlongkak
Rue Joseph Omgba Nsi
Place Etoa-Meki
Etoa-Meki
Rue Joseph Essono Balla
Av Ngu Foncha
Tsinga
Av du 27 Août
Blvd Sultan Njoya
Rue Hayabou Hammoa
Rue Zogo Fou da Ngono
Rue Sebastien Essomba
Av Giscard d'Estaing
Av de Gaulle
Av Churchill
Rue Djoungolo
Rue Frederic Foe
To Polyclinique André Fouda (700m)
Marché Mokolo
Messa
Rue Briqueterie
Briqueterie
Elig-Essono
Rue du Cercle Municipal
Rue de Narvik
Av Foch
Av de l'Indépendance
To Paroisse de N'Djong Melen (2km), Gare Routière Obili
Blvd Manga Bell
Gare Voyageurs (Central Train Station)
Rue Paul Martin Samba
Lake
Av Kennedy
Av Monseigneur Vogt
Av Ahidjo
Blvd du 20 Mai
Av Marchand (Av des Ministères)
Quartier du Lac
Melen
Rue Mpondo
Rue Melen
Akwa
Place Melen
University
Blvd Réunification
Plateau d'Atemengue
See Central Yaoundé Map p235
Rue Université
Place de la Réunification
Blvd de l'OCAM
Rue Joseph Tchoungui Akoi
Mvog-Mbi
Av Charles Atangana
To Central Voyages, Guaranti Express, Gare Routière Mvan & Transport to Kribi & Eastern Cameroon (1km), Art Batik (5km), Airport (18km) & Ebolowa (168km)
Rue Joseph Atemengué
To Quartier Damase & Musée Afhemi (6km)
0 250 500m
0 250 500yd
PLACES TO STAY
1 Hôtel Sipowa
9 Hôtel Laginaque
16 Sim's 1
24 Hôtel Idéal
29 Foyer International de l'Église Presbytérienne
PLACES TO EAT
13 Chez Wou
15 L'Atlantic
19 Africa Logik; Blessed Garden II Internet Café
20 La Forêt Dense
21 Resto Thifany
22 Restaurant Samovar
23 Mont Blanc
26 Le Globus
OTHER
2 Nigerian Ambassador's Residence
3 Ecofac Office (For Réserve du Dja)
4 Equatorial Guinean Embassy
5 Gabonese Embassy
6 Congolese Embassy
7 Consulate of Côte d'Ivoire
8 Congo (Zaïre) Embassy
10 Pharmacie Bastos
11 CAR Embassy
12 Orthodox Church
14 Chadian Embassy
17 WWF Office
18 Palais de Congrés
25 Pharmacie Lumière
27 Préfecture
28 Water Towers
30 Mosque
31 German Embassy
32 British High Commission
33 Supermarché Tigre
34 SGBC Bank & ATM; British Council
35 French Embassy

cool and green Mt Fébé, with a Benedictine monastery and museum at the top, a hotel on its slopes, and wide views over the city.

Information

Money Banks for changing money include Amity near the Hilton hotel, Crédit Lyonnais and Bicec, both just north of Place Ahmadou Ahidjo, Standard Chartered Bank on Av Foch and SGBC on Av Charles de Gaulle, next to the British Council. Amity is the only one we found that is sometimes willing to change travellers cheques without original purchase receipts. SGBC has an ATM.

Post & Communications The central post office is at Place Ahmadou Ahidjo.

There are many Internet cafés (most CFA800 per hour), including ICCNet in the arcade next to the Hilton hotel; the better ADT CyberCafé near the US embassy (go to the 2nd door down); and Blessed Garden II at Africa Logik in Bastos (see Places to Eat).

Travel Agencies Inter-Voyages (☎ 222 0361, 223 1005, fax 223 5642) about one block west of the US embassy and Safar Tours (☎ 222 8703, fax 222 8761, e safar@safartours.com) at the Hilton can book domestic and international air tickets and organise tours within Cameroon.

Cultural Centres Centre Culturel Français (☎ 222 0944) on Av Ahidjo, and British Council (☎ 223 3172) on Av Charles de Gaulle near Hôtel de Ville, provide schedules for films, concerts and other events.

Medical Services For medical emergencies, try Polyclinique de la Grace (☎ 222 4523) in Centre Ville near Abbia cinema on Rue Nachtigal or Polyclinique André Fouda (☎ 222 6612) in Elig-Essono southeast of Carrefour Nlongkak.

Well-stocked pharmacies include Pharmacie Bastos (☎ 220 6555) at Carrefour Bastos, and Pharmacie Lumière, at Carrefour Nlongkak.

Dangers & Annoyances Yaoundé has a growing reputation for crime, especially around the central market and at night. There's no need to be paranoid, but be careful. Conceal your valuables, and try not to carry a bag. At night, take a taxi.

Museums

The Benedictine monastery on Mt Fébé is home to the highly worthwhile **Musée d'Art Camerounais** *(admission CFA1000, but donations appreciated; open 3pm-6pm Thur, Sat & Sun)*, with an impressive collection of masks, bronzes and wonderful wooden bas-reliefs. There's an unusually ornate brass sculpture, the 'Great Maternal Figure', from the area around Bankim, northeast of Foumban. It represents *Nkam'si*, a revered counsellor and royal advisor. Note her elaborate coiffure, body tattoos and jewellery – all signs of her exalted status – as well as the pronounced navel, symbolising the link with the ancestors. To get the most from your visit, read the excellent English/French guidebook available at the entrance. The monastery's **chapel** (underneath the main church) is decorated with Cameroonian textiles and crafts, and kora are sometimes used to accompany the singing at Mass (11am Sunday). Take a shared taxi to Bastos and then change for Mt Fébé; chartered taxis from the city centre cost CFA2000.

The Musée National is closed, but some pieces are housed in the tiny **'musée'** *(admission CFA1000; open 8am-3.30pm Mon-Fri)* just left of the Ministry of Finance (Minefi) off Av Marchand in Quartier du Lac. The display is unorganised, and not really worth it.

Musée Afhemi *(☎ 231 5416, 994 4656; admission CFA3000; open 9am-8pm Tues-Fri, 10am-8pm Sat & Sun, but best to arrange an appointment)* is much better. It's in a private home, and showcases the owner's eclectic, but interesting personal collection of Cameroonian and regional artwork. With advance notice, you can arrange tours in English, and sometimes also lunch. It's in Quartier Damase, about 6km southeast of the centre, signposted to the left.

Markets

At Marché Central, security is bad – even some locals won't go. Better is Marché Mokolo, west of town, though you'll need to watch your pockets here as well.

Open-Air Mass

Although it's not done for tourism, the Ewondo language open-air mass outside the Paroisse de N'Djong Melen in Quartier Melen attracts many visitors. It begins at

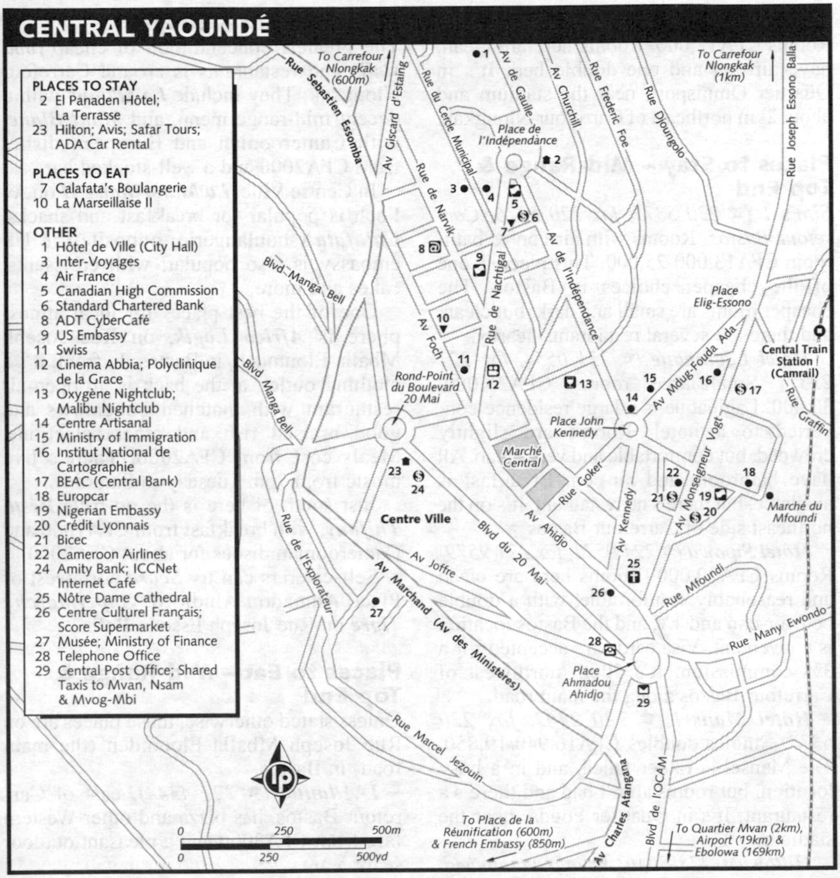
PLACES TO STAY
2 El Panaden Hôtel; La Terrasse
23 Hilton; Avis; Safar Tours; ADA Car Rental
PLACES TO EAT
7 Calafata's Boulangerie
10 La Marseillaise II
OTHER
1 Hôtel de Ville (City Hall)
3 Inter-Voyages
4 Air France
5 Canadian High Commission
6 Standard Chartered Bank
8 ADT CyberCafé
9 US Embassy
11 Swiss
12 Cinema Abbia; Polyclinique de la Grace
13 Oxygène Nightclub; Malibu Nightclub
14 Centre Artisanal
15 Ministry of Immigration
16 Institut National de Cartographie
17 BEAC (Central Bank)
18 Europcar
19 Nigerian Embassy
20 Crédit Lyonnais
21 Bicec
22 Cameroon Airlines
24 Amity Bank; ICCNet Internet Café
25 Nôtre Dame Cathedral
26 Centre Culturel Français; Score Supermarket
27 Musée; Ministry of Finance
28 Telephone Office
29 Central Post Office; Shared Taxis to Mvan, Nsam & Mvog-Mbi
To Carrefour Nlongkak (600m)
To Carrefour Nlongkak (1km)
Rue Sebastien Essomba
Av Giscard d'Estaing
Rue du Cercle Municipal
Av de Gaulle
Av Churchill
Rue Frederic Foe
Rue Djoungolo
Rue Joseph Essono Balla
Place de l'Indépendance
Rue de Narvik
Blvd Manga Bell
Rue de Nachtigal
Av de l'Indépendance
Av Foch
Place Elig-Essono
Central Train Station (Camrail)
Rond-Point du Boulevard 20 Mai
Av Mdug-Fouda Ada
Rue Graffin
Place John Kennedy
Marché Central
Av Monseigneur Vogt
Rue Goker
Av Kennedy
Marché du Mfoundi
Centre Ville
Av Ahidjo
Blvd du 20 Mai
Av Joffre
Rue de l'Explorateur
Av Marchand (Av des Ministeres)
Rue Mfoundi
Rue Many Ewondo
Place Ahmadou Ahidjo
Rue Marcel Jezouin
Av Charles Atangana
Blvd de l'OCAM
To Place de la Réunification (600m) & French Embassy (850m)
To Quartier Mvan (2km), Airport (19km) & Ebolowa (169km)
0 250 500m
0 250 500yd
CENTRAL YAOUNDÉ

9.30am on Sunday and includes African music, drums, dancing and a women's chorus. It's on the western side of town, and reached by shared taxi.

Places to Stay – Budget

Foyer International de l'Église Presbytérienne *(Presbyterian mission)* Dorm beds CFA2000, singles/twins with shared bathroom CFA4000/5000. This no-frills place is in quiet grounds behind the concrete water towers above Carrefour Nlongkak. Follow the dirt track around back for about 150m. It's spartan but friendly, and you can use the cooking facilities, but don't abuse their goodwill – pay for gas etc. It's quite dark around here at night – always take a taxi.

Hôtel Idéal *(☎/fax 220 9852, Carrefour Nlongkak)* Singles/doubles CFA6000/7000. Rooms here are clean and good value, with fan, bath and sometimes a balcony. The neighbourhood is noisy and a bit rough, but convenient and there are many cheap restaurants nearby.

Hôtel Sun Star *(☎ 951 3327)* Rooms CFA7500. Sun Star isn't as convenient, about 1.5km east of Carrefour Nlongkak in Elig-Edjoa, but rooms are clean and OK for the price. There's no food.

El Panaden Hôtel *(☎ 222 2765, Place de l'Indépendance)* Rooms with 1/2 double beds CFA10,000/13,000. El Panaden has attractive, spotless rooms with balcony, hot water, air-con and TV, and there's a good restaurant next door.

Hôtel Kaelly *(☎ 222 0594, 221 9096)* Rooms CFA12,000. Rooms here are clean, have air-con and one double bed. It's in Quartier Omnisport, near the stadium and about 2km northeast of Carrefour Nlongkak.

Places to Stay – Mid-Range & Top End

Sim's 1 *(☎ 220 5375, fax 220 5376, Carrefour Bastos)* Rooms with air-con & bathroom CFA13,000-25,000. This place is one of the cheaper choices in Bastos. The cheaper rooms are small and dark, but clean, and there are several restaurants nearby.

Hôtel Laginaque *(☎ 221 0554, fax 221 2332)* Small/large rooms CFA25,000/30,000. Laginaque is a large residence converted to a hotel. Rooms are slightly crowded, but comfortable and very clean. All have bathroom and air-con. Breakfast is available, but there's no restaurant. It's on the northeast side of Carrefour Bastos.

Hôtel Sipowa *(☎ 221 9571, fax 221 9579)* Rooms CFA20,000. Rooms here are clean and reasonably comfortable, with a double bed, air-con and TV, and the Bastos location is convenient. Visa cards are accepted for a 3% commission. It's 500m northwest of Carrefour Bastos along the main road.

Hôtel Mansel *(☎ 220 2462, fax 220 6373)* Singles/doubles CFA16,940/19,850. The Mansel is rather faded, and in a busy location, but rooms aren't bad and there's a restaurant. It's in Quartier Fouda, near the stadium.

Hilton *(☎ 223 3646, ⓔ info_yaounde@hilton.com, Blvd du 20 Mai, Centre Ville)* Singles/doubles from CFA122,000/132,000 plus 18.7% VAT; resident discounts available. This is Yaoundé's most upscale option, with a pool, gym and all the amenities.

Hôtel Mont Fébé *(☎ 221 4099, 221 1903, fax 221 6070)* Rooms with mountain/golf course view CFA48,000/56,000; discounts on weekends and for residents. Hôtel Mont Fébé is not quite up to the standards of the Hilton, but it's decent value and quite comfortable. It also has a wonderful location on the upper slopes of Mt Fébé – ideal for a respite from urban bustle. There's a pool (CFA2000 for nonguests) and a restaurant. The more expensive rooms have a small balcony and views over a nearby golf course and central Yaoundé in the distance.

Places to Eat – Budget

The greatest concentration of cheap ***food stalls*** and restaurants is around Carrefour Nlongkak. They include ***Le Globus*** with a decent mid-range menu, and ***Mont Blanc***, with Cameroonian and European dishes from CFA2000 and a well-stocked bar.

In Centre Ville, ***La Marseillaise II*** on Av Foch is popular for breakfast and snacks. ***Calafata's*** boulangerie, opposite the US embassy is also popular, with croissants, cakes and more.

One of the best places for local atmosphere is ***Africa Logik***, on Rue Joseph Mballa Eloumden, in Bastos. In front, it's a clothing outlet; at the back is an open-air restaurant with thatched bungalows and good braised fish and other selections. Meals cost from CFA2000. There's live music from 7pm Tuesday to Saturday.

Just south of here is the no-frills ***Resto Thifany***, with breakfast from CFA1000 and Cameroonian dishes for about CFA2000.

Self-caterers can try ***Score*** northwest of Place Ahmadou Ahidjo or ***Supermarché Tigre*** on Rue Joseph Essono Balla.

Places to Eat – Mid-Range & Top End

Unless stated otherwise, these places are on Rue Joseph Mballa Eloumden (the main road) in Bastos.

L'Atlantic *(☎ 221 4344)*, east of Carrefour Bastos, has pizza and other Western fare from CFA3000 and a pleasant outdoor seating area.

For Chinese food, try ***Chez Wou*** *(☎ 220 4679)*, with a nice porch, meals from CFA5000 and an all-you-can-eat Sunday buffet for CFA9800.

The popular ***La Terrasse*** *(☎ 222 1262, Place de l'Indépendance)* next to Le Panaden hotel has a good menu with Western and some Cameroonian dishes, and outdoor seating. It's open from 7am to 11pm daily.

For *poulet DG* (chicken with plantains and sauce), ndole and other Cameroonian dishes in an upscale environment, try ***La Forêt Dense*** *(☎ 220 5308)*. Most meals cost from CFA5500 to CF8000, though there are a few less-expensive selections.

Restaurant Samovar *(☎ 222 5528)* next door to La Forêt Dense serves good Italian dishes for about CFA4500.

Entertainment
Yaoundé's nightlife isn't as lively as that in Douala, but there are a few good places. For nightclubs, try ***Oxygène***, northwest of Place John Kennedy in Centre Ville, or the more expensive ***Malibu***, nearby.

Shopping
Centre Artisanal, off Place John Kennedy, has Cameroonian and regional crafts. The best place for batiks is Art Batik, about 5km south of the centre on the western side of the airport road. It's in an unmarked, light-blue multistorey building shortly after a petrol station. If you pass Base Arienne de Yaoundé on the opposite side of the road, you've gone too far.

Getting There & Away
Air
Camair has daily connections to Douala and Garoua, and flights several times weekly to N'Gaoundéré, Maroua and Bertoua. For information on international connections see the main Getting There & Away section, earlier in this chapter. Airlines with offices in Yaoundé include:

Air France (☎ 223 4379) Rue du Cercle Municipal, near Place de l'Indepéndance
Cameroon Airlines (☎ 223 0304, 223 4001) main office on Av Monseigneur Vogt; branch office at the Hilton hotel
Kenya Airways (☎ 223 3602) at the airport
Swiss (☎ 222 9737, fax 222 6329) Av Foch

Bus
To Douala (CFA3500), Central Voyages (☎ 230 3994) is the best bet, with departures throughout the day from 6.30am. It also has nonstop express service on its Prestige line, departing daily in each direction at 7am, noon and 4pm (CFA8000, three hours). Its office is south of the centre in Mvog-Mbi; unlike most companies, you can book 1st-class tickets a day in advance and they leave on time.

Guaranti Express also goes to Douala, as well as to Limbe. Its office is in Quartier Nsam, about 3km south of the centre.

Otherwise, all agency and nonagency transport for Kribi, Bertoua, Batouri and other destinations in southern, central and eastern Cameroon departs from Quartier Mvan, about 3km south of Place Ahmadou Ahidjo. For Kribi, look for La Kribienne. For Bertoua and points east, the main line is Alliance Voyages, departing at 9am daily to Batouri (CFA6000, at least eight hours).

Transport to Bafoussam (CFA3000, five hours) and points north departs from gare routière d'Etoudi, 5km north of Centre Ville, which is where most agencies have their offices; the best line is Binam. You can also find vehicles to Bamenda here – though it's often quicker to get something to Bafoussam and another vehicle from there to Bamenda. Transport to Bamenda also departs from gare routière d'Obili on the western edge of town.

Train
For details of train travel to N'Gaoundéré or Douala, see the main Getting Around section earlier in this chapter.

Getting Around
To/From the Airport Yaoundé's Nsimalen airport is about 18km south of town off the Ebolowa road (CFA3500 in a private taxi).

Car & Motorcycle Car rental agencies in Yaoundé include:

ADA (☎ 222 8703) Safar Tours, at the Hilton hotel
Avis (☎ 223 3646) Hilton hotel
Europcar (☎ 994 4983) just off Av Monseigneur Vogt, diagonally opposite the Nigerian embassy

Taxi Shared/charter taxis in town cost from CFA150/1000, more at night. Most drivers don't know street names; it's better to say the name of the quartier or nearby landmark. The best place to catch shared taxis to Nsam, Mvan and Mvog-Mbi (all CFA200) is the central post office.

Douala & South-West Province

The South-West Province is the most fertile part of Cameroon, with bustling markets and a colourful selection of produce. For travellers, attractions include Mt Cameroon, the beaches at Limbe, Korup National Park and – if you have time to get off the beaten track – Manengouba Crater Lakes near Bangem. Although Douala is part of neighbouring Littoral Province, the city is covered here as it's the most convenient starting point for visiting the southwest.

DOUALA

pop 1.4 million

Douala is Cameroon's largest city, the economic capital and industrial centre. With its humid climate, it has little to offer travellers. If you're in Cameroon only briefly, it's worth bypassing. However, if you stay around for longer, chances are Douala will begin to grow on you, with its good restaurants, lively nightlife, decaying tropical ambience and excellent fruits. It's also Cameroon's main air hub, and the easiest place in the country to change money and take care of business.

The city has a reputation for muggings and you need to be streetwise, especially at night, but it's not as bad as some people make out.

Orientation

The heart of town is Akwa, with many hotels, some Internet cafés and restaurants, most on or near Blvd de la Liberté. South of here along and near Rue Joss in Bonanjo is the administrative quarter with most banks, airline offices, government buildings, the central post office and more restaurants.

Information

Money For changing money, try Bicec, Crédit Lyonnais or CBC, all in Bonanjo, or Standard Chartered Bank in Akwa. SGBC has an ATM next to its building on the northwestern side of Rue Joss.

Post & Communications The central post office is at the western end of Rue Joss.

Cyberbao and ICCNet, opposite each other on Blvd de la Liberté in Akwa, have Internet connections for CFA800 per hour.

Travel Agencies BHC Business Centre (☎ 343 2705, ⓔ bhc@iccnet2000.com) at Hôtel Méridien helps with car rental, flight bookings and travel within Cameroon.

Bookshops & Cultural Centres Papyrus on Blvd de la Liberté in Akwa has a good selection of French books.

Centre Culturel Français (☎ 342 6996), also on Blvd de la Liberté, has frequent concerts and films.

Medical Services For medical emergencies, try Polyclinique Bonanjo (☎ 342 7936, 342 7983) on Av de Gaulle near Hôtel Ibis. For pharmacies, try Pharmacie du Centre on Blvd de la Liberté or Pharmacie de Douala on Blvd Ahidjo.

Things to See & Do

The clamorous **Marché de Lagos**, south of Ahmadou Ahidjo, is Cameroon's largest, though it's not for the faint-hearted and you'll need to watch your pockets.

More relaxing is spending an afternoon at one of the city's numerous **pools**. Best for laps is the 25m pool at Hôtel Akwa Palace (CFA4000 for nonguests) in Akwa. The pools at Hôtel Méridien and Hôtel Sawa in Bonanjo are similarly pricey, but extremely refreshing.

Places to Stay – Budget

Most budget places are in Akwa.

Centre d'Accueil Missionaire *(☎ 342 2797, ⓔ progemis.douala@camnet.cm, Rue Franceville)* Doubles/triples/quads CFA12,000/15,000/20,000, singles without/with shower CFA7000/8000. This place is good value, with clean, quiet air-con rooms, a swimming pool and secure parking. It's at the Procure Générale des Églises Catholique, just off Blvd de la Liberté; tell your taxi driver you're going to the 'Procure'. Reception is open 8.30am to 11.30am and 2.30pm to 5pm Monday to Saturday, and on Sunday morning; advance bookings are recommended.

Église Évangélique de Cameroun *(☎ 342 3611, ⓔ eec@wagne.net, Rue Alfred Saker)* Singles/doubles/triples CFA8000/10,000/15,000. This place is worth checking if Centre d'Accueil is full. Rooms are a bit run-down, but quiet and OK for the price, and there's a kitchen. It's southwest of Centre d'Accueil; look for the church steeple.

Foyer du Marin *(☎ 342 2794, ⓔ douala@seamannsmission.org, Rue Gallieni)* Singles/twins CFA10,000/13,500. Foyer du Marin, just off Rue Joffre, is the most popular budget/mid-range place, and good value. Rooms are comfortable, clean and secure, with air-con, bathroom and hot water. There's a small pool, beer garden and popular restaurant, and it's a good place to meet other travellers.

Hôtel Hila *(☎ 342 1586, Blvd de l'Unité)* Singles/doubles CFA9000/13,000. Hôtel

Hila is on a busy, dusty street northeast of Place Ahmadou Ahidjo, and worth checking only if everywhere else is full. The better rooms are on the upper floor, with air-con, bathroom and views over Douala.

Hôtel Sportif *(☎ 343 7640)* Room with fan & shared bathroom CFA8500, larger room with bathroom & air-con CFA18,000. This place south of Bonanjo in Bonapriso has very average rooms and no food, but will do in a pinch.

Places to Stay – Mid-Range & Top End

Unless stated otherwise, these places are in Bonanjo.

Hôtel La Falaise *(☎ 342 4646, fax 342 6891, Rue Kitchener)* Singles/doubles CFA24,000/28,000. Rooms here – most of which have air-con and bathroom – are nothing special, but staff are friendly and there's a restaurant. Don't confuse it with the Hôtel-Residence La Falaise on Blvd de la Liberté.

Hôtel Ibis *(☎ 342 5800, 994 8110, e hotel.ibis@camnet.cm, Rue Pierre Loti)* Doubles & twins CFA40,500, suites CFA65,000. Rooms here are decent value and the location is good – on a small side street off Av de Gaulle, convenient to banks and restaurants. There's a small pool, free transport from the airport and parking. Breakfast costs CFA4000.

Hôtel Akwa Palace *(☎ 342 2601, fax 342 7416, Blvd de la Liberté, Akwa)* Rooms in old/new wings from CFA35,000/65,000. The Akwa Palace used to be Douala's best. Now it's past its prime, but service is good and rooms in the newer wing are fine. Many people prefer it to the pricier Méridien. There's also a pool and a very good buffet breakfast.

Hôtel Sawa *(☎ 342 0525, fax 342 3871, Rue de Verdun)* Rooms CFA60,000. The Sawa is somewhat faded, but rooms are being renovated, there's a pool and garden, and the atmosphere is more relaxed than at the nearby Méridien.

Hôtel Méridien *(☎ 343 5000, fax 342 3507, W www.lemeridien-hotels.com, Av des Cocotiers)* Rooms from CFA80,000. This is Douala's most luxurious option, though it's a bit overpriced for what you get. There's a pool, pizza oven, garden area and views over the port.

Places to Eat

Apart from the cheap ***food stalls*** all over Akwa, Blvd de la Liberté has a wide range of cuisines and prices from which to choose. ***Garmary Restaurant*** is one of the better budget places, with Cameroonian and European dishes, most under CFA2000. The restaurant at ***Foyer du Marin*** (see Places to Stay) costs a bit more, but is still reasonably priced, with brochettes, grilled sausages and salads setting you back around CFA2500.

Back on Blvd de la Liberté, ***Le Glacier Modern*** has great ice cream, as well as reasonably priced pastries and light meals. It's open from 7.30am to 11pm daily. Just down the road opposite Hôtel Akwa Palace are the popular ***Méditerranée Restaurant***, with a relaxed atmosphere and meals from about CFA3000, and ***Dragon d'Or*** *(☎ 342 7488)*, open Monday to Saturday, which has good Vietnamese and Chinese dishes from CFA4000.

Another place for Chinese food is ***Restaurant Chinois*** *(☎ 342 3310)* next to the old US consulate building in Bonanjo. Meals start at about CFA4500 and there's a popular, but fairly pricey, Sunday buffet (CFA9000).

Boulangerie Zepol on Blvd de la Liberté has great baked items, yogurt, tempting pizza slices and a small grocery store. It's open around the clock.

For self-caterers, ***Mahima Supermarché*** on Blvd Ahidjo is well-stocked.

Entertainment

Douala is known for its nightlife, and the best way to sample it is with locals. Cover charges at most nightclubs range from CFA3000 to CFA8000, usually with ladies' night discounts, and things get going after 11pm. Places to check out include ***Byblos*** on Rue Joffre in Akwa, the more Western ***Ange Noir*** behind Hôtel Parfait Garden, and ***Le Sun Set*** on Av Charles de Gaulle in Bonanjo.

Shopping

The excellent **Centre Artisanal de Douala** at Marché des Fleurs, about 3km south of the centre along Av Charles de Gaulle, is surprisingly calm and one of the best places in Cameroon for crafts. Hard bargaining is always required here.

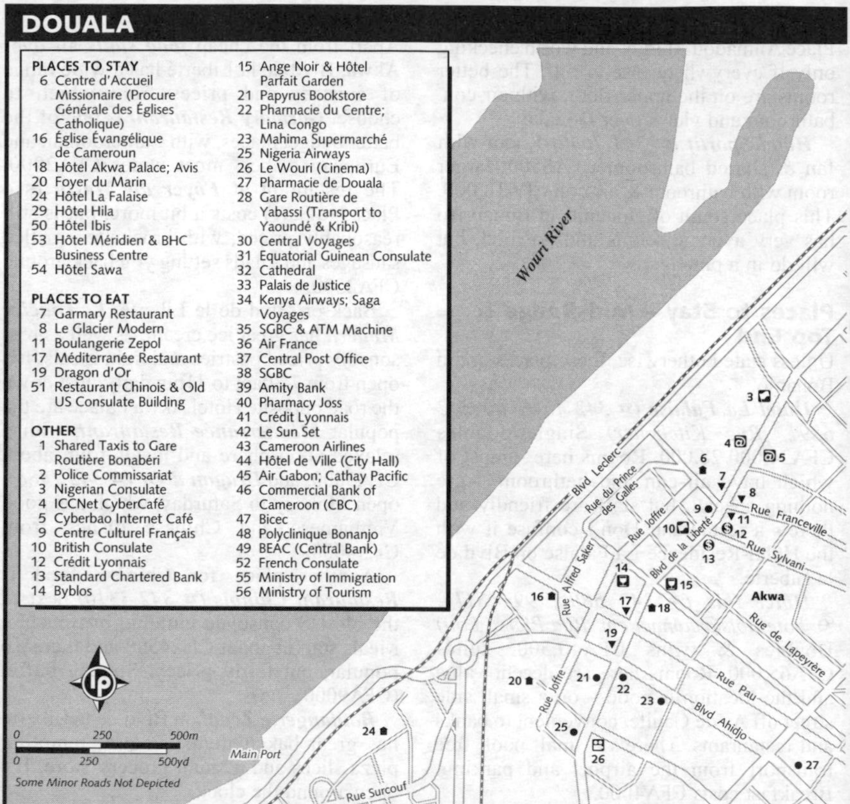
DOUALA
PLACES TO STAY
6 Centre d'Accueil Missionaire (Procure Générale des Églises Catholique)
16 Église Évangélique de Cameroun
18 Hôtel Akwa Palace; Avis
20 Foyer du Marin
24 Hôtel La Falaise
29 Hôtel Hila
50 Hôtel Ibis
53 Hôtel Méridien & BHC Business Centre
54 Hôtel Sawa
PLACES TO EAT
7 Garmary Restaurant
8 Le Glacier Modern
11 Boulangerie Zepol
17 Méditerranée Restaurant
19 Dragon d'Or
51 Restaurant Chinois & Old US Consulate Building
OTHER
1 Shared Taxis to Gare Routière Bonabéri
2 Police Commissariat
3 Nigerian Consulate
4 ICCNet CyberCafé
5 Cyberbao Internet Café
9 Centre Culturel Français
10 British Consulate
12 Crédit Lyonnais
13 Standard Chartered Bank
14 Byblos
15 Ange Noir & Hôtel Parfait Garden
21 Papyrus Bookstore
22 Pharmacie du Centre; Lina Congo
23 Mahima Supermarché
25 Nigeria Airways
26 Le Wouri (Cinema)
27 Pharmacie de Douala
28 Gare Routière de Yabassi (Transport to Yaoundé & Kribi)
30 Central Voyages
31 Equatorial Guinean Consulate
32 Cathedral
33 Palais de Justice
34 Kenya Airways; Saga Voyages
35 SGBC & ATM Machine
36 Air France
37 Central Post Office
38 SGBC
39 Amity Bank
40 Pharmacy Joss
41 Crédit Lyonnais
42 Le Sun Set
43 Cameroon Airlines
44 Hôtel de Ville (City Hall)
45 Air Gabon; Cathay Pacific
46 Commercial Bank of Cameroon (CBC)
47 Bicec
48 Polyclinique Bonanjo
49 BEAC (Central Bank)
52 French Consulate
55 Ministry of Immigration
56 Ministry of Tourism
Wouri River
0 250 500m
0 250 500yd
Some Minor Roads Not Depicted
Main Port
Blvd Leclerc
Rue du Prince des Galles
Rue Joffre
Blvd de la Liberté
Rue Franceville
Rue Sylvani
Rue Alfred Saker
Akwa
Rue de Lapeyrère
Rue Pau
Blvd Ahidjo
Rue Joffre
Rue Surcouf
Rue Kitchener
Place du Gouvernement
Rue Joss
Rue Gallieni
Bonanjo
Rue Lugard
Rue French
Rue Pierre Loti
Rue Koumassi
Rue Prince
Rue Bertaut
Av des Cocotiers
Bali
Av Douala Manga Bell
Rue de Verdun
Rue de Trieste
Av de Gaulle
Bell
Rue de New Bell
Rue Njonjo
To Marché des Fleurs, Centre Artisanal de Douala & Swiss (1km), Hôtel Sportif (1.5km) & Airport (4km)
To Europcar

CAMEROON

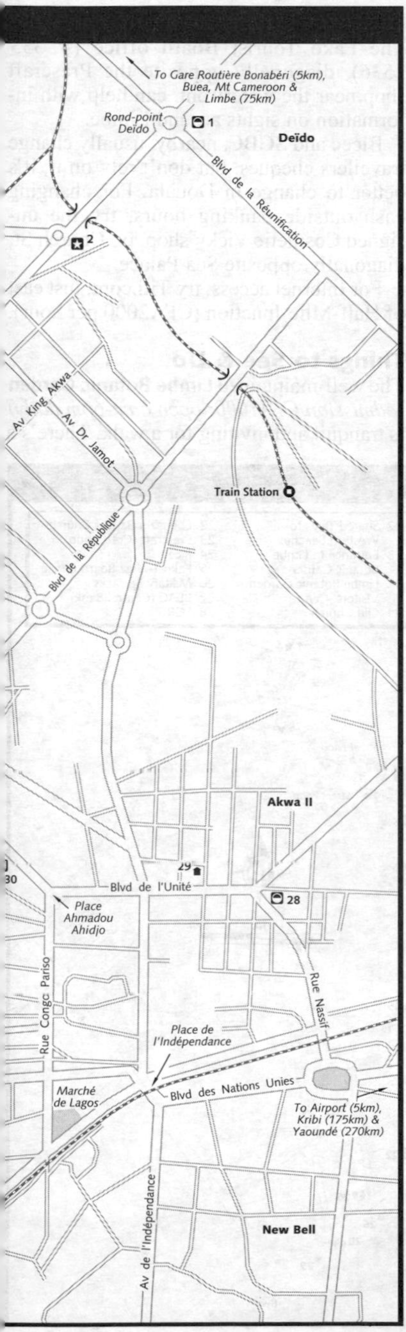
To Gare Routière Bonabéri (5km), Buea, Mt Cameroon & Limbe (75km)
Rond-point Deïdo
1
Deïdo
Blvd de la Réunification
2
Av King Akwa
Av Dr Jamot
Train Station
Blvd de la République
Akwa II
29
30
Blvd de l'Unité
28
Place Ahmadou Ahidjo
Rue Congo Pariso
Rue Nassif
Place de l'Indépendance
Marché de Lagos
Blvd des Nations Unies
To Airport (5km), Kribi (175km) & Yaoundé (270km)
Av de l'Indépendance
New Bell

Getting There & Away

Air Airlines in Doaula include:

Air France (☎ 342 1555) Rue Joss, Bonanjo
Air Gabon (☎ 342 4943) Rue French, one block east of Av de Gaulle, Bonanjo
Cameroon Airlines (☎ 342 2525, 342 3222) Rue Joss, Bonanjo; also with an office at the airport (☎ 342 2525), open 6.30am to 8pm daily
Cathay Pacific (☎ 343 0122) Rue French, next to Air Gabon
Kenya Airways (☎ 342 9691) Rue Joss at Saga Voyages, Bonanjo
Lina Congo Blvd de la Liberté, Akwa, next to Pharmacie du Centre
Nigeria Airways (☎ 342 7321) Blvd de la Liberté, Akwa
Swiss (☎ 342 2929) Marché des Fleurs, 3km south of the centre

Bus To Yaoundé, Central Voyages on Blvd Ahmadou Ahidjo is best, with express and regular services throughout the day from 6.30am. See Getting There & Away in the Yaoundé section for details. Buses also go every hour or two to Kribi (CFA2000, 2½ hours).

Agency and nonagency transport to/from Limbe, Bafoussam, Bamenda and points north uses the Bonabéri gare routière, 6km north of the city centre across the Wouri River bridge. To Limbe, look for Guaranti Express or Patience; for Bafoussam, try Binam.

If you arrive in Bonabéri, there will be charter taxis waiting to take you to town (CFA1000). Otherwise, walk out to the main road and get a shared taxi to Rond-point Deïdo (CFA150), where you'll need to get another shared taxi to wherever you're going. Charter taxis from Bonabéri to Central Voyages generally charge CFA2000.

Train For details of train services to/from Yaoundé and Kumba, see the main Getting There & Away section earlier in this chapter.

Getting Around

To/From the Airport Chartered taxis from Akwa or Bonanjo to the airport cost CFA2500 (CFA3000 at night).

Car & Motorcycle Avis (☎ 342 7056) is at Hôtel Akwa Palace, and Europcar (☎ 343 2126, 999 2189) is on Rue Njonjo, south of the centre. BHC Business Centre

(☎ 343 2705, ⓔ bhc@iccnet2000.com) at Hôtel Méridien also arranges vehicle rental.

Taxi Shared taxis anywhere in town cost CFA150; charters cost from CFA1000.

LIMBE

pop 40,000

Anglophone Limbe was founded in 1857 by British missionary Alfred Saker. It's a lively and manageable place with Mt Cameroon's lush slopes as a backdrop. It's also a popular weekend getaway from Douala – especially the attractive beaches northwest of town (see Around Limbe, following). The centre of activity is 'Half-Mile Junction' (the corner of Church St and Douala Rd) – look for Limbe's only traffic light.

Information

The Fako Tourist Board office (☎ 333 2536), diagonally opposite the Prescraft shop near the waterfront, can help with information on sights around Limbe.

Bicec and SGBC, nearby, usually change travellers cheques, but don't rely on it; it's better to change in Douala. For changing cash outside banking hours, try the unsigned Cosmetic Vicky shop, on Church St, diagonally opposite Sea Palace.

For Internet access, try Titi.com, just east of Half-Mile Junction (CFA2000 per hour).

Things to See & Do

The well-maintained **Limbe Botanic Garden** *(admission CFA1000; open 6am-6pm daily)* is tranquil and inviting for a walk. There's a

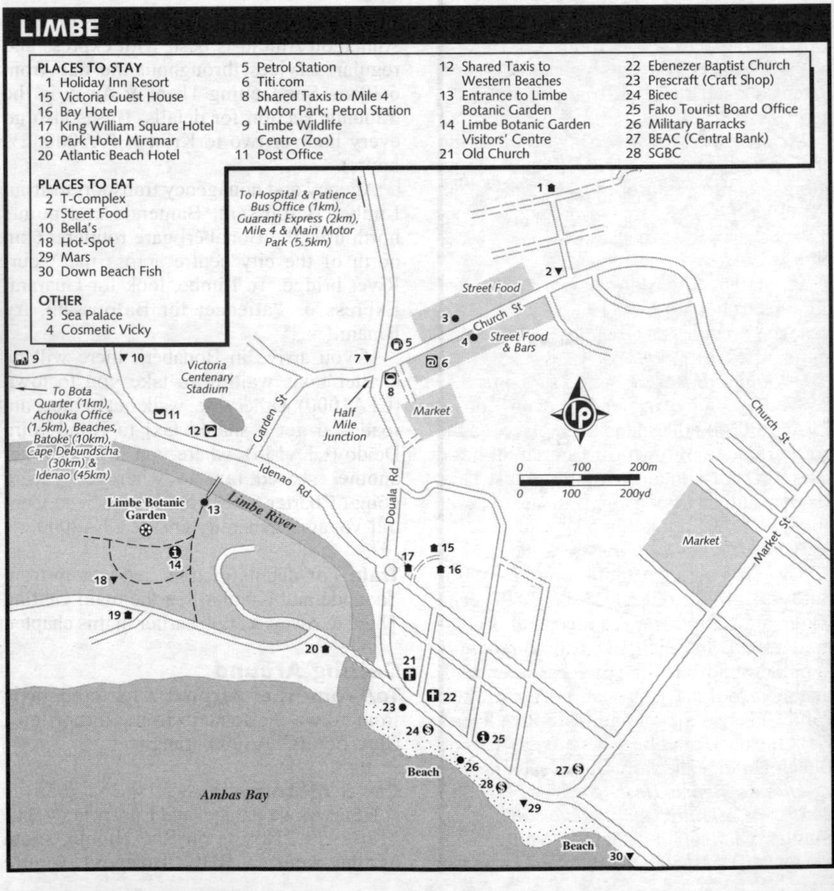
LIMBE
PLACES TO STAY
1 Holiday Inn Resort
15 Victoria Guest House
16 Bay Hotel
17 King William Square Hotel
19 Park Hotel Miramar
20 Atlantic Beach Hotel
PLACES TO EAT
2 T-Complex
7 Street Food
10 Bella's
18 Hot-Spot
29 Mars
30 Down Beach Fish
OTHER
3 Sea Palace
4 Cosmetic Vicky
5 Petrol Station
6 Titi.com
8 Shared Taxis to Mile 4 Motor Park; Petrol Station
9 Limbe Wildlife Centre (Zoo)
11 Post Office
12 Shared Taxis to Western Beaches
13 Entrance to Limbe Botanic Garden
14 Limbe Botanic Garden Visitors' Centre
21 Old Church
22 Ebenezer Baptist Church
23 Prescraft (Craft Shop)
24 Bicec
25 Fako Tourist Board Office
26 Military Barracks
27 BEAC (Central Bank)
28 SGBC
To Hospital & Patience Bus Office (1km), Guaranti Express (2km), Mile 4 & Main Motor Park (5.5km)
Street Food
Church St
Street Food & Bars
Victoria Centenary Stadium
To Bota Quarter (1km), Achouka Office (1.5km), Beaches, Batoke (10km), Cape Debundscha (30km) & Idenao (45km)
Garden St
Half Mile Junction
Market
Idenao Rd
Douala Rd
Limbe River
Limbe Botanic Garden
Market St
0 100 200m
0 100 200yd
Beach
Ambas Bay

small Visitors' Centre, and a library with materials on local flora and fauna. The entrance is opposite the stadium on Idenao Rd.

About 600m west of here is the **Limbe Wildlife Centre (Zoo)** *(admission CFA1000; open 9am-5pm daily)*, originally established to protect orphaned chimpanzees and now an internationally renowned primate sanctuary.

Places to Stay

Hotels fill up on weekends and holidays, so try to arrive early.

Just east of Limbe's main roundabout is a cluster of three budget hotels, although all are poor value compared with Park Hotel Miramar (see listing later), where you get a good setting and much more comfort for about the same price for a double.

Bay Hotel *(☎ 333 2332)* Rooms with 1 small bed & no window CFA6500, rooms with double beds CFA12,000. Bay Hotel is probably the best of the three in this area. Rooms have bathrooms, some have air-con, and there's a restaurant.

Victoria Guest House Small rooms with shared bathroom from CFA5000, better rooms with bathroom & fan from CFA10,000. Sheets are clean, but otherwise rooms are undistinguished. It's next to Bay Hotel.

King William Square Hotel Singles/doubles from CFA9000/10,000. This place, near the previous two listings, is of similar standard.

Holiday Inn Resort *(☎ 333 2290, fax 333 2179, e ngunjo@iccnet2000.com)* Rooms CFA12,000-20,000. This large place, on the northern edge of town off Church St, has a range of self-contained rooms. Most have air-con and bathroom and all are reasonably clean, though nothing special.

Park Hotel Miramar *(☎ 333 2332, 333 2689)* Singles CFA9500, doubles without/with air-con CFA11,500/13,500. The waterside setting is quite nice, and accommodation – in small, no-frills *boukarous* (small, round huts or cottages, often with thatched roofs) – is probably Limbe's best value. There's a pool and restaurant. Don't walk the back road from here to the Atlantic Beach Hotel, especially in the evenings.

Atlantic Beach Hotel *(☎ 333 2332, 333 2689, e atlanticbeachhotel@camnet.cm)* Singles CFA16,500, doubles without/with sea view CFA19,500/23,500. This is Limbe's most upscale option. There's a pool, a good waterside restaurant, and faded but comfortable air-con rooms.

Places to Eat

The best ***street food*** is around Half-Mile Junction, which fills in the evening with soya vendors and women grilling fish.

To sit down, try ***T-Complex*** on Church St, a bar-restaurant with meals from CFA2000. ***Mars***, on the waterfront, has a better ambience and views and serves good meals from CFA2000. It's also one of the best spots for sundowners. Just southeast of here is the unmarked ***Down Beach Fish***, with inexpensive grilled fish. Turn seawards at the sign for Mbonjo Beach Inn.

Hot-Spot, reached through the Botanic Garden, has a great setting overlooking the water and good meals for CFA2200 to CFA3500. ***Bella's***, just off Idenao Rd west of the stadium, is similarly priced, but with slower service and no sea views.

Getting There & Away

Bus & Taxi The main motor park is at Mile 4, about 5km from town on the Buea road. Minibuses depart from here to Buea (CFA400, 45 minutes), Douala (CFA1000, 1½ hours, 75km) and Kumba (CFA1500, 2½ hours). Before 6am and in the evening, transport departs from Half-Mile Junction, which is also where you can catch a shared taxi to Mile 4 (CFA100).

To Yaoundé, Guaranti Express and Patience, both on the Buea road, have one departure each around 8am daily (CFA5000). Otherwise, you'll need to go via Douala. Patience is opposite the hospital about 1km from the centre; Guaranti Express is about 1km further. Both lines also have one bus daily to Bafoussam (CFA4000) and Bamenda (CFA4000, seven to 12 hours), departing about 8am.

Shared taxis to the beaches at Batoke and Mile 11 (CFA400) depart from Idenao Rd near the stadium. To Mile 11, they take a while to fill; if you decide to charter, it should cost about CFA2500. Shared taxis for Batoke fill more quickly.

It's fairly common to charter taxis between Douala and Limbe. The fare is CFA10,000 to CFA15,000 for a drop, and about CFA20,000 for the entire day, though you'll often be quoted much higher.

Boat Sailing at least weekly – usually Monday – boats go to Malabo (Equatorial Guinea), although departures are often greatly delayed. For information, go to the Achouka office, signposted about 1.5km past the Botanic Garden on Idenao Rd. The boats have no comforts, and you'll need to bring your own food and drink. There are also occasional boats from Limbe to Oron (Nigeria), although departures are more frequent from Idenao, to the northwest. Achouka can provide information. Also see Boat in the main Getting There & Away section of this chapter.

AROUND LIMBE

Beaches

The better beaches (all with brown volcanic sand) are north of Limbe at Mile 8 (Batoke village – the best beach) and Mile 11. There's also a beach at Mile 6, though it's not quite as nice and you may have to fend off a band of aggressive monkeys. At all the beaches, check before plunging in as currents can be strong when the tide recedes. In the roadway near Mile 11, you can see the lava flow from Mt Cameroon's 1999 eruption.

Places to Stay All of these places are near the beach, but none have rooms on the water. There's no accommodation north of Mile 11.

Coastal Beach Hotel Rooms CFA15,000. This place near Mile 6 had just opened when we passed through, and we've heard some good reviews. All the rooms have bathroom and air-con, and there's a satellite TV.

Etisah Beach (☎ 998 3239, ⓔ etisah.beach@yahoo.fr) Rooms with fan CFA6000, rooms with 1/2 beds & air-con in main building CFA12,000/13,000. Etisah is a relaxing place set on a hill about 400m up from the beach at Mile 8. The cheaper rooms, in an annex, are nothing special and a bit dark, but the ones in the main building are clean, bright and good value. There's also a restaurant with meals from CFA3500. The hotel sometimes charges a CFA500 beach-use fee (CFA1000 per vehicle). North of Etisah along the beach is a military compound, so you can't take photos here.

Seme New Beach Hotel (☎ 333 2769, ⓔ camrevtour@camnet.cm) Rooms with shower/bath CFA19,500/23,800. This is the most upscale place, with large grounds, a restaurant and accommodation in modern attached cottages. Credit cards are accepted for a 10% commission. It's at Mile 11; there's a CFA500 beach-use charge.

Bota Islands

Offshore from Limbe are several tiny islands with steep cliff faces. They're now uninhabited, but important for traditional rituals. You can hire a pirogue to visit for about CFA2000 in Limbe's Bota Quarter, northwest of town off Idenao Rd. The main island has some carved stone stairs to climb to the top.

Mt Etinde (Petit Mt Cameroon)

Small but steep Etinde, a 1713m sub-peak on Mt Cameroon's southern slopes, is an extinct volcano and geologically older than its larger neighbour. Climbs can be arranged through the Mt Cameroon Ecotourism Project, either at its office in Buea (see the following section) or, easier, at the Visitors' Centre at Limbe Botanic Garden. It costs CFA6000 per guide plus a CFA3000 per person 'stakeholder' fee, and CFA1000 to CFA2000 for the local chief, whose permission you need to climb. You'll also need to bring a bottle of whisky along for the ancestral spirits.

It's possible to walk from Limbe to the mountain, in which case you should allow one long day for the entire trip. Otherwise take a shared taxi to Batoke, from where you can charter a taxi to either Ekonjo or Etumba (Etome), two villages at the mountain's base. From either of these, the climb should take about half a day. The idea with the whisky is that half is poured out at the summit as a libation for the spirits, while the other half is consumed. So be warned, as you still need to hike back down! Bring along insect repellent, sturdy shoes and whatever food and water you will need, and clarify before starting who is supplying food for the guide.

Cape Debundscha & Bomana Waterfalls

About 30km north of Limbe along the coast is Cape Debundscha. Together with an area in Assam (India) and part of the Hawai'ian Islands it's one of the three wettest places on earth, with 10m to 15m precipitation annually. There's an old German lighthouse here, and a crater lake. You'll need to charter a taxi to get here from Limbe. Further on, northeast of Idenao, is **Bomana Waterfalls**. It's a bit of an expedition to reach the falls, and you'll need a guide and permission from the local chief to enter onto the surrounding land, as well as vehicle transport as far as Idenao. The Limbe Botanic Garden Visitors' Centre can help with information on both destinations, and with arranging guides.

BUEA

Buea (boy-ah), on the lower slopes of Mt Cameroon, is a large, sprawling town and the starting point for climbing the mountain. From 1901, it was briefly the German colonial capital. To the south is the Tole Tea Factory; it's possible to walk to Limbe along the road leading past the factory (starting near Mermoz Hotel). There's a Nigerian consulate near Buea Mountain Hotel, but it generally issues visas only to Cameroonian residents.

Climbing Mt Cameroon

Mt Cameroon (4095m), known locally as Fako, is West Africa's highest mountain and one of its two active volcanos (the other is in Cape Verde). Mt Cameroon had eruptions in 1999 and 2000. Biologically, it is of great interest for its endemic plants and birds, and for the unique climatic conditions that make it a biodiversity 'hot spot'.

There are several routes to the top and numerous trails on the mountain's lower slopes. None require technical equipment, but warm clothes are essential near the

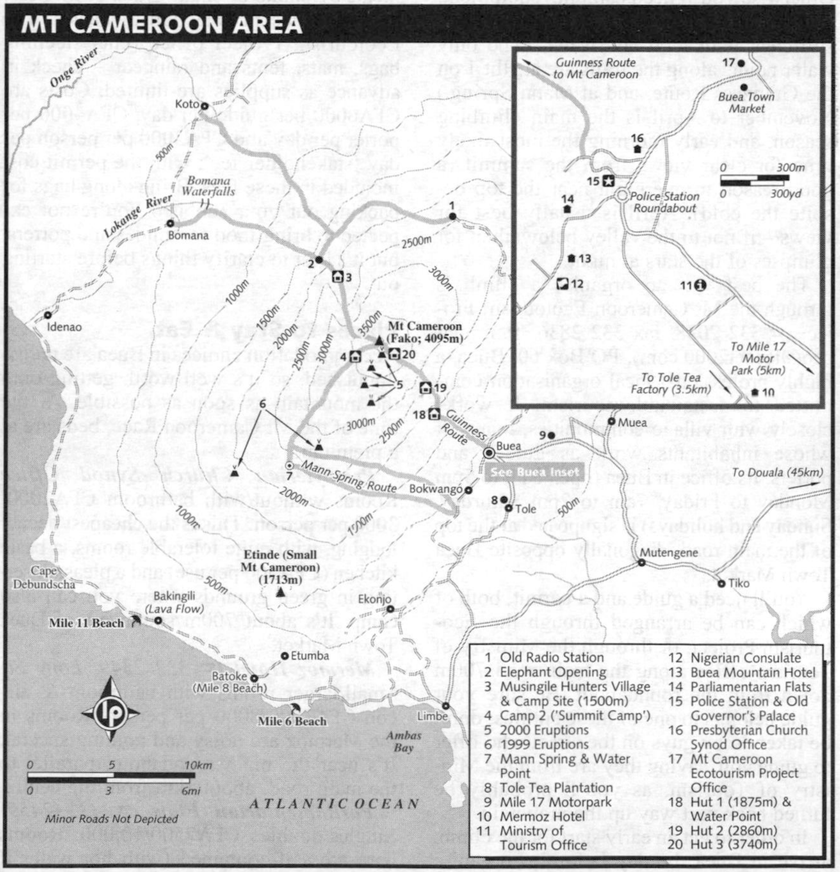
MT CAMEROON AREA
Onge River
Koto
500m
Bomana Waterfalls
Lokange River
Bomana
1
2500m
2
3
3000m
1000m
Idenao
1500m
2000m
2500m
3000m
3500m
Mt Cameroon (Fako; 4095m)
4
20
5
19
6
18
Guinness Route
3000m
2500m
7
Mann Spring Route
2000m
1000m
1500m
Bokwango
Buea
See Buea Inset
9
8
Tole
500m
Muea
To Douala (45km)
Mutengene
Tiko
Etinde (Small Mt Cameroon) (1713m)
Cape Debundscha
500m
Bakingili (Lava Flow)
Mile 11 Beach
Ekonjo
Etumba
Batoke (Mile 8 Beach)
Mile 6 Beach
Limbe
Ambas Bay
ATLANTIC OCEAN
0 5 10km
0 3 6mi
Minor Roads Not Depicted
Guinness Route to Mt Cameroon
17
Buea Town Market
16
0 300m
0 300yd
15
Police Station Roundabout
14
13
12
11
To Mile 17 Motor Park (5km)
To Tole Tea Factory (3.5km)
10
1 Old Radio Station
2 Elephant Opening
3 Musingile Hunters Village & Camp Site (1500m)
4 Camp 2 ('Summit Camp')
5 2000 Eruptions
6 1999 Eruptions
7 Mann Spring & Water Point
8 Tole Tea Plantation
9 Mile 17 Motorpark
10 Mermoz Hotel
11 Ministry of Tourism Office
12 Nigerian Consulate
13 Buea Mountain Hotel
14 Parliamentarian Flats
15 Police Station & Old Governor's Palace
16 Presbyterian Church Synod Office
17 Mt Cameroon Ecotourism Project Office
18 Hut 1 (1875m) & Water Point
19 Hut 2 (2860m)
20 Hut 3 (3740m)

summit and waterproof gear is advisable. The quickest is the 'Guinness Route', a straight up-and-down climb that can be easily done in 1½ days, though it's quite steep in parts. It's better to take at least two nights on the mountain to experience its ecosystems and explore less-travelled routes; if you have the time, there are set hikes of five days and more. One popular two-night, three-day combination is ascending via the Mann Spring route and descending via the Guinness Route. With more time, it's possible to descend via Musingile on the mountain's northern side, and from there through the forest to Koto (northwest of Idenao).

Along the Guinness Route are three poorly maintained huts (at 1875m, 2860m and 3740m) with plank beds and little else. Otherwise you'll need camping equipment, and for all routes you should be self-sufficient with food and water. (The only water points along the trails are at Hut 1 on the Guinness Route, and at Mann Spring.) November to April is the main climbing season, and early morning the most likely time for clear views from the summit (a good reason to overnight near the top despite the cold). April is usually best for views – if not to the valley below, then for glimpses of the stars at night.

The best way to organise a climb is through the Mt Cameroon Ecotourism Project (☎ 332 2038, fax 332 2836, e mountceo@iccnet2000.com), PO Box 60, Buea, a highly professional local organisation committed to sustainable tourism. It works closely with village communities, many of whose inhabitants work as guides and porters. Its office in Buea (open 8am to 5pm Monday to Friday, 7am to 2pm Saturday, Sunday and holidays) is signposted at the top of the main road, diagonally opposite Buea Town Market.

You'll need a guide and a permit, both of which can be arranged through the Ecotourism Project, or through the Ministry of Tourism office along the main road 700m down from the roundabout. Be sure your guide belongs to one of these entities; don't be taken in by guys on the street who offer to guide you, saying they are from the Ministry of Tourism, as you'll probably be turned back part way up the mountain.

In order to get an early start for the climb, arrive in Buea the day before to organise things, or at least make advance arrangements by phone or email. Buea Town Market has a decent selection of basics. The Ecotourism Project office rents sleeping bags, mats, tents and raingear – check in advance as supplies are limited. Costs are CFA6000 per guide per day, CFA4000 per porter per day and CFA3000 per person per day 'stakeholder fee', with the permit cost included in these fees. Bring along bags for packing out your rubbish. You're not expected to bring food for guides and porters, but it's best to clarify things before starting out.

Mt Cameroon Race

The Mt Cameroon Race ('Race of Hope') is held annually in February, and attracts an international group of competitors and many spectators. Competitors use the Guinness Route to reach the summit, with the winners usually finishing the approximately 40km course in an amazing 4½ hours for men and 5½ hours for women. For more information contact the Fédération Camerounaise d'Athlétisme (w www.gcnet.cm/fca/AscMt_Cmr.htm) or the IAAF Athletes Representative (☎ 222 4744, e kouohfr@yahoo.com), BP 353 Yaoundé.

Places to Stay & Eat

Accommodation choices in Buea are undistinguished, so it's well worth getting onto the mountain as soon as possible. At the time of the Mt Cameroon Race, beds are at a premium.

Presbyterian Church Synod Office Rooms without/with bathroom CFA2000/3000 per person. This is the cheapest decent lodging, with quite tolerable rooms, a basic kitchen (CFA500 per use) and a pleasant setting in green grounds where you can also camp. It's about 700m southwest of Buea Town Market.

Mermoz Hotel *(☎ 332 2349, Long St)* Small/larger rooms with bathroom & air-con CFA7000/8000 per person. Rooms in the Mermoz are noisy and nothing special. It's near the main roundabout, parallel to the main road, about 1km from the centre.

Parliamentarian Flats *(☎ 332 2459)* Singles/doubles CFA7500/10,000. Rooms here are self-contained (with hot water if

CAMEROON

you're lucky), though somewhat on the grubby side. Food can be arranged with notice. It's about 200m west of the main roundabout (to the left when entering town), and 1km from the town centre.

Buea Mountain Hotel *(☎ 332 2235)* Singles/doubles CFA9000/15,000, suites CFA20,000. The setting here is quiet and slightly rustic, and rooms are OK with clean sheets, though they've definitely seen better days. There's a restaurant, and, with luck, hot water. It's just after Parliamentarian Flats, on the opposite side of the road.

Getting There & Away

The motor park for shared taxis and minibuses to/from Limbe, Douala and Kumba is at Mile 17, about 6km from town along the Limbe road (CFA300 in a shared taxi).

KUMBA

Kumba is an important transport junction and the site of one of Cameroon's largest markets, with many goods from Nigeria. About 5km northwest is the attractive **Barombi Mbo** crater lake.

For inexpensive accommodation try ***Metropole Hotel***, west of the market off the Mundemba road, where rooms with fan cost from about CFA6000.

Several steps up in price and quality is ***Azi Motel***, along the Buea road, with rooms from about CFA10,000. There's a restaurant, and nonguests can make and receive telephone calls here.

For inexpensive fast food try ***Classy Burger***. Moses, the owner, is a good source of information on Kumba. It's several blocks north of the market.

For a respite from the streets, try the 'VIP lounge' at ***Tavern Motel*** near Azi Motel on the Buea road. The food is inexpensive, and if you befriend the bartender, you may be able to get your drinks from the (cheaper) non-VIP section. ***Western Inn***, near the stadium, also has inexpensive food.

Getting There & Away

Bus Several agencies go direct to Bafoussam and Bamenda, including Tonton Express and Symbol of Unity. All have offices near the market in the town centre. Transport to these destinations also leaves from Three Corners Motor Park in Fiango, on the northeastern edge of town, as does transport to Bangem (CFA3000, at least four hours), although for Bangem you may need to change vehicles at Tombel.

Transport to Douala (CFA1500), Limbe (CFA1500, 2½ hours) and Buea departs from the Buea road taxi park, on the southeastern edge of town.

To Yaoundé (CFA5000, seven hours), Tonton Express has a daily bus departing Kumba about 7am and Yaoundé about 3pm. Otherwise, you'll need to go via Douala.

To reach Barombi Mbo, take any shared taxi from the western side of town heading towards 'Upstation' and ask the driver to drop you at the junction, about 3km from town. From here, it's about 2km further and a nice walk; follow the 'new' road to the left from the junction. Otherwise, you can hire a taxi for the whole way.

Transport to Ekondo Titi (where you can find vehicles to Mundemba and Korup National Park) departs from Mbonge Road Motor Park on the southwestern edge of town.

Train There's a train four times daily between Douala and Kumba, though it's faster to take the bus from Douala to Mbanga, then the train from there to Kumba (CFA400, one to 1½ hours). Trains pass Mbanga every several hours from about 9am to 4pm.

BANGEM

Bangem is a pleasant town off the beaten path, and the centre of the Bakossi people. There are some nice hikes in the surrounding area, but the main reason to come is to visit the beautiful **Manengouba Crater Lakes**, set in a grassy caldera southeast of town. The lakes, known locally as Man Lake and Woman Lake, are the subject of various local superstitions. Swimming is permitted in Woman Lake, but not in Man Lake. A visit costs CFA1000, which you're supposed to pay at the police station in Bangem (get a receipt), though it's often easier to just pay the guy near the lakes who will approach you to collect it.

The lakes are about three hours uphill on foot from town; locals can point the way. Once you reach the rim, you'll need to hike through the caldera, past grazing cattle and Fulani herdsmen, to reach the lakes on the far side.

The basic but OK ***Prestige Inn*** is the best bet for accommodation in Bangem.

The most direct way from Kumba to Bangem is via Tombel, but the road is bad so it's faster and more comfortable to go first to Melong (about halfway between Kumba and Bafoussam), from where it's just CFA1500 and 45 minutes in a shared taxi to Bangem.

KORUP NATIONAL PARK

Korup protects an exceptionally biologically diverse patch of rainforest reported to be one of the oldest and richest in Africa. Within its 1259 sq km are more than 300 species of birds, 50 species of large mammals, more than 400 varieties of trees and over 90 medicinal plants. The vegetation is very dense and – apart from monkeys – you're unlikely to see animals, but visiting is a superb way to experience a rainforest ecosystem. Korup is also the easiest of Cameroon's protected rainforest areas to reach, and the one with the most developed infrastructure. There is more than 100km of marked walking trails within the park, well-trained English-speaking guides, and enough to keep you busy for at least two days.

The starting point for a visit is **Mundemba** village, about 8km before the park gate. There's an Information Centre (e korup@wwf.cm), which is open 7.30am to 5.30pm daily from November to May, 7.30am to 3.30pm Monday to Friday, and 7.30am to 8.30am and 4.30pm to 5.30pm Saturday and Sunday from June to September. You'll need to pay your park fees here (CFA 5000 per day) and arrange an obligatory guide (CFA4000 per day, plus CFA1000 per night). Porters can also be arranged (CFA2000 per day plus CFA1000 per night, maximum load 25kg), as can rental of sleeping bags, foam mats and cookware. Bring plenty of insect repellent. Basic supplies are available in Mundemba.

Places to Stay & Eat

There are three camp sites (CFA3000 per person) in the park's southern section: ***Iriba Inene***, about 2km from the entrance; ***Rengo*** (8km); and ***Chimpanzee*** (10km). Each has simple huts with wooden beds and mosquito screens, water for drinking and bathing, and a cooking area. You'll need to bring your own food, and a sleeping mat. You're not expected to supply food for guides and porters, but it's best to clarify this in Mundemba before setting off.

In Mundemba, the main place to stay is ***Iyas Hotel***, with simple but clean rooms with fan and bathroom for CFA5000/6000/8000 per single/double/twin.

Korup Park Hotel, near the post office, has a bar and restaurant and regular/large rooms with fan and bathroom costing CFA5000/7000.

The cheapest place is the rundown ***Vista Palace***, with rooms for CFA2500/4000 without/with bathroom. It's on a small side street to the right when entering Mundemba.

The best meals in town are at the friendly and reasonably priced ***Chez Contrôleur Touristic Café***, opposite Vista Palace.

Getting There & Away

There's usually at least one taxi brousse daily between Mundemba and Kumba (four hours, 120km), though you may need to change vehicles midway at Ekondo Titi.

From Mundemba to the park gate, you can either walk, or go with a park vehicle (CFA8000 per vehicle, 10 people maximum including guide and porters). The famous suspension bridge that crosses the Mana River at the park border is currently under repair, so you'll need to walk or boat across (included in the CFA8000, though), depending on the season.

If you have the money, a great way to depart or arrive in Korup is by boat along the Mana River. Staff can arrange pick-ups or drop-offs from as far south as Idenao through the disputed Bakassi Peninsula area (CFA200,000 to CFA250,000 one way per six-person boat). The boat can also be rented for shorter excursions along the river to explore the mangrove swamps or visit nearby Pelican Island (CFA100,000 to CFA150,000). All boat trips need to be arranged in advance.

There's another entrance to Korup at Baro, west of Nguti, which can be reached by taxi brousse from Mamfe during the dry season.

MAMFE

On the bank of the Cross River, Mamfe is the last major town before the Nigerian border at Ekok, 60km further west. Together with nearby Kembong village, it's also a regional centre for witchcraft and traditional medicine.

There's no bank at the border, so you'll need to ask at shops in Mamfe or at the market if you're looking for Nigerian naira. Bicec bank in Mamfe is occasionally willing to change cash euros (no travellers cheques), but shouldn't be relied upon.

If you're heading to Nigeria, it's worth stopping by the Office for Immigration and Emigration to make friends with the officer and ask for some names at Ekok. It's in the town centre between the main roundabout and Bayang Garage; locals can point you in the right direction.

Places to Stay & Eat

The best lodging is at ***Data Club Guest House*** on the northeastern edge of town, with air-con rooms from about CFA10,000 and a decent ***restaurant***. For something cheaper, try the more basic ***African City Hotel***, near the motor park, or ***Great Aim Hotel***, just to the north. Both have rooms for about CFA5000.

There are several good places to eat near the motor park, and there are also ***soya vendors*** scattered around the town during the evening.

Getting There & Away

Transport connections in all directions are good, although the roads are not. The main motor park is about 500m southwest of Mamfe's central intersection.

Transport goes daily, throughout the day, to Ekok, where you'll need to change vehicles after crossing the border. The main lines are Ali Baba and Tonton Express, and the price is CFA1500 in the dry season, though this can rise as high as CFA4000 during the rains, when you can expect to have to regularly get out and push.

The road from Mamfe to Bamenda (144km) is beautiful, dangerous – with perilous drop-offs – and only an option in the dry season. Expect to pay from CFA5000 to CFA10,000.

It's often better to take the longer southern route via Kumba (CFA5000, five to six hours, 180km), from where you can continue on to Bamenda (CFA6000, seven hours, 250km).

There's usually at least one vehicle daily between Mamfe and Nguti (for Korup National Park), although there's almost no traffic from Nguti into the park.

North-West Province

Anglophone North-West Province is one of Cameroon's most-pleasant areas, with an easy-going pace, friendly people and beautiful hill scenery. The climate in most places is relatively cool and you'll often need a jacket in the evenings, especially between November and February. Much of the North-West Province is very traditional, and the area is known for its witchcraft.

BAMENDA

pop 235,000

Bamenda is a large and sprawling place at more than 1000m altitude, capital of North-West Province, and a popular stop for travellers. While the town itself is not particularly attractive, the surrounding area is beautiful, and Bamenda makes a good base for exploring. It's also the centre of ongoing opposition to President Biya.

Orientation

Arriving from Bafoussam, you'll first reach Upstation, which overlooks Bamenda town and is home to various government buildings. From here, the main street winds down the cliff to Sonac St and City Chemists' Roundabout. From here, Commercial Ave (the main drag) leads south, while another road runs southwest towards Hospital Roundabout. Going northwest from Hospital Roundabout, you'll reach Ntarikon Motor Park and the road towards Bafut and Wum.

Note that many of Bamenda's streets have two names – the official names imposed by the government (shown on the map in parentheses), and the 'real' names used by everyone else.

Information

The tourist office, with some maps and information on the area, is in a pink building about three blocks west of Commercial Ave.

Amity Bank at City Chemists' Roundabout changes travellers cheques.

Mondial Computing near New Life Annex at Hospital Roundabout has Internet connection for CFA2400 per hour.

If you need medical treatment, try the 24-hour Mezam Polyclinic (☎ 336 1432) on Bali Rd.

CAMEROON

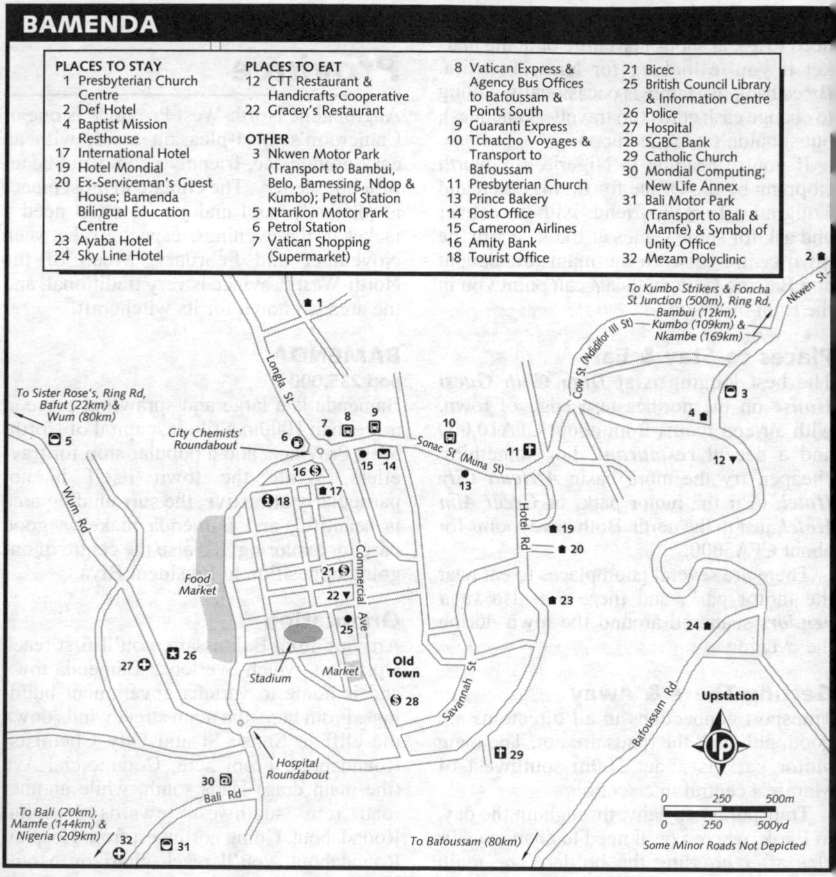
BAMENDA
PLACES TO STAY
1 Presbyterian Church Centre
2 Def Hotel
4 Baptist Mission Resthouse
17 International Hotel
19 Hotel Mondial
20 Ex-Serviceman's Guest House; Bamenda Bilingual Education Centre
23 Ayaba Hotel
24 Sky Line Hotel
PLACES TO EAT
12 CTT Restaurant & Handicrafts Cooperative
22 Gracey's Restaurant
OTHER
3 Nkwen Motor Park (Transport to Bambui, Belo, Bamessing, Ndop & Kumbo); Petrol Station
5 Ntarikon Motor Park
6 Petrol Station
7 Vatican Shopping (Supermarket)
8 Vatican Express & Agency Bus Offices to Bafoussam & Points South
9 Guaranti Express
10 Tchatcho Voyages & Transport to Bafoussam
11 Presbyterian Church
13 Prince Bakery
14 Post Office
15 Cameroon Airlines
16 Amity Bank
18 Tourist Office
21 Bicec
25 British Council Library & Information Centre
26 Police
27 Hospital
28 SGBC Bank
29 Catholic Church
30 Mondial Computing; New Life Annex
31 Bali Motor Park (Transport to Bali & Mamfe) & Symbol of Unity Office
32 Mezam Polyclinic
To Kumbo Strikers & Foncha St Junction (500m), Ring Rd, Bambui (12km), Kumbo (109km) & Nkambe (169km)
Nkwen St
Cow St (Ndidifor III St)
To Sister Rose's, Ring Rd, Bafut (22km) & Wum (80km)
Longla St
City Chemists' Roundabout
Sonac St (Muna St)
Hotel Rd
Wum Rd
Commercial Ave
Food Market
Stadium
Market
Old Town
Savannah St
Bafoussam Rd
Upstation
Hospital Roundabout
Bali Rd
To Bali (20km), Mamfe (144km) & Nigeria (209km)
To Bafoussam (80km)
0 250 500m
0 250 500yd
Some Minor Roads Not Depicted

Places to Stay

Baptist Mission Resthouse *(☎ 336 1285)* Rooms CFA2500. This is the best budget option. Rooms are clean and have sink, shared bathroom and two twin beds. It's on the eastern edge of town near Nkwen Motor Park.

Presbyterian Church Centre *(☎ 336 4070)* Dorm beds from CFA2000. Rooms here are more basic than those at the Baptist Mission Resthouse, but still good value, and the grounds are pleasant. There's no food. It's just off Longla St (the northern extension of Commercial Ave), about 1km from town.

Ex-Serviceman's Guest House Rooms CFA3000. It's a bit of a brothel here, and not for women alone, but it's clean enough and the location is convenient.

International Hotel *(☎ 336 2527)* Rooms from CFA6000. This place is better than the Ex-Serviceman's. Rooms have bathroom and hot water, and some have a balcony and views. It's near City Chemists' Roundabout in the town centre.

Def Hotel *(☎ 336 3748, Nkwen)* Rooms without TV CFA6000, nicer room with TV & hot water CFA10,000. The area here isn't great, just off busy Nkwen St near Foncha St junction, but rooms are fine for the price.

Hotel Mondial *(☎ 336 1832, fax 336 2884)* Singles/doubles CFA12,500/14,000. This is the best mid-range option, with clean and comfortable self-contained rooms and a good restaurant. The rooms facing the back are quieter. There are some basement rooms for CFA7500, but they're usually full. It's on the eastern side of town off Sonac St.

Sky Line Hotel *(☎ 336 1289, Bafoussam Rd, Upstation)* Rooms CFA14,000. Sky Line doesn't receive much business and is a bit rundown, though rooms aren't too bad. It's rumoured to have a decent restaurant as well. The main problem is the location about 3km from the centre overlooking town. If you don't have your own vehicle it can be difficult to find transport in the evenings.

Ayaba Hotel *(☎ 336 1356, ⓔ ayabahotel@refinedct.net, Hotel Rd)* Doubles/triples CFA18,000/25,000. The Ayaba has pretensions to grandeur but is very faded. Rooms are air-conditioned, with no mosquito nets. There's a restaurant, as well as a popular disco on weekend evenings.

Places to Eat

Gracey's Restaurant *(Commercial Ave)* This place has great omelettes and french fries from CFA700 for a large serving, but order at least an hour before you're hungry. It's just left of the Prescraft Centre; look for two wooden swing doors

CTT Restaurant & Handicrafts Cooperative Mains from CFA1500, pizza from CFA3000. The restaurant (on the basement floor) has Bamenda's best pizza (allow at least an hour for the order) and a range of good Cameroonian and standard Western meals.

Sister Rose's in Ntarikon, about 3km from the centre, is a Bamenda institution, and very popular. You get to choose your own fish (from about CFA4000), while the whole chicken (CFA5000) served on a platter with plantains and *njama njama* would easily feed several people. Take a shared taxi from Hospital Roundabout. The restaurant may move, but taxi drivers will know the new location.

Vatican Shopping, located at the City Chemists' Roundabout, is well-stocked for self-caterers.

Getting There & Away

Most agency offices for Bafoussam and points south are on Sonac St. To Douala and Yaoundé (both CFA4500, six to nine hours), Vatican Express is probably the best. To Yaoundé, it's faster to catch any vehicle going to Bafoussam (CFA1000, 1½ hours) and get a bus from there to Yaoundé.

For Limbe and the southwest, try Guaranti Express and Tchatcho Voyages, also on Sonac St.

To Wum (CFA2000, two hours), try Symbol of Unity; its office is diagonally opposite Mezam Polyclinic.

Kumbo Strikers Express goes to Kumbo from its office near Foncha St junction.

Main nonagency motor parks include Nkwen (for Belo, Bamessing, Ndop and Kumbo), Ntarikon (for Wum and Bafut) and Bali (for Bali and Mamfe).

AROUND BAMENDA

Bali

Bali is about 20km southwest of Bamenda, and makes a good day excursion. Along with Bafut and Kumbo, it's one of the most important traditional kingdoms in the area. It's possible to visit the **fon's palace** (although it's not as interesting as the one in Bafut) and have an audience with the fon himself, although he's frequently away. There's also an artisan centre, and an impressive *lela* (end-of-year festival, though it's not held every year) in late December, with traditional dancing and more. Shared taxis run frequently between Bamenda and Bali.

The Ring Road

The Ring Road is a 367km circular route commencing at Bamenda and passing – anticlockwise – Bambui (Bambili), Bamessing, Ndop, Kumbo, Nkambe, Wum and Bafut, as well as many smaller villages. It's a beautiful area of rolling hills, mountains, waterfalls and traditional kingdoms. This is also the heart of the Grassfields area – Cameroon's northwestern highlands where some of its most fascinating artwork originates. While there's little in the way of organised tourism, you could easily spend several weeks trekking from village to village. Unlike the rest of Cameroon, it's generally safe to camp here, usually with hospitable Fulani herdsmen or in village compounds (get permission first from the local village chief). Before setting out, visit the Institut National de Cartographie on Ave Monseigneur Vogt in Yaoundé for a topographical map.

For those heading east by vehicle, the road is in decent condition from Bamenda via Kumbo to Nkambe, while there's scarcely a discernible track from there to Wum and then a rough dirt road for much

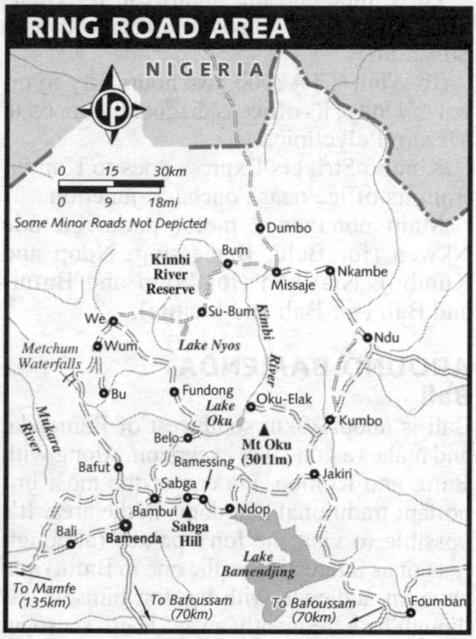
RING ROAD AREA
NIGERIA
0 15 30km
0 9 18mi
Some Minor Roads Not Depicted
Dumbo
Bum
Kimbi River Reserve
Nkambe
Missaje
Su-Bum
We
Kimbi River
Ndu
Metchum Waterfalls
Wum
Lake Nyos
Bu
Fundong
Lake Oku
Oku-Elak
Kumbo
Mukara River
Belo
Mt Oku (3011m)
Bafut
Bamessing
Jakiri
Sabga
Bambui
Ndop
Bali
Bamenda
Sabga Hill
Lake Bamendjing
To Mamfe (135km)
To Bafoussam (70km)
To Bafoussam (70km)
Foumban

of the remainder back to Bamenda. Several downed bridges mean that most of the stretch between Nkambe and Wum can only be done on foot.

Apart from in Kumbo and Nkambe, there is almost no infrastructure in this area, and nowhere to change money, so do this in Bamenda before setting off. In Kumbo, you can usually find shop owners willing to change cash.

Bamessing & Sabga-Ndop Bamessing (about 25km east of Bamenda) is a small village with a Prespot centre, where you can watch a group of skilled potters at work. About 500m after Prespot is the Handicrafts Training Centre, selling pottery, masks and wood carvings.

If you want to get a taste of the Ring Road but don't have time for longer exploration, Bamessing, together with the countryside around nearby Sabga village (about 3km west of Bamessing along the Bamenda road) makes an ideal day trip. The scenery along this stretch – actually for the entire way between Bambui to the west and Ndop to the east – is among the most impressive in the area, especially around September and October when the hills are green. Just east of Sabga is Sabga Hill, which you can climb in a few minutes for good views.

There is nothing in Sabga, and only a few local eateries in Bamessing, so if you'll be doing longer hikes from here, you'll need to be self-sufficient with food and water. If you get stuck for accommodation or want to do an overnight loop, try the basic ***Green Valley Resort*** in Ndop, about 10km east of Bamessing on the Ring Road. Rooms cost CFA4000 and there's a restaurant.

To reach Bamessing, take any vehicle heading towards Kumbo and ask the driver to drop you at the Prespot turn-off (about CFA500). To climb Sabga Hill, ask to be dropped off about 500m after Sabga village at the 10% grade sign. Another good point to start a walk is the dirt road branching left shortly after the police checkpoint before Sabga village.

Kumbo Situated at about 2000m altitude, Kumbo (Banso) is one of the largest towns in the northwest. It's home to the Banso people, one of the major traditional kingdoms in the Grassfields, and site of a famous horse-racing festival (usually in November). You can visit the **fon's palace**; there's no set fee, but CFA1000 to CFA2000 is expected for whoever shows you in. It's also worth visiting the market, especially the interior part with its section devoted to traditional medicine.

Two of Cameroon's better hospitals are here: Banso Baptist Hospital (BBH) in Kumbo and Shisong Catholic Hospital, just outside town.

Fomo 92 is the best place to stay, with reasonable self-contained rooms with hot water for CFA6000. Otherwise, there are several more basic and slightly less expensive places, including ***Central Inn***, near the motor park, with rooms from about CFA3000 and good views from the rooftop terrace, and the slightly pricier ***Merryland Hotel***.

There is transport several times daily between Kumbo and Bamenda (CFA1200, two hours), and during the dry season between Kumbo and Foumban. There are also daily departures to Nkambe, and westwards to Oku-Elak (for Mt Oku).

Nkambe to Wum Nkambe is the only town of any size between Kumbo and Wum. Like Kumbo, it is at altitude and has a cool climate. About halfway between Kumbo

Climbing Mt Oku

Mt Oku (3011m), in the centre of the Ring Rd area, is Cameroon's second-highest mountain. Although not nearly as popular as Mt Cameroon, it makes a rugged but satisfying climb. On its western slope is a crater lake, which is considered sacred, and the mountain is a centre for witchcraft. More mundanely, the Oku area is known for its honey.

The starting point for the climb is the village of Oku-Elak, reached by taxi brousse from Kumbo (CFA1000). Once there, you'll need to first go to the fon's palace to get permission. There's no charge, but it's not a bad idea to bring a bottle of whisky or other gift. The people at the palace will also help you arrange a guide; expect to pay between CFA2000 and CFA5000. If you get stuck for the night, there's basic accommodation in Oku-Elak.

The climb itself takes about six hours return, including some steep, rough sections. You'll need a good windcheater, as well as sufficient water. It's possible to descend via the mountain's western side, finishing near Belo, from where there's sporadic transport south to Bambui, and then to Bamenda. There is basic accommodation in Belo.

and Nkambe is **Ndu**, with a large tea plantation and basic ***guesthouse***.

Millennium Star Hotel, about a 20-minute walk or CFA500 in a shared taxi from the town centre, has basic but reasonable rooms for about CFA6500. Otherwise, the main choice is the cheaper and grubbier ***Divisional Hotel***, in the centre, with rooms for CFA2500. Allow about six hours by public transport between Bamenda and Nkambe.

At **Missaje**, about 20km west of Nkambe, the driveable road ends, and you'll need to continue on foot or mountain bike (it's all downhill from Nkambe to Wum). Allow a full day on foot between Missaje and We (13km northeast of Wum), assuming you don't get lost, but it's better to bring provisions to last two days. For much of this stretch, the road is nothing more than a rough track, and most travellers wind up hiring a Fulani herdsman to accompany them and point out the way. Many speak only Fulfulde. If you get stuck in Missaje, the only place to stay is in one of the very unappealing ***rooms*** behind the local bar.

En route between Nkambe and We and south of the Ring Road is **Lake Nyos**. The lake gained notoriety in 1986 when it was the site of a natural gas eruption, which resulted in around 1700 deaths.

Also en route to We, and before reaching Lake Nyos, is the seldom-visited **Kimbi River Reserve**, though you'll need your own vehicle to explore, and a tent if you plan to overnight. From We, there's occasional public transport to Wum, though you might end up walking at least part of the way.

Wum This is the only town of any size along the western side of the Ring Road, and the end of public transport if you're travelling in a clockwise direction. About 20km south of Wum just west of the road are some **waterfalls** on the Metchum River. Taxi drivers will often agree to a brief stop if you ask. Don't lean on the makeshift rail, as several visitors plunged to their deaths here some years ago. The falls are not visible from the road, so you'll need to ask someone to point out the spot.

There are several undistinguished guesthouses in Wum, the best of which is probably ***Morning Star Hotel***, with a restaurant and rooms for about CFA4000. It's at the southern end of town along the main road.

Symbol of Unity has daily buses between Wum and Bamenda. It's possible to go in a loop from Wum to We (13km north) and from there south to Bamenda via **Fundong** and Belo. In Fundong, there's inexpensive accommodation at ***Tourist Home Hotel***. Guaranti Express usually has a minibus daily between Fundong and Bamenda.

Bafut About 20km north of Bamenda is the large Tikar community of Bafut, traditionally the most powerful of the Grassfields kingdoms. The **fon's palace** here is home to a 700-year-old dynasty and is a fascinating insight into traditional culture. Most (but not all) years in late December, Bafut residents hold a huge four-day end-of-year celebration with masks, costumes and traditional dancing and drumming. Bafut is also the place where the naturalist Gerald Durrell wrote *The Bafut Beagles*, an amusing account of his animal-collecting expedition here during the 1950s.

The palace compound *(admission CFA1000, camera fee CFA1500, museum*

CFA2000) consists of numerous buildings, including the houses of the fon's many wives (about 40 of whom are presently in-residence), and the sacred **Achum**, which is off-limits to everyone except the fon and his close advisors. In front of the palace compound are several stones marking the burial sites of nobles who died while serving the fon, as well as a larger stone where only the fon is permitted to offer libations (to petition the ancestors to keep evil spirits from entering the palace). Around the palace, you'll see carvings of the lion, python, elephant and buffalo, all of which are symbols of the fon, and special protectors. According to traditional belief, the fon can turn himself into these, and thus acquire their particular protective characteristics. The museum, though, is poorly organised, and not worth the price.

The only accommodation is at the outwardly imposing 100-year-old ***resthouse***, formerly Gerald Durrell's residence. It costs CFA2000 per person for a basic room with bucket bath, or to camp; meals can be arranged with lots of advance notice. About 5km from the palace along the Bamenda road is ***Savanna Botanic Gardens (Saboga)***, with adequate self-contained rooms for CFA5000.

Getting There & Away Shared taxis go throughout the day between Bamenda and Bafut (CFA300 to the palace, 30 minutes). Ask the driver to drop you at the palace at the far end of the village. There's more transport on market day (every eight days).

West Province

Cameroon's Francophone West Province is dominated by the Bamiléké people around Bafoussam. East of here is Foumban, centre of the Bamoun people and a country highlight, with its Royal Palace, museum, market and crafts.

BAFOUSSAM

Bafoussam is a bustling commercial town, centre of the Bamiléké people and a major coffee- and cocoa-producing area. There's little here of interest, except for the large **chefferie** (chief's compound), about 15km south at **Bandjoun** *(admission CFA2000, camera fee CFA1500)*. The chefferie's main building is a good example of traditional Bamiléké architecture, with its square base, tall, conical roof and carved pillars resembling totem poles. It's primarily used for meetings; the chief lives in the more modern-looking building next door. There's also a less-interesting chefferie in Bafoussam, just off the main road at the southern end of town.

Information

For changing cash or travellers cheques, try Bicec on the southern end of Av Wanko or SBC-Crédit Lyonnais, near Carrefour Total, along the Foumban road.

For Internet access, try L'Excellence.net at the main junction in the town centre.

Places to Stay

Hôtel Fédéral *(☎ 344 1309, Route de Foumban)* Rooms CFA8000-9000. Rooms here are clean and good value, with hot showers, toilet and TV. The only disadvantages are that many have no exterior window and those to the front are noisy. There's a bar and restaurant.

Hôtel Le Continental *(☎ 344 1458, Av de la République)* Rooms CFA8000-9500. The Continental is on the busy main road, with faded but adequate rooms, clean sheets, a restaurant and a bar.

Hôtel Le Président *(☎ 344 1136)* Rooms without/with TV CFA8000/12,000 (but negotiable). This place has seen better days, but it's not bad value if you negotiate the price – it may go down to about CFA5000 when it's quiet, which is almost always. It's in an unsigned multistorey building on the small street behind Bicec bank.

Le Manoir *(☎ 344 4909)* Rooms for nonresidents CFA30,000-60,000 (though often negotiable to resident rates, which are 50% less). Le Manoir is the best hotel in Bafoussam. Rooms are modern, comfortable and clean, and good value if you can manage to get resident rates.

There's also a restaurant here. It's signposted off the main road, diagonally opposite the Douala gare routière at the southern end of town.

Hôtel-Residence Saré *(☎/fax 344 2599)* Rooms CFA15,000, apartments CFA25,000. Accommodation here is in pleasant attached chalets, and there's a restaurant. It's at the northern end of town, signposted off the Bamenda road.

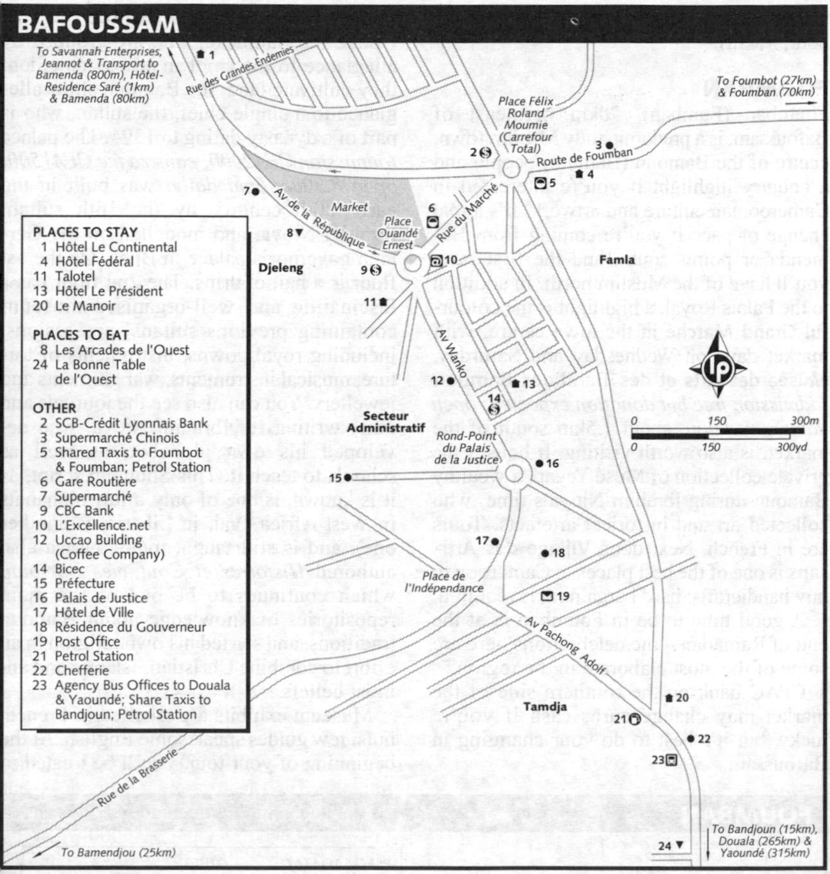
BAFOUSSAM
To Savannah Enterprises, Jeannot & Transport to Bamenda (800m), Hôtel-Residence Saré (1km) & Bamenda (80km)
Rue des Grandes Endemies
To Foumbot (27km) & Fouman (70km)
Place Félix Roland Moumie (Carrefour Total)
Route de Foumban
Av de la République
Market
Place Ouandé Ernest
Rue du Marché
Djeleng
Famla
Av Wanko
Secteur Administratif
Rond-Point du Palais de la Justice
Place de l'Indépendance
Av Pachong Adolf
Tamdja
Rue de la Brasserie
To Bamendjou (25km)
To Bandjoun (15km), Douala (265km) & Yaoundé (315km)
0 150 300m
0 150 300yd
PLACES TO STAY
1 Hôtel Le Continental
4 Hôtel Fédéral
11 Talotel
13 Hôtel Le Président
20 Le Manoir
PLACES TO EAT
8 Les Arcades de l'Ouest
24 La Bonne Table de l'Ouest
OTHER
2 SCB-Crédit Lyonnais Bank
3 Supermarché Chinois
5 Shared Taxis to Foumbot & Foumban; Petrol Station
6 Gare Routière
7 Supermarché
9 CBC Bank
10 L'Excellence.net
12 Uccao Building (Coffee Company)
14 Bicec
15 Préfecture
16 Palais de Justice
17 Hôtel de Ville
18 Résidence du Gouverneur
19 Post Office
21 Petrol Station
22 Chefferie
23 Agency Bus Offices to Douala & Yaoundé; Share Taxis to Bandjoun; Petrol Station

Places to Eat

There are plenty of ***food stalls*** and cheap ***cafés*** around Rue du Marché and Route de Foumban.

Les Arcades de l'Ouest opposite the market and just off Ave de la Républiqe, is the best place for cheap food, and it also has the cheapest beer in town (CFA350 for draught). There's live music on some Friday evenings.

La Bonne Table de l'Ouest *(☎ 344 1940)* Mains CFA1500-3000. This place, at the southern end of town along the main highway, is excellent value, with a pleasant atmosphere and local and Western cuisine.

Getting There & Away

Binam Voyages and other agency buses to Yaoundé (CFA3000) and Douala (CFA3500) have their offices at the southern end of town along the main road. Shared taxis to Bandjoun (CFA300) also leave from here throughout the day.

Savannah Enterprises, Jeannot and other agency buses to Bamenda have their offices on the Bamenda road, about 2km north of the centre. If you arrive from Bamenda and want to continue south, you'll need to take a taxi (CFA150) to the bus agency offices for Douala at the southern end of town.

Minibuses and shared taxis to Foumban depart from near the petrol station, just downhill from Carrefour Total. Agency vehicles doing this route include Butsis Voyages and Moungo Voyages. Most nonagency vehicles only go as far as Foumbot (CFA500, 30 minutes, 27km), where you'll need to change for Foumban (CFA500, one hour, 45km).

FOUMBAN

Foumban (Fumban), 70km northeast of Bafoussam, is a predominantly Muslim town, centre of the Bamoun (Bamum) people and a country highlight if you're interested in Cameroonian culture and artwork. It's a real change of pace if you're coming from Bamenda or points south, and the first taste you'll have of the Muslim north. In addition to the Palais Royal, a highlight is the colourful **Grand Marché** in the town centre, with market days on Wednesday and Saturday. **Musée des Arts et des Traditions Bamoun** *(admission free but donation expected; open 9am-5pm daily)*, about 1.5km south of the market, is also worth visiting. It houses the private collection of Mosé Yeyap, a wealthy Bamoun during Ibrahim Njoya's time, who collected art and historical artefacts. Tours are in French. Next door, **Village des Artisans** is one of the best places in Cameroon to buy handicrafts; hard bargaining is required.

A good time to be in Foumban is at the end of Ramadan – the celebrations here are some of the most elaborate in the region.

CPAC bank on the southern side of the market may change euros cash if you're lucky, but it's best to do your changing in Bafoussam.

Palais Royal (Royal Palace)

Unlike the Bamiléké, who are grouped by allegiance to the chief in whose chiefdom they cultivate land, the Bamoun show allegiance to a single chief, the sultan, who is part of a dynasty dating to 1394. The palace *(admission CFA2000; camera fee CFA1500; open 8.30am-6pm daily)* was built in the early 20th century by the 16th sultan, Ibrahim Njoya, and modelled on the German governor's palace in Buea. On the 1st floor is a hall of arms. The 2nd floor has a fascinating and well-organised **museum** containing previous sultans' possessions, including royal gowns, instruments of torture, musical instruments, war garments and jewellery. You can also see the journals and other writings of Ibrahim Njoya, who developed his own alphabet, as well as schools to teach it. This Shumom script, as it is known, is one of only a few alphabets in West Africa (Vai, in Liberia, is another one), and is still taught today. Njoya also authored *Histoires et Coutumes Bamoun*, which continues to be one of the main repositories of knowledge about Bamoun traditions, and started his own religion in an effort to combine Christian, Islamic and animist beliefs.

Museum exhibits are labelled in French, but a few guides speak some English. At the beginning of your tour, you'll be treated to

FOUMBAN

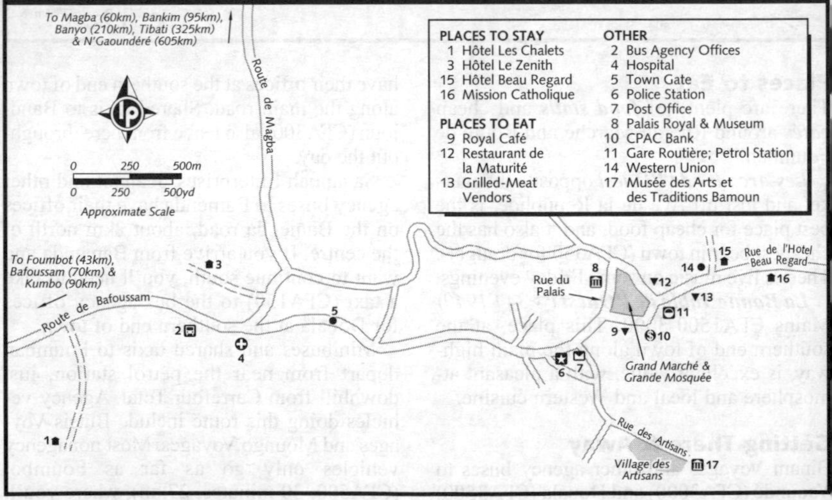
To Magba (60km), Bankim (95km), Banyo (210km), Tibati (325km) & N'Gaoundéré (605km)
Route de Magba
0 250 500m
0 250 500yd
Approximate Scale
To Foumbot (43km), Bafoussam (70km) & Kumbo (90km)
Route de Bafoussam
Rue du Palais
Rue de l'Hotel Beau Regard
Grand Marché & Grande Mosquée
Rue des Artisans
Village des Artisans
PLACES TO STAY
1 Hôtel Les Chalets
3 Hôtel Le Zenith
15 Hôtel Beau Regard
16 Mission Catholique
PLACES TO EAT
9 Royal Café
12 Restaurant de la Maturité
13 Grilled-Meat Vendors
OTHER
2 Bus Agency Offices
4 Hospital
5 Town Gate
6 Police Station
7 Post Office
8 Palais Royal & Museum
10 CPAC Bank
11 Gare Routière; Petrol Station
14 Western Union
17 Musée des Arts et des Traditions Bamoun

a demonstration of traditional musical instruments, which you'll then be encouraged to buy. Just outside the palace are a few artisan stalls, but it's better to shop at Village des Artisans at the southern end of town.

Places to Stay & Eat

Despite its cultural and historical interest, Foumban is not geared up for tourism (except for the craft vendors) and there is only a limited choice of accommodation.

Mission Catholique *(Rue de l'Hotel Beau Regard)* Dorm beds for a donation (CFA500 to CFA1000). Rooms here are decidedly grubby and there's no running water, but the location is convenient. It's a few blocks east of the market.

Hôtel Beau Regard *(☎ 348 2183)* Rooms without/with bathroom CFA4180/5225. Beau Regard, diagonally opposite the mission, has tolerable rooms, most of which open onto a shared balcony. There's a bar and nightclub but no restaurant.

Hôtel Les Chalets *(☎ 348 2412)* Rooms CFA8000. Rooms here are quieter and somewhat more appealing than those at the Beau Regard, but it's inconveniently located about 3km west of town, and 500m south of the main road (look for a faded signboard).

Hôtel Le Zenith *(☎ 348 2425)* Rooms with 1 double bed without/with TV CFA6000/7500. Better rooms with 2 beds CFA12,000. Standards here are similar to those at Les Chalets – adequate, but nothing special. The turn-off is signposted opposite the bus agency offices at the entrance to town.

The area just east of the gare routière is good for grilled meat and other street food.

Royal Café, on the southern side of the Grand Marché, has good meals from CFA2000 and a patio with views. It's down a flight of steps and is easy to miss; look for the white building and red signboard.

Restaurant de la Maturité, opposite the gare routière at the eastern end of the market, is cheaper than the Royal, with good avocado salads and omelettes.

Getting There & Away

All agencies to Bafoussam (CFA1000) have their offices on the main road at the entrance to town, west of the town gate and about 2km from the market. Shared taxis to the town centre cost CFA100. Moungo Voyages and Butsis Voyage have a few daily direct departures to Yaoundé (CFA3000, 382km) and Douala (CFA3500, 266km); otherwise you'll need to change vehicles in Bafoussam. Nonagency transport departs from the gare routière near the market.

During the dry season, there's transport between Foumban and Kumbo (at least six hours), which is a rough but interesting option if you want to combine the Ring Road area with Foumban.

It's also possible during the dry season to find vehicles going northeast to Banyo, from where you can continue to N'Gaoundéré via Tibati; you should allow several days for this journey.

Northern Cameroon

Northern Cameroon (consisting of North and Extreme North provinces) is an area of barren rocky outcrops, picturesque villages and striking beauty. It's also where you'll find most of Cameroon's Muslim population, especially in N'Gaoundéré, Garoua and Maroua. In the far north, in the mountainous areas bordering Nigeria, are animist peoples known collectively as 'Kirdi' (Fulani for 'pagan') who live in compounds clinging to terraced hillsides, where they cultivate millet and other crops. For tourists, the north is one of Cameroon's most-popular destinations and highly rewarding if you're able to get off the beaten track.

N'GAOUNDÉRÉ

Cool, leafy N'Gaoundéré is the terminus of Cameroon's main railway line and the first major town in northern Cameroon. It is at 1100m and makes a relaxing stop. Don't miss the **Palais du Lamido** *(admission CFA2000, plus CFA1000 per guide & CFA1000 photo fee)*, near the market, where the local chief resides with his numerous wives. The exterior isn't interesting, but some of the traditional buildings inside are. Next door is the **Grande Mosquée**. Among other things at the Palais, you can see where the Lamido holds court and conducts marriages, and where the royal barber plies his trade (the present Lamido apparently follows a rigorous twice weekly barbering routine). Friday (especially) and Sunday are the

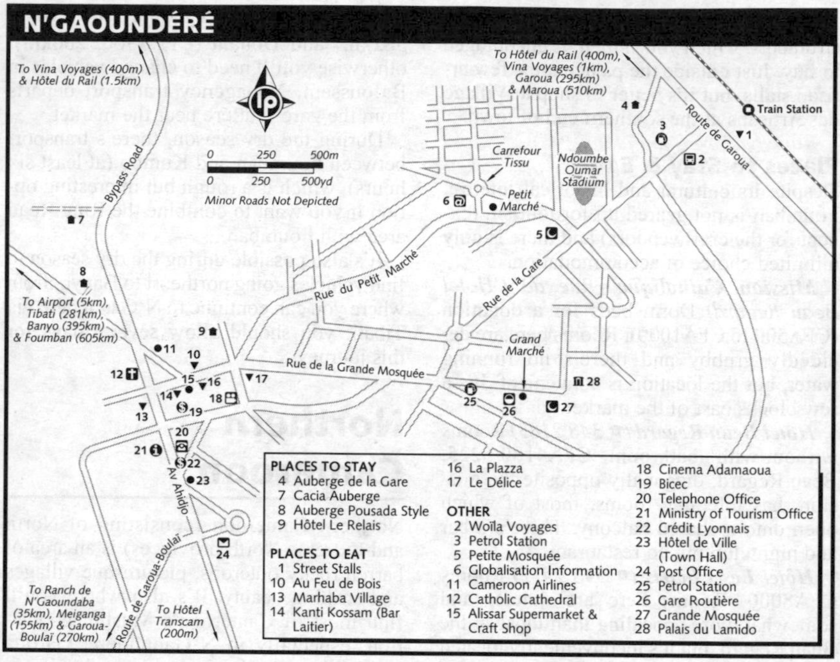
N'GAOUNDÉRÉ
To Vina Voyages (400m) & Hôtel du Rail (1.5km)
To Hôtel du Rail (400m), Vina Voyages (1km), Garoua (295km) & Maroua (510km)
Train Station
Route de Garoua
0 250 500m
0 250 500yd
Minor Roads Not Depicted
Bypass Road
Carrefour Tissu
Ndoumbe Oumar Stadium
Petit Marché
Rue du Petit Marché
Rue de la Gare
To Airport (5km), Tibati (281km), Banyo (395km) & Foumban (605km)
Grand Marché
Rue de la Grande Mosquée
Av Ahidjo
Route de Garoua-Boulaï
To Ranch de N'Gaoundaba (35km), Meiganga (155km) & Garoua-Boulaï (270km)
To Hôtel Transcam (200m)
PLACES TO STAY
4 Auberge de la Gare
7 Cacia Auberge
8 Auberge Pousada Style
9 Hôtel Le Relais
PLACES TO EAT
1 Street Stalls
10 Au Feu de Bois
13 Marhaba Village
14 Kanti Kossam (Bar Laitier)
16 La Plazza
17 Le Délice
OTHER
2 Woïla Voyages
3 Petrol Station
5 Petite Mosquée
6 Globalisation Information
11 Cameroon Airlines
12 Catholic Cathedral
15 Alissar Supermarket & Craft Shop
18 Cinema Adamaoua
19 Bicec
20 Telephone Office
21 Ministry of Tourism Office
22 Crédit Lyonnais
23 Hôtel de Ville (Town Hall)
24 Post Office
25 Petrol Station
26 Gare Routière
27 Grande Mosquée
28 Palais du Lamido

best days to visit, as you'll be able to see many nobles from the surrounding area who come to pay their respects.

Information

The Ministry of Tourism on Av Ahidjo is worth visiting for information on the surrounding area.

For Internet access try Globalisation Information on Carrefour Tissu. It costs CFA400 per minute, or CFA1500 per 30 minutes with a group (to divide the cost of the line). Bicec and Crédit Lyonnais, in the town centre, change cash and travellers cheques.

For reasonably priced, quality crafts, try the shop next to Alissar supermarket. For textiles, go to Carrefour Tissu.

Some areas of N'Gaoundéré are dangerous at night, particularly north of the stadium. Locals advise never to walk around after dark; moto-taxis anywhere cost CFA100.

Places to Stay

Auberge de la Gare *(☎ 225 2217)* Rooms CFA5000. Rooms here are tolerable, with fan and bathroom, and it's convenient to the train station.

Auberge Pousada Style *(☎ 225 1703)* Small/large rooms CFA4000/5000. The rooms at Auberge Pousada are similar to those at Auberge de la Gare, and with marginally better ambience. It's about 500m northwest of the cathedral, just off the main road.

Cacia Auberge Rooms CFA6000. Quiet Cacia Auberge is off the bypass road and a 15-minute walk from the town centre. It promises 'tranquillity, security and comfort, but no prostitution'. There's no food.

Hôtel Le Relais *(☎ 225 1138)* Rooms without/with TV CFA10,000/12,000. Le Relais, near the intersection of Rue du Petit Marché and Rue de la Grande Mosquée, has clean self-contained rooms and a restaurant.

Hôtel du Rail *(☎ 225 1013)* Rooms CFA9500/10,685 without/with TV. Staff here are friendly and the self-contained rooms are not bad at all, though we tripped over some bird-size cockroaches when checking things out. There's also a restaurant. It's convenient for the train station, but isolated from the rest of town.

Hôtel Transcam *(☎ 225 1252)* Rooms CFA24,000. This is N'Gaoundéré's best hotel, with comfortable self-contained rooms and a pricey restaurant. It's in a quiet setting 1.5km southwest of the centre.

Ranch de N'Gaoundaba *(☎ 225 2469, 999 3468, or book at Alissar supermarket)* Singles/doubles CFA9000/12,000, apartments CFA20,000. For a change of pace, try this old stone hunting lodge 35km southeast of N'Gaoundéré off the Meiganga road. Accommodation is in boukarous overlooking a crater lake. Breakfast/dinner costs CFA1500/4500, and camping can be arranged. Using public transport, you'll need to walk several kilometres from the main road to the ranch, and will probably have a long wait for transport back to N'Gaoundéré. Call before coming to be sure it's open.

Places to Eat

Cheap food is available from ***street stalls*** in the train station forecourt, around the Grand Marché and near the western end of Rue de la Grande Mosquée.

The friendly ***Le Délice***, off the western end of Rue de la Grande Mosquée, has meals for about CFA1500.

Marhaba Village at the cathedral junction has tables in an enclosed area off the street, and good grilled fish.

Au Feu de Bois, just east and down the road from Marhaba Village, has Cameroonian dishes from CFA1200. Just opposite, the popular ***La Plazza*** has good-value dining and outdoor tables. Meals cost from CFA3000 and there's a Sunday buffet (CFA5500).

Diagonally across the street is ***Kanti Kossam (Bar Laitier)***, with inexpensive snacks, and good *dakkéré*, a local yogurt and rice concoction.

Alissar supermarket is well-stocked. The main market is the Petit Marché; the Grand Marché only sells vegetables.

Getting There & Away

Air Camair has flights most days connecting N'Gaoundéré with Garoua, Maroua, Yaoundé and Douala. The airport is situated about 4km west of town (CFA1000 in a taxi).

Train The train is the best budget option if you're heading to Yaoundé, or to eastern Cameroon via Bélabo; see the main Getting Around section of this chapter for details.

Bus For Garoua (CFA3000, five hours, 296km) and Maroua (CFA5000, eight hours, 508km), Woïla Voyages is best, with several buses daily from about 6.30am; its office is near the train station.

To Garoua-Boulaï (CFA4000, 10 hours, 270km), there's at least one bus daily. There are also buses several times weekly (currently Saturday, Sunday and Tuesday) for Bertoua (CFA8000, 530km). Agency buses here are constantly changing, so get an update. Clandos on this route depart from the gare routière near the Grande Mosquée, but aren't recommended.

It's possible to go by road to Foumban via Tibati and Banyo, but the route is rough and seldom travelled, and you'll need to change vehicles several times; allow at least three days. There are sporadic departures towards Tibati from the main gare routière. The route from N'Gaoundéré to Yaoundé via Yoko is rarely used.

Getting Around

N'Gaoundéré is spread out, with the train station about 3km from the town centre. Moto-taxis are the main way of getting around (CFA100) and there are a few taxis.

Vina Voyages (☎ 225 2525) on the northwestern side of town rents vehicles.

GAROUA

pop 293,000

There's little of interest for tourists in Garoua, but it's a prosperous town, commercial hub of the north, and a convenient stop along the N'Gaoundéré-Maroua road. Garoua was former president Ahidjo's home town, which explains in part the modern buildings and large airport. The once-busy port is now only a shadow of its former self, and closes completely during the dry season.

For crafts, ask around for the Alliance Franco-Camerounais cooperative. On Saturday, there's a lively market.

Information

The Ministry of Tourism (☎ 227 1364) off Rue des Banques can help with information and accommodation for the parks.

Bicec and Crédit Lyonnais, both on Rue des Banques, change travellers cheques.

For car rental or organised tours, including to Parc National de la Bénoué or Parc National de Bouba Ndjida, try:

Norga Voyages (☎ 227 2617) at the southern end of town, near Cinéma Étoile
Lasal Voyages (☎ 227 2137) Rue des Banques

Places to Stay & Eat

Auberge Hiala Village *(☎ 227 2407)* Rooms CFA5000-7000. Near the port, it has decent self-contained rooms, and is arguably the best value in the budget range. There's off-street parking, and a good bar and restaurant.

Auberge de la Cité *(☎ 272493, Rue du Petit Marché)* Doubles with bathroom & fan/air-con CFA5000/7000. This auberge is probably the next best bet, though most locals will just shake their heads if you tell them you're staying here. Food is available.

Relais St-Hubert *(☎ 227 3033, Rue du Novotel)* Small/large boukarous CFA18,000/23,000, room in the 'Grand Bâtiment' CFA25,000. Rooms – all with one double bed – are either in pleasant boukarous or standard hotel-style, and there's a restaurant. Pool use is free for nonguests if you buy a drink. It's just north of the town centre.

Hôtel Bénoué *(☎/fax 227 1553, Rue du Novotel)* Twin/double rooms CFA18,000/25,000. The Bénoué, just up the road from Relais St-Hubert, has similar standards, although the rooms aren't quite as nice. Most have one double bed, shower and bath; a few have two twin beds and a shower. There's also a restaurant.

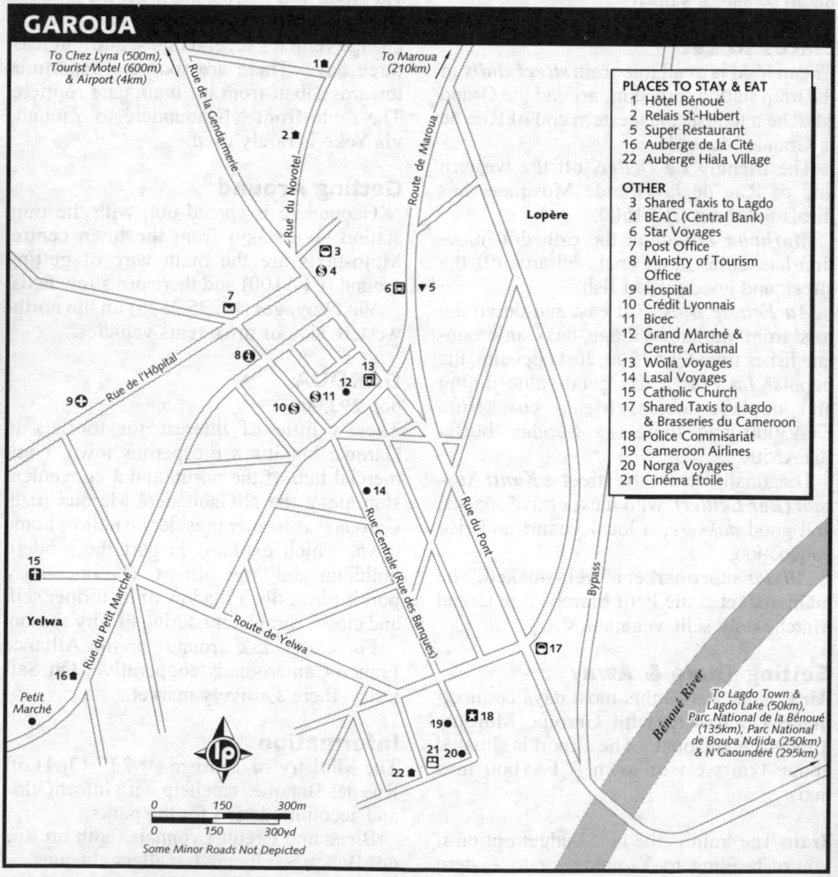
GAROUA
To Chez Lyna (500m), Tourist Motel (600m) & Airport (4km)
To Maroua (210km)
Rue de la Gendarmerie
Rue du Novotel
Route de Maroua
Lopère
Rue de l'Hôpital
Rue Centrale (Rue des Banques)
Rue du Pont
Bypass
Rue du Petit Marché
Route de Yelwa
Yelwa
Petit Marché
Bénoué River
To Lagdo Town & Lagdo Lake (50km), Parc National de la Bénoué (135km), Parc National de Bouba Ndjida (250km) & N'Gaoundéré (295km)
0 150 300m
0 150 300yd
Some Minor Roads Not Depicted
PLACES TO STAY & EAT
1 Hôtel Bénoué
2 Relais St-Hubert
5 Super Restaurant
16 Auberge de la Cité
22 Auberge Hiala Village
OTHER
3 Shared Taxis to Lagdo
4 BEAC (Central Bank)
6 Star Voyages
7 Post Office
8 Ministry of Tourism Office
9 Hospital
10 Crédit Lyonnais
11 Bicec
12 Grand Marché & Centre Artisanal
13 Woïla Voyages
14 Lasal Voyages
15 Catholic Church
17 Shared Taxis to Lagdo & Brasseries du Cameroon
18 Police Commisariat
19 Cameroon Airlines
20 Norga Voyages
21 Cinéma Étoile

Tourist Motel *(☎ 227 3244)* Rooms CFA25,000. This place has reasonably comfortable rooms, prices are often negotiable, and there's a pool. It's about 1.5km northwest of the centre.

Super Restaurant *(Route de Maroua)* is a breezy place with good juices (ask them to use bottled water) and large servings. For inexpensive local food, try ***Chez Lyna*** on Garoua's northern edge.

Getting There & Away

Camair flights connect Garoua with Douala and Yaoundé almost daily, and with N'Gaoundéré and Maroua several times weekly, sometimes via N'Djaména (Chad). The airport is 5km northwest of the centre.

Woïla Voyages has several buses daily to Maroua and N'Gaoundéré, departing from its office near the market.

Shared taxis to Lagdo depart from diagonally opposite Relais St-Hubert (behind BEAC and at the southern exit of town near Brasseries du Cameroon.

Moto-taxis are the main way to get around town.

AROUND GAROUA

At Lagdo Lake, 50km southeast of Garoua, you can enjoy a splurge at ***Lagon Bleu*** *(☎ 985 5353 or book at CDG Supermarché in Maroua)*. Lakeside boukarous (all triples) are CFA20,000/25,000 with fan/air-con. There's a restaurant (about CFA12,000 extra for full board) and swimming; locals claim the waters here are bilharzia-free.

Shared taxis to Lagdo town depart Garoua several times daily (CFA1000, one hour). Lagon Bleu is about 1km further on in Djibordé (CFA200 by moto-taxi).

PARC NATIONAL DE LA BÉNOUÉ & PARC NATIONAL DE BOUBA NDJIDA

These parks are primarily for hunting. Bénoué is also popular with anglers. Permits for both can be arranged with the Ministry of Tourism in Garoua. Parc National de Waza is much better for observing wildlife.

The Ministry of Tourism or travel agencies in Garoua can help organise trips and book accommodation. Entry to each park costs CFA5000, but fees are not being collected currently. Guides (obligatory) cost CFA3000 per day.

In Bénoué, ***Campement Grand Capitaine*** is a popular base for anglers. Boukarou-style accommodation costs CFA15,000 per room. Otherwise try the more rundown and somewhat cheaper ***Campement du Bufflé Noir***.

In Bouba Ndjida, there's a faded ***campement*** in the park centre. For both parks, you'll need to be self-sufficient with food and water, and you'll need your own 4WD.

MAROUA

pop 214,000

Maroua, Cameroon's northernmost major town, is popular with travellers and a good starting point for exploring the nearby Mandara Mountains. It has a lively **market**, especially on Monday when people from the surrounding region converge here to sell their wares. At the end of the market is the **Centre Artisanal**, with leatherwork and other crafts. Next door is **Musée d'Art Local de Diamaré** *(admission CFA500; open 9am-6pm daily)*. It's small and cluttered, but has a few interesting pieces.

Information

Bicec and Crédit Lyonnais change cash and travellers cheques.

You can send and receive emails on the 1st floor of the building opposite the Mobil petrol station just north of Pont de Founangué (CFA2000 per hour).

For medical emergencies, try Meskine Hospital, southwest of town off Garoua road.

Maroua has numerous tour operators who can arrange excursions to surrounding villages, trekking, and visits to Parc National de Waza. These include:

Extreme Nord Safaris (☎/fax 229 3356) BP 508, Maroua
Fagus Voyage (☎ 986 1871, e fagusvoyages@cameroun_online.com, w www.fagusvoyages.com)
Jean-Remy Zra Teri (☎ 229 2623, 229 2551)
Porte Mayo Voyages (☎ 984 1573, 870-761 856 569) through Relais de la Porte Mayo (see Places to Stay)

Hôtel Maroua Palace and (cheaper) Mizao Novotel also offer vehicle rental; see Places to Stay for contact details.

Places to Stay – Budget

Mission Catholique Djarengol Rooms CFA2500. Rooms here are clean and decent

CAMEROON

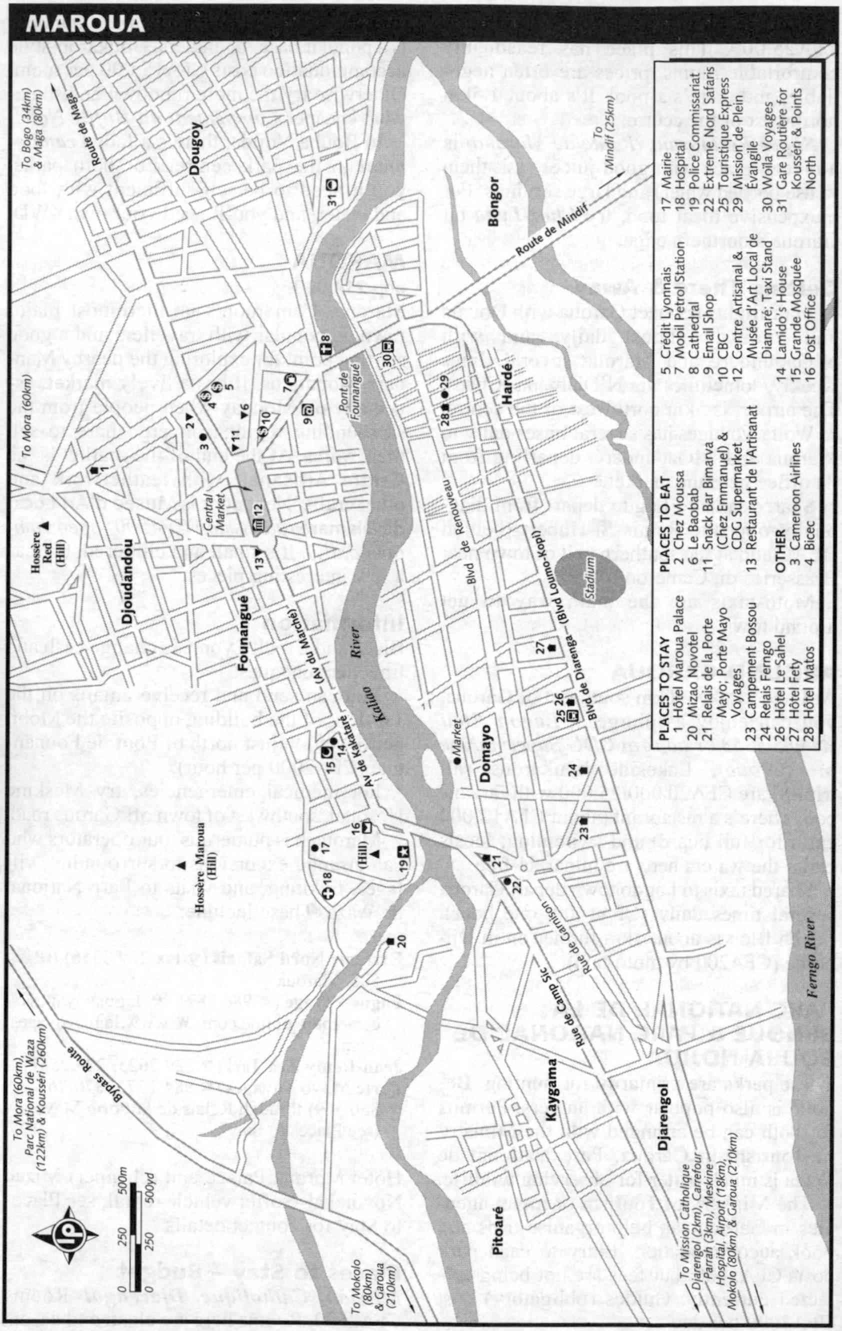
MAROUA
PLACES TO STAY
1 Hôtel Maroua Palace
20 Mizao Novotel
21 Relais de la Porte Mayo; Porte Mayo Voyages
23 Campement Bossou
24 Relais Ferngo
26 Hôtel Le Sahel
27 Hôtel Fety
28 Hôtel Matos
PLACES TO EAT
2 Chez Moussa
6 Le Baobab
11 Snack Bar Bimarva (Chez Emmanuel) & CDG Supermarket
13 Restaurant de l'Artisanat
OTHER
3 Cameroon Airlines
4 Bicec
5 Crédit Lyonnais
7 Mobil Petrol Station
8 Cathedral
9 Email Shop
10 CBC
12 Centre Artisanal & Musée d'Art Local de Diamaré; Taxi Stand
14 Lamido's House
15 Grande Mosquée
16 Post Office
17 Mairie
18 Hospital
19 Police Commissariat
22 Extreme Nord Safaris
25 Touristique Express
29 Mission de Plein Évangile
30 Woïla Voyages
31 Gare Routière for Kousséri & Points North
To Bogo (34km) & Maga (80km)
Route de Maga
To Mora (60km)
Dougoy
Hossère Red (Hill)
Djoudandou
Central Market
Fouangué
Pont de Founangué
To Mindif (25km)
Route de Mindif
Bongor
Hardé
Blvd de Renouveau
Blvd Loumo-Kopi
Blvd de Diarenga
Stadium
Kaliao River
(Av du Marché)
Av de Kakataré
Market
Domayo
Hossère Maroua (Hill)
(Hill)
Rue de Garnison
Rue de Camp Sic
Pitoaré
Kaygama
Djarengol
Ferngo River
Bypass Route
To Mora (60km), Parc National de Waza (122km) & Kousséri (260km)
To Mokolo (80km) & Garoua (210km)
To Mission Catholique Djarengol (2km), Carrefour Parrah (3km), Meskine Hospital, Airport (18km), Mokolo (80km) & Garoua (210km)
0 250 500m
0 250 500yd

CAMEROON

value, with shower and shared toilet. The main disadvantage is that it's about 4km south of the centre (along the Garoua road).

Campement Bossou Rooms CFA2480. The usually empty Campement Bossou, off Blvd de Diarenga, is closer, with basic boukarou-style rooms, bucket showers and shared toilets.

Relais Ferngo *(☎ 229 2153)* Camping CFA1000 per person, rooms CFA6000. Relais Ferngo, under the same management as Relais de la Porte Mayo, is a small step up. Accommodation is in spartan boukarous with cold-water shower and toilet. There's no food.

Hôtel Matos *(☎ 229 2913)* Rooms CFA6500. Matos is good value, with clean self-contained rooms and a small garden. It's off Blvd de Renouveau in Quartier Hardé, opposite Mission de Plein Évangile, and signposted. There's no food.

Hôtel Fety *(☎ 229 2913, Blvd de Diarenga)* Rooms CFA6500. Fety, under the same management as Hôtel Matos, is also good. Rooms are clean, with air-con and hot water. Persons of the same sex sharing a room pay CFA7750.

Places to Stay – Mid-Range & Top End

Relais de la Porte Mayo *(☎ 229 2692, fax 870-761 856 571)* Singles/twins CFA12,000/14,000. Porte Mayo is the town's most-popular hotel, and the only place that can be described as 'happening'. Accommodation is in simple, but very comfortable, air-con boukarous with bathroom and hot showers. There's a restaurant, an outdoor bar and a small craft shop.

Hôtel Le Sahel *(☎ 229 2960, Blvd de Diarenga)* Singles/doubles CFA13,800/17,990, suites CFA25,000. Le Sahel has small but clean rooms and a restaurant. It's next to Touristique Voyages.

Hôtel Maroua Palace *(☎ 229 3164, fax 229 1525)* Singles/doubles CFA20,000/22,000, suites CFA34,000. Located north of the market, this is the most upscale option in town. Rooms are sterile but fine and there's a pool (CFA1400 for nonguests), restaurant and travel agency.

Mizao Novotel *(☎ 983 2609)* Singles/doubles CFA22,000/27,000, apartments CFA37,600. Rooms here are faded but OK. However, the location, on a small side road just southwest of the hospital, is isolated unless you have your own vehicle. The clean pool costs CFA1500 for nonguests.

Places to Eat

Restaurant de l'Artisanat, opposite the main market entrance, has good meals from CFA1000, and yogurt.

Next to Cameroon Airlines, ***Chez Moussa*** is also good, especially for brochettes (CFA100) and juices (ask them to leave out the ice and use bottled water).

The popular ***Snack Bar Bimarva (Chez Emmanuel)***, next to CDG supermarket, is a step up, and has outdoor tables. It has good-value meals from CFA2000.

Restaurant Le Baobab, just down the road, has outdoor seating, good atmosphere and good food from CFA2000 (CFA4000 for the set menu). It's open from 7am to 11pm daily.

For upscale dining, ***Relais de la Porte Mayo*** (see Places to Stay) is the best option, though pricey. Main dishes cost from CFA4500; there's a less-expensive sandwich menu at the bar.

Getting There & Away

Air Camair (☎ 229 2019) has flights five times weekly to N'Gaoundéré, Yaoundé and Douala, sometimes via N'Djaména (Chad) or Garoua. The airport is 20km south of town along the Garoua road (CFA3000 in a chartered taxi).

Bus Woïla Voyages and Touristique Express are best for Garoua and N'Gaoundéré, with several buses daily; most departures are in the mornings, from about 6am. Woïla Voyages is just south of Pont de Founangué; Touristique is on Blvd de Diarenga. Nonagency transport south, and transport to Mokolo and Rhumsiki, departs from Carrefour Parrah in Djarangol at the southern end of town.

Transport north towards Kousséri departs from the gare routière on Maroua's eastern edge.

Getting Around

Maroua has a few taxis. They park at the market's western end. The main way of getting around is moto-taxi (CFA100 daytime, CFA150 night-time, extra for more-distant destinations).

CAMEROON

AROUND MAROUA

The area around Maroua is one of the most enjoyable places in Cameroon – rich in tribal culture, natural wonders and beautiful scenery. There are many fascinating villages and markets including **Rhumsiki** (striking mountain scenery); **Djingliya**, **Koza** and **Mabas** (all in picturesque settings near steep, terraced hillsides); **Oudjilla** (which has a traditional chief's compound); **Tourou**, known for the calabash hats worn by local women; and **Maga**, with its unique domed houses made entirely of clay. The Mandara Mountains themselves, which begin southwest of Mokolo, offer some excellent trekking.

Although Rhumsiki and some other villages here have become something of a tourist trap, tourist numbers in Cameroon are relatively low, so it's not all *that* bad. That said, it's not particularly rewarding for you or locals to be trotted from one village attraction to the next knowing the show will just continue when you leave. It's much better to linger longer, take the time to learn about the culture and explore off the beaten path.

There is accommodation in Waza, Maga, Rhumsiki, Mokolo, Mora and a few other villages, but otherwise, no infrastructure. Roads are rough and public transport infrequent, so if you're travelling independently allow plenty of time and plan to be self-sufficient with food and water. Moto-taxis are sometimes the only option for getting around. For those with limited time, travel agencies in Maroua can organise visits. Most charge CFA25,000 to CFA35,000 per day plus petrol for a vehicle with driver. One popular circuit goes from Maroua to Mora (with possible detours to Parc National de Waza and to Oudjilla), and then southwest via Koza, Djingliya and Mokolo to Rhumsiki, finishing in Maroua.

There's nowhere to change money outside Maroua. Petrol is available in Maroua and Mokolo. During the rainy season, when petrol supplies sometimes run short, expect public transport prices to rise.

Mokolo

Mokolo, centre of the Mafa people, is about 80km west of Maroua along a tarmac road. It's of little interest, but you'll probably pass through en route to other destinations.

Le Flamboyant Singles/doubles CFA8000/10,000, with air-con CFA11,000/13,000. This is the most comfortable place in town, with clean, self-contained rooms and a restaurant. It's just off the main road in the town centre.

Metcheme Bar Rooms about CFA2500. This bar has some grubby rooms in an annex with shared bathroom. Staff quote CFA5000, but it's usually negotiable to about half that.

If neither of these places suit, try the ***Catholic Mission*** at the northwestern edge of town, up past the market. It has simple rooms that are sometimes let to travellers for a donation.

Café Fait-Tous, just north of the main road at the entrance to town, has meals for about CFA1000. For something fancier, head to Le Flamboyant.

Getting There & Away Most transport departs from the market, in the town centre. Minibuses go frequently to Maroua (CFA1000, one hour), and at least once daily to Koza (CFA1500). Except on market day (Wednesday), when vehicles come into town, Rhumsiki transport departs from 'Tasha Haman Gaowa' at Mokolo's western end, where the tarmac road ends. You may be told by moto-taxi drivers in Mokolo that there are no vehicles to Rhumsiki, but this is only sometimes true.

Rhumsiki

Rhumsiki is on all the tourist itineraries and is definitely over-run. However, the surrounding countryside is beautiful and it's easy to leave Rhumsiki quickly behind and set out for more unspoiled areas on foot. Plus, if you've been in other areas of the north that have no infrastructure, Rhumsiki's modest amenities can be a nice change. Rising up from the valley just before the village is the much-photographed Rhumsiki Peak.

Rates for hikes start at about CFA8500 per day, including simple meals, accommodation in local homes, camping (with your own tent or on mats in the open) and a guide.

Most routes are between half a day and four days, and some cross into Nigeria, just 3km away; no visa is necessary, as long as you don't continue further into the country. Treks with horses can also be organised.

Places to Stay & Eat Except as noted, all places are along the main road, listed here

CAMEROON

in the order you reach them when arriving from Mokolo. All arrange trekking.

Kirdi Bar (BP 62, Mokolo) Camping CFA500 per person, rooms CFA1500 per person. Kirdi Bar is the best choice if you're on a shoestring budget. There's accommodation in no-frills boukarous with bucket baths, and meals for about CFA2500, including pizzas and excellent home-made bread. The English-speaking proprietor is knowledgeable about the surrounding area, makes every effort to please and organises reasonably priced treks (CFA8500 per person per day all-inclusive) and moto rental (CFA5000 per day plus petrol, with or without driver). It's at the town entrance, to the left of the road.

Campement de Rhumsiki (BP27, Mokolo) Singles/doubles/triples CFA7000/12,000/14,000. This is one of the more upscale options, with good views from the terrace, comfortable air-con boukarous with hot water, and a restaurant with meals for about CFA4000.

Auberge Le Kapsiki (La Casserole; ☎/fax 229 3356, ☎ 990 1878) Rooms with double bed & shower CFA5000, with double bed plus twin bed & bathroom CFA7500. Accommodation here is in spartan but adequate boukarous, and there's a good restaurant with meals costing from about CFA2500. The friendly English-speaking owner is experienced in organising treks in the surrounding area (CFA12,500 per person per day, or CFA10,000 if in a group or for multiday hikes; CFA20,000 per day for horse trekking).

Auberge Le Petit Paris Singles or doubles CFA8500, triple CFA12,000. Le Petit Paris, opposite La Casserole, is a new place with clean boukarou-style accommodation and a restaurant.

La Maison de l'Amitié (book through Lara Voyage in Maroua, ☎/fax 229 2113) Rooms CFA7500. This place is also new, with comfortable, modern boukarous and a restaurant. Trekking costs from about CFA15,000 per day plus food. It's at the far end of town, about 150m off the main road.

Getting There & Away Transport to/from Rhumsiki is best on Sunday, Monday and Wednesday. On Sunday, vehicles depart Mokolo about 6am for Rhumsiki, returning about 2pm. Vehicles depart Rhumsiki about 5.30am to 6am on Monday for Maroua (CFA3000) and on Wednesday for Mokolo (CFA1500), returning about 3pm. Travelling from Rhumsiki, it's best to reserve a seat the night before; if you miss the last vehicle out (usually departing by 2pm), you'll be stuck for the evening.

During the rest of the week, things are more sporadic, and it may take two days to get between Maroua and Rhumsiki, although there's usually at least one vehicle in each direction at least as far as Mokolo. Moto-taxis from Mokolo cost about CFA3000, though it's a long 50km on the back of a moto.

Tourou

Tourou is a quiet village in a picturesque setting, known primarily for the calabash hats worn by the local women. The designs on the hats often contain information such as whether the wearer is married or not, or whether she has children. The road from Tourou to Rhumsiki via Mabas isn't currently passable, and there are no vehicles between Tourou and Koza; the main way to reach Tourou is via Mokolo.

Djingliya & Koza

Djingliya, 15km north of Mokolo, is a tiny village perched on a hill with good views over the surrounding terraced countryside. ***Société Cooperative Artisanale de Djingliya*** *(BP 94, Mokolo)* sells local crafts and offers basic rooms with bucket bath for CFA3000; meals can be arranged, but you'll need to bring drinking water. Ask the caretaker for a

Market Day

Getting to/from villages in northern Cameroon (and elsewhere) via public transport is always easier on market day, as there are many more vehicles. Some local market days are as follows:

town	market day
Bogo	Thursday
Koza	Sunday
Maroua	Monday
Mogodé (north of Rhumsiki)	Friday
Mokolo	Wednesday
Mora	Sunday
Pouss (northeast of Maga)	Tuesday
Rhumsiki	Sunday
Tourou	Thursday

tour of a typical local housing compound. Vehicles between Mokolo and Koza will drop you, or take a moto-taxi from Mokolo.

Koza, 4km further north, marks the end of the scenic uphill route from Mokolo; from here to Mora, the terrain levels out. There's nowhere to sleep, but several places to eat.

There's at least one vehicle daily in each direction between Koza and Mokolo. On Monday there's also a vehicle direct to Maroua, departing Koza about 7am, and returning in the afternoon.

Mora

Mora, capital of the Wandala (Mandara) people, is situated 60km northwest of Maroua on the main road. It's known mainly for its Sunday market that attracts people from the surrounding area. About 11km west is **Oudjilla**, a touristy Podoko village. Apart from the scenery, the main attraction is the compound *(saré)* of the village chief and his many wives. To visit, and perhaps see a dance performance, costs CFA2000 to CFA3000. There's nowhere to sleep in Oudjilla.

Auberge Mora Massif Camping CFA1000 per person, rooms CFA3000. This is the best place in Mora, with clean boukarous and some less-appealing rooms. It's possible to camp in the compound, and meals can be arranged. It's 400m west of the main junction.

Campement Sanga de Podoko Rooms CFA4000. Campement Podoko has acceptable rooms with clean sheets. There's a bar and TV, and meals are available. It's signposted just east of the main road.

Minibuses go daily between Mora and Maroua. The main way to reach Oudjilla is by moto-taxi.

PARC NATIONAL DE WAZA

Waza *(admission CFA5000, plus CFA2000 per vehicle, camera fee CFA2000; open 6am-6pm daily)* is the most accessible of Cameroon's national parks and the best for viewing wildlife. While it can't compare with East African parks, you're likely to see elephants, hippos, giraffes, antelopes, many birds and – with luck – lions. Late March to April is the best time for viewing, as the animals congregate at water holes before the rains. Between about May and October, rains make some sections of the park inaccessible.

A guide (CFA3000) is obligatory in each vehicle. Walking isn't permitted.

Places to Stay

Waza can easily be done as a day trip from Maroua if you start early (bring a packed lunch). Otherwise, there are three places to stay near the park entrance.

Campement de Waza *(☎ 229 1646, 229 1165 in Maroua or 765 7717, 765 7558 in Waza)* Singles/doubles with air-con CFA14,800/16,000, room without air-con CFA12,500. This is the most luxurious option, with accommodation in reasonably comfortable boukarous. It's on a small hill about 700m from the park entrance, on the opposite side of the main road. Breakfast/picnic/dinner costs CFA2000/5000/6000.

Centre d'Accueil de Waza Camping per person including shower & toilet use CFA2500, rooms CFA7000. This simple place at the park entrance has accommodation in no-frills two-person boukarous with shared toilet facilities. Meals can be arranged (CFA2000) and it has a small kitchen.

GIC-FAC Café-Restaurant du IIme Millénaire The local women's group has a few very simple rooms that shouldn't cost more than about CFA4000, though no-one was around to tell us the price when we visited. Meals can be arranged. It's just off the main road along the park access road.

There's also basic ***accommodation*** in Waza village, just north of the park entrance.

Getting There & Away

The park entrance is signposted and about 400m off the main highway. Unless you have your own vehicle, the best way to visit is to hire a vehicle in Maroua (about CFA30,000 per day plus about CFA12,000 petrol). See the Maroua section earlier for listings of tour operators. A 4WD vehicle is best, and necessary during the rains.

Waza is also easily reached via public transport; catch any vehicle between Maroua and Kousséri and ask the driver to drop you at the park turn-off (about CFA1500, two hours). However, there's no vehicle rental at the park, so the only option is hitching – likely to involve a long wait.

During the dry season, it's possible to drive through the park and exit at Andrini, about 45km southeast of Waza village. The road from Andirni to Maroua via Bogo is only partially paved, and sometimes impassable during the wet season.

East Province

East Province is seldom visited by travellers, and is very much a destination for adventurers with plenty of time. Although some towns have experienced a boom in recent years – thanks to logging, pharmaceutical and mining interests – there's little infrastructure and travel throughout is rugged. The main attraction is the rainforest, now protected in Parc National de la Lobéké, Boumba-Bek and Nki forest reserves, and Réserve du Dja.

GAROUA-BOULAÏ

Garoua-Boulaï, near the CAR border, is a one-horse town with a few petrol stations and bars. Otherwise, it's undistinguished, except for its alarming HIV/AIDS rate, which is reported to be as high as 60% among some sectors of the population.

There are several unappealing and not recommended ***auberges*** with rooms for about CFA2000. Better is the ***Mission Catholique***, with dorm beds for a donation and a few rooms for about CFA5000. It's near the military checkpoint coming from the north.

The road is in tolerable condition from Garoua-Boulaï to N'Gaoundéré during the dry season, with at least one bus daily and many police checkpoints. Get an update on the security situation before setting out, as there have been sporadic instances of banditry along this route.

Vehicles go several times daily to Bertoua, and at least several times weekly direct to Batouri. For details on getting to CAR, see the main Getting There & Away section of this chapter.

BERTOUA

Bertoua, capital of East Province, is 345km east of Yaoundé. MTA Travel in the town centre can help with train and air tickets.

Places to Stay & Eat

Hôtel Montagne, near the gare routière, and ***Hôtel Alimentation*** (formerly Hotel Jenyf), nearby, both have cheap lodging. Bertoua's best place is ***Hôtel Mansa***, with air-con rooms for about CFA15,000 and a restaurant.

For food, try ***Café Moderne*** at the gare routière, with meals from CFA500. Other similarly inexpensive places include ***Madame Lumere*** (ask around town) or ***Chez Odette***, just off the road near La King textile store.

Getting There & Away

Camair has three flights weekly between Douala and Bertoua, sometimes via Yaoundé.

To Yaoundé, the main line is Alliance Voyages (CFA5000, about seven hours); most transport uses the southern route via Abong-Mbang and Ayos. The road is unpaved to Ayos, and tarmac from there to Yaoundé.

Minibuses go daily to Garoua-Boulaï, and on to N'Gaoundéré (CFA7500, 11 hours); the road is paved as far as Garoua-Boulaï. There's also daily transport to Batouri (CFA1200), along a reasonable road, and to Bélabo (CFA1000), where you can catch the Yaoundé–N'Gaoundéré train.

Most transport departs from the main gare routière near the market. Alliance Voyages' office is just west of here.

BÉLABO

Bélabo, on the Yaoundé–N'Gaoundéré train line 80km northwest of Bertoua, is the gateway to the east if you're travelling by rail. About 25km west of town off the road to Nanga Eboko is the privately run **Sanaga-Yong Chimpanzee Rescue Centre** *(admission free)*, which offers sanctuary to about 17 chimpanzees, and promotes local education efforts.

For accommodation, try ***La Girafe*** on the edge of town, with rooms from about CFA8000. There are a couple of cheaper places, including the very basic ***Hôtel de l'Est***, with rooms for about CFA2000. The best food is at ***Mama Etémé***, behind the health clinic.

Transport goes several times daily along the paved road between Bertoua and Bélabo (1½ hours). To get to the chimpanzee centre, you'll need to charter a taxi or moto, and ask the driver to wait.

The train reaches Bélabo between about 11pm and 1am in both directions, if it's on time. On arrival, hire a taxi or moto to take you to your hotel, or pay one of the vendors working at the station to walk with you; Bélabo is notorious for its dicey security, and going alone isn't safe. Minibuses to Bertoua meet the train, although security can be a problem on these, too. If you're departing Bélabo with a 1st-class train ticket, you can wait in the VIP lounge, rather than out on the street.

BATOURI

Batouri, 90km east of Bertoua, is the last major town before Berbérati in the CAR and the best place to break the journey if you're trying to make speed between Yaoundé and Yokadouma.

Budget accommodation is at ***Auberge Coopérant*** in the town centre. ***Hôtel Belle Etoile*** is a step up. Batouri's best is ***Hôtel Mont Pandi***, with a TV and restaurant.

Alliance Voyages has several buses daily to Bertoua, with the first at about 8am, and usually at least one bus daily to Yaoundé. To Yokadouma, there's daily transport departing in the morning; allow half a day, more in the wet season. There is also transport at least once daily to Kenzou and the CAR border, departing Batouri about 5am.

YOKADOUMA

Yokadouma is a bustling, fast-growing town with a 'Wild West' feel. The Ministry of Finance and the WWF both have branch offices here, the latter can help with arranging visits to Parc National de la Lobéké, and Boumba-Bek and Nki forest reserves.

The best place to stay is ***L'Elefant*** with rooms from about CFA6000. Otherwise, there are numerous cheaper and more basic choices, including ***Auberge Libértate***.

All transport departs early. To Moloundou, apart from hitching a ride in a comfortable Land Cruiser, the best bet is Alliance Voyages, with one bus daily in the dry season. It's best to reserve a seat in advance. During the wet season, the journey can take several days.

MOLOUNDOU

You'll need to pass through this border town if you're heading for Réserve de Nki or Ouesso (Congo).

There are two basic auberges, ***La Forestière*** and ***Jardin du Rose***, both with rooms for about CFA3000.

Alliance Voyages has one bus daily in the dry season to/from Yokadouma (CFA5000, about eight hours).

LOBÉKÉ, BOUMBA-BEK & NKI

These three areas protect large sections of southeastern Cameroon's rainforests. They are also the focus of a joint initiative between the Cameroon government and the WWF to halt timber exploitation and poaching and to protect the forests as well as local Baka communities (who depend on the forests for their livelihood) against further threat. Lobéké, with more than 2000 sq km, was declared a national park in 2001. It is part of the proposed Sangha Tri-National Park area, which also will encompass Dzanga-Sangha National Park (CAR), and Nouabalé-Ndoki Forest Reserve (Congo). Boumba-Bek and Nki are forest reserves, and slated to soon achieve national park status within a single 7500 sq km protected area.

Lobéké is the most accessible of the three areas, but all are difficult to reach, and you should only contemplate coming here if you have lots of time, as well as the patience and endurance necessary for discovering the rainforest. While the forests have many animals, including elephants, chimpanzees, gorillas and buffaloes, they are often difficult to see because of the dense vegetation. Camp site development is planned, but there is currently no tourist infrastructure other than some *miradors* (viewing platforms) in Lobéké. There are also no roads in any of the parks. Exploration is on foot, often through dense vegetation. The best time to visit is during the drier months between December and February. Also see the boxed text opposite 'A Guest in the Rainforest'.

To arrange a visit to Lobéké, you'll need to stop first in Yokadouma, where the Ministry of Finance branch office (check in here first) and the WWF office next door can provide you with information. Park fees (CFA5000 per person per day) and guide fees (CFA3000 per guide per day) are payable at the Ministry of Finance office; get a receipt to show at the entrance. From Yokadouma, take a shared taxi 160km south to Mambele (about CFA3000), where the WWF has a sub-office for arranging the logistics of park visits. Rates for transport eastwards into Lobéké had not yet been set at the time of research, but expect them to be equivalent of those for renting a vehicle elsewhere in Cameroon. Try to visit in a group to economise on costs, or be prepared to wait until a project vehicle with space is going to the park.

A Guest in the Rainforest

Here are a few tips if you plan to visit the southeastern reserves:

- Budget at least a week for a visit; travel from Yaoundé takes at least two days each way.
- Be prepared to be totally self-sufficient for food, drink and lodging. A good water purifier/filter is essential.
- Be sure all your vaccines and immunisations are up to date, take precautions for malaria and travel with a good first-aid kit.
- Bring a mosquito net and plenty of insect repellent, and wear clothing that covers your arms and legs, and a hat.
- Snake bites are a risk; wear sturdy, high-topped boots, and long trousers.
- Given the lack of infrastructure, you'll probably need to request assistance from conservation project staff, which they are usually more than willing to give. Keep in mind, however, that their primary responsibility is the protection of nature.
- Tread lightly; be patient; and wait for the rainforest to come to you. Remember that you are a guest.

If you get caught in Mambele for the night, there's accommodation at ***Le Bon Samariten***, which has basic rooms for about CFA2000. You can also find food and bottled water in town.

Réserve de Nki – the most pristine of the three areas – is accessed via Moloundou, then by boat westwards along the Dja River, and finally on foot into the forest. Project staff can assist with boat arrangements; plan on about CFA150,000 per five-person boat.

Boumba-Bek can be accessed via Ngola (north of Mambele on the Yokadouma road), from where you head west by vehicle and foot to reach the Boumba River and the reserve.

RÉSERVE DU DJA

The Réserve de Biosphère du Dja, as recognised by Unesco, protects about 526,000 hectares of rainforest, its animal inhabitants, including buffaloes, elephants, gorillas, chimpanzees, and more, though dense vegetation means that most of these are difficult to see. As with Lobéké and the other southeastern forest reserves, visiting here is a serious undertaking, and you'll need to be completely self-sufficient. Also see the guidelines in the boxed text 'A Guest in the Rainforest'. Although there are few people in the reserve area, there are Baka communities around its borders, particularly along the old road rimming Dja's northern edge, where they were forced in colonial days.

The reserve is currently being managed by Ecofac (☎/fax 220 9472, e ecofac@camnet.cm), which is where you should go for information and to arrange a visit. The office is in the Bastos section of Yaoundé, on the small street behind the Nigerian ambassador's residence.

The best starting point for a visit is Somalomo village, on the reserve's northwestern edge. There's a training centre here with basic ***rooms*** for CFA5000 per night (advance reservations necessary through Ecofac). Meals can be arranged with at least one week's advance notice (CFA18,000/25,000 for half/full board); otherwise you'll need to bring all food with you as there's nothing in Somalomo. You'll also need a good water filter. Guides (CFA3000 per day) are obligatory and can be arranged at Somalomo, as can porters (CFA2000 per day).

The main route from Somalomo into the reserve is a 30km hike south to Bouamir, where you can ***camp*** at the site of an old research base and then hike out again along the same path. Allow close to a week for a visit from Yaoundé, including a day each way to/from Somalomo, a day's hike in and out to Bouamir, and several days camping in the forest. You'll need your own tent. At Bouamir, you're likely to see buffaloes and many birds, including *picathartes oreas*, which nests here in May and June.

It's also possible to enter Dja from Lomié, to the east, although guides aren't as well-organised there as in Somalomo. Also, because of heavy poaching in the reserve's eastern section, it's more difficult to see animals. The best time to visit Dja is during the drier season between December and February, although visits are possible into June. From about August/September to November there is constant rain.

Getting There & Away

Buses between Yaoundé and Somalomo (CFA4000) depart Yaoundé three times weekly (currently about 9am Monday, Wednesday and Saturday) from the quarters of Mvog-Ada (ask the taxi driver to drop you at 'Fanta Citron, Mvog-Ada') and Nkoldongo, opposite the pharmacy. Allow a full day for the journey.

With your own vehicle, head from Yaoundé east to Mbama (30km east of Ayos), then turn south to Messamena and Somalomo. The road from Messamena to the south is difficult during the wet.

South Province

South Province is an area of lush vegetation, rainforests, 'Pygmy' villages, and beaches. Most travellers who come here do so to relax on the beaches at Kribi. You'll also need to pass through if you're heading overland to Equatorial Guinea or Gabon.

KRIBI

With its attractive beaches and good road access, Kribi has become Cameroon's main beach resort and the favoured weekend getaway for government ministers and Douala expats. It has also experienced a development boom in recent years, with the construction of the Chad-Cameroon oil pipeline, which will terminate just to the south. While you won't find the turquoise waters here that mark East Africa's coastal areas, the beaches make a relaxing break from the rigours of the road. Most are ideal for swimming, although check locally before plunging in as currents can be strong at times. On weekends and holidays, Kribi's roads fill with a steady stream of shiny Land Cruisers. During the rest of the week you'll probably have things to yourself.

The main beach area, with most hotels, begins at the southern end of town. There are also several attractive beaches to the north, including at Londji, about 15km from Kribi, but not many accommodation options.

Camping isn't safe here and don't walk along the beaches alone.

Information

There is nowhere to change money (Bicec here doesn't do foreign exchange). If you get stuck, MCG Supermarché in the town centre sometimes changes cash dollars, but at poor rates.

KRIBI

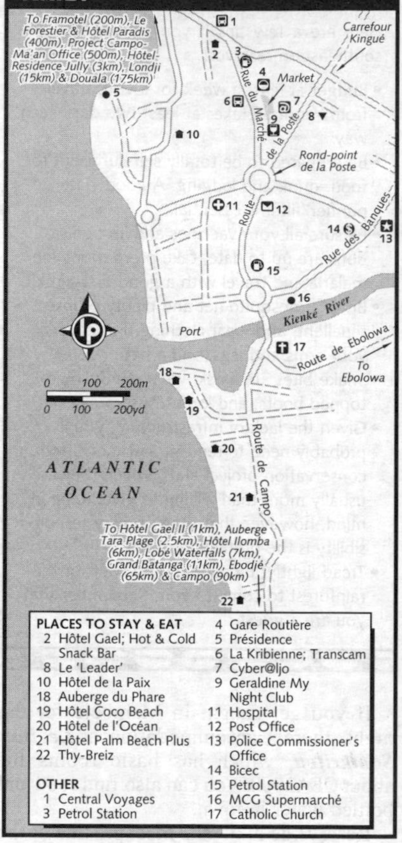
To Framotel (200m), Le Forestier & Hôtel Paradis (400m), Project Campo-Ma'an Office (500m), Hôtel-Residence Jully (3km), Londji (15km) & Douala (175km)
Carrefour Kingué
Market
Rue du Marché
Rue de la Poste
Rond-point de la Poste
Rue des Banques
Route de Kribi
Kienké River
Port
Route de Ebolowa
To Ebolowa
0 100 200m
0 100 200yd
ATLANTIC OCEAN
Route de Campo
To Hôtel Gael II (1km), Auberge Tara Plage (2.5km), Hôtel Ilomba (6km), Lobé Waterfalls (7km), Grand Batanga (11km), Ebodjé (65km) & Campo (90km)

PLACES TO STAY & EAT
2 Hôtel Gael; Hot & Cold Snack Bar
8 Le 'Leader'
10 Hôtel de la Paix
18 Auberge du Phare
19 Hôtel Coco Beach
20 Hôtel de l'Océan
21 Hôtel Palm Beach Plus
22 Thy-Breiz

OTHER
1 Central Voyages
3 Petrol Station
4 Gare Routière
5 Présidence
6 La Kribienne; Transcam
7 Cyber@ljo
9 Geraldine My Night Club
11 Hospital
12 Post Office
13 Police Commissioner's Office
14 Bicec
15 Petrol Station
16 MCG Supermarché
17 Catholic Church

Cyber@ljo, about 200m northeast of the post office roundabout, has a fast Internet connection (CFA1500 per hour).

The Project Campo-Ma'an office (☎/fax 346 2137, e campo-maan@gcnet.cm), for information on local tourism in the Campo-Ma'an region (see the Campo section later in this chapter), is about 1km north of town along the Douala road.

Lobé Waterfalls

About 8km south of Kribi are the picturesque, but commercialised, Lobé Waterfalls *(Chutes de la Lobé; admission free)*, which are reputed to be among the world's few falls flowing directly into the sea. There's a small ***restaurant*** here with grilled fish from CFA3500. You'll be besieged with offers to take a pirogue to see 'Pygmy villages' upstream on the Lobé River, or (in the dry season) hike around the falls. While the Pygmy villages are overrated and without much authenticity, the boat ride itself is worthwhile just to experience the river and vegetation. Expect to pay about CFA2500 per hour; a 'gift' is expected if you visit the villages.

Places to Stay – Budget

Hôtel de la Paix Rooms without/with shower CFA5000/7000. Sheets are clean, rooms grubby and the atmosphere sleazy, but it's one of Kribi's cheapest places. It's just west of the town centre along the road paralleling the water.

Hôtel Gael Rooms CFA12,500. Hôtel Gael has clean, modern rooms and a convenient location opposite Central Voyages bus office, but unless you're travelling early it's better to stay at the beach. There's no food.

The following beachside places are listed from north to south.

Auberge du Phare *(☎ 346 1106)* Rooms with fan/air-con CFA12,000/16,000, air-con suite CFA25,000. The long-standing Auberge du Phare has decent self-contained rooms, a nice setting and a good beachside restaurant with large servings from CFA3000. It's on the southern end of town, just west of the small bridge.

Thy-Breiz *(☎ 346 1499)* Rooms with fan & double bed from CFA10,000, rooms with air-con and 2 double beds from CFA30,000. Thy-Breiz (formerly Auberge Annette II) has a range of overpriced but OK rooms and a pleasant setting near the water, though most rooms don't face the sea. Prices can often be negotiated. It's about 1km south of the bridge.

Hôtel Gael II *(☎ 346 1620)* Rooms with fan/air-con CFA10,800/12,800. Gael II, under the same management as Hôtel Gael in town, has a beachside setting about 1.5km south of Thy-Breiz and clean rooms, although most open onto an interior corridor, or onto the backyard, rather than to the sea.

Auberge Tara Plage *(☎ 346 2083, 984 8928)* Camping & shower use CFA3000 per tent or CFA4000 per double (including tent rental), rooms with 1/2 double beds & fan CFA10,000/12,000, 4-person villa CFA20,000. Tara Plage is the best of the beachside budget places, with friendly owners, a good setting and relaxing atmosphere. The food is good, though pricey, at about CFA4000 per meal. It's about 400m off the coastal road and signposted, south of Gael II. Most rooms also have an extra (twin) bed, for which you'll pay an additional CFA2000 – good value if you don't mind crowding in.

North of Kribi, the options are more limited. ***Auberge Jardiniere***, the main place to stay in Londji, has rooms for CFA12,500. The setting is good, but the hotel has seen better days, and the location is isolated unless you have your own vehicle. It's about 500m off the main road and signposted (CFA2000 for a charter taxi from town).

Places to Stay – Mid-Range & Top End

Hôtel Coco Beach *(☎ 346 1584, 997 7496, fax 346 1819)* Rooms CFA20,000-24,000. This pleasant, family run place on the beach has seven well-maintained rooms (including many facing the sea), a European-style B&B atmosphere and a good restaurant. It's just southwest of the bridge, and has a tiny wading pool for children.

Hôtel de l'Océan *(☎ 346 1635, 990 0169)* Rooms with 1/2 double beds CFA20,000/24,000. Hôtel de l'Océan is just south of Hôtel Coco Beach. Accommodation is in simple but pleasant double chalets lined up along the beach, with a few more set back (about 300m). It's one of the few places in Kribi where most rooms actually face the water.

Hôtel Palm Beach Plus *(☎ 346 1447, fax 346 1832, ⓔ hotelpb@iccnet.cm)* Singles/doubles CFA25,000/35,000. This large, reasonably comfortable, but sterile complex is on the beach just south of Hôtel de l'Océan.

Hôtel Ilomba *(☎ 991 2923, 991 3236)* Singles/doubles CFA25,000/30,000, 4-/8-people suites CFA75,000/100,000. Hôtel Ilomba, in a good beachside setting about 7km south of town near Lobé Waterfalls, is Kribi's best. Accommodation is in comfortable boukarous, all with air-con, screened windows and mosquito nets. The suites are actually more like private houses. There's a good restaurant with meals from CFA4500 to CFA6000, and a daytime beachside grill. Day visitors are welcome, although there's limited public transport from here to town.

Hôtel-Residence Jully *(☎/fax 346 1962, ⓔ residencejully@iccnet.cm)* Singles/doubles

CFA23,000/27,000, suites CFA32,000. This new hotel, about 3.5km north of town on the Douala road, has rooms with TV and air-con, and a restaurant.

Framotel *(☎ 346 1640, 346 1840)* Rooms CFA17,000-21,000. If all the beachside places are full, the best option is Framotel, with accommodation in small but comfortable attached cottages set in green grounds. It's on the northern edge of town, about 300m east of the main road and signposted. There's a restaurant, and – on the western side of the Douala road – a beachside grill.

Places to Eat

The best place in town for ***street food*** is Carrefour Kingué, where you can get good grilled fish from CFA1000. After ordering, you can sit at one of the many nearby bars, and the fish will be brought to you.

Hot & Cold Snack Bar Snacks & fast food CFA500-1500. Hot & Cold, opposite Central Voyages bus office, is clean, efficient and reasonably priced. The menu includes good omelettes, chicken and chips, and sandwiches.

Le 'Leader' Meals CFA1000-2000. Le 'Leader' is the best choice for Cameroonian dishes, with authentic atmosphere, good ndole, and more. It's just south of Carrefour Kingué, down an unpaved side road.

For upscale dining in town, try ***Le Forestier*** at Hôtel Paradis, with meals from about CFA4000. It's at the northern end of town, a few hundred metres east of the Douala road and signposted.

All the beach hotels have restaurants; even at the budget places, expect to pay from CFA3000 per meal.

Getting There & Away

All agencies have offices on Rue du Marché in the town centre. Nonagency transport leaves from the main gare routière, on the same street.

To Douala (CFA2000, 2½ hours), Central Voyages is best, with buses throughout the day from about 5.30am.

To Campo, Transcam and (better) La Kribienne both have several buses daily (CFA1500, three to four hours). Both also have a daily bus to Yaoundé (CFA3500), departing about 8am.

To reach Lobé Waterfalls, you can walk along the beach (in a group!), catch a shared taxi going towards Grand Batanga (about CFA500, but few and far between) or charter a taxi (CFA2000). For charter taxis, it's worth paying extra so the driver will wait for you, as there's little public transport back.

GRAND BATANGA

Grand Batanga is a large village 12km south of Kribi. South of town towards Eboundja are some good and usually deserted **beaches**.

The only accommodation is at the ***Catholic Mission***, which is sometimes willing to put up travellers.

For food on the beach, locals will generally approach you to arrange grilled fish. Otherwise, you can place an order at the last small shop at the southern end of town, before the rain barrier. The only restaurant is the French-run ***Auberge Mimodo***, with good, pricey meals. The owners are building a few rooms, though for now there's no accommodation. It's signposted about 1km south of Grand Batanga.

CAMPO

Campo is the last town before the Equatorial Guinea border. The best accommodation is at ***Auberge Bon Course***, at Bon Course Supermarché at the main junction. There are three simple but decent rooms for CFA3000 each, and meals are available.

The Cameroon government together with the Netherlands Development Organisation (SNV) are trying to get some small tourism projects going in the Campo area. The main one is at **Ebodjé**, about 25km north of Campo along the main road, where you can stay in ***local homes*** and take guided tours of the area. Costs are CFA2000 per person for accommodation, CFA2000 per meal, CFA1000 per person environmental protection fee, and CFA2000 to CFA5000 per guide, depending on your programme; a portion of all fees goes to a village development fund. Although everything is still in the initial stages, the area is interesting to explore, and it's a good, low-key alternative if you want to get away from standard tourist sites and spend more time with Cameroonians. For more details, contact the Project Campo-Ma'an office in Kribi. Food is available in Ebodjé, but you'll need to bring your own water or filter, mosquito net and sleeping sheet.

Getting There & Away

There are daily minibuses between Campo and Kribi (CFA1500) that also stop at Ebodjé. Moto-taxis to Campo Beach (for Equatorial Guinea) cost CFA500. For information on crossing the border, see Land in the main Getting There & Away section of this chapter. There's a military base in Campo, and on leaving town you may be required to register at the military checkpoint.

PARC NATIONAL DE CAMPO-MA'AN & AROUND

Campo is the starting point for visiting the recently gazetted **Parc National de Campo-Ma'an** (2608 sq km), which protects rainforest, many plants and various animals, including buffaloes, elephants and mandrills. The animals are rarely seen because of the dense vegetation. There's no infrastructure, nowhere to stay and you'll need your own 4WD to get here. The CFA5000 entry fee should be paid at the forestry office *(poste forestier)* in Campo; get a receipt to show at the park entrance. Staff at the forestry office can also help you arrange a guide (obligatory, CFA3000 per day). You'll need to be self-sufficient with equipment and supplies. The road between Campo and Ma'an (east of the park) is being rehabilitated. For now it's only possible to drive as far as **Memve'ele Waterfalls**, just outside the park's eastern boundary.

EBOLOWA

Ebolowa, capital of Ntem district, is a bustling place and a possible stopping point en route between Yaoundé and Equatorial Guinea or Gabon.

The best accommodation is at ***Hôtel Porte Jaune*** in the town centre, with rooms from about CFA10,000 and meals. About 1km southwest of the centre is the similarly priced but rundown ***Hôtel Le Ranch***. There are several cheaper, undistinguished auberges near the main roundabout, including ***Hôtel Âne Rouge***, with rooms for about CFA4000.

During the dry season, there's at least one vehicle daily along the rough road between Ebolowa and Kribi. There are also several vehicles daily to Yaoundé (three hours).

Several vehicles depart in the morning for Ambam, where you can find transport towards Ebebiyin (Equatorial Guinea) or Bitam (Gabon).

Cape Verde

Situated about 445km off the African coast far into the Atlantic Ocean, the Cape Verde islands are a bit more than a stone's throw away from the continent. Geologically and culturally too, they're somewhat removed from the mainland; ethnically and historically, however, they're in closer proximity.

Despite the islands' name (meaning 'green cape'), when Charles Darwin visited them more than 100 years ago, he noted that such 'an utterly sterile land possesses a grandeur which more vegetation might spoil'. Though some islands are sterile, others are still green. It is this diversity that constitutes Cape Verde's main attraction.

On the islands you can find verdant valleys and mountains, long stretches of white sand, smoking volcanoes and dusty deserts, and pretty towns with cobbled streets. Additionally, there is Portuguese wine alongside local liquor, songs that are sad along with frenetic rhythms with a Latin beat, and exciting diving and windsurfing, along with hiking and fishing. Finally, the climate is pleasant, the water temperature agreeable, and the people are friendly and hospitable. Cape Verde may not be action-packed, but if the idea of islands with a Portuguese ambience, an African inspiration and a beauty all of its own intrigues, you'll be delighted with a visit here.

Cape Verde at a Glance

Capital: Praia
Population: 445,000
Area: 4035 sq km
Head of State: President Pedro Pires
Official language: Portuguese
Currency: Cape Verde escudo
Exchange rate: US$1 = CVE120
Time: GMT/UTC -1
Country telephone code: ☎ 238
Best time to go: Year-round

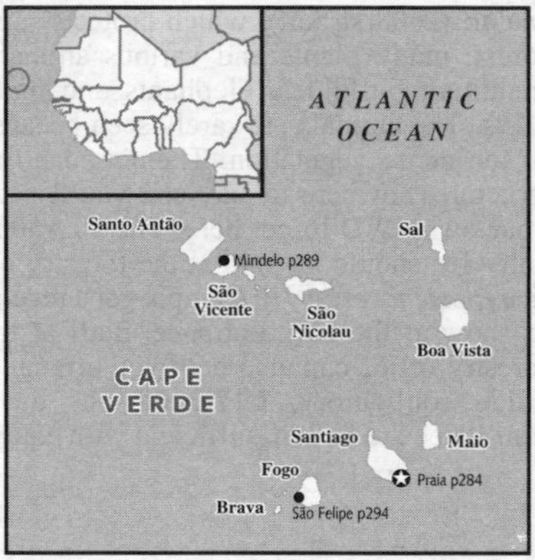

ATLANTIC OCEAN
Santo Antão
Mindelo p289
São Vicente
São Nicolau
Sal
Boa Vista
CAPE VERDE
Santiago
Maio
Fogo
Praia p284
Brava
São Felipe p294

Highlights

- Huffing and puffing to the top of Mt Fogo, an active volcano, still spouting its stuff
- Losing yourself in the colour and chaos of Mindelo's Mardi Gras, the country's most vibrant festival
- Plunging into the wide-open waters of the Atlantic and seeking out sharks, manta rays and whales
- Cooing over a *coladeira* or two sung by a talented local singer
- Vanishing into the verdant valleys and forests of beautiful Santo Antão island
- Gorging on Cape Verde's delicious fresh fish or famous lobsters

Facts about Cape Verde

HISTORY

When Portuguese mariners first landed on the Cape Verde islands in 1456, the islands were barren of people but not of vegetation. Returning six years later to the island of Santiago, the Portuguese founded Ribeira Grande (now Cidade Velha), the first European town in the tropics, and established vineyards and plantations. However, finding labourers to work the land proved more difficult and almost immediately slaves were imported from the West African coast. The islands additionally began to serve as a base for ships transporting slaves to Europe and the Americas. This prosperity attracted pirates to the islands, including England's Sir Francis Drake in 1585 (see the boxed text 'Cidade Velha – Slaves & Pirates' later in this chapter).

Cape Verde continued to prosper. In 1747, though, the islands were hit by the first (in

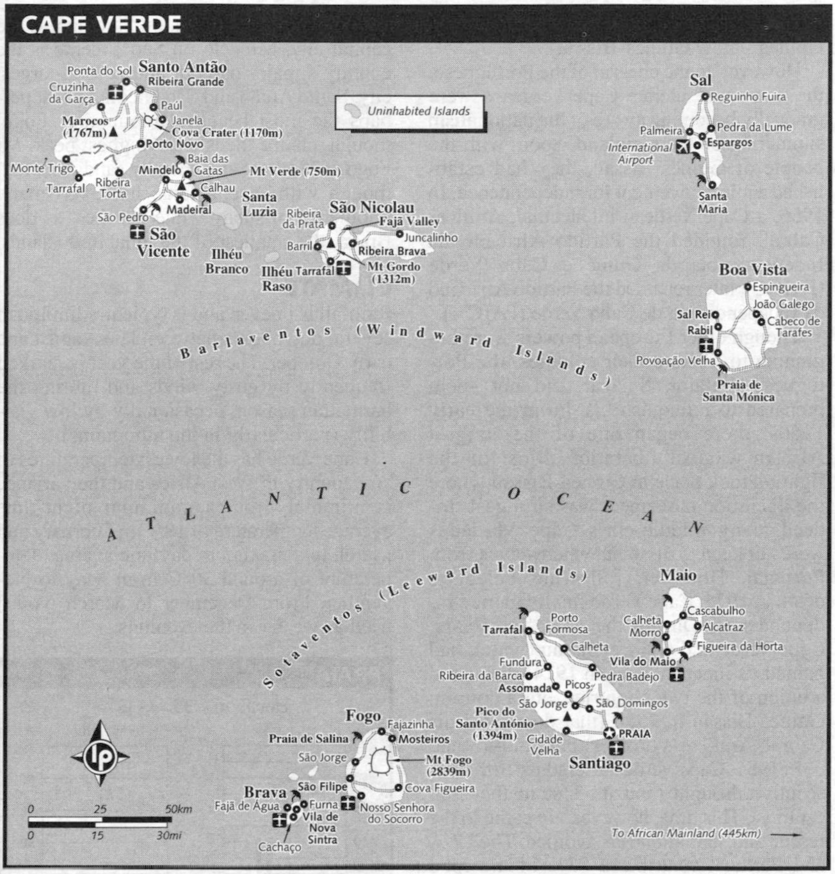
CAPE VERDE
Uninhabited Islands
Santo Antão
Ponta do Sol
Ribeira Grande
Cruzinha da Garça
Paúl
Janela
Marocos (1767m)
Cova Crater (1170m)
Porto Novo
Monte Trigo
Tarrafal
Ribeira Torta
Baia das Gatas
Mindelo
Mt Verde (750m)
Calhau
Madeiral
São Pedro
São Vicente
Santa Luzia
Ilhéu Branco
Ilhéu Raso
Ribeira da Prata
São Nicolau
Fajã Valley
Juncalinho
Barril
Ribeira Brava
Tarrafal
Mt Gordo (1312m)
Sal
Reguinho Fuira
Palmeira
Pedra da Lume
International Airport
Espargos
Santa Maria
Boa Vista
Espingueira
João Galego
Sal Rei
Cabeco de Tarafes
Rabil
Povoação Velha
Praia de Santa Mónica
Barlaventos (Windward Islands)
ATLANTIC OCEAN
Sotaventos (Leeward Islands)
Maio
Cascabulho
Calheta
Alcatraz
Morro
Figueira da Horta
Vila do Maio
Porto Formosa
Tarrafal
Calheta
Fundura
Ribeira da Barca
Pedra Badejo
Assomada
Picos
São Jorge
São Domingos
Pico do Santo António (1394m)
Cidade Velha
PRAIA
Santiago
Fogo
Fajazinha
Praia de Salina
Mosteiros
São Jorge
Mt Fogo (2839m)
São Filipe
Cova Figueira
Brava
Fajã de Água
Furna
Vila de Nova Sintra
Nosso Senhora do Socorro
Cachaço
0 25 50km
0 15 30mi
To African Mainland (445km)

recorded history) of many droughts that were to ravage the islands right up to recent years. Deforestation and overgrazing aggravated the situation. In the 100 years from 1773, three droughts killed more than 100,000 people, carrying off each time between 40% to 44% of the population. Yet the Portuguese colonisers sent little relief. The decline of the lucrative slave trade in the mid-19th century dealt another blow to the island's economy. Cape Verde's heyday was over.

With the advent of the ocean liner at the end of the 19th century, however, along with the islands' strategic position on the Atlantic shipping lanes, the islands' fortunes temporarily revived. Ships required fuel (imported coal), water and livestock, and soon the deep, protected harbour at Mindelo on São Vicente became an important commercial centre.

The droughts, however, continued. Between 1900 and 1948, around 15% of the population was wiped out each time in three more droughts. Starvation had become almost a way of life.

Independence

Cape Verde's population grew as a result of intermarriage between African slaves and Portuguese colonisers. Because of their ethnic make-up, the people fared slightly better than fellow-Africans in other Portuguese colonies. Cape Verde was the first Portuguese colony to have a high school, and a small minority received an education. By independence, 25% of the population could read (compared with 5% in Portuguese Guinea – now Guinea-Bissau).

However, to the chagrin of the Portuguese, the now more literate Cape Verdeans were gradually becoming aware of the nationalism simmering on the mainland. Soon, with the people of Guinea-Bissau, they had established a joint movement for independence. In 1956, a Cape Verdean intellectual, Amilcar Cabral, founded the Partido Africano da Independência da Guiné e Cabo Verde (PAIGC), later renamed the Partido Africano da Indepêndencia de Cabo Verde (PAICV).

Though other European powers were beginning to liberate their colonies, the Portuguese dictator, Salazar, did not seem prepared to relinquish his. From the early 1960s, there began one of the longest African wars of liberation. Most of the fighting took place in Guinea-Bissau where the liberation movement was strongest. Indeed many middle-class Cape Verdeans were not keen to dissociate themselves from Portugal. However, following Salazar's death in 1975, Cape Verde finally gained independence. During the next five years, Cape Verde and Guinea-Bissau (which had gained its independence in 1974) discussed a union of the two countries, but a coup in Guinea-Bissau in 1980 (that deposed Luis Cabral, Amilcar's brother) put paid to that.

In 1985, Cape Verde suffered its 17th consecutive drought (and its 31st in the 20th century). This time, however, aid came to the rescue and starvation was avoided. The USA and Portugal contributed 85% of the food deficit and continue to do so – food aid represents 50% of imports and 60% of GNP.

Cape Verde Today

After 1986, the weather proved more clement and crop yields more than doubled. However, after poor rains again in October–November 2001, hopes for a good harvest in 2002 were dashed. Cape Verde, it seems, is more than ever dependent on food aid. Because of these harsh environmental conditions, and despite the islanders' traditional attachment to their homeland, many inhabitants have left Cape Verde and now expats (a massive 700,000) outnumber the islanders.

GEOGRAPHY

Cape Verde consists of 10 major islands (nine of them inhabited) and five islets, all of volcanic origin. Praia, on Santiago, is the capital city. Mindelo on São Vicente is the country's major harbour and second-largest city. Santo Antão and São Nicolau boast perhaps the most beautiful mountains. Fogo, though, claims the islands' highest peak, Mt Fogo at 2839m. Sal, generally sandy and flat, though with several large hills, has many kilometres of sunny white beaches, as does Brava, the smallest of the inhabited islands.

CLIMATE

Rainfall is uneven and is typically limited to several downpours between late August and early October. The rest of the year is marked frequently by gusty winds and, during the harmattan season, occasionally by low visibility (particularly in the mountains).

Cape Verde has the lowest temperatures of any country in West Africa and the variance is minimal, from a minimum night-time average temperature of 19°C in February and March to a maximum daytime average temperature of around 30°C from May to November. From December to March, you'll need a sweater in the evenings.

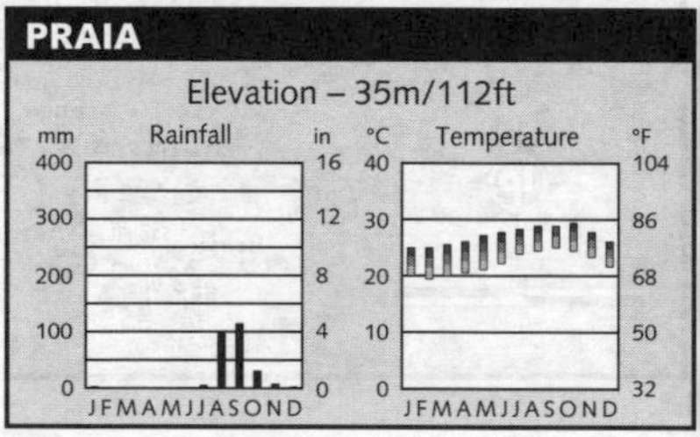
PRAIA
Elevation – 35m/112ft
mm
Rainfall
in
°C
Temperature
°F
400
16
40
104
300
12
30
86
200
8
20
68
100
4
10
50
0
0
0
32
JFMAMJJASOND
JFMAMJJASOND

ECOLOGY & ENVIRONMENT

The greatest threats to the environment today are deforestation, overgrazing (by goats) and, the major problem, soil erosion. Torrential rain, rapid water run-off and strong winds cause extensive erosion. Unsustainable cultivation has aggravated the problem. To combat these problems, more than 15,000 contour ditches and 2500km of dams have been constructed, and a major reforestation program was implemented in the 1970s.

FLORA & FAUNA

During the colonial period, the islands (with the exception of Sal, Maio and Boavista), were evidently much greener. Today, except

São Nicolau and Santo Antão, there is little to justify the Portuguese name: *Verde*. Only 20% of the land is arable. Of the 600 or so species of fauna, around 100 are endemic and the rest have been imported.

Cape Verde has less fauna than just about anywhere in Africa and mostly comprises domestic animals. Birdlife is a little richer (around 75 species), and includes a good number of endemics (38). Much sought after by twitchers are the frigate bird *(Fregata magnificens)* and the razo lark *(Alauda razae)*, one of the rarest birds in the world (only 250 specimens are thought to remain). One species more commonly seen is the grey-headed kingfisher *(Halycon leucocephala)*, unmistakable for its peculiarly strident call.

Flora of particular interest includes the indigenous *drageiro*, or dragon tree *(Dracanea draco)*, found particularly on São Nicolau.

If you take a ferry, look out for dolphins and flying fish and if you're very lucky, whales. Divers should see a good range of fish, including tropical species such as parrot fish and angelfish, groupers, barracudas, moray eels and, with much luck, manta rays, various species of sharks (including the nurse, tiger and lemon) and marine turtles. Five species of turtles visit the islands on their way across the Atlantic (the olive Ridley, green, leatherback, loggerhead and hawksbill). Nesting takes place throughout the year, but in particular from May to October.

GOVERNMENT & POLITICS

The year 1991 was significant for Cape Verde. It resulted in the first-ever direct presidential and multiparty parliamentary elections, the establishment of the right-of-centre Movimento Para a Democracia (MPD) – which ended the 15 years in power of the Marxist-inspired PAICV, and resulted in the start of economic liberalisation. Foreign investment was encouraged as well as the development of the service, fishing and tourism industries.

In February 2001, the PAICV swept back into power and Pedro Pires was elected president. During its current term (to 2006), the party is expected to introduce some measures of economic austerity (as a result of a growing fiscal deficit), bolster relations with its principal Western economic partners such as Portugal and the EU (on whom it is largely dependent for aid), while also maintaining good relations with other Lusophone African countries, such as Angola and Guinea-Bissau.

Following 11 September, Cape Verde was quick to condemn the attacks on the USA, as well as to offer the use of its airspace. In doing so, it has skilfully distanced itself from its previous socialist stance, curried favour with powerful Western donors, and reaffirmed ties between the islands and the USA (home to a large number of Cape Verdean expats).

Six political parties are currently registered, and 66 deputies are elected for five-year terms to the Assembléia Nacional by universal suffrage through proportional representation (six are elected by Cape Verdeans living abroad). Politically, the country is a stable democracy, has an outstanding human rights record (with no political prisoners) and is free of ethnic, religious and political violence.

ECONOMY

Based on the UN's quality-of-life index, Cape Verde comes out on top in West Africa, with health standards the highest on the continent. From 1975 to 1995, life expectancy leapt from 46 years to 66 years, 50% higher than the sub-Saharan African average. Cape Verde also boasts by far the highest GNP per capita (US$1060), though money received from relatives overseas (20% of GNP) contributes greatly to this.

Since 1991, the country has moved rapidly towards a free-market capitalistic system and by 2000, more than 25 state enterprises had been privatised, and tourism was counting more than 50,000 visitors per year. Although the country has been obliged to do some economic belt-tightening in 2001–02 (including the introduction of VAT in March 2002), real GDP growth is projected at a healthy 5% during 2002–03, as a result of increasing revenues gained from tourism, foreign investment and exports.

POPULATION & PEOPLE

Cape Verde's population of 445,000 enjoys the longest life expectancy in Africa, as well as one of the lowest growth rates. It is also the only country in West Africa with a population of primarily mixed European and African descent. The intermixing of the

Portuguese settlers and their African slaves (see Independence under History earlier in this chapter) forged a distinct Cape Verdean nationality with its own highly individual culture.

EDUCATION

Cape Verde's literacy rate of 68% is the highest in West Africa. Virtually all children of primary school age attend school, though attendance at secondary schools is considerably less.

ARTS

Craftwork

Traditional crafts include weaving, ceramics (mainly from Boa Vista, Maio, Santiago and Santo Antão), baskets (mainly from Santiago), mat making (from Brava, Fogo, Santiago and Santo Antão) and batik (mainly from São Vicente).

Literature

While Cape Verde has the smallest population of any country in West Africa, its literary tradition is one of the richest. Prior to independence, a major theme in Cape Verdean writing was the longing for liberation. As far back as 1936, a small clique of intellectuals founded a literary journal, *Claridade*, the aim of which was to express a growing sense of Cape Verdean identity. An attempt was also made to elevate Crioulo to a literary language by using it in some writing. After independence, the journal was replaced by *Raizes*.

The dominant themes of local literature have been the sea, oppression of the slave trade, and more recently, racial discrimination. The poet, Jorge Barbosa is known for his publication *Arquipélago*, which is laden with melancholic reflections on the sea, and longings for liberation.

Music

Many forms of music evolved as a kind of symbolic and collective protest against the ruling class and slavery. Some music forms, such as the *batuko*, have their roots in ancient African traditions. Cape Verdean music falls into three categories. The two oldest musical styles are *mornas* and *coladeiras*. Mornas are in essence mournful and express homesickness. With an emphasis on lyrics, they are similar to the Portuguese *fado* style, from where they may have originated. Their most famous proponent was Eugénio Tavares, born in 1867.

Coladeiras, in contrast, are more romantic love songs, but unlike mornas, can be upbeat. Among the best-known singers are Cesária Évora (see the boxed text) and Bana, as well as Tito Paris and Paulino Vieira. Other musicians to look out for include Marizia, Dina Medina, Chandinho Dédé, Lura, Ano Nobo, Kodé Di Dona, Chico Serra, Luis Morais and the group Tam-Tam 2000.

A newer style of music called *funaná* originated in the late 1970s with the group Bulimundo. It is a distinctive fast-paced music with a Latin rhythm and is great for dancing. It usually features players on the accordion and other musicians tapping two pieces of metal together. One of the leading singers today is Ildo Lobo. Leading funaná bands are Exitos de Oro and Ferro Gaita.

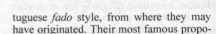

> **Cesária Évora**
>
> The undisputed star of *mornas* and *coladeiras* is Cesária Évora, who hails from Mindelo. She has made numerous international tours and has had international hits, particularly in France, where she records. In 1997, at the second annual all-African music awards ceremony held in South Africa, she ran away with three of the top 13 awards including top female vocalist. Cape Verdean music was vaulted out of the realms of the unknown. Despite her success, Évora is remarkably modest and continues living a fairly low-key life in Paris.

SOCIETY & CONDUCT

Though vestiges of Portuguese culture are much in evidence (such as in the islands' cuisine), local traditions are also conspicuous in handicrafts and music. Certain ceremonies, such as the *fazer cristao* (a kind of civil baptism) are adopted from an ancient African tradition. Music forms an essential part of Cape Verdean life (see also the Music of West Africa special section) and can be heard and seen in cafés, at public ceremonies, festivals and processions, nightclubs and private homes.

Cape Verdeans are a welcoming and hospitable people, particularly if you make the effort to learn a little Portuguese – or even better, Crioulo. If you get invited to someone's house, it's polite to take a small gift such as flowers or a box of pastries.

RELIGION

About 80% of the people are Roman Catholic. Despite the arrival of many Muslim slaves, Islam never took hold and today there are few Muslims.

LANGUAGE

Portuguese is the official language, but many, particularly in rural areas, speak Crioulo, an Africanised creole Portuguese. For some useful words and phrases in Portuguese and Crioulo, see the Language chapter.

Facts for the Visitor

SUGGESTED ITINERARIES

If you fly into Sal, you could relax or engage in some water sports on the beach at Santa Maria. Then, you could head for Mindelo, one of the country's most interesting towns. A ferry ride would take you over to Santo Antão, the best island for hiking, followed by a day in Praia, then, if there's time, a few days exploring the other islands.

If you have two weeks, you could spend longer hiking on Santo Antão or you could head for Fogo, where you could climb Mt Fogo, then spend a day in São Filipe. Later, you could head over to Brava by ferry for a couple of days hiking, before heading back to Praia. With three weeks at your disposal, you could do all of the above and also explore some of the less-visited islands such as São Nicolau (highly recommended for its scenery and tranquillity).

PLANNING

Maps

A good map of the islands is the German-produced AB Karten-Verlag *Cabo Verde* (1:200,000; 2001). An excellent hiking map for Santo Antão is the (also German) Goldstadt Wanderkarte (1:50,000; 2001) with around 40 suggested walks.

VISAS & DOCUMENTS

Visas & Visa Extensions

All visitors, except Cape Verdean nationals, require a visa. In the USA, mail your passport, one photo and US$20 to the Cape Verdean embassy in Washington, DC. Visas are issued routinely for stays of 30 days and more if you ask. Dakar, in Senegal, is one of the few places in West Africa where you can get a visa. If there's no Cape Verdean embassy, apply at the nearest Portuguese embassy. You'll need US$15 to US$20.

A tourist visa can be obtained on arrival at the airports and ports of Praia and Sal (and from mid-2002, Mindelo too). It costs CVE2000/4000 for single/multiple entry. They're usually valid for eight days only, though. After arriving, you'll need to go to a police station on any island, or the Direcção de Emigrãçao e Fronteiras, Rua Serpa Pinto on the Platô in Praia, and renew it (a maximum of 180 days). For an extension of more than a week, you need, in theory, to fill in a form, supply a photo and lodge the application, which will take a few days. In practice, visas are usually issued on the spot (particularly if you're polite and smiling!). Note that there's a fine of CVE12,000 if you let your visa expire.

Visas for Onward Travel In Cape Verde, you can get visas for Guinea, Guinea-Bissau and Senegal.

For visas to Guinea and Guinea-Bissau, go to the Ministry of Foreign Affairs on Praça Alexandre Albuquérquë.

For Senegal, visas cost CVE440 and take up to 48 hours to process.

Other Documents

Proof of yellow fever vaccination is only required if you are coming from an infected area (see Health later for more details).

EMBASSIES & CONSULATES

Cape Verdean Embassies & Consulates

In West Africa, there are Cape Verdean embassies in Guinea and Senegal. For more details, see the Facts for the Visitor section of the relevant chapter. Cape Verde has no diplomatic representation in the UK. Elsewhere, Cape Verdean embassies include:

Belgium (☎ 2-646 9025, fax 646 3385) Av Jeanne 29, 1050 Brussels

Canada

Honorary Consulate: (☎ 416-252 9881, fax 252 9924) 123 Yorkview Dr, Etobicoque, Toronto, Ontario M8Z 2G5

France (☎ 01 42 12 73 50, fax 01 40 53 04 36) Rue Jouffroy d'Abbans 80, 75017 Paris
Germany (☎ 30-2045 0955, fax 2045 0966) 43 Dorotheenstrasse, D-10117 Berlin
Italy (☎ 06-474 4678, fax 474 4643) Viale Giosué, Carduci 4, 00187 Rome
Netherlands (☎ 70-355 3651, fax 355 3678) 1930 Burgemeester Patijnlaan, 2585 CB The Hague
Portugal (☎ 21-301 6434, fax 304 1466) Avenida do Restelo 33, 1400 Lisbon
Spain
Consulate: (☎ 91-570 2568, fax 570 2563) Calle Capitán 51, 28020, Madrid
USA (☎ 202-965 6820, fax 965 1207) 3415 Massachusetts Ave, NW, Washington, DC 20007

Embassies & Consulates in Cape Verde

There are several embassies in Praia (Santiago island), including:

France (☎ 615589) Rua da Prainha, near Hotel Trópico, Prainha beach
Portugal (☎ 615602, 615603) Rua da Assembleia Nacional, Achada de Santo António
Senegal (☎ 615621) Rua Abilio Macedo, diagonally opposite the US embassy
USA (☎ 615616, fax 611353) 81 Rua Abilio Macedo, Platô

There are also embassies and consulates in Mindelo (São Vicente island), such as for France (Alliance Française) and Portugal (Avenida 5 de Julho).

MONEY

The unit of currency is the Cape Verde escudo (CVE), divided into 100 centavos. It's not a hard currency, but it's stable; in January 2002, it was pegged to the euro.

country	unit		escudo
euro zone	€1	=	CVE108
UK	UK£1	=	CVE175
USA	US$1	=	CVE120
West African CFA	CFA100	=	CVE17

Banks are found in all the main towns and islands and accept travellers cheques and cash in all the main currencies (except the West African CFA). Many also give cash advances with a Visa card (there are no ATMs yet in Cape Verde). Changing money on the black market is illegal and carries risks (US dollars and Portuguese escudos are often fakes), so avoid it unless you're desperate. Be careful not to get stuck with Cape Verdean escudos (not exchangeable outside the islands). The bank at Sal's airport and Banco Interatlântico in Praia should change escudos back into other currencies, but bring moneychanging receipts, your passport and air ticket, which may be requested.

POST & COMMUNICATIONS

The postal service is reliable and reasonably quick. A 20g letter or postcard costs CVE60 to anywhere outside the islands. Post offices *(correios)* are open from 8am to noon and 2.30pm to 5.30pm Monday to Friday, and Saturday mornings in some towns.

Telephone area codes are incorporated directly into the telephone number (the first two digits). Public telephone booths are fairly plentiful but you'll need a phonecard (available in CVE50/150 cards at any post office). Alternatively, call from a post office. Charges range from CVE180 per minute for the USA/Canada, CVE300 for Australia/New Zealand and CVE240-300 for Europe, depending on which country you're from.

In the larger towns, such as Praia and Mindelo, Internet cafés and access points are springing up (see those towns for more details). At the moment, only the larger hotels have Internet resources and email.

DIGITAL RESOURCES

Two sites to start with are W www.caboverde.com, with comprehensive tourism information in English, Portuguese and Italian; and W www.umassd.edu/specialprograms/caboverde/cvgeog.html, with educational articles on different aspects of Cape Verde (such as flora and fauna), maps and satellite photographs.

BOOKS

Publications in English about Cape Verde are scarce but include: *Cape Verde: Politics, Economics and Society* by Colm Foy, *Atlantic Islands* by Anne Hammick & Nicholas Heath and *The Fortunate Isles* by Basil Davidson. If you read Portuguese or Italian, or just want glossy photos for souvenirs, look out for *Cabo Verde Cruzamento do Atlântico Sul* by Federico Cerrone. If you're keen on birds, the *Aves de Cabo Verde*, a fairly basic BirdLife International brochure available at some tourism kiosks, contains around 12 pages of illustrations.

PHOTOGRAPHY & VIDEO

In general, Cape Verdeans are less likely to object to their photos being taken than people elsewhere in West Africa, but you should always ask permission first. Avoid photographing military installations. Film is readily available, and there are one-hour developing shops in Praia and Mindelo. See Photography & Video in the Regional Facts for the Visitor chapter for more general information.

HEALTH

A yellow fever vaccination is required if you have been in an infected area within the previous six days. Malaria has been almost eradicated from the islands bar one or two cases annually in Santiago (thought to have been contracted by immigrants from West Africa). See also Health in Regional Facts for the Visitor chapter.

The water in most towns is treated and is generally safe, although you're probably better off with bottled water, which is readily available. Hospitals in Cape Verde are fairly good by West African standards and pharmacies are fairly well stocked.

WOMEN TRAVELLERS

Cape Verde is one of the safest countries in West Africa for solo women travellers – problems are rarely encountered. For more general information and advice, see Women Travellers in the Regional Facts for the Visitor chapter.

DANGERS & ANNOYANCES

Praia (Santiago island) is probably the safest capital city in West Africa. Mindelo and other large towns are equally safe. Wallet snatchings, even in the country's most touristy town, Santa Maria (Sal island), are rare. However, pick-pocketing (particularly during festivities or carnivals) does occur.

BUSINESS HOURS

Business hours are from 8am to noon or 12.30pm, and 3pm to 6pm or 7pm, Monday to Friday, and 8am to noon or 1pm Saturday. Government offices are open from 8am to 2pm Monday to Friday. Banking hours are from 8am to 3pm Monday to Friday; closed weekends. When advertising opening hours, the Portuguese system is used, in which days are numbered from 1° to 7° (ie, 1° is Sunday; 7° Saturday etc).

PUBLIC HOLIDAYS & SPECIAL EVENTS

Public holidays include:

New Year's Day 1 January
National Heroes' Day 20 January
Labour Day 1 May
Independence Day 5 July
Assumption Day 15 August
All Saints' Day 1 November
Immaculate Conception 8 December
Christmas Day 25 December

Cape Verde's main festivals include the Mardi Gras, which is held all over Cape Verde in February or March, the largest occurring in Mindelo (São Vicente); Nhô São Filipe (Fogo), held on 1 May; and the Festival de Música, held in Baia das Gatas (São Vicente) in August.

ACTIVITIES

Windsurfing and kitesurfing, scuba diving and deep-sea fishing in Santa Maria (Sal island), plus trekking in the mountains, especially on Santo Antão, are major attractions.

Prices for diving are around CVE3000 to CVE3500 for one dive (cheaper for a series) plus CVE1000 extra per dive for full equipment rental. Courses cost from CVE35,000 to CVE63,100 (PADI Open Water Diver). Diving in Cape Verde is well known for the diversity of species seen. Dolphins, whales, sharks and rays are all occasionally seen. Because of the currents that can be encountered, not all sites are suitable for beginners or inexperienced divers. Note that there is currently no decompression chamber in Cape Verde. The best months are from March to November.

To hire an F2 windsurfer costs from around €15/18 per hour for board/board-wetsuit-harness and €45/53 per day. If you come in the high season, book boards in advance. Six hours of kitesurfing tuition costs around €150.

The best months are between mid-November to mid-May (and particularly January to March when winds are strong and constant). Because the winds can be strong and blow off-shore, conditions are not ideal for beginners.

April to November (especially June to October) is good for fishing (rays, barracudas, marlins, wahoos, sharks), and trekking and cycling are good year-round.

ACCOMMODATION

Good, clean budget hotels with rooms from US$10 to US$16 (CVE1000 to CVE1500) can be found almost everywhere. In some towns, you may find only a *pousada municipal* (town resthouse). There are no camp sites but camping on a remote beach is possible and generally safe. Hotels of international standing are springing up in Praia, Mindelo and Santa Maria.

FOOD & DRINKS

Cape Verdean food is heavily Portuguese-influenced, but some dishes are unique to the islands. The national dish is *cachupa*, a tasty stew of several kinds of beans plus corn and various kinds of meat (often sausage or bacon) or fish. Another common dish is *pastel de milho*, which is made with a mix of meat or fish, some vegetables, wrapped in a pastry made from boiled potatoes and corn flour, deep-fried and served hot. *Caldos* (soups) are also popular. One of the most common is *caldo de peixe* (fish soup). See the Glossary at the end of the book for a translation of common Portuguese dishes.

For drinks, there's *grogue* (grog), the local sugar-cane spirit; *ponch* (rum, lemonade and honey); and Ceris, a decent bottled local beer.

ENTERTAINMENT

Entertainment is limited primarily to bars and nightclubs, but don't miss the chance to hear live Cape Verdean music. This can be heard in different and changing venues from large hotels to grubby, no-name bars or even on the beach. Ask locals for recommendations. See also individual town sections.

SHOPPING

Apart from the traditional crafts (weaving, pottery, baskets and mats), there's not a great deal to buy. Good hunting-grounds for arts and crafts are the shops on or just off the Praça Amilcar Cabral in Mindelo.

Getting There & Away

AIR

All international flights, except those from West Africa (which arrive at Praia), land at Sal island.

TACV Cabo Verde Airlines has flights three to four times weekly from Lisbon, and one per week from Amsterdam, Basel, Fortaleza, Munich and Paris. TAP Air Portugal has daily flights from Lisbon (CVE52,700/57,040 return for low/high season). South African Airways flies from New York and Atlanta (CVE80,350), Johannesburg (CVE76,520) and Buenos Aires (CVE135,620).

From West Africa, TACV provides connections to Praia from Dakar (Senegal) three to four times weekly and to Bissau (Guinea-Bissau) once weekly. Air Senegal (☎ 617529, fax 615483) has three flights weekly to/from Dakar (CVE18,701/26,856 one way/return).

SEA

CS Lines (☎ 611206, fax 611175, ⓔ csline-praia-cv@cvtelecom.cv) based in Praia, has freighters that ply the following route: Cape Verde–Rotterdam–Leixões (Portugal)–Lisbon–Las Palmas–Cape Verde–Guinea-Bissau–Rotterdam. There's no passenger service on any of the vessels but talk with the captain – you might manage to get a berth. Other similar agencies to try are Seage (ⓔ seage@mail.cvtelecom.cv), and Temerosa (☎ 616 161, fax 616170), with vessels to the USA.

Getting Around

AIR

TACV serves all the inhabited islands, except for Brava (until landing facilities are eventually improved). Internal flights are slightly cheaper if you buy the ticket in Cape Verde. If you'll be taking two or more internal flights, you may want to purchase TACV's Cabo Verde AirPass (available from travel agencies abroad or in Cape Verde from TACV). But, in order to qualify for the AirPass, you must fly into Cape Verde with TACV; bring along your international ticket as proof.

Using the AirPass, flights to two/three/five or more islands costs US$120/150/180 (valid from 14 to 22 days depending on how many islands you visit). Flights (to Boa Vista, Fogo, Sal and São Vicente in particular) are often full particularly over the summer months, Christmas, New Year and the carnivals, so reserve as far in advance as possible. If flights are full, try putting yourself on stand-by at the airport as no-shows occur quite frequently.

Visa and MasterCard are usually accepted for payment, as is cash in US dollars, but travellers cheques are not. Confirmation is required for all flights (domestic and international).

TACV's only rival, Inter Island Airlines, folded in 2001.

MINIBUS, BUS & TAXI

Private vehicles (labelled *aluguer* – for hire) provide regular connections between the main towns. They pick up people at unmarked points around town (ask locals for directions), set off when they're full and drop passengers off on request.

Buses also serve the major routes on São Vicente, Santo Antão and Sal. Elsewhere, your choice may be limited to taxis and hitching. Hitching is easy (though one reader has claimed that it is officially discouraged in order to protect taxi drivers from losing revenue) and payment is sometimes expected. It's usually safe but see Truck & Hitching in the Getting Around West Africa chapter for a general warning on the possible risks of hitching.

CAR

Cars can be rented on many of the islands. The largest company is Alucar (e alucarst@mail.cvtelecom.cv), with offices in Praia, São Vicente, Sal and Boa Vista. Cars cost from CVE3899 per day (Opel Corsa) to CVE5753 (4WD Opel Frontera) all-inclusive with the first 100km free (CVE0.10 per kilometre thereafter). A deposit of CVE30,000 is required. Credit cards should be accepted.

BICYCLE

Cycling is a good way to get around the islands, but there are few places to rent them; think about bringing your own. See Bicycle in the Getting Around West Africa chapter for general information.

BOAT

There are ferry connections to all nine inhabited islands and prices are reasonable. However, journeys can be long (14 or more hours) and boats stop at many ports for only a few hours – making island-hopping difficult (unless you want to stay for more than a few days or take flights). There are also few creature comforts, you can get stuck on islands because of schedules or bad weather, and timetables change every week (making advance planning difficult).

Currently there are three passenger boats linking the islands. The *Barlavento* and *Sotavento* generally follow two circuits alternately: Santiago–Maio–Santiago–Boa Vista–Santiago–Brava–Fogo–Santiago. The newer *Praia d'Aguada* plies between Santiago–São Vicente–Santiago–Fogo–Brava–Santiago–Sal–São Nicolau–São Vicente. The freighter *13 Janeiro* accepts some passengers if there is enough demand and covers parts of the same routes, such as between Santiago, Fogo and Brava. To find out schedules, or book, head for the Arca Verde, which posts a new 10-day schedule in front of its various offices (see individual island sections for contact details).

Prices range from CVE1400 to CVE4900 for 1st-class cabins (a bunk in one of the four-berth cabins) to CVE700 to CVE2700 (for a 2nd-class salon – an overcrowded bench) and depend on distance travelled. There is a shared shower on the *Praia d'Aguada* but only basins on the other boat. There is usually a small bar that sells drinks and sandwiches. Get there one hour before departure.

Santiago

Santiago was the first island to be settled and with around 150,000 inhabitants (about 40% of the total population) is the major island of the Cape Verde archipelago. Principal attractions include the relaxed capital city, Praia, the old Portuguese settlement, Cidade Velha, superb beaches at Tarrafal and the mountainous interior.

PRAIA

pop 78,000

Praia is Cape Verde's largest city, has the country's most colourful food market and some good beaches. The town centre, on a large fortress-like plateau (*platô*; hence the name Platô) overlooking the ocean, is quite imposing.

Orientation

Around Platô, the town tumbles onto the land below: to the north is the commercial

PRAIA

PLACES TO STAY
8 Residencial Paraiso
24 Residencial Anjos
32 Residencial Praia Maria
35 Hotel Felicidade; Restaurante Panorama
40 Residencial Adega
52 Residencial Sol Atlântico
62 Hotel Marisol
69 Hotel América; Discoteca Macumba
75 Hotel Trópico
78 Hotel Praia Mar; Capital

PLACES TO EAT
1 Bar-Restaurante le Paris
4 Garden Grill Restaurante
15 Casa de Pasto Amélia
19 Pastelaria Vilu
22 Restaurante Flor de Lis
23 Lanchonette Aquarium
27 Restaurante Bar O Dragão
28 Restaurante Avis
29 Lanchonette Atryum
30 Sofia Fashion Café
50 Snack-Bar Cachito; Banco Interatlântico; Instituto da Biblioteca Nacional
58 Ártica
63 Restaurante Gamboa; Rentalauto
73 Restaurante Bar O Poeta
77 Bar-Restaurante A Falésia

OTHER
2 Church
3 Caixa Económica do Cabo Verde
5 Zéro Horas
6 Liceu
7 Police
9 Senegalese Embassy
10 Air Senegal
11 Sucupira Market; Minibus Station
12 Caixa Económica do Cabo Verde
13 Sal da Música
14 Arca Verde (Ferry Information)
16 Museum
17 US Embassy
18 Photo Quick
20 Bus Stop
21 Hospital
25 Praiatur
26 Orbitur
31 Platô Bus Stop
33 Cine-Teatro
34 Casa Felicidade
36 Verdean Tours
37 Minibus Stop & Taxis; Moneychangers
38 Termfrio
39 Banco do Cabo Verde
41 TACV (Head Office)
42 Direcção de Emigracão e Fronteiras (Immigration)
43 Cabetur
44 Swiss Consulate
45 Main Post Office
46 Centro Cultural Francês (French Cultural Institute)
47 Church
48 Tourist Information
49 Adega
51 Farmacia Modern
53 Banco Comercial do Atlântico
54 Ministry of Foreign Affairs
55 Palácio da República 56
56 Vehicles for Cidade Velha
57 Palácio do Governo
59 TAP (Air Portugal)
60 Alucar
61 Petrol Station
64 Italian Consulate
65 Banco Comercial do Atlântico
66 Supermercados Felicidades
67 TACV
68 Pharmacy
70 National Assembly
71 Promex; DHL
72 Portuguese Embassy
74 French Embassy
76 Spanish Honorary Consulate

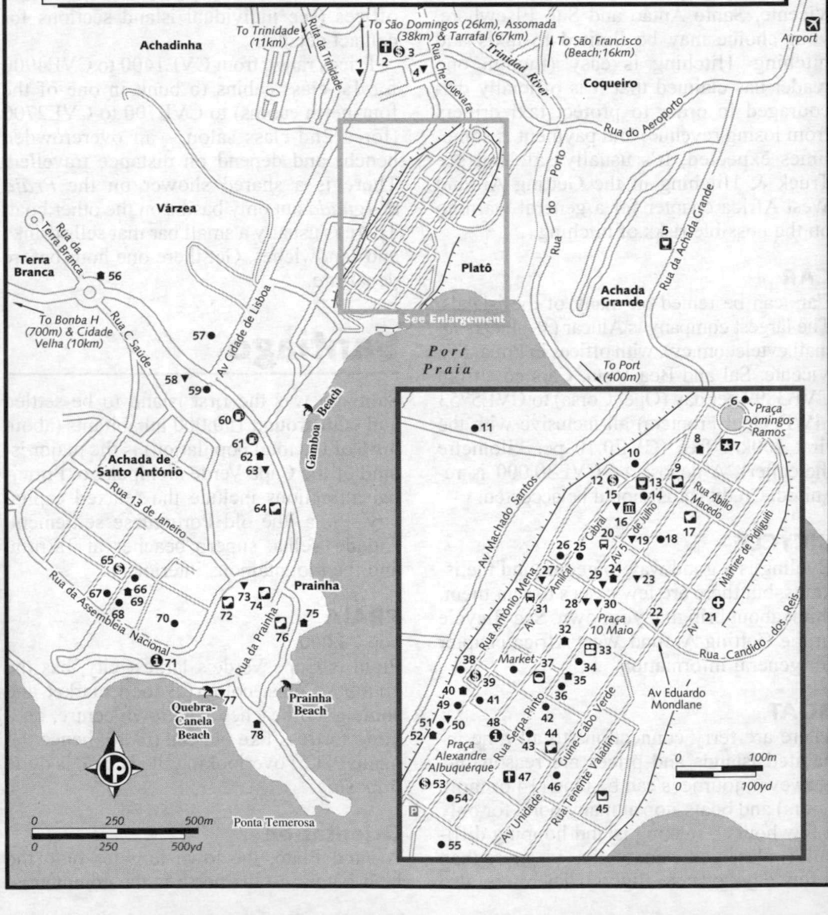
To Trinidade (11km)
Ruta da Trinidade
To São Domingos (26km), Assomada (38km) & Tarrafal (67km)
Rua Che-Guevara
Trinidad River
To São Francisco (Beach;16km)
Airport
Achadinha
Coqueiro
Rua do Aeroporto
Rua do Porto
Várzea
Rua da Achada Grande
Rua da Terra Branca
Terra Branca
Platô
Achada Grande
To Bonba H (700m) & Cidade Velha (10km)
Rua C Saúde
Av Cidade de Lisboa
See Enlargement
Port Praia
To Port (400m)
Gamboa Beach
Achada de Santo António
Rua 13 de Janeiro
Rua da Assembleia Nacional
Prainha
Rua da Prainha
Quebra-Canela Beach
Prainha Beach
Ponta Temerosa
0 250 500m
0 250 500yd
Praça Domingos Ramos
Av Machado Santos
Rua Abílio Macedo
Rua Cabral
Av 5 de Julho
Av Mártires de Pidjiguiti
Rua Amílcar
Rua Antonio Mena
Praça 10 Maio
Av Rua Candido dos Reis
Market
Av Eduardo Mondlane
Rua Serpa Pinto
Rua Guiné-Cabo Verde
Praça Alexandre Albuquérque
Rua Tenente Valadim
Av Unidade
0 100m
0 100yd

district of Fazenda; to the east Achada Grande and the port; and to the southwest, the more affluent, residential area of Achada de Santo Antoio, where the parliament building and some embassies are also found. Due south of the Platô, is the beachfront area, known as Prainha, where the pricier hotels, bars and some embassies are found.

Information

Tourist Offices The Promex office (☎ 622 621, fax 622737, ⓔ Promex@mail.cvtelecom .cv) is in Achada de Santo António.

Money Banco Comercial do Atlântico (☎ 612400), Banco do Cabo Verde (☎ 615 561) and Banco Interatlântico (☎ 618430) change cash and travellers cheques, and give Visa card cash advances. If the banks are closed, moneychangers are at the back of the market on the Platô. Caixa Económica do Cabo Verde (☎ 603560) near Air Senegal, organises Western Union transfers.

Post & Communications The post office is situated three blocks east of the main *praça* (park or square). DHL (☎ 623124) is next door to the Promex office. Sofia Fashion Café (on Praça 10 Maio) provides Internet access for CVE200 per 30 minutes.

Travel Agencies & Tour Operators The oldest travel agency is Cabetur (☎ 615551, fax 615553). Other agencies include Praatur (☎ 615746, fax 614500), Orbitur (☎ 615736, fax 613888) and Verdean Tours (☎ 608280, fax 613879). If you send a fax of your itinerary, agencies can organise flights, accommodation and car rental.

Bookshops The Instituto da Biblioteca Nacional (inside the Palácio da Cultura), next door to Snack-Bar Cachito, is good if you are looking for local publications, but most are in Portuguese.

Museum

The museum *(admission CVE100; open 10am-noon & 3pm-6pm Mon, Wed & Fri, 10am-1pm Tues),* on the Platô, is in a restored colonial house and has displays (with panels in Portuguese only) that recount the history of the islands and include items salvaged from wrecks (including canon shot, bracelets, pipes, vases and coins). There are examples of traditional agricultural and fishing tools, Portuguese-influenced porcelain and woven cloth (including shawls). If pressed for time, you can easily give this place a miss.

Beaches

The most popular beach is Praianha just east of Hotel Praia Mar. Better is the beach west of Hotel Praia Mar, Quebra-Canela, because it's not so packed and the body-surfing is good.

Places to Stay – Budget

***Residencial Sol Atlántico** (☎ 612872)* Singles/doubles without bathroom CVE1000/2000, with bathroom CVE1700/2700. This place is clean, centrally located and good value. Ask for a room overlooking the square.

***Residencial Adega** (☎ 615924, fax 615902)* Singles/doubles with bathroom CVE2800/3800. This is a pleasant and spacious place.

***Residencial Anjos** (☎ 617538, fax 615701)* Singles/doubles with telephone CVE2200/2700, with TV, air-con & minibar CVE2500/ 3000. This place is quite good value and is worth considering.

***Residencial Paraiso** (☎ 613539)* costs CVE2300/3500 for singles/doubles with bathroom and is in a peaceful location.

***Hotel Felicidade** (☎ 615585, fax 611289)* charges CVE2000/3200.

Places to Stay – Mid-Range & Top End

***Hotel América** (☎ 621431, fax 621432, Achada de Santo António)* Singles/doubles

São Francisco Beach

The best beaches on the southern side of Santiago island are at São Francisco, 16km northeast of Praia. There's no bus so you'll need to hitch (easiest on weekends) or take a taxi (CVE3000 return). Bring food and water as there are no drinks stalls or cafés. If you reserve in advance, you can stay at Kingfish (☎/fax 611661), which has simple but clean and spacious bungalows with bathroom and kitchen for 2/4/6 people from €65/75/105, plus food. This attractive hideaway on the beach caters mostly to Germans who made advance bookings.

with TV, telephone & air-con CVE5000/5500. Although it's very comfortable, this hotel is a bit far from the main drag.

Residencial Praia Maria *(☎ 618580, fax 618554)* Singles/doubles CVE4500/5600. This is also a good place to stay.

Hotel Marisol *(☎ 613460, fax 612538)* Singles/doubles CVE5200/6500. Rooms here have sea views, but some are on the small side and are a little overpriced.

Hotel Praia Mar *(☎ 613777, fax 612972)* Singles/doubles CVE8050/10,600. Relax and enjoy the pool, tennis court and nightclub.

Hotel Trópico *(☎ 614200, fax 615225, ⓔ hotel.tropico@mail.cvtelecom.cv)* Singles/doubles CVE9100/11,000. This is the city's top address.

Places to Eat

Most restaurants are open until around 10pm from Monday to Saturday; smaller restaurants and cafés from 7.30am to around 8pm.

City Centre For cheap snacks, try the little ***mobile kiosks*** on Praça Alexandre Albuquérque, which sell toasted sandwiches/hamburgers for CVE100/120.

Casa de Pasto Amélia *(☎ 614003)* Set menu CVE600. This is a simple but popular, family-run place offering good, local food. ***Restaurante Flor de Lis*** serves similar dishes at slightly lower prices.

Restaurante Gamboa Mains CVE750-2800. This is considered one of the best restaurants in town.

Restaurante Avis *(☎ 613079)* serves traditional mains for CVE500 to CVE1500 and is also a good place for coffee and cake (try the jam roll). ***Sofia Fashion Café*** *(☎ 614205)* has tables on Praça 10 Maio, and is a pleasant place for a drink and a snack in the evening.

Other places to try for cheap local fare (around CVE350 to CVE500) are ***Lanchonette Aquarium***, ***Lanchonette Atryum*** and ***Snack-Bar Cachito***, which has a good selection of local snacks as well as mains.

More upmarket is Hotel Felicidade's ***Restaurante Panorama***. The terrace here is also a good place for a beer in the evening. For Chinese food cooked by a Chinese chef, try ***Restaurante Bar O Dragão*** *(☎ 616972)*.

A good place for local snacks as well as slices of pizza, sandwiches and pastries, is ***Pastelaria Vilu***, diagonally opposite the Museum.

Suburbs Check out the smart dining room at ***Bar-Restaurante le Paris*** *(☎ 617553)* with a decent selection of reasonably priced meat and fish dishes for CVE450 to CVE1600.

Restaurante Bar O Poeta *(☎ 613800)* Mains CVE800-1200. This is considered one of the best restaurants in the city and it has sea views from its terrace.

Bar-Restaurante A Falésia Cocktails CVE270-400, milkshakes CVE250, ice cream CVE360-400, salads CVE600-800, seafood CVE1400-2400, traditional mains CVE800-1200. Not far from the Quebra-Canela beach, this place is attractively set above the ocean. Snacks are also available and it's a good spot for an evening beer.

Garden Grill Restaurante *(☎ 612050)* is set in a very pleasant, leafy courtyard. There's traditional music every night from around 8.30pm to midnight. The restaurant at ***Hotel Trópico*** is also considered good. You will pay CVE1000 or more for a meal here.

Ártica *(☎ 603302)* has great, home-made ice cream and cakes, as well as juices, snacks (such as pizzas and hamburgers) and mains.

Self-Catering For a picnic, try ***Termfrio***, with a selection of patés, hams and cheeses. Other supermarkets include ***Casa Felicidade*** on the Platô and ***Supermercados Felicidades*** in Achada de Santo António. Considered the best supermarket in the centre is ***Adega*** on Praça Alexandre Albuquérque.

Entertainment

Bars & Nightclubs For a popular local hang-out, try the small ***Restaurante Flor de Lis***. To hear great local music, head straight for ***5al da Música*** *(☎ 617282)*, where there's live music every night from around 10.30pm (except Tuesday). It also sells a good selection of CDs.

Most nightclubs charge around CVE200 to CVE300 from Monday to Thursday and CVE500 on Friday and Saturday. Those currently in favour are: ***Bonba H*** (around 1.7km out of town off the Cidade Velha road), ***Zéro Horas*** and ***Discoteca Macumba*** beneath Hotel América. A smarter place for a slightly older crowd, is ***Capital*** next to Hotel Praia Mar restaurant on Prainha beach.

:inemas The *Cine-Teatro* usually shows Iollywood films (with Portuguese subtitles) ıt 4.30pm, 6.30pm and 9.45pm. Tickets cost :VE250/400 for normal/balcony seats. *:entro Cultural Francês* (☎ *611196)* shows ilms in French at 8.30pm every Wednesday ıs well as staging concerts and exhibitions.

;etting There & Away

ʌir TACV's head office (☎ 608200, fax ,17528, at the airport ☎ 633982, ⓔ promo ao@tacv.com) is on Avenida Amilcar :abral. There are daily flights to Boa Vista CVE6256/10,694 one way/return, two ıours via Sal), one to two flights daily to 'ogo (CVE4842/8270, 20 minutes), three lights weekly to Maio (CVE3933/6856, 15 ninutes), six to 10 flights daily to Mindelo CVE8579/14,633, 45 minutes) and Sal CVE8579/14,633, 45 minutes), one flight veekly to Santo Antão (CVE 9084/15,340, ne hour) and daily flights to São Nicolau CVE7670/13,070, two hours).

ʌinibus There are private aluguer (for ire) minibuses to most towns that leave rom next to Sucupira market. Those for 'arrafal depart daily starting around 9.30am nd cost CVE250.

:oat Ferries leave from the port, but tickts and schedules can be obtained at Arca 'erde (☎ 615497, fax 615496) on the Platô. 'or ferry information, see the Getting ɹround section earlier in this chapter.

;etting Around

o/From the Airport A taxi from the airort to the centre (1.5km) costs around :VE250 (CVE300 to CVE400 at night). 'here are no buses.

:us Large Transcor buses connect the Platô ʼith all sections of the city and short joureys cost from CVE0.25. Destinations are ıarked on the windshields.

axi Fares are from CVE150 to CVE200 for short trip in town. If you're hiring a taxi by ıe hour, CVE500 to CVE600 is fair. If in oubt, ask the driver to switch on the meter hough they're not always 'working').

ar Rentalauto (☎ 613844, fax 613835) and ɹlucar (☎ 617324, fax 614900), both near Hotel Marisol, have reasonable cars at good prices (see the Getting Around section earlier in the chapter).

CIDADE VELHA

Cidade Velha, once called Ribeira Grande, is situated 10km west of Praia. It was the first town built by the Portuguese in Africa and is now a Unesco World Heritage site. The best-preserved structures are the ruins of the old cathedral, constructed in 1693 during the city's heyday, and the Pillory in the park where enslaved captives were chained up and displayed. A walk up the hill to Fort Real de São Filipe is worthwhile; it's remarkably well preserved and commands a great view of the village.

Getting There & Away

Buses from Praia (CVE70, 15 minutes) leave from Sucupira market. Finding a minibus back to Praia can take a while, so consider coming by taxi instead and having your driver wait.

PRAIA TO ASSOMADA

São Domingos is situated 25km north of the capital on the inland road to Tarrafal. The journey will give you an idea of what the formidable mountainous interior is like.

Facilities include ***Bar-Restaurant Morena*** (☎ *611252)* and the hotel ***Pousada Bela Vista*** (☎ *611475)*, although you may have trouble finding someone to open it.

> **Cidade Velha – Slaves & Pirates**
>
> In the late 16th century, Ribeira Grande, with its good harbour and reliable source of water, became the principal staging post for slave ships sailing between West Africa and the Caribbean. Some ships disembarked slaves, later to be sold and shipped away (usually to the West Indies). Ribeira Grande soon became the most important Portuguese settlement outside Portugal and for a number of pirates, including Englishman Sir Francis Drake, the prosperous Portuguese enclave was irresistible. In 1585, during one of his worldwide voyages, he plundered the town and forts. When one of his men was killed, Drake took revenge by setting the town aflame. The town was rebuilt, however, and continued to prosper through the following century.

In São Jorge dos Orgãos, 15km further on, there are good views of the island's highest peak, **Pico do Santo António** (1394m). There is good hiking in the area. Unfortunately, the one hotel in town, ***Rancho Relax***, has closed.

Further along is Picos, affording stunning views of an impressive basaltic outcrop nearby. The **Jardim Botanico Nacional** (botanical gardens) are lower down (around 2.3km off the main road) and are good for short walks or a picnic.

To get to any of these villages, take any bus to Assomada and get off en route.

ASSOMADA

Assomada, the largest town in the interior, has a lively market and some old colonial buildings. Just north of town is a monstrously large silk cotton tree, which is thought to be some 500 years old. To get there, head for Boa Entrada, a short walk north from town, then turn right and down into the valley.

Asa Branca *(☎ 652372)* Rooms with bathroom & meal CVE1500. This is a basic but clean place on the main street.

Café Paris *(☎ 653502)* Singles/doubles with bathroom CVE2200/2800. Not far away from Asa Branca, the rooms here are spotless.

In Praia, minibuses for Assomada (CVE200) leave from Sucupira market starting around 9.30am.

TARRAFAL

Around 68km north of Praia is Tarrafal's attractive, white-sand, palm-lined beach. From the bay on the northern side you can walk northward via a path leading up the cliffs.

Nest to Hotel Baia Verde, there's the German-run Dive Center Blue Adventure (☎/fax 661880). Around 1km outside Tarrafal, on the road to Praia, there's an old fort that is signposted. Admission costs CVE50, but it's not wildly interesting.

Places to Stay

Hotel Sol Marina *(☎ 661219)* Singles/doubles with bathroom CVE1500/1800. This place has rooms overlooking the bay.

Baia Verde *(☎ 661128, fax 661414)* Bungalows with TV & fridge for 1/2/4 people CVE2600/3000/6000. Set among coconut groves on the bay, Baia Verde offers well-furnished rooms and has a pleasant, tropica[l] ambience.

Pensão Mille et Nuits *(☎ 661463, fa[x] 661878)* Rooms CVE2500. Two block[s] south of the park this place also has [a] restaurant.

Pensão Tá-Tá *(☎ 661125)* Singles/double[s] with bathroom CVE1500/2000. Across th[e] street from Pensão Mille et Nuits, the Tá-T[á] has spotless rooms and a restaurant.

Hotel Tarrafal *(☎ 661785, fax 661787)* Singles/doubles CVE5000/6000. This hote[l] has a small pool and all rooms come wit[h] air-con, TV, telephone and minibar an[d] some have their own balcony.

Places to Eat

Casa de Pasto Sopa de Pedra *(☎ 661328)* Meals CVE250-300. This place, just sout[h] of the central park, is simple but popular.

Bar-Restaurant Graciosa *(☎ 661129)* Chicken/fish & rice CVE400. Near Casa d[e] Pasto Sopa de Pedra, this eatery has no se[t] menu, but serves cheap daily dishes.

Pensão Tá-Tá, one block south of th[e] Graciosa, is similar. The best restaurant is a[t] ***Hotel Baia Verde*** with mains for aroun[d] CVE800.

Getting There & Away

Minibuses from Praia (CVE250) depa[rt] from Sucupira market; from Tarrafal the[y] leave from the western end of the centra[l] park.

São Vicente

São Vicente is home to one of Cape Verde'[s] prettiest cities, Mindelo, and a small, sta[rk] mountainous interior that, although less i[n]teresting than that of nearby Santo Antão, i[s] only minutes away by taxi.

If you decide to travel inland, thre[e] places that are worth visiting include M[onte] Verde (750m), the island's highest peak[,] and the beaches at Calhau and at Baia da[s] Gatas, 15km east of Mindelo. A good tim[e] to come here is August when the Festival d[e] Música takes place. Attracting musicians o[f] all styles from around the islands, the fest[i]val runs over a weekend and comprises [a] heady mixture of dancing, singing, pe[r]forming, swimming...and lying exhauste[d] on the beach.

FRANCES LINZEE GORDON

JANE SWEENEY

ANTHONY HAM

ARIADNE VAN ZANDBERGEN

Sandy streets and secluded alleyways are typical of West African towns: the Cape Verde town of Porto Novo with its spectacular mountain backdrop (top); downtown Nouâdhibou, Mauritania (middle left); the famous Hôtel de l'Aïr in Agadez, Niger (middle right); brightly painted walls and narrow lanes on Île de Gorée, Senegal (bottom)

JOHN ELK III

JANE SWEENEY

ANTHONY HAM

DAVID ELSE

From urban sprawl to village huts, home takes many different forms in West Africa: dry and dusty Timbuktu, Mali (top); the rooftops of Kano from Dala Hill, Nigeria (middle left); a small family compound in Rhumsiki, Cameroon (middle right); mud-brick village on the banks of the Niger River, Mali (bottom)

MINDELO

pop 50,000

Mindelo is Cape Verde's deepest port and its liveliest town. Its heyday was in the late 19th century when the British operated a coaling station to fuel ships.

The city, with the sea on one side and tall barren hills on the other is picturesque enough and also features cobbled streets, lined with palms.

The town's Portuguese colonial houses are painted in pastel colours with white trim, and are very photogenic.

Much of what there is to see and do is on or off Rua de Libertad d'Africa. Praça Amilcar Cabral is vibrant from 6pm to 11pm. At weekends a band plays here from 7pm to 8.30pm.

Information

Tourist Offices The tourist kiosk on Avenida 5 de Julho has postcards, hotel prices, maps of the various islands and schedules of ferries to/from Santo Antão.

Money Banks in Mindelo offering the usual services include Banco Comercial do Atlântico on Rua de Libertad d'Africa and Caixa Económica on Avenida 5 De Julho.

Post & Communications The post office is inside the telecommunications building. It keeps normal business hours and is also open at weekends (8am to 11.30am and 3pm to 5pm on Saturday, and 8am to 11.30am Sunday). Telecommunications is open from 8am to 10pm Monday to Friday.

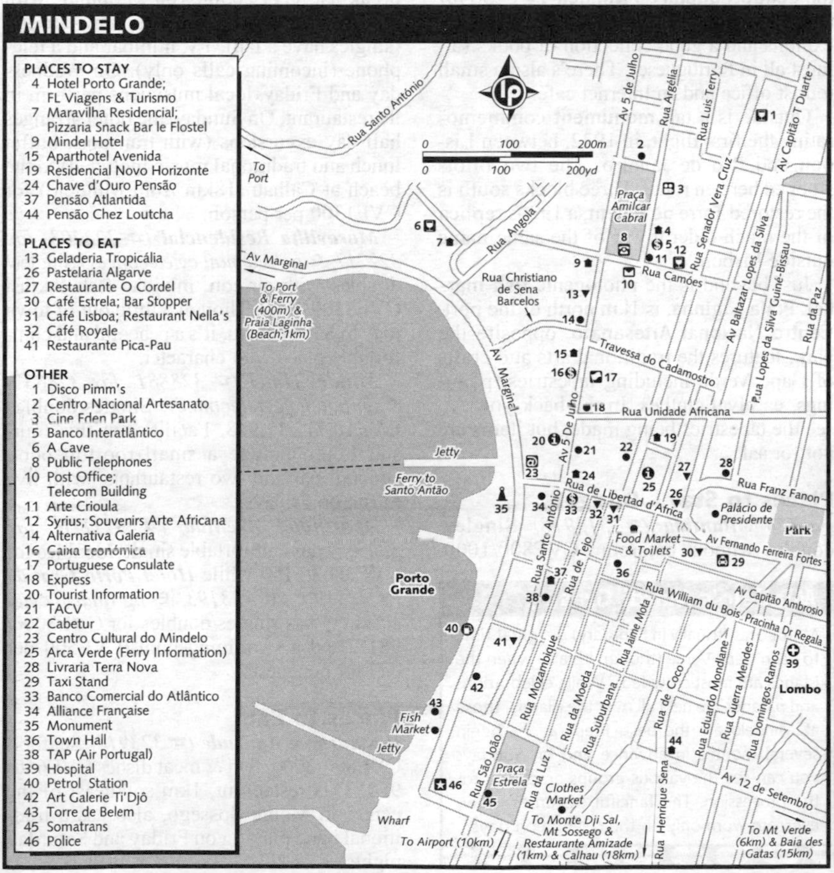
MINDELO
PLACES TO STAY
4 Hotel Porto Grande; FL Viagens & Turismo
7 Maravilha Residencial; Pizzaria Snack Bar le Flostel
9 Mindel Hotel
15 Aparthotel Avenida
19 Residencial Novo Horizonte
24 Chave d'Ouro Pensão
37 Pensão Atlantida
44 Pensão Chez Loutcha
PLACES TO EAT
13 Geladeria Tropicália
26 Pastelaria Algarve
27 Restaurante O Cordel
30 Café Estrela; Bar Stopper
31 Café Lisboa; Restaurant Nella's
32 Café Royale
41 Restaurante Pica-Pau
OTHER
1 Disco Pimm's
2 Centro Nacional Artesanato
3 Cine Eden Park
5 Banco Interatlântico
6 A Cave
8 Public Telephones
10 Post Office; Telecom Building
11 Arte Crioula
12 Syrius; Souvenirs Arte Africana
14 Alternativa Galeria
16 Caixa Económica
17 Portuguese Consulate
18 Express
20 Tourist Information
21 TACV
22 Cabetur
23 Centro Cultural do Mindelo
25 Arca Verde (Ferry Information)
28 Livraria Terra Nova
29 Taxi Stand
33 Banco Comercial do Atlântico
34 Alliance Française
35 Monument
36 Town Hall
38 TAP (Air Portugal)
39 Hospital
40 Petrol Station
42 Art Galerie Ti'Djô
43 Torre de Belem
45 Somatrans
46 Police
Rua Santo António
To Port
Rua Angola
Av Marginal
To Port & Ferry (400m) & Praia Laginha (Beach; 1km)
Rua Christiano de Sena Barcelos
Praça Amilcar Cabral
Av 5 de Julho
Rua Argélia
Rua Luis Terry
Av Capitão T Duarte
Rua Senador Vera Cruz
Rua Camões
Travessa do Cadamostro
Rua Unidade Africana
Rua de Libertad d'Africa
Rua Franz Fanon
Palácio de Presidente
Park
Av Fernando Ferreira Fortes
Food Market & Toilets
Jetty
Ferry to Santo Antão
Porto Grande
Rua William du Bois
Av Capitão Ambrosio
Pracinha Dr Regala
Lombo
Fish Market
Wharf
Praça Estrela
Clothes Market
Av 12 de Setembro
To Airport (10km)
To Monte Dji Sal, Mt Sossego & Restaurante Amizade (1km) & Calhau (18km)
To Mt Verde (6km) & Baia des Gatas (15km)

The Alliance Française (☎ 321149) has an Internet café that charges CVE150 per 30 minutes as does the Internet café at the Centro Cultural do Mindelo.

Travel Agencies & Tour Operators Cabetur (☎ 323847, fax 323842) and FL Viagens & Turismo (☎ 322844) can both arrange island tours. A day tour to São Vicente/Santo Antão, for example, including lunch costs CVE4120/6290 per person for one/three people.

Things to See & Do

From the old **Palácio de Presidente**, now the office of the island's governing council, you can walk down Rua de Libertad d'Africa to the restored old **food market**. Just beyond is the **Centro Cultural do Mindelo** *(☎ 325840)* at the harbour. The centre houses changing exhibits and a good collection of books (almost all in Portuguese). There's also a small tourist office and an Internet café.

Outside is a tall **monument** commemorating the first flight, in 1922, between Lisbon and Rio de Janeiro. The two pilots stopped here en route. Three blocks south is the restored **Torre de Belem**, a 1920s replica of the much older tower of the same name outside Lisbon.

Just beyond is the photogenic **fish market**. **Praia Laginha**, is 1km north of the port. **Centro Nacional Artesanato**, opposite the park, features the traditional arts and crafts of Cape Verde including tapestries, paintings, carnival clothes. In the back you can see the tapestries being made, but items are not for sale.

Places to Stay – Budget

***Pensão Atlantida** (☎ 313918)* Singles/doubles without bathroom CVE800/1000. This is a grubby and rundown place and is only for those on their last cent.

***Chave d'Ouro Pensão** (☎ 337050)* 2nd-floor singles/doubles CVE927/1200, singles/doubles without bathroom CVE1500/1750. The rooms here are old and colonial-like and the 2nd-floor rooms resemble an attic. It also has a good restaurant and the bathrooms are clean.

***Residencial Novo Horizonte** (☎ 323915)* Singles/doubles with bathroom & breakfast CVE1600/2000. This place is basic, but clean.

> **Mindelo's Mardi Gras**
>
> Mardi Gras (usually in February) is a great time to be in Cape Verde (though it's also when the islands are most crowded). While celebrations and parades are held all over the islands, those at Mindelo are the best. Preparations begin several months in advance and on Sundays you can see the various groups practising for the procession. The fanciful costumes, however, are worn only on the celebration days.

Places to Stay – Mid-Range & Top End

***Pensão Chez Loutcha** (☎ 321636, fax 321635)* Singles/doubles with bathroom & breakfast CVE2050/3160. Popular with readers, the Loutcha's rooms have air-con (singles have a fan), TV, minibar and a telephone (incoming calls only). On Wednesday and Friday, local musicians perform in its restaurant. On Sunday, the hotel arranges half-day excursions (with transport, buffet lunch and traditional music included) to the beach at Calhau (18km from Mindelo) for CVE1300 per person.

***Maravilha Residencial** (☎ 322203, fax 322217, e gabs@mail.cvtelecom.cv)* Singles/doubles with air-con, minibar & breakfast CVE3500/4500. Though a little out of town in Alto São Nicolau, it's a peaceful and comfortable place with character.

***Mindel Hotel** (☎ 328881, fax 328837, e mihotel@cvtelecom.cv)* Singles/doubles CVE10,712/11,948. Facilities at this four-star hotel include a small rooftop pool, cocktail bar and two restaurants (with live music on Fridays).

***Aparthotel Avenida** (☎ 321176, fax 322333)* has comfortable singles/doubles for CVE3863/5150 while ***Hotel Porto Grande** (☎ 323190, fax 323193, e pgrande@cvtelecom.cv)* has singles/doubles for CVE8000/9815, and a swimming pool (CVE500 per day for nonguests).

Places to Eat

***Restaurante Amizade** (☎ 323917)* Seafood CVE800-3000, fish & meat dishes CVE650-950. This restaurant, 1km southeast of the centre in Monte Sossego, also has a traditional band playing on Friday and Saturday nights.

Chave d'Ouro Pensão has a nice old-world atmosphere and serves good Cape Verdean food (from CVE500). Next door to the Maravilha Residencial is the newly opened ***Pizzaria Snack Bar le Flostel***, with good pizzas at decent prices (CVE300 to CVE500) as well as other mains (CVE350 to CVE400).

At ***Geladeria Tropicália*** you can get sandwiches, light meals and ice cream. ***Restaurante Pica-Pau*** *(☎ 328207)*, though simple, serves good food for around CVE500 to CVE700. The smarter ***Restaurante O Cordel*** *(☎ 322962)* has a French-Portuguese menu with dishes around CVE750 to CVE850. Another good place for seafood and fresh fish is ***Restaurant Nella's*** *(☎ 314321)*,situated above Café Lisboa. It also has live music sometimes at weekends. ***Pastelaria Algarve*** nearby is a good place for coffee and cake.

Entertainment

Bars & Nightclubs Unfortunately, ***Café Portugal*** has been renovated and has lost its charm, but ***Café Royale*** still draws crowds looking for a drink (and does good breakfasts too). The tiny ***Café Lisboa*** is better for espresso, but you can get a beer as well.

Syrius, A Cave *(☎ 327802)* and the intimate ***Disco Pimm's*** *(☎ 314597)* are currently considered the hottest places.

Cinemas Movie buffs should head for ***Cine Eden Park*** *(☎ 325354)*, which shows one film at 7.15pm daily (6.30pm and 9.30pm on Saturday). Normal/balcony seats cost CVE200/300.

Shopping

Alternativa Galeria *(☎ 315165)* sells unusual ceramics. ***Arte Crioula*** has quite a good selection of batiks, rugs and tapestries, clay pots and figurines, as well as postcards and fruit liquors from San Antaõ. ***Souvenirs Arte Africana***, next door to Syrius nightclub, has probably the best selection of batiks, jewellery, clothes and baskets.

Getting There & Away

Air TACV (☎ 321524, fax 323719, at the airport ☎ 323717) has six to 10 flights daily to and from Praia (CVE3933/6856 one way/return) and two to three flights daily to Sal (CVE8579/14,633, 45 minutes).

Sea Ferries connect Mindelo with most islands. For up-to-date prices and schedules, contact Arca Verde (☎ 321349, fax 324963). Tickets for ferries to Santo Antão are sold at the Somatrans agency. See also the main Getting Around section at the start of this chapter and the Santo Antão sections.

Getting Around

The taxi stand is on Avenida Fernando Ferreira Fortes. It costs CVE700 to the airport.

For car rental, Alucar (☎ 311150, fax 315169) is in Monte Dji Sal.

AROUND SÃO VICENTE

For views of Mindelo and the bay, take a taxi (6km) to **Mt Verde** (750m), the island's highest peak. Alternatively, it's a one-hour hike.

The most popular beach is at **Baia das Gatas**, 15km east of Mindelo. There's no bus service but on Sundays you may be able to hitch a ride (follow Avenida 12 de Setembro to the outskirts). A taxi there costs CVE1000 to CVE2000, depending on how long you stay. There is another beach at **Calhau**, 18km southeast of Mindelo.

Santo Antão

Santo Antão is Cape Verde's greenest island, with beautiful scenery, pine and cedar trees and a European-like climate. The verdant valleys leading down towards the ocean, provide magnificent views, making this the best island for hiking and mountain biking. The town of Paúl, dramatically set above the sea, also provides a good base for hiking.

RIBEIRA GRANDE & PORTO NOVO

Ribeira Grande, the administrative centre, is nothing special but the location – hemmed in by steep cliffs and the Atlantic Ocean – is impressive. Porto Novo, the major port 36km away on the eastern coast (CVE2500 by taxi one way), is somewhat less interesting. Both have a hospital, bank, travel agency and options for car hire. Porto Novo has a small but helpful tourist office just opposite the disembarkation point.

Places to Stay & Eat

Residencial Restaurante Antilhas *(☎ 221 193, Porto Novo)* Singles/doubles without

Hiking on Santo Antão

One of the most popular routes is up Ribeira Grande valley, which starts a few kilometres southwest of Ribeira Grande town. You can walk from Ribeira Grande (taking the road towards Cruzinha da Garça) or, to save an hour or so, take the occasional minibus that goes up the valley for several kilometres. A guide (around CVE1500) can be helpful but isn't essential. After several kilometres of flat road, take a left and start the climb. Initially, the slope is gentle and takes you through cultivated fields. You'll soon pass through a small village where you can get drinks. Houses, mostly stone, are spread out along the route. Further on, the gradient gets steeper. After an hour or so, you'll reach the cooler summit, with spectacular views if you aren't clouded in. Continue along the path and you'll eventually come to a dirt road. Take a left on this road and continue walking (northeast) along the plateau; within an hour or so you'll come to the trans-island road, where you can hitch to Ribeira Grande or Porto Novo. The hike takes at least half a day, usually longer. Some travellers arrange for taxis to pick them up at the top (about CVE2500).

A second popular hike is along the coastal road from Ribeira Grande east to Paúl and Janela (16km). Or hitch to Paúl (10km) and begin the hike there.

A third hike begins at Paúl and goes inland up the Vale do Paúl, an exceptionally verdant and lovely valley. The road passes by fields of sugar cane to Passagem (4km) and on up to Cova Crater (1170m) and the trans-island road. There's a small swimming pool (CVE100) in Passagem and a café open on weekends. That pretty village is where much of Cape Verde's grogue is distilled. You can also do this hike in the opposite direction.

A fourth hike is along the Ribeira das Fontainhas, departing westward from Ribeira Grande to Cruzinha da Garça via Fontainhas. You can stop en route at Ponta do Sol, a particularly picturesque village.

A fifth hike is up the trans-island road from Porto Novo to Cova Crater.

bathroom CVE1000/1400, with bathroom CVE1500/1800. This place is spotless, pleasantly furnished and good value.

Residencial Restaurante Pôr do Sol *(☎ 222179, fax 221166)* Singles with bathroom & breakfast CVE1500, doubles CVE2700-3400. Pôr do Sol is even smarter than the Antilhas and has good-value, bright, spacious rooms. It also has a restaurant.

Residencial Aliança *(☎ 211246, Ribeira Grande)* Rooms without/with bathroom CVE1200/1500. Rooms here vary, so ask to see them first. Better is ***Residencial 5 de Julho*** *(☎ 211345)* with rooms for CVE1500/2000 without/with bathroom.

Residencial Tropical *(☎ 211129, fax 212126)* Singles/doubles with bathroom, TV & minibar CVE2200/3200. The Tropical is situated at the far end of town and has very clean rooms as well as quite a pleasant terrace and restaurant.

Pensão Lizette *(☎ 251048, Ponta do Sol)* Singles/doubles with breakfast CVE1800/2600. Near the airport, this pension has clean rooms.

Residencial Vale do Paúl *(☎ 231319, Paúl)* Rooms without bathroom CVE1300. This place is set on the seafront and has simple but pleasant rooms and a restaurant.

Getting There & Away

TACV (☎ 211184) has weekly flights to/from Praia (CVE9084/15,340 one way/return, one hour) and weekly flights to São Vicente (CVE4236/7361 one way/return, 25 minutes).

Ferries (the *Ribeira Paúl* and the more comfortable *Mar Novo*) ply the route daily between Mindelo and Porto Novo (CVE500 one way, one hour). Schedules change, but in general, there are two ferries a day (but not Tuesday and Sunday when there's just one) in the morning and afternoon to/from Mindelo. Boats normally leave for Mindelo for Porto Novo either at 8am (9am Sunday), noon and 3pm and return at either 10.30am, noon and 5pm. Tickets can be bought at the Ribeira Paúl (at the ports) and Somatrans agencies in both Mar Novo and Mindelo. Crossings can be rough during December and January.

Fogo

The major attraction of this island is **Mt Fogo** (2839m; see the boxed text), a volcano that last erupted in 1995. A scenic cobbled road encircles the island and connects the pretty town of São Filipe and Mosteiros. The

Mt Fogo

The conical Pico do Fogo volcano sits on the floor of a huge depression with a diameter of some 8km, called Chã das Caldeiras (Plain of Craters). A crater with a precipitous cliff bounds all sides of this plain, where people farm and grow grapes, except on the eastern side where the *pico* (volcano) is located. If you hike up the crater, you'll see the black volcano in the distance. The depression was produced within the last 100,000 years when some 300 cubic kilometres of the island collapsed and slid into the sea to the east. Later, the eastern side was filled by the volcano.

The main cone has been inactive for more than 200 years. Subsequent eruptions have taken place on the sides of the volcano. The latest eruption, in 1995, occurred to the southwest of the cone, producing a long fissure to the south of the villages in Chã das Caldeiras. The northeastern end of that fissure still gives off gases, so be warned – don't get too close. The lava stopped short of the villages but covered some vineyards. Today, people are again growing crops here.

Despite the latest eruption, the volcano's cone remains intact and can still be climbed on the northern side. But the climb is now more difficult because the slopes are covered in slippery cinders, which can cause you to fall. Hiking boots are essential. The taxing ascent (a climb of 1000m up a 30° to 40° slope) takes three to four hours, but the view from the top is magnificent. Afterwards, you can run down in 45 minutes!

Make sure you get here early – you'll need to climb the volcano first thing in the morning to avoid the heat. This means departing São Filipe at around 5am. Alternatively, come the previous afternoon and camp. When you arrive you could visit part of the fissure that is still giving off gas (the 1995 vent) and arrange for a guide for the following day. The easiest route to the 1995 vent from the road is from the southeast (upwind of the fumarole), along the eastern edge of the recent lava flows.

A guide for the volcano (about CVE3000) is essential because the routes change monthly due to constantly falling ash. You'll find them in the villages of Portela and Bangaeira in the Chã das Caldeiras. Avoid climbing during or after rain because water can trigger rock falls. Instead, climb the huge crater around the volcano, starting from Fernan Gomes (for the northern rim) or from Curral Grande (for the western rim).

You can reach the southern rim from almost anywhere along the road between Achada Furna and Coxo. The climb, roughly 1500m, takes three or four hours (one down) and is a bit easier than climbing the volcano.

Simon Day

latter, at the northern tip of the island, is the nation's coffee capital. The route is punctuated by hamlets with lava block houses.

The eastern slopes of the volcano is where much of Fogo's coffee is grown, while on the northern slopes is the forest of Mt Velha, populated by pine and eucalyptus trees. Inside the crater and around Achada Grande you'll see vineyards. Fogo coffee and red wine, though not perhaps of world-class quality, are both hallmarks of the island, and are well worth trying for that reason alone.

SÃO FILIPE

Perched on a cliff with a black-sand beach below, São Filipe is also home to many praças and colourful houses. The town is divided into two sections with an old stone wall between them. The lower section includes the market, town hall and church. For centuries, the people on either side have made the wall a social division, like two clans vying for power. Walking around, you'll see old *sobrados*, homes of the town's elite.

If you're looking to take home some Cape Verdean music, head for Sons d'Afrique music shop.

A good time to visit São Filipe is 1 May, when the town's fiesta **Nhô São Filipe** takes place. The town's celebration of Mardi Gras is a festive time – see the boxed text 'Mindelo's Mardi Gras' in the Mindelo section earlier.

The beach far below the town is clean but the undertow is strong. **Praia da Salina** outside São Jorge, 17km to the north on the western route to Mosteiros, is better. If you're headed for Mosteiros, go to the market.

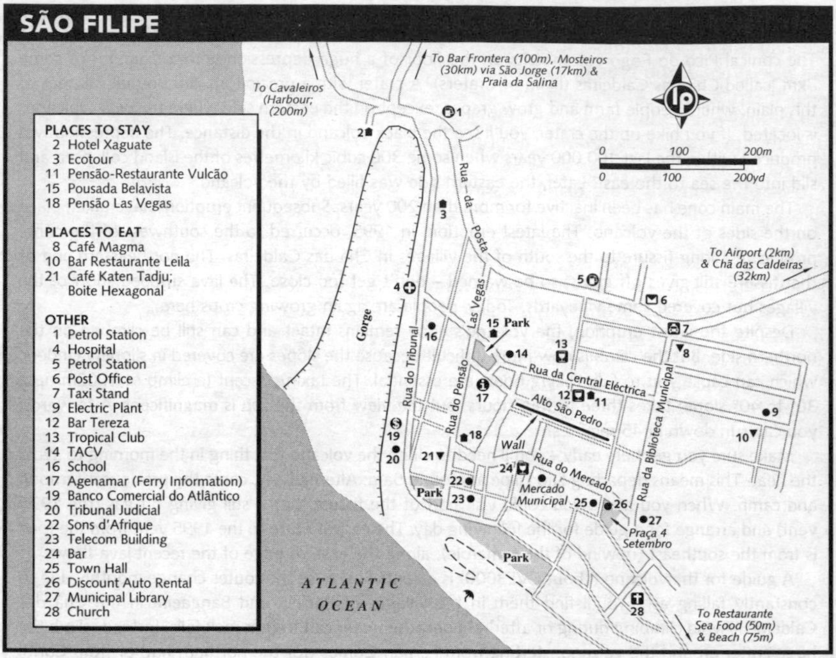
SÃO FILIPE
PLACES TO STAY
2 Hotel Xaguate
3 Ecotour
11 Pensão-Restaurante Vulcão
15 Pousada Belavista
18 Pensão Las Vegas
PLACES TO EAT
8 Café Magma
10 Bar Restaurante Leila
21 Café Katen Tadju; Boite Hexagonal
OTHER
1 Petrol Station
4 Hospital
5 Petrol Station
6 Post Office
7 Taxi Stand
9 Electric Plant
12 Bar Tereza
13 Tropical Club
14 TACV
16 School
17 Agenamar (Ferry Information)
19 Banco Comercial do Atlântico
20 Tribunal Judicial
22 Sons d'Afrique
23 Telecom Building
24 Bar
25 Town Hall
26 Discount Auto Rental
27 Municipal Library
28 Church
To Cavaleiros (Harbour; (200m)
To Bar Frontera (100m), Mosteiros (30km) via São Jorge (17km) & Praia da Salina
To Airport (2km) & Chã das Caldeiras (32km)
To Restaurante Sea Food (50m) & Beach (75m)
0 100 200m
0 100 200yd
Rua da Posta
Las Vegas
Gorge
Rua do Tribunal
Rua do Pensão
Rua da Central Eléctrica
Alto São Pedro
Rua da Biblioteca Municipal
Rua do Mercado
Wall
Park
Mercado Municipal
Praça 4 Setembro
ATLANTIC OCEAN

Places to Stay

Pensão-Restaurante Vulcão *(☎ 811896)* Singles/doubles without bathroom CVE1000/1100. Only stay at this place if you are on your last cent.

Pensão Las Vegas *(☎/fax 811281, ⓔ plasvegas@yahoo.com)* Singles/doubles with bathroom CVE2000/3000, with air-con, TV, telephone & minibar CVE3000/3500. The Las Vegas is a pleasant place and good value.

Hotel Xaguate *(☎ 811222, fax 811203)* Singles/doubles CVE5200/6400. The Hotel Xaguate is overpriced, but it has a pool (nonguests can use it for CVE300).

Ecotour *(☎ 812255, fax 811726, ⓔ ecotourfogo@hotmail.com)* Rooms without bathroom CVE2500, singles/doubles with bathroom CVE1800/3200. There is also Internet access here for CVE150 per 30 minutes. Car hire, excursions (including to the volcano) and fishing can also be organised.

Pousada Belavista *(☎ 811734, fax 811879)* Singles/doubles CVE1700/2500. The Belavista is an elegant, understated and well-run place with (for now) seven pleasant rooms that are good value. Prices sometimes drop a little in the off-season.

Pensão Restaurante Christina *(☎/fax 831045)* Singles/doubles without bathroom CVE1000/1600, with bathroom CVE1800/2500. Situated at Mosteiros, you can also get meals here for around CVE500.

Pousada Pedra Brabo *(☎ 618940)* Singles/doubles without bathroom CVE1900/2800. In Chã das Caldeiras, the Pedra Brabo is new and well designed.

Ponta Verde Pensão Restaurant *(☎ 841 135, Ponta Verde)* Singles/doubles with bathroom CVE1200/2000. The rooms here are very pleasant, spotless and well furnished. Breakfast is included.

Places to Eat & Drink

São Filipe is one of the best (and most reasonable) places in Cape Verde to try seafood.

Restaurante Sea Food *(☎ 812623)* Prawns CVE900, lobster CVE1000-1200. This is considered the best place in town. Another good place is ***Bar Restaurante Leila*** *(☎ 811 214)*. ***Tropical Club*** is a good place for a pre- or post-dinner drink or cocktail.

Pensão Las Vegas offers the usual fish and meat dishes (CVE600 to CVE1000) as well as local lobster (CVE1200). Snacks such as hamburgers (CVE250 to CVE450) are also usually available.

Café Katen Tadju is an open-air bar-café with a straw roof. Most people come for drinks and music, but you can get snacks. It's above ***Boite Hexagonal***, a popular nightclub.

Café Magma has cold drinks, espresso and snacks.

Getting There & Away

TACV (☎ 811228) has daily flights to/from Praia (CVE4842/8270 one way/return, 20 minutes) and one flight weekly to/from Sal (CVE9690/16,451 one way/return, one hour). A taxi from the airport into town (2km) costs CVE200; by truck it's CVE100. At the time of writing, the airport was supposed to reopen in Mosteiros at the end of 2002.

There's at least one minibus every morning to Mosteiros (around CVE300). For Mt Fogo, a taxi there and back will cost around CVE6000. For a car (CVE3500 to CVE4000 a day), try Discount Auto Rental (☎ 811 480). Check the conditions of the roads if you're planning to drive around Mt Fogo; rain sometimes destroys parts. There are few minibuses to and from Chã das Caldeiras, so you may be obliged to spend the night here.

For details of ferries that stop here, visit Agenamar (☎ 811012, fax 811312).

Sal

Sal is the island where tourism is most developed. Worth visiting is the salty crater, **Pedra da Lume** (CVE800 return by taxi), east of Espargos (the largest town, 2.3km from the airport in the centre of the island). Until the middle of the 20th century, the exportation of salt to West Africa and Brazil supported the islanders.

SANTA MARIA

Santa Maria, some 18km south of the airport, is the centre of tourism on Sal island. The small town overlooks the ocean, with the major tourist hotels spread out along the beach. The windsurfing here is superb (CVE700/1800 per hour/half-day rental). It's also a good place for deep-sea fishing, surf casting and scuba diving.

There are several good travel agencies, including the new Planeta, down from Pastelaria Relax towards the beach, Cabetur (☎ 421305) and CVTS on Rua Ngo Agostinho. The agencies can arrange fishing trips and tours of the other islands (though you'll need to be in a group to keep prices down). Trips cost from around CVE1700/3500 per person per half/full day. Sailing trips cost CVE4000/6500 per half/full day.

For scuba diving, various schools operate including the Portuguese-run Manta Diving (☎ 421540, fax 421550, e manta.diving@cvtelecom.cv), just beyond Hotel Belorizonte; the Italian-run Blueway Diving Center (☎ 421339) at Hotel Djadsal Holiday Club along the beachfront, which offers PADI courses; and the German-run Stingray Dive Center (☎ 421134, fax 421381, w www.stingraydive.com) inside the Odjo d'Água Hotel complex. Particularly recommended is the French-run Mares Dive Center (contact through the Morabeza hotel). Dive sites that come particularly recommended include Choclassa, Serra Negra, Cavala and Buracona.

At Funsystem (for more information and reservations, contact the head office in Germany; ☎ 49-6123-928791, e headoffice@fun-system.com), in front of Hotel Belorizonte, you can hire all the latest equipment for surfing, windsurfing and kitesurfing (including F2/Naish boards). Lessons are also available. For fishing trips, try Nautic Fishing Club (☎/fax 421617), which can arrange trawling (for wahoo, tuna and dorade) and high-sea fishing (for shark and blue marlin).

Centro de Artesanata is a good place for locally made souvenirs (ceramics, bead necklaces and woven cloth). **Mercado Municipa**, not far from Hotel Odjo d'Água, has a large range of mainland African-made souvenirs.

Places to Stay

Residencial Alternativa *(☎ 411237, fax 421165)* Singles/doubles without bathroom CVE1500/2250, with bathroom CVE2000/2600. You'll find this place on the main drag several blocks east of the windmill. It offers spotless, pleasant and excellent-value rooms with a ceiling fan.

Residencial Nhã Terra *(☎ 421109, fax 421534, e nhaterra@cvtelecom.cv)* Singles/doubles CVE3500/4500. Just east of the windmill, the Nhã Terra has good-value rooms.

Hotel da Luz *(☎ 421138, fax 421088)* Singles/doubles with bathroom, TV & telephone CVE3300/4500. This hotel is a five-minute walk from the centre of town and it has a small pool.

Les Alizés *(☎ 421446, fax 421008, ⓔ les alizes@cvtelecom.cv)* Singles/doubles with TV & telephone CVE3500/5000, high season CVE4200/6000. Opposite Restaurante Picador, this hotel is a pleasant option.

Hotel Odjo d'Ágau *(☎ 421430, fax 421430, ⓔ odjodagua@email.cvtelecom.cv)* Singles/doubles CVE5932/10,704, high season CVE7416/13,080. This newish hotel is a pleasant, peaceful place set right on the seafront at the eastern end of Santa Maria.

Along the beach is an entire row of large tourist hotels, popular with package tourists and all with pools, tennis courts, nightclubs etc. ***Morabeza*** *(☎ 421020, fax 421021, ⓔ hotel.morabeza@mail.cvtelecom.cv)* has singles/doubles from CVE6190/9654 (from CVE8234/13,742 in high season), and ***Hotel Belorizonte*** *(☎ 421045, fax 421210, ⓔ borizonte@cvtelecom.cv)* next door has singles/doubles costing CVE8380/11,030 (CVE10,050/14,340 in high season).

Places to Eat

Pastelaria Relax on the main drag has great sandwiches, snacks and good yogurt. ***Cocoricos*** below Les Alizés hotel is another good place. ***Vulcão d'Fogo***, though simple, is popular and offers reasonably priced dishes.

The open-air ***Mateus Restaurant*** *(☎ 421 313)* next to the park is often packed with people listening to the band that performs from Wednesday to Saturday. The nearby ***Restaurante Bar Esplanada Soleil*** and ***Restaurante Nhã Terra*** *(☎ 421109)* are also popular.

Restaurante Grill Por Do Sol, near the park overlooking the ocean, is good for beers and grilled fish. ***Restaurante Américo's***, facing the church, is also good for fish. ***Restaurante Piscador*** *(☎ 421010)* around the corner from the park is a more upmarket place with good fish. The open-air ***Cultural Café*** at the park with tables outside is a good place for a drink or a cocktail (CVE250). The excellent ***Blue Fish Restaurant*** *(☎ 421281)* on Rua Tanquinho is run by an Italian–Cape Verdean couple and specialises in barbecued fresh fish.

A very popular bar is ***Squeeze Bar***, next door to Restaurante Piscador. The more laid-back video-bar ***Galema*** is near Restaurante Américo's. The best club currently is ***Pirata Pizzaria Disco Pub***, just outside of town on the road to the airport, which is open until around 4am daily (except Sunday).

Getting There & Around

Taxis to Santa Maria cost CVE700 from the airport (CVE750 from Espargos). Minibuses ply the road between the two towns (CVE100), and from the airport, you can catch a minibus to Santa Maria (CVE100) from the road just outside. Mountain bikes can be hired at Hotel Djadsal Holiday Club (☎ 421170) along the beach for CVE300/1000 per hour/day. Cars can be hired from Alucar (based at Morabeza hotel).

ESPARGOS

Espargos is a small quiet town but in the evenings things liven up, especially around the central Praça 19 de Setembro. For good views, climb the large hill just outside of town (30 minutes from town to the top).

Places to Stay

Casa da Angela *(☎ 411327, Rua Abel Djassi)* Singles/doubles with bathroom CVE1700/2500. The rooms at Casa da Angela are spotless and quite homey, but there is no restaurant.

Residencial Central *(☎ 411366 fax 411610, ⓔ ccentral@mail.cvtelecom.cv)* Singles/doubles with bathroom & breakfast CVE2000/3000. Facing the main square this hotel has a slightly colonial feel to it, but rooms are pleasant and clean.

Hotel Atlántico *(☎ 411210, fax 411522)* Singles/doubles with TV CVE2678/3296. Nestled at the southern intersection, this place has upmarket rooms.

Paz e Ben *(☎ 411782, fax 411790)* Singles/doubles CVE2500/3500. Paz e Ben is similar to the Atlántico and has recently renovated rooms.

Places to Eat & Drink

Restaurante Salinas *(☎ 411799)* Grilled fish CVE460. On the main drag two blocks south of the park, this restaurant does great fresh fish.

Max Restaurant *(☎ 411913)*, around the corner from Angela's, advertises itself as a 'family place'. Near the central park, ***Restaurante Sivy***, has good for snacks and yogurt. A local favourite is the ***Churrasqueira Dinamica***. For groceries, try ***Supermercado Central*** facing the park.

Bar Violão *(☎ 411446)* near Casa da Angela has the best ambience in town and is a popular local hang-out. ***Bar Esplanada Recanto*** *(☎ 411567)* across the street from Bar Violão is a good place for drinks and music (live on Friday).

Getting There & Away

Air TACV (☎ 411268, fax 411320) has six to 10 flights daily to/from Praia (CVE8579/14,633 one way/return, 45 minutes), two to three daily to/from São Vicente (CVE8579/14,633, 45 minutes), one per week to Fogo (CVE9690/16,451, one hour), five to six flights weekly to Boa Vista (CVE3933/6856, 25 minutes) and three flights weekly to São Nicolau (CVE6255/10694, 35 minutes).

At the airport there are left-luggage facilities (CVE100 per bag per 24 hours), a bank, bureau de change (open 24 hours), tourist booth with maps, Cabetur travel agency (☎ 411545, fax 411098), airline offices (including TACV) and Rentalauto (☎ 413519) car hire. Taxis from the airport to town (2km) will charge CVE150/225/300 during the day/evening/after midnight, or you can hail a minibus on the highway in front of the airport (CVE100).

Minibuses to Santa Maria (CVE100), leave every 15 minutes from in front of the Cámera Municipal.

Sea Ferries stop at Palmeira, the port near Espargos. Inquire about schedules and bookings at the Agencia de Viagens e Turismo (☎ 411349) opposite Restaurante Salinas.

Other Islands

BRAVA

Brava is the smallest of the inhabited islands, but is relatively densely populated. It was settled in the late 17th century by refugees from Fogo, fleeing an eruption of the island's volcano. It gained fame in the 19th century as a source of whalers for American ships. Many of them eventually settled around Boston.

The mountainous landscape of the island offers numerous short hikes. The best of the beaches is at the western side of the island near the airport. Vila de Nova Sintra is the tiny capital in the centre (500m altitude). From there, you could hike 3km eastward down to Vinagre via Santa Barbara or, somewhat longer, westward to **Cova Joana** and then on to **Nosso Senhora do Monte** or **Lima Doce**, both nearby. To Fajã de Água (10km), hike or take a minibus (although there aren't many). A taxi costs around CVE800 one way.

Places to Stay & Eat

Pensão Restaurante Paul Sena *(☎ 851312)* in Vila de Nova Sintra has singles/doubles with bathroom for CVE1000/2000. ***Pousada Municipal*** *(☎ 811220, fax 811879)* has singles/doubles with bathroom costing CVE1700/2500.

Manuel Burgo Ocean Front Motel *(☎ 851321, fax 851321)* in Fajã de Água has singles/doubles with bathroom that will set you back CVE1500/2000.

For meals, try ***Esplanada*** or ***Pousada Bar Restaurante Português***.

Getting There & Away

TACV is not currently flying to Brava. Boats from Praia normally stop twice a week in Brava (sometimes stopping on the way back in Fogo). For ferry routes and details, see the main Getting Around section earlier in this chapter.

SÃO NICOLAU

With seven peaks at more than 500m, São Nicolau is a great place for hiking. The highest peak, **Mt Gordo** (1312m), is only 8km west, as the crow flies, from **Ribeira Brava**, the island's capital.

The island's most fertile area is the beautiful verdant **Fajã valley** just north of that peak. In many other areas, the landscape is rugged and dry.

Minibuses from Tarrafal, the port, for Ribeira Brava (CVE170, 26km) travel along a spectacular winding road that leads to the northern coast, skirting Mt Gordo and then back inland to Ribeira Brava. (You could get off halfway and hike in the Fajã valley or down a path eastward to Ribeira Brava.)

The best time to visit Ribeira Brava is in February or March during Mardi Gras as the celebrations here are second only to Mindelo's.

Places to Stay & Eat

Pensão da Cruz *(☎ 351282)* Singles/doubles without bathroom CVE1000/1200. Opposite the post office in Ribeira Brava, this pension has simple but clean rooms.

Pensão Jumbo *(☎ 351315)* Rooms without/with bathroom CVE1200/1400. The Jumbo is a little nicer than Pensão da Cruz.

Pensão Jardim *(☎ 351117)* Singles/doubles with bathroom & breakfast CVE2300/2800. Up on the hill overlooking town, the Jardim is pleasant and peaceful with its own terrace – an excellent place for an evening beer.

Residencial Alice *(Residencial Lidio Gomes Martins; ☎ 361187, fax 361693, Tarrafal)* Singles/doubles with bathroom CVE1000/1200. This place is set in very pleasant surroundings on the waterfront. It also does good home-cooking.

Residencial Natur *(☎/fax 361178)* has rooms with sea views for CVE1500.

Good restaurants include ***Restaurant Bela Sombra Dalila*** and the simpler ***Pizzeria Dora*** *(☎ 351930)* down a side street from the BCA bank (pizzas must be ordered in advance from the charming host and cook, Dora). ***Bar Evora*** does simple dishes for CVE150 to CVE300. The smarter ***Restaurante Patché*** has quite a good selection of mains for CVE480 to CVE600. ***Esplanada Tarrafal***, 20m from Residencial Alice, is not a bad bar.

Getting There & Away

TACV (☎ 351161, 351162) has daily flights to and from Praia (CVE7670/13,070 one way/return, two hours) and Sal (CVE6255/10,694, 35 minutes), and four times weekly to São Vicente (CVE4842/8270, 30 minutes). The airport is 5km southeast of Ribeira Brava (CVE400). About once a week you can get here by boat from Mindelo or Sal on the *Sotavento* or *Barlavento*. See the main Getting Around section earlier in this chapter for more details.

BOA VISTA

pop 5000

Tourism on Boa is growing. With the exception of the island's three mountains to the east, the island is flat and, apart from the north (a little greener), is pretty arid.

One of the best beaches is Santa Mónica on the southwestern side. An excursion there via the **Viana desert** and back to **Sal Rei**, the main town and island's capital, costs around CVE5500. A closer beach, which though smaller is just as pleasant, is **Praia de Chaves** (CVE2500 return from Sal Rei).

Another popular excursion is to the beached boat of *Cabo Santa Maria* (CVE2500). Cars can be rented from the Pousada Boa Vista for from CVE5500 per day all inclusive of taxes and insurance and for CVE5800 from the Santa Monica Tourist Agency (☎/fax 511445, ⓔ agsantamonica@mail.cvtelecom.cv) on the main square in Sal Rei. The latter can also organise horse riding, trekking, whale watching, fishing trips and island tours. It also offers Internet access (CVE250/450/600 per 15/30/60 minutes).

Also on the square is Boa Vista Watersport System (☎/fax 511392, ⓔ bws@bwscv.com), which offers diving, as does Alísios (☎ 924865) outside town. At Tortuga Beach Club, Happy Boa Vista (contact through Hotel Dunas – see Places to Stay & Eat following) is a German-run windsurfing club that charges CVE1700/5600 per hour/day for an F2 windsurfing board. Lessons per hour cost CVE3700, including equipment. Kitesurfers can also be hired.

Places to Stay & Eat

Residencial Boa Esperança *(☎ 511170, Rua Amizade Seixal)* has singles without bathroom for CVE750-1100, doubles for CVE1200-1600 and rooms with bathroom for CVE1800. Not far away, ***Residencial Bom Sossego*** *(☎ 511155)* has singles/doubles with bathroom for CVE2200/2500.

Hotel Dunas *(☎ 511225, fax 511384)* has singles/doubles with bathroom for CVE2350/2700. ***Pousada Boa Vista*** *(☎ 511 145, fax 511423 ⓔ pousadaboavista@cv telecom.cv)* offers very comfortable singles/doubles for CVE3800/4800.

Marineclub Boa Vista *(☎ 511285, fax 511390, ⓔ marineclub@mail.cvtelecom.cv)*, 1km from town on the beach, has comfortable single/double bungalows for CVE7000/9200. Half-board costs CVE9000/13,200. Two/three person apartments (CVE15,000/17,600) are also available. Prices rise by 20% in high season. There's a pool, and mountain bikes for hire at CVE250 per hour.

A local favourite is ***Restaurant Bar Rosy*** *(☎ 511242)* on Avenida Amilcal Cabral. The newish, Italian-run ***Esplanada de 5 Julha*** on Avenida dos Pescadores has a very pleasant shaded terrace. It does good pizzas (CVE300 to CVE350) as well as spaghetti, grilled fish etc.

Getting There & Away

TACV (☎ 511186, fax 511137) has daily flights to/from Praia (CVE6256/10,694 one way/return, two hours) and five to six flights weekly to Sal (CVE3933/6856, 25 minutes). Ferries sail to Boa Vista from Praia and Sal. For ferry details and routes, see the main Getting Around section earlier in the chapter.

MAIO

pop 5000

Maio is flat and desertlike. You may be the only traveller here and are likely to be well received. It was once an important salt-collecting centre controlled by the British; hence the main city and port, **Vila do Maio**, is commonly called Porto Inglés. There's a good beach, **Bitche Rotche**, just outside town. There are no buses, but ask around for car rental (around CVE3500 per day).

Hotel Bom Sossego *(☎ 551365, fax 551327)* has singles/doubles with bathroom with cold water for CVE1500/2500. For hot water, you'll pay CVE1700/2700.

Hotel Marilú *(☎ 551198)* has singles/doubles with bathroom for CVE2000/2800. Both hotels have good restaurants.

TACV *(☎ 551256)* has three flights weekly to/from Praia (CVE3933/6856) one way/return, 15 minutes). There's a ferry service that runs at least once a week between Praia and Vila do Maio.

Côte d'Ivoire

Côte d'Ivoire was once hailed as the economic miracle of West Africa and a role model for political stability in the region. Never completely breaking with their colonial masters, its post-independence leaders wooed French capital to build a modern infrastructure and the illusion of a generalised prosperity. The long-serving and charismatic first president, Houphouët-Boigny, managed to promote the notion of a happy amalgam of pragmatic Western capitalism with benign African values. However, the society he presided over was far from liberal and the dream ended with his death and ensuing difficulties in handing the baton to a successor. A consequent string of coups and popular insurgencies reverberated through 1999–2001; most of the huge French expat community jumped ship and foreign debt spiralled to one of the world's highest per capita.

Though the gloss has well and truly faded, this is nonetheless a rewarding country for the traveller. Communication facilities are still the region's best, the people are exceptionally warm-hearted and hospitable, and the country's cultural diversity has not suffered. It's a land rich in popular traditions due to a diverse ethnic mix that includes Dan, Lobi, Baoulé and Senoufo peoples.

There are also unique natural attractions. Parc National de la Comoë, in the northern savanna lands, is the largest in West Africa, while Parc National de Taï, in the southwest, preserves the country's last significant belt of rainforest. All along the Atlantic coast there are fine beaches and fascinating fishing villages.

Traditional architecture is displayed in Senoufo and Lobi villages and in 17th-century mud-brick mosques, and the colonial architecture of Grand Bassam, the original French capital south of Abidjan, has a faded charm. Yamoussoukro, the titular capital, is famed for its basilica, an astonishing replica of Rome's St Peter's, which epitomises the Houphouët-Boigny era and in some ways Africa's current place in today's world.

Abidjan, the true capital in all but name, is decidedly dog-eared these days, no longer justifying monikers such as 'Paris of West Africa', but its modern skyscrapers, upmarket restaurants, ATMs and beautiful

Côte d'Ivoire at a Glance

Capital: Yamoussoukro
Population: 16.4 million
Area: 322,465 sq km
Head of State: President Laurent Gbagbo
Official language: French
Main local languages: Mande, Malinké, Dan, Senoufo, Baoulé, Agni, Dioula
Currency: West African CFA franc
Exchange rate: US$1 = CFA694
Time: GMT/UTC
Country telephone code: ☎ 225
Best time to go: Year-round

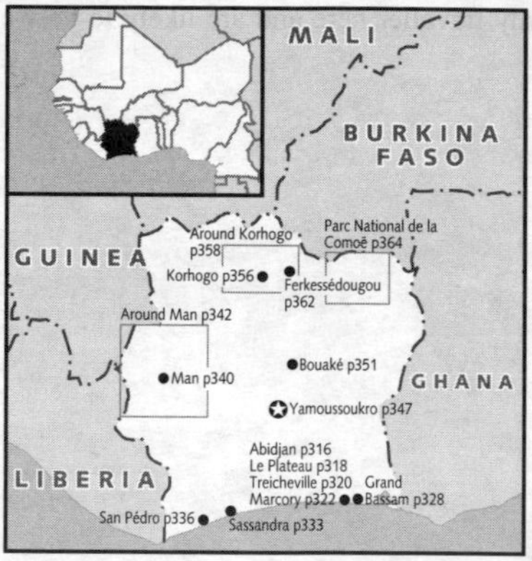
MALI
BURKINA FASO
GUINEA
GHANA
LIBERIA
Around Korhogo p358
Parc National de la Comoë p364
Korhogo p356
Ferkessédougou p362
Around Man p342
Man p340
Bouaké p351
Yamoussoukro p347
Abidjan p316
Le Plateau p318
Treicheville p320
Marcory p322
Grand Bassam p328
San Pédro p336
Sassandra p333

Highlights

- Experiencing the warmth and friendliness of Ivoirians
- Taking in a live performance of exhilarating music and masked dance in the Man area
- Soaking up the sun at rainforest-clad beaches, such as Monogaga, Grand-Béréby or Grand Lahou
- Communing with chimpanzees in the Parc National de Taï or with hippos at Parc National de la Comoë
- Exploring Grand Bassam's faded colonial charm
- Goggling at Yamoussoukro's colossal basilica

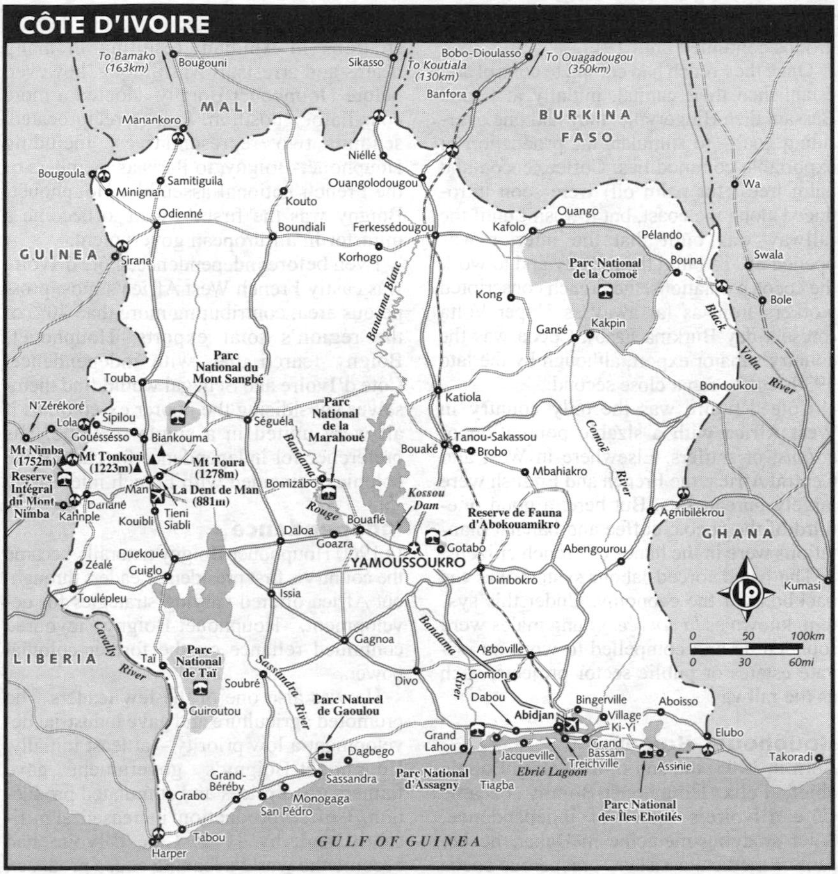
CÔTE D'IVOIRE
To Bamako (163km)
Bougouni
MALI
Sikasso
To Koutiala (130km)
Bobo-Dioulasso
To Ouagadougou (350km)
Banfora
BURKINA FASO
Manankoro
Niéllé
Bougoula
Samitiguila
Minignan
Kouto
Ouangolodougou
Wa
Odienné
Boundiali
Ferkessédougou
Kafolo
Ouango
Pélando
GUINEA
Sirana
Korhogo
Bouna
Swala
Parc National de la Comoë
Bandama Blanc
Kong
Bole
Black Volta River
Gansé
Kakpin
Parc National du Mont Sangbé
Touba
Bondoukou
N'Zérékoré
Katiola
Lola
Sipilou
Parc National de la Marahoué
Séguéla
Comoé River
Gouéssésso
Biankouma
Tanou-Sakassou
Brobo
Mt Nimba (1752m)
Mt Tonkoui (1223m)
Mt Toura (1278m)
Bouaké
Mbahiakro
Reserve Intégral du Mont Nimba
Man
La Dent de Man (881m)
Bomizabo
Kossou Dam
Danané
Bandama Rouge
Kahnple
Kouibli
Tieni Siabli
Bouaflé
Reserve de Fauna d'Abokouamikro
Agnibilékrou
Daloa
GHANA
Goazra
Gotabo
Abengourou
Duekoué
YAMOUSSOUKRO
Zéalé
Guiglo
Dimbokro
Kumasi
Issia
Toulépleu
Gagnoa
0 50 100km
0 30 60mi
Cavally River
Bandama River
Agboville
LIBERIA
Taï
Parc National de Taï
Sassandra River
Divo
Gomon
Soubré
Dabou
Bingerville
Aboisso
Guiroutou
Parc Naturel de Gaoulou
Abidjan
Village Ki-Yi
Grand Lahou
Grand Bassam
Elubo
Dagbego
Jacqueville
Treichville
Takoradi
Grand-Béréby
Sassandra
Parc National d'Assagny
Tiagba
Ebrié Lagoon
Assinie
Grabo
Monogaga
San Pédro
Parc National des Îles Ehotilés
Tabou
Harper
GULF OF GUINEA

lagoon setting will still astound if you're fresh off a bus from Burkina Faso.

Facts about Côte d'Ivoire

HISTORY

The major ethnic groups in Côte d'Ivoire all came relatively recently from neighbouring areas. The Krou (or Kru) people migrated eastward from Liberia around 400 years ago; the Senoufo and Lobi moved southward from Burkina Faso and Mali. It was not until the 18th and 19th centuries that the Akan people, including the Baoulé, migrated from Ghana into the eastern area and the Malinké (also called Mandingo) from Guinea moved into the northwest.

The Portuguese were the first Europeans to arrive. Compared with neighbouring Ghana, Côte d'Ivoire suffered little from the slave trade. European slaving and merchant ships preferred other areas along the coast with better harbours. France took no interest until the 1840s when the French, under their king, Louis-Philippe, enticed local chiefs to grant French commercial traders a monopoly along the coast. Thereafter, the French built naval bases to keep out non-French traders and began a systematic conquest of the interior. They accomplished this only after a long war in the 1890s against Malinké forces headed by the illustrious Samory Touré. Even then, guerrilla warfare by the Baoulé and other eastern ethnic groups continued until 1917.

Once the French had complete control and established their capital, initially at Grand Bassam then Bingerville, they had one overriding goal – to stimulate the production of exportable commodities. Coffee, cocoa and palm trees (for palm oil) were soon introduced along the coast, but it wasn't until the railway was built that the interior was opened up. To build the railway and to work the cocoa plantations, the French conscripted workers from as far away as Upper Volta (present-day Burkina Faso). Cocoa was the country's major export, although by the late 1930s coffee ran a close second.

Côte d'Ivoire was the only country in West Africa with a sizable population of *colons*, or settlers. Elsewhere in West and Central Africa, the French and English were largely bureaucrats. But here, a good one-third of the cocoa, coffee and banana plantations were in the hands of French citizens.

The hated forced-labour system was the backbone of the economy. Under this system, known as *la corvée*, young males were rounded up and compelled to work on private estates or public sector projects, such as the railway.

Houphouët-Boigny

Born in 1905, the son of a wealthy Baoulé chief, Félix Houphouët-Boigny became Côte d'Ivoire's father of independence. After studying medicine in Dakar, he became a medical assistant, prosperous cocoa farmer and local chief. In 1944 he turned to politics and formed the country's first agricultural trade union – not of labourers but of African planters. Opposing the colonial policy, which favoured French plantation owners, the planters united to recruit migrant workers for their own farms. Houphouët-Boigny soon rose to prominence and within a year, after converting the trade union into the Parti Démocratique de Côte d'Ivoire (PDCI), he was elected a deputy to the French parliament in Paris. A year later, he allied the PDCI with the Rassemblement Démocratique Africain (RDA), becoming the RDA's first president. That year the French abolished forced labour.

In those early years, Houphouët-Boigny was considered a radical. The RDA was closely aligned with international Marxist organisations and staged numerous demonstrations in Abidjan, resulting in many deaths and arrests. It wasn't long, however, before Houphouët-Boigny adopted a more conciliatory position. France reciprocated, sending two representatives, including Houphouët-Boigny, to Paris as members of the French national assembly. Houphouët-Boigny was the first African to become a minister in a European government.

Even before independence, Côte d'Ivoire was easily French West Africa's most prosperous area, contributing more than 40% of the region's total exports. Houphouët-Boigny feared that, with independence, Côte d'Ivoire and Senegal would find themselves subsidising the poorer ex-colonies if all were united in a single republic. His preference for independence for each of the colonies coincided with French interests.

Independence

In 1960 Houphouët-Boigny naturally became the country's first president. Leaders throughout Africa offered varying strategies for development. Houphouët-Boigny favoured continued reliance on the former colonial power.

He was also one of the few leaders who promoted agriculture and gave industrial development a low priority – at least initially. Houphouët-Boigny's government gave farmers good prices and stimulated production. Coffee production increased significantly and, by 1979, Côte d'Ivoire had become the world's leading cocoa producer, as well as Africa's leading exporter of pineapples and palm oil. The Ivoirian 'miracle' was foremost an agricultural miracle.

For 20 years, the economy maintained an annual growth rate of nearly 10%. The fruits of growth were widely enjoyed since the focus of development was on farming – the livelihood of some 85% of the people. Another reason was the absence of huge estates; most of the cocoa and coffee production was in the hands of hundreds of thousands of small producers. Literacy rose from 28% to 60% – twice the African average. Electricity reached virtually every town and the road system became the best in Africa, outside South Africa and Nigeria. Still, the numerous Mercedes and the posh African residences in Abidjan's Cocody quarter were testimony to the growing inequality of incomes.

Houphouët-Boigny ruled with an iron hand. The press was far from free. Tolerating only one political party, he eliminated opposition by largesse – giving his opponents jobs instead of jail sentences.

The Big Slump

The world recession of the early 1980s sent shock waves through the Ivorian economy. The drought of 1983–84 was a second body blow. From 1981–84 real GNP stagnated or declined. The rest of Africa looked on gleefully as the glittering giant, Abidjan, was brought to its knees for the first time with constant power blackouts. Overlogging finally had an impact and timber revenue slumped. Sugar had been the hope of the north, but world prices collapsed, ruining the huge new sugar-refining complexes there. The country's external debt increased 300% and Côte d'Ivoire had to ask the IMF for debt rescheduling. Rising crime in Abidjan made the news in Europe. The miracle was over.

Houphouët-Boigny slashed government spending and the bureaucracy, revamped some of the poorly managed state enterprises, sent home one-third of the expensive French advisers and teachers and, most difficult of all, finally slashed cocoa prices to farmers in 1989 by 50%.

The 1990s

In 1990 hundreds of civil servants went on strike, joined by students who took to the streets protesting violently, blaming the economic crisis on corruption and the lavish lifestyles of government officials. The unrest was unprecedented in scale and intensity, shattering Houphouët-Boigny's carefully cultivated personality cult and forcing the government to accede to multiparty democracy. The 1990 presidential elections were opened to other parties for the first time; however, Houphouët-Boigny still received 85% of the vote.

Houphouët-Boigny was becoming increasingly feeble, intensifying the guessing game of who he would appoint as his successor. Finally, in late 1993, after 33 years in power as Côte d'Ivoire's first and only president, 'le Vieux' died aged 88.

Houphouët-Boigny's hand-picked successor was Henri Konan-Bédié, a Baoulé and speaker of the national assembly. In 1995, Bédié achieved some legitimacy, receiving 95% of the vote in open presidential elections, while his party, the PDCI, won an overwhelming victory in legislative elections over a bickering and fragmented opposition. However, true democracy was stifled by the application of the new 'parenthood clause', which stipulated that both a candidate's parents must be Ivorian. After the elections, Bédié continued to discriminate against immigrants and their descendants who for decades had fuelled the country's agricultural expansion. This persecution was focused, in particular, on foreign Muslim workers in the north.

In December 1999 Bédié's unpopular rule was brought to an end by a military coup led by General Robert Guéi. However, having deposed Bédié on the basis of his discriminatory policies Guéi only pursued them further. The coup was quickly followed by military rebellion, violence and elections in 2000 in which Guéi was able to have his main opponent, Alasanne Ouattara, disqualified by the Supreme Court on the grounds that his parents were from Burkina Faso. When Guéi tried to steal the subsequent result from winner Laurent Gbagbo he was deposed by a popular uprising.

Côte d'Ivoire Today

While civilian rule has been re-established under Laurent Gbagbo, the country is still not politically stable. Scores of Ouattara's supporters were killed in the wake of their leader's call for a new election and, in January 2001, there was another, unsuccessful, attempt by the military to take power. Côte d'Ivoire's status as one of Africa's more stable countries is now a faded memory.

GEOGRAPHY

Côte d'Ivoire covers an area of about 322,465 sq km, which is about the size of Germany or New Mexico. The central area, where most of the coffee and cocoa grows, is a fairly uniform, flat or gently undulating plain. In the west and northwest the interior rises to a plateau averaging around 300m. Here Man, with its rolling hill country, is punctuated by several peaks over 1000m. Mount Nimba (1752m), on the Guinean and Liberian borders, is the country's highest peak. In the drier north, the land becomes savanna and sparse woodland, as in the Parc National de la Comoë.

Little remains of the dense rainforest that once covered most of the southern half of the country. The residue is mostly confined to the southwest, inland from the coast and towards the border with Liberia; the largest tract is protected within the spectacular Parc National de Taï.

A coastal lagoon with a unique ecosystem stretches from the Ghanaian border westward for nearly 300km.

CLIMATE

In the south annual rainfall is 1500mm to 2000mm, and there are two wet seasons: from May to July and October to November. In the drier northern half of the country the wet season extends from June to October, with no August dry spell. The south is very humid, with temperatures averaging 28°C. In the north, the average is 26°C from December to February with midday maximums regularly above 35°C and the harmattan, blowing in from the Sahara, greatly reducing visibility.

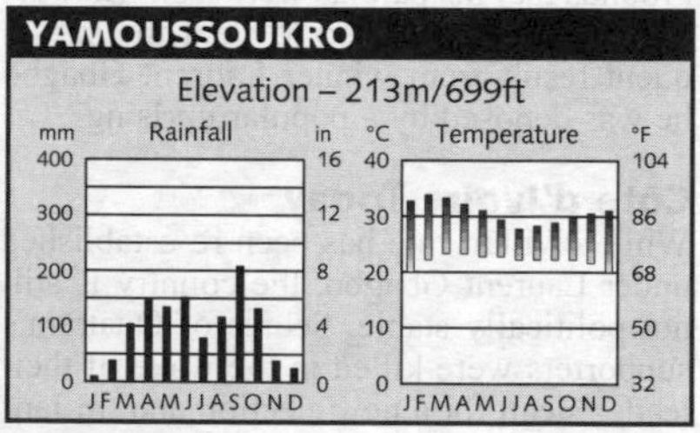
YAMOUSSOUKRO
Elevation – 213m/699ft
mm
Rainfall
in
°C
Temperature
°F
400
16
40
104
300
12
30
86
200
8
20
68
100
4
10
50
0
0
0
32
JFMAMJJASOND
JFMAMJJASOND

ECOLOGY & ENVIRONMENT

The major threat to Côte d'Ivoire's diverse flora and fauna is the expansion of agricultural lands (from 3.1 million hectares in 1965 to nearly eight million hectares in 1995). The rainforests are being cut down at a tragic rate; between 1977 and 1987 Côte d'Ivoire lost 42% of its forest and woodland – the highest rate of loss in the world. The corresponding figures for neighbouring Ghana and Liberia were 8% and 0%, respectively; for Brazil it was 4%. Since the late 1980s, the volume of timber exports has declined by about one-third, but hardwood exports are still on a level with those of Brazil, a country over 20 times larger. Wood exported includes mahogany, samba, sipo, bété and iroko. Around 64% of the country's electricity comes from a number of large hydroelectric schemes.

Much ecological damage has also been done by the damming of the Sassandra River at Buyo and the Bandama River at Kossou. There are also problems with water pollution from industrial and, in particular, agricultural effluent.

FLORA & FAUNA

The northern part of the country is savanna grassland interspersed with acacia and other bushes and trees. The south was once covered in dense tropical rainforest, but is now largely given over to coffee and cocoa production and massive groves of native palm, tapped for palm oil.

While Côte d'Ivoire has a large range of fauna, poaching and tragic habitat destruction mean numbers are small and the possibility of sightings limited. However, there are at least 11 species of monkey; chimpanzees; and 17 species of carnivore, including lions and leopards. There are giant pangolins, aardvarks, rock hyraxes, hippopotamuses, elephants, sitatungas, buffaloes, duikers, waterbucks, kobs, roan antelopes, oribi, bushpigs and warthogs.

Côte d'Ivoire has superb bird-watching potential, particularly in the Comoë (with over 500 species) and Taï national parks. Notable species include the white-breasted guineafowl, Nimba flycatcher, western wattled cuckoo-shrike and the yellow-throated olive greenbul. There are 10 species of heron, as well as yellow-billed egrets, ducks, raptors, plovers, francolins, hammerkops, black-winged stilts, four of the six West African stork species and five of the six West African vulture species. For a fascinating account of a birding field trip made to Côte d'Ivoire by Frank Rheindt in 2000, visit W worldtwitch.virtualave.net/ivory coast.htm.

National Parks & Reserves

None of the major parks are geared towards independent travel and access, and accommodation, where it does exist, comes at a premium.

Parc du Banco This is a rainforest park on the outskirts of Abidjan; it's very accessible.

Parc National d'Assagny This rainforest park is east of Grand Lahou.

Parc National de la Comoë The largest park in West Africa is in the savanna country of the northeast; there's a safari lodge here.

Parc National de la Marahoué This savanna and woodland park is northwest of Bouaflé.

Parc National de Taï In the southwest, this park includes the country's last remaining rainforest; there's an 'ecotel' here.

Parc National des Îles Ehotilés This is a marine park, east of Grand Bassam.

Parc National du Mont Sangbé A rainforest northeast of Mann, this park is currently closed to tourists.

Reserve de Fauna d'Abokouamikro This woodland park is northeast of Yamoussoukro.

Reserve Intégral du Mont Nimba This is a rainforest reserve on the western frontier with Guinea, but currently it's closed to tourists.

For up-to-date information on access and facilities, contact the Directorate of National Parks (☎ 20 22 53 66) in Abidjan.

GOVERNMENT & POLITICS

The head of state and commander in chief of the military is the president, who is elected by universal suffrage every five years. The president in turn appoints a council of ministers, including the prime minister. The legislature consists of a national assembly whose 175 members are also popularly elected to five-year terms. The ruling party, the PDCI, has operated for many decades, but multipartyism has existed only since 1990. There are now some 40 officially recognised opposition parties, the main ones being the Front Populaire d'Ivoire (FPI), the Parti Ivoirien des Travailleurs (PIT) and the Rassemblement des Républicains (RDR).

ECONOMY

In the agricultural sector, Côte d'Ivoire rates many superlatives – largest producer of cocoa in the world, largest producer of coffee in Africa (and third largest in the world) and largest producer of cotton in Francophone Africa. However, despite serious efforts at diversification (palm oil, rubber, bananas and pineapples in the south, and sugar cane and cotton in the north), coffee and cocoa still represent more than half of export earnings – about the same as in 1960. As a result of the collapse of the price of these commodities on world markets in the early 1980s, Côte d'Ivoire has become the world's largest debtor on a per capita basis owing $13.9 billion in 2000. In the same year negative growth of 0.3% resulted from difficulties in paying these debts, continued low-export prices and postcoup instability.

The infrastructure, the fruit of investment when the economy was more buoyant, is there and functioning, though. There are nearly 5000km of well-maintained tar roads linking all major towns, the interurban transport system is good and electricity reaches significantly more of the rural community than anywhere else in West Africa.

A bright prospect is the rise of oil and gas production. Two new offshore oil and gas fields will make the country self-sufficient in both. The fuel has begun to flow, but it's unlikely that it will ever be a bonanza.

POPULATION & PEOPLE

There are more than 60 tribes among the country's 16.4 million people. They can be divided, on the basis of cultural unity, into four principal groupings, each of which has tribal affiliations with members of the same group living in bordering countries.

The Akan (Baoulé and Agni primarily) live in the eastern and central areas and constitute about 42% of the indigenous population. The largest single group of Akan is the Baoulé, which separated from the Ashanti in Ghana around 1750 (following a dispute over the chieftaincy) and migrated west into the central area under the leadership of Queen Awura Pokou.

The Krou ethnic group (15% of the indigenous population) originated from the present-day Liberia. The Bété are its most numerous subgroup and the second-largest ethnic group in the country.

The savanna peoples can be divided into the Voltaic and Mande groups. The Voltaic group (17% of the indigenous population) includes the Senoufo, animists and renowned artisans who live in the north around Korhogo, and the Lobi, who straddle the borders with Burkina Faso and Ghana. The Mande (27%), who live in the north and west, include the Malinké (numerous around Odienné) and the Dan (renowned for their impressive masks and dancers on stilts) who inhabit the mountainous region around Man.

See also the special section 'Peoples of the Region' for more information on the Dan, Senoufo and other ethnic groups of Côte d'Ivoire.

There are also some 40,000 French, more than 25,000 Lebanese and an estimated two million immigrants from all over West Africa, predominantly from Burkina Faso.

The literacy rate is now 48.5% and the average life expectancy is a low 44.9 years. Around 11% of the population is infected with HIV and in urban areas the official unemployment rate is 13%.

ARTS

Arts & Craftwork

The art of Côte d'Ivoire is among the most outstanding in West Africa. Three groups stand out – the Baoulé, the Dan and the Senoufo. Among the traditional arts that are especially prized are Korhogo cloth (see the boxed text 'Korhogo Cloth' later in this chapter) from the northeast, Dan masks of wood or copper from the Man region and Senoufo statues, masks and traditional musical instruments in wood from the northeast. For more details, see the boxed text 'Art of Côte d'Ivoire'.

Although nowadays almost entirely factory produced, *pagnes*, the dazzling, brightly coloured lengths of cloth that women wear, reflect popular colour combinations and designs, and healthy experimentation is rife.

Literature

The doyen of Côte d'Ivoire's literature is Bernard Dadié, who is credited with writing the country's first play, first poetry anthology and first collection of short stories in French. He has a warm, simple style, even when expressing his dissatisfactions. One of his first novels, published in 1970, is *Climbié*, an autobiographical account of his childhood. Other works translated into English include *The Black Cloth* (1987) and *The City Where No One Dies* (1986).

Aké Loba is best known for *Kocoumbo* (abstracted in *African Writing Today*, 1967), an autobiographical novel of an impecunious, uprooted African in Paris being drawn towards militant communism.

Ahmadou Kourouma's first hit novel was *The Suns of Independence* (1981), the wry and humorous story of a disgruntled village chief, deposed following independence. His second novel, *Monné, Outrages et Défi*, written in 1990 after 22 years of silence and yet to be translated into English, took that year's Grand Prix Littéraire d'Afrique

Art of Côte d'Ivoire

Côte d'Ivoire has a greater variety of masks and woodcarvings than any other country in West Africa. Dan masks show a high regard for symmetry and balance, and are often highly expressive. Traditionally, they were carved spontaneously, inspired perhaps by a beautiful face. The most common mask is that of a human face, slightly abstract but with realistic features, a smooth surface, protruding lips, slit or large circular eye holes and a calm expression. These masks often have specific uses; a mask representing a woman, for example, is used to prevent women from seeing uncircumcised boys during their initiation into adulthood.

Other common Dan carvings include large rice-serving spoons that typically rest on two legs carved in a human form.

Baoulé masks typically represent an animal or a human face. The latter are often intended to portray particular individuals, who can be recognised by the mask's facial marks and hairstyles. Other Baoulé masks, however, are wholly works of the imagination. The *kplekple* horned mask, for example, represents a forest demon and is very stylised. The same is true of the painted antelope and buffalo masks called *goli*, which have large open mouths and are intended to represent bush spirits.

The Baoulé also carve figures. These often incorporate fine details and a shiny black patina. Baoulé *colon* carvings of people in European-style clothing are sold all over West Africa. Current opinion is that, far from portraying a colonial official, such figures represent a person's other-world mate – *blolo bian*, a wife from beyond, and *blolo bla*, a husband from beyond. Of course these days most are carved for the tourist trade and not necessarily by a Baoulé carver.

Senoufo masks are highly stylised, like the animal masks of the Baoulé. The most famous perhaps is the 'fire-spitter' helmet mask, which is a combination of antelope, warthog and hyena. Powerful and scary, it is said to represent the chaotic state of things in primeval times. The human face masks, on the other hand, can often have a very serene expression. One that you'll see everywhere in the tourist markets is the *kpelie* mask that features a highly stylised hairdo, thin eyes, small round mouth, various facial markings and two horns. The Senoufo also carve a great variety of statues, mostly female, which are used in divination and other sacred rituals.

Noire – Francophone Africa's premier literary prize.

Among younger writers, Bandama Maurice won the same honour in 1993 for his novel *Le Fils de la Femme Mâle*. Two Ivorian novelists and poets who are also widely read throughout Francophone Africa are Véronique Tadjo and Tanella Boni.

Music

Côte d'Ivoire's best-known musical export is Alpha Blondy, whose reggae style has achieved considerable international success. An early great, and probably his best recording, is *Apartheid is Nazism*. Other reggae stars are Serge Kassy, Ismael Isaac and Tiken Jah Fahkoly. Top female vocalists include Aïcha Koné, Monique Seka and Nayanka Bell. Gadji Celi plays more traditional Ivoirian music.

For the beat of the street, with in-your-face lyrics often counselling the country's political leaders, listen to wildly popular recordings such as Espoir 2000's *4éme Mandat*, Petit Yode & L'Enfant Siro's *Antilaléca* or Les Garagists' *Titrologues*.

RELIGION

Although the country has two of the largest Catholic cathedrals in the world, only about 12% of the people are Christian, including Protestant. Some 23%, mostly the Malinké and Dioula, are Muslims, living primarily in the north. The remaining 65% of the people practise traditional religions based upon ancestral worship, which can be loosely termed animist.

LANGUAGE

French is the official language. Principal African languages include Mande and Malinké in the northwest, Dan/Yacouba in the area around Man, Senoufo in and around Korhogo, Baoulé and Agni in the centre and south, and Dioula, the market language, everywhere. See the Language chapter later in this book for a list of useful phrases in French, Dioula, Senoufo and Dan.

Facts for the Visitor

SUGGESTED ITINERARIES

If you arrive directly from the developed world, consider saving Abidjan until last. That way, you'll appreciate its uniqueness in an African context.

If you're visiting Côte d'Ivoire for only a week – the minimum to get anything from it – plan on a couple of days in Abidjan, followed by two in one of the west-coast resorts, such as Sassandra, before heading north to Yamoussoukro (one day), with its amazing basilica, then back to Abidjan.

With three weeks or more at your disposal, we suggest the following circular tour. Before leaving Abidjan, spend a day or, better, stay overnight in the old colonial capital of Grand Bassam. Then head along the coast westwards. If you have transport and an ample budget, consider cosseting yourself for a day or two at the luxury hotels in Monogaga or Grand-Béréby. If you're travelling independently, aim for Sassandra or one of the rustic Robinson Crusoe beach camps to its west (three days). Nature lovers should build in a visit to Parc National de Taï – allow three days. From San Pédro, swing north to Man, the base for visiting some of the nearby villages of the Dan people, and the surrounding hills, ideal for a spot of hiking (three to four days). Then on to Korhogo, which merits another three to four days, and explore the nearby villages of the Senoufo people.

Korhogo is also the base for visiting, in December to May, Parc National de la Comoë (three days or more, including travelling time). From Korhogo, head south to Yamoussoukro, the titular capital (one or two nights), then back to Abidjan to soak up the remaining days.

PLANNING

Since the intercity roads are all tar, the rains shouldn't impede your travels too much. However, it's probably best to avoid the heaviest downpours in May, June and July.

The Michelin 1:800,000 map (No 957) gives the best coverage of Côte d'Ivoire. The tourist office in Abidjan has a useful, full-colour map of Abidjan (free).

VISAS & DOCUMENTS

Visas

Everyone except nationals of Economic Community of West African States (Ecowas) and US citizens need a visa. Visas are usually valid for three months and are good for visits of up to one month. The cost varies quite substantially depending on your nationality and where you are applying for it. You can't get a visa at the border and it's no longer possible to get one on arrival at Abidjan airport.

Visa Extensions Visas can be extended at the préfecture near the main post office in Le Plateau in Abidjan. An extension, valid for up to three months, costs CFA20,000 (plus two photos) and is ready the same day if you apply early. The visa section is open from 8am to noon and 3pm to 5pm Monday to Friday.

Visas for Onward Travel In Côte d'Ivoire, you can get visas for the following neighbouring countries. Note that the UK embassy issues visas to Sierra Leone and Kenya, and the French embassy issues visas to Togo.

Burkina Faso Three-month visas cost CFA13,000 and are issued within 24 hours. A consulate in Bouaké (☎ 31 63 44 31) also issues visas.

Ghana Four photos, CFA12,000 and 48 hours are required.

Guinea One-month visas cost CFA32,000 for all nationalities. You need three photos and visas are issued within 48 hours.

Liberia One-month visas, issued the same day, cost CFA20,000 for most nationalities and CFA25,000 for US and UK citizens.

Mali One-month visas cost CFA20,000 (issued within 24 hours). You will need two photos.

Other Documents

A yellow fever vaccination certificate is mandatory and will be requested when applying for a visa and on arrival. You need to have been vaccinated within the previous 10 years.

EMBASSIES & CONSULATES

Ivoirian Embassies & Consulates

In West Africa, Côte d'Ivoire has embassies or consulates in Burkina Faso, Ghana, Guinea, Liberia, Mali, Nigeria and Senegal. In other countries, embassies include the following:

Belgium (☎ 02-672 23 57, fax 672 04 91) 234 Av Franklin-Roosevelt, Brussels 1050
Canada (☎ 613-239 9919, fax 563 8287) Ave Marlborough, Ottawa, Ontario, K1N 8E6
France (☎ 01 45 01 53 10, fax 01 45 00 47 97) 102 Av R-Poincaré, 75116 Paris
Germany (☎ 089-714 10 63) Fürstenriederstr 276, D-81377 München
UK (☎ 020-7235 6991, fax 7259 5320) 2 Upper Belgrave St, London SW1X 8BJ
USA (☎ 202-797 0300) 2424 Massachusetts Ave, NW, Washington, DC 20008

Embassies & Consulates in Côte d'Ivoire

The following embassies and consulates in Abidjan are mostly in Le Plateau unless otherwise indicated:

Benin (☎ 22 41 44 13) Rue des Jardins, Les Deux Plateaux
Burkina Faso (☎ 20 21 13 13) Av Terrasson de Fougères; open 8am to 2.30pm Monday to Friday
Cameroon (☎ 20 21 33 31) Immeuble le Général, Rue Botreau-Roussel
Canada (☎ 20 21 20 09) Immeuble Trade Centre, Av Noguès; assists Australian nationals
France (☎ 20 20 05 05) Rue Lecoeur
Germany (☎ 20 21 47 27) Immeuble le Mans, Rue Botreau-Roussel
Ghana (☎ 20 33 11 24) Rue J95, Les Deux Plateaux; visa applications are accepted from 8.30am to 1pm Monday to Friday and visas are issued 1pm to 2.30pm Monday to Friday
Guinea (☎ 20 22 25 20) Immeuble Crosson Duplessis, Av Crosson Duplessis; open 9am to 3pm Monday to Friday
Liberia (☎ 20 32 46 39) Immeuble Taleb, Av Delafosse; open 9am to 11.30pm and 12.30pm to 3pm Monday to Friday
Mali (☎ 20 32 31 47) Maison du Mali, Rue du Commerce; open 7.30am to 4.30pm Monday to Thursday and 7.30am to 12.30pm Friday
Netherlands (☎ 20 21 31 10) Immeuble les Harmonies, Blvd Carde
Niger (☎ 21 26 28 14) Blvd Achalma, Marcory
Nigeria (☎ 20 21 19 82) Blvd de la République
Senegal (☎ 20 33 28 76) Immeuble Nabil, off Rue du Commerce
UK (☎ 20 22 68 50) Immeuble les Harmonies, Blvd Carde
USA (☎ 20 21 09 79) Rue Jesse Owens

MONEY

The unit of currency is the West African CFA franc.

country	unit		CFA
euro zone	€1	=	CFA656
UK	UK£1	=	CFA1024
USA	US$1	=	CFA694

Endeavour to bring a Visa card or euros, otherwise you'll find obtaining CFA costly and time consuming in Abidjan, and simply impossible in the provinces. Banks for changing money include Bicici (Banque Internationale pour le Commerce et l'Industrie en Côte d'Ivoire), BIAO (Banque Internationale pour l'Afrique Occidentale), SGBCI (Société Générale de Banques en Côte d'Ivoire) and Citibank.

In Abidjan, BIAO and Citibank honour Thomas Cook travellers cheques, Bicici honours American Express (AmEx) and SGBCI honours both varieties. The commission charged varies significantly from bank to bank. Travellers cheques in US dollars attract a flat CFA11,250 commission per transaction at SGBCI, 3.5% at BIAO and 9% at Bicici. Travellers cheques in euros attract 1% plus CFA5000 per transaction at SGBCI.

Changing euros into CFA generally attracts no commission. Commission on US dollars is similar to that charged on travellers cheques. In Abidjan there is a black market for changing US dollars; however, only the streetwise should use it. Hustlers can be found outside main banks in Le Plateau.

Bring plastic! SGBCI has ATMs throughout the country that reliably provide holders of Visa cards (and not MasterCards) with CFA. If you find your card does not open the door to ATM cubicles, just wait for a local to exit. In Korhogo the ATM can go offline from time to time – be patient and return later.

POST & COMMUNICATIONS

Post offices in Côte d'Ivoire are easy to recognise; they're all painted blue and white and are called SIPE (Société Ivoirienne de la Poste et de l'Épargne). An airmail letter costs CFA420 to Europe, CFA600 to the USA and CFA750 to Australia.

International telephone calls and faxes can be made from CI Telecom offices in major towns. They are open from 7.30am to 4pm Monday to Friday. A three-minute call costs CFA3000 to the UK, CFA3600 to the USA and CFA4200 to Australia. Phonecards are handy for local and international calls. Cards with 25/40/150 units cost CFA2500/4000/12,000.

With the exception of Man and Korhogo, most cities and regional centres have cybercafés with good connections. The cost is usually around CFA35 per minute or CFA1500 if you pay by the hour. However, be prepared to discover places with wildly inflated prices.

DIGITAL RESOURCES

Most of the better sites on Côte d'Ivoire are in French. One to start with is the official tourism website W www.tourisme.ci.

NEWSPAPERS

The main government newspaper is *Fraternité Matin*, while *La Voie* is very much the mouthpiece of the opposition FPI party. *Le Jour* steers an independent course between the two. All are in French.

HEALTH

You will need to have a yellow fever vaccination certificate to enter the country. A malaria risk exists throughout the country, year-round, so you should take appropriate precautions. For more information on health matters, see Health in the Regional Facts for the Visitor chapter.

There is a good clinic in Abidjan called the Polyclinique Internationale St Anne-Marie (☎ 22 44 51 32). While in the north of the country, a famous and excellent hospital exists in Ferkessédougou (or Ferké as its affectionately known), run by Baptist missionaries.

WOMEN TRAVELLERS

With the possible exception of the few coastal resorts, such as Grand Bassam, women travellers are unlikely to meet with special hassles. Dressing modestly, in the style of the locals, will help to minimise any unwanted attention. Be aware that many cheap hotels in Côte d'Ivoire double as brothels and should be avoided. In this chapter we only list brothels when alternative options are limited. Local women in Côte d'Ivoire are treated with more esteem and equality than is usual in the third world, and you will encounter many working or managing government offices, hotels, restaurants, bars and shops. Approaching and talking with local women, especially when they are with other women and in a business environment, is very easy: They are generally open, inquisitive and very friendly. For more general information and advice, see Women Travellers in the Regional Facts for the Visitor chapter.

DANGERS & ANNOYANCES

For assessment of the capital's security risks, see the boxed text 'How Safe is Abidjan?' in the Abidjan section later in this chapter. In general, Côte d'Ivoire, including its provincial cities, is as safe as anywhere else in West Africa.

The Atlantic has fierce currents and a ripping undertow and every year there are several drownings, often of strong, overly confident swimmers.

BUSINESS HOURS

Business hours are 8am to noon and 2.30pm to 6pm Monday to Friday, and mornings only on Saturday. Government offices are open 7.30am to noon and 2.30pm to 5.30pm Monday to Friday. Banking hours are from 8am to 11.15am and 2.45pm to 4.30pm Monday to Friday.

PUBLIC HOLIDAYS & SPECIAL EVENTS

Public holidays include:

New Year's Day 1 January
Easter March/April
Labour Day 1 May
Mothers' Day 28 May
Independence Day 7 August
Assumption Day 15 August
All Saints' Day 1 November
Fête de la Paix 15 November
National Day 7 December
Christmas Day 25 December

Various Islamic holidays are also celebrated – for a table of estimated dates for these holidays, see Public Holidays & Special Events in the Regional Facts for the Visitor chapter.

Côte d'Ivoire is rich in traditional festivals. Some particularly exuberant ones are:

February

Fêtes des Masques Held in the villages around Man. Masks are an integral part of Dan society and not simply superb works of art. The mask serves primarily as the community's collective memory and embodies a divine energy. The annual Fêtes des Masques brings together a great variety of masks and dances from the area and should not be missed if you are in the country at this time.

March/April

Le Carnaval de Bouaké One of Africa's largest carnivals, this celebration of friendship and life is held in March.

Fête du Dipri Held in Gomon, 100km northwest of Abidjan, in March or April. At midnight naked women and children carry out nocturnal rites to rid the village of evil incantations. Before dawn the village chief appears to the sound of drums, and villagers are sent into a trance. An animated frenzy carries on throughout the following day.

October/November

Fête de l'Abissa Held in Grand Bassam in October or November. A week-long, traditional carnival in which N'Zima people honour their dead and publicly exorcise evil spirits.

Fête des Harristes Held in Bregbo near Bingerville, 15km east of Abidjan, on 1 November, this is a major annual Harrist festival. Harrists have a 'born again' amalgam of Christianity and traditional beliefs. Their founder was William Wade Harris, who in 1913 began a preaching journey, walking barefoot from Liberia, through the Ivory Coast and on into the Gold Coast (modern Ghana).

ACTIVITIES

The area around Man is good for hiking. For swimming, there are unlimited possibilities all along the coast (see the East Coast and West Coast sections later in this chapter for details on the best beaches). Grand Lahou has great potential for surfing.

Côte d'Ivoire has a lot to offer birdwatchers. It's worth polishing your binoculars before visiting Taï and Comoë national parks or the last remaining coastal rainforest around San Pédro (see Flora & Fauna earlier in this chapter for details).

ACCOMMODATION

Accommodation is generally expensive and poor value for money. In Abidjan, you can find a clean, rudimentary double room with fan from CFA8000 and one with air-con and bathroom from CFA10,000. Anything less than CFA5000 is likely to be a *bordel* (brothel; look for tell-tail signs advertising the price for *passager*, meaning temporary use) and being dingy and squalid.

There's a good selection of mid-range hotels costing between CFA15,000 and CFA30,000.

Outside Abidjan, rates are slightly lower, although the choice, of course, is much more restricted. In some places, especially in the countryside, you may be offered accommodation in a *paillote* (a traditional, pole-and-thatch construction).

FOOD

There are three staples in Ivoirian cooking: rice, *foutou* and *attiéké*. Foutou is a dough of boiled yam, cassava or plantain, pounded into a sticky paste similar to mashed potato and so glutinous that it sticks to your palate. Attiéké is grated cassava with a subtle taste and texture very like couscous.

They're invariably served with a sauce, such as *sauce arachide*, which is made with groundnuts (peanuts); *sauce graine*, a hot sauce made with palm oil nuts; *sauce aubergine*, made with eggplant; or *sauce gombo* and *sauce djoumgbré*, both with a base of okra (ladies' fingers). In the sauce there will usually be some sort of meat, from chicken, pork or fish to more exotic offerings such as *hérrison* (hedgehog) or *biche* (antelope), which you may choose to avoid on environmental grounds.

Aloco, a dish of ripe bananas fried with chilli in palm oil, is a popular street food. *Kedjenou* – chicken, or sometimes guinea-fowl, simmered with vegetables in a mild sauce and usually served in an attractive earthenware pot – is almost a national dish. Many restaurants will serve you a whole chicken unless you specify that you only want half. While vegetarians are on the whole not well catered for, it is possible to find a variety of bean dishes and spicy vegetable stews containing yam, pumpkin and baby cabbage. Spinach stew is quite common and very delicious. (See the boxed text 'Eating Out in a Maquis'.)

Eating Out in a *Maquis*

The *maquis* is Côte d'Ivoire's contribution to eating in West Africa. Much copied by the country's Francophone neighbours, a typical maquis is a reasonably priced, open-air restaurant often housed in a *paillote* (a pole-and-thatch construction of varying degrees of sophistication). Open for lunch and dinner (though some are only open in the evening), they usually offer one or two of the standard sauces (aubergine, peanut or okra) containing chunks of meat or fish accompanied by some form of carbohydrate, usually rice, bread or *attiéké* (grated cassava). In the evenings, charcoal grills sizzle with meat, fish or poultry, normally served in an onion and tomato salad. On the coast the fish is superb and comes either whole or as *brochettes* (grilled on a stick).

DRINKS

Fizzy drinks are widely available. Youki Soda, a slightly sweeter version of tonic water, is a good thirst quencher. *Bandji* is the local palm wine, which is especially palatable when freshly tapped. Distilled, it makes a skull-shattering spirit known as *koutoukou*.

The standard beer is Flag, which locals order by asking for *une soixante-six*, a 660ml bottle. If you've a real thirst, go for *une grosse bière*, a hefty 1L bottle. For a premium beer, call for a locally brewed Tuborg. Unfortunately, the locally brewed Guinness doesn't taste like the version you're used to back home; it also contains almost double the alcohol content.

Getting There & Away

AIR

The main international airport is in Abidjan, at Port Bouët on the south side of town. There's a departure tax of CFA3000 on international flights. When you buy your ticket or reconfirm your flight, check whether this has been included in the ticket price.

Europe, the USA & Australia

There are only two carriers to/from Europe: Air France and KLM-Royal Dutch Airlines. Air France has daily flights to Paris for CFA453,500/616,900 one way in the low/high season; from Paris the price is around €710/895 return. KLM flies to Amsterdam three times weekly for CFA411,200/487,300 one way in the low/high season; from Amsterdam the price is around €830/655 return.

Royal Air Maroc flies from New York to Abidjan via Casablanca. A return flight in low/high season will be around US$1100/1350. If you can find a good deal on the trans-Atlantic leg of the trip, it can be marginally cheaper to buy one ticket to London or Amsterdam, and then a separate, discounted ticket onwards from there. Doing it this way (from the east coast) will cost about US$1000/1300.

There are no direct flights to Australia. It's cheapest to fly either via Egypt with

EgyptAir, or Johannesburg with South African Airways (SAA); in both cases a return flight in low/high season will be around A$2250/2450.

Africa

The combined services of small national airlines such as Air Burkina, Air Gabon, Ghana Airways, Air Guinée, Air Senegal and Air Mali ensure that there are daily flights between Abidjan and Accra (Ghana; CFA75,900 one way with Ghana Airways), Bamako (Mali; CFA92,500 with Air Senegal), Conakry (Guinea; CFA132,500 with Air Senegal) and Ouagadougou (Burkina Faso; CFA136,500 with Air Burkina). There are three flights a week to Liberia (Monrovia; CFA119,400 with Ghana Airways) and six flights weekly on Weasua Air Transport (CFA158,290/310,825 one way/return).

There are also daily flights further afield to Dakar (Senegal), Lagos (Nigeria) and Lomé (Togo), and at least three flights a week between Abidjan and Banjul (Gambia), Cotonou (Benin), Freetown (Sierra Leone), Niamey (Niger), Ethiopia (Addis Ababa) and Johannesburg (South Africa).

Middle East

EgyptAir flies once weekly to Cairo (CFA417,900 one way), and Middle East Airlines (MEA) twice weekly to Beirut (Lebanon) for around the same price.

LAND

Border Crossings

The frontier with Burkina Faso, at Ouangolodougou, is open between 8am and around 6.30pm daily. It's tar all the way.

The coastal road connecting Abidjan and Accra in Ghana is all tar and in good condition. There are lesser-used routes via Agnibilékrou and Ferkessédougou.

The main route to Guinea is via Gbapleu, but there are options available if you have time and scorn travelling in comfort.

To get to Liberia, the main route is from Danané to Ganta via Sanniquellie. People with their own transport can consider going along the Ivorian coast to Tabou and proceeding across the border to Harper.

From Abidjan to Bamako in Mali, the routes via Ferkessédougou or Odienné are tar all the way. The border is open between 8am and around 6.30pm daily.

Burkina Faso

Bus & Bush Taxi From Abidjan, bus company CTI (☎ 07 05 86 95), opposite the Treichville train station, has an 11am bus on Tuesday, Wednesday and Saturday to Bobo-Dioulasso (CFA15,000, 17 to 19 hours) and Ouagadougou (CFA21,000, 29 to 33 hours). Buses also run from Yamoussoukro to Bobo-Dioulasso (CFA11,000, 14 to 16 hours) and Ouagadougou (CFA17,000, 26 to 30 hours); from Bouaké to Bobo-Dioulasso (CFA11,000, 12 to 14 hours) and Ouagadougou (CFA17,000, 24 to 28 hours); and from Ferkessédougou to Bobo-Dioulasso (CFA9000, eight to 10 hours) and Ouagadougou (CFA15,000, 20 to 24 hours). In Bobo-Dioulasso connections can be made for Bamako in Mali.

Bush taxis make for a faster border crossing. A Peugeot bush taxi direct to Ouagadougou from Abidjan is CFA22,000, from Bouaké or Yamoussoukro CFA18,000 and from Ferkessédougou CFA16,000. Travel times can be two to four hours less than those of the bus.

Train The optimistically named express leaves Treichville train station in Abidjan for Ouagadougou on Tuesday, Thursday and Saturday morning. The 1st-/2nd-class fare is CFA20,700/16,500 to Bobo-Dioulasso (18 hours) and CFA26,000/21,500 to Ouagadougou (25 hours). If going from Bouaké the fare is CFA10,300/8300 to Bobo-Dioulasso (13 hours), CFA18,200/14,700 to Ouagadougou (20 hours). From Ferkessédougou it's CFA5300/1600 to Bobo-Dioulasso (nine hours) and CFA13,200/ 10,700 to Ouagadougou (16 hours). Only light snacks and drinks are available, although you can buy food and drink from vendors at stops en route.

This once-stylish train continues to deteriorate. All the same, consider travelling at least some of the journey by train – for instance the transfrontier leg, between Bouaké or Ferkessédougou and Banfora or Bobo-Dioulasso. The scenery is attractive and, on those occasions when the train's in motion, it fairly hurtles along.

Ghana

The best bus service between Abidjan and Accra is STIF's *Ecowas Express* (☎ 20 37 89 62). It departs Gare Routière d'Adjamé in Abidjan at 9am daily (CFA11,000, seven hours). It's far superior to the Ghanaian STC bus (☎ 21 35 84 07), which runs daily from its bus station south of Treichville. Leaving in principle – but rarely in practice – at 9.30am (though you must check in at 7am), it arrives 12 to 14 hours later depending on the delay at the border, which is always very long and tedious. The fare is CFA8000 plus CFA200 per kilogram for luggage and possibly a CFA1000 whip-round at the border (at Elubo) to cover bribes to border officials. Tickets must be purchased the day before departure.

Abidjan to Accra is cheaper and faster by bush taxi from the Gare de Bassam in Abidjan to Takoradi in Ghana (about CFA5000, four hours), from where there are frequent connections to Accra.

There are no direct buses if you choose to travel via Agnibilékrou, but you can do the journey in stages from Abidjan to Abengourou (CFA2500, three hours) then on to the border at Takikroum. Don't forget to collect an exit stamp from the police/immigration at Agnibilékrou. From the Ghanaian border there are bush taxis heading to Kumasi.

For the northernmost route, bush taxis go from Ferkessédougou to Bouna (CFA7500, eight to 12 hours) and from there to the border with Ghana (CFA1500, 1½ hours). From the border, there's a canoe that will take you across the Black Volta River for a standard fee. On the far bank are moneychangers (only change enough to get yourself to Tamale) and minibuses for Bole (39km). In Bole, there's a cheap, grubby motel without electricity or running water. A daily bus leaves Bole for Tamale at 6am.

Guinea

A bush taxi or minibus from Danané will drop you at the border at Gbapleu (CFA1500, 1½ hours), which is open 24 hours, from where you can catch transport to Lola and on to N'Zérékoré. Be sure to get your passport stamped at the commissariat at Danané.

There are a number of little-used alternative routes using roads in poor condition: via Odienné and Sirana to Beyla; via Minignan, Bougoula and Mandiana to Kankan; and via Biankouma and Sipilou to Beyla. Consider using these if you don't mind waiting long periods for very irregular, uncomfortable transport or have your own 4WD.

Liberia

Since the situation in Liberia is unstable, check first in Abidjan and again with the commissariat in Danané to find out if the border is open and whether it's safe to travel. The main route is from Danané to Ganta via Gbé-Nda, Kahnple and Sanniquellie. Minibuses from Danané to the border (CFA500, 30 minutes) leave when full.

If you have your own transport, you can also go along the Ivorian coast to Tabou and proceed to Harper, just beyond the frontier. From Harper, cut inland to Zwedru, Tappita and Ganta. This route takes three to four days and only expert drivers with 4WDs should attempt it from May to November, when the Liberian section becomes very muddy.

Mali

Several buses a week leave Abidjan for Bamako (CFA17,000, two days) going via Sikasso and Bougouni, but few travellers do this long, tedious journey in one hit.

Minibuses make the journey from Ferkessédougou to Bamako daily (CFA9000, 30 hours). There is a more frequent service as far as the frontier (CFA5000, 17 hours), beyond which you can pick up another vehicle for Sikasso.

There's only one direct bus a week between Odienné and Bamako (CFA6000, 15 hours). There are daily minibuses from Odienné to Manankoro on the border (CFA2500, two hours), from where you can pick up further transport to Bougouni.

Getting Around

AIR

As we went to press, Air Ivoire went to the wall. Rumour had it that Air France would come to its rescue. If this were to happen, flights to Korhogo, Man and Bouaké from Abidjan might be resurrected.

BUS

The country's large, relatively modern buses *(cars)* are around the same price, take the same time and are significantly more comfortable than bush taxis or minibuses. Most have fixed departure times and don't charge extra for luggage. The table on the next page shows journey times, typical fares and bus companies for routes between selected towns.

Bus Routes & Fares

from	to	distance (km)	duration (hours)	fare (CFA)	bus company & station
Abidjan					
	Aboisso	120	2	1500	STA from Gare Routière d'Adjamé or Gare de Bassam
	Bouaké	355	5	4000	STIF, MTT or UTB from Gare Routière d'Adjamé
	Ferkessédougou	590	9	5000	UTS, UTNA or Utrafer from Gare Routière d'Adjamé
	Grand-Bassam	45	1	600	UTAB from Gare Routière d'Adjamé via Gare de Bassam from where minibuses and bush taxis also leave
	Korhogo	640	10	4500	TCK from Gare Routière d'Adjamé
	Man	580	9	5000	Fandaso, BAN, UTB or CTM from Gare Routière d'Adjamé
	San Pedro	320	6	4500	A&M and SKT from Gare Routière d'Adjamé
	Sassandra	260	5	2500	A&M from Gare Routière Adjamé
	Yamoussoukro	200	3½	2500	MTT, UTB or STIF buses from Gare Routière d'Adjamé
Korhogo					
	Bouaké	285	5	2500	CTKS, UTB opposite the Grand Marché
	Ferkessédougou	55	1	1000	Utrako or minibus from Agip station
	Odienné	235	5	4000	postal van from post office daily (except Sunday) at 8am
Odienné					
	Man	275	5	4000	one minibus/bush taxi daily or the 7am daily (except Sunday) postal van from behind the post office
Yamoussoukro					
	Man	330	6	3500	CTM or STIF, from the depot on Av Houphouët-Boigny

BUSH TAXI & MINIBUS

Bush taxis (ageing Peugeots or covered pick-ups, known as *bâchés*) and minibuses cover major towns and outlying communities not served by the large buses. They leave at all hours of the day, but only when full so long waits may be required. These days their fares are around the same as those of buses.

TRAIN

The northbound express for Ouagadougou leaves Abidjan's Treichville station on Tuesday, Thursday and Saturday morning, calling in at Bouaké (1st/2nd class CFA6600/5400, five hours) and Ferké (CFA11,600/9400, nine hours) on the way and bypassing Yamoussoukro. It's slower than the bus or bush taxi.

CAR

At the time of writing petrol was CFA500 per litre (CFA510 for super, or premium) and diesel *(gasoil)* was CFA400. The road system is among the best in West Africa and highways between major towns are all tar. One exception is the road from Korhogo to Odienné, which is paved only as far as Boundiali and in a lamentable condition from there to Odienné.

LOCAL TRANSPORT

For details on taxi transport in Abidjan, see Getting Around in the Abidjan section. In most other towns, the fare for a ride in a *woro woro* (shared taxi) is CFA150. If your destination is far off the regular route, the driver may want you to hire the whole taxi, which will usually be expressed as *quatre places* – in other words, you are being asked to pay for four fares which, at CFA150 each, adds up to CFA600. In the same way, the driver may respond *deux places* or *trois places* when you state your destination.

ORGANISED TOURS

There are three companies offering tours; all are based in Abidjan. Pistes Africaines, with local reps in Korhogo and Man, can lay on an English-speaking guide. Other companies include Haury Tours and Ivoire Voyages Tourisme. (See Information under Abidjan for contact details of tour companies.)

Abidjan

Abidjan was an unimportant town until it became a major port in 1951, when the French finished the Vridi Canal connecting the Ébrié Lagoon with the ocean. Since then, its population has skyrocketed from 60,000 to 3.5 million people.

If you've just flown in from the USA or Europe, you won't fully savour the uniqueness of Le Plateau, the business district. But if you arrive after a few weeks of bus- and bush-taxi travel around West Africa, you'll gasp.

Your first glimpse of the city will probably be from across the lagoon. Water in the middle ground, offset by daring high-rises puncturing the sky. If you can ignore the dispossessed, the beggars and street hawkers who've slipped in from another world, the impression's sustained; smart hotels and boutiques, chic Ivorian ladies clacking along on high heels, on their way to restaurants of four-star Parisian quality – and prices to match – with their smooth escorts, talking in French. You'll sense the same atmosphere in the leafy residential areas of Cocody and Les Deux Plateaux.

But Abidjan has two faces. Adjamé, on the north side of town, plus Marcory and Treichville to the south of Le Plateau, linked by two major bridges, are areas in which rural immigrants have settled – they remain pure Africa in all its vitality and urban poverty.

Orientation

Abidjan spreads around the inlets and along the promontories of the large Ébrié Lagoon. Le Plateau, with its boulevards and skyscrapers, is the hub of the business and government districts.

Across a finger of the lagoon, east of Le Plateau, is the exclusive residential district of Cocody. North of Cocody lies the residential and restaurant district of Les Deux Plateaux.

To the north of Le Plateau is Adjamé and the main bus station, frantic Gare Routière d'Adjamé. South of Le Plateau, across two busy bridges are Treichville, full of vitality especially at night, and Marcory, of little interest in itself but safe at night and offering a selection of budget and mid-range hotels plus superb street food and *maquis* (open-air eateries).

The international airport and main marine port are at Port Bouët, further south, on the Atlantic Ocean.

Information

Tourist Offices The Office Ivoirien du Tourisme et de l'Hôtellerie (☎ 20 25 16 10) is opposite the main post office on Place de la République, Le Plateau. Work on a new visitor reception centre is under way. A good, free map of Abidjan is available.

Money The only places that will change money are the main branches of the banks in Le Plateau and those at the airport. If you're stuck with Central African CFA francs and

How Safe is Abidjan?

We felt quite safe in Abidjan. The once notorious petty-crime problem seems to have been improved by the employment of legions of young security guards who, dressed in yellow, stand vigil at every building of note and every major street corner. However, you should still take precautions. Avoid walking the streets at night, using the black market and buying drugs. The precincts of Treichville's nightclubs are a favourite haunt of no-gooders, the Gare Routière d'Adjamé is notorious for theft, and walking over either bridge between Treichville and Le Plateau is a risk, even during the day.

If you're attacked or lose anything, especially if you intend to claim insurance reimbursement, contact the commissariat du premier arrondissement, at the préfecture (☎ 20 21 58 33) in Le Plateau, Abidjan. Each certificate of theft costs around CFA7000.

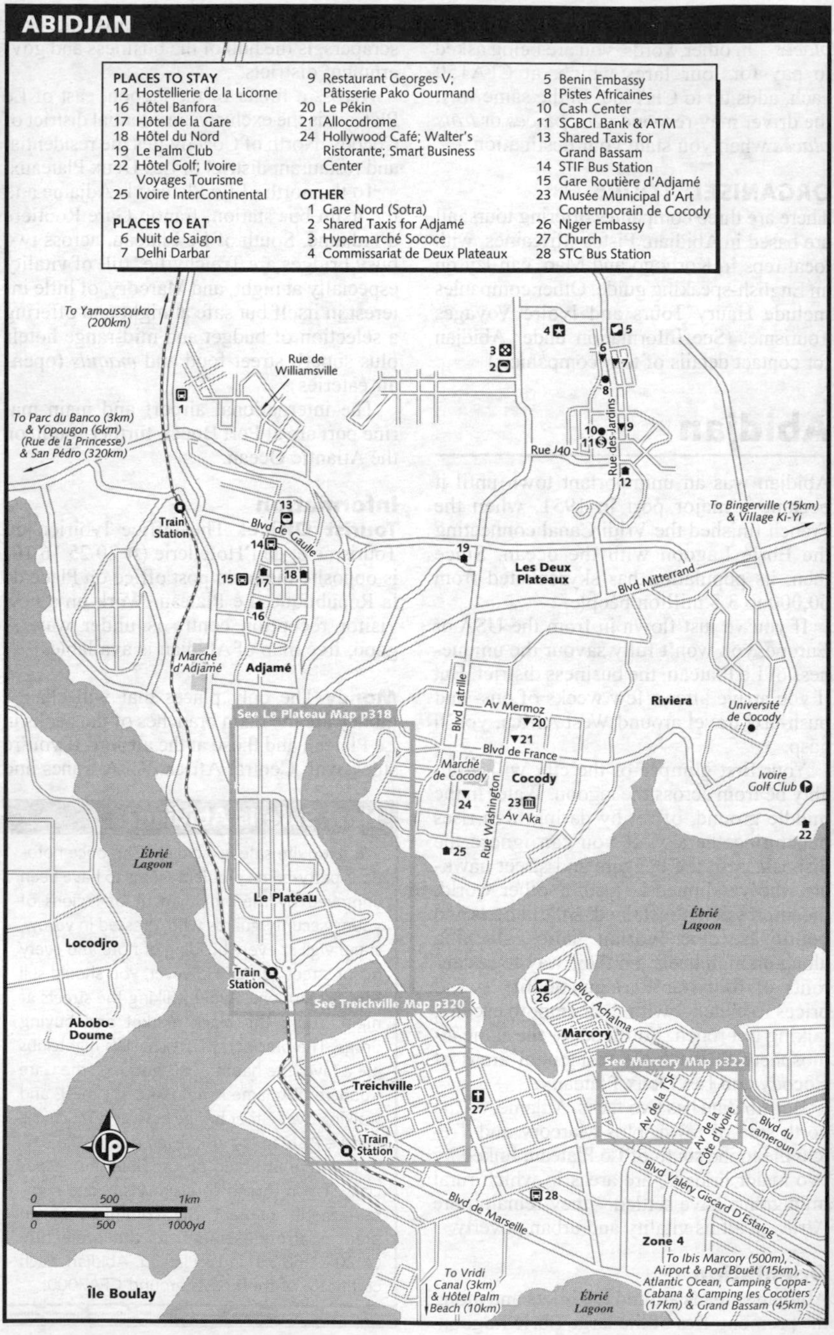
ABIDJAN
PLACES TO STAY
12 Hostellierie de la Licorne
16 Hôtel Banfora
17 Hôtel de la Gare
18 Hôtel du Nord
19 Le Palm Club
22 Hôtel Golf; Ivoire Voyages Tourisme
25 Ivoire InterContinental
PLACES TO EAT
6 Nuit de Saigon
7 Delhi Darbar
9 Restaurant Georges V; Pâtisserie Pako Gourmand
20 Le Pékin
21 Allocodrome
24 Hollywood Café; Walter's Ristorante; Smart Business Center
OTHER
1 Gare Nord (Sotra)
2 Shared Taxis for Adjamé
3 Hypermarché Sococe
4 Commissariat de Deux Plateaux
5 Benin Embassy
8 Pistes Africaines
10 Cash Center
11 SGBCI Bank & ATM
13 Shared Taxis for Grand Bassam
14 STIF Bus Station
15 Gare Routière d'Adjamé
23 Musée Municipal d'Art Contemporain de Cocody
26 Niger Embassy
27 Church
28 STC Bus Station
To Yamoussoukro (200km)
Rue de Williamsville
To Parc du Banco (3km) & Yopougon (6km) (Rue de la Princesse) & San Pédro (320km)
Rue J40
Rue des Jardins
To Bingerville (15km) & Village Ki-Yi
Train Station
Blvd de Gaulle
Les Deux Plateaux
Blvd Mitterrand
Marché d'Adjamé
Adjamé
See Le Plateau Map p318
Blvd Latrille
Av Mermoz
Riviera
Université de Cocody
Blvd de France
Marché de Cocody
Cocody
Rue Washington
Av Aka
Ivoire Golf Club
Ébrié Lagoon
Le Plateau
Ébrié Lagoon
Locodjro
Train Station
See Treichville Map p320
Blvd Achalma
Marcory
Abobo-Doume
See Marcory Map p322
Treichville
Av de la TSF
Av de la Côte d'Ivoire
Blvd du Cameroun
Train Station
Blvd Valéry Giscard D'Estaing
0 500 1km
0 500 1000yd
Blvd de Marseille
Zone 4
To Ibis Marcory (500m), Airport & Port Bouët (15km), Atlantic Ocean, Camping Coppa-Cabana & Camping les Cocotiers (17km) & Grand Bassam (45km)
To Vridi Canal (3km) & Hôtel Palm Beach (10km)
Ébrié Lagoon
Île Boulay

the banks turn their noses up at them, as they're likely to, try Air Gabon on Av Delafosse in Le Plateau.

AmEx is represented by Alize Voyages (☎ 20 32 24 36, fax 20 32 24 29) on Av Lamblin in Le Plateau. However, it will not change travellers cheques.

Post & Communications Poste restante at Abidjan's Le Plateau post office, opposite Place de la République, is open 7.30am to noon and 2.30pm to 5pm Monday to Friday. Letters cost CFA600 each to collect and are held for one month.

International telephone calls and faxes can be made easily between 7am and 6.30pm Monday to Saturday, and from 8am to noon Sunday, on the 1st floor of the CI Telecom office in the giant EECI building on Place de la République. It's CFA1000/1200/1400 per minute to Europe/USA/Australia. It's generally much cheaper to use the phone services of Internet cafés.

Baobab Communications Centre (☎ 20 32 02 52) on Rue du Commerce, Le Plateau, charges CFA2000 an hour for Internet use; the connection is fast. Cyber Espace (☎ 05 90 82 92) on Av Chardy, Le Plateau, charges CFA1500 per hour, but its connection is slow. Both are open 8am to 6pm daily.

Smart Business Center (☎ 22 44 13 02), behind the Marché de Cocody, charges CFA2000 per hour for Internet access. International calls can also be made here (CFA700/900/1100 per minute to Europe/USA/Australia). It's open from 7.30am to 9pm daily.

Restaurant Georges V (☎ 22 41 17 24) on Rue des Jardins in Les Deux Plateaux is a Lebanese Internet café. Online costs are CFA3000 per hour. It's open 9am to 11pm daily.

In Treichville there are any number of cybercafés along Av 16. The going rate for international calls can be as little as CFA250 a minute.

Travel Agencies & Tour Operators Pistes Africaines (☎ 22 41 17 18, fax 22 41 66 75, ⓔ pistesafricaines@aviso.ci) is on Rue des Jardins in Les Deux Plateaux. The very helpful Michael Thines speaks English and offers tailor-made group tours of the country, including fully equipped trekking and camping tours in national parks.

Haury Tours (☎ 20 22 18 15, fax 20 22 17 68, ⓔ haury@africaonline.co.ci), on the 2nd floor of the Chardy building in Le Plateau, is an affiliate of the French leisure giant, Nouvelles Frontières, and has several off-the-peg one-day tours from Abidjan, plus trips deeper into the provinces. It's open 8am to noon and 2pm to 6pm Monday to Friday and 8am to noon Saturday. Check its website at ⓦ www.haurytours.co.ci.

Ivoire Voyages Tourisme (☎ 22 43 01 74, fax 22 43 50 45, ⓔ IVT@africaonline.co.ci), based at Hôtel Golf, offers similar services. All three tour companies are highly professional and can provide personalised tours and car hire.

Saga Voyages (☎ 20 22 79 88, fax 20 32 38 42, ⓔ saga.agv@aviso.ci), on Av Anoma, opposite Air France, Le Plateau, has English- and French-speaking staff who can find discounted air fares. It's open 8am to 11.45am and 2.30pm to 6pm Monday to Friday and Saturday morning.

Bookshops Librairie de France (☎ 20 30 63 630) on Av Chardy in Le Plateau, is very good for French titles, but it also has a small collection of English-language classics. There are other smaller branches around the city.

Medical Services A recommended hospital in Abidjan is the Polyclinique Internationale St Anne-Marie (☎ 22 44 51 32) just off Blvd de la Corniche west of Cocody.

Musée National

Just more than 1km north of Le Plateau market is the Musée National *(☎ 21 22 20 56, Cnr Blvd Nangul Abrogoua & Av 13; admission free; open 9am-noon & 3pm-6pm Tues-Sat)*. It has a collection of over 20,000 objects, including wooden statues and masks, pottery, ivory and bronze. Many of the buses heading for Adjamé pass nearby.

Cathédrale St-Paul

Designed by the Italian Aldo Spiritom, this is a bold and innovative cathedral *(Blvd Angoulvant, Le Plateau; admission free; open 8am-7pm daily)*. The tower is a huge stylised figure of St Paul with the nave sweeping boldly behind him like trailing robes. Inside, the stained-glass tableaux are as warm and rich as those of the basilica in

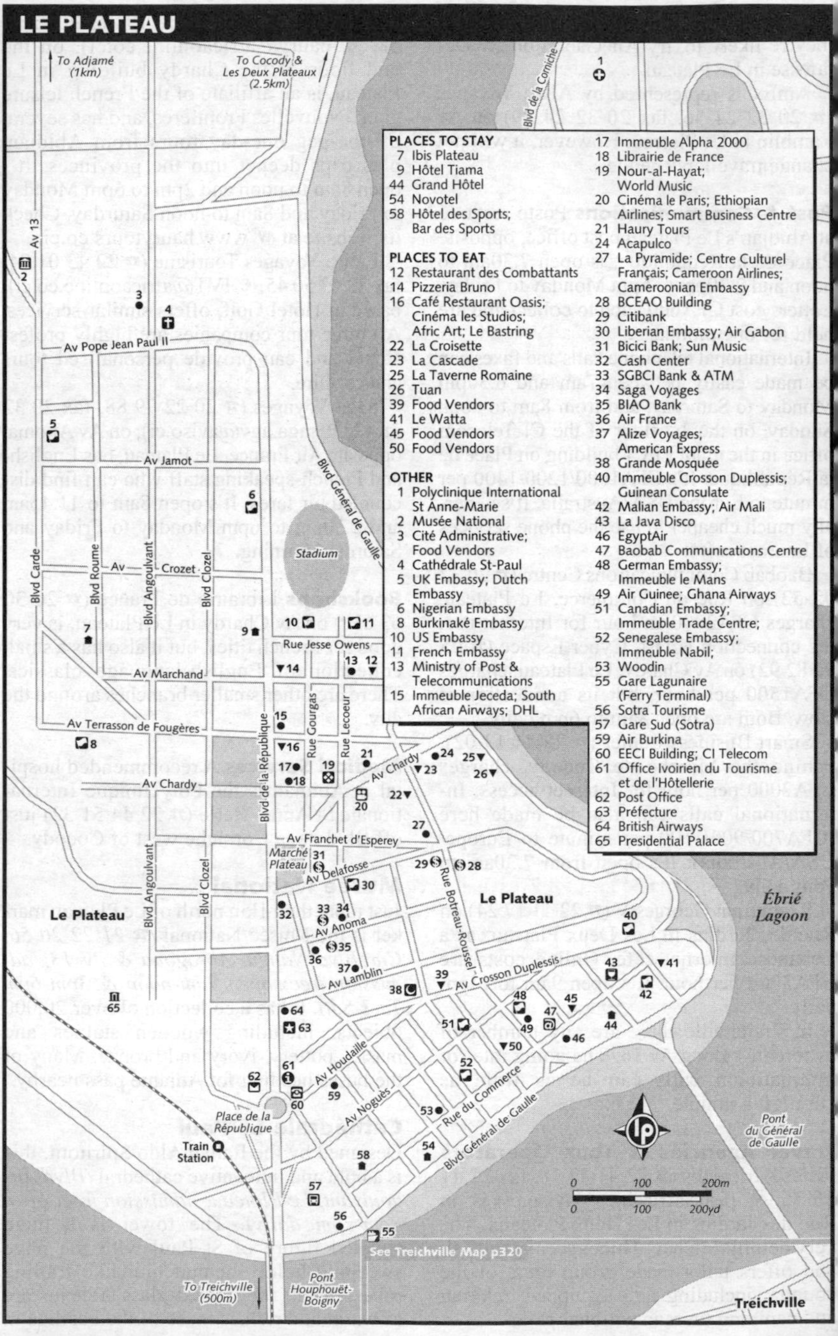
LE PLATEAU
PLACES TO STAY
7 Ibis Plateau
9 Hôtel Tiama
44 Grand Hôtel
54 Novotel
58 Hôtel des Sports; Bar des Sports
PLACES TO EAT
12 Restaurant des Combattants
14 Pizzeria Bruno
16 Café Restaurant Oasis; Cinéma les Studios; Afric Art; Le Bastring
22 La Croisette
23 La Cascade
25 La Taverne Romaine
26 Tuan
39 Food Vendors
41 Le Watta
45 Food Vendors
50 Food Vendors
OTHER
1 Polyclinique International St Anne-Marie
2 Musée National
3 Cité Administrative; Food Vendors
4 Cathédrale St-Paul
5 UK Embassy; Dutch Embassy
6 Nigerian Embassy
8 Burkinaké Embassy
10 US Embassy
11 French Embassy
13 Ministry of Post & Telecommunications
15 Immeuble Jeceda; South African Airways; DHL
17 Immeuble Alpha 2000
18 Librairie de France
19 Nour-al-Hayat; World Music
20 Cinéma le Paris; Ethiopian Airlines; Smart Business Centre
21 Haury Tours
24 Acapulco
27 La Pyramide; Centre Culturel Français; Cameroon Airlines; Cameroonian Embassy
28 BCEAO Building
29 Citibank
30 Liberian Embassy; Air Gabon
31 Bicici Bank; Sun Music
32 Cash Center
33 SGBCI Bank & ATM
34 Saga Voyages
35 BIAO Bank
36 Air France
37 Alize Voyages; American Express
38 Grande Mosquée
40 Immeuble Crosson Duplessis; Guinean Consulate
42 Malian Embassy; Air Mali
43 La Java Disco
46 EgyptAir
47 Baobab Communications Centre
48 German Embassy; Immeuble le Mans
49 Air Guinee; Ghana Airways
51 Canadian Embassy; Immeuble Trade Centre;
52 Senegalese Embassy; Immeuble Nabil;
53 Woodin
55 Gare Lagunaire (Ferry Terminal)
56 Sotra Tourisme
57 Gare Sud (Sotra)
59 Air Burkina
60 EECI Building; CI Telecom
61 Office Ivoirien du Tourisme et de l'Hôtellerie
62 Post Office
63 Préfecture
64 British Airways
65 Presidential Palace
To Adjamé (1km)
To Cocody & Les Deux Plateaux (2.5km)
Blvd de la Corniche
Av 13
Av Pope Jean Paul II
Av Jamot
Blvd Général de Gaulle
Stadium
Blvd Carde
Blvd Roume
Blvd Angoulvant
Blvd Clozel
Av Crozet
Rue Jesse Owens
Av Marchand
Av Terrasson de Fougères
Av Chardy
Blvd de la République
Rue Gourgas
Rue Lecoeur
Av Franchet d'Esperey
Marché Plateau
Av Delafosse
Rue Botreau-Roussel
Le Plateau
Ébrié Lagoon
Av Anoma
Av Lamblin
Av Crosson Duplessis
Av Houdaille
Av Nogues
Rue du Commerce
Place de la République
Train Station
Pont du Général de Gaulle
0 100 200m
0 100 200yd
See Treichville Map p320
To Treichville (500m)
Pont Houphouët-Boigny
Treichville

Yamoussoukro. Note in particular the one behind the altar depicting God blinding St Paul on the road to Damascus, the storm on Lake Galilee with Jesus pointing the way ahead as the disciples jettison the cargo and, opposite, the tableau of the first missionaries stepping ashore to a scene of African plenty – elephants, gazelles, luxuriant palms and smiling villagers.

Le Plateau

Step back and look up at some of the buildings of Le Plateau; they're as breathtaking close up as from a distance. **La Pyramide** on the corner of Av Franchet d'Esperey and Rue Botreau-Roussel, designed by the Italian architect Olivieri, was the first daring structure, although, now more than 25 years old, it's beginning to show its age. Poke your head next door into the airy **Centre Culturel Français** *(☎ 20 21 15 99, Av Franchet d'Esperey; open 10am-6pm Tues-Sat)*. It has regular art exhibitions, a library and, outside, an open-air café with copulating scrap-metal creatures.

Looming over the cathedral are the towers of the **Cité Administrative** on Blvd Angoulvant, giant copper-coloured slabs with fretted windows. The shimmering **Ministry of Post & Telecommunications** building situated on the corner of Av Marchand and Rue Lecoeur, all rounded angles and curves soaring skywards, contrasts with its cuboid, right-angled neighbours.

Parc du Banco

Only 3km from town to the northwest is the lush rainforest reserve Parc du Banco *(Autoroute de Nord)*. It has very pleasant walking trails, majestic trees and a lake, but little in the way of wildlife. Near the park entrance is Africa's largest outdoor laundrette, where hundreds of washermen scrub clothes in the Banco River and thrash them against the rocks (see the boxed text 'The Outdoor Laundrette'). Take bus No 20, 34 or 36 from the Gare Nord in Adjamé on the road north to Yamoussoukro, or bus No 20 from the Gare Sud in Le Plateau, south of Place de la République.

Ivoire InterContinental

In Cocody, pay a visit to the colossal Ivoire InterContinental *(☎ 22 40 80 00, fax 22 40 88 88, ⓔ ivoire@interconti.com, Blvd Latrille)*. It's West Africa's premier hotel and a small city in itself. It has 11 tennis courts, numerous swimming pools and restaurants, a bowling alley, cinema, pharmacy, bookshop, casino, grocery store, nightclub, sauna and a major craft shop. It also has an SGBCI bank with an ATM, which spits out CFA to those with cashed up Visa accounts. Take bus No 86 from Gare Sud, No 84 from Gare Nord or No 74 from Gare de Marcory.

The Outdoor Laundrette

Every day some 375 *fanicos* (washermen), mostly Burkinabé and none Ivorian, jam together in the middle of a small stream near the Parc du Banco, frantically rubbing clothes on huge stones held in place by old car tyres. Afterwards, they spread the clothes over rocks and grass for at least 500m (never getting them mixed up) and then iron them. Any washer not respecting the strict rules imposed by the washers' trade union, which allocates positions, is immediately excluded.

The soap is black and sold by women who make it from palm oil in small wooden sheds on the hills surrounding the stream. The activity starts at dawn when the fanicos head off on their rounds to collect the laundry; they begin arriving in single file at the stream around 6.30am. The best time to be here is between 10.30am and noon when the action is at its peak. You'll get some superb photos, although payment is expected. In the afternoon all you'll see is drying clothes.

Musée Municipal d'Art Contemporain de Cocody

It's an easy stroll east from Ivoire InterContinental in Cocody to this small museum *(☎ 22 44 83 54, Av Aka; admission free; open 9am-1pm & 3pm-6.30pm Tues-Sat)*. It has a thought-provoking, permanent collection of works by contemporary Ivoirian and other African artists and regularly mounts exciting, temporary exhibitions.

Activities

You can play **tennis** at the Ivoire InterContinental, and for CFA2000 nonguests can use the pools. You can **swim**, play **tennis** or hire **sailboards** at Hôtel Golf. For contact details for both, see Places to Stay – Top End.

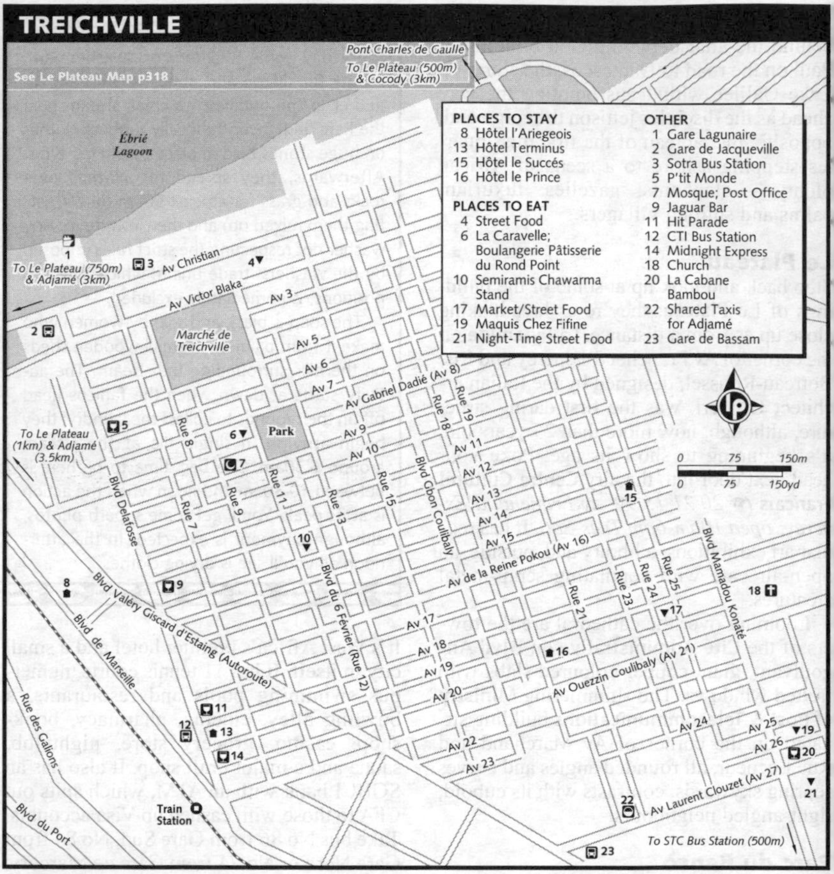
TREICHVILLE
Pont Charles de Gaulle
To Le Plateau (500m) & Cocody (3km)
See Le Plateau Map p318
Ébrié Lagoon
To Le Plateau (750m) & Adjamé (3km)
To Le Plateau (1km) & Adjamé (3.5km)
PLACES TO STAY
8 Hôtel l'Ariegeois
13 Hôtel Terminus
15 Hôtel le Succés
16 Hôtel le Prince
PLACES TO EAT
4 Street Food
6 La Caravelle; Boulangerie Pâtisserie du Rond Point
10 Semiramis Chawarma Stand
17 Market/Street Food
19 Maquis Chez Fifine
21 Night-Time Street Food
OTHER
1 Gare Lagunaire
2 Gare de Jacqueville
3 Sotra Bus Station
5 P'tit Monde
7 Mosque; Post Office
9 Jaguar Bar
11 Hit Parade
12 CTI Bus Station
14 Midnight Express
18 Church
20 La Cabane Bambou
22 Shared Taxis for Adjamé
23 Gare de Bassam
Av Christian
Av Victor Blaka
Marché de Treichville
Park
Av Gabriel Dadié (Av 8)
Av de la Reine Pokou (Av 16)
Av Ouezzin Coulibaly (Av 21)
Av Laurent Clouzet (Av 27)
Blvd Delafosse
Blvd Gbon Coulibaly
Blvd du 6 Février (Rue 12)
Blvd Mamadou Konaté
Blvd Valéry Giscard d'Estaing (Autoroute)
Blvd de Marseille
Rue des Galions
Blvd du Port
Train Station
To STC Bus Station (500m)
0 75 150m
0 75 150yd

Ivoire Golf Club (☎ *22 43 08 44, Blvd de France),* near Hôtel Golf, has the best 18-hole golf course in West and Central Africa.

Places to Stay

Accommodation is expensive and not always good value for money. Anything below CFA5000 is likely to be a brothel.

Places to Stay – Budget

About 17km east of Abidjan are two tiny neighbouring beachfront places, surrounded by cement walls, where you can camp or rent a basic room. These sites are on a frequent shared taxi (CFA500) route from the Gare de Bassam. ***Coppa-Cabana*** has camp sites for CFA1500 per person and singles/doubles with fan for CFA4000/5000. This a very simple but friendly facility with showers and a paillote bar-restaurant. Next door, the equally rudimentary ***Camping les Cocotiers*** also has camp sites for CFA1500 per person and offers doubles for CFA4500.

Treichville & Marcory Although the crime level has fallen, Treichville can be dangerous after dark, when it's prudent to take a taxi back to your hotel.

Hôtel le Prince *(☎ 21 24 17 38, Av 20)* Singles/doubles with air-con CFA6000/8000. The Prince has recently undergone a radical facelift. Plain rooms with shower and fan or air-con are excellent value. There's also a pleasant courtyard restaurant and bar.

Hôtel le Succés *(☎ 21 25 93 53, fax 21 25 81 53, Rue 25)* Singles without/with fan

BAKH★YAYE

ANDREW BURKE

CARL DRURY

NIUMI

DAVID ELSE

OLIVER STREWE

PAUL DYMOND

Getting from A to B is often more adventurous than arriving at your destination: touting for business from one of Dakar's *car rapides*, Senegal (top left); moped shop in Ouagadougou, Burkina Faso (top right); hitching a lift, Niger (middle right); ferries on the Gambia River between Banjul and Barra, Gambia (bottom left); hitching on an iron-ore train, Nouâdhibou, Mauritania (bottom right)

PATRICK SYDER

JANE SWEENEY

ARIADNE VAN ZANDBERGEN

DAVID ELSE

You don't always need a motor or wheels to get around in West Africa. Let a four-legged beast or the wind do the work: Tuareg man on a camel, Timbuktu, Mali (top left); a ride for two, Kiffa, Mauritania (top right); leaving the market by bullock cart, Djenné, Mali (middle right); taking advantage of the desert winds down the Niger River, Mali (bottom).

CFA1000/2000, doubles without/with fan CFA6000/10,000. This pink five-storey hotel near the corner of Rue 25 and Av 14 is a good option if the bottom line counts. All the dowdy rooms have showers. Ask for one with a balcony.

Hôtel l'Ariegeois *(☎ 21 24 99 68, Blvd de Marseille)* Singles/doubles CFA7000/14,000. This hotel, 500m north of Treichville train station, has unassuming rooms with air-con and bathroom.

Marcory is considerably safer than either Treichville or Adjamé.

Hôtel Pousada *(☎ 21 28 16 78)* Rooms without/with air-con CFA5000/CFA7000. The friendly Pousada, two blocks southeast of Av de la TSF, is a particularly active whorehouse. It has been warmly recommended – as a hotel, let's make it quite clear! – by several readers.

Hôtel le Souvenir *(☎ 21 35 12 56)* Rooms with fan/air-con & TV CFA5000/CFA7000. At the more conventional Souvenir, one block west of Gare de Marcory, all rooms have a bathroom. The larger rooms with air-con and TV are a bargain.

Adjamé This place is pretty hardcore, so a hotel with its own restaurant, where you can dine after dark, is an advantage.

Hôtel de la Gare *(☎ 20 37 75 34, Av 13)* Singles CFA4500-9000, doubles CFA9500. This hotel, across the less-than-tranquil road from Gare Routière d'Adjamé, has unexciting rooms with showers. There's a good, inexpensive restaurant next door.

Places to Stay – Mid-Range

A 20-minute drive south of the town centre will bring you to ***Hôtel Palm Beach*** *(☎ 21 27 42 16, fax 21 27 30 16, Rue de L'Océan)* with singles/doubles for CFA29,000/37,000. It is excellent value and has a good saltwater pool. Take bus No 18 or 24.

Treichville & Marcory Treichville's most comfortable option is ***Hôtel Terminus*** *(☎ 21 24 15 77, fax 21 24 04 24, Blvd Delafosse)*. With singles/doubles for CFA18,000/22,000 it is not great value for money, though.

Buses from Le Plateau and Treichville stop right outside the multistorey ***Hôtel Konankro*** *(☎ 21 28 33 98, Av de la TSF, Marcory)* where drab rooms with bathroom and fan/air-con are CFA7500/8500.

Hôtel le Repos *(☎ 21 26 32 57)* Rooms with fan/air-con & TV CFA7000/8000. At the surreal Repos, two blocks west of Gare de Marcory, unexceptional rooms are ranged around a colourful interior courtyard. It has a pleasant, active bar.

Adjamé Near Gare Routière d'Adjamé, ***Hôtel Banfora*** *(☎ 20 38 74 22, Rue Abrogoua)* is the best choice in this part of town. Singles/doubles are CFA10,500/12,500 and all rooms have air-con and a bathroom. There's a pleasant terrace restaurant with breakfast for CFA750.

Hôtel du Nord *(☎ 20 37 04 63, fax 20 37 56 48)* Rooms without/with bathroom CFA8000/10,000. This ageing establishment, off Blvd de Gaulle, has two small ground-floor rooms with air-con and less-cramped air-con rooms upstairs. There's also an inexpensive restaurant.

Le Plateau & Les Deaux Plateau The Abidjan classic ***Hôtel des Sports*** *(☎ 20 83 64 04, Rue du Commerce, Le Plateau)* offers the cheapest lodging in Le Plateau. It has large but sparsely furnished rooms with bathroom and air-con for CFA12,000 to CFA15,000. The staff are very friendly and there's a great bar-restaurant downstairs, generally full of fascinating characters; it's the ideal place to watch the world go by.

Grand Hôtel *(☎ 20 33 21 09, fax 20 32 98 60, Rue du Commerce, Le Plateau)* Singles/doubles CFA30,000/35,000. The Grand is getting a little long in the tooth. However, the price includes breakfast and the staff are accommodating.

In Les Deaux Plateau, the one-time Palme Industrie guesthouse, now known as ***Le Palm Club*** *(☎ 22 44 42 97, fax 22 44 44 54, Blvd Latrille)*, has rooms with bathroom for CFA20,000 and flats with two/three/four rooms for CFA50,000/70,000/90,000. The rooms are drab but good-value with air-con and TV. Renovations were under way when we visited. There are pleasant garden surrounds, two pools, a tennis court and an attractive paillote, which has a menu that changes daily.

The immaculate, friendly ***Hostellierie de la Licorne*** *(☎ 22 41 07 30, fax 22 41 09 98, Rue des Jardins, Les Deaux Plateau)* has singles/doubles for CFA30,000/50,000. It is down a side street, behind the Total petrol station, and has a great ambience, a garden and pool.

Places to Stay – Top End

Abidjan isn't short on luxury hotels.

Le Plateau The very popular ***Ibis Plateau*** *(☎ 20 21 01 57, fax 20 21 78 75, ⓔ ibisdg@africaonline.co.ci, Blvd Roume)* has a small swimming pool and rooms for CFA40,000. Some rooms have views of adjacent bat-infested trees which, if you like bats, is quite entertaining.

Novotel *(☎ 20 21 23 23, fax 20 33 26 36, 10 Av Général de Gaulle)* Singles CFA63,000-70,000, doubles CFA90,000-100,000. This superswish complex lacks nothing.

Hôtel Tiama *(☎ 20 31 33 33, fax 20 31 31 31, Blvd de la République)* Rooms CFA132,000-260,000. From its piano bar to its business centre, this is Abidjan at its plushest.

Elsewhere Handy to the airport, the ***Ibis Marcory*** *(☎ 21 24 17 30, fax 21 35 89 10, Blvd Valéry Giscard d'Estaing)* has prices and features much the same as its clone in Le Plateau.

Hôtel Golf *(☎ 21 43 10 44, fax 21 43 05 44, Blvd de France)* Singles/doubles CFA109,500/117,000. This relaxing hotel, in the Riviera area bordering the lagoon and a 15-minute taxi ride from the centre, has a pool and offers tennis and windsurfing.

Ivoire InterContinental *(☎ 22 40 80 00, fax 22 40 88 88, ⓔ ivoire@interconti.com, Blvd Latrille)* Singles/doubles CFA118,000/136,000, or CFA149,000/173,000 in the tower. Though it's well worn and overpriced, the 750-room Ivoire remains West Africa's most famous hotel.

Places to Eat

Street Food If you're staying in Treichville, one of the best areas for night-time ***street food*** is around La Cabane Bamboo nightclub. You'll also find open-air grills on Av Victor Blaka, just northeast of the market.

In Marcory, the seething area around the Petit Marché de Marcory is great for grilled fish and meat. On the other side of town the pulsating, 24-hour Rue de la Princesse in Yopougon is also excellent for a grilled feast.

In Cocody, the ***Allocodrome*** *(Rue Washington)* is a fantastic outdoors grill active from 4pm until late daily. Some 30 vendors barbecue fish, chicken and beef providing filling meals for around CFA1000.

Le Plateau, strangely enough, is superb for inexpensive African food, mainly at lunch time. ***Food vendors*** on the short street between Av Noguès and Rue du Commerce, or on Rue du Commerce diagonally opposite EgyptAir, are so popular that you'll

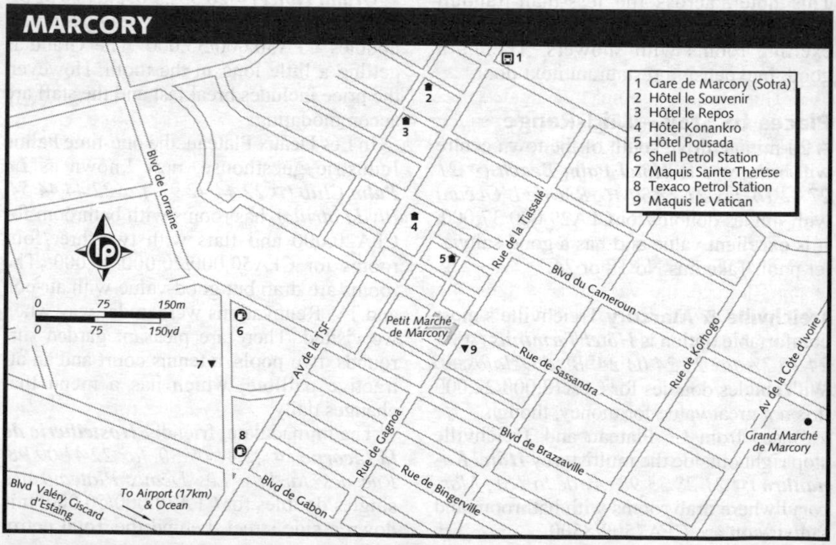
MARCORY
1 Gare de Marcory (Sotra)
2 Hôtel le Souvenir
3 Hôtel le Repos
4 Hôtel Konankro
5 Hôtel Pousada
6 Shell Petrol Station
7 Maquis Sainte Thèrése
8 Texaco Petrol Station
9 Maquis le Vatican
Blvd de Lorraine
Rue de la Tiassalé
Blvd du Cameroun
Petit Marché de Marcory
Av de la TSF
Rue de Sassandra
Rue de Korhogo
Av de la Côte d'Ivoire
Grand Marché de Marcory
Blvd de Brazzaville
Rue de Gagnoa
Rue de Bingerville
Blvd de Gabon
Blvd Valéry Giscard d'Estaing
To Airport (17km) & Ocean
0 75 150m
0 75 150yd

have to wait in line. There's also a cluster of small, highly recommended lunch-time food vendors at the base of the towers of the Cité Administrative on Blvd Angoulvant and others within the labyrinthine ***Marché Plateau*** (as well as bars selling Flagettes – small bottles of Flag beer – for CFA400). East of the Grande Mosquée, on Av Crosson Duplessis, a walled compound houses women with simmering pots of delicious sauces for CFA3000 each.

African As well as a bar in a paillote, the ***Restaurant des Combattants*** *(Av Marchand, Le Plateau)* has a relaxing barn-like dining hall out the back that seems a second home to the jovial female staff. Meals are around CFA4000 and it is open 7am to 9pm.

Café Restaurant Oasis *(Blvd de la République, Le Plateau)* Meals less than CFA2500. The Oasis is as its name suggests – a good place to take refuge from the busy streets outside. Afro-European food is served in diner-style cubicles.

Maquis Chez Fifine *(Av 26, Treichville)* Meals CFA1500. This place serves African dishes during the day and delicious grills at night.

Hôtel Banfora *(☎ 20 38 74 22, Rue Abrogoua, Adjamé)* Meals CFA1600-2200. The restaurant here serves basic African food in what feels like, given the area, a cheery oasis.

Espace 331 *(☎ 22 44 03 41, Rue 12, Cocody)* Meals around CFA1500-4000. Open 11.30am-4pm & 7pm-midnight Tues-Sun. This is a happening, tree-shaded outdoor joint. There are lunch-time sauce dishes and evening grills, such as *brochette d'escargots* (grilled snail kebabs) for CFA3000, as well as live music every Tuesday, Wednesday and Thursday night.

Maquis le Vatican *(Rue de la Tiassalé, Marcory)* Meals CFA3000-4000. With its upstairs terrace, the Vatican is perhaps the most pleasant of the area's maquis, although, strangely, it's often nearly empty. Try, in particular, its mouth-watering whole chicken kedjenou for CFA3000.

Maquis Sainte Thérèse *(North of Av de la TSF, Marcory)* Meals CFA2000-3000. A quiet, partially open-air place about 100m north of the Texaco petrol station, it's equally underpatronised and almost as good as the Vatican.

Asian & Indian There's no shortage of restaurants serving Chinese or Vietnamese cuisine.

Tuan *(☎ 20 21 63 80, Blvd du Général de Gaulle, Le Plateau)* Meals CFA5000-8000. Open daily. Tuan serves good food in a relaxing atmosphere.

Nuit de Saigon *(☎ 22 41 40 44, Rue des Jardins, Les Deux Plateaux)* Most meals CFA3000-6500. Open 11.30am-2pm & 7pm-11pm daily. This is arguably the best Vietnamese restaurant in Abidjan; the food is first rate and the decor swish. It specialises in duck and has an excellent French wine list.

Delhi Darbar *(☎ 22 41 31 62, Rue des Jardins, Les Deux Plateaux)* Meals CFA4000-7000. Open noon-2.30pm & 7pm-11.30pm Tues-Sun. The Delhi Darbar has very good, authentic Indian dishes served in tasteful surrounds. *Masala dosas* (savoury potato pancakes) cost CFA3500. This place is understandably popular with Abidjan's Indian community.

French & Italian French and local cuisine feature at ***Le Watta*** *(☎ 20 32 50 74, Rue du Commerce, Le Plateau)*. The food is good and reasonably priced (dishes CFA4000) and the restaurant is open at lunch time and in the evening until 11pm.

La Cascade *(☎ 20 21 71 07, Av Chardy, Le Plateau)* Meals CFA10,000. Open noon-3pm & 7.30pm-11pm Mon-Sat. The cuisine at Cascade is superb so it's usually packed. Try the *feuilleté de foi gras* (paté in puff-pastry) for a not-quite-African experience. A gushing waterfall and pond add to the ambience.

La Croisette *(☎ 20 21 27 86, Rue Botreau-Roussel, Le Plateau)* Meals CFA1200. Open noon-3.30pm & 7pm-11.30pm Mon-Sat. Excellent food is served here in airy, nautically inspired surroundings. The fish comes highly recommended.

Most Italian restaurants offer both Italian and French cuisine.

Pizzeria Bruno *(☎ 20 22 01 61, Blvd de la République, Le Plateau)* Pizzas CFA4500-5000. Open 7am-11pm daily. This popular pizzeria does big, wood-fired pizzas in apt surroundings, and real coffee to boot.

La Taverne Romaine *(20 21 89 51, Blvd du Général de Gaulle, Le Plateau)* Meals CFA4500-10,000. Open noon-3pm & 7pm-11pm daily. This place does great wood-fired pizzas for around CFA5000, and focaccias, the house speciality, are CFA6000.

Walter's Ristorante *(☎ 22 48 50 62, Marché de Cocody, Cocody)* Set menus CFA5500-8000. Open noon-3pm & 7pm-11pm daily. Behind the market, Walter's is the genuine article. Superb cuisine is served by Italian hosts in rustic surrounds; the coffee's to die for.

Lebanese You'll find Lebanese restaurants and chawarma outlets all over town.

Restaurant Georges V *(☎ 22 41 17 24, Rue des Jardins, Les Deux Plateaux)* Meals CFA600-3000. This is a friendly, inexpensive diner/takeaway. Felafels cost CFA600 and bottles of Flag are CFA700, and there are Internet and fax facilities.

Semiramis Chawarma Stand *(☎ 21 24 07 30, Av 13, Treichville)* Meals CFA750. The Semiramis is great for fresh chawarmas and takeaways.

La Caravelle *(24 96 89, Av 8, Treichville)* Meals CFA2500. This place has copious, all-inclusive meals. Its adjacent sweet shop produces delicacies as good as any sold in Beirut.

Patisseries The popular ***Pâtisserie Pako Gourmand*** *(☎ 22 41 30 55, Rue des Jardins, Les Deux Plateaux)* does sweet French fair superbly; cakes, pastries, buttery croissants and brilliant, real coffee. It's strongly recommended. It is open 6.30am to 10pm daily.

Boulangerie Pâtisserie du Rond Point *(☎ 21 34 20 46, Av 8, Treichville)* Despite the very down-to-earth surrounds, superb pastries are sold here.

Self-Catering Abidjan has two established supermarket chains in Le Plateau: ***Nour-al-Hayat*** and the cheaper, gaudier ***Cash Center***. The vast ***Hypermarché Sococe*** in Les Deux Plateaux is worth a visit for its own sake; you need to pinch yourself to confirm that you really are still in Africa.

Entertainment

Bars & Nightclubs The bar below Hôtel des Sports, ***Bar des Sports*** *(☎ 20 32 71 37, Rue du Commerce, Le Plateau)*, is a favourite watering hole for French expats and old-school Ivoirian professionals. With its bustle and French football-league tables posted on the wall it could have been transplanted from Marseille.

Acapulco *(☎ 20 22 26 17, Av Chardy, Le Plateau)* Acapulco is an expensive, cosy bar at night.

La Java Disco *(☎ 20 32 76 23, Rue du Commerce, Le Plateau)* Java belts it out till late.

Le Bastring *(☎ 20 22 04 37, Cnr Av Terrasson de Fougères & Blvd de la République, Le Plateau)* Le Bastring, near Cinéma les Studios, is a popular dance venue.

Ivoire InterContinental *(☎ 22 40 80 00, Blvd Latrille, Cocody)* From around 5pm to 10pm the lobby resonates with the sounds of a lively band.

Hollywood Café *(☎ 22 44 36 04, Next to Marché de Cocody)* Hollywood is open from noon to 3pm and 6pm till late on Monday to Thursday, and noon till late on Friday to Sunday. This café has surely been transported wholesale from a Los Angeles suburb. Complement your Budweiser with apple pie and ice-cream for CFA3500.

Play it safe and catch a taxi to the door of the following four bars in Treichville.

P'tit Monde *(☎ 03 01 04 37, Blvd Delafosse, Treichville)* This is a tastefully decorated, cheery little bar.

Jaguar Bar *(☎ 07 00 00 07, Blvd Delafosse, Treichville)* Further south down Blvd Delafosse, the Jaguar has live bands most nights.

Hit Parade *(☎ 21 24 13 90, Blvd Delafosse, Treichville)* Opposite the CTI bus station, but very upmarket, Hit Parade attracts a young, but predominantly expat crowd and has a particularly good restaurant upstairs.

Midnight Express *(☎ 21 25 63 40, Blvd Delafosse, Treichville)* Admission CFA4000. More downmarket, this place has full-length mirrors for the more narcissistic movers.

Cinemas All English-language movies are dubbed into French. The three best cinemas, all excellent, are: ***Cinéma Ivoire*** *(☎ 22 40 80 00, Ivoire InterContinental)* in Cocody, ***Cinéma le Paris*** *(☎ 07 89 74 05, Av Chardy)* and ***Cinéma les Studios*** *(☎ 07 90 45 66, Blvd de la République)* both in Le Plateau. Tickets are around CFA2500.

Traditional Music & Dance On the road to Bingerville, ***Le Village Ki-Yi*** *(☎ 22 43 37*

93/38 66, Blvd Mitterrand) offers a show with dinner that's very authentic. The singers, dancers and musicians of the resident troupe, Le Groupe Ki-Yi M'bock, enjoy national fame.

Le Watta *(☎ 20 32 50 74, Rue du Commerce, Le Plateau)* Cover charge CFA1000. Open from 7pm Friday night. *Spectacles Africaines* (dance, drumming and exhibits of art) can be seen at this restaurant.

Shopping

Markets Marché de Treichville, once a treasure trove, was burnt down. Its reconstruction was ongoing at the time of writing.

Marché d'Adjamé *(Blvd Abrogoua, Adjamé)* This, the cheapest market in Abidjan, caters primarily to locals, although it does have a good selection of fabrics.

Marché de Cocody *(Cnr Rue Washington & Blvd de France, Cocody)* This market is much more compact. Its top floor is geared more for the tourist market. It's a great place to hunt for beads, bronze and malachite and occasionally has fine woodcarving.

Marché Plateau *(Blvd de la République, Le Plateau)* There's a wonderful mix of food, hardware and craftwork here. There are also some intriguing places to eat and drink within it. Escape back to the real Africa for a few hours.

Art & Craftwork Apart from the markets, the best place for quality artisan goods is ***La Rose d'Ivoire*** *(☎ 22 44 22 55, Ivoire Inter-Continental, Cocody)*, which is open 9am to 12.30pm and 5pm to 9.30pm daily. Passing the quick-carve, off-the-peg items in the cabinet by the entrance, you descend into an Aladdin's cave of fine pieces. Don't expect any bargains.

Afric Art *(☎ 20 22 57 82, Blvd de la République, Le Plateau)* This gallery, behind Cinéma les Studios, also has some excellent pieces. Bargaining is possible.

For textiles, African print material is generally sold in a length of three pagnes, the quantity required to make a blouse, skirt and the wide strip that swathes a baby, bobbing on its mother's back. The cheapest is Fancy, from Ghana, which costs CFA9000 to CFA13,500 for three pagnes. Côte d'Ivoire wax cover prints are around CFA18,000, while block prints cost between CFA25,000 and CFA30,000.

Woodin *(☎ 20 33 25 93, Rue du Commerce, Le Plateau)* This outlet, one block east of the Novotel, is outstanding among the fabric shops. It's worth a visit for the sensual pleasure alone.

Music Abidjan, where many artists record, is about the best place in West Africa to buy African music.

World Music *(☎ 20 22 12 82, Av Chardy, Le Plateau)* In the Nour-al-Hayat shopping complex, this place has a wide selection.

Sun Music *(☎ 20 21 31 05, Av Delafosse, Le Plateau)* Near the Bibici bank, Sun is also worth a look.

In Treichville there are countless music shops along Av 16. Music cassettes sold on the street are cheap, but generally of good quality.

Getting There & Away

Air The airport is at Port Bouët on the south side of town. For details of international and domestic flights to/from Abidjan, see the Getting There & Away and Getting Around sections earlier in this chapter. For reconfirmation of flights and ticket sales, the following airlines have offices in Abidjan:

Air Burkina (☎ 20 32 89 19)
Air France (☎ 20 20 24 24)
Air Gabon (☎ 20 21 55 06)
Air Guinée (☎ 20 33 14 97)
Air Mali (☎ 20 32 19 62)
British Airways (☎ 20 32 00 55)
Cameroon Airlines (☎ 20 21 19 19)
EgyptAir (☎ 20 22 68 69)
Ethiopian Airlines (☎ 20 21 55 38)
Ghana Airways (☎ 20 32 42 21)
KLM-Royal Dutch Airlines (☎ 20 32 00 55)
South African Airways (☎ 20 21 82 93)
Wesua Air Transport (☎ 21 58 69 83)

Bus & Bush Taxi The main bus station is the shambolic Gare Routière d'Adjamé, some 4km north of Le Plateau. All buses and most bush taxis leave from here. There's frequent transport to all major provincial towns. You'll have less hassle if you decide in advance which bus company you want to travel with and head straight for its depot. For more information on fares, routes and bus companies, see the table in the Getting Around section earlier in this chapter.

Bush taxis and minibuses for destinations east along the coast such as Grand Bassam,

Aboisso and Elubo at the Ghanaian border, leave primarily from the Gare de Bassam at the corner of Rue 38 and Blvd Valéry Giscard d'Estaing, south of Treichville. A bush taxi costs CFA400 to Grand Bassam (35 minutes) and CFA1200 to Aboisso (1½ hours). Transport for Grand Bassam and Aboisso also departs from Gare Routière d'Adjamé and costs CFA100 more.

Buses for Jacqueville leave from the tiny, unmarked Gare de Jacqueville in Treichville, 200m east of Pont Houphouët-Boigny. The only company serving this route is 3A Express, which has frequent departures between 6am and 7pm (CFA1200, 1½ hours).

Train The main train station is in Treichville – from which the express to Ouagadougou in Burkina Faso departs three times a week, calling in at Bouaké (1st/2nd class CFA6600/5400, five hours) and Ferké (CFA11,600/9400, nine hours) on the way.

Getting Around

To/From the Airport Abidjan airport is no longer the threatening experience that travellers' tales would have you believe. Walk out, turn sharp left and continue for about 20m to a long line of waiting orange taxis. When your turn comes, ensure that the driver switches on his meter. If he refuses, establish a price, which shouldn't exceed CFA3000. If he won't accept this, make a show of getting out; you'll quickly reach an accommodation and, if not, there are plenty more behind him.

A metered taxi will cost about CFA2000 to Marcory, CFA2500 to Treichville, CFA2500 to Le Plateau and CFA3500 to Cocody (Ivoire InterContinental area). If you're travelling between midnight and 6am, rates double. Bus No 6 connects the airport with the central area; the cost is CFA400. If you reserve ahead, Hertz, Avis and Europcar will meet you with your car. There's a free shuttle service to major hotels.

Bus The city's Sotra buses tend to be crowded, but they're cheap – CFA400 for most destinations. They display their route number, which also features on bus-stop signs, but only rarely their destination. Even so, armed with the information below, it's not difficult to navigate around town.

The major Sotra bus station in Le Plateau is the Gare Sud, south of Place de la République. Other stations are the Gare Nord in Adjamé, 500m north of the train station; Gare de Marcory at the northern end of Av de la TSF in Marcory; and a Sotra bus station on Av Christian in Treichville. The buses on most lines operate from about 6am to between 9pm and 10pm daily. Routes include:

No 0/9 Gare Nord, Le Plateau (Cité Administrative, Blvd Clozel, Av Delafosse, La Pyramide building, Rue Botreau-Roussel), Gare de Marcory

No 2 Gare Nord, Marché d'Adjamé, Le Plateau (Musée National, Blvd Clozel, Blvd de la République, post office), Treichville (market and train station), Gare de Marcory

No 3 Gare Nord, Le Plateau (Musée National, Blvd Clozel, Av Delafosse, La Pyramide building, Rue Botreau-Roussel, Rue du Commerce, Av du Général de Gaulle), Marché de Treichville, Gare de Bassam, Gare de Marcory

No 6 Airport, Blvd de Marseille, Treichville hospital, Marché de Treichville, Gare Sud

No 12 Gare Nord, 220 Logements roundabout, Le Plateau (Cité Administrative, Blvd Clozel, Blvd de la République, Gare Sud), Marché de Treichville, Gare de Bassam, Port Bouët

No 14 Williamsville, Adjamé, Marcory

No 18 Gare Sud, Marché de Treichville, Gare de Bassam, autoroute, airport turn-off, Hôtel Palm Beach, Vridi Canal

No 21 Cocody, Le Plateau, Treichville

No 22 Gare Nord, Le Plateau (Cité Administrative, Blvd Clozel, Blvd de la République, post office), Treichville (market, Cinéma l'Entente)

No 24 Marché de Treichville, fishing port area, Vridi Canal, Hôtel Palm Beach, autoroute, Koumasi

No 25 Gare Sud, Av Christiani, Marché de Treichville, Gare Koumasi

No 26 Gare Koumasi, Le Plateau (Rue Botreau-Roussel, La Pyramide building, Av Delafosse, Blvd Clozel, Cité Administrative), Gare Nord

No 28 Le Plateau (Gare Sud, Blvd de la République, Blvd Clozel, Cité Administrative), Marché de Cocody, Université de Cocody, Riviera, Hôtel du Golf

No 31 Marché de Treichville, Gare de Marcory

No 35 Gare Nord, Av Reboul, Terminus Gobélé, Les Deux Plateaux

No 74 Gare de Marcory, Le Plateau (Rue Botreau-Roussel, La Pyramide building, Blvd Clozel, Cathédrale de St Paul), Marché de Cocody, Ivoire InterContinental

No 81 Gare Nord, Av Reboul, Université de Cocody, Route de Bingerville

No 82 Le Plateau (Gare Sud, Blvd de la République, Blvd Carde, Cité Administrative, Musée National), Av Reboul, Les Deux Plateaux

No 84 Gare Nord, Av Reboul, Marché de Cocody, Ivoire InterContinental
No 86 Le Plateau (Gare Sud, Rue Roussel, La Pyramide building, Blvd Clozel, Cité Administrative), Marché d'Adjamé, Gare Routière d'Adjamé, 220 Logements roundabout, Marché de Cocody, Université de Cocody

For travel between Marcory and Le Plateau, buses No 14 and 74 take the autoroute and are much quicker than the other options, which wind their way through Treichville.

Taxi Private taxis in Abidjan are reasonably priced. The fare from the Gare Routière d'Adjamé to Le Plateau, for example, is about CFA1500. Drivers generally switch on the meter without prompting. Do check, however, that it's set to tariff No 1. The more expensive No 2 rate only applies between midnight and 6am. Taxis by the hour cost about CFA3000 if you bargain.

Shared taxis cost between CFA300 and CFA500, depending on the length of the journey. They vary in colour according to their allocated area. Those in Treichville, for example, are red. One red route is between the Gare de Bassam in Treichville and Blvd du Général de Gaulle at the intersection just north of Gare Routière d'Adjamé. The fare is CFA300 in a shared taxi and CFA200 in a minibus. Grey-and-white taxis run from the Gare Routière d'Adjamé to Les Deux Plateaux, yellow taxis run between there and Cocody and there are green ones in Marcory and blue in Yopougon.

Car Hiring a car is expensive. The big multinationals are all represented: Europcar (☎ 21 25 12 27, fax 21 25 11 43) and Hertz (☎ 20 22 11 22) have offices at the Sofatel, and Avis (☎ 20 32 80 07) has an office at the Novotel. Their prices are almost identical. Typically, a small car costs CFA24,000 per day, including compulsory insurance, for use in Abidjan and CFA26,000 outside. CFA205 per kilometre is also charged. Add to this 20% taxes as well as the cost of petrol. A 4WD is CFA51,000 per day plus CFA435 per kilometre. To hire a driver costs CFA11,000 per day in Abidjan and CFA22,000 for outside.

Prices are somewhat lower at smaller agencies such as ETS Konaté (☎ 20 22 56 65, fax 20 22 07 70) or SORA (☎ 21 32 36 78). A relatively new car without driver and with unlimited mileage can, after very hard bargaining, cost CFA30,000 per day for travel outside Abidjan. A CFA300,000 deposit is usually required.

Boat Abidjan has a good ferry service on the lagoon. It goes from Treichville to Abobo-Doumé (across the lagoon, west of Le Plateau) to Le Plateau to Treichville again (in that sequence; it's a long ride from Treichville to Le Plateau). Taking a *bateau-bus* (ferry) is a great way to the see the city from a different perspective. It's also a way of avoiding the dangerous walk across one of the bridges linking Le Plateau and Treichville. The *gare lagunaire* (ferry terminal) in Le Plateau is 100m east of Pont Houphouët-Boigny. The fare from there across the lagoon to the Treichville ferry terminal, also east of Pont Houphouët-Boigny, is CFA400. There are several departures every hour from about 6am to 8.30pm.

AROUND ABIDJAN

Île Boulay

Sotra Tourisme *(☎ 20 32 17 37, Blvd Général de Gaulle)* offers a return trip (CFA1950, 1½ hours) across the lagoon to Île Boulay, southwest of Le Plateau. The boat leaves from the gare lagunaire in Le Plateau at 9.30am on Saturday and Sunday. You get a unique perspective of Abidjan's high-rises and also a sense of how immediate traditional Côte d'Ivoire, with its fishing villages, coffee, banana and cassava groves, is to the urban Gargantua. The boat chugs alongside the port and pokes its nose into the 2.7km-long Vridi Canal, whose completion in 1951 led to the city's phenomenal expansion.

East Coast

GRAND BASSAM

Grand Bassam, some 45km to the east of Abidjan, can be visited in a day, but its colonial buildings (some now being renovated) deserve more of your time. The narrow strip of land between ocean and lagoon, known as Ancien Bassam, is where the French first established their capital, distancing themselves from the locals, whose own settlement across the lagoon expanded as servants' quarters.

Grand Bassam was declared capital of the French colony in 1893, but a mere six years later, a major yellow-fever epidemic broke out, prompting the French to move their capital to Bingerville. Bassam, it seemed, was headed for oblivion. Construction of a wharf two years later, however, brought new life and substantial new construction. In 1931, when the French built another wharf in Abidjan, three golden decades came to an end. The *coup de grace* was the opening of the Vridi Canal.

Today, Grand Bassam is a schizophrenic sort of place. During the week, you'll almost have the place to yourself. At weekends, especially during the dry season, it seems as though half of Abidjan has fled the capital and fetched up here. In addition to the pull of its beaches and restaurants, visitors are also drawn by its boutiques, artisans and craft shops. Beware of the surf and the dangerous tides; every year someone drowns offshore.

The best time to visit is in late October or early November during the colourful week-long Fête de l'Abissa, when the N'Zima people honour their dead.

Information

There are good Internet connections at Taroko Service Internet (☎ 21 30 22 50). It costs CFA350 for three minutes. It's about 500m north of Place de Paix on Blvd Gouverneur Angoulvant and is open 7.30am to 6.30pm daily. The SGBCI bank, south of Place de Paix on Blvd Gouverneur Angoulvant, has an ATM that will accept your Visa card.

Colonial Buildings

Confident structures with spacious balconies, verandas and shuttered windows were the style of the day. Of the colonial-era buildings, mostly constructed between 1894 and 1920, the elegant former post office and the town hall *(mairie)* have been beautifully restored. The Musée National du Costume (formerly the governor's palace), with its imposing outer staircase, is currently being renovated and its reputation suggests it will be well worth a visit once reopened. Most of the remainder, including the old *palais de justice* (law courts), tax office, customs house, prison and hospital, are vacant now and in various stages of decay, although

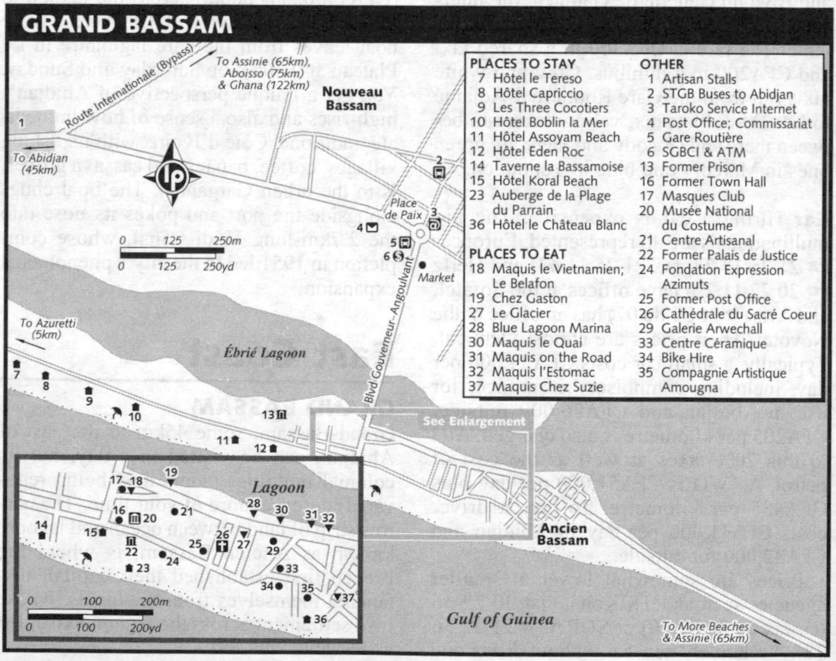
GRAND BASSAM
Route Internationale (Bypass)
To Assinie (65km), Aboisso (75km) & Ghana (122km)
Nouveau Bassam
To Abidjan (45km)
Place de Paix
Market
Blvd Gouverneur-Angoulvant
To Azuretti (5km)
Ébrié Lagoon
See Enlargement
Lagoon
Ancien Bassam
Gulf of Guinea
To More Beaches & Assinie (65km)
0 125 250m
0 125 250yd
0 100 200m
0 100 200yd
PLACES TO STAY
7 Hôtel le Tereso
8 Hôtel Capriccio
9 Les Three Cocotiers
10 Hôtel Boblin la Mer
11 Hôtel Assoyam Beach
12 Hôtel Eden Roc
14 Taverne la Bassamoise
15 Hôtel Koral Beach
23 Auberge de la Plage du Parrain
36 Hôtel le Château Blanc
PLACES TO EAT
18 Maquis le Vietnamien; Le Belafon
19 Chez Gaston
27 Le Glacier
28 Blue Lagoon Marina
30 Maquis le Quai
31 Maquis on the Road
32 Maquis l'Estomac
37 Maquis Chez Suzie
OTHER
1 Artisan Stalls
2 STGB Buses to Abidjan
3 Taroko Service Internet
4 Post Office; Commissariat
5 Gare Routière
6 SGBCI & ATM
13 Former Prison
16 Former Town Hall
17 Masques Club
20 Musée National du Costume
21 Centre Artisanal
22 Former Palais de Justice
24 Fondation Expression Azimuts
25 Former Post Office
26 Cathédrale du Sacré Coeur
29 Galerie Arwechall
33 Centre Céramique
34 Bike Hire
35 Compagnie Artistique Amougna

commendable efforts are at last being made to rescue what's still capable of being saved.

Handicrafts

To see a wide selection of artisan goods, visit the **Centre Artisanal** *(open 8am-5pm daily)* on the lagoon-side road heading to Ancien Bassam. It's a cooperative selling souvenir-quality items at reasonable prices.

At the **Centre Céramique** *(open 8am-5pm daily)* on the ocean road heading to Ancien Bassam, you can see potters at work and purchase their wares.

Dance

Compagnie Artistique Amougna *(☎ 21 30 32 88; admission CFA5000)* is an imaginative, contemporary dance troupe of young Bassam men and women. In their headquaters near Hôtel le Château Blanc they perform an original, high-energy blend of traditional and modern dance.

Pirogue Trips

Ask at any of the lagoon-side maquis in Ancien Bassam about dugout canoe trips, where you see traditional crab fishers, mangroves and birdlife. Boatman Amoussa asks for CFA4000 per person for three hours.

Places to Stay

At weekends, it's essential to ring and reserve. All hotels are on or just off the ocean-side road overlooking the Gulf of Guinea. The top-end hotels tend to vary their prices between the brief high season and the rest of the year; we quote the latter.

Places to Stay – Budget

Auberge de la Plage du Parrain *(☎ 21 30 15 41)* Rooms with fan CFA7500-9000, with air-con CFA10,000-12,000, bungalows with sea views & air-con CFA20,000. This hotel has an attractive paillote bar where meals are prepared to order (CFA2500 to CFA3500).

Les Three Cocotiers *(☎ 21 30 15 40)* Rooms with fan/air-con CFA8000/10,000. West along the beach strip, this place has musty but clean rooms and a private beach. The owner is friendly and there's a restaurant.

Places to Stay – Mid-Range

Hôtel Boblin la Mer *(☎/fax 21 30 14 18)* Rooms with fan/air-con CFA10,000/12,000. The ambience is great at this hotel, west of town where small rooms overlook the ocean. There's a decent restaurant and you can even have a massage from the qualified Italian co-owner. This place offers the best value for money in town.

Hôtel Capriccio *(☎ 21 30 18 02)* Rooms with fan/air-con CFA10,000/15,000. Capriccio is more downmarket than Boblin la Mer, but there's an authentic Italian restaurant.

Places to Stay – Top End

All the following have swimming pools and rooms with air-con and bathroom; they are listed from east to west:

Hôtel le Château Blanc *(☎ 21 30 39 95, fax 21 30 39 95, e chateaublanc@aviso.ci)* Rooms CFA25,000. This place is as much a private club as a hotel. Rooms look down onto a stage where there's great live jazz on Saturday evening and an extended Sunday lunch time. The food (CFA900 for the set menu) is French and great.

Hôtel Koral Beach *(☎ 21 30 19 08)* Singles/doubles/triples CFA20,000/22,000/25,000. This laid-back place with spacious rooms is the most African of the options (there's no shortage of wooden sculptures!). A good restaurant overlooks the ocean.

Taverne la Bassamoise *(☎ 21 30 10 62, fax 21 30 12 96)* Rooms CFA29,000. This is Grand Bassam's most expensive hotel. It's big on old-world charm, has a tennis court and its own beach.

Hôtel Eden Roc *(☎/fax 21 30 17 75)* Rooms CFA17,500-35,000. This new hotel has both air-con and terrace restaurants that specialise in seafood and Provençal cuisine, as well as live music on Saturday night.

Hôtel Assoyam Beach *(☎ 21 30 15 57, fax 21 30 14 74)* Doubles/triples CFA26,000/30,000. This place, with restaurant and attractive beach, has cosy rooms.

Hôtel le Tereso *(☎ 21 30 17 57, fax 21 30 17 97)* Singles/doubles CFA25,000/33,000. If you fancy something more strenuous than a sprawl on the beach, Grand Bassam's newest hotel, owned by the French travel giant, Nouvelles Frontières, offers a range of sporty, Club Med-like activities.

Places to Eat

Maquis Chez Suzie *(Ocean road)* Sauces CFA500. East of the Centre Céramique, Chez Suzie serves African food at African prices.

Maquis l'Estomac *(Lagoon-side road)* Estomac is a welcoming bar and eatery with excellent African dishes and prices.

Maquis on the Road *(Lagoon-side road)* This restaurant has a more comfortable ambience than its neighbour l'Estomac, but the prices are still low.

Maquis le Quai *(☎ 21 30 14 37, Lagoon-side road)* Meals CFA4000-5000. African and French dishes are served here in a relaxing lagoon-side setting.

Blue Lagoon Marina *(☎ 21 30 20 77, Lagoon-side road)* Meals CFA4000-5000. Next to Maquis le Quai, and similar, with African and French food served in a lovely setting.

Le Glacier *(☎ 21 30 29 50, Lagoon-side road)* Crepes from CFA2000. Opposite the Blue Lagoon, this creperie is upmarket and swanky. Ice cream is CFA500 a scoop and hamburgers CFA2000.

Chez Gaston *(☎ 07 82 02 53, Lagoon-side road)* Meals CFA3000-5000. Chez Gaston has a thatched roof and overlooks the lagoon; the food and service are first rate. *Crevettes sautées* (sauteed prawns) are CFA2000.

Maquis le Vietnamien *(☎ 21 30 10 09, Blvd Gouverneur Angoulvant)* Meals from CFA2000. Open Fri-Wed. At this eatery, on the first corner before the bridge over the lagoon, the authentic food and service are wonderful, and the menu extensive.

Le Balafon *(☎ 07 87 20 40, Blvd Gouverneur Angoulvant)* Pizzas from CFA4000. Le Balafon is a neighbour to Vietnamien and has a groovy bar; lobster is CFA5000.

Shopping

At the entrance to town, coming from Abidjan, in Nouveau Bassam, the highway is lined with 50 or more ***artisan stalls*** selling cane ware, cloth, carvings, masks and other crafts. Bargain hard and beware of imitation 'antiques'.

In Ancien Bassam, exciting, contemporary African oil paintings are on display at ***Fondation Expression Azimuts*** *(☎ 05 09 08 73, Ocean-side road)*, a modern art gallery.

There are several artisan shops on the lagoon-side road, including ***Galerie Arwechall***, facing Maquis le Quaim, which isn't pushy and has good-quality work.

Next to Le Balafon, ***Masques Club*** has a wide variety of artefacts and a knowledgeable owner.

Getting There & Away

Minibuses (CFA400, 40 minutes) and bush taxis (CFA500, 30 minutes) leave Abidjan from the Gare de Bassam and also leave from Gare Routière d'Adjamé (CFA500, one hour). UTAB has a bus service from Gare Routière d'Adjamé (CFA400 one hour). In Grand Bassam, the gare routière is beside the Place de Paix roundabout, north of the lagoon. From there, minibuses and bush taxis leave for Assinie (CFA1100, 1½ hours) and Aboisso (both CFA1100, one hour), on the way to Ghana.

Getting Around

The ideal way to get around Grand Bassam is on foot. Alternatively, bicycle hire (☎ 21 30 15 67) is available opposite the Centre Céramique.

ASSINIE

Some 85km east of Grand Bassam, Assinie, near the tip of a long sand spit where the Canal d'Assinie meets the mouth of the Abi Lagoon, has magnificent beaches. The preserve of rich weekenders from Abidjan and package tours from Europe, it has little to do with Africa.

Accommodation is exclusively top end and includes ***Assinie Plage*** *(☎ 21 30 93 84, fax 21 30 06 55)*, ***Les Palétuviers*** *(☎ 21 30 08 48)*, in nearby Assouindé, and the ***African Queen Lodge*** *(☎ 21 35 47 10, fax 21 35 92 70)*, 3km from Assinie. Prices for each are around CFA25,000/30,000 for half-board/full-board per person on the lagoon, or CFA30,000/35,000 for half-board/full-board per person on the seashore. Also in Assouindé, set well back from the ocean, you will find the beautiful ***Assouindé-Village*** *(☎ 21 35 36 85)*, which offers 45 bungalows for CFA25,000, half-board CFA45,000. Reservations are required.

From Abidjan, head first for Grand Bassam, from where there are irregular bush taxis to Assinie (CFA1100, 1½ hours). By car, take the right fork 28km east of Grand Bassam.

West Coast

JACQUEVILLE

Jacqueville, 50km west of Abidjan, is a small coastal community with a fine beach.

Today it retains few vestiges of either its time as an entrepot for the slave trade or its French heritage, except for several dilapidated colonial houses along the coast.

If you need a place to stay and price is your main concern, head to ***Hôtel Relax***, 600m from the bus station, which has rooms for CFA2000.

Campement de Jacqueville *(☎ 23 57 51 21)*, only a short walk from the bush-taxi stand, fronts onto a pleasant stretch of beach. It has attractive thatched-roof bungalows (CFA12,000) in addition to camping (CFA3000 per person), and there's an agreeable open-air restaurant.

Hôtel M'Koa *(☎ 23 57 72 08)* is a modern hotel, facing the lagoon. It features a pool, has a nearby private beach, and is the top establishment in town. There's a restaurant and all rooms (CFA20,000) have air-con.

Buses of the 3A Express company run to/from Abidjan several times a day. In Abidjan they leave from the tiny Gare de Jacqueville, just east of Pont Houphouët-Boigny; the fare is CFA1200 (1½ hours). If you're driving, be prepared for the 20-minute ferry crossing of the Ébrié Lagoon en route.

DABOU

Dabou, 49km west of Abidjan, is a potential rest stop for those en route to Tiagba or Grand Lahou.

If you get stuck in Dabou, ***Wrod Hôtel*** *(☎ 21 30 21 25)*, situated on the highway west of town, is clean, comfortable and has a bar and restaurant in a paillote. Bungalows cost around CFA14,000.

Le Fromager *(☎ 21 57 21 77)*, in the centre of town, does excellent fish dishes (CFA4000).

Buses connect Dabou with Gare Routière d'Adjamé in Abidjan (CFA700, 30 minutes).

TIAGBA

West of Dabou, old Tiagba is a fascinating village of houses on stilts on the Ébrié Lagoon. Hiring a pirogue for a trip around the lagoon is well worth the haggle.

Aux Pilotis de l'Ébieyé *(☎ 21 37 09 99)*, near the boat dock on the mainland, is the only accommodation option. It has four clean rooms (CFA4000) and its terrace bar facing the lagoon is a good place for a drink. It's closed during most of the wet season and reopens in August.

You could also ask villagers if you can stay in a local home. Aim for a price around CFA1500.

There's only one overcrowded minibus a day from Dabou to Tiagba (CFA850, 2½ hours) leaving about 5pm and returning the next morning at 6am. Expect to pay around CFA6000 for a private taxi – easily arranged in Dabou, but infrequently available in Tiagba. The Tiagba turn-off is about 30km west of Dabou on the road to Grand Lahou. From there, it's about the same distance on a rough dirt road through rubber plantations.

GRAND LAHOU

At the mouth of the Bandama River, Grand Lahou was occupied successively by the English, Germans and Dutch. In 1890, it was transformed into an important trading post by the French. After a brief period of prosperity, it virtually died. Today, it's a tranquil seaside village, similar to Grand Bassam except that the old colonial buildings are even more decaying and there are fewer palm trees. Modern Grand Lahou is 1km off the coast road, while the old town is on a thin sand bar facing the ocean a further 18km south.

Grand Lahou is a great place for nature lovers; on the opposite side of the Bandama River is **Parc National d'Assagny**, a dense rainforest, which is home to a large variety of birds and some of the country's few remaining forest elephants. It has observation decks for viewing and guards to accompany you on a walk through the park. The park office, where the admission fee (CFA2000) is payable and trips can be arranged, is in the modern town 500m north of the centre.

Places to Stay & Eat

Îles Ahonzo *(☎ 05 82 00 08)* Single/double paillotes CFA6000/8000. On a small and beautiful islet opposite old Grand Lahou, Îles Ahonzo offers seclusion and tranquillity. The crude but comfortable-enough huts have mosquito nets and are shrouded by palm trees.

Campement Hôtel les Roniers *(☎ 23 42 25 32, Lahou Plage)* Rooms CFA5000, full-board CFA10,000. Right on the beach, this place is clean and comfortable.

Getting There & Away

There are direct buses to Grand Lahou from the Gare Routière d'Adjamé in Abidjan

(CFA1300, two hours). You've also a reasonable chance of picking one up in Dabou.

To get to the old quarter facing the ocean, take a minibus from the modern town (CFA500, 30 minutes) and then a ferry across Tiagba Lagoon (CFA200, 15 minutes, from 7am to 6.30pm daily). If you're adventurous and are headed back to Abidjan, ask around for a *pinasse*. These large, motorised canoes usually travel at night and the trip takes about 10 hours.

SASSANDRA

Sassandra, 71km east of San Pédro, is a great base for visiting the spectacular beaches to its west – it helps considerably if you have your own transport. It's also an interesting Fanti fishing village on a scenic river estuary. (The Fanti, renowned as fishing people, are recent arrivals from present-day Ghana.) Sassandra was originally established by the Portuguese in 1472, who named it São Andrea. Settled successively by the British and the French, who developed it mainly as an outlet for timber from Mali, it went into swift decline once the port at San Pédro was constructed in the late 1960s. Today, you can still see several old colonial buildings, such as the governor's house, and the town is small enough to explore on foot.

Places to Stay

La Cachette du Wharf *(34 72 04 64)* Rooms CFA2500. If you can stand the stench of fish, this huddle of paillotes behind the fish market is the cheapest place to stay. It may be short on life's luxuries – rooms have a bare light bulb, bed and fan – but the fine view of the bay compensates.

Hôtel la Côtière *(☎ 34 72 01 20)* Singles with fan & mosquito net CFA6000, doubles with air-con but no nets CFA10,000. This is, you might say, a different kettle of fish. Strongly recommended, it sits on the estuary beneath coconut palms and a giant flame tree. Rooms are in cabins or small bungalows and all have bathroom.

Hôtel Grau *(☎ 34 72 05 20, fax 34 72 05 20)* Rooms CFA5000, with fan CFA6000, with air-con CFA10,000. The small Grau, on the road north out of town, is French-run. The bar is a popular watering hole with expats.

Le Campement *(☎ 34 72 04 15)* Singles/doubles/triples CFA15,000/18,000/20,000,

Bitter Harvest

Côte d'Ivoire produces 48% of the global cocoa supply, which comes from over 600,000 farms around the country. As you travel through the countryside you will often pass kilometre upon kilometre of plantations. However, hidden within the beautiful green canopy are untold stories of brutality and misery, for it's estimated that there are 15,000 child slaves working on cocoa plantations in Côte d'Ivoire. Indeed, the incidence of slavery has dramatically increased over recent years because of a slump in cocoa prices. In 2000, after prices for cocoa hit a 27-year low, many Ivorian producers increased their use of slaves to prop up flagging profit margins.

Most of the slaves are imported from Burkina Faso, Benin, Togo and Mali. The children are either lured over the border with promises of work or sold into bonded labour by debt-ridden parents; others are simply stolen as they play. Without money for transport or identity papers, even if they were to escape the often-isolated farms it would be almost impossible for them to make the long journey home.

Children working on plantations are usually aged 12 to 14 but can be as young as eight. They are forced to work from 80 to 100 hours a week, paid nothing, barely fed and regularly beaten. In Abidjan, where there is a slave market, the going rate for a child is around CFA37,500 – less than the amount the average person in the West spends on chocolate every year.

Under mounting public pressure, in October 2001 the chocolate industry announced a four-year plan to eliminate child slavery in cocoa-producing nations. The Harkin-Engel Protocol commits the industry to work with nongovernmental organisations and the International Labor Organization in monitoring and remedying abusive forms of child labour used in growing cocoa. Time will tell whether or not the measures are successful.

For more information, visit the Free the Slaves website 🅦 www.freetheslaves.net.

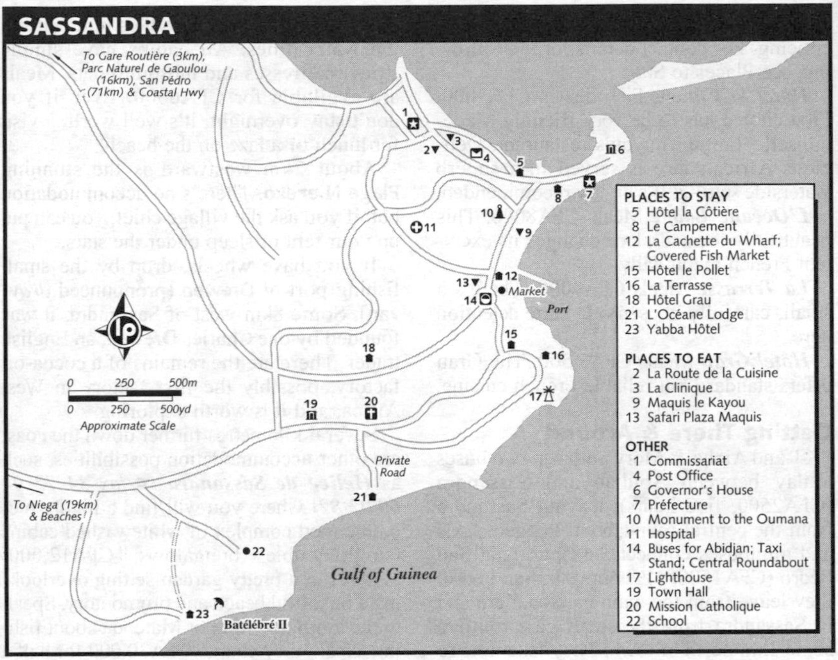
SASSANDRA
To Gare Routière (3km), Parc Naturel de Gaoulou (16km), San Pédro (71km) & Coastal Hwy
To Niega (19km) & Beaches
Private Road
Market
Port
Gulf of Guinea
Batélébré II
Approximate Scale
0 250 500m
0 250 500yd
PLACES TO STAY
5 Hôtel la Côtière
8 Le Campement
12 La Cachette du Wharf; Covered Fish Market
15 Hôtel le Pollet
16 La Terrasse
18 Hôtel Grau
21 L'Océane Lodge
23 Yabba Hôtel
PLACES TO EAT
2 La Route de la Cuisine
3 La Clinique
9 Maquis le Kayou
13 Safari Plaza Maquis
OTHER
1 Commissariat
4 Post Office
6 Governor's House
7 Préfecture
10 Monument to the Oumana
11 Hospital
14 Buses for Abidjan; Taxi Stand; Central Roundabout
17 Lighthouse
19 Town Hall
20 Mission Catholique
22 School

studios CFA30,000. Once splendid, Le Campement, on the road to the governor's house, is now showing its wrinkles, but it still has charm, the staff are pleasant and the beach is safe for bathing. All rooms have bathroom and air-con.

Hôtel le Pollet *(☎ 34 72 05 78)* Singles/doubles 15,000/16,000. This new and rather sterile hotel on the coastal road to the lighthouse, heading towards Niega, compensates with very clean rooms and exceptional views over Sassandra and the ocean.

L'Océane Lodge *(☎ 34 72 00 72, fax 34 72 05 00, ⓔ oceane@aviso.ci)* Single/double paillotes CFA25,000/30,000. This beautiful new complex of paillotes, opposite the Mission Catholique and overlooking a stunning beach, is run by an enthusiastic French couple. The immaculate cabins are stylish, but low key. The complex centres on a large and airy paillote that houses a fine restaurant. L'Océane Lodge has facilities and activities for children.

La Terrasse *(☎ 34 72 02 00, ⓔ marco@afnet.net, ⓦ www.sassandra.com)* Doubles/triples CFA25,000/30,000. La Terrasse, on the road to the lighthouse, has stupendous views of the port, sand bar, estuary and inland forest (look out for monkeys frolicking in the trees). Bungalows and cabins all have bathroom and air-con. It also has a restaurant and bar.

Places to Eat

There's plenty of ***street food***, including delicious fresh fish, around the market and central roundabout.

Safari Plaza Maquis Fish CFA2200-3000. Safari Plaza Maquis is just north of the central roundabout – you'll recognise it by the strings of dried coconuts hanging like shrunken heads from its breezy terrace. What's on offer, which may include barracuda or swordfish, depends on that day's catch. Help the survival of an endangered species by abstaining from the turtle steak.

La Clinique and ***La Route de la Cuisine*** Meals under CFA1000. These two simple maquis are opposite each other, southeast of the commissariat. They are also good drinking venues.

Maquis le Kayou Meals under CFA1000. The lagoon-side setting, on the road leading north of the port, gives this place its edge.

Hotel food in Sassandra is particularly enticing. For contact details for the following, see Places to Stay.

Hôtel la Côtière Fish dishes CFA3000. First choice has to be very friendly Mademoiselle Tantie Youyou's restaurant. Delicious African fare is served in a superb waterside setting. It's highly recommended.

L'Océane Lodge Meals CFA8000. This beautifully located place changes its excellent French menu daily.

La Terrasse Meals CFA9000. There's a small, carefully chosen à la carte selection here.

Hôtel Grau Meals CFA3,500. The Grau offers standard but reliable French cuisine.

Getting There & Around

SKT and Aicha & Mory both run two buses a day between Abidjan and Sassandra (CFA2500, five hours), leaving Sassandra from the central roundabout. Peugeot taxis and minibuses connect Sassandra and San Pédro (CFA1500, 1½ hours). In San Pédro, they leave from the main gare routière and in Sassandra from the small gare routière some 3km north of town. They take time to fill up.

Shared taxis around town cost CFA150, even for the longish journey to the gare routière for San Pédro.

AROUND SASSANDRA

Beaches

With one exception, all the beaches are west of Sassandra along a well-maintained dirt road. Accommodation is mostly Robinson Crusoe style – simple without electricity or running water. To reach all but the nearest, you'll have to take a taxi. The trip to Plage Niega, the furthest beach, costs around CFA6000. For the return journey, you need to make firm arrangements in advance with a taxi driver.

The nearest beach, **Batélébré II** (see the Sassandra map), requires a 45-minute walk towards the school, then about 10 minutes down a narrow footpath. Alternatively, you can take a shared taxi as far as the school (CFA150) or hire one all the way for CFA1500. Accommodation is available at ***Yabba Hôtel*** *(☎ 34 72 05 33)* where you can hire a cabin for CFA5000 to CFA10,000. Yabba has a magnificent setting right on the sandy beach, beneath palm trees and beside a small lake, where crocodiles lurk beneath the water lilies. All cabins have simple straw mattresses and mosquito nets. Meals are available for CFA6000. Even if you don't stay overnight, it's well worth a visit for lunch or a laze on the beach.

About 2km westward is the stunning **Plage Niezeko**. There's no accommodation but, if you ask the village chief, you can put up your tent or sleep under the stars.

If you have wheels, drop by the small fishing port of **Drewen** (pronounced *dray-***van**). Some 8km west of Sassandra, it was founded by one Charles Drewen, an English trader. There are the remains of a cocoa-oil factory, possibly the first factory in West Africa, and it is worth exploring.

Several kilometres further down the coast are other accommodation possibilities, such as ***Helice de Sassandra*** *(☎/fax 34 72 04 60/02 82)* where you will find a highly recommended complex of whitewashed cabins (single/double bungalows CFA12,000/15,000) in a pretty garden setting overlooking a beautiful beach and promontory. Speak to the animated Agat or Mateoda about fishing trips – they charge CFA30,000 for half a day or CFA22,000 per hour; all equipment is supplied. If you want to use a big boat it's CFA90,000 per day. Guided lagoon walks, with the possibility of seeing hippos, are also available for CFA25,000. Meals are available (CFA6000). If you call ahead the owners will pick you up from Sassandra (CFA5000).

About 200m further west there are two places, situated side by side and right on the magnificent beach, that cater to surfers. ***Spot Surfing*** and ***Pacific Surf*** *(☎ 34 72 02 15)* have very rudimentary palm huts, provisions and simple meals. Unfortunately, they don't provide surfboards; you will need to bring your own.

At **Plage Latéko**, about 10km further west, Raymond and his brothers hire out ***simple huts*** on the sand for CFA4000. It's a friendly, relaxing place and they'll cook meals on request.

There are also beachside accommodation possibilities several kilometres further west near the village of **Poly**. ***Chez Ousman*** has bamboo huts for CFA5000. Signed 'Camping Farafina Beach', unless the villagers have torn it down again, Ousman's beachside huts come with relatively clean toilets and mosquito nets. The young Ivoirian staff are friendly and their fish meals are delicious.

The final and brightest jewel in this necklace of beach paradises is **Niega**, about 4km further west, where the road ends. With its curling breakers, it's a popular surfing venue. Its other great attraction is the dense equatorial forest stretching inland. For a modest fee, the village boys will guide you along the narrow trails. ***La Cocoteraie** (☎ 34 72 00 08)*, a simple campement about 1.5km before the village, has rooms for CFA5000 to CFA10,0000 and is in a lovely, idyllic setting.

About 35km east of Sassandra, at **Dagbego**, there is a large resort complex called ***The Best of Africa** (☎ 34 72 07 74)* with bungalows for CFA40,000 to CFA50,000. This luxury holiday village is on the other side of the river to Sassandra.

Parc Naturel de Gaoulou

On a small island up the Sassandra River and 12km from town by road, a French couple, now departed, established a little paradise that is ideal for wildlife spotting. Unfortunately, accommodation in this beautiful place is no longer available. However, former staff have stayed on and for an admission fee of CFA2000 will give you a one-hour tour. There's an excellent chance of seeing hippos. Take the turn-off to the north opposite the Sassandra turn-off. It's about 8km to the park.

Other sites worth seeing, accessed by the same road, include an old 19th-century French-built **bridge**, Pont Weygand, that crosses the Sassandra River on what was the old coast road. There is also a **lemon factory** that produces lemon and bergamot essences.

MONOGAGA

Monogaga has great beaches with a backdrop of idyllic rainforest and here you will find an amazing place! ***La Langouste d'Or** (☎ 21 24 84 80, fax 21 24 81 97, ⓔ langoustedor@aviso.ci)* has rustic cabins with mosquito nets that are nestled in a superb jungle setting overlooking a wonderful beach. Single/double bungalows will set you back CFA16,500/22,500 and the price includes all meals (which heavily feature seafood, such as crab and lobster, and couscous). It's brilliant value for money.

On the other side of the fishing village, where the beach is equally as beautiful, there's a string of ***cabins***. Most charge CFA5000. Minibuses run to/from San Pédro's gare routière (CFA1000, 40 minutes) or take a taxi (CFA3000). To get here from San Pédro under your own steam, take the coastal highway eastwards towards Sassandra. After 27km, turn right at a clearly signed junction and continue for a further 11km.

SAN PÉDRO

Built from nothing in the late 1960s, San Pédro, 330km west of Abidjan, is the country's second-major port. Much of the country's timber, palm oil, rubber, coffee and cocoa is exported from here.

You may find yourself spending a night in town en route to either Sassandra, Grand-Béréby, Parc National de Taï, or Man and Dan territory. Your night won't be wasted. The Cité area in the heart of San Pédro throbs, particularly after dark. There's such a profusion of maquis that you could eat out for a month without revisiting the same place and enough dance venues to see you through to the dawn after next.

The main public **beach** is 1km west of the port. The commercial port has no interest, but the small, reeking area where the fishing boats moor is well worth a browse.

San Pédro caters well to all budgets.

Information

There's an SGBCI bank and Visa-card-friendly ATM on Rue de la République.

The Direction du Parc National de Taï (☎ 34 71 23 53, fax 34 71 17 79, ⓔ pnt.service@aviso.ci), where bookings for travel packages within the park can be made, is on Av Arthur Verdier, near the port (see Parc National de Taï later in this chapter).

Places to Stay – Budget

***Hôtel le Relais** (☎ 34 71 23 11, Rue B42)* Singles with fan/air-con CFA4000/5500, doubles with fan/air-con CFA5500/7000. The rooms at this hotel could do with a coat of paint, but they all have bathrooms. (There's only one room with fan, the rest have air-con.)

***Hôtel Bahia** (☎ 34 71 27 33, Rue Akossika)* Singles/doubles with fan CFA8000/9000, with air-con CFA13,000/14,000. At the

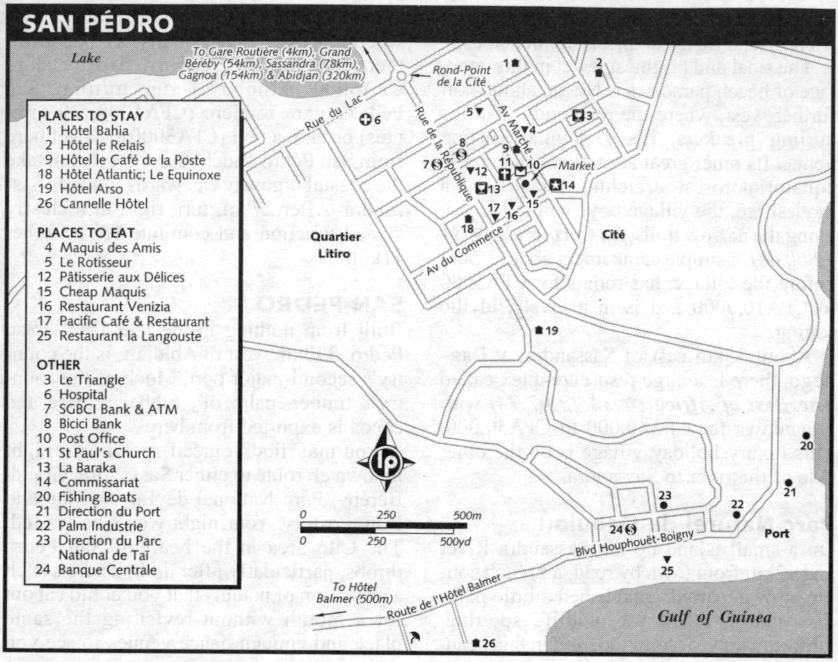
SAN PÉDRO
Lake
To Gare Routière (4km), Grand Béréby (54km), Sassandra (78km), Gagnoa (154km) & Abidjan (320km)
Rond-Point de la Cité
Rue du Lac
Rue de la République
Av Marché
Market
Av du Commerce
Quartier Litiro
Cité
Blvd Houphouët-Boigny
Route de l'Hôtel Balmer
To Hôtel Balmer (500m)
Port
Gulf of Guinea
0 250 500m
0 250 500yd
PLACES TO STAY
1 Hôtel Bahia
2 Hôtel le Relais
9 Hôtel le Café de la Poste
18 Hôtel Atlantic; Le Equinoxe
19 Hôtel Arso
26 Cannelle Hôtel
PLACES TO EAT
4 Maquis des Amis
5 Le Rotisseur
12 Pâtisserie aux Délices
15 Cheap Maquis
16 Restaurant Venizia
17 Pacific Café & Restaurant
25 Restaurant la Langouste
OTHER
3 Le Triangle
6 Hospital
7 SGBCI Bank & ATM
8 Bicici Bank
10 Post Office
11 St Paul's Church
13 La Baraka
14 Commissariat
20 Fishing Boats
21 Direction du Port
22 Palm Industrie
23 Direction du Parc National de Taï
24 Banque Centrale

Bahia in the centre of town the rooms are reasonable value at these prices.

Hôtel le Café de la Poste *(☎ 34 71 56 04, Av Marché)* Singles/doubles CFA10,000/15,000. There are well-furnished rooms here with clean, tiled bathroom and air-con. La Post is a cut above all others in this category.

Places to Stay – Mid-Range & Top End

Hôtel Atlantic *(☎ 34 71 18 14, fax 34 71 15 48, Rue de la République)* Rooms with fan CFA10,000, with air-con CFA12,000-18,000. The monolithic five-storey Atlantic is a rather forbidding place with a lobby hung with hunting trophies, but it has relatively generous-sized rooms that are cleaner than most in San Pédro.

Hôtel Arso *(☎ 34 71 24 74, fax 34 71 20 26, Av Burtel)* Doubles with fan only/air-con and shower/air-con and bathroom CFA5000/10,000/12,000. This is a tour-group favourite. The pool is without water these days and the restaurant menu is limited to a couple of dishes, but its cleanliness, the ample size of the rooms and the tranquil garden make it great value.

Cannelle Hôtel *(☎ 34 71 12 85, Blvd Houphouët-Boigny)* has doubles/triples for CFA25,000/30,000. This superior establishment with its palm grove and sea views is immaculate and represents the best value for money in the top-end category.

Hôtel Balmer *(☎ 34 71 22 75, fax 34 71 27 83, ⓔ ciebalmer@hotmail.com, Blvd Hôtel Balmer)* Singles/doubles CFA29,000/35,000. This place, 4km west of the port and a CFA1000 taxi ride from town, is the city's top establishment. It's ideally located in large, well-tended grounds on a rocky site overlooking the ocean and a safe, sandy beach. Prices for luxury bungalows vary according to season. It also has a very good restaurant.

Places to Eat

San Pédro is great for eating out. There are plenty of inexpensive places around the gare routière, and the Cité has a stomach-challenging variety of decent restaurants and maquis. There's a superb animated strip of ***cheap maquis*** and drinking places wedged one beside another on Av Marché in the same block as the market.

Maquis des Amis *(Av Marché)* Meals CFA1000-1500. This place stands out – though there are no frills, it's as friendly as its name implies, and the food is plentiful, delicious and popular.

Restaurant Venizia *(☎ 07 80 52 63, Av du Commerce)* Sandwiches CFA1000. Another slice of the West, this stylish place does salads and sandwiches, as well as first-rate coffee, to the sounds of country and western music (which feels a little peculiar).

Pâtisserie aux Délices *(☎ 34 71 48 26, Rue de la République)* Cakes CFA800. There are astonishingly authentic cakes and tarts for sale in this French-owned establishment. Why slum it up in Paris when Africa's your oyster?

Pacific Café & Restaurant *(☎ 34 71 52 10, Cnr Rue de la République & Av du Commerce)* Brochettes CFA2000-3000. The grilled meat dishes here are a little slow to arrive, but well and truly worth the wait.

Le Rotisseur *(34 71 25 26, Av B12)* Meals CFA3000. Imaginative African and European dishes are served on a terrace by a French manager in a pleasant walled garden.

Restaurant la Langouste *(☎ 34 71 19 00, Blvd Houphouët-Boigny)* Meals CFA4200-10,500. This restaurant has an attractive terrace overlooking the ocean. French-run, it serves fabulous seafood. Try the *tourte de pomme de terre a la langouste* (potato and lobster pie; CFA10,000), or *langouste rotie a l'orange* (roast lobster with orange sauce; CFA10,500).

Entertainment

Head for what locals call ***Le Triangle***, in the eastern part of the Cité, where you'll find half-a-dozen dance venues belting it out.

Le Equinoxe *(☎ 34 71 15 84, Rue de la République)* For something more structured – and expensive – try this place next to Hôtel Atlantic.

La Baraka *(☎ 34 71 11 87, Rue de la République)* Opposite Hôtel Atlantic, this place goes off after midnight.

Getting There & Away

Buses and bush taxis leave from the main gare routière, some 4km north of the Cité. It's at the northern limit of Rue de la République, beside Rond-point d'Abidjan. Buses to Abidjan (CFA4500, six hours) regularly run either via Gagnoa or follow La Côtière, the highway that parallels the coast, some distance inland.

UTB and CTM have three daily services each to Bouaké (CFA6000, eight hours) via Yamoussoukro (CFA4500, seven hours). UTB and CTM run one bus a day between San Pédro and Man (CFA6000, 10 hours). If you're aiming for Danané, near the border with Liberia, BST runs a daily minibus via Man. Buses and bush taxis travel west to Tabou (CFA2000, two hours) or Grand-Béréby (CFA1000, 45 minutes) en route, and also east to Sassandra (CFA1500, 1½ hours).

Getting Around

Shared taxis around town, including to the port or gare routière, cost CFA150.

GRAND-BÉRÉBY

Grand-Béréby, a fishing village some 50km west of San Pédro, has magnificent beaches. On the western side of its promontory is a protected bay with calm waters where reasonable snorkelling can be done. On the eastern side the surf is pretty good.

There are a number of hotels with restaurants next to each other on the steep palm-fringed beach with its crashing surf.

Le Python *(☎/fax 34 72 46 54, e python@aviso.ci)*, on the eastern side of the promontory, is a very hip bamboo warren that is great fun. Cabins are close set within a thick palm grove and have mezzanines (singles CFA7000, four-person without/with bathroom CFA10,000/12,000). There's a large central thatched paillote bar serving excellent *brochettes poisson* (grilled fish; CFA3000).

Baba Cool *(☎ 07 71 04 65)* The ambience is as the name suggests at this place, also on the eastern side of the promontory. Doubles with fan/air-con are CFA13,000/16,000. There's also a disco with mirrors on the wall and live music on Saturday night. At the restaurant the emphasis is on seafood (*sole meuniére* [fish dish]; CFA3000) and steaks (CFA5000).

Hôtel la Baie des Sirènes *(☎ 34 72 46 20, fax 34 72 46 32)* This luxury property on the western side of the promontory has 60 nice bungalows beside the ocean and backing onto a 40-hectare park. Singles/doubles are about CFA47,000/58,000. There's a long list of activities to indulge in, such as fishing, tennis and *pétanque*, of course.

Buses and bush taxis run to Grand Béréby from San Pédro (CFA1000, 45 minutes) and Tabou (CFA1500, one hour).

PARC NATIONAL DE TAÏ

Parc National de Taï with its 454,000 hectares, is one of the largest remaining areas of virgin rainforest in West Africa. You'll see trees over 45m high, with massive trunks and huge supporting roots. The trees block out the sun, preventing dense undergrowth from developing, thus making walking through the forest quite easy. It's a unique experience. The towering trees, hanging lianas, swift streams and varied wildlife create an enchanting environment. ***Ecotel Touraco** (☎ 05 95 20 26, Guiroutou)*, the park's only accommodation, allows you to experience the forest at close quarters.

The park is in a very rainy, humid area, so the best time to visit is from December to February, when there's a marked dry season. In these months, you can get there by car; at other times, travelling by 4WD is strongly recommended.

Because it's so special and so fragile, access to the park and the number of visitors are strictly controlled. To reserve in advance – which is essential – phone or fax the park's office in San Pédro (☎ 34 71 23 53, fax 34 71 17 79, e pnt.service@aviso.ci) on Av Arthur Verdier, or the Ecotel Touraco itself. You can also check out the park's website (w www.parc-national-de-tai.org). These days no special permit is needed, unless you are conducting research. For more information about the park's special conservation scheme, see the boxed text 'Conservation & Ecotourism: The Taï Example'.

There are a number of accommodation/trip options available. Simple singles/doubles/triples half-board at the ***Ecotel*** will cost CFA22,000/34,000/36,000. From there you can take guided trips to see the forest (CFA15,000 per person), the chimpanzees (CFA20,000 per person), or take pirogue trips (CFA7000 per person). Park admission costs a further CFA10,000 per day.

You can opt for all-inclusive, full-board packages. A two-day chimpanzee expedition costs CFA65,000 per person; a two-day ascent of Mont Niénokoué (396m, the highest point in the park) is CFA60,000; a three-day visit including chimpanzees and a mountain ascent is CFA95,000; or a four-day visit including monkeys, chimpanzees, a mountain ascent and pirogue trip is CFA125,000.

Conservation & Ecotourism: The Taï Example

The Parc National de Taï team has had remarkable success in preserving West Africa's largest rainforest from further destruction. The key has been to give a stake in its development to those who previously made a living from the forest. A proportion of the revenue from tourism is used to improve the quality of life of villagers by, for example, setting up a primary health care centre, improving drinking water and providing veterinary support for livestock. In Guiroutou, the villagers are being encouraged to share in the controlled development of tourism as owners of cafés and planned rural accommodation.

As a result, logging and encroachment by small landholders has ceased and poaching, controlled also by much stricter surveillance, has diminished significantly. Turning hunters into gamekeepers has meant that the locals now actively help in repelling the main threat – poachers who slip over the border from neighbouring Liberia.

Getting There & Away

If you left your car at home you'll need to take three bush taxis: San Pédro to Tabou, another on to Grabo and a third as far as Guiroutou, from where it's a 7km walk to the ecotel. The northern route is sparsely travelled and serviced, so it's probably easier for independent travellers to take a bus from Man to San Pédro, then head north again by bush taxi. If you want to try your luck from Man, take a CTN bus to Guiglo then do the Guiglo to Taï leg by the daily postal van *(courrier postal)*. From Taï to Guiroutou there are infrequent pick-ups.

With your own vehicle, from San Pédro go west to Tabou, from where a 145km dirt road via Grabo (68km) takes you to the park office at Guiroutou. If coming from the north, head for Duekoué. From there, it's tar to Guiglo and dirt to Taï and Guiroutou.

TABOU

Tabou is near the Liberian border. If you're headed for Liberia, you must get your passport stamped at the commissariat here.

Hôtel Campement *(☎ 34 72 49 82)* This friendly hotel with a garden and large veranda, has uninspiring but clean doubles with fan/air-con for CFA4000/8500. It is beside the beach at the eastern limit of town.

Hôtel Côtiére *(☎ 34 72 40 98)* The double bungalows with fan/air-con costing CFA5000/8000 are drab and musty, but are surrounded by a tranquil garden. It is inland from the beach at the eastern limit of town.

Regular buses and shared taxis run to San Pédro (CFA2000, two hours). There's one shared taxi a day to the Liberian border (CFA1000, 45 minutes), which starts filling in the morning. The border is the Cavally River, 27km further west. You will have to haggle over the price of a canoe to cross it. Independent travellers might be better off crossing via Danané, further north.

The West

MAN

Man, known as *la cité des 18 montagnes* (city of 18 mountains), nestles at the base of lush green hills and has the most beautiful location of any inland Ivoirian town. It's a good base for walking or for exploring the fascinating Dan villages nearby.

Man's main attraction, the covered market, burnt down in 1997. The market used to be a treasure-trove of fabrics, fetishes and woodcarvings, particularly masks. Until it is reconstructed, the merchants are dispersed around town (see Shopping later in this section).

The best time to be in the Man region is February, when you can see the masked dancing of the Fêtes des Masques.

Information

The Office Ivoirien du Tourisme et de l'Hôtellerie (☎ 33 79 06 90) on Route du Lycée Professionnel is open from 7.30am to noon and 2.30pm to 6pm Monday to Friday, and until 12.30pm on Saturday. The staff are very helpful and can arrange an official guide (about CFA8000 per day) and car hire. They'll also suggest and arrange tailor-made excursions to surrounding villages, as well as advise on local road conditions. Reservations can be made here to see dancing at nearby villages (see Around Man later in this section).

GSB (☎ 33 79 08 64), on Rue de l'Hôtel Leveneur opposite the Banque Central, charges CFA300 per minute for Internet access, but the connections are very poor.

The SGBCI bank on Rue de l'Hôtel Leveneur has an ATM, which yields cash to Visa-card holders.

Places to Stay – Budget

You can camp in the grounds of the ***Hôtel Beau-Séjour*** *(☎ 33 79 08 55)*, on the southwestern outskirts of town, for CFA1500 per person. This is favourite overnight spot for budget overland tours.

Hôtel Mont Dent *(☎ 33 79 03 94, Quartier Koko)* Rooms with shower CFA2500, singles/doubles with fan & bath CFA3000/6000. Although the rooms here are just so-so, Mont Dent is cheap and has clean beds and showers.

Hôtel CAA *(☎ 33 79 11 22, Quartier Koko)* Singles with fan/air-con CFA4500/6000, doubles with fan/air-con CFA6000/7000. The CAA, just up the hill from the Mont Dent, is distinctly superior and the best value in this category. Rooms are immaculately clean and cosy and there are fine views of Man and the surrounding hills. Don't be put off by the hotel's unfinished air – the result of an overly ambitious extension plan that ran out of cash.

Hôtel le Petit Coin *(☎ 33 79 03 91, Quartier CAFOP)* Rooms with shower/bathroom/air-con CFA2500/3500/5000. This hotel, east of the road out of town to Yamoussoukro, is uninspiring but OK value for the asking price.

Hôtel Leveneur *(☎ 32 79 14 81, Rue de l'Hôtel Leveneur)* Rooms with fan/air-con CFA5000/10,000. The Leveneur, northwest of the gare routière, is a little overpriced but conveniently central. There are stark air-con rooms with shower or bathroom. It has a pleasant enough restaurant and the terrace is a relaxing place to have a drink.

Places to Stay – Mid-Range

Hôtel du Guety *(☎ 33 79 29 50, fax 33 79 18 27, Quartier CAFOP)* Singles/doubles CFA12,000/16,000. This place is very clean and homely. It has a reasonable restaurant, attractive courtyard and possibly the most secure hotel in town.

Hôtel Beau-Séjour *(☎ 33 79 08 55)* Air-con bungalows CFA12,000. If you're mobile,

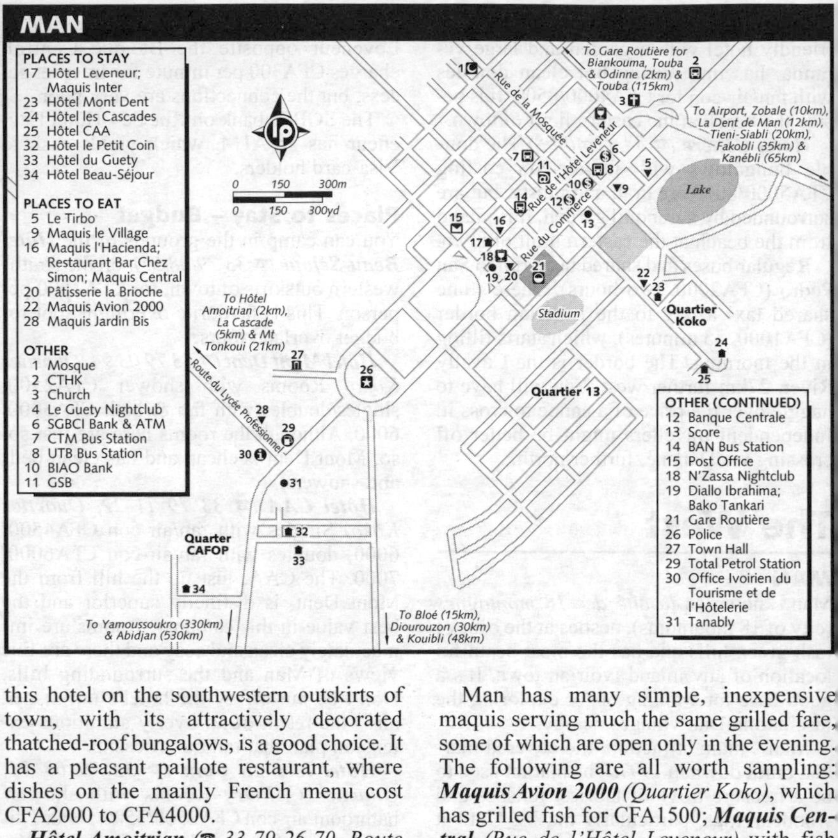
MAN
PLACES TO STAY
17 Hôtel Leveneur; Maquis Inter
23 Hôtel Mont Dent
24 Hôtel les Cascades
25 Hôtel CAA
32 Hôtel le Petit Coin
33 Hôtel du Guety
34 Hôtel Beau-Séjour
PLACES TO EAT
5 Le Tirbo
9 Maquis le Village
16 Maquis l'Hacienda; Restaurant Bar Chez Simon; Maquis Central
20 Pâtisserie la Brioche
22 Maquis Avion 2000
28 Maquis Jardin Bis
OTHER
1 Mosque
2 CTHK
3 Church
4 Le Guety Nightclub
6 SGBCI Bank & ATM
7 CTM Bus Station
8 UTB Bus Station
10 BIAO Bank
11 GSB
OTHER (CONTINUED)
12 Banque Centrale
13 Score
14 BAN Bus Station
15 Post Office
18 N'Zassa Nightclub
19 Diallo Ibrahima; Bako Tankari
21 Gare Routière
26 Police
27 Town Hall
29 Total Petrol Station
30 Office Ivoirien du Tourisme et de l'Hôtelerie
31 Tanably
0 150 300m
0 150 300yd
To Gare Routière for Biankouma, Touba & Odinne (2km) & Touba (115km)
To Airport, Zobale (10km), La Dent de Man (12km), Tieni-Siabli (20km), Fakobli (35km) & Kanébli (65km)
Rue de la Mosquée
Rue de l'Hôtel Leveneur
Rue du Commerce
Lake
Stadium
Quartier Koko
Quartier 13
To Hôtel Amoitrian (2km), La Cascade (5km) & Mt Tonkoui (21km)
Route du Lycée Professionnel
Quarter CAFOP
To Yamoussoukro (330km) & Abidjan (530km)
To Bloé (15km), Diourouzon (30km) & Kouibli (48km)

this hotel on the southwestern outskirts of town, with its attractively decorated thatched-roof bungalows, is a good choice. It has a pleasant paillote restaurant, where dishes on the mainly French menu cost CFA2000 to CFA4000.

Hôtel Amoitrian *(☎ 33 79 26 70, Route du Lycée Professionnel)* Singles/doubles CFA12,000/18,000. This new place is the best value for money in Man. Just west out of town, the rooms are immaculate, and there are great views, a pool and a first-rate restaurant (meals CFA3000 to CFA7000).

Hôtel les Cascades *(☎ 33 79 02 52, fax 33 79 02 11, Quartier Koko)* Singles/doubles CFA13,000/16,000. The Cascades offers exceptional value for money, despite its age. It's a perfectly preserved 1970s architectural classic. Air-con rooms are large, well appointed and very clean. Its pool (CFA1500 for nonguests) is the only one within easy reach of the town centre. There's a great view of Man and its corona of mountains.

Places to Eat

African The best place for cheap ***street food*** is around the main gare routière.

Man has many simple, inexpensive maquis serving much the same grilled fare, some of which are open only in the evening. The following are all worth sampling: ***Maquis Avion 2000*** *(Quartier Koko)*, which has grilled fish for CFA1500; ***Maquis Central*** *(Rue de l'Hôtel Leveneur)* with fish brochettes for CFA3500; ***Maquis Inter*** *(Rue de l'Hôtel Leveneur)*, which has chicken and chips for CFA3500; and ***Maquis le Village*** *(Rue du Commerce)*, which offers grilled chicken for CFA2500.

Maquis Jardin Bis *(Route du Lycée Professionnel)* Meals CFA2000-3000. This place, which has quickly built up a faithful local following, is especially recommended. It has fabulous brochettes (CFA3000) and French dishes, such as *cote d'agneau aux herbs des provençes* (side of lamb with herbs) for CFA1300.

Le Tirbo *(☎ 33 79 04 48)* Meals CFA1700-4500. One block southeast of SGBCI bank, Le Tirbo, with its covered terrace and bar, is a great place to relax.

French You'll eat well, and in agreeable surroundings, at the ***Restaurant Bar Chez***

Simon *(☎ 07 86 11 25, Rue de l'Hôtel Leveneur)*. It has a huge, lofty paillote in the heart of a quiet garden. The menu is mostly French with a few African selections. Dishes range from CFA2500 to CFA 3500.

Maquis l'Hacienda *(☎ 33 79 00 25, Rue de l'Hôtel Leveneur)* Meals CFA2000-4000. Nearby, this place serves simpler, less expensive but excellent meals in pleasant surrounds. Try the fish kedjenou (CFA3500).

Pâtisserie la Brioche *(☎ 33 79 03 65, Rue du Commerce)* Croissants CFA220. This French-managed patisserie is a great place for a terrace breakfast or morning coffee.

Entertainment

Man has two nightclubs, with two very different characters. Both have a first-drink charge of CFA2500.

Le Guety Nightclub *(☎ 33 79 06 64)* Admission CFA2500. Open nightly from 9.30pm. Le Guety, near the BAN bus station, has a vibrant, African energy. As in many other Ivoirian dance venues, mirrors seem to be the major attraction. Women gain free admission on Thursday night.

N'Zassa Nightclub Admission free. Open Mon-Sat. Opposite Hôtel Leveneur, N'Zassa is a more intimate place playing disco music and catering to rich Ivoirians.

Go out of your way to catch ***Tanably*** *(☎ 07 86 11 30, ⓔ ardeco@africaonline.com.ic)*. Based in Man, just east of the road to Yamoussoukro, this internationally famous dance troupe comprises 14 young and highly energetic male and female dancers and drummers. It performs a range of tribal dances using elaborate fetish masks and costumes. It is around CFA20,000 per show.

Shopping

There are around five craft shops worth exploring opposite Hôtel Leveneur. They include ***Diallo Ibrahima*** *(☎ 33 79 18 25)* and ***Bako Tankari***. Both have a wide selection of masks and woodcarvings, both new and antique, as well as cloth. Prices are negotiable (it may be possible to knock up to two-thirds off the first price quoted).

There are also shops facing Hôtel CAA and beyond Hôtel les Cascades.

For more information on Dan masks and woodcarvings, see the boxed text 'Art of Côte d'Ivoire' in the Facts about Côte d'Ivoire section.

Getting There & Away

Bus UTB (four blocks northeast of Hôtel Leveneur), BAN (Rue du Commerce) and CTM (three blocks northeast of the post office) run regular buses to Abidjan (CFA5000, nine hours), Yamoussoukro (CFA4000, five hours), Bouaké (CFA5000, 7½ hours), Odienné (CFA4000, five hours) and San Pédro (CFA6000, 10 hours). At 8am on Monday and Friday CTHK (200m northeast of the church) has a bus to Korhogo (CFA7000, 11 hours) via Yamoussoukro and Bouaké.

Bush Taxi The main gare routière for minibuses and bush taxis is on Rue du Commerce. Peugeot taxis travelling to Abidjan cost about CFA5000. Minibuses headed north to Biankouma (CFA1000, 45 minutes), Touba (CFA2500, 1½ hours) and Odienné (CFA4000, five hours) leave from the gare routière on the Touba road, 2km north of the centre, while those bound for Danané (CFA1500, one hour) leave from the central market.

Waiting for a minibus to Odienné to fill up can take hours. Much more punctual and reliable is the postal van that leaves at 8am daily except Sunday from the post office, arriving in Odienné some five hours later. It costs CFA4000, plus CFA500 for heavy luggage, and fairly flies along.

Getting Around

The tourist office can arrange car hire for about CFA15,000 per day, including driver but not fuel. Also ask at the Total petrol station opposite the tourist office.

AROUND MAN

La Cascade

Some 5km west of town on the road to Mt Tonkoui is La Cascade *(admission CFA500)*, which is a waterfall within a bamboo forest. A shared taxi seat costs CFA200 although, since it's off the regular routes, you may have to take all four places.

August to November are the months of fullest spate, when you can take a dip at the base of the waterfall. However, as the dry season progresses, from late December onwards, the water slows to scarcely a trickle. The site is very beautiful.

As you descend the steps to the waterfall, large, red, yellow and green butterflies will flutter around you.

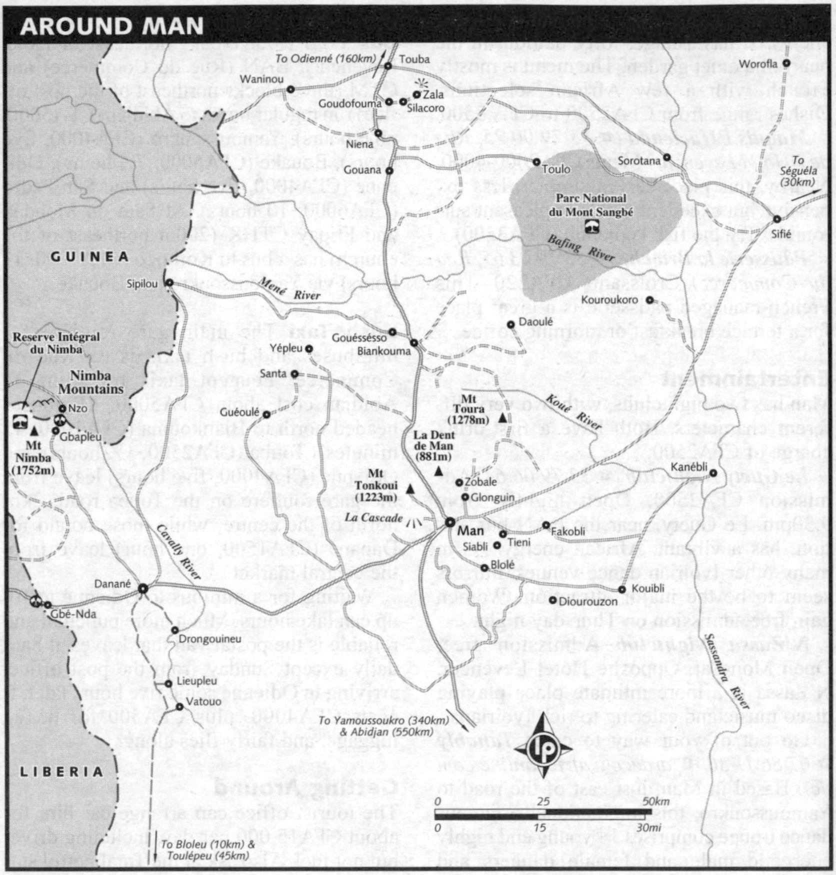
AROUND MAN
To Odienné (160km)
Touba
Waninou
Zala
Goudofouma
Silacoro
Niena
Gouana
Worofla
Toulo
Sorotana
To Séguéla (30km)
Parc National du Mont Sangbé
Bafing River
Sifié
GUINEA
Sipilou
Mené River
Kouroukoro
Daoulé
Reserve Intégral du Nimba
Nimba Mountains
Yépleu
Gouéssésso
Biankouma
Santa
Nzo
Gbapleu
Mt Nimba (1752m)
Guéoulé
Mt Toura (1278m)
Koué River
La Dent de Man (881m)
Mt Tonkoui (1223m)
Zobale
Glonguin
La Cascade
Kanébli
Man
Fakobli
Siabli
Tieni
Blolé
Cavally River
Danané
Gbé-Nda
Kouibli
Diourouzon
Drongouineu
Sassandra River
Lieupleu
Vatouo
To Yamoussoukro (340km) & Abidjan (550km)
LIBERIA
0 25 50km
0 15 30mi
To Bloleu (10km) & Toulépeu (45km)

Mt Tonkoui

Mt Tonkoui (1223m), topped by a giant communications tower, is the second-highest peak in Côte d'Ivoire and a further 16km of steep, winding road beyond La Cascade. Just before a T-junction where you turn left, about 3km before the summit, you'll see, on the right, a quinine plantation, established by an enterprising Ivoirian who returned from pharmaceutical training in France.

The views from the summit are breathtaking and extend as far as Liberia and Guinea, although not during the harmattan season (December to March).

If they're not too busy, the telecommunications engineers may let you go up the 325 steps to the observation balcony at the top of the tower.

La Dent de Man

For hikers, a major attraction is La Dent de Man (The Tooth of Man), a steep molar-shaped mountain (881m) 12km northeast of town. The walking track is much more interesting and challenging than the route up by road to Mt Tonkoui and the view from the crest is superb. Take a shared taxi (CFA300 per person) to the village of Zobale, 4km from town. There, the inhabitants ask for a CFA500 village tax.

From the village, strike due east to take a path that follows the contour line and southern flank of the hill that lies between you and La Dent. After 10 minutes of steep ascent, the track levels out as you stroll beside plantations of coffee, cocoa and bananas plus, at ground level, cassava, mountain rice and *gombo* (okra). In the distance you can see the coffee and rice-processing plant, the only building of significance to the southeast. After about 1¼ hours, take a minor track to the left. Here, the steep stuff begins – about 45 minutes of fairly gruelling ascent beneath shady trees. Allow four to 4½ hours for the round trip, including a breather at the summit. Carry lots of water and keep looking down at your feet and the stunning clouds of butterflies that they disturb.

Villages

The villages around Man, most of which charge an officially agreed fee of CFA500, are all accessible by car. They're well used to tourists. To diminish the hassle, ask for the village chief, who will usually impose a degree of order. If you need a place to stay, he can normally find you somewhere and someone to cook you a meal.

For travellers with wheels, an interesting circular route of around 250km to 300km, preferably with an overnight stop built into it, is to go north from Man to Biankouma (see following) and Gouéssésso, then west to Sipilou on the Liberian border, south to Danané, and back (east) to Man. However, be aware that this unmade road is bad and that, immediately after the rainy season (December), bridges may be washed out. The trip should therefore be undertaken with a 4WD well into the dry season.

Biankouma Some 44km north of Man, on the paved road to Touba, is Biankouma, famous for its acrobatic Goua dances, which usually take place on Sunday. The new part of town on the main highway is of no interest. In the old section, several kilometres away on a hillside, the traditional houses are noted for their decorative paintings in kaolin clay. The old part is also rich in fetishes. It is forbidden to photograph any of the 11 fetish houses, so you should ask before taking pictures. Look for houses surrounded by sacred yucca trees and interestingly shaped sacred rocks. To enter the village you will need to pay CFA500 to the chief.

For accommodation, try ***Chambres de Passage***, which is a brothel near the pharmacy, if cost is your major consideration. Rooms are CFA1500.

Those with lesser constitutions will be better off at ***Hôtel du Mont Sangbé*** (☎ *33 79 52 27*). It's clean and there is a pleasant and shady garden out the front. Doubles without/with fan are CFA3000/3500. Traditional meals are available (CFA2500). It is above the old village – the kids who trail you everywhere can lead you to it.

Minibuses run to Man (CFA1000, 45 minutes). Biankouma is the departure point for the Guinean border at Sipilou (although there is a more regularly used crossing at Gbapleu, reached via Danané). A minibus makes the trip to Sipilou daily (CFA1500, 1½ hours).

Bloé This village is 15km southeast of Man on the road to Kouibli. Arrangements can be made with the tourist office in Man to see masked dancing here. It costs CFA25,000 (CFA5000 for reserving and CFA20,000 for the performance) and involves a Yacouba dance performed by village girls wearing very old Goua masks. You will need to make a reservation early in the morning to see a dance in the evening. Transport can be arranged by the tourist office, or catch a minibus (CFA400, 45 minutes).

Diourouzon At this village, around 30km southeast of Man, child juggling can be seen (see the boxed text 'The Child Jugglers' later). Villagers will need advance warning (in the morning) in order to make the necessary preparations for the event (in the evening). Expect to pay CFA20,000. Take a minibus from Man (CFA700, two hours).

Kanébli About 64km east via Fakobli on the banks of the Sassandra River is Kanébli, where you can hire a pirogue for a river trip to view hippos and crocodiles. The village is renowned for the Tematé dance, performed by young Wobé girls at the end of the rice harvest. Take a minibus from Man (CFA1000, two hours).

Parc National du Mont Sangbé

At the time of writing the Parc National du Mont Sangbé, to the northeast, was closed. Ask at the tourist office in Man to find out if it has reopened. The park contains elephants, and tours may one day be available.

TOUBA & AROUND

This mainly Malinké town, 115km north of Man, has a colourful Saturday market. The

The Child Jugglers

No, we don't mean precocious Indian-club swingers but men of superhuman strength of the Guéré, Wobé and Dan (Yacouba) peoples, who literally juggle with young girls.

The preparation for both juggler and juggled is long and demanding. The juggler retires to the sacred forest, where he undergoes tests of endurance and learns the arcane secrets of his skill, which are handed down from father to eldest son. He remains isolated from all contact with the village. His food, prepared by a group of specially nominated young girls, is left at the edge of the forest. The girls, selected when they're only five years old, are kept apart from the rest of the village children and wear a special headdress to emphasise their separateness.

When the juggler returns from his isolation, he offers two sheep and four chickens to the families of the girls who will be his accomplices. In preparation for the ritual performance, the girls are washed in a liquid with secret medicinal properties and drink an equally secret concoction of roots and herbs to make them supple and light. Their lips are coated with a black substance, which, it's believed, encourages silence, for they mustn't utter a word or cry.

Four adolescent drummers and a sidekick, a junior juggler whose role is to highlight the greater skill of his superior, warm up the crowd. And then, as the girls roll their heads, trance-like, to stimulate the spirits, the performance begins. They're tossed high in the air, the juggler brandishes knives on which they seem certain to be impaled and the crowd becomes increasingly frenzied. But all the while, the countenances of the girls remain as still as death masks.

Child juggling can be seen in Diourouzon and further afield in Bloleu.

main attraction of Touba, however, is the stilt dancers who live in villages to the south.

Silacoro is the most celebrated village, mainly for its stilt dancing (see the boxed text 'Stilt Dancers'). If you wish to see dancing, ask at the village before noon. You can also hire an official guide from the Man tourist office for an excellent tour (CFA10,000) that takes in most of the attractions in the area and a stilt dance in the evening. The dancing costs CFA20,000; if you don't have your own wheels, car hire for the day costs CFA15,000.

An attractive village, Silacoro is worth visiting in its own right. It stands next to a sacred forest and consists entirely of mud houses with thatched, conical roofs. On the edge of the forest there is a muddy pond fed by a spring that is teeming with large, whiskered fish. The fish are said to be sacred and are thus not eaten by the villagers. Bring bread to feed the fish, which will slip and slide onto dry land for a mouthful.

To get to Silacoro, turn off the main highway 7km south of Touba or 20km north of Gouana. Silacoro is about 5km down the road, after the similarly attractive village of **Goudofouma**, where dancing can also be arranged and where there is also a sacred forest. Near the end of this road is **Zala**. Perched on a 500m-high rock, Zala has magnificent views of Touba and its environs. Beyond Zala the road ends atop an escarpment from which there are more panoramic views.

Back on the road to Man, **Niena** is renowned for its masked dancers. Arrangements to see a dance should be made with the village chief before noon for an evening performance.

A little further down the road, **Gouana** is famous locally for its enormous 200-year-old tree and its giant termite mound.

Places to Stay & Eat

There are two hotels in Touba.

Hôtel la Savanna *(☎ 33 70 73 63)* Singles without fan/with fan/with air-con CFA2000/2500/5000, doubles without fan/with fan/with air-con CFA3000/4000/8000. This modest place in the town centre is clean and quite reasonable at these prices. It also has a good restaurant that serves African food. On most days antelope features prominently at this and other eateries in Touba.

Hôtel l'Amitié Vraie *(☎ 33 70 71 01, fax 33 70 75 88)* Singles/doubles with bathroom & air-con CFA10,000/25,000. This is the best hotel in town and though a little gaudy, is a favourite with tour groups. It has spotless rooms and an excellent restaurant. Look for the blue minaret of the mosque. The call to prayer can be heard from the hotel's terrace. Unamplified, it drifts hauntingly over the surrounding savanna.

Stilt Dancers

In the mountain villages around Touba a select group of young Dan men perform heart-stopping masked dances atop 3m-high stilts. It's an exciting spectacle well worth going out of your way to experience, as much for the cultural setting as the dance itself. One such village is Silacoro, where circular mud-brick houses with conical thatched roofs are surrounded by a towering sacred forest. Some houses are fetish houses with sacred yucca plants and interesting-shaped sacred rocks.

The dance, which must be arranged in the morning to give villagers time to prepare, takes place as the sun is setting, when houses and compound walls are bathed in a radiant, ochre light. Most of the villagers participate in the cooperatively run performances. As kola nuts are passed round, proceedings begin with a chorus of young women singing and swaying to the beat of five young drumming men.

Eventually a beturbaned young woman, the village beauty, appears swinging a pair of tail-like brushes to the uplifted voices and drums. She represents the beauty of girls in traditional society. Individual dances by young men follow as the drumming becomes more and more frantic. By this stage the chief and other dignitaries have arrived and have seated themselves in the best vantage points. And then the stilt dancers make their appearance. Their costume is otherworldy; on their high stilts they don't resemble the human form in any way. Their frightening masks are of woven rafia dyed a dark indigo with tassels cascading from their mouths. Around their heads they wear cowrie shells and bells and their bodies are hidden beneath ballooning straw overcoats. As their swirling dance progresses the acrobatic feats become more and more outrageous until they are spinning at a terrific speed and hurtling themselves into the air, throwing their stilts over their heads then miraculously landing on them. The crowd goes wild. After each dangerous whirl the dancer approaches the chief and dignitaries howling like a demented wounded jungle bird until gifts of money are surrendered to their clutch.

Before they can dance publicly the dancers undertake three to five years of training. They tell no-one, not even their wives, what they're doing. Once initiated, they become empowered to communicate with the spirits who, during the dancing, direct their elaborate stunts.

Getting There & Away

There are minibuses travelling to/from Man (CFA2500, 1½ hours). You can also get here from both Man and Odienné on the daily postal van. Ask at the post office for details.

DANANÉ

For most who travel from Guinea or Liberia, Danané (about 80km west of Man) is the first major town you hit. Its two gares routières – east *(est)* for Man and west *(ouest)* for the Liberian and Guinean borders – are about 2km apart at opposite ends of town, so you may want to take a taxi (CFA200) from one to the other. When arriving or leaving, be sure to get your passport stamped by the police at the commissariat in the centre; otherwise you'll be sent back. There is an SGBCI bank in town (but no ATM) where cash (euros only) can be exchanged.

Places to Stay & Eat

For the budget option, choose ***Hôtel Tia Étienne*** *(☎ 33 70 00 97)*, 500m west of the eastern gare routière. Rooms are CFA4000 and crude at best, but it does decent meals for between CFA2000 and CFA2500.

Hôtel des Lianes *(☎ 33 70 01 65)* Doubles with bathroom & air-con CFA7000. Opposite the eastern gare routière, and owned by Simon, of Chez Simon fame in Man, these are the only digs of quality in town. The restaurant's quite good, too (meals CFA2500 to CFA6000, with green beans and mashed potatoes available!).

Maquis around town are inexpensive. Be aware that hérrison is hedgehog, and an acquired taste.

Getting There & Away

Minibuses and bush taxis to Man (CFA1500, one hour) go from the eastern gare routière. Minibuses leave for Gbapleu on the Guinean frontier (CFA1500, 1½ hours) and Liberian frontier (CFA500, 30 minutes) from the western gare routière when full. The asking price is US$450 to get from the Liberian frontier to Monrovia along what is a very bad road.

AROUND DANANÉ

Ponts de Lianes

Not far from Danané are some of Côte d'Ivoire's last remaining vine or creeper bridges, which cross the Cavally River. The major ones are near three villages south of town: Drongouineu (14km), Lieupleu (22km) and Vatouo (30km).

The bridge at Lieupleu (village tax, CFA500) is in the best condition and the easiest to get to; it's 2km east of the road to Toulépleu and signed. The bridge is sacred, and you should take off your shoes before crossing it. The cheapest way to get here is to catch a minibus from Danané (CFA650, 30 minutes) for Toulépleu and ask the driver to drop you off at the sign. Otherwise, a taxi costs about CFA6000 return.

Bloleu

At this village, around 60km south of Danané via Zéalé, child juggling can be seen. Villagers will need advance warning (in the morning) in order to make the necessary preparations for the event (in the evening). Expect to pay around CFA20,000.

The Centre

YAMOUSSOUKRO

The capital of Côte d'Ivoire – officially designated as such in 1983 – Yamoussoukro is a capital without embassies, ministries or significant commercial life. Originally a village called Ngokro with no more than 500 inhabitants, it has swollen to more than 100,000 people because of the whim of one man, Félix Houphouët-Boigny, who happened to be born hereabouts and who wanted to glorify himself, his family and his ancestors. With its lightly trafficked six-lane highways (bordered by more than 10,000 streetlights) leading nowhere in particular, and its grandiose monuments set just far enough apart to be inconvenient for walking, it's a lasting testament to Africa's greatest curse – the Big Boss, who can get away with anything.

The Habitat quarter, the original town, always resisted occupation. Here, the market bustles, the nightlife along Rue du Château d'Eau beats out and the tranquil lakeside maquis do good business. People are gradually humanising and reclaiming what the president usurped.

But let's not be churlish. Some of the overweening monuments are architecturally stunning, even if they owe little to Africa: the Basilique de Notre Dame de la Paix with its many superlatives, Hôtel Président and the complex of structures that constitute the Institut National Polytechnique Houphouët-Boigny.

Information

The staff at the tourist office (☎ 30 64 08 14), Av Houphouët-Boigny, can arrange visits to Institut National Polytechnique (CFA2000) and Baoulé dancing (CFA30,000) in Kondayaokro, which is 1km west of Bomizabo on the road to Bouaké.

SGBCI bank on Av Houphouët-Boigny has a 24-hour Visa-card-friendly ATM that will dispense CFA on demand.

Cyber Café Ivillage (☎ 30 64 39 88) on Av Houphouët-Boigny charges CFA1500 per hour, has a good Internet connection and is open 8am to 10pm daily.

The Cash Ivoire supermarket on Av Houphouët-Boigny in Habitat is well stocked. For medicines, Pharmacie de Yamoussoukro on Av Houphouët-Boigny in Habitat carries a wide range of products.

Basilique de Notre Dame de la Paix

One of the country's most astonishing sites is the basilica *(Route de Daloa; admission CFA2000, lift to the cupola CFA2000; open 8am-5pm Mon-Sat, 11.30am-5pm Sun)*. On the city's northwest fringe, the entrance to the lacquered aluminium leviathan is on the south side.

Don't forget to take your passport, which the uniformed guard holds until you leave. See the boxed text 'Yamoussoukro's Amazing Basilica' for more details.

Institut National Polytechnique

The institute consists of three colleges: the Institut National Supérieur de l'Enseignement Technique (Inset) trains applied scientists, the École Nationale Supérieure des Travaux Publics (ENSTP) engineers and the École Normale Supérieure Agronomique (ENMSA) agricultural specialists. Each building is a jewel of contemporary architecture. The tourist office can arrange guided visits.

Presidential Palace

Houphouët-Boigny's massive palace complex, where he is now buried, can be seen only from beyond its 5km perimeter wall. The lake on its southern side is home to a

YAMOUSSOUKRO

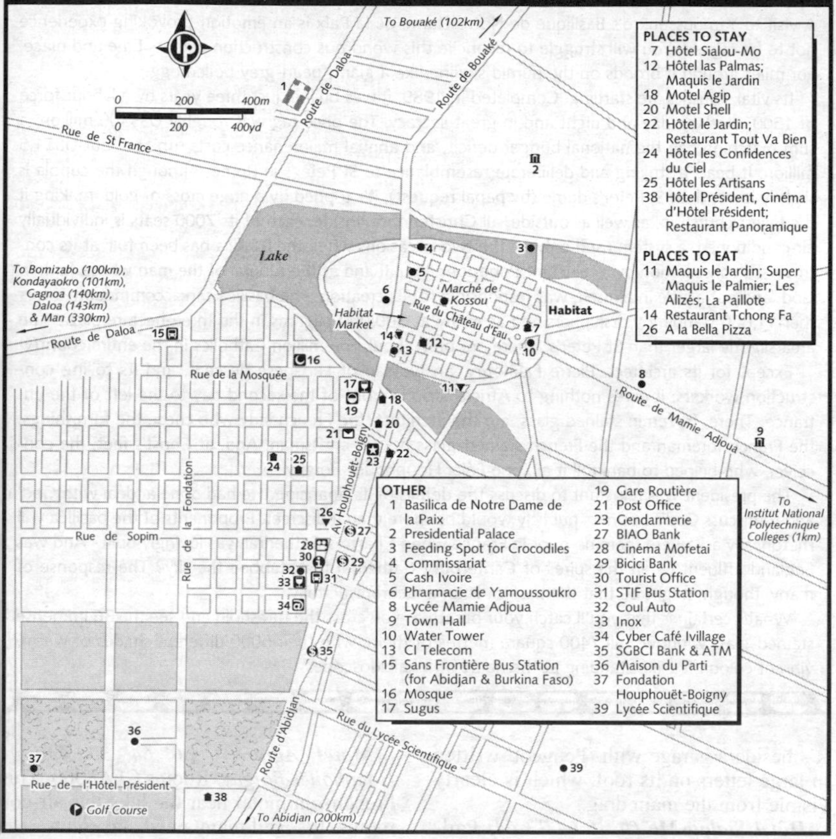

To Bouaké (102km)
0 200 400m
0 200 400yd
Route de Daloa
Route de Bouaké
Rue de St France
Lake
To Bomizabo (100km), Kondayaokro (101km), Gagnoa (140km), Daloa (143km) & Man (330km)
Route de Daloa
Rue de la Mosquée
Marché de Kossou
Habitat Market
Rue du Château d'Eau
Habitat
Route de Mamie Adjoua
Av Houphouët-Boigny
Rue de Sopim
Rue de la Fondation
Route d'Abidjan
Rue du Lycée Scientifique
Rue de l'Hôtel Président
Golf Course
To Abidjan (200km)
To Institut National Polytechnique Colleges (1km)
PLACES TO STAY
7 Hôtel Sialou-Mo
12 Hôtel las Palmas; Maquis le Jardin
18 Motel Agip
20 Motel Shell
22 Hôtel le Jardin; Restaurant Tout Va Bien
24 Hôtel les Confidences du Ciel
25 Hôtel les Artisans
38 Hôtel Président, Cinéma d'Hôtel Président; Restaurant Panoramique
PLACES TO EAT
11 Maquis le Jardin; Super Maquis le Palmier; Les Alizés; La Paillote
14 Restaurant Tchong Fa
26 A la Bella Pizza
OTHER
1 Basilica de Notre Dame de la Paix
2 Presidential Palace
3 Feeding Spot for Crocodiles
4 Commissariat
5 Cash Ivoire
6 Pharmacie de Yamoussoukro
8 Lycée Mamie Adjoua
9 Town Hall
10 Water Tower
13 CI Telecom
15 Sans Frontière Bus Station (for Abidjan & Burkina Faso)
16 Mosque
17 Sugus
19 Gare Routière
21 Post Office
23 Gendarmerie
27 BIAO Bank
28 Cinéma Mofetai
29 Bicici Bank
30 Tourist Office
31 STIF Bus Station
32 Coul Auto
33 Inox
34 Cyber Café Ivillage
35 SGBCI Bank & ATM
36 Maison du Parti
37 Fondation Houphouët-Boigny
39 Lycée Scientifique

dozen or more languid crocodiles, which supposedly lend protection. Every day around 5pm the guardian tosses them some 15kg of meat. Formerly, they gorged themselves on sacrifices of live chickens, but that practice has ceased in deference to tourists' sensibilities.

Fondation Houphouët-Boigny

The Fondation Houphouët-Boigny building *(Rue de l'Hôtel Président)*, on the southern side of town, was constructed as the headquarters of the largesse-distributing association established by the former president. On the weekend you can tour the foundation, an impressive four-storey structure with several auditoriums (including one with a capacity of 4500), huge air-con public spaces and marble floors. All it lacks is people. Nearby, the **Maison du Parti**, the old headquarters of the country's first political party, the PDCI, is closed to the public.

Places to Stay – Budget

Hôtel les Confidences du Ciel *(☎ 30 64 11 04)* Rooms with fan/air-con CFA2500/3500. The cheapest option, a few blocks south of the mosque, is now a brothel. Grubby rooms with fan and shower are cramped, but there are also larger, cleaner air-con rooms. The restaurant isn't always open.

Hôtel les Artisans *(☎ 30 64 02 27)* Rooms with bathroom & fan/air-con CFA4500/6000. Two blocks north of Rue de Sopim, and near the Confidences du Ciel, this hotel has spacious, clean rooms.

Yamoussoukro's Amazing Basilica

A visit to Yamoussoukro's Basilique de Notre Dame de la Paix is an emotion-provoking experience not to be missed. You will struggle to reconcile this wondrous construction with its time and place. For miles around it broods on the humid skyline like a giant, pearl-grey boiled egg.

Its vital statistics are startling. Completed in 1989, it was built in just three years by a labour force of 1500, working day and night and in great secrecy. The price tag was roughly US$300 million, a sum matching half the national budget deficit, and annual maintenance costs run at about US$1.5 million. It bears a striking and deliberate resemblance to St Peter's in Rome. Although the cupola is slightly lower than St Peter's dome (by papal request), it's topped by a huge cross of gold, making it the tallest church in, as well as outside, all Christendom. Inside, each of its 7000 seats is individually air-conditioned, a system used only on the two occasions when the basilica has been full: at its controversial consecration by a reluctant Pope John Paul II and at the funeral of the man whose faith in God, and not a little in himself, was responsible for its creation. The basilica can accommodate a further 11,000 standing worshippers and as many as 300,000 pilgrims in the three-hectare plaza – an area slightly larger than St Peter's. There are only about one million Catholics in the entire country!

Except for its architect, Pierre Fakhoury, an Ivoirian of Lebanese descent, and its toiling construction workers, it owes nothing to Africa. Stop in front of the second bay to the left of the entrance. There, frozen in stained glass, are the architect, the French lady who chose the furnishings, the French foreman and the French stained-glass master craftsman. And, at Christ's feet, the conceiver, who helped to bankroll it all, one Félix Houphouët-Boigny.

The president was reluctant to discuss the details of its financing. He had done a 'deal with God' and to discuss God's business publicly would be more than indiscreet. Proponents of the basilica will rhetorically ask, were there no poor in France when Chartres Cathedral was lovingly built? And was England affluent when the spires of Canterbury Cathedral first stabbed the sky? The response of many, though, might be that the basilica is an anachronistic folly.

What's certain is that you'll catch your breath as you cross the threshold and see the 36 immense stained-glass windows, all 7400 square metres of them, with their 5000 different shades of warm, vibrant colour. It's like standing at the heart of a kaleidoscope.

It's beside a garage with 'Peugeot' written in large letters on its roof, which is clearly visible from the main drag.

Hôtel Sialou-Mo *(☎ 36 64 13 64)* Paillotes CFA5000. The new Sialou-Mo (which means 'thanks, mother' in Baoulé), in the lively Habitat quarter, near the water tower, has attractive paillotes with fan and bathroom. They're the same price as the undistinguished, shower-only rooms in the main block. Like an African village in the suburbs, this is the fun place to stay.

Hôtel las Palmas *(☎ 30 64 02 73)* Rooms with fan CFA4000-5000, air-con rooms CFA6000. This small hotel, south of Rue du Château d'Eau, is clean and well located. It does, however, double as a brothel.

Places to Stay – Mid-Range & Top End

Rooms at all the mid-range hotels have bathroom and air-con. Several are clustered near the gare routière.

Motel Agip *(☎ 30 64 30 43, Av Houphouët-Boigny)* Rooms CFA8000. This French-run motel near the lake has air-con rooms. It's well maintained and clean.

Motel Shell *(☎ 30 64 11 27, Av Houphouët-Boigny)* Rooms CFA15,000. The Motel Shell, run by two brothers from Lyon, has attractive rooms, a bar that's popular with French expats, a sumptuous, if rather pricey restaurant and, in the garden, a veritable minizoo.

Hôtel le Jardin *(☎ 36 64 38 51, fax 36 64 34 39)* Singles/doubles CFA12,000/15,000. The relatively new Jardin, near the gendarmerie, has large rooms with big bathrooms (with bath!), new furniture and satellite TV. It's especially good value.

Hôtel Président *(☎ 30 64 15 82, fax 30 64 05 77, Route d'Abidjan)* Singles/doubles CFA31,000/36,000, superior luxury rooms CFA60,000. This place, to the east of the golf course, is the town's finest. It's now a member of the InterContinental hotel chain.

Places to Eat

African During the day, several shacks with ***street food*** around the Marché de Kossou on Rue du Château d'Eau in Habitat sell dishes such as sauce graine for CFA600 a plate. There's also an abundance of stalls near the gare routière, serving mostly snack food and brochettes. Yamoussoukro has some brilliant maquis.

Maquis le Jardin *(☎ 36 64 14 22)* Meals CFA2500-4500. This maquis, opposite Hôtel las Palmas, is upmarket and popular with well-heeled Ivoirians. It's more expensive than most, but the quality justifies the price.

Down by the lake's edge on the south side of Habitat, maquis cluster one beside another and several have pleasant terraces overlooking the water. There's no great difference between menus and prices. Ones which we and other travellers have enjoyed include, from west to east, the lakeside terrace at ***Maquis le Jardin*** (offering the same menu as its namesake but without the muzak), ***Super Maquis le Palmier***, ***Les Alizés*** and ***La Paillote***.

Other Cuisines The enticing and unpretentious ***Restaurant Tchong Fa*** *(☎ 36 64 27 43, Av Houphouët-Boigny)*, south of the Habitat market, has a wide selection of Chinese dishes at reasonable prices. It does takeaways, which you can order by phone.

Restaurant Tout Va Bien *(☎ 30 64 38 19)* Meals CFA4000-5000. This popular place near the gendarmerie is French run, and has paillotes and a great ambience. *Crevette sauce provençale* (prawns) is CFA3800.

A la Bella Pizza *(☎ 30 64 06 12, Cnr Av Houphouët-Boigny & Rue de Sopim)* Pizzas CFA2600-4200. Open Tues-Sun. French-owned A la Bella Pizza serves great pizzas. It's very popular with expats. You can also organise tours to the Reserve de Fauna D'Abokouamikro here.

Restaurant Panoramique *(☎ 30 64 15 82, Route d'Abidjan)* Meals CFA3500-6000. At Hôtel Président, the Panoramique, with its magnificent wraparound views, is great for a drink or meal.

Entertainment

Bars & Nightclubs At night, the liveliest area of town is around Rue du Château d'Eau in Habitat, where several modest bars blare out funky music.

Sugus *(☎ 30 64 02 91, Av Houphouët-Boigny)* Admission CFA2000. Open from 8pm daily. Appended to Hôtel le Bonheur II, this place starts jumping early.

Inox *(☎ 05 69 03 02, Av Houphouët-Boigny)* Admission CFA5000. Open nightly. This very classy nightclub, about to open when we visited, has yet to prove itself.

Cinema Recent releases are shown at the ***Cinéma d'Hôtel Président*** *(☎ 30 64 15 82, Route d'Abidjan)* at 6.30pm and 9pm nightly for CFA1500.

Cinéma Mofetai *(Av Houphouët-Boigny)* Admission CFA1000. This place also has recent releases, but it's more convenient, more downmarket and cheaper. Films are shown 4pm, 6.30pm and 9pm daily.

Getting There & Away

Onward travel in all directions is, in principle, easy from Yamoussoukro, which is a transport hub. However, many buses roll through full. Nevertheless, with a little patience you'll be on your way. Most transport leaves from the main gare routière (which is basically the first 100m of Av Houphouët-Boigny south of the lake), except Sans Frontière buses, which run to Abidjan and Burkina Faso and have their own station beside the Route de Daloa, and buses of the STIF company, which has its station near the tourist office on Av Houphouët-Boigny.

Day or night, buses leave for Abidjan (CFA2500, 3½ hours), Bouaké (CFA2000, 1½ hours), Korhogo and Ferké (CFA4000, six hours), Danané and Man (CFA4000, five hours) and San Pédro (CFA4500, seven hours). Bush taxis are about the same price.

Buses to Burkina Faso run via Bobo-Dioulasso (CFA15,000, 12 hours) to Ouagadougou (CFA17,000, 24 hours).

Buses to Mali leave from Motel Agip, at the main gare routière, and go via Sikasso (CFA8000, 18 hours) to Bamako (CFA12,000, 30 hours). Buses to Niamey (Niger; CFA25,000, four days) also leave from here.

Getting Around

A seat in a shared taxi is CFA125, even as far as the Institut National Polytechnique, although you'll have to pay more to get to the basilica in its splendid isolation. They're difficult to find after 9.30pm. By the hour, private taxis cost about CFA3000.

Coul Auto (☎ 30 64 38 91), opposite the tourist office, charges CFA30,000 per day for a car and driver (you pay for the fuel). A 4WD is CFA45,000 per day.

PARC NATIONAL DE LA MARAHOUÉ

There are several trails and four viewing towers in this park, 80km west of Yamoussoukro *(Park director in Bouaflé ☎ 30 68 93 73, fax 30 68 90 90; adult/child CFA3000/1500 per day, compulsory guides CFA3000; open year-round).* About one-quarter of the park's 1010 sq km is savanna woodland and the rest is dense forest. At the Marahoué River (also known as the Bandama Rouge), about 20km from the main entrance, you can hire a canoe or kayak and the chances of seeing hippos are good.

Baboons, too, are fairly plentiful and you may see some of the shy smaller forest elephants, of which there are about 25. Other animals include monkeys, chimpanzees, buffaloes, waterbucks, hartebeests and various kinds of antelope. Nearly 300 bird species have been recorded here, as well as more than 150 different plants and trees.

Though the park's open year-round, access is often cut during the rainy season. You can walk around freely. At the time of writing there was no longer accommodation available in the park. For the latest information, ask at Motel Shell in Yamoussoukro. Tours can be arranged at the Post de Gard in Goazra.

Getting There & Away

If you have transport, head west from Yamoussoukro on the road to Daloa. At Goazra, about 25km west of Bouaflé, take the well-signed dirt road leading north, which brings you to the park entrance after 7km. Alternatively, take any bus or bush taxi going towards Daloa and ask to be dropped off in Goazra, and then walk or hitch the remaining kilometres.

RESERVE DE FAUNA D'ABOKOUAMIKRO

In this park *(adult/child CFA2000/1000 per day, guides CFA3000 per day; open year-round),* 40km east of Yamoussoukro, there are rhinos, elephants, buffaloes, antelopes, monkeys and a variety of bird species. It comprises 15,000 hectares but, unfortunately, there is no longer any accommodation here.

To get here, take a minibus to Gofabo, nearby. Alternatively, day tours (CFA30,000 per group, including 4WD transport, admission and guide fees) can be arranged at A la Bella Pizza (☎ 30 64 05 81) in the town of Yamoussoukro.

BOUAKÉ

In the heart of Baoulé country, Bouaké, some 100km north of Yamoussoukro, is the country's second-largest city with a population of around half a million. Its numbers increased dramatically in the early 1970s when villagers, dispossessed of their lands by the waters from the giant Kossou Dam, headed for the big city.

Le Carnaval de Bouaké, one of Africa's largest carnivals, is held here in March. It's a celebration of friendship and life. Apart from that and Bouaké's extensive market, so many travellers give the city a cursory look and pass on. Bouaké sprawls, but the tree-lined and very pleasant Quartier du Commerce and the Koko district, where the Baoulé are concentrated, can be covered on foot. For more information about the Baoulé, see the special section 'Peoples of the Region'.

Orientation & Information

The main north-south highway is Av Houphouët-Boigny, in the centre of which is the Rond-point du Grand Marché. Southwest of the roundabout is the affluent Quartier du Commerce, while the much poorer Koko quarter is to the west. Wherever you are, you can use the tall telecommunications tower of the post office as a landmark.

Centre Voyages (☎ 31 63 13 52), on Av Gabriel Dadié, near Pâtisserie le Palmiers, is the city's top travel agency.

The SGBIC bank, on Av Gabriel Dadié, has an ATM that gives up CFA to Visa-card holders.

You can make international phone calls from the CI Telecom centre, near the train station.

We found ourselves well connected at Cyber Café S@H (☎ 31 64 00 23) on La Route de Carnival. It charges CFA35 per minute. There are cheaper places near the SGBCI bank, but the lines tend to drop out at inopportune times.

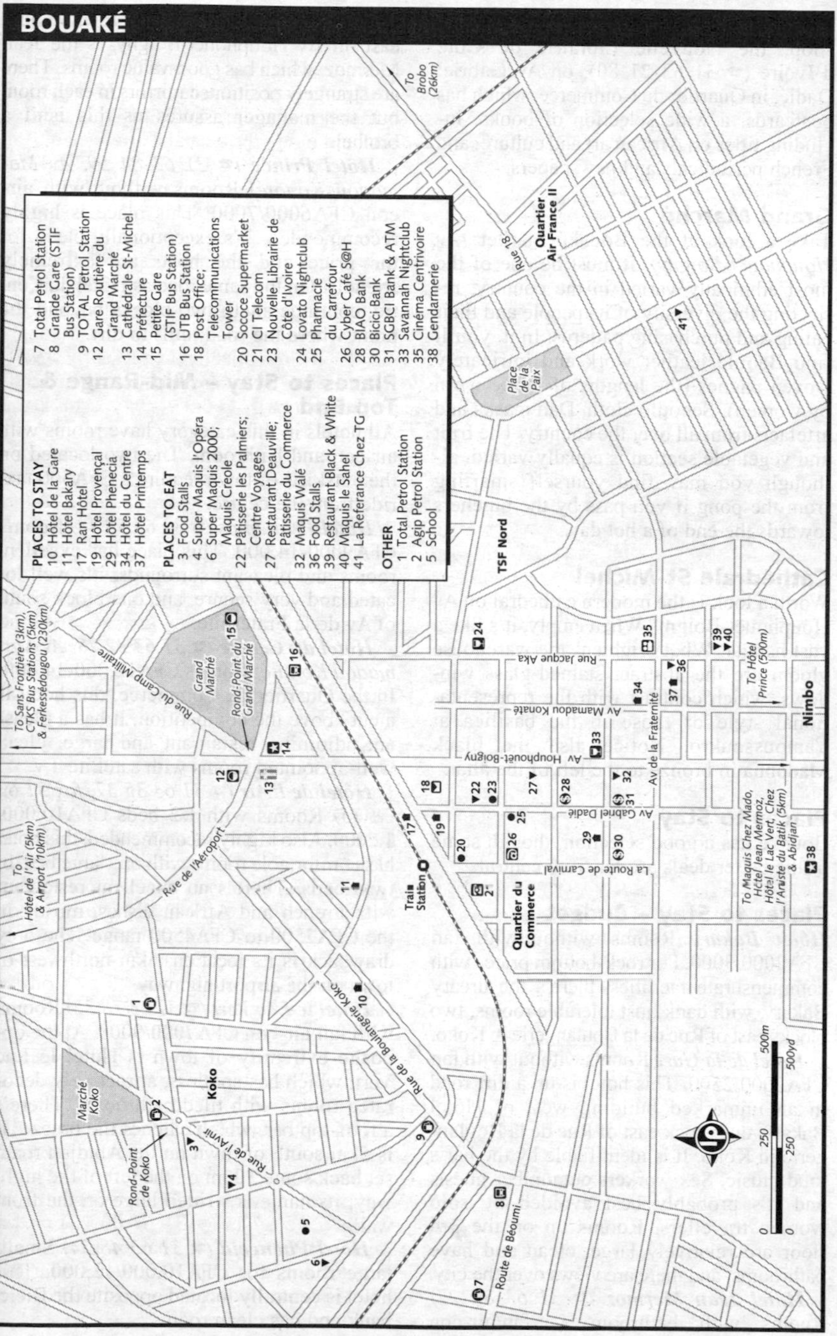
BOUAKÉ
PLACES TO STAY
10 Hôtel de la Gare
11 Hôtel Bakary
17 Ran Hôtel
19 Hôtel Provençal
29 Hôtel Phenecia
34 Hôtel du Centre
37 Hôtel Printemps
PLACES TO EAT
3 Food Stalls
4 Super Maquis l'Opéra
6 Super Maquis 2000; Maquis Creole
22 Pâtisserie les Palmiers; Centre Voyages
27 Restaurant Deauville; Pâtisserie du Commerce
32 Maquis Walé
36 Food Stalls
39 Restaurant Black & White
40 Maquis le Sahel
41 La Referance Chez TG
OTHER
1 Total Petrol Station
2 Agip Petrol Station
5 School
7 Total Petrol Station
8 Grande Gare (STIF Bus Station)
9 TOTAL Petrol Station
12 Gare Routière du Grand Marché
13 Cathédrale St-Michel
14 Préfecture
15 Petite Gare (STIF Bus Station)
16 UTB Bus Station
18 Post Office; Telecommunications Tower
20 Sococe Supermarket
21 CI Telecom
23 Nouvelle Librairie de Côte d'Ivoire
24 Lovato Nightclub
25 Pharmacie du Carrefour
26 Cyber Café S@H
28 BIAO Bank
30 Bicici Bank
31 SGBCI Bank & ATM
33 Savannah Nightclub
35 Cinéma Centrivoire
38 Gendarmerie
To Sans Frontière (3km), CTKS Bus Stations (5km) & Ferkessédougou (230km)
To Hôtel de l'Air (5km) & Airport (10km)
To Brobo (26km)
Rue du Camp Militaire
Grand Marché
Rond-Point du Grand Marché
Rue de l'Aéroport
Train Station
Marché Koko
Koko
Rond-Point de Koko
Rue de l'Avnir
Rue de la Boulangerie Koko
Route de Béoumi
Quartier du Commerce
TSF Nord
Place de la Paix
Quartier Air France II
Rue 18
Rue Jacque Aka
Av Mamadou Konaté
Av Houphouët-Boigny
Av Gabriel Dadié
Av de la Fraternité
La Route de Carnival
To Hôtel Prince (500m)
To Maquis Chez Mado, Hôtel Jean Mermoz, Hôtel le Lac Vert, Chez l'Artiste du Batik (5km) & Abidjan
Nimbo
0 250 500m
0 250 500yd

Bouaké has a particularly good bookshop, the Nouvelle Librairie de Côte d'Ivoire (☎ 31 63 21 80), on Av Gabriel Dadié, in Quartier du Commerce, which has postcards, a wide selection of books, including titles on African art and culture, and French periodicals and newspapers.

Grand Marché

Take a look at the Bouaké market *(Av Houphouët-Boigny)*. It must be one of the most ethnically varied in the country, reflecting the diversity of its people and their eating and purchasing patterns. In it, you'll find Baoulé leather work and intricately woven pagnes (the lengths of fabric worn by women), Senoufo cloth, Dan masks and artefacts from all over the country. The fruit and vegetable section is equally varied, although you may find yourself smarting from the pong if you pass by the butchers towards the end of a hot day.

Cathédrale St-Michel

Worth a look is the modern cathedral on Av Houphouët-Boigny. When empty, it's like a vast hangar. What brightens the warehouse gloom are the abstract stained-glass windows, which contrast with the representational style of those in the basilica at Yamoussoukro. Notice also the black Madonna in bronze to the left of the altar.

Places to Stay

Bouaké has a good selection, though some of the better deals are far from central.

Places to Stay – Budget

Hôtel Bakary Rooms without/with fan CFA2000/3000. For rock-bottom prices with commensurate facilities, there's the dreary Bakary, with dank, just tolerable rooms, two blocks east of Rue de la Boulangerie in Koko.

Hôtel de la Gare Rooms without/with fan CFA2000/2500. This hotel is up a dirt road in an unmarked building west of Hôtel Bakary, one block east of Rue de la Boulangerie in Koko. It is identifiable by the bar's loud music. Sex workers outnumber guests and it's probably best avoided by solo women travellers. Rooms up on the 3rd floor are relatively large, clean and have bathrooms, and there are views over the city.

Hôtel Jean Mermoz *(☎ 31 63 80 27)* Rooms with bathroom & fan/air-con CFA4000/7000. South of the town centre, east off Av Houphouët-Boigny, is the Jean Mermoz, which has good-value rooms. There are strangely positioned mirrors in each room but the manager assures us this isn't a brothel.

Hôtel Prince *(☎ 31 63 84 59, Av Mamadou Konaté)* Rooms without/with air-con CFA6000/7000. This place is highly recommended. It's exceptionally clean for the price and the hosts are extremely friendly. On the same road as Hôtel du Centre, continue south two blocks beyond the point where the road turns to dirt.

Places to Stay – Mid-Range & Top End

All hotels in this category have rooms with air-con and bathroom. The two located on the outskirts of town require a CFA500 taxi ride from the centre.

Hôtel Printemps *(☎ 31 63 58 13)* Rooms CFA9000-14,000. This place has excellent rooms and pleasant surrounds; it's well located and very secure, and one block south of Av de la Fraternité.

Hôtel du Centre *(☎ 31 63 32 78, Av Mamadou Konaté)* Rooms CFA12,000-14,000. In the Quartier du Commerce, this hotel is a cut above the competition. It has a pleasant adjoining restaurant and large, clean well-appointed rooms with satellite TV.

Hôtel de l'Air *(☎ 31 63 35 37, fax 31 63 28 15)* Rooms with 1/2 beds CFA10,000/12,000. Also highly recommended, this hotel has comfortable rooms with one large bed, or twin beds. There's an excellent restaurant with French and African dishes, mostly in the CFA2500 to CFA4500 range. The only drawback is its location, 5km northwest of town on the airport highway.

Hôtel le Lac Vert *(☎ 31 63 78 32)* Rooms with fan/air-con CFA7000/9000. At the opposite extremity of town is Hôtel le Lac Vert, which has spotless, attractively decorated rooms with tiled bathrooms. There's a roof-top bar, which catches the breeze. It is 5km south of town on the Abidjan road set back some 300m on the left of the highway; its name is written large on the front wall.

Hôtel Phenecia *(☎ 31 63 48 34)* Small/large rooms for CFA10,000/12,000. This hotel is centrally located opposite the Bicic bank and has clean rooms.

Hôtel Provençal *(☎ 31 63 34 91, Av Gabriel Dadié)* Singles/doubles CFA8500/10,500. Don't be deterred by the Provençal's dowdy exterior and tunnel-like corridors. The rooms, all with tiled bathroom and a balcony overlooking the street, opposite the post office, are surprisingly pleasant.

Ran Hôtel *(☎ 31 63 20 16, fax 31 63 40 32, e sipf-rhb@afrcaonline.co.ic, Route de Béoumi)* Doubles with shower/bath CFA23,000/25,000. The large, rather characterless Ran, beside the train station, has rooms with bathroom, satellite TV, and there's a large pool.

Places to Eat

African The area around the gare routière and market abounds with cheap, simple stalls. There are also ***food stalls*** in Koko, near the Agip petrol station and near the Cinéma Centrivoire.

In the Koko district, animated, rowdy maquis selling standard sauces are plentiful. Fill up for under CFA1000 at ***Super Maquis l'Opéra***, ***Super Maquis 2000*** or ***Maquis Creole***.

Maquis le Sahel *(☎ 31 62 38 59, Rue Jacque Aka)* Meals CFA1000-2500. This popular maquis in the Quartier du Commerce is a cut above the rest. Open for lunch and dinner, it charges CFA2500 for a whole grilled chicken with attiéké.

Maquis Walé *(☎ 31 63 41 46, Av Houphouët-Boigny)* Meals CFA4500. This maquis is a friendly, value-for-money place with a pleasant street-side terrace. The food and service are impressive.

La Referance Chez TG *(☎ 31 63 42 28, Quartier Air France II)* Meals CFA4000. This place has shady paillotes and is very popular. Food ranges from hedgehog and antelope to fish and chicken. The service is very good.

Other Cuisines For Chinese-Vietnamese food, ***Restaurant Deauville*** *(31 63 19 95, Av Houphouët-Boigny)* in Quartier du Commerce is reasonably priced (most dishes around CFA2000), despite its relatively luxurious ambience. Sit with your back to the window; their flashing neon sign is a veritable Chinese torture.

Near Maquis le Sahel, ***Restaurant Black & White*** *(☎ 31 63 14 68, Av Jacque Aka)* has both an air-con dining room and a small, intimate outdoor thatched area. The French menu is varied and ambitious. The house speciality is *confit d'agouti* (CFA6000) a type of antelope served with glazed fruit. There are crepes (CFA800 to CFA1800) and, for vegetarians, *soupe au pistou* (vegetable soup with basil; CFA2200). There's also pizza (CFA3000 to CFA4000).

A pleasant spot for breakfast or morning coffee is the ***Pâtisserie du Commerce*** *(☎ 07 80 69 41, Av Houphouët-Boigny)*. There are also sandwiches and Lebanese food. Croissants cost CFA200.

Pâtisserie les Palmiers *(☎ 31 31 63 98 37, Av Gabriel Dadié)* Croissants CFA250. This French-run place is unbeatable for French pastries and gateaux. It also does inexpensive ham baguettes and a first-rate quiche (CFA750/850/1300 according to size). The coffee here is exceptional and you can also lick your way through some delicious ice cream.

Entertainment

The street-side terraces of ***Hôtel Provençal*** and ***Hôtel Phenecia*** are pleasant for a drink. For earthier African bars, head for Koko, which has several.

Savannah Nightclub *(☎ 31 63 37 30, Av Houphouët-Boigny)* Admission CFA2000 on weekends. Open from 10pm daily. This nightclub has three dancing *pistes* (floors).

Lovato Nightclub *(☎ 31 63 08 58, Rue Jacque Aka)* Admission free. Open from 9pm daily. Look for the laser show in the night sky. Quite laid back, this place has chic but friendly staff.

Shopping

Chez l'Artiste du Batik Open daily. This small and well-marked concrete cube, about 5km from the centre on the road to Abidjan, is a good place for buying quality batik. Mamadou Diarra, a gentle Malian artist, has four photo albums full of his designs, which he'll make to order. Prices vary according to the complexity and originality of the design and the number of colours applied. Simple pieces start at around CFA1500.

Getting There & Away

Bus & Bush Taxi Most buses and bush taxis leave from Gare Routière du Grand Marché. UTB runs more than 15 buses a day to/from Abidjan from its own station south of the market. It also has three services a day for San Pédro and Man. STIF runs five buses to Abidjan via Yamoussoukro, which you can pick up at either its grande gare, west of the centre, or petite gare at the Grand Marché. It also has a daily bus to Danané via Man and three to Daloa via Yamoussoukro.

CTKS has four buses a day to Ferkessédougou and Korhogo, leaving from its station about 5km north of Rond-point du Grand Marché. Sans Frontière has a minimum of one departure a day for Burkina Faso. Its station is also on Av Houphouët-Boigny, about 3km north of the roundabout.

Standard fares are Abidjan CFA4000 (five hours), Yamoussoukro CFA2000 (1½ hours), Korhogo CFA4500 (10 hours), Ferké CFA3000 (four to five hours), Man CFA5000 (seven hours), Daloa CFA3000 (3½ hours), Danané CFA5500 (6½ hours) and San Pédro CFA6000 (eight hours). Peugeot taxis serve the same routes and charge the same.

Train The train for Abidjan, coming from Ouagadougou in Burkina Faso, calls in at Bouaké on Tuesday, Thursday and Saturday evening, or possibly early the next morning (1st/2nd class CFA6600/5400, five hours). Heading north for Ferké departures are on the same days (CFA5000/4000, four hours).

TANOU-SAKASSOU

Some 12km east of Bouaké on the road to Brobo, Tanou-Sakassou is one of several villages in the Bouaké area where the women specialise in pottery making.

The village is on the left and marked by a small artisans' cooperative sign. The pottery sculptures made here, in the form of animals or female heads, are very fine. You can buy a good example for around CFA2500. Take a minibus from Gare Routière du Grand Marché in Bouaké (CFA500, 30 minutes).

KATIOLA

About 55km north of Bouaké on the highway to Ferké, Katiola is the take-off point for the southern entrance to Parc National de la Comoë some 170km to the east. It has a huge pottery cooperative on the eastern outskirts. The pottery, heavily glazed and of tourist quality, is less interesting than seeing the women at work (for a fee) as they fashion perfectly symmetrical jugs without the aid of a pottery wheel.

Just off the highway, ***Hôtel de l'Amitié*** *(☎ 31 66 04 91)* is nothing to write home about, but it is reasonable value for money with rooms costing around CFA3000.

Hôtel Hambol *(☎ 31 66 05 25)*, on the north side of town, has more inspiring rooms with air-con for CFA9500 and there's a bar, restaurant, pool and nightclub.

The North

KORHOGO

A nine-hour bus ride north from Abidjan, Korhogo, dating from the 13th century, is the capital of the Senoufo, who are best known for their woodcarvings and cloth – coarse raw cotton, like burlap, with painted or woven designs (for more details, see the boxed text 'Korhogo Cloth' later in this chapter). They're also renowned for their skilled blacksmiths *(forgerons)* and potters *(potiers)*. (For more details on Senoufo art and culture, see the boxed texts 'Art of Côte d'Ivoire' in Facts about Côte d'Ivoire earlier this chapter, and 'The Lô Association' on the next page.) Korhogo is therefore a popular destination for travellers; not so much for the town itself, but as a base for visiting the nearby artisans' villages for which you'll need your own or hired transport. The heart of town is the bustling market, near which are the major bus company offices.

Despite advertising AmEx travellers cheques at their exchange desks, Korhogo's banks will not cash travellers cheques. The SGBCI bank has an ATM that miraculously pops out CFA for holders of solvent Visa accounts. You may have problems opening its security door; if so wait with the lizards sunning themselves on the wall, for a local user to open it with their standard bank account card. Euros are changeable at the Bicici bank for a 0.5% commission. If you have US dollars you will have to wait until Abidjan.

The helpful tourist office, the Délégation Régionale de Tourisme (☎ 36 86 05 84), is some 500m southwest of Place de la Paix. It can arrange Senoufou dance performances (see Around Korhogo for details).

There are many guides around town, some of whom are very competent. If someone offers their services, ask to see their *carte professionnelle de guide*, proof that they're recognised by the délégation and have completed its training course. French-speaking John Nagnama (contactable through Hôtel Chigata on ☎ 36 86 20 46) is recommended. A trip to his home village is a fascinating experience.

Musée Régionale Péléforo Gbon Coulibaly

The town's only museum is the small Musée Régionale Péléforo Gbon Coulibaly *(Av Coulibaly; admission by donation; open 8.30am-noon & 3pm-6pm Tues-Sat)*. It was the home of the famous Senoufo chief, Péléforo Gbon Coulibaly, until his death in 1962. Abandoned until 1987, it reopened as a repository for traditional Senoufo crafts in 1992. It has some interesting old photographs, chiefs' chairs, Korhogo cloth and fine wooden statues and masks. Donations are accepted – 'thanks for your gift', the box cheerily announces in English. In its grounds, visit the old man who fashions wax mask models, makes moulds from these out of termite-mound *banco* and then casts bronze at his little makeshift foundry.

Quartier des Sculpteurs

Most of the city's woodcarvers live and work in this small district. At its heart is the **Maison des Feticheurs**, three blocks north of the mosque, a small building dating from 1901 (for a price, the old man who guards this place may agree to let you see the fetishes inside). In the vicinity, you'll find woodcarvers at work, all keen to show you around their storerooms.

The Lô Association

The secret Lô association of the Senoufo, which is divided into the Poro cult for boys and the Sakrobundu cult for girls, is essentially a way of preparing children for adulthood. The goal is to preserve the group's folklore, teach children about their tribal customs so that they can take over the various social duties of the community and, through various rigorous tests, enable them to gain self-control. Their education is divided into three seven-year periods ending with an initiation ceremony involving circumcision, isolation, instruction and the use of masks. Each community has a 'sacred forest' where the training takes place. Many of the rituals involve masked dances; the uninitiated are never allowed to see them or the tests that the young people must undergo. However, some ritual ceremonies, such as the dance of the leopard men, occur in the village itself when the boys return from one of their training sessions, and these are open to all.

Places to Stay

Accommodation in Korhogo is among the country's best in terms of value for money, making an extended stay a good option.

Places to Stay – Budget

Hôtel Gon *(☎ 36 86 06 70)* Rooms with shared bathroom & without/with fan CFA2000/2500. One block east of the museum, the stark, two-storey Gon hasn't quite gone yet. Its bare rooms are quite tolerable – for the price.

Hôtel le Pélerin *(☎ 36 86 33 65, Route de Ferkessédougou)* Singles/doubles with fans & showers CFA2000/2500. This hotel next to the market has very worn rooms. However, it's dirt cheap, handy to the bus station and the staff are very friendly.

Mission Catholique *(☎ 36 86 03 31, Off Av Coulibaly)* Rooms without/with air-con CFA4000/5000. Accommodation at the friendly Catholic mission, east of the post office, is excellent value. Trim rooms have mosquito net and shower. However, it's often full so book ahead. The place is also worth a visit for its wacky, ultramodern open-air church.

Places to Stay – Mid-Range

Rooms in these hotels have bathroom and air-con unless stated otherwise.

Hôtel Chigata *(☎ 36 86 20 46, East of Route de Ferkessédougou)* Singles/doubles CFA8000/11,000, doubles with fan CFA6500. This is by far and away the best deal in town. The rooms are immaculate and cheery, the staff are attentive and there's a good restaurant in this new, French-run place. Highly recommended.

Hôtel Pacific *(☎ 36 86 00 85, Northwest of Route de Ferkessédougou)* Singles/doubles CFA7000/9000. Hot on the heels of the Chigata, the Pacific is a new pile in Petit Paris. Its rooms are also immaculate and there's an upstairs restaurant. The drawback is the location.

Motel Agip *(☎ 36 86 01 13, Route de Ferkessédougou)* Rooms CFA10,000. The

KORHOGO
To Natiokobadao (500m), Lataha (10km), Sinématiali (30km) & Ferkessédougou (53km)
To Koni (17km) & M'Bengue (75km)
0 200 400m
0 200 400yd
Petit Paris
Koko Nord
Servil Kaha
Quartier des Sculpteurs
To Kasoumbarga (23km), Boundiali (98km) & Odienné (230km)
Route de Boundiali
Route de Koni
Route de Ferkessédougou
Av Coulibaly
Market
Koro Sud
Dem
To Boundiali
Place de la Paix
Quartier Sinistre
Residential
Route de Sirasso
Route de Dikodougou
Route de l'Aéroport
To Waranienié (4km), Kanioraba (50km) & Sirasso (68km)
To Torgokaha (7km), Katia (10km), Napié (19km), Farkaha (35km) & Dikodougou (59km)
To Karakoro (19km)
PLACES TO STAY
1 Hôtel Pacific
2 Hôtel Kadjona
4 Hôtel Chigata
5 Hôtel le Vert Paradis
8 Motel Agip
9 Hôtel le Pélerin
20 Hôtel Gon
22 Mission Catholique
24 Hôtel Mont Korhogo; Le Poro Nightclub
32 Hôtel la Rose Blanche
PLACES TO EAT
6 Maquis l'Escale
18 Maquis le Katana
21 Chez Mousso
34 Chez Donald
35 La Bonne Cuisine
OTHER
3 Maison du Coulibaly Kassoum
7 Gare Routière (Ferké & Bouakè)
10 Gare Routière (Boundiali & Odienne)
11 Maison des Feticheurs
12 Mosque
13 Cinema
14 BIAO Bank
15 SGBCI Bank & ATM
16 TCK Bus Station
17 Pharmacie du Nord
19 Musée Régional Péléforo Gbon Coulibaly; Maquis les Lianes
23 Bicici Bank
25 Post Office; Postal Van to Odienné
26 CI Telecom
27 Commissariat
28 Centre Artisanal
29 Préfecture
30 Town Hall
31 Municipal Pool
33 Délégation Régionale de Tourisme

drab, French-run Agip is not the bargain it once was. However, the bar is homely and attractive and the garden restaurant has the best French cuisine in town.

Hôtel le Vert Paradis *(☎ 36 86 10 36, West of Route de Ferkessédougou)* Singles/doubles without air-con CFA3500/4000, with air-con CFA7500/8000. This central place has clean, reasonable rooms.

Hôtel la Rose Blanche *(☎ 36 86 06 13, North of Route de Sirasso)* Small singles/doubles CFA7500/9000, larger singles/doubles CFA10,000/13,000. The large rooms at the relaxing Rose Blanche have TV and carpets. It also has a decent restaurant.

Hôtel Kadjona *(☎ 36 86 20 87, Route de Ferkessédougou)* Singles/doubles CFA8500/11,000. The sprawling Kadjona has an endless supply of worn but clean rooms with TV. There's a large empty pool and a restaurant with an ambitious French menu. Kadjona is a forgotten, '80s time warp, but its tranquil grounds somehow make it endearing.

Hôtel Mont Korhogo *(☎ 36 86 02 93, fax 36 86 04 07, Blvd Houphouët-Boigny)* Singles/doubles CFA14,000/16,000. Most tour groups stay here in the city's top hotel. Within its extensive, well-maintained grounds, there's a pool (CFA800 for nonguests) and an excellent, if soulless restaurant.

Places to Eat

La Bonne Cuisine *(☎ 36 86 10 73)* Meals CFA1000-2500. This place, in the Quartier Sinistre east of Place de la Paix, serves top-notch sauce dishes. At night it becomes a maquis serving grilled chicken for CFA2500 and grilled fish for CFA1500 to CFA2000, according to size. Patron Mdme Marie likes a hearty laugh and the beers are very cold. La Bonne is warmly recommended.

Other maquis to try, all serving much the same African meals for less than CFA1000, include ***Maquis le Katana*** and ***Maquis les Lianes*** on either side of the museum. ***Chez Mousso***, an easy stroll east if you're staying at the Mission Catholique, has a breezy paillote, while ***Maquis l'Escale*** is convenient for guests at Hotel le Vert Paradis.

Chez Donald This is the place for chawarmas CFA700, steak and chips (CFA2000) and baby pizzas (CFA300). Tasty, safe ice cream is also available here. It is east of Place de la Paix.

Motel Agip *(☎ 36 86 01 13, Route de Ferkessédougou)* Set meal CFA4000. By far the best French restaurant in town, for both food and ambience, can be found at this motel. It offers a great three-course set meal plus à la carte dining.

Hôtel Mont Korhogo *(☎ 36 86 02 93, fax 36 86 04 07, Blvd Houphouët-Boigny)* Tourist menu CFA4200. The restaurant at this hotel does a three-course tourist menu in addition to its ambitious range of French dishes. Although the food's decent enough, the place is short on atmosphere and you may find yourself the only diner in its spacious dining room. The hotel's ***Le Poro Nightclub*** *(first drink CFA3000)* is active from 10pm nightly.

Shopping

Centre Artisanal *(Maison de l'Union des GVC d'Artisans du Nord)* Open 8am-noon & 2.30pm-6pm daily. This place west of Place de la Paix, on the road to Boundiali, stocks fine-quality Korhogo cloth plus Senoufo carvings, pottery and bronze castings of less merit. Prices are reasonable and fixed. It's an excellent place to start your shopping or simply to browse and get a feel for what to look for in the market and in the nearby artisans' villages.

Getting There & Away

Bus & Minibus TCK runs about four services a day between Korhogo and Abidjan (CFA4500, eight to 10 hours). To save a day of your life and a night's accommodation, muster some courage and take the evening bus. If you arrive before dawn, you can continue sleeping on board. All buses make a stop in Bouaké (CFA2500, five hours) and Yamoussoukro (CFA4000, six hours).

To Odienné, the best way to go is with the battered, windowless postal van (CFA4000, five hours), which leaves from the post office around 6.30am daily except Sunday.

Minibuses, by contrast, take an eternity to fill up. They run from the gare routière northeast of Motel Agip to Bouaké (CFA3000, four hours) and Ferkessédougou (CFA1200, one hour) and from west of the market to Boundiali (CFA2000, 1½ hours).

Getting Around

A seat in a shared taxi costs CFA125. You'll have trouble finding one after 10pm and, if you do, you'll have to pay more. By the hour, you should be able to get one for around CFA3000.

The tourist office can arrange car hire (CFA25,000 per day plus fuel) and provide an English-speaking guide (CFA10,000 per day). Alternatively, if you speak French, call Watara Salif (☎ 05 08 50 26). His grandson will take you on trips out of town, including to Parc National de la Comoë (CFA20,000 per day, plus fuel).

AROUND KORHOGO

The villages around Korhogo, where you can see artisans at work, are well accustomed to tourists and prices are generally no lower than in town. Main villages of interest are Waraniéné for weavers *(tisserands)* and dancing, Natiokobadao for dancing, Farkaha for painted Korhogo cloth, Lataha for dancing, Sinématiali and Kanioraba for potters, Koni and Kasoumbarga for blacksmiths (for more information about Senoufo blacksmiths, see the special section 'Peoples of the Region'), Niofouin for traditional Senoufo architecture and Torgokaha for basket makers *(vanniers)*. See following for more details on these places.

Dances can be arranged through the tourist office in Korhogo for around CFA25,000. Organising a performance independently involves speaking to the village chief, and may reduce the cost.

Without a vehicle, it's difficult to see all but the nearest villages. Negotiate a price that's exclusive of petrol; otherwise, the

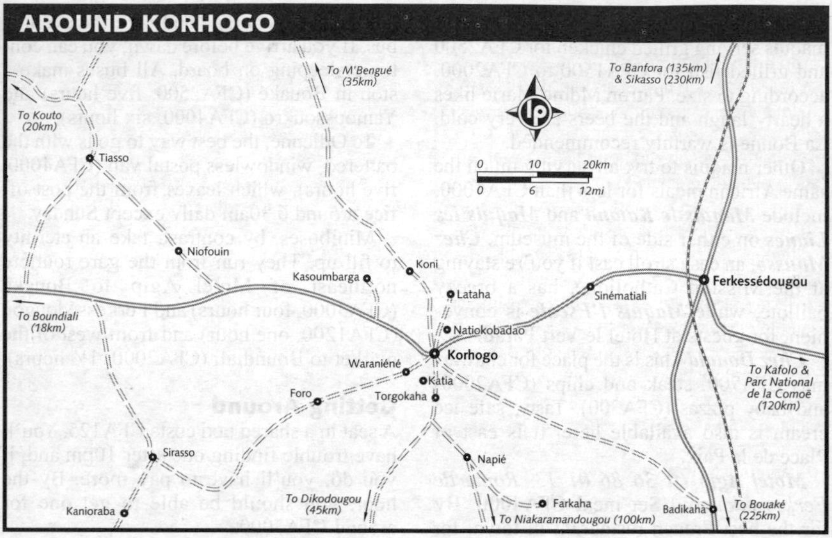
AROUND KORHOGO
To M'Bengué (35km)
To Banfora (135km) & Sikasso (230km)
To Kouto (20km)
Tiasso
0 10 20km
0 6 12mi
Niofouin
Koni
Kasoumbarga
Ferkessédougou
Sinématiali
Lataha
To Boundiali (18km)
Natiokobadao
Korhogo
Waraniéné
To Kafolo & Parc National de la Comoé (120km)
Katia
Foro
Torgokaha
Sirasso
Napié
To Dikodougou (45km)
Farkaha
Badikaha
To Bouaké (225km)
Kanioraba
To Niakaramandougou (100km)

driver will balk at every small detour. It's well worth investing in a guide, even if you have your own vehicle, for their knowledge, to avoid getting lost and to parry the sometimes overinsistent villagers. John, a guide based at Hôtel Chigata, can arrange tours on Peugeot mopeds (CFA4000 a day for hire, CFA14,500 per day guide's fee).

Waraniéné

The most touristy village is Waraniéné, in part because it's only 4km southwest of Korhogo on the route to Sirasso. As in all Dioula communities, men weave while the women spin and spool the threads. Look for the yarn strung out across a 500m-wide compound. The weavers' cooperative there has set prices, which are considerably less than those in Abidjan. Finished products include tablecloths (CFA6500) and smocks (CFA8000). You can also arrange to see a *boleye* (initiation dance) here, either independently or through the Korhogo tourist office.

Farkaha

The sleepy town of Farkaha, 35km southeast of Korhogo, makes most of the top-quality Korhogo cloth. As in Waraniéné, there's a cooperative, where bargaining is possible. To get here, take the old airport road to Napié (19km) and fork left for Farkaha, 16km further. At Katia, about halfway between Korhogo and Napié, several shops specialise in Korhogo cloth.

Sinématiali & Kanioraba

For pottery, head east for Sinématiali (30km on the tar road to Ferkessédougou) or, better still, southwest to Kanioraba (50km) via Sirasso. Although more difficult to reach, Kanioraba is a village of traditional round houses, while Sinématiali, once similar, now has ugly modern structures with metallic roofs.

Koni

At Koni, 17km northwest of Korhogo on the dirt road to M'Bengué, Senoufo blacksmiths make agricultural implements. If you're very lucky, you might see parts of the entire process in one visit: from mining the ore, by lowering men down shafts up to 20m deep, to smelting the iron and forging tools. Note that Senoufo smiths don't work on Friday.

Natiokobadao

On the northern outskirts of Korhogo, you can arrange to see a boleye, either independently or through the Korhogo tourist office.

Kasoumbarga

Kasoumbarga, 23km west of Korhogo, is another blacksmith centre. It also has a ruined

Korhogo Cloth

You'll find Korhogo cloth in all of Côte d'Ivoire's major hotels as bedspreads, wall hangings, napkins and tablecloths. It's easy to recognise the coarse, cream-coloured cotton with either woven geometrical designs or fantastical painted animals.

Its production illustrates the symbiotic relationship between two neighbouring, but very different, peoples. The Senoufo, animist and agriculturist, grow the cotton, which they sell in its raw form to the Dioula, who are Muslims and traditionally weavers and traders.

The Dioula women spin the cotton, which their menfolk weave into long strips. Being Muslim, they eschew anything figurative or representational, so they either weave in a variety of geometrical shapes or produce plain, unadorned cloth – which they sell back to the Senoufo.

Traditionally, the Senoufo painted this cloth for their hunters and dancers and for young people undergoing initiation. Nowadays, it's very much for the tourist trade but the technique remains the same and the dyes – brown, black and burnt red – are still made from natural, local products.

Brown is the base colour, brewed from the fermented leaves of the nangenmé tree. For black, maize (corn) or millet cobs are left to ferment. When the transparent liquid that trickles off is daubed over the brown base, it becomes black. The juice for the burnt-red colour comes from fermented sorghum stalks and is applied directly to the cream cloth. To complete the cycle, the Senoufo sell the finished dyed cloth back to the Dioula, who are also merchants.

Although some artisans have now moved to town, all weaving is traditionally done in the village of Waraniéné, 4km from Korhogo, while the dyes are applied in Farkaha, 35km to the southeast.

17th-century mosque, unusual in that it's round with a thatched roof. Take the tar Boundiali road for 14km then turn right (north). Kasoumbarga is 9km further.

Lataha

About 10km north of Korhogo, Lataha is another place to see a boleye, either independently or through the Korhogo tourist office.

Torgokaha

Torgokaha is 7km south of Korhogo on the road to Dikodougou and is noted for its basket and mat weavers.

NIOFOUIN

Around 60km west of Korhogo, Niofouin is interesting for its traditional Senoufo housing. Many of the mud-walled buildings with thick, straw roofs are in good condition. While some of the older structures may not be in perfect shape, they are less altered by incongruous modern features – such as metal roofs – than those of other villages. With its accentuated conical roof and decorated walls, the central fetish house is particularly interesting. The chief will require CFA500 for a tour.

Auberge Villageoise *(☎ 36 86 59 08)* This place is set in an attractive campement, north of the highway on the eastern side of town. The paillotes (CFA3000) have nets and fans and are great value.

Minibuses run to and from Korhogo (CFA1500, one hour) five times daily. With your own vehicle, take the Boundiali road west out of Korhogo for 45km then go right (northwest) on a dirt road for another 12km.

BOUNDIALI

Some 98km west of Korhogo, this Senoufo town in the heart of the country's cotton belt has a good market, and is a handy point of departure for visiting traditional Senoufo villages to see artisans at work.

Places to Stay & Eat

Hôtel Record *(☎ 36 86 04 36)* Rooms with bathroom & fan/air-con CFA3000/4500. This hotel situated near the market has relatively clean rooms.

Hôtel Dalaba *(☎ 36 86 50 54)* Paillotes with bathroom & fan/air-con CFA6000/8000. All paillotes at this hotel, south of the Shell petrol station, are in a pleasant garden.

Standard sauces are available at ***Maquis de l'Indenie*** on Av Jean-Baptiste-Mockey, ***Café/Restaurant Mama***, opposite the Shell petrol station, or ***Restaurant le Carrefour de la Paix***, diagonally opposite the Total petrol station.

Getting There & Away

Bush taxis and minibuses leave from the gare routière for Korhogo (CFA2000, 1½ hours) and, less regularly, Odienné (CFA3000, four hours). You may also find space on the postal vans, which pass through town in the late morning, for both destinations.

KOUTO & AROUND

Around 30km north of Boundiali, Kouto has a beautiful 17th-century mosque in the Sudanese style, with ancient banco walls. Inside there is a narrow stairway that leads onto the roof. The mosque is in a tranquil garden surrounded by lemon and other trees.

Accommodation is pretty rough at ***Hôtel Ma Cachet*** *(☎ 36 86 76 04)*, 500m northwest of the market. Rooms with fan/air-con cost CFA2500/5000.

En route to Kouto from Boundiali, you'll pass **Kolia**, a pottery crafts centre. Kolia and Boundiali are noted centres for blacksmiths, and you can watch them hauling the iron-rich earth from deep vertical shafts and washing it in the river before smelting.

Minibuses to Kouto run to and from Korhogo (CFA2500, 1½ hours) and Boundiali (CFA1000, 45 minutes).

ODIENNÉ

Odienné is in Malinké country and is predominantly Muslim. Historically, it's famous for its strong support for Samory Touré, the tenacious resistance fighter against the French. Take your bearings from the central roundabout and the four roads sprouting from it. The road north goes to Hôtel Kaoka, Hôtel Romani and Lake Savané. The post office is on the short southern spur, which ends at the police station. Off this are Maquis le Yancadi and the Campement. Along Bamako Rd, heading west, you'll find Restaurant les Étoiles and the Minhotel. Eastwards, the road heads towards Boundiali and Korhogo.

Near the large mosque is the **grave of Vakaba Tourié**, the Malinké warrior who founded the city.

Today, most of the town's traditional houses have been replaced by unattractive modern buildings. However, the setting in a valley, 12km east of the 800m-high **Massif du Dinguélé**, is attractive. You could hire a taxi (CFA15,000) to the foot of the mountain and do a half-day (return trip) hike to the summit, from where the view's spectacular.

At the Minhotel, you can get information about, and just possibly arrange a tour of, the nearby Zievasso and Diougoro **gold mines**.

At **Samatiguila**, 38km north, there's a well-preserved 17th-century **mosque**. The adjoining **museum** has a small display of weapons from the time of Samory Touré. According to local legend, he called by the mosque to pray before sacking the town. However, upon rising to his feet, he was incapable of finding his way out. Eventually, the imam of the mosque led him to the exit, against the solemn promise of Samory Touré that he'd spare the town.

Places to Stay

Campement Rooms with shower CFA3000, with bathroom & fan/air-con CFA4000/5000. The Campement, opposite Maquis le Yancadi, has gloomy, spartan rooms.

Hôtel Kaoka Singles/doubles CFA3000-4000. This place, 500m north of the roundabout, is distinctly superior to all the others.

Minhotel *(☎ 33 70 82 83)* Rooms CFA12,000-14,000. Single/double bungalows with air-con & bathroom CFA9000/10,000. Once the star of Odienné, Minhotel, 1km west of town, is beginning to slip. It has a pool (CFA1000 for nonguests).

Hôtel Romani *(☎/fax 33 70 05 06)* Rooms CFA9000-11,000. The Romani, 4km beyond the roundabout, beside the artificial Lake Savané, is an odd experience. You may be the only guest at this massive complex – apart, that is, from the geese, horses and strutting peacocks. Rooms have air-con and bathroom.

Places to Eat

There are several ***stalls*** selling street food on the north side of the roundabout and on either side of the road leading westward from it. On the southwest corner is the unsigned ***Chez Barry***, run by three friendly brothers and good for omelettes and simple snacks. Of the few maquis in town, ***Le Yancadi***, 300m southwest of the post office, and ***Les Etoiles***, about 1km west on the Bamako road, are popular with locals.

Minhotel has the best restaurant in town, offering mainly French cuisine. The menu of the day is CFA3500 and main dishes are between CFA1900 and CFA4000.

Getting There & Away

Buses and bush taxis all leave from the roundabout. Both EDT and Fecti have a daily run to Abidjan (CFA8000, 15 hours) via Man (CFA4000, five hours) and Yamoussoukro (CFA6000, 10 hours). The most reliable way of travelling to both Korhogo and Man is with the postal van, which leaves the post office around 6.30am daily except Sunday for each town. Either way, the trip costs CFA4000 and takes five to six hours.

For Manankoro and the Malian frontier there are up to four minibuses a day (CFA2500, two hours). For the Guinean border, the route is via Minignan (CFA1500, 1½ hours), Bougoula, Mandiana and Kankan. The crossing via Sirana to Beyla should only be considered by those with their own 4WD.

FERKESSÉDOUGOU

Ferké, 231km north of Bouaké, is a crossroads town where the route north, from Abidjan to both Mali and Burkina Faso, intersects with the east to west route, between Korhogo and Parc National de la Comoë. Should you overnight in transit, there's a good cluster of maquis and dance venues (active at weekends) near the Maquis la Primature and a large Thursday market. Ferké has one of the best hospitals in the country, run by Baptist missionaries, attracting patients from as far away as Ouagadougou and Bamako.

The town is essentially one long stem with side-shoots. The busiest area is the market and the roads bordering it to the west.

Places to Stay

Hôtel Koffikro *(☎ 07 66 93 86)* Singles without fan/with fan/with bathroom & air-con CFA2500/3000/5000, doubles without fan/with fan/with bathroom & air-con CFA3000/3500/5500. The Koffikro, two blocks west of the market, with its mosquito-netted windows and quiet compound, is one of the best budget options. The air-con rooms with bathroom are superior.

Hôtel la Paillote *(☎ 05 02 52 99)* Paillotes without/with fan CFA2000/2500. The paillotes here, west of the gendarmerie, built of brick and mortar not traditional materials, are by no means in their prime. However, the friendly staff, the verdant garden and the price make this a good budget option.

There are four comfortable but still very reasonable hotels off the Bouaké road, about 2km south of the market.

Hôtel la Muraille I *(☎ 07 98 45 64)* Rooms with bathroom & fan/air-con CFA2000/4500. This place, just west of the water tower, is a convivial-enough budget option. The clean rooms have an armchair or sofa. There's also a small restaurant.

Auberge de la Réserve *(☎ 36 86 82 62, Route de Bouaké)* Rooms with fan/air-con & TV CFA4500/6500. This sprawling hotel offers reasonable value for money and the restaurant is decent, with most dishes in the CFA1700 to CFA2500 range.

Hôtel la Pivoine *(☎ 36 88 03 90)* Rooms with air-con CFA8000. Here, south of the water tower, rooms have tiled floors. There's an overpriced restaurant. A relaxing 1st-floor terrace bar catches the evening breeze.

Hôtel Aguiè Koanin *(☎ 36 86 83 75, East of the water tower)* Rooms CFA7000. The Aguiè Koanin, also with bar and restaurant, is two blocks further east on a dirt road. The rooms are clean and well presented.

Places to Eat

In the cluster of places around Maquis la Primature, you can eat, drink and, at weekends, dance and be merry. ***Maquis la Primature*** *(☎ 36 86 86 34, Route de Bobo)* and its neighbour ***La Savane*** *(☎ 36 86 85 33, Route de Bobo)* serve standard maquis fare in a pleasant ambience. At the former, you can get a litre of ice-cold beer for CFA475.

Super Maquis le CFA Dishes CFA1000-3500. This maquis, a block away opposite the Agip petrol station, has a single large paillote and is earthier. The selections include braised fish/chicken for CFA1200/ 2500 and a whole chicken kedjenou for CFA3500.

La Bonne Auberge Pizzas CFA2000-4000. The pizzas here, north of Gare de Nord, are quite tasty.

Maquis Arc en Ciel *(☎ 05 62 19 46)* Meals CFA2000-4000. This oasis of calm is a great place to unwind after exploring the market. Chicken kedjenou is CFA3500.

Entertainment

Tribunal *(☎ 07 69 93 44)* Cover charge CFA1000. Open 8pm-6am nightly. The Tribunal, west of Route de Bobo, is especially lively at weekends.

Le Métro Cover charge free. The new and currently fashionable Métro is west of Route de Bobo, opposite Maquis la Primature, and open until late daily.

Le Phénix Cover charge CFA1000 Thur, CFA2000 Fri & Sat. West of the water

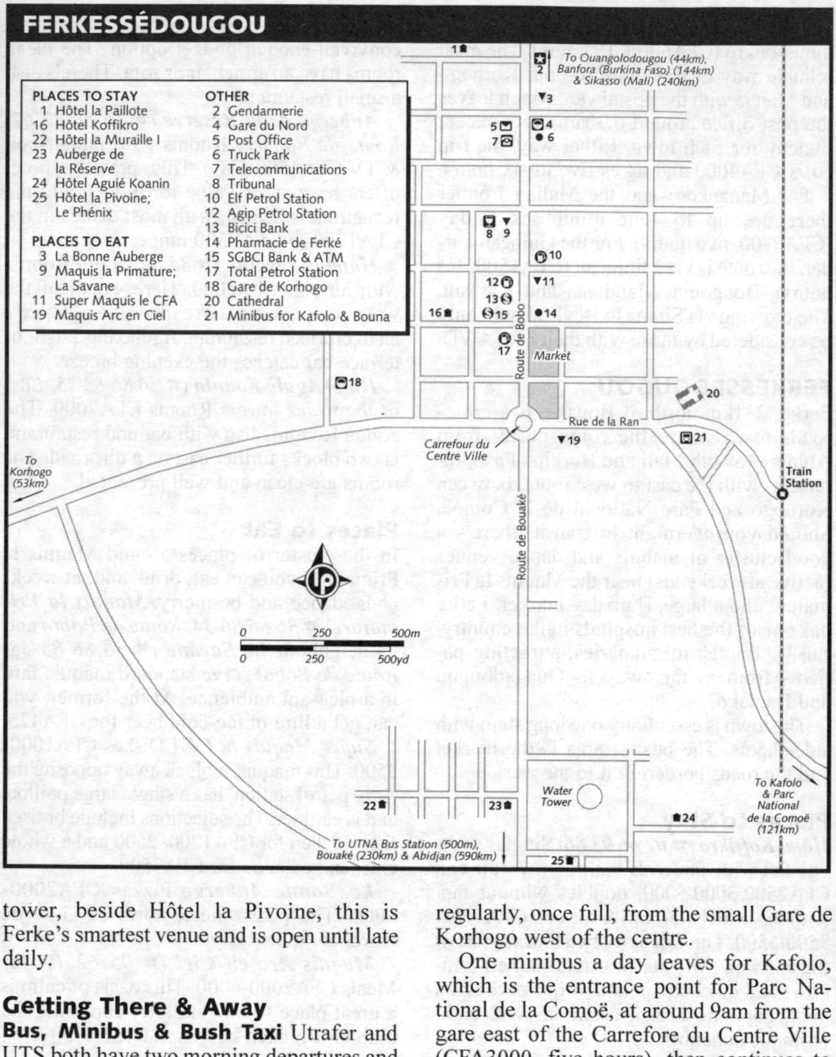
FERKESSÉDOUGOU
PLACES TO STAY
1 Hôtel la Paillote
16 Hôtel Koffikro
22 Hôtel la Muraille I
23 Auberge de la Réserve
24 Hôtel Aguié Koanin
25 Hôtel la Pivoine; Le Phénix
PLACES TO EAT
3 La Bonne Auberge
9 Maquis la Primature; La Savane
11 Super Maquis le CFA
19 Maquis Arc en Ciel
OTHER
2 Gendarmerie
4 Gare du Nord
5 Post Office
6 Truck Park
7 Telecommunications
8 Tribunal
10 Elf Petrol Station
12 Agip Petrol Station
13 Bicici Bank
14 Pharmacie de Ferké
15 SGBCI Bank & ATM
17 Total Petrol Station
18 Gare de Korhogo
20 Cathedral
21 Minibus for Kafolo & Bouna
To Ouangolodougou (44km), Banfora (Burkina Faso) (144km) & Sikasso (Mali) (240km)
Route de Bobo
Market
Rue de la Ran
Carrefour du Centre Ville
To Korhogo (53km)
Train Station
Route de Bouaké
0 250 500m
0 250 500yd
Water Tower
To Kafolo & Parc National de la Comoë (121km)
To UTNA Bus Station (500m), Bouaké (230km) & Abidjan (590km)

tower, beside Hôtel la Pivoine, this is Ferke's smartest venue and is open until late daily.

Getting There & Away

Bus, Minibus & Bush Taxi Utrafer and UTS both have two morning departures and one evening departure for Abidjan. These leave from Gare du Nord. UTNA has three morning departures from its bus station south of the water tower. All stop at Bouaké (CFA3000, five hours) Yamoussoukro (CFA4000, six hours), where you can pick up a connection to Man or San Pédro, before arriving in Abidjan (CFA5000, nine hours).

There are several minibuses a day to Korhogo (CFA1200, one hour), which leave irregularly, once full, from the small Gare de Korhogo west of the centre.

One minibus a day leaves for Kafolo, which is the entrance point for Parc National de la Comoë, at around 9am from the gare east of the Carrefore du Centre Ville (CFA3000, five hours), then continues to Ouango (CFA4000, nine hours) and Bouna (CFA7500, 12 hours).

Vehicles for Burkina Faso and Mali leave from Gare du Nord. To Burkina Faso, there are both bush taxis and buses to Bobo-Dioulasso (CFA9000, around eight hours) and Ouagadougou (CFA15,000, around 20 hours).

To Mali, there are buses and taxis to Sikasso (CFA5000, around 17 hours) and all the way to Bamako (CFA9000, around 30 hours).

Train From either Ouagadougou and Abidjan, trains are scheduled to arrive at about 8.30pm on Tuesday, Thursday and Saturday, but they're frequently about two hours late. Heading south, the 1st-/2nd-class fare is CFA5000/4000 to Bouaké (four hours) and CFA11,600/9400 to Abidjan (nine hours).

BOUNA

Bouna is a good base for visiting the nearby villages of the Lobi people, who are noted for their unique adobe architecture. Compounds, called *soukala*, are castle-like structures with inner courtyards. The most attractive soukala can be found at **Pélando**, a small village 18km northeast of Bouna, reachable only during the dry season.

In Bouna, you can stay at ***Hôtel Eléphant*** (about CFA3500 a room) or the small ***bar*** (around CFA2500) across the street. If you're heading for Ghana, you need to stop at customs in town. A bush taxi to the border with Ghana at the Black Volta River costs CFA750 and takes 1½ hours. There's a standard fee for crossing the river. For more details see Land in the main Getting There & Away section earlier in this chapter.

One minibus a day leaves Ferké at around 9am for Bouna (CFA7500, 12 hours) via Kafolo (CFA3000, five hours), which is the entrance point for Parc National de la Comoë, and Ouango (CFA4000, nine hours).

KONG

Kong, west of Parc National de la Comoë and 34km south of the road between Ferké and Kafolo, is an old Dioula village dating from the 12th century. Its Sahel architecture and flat-roofed buildings are reminiscent of Mali. Much of the town was razed in the late 19th century by Samory Touré during a battle with the French. The most impressive building standing today is the banco **Friday Mosque** with protruding wooden beams. Built originally in the 17th century, but restored after Samory's rampage and again more recently, it is very beautiful to behold. You'll also find an old Quranic school and traditional mud houses with roof terraces.

Kong's only hotel is the ***Auberge Villageoise*** *(☎ 36 86 85 55)*, 500m west of the market, where rooms with fan are CFA2500. Digs here are clean and excellent value at this price. Across the street ***Restaurant Pardon*** has good African fare.

Minibuses run once a day to Ferké (CFA1700, three to four hours).

PARC NATIONAL DE LA COMOË

Commanding 11,500 sq km, the largest wildlife reserve in West Africa is the Parc National de la Comoë *(admission CFA3000; open 15 Dec–30 May)*. It has several entry points: the most widely used are Kafolo (also called Petit Ferké) in the northwest, and Gansé and Kakpin in the south.

Sadly, it's no place for the budget traveller. While there's public transport to Kafolo, the southern entrances are not well served. Accommodation is expensive and, because walking in the park is prohibited out of respect for the lions, without private transport you're dependent on someone taking you on board.

A ride through the park takes you through savanna, forest and grassland. One of the most popular tracks broadly follows the Comoë River, which runs from Kafolo to Gansé. The whole trip, with frequent stops along the way, takes a full day. In the dry season, most of the wildlife is in this middle to western section of the park, where there's more water.

Lions, though, tend to be more abundant in the southern section, particularly in an area 30km north of Kakpin bounded by the Comoë River and the Iringou River.

There's a good chance of seeing elephants, of which there are an estimated 100 in the park. Other animals include pigs, green monkeys, hippos, Anubis baboons, black and white colobus monkeys, and many kinds of antelope including waterbucks, kobs and roans. Leopards also exist, but are rarely seen. Birds, on the other hand, are abundant. More than 400 species have been recorded here and one reader reported spotting 130 different types in three days.

Comoë Safari Lodge has vehicles that head out in the early morning and mid-afternoon, if there are enough clients. The cost for a full-day safari in a 4WD is CFA18,000 per person for a minimum of three.

Try to leave time for a pirogue trip on the Comoë River, interesting for both the scenery and the hippos. Comoë Safari Lodge offers this service for about CFA8000. Villagers won't do it for less, in fear of undercutting the chief's hotel trade.

PARC NATIONAL DE LA COMOË

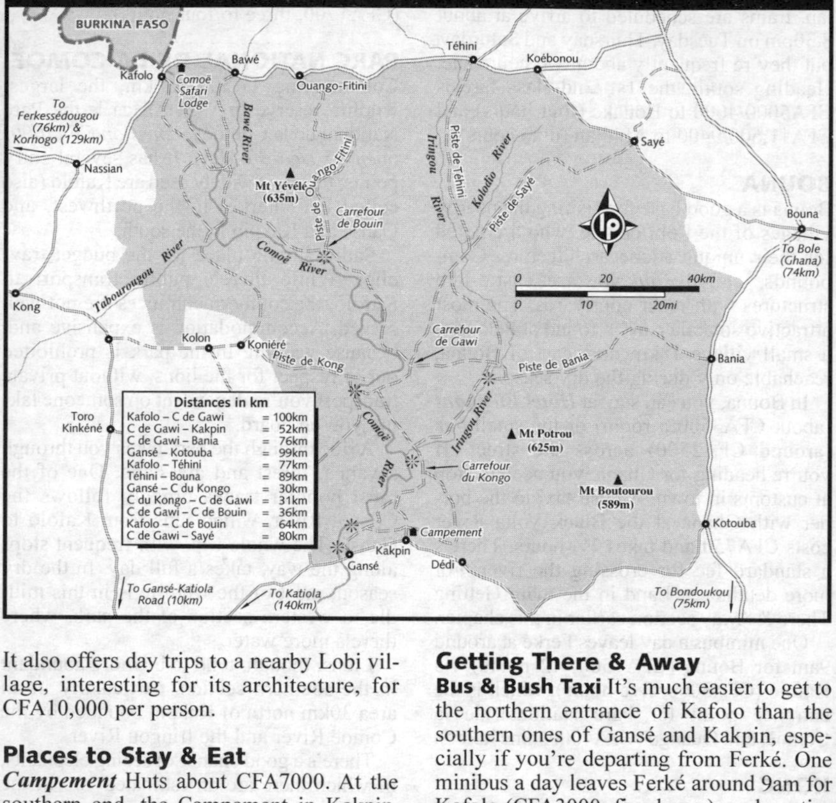
BURKINA FASO
Kafolo
Comoë Safari Lodge
Bawé
Ouango-Fitini
Téhini
Koébonou
To Ferkessédougou (76km) & Korhogo (129km)
Nassian
Bawé River
Piste de Ouango-Fitini
Mt Yévélé (635m)
Carrefour de Bouin
Piste de Téhini
Iringou River
Kolodio River
Sayé
Piste de Sayé
Bouna
To Bole (Ghana) (74km)
0 20 40km
0 10 20mi
Tabourougou River
Comoë River
Kong
Kolon
Konieré
Piste de Kong
Carrefour de Gawi
Piste de Bania
Bania
Distances in km
Kafolo – C de Gawi = 100km
C de Gawi – Kakpin = 52km
C de Gawi – Bania = 76km
Gansé – Kotouba = 99km
Kafolo – Téhini = 77km
Téhini – Bouna = 89km
Gansé – C du Kongo = 30km
C du Kongo – C de Gawi = 31km
C de Gawi – C de Bouin = 36km
Kafolo – C de Bouin = 64km
C de Gawi – Sayé = 80km
Toro Kinkéné
Iringou River
Mt Potrou (625m)
Carrefour du Kongo
Mt Boutourou (589m)
Kotouba
Campement
Kakpin
Gansé
Dédi
To Gansé-Katiola Road (10km)
To Katiola (140km)
To Bondoukou (75km)

It also offers day trips to a nearby Lobi village, interesting for its architecture, for CFA10,000 per person.

Places to Stay & Eat

Campement Huts about CFA7000. At the southern end, the Campement in Kakpin, 15km east of Gansé, has 17 traditional huts with bathroom but no air-con, and a thatched-roof bar-restaurant with very basic food such as spaghetti and tinned tomato sauce.

Comoë Safari Lodge *(in Abidjan ☎ 22 44 41 18, fax 22 44 13 91, ⓔ notroux@africaonline.co.ci)* Singles/doubles/triples with fan CFA17,000/21,000/25,000, singles/doubles/triples with air-con CFA22,500/26,000/31,500; an extra CFA8000 per person for half-board, CFA16,000 per person for full-board. The somewhat tired, 40-bungalow lodge is at the northern entrance near Kafolo. There's a pool and a collection of fenced animals.

Getting There & Away

Bus & Bush Taxi It's much easier to get to the northern entrance of Kafolo than the southern ones of Gansé and Kakpin, especially if you're departing from Ferké. One minibus a day leaves Ferké around 9am for Kafolo (CFA3000, five hours), and continues on to Bouna (CFA7500, 12 hours). The Katiola to Gansé route is not well travelled and finding a vehicle in Katiola is difficult.

Alternatively, hire a whole taxi in Korhogo (see Getting Around under Korhogo earlier in this chapter for details).

Car Driving from Abidjan takes about 10 and 12 hours to the southern and northern entrances, respectively. The turn-off points are Katiola (407km from Abidjan) for Gansé (160km further) and the southern entrance, and Ferkessédougou (584km from Abidjan) for Kafolo (121km) and the northern entrance. From either turn-off, it's jarring washboard roads the rest of the way.

The Gambia

Sunshine, warm weather and long golden beaches have long made Gambia a favourite getaway for Europeans, especially during winter. But to say Gambia is just sun and surf is a mistake. With minimal effort, and not much more time, you can flee the European- flavoured resorts that proliferate along the coast and take a good look at African-style wrestling matches, explore wildlife reserves, or climb through the ruins of long-abandoned slaving stations on the Gambia River. From an ornithological point of view, Gambia is blessed with so many species of birds in such a compact area that even those who struggle to identify a pigeon can't fail to be impressed. Its size, people and language make Gambia an ideal introduction to the region, and the choice of food, lodging and cheap flights from Europe is outstanding.

Just a note on nomenclature: you'll see the country referred to both as just 'Gambia' and 'The Gambia'. Although The Gambia's official name always includes 'The', this is often omitted in everyday usage. In this book we have usually omitted 'The' for the sake of simplicity and readability.

The Gambia at a Glance

Capital: Banjul
Population: 1.4 million
Area: 11,295 sq km
Head of State: President Yahya Jammeh
Official language: English
Main local languages: Mandinka, Wolof, Fula
Currency: dalasi (D)
Exchange rate: US$1 = D18.50
Time: GMT/UTC
Country telephone code: ☎ 220
Best time to go: December to February (best weather), May to October (fewer tourists)

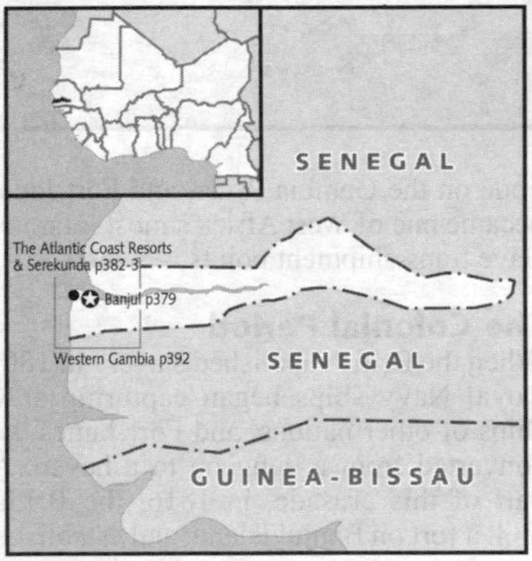
SENEGAL
The Atlantic Coast Resorts & Serekunda p382-3
Banjul p379
Western Gambia p392
SENEGAL
GUINEA-BISSAU

Highlights

- Watching the sun slide into the Atlantic from a beach hammock
- Spotting birds and monkeys at Abuko
- Paddling a pirogue on the Gambia River
- Negotiating a bargain in Albert market
- Tasting the anticipation at a traditional wrestling match

Facts about The Gambia

HISTORY

Ancient stone circles and burial mounds along the Gambia River indicate that this part of West Africa has been inhabited by organised societies for at least 1500 years. By the 13th century, the area had been absorbed into the empire of Mali, which stretched between present-day Senegal and Niger. It was during this period that migrating Mandinka traders introduced Islam, still the region's dominant religion.

The first Europeans to reach Gambia were Portuguese explorers in 1455. By 1650 they had been eclipsed by the British who established Fort James on an island 25km upstream from the mouth of the Gambia River. Twenty years later, the French built a rival fort at nearby Albreda, and during the 17th and 18th centuries the French and British vied for control of the region's trade. While the Europeans traded tobacco and gunpowder for ivory and gold, it was the purchase of slaves for shipment to the New World that most upset the traditional balance. Local chiefs, who had for years kept slaves for their own use, now set off on expeditions to round up as many slaves as they could. In 1783 Britain gained all rights to

THE GAMBIA

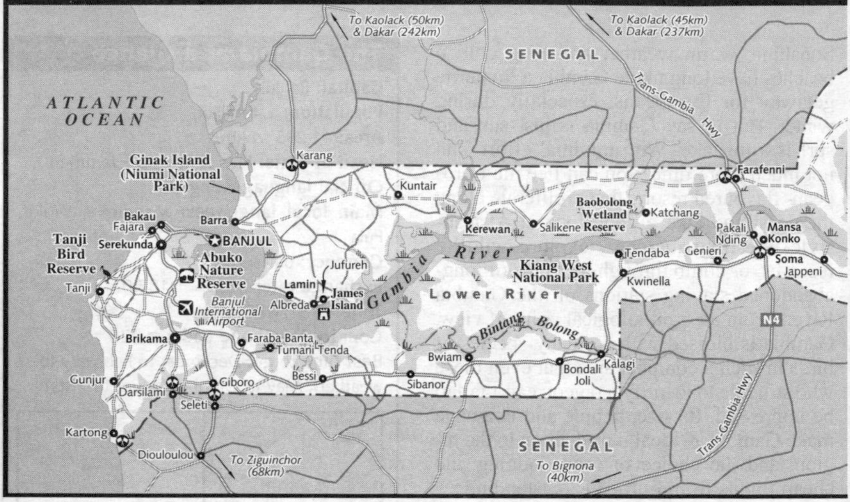
To Kaolack (50km) & Dakar (242km)
To Kaolack (45km) & Dakar (237km)
SENEGAL
Trans-Gambia Hwy
ATLANTIC OCEAN
Ginak Island (Niumi National Park)
Karang
Kuntair
Farafenni
Baobolong Wetland Reserve
Katchang
Bakau
Fajara
Barra
Kerewan
Salikene
Pakali Nding
Mansa Konko
Tanji Bird Reserve
Serekunda
BANJUL
Abuko Nature Reserve
Jufureh
Gambia River
Tendaba
Genieri
Soma
Jappeni
Kiang West National Park
Kwinella
Tanji
Lamin
Albreda
James Island
Lower River
Banjul International Airport
N4
Bintang Bolong
Brikama
Faraba Banta
Tumani Tenda
Bwiam
Kalagi
Bondali Joli
Gunjur
Bessi
Sibanor
Darsilami
Giboro
Seleti
Trans-Gambia Hwy
Kartong
SENEGAL
Diouloulou
To Ziguinchor (68km)
To Bignona (40km)

trade on the Gambia River, and Fort James became one of West Africa's most infamous slave trans-shipment points.

The Colonial Period

When the British abolished slavery in 1807, Royal Navy ships began capturing slave ships of other nations, and Fort James was converted from a dungeon to a haven. As part of this crusade, in 1816, the British built a fort on Banjul Island, and established a settlement that was named Bathurst.

The Gambia River protectorate was administered from Sierra Leone until 1888, when Gambia became a full colony, but for the next 75 years Gambia was almost forgotten, and administration was limited to a few British district commissioners and the local chiefs they appointed. Britain actually tried to trade Gambia for other colonial territories, but the French weren't interested.

In the 1950s Gambia's groundnut (peanut) plantations were improved as a way to increase export earnings, and other agricultural schemes were implemented. But there was little else in the way of services; by the early 1960s Gambia had fewer than 50 primary schools, and only a handful of doctors.

Independence

In 1960, when the rest of West Africa was busy gaining independence, Dawda Jawara founded the People's Progressive Party (PPP), but there was little else in the way of local political infrastructure and Britain doubted independence was feasible. Nevertheless, in 1965 Gambia became independent, and Jawara became prime minister, although Britain's Queen Elizabeth II remained head of state. Without any official explanation, Gambia was renamed The Gambia. More understandably, Bathurst was renamed Banjul.

A viable independent future still seemed unlikely, but during the next 10 years the world price for groundnuts increased and the number of tourists grew even more dramatically, from 300 in 1966 to 25,000 a decade later, enabling the tiny nation to survive and even prosper.

In 1970 Gambia became a fully independent republic, with Jawara as president. Opposition parties were tolerated, if not encouraged, and Jawara was accused of neglect and mismanagement.

The first major sign of discontent came in 1980 when disaffected soldiers staged a coup. In accordance with a mutual defence pact, the Senegalese army helped oust the rebels and, acknowledging this debt, Jawara announced that the armies of Gambia and Senegal would be integrated. In 1982 the Senegambian Confederation came into effect. Although political unity seemed a

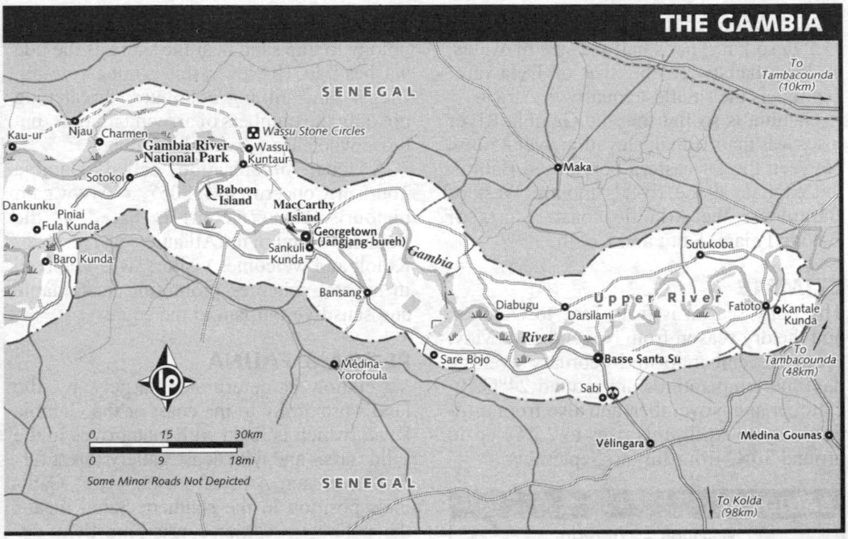
THE GAMBIA
SENEGAL
To Tambacounda (10km)
Kau-ur
Njau
Charmen
Wassu Stone Circles
Wassu
Gambia River National Park
Kuntaur
Maka
Sotokoi
Baboon Island
Dankunku
Piniai
Fula Kunda
MacCarthy Island
Georgetown (Jangjang-bureh)
Sankuli Kunda
Gambia
Sutukoba
Baro Kunda
Bansang
Diabugu
Upper River
Darsilami
Fatoto
Kantale Kunda
River
Sare Bojo
Basse Santa Su
To Tambacounda (48km)
Médina-Yorofoula
Sabi
Vélingara
Médina Gounas
0 15 30km
0 9 18mi
Some Minor Roads Not Depicted
SENEGAL
To Kolda (98km)

good idea, relations were never completely relaxed and by 1989 the confederation was dissolved.

Meanwhile groundnut prices began to fall, and restructuring by the International Monetary Fund (IMF) resulted in reduced agricultural subsidies and ever more dissatisfaction in rural areas. Despite this, and in the face of frequent allegations of incompetence and corruption, Jawara remained popular through the 1980s.

The 1990s

In April 1992 President Jawara and the PPP were re-elected for a sixth term. To the outside world, Jawara seemed to remain popular, so it came as some surprise when he was overthrown on 22 July 1994 in a reportedly bloodless coup led by young military officers. The coup leader, 29-year-old Lieutenant Yahya Jammeh, announced a new government headed by the Armed Forces Provisional Ruling Council (AFPRC). Ex-president Jawara was afforded refuge on a US warship that happened to be moored near Banjul and was later granted asylum in Senegal. Jammeh promised that the AFPRC would soon return to the barracks but when this promise went unfulfilled, aid donors such as the USA and the World Bank threatened to cut their support, and Gambia's tourist trade was badly affected.

In early 1995 Jammeh pragmatically announced that multiparty elections would be held the following year, and the British Foreign Office advised visitors that Gambia was safe once again. The 1996 elections were won by the APRC (now neatly renamed the Alliance for Patriotic Reorientation and Construction), and Jammeh was made president, completing his smooth transition from minor army officer to head of state in just over two years.

Despite being accused of taking backhanders himself, Jammeh recognised both public dissatisfaction with the corruption of the Jawara years and the key economic role of tourism. He launched an ambitious building programme, with schools, clinics and roads the priority. Despite a series of human rights abuses that included the shooting of several protesting students in 2001, many ordinary people grew to regard Jammeh as a force for good, and in October 2001 voted him into a second five-year term. This should mean stability at least until 2006.

GEOGRAPHY

Gambia's shape and position epitomise the absurdity of the colonial carve-up of Africa, with its territory and very existence determined by the Gambia River. About 300km long, but averaging only 35km wide, Gambia is entirely surrounded by Senegal, except for about 80km of coastline, and has an area of 11,295 sq km. That's half the size of Wales, or less than twice the size of Delaware. Gambia is the smallest country in Africa.

Gambia is so flat that the Gambia River loses less than 10m in elevation over 450km between the far eastern border and Banjul, the capital, at the river's mouth. West of Banjul are the Atlantic coast resorts of Bakau, Fajara, Kotu and Kololi.

CLIMATE

The rainy season is from June to October, and the dry season from November to May. From December to mid-February average daytime temperatures are around 24°C. In October and November, and also from mid-February to April, this rises to 26°C, up to around 30°C from July to September.

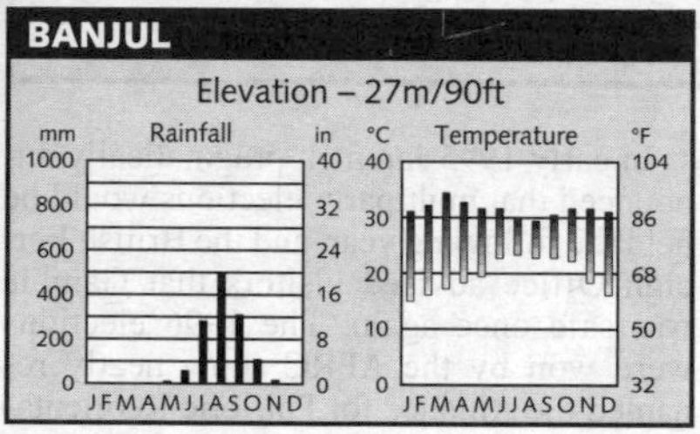
BANJUL
Elevation – 27m/90ft
mm
Rainfall
in
°C
Temperature
°F
1000
800
600
400
200
0
40
32
24
16
8
0
40
30
20
10
0
104
86
68
50
32
JFMAMJJASOND
JFMAMJJASOND

ECOLOGY & ENVIRONMENT

Not surprisingly, much of Gambia's ecology and environment revolves around the Gambia River. Spectacularly large mangroves line the river around Tendaba and are home to hundreds of bird species. But while the river and its estuaries remain fairly healthy, the same cannot be said for the coastal regions, which have thrown up several ecological challenges.

It's ironic that the very thing that originally brought tourists to Gambia now threatens to drive them away. The beaches of the Atlantic coast draw almost 100,000 tourists a year. But in order to accommodate those hordes, developers have dug thousands of tonnes of sand out of the coastline to be used in construction. The problem peaked in recent years with some beaches around Cape St Mary and Kololi literally disappearing. All that's left are ugly sandbags piled outside the resorts.

A US$20 million beach rejuvenation project was set to begin as this book went to press. The plan involves using Dutch technology to trap sand near the shore as the tide washes it in. However, this is not a cure-all. Illegal sand mining continues, threatening not only the numbers of arriving tourists, but those who earn a living from them.

A local organisation called Gambia Tourism Concern (☎ 462057, W www.gambiatourismconcern.com) is based at the Bakadaji Hotel in the Atlantic coast resort of Kololi and welcomes visitors. It is involved in several schemes promoting sustainable and sensitive tourism in the country.

FLORA & FAUNA

Vegetation is determined largely by the land's proximity to the coast or the Gambia River, which is lined with mangroves in the saline areas and with dense gallery forest further upstream. Away from the river, Gambia's position in the southern Sahel means that natural vegetation consists mostly of dry grassland or open savanna woodland.

Most of Gambia's large mammals have long since been shot out of existence, although warthogs and various antelope species can be seen in the national parks. However, plans are afoot to reintroduce elephants, giraffes and even big cats to reserves along the Gambia River. In the meantime, Gambia's primate populations, especially several species of monkeys, and a huge array of birds remain the most notable fauna.

Birds

A wide range of habitats in a compact area makes Gambia an important bird-watching destination, and more ornithologists come here than to any other country in West Africa. More than 560 species have been recorded (just 80 fewer than in Senegal which is almost 20 times larger), including the many migrants using the coast as a flight path between Europe and the tropics. There are no endemics, but 'specials', which get birders excited, include Egyptian plovers, swallow-tailed and red-throated bee-eaters, Abyssinian rollers, painted snipes and Pel's fishing owls. Good sites include all the protected areas listed under National Parks, following, plus some unexpected areas such as hotel gardens, sewage ponds and the mud flats in the scruffy part of Banjul. Upcountry, the Georgetown and Basse Santa Su areas are also particularly rewarding.

Finding a Guide

If organised tours aren't your bag, the best way to make the most of your bird-watching time is to employ a local guide. Seeing birds aside, there are several reasons to consider a local guide: you can forget about maps and language barriers, and expect to meet far more Gambians than you would on your own. Of course, guides aren't bad at directing you to the best viewing spots and identifying difficult species.

Some local guides have formed a group called Habitat Africa. Organised by Solomon Jallow (☎ 907694, ⓔ habitatafrica@hotmail.com), the group includes Aladin Jemeh, Tamba Jeffang, Sering Bojang, Osman Sayand, Buba Daffeh and Denbo. Solomon organises itineraries, transport and accommodation. Less formally, the bridge over Kotu Stream, near the Novotel in the Atlantic coast resort of Kotu, is a good bird-watching site and a traditional place to meet other birders and local guides looking for work.

When choosing a guide, get personal recommendations if you can, and go out with him for a few hours first to check his knowledge and approach. A fee of around D45 per hour, or D125 for a morning, is fair. Some guides offer week-long tours of the country for between D750 and D1500 per day, which includes a car and accommodation – but be warned that guides can overcharge wildly, or forget to mention that 'incidentals' (such as meals) are extra. Outright scams also happen.

It's worth checking out the Bird Safari Camp's website (ⓦ www.bsc.gm/guides.htm) where several guides have been 'reviewed' and their contact details listed. A couple even offer an online booking service.

National Parks

Gambia has six national parks and reserves protecting a good cross-section of habitat types. All except the Gambia River National Park (also known as Baboon Islands) are open to the public. Abuko Nature Reserve is a tract of gallery forest, while Kiang West National Park protects several habitats including mangroves, mud flats and dry woodland. Baobolong Wetland Reserve is on the north bank of the Gambia River. Niumi National Park and Tanji Bird Reserve are coastal, with dunes, lagoons, dry woodland and coastal scrub.

Several forest parks have been established to provide renewable timber stocks. However, one of these, Bijilo Forest Park, is primarily a nature reserve and a favourite with birders.

GOVERNMENT & POLITICS

The government is based on the British parliamentary system, and elections for the president and members of the national assembly are held every five years.

The dominant party, headed by President Yahya Jammeh, is the Alliance for Patriotic Reorientation and Construction (APRC), which took power in a coup in 1994, was elected in 1996 and was re-elected in 2001 in elections that were boycotted by much of the opposition. It holds 45 of the 48 elected seats in the national assembly. An additional five members are appointed by the president. The next elections are due in 2006.

ECONOMY

The Gambia is a poor country with an estimated gross domestic product of just US$456 per capita in 1998. Its economy is dominated by groundnuts (peanuts), which account for a staggering 70% of all export earnings. But a fall in world prices and ill-advised government interference in the groundnut industry are steadily eroding the power of the groundnut.

Gambia's balance of trade has been negative since 1975 and today foreign debt stands at around US$300 million. About one-third of food requirements, all fuel, transportation infrastructure, plant and machinery, and most manufactured goods are imported. To put all this in perspective, the United Nations' 2000 Human Development Index ranked Gambia 161st out of 174 countries.

The main economic activity besides groundnuts is tourism. But despite its high profile, tourism accounts for only 10% to 15% of gross national product, mainly because package tours are paid for in visitors' home countries.

POPULATION & PEOPLE

Estimates in 2001 put Gambia's population at around 1.4 million, with 45% of that total less than 14 years old. This total is growing by 3.1% a year, and the population density of around 115 people per square kilometre is one of the highest in Africa.

The main ethnic groups are the Mandinka (comprising about 42%), Fula (about 18%) and Wolof (about 16%). Smaller groups include the Sere and Jola. Intermarriage among the various ethnic groups is not uncommon, nor are cross-border unions with Senegalese.

ARTS

Unlike other countries in the region, Gambia is not noted for the use of wooden masks and statues; however, costumes made of plant fibre are used in initiation ceremonies. The growth of tourism has caused a boom in the production of poor-quality wooden carvings. Most of these are more inspired by the basic principles of commerce than by Gambian tradition.

Less commercial are Mandinka musical traditions. Islamic feast days, such as the end of Ramadan, and family celebrations, such as a wedding or circumcision, or even the arrival of a special guest, are seen as good reasons for some music and dancing. Traditional instruments include the kora and the *balafon* (a type of wooden xylophone; see the special section 'Music of West Africa'). Mandinka dances are based on common activities of everyday life, such as crop cultivation and fishing.

Gambian pop music is heavily influenced by the Sahel sounds of Senegal, Mali and Guinea, and most local artists who make it big soon disappear to the bright lights of Dakar. Popular Gambian musicians include Abdel Kabirr, kora guru Jaliba Kuyateh, and the ever-popular Ifang Bondi, the band whose most recent effort, *Gis Gis*, won a host of international awards including *Q Magazine's* best world music album of 2001.

SOCIETY & CONDUCT

Gambians are renowned for being very laid back and this makes their country one of the easiest places in Africa to visit, but it's still handy to be aware of some of the customs that are peculiar to Gambia. Greetings are important and you should expect to shake a lot of hands during your visit, both when you enter and when you leave a gathering. This is usually a ritual reserved for men, but Western women are often afforded the status of honourary man so any extraneous shaking is unlikely to cause offence.

If you find yourself visiting the home of a Gambian you will more than likely be offered sweet tea. It's served in three successive glasses over a period of up to two hours. It's important to note that by accepting the first glass you commit to the three or risk offending your hosts.

Gambians are not without their superstitions and taboos. Whistling after dark is forbidden, and after sunset you'll have difficulty if you want to buy soap, needles or charcoal, since all these things bring bad luck.

As in most of the region, public nudity, open displays of affection and outspoken criticism of the government are not advisable.

RELIGION

About 90% of Gambians are Muslim, 9% Christian and the remainder animist. See Religion in the Facts about the Region chapter for more details on Islam.

LANGUAGE

English is the official language. A number of African languages are spoken, the principal ones being Mandinka, Wolof and Fula. See the Language chapter for a list of useful phrases in these languages.

Facts for the Visitor

SUGGESTED ITINERARIES

Cheap charter flights and short flying times mean a trip to Gambia of just one week is a popular option for visitors from Europe. Overland travellers can easily spend a week in Gambia as part of wider travels around West Africa. You might want to combine a few days on the Atlantic coast beaches with time in Banjul, Gambia's small and dusty capital, and nearby places such as Bijilo and Abuko wildlife reserves, lively Serekunda or Jufureh (famous because of African-American writer, Alex Haley's *Roots*). If you cut out the resorts, you could head south to Tanji Bird Reserve or the fishing villages of Gunjur and Kartong, or even spend a few days following the Gambia River upstream to the old colonial outpost of Georgetown and the busy trading centre of Basse Santa Su.

With two weeks you'd have time to laze on the beach and tour the country. You could relax in the beautiful coastal area of Niumi National Park and if you go upcountry your first stop might be the mangroves and creeks of Tumani Tenda, or perhaps the colourful market at Farafenni. Wildlife fans should stop at Tendaba, the base for visiting Kiang West National Park and Baobolong Wetland Reserve. Further upcountry is peaceful Georgetown, from where you can reach Wassu Stone Circles or take a boat ride past Gambia River National Park, and the lively trading centre of Basse.

With three or four weeks in Gambia you could visit all the places listed earlier and also cross into Senegal, perhaps to Casamance or the Siné-Saloum Delta.

PLANNING

When to Go

The climate means the high season is from December to mid-February when conditions are dry and relatively cool. This is also the local trading season, when the harvest is completed and Gambians are more relaxed, perhaps with extra money to spend, making markets noticeably busier.

Low season is from May to October, and includes the rainy season from June to September. Some travellers prefer this as there are no crowds, hotels are cheaper, and rain only falls for a few hours each day, which means the vegetation is lush and the air clear.

Maps

Macmillan's *The Gambia Traveller's Map* is the best, but unavailable in Gambia itself. It's easy to read, with most roads marked, and has street maps of Banjul and the Atlantic coast resorts. International Travel Maps' *The Gambia* is available locally.

TOURIST OFFICES

Gambia is represented in Britain by Gambia National Tourist Office (☎ 020-7376 0093, e enquiries@gambiatourism.info, w www.gambiatourism.info) based at the Gambian high commission. It has a decent website, responds promptly to calls, faxes and emails, and will send a useful colour brochure anywhere in the world. Gambia Tourist Authority plans to open information booths at the coastal resorts.

VISAS

Visas are not needed by nationals of Commonwealth countries, Belgium, Germany, Italy, Luxembourg, the Netherlands, Spain or Scandinavian countries for stays of up to 90 days. For those needing a visa they are normally valid for one month, and are issued in two to three days for the equivalent of about US$45. You can find out whether you need a visa by emailing e enquiries@gambiatourism.info. An application form can be printed out from w www.gambia.com, though if you're applying by snail mail in the US you should allow at least two weeks for the process. It's best to get a visa before you land in Gambia, but if you arrive without one, take yourself to the Immigration Office (☎ 228611) on OAU Blvd in Banjul between 8am and 4pm, and 30 minutes later you'll be legal. Your visa can be extended at the same office for D250.

Visas for Onward Travel

In Gambia, you can get visas for the following neighbouring countries. For visa applications it's best to go to the embassy or consulate as early as possible. For locations, see Embassies & Consulates, following.

Guinea Visas cost CFA20,000, FF200 or US$40. If you arrive early you can collect it the same day.

Guinea-Bissau Visas cost D120 for 30 days or D150 for 60 days and take between 30 minutes and a day to issue.

Mali The consul here cannot issue tourist visas. There is an embassy in Dakar, or you can get a 72-hour transit visa at the border or the airport.

Mauritania The Gambia is the best place in West Africa to get a Mauritanian visa. One-month visas cost D300 and are issued the same day.

Senegal Visas are cheaper here than in Europe, but for some reason you can only apply on Monday and Wednesday. One month costs D57, three months multi-entry is D132, and they're issued in 48 hours.

Sierra Leone The high commission issues single-entry visas in 48 hours for US$45.

EMBASSIES & CONSULATES

Gambian Embassies & Consulates

The few West African countries with Gambian embassies include Guinea-Bissau,

THE GAMBIA

Nigeria, Sierra Leone and Senegal. See the Facts for the Visitor section of the relevant country chapter for more details. Elsewhere, Gambian embassies and consulates include the following:

Belgium (☎ 02-640 1049) 126 ave Franklin-Roosevelt, Brussels 1050
France (☎ 01 42 94 09 30) 117, rue Saint-Lazare, 75008 Paris
Germany (☎ 030-892 31 21, fax 891 14 01) Kurfurstendamm 103, Berlin
UK (☎ 020-7937 6316) 57 Kensington Court, London W8 5DH
USA (☎ 202-785 1399, e gamembdc@gambia.com) Suite 1000, 1155 15th St NW, Washington, DC 20005

The Gambia is also represented in Austria, Brazil, Canada, Italy, Japan, the Netherlands, Norway, Portugal, Spain, Sweden and Switzerland.

Embassies & Consulates in Gambia

Embassies and consulates in Banjul and the Atlantic coast resorts include those of:

Guinea (☎ 226862, 909964) Top floor, 78A Daniel Goddard St, Banjul; open 9am to 4pm Monday to Thursday, 9am to 1.30pm and 2.30pm to 4pm Friday; sometimes open Saturday
Guinea-Bissau (☎ 494854) Atlantic Rd, Bakau, above Distripharm; open 8am to 3pm Monday to Friday
Mali (☎ 226942) VM Company Ltd, Cherno Adama Bah St, Banjul
Mauritania (☎ 461086) Just off Badala Park Way, Kololi; open 8am to 4pm Monday to Friday
Senegal (☎ 373752, fax 373750) One block west of Kairaba Ave, Fajara, behind the mosque; open 8am to 2pm and 2.30pm to 5pm Monday to Thursday; to 4pm on Friday
Sierra Leone (☎ 228206) 67 Daniel Goddard St, Banjul; open 8.30am to 4.30pm Monday to Thursday, 8.30am to 1.30pm Friday
UK (☎ 495133/4, fax 496134) 48 Atlantic Rd, Fajara, opposite the Medical Research Council; open 8am to 3pm Monday to Thursday, 8am to 1pm Friday
USA (☎ 392856/8, 391971, fax 392475) Kairaba Ave, Fajara

For details of embassies not listed here, check the phone book (most telecentres have one).

CUSTOMS

There are no restrictions on the import of local or foreign currencies, or on the export of foreign currency, but you cannot export more than D100, not that you'd want to. The usual limits apply to alcohol (1L of spirits, 1L of wine) and tobacco (250 cigarettes).

MONEY

Currency

The Gambia's unit of currency is the dalasi. Notes are D5, D10, D25, D50 and D100. There is also a D1 coin. The dalasi is divided into 100 bututs. Many items can be paid for in CFA, but US dollars are usually accepted only in large hotels.

Exchange Rates

At the time of writing, US$1 bought D17.5, €1 bought D15 and UK£1 bought 25, even though the value has now fallen even further.

country	unit		dalasi
euro zone	€1	=	D16.50
UK	UK£1	=	D27
USA	US$1	=	D18.50
West African CFA	CFA1000	=	D25

Exchanging Money

Gambia's main banks are Standard Chartered, Trust Bank and IBC (formerly BICIS) and each has branches in Banjul, Serekunda and the Atlantic coast resorts. These towns also have several exchange bureaus and plenty of black-market traders.

Upcountry, banks are harder to find. Only Brikama, Farafenni and Basse Santa Su have branches. There's also a bank at the airport. If it's closed, the police will help you find an unofficial but tolerated money-changer (but they don't deal in travellers cheques). In and around Banjul, changing cash or travellers cheques is relatively quick and straightforward. Reconverting local currency into foreign currency is relatively straightforward, although rates are low.

ATMs These have begun to appear at Standard Chartered branches and a couple of petrol stations around the Atlantic coast. They are generally well stocked with crisp new D100 notes, but dispense them only to holders of Visa card. Despite the stickers on the machines, we met several unhappy travellers whose money was still 'earning interest' in their Plus, Cirrus, Maestro or Switch accounts. If you can't find an ATM, you can use

Visa, MasterCard and Eurocard to draw cash at any bank branch for a flat charge of D100.

POST & COMMUNICATIONS

Post

The postal service out of the country is reliable; most cards and letters arrive at their destinations in about a week. Letters to Britain and Europe cost D5, to North America D7 and Australasia D10. A 2kg package will cost D200 to Britain and Europe, D270 to North America, and D365 to Australasia. Poste restante is in the post office in Banjul.

Telephone & Fax

Efficient public telephone and fax offices are run by Gamtel (the state telephone company) and are open in the evening and at weekends. You'll also find privately owned 'telecentres' in all but the smallest of towns.

There are no telephone area codes in Gambia. Calls within Gambia cost around D8 for three minutes, and international calls outside Africa about D50 per minute at peak time (7am to 6pm). Calls are cheaper by about 33% between 11pm and 7am. Rates are also cheaper at weekends, when a call to Europe comes down to about D30 per minute. You can buy phonecards at Gamtel offices but you'll be lucky to find a cardphone that works.

For directory assistance dial ☎ 151. For the international operator dial ☎ 100.

Mobile Phones

Two GSM phone networks operate in Gambia. You can buy SIM cards for the government-run Gamcel (D500) from Gamtel offices, and for Africell (D450) from agents in Serekunda or Banjul. Prepaid calling cards cost D50, D100 and D150.

Email & Internet Access

Internet cafés are common in Banjul and on the Atlantic coast, and a couple of upcountry towns have also been wired into the Internet age. There are three main operators; CyberWorld, QuantumNET (W www.qanet.gm) and Gamtel. All charge about D30 an hour as a base rate. The service is generally reasonably fast; however, frequent power cuts have the potential to ruin your whole day.

Away from the coast, Net access is harder to find, slower and more expensive, though you can expect this to improve.

DIGITAL RESOURCES

You wouldn't describe Gambia as a powerhouse of Internet creativity, but if you're looking for predeparture tips there are a few sites worth a visit:

The Gambia Birding Group This is an excellent site for bird-watchers with reports on what birds are where, how to find a guide and links to birding tours.
W www.gambiabirding.org

The Gambia National Tourist Office This is a good site with general information and links to hotels and tour operators.
W www.gambiatourism.info

Gambia Tourist Support UK-focused, this website has links to gap year and working holiday information.
W website.lineone.net/~gambiagts/homep.html

Momodou Camara's site In English and Danish, Momodou offers a thorough insider's view of his home country. There's lots of cultural information plus links to news organisations and businesses.
W home3.inet.tele.dk/mcamara/index.html

Roots Festival The Roots Festival attracts members of the African diaspora to Gambia for a week-long celebration every two years. This is the official site and it includes a Roots Festival program.
W www.rootsfestival.gm

BOOKS

Useful locally produced books include *An Overview of Protected Areas in the Gambia* by the Department of Parks & Wildlife, and *Sites & Monuments of the Gambia* by the National Council for Arts & Culture, available at the National Museum in Banjul.

A Field Guide to Birds of The Gambia & Senegal by leading ornithologists Clive Barlow and Tim Wacher, with illustrations by award-winning artist Tony Disley, is undeniably the birder's bible. It lists over 660 species, with colour plates, detailed descriptions and in-depth background information. But this 400-page hardback is no featherweight, and costs UK£28 in Britain, US$42 in the US. It is also available in Gambia.

Lonely Planet's *The Gambia & Senegal* gives broader and more detailed coverage of the country.

NEWSPAPERS & MAGAZINES

There are several pamphlet-thin newspapers published in Banjul and distributed mainly in the west of the country. *The Gambia Daily* and *The Daily Observer* are closely aligned with the government. The *Point* is vaguely antigovernment while the twice-weekly *News & Report* and the *Independent* are probably the most provocative.

Day-old British papers can be found around the coastal resorts, especially during the high season. Timbooktoo on Kairaba Ave has a good range, with magazines such as *Time* and *Newsweek* also available. The US embassy is the best place to start looking for American papers.

RADIO & TV

When you consider that in 2000 Gambia was estimated to be home to just 5000 televisions, while more than 200,000 people owned radios, you start to understand the importance of the humble transistor. Radio stations include the government-run and rather staid Radio Gambia (648 MW or 91.4 FM), and Radio Syd (909 MW), with broadcasts in Swedish and German as well as English. FM stations include Sud FM (92.1 FM) and West Coast Radio (95.3 FM), with a heavy music weighting. The mainly music stations, Radio 1 FM (102.1 FM) and Citizen FM (105.7 FM), have been repeatedly harassed by the government for their aggressive reporting. You can hear the BBC on shortwave frequencies 15400 and 17830. Gambia's only TV station is the government-run GTV.

PHOTOGRAPHY & VIDEO

No permit is required, but the usual restrictions apply – see Photography & Video in the Regional Facts for the Visitor chapter for more general information.

HEALTH

Malaria kills a lot of people in Gambia, both locals and foreigners, and the risk exists year-round in the whole country – even short-stayers need to take prophylactics. For details see Health in the Regional Facts for the Visitor chapter. You'll need a yellow fever vaccination certificate if you're coming from an infected area.

The country's main government-run hospital is in Banjul, but there is a better selection of private clinics and doctors in the area around the Atlantic coast resorts (see the Atlantic Coast Resorts & Serekunda section later in this chapter for more information). Upcountry, you will find hospitals at Bansang and Farafenni.

EMERGENCIES

For the police dial ☎ 17. For the fire brigade or an ambulance dial ☎ 18.

LEGAL MATTERS

A combination of tourism and urban deprivation around Banjul and the tourist resorts means some drugs are cheap and readily available (a handful of grass can go for as little as D25), but despite what you may hear, no drug is legal in Gambia. If you're a smoker, be careful: some dealers are in cahoots with the police. Several tourists have been arrested (either by real policemen or impostors – it doesn't really matter) and forced to pay large bribes to avoid arrest and jail.

BUSINESS HOURS

Shops and businesses usually open from 8.30am to noon and 2.30pm to 5.30pm Monday to Thursday, and from 8am to noon Friday and Saturday. Most banks in Banjul city centre are open from 8am to 1.30pm Monday to Thursday, and 8am to 11am Friday. Banks in the Atlantic coast resorts and Serekunda open weekday afternoons and on Saturday, depending on the bank. See Money in the Atlantic Coast Resorts & Serekunda section later in this chapter for details.

PUBLIC HOLIDAYS & SPECIAL EVENTS

Public holidays include:

New Year's Day 1 January
Independence Day 18 February
Good Friday March/April
Easter Monday March/April
Workers' Day 1 May
Anniversary of the Second Republic 22 July
Assumption 15 August
Christmas Day 25 December

The Muslim holidays of Eid al-Fitr or Koraté (end of Ramadan), Tabaski, Muslim New Year and Mohammed's birthday are also celebrated. For a table of dates of Islamic holidays, see Public Holidays & Special Events in the Regional Facts for the Visitor chapter.

ACTIVITIES

Most major hotels have swimming pools that nonguests can use for a fee. Otherwise, you have several beaches to choose from, although large waves, steep shelves and a heavy undertow can make some of them dangerous. In tourist areas you can hire sailboards, or arrange other water sports. Fishing – either in the creeks or out on the ocean – is also available. Cycling is a great way to explore the Gambian countryside, and bikes can be hired at the Atlantic coast resorts. See the Getting Around section, later, for details on cycling in Gambia.

ACCOMMODATION

In Banjul and the Atlantic coast resorts there's plenty of choice in places to stay, from basic guesthouses to international-standard hotels. Upcountry you can choose between simple local places and more comfortable tourist-oriented establishments, but there is nothing too luxurious.

FOOD

Shoestringers should head for the cheap chophouses where plates of rice and sauce go for about D6, or visit an *afra*, where take-away grilled meat is sold at very reasonable prices. Even if you're not strapped for cash, it's well worth trying some local cooking. Traditional Gambian food is similar to Senegalese food (see Food in the Senegal chapter for more details), with the same ingredients and cultural background, although names and spellings may differ. Thick brown groundnut sauce called *mafay* is found everywhere. *Domodah* is another version, usually with meat or vegetables mixed in. Other meals include *benechin* (fish and rice), chicken *yasser* (marinated in onion and lemon sauce) and *yollof* rice – vegetables or meat cooked in a sauce of oil and tomatoes.

DRINKS

The local beer is JulBrew, served usually in 280ml bottles, but also as a draught beer in smarter bars and hotels. Prices for a bottle start at about D10 in the simplest watering hole, and range up to around D25 in posh restaurants. The common traditional 'beer' made from millet looks brown and gritty, but the most popular home-brew is palm wine.

SHOPPING

Keen shoppers can spend many happy hours browsing in Gambia's shops, stalls and markets. Woodcarvings vary in quality, but if you look hard enough you might find something that catches your eye. Tie-dyed or printed fabrics are also eye-catching, with vibrant designs and colours, but take care when you wash them. Very popular for tourists and locals are brightly coloured baggy trousers and 'Gambi-shirts'. Batiks are churned out in their thousands but you may have to search to find quality – there are some good stalls in Serekunda and the coastal resorts.

Getting There & Away

AIR

Gambia's main airport is Banjul international airport, about 20km from the city centre, and about 15km from the Atlantic coast resorts.

Apart from SN Brussels Airlines (the reincarnated Sabena), Gambia is served almost exclusively by charter operators. This is fine during the tourist season, but can be a problem in the quieter months. The departure tax from Gambia is usually included in the price of your ticket.

Europe

The only scheduled airline to fly regularly to Banjul from Europe is SN Brussels Airlines with five flights a week via Dakar. A return flight from Brussels to Banjul is €600, while flights from London to either start at UK£480. However, the best deals from Europe are on charter flights, available from holiday operators or travel agencies. Although these cater mainly for package tourists, independent travellers can get 'flight-only' deals. The leading British operator is The Gambia Experience (☎ 023-8073 0888, W www.gambia.co.uk) with one- or two-week flight-only deals from UK£335 return. Flights depart from Gatwick, Manchester, Bristol and Glasgow.

From Gambia to Europe, The Gambia Experience (☎ 460317), at Kairaba Hotel in Kololi, has one-way charter tickets from UK£300, sometimes less. This makes it one of the cheapest places to fly home from.

USA & Canada

The only direct flight between North America and West Africa is Ghana Airways'

THE GAMBIA

weekly service linking Washington and Accra via Dakar and Banjul. However, this has proved so unreliable that most people still prefer to take the roundabout route through Europe.

Africa

There are daily flights between Banjul and Dakar on Gambia International Airlines and Air Senegal International (D1104 one way). GIA also flies to Conakry via Freetown once a week. Ghana Airways flies twice weekly to Conakry for D1311, Abidjan (Côte d'Ivoire) for D5039 and Accra (Ghana) for D5825. Air Guinée has weekly flights between Banjul and Conakry via Labé in northern Guinea – perfect for reaching the Fouta Djalon. Bellview has twice-weekly flights to Lagos via Freetown for US$274 one way.

If you're heading for North Africa, it's better to go overland to Dakar (see the Getting There & Away section of the Senegal chapter).

LAND

Border Crossings

There are three main border points of interest for travellers: at Karang, north of Barra on the main road to/from Kaolack and Dakar; Seleti, south of Brikama, on the main road to Ziguinchor in southern Senegal; and Sabi, south of Basse Santa Su on the road to Vélingara. There are also major border crossing points just south of Soma, and just north of Farafenni where the Trans-Gambia Hwy cuts through Gambia. Along the border are several more minor crossing points, but aside from a dirt track from Brikama to Kafountine, these tend to be used mainly by local people.

At any border crossing there are usually a few kilometres of 'no man's land' between the Gambian and Senegalese border posts. Public transport usually stops at the border, where you continue your journey in another vehicle.

Senegal

The Gambia is completely surrounded by Senegal, and most vehicles running between the two countries are Senegalese, so drivers prefer to charge in CFA.

To reach Dakar from Banjul take the ferry across the Gambia River to Barra. There's an express bus to Dakar at 9am (D100 or CFA5000, five to six hours), but you have to be quick off the ferry to get a seat. The slower bus leaves between 10am and noon (D100 or CFA5000, seven to eight hours). If you miss these big buses you'll have to get to the border at Karang and organise a ride from there. A Peugeot taxi will cost CFA4500 (D90, about six hours), a minibus CFA3000 (D60, eight to nine hours) and a Mercedes bus, a white box into which about 35 people are jammed, costs CFA2500 (D50, 10 hours). A Peugeot taxi to Kaolack is CFA2000 (D40).

If you're coming from Dakar and think you might miss the last ferry across to Banjul (it leaves at 7pm), be aware that accommodation in Barra is limited to a couple of sleazy hotels. You'd be better off staying in Kaolack or Toubakouta (see the Senegal chapter) and getting the ferry from Barra to Banjul the next morning.

To get to Ziguinchor you must take a bush taxi from Serekunda to the border at Giboro (D25) and then change for a Senegalese taxi (D40 or CFA2000). Some also go from Brikama. If you're heading for Kafountine, you could get yourself to Diouloulou via Giboro, then change for Kafountine.

Easier, but with a greater risk of encountering men with guns (see the Senegal chapter), is to take a minibus from Brikama direct to Kafountine via a series of sandy back roads (D30, 1½ hours).

Heading east from Basse Santa Su, bush taxis go through Sabi to Vélingara (D20 or CFA1000). They leave when full, which can mean several hours of waiting. However, one taxi usually leaves at 7am (full or not). In Vélingara a horse-drawn *caleshe* (cart) costs CFA250 per person across town to the bush-taxi station for Tambacounda (CFA1500 by Peugeot taxi, CFA1100 by minibus).

SEA

Some travellers take sea-going pirogues (open wooden boats) that are used by local people, although these don't run to a set timetable and are notoriously unsafe. Options include Banjul to Ziguinchor, or Banjul to Djifer in the Siné-Saloum Delta. For details see the Getting There & Away section of the Senegal chapter.

Getting Around

BUS & BUSH TAXI

There are two main routes though Gambia: the potholed dirt road along the northern bank of the river, and the potholed tar road along the southern bank. The northern road has been described as 'dire' and few people use it by choice. The southern route is well served by bush taxis and large Gambia Public Transport Corporation (GPTC) buses. Fares are cheap – across the country by ordinary GPTC bus costs D75, or D85 on the express. Bush-taxi fares are slightly higher.

CAR & MOTORCYCLE

It's possible to hire a car in Gambia's resort areas, but you might also consider using a tourist taxi – see Taxi Tours later in this section. Despite Gambia's British heritage, its traffic drives on the right, as in most other countries in West Africa. Petrol costs D9.75 per litre, and diesel (called *gasoil*) D7.75 per litre.

BOAT

A company called River Gambia Excursions (☎ 497603, fax 495526, ⓔ mosa@qanet.gm) operates a boat between Tendaba Camp (in Tendaba) and Georgetown. The two-day trip usually leaves every second Thursday, but check this. A high-speed river boat between Banjul and Georgetown was due to begin service in 2002. Call Pleasuresports (☎/fax 462125, ☎ 962125) for details.

BICYCLE

If you've never cycled in Africa before, Gambia is an ideal place to start. We've heard from many travellers, particularly British, who take bikes on the cheap charter flights to Banjul and enjoy a couple of weeks cycling in the sun. The landscape is flat and the distances between major points of interest are not so great. Alternatively, hiring a bike for a few days or a week is a great way to get around. For general information on cycling in West Africa, see the Getting Around chapter.

LOCAL TRANSPORT

Local public transport, such as city minibuses and shared taxis, is pretty much limited to Banjul, Serekunda and the surrounding area. In the Atlantic coast resorts and at the airport you will also find green 'tourist taxis', which cater specifically for tourists. From some other towns around the country, local transport runs to outlying villages, but on no fixed schedule, and usually tying in with market days.

ORGANISED TOURS

Tour Companies

Taking an organised tour can be a good way to get around if time is short or money not a prime concern. All tour companies are based in the Atlantic coast resort area. Large hotels offer excursions but smaller independent companies usually have lower prices. This is a very small selection, but gives you an idea of prices and options:

Abaraka Jeep Safari (☎ 465847, fax 465544) Office above the Standard Chartered Bank in Kololi. Day trips to Makasutu (D450) or dolphin spotting (D400), or overnight to Tendaba (D1050).

Creek & River Fishing (☎ 495915) These folks are angling specialists; rates start at D500 per person per day, including tackle, tuition and lunch. More serious sport-fishing trips start at around D650 per person per day.

Pleasuresports (☎/fax 462125, ☎ 962125, ⓔ psg@qanet.gm) This is a boat-tour specialist aimed at groups, but independent travellers are welcome to book directly. A *Roots* tour costs D300 if you make your own way to the port.

Tropical Tours & Souvenirs (☎ 460536, fax 460546, ⓔ tropicaltour@gamtel.gm) This shop is at the entrance to Kairaba Hotel in Kololi. Informative and well organised without being pushy, the company's tours include: the *Roots* village of Jufureh by boat for D690, and a south-coast beach safari for D625. Trips focused on special interests (such as birding, brewing, bee keeping and traditional medicine) are also available.

Taxi Tours

Green tourist-taxi drivers offer tours at fixed prices but check carefully for any extras. Check the 'itinerary'; most drivers are reliable and considerate, but some like to go as fast as possible before leaving you stranded at a line of tacky souvenir stands. Some sample prices (per car) for a four-seater taxi from Bakau, Fajara, Kotu or Kololi are D300 to Lamin and Abuko, D1100 to Tendaba, and D1700 to Georgetown.

Several travellers have written to say their driver's local insights added considerably to

THE GAMBIA

their experience, and visits to far-flung family in country compounds can turn out to be the best part of all.

Banjul

pop 50,000

Banjul is one of the smallest, and perhaps least likely, capital cities in Africa. People are not flocking to Banjul, no new buildings are going up and there are no traffic jams.

All this makes Banjul well worth a visit. The bustling markets, the dusty museum, faded history and lethargic disposition combine to make this a truly African experience, all just 30 minutes from the plush resorts of the Atlantic coast. Many tourists come for Gambia's beaches and never bother to take in the capital – don't make the same mistake.

Orientation

Banjul was founded in 1816 and many of its streets were duly named after the English heroes of the Battle of Waterloo. Not any more. In one sweeping move recently the name of nearly every street in the city was changed – they're now named after heroes of a different time and a different place, the heroes of Gambia's independence.

We've included a list of some of the streets and their old names, but if you're still stuck, look for the addresses painted on the front of shops and businesses.

Changing Banjul Street Names

old name	new name
Anglesea St	Serign Sillah St
Buckle St	Ecowas Ave
Cameron St	Nelson Mandela St
Clarkson St	Rene Blain St
Cotton St	Cherno Adamah Bah St
Dobson St	Ma Cumba Jallow St
Grant St	Rev William Cole St
Hagan St	Daniel Goddard St
Hill St	Imam Lamin Bah St
Hope St	Jallow Jallow St
Independence Dr	July 22 Dr
Leman St	OAU Blvd
Marina Pde	Muammar al Gadhafi Ave
Orange St	Tafsir Ebou Samba St
Picton St	Davidson Carrol St
Wellington St	Liberation St

Banjul is small enough to walk around without too much trouble. The centre is July 22 Square (formerly MacCarthy Square), a dusty public park, from where several main streets run south. West of the October 17 Roundabout is the old part of Banjul – a maze of narrow streets and ramshackle houses where few tourists ever venture.

July 22 Drive runs west from July 22 Square, becoming the main road out of Banjul. On the edge of the city it goes under Arch 22 (see Things to See later) and turns into a dual carriageway which, after about 4km crosses Oyster Creek on Denton Bridge to reach the mainland. Only the president is allowed to drive through Arch 22 – all others must take a tedious detour.

Information

Money Standard Chartered and Trust Bank are both on Buckle St, and IBC is on Liberation St. The ATM at Standard Chartered takes Visa card. Black-market moneychangers can be found opposite the entrance to Albert market and at the ferry port. Several shopkeepers along Liberation St will also change money – a safer option.

Post & Communications The main post office and the Gamtel public telephone office are near Albert market; there's a reasonably reliable poste restante service at the post office. You can get online at either QuantumNET or Gamtel, both on Nelson Mandela St and open 9am to 8pm daily.

Travel Agencies Efficient agencies in Banjul include the Banjul Travel Agency (☎ 228813, ⓔ bta@qanet.gm) on Ecowas Ave, and Olympic Travel (☎ 223370/1, ⓔ olympictravel@gamtel.gm) on Nelson Mandela St. If these can't help you, you'll find more at the north end of Ecowas Ave, while others are listed in the Atlantic Coast Resorts & Serekunda section later in this chapter.

Medical Services The Royal Victoria Hospital (☎ 228223) on July 22 Drive is where you'd probably be taken if you were unfortunate enough to be involved in an accident, but the private establishments on the Atlantic coast are better for illnesses, minor injuries and malaria tests.

BANJUL

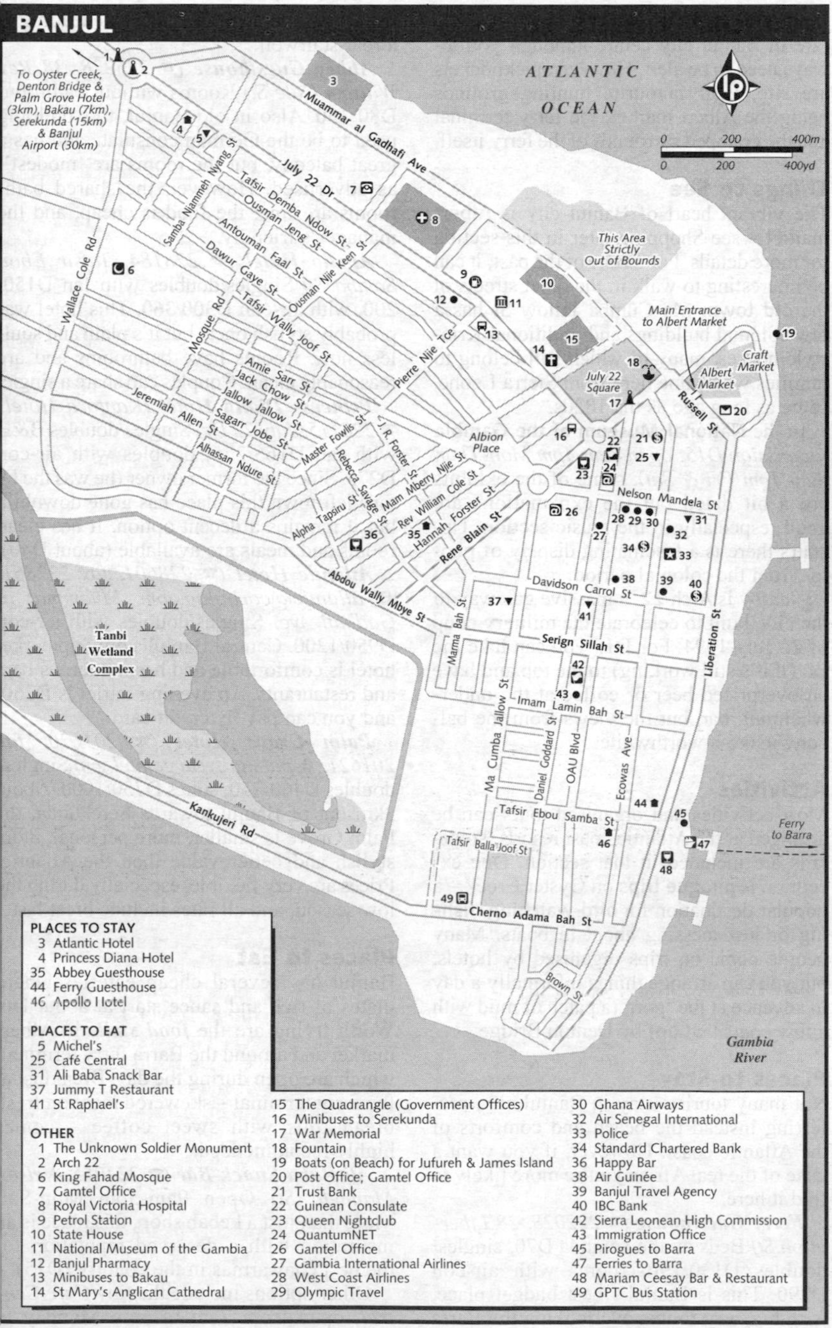
ATLANTIC OCEAN
0 200 400m
0 200 400yd
To Oyster Creek, Denton Bridge & Palm Grove Hotel (3km), Bakau (7km), Serekunda (15km) & Banjul Airport (30km)
Muammar al Gadhafi Ave
July 22 Dr
Tafsir Demba Ndow St
Ousman Jeng St
Antouman Faal St
Dawur Gaye St
Tafsir Wally Joof St
Ousman Njie Keen St
Samba Njammeh Nyang St
Wallace Cole Rd
Mosque Rd
Amie Sarr St
Jack Chow St
Jallow Jallow St
Jeremiah Allen St
Sagarr Jobe St
Alhassan Ndure St
Master Fowlis St
Rebecca Savage St
J. R. Forster St
Mam Mberry Njie St
Rev William Cole St
Hannah Forster St
Rene Blain St
Alpha Tapsiru St
Pierre Njie Tce
Abdou Wally Mbye St
Albion Place
This Area Strictly Out of Bounds
Main Entrance to Albert Market
Craft Market
Albert Market
July 22 Square
Russell St
Nelson Mandela St
Davidson Carrol St
Serign Sillah St
Imam Lamin Bah St
Liberation St
Marma Bah St
Ma Cumba Jallow St
Daniel Goddard St
OAU Blvd
Ecowas Ave
Tafsir Ebou Samba St
Tafsir Balla Joof St
Cherno Adama Bah St
Brown St
Ferry to Barra
Gambia River
Tanbi Wetland Complex
Kankujeri Rd
THE GAMBIA

PLACES TO STAY

3 Atlantic Hotel
4 Princess Diana Hotel
35 Abbey Guesthouse
44 Ferry Guesthouse
46 Apollo I lotel

PLACES TO EAT

5 Michel's
25 Café Central
31 Ali Baba Snack Bar
37 Jummy T Restaurant
41 St Raphael's

OTHER

1 The Unknown Soldier Monument
2 Arch 22
6 King Fahad Mosque
7 Gamtel Office
8 Royal Victoria Hospital
9 Petrol Station
10 State House
11 National Museum of the Gambia
12 Banjul Pharmacy
13 Minibuses to Bakau
14 St Mary's Anglican Cathedral
15 The Quadrangle (Government Offices)
16 Minibuses to Serekunda
17 War Memorial
18 Fountain
19 Boats (on Beach) for Jufureh & James Island
20 Post Office; Gamtel Office
21 Trust Bank
22 Guinean Consulate
23 Queen Nightclub
24 QuantumNET
26 Gamtel Office
27 Gambia International Airlines
28 West Coast Airlines
29 Olympic Travel
30 Ghana Airways
32 Air Senegal International
33 Police
34 Standard Chartered Bank
36 Happy Bar
38 Air Guinée
39 Banjul Travel Agency
40 IBC Bank
42 Sierra Leonean High Commission
43 Immigration Office
45 Pirogues to Barra
47 Ferries to Barra
48 Mariam Ceesay Bar & Restaurant
49 GPTC Bus Station

Dangers & Annoyances Muggings are rare in Banjul city centre although you always need to be alert. However, pickpockets are rife, their favourite hunting grounds being the Albert market, the ferry terminal and the cramped surrounds of the ferry itself.

Things to See

The vibrant heart of Banjul city is **Albert market** – see Shopping later in this section for more details. For a taste of the past, it can be interesting to walk in the quiet streets of the **old town**: Ma Cumba Jallow St has a few colonial buildings and traditional Krio-style houses, many of which still belong to families who came here from Sierra Leone, some as long ago as the 1820s.

THE GAMBIA

In the **National Museum of the Gambia** *(admission D15; open 8am-4pm Mon-Thur, 8am-1pm Fri & Sat)*, some of the exhibits are a bit dated but the explanations are good, especially in the music section. Upstairs there is a fascinating display of photos from the colonial period.

Nearby is **Arch 22**, a massive gateway to the city, built to celebrate the military coup of 22 July 1994. For D15 you can take the lift (if it's still working) to the top and have an overpriced beer or coffee at the underwhelming bar, but the views from the balcony make it worthwhile.

Activities

Most activities and organised tours can be arranged at the Atlantic coast resorts, so details are included in that section. One exception is **pirogue trips** on Oyster Creek – a popular destination for **bird-watching**, **fishing** or just messing about in boats. Many people come on trips organised by hotels, but you can arrange things informally a day in advance at the 'port' (a patch of mud with a few boats tied up) by Denton Bridge.

Places to Stay

Not many tourists stay in Banjul city, preferring instead the beach and comforts of the Atlantic coast. However, if you want a taste of the real Africa you're more likely to find it here.

Ferry Guesthouse *(☎ 222028, 28 Liberation St)* Beds on the veranda D70, singles/doubles D130/190, rooms with air-con D290. This is Banjul's best budget place, with big, airy rooms overlooking the Barra ferry terminal. Entry is via a lane leading to a rear stairwell.

Abbey Guesthouse *(☎ 225228, 38 Rev William Cole St)* Rooms without bathroom D80-150. Also in old Banjul, this building used to be the German consulate and has a great balcony, but the rooms are 'modest', as advertised. However, the shared bathrooms are fine, the food is cheap, and the manager's friendly.

Apollo Hotel *(☎ 228184, Tafsir Ebou Samba St)* Singles/doubles with fan D150/200, with air-con D300/360. This hotel was probably stylish once, but it's plain and soulless now. Rooms have bathrooms and are reasonably clean. Couples can share a single.

Princess Diana Hotel *(Kantora Hotel, ☎ 228715, July 22 Dr)* Singles/doubles B&B with fan D165/225, doubles with air-con D275. Since the former owner (he was the D fan) left town this place has gone downhill but it remains a decent option. It has clean rooms and meals are available (about D40).

Atlantic Hotel *(☎ 228601, fax 227861, ⓔ atlantic@corinthia.com, Muammar al Gadhafi Ave)* Singles/doubles with air-con D950/1200. Central Banjul's only upmarket hotel is comfortable and has numerous bars and restaurants. An evening buffet is D250 and you can pay by credit card.

Palm Grove Hotel *(☎ 201620, fax 201621, ⓔ palmgrove@gamtel.gm)* Singles/doubles D460/750, suites D750/1000. About 3km out of Banjul towards Serekunda, the Palm Grove is smaller, more personal, more stylish and better value than the Atlantic. Prices are very flexible, especially during the low season, and all rates include breakfast.

Places to Eat

Banjul has several cheap eateries where plates of rice and sauce start at about D6. Worth trying are the ***food stalls*** in Albert market and around the Barra ferry terminal, which are open during the day. Breakfast at the ferry terminal – skewered meat on fresh bread rolls with sweet coffee – comes highly recommended.

Ali Baba Snack Bar *(☎ 224055, Nelson Mandela St)* Open 9am-5pm Mon-Sat. More than just a kebab shop, this place is an institution with a deserved reputation for the best chawarmas in the country (D15).

Other options include the tiny ***Café Central***, open from 7am to 6pm Monday to

Saturday, around the corner from the Ali Baba. It serves local and European dishes for about D30, plus tasty sandwiches (D25 to D30) and beer (D9). Further south is ***Jummy T Restaurant*** *(☎ 222627, 7 Ma Cumba Jallow St)*, open 9am to 10pm Monday to Saturday, which is where to head if you fancy African dishes such as cow feet, *fufu* (mashed cassava) or comparatively boring domodah (all D10).

St Raphael's *(☎ 226324, 17 Davidson Carrol St)* Open 9am-midnight Mon-Sat. Once a snack bar, this place has graduated to restaurant status but seems to have forgotten to hike the prices. The large menu includes spicy seafood in foil (D20), pepper steak (D40) and spaghetti (D35).

Michel's *(☎ 223108, 29 July 22 Drive)* Open 8am-11pm daily. This new multicuisine restaurant is the classiest in town. The food and the prices will impress, from breakfast croissants (D8) to fish and steak dishes (D50 to D95). The paella (D60) and giant tiger prawns (D95) are both great value.

Entertainment

With the steady shift of people and businesses to the Atlantic coast resorts, most of Banjuls bars and nightclubs have closed.

Mariam Ceesay Bar & Restaurant *(☎ 226912)* Open 10am-7.30pm daily. Next to the ferry terminal, this is one of the few places you can reliably get a beer (D10).

Happy Bar *(Rev William Cole St)* Open 11am-2am daily. Here, 'if you are not happy, you can't come in'. This tiny joint serves the cheapest beer in town and Gambian and Ghanaian food.

Queen Nightclub *(Rene Blain St)* Admission costs D10. This is a pretty raw scene and could be intimidating for women on their own – if possible, take a Gambian friend.

Shopping

Walking through the main entrance of ***Albert market*** you'll pass stalls selling clothes, shoes, household and electrical wares, and just about everything else. Keep going and you'll reach the myriad colours and flavours of the fruit and vegetables market. Beyond here you'll find stalls catering mainly for tourists, usually called the ***Craft Market***, where you can browse through a wide range of carvings, fabrics, batiks, paintings, drums and other traditional musical instruments.

Kerewan Sound *(Russell St)* near the main entrance to Albert market (ask for directions when you get to the archway) is the best place for cassettes and CDs of African music.

Getting There & Away

Air For details of international flights to Gambia, see the main Getting There & Away section earlier in this chapter. A few airlines maintain offices in Banjul centre, including the following:

Air Guinée (☎ 223296, 903935) 72 OAU Blvd
Air Senegal International (☎ 472095) Ecowas Ave
Gambia International Airlines (☎ 223703/4, fax 223700, e gia-marketing@gamtel.gm) 78 Daniel Goddard St
Ghana Airways (☎ 228245, w www.ghana-airways-it.com) Nelson Mandela St
West Coast Airlines (☎ 201954, fax 201956) 7 Nelson Mandela St

Bus GPTC buses run several times a day between Banjul and Basse Santa Su (D75, about seven hours), with Soma (D37.50) and Georgetown (D62.50) en route. The buses leave from a wide piece of road GPTC likes to call a bus station on Cherno Adama Bah St, near the port. Ordinary buses leave at 6.45am, 7.30am, 9am, 10am and 1pm.

The express bus leaves at 8am, and costs D10 more to each destination. Reservations are not possible, so to be sure of a seat (particularly on the express), get the bus from the Jimpex Rd depot, in Kanifeng near Serekunda. The buses leave from here 30 minutes before they leave Banjul and cost an extra D2.

Bush Taxi Minibuses to Brikama, upcountry towns and southern Senegal all go from Serekunda garage (bush-taxi park). For more details see the Atlantic Coast Resorts & Serekunda section later in this chapter.

Boat Ferries are supposed to run between Banjul and Barra every one to two hours, from 7am until 7pm, but there are frequent delays and often one ferry is out of action. Get a ticket (D5) from the booth before going aboard. The ferries take vehicles, but car space is limited and it's not unusual for cars to wait hours for a place, while trucks regularly wait days! For information, call the ferry office (☎ 228205).

If the ferry isn't running, pirogues will be. The ride can be downright dangerous in choppy conditions, as was proven in February 2002 when a pirogue sank and 25 people drowned. The fare is D5 to D7 per person – always check before boarding. Pirogues also run at night, although the fare (and the risk) rises considerably.

Getting Around

To/From the Airport A green tourist taxi from Banjul international airport to Banjul is D180. The official fixed rates are painted on a board at the taxi rank, so bargaining is usually not required. Cheaper are the yellow taxis, which will take you to Banjul for about D120, or to the coast for D100. There is no airport bus but minibuses (see following) run along the main road between Brikama and Serekunda, passing the turn-off 3km from the airport.

Minibus & Shared Taxi Local minibuses run from near the Albert market in Banjul to Serekunda and Bakau, while yellow shared taxis run between Serekunda, Fajara and Bakau. The route between Serekunda, Kotu and Kololi is served by shared taxis and minibuses. Between Banjul and Fajara you have to change at Bakau or Serekunda. From Banjul to Bakau or Serekunda is D4, from Bakau or Serekunda to Fajara is D3.

Private Taxi If you take a yellow taxi by yourself it's called a town trip, and is more costly than a shared taxi trip in the same vehicle. A short ride across Banjul city centre costs about D20, but negotiation is required. From Banjul it's about D70 to Bakau, D80 to Serekunda and D90 to Fajara. Check the price with the driver first. Green tourist taxis also do town trips, but charge more.

Atlantic Coast Resorts & Serekunda

The Atlantic coast resorts of Bakau, Fajara, Kotu and Kololi are the heart of Gambia's

THE ATLANTIC COAST RESORTS

PLACES TO STAY
- 2 Cape Point Hotel; 911 Nightclub
- 9 Crocs Guesthouse
- 11 Bakau Guesthouse
- 20 Ngala Lodge
- 28 Francisco's Hotel & Restaurant
- 29 Leybato
- 30 Fajara Hotel
- 32 Bungalow Beach Hotel; Kombo Beach Novotel
- 34 Safari Garden Hotel; Flavours Restaurant
- 36 Friendship Hotel
- 48 Kanifeng YMCA Hostel
- 69 Praia Motel
- 73 Green Line Motel
- 79 Kololi Inn & Tavern
- 81 Bakadaji Hotel & Restaurant
- 85 Keneba Hotel
- 86 Balmoral Apartments
- 89 Senegambia Hotel; AB Rent-a-Car
- 90 Kairaba Hotel; The Gambia Experience Office; Tropical Tours & Souvenirs

PLACES TO EAT
- 3 Baobab Sunshine Bar
- 5 The Clay Oven
- 13 Buddies; Kumba's Bar
- 14 Buggerland
- 26 Weezo's
- 27 Eddie's Bar & Restaurant
- 31 The Sailor; Paradise Beach Bar
- 33 Gambia Etten
- 35 Golden Bamboo
- 41 Afra Kairaba
- 43 Le Palais du Chocolat
- 50 Come Inn
- 53 LK Fast Food
- 54 Safe Way Afra King
- 56 Sen Fast Food
- 64 C&B Grill
- 80 Village Gallery & Restaurant
- 84 Solomon's Beach Bar
- 91 Dolphin Bar & Restaurant

OTHER
- 1 Botanical Gardens
- 4 St Mary's Food & Wine Supermarket
- 6 One for the Road Bar
- 7 Lacondula International Pub
- 8 Gena Bes Batik Factory
- 10 Catholic Church
- 12 Minibuses to Banjul & Serekunda
- 15 Police
- 16 Trust Bank; Gamtel Office
- 17 IBC Bank
- 18 Guinea-Bissau Embassy
- 19 Standard Chartered Bank
- 21 UK Embassy
- 22 Medical Research Council
- 23 Olympic Travel
- 24 QuantumNET; Timbooktoo
- 25 SN Brussels Airlines Office
- 37 Shell Petrol Station; ATM
- 38 CyberWorld
- 39 St Mary's Food & Wine Supermarket
- 40 Harry's Supermarket
- 42 US Embassy
- 44 Afri-Swiss Travels
- 45 Senegalese Embassy

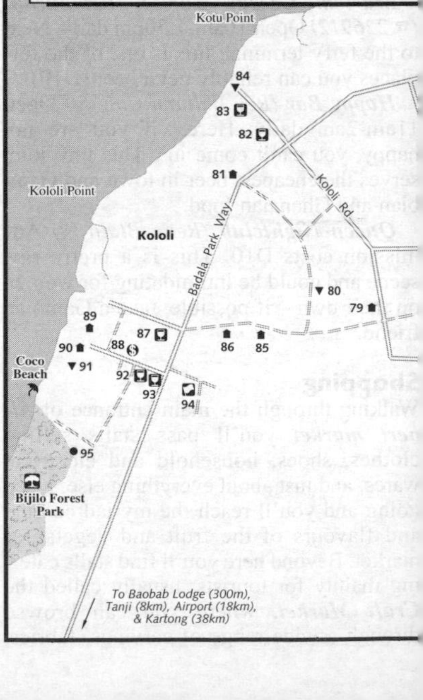
Kotu Point
84
83
82
81
Kololi Point
Kololi
Badala Park Way
Kololi Rd
80
79
89
87
86
85
90
88
91
92
93
94
Coco Beach
95
Bijilo Forest Park
To Baobab Lodge (300m), Tanji (8km), Airport (18km), & Kartong (38km)

& SEREKUNDA

OTHER (CONTINUED)
- 46 Jobort Laboratories
- 47 Mosque
- 49 Water Tower
- 51 Post Office
- 52 Jimpex Rd GPTC Bus Depot
- 55 Alliance Française-Gambienne
- 57 Standard Chartered Bank
- 58 Gamtel Office
- 59 Maroun's Supermarket
- 60 Minibuses to Banjul
- 61 Westfield Clinic
- 62 Jokor Nightclub
- 63 Mrs Musu Kebba
- 64 Drammeh's Batik Factory
- 65 Minibuses to Banjul
- 66 Serekunda Garage (Bush-Taxi Park)
- 67 IBC Bank; Shell Petrol Station
- 68 Trust Bank
- 70 Gamtel Office
- 71 Bobby's Choice
- 72 Petrol Station
- 74 Police
- 75 Asiamarie Cinema
- 76 Lana's Bar
- 77 Arena Babou Fatty
- 78 Hertz; Bakoteh Elf Petrol Station
- 82 Salz Bar
- 83 Churchill's
- 87 Spy Bar
- 88 Standard Chartered Bank; Abaraka Jeep Safari; Gamtel Office
- 92 The Pub
- 93 Waaw Nightclub
- 94 Mauritanian Consulate
- 95 Bijilo Forest Park Headquarters

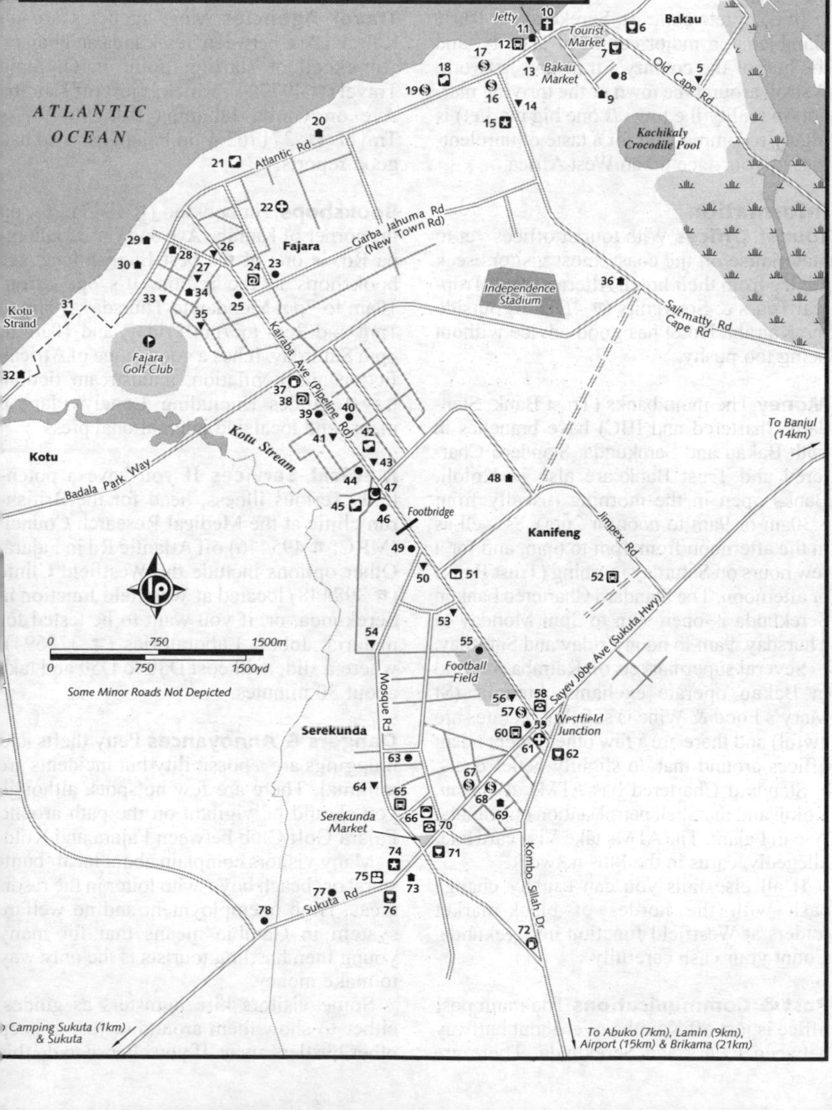

Cape Point
Bakau
Jetty
Tourist Market
Bakau Market
Old Cape Rd
Kachikaly Crocodile Pool
ATLANTIC OCEAN
Atlantic Rd
Garba Jahuma Rd (New Town Rd)
Fajara
Independence Stadium
Saitmatty Rd
Cape Rd
Kotu Strand
Fajara Golf Club
Kairaba Ave (Pipeline Rd)
Kotu Stream
Kotu
Badala Park Way
To Banjul (14km)
Footbridge
Kanifeng
Jimpex Rd
Sayer Jobe Ave (Sukuta Hwy)
0 750 1500m
0 750 1500yd
Some Minor Roads Not Depicted
Football Field
Westfield Junction
Mosque Rd
Serekunda
Serekunda Market
Sukuta Rd
Kombo Sillah Dr
To Camping Sukuta (1km) & Sukuta
To Abuko (7km), Lamin (9km), Airport (15km) & Brikama (21km)

THE GAMBIA

tourist industry, with about 20 hotels along this 10km-long series of beaches, and more planned. Back from the beach are more hotels, with restaurants, bars, nightclubs, souvenir stalls and all the other paraphernalia of tourism. The main tourist concentrations are at Kololi, which is referred to by most Gambians as 'Senegambia' after the hotel of the same name, and at Kotu. You won't have to look far to find pork pies or sauerkraut here.

In complete contrast, Serekunda is 100% Gambian – a major centre of activity, and the hub of the country's transport network. A stroll around the town or the thriving market (in reality the town *is* one big market) is highly recommended for a taste of unrelenting, in-your-face urban West Africa.

Information

Tourist Offices With tourist offices yet to materialise on the coast, most visitors seek advice from their hotel. Alternatively, Tropical Tours & Souvenirs (☎ 460536) outside the Kairaba Hotel has good advice without being too pushy.

Money The main banks (Trust Bank, Standard Chartered and IBC) have branches in both Bakau and Serekunda. Standard Chartered and Trust Bank are also in Kololi. Banks open in the morning (usually from 8.30am or 9am to noon or 2pm), as well as in the afternoon from 4pm to 6pm, and for a few hours on Saturday morning (Trust Bank) or afternoon. The Standard Chartered bank in Serekunda is open 9am to 3pm Monday to Thursday, 9am to noon Friday and Saturday.

Several supermarkets on Kairaba Ave and in Bakau operate exchange bureaus (St Mary's Food & Wine is safe but its rates are awful) and there are a few other independent offices around that do slightly better deals.

Standard Chartered has ATMs at Bakau, Kololi and the Shell petrol station on Kairaba Ave in Fajara. The ATMs take Visa card and, allegedly, cards in the Plus network.

If all else fails you can usually change cash with the hordes of black-market traders at Westfield Junction in Serekunda. Count your cash carefully.

Post & Communications The main post office is just off Kairaba Ave, about halfway between Fajara and Serekunda. There are Gamtel offices in Bakau, Kololi and Serekunda, and private telecentres everywhere, but especially in Serekunda.

There are more than a dozen Internet cafés along the coast. Kairaba Ave is a favourite, with QuantumNET, Gamtel and CyberWorld all here, all with fast connections and all for about D30 an hour. You can also get online in Kololi, Bakau and Serekunda.

Travel Agencies Most agencies are on Kairaba Ave between Serekunda and Fajara. An excellent starting point is Olympic Travel (☎ 497204), which is just off Kairaba Ave on Garba Jahumpa Rd. Afri-Swiss Travels (☎ 371762/4) in Fajara has also had good reports.

Bookshops Timbooktoo (☎ 494345/6), on the corner of Kairaba Ave and Garba Jahumpa Rd, is one of the best English-language bookshops in the region. It's open from 10am to 7pm Monday to Thursday, 10am to 1pm and 3pm to 7pm Friday, and 10am to 8pm Saturday. It has a good range of African fiction and nonfiction, mainstream fiction, travel guides (including Lonely Planet), maps, and local and international press.

Medical Services If you have a potentially serious illness, head for the British-run clinic at the Medical Research Council (MRC; ☎ 495446) off Atlantic Rd in Fajara. Other options include the Westfield Clinic (☎ 398448) located at Westfield Junction in Serekunda, or, if you want to be tested for malaria, Jobort Laboratories (☎ 375694), where a slide will cost D30 to D50 and take about 30 minutes.

Dangers & Annoyances Petty thefts and muggings are a possibility but incidents are minimal. There are few hotspots, although you should be vigilant on the path around Fajara Golf Club between Fajara and Kotu.

Many visitors complain about local 'bumsters' or 'beach boys' who loiter in the resort areas. High unemployment and no welfare system in Gambia means that for many young men hustling tourists is the only way to make money.

Some visitors hire bumsters as guides, either to show them around or just to keep other hustlers away. If you choose to do this it's best to use one of the official tourist guides (OTGs), who have had training in dealing with tourists. If you don't need help, be polite but firm when declining offers.

Things to See

Kachikaly Crocodile Pool *(admission D10)* in Bakau is a sacred site for the local people, who traditionally come here to pray – the crocodiles represent fertility. Success rates are apparently high, as many children in this area are named Kachikaly. Despite being a popular tourist spot, this place is usually quiet and well worth a visit. It's probably the nearest you'll get to a crocodile anywhere in Africa without having your leg chewed off – some people actually pet the more lethargic crocs. The largest croc is called Charley and seems completely resigned to being touched and photographed.

The **Bakau market** is a lively place full of bright colours and the strong smells of traditional foods. Opposite here a road leads down to a **beach** and a small jetty where fishing boats come and go while thousands of fish dry in the sun. Morning and late afternoon are the best times to visit. Further north is the **Botanical Gardens**, which is a peaceful, shady place and good for spotting birds.

Bijilo Forest Park *(admission D20)* is a small wildlife reserve on the coast, just a short walk from Kololi. It's a beautiful place to visit, and should be supported as it helps prevent more hotel development down the coast. A well-maintained series of trails of different lengths leads through the lush and shady vegetation, and you'll easily see monkeys and numerous birds. The monkeys are habituated to humans, mainly because visitors feed them. Birds are more easily spotted on the coast side. The dunes near the beach are covered in grass and low bush, with tall stands of palm just behind. Further back, away from the dunes, the trees are large and dense and covered in creepers. Many trees are labelled, and you can buy a small booklet (D15) that tells you a little about their natural history, traditional uses and so on.

Activities

If the Atlantic doesn't appeal, all the major hotels have **swimming pools**, while sailboards and other equipment can be rented on the beach from the **Fajara Watersports Centre** *(☎ 912002)*. The beaches are relatively safe, but people still drown every year, so it's best to swim between the flags where lifeguards are on patrol.

Fajara Golf Club has the country's main golf course, where an 18-hole round with clubs, balls and caddy is D275. Smooth grass is hard to grow here, so the holes are surrounded by well maintained 'browns', not greens! The club also has courts for tennis, squash and badminton.

Places to Stay

You'll find everything from plush resorts to grotty dives on the Atlantic coast, where competition is so intense that if you're there out of the peak season you'll almost always be able to negotiate a better deal. The list here is not exhaustive, but gives a good cross-section of options, especially for independent travellers. All rooms have bathrooms unless specified.

Places to Stay – Budget

Bakau Near Kachikaly Crocodile Pool, deep in the maze that is Bakau village, ***Crocs Guesthouse*** *(☎ 496654)* is the place to stay if you want to be in a typical urban Gambian environment. There are four large, self-catering rooms, singles/doubles cost D150/200. A local boy will show the way for about D5.

Bakau Guesthouse *(☎ 497460, 921854, Atlantic Rd)* Singles/doubles D180/250. Huge, clean, airy rooms with fan and fridge overlooking Bakau market or the beach make this guesthouse good value. However, expect prices to rise.

Friendship Hotel *(☎ 495830, ⓔ ifh@qanet.gm)* Singles/doubles with fan D195/225, with air-con D250/300. Next to (and associated with) the Independence Stadium, these spotless rooms with hot water and TV are a steal. The downsides are the location and the overly inquisitive staff.

Fajara East of Fajara, ***Kanifeng YMCA Hostel*** *(☎ 392647, fax 390793)* is a good budget option with simple but clean singles/doubles with shared bathroom for D80/120. Breakfast is an extra D10. Phone first to see whether there are vacancies.

Kololi About 1.5km from the beach, ***Kololi Inn & Tavern*** *(☎ 463410, fax 460486)* has a very African feel with bright thatched bungalows. Singles/doubles are D150/200, including breakfast. There is a small bar-restaurant, and a kitchen for guests.

Keneba Hotel *(☎ 460093)* Rooms D175 per person. In the same area as Kololi Inn, this place has small bungalows with bathroom; breakfast is included. You can get here on a minibus from Serekunda heading for Kololi; get off at the junction by the Spy Bar.

Serekunda On Sayer Jobe Ave, ***Green Line Motel*** *(☎ 394015)* is an old favourite but we don't know why. Singles/doubles are D200/300; they're hot and noisy, and the air-con and water supply are failing.

Praia Motel *(☎ 394887, 900902, Mame Jout St)* Rooms D200. A few minutes' walk off Sayer Jobe Ave, these simple but clean rooms in a very local part of Serekunda are worth your attention. Amiable Mr Ceesay is full of advice and serves cheap beer too. Air-con costs D50 more.

Sukuta Southwest of Serekunda, ***Camping Sukuta*** *(☎ 917786, ⓔ campingsukuta@yahoo.de)* has long been a favourite with overlanders and now offers comfortable rooms as well. Camp sites are D40 per person plus D10 per vehicle, singles/doubles cost D95/145 (add about D70 for a bathroom). Everything here is clean and organised with true German efficiency by the friendly owners, Joe and Claudia. These guys have spent a long time on the road and know about routes, spares, and where to buy and sell vehicles. From Serekunda, take any minibus towards Brufut or Gunjur, and get off near the junction where the roads to Gunjur and Brufut divide.

Places to Stay – *Mid-Range*

Several of the hotels in this range are small, owner-managed, and more used to dealing with individual travellers than the larger top-end establishments (although many also cater for groups). All rooms have their own bathroom and most hotels accept credit cards.

Bakau At the east end of Atlantic Rd, ***Cape Point Hotel*** *(☎ 495005, fax 495375)* has attractive gardens, a small pool and plenty of package tourists. Doubles with fan/air-con are D500/600, apartments with two double rooms and kitchen cost D700.

Fajara A small British-Gambian enterprise, ***Safari Garden Hotel*** *(☎ 495887, fax 497841, ⓔ geri@qanet.gm)* is popular as much for its friendly and efficient atmosphere as it is for its stylish rooms, lush garden and sparkling swimming pool. Singles/doubles/triples are D350/500/650, including breakfast. The well-trained staff are complemented by a management happy to answer your Gambia queries. Good value and highly recommended.

Leybato *(☎ 497186, fax 497562, ⓔ leybato47@hotmail.com)* Bungalows D350-400. This small Gambian guesthouse and restaurant (see Places to Eat) has one of the best locations anywhere on the coast. All the rooms are different and all prices negotiable. Leybato is reached along a dirt track opposite the end of Kairaba Ave.

Francisco's Hotel & Restaurant *(☎/fax 495332, Atlantic Rd)* Singles/doubles D550/680. These comfortable air-con rooms have a TV and fridge and come with a full English breakfast. It's good value.

Kotu & Kololi The extensive grounds at ***Bakadaji Hotel & Restaurant*** *(☎/fax 462307, ⓔ bakadajikn@hotmail.com)* open onto the beach and there's a flock of sheep to keep the grass short! Singles/doubles with breakfast are D300/450; self-catering bungalows (with two double rooms, lounge and kitchen) are D650.

Balmoral Apartments *(☎ 461079, mob 903634, ⓦ www.balmoral-apartments.com)* Self-catering apartments D450. East off Badala Park Way in Kololi, this small and homely place is good value.

Places to Stay – Top End

Most top-end hotels cater for groups of package tourists rather than independent travellers, so information here is cut to the bone. Prices for independent travellers may be reduced to half the advertised rate if you phone in advance, especially in the low season (when rates drop anyway). All rooms have air-con and most rates include breakfast. Nearly all hotels are on the beach and have a pool. Most accept credit cards.

Fajara If it wasn't on the beach you'd think ***Fajara Hotel*** *(☎ 495605, fax 495339)* was an army barracks. Singles/doubles will set you back D650/750.

Ngala Lodge *(☎ 497429, W www.ngala lodge.com)* Doubles US$140. In contrast, this place is small, stylish and exclusive, and has double suites. Be sure to book ahead.

Kotu A big place with stacks of facilities, ***Bungalow Beach Hotel*** *(☎ 465288, fax 466180, e bbhotel@qanet.gm)* offers self-contained singles/doubles for D700/900.

Kombo Beach Novotel *(☎ 465466, fax 465490, e kombo@gamtel.gm)* Singles/doubles D1000/1200. The Kombo is a favourite with 20-somethings and has hired help to 'jolly the punters' around the pool.

Kololi Claiming to be the best hotel in Gambia ***Kairaba Hotel*** *(☎ 462940, W www.kairabahotel.com)* isn't far wrong. Singles/doubles are D1840/D2240.

Senegambia Hotel *(☎ 462718/9, fax 461839, W www.senegambiahotel.com)* Singles D900-1060, doubles D1100-1360. Age has wearied the Senegambia a little, but you won't be uncomfortable.

Places to Eat

Mass tourism has made the area around the Atlantic coast resorts one of the best places to eat in West Africa. With new restaurants opening at a dizzying rate there's no shortage of cuisines to choose from. The greatest concentration of eateries is found in the Senegambia strip at Kololi, but for quality and individuality Fajara and Bakau are better bets. Of course, there's no shortage of local food either – try Serekunda and to a lesser extent Bakau if you came to Africa to eat more than burgers and pizzas. All the upmarket hotels have their own restaurants, and their evening buffets – usually D100 to D150 for all you can eat – might appeal.

Bakau At taxi ranks and the market there are usually women cooking rice and sauce, which goes for about D7 a plate, and other stalls selling fruit, nuts and other snacks.

Buggerland *(☎ 497697, 52 Saitmatty Rd)* Meals D30-50. Open 11am-midnight daily. We suspect the signwriter imbibed one too many JulBrews before he started work on this tiny burger joint. The 'buggers' and other not-so-fast food are pretty good, especially the fish and chips (D35).

Buddies *(☎ 495501)* Meals D40-90. Open 9am-2am daily. On Atlantic Rd near the market, this place does a good mix of Gambian and European dishes as well as afra (grilled meat). There's also a good all-day breakfast (D40).

Baoba Sunshine Bar Meals D25-40. Open until 8pm daily. Well worth checking out, this friendly, local-style bar is about 50m south along the beach from the Cape Point Hotel. Meals include shrimp sandwiches and Gambian dishes.

The Clay Oven *(☎ 496600)* Mains D90-120, side dishes D40-60. Open 7pm-11pm daily. Just off Old Cape Rd, this stylish place does excellent Indian food.

Fajara Hidden away in the back streets of Fajara, ***Golden Bamboo*** *(☎ 494213)* does good, cheap, Western-style Chinese food. Meals range from D40 to D70. Open 5pm to 11pm daily.

Eddie's Bar & Restaurant Meals D25-35. Open 8am-2am daily. Off Kairaba Ave, this local favourite offers afra and other good Gambian dishes. Guests at nearby top-end hotels have been known to sneak down for a taste of genuine Gambian cooking.

Flavours Meals D30-80. Open 8am-midnight daily. In the colourful courtyard of the Safari Garden Hotel (see Places to Stay – Mid-Range), this restaurant serves some of the most imaginative dishes in Gambia and will appeal to carnivores and vegetarians alike. Dining here allows you to use the swimming pool and there's a barbecue on Friday for D75.

Gambia Etten *(☎ 496754, 924205)* Meals D70-200. Open 8am-midnight daily. About 50m from the Safari Garden, this quiet, romantic restaurant in a garden setting gets good reports from locals. It's renowned for big pepper steaks (D85) and good service.

Leybato *(☎ 497186, fax 497562, e leybato47@hotmail.com)* Meals around D60. Open daily. The food here isn't the finest in town but it's hard to argue with the setting, right on the Atlantic Ocean – sunset here shouldn't be missed! On the menu you'll find steaks and seafood.

Kairaba Ave offers many more choices. The best thing to do is stroll down during the day and check out your options, but here are a few names to get you started.

Weezo's *(☎ 496918, W www.weezos.com, 132 Kairaba Ave)* Mains D130-150. Open

11am-3.30pm & 7pm-3am daily. This classy place morphs with the clock: it's a fusion-flavoured café for lunch, a smart Mexican cantina for dinner, and a trendy cocktail bar after 11pm. The food is great, and tapas (D50 to D70) is available all night.

Le Palais du Chocolat *(☎ 395397, 19 Kairaba Ave)* This café-patisserie does good coffee and English breakfast (D50), and great ice cream and imported chocolate. Enough to answer any calorie craving.

Afra Kairaba Meals D40. This eatery serves take-away grilled chicken and other meat in the evenings.

Kotu Readers have warmly recommended ***The Sailor*** *(☎ 4605210)* as one of the better beach bars on the coast. Burgers, pizzas and very fresh fish are all available (from D30 to D100) – the grilled fillet of barracuda in garlic and lime sauce (D90) is rather good. Open 9am to midnight daily.

Paradise Beach Bar *(☎ 466624)* Dishes D20-55. This place is more laid-back than The Sailor, with good Gambian dishes for D55.

Kololi Through the arch near the entrance to the Kairaba Hotel, you'll find all your favourite Euro-dishes, plus Gambian specialities and draft JulBrew at the ***Dolphin Bar & Restaurant*** *(☎ 460929)*. Meals range from D40 to D110. Open 9am to 11pm daily.

Scala Restaurant *(☎ 460813)* Meals from D110. If you're looking for a night out in your best holiday clothes, this place on the Senegambia strip is for you. The European food gets regular compliments, but don't forget to go to the bank first.

Solomon's Beach Bar *(☎ 460716)* Meals D40-80. Open 10am-midnight daily. At the north end of Kololi beach, this place is famous for its seafood grill and chips (D50) – try it.

Village Gallery & Restaurant *(☎ 460 369, e bahs@qanet.gm)* Meals D40-100. Open 10am-midnight daily. Surrounded by a gallery displaying local artworks, this visually stunning place serves excellent Gambian food. Meat dishes cost just D50, and a variety of vegetarian dishes are D40 to D50. The Saturday night Gambian buffet is great value at D100. This place can be hard to find – take a taxi (D15 to D20).

Serekunda There are several ***cheap eating houses*** around the market and taxi-park entrance, and several others scattered through the streets of Serekunda.

Heading up Kairaba Ave from Westfield Junction you'll find ***Sen Fast Food*** *(☎ 372 792)*, with omelettes (D20) and chawarmas (D15) standard fare. Further along is the similar ***LK Fast Food***. Both are open from 9am to midnight. Past LK is the ***Come Inn*** *(☎ 391 464)*, a German-style garden restaurant that serves tasty mains for about D70.

On Mosque Rd is the ***Safe Way Afra King*** *(☎ 391360)*, serving afra, sandwiches, fufu, 'cowfoot' and other African dishes from 5pm to midnight, all for less than D25. Further along is the ***C&B Grill*** *(☎ 375906)*, with similar fare at slightly higher prices.

Self-Catering The biggest supermarkets are found about halfway along Kairaba Ave. ***Harry's*** *(☎ 397444)*, open from 9am to 10pm Monday to Saturday, is probably the pick. There's a branch of ***St Mary's Food & Wine*** here too, and there are other branches in Bakau, on Cape Point Rd, and in Kololi, on the Senegambia strip. In Serekunda is ***Maroun's*** at Westfield Junction. All these stores are open from about 9am to 7.30pm Monday to Saturday and 10am to 1.30pm Sunday.

Entertainment

Many of the restaurants and hotels listed above have bars, some large and formulaic, others more personal, and a few in breathtaking locations. Of those with a sea view, ***Leybato*** in Fajara, ***The Sailor*** and ***Paradise Beach Bar*** at Kotu, and ***Solomon's Beach Bar*** at Kololi are all excellent spots for an afternoon ale. The bars mentioned following are generally smaller and more intimate affairs, more likely to have local patrons than purely package tourists.

Bakau & Fajara The shanty-like ***Lacondula International Pub*** *(☎ 495945, 21 Old Cape Rd)* plays reggae music and is worth investigating if you're up for a Gambian pub experience, or just want cheap beer. Nearby on Atlantic Rd is the ***One for the Road Bar***, a breezy place with just two tables, a fridge and owner-barman Sajo.

Nearer Bakau market on Atlantic Rd are ***Kumba's Bar*** *(☎ 496123)*, where beer is

D12 and decent food is on offer, and ***Buddies*** *(☎ 495501)*, where local bands play every night during the tourist season and pints of JulBrew cost D22. Both these places are open from 9am to 2am daily. For nightclubs, try ***911*** near the Cape Point Hotel. Most bars in Fajara are attached to hotels or restaurants.

Kololi The liveliest strip in the country is probably Senegambia Rd, where tourists, and to a lesser extent locals, have an impressive choice of drinking establishments. The ***Waaw Nightclub*** is popular, and there are several street-side bars and restaurants in the same area, though you'll constantly be fending off touts. ***The Pub*** has an upstairs terrace from where you can watch *other* people being hassled.

Towards Kotu is the vast ***Spy Bar*** nightclub. In stark contrast is the small and local ***Salz Bar*** *(☎ 460434)*, which opens at 9pm, earlier for big football matches. Nearer the beach is ***Churchill's***, the closest thing to an English pub in Gambia.

Serekunda Here you'll find bars with a more local feel. ***Lana's Bar*** *(☎ 395424)* is a small bar on a corner of Sukuta Rd and is ideal for refreshments during the day. Opposite the market, ***Bobby's Choice*** *(☎ 901 638)* affords a perfect view of the surrounding bustle, while ***Joker's Nightclub*** at Westfield Junction is the pick of the Serekunda clubs.

Spectator Sports

The Gambia's main sporting arena is ***Independence Stadium*** in Bakau, which is the site of major football matches and other sporting events. These are advertised locally on posters around town.

Traditional wrestling occasionally takes place at the Independence Stadium but it's more interesting, and much more fun, to see matches at one of the several smaller 'arenas' (open patches of ground) in Serekunda. These include the ***Arena Babou Fatty***, off Sukuta Rd, southwest of the Green Line Motel, and the ***Arena Tuti Fall Jammeh***, also on the west side of town, a couple of hundred metres south of Sukuta Rd. Matches take place in the late afternoon, usually on Sunday (less frequently in the dry season, and not during Ramadan). The entrance fee is usually about D15 for tourists. It's notoriously difficult to get notice of these matches. Ask a taxi driver or Gambian friend to keep an ear to the ground. Most wrestling goes on during November and December.

Traditional Wrestling

Watching a traditional wrestling match is a fascinating experience and great fun. The preliminaries can be as entertaining as the actual fights. Wrestlers enter the arena in full costume, a loincloth of bright, patterned material arranged with a tail falling behind, and their bodies and arms smothered in leather grigri (charms). They then slowly strut around the ring, sometimes preceded by griots beating drums.

There are usually many matches, as they last only a few minutes, until one contestant forces the other to the ground (technically one knee touching the ground ends the match). As many as four matches may be going on at once. And during the fight anything goes: biting, kicking, punching. No fancy hand-locks, technical throws, or points. Just get him down!

Shopping

At the entrance to the Kairaba Hotel in Kololi, ***Tropical Tours & Souvenirs*** *(☎ 460 536)* is worth checking out. It stocks an excellent selection of books, plus maps, postcards, clothing, film, batteries and craft items.

Bakau market has several stalls selling carvings, traditional cloth and other souvenirs. Opposite the Gamtel office is a particularly hassle-free ***shop*** selling batiks and brightly coloured clothing of good quality, at reasonable prices.

In the streets behind the Bakau market, near the Cinema Kachikaly (ask for Queen Amie), ***Gena Bes batik factory*** has a good selection of batiks and tie-dye cloth for around D60 per metre.

Readers have also recommended the tie-dye and ***batik factory*** *(☎ 960056)* in Serekunda owned by Mrs Musu Kebba Drammeh – all the taxi drivers know her place.

Getting There & Away

Peugeot taxis and assorted other bush taxis go from the garage (as the bush-taxi station is known) in Serekunda to upcountry towns south of the river (to Soma D35, Farafenni D40, Basse Santa Su D70), and to places on the South Coast (to Brufut D4, Tanji D5, Sanyang D6). Vehicles for Brikama leave from Westfield Junction and cost D5. For more information on transport options to places in southern Senegal see the main Getting There & Away section earlier in this chapter.

For details on transport between the Atlantic coast resorts and Banjul, see Getting Around in the Banjul section earlier in this chapter.

Getting Around

To/From the Airport A green tourist taxi from Banjul international airport to Serekunda is D100, and to any Atlantic coast resort D150. Yellow taxis cost about a third less, depending on your powers of negotiation. There isn't any public transport to the airport, but minibuses between Brikama and Serekunda can drop you at the turn-off 3km from the airport.

Minibus & Shared Taxi From Serekunda, outside the Gamtel office at the southern end of Kairaba Ave, you can get shared taxis to Bakau (D3). In Bakau, minibuses and shared taxis for Kololi (D3) and Banjul leave from near the northwest corner of the market.

Private Taxi Green 'tourist taxis' wait at ranks outside most large hotels. Prices are high and fixed. 'Town trip' destinations and fares from Bakau include Kololi (D120), the airport (D180) and Banjul city centre (D100/150 one way/return).

Car & Motorcycle Outside the Senegambia Hotel, AB Rent-a-Car (☎/fax 460926) has self-drive vehicles from D400 per day, or D350 per day for seven days. Add D100 to D150 for full insurance, and another 10% in tax. The rental and a D10,000 deposit can be paid in cash or by credit card. Hertz has an office at Bakoteh Elf petrol station (☎ 390041) but its rates are higher.

Bicycle Mountain bikes and traditional roadsters can be hired from some of the bigger hotels, but many people get better bikes for less money at the private outfits that tend to operate from under a shady tree in the tourist areas. You'll see them in Kololi and Kotu, and there's also an enterprising outfit near the Fajara Golf Club. Prices range from about D45 to D100 a day, depending on your negotiating prowess.

ABUKO NATURE RESERVE

For a park of only 105 hectares, Abuko *(☎ 472888; admission D31.50; open 8am-7pm daily)* has amazingly diverse vegetation, partly because a stream runs through the centre, allowing both gallery forest and savanna species to flourish. More than 250 species have been sighted here, making Abuko one of the best places in West Africa for bird-watching.

Abuko also has a small animal orphanage and education centre, housing hyenas, lions and bushbucks, and in the forest you can see monkeys, duikers, porcupines, bushbabies and ground squirrels. Pools are home to Abuko's population of approximately 20 Nile crocodiles.

Birders can enter the reserve from 6.30am, the early morning or late afternoon are best for bird-watching, although most of the hides face into the sun in the evening. Mid-morning is most popular for groups, and around midday is the quietest time. Birders will have a good chance of seeing the African goshawk, ahanta francolin, collared sunbird, western bluebill and green turaco. The main trail through the reserve takes about two hours, but there are a couple of shorter options indicated on the map at the main entrance gate.

A booklet on Abuko's flora and fauna can be bought at the ticket office for D35.

A private taxi to Abuko from one of the beach hotels costs about D220, including two hours of waiting time. Alternatively, take a minibus from Serekunda towards Brikama (D3). The reserve's entrance is on the right (west) of the main road (you pass the exit about 200m before reaching the entrance).

LAMIN

The village of Lamin is unremarkable, but ***Lamin Lodge*** *(☎ 497603, 900231, ⓔ gamriv@gamtel.gm)*, about 3km east of the village, is a unique restaurant built on stilts and overlooking a mangrove creek. Meals cost around D50, and the lodge is open from 7am to 8pm daily. The lodge is where tour groups come for their 'birds and breakfast' trip, as

The Monkeys of Abuko

Abuko is an excellent place to observe monkeys, especially in the morning or evening when they are most active. There are three types found here: the green (or vervet) monkey, the endangered western red colobus monkey and, less frequently, the patas monkey.

The green monkey has grey underparts and a light green-brown back with a black face surrounded by white fur. Instantly recognisable is the male's bright blue scrotum. The troops are adaptable and feed in either the savanna or the forest areas; their diet consists of leaves, roots, fruit, insects and bird eggs. Even small birds get gobbled up.

The western red colobus is, not surprisingly, red in colour, usually tending to black or dark brown on the back and a lighter russet on the underparts, and is larger than the green monkey. It prefers the higher parts of the gallery forest, rarely straying far from its territory, and can often be seen jumping from branch to branch. Unusually for a monkey, its diet consists largely of leaves.

The patas monkey is about the same size as the red colobus, although more slender, with longer legs and tail, and light brownish-red on the back and top of the head, with very light grey underparts and face, and dark bushy eyebrows.

The three species live in relative harmony. Territories frequently overlap, and they do not compete for food. You may even notice different species cooperating. Young colobus and green monkeys can be seen playing together, while their adult counterparts help each other groom. The green monkeys are the most alert and their warning cries are recognised by the other species. It is not unusual for the usually 'resident' colobus monkeys nearing maturity to leave their own troop and team up with a group of green monkeys to explore a wider area, before rejoining a new colobus troop to mate.

the surrounding swamps and rice fields seem as attractive to **birds** as the lodge is to tourists. You can hire small **motor boats** (D250 per hour) or go out in a **canoe** with a paddler for D100. A ride to Banjul costs D300, and to Denton Bridge D350.

The food is good here, and lunch times are often busy in the tourist season, so you might consider coming in the late afternoon. Lamin Lodge can be reached from the Atlantic coast resorts by private taxi (D150/270 one way/return), or combine Lamin Lodge with Abuko for D300. Alternatively, from Serekunda take any minibus towards Brikama, get off in Lamin village, then follow the dirt road to the lodge.

Western Gambia

The Gambia's western border is the coast, only 50km long as the pelican flies, but over 80km if all the bays and promontories are included. The coast is divided into northern and southern sections by the mouth of the Gambia River. Beyond the Atlantic coast resorts, the south coast proper begins.

SOUTH COAST

This stretch of the coast was long overlooked by travellers because of the diabolical state of the roads. But the completion of coastal highways from Serekunda and Kololi to Kartong is set to end this blissful seclusion. Most of the coastal towns offer somewhere to stay, meaning a visit here doesn't need to be rushed – you can wander through traditional fishing villages or enjoy the beaches long after the day-trippers have retreated to their hotels.

Tanji & Around

The main attraction is **Tanji River Bird Reserve**, an area of dunes, lagoons, palms, dry woodland and coastal scrub. The wide range of habitats supports a good variety of birds; almost 300 species have been recorded here. Although waders and water birds are the most obvious, this figure includes 34 raptor species. Animals include green, patas and red colobus monkeys (see the boxed text 'The Monkeys of Abuko' above), and porcupines. Nearby Bijol Island and the surrounding islets are part of the reserve. Trips to this important turtle-breeding area run twice weekly between October and March. There are places for only five people on each trip, so book early by calling the park manager on ☎ 919219.

The reserve could be combined with a visit **Brufut Beach** fishing centre, from where it's a 2km stroll to the bird reserve office.

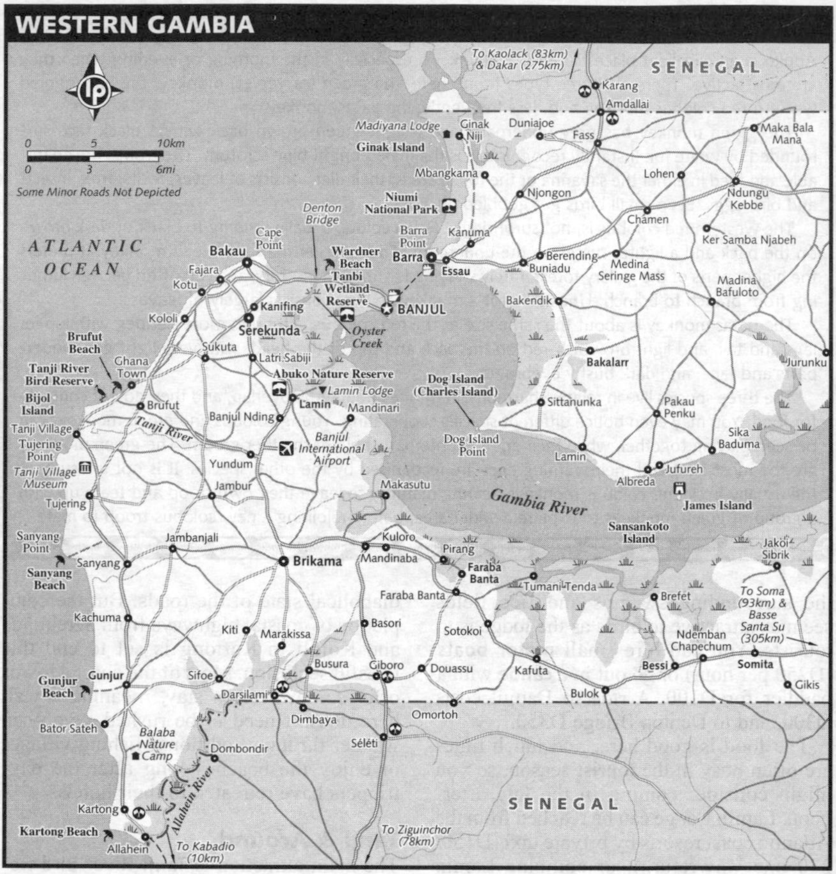
WESTERN GAMBIA
0 5 10km
0 3 6mi
Some Minor Roads Not Depicted
ATLANTIC OCEAN
To Kaolack (83km) & Dakar (275km)
SENEGAL
Karang
Amdallai
Madiyana Lodge
Ginak Niji
Duniajoe
Fass
Maka Bala Mana
Ginak Island
Mbangkama
Lohen
Njongon
Ndungu Kebbe
Niumi National Park
Chamen
Ker Samba Njabeh
Denton Bridge
Cape Point
Wardner Beach
Barra Point
Kanuma
Bakau
Barra
Berending
Medina Seringe Mass
Fajara
Essau
Buniadu
Madina Bafuloto
Kotu
Tanbi Wetland Reserve
Kanifing
BANJUL
Bakendik
Kololi
Serekunda
Oyster Creek
Brufut Beach
Sukuta
Ghana Town
Latri Sabiji
Bakalarr
Jurunku
Tanji River Bird Reserve
Abuko Nature Reserve
Lamin Lodge
Dog Island (Charles Island)
Bijol Island
Brufut
Lamin
Mandinari
Sittanunka
Pakau Penku
Tanji River
Banjul Nding
Tanji Village
Banjul International Airport
Sika Baduma
Tujering Point
Dog Island Point
Lamin
Yundum
Jufureh
Albreda
Tanji Village Museum
Makasutu
Tujering
Jambur
Gambia River
James Island
Sansankoto Island
Sanyang Point
Jambanjali
Kuloro
Jakoi Sibrik
Mandinaba
Pirang
Sanyang
Brikama
Faraba Banta
Sanyang Beach
Tumani Tenda
Faraba Banta
Brefet
To Soma (93km) & Basse Santa Su (305km)
Kachuma
Basori
Sotokoi
Ndemban Chapechum
Kiti
Marakissa
Busura
Giboro
Kafuta
Bessi
Somita
Gunjur Beach
Gunjur
Sifoe
Douassu
Gikis
Darsilami
Bulok
Dimbaya
Omortoh
Bator Sateh
Balaba Nature Camp
Séléti
Dombondir
Allahein River
SENEGAL
Kartong
Kartong Beach
To Ziguinchor (78km)
Allahein
To Kabadio (10km)

Admission to the bird reserve will set you back D31.50/15.75 for adults/children. To get there, take a bush taxi from Serekunda and ask to be let out at either Brufut Beach or the entrance to the reserve itself.

The village of **Tanji** is about 3km south of the reserve office. About a 15-minute walk away is the well-run ***Paradise Inn*** *(☎ 414 013, e paradiseinnlodge@gamtel.gm)*, with double bungalows set in a tropical garden for D260, including breakfast. About 2km further south is the fascinating **Tanji Village Museum** *(☎ 371007, W huizen.dds.nl/~tanje; admission D25; open daily)* with huts of various ethnic designs, displays of traditional artefacts, and an area with woodcarvers, blacksmiths and other artisans in action. There's a small ***bar-restaurant*** and accommodation in ***simple huts*** for D125 per person, including breakfast.

Further south is **Sanyang Beach**, one of the cleaner beaches on this stretch and a popular destination for day-trippers. About 1km inland is ***Sanyang Nature Camp*** *(☎ 497186)*, which has comfortable bungalows, but questionable water supply, in a pleasant setting for D150 per person including breakfast.

Gunjur Beach & Around

At Gunjur Beach there's a lot of activity: boats going in and out, nets being mended and fish being gutted. It's a good place for just sitting and looking – sunbathing is best done along the beach where you're less likely to upset the locals. Cheap food is available in the village where the road meets the beach, or you can head south to the European-style ***Gunjur Beach Motel*** *(☎ 486065, fax 486066)*, which has good meals from D55, camp sites for D25 per person plus D15 per tent, and bungalows for about D150 per person. The new road should make it simple to get to Gunjur Beach from Serekunda, but when we passed it was still easiest to come in a bush taxi from Brikama (D8).

About 3km south of Gunjur Beach is the hard-to-find and ultra-laid-back ***Balaba Nature Camp*** *(☎ 919012, W www.tribes.co.uk)*. Basic huts with open-air bathroom and full board cost D165 per person. Look for the yellow sign pointing left off the Kartong Hwy and follow the track.

Kartong

It used to take hours to get from Serekunda to Kartong, meaning few people bothered. Now it looks like the ideal launch pad into Casamance, but with no regular transport, no border post and a 10km hike on the Senegal side, you need to be keen.

Kartong itself is a village spread out under large shade trees. Not much English is spoken here, but head about 200m west along a dirt track to ***Morgan's Grocery*** and you'll find advice, food and beer. Along another dirt road leading west as you enter town is the low-key ***Follonko Resthouse*** with rooms at D75 per person. But you'd be stupid not to stay at the ***Boboi Beach Lodge*** *(fax 486026, e holiday@gambia-adventure.com)*, on the coast about 2km to the north – its beautiful beach setting and great food make it one of Gambia's budget gems. Large tents cost D50 per person, share bungalows D75 and double bungalows D175.

On the southern edge of Kartong, opposite the school, a track leads west for 300m to a sacred **crocodile pool**, with several deceptively soporific inhabitants, believed by locals to hold powers of fertility.

If you continue south, past the police post, you get to a fork in the road (2km from the village); keep right and pass through grassy dunes to reach the beach where fishing boats land. Go left at the fork to reach Kartong Fishing Centre and the Allahein River (also spelt Halahan), which marks the border with Senegal. If you do decide to enter Senegal here get your passport stamped at the police post, then cross the river by dugout canoe (D2). On the other side you'll be very lucky to avoid the 10km walk to Kabadio, between Kafountine and Diouloulou.

NORTH COAST & NORTH BANK

The north coast stretches all of 10km from the mouth of the Gambia River to the border with Senegal. In **Barra**, those with an interest in history may want to have a look at **Fort Bullen** *(admission D15)*, built by the British in the 1820s to help control slave shipping.

Ginak Island

The coastal island of Ginak (also spelt Jinak and often called 'Paradise Island' by tour operators) is part of **Niumi National Park**, where the range of habitats (beach, mud flats, salt marsh, dunes, mangrove swamps, lagoons, grassland and dry woodland) makes for excellent bird-watching. Dolphins are often seen from the shore and turtles nest on the beach. The park also protects small populations of manatees, crocodiles and clawless otters, plus monkeys and various small antelopes, although reports of the occasional leopard might be exaggerated.

On the beach, the only place to stay or eat is ***Madiyana Lodge*** *(☎ 494088, 920201, fax 495950)*, which has one of the most beautiful settings on the whole coast. Rooms cost D300, which includes breakfast and dinner. A day's tour costs UK£30 per person, and weekend trips are double. The booking agency is Tropical Tours & Souvenirs (see Organised Tours in the Getting Around section earlier in this chapter). Alternatively, a private taxi from Barra to the mainland opposite Ginak costs about D80, from where you go by dugout canoe (D2) across to the village of Ginak Niji and walk directly west across the island (20 minutes) to the lodge. Not as well located, but cheaper, is ***Coconut Lodge*** *(☎ 461152, 996905)*, near Niji.

Jufureh & Albreda

Jufureh became world famous in the 1970s following the publication of *Roots*, in which African-American writer Alex Haley describes how his ancestor Kunta Kinte was captured here and taken as a slave to America some 200 years ago. Today, Jufureh itself is nothing out of the ordinary – like many other villages along the Gambia River – but

The Roots Debate

Alex Haley based his research on recollections of elder relatives, who knew that their African forebear's name was Kinte and that he'd been captured by slavers while chopping wood for a drum outside his village. This later tied in with a story Haley was told by a griot at Jufureh. Critics have pointed out (quite reasonably) that the *Roots* story is flawed in many areas. Kinte is a common Mandinka/Malinké clan name throughout West Africa, and the griot's story of Kunta Kinte's capture would hardly have been unique. Also, as the slave stations of Albreda and James Island had been very close to Jufureh for some decades, it's unlikely that a villager from here would have been taken by surprise in this way.

The story of Alex Haley's ancestor is almost certainly true, but it's exceedingly unlikely that he actually came from here. Despite the inconsistencies, Haley seemed happy to believe he was descended from the Kintes of Jufureh, and the myth remains largely intact.

Detractors may delight in exposing fabrication, but there is a danger that the debate on the accuracy of Haley's story may obscure the much more serious, and undeniable, fact that the slave trade was immoral and inhuman, and had a devastating effect on Africa. Millions of men and women were captured by European traders, or by other Africans paid by Europeans, and taken to plantations in the Americas. Many historians also hold that their labour, and the slave trade itself, was fundamental to the economic development of Europe and the USA in the 18th and 19th centuries.

The Roots Festival attracts members of the African diaspora to Gambia, and Jufureh, for a week-long celebration every two years. For details see the website W www.rootsfestival.gm.

when the daily groups of tourists arrive things leap into action. Women pound millet at strategic points, babies are produced to be patted and filmed, artisans in the surprisingly good-value craft market crank into gear, and an old lady called Binde Kinte (descendant of Alex Haley's own forebear) makes a guest appearance at her compound.

Albreda, about 500m from Jufureh, is a slightly more peaceful place. The main things to see here are the ruined 17th-century 'factory' (fortified trading station) and **museum** *(admission D25; open 10am-5pm daily)* with a simple but striking exhibition describing the history of slavery. It's worth a visit.

You can do this trip in a day, but if you're making the effort to come all this way, you should consider staying overnight; both Jufureh and Albreda are at their best in the evening, when the light is soft and most of the tourist groups have left.

Places to Stay & Eat Behind the museum in Albreda is the ***Home at Last Motel***, which has cheap, clean singles/doubles for D80/D100, and food if you order far enough in advance.

Jufureh Resthouse *(☎ 398439, ask for Amadou; mob 907065)* is more lively, with cheap drumming lessons available if you call ahead. Facilities here are a bit run-down but it's hard to argue with the prices: singles/doubles D25/50, full board D125.

On the Square are the ***Rising Sun Restaurant***, which is home to freelance 'guides' and uninspiring meals for D40 to D60, and ***Mary's Restaurant***, where larger-than-life Mary serves traditional meals for D25.

Getting There & Away The usual (and easiest) way to visit Jufureh is by tourist boat (see Organised Tours in the main Getting Around section earlier in this chapter). Alternatively, take the ferry across to Barra, dodge the touts who try to get you into a private taxi, and find a shared taxi to Jufureh, which costs D15. If you want to do the trip in a day, you'll have to catch the first ferry.

If you can get a group together try hiring a pirogue from behind the Albert market in Banjul to take in Jufureh, Albreda and James Island before returning to Banjul. If you bargain well with the 'agent' on the beach in Banjul you'll get a 10-seater pirogue for six hours for D1100.

James Island

James Island is in the middle of the Gambia River, about 2km southwest of Jufureh and Albreda, and most boat tours stop here. On the island are the remains of **Fort James**, originally built in the 1650s and the site of numerous skirmishes in the following centuries (see History in the Facts about Gambia section for details). Today, the ruins are quite extensive, although the only intact room is a food store, which is often called the 'slave dungeon' because it sounds more interesting. The island itself is rapidly being eroded, and only the sturdy baobab trees seem to be holding it together. A good leaflet on the island is available at the National Museum in Banjul or the museum in Albreda for D15.

Upcountry Gambia

Upcountry Gambia is what locals call everywhere away from the coast, but it's only after you pass Brikama that its true charm is revealed. **Brikama** is Gambia's third-largest town but you'd have to look hard to find charm here. The much-hyped woodcarvers' market is disappointing – the almost complete lack of originality made worse by the unending hassle. Fortunately the main road bypasses this and most of the rest of Brikama, so you probably won't even know you were there.

At **Mandinaba** most traffic turns south for Ziguinchor, and the main road becomes surprisingly quiet as it winds through fields, rice paddies, palm groves and patches of natural forest. Every 10km or so there's a village or sleepy junction where a dirt track leads north towards the Gambia River, never far away, but always frustratingly out of view.

Places in this section are described west to east.

MAKASUTU

Makasutu means 'sacred forest' in Mandinka and after 10 years of effort by a couple of wandering souls from Britain it has developed into one of the most complete, and most popular, ecotourism sites in Gambia. Not far outside Brikama, ***Makasutu Culture Forest*** *(☎ 483335, ⓔ makasutu@hotmail.com)* occupies about 1000 hectares of land along Mandina Bolong. A day in the forest costs D320 and includes a large lunch, a demonstration of traditional dancing, a mangrove tour by pirogue, and guided walks through a range of habitats, including a palm forest where you can watch palm wine being tapped, and then taste the nectar. Even if you're not interested in wildlife it's worth a trip just to admire the stunning 'fusion' architecture and original artwork. Most people come on a tour arranged through one of the ground operators, but if you're making your own way it's best to take a taxi from Brikama for about D50.

TUMANI TENDA

Tumani Tenda camp *(☎ 903662, ⓔ tumanitenda@hotmail.com)* is about an hour from the coast on a *bolong* (creek) near the Gambia River. It's owned and operated by the residents of the neighbouring Taibatu village, who use the profits to fund community projects. There are five traditional-style huts, each maintained by a different family from the village, for D100 per person including breakfast. Other meals are D30. This is basic living, but for a taste of village life in a great location it's hard to beat.

Take a bush taxi from Brikama (D7) and ask to be dropped at the turn-off to Taibatu (look for the sign). From here it's a 2.5km walk.

TENDABA

Tendaba is a small village on the southern bank of the Gambia River, 165km upstream from Banjul and dominated by ***Tendaba Camp*** *(☎ 541024, ⓔ tendaba@qanet.gm)*. This is a popular destination for tour groups, especially bird-watchers, and although the crowds can be disturbing in the high season, Tendaba is undeniably an excellent base for visiting Kiang West National Park and Baobolong Wetland Reserve. Accommodation is in small bungalows costing D150/165 per person without/with bathroom. In the ***restaurant***, breakfast is bad value at D50, unlike the main meals at about D60 and the large evening buffet at D100.

Tours to Tendaba Camp arranged at the Atlantic coast resorts cost D900 to D1200 per person including transport, room, food and excursions. Green tourist taxis (carrying up to four people) charge about D800 to D1000 for the return trip. By bus, get off at Kwinella, from where the camp (signposted) is 5km along the dirt road. The manager promises to collect anyone who calls from Kwinella.

Kiang West National Park

Gambia's biggest and most important national park, Kiang West contains nearly all of the major animal species left in the country. You might see baboons, colobus monkeys, warthogs, marsh mongooses, bushbucks, roan antelopes and sitatungas (the bushbuck's aquatic cousin, adept at swimming and at crossing water vegetation on its wide hooves). Other species in the park, although very rarely seen, include hyenas, manatees, dolphins and crocodiles.

All of these animals live in the mangroves, creeks, mud flats, dry woodlands and grasslands that make up the park. If they're proving shy, you can always admire the view from the escarpment that runs parallel to the river: we're not talking Rift Valley here, but even 20m is significant in Gambia. Birdwatching is also rewarding, with more than 250 species recorded, including 21 raptors and some rarer birds such as the brown-necked parrot.

A popular place for viewing is **Toubab Kollon Point**, a promontory in the north-eastern part of the park. Behind the point, the escarpment runs close to the river bank, and 2km west is a viewing hide overlooking a water hole that attracts a good range of animals, especially in the dry season. Entry is D31.50, although this is included if you're on a tour from Tendaba.

From Tendaba, an excursion by 4WD vehicle to Kiang West costs D100 per person (with a minimum of six people). Boat rides around the creeks of the Baobolong Wetland Reserve are the same price (with a minimum of four).

Baobolong Wetland Reserve

Named after a tributary that enters the Gambia River upstream from Tendaba, the Baobolong (also spelt Baobolon) Wetland Reserve is in fact an area containing several other bolongs (creeks), mangroves and salt marshes, and is a Ramsar site. The giant mangroves here are some of the tallest in the region, growing to over 20m to become a virtual 'forest'. Birds are the major attraction (including the rare Pel's fishing owl) here, but the reserve also protects various aquatic mammal species, such as manatees, clawless otters and sitatungas. The best way to experience this wonderful maze of islands and waterways is on a boat, which most easily arranged at Tendaba Camp (see the Tendaba section earlier in this chapter).

SOMA & MANSA KONKO

Soma is a dusty, fly-blown junction town where the main road between Banjul and Basse Santa Su crosses the Trans-Gambia Hwy. Nearby is Mansa Konko, originally an important chief's capital (the name means 'king's hill'), then an administrative centre during the colonial era. Today it's a sleepy ghost town with a few reminders of the glory days, the most notable being the district commissioner's residence and a nearby colonial villa in the advanced stages of decay.

Places to Stay

If you get stuck in Soma, the lively ***Moses Motel*** *(☎ 531462)* on the north side of the main junction is the best option. Rooms without/with bathroom are D60/100. On the road north to Farafenni, what looks like a bungalow farm is actually the ***Trans Gambia Motel*** *(☎ 531402)*. Sparkling clean rooms are great value at D30 per person or D100 for a room with bathroom.

Getting There & Away

Buses between Banjul and Basse Santa Su stop at the GPTC compound in Soma. Other transport stops at the bush-taxi park in the town centre. If you're heading north from Soma, go to the Gambia River ferry by local bush taxi (D3), cross as a foot passenger (D3), then take another bush taxi to Farafenni (D3), where you'll find transport to Dakar.

FARAFENNI

Farafenni is on the Trans-Gambia Hwy north of the Gambia River. It's a busy little town and much more pleasant than Soma. The main *lumo* (market) is on Sunday, when people come from surrounding villages, and merchants come from as far as Mauritania and Guinea to sell their wares. If you're low on cash get to the Trust Bank. The border with Senegal is only 2km to the north and is open from 7am to midnight.

Places to Stay & Eat

Eddy's Hotel & Bar *(☎ 735225)* Singles/doubles with bathroom D150/200. This place has been a popular travellers' meeting point for many years. You can eat chicken and chips or benechin (fish and rice) for D35 to D45 in the shady garden courtyard while the apparently carefree Eddy shoots (unsuccessfully) at small birds with an air gun. Self-contained rooms come with either double beds or two beds, with air-conditioning an extra D50. There's also safe parking, cold beer and a disco at weekends.

Getting There & Away

Direct minibuses from Farafenni go to Serekunda most mornings for D40. For most other places you have to get to Soma (see Soma & Mansa Konko, earlier) and change. If you're heading for Dakar there are bush taxis for about CFA3000. If you're driving, bear in mind that you could face a lengthy wait for space on the ferry.

GAMBIA RIVER NATIONAL PARK

Upstream of Farafenni is the Gambia River's transition zone where it changes from salt to fresh water. The mangroves thin out, thick forest grows down to the water's edge and there are more islands. South of Kuntaur are five such islands, protected as the Gambia River National Park (also known as Baboon Islands National Park), the site of a privately funded project that takes chimpanzees captured from illegal traders and rehabilitates them to live in the wild.

Boat rides can be arranged in Georgetown (D800 to D1000 per day) or Kuntaur (D250), but visitors are not allowed to land or get close to the islands, partly because it interferes with the rehabilitation process, but mainly because the chimps can be very quick to attack humans, and males may vent their spleen on females and youngsters of their own troop.

Boats are permitted in the main channel between the islands and the east bank of the mainland, and are not allowed to approach the islands nearer than midstream. Boatmen try to please their passengers by getting closer, but this should be discouraged.

If you visit the area, it's best to go with the aim of having a good day out on this beautiful stretch of river. You'll quite likely see baboons and monkeys, and possibly hippos and crocodiles too, plus an excellent selection of birds. And if you do see any chimps it will be a bonus.

GEORGETOWN (JANGJANG-BUREH)

Under the British, Georgetown was a busy administrative centre and trading hub full of grand buildings. Today it's got a new (or should that be old?) name, a host of crumbling monuments and the sort of sluggish atmosphere that discourages all but the most necessary work – the perfect place to relax for a couple of days.

Located on the northern edge of MacCarthy Island in the Gambia River, about 300km by road from Banjul, the traditional and now officially reintroduced name for the town and island is Jangjang-bureh, but most people still call it Georgetown. The island is 10km long and 2.5km wide, covered with fields of rice and groundnuts, with ferry links to both river banks. There are no banks and only one available Internet-linked computer (at Alaka-bung Lodge).

Things to See

On the waterfront either side of the northern ferry landing are two crumbling warehouses. Imaginative local youths refer to the more intact building as the **slave house**, but although slaves were transported through Georgetown, these structures were built after slavery in British colonies was abolished in 1807. These same youths will politely but persistently offer to guide you around town, but this is unnecessary. However, the 'slave house' is more entertaining for the D1 commentary.

Other places to visit include the **stone circle** of Lamin Koto, 1km away from the north bank ferry ramp and worth a look. The passenger ferry (D1) runs on a fill-up-and-go basis.

Historians interested in exploration may want to head for **Karantaba Tenda** village, about 20km by road or river from Georgetown, where an obelisk marks the spot where the Scottish explorer **Mungo Park** started on his journey to trace the course of the Niger River.

Places to Stay

All of these places can arrange day trips to the Wassu Stone Circles, the Gambia River National Park and the Mungo Park Memorial. All rooms (even the tents) come with bathroom.

Alaka-bung Lodge *(☎ 676123, e alaka bung@qanet.gm, Owens St)* Twin bungalows D80 per person. Renovated and expanded, Alaka-bung is Georgetown's hippest and cheapest option. You'll find few package tourists, plenty of local drinkers and the only email access in town.

Baobolong Camp *(☎ 676133/51, Owens St)* Rooms D100 per person. This camp is set in lush gardens near the river and run by enthusiastic local bird-watchers. Breakfast and meals are D50; the buffet dinner is D80.

Bird Safari Camp *(☎ 676108, fax 674004, ⓔ bsc@gamtel.gm)* Single/double rooms or tents D275/475 B&B. About 1.5km outside town, this secluded and peaceful camp has good-quality rooms and luxury tents. It's popular with bird-watchers and boasts a resident ornithologist.

Jangjang-bureh Camp *(☎/fax 676182, in Banjul ☎ 497603, Ⓦ www.gre.gm)* Rooms D110 per person. On the north side of the river, this is an eclectic collection of rustic bungalows set in a maze-like garden. A large buffet breakfast is D55, and good meals around D30 to D80. Motorboat trips (for up to six people) cost D150 per hour. To reach Jangjang-bureh Camp, go to ***Dreambird Camp*** on MacCarthy Island, from where a transfer boat shuttles between the two – free for guests and diners. Dreambird has a few rooms at D75 per person.

Places to Eat & Drink

Few options exist outside the camps and lodges, especially after dark. There are a few cheap ***eating houses*** around the market, and near the ferry is the low-key ***Talamanca Bar/Restaurant***. Beer should be available at ***Tida's Bar***, a traditional compound run by the local school headmistress and reached through an unmarked green gate. If not, Alaka-bung is your best bet.

Getting There & Away

Most buses and bush taxis turn off the main road between Soma and Basse Santa Su to drop off passengers at the southern ferry ramp. Otherwise, you have to drop at Bansang, and take a bush taxi back (D5). The ferry costs D1 for passengers. On the far side pick-ups run across the island to Georgetown for D2.

WASSU STONE CIRCLES

The stone circles at Wassu might not be Stonehenge, but they are one of the best examples of the enigmatic megaliths that are scattered across the area, and one of the few remnants of ancient African cultures that have survived into the modern day. About 20km northwest of Georgetown, the circles each consist of about 10 to 24 massive, reddish-brown stones, between 1m and 2.5m high and weighing several tonnes. The site is complemented by a small but thorough **museum**.

From Georgetown, a bush taxi to Kuntaur (D9) waits most mornings at the north bank ferry ramp, but this only goes when full, and even if you reach Wassu in reasonable time there might be nothing coming back. To avoid these hassles we strongly recommend visiting on a Monday, the day of Wassu's particularly colourful market.

BASSE SANTA SU

Commonly called Basse, this is Gambia's easternmost town, a traditional trading centre and by far the liveliest of the upcountry settlements. The main market day is Thursday, but the streets are lined with shops and stalls and the whole place is always quite busy.

Trust Bank and Standard Chartered have branches in Basse that change travellers cheques and give credit card cash advances.

Down by the waterfront, an old colonial warehouse has been converted into a cultural centre and café called **Traditions** *(☎ 668533, ⓔ ann@qanet.com)*. The high-quality cloth and pottery work on show and for sale is a refreshing change from the tat sold on the coast. Owner Ann is a wealth of information about the crafts and the town.

Between June and February, Basse is also a good place to see the Egyptian plover, a rare species known locally as the crocodile bird. Boat rides to see the birds can be arranged with local boatmen.

For late-night action, the ***Plaza Nightclub*** is the pick. Entry is between D5 and D20 but the beer is cheap and the vibe is good.

Places to Stay & Eat

Basse is not blessed with a selection of fine hotels.

Basse Guesthouse Rooms D60. Overlooking the central square, this place is pretty basic but friendly enough.

Jem Hotel *(☎ 668356)* Singles/doubles D150/300. About 500m southeast of the town centre, this place is better but still a bit run down. It should have a new name by the time you arrive.

Lumos around Basse

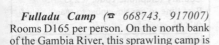

Several of Basse's surrounding villages have a weekly market, or *lumo*, all on a different day of the week. For example, at Lamwe, near Fatoto, the lumo is on Saturday; at Sabi, on the road towards Vélingara, it's Sunday; and at Sarengai on the north bank, it's Monday. Traders and shoppers come from other parts of Gambia, across the border from Senegal, and from as far as Mali, Guinea and Guinea-Bissau. Bush taxis from Basse run to wherever the lumo is that day.

Fulladu Camp *(☎ 668743, 917007)* Rooms D165 per person. On the north bank of the Gambia River, this sprawling camp is the best place to stay in Basse. Clean, comfortable bungalows and a decent restaurant make it worth the money.

It's worth eating at ***Traditions*** *(☎ 668 533, ⓔ ann@qanet.com)* for the views alone. This delightful place has tables on a balcony overlooking the river, and serves sandwiches or soups for D15 to D25. It's open from 9am to 6pm. Campers can pitch tents here for D50.

Around the garage are some tea shacks, and stalls and chop shops selling cheap bowls of rice and sauce; ***Fatu's*** domodah (D6) is highly recommended.

In town, cheap restaurants include ***Abdoulie's International Diner*** and ***Kekoi's Fast Food***, both of which are local hangouts with unpretentious meals from D5 to D20.

Getting There & Away

GPTC buses between Banjul and Basse leave throughout the day (see Getting There & Away in the Banjul section earlier in this chapter). From Basse, they go from the main road, not from the bush-taxi park. Bush taxis and minibuses go to Fatoto (D10), Georgetown (D18), Soma (D35) and Serekunda (D70).

For details on transport to Senegal, see the main Getting There & Away section earlier in this chapter.

Even further afield, a Peugeot taxi goes more or less daily (passengers depending) to Labé in northern Guinea. The fare is CFA15,000 and the trip takes around 24 hours.

Ghana

Ghana is one of the friendliest and easiest countries to get around in West Africa. Its vibrant cultural identity, historical monuments and wonderful diversity of natural attractions make it a first stop for many travellers to the region. On the coast, as well as magnificent beaches, Ghana has a string of old slaving forts, a fascinating and thought-provoking monument to a harrowing period of the region's history. Just inland are lush tropical forests and Kakum National Park, famous for its canopy walkway. Further in the interior, Kumasi is the heartland of the Ashanti, who ruled the most powerful kingdom in Ghana and still have the richest and most self-confident culture of all the Ghanaian peoples. Further north, the forests thin out into savanna; here Mole National Park offers superb wildlife viewing and, better still, is readily accessible to independent travellers. In the far north of the country is the semidesert of the Sahel. Here you can see Sahelian-style mud-and-pole mosques and experience the distinctive culture of the Dagomba and other peoples of the north. The east of the country is different again; it's dominated by the vast Lake Volta, the largest artificial lake in Africa. A boat trip up the lake is guaranteed to be an unforgettable experience. The rolling green hills between Lake Volta and the Togo border have a refreshingly cool climate, spectacular waterfalls and the highest mountain in Ghana, and offer great hiking opportunities.

Ghana at a Glance

Capital: Accra
Population: 18.8 million
Area: 238,537 sq km
Head of State: Dr John A Kufuor
Official language: English
Main local languages: Twi, Ga, Ewe
Currency: Cedi
Exchange rate: US$1 = C7922
Time: GMT/UTC
Country telephone code: ☎ 233
Best time to go: November to March, July & August

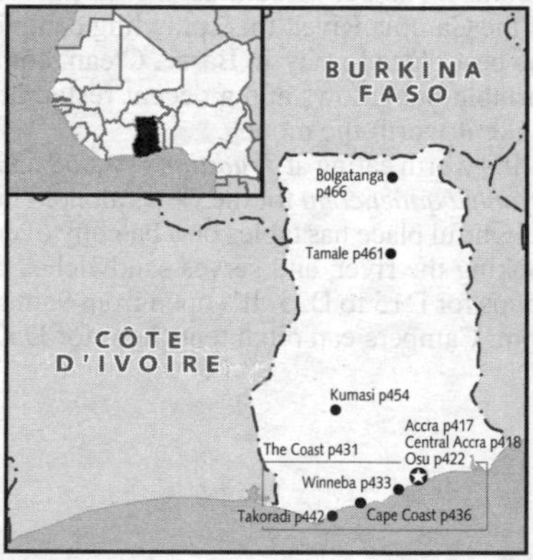

BURKINA FASO
Bolgatanga p466
Tamale p461
CÔTE D'IVOIRE
Kumasi p454
Accra p417
Central Accra p418
Osu p422
The Coast p431
Winneba p433
Takoradi p442
Cape Coast p436

Highlights

- Exploring the string of old coastal forts, a thought-provoking memorial to the slave trade
- Chilling out on sandy, palm-fringed beaches at Gomoa Fetteh, Busua or near Axim
- Seeing elephants at Mole National Park, hippos at Wechiau Hippo Sanctuary and primates at Tafi-Atome Monkey Sanctuary
- Taking a boat trip up Lake Volta, the largest artificial lake in Africa, surrounded by rolling green hills
- Experiencing the richness of Ashanti culture through the museums and vast open-air market at Kumasi
- Enjoying the friendliness, hospitality and courtesy of the Ghanaian people wherever you go

Facts about Ghana

HISTORY

Present-day Ghana has been inhabited since at least 4000 BC, although little evidence remains of its early societies. Successive waves of migration from the north and east resulted in Ghana's present ethnographic composition. By the 13th century, a number of kingdoms had arisen, influenced by the Sahelian trading empires north of the region, such as that of Ancient Ghana (which incorporated western Mali and present-day Senegal). Fuelled by gold, of which Ghana has substantial deposits, trading networks grew, stimulating the development of Akan

GHANA

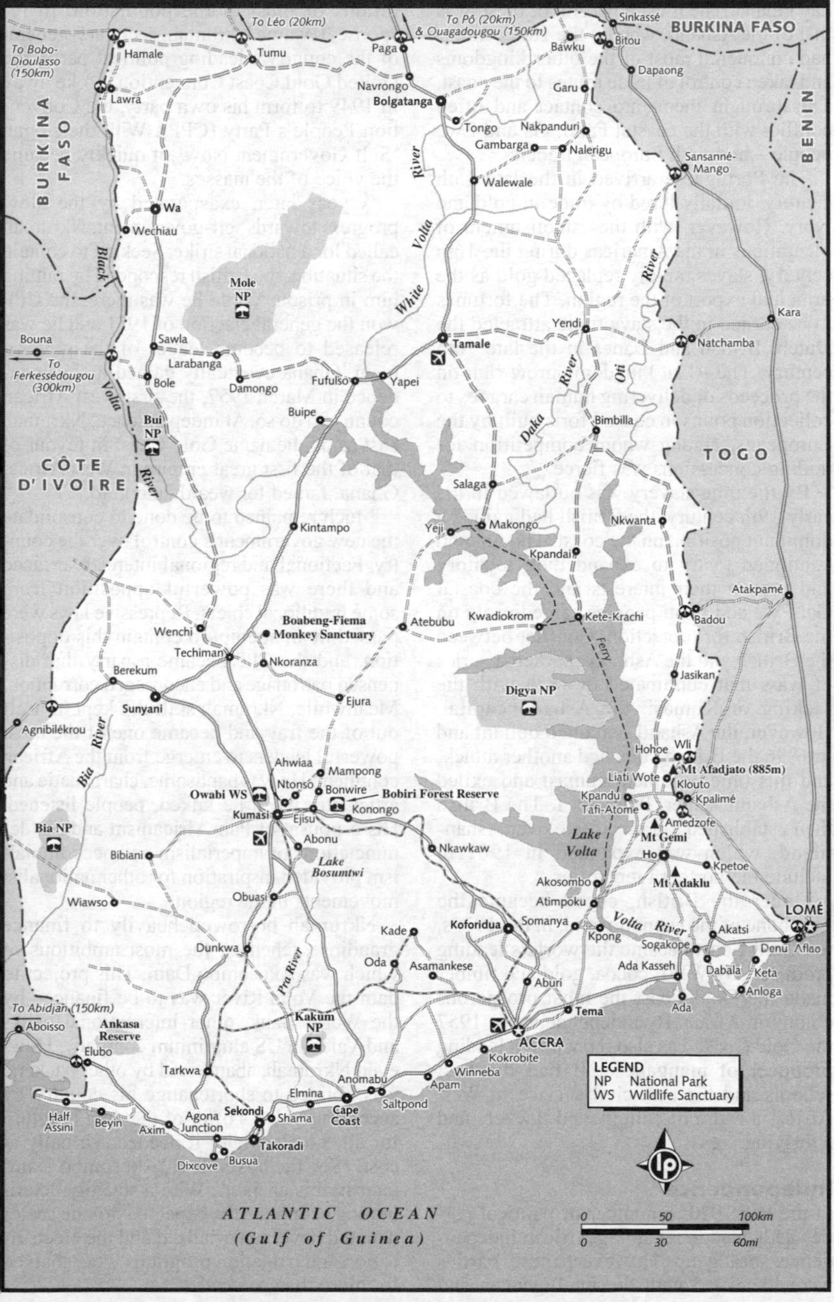
To Léo (20km)
To Pô (20km)
& Ouagadougou (150km)
BURKINA FASO
To Bobo-
Dioulasso
(150km)
Hamale
Tumu
Paga
Sinkassé
Bawku
Bitou
Dapaong
Navrongo
Lawra
Bolgatanga
Garu
BURKINA
FASO
BENIN
Tongo
Nakpanduri
Gambarga
Nalerigu
White
Volta
River
Sansanné-
Mango
Walewale
Wa
Wechiau
Black
Mole
NP
Oti
River
White
Volta
Kara
Yendi
Bouna
Sawla
Tamale
Natchamba
To
Ferkessédougou
(300km)
Larabanga
Volta
Bole
Damongo
Fufulso
Yapei
Daka
River
Oti
Buipe
Bimbilla
Bui
NP
TOGO
CÔTE
D'IVOIRE
River
Salaga
Kintampo
Yeji
Makongo
Nkwanta
Kpandai
Atakpamé
Boabeng-Fiema
Monkey Sanctuary
Wenchi
Atebubu
Kwadiokrom
Kete-Krachi
Badou
Techiman
Nkoranza
Ferry
Berekum
Jasikan
Sunyani
Ejura
Digya NP
Agnibilékrou
Bia
River
Ahwiaa
Hohoe
Wli
Mampong
Mt Afadjato (885m)
Liati Wote
Klouto
Ntonso
Owabi WS
Bonwire
Bobiri Forest Reserve
Kpandu
Kpalimé
Kumasi
Ejisu
Tafi-Atome
Konongo
Bia NP
Amedzofe
Lake
Volta
Mt Gemi
Abonu
Nkawkaw
Bibiani
Ho
Lake
Bosumtwi
Kpetoe
Mt Adaklu
Akosombo
Wiawso
Obuasi
Atimpoku
LOMÉ
Somanya
Volta River
Koforidua
Kpong
Kade
Akatsi
Sogakope
Denu
Aflao
Dunkwa
Ada Kasseh
Dabala
Oda
Asamankese
Keta
Pra River
Aburi
Anloga
Ada
To Abidjan (150km)
Tema
Aboisso
Ankasa
Reserve
Kakum
NP
ACCRA
Elubo
Kokrobite
LEGEND
NP National Park
WS Wildlife Sanctuary
Tarkwa
Winneba
Anomabu
Apam
Elmina
Saltpond
Cape
Coast
Half
Assini
Beyin
Agona
Junction
Sekondi
Shama
Axim
Takoradi
Dixcove
Busua
ATLANTIC OCEAN
(Gulf of Guinea)
0 50 100km
0 30 60mi

kingdoms in the centre and south of present-day Ghana. The most powerful of these was that of the Ashanti, who by the 18th century had conquered most of the other kingdoms and taken control of trade routes to the coast. This brought them into contact and often conflict with the coastal Fanti, Ga and Ewe people – and with European traders.

The Portuguese arrived in the late 15th century, initially lured by trade in gold and ivory. However, with the establishment of plantations in the Americas during the 16th century, slaves rapidly replaced gold as the principal export of the region. The fortunes to be earned in the slave trade attracted the Dutch, British and Danes in the late 16th century. The Akan kingdoms grew rich on the proceeds of delivering human cargoes to collection points in coastal forts built by the Europeans, among whom competition for trading concessions was fierce.

By the time slavery was outlawed in the early 19th century, the British had gained a dominant position on the coast. The Ashanti continued to try to expand their territory and protect their interests and the coastal Ga, Ewe and Fanti peoples came to rely on the British for protection. Conflict between the British and the Ashanti sparked a series of wars that culminated in 1874 with the sacking of Kumasi, the Ashanti capital. However, the Ashanti remained defiant and in 1896 the British launched another attack, and this time occupied Kumasi and exiled the Ashanti leader, Prempeh I. The British then established a protectorate over Ashantiland, which was expanded in 1901 to include the northern territories.

Under the British, cocoa became the backbone of the economy and, in the 1920s, the Gold Coast became the world's leading producer. By WWI, cocoa, gold and timber made the Gold Coast the most prosperous colony in Africa. By independence in 1957 the Gold Coast was also the world's leading producer of manganese. It had the best schools and the best civil service in West Africa, a cadre of enlightened lawyers and a thriving press.

Independence

In the late 1920s a number of political parties dedicated to regaining African independence sprang up. However, these parties were identified with the intelligentsia and failed to recognise the grievances and aspirations of most of the population. In response, Kwame Nkrumah, secretary-general of the country's leading political party, the United Gold Coast Convention, broke away in 1949 to form his own party, the Convention People's Party (CPP). With the slogan 'Self Government Now', it quickly became the voice of the masses.

A year later, exasperated by the slow progress towards self-government, Nkrumah called for a national strike. Seeking to contain the situation, the British responded by putting him in prison. While he was there, the CPP won the general election of 1951 and he was released to become leader of the government. Ghana eventually gained its independence in March 1957, the first West African country to do so. At independence, Nkrumah cast aside the name Gold Coast in favour of that of the first great empire in West Africa, Ghana, famed for wealth and gold.

Much remained to be done to consolidate the new government's control over the country. Factional and regional interests surfaced and there was powerful opposition from some traditional chiefs. Repressive laws were passed in an attempt to contain this opposition, and the CPP became a party that dispensed patronage and encouraged corruption. Meanwhile, Nkrumah skilfully kept himself out of the fray and became one of the most powerful leaders to emerge from the African continent. He was handsome, charismatic and articulate; when he talked, people listened. His espousal of Pan-Africanism and his denunciations of imperialism and neocolonialism provided inspiration for other nationalist movements in the region.

Nkrumah borrowed heavily to finance grandiose schemes, the most ambitious of which was Akosombo Dam. This project to dam the Volta River was to be financed by the World Bank, other international banks and Valco, a US aluminium company. However, Nkrumah, abandoned by other backers, was obliged to shortchange his country by accepting Valco's offer of the dam in return for all the electricity it needed, virtually at cost. (See the boxed text 'Akosombo Dam' later in this chapter.) With a steadily deteriorating economy, the expected private sector demand never materialised and the electrification and irrigation programs were shelved for more than a decade.

In the end, unbridled corruption, reckless spending on ambitious schemes, his anti-Western stance and unpaid debts to Western creditors were Nkrumah's undoing. Worst of all, he alienated the army by setting up a private guard answerable only to him. In 1966, while the president was on a mission to Hanoi, the army ousted him in a coup. Exiled to Guinea, Nkrumah died of cancer six years later.

The Rawlings Era

Neither the military regime nor the civilian government installed three years later and headed by Dr Kofi Busia could overcome the corruption and debt problems. In 1972, there was another coup, headed by Colonel Acheampong, under whose inept leadership the economy worsened still further. As the cedi became increasingly worthless, food staples and other basic goods became scarce. In 1979, in the midst of serious food shortages and demonstrations against army affluence and military rule, a group of young revolutionaries seized power. Their leader was a charismatic, half-Scottish 32-year-old air-force flight lieutenant, Jerry Rawlings, who quickly became the darling of the masses.

As he had promised, Rawlings' Armed Forces Revolutionary Council (AFRC) handed power over to a civilian government several months later after general elections. But not until some major 'house cleaning' had been done, resulting in the sentencing and execution of some senior officers, including Acheampong, and the conviction of hundreds of other officers and businessmen. The new president, Hilla Limann, unable to halt the country's downward spiral and uneasy with Rawlings' enormous grass-roots support, eventually accused him of attempting to subvert constitutional rule. This provoked a second takeover by the AFRC in January 1982, and this time Rawlings stayed for two decades.

Although Rawlings never delivered on his promised left-wing radical revolution, under his colourful leadership life became better for most Ghanaians. He yielded to World Bank and IMF pressure and carried out some tough free-market reforms, which included floating the cedi, removing price controls, raising payments to cocoa farmers and disposing of some unprofitable state enterprises. In return, the World Bank and the IMF rewarded Ghana amply with loans and funding. For a while, in the 1980s, Ghana was lauded as an economic success story, with an economic growth rate that was the highest in Africa.

In 1992, yielding to pressures from home and abroad, Rawlings announced a hastily organised referendum on a new constitution and lifted the 10-year ban on political parties. Opposition groups formed along traditional lines but divisions were deep. Without a united opposition front, Rawlings triumphed at the November 1992 presidential election, winning 60% of the vote. Independent election monitors concluded that the election was free and fair. Humiliated, the main opposition parties withdrew from the following month's parliamentary elections, so Rawlings' National Democratic Congress (NDC) won and Rawlings was sworn in as president.

During the 1990s, Ghana made mixed progress. On the one hand, Rawlings seemed to have achieved a respectable democratic mandate, economic growth was maintained and Ghana continued to attract praise from the IMF. On the other hand, however, all was not well with many Ghanaians. Austerity measures, lack of improvement in social services, rising inflation, increasing corruption within the NDC and a hurried attempt by the government to launch an unpopular value-added tax in 1995 led to major civil unrest. However, Rawlings' personal popularity was relatively unaffected and in December 1996 he was again elected as president in an election acknowledged as free and fair. At much the same time, the appointment of Ghanaian Kofi Annan as UN secretary general boosted national morale. In 1998, in an effort to improve tax collection and spread the burden more equitably, VAT was this time successfully introduced. However, a drought in the late 1990s led to morale-sapping electricity and water rationing throughout the country, while a fall in the world price of cocoa and gold diminished Ghana's foreign exchange earnings.

Ghana Today

Ghana is again on the upswing, with a slowly growing economy and a government cautiously joining the ranks of emerging African democracies.

The constitution barred Rawlings from standing for a third term in the December 2000 presidential elections. Despite the speculation, Rawlings did indeed stand down, nominating as successor his vice president, Professor John Atta Mills. The chief challenger for the presidency was Dr John Kufuor, leader of the well-established New Patriotic Party (NPP). In the parliamentary elections, the NPP won 99 of the 200 seats, against 92 won by the NDC. The result of the presidential election was even closer, resulting in a run-off election between the two candidates, won by Kufuor.

So far the changeover of government has been smooth. However, it's early days – Kufuor has inherited some tough economic and political challenges. Politically, Kufuor has every reason to tread carefully; Rawlings was in power for nearly 20 years and in many parts of the country, the state is synonymous with the NDC.

GEOGRAPHY

Ghana is about the size of Britain. It's generally flat or gently undulating, consisting of low-lying coastal plains punctuated by saline lagoons in the south, wooded hill ranges in the centre and a low plateau in the northern two-thirds. Keta Lagoon east of Accra, near the Togolese border, is Ghana's largest lagoon. Dominating the eastern flank of the country is Lake Volta, formed when the Volta River was dammed in the mid-1960s. It's the world's largest artificial lake, about twice the size of Luxembourg. The highest hills are part of the Akwapim range in the east, which runs from just north of Accra, then east of Lake Volta and into Togo.

CLIMATE

Ghana has a tropical equatorial climate, which means that it's hot year-round with seasonal rains. In the humid southern coastal region, the rainy seasons are from April to June, and during September and October. Throughout the year, maximum temperatures are around 30°C, dropping three or four degrees during the brief respite between rainy seasons. The humidity is constantly high, at about 80%. In the central region, the rains are heavier and last longer. In the hotter and drier north, there is one rainy season, lasting from April to October. Midday temperatures rarely fall below 30°C, rising to 35°C and higher during December to March when the rasping harmattan wind blows in from the Sahara. At this time, dust particles hang heavily in the air, making it constantly hazy, and temperatures plummet at night.

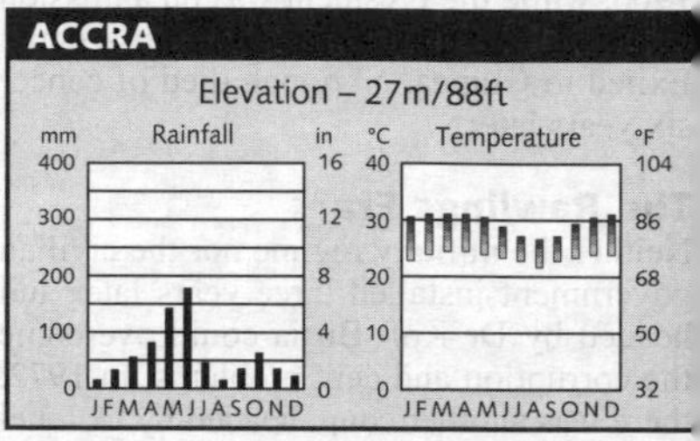
ACCRA
Elevation – 27m/88ft
mm
Rainfall
in
°C
Temperature
°F
400
300
200
100
0
16
12
8
4
0
40
30
20
10
0
104
86
68
50
32
JFMAMJJASOND
JFMAMJJASOND

ECOLOGY & ENVIRONMENT

As a result of logging, mining, the use of wood fuels, population pressures and deforestation for agriculture, Ghana's forests have been reduced from over eight million sq km in the early 20th century to less than two million sq km now. Marine and coastal areas are threatened by high coastal population concentrations, erosion and pollution. The formation of Lake Volta in 1966 swallowed up approximately 10,000 sq km of land and has increased the incidence of water-borne diseases such as bilharzia. As a result of unregulated mining practices around the gold-mining centre of Obuasi, rivers nearby have been poisoned by dangerous chemicals, the air is polluted by smoke containing arsenic and sulphur dioxide, and it's impossible to grow crops. In populated urban areas, waste and sewage disposal is probably the most pressing problem facing the country.

FLORA & FAUNA

In terms of vegetation, Ghana can be divided into three zones. The coastal region is savanna grassland with mangroves lining the river estuaries. Extending northwards from the coastline is a belt of forest, moist evergreen in the southwest corner and semi-deciduous elsewhere. Cocoa, introduced in the early colonial period, is grown across a wide band in this part of the country. The northern two-thirds of the country lies in the Sahel zone and the natural vegetation is dry grassland and open savanna woodland.

Ghana's national parks and reserves protect a variety of large mammals, including

Community-Based Conservation

If you want to experience some of the best of Ghana's natural attractions and traditional culture, while at the same time benefiting the local community, visit one of the growing number of ecotourism projects around the country. These projects are being established by traditional councils and district assemblies as part of a community-based venture, supported by the Ghana Tourist Board and the Peace Corps in collaboration with Ghana's Nature Conservation Research Centre.

A typical project is based in a village and will have a visitor centre where you can arrange activities such as guided walks, village tours, bicycle hire and basic accommodation in a guesthouse or with families. More and more communities, each with something special to offer, are joining the scheme. Projects that are up and running include the Tafi-Atome and Boabeng-Fiema Monkey Sanctuaries, Wechiau Hippo Sanctuary, Bobiri Butterfly Sanctuary, Mt Adaklu, Liati Wote Waterfalls and Domama Rock Shrine. For more details of these and other ecotourism sites, hit the Nature Conservation Research Centre website (W www.ncrc.org.gh) or contact the regional tourist office.

elephants, antelope species such as roan, kob, hartebeest, water buck, duiker and the endangered bongo, and primate species such as olive baboons, colobus and Mona monkeys and chimpanzees. The Black Volta River has a resident population of hippos; the best place to see them is at Wechiau Hippo Sanctuary near Wa. Nile crocodiles can be seen in various parts of the country but the crocodile ponds at Paga on the border with Burkina Faso are the best known. To see primates at close quarters, visit the sanctuaries at Boabeng-Fiema and Tafi-Atome, where villagers have traditionally venerated and protected the resident populations of black-and-white colobus and Mona monkeys.

Forested areas contain numerous species of butterflies. Kakum National Park, where some 400 species of butterflies have been recorded, and Bobiri Butterfly Sanctuary are some of the best places to see them.

The Volta estuary and coastal areas west of Accra (such as around Winneba) are important turtle-nesting sites for green, leatherback and olive Ridley turtles. Little is being done to protect the turtles, which are at their most vulnerable when they come to nest. Do your bit and don't eat turtle meat if it is offered to you.

Bird-watchers will find Ghana has much to offer, although there are no specialist guides or tours. In forested areas, birds such as hornbills, turacos, African grey and Senegal parrots and the rare white-fronted guinea fowl can be seen. The coastal wetlands around the Volta estuary and coastal lagoons are important resting and feeding grounds for some 70 species of indigenous and migratory water birds.

National Parks & Reserves

Ghana has five national parks and nine protected areas. Mole National Park in the northwest of the country protects savanna woodland and is the best place to see wildlife, including elephants, baboons and antelope species. Kakum National Park, just inland of Cape Coast, is known for its canopy walkway and is a good place to see rainforest habitat and birdlife. The three remaining national parks, Bui, Bia and Digya, aren't set up for visitors and aren't feasible to visit without your own transport. Of the protected areas, Ankasa Reserve near Elubo in the southwest has recently opened up to visitors and is noted for its rainforest habitat and forest elephants. Owabi Wildlife Sanctuary, near Kumasi, is one of several designated Ramsar wetlands conservation sites in Ghana.

GOVERNMENT & POLITICS

Since its 1992 constitution, Ghana has been a multiparty democracy with elections held every four years. Under it, the government is headed by an elected president and a 200-member national assembly, which is also elected. The NPP, led by President John Kufuor, currently holds the balance of power in the assembly by a narrow margin over the NDC, ex-president Rawlings' party. The next presidential and parliamentary elections are scheduled for 2004.

ECONOMY

Ghana's economy is based on gold, cocoa and, increasingly, tourism. As with other countries in the region, foreign debt is a major problem. Lauded an economic success story in the 1980s, falling prices of gold and cocoa compounded by rampant corruption and stalled reforms in the 1990s caused a massive devaluation of the cedi and precipitated Ghana into an economic crisis as it entered the 21st century. One of the new government's first acts has been to raise the price of fuel, previously heavily subsidised, and to loosen restrictions on the currency, allowing it to stabilise. More controversially, the government has accepted the Highly Indebted Poor Countries arrangement with the World Bank and IMF, giving Ghana relief on its US$5.8 billion foreign debt but causing a serious dent in national pride. Long-standing attempts to reduce Ghana's dependency on gold and cocoa have led to increasing interest in exports such as shea nut butter, tobacco, cotton and pineapples. Manganese, diamonds and bauxite are also mined for export. Despite recent difficulties, Ghana's economy continues to grow and attract investment and the outlook is brighter than in many other parts of Africa.

POPULATION & PEOPLE

Ghana's population of 18.8 million makes it one of the most densely populated countries in West Africa. Of this, 44% are Akan, a grouping that includes the Ashanti (also called Asante), whose heartland is around Kumasi, and the Fanti, who fish the central coast and farm its near hinterland. The Nzema, linguistically close to the Akan, fish and farm in the southwest. Distant migrants from present-day Nigeria, the Ga are the indigenous people of Accra and Tema. The southern Volta region is home to the Ewe.

In the north, the Dagomba heartland is around Tamale and Yendi. Prominent neighbours are the Gonja in the centre, Konkomba and Mamprusi in the far northeast, and, around Navrongo, the Kasena. The Sisala and Lobi inhabit the far northwest.

For more details on the Ashanti and Ewe people, see the Peoples of the Region special section.

ARTS

Arts & Craftwork

Ghana has a rich artistic heritage. Objects are created not only for their aesthetic value but as symbols of ethnic identity or to commemorate historical or legendary events, to convey cultural values or to signify membership of a group. The Akan people of the southern and central regions are famous for their cloth, goldwork, woodcarving, chiefs' insignia (such as swords, umbrella tops and linguist staffs), pottery and bead-making. The Ashanti in particular are famous for their kente cloth, with its distinctive basketwork pattern, which was originally worn only by royalty and is still some of the most expensive material in Africa. See the Ashanti Arts & Cuture special section for more details. The Ewe people of the southeast, who claim to have originally passed on the method of kente weaving to the Ashantis, produce both the Ashanti kente and their own Ewe kente, which is even more intricately woven. *Adinkra* cloth is characterised by its sombre colours and blockprinted symbols, which represent sayings and proverbs.

Akan stools are among the finest in West Africa and incorporate designs that are rich in cultural symbolism. Other objects carved from wood include the *akuaba* doll, used as a household fetish to protect against infertility. The Akan are skilled in the lost-wax method of metal casting, used to make exquisite brass objects, including weights used for measuring gold dust. Glass beads are made by grinding up glass of different colours and layering it in a mould to produce intricately coloured patterns. Around Bolgatanga in the north, fine basket weaving and leatherwork are traditional crafts.

Pop Music

Ghana is the birthplace of highlife music and you can pick up recordings by ET Mensah, Nana Ampadu, and The Sweet Talks. Ko Nimo, now in his early 60s, is Ghana's foremost exponent of acoustic guitar highlife (or palm wine music) and performs regularly with his band, the Adadam Agofomma Group, at many venues throughout Ghana. Gospel music is huge in Ghana, as is reggae; gospel rap is an immensely popular fusion of styles. Hiplife is Ghana's answer to hiphop. Ghanaian stars to look out for include the Genesis Gospel Singers, City Boys, Nana Acheampong, Kojo Antwi, Papa Yankson, Daddy Lumba, Nana Tuffuor, Blay Ambolley and George Darko.

SOCIETY & CONDUCT

The extended family is the foundation of Ghanaian society. The Akan people are unusual in that they are matrilineal – you belong to your mother's clan. Clans are grouped under a chief, who in turn is answerable to a paramount chief, who is the political and spiritual head of his people.

Age, education and wealth are afforded great respect and visitors are generally welcomed with friendliness. You'll probably be struck by how courteous Ghanaians are; it would be unthinkable not to reciprocate in the same vein. Greetings are extremely important and an essential prelude to social interaction of any kind. It's usual to shake the hand of anyone you meet. The Ghanaian handshake involves a fairly limp grasp of the hand followed by a snap of your index finger with the index finger of the person whose hand you're shaking (got it?). It's a tricky manoeuvre to perfect but you'll get plenty of practice. Religion is extremely important in Ghana; blasphemy or swearing of any sort is unacceptable.

If you're visiting a site, especially in a less-touristed area, you should ask to see the village chief to exchange greetings and to get his approval for your visit. He will probably then assign someone to accompany you as a guide. A dash (tip) or gift is required.

RELIGION

Religion of all kinds has a profound influence on every aspect of Ghanaian life. Christianity was introduced by European missionaries, who also were the first educators, and the link between religion and education persists. About 70% of Ghanaians are Christian, concentrated in the south. Pentecostal and charismatic denominations are well-represented, as are the Protestant and Catholic churches. About 15% of the population is Muslim, the majority being in the north, although there are also substantial Muslim minorities in southern cities such as Accra and Kumasi. The rest of the people practise traditional religions, which generally include a belief in a supreme being as well as in spirits and lesser gods who inhabit the natural world. Ancestor veneration is an important part of traditional beliefs. Most people retain traditional beliefs alongside Christian or Muslim beliefs.

LANGUAGE

English is the official language. There are at least 75 local languages and dialects. The most widely spoken language is Twi, which belongs to the Akan language group and is spoken in different versions throughout most of the central and southern parts of the country. The Ashanti version of Twi is not only spoken throughout the Ashanti homeland but also serves as a lingua franca for much of the country and especially in Accra. Fanti is spoken along much of the coast to the west of Accra. Other prominent languages are Ga in the Accra-Tema area, Ewe in the southeast and Mole-Dagbani languages in the north. See the Language chapter for useful phrases in Ga and Twi.

Facts for the Visitor

SUGGESTED ITINERARIES

If you've only got two weeks to spare, you could try doing a triangle bounded by Accra, Takoradi to the west, and, at the apex, Kumasi. Start in Accra (three to four days), then go to Cape Coast (three nights) and Elmina and on to Takoradi, taking in some of the coastal forts, villages and beaches (at least two nights) on the way. Take the night train from Takoradi to Kumasi, where you'll probably want to stay at least three nights, then back to Accra.

With four weeks to spare, you can do all of the above, adding in more days to explore the coast. Also, after reaching Kumasi, radiate northwards to Tamale (one night) and on to Mole National Park (three nights), back to Tamale (one night) and return to Accra via Kumasi or perhaps via Lake Volta. Then you could graft on a visit to the east: Ada Foah, (two nights), Akosombo (one night), on to Ho and Hohoe (three nights) and back to Accra. Alternatively, head directly to Hohoe from Tamale.

PLANNING

When to Go

In the south the dry months, November to March or July and August, are easier for travelling. In the north, avoid December to March, the hottest months, when the harmattan wind blows in from the Sahara.

Maps

The best map available outside Ghana is a 1:750,000 version of the country produced by International Travel Maps of Vancouver,

Canada. In Accra, the Survey Offices on Giffard Rd produces a series of four 1:500,000 maps (US$5 each) that cover the entire country. Other maps available in Ghana include the KLM-Shell map (US$7) with Accra on one side and, on the other, a rather out-of-date but adequate map of Ghana, and there's also the delightful *Tourist Map of Ghana* (US$7), which makes a nice souvenir. Both maps are available from bookshops at the major hotels and from the tourist office in Accra.

TOURIST OFFICES

There are no official tourist offices outside Ghana but the Ghana Tourist Board website (**W** www.africaonline.com.gh/tourism) has some useful information or try the Ghanaian diplomatic mission in your country. Within Ghana, the tourist board has a network of offices in the major regional capitals. Although a couple of the offices have a lot of information to offer, generally their usefulness is limited. Opening hours tend to be somewhat erratic and most offices are closed on Saturday and Sunday.

GHANA

VISAS & DOCUMENTS

Visas

Everyone except nationals of Ecowas countries needs a visa, which must be obtained before arriving in Ghana. Visas allow a stay of 60 days and can be single or multiple entry. They must be used within three months of the date of issue.

You can get visas in many countries in West Africa (see Visas & Documents in the Regional facts for the Visitor chapter) or elsewhere. Visa applications usually take three days to process and four photos are required. You often also need an onward ticket. In the UK, single/multiple entry visas cost UK£15/35. In the USA, they cost US$20/50.

Visa Extensions If necessary, visas can be extended at the immigration office in Accra (☎ 021-221667 ext 215) near the Sankara interchange. Applications are accepted between 8.30am and noon Monday to Friday. You need two photos, a letter stating why you need an extension, and an onward ticket out of Ghana. Your passport is retained for the two weeks it takes to process the application.

Visas for Onward Travel You need a visa for the following neighbouring countries.

Burkina Faso The embassy issues visas for three months on the same day if you get there early. You need three photos and it costs US$40 or CFA15,000 (not payable in cedis).

Côte d'Ivoire The embassy issues visas in 48 hours and you need two photos. A visa valid for up to a month costs US$4 (payable in cedis) for Australians and Americans or US$10 for British nationals.

Togo The embassy issues visas for one month on the same day. You need three photos and it costs US$20. Alternatively, you can get a visa for the same price at the border at Aflao but it's only valid for seven days.

Student & Youth Cards

With an international student card you can get discounts on admission to national parks, ecotourism projects and museums.

Vaccination Certificates

In theory, you need a yellow fever vaccination certificate to enter Ghana although it is rarely checked. It's more important to have it for onward travel to other countries.

EMBASSIES & CONSULATES

Ghanaian Embassies & Consulates

Ghana has embassies in Benin, Burkina Faso, Côte d'Ivoire, Guinea, Nigeria, Sierra Leone and Togo. For details, see Facts for the Visitor in the relevant country chapter.

Elsewhere, diplomatic missions include:

Australia (☎ 02-9223 5151) Level 8, 1 Chifley Square, Sydney 2000
Canada (☎ 613-236 0871) 1 Clemow Ave, The Glebe, Ottawa, Ont KLS 2A
France (☎ 01 71 10 14 02) 8 Villa Said, 75116 Paris
Germany (☎ 0228-35 20 01) Rheinalle 58, 53173 Bonn
Japan (☎ 03-409 3861) Azabu, PO Box 16, Tokyo
Netherlands (☎ 70-362 5371) Molenstraat 53, 2513 The Hague
UK (☎ 020-8342 8686) 104 Highgate Hill, London N6 5HE
USA
Embassy: (☎ 202-686 4520) 3512 International Dr NW, Washington, DC 20008
Consulate: (☎ 212-832 1300) 19 East 47th St, New York, NY 10017

Embassies & Consulates in Ghana

All embassies and consulates listed are in Accra (telephone area code ☎ 021). The Canadian high commission in Accra can assist Australians with consular services.

Benin (☎ 774860) Switchback Lane, Cantonments
Burkina Faso (☎ 221988) 2nd Mango Tree Ave, Asylum Down; open 8am to 2pm Monday to Friday
Canada (☎ 228555, fax 773792) 46 Independence Ave, Sankara interchange
Côte d'Ivoire (☎ 774611) 9 18th Lane, Osu; open 9am to 2.30pm Monday to Thursday
France (☎ 228571, fax 778321) 12th Rd, off Liberation Ave, Kanda
Guinea (☎ 777921) 4th Norla St, Labone
Germany (☎ 221311, fax 221347) 6 Ridge Rd, North Ridge
Japan (☎ 775616, fax 775951) 8 Josef Broz Tito Ave, off Jawaharlal Nehru Rd, Cantonments
Liberia (☎ 775641) Odoikwao St, Airport Residential Area
Mali (☎ 775160) Liberia Rd, West Ridge
Netherlands (☎ 231991, fax 773655) 89 Liberation Ave, Sankara Circle
Niger (☎ 224962) E104/3 Independence Ave, Ringway Estate
Nigeria (☎ 776158, fax 774395) 5 Josef Broz Tito Ave, Cantonments
Togo (☎ 777950) Cantonments Circle, Cantonments; open 8.30am to 3pm Monday to Friday
UK (☎ 221665, fax 221745) 1 Osu Link, Ringway Estate
USA (☎ 776601, fax 775747) Corner of 10th Lane and 3rd St, Osu

CUSTOMS

You're not supposed to export more than a handful of cedis, and you wouldn't want to anyway – once you're over the frontier no bank will look at them.

MONEY

Currency

The unit of currency is the cedi (C). There are C1000, C2000 and C5000 notes, as well as C100, C200 and C500 coins. Because of Ghana's high inflation and the until recently unstable exchange rate of the cedi, all prices in this chapter are expressed in US dollars.

Exchange Rates

At the time of printing, exchange rates for the cedi were as follows:

country	unit		cedi
euro zone	€1	=	C7880
UK	UK£1	=	C12,150
USA	US$1	=	C7922
West African CFA	CFA100	=	C1200

Exchanging Money

The best currencies to bring are US dollars, UK pounds or euros. For travellers cheques, it's best to bring a well-recognised brand, such as American Express (AmEx) or Thomas Cook. There are branches of Barclays and Standard Chartered Banks in all major towns. Exchanging travellers cheques or cash is a quick and efficient process at either bank and neither charges a commission. You can also change money at Ghana Commercial Bank. Foreign-exchange (forex) bureaus are dotted around most major towns, though there are fewer in the north. They usually offer a slightly better rate than the banks and have more convenient opening hours. However, they don't generally change travellers cheques. Most forexes offer a slightly better rate for larger notes than for smaller denominations.

Most Barclays and Standard Chartered Banks throughout the country have ATMs where you can get a cash advance in cedis (up to about C500,000 or US$70) on Visa or MasterCard. Credit cards, generally Visa and MasterCard, are only accepted by major hotels and travel agencies.

Don't change large amounts of money at a time because the largest note is C5000 (currently less than US$1). Bear in mind that you'll need something to put your wads of cedis in when you leave the bank, as they won't fit in a moneybelt.

Costs

Ghana is one of the cheaper countries in West Africa to travel in. Accommodation is the main expense; food and local transport is very cheap. If you're on a tight budget, you could get by on about US$10 a day. This would mean staying in cheap hotels, where a room with a ceiling fan and shared facilities costs about US$5, eating at food stalls for about US$2 per day, having the occasional beer for US$0.70 and getting around by public transport. A more comfortable budget would be about US$30 a day. On this you can get a basic room with air-con, fridge and bathroom for about US$10 to US$15, have meals at restaurants for about US$4 and take private taxis and more comfortable buses. A smarter double room at a more modern mid-range hotel costs about US$20. Top-end prices start at about US$50.

POST & COMMUNICATIONS

Post

Postcards cost US$0.20 to send anywhere. An airmail letter costs US$0.25 to the USA and Australasia, and US$0.17 to Europe. The main post offices in Accra and Kumasi have reliable post restante services.

Telephone

Every town and city has plenty of private 'communication centres' where you can make national and international calls and send and receive faxes. They're slightly more expensive than calling from a cardphone, but they're wonderfully convenient. Cardphones, operated by Ghana Telecom or Westel, are found throughout the country, and phonecards are readily available. The south and centre of the country has mobile phone coverage. Telephone calls (and faxes) cost about US$1.20 to Europe, US$1.10 to the USA and US$1.45 to Australasia.

Email & Internet Access

There are Internet centres in all major towns in the south and centre; they are more difficult to find in the north of the country. Access is cheap and costs around US$0.02 per minute. Connection speeds vary but outside Accra they can be very slow.

DIGITAL RESOURCES

The africaonline Ghana site (W www.africaonline.com/site/gh) is an excellent starting point for accessing all sorts of information about Ghana. Other websites that may be worth checking out include:

Ghana Tourist Board This site is a good resource, with (brief) information on the country's attractions categorised by region, as well as a summary, with dates, of the main festivals.
W www.africaonline.com.gh/tourism

Ghana.co.UK This UK-based site has plenty of good information about Ghana, from tourist attractions to history, culture and the latest news.
W www.ghana.co.uk

Ghanaweb This site has links to the major Ghanaian newspapers, including the *Daily Graphic*, as well as useful background information on the country
W www.ghanaweb.com

Ghana Review International This website has all the latest news and politics from Ghana.
W www.ghanareview.com

BOOKS

Albert van Dantzig's *Forts and Castles of Ghana*, although first published in 1980, remains the definitive work on the early European coastal presence and is slim enough to slip into your back pocket. The Ghana Museums & Monuments Board's *Castles & Forts of Ghana* has less text but some beautiful pictures. *Asante: The Making of a Nation* by Nana Otamakuro Adubofour, widely available in Kumasi, gives an insight into Ashanti history and culture. *The Making of Ada* by C Amate is an informative account of the little-known precolonial empire of Ada. It's available at the Manet Paradise Hotel in Ada Foah. *Two Hearts of Kwasi Boachi* by Arthur Japin explores the experiences of two Ashanti brothers who were sent to be educated in Holland in the early 19th century.

NEWSPAPERS & MAGAZINES

The national *Daily Graphic* is probably the best of the myriad English-language newspapers available, with reasonably good coverage of Ghanaian, African and international news. The broadsheet, *Ghanaian Times*, is also worth picking up. Of the rest, there's a wide selection of tabloids, many of which feature lurid headlines.

TV & RADIO

GTV is the national channel, available throughout the country. In Accra and Kumasi, you can also get TV3, which is very similar. GTV has nightly news in English at 7pm, which is worth catching, and shows a selection of educational programs, slapstick comedy shows (in Twi) and American soaps. On Sunday, sermons and gospel singing take centre stage. DStv is the main satellite channel.

Ghanaian radio is excellent value and extremely popular – you'll hear it everywhere, especially in taxis and cheap eateries. There's plenty of choice, and most programmes are at least partly in English. Talkback radio rules here and the feisty shows make fascinating listening. The national radio (FM 95.7) has world news in English

GHANA

on the hour, every hour. Other popular stations include Joy FM (99.7), Luv FM (99.5; in Kumasi), Gold FM (90.5), Groove FM (106.3) and Vibe FM (91.9).

HEALTH

Malaria exists year-round throughout Ghana so you'll need to get expert advice on prevention before you travel. Yellow fever is also endemic – make sure you are vaccinated against it. Bilharzia (schistosomiasis) exists throughout the country, including Lake Volta, so avoid bathing or paddling in freshwater rivers or lakes. The government is tackling the HIV/AIDS issue with public education programs – look out for the 'If it's not on it's not in' slogan on billboards and taxi windows. A medical-insurance policy is essential. For general information on these and other health matters, see Health in the Regional Facts for the Visitor chapter.

Medical services in major centres such as Accra and Kumasi are reasonably well-developed; elsewhere services are very basic. There are well-stocked pharmacies in the major centres and most medicines are available without prescription. Tap water (where it's available) is drinkable although to be on the safe side it's best to stick to bottled or sachet water, which is widely available, or purify it yourself.

DANGERS & ANNOYANCES

Ghana is one of the more stable countries in the region and, on the whole, very safe to travel around. Having said that, ethnic violence does sporadically flare up in the far northeast, around Bawku, so if you're heading that way, check with your embassy in Accra for the latest news. You need to take care on the beaches west of Accra – see the boxed text. Otherwise, reckless *tro-tro* (minibus or pick-up) drivers and open sewers are probably the main hazards you will encounter.

BUSINESS HOURS

Business hours are 8am to 12.30pm and 1.30pm to 5.30pm Monday to Friday, and 8.30am to 1pm Saturday. Government offices observe the same times during weekdays, but close Saturday. Banking hours are 8.30am to 2pm Monday to Thursday (to 3pm on Friday). A few bank branches are also open 8.30am to 1pm on Saturday, as are most forexes. Although streetside stalls and markets are open on Sunday, shops, many budget restaurants and most Internet centres are closed.

Be Beachwise

Ghana has around 500km of Atlantic coastline, an almost continuous palm-fringed, sandy stretch of beach. However, there's a sting to Ghana's tropical paradise beaches – offshore, the Atlantic has fierce currents and a ripping undertow and there are several drownings every year. Ask the locals for advice, respect what they tell you and stay well within your depth.

There's another sting – theft and the occasional muggings at knifepoint occur on and around beaches frequented by tourists. Most fishing villages along the coast are extremely poor and local people don't benefit from tourism as resorts tend to be run by outsiders, so tourists are a temptation for some elements in the community. It makes sense not to take any valuables onto the beach with you and to avoid being alone on isolated stretches. If you're walking along the beach or a coastal path, do what the locals do and take a guide with you – not only to show you the way but also as protection against possible muggings. As a way of helping make a difference, try to patronise community-run businesses as far as possible.

Most beaches near settlements are working beaches from which the important business of fishing is carried out. They also function as the village toilet. If you don't want to feel a squelch underfoot, stick either to resort beaches, for which you usually pay a small fee, or to beaches away from settlements.

PUBLIC HOLIDAYS & SPECIAL EVENTS

Public holidays include:

New Year's Day 1 January
Independence Day 6 March
Easter March/April
Labour Day 1 May
Republic Day 1 July
Farmers' Day 1st Friday in December
Christmas Day 25 December

Ghana also observes the Muslim festivals of Eid al-Fitr, at the end of Ramadan, and Eid al-Adha, both of which are determined by the lunar calendar. See Public Holidays & Special Events in the Facts for the Visitor chapter for a table of Islamic holidays.

Ghana has colourful festivals and events, including Cape Coast's Fetu Afahye Festival (first Saturday of September), Elmina's Bakatue Festival (first Tuesday in July), the Fire Festival of the Dagomba people in Tamale and Yendi (dates vary according to the Muslim calendar) and various year-round Akan celebrations in Kumasi. Ghana's most famous festival – Aboakyer (Deer Hunt) – is celebrated in Winneba on the first weekend in May. Accra's tourist office sells an informative booklet on Ghana's festivals. Panafest is celebrated annually in Cape Coast, Accra and Kumasi.

ACTIVITIES

Ghana's coast is famous for its beaches, although the currents and undertow make many unsafe for swimming. Water sports are available at many of the beach resorts. Ghana offers some good hiking; the best areas are in the Volta Region around Ho and Hohoe in the east and in the Tongo Hills near Bolgatanga in the north. For drumming and dancing lessons, contact the Academy of African Music & Arts Ltd (AAMAL) in Kokrobite; many of the community-based tourism projects around the country also offer lessons.

Emancipation Day & Panafest

In 1998 Ghana became the first country in Africa to host an Emancipation Day celebration. As a major centre of the slave trade and also the first West African country to gain independence (in 1957), Ghana was an appropriate venue. The celebrations included a symbolic march along the route the slaves took from the interior before being shipped across the Atlantic, and the burial of the remains of two slaves from Jamaica and the USA. The remains were received at Independence Square in Accra before being transported by sea to Cape Coast Castle. Here, in an intensely symbolic gesture, they passed through the Door of No Return, later renamed the Door of Return in commemoration. Later the remains were buried at an old slave market in Assin Manso.

Emancipation Day is now celebrated as part of the Pan-African Historical Theatre Festival (Panafest), an annual arts and culture festival dedicated to Pan-Africanism and the development of Africa and Africans. First held in 1992, Panafest features music and theatre performances as well as activities commemorating slavery and the diasporic heritage. It's usually held in July and August and is based in Cape Coast, Accra and Kumasi. For a program of events, check out the Panafest website at **W** www.panafest.org.

ACCOMMODATION

The major towns in the south and centre offer a wide selection of accommodation in the mid-range to top-end bracket and a smaller selection of budget accommodation. Prices are generally higher in Accra than elsewhere in the country. Outside the main centres, options are much more limited. Off the tourist trail there are very few hotels and guesthouses but it's usually possible to arrange to sleep on a floor somewhere. Most of the ecotourism projects offer overnight stays in simple guesthouses or at homestays. Along the coast, there are some fabulous beach resorts, many of which are within reach of a mid-range budget. Camping is a possibility at some of these resorts and also at national parks and reserves. A few of the coastal forts offer extremely basic guesthouse accommodation (bucket showers).

Many Ghanaian hotels don't have single rooms as such but offer the choice of double or twin rooms. Double rooms have one double bed and can sleep one or two people; twin rooms are usually more expensive and have two single beds. Mid-range and top-end hotels usually quote prices in US dollars but you can pay in cedis or US dollars.

FOOD

A typical Ghanaian meal consists of a starch staple such as rice, *fufu* (mashed cassava, plantain or yam), *kenkey* or *banku* (fermented maize meal) eaten with a sauce or stew. It's good, sturdy food that will fill you up. Common sauces (called soups) include groundnut, *palaver* (made from greens) and light soup (egg and tomato soup with fish or meat). Other menu regulars are fried rice with chicken or vegetables, *jollof* rice (the West African paella) and *red red*, bean stew with meat or fish, often served with fried plantains. The meat used is usually chicken,

GHANA

goat or beef; guinea fowl replaces chicken in the north of the country. Grasscutter, a large rodent, is also popular. Fish, usually dried and smoked, is a common component of meals. *Omo tuo*, a special dish served only on Sunday, are mashed rice balls with a fish or meat soup.

Breakfast is usually iced kenkey, a sort of liquid porridge made from fermented maize, with a hunk of bread, or bread and an omelette. Ghanaian bread is soft and white; varieties include sugar bread (very soft and sickly sweet), tea bread (less sweet), milk bread (slightly richer) and cinnamon bread.

The cheapest food is sold at street stalls. Look out for women doling out rice, pasta and sauce from huge covered bowls set up on a wooden table. You can either eat it at the stall or take it away in a plastic bag or plantain leaf parcel. Other food-stall staples include egg salad with rice, roast yam with spicy sauce, roast plantain with groundnuts, omelette in bread, and spicy kebabs. Inexpensive food is also available from chop bars, which serve up a selection of dishes, usually with daily specials. Cheap places to eat are also referred to as 'catering services' and 'canteens'.

In Accra and other major centres you'll find a variety of cuisines, commonly Lebanese, Chinese and West African, but also Italian, French and Indian. Western fast food (burgers, fried chicken etc) is hugely popular and there are plenty of outlets in Accra and other centres in the south. Most restaurants offer a choice of Western and Ghanaian dishes.

DRINKS

Cold water is sold everywhere in plastic sachets or plastic bags for about US$0.03. The stuff in sachets (called 'pure water') has been filtered, whereas the stuff tied up in plastic bags (called 'ice water') is just ordinary water. A delicious home-made ginger ale is sold in some areas. As well as the usual soft drinks, bottled pure pineapple juice is available in some places. Generally, though, fresh fruit juice is difficult to find and expensive compared with the bottled drinks. Ghanaian tea is drunk from a huge mug with lots of evaporated milk and heaps of sugar.

Bars in Ghana are often referred to as a 'spot'. Decent, locally made beer is widely available. Popular brands include Star (slogan: 'The Taste of a Lifetime'), Club, Gulder ('The Ultimate in Beer') and Guinness ('Brings out the Power in You'). Be prepared for a withering look if you order a wimpy 'mini' (250ml) beer.

Among home-brew alcoholic drinks, *pito* (millet beer) is the drink of choice in the north. Palm wine, which is more subtle, is the preferred tipple in the south. Catch it when it's young. 'Tap before seven, drink before eleven', goes the local saying. As the day grows older the wine becomes less refreshing, more sour – and more seriously alcoholic. *Akpeteshie* is a fiery local spirit.

SHOPPING

Traditional arts and crafts include batik, kente and adinkra cloth, stools and woodcarvings, beads, pottery, brasswork, leatherwork and baskets. You'll find crafts from all over Ghana at the Centre for National Culture (Arts Centre) in Accra; other good places to shop are the markets in Kumasi and Bolgatanga and the craft villages around Kumasi.

Getting There & Away

AIR

Ghana's only international airport is Kotaka international airport in Accra. The national carrier, Ghana Airways has a reputation for overbooking and random cancellations. It connects Accra with other West African capitals, South Africa, some European centres (London, Dusseldorf and Rome) and New York. Other airlines that regularly link Accra with Europe include Alitalia, British Airways, KLM and Lufthansa. South African Airways links Ghana with Perth in Australia, via Johannesburg.

The US$50 airport departure tax (payable in US dollars) is usually included in the price of tickets, whether bought in Ghana or overseas.

LAND

Border Crossings

Ghana has land borders with Côte d'Ivoire to the west, Burkina Faso to the north and west, and Togo on the east. The main border crossing into Côte d'Ivoire is at Elubo; here are less-travelled crossings between Sunyani and Agnibilékrou and between Bole and Ferkessédougou. Into Burkina the main crossing is at Paga, with other crossings at Tumu, Hamale and Lawra. The main crossing into Togo is at Aflao, just outside Lomé. Note that Ghana's borders all close promptly at 6pm.

Burkina Faso

Between Accra and Ouagadougou, the usual route is via Kumasi, Tamale, Bolgatanga, Paga and Pô. A direct VanefSTC bus runs to Ouagadougou from Accra (US$10, 24 hours) once daily Monday to Saturday and from Kumasi (US$7.50, 20 hours) every Wednesday evening. Going the entire distance in one sitting, though, can be excruciating and most people do the trip in stages. From Bolgatanga, there are frequent tro-tros to the border at Paga (US$0.70, 40 minutes), from where you can get onward transport to Pô, 15km beyond the border, and Ouagadougou.

You can also enter Burkina Faso from the northwest corner of Ghana, crossing between Tumu and Léo or from Hamale or Lawra and onto Bobo-Dioulasso. You can reach Tumu most easily from Bolgatanga, Hamale from Bolgatanga or Wa, and Lawra from Wa. However, traffic is relatively scarce on all these routes.

GHANA

Côte d'Ivoire

VanefSTC buses run between Accra and Abidjan (US$6.50, 12 hours) via Elubo once daily Monday to Friday, leaving in the morning. The Ecowas Express, run by STIF, a company from Côte d'Ivoire, does three runs a week between Neoplan motor park in Accra and Abidjan. From Takoradi, Peugeot bush taxis (US$1) make a daily trip to Abidjan. Otherwise, make your way to Elubo in stages, cross the border on foot and take onward transport from there.

Other less commonly used crossings are from Kumasi via Sunyani and Berekum to Agnibilékrou (you'll have to do this in short stages as there are no direct buses) and between Bole and Bouna to Ferkessédougou. However, on this route you have to cross the Black Volta River (the border) by canoe and readers report being at the mercy of dash-hungry border officials. Onward transport from Bouna to Ferkessédougou takes eight to 12 hours.

Togo

Tro-tros and buses regularly ply the coastal road between Accra and Aflao (all about US$2, three hours). VanefSTC buses leave from the smaller Tudu bus station in Accra. The border at Aflao is open from 6am to 10pm daily but you should cross between 9am and 5pm if you need a Togolese visa at the border. Public transport from Ghana doesn't cross the border, which is only 2km from central Lomé. Other crossings are at Wli near Hohoe and between Ho and Kpalimé. In the north, you can cross from Tamale via Yendi to Sansanné-Mango or Kara but transport is scarce on this route.

SEA

Occasional ships connect Tema, the major port east of Accra, with numerous countries, including Nigeria, Côte d'Ivoire, Gabon, Cameroon and South Africa. Contact the Black Star Line's office in Tema (☎ 022-202888) for information.

Getting Around

AIR

Currently, the only domestic flights are with Airlink, operated by Ghana Air Force. It flies three times a week between Accra and Kumasi (US$28), and between Accra and Tamale (US$44). Ghana Airways, Expertravel & Tours in Accra and M & J Travel & Tours (☎ 773153) in Accra and Kumasi sell Airlink tickets. You can't reserve a seat so you have to arrive at the airport uncomfortably early if you're to be sure of a seat. The departure tax for internal flights is US$0.30 (payable in cedis).

BUS

The best bus service in the country is provided by VanefSTC (W www.vanef-stc.com), the old State Transport Corporation now owned by Greyhound. It runs reliable, frequent and very popular services between the major centres in Ghana, linking Accra, Kumasi, Takoradi, Cape Coast, Tamale and Bolgatanga, among other places. Seats can generally be booked one day in advance, which is essential for long-haul routes especially during busy holiday periods. Other operators, which may have the only buses on some routes (such as between Tamale and Mole National Park), include OSA, Kingdom Transport Services, City Express and GPRTU. Where they share routes, fares are less than with VanefSTC, but the buses tend to be older and less comfortable.

You have to pay extra for luggage. On VanefSTC buses, your luggage is weighed and you're charged about US$0.06 per kilogram. Avoid the flip-down aisle seats which can be real backbreakers on a long journey.

TRO-TRO & TAXI

Tro-tro is a catch-all category that embraces any form of transport that's not a bus or taxi. They cover all major and many minor routes and, without them, Ghana would simply grind to a halt. Except on real backcountry routes, tro-tros are minibuses of all shapes, sizes and degrees of dilapidation. They don't work to a set timetable but leave when full, having squeezed in as many passengers as they can. The beauty of tro-tros is that you can pick them up anywhere along a route and they're incredibly cheap (about US$0.01 per kilometre). For long journeys, though, buses are more comfortable and safer. Most tro-tro drivers demand a negotiable luggage fee – bargain hard.

Most towns have an area where tro-tros and buses congregate, usually in or near the market. These are called lorry park or motor park (the terms are used interchangeably) or, quite often, station. You may hear the term tro-tro used but taxis and minibuses are often just called 'cars'.

Within towns and on some shorter routes between towns, shared taxis (called passenger or line taxis) are the usual form of transport. Line taxis run on fixed routes, along which they stop to pick up and drop off passengers. Passenger taxis run on routes between towns and will set you down wherever you want to go. Shared taxis are more expensive than tro-tros but still very cheap.

Private or 'dropping' taxis don't have meters and rates are negotiable. Taxis can be chartered for an agreed period of time from one hour to a day for a negotiable fee.

TRAIN

Ghana's railway links Accra, Kumasi and Takoradi. The rolling stock is good and, like so many tro-tros and buses, was imported second-hand from Germany. But the trains creep along and are much slower and no cheaper than motorised transport. There are daily passenger services in either direction between Accra and Kumasi (US$2/1.60 in 1st/2nd class; about 12 hours) and a nightly service between Accra and Takoradi, which costs about the same and takes at least 12 hours, but these are really only for masochists and train enthusiasts. However, the line between Kumasi and Takoradi is worth considering, both as a change from road transport and for the experience in itself. On this line, there are two trains daily, leaving at 6am and 8.30pm. Fares are US$2.50/2 in 1st/2nd class and on the night train this gets you either a two- or four-person sleeper. The journey in theory takes eight hours but it's usually more like 12 in practice, especially on the night train. No food is available on the train, although you can get food at stops along the way. Take some supplies just in case.

CAR & MOTORCYCLE

Driving is on the right in Ghana. Most main roads in Ghana are in good condition apart from some potholed stretches between Kumasi and Tamale and on the coastal road between Accra and Aflao. Almost all secondary roads are unsealed. The frequent police checkpoints along the road are usually angling for a dash. Self-drive car rental is available in Accra but not recommended unless you are used to driving the West African way. Car hire with a driver is a good option if you have limited time; it costs anything from US$50 to US$100 per day. The estimated cost is generally payable in advance in cash or by major credit card. Rental companies in Accra include:

Hertz (☎ 021-223389) Golden Tulip Hotel, Liberation Ave, Airport Residential Area
Europcar (☎ 021-667546) Golden Tulip Hotel, Liberation Ave, Airport Residential Area
Avis (Speedway Travel & Tours; ☎ 021-227744, fax 228799) 5 Tackie Tawiah Ave
Vicma Travel & Tours (☎ 021-232294, fax 234843) Liberia Rd North

BOAT

A passenger boat, the *Yapei Queen*, runs along Lake Volta between Akosombo and Yeji, stopping at the town of Kete-Krachi and a few villages along the way. The journey winds past beautiful hills and is an experience in itself as well as a great alternative to road travel. It leaves the port at Akosombo at 4pm on Monday and arrives in Yeji on Wednesday morning. The southbound service leaves Yeji around 4pm on Wednesday and arrives in Akosombo on Friday morning. Tickets cost US$8/3.50 in 1st/2nd class, and food and drinks are available on board. If you want one of the two 1st-class cabins (recommended), you have to reserve at least two weeks in advance – call ☎ 0251-20686 in Akosombo to make a booking.

Accra

☎ 021 • pop 2 million

Accra is the capital of Ghana and its largest city. Originally a scattering of villages controlled by Ga chiefs, today it's a sprawling city that extends eastwards almost to the neighbouring city of Tema, 25km away. It's a city of contrasts, vibrant shanty town in parts, genteel leafy suburbia in others. Chop bars and food stalls vie with pizza joints and ice-cream parlours; chauffeur-driven cars edge through streets congested with market stalls; immaculately coiffured women draped in exquisite fabrics sail like galleons along dusty streets lined with open sewers.

Accra is a low-key capital, with no high-rise business district, but it's a friendly and self-assured city, where visitors are welcomed but not overwhelmed. Although there's not a lot to see in Accra itself, if you've just arrived in Ghana a short stay here makes an excellent introduction to the rest of the country. If you've been upcountry for a while, Accra is a great place for relaxing and indulging.

Orientation

The action area of Accra is bounded by a semicircular road called Ring Road West, Ring Road Central and Ring Road East, whose four major circles and interchanges are, from west to east, Lamptey, Nkrumah, Sankara and Danquah. Accra's vibrant commercial heart is Makola Market, the city's chaotic main market. South of Makola, High St runs along the sea front. West of the city centre are the shanty-town areas of James Town and Ussher Town, bordered by Korle Lagoon. East of the city centre is the beachside suburb of La. North of Makola, the commercial district extends along Nkrumah Ave and Kojo Thompson Rd, two parallel north-south highways that connect High St with the Nkrumah Circle area. The district of Adabraka, south of Nkrumah Circle is where you'll find budget hotels and inexpensive bars and restaurants. East of Adabraka, the leafy residential area of Asylum Down has some good accommodation options, and is another popular base for travellers. Accra's most happening area is Osu, south of Danquah Circle, which has heaps of fast-food joints, restaurants, Internet centres and more-expensive hotels. On the northern and eastern side of Ring Road East are the upmarket residential areas of Cantonments, Labone and Airport, with embassies and upmarket hotels.

Maps The best and most up-to-date map available is the KLM *Guide Map of Accra* (US$6). It's on sale at Koala supermarket on Cantonments Rd, Osu, and at most of the upmarket hotels. Although the map itself isn't entirely accurate, on the flip side is an aerial photo of the city. An older version of this map, produced by KLM in conjunction with Shell, is also widely available at tourist sites and hotel bookshops in Accra for about the same price.

Information

Tourist Offices The tourist office (☎ 231 817), open from 8am to 4pm Monday to Friday, is 50m down Education Close, off Barnes Rd. The friendly staff can supply you with free leaflets but cannot help with a lot of practical information. There is a small but helpful tourist information counter (☎ 776171 ext 1314) in the international arrivals hall at the airport.

No Worries! The Indispensable Insiders' Guide to Accra, published by the North American Women's Association and targeted at expats, is a mine of practical information about Accra. It is, in theory, available from upmarket hotels, major supermarkets and Mobil petrol stations but in practice it's hard to track down.

Money There are plenty of options for changing cash or travellers cheques in

ACCRA

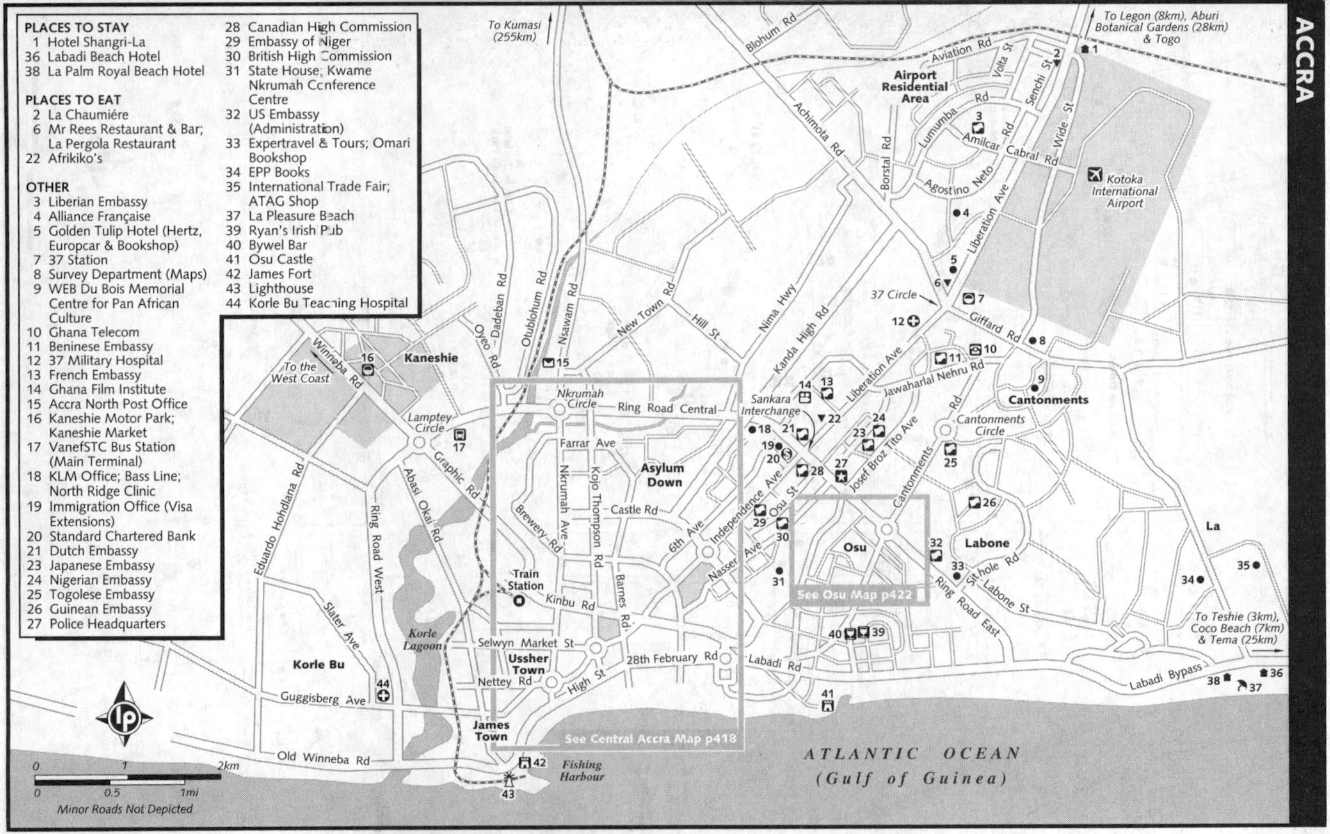
To Kumasi (255km)
To Legon (8km), Aburi Botanical Gardens (28km) & Togo
Blohum Rd
Aviation Rd
Volta St
Senchi St
Wide St
Airport Residential Area
Lumumba Rd
Amilcar Cabral Rd
Agostino Neto Rd
Achimota Rd
Borstal Rd
Liberation Ave
Kotoka International Airport
37 Circle
Giffard Rd
Nima Hwy
Kanda High Rd
New Town Rd
Hill St
Dadeban Rd
Otublohum Rd
Nsawam Rd
Oyeo Rd
Kaneshie
Winneba Rd
To the West Coast
Lamptey Circle
Graphic Rd
Abasi Okai Rd
Eduardo Hohdlana Rd
Ring Road West
Slater Ave
Korle Bu
Guggisberg Ave
Old Winneba Rd
Korle Lagoon
Nkrumah Circle
Ring Road Central
Farrar Ave
Nkrumah Ave
Kojo Thompson Rd
Asylum Down
Castle Rd
Brewery Rd
Train Station
Kinbu Rd
Barnes Rd
6th Ave
Independence Ave
Osu St
Nasser Ave
Selwyn Market St
Ussher Town
Nettey Rd
High St
28th February Rd
James Town
See Central Accra Map p418
Fishing Harbour
Sankara Interchange
Jawaharlal Nehru Rd
Josef Broz Tito Ave
Cantonments Rd
Cantonments Circle
Cantonments
Osu
See Osu Map p422
Labone
Sithole Rd
Labone St
Ring Road East
Labadi Rd
La
Labadi Bypass
To Teshie (3km), Coco Beach (7km) & Tema (25km)
ATLANTIC OCEAN
(Gulf of Guinea)
0 1 2km
0 0.5 1mi
Minor Roads Not Depicted

PLACES TO STAY

1 Hotel Shangri-La
36 Labadi Beach Hotel
38 La Palm Royal Beach Hotel

PLACES TO EAT

2 La Chaumiére
6 Mr Rees Restaurant & Bar; La Pergola Restaurant
22 Afrikiko's

OTHER

3 Liberian Embassy
4 Alliance Française
5 Golden Tulip Hotel (Hertz, Europcar & Bookshop)
7 37 Station
8 Survey Department (Maps)
9 WEB Du Bois Memorial Centre for Pan African Culture
10 Ghana Telecom
11 Beninese Embassy
12 37 Military Hospital
13 French Embassy
14 Ghana Film Institute
15 Accra North Post Office
16 Kaneshie Motor Park; Kaneshie Market
17 VanefSTC Bus Station (Main Terminal)
18 KLM Office; Bass Line; North Ridge Clinic
19 Immigration Office (Visa Extensions)
20 Standard Chartered Bank
21 Dutch Embassy
23 Japanese Embassy
24 Nigerian Embassy
25 Togolese Embassy
26 Guinean Embassy
27 Police Headquarters
28 Canadian High Commission
29 Embassy of Niger
30 British High Commission
31 State House; Kwame Nkrumah Conference Centre
32 US Embassy (Administration)
33 Expertravel & Tours; Omari Bookshop
34 EPP Books
35 International Trade Fair; ATAG Shop
37 La Pleasure Beach
39 Ryan's Irish Pub
40 Bywel Bar
41 Osu Castle
42 James Fort
43 Lighthouse
44 Korle Bu Teaching Hospital

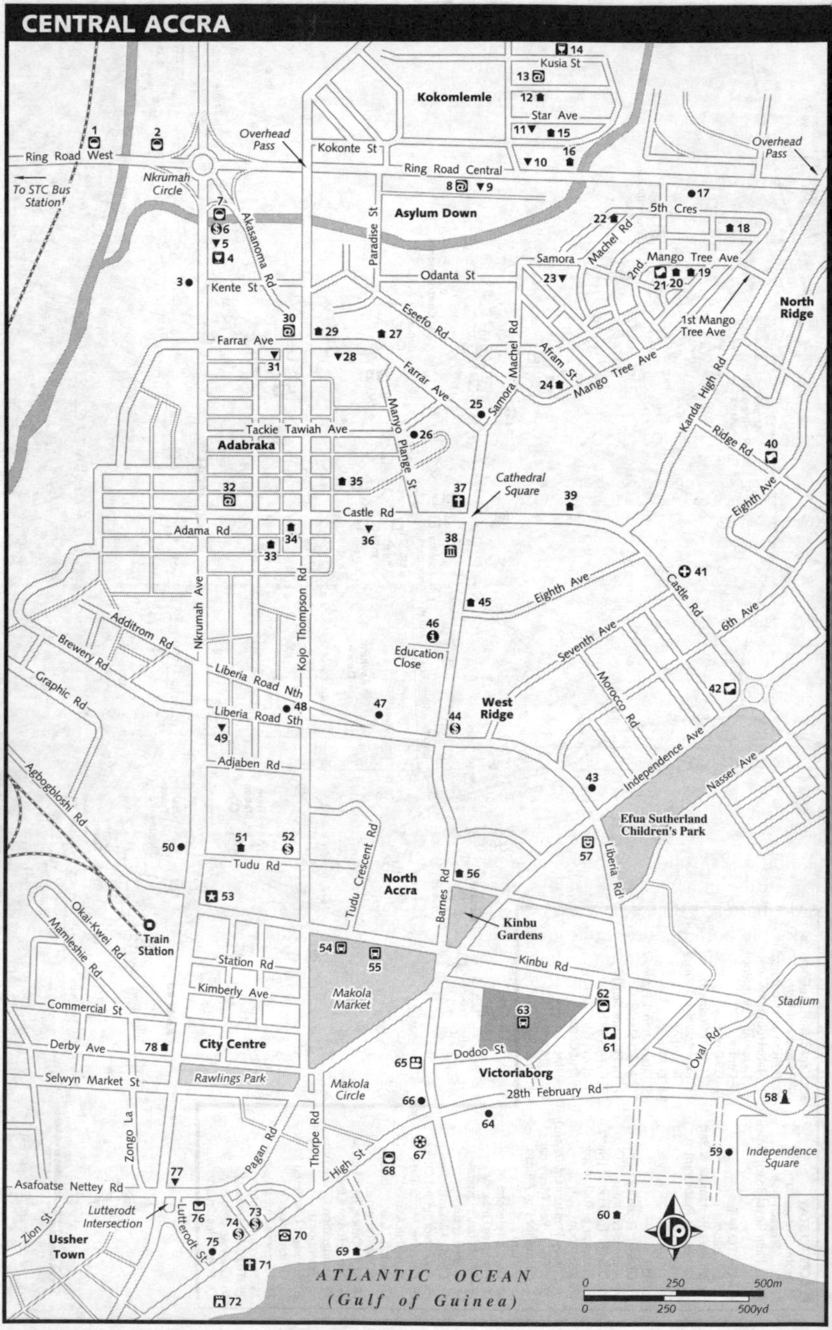
CENTRAL ACCRA
Kokomlemle
Kusia St
Star Ave
Overhead Pass
Kokonte St
Ring Road West
Nkrumah Circle
To STC Bus Station
Ring Road Central
Asylum Down
Akasanoma Rd
Paradise St
5th Cres
Samora Machel Rd
Mango Tree Ave
2nd
Odanta St
Kente St
Eseefo Rd
North Ridge
1st Mango Tree Ave
Farrar Ave
Afram St
Manyo Plange St
Kanda High Rd
Tackie Tawiah Ave
Adabraka
Ridge Rd
Cathedral Square
Eighth Ave
Castle Rd
Adama Rd
Nkrumah Ave
Kojo Thompson Rd
Additrom Rd
Brewery Rd
Graphic Rd
Education Close
Seventh Ave
6th Ave
Liberia Road Nth
Liberia Road Sth
Morocco Rd
West Ridge
Adjaben Rd
Agbogbloshi Rd
Independence Ave
Nasser Ave
Efua Sutherland Children's Park
Tudu Rd
Tudu Crescent Rd
North Accra
Barnes Rd
Liberia Rd
Kinbu Gardens
Okai-Kwei Rd
Mamleshie Rd
Train Station
Station Rd
Kimberly Ave
Makola Market
Kinbu Rd
Stadium
Commercial St
Derby Ave
City Centre
Dodoo St
Victoriaborg
Oval Rd
Selwyn Market St
Rawlings Park
Makola Circle
28th February Rd
Zongo La
Pagan Rd
Thorpe Rd
High St
Independence Square
Asafoatse Nettey Rd
Lutterodt Intersection
Lutterodt St
Zion St
Ussher Town
ATLANTIC OCEAN
(Gulf of Guinea)
0 250 500m
0 250 500yd

CENTRAL ACCRA

PLACES TO STAY
12 Kokomlemle Guesthouse
15 New Haven Hotel
16 Paloma Hotel & Suites; Paloma Shopping Mall; Champs Sports Bar
18 Gye Nyame Hotel
19 Korkdam Hotel
20 Lemon Lodge
22 Pink Hostel International
24 Times Square Lodge
27 Hotel President
29 Niagara Hotel
33 Date Hotel
34 Hotel de California
35 St George's Hotel
39 YMCA
45 Calvary Methodist Church Guesthouse
51 Gasotel
56 Novotel
60 Riviera Beach Hotel & Restaurant
69 Akuma Village
78 Danotel

PLACES TO EAT
5 Palma Nova Restaurant & Bar
9 Bus Stop Restaurant; Next Stop
10 Joysco Bar & Restaurant
11 Tasha Food
23 Spicy Chicken
28 The Orangery; Fox Trap
31 White Bell
36 YWCA
49 Elbi's Snack Bar
77 Backpass Bar & Restaurant

OTHER
1 Neoplan Motor Park
2 Tro-Tro Park
3 The Loom
4 Waikiki Restaurant & Nightclub
6 Barclays Bank
7 Taxi Station (for La, Osu & Airport)
8 Surfers Paradise; Standard Chartered Bank
13 Internet Centre
14 Slyfoks Garden
17 Alitalia Office; South African Airways Office; Lufthansa Office
21 Burkinabé Embassy
25 Trust Towers (Afro Wings Limited)
26 Speedway Travel & Tours; Avis
30 Ghana Internet Centre
32 Omari Internet Centre
37 Catholic Cathedral
38 National Museum; Edvy Restaurant
40 German Embassy
41 Ridge Hospital
42 US Embassy, Public Affairs Section
43 British Council
44 Standard Chartered Bank
46 Tourist Office
47 Vicma Travel & Tours
48 British Airways Office
50 Cocoa House (Ghana Airways, Air Ivoire)
52 Standard Chartered Bank
53 Police Station
54 Tudu Bus Station
55 VanefSTC Bus Station (to Ho and Aflao)
57 National Theatre; Trafix Courtyard Restaurant
58 Independence Arch
59 Wildlife Department
61 Malian Embassy
62 Ho Station
63 Tema Station
64 Centre for National Culture (Arts Centre)
65 Rex Cinema
66 Former Parliament House
67 Kwame Nkrumah Memorial Park
68 Labadi Lorry Park
70 Ghana Telecom
71 Holy Trinity Cathedral
72 Ussher Fort
73 Standard Chartered Bank (Head Office)
74 Barclays Bank (Head Office)
75 Multistores
76 Main Post Office

Accra. The head offices of Barclays and Standard Chartered are both on High St and there are several branches around town, including on Nkrumah Ave and Cantonments Rd. All the branches of Barclays and Standard Chartered Banks have ATMs. There is also a plethora of forexes around town, especially in the area around Makola Market and along Kojo Thompson Rd in central Accra and along Cantonments Rd in Osu. Afro Wings Ltd (☎ 235420), in the Trust Towers complex on Farrar Ave, is the representative of AmEx.

Post The main post office (for poste restante) is in Ussher Town, on the Lutterodt intersection. It's open 8am to 5pm Monday to Friday and 9am to 2pm Saturday. Poste restante can be collected between 8.30am and 5pm Monday to Friday. The Accra North post office on Nsawam Rd, just north of Nkrumah Circle, is handy if you're staying in Asylum Down or Kokomlemle.

Telephone & Fax Making a telephone call is probably the easiest thing you can do in Accra; there are plenty of cardphones for direct dialling and every street corner seems to have a communication centre. You can buy phonecards and make telephone calls from the Ghana Telecom offices on High St in central Accra or on Nehru Rd, Jawaharlal. You can also buy phonecards from many stalls around town; just look for the sign. To send a fax, it's simplest to use one of the communication centres.

Email & Internet Access Internet centres have mushroomed in Accra over the last few years. Prices are around US$0.01 per minute online and most places are open 8am to 9pm Monday to Saturday.

If you're staying in or around Asylum Down, the Internet centre at Paloma complex is convenient, not too crowded and has Arctic air-con. There's also a basic centre opposite the Kokomlemle Guesthouse, as well as the huge Surfer's Paradise on Ring Road Central. In Adabraka, the small and basic Ghana Internet Centre is opposite the Niagara Hotel on Farrar Ave, or try Omari Internet Centre on Castle Rd.

Along and just off Cantonments Rd in Osu there are almost as many Internet cafés as there are fast-food joints. Cyberia 1, above Fusion at the Danquah Circle end of Cantonments Rd, and Cyberia 2, opposite Frankie's, are two of the longest-established centres in Accra and some of the very few places that are actually Internet 'cafés' as opposed to centres. Other recommended alternatives include Besnet, down 14th Lane, opposite the Niagara Plus Hotel or, if you want to combine browsing with bratwurst and a stein of beer, go to the German theme pub Aquarius on Osu Cresent.

Travel Agencies Travel companies with a proven track record for arranging local tours and international flights include Expertravel & Tours on Ring Road East (☎ 775498, fax 773937), Speedway Travel & Tours (☎ 227 744, fax 228799) on Tackie Tawiah Ave and M & J Travel & Tours (☎ 773153, fax 774338), on 11th Lane in Osu.

Bookshops & Libraries Books for Less, on 17th Lane in Osu, has the best range of second-hand novels in the city. Less convenient is Omari bookshop on Ring Road East, which carries several mildly interesting books on Ghana plus a limited range of fiction. If you're looking for books about Ghana, the best bookshop is the one out at the University of Ghana in Legon, although it's a long way to get there. EPP Books in Labadi, opposite the Trade Fair, also has a good selection. Of the hotel bookshops, the best by far is the one at the Golden Tulip Hotel near the airport.

A limited selection of foreign magazines and newspapers is available at bookshops at upmarket hotels and supermarkets in Osu.

The British Council on Liberia Rd has an air-con library open to the public where you can drop in to cool down and catch up with English newspapers and magazines.

Cultural Centres In Accra these include:

Alliance Française (☎ 773134, fax 760279, e alliance@ghana.com) Liberation Link, Airport Residential Area

British Council (☎ 244744, fax 240330, w www.britishcouncil.org/ghana)

Goethe Institut (☎ 776764, fax 779770, e goetheil@ncs.com.gh) 30 Kakramadu Rd, Cantonments

Public Affairs Section, US embassy (☎ 229179) African Liberation Square, off Independence Ave

Medical Services Your embassy can generally provide you with a list of recommended doctors and specialists. One recommended private hospital where you can see a general practitioner is The Trust Hospital (☎ 776787, 777137) on Cantonments Rd in Osu. It also has a laboratory if you need a medical test. The North Ridge Clinic (☎ 227328, 024-355366) near the KLM office at the eastern end of Ring Road Central also offers a general practitioner service. The main public hospitals in Accra are Korle Bu Teaching Hospital (☎ 665401) on Guggisberg Ave in Korle Bu; 37 Military Hospital (☎ 776111) near 37 Circle on Liberation Ave, recommended for traumatic injuries; and Ridge Hospital (☎ 228382) on Castle Rd. There are plenty of pharmacies throughout town or try the supermarkets in Osu.

Emergency In an emergency, try phoning the following:

ambulance ☎ 193
fire ☎ 192
police ☎ 191

Dangers & Annoyances On the whole, Accra is a remarkably safe city to travel around. If you're on foot, the traffic is probably the most significant hazard you'll face. If you've been for a ride in a taxi, you'll know to be extremely cautious at any pedestrian crossing. Potholes, uneven surfaces and open sewers make the streets particularly treacherous at night, when there is little street lighting.

As in any big city, it makes sense to take the usual precautions against pickpockets, especially in busy areas such as the markets and bus stations. Other areas that it's worth taking care around are Independence Square, James Town and Nkrumah Circle. Take extra care at the beaches – petty theft and even the occasional mugging are real possibilities. Never leave any valuables on the beach and avoid solitary strolls after dark.

Be particularly cautious of taking photos near Osu Castle, the president's office (which bristles with nervy soldiers) who may view you as a spy or, worse, a journalist.

National Museum

This museum *(☎ 221633, Barnes Rd; admission US$1.40, camera fee US$0.70; open 9am-6pm daily)* has fascinating displays on various aspects of Ghanaian culture and history, housed in a large, airy and gently decaying building set in shady grounds. The displays on royal stools, state umbrellas, swords and linguist's staffs *(akyeamepoma)* are excellent. There is some fine brasswork, including weights used by Ashanti goldsmiths for measuring gold and the spoons they used for loading the scales with gold dust. There are informative displays explaining local iron-smelting techniques, the lost-wax method for casting metal sculptures and how glass beads are made. Smaller displays feature masks, drums, wooden statues and the artefacts of other African cultures, such as the Baoulé and Senoufo peoples. When we visited there was also an excellent but harrowing exhibition on the slave-ship Fredensborg whose story is typical of the many ships that took slaves from the Gold Coast to the Americas in the 18th century.

In the museum grounds is a shady open-air restaurant (see Places to Eat, later for more details).

Makola Market

For an intense and colourful introduction to Ghanaian life, customs and humour, weave your way through and around the city's central market, Makola. Hundreds of stalls and vendors line the pavements with their wares: handkerchiefs, flat irons, pumpkin-sized bras, hair extensions, cooking utensils, gaudy fake-gold trinkets, sachets of washing powder, bars of soap and, everywhere, piles on piles of second-hand clothes and shoes. The food vendors have some of the most fascinating displays – pungent-smelling smoked fish, mountains of bread, painstakingly arranged piles of tomatoes and shallots, pyramids of rice, maize and millet, roast plantain and vast arrays of sweets, toffees and chewing gum. Just allow yourself to be swept along by the crowd, and let your senses be assaulted by the smells, sights and sounds of Ghana.

Independence Square & Osu Castle

Sometimes called Black Star Square, Independence Square is to Accra what Red Square is to Moscow, only more aesthetically challenging. This vast expanse of baking-hot concrete, backed by the sea, can hold 30,000 people, though you are more likely to find it deserted. It marks the spot where, in colonial times, three ex-servicemen were shot while attempting to present grievances to the governor in a peaceful demonstration. Its focal point, on 28th February Rd, is Independence Arch, a monolithic replica of the Arc de Triomphe, beneath which the Eternal Flame of African Liberation, lit by Nkrumah, still flickers. Opposite the arch, in the square, is the memorial to the Unknown Soldier.

From the square, looking east along the coast towards La, you can see Osu Castle. Built by the Danes around 1659 and originally called Christiansborg Castle, it's now the seat of government and is off limits to the public.

Centre for National Culture

At this centre *(☎ 664099, 662581, 28th February Rd; open 9am-5pm daily)*, also known simply as the Arts Centre, there's a large arts and crafts market as well as an art gallery and performance area. At the market you'll find good-quality handicrafts from all over Ghana, including batik, kente and other fabrics, beads, masks, woodcarvings, drums, brass and leatherwork. This is the closest thing Accra has to a tourist trap – the pressure to buy is intense and the level of hassle is high.

The small art gallery *(admission free; open 9am-5pm Sun-Fri)* displays and sells paintings by local artists and is worth dropping into. There's also a small post office and a forex within the complex. On Thursday to Sunday afternoons performances are often held at the centre, including music, drumming, traditional dance and theatre. Check the chalkboard at the main entrance for what's on.

Kwame Nkrumah Memorial Park

About 250m west of the Arts Centre is this park *(High St; admission US$0.70, camera fee US$0.40; open 10am-6pm daily)*, the resting place of the founder of Ghana, laid out in the early 1990s as a gesture of rehabilitation.

Kwame Nkrumah's effigy, carved big, with arm outstretched and pointing the way forward, stands beneath a huge marble pile. With the playing fountains, the swathe of grass and the twin ranks of musicians at his feet, it's all on the monumental scale that he favoured and would have appreciated. There's also a small air-conditioned museum, with photos and artefacts from Nkrumah's life.

James Town & Ussher Town

A visit to the sprawling, vibrant shantytown area of James Town, west of the city centre, is recommended, if only for the contrast it provides to Accra's leafy northern suburbs. For a great view of the city (haze and pollution permitting), climb to the top of the old **lighthouse** (give the lighthouse keeper a dash) near James Fort and the busy and colourful fishing harbour.

From the lighthouse, walk back to the centre along Cleland Rd, which becomes High St, perhaps taking a detour along Hansen Rd to see the **Timber Market** (it's hard to find so you'll need to ask someone to show you where it is). The fetish section is fascinating, with its animal skulls, live and dead reptiles, strange powders, charms, bells, shakers, leopard skins, teeth, porcupine quills and *juju* figurines. If your energy levels are wavering at this stage, stop off for a drink or bite to eat at the Backpass Bar & Restaurant on the Lutterodt intersection. Alternatively, head on to the **Holy Trinity Cathedral**, opposite Barclays on High St, which has a shady garden and, inside, a magnificent wooden barrel-vaulted roof.

WEB Du Bois Memorial Centre for Pan African Culture

Dr Du Bois was an academic, who championed civil rights and African unity. Towards the end of his life, he was invited to Ghana by Nkrumah to begin work on an encyclopaedia of Pan-Africanism. This centre *(☎ 776502, 1st Circular Rd, Cantonments; admission US$0.70; open 8.30am-4.30pm Mon-Fri)*, where Du Bois spent the last two years of his life, houses a research library for students of Pan-Africanism and memorabilia from his life, including a photographic display of leading black personalities and political leaders. In the grounds is the burial

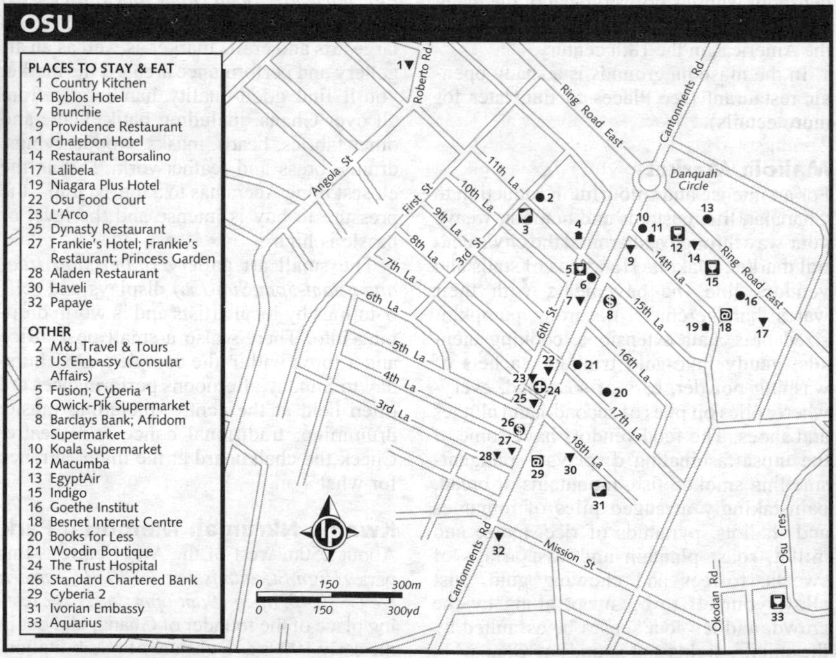
OSU
PLACES TO STAY & EAT
1 Country Kitchen
4 Byblos Hotel
7 Brunchie
9 Providence Restaurant
11 Ghalebon Hotel
14 Restaurant Borsalino
17 Lalibela
19 Niagara Plus Hotel
22 Osu Food Court
23 L'Arco
25 Dynasty Restaurant
27 Frankie's Hotel; Frankie's Restaurant; Princess Garden
28 Aladen Restaurant
30 Haveli
32 Papaye
OTHER
2 M&J Travel & Tours
3 US Embassy (Consular Affairs)
5 Fusion; Cyberia 1
6 Qwick-Pik Supermarket
8 Barclays Bank; Afridom Supermarket
10 Koala Supermarket
12 Macumba
13 EgyptAir
15 Indigo
16 Goethe Institut
18 Besnet Internet Centre
20 Books for Less
21 Woodin Boutique
24 The Trust Hospital
26 Standard Chartered Bank
29 Cyberia 2
31 Ivorian Embassy
33 Aquarius
Roberto Rd
Ring Road East
Cantonments Rd
Danquah Circle
Angola St
First St
11th La
10th La
9th La
8th La
7th La
6th La
5th La
4th La
3rd La
3rd St
6th St
14th La
15th La
16th La
17th La
18th La
Mission St
Okodan Rd
Osu Cres
0 150 300m
0 150 300yd

place of Du Bois and his wife, built in the form of a traditional chief's compound. It's a peaceful and inspiring place to visit.

Beaches

There are some beautiful sandy beaches around Accra. **La Pleasure Beach** *(admission US$0.70)*, also known as Labadi Beach, is about 8km east of central Accra and easily reached by public transport. The well-guarded entrance is at the end of a short dirt track off the main road, just before the Labadi Beach Hotel. There are showers and a lifeguard, as well as some decent beachside eating places and bars. Tourist leeches can sometimes spoil the ambience here. Take a shared taxi or tro-tro (US$0.30) from Tema station, Nkrumah Circle, any of the stops along Ring Road Central or Labadi lorry park on High St. Alternatively, charter a taxi for about US$2.50.

At **Coco Beach**, about 7km further east towards Nungua, access to the beach is free or you can base yourself at the New Coco Beach Hotel, which has a swimming pool, bar and restaurant and overlooks the shore. Take a taxi or tro-tro (US$0.50) to Nungua and walk (about 20 minutes) or charter a taxi for the whole way (about US$4).

Places to Stay – Budget

Good-value budget accommodation is available around the junction of Castle and Kojo Thompson Rds in Adabraka, in the quiet residential area of Asylum Down and in Kokomlemle, north of Ring Road Central. There's also one good budget option on the cliffs near the city centre and, if you don't mind dorm accommodation, the YMCA.

YMCA *(☎ 224700, Castle Rd, West Ridge)* Dorm beds US$1.50. This basic hostel is 250m east of the Catholic cathedral, but accepts men only (including nonmembers).

Akuma Village *(☎ 660573)* Singles/doubles with fan US$6.50/8. This groovy place has a great location, perched on the edge of the cliff, overlooking the ocean and within striking distance of the Arts Centre. It's well signposted off the ocean side of High St near the Kwame Nkrumah Mausoleum. Rooms are extremely basic but clean, as are the shared toilets and showers. Tourist leeches can be a problem in the bar area.

Date Hotel *(☎ 228200, Adama Rd, Adabraka)* Singles/doubles with fan US$4/4.50, doubles with bathroom US$5. The tranquil Date Hotel is one of the best budget options in Accra. Rooms are large, old-fashioned and clean and it has a lovely shady terrace bar and restaurant.

Hotel de California *(☎ 226199, Cnr Kojo Thompson & Castle Rds, Adabraka)* Singles with fan US$4, doubles with fan/air-con US$6/7. This long-time backpackers favourite, housed in an airy, high-ceilinged, colonial-era house, retains a certain charm, although it has been getting mixed reviews recently. Rooms (shared bathroom) are a reasonable size and there's a nice veranda bar area.

Gasotel *(☎ 660536, Tudu Rd, Adabraka)* Doubles with fan US$6. This well-worn hotel, on a road running between Nkrumah Ave and Kojo Thompson Rd, has noisy but good-sized rooms with bathroom and a central location.

St George's Hotel *(☎ 224699, Amusudai Rd, Adabraka)* Singles/doubles with air-con US$13/19. One block north of Castle Rd, opposite a school, this delightful hotel has a pleasant location and is excellent value, with large, cheerful rooms.

Hotel President *(☎ 223343, Farrar Ave, Adabraka)* Singles with fan US$15, doubles with air-con US$19. In a distinctive purple multistorey building, this hotel is reasonably priced, with clean, pleasant rooms and a good central location.

Calvary Methodist Church Guesthouse *(☎ 234507, Barnes Rd, West Ridge)* Singles/doubles with air-con US$6.50/8. On the top floor of Reverend Gadiel Acquaah House on the eastern side of Barnes Rd, this guesthouse is a great bargain and often full. The pleasant rooms are spotlessly clean and have a small balcony and bathroom. Breakfast is US$0.70 and a filling lunch or dinner is US$1.40. It's basically for visiting pastors and you'll need to behave with decorum.

Times Square Lodge *(☎ 222694, Cnr Mango Tree Ave & Afram Rd, Asylum Down)* Doubles with fan US$4. In a quiet residential area, this friendly lodge is excellent value for money, with spotless, attractive rooms with shared bathroom.

Lemon Lodge *(☎ 227857, 2nd Mango Tree Ave, Asylum Down)* Doubles with fan US$5. Also in Asylum Down and set in a leafy garden, this charming place is a long-standing travellers' favourite. It's often full, especially over holiday periods, so ring ahead.

Korkdam Hotel *(☎ 223221, fax 223424, ⓔ korkdam@africaonline, 2nd Mango Tree Ave, Asylum Down)* Singles/doubles with fan US$8/13, doubles with air-con US$20. Next door to Lemon Lodge is the Korkdam. The rooms are run-down and the sound-proofing is lousy, but it's still popular.

Kokomlemle Guesthouse *(☎ 224581, Oroko St, Kokomlemle)* Singles/doubles with fan & bathroom US$4/5. North of Ring Road Central, this exceptionally friendly place is a favourite with nongovernmental organisation (NGO) workers. Rooms are small and basic but comfortable, and you can get meals and cold drinks on the terrace at the front.

New Haven Hotel *(☎ 222053, Kokomlemle)* Singles/doubles with fan & bathroom US$5/8, doubles with air-con US$9. On a dirt road that runs parallel to and between Star Ave and Ring Road Central, this hotel has pleasant rooms set around a leafy courtyard bar area. Solo women might want to give this place a miss as there have been reports of harassment of women guests by drunken members of staff.

Places to Stay – Mid-Range

Most hotels in this category have rooms with air-con, private bathroom, TV and fridge.

City Centre Off 28th February Rd near the Arts Centre is ***Riviera Beach Hotel & Restaurant*** *(☎ 662400)*, which has singles/doubles with fan for US$25/28.50. This gently decaying but charming hotel has a superb location overlooking the ocean. Rooms are run-down but are a good size and have magnificent sea views.

Asylum Down & Adabraka Set within a leafy garden, ***Gye Nyame Hotel*** *(☎ 223321, fax 226486, 5th Crescent, Asylum Down)* has singles/doubles for US$50/60. It is warmly recommended for its immaculate and well-furnished rooms, shady 1st-floor veranda and comfortable sitting area – shame it's somewhat overpriced but you may be able to negotiate a discount. Meals are available.

Pink Hostel International *(☎ 256710, fax 256712, ⓔ pinkhostel@ghana.com, 5th Crescent, Asylum Down)* Singles US$40, doubles/triples US$60/70 per person, student price US$15. This new, well-equipped hostel is way overpriced unless you can take advantage of the student/NGO rate, which makes it good value. Rooms are plainly furnished but spotless and most have bunk beds. Within the hostel is an Internet centre and a stylish restaurant serving pricey Mediterranean food.

Niagara Hotel *(☎ 230118, fax 230119, Kojo Thompson Rd, Adabraka)* Singles/doubles US$66/88. On the corner of Farrar Ave and Kojo Thompson Rd, the upbeat and well-established Niagara has comfortable, modern rooms. It offers car-hire services and has a good Lebanese restaurant.

Paloma Hotel & Suites *(☎ 228700, 228723, fax 231815, ⓔ paloma@africaonline.com.gh, Ring Road Central)* Singles/doubles US$50/70, suites US$95. Part of the Paloma Shopping Mall complex on the northern side of Ring Road Central, this smart hotel has large, modern rooms and is popular with the expat crowd. Also in the complex is a garden bar, several restaurants and an Internet centre.

Osu On 14th Lane, just round the corner from Koala supermarket is ***Ghalebon Hotel*** *(☎ 778897, 14th Lane)* with singles/doubles for US$35/50. It's a lovely, friendly place with pleasant rooms and a great location. Phone ahead as it's often full.

Niagara Plus Hotel *(☎ 772428, fax 772402, 14th Lane)* Doubles US$55. Under the same management as the Niagara Hotel, this friendly place is good value and willing to offer discounts. It's down 14th Lane, about 200m from Cantonments Rd. The comfortable, modern rooms have large bathrooms with hot water and it has a pleasant courtyard pizza restaurant.

Byblos Hotel *(☎ 782250, fax 782320, 11th Lane)* Singles/doubles US$45/60. This stylish hotel near Danquah Circle has attractively furnished rooms with huge bathrooms.

Frankie's Hotel *(☎ 773567, fax 773569, ⓔ frankies@frankiesghana.com, Cantonments Rd)* Singles/doubles US$65/88. Above Frankie's restaurant, this slick place has characterless motel-style rooms but a great location.

Coco Beach ***Akwaaba Beach Guesthouse*** *(☎ 717742, ⓔ akwaaba21@hotmail.com, Nungua)* Doubles with fan/air-con US$35/52, suites US$90. Out at Coco Beach, about a five-minute walk from the New Coco Beach Hotel, this delightful guesthouse is set in a garden overlooking the sea. The rooms are beautifully decorated with great attention to detail.

New Coco Beach Hotel *(☎ 717237, Nungua)* Singles/doubles US$70/90, suites with air-con US$120. Under new management, this beachside resort about 15km east of central Accra has been given a makeover. Camping is no longer allowed and facilities include a gym and a swimming pool.

Places to Stay – Top End

All hotels in this category have swimming pools and rooms with air-con, bathroom, TV and fridge; rates include breakfast. They all provide free airport transfers.

Danotel Hotel *(☎ 676263, fax 676262, ⓔ danotel@africaonline.com.gh, Derby Ave, Accra City Centre)* Singles/doubles US$100/120. Although good taste was clearly in short supply when the Danotel was created, it has an incredible location in the heart of central Accra.

Hotel Shangri-La *(☎ 762590, 761112, fax 774873, ⓔ shangri@ncs.com.gh, Liberation Ave, Airport Residential Area)* Singles US$100, doubles US$120-170. Out past the airport, near Tetteh Quarshie Circle, the Shangri-La is something of an Accra institution and is very popular with residents. The traditionally Ghanaian decorations and artefacts on show around the hotel give it a warm feel, and it has a good swimming pool, a couple of restaurants and a pizzeria.

Novotel Hotel *(☎ 667546, fax 667533, Barnes Rd, Accra North)* Singles/doubles US$170/ 200. This hotel, part of an international chain, forms a green oasis of air-con calm in Accra's frenzied central area. It has characterless, modern rooms with beautiful views.

Labadi Beach Hotel *(☎ 772501, fax 773110, ⓔ labadi@ncs.com.gh, Labadi Bypass, La)* Singles/doubles US$240/270, suites US$525. Overlooking Labadi Beach, this sumptuous five-star hotel is arguably Accra's finest, with superb landscaped gardens surrounding the swimming pool and tasteful, understated decor throughout.

La Palm Royal Beach Hotel *(☎ 771700, fax 771717, ⓔ mail@goldenbeachhotels.net, La)* Rooms US$200-350. This glitzy new five-star resort is just next door to the Labadi Beach Hotel and has much the same facilities as its rival but no direct access to the beach.

Places to Eat

Accra has the best choice of restaurants in the country, with plenty to suit all tastes and budgets. If you're on a really tight budget, you can eat cheaply and well at chop bars and food stalls, especially around the transport terminals and major circles such as Nkrumah and Danquah. Osu has the widest selection of eateries in the capital, from Western-style fast-food joints to upmarket restaurants serving fine African, French, Italian and Chinese cuisine. This selection will give you an idea of what's on offer.

City Centre On the north side of the Lutterodt intersection, the popular ***Backpass Bar & Restaurant*** has mains for US$2 to US$3. This 1st-floor terrace restaurant is accessed up a flight of stairs at the back of the building, hence the unfortunate name. The Ghanaian dishes are good, the terrace is cool and you can watch the bustle on the street below.

Riviera Beach Hotel & Restaurant (See Places to Stay) Mains US$1-3. The empty swimming pool is a forlorn reminder of past glories but the deep terrace restaurant catches the sea breeze and has a relaxed, friendly ambience. It's a great place to chill out on a hot afternoon and the food's good too – try the excellent toasted sandwiches or the chicken and rice dishes.

Adabraka & West Ridge Along Kojo Thompson Rd and Nkrumah Ave, and in the backstreets running between them, you'll find plenty of small chop bars selling rice, fufu, banku and sauce. ***Elbi's Snack Bar*** on Liberia Rd Sth in Adabraka is one recommended place, briskly serving up good rice-and-sauce dishes in a clean setting for about US$1.

YWCA *(Castle Rd)* Mains US$0.50. The excellent canteen at the YWCA is open to all for lunch and offers generous servings of fufu and rice dishes.

White Bell *(Farrar Ave)* Mains US$1.50-2.50. Popular with travellers, this upstairs restaurant has huge, tasty hamburgers as well as the usual Ghanaian dishes. In the evening it transforms into a great music and dancing spot.

Palma Nova Restaurant & Bar *(☎ 232 160, Nkrumah Ave)* Mains US$2-3. Don't be put off by the rather grim concrete bar area at the front; behind is a lovely garden restaurant offering a good range of Ghanaian, Western and Chinese dishes.

The Orangery *(☎ 232988, Farrar Ave)* Mains US$2.50-5. Popular with homesick expats and travellers with cedis to burn, this classy place specialises in sweet and savoury pancakes but has other yummy offerings such as muffins, pies and sandwiches.

Trafix Courtyard Restaurant *(☎ 672411, Independence Ave)* Mains US$2-3.50. Within the National Theatre complex, this canteen gets very busy at lunch time. The food (Ghanaian, Chinese and Western dishes) isn't fancy but it fills a gap.

Edvy Restaurant *(Barnes Rd)* Mains US$2-3.50. Open 9am-4pm daily. This place has a nice, shady garden setting in the grounds of the National Museum. It has a relaxed atmosphere and delicious Ghanaian food. Opening hours are somewhat erratic.

Asylum Down & Kokomlemle Along Ring Road Central, west of the Paloma complex, are several eateries with similar menus and prices. ***Bus Stop Restaurant*** is a long-standing favourite that has a range of basic Ghanaian and Western dishes, including chicken and rice, burgers and club sandwiches for around US$2. Also on Ring Road Central and with similar menu and prices is ***Joysco Bar & Restaurant***.

On Samora Machel Rd in Asylum Down, ***Spicy Chicken*** is another cheap and cheerful place serving up crispy fried chicken and other fast-food staples.

Tasha Food *(Star Ave)* Mains US$1-2. In Kokomlemle is this small, friendly eatery. You can get a full English breakfast here as well as delicious Ghanaian food at lunch and dinner.

Paloma Shopping Mall *(☎ 228142, Ring Road Central)* Mains US$2.50-5. Not so much a shopping mall as a hotel and restaurant complex, this place is very popular with expats and locals alike. It has a garden bar and restaurant area (you can also eat inside) serving a variety of food, including pizzas, Lebanese food and Ghanaian dishes.

Osu Listed here is a small selection of what Osu has to offer.

Papaye *(Cantonments Rd)* Burgers US$1.50, fried chicken US$2.50. At the junction with Mission St, Papaye provides a takeaway service and features what many claim to be the best charcoal-grilled chicken in Accra.

Aladen Restaurant *(☎ 782236)* Mains US$2-3. Just off Cantonments Rd, around the corner from Frankie's is this gem of a place, serving tasty, inexpensive Lebanese food.

Osu Food Court *(☎ 783444, Cantonments Rd)* Mains US$3-3.50. Accra's first food court is a roaring success. It has an excellent coffee shop and bakery, a pizza joint and a couple of fried-chicken places. Sit at the upstairs terrace bar and watch the mayhem in the parking lot below.

Brunchie *(Cantonments Rd)* Mains US$3-3.50. Popular with rich kids, lunching expats and pool enthusiasts, this place has pizza, baguettes, salads and pasta dishes, as well as ice cream and pool tables.

Frankie's *(☎ 773567, Cantonments Rd)* Mains US$2-4. An Accra institution, this well-established place has a takeaway outlet, an ice-cream shop and a bakery and patisserie, while upstairs is an air-con restaurant. You can get burgers, pizzas and fried chicken, as well as salads, baguettes and sandwiches in Lebanese bread.

Providence Restaurant *(☎ 773696, Cantonments Rd)* Mains US$3-4.50. Open 8am-6pm Mon-Sat. This is a fairly classy place that serves excellent Ghanaian food in pleasant surroundings.

Country Kitchen *(☎ 229107, Roberto Rd)* Mains US$3-4.50. Open noon-10pm daily. This place has a reputation for the best Ghanaian food in Accra, and is a lunch-time favourite during the week. The atmosphere's pleasant, the service is good, the food is fresh and it's excellent value.

Lalibela Mains US$5-5.50. Serving traditional Ethiopian dishes, including vegetarian options, this attractive garden restaurant offers a change from fufu and fried rice. You can either approach it directly from Ring Road East, or follow the signs down 14th Lane, past Chez Lien restaurant.

Restaurant Borsalino *(Ring Road East)* Mains US$4-6. Just off Danquah Circle, this place offers superb Italian food in relaxed surroundings.

L'Arco *(☎ 778949, 6th St)* Mains US$4-7. A little piece of Italy in Accra, this classy new restaurant has a range of Italian dishes and an extensive wine list.

Haveli (☎ 774714, 18th Lane) Mains US$4-6. This is the best Indian restaurant in town and worth a look just for its magnificent palace door.

Princess Garden (☎ 774991, Cantonments Rd) Set lunch US$6, set dinner US$10-12. Next to Frankie's and one of several good Chinese restaurants in Osu, this one is not quite as expensive as the others but still has excellent food.

Dynasty Restaurant (☎ 775496, Cantonments Rd) Set menu US$10-14. This vast restaurant specialises in Peking cuisine and is incredibly grand – you'll probably feel rather out of place here if you don't arrive in a 4WD with diplomatic plates.

Kanda & Airport Residential Area Run by the friendly Mr Rees and popular with expats, ***Mr Rees Restaurant & Bar*** has dishes for US$1.50 to US$2. It has a large, shady outdoor eating area and serves generous portions of tasty Ghanaian food. In the evening, it transforms into a lively drinking and dancing spot. It's about 100m north of 37 Circle.

La Pergola Restaurant (☎ 778664) Despite its unpromising location beside the Elf station just north of 37 Circle, the African food (Ghanaian, Ivoirian and Togolese) at this place is surprisingly good.

Afrikiko's (☎ 761028, Liberation Ave) Mains US$3-5. A popular expat haunt, this large garden restaurant serves excellent pizzas as well as Ghanaian dishes. Also within the complex is a café where you can get pastries and ice cream during the day. It has a dance floor and live music Thursday to Saturday.

La Chaumière (☎ 772408) Mains US$6-7. Opposite the Hotel Shangri-La, La Chaumière is a well-established restaurant serving fine French food.

La & Coco Beach Off the Tema road about 2km east of the Labadi Beach Hotel, ***Next Door Restaurant & Bar*** is a large restaurant with a fabulous seaside location. It's a friendly, popular place, great for a lazy weekend lunch, with a varied menu but strong on seafood (mains US$3-3.50). It's also one of the best places in Accra for live music and dancing, with the big nights being Friday and Saturday. Any tro-tro heading down this road towards Teshie should be able to drop you here or you can charter a taxi.

Self-Catering For basic provisions such as biscuits, bread, margarine, bananas, tinned sardines and baked beans, there are plenty of ***food stalls*** and small shops around town. For imported goods, the supermarkets in Osu are best, especially ***Koala***, just off Danquah Circle at the top of Cantonments Rd. In the city centre area, ***Multistores*** on High St has a good selection.

Entertainment

Bars Accra has no shortage of places where you can enjoy an icy-cold beer in congenial surroundings at any time of the day or night. Bars are rarely just places for a drink; they're usually also restaurants, at least during the day, and you often find that a popular lunch-time restaurant transforms into a lively bar with music and dancing at night. As well as the selection listed here, see Places to Eat earlier for more possibilities.

Akuma Village This groovy open-air place (see Places to Stay) on the cliff edge is good for a beer any time but especially on Friday when it has live music.

Next Stop (Ring Road Central, Asylum Down) Upstairs, next door to the Bus Stop Restaurant, this tiny place attracts a friendly young crowd for dancing and music at the weekends.

Slyfoks Garden (Kuasi St, Kokomlemle) In a shady garden setting, on a street running parallel to Star St, this laid-back bar and restaurant is a pleasant spot for a drink or a simple meal.

Bywel Bar (Cantonments Rd, Osu) At the southern end of Cantonments Rd, opposite the Sotrec stores, is this bar, which is fun on a Thursday or Friday night when a live band plays.

Ryan's Irish Pub (☎ 762334) Off Cantonments Rd in the south of Osu and well-signposted, this is the only place in Ghana with draught Guinness. Extremely popular with the expat crowd, it has a large garden bar area as well as an indoor pub. It has live music at the weekends and serves pub-style food.

Fusion (11th Lane) In Osu, this upmarket cocktail bar and restaurant attracts a well-heeled expat crowd. It's fun on a karaoke night, usually Wednesday, but it's liveliest at the weekends.

Aquarius *(Osu Crescent, Osu)* If you have a hankering for German beer (draught or bottled), check this place out. It also has pricey but good German food, as well as a pool table, pinball, darts, table football and Internet access.

Champs Sports Bar *(☎ 228937, Ring Road Central)* In the Paloma Shopping Mall, this theme pub shows the big matches live on Friday and Saturday and an English-language film every Sunday. It serves the only Mexican food in Accra.

Clubs Thursday, Friday and Saturday are the big nights and although clubs open from about 8pm, the action rarely starts before 10pm or 11pm. Osu is where most of the trendiest clubs are but there are also some popular, inexpensive places around Nkrumah Circle. Most clubs have an entry fee of about US$3. At any one of them you may be offered cocaine, gold smuggling, marriage, sex and several other deals best refused.

Waikiki Restaurant & Nightclub *(Nkrumah Ave)* Near Nkrumah Circle, this well-established nightclub attracts a brash, down-to-earth, young crowd and plays a good mix of music.

Fox Trap *(Farrar Ave, Adabraka)* Popular with the 30 to 45 age group, this smart place plays plenty of highlife.

Indigo *(Ring Road East)* Near Danquah Circle, this stylish new place is housed in an old embassy building and attracts Accra's trendsetters. Friday and Saturday are the best nights.

Macumba *(Ring Road East)* Also near Danquah Circle, Macumba is one of Accra's best-known and long-standing clubs, and caters very much for the European disco set.

Bass Line *(Ring Road Central)* This hip club to the west of Kanda High Rd, near the junction with Kanda High Rd reeks of atmosphere and plays great jazzy, bluesy live music most nights from late.

Theatre & Cinema The impressive Chinese-built ***National Theatre*** *(☎ 666986, Liberia Rd)* looms against the sky like the keel of a huge schooner. It puts on performances by West African playwrights – check the billboards for future activities. One regular weekly event is the Saturday afternoon Concert Party (admission a bargain US$0.70), a Ghanaian music hall, or vaudeville, with sketches, songs and stand-up comedians. Even though most of it's in Twi, it's a fun afternoon out, where the audience reaction is as interesting as what's happening on stage. The various cultural centres (see Information earlier) also offer regular concerts and exhibitions.

Ghana Film Institute *(☎ 763462; admission US$2)*, off Liberation Ave, across from the French embassy, shows the latest Ghanaian films and foreign releases and is often packed. It has two nightly showings plus an extra Saturday session. In the city centre, the ***Rex Cinema*** *(Barnes Rd)* shows recent Western films in English.

Shopping

The ***Arts Centre*** (Centre for National Culture) on 28 February Rd has the widest selection of arts and crafts from all over Ghana, as well as from neighbouring countries, but you have to look hard for good-quality work and bargain even harder for good prices. The small shop beside the art gallery has a small but eclectic selection of music.

Makola Market and the area around is particularly rich in fabrics, including batiks and tie-dyes. Zongo Lane, not far from the post office, has rows of small shops offering colourful prints. Expensive Dutch wax cloth is everywhere, but you can also find almost identical cloth made by Akosombo Textile Co that is almost as good and much cheaper. The market is also good for glass beads, and you'll find second-hand clothing everywhere, sold for a snip.

Accra's second major market, **Kaneshie Market** on Winneba Rd on the western side of the city, is also a good place to look for beads and textiles (on the 1st level) as well as basic goods and foodstuffs.

As well as the Arts Centre and the markets, look out for roadside stalls selling crafts, such as pottery and cane chairs near 37 Circle, tie-dye clothes and woodcarvings around Danquah Circle and along Cantonments Rd in Osu and woodcarvings near La Beach.

For superb-quality, fixed price crafts, try the Aid to Artisans Ghana (ATAG) at the Trade Fair Centre in La. ATAG is a NGO that offers practical assistance to Ghanaian artisans. ***The Loom***, 200m south of the Nkrumah Circle, is an upmarket art gallery that specialises in fabrics and clothes as well as woodcarvings, paintings and statues. ***Woodin Boutique*** on Cantonments Rd in Osu is a chic fabric shop that's worth a look.

If you're interested in contemporary Ghanaian painting, check out the ***Artist's Alliance Gallery***, run by one of Ghana's top artists, Professor Ablade Glover. It's on the road to Tema, a few kilometres past the Labadi Beach Hotel. Also on the Tema road, in Teshie, is the famous ***coffin shop***, where fantastic coffins are fashioned in the shape of fish, cars, aeroplanes, whatever is meaningful for the client.

Getting There & Away

Air Kotoka international airport is served by Ghana Airways and several major airlines, including Alitalia, British Airways, KLM-Royal Dutch Airlines, Lufthansa and South African Airways. Airline offices in Accra include:

Air Ivoire (☎ 241461) Cocoa House, Nkrumah Ave
Alitalia (☎ 239315) Ring Road Central, Asylum Down
British Airways (☎ 240386) Kojo Thompson Rd, Adabraka
EgyptAir (☎ 773537) Ring Road East, Osu
Ghana Airways (☎ 221000) Cocoa House, Nkrumah Ave
KLM-Royal Dutch Airlines (☎ 224020) Ring Road Central
Lufthansa (☎ 243893) Fidelity House, off Ring Road Central
South African Airways (☎ 230722) Ring Road Central, Asylum Down

Bus & Tro-Tro There are two VanefSTC bus stations in Accra. The main one (☎ 221 414, 227373) is just east of Lamptey Circle and serves destinations to the west and north. Buses leave hourly for both Kumasi (US$3, four hours) and Takoradi (US$2, four hours) between 3am and 5.30pm, twice a day to Cape Coast (US$1.40, three hours) and three times a day for Tamale (US$5.70, 12 hours). In addition, two express services a day run between Accra and Kumasi (US$5.70); these clip more than an hour from the standard journey time. The second, smaller VanefSTC terminal is next to Tudu station, at the northern end of Makola Market. From there, buses head east, serving towns such as Ho (US$1.20; once a day), Hohoe (US$1.70; twice daily) and Aflao, on the Togo border (US$2; three times a day).

Private buses and tro-tros leave from four main motor parks. Those for Cape Coast, Takoradi and other destinations to the west leave from Kaneshie motor park, 500m northwest of Lamptey Circle. Neoplan motor park, 250m west of Nkrumah Circle, has buses to north points such as Kumasi and Tamale. From Tema station east of Makola market, tro-tros leave for local destinations as well as Tema and Aburi. From the chaotic Tudu station at the northeast corner of Makola Market, tro-tros leave for destinations such as Aflao, Ada, Keta, Hohoe and Akosombo. In addition, there's a small station tucked in behind Tema station from which tro-tros go to Ho and Hohoe (again).

Train

There are train services between Accra and both Kumasi and Takoradi but these take forever and are really only for train enthusiasts. For more details, see Train under Getting Around earlier in this chapter.

Getting Around

To/From the Airport When you step outside Accra's Kotoka international airport, you'll be ushered to a private (or 'dropping') taxi, which has a fixed rate of US$6 for the journey into central Accra. Tro-tros and shared taxis (around US$0.30) also leave from the small, well-organised station within the airport compound. From the city centre to the airport, a private taxi costs much less (around US$3). Alternatively, get a shared taxi from the taxi parks at Nkrumah Circle or Sankara interchange or a tro-tro from Tema station.

Line Taxi & Tro-Tro Line taxis and tro-tros travel on fixed runs from major landmarks or between major circles, such as Danquah, 37 and Nkrumah (usually just called 'Circle'). Fares are fixed and are typically about US$0.20. Major routes include Circle to Osu via Ring Road; Circle to the central post office via Nkrumah Ave; Tudu station to Kokomlemle; 37 Circle to Osu; Makola Market to Osu; and Circle to the airport. Major shared taxi and local tro-tro parks include Tema station and the ones at Nkrumah Circle and 37 Circle. In addition, transport to La leaves from the taxi park at Nkrumah Circle or from Labadi lorry station on High St.

At the stations, tro-tros and shared taxis often have the destination written on a placard. Elsewhere, flag one down and shout your destination – if they're going your way, they'll stop and pick you up. For Nkrumah Circle, there's a special convention: point the index finger of your right hand towards the ground and make a circular motion.

Private Taxi Finding a private taxi in Accra is easy enough – just flag any taxi that passes and see if it stops – but finding a taxi driver who knows Accra well can be difficult. Taxis don't use meters so rates are negotiable. A journey within town usually costs around US$1.50.

AROUND ACCRA

University of Ghana

The university, founded in 1948, is in Legon, on the northern fringes of Accra and 14km from the city centre. Its **Balme Library** *(open 8am-4.30pm Mon-Sat)* has a rich collection dating from the colonial era. Its botanical gardens are sadly run-down but they're a pleasant place for a stroll. The other reason for making the trip out here is to visit the university bookshop, the best in the country. Tro-tros (US$0.15) leave from Tema station in Accra or from the Sankara interchange.

Aburi Botanical Gardens & Akwapim Hills

Aburi, originally built by the British as a health and hill station, is on a ridge 34km north of Accra. It offers fine views and on a clear day you can make out Accra in the plains below. The botanical gardens *(admission US$0.70, open 8am-6pm daily)*, about 200m up from the tro-tro station, are a popular weekend retreat; they're more peaceful but less fun during the week. Established in 1890 with seedlings from all over the British Empire, they're home to an impressive variety of tropical and subtropical plants and trees. The oldest tree, more than 150 years old, is a huge kapok tree facing the headquarters building. It's the only indigenous one the British didn't cut down.

Although the botanical gardens are the obvious tourist focus, the entire Akwapim Hills area is stunningly beautiful and worth exploring further. At the southern entrance of the gardens is ***Aburi Bike Tours & Rentals*** *(☎ 024-267303, W www.aburibike.ch)* offering bicycle tours and hikes throughout the area.

Places to Stay & Eat In the middle of the gardens, the old colonial-style ***Aburi Botanical Gardens Resthouse*** *(☎ 0876-22037)* has rooms for US$8 and bungalows for US$11. The bungalows are incredibly run-down and there's no running water, but for atmosphere and tranquillity, it's hard to beat. The rooms in the resthouse have good views and are a better option than the bungalows. Book in advance as it's incredibly popular.

Olyander Guest House *(☎ 0876-22058)* Doubles with fan & bathroom US$4-11. About 100m up the hill from the northern gate of the gardens is this homely, peaceful guesthouse. It's pleasantly decorated and the chef prepares wonderful family-style meals.

May Lodge & Restaurant *(☎ 0876-22025)* Singles/doubles US$7/8. Coming from Accra, this lodge is about 2km before the entrance to the gardens. It's a relaxing place with good views and decent meals at reasonable prices. It has only four guest rooms, which are rather run-down but are pleasant enough and open onto a small balcony.

Rose Plot Restaurant, attached to the resthouse, prepares basic fare for approximately US$2.

Royal Botanical Gardens Restaurant, just down the hill from the resthouse, has better food than the Rose Plot and superb views, but is pricier. Note that both restaurants open at 7am and close at 7.30pm.

Getting There & Away Tro-tros to Aburi (US$0.40, 45 minutes) leave regularly from the far eastern end of Tema station in Accra. You may have to wait a while for transport to Accra on a Sunday. Regular shared taxis run north from Aburi to towns such as Mampong, Adukrom and Somanya, from where you can get connections to Kpong (for Akosombo and Ho) and Koforidua.

The Coast

KOKROBITE

☎ 027

People come to Kokrobite, 32km west of Accra, for one or both of two reasons: to

GHANA

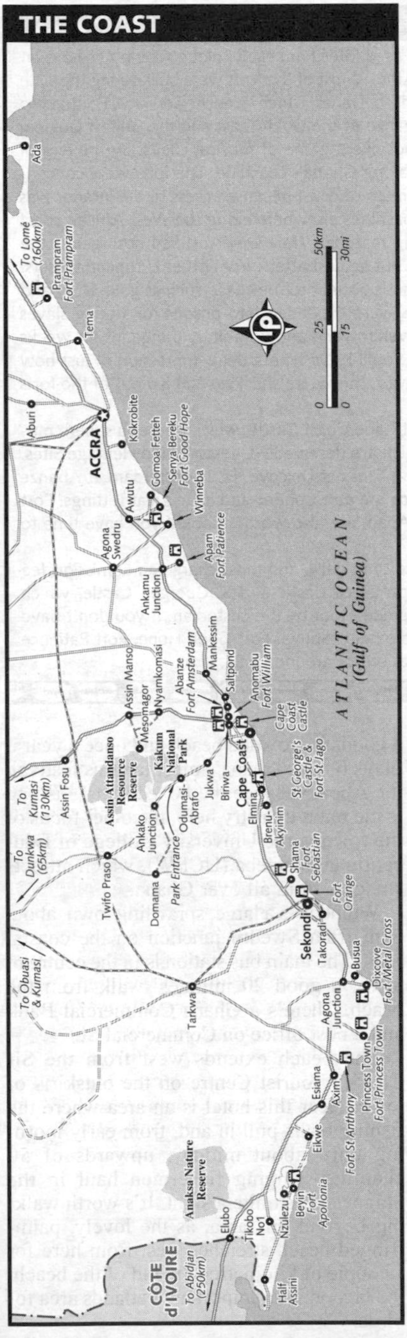
THE COAST
Ada
To Lomé (160km)
Prampram
Fort Prampram
Tema
Aburi
ACCRA
Kokrobite
Gomoa Fetteh
Senya Bereku
Fort Good Hope
Awutu
Winneba
Agona Swedru
Apam
Fort Patience
Ankamu Junction
Mankessim
Abanze
Fort Amsterdam
Saltpond
Anomabu
Fort William
Cape Coast Castle
ATLANTIC OCEAN
(Gulf of Guinea)
0 25 50km
0 15 30mi
Assin Manso
Nyamkomasi
Mesomagor
Kakum National Park
Assin Attandanso Resource Reserve
Assin Fosu
To Kumasi (130km)
Jukwa
Biriwa
Cape Coast
Elmina
St George's Castle & Fort St Jago
Odumasi-Abrafo
Ankako Junction
Park Entrance
Brenu-Akyinim
Shama
Fort Sebastian
To Dunkwa (65km)
Twifo Praso
Domama
Fort Orange
Sekondi
Takoradi
Busua
Dixcove
Fort Metal Cross
Agona Junction
Princess Town
Fort Princess Town
Tarkwa
To Obuasi & Kumasi
Esiama
Axim
Fort St Anthony
Eikwe
Ankasa Nature Reserve
Elubo
Tikobo No1
Nzulezu
Beyin
Fort Apollonia
CÔTE d'IVOIRE
To Abidjan (250km)
Half Assini

laze on the superb beach or to drum and strum at the renowned Academy of African Music & Arts Ltd (Aamal). Founded by legendary drummer Mustafa Tettey Addy, the academy offers courses (from two hours to three months) in traditional African music, drumming and dance. On Saturday and Sunday afternoons you can groove to the beat by listening to live music and drumming performances.

Big Milly's Backyard Camping US$1.50 per person, single/double huts US$5/6. Also known as Wendy's, this friendly, laid-back place is on the beach and is extremely good value. Meals, mainly fish and vegetarian food, are excellent and cost around US$2.

Kokrobite Beach Resort *(☎ 554042)* Huts US$4.50/6.50, bungalows with bathroom US$12. Run by Aamal and on the same site, this resort is a 15-minute walk west along the beach from Big Milly's and has a pricey bar and restaurant on site.

Franco's Mains US$2.50-3. This Italian restaurant, behind Big Milly's, has good food in pleasant surroundings.

Tro-tros (US$0.30, 45 minutes) to Kokrobite go from the western end of Kaneshie motor park in Accra. Private taxis are US$9.

GOMOA FETTEH & SENYA BEREKU

☎ 027

The main reason to visit Gomoa Fetteh, an attractive fishing village set on a hill on the coast between Accra and Winneba, is for its magnificent beaches. Senya Bereku, about 5km west, is the site of the impressive **Fort Good Hope** *(admission US$0.70)*, built by the Dutch in 1702. Originally intended for the gold trade, the fort was expanded in 1715 when it was converted into a slave prison. Well-restored, it sits on the edge of a cliff above the beach and has good views. Shared taxis (US$0.20) ply regularly between the villages or you could walk (with a guide).

Fort Good Hope Doubles with fan US$7. Rooms are extremely basic with shared bathrooms (bucket showers) but there's a nice, breezy sitting area upstairs. Simple meals are prepared on request (US$2.50) or bring your own supplies. Lone women would not feel comfortable here.

Till's No 1 Hotel *(☎ 550480, fax 558247)* Singles/doubles with air-con US$35/40. On a good beach, this serene resort has good-value

GHANA

The Coastal Forts

The chain of forts and castles (the terms tend to be used interchangeably) along Ghana's coast is an extraordinary historical monument, unique in West Africa. Most of the forts were built during the 17th century by various European powers, including the British, Danes, Dutch, French, Germans, Portuguese and Swedes, who were vying for commercial dominance of the Gold Coast and the Gulf of Guinea. Competition was fierce and the forts changed hands like a game of musical chairs. By the end of the 18th century, there were 37 such fortifications along Ghana's coastline. The forts were concentrated along this relatively short (around 500km) stretch of coast because access to the interior was relatively easy compared with the more swampy coastlines elsewhere along the West African coast and also because the rocky shore provided building material. They were fortified not against the local population, with whom they traded equitably, but against attack from other European traders.

Originally established as trading posts to store goods bought to the coast, such as gold, ivory and spices, later, as the slave trade took over, the forts were expanded into prisons for storing slaves ready for shipping. Slaves were packed into dark, overcrowded and unsanitary dungeons for weeks or months at a time. If you tour some of the forts, you'll leave with a deep impression of just how brutally the captives were treated. When a ship arrived, they were shackled and led out of the forts to waiting boats through the Door of No Return.

If your time is limited, make sure you visit at least Cape Coast Castle, which houses a superb museum, and St George's Castle at Elmina, both of which are deservedly Unesco World Heritage Sites. With a bit more time, you could also visit Fort Metal Cross at Dixcove, Fort Amsterdam at Abanze and Fort Princess Town at Princess Town, all of which are atmospheric and have great settings. Fort Good Hope at Senya Bereku and Fort Patience at Apam are also worth a look if you have time to spare; both overlook busy fishing harbours.

Most forts are open to the public, usually 9am to 5pm daily, and most charge an admission fee of around US$0.70, apart from a few such as Cape Coast Castle and St George's Castle, which charge more. The admission fee usually includes a guided tour by the custodian. If you don't have any qualms about staying in a fort where slaves were held captive, Fort Good Hope, Fort Patience and Fort Princess Town offer very basic accommodation for around US$4.

rooms with balconies and a sea view. It's signposted as you enter Gomoa Fetteh.

White Sands Beach Club *(☎ 550707, fax 021-774064, ⓔ whsands@ighmail.com)* Doubles US$100, day use US$3. This resort at Fetteh is on a spectacular stretch of beach backed by a lagoon. It's mainly a day resort, although some accommodation is available. Bear left as you enter Fetteh and follow the main road down through the village until you reach the resort gates.

From Kaneshie motor park in Accra, there are direct tro-tros to Senya Bereku (US$0.40, one hour). Tro-tros also ply the scenic but bumpy cross-country route between Winneba and Senya Bereku (US$0.60, 40 minutes). For Gomoa Fetteh, take a Winneba-bound tro-tro from Accra and drop at Awutu junction on the main road from where you can get a tro-tro direct to the village.

WINNEBA

☎ 0432

Winneba, 64km west of Accra, is the main town between Accra and Cape Coast. It has a good, uncrowded beach and once a year it plays host to Ghana's most famous festival, the Aboakyer (see the boxed text). Fishing is the main industry here; the other focus of the town is the University College of Education at Winneba (UCEW), which attracts students from all over Ghana.

Winneba is a large, sprawling town, about 6km from Swedru junction on the coastal road. The main bus station is in the centre of town, a good 20 minutes' walk from the beach. There's a Ghana Commercial Bank and a post office on Commercial St.

The beach extends west from the Sir Charles Tourist Centre on the outskirts of town. Near this hotel is an area where the fishing boats pull in and, from early morning until about midday, upwards of 50 chanting, singing fishermen haul in the dragnets. It's quite a sight. It's worth walking beyond this area, as the lovely, palm-fringed beach stretches west from here for a couple of kilometres. Inland of the beach, the lagoon is an important wetlands area for birds.

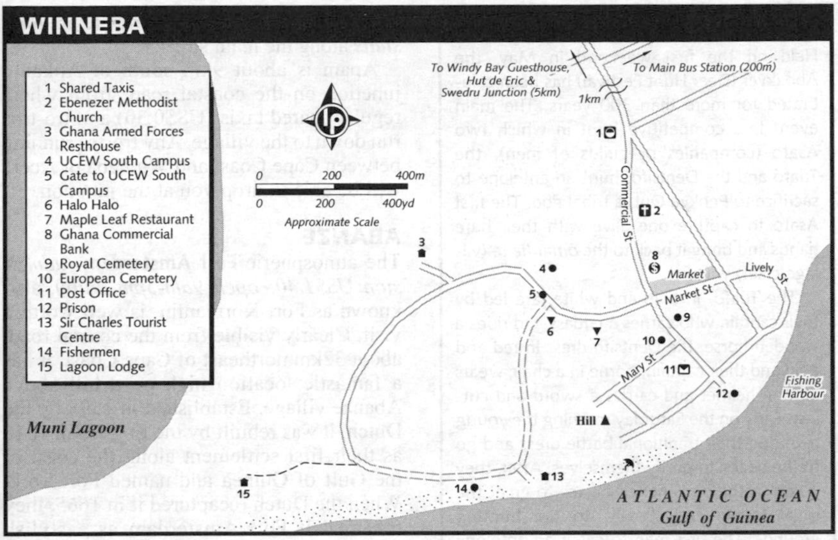
WINNEBA
1 Shared Taxis
2 Ebenezer Methodist Church
3 Ghana Armed Forces Resthouse
4 UCEW South Campus
5 Gate to UCEW South Campus
6 Halo Halo
7 Maple Leaf Restaurant
8 Ghana Commercial Bank
9 Royal Cemetery
10 European Cemetery
11 Post Office
12 Prison
13 Sir Charles Tourist Centre
14 Fishermen
15 Lagoon Lodge
0 200 400m
0 200 400yd
Approximate Scale
To Windy Bay Guesthouse, Hut de Eric & Swedru Junction (5km)
1km
To Main Bus Station (200m)
Commercial St
Market
Market St
Lively St
Mary St
Hill
Fishing Harbour
Muni Lagoon
ATLANTIC OCEAN
Gulf of Guinea

Places to Stay & Eat

Sir Charles Tourist Centre *(☎ 22189)* Singles/doubles US$4/5. This huge, crumbling concrete ruin of a complex somehow manages to cling to life. People stay here because it's friendly, cheap and it has a terrific location right along the beach. The rundown chalets have a small sitting area and bathroom. Simple meals (US$2 to US$2.50) can be ordered in advance at the echoing restaurant.

Ghana Armed Forces Resthouse *(☎ 22 208)* Doubles with fan US$5. Up on a hill, in a peaceful garden setting overlooking the lagoon, this delightful place has spotlessly clean rooms. It's hard to find – follow the road up past the UCEW South Campus and, where it forks, take the road on the right.

Lagoon Lodge *(☎ 020-8162034)* Singles/doubles with fan US$5/8.50. This attractive new hotel is in a tranquil setting on the edge of the lagoon. It has smart, modern rooms and a terrace restaurant and bar. It's reached by heading down a winding track through the fields, signposted off the beach road past the turn-off to Sir Charles Tourist Centre.

Windy Bay Guesthouse *(☎ 22242)* Singles/doubles US$13/25. Just south of the junction, and signposted off the road into Winneba, this upmarket place has tasteful, modern rooms and a good restaurant.

Along the road leading off Commercial St towards the UCEW South Campus are plenty of ***food stalls***, as well as a few ***chop bars*** serving up basic Ghanaian food for around US$1.50 to US$2.

Halo Halo attracts a hip young crowd who come here for its icy beers, tasty food and mind-numbingly loud music. On the same side of the street, the small ***Maple Leaf Restaurant*** offers a few vegetarian dishes. At the junction, ***Hut de Eric*** is more upmarket, with comfortable outdoor seating. It offers Ghanaian dishes and grills for US$2 to US$3, as well as fresh juices and ice cream.

Getting There & Away

There's a bus station in Winneba town but the main transport hub is at the junction on the coastal road. Regular shared taxis (US$0.20) run between the junction and Winneba town. Tro-tros to Winneba leave from Kaneshie motor park in Accra (US$0.70, 1¼ hours) or from the Accra station in Cape Coast (US$0.70, one hour). From the junction, plenty of transport runs in both directions.

APAM

☎ **0432**

Some 20km west of Winneba, Apam is a busy fishing village and the site of **Fort**

Aboakyer

Held on the first weekend in May, the Aboakyer (Deer Hunt Festival) has been celebrated for more than 300 years. The main event is a competitive hunt in which two Asafo (companies or guilds of men), the Tuafo and the Dentsifo, hunt an antelope to sacrifice to Penkye Out, a tribal god. The first Asafo to capture one alive with their bare hands and bring it back to the *omanhene* (village chief) wins.

The Tuafo, in blue and white, are led by their captain who carries a cutlass and rides a wooden horse; the Dentsifo dress in red and gold and their captain, borne in a chair, wears an iron helmet and carries a sword and cutlass. Early on the Saturday morning the young men don their traditional battle dress and go to the beach to purify themselves. After, they go on to the omanhene's palace to greet the royal family and, finally, to the hunting grounds. The first man to catch an antelope alive rushes with his company to the omanhene's dais, singing and dancing along the way and hurling taunts at their opponents.

Next day the companies assemble before the Penkye Otu deity to question the oracle. The priest draws four parallel lines on the ground, in white clay, red clay, charcoal and salt. A stone is rolled down from the fetish. If it falls upon the white clay line, there will be a great drought. If it stops at the charcoal lines, this portends heavy rains. Landing on the salt line indicates that there will be plenty of food and fish, while settling upon the red line augurs war and strife. The hapless antelope is then sacrificed and cooked, the priest taking some of the hot soup with his bare hands and placing it on Penkye Otu. This offering is the *raison d'être* of the hunt and the festival concludes.

Patience *(admission US$0.70)*, built by the Dutch in 1697. The fort is set on a hill overlooking the village and from the ramparts you get a fantastic view over the picturesque fishing harbour at one end of a wide sandy bay. Near the harbour is a great three-storey **posuban** (shrine), with mounted horsemen overlooked by a white-robed Jesus.

The fort also functions as a ***guesthouse.*** Very basic rooms with shared bathroom (bucket shower) cost US$3.50. Simple meals can be prepared on request or there are ***food stalls*** along the main street.

Apam is about 9km south of Ankamu junction on the coastal road, from where regular shared taxis (US$0.30) and tro-tros run down to the village. Any tro-tro running between Cape Coast and Winneba or Accra will be able to drop you at the junction.

ABANZE

The atmospheric **Fort Amsterdam** *(admission US$1.40; open 9am-5pm daily)*, also known as Fort Kormantin, is well worth a visit. Clearly visible from the coastal road, about 32km northeast of Cape Coast, it has a fantastic location high on a hill above Abanze village. Established in 1598 by the Dutch, it was rebuilt by the English in 1645 as their first settlement along the coast of the Gulf of Guinea and named Fort York. When the Dutch recaptured it in 1665, they renamed it Fort Amsterdam as a stylish thumbing of the nose at the English who, the previous year, on the other side of the Atlantic, had taken possession of New Amsterdam and re-christened it New York. Louis Armstrong, the legendary 'Satchmo' himself, reckoned that his ancestors had been despatched as slaves from this fort. The fort is only partially restored, giving it a poignancy that many of the whitewashed castles elsewhere along the coast lack. The views from the ramparts are tremendous.

Transport going west to Cape Coast can drop you at Abanze. From Cape Coast, take a tro-tro (US$0.25, 20 minutes) from Kotokuraba station as you head towards Mankessim and get off when you see the fort up on the hill to your right, just before Abanze. Returning to Cape Coast you may have to wait a while for an empty seat.

ANOMABU

☎ 042

The small fishing town of Anomabu, about 18km northeast of Cape Coast, has a handsome fort (not open to the public), some good posubans and an excellent beach resort at its western limit. **Fort William**, on the seafront in the centre of town about 150m from the coastal road, was built by the British in 1753 and is now a prison. You can walk around it but you can't go inside and photos are forbidden. More interesting are Anomabu's seven posubans. The easiest to find is Company No 3's, which features a collection of animals, and is about 50m from the main road, opposite the Ebeneezer Rest Stop & Hotel. The most spectacular shrine is the one in the form of a large painted ship, which is in the area just west of the fort.

Anomabu Beach Resort *(☎ 33801, ⓔ anomabu@hotmail.com)* Camping own/rented tent US$3/9, doubles without/with air-con US$24/45. Simple but comfortable huts are set within a shady grove of coconut palms on a wonderful sweep of sandy beach at this good new resort. Pricey meals are available at the beachside restaurant.

From Cape Coast, take a tro-tro (US$0.20, 15 minutes) from Kotokuraba station heading for Mankessim and ask to be dropped at the Ebeneezer Rest Stop for Anomabu town or at the turn-off for the beach resort, which is about 2km west of the Ebeneezer. From the turn-off, it's about 500m to the resort gates. The main tro-tro and shared taxi stop in Anomabu is just east of the Ebeneezer and plenty of vehicles run in both directions along the coastal road.

BIRIWA

☎ 042

Just to the west of the fishing village of Biriwa, 13km northeast of Cape Coast, is a fine sandy beach, accessed from the bluff above via ***Biriwa Beach Hotel*** *(☎ 33333, fax 33444, ⓔ bbh@ghana.com)*. Comfortable singles/doubles here with air-con are US$54/60, although the hotel has definitely seen better days. The shady terrace restaurant at the hotel has superb views and is a popular lunch spot at weekends, specialising in seafood and German dishes (US$4 to US$5). The hotel is well signposted off the main coastal highway; any tro-tro heading along the coastal road can drop you at the junction, from where it's a five-minute walk uphill to the hotel. A private taxi from Cape Coast costs about US$3.

Posubans

In the Fanti villages clustered around the coastal forts, you may stumble across strange groupings of painted, sculpted figures representing animals, European ships, policemen, soldiers and even Adam and Eve. These are posubans, which serve as religious shrines and gathering places for Asafo meetings and rituals, while the often fantastical figures identify and advertise each company. In the past, Asafo were primarily military groups devoted to the defence of the state. These days they're primarily social groupings, which also exert political clout through, for example, their participation in the selection and enstoolment of the area chief. Each Asafo is numbered and named and has its own individual emblems and regalia.

Ingrid Roddis

CAPE COAST

☎ 042

Cape Coast, capital of the Central Region, is a lively, upbeat town with a wonderful location. Originally the British colonial capital until the administration moved to Accra in 1876, it's renowned in Ghana as a centre for education. The main attraction for visitors is Cape Coast Castle, a Unesco World Heritage Site, but it's also the starting point for trips to Kakum National Park and makes a good base for exploring the surrounding area.

Orientation & Information

Cape Coast sprawls over a hilly area, its outer extents bound by the coastal road bypass. The focus of the town is the intersection of Commercial St and Ashanti Rd, marked by a small statue of a crab, the town's traditional symbol. South from here, Commercial St leads down to the shoreline and the castle.

The tourist office (☎ 30265), open 8am to 5pm Monday to Friday, is on the 1st floor of Heritage House, a restored colonial-era building. The staff here can arrange guided walking tours of the town (US$3 for one hour) but can't provide a lot more information.

Standard Chartered Bank in Chapel Square near the tourist office and Barclays Bank on Commercial St can change travellers cheques and cash. Both banks have ATMs. There are several forexes around town, including Coastal Forex on Jackson St and one opposite the Accra bus station.

The post office is on Attebury Rd. For email facilities, Cyber City is on Commercial St, a couple of blocks north of Cape Cafe. It's open from 7.30am to 9.30pm Monday to Saturday and access costs US$0.03 per minute.

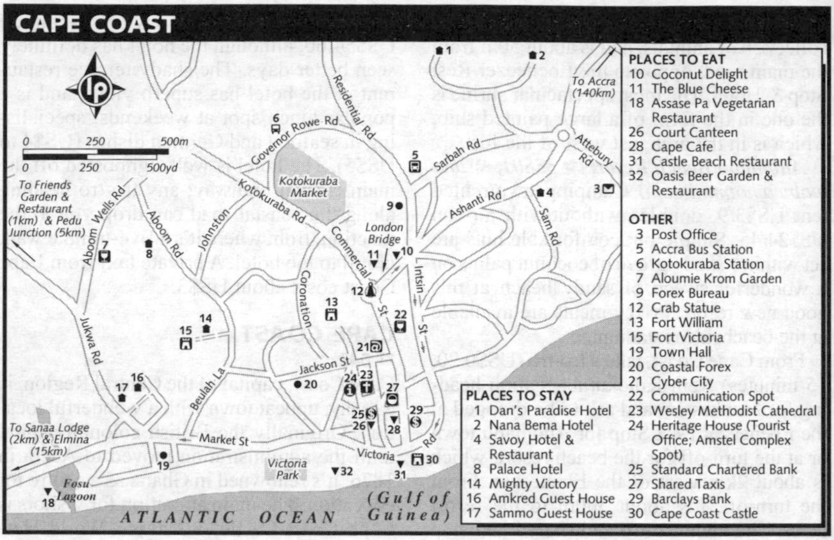
CAPE COAST
0 250 500m
0 250 500yd
To Friends Garden & Restaurant (1km) & Pedu Junction (5km)
To Accra (140km)
To Sanaa Lodge (2km) & Elmina (15km)
Governor Rowe Rd
Residential Rd
Sarbah Rd
Attebury Rd
Ashanti Rd
Sam Rd
Kotokuraba Market
Kotokuraba Rd
Aboom Wells Rd
Aboom Rd
Johnston
Commercial St
London Bridge
Intsin St
Coronation
Jukwa Rd
Beulah La
Jackson St
Market St
Victoria Park
Victoria Rd
Fosu Lagoon
ATLANTIC OCEAN
(Gulf of Guinea)
PLACES TO EAT
10 Coconut Delight
11 The Blue Cheese
18 Assase Pa Vegetarian Restaurant
26 Court Canteen
28 Cape Cafe
31 Castle Beach Restaurant
32 Oasis Beer Garden & Restaurant
OTHER
3 Post Office
5 Accra Bus Station
6 Kotokuraba Station
7 Aloumie Krom Garden
9 Forex Bureau
12 Crab Statue
13 Fort William
15 Fort Victoria
19 Town Hall
20 Coastal Forex
21 Cyber City
22 Communication Spot
23 Wesley Methodist Cathedral
24 Heritage House (Tourist Office; Amstel Complex Spot)
25 Standard Chartered Bank
27 Shared Taxis
29 Barclays Bank
30 Cape Coast Castle
PLACES TO STAY
1 Dan's Paradise Hotel
2 Nana Bema Hotel
4 Savoy Hotel & Restaurant
8 Palace Hotel
14 Mighty Victory
16 Amkred Guest House
17 Sammo Guest House

Cape Coast Castle

This majestic castle *(admission without/with guided tour US$2/4, camera fee US$0.70; open 9am-5pm daily)* is in the heart of town overlooking the sea. First converted into a castle by the Dutch in 1637 and expanded by the Swedes in 1652, the castle changed hands five times over the 13 tumultuous years that followed until, in 1664, it was captured by the British. During the two centuries of British occupation, the castle was the headquarters for the colonial administration until the capital was moved to Accra in 1877. Extensively restored, the whitewashed castle now houses a superb **museum**. The introductory video show at the museum is a little cheesy but the displays on the history of Ghana, the slave trade and the culture of the Akan people are excellent. The castle buildings, constructed around a trapezoidal courtyard facing the sea, and the dungeons below provide a horrifying insight into the workings of a Gold Coast slaving fort. It's not essential to take the guided tour; an informative booklet guide with a plan of the castle costs an additional US$0.70 from the ticket office. Allow a couple of hours for going around the museum and the castle.

Other Attractions

Overlooking the town are **Fort William**, which dates from 1820 and now functions as a lighthouse, and **Fort Victoria**, originally built in 1702 and heavily restored in the 19th century. The castle and the two forts originally formed a triangular lookout system between which signals could be passed. You can't go inside either of the forts, but the panoramic views make the short ascent to their terraces worthwhile. There are several other historic buildings in Cape Coast; if you're interested ask at the tourist office about a guided walk around the town.

To experience present-day Cape Coast at its vibrant best, take a wander round bustling Kotokuraba Market or walk down Intsin St after dark, when everyone comes out to promenade and to sample the food offered at numerous lantern-lit stalls lining the street.

Special Events

Cape Coast's Fetu Afahye Festival, a raucous carnival, takes place on the first Saturday of September. The highlight is the slaughter of a cow for the gods of Oguaa (the traditional name for Cape Coast). The biennial Panafest celebration is held in Cape Coast (see the boxed text 'Emancipation Day & Panafest' earlier in this chapter).

Places to Stay

Palace Hotel *(☎ 33556, Aboom Rd)* Singles/doubles with fan US$4/5, doubles with fan

& bathroom US$6. The grubby rooms at this gloomy place are the cheapest in town.

Sammo Guest House *(☎ 33242, Jukwa Rd)* Singles US$3, doubles without/with bathroom US$7/8. Popular with travellers, this place has good, clean rooms with fan, some with balconies, a nice courtyard restaurant and a rooftop terrace.

Amkred Guest House *(☎ 32868)* Doubles with fan/air-con US$9/11. Just behind Sammo's, down a lane, this place is also recommended. Rooms with TV are quiet and comfortable, and there is a dining room for guests (order in advance).

Savoy Hotel & Restaurant *(☎ 32805, fax 32804, Sam Rd)* Doubles with fan/air-con US$9/11. The endearingly eccentric Savoy complex offers a range of spotlessly clean rooms. The rooms with fan are larger but noisier than the air-con rooms, which are a bit gloomy. There's a reasonably priced restaurant attached to the hotel.

Mighty Victory *(☎ 30135, Aboom Close)* Singles/doubles with fan US$9.50/11. This friendly new place has smart rooms and a great location, set on a hill just below Fort Victoria. It's off Aboom Rd about 100m north of the junction with Beulah Lane. Meals are available on request.

Dan's Paradise Hotel *(☎ 32942)* Doubles with air-con US$10-11.50. At the top of a steep hill off Sarbah Rd north of the Accra bus station, this luridly decorated multistorey hotel has reasonable rooms with huge beds. On Saturday nights it hosts a popular nightclub.

Nana Bema Hotel *(☎ 32103, fax 32616, Nana Bema Hill)* Doubles with air-con US$11-25. Near Dan's Paradise, up another steep hill, this smart, modern hotel has great views and comfortable rooms. It has a small restaurant serving good meals for US$2 to US$3.

Sanaa Lodge *(☎ 32570, fax 32898)* Singles/doubles US$65/70. This tranquil place on a hill near the westernmost entrance to town is Cape Coast's best hotel, with classy rooms, a swimming pool and good restaurant.

Places to Eat & Drink

You can get good ***street food*** either around Kotokuraba Market, around the intersection of Commercial St and Ashanti Rd and along Intsin St.

Coconut Delight Juices US$0.70. This tiny chop bar on Ashanti Rd, near London Bridge, does wonderful fresh fruit juices as well as snack food. A couple of doors along is another tiny place selling home-made ice cream.

The Blue Cheese Mains US$1.50-2. Opposite the crab statue, this outdoor bar and restaurant has basic food at lunch time and is an immensely popular drinking spot at night.

Court Canteen Mains US$1.50-2. This functional canteen has a limited range of cheap and tasty meals. It's at the back of the law courts building, near the castle.

Amstel Complex Spot Mains US$1.50-2. Within the Heritage House complex is a pleasant courtyard canteen serving the usual Ghanaian fare.

Cape Cafe Mains US$1.50-3.50. On the busy main street this well-signposted café is on the 1st floor of the Women's Centre building, above the Methodist bookshop. It's a friendly place with a relaxed atmosphere and an extensive menu that includes pancakes and French toast for breakfast, as well as Ghanaian dishes and a good vegetarian selection. It's cool and breezy and a great place to sit and watch the bustle below. Smoking is not allowed and no alcohol is served. Proceeds from the café and the batik shop on the premises go to help needy women in the community.

Castle Beach Restaurant Mains US$1.50-2.50. Next to the castle and overlooking the beach, this open-air restaurant specialises in seafood. Service is incredibly slow but it's an agreeable place to just have a drink, watch the waves and let the sea breeze play.

Oasis Beer Garden & Restaurant Mains US$3-4. This large garden restaurant, near Victoria Park and with access to the beach, is popular with expats and travellers. It has a varied menu that includes plenty of seafood as well as a few vegetarian options. Service is fast and efficient and the food isn't bad.

Assase Pa Vegetarian Restaurant Mains US$1.50-2.50. Possibly the only restaurant of its kind in Ghana, Assase Pa has a fantastic location, on a promontory overlooking the sea just across the bridge over the lagoon. On offer is a varied menu that includes vegetarian versions of Ghanaian dishes. Most afternoons there are live-music and dance sessions at the practice ground next door.

Friends Garden & Restaurant Mains US$2-2.50. Off Jukwa Rd, by the side of the lagoon, this pleasant garden bar and restaurant is a popular place for a drink or a meal.

Aloumie Krom Garden *(Aboom Wells Rd)* Mains US$2-2.50. North of the intersection with Jukwa Rd is this shady garden restaurant and bar. It has a groovy, laid-back atmosphere during the day and is a lively spot for a drink in the evening.

Communication Spot *(Commercial St)* This upstairs drinking spot is a cheerful and breezy place to sink a cold beer.

Getting There & Away

The VanefSTC bus station is at Pedu junction, about 5km northwest of the town centre. There are buses twice a day to/from Accra (US$1.40, three hours) and Takoradi (US$0.70, one hour) and once a day to/from Kumasi (US$2.50, five hours). Passenger taxis to Pedu junction leave from Commercial St, opposite Cape Cafe.

There are two main motor parks in Cape Coast. The Accra bus station, at the junction of Sarbah and Residential Rds, serves long-distance routes, such as Accra and Kumasi. Kotokuraba station, on Governor Rowe Rd, near the market, serves destinations around Cape Coast, such as Abanze, Anomabu, Kakum National Park and Takoradi. Shared taxis to Elmina (US$0.20, 15 minutes) leave from the station on Commercial St, opposite Cape Cafe.

KAKUM NATIONAL PARK

☎ 042

This national park *(☎ 33278, 33042, admission US$0.10, open 8am-5pm daily)*, 33km north of Cape Coast, is one of Ghana's major tourist attractions. The much-hyped highlight of the park is its canopy walkway, which is unique in Africa and one of only four in the world.

Together with the neighbouring Assin Attandanso Resource Reserve, the park protects 357 sq km of diverse and dense vegetation, a mixture of true rainforest and semideciduous forest. It's home to 40 species of larger mammals (including elephants, colobus monkeys and antelopes), about 300 species of birds and a staggering 600 varieties of butterfly, including one species that was discovered at Kakum. The park is an important refuge for several endangered species, including forest elephants, bongos and yellow-backed duikers. However, if you come here expecting great wildlife viewing, you'll almost certainly be disappointed. Visitors see just a tiny percentage of the park's total area, and most of the wildlife understandably chooses to stay well away from the action areas. Instead, come here for the unique perspective of the canopy walkway and to learn about the rainforest environment. For the best chance of seeing any wildlife, get here when the park opens at 8am or take a night hike (see later).

The 350m rope and cable **canopy walkway** *(adults/students US$8.50/2)* was constructed in 1996. It consists of seven viewing platforms linked by a circuit of narrow suspension bridges, along which you sway, 30m above the forest floor. It gives you a bird's-eye view of the forest, although as you bounce along it's hard to concentrate on anything except how flimsy the ropes seem and what a vast distance it is from the forest floor.

Although the hype can make it seem as if the walkway *is* the park, there are other activities. A guided hike costs US$3/1 per hour for adults/students and is a good way to learn about the rainforest flora and its traditional uses. A guided night walk costs US$2 for two people for one hour and needs to be arranged in advance (☎ 30265, fax 33042).

In the park's visitor centre, there's a superb, ecologically sensitive display, a masterpiece of gentle didacticism.

An interesting alternative option is to visit the park from Mesomagor on its eastern outskirts. You can arrange guided walks and there's a good chance of seeing wildlife such as forest elephants. Mesomagor is also the home of the famous **Kukyekukyeku Bamboo Orchestra** and it may be possible to hear a performance. For more details, contact the park or ask at the tourist office in Cape Coast.

Places to Stay & Eat

Most people visit Kakum as a day trip from Cape Coast but if you want to stay, you can sleep on a ***tree platform*** at the camp site near the park headquarters for US$1.40 per person. You will need to bring your own equipment (sleeping bag and mosquito net or tent) and food. No camp fires are allowed. Simple ***homestay accommodation*** is also available in Mesomagor, on the eastern outskirts of the park.

Another possibility is to stay at ***Hans Cottage Botel*** *(☎ 33621, fax 33623)*, on the road to Kakum, about 10km north of Cape Coast. Singles/doubles US$19/24, suites US$26. With its crocodile pond, sunbirds, squabbling weaverbirds, monkeys and restaurant overlooking an artificial lake, it's enjoyably eccentric. Any tro-tro heading along the Jukwa road towards Kakum can drop you at the hotel.

There's a shady picnic area just inside the park entrance and another at the park headquarters. Also at the headquarters is ***Kakum Rainforest Cafe***, which is open for breakfast (US$2) and has a selection of Ghanaian dishes (US$4) at lunch time.

Getting There & Away

From Cape Coast, tro-tros (US$0.20, 45 minutes) that go past the entrance to the park leave from Kotokuraba station on Governor Rowe Rd. It's a five-minute walk from the main road to the park headquarters. Alternatively, you could charter a taxi for about US$4. To get to Mesomagor, take a tro-tro from Cape Coast to Nyamkomasi and a shared taxi from there to the village.

DOMAMA ROCK SHRINE

A visit to this awesome natural rock formation near the small village of Domama, northwest of Kakum National Park is usually combined with a canoe trip on the Pra River, a highlight in itself. Domama is part of a community-based tourism project. The tour costs US$3, including a guided trek and canoe trip, and takes about six hours if you are on foot or about four hours if you have your own transport. Simple accommodation (US$3 for doubles; bucket showers, no electricity) and food (about US$0.70) is available at the ***guesthouse*** in Domama. Most visitors stay overnight so that they can get an early start in the morning. No tours are available on Wednesday, when it's taboo for the villagers to work.

From Cape Coast, take a tro-tro from Kotokuraba station to Ankako junction (US$0.35) on the road to Twifo Praso, past the entrance to Kakum National Park. From Ankako, it's 17.5km down a bumpy but scenic dirt road to Domama village. Tro-tros run sporadically from the junction to Domama for about US$0.20. Transport from Domama back to the junction can be a problem, but something generally turns up.

ELMINA

☎ 042

The quiet backwater of Elmina (population 20,000), about 15km west of Cape Coast, is the site of St George's Castle, the oldest European structure still standing in sub-Saharan Africa. It's also one of the more picturesque towns in Ghana and has a lively fishing harbour. Most people visit Elmina as a day trip from Cape Coast or one of the nearby beach resorts but it's worth staying overnight to savour the atmosphere.

Known as Edina in the local language, the name Elmina is most likely derived from the name the Portuguese gave this stretch of the coast, Mina d'Ouro (Gold Mine). On a narrow peninsula between the Atlantic Ocean and Benya Lagoon, Elmina has one of the best natural harbours on the coast, which was what attracted first the Portuguese here and later the Dutch and the British.

St George's Castle & Fort St Jago

At the end of a rocky peninsula, St George's Castle *(admission without/with guided tour US$2/4, camera fee US$0.70; open 9am-5pm daily)* is irresistibly photogenic. Now a Unesco World Heritage Site, it was built in 1482 by the Portuguese. The Dutch captured the castle in 1637, and from then until 1872, when they ceded it to the British, the castle served as the African headquarters of the Dutch West Indies Company. It was expanded when slaves replaced gold as the major object of commerce, and the storerooms were converted into dungeons. The informative guided tour takes you around the incredibly grim slave dungeons, the punishment cells (even worse than the dungeons) and the turret room where the British imprisoned the Ashanti king, Prempeh I, for four years. The Portuguese Catholic church, converted into slave auctioning rooms by the Protestant Dutch, now houses a museum with excellent displays on the history and culture of Elmina.

Facing the castle across the lagoon is the much smaller Fort St Jago *(admission US$0.70; open 9am-5pm daily)*, also a Unesco World Heritage Site, built by the Dutch between 1652 and 1662 to protect the castle. Controversial plans to convert the fort into a guesthouse have ground to a halt and for the moment it remains in a state of partial ruin. The views of the town and St George's Castle from the ramparts are superb.

Other Attractions

The crowded Mpoben port and the vast fish market on the lagoon side are fascinating to watch, particularly when the day's fishing catch is being unloaded in the afternoon. There are a few interesting posubans in town and a well-kept Dutch cemetery. To get to the cemetery from the castle take a left turn over the bridge and follow the road around. Getting to either of these sites takes you past some of the posubans.

Special Events

Elmina's colourful Bakatue Festival takes place on the first Tuesday in July. A joyous harvest thanksgiving feast, one of its highlights is watching the priest in the harbour waters casting a net to lift a ban on fishing in the lagoon.

GHANA

Places to Stay

There are just two accommodation options in the centre of Elmina, at either end of the price scale.

***Nyansapow Hotel** (☎ 33955, Lime St)* Singles/doubles with fan & bathroom US$5.70/6.40. At this friendly, quiet place, simple rooms open onto a pleasant courtyard. It's signposted off the main road into town.

***Coconut Grove Bridge House** (☎ 34557, Liverpool St)* Doubles with air-con US$30-50. The only other hotel in central Elmina, it's run by the Coconut Grove Beach Resort and has a dream location in a converted old mansion opposite St George's Castle. However, the modern rooms are characterless and the hotel is surprisingly without any real atmosphere.

***Elmina Beach Resort** (☎ 33105, fax 34259, ⓔ ebr@africaonline.com.gh)* Singles/doubles from US$54/59. You can really pamper yourself at this slick and luxurious option, which is on the ocean side of the main road, about 2km out of the centre towards Cape Coast. Facilities include tennis courts, a swimming pool and an excellent restaurant. Despite its name, it has no direct access to the beach, although it has a shuttle service to Brenu beach nearby.

***Harmony Beach Hotel** (☎ 33678, fax 33681)* Doubles US$30-45. Modern, well-equipped rooms are good value at this friendly place, which is off the main road about 2.5km east of Elmina although it has no access to a beach.

***Coconut Grove Beach Resort** (☎ 33646, ⓔ coconut@africaonline.com.gh)* Rooms US$75/95. This luxurious resort has a beachside location 4km west of Elmina (follow the signs across the bridge over the lagoon) and offers a variety of smart rooms as well as a swimming pool and golf course.

Places to Eat

The area around the harbour and along Liverpool St is the best place to look for ***food stalls***.

***Gramsdel J** (High St)* Mains US$2-2.50. This eatery has a restaurant area serving good, cheap meals and, across the road on the beach, a raised platform bar area. It's about 1.5km from the bridge.

Castle Restaurant Mains US$2.50-3. Within the castle complex but with its own entrance, this pleasant terrace restaurant overlooks the harbour and is a great place for a drink or a meal.

Coconut Grove Bridge House Mains US$2.50-3. During the heat of the day, you can eat in air-conditioned calm inside, but once it has cooled down outside you can sit on the terrace overlooking the castle. It serves a selection of Ghanaian and Western dishes.

Getting There & Away

The main taxi and tro-tro station is outside the Wesley Methodist Cathedral. From here you can get tro-tros to Takoradi (US$0.40) or passenger taxis to Cape Coast (US$0.15). In Cape Coast, shared taxis (US$0.20, 15 minutes) to Elmina leave from the station on Commercial St, a block north of Barclays Bank. From Takoradi, take a tro-tro (US$0.50, one hour) from the Cape Coast station.

BRENU-AKYINIM

About 10km west of Elmina is a fabulous stretch of sandy beach at the village of Brenu-Akyinim. Part of the beach has been cordoned off to form the Brenu Beach Resort, where the sand is clean and there's a good restaurant and other facilities. A small fee (US$0.50) is charged for admission to the resort. You can stay in basic ***rooms*** at the resort for about US$10 or in the village for about US$4. At the junction on the main road is a simple eatery with a great name, ***Ocean Style Restaurant***.

From Elmina or Cape Coast, take a tro-tro west towards Takoradi and ask to be let off at the junction for Brenu-Akyinim (US$0.20). From here you should be able to get a passenger taxi to the village (US$0.20; 5km).

SHAMA

☎ 031

Fort Sebastian *(admission US$0.70, camera fee US$0.25)* at Shama was built by the Portuguese in about 1550. Where the Pra River joins the ocean, there's a colourful fish market from around 9am to 6pm daily except Tuesdays. Nearby, on the long peninsula, there's a beautiful sandy beach. Boatmen on the town side will ferry you across for a small fee or take you on longer excursions up the river.

The monolithic ***Hotel Applause*** *(☎ 23 941)* – yet another coastal white elephant, echoing and empty – is good value. Singles/doubles with fan and bathroom cost US$4/4.20.

Shama junction is about 18km east of Takoradi, off the main coastal road. The town is 4km south of the junction. Any vehicle travelling between Takoradi and Cape Coast or Elmina can drop you at the junction, from where there are regular shared taxis into Shama. Alternatively, you can get a tro-tro direct to Shama (US$0.20) from the Cape Coast station in Takoradi.

SEKONDI-TAKORADI

☎ 031

The twin cities of Sekondi-Takoradi don't have much in the way of tourist sights but Takoradi is a major transport hub and most travellers end up spending at least a night here. On the plus side, Takoradi has a huge selection of hotels, several good eateries, banks for changing money, a vibrant market and an attractive beach area.

Takoradi was just a fishing village until it was chosen as Ghana's first deep-water seaport; since then it has prospered. Sekondi, the older of the two settlements, is about 10km northeast of Takoradi. The only reason you might venture into Sekondi is to take a quick look at **Fort Orange**, built by the Dutch in 1640 and now a lighthouse.

The heart of Takoradi is the busy Market Circle, around which you'll find the motor parks, most of the cheap hotels and restaurants, banks and forexes. The port is about 2km southeast of Market Circle. Near it is the train station and head offices of banks. West of the port area is a green residential area, bordered to the south by a golf course and the beach.

The tourist office (☎ 22357, fax 23601), open 9am to 5pm Monday to Friday, is in the SIC Building on Harbour Roundabout. Both the Standard Chartered Bank and the Barclays Bank on the south side of Market Circle, have ATMs. There are several forexes near Market Circle, including Bethel Forex next to the Mosden Hotel and Esam Forex on John Sarbah Rd. For email access, try the Internet centre at the Ahenfie Hotel or WestCom Internet Café on Obuasi Rd.

At the far (northeastern) end of John Sarbah Rd, across the Cape Coast road, is a wooded hill that is home to a quickly diminishing population of colobus and spot-nosed monkeys. There are plans to make this area into a reserve to protect the monkeys.

Places to Stay – Budget

Amenla Hotel *(☎ 22543, John Sarbah Rd)* Singles/doubles with fan US$3.40/3.50, doubles with fan & bathroom US$4.50. This friendly hotel, southwest of Market Circle, has simple, clean rooms as well as a pleasant bar and restaurant.

Zenith Hotel *(☎ 22359, Kitson Rd)* Rooms with fan US$3/3.50, doubles with fan & bathroom US$6. The Zenith, east of Market Circle, is in a big old multistorey building, with clean rooms arranged around a central courtyard. The nightclub on the ground floor was due to reopen, which will make this a noisy option on Saturday nights.

Arvo Hotel *(☎ 21530, Ashanti Rd)* Rooms without/with bathroom US$4.50/6.50. The Arvo is unexciting but good value, especially the rooms with bathroom.

Mosden Hotel *(☎ 22266, Axim Rd)* Doubles with bathroom & fan/air-con US$8/10. On the 1st floor of Mankessim White House, conveniently close to the VanefSTC bus station, this is one of the best budget options in

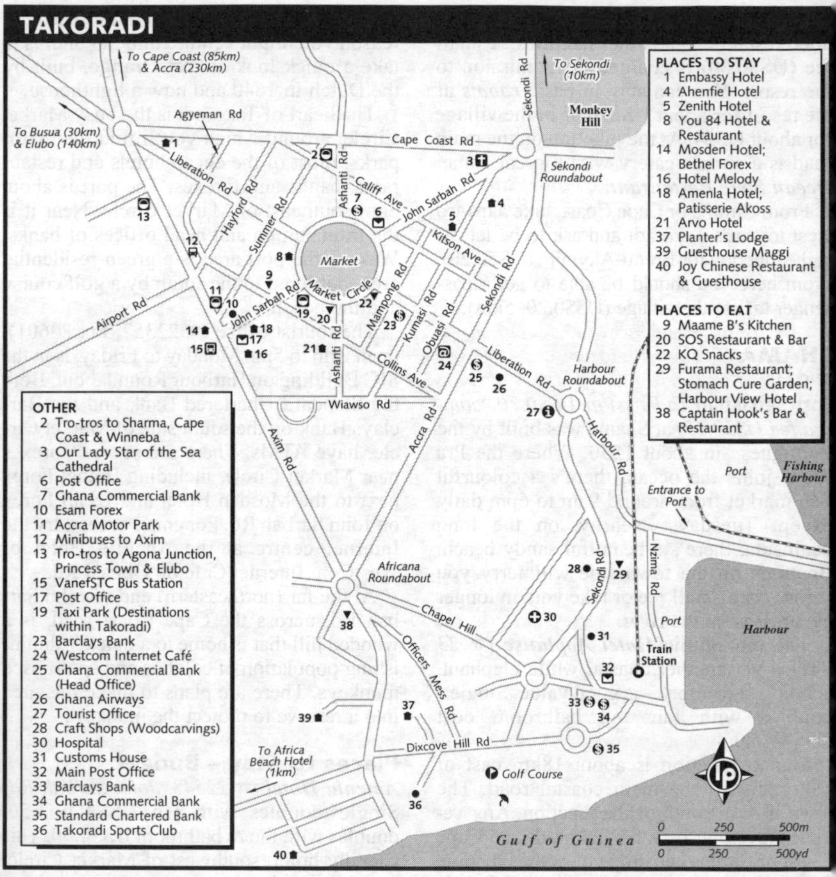
TAKORADI
To Cape Coast (85km) & Accra (230km)
To Busua (30km) & Elubo (140km)
To Sekondi (10km)
Monkey Hill
Agyeman Rd
Cape Coast Rd
Liberation Rd
Hayford Rd
Summer Rd
Ashanti Rd
Califf Ave
John Sarbah Rd
Kitson Ave
Sekondi Rd
Sekondi Roundabout
Market
Market Circle
Mampong Rd
Kumasi Rd
Obuasi Rd
Airport Rd
Collins Ave
Wiawso Rd
Axim Rd
Accra Rd
Harbour Roundabout
Harbour Rd
Port
Fishing Harbour
Entrance to Port
Nzima Rd
Harbour
Train Station
Africana Roundabout
Chapel Hill
Officers Mess Rd
Dixcove Hill Rd
To Africa Beach Hotel (1km)
Golf Course
Gulf of Guinea
0 250 500m
0 250 500yd
PLACES TO STAY
1 Embassy Hotel
4 Ahenfie Hotel
5 Zenith Hotel
8 You 84 Hotel & Restaurant
14 Mosden Hotel; Bethel Forex
16 Hotel Melody
18 Amenla Hotel; Patisserie Akoss
21 Arvo Hotel
37 Planter's Lodge
39 Guesthouse Maggi
40 Joy Chinese Restaurant & Guesthouse
PLACES TO EAT
9 Maame B's Kitchen
20 SOS Restaurant & Bar
22 KQ Snacks
29 Furama Restaurant; Stomach Cure Garden; Harbour View Hotel
38 Captain Hook's Bar & Restaurant
OTHER
2 Tro-tros to Sharma, Cape Coast & Winneba
3 Our Lady Star of the Sea Cathedral
6 Post Office
7 Ghana Commercial Bank
10 Esam Forex
11 Accra Motor Park
12 Minibuses to Axim
13 Tro-tros to Agona Junction, Princess Town & Elubo
15 VanefSTC Bus Station
17 Post Office
19 Taxi Park (Destinations within Takoradi)
23 Barclays Bank
24 Westcom Internet Café
25 Ghana Commercial Bank (Head Office)
26 Ghana Airways
27 Tourist Office
28 Craft Shops (Woodcarvings)
30 Hospital
31 Customs House
32 Main Post Office
33 Barclays Bank
34 Ghana Commercial Bank
35 Standard Chartered Bank
36 Takoradi Sports Club

town. It has clean, good-sized rooms and a restaurant.

***You 84 Hotel & Restaurant** (☎ 22945, Market Circle)* Doubles with bathroom & fan/air-con US$8.50/11.50. This intriguingly named hotel is upstairs on the western side of Market Circle. Despite the rather grim reception area, the rooms, some of which open onto a balcony, are good value.

Places to Stay – Mid-Range & Top End

Unless otherwise indicated, all rooms in this category contain air-con and private bathrooms.

***Ahenfie Hotel** (☎ 22966, Kumasi Rd)* Singles with fan/air-con US$8/17, doubles with fan/air-con US$12/19. Although this hotel is a bit out of the way, at the northern end of Kumasi Rd near Sekondi Roundabout, the large, smart rooms with TV and fridge are comfortable and good value. The hotel complex includes an attractive air-con restaurant, a nightclub and disco and an Internet centre.

***Joy Chinese Restaurant & Guesthouse** (☎ 30347, fax 27418, Beach Rd)* Doubles US$11. This newly completed guesthouse, just around the corner from the Joy Chinese Restaurant, has a fabulous location, perched on the edge of the cliffs overlooking the sea at the far end of Beach Rd. Rooms are small but charming and are excellent value.

***Hotel Melody** (☎ 24109, Axim Rd)* Doubles US$22-26. Conveniently located opposite the VanefSTC station, this hotel has large comfortable rooms and a reasonable if pricey, restaurant. The pink padded toilet seats are an unexpected treat.

Guesthouse Maggi *(☎ 22575, fax 30183, Off Axim Rd)* Doubles US$21-28. This friendly hotel has a peaceful location in the midst of a grove of plantains and looks as if it should be much more expensive than it is. Pleasant, modern rooms overlook the lush garden. The hotel, south of the Africana Roundabout, is well-signposted.

Planter's Lodge *(☎ 22233, fax 22230, e planters@africaonline.com.gh, Off Dixcove Hill Rd)* Bungalows US$65. This gorgeous hotel has comfortable chalets set within beautiful landscaped grounds. It also has a nice open-air restaurant and a swimming pool (US$2.50 for day use).

Africa Beach Hotel *(☎ 23466, fax 21666)* Bungalows US$70. On the western edge of town, this resort hotel has an attractive beachside setting.

Places to Eat & Drink

Good ***street food*** is on offer around Market Circle and the motor parks. There are also several good-value eateries and lively drinking spots along Axim Rd, around Market Circle and on Liberation Rd.

SOS Restaurant & Bar *(Cnr Ashanti Rd & Market Circle)* Mains US$1.50-2. On the southern side of Market Circle, this small restaurant has a breezy balcony upstairs overlooking the action on Market Circle. It serves basic Ghanaian food, snacks and cold drinks.

KQ Snacks *(Cnr Liberation Rd & Market Circle)* Snacks US$0.70-1. This is a good place to get snacks such as meat pies and sandwiches.

Patisserie Akoss *(John Sarbah Rd)* Delicious baking smells emanate from this patisserie and coffee shop next to the Amenla Hotel. It has a selection of bread and cakes.

Maame B's Kitchen *(John Sarbah Rd)* Mains US$2.50-3. About 100m west of Market Circle, this air-con restaurant has a good selection of fast food (such as burgers and kebabs) and Ghanaian dishes.

Furama Restaurant *(Sekondi Rd)* Mains US$2.50-3.50. Underneath the Harbour View Hotel, this restaurant has a tasty selection of Chinese and Western dishes. ***The Stomach Cure Garden*** is a terrace bar next to the Harbour View, overlooking the port area. It's a popular if somewhat sleazy spot for a drink (beware the hustlers) and it serves food from the Furama downstairs.

Joy Chinese Restaurant *(Beach Rd)* Mains US$3.50-4. This restaurant has a superb location overlooking the sea and serves delectable Chinese food. The terrace is a wonderful place to watch the sun set over the sea.

Captain Hook's Bar & Restaurant *(Africana Roundabout)* Mains US$4.50-6. The best restaurant in town, Captain Hook's has a maritime theme and plenty of ambience. Not surprisingly, seafood is the speciality but it does a mean pizza too.

Getting There & Away

Bus & Tro-Tro The VanefSTC bus station (☎ 23351/2/3) is on Axim Rd, opposite the junction with John Sarbah Rd. It has regular buses to Accra (US$2.50, four hours) between 3am and 5.30pm, as well as a daily air-con express service (US$4) at 8.30am. There are two buses per day to Kumasi (US$2.50, six hours) at 6.30am and 1pm. The Accra bus can drop you at Pedu junction (for Cape Coast) or Anomabu, but you will have to pay the full Accra fare. If you're heading for Abidjan, it's possible to pick up the bus from Accra as it passes through but you'll need to arrange this in advance; it's easier get transport to Elubo and continue from there.

Opposite the VanefSTC bus station is the Accra motor park, from where you can get OSA and City Express buses and GPRTU minibuses to Accra. At the top of Axim Rd, near the traffic circle, is a tro-tro park serving destinations west of Takoradi, including Agona junction (US$0.20, 30 minutes; for Busua and Dixcove), Axim, Beyin and Elubo (US$1.70, three hours). This is also where you can get tro-tros and Peugeot taxis (US$1) to Abidjan. Tro-tros to destinations east of Takoradi leave from the Cape Coast tro-tro station north of Market Circle. Destinations include Shama (US$0.20), Cape Coast (US$0.60) and Winneba (US$1).

Train There are passenger trains from Takoradi to Kumasi and Accra. For more details, see Train in Getting Around earlier.

Getting Around

Takoradi is very spread out and, apart from the Market Circle area, it's not really feasible to get everywhere by foot. Fortunately,

GHANA

it's well served by a network of line taxis. Useful routes are along Axim Rd and between Market Circle and the port area. For Sekondi (US$0.20), shared taxis leave from the taxi park near the Zenith Hotel.

BUSUA & DIXCOVE

☎ 031

For years Busua and Dixcove, about 30km west of Takoradi, were a mecca for beach-lovers and budget travellers in the know. Now that they're an easy drive from Accra, they've lost their off-the-beaten-track exclusiveness but are still worth a visit to see what the fuss was all about. Be prepared, though, to deal with a higher level of hassle here than you'll probably encounter anywhere else in Ghana.

The long, sandy beach at Busua is one of the finest in Ghana, and unlike other beaches along this coastline, the sea is shallow for a long way out. At the far western end of the beach, segregated from the tourists, is Busua's fishing harbour, usually a colourful and busy scene. You can hire a boat to go out to the offshore island.

On the shore of a rocky cove, Dixcove is an animated fishing village. Its natural harbour is deep enough for small ships to enter – one of the reasons why it became the site of the picturesque **Fort Metal Cross** *(admission US$0.70, camera fee US$0.15; open 9am-5pm daily)*, which overlooks the port. Built in 1696 by the British, it got its name from the metal brand used on the slaves who passed through here. The post office in the first courtyard has been here since the British occupation and is still the only post office for the entire Busua-Dixcove area. From the ramparts there are magical views over the harbour and the village.

If you head east along the beach from Busua, after about 2km you'll reach the settlement of Butre, site of the ruined Fort Batenstein.

Dixcove is about 2km around the coast west of Busua, an undemanding 20- to 30-minute walk over the headland to the west. There have been several reports of muggings along this track and locals will warn against walking it alone. It's best to follow their advice and take a local guide (for a small fee); don't take any valuables with you. Alternatively, you can get a shared taxi back to Agona junction then another from there to Dixcove. There's no direct transport between Dixcove and Busua.

Places to Stay

Busua is better set up than Dixcove for travellers, and most people stay there and visit Dixcove as a day trip. Several villagers in Busua rent out simple ***rooms*** in the family compound for about US$5. Ask around to see who's offering what. ***Sabina's Guesthouse***, opposite Dadson's Lodge, is more formal these days and offers clean rooms around a courtyard. ***Elizabeth's***, signposted on the right as you come into town, has a few agreeable rooms at the top of the house. All these options, given enough notice, will prepare you a meal for under US$2. Otherwise, there are three beachside accommodation options, reached by turning left as you enter the village.

Dadson's Lodge Singles/doubles with fan from US$4.50/6.50. In a converted private house, Dadson's has a selection of rooms with bucket showers – the large-size rooms have a huge sitting area and are particularly good value. Avoid the rooms at the front, which can be very noisy.

Alaska Beach Club Rondavels US$6.50. This place has a wonderful beachside setting and a good restaurant and bar. Accommodation is in simple round huts with thatched roofs. The shared facilities are kept spotlessly clean. It's a popular stop-off for overland trucks. Opinion is somewhat divided over this place; it can get noisy at night when the bar livens up and theft from the huts has been a problem.

Busua Beach Resort *(☎ 21210, fax 21858, ⓔ bbr@ghana.com)* Rooms with air-con from US$40/50, budget rooms with fan/air-con US$5/10. Set in landscaped gardens, this resort has attractive bungalow accommodation. The budget accommodation is a possibility but only if you don't mind staying opposite the staff canteen and next to the hotel laundry, a long walk from the rest of the hotel.

Quiet Storm Hotel Doubles with fan US$7. Your only option in Dixcove is the curiously named Quiet Storm, a vast crumbling multistorey building that has musty rooms with shared facilities. You can't miss it – it's the large blue building on the hill to your right as you come into Dixcove by road.

Places to Eat

Dixcove and Busua are known for their lobsters and you'll find no shortage of locals who will offer to cook their day's catch. In Busua, the other must-have menu item is pancakes. You can get a good selection of ***street food*** along Busua's main drag and around the harbour area in Dixcove. There are also several small, inexpensive eateries between Dadson's Lodge and the Alaska Beach Club in Busua, including ***Daniel the Pancake Man*** who serves up all sorts of sweet and savoury pancakes, as well as meals such as lobster and rice and some vegetarian options for around US$2.

Alaska Beach Club Mains US$1.50-2. With its beachside location, this restaurant is a great place for a meal or just to chill out with a beer and watch the moonlight on the water.

Black Mamba Corner Mains US$5-6. This unusual restaurant is on the terrace of a private house up on a hill at the far western end of the beach. It offers a varied menu, with pizzas as a speciality. It's not cheap but the setting is lyrical and the food is good. To get to it, walk past the fishing harbour, right to the end of the beach and look for the sign across the water.

Getting There & Away

Busua and Dixcove are each about 12km from the main coastal road. There's no direct transport to/from either Busua or Dixcove; you have to get to Agona junction on the main road and then take a tro-tro or shared taxi from there. From Takoradi, regular tro-tros (US$0.20, 30 minutes) leave for Agona junction from the station at the top of Axim Rd. From Agona junction there is frequent transport (US$0.20) to Busua and Dixcove.

PRINCESS TOWN

With its fine castle and magnificent beach, Princess Town has become a focus for travellers looking to get away from the resort trail. It's harder to get to than Busua, which is part of the attraction. **Fort Princess Town** *(admission US$0.70; open 9am-5pm daily)*, on top of a hill on the eastern edge of the village, was originally called Gross Friedrichsburg by the Prussians who built it in 1683.

The partly restored fort is made from greyish local stone and this, together with the lush vegetation surrounding it, makes it one of the most attractive forts on the coast. There are superb views from the ramparts over the sandy bay and towards Cape Three Points, Ghana's southernmost point. The fort's caretaker can help arrange excursions in the area, such as canoe trips on the nearby lagoon, and trips up the River Kpani to visit a palm-wine distillery.

The only accommodation in Princess Town is at the fort, where simple ***rooms*** with shared bathroom (bucket showers) cost US$7. Just down the hill from the fort is a pleasant terrace ***bar and restaurant*** where you can get cold drinks and cheap, tasty meals, including lobster. Watch out for tourist leeches here.

The junction for Princess Town is about 15km west of Agona junction; any tro-tro heading west from Agona can drop you there (US$0.70). From here, it's about 18km to Princess Town along a scenic but rough road. Shared taxis run reasonably regularly between the junction and the town and cost about US$0.50. There are also direct tro-tros from Agona to Princess Town but they take forever to fill up.

AXIM

☎ 0342

The largest town on the coast west of Takoradi, Axim is a pleasant, friendly place, of interest mainly for its fort and for being near two excellent beach resorts. **Fort St Anthony** *(admission US$0.70, camera fee US$0.20)*, the second-oldest fort on the Ghanaian coast, was built by the Portuguese in 1515. It's in the centre of town, behind the soccer pitch.

Frankfaus Hotel *(☎ 222291)* Doubles without/with bathroom US$6.50/8. Up the hill from the fort, this agreeable place has pleasant, breezy rooms with fan, although the lurid-pink decor hurts your eyes somewhat, The Frankfaus doesn't have food but you can eat at Friends Snack Bar around the corner.

Axim Beach Hotel *(☎ 22260, e info@aximbeach.com)* Single/double bungalows with fan US$16/18.50. This new resort has a wonderful location on a low hill a couple of kilometres east of Axim town centre. The attractive bungalows are perched on the cliff edge and all have sea views. The shady restaurant has tasty meals (including lobster) for US$3 to US$4 and is a great place to mellow out any time of the day. There's a fine beach below the resort, although here like elsewhere along the coast, the coconut palms have been affected by a blight and there isn't a lot of shade. Activities can be arranged, such as canoe trips to Princess Town and Cape Three Points, drumming and dancing courses and tours to Nzulezu and Ankasa Nature Reserve. A private taxi to the resort from the station opposite the fort is about US$0.70.

Ankobra Beach Hotel *(☎ 22400, 22368, fax 22398, ⓔ ankobra_beach@hotmail.com)* Bungalows with fan US$25-29, rooms with fan US$11.50. This gem of a place has simple but comfortable bungalows set within a grove of palms on a stunning beach. Meals at the pleasant restaurant cost around US$5 to US$6. Activities such as canoe trips up the nearby Ankobra River and tours to Nzulezu and Ankasa can be arranged. Ankobra Beach is signposted off the main Elubo road, about 5km from the turn-off to Axim. From the main road, it's about 500m to the resort. A dropping taxi from Axim costs around US$2.

Getting There & Away

Axim is 69km west of Takoradi, off the main Elubo road, which bypasses it. Axim's well-organised motor park is in the centre of town, across from the soccer pitch in front of the fort. There are regular tro-tros to Takoradi (US$0.50, 1½ hours), which can drop you at Agona junction (for Busua and Dixcove) or the Princess Town junction. Heading west, for Elubo and Ankasa you may have to get a tro-tro to Esiama, a big transport hub on the coastal road about 10km from Axim, and get onward transport from there. To Beyin (US$0.70), you'll have to get a tro-tro to Eikwe and then transport on from there.

BEYIN & NZULEZU

About 65km west of Axim, is the village of Beyin. It's the site of **Fort Apollonia**, the last of the coastal forts west of Accra, but, much more exciting, it's the departure point for visits to the Amansuri Lagoon and the stilt village of Nzulezu. This village is reached by canoe, which takes about an hour each way. At the Ghana Wildlife Society office on the outskirts of Beyin, you register and pay a fee of US$4.50 per person (US$0.70 for a camera), which includes the canoe trip and entry to the village. There's no shade on the lagoon so the earlier in the day you leave the better, and take plenty of water and a hat with you.

You can stay overnight in Nzulezu in a tranquil room over the water for US$4.50. Simple meals can be arranged for around US$1. Let them know you want to stay over when you are arranging your trip.

Beyin is on a rough dirt road that leaves the main Elubo road about 20km west of Esiama. From there it's about 15km to Eikwe and then the road follows the coast to Beyin. From Takoradi, you may be able to get a direct tro-tro from the station at the top of Axim Rd but it's probably quicker to get a tro-tro to Esiama and then transport on from there. From Axim, there are a few tro-tros to Eikwe, from where you can get onward transport to Beyin. Alternatively, Axim Beach Resort and Ankobra Beach Hotel can charter a taxi to take you there and back for about US$20. Heading to Elubo, you can get transport east from Beyin to Tikobo No 1 and onward transport from there.

ANKASA NATURE RESERVE

This reserve *(admission US$2)*, near the border with Côte d'Ivoire and newly developed for visitors, offers reasonable wildlife-viewing opportunities in tranquil surroundings, although facilities are still very basic. Together with the neighbouring Nini-Suhien Reserve, Ankasa covers 490 sq km of wet rainforest. Mammals such as forest elephants, bongos and several monkey species have been identified and the area is particularly rich in birdlife, including parrots, hornbills and the rare white-fronted guinea fowl.

The park headquarters is at the main Ankasa Gate, where you pay the entrance fee and can arrange guided hikes. Overnight accommodation is available in the park in ***camps*** (US$1.20) within walking distance of the main Ankasa Gate. You'll need to bring your own mosquito net or tent, sleeping bag and food, although a restaurant may be up and running soon.

Ankasa Gate is about 6km north of the main Elubo road, about 20km southeast of Elubo. Direct transport can be difficult so it may be better to take any transport along the main road and ask to be dropped at the junction.

The East

ADA

☎ 0968

Ada, 120km east of Accra, is a quiet backwater, visited for its beautiful setting on the Volta estuary, its fine ocean-side beach and its water-sports facilities. The beach is also a turtle nesting site and it may be possible to see the turtles when they come ashore between November and February.

Ada consists of three parts: Ada Kasseh at the junction on the main Accra to Aflao highway, Big Ada about 15km south and Ada Foah on the estuary. There's a small community-run tourist centre near the motor park in Ada Foah, which is open from 10am to 6pm Monday to Saturday. Boat trips on the river can be arranged at the tourist office or Cocoloko Beach Resort and cost US$3.50 for one hour; the trips are more expensive if organised from the Manet Paradise Hotel.

One warning – swim in the ocean as there's a chance of picking up bilharzia in the estuary.

Places to Stay & Eat

***Cocoloko Beach Resort** (☎ 22023)* Camping US$2 per person, singles/doubles US$5.50/8. Run by the local community and built to replace the popular Estuary Beach Camp, which was washed away in a storm in 1998, this resort lacks the charm of the original but is still good value. Accommodation is in simple round huts, some with electricity, set on the sand. It's about 2km from the centre of Ada Foah.

***Manet Paradise Beach Hotel** (☎ 22275, e manet@ghana.com)* Singles/doubles US$75/88. It's not quite paradise but this upmarket hotel has a great location near the mouth of the estuary, about 1.5km from the town centre. It has comfortable but characterless rooms, a swimming pool and plenty of water-sports facilities. The air-con restaurant is good and the terrace overlooking the estuary mouth is an agreeable place to sip a cold beer and watch the sun set.

Two popular spots where you can drink pleasurably and eat simply are ***Midas*** in the town centre and the wondrously named ***Hushie Hushie Bar*** on the road out to the Manet Paradise Hotel.

Getting There & Around

Any transport heading in either direction along the Accra to Aflao highway should be able to drop you at the junction, Ada Kasseh, from where regular passenger taxis run to Ada Foah (US$0.20). From Accra, tro-tros (US$0.75) to Ada leave from Tudu station. To get to Ho from Ada, you'll need to change vehicles at Sogakope or, possibly, Akatsi junction. If you're headed to Akosombo, it's probably easiest to take any vehicle to Tema and change there.

From the lorry park in Ada Foah, private taxis cost US$0.70 to the Manet Paradise and US$1 to Cocoloko.

KETA

☎ 0966

East of Ada, towards Keta, you'll find a relatively untouristed area with superb sandy beaches and, just inland, Keta Lagoon, an important wetlands zone with great bird-watching potential. The strip of land between the sea and the lagoon is narrow, especially around Keta, and much of the town has been washed away by the sea. At Keta you can visit the ruins of Fort Prinzenstein, built in 1784 by the Danes. Just on from the fort is the beach; other beaches are at Tegbi, Woe and Anloga on the road to Keta. You can arrange canoe trips at these places.

Places to Stay & Eat

***Keta Beach Hotel** (☎ 42288)* Singles US$7, doubles without/with air-con US$8/16. This friendly place has plenty of character and a lovely garden setting. It's near the beach and has a restaurant and bar. It's clearly signposted off the main road, about 2km before the motor park in Keta.

Tsisa Guesthouse Doubles with fan US$6.50. About 500m from the Keta Beach Hotel, on the opposite side of the road, the Tsisa looks dingy on the outside but has smart, comfortable rooms inside. Meals are available on request.

Larota Guesthouse Singles/doubles with fan US$5/6. In Tegbi, about 4km south of the Keta Beach Hotel, this is a nice, friendly place with lovely, spacious rooms with bathroom. Meals are available on request.

***Abutia Lodge** (☎ 22239)* Rooms US$5/6. On the edge of the lagoon in Woe, about 8km south of the Keta Beach Hotel and clearly signposted off the main road, this is a tranquil place. The lovely garden and friendly owners make up for small, hot rooms and uncomfortable beds. Simple, tasty meals are provided.

Lorneh Lodge *(☎ 42162, fax 42160)* Singles/doubles US$21/26. The only upmarket option in the area, Lorneh Lodge is near the sea in Tegbi, about 4km from the Keta Beach Hotel. Everything about this place is tacky but the rooms are comfortable and well-equipped. It has a swimming pool, a pricey restaurant and an Internet centre.

Getting There & Away

Tro-tros to Keta leave from Tudu station in Accra (US$0.85, three hours). From Ada, you may need to change vehicles in Sogakope and again at Dabala. From Ho, infrequent tro-tros head to Keta but it's quicker to go to Akatsi junction and on from there. East of Keta towards Aflao and the Togo border, the sea has encroached on the road. Occasional 4WDs make the trip; otherwise you'll need to get a boat across and onward transport from there. Although there is a motor park near the fort in Keta, the main transport hub is at Anloga, about 15km southwest. Tro-tros and shared taxis connect the settlements between Anloga and Keta.

AKOSOMBO

☎ 0251

Akosombo, 104km northeast of Accra, is the town at the dam holding back Lake Volta, the world's largest artificial lake. The views of Lake Volta and the beauty of the surrounding area are reason alone to visit the town; it's also the terminus for a passenger-boat service north to Yeji. The town was originally built to house construction workers and it retains a tidy orderliness.

Akosombo is about 6km north of the Accra to Ho road, 2km before the dam and 6km before the port. In town there are two hotels, a Ghana Commercial Bank, post office and small visitor centre on the main road near the motor park. A wider selection of accommodation and eating options are available in Atimpoku, to the south of Akosombo, where the Ho road crosses the Volta at a particularly impressive suspension bridge.

For a wonderful view of the dam, head for the lookout halfway up the drive to the Volta Lake Hotel. To get to it, take a shared taxi to 'Mess' and get off at the foot of the drive. The Volta River Authority arranges tours of the dam (ask at the visitor centre or the Volta Hotel). On Sunday, a fun day out

GHANA

Akosombo Dam

In 1915 an engineer called Albert Kison realised that the Kwahu plateau was a rich bauxite deposit, that damming the Volta River at Akosombo could generate enough electricity for a huge foundry and that Tema could be converted into a deep-water port to export the aluminium. His conclusions gathered dust for 40 years until Nkrumah, keen to industrialise Ghana, picked up the idea. To finance the project, he had to accede to the harsh terms of Valco, the US company most interested in the project. Under these terms, in return for building the dam, Valco would receive over two-thirds of the electricity generated, at cost price, for its aluminium smelter at Tema for the foreseeable future.

The project proved so expensive that it was decided to import the necessary raw material for the foundry rather than to extract it from the Kwahu Plateau. Costs immediately escalated. Some 84,000 people had to be relocated and, at Tema, a new port and town had to be constructed. The dam was eventually inaugurated in 1966; a month later Nkrumah was gone, ousted by the military.

For years, the economy spiralled downward and Valco's savage terms allowed little potential for earning money from power generation, for realising the dam's potential for electrifying the country or irrigating nearby farmland. Only now, partly due to Valco's terms being renegotiated, is the country truly beginning to benefit, but the dam's full potential is still far from realised.

The dam is 124m high and 368m wide and can generate 912,000 kW of power. Except after severe droughts, there's potentially enough electricity to power all Ghana plus a good portion of Togo and Benin. Because of the earthquake risk, the dam's not built of solid concrete but has a central nucleus of clay covered by a layer of crushed rock and outer walls covered with huge boulders. Lake Volta, which flooded 850,000 hectares of land (7% of Ghana's land surface), stretches north from Akosombo for 402km. Much more remains to be done to compensate people for the loss of their land.

ANTHONY HAM

SIEGE A.D.I.D

JANE SWEENEY

KIM WILDMAN

ARIADNE VAN ZANDBERGEN

There's a vast array of architectural styles in West Africa, but there's always one common theme – beating the heat: mud-brick Tuareg house in Agadez, Niger (top); traditional architecture, Djenné, Mali (bottom left); Tata compounds in the Tamberma Valley, Togo (middle right); Posuban shrine, Elmina, Ghana (bottom right)

ARIADNE VAN ZANDBERGEN

ARIADNE VAN ZANDBERGEN

DAVID ELSE

ANDREW BURKE

JANE SWEENEY

DAVID ELSE

ANTHONY HAM

Clockwise from top left: The mosques at Djenné, Mali; Larabanga, Ghana; and Diourbel, Senegal are impressive structures. Clockwise from middle left: Other places of religious or royal significance include the stone circles of Wassu, Gambia; the Emir's Palace, Kano, Nigeria; a Fula palace, Bandiagara, Mali; and this Muslim chief's palace in Maroua, Cameroon.

is to take a cruise (US$6) to nearby Dodi Island on the infelicitously named *Dodi Princess*. Leaving at 10am, the trip takes six hours, with two hours on the island. It leaves from a well-signposted jetty beyond the dam, before the port. Any shared taxi heading for the port from the motor park can drop you at the jetty.

Places to Stay & Eat

Benkum Motel Doubles US$5. The only real budget hotel near Akosombo, this place is in Atimpoku, south of the suspension bridge. It looks unpromising on the outside, but inside it has clean, basic rooms with shared bathrooms.

Zito Guesthouse *(☎ 20474)* Doubles with fan/air-con US$7/10. About 800m up the hill from the motor park past the market, this popular place is the only budget option in Akosombo. The cool rooms have huge beds and are good value.

Adomi Hotel & Restaurant Doubles with fan/air-con US$10/17. In Atimpoku, this new hotel is on the roundabout opposite the suspension bridge. It has smart, modern rooms away from the traffic noise and a stylish terrace restaurant.

Aylo's Bay *(☎ 20901, W www.aylosbay.com)* Doubles with fan US$20. This delightful place, next to the Akosombo Continental Hotel, has riverside frontage and a tranquil, shady garden. As well as a garden bar and restaurant (mains US$2 to US$3), it has five exquisite rooms overlooking the river. You can also camp here for a small fee.

Akosombo Continental Hotel Doubles with air-con US$60. On the riverfront, just beyond the suspension bridge, this large resort complex is a favourite with day-trippers and tour groups. It has beautiful landscaped gardens, swimming pool (day use US$2) and a good restaurant (mains around US$5 to US$6). Hotel accommodation was in the process of being built when we visited but should be available by the time you read this.

Sound Rest Motel *(☎ 20288)* Singles US$5, doubles with fan/air-con US$6/10. Just off the main road, about halfway between Atimpoku and Akosombo is this quiet hotel with rooms, some with bathroom, set around a garden courtyard.

Volta Hotel *(☎ 021-662639, fax 663791)* Singles/doubles US$95/105. This classy hotel is perched on a hill with sweeping views of the lake, dam and surrounding Akwamu highlands.

You'll find excellent and exotic ***street food*** in Akosombo and Atimpoku. Specialities include fried shrimp sold in plastic bags and 'one man thousand' (minute fried fish). In Akosombo town, try the ***Kokoo-Ase Spot*** near the motor park for a drink or bite to eat. About 500m beyond Akosombo port (and signposted) is the ***Maritime Club***, a groovy place set on the edge of the lake. Mains cost US$3 to US$4 and it's open Thursday to Tuesday. Take a shared taxi to the port and walk from there.

Getting There & Around

The main transport hub is at Kpong, on the Accra to Ho road 10km south of Atimpoku. Regular tro-tros travel between Kpong, Atimpoku and Akosombo. From Accra, tro-tros for Kpong/Akosombo (US$1) leave from Tudu station. Alternatively, get any transport to Ho from Accra or to Accra or Kpong from Ho and get off at the suspension bridge at Atimpoku.

For details about the boat between Akosombo and Yeji, see Boat under Getting Around earlier in this chapter.

Regular shared taxis leave the motor park in Akosombo for places in and around town for around US$0.20. For the port, get one to 'Marine'.

HO

☎ 091

Capital of Volta Region, Ho is about 75km northeast of Akosombo. It nestles at the base of a range of hills with the distinctive Mt Adaklu forming a backdrop to the south. Although unexciting in itself, Ho has a good range of accommodation and transport connections and is the obvious base for exploring this part of the Volta Region.

Ho's main street, along which you'll find banks, the post office and the VanefSTC bus station, extends for about a kilometre south from the junction with the Accra road. The main lorry park is on a parallel road, a couple of blocks east of the Accra road junction.

There's a small, helpful tourist office (☎ 26560) in the State Insurance Corporation (SIC) building on the Accra road. Barclays Bank is on the main drag, just up from the junction with the Accra road. If you're after

Internet access, try the centre beside the White House drinking spot or the one near Mother's Inn.

The small **Volta Regional Museum** *(admission US$0.70; open 9am-5pm Tues-Sun)*, behind the hospital on the western side of town, is worth a quick look.

Places to Stay

EP Church Social Services Centre *(☎ 26 670)* Dorm beds US$1.60, doubles with fan/air-con US$7/8. Part of a complex of church buildings on the southern outskirts of town, this guesthouse offers basic accommodation. From the lorry park, head south for about 1.5km, following the signs to Mt Adaklu, until you get to a petrol station at a large intersection. From here, head uphill towards the large church building.

Fiave Lodge *(☎ 26412)* Doubles US$3-5. At this small guesthouse, you feel like a guest in someone's home. A selection of rooms is available, some with private bathrooms. It's situated on the Kpalimé road, about 200m beyond the motor park towards Kpalimé. There are meals available upon request.

Hotel de Tarso Doubles with fan US$6. This charming but very run-down hotel, once Ho's finest, may not have the best rooms in town but it's inexpensive and the staff are very hospitable. Meals can be arranged with advance notice. The Tarso is set back from the main street, about 500m south of the post office, on the left just past the bridge.

Freedom Hotel *(☎ 28158)* Doubles without/with bathroom US$4/6.50, with air-con US$17. This upbeat, smart complex has a wide variety of spotlessly clean rooms as well as a pleasant terrace bar and restaurant. It's on the Kpalimé road, about 500m out of town from the motor park.

Taurus Hotel *(☎ 26574)* Singles/doubles US$5.50/8.50. This pleasant place, opposite the Total petrol station about 1km out of town on the Accra road, is excellent value. It has large, airy rooms with views.

Chances Hotel *(☎ 28344, fax 27083)* Doubles/chalets US$40/48. On the Accra road about 3km before the centre, this is Ho's only top-end option. It has attractive, modern rooms set within landscaped gardens, a good restaurant (mains US$3 to US$4) and an Internet centre.

Places to Eat & Drink

Around the motor park and the VanefSTC bus station on the main street are lots of ***food stalls*** selling tasty, filling food.

Lord Restaurant Mains US$1.50-2. Serving good, solid local food, this established eatery is just off the main street near the junction with the Accra road.

Phil's Country Kitchen Mains US$1.50-2.50. Out on the Kpalimé road, before you get to the Freedom Hotel, is this pleasant garden restaurant serving a good selection of Ghanaian and Western dishes.

The White House A short way up the hill from the Hotel de Tarso, this is a lively place for a drink, especially at the weekend.

Mother's Inn Mains US$2-3. A popular drinking spot, if you don't mind the traffic noise, this bar on the southern outskirts of town offers simple, local food. To get to it, head up the hill from The White House and turn right at the traffic circle. Mother's Inn is about 200m along the busy road, on the right.

Getting There & Away

Ho's busy main lorry park is well organised. From here, regular tro-tros run between Ho and Hohoe (US$1, two hours) throughout the day. Other destinations include Accra (US$1.30), Amedzofe (US$0.60), Akatsi and Keta.

VanefSTC runs one bus a day (US$1.30, three hours) between Ho and Accra, leaving from the VanefSTC station on the main street in Ho at 4am. In Accra, buses for Ho leave from the smaller VanefSTC bus station near Tudu station. Tro-tros for Ho depart from the small terminal near Tema station.

OSA has a daily bus from Ho to Kumasi (US$2.50) via Koforidua leaving from opposite the lorry park early in the morning.

AROUND HO

Mt Adaklu

The views from the top of this impressive mountain, about 12km south of Ho, are spectacular. Surrounded by nine villages, the Adaklu area is part of a community-based tourism project. At the visitor centre in the village of Helekpe at the foot of the mountain, you pay a fee of US$2 and are assigned a guide. It's a challenging two- to four-hour climb return and you need appropriate footwear and plenty of water with you. There's a basic ***guesthouse*** (rooms

US$1.70) in Helekpe or you can *camp* on the mountain. Tro-tros leave sporadically (but not on Sunday) for Helekpe (US$0.20, 30 minutes) from the motor park in Ho; another place to pick up transport is on the Adaklu road just south of the town. Return transport can be a problem, but something can usually be arranged.

Amedzofe

This mountain village is the main centre in the Avatime Hills, an area that offers breathtaking vistas, a waterfall, forests, cool climate and plenty of hiking opportunities. In Amedzofe there's a community-run visitor centre where you pay a flat fee of US$2 and can arrange hikes. Popular hikes include a 45-minute walk to Amedzofe Falls and a 30-minute walk to the summit of Mt Gemi, one of the highest mountains in the area, with stunning views. Accommodation is available in the ***government resthouse*** for about US$5 or you can arrange a ***homestay*** for about US$2.

Infrequent tro-tros head for Amedzofe (US$0.60, one hour) from the motor park station in Ho but transport of any kind is unlikely on a Sunday. If you're planning to head to Amedzofe from Hohoe, note that the route between Fume and Amedzofe (about 8km) is passable by foot only.

Kpetoe

Kpetoe, a 15-minute tro-tro ride to the southeast of Ho, near the Togo border, is a major kente weaving centre. The Ga-Adangbe people of this area claim to have introduced the art of kente weaving to the Ashanti. Two types of kente are woven: the Ashanti version and the Ewe version, which is more difficult to make.

Tafi-Atome Monkey Sanctuary

At Tafi-Atome, about 25km north of Ho, the villagers have created a sanctuary around the village to protect the sacred Mona monkeys that live in the surrounding forest. The monkeys are habituated to humans and roam around the village in the early morning and late afternoon. A superb example of ecotourism, various activities are offered, the main one being a guided tour of the sanctuary, which costs US$1 in addition to the admission fee of US$2. You can also go on a tour of the village, rent a bicycle to visit other sites in the area or stay for drumming, dancing and story-telling sessions in the evening. Basic accommodation and meals are available at the ***guesthouse*** (US$3 per person) or at the ***homestays*** (US$1.50 per person).

Tafi-Atome is about 5km west of Logba Alakpeti on the main road between Ho and Hohoe. Any tro-tro running between Ho and Hohoe can drop you at Logba Alakpeti (US$0.70), from where you can either walk or wait for transport – infrequent except on market day.

HOHOE

☎ 0935

This busy district capital makes a good base for visiting the waterfalls and hills nearby. It's also a staging point for travel across the border into Togo and north to Tamale via Bimbilla and Yendi.

The action area of Hohoe (ho-ho-**we**) is the Accra road, which becomes the road to Jasikan and Bimbilla as it heads north out of town. Along here, south to north, you'll find the motor park and market, a Ghana Commercial Bank, the post office, Ghana Telecom and several chop bars. The road to Wli and the Togo border turns off the main road at the Bank of Ghana about 1km from the motor park; there's a Barclays Bank for changing money a short distance down this road. For Internet access, try the Internet centre opposite Taste Lodge.

Places to Stay & Eat

Grand Hotel *(☎ 22053)* Singles/doubles with fan US$4/6. A good, central budget option, the Grand has neat, basic rooms set around a courtyard and clean communal bathrooms. The pleasant courtyard restaurant serves tasty food (mains US$2 to US$2.50). It's on the main street, opposite the Bank of Ghana.

Pacific Guesthouse *(☎ 22146)* Rooms US$5/5.50, with air-con US$6.50. The Pacific has good-value, clean rooms and is popular with travellers. It has a bar and meals can be arranged. It's about 750m from the motor park, signposted down a dirt road opposite.

Geduld Hotel *(☎ 22177)* Rooms with air-con US$4/9. About 1.5km from the motor park (follow the signs for the Pacific and keep going), this two-storey house has a

GHANA

pleasant, shady setting and OK rooms. It has a garden bar and restaurant.

Matvin Hotel *(☎ 22134)* Singles US$5, doubles US$7-13. On the northern outskirts of town, off the Jasikan road, this vast echoing complex has large, airy, good-value rooms and a pleasant garden bar and restaurant overlooking the river.

Taste Lodge *(☎ 22023, fax 22025)* Doubles US$10. The most upmarket hotel in town, this friendly place has five comfortable – if small – rooms opening onto a shady courtyard and a good restaurant. To get to the Taste Lodge, walk north up the main street from the main lorry station for about 500m until you get to the post office and take the turning off on the right. The Taste is just on the left, about 250m from the intersection.

At night, you'll find a selection of ***food stalls*** along the main street especially around the post office. There are also several good-value chop bars (all closed on Sunday) and lively evening drinking spots. Try the delightfully named ***Peace & Love Special Chop Bar*** on the road to the Taste Lodge, the lively ***Eagle Canteen & Communication Centre*** near the Grand Hotel, the hip ***LIPS drinking spot***, near the Pacific Guesthouse, or the loud ***Club Havana Spot*** opposite the post office.

Getting There & Away

From the well organised main lorry station, tro-tros leave regularly for Accra (US$1.70, four hours), Ho (US$1, two hours) and the Togo border at Wli (US$0.30, 40 minutes). There's a daily VanefSTC bus between Hohoe and Accra, which leaves from the smaller Tudu station in Accra and from the main street in Hohoe, just north of the post office. Heading north, tro-tros to Jasikan and Nkwanta (for Bimbilla and Tamale) leave from a stop on the Jasikan road, north of the post office. Tro-tros to Liati Wote (see Around Hohoe) leave from Fodome station in front of the post office (US$0.30).

GHANA

AROUND HOHOE

Wli (Agumatsa) Falls

About 20km east of Hohoe are these spectacular falls within the Agumatsa Wildlife Sanctuary. At the Wildlife Office in Wli (pronounced vlee) village, you pay a fee of US$4, which includes a mandatory guide. It's a scenic, undemanding 40-minute walk to the falls along a stream. The falls cascade some 40m down from a horseshoe of cliffs that are home to an estimated half a million fruit bats. You can brave the icy water and swim in the plunge pool if you want. A hike to the upper falls is a more demanding 1½-hour climb (US$3). Wli is an easy day trip from Hohoe, but if you want to stay overnight, you can ***camp*** near the falls (US$0.70) or you can stay in Wli village at one of two simple ***guesthouses*** (with bucket showers) for about US$2 to US$3 – ask at the Wildlife Office.

Regular tro-tros (US$0.30, 40 minutes) make the scenic run between Wli and Hohoe throughout the day. If you're heading for Togo, the Ghanaian border post is on the eastern side of Wli (turn left at the T-junction as you enter the village). From there, it's a 10-minute walk to the Togolese side.

Liati Wote & Mt Afadjato

This pretty village, 21km south of Hohoe, lies on the foothills of Ghana's highest mountain, Mt Afadjato (885m). Liati Wote is part of another community-based ecotourism initiative – check in at the visitor centre when you arrive to pay your fees and arrange a hike. It's a reasonably challenging two-hour climb to the summit of Mt Afadjato, which offers stupendous views of Lake Volta and the countryside below. There are also a couple of easier walks, including to Tagbo Falls, a 45-minute hike from the village through coffee and cocoa fields. Tro-tros leave for Liati Wote (US$0.30, one hour) from Fodome station in Hohoe.

KETE-KRACHI

☎ 0953

This town is one of the main ports on Lake Volta and a stop on the boat trip between Akosombo and Yeji. The original town of Kete-Krachi, once an important stop on slave trading routes, was flooded when Lake Volta was created. The ferry dock is a 15-minute ride from town. The only accommodation option is the spartan ***Simon Hotel***, about 2km from the lake, where rooms with fan cost US$5.

There are tro-tros between Kete Krachi and Tamale, Ho, Hohoe and Bimbilla. To/from Tamale, you may have to do the journey in short stages. Alternatively, there's a morning ferry between Kete-Krachi and Kwadiokrom on the west bank, from where you can get transport to Kumasi (256km).

For details about the Lake Volta ferry from Akosombo or Yeji, see Boat under Getting Around earlier in this chapter.

The Centre

KUMASI

☎ 051 • pop 1 million

Once the capital of the rich and powerful Ashanti kingdom, Kumasi is still a major cultural and economic centre. Founded in 1695, little remains of the original city which was razed by the British in 1874 during the Fourth Ashanti War. With its rich historical and cultural heritage, busy streets, permanent traffic jams and the largest market in Ghana (and possibly in West Africa), Kumasi is a vibrant and fascinating place to explore.

Orientation

Kumasi sprawls over a vast hilly area. The heart of town is Kejetia Circle, a vast traffic-clogged roundabout. On the eastern side of the circle is Kejetia Market, which spills over onto the roads around it. West of the circle is the vast Kejetia motor park, the city's main transport park. South of the circle, the parallel Guggisberg and Fuller Rds lead past the train station. The district of Adum, just south of the circle, is the modern commercial district, where you'll find the major banks and shops. The VanefSTC bus station is on the southern edge of this district, a 10-minute walk from Prempeh II Roundabout.

Information

Tourist Offices The helpful tourist office (☎ 26243) is within the National Cultural Centre complex to the west of Kejetia Circle. It's open 9am to 5pm Monday to Friday and until noon on Saturday. The friendly staff can arrange guided tours of the city and surrounding craft villages.

Money The head offices of Barclays and Standard Chartered Banks are on Prempeh II Roundabout. Both banks change travellers cheques and have ATMs. There are also plenty of forexes dotted over town for changing cash.

Post & Communications The main post office, on Stewart Ave opposite the Armed Forces Museum, is open from 8am to 5pm Monday to Friday. Poste restante shuts at 4.30pm, though. Next door is Ghana Telecom with a bank of cardphones in front of it.

Several places around town offer Internet access. In the centre of town, just off Prempeh II Roundabout, is Vic Baboo's Café, open 11am to 9pm Monday to Saturday, where access costs US$0.85 per half-hour. Other possibilities are CPC Ltd (☎ 24377), just south of 24 February Rd near Asafo Roundabout, and Spirit Cybercafe, in the ground floor of Spirit FM radio station at the southern end of Hudson Rd.

Medical Services Okomfo Anokye Teaching Hospital on Bantama Rd, out past the National Culture Centre, is Kumasi's main public hospital. There are plenty of pharmacies dotted around town.

Kejetia Market

Seen from above, the rusting tin roofs of this huge market give the appearance of a vast shanty town. But below, it's throbbing, vital and infinitely confusing. On sale within its narrow alleyways is everything from foodstuffs, second-hand shoes, clothes and plastic knick-knacks to kente cloth, glass beads, Ashanti sandals, batik and bracelets. You may also see fetish items, such as vulture heads, parrot wings and dried chameleons.

Kente cloth, made locally, is a particularly good deal here. It's usually sold in standard lengths of 12m and price varies according to the composition of the material (cloth containing a mixture of cotton, silk and rayon is more expensive than all-cotton, for example) and weave (double weave is, naturally, more expensive than single). You can get cloth made up cheaply and expertly into whatever you want by dressmakers in the market.

The best way to experience the market is just to take a deep breath, dive in through one of the many entrances and wander at random through the alleyways. If you want to be sure of finding something in particular, such as kente cloth, ask a child to show you for a small dash.

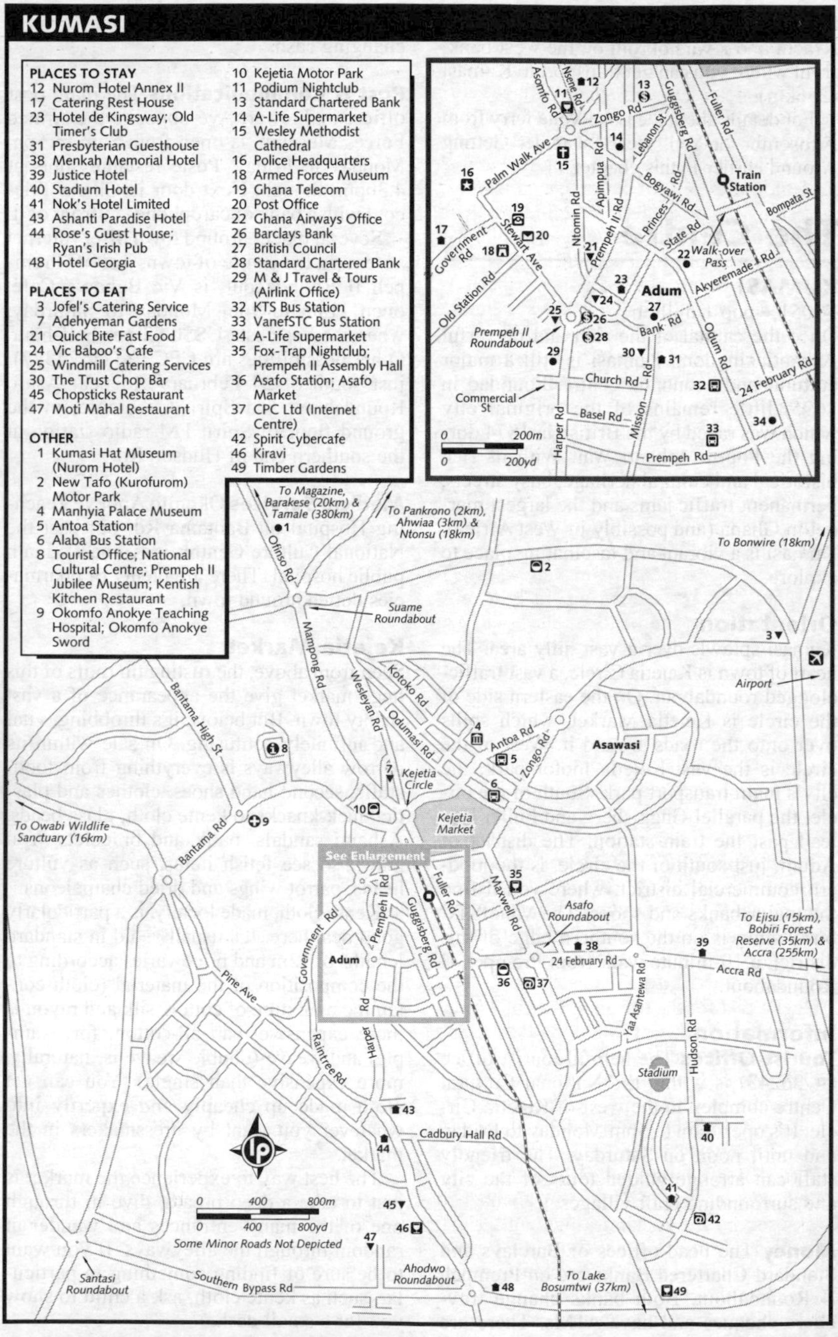
KUMASI
PLACES TO STAY
12 Nurom Hotel Annex II
17 Catering Rest House
23 Hotel de Kingsway; Old Timer's Club
31 Presbyterian Guesthouse
38 Menkah Memorial Hotel
39 Justice Hotel
40 Stadium Hotel
41 Nok's Hotel Limited
43 Ashanti Paradise Hotel
44 Rose's Guest House; Ryan's Irish Pub
48 Hotel Georgia
PLACES TO EAT
3 Jofel's Catering Service
7 Adehyeman Gardens
21 Quick Bite Fast Food
24 Vic Baboo's Cafe
25 Windmill Catering Services
30 The Trust Chop Bar
45 Chopsticks Restaurant
47 Moti Mahal Restaurant
OTHER
1 Kumasi Hat Museum (Nurom Hotel)
2 New Tafo (Kurofurom) Motor Park
4 Manhyia Palace Museum
5 Antoa Station
6 Alaba Bus Station
8 Tourist Office; National Cultural Centre; Prempeh II Jubilee Museum; Kentish Kitchen Restaurant
9 Okomfo Anokye Teaching Hospital; Okomfo Anokye Sword
10 Kejetia Motor Park
11 Podium Nightclub
13 Standard Chartered Bank
14 A-Life Supermarket
15 Wesley Methodist Cathedral
16 Police Headquarters
18 Armed Forces Museum
19 Ghana Telecom
20 Post Office
22 Ghana Airways Office
26 Barclays Bank
27 British Council
28 Standard Chartered Bank
29 M & J Travel & Tours (Airlink Office)
32 KTS Bus Station
33 VanefSTC Bus Station
34 A-Life Supermarket
35 Fox-Trap Nightclub; Prempeh II Assembly Hall
36 Asafo Station; Asafo Market
37 CPC Ltd (Internet Centre)
42 Spirit Cybercafe
46 Kiravi
49 Timber Gardens
Asomfo Rd
Nsene Rd
Zongo Rd
Guggisberg Rd
Fuller Rd
Lebanon St
Palm Walk Ave
Apimpua Rd
Train Station
Bogyawi Rd
Bompata St
Ntomin Rd
Prempeh II Rd
Princes Rd
Government Rd
Stewart Ave
State Rd
Walk-over Pass
Akyeremade Rd
Old Station Rd
Adum
Bank Rd
Prempeh II Roundabout
Odum Rd
Church Rd
24 February Rd
Commercial St
Basel Rd
Mission Rd
Harper Rd
Prempeh Rd
200m
200yd
To Magazine, Barakese (20km) & Tamale (380km)
To Pankrono (2km), Ahwiaa (3km) & Ntonsu (18km)
To Bonwire (18km)
Ofinso Rd
Suame Roundabout
Mampong Rd
Airport
Bantama High St
Wesleyan Rd
Kotoko Rd
Odumasi Rd
Antoa Rd
Zongo Rd
Asawasi
Kejetia Circle
To Owabi Wildlife Sanctuary (16km)
Bantama Rd
Kejetia Market
See Enlargement
Fuller Rd
Maxwell Rd
Asafo Roundabout
To Ejisu (15km), Bobiri Forest Reserve (35km) & Accra (255km)
Prempeh II Rd
Government Rd
Guggisberg Rd
Adum
24 February Rd
Accra Rd
Yaa Asantewa Rd
Pine Ave
Harper Rd
Raintree Rd
Stadium
Hudson Rd
Cadbury Hall Rd
800m
800yd
Some Minor Roads Not Depicted
Ahodwo Roundabout
To Lake Bosumtwi (37km)
Santasi Roundabout
Southern Bypass Rd

National Cultural Centre

This complex *(admission free; open 8am-5pm daily)* is set within spacious grounds and includes a model Ashanti village; craft workshops where you can see brassworking, woodcarving, pottery making, batik cloth dyeing and kente cloth weaving (as well as buy their products, of course); a gallery and gift shop; the regional library; and the small Prempeh II Jubilee Museum. This is also where you'll find the tourist office. The craft workshops aren't always active, especially on Sunday, and it's all rather low-key but the grounds are pleasant and shady and it's an agreeable place to spend an afternoon, perhaps having had lunch first at the restaurant in the complex. If you are looking to buy crafts, what's on offer is on the whole good quality and prices are reasonable.

Prempeh II Jubilee Museum *(admission US$0.60; open 2pm-5pm Mon, 9am-5pm Tues-Fri, 10am-4pm Sat & Sun)* may be small but it has an excellent display of artefacts relating to the Ashanti king Prempeh II that give a fascinating insight into Ashanti culture and history. These include the king's war attire, ceremonial clothing, jewellery, protective amulets, personal equipment for bathing and dining, furniture, royal insignia and some fine brass weights for weighing gold. Constructed to resemble an Ashanti chief's house, it has a courtyard in front and walls adorned with traditional carved symbols. Among the museum's intriguing photos is a rare one of the famous Golden Stool (see The Golden Stool in the Ashanti Arts & Culture special section). The museum also contains the fake golden stool handed over to the British in 1900.

Manhyia Palace Museum

To get a feel for the life and times of a modern Ashanti ruler, visit Manhyia Palace and its museum *(adult/student US$2.25/1; open 9am-noon & 1pm-5pm daily)* off Antoa Rd, up the hill north from Kejetia Circle. The palace was built by the British in 1925 to receive Prempeh I when he returned from a quarter of a century of exile in the Seychelles to resume residence in Kumasi. It was used by the Ashanti kings until 1974. On display is the original furniture, including Ashantiland's first TV, and various artefacts from the royals, including china, gold and silver ornaments, medals awarded to Prempeh II by various overseas governments, and evocative photos of the time. More striking are the unnervingly lifelike, life-size wax models of the two kings and their mothers and of the most redoubtable queen mother, Yaa Asantewaa, who led the 1900 revolt against the British and who died in exile in the Seychelles.

Inquire here or at the tourist office if you'd like an appointment with the present *asantehene* (king), Otumfuo Opoku Ware II. If you're lucky enough to get an audience, etiquette demands presentation of a bottle or two of schnapps when meeting the royals. This curious custom is a legacy from the days when the Dutch traded with the Ashantis and would present the chiefs with schnapps as a token of good will. It's very important to take the right number of bottles – too few and you'll get a cool reception.

Okomfo Anokye Sword

The Okomfo Anokye Teaching Hospital on Bantama Rd is the unlikely setting for this small museum *(admission US$0.30; open 9am-5pm Mon-Fri, 9am-noon Sat)* housing the Okomfo Anokye Sword, an important Ashanti monument. The sword has been in the ground for three centuries and has never been pulled out. According to Ashanti legend, it marks the spot where the Golden Stool descended from the sky to indicate where the Ashanti people should settle. The sword is a symbol of the unity and strength of the Ashanti people and if anyone ever pulls it out, their kingdom will collapse. To find the museum, go through the main hospital gate, walk past the main entrance and then through into a courtyard, behind Block C (you still with us?).

Armed Forces Museum

Fort St George and its museum *(admission US$1.50; open 8am-5pm Tues-Sat)* on Stewart Ave merit a visit. The fort was originally constructed by the Ashanti in 1820. In 1873, during the Fourth Ashanti War, it was razed by the British, who built the present structure in 1896. The most interesting section relates to the British-Ashanti war of 1900, when the Ashanti, led by their queen mother, Yaa Asantewaa, temporarily besieged the fort, starving the British residents. The museum's major part is an extraordinary and diverse collection of booty amassed by the

West Africa Frontier Force, forerunner of today's Ghanaian army, with items looted from the Germans in Togo during WWI and, in WWII, from the Italians in Eritrea and Ethiopia and from the Japanese in Burma.

Kumasi Hat Museum

The top floor of the Nurom Hotel on Ofinso Rd is a monument to one man's obsession with hats. The owner, Chief Nana Kofi Gyemfi II, has assembled an amazing personal collection of more than 2000 hats from all over the world. Beginning with his first headgear, back in 1928, he now has an astounding, if dusty, collection of fedoras, sombreros, boaters, bowlers and much more. The hotel is in the Suame district on the northern outskirts of town. To get there, take any tro-tro heading north from Kejetia Circle to Suame Roundabout or catch a taxi.

Magazine Area

Kumasi is made up of a collection of districts, each of which used to perform a specific role for the Ashanti king. The Magazine area in Suame district was originally where artillery was made; now, however, it's a vast used-car workshop where rusty old wrecks are miraculously brought back to life. Piles and piles of rusting engine parts line the sides of the roads and the air is filled with the chinking sound of metal hitting metal. It's an amazing sight, worth a look as you pass through on your way north.

GHANA

Special Events

The 42-day cycle of the Ashanti religious calendar is marked by Adae festivals, a public ceremony involving the asantehene. The tourist office has a list of exact dates. The Odwira festival is an important annual celebration. For more details, see the Ashanti Arts & Culture special section.

Places to Stay – Budget

Unless we've indicated otherwise, all rooms in this category have fans.

Presbyterian Guesthouse *(☎ 23879, Mission Rd)* Doubles US$7. This two-storey colonial-style guesthouse, all deep wooden balconies and high ceilings, has long been the budget travellers' favourite. For atmosphere and a location, close to the city centre, it's hard to beat. The huge rooms are basic but quiet and you get use of a kitchen. On the downside, there is just one shower and the running water is very sporadic. It's possible to camp here if the rooms are full.

Nurom Hotel Annex II *(☎ 32324, Nsene Rd)* Singles/doubles US$3/4.50. This hotel is a reasonable central option, although rooms can be noisy at times.

Menkah Memorial Hotel *(☎ 26432, 24 February Rd)* Doubles without/with bathroom US$4/5. This hotel is better than the outside suggests but get a room at the back for a peaceful night.

Justice Hotel *(☎ 22525, Accra Rd)* Singles/ doubles with fan & shared bathroom US$5/6.50, doubles with bathroom US$9.50, rooms with air-con US$14/15. This friendly place is good value, with comfortable rooms. It has a cool and shady courtyard, a restaurant and a bar. Regular shared taxis run along Accra Rd into the centre.

Hotel de Kingsway *(☎ 26228)* Singles with shared bathroom US$7, doubles with bathroom US$9-14. This hotel, in a side street off the Prempeh II Roundabout end of Prempeh II Rd, is an old colonial place with plenty of charm. It's a popular central option and the clean rooms are a good size.

Ashanti Paradise Hotel *(☎ 24222)* Doubles with fan/air-con US$11.50/14. This hotel has an attractive garden setting away from traffic noise and good rooms. It's down a small lane off Harper Rd just north of Cadbury Hall Rd. Meals are available with advance notice.

Places to Stay – Mid-Range & Top End

All hotels in this category have air-con and most are outside the city centre.

Stadium Hotel *(☎ 23647, 23730, fax 26374, 8th St)* Singles/doubles US$17/21. This hotel is excellent value, with comfortable modern rooms and a good restaurant and bar. It's near the stadium in the quiet residential area of Asukwa.

Catering Rest House *(☎ 26506, Government Rd)* Doubles US$16-32. This delightful place has an old block that is a bit dowdy but full of character and superb new bungalow-style rooms. Also on site is an excellent restaurant and an air-con bar.

Nok's Hotel Limited *(☎ 24438, fax 24162)* Doubles US$26-28. On a side street off the southern end of Hudson Rd, set in quiet leafy surroundings, this interesting place has comfortable rooms with 1970s decor.

Rose's Guest House *(☎ 24072, ☎/fax 23500, Harper Rd)* Rooms US$29. This small, friendly hotel with a garden setting has pleasant rooms and has long been a popular option in this price range. It now has a Ryan's Irish Pub attached to it, a younger sibling of the Irish theme pub in Accra, which is either an attraction or a deterrent, depending on your point of view.

Hotel Georgia *(☎ 24154, fax 24299)* Singles/doubles US$70/80. The multistorey Georgia, just east of Ahodwo Roundabout, is rather run-down and a bit tacky, but the rooms are fine and it has a nice swimming pool and a terrace restaurant.

Places to Eat

For ***food stalls***, good areas are near the train station, around Kejetia Circle and on the Hudson Rd side of the stadium. There are several small chop bars along Prempeh II Rd, including the aptly named ***Quick Bite Fast Food***.

The Trust Chop Bar *(Mission Rd)* Mains US$1. This tiny place opens early and is handy for breakfast or a basic lunch if you're staying at the Presbyterian Guesthouse opposite.

Windmill Catering Services Mains US$1.50-2. On the eastern side of Prempeh II Roundabout, in a courtyard off the main road, Windmill is both a restaurant and a bakery. It serves tasty meals at lunch time and is a possible breakfast option if you're staying at the Presby.

Kentish Kitchen Restaurant Mains US$2-3. Open breakfast-6pm. This open-air restaurant within the National Cultural Centre serves a variety of Ghanaian dishes, as well as snacks such as kebabs and meat pies. It's a pleasant spot to just sit and sip a drink between bouts of exploring the centre.

Jofel's Catering Services Mains US$3-3.50. Out on the airport roundabout, Jofel's is a large, two-storey eatery with a terrace bar. It does good Ghanaian and Western food.

Adehyeman Gardens *(Wesleyan Rd)* Mains US$2-3. Overlooking Kejetia Circle and the motor park, this place serves tasty Ghanaian and Chinese cuisine. The fruit bats that fill the trees just to the north of Kejetia Market sometimes take up residence here, often provide guests with a bit of evening entertainment.

Vic Baboo's Cafe *(Prempeh II Rd)* Mains US$4-6. This cheerful café just down from Prempeh II roundabout is a mecca for travellers. It offers a wonderfully varied menu, including sandwiches, pizza, fast food and Indian, with several veg options. It also has ice cream, cashew nuts and popcorn. Unfortunately for early breakfasters, it doesn't open until 11am.

Chopsticks Restaurant *(☎ 23221, Harper Rd)* Mains US$5-7. One of the city's top restaurants, this place serves succulent Chinese food, for which it is deservedly popular. In a fine example of multiculturalism, there's now a pizzeria as well as the Chinese restaurant.

Ryan's Irish Pub *(Harper Rd)* Mains US$5-7. If it's liver and onions you're after, then this is the place for you.

Moti Mahal Restaurant Mains US$3-4. This place serves wonderful Indian cuisine in a pleasant setting. It's off the Southern Bypass Rd – most taxi drivers know where it is.

Self-caterers can find basic provisions at the many food shops along Prempeh II Rd. The best supermarket is the ***A-Life*** chain, which has three stores in town, including a branch on Prempeh II Rd and a large branch (with a café outside) on Guggisberg Rd.

Entertainment

For drinking spots, you've plenty of choice. Popular places include ***Adehyeman Gardens*** and ***Jofel's Catering Services*** (see Places to Eat earlier), both of which have live music on Saturday evenings; ***Timber Gardens***, at the junction of Lake Rd and Southern Bypass Rd, which is a lively outdoor spot for a drink or a bite to eat; ***Ryan's Irish Pub***, which is something of an expat haunt; ***Kentish Kitchen*** at the National Culture Centre (for day-time drinking only); and the bar at ***Hotel de Kingsway***.

For highlife music, it's got to be the ***Old-Timers Club*** on a Saturday evening at the Kingsway. It attracts crowds, many in traditional dress. The dancing starts early, around 6pm, and lasts until 2am.

Among the clubs, enduring favourites include the ***Podium Nightclub***, on Nsene Rd in the centre, which serves ice cream and fast food during the day and mutates into a nightclub on Wednesday to Saturday evenings;

the ***Fox-Trap Nightclub***, next to Prempeh Assembly Hall on Maxwell Rd, which has a large dance floor; and the classy ***Kiravi*** on Harper Rd near Chopsticks. Most are open from Thursday to Sunday only.

Getting There & Away

Air Kumasi airport is on the northeastern outskirts of town, about 6km from the centre. Airlink has flights between Kumasi and Accra three times a week for US$28 one way. There are northbound flights to Tamale (US$42), also three times a week. For information and reservations, go to the airport or to M&J Travel & Tours (☎ 29337) in SSNIT House on Harper Rd.

Bus & Tro-Tro Kumasi's transport system is confusing to work out; if in doubt, hop in a taxi and tell the driver where you're aiming for – taxi drivers generally know which motor park to take you to.

The huge Kejetia motor park is the city's main transport hub, from where you can get tro-tros to most regional destinations as well as non-VanefSTC buses to Accra and other points south. At the time of writing, Kejetia was undergoing major renovations, resulting in head-spinning chaos in this area. However, it should be finished by the time you read this, and the new park looks to be well organised, with destinations and timetables clearly signposted. In addition, transport for Accra (again), Sunyani, Cape Coast, Takoradi and local destinations such as Lake Bosumtwi leave from Asafo station east of Asafo Roundabout.

Large buses to Tamale, Bolgatanga, Bawku and Ouagadougou (Burkina Faso) leave from New Tafo (Kurofurom) station in Dichemso, about 2km north of Kejetia market. Smaller buses to Tamale (again) and destinations in the Upper West region leave from Alaba bus station off Zongo Rd, on the northwestern side of the market. The VanefSTC bus station (☎ 24285 for information) is on Prempeh Rd. Buses to Accra (US$3, four hours) leave regularly between 6am and 6pm. There are two air-con express services (US$3.40) at 8am and 1pm. VanefSTC buses also leave daily for Cape Coast (US$2, five hours) and Takoradi (US$2.60, five hours), and three times a week to Tamale (US$3.40, eight hours). There are infrequent services to Bolgatanga and Wa. Kingdom Transport Services (KTS), on Odum Rd near the VanefSTC bus station, has regular services to Accra and less frequent services to Bolgatanga and Bawku. Vehicles for Bonwire and Yeji leave from Antoa station, on Antoa Rd near the Manhyia Palace.

Train For details of the train service to Takoradi and Accra, see Train under Getting Around earlier in this chapter.

Getting Around

Most taxi lines start at Kejetia motor park and across the street at the intersection of Prempeh II and Guggisberg Rds. From Ntomin Rd, shared taxis head south along Harper Rd, serving the areas of town beyond Ahodwo Roundabout. The standard fare is about US$0.20. A 'dropping' taxi normally costs about US$1 to US$2 within town. Taxis are often reluctant to cross Kejetia Circle (because the traffic is so bad) so consider breaking a long journey into shorter stages.

AROUND KUMASI

Craft Villages

There are several villages specialising in traditional crafts within a 30-minute drive of Kumasi. They're very much on the tourist trail, so be prepared for a fair amount of hassle. If you want to try your hand at some of the crafts, the tourist office in Kumasi can arrange workshops.

There are two villages on the outskirts of Kumasi, on the Mampong road beyond Suame Roundabout. **Pankrono** is a major pottery centre. One kilometre further is **Ahwiaa**, known for its woodcarving. **Ntonso**, 15km further, is the centre of adinkra cloth printing. **Bonwire**, 18km northeast of Kumasi, is the most famous of several nearby villages that specialise in weaving kente cloth (listen out for the clack-clack of weavers as you drive through). At the visitor centre here weavers demonstrate their craft and examples of their work are on sale.

Other less-visited kente villages include Wonoo and Adanwomase, near Bonwire, and, further north, Bepoase. Several villages northwest of Kumasi on the Barekese road specialise in bead-making, including Asuofia and Pasoro.

The easiest way to visit these villages is probably to hire a private taxi (about US$20 for a half-day) or to arrange a tour through the tourist office. Alternatively, you can get a tro-tro from Kejetia motor park for the villages on the Mampong road or from Antoa station for Bonwire (US$0.25).

Owabi Wildlife Sanctuary

This small sanctuary *(admission US$0.70; open 9am-5pm daily)* 16km northwest of Kumasi, just off the Sunyani road, is a designated Ramsar site and protects an area of forest around the Owabi reservoir. It's an important refuge for birds and mammals such as colobus and Mona monkeys in the forest. You have to be accompanied by a guide, which you can arrange at the entrance gate. Take a tro-tro from Kejetia motor park to Akropong on the Sunyani road, from where it's a 3km walk. You may be able to hitch a ride.

Ejisu

The small junction town of Ejisu, about 20km east of Kumasi on the Accra road, is best known for being the home of Yaa Asantewaa, queen mother and chief of Ejisu, who resisted the British and was responsible for preventing the revered Golden Stool falling into their hands. The recently opened **Nana Yaa Asantewaa Museum** *(admission US$0.70; open 9am-5pm daily)* is well worth a visit. Built in the form of a traditional queen mother's palace, it houses a fascinating display of artefacts from Yaa Asantewaa's life. Also recommended is a visit to the **shrine** *(admission US$0.70; open 9am-5pm daily)* at nearby Besease. Recently restored with help from Unesco, this was the shrine Yaa Asantewaa consulted before launching her attack against the British. Inside is an excellent display on traditional Ashanti shrines.

Regular tro-tros to Ejisu (US$0.30, 30 minutes) leave from Asafo motor park in Kumasi. The museum is about 1.5km from the motor park in Ejisu and Besease is about 2km further along the Accra road. You can either walk or get a dropping taxi.

Lake Bosumtwi

For a break from the bustle and choking pollution of Kumasi, take a trip to tranquil Lake Bosumtwi, 38km southeast of Kumasi. A crater lake, it's ringed by lush green hills in which you can hike, visiting some of the 20 or so small villages around its perimeter. The lake is a popular weekend venue for Kumasi residents, who come here to relax, swim (the water is said to be bilharzia free), fish and take boat trips. You can cycle around the lake's 30km circumference. One downside is the high level of hassle in Abonu, the lakeside village.

Not only is Bosumtwi the country's largest and deepest natural lake (86m deep in the centre), it's also sacred. The Ashanti believe that their souls come here after death to bid farewell to their god Twi. One interesting taboo is any form of dugout canoe, which is believed to alienate the lake spirit. Instead the fishermen head out on specially carved wooden planks, which they paddle either with their palms or with calabashes cupped in their hands.

Places to Stay & Eat It's possible to stay in basic ***rooms*** in Abonu – you'll be assailed by offers as soon as you step out of your vehicle. If you have a tent, ***camping*** beside the lake is possible providing you ask permission from the local chief.

Bagda Guesthouse *(Reservations ☎ 20 146 or call the tourist office in Kumasi ☎ 26 243)* Rooms US$7. Perched on the edge of the hill, just before the (hair-raising) descent to the lake is this guesthouse and restaurant, which has fabulous views over the lake below. Even if you don't stay here, it's worth stopping for a drink and to admire the views.

Lake Bosomtwe Paradise Resort Singles/doubles with air-con US$32/39. This is a beautiful new resort on the lake's edge about 2km east of Abonu and it's well-signposted as you enter the village. The modern, well-equipped rooms all have lake views. On the lake front is a pleasant restaurant and bar area.

Getting There & Away Occasional tro-tros run direct to Abonu (US$0.70) from Asafo motor park in Kumasi; alternatively, take a tro-tro to Kuntanase and a passenger taxi from there.

Bobiri Forest Reserve

This reserve protects a parcel of virgin, unlogged forest about 35km east of Kumasi. The main goal for visitors is **Bobiri Butterfly Sanctuary** *(admission US$0.70)*, home to more than 300 species of butterfly and an arboretum. Even if you don't see any butterflies, this is a serene and beautiful place in which to rest up for a while. Guided walks of varying length are available or you can hike unaccompanied on some of the trails. The ***guesthouse*** at the sanctuary is a bit run-down but the rooms with fan and bathroom (US$6/6.50) are very comfortable. Simple meals are available.

From Kumasi or Ejisu, take any vehicle going to Konongo or further south, and ask to be dropped at Kubease (about US$0.50), from where Bobiri is a pleasant 3km walk.

BOABENG-FIEMA MONKEY SANCTUARY

This sanctuary *(admission US$3)*, a superb example of community-based conservation, is between the twin villages of Fiema and Boabeng, 165km north of Kumasi. The villagers have traditionally venerated and protected the black-and-white colobus and Mona monkeys, which live in the surrounding forest. The animals are accustomed to humans and roam the streets, looking for food from the villagers.

As well as viewing the monkeys, you can go on guided walks through the forest. There's a simple ***guesthouse*** (doubles US$5) in Fiema; camping is also possible here.

From Kumasi, take a tro-tro to Techiman from Alaba station. From there, take a shared taxi to Nkoranza, 25km east. There are regular passenger taxis from Nkoranza to Fiema, about 20km away. The whole journey shouldn't cost more than about US$2.

YEJI

One of the main port towns on Lake Volta and the last stop for the Lake Volta ferry, Yeji is 216km northeast of Kumasi on the old Tamale road. There's nothing to keep you here but if you have to stay overnight, you can get basic ***accommodation*** in town for about US$4.

Tro-tros run between Yeji and Antoa station in Kumasi (US$1.50, four hours) For Tamale, take the twice-daily ferry (US$0.70, 45 minutes) across to Makongo on the east bank. Tro-tros run between Makongo and Tamale (US$1.75, five hours).

For details of the ferry service to Akosombo, see Boat under Getting Around earlier in this chapter.

The North

TAMALE

☎ 071

Tamale, 380km north of Kumasi, is the capital of the Northern Region. It's a hot, busy and incredibly dusty place. It doesn't have much in the way of tourist sights but it's a major transport hub and most travellers end up stopping over here. The heart of town is the central market and motor park, marked by the tall radio antenna near the VanefSTC bus station.

The tourist office (☎ 24835), open 9am to 5pm Monday to Friday, is about 1.5km east of the centre, in the administration buildings. You can change money at Barclays Bank on Salaga Rd near the Giddipass Restaurant or at Standard Chartered Bank on Salaga Rd opposite the market. Both banks have ATMs. For Internet access, the small 2nd Sight Ent Internet centre next to Standard Chartered Bank is the best central option, although the connection is painfully slow. Access will set you back US$0.03 per minute.

If you've got time on your hands, the compact central **market** is fascinating to wander around and a good place to look for the local striped cloth, usually made up into men's smocks. The **National Cultural Centre**, off Salaga Rd, has an echoing auditorium where music and dance performances are occasionally put on; there are a few craft shops around the back that might be worth a quick look.

The Dagomba **Fire Festival** takes place in July. According to legend a chief lost his son and was overjoyed when he found him asleep under a tree. Angry that the tree had hidden his son, he punished it by having it burnt. On the night of the festival young men rush about with blazing torches.

Places to Stay – Budget

Al Hassan Hotel *(☎ 23638)* Singles/doubles with fan US$3/4. The Al Hassan Hotel's convenient central location makes it a firm favourite with many travellers even though rooms are furnace-like, noisy and none too clean. On the plus side, it has a surprisingly good restaurant that serves great breakfasts.

Marcos Hotel Rooms US$2.50/3.50. This friendly hotel, signposted off Bolgatanga Rd about 1.5km north of the town

GHANA

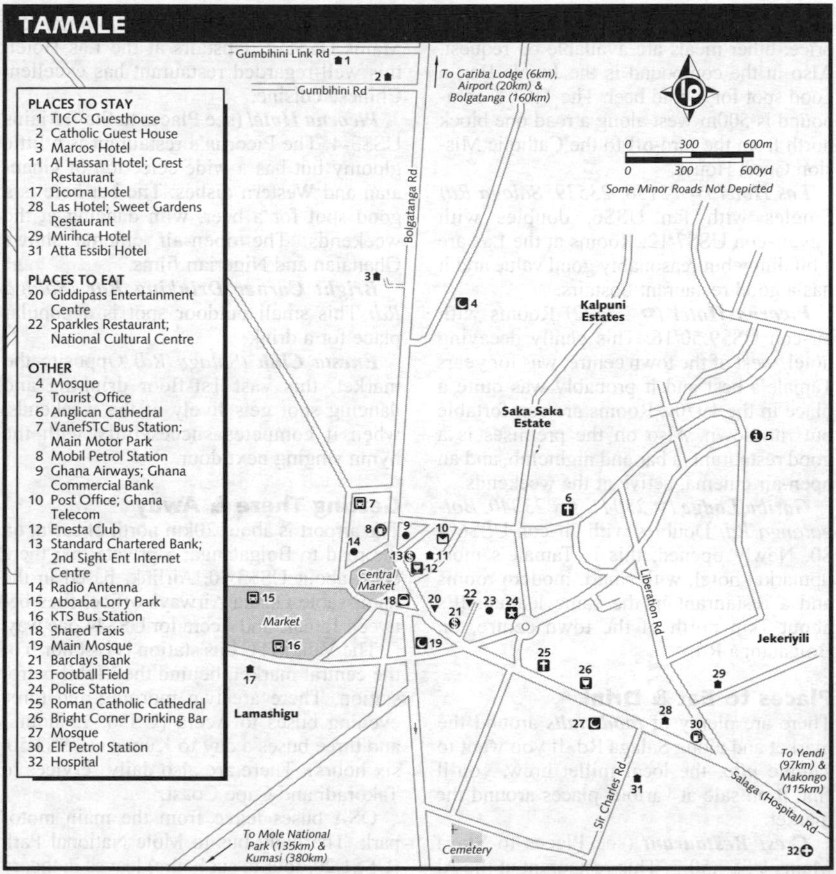
TAMALE
PLACES TO STAY
1 TICCS Guesthouse
2 Catholic Guest House
3 Marcos Hotel
11 Al Hassan Hotel; Crest Restaurant
17 Picorna Hotel
28 Las Hotel; Sweet Gardens Restaurant
29 Mirihca Hotel
31 Atta Essibi Hotel
PLACES TO EAT
20 Giddipass Entertainment Centre
22 Sparkles Restaurant; National Cultural Centre
OTHER
4 Mosque
5 Tourist Office
6 Anglican Cathedral
7 VanefSTC Bus Station; Main Motor Park
8 Mobil Petrol Station
9 Ghana Airways; Ghana Commercial Bank
10 Post Office; Ghana Telecom
12 Enesta Club
13 Standard Chartered Bank; 2nd Sight Ent Internet Centre
14 Radio Antenna
15 Aboaba Lorry Park
16 KTS Bus Station
18 Shared Taxis
19 Main Mosque
21 Barclays Bank
23 Football Field
24 Police Station
25 Roman Catholic Cathedral
26 Bright Corner Drinking Bar
27 Mosque
30 Elf Petrol Station
32 Hospital
Gumbihini Link Rd
Gumbihini Rd
To Gariba Lodge (6km), Airport (20km) & Bolgatanga (160km)
0 300 600m
0 300 600yd
Some Minor Roads Not Depicted
Bolgatanga Rd
Kalpuni Estates
Saka-Saka Estate
Liberation Rd
Central Market
Market
Jekeriyili
Lamashigu
Sir Charles Rd
Salaga (Hospital) Rd
To Yendi (97km) & Makongo (115km)
Cemetery
To Mole National Park (135km) & Kumasi (380km)

centre, has simple, clean rooms with shared bathroom. Meals can be arranged with advance notice.

Atta Essibi Hotel *(☎ 22569, Sir Charles Rd)* Singles US$2, doubles without/with bathroom US$3/5. About 150m down a road leading off Salaga Rd opposite the Las Hotel, is the neat Atta Essibi, run by the exceptionally friendly Sister Mary.

Mirihca Hotel *(☎ 22935, Off Liberation Rd)* Singles/doubles with fan US$5.50/8, doubles with air-con US$9.50. The best option in this price range, the Mirihca has cool, quiet rooms around a shady courtyard. It also has a restaurant and a pleasant outdoor bar area.

Catholic Guest House *(☎ 22265, Gumbihini Rd)* Rooms with fan US$5/6.50, doubles with air-con US$11. Off Bolgatanga Rd, about 2.5km north of the centre, is this popular guesthouse set in a leafy compound. The air-con rooms are particularly good value. Breakfast is served at 7.30pm sharp; other meals are available on request. It has a lovely garden bar area. Internet access is available within the complex.

Places to Stay – Mid-Range & Top End

All rooms in this category come with private bathroom.

TICCS Guesthouse *(☎ 22914, fax 22836, ⓔ TICCS@africaonline.com.gh, Gumbihini Link Rd)* Singles with fan/air-con US$7/10, doubles with air-con US$14. Run by a Catholic institution, this place has good-value rooms. Breakfast is included in the room price; other meals are available on request. Also in the compound is the Jungle Bar, a good spot for a cold beer. The TICCS compound is 500m west along a road one block north from the turn-off to the Catholic Mission Guest House.

Las Hotel *(☎ 22158, 23539, Salaga Rd)* Singles with fan US$6, doubles with fan/air-con US$7/12. Rooms at the Las are a bit dingy but reasonably good value and it has a good restaurant upstairs.

Picorna Hotel *(☎ 22672)* Rooms with air-con US$9.50/16. This gently decaying hotel, west of the town centre, was for years Tamale's best and it probably was quite a place in the 1970s. Rooms are comfortable but run-down. Also on the premises is a good restaurant, a bar and nightclub, and an open-air cinema, active at the weekends.

Gariba Lodge *(☎ 23041, fax 23040, Bolgatanga Rd)* Doubles with air-con US$60-80. Newly opened, this is Tamale's most upmarket hotel, with smart, modern rooms and a restaurant in the same league. It's about 7km north of the town centre, on Bolgatanga Rd.

Places to Eat & Drink

There are plenty of ***food stalls*** around the market and along Salaga Rd. If you want to sample *pito*, the local millet brew, you'll find it on sale at various places around the market.

Crest Restaurant (see Places to Stay) Mains US$2.50-3. This restaurant at the Al Hassan Hotel doesn't have much atmosphere but it does have tasty Ghanaian and Western food, as well as an excellent breakfast menu that includes fresh orange juice.

Sparkles Restaurant Mains US$2.50-3.50. Sparkles, in the National Cultural Centre compound has a variety of Ghanaian and Chinese dishes and is a pleasant spot away from the hustle and bustle of the centre.

Giddipass Entertainment Centre *(Salaga Rd)* Mains US$2.50-3.50. The Giddipass (can you resist such a name?) is enormously popular with expats, travellers and locals. The restaurant offers a reasonable selection of Ghanaian and Chinese food, but you'll wait a long time for it to arrive. The rooftop terrace, which is open to the skies, makes a wonderful spot for a late-afternoon or evening beer.

Sweet Gardens Restaurant *(Salaga Rd)* Mains US$5-7. Upstairs at the Las Hotel, this well-regarded restaurant has excellent Chinese cuisine.

Picorna Hotel (see Places to Stay) Mains US$3-4. The Picorna's restaurant is a little gloomy but has a wide selection of Ghanaian and Western dishes. The bar here is a good spot for a beer, with dancing at the weekends. The open-air cinema shows Ghanaian and Nigerian films.

Bright Corner Drinking Bar *(Salaga Rd)* This small outdoor spot is a popular place for a drink.

Enesta Club *(Salaga Rd)* Opposite the market, this vast 1st-floor drinking and dancing spot gets lively at the weekends, when it competes successfully with the hymn singing next door.

Getting There & Away

The airport is about 20km north of town, on the road to Bolgatanga; a private taxi there costs about US$3.50. Airlink, based in the unmissable Ghana Airways office, flies between Tamale and Accra for US$44 one way.

The VanefSTC bus station is just north of the central market, behind the Mobil petrol station. There are two morning and three evening buses to Accra (US$6, 12 hours) and three buses a day to Kumasi (US$3.50, six hours). There are also daily services to Takoradi and Cape Coast.

OSA buses leave from the main motor park. The daily bus to Mole National Park (US$1.20, four to six hours) leaves in theory at 2.30pm but in practice a lot later. Get to the bus station well before its scheduled departure time to be sure of a seat. There's also a daily service to Wa (US$3, eight hours), leaving at 5.30am. The KTS bus station is opposite the Picorna Hotel; KTS has services to Accra, Kumasi, Sunyani and Takoradi.

Regular tro-tros leave the motor park throughout the day heading to Bolgatanga (US$2.50, two hours). For details of services to the Volta Region via Yendi and Bimbilla, see the Tamale to Hohoe section.

TAMALE TO HOHOE

The route between Tamale and the Volta Region via Yendi and Bimbilla is rough and there are few facilities for travellers but it offers a rewarding off-the-beaten-track experience and some magnificent scenery.

This route can be done in either direction and takes a minimum of two days but if you've got time, it's worth breaking the journey up. Transport is generally infrequent so be prepared for long waits. Apart from a short tarred section just outside Tamale and again before Hohoe, the road is dirt and very bumpy.

Yendi

Yendi, 97km east of Tamale, is the home of the paramount Dagomba chief, the Ya-Na, who has 22 wives distinguished by their shaven heads. It's a dusty small town notable for its palace, an interesting fusion of Moorish and Sahelian styles. Yendi, like Tamale, is a good place to see the Dagomba Fire Festival.

If you want to break your journey here, you may be able to stay at the ***Norrip compound*** but check with Norrip in Tamale (☎ 071-23901) before you leave. ***Street food*** is available around the motor park and petrol station in Yendi.

Tro-tros to Yendi (US$0.70, two hours) leave from the main motor park in Tamale; at least one tro-tro heads daily from Yendi to Bimbilla (US$0.70, two hours).

Bimbilla

This flat, dusty district capital is about 100km from Yendi and a convenient place to break your journey. Like Yendi, it has an interesting palace, home to Bimbilla's chief. Just off the main drag, clearly signposted, is the ***Work & Happiness Guesthouse***, where basic rooms with shared bathrooms (bucket shower) cost US$3. Meals can be prepared for you at the ***Work & Happiness Bar*** on the main road. The main lorry station is on the southern edge of town. From here, there's a daily bus each to Tamale via Yendi (US$1.50, four hours) and Accra via Hohoe (US$3 to Hohoe, seven hours), although transport can be scarce on Monday. Tro-tros to Accra leave at around 11am but get there a little after 6.30am to be sure of a seat. **Nkwanta**, a pretty little village with a scenic mountain backdrop, about halfway between Bimbilla and Hohoe is another possibility for breaking your journey.

LARABANGA

Apart from being the turn-off to Mole National Park, Larabanga is known for its picturesque whitewashed mud-and-pole mosque, the oldest of its kind in Ghana, said to have been founded in the 15th century. The mosque is impressive, although you can't go inside. Photography is allowed. At the information post opposite it, you can register for a guided tour of the mosque (US$0.70) and the village's other sight, the Mystic Stone. In addition to this fee, you have to give a donation (about US$0.70) to the imam. In the village you'll see some fine examples of the mud-walled domestic compounds decorated with geometric two-tone patterns that are a feature of northern Ghana.

On the eastern outskirts of the village a replica of the mosque houses a tourist office, part of a community-based project set up by a pair of villagers, the Salia brothers, to help the village benefit from tourism to nearby Mole. You can rent bicycles from the tourist office for the 6km ride to the park, as well as binoculars and bird-identification kits. The Salia brothers also run a small ***guesthouse***, where simple rooms cost US$1.40. Meals are available on request. A new guesthouse is under construction on the road to Mole, which may be up and running by the time you visit.

There isn't a lot of traffic through Larabanga. To Tamale, there's the daily bus from Mole and a daily bus from Wa, both of which pass through town early in the morning; heading east, there are two daily buses to Bole, in the early afternoon and a daily bus to Wa at around 9.30am. Tro-tros from the junction town of Sawla on the Kumasi to Wa road occasionally pass through on the way to Tamale. To get to Mole, you can walk (not advisable in the heat of the day), hire a bicycle or try to hitch (you'll be in for a long wait).

MOLE NATIONAL PARK

☎ 0717

This national park *(adults/children/students US$2/0.70/0.40, camera fee US$0.20)* is Ghana's largest at 4840 sq km and the best for seeing wildlife. It's also relatively easily accessed by public transport and has motel accommodation. Established in 1958, it was formally recognised as a national park in 1971. It consists for the most part of flat savanna, with gallery forests along the rivers and streams. There's one main escarpment, on which the motel and park headquarters are situated. The park protects some 90 mammal species and you've a good chance of seeing elephants, water bucks, wart hogs, antelopes and olive baboons. More than 300 bird species have been recorded here. The best time for seeing wildlife is during the harmattan season from January to March, but it's worth a visit any time of the year, even if it's just to admire the green landscape during the rains (July to September).

The park entrance gate is about 4km north of the turn-off in Larabanga. The park headquarters and the motel are a further 2km into the park. Guided walks are offered twice daily, at 6.30am and 3.30pm and cost US$0.70 per person for one hour (the walks usually last two hours). The walks are excellent value – the guides are informed and you'll see plenty of wildlife at close quarters, although the electricity generator by the main water hole spoils the ambience somewhat. You are not permitted to walk (or drive) in the park unless you're accompanied by an armed ranger. You are, however, allowed to walk unaccompanied along the road back to Larabanga – perhaps potential predators ignore sweat-drenched backpackers. Day visitors can swim in the motel's pool for US$1.40.

Places to Stay & Eat

Mole Motel (☎ 22045) Camping own/rented tent US$1.50/3 per person, doubles US$16, chalets US$22. This is the only place to stay within the park; book ahead as it gets very busy in the dry season. Perched on the edge of a low escarpment overlooking a water hole where animals gather, with baboons socialising in the trees outside your window, it has a superb setting. This just about compensates for the run-down rooms, lacklustre service, lack of running water and limited electricity supply. The camp site, however, has a view to die for and is good value. Alternatively, you can stay in Larabanga and cycle into the park for the day.

If you're hungry, you can either chance the glacier-like service at the motel restaurant (meals around US$3 to US$4) or bring your own provisions.

Getting There & Away

The reserve is 135km west of Tamale, off the dirt road that connects Fufulso on the Kumasi to Tamale road with Sawla on the Kumasi to Wa road. The turn-off to the park is in Larabanga, 15km west of Damongo, a busy transport and market centre.

A daily OSA bus runs from Tamale (US$1.20, four to six hours), leaving some time after 2.30pm, once it's packed to the gunwales, and arriving at the park motel about 7pm. The same bus returns to Tamale the next day, leaving the park at 5.30am. When we were there, the OSA bus had broken down and wasn't running, which seemed to be a fairly regular occurrence. The alternative is to take any bus from Tamale heading to Bole or Wa and get off at Larabanga, then walk, cycle or try to hitch (very difficult). Leaving Mole, your options are to take the OSA bus from the motel to Tamale or to make your way to Larabanga, from where there is infrequent transport in either direction.

WA

☎ 0756

Capital of Upper West Region, Wa is tucked away in the far northwestern corner of the country near the border with Burkina Faso and is very much off the beaten track. If you have time, it's well worth a visit to experience a very different part of Ghana. It's also the departure point for visits to the hippo sanctuary at Wechiau.

Wa's main drag extends west from the roundabout near the VanefSTC bus station for 1km or so to the motor park and market. The tourist office (☎ 22431) is in the Admin Block near the fire station at the roundabout. On the main drag, near the roundabout, is the post office and Ghana Telecom. Further down, on the same side, is the Ghana Commercial Bank.

The palace of the Wa Na (as the chief is called) is Wa's best-known attraction. Built in the traditional Sahelian mud-and-pole style, it's a magnificent structure. Unfortunately, it's in a sorry state at present while a succession battle between two opposing family factions remains unresolved. An armed guard watches over its melancholy decline and will take you on a quick tour of the crumbling remains inside. The palace is in behind the post office and Ghana Telecom complex, about 150m from the main road.

Also worth a look are the relatively new and impressive Great Mosque and, behind it, an older mud-and-pole mosque. You'll be taken to pay your respects (and a small donation) to the imam, an interesting character, who will expect you to sign his visitors book.

About 5km past the Upland Hotel is the small village of Nakori, which has an impressive mud-and-pole mosque. There's no public transport; you'll have to either take a private taxi from the motor park or it makes a pleasant walk (allow a good hour one way from the Upland Hotel).

Places to Stay & Eat

Seinu Hotel *(☎ 22010)* Doubles without/with bathroom US$3.50/4. This centrally located hotel, a five-minute walk north of the motor park, has clean, basic rooms but no restaurant.

Numbu Hotel Doubles US$3.50. This pleasant hotel has large airy rooms with shared bathroom. It's a short walk west of the market.

Hotel du Pond *(☎ 20018)* Singles/doubles US$2/5, rooms with air-con US$8. This friendly place is popular with budget travellers. Rooms are a bit dark and dingy but it's hard to argue with the price or its location near the motor park.

Kunateh Lodge *(☎ 22102)* Rooms US$3/4. Rooms here are a bit grubby but it's a friendly place and it's a five-minute walk from the VanefSTC and City Express bus stops.

Upland Hotel *(☎ 22180)* Doubles with fan/air-con US$8/12. Wa's best, this hotel is about 3km west of the town centre. It has large, comfortable rooms in a peaceful garden setting, a good restaurant and a pleasant garden bar.

There are plenty of ***food stalls*** and ***chop bars*** in and around the market area.

Getting There & Away

OSA has a daily service to and from Tamale (US$3, seven hours) via Larabanga (for Mole National Park). OSA buses leave from the empty lot next to the post office and Ghana Telecom. City Express has daily buses to Bolgatanga (US$2.30, six hours) via Tumu. VanefSTC has services to Accra. The VanefSTC and City Express buses leave from the main roundabout, opposite the police station. Other transport, including buses to Kumasi (US$3) and tro-tros to Bole, Sawla, Hamale, Lawra and Tumu leave from around the motor park. For Wechiau (US$0.50), tro-tros leave from within the motor park. If you're headed for Burkina Faso, border crossings can be reached via Hamale, Lawra and Tumu.

WECHIAU COMMUNITY HIPPO SANCTUARY

Part of an ecotourism project, this sanctuary *(day tour US$4)* protects a stretch of riverine habitat along the Black Volta River which is home to a population of hippos as well as many species of birds. Basic ***guesthouse accommodation*** is available and you can arrange canoe trips to see the hippos. Meals can be prepared if you bring your own provisions. Wechiau village is reached easily by tro-tro (US$0.50, one hour) from the main lorry park in Wa. The sanctuary is about 20km from Wechiau – you can hire a bicycle for the day for US$1.20.

BOLGATANGA

☎ 072

Bolga, as it's known to locals, is the fast-growing capital of the Upper East Region and the major town between Tamale and the border with Burkina Faso. It's a bustling, friendly place that makes both a good stopover and a convenient base for exploring the surrounding area.

There's a helpful tourist office (☎ 23416, fax 23578), open 9am to 5pm Monday to Friday, on Navrongo Rd across from SSNIT House. Your best bet for changing money is the Standard Chartered Bank on Commercial Rd.

Bolga's fascinating **market** is known in Ghana as a centre for crafts, including textiles, leatherwork (sandals, handbags, wallets and day packs) and baskets. The multicoloured baskets, prized throughout Ghana, are tightly woven from raffia and are available in a wide range of sizes. You'll also find fans and the famous Bolga straw hats. For baskets, you could also try the shop on Commercial Rd near the intersection with Bazaar Rd, where baskets are woven and sold. A medium-sized basket costs around US$1; a nest of three baskets costs around US$3.

The small **museum** *(admission US$0.70; open 9am-5pm daily)*, off Navrongo Rd behind the Catholic mission, has a small display on the ethnology and culture of the northeast.

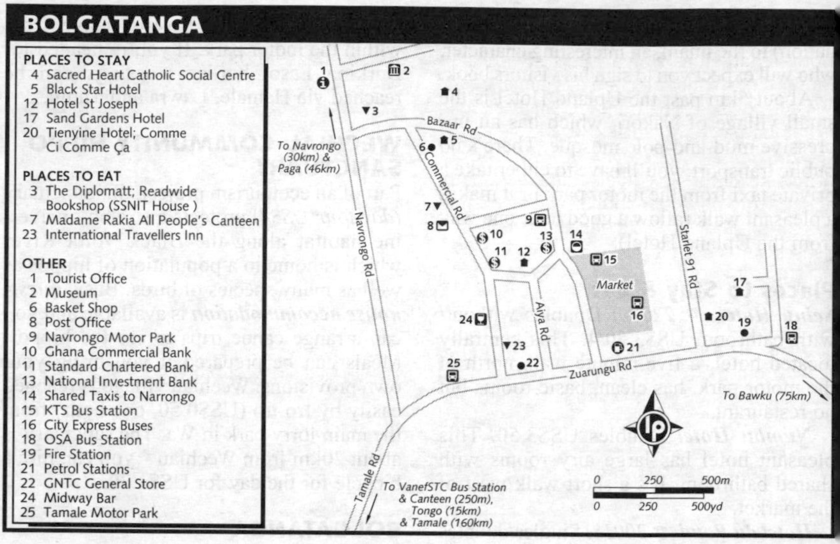
BOLGATANGA
PLACES TO STAY
4 Sacred Heart Catholic Social Centre
5 Black Star Hotel
12 Hotel St Joseph
17 Sand Gardens Hotel
20 Tienyine Hotel; Comme Ci Comme Ça
PLACES TO EAT
3 The Diplomatt; Readwide Bookshop (SSNIT House)
7 Madame Rakia All People's Canteen
23 International Travellers Inn
OTHER
1 Tourist Office
2 Museum
6 Basket Shop
8 Post Office
9 Navrongo Motor Park
10 Ghana Commercial Bank
11 Standard Chartered Bank
13 National Investment Bank
14 Shared Taxis to Narrongo
15 KTS Bus Station
16 City Express Buses
18 OSA Bus Station
19 Fire Station
21 Petrol Stations
22 GNTC General Store
24 Midway Bar
25 Tamale Motor Park
Bazaar Rd
Commercial Rd
Navrongo Rd
Starlet 91 Rd
Aiya Rd
Zuarungu Rd
Tamale Rd
Market
To Navrongo (30km) & Paga (46km)
To Bawku (75km)
To VanefSTC Bus Station & Canteen (250m), Tongo (15km) & Tamale (160km)
0 250 500m
0 250 500yd

Places to Stay

Sacred Heart Catholic Social Centre *(☎ 23 216)* Dorm beds US$1.10, singles/doubles with fan US$3.50/5. Over the road from the Black Star Hotel and set back from the road, the friendly Catholic mission has comfortable, quiet rooms with shared facilities set around a pleasant courtyard. Meals are available with advance notice.

Hotel St Joseph *(☎ 23214)* Doubles US$4-13. In behind the National Investment Bank, at the back of the Navrongo motor park, this hotel is the most central option in town. It has a variety of small, dark rooms with and without bathrooms, some with air-con. On the plus side, it has a popular bar and a good restaurant serving tasty kebabs and filling meals.

Sand Gardens Hotel *(☎ 23464)* Doubles US$5-11. This hotel currently offers the best-value accommodation in Bolga. It's an upbeat, friendly place with a variety of cool, comfortable rooms with fan or air-con set at the back of a large shady garden bar and restaurant area. To get to it, head east down Zuarungu Rd until you reach the fire station (about 1.5km from the centre); keep left on the dirt track that leads off the main road, and Sand Gardens is about 150m further from the road.

Black Star Hotel *(☎ 22346, fax 23650, Bazaar Rd)* Singles/doubles US$6.50/13-16. This well-established hotel has plenty of character, labyrinthine corridors and grubby rooms.

Tienyine Hotel *(☎ 22355)* Doubles US$19/21. The long-standing and popular Comme Ci Comma Ça restaurant has an attached hotel complex with good-value rooms, some of which are arranged, traditional style, in a circular compound.

Places to Eat & Drink

There are plenty of ***food stalls*** on the stretch of Zuarungu Rd east of the intersection of Navrongo and Commercial Rds. If you happen to be at the VanefSTC bus station, the ***canteen*** there is excellent.

Madam Rakia All People's Canteen *(Commercial Rd)* Mains US$1-1.50. Just north of the post office this canteen has good, sturdy food such as TZ, the local millet-based staple, and guineafowl stew.

International Travellers Inn *(Commercial Rd)* Snacks US$0.50-70. This grandly named place is basically a well-stocked food shop where you can get snacks and cold drinks.

The Diplomatt *(Cnr Bazaar & Navrongo Rds)* Mains US$2.50-3. At SSNIT House, this popular restaurant has something of the look of an English tearoom. It's comfortable and pleasant and serves good solid Ghanaian food.

Comme Ci Comme Ça Mains US$2.50-3. Long regarded as Bolga's best, this restaurant offers a wide selection of Ghanaian and Western dishes. The tranquil, shady garden is a good place for a drink.

Midway Bar *(Commercial Rd)* For a drink, head for this lively bar, diagonally across from the International Travellers Inn. It's an outdoor place facing the street with decent music and grilled-meat vendors nearby.

Getting There & Away

Tro-tros to Tamale (US$2.70, two hours) leave from the motor park on Zuarungu Rd east of the intersection with Navrongo and Tamale Rds. Tro-tros to Navrongo (US$0.35, 30 minutes) and buses to Kumasi and Accra leave from the Navrongo motor park on Bazaar Rd. Passenger taxis to Navrongo leave from the taxi station diagonally opposite the National Investment Bank. The VanefSTC bus station is on Tamale Rd, about 800m south of the intersection with Navrongo and Zuarungu Rds. From here, buses leave daily for Accra (US$6.50, 15 hours) and Kumasi (US$4.20, six hours). Behind the market, in the block between Zuarungu and Bazaar Rds, is a vast motor park. In the far northwest corner is the KTS bus station, with buses to Accra and Kumasi. In the southeast corner is the City Express bus station. From here, there's an early morning (5.30am) service to Wa via Tumu on Monday to Saturday.

If you're headed for Ouagadougou in Burkina Faso, take a tro-tro to the border at Paga (US$0.70, 40 minutes). To cross into Togo, take a tro-tro from the motor park behind the market to Bawku from where you can catch vehicles to the border (30km) and on to Dapaong (Togo), 15km further east.

AROUND BOLGATANGA

A worthwhile side trip is to the **Tongo hills** southeast of Bolga, known for their balancing rock formations, panoramic views and the whistling sound the rocks make during the harmattan season. A popular goal is Tenzuk Shrine, about an hour's (steep) hike from Tongo village, 9km from Bolgatanga. Tro-tros run regularly to Tongo (US$0.35) from the main motor park behind the market. Tongo is being developed as an ecotourism project.

The **Red Volta River Valley**, between Bolgatanga and Bawku, is potentially a fascinating area to explore, with opportunities for learning about the distinctive local culture and architecture, hiking, canoeing and wildlife viewing (it's a migration corridor for elephants and other wildlife). Although there are few facilities for visitors at present, it's being developed as an ecotourism project.

GAMBARGA ESCARPMENT

Southeast of Bolga, the Gambarga Escarpment extends towards the Togolese border. Along it is Gambarga, ancient capital of the Mamprusi kingdom; Nalerigu, the modern district capital; and Nakpanduri, the goal of most travellers to the area. A sleepy, unspoilt village of neatly thatched huts, perched on the edge of the escarpment, Nakpanduri has magnificent views and offers some fine hiking. You can stay at the ***Government Rest House***, which has basic rooms for about US$2.

Nakpanduri and the other towns along the escarpment can be difficult to get to by public transport. Your best bet is probably to do the journey in stages: from Bolga, get any transport heading to Tamale and drop at Walewale, where the road to Gambarga turns off the Tamale road. From there, you should be able to get a tro-tro to Nalerigu, and from there to Nakpanduri, although it may take a while.

NAVRONGO

The small town of Navrongo is 30km northwest of Bolgatanga. It's a quiet, pleasant place but there isn't much reason to stop here except perhaps to have a look at the Our Lady of Seven Sorrows Cathedral, which dates from 1906. It's unusual in that it was constructed of *banco* (clay or mud) in the traditional Sahel style and claims to be the world's largest cathedral built of mud – although how intense, you wonder, is the competition? The main point of interest is the colourful frescos that decorate the interior.

If for some reason you decide to stay overnight, the only hotel in town is the ***Hotel Mayaga*** *(☎ 22327)*, about 500m west of the bus station, off the road to Wa, which has doubles with fan for US$5 to US$8.50. The ***guesthouse*** at the Catholic mission, near the cathedral, has clean, cool singles/doubles with bathroom for US$2/3.50, but doesn't offer meals. Stalls around the bus station have a small selection of ***street food*** or there are a couple of ***chop bars*** on the main drag.

Getting There & Away

Regular shared taxis throughout the day make the short journey to Paga (US$0.20, 15 minutes) for the border with Burkina Faso and to Bolgatanga (US$0.35, 30 minutes). If you're heading south, you're better off getting to Bolgatanga, which has much better transport connections. If you're heading west towards Tumu and Wa, the bus from Bolga to Wa passes through Navrongo but it's usually jam-packed by the time it reaches here, so it's better to pick it up from Bolga instead.

PAGA

As well as being the main border crossing into Burkina Faso, Paga is known for its **crocodile ponds**. Chief Pond is visible from the road, about 1km from the main motor park towards the Burkinabé border, while Zenga Pond is signposted off the main road, just after the motor park. Since Paga has been involved in an ecotourism project, visiting the crocodile ponds has become a more sanitised process. At Chief Pond, you'll find official guides and a good informative booklet on the ponds. on the ponds. It costs US$7 for groups of two to five people to see the crocs, plus US0.70 for the crocs' chicken. More interesting, and highly recommended, is a tour of the chief's compound, the Paga Pio's Palace, a traditional homestead of the local Kasena people. There's no set fee for the tour but a donation is required. You can also arrange tours by bicycle of villages in the surrounding area through ***Alhassan Village Tours***, opposite Chief Pond. Tour prices depend on your itinerary but typically cost around US$6 per person. Alhassan offers the only ***accommodation*** in Paga; you can sleep on the roof of mud huts for US$3.50. Meals can be arranged.

At the other end of the village, near the lorry station, is the ***Black Heritage Gate Pimms Club***, an attractive garden bar, which is a good spot for a drink or bite to eat.

Regular shared taxis and tro-tros run between Paga and both Navrongo (US$0.20) and Bolgatanga (US$0.70). From the motor park in Paga, you can either walk the 2km to the border post or you can pay an extortionate US$2 for a private taxi.

ASHANTI ARTS & CULTURE

Ashanti culture is Ghana's richest and most self-confident. The Ashanti have a matrilineal social system and trace descent through the female line. Ashanti women are known for their independence, business acumen and influence in traditional politics. The *asantehene* (king) can have as many wives as he likes, although the present incumbent has just one. The Queen Mother, who can be the asantehene's sister, niece, aunt or mother, exerts considerable power. She is the only person who can criticise the asantehene.

Funerals, rather than marriages or naming ceremonies, are the occasions that bring together family, townspeople and distant relatives, which is consistent with the ancestor-focused nature of Ashanti traditional religion. The streets of Ashanti towns teem with mourners and sympathisers wearing the distinctive funeral colours of black, red and shades of reddish brown. Expenditure is lavish and there's plenty of socialising and drinking.

Inset: Statue of the 14th Asantehene Nana Osei Agyeman Prempreh II. The asantehene is the Ashanti king, who lives in a palace in Kumasi, the Ashanti capital . (Photo by Ariadne van Zandbergen)

Right: A young boy holds a golden sceptre during the Adae Festival. During the festival the king's subjects pay homage to him at the Manhyia Palace.

ARIADNE VAN ZANDBERGEN

Wealth is important in Ashanti culture; when Ashantis make money they build a fine house in their home town or village, however remote that may be. Many small Ashanti towns boast a few houses whose magnificence is almost incongruous in simple villages ill-served with basic facilities.

Arts & Crafts

Some of the best-known African artefacts and symbols in Europe and North America are Ashanti, including kente cloth, carved stools and adinkra symbols. The Ashanti have a long tradition of skilled artisanship in gold, iron, brass and textiles, producing items that befitted the power and historical significance of their kingdom. As an expression of his power and wealth, when the asantehene makes a public appearance, he shimmers with gold: he wears bracelets and gold rings so heavy that his arms have to be supported, a gold necklace, gold anklets and sandals embossed with small golden ornaments. The king's stool is entirely covered in gold and displayed under a magnificent umbrella.

Stools feature prominently in Ashanti culture. There's an Ashanti saying: 'There are no secrets between a man and his stool', and when a chief dies his people say 'The stool has fallen'. Ashanti stools are among the most elaborate in Africa. They are carved from a single piece of wood and the basic form is the same – a curved seat set on a central column with a flat base. Historically, certain designs, such as the seat supported upon the image of a leopard or elephant, were restricted to particular ranks within Ashanti society. The higher a person's status, the larger and more elaborate the stool.

Stools have a variety of functions and meanings. In official ceremonies, stools act as symbols of authority; on the death of their owner, consecrated stools are worshipped as homes to ancestral spirits; in most households, stools are articles of everyday use. A stool is the first gift of a father to his son, and the first gift bestowed by a man on his bride to be. Women's stools are different from men's. After death, the deceased is ritually washed upon a stool, which is then placed in the

ARIADNE VAN ZANDBERGEN

Left: An ancient stool displayed in the Yaa Asantewaa Museum. Stools are an important feature of Ashanti culture and have a variety of functions and symbolic meanings.

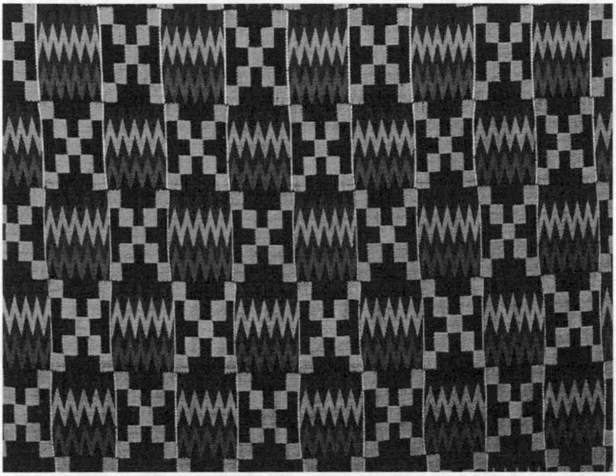

Right: Ashanti Kente cloth is one of the best-known – and most expensive – West African textiles. Its orange-yellow hues are indicative of the wealth of the wearer and its intricate geometric patterns have symbolic meaning.

ARIADNE VAN ZANDBERGEN

room for ancestral worship. Chiefs consider stools to be their supreme insignia. There are as many stool designs as there are chiefs, and the symbols are infinite.

State swords, which have a carved wooden handle coated in gold or silver and a metal blade, are an important part of a chief's regalia. Umbrellas are another symbol of chiefly office. The carved umbrella tops are usually coated in silver or gold and represent traditional proverbs, qualities the chief is supposed to possess or historical events. At gatherings of chiefs, the umbrella tops help the audience to distinguish one chief from another.

Traditionally, the chief speaks only through his spokesperson, who holds a staff that distinguishes his office. The linguist answers on the chief's behalf, with a long speech laced with proverbs. The staffs are decorated with creative designs that represent sayings or other meaningful symbols. The post of linguist is hereditary, open to the talented within the matrilineage of the linguist.

The colour and design of the cloth worn is yet another way of indicating status and clan allegiance. Different cloth is worn according to what the occasion requires. Ashanti kente cloth is one of West Africa's most famous textiles. It is traditionally worn by high-ranking men at ceremonies to display their wealth and status; originally, it was for royalty only. Kente is woven on treadle looms by men only in long thin strips that are sewn together. Its intricate geometric patterns are full of symbolic meaning while its orange-yellow hues indicate wealth. In contrast, *adinkra* cloth is worn primarily on solemn occasions by both men and women. The symbolic designs are printed in black on cotton cloth that is usually dark grey, dark red or white.

The Golden Stool

The Golden Stool is the Ashanti's most sacred object. According to legend, the powerful priest Okomfo Anokye drew the Golden Stool down from the heavens, through the dark clouds of thunder and dust, to rest upon the knees of Osei Tutu, chief of Kumasi, who became the first asantehene. Anokye collected nail and hair clippings from the chiefs and queen mothers and mixed these symbolic carriers of vital energy into a concoction he smeared over the stool. The soul of the Ashanti people now resided in the stool and Anokye warned that if the stool was ever destroyed, this would signal the end of the Ashanti nation. This is why the Ashanti were ready to hand over their chief, Prempeh I, to the British to be exiled but not their stool, and fought a bloody war to defend it. The war was lost and a fake Golden Stool was handed over to the British. The real Golden Stool was hidden, uncovered years later by road builders who tragically melted down its precious ornaments. The stool was eventually restored and is now kept at the palace in Kumasi where it is occasionally brought out for sacred rituals.

Architecture

Very few examples remain of the distinctive architectural style of the Ashanti as many traditional buildings were destroyed during the long wars with the British. Most of the surviving examples are shrines in the area around Kumasi. Houses were built around a courtyard and were made of mud with steeply pitched roofs covered in thatch. The upper parts of the walls were painted white whereas the timbers and lower parts of the walls were covered in red laterite. Significant buildings such as chief's palaces and shrines were covered in intricate bas-relief decorations that can still be seen on some of the shrines.

Festivals

The Ashanti calendar is divided into nine cycles of 42 days called Adae, which means resting place. There are two special days of worship within each Adae when a celebration is held and no work is done. The most important annual festival is the Odwira festival, which marks the last or ninth Adae.

Adae

On the day before Adae, horn-blowers and drummers assemble at the chief's house and play until late at night. Early next morning, the chief's head musician goes to the stool house where the sacred stools are kept and he drums loudly. Eventually the chief arrives and he and his elders go into the stool house to ask their forefathers for guidance. Ritual food of mashed yam, eggs and chicken is then brought into the room; the chief places portions on each of the sacred stools inside. A sheep is sacrificed and the blood is smeared on the stools. The sheep is then roasted and offerings of meat are placed on each stool. The queen mother prepares *fufu* (mashed cassava, plantain or yam) and places some on the stools.

A bell is sounded, indicating that the spirits are eating. Gin or schnapps is poured over the stools and the rest is passed around. When the ritual is over, the chief retires to the courtyard and the merrymaking begins; drums beat and horns blast. The chief dons his traditional dress with regalia and sits in court, receiving the homage of his subjects. On some occasions, he is then borne in public in a palanquin shaded by a huge canopy, and accompanied by lesser chiefs.

Odwira

On Monday, the path to the royal mausoleum is cleared. On Tuesday, the ban on eating the new yam is lifted and tubers are paraded through the streets while the chief sexton proceeds to the royal mausoleum with sheep and rum to invoke the Odwira spirit. He then returns to the chief and is blessed. Wednesday is a day of mourning and fasting. People wear sepia-coloured attire and red turbans and there's lots of drinking and drumming all day long. Thursday is for feasting. Ritual food, including yam fufu, is borne in a long procession from the royal house to a shrine where it's presented to the ancestors. That night, when the gong strikes, everyone must go indoors; no one but the privileged few may see the procession of the dead, when the sacred stools are borne to the stream for their yearly ceremonial cleansing.

The climax is Friday, when the chief holds a great durbar, a grand meeting, at which all the subchiefs and his subjects come to pay their respects. The highlight is a great procession of elegantly dressed chiefs, the principal ones being borne on palanquins and covered by multicoloured umbrellas.

Katie Abu, Alex Newton, Miles Roddis & Isabelle Young

Guinea

Guinea used to suffer under one of the most oppressive regimes in Africa. But, following the death of President Sekou Touré in 1984, things began to change; today, although it's still struggling, the country exudes a marked peppiness and economic vitality.

One of Guinea's major attractions is the vibrancy of its culture. Across the country, there's a strong tradition of music and dance. Added to this is Guinea's spectacular landscape. The country has some of the world's few remaining tropical dry forests, and the rainforests of the southern region are lush and verdant. The Fouta Djalon plateau in the west of the country has breathtaking scenery and is an excellent area for hiking.

Despite these attractions, Guinea is not prepared for tourism. Outside the capital Conakry, most accommodation is basic, and journeys by road can be long and hard. If you like your creature comforts you may not enjoy Guinea. But if you're prepared to rough it, a visit here can be very rewarding.

Guinea at a Glance

Area: 245,855 sq km
Population: 7.6 million
Capital: Conakry
Head of State: President General Lansana Conté
Official language: French
Main local languages: Malinké, Pulaar (Fula), Susu
Currency: Guinean franc
Exchange rate: US$1 = GF1963
Time: GMT/UTC
Country telephone code: ☎ 224
Best time to go: Mid-November

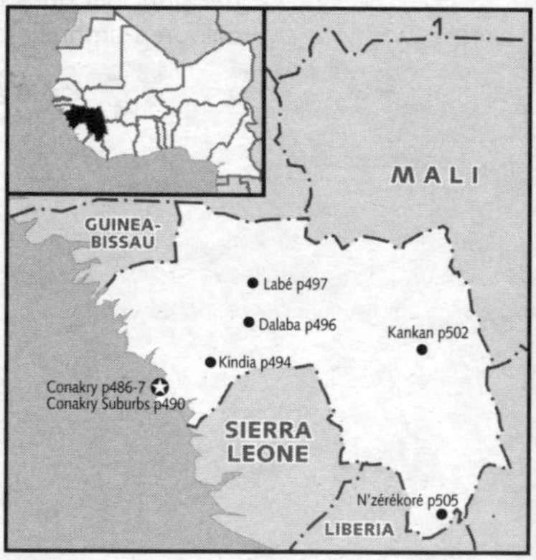
MALI
GUINEA-BISSAU
Labé p497
Dalaba p496
Kankan p502
Kindia p494
Conakry p486-7
Conakry Suburbs p490
SIERRA LEONE
N'zérékoré p505
LIBERIA

Highlights

- Hiking in the Fouta Djalon
- Listening to live music in Conakry
- Discovering interesting mosques and Islamic history in Conakry and Dinguiraye
- Lazing on the beaches of Room and Bel Air
- Exploring the Forest Region's lush scenery
- Learning about the fascinating ecosystems of Forêt Classé de Ziama, Parc Transfrontalier Niokolo-Badiar and Parc National du Haut Niger

Facts about Guinea

HISTORY

Rock paintings found in the Fouta Djalon indicate that Guinea was inhabited as early as 30,000 years ago. By 2000 years ago, the Coniagui, Baga and other smaller tribes had established isolated farming and fishing settlements along the coast and in the northwest. These were gradually pushed aside by influxes of Susu and Malinké following the fall of the Empire of Ghana. From the 13th century AD, the Malinké established dominance over much of Upper Guinea and by the 14th century all of Guinea had been incorporated into the powerful Empire of Mali. (For more information about this and other early empires, refer to the History section in the Facts about West Africa chapter.) Around the 15th century – about the same time that Portuguese navigators first reached the Guinean coast – Peul (also called Fula) herders started migrating into the area and settled in the mountainous Fouta Djalon region where they established an influential theocracy.

In the 19th century, the Guinean hero Samory Touré led the fight against French colonialists. He was captured in 1898 and resistance gradually withered. Once the train line from Conakry to Kankan was completed, France began serious exploitation of the area, which by then had become part of French West Africa.

GUINEA

SENEGAL
To Tambacounda (194km)
Parc National du Niokolo-Koba
Gambia
River
MALI
Kita
Sambaïlo
Kedougou
Gabú
Saréboïdo
Bafatá
Koundara
Massif du Tamgué
BAMAKO
GUINEA-BISSAU
Parc National du Badiar
Mali-ville
Koumbia
Buba
Gaoual
Kourémalé
Niger River
Source of the Gambia
Bankan
Labé
Bafing River
Dinguiraye
River
Siguiri
Pita
Boké
Fouta Djalon
Télimélé
Tinkisso
Niani
Kamsar
Dalaba
To Bougouni (50km)
Lower Guinea
Fria
Dabola
Kouroussa
Mandiana
Konkouré River
Mamou
Parc National du Haut Niger
Cape Verga
Boffa
Kankan
Kilomètre 36
Kindia
Faranah
Upper Guinea
Dubréka
Milo
Conakry
Coyah
To Odienné (30km)
Forécariah
Kabala
To Odienné (20km)
Îles de Los
Pamelap
Kérouané
Kambia
Forokonia
Source of the Niger
Kissidougou
River
ATLANTIC OCEAN
Makeni
Forest Region
Guéckédou
Sinko
Beyla
Macenta
Freetown
Koindu
Kailahun
Voinjama
Touba
Bo
Kenema
SIERRA LEONE
Zorzor
N'zérékoré
Lola
Nzo
Biankouma
Bossou
Yekepa
Nimba Mountains
Diéké
Man
0 50 100km
0 30 60mi
LIBERIA
Ganta
Sanniquellie
Danané
CÔTE D'IVOIRE

The most famous Guinean of all was Sekou Touré, a descendant of Samory Touré who was born into a poor Malinké family. After becoming the foremost trade unionist in French West Africa he led the fight for independence; in 1956 he led a breakaway movement from the French parent union to form a federation of African trade unions.

Independence

In 1958, Charles de Gaulle offered the French colonies in West Africa a choice between autonomy as separate countries in a Franco-African community or immediate independence. Sekou Touré declared that Guinea preferred 'freedom in poverty to prosperity in chains' and was the only leader to reject de Gaulle's proposal. Thus, Guinea became the first French colony to gain independence. Sekou Touré became an African legend in his own time and, as leader of Guinea's only viable political party, the country's first president.

De Gaulle, infuriated, immediately withdrew the French colonial administration. French private citizens fled with massive amounts of capital, precipitating an economic collapse in Guinea.

Wanting nothing more to do with the CFA franc, which was linked to the French franc, Touré introduced a new currency, the syli. But with French economic assistance gone, the new country badly needed foreign aid. Touré turned to the USSR, but the link was short-lived.

The government continued on a socialist road, however, and in 1967 commenced a campaign of cultural revolution on the Chinese model, with state-run farms and weekly meetings of revolutionary units. It was an unmitigated disaster. As many as one million Guineans fled into neighbouring countries, while remaining farmers were able to work only one-quarter of the country's cultivable land.

Reign of Terror

Sekou Touré appointed Malinké to all major government positions and treated his political opponents with cruelty. Following an unsuccessful Portuguese-led invasion in 1970, he became paranoid, often speaking of a plot against his regime. Waves of arrests followed; prisoners were sentenced to death, and torture became commonplace. In 1976, Touré charged the entire Peul population with collusion in an attempt to overthrow the government. Thousands of Peul went into exile.

Towards the end of his presidency, Touré changed many of his policies. A major influence was the Market Women's Revolt of 1977, in which several police stations were destroyed and three governors were killed, as part of the fight against state plans to discourage private trade.

Sekou Touré died of heart failure in 1984. Days later a military coup was staged by a group of army colonels, including Diarra Traoré, who became prime minister, and Lansana Conté. They denounced Touré and promised an open society and restoration of free enterprise.

A New Beginning

The change of government opened up Guinea, but tensions among leaders led to more problems. Following a failed coup attempt in 1985 by Traoré, Conté was forced to face the urgent matter of reforming the economy. He introduced austerity measures to secure International Monetary Fund (IMF) funding, and a new currency, the Guinean franc.

In 1991, Conté seemed to be moving towards democracy when he agreed to a multiparty political system. Within months there were 34 legalised parties, and eight presidential candidates for the 1993 election. After a tense pre-election period, Conté won with just over 50% of the total ballot against a divided opposition and in the face of accusations of fraud and vote-rigging.

Conté's control was challenged in 1996, when an army mutiny, instigated by soldiers protesting about poor salaries, threatened to become a full-blown coup. With considerable political savvy, Conté quickly quelled the uprising, but several dozen civilians were killed in the intervening 48 hours.

The 1998 presidential elections were considered more transparent than those of 1993, but proceeded in much the same vein; the campaign period was marred by widespread violence, military interference of opposition party rallies, and arrests of opposition supporters. On election day itself, the country's borders were closed and irregularities (generally favouring Conté) were evident in polling stations. The following day, Alpha Conde, candidate of the leading opposition party, was arrested in Lola and charged with a slew of offences – including, ironically, attempting to overthrow the government. Two other opposition candidates were placed under house arrest while the results were announced: Conté had won again with 56% of the vote. The results were disputed by most observers.

Guinea Today

With its sketchy efforts at democracy and reputation for corruption, the government inspires little optimism in most Guineans. Despite a wealth of resources, life here remains hard for the majority. Life expectancy (46 years) and the rate of adult literacy (36%) are among the lowest in the world; under the UN's quality-of-life index, Guinea has ranked at or near the bottom every year since 1990.

In addition, the country has suffered from the instability of its neighbours. It was plagued with violence in 1998 and 1999, when cross-border raids by Sierra Leonean and Liberian rebels (and possibly Guinean dissidents) in the southeastern Forest Region resulted in dozens of deaths. Tension continued into 2000, when unidentified men from across the border in Liberia attacked the Guinean border town of Massadou, killing almost 50 people. The situation got the world's attention when a UNHCR employee was killed, along with several others, in a raid on Macenta days later. By December,

Guéckédou was a veritable battle zone, and attacks on Macenta, Kissidougou and other small towns along the border were frequent. The crisis was compounded by the fact that refugee camps in the area were either destroyed in the process or else deliberately targeted by Guineans in retribution for the attacks. Thousands of refugees were trapped in the bush, while others were sent fleeing further north into Guinea and south into Sierra Leone. The situation gradually quietened down in 2001 and, as of early 2002, was completely peaceful, but more than 1000 people, by the Guinean government's count, were killed in the fighting.

GEOGRAPHY

Guinea has four zones: a narrow coastal plain, the Fouta Djalon plateau, northeastern dry lowlands and the forests of the southeast. The Fouta Djalon plateau, rising to over 1500m, is the source of the Gambia and Senegal Rivers and of much of the Niger (although the actual source of the Niger River lies south of the Fouta Djalon, near the Sierra Leone border). Southeastern Guinea is hilly and heavily vegetated, although little virgin rainforest remains.

CLIMATE

Guinea is one of the wettest countries in West Africa. Rainfall along the coast averages 4300mm a year, half of which falls in July and August, while the central mountainous region receives about 2000mm, more evenly distributed between May and October. Temperatures average 30°C along the coast, are somewhat cooler inland, and can fall to 10°C and below at night in Maliville and other high areas.

ECOLOGY & ENVIRONMENT

One of the major environmental concerns in Guinea is deforestation, although environmental exploitation has been mostly small-scale due to limited mechanisation. However, this is rapidly changing as the improved road system enables wood to be shipped out more easily, and as population pressures from some 500,000 refugees take their toll.

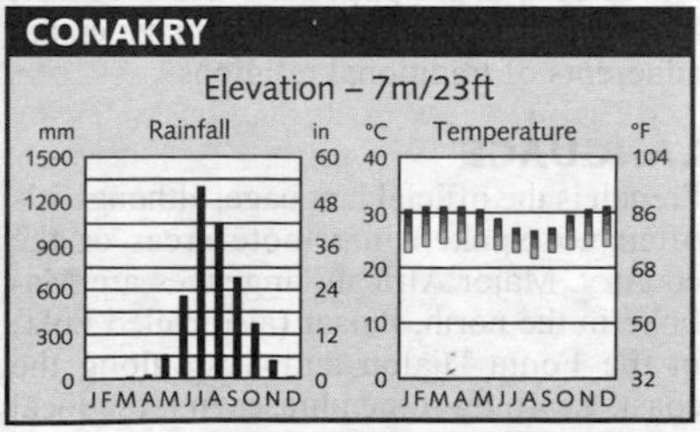
CONAKRY
Elevation – 7m/23ft
mm
Rainfall
in
°C
Temperature
°F
1500
1200
900
600
300
0
60
48
36
24
12
0
40
30
20
10
0
104
86
68
50
32
JFMAMJJASOND
JFMAMJJASOND

NATIONAL PARKS & RESERVES

Guinea has many designated protected areas *(forêts classée)*, although in practice there is little enforcement of environmental regulations. The country also has two national parks, Parc Transfrontalier Niokolo-Badiar near Koundara and Parc National du Haut Niger, northeast of Faranah, which are in the early stages of development but worth a visit if you have your own transport. Two new parks, on the borders of Guinea-Bissau and Mali, are in the planning stages. Guinea is, in a sense, still getting to know its own plants and wildlife; during the Sekou Touré reign, scientific research was discouraged and restrictions on areas protected under colonial rule were lifted. The national parks came into existence only after Touré's death. The result is that today animal populations are just beginning to recover and that even basic data on flora and fauna have yet to be gathered.

GOVERNMENT & POLITICS

President Conté's Parti de l'Unité et du Progrès (PUP) dominates the government, although with 62% of the national assembly, it's one seat short of the majority required to make constitutional amendments. In addition to support from Susus (President Conté is a Susu), the PUP is supported by Guerzé, Toma, Kissi and other smaller groups in the Forest Region. The strongest opposition group is the Rassemblement du Peuple de Guinée (RPG), headed by Professor Alpha Conde. The RPG's main support comes from Malinké. The Union pour la Nouvelle République (UNR), the other major opposition, is headed by Mamadou Bah and supported primarily by Guinea's Peuls.

While the opposition has been strong enough to influence some parliamentary votes, Guinea is essentially a one-man state, with authority in the hands of the president. During his term in office, Conté has consolidated control of several key areas and issued decrees enabling him to bypass his ministers. In November 2001 a constitutional referendum was passed (with an staggering 98% approval) extending the presidential mandate from five to seven years and removing the limit on the number of terms a president can serve.

ECONOMY

Although the economic situation has improved since President Conté took over, Guinea remains one of the world's poorest nations. The rate of inflation has fallen to about 6%, and average annual growth rates have stabilised at around 5%. But about 40% of Guineans live below the poverty line and rates of unemployment and underemployment are high. Rampant corruption, along with the instability of neighbouring countries, discourages much-needed foreign investment.

Guinea has abundant natural resources, including large mineral deposits. Agriculture, much of it at subsistence level, and mining (particularly bauxite, used in the manufacture of aluminium) are the mainstays of the economy. Guinea is the second-largest producer of bauxite in the world, with an estimated 30% of the reserves. The country also has impressive reserves of diamonds, gold, iron, copper, manganese and uranium, although revenue potentials have not been realised in these resources. Lack of infrastructure and, in the case of diamonds and gold, illegal export have been major obstacles.

POPULATION & PEOPLE

Guinea's population is approximately 7.6 million, including about 500,000 refugees from Sierra Leone and Liberia. Major ethnic groups are Peul (about 40% of the population), Malinké (about 30%) and Susu (about 20%). There are 15 other ethnic groups that constitute the rest. Susu predominantly inhabit the coastal region, Peul the Fouta Djalon and Malinké the north and centre. Guinea's refugee population is concentrated in the southeast and in Conakry.

ARTS

Traditional music and dance have flourished in Guinea, due in part to government subsidisation during the Sekou Touré era. Guinea has a thriving local music industry (for more details, see the special section 'Music of West Africa' earlier in this book). It also has several widely renowned dance troupes. This cultural heritage is most accessible to visitors in Conakry, where music and dance performances are often held at the Palais du Peuple and the Centre Culturel Franco-Guinéen.

The country's most famous cultural figure, however, is Camara Laye, author of *L'Enfant Noir*. Laye's book, considered one of the pre-eminent pieces of African literature, is full of fascinating insights into the traditions and daily life of Guinea's Malinké.

SOCIETY & CONDUCT

One of the best times to experience traditional Guinean culture is on Eid al-Fitr, which marks the end of Ramadan and is one of Guinea's most important holidays. Families start preparing well in advance. On the day itself, everyone from grandparents to children dresses in their colourful best and heads for the mosques. You'll often see groups of young girls walking down the street, all wearing matching elaborate *boubous* (traditional dresses), or gatherings of boys with their fathers and grandfathers, all in new outfits. Griots wander the streets, playing music for *cadeaux* (gifts), while prayer mat and jewellery vendors are out in full force. Afterwards, family celebrations last until well into the night.

As Guinea is a traditional Muslim country, travellers should respect local sensibilities by not wearing shorts; long skirts (for women) or trousers are preferable. For men, going without a shirt is not acceptable. Overall, the better dressed you are, the more respect you will enjoy and the easier time you'll have in encounters with local authorities. During the Ramadan fasting period, show respect for locals by not eating or drinking in public.

RELIGION

About 85% of the population are Muslims, 8% are Christians, and the remainder are adherents of traditional religions.

LANGUAGE

French is the official language, although it's often not spoken in remote areas of the country. Major African languages are Malinké in the north, Pulaar (also called Fula) in the Fouta Djalon and Susu along the coast. Learning some phrases in these local languages is essential if you'll be spending time off the main routes. See the Language chapter at the end of this book for a list of useful phrases in French, Malinké, Pulaar (Fula) and Susu.

Facts for the Visitor

SUGGESTED ITINERARIES

If you have a week or less in Guinea, a good option would be to spend two days in Conakry getting oriented, then to head to Kindia and spend a couple of days there exploring the town and visiting nearby attractions. Alternatively, you could fly from Conakry to Labé, then travel by road through the Fouta Djalon back to Conakry, with stops at Dalaba and Kindia en route. If you don't have time to leave Conakry, at least try to take a half-day excursion to Coyah or Dubréka; upcountry Guinea is quite a contrast from the capital.

If you have two weeks, head east from Kindia to Mamou and then north to the Fouta Djalon, where you could easily spend five to six days or longer walking between the villages, or doing day excursions based in Dalaba.

For those fortunate enough to have a month or more, add northeastern and southeastern Guinea to the itinerary: from the Fouta Djalon region, head east towards Dabola and Kankan. It's well worth pausing in Kankan for a few days before heading south towards Kissidougou. From Kissidougou, head east towards Macenta and N'zérékoré. The region around N'zérékoré can keep you busy for up to a week, including excursions to nearby Lola and Mt Nimba. From N'zérékoré you could fly back to Conakry or continue by road into Côte d'Ivoire. To make this grand loop with the minimum of backtracking, fly from Conakry to N'zérékoré. From N'zérékoré head towards Kankan via Macenta and Kissidougou, then continue from Kankan towards Dabola and Mamou. Alternatively, from Dabola, you could go south to Faranah and then on to Mamou. From Mamou, go north through the Fouta Djalon to Labé. From Labé you could continue to Mali-ville or Koundara and on into Senegal or Guinea-Bissau, or you could fly or return by road to Conakry.

PLANNING

The best time to visit is mid-November, after the rains and before the dusty harmattan winds spoil the views.

Institut Géographique Nationale's (IGN) map of Guinea is good, though much of the road information is outdated. It's on sale at IGN, at several stationery stores in Conakry, and on the street (GF10,000). The IGN also sells black and white or colour copies of topographical maps (scales 1:50,000 to 1:500,000) covering individual regions of the country for GF10,000 to GF20,000.

TOURIST OFFICES

Guinea's Office National du Tourisme in Conakry can provide information on travel throughout the country.

For details of local events, *Dyeli* is a listings magazine available free at the Centre Culturel Franco-Guinéen and at some hotels and travel agencies in Conakry.

VISAS & DOCUMENTS

Visas

All visitors, except nationals of Economic Community of West African States (Ecowas) countries, need a visa. Visas are not available at airports or land borders. Visas issued by embassies in Africa are usually valid for one month; visas issued outside Africa are usually valid for up to three months.

Visa Extensions Visas can be extended for up to three months at the Bureau of Immigration in Conakry for GF80,000. Extensions are supposed to be processed within 72 hours. For longer stays, you'll need a residency permit (valid for up to one year), which requires two photos, GF400,000 and a good reason.

Visas for Onward Travel In Guinea, you can get visas for the following neighbouring West African countries:

Côte d'Ivoire One month single-entry visas cost GF34,500 to GF87,000, depending on nationality, plus two photos, and are issued in three days.

Guinea-Bissau One-month single-entry visas cost GF40,000 (GF125,000 for three-month multiple-entry visas). You need two photos and visas are issued within two days.

Liberia Three-month single-entry/multi-entry visas cost GF50,000/75,000 for most nationalities; US and Canadian citizens must pay GF95,000 (multiple entry). You need two photos and visas are ready within two days.

Mali One-month single-entry visas cost GF13,650 plus two photos, and can be ready the same day if you go early.

Senegal One-month/three-month single-entry visas cost GF8500/18,600 plus three photos and are ready within 48 hours.

Sierra Leone One month single-entry visas cost GF42,000 to GF100,000, depending on nationality, and are ready within 24 hours.

Vaccination Certificates

A certificate with proof of a yellow fever vaccination is required of all travellers.

EMBASSIES & CONSULATES

Guinean Embassies & Consulates

Guinea has embassies in Côte d'Ivoire, Gambia, Ghana, Guinea-Bissau, Liberia, Mali, Nigeria, Senegal and Sierra Leone. Guinea also has embassies in the following countries:

Belgium (☎ 02-771 01 26) 75 ave Vandendriessche, Brussels 1150
France (☎ 01 47 04 81 48) 51 rue de la Faisanderie, 75016 Paris
Germany (☎ 0228-23 10 98) Rochusweg 50, 53129 Bonn
UK (☎ 020-7333 0044) 20 Upper Grosvenor St, London W1K 7PB
USA (☎ 202-483 9420) 2112 Leroy Place, NW, Washington, DC, 20008

Guinea also has embassies in Canada, Italy and Japan. In addition, there are consulates in Hamburg and Munich in Germany and in New York in the USA.

Embassies & Consulates in Guinea

Embassies in Conakry include:

Belgium (☎ 41 28 31) Corniche Sud, Kouléwondy
Benin (☎ 46 17 47) Madina, Matam
Canada (☎ 46 32 91) Corniche Sud, Coléah
Cape Verde (☎ 22 17 44) Ratoma Mosquée
Côte d'Ivoire (☎ 45 10 82) Blvd du Commerce; open 8.30am to 3pm Monday to Thursday and 8.30am to 2pm Friday
France (☎ 41 16 55) Blvd du Commerce; processes visas for Burkina Faso
Germany (☎ 41 15 06) Almamya, Kaloum
Ghana (☎ 46 15 12) Super V Complex, Route du Niger, Coléah
Guinea-Bissau (☎ 42 21 36) Route de Donka, 500m northeast of Carrefour Bellevue; open 8am to 2.30pm Monday to Thursday and 8am to 1pm Friday
Japan (☎ 41 36 07) Corniche Sud, Coléah
Liberia (☎ 46 20 59) Corniche Nord, Cité Ministérielle; open 9am to 4pm Monday to Friday
Mali (☎ 46 14 18) Blocs des Professeurs, Camayenne; open 8am to 4pm Monday to Thursday and 8am to 1pm Friday
Nigeria (☎ 46 13 41) Corniche Nord, Almamya, Kaloum
Senegal (☎ 46 29 30) Corniche Sud, Coléah; open 9am to 12.30pm and 1.30pm to 5pm Monday to Friday
Sierra Leone (☎ 46 40 84) Carrefour Bellevue; open 9am to 3pm Monday to Friday
UK (☎ 45 58 07) Blvd du Commerce, Almamya, Kaloum
USA (☎ 41 15 20/1) Off Corniche Nord, Almamya, Kaloum

CUSTOMS

You're not allowed to export more than GF5000 in local currency; additional amounts will be confiscated on departure. There are no limits on the import or export of foreign currency. Currency declarations are only occasionally given out at the airport, and are rarely checked.

To export art objects (interpreted to include anything made of wood), you'll need a permit from the Musée National in Conakry. Cost varies, but averages 10% of the value for items worth less than GF50,000, and up to 20% of the value for more expensive pieces. It's best to do this a day before departure and to bring purchase receipts.

MONEY

The unit of currency is the Guinean franc (GF).

country	unit		GF
euro zone	€1	=	GF1945
UK	UK£1	=	GF3009
USA	US$1	=	GF1963
West African CFA	CFA100	=	GF297

Most banks outside Conakry exchange only cash; if you're arriving overland carry some US dollars, euros or CFA as they're easily

GUINEA

DAVID ELSE

ARIADNE VAN ZANDBERGEN

DAVID ELSE

ARIADNE VAN ZANDBERGEN

Architecture in West Africa is heavily influenced by the region's pre-independence past: Mediterranean-style architecture on Île de Gorée, Senegal (top left); the 17th-century Portuguese Fort Metal Cross, Dixcove, Ghana (top right); French-colonial-style train station at Dakar, Senegal (middle right); and the eerie interior of the slave house, Georgetown, Gambia (bottom)

DAVID ELSE

ARIADNE VAN ZANDBERGEN

ANTHONY HAM

KIM WILDMAN

Only the Gambian president may drive through Arch 22 in Banjul (top); all others must make a tedious detour. The Grand Mosquée in Niamey, Niger (middle right), however, is open to visitors. The monument on Île de Gorée, Senegal (bottom left) honours the dead from WWII, while The Point of No Return memorial in Ouidah (bottom right) is a reminder of Benin's horrific slave history.

changed almost everywhere. Black market dealers are widely used throughout Guinea (cash only); their rates are generally about 8% better than the bank rate.

The exchange counter at the airport is rarely open and offers extremely low rates. Neither this bank nor any other will change Guinean francs back into hard currency when you leave Guinea, even if you have your exchange receipts. Moneychangers can help you out, though. They work in the open, but you should still be discreet when dealing with them.

POST & COMMUNICATIONS

International mail is usually dependable; however Guinea's separate express mail service is not.

All major cities and towns have a telecommunications centre (PTT) where you can make domestic and international phone calls, though line quality is sometimes poor. Becoming increasingly popular are Internet phone connections but, once again, a good line is extremely difficult to find.

Area codes were recently introduced for certain Conakry numbers, and though they're not always necessary, they can sometimes help make the connection. The code 013 precedes numbers beginning with 21, 22, 23, 25, 26 and 27; 012 precedes 66, 67 and 69 numbers; and 013 goes with numbers starting with 40.

Internet services are easy to come by in Conakry and are rapidly increasing in the major towns.

DIGITAL RESOURCES

The vast Ⓦ www.guinee.net is a comprehensive resource on Guinean culture, politics, history and just about anything else you can think of. It's mostly in French, with a smattering of English articles. The small site with the long name, Ⓦ www.arts.uwa.edu.au/AFLIT/countryguineaen.html, summarises the work and lives of some Guinean women authors.

BOOKS

Guinea Today by Mylène Rémy has good historical background. You can pick up a copy for GF25,000 in Conakry at Soguidip, two blocks south of Av de la République, and also at the tourist office.

NEWSPAPERS & MAGAZINES

English-language magazines and the *International Herald Tribune* are on sale at Super-Bobo Supermarket.

PHOTOGRAPHY & VIDEO

Photo permits are not required, although police officers will often insist that they are and hassles are frequent. Don't snap government buildings, airports, bridges and military installations, and it's best not to use a camera at all in cities and towns unless you're sure the police aren't watching and locals don't object. Copies of a government decree expressly permitting tourist photos are available at the tourist office and at some prefectures and hotels. The same restrictions apply to video.

Konica and Tudorcolor film are available in Conakry. For developing, the best place is Labo Photo on Av de la République in Conakry, although quality is erratic. For more general information, see the Photography & Video section in the Regional Facts for the Visitor chapter.

HEALTH

A yellow fever vaccination certificate is required from all travellers. Malaria risk exists year-round throughout the whole country, so you should take appropriate precautions. For more general information on these and other health matters, see the Health section in the Regional Facts for the Visitor chapter.

WOMEN TRAVELLERS

Women travellers are unlikely to experience any special problems in Guinea. For more general information and advice, see the Women Travellers section in the Regional Facts for the Visitor chapter.

DANGERS & ANNOYANCES

Hassling and demands for bribes by soldiers and customs officials, particularly at road checkpoints and the airport, are the major annoyances faced by travellers in Guinea. As long as your documents are in order, there is no need to pay these guys anything. Maintaining a respectful but relaxed and friendly attitude – and, for women, covering your hair – generally helps.

Overall, travel in Guinea is relatively safe. However, bush taxis often drive at breakneck speeds and road accidents are common. Don't be afraid to ask your driver to slow down – a simple *'chauffeur, doucement'* often does the trick. Take care when walking near traffic.

BUSINESS HOURS

Government offices are open from 8am to 4.30pm Monday to Thursday and 8am to 1pm Friday. Some businesses (particularly airline offices) work government hours. Others are open from 8am to 6pm Monday to Saturday, except Friday, when they close at 1pm. Many businesses also close between 12.30pm and 2pm for lunch or on Saturday afternoon. Banking hours are from 8.30am to 12.30pm and 2.30pm to 4.30pm Monday to Thursday, and 8.30am to 12.30pm and 2.45pm to 4.30pm Friday.

PUBLIC HOLIDAYS & SPECIAL EVENTS

Public holidays include:

New Year's Day 1 January
Easter March/April
Declaration of the Second Republic 3 April
Labour Day 1 May
Market Women's Revolt 27 August
Assumption Day 15 August
Independence Day 2 October
Armed Forces Day 1 November
Christmas Day 25 December

Islamic holidays are also observed, and Ramadan is one of the biggest holidays; see under Religion in the Regional Facts for the Visitor chapter for a table of dates.

ACTIVITIES

The Fouta Djalon region is great for walking and biking; the Forest Region in the southeast is good for biking. Anglers should bring a rod; there are streams and rivers everywhere and deep-sea fishing is possible off the coast by Conakry. If you have more time, you can easily find teachers of traditional dance and music across the country.

ACCOMMODATION

In Conakry, budget lodging is limited. Upcountry, most towns have at least one place to stay, often with basic but cheap facilities, while larger towns generally have a range of hotels. Many places upcountry have no electricity from about February to May. Expect to pay up to GF10,000 for budget lodging, and from GF15,000 for a room with amenities (usually bathroom and fan). Bathrooms, however, often have bucket water only.

A tourism tax of GF2000 per person applies to top-end and some mid-range hotels.

FOOD

Street food throughout Guinea is generally good, and there's at least one rice bar in every town. Shoestring travellers can keep their food budget under GF5000 per day. For those able to spend more, there are decent restaurants in most larger towns where you can eat well for GF6000 to GF15,000.

DRINKS

Although Nescafé is available everywhere, Guinea is fortunate enough to have a real coffee tradition: *café noir* is a bit like espresso, and is served in small cups with lots of sugar. Guinea has two beers – Skol, a light lager, and Guiluxe, a darker brew. European beers are available at some Conakry bars and restaurants.

Getting There & Away

AIR

Guinea's only international airport is the Conakry-Gbessia airport, 13km from the centre of town. Regional flights leave from the *aérogare nationale*, next to the international airport. Be prepared for frequent cancellations and delays when travelling with the national carrier, Air Guinée.

Departure tax for international flights is usually included in the ticket; otherwise it's GF30,000. For regional flights, departure tax is GF20,000.

The only international airlines serving Conakry are Air France (via Paris), Aeroflot (via Moscow), Ghana Airways (via Accra) and Royal Air Maroc (via Casablanca).

The table on the next page lists flights between Conakry and West African destinations. You can also connect to Bamako (Mali) and Nouakchott (Mauritania) on Air France. For southern and East Africa, you can connect to Johannesburg via Abidjan (Côte d'Ivoire) or Accra (Ghana), and to Addis Ababa (Ethiopia) or Nairobi (Kenya) via Abidjan.

Flights from Conakry (within West Africa)

destination	flights per week	airline	one-way/ return fare (GF)
Abidjan (Côte d'Ivoire)	5	Ghana Airways, Air Senegal, Air Guinée, InterTropic	325,000/460,000
Accra (Ghana)	3	Ghana Airways, Air Senegal, InterTropic	600,000/820,000
Bamako (Mali)	3	Air Guinée, Air France	370,000/420,000
Banjul (Gambia)	3	Air Dabia, Ghana Airways, Guinée Paramount, InterTropic	260,000/325,000
Bissau (Guinea-Bissau)	2	Air Senegal	580,000/680,000
Dakar (Senegal)	5	Air Senegal, Air Guinée, Ghana Airways, Royal Air Maroc	250,000/380,000
Freetown (Sierra Leone)	7	Air Guinée, Guinée Paramount, UTA/West Coast Airways, InterTropic	135,000/250,000
Monrovia (Liberia)	2	Air Guinée, Ghana Airways	260,000/375,000
Praia (Cape Verde)	1	Air Senegal	350,000/570,000

LAND

Border Crossings

Guinea shares borders with Côte d'Ivoire, Guinea-Bissau, Liberia, Mali, Senegal and Sierra Leone. Into Côte d'Ivoire, the main crossing is between Lola and Man; for Guinea-Bissau, the main crossing is between Conakry and Bissau via Labé, Koundara and Gabú; for Liberia, between N'zérékoré and Ganta via Diéké; at Kouré-malé for Mali; and for Senegal from Labé via Koundara to Tambacounda. Border crossings into the troubled country of Sierra Leone were just beginning to reopen at the time of writing.

Côte d'Ivoire

The most frequently travelled route is between Lola and Man either via Nzo and Danané or via Tounkarata, Sipilou and Biankouma. Alternatively, you can go from Kankan to Odienné via Mandiana. Bush taxis run from Kankan to Mandiana and Noumoudjila, where you can find transport to Mininian and from there, onwards to Odienné.

There's also a route between Beyla and Odienné (via Sinko). To/from Beyla you can get transport to N'zérékoré or to Kankan. It's better to cover as much distance as possible on the Côte d'Ivoire side, as many secondary roads in Guinea's Forest Region are in bad shape.

Guinea-Bissau

The most popular route between Conakry and Bissau is via Labé, Koundara and Gabú, although the 100km stretch of road between Koundara and Gabú is in bad condition. From Koundara, there are direct bush taxis to Gabú, though it's often faster to travel in stages, first to Saréboïdo, then change to border transport.

On the Guinea-Bissau side, there's usually at least one pick-up a day between Gabú and the border. Your best chance for good connections is to coordinate your travels with Saréboïdo's Sunday market: vehicles from Gabú and Koundara go there on Saturday, returning on Sunday or Monday.

Another route from Conakry to Bissau is via Boké and Koumbia to Gabú, but you often must change vehicles at the border. The Boké to Koumbia road is in bad condition.

Liberia

The route with the best road conditions is from N'zérékoré to Ganta via Diéké. Bush taxis go frequently from N'zérékoré to the border, where you can change cars or walk the remaining 2km to Ganta. This border closes from time to time depending on the prevailing political climate, so check before starting out.

Another route goes from Lola via Bossou to Yekepa (GF4500). There's sporadic transport between Yekepa and Sanniquellie.

From Macenta, bush taxis go via Daro to the border and occasionally on to Voinjama, although the Voinjama road is often impassable. It's better to go from Macenta to Koyama, where you can find transport to Zorzor and on to Monrovia, although the Zorzor road is also in bad condition; allow two days to Monrovia. Both routes are only feasible in the dry season (November to April). At the time of writing, fighting in Liberia's Lofa County made this route unsafe for travel, so check locally about the current situation.

Mali

There's frequent transport to the border at Kourémalé from both Kankan (GF15,000) and Siguiri (GF7000). A few times a week another direct service goes from both towns direct to Bamako (about an extra GF6000). There's also a direct bush taxi daily from Conakry's Siguiri station to Bamako (GF60,000). Bush taxis from Siguiri to Bamako sometimes take a less-travelled route (a better option for cyclists) paralleling the Niger River via Bankan. You can also go from Kankan via Mandiana to Bougouni, but you'll have to travel it in stages.

Senegal

The main route between Guinea and Senegal goes from Labé via Koundara to Tambacounda and Dakar (GF50,000, 25 to 35 hours). During the rainy season (May to October) the stretch between Labé and Koundara is slow or impassable for 2WD, although trucks ply the route frequently. From Koundara, there are several cars a week to the border, from where there is frequent transport to Tambacounda.

There is a road between Mali-ville and Kedougou, but the road is often impassable, even for 4WD and most people end up walking. See Mali-ville later in this chapter for more details.

Sierra Leone

Many of the following routes were just beginning to reopen at the time of writing. Seek local advice before setting out.

Bush taxis run from Conakry to Freetown (GF20,000, 10 hours, 330km). The road is sealed except for a 70km stretch near the border. Alternatively, you can take a bush taxi to the border at Pamelap (GF6000), then connect with vehicles on the other side. There are numerous checkpoints on this route; those in Guinea are particularly onerous.

You can also enter Sierra Leone from Faranah via a sparsely travelled road to Gberia-Fotombu on the border; from there you may find a truck heading for Kabala. It's possible to reach Makeni in Sierra Leone from Kindia via Medina Oula (written Medina Dula on some maps) and Kamakwie. Bush taxis run from Kindia to the border; sometimes there's transport all the way to Kamakwie. In Sierra Leone, vehicles run between the border and Kamakwie, from where there's a daily bush taxi to Makeni.

SEA & RIVER

Pirogues go from Kamsar (southwest of Boké) to Cacine in Guinea-Bissau (five hours), but the boats follow no set schedules.

Every couple of days the ferry goes to Freetown in Sierra Leone from Conakry's main port near the bus station. Tickets will setyou back GF40,000 and no advance reservations are necessary; inquire at the port for more information.

Depending on the river level, a barge runs once a week between Siguiri and Bamako in Mali. See Getting There & Away in the Mali chapter for more details.

Getting Around

AIR

Domestic flights use the aérogare nationale, next to the international airport. For information on domestic flight fares and schedules, see the Conakry Getting There & Away section. Departure tax for domestic flights is GF5000.

BUS

Private buses sometimes run between Conakry and Boké, Kindia, Mamou, Labé, Kankan and N'zérékoré. Although the buses are fairly comfortable and less expensive than bush taxis, they're slow and break down often. Postal buses are a good alternative.

For information on bus schedules, go to the Gare Voiture de Madina in Conakry. In Guinea, the term *gare voiture* is used for the bus and taxi station.

BUSH TAXI & MINIBUS

Bush taxis are the major form of transport in Guinea. They're usually Peugeot 504s, with nine passengers. If you want to charter *(déplacer)* a bush taxi for yourself, the cost should be a little less than the fare for one seat multiplied by the number of seats in the car. In general, transport is cheaper, faster and more frequent on or around market days. Ferry crossings and road checkpoints – the bane of travellers' lives in Guinea – can add several hours on to journeys. Sample bush taxi fares and journey times are listed in the table.

The cheaper but more crowded and dangerous minibuses cover the same routes as bush taxis and are best avoided unless there's no alternative.

CAR & MOTORCYCLE

If you're driving your own or a rented vehicle in Guinea, be sure the insurance and registration papers are in order as they will be checked frequently. They'll also sometimes be held for bribes – remember that amounts are always negotiable and you may not have to hand over your papers at all if you pay, say, CFA1000 upfront. Petrol averages GF1200 per litre.

The main road east from Conakry to N'zérékoré via Mamou and Kissidougou is tar and in reasonable condition, except for the stretch between Kissidougou and Macenta.

The coastal road from Conakry is tar and in excellent condition as far as Boké; from there it's dirt. There's a ferry over the Pongo River at Boffa.

Bush Taxi Fares & Journey Times

from	to	fare (GF)	duration (hours)
Conakry	Boké	13,000	5*
	Kankan	28,000	13
	Kissidougou	25,000	11
	Labé	16,000	9
	Mamou	10,000	6
	N'zérékoré	42,000	20
	Siguiri	35,000	15*
Kissidougou	Kankan	8000	5

*Timings are dependent on ferry crossings

From Mamou north, the road is tar as far as Labé; it's in bad condition thereafter. There's a ferry crossing between Labé and Koundara.

In Upper Guinea, the Mamou–Dabola–Kankan road is tar and in excellent condition. From Kankan to Siguiri (two ferry crossings), the road is dirt but OK; the road south from Kankan to Beyla is rough, and the road from Kankan to Kissidougou is paved but riddled with potholes.

Secondary roads can get bad during the rainy season, especially in the southeast, although bush taxis usually find a way through. Conditions vary depending on how recently a road has been graded. When we visited, the dirt roads from Dabola to Faranah and from Konsankoro to Macenta were in good shape, while those in most directions from Beyla were in bad condition.

BICYCLE

Although Conakry is too congested for cycling, many areas upcountry are excellent for mountain biking. Villages are spaced closely enough that lodging and food are seldom a problem on longer trips. You'll need to be fully equipped with spare parts, as you won't find fittings for Western-made cycles anywhere. Most towns have at least one shop that can mend flat tyres and take care of other basics.

Conakry

Conakry is a lively city on the upswing, with glitzy new shops, restaurants and nightclubs constantly appearing. If you walk around side streets on a Sunday, chances are you'll see a street celebration or two, and dozens of neighbourhood football (soccer) matches. Offshore are the Îles de Los with palm-fringed beaches.

Historically, Conakry was one of colonial France's major ports in West Africa and in its heyday was known as the 'Paris of Africa'. Until the end of the 19th century, what is now downtown Conakry was an island, separated from the mainland by a marshy channel (later bridged at the site of the Palais du Peuple).

Conakry's many good restaurants, friendly people, live music and vibrant neighbourhood life make it well worth

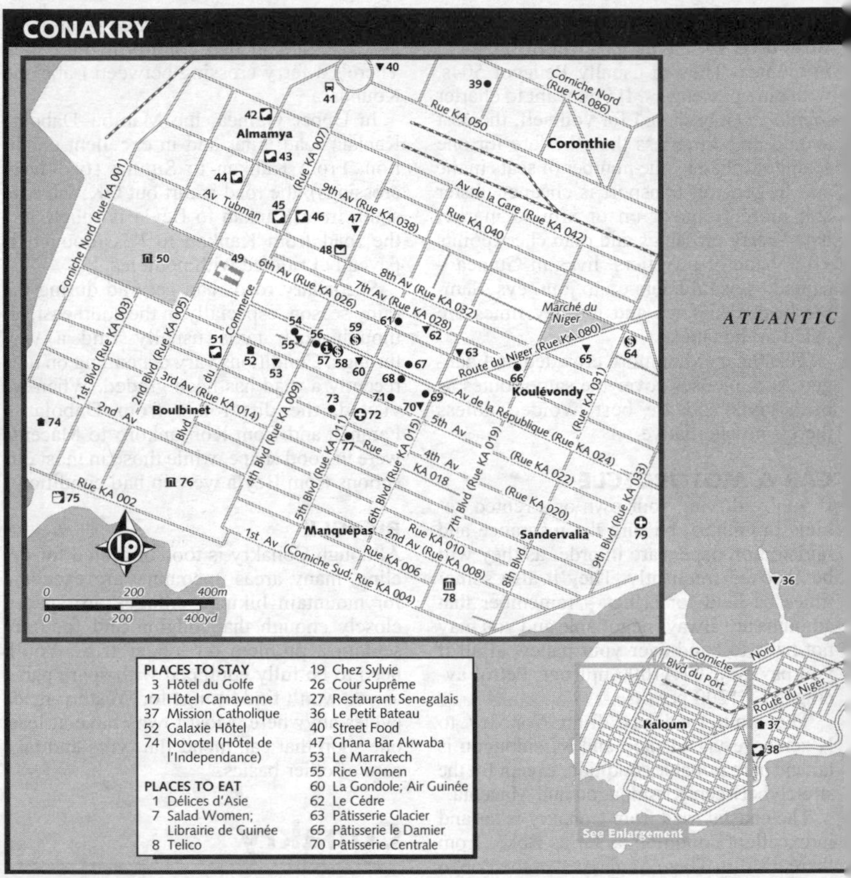
CONAKRY
ATLANTIC
Corniche Nord (Rue KA 086)
Rue KA 050
Coronthie
Almamya
Av de la Gare (Rue KA 042)
Rue KA 040
9th Av (Rue KA 038)
Av Tubman
8th Av (Rue KA 032)
7th Av (Rue KA 028)
6th Av (Rue KA 026)
Corniche Nord (Rue KA 001)
Marché du Niger
Route du Niger (Rue KA 080)
Koulévondy
Av de la République (Rue KA 024)
5th Av
4th Av
Rue KA 018
(Rue KA 022)
(Rue KA 020)
Boulbinet
1st Blvd (Rue KA 003)
2nd Blvd (Rue KA 005)
3rd Av (Rue KA 014)
2nd Av
Blvd du Commerce
4th Blvd (Rue KA 009)
5th Blvd (Rue KA 011)
6th Blvd (Rue KA 015)
7th Blvd (Rue KA 019)
8th Blvd
9th Blvd (Rue KA 033)
(Rue KA 031)
Rue KA 002
Manquépas
Sandervalia
Rue KA 010
2nd Av (Rue KA 008)
Rue KA 006
1st Av (Corniche Sud; Rue KA 004)
0 200 400m
0 200 400yd
Corniche Nord
Blvd du Port
Route du Niger
Kaloum
See Enlargement
PLACES TO STAY
3 Hôtel du Golfe
17 Hôtel Camayenne
37 Mission Catholique
52 Galaxie Hôtel
74 Novotel (Hôtel de l'Independance)
PLACES TO EAT
1 Délices d'Asie
7 Salad Women; Librairie de Guinée
8 Telico
19 Chez Sylvie
26 Cour Suprême
27 Restaurant Senegalais
36 Le Petit Bateau
40 Street Food
47 Ghana Bar Akwaba
53 Le Marrakech
55 Rice Women
60 La Gondole; Air Guinée
62 Le Cèdre
63 Pâtisserie Glacier
65 Pâtisserie le Damier
70 Pâtisserie Centrale

spending a few days here before you explore upcountry Guinea.

Orientation

Conakry's location on a narrow peninsula means that the city – now home to 20% of Guinea's population – has nowhere to expand but inland, making it increasingly difficult to travel from one end to the other. This trip can take up to an hour in rush-hour traffic.

La ville (downtown) centres on Av de la République; banks, airline offices and several restaurants are on or around this street. About 10km northeast is the colourful Taouyah *quartier* (neighbourhood), which is livelier than the city centre at night. Further out still is well-to-do Ratoma with a number of hotels and restaurants, and beyond here the rapidly expanding quartiers of Kipé and Kaporo.

The city is divided into five main zones: Kaloum comprises all of downtown; Dixinn runs from Cameroun to Minière; Ratoma, a sprawling district that includes the Taouyah, Ratoma, Kipé and Kaporo quartiers; Matam, on the southern side, contains Coléah and Madina; and Matoto is out by the airport and continues far inland to Kissosso.

The main streets are the Autoroute, the Route du Niger and the Route de Donka. Route du Niger runs into Av de la République in town and into the Autoroute at the airport, and Route de Donka branches off the Autoroute at the Centre Culturel

GUINEA

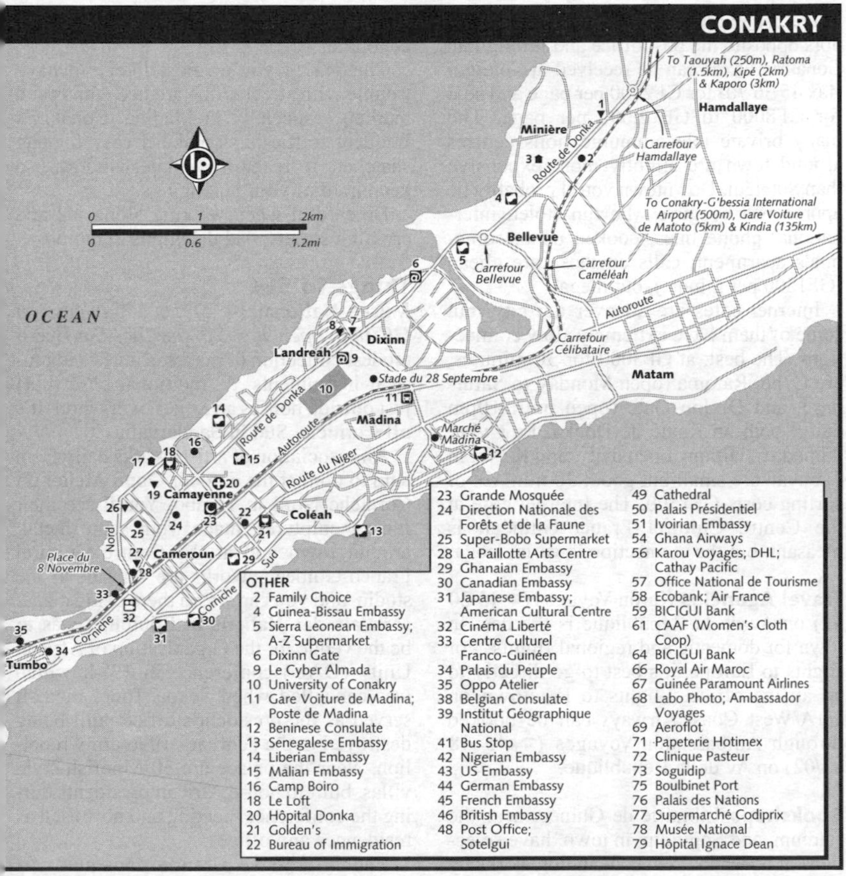
CONAKRY
To Taouyah (250m), Ratoma (1.5km), Kipé (2km) & Kaporo (3km)
Hamdallaye
Minière
Route de Donka
Carrefour Hamdallaye
To Conakry-G'bessia International Airport (500m), Gare Voiture de Matoto (5km) & Kindia (135km)
Bellevue
Carrefour Bellevue
Carrefour Caméléah
Autoroute
Carrefour Célibataire
OCEAN
0
1
2km
0
0.6
1.2mi
Landreah
Dixinn
Stade du 28 Septembre
Matam
Madina
Marché Madina
Route du Niger
Camayenne
Coléah
Cameroun
Place du 8 Novembre
Nord
Sud
Corniche
Tumbo
OTHER
2 Family Choice
4 Guinea-Bissau Embassy
5 Sierra Leonean Embassy; A-Z Supermarket
6 Dixinn Gate
9 Le Cyber Almada
10 University of Conakry
11 Gare Voiture de Madina; Poste de Madina
12 Beninese Consulate
13 Senegalese Embassy
14 Liberian Embassy
15 Malian Embassy
16 Camp Boiro
18 Le Loft
20 Hôpital Donka
21 Golden's
22 Bureau of Immigration
23 Grande Mosquée
24 Direction Nationale des Forêts et de la Faune
25 Super-Bobo Supermarket
28 La Paillotte Arts Centre
29 Ghanaian Embassy
30 Canadian Embassy
31 Japanese Embassy; American Cultural Centre
32 Cinéma Liberté
33 Centre Culturel Franco-Guinéen
34 Palais du Peuple
35 Oppo Atelier
38 Belgian Consulate
39 Institut Géographique National
41 Bus Stop
42 Nigerian Embassy
43 US Embassy
44 German Embassy
45 French Embassy
46 British Embassy
48 Post Office; Sotelgui
49 Cathedral
50 Palais Présidentiel
51 Ivoirian Embassy
54 Ghana Airways
56 Karou Voyages; DHL; Cathay Pacific
57 Office National de Tourisme
58 Ecobank; Air France
59 BICIGUI Bank
61 CAAF (Women's Cloth Coop)
64 BICIGUI Bank
66 Royal Air Maroc
67 Guinée Paramount Airlines
68 Labo Photo; Ambassador Voyages
69 Aeroflot
71 Papeterie Hotimex
72 Clinique Pasteur
73 Soguidip
75 Boulbinet Port
76 Palais des Nations
77 Supermarché Codiprix
78 Musée National
79 Hôpital Ignace Dean

Franco-Guinéen and then continues into Ratoma.

Papeterie Hotimex in town sells an excellent atlas of Conakry for GF16,000. Maps of the city are also sold by vendors on Av de la République for about GF10,000.

Information

Tourist Offices The Office National du Tourisme is on the 2nd and 3rd floors of the Karou Voyages building on Av de la République. It's more of an office than a welcome centre, but the folks there are friendly.

Money The best bank for changing money is Banque Internationale pour le Commerce et l'Industrie de la Guinée (BICIGUI). The main branch on Av de la République accepts Thomas Cook, Visa and American Express travellers cheques, and will give cash advances against a Visa card. Ecobank, just across the street, has better hours (open Saturday) but a higher commission.

Post & Communications The main post office is three blocks north of Av de la République; it's open from 8am to 4pm Monday to Thursday, until 1pm Friday and until noon Saturday. The unorganised poste restante charges GF500 per collected letter and will hold mail indefinitely.

Sotelgui (Guinea telecom), across the street from the main post office, is open from 8am to 8pm Monday to Saturday. International calls average GF4000 per minute.

There are cardphones and phonecard vendors opposite the post office and throughout Conakry. Faxes can be received at Sotelgui (fax 45 36 70) for GF2000 per page and sent for GF8000 to GF12,000 per page. The many private telecommunications centres around town are slightly more expensive than Sotelgui. Downtown you'll probably be approached by guys who run stolen international phone lines, hooked up in someone's apartment; calls on these are cheap (GF1500 per minute), but illegal.

Internet cafés are all over the city, but some of them have extremely slow connections. The best, at GF3000 for 30 minutes, are Cyber Ratoma (open Monday to Saturday), and Dixinn Gate (open until 10pm daily) both on Route de Donka. Le Cyber Almada in Dixinn, open daily, and K-Net in Taouyah are small but good; 30 minutes of surfing costs GF1500. The Internet café at the Centre Culturel Franco-Guinéen is pleasant, but the connection is variable.

Travel Agencies Karou Voyages (☎ 45 20 42) on Av de la République is the best in town for domestic and regional flights. For flights to Europe, it's best to go directly to an airline office. Flights to Freetown on UTA/West Coast Airways can be booked through Ambassador Voyages (☎ 45 38 01/02) on Av de la République.

Bookshops Librairie de Guinée, near the stadium, and Soguidip, in town, have selections of books in French, including works by Guinean authors. Soguidip also has many French magazines and some in English.

Medical Services Clinique Pasteur (☎ 41 25 55) is recommended for emergencies. Pharmacies in Conakry are fairly well stocked.

Dangers & Annoyances After 11pm, checkpoints are set up all over the city, and it's common for the soldiers manning them to seek bribes. As long as you have all your papers, you shouldn't have to pay anything if you're riding in a taxi. In your own car, you may have to pay up to GF5000 to pass (many people simply pay GF1000 upfront to avoid protracted discussion). If you don't have your passport with you or it's not in order, you'll definitely have to pay a fine; but remain calm and good humoured and negotiate.

The places you're most likely to have trouble with street crime are taxi stands and markets, especially in Madina. Conakry's frequent traffic jams make it easy for bag snatchers to reach in vehicle windows, so keep hold of your belongings.

Be careful when walking alongside and crossing streets; bad driving is common.

Things to See

Musée National *(☎ 41 50 60; admission GF1000; open 9am-5.30pm Tues-Sun)* has a modest collection of masks, statues and musical instruments. A traditional *case* (hut) just outside houses an artists' workshop. It's off Corniche Sud in Sandervalia.

An association of artists works daily from 8am to 6pm at the outdoor **Oppo Atelier** on Corniche Nord in Tumbo. You'll see their funky sculptures, made from scrap metal, around town and at the Centre Culturel Franco-Guinéen. Works are for sale at the studio, and you can watch them being made.

Palais des Nations in Boulbinet was to be the venue for the Organisation of African Unity (OAU) conference in 1984, which was cancelled when Sekou Touré died. It served as the president's office until being destroyed in the February 1996 army rebellion. Near the palace are 50 Moorish-style villas, built to house African presidents during the conference meeting and now used as residences and offices.

The impressive **Grande Mosquée**, financed primarily by Saudi Arabia and inaugurated in 1984, has an inner hall capable of accommodating 10,000 worshippers. Although visitors are not usually allowed inside, you can inquire at the Islamic Centre next door about arranging a tour. Sekou Touré's grave is in a small gazebo on the grounds.

It's worth stopping at the **university** to see its two large and interesting mosaics.

If you're getting a visa for Guinea-Bissau, take a look at **Amilcar Cabral's house** on the grounds. This was his revolutionary party's headquarters during the war for Guinea-Bissau's independence and the place where he was eventually assassinated.

Conakry's biggest **market** is the hectic Marché Madina, but the best is Marché du Niger.

Camp Boiro

Although almost 20 years have passed since Sekou Touré's death, his legacy continues to influence Guinean life. Some knowledge of his era is important if you want to understand present-day Guinea.

A good place to start is Camp Boiro, in the centre of Conakry on Route de Donka, tactfully called Garde Républicaine on some maps. Originally constructed as a military camp, Boiro rapidly became synonymous with the worst atrocities carried out during Touré's 'reign of terror'. From 1960 until Touré's death in 1984, thousands of prisoners were tortured or killed at Camp Boiro, including many prominent figures. Every sector of society was affected, and most Guineans you meet can tell of a family member or friend who was there. Many prisoners were held for years in isolation; others were kept in a horrifying cement holding-pen open to the elements until they died.

Boiro was not the only camp of this kind in Guinea; there was another notorious one in Kindia, as well as smaller camps throughout the country. The bodies of many of those who died at Boiro have been lost. Others are buried in unmarked graves at the overgrown Nongo cemetery on the outskirts of town beyond Kaporo. The present government is not eager to discuss this part of Guinea's history, and Camp Boiro is not open to the public. But in 1998 a group of organisations associated with family members of victims succeeded in walling off a cemetery in Boiro to commemorate those who died.

For further reading on this era, check out W www.guinee.net.

Places to Stay – Budget

Inexpensive lodging is scarce in Conakry, and most of what exists is in the suburbs, a 10-minute taxi ride from the city centre.

Mission Catholique Singles/doubles with fan GF16,500/21,500, with air-con GF20,000/25,000. This is the best of the budget accommodation and, unusually, it is right in the centre of town, near the Marché du Niger. Rooms at the back face a tranquil yard.

Résidence Horeka Kaporo *(☎ 21 61 60)* Rooms with fan/air-con GF30,000/45,000. This hotel, 13km from the centre on Route de Donka, is spotless and safe, although rooms don't have bathrooms.

Hôtel Mixte Rooms with fan/air-con GF15,000/20,000. Most clientele rent by the hour at this place in Kipé, but rooms are tolerable.

Guesthouse Deborah *(☎ 42 19 01)* Rooms with fan/air-con GF35,000/40,000. Rooms here are nice and spacious, and it's a friendly place. The rooftop terrace has sea views. It's at the turn-off to the Mariador hotels in Ratoma.

Pension La Maison Blanche Rooms with fan/air-con GF20,000/25,000. This new hotel is in a quiet location in Kipé and is excellent value.

Auberge Kakimbo *(☎ 22 21 27)* Rooms GF25,000-40,000. This place in Ratoma has good rooms, most with air-con. Some GF40,000 rooms on the upper floors have great views of the ocean, but no air-con.

Kakilambe Bruss Rooms GF35,000. Though out of the centre in Kaporo, this hotel has a couple of beautiful rooms overlooking the Kakimbo inlet. All rooms are nicely decorated and clean.

Places to Stay – Mid-Range

Auberge Irena *(☎ 42 10 63)* Rooms GF60,000-80,000. This auberge in Ratoma is OK; rooms have air-con, bathroom, TV and telephone and rates include breakfast.

Hôtel du Golfe *(☎ 41 13 94)* Singles GF45,000-55,000, doubles GF60,000-80,000. This place in Minière has OK but overpriced rooms with TVs. The whole establishment is very clean and professional.

Hôtel César *(☎ 22 10 67)* Main building/annexe rooms GF45,000/60,0000. The César, 500m from the Mariador Park in Taouyah, has nice air-con rooms with bathroom, and a small pool.

Hôtel Mariador Résidence *(☎ 27 06 22)* Rooms GF65,000-85,000. This Taouyah hotel has a seaside terrace, a pool and comfortable rooms.

Hôtel Mariador Park *(☎ 22 97 40)* Rooms GF58,200-76,450. The Mariador Park is a step down from the Résidence, but not bad. Rooms are spacious and clean.

Le Galion *(☎ 42 20 22)* Singles/doubles GF88,500/100,300. The setting, among palm trees on the coast in Ratoma, is hard to beat. Rates include breakfast.

Galaxie Hôtel *(☎ 45 10 03)* Singles/doubles GF70,000/100,000. The Galaxie, off Av de la République, has fully equipped

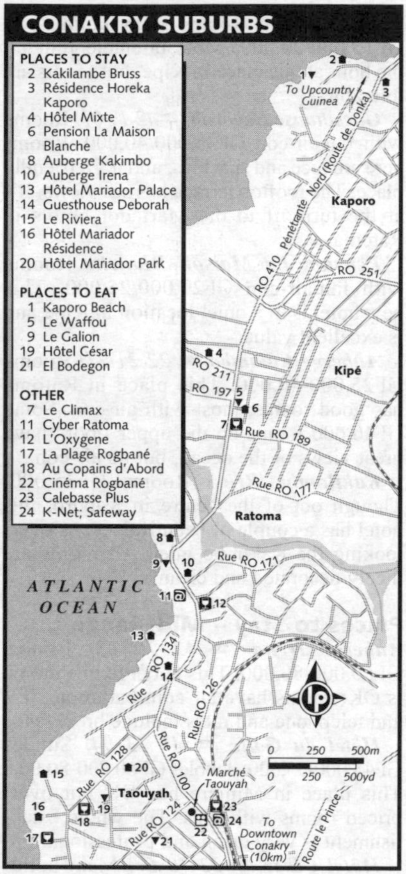
CONAKRY SUBURBS
PLACES TO STAY
2 Kakilambe Bruss
3 Résidence Horeka Kaporo
4 Hôtel Mixte
6 Pension La Maison Blanche
8 Auberge Kakimbo
10 Auberge Irena
13 Hôtel Mariador Palace
14 Guesthouse Deborah
15 Le Riviera
16 Hôtel Mariador Résidence
20 Hôtel Mariador Park
PLACES TO EAT
1 Kaporo Beach
5 Le Waffou
9 Le Galion
19 Hôtel César
21 El Bodegon
OTHER
7 Le Climax
11 Cyber Ratoma
12 L'Oxygene
17 La Plage Rogbané
18 Au Copains d'Abord
22 Cinéma Rogbané
23 Calebasse Plus
24 K-Net; Safeway
To Upcountry Guinea
Nord (Route de Donka)
Pénétante
RO 410
RO 251
Kaporo
Kipé
RO 211
RO 197
Rue RO 189
Rue RO 177
Ratoma
Rue RO 171
ATLANTIC OCEAN
RO 134
Rue
Rue RO 126
Rue RO 128
Rue RO 100
Rue RO 124
Taouyah
Marché Taouyah
Route le Prince
To Downtown Conakry (10km)
0 250 500m
0 250 500yd

air-con rooms in a convenient location near the city centre.

Places to Stay – Top End

Hôtel Camayenne *(☎ 41 40 89)* Rooms GF276,000. The Camayenne has comfortable rooms with all the amenities you'd expect, and the pool and bar area are pleasant, and catch the sea breezes.

Novotel *(☎ 41 50 21)* Rooms GF237,000. At the tip of Kaloum peninsula Novotel has fully equipped rooms, tennis courts and a pool.

Hôtel Mariador Palace *(☎ 42 40 00)* Singles/doubles GF197,000/257,000. Rooms are luxurious and airy; many have sea views.

Le Riviera *(☎ 66 11 98)* Rooms GF137,000. This new hotel on the water has elegant rooms with TVs and kitchens. Breakfast is included in the room rate.

Places to Eat

Places with good ***street food*** for less than GF1500 include Marché du Niger and the stalls at the intersection of Corniche Nord and Blvd du Commerce. At lunch time, you'll find a slew of women serving rice just south of Av de la République in town. At night, women prepare salad (not washed in purified water) meals near the stadium.

Chez Sylvie Meals GF5000. Opposite Hôtel Camayenne is Chez Sylvie, which is actually a row of women who prepare the best-quality *attiéké* (cassava) in town (evenings only).

La Gondole *(☎ 41 15 40)* Meals GF4000-8000. La Gondole has chawarmas, ice cream and delicious vegetarian pizza.

Ghana Bar Akwaba Meals GF1000-2500. This Ghanaian restaurant serves *fufu* (pounded cassava) and rice balls.

Pâtisserie Centrale *(☎ 41 18 42)* Meals GF6000-10,000. This place has hamburgers, sandwiches and ice cream.

Pâtisserie Glacier *(☎ 41 27 48)* Meals GF6000-10,000. Though a bit sterile, this café has good pastries, pizzas and satellite TV.

Le Marrakech *(☎ 29 48 64)* Meals GF6000-16,000. The atmospheric Marrakech has a selection of Moroccan and European dishes.

Le Cédre *(☎ 41 44 73)* Meals GF6000-15,000. For the best Lebanese food in town, try this place off Route du Niger.

Pâtisserie le Damier *(☎ 41 17 86)* Meals GF10,000. This pastry shop has excellent French food as well as breads and pastries to take away.

Le Petit Bateau *(☎ 41 28 85)* Meals GF15,000. The food here is OK and the restaurant is worth visiting for its relaxing setting out on a pier.

La Paillotte Arts Centre Meals GF1000-2000. The restaurant here serves simple but unusually good rice and other dishes.

Cour Suprême Meals GF1500. Open Mon-Fri lunch only. The Supreme Court cafeteria serves up delicious *thiéboudjenne* (rice cooked in fish sauce) and other Senegalese dishes.

Restaurant Senegalais Meals GF1000-2000. This tiny Senegalese restaurant serves excellent dishes for a song.

Telico Meals GF2500-5000. The no-frills Telico has cheap food and satellite TV.

Délices d'Asie *(☎ 41 21 22)* Meals GF9000. Délices d'Asie in Minière has good but expensive Vietnamese food.

El Bodegon *(☎ 26 85 35)* Meals GF7000. This Hamdallaye restaurant is a friendly place with occasional live music.

Hôtel César *(☎ 22 10 67)* Meals GF6000-12,000. César's in Taouyah serves up pizzas and pasta dishes by the pool on its back porch.

Le Galion *(☎ 40 32 82)* Meals GF10,000-14,000. The seaside setting here is worth a visit; diners can use the pool.

Le Waffou *(☎ 25 57 01)* Meals GF2000-8000. Le Waffou serves delicious Ivoirian food, including banana fufu.

Kaporo Beach *(☎ 25 10 83)* Meals GF9000-15,000. The pizzas and salads here are good, but most people come for the view of the ocean and the nice pool.

Well-stocked (but expensive) supermarkets include ***A-Z Supermarket*** at Carrefour Bellevue, ***Super-Bobo Supermarket*** in Camayenne, ***Family Choice*** in Minière, ***Safeway*** in Taouyah, and ***Supermarché Codiprix*** downtown.

Entertainment

Bars & Nightclubs Conakry has many night spots, although most are in the suburbs. None get lively before 11pm. Cover charges start around GF5000, more on weekends. Thursday and Saturday are the biggest nights. Many bars popular with Western men are also frequented by prostitutes, but they're not usually very sleazy.

La Paillotte Arts Centre The nightclub here has good music and is always crowded.

Golden's There are quite a few prostitutes here, but it's worth visiting for the dancing. It's also known as Trente-six/Quinze.

Le Loft This unusually hip lounge has velvet-covered chairs and dim lighting.

Le Climax This Kipé nightclub has great pizzas and music. Wednesday is ladies' night.

Calebasse Plus Musicians play at this Taouyah spot on Thursday and Saturday nights.

L'Oxygene Open Wed-Mon. L'Oxygene in Ratoma is very lively at weekends, when the cover charge goes up to GF10,000.

Au Copains d'Abord The live music at this Taouyah bar goes well with the pizzas (GF6000).

La Plage Rogbané This stretch of beach in Taouyah was cleaned up so people could use it. You can watch the sunset from the bar.

Music Venues For live music, check out ***La Paillotte***, the local arts centre for Guinea's old-school stars. There are no set schedules: just turn up and see what's happening. It's just north of Place du 8 Novembre. The dance and drum troupe ***Faréta*** rehearses every afternoon (except Sunday) at the former Ciné-Club, near Carrefour Célibataire in Bellevue.

Palais du Peuple There are often performances by local artists here. Look for advertisements at the Palais or in the free magazine, *Dyeli*.

Centre Culturel Franco-Guinéen Every Wednesday is Café Concert night, with free live music. The centre also puts on performances by local and visiting artists.

Cinemas Near the Taouyah market, ***Cinéma Rogbané*** has shows most evenings. Admission is GF1000. ***Cinéma Liberté*** on the Autoroute is another place to try. The ***Centre Culturel Franco-Guinéen*** shows French and African films; stop by for a schedule.

Shopping

For African print material, ***Marché Madina*** is the best. The ***Centre d'Appui à l'Autopromotion Féminine (CAAF)*** women's co-operative outlet has interesting tie-dyed cloth. The ***vendors*** opposite Hôtel Camayenne sell crafts of average quality, though occasionally they have unusual pieces. Slightly better are the shops and stands clustered around the CAAF. In general, it's better to buy baskets, textiles and other crafts upcountry as quality is higher and prices are lower.

The stalls in ***Marché du Niger*** and along ***Av de la République*** stock tapes and CDs of current stars. ***Enima*** inside the Palais du Peuple has a selection of older recordings.

Getting There & Away

Air All domestic flights use the aérogare nationale near the international airport, 13km from town. At the time of writing, only UTA/West Coast Airlines was running domestic flights, and only to N'zérékoré (GF120,000). Air Guinée and Guinea Air Service will probably resume flights from Conakry to Labé, Siguiri, N'zérékoré, Kissidougou and Kankan. Guinée Paramount Airlines should commence flying to Kankan (GF80,000), Siguiri (GF60,000) and N'zérékoré (GF120,000) shortly. On all of these airlines, schedules change constantly and prices vary. Be sure to confirm your seat a few days in advance; having a ticket does not necessarily guarantee your seat on the plane. The planes are not the most luxurious and cancellations and delays are frequent.

For details of regional and intercontinental flights to/from Conakry see Getting There & Away earlier in this chapter.

In Conakry, most airline offices are on or near Av de la République, and include:

Aeroflot (☎ 41 41 43)
Air France (☎ 43 10 46)
Air Guinée (☎ 45 46 09)
Cathay Pacific (☎ 41 47 38)
Ghana Airways (☎ 41 41 73)
Guinea Air Service (☎ 45 20 42; through Karou Voyages)
Guinée Paramount Airlines (☎ 45 46 69)
Royal Air Maroc (☎ 41 38 96)
UTA/West Coast Airways (☎ 45 38 01; through Ambassador Voyages)

Bus Long-distance buses leave from Gare Voiture de Madina, 6km from the centre (GF250 by shared taxi). Buses to Kindia and Mamou usually go daily and to Labé and Kankan a few times a week. The luggage fee for large bags is GF3000.

Bush Taxi & Minibus Bush taxis and minibuses for most upcountry destinations leave from Gare Voiture de Madina. Bush taxis for Siguiri and Bamako leave from the Ligne de Siguiri, near the gare voiture. Bush taxis for Sierra Leone leave from Gare Voiture de Matoto, 18km east of the city centre, and from the Madina station for the border at Pamelap. There's a postal bus from the Poste de Madina to Kankan (GF22,000; Wednesday and Friday), Labé (GF14,000; Tuesday and Saturday) and Kamsar (GF13,000; Monday and Thursday); go to the post office the day before to confirm departure times.

Note that bush taxis going into Conakry don't enter the city at night, but stop at Kilomètre 36 and wait until dawn before finishing their journey.

Getting Around

To/From the Airport Taxis from downtown to the airport shouldn't cost more than GF5000. From the airport into town costs GF3000 to GF6000, depending on your bargaining powers and where you're going.

Alternatively, catch a shared taxi (GF500) from just outside the airport or take the bus into the centre (GF300).

Bus Though the bus is not the most efficient way to get around, there are two main lines in the city, run by Futur-Transport and Béa Diallo: the 'C' line from the centre to Kaporo, and the 'A' line from the centre to Matoto beyond the airport. Fares range from GF150 to GF450, and both lines start at the roundabout opposite the port.

Taxi A seat in a shared taxi around town costs GF250 per zone, with the downtown zone ending at Dixinn (on the Route de Donka) and Madina (on the Route du Niger and Autoroute). To catch one, stand on the appropriate side of the road and yell your destination as the taxi passes. There's also a tricky hand-signal method, by which you point in the direction that the taxi takes at the major roundabouts. A charter taxi costs a minimum of GF1000, although that won't take you far; from downtown to Taouyah, for example, will cost around GF3500 during the day, GF5000 at night. To charter a taxi by the hour should cost GF6000, if you bargain.

Car All the companies listed have base rates of about GF60,000 per day plus mileage and chauffeur charges, except EGLPS which offers cheaper rates and a range of related services for long-term visitors.

A Tout Service (☎ 21 50 60) Hôtel Camayenne
Avis (☎ 45 45 71) Novotel
EGLPS (☎ 46 37 92) Opposite the Super-Bobo Supermarket
Europcar (☎ 45 19 80) Novotel
Hertz (☎ 43 07 45) Av de la République

AROUND CONAKRY

Îles de Los

The Îles de Los are a group of small islands about 10km southwest of Conakry, used as

GUINEA

a way station for the slave trade and later by the British (who controlled the islands during much of the 19th century) to resettle freed slaves. They're now popular for weekend excursions.

Tiny **Room** has a tranquil beach, which is good for swimming, and a pretty hotel, ***Le Sogue***, with singles from GF71,000 to GF119,000 and doubles from GF181,000 to GF218,000 (more at weekends), including transport and meals. Make reservations at Karou Voyages in Conakry. Le Sogue closes from mid-June to mid-October. ***Foré-Foté*** in the village has basic rooms for around GF20,000 (negotiable). Ask at the beach for Sinny or Kalla, who run the place along with their drumming school.

Kassa is closer to Conakry and large enough to walk around. Near Soro, the attractive main beach (admission GF1000), are some ***bungalows*** *(☎ 41 51 30)* for GF25,000 and a restaurant. ***Le Magellan*** is a fancy place with a pool on the other side of the island with air-con singles/doubles for GF85,000/95,000. Make reservations at Le Galion (☎ 42 20 22) in Conakry (see Places to Stay – Mid-Range in Conakry earlier in this chapter).

Tamara, used by the French and later by Sekou Touré as a penal colony, is not as popular with tourists as its beaches aren't particularly good, although it offers some interesting hikes. Fotoba, with its small Anglican church, is the main village; it doesn't have any restaurants.

Getting There & Away A motorised pirogue leaves for Room (GF14,000) from Hôtel Camayenne at 9.30am on Saturday. You can also hire your own pirogue for any of the islands from Boulbinet Port near the Novotel, though it's unlikely you'll pay less than GF25,000 for the day (don't pay the full amount upfront). Alternatively, overcrowded pirogues leave regularly for Soro (GF500), Fotoba (GF1000) and Room (GF1000), but return trips are erratic.

Coyah

Coyah, about 50km from Conakry, is where Guinea's bottled mineral water comes from; it's a possible place to stay if you want to avoid arriving late in the capital from upcountry. ***Môtel le Palmier*** *(☎ 21 38 84)* has air-con rooms for GF30,000 and GF40,000. ***Chez Claude*** *(☎ 22 93 28)* is a good French restaurant with a selection of delicacies from GF8000. If you've got transport, it makes a nice day excursion from Conakry.

From Coyah, it's GF5000 in a bush taxi to Pamelap, GF3000 to Kindia, GF2000 to Forécariah and GF700 to Conakry.

Dubréka

Dubréka, 5km from Dubréka junction on the Boffa highway, is President Lansana Conté's home town and the starting point for excursions to several natural attractions. Near the town are mangrove swamps with a rich variety of bird and animal life. You can hire a pirogue locally, but be sure it's in good condition as it takes several hours to really get into the swamps.

Les Cascades de la Soumba make a good outing (except from February to May, when they dry up to a trickle). The falls were held sacred by locals and were a site for sacrifices. Beneath the falls is a refreshing pool where you can swim. There's a nice ***restaurant*** here with meals for GF10,000 and, nearby, six fully equipped single/double ***bungalows*** for GF50,000/65,000, including breakfast. The owner can organise hikes into the surrounding area. The signposted turn-off to the falls is 11km after Dubréka junction on the Boffa highway; the falls are 5km further down a dirt road. To charter a taxi for the day from Dubréka junction costs about GF10,000.

About 10km east of Dubréka **Mt Kakoulima** (1011m) offers some good day hikes, and there are rock formations nearby, including one called **Le Chien Qui Fume**.

Kindia

Bustling Kindia is a good introduction to upcountry Guinea. It's a small town with a pleasant ambience and it's a good place to look for indigo cloth and other woven fabrics. You can see how the indigo cloth is made at the **Coopérative des Teinturières**. About 5km north of town is the interesting **Institut Pasteur** *(open daily)*, where research into snake venom is done; adjoining is a sad little zoo.

Voile de la Mariée *(Bridal Veil Falls; admission GF1000)*, 12km out of town, are worth a visit, especially during the rainy season. There are bungalows at the falls (GF25,000) and a restaurant is planned.

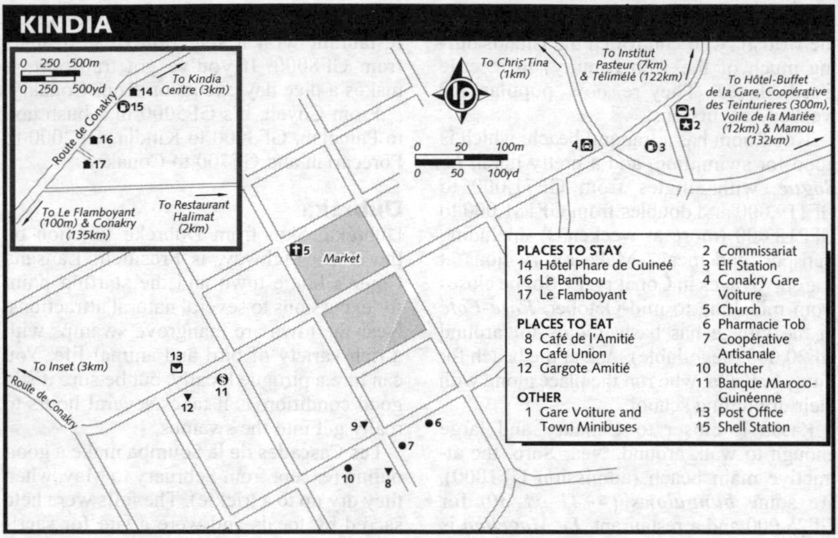
KINDIA
0 250 500m
0 250 500yd
To Kindia Centre (3km)
Route de Conakry
To Le Flamboyant (100m) & Conakry (135km)
To Restaurant Halimat (2km)
To Chris'Tina (1km)
To Institut Pasteur (7km) & Télimélé (122km)
To Hôtel-Buffet de la Gare, Coopérative des Teinturieres (300m), Voile de la Mariée (12km) & Mamou (132km)
0 50 100m
0 50 100yd
Market
To Inset (3km)
Route de Conakry
PLACES TO STAY
14 Hôtel Phare de Guineé
16 Le Bambou
17 Le Flamboyant
PLACES TO EAT
8 Café de l'Amitié
9 Café Union
12 Gargote Amitié
OTHER
1 Gare Voiture and Town Minibuses
2 Commissariat
3 Elf Station
4 Conakry Gare Voiture
5 Church
6 Pharmacie Tob
7 Coopérative Artisanale
10 Butcher
11 Banque Maroco-Guinéenne
13 Post Office
15 Shell Station

Shared taxis (GF600) head there daily or it costs about GF5000 to charter your own.

Places to Stay & Eat Rooms at the ***Hôtel Buffet de la Gare*** *(☎ 61 10 20)* will cost GF10,000/ 20,000 without/with fan and GF25,000/30,000 with air-con. They're somewhat dingy but tolerable.

Hôtel Phare de Guinée *(☎ 61 05 31)* Rooms with shared bathroom GF10,000, with bathroom GF20,000-30,000. Much better, although inconveniently located 3km from town, is the Phare de Guinée, with good, clean rooms.

Le Bambou *(☎ 61 08 39)* Rooms GF20,000. Also out of town, this is a friendly place with clean, comfortable rooms with fan and bathroom.

Le Flamboyant *(☎ 61 02 12)* Rooms with fan GF25,000, with air-con GF30,000-40,000. This hotel is in a tranquil setting and has beautiful, spotless rooms with bathroom. There's also a restaurant and a small pool. Rates include breakfast.

Kindia has a number of good hole-in-the-wall cafés in town. Café de l'Amitié and Café Union both have good coffee and a warm atmosphere.

Restaurant Halimat Meals GF6000-10,000. Halimat cooks up French and African cuisine as well as pizzas, although the restaurant is out of town.

Gargote Amitié *(☎ 61 06 03)* Meals GF3000-6000. This laid-back place has simple comfort food.

Chris'Tina Meals GF10,000. Chris'Tina is Kindia's most popular nightclub (GF5000 entry). You'll need to charter a taxi to find the place and to get back; it'll cost you GF3000 to GF6000 each way.

Getting There & Away Daily taxis leave the gare voiture for Télimélé (GF7000), the Sierra Leone border (GF2500), Mamou (GF5500), Coyah (GF2000) and Conakry (GF4000). Buses travel several times weekly to Mamou (GF5000) and Conakry (GF2500). There's a bypass road around town which avoids the centre.

Fouta Djalon

The Fouta Djalon plateau – an area of green rolling hills, 1000m peaks, orchards and farmland – is one of the most scenic areas of Guinea and the heartland of the country's Peul population (the language spoken is Pulaar). It's also one of the better hiking places in West Africa, especially from November to January when temperatures are cooler and the sky is not too dusty.

The towns included in this section are listed in order of distance from Conakry.

Hiking in the Fouta Djalon

The Fouta Djalon is excellent for hiking (and mountain biking), as – unlike many other places in West Africa – you can essentially go at will. It's suitable either for an extended series of day trips based in one of the towns, or for village to village walking (the villages are closely spaced).

Lodging is basic (with villagers) and cheap, and limited food is available en route, although you should carry your own supplies as well as water-purifying tablets. Bring a jacket, as it gets chilly at night, especially near Mali-ville. It's advisable to use topographical maps from the IGN in Conakry (see Planning in Facts for the Visitor earlier in this chapter for more details).

The terrain is hilly, but not overly strenuous (except near Mali-ville, where there are some steep sections if you're climbing up the escarpment from Senegal). The landscape is pastoral, with wide views over rolling hills and small mountains.

Outside the major towns (all of which, except Mali-ville, have a range of hotels and restaurants), there is no infrastructure and the area is not much visited, although tourism is increasing. Even so, you'll probably be the only tourist on the back paths.

MAMOU

Mamou, sometimes called the gateway to the Fouta Djalon, is a lively town with an interesting mosque. There are several vine bridges nearby, including one at Soumayereya south of Marella (about halfway between Mamou and Faranah). ***Auberge Mongo*** in Marella has good rooms. Also near Mamou is **Timbo**, former capital of the Fouta Djalon and, together with Fougoumba near Dalaba, an important religious centre for Guinea's Peuls. Closer to town is École Forestière (Enatef), a forestry school perched on the edge of a wooded reserve; trails through the woods are open to visitors.

Places to Stay

Hôtel Luna *(☎ 68 07 39)* Rooms with shared bathroom GF5000-10,000, with private bathroom GF15,000-20,000. This hotel, located on the Dalaba road, is the cheapest place to stay. Rooms have electricity at night only.

Hôtel Rama *(☎ 68 04 30)* Rooms GF17,000-30,000. The restaurant here has good food and a TV, and the rooms are clean and comfortable. The nightclub next door can get noisy.

École Forestière *(☎ 68 06 34)* Dorm beds GF7000, cabins GF18,000. Set in a pretty forest reserve about 3km from town on the Conakry road, this forestry school has rooms with three single beds each and clean shared bathrooms, as well as some nice cabins, with sitting area and kitchen.

Hôtel Africa Rooms GF17,000. This is the nicest place to stay in town, with clean, airy rooms and a cosy parlour with TV. It's in a tranquil spot just down the road from the Rama hotel.

Mariador Hôtel Linsan *(☎ 41 45 44)* Rooms GF40,000-52,000. This fancy place is in the village of Linsan, about 40km from Mamou on the Kindia road. Rooms are fully equipped, and there's a small pool.

Places to Eat

La Pergola Meals GF1000-5000. Situated in Quartier Petel, about 2km from the centre on the Dalaba road (GF250 in a shared taxi), is this popular bar-restaurant. Inexpensive dishes include chicken (GF12,000; enough for four people).

Restaurant Luna Meals from GF200. The cheap Restaurant Luna, across from the hotel of the same name, has a limited menu of brochettes and bouillon. Just next door to the restaurant a woman often sells *foneo* (millet) for GF200 a plate.

Getting There & Away

Mamou is a major transport junction. Frequent bush taxis to Conakry (GF10,000), Kindia (GF5000), Dalaba (GF2500), Labé (GF8500), Faranah (GF8000), Dabola (GF8000) and Kissidougou (GF15,000) depart from the gare voiture, next to the Elf petrol station.

DALABA

Dalaba, with its pretty pine groves and interesting nearby villages, makes a superb base for hiking or biking in this region. Before independence, the town was a therapeutic centre for colonial administrators, and many buildings from the era remain.

There's an excellent tourist office in the Chargeur Quartier with informative booklets

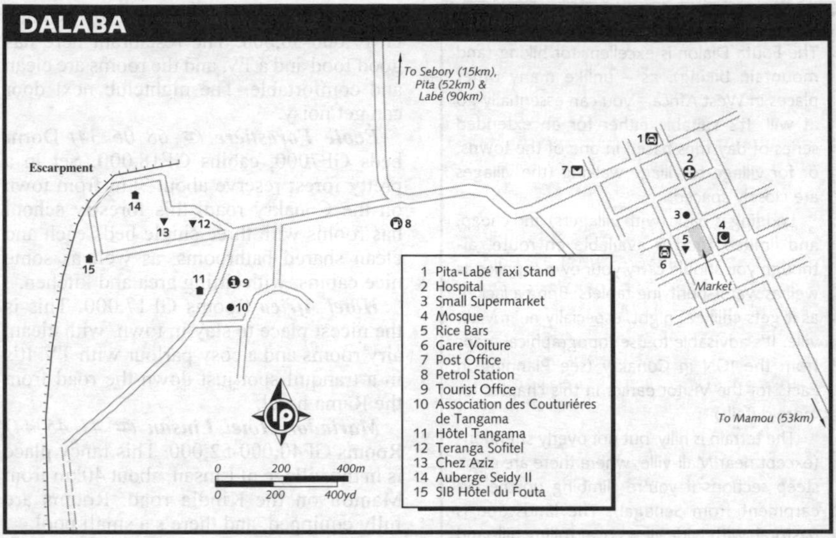
DALABA
To Sebory (15km), Pita (52km) & Labé (90km)
Escarpment
Market
To Mamou (53km)
1 Pita-Labé Taxi Stand
2 Hospital
3 Small Supermarket
4 Mosque
5 Rice Bars
6 Gare Voiture
7 Post Office
8 Petrol Station
9 Tourist Office
10 Association des Couturiéres de Tangama
11 Hôtel Tangama
12 Teranga Sofitel
13 Chez Aziz
14 Auberge Seidy II
15 SIB Hôtel du Fouta
0 200 400m
0 200 400yd

detailing places of interest in and around Dalaba. They can help plan routes and arrange a guide if you want one, though it's not necessary. They can also set you up with local accommodation. It can be difficult to change money in Dalaba, especially on Monday when many shops are closed. Market day is Sunday.

The Dalaba region is good for crafts. Places worth visiting include the Association des Couturières de Tangama for batiks and tie-dyed fabric, and the Group Artisanal Feminin Vanerie in Sebory (15km northwest of town) for baskets.

Places to Stay & Eat

Hôtel Tangama *(☎ 69 11 09)* Rooms with shared bathroom GF15,000, singles/doubles with bathroom GF20,000/25,000. The rooms at this pleasant pension are simple and clean. The restaurant serves breakfast for GF2000 and a main meal will cost GF4500 or GF6000.

Auberge Seidy II *(☎ 69 10 63)* Rooms GF15,000. This place has four clean rooms with bathroom; the two on the 2nd floor have great views. Meals (GF4500 to GF6000 for dinner) need to be ordered in advance.

SIB Hôtel du Fouta *(☎ 69 71 10)* Rooms GF35,000. The SIB is Dalaba's luxury accommodation option, with fully equipped rooms. Even if you don't stay here, swing by for a drink at sunset; the views of the valley from the terrace are not to be missed.

Chez Aziz Meals GF2000. Close to the hotels, Chez Aziz has inexpensive local fare.

Teranga Sofitel Mains GF5000. The friendly couple who run this place make good Senegalese dishes. Be sure to check out the drawings on the wall.

Near the gare voiture are several good ***rice bars***. You can also find *attiéké* in the neighbouring alleys.

Getting There & Away

Bush taxis for Pita (GF2500), Labé (GF4000), Mamou (GF2500) and Conakry (GF14,000, seven hours) leave from the gare voiture near the market.

PITA

Pita's major attraction is the **Chutes du Kinkon**. To get there, take the main road north out of town for 1km, then head left 10km down a dirt road to the falls. It's a good walk or an easy bike ride. The setting is not ideal as the falls are below a hydroelectric plant, but they're still worth a visit. Camping is prohibited. Before visiting, you'll need to get a permit from the police station in Pita; it's free and usually not a hassle to obtain.

Places to Stay & Eat

Auberge de Pita has clean and spacious rooms with bathroom for GF15,000. The bar/lounge has a TV and a friendly atmosphere. Just around the corner from the hotel is an outdoor weaving centre, with looms lined up in the shade of the trees. The Auberge is off the main road at the southern end of town.

Centre d'Accueil, behind the prefecture, has run-down rondavels (huts) for GF5000 and better rooms in the main building for GF15,000 and GF20,000.

Pita has a wealth of good cafés, rice and coffee bars, and street food. ***Bar Café 109*** has the usual brochettes and omelettes (GF2000) served here in a comfy setting at the northern end of town.

Although meals are only available at ***Oury's Cool & Cozy Café*** with advance notice, it's worth visiting for the *café noir* and for a chat with Oury, who speaks English and has a wealth of information on the area. Stop by before setting off on any excursions. He can arrange guides for hikes to the falls and can help you find accommodation with locals. Oury's Cool & Cozy Café is behind Bar Café 109.

Getting There & Away

The postal bus from Labé usually saves a few seats for passengers heading for Pita. Bush taxis leave from the Rex Cinéma to Labé (GF2000) and Dalaba (GF3000) throughout the day, and twice a week to Télimélé (GF11,000).

AROUND PITA

The three-tiered **Chutes de Kambadaga** are about 35km from Pita and are rough to reach; you'll need transport. To get there, follow the dirt road from Pita to Kinkon, then branch right. It's a steep hike down to the bottom. There's a small bungalow where you can overnight for about GF5000; bring your own food and water-purifying tablets.

About 50km from Pita on the Télimélé road is the village of Doucké (part of Donghol Touma), where the friendly Hassan Bah runs a guesthouse of sorts – it's a luxurious hut equipped with gas stove and queen-size bed on, as one reader put it, 'the edge of Guinea's Grand Canyon'. Doucké is marked, oddly enough, by a stop sign; ask at the telecommunications centre for Hassan.

LABÉ

The largest town in the Fouta Djalon, Labé is also the region's administrative capital. There are several indigo-cloth cooperatives downtown; one to try is Teinture-Promotion Labé. Although Labé has two banks, they're often reluctant to change money (much less travellers cheques); shop owners may be able to help you out.

For email, visit CFIT next door to the Hôtel de l'Indépendance, where 30 minutes online costs GF3000. Cyber Fouta costs the same and has more computers, but connection is slower.

There are many hikes and excursions in the Labé area, including the **Chutes de Saala**, which are about an hour's drive down a rugged road off the Route de Koundara. Expect to pay about GF30,000 for a chartered taxi from the main gare voiture. Be sure to visit the falls at both the main entrance – where you can picnic and swim – and at the lookout point (veer right at the fork in the road as you approach).

About 20km out of town on the Mali-ville road is the signposted turn-off for the source of the Gambia River.

LABÉ
1 Church
2 Mosque
3 Le Petit Dakar; Shared Taxis for Gare Voiture Daka
4 Le Zephyr
5 Cyber Fouta
6 BICIGUI Bank
7 Air Guinée; Labo Photo
8 Teinture-Promotion Labé
9 Restaurant
10 College Hugo M'Bouro
11 Restaurant
12 Bar Americain le Relaxe
13 Hôtel de l'Indépendance & Annexe; CFIT
14 Main Gare Voiture
15 Rice Bars
16 Post Office
17 BCRG Bank
18 Petrol Station
19 Keur Samba
0 100 200m
0 100 200yd
Market
To Gare Voiture Daka (2km) & Mali-ville (120km)
To Koundara (265km)
Route de Koundara
Rue de la Poste
To Hôtel Salam (1km)
To Hôtel Provincial & Hôtel Saala (3km), Hôtel Safatou (5km), Pita (38km), Mamou (141km) & Conakry (408km)
To Hôtel Tata (1km)

Places to Stay

Hôtel de l'Indépendance *(☎ 51 10 00)* Annexe/main building rooms GF5000/20,000. The cheapest lodging in Labé is in the annexe here near the main gare voiture, but the rooms are depressing. Rooms in the main part of the hotel across the street are better and have bathrooms.

Hôtel Saala *(☎ 51 07 31)* Rooms without/with bathroom GF7000/13,000, or villas GF18,000/23,000. The Saala, 3km outside town, is good value, with basic clean rooms. Behind the main building are pretty villas.

Hôtel Salam *(☎ 51 16 81)* Rooms without/with bathroom GF10,000/20,000. Not to be confused with Hôtel Saala, the Salam is a bit closer to town in a quiet *quartier*. Rooms are spotless and spacious.

Hôtel Provincial Rooms without/with bathroom GF10,000/22,000. The garden setting here is tranquil and the hotel, a bit out of town, has good live music on weekends. Mouctar Paraya, among other well-known Guinean musicians, often performs here.

Hôtel Tata *(☎ 51 05 40)* Huts GF17,000, rooms GF30,000. The nicest place in Labé, the Tata has comfortable, good-value rooms with attractive tilework, and cosy *cases* (huts) with bathrooms. Madame Raby, the owner, has lots of information on the area and can organise excursions or arrange transport (including bicycle rental).

Hôtel Safatou *(☎ 51 11 09)* Singles/doubles GF35,000/40,000. The glitzy Safatou, as you enter Labé, has fully equipped rooms, but it's an inconvenient 5km from the centre. Rates include breakfast.

Places to Eat

Labé has good ***street food***. You'll find stands everywhere selling beans, fried sweet potatoes and brochettes for under GF1000. There are ***rice bars*** along the length of the gare voiture as well as a couple of great nameless restaurants down the street from the station as you head into town. ***Bar American Le Relaxe*** is one of many cute bars in town.

Keur Samba *(☎ 51 09 10)* Meals GF6000. The restaurant at the Hôtel de Tourisme has a friendly atmosphere and a limited menu of delicious European-style dishes.

Le Zephyr Meals GF2000. Le Zephyr has the usual brochettes, omelettes, and peas and green beans.

Le Petit Dakar Meals GF2000. This little café is good for coffee, sandwiches and people-watching.

Hôtel Tata Meals GF7000. The Tata has excellent pizzas and a selection of Italian and other dishes.

Getting There & Away

Air Guinée makes a loop between Conakry, Labé, Dakar, Banjul, Labé and Conakry once a week. The Labé to Conakry leg costs GF45,000, but was temporarily suspended at the time of writing.

Labé is an important road transport junction, and the end of the tar road for onward transport to Senegal and Guinea-Bissau. Bush taxis for Mali-ville (GF7500, four hours) and Koundara (GF16,000, eight hours) leave from Gare Voiture Daka 2km north of town. Shared taxis (GF250) for Gare Voiture Daka leave from Le Petit Dakar, in the town centre. Bush taxis for Conakry (GF16,000, nine hours) and other destinations leave from the main gare voiture near Hôtel de l'Independance.

The postal bus to Conakry (GF14,000) departs from the post office at 7am Wednesday and Sunday. Reserve a spot in advance as it tends to fill up.

MALI-VILLE

Mali is the proper name of this town, but the name Mali-ville is often used to distinguish it from the country Mali. Mali-ville is perched on the edge of the spectacular Massif du Tamgué just before its precipitous drop towards Senegal and the plains below. At over 1300m it's the highest town in the Fouta; the climate is cool and the scenery superb. If you don't mind roughing it a bit, it makes an excellent base for hiking and mountain biking excursions into the surrounding area. There's no electricity or running water in town, and only basic provisions.

On Sunday, Mali-ville has a good market. Look for the honey vendors; they gather the honey from the baskets you see in the trees lining the road to Labé. Opposite the market is the Centre d'Appui à l'Auto-Promotion Féminine (CAAF), a cloth-weaving cooperative with a small boutique. Just around the corner is Mali-ville's unofficial tourist office, staffed by the friendly Monsieur Souaré, who runs Campement Bev and organises excursions in the area.

Mali-ville's best-known attraction is **Mt Loura** which has the **Dame de Mali** rock formation on its side. The top (look for the radio antenna) is 7km from town by bike (shorter if you hike), and offers unparalleled views. On a clear day you can see the Gambia River and Senegal. No permits are necessary to climb Mt Loura, despite what the police may tell you.

Mt Lansa is another good excursion. It's a three-hour hike to the top, from where there are excellent views over the surrounding countryside. You'll need a guide on the upper section of the mountain; ask him to point out the stone platform used for drumming messages to the villages below.

Places to Stay & Eat

The only place in town with electricity (solar powered), ***L'Auberge Indigo*** has cute little rooms. The staff have all sorts of information on the area and can connect you with folks who prepare meals (otherwise there are a few rice bars in town). Singles/doubles are GF8000/12,000.

La Dame du Mali Rooms GF5000. This place has dingy rooms with bathroom; meals are available if you order in advance.

Campement Bev Rooms/huts GF5000/7000. You'll definitely want to stay in one of the four huts here, each of which has a comfy double bed. It is set in the friendly village of Donghol-Teinseire and is perfectly aligned with La Dame de Mali's profile. Meals are available.

The ladies at the ***CAAF*** make the best dishes in town but if you want dinner, you must order in the morning.

Getting There & Away

There's at least one vehicle daily between Mali-ville and Labé (GF7500, 120km, four hours). There's generally one or two vehicles per week to Kedougou (Senegal; GF14,000) in the dry season. In the other direction, travellers occasionally end up walking from the border. Boys will be around to help carry your luggage; it takes up to 12 hours.

The Mali-ville to Koundara road is very bad; transport is only feasible on Saturday, market day in Madina Woura, or Sunday, market day in Termessé. You'll have to change vehicle in these towns. Alternatively, you can go via Labé.

KOUNDARA

Koundara is the starting point for visits to **Parc Transfrontalier Niokolo-Badiar**, which consists of Guinea's Parc National du Badiar and Senegal's Parc National du Niokolo-Koba. Together they encompass a 950,000-hectare protected area, of which about 50,000 hectares are in Guinea. Development on the Guinean side lags well behind that in Senegal, but it's coming along, with huts and a restaurant 7km into the park due to be finished soon. Park headquarters are in Sambaïlo, and the folks there are friendly and knowledgeable. You can't walk or ride mopeds in the park so if you don't have a car, you'll have to charter one in Koundara.

Animals you might see include bushbucks, roan antelopes, wart hogs and western red colobus and patas monkeys. There are also chimpanzees and hippopotamuses in the region. The best months for spotting animals are February and March, but even if you don't see any animals, there are some interesting birds here and the landscape alone makes for a nice drive. The park is officially closed during the rainy season, from June to November. In Conakry, information on the park is available from the Direction Nationale des Forêts et de la Faune on Route de Donka in Camayenne.

There are many ethnic groups in this area, including the Badiaranké, Bassari, Peul and Coniagui, and the colourful mixture makes Koundara an interesting place to visit. About 45km from Koundara on the Bissau border is **Saréboïdo**; it has a good Sunday market.

Places to Stay & Eat

Hôtel Gangan Rooms GF10,000. The Gangan has basic rooms with shared bathrooms. There's electricity at night, if enough people are staying here.

Hôtel Mamadou Boiro Rooms without bathroom GF4000-7000, with bathroom GF8000. This place has rooms of about the same standard as the Gangan, but there's no running water.

Hôtel Skanté Rooms GF5000. The Skanté is good for the money, and has rooms with shared bathrooms. There's a decent restaurant here and a nightclub that can get noisy on Thursday and Saturday night.

There are several ***rice bars*** near the gare voiture. In the mornings, look for *gosseytiga*, a rice porridge with ground peanuts and sugar that is a speciality of the region. The ***Niokolo-Badiar Café*** near the Saréboïdo taxi stand has good coffee, and the ***Café Oriental*** has good omelettes. Thanks to Koundara's proximity to Bissau, you can usually find Superbock beer here.

Getting There & Away

Bush taxis run frequently to Sambaïlo (GF1300) and Saréboïdo (GF2000). There are daily bush taxis to Labé (GF16,000, eight hours), and a direct taxi once a week to Conakry (GF30,000, 20 hours). For those driving their own vehicle, there's a ferry (GF2500) over the Koumba River between Kounsitél and Dinguétéri.

The best way to get to Boké is via Saréboïdo after its Sunday market; you'll need to change vehicle in Saréboïdo.

A bush taxi generally heads daily for the Senegal border, from where there's transport on to Tambacounda.

Upper Guinea

In Upper Guinea (Haute Guinée), the hills and greenery of the Fouta Djalon give way to the reds and browns of the country's grassy, low-lying savanna lands. Although few tourists make it to this region, there's much of interest and it's an area well worth exploring.

DABOLA

Dabola is a peaceful town set amid hills. The town's main attraction is the **Barrage du Tinkisso**, which supplies electricity for Dabola, Faranah and Dinguiraye. At the bottom is a picnic area, which is popular on weekends. You can also cross over the stream, where there's a beach and a small waterfall. The dam is 8km from town, signposted on the Conakry road.

Tinkisso Bungalows/rooms GF15,000/30,000. Just out of town on the Conakry road, this is Dabola's best hotel, with spotless air-con rooms with bathroom. The bungalows have electricity and bathrooms but are in an isolated area 2km behind the main building.

Hôtel Le Mont Sincery Rooms with fan/air-con GF17,000/20,000. This friendly place, signposted off the Conakry road, has very clean rooms with bathroom. Meals are available in a pretty restaurant for around GF5000.

Chez Marie Meals around GF5000. Opposite the Tinkisso hotel, Chez Marie has a limited menu, but the food is quite amazing (be sure to try the vinaigrette). Marie can prepare special dishes if you order in the morning.

Chez Fatou Yebhe Barry Rice and salads at this place in town are good and cheap.

Bush taxis leave every day to Faranah (GF7000, 3½ hours), Mamou (GF8000), Kankan (GF15,000) and Conakry (GF18,000).

DINGUIRAYE

This is a small town whose main claim to fame is its **mosque** – until recently one of the largest thatched structures in Africa. Although renovations have replaced the thatching with more modern materials, it's still significant as the seat of an important regional Islamic sect founded in the mid-19th century by El Hadj Omar Tall.

For a place to stay, try ***Madame Sow*** who rents out basic rooms for GF5000. The ***Hôtel de l'Amitié*** has decent rooms for GF15,000. Bush taxis from Dabola will set you back GF7000.

FARANAH

President Sekou Touré hailed from this region, and Faranah still bears his marks. There's a conference centre (now a dirty old hotel), an airstrip built to accommodate Concorde, and an oversized abandoned villa. It's also the highest point on the Niger River that is easily accessible, just 150km from the river's source. The main reason to come here is to visit the **Parc National du Haut Niger** (see the boxed text on the next page). Behind Hôtel Cité de Niger is the house of renowned Guinean drummer Fadoubah Oularé; serious students can arrange lessons for a fee.

Between Faranah and Kissidougou, a dirt road branches south towards the village of **Forokonia** (72km from the main road), which you can use as a base if you wish to visit the source of the Niger River, 7km further, which is considered sacred by locals.

Places to Stay & Eat

Hotels in Faranah are nothing to write home about. None have running water, and electricity is only on at night.

Parc National du Haut Niger

The Parc National du Haut Niger protects one of West Africa's last remaining dry-forest ecosystems. The park's 554-sq-km core area (there are 6500 sq km of inhabited buffer zones) has an interesting assortment of wildlife that is easy to spot, including waterbucks, bushbucks, buffalos, duikers, Nile crocodiles, hippos and an array of monkeys. It's less likely that you'll see the panthers and lions that live here, but you might spot their tracks.

The park headquarters and an interesting botanical garden are in Sidakoro, 45km from Faranah on a rough road. There are some nice rooms here for GF10,000 per person, as well as a restaurant (though it's better to bring your own food). You can also camp here for GF5000. No bottled water is available.

The park has some pirogues that you can take up the Niger (GF20,000) from Somoria, the gateway to the core area, about 30km into the park. The small *campement* (camp) here has huts with bathroom for GF15,000 a person. There's running water, but no restaurant. Somoria also has a chimpanzee centre, where chimps rescued from domesticity are trained to re-enter the wild.

To visit the park, you'll need your own transport. Permits for entering the park cost GF15,000 per person per day, with a GF10,000 additional charge for the mandatory guide. Visit the Direction Nationale des Forêts et de la Faune on Route de Donka in Conakry for more information.

Hôtel Camaldine Rooms GF20,000. Though overpriced, rooms here are acceptable. The hotel is unmarked, 2km from the centre off the Dabola road. The restaurant here is pleasant; meals cost around GF5000.

Le Bas-Fond Rooms GF5000. This place, in a rural setting about 1km from the centre on the Mamou road, has basic rooms with bathroom.

Hôtel Bati Rooms GF10,000. The Bati has decent rooms with shared bathroom and one of Faranah's better restaurants. Meals are about GF5000.

Restaurant Bantou Meals GF1000-5000. This lively outdoor bar/restaurant is just next to the Bati. Meals here are usually available on request.

Getting There & Away

The bush-taxi stand is on the main street next to the petrol station. Vehicles go daily to Kissidougou (GF7000), Mamou (GF9000), Dabola (GF7000) and Conakry (GF19,000).

KANKAN

Guinea's second city and a university town, Kankan is a pleasant place with a Sahelian feel, set on the banks of the Milo River (a large tributary of the Niger River). The capital of the ancient Empire of Mali was at **Niani**, 130km northeast of here, and today it's still an unofficial 'capital' for Guinea's Malinké people. Nearly every Malinké you meet, even as far away as Senegal and Gambia, regards Kankan as their spiritual home. Just over the river is the hill from which Samory Touré's famed siege of Kankan and later standoff against the French colonialists took place.

The main sights are the colourful markets and the Grande Mosquée. The caretaker at the mosque will be glad to show you around for a small fee. Also worth a visit is the old presidential palace, Villa Syli, overlooking the river. It's closed now, although you can still walk around the grounds (no photos are allowed).

In the post office annexe is a Sotelgui office where you can sometimes log onto the Internet. The fee costs about GF3000 per session.

Quiet **Kouroussa**, about 65km from Kankan on the Dabola road, is the birthplace of Guinean author Camara Laye, known in particular for his autobiographical *L'Enfant Noir* (often translated as *The African Child* or *The Dark Child*) about coming of age among the Malinké people. You can visit the family compound here, and there's a fancy hotel if you want to overnight.

Places to Stay

Le Refuge *(☎ 71 05 41)* Rooms GF10,000. Also known as Chez Marie, Le Refuge has a peaceful courtyard and simple, clean rooms with bathroom. It's 2.5km from town on the Kissidougou road.

Centre d'Acceuil Diocesan Rooms GF20,000. This new Catholic mission guesthouse is so clean you could eat off the floor. Rooms have showers and sinks (toilets are down the hall), mosquito nets, ceiling

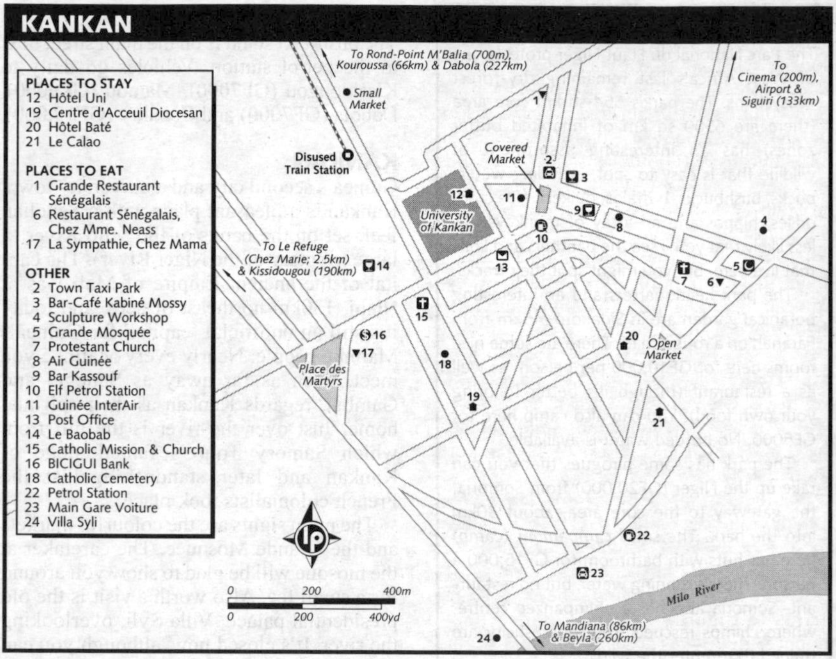
KANKAN
PLACES TO STAY
12 Hôtel Uni
19 Centre d'Acceuil Diocesan
20 Hôtel Baté
21 Le Calao
PLACES TO EAT
1 Grande Restaurant Sénégalais
6 Restaurant Sénégalais, Chez Mme. Neass
17 La Sympathie, Chez Mama
OTHER
2 Town Taxi Park
3 Bar-Café Kabiné Mossy
4 Sculpture Workshop
5 Grande Mosquée
7 Protestant Church
8 Air Guinée
9 Bar Kassouf
10 Elf Petrol Station
11 Guinée InterAir
13 Post Office
14 Le Baobab
15 Catholic Mission & Church
16 BICIGUI Bank
18 Catholic Cemetery
22 Petrol Station
23 Main Gare Voiture
24 Villa Syli
To Rond-Point M'Balia (700m), Kouroussa (66km) & Dabola (227km)
Small Market
Disused Train Station
To Le Refuge (Chez Marie; 2.5km) & Kissidougou (190km)
Covered Market
University of Kankan
Place des Martyrs
Open Market
To Cinema (200m), Airport & Siguiri (133km)
Milo River
To Mandiana (86km) & Beyla (260km)
0 200 400m
0 200 400yd

fans and electricity at night. A simple breakfast is included in the room rate.

Le Calao *(☎ 71 27 97)* Rooms GF30,000. Le Calao has clean air-con rooms with bathroom, TV and fridge. The restaurant has good food; meals cost GF5000 to GF7000.

Hôtel Baté *(☎ 71 26 86)* Singles GF42,000, doubles GF52,000-62,000, annexe rooms with fan/air-con GF25,000/30,000. The luxurious rooms here have all the fittings, and rates include breakfast. The cheaper rooms in the annexe are nice enough; rates for these don't include breakfast. Note that two people of the same gender may have trouble sharing a room here.

Hôtel Uni *(☎ 71 06 28)* Rooms GF35,000-40,000. Rooms here have all the amenities of the rooms at the Baté but are also equipped with Internet capability. But again, two travellers who are not 'Madame et Monsieur' may have to negotiate to share a room. Rates include breakfast.

Places to Eat

Kankan has good street food and many rice bars. One of the best is ***Grande Restaurant Sénégalais***, with rice and sauce for GF300.

Restaurant Sénégalais, Chez Mme. Neass Meals GF1000-5000. Mme Neass makes a great *yassa* (onion and lemon sauce) and can prepare just about any African dish with advance notice.

La Sympathie, Chez Mama Meals around GF1000. La Sympathie has inexpensive and inspired meals. Mama's a spunky lady who speaks English and knows Kankan inside out.

Entertainment

Le Baobab In the field behind the university – look for the two baobab trees – is this bar, popular with students in the afternoon.

Bar Café Kabiné Mossy This little drinking spot occasionally has sandwiches and other simple food.

Bar Kassouf Kankan's most popular bar is usually crowded and lively. Most nights of the week you can get grilled fish and salad outside for GF2500.

Getting There & Away

At the time of writing there were no flights to Kankan, but Guinée Paramount was planning to resume service from Conakry (GF80,000).

Bush taxis for all destinations, including places like Conakry (GF29,000), Kissidougou (GF12,000), Beyla (GF20,000) and N'zérékoré (GF22,000), leave from the main gare voiture near the bridge. There's also a smaller taxi stand near Rond-Point M'Balia for Kouroussa (GF5000). The postal bus goes from Kankan to Conakry (GF22,000) on Thursday and Saturday morning, but seats fill up fast so book in advance.

Bush taxis to Côte d'Ivoire go via Mandiana to Noumoudjila (GF15,000), where you can find transport to Mininian and from there onwards to Odienné.

SIGUIRI

Siguiri is the last major town en route to Mali. There are some good walks outside the centre which offer views of the Tinkisso and Niger Rivers.

For lodging, try ***Hôtel Tam Tam*** on the Kankan road which has rooms with fan for about GF10,000. ***Hôtel de la Paix***, near the radio mast, is slightly cheaper.

At the time of writing, there were no flights to Siguiri, although Guinée Paramount Airlines was preparing to start flights from Conakry for GF70,000. From Siguiri, two roads lead to Mali. Bush taxis generally go via Kourémalé to Bamako (seven hours). The secondary route along the Niger River makes a great bike trip during the dry season. Bush taxis also leave daily for Kankan (GF10,000) and Conakry (GF40,000).

Forest Region

Guinea's Forest Region (Guinée Forestière), in the southeastern corner, is a beautiful region of hills, lush forests and streams, although deforestation is taking its toll. The area is close to Liberia and Sierra Leone and was hit hard in 2000 and 2001 by spill-over fighting from the wars in these countries. At the time of writing, however, the Forest Region was peaceful, if a bit shell-shocked, and many Sierra Leonean refugees have begun to return home.

KISSIDOUGOU

Kissidougou is a friendly town and the surrounding area, with gently rolling hills and many villages, is perfect for exploring by bicycle.

For food and lodging, the nicest place is ***Hôtel Savannah*** *(☎ 98 10 40)*, with fan/air-con rooms for GF25,000/30,000. The restaurant is beautifully decorated; meals are around GF8000. ***Hôtel Nelson Mandela*** *(☎ 98 13 05)*, signposted on the Kankan road, has decent rooms from GF15,000 and a restaurant with meals from GF2000 to GF6000. ***Hôtel de la Paix*** is not as nice, but is cheaper at GF10,000 per room. ***Hôtel Béléfé*** *(☎ 98 12 34)*, signposted 500m from the market, has clean, well-equipped rooms for GF15,000, though most have only interior windows.

There's an airport in Kissi, but usually no flights. Bush taxis go daily to Faranah (GF7000), Conakry (GF25,000) and Kankan (GF12,000, five hours). The scenic Kankan road is very potholed. For cyclists, Tokounou (where Friday is market day) makes a good stop; you can get basic supplies and arrange lodging with locals.

LOLA

Lola, near the borders of Liberia and Côte d'Ivoire, is the starting point for hiking up Mt Nimba (see the boxed text 'Hiking on Mt Nimba'). There are several mud-cloth cooperatives in town, including Cooperative Laanah des Teinturières, 2km from the centre on the N'zérékoré road. In the past, Lola was known as a centre for traditional medicine; the staff at Hôtel Heinoukoloa can introduce you to local herbalists, if you're interested. Lola is also home to the endangered African grey parrot, which, because of its ability to imitate sounds, is often caught and sold into captivity. There are some places (called *dortoits*) around town where the birds sing daily at dawn (6am) and dusk (5pm).

Hôtel Heinoukoloa has basic but acceptable rooms without bathroom for GF6000 to GF10,000 or with bathroom for GF15,000. It's about 1km off the main road. En route is the newer ***Hôtel Nouketi***, where rooms without bathroom cost GF6000 to GF10,000 and with bathroom GF15,000; prices are negotiable.

About 18km from Lola is **Bossou**, the site of a chimpanzee research centre. The fee for entering the forest for a few hours to see the chimps is a steep GF40,000 per person (including guide), but it's a scenic hike through the woods and you're likely to see the animals (note that they take a midday nap between noon and about 2.30pm). There's one ***hotel*** in Bossou, at the base of the big hill, with simple but surprisingly decent rooms for GF5000. The research centre also has rooms, each with a single bed and shared bathroom; the price isn't fixed but should be around GF10,000.

From Lola, bush taxis head to N'zérékoré (GF2500), Bossou (GF2000) and Nzo (GF2500). To the Côte d'Ivoire border, you can go via Nzo to Danané or via Tounkarata to Sipilou and Man. Bush taxis to Yekepa in Liberia cost GF4500.

MACENTA

Macenta is set in a scenic area of hills and streams. In the centre of the market is a theatre which puts on occasional performances by local dance groups.

Hôtel Bamala, 3km from the centre off the N'zérékoré road, has clean rooms with bathroom from GF20,000 (GF25,000 with air-con) and meals by request.

Hiking on Mt Nimba

Mt Nimba, Guinea's highest peak at 1752m, is part of the mountain range straddling Guinea, Côte d'Ivoire and Liberia. The summit offers excellent views of surrounding peaks in all three countries. The hike follows an old logging road, and you can ascend and descend in a day, if you start out early enough.

From Lola, take a bush taxi towards Nzo and disembark after 18km at the village of Gbakoré. The hike begins behind the health centre. It's a steep, winding four-hour trek to the top.

If you want to overnight on the mountain, you can stay in abandoned forest ranger cabins (known as La Cité) about one-third of the way up for GF10,000. Monsieur Pierre has the key to the cabins; ask for him in Gbakoré. Bring your own food and water-purifying tablets; there's electricity and running water at La Cité and a stream about halfway between there and the top.

The Nimba mountains host a rich variety of unique plant and animal life, including a rare frog. The range is under special Unesco protection – to the dismay of some sectors of the Guinean government, who are more interested in realising earnings from its iron-ore reserves.

Cheaper, but dirty, is ***Hôtel Palm*** near the market, with rooms from GF6000 and meals on request from GF1000. ***Hôtel le Magnétic*** is similarly grungy, but it's right at the gare voiture and is tolerable (and cheap). Rooms without bathroom are GF5000.

Bush taxis to Kissidougou are GF12,000; it's GF10,000 to N'zérékoré. Taxis go via Daro to the Liberian border and on to Voinjama. However, if you're heading to Monrovia, it's often faster to go from Macenta to Koyama and from there over the border to Zorzor as the Voinjama road is terrible.

N'ZÉRÉKORÉ

N'zérékoré, the major city in Guinea's Forest Region, is a pleasant place and a good base for exploring the surrounding area. Market day is Wednesday.

There's a mud-cloth cooperative at the artisanal village where you can watch women dyeing the cloth with kola nuts. A variety of woodcarvings, baskets and other crafts are also for sale. **Musée Ethnographique** *(open daily)* has a small but fascinating collection of masks, fetishes and other objects of traditional forest culture. The museum director is a spritely old man who tells good stories about the forest.

The area around N'zérékoré offers endless possibilities for exploration by bicycle. Many villages have vine bridges, particularly those along the Oulé River. There's a more accessible vine bridge over the Diani River 3km off the main road at **Silisu**, 45km northwest of N'zérékoré. About 50km further on, near **Sérédou**, is Forêt Classée de Ziama, one of Guinea's few remaining rainforests. Elephants are easy to spot here, and you don't need a car to enter the forest. You can get a guide and information at the new park headquarters in Sérédou. In town, ***Hôtel de l'Unité*** has cheap rooms.

Places to Stay & Eat

Hôtel Bakoly *(☎ 91 07 34)* Rooms GF4000-8000. This hotel near the market is the cheapest place to stay, with basic rooms and shared bathrooms; those in the annexe are more expensive but they're smelly.

Hôtel Bohema *(☎ 91 10 95)* Rooms GF15,000. The much nicer Bohema is friendly and good value with clean rooms with bathroom. The restaurant is pleasant and has dishes for about GF4000.

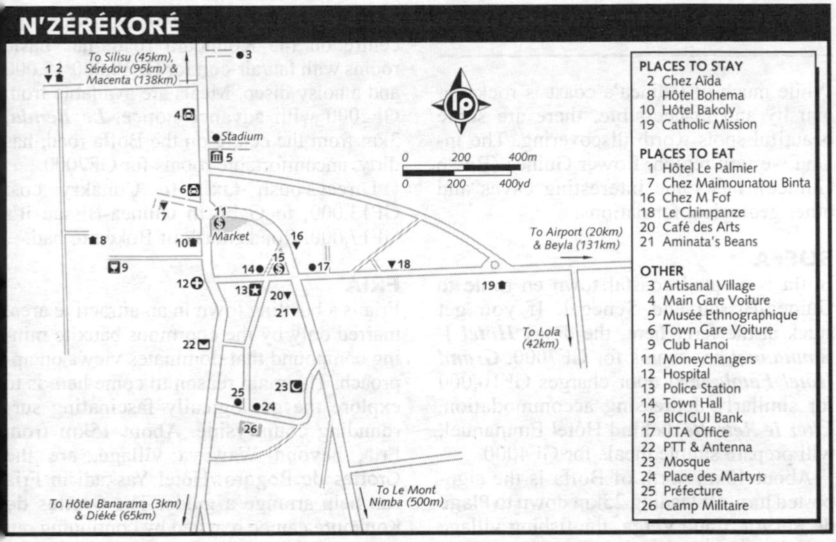
N'ZÉRÉKORÉ
To Silisu (45km), Sérédou (95km) & Macenta (138km)
Stadium
Market
To Airport (20km) & Beyla (131km)
To Lola (42km)
To Hôtel Banarama (3km) & Diéké (65km)
To Le Mont Nimba (500m)
0 200 400m
0 200 400yd
PLACES TO STAY
2 Chez Aïda
8 Hôtel Bohema
10 Hôtel Bakoly
19 Catholic Mission
PLACES TO EAT
1 Hôtel Le Palmier
7 Chez Maimounatou Binta
16 Chez M Fof
18 Le Chimpanze
20 Café des Arts
21 Aminata's Beans
OTHER
3 Artisanal Village
4 Main Gare Voiture
5 Musée Ethnographique
6 Town Gare Voiture
9 Club Hanoi
11 Moneychangers
12 Hospital
13 Police Station
14 Town Hall
15 BICIGUI Bank
17 UTA Office
22 PTT & Antenna
23 Mosque
24 Place des Martyrs
25 Préfecture
26 Camp Militaire

Catholic Mission *(☎ 91 07 93)* Rooms GF15,000. The Catholic Mission, at the other end of town, has simple but clean rooms with shared bathroom and mosquito net.

Chez Aïda *(☎ 91 07 47)* Rooms GF20,000. Aïda has clean and spacious rooms with bathroom and an excellent restaurant with dishes for GF6500.

Hôtel Banarama *(☎ 91 13 37)* Rooms GF25,000. The Banarama has large, airy rooms with bathroom. The only drawback is its location 3km from town. The restaurant alone is worth the trip; meals are GF3000 to GF4000.

Le Mont Nimba *(☎ 91 15 57)* Rooms GF80,000-180,000. If you have money to burn, the Mont Nimba is a nice place. Rooms have air-con and bathroom and there's a casino and a pool which nonguests can use for GF5000.

N'zérékoré has excellent ***street food*** – some places to try are ***Aminata's Beans*** south from the BICIGUI bank, and the ladies near the gare voiture who sell rice with *arachide* (peanut) sauce. ***Mouminatou Binta*** whips up a mean rice with peanut sauce at her place, which is hidden behind the Sougué Boutique near the market.

Hôtel Le Palmier Meals GF2500-6000. Dishes at Le Palmier next to Chez Aïda are simple but fresh – try the spaghetti with tomato sauce (GF2500).

Le Chimpanze Meals GF500-1000. This cute little diner has African basics such as *fonio* (millet) and *riz gras* (rice cooked in sauce) in a colourful setting.

Café des Arts The owner, Monsieur Kourouma, is a Bureau of Tourism representative and he makes a good *café noir*. The café is a pretty place, with lots of plants.

Chez M Fof This little supermarket is worth a visit for Pringles and Ivoirian chocolate bars.

Entertainment

Club Hanoi Admission GF5000-8000. This club near the market is the best dance spot. The cover charge is often waived.

Getting There & Away

There are flights once or twice a week between Conakry and N'zérérékoré on UTA for GF120,000.

N'zérékoré's well-organised gare voiture is near the petrol station on the Macenta road. Bush taxis depart daily for Macenta (GF8000), Beyla (GF7000) and Conakry (GF42,000). There's also a private bus to Conakry for GF32,000 daily.

If you're heading for Liberia via Diéké, note that sometimes the Diéké border crossing is closed; inquire locally before setting out.

Lower Guinea

While much of Guinea's coast is rocky or marshy and inaccessible, there are some beautiful spots worth discovering. The inland western region, Lower Guinea (Basse Guinée), has some interesting caves and other geological formations.

BOFFA

Boffa is a small coastal town en route to Guinea-Bissau and Senegal. If you get stuck at the ferry here, the dingy ***Hôtel V Emmanuel*** has rooms for GF7000. ***Grand Hôtel Fatala*** next door charges GF10,000 for similarly depressing accommodation. ***Chez le Retraite,*** behind Hôtel Emmanuel, will prepare simple meals for GF4000.

About 40km north of Boffa is the signposted turn-off leading 25km down to **Plage de Bel Air**, **Cape Verga**, the fishing village of **Kokoudé** and a beautiful coastline. Without your own transport, you'll need to charter a taxi in Boffa or be prepared for a long wait at the junction for the occasional pickup truck plying the route (GF1000).

Basic ***beach huts*** can be rented from the residents of **Bel Air** village, 2km inland from the beach; they shouldn't cost more than GF5000 a night. Meals can also be arranged.

If you're driving your own vehicle, inquire in Conakry whether the Boffa ferry is working. Otherwise, bush taxis will be waiting on either side of the Pongo River (GF5000 to Conakry, GF7000 to Boké). The ferry costs GF500 per person or GF5000 per vehicle; the last boat leaves around 9pm.

BOKÉ

Boké, a sprawling town with views over the surrounding countryside, is a major junction for transport to/from Guinea-Bissau and Senegal. Near the taxi stand is the **Fortin de Boké** *(admission free; open daily)*, once a slaving fort but now a museum with a small collection of artefacts. You can also see the horrifying holding cells where slaves were kept before they were taken down river to the coast.

Le Chalet *(☎ 31 02 05)*, 2km from the centre on the Koundara road, has basic rooms with fan/air-con for GF10,000/15,000 and a noisy disco. Meals are available from GF2000 with advance notice. ***Le Benda***, 3km from the centre on the Boffa road, has dirty, uncomfortable rooms for GF7000.

Direct bush taxis to Conakry cost GF13,000; to Gabú in Guinea-Bissau it's GF17,000. Roads north of Boké are bad.

FRIA

Fria is a bustling town in an attractive area, marred only by the enormous bauxite mining compound that dominates views on approach. The main reason to come here is to explore the geologically fascinating surrounding countryside. About 15km from Fria, beyond Wawaya village, are the **Grottes de Bogoro**. Hôtel Yaskadi in Fria can help arrange a guide. The **Grottes de Konkouré** can be reached by continuing out of town on the airport road and then down about 4km on a very rough road (best on bike or foot) to the Konkouré River. From there, it's an additional 10km or so to the Troisième Plage where you can arrange a pirogue and a local guide to visit the grottoes. The trip is best done in the dry season when the river is calmer.

There are also interesting caves in **Tormélin**, between Fria and the Boffa highway; they're about a 6km walk from the Tormélin mosque.

Hôtel Mariam *(☎ 24 09 55)* Rooms with fan/air-con GF15,000/25,000. The pleasant Mariam on Route Unite-III is the best choice in town.

Hôtel Yaskadi *(☎ 24 09 84)* Rooms with fan/air-con GF15,000/20,000. The Yaskadi, 1km off Route Unite-III, has clean, decent rooms.

La Teranga Meals GF3000-5000. At the end of the airport road, this place has good Senegalese and Guinean dishes.

Getting There & Away

Bush taxis go daily to Conakry (GF4000) and to Télimélé (GF10,000), from where you can continue on to Gaoual and Koundara. Transport from Fria to the Boffa highway junction costs GF2000.

Guinea-Bissau

Warning

Since the 1998–99 coup, Guinea-Bissau has been mostly peaceful. However, political problems are profound and President Koumba Yala's popularity has fallen drastically since he took office. Many Western countries warn their citizens against travel here for fear of further unrest, which cannot be ruled out. You are strongly advised to check the latest situation before entering Guinea-Bissau.

For travellers, Guinea-Bissau is a joy. It's home to some of the friendliest people on the continent, and its towns are small, with wide streets, flowering trees and rarely a tourist in sight. Bissau, the capital, is on the rebound after a few rough years during the war and has colourful markets alongside pastel-coloured Mediterranean-style buildings.

The Arquipélago dos Bijagós, off the coast, has azure waters, fine empty beaches and a fascinating culture, while the mainland offers many pristine natural areas with rich ecosystems.

Facts about Guinea-Bissau

HISTORY

The great Sahel Empire of Mali, which flourished between the 13th and 15th centuries AD, included part of present-day Guinea-Bissau. For more information on the precolonial history of this part of West Africa, see History in the Facts about West Africa chapter.

Guinea Who?

Causing no end of confusion to visitors, people from Guinea-Bissau refer to themselves as Guinéan and to the country as Guiné, while that southerly neighbour known to the rest of the world as Guinea is here demoted to Guiné-Conakry. You may also hear people from Guinea-Bissau referred to as Bissau-Guinean. For this book, we use the term Guineans.

Guinea-Bissau at a Glance

Capital: Bissau
Population: 1.3 million
Area: 36,125 sq km
Head of State: President Koumba Yala
Official language: Portuguese
Main local language: Crioulo
Currency: West African CFA franc
Exchange rate: US$1 = CFA694
Time: GMT/UTC
Country telephone code: ☎ 245
Best time to go: Late November to February

SENEGAL
Gabú p522
Bafatá p521
Bissau p517
Bubaque Town p525
GUINEA

Highlights

- Viewing the flora and fauna of the Arquipélago dos Bijagós
- Experiencing Bissau's February Carnival, with music, masks, parades and dancing
- Hiking and observing wildlife in the south's sacred forests
- Checking out interesting Portuguese colonial architecture throughout the country
- Relaxing on the pristine beaches of the Arquipélago dos Bijagós, and at Varela and Cassumba

European Arrival

The first Europeans to arrive in Guinea-Bissau were Portuguese navigators, who had been exploring the coast of West Africa since the early 15th century. By around

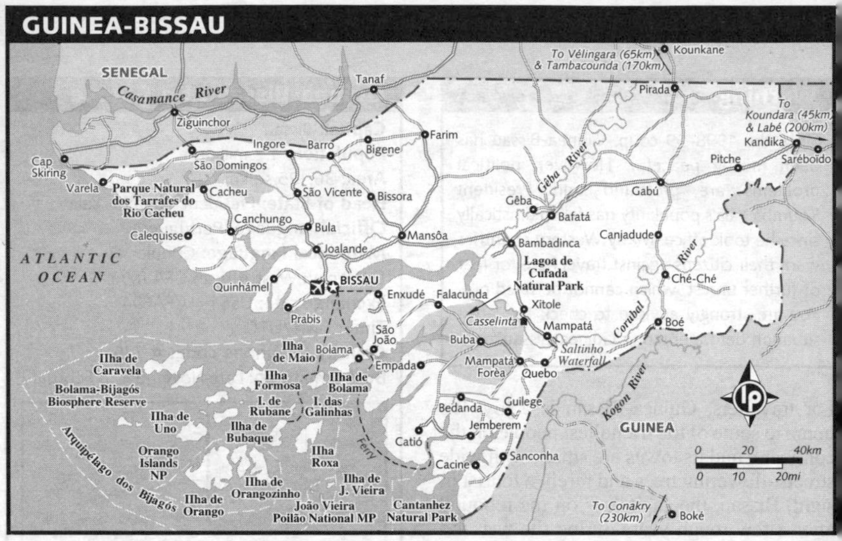
GUINEA-BISSAU
SENEGAL
Casamance River
Tanaf
To Vélingara (65km) & Tambacounda (170km)
Kounkane
Pirada
To Koundara (45km) & Labé (200km)
Kandika
Saréboïdo
Pitche
Gabú
Ziguinchor
Ingore
Barro
Bigene
Farim
Cap Skiring
Varela
São Domingos
Parque Natural dos Tarrafes do Rio Cacheu
Cacheu
São Vicente
Bissora
Géba River
Gêba
Bafatá
Canchungo
Bula
Calequisse
Mansôa
Bambadinca
Canjadude
Joalande
ATLANTIC OCEAN
Lagoa de Cufada Natural Park
Ché-Ché
Quinhámel
BISSAU
Enxudé
Falacunda
Xitole
Corubal River
Casselinta
Mampatá
Boé
Prabis
São João
Buba
Ilha de Maio
Bolama
Ilha de Caravela
Saltinho Waterfall
Empada
Mampatá Forèa
Quebo
Ilha Formosa
Ilha de Bolama
Bolama-Bijagós Biosphere Reserve
I. de Rubane
I. das Galinhas
Guilege
Bedanda
Kogon River
GUINEA
Ilha de Uno
Ilha de Bubaque
Jemberem
Catió
Ferry
Orango Islands NP
Ilha Roxa
Sanconha
Cacine
Arquipélago dos Bijagós
Ilha de Orangozinho
Ilha de J. Vieira
Ilha de Orango
João Vieira Poilão National MP
Cantanhez Natural Park
To Conakry (230km)
Boké
0 20 40km
0 10 20mi

1450 their ships had reached Guinea-Bissau and other areas along the coast, and they began trading with the inhabitants for slaves, gold, ivory and pepper.

The Portuguese built many forts and trading stations along the coast but their trade monopoly ended in the late 17th century when British, French and Dutch merchant adventurers entered the slave trade with notable enthusiasm. Over the following centuries, the surrounding territories became British or French possessions, but Portugal kept hold of what became known as Portuguese Guinea.

Portugal was content to trade on the coast and didn't lay claim to the interior until the 1880s, when the European powers carved up the continent. Even so, Portugal was unable to gain full control of the area until 1915, after a long series of wars with the local people, and Portuguese Guinea ended up with the most repressive and exploitative of all the colonial powers.

Colonial Period

While Britain and France developed their West African colonies for the exportation of crops, the Portuguese administration here was weak and lethargic. Companies from other European countries were allowed to lease land for plantations, mainly to produce groundnuts (peanuts) and palm oil, but this changed in 1926 when the dictator Salazar came to power in Portugal and imposed restrictive customs duties on foreign companies. Direct Portuguese rule resumed, and it was simple: if you were a peasant, you planted groundnuts, like it or not. The oppressive regime was most notably characterised by the Pidjiguiti massacre of 1959, a pivotal event in Guinea-Bissau's recent history, when 50 striking dockworkers were shot by police at the Pidjiguiti pier in Bissau.

By the early 1960s, many African countries were gaining independence from their European colonial rulers. Britain and France changed fairly smoothly from being colonials to neocolonials and still profited from trade with their former colonies. But Portugal's own weakness made Salazar refuse to relinquish his hold on the colony.

War of Liberation

The result was the longest liberation struggle in the history of Africa: a guerrilla war waged by the Partido Africano da Independência da Guiné e Cabo Verde (PAIGC) with significant help from the Soviet Union and Cuba. Many PAIGC leaders were better-educated Cape Verdeans, including the leader and co-founder of the party, Amilcar Cabral. But it was from the mainland of Portuguese Guinea that the movement drew its strongest grass-roots support.

In 1961, the PAIGC entered Portuguese Guinea from neighbouring Guinea and started arming and mobilising the peasants. As the PAIGC's numbers grew to about 10,000 the Portuguese responded by increasing their troops to 25,000 plus 10,000 conscripted Africans. Despite this, within five years half the country was in PAIGC hands. Internationally, Portugal became isolated. Foreign politicians and journalists visited the liberated area, and the struggle became front-page news during the early 1970s.

The Portuguese continued to hold out in refugee-swollen Bissau, a few smaller towns and pockets in the northeast where some Fula (one of the country's main ethnic groups) collaborated with the Portuguese in an attempt to preserve their social privileges. Their agents in Conakry (Guinea), where Amilcar Cabral the PAIGC leader was based, assassinated him in early 1973.

But the movement was too strong. The PAIGC organised nationwide elections in the liberated areas and proclaimed independence, with Amilcar Cabral's half-brother, Luiz (also a Cape Verdean), as president. Eighty countries quickly recognised the new government, but it still took Salazar's overthrow the following year for Portugal to do the same.

Independence

Once in power, the new PAIGC government had more than a handful of problems. The Portuguese had seen Guinea-Bissau as little more than a cheap source of groundnuts, and had done almost nothing to develop the country. Only one in 20 people could read, life expectancy was 35 years and 45% of children died before the age of five. During the war of independence, rice production had fallen by 71% and rice had to be imported for the first time ever.

Politically, the PAIGC wanted a unified Guinea-Bissau and Cape Verde. However, this idea was dropped in 1980 when President Cabral was overthrown in a coup while he was visiting Cape Verde to negotiate the union. João (Nino) Vieira took over and became president.

Despite the change of leader, Guinea-Bissau continued to follow a socialist path. The state controlled most major enterprises, Marxist literature was everywhere and political dissent was banned, although behind the dogma Vieira encouraged pragmatism and political neutrality. The Soviet Union provided arms and advisers while the West provided nonmilitary aid.

But life remained hard for most people. Bissau's shops were almost empty and in rural areas foreign products were even more scarce. Vieira realised that Guinea-Bissau was making no progress under Marxism, and in 1986, following a serious coup attempt the previous year, the government completely reversed its policies, devalued the currency and began selling off state enterprises.

The 1990s

Vieira proved to be a shrewd politician, surviving three coup attempts while keeping the PAIGC in power. He won the 1994 presidential elections, although 52% of the vote was hardly a landslide victory and many Guineans questioned the results. Opposition leader Koumba Yala accepted defeat and appealed for national unity.

Away from the political machinations, things improved on the domestic front for most people. Unusually for an African nation, rural inhabitants had enjoyed a slight improvement in living conditions since the 1970s. Output from farmers increased, while local produce and foreign goods were more readily available in shops and markets. Overall, however, Guinea-Bissau's social and economic situation remained dangerously poor. Cracks began to show in 1997, when teachers, health workers and other state employees went on strike to

The PAIGC

The Partido Africano da Independência da Guiné e Cabo Verde (PAIGC) is viewed as a model for revolutionary armies in many parts of the world. The movement was successful largely because of its political strategy during the war of liberation. As each part of the country was liberated, the PAIGC helped villagers build schools, provided medical services and encouraged widespread political participation. Amilcar Cabral insisted on a war of revolution, not of revolt, and he realised that society had to be completely reorganised if the people were ever to be genuinely free. From the very start of the war, the people of Guinea-Bissau believed in what they were fighting for.

protest about, among other things, foreign aid money that had gone 'missing' in the hands of the government.

Things suddenly came to a head on 7 June 1998, with an attempted coup led by General Ansumane Mane, former head of the army. Mane had been sacked the day before by Vieira, for allegedly supplying arms to the Mouvement des Forces Démocratiques de Casamance (MFDC), the separatist rebel group in neighbouring Senegal. Mane's coup was backed by a majority of Guinean soldiers and, reportedly, by the MFDC. Loyal government troops were supported by regiments sent in from Senegal and Guinea. As the two sides shelled and bombed each other, the surrounding residential districts were caught in the crossfire, and many people were killed. Fighting continued through the rest of June and into July, and spread to other parts of Guinea-Bissau. The capital and most parts of the country were in a state of chaos. The airport and the border with Senegal were effectively closed.

The rebels, known as the Junta Militar, were reported to have support from the people of Guinea-Bissau, and this apparently made civilians legitimate targets in the eyes of the government troops and their allies. News reports from mid-July told of towns and villages being attacked, many people killed and atrocities committed. Food production and harvesting were interrupted and, by late July, 300,000 people were displaced. Bissau was a ghost town as residents fled to rural areas or tried to leave the country.

In August 1998, a tentative cease-fire was agreed to, and peace negotiations were brokered by Portugal, other nations of the Portuguese-speaking community and several Economic Community of West Africa (Ecowas) states. Despite some cautious optimism, outbreaks of fighting in various parts of Guinea-Bissau continued for a few more weeks.

By October, all-out fighting resumed, with the rebels taking control of most of the country. Despite another peace accord in November, fighting erupted in late January 1999 and then again in May, when the Junta at last conquered all of Bissau and personally escorted Vieira to the Portuguese embassy. With the Junta's claim that they had no interest in power, the president of the national assembly became interim president.

Guinea-Bissau Today

Transparent presidential and legislative elections were held in November, and a presidential run-off in January 2000 made Koumba Yala the president of the new civilian government. Tension between the government and the military was high, however, with the military frequently challenging presidential decisions. When Yala issued promotions to army members in November 2000, Ansumane Mane rejected his new title, saying that Guinea-Bissau already had too many generals, and declared himself supreme chief of the armed forces. Shooting broke out between Mane's men and those loyal to the existing administration, and Mane found himself on the run. He was later killed in a shoot-out at Quinhámel, 40km from the capital. With Mane's death, Yala declared true peace and democracy and an end to any involvement with the MFDC, whom Mane was thought to support, counter to government policy.

Yala's problems with the military had now tapered off, but it wasn't long before his relations with other sectors of the government, as well as with civic groups and the media, were strained. In 2001 and 2002, Yala seemed to seek out controversy: he had journalists arrested for criticising the government; issued a decree deporting members of an Islamic group and then sacked members of the Supreme Court who ruled the decree unconstitutional (a move which was in itself unconstitutional); laid off half the country's civil servants and replaced them with members of his own party; and often angered the national assembly by his constant firing and manipulation of staff. In October 2001, the assembly passed a no-confidence motion against Yala, which was followed two months later by an alleged coup attempt (charges, however, were unsubstantiated, and many doubt it ever happened).

Although most of the country remains optimistic, and few want a return to war, faith in the government is low and the prospect of renewed fighting, or disturbances brought on by nationwide disruption, cannot be ruled out. The future for Guinea-Bissau is still far from certain.

GEOGRAPHY

Guinea-Bissau has an area of just over 36,000 sq km (about the size of Switzerland), making it one of West Africa's smaller countries. The coastal areas are flat, with estuaries, mangrove swamps and patches of forest. Inlets indent the coast and high tides periodically submerge the lowest areas, sometimes covering up to a third of the land surface. Inland, the landscape remains flat, with the highest ground, near the Guinean border, just topping 300m above sea level. Off the coast is the Arquipélago dos Bijagós, consisting of 18 main islands.

CLIMATE

The rainy season is from June to October; rainfall is almost twice as much along the coast as it is inland. Conditions are especially humid in the months before the rains (April and May), when average maximum daytime temperatures rise to 34°C. Although daily maximums rarely fall below 30°C, this is quite bearable in the months after the rains, especially on islands that catch the sea breeze.

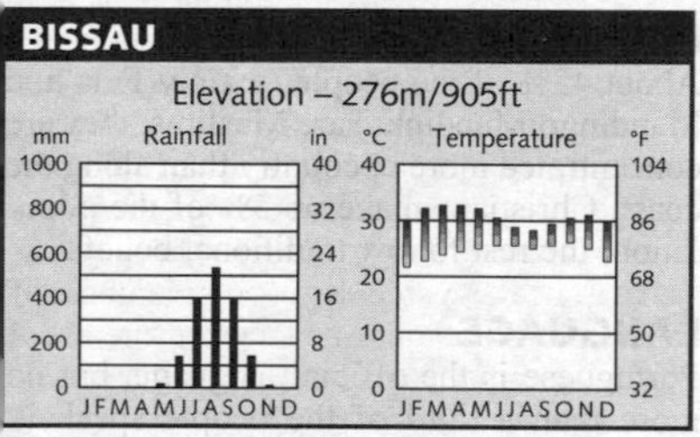
BISSAU
Elevation – 276m/905ft
mm
Rainfall
in
°C
Temperature
°F
1000
800
600
400
200
0
40
32
24
16
8
0
40
30
20
10
0
104
86
68
50
32
JFMAMJJASOND
JFMAMJJASOND

ECOLOGY & ENVIRONMENT

A major environmental issue is the destruction of mangroves – some of the most important in Africa – on the coast, due to the expansion of rice production in seasonally flooded areas. The increase in groundnut production also creates problems – the plants rapidly exhaust soil nutrients and farming methods lead to erosion. Offshore, Guinea-Bissau has rich fishing waters, but overfishing may become an issue if controls are not introduced. The UICN (World Conservation Union) and several other bodies are working to protect Guinea-Bissau's natural environment.

FLORA & FAUNA

The natural vegetation of the inland areas is lightly wooded savanna, but much of it is under cultivation. You'll see rice fields and plantations of groundnuts, maize and other crops. The coastal zone is very low-lying and indented by many large creeks and estuaries, where mangroves are the dominant vegetation. Off the coast, the islands of the Arquipélago dos Bijagós are also low-lying, and the vegetation is a combination of light woodland and mangroves.

Guinea-Bissau has several protected areas, including the flagship Bolama-Bijagós Biosphere Reserve, which contains the Orango Islands National Park and the João Vieira Poilão National Marine Park. On the mainland, the Parque Natural dos Tarrafes do Rio Cacheu, near the border with Senegal, protects a vast area of mangroves. In the south of the country, near Buba, the Lagoa de Cafada Natural Park protects a freshwater wetland area. South of here the Cantanhez Natural Park is planned to protect estuarine mangroves and several sacred forests that have cultural significance. Despite this impressive collection, tourist facilities in most parks are still limited or nonexistent.

GOVERNMENT & POLITICS

Guinea-Bissau was ruled by the PAIGC, the sole political party, until 1991 when multiparty democracy was approved by the government. Members are elected to a 102-seat national assembly, with the president elected separately. The prime minister is appointed by the president, subject to the approval of the assembly, which in Yala's case has resulted in three prime ministers so far. The Partido da Renovacão Social (PRS), Yala's party, holds 37 seats in the assembly, followed by the Resistencia da Guiné-Bissau (RGB) with 27 and the PAIGC with 25. The assembly is often divided among itself, and shifting coalitions make government unity – not to mention progress – a constant struggle.

ECONOMY

On paper, Guinea-Bissau is one of the world's poorest countries but, unlike many other West African nations, its huge economic dependency on agriculture means people in rural areas normally survive relatively well. Guinea-Bissau is the world's sixth-largest producer of cashew nuts, which are exported along with groundnuts, palm kernels, timber and fish, and the country is virtually self-sufficient for rice. Guinea-Bissau is highly dependent on overseas aid, however, especially since the 1998–99 war, which severely damaged the economy.

POPULATION & PEOPLE

Current estimates put the population at about 1.3 million, made up of 23 ethnic groups. The main groups are Balante (30%) in the coastal and southern regions and Fula (20%) in the north. Other groups are the Manjaco (or Manjak), Papel, and Fulup (closely related to the Diola of Senegal) in the northwest, and the Mandingo/Mandinka in the interior. The offshore islands are mostly inhabited by the Bijago people. There's also a significant minority of people of mixed European and African descent.

For more information on Fula and Mandingo cultures, see the special section 'Peoples of the Region'.

ARTS

While mainland Guinea-Bissau is not noted for the use of sculpted figures and masks, the Bijago people, due to their isolation, continue to maintain these traditions. Statues representing Iran, the great spirit, are used in connection with agricultural and initiation rituals. These are carved as seated figures, sometimes wearing a top hat. Initiation masks are also carved, the best known being the Dugn'be, a ferocious bull with real horns. Other masks represent sharks, sawfish and hippos. The hippo masks are so massive that the dancer supports the mask with a pair of sticks carved as legs. One of the best times to see masks is in Bissau at Carnival time (usually February).

On the mainland, traditional dance and music are influenced by the Mandingo/Mandinka and Diola people of neighbouring Gambia and Senegal. The harp-like *kora* and the xylophone-like *balafon* are played, while women take turns dancing in front of a circle of onlookers. The traditional Guinean beat is *gumbé*.

Modern music shares the same roots, and the Portuguese colonial legacy has given it a Latin edge, especially among the larger orchestras. On the street and in bush taxis you'll hear little Sahelian-style music and more salsa and Latin sounds. One of Guinea-Bissau's most popular groups is Super Mama Djombo, along with Dulce Maria Neves, N'Kassa Cobra, Patcheco, Justino Delgado, Rui Sangara, and Ramiro Naka. These singers perform occasionally in some of Bissau's nightclubs.

SOCIETY & CONDUCT

The mainland people share many cultural aspects with similar groups in neighbouring Senegal and Guinea. Bijago customs are particularly interesting. On several islands, beliefs about death mean that bodies are taken to another island for burial so that their spirits do not haunt the living. On some of the islands, as soon as a girl reaches puberty the young men venture forth with as much rice and other goods as they can afford in the hope of buying their way into her favour. She chooses a suitor, but if she's not pregnant within a year, or if someone makes a better bid, she can ditch her man and choose another. The man usually stays around only until she gives birth, and then returns home and becomes eligible for other liaisons. Children take the mother's name and are rarely able to identify their father.

RELIGION

About 45% of the people (mainly Fula and Mandingo/Mandinka) are Muslims; they are concentrated more upcountry than along the coast. Christians make up 5% of the population; the rest follow traditional beliefs.

LANGUAGE

Portuguese is the official language, but no more than a third of the people speak it. Each group has its own language, but the common tongue is Crioulo – a mix of medieval Portuguese and local words. As Guinea-Bissau gets increasingly drawn into the Afro-Francophone world, more and more people understand French. See the Language chapter for some useful phrases.

Facts for the Visitor

SUGGESTED ITINERARIES

Most travellers with only a week to spare spend a day or two in the capital Bissau. There's little in the way of 'sights', but the city has a pleasant, relaxing feel. This could be combined with a few days visiting the country's major attraction, the Arquipélago dos Bijagós, southwest of Bissau. The island of Bubaque is the easiest to reach, with good beaches and a range of places to stay.

If you have two or three weeks to spare, you could simply spend more time on Bubaque, or visit some of the smaller islands, such as Galinhas or Orango. Alternatively, you could combine Bissau and the islands with time in the country's interior, heading northwest to the region around Canchungo, or south to the fascinating forested areas around Buba and Catió. Another option is Gabú, a lively market town from where you can get onward transport to Guinea.

PLANNING

The rainy season is from June to October, and the best time to visit is from late November to February, when conditions are dry and relatively cool. February is also Carnival time in Bissau, although smaller festivals take place in many towns to celebrate the end of harvest in November and December.

The best map of Guinea-Bissau is produced by Institut Géographique National (IGN), but it's unavailable in the country. Papelaria GMS sells an old map of the country that's good for getting your bearings.

VISAS & DOCUMENTS

Visas

All visitors, except nationals of Ecowas countries, need visas. These are normally valid for one month and are issued for around US$20 at embassies. They are not issued at land borders, but may be issued at the airport if you come from an African country where visas are not available. To avoid hassles, get one before you arrive.

Visa Extensions These are easy to obtain at Serviço de Estrangeiros, behind the main Immigration building across from the Mercado Bandim. For all nationalities, 45-day visa extensions cost a mere CFA2000 and are ready the same day if you apply early.

Visas for Onward Travel Visas for the following neighbouring countries can be obtained at their embassies in Bissau.

Gambia Three-month single-entry visas cost CFA15,000 and require one photo; they're ready the same day if you go early.

Guinea Two-month multiple-entry visas cost US$40 plus two photos and take a day or two to issue.

Senegal One-month multiple-entry visas cost CFA3000 with four photos and are issued in two days.

Vaccination Certificates

A certificate with proof of a yellow fever vaccination is required of all travellers.

EMBASSIES & CONSULATES

Guinea-Bissau Embassies & Consulates

In West Africa, you can get visas for Guinea-Bissau in Cape Verde, Gambia, Guinea, Mauritania and Senegal. For more details see the Facts for the Visitor section of the relevant chapter. Outside Africa, Guinea-Bissau has very few embassies or consulates. These are more or less limited to the following:

Belgium (☎ 02-647 13 51) 70 Av Franklin-Roosevelt, Brussels 1050
France (☎ 01 45 26 18 51) 94 rue Saint Lazare, 75009 Paris
Portugal (☎ 303-04 40) Rua Alcolena, 17, Lisbon 1400
USA (Permanent Mission to the UN; ☎ 212-687 8115) 211 E. 43rd St, NY, NY 10017

Embassies & Consulates in Guinea-Bissau

All embassies and consulates are in Bissau, some in the centre, others along the road towards the airport.

France (☎ 201312) Avenida de 14 Novembro, corner of Avenida do Brazil
Gambia (☎ 251099) Avenida de 14 Novembro, 1km northwest of Mercado de Bandim; open 8.30am to 3pm Saturday to Thursday and 8.30am to 12.30pm Friday
Guinea (☎ 201231) Rua 12, east of the central stadium; open 8.30am to 3pm Saturday to Thursday and 8.30am to 1pm Friday
Mauritania (☎ 203696) Rua Eduardo Mondlane, south of the central stadium
Nigeria (☎ 201018) Avenida Francisco Mendes, opposite the stadium
Senegal (☎ 212944) southwest of Praça dos Heróis Nacionais; open 8am to 5pm daily

The consul for the UK and for the Netherlands is Jan van Maanen (☎ 201224, 211529, fax 201265), at the Mavegro supermarket on Rua Eduardo Mondlane. The French embassy handles visas for Benin, Côte d'Ivoire and Togo.

MONEY

The unit of currency is the West African CFA franc.

country	unit		CFA
euro zone	€1	=	CFA656
UK	UK£1	=	CFA1024
USA	US$1	=	CFA694

The principal bank of Guinea-Bissau is the Banco da Africa Ocidental (BAO), although they don't change travellers cheques. In Bissau you can change cash at BAO or at the forex bureaus in town; you can also change cash and travellers cheques at Mavegro supermarket. Outside Bissau, there are few banks, so most travellers change money in Bissau. Credit cards are useless and ATMs are nonexistent in Guinea-Bissau.

POST & COMMUNICATIONS

The postal service out of the country is reliable but slow – you're probably better off posting mail home from Senegal or Gambia. If you decide to make a go of it, airmail letters cost CFA450. Travellers report that the poste restante in Bissau is unhelpful and unreliable. The best place for email or international phone calls is Bissau, though the latter are quite expensive.

RADIO & TV

The national radio and TV stations broadcast in Portuguese. Most interesting for travellers is Radio Mavegro FM (100.0MHz), which combines music with hourly news bulletins in English from the BBC.

PHOTOGRAPHY & VIDEO

Photo permits are not required, but the usual restrictions apply. For more information see Photography & Video in the Regional Facts for the Visitor chapter.

HEALTH

Have a yellow fever vaccination before you come. You should take also precautions against malaria, as it exists throughout the year in the whole country. For more information on these and other health matters, see Health in the Regional Facts for the Visitor chapter.

Health care in Guinea-Bissau is extremely limited; most people who can afford to head for Dakar in Senegal for treatment. Otherwise, Bissau, Bafatá and Canchungo have hospitals.

WOMEN TRAVELLERS

The combined legacy of Portuguese assimilation and the role of women fighters in the liberation war, plus limited Islamic influence, means local women enjoy a certain degree of freedom. If you've travelled through Senegal or Mali, the sight of women in trousers, couples holding hands in public, or men and women simply socialising comfortably together, makes a refreshing change. Although the atmosphere is relaxed, in rural areas women visitors may be more comfortable behaving and dressing conservatively. For more information, see Women Travellers in the Regional Facts for the Visitor chapter.

DANGERS & ANNOYANCES

Guinea-Bissau's political stability is precarious; see the Warning box at the start of this chapter. The conflict in Casamance (see the Senegal chapter for more details) occasionally spills over the border into northern Guinea-Bissau. Travellers heading for Varela should check the latest security situation.

BUSINESS HOURS

Shops, offices and banks are open from 8am to noon and 3pm to 6pm Monday to Friday, or from 8am to 2pm – or any variation on these hours. Shops are also open on Saturday morning. Post offices are generally open Monday to Friday mornings only, but the main one in Bissau is open 8am to 6pm Monday to Saturday.

PUBLIC HOLIDAYS & SPECIAL EVENTS

Public holidays include:

New Year's Day 1 January
Anniversary of the Death of Amilcar Cabral 20 January
Women's Day 8 March
Easter March/April
Pidjiguiti Day 3 August
Independence Day 24 September
Christmas Day 25 December

Islamic feasts such as Eid al-Fitr (at the end of Ramadan) and Tabaski are also celebrated. See Public Holidays & Special Events in the Regional Facts for the Visitor chapter for a table of dates of Islamic holidays.

Guinea-Bissau's main event is Carnival which takes place in Bissau every February. Music, masks, dancing, parades and all-around good times are the order of the day. Small festivals are held in other towns around the country at about the same time of year, although dates are not fixed so you need to ask locally for details.

ACTIVITIES

On the islands of the Arquipélago dos Bijagós the sandy beaches are good for swimming, while several hotels offer deep-sea fishing and other water sports. On the islands, and in some of the remoter parts of Guinea-Bissau, cycling is an excellent way to get around. Roads are quiet and distances between towns are not too long. There are no formal hire outlets, but you can usually arrange something just by asking around. For more serious exploration, consider bringing your own bike (for more information, see the Getting Around West Africa chapter).

ACCOMMODATION

In Bissau, the number of upmarket hotels is on the increase, but the choice in the budget range has shrunk in recent years. For this reason, many travellers head inland or to the islands, where accommodation is more reasonably priced. Specialist hunting and fishing camps are scattered around the country, catering for upmarket visitors flying in from France and Portugal.

FOOD & DRINKS

In Bissau, street food is surprisingly hard to find. Even coffee and bread stalls take some determined tracking down. However, in the last few years, Bissau's choice of patisseries has grown considerably, and several smarter restaurants serve good seafood. In rural areas, meat dishes may be monkey *(macaco)*, so ask before ordering if chimp is not to your fancy.

Canned soft drinks and beers imported from Portugal are easy to find. Local brews include palm wine, as in many other West African countries. For a stronger home-brew, you may be offered *caña* (rum), which is 60% proof. You may also come across *caña de cajeu* (cashew rum), equally strong and made not from the nuts, but from the fruit of the cashew-nut tree.

Getting There & Away

AIR

Guinea-Bissau's only international airport is on the outskirts of Bissau. The main airlines flying to/from Guinea-Bissau are TAP Air Portugal, TACV Cabo Verde Airlines (which works in cooperation with the new Guinea-Bissau Airlines) and Air Senegal. Departure tax for international flights is US$20, but this is usually included in the ticket price.

TAP Air Portugal is the only airline with direct flights from Europe to Bissau. A ticket from Lisbon costs US$580 return; from London it's US$720 one way. TACV Cabo Verde Airlines has flights to Bissau from Amsterdam, Basel, Munich and Paris, via Cape Verde and Dakar (Senegal). Alternatively, get any flight from Europe to Dakar and change to a regional airline.

Between them, Air Senegal and TACV Cabo Verde Airlines operate seven flights per week between Bissau and Dakar (CFA100,000 one way). To fly between Bissau and anywhere else in Africa, you'll have to get a connecting flight in Dakar.

LAND

Border Crossings

The busiest crossing point to/from Senegal is at São Domingos, on the main route between Ingore and Ziguinchor. There are also crossing points between Tanaf and Farim, and near Pirada, north of Gabú on the route to/from Vélingara and Tambacounda.

To/from Guinea, most traffic goes via Kandika and Saréboïdo on the road between Gabú and Koundara. A less-travelled route, open only in the dry season, links south-eastern Guinea-Bissau and western Guinea via Quebo and Boké.

Guinea

Bush taxis usually go daily to the border from Gabú and Koundara for GF6000 (about CFA2400). It can take all day to cover this 100km stretch, although the winding road through the Fouta Djalon foothills is beautiful. If you have to change transport at Saréboïdo, tying in with the weekly Sunday market will improve your options.

Another option in the dry season is to take the Land Cruiser that goes daily from Gabú to Boké (CFA8000); from here transport goes on to Conakry. You can also get to Boké from Quebo, but this route is slow, unless you tie in with Boké's market (Wednesday).

For the adventurous, a *canoa* (motorised canoe) goes every few days from Cacine in the far southeast to Kamsar (about a five-hour trip), from where you can find onward transport to Boké or Conakry.

Senegal

The main Ziguinchor to Bissau route goes via the border at São Domingos, Ingore and Bula, and costs CFA3500. However, a bridge is under construction at Joalande, which means that vehicles currently go via the tar road through Ingore, Barro and Bissora for CFA4500. When the bridge is completed, the route will again pass by São Vicente, and the ferry crossing here will be the only one holding you up. Passengers have to pay CFA100 for the ferry.

You can also cross the border between Farim and Tanaf by bush taxi. Another option is to go via Gabú, from where a daily bush taxi goes to Tambacounda (via Vélingara) in Senegal for CFA12,500. On Tuesday, an old bus goes directly from Gabú to Dakar – a two-day, CFA7500 trip that will surely make you or break you.

Getting Around

AIR

There are no domestic flights on the mainland. For details of flights to the islands see Getting There & Away in the Ilha de Bubaque section later in this chapter.

MINIBUS & BUSH TAXI

The main roads between Bissau and the towns of Gabú, Cacheu, Buba and Farim, and to the Senegal border at São Domingos, are all tar, although potholed on some stretches. Other roads are not as good and can be impassable in the rainy season. There are few bridges in Guinea-Bissau, so many road journeys involve ferry crossings.

Public transport around the country consists mainly of minibuses and Peugeot 504 bush taxis on the main roads, and *kandongas* (trucks or pick-ups) on rural routes. Mornings are always the best time to get transport. For an idea of fares across the country, from Bissau to Gabú (around 200km) is CFA2500 by Peugeot 504, CFA2000 by minibus and CFA1500 by kandonga.

BOAT

From Bissau, public passenger boats, smaller boats and canoas go from Bissau to the islands of Rubane, Bubaque, Galinhas and Bolama, and to Enxudé, Cacine and Catió on the mainland. Departure times vary with the tide.

Bissau

Before the war, Bissau was slowly livening up or, as some say, becoming more 'Senegalised.' However, things have quietened down considerably since then, so much so that you might forget you're in a capital city. But the streets are clean, people are generally friendly, and hassling of tourists is practically nonexistent. The city is slowly coming around, too; despite the frequent blackouts, bars, nightclubs, restaurants and shops selling imported goods are thriving, and people are generally optimistic about the future of this small-town city.

Orientation

Bissau's main drag is the wide Avenida Amilcar Cabral, running between the port and the Praça dos Heróis Nacionais. A block west on Avenida Domingos Ramos is the main market, the Mercado Central, and Praça Ché Guevara (better known as Baiana), which has some bars and restaurants. On the northwestern edge of the centre is the Mercado de Bandim. From here Avenida de 14 Novembro leads northwest to the main *paragem* (bus and taxi park), the airport nearby and most inland destinations.

Information

Tourist Offices The people at the Ministry of Tourism on Avenida Pansau Na Isna are friendly enough, but for information on hotels and private transport, you're better off at a travel agency or tour operator.

Money Travellers cheques and credit cards will do you little good in Guinea-Bissau. BAO near the port was the only bank at the

BISSAU

PLACES TO STAY
1 Hotel 24 de Setembro
11 Chez Jean
12 Hotel Caracol
13 Tambarina
39 Unnamed Hotel
43 Residencial Coimbra
45 Aparthotel Jordani
51 Pensão Centrale
62 Apartmentos Proquil
63 Hotel Ta-Mar

PLACES TO EAT
2 Dona Fernanda
5 Ganaan
17 Water Tower; 6 Mil
20 Papa Louca Fast Food
31 Santa Rosa
35 Bate Papo
36 Restaurant Asa Branca
37 Restaurant Magui
41 Gelataria Baiana; Morabeza
44 Guiné-Serviço
47 O Bistro
49 Pastelaria Dias & Dias
53 Restaurant Trópico; TACV Cabo Verde Airlines, Guinea-Bissau Airlines; Rodofluvial
57 Rice Bars
59 Fortaleza d'Amura Café
67 Cais Bar
68 Galáxia
69 Brisa do Mar

OTHER
3 Verda Tropical Nightclub
4 Coquiero
6 Mosque
7 Mosque
8 Centro Artistico Juvenil
9 Gambian Embassy
10 Church
14 Immigration Office; Serviço de Estrangeiros
15 Petrol Station
16 French Embassy
18 UICN Office
19 Nigerian Embassy
21 Papelaria GMS
22 Former Presidential Palace
23 Ministry of Tourism
24 TAP Air Portugal
25 Senegalese Embassy
26 Confeitaria Imperio
27 UDIB Cinema
28 Hospital Simão Mendes
29 Guinetours
30 Guinean Embassy
32 Surire Tours
33 Dr Kassem Dahrouge
34 Pharmacie Moçambique
38 Mauritanian Embassy
40 X Club
42 Bar Galeon; Churasquiera a Braza
46 Tropicana
48 Mavegro Supermarket; British and Dutch Consul
50 Cathedral
52 Correio (Post Office); Telephones
54 Air Senegal; Supermercado Bonjour
55 Forex Bureaus
56 BCEAO
58 Petrol Station
60 MultiArte
61 Fortaleza d'Amura
64 BAO
65 Electrodata
66 Pidjiguiti Monument
70 Canoas to Enxudé

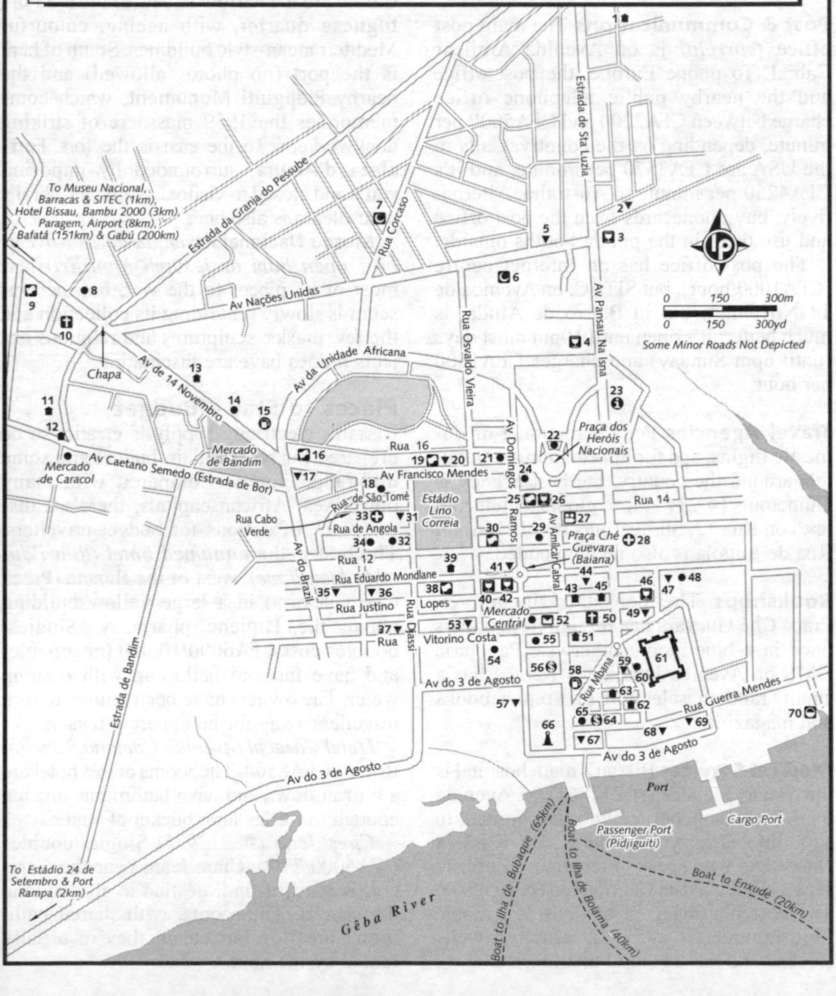

To Museu Nacional, Barracas & SITEC (1km), Hotel Bissau, Bambu 2000 (3km), Paragem, Airport (8km), Bafatá (151km) & Gabú (200km)
Estrada da Granja do Pessube
Rua Corcaso
Estrada de Sta Luzia
Av Nações Unidas
Av da Unidade Africana
Av de 14 Novembro
Chapa
Rua Osvaldo Vieira
Av Pansau Na Isna
0 150 300m
0 150 300yd
Some Minor Roads Not Depicted
Mercado de Bandim
Mercado de Caracol
Av Caetano Semedo (Estrada de Bor)
Rua 16
Av Francisco Mendes
Rua de São Tomé
Estádio Lino Correia
Av Domingos Ramos
Praça dos Heróis Nacionais
Rua 14
Rua Cabo Verde
Rua de Angola
Rua 12
Av do Brazil
Rua Eduardo Mondlane
Rua Justino Lopes
Rua Dassi
Rua Vitorino Costa
Av Amilcar Cabral
Praça Ché Guevara (Baiana)
Mercado Central
Rua Mbana
Rua Guerra Mendes
Av do 3 de Agosto
Estrada de Bandim
Port
Cargo Port
Passenger Port (Pidjiguiti)
Boat to Ilha de Bubaque (65km)
Boat to Ilha de Bolama (40km)
Boat to Enxudé (20km)
To Estádio 24 de Setembro & Port Rampa (2km)
Gêba River

time of writing that had any money. However, it doesn't change travellers cheques and is reluctant to change US dollars (euros are preferred). The forex bureaus near the Mercado Central offer mostly OK rates and quick service. The quickest and safest place to change money is at the Mavegro supermarket on Rua Eduardo Mondlane. All currencies, cash or travellers cheques, are exchanged here at bank rates with no commission (when they have enough money). Outside business hours, you could deal with the moneychangers who loiter near Mercado Central, but this should be as a last resort.

Post & Communications The main post office *(correio)* is on Avenida Amilcar Cabral. To phone Europe, the post office and the nearby public telephone office charge between CFA2200 and CFA5000 per minute, depending on the country. Calls to the USA are CFA3570 per minute, and it's CFA4250 per minute to Australia. Alternatively, buy phonecards from the post office and use them in the public booths outside.

The post office has an Internet centre (CFA1000/hour), but SITEC, on Avenida de 14 Novembro out in Bairro de Ajuda, is much better; it's open until 10pm most days (until 6pm Sunday) and charges CFA1500 per hour.

Travel Agencies For international or domestic flights, and for information about hotels around the country, the best agency is Guinetours (☎ 214344, ⓔ gtours@gtelecom.gw) on Rua 12. Surire Tours (☎ 214166) on Rua de Angola is also recommended.

Bookshops The bookstall situated on Praça Ché Guevara has foreign newspapers once in a blue moon; otherwise Papelaria GMS on Avenida Domingos Ramos has a small, random selection of French books and magazines.

Medical Services Bissau's main hospital is the Simão Mendes (☎ 212861) on Avenida Pansau Na Isna, but facilities are limited, to say the least. Alternatively, Dr Kassem Dahrouge, who speaks French and English, runs a clinic on Rua Cabo Verde (☎ 203297). The best pharmacy in town is Pharmacie Moçambique (☎ 205513), which is well-stocked and has a helpful pharmacist.

Dangers & Annoyances Walking around at night is safer in Bissau than in just about any other African capital city. Nevertheless, crime is slowly increasing, so take the usual precautions. Avoid side streets and the port area at night.

Things to See

The former **Presidential Palace** dominates Praça dos Heróis Nacionais at the northern end of Avenida Amilcar Cabral, but the war left it with an enormous hole in its roof. The new presidential palace is nearby.

Off the southern end of Avenida Amilcar Cabral are the narrow streets of the **old Portuguese quarter**, with ageing, colourful Mediterranean-style buildings. South of here is the port (no photos allowed) and the nearby **Pidjiguiti Monument**, which commemorates the 1959 massacre of striking dockworkers. To the east is the fort, **Fortaleza d'Amura**, surrounded by imposing walls and closed to visitors. Amilcar Cabral's mausoleum is also here.

Museu Nacional *(Avenida de 14 Novembro; open 8am to 1.30pm Mon-Fri)* lost most of its pieces to the war, but the museum is slowly rebuilding its collection and the few masks, sculptures and religious objects it does have are fascinating.

Places to Stay – Budget

Bissau's electricity supply is erratic, so be prepared for blackouts in budget and some mid-range hotels. Compared with many other West African capitals, there's a distinct lack of options for budget travellers. The best is the ***unnamed hotel*** *(Rua Eduardo Mondlane)*, west of the Baiana (Praça Ché Guevara) in a large yellow building above the Higiene pharmacy. Singles/doubles cost CFA6000/10,000 (negotiable) and have fan and bathroom with running water. The owners have been known to turn travellers away for no apparent reason.

Hotel Caracol *(Avenida Caetano Semedo)* Rooms CFA8500. The rooms at this hotel are a bit run-down and have bathrooms just big enough to fit the large bucket of water.

Chez Jean *(☎ 212935)* Singles/doubles CFA5000/7700. Chez Jean, near the Caracol, is hard to find, nestled as it is among the shacks. The rooms, with shared bathroom, are tiny but clean; they're usually rented by the hour.

Hotel Ta-Mar Rooms CFA10,000. The Ta-Mar in the quiet, narrow streets near the port, is a good deal; rooms have bathroom, air-con, fridge and character.

Tambarina *(Avenida de 14 Novembro)* Doubles with bucket/running water CFA7500/12,000. The rooms at this bar-restaurant are mostly rented for quickies, but they're clean and have 24-hour electricity.

Places to Stay – Mid-Range

Pensão Centrale *(Avenida Amilcar Cabral)* Rooms CFA20,000. This place is a longtime favourite with heaps of character but it's overpriced. The shared bathrooms have bucket water.

Aparthotel Jordani *(☎ 201719, Avenida Pansau Na Isna)* Singles/doubles CFA25,000/40,000. The overpriced Jordani has nice rooms with bathroom but bucket water only. Room rates include breakfast.

Apartmentos Proquil *(☎ 213069)* Rooms with fan/air-con CFA15,000/20,000. The Proquil near the port is just above an export business of the same name. Rooms with bathroom are clean and comfortable, and the decor is 1960s airport.

Places to Stay – Top End

All top-end hotels have rooms with bathroom, air-con and running water. Room rates include breakfast; a 15% tax is levied on the rates.

Hotel 24 de Setembro *(☎ 221034/37, fax 221002)* Singles/doubles CFA20,000/35,000. This hotel, 1.5km north of the centre, has a country-club feel, with clean white buildings sprawled out among pretty gardens.

Hotel Bissau *(☎ 251251, fax 251152, Avenida de 14 Novembro)* Singles/doubles CFA38,500/49,500. Formerly (and still known as) the Sheraton, this is Bissau's business hotel. The exterior's bland, but the rooms are a step up from the 24 de Setembro. It's about 3km northwest of the centre.

Residencial Coimbra *(☎ 213467, Avenida Amilcar Cabral)* Singles/doubles CFA45,000/55,000. This place offers a few tastefully decorated rooms on the 2nd floor of an inconspicuous building.

Places to Eat

Street food is hard to come by in Bissau. During the day the ***rice bars*** in the area around the port are your best bet, with rice and meat or fish for CFA500. If you're here in the months following Carnival, head for Bairro de Ajuda, where dozens of women set up makeshift bar/restaurants, ***barracas***, serving excellent grilled fish and salad, and sometimes other dishes, for around CFA1000. Our favourites are ***Mana Fatima's place*** and ***Africa People***, the latter as much for the name as for the food!

Papa Louca Fast Food *(Avenida Francisco Mendes)* Meals CFA800-3000. Papa Louca has good chawarmas (CFA900), hamburgers (CFA1300) and pizza (CFA1500), and the staff wear red-check uniforms with chickens on them.

Bate Papo *(Rua Eduardo Mondlane)* Meals CFA1000-3500. This upmarket place has the best pizza in town (CFA3000) at night, and good pastries and coffee in the morning.

Cais Bar Sandwiches CFA300-800. This cute little café down by the port has sandwiches and fresh fruit juices (CFA300).

Brisa do Mar *(Avenida de 3 Augusto)* Meals CFA1000-3000. The open-air Brisa do Mar is a cheap place with good atmosphere and music.

Morabeza *(Baiana)* Meals CFA500-2500. This local expat haunt has good food and ambience, with party lights at night.

Pensão Centrale *(Avenida Amilcar Cabral)* 3-course meal CFA4000. The restaurant here offers a filling three-course Portuguese meal that's one of the best deals in town.

Restaurant Trópico *(Rua Osvaldo Vieria)* Meals CFA3500-6000. The Trópico has a very pleasant garden where meals are served in the evening.

Santa Rosa Meals CFA600-2000. Santa Rosa, west of the stadium, is primarily a chicken place. It's lively at night, with loud music and lots of people.

Restaurant Asa Branca *(Rua Justino Lopes)* Meals CFA4000-6000. Asa Branca serves traditional Portuguese fare and is particularly noted for its seafood.

Dona Fernanda Meals CFA2500-5000. This place, east of Estrada de Santa Luzia, has good atmosphere, with plants, dim lights, and grass skirts from the Bijagós on the walls.

O Bistro *(☎ 204444, Rua Eduardo Mondlane)* Meals CFA3000-5000. The popular O Bistro has decent French dishes. The owner has also opened ***6 Mil***, a casino-pizzeria out by the Mercado de Bandim.

Restaurante Galáxia Meals CFA1000-3000. A vegetarian's paradise (relatively speaking), the Galáxia has excellent hummus and falafel. It's down by the port.

Restaurant Magui *(Rua Vitorino Costa)* Meals CFA2000-2500. Some of the best lunch in town is cooked up at this Senegalese spot, unmarked behind an aqua-and-white house.

Pastry Shops Pastry shops worth visiting include ***Pastelaria Dias & Dias***, north of the fort; ***Ganaan*** on Avenida Nações Unidas; and ***Gelataria Baiana*** on Baiana (Praça Ché Guevara). ***Guiné-Serviço***, under an enormous red umbrella on Rua Justino Lopes, and ***Fortaleza d'Amura Café***, across from the fort, are both good for espresso (CFA250) and a sandwich (CFA500).

Self-Catering Upscale supermarkets are as abundant in Bissau as street food is scarce. ***Mavegro*** supermarket on Rua Eduardo Mondlane sells all kinds of imported items, from car tyres to shampoo, plus many kinds of food. ***Supermercado Bonjour*** near the Air Senegal office also has a good selection of food. For a more colourful experience, you can buy fruit at the ***Mercado Central***, but the ladies here will rob you blind if you don't know your papayas. ***Mercado de Bandim*** has more fresh produce and more buzz.

Entertainment

Several of the restaurants listed earlier are also bars; ***Brisa do Mar*** and the ***barracas*** are some of the best. More upmarket is ***Bar Galeon*** on Baiana (Praça Ché Guevara), which is also a restaurant and casino, and the ***Churasquiera a Braza*** just next door. ***Confeitaria Imperio*** on the Praça dos Heróis Nacionais is a good spot for a drink (CFA500) and people-watching.

To the north in Santa Luzia is the lively ***Verda Tropical Nightclub***, and just south, the sedate ***Coquiero*** with a garden terrace for drinks, plus a snack bar and restaurant.

Nightclubs in the centre include ***Tropicana*** near Mavegro's, ***Galáxia*** near the port, and ***X Club*** (pronounced 'sheesh club') on Rua Osualdo Vieira. ***Bambu 2000*** is perhaps Bissau's most popular spot; it's out on Avenida de 14 Novembro near Hotel Bissau.

Shopping

The best place for arts and crafts is the ***Centro Artistico Juvenil*** *(Avenida de 14 Novembro)*, which is a training centre for young artists. The fixed prices are reasonable, and there's no pressure to buy. It's open Monday to Saturday. Woodcarvings are also sold at ***stalls*** on the footpath outside the Pensão Centrale and at ***MultiArte*** on the western side of the Fortaleza d'Amura. Clothing and fabrics are sold outdoors on Avenida Amilcar Cabral, one block north of the post office.

Getting There & Away

Air Airlines represented in Bissau include Guinea-Bissau Airlines and TACV Cabo Verde Airlines (☎ 204894) on Rua Osualdo Vieira, Air Senegal (☎ 202400) on the same street, and TAP Air Portugal (☎ 201359) on Praça dos Heróis Nacionais.

Bush Taxi & Minibus All bush taxis and minibuses leave from the paragem on Avenida de 14 Novembro. It's hidden about 500m south of the road, out by the airport. It's always best to get transport in the morning. To get here take a *toca-toca* (minibus) from the Mercado de Bandim (CFA100) or a taxi (about CFA1000) from anywhere in town.

Boat Guinea-Bissau has one ferry operated by Rodofluvial (☎ 212350, 212376). Sailing days and times are posted at their office near the port on Rua Vitorino Costa. It may also be able to advise on boats to Cacine. More information on boats to Bubaque, Galinhas, Enxudé, Bolama and Catió is given in the relevant sections later in this chapter.

Getting Around

To/From the Airport The airport is about 10km from the centre. Taxis meet most flights, and it should cost no more than CFA2000 to get into town. To get a minibus, walk 200m to the roundabout at the start of Avenida de 14 Novembro, the road into the city.

Toca-Toca These are small minibuses painted blue and yellow that run around the city. Most rides cost CFA100. The most useful route for visitors goes from Mercado de Bandim along Avenida de 14 Novembro towards the paragem and airport.

Taxi Shared taxis are painted blue and white and cost CFA150 per person for a short ride across town or CFA300 (for one or two people) from downtown (Praça) to Bairro de Ajuda.

Car There haven't been any car rental agencies in Bissau since the war. However, a guy affiliated with the Hotel 24 de Setembro (☎ 221034/7, fax 221002) rents his red Mercedes with driver for CFA30,000 a day.

The North

BAFATÁ

The birthplace of Amilcar Cabral, Bafatá is on a hill overlooking the Gêba River. The western part of town has some interesting old colonial architecture. We heard from a traveller who hired a bicycle in Bafatá and cycled through 'fields, villages and beautiful jungle' to reach a ruined Portuguese outpost at **Gêba**.

The nicest place to stay in Bafatá is ***Hotel Maimuna Capé***, which has airy, spotless rooms with bathroom for CFA12,000 (fan) or CFA17,000 (air-con). French meals are served for CFA2800 to CFA5000. ***Apartmento Fao***, hidden among some houses, has basic rooms for CFA5000. There are several cheap ***food stalls*** by the petrol station and a couple of nicer Portuguese restaurants further west: ***Restaurante Ponto de Encontro*** has excellent dishes for around CFA3500 and beer on tap (CFA400), and the popular ***Cantinho do Ceu*** has an outdoor terrace and good food for CFA3000.

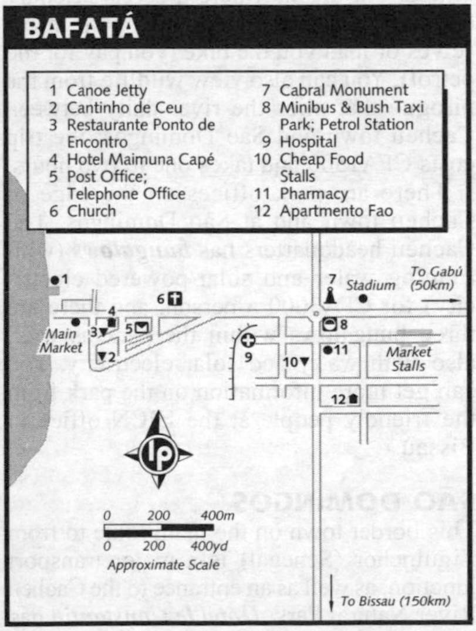
BAFATÁ
1 Canoe Jetty
2 Cantinho de Ceu
3 Restaurante Ponto de Encontro
4 Hotel Maimuna Capé
5 Post Office; Telephone Office
6 Church
7 Cabral Monument
8 Minibus & Bush Taxi Park; Petrol Station
9 Hospital
10 Cheap Food Stalls
11 Pharmacy
12 Apartmento Fao
Main Market
Stadium
To Gabú (50km)
Market Stalls
0 200 400m
0 200 400yd
Approximate Scale
To Bissau (150km)

Minibuses to Bissau (CFA1500), Gabú (CFA500) or Buba (CFA1500) depart from the petrol station area.

GABÚ

Gabú is a lively town, especially in the evening when the large market and food stalls come alive, and a major transport hub for travel between Guinea-Bissau, Guinea and Senegal. It's a good place to stay for a day or two and get a feel for upcountry life. If you crave activity, about 40km south of Gabú on the road to Boé is **Canjadude**, where you can hike up several rocky hillocks rising from the plain and get good views of the surrounding area. Further south at **Ché-Ché** is a group of standing stones.

Places to Stay & Eat

Pensão Miriama Sago Rooms CFA4500. One of the cheapest places to stay is this unmarked *pensão* (guesthouse) near the market, which has good basic rooms.

Jomav Rooms CFA8000. Spotless rooms at this bar/restaurant/disco have fan and bathroom. You won't get much sleep here when the disco's open.

Hotel Visiom *(☎ 511484)* Rooms with fan/air-con CFA8000/15,000. Out in a quiet spot north of town, the Visiom is good value, with clean rooms with bathroom.

Residencial Djaraama *(☎ 511382)* Rooms CFA12,500. Rooms here are overpriced, but it's almost worth staying here just for the wacky decor which includes a 4m-long snakeskin and an inflatable reindeer in the salon.

You can get ***street food*** and roast meat in the evening in the area around the market.

Restaurant Binta Senegaless Meals CFA500. Binta is a feisty Dakar lady who makes a hell of a peanut sauce.

Restaurante-Bar Fa-Do *(☎ 511242)* Meals CFA1000-3000. Fatima and Do have fresh juices and standard local fare in a pseudo-naturalistic setting.

Pó di Terra Meals CFA1000-2000. The Pó di Terra has outdoor seating in a pleasant garden on the north side of town.

GABÚ
1 Hotel Visiom
2 Restaurante Bar Pòdi Terra
3 Guiné Telecom
4 Residencial Djaraama
5 Bar Tudo na Iskina
6 Jomav
7 Police
8 Street Food Stalls
9 Church
10 Bush Taxi & Minibus Park
11 Restaurant Binta Senegaless
12 Pensão Miriama Sago; Restaurante-Bar Fa-Do
0 100 200m
0 100 200yd
To Bafatá (50km) & Bissau (200km)
Market
To Guinea (66km)

Bar Tudo na Iskina This outdoor spot is the best place for a drink, with low lights, cheerful management and good music.

Getting There & Away

Minibuses go regularly to Bissau (CFA2000, 200km, four hours). If you're heading for Guinea or Senegal, see Getting There & Away earlier in this chapter for details of transport options from Gabú. You can easily change CFA into Guinean francs at the bush taxi and minibus park.

CANCHUNGO

This small, gritty town, northwest of Bissau, is a good stepping-off point for exploring the surrounding area. You can eat at the couple of small ***restaurants*** here; one of them also has cheap ***rooms***. Minibuses run direct from Bissau to Canchungo (CFA950), although you may have to change vehicles at the Joalande River crossing if the bridge has not been completed.

CALAQUISSE

This peaceful and beautiful place is about 25km west of Canchungo on the coast. There's a daily bush taxi here from Canchungo (CFA500, 1½ hours), and Calaquisse has a small and friendly ***hotel***, with rooms for CFA3500. From here you can take walks through the surrounding woodland or reach a small port on the estuary about 2km away and stroll on the edge of the mangroves and salt marsh.

CACHEU

The small riverside town of Cacheu (**cash**-ay-ou), north of Canchungo, was once a major Portuguese slave-trading centre from which the infamous English pirate Sir Francis Drake was repulsed in 1567. You can visit the fort and see the cannons and some large bronze statues stacked in a corner and seemingly forgotten. Most visitors, though, come to visit the nearby park (see the following entry). Minibuses run to/from Canchungo (CFA500) and Bissau (CFA2000).

PARQUE NATURAL DOS TARRAFES DO RIO CACHEU

The Cacheu River Natural Park was established to protect some large areas of mangrove (for more information on mangroves, see the boxed text 'Mangroves' in the Senegal chapter), though it also includes some sacred forests. The diverse array of wildlife includes over 200 bird species, among them flamingos, Senegal parrots and African giant kingfishers, and a number of different monkeys. Alligators, hippos, manatees, panthers, gazelles and hyenas also live here.

You can explore the park by car, if you have one. Motorbikes are not officially rented, but the staff here are very friendly and can either take you in the park themselves or loan you the bike (you pay for the petrol). You can also view wildlife from the pirogue that plies the river daily between Cacheu town and São Domingos; the trip costs CFA1500 and takes one to two hours.

There are park offices on the edge of Cacheu town and at São Domingos. The Cacheu headquarters has ***bungalows*** (with running water and solar-powered electricity) for CFA3000 a person, and there are three bungalows within the park as well, also with water and solar electricity. You can get more information on the park from the friendly people at the UICN office in Bissau.

SÃO DOMINGOS

This border town on the main route to/from Ziguinchor (Senegal) is a major transport junction, as well as an entrance to the Cacheu River Natural Park. ***Hotel le Constantin*** has rooms for CFA3500, and there are ***food shacks*** near the immigration office. If you're going to Varela, note that bush taxis go from outside the border post. A shared taxi here from Bissau costs CFA2500.

VARELA

Varela is a village on the coast, about 50km west of São Domingos. The magnificent beaches here are just as good as at Cap Skirring in Senegal, only a few kilometres away, but without the people. You can ***camp*** on the beach or stay at ***Chez Helene*** about 1km away, with rooms for CFA10,000. Bring your own food and water, though, as both are sometimes hard to find. There's a kandonga (CFA500) once a day between São Domingos and Varela. Be sure to check the security situation in neighbouring Casamance before coming here; fighting has spilled over into Varela in the past.

The South

Moving into southern Guinea-Bissau you leave the Sahel well behind and enter a beautiful region of forests and waterways. The bird and monkey populations are impressive, and this is the home of Africa's most westerly chimpanzee populations.

You can reach the region by the Tuesday boat from Bissau via Bolama to Catió; the trip is around eight hours and the boat returns on Friday. Alternatively, the boat from Bissau to Enxudé (en-shu-day) runs daily except Sunday, stays an hour and then returns. You can also get a canoa to Enxudé from the jetty east of the main port in Bissau – there's usually at least one every morning. Returning to Bissau by road, via Buba and, if you choose, Saltinho, is straightforward.

BUBA

Buba is a lively junction town on the way to points further south and east. Connections here can be erratic, but if you get stuck it's no hardship. ***Barracudas de Buba*** *(☎ 611 120)* has pretty single/double bungalows, with bathroom, on the water for CFA12,500/17,500, including breakfast. It caters primarily to anglers from overseas. ***Belo Ocanto*** has basic rooms with shared bathroom for CFA3500. The rooms at ***Berço do Rio*** *(☎ 611118)* are a step up, with bathroom, and cost CFA8000. Both these hotels have restaurants, and there's a couple of others in town serving cheap bowls of fish and rice. A minibus from Bissau is CFA2500 – there's usually one each way every morning.

CATIÓ

A weekly boat goes every Tuesday from Bissau via Bolama to Catió (around eight hours) and the boat returns on Friday. You can reach Catió on the daily minibus (CFA3000) from Bissau (though you may have to go from Bissau to Buba by minibus (CFA2500) and change to a kandonga for the section to Catió. From Catió to Jemberem there's a kandonga every morning, which takes you across to the ferry.

JEMBEREM

Jemberem is a small village 22km east of Catió, and the centre of a community-based conservation scheme connected with the proposed **Cantanhez Natural Park**, which is a good place to see birds and monkeys. The local women's association has set up the small and inexpensive ***Raça Banana guesthouse***. Through them or the local chief you can arrange a guide (essential) to show you through the nearby sacred forest. A colourful booklet called *Cantanhez Forêts Sacrées* (in French), produced by an organisation called Tiniguena (☎ 251907), is available in Bissau at its offices behind the Gambian embassy.

There's a daily kandonga in the morning between Catió and Jemberem, which takes you across to the ferry.

CACINE

From Jemberem, you can reach the pretty jungle town of Cacine (from where you can also catch a canoa to Kamsar in Guinea). Cacine is a good base to see some interesting *lumos* (markets) in the nearby villages of **Camaconde** (Wednesday) and **Sanconha** (Saturday), or to visit the pristine beach at **Cassumba**. There's no established hotel in Cacine, but locals can set you up with something.

You can easily find transport to Bissau from Camaconde or Sanconha on market days. To get to Cacine from Jemberem, take a boat directly or get a minibus or kandonga to Canabine and from there, a boat to Cacine.

SALTINHO

About 25km southeast of Xitole, the main Bissau-Buba road crosses the Corubal River near the **Saltinho waterfall** *(cascata)*. The upscale ***Pousada do Saltinho*** *(☎ 202901)* has singles/doubles with air-con and bathroom for CFA20,000/25,000 and outstanding views of the falls. The hotel is popular with European hunters. Even if you don't stay here, come for a drink or just for a swim. The forest here is full of birds, monkeys and other wildlife.

The ***Ilha Hotel Surire*** is in another beautiful spot on a nearby island. Comfortable air-con cabins cost CFA15,000/20,000 and have bathrooms with hot water. To arrange transport, it's easiest to contact Surire Tours (☎ 214166) in Bissau before you go.

Arquipélago dos Bijagós

The Arquipélago dos Bijagós is the island group off the coast of Guinea-Bissau. Several of the islands are uninhabited, while others are home to small farming and fishing communities. The whole archipelago has been declared a Biosphere Reserve, and the southern Orango group of islands and the eastern João Vieira group are national parks. The islands are renowned for their many rare bird and plant species, and for their endangered populations of sea turtle. The UICN and several other bodies are working to protect the natural environment and improve conditions for the islands' populations.

Before you go to any beach, check the tides. When it's low the sea is miles away and you'll have to wade through thigh-deep mud to get a swim.

The main transportation from Bissau to the islands is by one of the small boats or canoas that go frequently (usually to transport fish). They're slow, unreliable and probably terribly safe, but you'll make friends on the trip. They leave Bissau from Port Rampa, the fishermen's port near the Estádio 24 de Setembro. The top-end hotels and fishing camps have fancy speedboats to Bubaque and some of the other islands; ask at a travel agent in Bissau if you're interested.

For something more exclusive, you might consider a tour around the archipelago on the luxurious *African Queen*. An all-inclusive one-week trip is CFA350,000 (shorter trips are CFA50,000 a day). For more information, see Jean-Claude at O Bistro (see Bissau Places to Eat) on Rua Eduardo Mondlane in Bissau.

ILHA DE BOLAMA

Bolama, about 40km south of Bissau, was the seat of the country's capital during early colonial days, but the town has been slowly crumbling away since 1941 when everything was transferred to Bissau. Today it's eerily beautiful; the once-majestic pastel-coloured buildings are weathered in interesting ways, while papaya trees grow in their rooms and women braid hair on their porches. The island is a great place to bring a bicycle and explore. The closest beach is about 4km south of Bolama town, but the best beaches are along the far southwestern end of the island, about 20km from town.

Residencial Rui Ramos *(☎ 811136)* is the only place to stay, with basic rooms for CFA8000. ***Mercearia Bar,*** also known as Cantinho da Pedra, serves grilled fish and salad for CFA500.

Getting There & Away

A decrepit ferry run by Rodofluvial leaves Bissau every Tuesday for Bolama (on its way to Catió) and returns on Friday; it goes again on Saturday, returning on Sunday. The fare is CFA2000 each way. Visit the office in Bissau for departure times. You can also go via Enxudé, from where you can catch a bush taxi to São João and then a canoa to Bolama.

ILHA DE BUBAQUE

At the centre of the Arquipélago dos Bijagós, Bubaque is the hub of the islands' transport system (such as it is) and the best place to find a boat to other islands. The island has a range of places to stay and is an ideal place to slow down for a few days or weeks. UICN runs the small **Casa do Ambiente e da Cultura**, which has displays on local people and the islands' wildlife.

You can walk through the forest, palm groves and fields around the town, but most visitors come for the beaches; there's a little one near Club des Dauphins, but much better is **Praia Bruce** at the southern end of the island, about 18km from town. Some

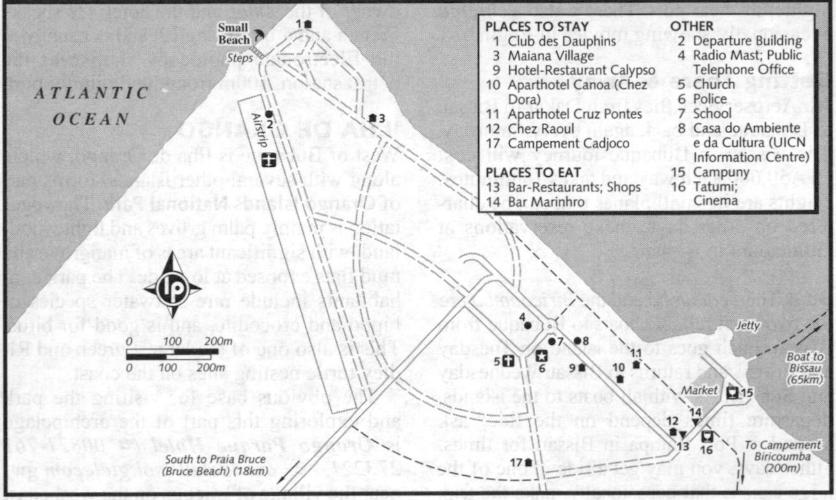
PLACES TO STAY
1 Club des Dauphins
3 Maiana Village
9 Hotel-Restaurant Calypso
10 Aparthotel Canoa (Chez Dora)
11 Aparthotel Cruz Pontes
12 Chez Raoul
17 Campement Cadjoco
PLACES TO EAT
13 Bar-Restaurants; Shops
14 Bar Marinhro
OTHER
2 Departure Building
4 Radio Mast; Public Telephone Office
5 Church
6 Police
7 School
8 Casa do Ambiente e da Cultura (UICN Information Centre)
15 Campuny
16 Tatumi; Cinema
ATLANTIC OCEAN
Small Beach
Steps
Airstrip
Jetty
Boat to Bissau (65km)
Market
To Campement Biricoumba (200m)
South to Praia Bruce (Bruce Beach) (18km)
0 100 200m
0 100 200m
BUBAQUE TOWN

hotels arrange transport to the beach or you can hire a bicycle. The road has a hard surface of shells and cement, making it suitable for bicycles.

Places to Stay – Budget

All the rooms in this category have shared bathroom with bucket shower.

Chez Raoul Rooms CFA4000. This place, run by a spritely Senegalese family, has basic rooms with an African feel.

Campement Cadjoco Singles/doubles CFA5000/7000. About 200m southwest of the Cruz Pontes, this *pensão* has clean rooms in a lush garden setting.

Campement Biricoumba Rooms around CFA5000. At the time of writing, this cheapie was scheduled to open soon. Rooms are in huts on the eastern edge of town.

Places to Stay – Mid-Range & Top End

Aparthotel Cruz Pontes *(☎ 821135)* Rooms CFA10,000. Paulino, the owner here, is a friendly guy who can advise on boat travel. Rates here include breakfast and may be negotiable.

Aparthotel Canoa Singles/doubles CFA10,000/12,000. The Canoa, known to all as Chez Dora, is good value; spotless, pretty rooms in huts have bathrooms and running water, and rates include breakfast. The bar/restaurant serves Portuguese or African meals from CFA4000.

Hotel-Restaurant Calypso *(☎ 821116)* Singles/doubles CFA12,000/15,000. This French family-run place has cool bungalows around a pool and includes breakfast.

Maiana Village *(☎ 821125)* Singles/doubles CFA10,000/12,000. West of town, the Maiana has a small private beach. Boats and angling gear can be hired, and the place caters mainly to fishing groups from Europe.

Club des Dauphins *(☎ 821156)* Singles/doubles CFA15,000/20,000. This place has a macho fishing atmosphere and is almost identical to the Maiana. It has comfortable rooms in huts on the water.

Places to Eat

Around the port area are several workers' ***bar/restaurants*** serving cheap beers and bowls of rice and sauce. ***Bar Marinhro*** is one of the better ones.

Chez Raoul Meals CFA750-2500. This place serves the best food in town. Dinners include dishes such as clams with green papaya (CFA2500); lunch might be Senegalese-style *thiéboudjenne* (rice baked in fish sauce) for CFA750.

Entertainment

The ***bar/restaurants*** mentioned earlier are good places for a beer. For a drink in lively surroundings, try ***Tatumi*** or ***Campuny***, two nightclubs near port. There's also a ***cinema*** occasionally showing movies in English.

Getting There & Away

Air Aeroservices flies from Dakar to Bissau to Bubaque and back again every Saturday. The Bissau to Bubaque journey will cost CFA50,000 each way and takes 15 minutes. Flights are in small planes that can be chartered on other days; make reservations at Guinetours in Bissau.

Boat The *Téamanhá* and the *Biricoumba* are the two most reliable boats to Bubaque from Bissau. Each goes to the island on Tuesday and Friday, and returns to Bissau Wednesday and Sunday. As with all boats to the islands, departure times depend on the tide; ask around at Port Rampa in Bissau for times. Other days, you may get a ride in one of the large canoas that occasionally make the trip. Whatever boat you catch, it costs CFA2500. The trip is meant to take five hours.

ILHA DAS GALINHAS

The island of Galinhas is between Bolama and Rubane, about 60km south of Bissau. There are a few small villages on it, and people grow crops on plots among the trees. The island is also the site of the old Portuguese prison and governor's house; you can walk across the island to see the crumbling building now gradually being consumed by the lush vegetation.

Hotel Ambancana Bungalows without/with bathroom CFA7500/10,000. This friendly, low-key hotel is the only place to stay on Galinhas. Rooms are on the beach and look out on wonderful sunsets; rates include breakfast. Meals are CFA3000. You can buy beers and other drinks, but as there are no shops or markets on the island, the hotel occasionally runs out of things. But it's a marvellous place; we've heard from people who planned to go for a couple days and stayed for a week. Some money from the hotel supports the local village school.

Getting There & Away

The hotel's boat *Amor* goes from Bissau to Galinhas on Thursday or Friday and returns Sunday (and sometimes other days). The return fare is CFA5000. If you're heading to/from Bubaque, you may be able to arrange something with the friendly Mr Sulai, the owner of the *Amor* and the hotel. He speaks French and a bit of English and is usually at the Electrodata photocopy shop near the petrol station, 100m from the Pidjiguiti port.

ILHA DE ORANGO

West of Bubaque is Ilha de Orango, which, along with several other islands, forms part of **Orango Islands National Park**. The vegetation is mainly palm groves and light woodland, with significant areas of mangrove and mud flats exposed at low tide. The park's inhabitants include rare saltwater species of hippo and crocodile, and is good for birds. This is also one of the largest green and Ridley turtle nesting sites on the coast.

The obvious base for visiting the park and exploring this part of the archipelago is ***Orango Parque Hotel*** *(☎ 00871-761 273221, e orangotel@sol.gtelecom.gw)* near the village of Eticoga on the west coast of Orango. Good quality local-style singles/doubles are CFA10,000/18,000; meals are around CFA5000. There are also some ***cheap huts*** for rent at the park headquarters. Bird-watching and fishing can be arranged.

OTHER ISLANDS

Some of the other islands in the Arquipélago dos Bijagós have hotels or tourist facilities, but the majority remain almost completely untouched by modern civilisation (only a small percentage of the islanders even use money). Where you get to depends on the time and money available to you, but wherever you go tread lightly: the Bijagós culture is fragile.

Ilha de Rubane is easily reached by canoa or small boat from Bubaque town. On the island is the upmarket ***Acaja Club***, totally devoted to fishing. The nearby ***Tubaron Club*** is similar. These places cater to upmarket visitors who book their vacations from Europe. If you fancy some luxurious living and fishing in a predominantly French atmosphere, you can make reservations at Guinetours in Bissau. On **Ilha de João Vieira** is another fishing camp, ***Le Tytéline*** *(☎ 00881-631 413199)*, but the owner here is trying to encourage more independent travellers to stay. Rooms in huts with electricity and water go for CFA15,000. The island is part of the João Vieira Poilão National Marine Park and is an important turtle-nesting site.

Liberia

Warning

Although more than six years have passed since the signing of a peace accord, Liberia's security situation continues to be fragile. Since 1999, there has been fighting in Lofa County along the Guinean border, and as this book went to press, hit-and-run style attacks were being reported around Tubmanburg and other areas closer to Monrovia. While travel is possible, it's unwise to set off outside Monrovia without official or business backing, and independent travel in many areas is dangerous. Get an update from your embassy before planning a visit.

Liberia at a Glance

Capital: Monrovia
Population: 2.95 million
Area: 111,370 sq km
Head of State: President Charles Ghankay Taylor
Official language: English
Major local languages: Bassa, Kpelle, Kru, Grebo
Currency: Liberian dollar (L$)
Exchange rate: US$1 = L$55
Time: GMT/UTC
Country telephone code: ☎ 231
Best time to go: November to April

MALI
GUINEA
SIERRA LEONE
CÔTE D'IVOIRE
Ganta p545
Monrovia p538
Central Monrovia p539
Buchanan p543
ATLANTIC OCEAN

Highlights

- Relaxing at Kendeja Beach just southeast of Monrovia
- Getting to know Liberians
- Exploring the rainforest in Sapo National Park

Since 1996, a tenuous calm has prevailed in Liberia, following years of brutal civil war. However, many areas remain factionalised and remote, and the country is not yet a place for independent travellers. The security situation is particularly precarious in the north and west, along the borders with Guinea and Sierra Leone, where rebels have been waging low-level combat since 1999. If peace consolidates and travel opens up, Liberia offers much to discover, including friendly people, lush landscapes and some of the last remaining rainforest in West Africa.

Facts about Liberia

HISTORY

The area that is now Liberia has probably been populated for more than 2000 years, although little is known of its early history. Many present-day Liberians trace their ancestry to peoples who migrated southeast from the Sahel following the fall of the Mali Empire in the 15th century. However, settlement of the area remained sparse because of the dense and inhospitable forests covering most of the country, and no great cities developed.

European contact with Liberia began in the 1460s with the arrival of Portuguese navigators who named several coastal features, including Cape Mesurado (Monrovia) and Cape Palmas (Harper). Because of the trading success of a pepper grain, the area soon became known as the 'Grain Coast'.

In the early 19th century, the Grain Coast rose to the forefront of discussions within the abolitionist movement in the USA as a suitable place to resettle freed American slaves. After several failed attempts at gaining the agreement of local chiefs, officials of the American Colonization Society (ACS) forced a treaty upon a local king at Cape Mesurado. Despite resistance by the indigenous people, settlement went ahead, and in April 1822, an expedition with the first

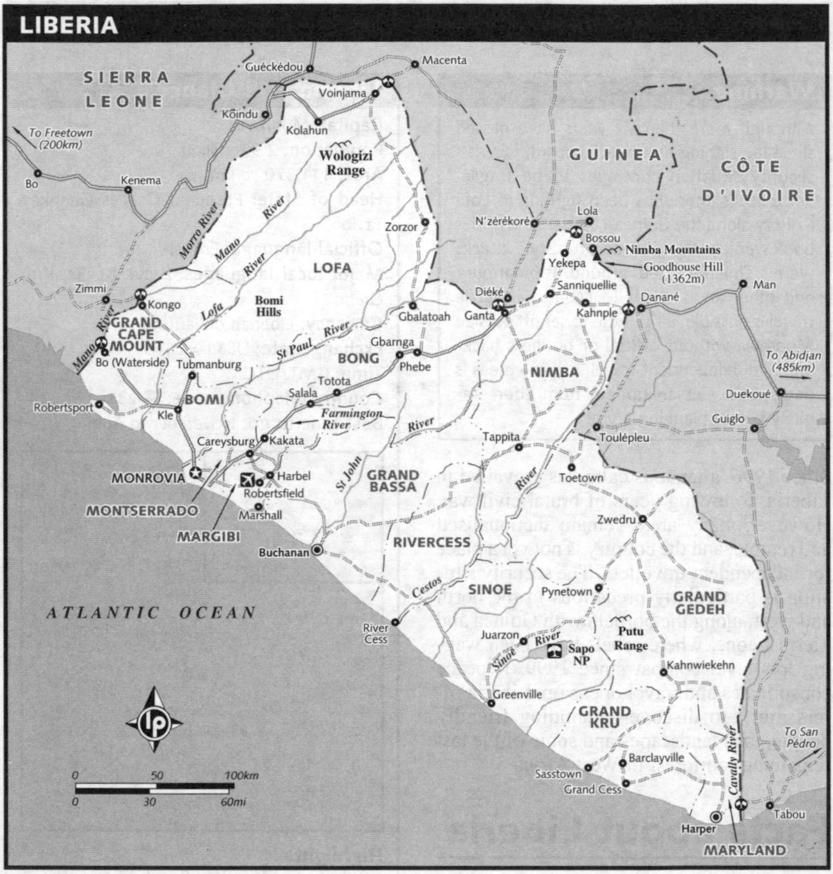
LIBERIA
SIERRA LEONE
To Freetown (200km)
Bo
Kenema
Guéckédou
Kõindu
Kolahun
Voinjama
Macenta
Wologizi Range
Morro River
Mano River
Mano River
Zorzor
LOFA
Zimmi
Kongo
Lofa River
Bomi Hills
GRAND CAPE MOUNT
Mano River
Bo (Waterside)
Tubmanburg
St Paul River
Gbalatoah
Gbarnga
Phebe
BONG
Robertsport
BOMI
Kle
Totota
Salala
Farmington River
Careysburg
Kakata
MONROVIA
Harbel
Robertsfield
Marshall
MONTSERRADO
MARGIBI
St John River
GRAND BASSA
Buchanan
RIVERCESS
GUINEA
CÔTE D'IVOIRE
N'zérékoré
Lola
Bossou
Nimba Mountains
Yekepa
Goodhouse Hill (1362m)
Sanniquellie
Diéké
Ganta
Kahnple
Danané
Man
NIMBA
To Abidjan (485km)
Duekoué
Guiglo
Tappita
Toulépleu
Toetown
River
Zwedru
ATLANTIC OCEAN
Cestos River
SINOE
Pynetown
GRAND GEDEH
River Cess
Juarzon
Sinoe River
Sapo NP
Putu Range
Kahnwiekehn
Greenville
GRAND KRU
To San Pédro
Cavally River
Barclayville
Sasstown
Grand Cess
Harper
Tabou
MARYLAND
0 50 100km
0 30 60mi

group of black-American settlers arrived at Providence Island in present-day Monrovia. Within a short time, under the leadership of the American Jehudi Ashmun, the foundations for a country were established. Additional settlements were founded along the coast, notably at Greenville and Harper.

In 1839, Thomas Buchanan was appointed first governor of the new territory. He was succeeded in 1841 by Joseph Jenkins Roberts, who expanded its boundaries and encouraged cooperation among the various settlements. In 1846, the settlement at Cape Mesurado merged with others along the coast, and a declaration of independence and a constitution were drafted. Both were modelled on those of the USA. In 1847 Liberia declared itself an independent republic, although – fatally for its future history – citizenship excluded indigenous peoples. Roberts was elected the first president. Every successive president until 1980 was of American freed-slave ancestry.

By the mid-19th century, about half of the 5000 black Americans who had originally migrated to Liberia had either died or returned to the USA. The remaining settlers, the citizens of the new republic, came to be known as Americo-Liberians. They saw themselves as part of a mission to bring civilisation and Christianity to Africa, and although constituting only a tiny fraction of Liberia's total population, they dominated the indigenous peoples. The Masonic Order, established in the country in 1851, came to be a symbol of Americo-Liberian solidarity and five presidents, starting with Roberts, were grand masters.

For nearly a century, Liberia foundered economically and politically while indigenous populations continued to be repressed, suffering under a form of forced labour that anywhere else would have been called slavery. In 1930 Britain and the USA cut off diplomatic relations for five years because of the sale of human labour to Spanish colonialists in what was then Fernando Po (now Bioko in Equatorial Guinea).

The Era of Prosperity & the Coup

The True Whig Party monopolised power from early in Liberia's history. Despite the country's labour-recruitment policies, the party was able to project an image of Liberia as Africa's most stable country. During William Tubman's presidency (1944–71), this image led to massive foreign investment, and for several decades following WWII Liberia sustained the highest growth rate in sub-Saharan Africa. Firestone and other American companies made major investments and Tubman – to whom much of the credit was due – earned praise as the 'maker of modern Liberia'. In the 1960s, iron ore–mining operations began near Yekepa by Lamco (Liberian-American Swedish Minerals Company), which became the largest private enterprise in sub-Saharan Africa.

The huge influx of foreign money soon began to distort the economy, resulting in exacerbation of social inequalities and increased hostility between Americo-Liberians and the indigenous population. Viewing this development with alarm, Tubman was forced to concede that the indigenous people would have to be granted some political and economic involvement in the country; one of his concessions was to enfranchise them. Until this point (1963), 97% of the population had been denied voting rights.

William Tolbert succeeded Tubman as president in 1971. While Tolbert initiated a series of reforms, the government continued to be controlled by about a dozen related Americo-Liberian families and corruption was rampant. Tolbert established diplomatic relations with Communist countries such as the People's Republic of China, and at home clamped down harshly on opposition.

Resentment of these policies and of growing government corruption grew. In 1979 several demonstrators were shot in protests against a proposed increase in rice prices. Finally, in April 1980, Tolbert was overthrown in a coup led by an uneducated master sergeant, Samuel Doe. In the accompanying fighting, Tolbert and many high-ranking ministers were killed. For the first time, Liberia had a ruler who wasn't an Americo-Liberian, giving the indigenous population a taste of political power and an opportunity for vengeance. The 28-year-old Doe shocked the world by ordering 13 ex-ministers to be publicly executed on a beach in Monrovia.

Although the coup turned over power to the indigenous population, it was condemned by most other African countries and by Liberia's other allies and trading partners. Over the next few years, though, relations with neighbouring African states gradually thawed. However, the flight of capital from the country in the wake of the coup, coupled with ongoing corruption, caused Liberia's economy to rapidly decline. During the 1980s, Liberia recorded the worst economic performance in Africa; real incomes fell by half, the unemployment rate in Monrovia rose to 50% and electricity blackouts became common.

Doe struggled to maintain his grip on power by any means available, including a sham 'election' held in 1985, largely to appease his major creditor, the USA. By the late 1980s, however, it was clear that opposition forces had had enough and were determined to topple him. Following a foiled post-election coup attempt, members of Doe's Krahn tribe began killing and torturing rival tribespeople, particularly the Gio and Mano in Nimba County.

Civil War

On Christmas Eve 1989, several hundred rebels led by Charles Taylor (former head of the Doe government's procurement agency) invaded Nimba County from Côte d'Ivoire. Doe's troops arrived shortly thereafter and indiscriminately killed hundreds of unarmed civilians, raped women and burned villages. Thousands of civilians fled into Côte d'Ivoire and Guinea.

Shortly after the invasion, Prince Johnson of the Gio tribe broke away from Taylor and formed his own rebel forces. By mid-1990, Taylor's forces controlled most of the country while Johnson's guerrillas had seized most of Monrovia; Doe was holed up with some loyal troops in his mansion. Meanwhile, Liberia lay in ruins. Refugees were streaming into neighbouring countries, US warships were anchored off the coast and an Ecowas peacekeeping force (known as Ecowas Monitoring Group or Ecomog) was despatched in an attempt to keep the warring factions apart.

It was all to no avail. Refusing to surrender or even step down as president, Doe and many of his supporters were finally wiped out by Johnson's forces. With both Johnson and Taylor claiming the presidency, Ecomog forces installed their own candidate, political-science professor Amos Sawyer, as head of the Interim Government of National Unity (IGNU). Meanwhile, Taylor's National Patriotic Front of Liberia (NPFL) forces continued to occupy about 90% of the country, while remnants of Doe's former army and Johnson's followers were encamped within Monrovia itself.

After a brutal assault by Taylor on Monrovia in October 1992, Ecomog increased its forces and in August 1993, the protagonists finally hammered out a peace accord at a UN-sponsored meeting in Geneva. The accord, known as the Cotonou Agreement, called for installation of a six-month transitional government representing IGNU, NPFL and the third major player, Ulimo (United Liberation Movement for Democracy), Doe's former soldiers. When its mandate expired in September 1994 a new agreement, the Akosombo Amendment, was signed. It called for the formation of a new five-member Council of State to replace the IGNU. The amendment was rejected by the IGNU, though, which extended its own life span until mid-1995.

In August 1995, yet another peace agreement (the Abuja Accord) was signed by leaders of the main warring factions. This one lasted until 6 April 1996, when fighting erupted in Monrovia between NPFL and Ulimo. During April and May there was widespread looting, large sections of Monrovia were severely damaged, and nearly all resident foreigners and UN staff were evacuated.

August 1996 resulted in the negotiation of an amended Abuja Accord, which provided for a cease-fire, disarmament and demobilisation by early 1997, followed by elections. At the same time, Ruth Perry, a former senator, was appointed to head the Council of State. Despite serious cease-fire violations and an incomplete disarmament process, elections took place on 19 July. Charles Taylor and his National Patriotic Party (NPP) won an overwhelming majority (75%) – in part because many Liberians feared the consequences if he lost – and the voting was declared by international observers to have been free and transparent.

Following the elections, things picked up markedly in Liberia, especially in Monrovia where shops were once more well-stocked and street life recovered its vibrancy. Even upcountry, some of the thousands of refugees from the earlier fighting began to return to Liberia and daily life started to regain its normal rhythms.

However, the political scene continued to be fragile. By late 1998, all former faction leaders except Taylor were living in exile and power became increasingly consolidated in the presidency. In 1999 dissident groups led by the Liberians United for Reconciliation and Democracy (LURD) launched armed incursions in Lofa County near the Guinean border, setting off a new round of low-level fighting. LURD – whose members include many former Ulimo fighters – has stated its determination to topple Taylor's government. The government says it is hampered in dealing with the situation by UN sanctions imposed in May 2001 to force Liberia to sever ties with Sierra Leone's Revolutionary United Front (RUF) rebel group. Meanwhile, in the centre of things and fuelling regional brutalities and international terrorism is the lure of profits from the diamond fields in the area where the Liberian, Guinean and Sierra Leonean borders meet.

As this book went to press, the outlook for Liberia's future was clouded. The only effective authority is wielded by those with access to guns or money, and the ever-present threat of instability and further violence continues to hinder reconstruction and economic development. While hopes persist that the situation will stabilise, they are tempered by the tragic realities of Liberia's recent past, and a durable peace remains elusive.

GEOGRAPHY

With barely three million people within its 111,000 sq km, Liberia is sparsely populated in comparison with its neighbours and large tracts of the country are uninhabited. The main population centres are around Monrovia on the coast, in the centre near Gbarnga and Ganta, in the northwest near the Sierra Leone border and in the southeast near Harper.

The country's low-lying coastal plain is intersected by marshes, tidal lagoons and at least nine major rivers, the largest of which is the St Paul. Inland is a densely forested plateau rising to low mountains in the northeast, in Lofa and Nimba counties.

CLIMATE

Monrovia is one of the two wettest capital cities in Africa (Freetown in Sierra Leone is the other), with rainfall averaging more than 4500mm per year along much of the Liberian coast. Inland it's less – in some areas only about 2000mm annually. Temperatures range from 23°C to 32°C in Monrovia, and slightly higher inland. However, humidity levels of more than 85% in the dry season (November to April) and more than 90% in the rainy season (May to October) often make it feel much warmer. There is little seasonal temperature variation.

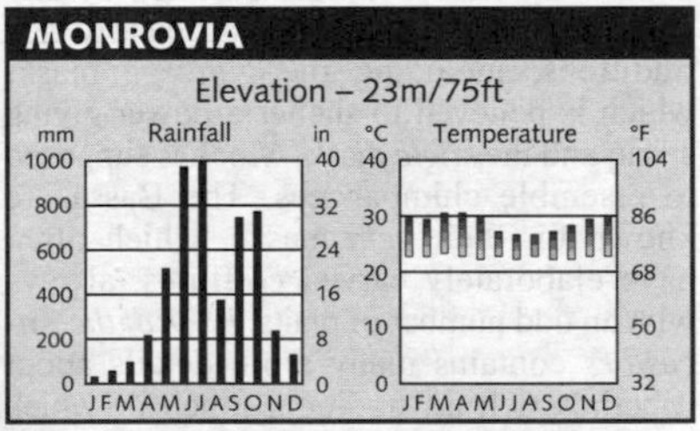
MONROVIA
Elevation – 23m/75ft
mm
Rainfall
in
°C
Temperature
°F
JFMAMJJASOND
JFMAMJJASOND

ECOLOGY & ENVIRONMENT

Liberia is one of the last West African countries with significant areas of rainforests. Originally found throughout the country, the rainforests now cover about 40% of total land area, primarily in the northwest near the Sierra Leone border and in the southeast by Sapo National Park. The forests, however, are under threat. About two-dozen logging companies are operating in the country, primarily in the southeast. Timber exports constitute over half of Liberia's total exports, and effective regulation is weak to nonexistent.

Among the bright spots are the activities of the small but dedicated Society for the Conservation of Nature of Liberia (SCNL; ☎/fax 227 058, ☎ 226 888, ext 330 414), PO Box 2628, based at Monrovia Zoo in Larkpase. In addition to striving to get the zoo back on its feet, SCNL is sponsoring a tree project in which acacia seedlings are planted at various sites around the capital. It is also working to keep attention focused on Sapo National Park. SCNL's informative newsletter, the *Pepperbird*, is available through its office.

The Forestry Development Authority on the 4th floor, Ministry of Finance building, at the corner of Broad and Mechlin Sts, is another good source of information on Liberian environmental issues.

GOVERNMENT & POLITICS

Liberia's government is modelled on that in the USA, with popularly elected executive and legislative branches and a court system, although the present legislature was elected under a special proportional-representation formula mandated by the peace accord provisions. The ruling NPP holds a large majority in the legislature and power rests in the hands of the president. The next presidential and legislative elections are scheduled for 2003.

ECONOMY

Liberia has abundant natural resources, including timber, gold, diamonds and iron ore, although potential revenues have never been realised. The economy, weak before the war, is now in a shambles and World Bank data rank the country as one of Africa's poorest.

Agriculture has been the traditional mainstay of the economy, with major crops including coffee, cocoa, rubber, palm trees, fruit, rice and cassava. However, the number of Liberians involved in this sector dropped significantly during the past decade because of massive wartime displacement of rural communities; only slowly is this trend beginning to reverse.

Apart from resettling displaced populations, restarting an educational system, and reintegrating thousands of former fighters, Liberia is faced with the task of rebuilding almost all infrastructure. A small but steady stream of outside investors has been visiting the country, but serious investment is hampered by fears of further instability and corruption. Under any scenario, Liberia will

Sapo National Park

While Liberia has several designated conservation areas, Sapo is the only official national park. Within its 1308 sq km, it contains some of West Africa's last remaining primary rainforest, as well as a variety of wildlife, including forest elephants, pygmy hippos, chimpanzees and antelopes. Surrounding the park is a 1.6km-wide buffer zone, which before the war was the site of agro-forestry projects aimed at sustainably balancing community needs with protection of the park's ecosystems. Some of these projects are now being revived on a limited scale. Efforts are also underway to increase community involvement in park management and there's a strong network of private support, primarily in Liberia and the USA, to get Sapo going again.

Currently, there are no commercial tours into the park, although given an improved political situation, this could quickly change. In the meantime, there are plans to re-establish a tented camp outside the park boundary and there are several temporary camps on the river. If you are interested in visiting, the best contacts are SCNL and the Forestry Development Authority (see Ecology & Environment, for contact details). Allow a full day to reach Sapo from Monrovia by 4WD along the road paralleling the coast, and at least two days if you go via Zwedru. Once at the park, you can arrange guided hikes and canoe rides.

In addition to SCNL and the Forestry Development Authority, you can obtain information on Sapo through Conservation International's local office in Monrovia, through the Philadelphia Zoo in the USA (e conservation@phillyzoo.com) and through the Ministry of Information, Cultural Affairs and Tourism in Monrovia (see Tourist Offices later in this chapter).

remain heavily dependent on international aid for the foreseeable future. The unemployment rate is estimated at well over 70%.

POPULATION & PEOPLE

Liberia's population of 2.95 million (including several hundred thousand refugees still outside the country) consists overwhelmingly of people of indigenous origin. There are more than a dozen major ethnic groups, including the Kpelle in the centre, the Bassa around Buchanan, the Krahn in the southeast, the Mandingo (also called Mandinka) in the north and the Kru along the coast. The Kpelle and the Bassa are the most numerous, making up about 20% and about 15% of the population, respectively. Americo-Liberians account for less than 3% of the total population. There's a large Lebanese community in Monrovia who wield a disproportionate share of economic power.

Large parts of Liberia are uninhabited or have very scattered populations, especially in the southeast. Almost 50% of Liberians were displaced from their homes in the war.

ARTS

The arts of Liberia are well described in *Rock of the Ancestors* by William Siegmann with Cynthia Schmidt. These authors note that masks have traditionally been one of Liberia's most important art forms. Masks are viewed as having religious and moral significance and are used both to teach lessons and to entertain. The Gio in Nimba County to the northeast have some particularly rich traditions, including the *gunyege* mask, which is believed to shelter a power-giving spirit, and the *kagle* mask, which is supposed to resemble chimpanzees. The Bassa are known for their *gela* masks, which often have elaborately carved coiffures, always with an odd number of plaits. *Rock of the Ancestors* contains many more details about Liberia's rich art tradition, much of which was unfortunately destroyed during the war.

One of the most well-known musical instruments – although not uniquely Liberian – is the 'talking drum', an hourglass-shaped instrument whose upper and lower ends are connected by tension strings. When these are compressed by the drummer while holding it under one arm next to his body, the pitch increases producing a variable tone, giving the drum its name. It is beaten with a stick and not with the hands. See the 'Music of West Africa' special section.

RELIGION

Almost half the population is Christian, close to 20% is Muslim and the remainder follows traditional religions.

> **Secret Societies**
>
> Among the most distinctive features of Liberian culture are secret societies, called Poro for men and Sande for women. They are found throughout the country, except in the southeast, and they are strongest in the northwest. Each has rites and ceremonies aimed at educating young people in the customs of the tribe, preserving the folklore, skills and crafts, and instilling discipline. Their contribution in preserving traditional ways has proved quite significant.
>
> Initiations, which used to involve as many as four years of training, now usually less, take place when children approach puberty. Initiates are easily recognised by their white painted faces and bodies and their shaved heads.
>
> Hierarchies prevail; the most extreme example is the Poro among the Vai, which traditionally had 99 levels. Lower-ranking members cannot acquire the esoteric knowledge of higher-ranking members or attend their secret meetings. Ascending the ranks depends on birth (leadership is frequently restricted to certain families), seniority and the ability to learn the societies' beliefs and rituals.
>
> The role of these societies has traditionally gone beyond religion and the education of the young, with *zoes* (Poro society leaders) wielding important political influence. The societies also control the activities of indigenous medical practitioners, and they often judge disputes between members of high-ranking families or punish people for things such as theft and murder. A village chief who doesn't have the support of the Poro on important decisions can expect trouble enforcing them.

LANGUAGE

More than 20 African languages are spoken in Liberia, including Kpelle in the north-central region, Bassa and Kru along the coast, and Grebo in the southeast. English is the official language, although travellers often have difficulty understanding the local version. The following will help you get started:

dash	bribe
coal tar	tar road
waste	discard (waste the milk) or splash (waste water)
I beg you	please (with emphasis)
carry	give a ride to
wait small	just a moment please
kala kala	crooked, corrupt

Facts for the Visitor

PLANNING

The best time to visit Liberia is during the dry season, between November and April.

In Monrovia, the Cartographic Section on the ground floor of the Ministry of Planning and Economic Affairs building on Randall St, has dated maps of the capital and most other towns, which it will copy for you for a negotiable fee.

There are no recent commercially printed maps of Monrovia or Liberia on the market.

TOURIST OFFICES

The Ministry of Information, Cultural Affairs and Tourism (☎ 227 349, fax 226 544, Ⓦ www.micat.gov.lr) in Monrovia is the entity to contact with any questions, although they have no specific tourist information. Outside Liberia, embassies can provide general information.

VISAS & DOCUMENTS

Visas

Visas are required by all except nationals of Ecowas countries and cost US$40 (US$45 for US citizens), plus two photos. Fees may be higher depending on where you apply. Regardless of the duration of your visa, you'll be given 48 hours on arrival during which you must report for an extension to the Bureau of Immigration (open 9am to 5pm Monday to Friday and to 3pm on Saturday) on Broad St in Monrovia. Once there, you will need to pay US$25 plus two photos for your initial 30-day stay.

Visas for Onward Travel In Liberia, you can get visas for Côte d'Ivoire (previously US$50 plus one photo for a three-month visa) and possibly also for Sierra Leone and Guinea. Embassies are generally open for applications from 9am to noon and visas are generally issued within one to two days.

Other Documents

Proof of vaccination against yellow fever and cholera is obligatory and will be scrutinised on arrival.

EMBASSIES & CONSULATES

Liberian Embassies & Consulates

In West Africa, Liberia has embassies or consulates in Cameroon, Côte d'Ivoire, Gambia, Ghana, Guinea, Nigeria and Sierra Leone. See the Facts for the Visitor section of the relevant country chapter for more details. Elsewhere, embassies and consulates include the following:

Belgium (☎ 02-414 73 17, 664 16 53) 50 Av du Château, 1081 Brussels
France (☎ 01 47 63 58 55) 12 Place du General Catroux, 75017 Paris
Germany (☎ 0228-34 08 22) Mainzerstrasse 259, 53179 Bonn
UK (☎ 020-7221 1036) 2 Pembridge Place, London W2 4XB
USA (☎ 202-723 0437, W www.liberiaemb.org) 5201 16th St, NW, Washington, DC 20011

There are embassies or consulates in Egypt, Ethiopia, Japan and several other countries.

Embassies & Consulates in Liberia

Embassies and consulates in Monrovia include the following:

Belgium (☎ 224 109, 226 209) Bushrod Island Rd (honorary consul)
Côte d'Ivoire (☎ 227 436) 8th St, Sinkor, near St Joseph's Construction
Ghana (☎ 227 448) 15th St, Sinkor, Monrovia
Guinea Cnr 24th St and Tubman Blvd, Sinkor
Nigeria (☎ 227 345, 227 346) Nigeria House, Tubman Blvd, Congo Town
Sierra Leone (☎ 226 250, 225 618) Hotel Africa compound, Villa 18
Spain (☎ 226 854) Broad St, at the Weasua-KLM office
UK (☎ 226 516) European Union Office, Mamba Point (honorary consul, emergency assistance only)
USA (☎ 226 370) United Nations Dr, Mamba Point

China, Egypt, India, Lebanon and Libya also have diplomatic representations in Monrovia. Australian citizens who need assistance should contact the Canadian embassy in Abidjan (Côte d'Ivoire) or the Australian high commission in Lagos (Nigeria); see those chapters for contact details.

CUSTOMS

Up to US$7500 can be exported in foreign currency notes. For sums above this, you will need to use bank drafts, cheques etc. There are no limits on the import of foreign currency, but cash totalling more than US$10,000 must be declared on arrival. Unless you have a bank account in Liberia, over-the-counter wire transfers are limited to US$5000 per transaction, with a maximum of two transactions per month.

For exporting artwork, permits are only required for quantities deemed in excess of normal tourist purchases or for items of exceptional value. Permits are available from Customs & Excise on the 3rd floor of the Ministry of Finance on the corner of Mechlin and Broad Sts in Monrovia. The cost of these depends on quantity and value.

MONEY

The unit of currency is the Liberian 'unity' dollar (L$). US dollars are also widely accepted.

country/region	unit		L$
euro zone	€1	=	L$50
UK	UK£1	=	L$35
USA	US$1	=	L$55
West African CFA	CFA100	=	L$7

Because of the fluctuations of the Liberian dollar, all prices in this chapter are expressed in US dollars.

Exchanging Money

Money can be changed at the airport, at one of the several foreign-exchange bureaus in Monrovia, and at a bank. Avoid changing money on the street. The best exchange rates are for the US dollar. It's also possible to exchange other major currencies, including euros and British pounds, though at less favourable rates. Travellers cheques are virtually useless, although if you're stuck some shop owners may accept payment for purchases in travellers cheques and give you the change in local currency. Credit cards are not accepted anywhere.

POST & COMMUNICATIONS

The Liberian postal system's express service is OK for letters, although 'express' is an exaggeration. Sending parcels through the Liberian post is not reliable. There's no poste restante. For anything important, use DHL or one of the other courier services in Monrovia.

There are no telephones upcountry. In Monrovia international calls can be made from the Liberia Telecom building on Lynch St, open daily between 8am and 10pm. Rates are about US$3 per minute to the USA and US$4 to Australia and Europe; there's a three minute minimum charge and a deposit is required. Some Internet cafés offer Internet dialling, though it's less reliable. The only place to make collect calls is at the Liberia Telecom branch office on Nelson St.

There are several Internet cafés in Monrovia. Most charge about US$5 per 15 minutes. Connections through local servers are often very slow, especially during the day when the lines are overloaded.

DIGITAL RESOURCES

Some useful websites include the following:

University of Pennsylvania This comprehensive site has many useful links.
W www.sas.upenn.edu/African_Studies/Country_Specific/Liberia.html

Friends of Liberia This good site, started by former Peace Corps volunteers, highlights the activities and projects of the nonprofit Friends of Liberia group.
W www.fol.org

Allaboutliberia.com This site offers an attractive, but idealistic, view of tourism in Liberia and news with a decidedly pro-government slant.
W www.allaboutliberia.com

BOOKS

There's a wealth of English-language material on Liberia, much focused on post-1989 history, and most not available within Liberia. For interesting reading on Liberian art and culture, look for *Rock of the Ancestors* by William Siegmann with Cynthia Schmidt. It's actually a catalogue based on museum exhibits, but has some fascinating information on traditional Liberian artwork. See Arts earlier in this chapter for details.

J Gus Liebenow's series of writings about Liberia (*Liberia, 1969 through 1987*) are a fascinating account of the country's history.

One of the best articles on the war is *The Final Days of Dr Doe* by Lynda Schuster (published in *Granta* 48, 1994).

PHOTOGRAPHY & VIDEO

Photo permits are issued by the Ministry of Information, Cultural Affairs and Tourism in Monrovia. Government policy on photo permits is not clear, although police officers on the street will insist you need one. In any case, use a high degree of caution. Don't photograph government buildings, airports, bridges and military installations, and it's best not to use a camera at all in cities and towns unless you're absolutely sure the police aren't watching and locals have no objection.

Kodak film is available at supermarkets in Monrovia.

ELECTRICITY

Unlike the rest of West Africa, voltage in Liberia is 110V. However, many buildings are also wired with 220V. Sometimes outlets are marked, and sometimes not, so ask before connecting appliances. Most plugs are US-style (two flat pins).

Much of Monrovia now has power, but blackouts and power surges are common. There's no power outside the capital.

HEALTH

You need a yellow fever vaccination certificate and proof of cholera vaccination. Malaria is wide spread year-round, so take appropriate precautions. For more information, see Health in the Regional Facts for the Visitor chapter.

St Joseph's Catholic Hospital (☎ 226 207) in Monrovia is the best for emergencies. Upcountry, your best option is Phebe Hospital near Gbarnga. Monrovia has several well-stocked pharmacies.

WOMEN TRAVELLERS

Liberia presents no specific problems for women travellers. For general information, see Women Travellers in the Regional Facts for the Visitor chapter.

DANGERS & ANNOYANCES

The security situation in Liberia is extremely fragile and there are still many weapons around. In general, independent travel outside of Monrovia is unsafe and almost completely unheard of in the present political climate. If you are thinking of setting off, get a complete briefing first from people who know the situation; embassies and resident expats are the best sources. Overall, land mines are not a problem, though some have been found in areas of Firestone Plantation, and along the beach south of Buchanan.

BUSINESS HOURS

Government offices are open 8.30am to 4pm Monday to Friday. Most businesses operate from 9am to 5pm Monday to Friday (often with a break between noon and 2pm) and from 9am until 1pm on Saturday. Banking hours are 9.30am to noon Monday to Thursday and until 12.30pm on Friday.

PUBLIC HOLIDAYS & SPECIAL EVENTS

Public holidays include:

New Year's Day 1 January
Armed Forces Day 11 February
Decoration Day 2nd Wednesday in March
JJ Roberts' Birthday 15 March
Fast & Prayer Day 11 April
National Unification Day 14 May
Independence Day 26 July
Flag Day 24 August
Thanksgiving Day 1st Thursday in November
Tubman Day 29 November
Christmas Day 25 December

ACCOMMODATION

Hotels are operating in Monrovia, although anywhere with a generator and water will be expensive. There are almost no hotels upcountry and those that do operate are generally very basic. Often the only accommodation is with missions or aid organisations, although these usually do not have sufficient facilities to accommodate independent travellers. If you seek lodging in villages, most locals will be very welcoming and provide a space for you to set down a mat. Remember, though, that almost half of the Liberian people were displaced from their homes during the war.

FOOD

Monrovia is the only city offering a variety of dining options; elsewhere, you'll have to rely on chop bars or simple meals or be prepared to be self-sufficient with food.

Traditional Liberian food consists of rice or a cassava-based staple (*fufu*, *dumboy* or GB) eaten with a soup or sauce, generally with greens and palm oil, and often with meat or fish. Popular dishes include *togborgee* (a Lofa County speciality made with *bitterbuoy* or *kittaly*, vegetables and country soda), *palava* sauce (made with *plato* leaf, dried fish or meat and palm oil) and palm butter (a sauce traditionally from Maryland and Grand Kru counties and made from palm nuts).

SHOPPING

Liberia was traditionally a good place to buy masks, baskets and textiles, and craft-making is slowly reviving. In general, you'll find better items upcountry, but the selection is scanty everywhere.

Getting There & Away

AIR

There are no flights from Europe or the USA direct to Liberia. The best connections are through Abidjan (Côte d'Ivoire) on Weasua Air Transport (US$220/432 one way/return, six times weekly). There are also connections to/from Accra (Ghana) on Ghana Airways (US$315 one way, four times weekly), Freetown (Sierra Leone) on both Weasua and Ghana Airways (US$165/322, three times weekly) and Conakry (Guinea), weekly on Ghana Airways. In all directions, Weasua is reliable and the only recommended airline.

All flights arrive and depart from Roberts international airport (Robertsfield), 60km southeast of Monrovia. Departure tax is US$40 (which includes a US$15 airport development fee).

LAND & SEA

Border Crossings

For Sierra Leone, the main crossing is at Bo (Waterside). There's also a border post north of Bo (Waterside) at Kongo, and one northwest of Kolahun (near Voinjama), although this area is completely off-limits.

For Guinea, there are border posts just north of either Ganta, Voinjama and Yekepa. The border at Voinjama is closed, and the situation at the other two was uncertain as this book went to press, so you'll need to get an update.

Border crossings with Côte d'Ivoire are just beyond Sanniquellie, and east of Harper, towards Tabou.

Côte d'Ivoire

There's a bus several times weekly from Monrovia to Abidjan and on to Accra via Sanniquellie. It's US$40 to Abidjan and

US$60 to Accra, plus approximately US$20 for border fees etc. Schedules are irregular; inquire at the bus companies' office (☎ 226 588) opposite the Belco building 50m beyond Bong Mines Bridge.

There are also daily bush taxis from Monrovia to Ganta and Sanniquellie near the border from where you can get transport to Danané and Man. Monrovia to Man takes 12 to 15 hours.

In the south, a road connects Harper with Tabou; you'll have to cross the Cavally River in a ferry (or canoe, if the ferry isn't operating). Service is erratic during the rainy season. Once over the river, you'll find taxis to Tabou, from where you can get transport to San Pédro and Abidjan.

Guinea

Get an update on all Guinean border crossings before setting off.

Bush taxis run daily from Monrovia to Ganta (US$15), where you can find transport to N'zérékoré.

If peace returns, it's possible to go in the dry season via Voinjama to Macenta along bad roads and changing vehicles at the border. However, this area is off-limits now.

From Yekepa it's a few kilometres walk to the border, where you'll find Guinean vehicles to Lola. From the border to Lola costs GF1500 (US$1).

For information on boats between Conakry (Guinea) and Monrovia, inquire at the Freeport about 4km northeast of central Monrovia. Allow at least 36 hours for the journey. Fishing boats run sporadically between Harper and San Pédro (Côte d'Ivoire).

Sierra Leone

The main crossing is at Bo (Waterside), although it was closed at the time of research due to nearby rebel activity. Depending on the security situation on both sides of the border, you can go via bush taxi between Monrovia and Freetown (about US$30, 15 hours, 650km). The road is tar the whole way except for a bad section between the border and Kenema.

Apart from unofficial canoe crossings over the Mano River, there's another border post north of Bo (Waterside) at Kongo, although it's rarely travelled by bush taxis. The road on the Liberian side is in poor condition; allow a full day from Tubmanburg.

Getting Around

AIR

There are no regularly scheduled flights within Liberia. Weasua is available for charters.

BUSH TAXI & MINIBUS

Independent road travel is not safe at the moment and much of Lofa County in northern Liberia is completely off-limits because of fighting.

Once things settle down, the main form of public transport is bush taxis, which go daily from Monrovia to Buchanan, Gbarnga, Ganta, Sanniquellie and the Sierra Leone border, as well as to numerous other destinations. Several bush taxis weekly link the capital with almost everywhere else, although many routes (especially those connecting Zwedru with Greenville and Harper) are restricted during the rainy season. Minivans (called 'buses') also ply most major routes, although they're more crowded and dangerous than bush taxis, and best avoided. Some sample journey times and approximate fares: Monrovia to Buchanan (US$5, three hours, 150km); Monrovia to Bo (Waterside; US$5, 2½ hours, 140km); Monrovia to Sanniquellie (US$16, six hours, 305km). On most journeys the luggage surcharge should not exceed US$1 for a standard backpack. To charter a bush taxi, the price should be equivalent to the price for a single fare times the number of seats (five for small cars, nine for station wagons).

CAR & MOTORCYCLE

Most roads are dirt and many become nearly impassable during the rainy season. Major exceptions are the tarmac routes connecting the capital with Bo (Waterside), Tubmanburg, Ganta and Buchanan, although there are some deteriorated stretches on the Buchanan road.

Vehicle rental can be arranged through top-end hotels and sometimes through shop owners; prices (including driver) average about US$100 per day for 4WD.

BOAT

For those with time and a sense of adventure, fishing boats link most coastal cities, and are sometimes faster than road travel.

There are also frequent charter boats from Monrovia along the coast that sometimes have room for passengers. For more information on connections from Monrovia, see Getting There & Away in the Monrovia section. There has been talk of a regular passenger service starting between Buchanan and Harper, via Greenville, but nothing concrete has happened yet.

Monrovia

Monrovia suffered badly during the war. Infrastructure was largely destroyed and most buildings gutted. During the recent years of peace, there have been many improvements, although there's still a long way to go. However, despite the state of its infrastructure, Monrovia has pep. It's also one of the friendliest capitals you are likely to visit in Africa. Pick a day when it's not raining, find some Liberian friends, and soon you'll forget you're walking around in what was only recently a war zone.

Information

Money There are foreign exchange bureaus and banks on and near Broad St.

Post & Communications The main post office, on the corner of Randall and Ashmun Sts, is open 8am to 4pm Monday to Friday and 10am to noon on Saturday.

There are several Internet cafés, including DataTech on Broad St near the cathedral,

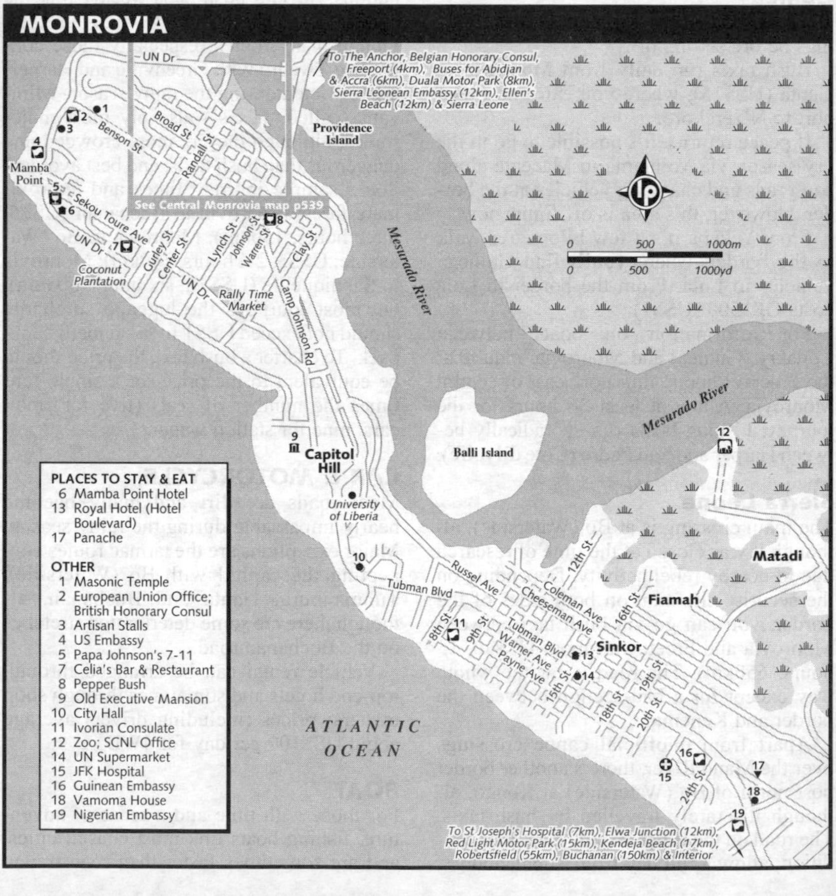
MONROVIA
UN Dr
To The Anchor, Belgian Honorary Consul, Freeport (4km), Buses for Abidjan & Accra (6km), Duala Motor Park (8km), Sierra Leonean Embassy (12km), Ellen's Beach (12km) & Sierra Leone
Broad St
Randall St
Benson St
Providence Island
Mamba Point
Sekou Toure Ave
UN Dr
See Central Monrovia map p539
Lynch St
Johnson St
Warren St
Clay St
Gurley St
Center St
Coconut Plantation
UN Dr
Rally Time Market
Camp Johnson Rd
Mesurado River
0 500 1000m
0 500 1000yd
Mesurado River
Balli Island
Capitol Hill
University of Liberia
Tubman Blvd
Russel Ave
12th St
Coleman Ave
Cheeseman Ave
16th St
Tubman Blvd
Warner Ave
Payne Ave
8th St
9th St
15th St
18th St
19th St
20th St
24th St
Matadi
Fiamah
Sinkor
ATLANTIC OCEAN
To St Joseph's Hospital (7km), Elwa Junction (12km), Red Light Motor Park (15km), Kendeja Beach (17km), Robertsfield (55km), Buchanan (150km) & Interior
PLACES TO STAY & EAT
6 Mamba Point Hotel
13 Royal Hotel (Hotel Boulevard)
17 Panache
OTHER
1 Masonic Temple
2 European Union Office; British Honorary Consul
3 Artisan Stalls
4 US Embassy
5 Papa Johnson's 7-11
7 Celia's Bar & Restaurant
8 Pepper Bush
9 Old Executive Mansion
10 City Hall
11 Ivorian Consulate
12 Zoo; SCNL Office
14 UN Supermarket
15 JFK Hospital
16 Guinean Embassy
18 Vamoma House
19 Nigerian Embassy

and the Internet Café on the corner of Center and Carey Sts.

Travel Agencies Monrovia has several good, reliable travel agencies.

Weasua-KLM (☎ 227 544) on Broad St can book Weasua flights, as well as international connections on KLM.

Karou Voyages (☎ 226 508) and Gritaco Travel (☎ 226 854), both on Broad St, can also help with booking regional flights on Weasua or Ghana Airways and with international connections. Karou Voyages is the agent for Swiss airlines.

Bookshops Monrovia is not a good place to stock up on reading material; most books were lost during the war and those remaining are expensive. Occasionally, however, you'll find some decent second-hand books. A good place to start is the African Books & Stationery Store on the corner of Benson and Newport Sts, which has Liberian history texts and some books by Liberians on Liberia.

Medical Services Pharmacies with a good selection of European and US items include the American Drug Store & Pharmacy on Benson St and the Charif Pharmacy on Randall St. See the hospital recommendation under Health, earlier in this chapter. St Joseph's Catholic Hospital (☎ 226 207), about 7km southeast of town on the extension of Tubman Blvd, is the best hospital for emergencies.

Dangers & Annoyances Use caution when going out in the evening, and get an update on security when you arrive from your embassy or resident expats.

Things to See & Do

National Museum *(Broad St; admission free; open 8am-5pm Mon-Sat)* is only a shadow of its former self. Much of the collection was destroyed or looted and all that remains is a handful of masks, drums and paintings accompanied by some interesting descriptions. However, it's still worth a visit; upstairs are a few dedicated and knowledgeable employees who will be happy to show you around.

Providence Island is where the first expedition of freed American slaves landed in 1822. There's not much to see now, although hopes are that the cultural centre will one day re-open.

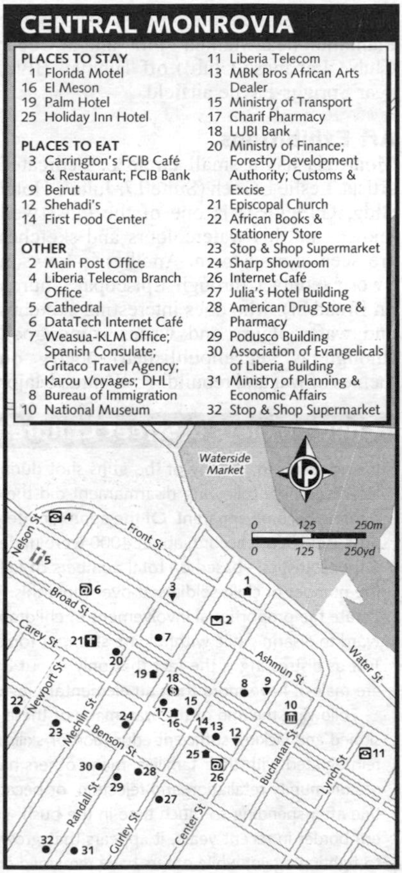
CENTRAL MONROVIA
PLACES TO STAY
1 Florida Motel
16 El Meson
19 Palm Hotel
25 Holiday Inn Hotel
PLACES TO EAT
3 Carrington's FCIB Café & Restaurant; FCIB Bank
9 Beirut
12 Shehadi's
14 First Food Center
OTHER
2 Main Post Office
4 Liberia Telecom Branch Office
5 Cathedral
6 DataTech Internet Café
7 Weasua-KLM Office; Spanish Consulate; Gritaco Travel Agency; Karou Voyages; DHL
8 Bureau of Immigration
10 National Museum
11 Liberia Telecom
13 MBK Bros African Arts Dealer
15 Ministry of Transport
17 Charif Pharmacy
18 LUBI Bank
20 Ministry of Finance; Forestry Development Authority; Customs & Excise
21 Episcopal Church
22 African Books & Stationery Store
23 Stop & Shop Supermarket
24 Sharp Showroom
26 Internet Café
27 Julia's Hotel Building
28 American Drug Store & Pharmacy
29 Podusco Building
30 Association of Evangelicals of Liberia Building
31 Ministry of Planning & Economic Affairs
32 Stop & Shop Supermarket
Waterside Market
0 125 250m
0 125 250yd
Nelson St
Front St
Broad St
Carey St
Newport St
Mechlin St
Benson St
Randall St
Gurley St
Center St
Ashmun St
Buchanan St
Lynch St
Water St

Now in ruins, the **Masonic Temple** *(Benson St)* was once Monrovia's major landmark. Since most Masons were Americo-Liberian descendants of the original settlers, the Temple was a prominent symbol of previous regimes. It was vandalised after the 1980 coup when the Masonic Order was banned. A grand master's throne from the temple, once used by William Tubman, is now a dusty exhibition at the National Museum.

Waterside Market, spread out on Water St on the northern end of town, is fun to walk around. You'll find everything here, but you'll need to search for the good buys.

There are **swimming pools** at Coconut Plantation near Mamba Point, and at Cedar Club ('Lebanese Club') off Tubman Blvd, near Spriggs-Payne airfield.

Art Exhibitions

Monrovia has a small circle of dedicated artists. Leslie Lumeh (Suite 17, Julia's Hotel Bldg, Gurley St) is one of the most well known, and his watercolours and sketches are seen around town. Another is Lawson Sworh (contact through Episcopal Church on Broad St), who does interesting sketches and watercolours and writes some good (though as yet unpublished) poetry on themes of war and rebuilding. Wantue Major does political cartoons and paintings; some of his works are at Mamba Point Hotel.

Places to Stay

Good budget lodging is almost nonexistent in Monrovia.

Florida Hotel *(Front St)* Rooms US$16. This is the only inexpensive place worth considering. It's reasonably clean, has a generator at night and simple rooms, most with fans.

El Meson *(☎ 227 871, Carey St)* Singles/doubles US$40/60. The long-standing El Meson has decent rooms, some with air-con. There's running water for a few hours each morning and evening and a generator.

Child Soldiers & Street Children

It's no secret that many of the guns shot during Liberia's civil war were wielded by young people. However, only following disarmament did the extent to which children were used in the factional fighting become apparent. Of the approximately 20,000 former combatants disarmed under the August 1996 peace accord, about 4000 were under 17, and about half of these were aged 15 or under. Other statistics – based on total numbers of fighters, and not just those who were disarmed – place the number of child soldiers at over triple this figure. Although the disarmament figures may exaggerate the proportional involvement of children in the war (since many factions pushed youths forward to disarm while withholding stronger forces), the numbers are distressingly high by any count. Just as distressing is the fact that only about 8% of the former combatants (about 97% of whom are males), have more than an elementary level of schooling.

Following the end of the war, many of these disenfranchised youths turned to the streets – disillusioned and lacking sufficient education or skills to move to happier circumstances. While some were reintegrated with their families, many others have been unwilling or unable to return either for fear of community retaliation and rejection, or because of the difficulty of fitting into an established routine after spending so much time in the bush. With the resumption of fighting along Liberia's northern border in recent years, it appears that growing numbers of these youths have been forced back to fighting again, while others have remained on the streets, trying to eke out a meagre living.

The former combatants actually make up only a relatively small proportion of the overall number of young Liberians who are estranged from family or community. The near total suspension of schooling during the war, coupled with massive community displacement and wartime deaths or separations from family members, have led many hundreds more youths onto the streets, particularly in Monrovia.

There are several groups working to assist these boys and girls. The Monrovia branch of the UK-based Save the Children organisation is one. Among other things, their projects aim to reunite children with their families, assist community reintegration, and provide health care and other support. Another is the missionary-run Don Bosco Program, based in Sinkor. At any one time, this programme is in touch with approximately 2000 youths in Monrovia alone, and more at several centres up-country. In addition to providing temporary night shelters, staff work to reunify children with their families, provide skills training and facilitate community reintegration. For the girls, many of whom have turned to prostitution, health advice and counselling are offered as well as basic small-business training to help them find an alternative livelihood. Some skills-training projects you may see around Monrovia include a pastry baking school and woodworking and craft centres. Many of the young boys you'll meet by the supermarkets and on the street in downtown Monrovia are enrolled in the program. If you want to give them some support, speak to staff at the Sinkor headquarters off Tubman Blvd in Monrovia, or just give them a few minutes of your time and attention.

***Palm Hotel** (☎ 227 278, Cnr Broad & Randall Sts)* Singles/doubles US$55/75, including breakfast. This place, opposite LUBI Bank, has reasonable rooms.

***Holiday Inn** (☎ 224 332, fax 226 886, Carey St)* Singles/doubles US$75/100 plus 10% tax. Rooms here are a bit dark, but OK, and meals can be arranged. Significant discounts are available for longer stays.

***Metropolitan Hotel** (☎ 226 693, Broad St)* This hotel, towards the southeastern end of Broad St is reported to be a reliable mid-range hotel, with rooms for about US$70 and a reasonably priced restaurant.

***Mamba Point Hotel** (☎ 226 693, fax 226 050, United Nations Dr)* Singles/doubles US$120/150, suites US$165 plus 10% tax. This hotel on Mamba Point is Monrovia's best. Rates include a buffet breakfast and comfortable rooms with all the amenities; some have views of the sea.

***Royal Hotel** (☎ 226 590, Cnr 15th St & Tubman Blvd, Sinkor)* Singles/doubles US$105/125, suites from US$140, all plus 10% tax, all prices negotiable. The Royal Hotel (formerly Hotel Boulevard) is also popular, with comfortable rooms, an Internet connection, a restaurant, and sometimes music and dancing. It was undergoing renovations as this book went to print, so expect some price changes.

Places to Eat

A popular lunch-time place for Liberian dishes is ***Auntie Nana***, with good local food from about US$5. It's not far from the cathedral; any taxi driver will be able to point out the way. Another place to try is ***Carrington's FCIB Café & Restaurant** (Cnr Mechlin & Ashmun Sts)*, with a different local speciality daily. It's directly behind FCIB bank, and open from about 11.30am to 4pm Monday to Saturday.

For Lebanese and Middle Eastern food, two good places are ***Shehadi's** (☎ 227 130, Center St)*, with sandwiches, light meals and takeaways from US$5 (closed Sunday), and the similarly-priced ***First Food Center** (☎ 223 997, Gurley St)*. ***Beirut** (☎ 227 299, 222 891, Center St)* is more upmarket, with delicious Lebanese food from about US$20.

The Anchor on Bushrod Island (follow signs to Island Hospital) has seafood, lobster, burgers and similar fare in large portions from about US$10 and a Friday evening happy hour. It's open evenings only (closed Monday).

***Panache** (☎ 226 629)* doesn't have much atmosphere, but the food (seafood, pepper steak, chicken and other choices from US$20 per meal) is good and it's popular with groups. There's also a less-expensive Liberian daily special. The restaurant is in Sinkor; from the city centre, branch left off Tubman Blvd on the airport shortcut road; it's a few hundred metres down on the left.

Another upmarket choice is the restaurant at ***Mamba Point Hotel*** (see Places to Stay), with good pizza, decent meals from about US$25, and a terrace overlooking the sea.

For self-caterers, ***Stop & Shop***, with outlets on Benson and Randall Sts, has a wide range of goods from the USA. ***UN Supermarket*** on Tubman Blvd in Sinkor is also good, but with a more limited selection.

Entertainment

The terrace bar at ***Mamba Point Hotel*** is popular for sundowners and there's a Thursday evening happy hour. For more local flavour, try ***Porch*** off Benson St, or see if the unassuming ***Papa Johnson's 7-11*** on Mamba Point is still operating.

Pepper Bush, on Warren St near Carey St, is a popular nightclub that gets going after midnight. The disco at ***Holiday Inn*** (see Places to Stay) also attracts a steady crowd.

Spectator Sports Soccer games always draw a crowd. Liberia's national team, the Lone Stars, plays at the stadium near Elwa Junction, 12km southeast of town.

Shopping

There are some ***artisan stalls*** diagonally opposite the US embassy on United Nations Dr. Many items are imported or of average quality, but sometimes they have good pieces. Another place to check is ***MBK Bros African Arts Dealer** (Carey St)*, which sells (mostly imported) woodcarvings, musical instruments and stone statues.

Textiles are sold by the *lapa* (2m) – the best place to look is ***Waterside Market*** near Gurley St.

Getting There & Away

Air For details on flights to/from Monrovia see the Getting There & Away section earlier in this chapter.

Bush Taxi & Minibus Bush taxis for Tubmanburg and the Sierra Leone border leave from Duala motor park, 9km northeast of the town centre. Transport for most other upcountry destinations, including the borders of Guinea and Côte d'Ivoire, leaves from Red Light, Monrovia's main motor park 15km northeast of the centre. Buses for Accra and Abidjan depart from near Bong Mines Bridge.

Boat Sam Kazouh (☎ 227 303) on the 1st floor of the Association of Evangelicals of Liberia building, opposite Podusco on Randall St, runs a weekly boat to Greenville (US$30, deck seating only, 12 to 15 hours); days of departure vary. The boat leaves in the evening and then stays a day or two in Greenville before returning. If there are sufficient passengers, the boat continues to Harper (from Monrovia US$50, 22 to 25 hours).

There's a sporadic speedboat between Monrovia and Harper (US$60, 36 hours). Inquire at the 'fishing pier' at the freeport.

Getting Around

To/From the Airport Taxis charge about US$30 from Robertsfield into Monrovia.

Taxi Shared taxis are the primary means of public transport in Monrovia and can be a lot of fun. They operate on a zone system with prices ranging from US$0.10 to US$0.50. It's US$0.20 from the centre to Duala motor park and US$0.50 to Red Light motor park.

Chartering a taxi within central Monrovia costs about US$1.35. Good places to catch one include Waterside Market, Duala motor park and Broad St.

Car Mamba Point Hotel and Holiday Inn can both arrange vehicle hire; otherwise, shopkeepers often have connections who can help. The cost for renting a 4WD with driver is about US$100 per day. Petrol costs about US$3 per gallon.

AROUND MONROVIA

Liberia has some beautiful beaches stretching both south and north of Monrovia. You'll have most to yourself except on weekends, when those close to the capital fill up. Before jumping in, get local advice as currents can be dangerous; there have been several drownings.

Ellen's Beach

Ellen's Beach, just beyond the now-closed Hotel Africa compound at Monrovia's northern edge, is popular at weekends. It has large rocks offshore and a kiosk selling drinks.

Kendeja

Kendeja Beach *(admission US$0.50)* is 15km southeast of central Monrovia on the Buchanan road. It's prettier than Ellen's Beach, better for walking and there are many drink vendors.

Behind the beach is **Kendeja Cultural Center** *(admission around US$1)*. It holds frequent dance performances complete with traditional costumes.

About 1km beyond Kendeja, ***Thinker's Village*** *(☎ 227 412)* is the only beachside place for food and lodging. Air-con rooms with bathroom cost about US$50 and meals cost about US$10.

Marshall

Marshall, about a one-hour drive southeast from Monrovia, at the confluence of the Junk, Farmington and Little Bassa Rivers with the sea, has a lagoon and an attractive stretch of deserted beach.

Firestone Plantation

Firestone – the world's largest rubber plantation – was established in 1926 when the Firestone tyre company secured one million acres of land in Liberia at an annual rent of only US$0.06 per acre. In its heyday, the company employed 20,000 workers, more than 10% of Liberia's labour force; Liberia was once known as the Firestone Republic.

After lying dormant during the war, Firestone is again operating, although at reduced capacity. There are no regular tours, but you can usually find employees on the grounds who can show you around and explain the tapping process. Stick to the beaten path, as Firestone is one of several areas in Liberia where land mines have been found.

The plantation is in Harbel, near Robertsfield airport. You'll need private transport to get here.

The Coast

ROBERTSPORT

Once a relaxing beach town, Robertsport was completely destroyed during the war. No infrastructure remains, although the beaches are still beautiful. They are said to offer some of the best surfing along the West African coast. During World War II, Robertsport was used as an Allied submarine base; you can still see relics of this era.

Lake Piso, separating Robertsport from the mainland, often flows onto the road during the rainy season; inquire first in Monrovia about conditions before heading there.

There is no lodging at Robertsport. There's a small fishing village in town with basic provisions.

BUCHANAN

Buchanan is Liberia's second port and the capital of Grand Bassa County. During the early 1990s, the town was inundated by refugees fleeing fighting in the surrounding countryside, although infrastructure within its borders remained relatively intact.

Stick to the beaten path on the outskirts of Buchanan and in the vegetated strip bordering the beaches as some areas were mined during the war.

Things to See & Do

Southeast of the port are some beautiful **beaches**. Follow the port road to the old Lamco Compound, then ask locals the way.

There's a large Fanti community in Buchanan. Northwest of the centre is their lively **fishing village** (Fanti Town); you'll feel like you're in Ghana.

Places to Stay & Eat

Apart from private guesthouses, there is really nowhere to stay. ***NGOs Center***, 2km north of the centre, may be able to fix you up with something basic for about US$10 per person. Meals can be arranged for a reasonable fee if you supply the food. It's signposted and is 1.5km from the main road.

For inexpensive local meals, try ***Franmah's Bar & Restaurant*** on Tubman St, or ***Capital Hill***, about 1km northeast of town on the main road. ***Gbehzon***, near the port, has grilled fish, but allow lots of time.

BUCHANAN

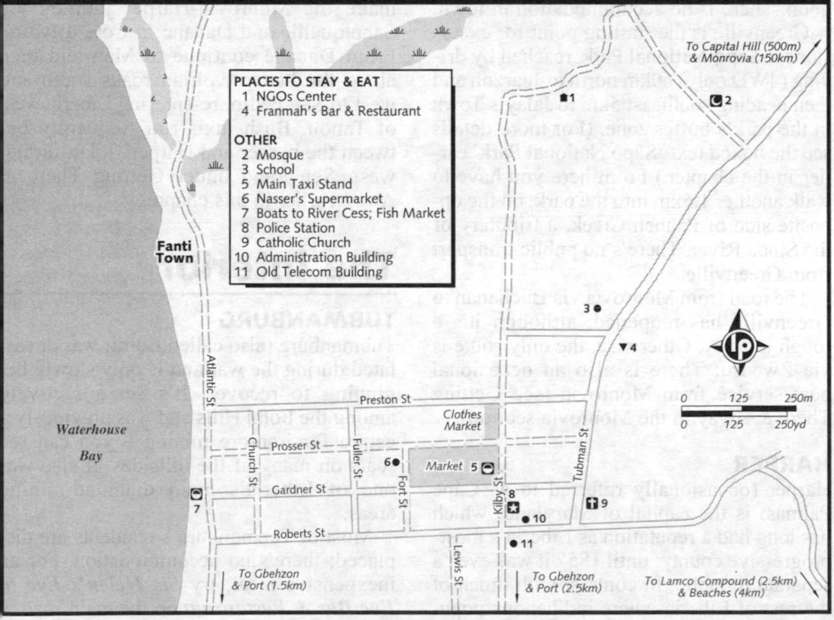
PLACES TO STAY & EAT
1 NGOs Center
4 Franmah's Bar & Restaurant
OTHER
2 Mosque
3 School
5 Main Taxi Stand
6 Nasser's Supermarket
7 Boats to River Cess; Fish Market
8 Police Station
9 Catholic Church
10 Administration Building
11 Old Telecom Building
To Capital Hill (500m) & Monrovia (150km)
Fanti Town
Waterhouse Bay
Atlantic St
Church St
Fuller St
Fort St
Kilby St
Lewis St
Tubman St
Preston St
Prosser St
Gardner St
Roberts St
Clothes Market
Market
To Gbehzon & Port (1.5km)
To Gbehzon & Port (2.5km)
To Lamco Compound (2.5km) & Beaches (4km)
0
125
250m
0
125
250yd

Nasser's Supermarket on Fort St has a modest selection of basics.

Getting There & Away

Bush taxis run daily to Monrovia (US$5, three hours). From Monrovia, it's better to get one at Elwa Junction than at the hectic Red Light motor park.

During the dry season at least several vehicles weekly travel to River Cess. It's also possible to take a fishing boat, although safety can be a serious concern with these. There are no set fees or schedules; boats leave from Fanti Town and from the beach west of the town centre.

Bush taxis for all destinations depart from the main taxi stand near the market; some also leave from the junction on the Monrovia road several kilometres northeast from town.

GREENVILLE

Greenville (sometimes called Sinoe) is the capital of Sinoe County. It was completely destroyed during the war, but the future is likely to be brighter thanks to its port and to significant logging interests in the area. Greenville has a beach, but to reach the open sea you need to cross a shallow lagoon. There is no accommodation in town.

Greenville is the starting point for excursions to **Sapo National Park**, reached by driving (4WD only) 60km north to Juarzon and then heading southeast 5km to Jalay's Town in the park's buffer zone. (For more details see the boxed text 'Sapo National Park' earlier in the chapter.) From here you have to walk another 1.5km into the park, on the opposite side of Pahneh Creek, a tributary of the Sinoe River. There's no public transport from Greenville.

The road from Monrovia via Buchanan to Greenville has reopened, although it's a rough journey. Otherwise, the only route is via Zwedru. There is also an occasional boat service from Monrovia (see Getting There & Away in the Monrovia section).

HARPER

Harper (occasionally referred to as Cape Palmas) is the capital of Maryland, which has long had a reputation as Liberia's most-progressive county; until 1857 it was even a separate republic. In contrast with much of the rest of Liberia where indigenous populations were severely repressed, in Harper, settlers worked to cultivate a more cooperative relationship with the local residents, and there is a monument in town commemorating the original accord between settlers and locals. Harper was also the seat of Liberia's first university (Cuttington, since transferred to Gbarnga) and the traditional centre of education in the country. Now Harper is just a shell of its former self and only ruins remain of the many fine old houses that once graced its streets, including former president William Tubman's residence. The surrounding area, however, is very attractive.

While there's no accommodation in Harper, food and other basics are available.

A boat runs sporadically between Harper and Monrovia (see Getting There & Away in the Monrovia section).

Road access from Monrovia is via Tappita and Zwedru, then southeast to the coast. There is no public transport. Under good conditions, it's a three-day journey in a 4WD; during the rainy season the road from Zwedru becomes impassable. There's no accommodation en route, other than what locals may offer, and you'll need to be self-sufficient with food and water. Although longer, many Liberians prefer to make the Monrovia-Harper journey via Sanniquellie and Danané in Côte d'Ivoire. From Danané continue to Man and then along the better Ivoirian roads south and west to San Pédro, re-entering Liberia west of Tabou. Bush taxis run frequently between the border and Harper, 20km further west. See Land under Getting There & Away earlier in this chapter.

The Interior

TUBMANBURG

Tubmanburg (also called Bomi) was devastated during the war and is only slowly beginning to recover. It's set attractively among the **Bomi Hills** and was previously a centre for iron-ore mining – you can see scars on many of the hillsides. It also was one of Liberia's main diamond-mining areas.

Most of Tubmanburg's residents are displaced; there's no accommodation. For an inexpensive meal, try ***Sis Helen's Eye to Eye Bar & Restaurant*** on the main road.

At the end of town is an immigration checkpoint where you can get both entry and exit permits.

Bush taxis cost US$3 to Monrovia. There is also occasional transport to the Sierra Leone border, usually via Bo (Waterside).

GBARNGA & PHEBE

Gbarnga was Charles Taylor's centre of operations during the war and became virtually the second capital of Liberia.

About 10km from Gbarnga on the Monrovia road is Phebe, site of Cuttington College. On campus are ruins of the old Africana Museum, which once had a good collection of 3000 pieces. Now, thanks to looting and the war, only fragments remain, and pieces from the original collection have been found in places such as Brooklyn, New York.

About 30km northwest of Phebe are the pretty **Kpatawe Falls**; take the dirt road opposite Phebe Hospital. You'll need either a bicycle or a 4WD; there are no taxis. There's a village before the falls, but no accommodation or restaurants.

About 40km north of Gbarnga on the Voinjama road, near Gbalatoah and just before the bridge over the St Paul River, is the site of former President Tolbert's house, **Tolbert Farms**, with beautiful views over the surrounding area.

Places to Stay & Eat

Jalk Enterprises Restaurant & Store *(Josephine's)* Rooms US$20. This place in Phebe has adequate rooms with fan and shared bathroom and a nice restaurant (closed Sunday lunch) offering one or two daily dishes.

Villa de Via Classique Rooms US$25. If Jalk Enterprises Restaurant & Store is full, try this place, a few kilometres further down the Monrovia road, which is said to have tennis courts.

In addition to the restaurant at Josephine's, Gbarnga has several ***chop bars***.

CooCoo Nest *(Also known as Tubman Farms)* Rooms US$35, or US$50 when the generator is working. CooCoo Nest, on the main road, about 60km southwest of Gbarnga between Totota and Salala, was former president Tubman's private residence and is now a hotel with relatively comfortable self-contained rooms. The name is said to come from Tubman's term of endearment for his daughter. When the generator works, there's also a disco and a restaurant. Across the road is a small ***coffee shop*** and a base for Charles Taylor's radio station.

Getting There & Away

Bush taxis go frequently from Gbarnga to Monrovia (US$10, six hours). Taxis from Gbarnga to Phebe Junction (US$0.60) leave from the taxi union parking lot at the top of the hill just off the highway. You need your own transport to get to CooCoo Nest.

GANTA

Ganta is a pleasant, bustling town 2km from the Guinean border. Its official name (and the one you'll still see on some maps) is Gompa City.

On a street running north off the main road there's an interesting **mosque**, the design of which is said to be unique in Liberia. Just out of town on the Sanniquellie road is a good **craft shop** *(open 8am-6pm Mon-Sat)* with basketry and woodcarvings.

Places to Stay & Eat

Mid-Nite Fever Motel Singles/doubles US$7/9. This place on the Tappita road is the only hotel in town. Rooms are basic, but with clean sheets and (if the generator is working) fan. Bring your own mosquito net.

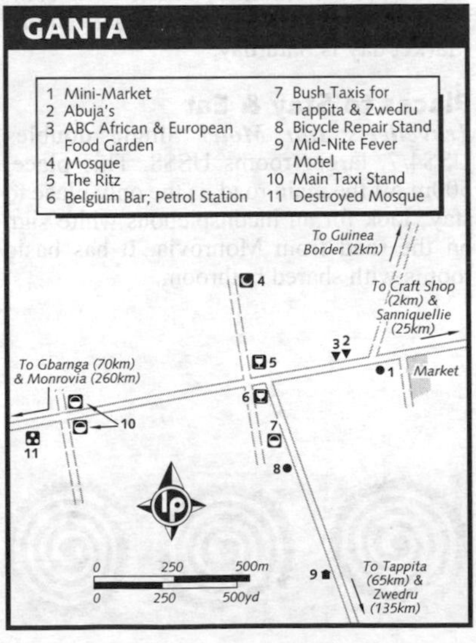
GANTA
1 Mini-Market
2 Abuja's
3 ABC African & European Food Garden
4 Mosque
5 The Ritz
6 Belgium Bar; Petrol Station
7 Bush Taxis for Tappita & Zwedru
8 Bicycle Repair Stand
9 Mid-Nite Fever Motel
10 Main Taxi Stand
11 Destroyed Mosque
To Guinea Border (2km)
To Craft Shop (2km) & Sanniquellie (25km)
To Gbarnga (70km) & Monrovia (260km)
Market
To Tappita (65km) & Zwedru (135km)
0 250 500m
0 250 500yd

ABC African & European Food Garden Meals from US$2.50. Anthony Buster Clinton's place has chicken and other meals.

Abuja's Meals around US$1. Abuja's, next door to ABC, is a more basic chop bar with rice dishes and drinks.

The ***Mini-Market*** opposite the market has the best selection of basics.

For cold drinks and dancing try ***The Ritz***, opposite Tappita road. Opposite is ***Belgium Bar***, also good for a drink.

Getting There & Around

Bush taxis leave several times daily from the main taxi stand to Gbarnga (US$3, 1½ hours), Monrovia (US$13, five hours) and Sanniquellie (US$3, one hour). A few weekly bush taxis go to Tappita and Zwedru.

Bush taxis from the centre to the Guinean border cost US$0.30; from the border there's daily transport to Diéké (US$1).

For bike rentals (US$1 per hour), check at the bicycle repair stand on the Tappita road.

SANNIQUELLIE

Sanniquellie is important historically as the birthplace of the Organisation of African Unity. On the main road into town is the building where William Tubman, Sekou Touré and Kwame Nkrumah met in 1957 to discuss a union of African states – a concept which was formalised in 1958 with the drafting of a preliminary charter. The compound is now used to house official visitors. Market day is Saturday.

Places to Stay & Eat

Traveller's Inn Motel Singles/doubles US$4/7, larger rooms US$8. This place, 500m off the main road, is the only place to stay; look for an inconspicuous white sign on the road from Monrovia. It has basic rooms with shared bathroom.

There are a few undistinguished ***chop houses*** along the main road and a few reasonably well-stocked shops.

Getting There & Away

Bush taxis for the Côte d'Ivoire border (US$4) via Kahnple and sporadically onto Yekepa (US$3) congregate north of the market, while those for Ganta (US$3) and Monrovia (US$16) leave from the other end.

YEKEPA

Yekepa, near the Guinean border and about 350m above sea level, has a pleasant climate and good views of the lush surrounding mountains, although the town itself has been completely destroyed. Given increased stability and infrastructure, the area holds potential for some good hiking, although you'll need a machete to hack through the underbrush. Nearby is **Guesthouse Hill** in the Nimba range, Liberia's highest peak at 1362m.

Before the war, Yekepa was the company town of Lamco and site of some of the world's richest iron-ore deposits.

Places to Stay & Eat

There is no accommodation in Yekepa, although locals living in the old Lamco houses are sometimes willing to rent out rooms. ***Ma Edith's*** on the central market square is friendly and the best bet for a meal. Otherwise, try ***Zay Duan Lay Food Center*** near the market.

Getting There & Away

The Guinean border is just a few kilometres away; you'll have to walk as there's no transport. Transport from the border to Lola (Guinea) costs US$1.50. For Côte d'Ivoire, you'll need to go to Sanniquellie first.

Mali

If Mali is famous for anything then it's Timbuktu (you know, that place you've always heard about, but can never find on the map). However, this belies that fact that Mali is a country with a proud and fascinating history. You can explore the fringes of the Sahara, journey down the great Niger River, watch nomads guide camel caravans across the Sahara and visit beautiful, mud-brick mosques dating from medieval times. The wonderful, bustling river port of Mopti (the centre of Mali's fledgling tourist industry) and vibrant capital Bamako (*the* place to see Mali's world-famous musicians) may be modern by Malian standards, but walking through the market at the ancient town of Djenné is a step back in time.

Away from the towns, adventures around the Niger Inland Delta, into the Sahara or along the spectacular sandstone Falaise de Bandiagara (Bandiagara Escarpment) in Dogon Country are all possible.

Mali at a Glance

Capital: Bamako
Population: 10.2 million
Area: 1,240,140 sq km
Head of State: Amadou Toumani Touré
Official language: French
Main local languages: Bambara, Fula, Tamashek, Dogon, Bozo, Songhaï
Currency: West African CFA franc
Exchange rate: US$1 = CFA694
Time: GMT/UTC
Country telephone code: ☎ 223
Best time to go: November to February

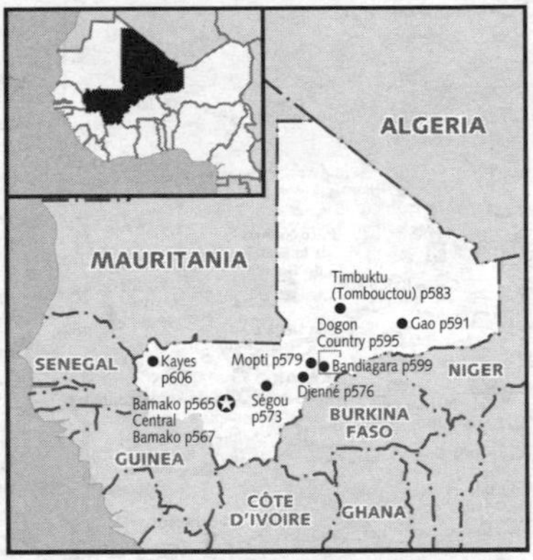

ALGERIA
MAURITANIA
Timbuktu (Tombouctou) p583
Dogon Country p595
Gao p591
SENEGAL
Kayes p606
Mopti p579
Bandiagara p599
NIGER
Djenné p576
Bamako p565
Central Bamako p567
Ségou p573
BURKINA FASO
GUINEA
CÔTE D'IVOIRE
GHANA

Highlights

- Looking at Djenné's mosque, the largest mud-built building in the world
- Experiencing Mopti's port; salt slabs arrive from Timbuktu on one side, while new *pinasses* (motorised boats) are constructed on the other
- Cruising down the Niger River into the inland delta, an area rich in birdlife
- Trekking the Falaise de Bandiagara, dramatic sandstone cliffs rising out of the plains
- Climbing La Main de Fatima with the nearby Hombori Tondo as a backdrop
- Exploring Timbuktu's dusty labyrinth of streets, and standing on the edge of the Sahara watching a salt caravan arrive – an experience like stepping back centuries

Facts about Mali

HISTORY

Archaeological evidence (rock paintings and carvings, which can be seen in the Gao and Timbuktu regions) suggests that northern Mali has been inhabited since 50,000 BC when the Sahara was fertile grassland. There's evidence that, by 5000 BC, farming was taking place and the use of iron began around 500 BC. By 300 BC large organised settlements had developed, most notably at Djenné and by the 6th century AD there was a secure foundation for the trade that powered Mali's three great empires. Each empire was formed by a different ethnic group and all grew rich and powerful facilitating the trans-Saharan trade in gold, salt and slaves.

The Empire of Ghana (unrelated to present-day Ghana) covered much of what is now Mali and Senegal until the 11th century. It was followed by the great Empire of Mali, which, in the 14th century stretched from the Atlantic Ocean to present-day Nigeria. Timbuktu was developed as a great centre of commerce and Islamic culture. The Empire of Songhaï came next, but was destroyed by a Moroccan mercenary army in the late 16th

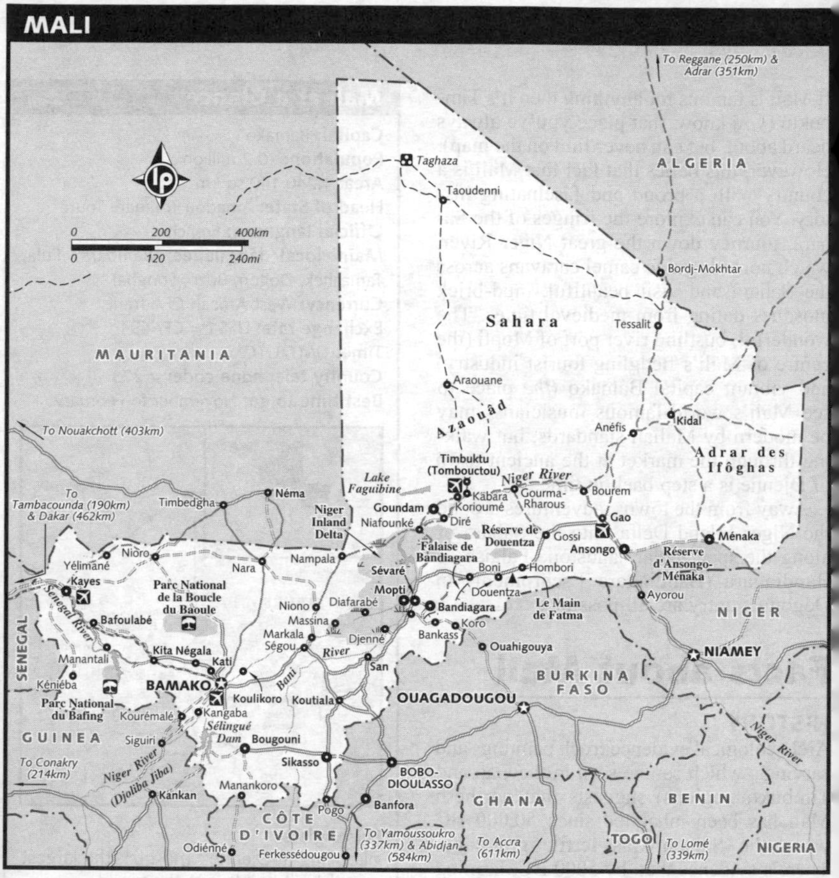
MALI
To Reggane (250km) & Adrar (351km)
Taghaza
ALGERIA
Taoudenni
0 200 400km
0 120 240mi
Bordj-Mokhtar
Sahara
Tessalit
MAURITANIA
Araouane
Kidal
Azaouâd
Anéfis
To Nouakchott (403km)
Adrar des Ifôghas
Timbuktu (Tombouctou)
Niger River
Lake Faguibine
Kabara
Gourma-Rharous
Bourem
To Tambacounda (190km) & Dakar (462km)
Timbedgha
Néma
Korioumé
Niger Inland Delta
Goundam
Niafounké
Diré
Gao
Réserve de Douentza
Gossi
Ménaka
Falaise de Bandiagara
Ansongo
Réserve d'Ansongo-Ménaka
Nioro
Yélimané
Nara
Nampala
Sévaré
Boni
Hombori
Kayes
Parc National de la Boucle du Baoule
Mopti
Douentza
Le Main de Fatma
Ayorou
Niono
Diafarabé
Bandiagara
NIGER
Bafoulabé
Massina
Koro
Markala
Djenné
Bankass
SENEGAL
Senegal River
Ségou
River
Manantali
Kita
Négala
Ouahigouya
NIAMEY
Kati
San
Kéniéba
BAMAKO
Bani
BURKINA FASO
Parc National du Bafing
Koulikoro
Koutiala
OUAGADOUGOU
Kourémalé
Kangaba
Sélingué Dam
GUINEA
Siguiri
Bougouni
Niger River
To Conakry (214km)
Niger River
Sikasso
BOBO-DIOULASSO
(Djoliba Jiba)
Manankoro
GHANA
BENIN
Kankan
Banfora
Pogo
CÔTE D'IVOIRE
To Yamoussoukro (337km) & Abidjan (584km)
To Accra (611km)
TOGO
To Lomé (339km)
NIGERIA
Odienné
Ferkessédougou

century. At the same time European ships were arriving at the coast of West Africa thus circumventing the trans-Saharan trade routes and breaking the monopoly and power of the Sahel kingdoms and northern cities.

Later the Bambara Empire of Ségou rose briefly to control huge swathes of Mali, before being usurped by two waves of Fula-led Islamic jihad, the second originating from the Tukulor Empire of northern Senegal. The Tukulor were still around when the French expanded east into Mali during the mid-19th century.

For more information about Mali's precolonial history see the Facts about West Africa chapter.

By the end of the 19th century, Mali was part of French West Africa. Remnants of this colonial era visible today include the huge Office du Niger irrigation scheme near Ségou and the 1200km Dakar-Bamako train line, the longest rail span in West Africa. Both were partially built with forced labour. However, Mali remained the poor neighbour of Senegal and Côte d'Ivoire as France's chief interest was in 'developing' Mali as a source of cheap cash crops (rice and cotton) for export.

Independence

Mali became independent in 1960 (for a few months it was federated with Senegal) and its first president, Modibo Keita, embarked on an unsuccessful period of one-party state socialism. Newly formed state corporations took control of the economy, but all except the cotton enterprise soon began losing money. Ambitious planning schemes went awry, the economy wilted and Keita was forced to ask the French to support the Malian franc, something of a humiliation. Eventually in 1968 Keita was overthrown by a group of army officers led by Moussa Traoré.

While the rest of the world was embroiled in the Cold War, Mali continued to develop Soviet-style socialism. However from 1970 to 1990 five coup attempts were made against Traoré and the early eighties were characterised by strikes, often violently suppressed. Continual food shortages were conveniently blamed on droughts (which devastated the northern regions in 1972–74 and again in 1984–85), but were largely due to government mismanagement.

In 1979 Mali was officially returned to civilian rule, although it remained a one-party state with Moussa Traoré head of state. During the 1980s Soviet influence waned, a free enterprise system was reinstalled and Mali joined the Communanté Financière Africaine (CFA) group. Thanks to market liberalisation (and adequate rainfall) by 1987 Mali had produced a grain surplus.

However, trouble began brewing for Traoré with the first talk of multiparty democracy in 1989. The Tuareg uprising began in 1990 (see the boxed text 'Plight of the Tuareg' later in this chapter) and later that year a peaceful pro-democracy demonstration attracted about 30,000 people onto the streets of Bamako. This action was followed by strikes and further demonstrations culminating on 17 March 1991 when security forces met students and other demonstrators with machine-gun fire. Three days of rioting followed, during which 150 people were killed. The unrest finally provoked the army, led by General Amadou Toumani Touré (General ATT as he was known as) to take control. Moussa Traoré was arrested, and around 60 senior government figures were executed.

Touré established an interim transitional government, and gained considerable respect from Malians and the outside world, when he resigned a year later and kept his promise to hold multiparty elections.

The 1990s

Alpha Oumar Konaré (a scientist and writer) was elected president in June 1992 and his party Alliance for Democracy in Mali (Adema) won a large majority of seats in the national assembly. Though a widely respected and capable leader who oversaw considerable political and economic liberalisation, during the 1990s Konaré had to deal with a 50% devaluation of the CFA (which resulted in rioting and protest) and an attempted coup.

Presidential and national assembly elections were held in 1997, but were marred by irregularities and the withdrawal of opposition parties. Konaré and his party were duly re-elected. Nevertheless, as a democrat, diplomat and advocate of negotiation and compromise he appointed opposition figures to his cabinet and made genuine attempts to democratise and decentralise Mali.

Mali Today

In sharp contrast to many African leaders, Konaré stood down in 2002 as the new constitution he helped draft dictated. Former general Amadou Touré was elected as president in April 2002.

Mali is still very dependent on good rains, and widespread corruption remains a problem, but economically and politically things look pretty rosy. Increased privatisation is necessary and gold revenues need to be spent wisely, but on the whole Malians seem to like the political direction their country is heading. Peace in the north is holding strong, but banditry is still a problem in some places and some observers fear that if aid funds dry up there will be problems. However, while other West African nations stumble, Mali looks pretty secure.

GEOGRAPHY

Mali is the largest country in West Africa, covering more than 1.2 million sq km of generally flat land. Mali is occasionally punctuated by sandstone plateaus and escarpments, but is characterised by five different environments. The north is covered by the Sahara desert, the south is relatively flat and well-watered agricultural land, the west is a hilly and well-wooded extension of the Futa Djallon highlands of Guinea, the central band is semi-arid scrub savanna (the Sahel) and the Niger Inland Delta is a maze of channels, swamps and lakes.

The Niger River is the major geographical marvel of Mali. It flows 1626km through the country, sweeping up from Guinea in the southwest to Timbuktu and the edge of the Sahara before heading southeast through Niger and Nigeria to the Atlantic. It is the country's lifeline.

CLIMATE

The rainy season cuts loose from June to October. It's characterised by torrential downpours and thunderstorms normally preceded by very strong winds. It rains most in the south (Sikasso gets 1120mm) and least in the north (Timbuktu gets 140mm and Tessalit just 54mm). July and August are wet.

Mali's hottest season occurs shortly before the rains – between April and July temperatures frequently exceed 40°C. There is another hot spell in September and October. Unsurprisingly the northern Saharan towns are hottest, but also get coldest at night.

The dry season lasts from November to June and is characterised by a couple of prevailing winds. From November through January the *alize* blows cooler air from the northeast. This keeps daytime temperatures in the 30s, but makes sleeping out at night chilly. Malians refer to this period as the cold season! The harmattan then blows until June.

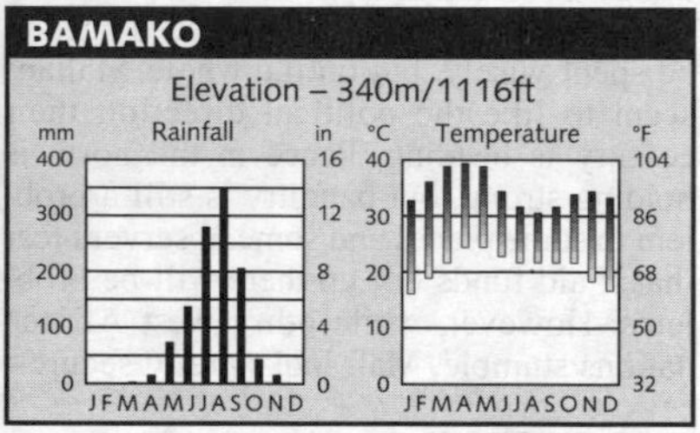
BAMAKO
Elevation – 340m/1116ft
mm
Rainfall
in
°C
Temperature
°F
400
16
40
104
300
12
30
86
200
8
20
68
100
4
10
50
0
0
0
32
JFMAMJJASOND
JFMAMJJASOND

ECOLOGY & ENVIRONMENT

Mali's most urgent environmental issues are deforestation, overgrazing and desertification. The three problems are inextricably linked and, between them, threaten much of the country. In the Sahel trees are felled for cooking fuel and building materials, while elsewhere overgrazing is leaving areas barren. Both factors lead to erosion and desertification. The increasing population only exacerbates these problems.

FLORA & FAUNA

Mali is one of the Sahel countries of West Africa – for more details about vegetation in the Sahel, see the boxed text 'The Sahel' in the Facts about West Africa chapter.

Mali is not a major wildlife destination, although a few large mammals can be found.

Mali's Birds

Mali is an underrated birding destination mainly because accessibility to birding sites is difficult. Yet Mali has some excellent savanna and wetland habitats and more than 655 bird species have been recorded, including six threatened species.

In the Niger Inland Delta (and the Office du Niger region) Egyptian plovers, hammerkops (which make an enormous nest), jaçanas (lily trotters), pied kingfishers, cattle egrets and majestic crowned cranes can be seen year-round. However, February is the best time to visit when over-wintering species such as greenshanks, black-winged stilts, marbled teal and ferruginous duck are resident.

The marshes and flooded forests beside the Kayes-Yélimané and Bamako-Kangaba roads can also be rewarding for migratory and water birds.

The sandstone cliffs of the Falaise de Bandiagara are good for large raptors, while in the wooden savanna at the base are Abyssinian and blue-bellied rollers and a colourful variety of bee-eaters, finches, weavers, parrots and numerous small raptors.

In urban areas look out for black kites (with a yellow bill and forked tail), purple glossy starlings, black-faced firefinches and Malian ground doves. The Mali firefinch inhabits the dry grassland and thickets of the Sahel, not just in Mali. The scavenging cape vulture is Mali's most common vulture.

National Parks & Reserves

Mali has four national parks and reserves, although much of the wildlife has gone. Despite this, and although the parks are not easily accessible, they are worth visiting.

Northwest of Bamako, the vast **Parc National de la Boucle du Baoulé** is mostly wooden savanna with pockets of riverine forest. Bird-watching is reported to be good, but you will see few animals. The park also contains more than 200 archaeological sites. Bordering the lake formed by Manantali dam, west of Kita, **Parc National du Bafing** protects a number of primate species including chimpanzees, which are the focus of a small chimp-tourism project.

The **Réserve d'Ansongo-Ménaka** lies southeast of Gao next to the Niger River and is extremely isolated. Much of the wildlife has gone but the Niger still has hippos. Of most interest to visitors, although difficult to reach, is the **Réserve de Douentza**, a vast area of semidesert north of the main road between Mopti and Gao, through which a herd of hardy desert elephants migrate.

GOVERNMENT & POLITICS

In 1991 Mali's constitution was changed to allow a multiparty political system. Now 147 assembly members stand for election (by universal suffrage) every five years.

Head of state is the president, currently Amadou Touré. The opposition Alliance for Democracy in Mali (Adema), dominates the government, and has popular support.

There remains a genuine desire to democratise the political process and the constitutional court remains safely independent of the government. The presidential council includes representatives from a number of political parties, allowing them a platform denied by the Adema-dominated national assembly. There are few press restrictions, and government corruption is being tackled.

ECONOMY

Mali is among the 10 poorest countries in the world with a per capita GDP or around US$277. The economy is dominated by agriculture, which accounts for 47% of GDP. Cotton (40% of exports) and cereal production (millet and rice) are increasing. Mali is Africa's third-largest gold producer and gold revenues are what keep government finances relatively healthy. The national debt of US$3 billion costs the government US$64 million a year (even after recent international debt relief), about as much as it spends on education.

POPULATION & PEOPLE

In 2001 Mali's population was 10.2 million and it's growing by 2.9% per year. This figure would be higher, but Mali has the fourth-highest child mortality rate in the world – around 24% of babies will perish before their fifth birthday. By African standards the HIV infection rate is low (about 2% of the population).

About 80% of Malians are tied to the land directly or indirectly, which partly explains why only around 50% of men and 30% of women are literate.

Most of the population live in Mali's fertile south, while the vast northern desert and semidesert (60% of Mali) contains just 10% of the population (the same percentage of people live in Bamako).

Concentrated in the centre and south of the country, the Bambara are Mali's largest ethnic group (33% of the population) and they hold much political power. They are renowned for their carving and artistic ability. Together with the Soninké and Malinké (who dominate western Mali) they make up 50% of Mali's population.

Fula (17%) pastoralists are found throughout Mali where there is grazing for their livestock, particularly around Massina in the Niger Inland Delta. The farmlands of the Songhaï (6%) are concentrated along the 'Niger Bend', the stretch of river between Niafounké and Ansongo, while the Sénoufo (12%) live in the region around Sikasso and Koutiala. The Dogon (7%) live on the Falaise de Bandiagara in central Mali. The lighter-skinned Tuareg and Moor (6%), traditionally pastoralists and traders, respectively, inhabit the fringes of the Sahara and range along the northern border with Mauritania.

Other groups include the Bozo fisher people of the Niger River and the Bobo (2.5%), farmers who live close to the border with Burkina Faso.

There is considerable intermarriage between people of different ethnic groups, the common tie being Islam. However, it's taboo for some groups to intermarry (eg, between Dogon and Bozo).

Over the centuries many of Mali's ethnic groups have carved out huge kingdoms, which usually meant the subjugation and enslavement of other ethnic groups. But instead of being a bone of contention between former enslavers and slaves, a *cousinage* or 'joking cousins' relationship exists. People from different groups commonly tease and poke fun at ethnic stereotypes and past deeds.

ARTS

Music

Mali's cultural diversity affords a wealth of great music, not only from the Bambara who dominate the scene, but also from the Tuareg, Songhaï, Fula, Dogon and Bozo people. Best known are the griots (also called *jalis*), a hereditary caste of musicians who fulfil many important functions in Malian society. You can easily tell whether a musician or singer comes from a griot family by their name: Diabaté, Kouyaté and Sissoko are the most common. Many of Mali's modern singers are members of the griot caste. The female griots of Mali are famed throughout West Africa for the beauty and power of their voice; some of the most famous singers include Ami Koita, Fanta Damba, Tata Bambo Kouyaté and Mariam Kouyaté.

After independence Malian cultural and artistic traditions were encouraged and several state-sponsored 'orchestras' were founded. Some of the greatest pop music to come out of Africa was produced by these orchestras who influenced a generation of musicians. Top of the heap were the legendary Rail Band de Bamako (actual employees of the Mali Railway Corporation!), although one of its ex-members, Salif Keita, went onto even greater heights. See the boxed text for more information.

Mali's wealth of talented female singers makes it difficult to pick out the best, however, as far as popularity in Mali goes, Oumou Sangaré would easily win. Her songs deal with contemporary social issues, and she addresses topics such as polygamy and arranged marriages. Her music is influenced by the musical traditions of the Wassoulou region of southwestern Mali, and features the *kamelen-ngoni*, a large six-stringed harp-lute. If you like her music, also look out for recordings by Sali Sidibé and Kagbe Sidibé.

The enigmatic Ali Farka Touré is perhaps Africa's best-known modern musician, although he's far more popular abroad than at home (look out for albums *The River* and *Radio Mali*). His blues-influenced sound highlights similarities between the music of Africa and the Mississippi delta (some scholars believe that the roots of American blues lie with the Malian slaves who worked in US plantations).

Some of Mali's other popular artists include Les Amdassadeurs, Super Biton de Ségou, Zani Diabaté, Toumani Diabaté and Lobi. Rising Malian stars include Tinariwen, Djenaba Seck, Nahawa Doumbia, Teningnini Demba, Fantani Touré, Souleymane Traoré and Kon Kan Kon Sata.

Salif Keita

Salif Keita is perhaps the most famous singer in West Africa. A direct descendant of Sundiata Keita, the founder of the Empire of Mali in the 13th century, Salif chose his career in music against the wishes of his family who considered such an occupation to be beneath their noble standing. In 1970 he joined the Rail Band de Bamako and later he left to form Les Ambassadeurs. In 1978 Salif left Mali for Côte d'Ivoire and created a new band, Les Ambassadeurs Internationaux, whose first release *Mandjou* was a great success. Playing the role of a griot in Mandjou, Salif sang the praises of the Touré family. The former president of Guinea, Sekou Touré, was so moved by it that he made Salif an Officer of the National Order. Salif's solo career began with the album *Soro*, a masterpiece that launched him onto the international stage, and which was one of the most influential recordings of African music in the 1980s. His later album *Ko-Yan* is another landmark in World Music.

An outspoken opponent of racism, a man 'with white skin and black blood' (he is albino), Salif now performs concerts in all corners of the world, returning to Mali regularly for inspiration.

Graeme Counsel

Arts & Craftwork

Mali's famous sculptural traditions date back to the 12th century, when figures in terracotta, bronze and gold were created by the inhabitants of Djenné and surrounding towns. These sculptures usually depict a kneeling person with stylised eyes.

Woodcarvings made by the Bambara people are noted for their angular forms. Figures called *flanitokele* are carved in a rigid posture with an elongated torso, arms held stiffly to the side, often with palms out, and conical breasts. Bambara masks are usually bold and solid, with human and animal features incorporated into the design, and are often used in secret society ceremonies. The best known (and frequently used as a symbol of West Africa) is the *chiwara*, a headpiece carved in the form of an antelope, and used in ritualistic dances.

MALI

The Bozo sculpt a mask representing a sacred ram called *saga* and are believed to have begun the tradition of marionette theatre, where human and animal figures are used to act out scenes from history and everyday life. The Bambara, Malinké and Soninké have adopted this tradition and there are annual marionette festivals in Diarabougou (20km east of Koulikoro) and Markala.

The Bambara also produce striking *bogolan* or mud cloth (see the 'Arts & Craftwork' special section in the Regional Facts for the Visitor chapter).

The Dogon are renowned for their carved doors, sculpture and masks (see the 'Dogon Arts & Culture' special section later in this chapter).

SOCIETY & CONDUCT

Malian societies are highly stratified, with hereditary nobles at the top and castes of hunters and blacksmiths at the bottom. In former centuries slavery was universal and subtribes of former slaves exist in some societies.

For centuries the diverse peoples of Mali have shared a country that is not always bountiful agriculturally or materially. While many are proud of their individual group's success in the competition for land and resources (eg, empire building), they are also tolerant and welcoming of other peoples.

Greeting people in Mali is very important and one of the rudest things you can do to a Malian is ignore them. People think it very impolite to ask for directions to the nearest bank before saying hello or enquiring about their health. If you are introduced, shaking hands is polite – but be aware that some Muslims are uncomfortable doing this with a non-Muslim woman.

Although Mali has a higher number of female government ministers than France, and progress towards equality is being made in the higher echelons of society, rural women have few rights over the fruit of their labours and are generally marginalised.

Several mosques are open to respectfully dressed, bare-footed non-Muslims (apart from at prayer times), but never push someone into letting you in.

RELIGION

Between 80% and 90% of Malians are Muslim and 2% Christian. The remainder retain animist beliefs, which often blur with Islamic and Christian practices, especially in rural areas.

Mali is a secular state, but Islam here is conservative and reasonably influential. In recent years some powerful *imams* have called for more Islamic influence in the running of the country and less Westernisation. However, despite the odd Bin Laden T-shirt in the market, there is very little anti-Western sentiment in Mali.

LANGUAGE

While French is the official language, the most widely spoken African language is Bambara, similar to the Mandinka/Malinké spoken in Senegal and Gambia, and the Dioula spoken in several countries to the south. In contrast, the Dogon language is spoken in a relatively compact area, but even so it is divided into dozens of dialects, Sangha being a major one. Other languages include Bozo and Fula along the Niger River, and Songhaï around Gao and Timbuktu. See the Language chapter for useful phrases in French and Bambara.

Facts for the Visitor

SUGGESTED ITINERARIES

If you've only got one week, head for the lively port town of Mopti, an excellent base for visiting the great mud-mosque and market at Djenné and for launching trips into Dogon Country. This journey would be better spread over two weeks, though, and would enable you to visit Timbuktu (consider flying).

A one-month itinerary could include two days in Djenné, a relaxing three- or four-day boat trip down the Niger River to Timbuktu, and anything from three to 10 days of outstanding trekking in Dogon Country. You could spend a day or two in Bamako wandering around the lively streets and markets and seeing some live music, or stop off at the pleasant town of Ségou. If you're travelling east, head for Gao, from where transport continues to Niger. If you're heading south go to Sikasso for transport into Côte d'Ivoire or Burkina Faso. If Senegal is your next stop, take the train and break the journey at the rarely visited towns of Kita and Kayes.

With the luxury of two months, pick and choose from the previous suggestions and head for hard-to-reach places out west, such as the near-inaccessible Parc National du Bafing. Upcountry, explore the stunning scenery around Hombori, and in February and March look for desert elephants near Gossi and Douentza, or stop in the tiny villages of the Niger Inland Delta.

PLANNING

When to Go

Mali is wettest between July and August and hottest between April and June. The harmattan blows from January to June making October to February the best time to visit. However, December and January are the busiest tourist months and many travellers visit at other times with no problems.

Maps

The French IGN produces the excellent *Mali* (1:2,000,000), but it's not available in Mali itself. Michelin's 953 *Africa North and West* (1:4,000,000) is large scale, but shows Mali's minor roads accurately.

Institute Geographique du Mali (☎ 202 840, ⓔ igm@cefib.com), off Av de l'OUA, Badalabougou Est in Bamako, holds basic country and town maps (CFA12,500) plus 1:200,000 topographical maps (CFA5000).

MALI

RESPONSIBLE TOURISM

Increased tourism (and Westernisation) has resulted in cultural change in Mali. There is now a huge foreign market for Malian art and craft and many precious cultural objects are sold to tourists – a classic example are carved Dogon granary doors, now rarely seen on granaries. You should buy newly carved pieces only and preserve Mali's history while also managing to stimulate the carving industry.

Tourists create tremendous amounts of rubbish, particularly nonbiodegradable packaging such as plastic bags and water bottles, which cannot be disposed of easily. Piles of this detritus is a tremendous problem in small Dogon villages where traditionally all rubbish simply decomposed. So purify your own drinking water, re-use your own shopping bags and cut down on 'Western' products that have layers of packaging.

Likewise latrines and shower blocks built for tourists are sometimes dug too shallow or are badly located. These can pollute watercourses and spread disease. Select your *campement* (encampment or camp) wisely and use environmentally friendly cleaning products.

An effort to respect local tradition and etiquette will always bring greater rewards for the traveller. The dress code is pretty relaxed in Bamako, but Mali is a Muslim country so dress conservatively, especially in rural areas. Shorts are seen as offensive (or humorous) almost everywhere in Mali except in Dogon country.

Always ask permission to photograph people and always respect the wish of anyone who declines. People in tourist areas will often ask for money. Public displays of affection are culturally inappropriate. See Society & Conduct earlier in this chapter for more details of appropriate behaviour.

VISAS & DOCUMENTS

Visas

Visas are required by everyone. If there's no Malian embassy in your home country it's best to contact the embassy in Brussels or Washington, DC, or get a get the visa while you're travelling through West Africa. If obtained overseas, visas are issued in three to five days and valid for three months before entry.

The Malian embassy in Brussels charges €30 plus €5.50 for postage, money which must be sent in *cash* with two copies of the application form, two photos, a yellow fever vaccination certificate and printed flight itinerary. Forms can be requested over the phone.

The Malian embassy in the USA has the same requirements (US$40; cashier's check or money order only) and offers a range of return mailing/courier options. See their website (ⓦ www.maliembassy-usa.org) for further details and to download an application form.

Visas are not available at the airport or land borders, although it's been reported that temporary visas are sometimes issued at remote crossings. *Don't* bank on it.

Visa Extensions These cost CFA2500 per month, require two photos and are only available at the Sûreté buildings in Bamako and Mopti. Extensions are granted one month at a time.

Visas for Onward Travel In Mali, you can get the following visas for neighbouring countries.

Burkina Faso The embassy gives same-day service if applications are made before 9am. Three photos are required and visas (CFA13,500) are valid for three months.

Côte d'Ivoire The embassy will issue visas (CFA30,000) in three days if delivered between 9 and 11am Monday and you will need two photos. Proof of yellow fever and meningitis vaccinations is required. Numerous other requirements and processing problems are common. Get a visa elsewhere.

Ghana TAM Voyages in Bamako deals with applications (CFA12,000) that are flown out and processed in 14 days. Four photos are required. Get a visa elsewhere.

Guinea The embassy issues one-/two-month visas for CFA20,000/60,000 in 48 hours. Two photos plus a photocopy of your passport are required.

Mauritania The embassy will issue visas (CFA14,000) in 48 hours. Three photos are required.

Senegal The embassy issues one-/three-month visas for CFA3000/7000 in 24 hours.

Togo The French embassy no longer issues visas for Togo. Get them at the border or Lomé airport.

Registration

During the troubles in the north in the mid-1990s, foreigners had to register with the police in Mopti, Gao and Timbuktu. This is no longer necessary, although some police officers still try to enforce the old rule and 'fine' travellers not registered. This has been reported around Mopti, Timbuktu and Djenné.

EMBASSIES & CONSULATES

Malian Embassies & Consulates

All embassies issue visas and in West Africa Mali has embassies in Burkina Faso, Côte d'Ivoire, Ghana, Guinea, Senegal and Niger. For details, see Facts for the Visitor in the relevant country chapters. Outside Africa, Malian embassies or consulates include:

Belgium (☎ 02-345 74 32, fax 344 57 00) 487 Av Molière, Brussels 1060
Canada (☎ 613-232 1501, 232 3264, fax 232 7429) 50 Avenue Goulburn, Ottawa, Ontario K1N 8C8
France (☎ 01 45 48 58 43, fax 01 45 48 55 34) 89 Rue du Cherche Midi, Paris 75006
Germany (☎ 030-319 98 83, fax 319 98 84) Kurfurstendamm 72, 10709 Berlin
Italy (☎ 06-4425 4069, fax 4424 4029) Via Antonia Bosion, Rome 200 161
USA (☎ 202-332 2249, fax 332 6603, ⓔ info@maliembassy-usa.org) 1900L St NW, Washington, DC 20036

Embassies & Consulates in Mali

All embassies are in Bamako.

Belgium *Consulate:* (☎ 219622, fax 211279, ⓔ ambelba@cefib.com) Place du Souvenir, Central Bamako
Burkina Faso (☎ 223171, fax 219266, ⓔ ambfaso@datatech.toolnet.org) Rue 224, Hippodrome; open 7.30am to 12.30pm and 2pm to 4pm Monday to Friday
Canada (☎ 212236, fax 214362, ⓔ bmako@dfait-maeci.gc.ca) Route de Koulikoro, opposite Luna Parc; also assists Australian nationals
Côte d'Ivoire (☎ 222289, fax 211376) Above TAM Voyages, Square Lumumba; open 9am to 12.30pm and 1.30pm to 4pm Monday to Friday
France *Consulate:* (☎ 216246, 218953, fax 210 329) Square Lumumba; assists Austrian, Spanish, Greek, Italian and Portuguese nationals
Germany (☎ 223715, emergency ☎ 223299, fax 229650, ⓔ allemagne.presse@afribone.net.ml) Badalabougou Est, close to Pont des Martyrs
Ghana (☎ 219210, ⓔ tamvoyage@cefib.com) TAM Voyages, Square Lumumba; open 8am to 5pm Monday to Friday
Guinea (☎/fax 210806) Blvd du Peuple, Medina Coura; open 8am to 5pm Monday to Friday
Mauritania (☎ 214815) Off Route de Koulikoro, Rue 213, Hippodrome; open 8am to 3.45pm Monday to Friday
Netherlands (☎ 215611, fax 213617, ⓔ nlgovbam@afribone.net.ml) Off Route de Koulikoro, Rue 437, Hippodrome
Senegal (☎ 218273/74, fax 211780) off Av de l'Yser, Rue 287, Hippodrome; open 7.30am to 1pm and 1.30pm to 4pm Monday to Friday
UK (☎/fax 233412, ⓔ info@britembmali.org) Badalabougou l'Ouest, turn right past the Palais de la Culture and continue west for 1km beside the river then turn left at the sign for British embassy; open 8am to 4.30pm Monday to Thursday and to 2pm Friday. Assists New Zealand, Republic of Ireland and unrepresented Commonwealth nationals.
USA (☎ 225470, ⓔ cons@usa.org.ml) Cnr Rues de Rochester and Mohammed V

CUSTOMS

Theoretically there's a limit on the amount of CFA francs that you can take out of the country, but this is rarely enforced.

MONEY

The unit of currency is the CFA franc.

country	unit		CFA
euro zone	€1	=	CFA656
UK	UK£1	=	CFA1024
USA	US$1	=	CFA694

Most of Mali's banks change foreign cash and travellers cheques, but services and commission rates vary wildly between branches and towns. The Bank of Africa offers a reliable and efficient service, while Banque National de Développement Agricole (BNDA) and Banque Internationale du Mali (BIM) usually charge around 2% to change travellers cheques.

The switched-on Ecobank is another possibility (some branches open on Saturday), but branches often levy high commissions. Banque Internationale pour le Commerce et l'Industrie du Mali (Bicim) in Bamako has Mali's only international ATM (Visa only).

Changing money in a bank (even cash) can take up to an hour, but some Western-orientated businesses such as supermarkets, big expensive cafés etc (all Lebanese owned) will happily change cash and sometimes travellers cheques. Euros are the best currency to carry. Dollars are OK, but commissions are quite often higher and nonbank exchange rates appalling.

Many banks and post offices, and even the odd petrol station, are agents for Western Union, the international money transfer company (see the Regional Facts for the Visitor chapter for details).

Visa cards are accepted in a few ritzy hotels, restaurants and businesses in Bamako.

POST & COMMUNICATIONS

Post

Letter and parcel post from Mali's cities is reasonably reliable, but letters can still take weeks to arrive. A postcard to Europe/North America costs CFA385/395 and a letter CFA475/505.

Parcels do go missing, but usually only items sent from overseas. However, anything of real value should be sent by DHL (☎ 226376, Av Ruault, Bamako).

Poste restante is available at all major post offices. Some charge CFA300 per letter upon collection.

Telephone & Fax

Sotelma, the national telephone company, no longer operates many operator-assisted call centres and has installed cardphones instead. Local calls cost CFA100 per minute, national calls CFA300 to CFA500, calls to Europe CFA1825 and CFA3000 to the USA. However tariffs are reduced by 25% after 5.30pm, 40% between 12.30am and 7am Monday to Friday and then 50% between 5.30pm and 7am on weekends. There are no area codes. Mobile phones begin with 77 and are more expensive to call.

Phonecards are widely available, but prepaid calling cards (that can be used from any phone) are not.

Most towns have privately owned *télécentres* or *cabine téléphonique*, which allow easy (though a little more expensive) telephone and fax communication.

Malitel offers a limited GSM cell (mobile) phone service in Bamako. There are plans for expansion.

Email & Internet Access

Internet access is widely available in Bamako and is possible in Sikasso, Mopti and Timbuktu. In other towns Sotelma's ancient exchanges make connecting very difficult and expensive.

DIGITAL RESOURCES

Try the following websites for extra information about Mali:

Afribone Mali General information on Mali.
W www.afribone.com

Time for a Change

As this book was going to press Sotelma announced changes to Mali's telephone numbering system. From July 2002 all Malian six-digit, fixed-line phone numbers were prefixed with a two. A six was added to the front of Malitel GSM mobile (cell)-phone numbers, while mobile-phone numbers starting with 77 were prefixed with a two, just like all fixed-line numbers.

MALI

Cefib Internet Mali This website provides general information on Mali.
W www.cefib.com

Contemporary Africa Database An online database enabling users to search for general information on Mali.
W www.africaexpert.org

Journée Nationale des Communes Government website.
W www.journee-nationale-communes.org

BOOKS

Ségu by Maryse Condé is an epic novel following the generations of a family living in the Niger River trading town of Ségou. It has inspired many Dutch and French travellers to visit Mali.

Lieve Joris captures the essence of the country in *Mali Blues*, published in Lonely Planet's travel literature series, Journeys. Lieve travelled to Bamako, Kayes and Dogon Country accompanied by famed Malian musician Boubacar 'Kar Kar' Traoré. *The Blue Man: Tales of Travel, Love & Coffee* by Larry Buttrose is an entertaining read and includes a personal account of hiking in the Dogon Country.

NEWSPAPERS & MAGAZINES

Several daily papers (all in French) are available in Bamako and other large towns. *Le Soir* and *Le Malien* are among the best. Only French foreign newspapers (such as *Le Figaro* and *Le Monde*) are widely available, although hawkers in Bamako often have US publications such as *Herald Tribune*, *Time* and *Newsweek*.

PHOTOGRAPHY & VIDEO

Photo permits are not required, but restrictions on photography do apply in Mali – see the Photography & Video section in the Regional Facts for the Visitor chapter for general information.

HEALTH

All visitors require a yellow fever vaccination certificate and should be aware that malaria exists throughout the country, year-round, and drug resistance is common. See Health in the Regional Facts for the Visitor chapter for more information and advice on disease prevention.

Most large towns have a hospital and pharmacy, although standards and supplies are sometimes limited. The best services are in Bamako.

WOMEN TRAVELLERS

Most of the time women travellers have no special problems in Mali. Sometimes being a woman is a distinct advantage, as Malians will readily offer you protection and support.

Sexual harassment is less of a problem for women travellers in Mali than in some parts of the world, but an unaccompanied foreign woman is sometimes seen as a ticket to a better life and you may become the focus of unwanted amorous attention – proposals of marriage are pretty standard.

Always dress modestly, a wedding ring is a useful accessory and wearing dark glasses a good way to avoid unwanted eye contact. If a man shakes your hand and tickles your palm with his index finger it's a highly suggestive action – a good-humoured '*non mercie*' is often more effective than abuse.

Meeting Malian women can be a weird experience for some female travellers. In rural areas few women will understand why you haven't got hoards of kids and are not (necessarily) travelling with your husband. If you are travelling with your husband don't be surprised if all the questions and conversation is directed towards him.

DANGERS & ANNOYANCES

Crime is not a big problem in Mali, however passengers at the train stations in Kayes and Bamako are targeted by thieves (see Information under Bamako later in this chapter for more details).

Security in the North

Although the Tuareg rebellion ended in 1996, there have been a few recent instances of banditry and 4WD hijackings north of the Niger River, some of which have resulted in deaths. Toyota Land Cruisers (4WDs) are the most common target and passengers of hijacked vehicles are robbed before being dumped a few kilometres from a settlement. The Gao region seems to be the most insecure (4WDs have been stolen from compounds in Gao itself) and the Gao-Timbuktu road is certainly not recommended. It's vital to get up-to-date security information from local authorities or your embassy before setting out.

MALI

The main annoyance for visitors are the young men who lurk outside hotels in Bamako and other tourist towns, offering their services as guides (see the boxed text 'Guides in Mali' later in this chapter).

BUSINESS HOURS

Government offices are open from 7am to noon and 2pm to 4.30pm weekdays, except on Friday when they're closed (or as good as) after noon. Business and bank hours are from 8am to noon and 3pm to 5pm (approximately) on weekdays, and from 8am to noon on Friday. Many shops and businesses open on Saturday and some on Sunday.

PUBLIC HOLIDAYS & SPECIAL EVENTS

Public holidays include:

New Year's Day 1 January
Army Day 20 January
For the Martyrs of the 1991 revolution 26 March
Easter March/April
Labour Day 1 May
African Unity Day 25 May
Independence Day 22 September
Christmas Day 25 December

For a table of Islamic holiday dates, see Public Holidays & Special Events in the Regional Facts for the Visitor chapter.

Special events include the Biennal (September in even years), a national sport and cultural festival held in Bamako. Lots of regional bands enter the competitions, and it's an excellent opportunity to hear live music. There are also annual Dogon ceremonies (usually held from March to May), which include masked dances. Annual Fula cattle crossings take place November to December.

ACTIVITIES

Trekking in Dogon Country is the most popular activity in Mali and camel trekking north of Timbuktu is possible.

There's world-class rock climbing near Hombori and some routes near Sibi, not far from Bamako. It's all on sandstone.

COURSES

The Asfit Language School (☎ 290496, ⓔ bbocoum2001@yahoo.fr) offers individual tuition in a large number of Mali's indigenous languages (around CFA5000 per hour).

Djembe (drumming) and dance tuition is available in several towns. In Bamako try the Carrefour des Jeunes or Maison des Jeunes.

WORK

The American International School Bamako (☎ 224738, fax 220853, ⓔ aisb@aisb-ml.org) often requires well-qualified, English-speaking teachers. Contracts are usually for two years.

ACCOMMODATION

Mali's hotels are generally poor value for money. Most large towns have accommodation ranging from back-street brothels to smart hotels. Between these two extremes are campement or *centre d'accueil* (welcome centre) where accommodation is simple, but adequate.

Sleeping on flat roofs (mattresses are often provided) is the cheapest accommodation option in Mali, but you'll need a mosquito net.

Some places add CFA500 per person tourist tax to room costs – wherever possible, this is included in the rates we quote.

FOOD & DRINKS

Food in Mali is generally similar to that found in Senegal, with *poulet yassa* (chicken in an onion and lemon sauce) and *riz yollof* (rice with vegetables and/or meat) featuring on many menus. All along the Niger River, restaurants also serve grilled or fried *capitaine* (Nile perch).

Around markets and bus stations you'll find stalls selling tea, coffee (both made with condensed milk) and maybe egg sandwiches. Street food is usually excellent and widely available. Look out for beef brochettes, fried fish, corn on the cob, fried bananas, sweet potato chips and plates of rice and sauce.

If you order 'breakfast' in a hotel or restaurant you'll rarely get more than bread and a cup of tea or coffee.

Coke and Fanta are omnipresent, but local drinks such as ginger juice or red *bissap* or *djablani* juice (which is brewed from hibiscus petals then chilled) and orange squash are sometimes available (but are not always sterile).

Although Mali is predominantly Muslim, most towns have at least one bar or hotel where you can buy Castel, Malian lager.

Flag, from Senegal, is also available in Bamako and Mopti.

Thick, brown and bubbling millet beer is brewed in Christian communities and in Dogon Country, while palm wine is sometimes available in southern Mali.

ENTERTAINMENT

Every decent-sized town has a *carrefour* or *maison des jeunes* or *maison des arts* where dancers and musicians practice and perform and when spectaculars (cultural events, magic shows etc) are held.

SPECTATOR SPORTS

Going to football matches in Mali is a great experience although large crowds of celebrating supporters can get carried away – crushes and small riots are not unheard of.

Mali CAN

Mali spent US$150 million to host the 2002 Cup of African Nations soccer tournament. This is more than the country's education and health budgets combined, although much of the money came as part of an 'aid' package from the Chinese government. Needless to say, there was a little resentment about this expenditure, especially on buses delayed at roadblocks for 'voluntary' contributions towards the cost of stadium construction.

Despite these criticisms Mali did make some serious improvements to its infrastructure (be they localised and some left unfinished when the first ball was kicked) and got five new stadia as well as huge number of bizarre new monuments.

The competition itself was a qualified success and the Mali Eagles showed great promise until being beaten like a gong in the semi-final by Cameroon (Malians claim this was because Cameroon's coach threw a fetish onto the pitch before kick off). Cameroon went on to beat Senegal on penalties in the final.

Getting There & Away

AIR

With the exception of a few charter flights, international flights go to/from Bamako's Sénou international airport. The airport tax here costs CFA8000/10,000 for continental/intercontinental flights.

Europe & the USA

Return flights from Europe cost US$600 to US$1000 return (€680 to €1150). Air France is the only European carrier with scheduled flights to Mali, from Paris. Numerous African carriers fly between Paris and Bamako, while NAS Air has a weekly flight to/from Brussels. Both Air Algéria and Royal Air Maroc (RAM) have weekly connections to Bamako from destinations across Europe. If you are thinking of travelling through Europe and Morocco before arriving in Mali, a Casablanca-Bamako flight is around US$350 (€400).

Between November and February Point Afrique (w www.point-afrique.com) fly to Gao from Paris and Marseille (US$175 to US$225 or €200 to €260 one way).

From the USA you can take RAM from New York via Casablanca. Alternatively go via Europe.

From Mali to Europe one way/return fares of around CFA215,000/CFA350,000 (€330/€535 or US$290/US$470) are not unheard of.

Africa

One-way fares are quoted here unless otherwise stated.

There are daily flights to Dakar in Senegal (CFA85,000), Abidjan in Côte d'Ivoire (CFA110,000) and Ouagadougou in Burkina Faso (CFA100,000), and numerous flights to Lagos in Nigeria (CFA240,000). Three or four times a week there are flights to Nouakchott in Mauritania (CFA250,000), Accra in Ghana (CFA200,000), Johannesburg in South Africa (CFA600,000), Douala in Cameroon (CFA400,000 return), Addis Ababa in Ethiopia (CFA550,000) and Algiers in Algeria (CFA230,000).

You will also be able to find flights to Conakry in Guinea (CFA100,000), Casablanca in Morocco (CFA240,000), Libreville in Gabon (CFA400,000), Banjul in Gambia (CFA63,000) and to Khartoum in Sudan (CFA611,900).

LAND & RIVER

Border Crossings

You can cross into Burkina Faso easily just south of Kouri (southwest of Koutiala) or

Air Maybe

Air Mali's international fares to Europe are among the world's cheapest, but in the past the company has been poor at keeping certified maintenance records (the two facts are apparently unrelated). US government employees were not permitted to fly with Air Mali at the time of writing. However, after the acquisition of a new (to them) 737 and Airbus 300 the situation was under review.

along dirt roads east of Sikasso (to Koloko) or via Koro (east of Dogon Country).

The best way to drop into Côte d'Ivoire is along the tarmac road at Zégoua south of Sikasso. Kourémalé is the main border crossing for Guinea, but some traffic takes the back roads via Bougouni, Sélingué or Kéniéba.

The crossing to/from Senegal is at Kidira, west of Kayes. The main access points to Mauritania are north of Nioro or Nara, but it's possible to travel direct to Sélibabai from Kayes.

The Tanezrouft trans-Saharan route through Algeria is effectively closed to travellers. Go via Niger crossing the border at Labbéganza, east of Gao.

Burkina Faso

Buses leave Bamako's Sogoniko gare routière daily for Ouagadougou (CFA13,500, 20 to 24 hours) via Bobo-Dioulasso (CFA8500, 15 hours) and Kouri. Buses also go to Bobo-Dioulasso from Ségou, Sikasso, Mopti and Koutiala. A daily bus links Koro with Ouagadougou.

Côte d'Ivoire

At the time of writing the volume of transport from Mali to Côte d'Ivoire had dropped off due to their political troubles. However, buses to Abidjan leave daily from Bamako (CFA20,000, 36 to 48 hours). Buses for Côte d'Ivoire also leave from Sikasso.

Guinea

Peugeot taxis or minibuses run most days from Bamako's Djikoroni gare routière to the border at Kourémalé (CFA3000, three hours) and then to Siguiri (CFA5000). There's occasionally transport to Kankan (CFA7500) and Kissidougou (CFA12,500), while on Thursday a coach continues all the way to Conakry (CFA22,000).

When the Niger River is high enough (July to November) a passenger-carrying barge makes an occasional journey between Jukuroni (upstream from Bamako) and Siguiri in Guinea (around CFA6000). The trip *should* take four days. For details ask at the Comanav office in Koulikoro.

Mauritania

Battered 4WDs and trucks are the usual transport. There are daily departures from Kayes to Sélibabai (CFA10,000, eight hours) and Nioro to Ayoûn el Atroûs (CFA15,000). The latter option gets you onto the paved road leading to Nouakchott. All these routes are sandy in the October to May dry season, best travelled between November and February before the harmattan, and extremely difficult in the wet season from June to October. The road from Nioro and Nara to Bamako is rough, but OK in the dry season.

Niger

Truck-buses travel from Gao to Niamey (CFA8500, 16 to 24 hours on Wednesday, Friday and Saturday.

Transport leaves Niamey for Gao on Monday, Wednesday and Thursday, and you'll probably end up sleeping at the border. The road on the Nigérien side is bad, but the road between Ansongo and Gao is terrible. All passport formalities must be completed at the main police station in Gao the day before departure/upon arrival. If you want to split your journey and spend time in Ansongo make this clear to immigration officials.

Senegal

Most travellers take the train between Bamako and Dakar, but the new tarmac road between Kidira and Dakar has made road transport a more appealing prospect. Most road traffic crosses the border here.

Bush Taxi From Kayes there's regular transport to Diboli (CFA3000, two hours). Some transport continues over the bridge to Kidira in Senegal from where there's transport to Tambacounda (CFA2300 to CFA4000). Alternatively, there's an overnight bus direct to Dakar from Kayes (CFA13,000) on Wednesday and Saturday.

Train The train departs Bamako for Dakar (CFA34,620/25,480 1st/2nd class, 35 hours) at 9.15am Wednesday and Saturday and from Dakar at 10am. For the lowdown on this ride see Getting There & Away in the Senegal chapter. Couchettes are available to 1st-class ticket holders for an extra CFA18,000.

Slower and cheaper (by about 40%) autorail and weekend trains go between Bamako and Kayes (two hours from the Senegalese border). Ticket reservations cost CFA375. See the Getting Around section for more details.

Car & Motorcycle The best route to Bamako is currently via Bafoulabé, Manantali and Kita. The first quarter is pretty rough, but once in Bafoulabé it's pretty reasonable all the way to Bamako. There's again talk of improving the whole route between Bamako and Kayes.

You can put your vehicle on the train at Bamako or Kayes. However, this is a real headache and fiercely expensive for vehicles (at least CFA100,000), but affordable and a little more straightforward for motorbikes (CFA9615) and bicycles (CFA3140). However, expect 'labour', 'paperwork' and other incidentals/bribes to double your costs. Carriage between Bamako and Dakar is roughly double again.

Getting Around

AIR

It's relatively easy to fly into Mopti, Timbuktu or Kayes, but more difficult to fly to Yélimané, Goundam or Kéniéba and just about impossible to fly to Nioro, Manantali and Niafounké without chartering some or all of a plane. The domestic carriers are:

African Airlines (☎ 238601, ⓔ fatimakin@hotmail.com)
Air Mali (☎ 229394)
Sahel Aviation Service (☎ 229826) It provides small-plane charters, all-important if you need medical evacuation.
Société Avion Express (SAE; ☎ 212246)
Société Transport Aérienne (STA; ☎ 238339)

SAE flies to/from Bamako to Timbuktu on Tuesday and Saturday, while Air Mali and African Airlines fly the Timbuktu route on Saturday. SAE's Tuesday flight is via Goundam, but there's a week wait for flights back out (via Timbuktu). All other flights return to Bamako the next day, most via Mopti.

SAE flies between Bamako and Kayes via Yélimané on Monday and Thursday, and via Kéniéba on Saturday. All flights return the same day. STA flies direct between Bamako and Kayes on Monday, Tuesday, Thursday and Saturday and African Airlines on Monday and Thursday.

Standard fares vary little between airlines, although African Airlines was the cheapest carrier at the time of writing. As a rule of thumb, one-way fares to/from Bamako are: Timbuktu and Goundam CFA95,000, Mopti CFA55,000, Kayes, Kéniéba and Yélimané CFA65,000. Return fares are double.

Make sure that you confirm your reservation 72 hours before the flight. You should also check on the status and time of your flight the day before (Air Mali is especially unreliable).

Domestic departure tax is CFA2750 and the luggage allowance 20kg.

BUS & BUSH TAXI

Journey times vary hugely depending on the gung-ho nature of the driver (most are pretty 'keen'), the fitness of the vehicle, the state of the roads and the time taken at police and customs. Sometimes these checkpoints can take two minutes, sometimes 42 minutes. As a rough guide bank on at least 2¼ hours per 150km on sealed roads.

Companies Bani (☎ 206081), Binke (☎ 205683), Bittar (☎ 201205) and Somatra (☎ 209932) run reasonably safe and comfortable buses along routes between the main towns south of the Niger River. Fares work out at around CFA10 per kilometre, for example, Bamako to Ségou is CFA2500 (235km), Bamako to Mopti CFA7000 (640km) and Bamako to Gao CFA11,000 (1200km). At major towns, all new passengers are called by name from a list. Booking a ticket in advance puts you further up the list and thus ensures a good seat.

North of the Niger River, the roads can be terrible and 4WDs, fortified truck-buses and standard trucks are used as public transport. The cost can be as much as CFA30 per kilometre.

Bush taxis and minibuses run on some long routes and are generally slightly more expensive than buses (you're likely to be charged a CFA500 luggage fee). On shorter routes, bush taxis are usually the only option: either Peugeot 504s carrying nine people or *bâchés* (pick-ups) with about 16 passengers.

Bâchés are slower, but about 25% cheaper than 504s. Bus stations in Mali are called gares routières.

TRAIN

The train is the best way to travel through western Mali. The cheapest is the *autorail* that leaves Bamako and Kayes at 7.20am daily except Wednesday and Saturday and arrives 10 to 14 hours later. Examples of some fares in CFA francs (including seat reservation) are:

from	to	1st class	2nd class
Bamako	Kayes	11,670	6960
Bamako	Mahina	9050	5435
Bamako	Kita	4625	2850

The *weekend* or night train is fractionally more expensive, but has a restaurant car and *couchettes* (CFA6065, but you must have a 1st-class ticket). It leaves Bamako at 7.30pm on Tuesday and Friday and returns from Kayes at 7.45pm on Wednesday and Sunday.

The *autorail omnibus* or *petit train* runs between Bamako and Kita (six hours). A service leaves Bamako at 3.30pm and Kita at 5am daily.

Seat reservations will set you back CFA375 and more information is available at W www.rcfm.com.

CAR

Self-drive car rental is rare, and not recommended because accident insurance for foreigners can be ineffective (even if you're not at fault) and the correct roadblock/bribe etiquette takes a while to master. However, 4WDs with drivers are easy to arrange through tour operators in all major cities. Rates begin at CFA50,000 per day for a 4WD with unlimited mileage. Some companies also levy a charge per kilometre. Hiring a salon car is rarely cheaper.

On main routes diesel/petrol was CFA325/425 per litre at the time of writing, although these prices were up to 10% higher in out-of-the-way places.

BOAT

Passenger Boat

Three large passenger boats (the *Kankan Moussa* is the best), operated by the Compagnie Malienne de Navigation (Comanav), ply the Niger River between Koulikoro (50km west of Bamako) and Gao, stopping at numerous riverside towns including Mopti and Korioumé (for Timbuktu). They run usually from August to November, when the river is high. In theory, one boat heads downstream from Koulikoro every Tuesday and arrives in Gao the following Monday, while another boat heads upstream from Gao every Thursday and arrives at Koulikoro a week later. The journey from Koulikoro to Mopti should take three days and from Mopti to Gao it should be four days, but schedules are very unreliable and each section can take twice as long.

Despite the vagaries of the timetable, the journey provides some insight into village life along the Niger, but it's not for everyone. The boats are more like floating villages than Caribbean cruise ships. People and cargo are everywhere, the cabins are sweltering, the toilets flooded and the food, well it ain't cordon bleu. Don't let this put you off – many travellers rate the river journey as one of the highlights of their trip. Some travellers suggested getting a group together, hiring a small cabin for everyone's kit and then going 4th class, which means sleeping on the roof (cabins can be hot and stuffy anyway).

It's not essential to do the whole trip and the two-day section from Mopti to Korioumé (about 400km) is arguably the most interesting, although from Koulikoro to Mopti is less crowded. Fares in CFA for popular sectors, in either direction, are listed in the table on the next page.

The 'luxe' cabins have a bathroom and air-con, 1st-class cabins have two bunk beds, toilet and washbasin and 2nd-class cabins are four-berth with a washbasin and shared toilets. Third class is an eight-berth cabin and in 4th class you get to fight for a space on deck and don't get meals.

Booze, food and water are all available, but it's a good idea to take extra supplies as you may get stranded.

Pirogue & Pinasse

Pirogues are small canoes, either paddled by hand or fitted with a small outboard

Passenger Boat Fares (CFA)

route	luxe	1st	2nd	3rd	4th
Koulikoro to Ségou	95,104	20,850	16,139	9130	5651
Ségou to Mopti	70,208	36,829	27,222	16,013	3750
Mopti to Koriouméé	85,915	45,156	33,350	19,535	4521
Koriouméé to Gao	88,565	35,708	33,748	20,016	4632

motor. They're usually the slowest form of river transport. *Pinasses* are larger motorised boats, carrying cargo and anything from 10 to 100 passengers. Some are large enough to have an upper deck and a couple of basic cabins; smaller pinasses make do with a reed mat roof to keep off the sun. Pinasses can be faster than the Comanav passenger boat, but they are equally unpredictable and can be extremely crowded and overloaded – the gunwales often hover just above the surface of the water.

However, by using this mode of transport common on the Niger and Bani Rivers (especially around the Niger Inland Delta), you'll get an experience of river life impossible to achieve on the bigger boat. To avoid getting seriously stranded, use the various market days (when there's more river transport).

The table below lists some of the bigger markets along the Niger River:

market day	town
Monday	Danga, Diafarabé, Ségou
Tuesday	Diré
Wednesday	Gourma-Rharous
Thursday	Mopti, Niafounké, Ténenkou
Friday	Massina
Saturday	Youvarou
Sunday	Gao, Markala, Tonka

ORGANISED TOURS

Tailor-made tours of Mali are easily arranged in Bamako or other cities, but can be expensive; it's always worth enquiring if you can join an existing trip. For specialist desert adventures through Mali and Mauritania contact:

Chameau Vert (☎ 02 40 22 60 40, fax 40 22 60 33, ⓔ takouba@club-internet.fr) 18 Rue de la Paix, 44600 St Nazaire, France. This company conducts 4WD tours.

Nomade Voyage (☎ 217513, fax 227513, ⓔ nomade@cefib.com) This company also runs fixed-date trips including Dogon Country, pinasse tours and Timbuktu.

Point Afrique (☎ 08 20 83 02 55, ⓦ www.point-afrique.com) 2 Rue de la Roquette, 75011 Paris. It offers the usual Dogon/Timbuktu trips plus some adventurous itineraries around Gao. This is our best bet for cheap flights from France.

Sahara Passion (☎/fax 820187, ⓔ spassion@bluewin.ch) This company offers tours into the Sahara north of Gao and Timbuktu.

Shorter tours (boat trips and Dogon treks for example) can be arranged in many Malian towns and are mentioned throughout this chapter.

Bamako

Most travellers leave Mali's rather gritty capital as quickly as possible. In the rainy season roads flood and sewers overflow, while in the dry season, clouds of dust and pollution clog the air. It's a busy, hard-working city and the streets are full of people, cars and buzzing flocks of *mobylettes* (mopeds). Bamako may not be geared towards tourists,

Guides in Mali

In Bamako you may be approached by guides offering tours of the country, for which you pay a daily fee. They'll tell you horror tales of thieves and complex travel arrangements, but it's all hot air. If you're new to travel in Africa, booking a specific trip with a tour operator is worth considering, but you certainly don't need a constant companion or intermediary to get around Mali.

By contrast, in such places as Djenné or Timbuktu, a knowledgeable and informative guide, hired on the spot for a few hours, can greatly enhance your visit, though Dogon Country is the only place for which guides are highly recommended.

but it's a friendly and safe introduction to West Africa and the city centre is one big market, with stalls on every pavement, music blasting away in shop doorways and traders selling everything under the sun.

There's enough money around to support a few decent restaurants and hotels, and at the weekend the city jumps to the beat of music from all over Mali – there's no better place in the country to hear live music.

History

In 1806, when explorer Mungo Park passed by, Bamako was a Bozo fishing and trading community of about 6000 people. In 1883 the French captured the town and in 1908 they transferred their regional seat of power from Kayes to Bamako. When Mali became independent in 1960 Bamako was chosen as the capital.

Orientation

Bamako's city centre is on the north bank of the Niger River, focused on the triangle formed by Av Kassa Keita, Blvd du Peuple and the train tracks.

South of Av Kassa Keita is Square Lumumba and, just beyond, Pont des Martyrs, which leads to Route de Ségou (also called Av de l'Unité Africaine, OUA), the main road out of town – the Sogoniko gare routière is about 6km along this road. The Pont du Roi (west of Pont des Martyrs) carries a new highway that leads to Sénou International Airport (17km).

Information

Tourist Offices The Office Malien du Tourisme et de l'Hôtellerie (Omathma; ☎ 225 673, fax 225541, w www.tourisme.gov.ml) on Rue Mohammed V is not set up for independent travellers, but the staff are friendly and have a few brochures.

Available free at some travel agencies and hotels is *Le Dourouni*, a monthly listings magazine with advertisements for local events, nightclubs and restaurants, plus listings for hotels and emergency services. Similar is *Senou Air Affaires*, which also contains details of flights in and out of Bamako.

Clean public toilets are hard to find in Bamako – use a restaurant.

Money Banks for changing money include the BIM on Av de l'Indépendance, Banque de Développement du Mali (BDM) on Av Modibo Keita and Bicim in Immeuble Nimagala, Blvd du Peuple. Bicim hosts Mali's only international ATM (Visa only). Western Union offices are found in most banks and post offices.

Travellers cheques can be purchased with an AmEx card at ATS Voyages, the American Express Agent (☎ 224435, e ats@malinet.ml), Av Modibo Keita.

Moneychangers deal openly outside the banks and at the airport. Most offer good rates with no commission and the process is quick. However, rip-offs are not unheard of.

Post & Communications The main post office is on Rue Karamoko Diaby. Poste restante is fine for letters (CFA300 to collect), but unreliable for packages. .

There are numerous *cabine téléphonique* (private telephone offices) around Bamako; some are marked on the map.

Two of the best places for Internet access are Smint on Place OMVS (CFA1000 to CFA2000 per hour) and Bamako Net on Av du 22 Octobre 1946 (CFA2000 per hour).

Visa Extensions These are processed in 48 to 72 hours at the Sûreté Nationale building 200m northeast of Rond-point de l'Unité Africaine.

Travel Agencies & Tour Operators There are several agencies dealing in international and domestic flights. Probably the best is ESF (☎ 225144, e esf@cefib.com) on Place du Souvenir where staff speak English and know the best deals. Also switched on are ATS Voyages (☎ 224435, e ats@malinet.ml) on Av Modibo Keita and TAM Voyages (☎ 219210, e tamvoyage@cefib.com) on Square Lumumba.

Of Bamako's tour operators try the following. All are used to English-speaking clients and create tailor-made itineraries:

Bambara Tours (☎ 292377, fax 290377, e bambara@bambara.com)
Tam Tam Tours (☎/fax 236671) Rue 533, Quinzambougou, south of the river
Toguna Adventure Tours (☎ 237853, e togunaadventure@afribone.net.ml) Off Av de l'OUA, Quizambougou, south of the river

Bookshops There's a good selection of French books, magazines and newspapers at

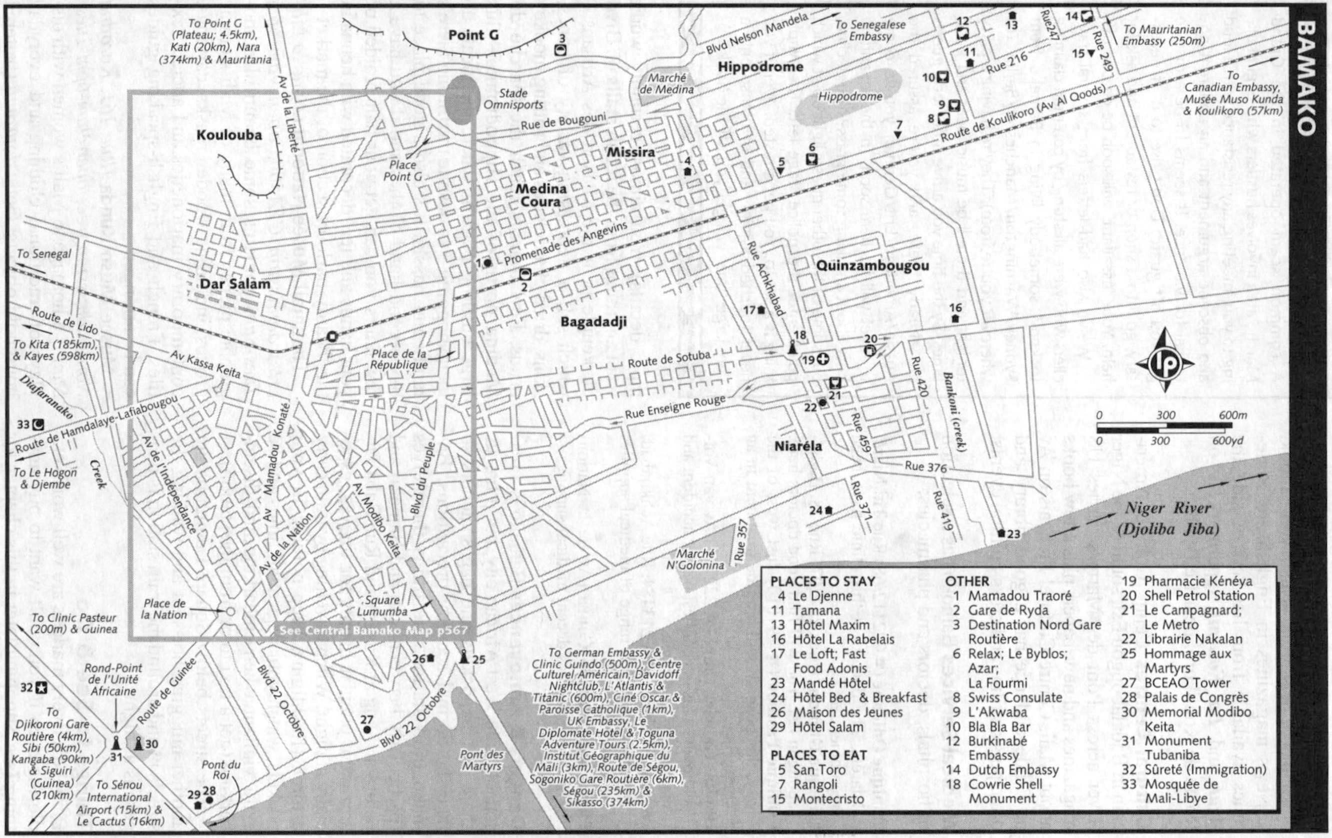

BAMAKO
PLACES TO STAY
4 Le Djenne
11 Tamana
13 Hôtel Maxim
16 Hôtel La Rabelais
17 Le Loft; Fast Food Adonis
23 Mandé Hôtel
24 Hôtel Bed & Breakfast
26 Maison des Jeunes
29 Hôtel Salam
PLACES TO EAT
5 San Toro
7 Rangoli
15 Montecristo
OTHER
1 Mamadou Traoré
2 Gare de Ryda
3 Destination Nord Gare Routière
6 Relax; Le Byblos; Azar; La Fourmi
8 Swiss Consulate
9 L'Akwaba
10 Bla Bla Bar
12 Burkinabé Embassy
14 Dutch Embassy
18 Cowrie Shell Monument
19 Pharmacie Kénéya
20 Shell Petrol Station
21 Le Campagnard; Le Metro
22 Librairie Nakalan
25 Hommage aux Martyrs
27 BCEAO Tower
28 Palais de Congrès
30 Memorial Modibo Keita
31 Monument Tubaniba
32 Sûreté (Immigration)
33 Mosquée de Mali-Libye
0 300 600m
0 300 600yd
Point G
Koulouba
Dar Salam
Missira
Medina Coura
Bagadadji
Hippodrome
Quinzambougou
Niaréla
Niger River (Djoliba Jiba)
To Point G (Plateau; 4.5km), Kati (20km), Nara (374km) & Mauritania
To Senegalese Embassy
To Mauritanian Embassy (250m)
To Canadian Embassy, Musée Muso Kunda & Koulikoro (57km)
To Senegal
To Kita (185km), & Kayes (598km)
To Le Hogon & Djembe
To Clinic Pasteur (200m) & Guinea
To Djikoroni Gare Routière (4km), Sibi (50km), Kangaba (90km) & Siguiri (Guinea) (210km)
To Sénou International Airport (15km) & Le Cactus (16km)
To German Embassy & Clinic Guindo (500m), Centre Culturel Américain, Davidoff Nightclub, L'Atlantis & Titanic (600m), Ciné Oscar & Paroisse Catholique (1km), UK Embassy, Le Diplomate Hotel & Toguna Adventure Tours (2.5km), Institut Géographique du Mali (3km), Route de Ségou, Sogoniko Gare Routière (6km), Ségou (235km) & Sikasso (374km)
See Central Bamako Map p567
Blvd Nelson Mandela
Route de Koulikoro (Av Al Qoods)
Rue de Bougouni
Promenade des Angevins
Rue Achkhabad
Route de Sotuba
Rue Enseigne Rouge
Route de Lido
Av Kassa Keita
Route de Hamdalaye-Lafiabougou
Av de l'Indépendance
Av Mamadou Konaté
Av de la Nation
Av Modibo Keita
Blvd du Peuple
Av de la Liberté
Blvd 22 Octobre
Route de Guinée
Stade Omnisports
Marché de Medina
Hippodrome
Place Point G
Place de la République
Place de la Nation
Square Lumumba
Marché N'Golonina
Rond-Point de l'Unité Africaine
Pont des Martyrs
Pont du Roi
Diafaranako
Creek
Bankoni (creek)
Rue 216
Rue 247
Rue 249
Rue 420
Rue 459
Rue 376
Rue 371
Rue 419
Rue 357

the Grand Hôtel bookshop; Librairie Nakalan, out in Niaréla, is also worth a look.

News magazines in English are sometimes available from hawkers outside the ***Azar*** and ***La Fourmi*** supermarkets on Route de Koulikoro, near Le Byblos.

Cultural Centres Centre Culturel Américain in Badalabougou Est, south of the Niger River across Pont des Martyrs carries US magazines and newspapers plus a few books about Mali. Centre Culturel Français on Av de l'Indépendance has a good library and often puts on films and cross-cultural events.

Medical Services Bamoko has a selection of hospitals, doctors and pharmacies:

Clinique Odiénné (☎ 222112/68) Rue Titi Niaré, Niaréla. The doctors at this clinic have been recommended.
Clinique Guindo (☎/fax 222207) Rue 18, Badalabougou Est. You will find good doctors here.
Clinique Pasteur (☎ 291010) Just west of the city, this hospital will provide treatment in an emergency.
Hôpital Gabriel Touré (☎ 222712) Av van Vollenhoven. This is your best bet for accident and emergency treatment.
Pharmacie Kénéya (☎ 213484, Rue Achkhabad, Quinzambougou) A range of medical supplies are found here.
Pharmacie Officine Coura (Av de la Nation) This pharmacy has decent medical supplies.

Dangers & Annoyances Bamako is a reasonably safe West African city, but it has its share of pickpockets and bag snatchers so take the normal security precautions. Bamako train station, the trains themselves (particularly between Kati and Bamako and before arriving at Kayes) and Rue Baba Diarra are a popular haunts for thieves, especially at night. When travelling by train carry a torch (flashlight), keep nothing in your pockets, watch your bags at all times and be extra vigilant when embarking and disembarking (get a taxi to or from the station).

The streets below Square Lumumba are another mugging hot-spot and walking the streets in and around the train station is dangerous at night.

Things to See & Do

Bamako's lively **markets** are well worth exploring even if you don't want to buy anything (see Shopping later in this chapter for more details). You almost certainly won't want anything from the **fetish stalls** on Blvd du Peuple near the Maison des Artisans – which sell a depressing variety of bones, skins, dried chameleons and rotting monkey heads. Few tourists reach the **Marché de Medina** north of the Hippodrome – this large bustling place is where the locals do their shopping – so despite the throng there's rarely any hassle. It's also a good place to buy second-hand clothes and if you have a few hours you can get your hair braided or your hands and feet decorated with henna in the 'beauty parlour' section of the market.

The small **Musée National** *(Av de la Liberté; admission CFA500; open 9am-6pm Tues-Sun)* contains some beautiful ethnographic pieces from many of Mali's ethnic groups, including wooden masks, carvings, contemporary marionettes and ancient textiles. French and English-speaking guides can be arranged.

Musée Muso Kunda *(Rue 161, Korofina Nord; admission free; open 9am-6pm Tues-Sun)* is a homage to Mali's women with displays of traditional clothing and everyday household objects. Get a *dourouni* (battered

Bamako Scams

A common scam operated in the Grand Marché area involves hustlers who begin talking to you, meeting any resistance with a loud and obscene argument and an apparent potential for violence. It seems to be a ruse to get you off guard. Don't rise to it. If necessary, go into a shop or restaurant and ask for help. Your 'assailant' will soon be chased off.

We've also had letters from several travellers who were all stung by con men claiming to know somebody living in Bamako from Sydney/Washington/Manchester/Berlin (or wherever you're from). They're having a party tonight and there'll be music, beer and good times. By the time you arrive other local guests are already there, and you're assured the Aussie/American/Brit/German you've come to meet will be here soon. In the meantime how about smoking some grass? You decline, but some of the other guests light up at which point enter the police stage left. The whole thing is a setup. You get arrested, even if you never touched a joint, and of course only a very large 'fine' will get you off the hook.

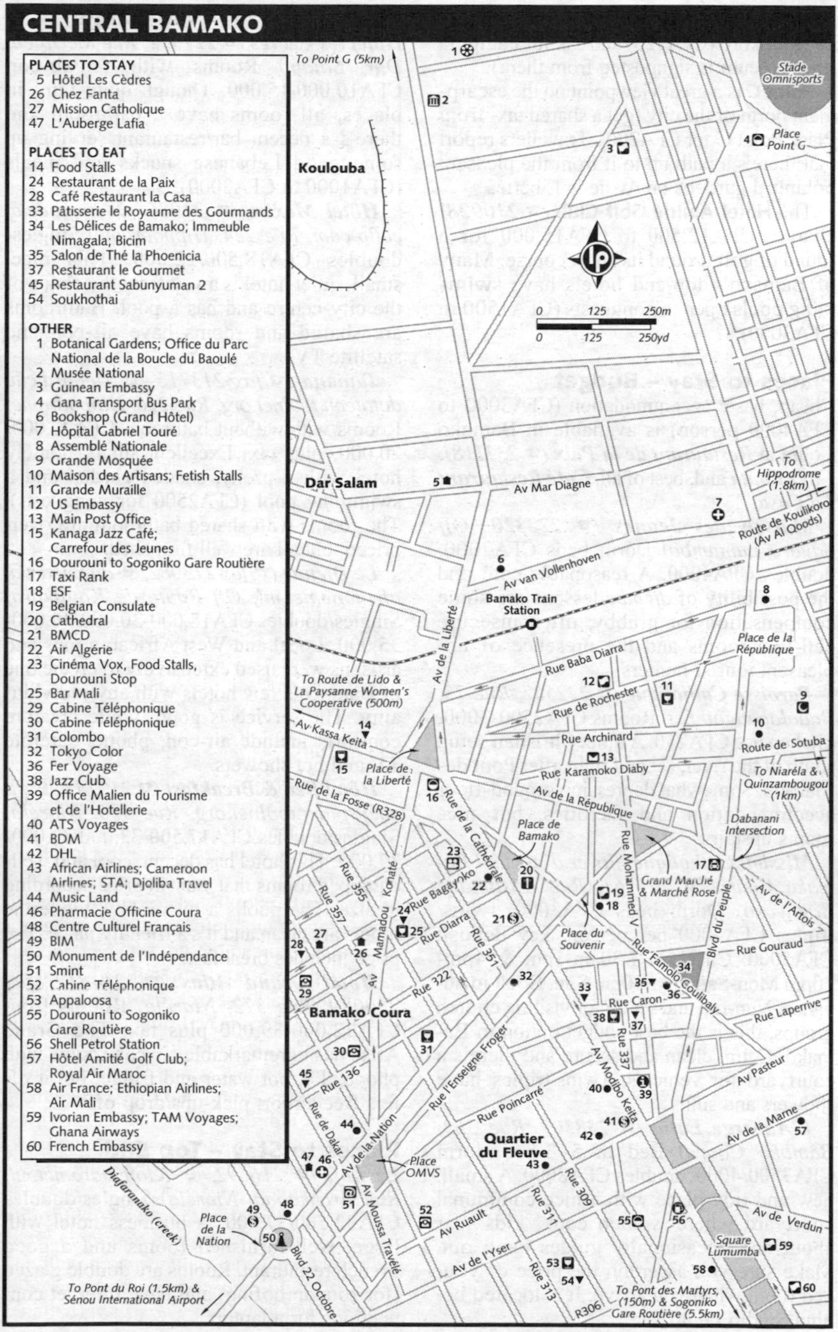
CENTRAL BAMAKO
PLACES TO STAY
5 Hôtel Les Cèdres
26 Chez Fanta
27 Mission Catholique
47 L'Auberge Lafia
PLACES TO EAT
14 Food Stalls
24 Restaurant de la Paix
28 Café Restaurant la Casa
33 Pâtisserie le Royaume des Gourmands
34 Les Délices de Bamako; Immeuble Nimagala; Bicim
35 Salon de Thé la Phoenicia
37 Restaurant le Gourmet
45 Restaurant Sabunyuman 2
54 Soukhothai
OTHER
1 Botanical Gardens; Office du Parc National de la Boucle du Baoulé
2 Musée National
3 Guinean Embassy
4 Gana Transport Bus Park
6 Bookshop (Grand Hôtel)
7 Hôpital Gabriel Touré
8 Assemblé Nationale
9 Grande Mosquée
10 Maison des Artisans; Fetish Stalls
11 Grande Muraille
12 US Embassy
13 Main Post Office
15 Kanaga Jazz Café; Carrefour des Jeunes
16 Dourouni to Sogoniko Gare Routière
17 Taxi Rank
18 ESF
19 Belgian Consulate
20 Cathedral
21 BMCD
22 Air Algérie
23 Cinéma Vox, Food Stalls, Dourouni Stop
25 Bar Mali
29 Cabine Téléphonique
30 Cabine Téléphonique
31 Colombo
32 Tokyo Color
36 Fer Voyage
38 Jazz Club
39 Office Malien du Tourisme et de l'Hotellerie
40 ATS Voyages
41 BDM
42 DHL
43 African Airlines; Cameroon Airlines; STA; Djoliba Travel
44 Music Land
46 Pharmacie Officine Coura
48 Centre Culturel Français
49 BIM
50 Monument de l'Indépendance
51 Smint
52 Cabine Téléphonique
53 Appaloosa
55 Dourouni to Sogoniko Gare Routière
56 Shell Petrol Station
57 Hôtel Amitié Golf Club; Royal Air Maroc
58 Air France; Ethiopian Airlines; Air Mali
59 Ivorian Embassy; TAM Voyages; Ghana Airways
60 French Embassy
To Point G (5km)
Stade Omnisports
Place Point G
Koulouba
0 125 250m
0 125 250yd
Dar Salam
Av Mar Diagne
To Hippodrome (1.8km)
Route de Koulikoro (Av Al Qoods)
Av van Vollenhoven
Bamako Train Station
Av de la Liberté
Place de la République
Rue Baba Diarra
Rue de Rochester
To Route de Lido & La Paysanne Women's Cooperative (500m)
Av Kassa Keita
Rue Archinard
Route de Sotuba
To Niaréla & Quinzambougou (1km)
Place de la Liberté
Rue Karamoko Diaby
Av de la République
Rue de la Fosse (R328)
Rue de la Cathédrale
Place de Bamako
Dabanani Intersection
Rue Mohammed V
Grand Marché & Marché Rose
Av de l'Artois
Blvd du Peuple
Rue 355
Rue 357
Mamadou Konaté
Rue Bagayoko
Rue Diarra
Rue 351
Place du Souvenir
Rue Famolo Coulibaly
Rue Gouraud
Av Mamadou Konaté
Rue 322
Rue Caron
Rue Laperrive
Bamako Coura
Rue 337
Rue l'Enseigne Froger
Av Modibo Keita
Av Pasteur
Rue 136
Rue de Dakar
Av de la Nation
Rue Poincarré
Av de la Marne
Quartier du Fleuve
Place OMVS
Diafaranako (creek)
Place de la Nation
Av Moussa Travélé
Rue 309
Rue 311
Av Ruault
Av de Verdun
Square Lumumba
Av de l'Yser
Rue 313
Blvd 22 Octobre
To Pont du Roi (1.5km) & Sénou International Airport
To Pont des Martyrs, (150m) & Sogoniko Gare Routière (5.5km)
R306

green minibus) from the west end of Route de Koulikoro (CFA125) and ask for Fagigula (the museum is signposted from there).

Point G is a great viewpoint on the escarpment north of the city (get a shared taxi from Place Point G for CFA200). Travellers report that there's a path up to it from the pleasant **botanical gardens** on Av de la Liberté.

The **Hôtel Amitié Golf Club** *(☎ 210928)* charges CFA12,500 to CFA15,000 for a round of golf around its short course. Many of Bamako's top-end hotels have **swimming pools** open to nonguests (CFA1500 to CFA3000).

Places to Stay – Budget

Cheap, basic accommodation (CFA3000 to CFA4000 person) is available in Bamako Coura at ***Restaurant de la Paix*** *(☎ 231118)*, ***Chez Fanta*** and, best of all, ***Café Restaurant La Casa***.

Maison des Jeunes *(☎ 222320, Off Square Lumumba)* Dorm beds CFA2000, doubles CFA4000. A reasonable café and the possibility of *djembe* lessons are some compensation for grubby, often insecure cell-like rooms and the presence of unpleasant tourist-hunters.

Paroisse Catholique *(☎ 222557, Rue 73, Badalabougou Est)* Rooms CFA2500-3000, kitchen use CFA250. A quiet Christian setup south of the river, second right after Pont des Martyrs. Somewhat depressing ground-floor accommodation and facilities, but nice rooms upstairs.

Mission Catholique *(Foyer d'Accueil Bamako Coura; ☎ 227761, Rue Ousamane Bagayoko)* Dorm beds CFA3000, twins/triples CFA4000 per person, key deposit CFA5000. Check-in 7.30am-1pm & 4pm-10pm Mon-Sat, 5pm-10pm Sun. Book in advance. Nun-run and set up for visiting church groups, this is the best budget option in Bamako. Calm, clean and secure and there's a courtyard for vehicles. Twins/triples have showers and sinks.

L'Auberge Lafia *(☎ 238309, Rue 364, Bamako Coura)* Bed in 5-/3-bed dorm CFA3500/4000, doubles CFA8000. A small, new and tidy place with a nice communal courtyard where women cook, kids tear about and occasionally guides hang out. Make sure you ascertain the price of your bed/room when you arrive. It is located behind Studio Photo.

MALI

Places to Stay – Mid-Range

Hôtel les Cèdres *(☎ 227972, Rue Meridien, Dar Salam)* Rooms with fan/air-con CFA10,000/15,000. Though quite tatty in places, all rooms have a bathroom and there's a decent bar/restaurant serving up some good Lebanese snacks and meals (CFA1000 to CFA3000).

Hôtel Maxim *(☎ 21986, ⓔ nomade@cefib.com, Rue 224, Hippodrome)* Singles/doubles CFA18,500/22,000. This nice, small, quiet hotel is away from the chaos of the city centre and has a pool. Bathrooms are shared and rooms have air-con and satellite TV.

Tamana *(☎/fax 213715, ⓔ richard.c@datatech.toolnet.org, Rue 216, Hippodrome)* Rooms with/without bathroom CFA22,000/20,000, plus tax. Excellent small, homely hotel with a pretty, shaded garden and a swimming pool (CFA2500 for nonguests). The rooms with shared bathroom are overpriced, but all are well furnished.

Le Djenne *(☎/fax 213082, ⓔ djenneart@afribone.net.ml, Off Route de Koulikoro)* Singles/doubles CFA18,000-30,000/30,000-35,000. Local and West African artists and artisans were used extensively to create one of Bamako's few hotels with any individuality. The service is good, while creature comforts include air-con, phone, satellite TV and hot showers.

Hôtel Bed & Breakfast *(☎ 210144, ⓔ paco@spider.toolnet.org, Rue 326, Niaréla)* Singles/doubles CFA17,500-33,000/33,000-37,000. This hotel has decent, cool and well-equipped rooms that vary in price according to size. The pool's a bit grubby, while the rooms are clean and it's a friendly place. The price includes breakfast.

Hôtel Grand Atlas *(☎ 214817, fax 210089, Rue 372, Niaréla)* Rooms from CFA32,000-39,000 plus tax. The Grand Atlas has unremarkable air-con rooms with phone, TV, hot water and fridge, but it offers free airport pick-ups/drop-offs.

Places to Stay – Top End

Le Loft *(☎ 216692, ⓔ leloft@arc.net.ml, Rue Archkabad, Niaréla)* Singles/doubles CFA32,500/37,000. A business hotel with large, well-furnished rooms and a good French restaurant. Rooms are double glazed (for soundproofing) and have Internet connections for a laptop.

Mandé Hôtel *(☎ 231993, e mande hotel@spider.toolnet.org, Rue Niaréla)* Rooms CFA40,500-47,000. This hotel has a great location on the banks of the river with the restaurant-bar jutting over the water. Rooms are well equipped and there's a pool.

Hotel La Rabelais *(☎ 215298, e rabe lais@datatech.toolnet.org, Route de Sotuba, Quinzambougou)* Rooms from CFA41,500-58,000. A very pleasant and together hotel. Individually styled rooms have fridges, safes and video machines (there's a hotel film library). La Rabelais has a beautiful pool (CFA2500 nonguests) and there's a good bar and restaurant – the French cuisine is very good (dinner CFA9500).

Le Diplomate *(☎ 233853, e ledip@le mali.com, Off Av de l'OUA, Badalabougou Est)* Rooms CFA40,000-60,000. This is a well-equipped business hotel with Internet access and the usual four-star mod cons. Some of the beautiful furnishings look out of place, but there's a nice garden/pool area and fine Mediterranean cuisine (CFA3000 to CFA6000).

Hôtel Salam *(☎ 221200, e salam@ cefib.com, Next to Pont du Roi)* Rooms CFA65,500-91,000. Salam is easily Bamako's best-equipped hotel. Perhaps it lacks a little personality and warmth, but what the hell – it's got a swimming pool, tennis courts, gym, shops, bars and a reasonable restaurant.

Places to Eat

Cheap Eats Snacks like *brochettes* (grilled pieces of meat on a stick) and chips are cooked on small barbeques all around town. At the dourouni ranks near the Cinéma Vox, as well as west of Place de la Liberté across from Carrefour des Jeunes there are ***food stalls*** serving cheap rice and sauce.

In Bamako Coura, ***Restaurant de la Paix*** and ***Restaurant Sabunyuman 2*** are good, simple places serving spicy Senegalese dishes for around CFA1000.

Restaurant le Gourmet *(Rue Caron, off Rue Mohammed V)* Meals CFA600-1000. Open 7am-6pm Mon-Sat. This is small and simple offering only two or three dishes per day (often rice with a stew or sauce). It's a pretty safe bet downtown.

Café Restaurant la Casa *(Opposite Mission Catholique, Bamako Coura)* Meals CFA750-1000. This is a fine, relaxed backpacker hang-out. There's just one dish in the evening (often vegetarian) and it's usually a goodie. Rooms (CFA4000 per person), bicycle hire (CFA3000 per day) and a 4WD are also available.

Fast Food Adonis *(Rue Achkabad)* Meals CFA2500-3000. Adonis has impressive fast food (some good Lebanese specialities) with beautiful service. It can be found below Le Loft.

Salon de Thé la Phoenicia *(Rue Mohammed V)* Snacks & meals CFA750-CFA2500. This place falls somewhere between a snack bar and patisserie. It's OK, and has air-con.

Cafés & Patisseries The best patisserie in downtown Bamako is ***Pâtisserie le Royaume des Gourmands*** *(Av Modibo Keita)*. Here you will find good croissants, coffee and fresh orange juice served with a smile in clean, air-conditioned surroundings. Meals range from CFA1000 to CFA3000 and pastries and cakes from CFA250 to CFA700.

Les Délices de Bamako *(Immeuble Nimagala, Rue Famolo Coulibaly)* Meals CFA750-4000, pastries & cakes CFA250-600. This is a friendly and popular choice with cake eaters.

Relax *(Route de Koulikoro)* Meals CFA2000-CFA3000, pastries CFA250-700. Relax is open all hours to tempt you with rich cakes and some excellent pastries. Some of the meals can be a little off beam (especially the hamburgers).

Restaurants One of Mali's best restaurants is ***Soukhothai*** *(☎ 222448, Rue 311, Quartier du Fleuve)* It has a cosy atmosphere, switched-on service and authentic Thai cuisine. Bookings are essential at weekends. Meals range from CFA2500 to CFA10,000.

San Toro *(☎ 213082, Route de Koulikoro, Missira)* Malian specialities CFA4500. No alcohol is served here (it has a range of delicious juices instead) and the food is usually worth the wait. The surroundings are exquisite and *kora* (harp-like musical instrument) musicians play in the evening. There's also a gallery selling fine art and craftwork.

Rangoli *(☎ 745047, Route de Koulikoro, Hippodrome)* Meals CFA3000-6000. Rangoli is Bamako's only Indian restaurant and it is a real goodie. The select menu is high on quality with a great variety of sauces and chutneys. It also does takeaways!

Montecristo *(☎ 211296, Rue 249, Hippodrome)* Meals CFA4000-13,500. This is a top-quality restaurant dishing out delicious continental cuisine with impeccable service. Mains are quite reasonably priced, but thanks to a decent wine list bills can get out of hand (Visa is accepted).

Self-Catering For imported food and wine, try ***Azar*** and ***La Fourmi*** supermarkets on Route de Koulikoro or ***Le Metro*** in Niaréla.

There are good fruit and vegetable stalls at the dourouni rank near the Cinéma Vox and on Place OMVS.

Entertainment

Bars For a serious drinking den (read brothel) try ***Bar Mali***, on Av Mamadou Konaté. Very lively, although not for the faint-hearted, is ***Grande Muraille*** off Rue de Rochester – a bar-restaurant (serving cheap beer and Chinese food) and another unashamed brothel.

L'Akwaba *(Rue 235, Hippodrome)* Meals CFA2000-3000, big beers CFA1500. This is a restaurant and open-air nightclub with occasional live bands.

Appaloosa *(Rue 311, Quartier du Fleuve)* Meals CFA1750-4000, beers CFA1000-3000. A Tex-Mex theme bar is kind of weird for Bamako, but nice for an evening of escapism. There's a smaller local bar next door if you want to get liquored on the cheap before the karaoke on Wednesday.

Bla Bla Bar *(Rue 235, Hippodrome)* Small beers CFA1000. As chic and sophisticated a bar as you'll find in Mali. It's filled with the bold and the beautiful at weekends and it plays some good Latin tunes.

Le Campagnard *(Above Le Metro Supermarket, Niaréla)* Meals CFA2500-5000, small beers CFA1000. Popular with expats, there's a free pool table and an extensive restaurant menu.

Le Cactus *(e acharmaca@yahoo.com, Near Kabala 16km west of Bamako, south bank of the Niger)* This low-key place has the kind of comfortable, eccentric bar that you can spend days unwinding in. Food (CFA2000 to CFA3000) and accommodation (CFA10,000 to CFA12,500 per person) are available. Catch a dourouni to Kalanban-Coura from near Square Lumumba, then another to Kabala. Ask to be dropped at the soccer training ground.

Live Music & Nightclubs Clubs don't get going before midnight and close around 5am. Friday and Saturday things are really jumping and most clubs also open Thursday and Sunday. Cover charges usually include a drink. After that drinks cost CFA1000 to CFA3000.

Kanaga Jazz Café *(Carrefour des Jeunes, Av de l'Oyako)* Admission free or CFA1000. This place is friendly and inexpensive, and the roof-top terrace (or open-air stage) is a great place to see live bands. Dance troupes and musicians often practice here early evening. Drumming and dancing tuition is available.

Le Hogon *(☎ 230760, N'Tomi Korobougou)* Admission free. Le Hogan is a fine open-air music venue 2km west of the city. Wednesday is big band night, Friday is devoted to kora music and on Saturday, traditional Malian music is played.

Jazz Club *(Rue 337)* Admission CFA1000. This is a local-orientated place with West African music, sometimes live. It can get quite frantic.

Djembe *(Lafiabougou)* is an excellent live music venue – lots of Guinean musicians play here. Admission is CFA2000.

Colombo *(Av de la Nation)* Admission CFA2500. This is a local booze-free nightclub playing a mix of African and cheesy disco music for a young crowd.

Le Byblos *(Route de Koulikoro, Hippodrome)* Admission CFA5000. Open daily. This is a glitzy disco popular with male expats and beautiful working women.

Davidoff Nightclub *(Off Av de l'OUA, Badalabougou Est)* Admission CFA5000. Like Le Byblos, but with more elbow room and a garden. There are some reliably cheap bars opposite.

L'Atlantis *(Off Av de l'OUA, Badalabougou Est)* Admission CFA5000 Fri-Sun. L'Atlantis is a popular nightclub. The garden bar ***Titanic*** *(admission CFA1500; open Fri-Sun)* is next door – Malian bands sometimes play here.

Cinemas For karate flicks and Indian movies try the ***Cinéma Vox*** *(Rue Bagayoko)*. ***Centre Culturel Français*** shows French movies, while ***Ciné Oscar*** *(Army officers*

MALI

mess, near Paroisse Catholique, Badalabougou Est) is mainstream.

Shopping

The rather pink ***Marché Rose*** mainly houses shoe stores, while the surrounding streets are jam-packed with stalls selling tie-dyed fabrics and indigo cloth, traditional blankets and rugs, brass, incense, spices and local medicines.

Maison des Artisans *(Blvd du Peuple)* Leather goods and woodcarvings are made and sold here and there are several jewellers, gold and silver objects, which are sold by weight (watch out for gold-plated brass). Bargaining is tough. Several more ***jewellers*** are located in Bamako Coura.

La Paysanne Women's Cooperative *(West of city centre, off Av Kassa Keita)* A friendly place selling some great fabrics, designed and printed by women from the surrounding area. Prices are slightly higher than what you can get at the market, and the clothes are more adapted to Western tastes or made to order.

Mamadou Traoré *(☎ 212885, Rue Alcott, Porte 695, Medina Coura)* This wholesaler of crafts and antiquities has an enormous variety of stuff at reasonable prices.

Music Land *(☎ 746305, ⓔ music-land@mali-music.com, Av Mamadou Konaté)* Music Land is a stockist of all kinds of Malian and West African music. Pirated tapes and CDs are widely available, but unfortunately do serious damage to Mali's local music industry.

Bamako's best places for print film and processing is ***Tokyo Color*** *(☎ 223498, Av de la Nation)*.

Getting There & Away

Air Numerous airlines fly into Bamako and those with offices there include:

Air Algérie (☎ 223159)
Air Burkina (☎ 210178)
Cameroon Airlines (☎/fax 238285, ☎ 229400)
Ethiopian Airlines (☎/fax 226036)
Air France (☎ 222212, fax 224734) You can check-in your luggage at the office between 11am and 1pm on the day of departure.
Ghana Airways (☎ 219210)
Air Guinée (☎ 292485)
Air Mali (☎ 228439, 229400)
Air Mauritanie (☎ 225605)
Royal Air Maroc (☎ 226105)

Bus Long-distance transport for destinations south of the Niger River leaves from the Sogoniko gare routière, 6km south of the city centre on the left-hand side of the road heading south (CFA2000 by taxi, CFA125 by dourouni).

Buses for Sikasso via Bougouni leave almost hourly with either Somatrie, Kenedougou YT or Kenedougou Voyagers.

In the centre of the gare routière is Bani's (☎ 206081) bus park, while just outside are Bittar (☎ 201205) and Somatra (☎ 209932). About 2km back towards town is the new Binke (☎ 205683) bus park. Between them these companies have dozens of services heading north along the Bamako-Gao road (at least as far as Mopti).

Transport for destinations north of the Niger River leaves from Destination Nord gare routière (below Point G) or around Marché de Medina. Truck-buses to Kita leave at least three times a day, while services to Nioro, Nara and Timbuktu (only in the dry season) leave a couple of times a week. Transport to Koulikoro (CFA1000) and Kati (CFA250) leave daily when full.

Also handy for Koulikoro, Timbuktu and Kangaba is the Gana Transport (☎ 210978) bus park at Place Point G.

Bâchés and minibuses to Sibi (CFA1000) and Kangaba (CFA1750) leave daily from Djikoroni gare routière on Route de Guinea, 5km southwest from the centre – take a dourouni (CFA100) from opposite the Vox Cinéma.

Sample fares in CFA and travel times in hours from Bamako are as follows:

Bamako to	fare (CFA)	duration (hrs)
Bandiagara	8000	9–11
Bougouni	2000	2½
Douentza	9000	10–12
Gao	14,000	16–20
Kita	2500	4
Mopti	7000	7–10
Nioro	10,000	24–28
Ségou	2500	3
Sikasso	4000	3
Timbuktu	15,000	24–30

Train Tickets can be bought in advance from the station office (☎ 225566), but queues can be very long. Tickets bought from touts may not be valid.

MALI

Fer Voyage (☎ 220514, Rue Famolo Coulibaly) sells train tickets to Kayes and Dakar. You can buy your ticket a day in advance and avoid the scrum at the station.

Arrive at the station 30 minutes before departure and beware of thieves.

Boat The big boats leave from Koulikoro some 50km downstream of Bamako. For details on the Niger River boat service see Getting Around earlier in this chapter.

Getting Around

Bamako to the airport by taxi costs from CFA6000 to CFA7500.

Dourounis run from central Bamako to the gare routières and the outer suburbs for CFA75 to CFA150. Important stops are marked on the map.

Most taxis in Bamako are yellow. Those with a 'taxi' sign on the roof are shared – the driver may pick up other passengers going your way, but the fare is cheaper. Those without signs are for private hire *(déplacement)* only. Tourists will be charged a minimum of CFA750 for a short journey and from CFA1000 to CFA1500 for a trip across town.

AROUND BAMAKO

Koulikoro

Koulikoro may have been an important place in colonial days when the train from Dakar terminated here, but today most visitors only come here to catch the Comanav boat to Timbuktu. However, the surrounding rocky hills may offer some good hiking and, in November, there's an annual marionette festival at Diarabougou roughly 20km east of town.

***Motel le Saloon** (☎ 262024)* is the most pleasant place to stay (air-con doubles CFA12,500), while close to the river to the east of town ***Centre d'Accueil Regional** (☎ 262261)* has rooms for CFA9000.

Plenty of transport leaves from Koulikoro market for Bamako's Destination Nord gare routière (CFA1000). Gana Transport has four buses a day from Place Point G.

The Comanav office (☎ 262095, fax 262009) is situated on the western outskirts of town.

Sibi

This small village at the edge of the Monts Manding, an area of hill country 50km southwest of Bamako, is a great excursion from the city. A 75-minute walk uphill from Sibi is Kamadjan a fantastic **rock arch**. **Grottes de Fanfaba**, a huge cave with a permanent spring, is north of Sibi's school and **Cascades Danda** are 4km further east along the Bamako road.

The small tourist bureau has plenty of advice for visitors and you must pay your tourist tax (CFA2000) here.

Sibi's basic accommodation is limited to the family-run ***Segou Kamara*** (CFA1500 per person) where you'll be well looked after and the purpose-built ***Kamadjan Village Campement*** (CFA2500 per person).

Good ***food stalls*** are dotted around the village, which comes to life on market day (Saturday) when there are more than the usual two or three bâchés to Bamako's Djikoroni gare routière (CFA1000).

The Niger River Route

The classic journey through Mali follows the Niger River, either by road or by boat, as it carves a huge arc through the Sahel.

SÉGOU

Ségou is a large, sleepy town on the banks of the Niger River about 230km east of Bamako. Often overlooked by visitors as they rush east to Mopti and Djenné, Ségou was important in colonial days as the headquarters of the vast Office du Niger irrigation scheme. The wide avenues and several imposing colonial buildings remain and it's an interesting place to stop for a night or two.

Information

The BDM on Blvd de l'Indépendance changes cash and travellers cheques.

Cybercafé La Corniche at Hôtel de l'Esplanade has Internet access for CFA1500 per hour.

Pharmacie Officine Sarakole on Blvd El Hadj Amar Tall and Pharmacie Officine Adam (☎ 320643) on Blvd de l'Indépendance are both competent.

Balazan Tours was awaiting new premises at the time of writing. Many of the guides employed by the agency hang out beside L'Auberge.

MALI

Things to See & Do

From the waterfront, pirogues can take you on excursions to a number of nearby sites on the river. For example, pottery is produced at **Kalabougou** (and fired at weekends) and **Farako** is a centre for mud-cloth making. Trips cost CFA15,000 to CFA20,000 per boat.

The historic and beautiful village of **Ségou Koro** lies 9km upstream, just off the main Bamako road. In the 18th century it was the centre of Biton Mamary Coulibaly's Bambara empire and the great man is buried here. Wonderful examples of **Bambara architecture** and **ancient mosques** are found in the village. Introduce yourself to the chief who collects the CFA2500 tourist tax. A taxi to/from Ségou costs around CFA10,000 and a guided tour around CFA2500.

Places to Stay

***Hôtel-Restaurant Balely Agne** (3.5km along Route de Mopti, opposite a water tower)* Singles/doubles with bathroom & fan CFA4000/6500. One of Ségou's better budget options, this place was being renovated at the time of writing (looks promising).

***Motel Savanne** (☎ 320974, Off Blvd de l'Indépendance)* Rooms with bathroom & fan CFA7500-12,250, air-con CFA14,000-21,000. Savanne is a nice place with round bungalows, a shaded restaurant/bar area and some rooms with hot water.

***Kaarta Hôtel** (☎/fax 321080, Rue 100, Médine, opposite radio/TV transmitter)* Rooms with bathroom & fan CFA10,000, with air-con CFA12,500-17,500. Most rooms here surround a pleasant courtyard and are good value; there's also a bar and restaurant.

***L'Auberge** (☎ 321731, e hotelauberge@cefib.com, Rue 21)* Rooms with fan CFA15,000, air-con CFA20,000-35,000. All rooms have bathrooms and satellite TV. Some also have hot water and phones. It's a little overpriced, though the sparkling swimming pool (CFA1500 for nonguests), fine bar and restaurant (meals CFA1800 to CFA3000) are fair compensation. Their sister hotel, ***Hôtel de l'Indépendance** (☎ 321 733)* is on Route de Mopti.

***Hôtel de l'Esplanade** (☎/fax 320127, The waterfront)* Singles CFA20,000-24,000, doubles CFA24,000-27,000. This hotel is in a great location, but it was undergoing

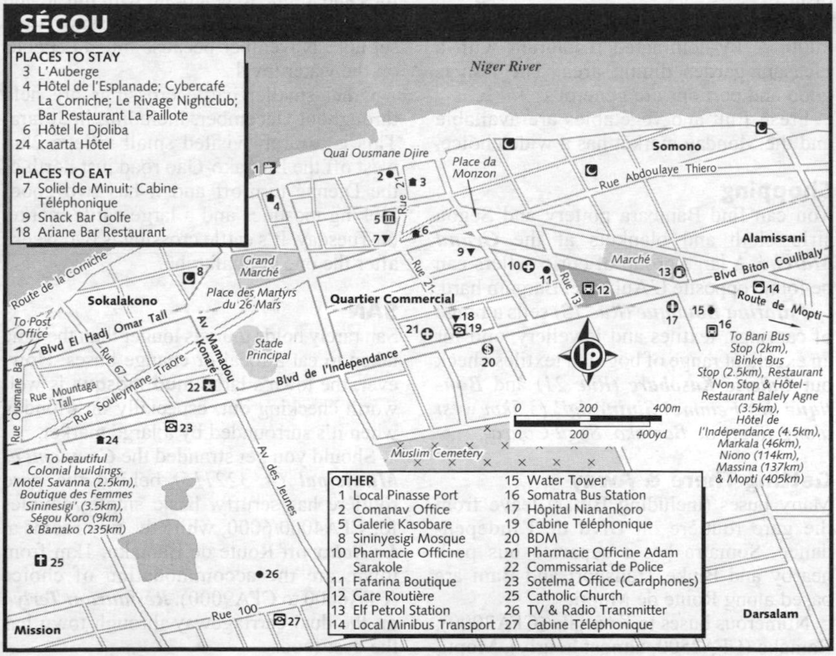
SÉGOU
PLACES TO STAY
3 L'Auberge
4 Hôtel de l'Esplanade; Cybercafé La Corniche; Le Rivage Nightclub; Bar Restaurant La Paillote
6 Hôtel le Djoliba
24 Kaarta Hôtel
PLACES TO EAT
7 Soliel de Minuit; Cabine Téléphonique
9 Snack Bar Golfe
18 Ariane Bar Restaurant
Niger River
Quai Ousmane Djire
Place da Monzon
Somono
Rue Abdoulaye Thiero
Alamissani
Marché
Blvd Biton Coulibaly
Route de Mopti
Rue 21
Rue 13
Grand Marché
Place des Martyrs du 26 Mars
Quartier Commercial
Sokalakono
Route de la Corniche
To Post Office
Blvd El Hadj Omar Tall
Rue 67
Av Mamadou Konaré
Stade Principal
Blvd de l'Indépendance
Rue Mountaga Tall
Rue Souleymane Traore
Rue Ousmane Ba
Av des Jeunes
Muslim Cemetery
To Bani Bus Stop (2km), Binke Bus Stop (2.5km), Restaurant Non Stop & Hôtel-Restaurant Balely Agne (3.5km), Hôtel de l'Indépendance (4.5km), Markala (46km), Niono (114km), Massina (137km) & Mopti (405km)
To beautiful Colonial buildings, Motel Savanna (2.5km), Boutique des Femmes Sininesigi' (3.5km), Ségou Koro (9km) & Bamako (235km)
0 200 400m
0 200 400yd
Rue 100
Mission
Darsalam
OTHER
1 Local Pinasse Port
2 Comanav Office
5 Galerie Kasobare
8 Sininyesigi Mosque
10 Pharmacie Officine Sarakole
11 Fafarina Boutique
12 Gare Routière
13 Elf Petrol Station
14 Local Minibus Transport
15 Water Tower
16 Somatra Bus Station
17 Hôpital Nianankoro
19 Cabine Téléphonique
20 BDM
21 Pharmacie Officine Adam
22 Commissariat de Police
23 Sotelma Office (Cardphones)
25 Catholic Church
26 TV & Radio Transmitter
27 Cabine Téléphonique

renovations at the time of writing. Rooms have bathroom and air-con. Le Rivage Nightclub and riverside Bar Restaurant La Paillote (with unexceptional European staples CFA2900 to CFA4000) are attached.

Hôtel le Djoliba *(☎/fax 321572, ⓔ zarth@afribone.net.ml, Cnr Rue 21 & Blvd El Hadj Omar Tall)* Singles/doubles with bathroom, air-con & satellite TV CFA20,000/22,500. This smart hotel has an intimate, European feel to it. The restaurant (meals CFA2000 to CFA5000) and bar are excellent and there's a pizza night on Saturday. A backpacker's dorm (CFA4000 per person) is planned.

Places to Eat

There are a couple of cheap ***restaurants*** at the gare routière, ***food stalls*** at the Grand Marché area behind Hôtel de l'Esplanade and some hotels do good meals.

Restaurant Non Stop *(2km along Route de Mopti)* Meals CFA1100-2500. Of the European-style food, the fried chicken and pizza reign supreme.

Soleil de Minuit Meals CFA1500-2500. Slightly more imaginative than most places, with some vegetarian options and good fish dishes.

Ariane Bar Restaurant Meals CFA1500-3000. A TV-dominated restaurant with a pleasant garden dining area. The fish is good and portions are generous.

Fresh fruit and vegetables are available and the Monday market has a wide choice.

Shopping

You can find Bambara pottery and Ségou strip cloth and blankets at the ***Grand Marché***. A large group of curio sellers can be found opposite L'Auberge. Bargain hard.

Fafarina Boutique *(Rue 13)* sells a range of carvings, textiles and jewellery, and for an excellent range of bogolan textiles check out ***Galerie Kasobare*** *(Rue 21)* and ***Boutique des Femmes Sininesigi'*** *(3.5km west along Route de Bamako, Segu Coura)*.

Getting There & Away

Many buses (including Bittar) leave from the gare routière on Blvd de l'Indépendance. Somatra has a separate bus park nearby and Binke Transport and Bani are based along Route de Mopti.

Numerous buses to Koutiala (CFA2000), Bamako (CFA2500, almost hourly), Mopti/Sévaré (CFA4500) and Sikasso (CFA3500) pass through Ségou daily. A few buses head up to Gao (CFA8500), though there is a designated service on Monday and Thursday.

Minibuses to local destinations collect on the dirt road behind the Elf petrol station. Transport to Markala (CFA750) is frequent, and leaves around noon for Massina (CFA2500).

AROUND SÉGOU

Markala, north of Ségou, is the gateway to the Office du Niger irrigation scheme and has an amazing bridge/dam and an interesting market. From the pleasant Fula village of **Massina** you can start a trip along the Niger by public pinasse. A good first stop is **Diafarabé** (CFA1000 to CFA1500). There are places to stay in all three villages.

Every December, in a rite that goes back almost 200 years, Diafarabé is transformed into a hive of activity as hundreds of thousands of cows are driven southwards across the Niger to greener pastures. It's a happy time for the Fula herders, who have been in the fringes of the Sahara for many months. The crossing means reunion with their families and a time to celebrate with music and dance. The exact date of the crossing is not set until November because much depends on the water level.

Other smaller cattle crossings are held throughout December, including in **Sofara**. This is a rarely visited small village 2km west off the Bamako-Gao road just north of the Djenné turn-off and it has two good-looking mosques and a large cattle market on Tuesday. It's cattle crossing is two weeks after the one at Diafarabé.

SAN

San rarely holds tourists longer than the time taken to eat a meal or change buses. However, the town's large **mud mosque** is well worth checking out, especially on Monday when it's surrounded by a large market.

Should you get stranded the ***Campement Municipal*** *(☎ 322115)* behind the gare routière has scruffy, basic singles/doubles for CFA4000/6000, while the tidy rooms at ***Le Relax*** off Route de Bamako, 1km from town, are the accommodation of choice (CFA6000 to CFA9000). ***Restaurant Teriya*** on the dual carriageway through town has the best food.

DJENNÉ

Djenné sits on an island in the Bani River about 130km southwest of Mopti. It is unquestionably one of the most interesting and picturesque towns in West Africa, and one of the oldest. Little has changed since its heyday during the 14th and 15th centuries when it profited, like Timbuktu, from the trans-Saharan trade. But while Timbuktu declined, Djenné remained wealthy.

Most of Djenné's houses and the world-famous mosque are skilfully built with mud bricks and rendered in traditional Sahel style. There's only a little encroachment by modern construction techniques. Djenné's Monday market is incredibly large and lively, so come on this day, if you can, then stay on for a day or two to enjoy the narrow, winding streets and sleepy atmosphere virtually undisturbed.

The Mosque at Djenné

Djenné's elegant mosque is a classic example of Sahel-style (or Sudanese) mud-brick architecture – in fact, it's the largest mud-brick building in the world and a Unesco World Heritage Site. However, the current mosque was constructed in 1907, though it's based on the design of the Grande Mosquée that once stood on the site. The Grande Mosquée was famous throughout the world. It was built in 1280 after Koi Konboro, the 26th king of Djenné, converted to Islam and it remained intact until the early 19th century when the fundamentalist Islamic warrior-king Cheikou Amadou let it fall to ruin.

The wooden spars that jut out from the walls not only form part of the structure, but also support ladders and planks used during the annual repairs to the mud-render. Overseen by specialist masons this work takes place at the end of every rainy season when up to 4000 people volunteer to help.

Inside, a forest of wooden columns supporting the roof takes up almost half of the floor surface. A lattice of small holes in the roof allow beams of light to penetrate between the columns (in the rainy season they're covered with ceramic pots).

Non-Muslim visitors cannot go inside (apparently after a European advertising company filmed scantily clad women here). Excellent views of the mosque are to be had from the roofs of surrounding houses (usually for CFA500) or the Petit Marché. Beside the mosque are the tombs of great Islamic scholars, including one of a former imam of Djenné who died in 1724.

Information

There are no banks in Djenné. You may be able to change euros or dollars at Le Campement or Auberge le Maafir. Phone calls can be made at the post office. There's a CFA1000 fee for tourists entering Djenné.

The hospital is on the western edge of town and Pharmacie Alafia is opposite Restaurant Kita Kouraou.

Djenné's status as a tourist town has brought inevitable downsides. Many of the streets are litter-strewn and as a tourist you will be the focus of attention for would-be guides and begging children.

Things to See & Do

Before touring the town properly it's worth visiting the **Mission Culturelle** (close to the roadblock at Djenné's entrance) which gives an excellent background to Djenné and the surrounding region. The well-informed staff can recommend good guides.

Guides are not essential in Djenné, though hiring a good one will open your eyes to aspects of Djenné you'd otherwise miss. Some guides speak English and fees are negotiable (aim for CFA3000 per person).

Top of the sightseeing list are the **Grande Mosquée** and **Grand Marché**, which covers the wide, open area in front of the mosque every Monday. Thousands of traders and customers come from miles around and it's very much a local's market with little on sale for tourists. The sights, sounds and smells of the market with the awesome mosque as a backdrop, make this a highlight of any visit to Mali. Nearby is the **Petit Marché**, which sells fruit and vegetables daily.

Many of Djenné's mud-brick houses are over a storey high; traditionally, the top part was for the masters, the middle floor for the slaves and the bottom floor for storage and selling. The porches of the houses are lined with wooden columns and the wooden window shutters and doors are painted and decorated with metal objects. Several of the most impressive houses once belonged to **Moroccan traders** and are decorated in a Moorish style.

Jenné-Jeno

About 3km from Djenné are the ruins of Jenné-Jeno, an ancient settlement that dates back to about 300 BC. Implements and jewellery have been discovered that suggest it may have been one of the first places in Africa where iron was used, and this discovery certainly exposed the myth that no organised cities existed in West Africa before trade began and external influences were brought to bear upon it. In the 8th century AD Jenné-Jeno was a fortified town with walls 3m thick, but around 1300 it was abandoned. Today, there is nothing much to see – some mounds and millions of tiny pieces of broken pottery – so a visit is likely to be of interest only to archaeologists.

On a stroll through the dusty streets you will pass a few **madrassas**, schools where young children learn the Quran. There are more madrassas in Djenné than in any other town in Mali. With the help of a guide, you can also see the **old well** and the beautiful **house of the traditional chief**, whose role today is mainly as an adjudicator in local disputes.

On the southern edge of town is **Tapama Dienepo**, the tomb of a young girl sacrificed here in the 9th century after a local religious leader decided the town was corrupt.

Welingare and **Roundessirou** are two interesting Fula villages a few hundred metres north of Djenné and well worth the walk. **Sirung**, a beautiful Bozo village with a stunning mud mosque, is roughly a 20-minute moped ride southwest from Djenné.

Hire of bicycles (CFA3500 per day) and mopeds (CFA6000 per day including fuel) can be arranged at most hotels.

Places to Stay & Eat

Restaurant Kita Kouraou *(☎ 420138)* Mattress on roof CFA1500, rooms CFA2500 per person. The rooms (without windows) in this friendly place are simple and clean. The restaurant offers tasty, traditional Malian and European staples (meals CFA2000). A nice bolt-hole.

Chez Baba Camp sites per person CFA2000, rooms CFA3000. This is a lovely compound, looked over by very basic rooms. It offers appealing, but surprisingly expensive food (meals CFA1200 to CFA2800), and is a good place to meet prospective guides.

Hotel Tapama Mattress on roof CFA2000, rooms with bathroom & fan CFA7000. This is a large hotel built around an internal courtyard, Moroccan style. There's a nice feel to the place, but it's a little expensive.

Le Campement *(☎ 420497)* Mattress on roof CFA2000, singles/doubles with fan CFA8500/10,000, with fan & bathroom

DJENNÉ

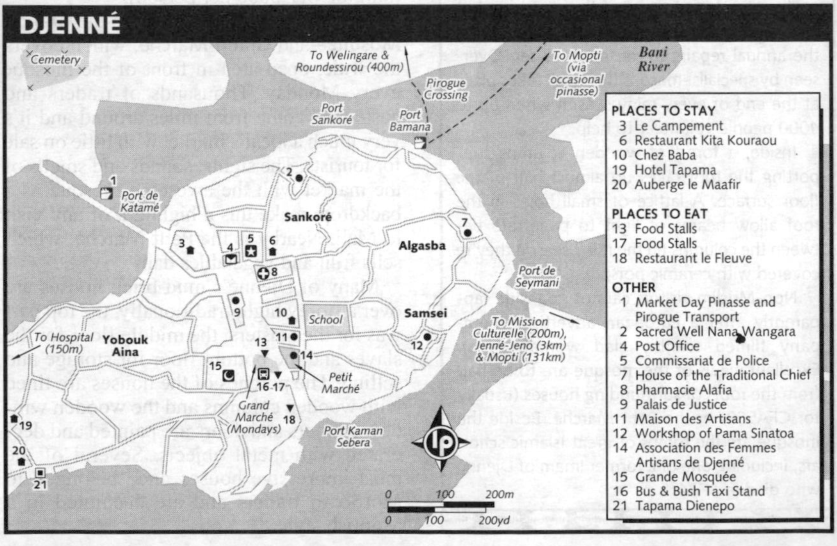
Cemetery
To Welingare & Roundessirou (400m)
To Mopti (via occasional pinasse)
Bani River
Pirogue Crossing
Port Sankoré
Port Bamana
Port de Katamé
Sankoré
Algasba
Port de Seymani
Samsei
School
To Mission Culturelle (200m), Jenné-Jeno (3km) & Mopti (131km)
To Hospital (150m)
Yobouk Aina
Petit Marché
Grand Marché (Mondays)
Port Kaman Sebera
0 100 200m
0 100 200yd
PLACES TO STAY
3 Le Campement
6 Restaurant Kita Kouraou
10 Chez Baba
19 Hotel Tapama
20 Auberge le Maafir
PLACES TO EAT
13 Food Stalls
17 Food Stalls
18 Restaurant le Fleuve
OTHER
1 Market Day Pinasse and Pirogue Transport
2 Sacred Well Nana Wangara
4 Post Office
5 Commissariat de Police
7 House of the Traditional Chief
8 Pharmacie Alafia
9 Palais de Justice
11 Maison des Artisans
12 Workshop of Pama Sinatoa
14 Association des Femmes Artisans de Djenné
15 Grande Mosquée
16 Bus & Bush Taxi Stand
21 Tapama Dienepo

CFA13,000/15,000, with air-con & bathroom CFA15,000/17,5000. The food's pretty good (meals CFA1500 to CFA2000) and the accommodation is clean and tidy, but nothing special.

Auberge le Maafir Rooms with bathroom, fan & breakfast CFA20,000. This is more like it. The well-furnished, clean rooms are set around a courtyard. It's easily the best place to stay.

There are number of ***food stalls*** near the market in the early evening or you could try ***Restaurant le Fleuve*** whose simple Malian dishes (CFA750 to CFA2000) are best ordered in advance.

Shopping

Djenné is famous for bogolan, or mud-cloth (see the special colour section 'Arts & Craftwork' in the Regional Facts for the Visitor chapter). The most famous female artisan is ***Pama Sinatoa*** whose workshop is near the town entrance. There are several other workshops in the same area and numerous ***craft stalls*** in the city centre.

Getting There & Away

Bus & Bush Taxi Very little transport goes into Djenné except on Monday (market day). Most transport will drop you at the junction on the Mopti-Bamako road 30km from Djenné itself. You may have a long wait for a lift into town.

Transport to Djenné is easiest from Mopti's bâché gare – bâchés (CFA1750) and Peugeot taxis (CFA2000) leave from here most mornings and then return in the afternoon. The journey takes about two hours.

Transport from San (CFA2000), Koutiala (CFA4500), Sikasso (CFA6000) and Ségou (CFA4500) arrives Monday morning and leaves in the afternoon. A minibus to Bamako (CFA6000) leaves noon Thursday. Reserve or buy your ticket the night before travel to be sure of a place.

Just before Djenné there's a short ferry crossing.

Boat There's no regular river transport between Djenné and Mopti as nearly everything goes by road. However, when the Bani River is high enough it's possible to reach Djenné by public pinasse (CFA3000) leaving Mopti Sunday.

MOPTI

Like many Malian settlements, Mopti is an agglomeration of quarters made up of several ethnic groups. The town lies at the junction of the Niger and Bani Rivers and is surrounded by water and rice fields. This region is one of the most interesting parts of West Africa. Traditionally the Bozo and Fula peoples met here to trade, but until the 20th century Mopti was largely overshadowed by Djenné and Timbuktu. During the colonial period, commerce along the Niger River increased and Mopti's position between Bamako and Gao gave it a distinct advantage.

Mopti remains dependent on the river and has a large, thriving market, a beautiful mosque and the most vibrant port in Mali. The ancient town of Djenné and Dogon Country are only a day's journey away and Mopti is also a starting point for a trip to Timbuktu. Sévaré and the Bamako-Gao road are linked with Mopti by a 12km-long causeway.

Information

Tourist Office The Bureau Régional du Tourisme (☎ 430506) is 50m north of Hôtel Kanaga.

Money BIM on Blvd de l'Indépendance changes cash, charges CFA3450 to change travellers cheques and is a Western Union agent. Some hotels and tour companies will change cash and travellers cheques.

Post & Communications The post office is on Rue 68, the Sotelma office next door has three cardphones.

Perhaps the most expensive (and unreliable) Internet access in Mali is available at Le Palais Pret à Porter and Cybercafé Mopti (CFA100 per minute).

Visa Extensions These are possible (after a 15-minute wait) at a small office next to the police station (☎ 430020).

Travel Agencies & Tour Operators The following companies can assist with travel reservations, hire 4WDs and run a range of river trips and Dogon treks:

Ashraf Voyages (☎ 430279, fax 430924) Av de l'Indépendance. Ashraf also offers mountain bike hire for CFA6000 per day.

MALI

Bambara Tours (☎/fax 430080, ⓔ bambara@bambara.com) Rue 68. Bambara also has another office at Hôtel Kanaga.

Djoliba Travel (☎ 430781, 430133, fax 430924) Rue 64. Djoliba is good for 4WD hire and pinasse charters up to Timbuktu.

Medical Services The hospital (☎ 430 441) on Av de l'Indépendance offers basic health care, while Pharmacie Officine de La Venise (☎ 430377) beside Marché des Souvenirs, and Pharmacie Officine du Carrefour (☎ 430422) on Av de l'Indépendance have decent medical supplies.

Dangers & Annoyances Mopti is the centre of Mali's tourist industry and your visit can be ruined by local youths continually offering their services as guides, or simply trying to sell you postcards and souvenirs. If you don't need their services, politely tell them you've already got something booked.

If you want a guide to show you around Mopti or organise a boat trip, get some personal recommendations from other travellers. Remember that trips around Dogon Country are best arranged *in* Dogon Country.

Things to See

Mopti's **port** is a lively place, where boats from up and down the river unload their cargoes. You'll see slabs of salt from Timbuktu, dried fish, firewood, pottery, goats, chickens and much more. **Boat building** happens next to Restaurant Bar Bozo.

The classic Sahel-style **Misire Mosquée** or Grand Mosquée, built in 1933, towers over the old part of town. Just before the rains in May or June the lower, mud-covered part of the mosque is re-rendered. The mosque is off limits to non-Muslims, but money (CFA500 to CFA1000) can buy you a good view from a nearby rooftop.

East of the mosque is the old town, where tourists rarely venture. It's an interesting place to wander around and has separate Fula, Bella, Bobo and Mossi quarters.

At the **Marché Souguni** are traders selling fruit, vegetables, salt, fish and meat downstairs and art and crafts upstairs. A **smaller market** sells herbs, spices, traditional medicines and food stuff, and nearby at the corner of Rues 271 and 282 is a small Bobo bar. **Bellaphone music** is sometimes played here and it continues as long as people keep drinking millet beer.

Pin-hole photographers set up cameras on Rue 62 beside Mission Catholique Saint Joseph. Portraits cost CFA1000 to CFA2000.

Cinéma Osenam de Mopti, 20m off Av de l'Indépendance, Mossinkoré, shows trashy movies (CFA250 to CFA300) at 8pm most evenings.

River Trips

Dusk is a good time to take a short boat trip. There are numerous Fula and Bozo villages along the river. **Kotaka** is a Fula village well known for its pottery and the Bozo village of **Kakalodaga** really comes alive at dusk, with women cooking, kids playing and men repairing their nets and building boats. A little further afield is **Konna**, which has a beautiful mosque (but sits on the Bamako-Gao road) and then there's always a river trip to **Djenné**. Sailing to **Lake Debo** takes a day. This enormous lake is an important overwintering place for migratory birds and has several Fula and Bozo villages on its shores.

Lake Debo is visited on any pinasse trip to **Timbuktu**. Many tour companies offer this as a three-day journey, but it's a rush and you'll be travelling constantly while it's light. Four to five days allows time for exploration of settlements and environments en route. Each night you'll sleep on the sandy river banks or in a village.

Before signing up to any river trip, check exactly where you're going, how much time you'll have sightseeing, what's included and what the boat looks like (some pinasses have little more than planks covered in thin foam mats to sit on).

Tour companies charge around CFA15,000 per person for a half-day pinasse hire (with a motor) and around CFA10,000 per person for a smaller pirogue (without a motor).

To charter a larger boat to Timbuktu, you won't get much change out of CFA500,000, and that's before food costs.

Arranging a trip directly through a boat owner may get you cheaper rates, but negotiations can be difficult.

Places to Stay

Good accommodation is scarce in Mopti. Also check listings in the Sévaré section.

Mission Catholique Saint Joseph *(The waterfront)* Dorm beds CFA2000, rooms CFA5000. This is a fantastic location and the clean, quiet and cool rooms are always busy.

MALI

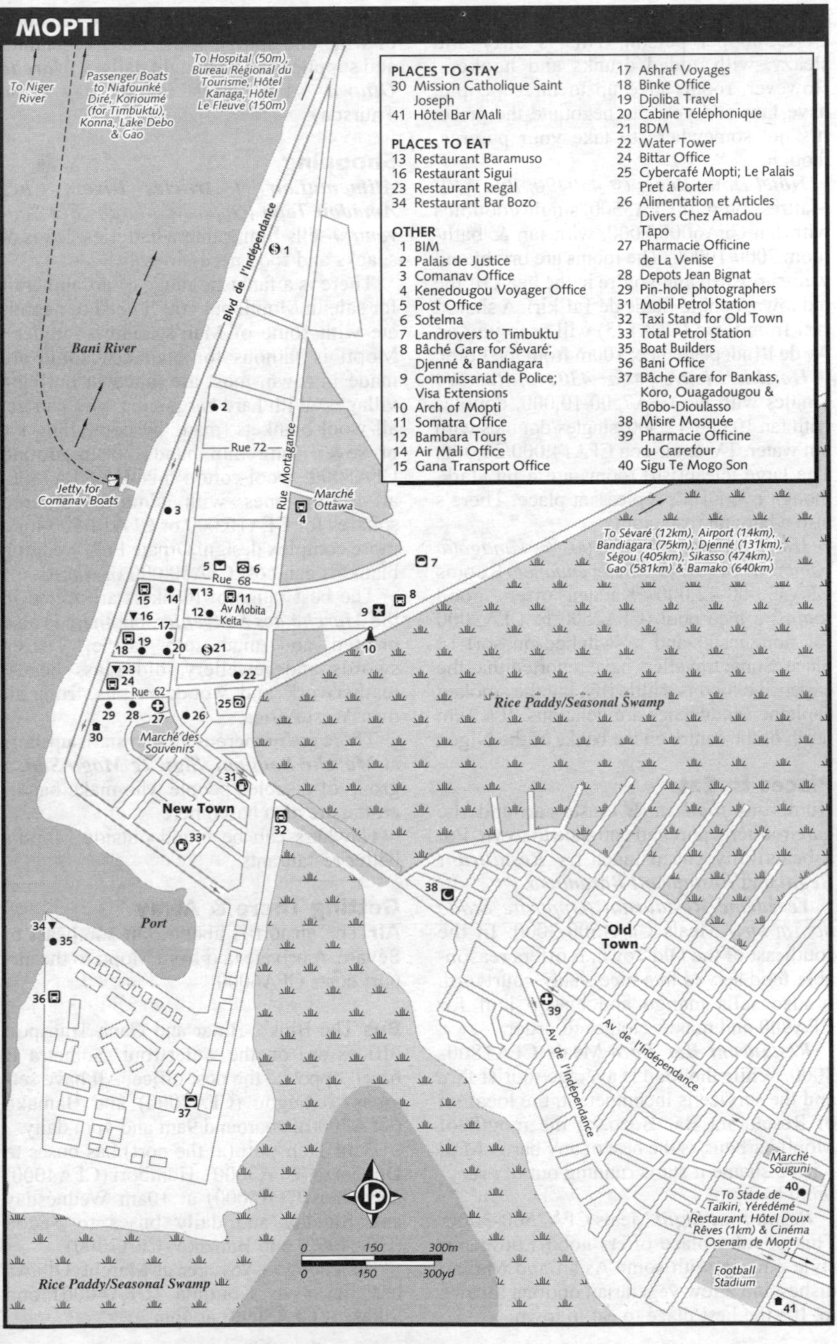
MOPTI
PLACES TO STAY
30 Mission Catholique Saint Joseph
41 Hôtel Bar Mali
PLACES TO EAT
13 Restaurant Baramuso
16 Restaurant Sigui
23 Restaurant Regal
34 Restaurant Bar Bozo
OTHER
1 BIM
2 Palais de Justice
3 Comanav Office
4 Kenedougou Voyager Office
5 Post Office
6 Sotelma
7 Landrovers to Timbuktu
8 Bâché Gare for Sévaré; Djenné & Bandiagara
9 Commissariat de Police; Visa Extensions
10 Arch of Mopti
11 Somatra Office
12 Bambara Tours
14 Air Mali Office
15 Gana Transport Office
17 Ashraf Voyages
18 Binke Office
19 Djoliba Travel
20 Cabine Téléphonique
21 BDM
22 Water Tower
24 Bittar Office
25 Cybercafé Mopti; Le Palais Pret á Porter
26 Alimentation et Articles Divers Chez Amadou Tapo
27 Pharmacie Officine de La Venise
28 Depots Jean Bignat
29 Pin-hole photographers
31 Mobil Petrol Station
32 Taxi Stand for Old Town
33 Total Petrol Station
35 Boat Builders
36 Bani Office
37 Bâche Gare for Bankass, Koro, Ouagadougou & Bobo-Dioulasso
38 Misire Mosquée
39 Pharmacie Officine du Carrefour
40 Sigu Te Mogo Son
To Niger River
Passenger Boats to Niafounké Diré, Korioumé (for Timbuktu), Konna, Lake Debo & Gao
To Hospital (50m), Bureau Régional du Tourisme, Hôtel Kanaga, Hôtel Le Fleuve (150m)
Bani River
Blvd de l'Indépendance
Rue Mortagance
Rue 72
Rue 68
Rue 62
Av Mobita Keita
Jetty for Comanav Boats
Marché Ottawa
Marché des Souvenirs
To Sévaré (12km), Airport (14km), Bandiagara (75km), Djenné (131km), Ségou (405km), Sikasso (474km), Gao (581km) & Bamako (640km)
Rice Paddy/Seasonal Swamp
New Town
Port
Old Town
Av de l'Indépendance
Marché Souguni
To Stade de Taïkiri, Yérédémé Restaurant, Hôtel Doux Rêves (1km) & Cinéma Osenam de Mopti
Football Stadium
0 150 300m
0 150 300yd
Rice Paddy/Seasonal Swamp

Hôtel Bar Mali *(Rue 157, Gungal)* CFA5500 per person. This is dirty and sleazy, with added drunks and hookers. However, rooms take up to three people, have fans and you can negotiate the price. It's not somewhere to take your parents, though.

Hôtel Doux Rêves *(☎ 430490, Rue 540)* Mattress on roof CFA3500, singles/doubles with fan CFA6000/8000, with fan & bathroom 7000/10000. The rooms are bright and well-furnished and you're in the heart of the old town, behind Stade de Taí'kiri. A shared taxi from town (CFA125) will drop you on Av de l'Indépendance, 100m from the hotel.

Hotel le Fleuve *(☎/fax 430246, Rue 86)* Singles with fan CFA7500-10,000, doubles with fan 10,000-12,500, singles/doubles with hot water, TV & air-con CFA14,000/20,000. The large, clean(ish) rooms are a bit stark, though overall it's a pleasant place. There's also a bar and restaurant.

Hôtel Kanaga *(☎ 430500, ⓔ kanaga@bambara.com, Av de l'Indépendance)* Rooms CFA33,000-42,000. Kanaga offers good rooms, a nice pool (CFA2500 to CFA3000 for nonguests) and a switched-on sort of place. Some travellers have reported that the expensive food is a little iffy, but the smoked capitane sandwiches are delicious. It's 1km north of the centre on the banks of the Niger.

Places to Eat

Numerous ***food stalls*** cluster around the gare routière, port and entrance to town. For a beautifully cheap lunch try ***Restaurant Regal*** and ***Restaurant Baramuso***.

Yérédémé Restaurant *(Opposite Stade de Taí'kiri)* Meals CFA1500-3000. In the southeast of the Old Town, it offers reasonable food served in a nice shady courtyard. It also sells mango and bissop jam for CFA900 and makes clothes to order.

Restaurant Bar Bozo Meals CFA1800-3000. While the food is average tourist fare and the service is incompetent, the location of Restaurant Bar Bozo, at the mouth of Mopti harbour, is the best of any bar in Mali – it's a shame it starts running out of *everything* by 8pm.

Restaurant Sigui Meals CFA2500-3000. This popular place offers good European-style cuisine with some Asian and Malian dishes and a few vegetarian options thrown in. It's the best place to eat in town.

Depots Jean Bignat has a good selection of wine and spirits, while fruit, vegetables and supplies can be bought daily at ***Marché Ottawa*** – the busiest market day is on Thursday.

Shopping

Alimentation et Articles Divers Chez Amadou Tapo *(Opposite Marché des Souvenirs)* sells film, camera batteries, loads of snacks and food necessities.

There is a fantastic range of art and craft for sale in Mopti, but you'll need to negotiate with some of Mali's toughest traders. Mopti is famous for blankets, some are made in town, most are made in outlying villages. With hard bargaining, you can get all-wool blankets (made by combining six or seven long thin bands) from around CFA5000, wool-cotton mix for CFA7500, all-cotton ones with simple coloured squares for CFA10,000 or CFA12,500 for a more complex design. Ornate Fula wedding blankets can cost CFA50,000 or more.

The best range of blankets are found in the ***Marché des Souvenirs***, but there is also printed and mud-cloth fabric, Tuareg swords and jewellery, old glass beads, leatherwork and woodcarvings from all over West Africa.

There are numerous artisan stalls upstairs at ***Marché Souguni***. ***Sigu Te Mogo Son***, a group of disabled people who make handicrafts, are also based here.

Hawkers can be found outside Mopti's better restaurants.

Getting There & Away

Air The airport is about 2km southeast of Sévaré. A private taxi from Mopti to the airport costs CFA6000.

Bus The Binke, Bittar and Gana Transport offices are on the waterfront. Somatra is based opposite the post office. All have services to Ségou (CFA4000) and Bamako (CFA7000), at around 9am and 4pm daily.

Bani Transport (at the port) has buses to Douentza (CFA3000), Hombori (CFA4000) and Gao (CFA5000) at 10am Wednesday and Sunday and daily buses to Ségou (CFA4000) and Bamako (CFA7000).

Kenedougou Voyager at Marché Ottawa has buses to Koutiala (CFA4000) and Sikasso (CFA5000) at 4pm.

Buses to Bobo-Dioulasso (CFA6500) in Burkina Faso depart from the port daily when full. Alternatively go to Koro or Koutiala (CFA4000) first and arrange transport from there.

Bush Taxi Bâchés (CFA175) and Peugeot taxis (CFA210) cover the 12km between Mopti and Sévaré between 7am and 8pm daily. They leave from the bâché gare at the town entrance. Transport also leaves here every morning for Djenné (CFA1750 to CFA2000) and Bandiagara (CFA1400).

Bâchés and Peugeot taxis leave the port every morning for Bankass (CFA2500 to CFA 3000) and Koro (CFA3500 to CFA5000), from where there's a bus to Ouagadougou and Bobo-Dioulasso (CFA8000, 12 to 15 hours). Occasionally there is a direct minibus from the Port to Bobo-Dioulasso and Ouagadougou (CFA6500).

To Timbuktu (CFA12,500 to CFA15,000, 12 hours at best), 4WDs leave infrequently from behind the bâché gare. It's more expensive to travel in the rainy season and in the cab with the driver (the most comfortable seats). It's a hard journey.

Boat From Mopti many travellers head for Korioumé (Timbuktu's port) by boat. Comanav (☎ 430006) has an office on the waterfront, though tickets can sometimes be hard to come by as this is the busiest sector on the boat's itinerary.

Getting a ride on a large *pinasse transporteur* (cargo pinasse) is an option for Mopti to Korioumé (CFA10,000), which takes about two days. Bakaye Minedou Traore (☎ 430104) operates a big pinasse to Timbuktu, while the 80m-long *Baba Tigamba* (known as *Petit Baba*) makes the journey on Friday afternoon. It has proper seats and even a small upper deck called the *cabine luxe*!

Smaller pinasses take about three days from Mopti to Korioumé (CFA7500), but with breakdowns and cargo stops they can take up to six.

This local pinasse transport is a great way to explore the Niger Inland Delta, but getting a cheap passage requires some hard bargaining. From Mopti aim for the following prices: north to Diré (CFA5000), Tonka (CFA4000) and Niafounké (CFA3000). South to Kouakourou (CFA2000), Djenné (CFA3500 along River Bani), Diafarabé (CFA2500) and Massina (CFA3500).

SÉVARÉ

This bustling little town is a good staging post for trips to Dogon Country and exploration of the Niger Inland Delta. Mopti is only 12km away and Bandiagara 63km.

Information

BNDA on Route de Mopti charges 2% commission on travellers cheques and cash. There's a Western Union office at the post office also on Route de Mopti.

Tokyo Color at the main crossroads sells slide and print film.

Places to Stay & Eat

Thanks partly to the numerous nongovernmental organisations (NGOs) based there, Sévaré has some reasonable hotels and bars.

Teranga Auberge *(Route de Bamako)* Mattress on roof CFA2500, doubles CFA8000, twins/triples CFA10,000/12,500. The basic rooms (which are a bit tatty) are redeemed by the pleasant garden restaurant/bar and good Senegalese and Moroccan dishes (CFA1000 to CFA4000).

Mac's Refuge *(c/o ☎ 420449, ⓔ melm@maf.org, Rue 124)* Mattress on roof CFA4500, rooms with fan CFA7000, with bathroom CFA8500, singles/doubles with air-con CFA10,500/18,000. Mac's is a good-value little place, with a homely atmosphere and excellent food – the room prices include an excellent breakfast and the three-course evening meal (CFA4800) is well worth staying in for. There's a small pool (CFA1500 for nonguests) and Mac is a fountain of knowledge about the region. Bicycles are available for guests, and there's a book swap, reference library and video. Massage therapy is also available for CFA7500 per hour. Turn left off the Bamako-Gao road near the airport and continue west for 800m.

Hôtel Oasis *(☎ 420498, fax 420415, Off Route de Mopti)* Mattress on roof CFA2500, singles/doubles with fan CFA7500/12,000, with air-con CFA12,000/14,000. This is generally not a bad choice. The rooms in the nearby annexe are cleaner and brighter than those in the main hotel.

Hôtel Byblos *(☎ 430457, Off Route de Bamako)* Singles/doubles with air-con & bathroom CFA14,000/17,000. The rooms here are clean and well decorated and the funky(ish) outside bar/restaurant (meals CFA1500 to CFA2500) is deservedly popular.

Mankan Te *(☎ 420193, ⓔ mankante@gmx.net, East of Route de Bamako)* Singles/doubles with air-con CFA15,500/17,500, with air-con & bathroom CFA19,500/21,500. The rooms in this hotel are spacious and smart and there are relaxing gardens and a roof terrace.

Around the main crossroads and bus offices are loads of ***food stalls***, while behind the cathedral ***Le Soleil du Minuit*** has some excellent simple food. ***Mini Prix*** *(Route de Mopti)* has a good range of supplies.

Things to Buy

Farafina Tigne *(☎ 420449, ⓦ www.farafina-tigne.com, Route de Bamako)* is a great place to buy Malian arts and crafts. Prices are a little more than elsewhere, but the huge selection and lack of sales pressure makes up for it. There's a small bead museum upstairs.

Getting There & Away

Bus Sévaré is on a busy transport route so getting there is usually no problem, but reserving a seat in advance will help you get out. Buses stop at the main crossroads.

Occasional minibuses go to Bandiagara (CFA1750) and Bankass (CFA2500). Bâchés head to and from Mopti (CFA175) between 7am and 8pm.

MALI

AROUND SÉVARÉ

The ruins of **Hamdallaye**, the capital of Cheikou Amadou's 19th-century Fula empire, are found 17km from Sévaré on the Route de Bamako. The site is about 3km across, but the mud walls that once encircled Hamdallaye have eroded down to small banks of earth, and this is all that now remains of the once grand buildings. The high stone wall that once surrounded a mosque now encircles the simple tombs of Cheikou Amadou and his son Alaye Cheikou. A few nomadic Fula set up camp here from time to time, and there are plans to build a large new mosque at this important Fula pilgrimage site.

For details on places to see along the road to Gao, see the boxed text 'The Road from Gao to Mopti' later in this chapter.

The North

TIMBUKTU (TOMBOUCTOU)

Strategically located on the southern edge of the Sahara and at the top of the 'Niger bend', Timbuktu is the terminus of a camel caravan route that has linked West Africa and the Mediterranean since medieval times. Today Timbuktu is a shadow of its former self, a sprawl of low, often shabby, flat-roofed buildings that only hint at former grandeur, while all the time the streets fill up with sand blown in from the desert.

For centuries Timbuktu has been a byword for inaccessibility and mystery, but for some the physical nature of Timbuktu can be a let down. To get the most out of the place, give yourself time to understand the significance of this town – its isolation, its history and its continuing importance as a trading post on the salt-trade route.

Information

Every visitor to Timbuktu must pay a CFA5000 tourist tax, but this does include entry to some of the town's attractions.

The Bureau Régional du Tourisme (☎ 924 035) in the centre of town is open 7.30am to 4pm daily. It has a list of recommended guides and can advise on trips further afield and security.

Fula Earrings

In Djenné, Mopti and other towns along the Niger, you will sometimes see well-to-do Fula women dressed very elaborately, with large bracelets of silver and necklaces of glass beads. Most spectacular, however, are the huge gold earrings called *kwotenai kanye*, worn by the wealthiest women. They are so heavy that the top of each earring is bound with red wool or silk to protect the ear, and sometimes supported with a strap over the top of the woman's head. Earrings are given as wedding gifts from the woman's husband, who will have had to sell off several cows to afford them, but Fula women remain financially independent of their husbands and so gold and jewellery is often passed down from mothers to daughters.

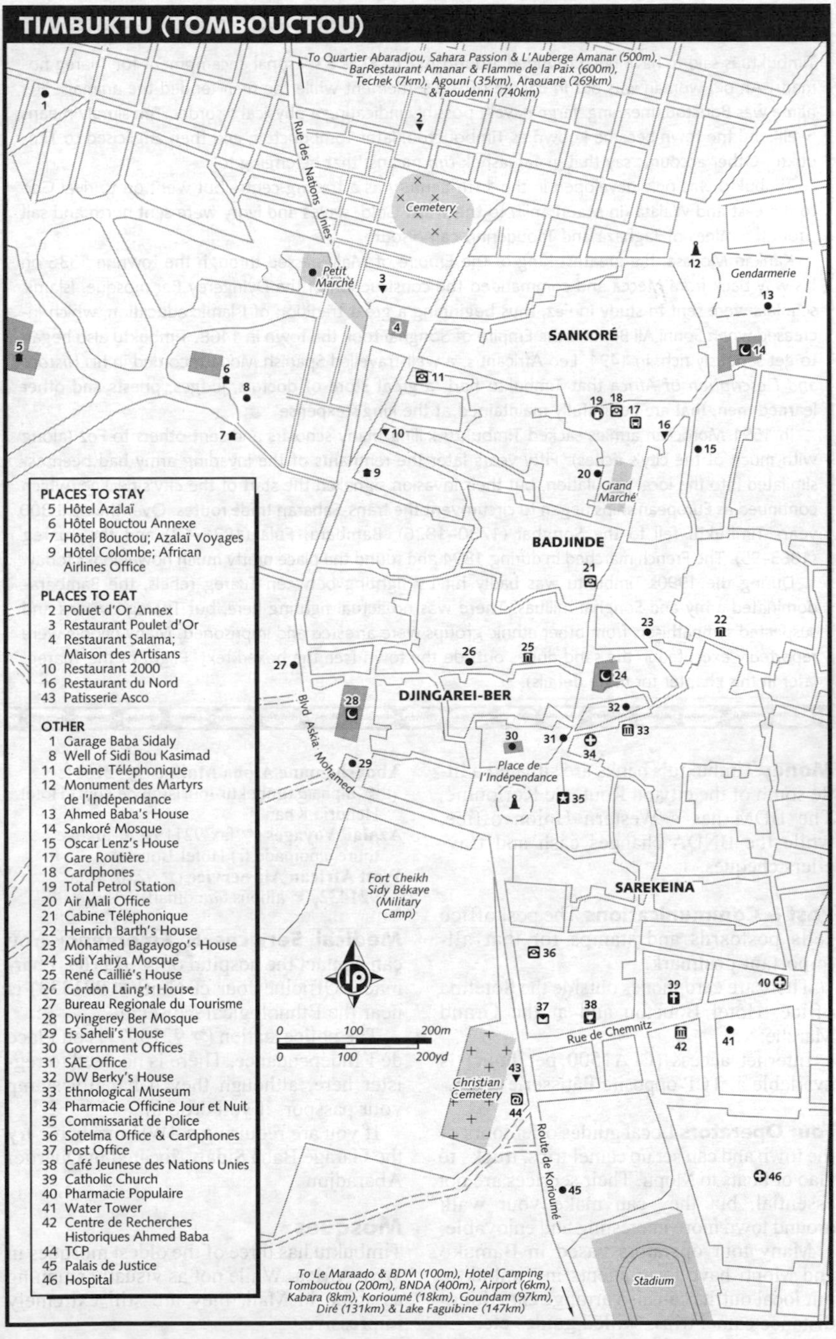
TIMBUKTU (TOMBOUCTOU)
To Quartier Abaradjou, Sahara Passion & L'Auberge Amanar (500m), BarRestaurant Amanar & Flamme de la Paix (600m), Techek (7km), Agouni (35km), Araouane (269km) &Taoudenni (740km)
Rue des Nations Unies
Cemetery
Petit Marché
SANKORÉ
Gendarmerie
Grand Marché
BADJINDE
DJINGAREI-BER
Blvd Askia Mohamed
Place de l'Indépendance
SAREKEINA
Fort Cheikh Sidy Békaye (Military Camp)
Rue de Chemnitz
Christian Cemetery
Route de Korioumé
Stadium
To Le Maraado & BDM (100m), Hotel Camping Tombouctou (200m), BNDA (400m), Airport (6km), Kabara (8km), Korioumé (18km), Goundam (97km), Diré (131km) & Lake Faguibine (147km)
0 100 200m
0 100 200yd
PLACES TO STAY
5 Hôtel Azalaï
6 Hôtel Bouctou Annexe
7 Hôtel Bouctou; Azalaï Voyages
9 Hôtel Colombe; African Airlines Office
PLACES TO EAT
2 Poluet d'Or Annex
3 Restaurant Poulet d'Or
4 Restaurant Salama; Maison des Artisans
10 Restaurant 2000
16 Restaurant du Nord
43 Patisserie Asco
OTHER
1 Garage Baba Sidaly
8 Well of Sidi Bou Kasimad
11 Cabine Téléphonique
12 Monument des Martyrs de l'Indépendance
13 Ahmed Baba's House
14 Sankoré Mosque
15 Oscar Lenz's House
17 Gare Routière
18 Cardphones
19 Total Petrol Station
20 Air Mali Office
21 Cabine Téléphonique
22 Heinrich Barth's House
23 Mohamed Bagayogo's House
24 Sidi Yahiya Mosque
25 René Caillié's House
26 Gordon Laing's House
27 Bureau Regionale du Tourisme
28 Dyingerey Ber Mosque
29 Es Saheli's House
30 Government Offices
31 SAE Office
32 DW Berky's House
33 Ethnological Museum
34 Pharmacie Officine Jour et Nuit
35 Commissariat de Police
36 Sotelma Office & Cardphones
37 Post Office
38 Café Jeunese des Nations Unies
39 Catholic Church
40 Pharmacie Populaire
41 Water Tower
42 Centre de Recherches Historiques Ahmed Baba
44 TCP
45 Palais de Justice
46 Hospital

MALI

Timbuktu – Some Snippets of History

Timbuktu is said to have been founded around AD 1000 as a seasonal encampment for Tuareg nomads. An old woman was put in charge of the settlement while the men tended the animals. Her name was Bouctou, meaning 'large navel', possibly indicating a physical disorder. Tim simply means 'well' and the town became known as Timbouctou, later Tombouctou, and then anglicised to Timbuktu. Other accounts say that in Tamashek *tim* means 'that belonging to'.

Timbuktu was only developed in the 11th century as a trading centre but went on to rival Gao to the east and Walata (in Mauritania) to the west. Gold, slaves and ivory were sent north and salt (from the mines of Taghaza and Taoudenni) came south.

Kankan Moussa, the greatest King of the Empire of Mali, passed through the town in 1336 on his way back from Mecca and commanded the construction of the Dyingerey Ber mosque. Islamic scholars were sent to study in Fez, thus beginning a great tradition of Islamic education, which increased when Sonni Ali Ber and the Empire of Songhaï took the town in 1468. Timbuktu also began to get seriously rich. In 1494, Leo Africanus, a well-travelled Spanish Moor, recorded in his *History and Description of Africa* that Timbuktu had 'a great store of doctors, judges, priests and other learned men, that are bountifully maintained at the king's expense'.

In 1591 Moroccan armies sacked Timbuktu killing many scholars and sent others to Fez (along with much of the city's riches). Fifty years later the remnants of the invading army had been assimilated into the local population, but their invasion signalled the start of the city's decline, which continued as European ships began to circumvent the trans-Saharan trade routes. Over the next 300 years Timbuktu fell to the Songhaï (1780–1826), Bambara, Fula (1826–63) and the Tuareg (1863–95). The French marched in during 1894 and found the place pretty much how it looks today.

During the 1990s Timbuktu was badly hit by fighting between Tuareg rebels, the Bambara-dominated army and Songhaï militias. There was no actual fighting here, but Tuareg civilians and suspected sympathisers from other ethnic groups were arrested and imprisoned. Many people were reportedly executed in the sand dunes outside the town (see the boxed text 'Plight of the Tuareg' later in this chapter for more details).

Money Timbuktu's banks are situated a little south of the city on Route de Korioumé. The BDM has a Western Union office, while the BNDA changes cash and travellers cheques.

Post & Communications The post office sells postcards and stamps for that all-important postmark.

There are cardphones outside the Sotelma office, Hôtel Bouctou and at the Grand Marché.

Internet access (CFA1500 per hour) is available at TCP opposite Pâtisserie Asco.

Tour Operators Local guides offer tours of the town and can set up camel trips, trucks to Gao or boats to Mopti. Their services are not essential, but they can make your walk around town more interesting and enjoyable.

Many tour operators based in Bamako and Mopti have local agents in Timbuktu, but local outfits can also arrange cars, long-distance camel trips, skilled guides etc.

Abderhamane Alpha Maí'ge (☎ 921681, ⓔ alpha@timbuktu-touristguide.com) Hotel Hendria Khan
Azalaí' Voyages (☎/fax 921199, ⓔ alkoye toure@nomade.fr) Hôtel Bouctou
West African Air Service (☎ 921079, fax 921432, ⓔ alhous.t@nomade.fr)

Medical Services & Emergency You can contact the hospital on ☎ 921169. Pharmacie Officine Jour et Nuit (☎ 921333) is near the Ethnological Museum.

The police station (☎ 921007) is on Place de l'Indépendance. There is no need to register here, although they'll happily stamp your passport if you drop in.

If you are requiring a 4WD mechanic try the Garage Baba Sidaly, located in Quartier Abaradjou

Mosques

Timbuktu has three of the oldest mosques in West Africa. While not as visually stunning as some in Mali, they are still extremely impressive.

The oldest, dating from the early 14th century, is **Dyingerey Ber Mosque** *(West of Place de l'Indépendance; admission CFA1000 or part of town entry charge)*. You can go in, but sometimes only with a guide.

Named after one of the city's saints (it's said that 333 saints have lived in Timbuktu) is **Sidi Yahiya Mosque** *(North of Place de l'Indépendance)*. It was constructed in 1400, but you can't go inside.

Built a century later than Sidi Yahiya was the **Sankoré Mosque** *(Northeast of the Grand Marché)*. It also functioned as a university, which by the 16th century was one of the largest schools of Arabic learning in the Muslim world, with some 25,000 students. Alas, nowadays all you can do is observe from the outside.

Museums

The **Ethnological Museum** *(Near Sidi Yahiya Mosque; admission CFA1000 or part of town entry charge; open 8am-5pm daily)* contains not only the well of Bouctou, from where the city's name originates, but also a good variety of exhibits including clothing, musical instruments, jewellery and games. There are also some interesting colonial photographs and pictures of the ancient rock carvings at Tin-Techoun that have since been stolen or destroyed.

An amazing collection of ancient manuscripts and books are kept at the **Centre de Recherches Historiques Ahmed Baba** *(Cedrhab; ☎ 921081, ⓔ cedrhab@tombouctou.org.ml, Rue de Chemnitz; admission CFA1000; open daily)*. Islamic religious, historical and scientific texts from all over the world are kept here with documented family histories (often over 400 years old) of Timbuktu's most famous clans. The oldest manuscript is a copy of Islamic law dating back from 1204.

Timbuktu has a few other **private libraries** containing ancient manuscripts and books.

Explorers' Houses

Between 1588 and 1853 at least 43 Europeans tried to reach this fabled city; only four made it.

The house where **Gordon Laing** *(West of Sidi Yahiya Mosque)* stayed is very small. He was the first European to reach Timbuktu, but was then murdered heading north across the Sahara. You can't go inside.

Lightning Tours of Timbuktu

The Comanav passenger boat stops from four to 12 hours at Korioumé, so if you're travelling between Gao and Mopti, it's possible to make a mad dash to Timbuktu, 18km north. The going rate for a round-trip tour in a chartered taxi is around CFA20,000 – there's no time to take a shared one.

René Caillié spent a year learning Arabic and studying Islam before setting off for Timbuktu disguised as a Muslim. The house *(West of Sidi Yahiya Mosque)* where he stayed in 1828 is in a tumbledown condition and you cannot enter. Caillié's research paid off and he was the first European to reach Timbuktu and live to tell the tale.

Heinrich Barth's incredible five-year journey began in Tripoli and took him first to Agadez, then through Nigeria and finally, in September 1853, he reached Timbuktu disguised as a Tuareg. He stayed for the best part of a year before narrowly escaping with his life and eventually returning to Europe. The house *(East of Sidi Yahiya Mosque; admission CFA1000; open 8am-6pm daily)* where he stayed is now a tiny museum containing reproductions of Barth's drawings and extracts of his writings.

All that remains of **Oscar Lenz's** house is a pile of mud bricks. A plaque on a nearby building identifies the spot where he stayed in July 1880 after travelling down from Morocco.

The house of **DW Berky** – leader of the first American Trans-Saharan Expedition of 1912 – is opposite the Ethnological Museum.

Markets

The **Grand Marché** is the large covered building in the centre of town. It's not particularly grand, but is very busy and not a bad place to buy salt. The **Petit Marché** is further west by the old port (see Waterways & Desert Wells following), while the **Maison des Artisans** (where local artisans produce and sell their wares) is close by at the end of Blvd Askia Mohamed.

Waterways & Desert Wells

Thirty years ago an offshoot of the **Niger River** ran past Hôtel Bouctou and there was a small port where the Petit Marché now stands. The channel needed constant dredging and in the early 1980s it was finally overwhelmed by the desert.

Also near the hotel is the sacred, funnel-shaped **well of Sidi Bou Kasimad**. It's about 50m across at the top (a conventional one would collapse in this soil) and its discovery is said to have saved the town from drought. However, with the advent of piped water it has fallen into disrepair.

Camel Rides & 4WD Tours

Visitors will receive numerous offers of camel trips into the surrounding desert during a stay in Timbuktu. Basically speaking these can be divided into short afternoon trips to nearby dunes/Tuareg encampments (CFA6000 to CFA7000 per person), overnight trips that involve dunes at sunset and a night under the stars, often at a Tuareg encampment (CFA15,000 to CFA20,000 per person including a traditional meal) and one-day or extended, unsupported treks (CFA20,000 per person per day). No prices are cast in stone and opening prices can be 10 times higher than these!

For extended trips there are a number of interesting options. **Techek** (7km away) and **Agouni** (35km away) are both popular destinations (salt caravans muster at Agouni before entering Timbuktu), while more far-flung destinations include **Lake Faguibine** (see Around Timbuktu later in this chapter), **Araouane** or even **Taoudenni**.

Options for 4WD excursions are endless and you're looking at CFA70,000 to CFA100,000 per vehicle per day including guide, driver and food. Straightforward 4WD hire is CFA50,000 to CFA70,000. Obviously a vehicle gives you great range (in two days you'll reach Taoudenni), but this is only useful if your guide knows the desert well.

On any trip you'll be given strong sweet Arab tea, and undoubtedly offered knives, jewellery or leatherwork to buy, but watch out for sharks. Some travellers have been trapped in tents and submitted to hours of hard-sell. Others have reported being taken for just a 30-minute ride, not even reaching the dunes, while still others have been left waiting in the desert for hours or had week-long trips cut short. To prevent this happening to you make it clear from the start what you want, pay for the trip on your return and, ideally, go with a guide who's been recommended by other travellers.

If you're short of cash for a trip, it's easy to walk northwest past the Flamme de la Paix monument out into the dunes. This monument was built on the spot where 3000 weapons were ceremonially burnt at the end of the Tuareg rebellion (see the boxed text 'Plight of the Tuareg' later in this chapter).

The Toughest of Treks

It's still possible to join one of the salt caravans travelling between Timbuktu and Taoudenni. The return trip takes between 36 and 40 days. These are commercial operations and trips are very tough and not to be taken lightly – there's no escape if you find you can't hack it or get sick. Expect to spend at least 14 hours a day on the move with no rest days.

Making the trip with a guide and your own camels gives you a few more options and you'll be able to negotiate rest days before departure.

Either option costs about CFA600,000. This gets you a guide, food and three camels. You'll be living on dates, peanuts, dried goat meat and rice; most meals are taken on the move.

November and December are the ideal months to travel – the desert is not too hot and the harmattan has not begun. Sand storms are a problem in January and February.

Places to Stay

Accommodation doesn't come cheap in Timbuktu; try ***Restaurant Poulet d'Or Annexe*** and ***Pâtisserie Asco*** for really cheap rooms.

Hotel Camping Tombouctou *(☎ 924032, Route de Korioumé)* Camp sites per person CFA2500, dorm beds CFA3500, singles/doubles CFA6500/9000. The simple rooms (with mosquito nets) of this good cheap option are kept cool by thick walls and fans, and there's a nice communal area.

Hôtel Bouctou *(☎ 921012)* Dorm beds/mattress on roof CFA6500, rooms with fan CFA9500-19,000, singles/doubles with air-con & bathroom CFA18,000/21,500. This hotel is not stunning value and is showing its age in places, although it's clean and generally OK. The main restaurant/bar area is a popular guide/hawker hang-out, while the annexe offers the nicest accommodation. Be

MALI

sure to clarify prices. The overpriced restaurant is geared towards tour groups and is not blessed with a talented chef.

Sahara Passion *(☎ 921394, ⓔ spassion@malinet.ml, Near Flamme de la Paix)* Mattress on roof CFA5000, rooms with fan CFA10,000-17,000. The simplest rooms here verge on stark, but it's a quiet, friendly and relaxed place and close to Amanar Restaurant, which is reason enough to consider it. There is secure parking.

L'Auberge Amanar *(☎/fax 921285, ⓔ amanar@dromadaire.com, Near Flamme de la Paix)* Mattress on roof CFA7500, singles/doubles with fan CFA12,500/15,000, with air-con CFA18,000/22,000. This little hotel is of the same high standard as the restaurant just down the road. Rooms may not have any windows, but they are cool and nicely furnished. The roof terrace is a pleasant place to sit, although a ridiculously expensive place to sleep. There is secure parking.

Hôtel Azalaï *(☎/fax 921163)* Singles/doubles CFA26,100/32,000. Though the place is a little old and soulless (blame the 1970s), the rooms, all with air-con and bathroom (including hot water), are clean and decent and the restaurant's OK (mains CFA2500, three-course menu CFA5000). Probably the best place to stay, but don't get your hopes up. There is secure parking.

Places to Eat

Rotisseries are found all over town.

Restaurant du Nord *(Near the Grand Marché)* Meals CFA1000-1750. This place is not bad for omelettes, bread and coffee, but not much else.

Restaurant 2000 *(Near Hôtel Colombe)* Meals CFA1000-2000. This is grubby, yet popular, and has perhaps the best cheap eats (rice and sauce dishes) in town.

Restaurant Salama *(Maison des Artisans)* Meals CFA1000-2000. For simple things, service at the Salama is speedy; more elaborate dishes are best ordered in advance – good local specialities include *fakohoye toukassou* (steam cooked bread with a meat sauce) and *kaata* (a traditional Songhaï pasta).

Patisserie Asco *(☎ 921168, Route de Koriomé)* Meals CFA1000-2000. This is a popular restaurant serving a variety of European and local dishes, but the pastries are disappointing. The friendly manager sometimes offers a couple of basic rooms (CFA2500).

Restaurant Poulet d'Or, *(☎ 921913, Near the Petit Marché)* Meals CFA1000-2500. At this restaurant, expect the usual chicken and chips, brochettes, rice, meat and sauce, but look out for some more adventurous dishes (like roast goat), which might need ordering in advance. The ***Poulet d'Or Annex*** also serves good food and has a few cheap rooms (CFA2500 per person).

Le Maraado *(Route de Koriomé)* Meals CFA1500. This is a bar that hosts the occasional evening soirée. Food is available with advance notice.

Bar Restaurant Amanar *(☎ 921285, Opposite Flame de la Paix)* Meals CFA1500-3600. Timbuktu's top restaurant is well situated on the edge of town, close to where salt caravans arrive. It serves delicious food (European in style) and excellent service. There's also a nice little bar with a dance floor that gets lively some evenings.

Getting There & Away

Getting out of Timbuktu is often harder and more expensive than getting in. Start planning and negotiating your departure early.

Air The flash new airport (☎ 921320) is 6km (CFA3000 by 'taxi') from Timbuktu. Air Mali (☎ 921091), African Airlines (☎ 921 079) and SAE (☎ 921121) all fly to Bamako via Mopti.

Land In the dry season, battered Land Rovers run from Mopti to Timbuktu (CFA12,500 to CFA15,000) a few times per week. The road is bad; waterlogged and muddy after the rains, sandy and dusty in the dry. It's a very uncomfortable journey, often with a night under the stars, and many tourists either pay extra for the front seat or group together and hire a 4WD themselves (aim for CFA125,000). The journey should take around 12 hours but can take 24 after breakdowns, river crossings and other hold-ups (no pun intended). Trucks sometimes run this route, but take even longer.

The most-used route from Mopti goes via Douentza to Bambara-Maounde then to another ferry directly south of Timbuktu (CFA4000 per vehicle). In the dry season some vehicles head north off the Bamako-Gao road at Konna heading for Niafounké then northeast via Goundam to Timbuktu, which involves two river crossings.

The route via Gourma-Rharous and Gossi has fallen out of favour because of security problems.

In the dry season there are truck-buses from Bamako to Timbuktu (CFA15,000, 24 hours, but can take two days), with Gana Transport and Alfarouk Transport. Buses leave Bamako Place G and Medina Coura, respectively, while they depart from Timbuktu on Sunday and Monday. The journey goes via Ségou, Nampala and Niafounké.

If you're heading east, trucks also run a couple of times each week between Timbuktu and Gao (CFA10,000 to CFA15,000) along the north side of the river. Sometimes 4WDs make the trip, but vehicles have been hijacked along this route. Ask around at the Grand Marché and steel yourself for a tough two-day trip.

There's some transport to and from Diré on Tuesday (CFA3000 to CFA4000) and the occasional bâché travelling to Goundam (CFA3000) and Niafounké (CFA6000) at the weekend.

Touring the hotels looking for other tourists with a vehicle/who want to share a vehicle, is a good ploy.

Boat Between late July and late November, the large Comanav passenger boats stop at Korioumé, Timbuktu's port. Alternatively, you can reach Timbuktu by pinasse, see Getting There & Away under Mopti earlier in this chapter.

If you want to leave Timbuktu on the Comanav boat, the ticket office is in Kabala (the old port). Azalaï Voyages can reserve a ticket for a small fee. If you're waiting for the boat, Korioumé has some ***food stalls*** and ***basic eateries***. ***Rooms*** can be found for the desperate.

Pinasses go to Diré (about CFA2500) a few times a week, especially Monday and return Tuesday afternoon (after the market); other pinasses go on to Mopti (around CFA4000).

There's very little transport to/from Gao, although an occasional pinasse goes to Gourma-Rharous where you might find another pinasse going to Gao or (more likely) a place in a truck.

You can charter a pinasse to Mopti or Gao (boats loaded with tourists regularly come from these destinations). This can be arranged in advance or you can take pot luck in Timbuktu and hope to pick one up that's returning empty to its home port. For an idea of prices, see the Mopti section – and beware of guides charging you for a chartered pinasse and then putting you on a public one carrying cargo and dozens of other passengers.

Getting Around

A private taxi/bâché to Kabara costs CFA5000/250 and to Korioumé, CFA6000/500, but you may be charged five times as much. There are no taxis as such, just guys with underused vehicles.

AROUND TIMBUKTU

Diré

Diré, southwest of Timbuktu, is a good place to change boats/pick up some road transport and stock up with supplies (market day is Tuesday).

Campement Diré *(☎ 931043)* Mattress on roof & camping CFA3500, doubles with bathroom & breakfast CFA10,000. This is a pretty respectable hotel for the middle of nowhere.

Road transport leaves from near the market to Goundam (CFA1500), Niafounké (CFA3500), Nampala (CFA8000) and Bamako (CFA10,000 to CFA11,000).

Pinasses to Timbuktu/Mopti will set you back CFA2500/5000.

Niafunké

Another good place to break your journey is Niafounké. Ali Farka Touré owns the only ***hotel*** in town. It has pretty respectable rooms for CFA6500 and is close to the market (market day is Thursday).

Trucks leave each week to Diré (CFA3500), Timbuktu (CFA6000) and elsewhere. You'll find plenty of river transport heading to Timbuktu (CFA3000) and to Mopti (CFA3000)

Lake Faguibine

When the Empire of Ghana was at its height this lake (about 50km north of Goundam) was one of the most impressive in West Africa. However, it's been dry since the end of the 1980s. The cliffs on the northern shore and landscape are very impressive – cave paintings are found at Farach.

MALI

The Timbuktu Salt Trade

Throughout the cool season, from October to March, a camel caravan from the salt mines at Taoudenni (about 740km north of Timbuktu) arrives in Timbuktu every few days.

Each caravan consists of 60 to 300 camels, and every camel carries four to six slabs of salt weighing about 60kg. The journey takes about 16 days, and because of the intense heat the caravans often travel at night, with camels unloaded and rested during the day. On arrival in Timbuktu the salt is sold to merchants who transport it up-river to Mopti, where it is sold again and dispersed all over West Africa. Salt is a valuable commodity that used to be traded weight for weight with gold. Nowadays, a good-quality slab will fetch up to CFA5000 in Timbuktu, with its value increasing as it heads south.

The salt comes from the beds of ancient lakes, which dried out many millennia ago. The salt starts about 1m below the surface and is reached by a system of trenches and tunnels up to 6m deep and up to 200m long. The salt is dug out in large blocks and split into slabs on the surface.

Work in the mines is appallingly paid and dangerous; each man earns about CFA30,000 for six months work, and is allowed to keep one in every four bars mined. But they don't bring many back to Timbuktu where they can be sold: The nearest oasis to the mines is a three-day camel journey away, and the masters provide water to their workers in exchange for salt. One guerba of water (about 30L) costs two slabs.

The salt caravans unload on the northern side of Timbuktu, where the Bella live in temporary camps, but the Tuareg and Arab traders do not welcome visitors. If you really want to see more, go with a reputable guide who knows the traders.

ARAOUANE

The sand-drowned oasis village of Araouane is over 250km north of Timbuktu. It was once a place of great learning; clan histories and Islamic texts dating back centuries are still kept by local families. It's still a major staging post on the camel caravan route from the salt mines of **Taoudenni**. Some local people started a project called Arbres pour Araouane (Trees for Araouane; ☎/fax 921253). Unfortunately, much of their good work was destroyed during the Tuareg rebellion.

Araouane is about nine days from Timbuktu by camel or 12 hours by 4WD. There are two routes to Araouane. The eastern route takes in an ancient mosque now almost completely buried (only the minaret now protrudes from the sand). Further along the route rock paintings can be seen on a desolate outcrop.

GAO

For a city on the edge of one of the world's most inhospitable and sparsely populated regions, Gao's a fairly busy place, though at times it feels like a collection of Songhaï and Tuareg encampments that have absent-mindedly grown together (temporary camps are found across the city).

Over recent years Gao has seen few visitors, firstly because of continued security problems on the Tanezrouft trans-Saharan route and then because of the Tuareg rebellion. It also has the shortest tourist season in Mali, November and March. This is when Point Afrique's weekly charter flights from France start arriving (see the Getting There & Away chapter for further information).

This lack of visitors is a shame because the city and surrounding region has plenty to offer the traveller and although the mixture of cultures, aspects of history and network of sandy streets is similar to Timbuktu, somehow Gao has a completely different atmosphere. Perhaps this has something to do with the vibrant port and market, which can be as lively as any in Mali.

Gao lies on the north bank of the Niger, while the long tarmac road from Bamako terminates on the southern side; a ferry makes the crossing.

History

Gao was probably established in AD 650 and by the beginning of 1000, before Timbuktu had even been created, Gao was a well-established city-state and gateway to the eastern trans-Saharan trade routes. Gao became the capital of the Empire of Songhaï around 1020 shortly after Dia Kossi, the then ruler, converted to Islam. Over the next 300 years, Gao became rich and powerful, and although it eventually fell to the mighty Mali empire in 1324, its people were subjugated for less than 20 years (though accounts vary).

One of the greatest leaders of the Songhaï was Sunni Ali Ber, a ruthless military tactician most content when waging war to expand the empire, which soon included Djenné and Timbuktu. Alas his son wasn't a patch on his father and was overthrown by Askia Muhammad Touré. Askia was a devout Muslim and immediately set about restoring the prestige of Gao's Islamic institutions (he now lies in the Tomb of Askia in the north of the city). Then, 53 years after his death, Gao was smashed and looted by invading Moroccan armies and it never regained its former glory.

Information

Both the BDM (an agent of Western Union) and BNDA banks will change cash and travellers cheques.

Guides are really surplus to requirement for the city, but handy for the desert, obviously. Members of the Association Askia Guide (☎ 820130) usually hang out around Hótel Atlantide and charge CFA6000 per day.

Sahara Passion (☎/fax 820187, ⓔ spassion@bluewin.ch) is your best bet for 4WD hire (CFA70,000 per day) and brief, slightly lame trips into the desert. The best place for Toyota spares is SMF (☎/fax 820199), off Av des Askia. It can help with other marques.

Gao's new hospital (☎ 820254) is on Route de l'Aéroport. In the centre of town are Pharmacie Attibey (☎ 820441) on Rue Aldousseini O Touré and Pharmacie Populaire du Mali (☎ 820402) on Av des Askia.

Things to See & Do

The **Grand Marché** and **port** are interesting and well worth checking out on Sunday (market day).

Musée du Sahel *(Rue 224, Sosso-Kiora; admission CFA1000; open 7.30am-noon & 3pm-6pm Tues-Sun)* is a wonderful museum that tells the story of the Songhaï and Tuareg people, and the prehistoric sites in the surrounding region.

Tomb of the Askia *(admission CFA1000; open Sat-Thur)* was built in 1495 by Askia Muhammad Touré whose remains lie within. It's an amazing building and it's possible to climb the 10m-high tomb for good views of the city and river.

You can rent a pirogue around dusk and watch the dunes turn orange as you drift along, or go further upstream to **La Dune Rose** and the large sand dunes at Quema and Hondo – a three-hour trip that costs around CFA3000 per person or CFA10,000 for the boat.

River-trip prices are somewhat inflated, but hippo and manatee spotting is possible (CFA75,000 per day) or you can hire a

MALI

Plight of the Tuareg

During the extended droughts of 1972–74 and 1984–85 the Tuareg lost huge numbers of livestock. Many felt that the Malian government had ignored their hardship and that government officials had embezzled aid money. Calls began for an independent Tuareg state.

In 1990 a group of Tuareg separatists attacked government offices in the Gao region, and the heavy-handed retaliation by Malian soldiers led to a widespread Tuareg uprising. Peace initiatives were quickly made and President Alpha Konaré allowed more Tuareg representation in the army, civil service and government in 1992 as part of his National Pact. However, in 1994 there was large Tuareg assault on Gao, which in turn led to bloody reprisals by the Malian army and the creation of the Ghanda Koi, a Songhaï militia. By the middle of the year, Mali was in a state of virtual civil war. Hundreds of people were killed and bandits exploited this unrest to cause further chaos in the north.

Things calmed in 1995, after moderate representatives from the Songhaï and Tuareg communities came together to push towards a lasting peace. This culminated in the ceremonial burning of 3000 weapons in Timbuktu on 27 March 1996. The Flamme de la Paix (Flame of Peace) monument now stands on the site of the pyre, a memorial to those who died in the conflict.

Huge amounts of aid money has since been pumped into the region and Tuareg refugees have returned from Mauritania, Algeria and Libya (who had armed and trained many of the insurgents). However, for many the traditional nomadic lifestyle, pivotal to the Tuareg's cultural identity, is now a thing of the past.

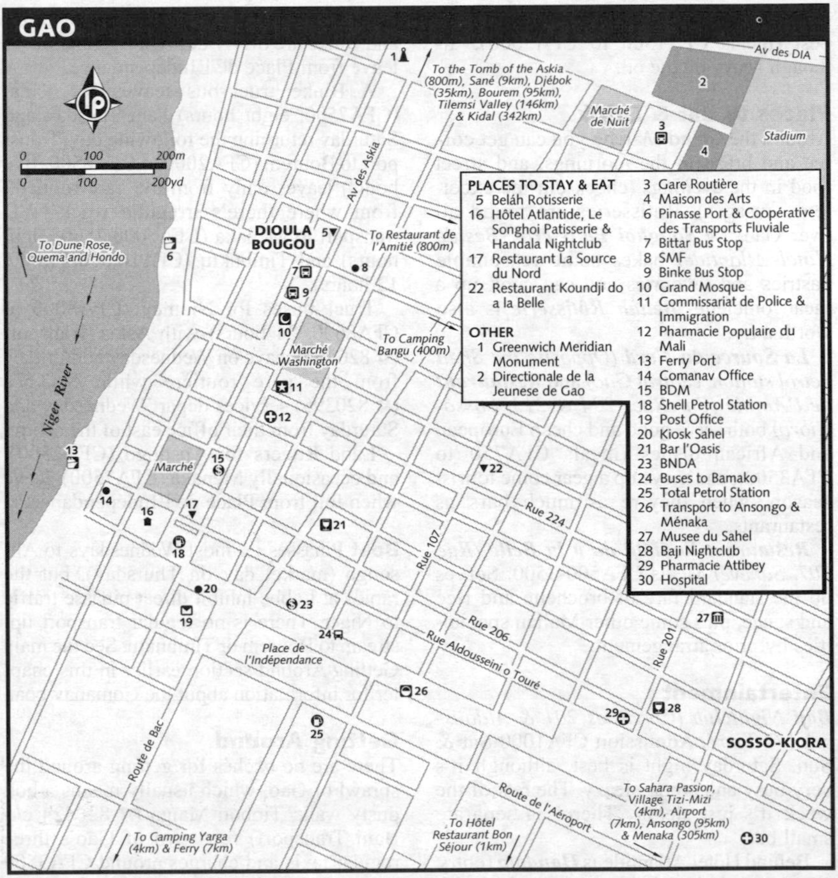
GAO
Av des DIA
To the Tomb of the Askia (800m), Sané (9km), Djébok (35km), Bourem (95km), Tilemsi Valley (146km) & Kidal (342km)
Marché de Nuit
Stadium
0 100 200m
0 100 200yd
Av des Askia
DIOULA BOUGOU
To Restaurant de l'Amitié (800m)
To Dune Rose, Quema and Hondo
To Camping Bangu (400m)
Marché Washington
Niger River
Marché
Rue 224
Rue 107
Rue 206
Rue 201
Rue Aldousseini o Touré
Place de l'Indépendance
Route de Bac
Route de l'Aéroport
SOSSO-KIORA
To Sahara Passion, Village Tizi-Mizi (4km), Airport (7km), Ansongo (95km) & Menaka (305km)
To Hôtel Restaurant Bon Séjour (1km)
To Camping Yarga (4km) & Ferry (7km)
PLACES TO STAY & EAT
5 Beláh Rotisserie
16 Hôtel Atlantide, Le Songhoi Patisserie & Handala Nightclub
17 Restaurant La Source du Nord
22 Restaurant Koundji do a la Belle
OTHER
1 Greenwich Meridian Monument
2 Directionale de la Jeunese de Gao
3 Gare Routière
4 Maison des Arts
6 Pinasse Port & Coopérative des Transports Fluviale
7 Bittar Bus Stop
8 SMF
9 Binke Bus Stop
10 Grand Mosque
11 Commissariat de Police & Immigration
12 Pharmacie Populaire du Mali
13 Ferry Port
14 Comanav Office
15 BDM
18 Shell Petrol Station
19 Post Office
20 Kiosk Sahel
21 Bar l'Oasis
23 BNDA
24 Buses to Bamako
25 Total Petrol Station
26 Transport to Ansongo & Ménaka
27 Musee du Sahel
28 Baji Nightclub
29 Pharmacie Attibey
30 Hospital

pirogue (CFA50,000 per day) and potter around on the river.

Places to Stay

Advanced booking of accommodation (which is mostly far from central Gao) is a good idea between November and February.

Camping Bangu *(Cnr Rues 227 & Tiemoko Fadiala Sangare [TFS], Sosso-Kiora)*, ***Camping Yarga*** *(Off Route de Bac, 4km south of central Gao)* and ***Village Tizi-Mizi*** *(☎ 820440, 4km along Route de l'Aéroport)* offer basic camping and simple dorm accommodation for CFA2000 to CFA5000. Village Tizi-Mizi is easily the most together place with decent rooms and a good bar. Camping Yarga has a low-key, laid-back atmosphere.

Hôtel Restaurant Bon Séjour *(☎ 820338, Opposite the water tower)* Mattress on roof CFA1500, rooms CFA7500-15,000. This is not exactly four-star (well, not even close), but not bad and one of the closest places to the centre. The food (meals CFA1500 to CFA2250) is pretty good and it sells beer.

Hôtel Atlantide *(☎ 820130)* Rooms CFA10,000-17,500. This is an old, colonial place with a past more glorious than its present, but the rooms are clean and tidy and those with fans are pretty good value. It's not a bad place for a beer.

Sahara Passion *(☎/fax 820187, ⓔ spassion@bluewin.ch, Off Rue 381)* Rooms with fan CFA13,500-16,000, with air CFA15,500-23,000. The Sahara is done, but overpriced. However, the

is pleasant and the restaurant is one of Gao's best (meals CFA1500 to CFA3000), although heavy on the oil.

Places to Eat & Drink

Around the **Grand Marché** you can get coffee and bread in the mornings, and street food in the evenings (check out the excellent sausages). Rotisseries are found all over Gao. ***Le Songhoi Pâtisserie*** *(Beside Hôtel Atlantide)* bakes some reasonable pastries and savouries and can cook up a mean omelette. ***Bellàh Rôtisserie*** is also worth a try.

La Source du Nord *(Opposite the Shell petrol station, central Gao)* and ***Restaurant de l'Amitié*** *(Cnr Rues 234 & 213, Sosso-Kiora)* both serve good and cheap European and African dishes (meals CFA750 to CFA3500), and move up a gear come tourist season, when they're as much bars as restaurants.

Restaurant Koundji do a la Belle *(Rue 107, Saneye)* Meals CFA500-3500. Serves up the standard fare of brochette and rice and sauce, plus some other Malian specialities by prior arrangement.

Entertainment

Baji Nightclub *(Cnr Rues 201 & Aldousseini O Touré)* Admission CFA1000 Sat & Sun. Saturday night is best, although it's very busy and pretty sleazy. The rest of the week it's just sleazy. There's a separate small bar.

Behind Hôtel Atlantide is ***Handala*** (entry CFA1500), which is more popular with Gao's younger, less whore-hungry crowd.

Bar l'Oasis is just one of a few spit-and-sawdust drinking dives.

For music, performances and spectaculars, or just to watch musicians practise, head to the ***Maison des Arts*** and ***Directionale de la Jeunesse de Gao*** close to the gare routière. The ***marché de nuit*** also stages the occasional event.

Getting There & Away

Air Only Point Afrique and aircraft chartered by NGOs arrive at Gao's airport.

Bus Departures to Bamako (CFA10,000 to CFA11,000, 16 to 20 hours) via Sévaré (CFA5500, eight hours) and Ségou (CFA8000 to CFA9000, 12 hours) leave around 5am and 3pm. The offices of Bittar and Binke are off Av des Askia. Other buses leave from Place de l'Indépendance.

A Binke truck-bus leaves for Kidal (CFA7500, eight hours) 8am Tuesday and Saturday returning the following day. Transport to Bourem (CFA2000 to CFA2500, five hours) leaves daily from the gare routière, from where there's irregular truck/4WD transport to Ménaka (CFA5000/7500, eight hours) and Timbuktu (CFA10,000/15,000, 12 hours).

Truck-buses for Niamey (CFA8000 to CFA8600, 24 hours) with Askia Transport (☎ 820464) leave on Wednesday and Friday, from the gare routière while SNTN's (☎ 820395) services depart Wednesday and Saturday from their office east of the centre.

Land Rovers for Ansongo (CFA2500), and occasionally Ménaka (CFA7500), leave when full from Place de l'Indépendance.

Boat Pinasses go most Wednesdays to Ansongo (market day on Thursday), but the rapids at Labbe inhibit direct pinasse traffic to Niger. There is no regular transport upstream to Bourem or Timbuktu. See the main Getting Around section earlier in this chapter for information about the Comanav boat.

Getting Around

There are no bâchés for getting around the sprawl of Gao, which usually means a hot, dusty walk. Tiobou Maïga (☎ 820424 c/o Bani Transport) runs two of Gao's three regular taxis and charges around CFA3500 per hour (you'll need to negotiate for single trips).

AROUND GAO

To explore the region you'll need a 4WD, but be aware that many 4WDs have been hijacked in the region. Point Afrique runs tours in the area.

There's a huge cattle market at **Djébok** on Monday (transport from Gao CFA750) and the archaeological remains of ancient Gao lie at **Sané** (though there's not much to see). The **Tîlemsi Valley** is said to be beautiful and **Neolithic rock paintings and carvings** can be seen in the **Adrar des Ifôghas** region around **Kidal** (where the landscape is stunning). **Stone tablets** inscribed with historic and Quranic texts have been found near **Ménaka**, which is utterly remote, while the

MALI

The Road from Gao to Mopti

The long bus journey between Gao and Mopti can be dull and uncomfortable. Happily there are a few places en route worth visiting and transport heading north and south is reasonably easy to pick up (especially on market days).

About 100km southwest of Hombori is **Gossi** a sandy town sprawled on the fringes of a muddy lake. The basic campement and Sunday market is quite a hike from the tarmac road and the lake is good for **bird-watching**. **Desert elephants** (see the boxed text later in this chapter) pass close to the town on their annual migration. **Hombori**, about 100km further southwest is a major destination (see following).

Some people call the 80km stretch of road between Hombori and Douentza Mali's monument valley. The rock formations and sheer cliffs of the **Gandamia Plateau** (great trekking potential) are truly beautiful. **Boni** lies halfway between Hombori and Douentza in a wide pass 5km south of the main road. It's a beautiful setting and on Thursday there's a huge cattle market.

Douentza is the launching point for treks into northern Dogon Country. Members of the **guide association** (☎ 452002, fax 452044) hang out at Auberge Gourma (☎ 452031) a basic but decent place to stay (CFA2000 to CFA2500 per person). Guides here can also advise about exploring the nearby Réserve de Douentza (and provide 4WD hire). There's a Sunday market.

Réserve de Douentza is of great interest to visitors, although it's difficult to reach. It is a vast area of semidesert north of the main road between Mopti and Gao, through which a herd of hardy desert elephants migrate.

About 100km north of Sévaré is **Boré**, which has a beautiful Sahel-style mud-brick mosque that tourists can enter (for CFA500). The views from the roof are worth the climb especially on Saturday, market day.

area around **Ansongo** is said to be extremely beautiful (**hippos and manatees** can be seen here) and it's also the gateway for the Réserve d'Ansongo-Ménaka.

The **Réserve d'Ansongo-Ménaka** is situated next to the Niger River and is extremely isolated. Much of the wildlife has gone but with considerable luck you may see red-fronted gazelles and the Niger River still contains hippos. Access (via Ansongo) is difficult. You'll require a well-equipped 4WD and an informed guide who keeps himself up to date with the local security situation.

Of course, you can also opt for pure desert exploration.

HOMBORI

Hombori is a large village on the main road between Mopti and Gao. The new part of the village straddles the tarmac road, while the old, picturesque part climbs the hillside to the south. Elephants pass close to Hombori in February and March.

Hombori contains a couple of guides (CFA5000 per person per day), but there is no telephone, post office or hospital. Fuel is sold out of a barrel here.

Things to See & Do

A series of magnificent sandstone buttresses or 'mesas' punctuate the semidesert landscape in this area and offer some great **climbing** and **walking**. These huge lumps of rock culminate north of town with **Hombori Tondo**, which rises from the plains to 1155m (the highest point in Mali). To reach the wide summit plateau (reportedly inhabited by monkeys) you'll need some climbing ability and equipment, but **La Clé de Hombori** ('Key to Hombori'), a separate jagged spire at the southwestern end of the massif, can be climbed without ropes in about four hours.

Kissim, **Fada**, **Barcousi** (where Tellem caves can be seen) and **Wari** *tondos* (hills) due south of Hombori offer at least two days of walks and the summits of Fada, Barcousi and Wari (where a CFA1500 tourist tax must be paid) can be reached without ropes.

About 13km south of town is **La Main de Fatima** (The Hand of Fatima) whose narrow, finger-like towers reach up 600m from the plains and provide world-class technical rock climbing. Several routes have been established, most of very high and demandir standard (British grades around E4, Fre grades around 7a). There is a 12n boulder (with protected routes marked out from 6a to 8a) where the road passes closest to La Main de Fatima and nearby is an area for ***camping*** (CFA2000 per person, the guardian will find you).

A spectacular walking trail passes left (south) of Fatima's northern-most digit to a wonderful ***camp site*** before descending to Garmi Tondo, a picturesque, stone-built village (with a water pump) close to the Gao-Bamako road where all visitors to the rock should pay a CFA1500 tourist tax.

Anyone wanting to climb here should contact a Spanish climber called Salvador Campillo (☎/fax 0034-93 835 7328, Plà de la Botxes, s/n 08296 Castellbell, El Vilar), who lives in the area for part of the year and arranges climbing tours. Some details on the region are available from the October 1998 issue of *High* magazine (back issues are available from W www.planetfear.com/climbing/highmountainmag).

A 45-minute walk north of Hombori is an impressive **dune system**, Hondo Miyo. It's a great place to watch the sunset.

Places to Stay & Eat

Campement Hôtel Mangou Bagni Camp site per person/mattress on roof CFA2000, singles/doubles CFA3000/4500. This is a simple, really quite a nice place to stay and eat.

There's another very simple ***campement*** on the main road just west of Hombori's two rather good ***Senegalese restaurants***.

Dogon Country

On everybody's list of the top 10 places in West Africa, is the homeland of the fascinating Dogon people, the huge Falaise de Bandiagara that extends some 150km through the Sahel to the east of Mopti. The landscape is stunning, and the Dogon people are noted for their complex and elaborate culture, art forms and unique houses and granaries – some clinging to the bare rock face of the escarpment. For more details on the Dogon people, see the Dogon Arts & Culture special section.

Before the Dogon reached the escarpment, it was inhabited by the Tellem people. The origins of the Tellem are unclear – Dogon tradition describes them as small and red skinned – and none remain today. The vertical cliff is several hundred metres high, yet the Tellem managed to build dwellings and stores in the most inaccessible places. Most cannot be reached today, and the Dogon believe the Tellem could fly, or used magic powers to reach them. Another theory suggests that the wetter climate of the previous millennium allowed vines and creepers to cover the cliff, providing natural ladders for the early inhabitants. The Tellem also used the caves to bury their dead, and many are still full of ancient human bones.

The best way to see Dogon Country (Pays Dogon) is on foot. Treks along the escarpment are possible for anything from between

Desert Elephants

It comes as a surprise to most visitors to learn that Mali is the part-time home to large herds of migratory elephants, especially as the Sahel seems unable to produce enough food even for people and their livestock. Mali's elephants have longer legs and shorter tusks than their East African cousins and inhabit the Gourma region between the Niger River and the border with Burkina Faso. During the rainy season they fatten themselves up in the relatively lush southern area, and around November to January, as the vegetation withers, they move north to a chain of reliable water holes and survive on relatively little food for the duration of the dry season.

The easiest place to see them is near Gossi, where they drink at the large lake. They move south again in June, a welcome sign for local people of coming rain, often passing near the town of Boni. This annual 1000km circuit is the longest elephant migration in Africa.

For centuries the elephants have coexisted with Fula pastoralists and sedentary farmers, happy to share their water resources and have the elephants fertilise their lands. Nomadic pastoralists even trail the elephants in order to find the best pasture and water sources. But conditions in the Sahel have become very hard for farmers in recent years and as the population grows so pressure on the land increases. Also, after the Tuareg rebellion, firearms are now widely available, but hopefully the easy coexistence between man and beast will continue.

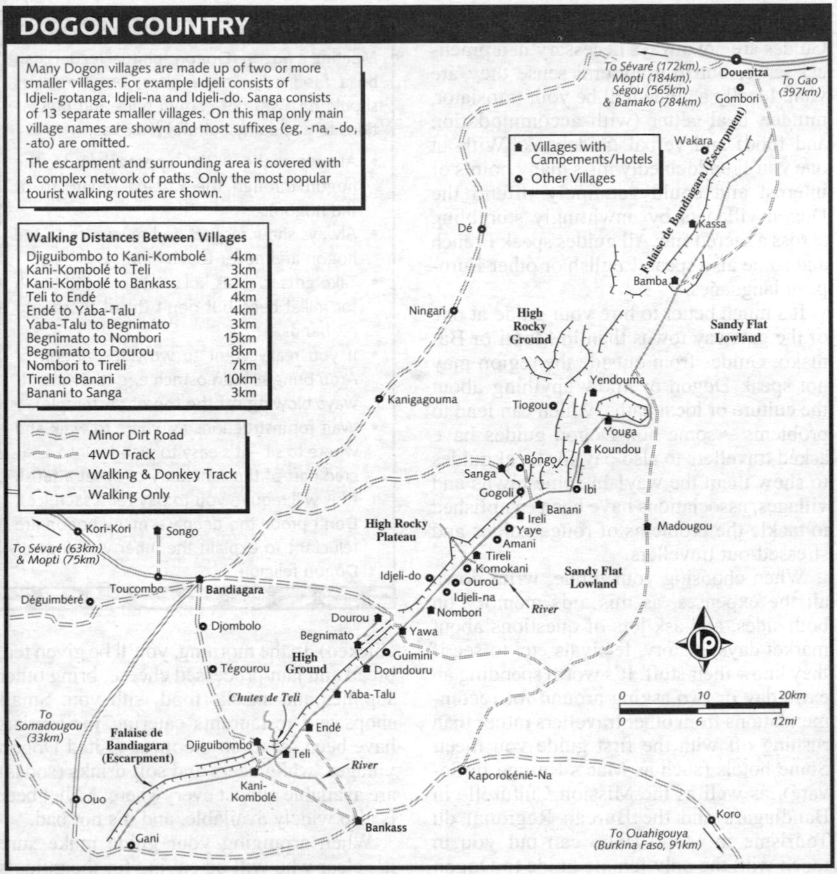
DOGON COUNTRY
Many Dogon villages are made up of two or more smaller villages. For example Idjeli consists of Idjeli-gotanga, Idjeli-na and Idjeli-do. Sanga consists of 13 separate smaller villages. On this map only main village names are shown and most suffixes (eg, -na, -do, -ato) are omitted.
The escarpment and surrounding area is covered with a complex network of paths. Only the most popular tourist walking routes are shown.
Walking Distances Between Villages
Djiguibombo to Kani-Kombolé 4km
Kani-Kombolé to Teli 3km
Kani-Kombolé to Bankass 12km
Teli to Endé 4km
Endé to Yaba-Talu 4km
Yaba-Talu to Begnimato 3km
Begnimato to Nombori 15km
Begnimato to Dourou 8km
Nombori to Tireli 7km
Tireli to Banani 10km
Banani to Sanga 3km
Minor Dirt Road
4WD Track
Walking & Donkey Track
Walking Only
Villages with Campements/Hotels
Other Villages
To Sévaré (172km), Mopti (184km), Ségou (565km) & Bamako (784km)
Douentza
To Gao (397km)
Gombori
Falaise de Bandiagara (Escarpment)
Wakara
Kassa
Dé
Bamba
Ningari
High Rocky Ground
Sandy Flat Lowland
Yendouma
Kanigagouma
Tiogou
Youga
Koundou
Bôngo
Sanga
Gogoli
Ibi
Banani
Ireli
Madougou
Yaye
Amani
Tireli
High Rocky Plateau
Kori-Kori
Songo
To Sévaré (63km) & Mopti (75km)
Komokani
Sandy Flat Lowland
Idjeli-do
Ourou
Toucombo
Bandiagara
Idjeli-na
Déguimbéré
Nombori
River
Dourou
Djombolo
Begnimato
Yawa
High Ground
Guimini
Tégourou
Doundourou
Yaba-Talu
Chutes de Teli
0 10 20km
0 6 12mi
To Somadougou (33km)
Falaise de Bandiagara (Escarpment)
Endé
Djiguibombo
Teli
River
Kaporokénié-Na
Ouo
Kani-Kombolé
Koro
Bankass
Gani
To Ouahigouya (Burkina Faso, 91km)

two days and three weeks. Ancient tracks link village with village and the plateau with the plain. In places, carefully laid stones create a staircase up a fissure in the cliff face, while elsewhere ladders provide a route over a chasm or up to a higher ledge.

On standard treks, daily distances are often short allowing plenty of time to appreciate the people and landscape, while avoiding heat in the middle of the day.

TREKKING PRACTICALITIES

When to Go

From March to May, with temperatures touching 40°C, it's really too hot for trekking, although the first few hours of the morning are OK and a number of festivals take place in May. The rainy season from June to September is not usually popular, but downpours only last an hour or two, the air is clear and the waterfalls over the escarpment are spectacular. November to February is therefore the best time to trek, although daytime temperatures are still well over 30°C. December and January are the busiest tourist months.

Starting Points

Three towns, Bandiagara, Bankass and Douentza, provide gateways to Dogon Country. From these towns transport to the actual trailheads must be arranged (although Douentza is only about 5km from Dogon Country). Of the numerous possible trailheads, Kani-Kombolé, Djiguibombo, Endé, Dourou and Sanga are the most popular.

Guides

Guides are not always necessary in a practical sense, but in a cultural sense they are vital. Ideally a guide will be your translator, minder, deal-getter (with accommodation and food) and verbal guidebook. Without one you'll undoubtedly miss many points of interest and could genuinely offend the Dogon villagers by unwittingly stumbling across a sacred site. All guides speak French and some also speak English or other European languages.

It's much better to hire your guide at one of the gateway towns than in Mopti or Bamako. Guides from outside the region may not speak Dogon or know anything about the culture or local paths, which can lead to problems – some non-Dogon guides have asked travellers to also pay for local guides to show them the way! In some towns and villages, associations have been established to tackle the problems of rouge guides and stressed-out travellers.

When choosing your guide, write down all the expenses, as this aids memory on both sides, and ask lots of questions about market days, history, festivals etc, to see if they know their stuff. It's worth spending an extra day or two asking around for recommendations from other travellers rather than rushing off with the first guide you meet. Some hotels (such as Mac's Refuge in Sévaré), as well as the Mission Culturelle in Bandiagara and the Bureau Regional du Tourisme in Mopti (who can put you in touch with the only female guide to Dogon Country) have lists of knowledgeable and culturally aware guides.

Tour operators are worth considering if you're planning a long trek with a large group. Respected operators are listed in the main Getting Around section earlier in this chapter, and in the Mopti section.

Accommodation & Food

You'll find food and lodging in most Dogon villages, be it in a family house with some extra space or a ***campement*** especially built for tourists. Rooms are usually available, but sleeping on the flat roof of a house under the stars can be a wonderful experience. The sights and sounds of the village stirring in the early morning light are unforgettable.

Evening meals are usually rice with a sauce of vegetables or meat (usually chicken). In the morning, you'll be given tea, bread and jam/processed cheese; bring other supplies and snacks food with you. Small shops and restaurants catering for tourists have been set up in the most visited Dogon villages, while beers and soft drinks (sodas) are available almost everywhere. Millet beer is also widely available, and it's not bad.

When arranging your guide make sure it's clear who will be paying for the guide's meals and lodging. It is usual for these to be covered by the fee you pay them.

Hogon Etiquette

Meeting a *hogon* (Dogon spiritual leader) can be a fascinating experience, but travellers should be aware of certain rules and regulations to avoid any cultural *faux pas*:

- Always make initial approaches to the hogon through the *kadana* (guardian of the hogon).
- Always show respect and reverence to the hogon and never touch him.
- Take gifts such as kola nuts or a little cash for millet beer, but don't thrust these into his hands.
- If you really want to wow the hogon of Arou bring him an ostrich egg (they are always blowing off the top of his temple).
- Wait for instructions as where to walk and where to sit – it's easy to wander into a sacred part of the sanctuary or upset a fetish (this will require you to pay for a sacrifice).
- Don't probe too deeply – many hogon are reluctant to explain the inner workings of Dogon religion.

Equipment

The general rule is to travel as lightly as possible because paths are steep or sandy in places. Footwear should be sturdy, but boots are not essential. It is vital to have a sunhat and a water bottle, as otherwise heatstroke and serious dehydration are real possibilities. You should always carry at least a litre of water. Re-useable bottles can be bought in Mopti market, and you can get water from village pumps (always preferable to a well) along the way – although it needs to be purified. Tents are not required, although a mosquito net is a good idea, especially after the rains. Nights are warm, although a lightweight sleeping bag will keep off the predawn chill from November to February. Dogon villages are dark at night, so a torch (flashlight) is useful and you'll need toilet paper. Wearing shorts for trekking is OK, as they do not offend Dogon culture, although women will feel more comfortable wearing a skirt or long trousers when staying in a village, especially in remote areas.

Costs

Visitors to Dogon Country must pay for the privilege. Fees for visiting a village are reasonable (CFA500 to CFA1000 per person, nothing if you're just passing through) and provide the local people with a much-needed source of income. The fee should allow you to take photos of houses and other buildings (but *not* people – unless you get their permission), and to visit nearby cliff dwellings. If possible, pay this fee directly to the village headman, not to your guide.

To sleep at a campement or private house costs CFA1000 to CFA2500 per night. Food is CFA500 for breakfast and between CFA1000 to CFA2000 for dinner.

Fees for guides vary hugely. Guide associations have tried to set up a fixed-rate tariff system, but these rates are widely ignored and you can pay anywhere between CFA5000 and CFA10,000 per person per day, although reductions are possible for large groups and long treks. Generally speaking you get what you pay for and top guides can charge CFA15,000 per day. Cooks and porters can be hired for around CFA5000 per day for the group.

Many guides offer all-inclusive 'packages' offering all transport, food, accommodation, village fees, etc for a flat fee (often CFA10,000 to CFA17,500 per person per day). These can make life easy and sometimes only costs a little more than organising everything yourself. However, make sure absolutely everything (with the exception of soft drinks and snacks) is covered (including accommodation on the last day of your trek) before sealing the deal.

Your only other cost is reaching the escarpment. From Bandiagara, a local taxi to any of the local trailheads will cost CFA10,000 to CFA20,000. If you're alone it might be cheaper for you and the guide to hire mopeds.

From Bankass to the escarpment at Endé or Kani-Kombolé (12km) by horse and cart is CFA3000 to CFA5000. (The track is too sandy for mopeds.) Of course, you can save money by walking this section.

Your last cost is to cover payments to take photos of people (with permission of course) or to visit a village's *hogon* (spiritual leader). It's usual to give him a small gift of around CFA500. Another good gift is kola nuts, which can be bought in Mopti or Bandiagara – but not always in Bankass or Sanga.

Hiking & Trekking Routes

Time and money usually decide the length and starting point for a trek, but also consider how much energy you want to exert. Simple routes will take you along the bottom (or top) of the escarpment, while the more interesting routes head up and down the cliff itself, winding through caves, scrambling on all fours, leaping from boulder to boulder or using ladders carved from logs to cover the steepest sections. People with no head for heights may feel a bit shaky, and routes of this nature usually involve walking a little longer each day. The best source of information is other travellers, so ask around before finalising anything.

One Day If you are very short of time there are three circular walks from Sanga, aimed at tour groups on tight schedules who arrive by car. (With public transport it can easily take two or three days just getting to/from Sanga.) The Petit Tour goes to Gogoli (7km), the Moyen Tour goes to Gogoli and Banani (10km), and the Grand Tour goes to Gogoli, Banani and Ireli (15km).

Two Days Spending a night in a Dogon village gives you a much better impression of life on the escarpment than you'll ever get on a one-day trip. From Bandiagara, with a lift to Djiguibombo (pronounced Jiggy-boom-bo) you can walk down to the plains, spend the night in either Kani-Kombolé, Teli or Endé and return by the same route. You could also do a circular route from Dourou to Nombori. From Bankass, a short, but rewarding circuit takes you to Kani-Kombolé, through Teli to Endé (spending the night at either) and then back.

Three to Five Days A good three-day trek from Bandiagara starts with a lift to Djiguibombo. You descend to Teli for the first

MALI

night and trek northwards to Begnimato (second night). On the third day continue to Yawa, then up the escarpment to Dourou, where you can either stay and walk back to Bandiagara on day four or arrange for a lift. You can add an extra day by diverting northward to Nombori. An easier trip from Bandiagara would be Djiguibombo, Teli and Endé, returning by the same route.

From Bankass, you can get to Teli or Endé and then walk northwards to Begnimato, Yawa or Nombori, before retracing your route.

Another option to avoid backtracking is to start from Bandiagara, go to Dourou, trek south to Endé or Teli and then continue southwards to Bankass, from where you can get transport back to Mopti or on towards Burkina Faso. Alternatively, start this route in Bankass and end at Bandiagara – the views are better this way.

From Sanga, a good four-day route descends first to Banani then heads north to Kundu (first night), Youga (second night) and Yendouma (third night). On the fourth day go up the cliffs to Tiogou and return over the plateau to Sanga. The escarpment is less well defined north of Banani, but unlike areas further south, it's rarely visited.

Six Days or More If you have plenty of time, any of the routes described above can be extended and combined, and routes in from Douentza exploring the north are possible. For example, from Douentza to Sanga takes at least seven days and takes in Gombori, Wakara, Kassa and Bamba. From Sanga and Banani you can head southwards via Tireli and Yawa to reach Dourou (after three days) or Djiguibombo (after another two or three days), and then end your trek at Bandiagara or Bankass. This trek can also be done in reverse: to Djiguibombo, first night in Teli, second night in Begnimato, third night in Nombori, fourth night in Tireli and fifth night in Banani before going up the escarpment to Sanga.

MALI

Things to See & Do

The following information may be helpful for deciding your route. Working roughly south to north, **Kani-Kombolé** has an interesting mosque, while **Teli** and **Endé** are very picturesque and have waterfalls nearby. Endé and **Nombori** are also good places to visit the village hogon. **Begnimato** and **Dourou** offer spectacular views of the plains, and picturesque **Tireli** is known for its pottery. At **Daga-Tireli**, on top of the escarpment, a large area of vegetable plots surrounds a dam. **Amani** has a sacred crocodile pool, and **Ireli** is a classic Dogon village with cylindrical granary towers at the foot of the cliffs, and a mass of ancient Tellem houses. **Banani-kokorou** can be overrun by souvenir sellers, while **Banani-ama**, which sits under an amazing overhanging cliff, is full of wonderful Tellem buildings. **Bongo** has spectacular views of the plains and an enormous natural tunnel. **Arou** is where the most powerful hogon in Dogon Country lives (the temple is marvellous) and has a nice rock arch. The **Koundou** villages stretch from the top to the bottom of the escarpment making for an excellent walk, while the **Youga** villages that lie on a separate hill out on the plains, are quite traditional, animist and beautiful. **Kassa** in the north has numerous springs and is very attractive, while **Wakara** is one of the highest villages in the area.

BANDIAGARA

This small, dusty town lies 63km east of Sévaré and about 20km from the edge of Falaise de Bandiagara. Once a major administrative centre, tourism is now the main show in town and the attention of numerous would-be guides as soon as you arrive can be quite intimidating.

Information

There's a CFA500 tax on tourists entering Bandiagara.

In the heart of town is the market (market day is Monday) and supplies can be purchased from here and a number of outlets nearby (try Alimentation Niang Ibrahim).

Guides in Bandiagara are developing a reputation for aggressive salesmanship, but you can contact the guide association on ☎ 420461. The staff of the Mission Culturelle (☎/fax 420263) can provide cultural information and recommend guides.

Centre de Médecine Traditionnelle (☎ 420 006, e crmt@afribone.net.ml) is as well known for its *maisons sans bois* (houses without wood) architecture as it is for its work with medicinal plants. Visits are free, although donations are appreciated.

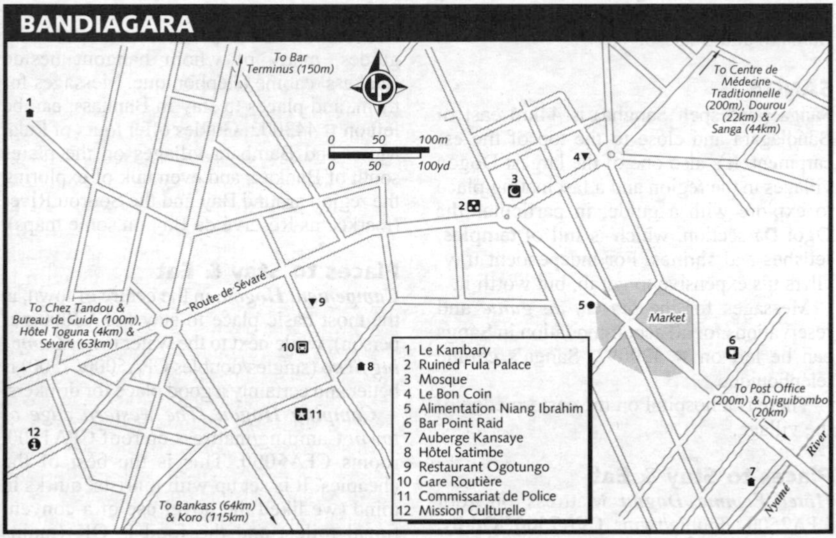
BANDIAGARA
To Bar Terminus (150m)
To Centre de Médecine Traditionnelle (200m), Dourou (22km) & Sanga (44km)
0 50 100m
0 50 100yd
Route de Sévaré
To Chez Tandou & Bureau de Guide (100m), Hôtel Toguna (4km) & Sévaré (63km)
Market
To Post Office (200m) & Djiguibombo (20km)
Nyamé River
To Bankass (64km) & Koro (115km)
1 Le Kambary
2 Ruined Fula Palace
3 Mosque
4 Le Bon Coin
5 Alimentation Niang Ibrahim
6 Bar Point Raid
7 Auberge Kansaye
8 Hôtel Satimbe
9 Restaurant Ogotungo
10 Gare Routière
11 Commissariat de Police
12 Mission Culturelle

Places to Stay & Eat

Hôtel Satimbe *(Gare routière)* CFA2500 per person. This tranquil oasis has a nice shady garden, simple beds with nets and reasonable food.

Auberge Kansaye *(☎ 420487, Off the southern end of the main street overlooking the river)* CFA3000 per person. Rooms are clean and spartan and there's a good travellers' atmosphere – consequently the wildly decorated restaurant/bar (meals CFA1000 to CFA3000) and pleasant shady garden are busy with local guides. To leave baggage costs CFA1000.

Hôtel Toguna *(☎ 420159, Road to Sévaré)* Camp sites per person CFA2000, rooms per person CFA3500-5000. This is a shady, nicely laid out placc that benefits from being a little way out of town (it's 4km west). The staff are helpful and there's a restaurant – try the good fried chicken (meals CFA500 to CFA2500).

Le Kambary *(Restaurant Cheval Blanc; ☎/fax 420388)* Singles/doubles with fan CFA12,000/17,000, with air-con CFA27,000/29,000-32,000. This upmarket hotel/restaurant, made from a collection of stone domes, is a pleasant place to stay, if not really stunning value. The rooms are cool and well appointed. The French- and European-style cuisine (meals CFA1500 to CFA3000) is the best in town, but customer service is not a priority. You can arrange 4WD hire here (roughly CFA50,000 per day).

Street food is also available around the market and gare routière in the evening.

Restaurant Ogotungo *(Gare routière)* Meals CFA300-500. This is a friendly place and cheap as chips (cold drinks too).

Chez Tandou *(Off the road to Sévaré)* Mains CFA500-2500. This is another good cheapie, doling out the usual range of eats from rice and sauce to beef hues.

Also try ***Le Bon Coin*** and ***Bar Point Raid*** for cheap beer (primarily) as well as for Western staples such as steak or spaghetti bolognaise for CFA2000.

Also worth a shout on the beer front is ***Bar Terminus*** on the road north to Kalikombo, while you could also track down ***Galaxy Bar*** and look for music at ***Foyer des Jeunes***.

Getting There & Away

Most transport leaves Bandiagara around 7am or 5pm. There's a lot of transport to Sévaré/Mopti (around CFA1400), but getting to Bankass (CFA1500) or Koro (CFA3000) can be a nightmare. It's easier from Mopti.

Somatra's Bamako service (CFA8000) arrives on Sunday and Thursday and returns Monday and Friday, usually around 4pm. Buses to Bamako and Sikasso (CFA4500) pass through on Tuesday evening or Wednesday morning.

In the dry season there are more buses to Bamako and Sikasso.

SANGA

Sanga (also spelt Sangha) is 44km east of Bandiagara and close to the top of the escarpment. It's also one of the largest Dogon villages in the region and a fascinating place to explore with a guide, in particular the **Ogol Da** section, which is full of **temples**, **fetishes** and **shrines**. For independent travellers it's expensive to get to, but worth it.

Messages for the *bureau de guide* and reservations for all accommodation in Sanga can be left on ☎ 420092, Sanga's cabine téléphonique.

There is a hospital on the eastern edge of the village.

Places to Stay & Eat

Hôtel Femme Dogon Mattress on roof CFA2500, double/twins CFA7500. Oddly, this place looks and feels slightly like a French refuge, though a little shabbier. However, it's a nice (if overpriced) setup with a popular bar and restaurant and running water. Treks and 4WD hire can be arranged here, but you'll need to bargain hard.

Campement-Hôtel Guinna Singles/doubles with bathroom & fan CFA15,000/17,500. This is a tour-group favourite, but don't expect too much. After a week's trekking the food is good (CFA1000 to CFA5000) and cold beer fantastic.

Try the cheap rooms at ***Hôtel Guirou Yam,*** off the road to Bandiagara, and food at ***Le Grand Castor Dogon*** in Ogol Leoi.

Getting There & Away

There's no regular public transport to Sanga so hitching might be your best bet. However, you may find transport heading in either direction on Sanga's or Bandiagara's market day, and Monday, respectively. Chartering a bush taxi costs CFA15,000 to CFA20,000 or getting a moped to drop you off costs CFA7500 (including petrol).

BANKASS

Bankass is 64km south of Bandiagara along the new dirt road to Burkina Faso. The Falaise de Bandiagara is about 12km away, which makes it a good gateway to southern Dogon Country, particularly if you're coming from Burkina Faso.

Information

Association Bandia represents Bankass' guides, many of whom hangout beside Bankass' cabine téléphonique. Messages for them, and places to stay in Bankass, can be left on ☎ 443002. Guides offer tours of Fula, Mossi and Bambara villages on the plains south of Bankass and even talk of exploring the region around Bay and the Sourou River (marked as Réservé de Bay on some maps).

Places to Stay & Eat

Campement Hogon, in the centre of town, is the most basic place to stay (CFA3000 per person), while next to the water tower ***Camping Seno*** (singles/doubles CFA5000/ 7500) is better and certainly a good place for drinkers.

Camping Hogon *(The western edge of town)* Camping/mattress on roof CFA1500, rooms CFA5000. This is the best of the cheapies. It is set up with tourists' quirks in mind (we liked the novel use of a conventional toilet) and the food is OK (mains CFA2500 to CFA3500). Readers have also recommended treks organised here.

Hôtel les Arbres *(Eastern edge of town)* Camp sites per person CFA1500, mattress on roof CFA3500, rooms CFA5000- 20,000. Rooms with air-con are OK, if overpriced, but the so-called 'Dogon Rooms' should be avoided. This hotel is decaying.

Getting There & Away

There are daily Peugeot taxis and minibuses to Bandiagara (CFA1500), Mopti (CFA2500) and Koro (CFA1000).

Buses to Bamako (CFA6500) leave on Tuesday and to Sikasso (CFA5000) on Tuesday or Wednesday.

Koro & Burkina Faso

Koro has a nice mosque but little else to offer apart from an impressive baobab tree, the Saturday market and a bus to Ouagadougou (CFA5000, seven hours) that leaves Koro around 2pm daily. Passport and customs formalities must be completed in Koro and Tiou (in Burkina Faso). Peugeot taxis and minibuses ply the route between Koro and Mopti (CFA3500) daily. There are buses to Bamako (CFA7500) on Tuesday and to Sikasso (CFA6000) on Tuesday or Wednesday.

[Continued on page 605]

MALI

DOGON ARTS & CULTURE

The Dogon were first brought to the attention of the outside world through the work of French anthropologist Marcel Griaule, whose influential book *Dieu d'Eau: Entretiens avec Ogotemmêli* (published in 1948) was the result of many years living and studying near the village of Sanga. Griaule died in France in 1956, and a plaque near a dam he helped build marks the spot where the Dogon believe his spirit resides. Griaule's book was published in English under the title *Conversations with Ogotemmêli* in 1965 and is still available.

Dogon religion and culture (the two are inextricably linked) are incredibly complex and very difficult for outsiders to appreciate. This section is therefore a very simplified introduction. For more details read *African Art of the Dogon* by Jean Laude or *Dogon – Africa's people of the Cliffs* by Stephenie Hollyman & Walter van Beek.

Religion & Cosmology

The Dogon believe that the earth, moon and sun were created by a divine male being called Amma. The earth was formed in the shape of a woman, and by her Amma fathered twin snake-like creatures called the Nommo, which Dogon believe are present in streams and pools.

DAVID ELSE

Inset: Hand-woven
askets containing millet,
the staple food of the
ogon people. Millet also
ays an important role in
)ogon culture, especially
during ceremonies and
even in traditional
architecture.
(Photo by David Else)

ight: A Malian *togu-na*,
a traditional meeting
place for village elders

Later, Amma made two humans – man and woman – who were circumcised by the Nommo and then gave birth to eight children, who are regarded as the ancestors of all Dogon.

Amma is also credited with creating the stars, and a major feature of Dogon cosmology is the star known in Western countries as Sirius or the Dog Star, which was also held to be auspicious by the ancient Egyptians. The Dogon are able to predict Sirius' periodic appearance at a certain point above the skyline, and have long regarded it as three separate stars – two close together and a third invisible. The movements of these stars dictate the timing of the major Sigui festival, which takes place about every 60 years. Although modern astronomers knew Sirius to be two stars, it was only in 1995 that powerful radio telescopes detected a third body of super-dense matter in the same area.

Aspects of Dogon religion readily seen by visitors are the *omolo* or 'fetishes', sacred objects that are dotted around most villages. Most are usually a simple dome of hard-packed mud and their function is to protect the village against certain eventualities. To strengthen their power, sacrifices are made to these omolo on a regular basis. This usually means pouring millet porridge over them, although sometimes the blood of a chicken is used.

Masks & Ceremonies

Masks are very important in Dogon culture, and play a significant role in religious ceremonies. The most famous ceremony is the Sigui, performed every 60 years (most recently during the 1960s), which features a large mask and headdress called the *iminana*, which is in the form of a prostrate serpent, sometimes almost 10m high. During the Sigui, the Dogon perform dances recounting the story of their origin. After the ceremony, the iminana is stored in a cave high on the cliffs.

The iminana is also used during a major 'funeral' ceremony that takes place every five or so years. According to Dogon tradition, when a person dies their spirit wanders about looking for a new residence. Fearful that the spirit might rest in another mortal, the Dogon bring out the iminana and take it to the deceased's house to entice the spirit to reside in the mask. The accompanying ceremony can last up to a week and celebrates the life of the dead person and the part they played in village life.

When important village members die, they are interred in a cave high on the cliffs (sometimes appropriating a Tellem cave), usually on the same day or the day after they die. The body is wrapped in colourful cloth and paraded head-high through the village, then lifted with ropes up to the cave. A smaller funeral ceremony takes place about five days later.

Other masks used by the Dogon include the bird-like *kanaga*, which protects against vengeance (of a killed animal), and the house-like *sirige*, which represents the house of the *hogon*, who is responsible for passing on Dogon traditions to younger generations. Most Dogon ceremonies, where you may see masks, take place from April to May. These include Agguet, around May, in honour of the ancestors, and Ondonfile and Boulo (the rain welcoming festival), which takes place in the period leading up to the first rains.

Architecture

When the Dogon first moved into this area, they built their houses on the high cliffs of the escarpment for protection. These houses were made of mud on a wooden frame with a flat roof supported by wooden beams, while the smaller granaries had conical roofs. In recent, safer times, many of the cliff dwellings have been abandoned as more Dogon moved down to the better farmland on the plains.

The design of Dogon houses is unique. Each house is collectively built of rock and mud and set in a compound that contains one or two granaries. Single-sex dormitories are constructed for those who have been circumcised, but not yet married and slight architectural variations occur across Dogon Country.

The granaries, with their conical straw roofs, stand on stone legs to protect the maize or other crops from vermin. At one time their most notable features were the elaborately carved doors and shutters, but, sadly, many have been sold to unscrupulous tourists and replaced with plain wooden doors.

The focal point of any village is the *togu-na*, a low-roofed shelter that is the meeting place for older men, where they discuss the affairs of the village or simply lounge, smoke, tell jokes and take naps. Nine pillars support the roof made from eight layers of millet stalks and the outside pillars are sometimes carved with figures of the eight Dogon ancestors. Women are allowed into some togu-na, although by no means all.

Each clan in the village has a clan house called a *guina*, that usually contains a shrine. The most impressive of these are characterised by rows of holes, like compartmentalised shelves, and geometric decoration.

Women stay in *yapunu guina* (menstruation houses) during menstruation, as this is considered an unclean time.

The *taï* is a village's central square and the place where most ceremonies take place. There is often an important togu-na close by.

ARIADNE VAN ZANDBERGEN

ght: A village in Dogon Country with traditional mud-brick dwellings, built on the Bandiagara escarpment

Agriculture

The Dogon are traditionally farmers and both men and women are very industrious, as work is a central feature of Dogon society. A man must spend time working hard in fields belonging to his intended wife's parents before permission to marry is granted.

Crops such as millet are planted in the fields below the escarpment and on terraces created on the lower slopes (where water and soil must be brought up from the plains below). In some areas dams have enabled the creation of irrigated market gardens on the solid rock of the plateau.

Unsurprisingly many Dogon now choose to farm down on the plains, where traditionally there had been conflict with the Fula and Mossi. Now Fula groups bring their cattle to graze on harvested Dogon fields, thus providing fertiliser for the following year's crop.

Weekdays & Markets

The traditional Dogon villages keep a five-day week, while those on the plateau tend to keep a seven-day week. Dogon markets are always lively affairs, although they don't get going until about noon, and the following table should help you attend one.

Dogon Market Days

five-day week	Dourou cluster	Sanga cluster	others
1	Dourou	Tireli	Ibi
2	Gimini, Nombori	Banani, Tiogou	
3	Idjeli, Pelou, Amani		Yendouma
4	Konsongou, Komokani	Sanga	
5	Djingorou (near Begnimato)	Ireli, Kama	

seven-day week	village
Monday (big) and Friday (small)	Bandiagara
Tuesday	Bankass
Wednesday	Djiguibombo
Thursday	Kani-Kombolé
Saturday	Bamba
Sunday	Douentza, Endé

DAVID ELSE

The Sanga market held once every five days on the Bandiagara escarpment.

[Continued from page 600]

The South

SIKASSO

The Sikasso region is relatively lush, compared to the Sahel, and is the market garden of Mali. Most travellers heading to Côte d'Ivoire or Burkina Faso just race through town, but it's well worth stopping.

Physical evidence of Sikasso's fascinating history has eroded over time, although the mud-brick **tata** (town wall), that fell to French cannons in 1898 is still visible in places. Sikasso was the last Malian town to resist French colonialism and King Babemba Traore chose to kill himself rather than surrender. The beautiful **Palais du Dernier Roi** still stands on the western side of town and in the centre is the **Mamelon,** a small hill that was sacred to the Kénédougou kings on which a French colonial tower still stands.

Information

The Bank of Africa, off Av Mamadou, changes major foreign currencies and travellers cheques.

Sikasso's hospital (☎ 620001) is on Av du Gouverneur Jacques Fousset. Pharmacie du Souvenir (☎ 620119) on Blvd Coffet is open 24 hours daily or you can try Pharmacie Officine Kenepharm (☎ 320033) on Rue Fôh Traore.

Places to Stay & Eat

Hotel Lotio *(☎ 621001, Blvd Coiffet)* Singles CFA5000-6000, doubles CFA6500-7500. This is a friendly, rough-and-ready place with basic rooms with fans.

Hôtel Mamelon *(☎ 620044, Av Mamadou Konate)* Rooms with bathroom CFA8000-19,000. The air-con still functions in a few of the neglected rooms of this friendly, once-lovely hotel that's still worth checking out.

Zanga Hôtel *(☎ 620431, 100m north of gare routière)* Singles/doubles with fan CFA10,000/14,000, with air-con & bathroom CFA19,500/23,500. Zanga is a fairly flash place with a pool. However, the cheaper rooms with fans are not good value.

Blvd Coiffet has several cheap eateries serving good filling meals for around CFA500 to CFA1500. ***La Vieille Marmite*** and ***Restaurant Kenedougou,*** both on Blvd Coiffet, provide good Malian fare and the enormous Sunday market is a real bonus for street-food fans.

Getting There & Away

The gare routière is a 15-minute walk (CFA200 in a shared taxi) from the town centre. There are daily buses to Bamako (CFA4000), Koutiala (CFA2500), Mopti (CFA5000) and Ségou (CFA3500).

There's daily transport to Burkina Faso (Bobo-Dioulasso CFA4000; Ouagadougou CFA7500) and south into Côte d'Ivoire (Ferkessédougou CFA5000; Abidjan CFA8500).

AROUND SIKASSO

Riddled with chambers and tunnels, the fascinating **Grottes de Missirikoro**, a lump of limestone roughly 12km south-west of Sikasso, is important to local animists *and* Muslims. A taxi tour from Sikasso costs around CFA7500.

The beautiful waterfalls, **Les Chutes de Farako**, lie about 27km east of Sikasso, and are easily accessible from the Route de Burkina Faso.

KOUTIALA

This bustling town is Mali's cotton-growing capital and a good place for transport to Burkina Faso (Bobo-Dioulasso CFA4500). The Bank of Africa, 80m west of Pont Lumumba, changes foreign currency and travellers cheques.

Motel La Chaumière *(☎ 640220)* Singles/doubles with fan & bathroom CFA9500-11500, with air-con CFA14,500-16,500. This is the best hotel in town. It offers clean, good-value rooms with satellite TV and a reasonable restaurant (meals CFA900 to CFA3000).

There are basic rooms near the gare routière at ***La Fourchette*** for CFA5000 and across Pont Lumumba at ***Auberge Poulet Vert*** *(☎ 64022)* for CFA6750.

The West

KAYES

Kayes is the principal settlement in the west of Mali. Many travellers just pass through on the express between Bamako and Dakar, but this hot and dusty town is worth a stopover. Kayes was the first place the French settled in Mali and several colonial buildings remain.

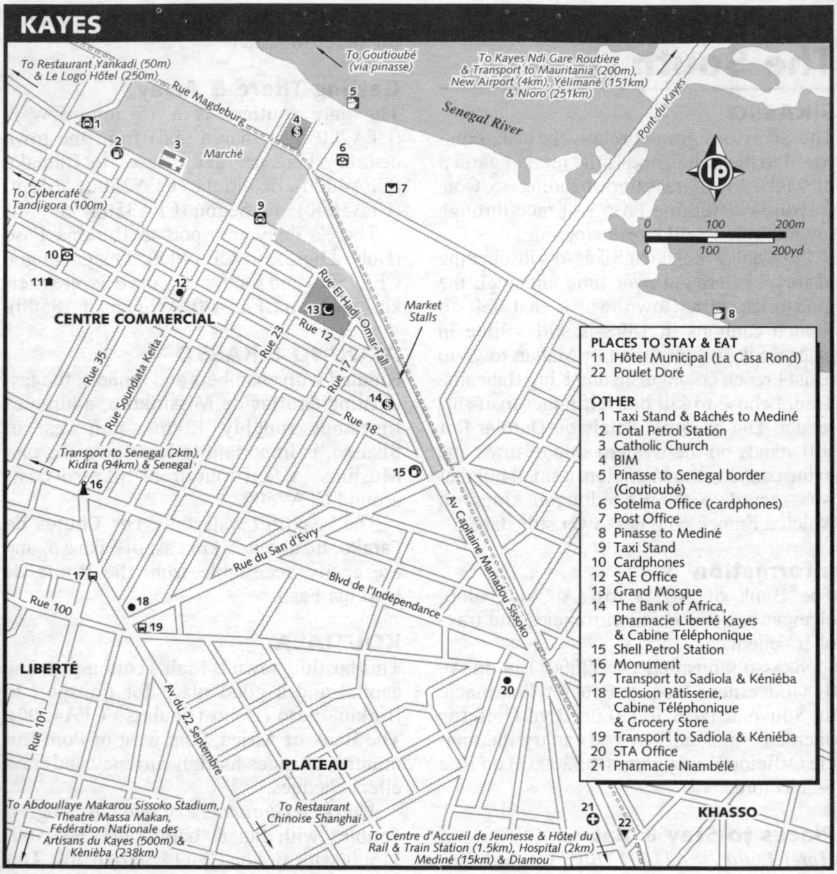
KAYES
To Restaurant Yankadi (50m) & Le Logo Hôtel (250m)
To Goutioubé (via pinasse)
To Kayes Ndi Gare Routière & Transport to Mauritania (200m), New Airport (4km), Yélimané (151km) & Nioro (251km)
Senegal River
Pont du Kayes
Rue Magdeburg
Marché
To Cybercafé Tandjigora (100m)
0 100 200m
0 100 200yd
CENTRE COMMERCIAL
Market Stalls
Rue El Hadji Omar Tall
Rue 12
Rue 23
Rue 17
Rue 18
Rue 35
Rue Soundiata Keita
Transport to Senegal (2km), Kidira (94km) & Senegal
Rue du San d'Evry
Blvd de l'Indépendance
Av Capitaine Mamadou Sissoko
Rue 100
LIBERTÉ
Rue 101
Av du 22 Septembre
PLATEAU
KHASSO
To Abdoullaye Makarou Sissoko Stadium, Theatre Massa Makan, Fédération Nationale des Artisans du Kayes (500m) & Kènièba (238km)
To Restaurant Chinoise Shanghai
To Centre d'Accueil de Jeunesse & Hôtel du Rail & Train Station (1.5km), Hospital (2km) Mediné (15km) & Diamou
PLACES TO STAY & EAT
11 Hôtel Municipal (La Casa Rond)
22 Poulet Doré
OTHER
1 Taxi Stand & Báchés to Mediné
2 Total Petrol Station
3 Catholic Church
4 BIM
5 Pinasse to Senegal border (Goutioubé)
6 Sotelma Office (cardphones)
7 Post Office
8 Pinasse to Mediné
9 Taxi Stand
10 Cardphones
12 SAE Office
13 Grand Mosque
14 The Bank of Africa, Pharmacie Liberté Kayes & Cabine Téléphonique
15 Shell Petrol Station
16 Monument
17 Transport to Sadiola & Kéniéba
18 Eclosion Pâtisserie, Cabine Téléphonique & Grocery Store
19 Transport to Sadiola & Kéniéba
20 STA Office
21 Pharmacie Niambélé

There's a thriving, chaotic market, the town is largely hassle free and a number of interesting excursions are possible.

Information

The Bank of Africa on Rue 14 changes travellers cheques and cash.

Internet access *might* be available at Cybercafé Tandjigora on Rue 134 in Légal Ségou for CFA2000 per hour.

Call the hospital, south of the train station, on ☎ 521232. Pharmacies Niambélé and Liberte Kayes (☎ 521491) are both on Av du Capitaine Mamadou Sissoko.

Places to Stay & Eat

Centre d'Accueil de Jeunesse *(Near the train station)* Camp sites per person/mattress on roof CFA2000, singles/doubles CFA4250/6500. This is a real late-night, let's-just-crash sort of place, with a bar.

Hôtel Municipal *(Le Casa Rond; ☎ 521 947, Rue 18)* Singles/doubles with fan CFA4000/6000. This hotel has small, basic rooms and a good central location.

Hôtel du Rail *(☎ 521233, Opposite the train station)* Rooms with bathroom and air-con CFA17,880-29,140. Despite the overpriced rooms in a tired colonial building, it's still a nice place to stay! The food here is good (three-course menu CFA5760) while the garden's an ideal place to wait for trains. You'll find Le Logo off Rue Magdeburg.

Le Logo Hôtel *(☎ 521381, Rue 139 Légal Ségou)* Singles/doubles with air-con, bathroom & breakfast CFA12,500/17,500. This is a friendly place. There is good food (meals CFA1500 to CFA3500) and a decent bar.

There are several cheap ***food stalls*** near the train station and in the market. ***Restaurant Yankadi*** *(Rue 122, near the junction with Rue Magdeburg)* is a popular place serving excellent simple meals (CFA250 to CFA700) and ***Poulet Doré*** *(Av du Capitaine Mamadou Sissoko)* serves excellent roast chicken (whole chicken CFA3000).

Restaurant Chinoise Shanghai *(Southern end of Av du 22 Septembre)* Meals CFA1250 to CFA3750. This restaurant serves authentic Chinese cuisine, freshly prepared in front of your eyes. The portions are tasty, but a little small.

All Kayes' pâtisseries are open daily until late and serve meals (CFA1000-3500) as well as pastries (CFA200-500). ***Pâtisserie Eclosion*** *(Av du 22 September)* is pretty reliable and has some interesting murals, although the cake selection is limited. ***Pâtisserie Thilambeya*** *(Av du Capitaine Mamadou Sissoko)* doles out unoriginal but tasty meals and rather doughy pastries in aircon comfort (satellite TV included!). ***Pâtisserie Médine*** *(Rue Magdeburg)* is the most upmarket option. It serves decent European-style dishes in a cavernous restaurant.

Shopping

The excellent market is busy on Saturday. ***Fédération Nationale des Artisans du Kayes*** *(☎ 522445, Beside the stadium)* puts you in touch with local artisans producing excellent textiles.

Getting There & Away

Air At the time of writing a new airport was being built north of the Senegal River on the road to Yélimané.

Bush Taxi The route to Bamako via Nioro, is long, bad and indirect. However, transport leaves daily from Kayes Ndi, on the north side of the river, to Nioro (CFA7500 to CFA9000) and Yélimané (CFA5000). Old Land Rovers go to Sélibabai (CFA10,000) in Mauritania directly from Kayes Ndi.

Transport to Senegal leaves from Blvd de l'Indépendance, about 2km west of the town centre – there are daily bush taxis to Diboli (CFA3000, two hours) and a coach to Dakar (CFA13,000, 24 hours) at 2pm Wednesday and Saturday.

Train You have a choice between the express, autorail and weekend trains to Bamako, while the express trains cross the border into Senegal – for more details see the main Getting There & Away and Getting Around sections earlier in this chapter.

Boat Pinasses to the Senegal border at Goutioubé (CFA2500) leave around 3pm daily. Some go on to Bakel (CFA10,000).

AROUND KAYES

The **Fort de Médine**, about 15km upstream from Kayes, was part of the chain of defence posts built along the Senegal River in French colonial times and was besieged by El Hadj Omar Tall in 1855. The crumbling buildings hold a real sense of history and the old train station is particularly beautiful. You may be able to stay with a local family; ask either of the guides at Fort de Médine or at the mayor's office just beside it.

The **Chutes de Felou** are a set of rapids and waterfalls about 2km south from Médine.

Pinasses to Médine (CFA750) leave from opposite the Total petrol station in Kayes around 6.30am and 1.30pm daily, and return around 8am the following morning. A taxi there and back costs around CFA10,000.

Pirogues to Médine (CFA750) leave around 3pm daily and return to Kayes the following morning.

YÉLIMANÉ

The new dirt road between Yélimané and Kayes makes the interesting journey to this little Sahelian town easy. The compact hilltop centre of Yélimané is worth exploring, but the real attractions are out of town.

After the wet, dozens of lily-covered seasonal lakes and flooded forests appear along the course of the Kolinbiné River providing feeding grounds for migratory and Malian water birds. Many of these lakes are visible north of the Kayes-Yélimané road.

Mare de Goumboko is the closest lake to Yélimané (10km west), while **mares de Garé, Lebé** and **Toya** are harder to get to. The former two are best reached via **Komolo** (signposted from the Kayes road around 45km west of Yélimané). Mare de Toya is reached via **Yaguine** (22km west of Yélimané). You are advised to seek out the chief of both villages and take a guide to see you safely along the often-confusing 4WD tracks.

East of Yélimané is a region of **hill-country** and **escarpments** (best explored via **Nougoméra**). Slightly away from the escarpment **Colline Kasa** can be climbed. Mules and guides can be organised in town.

Maison de l'Amitié *(☎ 522251)* offers good, cheap (CFA1500 per person) accommodation. It's just north of the market and 150m south of the huge airport terminal.

DIAMOU

This tiny rail-side town has nothing much to offer travellers, but the surrounding landscape is stunning. The Senegal River flows through a cluster of large sandstone mesas (scenery that looks like it was ordered for the set of a cowboy movie) creating potentially great trekking/mountain biking country. One good objective is the **Chutes de Gouina**, a 200m wide, 10m high set of waterfalls located about 24km upstream from Diamou. The surrounding hills and Sahelian scrub make for a fine few days exploration, although you'll need to be totally self-sufficient.

An access road used during the construction of the power line between Bafoulabé (a small town at the meeting point of Bafing and Bakoy Rivers) and Kayes provides a direct route to the falls, but there is no regular transport. Follow the old tarmac road 6km out of Diamou to a junction just past the defunct cement factory. Turn right onto the dirt road (signposted to 'Gouina and Bafoulabé') and in 18km, just after passing the ruins of a French Mission, you'll see the spray of the falls through the scrub.

Back in Diamou, ***Bar Le Khasso*** (across the tracks from the train station) offers very simple accommodation in huts, should you miss the day's train.

Trains between Bamako and Kayes stop here. There is little road transport to Kayes but, if you have a vehicle, head east through the town centre to hit the track going north.

KÉNIÉBA

This neglected town may be something of a dog's breakfast, but the surrounding escarpments and hills are dramatic and picturesque. There's also a fair amount of wildlife in the region so if you go walking (and you really should) your chances of actually seeing some are not bad. Just make sure that if you are with a guide they don't try to kill it.

The town was once the centre of a gold-producing area and is the starting point for little-used routes into Guinea and Senegal.

The ***Casa Ronde*** campement provides the only basic, grubby and rather depressing accommodation (singles/doubles CFA2500/4000), and the simple food is OK. ***Restaurant Wassa*** has better grub. It's located beside Pharmacie Abdoul Wahab, just up from the Total petrol station.

On the same road as Casa Ronde you'll find the post office and market.

Getting There & Away

SAE fly into Kéniéba from Bamako and Kayes and there's usually one vehicle per day for Kayes (CFA6000 to CFA7500) and Manantali (CFA6000) or Kita (CFA12,500). Regular departures are chalked up on a board in the square next to the mayor's office.

Transport into Guinea is not high volume. You can hire a motorcycle to the border village of Kali (CFA7500) – there's a vehicle from Kali to Labé in Guinea (CFA7500) on Wednesday – or wait until Monday or Tuesday and pick up transport to Dinguiraye (CFA7500), a Guinean town with a Wednesday market (transport heads back the next day).

Between December and May it's possible to cross the Falémé River into Senegal. When the river is low 4WDs are occasionally used, but going by motorbike (around CFA15,000 per person) is more common.

All international transport leaves from just past the post office.

PARC NATIONAL DU BAFING

Bordering the lake formed by Manantali dam, west of Kita, this park protects a number of primate species including chimpanzees, which are the focus of a small NGO chimp-tourism project. Access is via Kounjdan (CFA2000, bush taxis leave from Manantali on Friday mornings), 45km from Manantali on the route to Kéniéba. From Kounjdan, take the road south to Makandougou where two huts have been built. Be warned, the road is terrible and you'll probably have to walk the 25km from Kounjdan. Once you arrive ask for Famakan Dembele, a forestry worker. Manantali makes a good base for exploring the region. There are several places to stay and good connections to Mahina (for the Kayes-Bamako train) and Kita.

CARL DRURY

ANTONY GIBLIN

KIM WILDMAN

ANTONY GIBLIN

ARIADNE VAN ZANDBERGEN

ANTHONY HAM

Most West African communities have a local market offering a huge variety of goods, from everyday practical items to the unusual: fresh fruit and vegetables, saucepans, pottery, beaded jewellery, and animal bones and skulls. Hard bargaining is often required between the trader and the prospective buyer, with the best results usually coming from a spirited, but friendly, exchange.

DAVID WALL

INGRID RODDIS

ARIADNE VAN ZANDBERGEN

DAN HERRICK

ARIADNE VAN ZANDBERGEN

Markets in West Africa are large, vibrant, colourful and always fascinating. There are two main types of market. The most common are those where local people come to buy and sell everyday goods such as fruit, vegetables, clothes and farm tools. Other markets are aimed more at tourists and offer arts and crafts and other souvenirs.

Gold Mining

Gold may be a vital part of Mali's economy today, but individual prospectors have mined gold in Mali for at least 1500 years. Initially gold 'pits' were dug in the Bambouk region in western Mali, an area roughly west of the Falaise Tambaoura and east, south and north of the Falémé, Sanokolé and Bafing Rivers, respectively. At this time gold was traded for salt and other goods in a system of 'dumb barter'. Barrels of salt and other goods were crudely exchanged for gold in a process almost devoid of direct contact (the actual source of the gold was always a closely guarded secret).

Portuguese prospectors reached Bambouk in 1550, but quickly died off, and French attempts at trading (through forts on the Falémé River) started in 1714, but only lasted for 20 years. In any case, by the 11th or 12th century an area known as Bouré that surrounds present-day Siguiri in Guinea and stretches along the Niger River into Mali, had become the greatest source of gold in the region.

In the 20th century there was little commercial mining. However, economic and political liberalisation in the 1990s, and a revision of the mining code, has attracted a host of multinational mining companies in recent years. The government is a stakeholder in all mines and levies taxes on revenues, but the profits of these companies are easily large enough to offset start-up costs of hundreds of millions of dollars.

Gold mining in Mali is no longer a matter of looking for nuggets; now all mines are open-cast operations where gold particles are leached from crushed rock using cyanide. But some things don't change. The areas most interesting to the multinationals are still Bambouk and Bouré where, for centuries, locals have dug for gold with picks and shovels.

KITA

Kita is on the train line between Kayes and Bamako. A large multinational company established a massive cotton enterprise here in the mid-1990s, and Kita became a boom town for a few short years before the world price of cotton fell. Today it's a bit of a backwater. Catholic pilgrims drop by between 18 and 21 November for a huge festival, but the rest of the year Kita has few visitors. On the western side of the sacred mountain, **Kita Koura** (637m), is **Kita Kayamba**, which has some wonderful sandstone caves with geometric cave paintings, but there are burial sites here so a guide is essential.

Places to Stay & Eat

Close to the station are the cheap and sleazy ***Restaurant Senegalese*** and ***Hotel Restaurant Appia***. A five-minute walk from the station is the more upmarket ***Relais Touristique*** *(☎ 573094)*, which has singles/doubles with fan and bathroom for CFA7500/8500. Inquire about guides here.

There are numerous cheap ***food stalls*** near the station; near the market try ***Restaurant Damoum*** *(Chez Issa)* and ***L'Oasis***, which both serve good local dishes (CFA250 to CFA1000). The excellent market is busiest on Wednesday and Sunday.

Getting There & Away

The train is the quickest option for travelling out of Kita as the roads are poorly maintained.

Daily road transport to Bamako (CFA2500) leaves from the centre of town and for Manantali (CFA3500) from outside the train station.

There's weekly transport to Siguiri (CFA12,500) in Guinea.

PARC NATIONAL DE LA BOUCLE DU BAOULÉ

This vast park once contained many of the species that you'd see on a Kenyan safari. However, most of the large herbivores have been hunted out, their demise signalling the end for many large carnivores. Northwest of Bamako, the park lies between two large bends on the Baoule River and is mostly wooden savanna with pockets of riverine forest. Bird-watching is reported to be good, but you will see few animals. Optimists may hope to see a roan antelope or lion, but you'll be lucky to see a even a bush pig or baboon. The park is probably of more interest to archaeologists than zoologists as over 200 archaeological sites have been found here.

Access to the park is best via Négala, a small village 60km northwest of Bamako. You'll need a 4WD and be completly self-sufficient. For more information contact Office du Parc National de la Boucle du Baoulé (☎ 222498), which is next to Bamako's botanical gardens.

Mauritania

Mauritania is a place apart; it's a transition between the North African Arab countries and black Africa, yet it doesn't really belong to either. If ancient Saharan caravan towns, riding camels among sand dunes and travelling through spectacular desert landscapes are your thing, then you'll love Mauritania. It's also one of the best bird-watching areas in the world. For many, arriving in Mauritania will herald the successful crossing of the Sahara from the north and is a gentle introduction to sub-Saharan Africa.

Mauritania at a Glance

Capital: Nouakchott
Population: 2.5 million
Area: 1,030,700 sq km
Head of State: Colonel Maaouya Sid'Ahmed Ould Taya
Official language: Arabic
Main local languages: Hassaniya, Fula, Wolof, Soninké
Currency: Ouguiya
Exchange rate: US$1 = UM275
Time: GMT/UTC
Country telephone code: ☎ 222
Best time to go: November to February

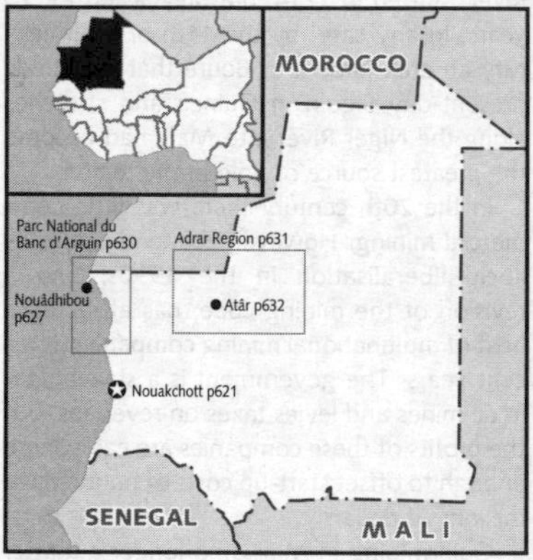
MOROCCO
Parc National du Banc d'Arguin p630
Adrar Region p631
Nouâdhibou p627
Atâr p632
Nouakchott p621
SENEGAL
MALI

Highlights

- Imagining when Chinguetti was a great Saharan city, and taking a camel ride in the surrounding dunes
- Exploring the enchanting old city of Ouadâne
- Bird-watching in the remote Parc National du Banc d'Arguin
- Lazing under the palm trees of the idyllic oasis of Terjît
- Travelling on the longest train in the world from Nouâdhibou to Choûm

Facts about Mauritania

HISTORY

Mauritania was once covered with large lakes, rivers and enough vegetation to support plenty of elephants, rhinos and hippopotamuses. Neolithic rock paintings and arrowheads also attest to early human habitation that came to an end when the Sahara started spreading, about 10,000 years ago.

From the 3rd century AD, the Berbers established trading routes all over the Western Sahara, including Mauritania. By the 9th and 10th centuries the gold trade, as well as slavery, had given rise to the first great empire in West Africa, the Soninké Empire of Ghana (the capital of which is believed to have been at Koumbi Saleh in southeastern Mauritania).

With the spread of Islam in the 7th century, the Almoravids established their capital in Marrakesh (Morocco), from where they ruled the whole of northwest Africa, as well as southern Spain. In 1076 they pushed south and, with the assistance of Mauritanian Berber leaders, destroyed the Empire of Ghana. That victory led to the spread of Islam throughout Mauritania and the Western Sahara. The Mauritanian part of the empire was subjugated by Arabs in 1674, after which virtually all Berbers adopted Hassaniya, the language of their conquerors.

The Colonial Period & Independence

As colonialism spread throughout Africa, France stationed troops in Mauritania to protect the rest of French West Africa from raids by neighbours and ambitious European powers, but did nothing to develop the area. They also used the region as a place of exile for political prisoners.

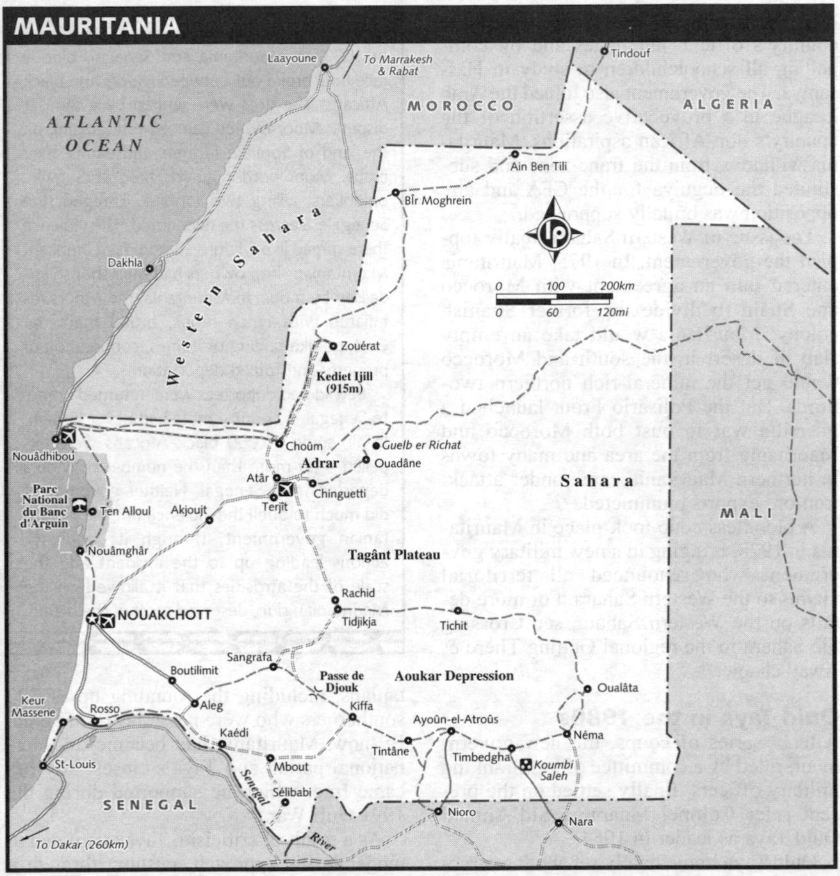
MAURITANIA
Laayoune
To Marrakesh & Rabat
Tindouf
ATLANTIC OCEAN
MOROCCO
ALGERIA
Ain Ben Tili
Bîr Moghrein
Western Sahara
Dakhla
0 100 200km
0 60 120mi
Zouérat
Kediet Ijill (915m)
Nouâdhibou
Choûm
Guelb er Richat
Adrar
Ouadâne
Atâr
Chinguetti
Terjît
Sahara
Parc National du Banc d'Arguin
Ten Alloul
Akjoujt
MALI
Nouâmghâr
Tagânt Plateau
Rachid
NOUAKCHOTT
Tidjikja
Tichit
Sangrafa
Boutilimit
Passe de Djouk
Aoukar Depression
Oualâta
Keur Massene
Rosso
Aleg
Kiffa
Ayoûn-el-Atroûs
Néma
Kaédi
Tintâne
Timbedgha
Koumbi Saleh
St-Louis
Mbout
Sélibabi
SENEGAL
Senegal River
Nioro
Nara
To Dakar (260km)

In 1814, the Treaty of Paris gave France the right to explore and control the Mauritanian coast, but it was not until 1904 that, having played one Moorish faction off against another, the French finally managed to make Mauritania a colonial territory; it took the French another 30 years to subjugate the Moors in the north.

Mauritania was a political backwater in the lead up to independence with its politicians resisting the anticolonial trend sweeping West Africa, instead siding with the French. When, in 1956, an independent Morocco began claiming much of Mauritania as part of a 'greater Morocco', Mauritania's first political party, the Union Progressiste Mauritanienne, was formed and in 1957 won most of the seats in the territorial assembly elections.

Independence came quickly. On 28 November 1958, Mauritania became an autonomous republic within the French community. The Parti du Regroupement Mauritanien, led by Mokhtar Ould Daddah, won every seat in the new national assembly and Ould Daddah became prime minister. When full independence came in 1960, Ould Daddah became the new president. The Moors declared Mauritania an Islamic republic and hastily set about building a new capital at Nouakchott. At the same time both a 675km railway line from Zouérat to the coast and a mining port at Nouâdhibou were established to take advantage of Zouérat's sizable iron-ore deposits.

During the late 1960s, Ould Daddah alienated the (mainly black African) southerners by making both Hassaniya and French the country's official languages and by compelling all schoolchildren to study in Hassaniya. The government also joined the Arab League in a provocative assertion of the country's non-African aspirations. Mauritania withdrew from the franc zone and substituted the ouguiya for the CFA and any opposition was brutally suppressed.

The issue of Western Sahara finally toppled the government. In 1975, Mauritania entered into an agreement with Morocco and Spain to divide the former Spanish colony: Mauritania would take an empty slab of desert in the south and Morocco would get the mineral-rich northern two-thirds. But the Polisario Front launched a guerrilla war to oust both Morocco and Mauritania from the area and many towns in northern Mauritania came under attack; iron-ore exports plummeted.

A bloodless coup took place in Mauritania in 1978, bringing in a new military government who renounced all territorial claims to the Western Sahara. For more details on the Western Sahara, see Crossing the Sahara in the regional Getting There & Away chapter.

The 1989 Race Riots

In 1989, in Mauritania and Senegal, bloody race riots broke out between Moors and black Africans. The riots were ignited by a familiar dispute: Moor-owned camels were grazing on the land of Soninké farmers and eating their crops. Moor border guards fired at Soninké onlookers, killing two farmers. Enraged, the Senegalese across the river rioted. The violence there spread like wildfire; hundreds of innocent Mauritanian shop owners had their shops vandalised by mobs. In Mauritania, the Moors retaliated with lynch mobs, brutal maiming, Gestapo-like raiding of homes, confiscation of property and forced deportation.

Bewildered deportees were 'returned home' to Senegal, a country most had never known. In all, some 70,000 black Africans were expelled – far more than the number of Moors deported from Senegal. Neither government did much to quell the violence but the Mauritanian government, through its antiblack actions leading up to the incident and the scale of the atrocities that it allowed on the Mauritanian side, deserved most of the blame.

Ould Taya in the 1980s

After a series of coups, the new government, ruled by a committee of high-ranking military officers, finally settled on the present ruler Colonel Maaouya Sid'Ahmed Ould Taya as leader in 1984.

Ould Taya immediately set about restructuring the economy, with an emphasis on agricultural development, fishing and tentative moves towards democratisation. However, it is for the persecution of black Africans that Ould Taya's early years of power will be remembered. In 1987, he jailed various prominent southerners and the subsequent rioting in Nouakchott and Nouâdhibou was partly quelled through the introduction of strict Islamic law. Later that year, the government dismissed some 500 Tukulor soldiers from the army and soon after, the jailed author of an antiracist manifesto died in prison.

Mauritania in the 1990s & Today

An unrepentant Taya spent the early 1990s continuing the persecution of black Mauritanians, including the rounding up of 300 southerners who were never heard of again. By now, Mauritania had become an international pariah and Taya's closest ally became Iraq, which he supported during the 1991 Gulf War.

As a result of criticism, Taya attempted to moderate his approach, pushing through a new constitution permitting opposition political parties. In early 1992, in the country's first presidential elections, Taya was re-elected with 63% of the vote, but electoral fraud was massive and the hotly contested election results won him little international respect. Opposition parties consequently boycotted the general elections later in the year.

Bread riots in 1995, stemming from a new tax on bread, led to the arrest of Taya's principal political opponents, Ould Daddah and Hamdi Ould Mouknass – another sign that the crossover to a civilian government had yet to materialise.

In December 1997, the four main opposition groups boycotted the presidential elections fearing massive vote-rigging, while the remaining four candidates had no serious backing.

Today, the question of repatriation and the culture of impunity still haunt the country. Although direct attacks have ceased, black Mauritanians continue to have difficulty recovering their land and obtaining jobs, identity cards and bank loans. They live in fear and are denied their civil rights. In 1993, many high-ranking government officials linked to past crimes were granted amnesty by the government.

In late 2000, electoral reforms were introduced under which political parties were to receive funds according to their electoral performance. Such changes will remain largely cosmetic as long as the harassment and arrest of opposition figures continues. To no-one's surprise, in October 2001 the ruling Parti Républicain Démocratique et Social (PRDS) won 64 out of the 81 National Assembly seats in elections.

GEOGRAPHY

Mauritania is about twice the size of France. About 75%, including Nouakchott, is desert, with huge expanses of flat plains broken by occasional ridges, rocky plateaus and sand dunes. Moreover, the desert is expanding southward. One of the highest plateau areas (over 500m) is the Adrar, 450km northeast of Nouakchott, with its towns of Chinguetti and Ouadâne. These plateaus are often rich in iron ore, and there are especially large deposits at Zouérat about 200km north of Chinguetti. The highest peak is Kediet Ijill (915m) near Zouérat. Mauritania has some 700km of shoreline, including the Banc d'Arguin. The south is mostly flat scrubland.

CLIMATE

In the Sahara region of the country, annual rainfall is usually less than 100mm. In the south, rainfall increases to about 600mm per year, mostly occurring during the short rainy season from July to September and enabling the narrow 400km strip of arable land to support cultivation.

It is extremely hot from April to October, especially from June to August when hot winds *(rifi)* from the north send temperatures soaring to 45°C and above. However, along the coast, the trade winds *(alizé)* blow from the ocean, causing average highs to be 5°C lower. From December to March, temperatures are much more pleasant and can even get quite cool.

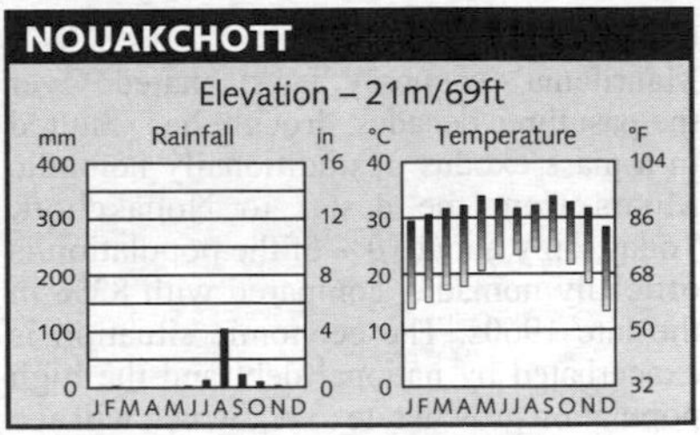
NOUAKCHOTT
Elevation – 21m/69ft
mm
Rainfall
in
°C
Temperature
°F
400
300
200
100
0
16
12
8
4
0
40
30
20
10
0
104
86
68
50
32
JFMAMJJASOND
JFMAMJJASOND

ECOLOGY & ENVIRONMENT

Desertification looms as the greatest environmental problem. Nearly 75% of Mauritania's land surface is desert or near-desert and this is increasing. Augmented livestock herds, as a result of additional wells and human population growth, contribute to overgrazing. Wood has become so scarce that most cooking is now done on kerosene stoves.

FLORA & FAUNA

The uninhabited eastern desert is home to the addax antelope, an endangered species. Giraffes and lions have long gone – victims of desertification and the bullet. The last troop of elephants meanders in the hilly terrain between Kaédi and Ayoûn-el-Atroûs. One endangered species that you might see if you're lucky is the monk seal, off Cape Blanc near Nouâdhibou. Between there and Nouakchott is Parc National du Banc d'Arguin, where hundreds of thousands of birds migrate from Europe in the winter. It is one of the world's major bird-breeding grounds and is on Unesco's list of World Heritage natural sites.

GOVERNMENT & POLITICS

Mauritania is in the process of what it calls 'controlled democratisation'. The 1991 constitution legalised political parties but prohibited them from being organised on racial or regional lines or to be opposed to Islam. Some 16 political parties, including the president's party, the PRDS, are now registered. The two major opposition parties are the Union des Forces Démocratiques (UFD) and the Union pour la Démocratie et le Progrès (UDP) led, respectively, by Taya's old foes, Ould Daddah and Ould Mouknass.

Parliament consists of an 81-member chamber of deputies and a 56-member senate elected every five and six years, respectively. The presidential term is six years.

ECONOMY

Mauritania's economy has stagnated. Over the past three decades, drought has resulted in a mass exodus of traditionally nomadic Moors from the desert to Nouakchott. Today, only about 10% of the population is officially nomadic, compared with 83% in the late 1960s. The economic situation is exacerbated by national debt and the high population growth rate (3%), which will see Mauritania's population double in the next 20 years.

GNP per capita is just over US$500, relatively high for West Africa. Agriculture along the Senegal River contributes to one-third of GNP, making this land a focal point for development. While irrigation there is increasing, the government encourages cattle-raising and rain-fed farming methods, traditionally Moorish activities, which is to the detriment of black Mauritanians.

Fishing and the iron-ore industry account for over 90% of export earnings. The waters off Mauritania are among the world's richest but over-fishing has devastated stocks. Mauritania has one of the world's largest reserves of iron ore, mainly around Zouérat, but falling world prices have affected exports. On a brighter note, gold-extracting operations began in 1992 in Akjoujt. Texaco and Amoco are also conducting oil exploration.

POPULATION & PEOPLE

Of Mauritania's 2.5 million inhabitants, about 60% are Moors of Arab and Berber descent. Moors of purely Arab descent, called 'Bidan', account for 40%.

The other major ethnic group are black Africans, ethnically split into two groups. The Haratin, or black Moors, the descendants of people enslaved by the Moors, have assimilated the Moorish culture and speak Hassaniya, an Arabic dialect. Culturally, they have little affinity with black Mauritanians living in the south along the Senegal River, the 'Soudaniens'. The Soudaniens constitute 40% of the total population and are mostly Fulani (sedentary or nomadic, also known as Peul) or the closely related Tukulor. These groups speak Pulaar (Fula) and are known jointly in Mauritania as Hal-Pulaar. There are also Soninké and Wolof minorities. Mauritania has one of the lowest population densities in the world, with just 2.2 persons per sq km.

The Haratin & the Bidan

The Moors have one of the most stratified caste systems in Africa. The system is based on lineage, occupation and access to power, but colour has become an increasingly popular determinant of status. At the top are the upper classes, the typically light-skinned Bidan Moors descended from warriors and men of letters. Below them are commoners, mostly of Berber-Negroid stock. The lowest castes traditionally consisted of four groups: the Haratin Moors, artisans and griots who have very few rights, and slaves, who have none at all. The Haratin do most of the menial work.

Only in 1980, when there were an estimated 100,000 Haratin slaves in Mauritania, did the government finally declare slavery illegal. International human rights agencies continue to express concern that pockets of slavery still exist in the country and there are regular roundups of antislavery activists, suggesting that the issue remains a matter for great concern.

EDUCATION

While formal education is not compulsory, some 51% of school-age children attend primary school and about 15% go on to secondary school. The adult literacy rate is still only around 37%, well below the sub-Saharan average of 51%.

ARTS

Arts & Craftwork

Mauritania has a strong tradition of arts and craftwork, especially silverwork. Most prized are wooden chests with silver inlay, but there are also silver daggers, silver and amber jewellery, earth-tone rugs of camel and goat hair from Boutilimit, hand-painted Kiffa beads, hand-dyed leatherwork including colourful leather cushions and leather pipe pouches, camel saddles and sandals. Kaédi is famous for its colourful batik cloth.

Music

The traditional music of Mauritania is mostly Arabic in origin, although along its southern border there are influences from the Wolof, Tukulor and Bambara. If Arabic music is your preferred style, you'll enjoy the power of Mauritanian singers. Mauritanian instruments include the *ardin* (harp) and the *tidnit*, a four-stringed plucked lute, similar to the *xalam* of the Wolof over the border in Senegal. Several singers with a more modern African inspiration have hit the international scene, including Malouma, as well as Khalifa Ould Eide and Dimi Mint Abba.

SOCIETY & CONDUCT

The majority of Moors were traditionally nomads who made their living from raising cattle and sheep and from commerce, particularly transport with camel caravans. This came to an end for many after the severe droughts of the 1970s and early '80s and today most Moors live in cities and towns. The men characteristically wear long light-blue robes. Many have the name Ould (son of), eg, Ahmed Ould Mohamed. For women it's Mint (daughter of). Women are in a very disadvantaged position. Only a third as many women as men are literate and few are involved in commercial activities other than selling food and crafts.

Elaborate greetings are traditional in Moorish society. Social activities revolve around tea, which is invariably strong and sweet. It's almost obligatory to accept the first three glasses, but declining the fourth is not impolite.

RELIGION

Over 99% of the population are Sunni Muslims. Islamic fundamentalists are growing in number but remain a minority.

LANGUAGE

Arabic is the official language, but French is still spoken in all government sectors and is widely used in business. The everyday language of the Moor majority is a Berber-Arabic dialect called Hassaniya. In the south, other languages are spoken, including Fula (Pulaar), Wolof and Soninké. See the Language chapter for a list of useful phrases in French, Hassaniya, Fula and Wolof.

Facts for the Visitor

SUGGESTED ITINERARIES

If you have only a week to visit Mauritania, you should plan on spending your time in the Adrar region. It is possible to fly direct from Europe to Atâr and there arrange transport to Chinguetti and Ouadâne. Plan at least a day-and-a-half in Chinguetti so that you can enjoy a day's camel ride out into the desert.

If you have two weeks, you could also try the three-day overland route from Atâr to Tidjikja along the panoramic Tagânt plateau. An alternative would be to spend a few days exploring the Parc National du Banc d'Arguin on Mauritania's remote Atlantic coast.

Additional weeks could be spent exploring southern Mauritania or undertaking a longer camel ride in the northeast.

VISAS & DOCUMENTS

Visas

Visas are required for all except nationals of Arab League countries, some African countries, France and Italy, although check that these exceptions haven't changed. The standard visa is valid for three months and good for a stay of one month from the date of entry.

In most places, Mauritanian embassies require a letter of recommendation from your embassy and an onward air ticket (or at least an itinerary). This is the case at most embassies in Europe as well as Morocco. It is common practice for an overland traveller to buy an airline ticket in Rabat for the purpose of obtaining a visa and to sell (or refund) the ticket once the visa is issued. The visa will indicate that it's valid for entry at Nouakchott airport but border officials routinely ignore this. Visas can cost anywhere from US$10 to US$120.

In countries where Mauritania has no diplomatic representation, including Australia and many countries in West Africa, French embassies will issue visas with a minimum of fuss for around US$25.

Visa Extensions Visa extensions can be obtained from the *commissariat central* on Av Abdel Nasser in Nouakchott.

Visas for Onward Travel In Mauritania you can get visas for the following neighbouring countries.

Mali Visas cost UM2000 and are issued in 24 hours. You need two photos and a photocopy of the information pages of your passport.

Morocco Single-/double-entry visas cost UM4800/7200 and are issued in 48 hours. You need two photos and photocopies of your passport and air ticket.

Senegal One-/two-month visas (UM1015/2030) are issued in 24 hours. You need to supply two photos.

Other Documents

You may need proof of vaccination against yellow fever (if you're coming from an infected area).

Those driving officially need a *carnet de passage en douane*, although some travellers have reported that Mauritanian officials often waive the requirement, instead entering details of the car in your passport, which is then checked on departure from the country. Many European car-insurance companies will only issue policies for as far south as Morocco; in Mauritania expect to pay around US$25 for 10 days. An International Driving Permit (IDP) is not required.

EMBASSIES & CONSULATES

Mauritanian Embassies & Consulates

In West Africa, Mauritania has embassies in Côte d'Ivoire, Gambia, Mali, Nigeria and Senegal, and a consulate in Niger. For more details, see the Facts for the Visitor section of the relevant country chapter.

Elsewhere, Mauritania has embassies and consulates in the following countries:

Belgium (☎ 02-672 47 47) Colombialaan, 6, Brussels 1000
France (☎ 01 45 48 23 88) 89 Rue du Cherche-Midi, 75006 Paris
Germany (☎ 030-20 65 88 30) Axel Springer Strasse 10117 Berlin
Morocco (☎ 07-75 68 28 or 65 66 78) 1 Rue de Normandie, Souissi, Rabat
Spain (☎ 91-575 7007, fax 435 9531) Velasquez 90, 28224 Madrid
USA (☎ 202-232 5700, fax 232 5701) 2129 Leroy Place, NW, Washington, DC 20008

Mauritania also has embassies in Canada, and consulates in Austria, the Canary Islands, Germany, Switzerland and an honorary consul in the UK (☎ 0208-343 2829).

Embassies & Consulates in Mauritania

The following countries are represented in Nouakchott:

France (☎ 525 23 37) Rue Ahmed Ould Mohamed, just before the Monotel Dar-el-Barka
Germany (☎ 525 17 29) Rue Abdallaye
Mali (☎ 525 40 81, 525 40 78) 700m north of Rue de l'Ambassade du Sénégal
Morocco (☎ 525 14 11) Av du Général de Gaulle
Senegal (☎ 525 72 90) Rue de l'Ambassade du Sénégal
USA (☎ 525 26 60, fax 525 15 92) Rue Abdallaye

CUSTOMS

It is illegal to bring any alcohol into the country and heavy fines are levied. There are no longer currency declaration forms and there is no restriction on the amount of foreign currency you can bring in. Local currency cannot be imported or exported.

MONEY

The unit of currency is the ouguiya (UM), which equals five khoums. Exchange rates are as follows:

country	unit		UM
euro zone	€1	=	UM260
UK	UK£1	=	UM407
USA	US$1	=	UM275
West African CFA	CFA100	=	UM40

There is no longer a huge difference between the black-market rate and those offered by bureaus de change (in larger towns and Nouakchott airport). For the best black-market rates, try the market and always conduct your transactions discreetly. Rates outside Nouakchott are considerably lower than in the capital.

The preferred currencies are US dollars, UK pounds and euros. Some bureaus de change in Nouakchott and the south will exchange CFAs. Travellers cheques are usually exchangeable at bureaus de change, although the commission exacted can be as high as 5%. Hotels usually won't accept travellers cheques.

The banks are only good for exchanging money as a last resort as they have the worst rates. The Banque Mauritanienne pour le Commerce International (BMCI) and Banque Nationale de Mauritanie (BNM) are your best bet. No banks give cash advances on credit cards. Credit cards are accepted only at top-end hotels.

POST & COMMUNICATIONS

Letters from here to Europe take about a week, sometimes more. The poste restante (in Nouakchott) is generally efficient.

You can make international calls and send faxes at post offices. The many privately run phone shops in the major cities and towns cost about the same and are open late. The cost is about UM450 a minute to the USA or Europe and 25% less for calls within West Africa.

There are no telephone area codes.

DIGITAL RESOURCES

It's not the most exciting Web site, but for some good information on culture, language and more, try W www.arab.net/mauritania/mauritania_contents.html.

PHOTOGRAPHY & VIDEO

Photo permits are not required. However, a police officer could cause problems if you are caught photographing something other than a tourist site. Taking photographs of government buildings including post offices, airports, ports, radio antennas and military installations is strictly forbidden. Some Mauritanians are delighted to have their photos taken, others are not, so it's best to always ask first.

HEALTH

Malaria is a risk year-round, although the dangers are less the further north you go. Be particularly careful during the wet season. The risk is minimal in Nouâdhibou. See Health in the Regional Facts for the Visitor chapter for more information on these and other health matters.

The water in rural areas is generally safe, as it comes from deep bore holes, but treating water is still recommended. In urban areas, the water can become contaminated by leaks in the pipes. In general, it's the unsanitary handling of the food that causes most stomach problems.

In an emergency, the hospital in Nouakchott (☎ 525 21 35) has French doctors. There are also hospitals in Nouâdhibou, Atâr and Rosso. Pharmacies are quite well stocked.

WOMEN TRAVELLERS

Mauritania is a conservative Muslim country but by no means the most extreme in this regard. It is not unusual to find women working in public offices and driving; most wear a headscarf rather than a veil covering the face. The best way to meet local women is to hope for an invitation home from a family or to spend some time talking with stallholders, most of whom are women, in local markets. Women travellers can be subjected to sexual harassment, especially when alone or with other women, although most women encounter no problems. It's a good idea for women to dress conservatively, as miniskirts, shorts and swimsuits are offensive to many Mauritanians, especially outside Nouakchott.

DANGERS & ANNOYANCES

Nouakchott remains one of the safest capital cities in Africa.

There are thousands of land mines buried along the Mauritanian side of the border with the Western Sahara, even as close as a few kilometres from Nouâdhibou. People have been killed here, so always take a local guide when heading out of Nouâdhibou. There have been isolated incidents of bandits attacking single cars travelling overland to Mali, especially around Néma, so always travel in a group.

BUSINESS HOURS

Business hours are from 8am to noon and 3pm to 6pm Sunday to Thursday; closed Friday and Saturday. Some businesses are open on Saturday mornings, and many shops are open every day. Government offices are open from 8am to 3pm; Thursday 8am to 1pm Saturday to Wednesday. Banking hours are from 7am to 12.30pm Sunday to Thursday.

Post offices are open from 8am to noon and 3pm to 6pm and are usually closed on Friday and Saturday. However, the office in Nouakchott is open seven days a week.

PUBLIC HOLIDAYS & SPECIAL EVENTS

Public holidays include:

New Year's Day 1 January
National Reunification Day 26 February
Workers' Day 1 May
African Liberation Day 25 May
Army Day 10 July
Independence Day 28 November
Anniversary of the 1984 Coup 12 December

Mauritania also celebrates the usual Islamic holidays – see Public Holidays & Special Events in the Regional Facts for the Visitor chapter for a table of estimated dates of these holidays.

ACCOMMODATION

Finding inexpensive accommodation (in the US$5 to US$10 range) is easy in cities and major towns. There are also air-con hotels meeting international standards in Nouakchott and, to a lesser extent, Nouâdhibou and Atâr. Elsewhere, people will frequently offer you a bed, and most restaurants will allow you to sleep on the floor if you buy a meal. Camping in the open spaces of the desert is legal.

FOOD & DRINKS

The desert cuisine of the Moors wins no culinary awards. Dishes are generally bland and limited to rice, mutton, goat, camel or dried fish. Unsweetened, curdled goat or camel milk often accompanies meals served in private homes. Mauritanian couscous, similar to the Moroccan variety, is delicious. A real treat is to attend a *méchui*, a traditional nomad's feast, where an entire lamb is roasted over a fire and stuffed with cooked rice. Guests tear off bits of meat with their hands.

The cuisine of southern Mauritania, essentially Senegalese, is excellent, with much more variety, spices and vegetables. Most cheap African restaurants, even in the north, are operated by Tukulors and Fulani from the south. Two of the most popular dishes are rice with fish and Senegalese *mafé* (a peanut-based stew), typically UM150 to UM200.

Soft drinks are available everywhere, and alcohol is available at some hotels and restaurants in Nouakchott and Nouâdhibou.

MAURITANIA

Getting There & Away

AIR

Nouakchott, Nouâdhibou and Atâr have international airports and it's a good idea to reconfirm flights. There is no airport departure tax.

Europe & the USA

Air France has three weekly flights to/from Paris (with connecting flights to other destinations in Europe and the USA). From Nouakchott, undiscounted return fares (cheaper than one way) are UM136,190.

You can also fly to Paris (UM203,000 return) via Casablanca (UM85,010) once a week on Royal Air Maroc, or to Paris (UM132,000) via Tunis (UM87,230), once a week on Tunis Air.

Air Mauritanie flies from Nouakchott to Las Palmas (Canary Islands; UM93,610 return) three times a week via Nouâdhibou; from Nouâdhibou the fare is UM65,180/70,600 one way/return.

Point Afrique (W www.point-afrique.com) has two flights a week from Paris to Atâr as well as one from Marseilles. Return fares start at around €410 plus taxes.

Africa

You can fly between Nouakchott and Dakar (Senegal) three times a week on Air Mauritanie (UM34,000 one way) and twice a week on Air Sénégal (UM36,000). Banjul (UM66,360) in Gambia is served by Air Sénégal International via Dakar. There are twice weekly Air Mauritanie flights to Abidjan (UM86,150) in Ghana via Bamako (UM76,660) in Mali. Air Mauritanie also flies to Cotonou (UM144,190; twice weekly) in Benin. Air France flies to/from Conakry in Guinea three times weekly for UM89,240. For Praia (Cape Verde; UM89,970), connections are via Dakar on Air Sénégal International. For Tunis and Casablanca from Nouakchott, see Europe & the USA earlier. Air Mauritanie also flies to Casablanca and the fare from Nouâdhibou is UM64,350/78,880 one way/return.

LAND

Border Crossings

The main border crossing for Senegal is south of Rosso, while for Morocco, it's north of Nouâdhibou.

For Mali, most people cross at Néma, Timbedgha (both connecting with Nara in Mali), Ayoûn-el-Atroûs, Tintâne and Kiffa (all connecting with Nioro in Mali). The route via Tintâne is popular with drivers as it avoids the worst of the dunes.

If driving into Mauritania, see also Other Documents earlier in this chapter.

Mali

If crossing into Mali, have your passport stamped by police at the first town you reach after crossing the border. You must also clear customs, which is done in Néma.

From Nouakchott, you can catch bush taxis to Néma (UM5000 to UM5500, two days) and Ayoûn (UM3700 to UM4200, 15 hours). From these places you can catch transport into Mali.

There are two routes between Nioro and Ayoûn if you're travelling by car; the westward route is better. If you cross via Timbedgha, check out the excavations at Koumbi Saleh on the way. The trip, by whichever route, is roughly 230km and usually takes 1½ days (one day if you really push it). It's easy to lose the track, so take a compass.

Petrol is usually available in Nioro, Nara, Néma, Ayoûn (three stations) and Kiffa. Take everything you'll need, as petrol and supplies are not available en route.

Morocco

If going to Morocco, note that the trail is still primarily a one-way route – for more details, see Crossing the Sahara in the regional Getting There & Away chapter. Mauritania considers the border dangerous because of land mines and does not permit crossings northward without special permission, although this has been relaxed in recent years and you may find the occasional vehicle heading north. If you do decide to try, it would be foolhardy to go without a guide (around UM25,000; try the Fedération Mauritanienne de Guides Touristique on ☎ 574 56 17) to assist in both avoiding land mines and finding the Moroccan border post, where you wait for the Moroccan army officer accompanying the convoy southward from Dakhla.

Senegal

When crossing into Senegal at Rosso, note that immigration is only open on the Mauritanian side from 8am to noon and 3pm to 6pm. The border crossing here, while easy for most travellers, is often a nightmare for vehicle owners; ignore requests from customs officials for an 'exit tax'.

Bush Taxi From Dakar to Nouakchott usually takes from 11 to 13 hours depending on the wait at Rosso. Most minibuses and bush taxis leave Dakar before 10am to be sure of arriving in Rosso well before the border closing time (6pm). At Rosso, most travellers without vehicles cross by pirogue (five minutes; UM200/CFA500) as the ferry crosses only four times daily.

Car & Motorcycle The Dakar to Nouakchott route involves crossing the Senegal River at Rosso, which takes only 10 minutes by ferry *(bac)*. The ferry departs from the Mauritanian side at 9am, 11am, 3pm and 5pm, and from the Senegalese side some 45 minutes later. It costs UM2500 (CFA7000) for cars and UM2700 (CFA7500) for a Land Rover.

Getting Around

AIR

Air Mauritanie, one of the better airlines in West Africa, flies from Nouakchott to:

destination	frequency	fare (one way/ return)
Nouâdhibou	twice daily	UM13,140/26,070
Néma	Fri	UM14,550/28,140
Zouérat	Sun & Thur	UM14,940/28,920
Tidjikja	Wed	UM9880/18,800
Kiffa	Wed	UM9900/18,840

At the time of writing, the runway at Ayoûn-el-Atroûs was in need of repair and flights had been suspended.

Another private airline, Compagnie Mauritanienne de Transport Aérian, also connects Nouakchott with Nouâdhibou (UM11,400, four weekly), Atâr (UM11,000, Monday), Kiffa (UM9200, Friday) and Sélibabi (UM10,200, Sunday).

BUSH TAXI

Peugeot taxis (Peugeot 504s), Land Rovers, minibuses and pick-ups *(bâchés)*, in descending order of cost, are the four types of public transport. Overcharging is rare except with the baggage fee, which requires bargaining. Bush taxis go to all the major towns daily, but finding one for small villages is challenging.

Peugeot bush taxis are uncomfortable because you're crammed in four to a row, so consider paying for two seats to avoid the misery. The front two seats are less cramped but they're also more expensive. Note that a *taxi course* is a taxi that you have all to yourself.

The Iron-Ore Train

The Zouérat to Nouâdhibou train is the longest in the world – typically 2.3km long. When it arrives at the 'station' in Nouâdhibou, an unmarked place in the open desert, a seemingly endless number of ore wagons pass before the passenger carriage at the rear appears. Then the stampede to get on board begins. The lucky ones find a place on one of the two long benches; the rest stand or sit on the floor, or perch on the roof for free. There's little to see, as the windows are small and many are shut. The train stops in the middle of nowhere every hour or so to let people off. The atmosphere can be quite jovial, with people playing cards on the floor. In the late afternoon, many men find space on the floor to pray and at dusk when the cabin becomes totally dark, chanting begins. Take enough clothes to keep warm, as it can get very cold at night.

TRAIN

The Nouâdhibou-Zouérat train is a great adventure. It's an iron-ore train with no passenger terminals, but it has become a passenger train for lack of alternatives. The trip takes 16 to 18 hours, but most travellers get off at Choûm, 12 hours from Nouâdhibou. You can put your car on board.

CAR & MOTORCYCLE

Petrol was UM114 per litre at the time of writing. There's a new Japanese-financed road to Atâr, so driving there from Nouakchott is now six hours nonstop. The road from Atâr to Choûm and Chinguetti (both two hours) is reasonably good and doesn't require 4WD. Petrol is usually available in both towns but can be pricey if there's a shortage. You can also make it to Ouadâne without 4WD if you travel along the northern plateau road, but not if you travel from Chinguetti via the more interesting but sandy southern route. You'll also need a 4WD for Tidjikja.

The overland trip from Nouakchott to Nouâdhibou (525km) takes 22 to 24 hours and requires a 4WD. This route is far worse than any other section of the trans-Saharan route through Morocco and Mauritania. The first 155km from Nouakchott north to Cape Timiris is along the beach and passable only during low tide. Thereafter you enter the worst section, full of dunes for almost 300km. There are poles every 5km between Nouâmghâr, the fishing village at Cape Timiris, and just before the railway track in the north, but they will not keep you from getting lost if you have no guide. The last 70km southwestward alongside the railway tracks is flat and easy but don't stray from the track as mines abound.

For safety reasons (it's easy to get lost) go with at least one other vehicle and a guide (typically UM25,000; in Nouâdhibou, try the Fedération Mauritanienne de Guides Touristique ☎ 574 56 17). Make sure you take sufficient food, water and warm clothes.

The Route de l'Espoir from Nouakchott to Néma (around 1100km) has deteriorated and now only the first one-third counts as a road. For the rest of the way, the tracks on either side are marginally better and the 250km stretch between the Passe de Djouk and Aleg is appalling.

Rental

If you don't have a vehicle and you want more freedom than a tour can offer (most companies won't run tours for less than four people), consider renting a 4WD and driver. The standard Toyota Hilux usually costs around UM20,000 per day for the vehicle, plus petrol. A five-day round trip to/from Nouakchott taking in Terjît, Atâr, Chinguetti, Ouadâne, and a few small detours along the way, should costs no more than a total of UM100,000 plus UM20,000 petrol.

ORGANISED TOURS

There are numerous travel agencies in Nouakchott that offer tours around the country (see Nouakchott for more details). Travel is usually by 4WD. Standard tours include an eight-day tour to Atâr, Chinguetti, Ouadâne, Guelb er Richat and Terjît, the Tagânt plateau, or six-day excursions to the Banc d'Arguin. If there are at least four travellers, prices should average around UM15,000 per person per day.

Nouakchott

pop 735,000

Nouakchott, meaning 'Place of the Winds' in Hassaniya, was hastily constructed in 1960 at independence. St-Louis, which was the

NOUAKCHOTT

PLACES TO STAY
6 Hôtel-Restaurant Casablanca
8 Hôtel du Petit Paris; Phone Office
10 Auberge du Désert
11 Monotel Dar-el-Barka
12 Hôtel Halima
30 Auberge la Dune
43 Hôtel El Amane; Artisan Stall
52 Hôtel Chinguetti
55 Auberge de Jeunesse l'Amitié
63 Hôtel Mercure (Marhaba); GCAL – Tourisme Europcar
69 Auberge al Jezira
70 Hôtel Adrar; Auberge El Ahram

PLACES TO EAT
5 Welcome Burger
7 Pizza Lina; Naf
9 Parma Burger
20 Restaurant Le Guervoum; Cyber Valley
21 La Brioche Dorée; Taska Karaoke
25 Restaurant El-Bahdja
28 Le Bambou
37 Ali Baba
38 Snack Irak; Bakery; Supermarkets
39 Le Prince; Fruit Stands
51 Restaurant Phenicia
54 Rimal
71 Restaurant Taiba
72 Restaurant Zoubeida

OTHER
1 Elf Petrol Station
2 Petrol Station
3 Hi Net Cyber Café
4 Senegalese Embassy
13 Post Office
14 Airport
15 US Embassy
16 Spanish Embassy
17 German Embassy
18 Compunet
19 Moroccan Embassy
22 French Embassy
23 French Cultural Centre
24 St Joseph Cathedral
26 Artisan Shops
27 Kommunik
29 Air France
31 Tunis Air; Librairie Vents du Sud
32 Librairie
33 Randonée Tours; Savana Tours
34 Hadya Change
35 Mosquée Saudique (Grande Mosquée)
36 Petrol Station
40 La Nouvelle Boucherie
41 Car & 4WD Rental Agencies
42 BNM Bank; National Car Rental
44 Soprage; Atlas Voyages
45 Phone Shop
46 La Gazelle du Désert
47 Petrol Station; Air Algérie
48 Mauritanie Air Service
49 Compagnie Mauritanienne de Transport Aérian
50 ATV; Soreci Voyages
53 Bureau de Change
56 BMCI Bank
57 Main Post Office
58 Commissariat Central
59 Air Mauritanie
60 Royal Air Maroc
61 Friday Mosque
62 Petrol Station
64 Musée National
65 Cyber M@g
66 Hospital
67 Stade de la Luttes
68 L'Artisanal Féminin
73 Moroccan Mosque
74 4WDs for Eastern Mauritania

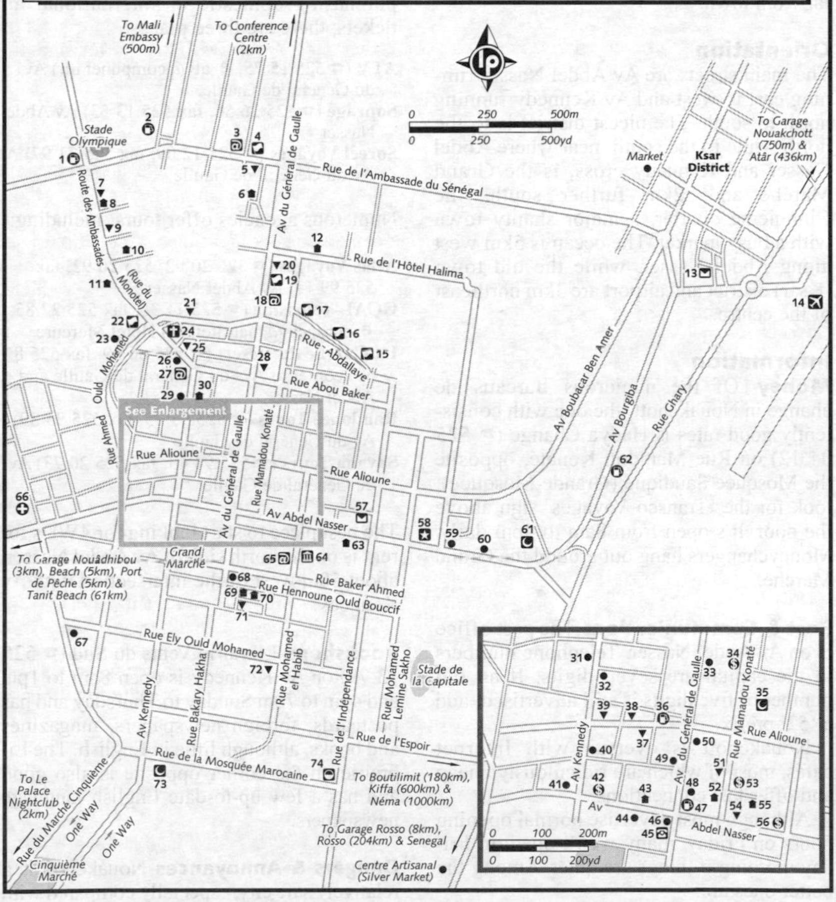
To Mali Embassy (500m)
To Conference Centre (2km)
0 250 500m
0 250 500yd
To Garage Nouakchott (750m) & Atâr (436km)
Market
Ksar District
Stade Olympique
Rue de l'Ambassade du Sénégal
Route des Ambassades
Av du Général de Gaulle
Rue de l'Hôtel Halima
(Rue du Monotel)
Rue Abdallaye
Rue Abou Baker
Ould Mohamed
Rue Ahmed
See Enlargement
Rue Alioune
Rue Mamadou Konaté
Av Abdel Nasser
Av Boubacar Ben Amer
Av Bourgiba
Rue Ghary
Grand Marché
Rue Baker Ahmed
Rue Hennoune Ould Bouccif
To Garage Nouâdhibou (3km), Beach (5km), Port de Pêche (5km) & Tanit Beach (61km)
Rue Ely Ould Mohamed
Av Kennedy
Rue Bakary Hakha
Rue Mohamed el Habib
Rue de l'Independance
Rue Mohamed Lemine Sakho
Stade de la Capitale
Rue de l'Espoir
Rue de la Mosquée Marocaine
To Boutilimit (180km), Kiffa (600km) & Néma (1000km)
To Le Palace Nightclub (2km)
Rue du Marché Cinquième
One Way
One Way
To Garage Rosso (8km), Rosso (204km) & Senegal
Cinquième Marché
Centre Artisanal (Silver Market)
Rue Alioune
Av Abdel Nasser
0 100 200m
0 100 200yd

MAURITANIA

administrative centre of the French territory Senegal-Mauritania, ended up on the Senegalese side, leaving Mauritania without a major city. Nouakchott is a strange place, built unusually 5km inland from the coast and, reflecting the desert origins of Mauritania's dominant Moors, its orientation is more towards the desert than the Atlantic; the town is surrounded by rolling sand dunes.

Designed for 200,000 inhabitants, the city was planned with wide streets and space around public buildings and houses – quite unlike a typical African city. Today, surrounded by shanty towns, it has nearly quadruple that number. In 1990, in order to free land for middle-class Moors, the government moved the poor to new settlements far from town.

Orientation

The main streets are Av Abdel Nasser running east to west and Av Kennedy running north to south. The nicest district is to the north while to the south, near where Abdel Nasser and Kennedy cross, is the Grand Marché and, 2km further south, the Cinquième quarter, a major shanty town with a busy market. The ocean is 5km west along Abdel Nasser, while the old town (Ksar) district and airport are 3km northeast of the centre.

Information

Money Of the numerous bureaus de change in Nouakchott, the one with consistently good rates is Hadya Change (☎ 525 04 12) on Rue Mamdou Konaté, opposite the Mosquée Saudique (Grande Mosquée); look for the 'Transco Voyages' sign above the door. It's open from 8am to 4pm daily. Moneychangers hang out around the Grand Marché.

Post & Communications The post office is on Av Abdel Nasser. Telephone numbers in the capital are seven digits. If an old number of five digits is still advertised, add a '52' prefix.

Nouakchott is overrun with Internet cafés, most of which are ridiculously cheap and offer fast connections.

Although most advertise normal opening hours on Friday, many won't open on Friday morning if things are quiet. Among the better ones are:

Compunet (☎ 525 90 17) Av du Général de Gaulle. Open 8am to 11pm Saturday to Thursday, 3pm to 11pm Friday. It charges UM200 per hour.

Cyber M@g (☎ 525 56 89) Rue Mohammed el-Habib. Open 8am to 1am daily. UM200 per hour.

Cyber Valley (☎ 529 34 78) Av du Général de Gaulle, near Restaurant Le Guervoum. Open 9am to 1pm daily. Students/adults UM200/300 per hour.

Hi Net Cyber Café (☎ 631 62 27) Rue de l'Ambassade du Sénégal. Open 9am to 2am daily. UM300 per hour.

Kommunik (☎ 525 27 03, fax 525 32 65) Av Kennedy. Open 8am to 2.30am daily. UM300 per hour.

Travel Agencies & Tour Operators For purchasing domestic or international air tickets, there are three places:

ATV (☎ 525 15 75, e atv@compunet.mr) Av du Général de Gaulle

Soprage (☎ 525 26 56, fax 525 13 53) Av Abdel Nasser

Soreci Voyages (☎ 525 12 09, fax 525 71 97) Av du Général de Gaulle

Numerous agencies offer tours, including:

Atlas Voyages (☎ 525 20 92, 525 20 92, fax 525 99 17) Av Abdel Nasser

GCAL-Tourisme (☎ 525 11 36, fax 525 22 85, e europcar@mauritel.mr) Hôtel Mercure

La Gazelle du Désert (☎ 525 06 69, fax 525 81 62) corner of Avs du Général de Gaulle and Abdel Nasser

Randoneé Tours (☎ 525 95 35, fax 525 95 39) Av du Général de Gaulle

Savana Tours (☎ 525 94 43, fax 525 20 73) Av du Général de Gaulle

The best place to start looking for 4WDs for rent is on the north side of Av Abdel Nasser, about 50m west of the intersection with Av Kennedy.

Bookshops Librairie Vents du Sud (☎ 525 13 79) on Av Kennedy is open 8am to 1pm and 4pm to 7pm Sunday to Thursday and has postcards, foreign newspapers, magazines and books, although little in English. The Librairie on the corner opposite is also good and has a few up-to-date English language newspapers.

Dangers & Annoyances Nouakchott is a relatively safe city, especially compared with other capital cities in the region. It's a late-night city, with many people walking around even at 11pm. Even at those hours walking is generally safe for men. The worst area is along the beach near the city; no-one, especially women, should walk along the beach at night as muggings there are common. Avoid driving the major streets in the late afternoon as the traffic jams can quickly descend into stalemate.

Musée National

The museum *(admission UM300; open 9am-3.30pm Sun-Thur)*, southwest of Hôtel Mercure, is worth visiting, although it focuses on the culture of the Moors, excluding that of the black southerners. On the first level is a prehistoric gallery with archaeological exhibits while the second level is taken up with more recent ethnographic displays from Moorish society. Admission is officially UM300 but you may be charged UM500. The building is labelled as the Ministry of Culture.

Mosques

The **Grande Mosquée** (better known as the Mosquée Saudique) in the centre on Rue Mamadou Konaté was donated by Saudi Arabia. The two other principal mosques are the **Friday mosque** *(Av Abdel Nasser)* and the new **Moroccan mosque** near the Cinquième district.

Port de Pêche

It's definitely worth checking out the small wharf and fish market, Port de Pêche; the best time is between 4pm and 6pm, when the fishing boats return. You'll see teams of men dragging in heavy hand-knotted fishing nets. Small boys hurry back and forth with trays of fish, which they sort, gut, fillet and lay out on large trestles to dry. The fishers, mostly Wolof and Fula, are friendly and will explain techniques, the different types of fish they catch and the going prices.

The cheapest way to get here is by shared taxi (around UM100 from the centre). A 'taxi course' from the centre of town to the fish market costs about UM300.

Le Ksar

This Moorish settlement is the oldest part of town but lost much of its interest and old buildings when it was destroyed by flood in 1950. If you're driving over the desert and need spare parts, the Ksar is the place to look and there are some good markets.

Swimming

The nearest beach to Nouakchott is 5km west of the centre. There's no shade, so bring sunscreen. On weekday mornings the beaches are relatively deserted. If you have a 4WD, head for the unmarked, secluded **Tanit beach**, 61km to the north, where there's a good camping spot. Hôtel Mercure's **swimming pool** can be used by nonguests for UM500.

Places to Stay – Budget

Auberge de Jeunesse l'Amitié *(☎ 525 44 19, Off Rue Mamadou Konaté)* Dorm beds UM1000. This friendly youth hostel is a down-to-earth place with clean four- to six-bed rooms, hot water showers, a kitchen and secure parking. It's a good place to get advice on travelling in Mauritania.

Hôtel Adrar *(☎ 525 29 55, Off Rue Hennoune Ould Bouccif)* Rooms UM2000. The friendly Adrar, southeast of the Grand Marché, offers simple, clean rooms with hot water showers and fan.

Auberge du Désert *(☎ 525 87 01)* Singles/doubles with shared bathroom UM2000/3000. This place is on the next road to the right beyond the Monotel and the third building in on your left – an unmarked two-storey house.

Hôtel du Petit Paris *(☎ 525 66 21, Route des Ambassades)* Rooms UM1500 per person. Hôtel du Petit Paris, near Auberge du Désert, has a common room with mattresses and a shower (see also Places to Stay – Mid-Range).

Auberge la Dune *(☎ 525 37 36, fax 525 70 43, Rue Abou Baker)* Singles/doubles with fan UM2500/5000, with fan & bathroom UM3000/5800, with air-con & shared bathroom UM3500/7000. This highly recommended place, run by an ex-guide who is a good source of information, has a nice family feel (complete with Phoenix the dog) and offers good, clean rooms and secure parking. Meals are good especially on the pleasant upstairs terrace. Breakfast costs UM700.

Places to Stay – Mid-Range

Hôtel du Petit Paris *(☎ 525 66 21, Route des Ambassades)* Rooms with bathroom &

fan/air-con from UM4000/6800. This pleasant French-run hotel, beyond the Monotel, has reasonably priced rooms that are tidy and spacious; prices are negotiable if things are quiet.

Auberge el-Ahram *(Rue Hennoune Ould Bouccif)* Rooms with bathroom & fan/air-con from UM4000/6000. Run by a friendly Syrian family, the rooms here are simple but reasonable value for Nouakchott. The downstairs restaurant serves decent meals for UM500 to UM1900.

Auberge al-Jezira *(☎ 529 25 30, Off Rue Hennoune Ould Bouccif)* Singles/doubles UM5000/6000. The spacious and attractive rooms here are much better value than the exterior suggests and come with bathroom, satellite TV, fridge, sitting room and balcony.

Hôtel Chinguetti *(☎ 525 35 37, Rue Mamadou Konaté)* Singles/doubles with bathroom UM5500/6200. The Chinguetti has spacious but sterile rooms. Still, it's central and not bad value.

Hôtel-Restaurant Casablanca *(☎ 525 59 65, Off Rue de l'Ambassade de Sénégal)* Rooms with air-con without/with bathroom UM10,000/12,000. The somewhat remote Casablanca has very pleasant rooms, an enclosed garden area, bar and restaurant. Staff can be a bit offhand, but it's a good choice.

Hôtel El Amane *(☎ 525 21 78, fax 525 70 43, e elamane@toptechnology.mr, Av Abdel Nasser)* Singles/doubles with air-con UM10,000/11,500. The tidy but unspectacular rooms are a tour-group favourite and it's certainly a well-run establishment. The rooms at the front have a balcony but are also noisier. Breakfast costs UM600 to UM1200.

Places to Stay – Top End

All these hotels accept credit cards and have satellite TVs.

Hôtel Mercure *(Marhaba; ☎ 529 50 50, fax 529 50 55, e mercuremarhaba.bc@compunet.mr, Av Abdel Nasser)* Singles/ doubles UM17,900/19,800, suites UM29,800. Arguably Mauritania's finest, the Mercure has a good restaurant, bar, swimming pool and very comfortable rooms.

Hôtel Halima *(☎ 525 79 21, fax 525 79 22, Rue de l'Hôtel Halima)* Singles/doubles UM15,000/17,000, suites UM35,000. The well-run Halima also has a touch of class, with tastefully decorated rooms as well as a good restaurant and bar.

Monotel Dar-el-Barka *(☎ 525 35 26, fax 525 18 31, e info@monotel.mr, Route des Ambassades)* Singles/doubles UM15,300/18,200, suites UM36,540. The rooms here are large and well appointed but the whole place is a little tired and is now running behind the other two. There's a boutique, bar, restaurant, swimming pool and cybercafé.

Places to Eat

Cheap Eats There are many fast-food establishments on Rue Alioune between Av Kennedy and Av du Général de Gaulle. Open until 11pm or later, most have a Lebanese bent.

Le Prince and ***Ali Baba*** offer chawarma sandwiches, hamburgers and chicken sandwiches for UM300. ***Snack Irak*** *(☎ 525 12 23)* is also a perennial favourite of budget travellers. To the north, ***Welcome Burger*** is opposite the Senegalese embassy, while ***Naf*** and the excellent ***Parma Burger***, where burgers cost UM400 to UM600 and pizzas start at UM900, are along Route des Ambassades. ***La Brioche Dorée*** *(☎ 525 44 58, Rue Abdallaye)* is also good for cheap snacks.

Restaurant Taiba *(Off Rue Hennoune Ould Bouccif)*, near Hôtel Adrar, serves couscous for UM250 and rice with fish or meat for UM250. It's open until late.

African & Moroccan The friendly ***Restaurant Le Guervoum*** *(☎ 525 60 36, Av du Général de Gaulle)* is an excellent, reasonably priced choice. The menu owes a lot to the owner's Cameroonian origins, including *sauce feuille* and *sauce gombo* (UM700) and *n'dole viande* (UM1000). There's also a good selection of fish dishes for UM1400 to UM2500. Entrees range from UM600 to UM900 and mains start at UM850. It is open 11am to 3pm and 7pm to 11pm Saturday to Thursday, and 7pm to 11pm Friday.

One of Nouakchott's best choices is ***Restaurant El-Bahdja*** *(☎ 630 53 83, Off Rue des Ambassades)* Run by a friendly Moroccan family, this pleasant place has a varied, predominantly Moroccan menu at very reasonable prices. Sandwiches range from UM200 to UM500, soups are UM500, and mains range from UM800 to UM1500. It is open 12.30pm to midnight daily.

Restaurant Zoubeida *(☎ 525 21 84, Rue Ely Ould Mohamed)*. Mains from UM300.

Open noon-11pm daily. For something different, try the Zoubeida. There's a carpeted room at the back where customers, usually all men, lounge on worn cushions. It serves Moroccan couscous (UM250) and Senegalese rice with fish sauce (UM200).

European Near Hôtel du Petit Paris, the air-con ***Pizza Lina*** *(☎ 525 86 62, Route des Ambassades)* is extremely popular with expats and locals alike. The service is good, the dining area has a pleasant modern ambience and it serves alcohol. Pizzas range from UM900 to UM1500, other mains are UM1500 to UM2400 and salads range from UM1200 to UM1900. It is open noon to midnight daily.

Hôtel El Amane *(☎ 525 21 78, fax 525 70 43, ⓔ elamane@toptechnology.mr, Av Abdel Nasser)* Entrees UM900-1900, mains UM2200-2500. Open noon-3pm & 7pm-10.30pm daily. This place serves expensive but high-quality French cuisine, which comes in huge servings. The fish dishes are especially good.

Hôtel du Petit Paris *(☎ 525 66 21, Route des Ambassades)* Open 7pm-10pm daily. This hotel has a limited menu but what it does it does well; spaghetti or roast chicken and chips cost UM550.

Lebanese & Asian Cheap, cheerful and not bad value, the ***Rimal*** *(☎ 525 48 32, Av Abdel Nasser)* has main meals from UM600 and is open from noon to 11pm Saturday to Thursday.

Restaurant Phenicia *(☎ 525 25 75, Rue Mamadou Konaté)* Sandwiches UM200, mains UM400-1100. Open 11.30am-11pm daily. Spacious and plain, the lively Phenicia is a popular lunch and dinner spot right in the centre of town. The food is patchy but it's probably the best Lebanese you'll get for the price.

Hôtel-Restaurant Casablanca *(☎ 525 59 65, Off Rue de l'Ambassade de Sénégal)* Mains from UM1600. Open noon-3pm & 7pm-11pm daily. The air-con Casablanca serves alcohol and specialises in good but expensive Lebanese and French cuisine.

The simple ***Le Bambou*** *(☎ 634 27 72, Av du Général de Gaulle)* serves good, moderately priced Chinese and Vietnamese food. Entrees start at UM600. It is open noon to 3pm and 7pm to 10.30pm daily.

Self-Catering On Av Kennedy and Rue Alioune are shops with tinned goods and drinks and stalls stacked with fresh fruit. Vendors are open until around 11pm and prices are reasonable.

La Nouvelle Boucherie *(☎ 525 1303 Av Kennedy)* Open 8am-1pm & 4pm-7pm Sat-Thur. This small French-run supermarket has imported cheeses, bread, pastries, meats and tinned goods.

Entertainment

Bars The top-end hotels, as well as ***Pizza Lina*** and ***Hôtel-Restaurant Casablanca***, serve alcohol. A beer costs UM500.

Taska Karaoke *(Rue Abdallaye)* Admission UM1500. Open from 7pm. The Taska Karaoke (or Karaoke Club), near the French embassy and next door to La Brioche Dorée (see Places to Eat), has lively music, enthusiastic singers and serves good food.

Le Palace Admission UM2000. Open from 10pm Tues & Thur. Le Palace features a dance floor and video screen. It's at Ceinture Verte and you'll need a taxi to get there. If you're coming from the TV station heading west, turn left when you pass the *palais du congrès*; the house-like disco is at the end.

Cinemas French films are shown at the ***French Cultural Centre*** *(Rue Ahmed Ould Mohammed)*; its programme is outside.

Wrestling Occasionally on Saturday afternoons there are wrestling matches at the ***Stade de la Luttes*** (wrestling arena), at the western end of Rue Ely Ould Mohamed.

Shopping

L'Artisanal Féminin Open 8am-11am & 4pm-6pm daily. This women's cooperative, near the Grand Marché, sells tablecloths, clothes, purses, pillows, camelhair rugs, colourfully painted leather cushions, nomad tents and fine straw mats at fixed prices.

Grand Marché (also called Marché Capital) offers a bit of everything. Potential souvenirs include brass teapots, silver jewellery, traditional wooden boxes with silver inlay, pipes, leather bags, sandals, cushions, beads and *grisgris* (charms) such as dried frogs and bird claws. You'll find dress material, colourful Soninké tie-dyed material, Senegalese batiks and the inexpensive, crinkly *malafa* that Moor women use as veils.

Cinquième Marché is good for browsing through and people-watching, and has good vegetables, household wares and tailors. To get there, look for a green minivan along Av Kennedy and ask for 'le Cinquième'; the cost is about UM30.

For wooden boxes with silver inlay, daggers and jewellery, check outside ***Hôtel El Amane*** or northeast of the corner of Av Kennedy and Route des Ambassades; prices are high, and hard bargaining is required. Also check the ***Centre Artisanal*** (or 'silver market'). Obscure and sometimes moribund, it's unmarked and not easy to find. Head south on the highway to Rosso – it's beyond the roundabout intersection for Boutilimit and on your right.

Getting There & Away

Air For details of international and domestic flights to/from Nouakchott, see the Getting There & Away and Getting Around sections earlier in this chapter. The following airlines have offices in Nouakchott:

Air Algérie Cnr Avs du Général de Gaulle and Abdel Nasser
Air France (☎ 525 18 08) Av Kennedy
Air Mauritanie (☎ 525 22 12 or 525 25 45) Av Abdel Nasser
Compagnie Mauritanienne de Transport Aérian (☎ 529 80 67) Av du Général de Gaulle
Royal Air Maroc (☎ 525 36 48) Av Abdel Nasser
Tunis Air (☎ 525 87 63) Av Kennedy

Bush Taxi The main Garage Nouakchott is on the road to Atâr, about 1km north of the airport. Vehicles to most destinations leave in the morning from around 9am, but for Rosso (UM1000 to UM1250, 3½ hours) you may be able to find earlier ones. Transport to Atâr costs UM2800 to UM3500 (seven hours).

There are also specific garages for Mauritania's various regions that are worth trying if nothing's happening at the main garage. For Nouâdhibou (UM3000 to UM5000, 15 to 20 hours), the Garage Nouâdhibou is about 3km west of the town centre, the Garage Rosso is almost 10km south of the centre, and 4WDs for the east of the country leave from an open area at the corner or Rues de l'Independance and la Mosqué Marocaine. Departures include Kiffa (UM3000 to UM3500, ten hours), Ayoûn-el-Atroûs (UM3700 to UM4200, 15 hours) and Néma (UM5000 to UM5500, up to two days).

Getting Around

To/From the Airport The airport is in the Ksar district. The standard taxi fare to the centre is UM700. It's cheaper to hail a shared taxi from the highway nearby (UM150).

Minibus & Taxi Green minibuses run throughout the city (UM30) and can be hailed anywhere along the main thoroughfares.

Taxis come in all colours and spotting them is fairly easy. You need to specify clearly whether you want a shared taxi or a taxi course. Fares start from UM100 for a seat in a shared taxi, and from UM500 for a short trip anywhere around town in your own taxi. Expect to pay UM1500 to rent a taxi by the hour.

Car All the agencies listed earlier under Travel Agencies & Tour Operators also rent cars with drivers. For European-standard service, try Europcar (☎ 525 11 36, fax 525 22 85), in Hôtel Mercure on Av du Général de Gaulle; or National (☎ 525 4309, fax 529 20 33, ⓔ c.m.t@compunet.mr), near BNM bank, also on Av du Général de Gaulle. The cheapest Toyota Corolla/Hilux (4WD) cost UM4800/9600 per day plus UM108/150 per km. Costs quickly escalate once you add insurance, driver and petrol.

The North Coast

NOUÂDHIBOU

pop 72,000

Called Port-Étienne during colonial days, Nouâdhibou is on the Baie du Lévrier, in the middle of a narrow 35km-long peninsula. The eastern half of the peninsula is Mauritania and the western half, the Atlantic Ocean side, is Western Sahara. Be warned – there are many land mines planted in the sands on the western side, and this area is strictly off limits.

The sea on both sides is chilled by the Canary current, and it has one of the world's highest densities of fish. As a result, Nouâdhibou is famous for its fishing and ships come here from all over the world.

Orientation

The city's main street, running north-south, is Blvd Médian. The northern side of town is Numerowat, while the older fishing quarter, east of the stadium, is Tcherka. The latter was once a settlement of people from the Canary Islands. Today, it's a shanty town crammed with fishers. At the southern edge of town is the Port de Pêche Moderne (the container port) and 8km further south is Cansado. Port Minéralier, 3km further, is where the train line ends and ore is loaded onto ships, while 4km beyond is Cape Blanc, the southern tip of the peninsula. (For a map of the area around Nouâdhibou see the Parc National du Banc D'Arguin map later in this chapter.)

Information

Money There are bureaus de change along Blvd Médian. Alternatively, ask discreetly around the market. Rates here are considerably lower than in Nouakchott.

Registration Overland travellers must get their passports stamped at the *sûreté* (☎ 574 50 72), which closes at 2.30pm. Those with vehicles must buy insurance. The entire process usually takes four to six hours.

Post & Communications The post office is east off Blvd Médian. Nouâdhibou has a number of Internet cafés that charge UM300 an hour. Connections are much slower than in Nouakchott or even Atâr. Places to try along Blvd Médian include:

Cyber Éspace (☎ 574 51 50) Open 8am to midnight Saturday to Thursday and 1pm to midnight Friday.

Top Net Cyber Café (☎ 574 91 88) Open 8.30am to 2.30am Saturday to Thursday and 3pm to 2.30am Friday.

Top Technology (☎ 574 56 43) Open 8am to midnight Saturday to Thursday and 1pm to midnight Friday.

If any of the old five-digit telephone numbers are still advertised, add a '57' prefix.

Travel Agencies For purchasing air tickets, reliable agencies along Blvd Médian include Soreci Voyages (☎ 574 63 25), Sogetra (☎ 574 54 58) and NVT (☎ 574 52 80). The latter advertises fares to Australia, but sadly they can't deliver.

Things to Do

For **fishing**, head to the fishing centre at Oasian Hôtel, about 10km south of the

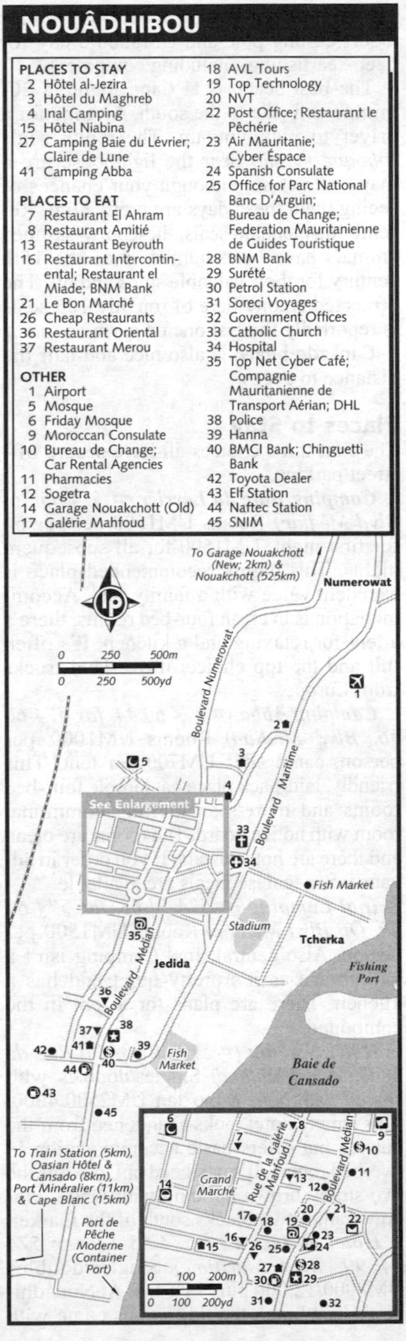
NOUÂDHIBOU
PLACES TO STAY
2 Hôtel al-Jezira
3 Hôtel du Maghreb
4 Inal Camping
15 Hôtel Niabina
27 Camping Baie du Lévrier; Claire de Lune
41 Camping Abba
PLACES TO EAT
7 Restaurant El Ahram
8 Restaurant Amitié
13 Restaurant Beyrouth
16 Restaurant Intercontinental; Restaurant el Miade; BNM Bank
21 Le Bon Marché
26 Cheap Restaurants
36 Restaurant Oriental
37 Restaurant Merou
OTHER
1 Airport
5 Mosque
6 Friday Mosque
9 Moroccan Consulate
10 Bureau de Change; Car Rental Agencies
11 Pharmacies
12 Sogetra
14 Garage Nouakchott (Old)
17 Galérie Mahfoud
18 AVL Tours
19 Top Technology
20 NVT
22 Post Office; Restaurant le Pêchérie
23 Air Mauritanie; Cyber Éspace
24 Spanish Consulate
25 Office for Parc National Banc D'Arguin; Bureau de Change; Federation Mauritanienne de Guides Touristique
28 BNM Bank
29 Sureté
30 Petrol Station
31 Soreci Voyages
32 Government Offices
33 Catholic Church
34 Hospital
35 Top Net Cyber Café; Compagnie Mauritanienne de Transport Aérian; DHL
38 Police
39 Hanna
40 BMCI Bank; Chinguetti Bank
42 Toyota Dealer
43 Elf Station
44 Naftec Station
45 SNIM
To Garage Nouakchott (New; 2km) & Nouakchott (525km)
Numerowat
0 250 500m
0 250 500yd
Boulevard Numerowat
Boulevard Maritime
See Enlargement
Fish Market
Stadium
Tcherka
Fishing Port
Jedida
Boulevard Médian
Fish Market
Baie de Cansado
To Train Station (5km), Oasian Hôtel & Cansado (8km), Port Minéralier (11km) & Cape Blanc (15km)
Port de Pêche Moderne (Container Port)
Grand Marché
Rue de la Galerie Mahfoud
Boulevard Médian
0 100 200m
0 100 200yd

centre. Count on paying about UM1500 for a surf casting pole and UM8500 a day for deep-sea fishing, including equipment.

The best beach is at **Cape Blanc**, a 20-minute taxi ride to the south. Arrange for a driver to pick you up. The monk seals *(phoque moine)* near the lighthouse are a major attraction, although your chances of seeing them these days are pretty slim. Resembling elephant seals, these grey-skinned animals have been hunted since the 15th century for their valuable skins and oil. The protected colony here of roughly 100 seals is reportedly the last one on earth.

Cansado beach is also nice and half the distance to get to.

Places to Stay

The first three choices all have secure off-street parking.

Camping Baie du Lévrier *(☎ 574 65 36, Blvd Médian)* Rooms UM1500 per person for first night, UM1500 for all subsequent nights. This highly recommended place is excellent value with a family feel. Accommodation is in clean four-bed rooms, there's a tent for relaxing and a kitchen. It's often full and the top choice of overland trucks from Europe.

Camping Abba *(☎ 574 60 44, fax 574 60 56, Blvd Médian)* Rooms UM1000 per person, camp sites UM700 per tent. This friendly, laid-back place has simple four-bed rooms and there's an inviting communal room with notice board. The rooms are clean and there are hot showers. If you order in advance, Senegalese meals are available.

Inal Camping *(☎ 574 54 63, fax 574 64 69, Off Blvd Médian)* Rooms UM1500 per person. Also central, Inal Camping isn't a bad choice as it's pretty quiet and has a kitchen. There are plans for a tent in the compound.

Hôtel Niabina *(☎ 574 59 83, Off Rue de la Galérie Mahfoud)* Singles/doubles with shared bathroom & no fan UM2500/4000. This simple hotel looks abandoned from the outside but offers basic accommodation in two-bed rooms. It's unsigned but look for the two-storey brown building with white window frames two blocks south of the market.

Hôtel al-Jezira *(☎ 574 53 17, fax 574 54 99, Blvd Maritime)* Singles/doubles UM8000/12,000 plus 14% tax. At Nouâdhibou's best hotel, the tidy rooms come with air-con, hot-water bathroom and satellite TV. The restaurant offers good service but disappointing food.

Hôtel du Maghreb *(☎ 574 55 44)* Singles/doubles UM5000/6000. On the road to the airport, the Maghreb has an abandoned air, the simple rooms don't come with a fan and there isn't a restaurant. There is, however, a reasonably stocked bar.

Oasian Hôtel *(☎ 574 90 29, fax 574 90 53)* Singles/doubles with air-con UM7980/10,830. The Oasian in Cansado about 10km south of the centre of town has excellent rooms. It accepts credit cards and has a deep-sea fishing centre and a beach nearby.

Places to Eat

In the centre, you'll find a number of very cheap restaurants along Rue de la Galérie Mahfoud including ***Restaurant Amitié***, little more than a hole in the wall but from where you'll leave well fed on cheap stews and chicken. Others worth trying include ***Restaurant Intercontinental*** and ***Restaurant el Miade***, while cheap chop houses also abound around the perimeter of the market. All charge around UM200 or less for a filling meal.

Restaurant Beyrouth *(☎ 574 52 06, Rue de la Galérie Mahfoud)* Sandwiches & omelettes UM200-800, other mains UM450-1800. Open 10am-3.30pm & 6pm-2am Sat-Thur. This is one of the better Lebanese restaurants around Nouâdhibou. It's a block east of the market and run by a friendly Lebanese family who cook excellent chicken and fish/seafood dishes.

Restaurant El Ahram *(☎ 574 50 18)* Meals UM300-500. On the north side of the market, and also Lebanese, El Ahram is a cheerful place with decent meals, including a few North African dishes such as couscous.

Restaurant le Pêchérie *(Off Blvd Médian)* This restaurant next to the post office is highly recommended. Servings are huge – a filling shrimp dinner costs UM350.

Claire de Lune *(☎ 641 95 85, Blvd Médian)* Snacks from UM150, salads UM500-1000, mains UM500-800. Open 7.30am-midnight. This popular, spotlessly clean place right in the heart of town near Camping Baie du Lévrier is great any time of the day. Good breakfasts start from UM500, while there are excellent pastries, brochettes and other mains. You can also get sausage rolls, spring rolls, ice cream and espresso coffee.

Restaurant Merou *(☎ 574 59 80, fax 574 64 78, Blvd Médian)* Entrees UM500-1000, mains UM1500-2500. Open 11.30am-3.30pm & 6.30pm-11.30pm daily. This is arguably the best restaurant in Nouâdhibou. The chef is Korean, the cuisine is Korean and French and the menu is also written in Spanish and Chinese. The plate of grilled seafood (UM1500) is the stuff of which cravings are made. Sadly, the owner is reportedly considering closing down the place so get there before it goes.

Restaurant Oriental *(☎ 574 58 77, Off Blvd Médian)* Soups UM300-700, mains UM900-2800. Open noon-4pm & 7pm-11pm Sat-Thur. The Oriental is a cosy little place with eccentric but attentive service and the Franco-Oriental cuisine is thoughtfully prepared with a decent range of chicken and seafood dishes.

Le Bon Marché *(☎ 574 56 30, Blvd Médian)* Of the many small grocery stores around town, Le Bon Marché, right in the centre of town, is probably the pick.

Getting There & Away

Air For details of international flights, see the main Getting There & Away section earlier in this chapter. Air Mauritanie (☎ 574 54 50) has two flights on most days to/from Nouakchott (UM13,140/26,070 one way/return), as well as a Sunday flight to Zouérat (UM12,640).

Compagnie Mauritanienne de Transport Aérian (☎/fax 574 83 18, ⓔ cmt@toptechnology.mr), Blvd Médian, has four flights weekly to/from Nouakchott for UM11,400 and a Monday flight to Atâr for UM11,000). It offers discounted fares during Ramadan.

Train The 'train station' is about 5km south of town, 3km before Cansado. There's no building, just a spot in the desert near the tracks where you can buy tickets and a few meagre snacks. On board, a man sells tea and cheap snacks. The train with a passenger car leaves around 2.30pm daily, arriving in Choûm (UM800) around 2am (where pick-up trucks for Atâr will be waiting) and Zouérat (UM1000) around 7am. For more details, see the boxed text 'The Iron-Ore Train' in the main Getting Around section earlier in this chapter.

Car There are two routes to Nouakchott – via Choûm and Atâr (usually involving shipping your car on the train) or directly south along the beach. For details of this latter route, see Car & Motorcycle in the main Getting Around section earlier in the chapter.

Alternatively, ship your vehicle by train to Choûm, and drive from there to Nouakchott, a day's drive. You must make arrangements with SNIM (the company that operates the train) at least a day in advance at the Cité SNIM building (☎ 574 51 74, fax 574 53 96). It costs UM6500 to UM11,000, depending on vehicle size.

Bush Taxi Bush taxis ply daily between Nouâdhibou and Nouakchott. The route is partially along the beach and when the tide is high, vehicles must wait for it to recede. The trip usually takes 15 to 20 hours depending in part on the tides. Vehicles (pickups and Land Rovers) leave Nouâdhibou from the new Garage Nouakchott, 5km north of the market, although some still leave from the old Garage behind the market. Departures are usually between 8am and 11am and again around 5pm. The fare is UM5000 (UM3000 in the back of a pick-up).

Getting Around

Taxi Shared taxis are plentiful. Fares are fixed: UM50 within the centre and up to Numerowat, UM70 to the Port de Pèche Moderne and UM100 to the train station and Cansado. Chartered black-and-yellow taxis charge UM500 from the airport to the centre (less if you share) and at least UM600 by the hour.

Car AVL Tours (☎ 574 53 34), opposite Galérie Mahfoud, rents cars for travel around town (UM7500). For the Parc National du Banc d'Arguin, Hanna (☎ 574 62 42) on Blvd Maritime charges UM50,000 for a standard two-day tour. However, to tour the park properly you need at least three days because the trip there takes seven hours. Three-day trips are negotiable. Hanna asks UM80,000 (which includes petrol, driver, guide and tents).

PARC NATIONAL DU BANC D'ARGUIN

This park *(Park office in Nouâdhibou, ☎ 574 67 44, Blvd Médian; admission UM800 per person per day)* is an important stopover and breeding ground for multitudes of birds migrating between Europe and Southern Africa. Over two million broad-billed sandpipers *(limicoles)* have been recorded here in the winter. Other species include pink flamingos *(flamant rose),* white pelicans *(pélican blanc),* grey pelicans, royal terns *(sternes royales),* gull-billed terns *(spatule blanche),* black terns *(sterne bridée),* white-breasted cormorants, spoonbills and several species of herons, egrets and waders.

The park extends 200km north from Cape Timiris (155km north of Nouakchott). Most birds are found on sand islands in the shallow ocean. The best viewing time is December and January, which is also the mating season. During this period, you can't get too close to the birds because the slightest disturbance can cause them to fly away and abandon their eggs. The only way to see them is by small boat. The main island, 30km long, is Tidra, and just to the west of the northern tip are two tiny islands, Niroumi and Nair. There are other sandbanks but these three are the most accessible. The principal launching point is **Twik**, a fishing village on the mainland 6km northeast of Tidra. You can find boats here; they cost UM10,000 whether you stay out all day or only a few hours.

After, you could head to **Cape Tagarit**, 40km north of Tidra. You can fish, snorkel and ***camp*** here without government permission or a guide. The view from the cape is magnificent and the water is crystal clear, perfect for viewing fish. A catch of trout, sea bass and sea bream is almost guaranteed; just don't let the eerie wailing of jackals, or their presence near camp, bother you.

Park permits are issued in Nouâdhibou at the park headquarters which organises trips for large groups and is open 8am to 4pm Saturday to Thursday. It also sells a number of brochures for UM1000 to UM4000.

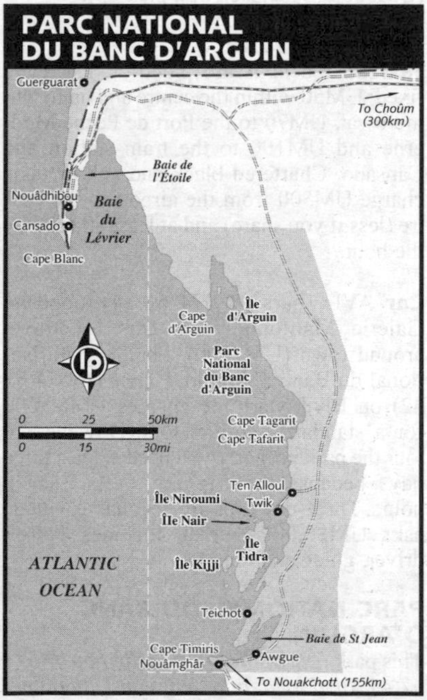
Guerguarat
To Choûm (300km)
Baie de l'Étoile
Nouâdhibou
Baie du Lévrier
Cansado
Cape Blanc
Île d'Arguin
Cape d'Arguin
Parc National du Banc d'Arguin
0 25 50km
0 15 30mi
Cape Tagarit
Cape Tafarit
Ten Alloul
Île Niroumi
Twik
Île Nair
Île Tidra
Île Kijji
ATLANTIC OCEAN
Teichot
Baie de St Jean
Cape Timiris
Nouâmghâr
Awgue
To Nouakchott (155km)
PARC NATIONAL DU BANC D'ARGUIN

Getting There & Away

To get to Twik, head for the fishing village of Ten Alloul, which is roughly halfway between Nouâdhibou and Nouakchott. You can rent a vehicle in either city or, cheaper, take a bush taxi; most of those plying the Nouakchott to Nouâdhibou route stop here. You must pay the full fare, though (UM5000). From Ten Alloul it's 14km southwest along the coast and down a small peninsula to Twik.

If you're driving from Nouâdhibou, see Car & Motorcycle in the main Getting Around section earlier in this chapter. Coming from Nouakchott, it's another 70km from Cape Timiris on a good sand track to where the track divides; take the left track towards the sea for roughly 25km more to Twik. If you're headed for Cape Tagarit, though, continue northwards along the track. At 106km north of Cape Timiris, you'll reach two low rocky hills bisecting the track; head directly west by compass over sand dunes for 25km to Cape Tafarit. The smaller Cape Tagarit is 5km to the north and better for camping.

The North

If you have time to visit only one area in Mauritania in depth, head for the Adrar region. Highlights include the ancient Saharan caravan towns of Chinguetti and Ouadâne, the oasis of Terjît and superb desert scenery.

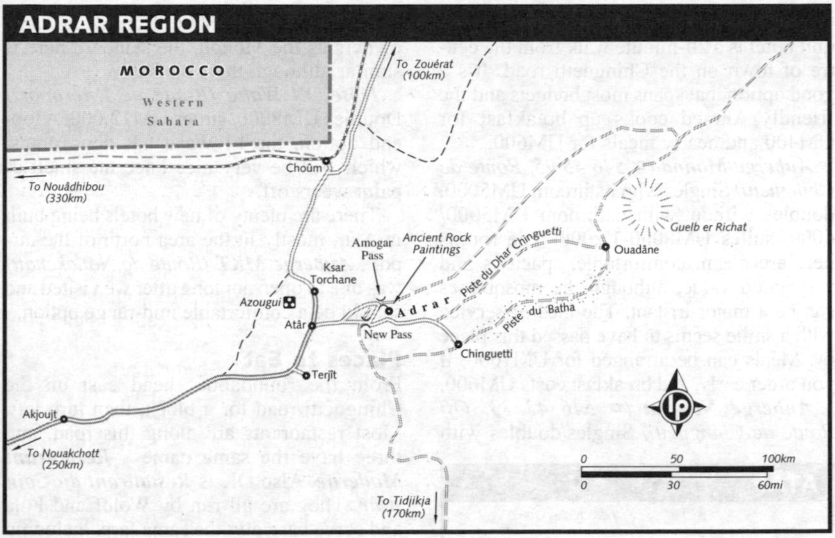
ADRAR REGION
MOROCCO
Western Sahara
To Zouérat (100km)
Choûm
To Nouâdhibou (330km)
Guelb er Richat
Ancient Rock Paintings
Amogar Pass
Ksar Torchane
Piste du Dhar Chinguetti
Ouadâne
Azougui
Adrar
Atâr
Piste du Batha
New Pass
Chinguetti
Terjît
Akjoujt
To Nouakchott (250km)
0 50 100km
0 30 60mi
To Tidjikja (170km)

ATÂR

pop 20,000

Atâr is the major northern commercial centre. It's a town with little of interest but is the starting point for several interesting side trips. With the arrival of regular flights direct from France, the town has become quite a competitive place and, unlike the rest of Mauritania, you're likely to encounter your fair share of touts and hustlers.

A large rond-point (roundabout) marks the centre of Atâr and the market is just north of it. The area around the market is good for changing money (US dollars and euros), although the bureaus de change around the main roundabout offer similarly poor rates. The small maze-like Ksar district, west of the market, is a good place to explore. It's the old residential quarter, with narrow winding streets, brick walls and carved doorways.

Atâr has at least two Internet cafés; one hour costs UM300. MDI Cyber Café (☎ 633 42 51) is open 8am to 1pm and 4pm to 11pm Saturday to Thursday; it's upstairs in the two-storey building just north of the Route de Chinguetti. Sodeq Cyber Café (☎ 645 11 61), opposite Salima Voyages, is open 9am to noon and 4pm to 6pm Saturday to Thursday.

Places to Stay

Bab Sahara *(☎ 647 39 66, fax 546 46 05, ⓔ justus_buma@yahoo.com, Off Route de Azougui)* Bed in tent UM1200 per person, 2-person stone hut UM1500 per person. Bab Sahara is probably the best value in town and is well run by a Dutch/German couple, Justus and Cora, long-term residents of Atâr. The toilets and showers are excellent, as are the meals for UM750 to UM2000, although there are cheaper sandwiches available from UM500. Scattered around the courtyard are old wooden doors from Atâr, which have been rescued from wreckers and Western antique dealers. Justus can arrange alternative tours into the desert and even a few secret hideaways, but hold firm if you really do want to go to Chinguetti or Ouadâne. It costs UM300/500 to park your car/truck.

Auberge Ederg Atâr *(☎ 632 58 49, Off Route de Chinguetti)* Mattress in communal room UM1200. This place is cheap but has few other virtues and is pretty down at heel.

Auberge des Caravanes *(☎ 546 42 72)* Room UM1200 per person, half board (no lunch) UM2800, full board UM3800. One of the newer places in town, this place offers the same hospitality that travellers to Terjît, Chinguetti and Tidjikja have come to expect from the hotels of the same name (and owner).

Hôtel Dar Salam *(☎ 546 42 22, Route de Chinguetti)* Rooms for 5 people with air-con UM5500, without electricity UM3500, 2-person *tigit* (conical straw hut) UM2000, sofa or mattress on roof UM1000. This tranquil hotel is a 20-minute walk from the centre of town on the Chinguetti road. It's a good option that spans most budgets and the friendly Ahmed cooks up breakfast for UM400 and hearty meals for UM600.

Auberge Monod *(☎ 546 45 95, Route de Chinguetti)* Singles with bathroom UM5000, doubles without/with bathroom UM5000/6000, suites UM8000-12,000. The rooms here are clean, comfortable, spacious and very good value, although the mosquitoes can be a major irritant. The idea of service with a smile seems to have passed this place by. Meals can be arranged for UM1000, if you order early, and breakfast costs UM600.

Auberge Nouzha *(☎ 546 43 33, Off Route de Chinguetti)* Singles/doubles with bathroom UM5000/6000. Run by the same owners as the Monod, the standard here is similar although there's a bar.

Hôtel El Waha *(Route de l'Aéroport)* Doubles UM8000, suites UM12,000. A top-end option, the El Waha has new rooms, which will be very nice once the smell of paint wears off.

There are plenty of new hotels being built in Atâr, mostly in the area north of the airport. ***Auberge MKT*** *(Route de Nouakchott)* was due to open not long after we visited and should be a comfortable mid-range option.

ATÂR

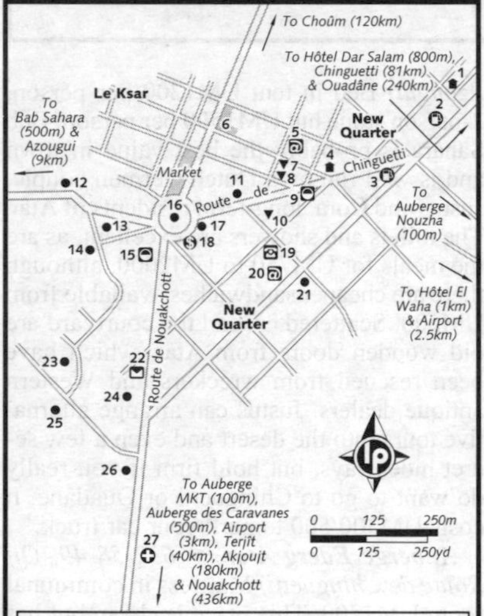
To Choûm (120km)
To Hôtel Dar Salam (800m), Chinguetti (81km) & Ouadâne (240km)
Le Ksar
To Bab Sahara (500m) & Azougui (9km)
New Quarter
Market
Route de Chinguetti
To Auberge Nouzha (100m)
To Hôtel El Waha (1km) & Airport (2.5km)
New Quarter
Route de Nouakchott
To Auberge MKT (100m), Auberge des Caravanes (500m), Airport (3km), Terjît (40km), Akjoujt (180km) & Nouakchott (436km)
0 125 250m
0 125 250yd

PLACES TO STAY
1 Auberge Ederg Atâr
4 Auberge Monod; Agence Bivouac Tours

PLACES TO EAT
7 Restaurants Moderne; Cheap Restaurants
8 Restaurant du Coin Atâr
10 Restaurant Terjît Vacanes; Restaurant Oualâta

OTHER
2 Petrol Station
3 Petrol Station
5 MDI Cyber Café
6 Small Artisan Workshops
9 Garage de Chinguetti; Street Food
11 Pharmacy
12 Hôtel de Ville (Town Hall)
13 School
14 Regional Governor's Residence
15 Gare Routière; Taxi Stand
16 Rond Point
17 Grocery Stores
18 Money Exchange; Telephone Shop; Artisan Shops
19 Telephone Shop
20 Sodeq Cyber Café
21 Salima Voyages
22 Post Office
23 Water Tank
24 TV Relay Station
25 Military Camp
26 French Cemetery
27 Hospital

Places to Eat

From the roundabout head east on the Chinguetti road for a block, then turn left. Most restaurants are along this road, and three have the same name – ***Restaurant Moderne***. Also OK is ***Restaurant du Coin Atâr***. They are all run by Wolof and Fula and serve basically the same fare, including spaghetti, rice, fish and Senegalese *mafé* (peanut sauce) for UM150 to UM200. The best ***brochettes*** are sold in the evening outside Garage de Chinguetti, two blocks east of the roundabout.

Restaurant Terjît Vacanes *(Route de Chinguetti)* Sandwiches UM200, mains UM500-800. Food here is simple and the service is friendly. Rice or spaghetti with a sauce costs UM500, while grilled chicken is UM800.

Restaurant Oualâta *(Off Route de Chinguetti)* Sandwiches UM200, mains UM500-800. Just around the corner, this also offers similarly simple food and friendly service.

There is a concentration of grocery stores in the streets leading out from the main roundabout, and most are pretty well stocked.

Getting There & Away

Air Compagnie Mauritanienne de Transport Aérian has a Monday flight between Nouâdhibou and Atâr for UM11,000. Point Afrique (🅦 www.point-afrique.com) has two flights a week from Paris to Atâr as well as one from Marseilles. Return fares start at around €410 plus taxes.

Bush Taxi & Truck The main gare routière, opposite the roundabout, is where you can get vehicles, mostly pick-ups, for Choûm

(UM1000, two hours) and Nouakchott (UM2800 to UM3500, seven hours).

Battered Land Rovers and pick-ups headed for Chinguetti (UM1500, three hours) and Ouadâne (UM2000, five hours) leave from Garage de Chinguetti east of the roundabout mid-morning to late afternoon.

Car To rent a vehicle to Chinguetti, count on paying up to UM20,000 per day for a Toyota Hilux plus petrol, although you'll have to bargain hard and you may have to pay for food and lodging for the driver.

Agence Bivouac Tours (☎ 546 45 95), near Auberge Monod, is a very professional agency, and Salima Voyages (☎/fax 546 43 47), two blocks south of the Chinguetti road, is quite good. It's worth asking around Bab Sahara and Auberge des Caravanes (see Places to Stay) to see what can be arranged.

For details of the route from Atâr, see Getting There & Away under Chinguetti later in the chapter. If you wish to take the Amogar Pass (it's easier and more spectacular coming the other way), the turn-off to the left is 10km out of Atâr.

AZOUGUI

A good side trip from Atâr is to Azougui, 10km northwest. It was from here in the 11th century that the Berber Almoravids launched their attacks on the capital of the Empire of Ghana, Koumbi Saleh, leading to the spread of Islam throughout West Africa. It was once an oasis of 20,000 palms, and one of the premier cities in the region, before the rise of Chinguetti and Ouadâne. The moderate ruins consist of a fort's foundations and, 300m beyond the archaeological site, the mausoleum of the warrior hero Imam Hadrami, who is revered by the Moors. His grave is still a place of pilgrimage.

Auberge Oued Tillige a Azougui Rooms, tents or tigits UM1200 per person. This is an excellent, quiet alternative to staying in Atâr and has wonderful views down the valley. It's all very well maintained and there are freshly whitewashed huts, tents or the traditional tigits in which to sleep. Breakfast/meals cost UM600/1000 and it can be found 300m beyond the mausoleum.

TERJÎT

Some 40km south of Atâr as the crow flies is Terjît, an unusually verdant oasis. What's special here is a natural pool in which you can swim. This lush place at the end of a narrow canyon is wonderful – you'll think you're in the tropics. You pay UM700 to enter the site.

The main spring has been taken over by ***Oasis Touristique de Terjît***, where a mattress in a tent by the trickling stream costs UM1500, while breakfast/meals go for UM600/1500.

The only other place to stay is the ***Auberge des Caravanes***, which is very reasonable – UM1000 per person and UM3000 per day for food. There's also a protected area for parking.

To get here by private car, drive 40km south of Atâr on the road to Nouakchott, then turn left at the checkpoint and follow a sandy track for 13km. The trip takes 1½ hours. By public transport, take anything headed towards Nouakchott and hitch a ride from the checkpoint.

The Guedra

In the Adrar region, a real treat is to see a performance of the Guedra, a ritual dance of love performed by women. Sometimes the dancer stands, but more often she squats, covered in a black veil. The dance is a ballet of complex movements of the hands and feet on which the women paint intricate designs with henna to draw attention to them. The dancer's hair is sumptuously decorated; every plait is embellished with pendants, talismans, carved shell discs and green and red glass beads.

CHINGUETTI

pop 4000

Chinguetti is the seventh-holiest city of Islam. Once famous for its Islamic scholars, it was the ancient capital of the Moors, and some of the buildings date from the 13th century. In its heyday, Chinguetti had 12 mosques, 25 madrases and was home to 20,000 people. Epic *azalais* (caravans) of 30,000 camels laden with salt once travelled between Chinguetti and Morocco, St Louis in Senegal (each 30 days), Nioro in Mali (45 days) and Timbuktu (55 days). It was also the assembly point for Moors joining the annual caravan to Mecca.

Surrounded by sand dunes up to 20m high, Chinguetti is now a shadow of its former self and the old town is in urgent need of restoration. That said, it is still one of the more attractive of the ancient caravan towns in the Sahara and it's the sort of place worth lingering in for a few days. The modern town, which has a delightfully sleepy market remarkable for how little produce is available, is separated from the old town (Le Ksar) by a broad, flat wadi where palm trees grow.

Chinguetti is a place where the streets have no name, there is only generator-powered electricity and, blissfully, there are no telephones.

Le Ksar

The old quarter's structures are mostly stone and most are in ruins and unoccupied. The principal attraction is the 16th-century stone **mosque** (no entry to non-Muslims). Also of great interest are the five old **libraries**, which house the fragile-as-dust ancient Islamic manuscripts of Chinguetti. In these libraries are the stories of Chinguetti's golden age. The libraries include the **Bibliothèque Ehel Hamoni**, **Bibliothèque Moulaye**, and **Fondation Ahmed al Mahmoud** (admission to each UM300) and each has an attached museum (UM200) containing items from the old caravans. None of the libraries keep regular opening hours and your best bet is to ask at your hotel for the man with the key.

Camel Rides

The sand dunes around Chinguetti are perfect for exploring by camel and prices are reasonable – UM1000 to UM1500 for a camel for the day. Each trip must be accompanied by a guide (UM2500). Plan on a full day's ride as you'll see little of the dunes in half a day. Possible trips (probably with tea at a nomad camp) include to the oases of Abeir (3km), Tendewalle (5km), Legueilla (12km) or a four-day return trip to Tenauchert (45km). The best places to start asking are Auberge des Caravanes or Auberge La Rose des Sables (see Places to Stay & Eat).

Places to Stay & Eat

All the places listed below have terraces on the roof overlooking town, all have shared shower and toilet unless stated otherwise. The first five are in the new part of town.

Auberge des Caravanes *(☎/fax 546 42 72, Atâr)* Room UM1200 per person, half board (no lunch) UM2800, full board UM3800. This place, right in the centre of town, catches most arrivals in town, especially tour groups and is thus a good place to meet other travellers. It's well run, clean and there's an equally pleasant extension at the western end of the old town.

Auberge La Rose des Sables Room UM1000 per person, tents UM700 per person. Next to the market, this highly recommended place is run by the amiable Cheikh Ould Amar, who is also an experienced guide and a good man with whom to explore the desert. The auberge has a homely, hospitable feel and you can get breakfast/meals for UM400/800.

Hôtel Nouâtil *(☎ 529 02 99, fax 525 48 36, Nouakchott)* Room UM1200 per person, half board (no lunch) UM2800, full board UM3800. The first building you come to if you're arriving from Atâr and a 10- to 15-minute walk into town, the Nouâtil is also well run and wonderfully quiet. Ask to see the family's old Islamic manuscripts.

Auberge de Zarga Mattress on roof UM500, in tent UM700, in communal room UM1000. The Zarga is about 300m off to the left as you come from Atâr. It overlooks the wadi and, while fairly rough and ready, is friendly enough. Meals are available for UM700.

Hôtel Fort Saganne *(☎ 525 99 58, fax 525 24 55, Nouakchott)* Mattress in 5-bed room UM2000, singles/doubles with bathroom UM3000/6000, suites UM10,000. Renovated in 2000, this old fort is the closest that Chinguetti comes to having a top-end hotel. The rooms are tidy and spacious and the suites have a dizzyingly large circular bathroom. The ***Restaurant La Porte du Desert*** (Meals UM500 to UM800) in the courtyard has both an indoor dining room and a lovely tent. It's well signposted in the centre of town.

In the old town, there are a cluster of cheap auberges.

Auberge de Bien Être de Chinguetti UM1000 per person, full board UM3500. This tranquil auberge has rooms with a mattress on the floor. It features a lovely courtyard and a nomad's tent for relaxing.

Also cheap, but a touch more run-down, are ***Auberge des Oasis*** and ***Auberge La Vieille Ville***, which is close to the mosque and libraries.

MAURITANIA

Getting There & Away

Car & Pick-up There is at least one vehicle a day to/from Atâr (UM1500 in the back of a pick-up, three to four hours). They leave from just behind the market; you'll need to ask around as the driver often goes off looking for his full complement of eight to ten passengers.

For those with their own vehicle, there are two routes to Atâr. The faster route (81km, two hours) is via the New Pass and the lunar-like Adrar plateau while the other (91km, three to four hours) leads up to the **Amogar Pass,** which is slow going but offers spectacular views. If you're coming from Chinguetti, the turn-off for the Amogar Pass is at the signpost to the faintly discernible Neolithic rock paintings (including giraffes, cows and people in a grassy landscape).

There are also two routes to Ouadâne – via the plateau or, more picturesque, across the sand dunes to the east of town.

Camel An excellent alternative to motorised transport is to travel by camel from Chinguetti. Possible destinations include Ouadâne (five to six days), Terjît (six days) and Tidjikja (13 to 15 days). Standard costs start from UM4200 per person per day for the camel, food and guide although up to UM5000 is reasonable.

OUADÂNE

Ouadâne was founded in 1147 by Berbers, and sits on the edge of the Adrar plateau, 120km northeast of Chinguetti. For 400 years, it was a prosperous caravan centre and a transit point for dates, salt and gold – the last stopover for caravans heading to Oualâta in the southeastern corner of the country. The decline began in the late 16th century when the powerful Moroccan prince Ahmed el Mansour gained control of this trans-Saharan route and diminished Ouadâne's commercial role.

Upon arrival in the town you must register at the *gendarmérie* at the top of the hill.

The most interesting section is the old quarter, **Le Ksar el Kiali**.

Le Ksar al Kiali

The old quarter of Ouadâne is one of the most enchanting semighost towns of the Sahara. As you arrive across the sands or plateau from Atâr or Chinguetti, the stone houses seem to tumble down the cliff like an apparition, and they change colour depending on the time of day. From the base of the town, the lush gardens of the oasis stretch out before the desert again takes hold. The top of the hill is dominated by the minaret of the **new mosque**, which is a mere 200 years old while at the western end at the base of the town is the 14th-century **old mosque**, which was being restored when we visited. At the height of Ouadâne's power, the two mosques were connected by the **Street of 40 Scholars (savant)** and houses along either side were only allowed to be occupied by Ouadâne's considerable intelligentsia. In between, many of the crumbling structures are built into the escarpment with which, from a distance, they can seem to blend to form a massive stone wall. Only 20 to 30 families still live in the old town.

The friendly, French-speaking guide Mohamed Lemine Kettab (UM1000) is knowledgeable about his town's history and can really enhance your visit. He is also the caretaker of the museum. He will probably have found you long before you start looking.

Maison de la Culture

Like Chinguetti, Ouadâne was a place of scholarship and is home to over 3000 manuscripts held in 23, mostly private, libraries. At the time of research, the only one open to the public was the Maison de la Culture (UM500) in a French-built eyesore at the eastern end of town atop the hill. There are a number of interesting manuscripts as well as museum items from the ancient caravans. Unesco has plans to consolidate the town's collection by restoring one of the old houses as a library. To enter the Maison de la Culture, ask around for Mohamed Lemine Kettab (see Le Ksar al Kiali).

Places to Stay & Eat

Auberge Vereny Rooms or tent UM1200 per person. Directly opposite the gendarmérie, this is the only place to stay atop the rocky bluff and is an easy walk to the top of the old town. The owners are eager to please and can arrange breakfast/meals for UM600/1000.

The following places are down on the plateau.

Auberge Ouadâne Agoueidir *(☎ 525 07 91, Nouakchott)* Rooms or tents UM1200 per person. Many travellers stay at this excellent auberge, which is at the entrance to town coming over the dunes from Chinguetti. It has plenty of tidy rooms and tents set around a pleasant courtyard. Breakfast/meals cost UM1000 and you may be invited for tea with the family.

Auberge Waranel Ouadâne *(☎ 546 46 04, Atâr,* e *mzwaranel12000@yahoo.fr)* Rooms or tents UM1200 per person. On the plateau road in from Atâr, this place is also a decent choice and you could have the place to yourself. The dining tent, where breakfast/meals cost UM600/1000, is pleasant.

Auberge Vasque Ouadâne Tents UM1000 per person. This is the least attractive, but cheapest, of Ouadâne's four options. It's at the base of the track leading up to the bluff and is fine if you don't mind sleeping on a slope. Breakfast/meals cost UM600/1000.

Getting There & Away

Finding transport to Ouadâne is not easy. Atâr is a much better place to look than Chinguetti, as vehicles go between Atâr and Ouadâne every few days, but next to never from Chinguetti. The trip (UM2000) normally takes about six hours (four hours by private car).

If driving you have two alternatives: the southerly Piste du Batha, which passes through sand dunes and definitely requires a guide, and the northerly Piste du Dhar Chinguetti along the plateau, which is in good condition. The latter departs the Atâr-Chinguetti road 18km before Chinguetti.

AROUND OUADÂNE

The **Guelb er Richat** crater is 40km to the northeast. En route, stop at **Tin Labbé** (7km), a unique settlement where the large boulders prevalent in this area have been incorporated into the villagers' homes.

MAURITANIA

The Eastern Desert & The South

Exploring this region is not possible without your own vehicle or camel.

TIDJIKJA

pop 6000

Tidjikja is the capital of the Tagânt region. Founded in 1680 and now surrounded by sand dunes, the town supports one of the country's more important palm groves (which dates from the 18th century), a busy market, numerous shops and Fort Coppolani (an old French military fort used in subduing the Moors).

The town is split in the middle by a spacious sandy wadi. You'll arrive at the 'modern' southwestern section with wide streets and administrative buildings, including the police. The old quarter to the northeast is where you'll find the ancient palm grove, an old mosque and traditional houses (some are vacant and easily visited). Notice the decorative niches with geometric designs, the flat roofs with gargoyle-decorated drains for rainwater and double-panelled doors in place of windows.

A good side trip can be made to **Rachid**, 35km north on the track to Atâr. High up a cliff, it's one of the most beautiful spots in Mauritania and was once used as a site for launching attacks on passing caravans.

Places to Stay & Eat

Auberge des Caravanes de Tidjikja *(☎ 569 92 25)* Full board UM3800. Part of a small chain of homely auberges across Mauritania's desert region, this place is typically good value. It's in the new quarter of town on your left as you arrive from Nouakchott. For food, there are also some small grocery shops and the ***market***.

Getting There & Away

Air Mauritanie flies to Tidjikja on Wednesday (UM9880).

If you're driving from Nouakchott, be prepared to get stuck in the sand on the final 205km leg. There's petrol in Tidjikja but it can never be guaranteed, so carry plenty.

It's possible to drive from Tidjikja to Atâr (470km). A guide is essential and attempting it with only one vehicle inadvisable.

TICHIT

If you're adventurous and want to see a ghost town in the making, head for the isolated, ancient town of Tichit, 255km east of Tidjikja. Driving here, you'll pass through barren landscape – the trees are bare, the scrub is twisted, and the ground is littered with the bleached bones of camels and goats. You should report to the police when you arrive.

The town once furnished water and precious supplies to desert caravans and boasted over 6000 people and 1500 houses. Today, fewer than 300 houses remain and only about half are inhabited. The main mosque is impressive, as are the old houses, which are made of local stone of different hues. They have decorative motifs on the exterior and solid, ornate doors with wooden latches, like those of the Dogon people in Mali.

A guide is essential and you'll need your own transport. The tracks frequently disappear and there are few landmarks, so you'll need enough petrol for a return trip, including unplanned detours. Bring some food.

ROSSO

pop 28,000

Rosso is a busy little town with a Senegalese flavour but not much to see. Most travellers cross the border here and head on. For more details, see Land in the main Getting There & Away section earlier in this chapter.

Restaurant du Fleuve, near the ferry wharf, has rooms (UM2000) with bare mattresses on the floor and shared bathrooms. For a little more, try ***Hôtel Union*** *(☎ 556 90 29)*, 150m north of the gare routière, where singles/doubles with air-con and bathroom cost UM3500/4500. For cheap food, try ***Restaurant Marie***.

Peugeot bush taxis from Nouakchott cost UM1250 (UM1000 by minibus). The trip takes at least 3½ hours, more by minibus. The onward trip to Dakar costs CFA3000 by minibus and CFA4500 by Peugeot taxi.

KAÉDI

pop 35,000

Southeast of Nouakchott on the Senegal River, Kaédi is the country's fourth-largest city, with a mostly Tukulor population. It has become a site for development projects, including SNIM's extraction of high-grade ore from a nearby reserve. The market is good for Tukulor crafts and authentic Senegalese batik cloth.

For a room, try the rustic ***Sonader Case de Passage*** near the centre or the ***UNDP Guesthouse***. The latter has air-con rooms (UM5000), a dining room and a pool, and it's definitely worth the price.

Minibuses (UM2000) and pick-ups go daily to/from Nouakchott (437km).

THE ROAD TO MALI

For more details on reaching this area by public transport, see Getting There & Away in the Nouakchott section and under Land in the main Getting Around section earlier in this chapter.

The first major town on the road to the Malian border is **Kiffa** (population 29,000), the capital of the southern Assabe region and an important regional trading centre and crossroads. Much of the activity of this vibrant place centres on the active market. The city is famous for its glass beads – check them out in the market, where they're made. The most popular place to stay is ***Hôtel de l'Amitié et du Tourism,*** in the centre, with basic singles/doubles with mattresses on the floor and fans for UM2000/3000. Meals are available here, or at ***Brahims*** where the mutton and couscous are good.

The next town of note is **Ayoûn el-Atroûs**, which is a good place to spend your last ouguiyas before crossing into Mali (see Land in the main Getting There & Away section earlier in this chapter). For accommodation, try ***Hôtel Ayoûn*** *(☎ 559 00 79)*, which is in the centre and surprisingly nice

Diabandé – the Art of Home Decoration

If you make it to Sélibabi, south of Mbout (on the road between Kaédi and Kiffa), try to visit **Tachott Botokholo**, 30km to the south. It and other Soninké villages in the area are famous for their colourfully painted houses. Several decades ago, the women, given free rein over their homes as their husbands looked for work in Senegal, began painting the inside of their houses, a practice called *diabandé*. The designs have evolved over the years: in the 1970s the fad was for simple, bold checks painted in white, ochre and black, and covering entire walls. Today, some rooms may be painted in bold, wide strips, others in geometric shapes with abstract drawings. The white is made from limestone, the ochre from soil and the black from red clay mixed with cow dung. The grinding and mixing can take days and when it comes time to paint, five or six women may work together for a week on a single room. The overall effect is truly splendid.

Koumbi Saleh

The legendary capital of the Empire of Ghana, West Africa's first medieval empire, Koumbi Saleh is one of the best-known archaeological sites in West Africa. Traces of the town were uncovered in 1913, and although several digging campaigns have been carried out since then these have only scratched the surface. Large stone houses and a huge imposing mosque have been partially excavated, attesting to the large number of people, estimated in the tens of thousands, who once lived here. From Timbedgha (106km west of Néma), head south on the route to Nara in Mali for 65km, then head a few kilometres east.

(UM2000/3000 for singles/doubles with fan and bathroom).

A turn-off at Timbedgha leads to **Koumbi Saleh** (see the boxed text).

Néma offers travellers little more than a small market, a petrol pump and a police station at which you can get your passport stamped.

OUALÂTA

Dating from 1224, Oualâta, about 100km north of Néma, used to be the last resting point for caravans heading for Timbuktu. Ransacked on several occasions, the town has suffered considerably and its mosque is in a lamentable shape. Most interesting, however, is the decorative painting on the exterior and interior of the houses. If you're lucky, you may get invited inside one of them. The women paint geometric designs with dyes, typically red or indigo.

There's a ***hotel-restaurant*** owned by the mayor of the town; rooms cost about UM800. Pick-ups and Land Rovers ply between Néma and Oualâta, but count on waiting a few days.

MAURITANIA

Niger

Niger sits precariously on the edge of the Sahara, a barren windswept land ravaged by drought and colonial conquest, yet somehow surviving against the odds. Its people are among the poorest on earth and their stoic and resilient nature in this harsh place creates a lasting impression. The nation's vibrant mix of people meet in the old market towns, which once stood proudly on the trans-Saharan trade routes, with the markets of Niamey and Zinder as colourful as you'll find anywhere in Africa. But it is for the desert and ancient caravan town of Agadez that most people come to Niger. Agadez is one of the most fascinating and best-preserved towns anywhere in the Sahara and a gateway to the stark beauty of the Aïr Massif and Ténéré Desert.

Facts about Niger

HISTORY

As difficult as it is now to imagine, Niger's arid landscape once supported some of the great empires of West Africa, fed by the lucrative trans-Saharan trade in gold, salt and slaves.

Hunters and herders lived in the then grassland plateaus of the north about 4000 BC (see the boxed text 'The Rock Art of the Aïr' later in this chapter for more details). As the Sahara became drier, these people moved progressively south and, towards the end of the 1st millennium BC had learnt the skills of metalwork and developed complex social organisations and forms of trade.

The Kanem-Borno Empire flourished in the east around Lake Chad between the 10th and 13th centuries AD, remaining a significant force until the 19th century. During the same period, the large Hausa population expanded into southern Niger from the north of present-day Nigeria. They were followed, in the 17th century, by groups of Djerma people, descendants of the great Songhaï Empire.

Although the slave trade had been abolished in most other parts of West Africa, it was still going strong in Niger and Chad in the 1850s. With an army of 12,000 soldiers, the Sultan of Zinder had little trouble attacking villages in his own kingdom, to capture the inhabitants and sell them into slavery as a means of supporting his 300 wives and numerous children. Agadez, once a

Niger at a Glance

Capital: Niamey
Population: 9.9 million
Area: 1,267,000 sq km
Head of State: President Mamadou Tandja
Official language: French
Main local languages: Hausa, Djerma, Fula, Tamashek
Currency: West African CFA franc
Exchange rate: US$1 = CFA694
Time: GMT/UTC +1
Country telephone code: ☎ 227
Best time to go: December to February

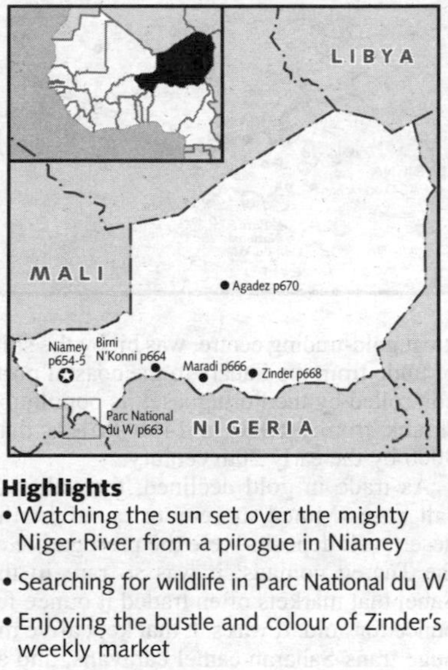
LIBYA
MALI
Agadez p670
Niamey
p654-5
Birni
N'Konni p664
Maradi p666
Zinder p668
Parc National
du W p663
NIGERIA

Highlights

- Watching the sun set over the mighty Niger River from a pirogue in Niamey
- Searching for wildlife in Parc National du W
- Enjoying the bustle and colour of Zinder's weekly market
- Exploring the labyrinthine old mud-brick quarters of Zinder and Agadez
- Hearing the stories of the Tuareg around the campfire or beneath the rock art of the Aïr Mountains
- Seeking out the silent gravitas of deserted villages and vast sand dunes of the Ténéré Desert and Djado Plateau in the Sahara

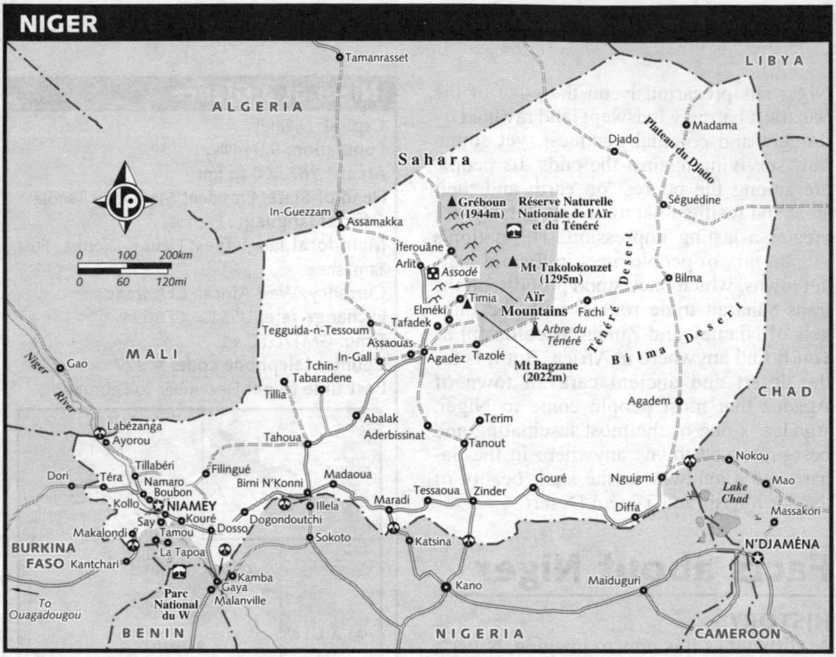
NIGER
ALGERIA
LIBYA
MALI
CHAD
BURKINA FASO
BENIN
NIGERIA
CAMEROON
Sahara
Ténéré Desert
Bilma Desert
Plateau du Djado
0 100 200km
0 60 120mi
Tamanrasset
In-Guezzam
Assamakka
Iferouâne
Arlit
Assodé
Timia
Elméki
Tafadek
Tegguida-n-Tessoum
Assaouas
In-Gall
Agadez
Tazolé
Tchin-Tabaradene
Tillia
Abalak
Aderbissinat
Tahoua
Filingué
Birni N'Konni
Madaoua
Illela
Dogondoutchi
Sokoto
Maradi
Tessaoua
Zinder
Gouré
Katsina
Kano
Terim
Tanout
Gréboun (1944m)
Réserve Naturelle Nationale de l'Aïr et du Ténéré
Mt Takolokouzet (1295m)
Aïr Mountains
Arbre du Ténéré
Mt Bagzane (2022m)
Fachi
Bilma
Djado
Madama
Séguédine
Agadem
Nguigmi
Nokou
Mao
Lake Chad
Diffa
Massakori
N'DJAMÉNA
Maiduguri
Gao
Niger River
Labézanga
Ayorou
Tillabéri
Dori
Téra
Namaro
Boubon
Kollo
NIAMEY
Say
Kouré
Tamou
Dosso
Makalondi
La Tapoa
Kantchari
Kamba
Gaya
Malanville
Parc National du W
To Ouagadougou

great gold-trading centre, was hit by the shift of trade from the Sahara to the coastal ports controlled by the Portuguese; its population shrank from 30,000 in 1450 to less than 3000 by the early 20th century.

As trade in gold declined, the value of salt rose. Mined at remote oases in the desert, salt deposits were the prerogative of the Tuareg nomads; it was so rare in the Sahel that markets often traded it ounce for ounce for gold. It was salt that kept alive the huge trans-Saharan camel caravans, and as recently as 1906 a 20,000-camel caravan left Agadez to collect salt at Bilma, an oasis some 610km to the east.

The empires survived the arrival of Islam during the 10th and 11th centuries, but not that of the Europeans. Europe's first intruder was a Scot, the celebrated Mungo Park, who disappeared in the Niger River in 1806.

French soldiers came next. When they encountered stronger-than-expected resistance from the local inhabitants, the French authorities quickly lost patience. The punitive Voulet-Chanoîne expedition laid waste to much of southern Niger in 1898–99. The massacre in Birni N'Konni in particular is one of the most shameful episodes in French colonial history. Although successive Tuareg revolts in the north continued, culminating in the siege of Agadez in 1916–17, French control over the territory had now been assured.

French rule was not kind to Niger. The colonial administration selectively cultivated the power of traditional chiefs whose abuses were tolerated if not encouraged as a means of de facto control. The replacement of local currency with the French franc (in which taxes had to be paid) drove many agricultural workers from their farms and into the cities in search of work. The enforced shift from subsistence farming to cash crops further cemented French dominance by reorienting trade away from traditional trans-Saharan routes towards coastal markets controlled by European powers. Fallow periods, which had previously preserved a fragile ecological balance, were replaced with high density farming, the effects of which are seen today in the ongoing march of the Sahara.

Niger received much less investment than other French colonies – by the time of independence in 1960, the French had built

JANE SWEENEY

JANE SWEENEY

ARIADNE VAN ZANDBERGEN

ERIC L WHEATER

ARIADNE VAN ZANDBERGEN

ANTONY GIBLIN

With so many religious beliefs, ceremonies and festivals play an important role in West African life: Durbar festival, Kano, Nigeria (top left & top right); playing traditional ivory horns (middle left) at the Adae festival, Ghana (bottom left); Tuareg men dancing at Ramadan celebrations, Niger (middle right); Bororo Fula men at the Cure Saleé (Salt Cure) festival, Niger (bottom right)

JEFF WILLIAMS

ARIADNE VAN ZANDBERGEN

PATRICK SYDER

CHRIS BEALL

KIM WILDMAN

Village festivals may be held to honour dead ancestors or local traditional deities and to celebrate the end of the harvest. Some festivals include singing and dancing, while some favour parades. Ceremonies are also important in West Africa as they reinforce social structures. Much of the region's cultural life revolves around events such as baptisms, circumcisions, weddings and funerals.

1032km of paved roads in West Africa, only 14km of which were in Niger.

Independence

In 1958, Charles de Gaulle offered the 12 French colonies in West Africa a choice between self-government in a French union or immediate independence. Hundreds of thousands of votes conveniently went missing enabling the French to claim that Niger wished to remain within the French sphere of influence.

Djibo Bakari and the radical Sawaba party campaigned for complete independence, and the infuriated government banned the party and sent Bakari into exile. This left Hamani Diori, leader of the Parti Progressiste Nigérien (PPN), in complete control and the only candidate for president when full independence arrived in 1960.

Diori's repressive one-party state maintained close ties with the French. Despite several unsuccessful coups, Diori survived until the great Sahel drought of 1968–74. Niger was probably the worst hit country of all: over 60% of livestock was lost. Stocks of food were discovered in the homes of several of Diori's ministers and, soon after, Lt Col Seyni Kountché overthrew Diori in a bloody coup and set up a military council to rule the country, with himself as president.

The Post-Independence Period

Kountché was lucky to survive a number of coup attempts. He was lucky in other ways, too. Uranium had been discovered in 1968 in the far northeast of the country, and from 1974 to 1979, world prices for uranium quintupled. Kountché embarked on a number of ambitious projects, including the construction of a 'uranium highway' to Agadez and Arlit. Not everyone was smiling, however; the cost of living rose dramatically and the poorest of the poor were worse off than ever.

In the early 1980s, government revenues from uranium took a nose dive and the construction boom was over. In 1983–84, another great drought hit. For the first time in recorded history, the Niger River stopped flowing. Kountché's reputation for honesty helped him weather the resulting dissatisfaction, including a third unsuccessful coup attempt in 1983. But in 1987 he died after a long illness and was replaced by his chosen successor, Ali Saïbou.

Saïbou immediately embarked on a process of constitution-making. In 1989 he formed a new political organisation called

Tuareg Rebellion

The Tuareg form minorities in many Saharan countries, including Niger, Algeria, Burkina Faso, Chad, Libya, Mali, Mauritania, Senegal and Tunisia. Being a minority has put them at a disadvantage with the majority groups when it comes to getting their fair share of the respective national budgets, and they have been marginalised politically and economically. Their difficulties have been compounded by the droughts in the 1970s and 1980s, which decimated livestock and altered the way of life of these traditionally nomadic herders, not to mention increasing desertification and population growth, which thrust them into conflict with other pastoral groups such as the Arabs and Fulani.

In 1992 the Tuareg in Niger launched a raid on a police post at Tchin-Tabaradene. The raid reflected Tuareg frustration over the lack of assistance given to Tuaregs who had recently returned from Algeria and the misappropriation of funds promised to them following Saïbou's accession to power. They were also seeking the right for Tuareg children to learn Tamashek in schools. Brutal government reprisals followed, sparking a protracted conflict in which hundreds of rebels, police and civilians were killed.

The Tuareg demanded a federal country, with an autonomous Tuareg region in the north. During the conflict, the government banned travel in Niger's north and closed its main border with Algeria, halting the tourist flow across one of the Sahara's oldest routes and stifling Niger's tourist industry.

In early 1994, the Tuareg Front de Libération de l'Aïr et l'Azouack (FLAA) and Front de Libération Tamouist (FLT) agreed to an uneasy truce. A peace accord was signed in 1995 after the government and the Organisation de la Résistance Armée (ORA), representing the Tuareg groups, met in Ouagadougou. A final peace accord was signed with the last rebel group in 1998 and programmes are currently underway to integrate former Tuareg rebels into the armed forces.

the Mouvement National pour une Société de Développement (MNSD), but at the same time upheld the ban on political parties that Kountché had reintroduced after the 1974 coup. He then stood for presidential election, but with himself as the sole candidate in the interests of national unity. Strangely enough, he won.

Keenly aware of the profound political changes sweeping across West Africa, the people of Niger weren't satisfied with Saïbou's cosmetic alterations. In February 1990, there were mass student demonstrations and strikes by workers. Students at Niamey University staged a demonstration calling for democratic reform. Several people were killed when security forces opened fire and the ensuing public outcry forced a reluctant Saïbou to convene a national conference. The conference, held in July 1991, produced an interim government that ruled until the first multiparty elections in early 1993. At these elections Mahamane Ousmane became the country's first Hausa head of state, power having been monopolised by the Djermas since colonial times.

His (and democracy's) reign was short-lived. A military junta, led by Colonel Ibrahim Bare Mainassara, staged a successful coup in January 1996. Elections held in July were won by Mainassara – a hardly surprising result given that he dissolved the independent election commission and confined his four main opponents to house arrest.

In April 1999, against the backdrop of widespread strikes and economic stagnation, Mainassara was assassinated by the commander of the presidential guard. The prime minister at the time described the death of the president, without any apparent attempt at irony, as 'an unfortunate accident'. The leader of the coup, Major Daoud Mallam Wanke, quickly set about a return to democratic rule. In peaceful elections in October and November 1999, Mamadou Tandja was elected with over 59% of the vote. In the 83-seat national assembly (with only one female MP), Mamadou forged a coalition majority with supporters of former President Ousmane.

A decreasing GDP since 1990, a heavy reliance on imports, shrinking areas of arable land and falling uranium prices have all helped to impoverish Niger. In 2001, Niger ranked second to last on the UN's Human Development Index, a statistic manifested in low life-expectancy and high infant mortality. Simmering discontent from students, Islamic groups, soldiers and civil servants, many of whom have not been paid in years, continues. More than 60% of the population live on less than US$1 a day. While the population of Niger can take pride in the impressively smooth transition from military to democratic rule, the task that confronts the present government is enormous.

GEOGRAPHY

Niger is West Africa's second-largest country, more than twice the size of France. It is landlocked, being more than 650km from the sea. The Niger River, Africa's third-longest river, flows for about 300km in the southwestern corner of the country. Lake Chad no longer exists on Niger's side of the border.

Niger's most remarkable area is the Aïr Mountains in the northeast. Rising more than 2000m and comprising dark volcanic formations, culminating in the Bagzane peaks, the mountains are breathtakingly beautiful. Beyond the massif to the east is the Ténéré Desert, which has some of the most spectacular sand dunes in the Sahara.

CLIMATE

The hottest part of the year is March to June, the worst month being April when daytime temperatures reach 45°C (113°F) or more (especially in the north), with the heat becoming so intense that rain evaporates before reaching the ground. December to February is the coolest period, when temperatures in the desert can drop to freezing at night.

The harmattan winds, however, usually come before the rains and blow a fine dusty fog that envelops everything. Visibility is cut to less than 1km. In late May, the rains come to the southern parts of the country. The annual total rainfall in the south is usually

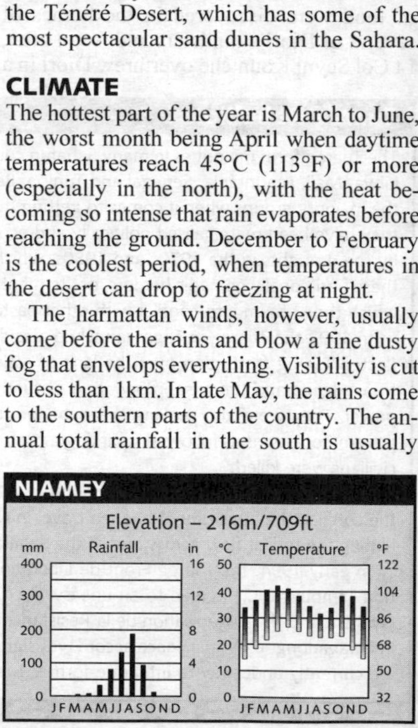
NIAMEY
Elevation – 216m/709ft
mm
Rainfall
in
°C
Temperature
°F
400
300
200
100
0
16
12
8
4
0
50
40
30
20
10
0
122
104
86
68
50
32
JFMAMJJASOND
JFMAMJJASOND

550mm. In contrast, the northern parts receive less than 150mm of rainfall annually, even in the best of years.

ECOLOGY & ENVIRONMENT

Today, two-thirds of Niger is desert and the rest is Sahel (the semidesert zone south of the Sahara). Desertification is Niger's greatest environmental problem and is mostly due to overgrazing and deforestation as people cut wood to use as fuel for cooking. The high quartz level in the sandy soil makes high-yield crops unsuitable in many places and also prevents the anchoring of top soil, causing erosion.

In 1980, the community-based Guesselbodi National Forest Project was launched not far from Niamey in an attempt to enable reafforestation by encouraging villagers to build windbreaks and establish nurseries. While the project has been a success at a micro level in reducing soil depletion, it may be too late for widespread application throughout the country. Irrigation projects in the north have also brought life back to once-barren soil with the village of Azad now among those supplying Agadez with fruit.

To help rebuild livestock herds (after they were decimated by the droughts in the early 1990s) and generate income, one aid scheme 'loans' young goats to farmers who then tend the animals until they mature and reproduce. The animals' offspring are then 'repaid' to the aid scheme. However, it's a fragile balancing act to prevent herds growing too large and hence taking them beyond the land's carrying capacity.

The Last Giraffes in West Africa

In the second half of the 1990s, the government of Niger and international conservation groups launched a campaign to save the last wild giraffes left in West Africa. The population, concentrated around Kouré just 60km east of Niamey, had fallen to just 100 from more than 3000 a few decades ago. The threats to the giraffes came from the destruction of their habitat through desertification and deforestation, as well as disease and poaching. It also didn't help that from April to August 1996, soldiers shot around a dozen giraffes while trying to carry out a presidential order to capture giraffes for presentation as gifts to friendly foreign leaders.

But the giraffes are again under threat. Reports began circulating when we were in Niger that the government project protecting this endangered species is unlikely to be renewed. With some estimates putting the population at just 40 animals, the threats from traditional sources, as well as road accidents and farmers killing them to protect their crops, may just prove too much for this brave and lonely herd unless urgent measures are taken.

FLORA & FAUNA

The zoo that forms part of Niamey museum is one of the most appalling abuses of animal welfare that we've seen, with lions, cheetahs, monkeys and other wildlife kept in squalid and impossibly cramped conditions.

Elsewhere there has been a concerted attempt to preserve the remaining wildlife of the southwest, especially in Parc National du W. In the park can be found antelopes, elephants, lions, leopards, cheetahs, baboons, Nile crocodiles, hyenas and jackals, as well as more than 300 bird species.

In the desert regions, the camel is the most common animal that visitors will come across, but there are still herds of gazelle in remote areas (the dorcas gazelle is the most common) and the nocturnal fennec (a small fox with large ears) can be glimpsed if you're lucky. The Saharan cheetah is very rare.

GOVERNMENT & POLITICS

The constitution provides that the president is elected by universal suffrage and serves for a five-year term. Elections are next scheduled for 2004. The president appoints the prime minister, who heads the national assembly. The assembly has 83 members, elected by popular vote, for five-year terms.

ECONOMY

Niger's economy is doing very badly. It has recorded a declining GDP ever since 1990 and was one of the countries worst hit by the devaluation of the CFA franc in early 1994. The country would be economically lost without its uranium. It owns about a fifth of the world's total uranium deposits and, despite the devastating collapse in world prices during the 1980s, uranium still accounts for about three-quarters of export earnings.

While only 3% of Niger's land is arable and rainfall is unpredictable, subsistence

Suffer the Children...

Niger's statistics are suitably dire for what is arguably the world's poorest country. The indicators are particularly horrifying for children under five: the infant mortality rate is 113 per 1000 live births; 32% are stunted; 16% are badly malnourished; 36% are underweight; and one-third of Niger's children die before they reach the age of five. Studies in villages around Niamey have revealed that micronutrient deficiencies in pregnant women and school children are rife – 60% are anaemic (iron deficient) and iodine deficient, and vitamin A deficiency – the cause of xerophthalmia (night blindness) – is widespread.

Further facts point to the desperation of the situation – maternal mortality is one in 20, compared with one in 1000 in developed countries; each woman has, on average, seven children; only 15% of the births are aided by trained health workers (and only in Niamey); and in rural areas there is little or no prenatal or postnatal care; some 40% of women have given birth by the age of 17; and only 4% use some form of contraception.

The problems have been compounded by the cycle of droughts that regularly ravage this part of the Sahel. Urban migration has decimated rural communities and led to dislocated populations of urban poor living without adequate infrastructure on city fringes.

Already meagre government resources are drained further by the country's crippling foreign debt. As a result there are no funds left to put in place preventative health programs or provide basic medicines. Failure to take preventative measures against diseases such as measles, meningitis and malaria claims the majority of children.

The *soudure* (hungry period), which usually lasts from May to June, has lengthened in recent years. As a result, cereal prices are 150% higher than in 1997 and farmers are forced to sell their grain early to pay taxes and then repurchase it during *soudure* at higher prices. It is believed that the current crisis affects three million (about one-third) of the population.

One of the frightening consequences of the malnutrition has been the re-emergence of 'grazer' or noma, a severe gangrene of the tissues of the mouth and face – often described as the 'African disease' and most prevalent in children. A minor case of gingivitis (gum infection), for example, caused by commonplace bacteria, can develop into gangrene, when the flesh of the face is literally eaten away.

The noma could easily be prevented with adequate nutrition and antibacterials (mouthwash, ointments or antibiotics). The parents of the children, though, are often starving themselves and have no money to buy these. Survivors are hidden away where no-one can see their faces. High-profile cases of aid agencies flying children to Europe for surgery do not hide the fact that this could easily be prevented given adequate resources and international commitment.

If you want to help, information about making donations to, or volunteering with, the international medical aid organisation Médecins Sans Frontières (MSF) can be found by checking out its website (W www.msf.org).

farming and stock rearing contribute around 40% of GDP, and 90% of the labour force is employed in this sector. Exports include cotton, cowpeas (black-eyed peas), onions and groundnuts (peanuts). Principal subsistence crops are millet, sorghum, cassava and rice.

POPULATION & PEOPLE

More than 90% of the population lives in the south, mostly in the southwest.

The population, growing at 3% annually, almost doubles every 20 years. Life expectancy is estimated to be less than 42 years.

The main ethnic group in Niger's diverse population is the Hausa, who make up 56% of the population. The second-largest group (22%) is the Songhaï-Djerma along the Niger River and in Niamey, followed by the Fulani (also called Peul-Fulani; 8.5%) and the Tuareg in the north (8%). Other groups include the Kanouri in the east, between Zinder and Chad, and the Toubou in the north. Niger also has a minority of Arabs in parts of the country's northeast, related to groups in Libya and Chad.

The Tuareg are Muslim, but although they celebrate most Muslim holidays, some ignore the annual Ramadan fast in recognition of the harsh dictates of desert life. The Tuareg are also one of the few groups in Africa who traditionally eat with utensils – a large wooden spoon – rather than their hands. Tuareg women traditionally do no livestock-keeping (although that is changing with the exodus of many Tuareg men to the cities) or domestic work. While the Tuareg are effectively monogamous, women enjoy a degree of independence, owning their own livestock and spending the income on themselves, while men have to provide for the home. Chieftaincy is passed to men through the female line. The young have a choice in whom they marry and courtship is an established art involving instrumental music, songs and poetry.

The Songhaï were once known as traditional administrators and warriors. About 400 years ago, they migrated south and settled along the Niger River. Today, they constitute over half the population of Niamey. The Djerma (or Zarma) have common origins and speak the same language as the Songhaï. They are found in Dosso and south of Niamey.

The Fulani are the second-largest nomadic group in Niger (after the Tuareg). The best known are the Bororo Fula, or Wodaabé, from the Dakoro-Tanout region west of Agadez. Their annual Cure Salée festival in September, known as the Gerewol, is famous throughout Africa. For more details, see the boxed text 'La Cure Salée' later in this chapter.

EDUCATION

Niger ranks at the bottom of the world in terms of schooling for children. Education is available in most major towns and is compulsory and free of charge, but only 17% of school-age children attend school, one of the lowest rates in the world. Literacy rates are 13.6% (just 6.6% for women). University-level education is faring no better. The University of Niamey went bankrupt in 1993. Today, the average length of schooling for adults is less than two months – the lowest in the world. About 10% of government expenditure is spent on education.

> **In the Eye of the Beholder**
>
> In a land where beauty and fashion contests have sparked violent protests (see boxed text 'The Night of Fire' later in this chapter), one beauty contest with a difference appears to have the sanction of Islamic fundamentalists. As part of the *Hangandi* festival, Djerma women compete to become the heaviest and hence the most beautiful. Training for the event involves eating as much millet as possible and drinking large quantities of milk and water. The heaviest woman is declared the winner and given the prize of more food, not to mention great public admiration.

ARTS

Best known, perhaps, is the art and craftwork of the Tuareg, especially their silverwork, including jewellery. The most unusual item is the *croix d'Agadez*, but every town and region with a significant Tuareg population has its own unique version of the cross of stylised silver with intricate filigree designs. Although European explorers saw the design as evidence of prior Christianity, traditional Tuareg see them as powerful talismans that are designed to protect against ill-fortune and the evil eye. Some serve as fertility symbols. At other times, the crosses are worn by wives as a sign of wealth.

Other silver items include: a wide range of silver necklaces; striking square silver amulets, which are worn around the neck by elders as a symbol of status; and ornamental daggers made of silver with a leather hilt.

Leather items include saddle-bags, cushions and tasselled pouches that are worn around the neck by men and used to carry tobacco or money.

RELIGION

Over 80% of the population is Muslim and only a small percentage of urban dwellers are Christian. A few rural communities continue to practise the traditional animist religions.

LANGUAGE

French is the official language. The principal African languages are Hausa, spoken mainly in the south, and Djerma (also spelt Zarma), spoken mostly in the west, including around Niamey. Other languages include Fula and Tamashek (also spelt Tamachek and Tamasheq), the language of the Tuareg. See the Language chapter for useful phrases in French, Hausa, Fula and Tamashek.

Facts for the Visitor

SUGGESTED ITINERARIES

Niamey is an interesting town to explore, with a delightful riverside location and some good markets, and is also a decent place to recharge the batteries if you've been on the road a while. Allow two to three days here. Possible one-day excursions include trips to the Sunday markets at Ayorou and Filingué. Allow another three to four days for visiting Parc National du W in the south.

Very few people visit Niger without visiting Agadez – allow another week for this. Plan on two days for the return journey to Niamey, a couple of days in Agadez itself and a minimum three days for an excursion to the Aïr Mountains, or up to five weeks in total if you also visit the Ténéré Desert and Djado Plateau. As an alternative route to Agadez, you could take in Zinder, which has a vibrant Thursday market.

PLANNING

December to February is the best time to be here even though the harmattan can ruin photos and cause respiratory problems. From May to August it is just too hot to travel in the desert.

The French-based Institut Géographique National publishes the 1:2,000,000 *Niger*, while Michelin's Map 953 *Africa – North & West* is also excellent.

TOURIST OFFICES

The Office National du Tourisme (ONT) has an outlet on Av du Président Heinrich in Niamey.

VISAS & DOCUMENTS

Visas

Visas are required by almost everyone. Requirements change all the time, however, so check with a Nigerien embassy. French visitors do not need visas except for stays of more than three months.

Getting a visa is generally straightforward, although you may have to provide up to three photos, proof of yellow-fever vaccination and a copy of your airline ticket proving onward travel (although this can usually be a ticket for departing some months later from another African country). In France, Niger's embassy in Paris is open from 9.30am to 12.30pm Monday to Friday, charges around €50 for three-month multiple-entry visas and usually gives 24-hour service.

If you're travelling overland, note that Niger has few embassies in West Africa, so getting a visa requires careful planning. Most of Niger's embassies do not impose an onward ticket requirement on overland travellers. Visas are easy to obtain in Benin (Cotonou or Parakou), Nigeria (Lagos or Kano), Côte d'Ivoire, Ghana and Chad, but *not* in Mali or Burkina Faso.

If you are entering from a country without any Nigerien diplomatic representation (eg, Burkina Faso), you can have your passport stamped at the border and the full visa is issued in Niamey. That said, you're better off arriving in Niger with the visa already in your passport as getting through at the border leaves you open to, often substantial, bribes.

Visa Extensions For a visa extension, go to the *sûreté* just off Place de la République in Niamey; it costs CFA10,000 and takes 24 hours to issue.

Visas for Onward Travel In Niger, you can get visas for the following neighbouring countries:

Algeria If you're lucky, the Algerian embassy in Niamey or the consulate in Agadez may issue you with a visa, but we've heard of few such cases. Most travellers wait up to a month for an answer from Algiers before giving up.

Benin The embassy usually issues visas the same day (bring two photos). Transit visas cost CFA10,000, three-month single-entry visas are CFA12,000, while three-month multiple-entry visas go for CFA20,000. You can also get a transit visa (CFA4000) at the border in Malanville, but it's good only for 48 hours (though you can renew it in Cotonou).

Burkina Faso, Côte d'Ivoire & Togo The French consulate, which issues visas to these countries, offers a same-day service. One-month visas cost CFA16,400 (one photo required). For Togo, though, the consulate can only issue two-day transit visas, which need to be extended in Lomé.

Chad One-month visas can cost anywhere between CFA15,000 and CFA50,000, and are either granted on the spot or refused altogether depending on the whim of the official and your nationality. You'll need three photos.

Mali One-month visas cost CFA20,000, require one photo and are issued in 24 hours.

Nigeria The embassy will *not* issue visas to anyone who is not a resident of Niger without an exceptionally good reason. On occasion, travellers have been successful in getting around this requirement, but you shouldn't come here counting on it.

Registration
It is no longer necessary to register with the police when you arrive in major towns in Niger.

Other Documents
To enter Niger, you need a yellow-fever vaccination certificate, which you must show at the airport if you fly in. Proof of cholera vaccination may also be asked for. Entering overland, a check usually depends on the mood of border officials.

EMBASSIES & CONSULATES
Nigerien Embassies
In West Africa, Niger has embassies in Benin, Côte d'Ivoire, Ghana and Nigeria. For more details see the Facts for the Visitor section of the relevant country chapter. Embassies elsewhere include the following:

Belgium (☎ 02-648 6140) 78 Av Franklin-Roosevelt, Brussels 1050
France (☎ 01 45 04 80 60) 154 Rue de Longchamp, 75016 Paris
USA (☎ 227-483 4224) 2204 R St NW, Washington, DC 20008

Niger does not have diplomatic representation in the UK.

Embassies & Consulates in Niger
All embassies and consulates are in Niamey unless stated.

Algeria
Embassy: (☎ 75 30 97) Blvd de la République, 6km west of city centre
Consulate in Agadez: (☎ 44 01 17) 800m east of SNTV bus station
Benin (☎ 72 28 60) Rue des Dallois, 2km northwest of the centre; open 8am to 12.30pm and 4pm to 6pm Monday to Friday
Canada (☎ 75 36 86, fax 75 31 07) Off Blvd Mali Bero
Chad (☎ 75 34 64) Av du Général de Gaulle; open 9am to noon Monday to Friday
France
Consulate: (☎ 72 27 22, fax 73 40 12) Place Nelson Mandela; open 8.30am to 11.30am Monday to Friday
Mali (☎ 74 42 90) Off Av Mali, 6km northwest of the city centre; open 9am to 12.30pm Monday to Friday
Nigeria (☎ 73 24 10) Blvd de la République, 1km past the US embassy; open 10am to 1pm Monday to Thursday
USA (☎ 72 26 61 or 64, fax 73 31 67, e usemb@intent.ne) Rue des Ambassades, 5km northwest of the centre, BP 11201

There is no UK diplomatic representation in Niger.

CUSTOMS
The thoroughness of searches by customs officials varies greatly, though foreign travellers are rarely targeted for a total going-over. Ignore requests for 'special taxes'. There is no limit on the import or export of foreign currencies.

MONEY
The unit of currency is the West African CFA franc.

country	unit		CFA
euro zone	€1	=	CFA656
UK	UK£1	=	CFA1024
USA	US$1	=	CFA694

Banks that change money include the Banque Internationale pour l'Afrique – Niger (BIA-Niger), Eco Bank, the Bank of Africa Niger (BAN) and the Banque de Développement de la République du Niger (BDRN).

In Niamey it's quicker and easier to change cash. At all banks, staff find euros easiest to deal with, although US dollars are generally no problem. UK pounds and some other hard currencies are also accepted in the BIA-Niger and Eco Bank, but not at the BAN. Banks in Niamey will also change travellers cheques, but commissions can be high and rates are often extremely variable.

Outside Niamey, finding a bank that accepts travellers cheques can be difficult. Banks here are more likely to give bad rates and levy ridiculously high commissions (typically a flat rate of around CFA4000, but sometimes a percentage).

POST & COMMUNICATIONS

Postal services outside the capital are slow and unreliable, so you should send everything from Niamey. As an example of rates, a 10g letter to Europe costs CFA450.

DIGITAL RESOURCES

One good website is W www.txdirect.net/users/jmayer/fob.html. It's run by a former Peace Corps volunteer, and has a variety of links and weekly news summaries.

NEWSPAPERS & MAGAZINES

With a literacy rate of just 13.6%, newspapers are not big business. The local French-language newssheet *Le Sahel* is available from a few roadside stalls and bookshops, but offers little in the way of real news. For international French-language (and the occasional English-language) newspapers and magazines, try the American or French cultural centres in Niamey (see Cultural Centres in the Niamey section later in the chapter) or the postcard stall right outside the door of the Score supermarket.

PHOTOGRAPHY & VIDEO

A photo or video permit is not required. The usual etiquette for photographing or video taping people and places applies – for more details see Photography & Video in the Regional Facts for the Visitor chapter. You shouldn't take photos of Kennedy Bridge in Niamey, nor of people bathing in the river.

HEALTH

A yellow fever vaccination certificate is required to enter Niger. Proof of cholera vaccination may also be asked for. Vaccination against meningitis is also highly recommended – hundreds of people die from the disease in Niger every year. Malaria is a risk year-round in the whole country, so you should take appropriate precautions. Dehydration and heat stroke are real risks here, especially in the hot season, so make sure you drink plenty of purified or bottled water. Bring your own water purification tablets, as they are generally unavailable here.

For more information see Health in the Regional Facts for the Visitor chapter.

WOMEN TRAVELLERS

Generally women have little trouble when travelling in Niger. It is nonetheless important to be aware that this is a Muslim country, where dress is taken very seriously. Shorts or singlets for either women or men show a lack of sensitivity and are not advised. For more general information and advice, see Women Travellers in the Regional Facts for the Visitor chapter.

BUSINESS HOURS

Business hours are from 8am to 12.30pm and 3pm to 6.30pm Monday to Friday, and from 8am to 12.30pm on Saturday. Government offices are open from 7.30am to 12.30pm and 3.30pm to 6.30pm Monday to Friday. Banking hours are generally from 8am to 11.30am and 3.45pm to 5pm Monday to Friday.

PUBLIC HOLIDAYS & SPECIAL EVENTS

Public holidays include:

New Year's Day 1 January
Easter March/April
Labour Day 1 May
Independence Day 3 August
Settlers' Day 5 September
Republic Day 18 December
Christmas Day 25 December

Niger also observes the usual Islamic holidays – for a table of estimated dates of these holidays see Public Holidays & Special Events in the Regional Facts for the Visitor chapter.

ACTIVITIES

There aren't really any hiking options in Niger, although you can go for trips in the desert by 4WD or camel. Alternatively, you can hire a pirogue along the Niger River, perhaps combining it with a walk through some of the riverside villages.

ACCOMMODATION

Budget places are relatively expensive in Niger, with the cheapest single rooms costing around CFA3000, and the quality is often very low. However, camping (which normally costs about CFA2000 per person) is possible in Niamey, Tahoua, Birni N'Konni and Parc National du W.

Mid-range hotels in Niger are more expensive than in most neighbouring countries, although on a par with Mali, with prices starting from CFA11,000 for a double

La Cure Salée

One of the most famous annual celebrations in West Africa is the Cure Salée (Salt Cure). It is held in the vicinity of In-Gall, particularly around Tegguidda-n-Tessoum.

Each group of herders has its own Cure Salée, but that of the Wodaabé people is famous throughout Africa. The festival lasts a week, usually during the first half of September, and the main event happens over two days.

The Wodaabé are a unique sect of nomadic Fulani herders. When the Fulani migrated to West Africa centuries ago, possibly from the Upper Nile, many converted to Islam. For the Fulani who remained nomads, cattle retained their pre-eminent position. Valuing their freedom, the nomadic Fulani despised their settled neighbours and resisted outside influences. Many called themselves 'Wodaabé' meaning 'people of the taboo' – those who adhere to the traditional code of the Fulani, particularly modesty. The sedentary Fulani called them 'Bororo', a name derived from their cattle and insinuating something like 'those who live in the bush and do not wash'.

The Wodaabé men have long, elegant, feminine features, and they believe they have been blessed with great beauty. To a married couple, it is of primary importance to have beautiful children. Men who are not good-looking have, on occasion, shared their wives with more handsome men to gain more attractive children. Wodaabé women have the same fine, elegant features and enjoy great sexual freedom before marriage.

During the year, the nomadic Wodaabé are dispersed, tending to their animals. As the animals need salt to remain healthy, the nomads bring their animals to graze in the area around In-Gall (known for its high salt content) when the grass can support large heards at the height of the rainy season. During the Cure Salée, you'll see men on camels trying to keep their herds in order and camel racing. The event serves, above all, as a social gathering – a time for wooing the opposite sex, marriage and seeing old friends.

For the Wodaabé, the Cure Salée is the time for their Gerewol festival. To win the attention of eligible women, single men participate in a 'beauty contest'. The main event is the Yaake, which is a late-afternoon performance when the men dance, displaying their beauty, charisma and charm. In preparation they will spend long hours decorating themselves in front of small hand mirrors. They then form a long line and are dressed to the hilt with blackened lips to make the teeth seem whiter, lightened faces, white streaks down their foreheads and noses, star-like figures painted on their faces, braided hair, elaborate headware, anklets, all kinds of jewellery, beads and shiny objects. Tall, lean bodies, long slender noses, white, even teeth and white eyes are what the women are looking for.

After taking special stimulating drinks, the men dance for long hours. Their charm is revealed in their dancing. Eventually, the women, dressed less elaborately, timidly make their choices. If a marriage proposal results, the man takes a calabash full of milk to the woman's parents. If they accept, he then brings them the bride price, three cattle, which are slaughtered for the festivities that follow.

Rivalry between suitors can be fierce, and to show their virility the young men take part in the Soro, an event where they stand smiling while others try to knock them over with huge sticks. At the end of the festival, the men remove their jewellery, except for a simple talisman. All of this is magnificently recorded in *Nomads of Niger* by Carol Bcckwith and Marion Van Offelen.

room with fan and another CFA5000 if you want air-con. There are decent mid-range hotels in Niamey, Agadez, Zinder, Maradi and Parc National du W.

Niamey and Agadez have upmarket hotels, where rooms cost between CFA30,000 and CFA75,000.

FOOD & DRINKS

The traditional food of Niger is nothing to write home about. In the north, dates, yogurt, rice and mutton are standard fare among the nomadic Tuareg. In the south, rice and sauce is the most common dish. Couscous and ragout are also popular. On most occasions, you'll probably be eating in some open-air place, with your feet in the sand and, at night, the starlit heavens above you. Standard fare at restaurants is usually grilled fish or chicken with chips, or beef *brochettes* and rice. You can get vegetarian dishes at one of Niamey's Chinese restaurants.

For drinks, you have a choice of tea or a Flag beer. The local beer, Bière Niger, isn't bad. Bottled water and soft drinks are also available.

Getting There & Away

AIR

Niamey has the only international airport in Niger, although this will change when flights resume between France and Agadez. Airport departure tax is CFA2500 for flights within West Africa (CFA9000 for other international flights). Some long-haul airlines have the tax included in the price for the ticket.

Europe & the USA

Air France has a weekly service between Niamey and Paris, with connections on to other European destinations. Undiscounted economy-class return fares cost CFA369,300.

The other option is Royal Air Maroc, which charges CFA417,000 to Paris return via Casablanca, and CFA590,000 for a return ticket to New York, also via Casablanca.

Point Afrique (W www.point-afrique.com) operates one flight a week from Paris/Marseilles to Niamey. Return fares start from €410 plus taxes. When the runway in Agadez has been repaired, Point Afrique flights will also resume from Paris/Marseilles to Agadez.

Africa

Royal Air Maroc flies weekly between Niamey and Casablanca for CFA346,500 return. Air Burkina flies once a week between Ouagadougou and Niamey for around CFA90,000 return.

LAND

Border Crossings

One of the great border crossings – from Assamakka (Niger) into Algeria – has reopened, although only a trickle of travellers pass this way. With the stabilising of the situation in southern Algeria, this is an increasingly popular way of crossing the Sahara.

The four main entry points into Nigeria – east of Gaya, Birni N'Konni, Maradi and south of Zinder – all tax the patience of even the most hardened of travellers. The Nigerian authorities have a field day, with about five standard checks (customs, immigration, luggage, drugs and bribe check).

The crossing into Benin (between Gaya and Malanville) is relatively painless.

Not many travellers cross into Mali or Chad from Niger. Crossing into Burkina Faso, usually via Makalondi, is a breeze, but note that there is a time change.

Benin

The road from Niamey to Cotonou via Gaya is tar all the way; the border between Niger and Benin closes at 7.30pm.

Peugeot taxis leave from the Wadata *Autogare* in Niamey to Malanville (CFA4600, four to six hours), Parakou (CFA8600, eight to 10 hours) and Cotonou (CFA12,350, 13 to 15 hours). Minibuses do the same trip for CFA3500, CFA7350 and CFA10,850, respectively, but they take forever.

Burkina Faso

Bus & Bush Taxi Only large buses and minibuses can cross the border, making direct connections between Niamey and Ouagadougou. Société Nigérienne de Transports de Voyageurs (SNTV) and Sotrao have one service a week each between Niamey and Ouagadougou (CFA7500, 12 to 14 hours, Wednesday and Friday). Buses are reasonably comfortable and fairly punctual. Checks at the border can take two hours. Tickets must be purchased a day or so in advance.

Despite what drivers may tell you, Peugeot taxis do not cross the border and you must change at Kantchari. By bush taxi, Niamey to the border at Kantchari or Makalondi is about CFA2000 (two hours, 130km). You can travel from Niamey to Ouagadougou by bush taxi in a long day, if you leave early and make fairly quick connections at the border. To find a bush taxi from Niamey heading to the border, go to the gare routière on the west side of the Niger River (across the Kennedy Bridge). Follow the Burkina Faso road – the gare routière is about 1km before the Rive Droite customs.

Minibuses leave from Niamey's Wadata Autogare, 4km east of the centre, for Ouagadougou most days (CFA7600, 15 to 18 hours).

Car & Motorcycle The main road from Niamey to Ouagadougou is tar, and the trip usually takes about 10 hours. For an alternative, try the route via Farié (62km northwest of Niamey), over the river by ferry, and Téra towards Dori and Ouagadougou. Bear in mind that the Niger-Burkina border closes at 6.30pm Nigerien time (Niger is one hour ahead of Burkina Faso).

Chad

There is no public transport travelling across this border.

In Niger, the closest you can get to the border is 100km away, at Nguigmi. Nguigmi is linked to Zinder most days by bush taxi (CFA8500, 16 hours) and a weekly SNTV bus (CFA8000). The trip between Diffa (between Zinder and Nguigmi) and Zinder by bush taxi costs CFA6000 (12 hours). Trucks and pick-ups trundle between Nguigmi and Nokou once every few days and take passengers for about CFA11,000.

On the Chadian side there's no public transport. After more waiting, you can find something between Nokou and Mao for about CFA3500, and from there you might be able to find something on to N'Djaména, probably after another few days of waiting.

Don't forget to get your passport stamped in Diffa and remember that, in Chad, they use Central African CFA francs.

Mali

SNTV has a bus (actually a truck with a cabin on the back) that goes between Niamey and Gao each Monday (CFA12,000, up to 30 hours). The road from Niamey to Ayorou is tar; from there it's sandy all the way to Gao. From July to September, the route is muddy and the journey has been described by one reader as 'a horrific journey of hassles, bureaucracy, time-wasting and general lunacy'. Take plenty of water. In addition, one private bus leaves most days from the Wadata Autogare.

There are no bush taxis ploughing the entire distance between Niamey and Gao. Consider going to Mali via Burkina Faso.

Nigeria

The cheapest way to get from Niamey to Nigeria is via Gaya; take a bush taxi from the Wadata Autogare (CFA4100, four hours). At the junction 10km before Gaya, motorcycle-taxis (moto-taxis) will be waiting to whisk you across the border to Kamba for about CFA1000. From Kamba, you can catch a bush taxi (bush taxis are much cheaper in Nigeria) almost immediately for Sokoto (three to five hours). Minibuses to Niamey from Kamba take four to six hours (CFA3500).

You can also cross into Nigeria from Birni N'Konni, Maradi and Zinder. From Konni, you can take a motorcycle taxi to the border, while from Maradi and Zinder you have to take a bush taxi.

Getting Around

AIR

There are no scheduled flights within Niger. Nigeravia (☎ 73 33 90, fax 74 18 42), though, runs 10-seater charter flights, including a semiregular service on Tuesday and Thursday from Niamey to Agadez (CFA185,500 for a seat), but you'd have to be lucky and the long-term viability of the service is an issue. Ask at the Nigeravia office on Av du Président Heinrich, near the Grand Hôtel in Niamey, to see if there's anything going, or check the noticeboards at top-end hotels.

BUS

The government's recently overhauled, large SNTV buses are the best (but most expensive) way to travel around Niger because they cover all the major routes, are comfortable, relatively fast and punctual. Seats must be reserved in advance. In each major town, SNTV has its own bus station.

You can save about 20% by taking a private bus. These tend to have more frequent departures from the gares routières (also called autogares in Niger), although they have later departure times and the driving time is typically 50% longer.

BUSH TAXI

Bush taxis are cheaper and leave more frequently than the buses, although they are often very crowded. There are two types of bush taxi: Peugeot 504 seven-seater station wagons, which normally carry about 12 people; and minibuses, which carry 30 people or more. The seven-seaters are preferable because they fill faster and stop less often.

Bush taxis cover all but the most remote villages, although there's next to no public transport in the Sahara. In rural areas, you can also find converted trucks and pick-ups, called *fula-fulas*. These are cheap, but slow and terribly uncomfortable. Note that baggage charges are sometimes levied; they are usually about 10% of the passenger fare.

CAR & MOTORCYCLE

Main roads in Niger are generally good, although the sections between Niamey and Dosso, and Niamey and the border with Burkina Faso, were in desperate need of repair when we visited. From Niamey to Arlit via Agadez, Nguigmi via Zinder, and to the Burkinabé border, the roads are all tar.

The central section of the road between Zinder and Agadez has been engulfed by the desert – it's 4WD only, as the promised repairs have never been carried out. SNTV buses take on armed soldiers between Tahoua and Agadez and private vehicles should never travel this stretch of road at night due to the risk of banditry.

Private cars must pay a toll *(péage)* to use the main routes. You buy a ticket before travelling from a checkpoint on the edge of each town, either for a whole trip, eg, Niamey to Agadez (CFA1000), or in sections, eg, Niamey to Tahoua (CFA500), then Tahoua to Agadez (CFA500). If you don't have a ticket when it's asked for at a checkpoint, you're fined on the spot.

ORGANISED TOURS

Your only choice in order to visit Parc National du W or the desert areas around Agadez may be to take an organised tour. For more details see Information in the Niamey and Agadez sections later in this chapter.

Niamey

pop 700,000

Since becoming the capital, Niamey has experienced fantastic growth – from around 2000 people in the 1930s to more than 700,000 today. However, the city is fairly spread out and uncongested, which means that getting around requires a little more walking than in other Sahel capitals.

Niamey can feel like the end of the earth – in summer the dust never settles and, as the capital of one of the world's poorest countries it can be a desperate place where Africa's pain is everywhere on show. And yet, many travellers enjoy Niamey as a laid-back capital with an attractive riverside atmosphere.

If you've arrived from Ouagadougou or Bamako, you may be struck by the number of smart government buildings in the centre, a reminder of the time when uranium prices were sky-high. And yet, Niamey still has a traditional African ambience that gives the city its charm. It is most noticeable on the eastern bank of the Niger River, spanned by the Kennedy Bridge. Dusk is the time to have a drink nearby and watch the activity. If you wait long enough, you are bound to see a camel or two crossing over it. At night, finding a place to eat, drink and chat under the stars is easy; and, as with anywhere in the desert, that's when you'll most appreciate being here.

Orientation

Like many African cities, street names in Niamey are virtually useless as nobody knows them, even though most streets have signs. The street pattern, however, is easier to understand than it looks. The two principal arteries intersect at the Grand Marché: Rue de Coulibaly Kalleye, running from the northeast to the southwest (towards Kennedy Bridge) and Blvd de la Liberté. Rue de Coulibaly Kalleye is the main commercial drag, becoming Rue du Gaweye (also known locally as Rue du Commerce) near the Niger River.

The other major axis, Blvd de la Liberté, runs alongside the market and heads southeast towards the airport and out of town (to Agadez, Zinder and Benin) and northwest towards the equally wide Route de Tillabéri. The latter route, also called Blvd de l'Indépendance, leads out through the smart Plateau *quartier* (suburb) to Rond-point Yantala on the northwestern edge of town.

Information

Tourist Offices The ONT (☎ 73 24 47, fax 72 39 40) is on Av de Président Heinrich. Although it still has limited resources, it has got its act together since we last visited and has a few books and brochures for sale, including a field guide to the animals of Park National du W.

Money BIA-Niger (☎ 73 31 01), on Rue du Commerce/Gaweye, charges between 1%

and 2% to change travellers cheques, plus a handling charge per cheque. It gives quick service and also handles Visa cash advances (although it has been known to charge a fee of up to CFA10,000) and cash transfers by Western Union. The Eco Bank on Blvd de la Liberté efficiently changes cash and travellers cheques and is open between the convenient hours of 8.30am to 5.30pm Monday to Friday and 9am to 1pm on Saturday.

Post & Communications There are two main post offices; in the centre of town (Grande Poste) and in Plateau. The post office in Plateau has a poste restante service, which is quick and reliable; letters are kept for up to four months.

Cheap telephone calls (and telexes) can be made from either of the post offices. Three minutes (the minimum charge) to Europe costs about CFA5000, plus CFA1600 per subsequent minute. Maison de l'Internet, on Rue du Gaweye in the Immeuble el-Nasr building, is a good place to make really cheap international calls (as low as CFA600 per minute to Europe). Faxes are also charged by the minute. The central post office also operates a 'fax restante' service; you can have faxes sent to you (fax 73 44 70) and pick them up free of charge.

Email & Internet Access At the time of research, there were three public internet offices. Cyberéspace at the Centre Culturel Franco-Nigerién (☎ 73 48 34), opposite the Museum entrance, was the cheapest at CFA1500 per hour, but there's often a queue and connections are slow. It's open 9am to 4.30pm Monday, and 9am to 12.30pm and 3.30pm to 6.30pm Tuesday to Saturday. Maison de l'Internet (☎ 73 59 79), in the Immeuble (Building) El Nasr, is more expensive (CFA3000) but the connections are faster. It's open 8am to 1pm and 3.30pm to 9pm Monday to Saturday, as well as 10am to noon and 5pm to 9pm on Sunday. The small telecentre (☎ 73 23 78) outside the ONT tourist office is outrageously expensive (CFA175/9000 per minute/hour), but connections are lightning fast and it's open from 8.30am to 11pm daily.

Travel Agencies & Tour Operators Most companies run tours to Parc National du W (and other destinations around Niamey).

One of the best and most-expensive agencies is Niger-Car Voyages (☎ 73 23 31, fax 73 64 83) on Av de l'Afrique. Their tours include Filingué and Baleyara, Ayorou, pirogue journeys, the giraffes at Kouré and Parc National du W. Although it runs tours for as few as two people, the per-person rate almost halves if there are six or more of you.

For air tickets, look no further than the efficient and reliable Satguru Travels and Tours Service (☎ 73 69 34, ⓔ stts-nim@intenet.ne) on Rue de la Copro.

Cultural Centres The Centre Culturel Franco-Nigérien (☎ 73 48 34, fax 73 42 40, ⓔ ccfndir@intnet.ne) faces the northern side of the museum off Av de la Mairie. Its library is open to everyone and there's a busy schedule of lectures, exhibits, dance and theatre. It also regularly screens excellent French, American and African films at CFA500 per person (commencing at 8.30pm).

The American Cultural Center (☎ 73 31 79) is off Av du Général de Gaulle in the Plateau district. It's a good place to catch US TV news and newspapers.

Centre Culturel Oumara Ganda (☎ 74 09 03), named after a famous film maker, near the Grande Mosquée, which is east of the city centre, sponsors a variety of African cultural activities that include wrestling, dancing, films by local film makers, concerts and art exhibitions.

Medical Services The best hospital is Clinique de Gamkalé (☎ 73 20 33) on Corniche de Gamkalé about 2km southeast of Rond-point Kennedy. The standard fee is CFA11,000 per consultation. It's open 8.30am to 12.30pm and 3.30pm to 6.30pm weekdays and 8.30am to 12.30pm Saturday.

Otherwise, there are plenty of pharmacies around town. Among the best are Pharmacie Grand Marché (☎ 73 40 78) on Blvd de la Liberté and Pharmacie El Nasr (☎ 73 47 72) in the Immeuble El Nasr.

Dangers & Annoyances Crime has become a significant problem in Niamey. The most dangerous areas are the Petit Marché (where pickpockets are also a problem), Kennedy Bridge and the two Corniche roads running parallel to the river on the city side, including the area around Hôtel Gaweye Sofitel. There have been frequent

NIAMEY

PLACES TO STAY
1 Camping Touristique (Yantala Camping)
7 AFVP Rest House
14 Mission Catholique
28 Hôtel Gaweye Sofitel; La Potiniére; La Croix du Sud
31 Hôtel Maourey
59 Grand Hôtel
66 Hôtel Ténéré
69 Hôtel Terminus
70 Hôtel du Sahel
75 Hôtel Moustache

PLACES TO EAT
2 Food Stalls
4 Le Shanghai
12 Restaurant Le Pilier
20 L'Hippopotame Bleu
33 Le Hilly
34 Le Groto Club
36 Restaurant Bamba
37 La Cascade
41 Le Caramel
46 La Cloche; Niamey Club
47 La Pizzeria; Hi Fi Nightclub; Le Méridien
49 Suya Stalls
60 Le Dragon d'Or
62 Bar Teranga
63 Maquis 2000
71 Le Diamangou (Le Bateau)
74 Restaurant Chez Pinda

OTHER
3 Bush Taxi Stop
5 Canadian Embassy
6 Mobil Petrol Station
8 Beninese Embassy
9 Chadian Embassy
10 Jo Jos Mini Market
11 Total Petrol Station
13 American Cultural Center
15 Cathedral
16 BCEAO Bank (Central Bank)
17 Poste du Plateau
18 French Consulate
19 Presidential Palace
21 Hospital
22 Co-opérative des Métiers d'Arts
23 Centre Culturel Franco-Nigérien; Cyberéspace (Internet)
24 Musée National; Zoo; Artisan Workshops
25 SNTV Bus Station
26 Palais du Congrès
27 Maquis la Rivière
29 Sonibank
30 Le Chant du Monde (Music Store)
32 Satguru Travels and Tours Service
35 Pharmacie du Grand Marché
38 Le Studio Cinema
39 Score Supermarket
40 Ciné Vox
42 Supermarket Haddad
43 Jet Set Nightclub
44 Shell Petrol Station
45 Artisan Stalls
48 BIA-Niger Bank

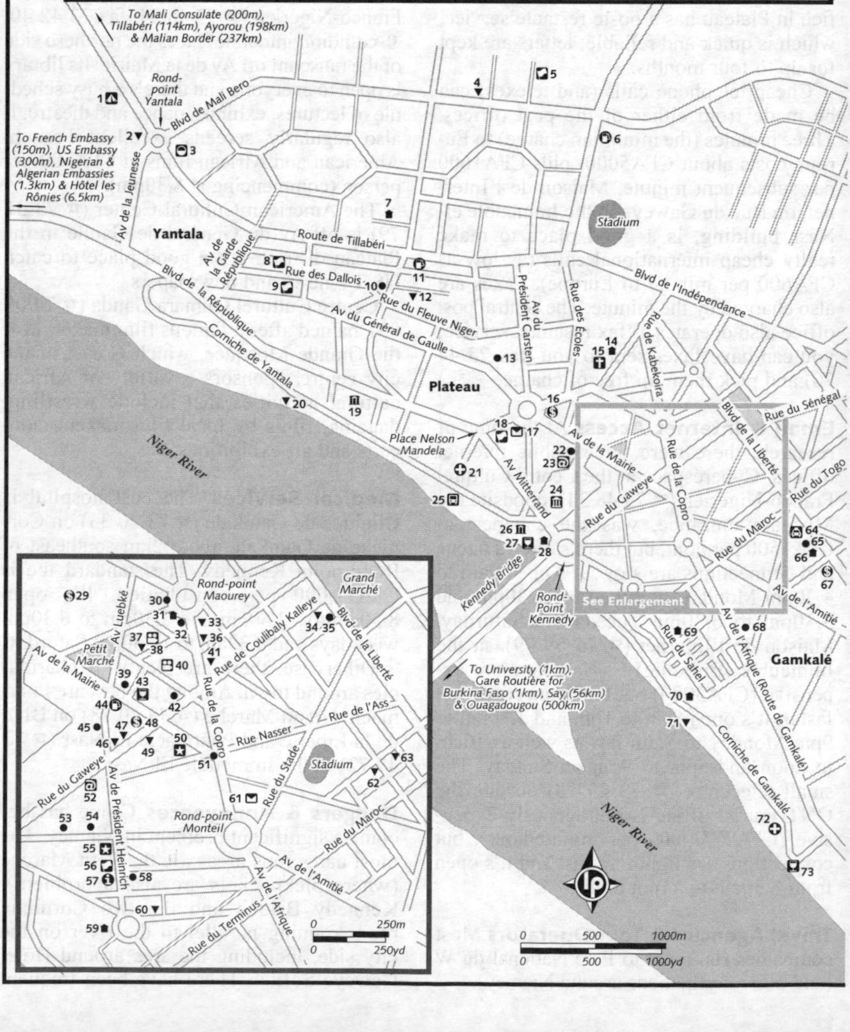

To Mali Consulate (200m), Tillabéri (114km), Ayorou (198km) & Malian Border (237km)
Rond-point Yantala
Blvd de Mali Bero
To French Embassy (150m), US Embassy (300m), Nigerian & Algerian Embassies (1.3km) & Hôtel les Rônies (6.5km)
Av de la Jeunesse
Yantala
Av de la Garde République
Route de Tillabéri
Rue des Dallois
Blvd de la République
Rue du Fleuve Niger
Av du Général de Gaulle
Corniche de Yantala
Stadium
Blvd de l'Indépendance
Av du Président Carsten
Rue des Écoles
Rue de Kabekoira
Plateau
Place Nelson Mandela
Av de la Mairie
Av Mitterrand
Rue du Gaweye
Rue de la Copro
Blvd de la Liberté
Rue du Sénégal
Rue du Togo
Rue du Maroc
Av de l'Amitié
Kennedy Bridge
Rond-Point Kennedy
See Enlargement
Rue du Sahel
Av de l'Afrique (Route de Gamkalé)
Gamkalé
Corniche de Gamkalé
Niger River
To University (1km), Gare Routière for Burkina Faso (1km), Say (56km) & Ouagadougou (500km)
Rond-point Maourey
Grand Marché
Av Luebké
Petit Marché
Rue de Coulibaly Kalleye
Rue de l'Ass
Rue Nasser
Rue du Stade
Av de Président Heinrich
Rond-point Monteil
Rue du Terminus
Av de l'Afrique
0 250m
0 250yd
0 500 1000m
0 500 1000yd

OTHER (CONTINUED)
- 50 Sûreté
- 51 Place de la République
- 52 Immeuble El Nasr; Royal Air Maroc; Pharmacie El Nasr; Maison de l'Internet; Air Algérie; Extase Nightclub
- 53 Immeuble Sonara I; Air France
- 54 Immeuble Sonara II; Bank of Africa
- 55 Prefecture
- 56 Moroccan Embassy
- 57 Office National du Tourisme (ONT); Internet Telecentre
- 58 Nigeravia (Airline)
- 61 Grande Poste (PTT)
- 64 Airport Taxi Station
- 65 DHL
- 67 Eco Bank
- 68 Niger-Car Voyages
- 72 Clinique de Gamkalé
- 73 Isangani
- 76 Moped Rentals
- 77 Grande Mosquée
- 78 Pharmacie du Grande Mosquée
- 79 Centre Culturel Oumarou Ganda
- 80 Stade de la Lutte Traditionelle (Traditional Wrestling)
- 81 Wadata Autogare; EHGM Bus Station; Village Artisanal de Wadata

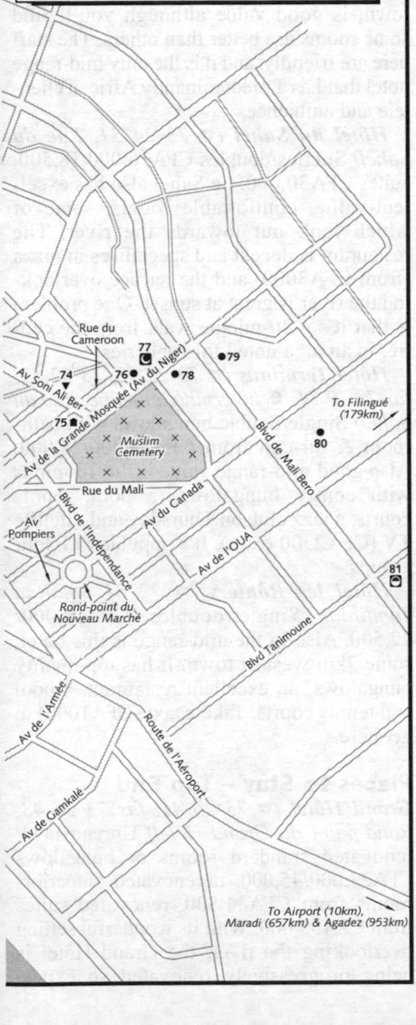
Rue du Cameroon
77
79
74
76
78
Av Soni Ali Ber
Av de la Grande Mosquée (Av du Niger)
To Filingué (179km)
75
Muslim Cemetery
80
Blvd de Mali Bero
Rue du Mali
Blvd de l'Indépendance
Av du Canada
Av Pompiers
Av de l'OUA
81
Rond-point du Nouveau Marché
Blvd Tanimoune
Av de l'Armée
Route de l'Aéroport
Av de Gamkalé
To Airport (10km), Maradi (657km) & Agadez (953km)

muggings and even knife-slashings in these areas, which should be avoided after sunset, especially if you are alone and on foot. Crime can also be a problem in the northern areas of Niamey, including Yantala.

Markets

The **Grand Marché**, on Blvd de la Liberté, has a colourful array of clothes, food and household goods lining its narrow lanes, which are invariably filled with a heady aroma of spices. The considerable trade-off for the lack of elbow room is the bustling African ambience.

The **Petit Marché** on Av de la Mairie is closer to the river and mainly a food market, but it too merits a visit (make sure you watch your valuables, though).

Grande Mosquée

This impressive mosque *(Av de la Grande Mosquée)*, financed by CFA500 million of Libyan money, is 1.5km east of the Grand Marché. Open to both male and female visitors (although women are theoretically denied entry if they are having their period), it has workers and guards who, if shown a little politeness, are often glad to give a short tour. A tip will be expected so agree to a price before you start; up to CFA2500 is reasonable if the tour includes a climb to the top of the minaret. The mosque is especially busy from late Friday morning.

Musée National du Niger

Built in 1959, this museum *(☎ 73 43 21, fax 73 64 83; admission CFA1000, camera/video fee CFA500/1000; museum & zoo open 8am-noon & 4pm-6.30pm Tues-Sun)*, between Av de la Mairie and Rue du Gaweye, is well worth a visit. You'll find life-sized models of traditional dwellings of the Tuareg, Hausa, Djerma, Fula and Toubou peoples, along with life-sized models in typical dress – a quick way to train the eye for detecting the differences in ethnic groups as you travel around the country. In addition, there is a series of pavilions, each with a different thematic display such as handicrafts, weapons and costumes. One pavilion contains an intact 100-million-year-old dinosaur skeleton (an iguanadon), found by uranium prospectors near Agadez, and other palaeontological treasures as well as a fragment of the infamous Arbre de Ténéré.

The depressing **zoo**, where lethargic and neurotic animals are kept in appallingly cramped conditions, is, sadly, likely to be your most enduring memory of a visit here.

At the artisans' centre in the musuem, you can see how the various crafts are made. You can also purchase silver, leather and wood items direct from the artisans.

Swimming

The top-end hotels have pools, with fees ranging from CFA500 to CFA2000 at Hôtel Gaweye Sofitel. Hôtel Ténéré and Grand Hôtel charge CFA1000. See Places to Stay for contact details.

Pirogue Trips

Niger-Car Voyages (☎ 73 23 31) on Av de l'Afrique can arrange pirogue rides along the river to see Niamey at sunset. Rates start at about CFA5000 per person for an hour-long trip, or you can arrange your own trip by going direct to the piroguers at the waterfront near the SNTV bus station. These boats only take four people in safety (around CFA5000 per hour for a boat would be reasonable).

Places to Stay – Budget

Camping Touristique *(Yantala Camping; ☎ 75 44 89, fax 75 45 78, Route de Tillabéri)* Camping CFA2000 per person plus CFA1000 per vehicle. It's a fair hike to the centre of town (CFA200 in a shared taxi) and you may have the place to yourself, but this dusty camp site has improved in recent years. It also has reasonably clean showers and toilets. The restaurant becomes a noisy bar at night.

AFVP Rest House *(☎ 75 28 58, Off Route de Tillabéri)* Bed in 3-person room CFA2500. This place, run by the Association of French Volunteers for Progress, is highly recommended and the tidy rooms are by far the cheapest you'll find in Niamey.

Mission Catholique *(☎ 73 32 03)* Rooms with bathroom CFA5000. This mission has been reluctant to take travellers for some years, but occasionally we hear of someone who is allowed to stay. It's well worth asking because the rooms are good and it's a quiet place.

Hôtel Moustache *(☎ 73 33 78, Av Soni Ali Ber)* Rooms with fan CFA5000, with fan & bathroom CFA7500, with air-con & bath CFA10,000. Service is definitely the name of the game here although probably not quite the kind you're after. The rooms are kept clean, but the cheapest ones are usually reserved for liaisons with the hotel's large population of prostitutes. The delightfully seedy bar attracts all manner of seedy characters – always lock your door – and bumps and grinds until 2am.

Places to Stay – Mid-Range

Hôtel Maourey *(☎ 73 28 50, fax 73 20 54, Rond-point Maourey)* Singles/doubles with bathroom & air-con CFA15,000/18,500, suites CFA25,000. This hotel, in the heart of town, is good value although you'll find some rooms are better than others. The staff here are friendly, and it is the only mid-range hotel that has a predominantly African clientele and ambience.

Hôtel du Sahel *(☎ 73 24 31, Rue du Sahel)* Singles/doubles CFA16,000/18,500, suites CFA30,000. Le Sahel also has excellent-value, comfortable rooms, some of which look out towards the river. The restaurant is decent and specialises in pizza (from CFA3000) and the terrace overlooking the river is great at sunset. One problem is that it's a 20-minute walk from the centre, in an area noted for robberies.

Hôtel Terminus *(☎ 73 26 92, 73 22 52, fax 73 39 74, ⓔ hotermi@intnet.ne, Rue du Sahel)* Single/double bungalows with bathroom & air-con from CFA24,000/28,000. Also good mid-range value is the Terminus with comfy bungalows, a pool, tennis courts, a jazz club on Thursday and satellite TV (CFA2500 extra). It's popular with tour groups.

Hôtel les Rôniers *(☎ 72 31 38, Rue Tondibia)* Singles/doubles CFA19,000/22,500. Also in the mid-range is this hotel, some 7km west of town. It has top-quality bungalows, an excellent restaurant, a pool and tennis courts. Take a taxi (CFA1000) to get here.

Places to Stay – Top End

Grand Hôtel *(☎ 73 26 41, fax 73 26 43, Rond-point du Grand Hôtel)* Unrenovated/renovated standard rooms or bungalows CFA27,000/45,000, unrenovated 'superior' rooms from CFA34,500, renovated suites from CFA55,000. With its wonderful setting overlooking the river, the Grand Hôtel is being progressively renovated so expect prices to increase. The standard of rooms (with satellite TV) is high, there's a good swimming pool and the terrace is a great place for a meal, a beer or just taking in the sunset. It accepts AmEx and Diners Club.

Hôtel Ténéré *(☎ 73 30 55, 73 20 20, 73 30 55, Blvd de la Liberté)* Singles/doubles CFA25,500/30,000, suites CFA35,500. The rooms here are spacious and comfortable if a little rundown. All rooms have satellite TV and there's a clean swimming pool.

Hôtel Gaweye Sofitel *(☎ 72 27 10, fax 72 33 47, ⓔ gaweye@intnet.ne, Av Mitterand)* Rooms with city/river view CFA70,000/75,000, suites from CFA100,000. Built during the uranium boom, this hotel, adjacent to the Palais du Congrès, is Niamey's finest and most impressive hotel. It has a pool, tennis courts, boutiques and a nightclub. It accepts Visa, AmEx and Diners Club.

Places to Eat

Cheap Eats The best place for really cheap food is around the Petit Marché on Av de la Mairie. ***Street stalls*** and basic ***eating houses*** serve *riz sauce* (rice with meat or chicken) for around CFA600, or Nescafé, bread and fried-egg sandwiches in the morning until around 9.30am and again in the evening from around 6.30pm. The food stalls on Rond-point Yantala are similar.

Just along Hôtel Moustache on Av Soni Ali Ber is the simple ***Restaurant Chez Pinda***, which offers hearty servings of couscous (CFA500; CFA1000 with chicken or fish).

If you are out partying along the disco strip of Rue du Gaweye in the centre of town, there are some great ***suya stalls*** (*suya* is Hausa for brochette) opposite the nightclubs; CFA500 will see you well fed. Fast food of all sorts is available from ***Le Méridien***, including omelettes or sandwiches (from CFA500) and hamburgers (from CFA750).

Restaurant Bamba *(Rue de la Copro)* Meals from CFA500. This cheap and sometimes cheerful shack serves hearty Senegalese meals.

Le Hilly *(Rue de la Copro)* This animated eatery, with bare tables and loud music, serves food until around 10pm and drinks until midnight or !ater.

Le Caramel *(☎ 73 40 40, Rue de la Copro)* Meals from CFA450, pastries from CFA175. Open 6am-2pm & 4pm-midnight Mon-Sat, 6am-1pm & 4pm-10.30pm Sun. If you're still on your way home the following morning, Le Caramel has good croissants, and, for later in the day, it also has a basic menu with omelette and chips (CFA450), sauté chicken and french fries (CFA1600), and riz sauce (CFA600).

Bar Terenga *(Off Rue du Maroc)* Open noon-11pm. It's mainly a watering hole and the beers are cheap (from CFA300), but the outdoor tables are also a good place to down a plate of rice or spaghetti with sauce (CFA200) or with chicken or fish (CFA400).

African & Middle Eastern The highly recommended ***Maquis 2000*** *(☎ 73 55 56, Off Rue du Maroc)* is an Ivoirian-style open-air restaurant with a varied menu that includes *brochette de capitaine* (fish brochette; CFA2500), *crevette grillé* (grilled prawns; CFA2900) and, if you're game, the *agouti braisé* (grilled grasscutter; CFA3500). It also has ice creams (CFA2300), fruit juices (CFA800) and beer (from CFA600). It's open from noon to 3pm and 6pm to 11.30pm daily.

Le Groto Club *(Rue de Coulibaly Kalleye)* Meals from CFA1500. Open noon-3pm & 6pm-11.30pm daily. Almost opposite the Grande Marché, Le Groto's interior courtyard is a pleasant place to eat, especially on Friday and Saturday night when you can follow your meal with great music and plenty of dancing until late.

La Cloche *(Av Luebké)* Meals from CFA1000. Open noon-midnight daily. Expats swear by La Cloche, exhorting that it serves the best chawarma, humous and tabouleh in town; it's OK but we feel it doesn't deserve the rave.

Asian The excellent ***Le Dragon d'Or*** *(☎ 73 41 23, Rue de Grand Hôtel)* serves a mix of Vietnamese and Chinese food, has a pleasant garden setting and over 100 menu selections. Entrees cost from CFA1000, mains from CFA2500. The speciality here is the filling, delicious *pho* (a noodle soup with coriander, bean sprouts and beef; CFA1500). The rice-paper rolls (CFA1400), served with lettuce, mint and fish sauce are as good as you'll get anywhere. The buffet on a Saturday night (CFA7500 plus drinks) is superb. It's open noon to 2.30pm and 7pm to 11pm daily.

Le Shanghai *(☎ 75 38 29, Blvd de Mali Bero)* Entrees from CFA1000, mains from

CFA2500. Open noon-2.30pm & 7pm-11pm Tues-Sun, 7-11pm Mon. With the same owners as Le Dragon D'Or, this place is of a similarly high standard.

European Two of the top French restaurants are at hotels. ***La Croix du Sud*** at Hôtel Gaweye Sofitel, with mains from CFA3000, (open 7pm to 11pm Monday to Saturday) and the restaurant in ***Hôtel les Rôniers***, with mains from CFA2500, (open noon to 2.30pm and 7pm to 10.30pm daily), are about as good as you'll find anywhere.

Le Diamangou *(Le Bateau; ☎ 73 51 43, Corniche de Gamkalé)* Mains from CFA2200. Open 7pm-11pm Sat-Thur. At this place, about 1.5km east of Kennedy Bridge, you can dine by the riverside or on board the boat. The main attraction is the pleasant setting overlooking the river, although the food, mainly European, is good.

La Cascade *(☎ 73 40 50, Off Av Luebké)* Mains from CFA3000. Open noon-2.30pm & 7pm-11pm daily. The French and Italian food here is good and the owners are friendly, but prices are on the high side (fish soup is CFA3600, large salads are CFA3700 and fish platters from CFA4000).

Niamey has plenty of places where the pizza is good.

L'Hippopotame Bleu *(Corniche de Yantala)* Pizzas from CFA2500. Open 5pm-late Tues-Sat, noon-late Sun. Expats in Niamey claim that this place has the best pizzas in Niger. The setting on the riverbank is also lovely and you may see hippos. Apart from pizzas it does *brochettes*, fish and decent salads. There's a bar with cocktails and dance floor with good music.

Of the hotel restaurants, pizzas at ***Grand Hotel*** (from CFA4000) are good and ***La Potinière***, the informal pool-side restaurant at Hôtel Gaweye Sofitel is hardly cheap, but the pizzas (from CFA3500) are first-rate.

Le Pizzeria *(☎ 72 12 40, Rue du Gaweye)* Pizzas from CFA3000. Open 7pm-11.30pm daily. The pizzas here are also excellent and it's a good place to line the stomach before dancing the night away.

Restaurant Le Pilier *(☎ 72 24 86)* Mains from CFA2600. Open noon-2.30pm & 7pm-11pm Wed-Mon. This place, east of Rue des Dallois in Plateau, is highly recommended for quality Italian cuisine and the service is good.

Self-Catering Niamey's largest supermarket, ***Score*** *(Av Luebké)*, is in the heart of town, facing the Petit Marché. It's large and loaded with groceries from France. It's open 8am to 12.30pm and 3pm to 6.30pm weekdays, and 8am to 12.30pm Saturday.

Supermarket Haddad *(☎ 73 61 60, Rue de Gaweye)* Open 8am-12.30pm & 3pm-6.30pm Mon-Fri, 8am-12.30pm Sat. This is another well-stocked choice in the centre of town.

There are also smaller Lebanese-owned stores that carry many products from the Arab world. For fresh produce, the best place is the ***Petit Marché***.

Entertainment

Bars & Nightclubs The lively ***Niamey Club*** *(Rue de Gawaye)* is a long-time Niamey favourite and is popular with locals and expats alike. It has cheap drinks and tasty meals, and, occasionally, live music at night.

Le Hilly For an open-air bar with a rustic African feel, try this lively place, south of Rond-point Maourey.

The poolside terrace at ***Grand Hôtel*** provides the best views over the river; it has inexpensive *brochettes* and other snacks, as well as beers.

Maquis la Rivière Another place for a beer at sundown on the river's edge is Maquis la Rivière, behind the Palais du Congrès. It's a great place to meet friends for a drink and a light lunch (chicken couscous is CFA2500).

Nightlife in Niamey is centred on the Rue du Commerce, a section of street squeezed between Rue du Gaweye and Rue de Coulibaly Kalleye. Here you will find the perennial ***Hi-Fi Club***, one of those glitterball fantasias. ***Extase Nightclub*** *(☎ 73 30 70, Immeuble El Nasr)* is expensive (cover charge CFA2000), but it's not bad.

Jet Set Nightclub *(☎ 73 61 61, Av de la Mairie)* Cover charge CFA3000. *The* disco in Niamey is Jet Set; drinks are expensive (from CFA1500).

When we were there, ***Isangani***, at the eastern end of the Corniche de Gamkalé, was also 'in'; drinks cost CFA2500.

Cinemas The air-con ***Le Studio*** cinema, in the centre on the street behind Score supermarket, is the best in town. ***Ciné Vox*** is a block away and worth checking, too. Films are also shown at the ***Centre Culturel Franco-Nigérien***, the ***Palais du Congrès*** and the ***American Cultural Center***.

Spectator Sports

On some Sundays, you may have the opportunity to see African-style wrestling matches at ***Stade de la Lutte Traditionelle***, a block northwest of the Wadata Autogare on Blvd de Mali Bero, 3km east of the Grand Marché. The crowds are very enthusiastic and the matches, held in an arena surrounded by a covered viewing stand, are definitely worth seeing.

Shopping

Art & Craftwork At the ***Grand Marché*** there's a selection of goods, including Tuareg and Hausa leatherwork, silver jewellery, batiks, tie-dyed cloth and Djerma blankets. Look out for *les couvertures Djerma*, large, bright strips of cotton sewn together into a large cloth, which are truly spectacular and unique to Niger.

Also worth trying are ***Village Artisanal de Wadata***, near the autogare, although this has a less-extensive selection.

Also highly recommended is the ***artisan workshop*** inside the museum (open 8am-noon & 4pm-6.30pm Tues-Sun) and the ***Coopérative des Métiers d'Arts*** (☎ *73 50 34*), open 9am-noon & 4pm-6pm Mon-Sat, just up the road. Also worth a look are the ***artisan stalls***, south of Petit Marché on Av de Président Heinrich.

Music Cassettes of local and Western music (originals and bootlegs) can be bought from several of the stalls in the ***Grand Marché***. Other places to try include ***Le Chant du Monde*** at Rond-point Maourey. It has an extensive selection and is open from 8.30am to 1pm and from 4pm to 9pm daily.

Getting There & Away

Air For details of international flights to/from Niamey, see the main Getting There & Away section earlier in this chapter. Airlines with offices in Niamey include:

Air Algérie (☎ 73 32 14) In Immeuble El Nasr
Air France (☎ 73 30 11) In Immeuble Sonara I on Rue du Gaweye
Royal Air Maroc (☎ 73 28 85) In Immeuble El-Nasr

Bus The SNTV bus station (☎ 72 30 20) is on Corniche de Yantala, northwest of Kennedy Bridge. The ticket office is open from 7.30am to 12.30pm and 3.30pm to 6.30pm weekdays, 8am to 9am Saturday and 8am to noon Sunday; your best bet is to book 8am the day before you want to travel. One-way fares from Niamey with SNTV include the following.

destination	fare (CFA)	frequency	duration (hours)
Agadez	15,570	Tues, Thur, Sat	12
Birni N'Konni	6600	Mon, Tues, Thur, Sat	6
Dogondoutchi	4860	Mon, Tues, Thur, Sat	4
Dosso	2440	Mon, Tues, Thur, Sat	2
Maradi	9565	Mon, Tues, Thur, Sat	9
Tahoua	8750	Tues, Thur, Sat	8
Zinder	12,625	Mon, Tues, Thur, Sat	12

Note that the days of travel are subject to change.

Large private buses leave from the Wadata Autogare (note that it's autogare and not gare routière) on Blvd de Mali Bero, east of the city centre. Private buses are about 20% cheaper than the SNTV buses. A cut above the other private companies is EHGM, which has a bus between Niamey and Zinder (CFA12,200, 12 hours), via Maradi (CFA8200, nine hours), departing at 7am on Monday and Friday.

Bush Taxi At least one Peugeot taxi leaves Niamey's Wadata Autogare daily for the following places. Fares are for one-way travel.

destination	fare (CFA)	destination	fare (CFA)
Agadez	15,100	Gaya	4100
Ayorou	3000	Maradi	9000
Birni N'Konni	5500	Tahoua	7800
Dogondoutchi	4400	Téra	3000
Dosso	2600	Tillabéri	1900
Filingué	2750	Zinder	11,600

Travel times vary widely, to which must be added time spent waiting for the bush taxi to fill. Minibuses are cheaper, but take a lifetime to leave and another to arrive.

For details of getting to Burkina Faso or Benin, see the main Getting There & Away section earlier in the chapter.

Getting Around

To/From the Airport A private taxi from the airport to the city centre (12km) costs about CFA5000, but this depends on your bargaining powers and the time of day; going the other way costs around half that. Shared taxis (CFA250 to the centre) run along the highway nearby.

Car Rental The major car-rental agency is Niger-Car Voyages (see Travel Agencies). For the smallest car without air-con, it charges around CFA13,500 a day, plus CFA2000 per day for insurance, CFA130 per kilometre and tax (about 20%). Vehicles can only be used around town.

For travel outside Niamey, the cheapest car is a Toyota Corolla, which costs CFA15,000 per day, plus CFA2000 insurance, CFA130 per kilometre, obligatory chauffeur (at CFA6000 a day) and tax. This comes to almost CFA50,000 a day if you travel around 200km, not including petrol.

Taxi Taxis around town don't have meters and are mostly shared, simply heading off in the direction requested by the passenger and picking up other passengers heading in the same general direction en route. To hail a taxi, simply call your destination in through the window as the taxi slows and the driver will decide if he wants to take you. Shared taxi fares are usually CFA250 for most destinations around Niamey.

A taxi to yourself *(déplacement)* will cost from CFA1000 for a short ride across town, say from the centre to the Wadata Autogare, or about CFA2500 per hour and CFA20,000 per day. You can find them at the Grand Marché, Petit Marché and at the big hotels (although they charge higher rates). From 10pm, taxis are scarce and charge more.

AROUND NIAMEY

Boubon

The best time to come to Boubon, 25km northwest of Niamey, is on Wednesday, when there's a marvellous market. But even better is simply being so close to the Niger River. You can hire a pirogue (around CFA5000) for a trip along the river. There's an outdoor restaurant on the small island 200m from the village (you'll find someone with a pirogue to take you over). ***Le Campement Touristique Boubon*** *(☎ 73 24 27)* is also on the island with thatched-roof cabins for around CFA5000, a restaurant and a clean pool. Boubon is on the tar road to Tillabéri.

Kouré

About 60km east of Niamey, Kouré is the place to go to see Niger's (and West Africa's) last remaining giraffe herd (see boxed text 'The Last Giraffes in West Africa' earlier in the chapter). It's an easy half-day trip from the capital. If you don't have your own vehicle, it's easiest to rent a taxi in Niamey (bargain hard but expect to pay around CFA25,000 for the return journey). The turn-off to the giraffes is well-marked with signs on the main highway. There's also a police checkpoint here where you'll need to pay the CFA3000 entry fee and take on the compulsory guide (around CFA2500) who'll help you track down the remarkably tame herd. Entrance fees are subject to change.

Niger-Car Voyages in Niamey (see Travel Agencies in that section) runs a range of tours to see the giraffes with the standard tour starting from CFA25,000 per person for six or more people; the price includes a picnic lunch.

North of Niamey

From Niamey, one main road leads northwest along the Niger River, towards the Malian border. See the main Getting There & Away section of this chapter for details on getting to Burkina Faso or Mali.

TILLABÉRI

Tillabéri (also spelt Tillabéry) is one of Niger's biggest rice-growing areas. If you're driving to Mali, get your passport stamped here. The most interesting day to visit is market day on Sunday. The only place to stay in town is the ***Relais Touristique***, which was closed for renovations when we visited but should have reopened by now. It's near the river on the northern side of town. There are bush taxis between Niamey's Wadata Autogare and Tillabéri (CFA1900).

AYOROU

If you have a car, or can rent one for the day, Ayorou is an interesting one-day excursion from Niamey and highly recommended. The major attraction of the town, particularly from November to April, is the livestock **market** (for cattle, camels, sheep and goats) held every Sunday. You'll see Tuareg, Fulani, Bella and Mauritanian Moors, all in traditional dress. The market doesn't really warm up until around noon, so if you're there in the morning, go to the river to watch the cattle swimming across. Guides and piroguers can be persistent around town, but it's not a bad idea to hire a guide (CFA3500 per day) as they will arrange photo permissions.

Make sure you leave time afterwards to take a trip on the river. You can rent pirogues in Ayorou or, more cheaply, in **Firgoun**, a small, rarely visited fishing village 11km to the north. A fee of CFA4000 for the boat is a fair price.

If it's still open, try the ***Campement***, which has some dirt-cheap huts where you can sleep on the floor, or you may find lodging with a local. Better is ***Hôtel Amenokal*** *(Book with Niger-Car Voyages ☎ 73 23 31, Niamey)* on the riverbank. The once-good singles/doubles start from a highly negotiable CFA12,000/14,000, as there's no running water and the pool's empty. There's a bar and restaurant.

For meals, you could also try ***Restaurant à la Pirogue***. Otherwise, bring food with you, as there's little in town.

There are bush taxis between Niamey's Wadata Autogare and Ayorou (CFA3000).

FILINGUÉ

Filingué is 185km northeast of Niamey on a tar road, and another interesting place for a day excursion. The market on Sunday, used primarily by the Fulani and Songhaï-Djerma, is surprisingly active for such a small town and there are some good examples of traditional architecture here. It's at the base of a hill, which you can climb to get an excellent view of the town and the Dallol Bosso, a valley with a dry riverbed.

If you come on a Sunday, don't fail to stop in **Baleyara** (meaning 'where the Bella meet'), roughly halfway between Niamey and Filingué. Its Sunday market is picturesque, being under a canopy of shady trees – the animal bartering, which takes place on the town side of the market, is particularly worth seeing.

In Filingué, the rudimentary ***Campement*** is on your right as you enter town from Niamey, next to the fort. Singles cost about CFA3000 and the beds are big enough for two people. There's also a shower but no fans.

There are bush taxis between Niamey's Wadata Autogare and Filingué (CFA2750).

The South

Niger's main arterial road leads from Niamey eastward along the southern edge of the country towards Chad, running roughly parallel to the Nigerian border. For details on getting to the Beninese, Nigerian or Chadian border, see the main Getting There & Away section earlier in this chapter.

DOSSO

Some 136km southeast of Niamey, Dosso is the first major settlement reached on the main southern road. The name comes from 'Do-So', a Djerma spirit. Dosso was once an important Islamic centre and the home of the Djermakoye, the most important Djerma religious leader. Today Dosso is a crossroads, south to Benin and west to Nigeria.

Musée Regional de Dosso and **Centre Artisanal** *(☎ 65 03 21; admission CFA1000, camera/video fee CFA500/1000; open 8am-noon & 4pm-6.30pm Tues-Sun)* are housed in the same building and the ethnographic exhibits are worth a quick browse.

Places to Stay & Eat

Sous les Palmiers Rooms CFA3500 per person. This place has the cheapest beds in Dosso, although the rooms are pretty basic. It's off the main road that runs from the Hôtel Djerma towards Niamey. Cheap meals are also on offer here.

Auberge du Carrefour *(☎ 65 00 17)* Doubles with fan/air-con CFA4500/6500. This renovated and good-value auberge is on the right as you enter town from Niamey, not far from the autogare. It has a nice courtyard restaurant.

Hôtel Djerma *(☎ 65 02 06)* Rooms with air-con & bathroom from CFA12,000. This hotel, behind the Mobil petrol station on the main drag in the centre of town, has excellent rooms with showers that try very hard to be hot. The rooms at the back, away from the lively bar, are quieter. The hotel has an OK restaurant, serving couscous, spaghetti (CFA1500) and steak with chips, plus a beer garden. The pool may even be filled one day.

Cheap ***street food*** can be found along the main road, particularly at the autogare. Also, at night, the road running out from opposite Hôtel Djerma is alive with gas lanterns, diesel fumes and good street food. If you're self-catering, the ***Mini-Bazaar*** grocery store on the main east-west drag has a variety of goods.

Near the Grand Marché, ***Chez Rita*** has meals that are good and cheap, but the star attraction is Rita herself.

Getting There & Away

Dosso sits at the junction of the main roads between Niamey and Zinder and south to Gaya (for Benin and Nigeria), so there are always plenty of bush taxis. Bush taxis to/from Niamey cost CFA2600 and around CFA2000 to/from Gaya.

GAYA

Gaya is the only border town for Benin and one of four for Nigeria. The only place to stay is ***Hôtel Dendi***, very near the market. Singles/doubles are CFA3000/4000 with electricity, fan and bucket shower. For cheap food, try the ***Restaurant la Joie d'Été***, next to the market. For a beer, try the rustic ***Bar Station*** across from the bus park.

Minibuses/Peugeot taxis run from Niamey to Gaya (CFA3500/4100).

PARC NATIONAL DU W

This excellent national park *(adult/child CFA3500/2000 per day; open 1 Dec-late May)* is on the west bank of the Niger River in an area of dry savanna woodland, a transition zone between the Sahel and moister savannas to the south. The 'W' (pronounced du-blay-vay) in the name comes from the double bend in the Niger River at the park's northern border. The park straddles three countries – Niger, Benin and Burkina Faso.

Although there's a wide variety of wildlife, their total numbers, with the exception of antelopes, are very small. Elephants number around 100 or less. Carnivores include lions, leopards, cheetahs, baboons, Nile crocodiles, hyenas and jackals. Migratory birds arrive between February and May. There are also more than 300 species of birds present in the park.

The best wildlife-viewing time is towards the end of the dry season (March to May) when the animals congregate around water holes. This is also the time of year when the park is most barren-looking. In the dry season, one of the favoured elephant haunts is the river near the park lodge.

There are more than 500 plant species in the park.

The entrance to the park is at La Tapoa, 145km south of Niamey. A map is available. A guide costs from CFA3500 to CFA6000 a day. Guidebooks can be purchased at the park (CFA5000).

Places to Stay & Eat

Camping inside the park or in one of the adjoining protected reserves is prohibited. A ***camp site***, just before the River Tapoa, may be open (CFA2500 per person).

The only alternatives are finding someone in La Tapoa village to put you up for the night, or staying at the 35-room lodge called ***Relais de la Tapoa*** next to the camp site and the river. The lodge is open for the same months as the park.

The cost of single/double bungalows with half board (bed, breakfast and dinner or lunch) is CFA17,500/27,000 (CFA20,000/31,500 with air-con). There's also a bar and swimming pool. You can make a reservation at Niger-Car Voyages (☎ 73 23 31, fax 73 64 83) in Niamey.

Getting There & Away

Access by public transport is very difficult. From the small gare routière on the western side of Kennedy Bridge in Niamey, you can take transport to Say, then on to Tamou. From Say or Tamou you may find transport to La Tapoa, but don't count on it. Remember that the only way into the park is by vehicle, and walking around the park is not permitted because of lions.

Niger-Car Voyages runs two-day tours to the park for CFA145,000 per person for two people but the price drops to CFA75,000 per person if there are six or more people.

PARC NATIONAL DU W

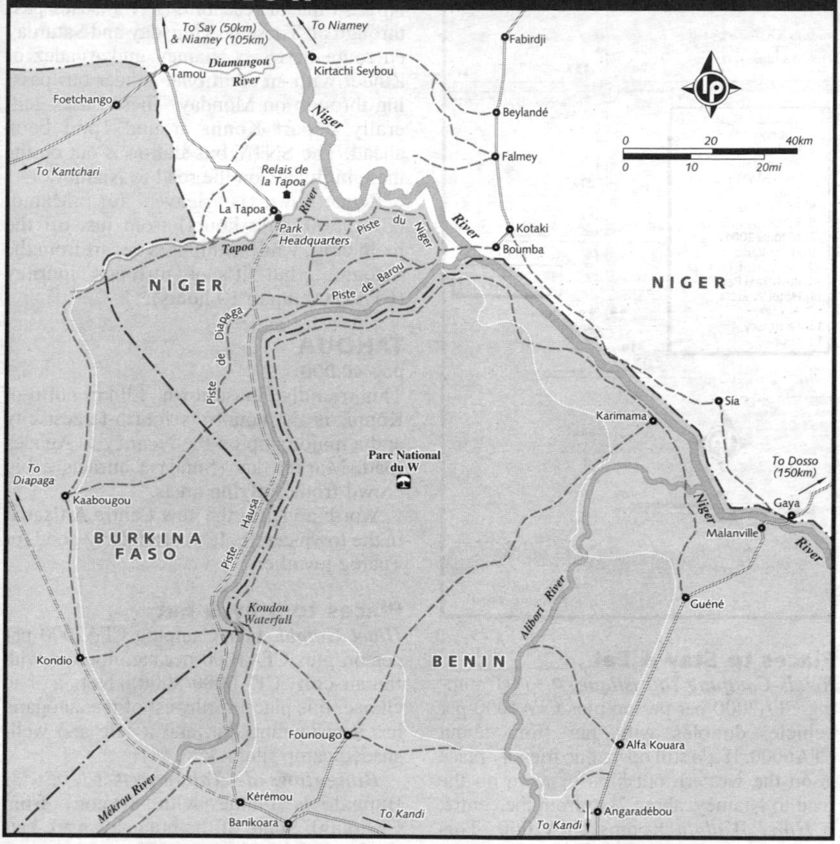
To Say (50km)
& Niamey (105km)
To Niamey
Fabirdji
Tamou
Diamangou
River
Kirtachi Seybou
Foetchango
Niger
Beylandé
Falmey
0
20
40km
0
10
20mi
To Kantchari
Relais de
la Tapoa
La Tapoa
River
Park
Headquarters
Piste du Niger
River
Kotaki
Boumba
Tapoa
NIGER
Piste de Barou
NIGER
Piste de Diapaga
Sía
Karimama
Parc National
du W
To Dosso
(150km)
To
Diapaga
Kaabougou
Niger
Gaya
Malanville
River
BURKINA
FASO
Piste Hausa
Guéné
Alibori River
Koudou
Waterfall
Kondio
BENIN
Founougo
Alfa Kouara
Mékrou River
Kérémou
To Kandi
Banikoara
Angaradébou
To Kandi

The price includes accommodation, transport, admission to the park and food.

If you're going by car, from Niamey take the conversation-stopping washboard road south to Say (50km) and on to Tamou (55km) at the border with Burkina Faso, then 40km further south to La Tapoa.

DOGONDOUTCHI

'Doutchi' is a small town on the main road, about halfway between Dosso and Birni N'Konni. The nearby area is picturesque and the town is pleasant. Just outside the town is a small hill, which you can walk up, and about 15km away is an impressive escarpment *(falaise)* that offers good views.

The only place to stay is ***Hôtel Magama*** *(☎ 282)*, well signposted near the centre of town. Rooms in pleasant bungalows cost CFA4000 and an air-con double is CFA9000. The shady restaurant serves meals for between CFA700 and CFA1500, and there's secure parking. To get to Dogondoutchi, take a bush taxi travelling between Dosso and Birni N'Konni.

BIRNI N'KONNI

About 420km east of Niamey, Birni N'Konni (or simply 'Konni') is one of the four major border crossings with Nigeria. The two principal streets form a crossroads, with the east-west highway between Niamey and Zinder about 750m north of the town centre, meeting the main road to Sokoto in Nigeria, which extends south from it. Moneychangers are everywhere.

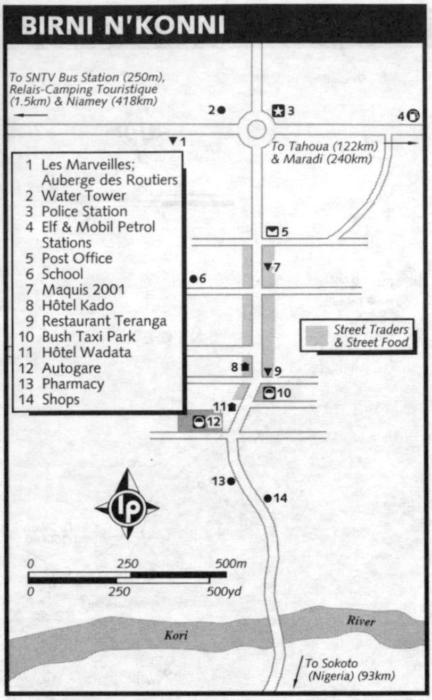
BIRNI N'KONNI
To SNTV Bus Station (250m), Relais-Camping Touristique (1.5km) & Niamey (418km)
To Tahoua (122km) & Maradi (240km)
1 Les Marveilles; Auberge des Routiers
2 Water Tower
3 Police Station
4 Elf & Mobil Petrol Stations
5 Post Office
6 School
7 Maquis 2001
8 Hôtel Kado
9 Restaurant Teranga
10 Bush Taxi Park
11 Hôtel Wadata
12 Autogare
13 Pharmacy
14 Shops
Street Traders & Street Food
0 250 500m
0 250 500yd
Kori
River
To Sokoto (Nigeria) (93km)

Places to Stay & Eat

***Relais-Camping Touristique** (☎ 338)* Camping CFA2000 per person plus CFA1000 per vehicle, doubles with fan from about CFA6000. If it's still open, this friendly place is on the western outskirts of town on the road to Niamey, about 2km from the centre.

Hôtel Wadata Rooms CFA2000. This hotel with basic rooms is in the centre of town on the main north-south drag.

***Hôtel Kado** (☎ 296)* Rooms with bathroom & fan/air-con CFA6500/9800. The Kado, one block north of the Wadata, is the best hotel – although that's not saying much. The staff are generally friendly and helpful, but the rooms have a dusty, neglected air. The shady restaurant is good for a simple meal (from CFA1000).

Along the main street and in the autogare you'll find plenty of ***food stalls*** selling rice, meat and sauces. Both ***Restaurant Teranga*** (Senegalese) and ***Maquis 2001***, on the main street, are breezy and the food isn't bad. A few hundred metres west of the main intersection, out along the highway, ***Les Marveilles*** and ***Auberge des Routiers*** are decent cheapies.

Getting There & Away

At the time of research, SNTV buses pass through on Tuesday, Thursday and Saturday en route between Niamey and Agadez or Zinder with an additional Zinder bus passing through on Monday. These buses generally depart Konni around 1pm; book ahead. The SNTV bus station is out on the main highway, on the road to Niamey.

Peugeot taxis leave for Maradi (CFA3500, four hours) from just off the main drag, while minibuses depart from the autogare, but it's a tortuous journey (CFA2500, up to 10 hours).

TAHOUA

pop 40,000

This friendly Hausa town, 130km north of Konni, is the country's fourth-largest city and a major stop on the Niamey to Agadez road. Market day (Sunday) attracts a big crowd from outlying areas.

Worth a visit is the new **Centre Artisanal** in the town centre. It's particularly good for Tuareg jewellery.

Places to Stay & Eat

Hôtel Galabi Ader Camping CFA2000 per person plus CFA1000 per car, doubles with fan/air-con CFA6000/8000. Not a bad choice, this place northwest of the autogare, has a restaurant, bar, and a safe and well-shaded camp site.

***Bungalows de Tahoua** (☎ 61 05 53)* Bungalows (some with air-con) from CFA6000. Some of the bungalows are better than others (the ones with carpet have a mosquito problem) and it's worth bargaining. It's a 10-minute walk northeast of the SNTV bus station, opposite the Mairie.

***Hôtel l'Amitié** (☎ 61 01 53, Route de Niamey)* Doubles with air-con CFA10,000. If it's still open, the clean and well run Hôtel l'Amitié is well worth trying. It's just 200m back from the SNTV bus station on the main highway – look for the giraffes outside. There's a friendly bar and restaurant with meals from CFA2000.

There are plenty of ***food stalls*** opposite the entrance to the SNTV bus station, some of which do sandwiches (CFA200).

***Restaurant les Délices** (Jardin Publique)* Meals less than CFA2500. Open noon-10.30pm daily. With an extensive menu and a lovely garden setting, les Délices, next to

Bungalows de Tahoua, is the pick of Tahoua's restaurants. However, the Donald Duck signs advertising its existence around town are an irritating.

Chez Fatima For traditional African food, head for the popular Chez Fatima at the roundabout, just east of the BIA-Niger bank.

Getting There & Away

The SNTV buses between Niamey and Agadez stop here on Tuesday, Thursday and Saturday, sometime between 1pm and 3pm. Book ahead for a seat to Niamey (CFA8750, eight hours) or Agadez (CFA6800, five hours). Bush taxis to/from Niamey charge CFA7800 and can easily take 14 hours.

If you're in your own vehicle and plan on travelling to Agadez, avoid doing so at night as banditry is common under cover of darkness. The SNTV bus takes on soldiers as escorts for this section.

MARADI

pop 70,000

Maradi, the country's third-largest city, remains the administrative capital and commercial centre for agriculture, although it was hit particularly hard by the economic slowdown of 1990s. It's a conservative place with a troubled recent history.

Information

To change money, try BIA-Niger on Rue de la Sûreté or Sonibank on Route de Niamey, across the road from the market. For changing naira (for Nigeria), try the gare routière 200m north of Sonibank.

The only Internet cafés in Maradi at the time of research were: Sareli Internet (☎ 41 12 03), on the south side of the market; and Public Services Informatique (☎ 41 11 16) on Rue de la Sûreté. Both charge CFA200 per minute (hourly rates are negotiable) and are open 8am to 7pm Saturday to Thursday.

Things to See & Do

Don't miss the **market** in the heart of town on the main north-south drag; Friday is market day. Also worth seeing is the **Maison des Chefs** at Place Dan Kasswa on the western side of town, which, with its traditional geometric designs, is a fine example of Hausa architecture. The **Maison de la Culture Bawa Dan Wardanga**, south of the Jardin Publique, hosts cultural events and exhibitions.

The Night of Fire

The social landscape of southern Niger is heavily influenced by its overbearing neighbour, Nigeria. The push towards Islamic conservatism and the imposition of Islamic sharia law in northern Nigeria has found a ready audience in Maradi. The Government of Niger has rejected calls for sharia to be introduced, arguing that Niger is a secular state. Undaunted, fundamentalist Muslims in Maradi decided to take matters into their own hands.

On 11–13 November 2000, Niger hosted an international fashion festival intended to herald a new era of African and European cooperation and the reinforcement of Niger's status as a modern African nation. The festival sparked anger among conservative clerics, who saw the festival as un-Islamic. While the majority of protests were peaceful, those in Maradi turned nasty with mobs of fundamentalist thugs roaming the streets targeting businesses perceived to be engaged in un-Islamic practices. These included bars, restaurants and hotels, which were either burned to the ground or forced to close under threat of attack. While casualties were remarkably low, the scars remain from a night of fire when the townspeople learned who really controlled Maradi.

Centre Artisanal *(☎ 41 01 02)*, on the main road north of town where the roads from Niamey and Zinder meet, is worth a visit.

Places to Stay

Hôtel Liberté *(☎ 41 03 80)* Singles with fan & shower CFA3000, doubles/twins with bathroom CFA4500/5000, doubles with bathroom & air-con from CFA7000. Some of the rooms here are bad, a tad grubby and the beds terrible, but it's the cheapest place to stay. The courtyard is pleasant and meals are available for CFA1000 to CFA1500. It's located to the southwest of the market.

Hôtel Larewa *(☎ 41 08 13, Off Route de Niamey)* Rooms with fan/air-con from CFA4300/7300. The Larewa is quiet and not bad value by Niger standards, although it's a little rundown these days. The rooms are large and generally clean.

Hôtel Jangorzo *(☎ 41 01 40, Route de l'Aéroport)* Small rooms with shower

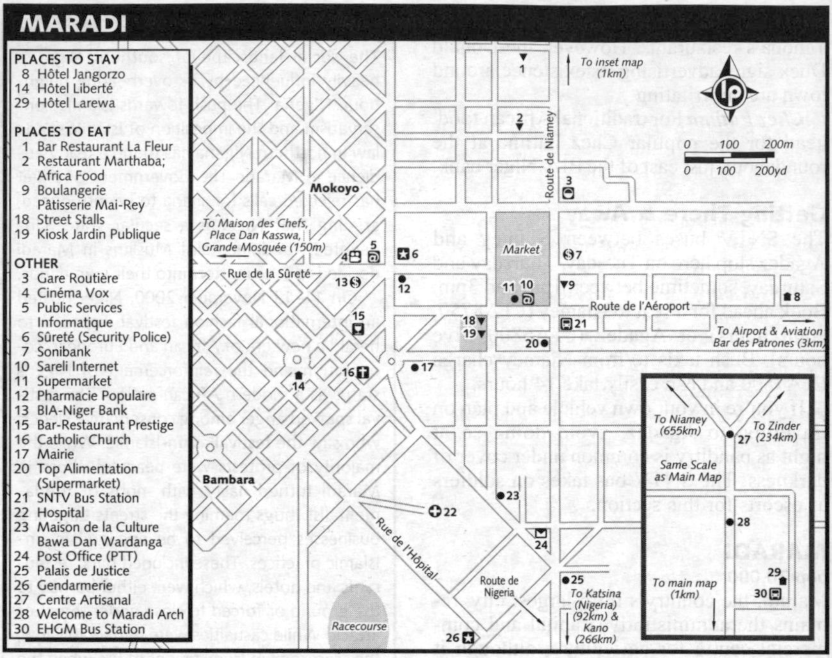
MARADI
PLACES TO STAY
8 Hôtel Jangorzo
14 Hôtel Liberté
29 Hôtel Larewa
PLACES TO EAT
1 Bar Restaurant La Fleur
2 Restaurant Marthaba; Africa Food
9 Boulangerie Pâtisserie Mai-Rey
18 Street Stalls
19 Kiosk Jardin Publique
OTHER
3 Gare Routière
4 Cinéma Vox
5 Public Services Informatique
6 Sûreté (Security Police)
7 Sonibank
10 Sareli Internet
11 Supermarket
12 Pharmacie Populaire
13 BIA-Niger Bank
15 Bar-Restaurant Prestige
16 Catholic Church
17 Mairie
20 Top Alimentation (Supermarket)
21 SNTV Bus Station
22 Hospital
23 Maison de la Culture Bawa Dan Wardanga
24 Post Office (PTT)
25 Palais de Justice
26 Gendarmerie
27 Centre Artisanal
28 Welcome to Maradi Arch
30 EHGM Bus Station
To inset map (1km)
0 100 200m
0 100 200yd
Route de Niamey
Mokoyo
To Maison des Chefs, Place Dan Kasswa, Grande Mosquée (150m)
Rue de la Sûreté
Market
Route de l'Aéroport
To Airport & Aviation Bar des Patrones (3km)
Bambara
Rue de l'Hôpital
Route de Nigeria
To Katsina (Nigeria) (92km) & Kano (266km)
Racecourse
To Niamey (655km)
To Zinder (234km)
Same Scale as Main Map
To main map (1km)

CFA5500, singles/doubles with air-con CFA13,500/16,000, suites CFA30,000. The sprawling Jangorzo is arguably the nicest hotel, but its standards are slipping. The small rooms are a bit cell-like, but the remainder are spacious and airy. It's also reasonably central and the restaurant serves breakfast/meals from CFA1000/3500.

Places to Eat

At night you'll find delicious grilled chicken and other snacks at ***street stalls*** around the Jardin Publique, while there are also cheap meals and beer available from the ***kiosk*** inside the gate of the Jardin.

Restaurant Marthaba *(☎ 41 01 18, Off Route de Niamey)* Mains from CFA500, half/full chicken CFA800/1600. Open 8am-11.30pm Sat-Thur, 4pm-10pm Fri. This sleepy outdoor place isn't bad provided the staff can find the cook.

Africa Food is a simple chop house next door to the Marthaba.

Bar-Restaurant La Fleur Mains from CFA500, half/full chicken CFA800/1600. Open 8am-11.30pm Sat-Thur, 4pm-10pm Fri. The food at La Fleur, west off Route de Niamey, is similar to that at the Marthaba, but this open-air place is more lively in the evening.

Boulangerie Pâtisserie Mai-Rey *(☎ 41 01 81, Route de Nigeria)* Pastries & bread from CFA200. Open 8am-11.30pm Sat-Thur, 4pm-10pm Fri. The selection here is fairly meagre, but it's still good for a snack, especially during Ramadan when it's one of the few places open during the day.

Entertainment

Maradi has suffered badly from the zeal of Islamic heavies but a couple of resilient places survive.

Bar-Restaurant Prestige Cover charge CFA300. Beers from CFA500. Open 8pm-late daily. This defiantly hedonistic place, to the west of Jardin Publique, was the most popular in town when we visited. It's one of the few places in Maradi that hosts live music; bands usually strike up some time after 10pm. It doesn't serve meals.

Aviation Bar des Patrones *(Maradi Airport)* Cover charge CFA300. Beers from CFA500. Open 9pm-1am daily. This is the other bar of choice for Maradi's youth and, while there's no live music, it does serve meals.

Getting There & Away

There are four SNTV (☎ 41 03 26) buses a week in each direction between Niamey and Zinder via Maradi. Heading east, the buses leave Maradi around 4pm, while in the other direction it's around 10am. The fare for Niamey is CFA9565 (nine hours) while the three-hour journey to Zinder costs CFA4500.

EHGM (☎ 41 13 40) also has a bus between Niamey (CFA8200, nine hours) and Zinder (CFA3000, three hours) via Maradi, on Monday and Friday. It's depot is just off Route de Niamey at the northern end of town; take the turn-off for Hôtel Larewa.

Bush taxis/minibuses depart from the gare routière for Zinder (CFA3100/2500, three/five hours) and Konni (CFA3100/2500, three/five hours) at reasonably regular intervals throughout the day. If you're leaving (or changing vehicles) at night, you'd be better off trying the checkpoint about 5km out along the road to Zinder.

At the gare routière, you'll find bush taxis heading for Katsina (CFA1400, 92km) or Kano (CFA2700, 266km) in Nigeria; travel times depend on your luck (or lack of) with Nigerian officials at the border.

ZINDER

pop 85,000

When the French arrived in Niger at the end of the 19th century, the only significant city they found in the area was Zinder (zen-**dair**), a city on the old trans-Saharan caravan route. So they made it the capital until 1926, when the administrative offices were transferred to Niamey. Zinder was founded two centuries earlier by Hausa people emigrating from the Kano area. They were soon joined by the Kanouri from the north. By the mid-19th century, Zinder was in its prime. The importance of this old Hausa trading town, now Niger's second largest, was brought about by its location on the trade route between Kano and Agadez.

For Nigerian naira, look for moneychangers around the gare routière. Moneychangers in Kano give better rates for US dollars.

Things to See & Do

A stroll through the narrow streets of the **Birni Quartier**, the picturesque old quarter to the southeast of the centre, is highly recommended. You'll find small gardens, friendly people and some fine examples of traditional **Hausa architecture**. Even in Nigeria you won't see such a well-preserved area of traditional Hausa buildings. The old *banco* (mud brick) houses are everywhere, easily identified by geometrical designs in relief, usually colourfully painted. A good place to start is the **Grande Mosquée**, as there are some fine examples nearby. Behind it is the **Sultan's Palace**, built in the mid-19th century, reportedly still with the bones of the Sultan's enemies within its fortified walls.

The other old section, the **Zengou Quartier** on the northern side of town, has lots of commercial buildings as well as more mud-brick houses.

Also worth checking out are the **markets**, which are some of the liveliest in Niger – the big day is Thursday. Look for leather goods as the best *artisans de cuir* in Niger are here. Thursday is also the day for the big animal market outside the city, but close to the Sultan's Palace.

The building housing the **Musée Régional de Zinder** *(admission CFA1000, camera/video fee CFA500/1000; open 8am-noon & 3pm-6pm Tues-Sun)* is a fine reproduction of traditional Hausa design. It also has a wonderful wooden door from the Sultan's Palace embossed with bronze, and there is a range of other ethnographic and archaeological exhibits.

Places to Stay

Hôtel Malem Kalkadanu *(☎ 51 05 68, Av de la République)* Rooms with fan without/with shower CFA3100/4100, with fan & private bathroom CFA6100. This homely option, with a friendly owner and clean rooms, is on the main drag, 700m north of the town centre. It's excellent value. Simple meals are available and there are plans for a restaurant in the pleasant courtyard.

Hôtel Central *(☎ 51 20 47, Av de la République)* Doubles with fan/air-con CFA6500/9500. Once the favourite of overlanders, Hôtel Central has recently taken a downward slide. The rooms are mediocre and noisy; the hotel courtyard is the city's most popular rendezvous in the evenings for expats, prostitutes and locals.

Hôtel Damagaram *(☎ 51 00 69, Av des Banques)* Singles/doubles/twins with air-con

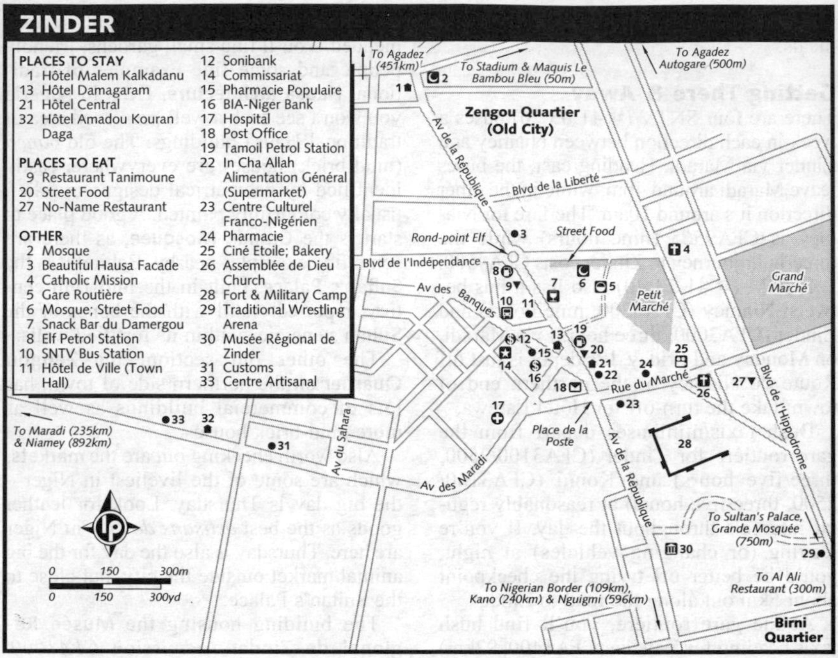
ZINDER
PLACES TO STAY
1 Hôtel Malem Kalkadanu
13 Hôtel Damagaram
21 Hôtel Central
32 Hôtel Amadou Kouran Daga
PLACES TO EAT
9 Restaurant Tanimoune
20 Street Food
27 No-Name Restaurant
OTHER
2 Mosque
3 Beautiful Hausa Facade
4 Catholic Mission
5 Gare Routière
6 Mosque; Street Food
7 Snack Bar du Damergou
8 Elf Petrol Station
10 SNTV Bus Station
11 Hôtel de Ville (Town Hall)
12 Sonibank
14 Commissariat
15 Pharmacie Populaire
16 BIA-Niger Bank
17 Hospital
18 Post Office
19 Tamoil Petrol Station
22 In Cha Allah Alimentation Général (Supermarket)
23 Centre Culturel Franco-Nigérien
24 Pharmacie
25 Ciné Etoile; Bakery
26 Assemblée de Dieu Church
28 Fort & Military Camp
29 Traditional Wrestling Arena
30 Musée Régional de Zinder
31 Customs
33 Centre Artisanal
To Agadez (451km)
To Stadium & Maquis Le Bambou Bleu (50m)
To Agadez Autogare (500m)
Zengou Quartier (Old City)
Av de la République
Blvd de la Liberté
Street Food
Rond-point Elf
Blvd de l'Indépendance
Av des Banques
Grand Marché
Petit Marché
Rue du Marché
Blvd de l'Hippodrome
Place de la Poste
Av du Sahara
Av des Maradi
To Maradi (235km) & Niamey (892km)
To Sultan's Palace, Grande Mosquée (750m)
To Al Ali Restaurant (300m)
To Nigerian Border (109km), Kano (240km) & Nguigmi (596km)
Birni Quartier
0 150 300m
0 150 300yd

& bathroom CFA13,500/16,500/18,500. The Damagaram is ageing rapidly, but is still the best option in the heart of town. It can be noisy at weekends, but the rooms are spacious with enormous beds; you may need to ask them to turn on the hot water, though.

Hôtel Amadou Kouran Daga *(☎ 51 07 42, Av des Maradi)* Singles/twins with fan & bathroom CFA7500/9500, singles/doubles/twins with air-con & bathroom CFA13,500/16,500/18,500. With probably the best rooms in Zinder, this place is a bit out on a limb on the road to Niamey. It is, however, quiet and has a good restaurant and a pleasant terrace bar.

Places to Eat & Drink

Some of the best ***street food*** can be found in the square in front of Hôtel Central and on Blvd de l'Indépendance by the gare routière. There is a good ***bakery*** *(Rue du Marché)* next door to the Ciné Etoile, or for a cool drink try the ***Snack Bar du Damergou***, almost opposite Hôtel Le Damagaram, where the drinks menu includes a condom for CFA50. The simply named ***Restaurant*** on Blvd de l'Hippodrome, opposite the southwest corner of the market, does large servings, but doesn't do dinner.

Al Ali Restaurant *(☎ 51 02 37)* Mains CFA1000-1750, salads CFA500. Open noon-3pm & 6pm-11pm Sat-Thur, 6pm-11pm Fri. All your African favourites (especially rice and couscous with sauce) can be tasted underneath the pleasantly down-at-heel *paillotes* (thatched sun shelters often serving cheap food and drink) at Al-Ali, southeast of the town centre. There are also steak dishes and spaghetti.

Maquis Le Bambou Bleu *(☎ 51 04 87, Sports Stadium)* Sandwiches CFA300, mains CFA1000. Open noon-3pm & 6pm-11pm Sat-Thur, 6pm-11pm Fri. The pleasant garden setting is complemented by good food (especially couscous) and reasonable prices. It's at the back of the stadium car park.

Restaurant Tanimoune *(Av de la République)* Mains from CFA1200, snacks up to CFA1000. Open 8am-midnight daily. This is arguably the best place to eat in Zinder. The balcony overlooks the main street and the menu includes fish, salads, omelettes, chicken, couscous and rice, and cornflakes with milk (CFA2000) for breakfast.

Getting There & Away

SNTV buses (☎ 51 04 68) run four times a week in each direction between Niamey and Zinder (CFA12,625, 12 hours, 6.30am departure). The SNTV bus station is on Av des Banques, a couple of blocks northwest of Hôtel Central. Bush taxis run daily between Zinder and Niamey for CFA11,600 (up to 14 hours); they leave from the gare routière near the Petit Marché.

SNTV trucks leave for Agadez (CFA6700, 10 hours) on Saturday (luggage is about CFA500). There's usually one daily private bus to Agadez from the Agadez autogare but the departure time (early morning or evening) depends on when it arrives from across the desert.

SNTV also has a twice weekly service to Nguigmi (CFA9500). Bush taxis run between Zinder and Diffa, on the road to Chad, for CFA6000. Some go on to Nguigmi and charge CFA8500 for the whole trip.

If you're heading to Kano in Nigeria, you'll have no problem finding a bush taxi in the morning. The Zinder to Kano price is CFA3500, although it's often cheaper to change at the border.

NGUIGMI

Nguigmi is a small town in the far east of Niger, at the end of the tar road, and the last settlement of any size before you reach Chad. The town has no hotels. There is a lively market area to the south of town where you can buy *brochettes*.

There are a few bush taxis between Zinder and Nguigmi, charging CFA8500. For transport to/from Chad, see the main Getting There & Away section earlier in this chapter.

The North

AGADEZ

pop 30,000

Agadez, like Timbuktu, is one of the great, ancient trading towns of the Sahara. Its sandy streets, distinctive mud-brick architecture, and predominantly Tuareg population make for a fascinating experience that's likely to be one of the highlights of any visit to Niger.

In the 16th century, with a population of 30,000 people, Agadez thrived off the caravans *(azalai)*, plying between Gao (in Mali) and Tripoli (in Libya). Some were as large as 20,000 camels laden with gold, salt and slaves. Although the town's fortunes have waxed and waned over the centuries and its economy is heavily dependent upon a fickle flow of tourists (complete with plenty of persistent hustlers), Agadez is a resilient city and it remains the principal supply stop for trucks crossing the Sahara.

Agadez should not be missed. Standing as it does on the frontier of the Sahara, it's the main jumping-off point for expeditions into some of the most spectacular desert and mountain scenery in Africa.

Information

The absence of a competent tourist office in Agadez makes getting information difficult. Thankfully, there are plans among the private tour agencies to fill this gap by setting up a Syndicat du Tourisme (BP 248) in the form of a visitors centre and museum. The visitors centre will also provide information on the necessary procedures for visiting the mosque and the houses of the Vieux Quartier. For details on how this plan is progressing, speak with Akly Joulia-Boileau at the Auberge D'Azel.

Money The Bank of Africa and BIA-Niger, both opposite the Grand Marché, usually charge only 1% commission on US dollars travellers cheques.

Travel Agencies & Tour Operators There are more than 50 travel agencies in Agadez, although many are little more than one man with a camel. There are two main options as to the type of journey.

Budget travellers usually make the arrangements through an independent guide, who charges around CFA20,000/60,000 per person per day including all transport via camel/4WD, food, sleeping arrangements and permits. Highly recommended among the many guides roaming Agadez are Moussa Touboulou and Sidi Mohamed, who are wonderful companions in a desert region they love. This is a good option if you're on your own as most other tour operators require a minimum four people. It is a great way to explore the Aïr Mountains, especially as you'll sleep in Tuareg villages, and both men are concerned to minimise your impact on what is a fragile society. The two men are

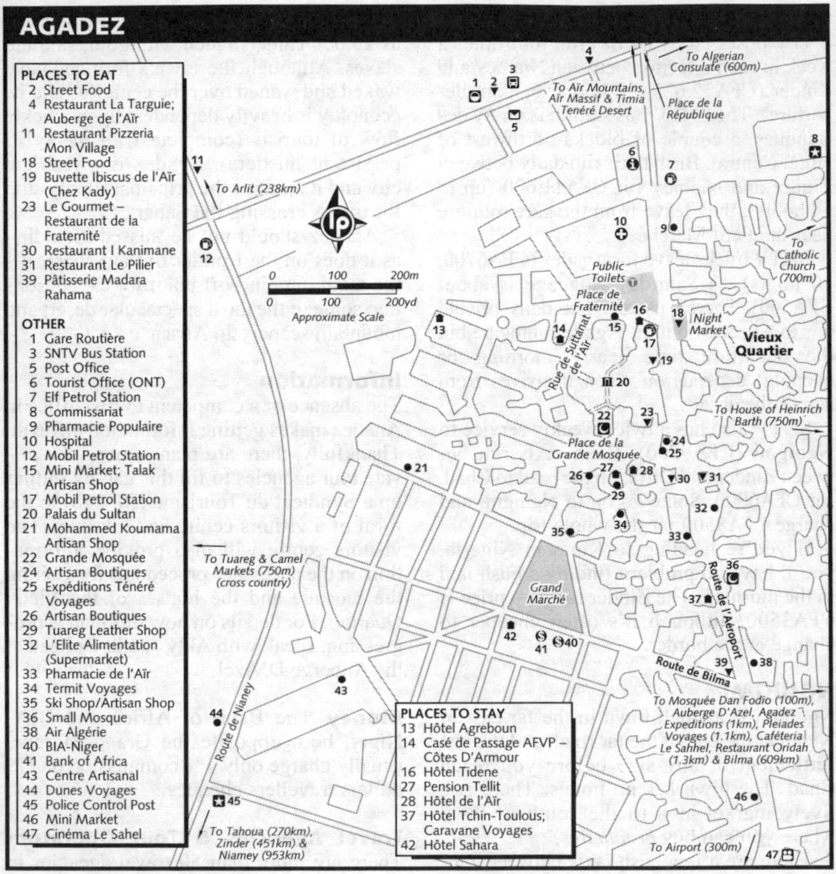
AGADEZ
PLACES TO EAT
2 Street Food
4 Restaurant La Targuie; Auberge de l'Aïr
11 Restaurant Pizzeria Mon Village
18 Street Food
19 Buvette Ibiscus de l'Aïr (Chez Kady)
23 Le Gourmet – Restaurant de la Fraternité
30 Restaurant I Kanimane
31 Restaurant Le Pilier
39 Pâtisserie Madara Rahama
OTHER
1 Gare Routière
3 SNTV Bus Station
5 Post Office
6 Tourist Office (ONT)
7 Elf Petrol Station
8 Commissariat
9 Pharmacie Populaire
10 Hospital
12 Mobil Petrol Station
15 Mini Market; Talak Artisan Shop
17 Mobil Petrol Station
20 Palais du Sultan
21 Mohammed Koumama Artisan Shop
22 Grande Mosquée
24 Artisan Boutiques
25 Expéditions Ténéré Voyages
26 Artisan Boutiques
29 Tuareg Leather Shop
32 L'Elite Alimentation (Supermarket)
33 Pharmacie de l'Aïr
34 Termit Voyages
35 Ski Shop/Artisan Shop
36 Small Mosque
38 Air Algérie
40 BIA-Niger
41 Bank of Africa
43 Centre Artisanal
44 Dunes Voyages
45 Police Control Post
46 Mini Market
47 Cinéma Le Sahel
PLACES TO STAY
13 Hôtel Agreboun
14 Casé de Passage AFVP – Côtes D'Armour
16 Hôtel Tidene
27 Pension Tellit
28 Hôtel de l'Aïr
37 Hôtel Tchin-Toulous; Caravane Voyages
42 Hôtel Sahara
To Algerian Consulate (600m)
To Aïr Mountains, Aïr Massif & Timia Ténéré Desert
Place de la République
To Arlit (238km)
To Catholic Church (700m)
0 100 200m
0 100 200yd
Approximate Scale
Public Toilets
Place de Fraternité
Rue de Suttanat de l'Aïr
Night Market
Vieux Quartier
To House of Heinrich Barth (750m)
Place de la Grande Mosquée
To Tuareg & Camel Markets (750m) (cross country)
Grand Marché
Route de l'Aéroport
Route de Bilma
Route de Niamey
To Mosquée Dan Fodio (100m), Auberge D'Azel, Agadez Expéditions (1km), Pleiades Voyages (1.1km), Caféteria Le Sahhel, Restaurant Oridah (1.3km) & Bilma (609km)
To Tahoua (270km), Zinder (451km) & Niamey (953km)
To Airport (300m)

well known around town, but the best place to start asking is Hôtel Agreboun.

The alternative is to go through one of the larger local tour operators who cost more (from CFA65,000 per day), but also offer a complete, fully equipped service. Agencies that we recommend, or which have been recommended to us, include:

Agadez Expéditions (☎/fax 44 01 70, ⓔ azel.auberge@caramail.com or az-tours@intnet.ne) Route de Bilma. Based at Auberge D'Azel, this is arguably the most-professional agency in Agadez; it charges about CFA70,000 to CFA75,000 per person per day, including tents, tables and Akly Joulia-Boileau, the experienced and enthusiastic leader.

Expéditions Ténéré Voyages (☎ 44 01 54) An experienced agency, located near the Grande Mosqée, that works primarily with French tour groups

Caravane Voyages (☎ 44 04 59, fax 73 20 06) Based at Hôtel Tchin-Toulous, its director is Mahamadou Souleymane.

Dunes Voyages (☎ 44 05 83) Route de Niamey

Pleiades Voyages (☎ 44 05 41) Route de Bilma

Termit Voyages (☎ 44 00 24) Behind Pension Tellit

The list of potential routes is as vast as the Sahara itself, but standard excursions include the following: an eight-day circuit of the Aïr Mountains (including the dunes at Temet); a tour of the Aïr and Ténéré (eight to 12 days); a circuit of the Aïr/Ténéré and the ghost towns of the Djado Plateau (14 to 15 days); while an extra week will enable you to explore all of the above plus the

Grand Ténéré and the dinosaur fossils at Termit.

If you have your own vehicle, expect to pay CFA15,000 per day for a compulsory guide and CFA7000 per day if you want a driver. To this, petrol costs must be added.

Finally, the most adventurous option is to take one of the trucks from Agadez to Bilma and return either by truck or, with one of the much smaller camel caravans that still cross the desert (18 to 40 days) from time to time. Either way, it's an arduous journey, but one that captures the true spirit of Saharan travel. To make this journey, you would need to be in Agadez no later than mid-October although exact departure dates are a notoriously inexact science. To find out more, talk with Sidi Mohamed, one of the independent guides listed earlier.

Grande Mosquée & Palais du Sultan

The Grande Mosquée dates from 1515, but was totally rebuilt in 1844. Its pyramid-like minaret with wooden scaffolding is a classic of Sahel/Sudanic-style architecture and was described by Bruce Chatwin as 'bristling with wooden spires like the vertebra of some defunct fauna'. Climbing to the top is possible, but unless you want to attract swarms of hangers-on, ask someone from your hotel or your Saharan guide to make the arrangements. A CFA1000 cadeau is often sufficient to persuade the guardian to let you climb 27m to the top for photographs. It's well worth the hassle with the summit affording breathtaking views across the Sahara and Aïr Mountains. Under the minaret, the unadorned prayer hall with low ceilings and pillars is simplicity itself. The side room, equally undecorated, is reserved for the sultan.

The three-storey building just north of the mosque is the Palais du Sultan, the residence of the city's traditional ruler, but it's not open to visitors.

Markets

The **Grand Marché** south of the mosque is the most animated place in town. The variety of people here, many dressed in traditional desert costumes, is at least as interesting as what's for sale. You can find a wide range of art and craftwork here, including rugs and Tuareg leatherwork.

There is also a **Tuareg market** on the western outskirts of town where the Tuareg will trade just about anything with you. Sitting down for endless cups of tea is a highlight, but don't pay more than CFA1500 for 1kg of desert 'Tuareg tea' (in spite of what the touts and others tell you). If you wish to take photographs, request permission from the chief of the market and expect to pay (perhaps CFA2500).

The marvellous **camel market**, part of the Tuareg market, is another must-see. It has wonderful colours – and not so wonderful smells emanating from the camels, goats and other animals for sale. Sunrise and sunset are the best times to visit.

Vieux Quartier

The Vieux Quartier, the old section of town, is an enchanting maze of small crooked streets, tiny shops and fascinating mud-brick architecture of Tuareg and Hausa inspiration. Ask especially to see the houses with '*les belles façades*' (meaning 'beautiful facades'). To enter the houses, some of which date back 150 years, permission from the owner and a cadeau (CFA500 to CFA1000) is required. You'll also find all kinds of artisan shops, including silversmiths making the famous croix d'Agadez, leatherworkers producing Tuareg *samaras* (sandals), *coussins* (cushions) and magnificent *selles de chameau* (camel saddles), and bronzesmiths making a variety of objects, including jewellery. You can usually take photographs of the artisans at work, but ask first. If possible, explore the old quarter once with a local to ensure you don't miss the best areas, and once on your own, simply losing yourself in the labyrinth.

Definitely worth a visit is the **House of Heinrich Barth**, one of the greatest Saharan explorers who lived in Agadez in the 1850s. In 1851 Barth was one of the first Europeans to witness the dramatic departure from Agadez of the salt caravans, describing it as 'a whole nation in motion'. The house is now a small museum containing some of Barth's possessions and items carried with him on his Saharan journey. A cadeau (up to CFA1000) to the old caretaker is appropriate.

Unlike many old towns across the Sahara, the old quarter of Agadez remains inhabited and thus stands a good chance of surviving the ravages of time. Urgent restoration work

Camel Racing

Camel racing is a favourite Tuareg sport. The usual routine involves a champion rider taking an indigo scarf from a woman and heading off into the desert. The other riders try to catch him and grab the scarf. Whoever succeeds is the winner. During the race, women decked out in their best silver jewellery cheer on the riders, singing and clapping to the sound of drums.

The best time to be in Agadez is during one of the Muslim holidays, especially Tabaski. Following the feast, you can see one of the great spectacles of the desert – the 'cavalcade', a furious camel race through the narrow crowded streets to the square in front of the Palais du Sultan.

is nonetheless required and the absence of an integrated approach to preserving the old town concerns many of the town's residents. For more information on efforts being undertaken to preserve old Agadez, talk with Céline and Akly Joulia-Boileau at Auberge D'Azel.

Places to Stay – Budget

Hôtel Agreboun *(☎ 44 03 07)* Room without/with shower CFA4000/5000. It's hard to beat this friendly hotel, on the western edge of town, several blocks from the mosque. Rooms are simple, but clean, and there are two very pleasant courtyards in which to sit out the day's heat.

Casé de Passage AFVP – Côtes D'Armour *(☎ 44 05 29, Rue de Sultanat de l'Aïr)* Rooms CFA2500 per person. Run by the French charity, AFVP, this place offers cheap beds in clean rooms and in a good location near the mosque.

Restaurant Oridah *(Route de Bilma)* Rooms with shower CFA5000. In a quiet area of town, the Oridah has simple rooms that are kept tidy, despite not getting much business.

Hôtel Sahara *(☎ 44 04 80)* Rooms with fan without/with bathroom CFA5000/7500, with air-con & bathroom CFA15,000. The rooms at this rambling place, southwest of the Grand Marché, are perfectly habitable, but it has always had a dodgy feel with hustlers, prostitutes and groups of young men loitering in the shadows. This should be a last resort and even then only for men.

Places to Stay – Mid-Range & Top End

Hôtel Tidene *(☎ 44 04 06, fax 44 05 78, Off Route de l'Aéroport)* Singles/doubles with fan & shared bathroom CFA9500/13,000. This excellent choice has a lovely feel about it. The rooms are nice and tidy, and there's a good restaurant and bar.

Hôtel de l'Aïr *(☎ 44 01 47)* Rooms with fan/air-con & bathroom CFA10,000/12,500. If you're into history and atmosphere, the best place to stay is the famous and once-elegant Hôtel de l'Aïr, in the centre of town with a perfect view from its terrace of the Grande Mosquée. Architecturally fascinating, with 1m-thick walls, the Aïr was formerly a Sultan's (Kaocen's) residence. Today, the rooms in the annexe are quite plain, but it's still good value for money.

Hôtel Tchin-Toulous *(☎/fax 44 04 59, ⓔ caravane@bow.intnet.ne, Route de l'Aéroport)* Rooms with shared bathroom from CFA10,000, with air-con & bathroom CFA20,000. The cheaper rooms here are small and airless, while those with air-con aren't bad value and open onto a terrace overlooking the town. The loose pebbles on the floor are a nice touch.

Auberge D'Azel *(☎/fax 44 01 70, Route de Bilma)* Rooms with air-con & bathroom CFA30,000. This is one of two high-quality hotels in Agadez with very comfortable and tastefully decorated rooms, sparklingly clean bathrooms and a good restaurant and bar. Not surprisingly, it's a popular place and you should book ahead. The Tuareg/French couple, Akly and Céline, are delightful hosts.

Pension Tellit *(☎/fax 44 02 31, Place de la Grande Mosquée)* Rooms with bathroom & air-con from CFA18,000, suites from CFA28,000. This Italian-run place in the centre of town is another superb choice, with comfortable rooms decorated in traditional style. The best room is No 4, a delicious suite (CFA38,000) with a window looking out on the Grande Mosquée.

Places to Eat

For ***street food***, check out the main northern road near the gare routière, which is lined with cheap chop houses. Further west are more chop houses, including ***Restaurant La Targuie*** and ***Auberge de l'Aïr***, which is arguably the best; sandwiches cost CFA150 and couscous starts from CFA700.

Also good along the main Route de l'Aéroport are ***Restaurant I Kanimane***, opposite L'Elite Alimentation, where rice or couscous cost around CFA300, and ***Buvette Ibiscus de l'Aïr*** (also known as Chez Kady), where the prices are similar. In the evenings, the ***night market***, almost opposite Place de la Fraternité, is great for ambience and a hearty selection of stews, *igname* (pounded yams baked in a doughy bread-like mix) and/or spaghetti ensure you'll be well-fed for under CFA400. You could also try the goat's head.

Pâtisserie Madara Rahama *(☎ 44 02 97, Route de l'Aéroport)* Pastries from CFA250. Open 8am-10pm daily. This friendly little pâtisserie also makes its own yogurt (CFA150), which is refreshing on a hot day.

Le Gourmet – Restaurant de la Fraternité *(Place de la Grande Mosquée)* Main dishes CFA500-1500. Open 8am-11pm daily. For tasty food in plentiful servings and simple surrounds, it's hard to beat this place. Its *steak garni* (CFA1500) is a cut above the rest, the Spanish omelette (CFA1000) is a good way to start the day and the mixed salad (CFA1000) is great. Abu Bakr, the Togolese owner, and his family are also friendly.

Restaurant Pizzeria Mon Village *(Route de Arlit)* Mains from CFA500. Open noon-10pm daily. Since its move from the centre of town, this place is a bit out on a limb but it still serves decent food, with bolognese sandwiches (CFA500) among the highlights.

Restaurant Oridah *(Route de Bilma)* Mains from CFA1000. Open noon-3pm & 6pm-10.30pm daily. The simple fare here usually revolves around couscous, spaghetti or steak frite (CFA1500).

If you're in the same area and just fancy an omelette sandwich (CFA300), try ***Cafeteria Le Sahel***, a palm-frond shack outside the Oridah.

Restaurant Le Pilier *(☎ 44 02 31, Route de l'Aéroport)* Mains from CFA2600. Open 10am-2pm & 6pm-11pm daily. One of the few fine-dining options in Agadez, Le Pilier does quality Italian cuisine as well as a few local dishes. The service is attentive and the traditional architecture superb. This place is highly recommended.

Auberge D'Azel *(Route de Bilma)* Entrees CFA1500-3500, mains from CFA3500. Open noon-3pm & 7pm-11pm daily. The restaurant here is also warmly recommended. With a terrace as well as summer and winter dining rooms, the ambience is lovely and the food good. The varied menu includes pasta as well as local specialties such as *mouton targui* (Tuareg mutton; CFA3500). Set menus can be arranged for groups (from CFA6000 per person). It also stocks a good selection of drinks.

Of the other hotel restaurants, ***Hôtel Tidene*** is good, with main dishes from CFA2500.

Self-caterers could try ***L'Elite Alimentation*** *(☎ 44 03 71, Route de l'Aéroport)* or the ***mini-market*** just along from Hôtel Tidene.

Entertainment

The quiet bar at ***Hôtel Tidene*** has an eclectic drinks selection; the *whisky au gingembre* (whisky with ginger; CFA1600) is surprisingly good. The bar at ***Hôtel Sahara*** is good for dancing, but attracts a rough crowd. For the latest 'in' nightspot, ask a local friend for a recommendation, as places come and go here with monotonous regularity.

Shopping

For buying jewellery and seeing silversmiths at work, check out the ***Centre Artisanal*** on the southwestern edge of town, or the excellent collection of renowned silversmith ***Mohamed Koumama*** *(☎/fax 44 04 96)*, 250m northwest of the Grand Marché. Elsewhere there are loads of small artisan boutiques around town, especially around Place du Grande Mosquée, the market and immediately north of the Sultan's Palace. Bargaining is always required.

If you're after a turban for a desert expedition, expect to pay CFA500 per metre in the market (indigo costs more); 3m should suffice.

Getting There & Around

Air The runway at Agadez airport is supposed to be repaired some time in 2002, but work keeps on being delayed. As a consequence Point Afrique flights between Paris/Marseilles and Agadez were suspended at the time of research.

Bus, Bush Taxi & Motos SNTV (☎ 44 02 07, 44 00 16) has three buses a week to Niamey (CFA15,470, 12 hours). At the time of research, departures were at 9.30am on Monday, Thursday and Saturday. There is also a

Tuesday departure to Zinder (CFA6700, 10 hours), which leaves at 11.30am. For Arlit (CFA4000, two hours) a bus leaves Agadez after 8pm Tuesday, Thursday and Saturday.

A shared taxi/minibus between Niamey and Agadez costs CFA12,500/11,850, but could take two days to arrive once you factor in breakdowns, detours to visit friends and stops in the middle of nowhere.

There are *motos* (ideal for the narrow lanes of the Vieux Quartier) or regular private taxis that should cost no more than CFA200 for most journeys around town, more from the airport.

AÏR MOUNTAINS & TÉNÉRÉ DESERT

For more details on exploring these regions, see Travel Agencies & Tour Operators in the Agadez section.

Aïr Mountains

The Aïr Mountains are among of the most spectacular sights in West Africa. Covering an area the size of Switzerland, these mountains are of dark volcanic rock (often granite) capped with unusually shaped peaks, the highest being Mt Bagzane (2022m), 145km from Agadez. The mountains aren't as bare as the Hoggar Mountains in Algeria.

From Agadez the road goes 45km northeast to a fork in the road, called Téloua. The left fork takes you to the hot thermal springs at **Tafadek**; the right fork takes an anticlockwise route that rejoins the main road just before Elméki. On taking the left fork, after about 15km the road forks again; the left one goes to Tafadek and the right goes to Elméki, 65km to the northeast.

After Elméki is Kreb-Kreb, then the lovely green oasis of **Timia**, some 110km from Elméki. Timia is the second-major destination on many tours and the waterfalls near town are a 'don't miss' attraction. The next oasis further north is Assodé, then **Iferouâne**, 180km north of Timia and 160km east of Arlit. This is a good place to stop as the oasis is beautiful and there are some interesting prehistoric sites in the area. ***Hôtel Tellit*** (☎ 44 02 31 in Agadez) is run by the same owners as the Pension Tellit in Agadez and is of a similarly high standard; prices are similar. Northeast of Iferouâne, on the eastern boundary of the Aïr, the sand dunes at **Temet** are also well worth a visit.

Ténéré Desert

The Ténéré Desert, some 500km as the crow flies east and northeast of Agadez, is an area of sand dunes and monotonous flat areas of hard sand. The desert is reputed to have some of the most extraordinarily beautiful sand dune areas in the entire Sahara. You'll need several days to reach them, so at a minimum it's a one-week trip, preferably more. At least two vehicles are required for safety reasons. There are two main routes, both notoriously difficult: east towards Bilma and then north, or north to Iferouâne and Tadéra, then east.

Heading east from Agadez towards Bilma, you'll come to Tazolé after 100km. To the south is a **dinosaur cemetery**, one of the world's most-important ones. The fossils are spread over a belt 150km long. Continually covered and uncovered by the sand, they are silent witness to the fact that the whole Sahara Desert was once green and fertile. You may see fossils of a number of species, maybe even the fossilised Super Croc.

After another 179km, you'll pass the famous **Arbre du Ténéré**, the only tree in Africa marked on the Michelin map – except it no longer exists. This sole tree in the middle of the desert, over 400km from the next nearest tree – the last acacia of the once great Saharan forests – was hit in 1973 by a Libyan truck driver. Incredible. All you'll see is a metal replica; the remnants of the real thing are in the museum in Niamey.

Some 171km further east is the salt-producing oasis of Fachi and, 610km from Agadez, **Bilma**, which is truly the end of the earth. This town satisfies every thought you ever had of an exotic oasis in the middle of a forbidding desert. It is fortified and surrounded by palm trees and irrigated gardens – everywhere are piles of salt destined for the market towns of southern Niger and northern Nigeria. You'll see how salt is purified and poured into moulds made from large palm trunks, giving the salt its loaf-like form (in contrast, for example, to the door-like slabs from Mali).

If you continue on to the **Djado Plateau**, some 1000km from Agadez via Bilma, you'll see some of the prehistoric cave paintings of antelopes, giraffes and rhinos for which the area is noted, not to mention deserted old towns, forts atop rocky crags and forbidding mountain scenery.

The Rock Art of the Aïr

The Aïr Mountains are a treasure trove of Neolithic art, although few visitors are aware that they are visiting one of the world's most remote open-air galleries.

Until about 4000 BC, rivers ran through grassy plateaus in parts of northern Niger that are now desert, and the region was populated by hunters, herders and a rich variety of wildlife. As the Sahara became drier around 2500 BC, these people migrated southwards and the Aïr came to be dominated by the ancestors of the modern Tuareg.

The art of the Aïr predominantly consists of carvings or petroglyphs. The carvings were rendered through a method known as 'pecking', which involved the use of a heavy, sharp stone. A second stone was sometimes used to bang the sharp stone like a pick. The outline was usually completed first, often by scratching and, on occasion, the rock face was smoothed first as a form of preparation. Upon completion, some of the lines were ground smooth. After metal was introduced to the Sahara around 1200 BC, a metal spike may have been used.

It is thought that the oldest rock art in the Aïr dates back to 6000 BC. The majority of the carvings date from the Pastoral Period (5500–2000 BC), a period characterised by depictions of domesticated cattle and dominant human figures, or the later Horse or Camel Periods (1000 BC to the arrival of Islam). This latter period of rock art is also known as the Libyan Warrior Tradition. Chariots are a feature of this latter period, as are human figures represented by two triangles.

The most common subjects depicted in the Aïr are people, horses, cows, camels, giraffes, ostriches, gazelles, elephants and rhinos. The best sites are at Iwelene, Arakaou, Tanakom and Anakom, all of which are at the mouths of wadis running into the Ténéré. In the northern Aïr, there are some fine sites around Iferouâne while, to the west, Dabous is especially rich in carvings. Perhaps the most famous carving is the 5.4m high giraffe at Dabous, discovered in 1999 and some 500km from the nearest similar work. A moulding of the giraffe is now on display at Agadez airport and in 2000 the site was listed by Unesco as one of the world's most endangered monuments.

If you are fortunate enough to see some of the art, remember a few simple rules. Whatever you do, please leave the carvings as you find them. Throughout the Sahara, travellers have chipped away sections of the rock wall or thrown water on the paintings to enhance the light for taking photographs, causing irreparable damage to these ancient sites.

If you want to learn more about Saharan rock art or about efforts being undertaken to preserve rock art across Africa, contact the Trust for African Rock Art (TARA; ☎/fax 254-2-884467, e tara@swiftkenya.com, w www.tara.org.uk), PO Box 24122, Nairobi, Kenya. In addition to a wealth of historical information, it also has a nine-point Recommended Code of Conduct for viewing the art. A superb resource is also *African Rock Art* by David Coulson and Alec Campbell.

ARLIT

Uranium was discovered here in 1965. Six years later, Somair, the uranium mining company, created Arlit, Niger's most northern major town. Since then, this dusty mining settlement has grown considerably. Very few travellers would bother passing through Arlit were it not for the fact that it's the first town of any size in Niger if crossing the Sahara from Tamanrasset (Algeria).

Hôtel l'Auberge la Caravane *(☎ 45 22 78)* Doubles with fan CFA7500, with air-con CFA11,000. Right in the centre of town to the west of main street, this isn't a bad choice.

Hôtel Tamesna *(☎ 45 23 30, 45 23 32)* Around the corner is the Tamesna, which functions primarily as a bar and nightclub, but may have a few beds available.

Behind the Tamesna you'll find ***Café des Arts*** doing excellent meals for around CFA1500. Two other recommended bar-restaurants are ***Au Bon Coin*** and ***Le Refuge***, both of which serve inexpensive European and African dishes. The bar-dancing ***Sahel 2*** is also a good place to enjoy a desert evening.

SNTV buses run between Niamey and Arlit on Tuesday, Thursday and Saturday for around CFA18,000 and take 15 hours.

Nigeria

Nigeria is the veritable giant of West Africa. Recognised as the region's most influential country economically and militarily, Nigeria has more than half of West Africa's population and one of its most highly educated workforces. The country is also off most travellers' lists as a place to visit: its sights are only accessible to the ascetic or the truly masochistic voyager. And yet, if you don't visit, you can hardly say you've been to West Africa. Do remember, however, before you rush to pack your bags, that Nigeria was rated the world's most corrupt country (out of 52) in a Corruption Perception Index compiled by a Berlin company.

No visit to Nigeria is complete without some time in Lagos – West Africa's largest city and, by many criteria, Africa's worst, with one of the highest crime rates. The current harsh penalties meted out to armed robbers (death by firing squad with the scantiest of trials) and the accompanying 'Operation Sweep' have made conditions a little safer for travellers and locals. The biggest problems throughout the country are frequent fuel shortages, which give rise to riots; a lack of transport between cities; economic depression; and political and social instability.

Places such as Kano, Katsina, Zaria, Jos, Sokoto, Calabar, Abraka, Maiduguri, villages in the delta states of Bayelsa and the rivers and mountains in the far east along the Cameroonian border, are respites for those who don't appreciate the overwhelming bustle of Lagos and Ibadan. However, these places also have periodic flares of violence, lawlessness, curfews and frequent rough military intervention.

Nigeria at a Glance

Capital: Abuja
Population: 126.6 million
Area: 924,000 sq km
Head of State: Olusegun Obasanjo
Official language: English
Main local languages: Hausa, Igbo, Yoruba
Currency: naira (N)
Exchange rate: US$1 = N120
Time: GMT/UTC +1
Country telephone code: ☎ 234
Best time to go: Year-round

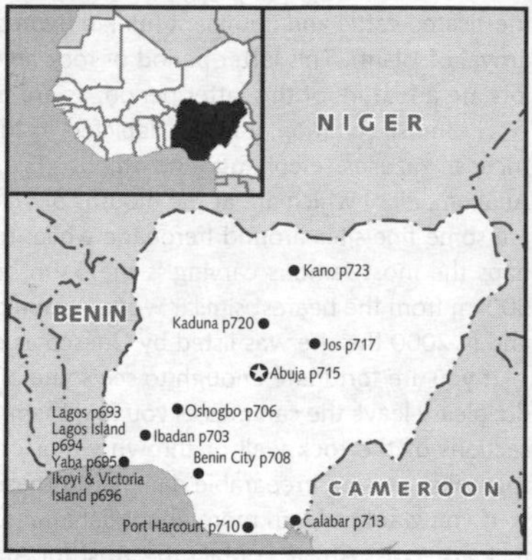
NIGER
BENIN
CAMEROON
Kano p723
Kaduna p720
Jos p717
Abuja p715
Lagos p693
Oshogbo p706
Lagos Island p694
Ibadan p703
Yaba p695
Benin City p708
Ikoyi & Victoria Island p696
Port Harcourt p710
Calabar p713

Highlights

- Viewing wildlife at Yankari National Park
- Club-hopping in Lagos
- Visiting the ancient city in Kano
- Exploring the Niger Delta
- Living to tell about it!

Facts about Nigeria

HISTORY

Northern and southern Nigeria are essentially two different countries, and their histories reflect this disparity. The first recorded empire to flourish in this part of West Africa was Kanem-Borno in the north around Lake Chad. Its wealth was based on control of the important trans-Saharan trade routes from West Africa to the Mediterranean and the Middle East. Islam became the state religion quite early in Kanem-Borno's history. A number of Islamic Hausa kingdoms also flourished between the 11th and 14th centuries, based around the cities of Kano, Zaria and Nupe.

In the southwest, a number of Yoruba kingdoms sprang up between the 14th and 15th centuries, centred in Ife, Oyo and Benin City, which became important centres of trade. The most famous was the Kingdom of Benin, which produced some of the finest bronze artwork in Africa. The

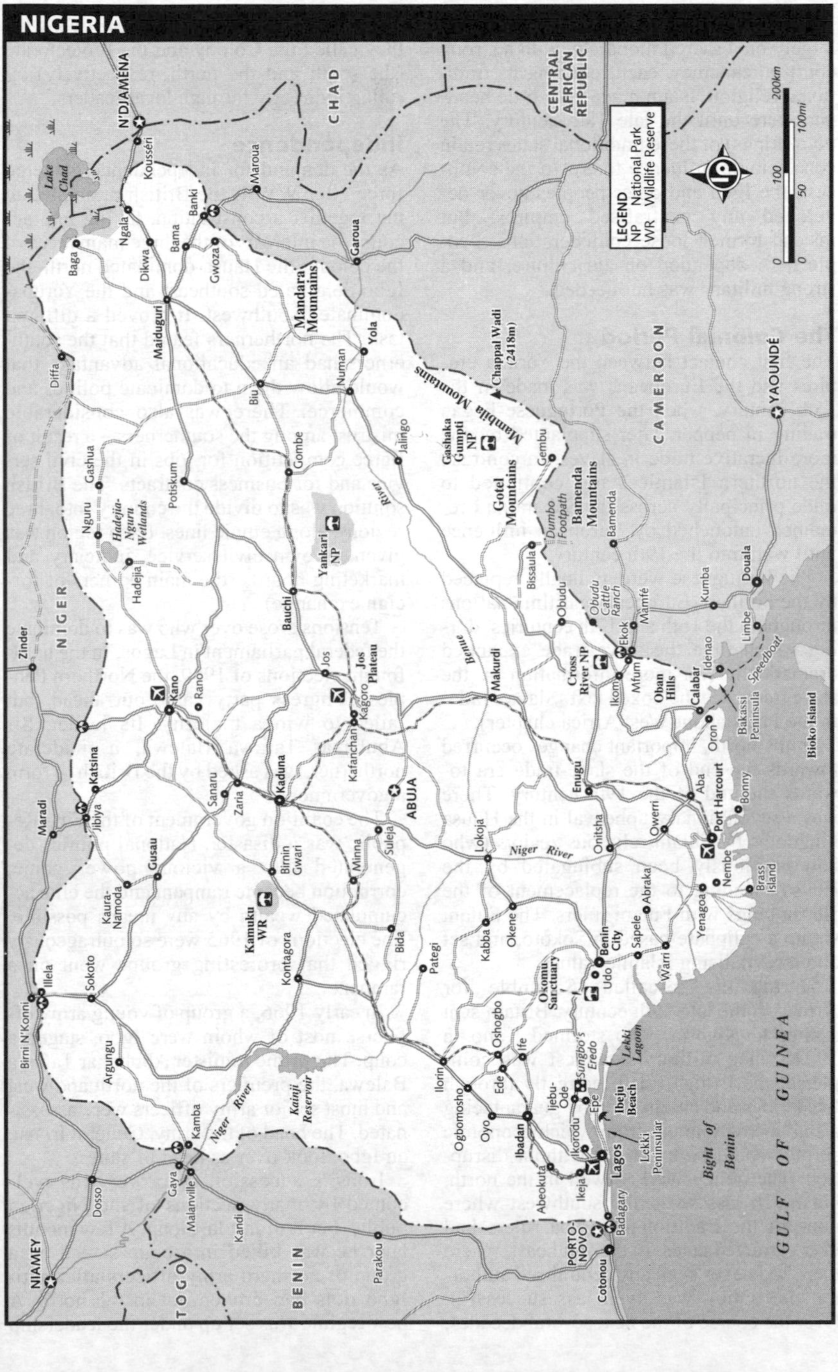
NIGERIA
N'DJAMENA
CHAD
CENTRAL AFRICAN REPUBLIC
Lake Chad
Kousséri
Maroua
Ngala
Banki
Bama
Dikwa
Gwoza
Baga
Maiduguri
Mandara Mountains
Garoua
Yola
Diffa
Biu
Numan
Mambilla Mountains
Chappal Wadi (2418m)
Gashaka Gumpti NP
Jalingo
Gombe
Gashua
Nguru
Hadejia-Nguru Wetlands
Potiskum
Hadejia
Yankari NP
Bauchi
Jos
Jos Plateau
Zinder
NIGER
Kano
Rano
Katsina
Maradi
Jibiya
Kaduna
Zaria
Sanaru
Kafanchan
Kagoro
ABUJA
Suleja
Minna
Birnin Gwari
Gusau
Kaura Namoda
Kamuku WR
Kontagora
Bida
Pategi
Lokoja
Niger River
Benue River
Makurdi
Gotel Mountains
Gembu
Bamenda Mountains
Bamenda
Dumbo Footpath
Bissaula
Obudu
Obudu Cattle Ranch
Mamfe
Ekok
Mfum
Ikom
Cross River NP
Oban Hills
Calabar
Idenao
Limbe
Kumba
Douala
YAOUNDÉ
CAMEROON
Speedboat
Bakassi Peninsula
Oron
Bioko Island
Enugu
Aba
Port Harcourt
Bonny
Owerri
Onitsha
Nembe
Brass Island
Yenagoa
Abraka
Sapele
Warri
Okene
Kabba
Benin City
Udo
Okomu Sanctuary
Ilorin
Oshogbo
Ife
Ede
Sungbo's Eredo
Lekki Lagoon
Ijebu-Ode
Epe
Ibeju Beach
Ibadan
Oyo
Ogbomosho
Ikorodu
Lagos
Lekki Peninsular
Ikeja
Abeokuta
Badagary
PORTO-NOVO
Cotonou
Bight of Benin
GULF OF GUINEA
Sokoto
Illela
Birni N'Konni
Argungu
Kainji Reservoir
Kamba
Gaya
Malanville
Dosso
NIAMEY
Kandi
Parakou
BENIN
TOGO
LEGEND
NP National Park
WR Wildlife Reserve
0 50 100 200km
0 100mi

political systems of these states rested largely on a sacred monarchy with a strong court bureaucracy, each retaining its traditional religion. Islam made very little headway here until the late 18th century. The *obas* (kings) of these traditional states retain considerable influence today. In the southeast, the Igbo and other peoples never developed any centralised empires, but instead formed loose confederations. People here depended on agriculture, and a strong military was not needed.

The Colonial Period

The first contact between the Yoruba empires and the Europeans was made in the 15th century, when the Portuguese began trading in pepper, later supplanted by the more lucrative trade in slaves. In contrast, the northern Islamic states continued to trade principally across the Sahara and remained untouched by European influence until well into the 19th century.

The Portuguese were gradually replaced by the northern European maritime nations throughout the 16th and 17th centuries, during which time the slave trade expanded dramatically (for more information on the slave trade, see the boxed text 'Slave Trade' in the Facts about West Africa chapter).

In the north, important changes occurred towards the end of the slave-trade era towards the end of the 19th century. There was a revolutionary upheaval in the Hausa kingdoms by Fulani religious zealots (who had previously been subjugated by the Hausa), leading to the replacement of the Hausa kings with Fulani rulers. The Fulani set up a caliphate based in Sokoto, and set about revitalising Islamic values.

During the so-called 'Scramble for Africa' in the late 19th century, Britain sent armies to Nigeria, who stormed Kano in 1902. Once military conquest was completed, the British ruled indirectly through local kings and chiefs, thereby guaranteeing a stable environment from which economic surplus could be extracted without disruption. The policy worked well in the north, but much less so in the southwest where none of the traditional Yoruba rulers had ever extracted taxes. In the southeast, where there had never been any centralised authority, the policy was even less successful. Over the course of the next several decades, the British consolidated their hold over what they called the Colony and the Protectorate (the south and the north, respectively) by ruling indirectly through local leaders.

Independence

As the demand for independence gathered force after WWII, the British attempted to put together a constitution, taking into account the interests of the three main areas of the colony: the Hausa-dominated north, the Igbo-dominated southeast and the Yoruba-dominated southwest. It proved a difficult task. The northerners feared that the southerners had an educational advantage that would allow them to dominate politics and commerce. There was also considerable mistrust among the southerners – a result of fierce competition for jobs in the civil service and for business contracts. The British solution was to divide the country into three regions, along ethnic lines. Each region was given its own civil service, judiciary and marketing boards (the main earners of foreign exchange).

Tensions arose over who was to dominate the federal parliament in Lagos. In the hard-fought elections of 1959, the Northern Peoples Congress party came out ahead, but failed to win a majority. Its leader, Sir Abubakar Tafawa Balewa, a moderate northerner, was asked by the British to form a government.

The coalition government of the First Republic was a disaster. National politics degenerated into a vicious power game, corruption became rampant and the elite accumulated wealth by any means possible. The elections of 1965 were so outrageously rigged that protesting groups went on a rampage.

In early 1966, a group of young army officers, most of whom were Igbo, staged a coup. The prime minister Abubakar Tafawa Balewa, the premiers of the north and west and most senior army officers were assassinated. The head of the army, General Ironsi, an Igbo, took over as head of state.

Ironsi's accession to power was welcomed by many sections of the Nigerian public, but it didn't last long. A few months later he was killed in a coup staged by a group of northern army officers after anti-Igbo riots had broken out in the north. A new regime was set up under the leadership of Lt Colonel Yakabu Gowon, a Christian from a minority group in the north.

The coup was viewed with horror in the east and the military commander of the area, Lt Colonel Ojukwu, refused to recognise Gowon as the new head of state. His antipathy to the new regime was sealed when large-scale massacres of Igbo again took place in the north, triggering a return to the east of thousands of Igbo from all over the country. In May 1967, Ojukwu announced the secession of the east and the creation of the independent state of Biafra. A civil war began.

Seeing an opportunity to secure drilling rights in oil-rich Biafra, France and other countries threw their support behind the republic. Washington supported the federal government, but the international press was pro-Biafra, and broadcast scenes of mass starvation; Biafra was recognised by only a handful of African countries. The civil war dragged on for three years, as the Igbo forces fought tooth and claw for every inch of territory that the federal forces took back. By early 1970, as a result of the blockade imposed by the federal government, Biafra faced famine and its forces were forced to capitulate. Somewhere between 500,000 and two million Biafran civilians had died in this three years, mainly from starvation.

The Oil Boom

Reconciliation was swift and peaceful, and the horrors of civil war were eclipsed in part by the oil boom. Oil production increased sevenfold between 1965 and 1973, and world prices rocketed. By 1975, Nigeria found itself with a US$5 billion surplus. The military government under Gowon went on a spending spree. Foreign contractors rushed to Lagos. Corruption was rife, and crime was rampant – the chaos became unbearable. In July 1975, Gowon was overthrown in a bloodless coup led by General Murtala Mohammed.

The new government launched a clean-up of the civil service, the judiciary and the universities. However, despite his widespread popularity, Mohammed was assassinated in a coup attempt in early 1976; other members of the regime survived and continued to implement Mohammed's policies. In 1979, the military leaders declared they would adopt a US-style constitution and handed power back to a civilian government following elections in 1979. A northerner, Shehu Shagari, was sworn in as president.

Within four years, the Second Republic had fallen. When Nigeria was at the height of its political influence, Shagari squandered the country's wealth on grandiose and ill-considered projects until the next crisis loomed in the early 1980s, when the price of oil plummeted and the supply of easy money dried up.

Unpaid contractors packed up and left. In an attempt to shore up the crumbling edifice, Shagari turned to bartering oil for essential commodities such as foodstuffs and transport. Next he turned on the millions of West Africans who had flocked to Nigeria in search of work during the oil boom. Some three million of these immigrants were suddenly expelled, causing massive disruption, unemployment and food shortages in neighbouring countries. Nigeria's action almost destroyed the Economic Community of West African States (Ecowas). On New Year's Eve in 1983 Shagari was overthrown in a military coup that was headed by General Mohammed Bahari.

Bahari clamped down heavily on corruption and made bold moves to get the country back on track economically. Many of Shagari's grandiose projects were postponed or cancelled. However, during Bahari's rule there were widespread abuses of civil liberties: torture, arbitrary arrests and incarceration without trial became common. In 1985, he was overthrown in yet another coup – the sixth since independence – led by the army's chief of staff, General Ibrahim Babangida.

The Babangida Years

Babangida, the new head of state, gained instant popularity by releasing political prisoners, and by lifting press controls. Babangida also started something of an economic revolution. Going further than the IMF dared recommend, he devalued the naira fourfold, dismantled many of the major marketing boards and privatised unprofitable public enterprises.

But devaluation and the other economic measures bore little fruit. Oil revenues dropped again and the country's debt rose to US$20 billion. Crime increased, with police and soldiers often being the worst culprits. The country was broke.

In 1990, a year after taking office, Babangida announced he would hand over power to a civilian government. In 1989, in the Abuja Declaration, he lifted the ban on political parties, declaring that there could be two parties. As a result, the Social Democratic Party (SDP) and the National Republican Convention (NRC) were formed.

Return to civilian rule was postponed twice. Support for Babangida dwindled amid continuing economic difficulties and fuel shortages, which caused riots throughout the country.

The much delayed presidential elections finally went ahead in June 1993. The SDP candidate, Moshood Abiola, a wealthy Yoruba Muslim from the south, claimed victory. Two weeks later Babangida annulled the results, and announced that another election would be held, which resulted in widespread rioting.

Had the election results been allowed, Abiola would have become the first Yoruba to beat a Hausa candidate to the presidency. For the first time in Nigeria's history, people had voted across ethnic and religious lines – a momentous break from past elections. The military, on the other hand, continued to be dominated by the Hausa, and its resistance to Abiola was viewed by many Yoruba as indicative of Hausa reluctance to share power.

Pressured by fellow army officers to hand over power, Babangida stepped down in August 1993 and appointed Ernest Shonekan as head of an interim civilian government, the Transitional Council. Shonekan's first priority, he claimed, was to hold 'democratic' elections. He and the newly appointed Vice President General Sani Abacha urged Nigerians to be patient, but violent rioting broke out around the country. Abiola, who by this time had fled the country, denounced the puppet government.

Shonekan lasted all of three months. Preempting an uprising by junior ranks, Abacha seized control in a bloodless coup in November, forcing Shonekan to announce his government's resignation and reinstating military rule. Abacha abolished all 'democratic' institutions, including the two political parties, the national and state assemblies and local governments. Establishing a Provisional Ruling Council and appointing himself chairman, Abacha created a tightly constructed power base from which he could rule. In a surprise move, he chose a mainly civilian cabinet that included Abiola's running mate. Abiola, who had returned to Nigeria to claim the presidency, was arrested and charged with treason.

Under Abacha's rule corruption flourished once again. In Abacha's attempt to maintain his grip on power, many leading Nigerian politicians, intellectuals, labour leaders, politicians, prodemocracy leaders and retired military leaders were arrested. Crackdowns on the opposition also resulted in dozens of newspapers being shut down.

Among the victims was one of Nigeria's most prized authors and the first African to win the Nobel Prize, Wole Soyinka. He had to flee Nigeria in November 1994 to avoid arrest. Ken Saro-Wiwa, the poet and activist, was not so fortunate: He was executed in November 1995 for allegedly plotting to overthrow the government (see the boxed text 'Ken Saro-Wiwa' later in this section). There was worldwide condemnation of this action, leading to the expulsion of Nigeria from the Commonwealth.

Abacha dissolved his cabinet in November 1997, later allowing the formation of five political parties (rejecting another 10 because they were likely to oppose him). However, no-one will ever know if Abacha really intended a return to civilian rule: In June 1998, he unexpectedly died of a heart attack, aged 54 (and estimated to be worth US$10 billion). His defence chief, Abdulsalam Abubakar, was sworn in as his successor. There were immediate calls for a return to a genuine democratic process, including democratic elections. Abubakar released some political prisoners and promised reforms. It seemed probable that he also intended to release Abiola, who was still in prison. However, Abiola died unexpectedly in July 1998, shortly after a visit by UN representatives.

Nigeria Today

True to his word, Abubakar allowed elections to proceed, and on 27 February 1999, Olusegun Obasanjo, a southern Yoruba Christian, was elected president with 63% of the vote. Obasanjo, of the People's Democratic Party (PDP), was a former general who fought in the civil war and was head of state from 1976 to 1979. He was one of the many arrested under the Abacha regime and released by Abubakar. The fact that Niger-

Safety in Nigeria

Lagos is one of the most dangerous cities in West Africa (Abidjan in Côte d'Ivoire and Dakar in Senegal are others). More than one expatriate living in Lagos has said that it's not uncommon to see bodies on the sides of the road on their morning commute to work. For travellers, armed thieves are the major problem. Taxi drivers seem to be involved in most of the thefts involving foreigners, so be careful when choosing a driver at Murtala Mohammed international airport, particularly if you are arriving at night (to be avoided if at all possible). Your best bet is to arrange to have someone meet you at the airport with a car. If you don't know anyone in Lagos and it's your first trip there, it is well worth the money to reserve a room in advance and arrange to have the hotel's car pick you up. Your driver should be standing outside the main airport entrance with your name on a placard. If you must take a taxi, make a point of writing down the number of the taxi's licence plate and if you change money at the airport, do it inside the car with the doors locked. Also, avoid taxis where there is a second person riding along for some unknown reason. Carry your passport at all times – police stops are frequent – but keep it well hidden.

Bribery is everywhere. If the police stop you on the road and ask you to 'settle' the problem, they want money (known locally as a *dash*), not an explanation. In Nigeria, there's one law for the rich and another for the poor. Money can 'settle' anything.

There seems to be few places immune to random violence, demonstrations, mishaps and military action. During our research in Nigeria, every city we visited (except Kano and Kaduna) experienced some sort of large-scale violence or catastrophic tragedy that led to violence. The rule of thumb is to never let your guard down and be prepared to change your plans at a moment's notice. Nigeria may now be a democracy, but it often feels like a war zone.

ians had elected a former military ruler as their new democratic president didn't dampen their expectations of his administration. Nearly four years after his election, there's little tangible evidence that democracy is working much better for Nigerians than military rule did. Ethnic conflicts continue to flair in the Niger Delta and, most recently, in Lagos, where a Yoruba street gang has terrorised the Hausa population for more than a year.

Adding to the trouble is the adoption of strict Islamic sharia in a number of northern Hausa states, a development that threatens to further rend the north from the south. Indeed, Nigeria now seems more like two countries than ever, with Islamic-led states enforcing sometimes brutal punishments on Muslims convicted of drinking beer or engaging in premarital sex. Obasanjo has so far done little to address the fears of Christians living in the north, and almost nothing to address the concerns of southerners who continue to clamour for a more equitable distribution of Nigeria's oil wealth.

The next round of elections is scheduled for March 2003 and the setting is ripe for them to be marred by further sectarian violence, if not an outright coup.

GEOGRAPHY

More than three times the size of the UK, Nigeria occupies 15% of West Africa (but has 56% of its people). Nigeria's only mountains are in the far east along the Cameroonian border. They're spectacular, but are too far off the beaten path for most people. In the centre around Jos is a plateau area (1500m), with the most pleasant climate in the country. With short grass and open scenery, this central savanna area offers some impressive sights. The north borders the Sahel and is largely savanna, with a drier climate. Cutting northwest to south is the Niger River, Africa's third-longest river. It forms a huge delta in the region around Port Harcourt. The Benue River flows west from Cameroon, emptying into the Niger near Lokoja.

The coastal oil-producing region is almost a different country, with lagoons, mangrove swamps, sandy beaches, innumerable streams and, as you move inland, thick forests.

CLIMATE

Nigerian weather patterns differ substantially in the north and the south. In the north, the climate is like that of the Sahel – hot and dry, with one long rainy season from late May to the end of September. Between March and May temperatures reach around 40°C. Along the coast, temperatures average 5°C to 10°C less, but the humidity can be unbearable. In the coastal regions, it rains most heavily between April and July, peaking in June; September to October is a second, shorter, rainy season. The harmattan season, from mid-November to April, is truly something to behold; in the north, low-grade sandstorms and 500m visibility on the clearest of days is the norm. Conditions are better in the south, where it's more humid, but thick dust and hazy conditions are still typical.

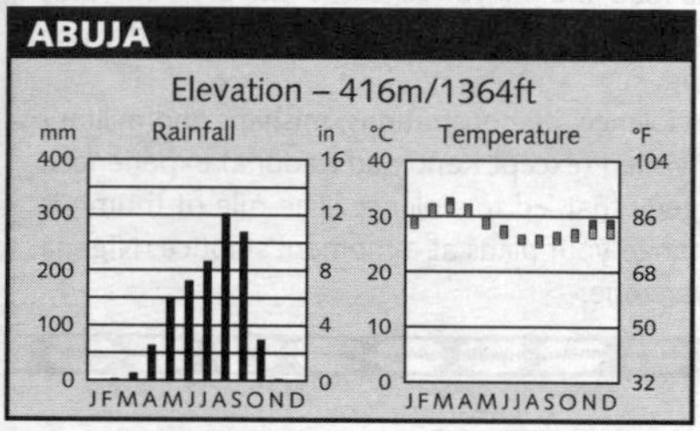
ABUJA
Elevation – 416m/1364ft
mm
Rainfall
in
°C
Temperature
°F
400
300
200
100
0
16
12
8
4
0
40
30
20
10
0
104
86
68
50
32
JFMAMJJASOND
JFMAMJJASOND

ECOLOGY & ENVIRONMENT

Nigeria has extraordinary biological diversity. Most of it, however, is on a swift path to destruction. Nigeria's major environmental problems stem in large part from its rapidly increasing population. One consequence of this is deforestation. Between 1983 and 1993, Nigeria's forest cover decreased by 20%, second only to Côte d'Ivoire in West Africa. Overall, Nigeria has logged 95% of its original forests. Moreover, very little land in Nigeria is protected, allowing the destruction of animal habitats by human activity to go unabated.

A further problem is pollution in the oil-producing regions of the delta. In 1999, it was estimated that over 123,000 barrels of crude oil were spilled in the Delta, very little of which has been satisfactorily cleaned up. The economies of whole groups of villages have been wiped out, especially by pollution of rivers and estuaries, and little has been given in the way of compensation. For more information on the fight to stop the pollution, see the boxed text 'Ken Saro-Wiwa' later in this section.

In addition to the Nigerian Conservation Foundation, another group involved in national parks and environmental matters is the British Voluntary Service Overseas (VSO). Its main office is in Kano, and it can provide travellers with information about current programmes.

FLORA & FAUNA

While Nigeria doesn't have a huge population of large mammals, you can still see a wide variety of wildlife (mostly ungulates), and the bird-watching is excellent. Yankari National Park, northeast of Abuja, is the best-known Nigerian park and the most developed; it's home to lions, elephants and waterbucks. At Cross River National Park (in the far east near Obudu Cattle Ranch), gorillas have been spotted recently. Gashaka Gumpti National Park, 200km southwest of Yola, is the largest national park in Nigeria and has the most diverse wildlife and terrain.

The Okomu Sanctuary, west of Benin City, has a patch of rainforest. Kamuku Wildlife Reserve, west of Kaduna, is a great place for bird-watchers, as is the Hadejia-Nguru Wetlands near Nguru, about 200km northeast of Kano.

GOVERNMENT & POLITICS

Nigeria is still struggling to emerge as a democracy after nearly 30 years of military dictatorships. There are 36 states, plus the Federal Capital Territory based on Abuja. The governors of most states are all former high-ranking military officials, with close ties to the dictators of old. Nigeria has a bicameral legislature as in the USA, with an elected president, senators and members of the House of Representatives.

ECONOMY

With such a turbulent political climate, Nigeria's economy has suffered. As the world's 12th-largest oil producer, Nigeria is frighteningly dependent on revenue from oil. Oil accounts for 20% of the country's gross domestic product (GDP), 95% of Nigeria's foreign exchange earnings and 65% of its budgetary revenues; and yet, in 1960, food accounted for 70% of Nigeria's exports and the country was the largest producer of palm kernels and palm oil. Nigeria now imports cooking oil and food imports cost billions of dollars.

By mid-1994 Nigeria's foreign debt had grown from US$20 billion to a shocking

US$34 billion, while the price of oil had dropped by more than one-third. With fraud and mismanagement running rampant in the government and oil industry, and frequent oil strikes, there is little hope that the country can soon shrug off its debts. Obasanjo has recently been clamouring to Western governments to intervene and argue on Nigeria's behalf for foreign-debt relief. Nigeria currently owes over US$13 billion, but will pay more than US$43 billion in debt-servicing over the next 20 years. It remains to be seen whether substantial international debt relief will happen or not. Thousands of barrels of local petrol are smuggled out of the country every day with the collusion of government officials and the army.

In summary, the situation continues to spiral out of control. Inflation is rampant: Real incomes are at least one-third less than they were in 1974, and per capita gross national product (GNP) dropped from US$860 in 1982 to US$280 in 1996. By some estimates, this is lower than it was in 1965, before Nigeria's oil began flowing. Although the per capita GNP has improved substantially, to about US$950 in recent years, most Nigerians face a very grim economic future, with 45% of the population living in poverty.

POPULATION & PEOPLE

Almost one in two West and Central Africans is Nigerian. Nigeria has a population of approximately 127 million, a guesstimate given the lack of census information. The population is increasing by 2.6% annually (the fifth-highest growth rate in Africa) and is doubling every 19 years. By 2025, with an estimated 285 million people, Nigeria will be the third most densely populated place, behind India and China, and ahead of the USA.

It is a scenario that does not bode well for the country's future. During the late 1980s, the US government poured more money into population-control programmes in Nigeria than into any other country in the world. Unlike similar programmes in Asia and Latin America, the effort has had minimal impact. The number of couples using contraception is universally thought to be very low and the current birth rate outpaces the death rate by almost three to one, even with an average life expectancy of only 51 years.

Nigeria has more than 250 ethnic groups, most with their own language, but the three main groups (comprising 68% in total) are the Hausa in the north, the Igbo in the southeast and the Yoruba in the southwest, around Lagos and Ibadan. Countless smaller linguistic groups (Ido, Nupe, Efik, Idoma, Nembe) make up the rest of the population. In some ways, it is these minorities that help unify Nigeria as a nation: As none could be politically viable independently, they tend to forge alliances in order to suit their interests, and thereby blurring tribal-political divisions.

There have always been these three major divisions, and ethnic rivalries between them are as fierce as ever. In large part this is due to the scramble for national resources. The country's vast oil wealth is pooled at the centre and redistributed among the 36 states. The states compete for the federal government's favour, thus reinforcing the respective groups' strong community and ethnic identities. And political patronage – the bedrock of Nigerian politics – has in turn fed off these regional rivalries, further undermining national solidarity.

ARTS

Nigeria's vast and rich art heritage is unequalled anywhere in West Africa.

Music

Some of Africa's best-known singers come from Nigeria. Foremost among them are the late Fela Anikulapo Kuti (see the boxed text 'Fela Kuti – The Legend Lives On' later in this chapter), Femi Kuti (Fela's son) and King Sunny Ade, followed by Sonny Okosun, Ebenezer Obey and the group Ghetto Blaster. Another well-known Nigerian singer is Chief Stephen Osita Osadebe. Sunny Ade is king of *juju* music, one of Nigeria's most popular styles (for more details, see the special section 'Music of West Africa'). His recordings with Onyeneka Onwenu, Choices and Wait For Me, encourage family planning.

Similar to Afro-Soul, *fuji* incorporates elements from juju and a range of other musical styles and instruments. Chief Sikiru Ayinde Barrister and King Wasiu Ayinde Marshal II are the main exponents of fuji.

Literature

Nigeria seems to have as many writers as the rest of Africa combined. Chinua Achebe

Ken Saro-Wiwa

Ken Saro-Wiwa, the distinguished Nigerian novelist, playwright and political activist, was hanged in November 1995, along with eight other Ogoni people, on the order of the military head of state General Sani Abacha. A hand-picked military tribunal found Saro-Wiwa guilty of complicity in the murder of four pro-government Ogoni chiefs. The trial was marked by numerous irregularities, the intimidation of witnesses and the refusal of the prosecution to present vital evidence.

Saro-Wiwa's conflict with the Nigerian government began in 1993 with his formation of a peaceful resistance organisation, the Movement for the Survival of the Ogoni People (Mosop). The Ogoni, a minority tribal group of 500,000 people, inhabit a region of Rivers State, which for decades has born the brunt of oil-drilling operations by Anglo-Dutch company Shell, which extracts about one million barrels per day from wells in the delta.

The environmental damage to the Ogoni territory has been severe and has rendered much of the land unusable. Between 1976 and 1991, there were almost 3000 oil spills, averaging 700 barrels each. Clean-up operations, when they have taken place at all, have been inordinately slow. In addition, gas flares, burning 24 hours a day (some of them for the past 30 years), are often near Ogoni villages, resulting in acid rain, massive deposits of soot, and respiratory diseases in the surrounding community.

It was against this background that Mosop was formed. Saro-Wiwa campaigned vigorously. Every protest mounted (several of which involved hundreds of thousands of people) by the Ogoni was met with violence from the armed forces. Hundreds of Ogoni have been killed, many more maimed, and tens of thousands have been rendered homeless by pro-government vandalism.

Saro-Wiwa's execution provoked international outrage, particularly after numerous appeals for clemency had been expressed by many world leaders, including Nelson Mandela. It led to Nigeria being expelled from the Commonwealth and to sanctions being applied by the USA and several European countries.

is probably Nigeria's most famous author, although he faces strong competition from Wole Soyinka, Ben Okri, Amos Tutuola, Cyprian Ekwensi and the late Ken Saro-Wiwa. For details of these and other West Africa writers, see Arts in the Facts about West Africa section chapter.

Another notable writer is Flora Nwapa, an Igbo teacher and administrator, who was the first Nigerian woman to have a novel published. Most of her stories focus on the problems women face in marriage and with children. She has since formed her own publishing company, Flora Nwapa & Co, and published 12 books, seven of which she wrote herself.

Scuplture

The oldest sub-Saharan sculptures discovered are the 2000-year-old terracottas found near Nok village. Ancient cultures renowned for sculpture include those of the Igbo-Ukwe, Ife, Owo and Benin – examples of are seen at the National Museum in Lagos.

Many tribal groups still produce fine sculptures and masks. The best known are those made by the Yoruba, whose small twin figures, *ibeji*, are world famous. The Yoruba also carve figures of the many deities and cults that make up their religion. A figure with a carved double axe balanced on its head represents Shango, the god of thunder. A kneeling couple portray Eshu, the representative of Olurin, the supreme or sky god. For the cults of *epa* and *gelede*, masks are carved with elaborate superstructures incorporating human and animal groups. The Yoruba are also known for their bronze casting and iron herbalist staffs that depict a large bird surrounded by many smaller birds.

The Igbo carve personal shrine figures called *ikeng*, which feature a horned man holding a sword in one hand and a severed head in the other. The Igbo also carve masks with openwork crests, representing a beautiful maiden. The Ekoi (or Ejagham), who live near the Igbo, use similar masks covered in animal skin, which are unique to West Africa. In the northeast, the Mumuye are renowned for their cubist approach to the human form, expressed in their figure carvings of ancestors.

The soapstone figures from the Esie people, the pottery, metalwork and glass-making of the Nupe, and the applique banners and phenomenal beadwork of the Yoruba are just a few of the great reflections of precolonial Nigeria.

SOCIETY & CONDUCT

In the Muslim north, strict sharia laws apply for Muslims: It is forbidden to drink, smoke or engage in premarital sex, among a number of other things. The rules are enforced by special sharia police in places such as Kano, Kaduna, Katsina and other sharia states. Punishments for violating these laws often involve brutal public canings or, in one case, death by public stoning. Many hotels and tourist spots in the north, however, seem to realise the negative effects sharia can have on tourism and bend over backward to make non-Muslim visitors feel comfortable, so there is no lack of bars or social centres. Still, it's advisable that visitors dress and behave conservatively when travelling in the north (for women, that means covering arms and legs). Smoking and drinking in public – except in designated bars and lounges – isn't advisable.

In the south, dress standards are much more relaxed and Lagos is *the* place to dress up – or down.

If someone is late for an appointment, they are probably delayed in a 'go slow' (a Nigerian term for an impregnable traffic jam) or are operating on 'African time' – it's nothing to get upset about.

RELIGION

Three primary religions are practiced in Nigeria: Christianity, Islam and animism. In addition, there are countless cults and syncretic religions that combine, for example, Christianity with the worship of local spirits and guardians.

Islam dominates in the north; Christianity dominates in the south, although the Yoruba (and some Igbo groups) in the south practice animism. Islam expanded into Nigeria via the trans-Sahara trading caravans and various holy wars. Today, evidence of its influence is seen in every aspect of life in the north. Christianity arrived much later, with the colonial powers.

LANGUAGE

English is the official language in Nigeria. The three principal African languages are Hausa in the north, Igbo in the southeast and Yoruba in the southwest, around Lagos. See the Language chapter for some useful words and phrases in these languages.

Facts for the Visitor

SUGGESTED ITINERARIES

Most people would advise getting out of Lagos as soon as possible and bypassing Ibadan on your way out. However, if you have at least a week to explore the country the brave should allow a few days in Lagos, in part because one of the major highlights of any trip to Nigeria is an evening at one of the city's great nightclubs that feature live music.

Although Benin City has an interesting museum and the nearby Okomu Reserve, and Abraka has white-water rafting and diving, cities in the southern half of the country have little to offer travellers. For those on a one-week trip, a good schedule would be to spend a few days in Lagos, then fly to Kano or Port Harcourt. Port Harcourt, while incredibly polluted and intimidating, is a good launching-off point for exploring the smaller villages of the delta, a worthwhile endeavour if only to see how simple life has been practically ruined by oil exploration.

The north is far more interesting than the south, especially Jos, which has an excellent museum, good climate and friendly people; Kano, which has a fascinating history; and the must-see Yankari National Park, where elephants, waterbucks and baboons wander freely through the tourist compound. A month-long trip can easily encompass all these areas and give an excellent taste of Nigeria's diversity.

PLANNING

Nigeria can be visited at any time when the political situation is stable. Since that seems to change on a day-to-day basis, chances are that one or more major regions will be off limits. At the time of our visit, there were two police strikes that brought traffic to a dead halt across the country, an explosion at a Lagos ammunition dump that killed over 1000 people, running gun-battles between the Yoruba and the Hausa in Lagos, a police riot in Abuja, violent demonstrations in Jos and Port Harcourt over a CNN report and a military blockade around Katsina. That this is a fairly typical state of affairs was illustrated when we mentioned to a Lagosian that we were visiting Nigeria at a bad time. Her response was 'How so?'. There were several areas that were impossible to visit and are noted in the relevant sections. Expect your itinerary to change almost hourly.

When summers (between March and May) are very hot and muggy along the coast, you can escape to the plateau and Jos.

WAPB Street Maps Lagos 1992 is the latest street guide to Lagos. The *Spectrum Road Map Nigeria* (1994) has contour colouring; the scale is 1:1,500,000.

VISAS & DOCUMENTS

Visas

Everyone needs a visa to visit Nigeria. Most Nigerian embassies (including the high commissions in the UK and Australia, and the embassies in Benin and Togo) issue visas only to residents and nationals of the country in which the embassy is located. The Nigerian embassy in Washington, DC well as the consulates in New York and San Francisco, issue single-entry visas (valid for a month's stay) free of charge, and process applications in two days. Nigerian embassies generally require forms in triplicate, evidence of a round-trip airline ticket and a letter of invitation from a person/company in Nigeria detailing the reason for your visit. All applications require plenty of photos.

The cost of a visa depends on your nationality. For most it's about US$45 (or the equivalent) but it's a huge US$200 for UK citizens (a quid pro quo for visa restrictions placed on Nigerians by the British government). For Australians it costs A$36 and for New Zealanders it costs a mere A$8. Processing takes from one to two weeks.

Visas usually allow for a stay of up to one month and remain valid for three months from the date of issue, not the date of arrival.

Visa Extensions A visa extension can be obtained in all the state capitals from the immigration department of the Federal Secretariat. Extensions cost N800 and you will need a letter from a local citizen or resident vouching for you; in Kano you can get this from the manager of the Kano State Tourist Camp. A *dash* (bribe) will speed up the process considerably.

Visas for Onward Travel In Nigeria, you can get visas for the following neighbouring countries (note that you usually need at least two photos for each application).

Benin The Beninese embassy in Lagos provides same-day service (collection is at 2pm). Visas (N600) are valid for 15 days but are easily renewable in Cotonou.

Cameroon The Cameroonian embassy issues 90-day, multiple-entry visas (N5000) in 24 hours. You'll need an onward air ticket. You can also get visas with much less hassle in Calabar in 24 hours; the consulate is at 21 Ndidan Usang Iso Rd (formerly Marian Rd); you may not be asked for an onward ticket.

Niger The Nigerien embassy issues visas (N3000 for one-month visas) in 24 hours. You can also get visas to Niger in Kano (same cost); the consulate (☎ 645274) is at 12 Aliyu Ave (just off Murtala Mohammed Way) near Airport Roundabout.

Other Documents

You need proof of vaccination against yellow fever to enter Nigeria.

EMBASSIES & CONSULATES

Nigerian Embassies & Consulates

In West Africa, Nigeria has embassies in all countries, except Cape Verde. For more details, see the Facts for the Visitor section of the relevant country chapter.

Elsewhere, there are embassies in most European Union member states, as well as in the following:

Australia (☎ 02-6286 1222) 7 Terrigal Crescent, O'Malley, ACT 2606
Belgium (☎ 02-735 40 71) 3B Av de Tervueren, Brussels 1040
France (☎ 01 47 04 68 65) 173 Av Victor Hugo, 75016 Paris
Germany (☎ 0288-32 20 71, 32 20 72) Goldbergweg 13, 53177 Bonn
UK (☎ 020-7353 3776) 76 Fleet St, London EC4Y
USA (☎ 202-822 1500) 2201 M St NW, Washington, DC 20037; also in New York (☎ 212-370 0856)

Embassies & Consulates in Nigeria

The majority of foreign embassies and consulates are in Lagos, on Ikoyi or Victoria Island (VI).

Australia (☎ 261 8440, 261 8875, 90-404 980, fax 261 8703) 2 Ozumba Mbadiwe Ave, VI
Benin (☎ 261 4411) 4 Abudu Smith St, VI; open 9am to 11am Monday to Friday
Burkina Faso (☎ 268 1001) 15 Norman Williams St, Ikoyi
Cameroon (☎ 261 2226) 5 Femi Pearse St, VI; open 8am to 11am Monday to Friday
Côte d'Ivoire (☎ 261 0963) 5 Abudu Smith St, VI
France (☎ 260 3300) 1 Oyinkan Abayomi Rd, Ikoyi
Germany (☎ 261 1011) 15 Walter Carrington Crescent, VI
Ghana (☎ 263 0015) 23 King George V St, Lagos Island
Niger (☎ 261 2300) 15 Adeola Odeku St, VI; open 9am to 2.30pm Monday to Friday
Togo (☎ 261 1762) Plot 976 Oju Olobun Close, VI
UK (☎ 261 1551) 11 Walter Carrington Crescent, VI
USA (☎ 261 0050) 2 Walter Carrington Crescent, VI

Chad, Italy, Kenya and Russia also have embassies in Lagos.

Although Abuja is the official capital, few countries have relocated their offices there. Some that can be found in Abuja include the European Community House (☎ 523 3144) at 63 Usuma St, which serves the diplomatic needs of citizens of many European countries, the British high commission (☎ 523 2010) on North Shehu Shagari Way, which attends to the needs of Commonwealth citizens, and the US embassy (☎ 523 0916) at 9 Mambilla Way in Maitama.

CUSTOMS

It is illegal to import or export any more than N50. Nigeria strictly enforces its laws against exporting Nigerian antiquities; anything that looks old may be confiscated by customs unless you have either a certificate from the National Museum in Lagos or a dash.

MONEY

The unit of currency is the naira (N).

country	unit		naira
euro zone	€1	=	N118
UK	UK£1	=	N183
USA	US$1	=	N120
West African CFA	CFA100	=	N18

Many visitors regret bringing travellers cheques instead of cash. Many bureaus de change won't accept travellers cheques, and some banks won't either. If you're very lucky, you might get an exchange rate about 5% to 7% less than that for cash; but you may waste an entire morning at the bank. Among the banks, try the First Bank of Nigeria (FBN); it gives better rates and its commissions are low.

Credit cards are virtually useless except at major hotels in Lagos and Abuja. Elsewhere, hotels don't accept them. Money transfers from overseas are confined to Western Union, which has offices in most major banks in large cities. There is one ATM in the entire country, at the Mega Plaza on VI (14 Idowu Martins St) but you need a Nigerian bank card to use it.

Changing money on the black market is a widespread practice in just about every town of any size. In Lagos, for example, you can drive by the Bristol or Federal Palace Hotels in a taxi and do your transaction in the taxi quickly, but discretion and care is the key. US dollars are the hot favourites, particularly US$100 bills, but UK pounds and euros are all readily accepted in Lagos; outside Lagos and Abuja US dollars are best.

The major banks for changing money are the FBN, the International Bank for West Africa (IBWA), the Société Générale Banque Nigeria (SGBN), the Union Bank of Nigeria (UBN) and the United Bank for Africa (UBA).

POST & COMMUNICATIONS

Post

Postal rates are low – N50 a letter and N40 for an aerogram – but the service is questionable. Alternatively, try the EMS or DHL courier services; the documents are insured and are almost guaranteed to arrive at their intended destination. The cost to Europe is N1000 per 100g for these services.

Telephone

Telephone services tend to be erratic, although the global system for mobile communications (GSM) service seems to work very well across Lagos and in many of the major towns. International telephone, fax and telex facilities are generally quite good and efficient; they are available at Nigeria Telecom's (Nitel) principal office in Lagos (14 Marina St) and at Nitel's offices throughout the country. The charges are reasonable: for example, it costs N1350 for a three-minute call to North America.

Email & Internet Access

Public Internet services are springing up everywhere in Nigeria and there's no lack of places to send or receive email in Lagos.

If you're checking email from your hotel room, America Online and Compuserve use the same number (☎ 062-154000) for access all over Nigeria.

DIGITAL RESOURCES

Before heading to Nigeria, travellers can check the pulse of the country by visiting W www.allafrica.com, an African news resource that publishes daily news items from many of the country's newspapers. Mosop has a helpful website with background on oil pollution in the Niger Delta at W www.mosopcanada.org; for an alternate view of the same topic, check out W www.shellnigeria.com. A plethora of travel information about Lagos can be found at W www.lagos-online.com.

BOOKS

The hefty tome *Yoruba: Nine Centuries of African Art & Thought* by Henry John Drewal, John Pemberton III & Rowland Abiodun is a must for the art enthusiast. It covers the art of the Yoruba in detail, and has excellent photos. Other specialist art books include *Royal Benin Art* by Brian Freyer (1987) and *The Art of Benin* by Paula Girshick & Ben Amos (1995).

Nigeria: Giant of Africa by Peter Holmes (1985) is an excellent coffee-table book.

Enjoy Nigeria by Ian Nason (1993) is good for information on less-travelled roads and little-known towns, natural wonders and celebrations; it's available in Lagos.

This House Has Fallen by Karl Maier (2000) is an excellent primer on modern Nigerian politics and is practically required reading for anyone visiting the country who wants to hold an informed conversation about the one topic everyone talks about: politics.

PHOTOGRAPHY & VIDEO

No permit for photography or video use is required, but exercise great caution: You may find lots of people will be offended by being photographed. The usual restrictions on photographing military locations, government buildings etc apply – see the boxed text 'Photography Hints' in the Regional Facts for the Visitor chapter for more information. Be careful: The police are often looking for ways to extort bribes.

HEALTH

A yellow fever vaccination certificate is required of all travellers to Nigeria. Malaria is a risk year-round throughout the whole country, so you should take appropriate precautions. See also Health in the Regional Facts for the Visitor chapter.

WOMEN TRAVELLERS

Apart from the usual security concerns for anyone travelling in Nigeria, women will probably like travelling in the south. This is a nation where women have made more gains than in most African countries (but there is still a lot to achieve before any lofty claims of gender equality can be made).

For more general information and advice, see the boxed text 'Tips for Travellers in Islamic Countries' in the Facts about West Africa chapter, and Women Travellers in the Regional Facts for the Visitor chapter.

BUSINESS HOURS

Business hours are from 8.30am to 5pm Monday to Friday. Government offices are open from 7.30am to 3.30pm Monday to Friday and 7.30am to 1pm Saturday. Banking hours are from 8am to 3pm Monday to Thursday and 8.30am to 1pm Friday.

Sanitation day (when people are theoretically required to clean up the country) is the last Saturday of the month. You aren't officially allowed on the streets from 7am to 10am.

PUBLIC HOLIDAYS & SPECIAL EVENTS

Public holidays include:

New Year's Day 1 January
Easter March or April
May Day 1 May
National Day 1 October
Christmas 25 December
Boxing Day 26 December

Islamic holidays are observed in Nigeria, even in the south – for a table of estimated dates of these holidays, see Public Holidays & Special Events in the Regional Facts for the Visitor chapter.

Of all the festivals in West Africa, the most elaborate are the celebrations in northern Nigeria, in particular in Kano, Zaria and Katsina, for the two most important Islamic holidays – the end of Ramadan and Tabaski, 69 days later. The principal event is the durbar, a cavalry procession that features ornately dressed men mounted on colourfully bedecked horses. The horsemen wear breastplates and coats of flexible armour and, on their scarlet turbans, copper helmets topped with plumes. The emir (ruler), draped in white and protected by a heavy brocade parasol embroidered with silver, rides in the middle of the cavalry, which is dressed in blue. He may be followed by traditional wrestlers flexing huge biceps, and lute players with feathered headdresses decorated with cowrie shells.

Around mid-February, the three-day Argungu Fishing & Cultural Festival takes place on the banks of the Sokoto River in Argungu, 100km southwest of Sokoto. The fishers' customs and traditions are closely tied to Islamic religious practices. Several months before the festival, the Sokoto River is dammed. When the festival begins, hundreds of fishers jump into the river with their nets and gourds. Some come out with fish weighing more than 50kg. It's quite a sight.

Around August, don't miss Nigeria's most photographed festival – the Pategi Regatta. Pategi is on the Niger River, halfway between Ibadan and Kaduna. There's swimming, traditional dancing, acrobatic displays, fishing and a rowing competition.

On the last Friday in August, the Oshun Festival takes place in Oshogbo, 86km northeast of Ibadan. It has music, dancing and sacrifices, and is well worth seeing.

The Igue/Ewere Festival, held in Benin City, usually in the first half of December, has traditional dances, a mock battle and a procession to the palace to reaffirm loyalty to the oba.

ACCOMMODATION

Hotel room bills are subject to a hefty 15% tax; prices quoted in this chapter include this tax. Almost all hotels require a deposit, which is refundable, but is often twice the room rate. Many hotels have a resident and nonresident rate; if you make it a habit of asking for the resident rate you can sometimes get lucky.

Hotels in Nigeria are reasonably priced just about everywhere except Lagos and Abuja. Even in Lagos, however, if you're willing to stay in one of the suburbs – which isn't recommended – you can sleep cheaply (if tensely). Elsewhere, Nigeria's large cities have hotels to suit all budgets, and you should be able to get a room for under US$10 or N1200. In some cities, such as Jos, Sokoto, Ibadan and Kano, there are mission guesthouses with rooms at bargain prices. Few cities have camping facilities.

FOOD

Nigerian food is nothing to write home about. In fact, you'll be lucky to find more than the ubiquitous chicken and rice (or for a twist, chicken and chips) in most restaurants, despite the extensive menu you'll be given. Soup is a common lunch-time food in Nigeria. It's usually eaten by scooping it up with a closed hand in the form of a spoon. As in most of Africa, you only eat with your right hand. Vegetarians may be hard pressed to find more than pounded yams and cassava – which are used to dip into and scoop up soup – rice and groundnut stew.

In the south, two favourites of the Yoruba are *egusi*, a fiery-hot yellow stew made with meat, red chilli, ground dried prawns and bits of green leaves, and palm-nut soup (a thick stew made with meat, chilli, tomatoes, onions and palm-nut oil).

Other favourites include fish pepper soup, bitter leaf soup (made with greens and various types of meats and usually eaten with pounded yams), groundnut soup and *ikokore* (a main course made with ground yams and various types of fish, popular in the west of the country). Then there's *ukwaka* (a steamed pudding based on corn and ripe plantains), various okra-based stews (which are usually very spicy and tasty), brown beans, *jollof* (a paella-like rice dish), and *moin-moin* (a steamed cake of ground dried beans with fish or boiled eggs eaten with *gari* – dried manioc flour – or yams).

You'll also find lots of snack food, including fried yam chips, fried plantains, boiled groundnuts, meat pastries, *akara* (a puffy deep-fried cake made with black-eyed peas and sometimes eaten with chilli dip), *kulikuli* (small deep-dried balls made of peanut paste), *suya* (a hot spicy kebab) and a few sweets such as *chinchin* (fried pastry in strips).

Getting There & Away

AIR

There are four international airports: in Lagos, Abuja, Port Harcourt and Kano. Getting in and out of Murtala Mohammed international airport in Lagos will probably be one of your hardest travel experiences ever. It's worth considering flying to Kano, Port Harcourt or Abuja instead, so that you can overcome the 'Nigeria shock' before setting out on your travels and avoid getting robbed or worse in your first five minutes in the country (see the boxed text 'Safety in Nigeria' earlier in this chapter).

The departure tax of US$35 for international flights from all four airports is already included in your ticket price. Check, and on no account pay departure tax to anyone at the airport – you will be asked!

Europe & the USA

There are flights to Lagos from Amsterdam, Brussels, Frankfurt, Geneva, London, Madrid, Moscow, New York, Paris, Rome and Zurich.

Nigeria Airways has resumed flights between London and Lagos after suspending them due to safety concerns. British Airways, Virgin Atlantic, KLM-Royal Dutch Airlines and Lufthansa have daily flights between London Gatwick and Lagos (average price US$684 one way). Air France flies from Paris to Lagos five times a week and once a week to Port Harcourt; the standard fare is US$828 return. KLM and Swiss also fly to Lagos from Paris. EgyptAir has regular flights to and from Kano via Cairo.

Nigeria Airways, Northwest Airlines/KLM and Air France have direct flights to Lagos from New York (prices range from US$633 to US$1846).

Africa

There are daily flights between Lagos and Abidjan (Côte d'Ivoire), Accra (Ghana), Cotonou (Benin), Lomé (Togo), Johannesburg (South Africa), Niamey (Niger), Yaoundé and Douala (both in Cameroon), and four flights weekly to/from Dakar (Senegal). Most of these flights are on Nigeria Airways or Ghana Airways. South African Airways has a twice weekly service between Johannesburg and Lagos.

Flights also operate to Nairobi with Nigeria Airways, Ethiopian Airlines, Kenya Airways and Bellview (all cost about US$500). Foreigners must pay in hard currency and not naira.

LAND & SEA

Border Crossings

No border crossing into Nigeria is going to be easy. Those in the north (to/from Benin and Niger) seldom see Western travellers, and after the initial shock, a series of luggage searches is usually carried out designed to get bribes. Your passport stamp can be delayed for up to half a day if you don't pay the bribe.

The Beninese border crossing on the Cotonou-Lagos road in the southeast is probably the least difficult, because officials are more used to seeing Western travellers.

The most used crossing into Cameroon is east of Mfum.

Benin

You can catch direct bush taxis from Cotonou to Lagos Island. You can also board a ferry on Lagos Island to Mile-2 (west of Apapa in Lagos), and catch Benin-bound vehicles from the Mile-2 Motor Park (bus and bush taxi station) just to the north. Bush taxis charge N300 to Cotonou; the trip takes three hours in Peugeot taxis, and up to six hours in cheaper minibuses, which tend to be stopped frequently by police. The coastal border with Benin is open 24 hours.

Cameroon

You can take a bush taxi in Ikom for the 25km trip to the Cameroonian border (Mfum). There are bush taxis in Ekok (Cameroon) for other points in Cameroon.

Depending on the security situation in the disputed Bakassi Peninsula area, it's usually possible to travel to Cameroon by boat from Oron, a short ferry ride from Calabar. For more information, see the main Getting There & Away section in the Cameroon chapter.

Niger

There are four major entry points into Niger. From east to west they are Kano to Zinder, Katsina to Maradi, Sokoto to Birni N'Konni and Kamba to Gaya. This latter route is usually the least-expensive way to get to Niamey, as you travel further in cheap Nigeria and less in expensive Niger. If you are in a bush taxi, feel for your fellow passengers who may have to wait as the customs, immigration, police and army stop the vehicle every time they see a tourist.

Getting Around

AIR

For air travel within Nigeria, the service on Nigeria Airways is sometimes good, but the private airlines – ADC Airlines, Albarka Air, Kabo Airlines, Okada Air, Bellview Airlines, EAS Airlines, Skyline and Chanchangi – are often better and their planes are more comfortable. They all have offices at Terminal 2 at the domestic airport, and at various locations around Lagos (see Getting There & Away under Lagos later in this chapter). You may find you cannot book a ticket in advance with most domestic airlines – buy it at the airport, and anticipate wasting lots of time as the departure schedules are a joke. A number of expediters will offer to get you your ticket, but beware – many are crooks.

In Lagos, domestic flights do not leave from Murtala Mohammed international airport, but rather from an older domestic airport 10km away. It's dusty, cramped and filled with baggage handlers looking for massive dashes for everything from carrying your bags to letting you leave the bathroom. Keep on your toes here.

Flights within Nigeria are cheap: Most airlines charge around N6000 to N7000 for each domestic leg, but keep in mind that it's almost impossible to fly between the smaller cities without first going through Lagos. Therefore, a flight from Kaduna to Port Harcourt, for example, will cost N14,000 because you pay for each leg to/from Lagos.

A N50 airport tax applies for all Nigerian domestic flights.

BUS & BUSH TAXI

Travel by bus is safer, more comfortable (depending upon the condition of the bus) and cheaper than bush taxis on long-haul routes. Buses connect all the main cities. Each bus company has its own offices, but they're often not at the motor park, so finding them isn't always easy. However, most companies tend to have their offices in the same general area.

The main advantage of bush taxis (Peugeot taxis) is that they leave at all hours. Nigeria's bush-taxi system is unquestionably the fastest and most comfortable in West Africa – but it's dangerous. Two types of bush taxis are used – the Peugeot 504s that take five passengers (and are more expensive), and the 504 station wagons that take up to nine passengers. Bush taxis are cheaper in Nigeria than in any other country in West Africa – for example, it costs around N1200 from Lagos to Kano (1028km).

Minibuses are slower and generally at least 25% cheaper than bush taxis, but they're far more dangerous, accounting for the vast majority of traffic fatalities on Nigeria's highways. In fact, even Nigerians call them maulers, in reference to what will happen to you if one crashes.

TRAIN

More often than not the trains are not running; don't let the schedules fool you as trains *never* arrive on time. Contact the now almost defunct Nigerian Railway Corporation (☎ 283 4302) to learn more.

There are three railway lines: one connects Lagos with Ibadan, Kaduna and Kano; another connects Port Harcourt with Maiduguri, passing through Enugu, Jos and Bauchi; and the third links Kaduna and Kafanchan.

CAR & MOTORCYCLE

The road system in Nigeria is excellent. However, driving is dangerous, especially on the expressway between Lagos and Ibadan, where it's like playing bumper cars at the carnival. Drive only during the day and be aware of frequent police roadblocks – often consisting of a nail-studded board across the road. Should you need help with car towing or a repair (and you are a member), contact the Automobile Club of Nigeria (☎ 296 0514) at 24 Mercy Eneli St, Surulere, Lagos – but don't hold your breath.

Commercial motorcycles, called *okadas*, are a cheap and easy way to get around in almost all cities. Just flag down an okada without any passengers, and hold on. Most okada drivers seem to have a fatalist's view of their own mortality, however, so consider this if you're only going a short distance or if a go slow makes car travel impossible. A trip around town on a motorcycle shouldn't cost more than N50 anywhere in Nigeria.

HITCHING

Hitchhiking in Nigeria is very dangerous, and cannot be recommended. If you do resort to it, be careful. Remember that there is little that you can do if the driver produces a gun – cheerily hand over everything and you may live to tell your story. See Truck & Hitching in the Getting Around West Africa chapter for more on the dangers of hitching.

Lagos

☎ 01

Most travellers detest Lagos, and for good reason. The city's reputation for crime and sectarian violence is known worldwide. Its number of inhabitants – perhaps 13 million – doesn't help. In the last 30 years, the population has grown 20-fold, a world record for cities of more than one million people. About half of Lagos' inhabitants are under the age of 16. By 2025, Lagos is predicted to become one of the world's five largest cities.

Wide expressways connect the airport with the city centre and encircle Lagos Island (the heart) and nearby Ikoyi and Victoria Island, universally referred to as VI, where you'll find the top-end hotels and posh residences. Underneath the freeways you'll find another city inhabited by people living in dilapidated cardboard shacks.

Lagos' attraction is its music – Sunny Ade, Lagbaja, Shina Peters and Femi Kuti (son of the late, great Fela Kuti) all have their nightclubs here. Nonetheless, this hardly makes up for the city's faults – hassles with taxi drivers and police, high prices and violent crime. If you hear of people liking Lagos, the chances are they made Nigerian friends; this seems to be the only way to enjoy it.

Orientation

The heart of Lagos is Lagos Island, where the major banks, department stores and large commercial establishments are found.

Fela Kuti – The Legend Lives On

Fela Kuti, born in 1938 in Abeokuta, 100km north of Lagos, is one of Africa's most famous musicians. Immensely popular in Nigeria, Kuti was also vocal politically. When he travelled to Los Angeles in 1964, Kuti met Malcolm X, who stirred black consciousness in him; on the musical front, James Brown influenced Kuti greatly. On his return to Nigeria, Kuti mixed Brown's soul music with the many intricacies of Nigerian music to create Afro-beat.

During the 1970s, he formed the Kalakuta Republic, a commune for playing music. Government forces burnt it down in 1977, resulting in the death of Fela's mother. Kuti was exiled in Ghana from 1978 to 1980; when he returned to Nigeria he continued to play music with lyrics critical of the regime. In 1985 he was jailed on currency-smuggling charges, then released a year later when the judge admitted Kuti had been framed. Kuti was also accused in 1993 of killing a man; Kuti and his brother, a key figure in the group Campaign for Democracy, rebutted the charge as being politically motivated. Fela avoided the authorities throughout the 1990s, mainly because he produced very little new music and retired to a quiet life of performing only twice a week at The Shrine, his Lagos nightclub. He died of an undisclosed illness in 1997.

The major road is Broad St, which passes Tinubu Square, a major intersection near the centre of the island, and ends at Tafawa Balewa Square, a large commercial complex. You'll find most of Lagos' airline offices and travel agencies on the southern side of Tafawa Balewa Square, and shops and restaurants on the northern side; the national museum is just to the southeast, in Onikan. Within several blocks of the corner of Martin and Broad Sts are most banks, airline offices and black marketers.

Running roughly parallel with Broad St is Marina St, which overlooks the harbour and is home to numerous large commercial establishments. The entire island is encircled by Ring Rd, a major expressway.

Most of the embassies and big houses are on VI and Ikoyi, both just to the southeast of Lagos Island. At the end of VI are the two leading central hotels – the Eko and the Kuramo Lodge. On Ikoyi, the wide Kingsway Rd leads up to the Ikoyi Hotel.

LAGOS

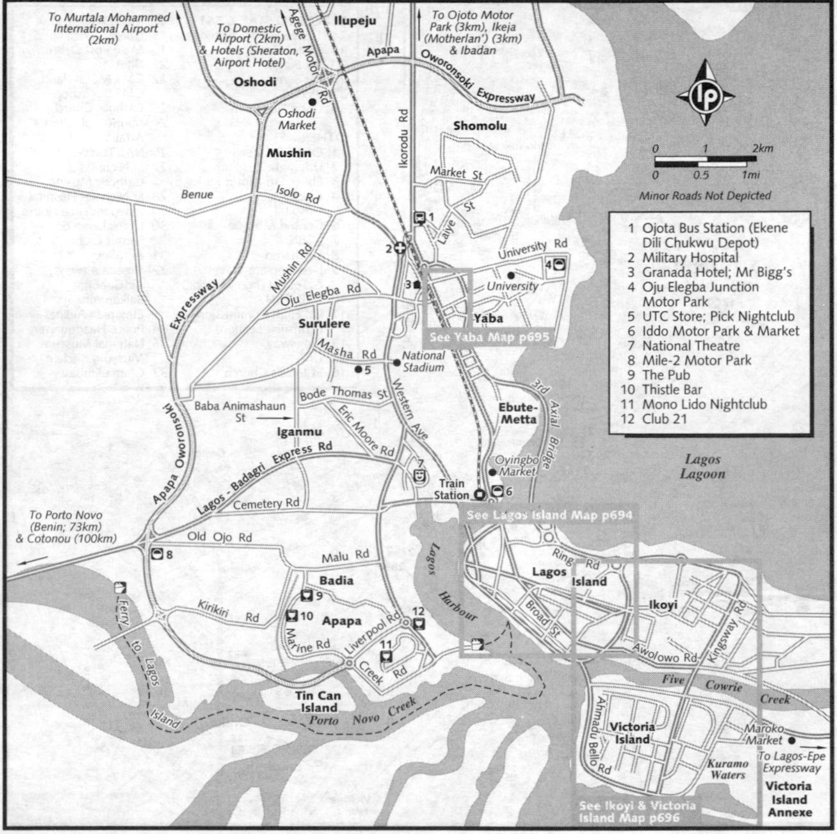
To Murtala Mohammed International Airport (2km)
To Domestic Airport (2km) & Hotels (Sheraton, Airport Hotel)
To Ojoto Motor Park (3km), Ikeja (Motherlan') (3km) & Ibadan
Agege Motor Rd
Ilupeju
Apapa
Oworonsoki Expressway
Oshodi
Oshodi Market
Ikorodu Rd
Shomolu
Mushin
Market St
Benue
Isolo Rd
Laiye St
0 1 2km
0 0.5 1mi
Minor Roads Not Depicted
1 Ojota Bus Station (Ekene Dili Chukwu Depot)
2 Military Hospital
3 Granada Hotel; Mr Bigg's
4 Oju Elegba Junction Motor Park
5 UTC Store; Pick Nightclub
6 Iddo Motor Park & Market
7 National Theatre
8 Mile-2 Motor Park
9 The Pub
10 Thistle Bar
11 Mono Lido Nightclub
12 Club 21
Mushin Rd
University Rd
University
Expressway
Oju Elegba Rd
Yaba
Surulere
See Yaba Map p695
Masha Rd
National Stadium
3rd Axial Bridge
Bode Thomas St
Western Ave
Baba Animashaun St
Eric Moore Rd
Ebute-Metta
Apapa Oworonsoki
Iganmu
Lagos - Badagri Express Rd
Oyingbo Market
Lagos Lagoon
Train Station
To Porto Novo (Benin; 73km) & Cotonou (100km)
Cemetery Rd
See Lagos Island Map p694
Old Ojo Rd
Ring Rd
Malu Rd
Lagos Island
Lagos Harbour
Badia
Ikoyi
Broad St
Kirikiri Rd
Apapa
Liverpool Rd
Kingsway Rd
Ferry to Lagos Island
Marine Rd
Awolowo Rd
Creek Rd
Five Cowrie Creek
Tin Can Island
Porto Novo Creek
Ahmadu Bello Rd
Victoria Island
Maroko Market
To Lagos-Epe Expressway
Kuramo Waters
Victoria Island Annexe
See Ikoyi & Victoria Island Map p696

The liveliest street is Awolowo Rd, where there are many restaurants.

Most of the city's residential quarters are to the north, in the direction of the airport, and are connected to Lagos Island by three bridges. From east to west they are 3rd Axial Bridge, Carter Bridge and Eko Bridge. Yaba, about 5km north of Lagos Island, and Surulere, northwest of Yaba, are major nightclub areas. Two major expressways, Agege Motor Rd (leading to the airports) and Ikorodu Rd, intersect in Yaba. Ikorodu Rd eventually intersects with the Lagos-Ibadan Expressway, which leads to all points north.

Information

The major hotels may be able to provide some information on the city. Merchants in VI publish a free, slick monthly guide to restaurants and attractions, *ViiP*. It can be found in most top-end hotels and restaurants. The twice-monthly *Lagos City Guide* (N100) is also a good source of information and can be found in most bookstores and top-end hotels.

Money Lagos has more than 50 banks; the three largest are the FBN (☎ 266 5900) at 35 Marina St, which changes travellers cheques and gives advances on MasterCard; the UBN (☎ 266 5439) at 40 Marina St; and the UBA (☎ 266 7410) at 97 Broad St.

Moneychangers hang out along Broad St, around Bristol Hotel and in front of the Federal Palace Hotel and Kuramo Lodge on VI.

PLACES TO STAY & EAT
14 Tastee Fried Chicken
15 Bristol Hotel
20 Mr Bigg's
26 Mr Bigg's
33 YWCA
35 Chop Houses
OTHER
1 Oba's Palace
2 Udumata Bus Stop
3 Ebute Ero Motor Park
4 Clocktower
5 Hospital
6 Central Mosque
7 SGBN
8 Lufthansa
9 L'Aristocrate Travel & Tours (Thomas Cook)
10 UTB; FBN
11 UK High Commission (Consular Section)
12 Kingsway
13 UBA
16 St John's Church
17 Mandilas Travel
18 UBN
19 Main Post Office
21 Nitel
22 CMS Motor Park; CMS Bookshop
23 Catholic Church
24 Ministry of External Affairs
25 NAL Towers
27 St Nicholas Catholic Mission
28 St Nicholas Hospital
29 Independence House
30 Lagos Lawn & Tennis Club
31 Aeroflot
32 Nigeria Airways; Air Gabon; Balkan Airways; Ethiopian Airlines
34 Police Headquarters
36 National Museum; Museum Kitchen
37 Ghana Embassy
To Yaba (5km)
Eko Bridge
To Iddo Motor Park & Yaba
Carter Bridge
3rd Axial Bridge
Ring Rd
Ebute Ero Market
Adeniji
Adele Rd
Islae Eko Market
Upper King St
Princess St
Bridge St
Apongbon St
Kosoko St
Idowolu St
Yin St
Isale Gangan
Bankole
Alhaji Issa William St
Martin St
Balogun St
Balogun Market
Idumagbo Ave
Okoya St
Jankara Market
Breadfruit St
Clothing Market
Mmamadi Azikiwe St
Ita Faji Market
Apatira St
Odunfa St
Okepopo St
Rd
Broad St
Taiwa St
Smith St
Massey St
Tinubu Square
Kakawa
Odunlami St
Tokunbo St
Massey Bambgbashe St
Glover St
Freeman St
Cemetery
Becroft St
Simpson St
Pike St
Okesuna St
Marina St
Campos St
Campbell St
Catholic Mission St
Joseph St
Hospital Rd
Igbosere Rd
Hawley St
Lewis St
Apongbon St (Elevated)
Apongbon St (Ground Level)
Cable St
Tafawa Balewa Square
Tafawa Balewa Sq
Maloney St
Araromi St
Macarthy St
Onikan
Ring Rd
Force Rd
Awolowo Rd
Onikan Stadium
Yoruba Tennis Club Rd
To Ikoyi
To Victoria Island
Ferry
Lagos Harbour
0 250 500m
0 250 500yd
See Ikoyi & Victoria Island Map p696
LAGOS ISLAND

Post & Communications The main post office is on Marina St on Lagos Island, a couple of blocks southwest of Tinubu Square. There are smaller branches on Ikoyi, about 200m east of the intersection of Kingsway and Awolowo Rds, and on VI, on Adeola Odeku St. They are all open weekdays only. The major hotels can organise air freight; DHL (☎ 268 1106) is at 1 Sumbo Jibowu St on Ikoyi.

For phone calls, your best bet is to call from your hotel (most hotels have direct-dialling facilities).

There are plenty of Internet cafés in Lagos. The most comfortable and reliable place is on the 3rd floor of the Mega Plaza, 14 Idowu Martin St, VI. Expect to pay N10 per minute for Internet time.

Travel Agencies There are many travel agencies on the southern side of Tafawa Balewa Square on Lagos Island. Many of the airline offices are in this area too. L'Aristocrate Travels & Tours (☎ 266 7322) at the corner of Davies and Broad Sts, is the agent for Thomas Cook. Mandilas Travel (☎ 266 3339) on Broad St, two blocks southeast of Martin St, is the agent for American Express and Hertz. On Ikoyi, Bitts Travel & Tours (☎ 268 4550) is at Falomo Shopping Centre.

Cultural Centres The British Council (☎ 269 2188, 269 2192), 11 Kingsway Rd on Ikoyi, carries various newspapers and magazines in its reading room; it's open from 10am to 6pm. The Centre Culturel Français (☎ 261 5592), just off Idowu

Taylor Rd in VI, screens films at 7pm every Thursday. The Goethe Institut (☎ 261 0717) is on Maroko Rd in VI.

Medical Services For emergencies, the best hospitals in Lagos are St Nicholas Hospital (☎ 263 1739) at 57 Campbell St on Lagos Island, and the clean, modern Medical Consultants Group, Flat 4, Eko Court Annexe, Kofo Abayomi Rd on VI.

Dr CO Da Silva (☎ 263 6997) is a general practitioner who accepts emergency cases without appointment. Drs M and D Seeman (☎ 268 4125) and Dr BR Bahl (☎ 268 3127) are also recommended. If you have a medical problem, it might be worth contacting your diplomatic representatives for a list of reputable medical practitioners.

Dangers & Annoyances Lagos is infamous for its violent crime. In some areas of the city home-owners take turns guarding their neighbourhoods. Walking alone at night anywhere in Lagos is extremely risky and should be avoided, particularly around hotels and other areas frequented by foreigners. For a more general discussion of safety issues in Nigeria, see the boxed text 'Safety in Nigeria', earlier in this chapter.

National Museum

The museum *(Awolowo Rd; admission N100; open 9am-5pm daily)* is definitely worth seeing. The star attractions are the Nigeria bronzes from Benin City and ivory carvings. Equally memorable is the bullet-riddled car in which Murtala Mohammed was assassinated in 1976. Architectural buffs will enjoy the numerous wooden doorways and house posts, and those interested in crafts should check out the craft shop here for a demonstration of *adire* cloth making.

The museum is on Lagos Island, 150m southeast of Tafawa Balewa Square.

Markets

In Lagos the many markets are by far the best attractions, but definitely consider hiring a guide to show you around; the markets have also been the scene of violence between Hausa and Yoruba gangs. A definite favourite is the labyrinthine **Balogun Market**, northwest of Bristol Hotel; you can really get lost in this busy maze that's reminiscent of Cairo's markets. Other

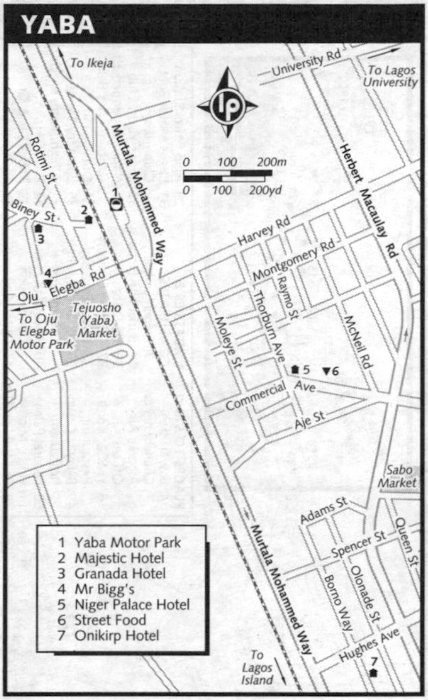
YABA
To Ikeja
University Rd
To Lagos University
0 100 200m
0 100 200yd
Rotimi St
Murtala Mohammed Way
Herbert Macaulay Rd
Biney St
Harvey Rd
Montgomery Rd
Elegba Rd
Oju
To Oju Elegba Motor Park
Tejuosho (Yaba) Market
Thorburn Ave
Raymo St
Moleye St
McNeil Rd
Commercial Ave
Aje St
Sabo Market
Adams St
Queen St
Spencer St
Olonade St
Borno Way
Hughes Ave
To Lagos Island
1 Yaba Motor Park
2 Majestic Hotel
3 Granada Hotel
4 Mr Bigg's
5 Niger Palace Hotel
6 Street Food
7 Onikirp Hotel

Lagos Island delights are **Isale Eko Market**, **Jankara Market** and **Ebute Ero Market**. Thanks to the go slow, most market offerings are available as you wait in the embroilment of choked traffic.

In the south of VI, along Bar Beach, is the grimy and depressing Bar Beach Market. East of VI, on the way to Lekki Peninsula, are **Morocco I** and **Morocco II**, huge lively evening markets that have to be seen to be believed.

The **Ekpe Fish Market**, east of the city, is vast, but the smell will blast away the most hardened traveller.

Other Things to See

Tafawa Balewa Square is a huge arena adorned by statues of gargantuan horses. In the square is Remembrance Arcade, featuring memorials to Nigeria's WWI, WWII and civil-war victims; the guard changes on the hour. Across the road is the 26-storey **Independence House**, built in 1963 to commemorate Nigeria's independence.

The **Brazilian Quarter** is a collection of distinctive houses built by former slaves and descendants who returned from Brazil;

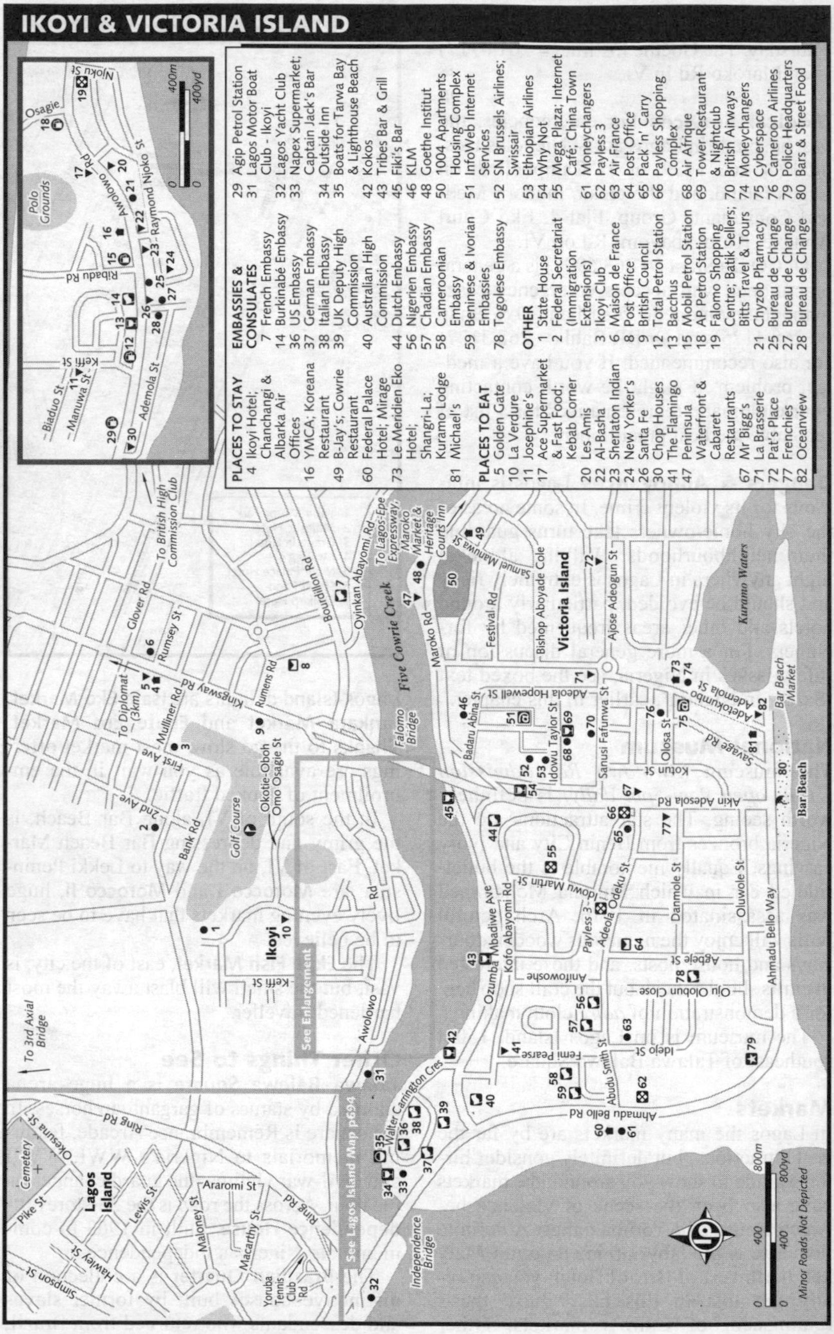
IKOYI & VICTORIA ISLAND
PLACES TO STAY
4 Ikoyi Hotel; Chanchangi & Albarka Air Offices
16 YMCA; Koreana Restaurant
49 B-Jay's; Cowrie Restaurant
60 Federal Palace Hotel; Mirage
73 Le Meridien Eko Hotel; Shangri-La; Kuramo Lodge
81 Michael's
PLACES TO EAT
5 Golden Gate
10 La Verdure
11 Josephine's
17 Ace Supermarket & Fast Food; Kebab Corner
20 Les Amis
22 Al-Basha
23 Sherlaton Indian
24 New Yorker's
26 Santa Fe
30 Chop Houses
41 The Flamingo
47 Peninsula Waterfront & Cabaret Restaurants
67 Mr Bigg's
71 La Brasserie
72 Pat's Place
77 Frenchies
82 Oceanview
EMBASSIES & CONSULATES
7 French Embassy
14 Burkinabé Embassy
36 US Embassy
37 German Embassy
38 Italian Embassy
39 UK Deputy High Commission
40 Australian High Commission
44 Dutch Embassy
56 Nigerien Embassy
57 Chadian Embassy
58 Cameroonian Embassy
59 Beninese & Ivorian Embassies
78 Togolese Embassy
OTHER
1 State House
2 Federal Secretariat (Immigration Extensions)
3 Ikoyi Club
6 Maison de France
8 Post Office
9 British Council
12 Total Petrol Station
13 Bacchus
15 Mobil Petrol Station
18 AP Petrol Station
19 Falomo Shopping Centre; Batik Sellers; Bitts Travel & Tours
21 Chyzob Pharmacy
25 Bureau de Change
27 Bureau de Change
28 Bureau de Change
29 Agip Petrol Station
31 Lagos Motor Boat Club - Ikoyi
32 Lagos Yacht Club
33 Napex Supermarket; Captain Jack's Bar
34 Outside Inn
35 Boats for Tarwa Bay & Lighthouse Beach
42 Kokos
43 Tribes Bar & Grill
45 Fiki's Bar
46 KLM
48 Goethe Institut
50 1004 Apartments Housing Complex
51 InfoWeb Internet Services
52 SN Brussels Airlines; Swissair
53 Ethiopian Airlines
54 Why Not
55 Mega Plaza; Internet Café; China Town
61 Moneychangers
62 Payless 3
63 Air France
64 Post Office
65 Pack 'n' Carry
66 Payless Shopping Complex
68 Air Afrique
69 Tower Restaurant & Nightclub
70 British Airways
74 Moneychangers
75 Cyberspace
76 Cameroon Airlines
79 Police Headquarters
80 Bars & Street Food
Lagos Island
Ikoyi
Victoria Island
Five Cowrie Creek
Kuramo Waters
Bar Beach
Bar Beach Market
Golf Course
Polo Grounds
Cemetery
Independence Bridge
Falomo Bridge
To 3rd Axial Bridge
To Diplomat (3km)
To British High Commission Club
To Lagos-Epe Expressway; Maroko Market & Heritage Courts Inn
See Lagos Island Map p694
See Enlargement
Yoruba Tennis Club Rd
Awolowo Rd
Ademola St
Raymond Njoko St
Ribadu Rd
Keffi St
Biaduo St
Manuwa St
Njoku St
Osagie
Walter Carrington Cres
Ozumba Mbadiwe Ave
Kofo Abayomi Rd
Ahmadu Bello Rd
Ahmadu Bello Way
Maroko Rd
Oyinkan Abayomi Rd
Bourdillon Rd
Kingsway Rd
Glover Rd
Rumsey St
Rumens Rd
Mulliner Rd
First Ave
2nd Ave
Bank Rd
Okotie-Oboh
Omo Osagie St
Ring Rd
Simpson St
Hawley St
Pike St
Okesuna St
Lewis St
Maloney St
Araromi St
Macarthy St
Badaru Abina St
Festival Rd
Samuel Manuwa St
Bishop Aboyade Cole
Adeola Hopewell St
Idowu Taylor St
Sanusi Fafunwa St
Ajose Adeogun St
Idowu Martin St
Adeola Odeku St
Payless 3
Anifowoshe
Femi Pearse
Abudu Smith St
Idejo St
Oju Olobun Close
Agbeje St
Danmole St
Oluwole St
Akin Adesola Rd
Kotun St
Olosa St
Savage Rd
Adetokumbo Ademola St
0 400 800m
0 400 800yd
0 400m
0 400yd
Minor Roads Not Depicted

have a look along Kakawa and Odunfa Sts on Lagos Island.

The **National Theatre** (☎ *283 0200)* is the huge round building you can't miss on the drive in from the airport. It has galleries of modern Nigerian art, Nigerian crafts and other African arts. The best time to visit is between 10am and 3pm Tuesday to Saturday, when all three galleries are open.

Beaches

Some weekend favourite alternatives are **Palasides Beach**, **Lekki Beach**, **Tarkwa Beach** (which has no undertow) and, nearby, **Lighthouse Beach** (which has a strong undertow).

The beaches are a delightful half-hour trip by water taxi through the port, across the lagoon and past fishing villages. Launches are available most readily on weekends and holidays. You'll find them on VI along Walter Carrington Crescent. The price is negotiable, with N600 per person (return) the maximum. Make arrangements to be picked up in the afternoon and don't pay beforehand. Ilekki Beach, 50km east of Lagos off the Ilekki-Epe Expressway, is also popular.

Places to Stay – Budget

Ikoyi & Lagos Island For women only, the ***YWCA*** *(Cnr Moloney St & Yoruba Tennis Club Rd)* has dorm beds for N3500, including breakfast. The YWCA is on Lagos Island, a block east of Tafawa Balewa Square. Unlike the YMCA, it's still good value.

Ritz Hotel *(☎ 252 3148, 41 George V St)* Singles/doubles with air-con N1250/3000. Once a reasonable place to stay, the Ritz embodies almost the opposite to what its name suggests. The rooms are filthy, the service could be better and it has a bar that has been described as 'cool and sleazy' – we agree.

The Mainland Yaba, 5km north of Lagos Island and easily reached by shared taxis, is livelier and much cheaper than the centre.

Majestic Hotel *(14 Popo St)* Singles with fan/air-con N1550/3500. The old Majestic is two blocks north of Tejuosho (Yaba) Market. It has decent singles; the beds are wide enough for two people. The building is dilapidated, but the staff are friendly.

Granada Hotel *(☎ 284 7980, 29 Biney St)* Singles/doubles N1250/3500. The Granada, near the Majestic, has excellent air-con rooms with bathroom.

Places to Stay – Mid-Range & Top End

Lagos Island Most of the pricier hotels require deposits, which are sometimes double the cost of the room.

Bristol Hotel *(☎ 266 1204, Martin St)* Singles/doubles N1400/2000, plus N4000 deposit. This Nigeria Hotels Ltd (NHL) property, near the corner of Martin and Broad Sts, was once the most famous hotel in Lagos. It's fallen on bad times: The lift is slow or not working and the restaurant is a shocker, but the terrace bar is atmospheric (as it overlooks the heart of town).

The Mainland As with the cheap hotels, you'll get better value here than on Lagos Island.

Niger Palace Hotel *(☎ 280 0010, 1 Thurburn Ave)* Doubles N3500, plus N4000 deposit. This hotel, on the corner of Thurburn and Commercial Aves, is a bit pricey. Rooms have carpet, TV and bathroom.

Stadium Hotel *(☎ 283 3593, 27 Iyun St)* Twin share with TV & air-con N3500. The well-known Stadium Hotel is just north of the national stadium in Surulere; it is often full. The Stadium has one of Lagos' best highlife venues, and a nightclub that features a great floor show.

Onikirp Hotel *(328 Borno Way)* Singles/doubles N1750/2250. The Onikirp has clean, quiet air-con rooms.

Mainland Hotel *(☎ 280 3306, 2/4 Murtala Mohammed Way)* Doubles N3630. You could try the austere but comfortable and clean Mainland Hotel, just to the north of Iddo Motor Park (and convenient if you arrive in Lagos late).

Ikoyi & Victoria Island Prices in this section are given in US dollars because this is what tourists usually have to pay. Only the top-end places take credit cards; ring them to find out which cards are in favour. The benefit of staying in Ikoyi or VI is that these areas are generally much more secure than Lagos Island or the mainland.

Ikoyi Hotel *(☎ 269 1522, 269 1531, Kingsway Rd)* Singles/doubles nonresidents US$110/115, residents N5000/7000. This NHL property in Ikoyi looks better than it actually is. There is a filthy pool, casino, magazine stand, one poor restaurant and another overpriced Chinese restaurant (meals start at N900). Chanchangi and Albarka Air airlines have offices here.

Diplomat Hotel *(40C Agodogba Ave)* Doubles/minisuites US$90/125. If you really want to forget you're in Lagos, the Diplomat is the place to retreat to. Rooms are shockingly luxurious and good value for the price. The hotel is located in a quiet gated residential neighbourhood. A business centre with Internet access, a good pool and an overpriced restaurant round out the experience.

Federal Palace Hotel *(☎ 262 3116, 262 3125, Cnr Ahmadu Bello Rd & Abudu Smith St)* Deluxe singles/doubles US$180/300 nonresidents, N7000/10,000 residents. This huge hotel on VI looks as depressing as it is. The desk staff are unhelpful and the dreadful lobby bar and its lack of ambience makes you wish you were somewhere else – even though it overlooks the sea. The pool costs N750 for nonguests.

B-Jay's *(☎ 261 2391, 24 Samuel Manuwa St)* Standard/executive doubles US$100/115 nonresidents, N7600/8300 residents. Once a well-priced alternative to the more expensive places, B-Jay's is a victim of inflation and is no longer as good value as it used to be. This friendly place offers rooms with cable TV, shower and fridge.

Michael's *(Adetokumbo Ademola St)* Singles/doubles for nonresidents US$65/90. This quiet place south of Le Meridien Eko has clean, tidy but small rooms with air-con and TV. A nice pool and restaurant make it a worthwhile place.

Le Meridien Eko Hotel *(☎ 262 4600, fax 261 5205, Adetokumbo Ademola St)* Standard rooms/doubles US$190/210. It costs big bucks to stay at the Meridien; it's the haunt of the company-credit-card set. It has a casino, pool, sports bar and pleasant outside bar that's good for a quiet drink at night. Also good is the adjoining ***Kuramo Lodge***, which has top-quality rooms for US$120, and includes access to all facilities; make reservations to ensure a lower price.

Airport Area For those in transit, staying in the airport area (Ikeja), 22km from the centre, only makes sense if you have a lot of money to waste on mediocre rooms. It's well worth the time, effort and money to pay less and get more from hotels in VI or Ikoyi.

Airport Hotel *(☎ 490 1001, Obafemi Awolowo Rd)* Doubles/business suites for nonresidents US$180/230, residents N8800/11,300. This huge old hotel 3km northeast of the domestic terminal is obscenely expensive and hardly worth its proximity to the airport. It has a pool, tennis court, bookshop, nightclub and car rental. You should be able to get a taxi from here to the airport for N200.

Sheraton *(☎ 490 0930, 497 0321, 30 Mobolaji Bank, Anthony Way)* Rooms from US$180. The Sheraton, 3km due east of the domestic terminal, exists for those uncomfortable with going into town. The rooms are also ridiculously expensive, considering that you are far removed from the excitement of Ikoyi, VI or Apapa. There is a kitsch English-style pub here, the Goodies.

Places to Eat

Ikoyi The area with the highest concentration of good restaurants in Lagos is the 1km stretch along Awolowo Rd on Ikoyi, which has restaurants in all price ranges. The street's numbering system is confusing.

Ace Supermarket & Fast Food *(99 Awolowo Rd)* is among the cheapest of the Awolowo Rd food places, and is 100m east of the YMCA. Across the street from the Ace Supermarket at No 160 is the popular ***Les Amis***, which has Lebanese specialties, including falafel and kofta sandwiches (N250) and burgers (N600).

Al-Basha *(126 Awolowo Rd)* has good pizzas from N550 and falafels from N300.

Josephine's *(10 Keffi St)* serves basic fare such as rice and soup.

The inexpensive ***Sherlaton*** *(108 Awolowo Rd)* has been around for years; it's considered the city's best Indian restaurant.

Santa Fe Saloon *(144 Awolowo Rd)* reportedly has some of the best Italian food in Lagos, despite its name.

Koreana Restaurant *(81 Awolowo Rd)* has excellent Korean, Japanese and Chinese dishes from N600.

New Yorker's *(59 Raymond Njoko St)* is one of those imitation American diners; it's said to have the best hamburgers (N400) in Lagos.

La Verdure *(Ribadu Rd)* is a large, fancy place with a predominantly French menu; the bar is popular with expats.

Planet 44 Restaurant *(44 Awolowo Rd)*, also referred to as 'double 4', is an attractive upmarket café with pizzas (N500) and Lebanese dishes, among other things.

Victoria Island For a fast-food fix, try ***Mr Bigg's*** *(Akin Adesola Rd)* or ***Frenchies*** *(29A Akin Adesola St)*, a popular pastry shop with éclairs (N250) and other cakes, bread, pizza (N450) and sandwiches (N200).

Some of the best Chinese and Thai cuisine can be found at the expensive ***China Town*** *(3rd floor, Mega Plaza, 14 Idowu Martin St)*. Filling meals start at N900.

Cowrie Restaurant is an excellent restaurant at B-Jay's and has the best African food in town. It is expensive (the chef's salad is N750). The Cowrie has bands on Friday and Saturday nights.

Mirage at Federal Palace Hotel is, unlike the hotel, maintaining its high standards.

Shangri-La Meals N1600-2000. This Chinese restaurant on the 14th floor of Le Meridien Eko Hotel has good food, atmosphere and views.

Golden Gate *(Kingsway Rd)*, 200m north of Mulliner Rd, is well worth a splurge if you have bulging pockets.

Two places that combine Chinese and Indian food are the casual ***La Brasserie*** *(52 Adetokumbo Ademola St)* and ***The Flamingo*** *(10 Kofo Abayomi Rd)*, which is more dressy and serves dishes for around N700.

Pat's Place *(292C Ajose Adeogun St)* is popular with expats, and serves excellent pizzas (N1200) and burgers (N750). It has a well-stocked selection of imported American and European beers.

Lagoon Restaurant *(Ozumba Mbadiwe Ave)* has European food and a cheaper section for takeaway pizza and banana splits.

Oceanside Restaurant *(Cnr Adetokumbo Ademola St & Ahmadu Bello Way)* is an expensive restaurant at the far south end of the Eko Meridien complex and has seafood and continental dishes.

Lagos Island On Lagos Island (and indeed all over Lagos) you will find chop houses, locally called ***suya stalls***, under nearly every highway overpass, and on the fringe of markets and motor parks. Favourites are the Cameroonian places scattered around the corner of Martin and Broad Sts near Bristol Hotel, and other stalls near Balogun Market.

For fast food, try ***Mr Bigg's*** outlets at the junction of Marina and Odunlami Sts (look for the red-and-yellow sign) and on Joseph St; for fowl, try ***Tastee Fried Chicken*** on Broad St. The snack bars at the large stores serve snacks and Nigerian fare, and include ***UTC*** on Broad St and ***Kingsway*** at the southern end of Martin St.

Museum Kitchen, at the National Museum in Onikan, has Nigerian specialties, including *gwaten doya* (yam soup), ikokore, pepper soup and groundnut soup. Expect to pay N500 for *edikang ikong* (bitter leaf soup with beef); add another N300 for a piece of stockfish or some large snails.

Bagatelle *(☎ 266 2410, 4th floor, 208 Broad St)* Open Mon-Sat. Bagatelle has been a Lagos institution for over 35 years. It has excellent harbour views and is an elegant place; men need to wear ties.

Club Panache Open Mon-Sat. Readers recommend this Chinese restaurant for good-value meals; it's at Mainland Hotel near Iddo Motor Park.

Yaba & Airport Area In Yaba, there is a ***Mr Bigg's*** restaurant across from Tejuosho (Yaba) Market, and many ***chop houses*** along Oju Elegba Rd and Commercial Ave.

Taj Mahal Indian Restaurant *(Mobolaji Bank, Anthony Way)* is handy for those staying at or near the Sheraton.

The Sheraton has four restaurants, including the good ***Pili Pili Restaurant*** and an Italian place with meals from N1400 to N2000.

Self-Catering For basic provisions on Lagos Island, try ***Kingsway***.

On Ikoyi, head for Awolowo Rd, particularly the ***Falomo Shopping Centre*** *(Cnr Awolowo Rd & Njoku St)*, and the small ***Ace Supermarket & Fast Food*** *(99 Awolowo Rd)* 350m further west. ***Bhojosons Supermarket*** *(77 Awolowo Rd)* is well stocked.

On VI the ***Napex Supermarket*** *(Walter Carrington Crescent)* is opposite the US embassy, ***Payless 3*** *(Ahmadu Bello Rd)* is across from Federal Palace Hotel, and there's also another ***Payless 3*** shopping complex *(Adeola Odeku St)*. The best place to shop in VI is the modern ***Mega Plaza*** *(14 Idowu Martins St)*, where you can buy everything from gasoline generators and kitchen appliances, to new eyeglasses and Viagra.

Entertainment

Victoria Island & Ikoyi A 'respectable brothel bar' is ***Kokos*** where a beer will set you back N120; a live band plays here on Friday and Saturday nights.

Outside Inn *(☎ 261 4216)* has an air-con 'inside' bar and an 'outside' bar; it has a good selection of ice-cold beers. In the same category is ***Why Not*** *(Alakija St)*, which has loud music, lots of locals and pool tables.

Tower Restaurant & Nightclub *(18 Idowu Taylor St)* Cover charge N350. This place is popular with the young expat set; the music tends to be loud rap.

Tribes Bar & Grill *(20–24 Ozumba Mbadiwe St)* seems to be the place for the crowd at Pat's Place to migrate when closing time hits. There's a popular happy hour from 4pm to 9pm Friday nights when all drinks are half price.

Another popular place is ***Cheers Bar*** *(Bollywood; 10 Kofo Abayomi St)*, which describes itself as an 'Indian Hollywood-style bar, restaurant and nite club'.

Bacchus *(57 Awolowo Rd)* Cover charge N500. This popular place is a dressy affair on Saturday; the dancing is the attraction.

The Mainland Every taxi driver knows the following three famous clubs.

Shrine Cover charge N100. The star nightclub in Lagos is the late Fela Kuti's Shrine, in Ikeja. It's 500m east of Agege Motor Rd Expressway at the point where it intersects with the road from the domestic airport. It lacks Fela (who died in 1997), but the mantle has been assumed by his son Femi Kuti.

Ariya Nightclub *(15 Ikorodu Rd, Yaba)* Cover charge N200. Open until late Tues-Sun. The second famous club, where juju music reigns, is King Sunny Ade's Ariya Nightclub. It's on the major expressway towards the airport, a 15-minute ride north from Lagos Island. Don't arrive before 11pm unless you're coming to eat. King Sunny Ade may play here Wednesday and Saturday.

Shina Peters, the Afro-juju master, performs periodically at ***Stadium Hotel*** *(☎ 283 3593, 27 Iyun St)*, the famous third club (see Places to Eat earlier). Peters usually sings on Thursday nights, but call to check.

Motherland *(Opebi Rd)* is Lagbaja's club.

Pick Nightclub *(Adeniran Ogunsanya St)* is in Surulere (near the UTC Store) and is one of those places where you have to dress up – drinks are priced accordingly.

The entertainment capital of the 'mainland' is Apapa, the port city; most places have a small entry fee if there is live music.

Wazobia is one of the best venues to meet locals. It's near the UTC Store and buzzes with live music on Friday and Saturday.

Mono Lido Nightclub is a famous nightclub, known to every sailor who visits Lagos.

Caesar's Palace is a Lebanese-run place near the Calcutta Rd Roundabout.

On Marine Rd there are two good bars – the best is ***Thistle Bar*** (also known as Avondelle) at No 36, because of its live music. Equally popular, especially with expats, is the aptly named ***The Pub***.

Shopping

Arts & Craftwork The best place for batiks is Njoku St, on the western side of Falomo Shopping Centre in Ikoyi. They're sold on the street and the selection is extensive.

The ***National Museum*** has a nonprofit crafts centre with batik, calabashes, woodcarvings and textiles at fixed prices.

Jankara Market *(Adeniji Adele Rd)* is the largest market in Lagos. You'll find traditional tie-dyed and indigo cloth, trade beads, jewellery and pottery. There is also a fetishes market you can buy various medicines.

At the eastern end of Bar Beach on VI is a ***market*** where traders sell batik, baskets and calabashes.

Getting There & Away

Air International flights leave from Murtala Mohammed international airport and domestic flights leave from the older airport; both are 10km north of Lagos Island by road. Nigeria's major private airlines all have their offices at Terminal 2 of the domestic airport, including Albarka Air, Chanchangi (☎ 493 9755), Okada Air (☎ 496 3881), Kabo Airlines (☎ 497 0449) and Skyline (☎ 493 4440). Offices for Albarka Air and Chanchangi can also be found at Ikoyi Hotel.

Airline offices on Lagos Island and the mainland include the following:

Aeroflot (☎ 263 7223) 36 Tafawa Balewa Square
Air Gabon (☎ 263 2827) 29 Tafawa Balewa Square
Air Guinée (☎ 584 8689) Murtala Mohammed international airport, Ikeja
Balkan Airways (☎ 263 5267) 18 Tafawa Balewa Square
Ethiopian Airlines (☎ 263 2690) 20 Tafawa Balewa Square
Nigeria Airways (☎ 490 0810) Airways House, Ikeja

Airline offices on Victoria Island and Ikoyi include:

Air France (☎ 262 1456) 4th floor, ICON Bldg, Idejo St, VI
British Airways (☎ 261 3004) Near the corner of Sanusi Fafunwa and Oloshore Sts, VI
Ghana Airways (☎ 266 1808) 130 Awolowo Rd, Ikoyi
SN Brussels Airlines & Swiss (☎ 261 1655) Plot PC10, Engineering Close, VI

Bus Various bus companies connect Lagos with major cities in the country, and each has its own station. A major company serving the south (Benin City, Onitsha and Enugu) is Ekene Dili Chukwu, which has its station in Otoja on Ikorodu Rd. Many other bus companies, including those running to Kano, are near Iddo Motor Park on the mainland, just north of Lagos Island. ABC buses serving the southeast (Calabar and Port Harcourt) leave from Oju Elegba Junction Motor Park in Surulere. For details of prices, see the individual sections.

Bush Taxi From north to south, the main motor parks are: Ojota Motor Park (Ibadan, Oshogbo, Ife) on Ikorodu Rd in Ojota, roughly 10km north of Lagos Island; Oju Elegba Junction Motor Park (Benin City, Onitsha, Enugu, Port Harcourt, Calabar) on Western Ave, at the intersection with Oju Elegba Rd in Surulere; Iddo Motor Park (Kano, Kaduna, Jos, Sokoto, Zaria) on Murtala Mohammed Way on the mainland; and Ebute Ero Motor Park (Cotonou and Lomé) on the northern tip of Lagos Island between Carter and Eko Bridges.

Typical fares are N100 to Ibadan, N300 to Benin City, N700 to Calabar, N800 to Kano and N700 to Jos.

Train The train station (☎ 283 4302) is on the mainland just north of Lagos Island, near Iddo Motor Park.

Getting Around

To/From the Airport Murtala Mohammed international airport has a restaurant and a Hertz agency, but no bureau de change, so you'll probably have to negotiate a taxi fare in dollars or carefully change some cash with one of the black marketers. Better yet, make hotel reservations in advance and arrange to have the hotel send a driver to collect you. You may end up paying slightly more than you would with a cab, but it's probably the safest way to negotiate the airport.

At the airport, taxis licensed to carry passengers will show you their identity cards; they are generally more reliable and safer than those not licensed to carry passengers. Haggle over the fare. A taxi from the international airport should cost less than N1000. However, you'll probably end up paying US$20 to US$30 (N2000 to N3000) to Lagos Island (22km) or nearby VI and Ikoyi, N500 to the domestic airport and N1000 to the Sheraton. A minibus from Agege Motor Rd to Lagos Island is N10, but it would be suicide to try this with your luggage in tow.

Taxi & Minibus Minibuses provide the cheapest transport around Lagos; most go on fixed routes. They can cost as little as N10. The CMS Motor Park is on Ring Rd in Lagos Island. There are no longer any shared taxis in Lagos so you must charter a taxi and haggle like crazy. A taxi costs N300 to go anywhere on Lagos Island and up to N500 to VI and Ikoyi from Lagos Island.

Car Self-drive rental cars are virtually unavailable in Lagos: most hire cars come with driver. By the hour, expect to pay about N800 with a driver. (Taxis by the hour are less than half this.) Hertz, Budget and Europcar have offices at the international airport. Hertz is also handled by Mandilas Travel at Broad St, Lagos Island; and Avis by Nigerian Rent-a-Car (☎ 284 6336) at 225 Apapa Rd, Inganmu.

Ferry Ferries provide the cheapest and quickest transport from Lagos Island to Apapa and to Mile-2, on the western side of town. The ferry fare is N20. The ferry terminal is to the southwest side of Lagos Island, just south of Ring Rd.

AROUND LAGOS

Lekki Conservation Centre

A mere 20-minute drive east from Lagos on the Lagos-Epe Expressway, opposite the Chevron Plant, is the Lekki Conservation Centre *(admission free; open daily)*. Run by the Nigerian Conservation Foundation, it has 78 hectares of wetlands that have been set aside for viewing wildlife. Raised walkways enable you to see monkeys, crocodiles and various birds; early morning is the best time to visit. There is a conservation/visitors centre and a library.

The easiest way to get there is to flag down a bus on VI along Maroko Rd; the cost is around N100.

Abeokuta

☎ 039

Abeokuta, 70km north of Lagos, translates as 'under the rock'; it's famous not only for being the birthplace of the late musician Fela Kuti and the writer Wole Soyinka (who lives in exile), but also for the Olumo rock. This chunk of granite is considered sacred and is used in various celebrations and rituals. Guides will take you to the top of the rock for commanding views of Lagos and the surrounding country. There are also **caves** and a **shrine** in the area. At the market you can buy adire cloth and plenty of juju material such as *grisgris* (charms).

Bush taxis leave from Ojota Motor Park in Lagos (N350, two hours).

The South

IBADAN

☎ 022 • pop 8 million

Roughly half the size of Lagos, Ibadan is an ugly, congested and sprawling Yoruba city. The capital of Oyo State, geographically it's thought to be the largest city in Africa, and it's the second most populous city in West Africa after Lagos (it was the most populous city from the late 1800s to the 1960s, which makes it all the more surprising that there's so little of interest to travellers).

The major sights are the huge, sprawling Dugbe Market, the University of Ibadan (UI) and the International Institute of Tropical Agriculture (IITA). Two interesting markets that are notably less hectic than Dugbe are Oje and Bode. Bode is the most fascinating because of its fabulous juju section.

Orientation

The commercial heart of town is the block-size triangle formed by Dugbe Market, the train station and Cocoa House. UI is on the northern outskirts of town and is connected to the centre (5.5km away) by Oyo Rd, which leads southwest to eventually become Fajuyi Rd and, near the market, Dugbe Rd. Further southwest beyond the train station, it becomes Yaganku and Abeokuta Rds. Bodija Rd leads directly south from UI, becoming Ogunmola St and eventually Lagos Rd.

Three major connecting roads running roughly east-west are (from north to south): Queen Elizabeth II Rd, which connects the southern end of Oyo Rd with Bodija Rd; Commercial St, which connects the central triangle with Lagos Rd; and Ring Rd, which connects the southern end of Yaganku Rd with Lagos Rd. Further south on Lagos Rd is New Garage Motor Park, for Lagos and points east (including Benin City and Port Harcourt).

Cocoa House is the only high rise in Ibadan and is a good downtown reference point.

Information

There is no tourist information office in Ibadan, and the map in this book is as good as you will find. Otherwise, rely on your taxi driver to negotiate a way through the labyrinth.

Money The National Bank of Nigeria, UBA, UBN and a bureau de change are all on Lebanon Rd next to Dugbe Market; FBN is one block to the south, on New Court Rd; New Nigeria Bank is two blocks to the south, on Commercial St. The reliable Safe Bureau de Change is across from UI, to the north.

Post & Communications The post office is chaotic; it's on Abeokuta Rd, and it's open from 8am to noon and 2pm to 4pm Monday to Friday.

Cultural Centres The American Cultural Center is on Bodija Rd, near PI Hostel. The Alliance Française is in the centre of town at 7 Lebanon Rd; there is also a branch near the junction of Oshontokun Ave and Bodija Rd. The British Council library is on Magazine/Jericho Rd, 500m northwest of the train station.

Medical Services If you need medical help contact the IITA (☎ 241 2626) for a list of recommended doctors and clinics.

Things to See & Do

The **International Insitute of Tropical Agriculture** is Nigeria's accommodation oasis, if

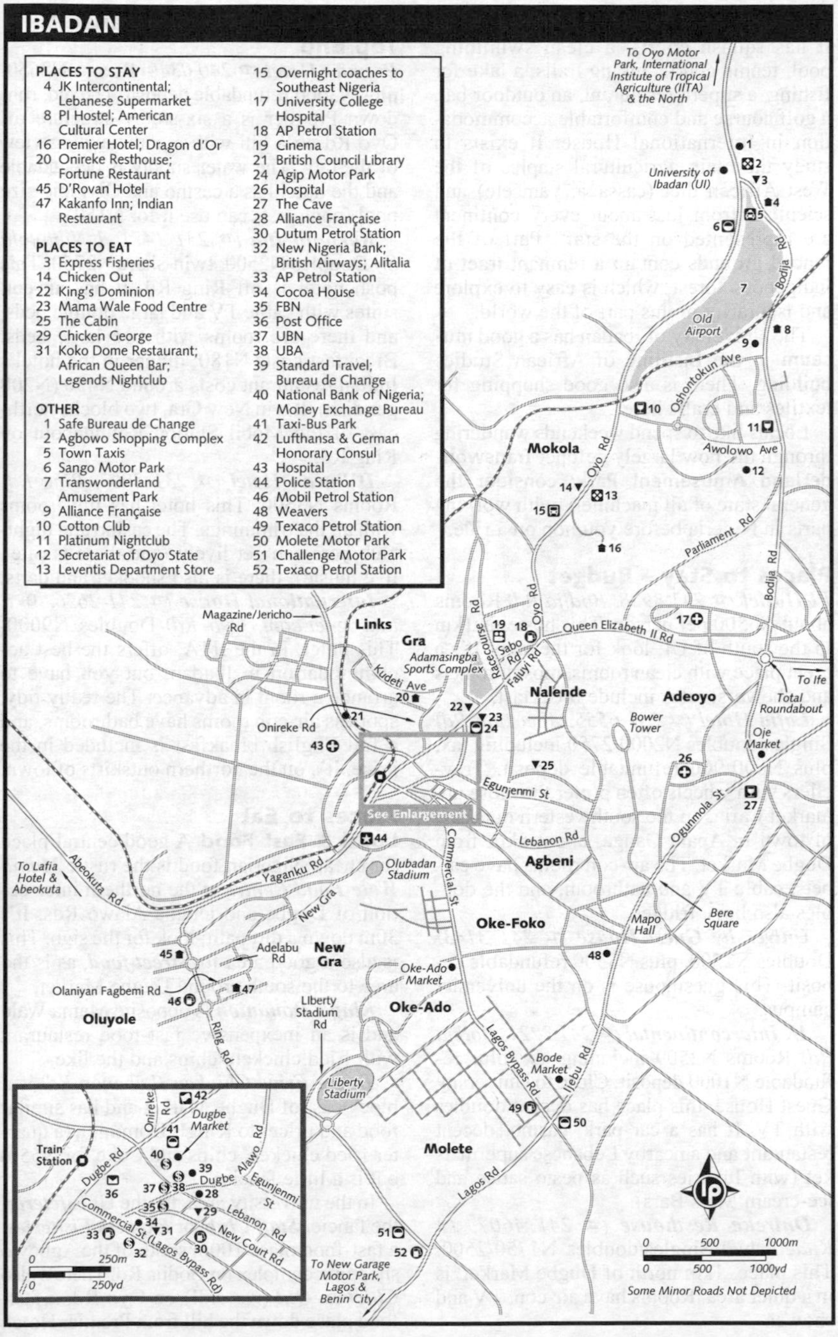
IBADAN
PLACES TO STAY
4 JK Intercontinental; Lebanese Supermarket
8 PI Hostel; American Cultural Center
16 Premier Hotel; Dragon d'Or
20 Onireke Resthouse; Fortune Restaurant
45 D'Rovan Hotel
47 Kakanfo Inn; Indian Restaurant
PLACES TO EAT
3 Express Fisheries
14 Chicken Out
22 King's Dominion
23 Mama Wale Food Centre
25 The Cabin
29 Chicken George
31 Koko Dome Restaurant; African Queen Bar; Legends Nightclub
OTHER
1 Safe Bureau de Change
2 Agbowo Shopping Complex
5 Town Taxis
6 Sango Motor Park
7 Transwonderland Amusement Park
9 Alliance Française
10 Cotton Club
11 Platinum Nightclub
12 Secretariat of Oyo State
13 Leventis Department Store
15 Overnight coaches to Southeast Nigeria
17 University College Hospital
18 AP Petrol Station
19 Cinema
21 British Council Library
24 Agip Motor Park
26 Hospital
27 The Cave
28 Alliance Française
30 Dutum Petrol Station
32 New Nigeria Bank; British Airways; Alitalia
33 AP Petrol Station
34 Cocoa House
35 FBN
36 Post Office
37 UBN
38 UBA
39 Standard Travel; Bureau de Change
40 National Bank of Nigeria; Money Exchange Bureau
41 Taxi-Bus Park
42 Lufthansa & German Honorary Consul
43 Hospital
44 Police Station
46 Mobil Petrol Station
48 Weavers
49 Texaco Petrol Station
50 Molete Motor Park
51 Challenge Motor Park
52 Texaco Petrol Station
To Oyo Motor Park, International Institute of Tropical Agriculture (IITA) & the North
University of Ibadan (UI)
Bodija Rd
Old Airport
Oshontokun Ave
Awolowo Ave
Mokola
Oyo Rd
Parliament Rd
Bodija Rd
Queen Elizabeth II Rd
Magazine/Jericho Rd
Links
Gra
Adamasingba Sports Complex
Kudeti Ave
Racecourse Rd
Sabo Rd
Fajuyi Rd
Nalende
Adeoyo
To Ife
Total Roundabout
Onireke Rd
Bower Tower
Oje Market
Egunjenmi St
See Enlargement
Commercial St
Ogunmola St
Lebanon Rd
Agbeni
To Lafia Hotel & Abeokuta
Abeokuta Rd
Yaganku Rd
New Gra
Olubadan Stadium
Oke-Foko
Mapo Hall
Bere Square
Adelabu Rd
New Gra
Oke-Ado Market
Olaniyan Fagbemi Rd
Oluyole
Liberty Stadium Rd
Oke-Ado
Ring Rd
Lagos Bypass Rd
Ijebu Rd
Bode Market
Liberty Stadium
Molete
Lagos Rd
Onireke Rd
Dugbe Market
Train Station
Dugbe Rd
Alawo Rd
Egunjenmi St
Dugbe
Lebanon Rd
New Court Rd
Commercial St (Lagos Bypass Rd)
To New Garage Motor Park, Lagos & Benin City
0 250m
0 250yd
0 500 1000m
0 500 1000yd
Some Minor Roads Not Depicted

you are lucky enough to be invited to stay. It has squash courts, a clean swimming pool, tennis courts, hiking trails, a lake for fishing, a superb restaurant, an outdoor bar, a golf course and comfortable accommodation in International House. It exists to study the main agricultural staples of the West African diet (cassava, yam etc) and scientists from just about every continent are represented on the staff. Part of the fenced grounds contain a remnant tract of indigenous forest, which is easy to explore and is a rarity in this part of the world.

The University of Ibadan has a good **museum** in the Institute of African Studies building. There is also good shopping for textiles and crafts here.

Locals like to spend weekends wandering through the now largely defunct **Transwonderland Amusement Park**; consider the general state of all machinery with working parts in Nigeria before you hop on a ride.

Places to Stay – Budget

PI Hostel *(☎ 241 3928, Bodija Rd)* Rooms about N6500 per person. This hostel is 1km to the south of UI; look for the sign. It's a great place with clean rooms, mosquito nets and showers; rates include breakfast.

Lafia Hotel *(☎ 231 6555, Abeokuta Rd)* Singles/doubles N2000/2750 including tax, plus N600/900 refundable deposit. Travellers with wheels often prefer the more upmarket Lafia, on the southwestern outskirts of town in Apata Ganga, about 5km from Dugbe Market. The air-con rooms have carpets, cable TV and bathroom, and the doubles also have fridges.

University Guest House *(☎ 241 3143)* Doubles N2500, plus N3500 refundable deposit. This guesthouse is on the university campus.

JK Intercontinental *(☎ 241 2221, Bodija Rd)* Rooms N2500 including tax, plus refundable N1000 deposit. Close to University Guest House, this place has decent doubles with TV. It has a car park, casino, decent restaurant and a nearby Lebanese supermarket (with luxuries such as pesto sauce and ice-cream Mars Bars).

Onireke Resthouse *(☎ 241 4607, 13 Kudeti Ave)* Singles/doubles N1750/2500. This place, 1km north of Dugbe Market, is in a quiet area. Rooms have air-con, TV and shower.

Places to Stay – Mid-Range & Top End

Premier Hotel *(☎ 240 0340)* Rooms N2650, plus N3000 refundable deposit. The old, rundown Premier is a six-storey structure off Oyo Rd on a hill with a commanding view of the city. The water supply is dependable and the hotel has a casino and Olympic-size pool (nonguests can use it for N150).

Kakanfo Inn *(☎ 231 1471, 1 Nihinlola St)* Doubles N2500, twin-share N2750. This posh hotel is off Ring Rd. It has air-con suites with cable TV and large double beds, and there are rooms with two large beds. Breakfast costs N180; dinner in the hotel's Indian restaurant costs around N450 (N200 per dish). It's in New Gra, two blocks northeast of the Mobil Station Roundabout on Ring Rd.

D'Rovan Hotel *(☎ 231 2907, Ring Rd)* Rooms N3500. This hotel has tiny rooms with all the trimmings. The casino and nightclub here can get lively (and there is often live music); there is also snooker and darts.

International House *(☎ 241 2626, e iita@cgnet.com, Oyo Rd)* Doubles N9000. This hotel, in the IITA, offers the best accommodation in Ibadan, but you have to arrange a room in advance. The really tidy, spotless air-con rooms have bathrooms, and a full English breakfast is included in the price. It's on the northern outskirts of town.

Places to Eat

Local & Fast Food A good central place for cheap Nigerian food is the rustic ***Mama Wale Food Centre*** at the northern intersection of Dugbe and Dugbe Alawo Rds. It's 30m down a dirt path; look for the sign. This is also a good area for ***street food***, as is the area to the south around Dugbe Market.

King's Dominion is opposite Mama Wale and is an inexpensive fast-food restaurant with fried chicken, chips and the like.

Tastee Fried Chicken *(Lebanon Rd)* is a block east of Dugbe Market and has similar food and prices to King's Dominion (a quarter fried chicken, chips and Coke for N550) but is a little fancier.

In the university area, try the UI ***cafeteria***, the fancier ***Staff Club***, or ***Express Fisheries***, a fast-food place 100m south of the Agbowo shopping complex on Bodija Rd. There's also ***Chicken Out*** (we did!) on Oyo Rd, a fast-food place down the hill from Premier Hotel.

ARIADNE VAN ZANDBERGEN

ARIADNE VAN ZANDBERGEN

ARIADNE VAN ZANDBERGEN

JOHN ELK III

Costume and clothing is often elaborate and colourful and varies across tribal groups. Women choose their head-dress carefully and wear it with pride: marriage dress, Soma, Gambia (top left); matching patterns, Banjul, Gambia (top right); Wolof woman in traditional blue, Banjul, Gambia (bottom left); fashionable threads, Mopti, Mali (bottom right).

ARIADNE VAN ZANDBERGEN

JOHN ELK III

ARIADNE VAN ZANDBERGEN

ARIADNE VAN ZANDBERGEN

FRANCES LINZEE GORDON

There are two striking aspects of traditional West African costume – unique style and colour: Tuareg woman, Timbuktu, Mali (top left); Tuareg girl covered head to toe, Mali (top right); Peul man, Djenné, Mali (bottom right); Peul woman wearing traditional earrings, Djenné, Mali (bottom left); Dogon man, Mali (middle left)

Restaurants The best European food in town is found at the IITA's ***restaurant***. For about N1300 you can get a three-course meal – soup, roast and vegetables, and desserts. Every now and then there is live entertainment or theme nights, for example French night, when cheese, wine and regional delicacies are provided.

Fortune Restaurant *(27 Kudeti Ave)* Meals around N900. Open lunch & dinner Mon-Fri, dinner Sat. The Fortune, one of Ibadan's best restaurants, serves Chinese cuisine. It's 150m beyond the Onireke Guesthouse.

Dragon d'Or is a Chinese restaurant at Premier Hotel that is also quite good; it has similar prices to the Fortune Restaurant.

Koko Dome Restaurant is a pleasant and moderately priced restaurant, near Cocoa House. It has Middle Eastern and European selections for N600 per plate (the African dishes are a little more expensive). It also has a snack bar by the pool.

The Cabin is another good place for Lebanese food. It's on the street north of Egunjenmi St and is known for its excellent mezzes.

Entertainment

Ibadan is a quiet place most of the time.

The Cave *(Ogunmola St)* features live music every night, usually a highlife or juju outfit. Watch for curious additions to your bill, usually ordered by female 'friends' who have ordered drinks on your tab; beers are otherwise cheap.

Cotton Club *(Awolowo Ave)*, east of Oyo Rd, is a good bar and has pool tables, TV and Western-style food.

Koko Dome Restaurant has the ***African Queen Bar*** downstairs and the ***Legends Nightclub*** upstairs; both are haunts of Lebanese businesspeople.

Getting There & Away

Bush Taxi There are bush taxis and minibuses for Lagos and points east leaving from New Garage Motor Park on the southern outskirts of town off Lagos Rd; they also leave from Challenge Motor Park near the junction of Lagos and Ring Rds.

Vehicles leave every few minutes for Lagos (N80 to N100), which is just over an hour away. Vehicles travelling to Benin City (N300), Onitsha and other points east take longer to fill. Ojoo Motor Park, which also serves Lagos and is on the northern outskirts of town, has a greater variety of vehicles, including Peugeot taxis (N110).

Vehicles headed for Kaduna, Kano and other points north leave from Sango Motor Park on Oyo Rd. Peugeot taxis to Kano (N1100, 11 hours) and Abuja (N900, eight hours) usually leave by 7am. Bush taxis for Ife (N80) and Oshogbo (N80) leave from Egbede Motor Park on the southeast side of town at the junction of Ife and Lagos Rds.

To get here from Lagos, catch bush taxis (N100) at Iddo Motor Park.

Train The train system is so unreliable you would have to be studying the inefficiencies of rail transport in Nigeria first hand to want to use it. Ask for details of services at the train station, which is one block west of Dugbe Market.

Getting Around

You'll find plenty of inner-city minibuses and taxis on Dugbe Rd across from the market; get a shared taxi to take you there (N10 to N20).

OSHOGBO

☎ 035 • pop 500,000

This quiet but unattractive town, the capital of Osun State, was once one of the most creative and artistic places in Africa. Unfortunately, the art attractions and related centres are looking decidedly tired these days. On the last Friday in August, the town hosts the colourful Oshun Festival.

Osun Sacred Forest

Oshogbo is also famous for its Sacred Forest on the outskirts of town, a half-hour walk from the Oba's Palace. This collection of sacred shrines to various Yoruba gods appears to be reverting to the forest as its cement and laterite mix crumbles and vines encroach into the inner sanctums. However, much work is being done to maintain the shrines (see the boxed text 'The Sacred Forest' later). For a tour, ask the caretakers (priestesses), although they seem to require donations at every shrine.

Things to See & Do

In its heyday, Oshogbo was the flourishing centre of the Oshogbo School of Art, a

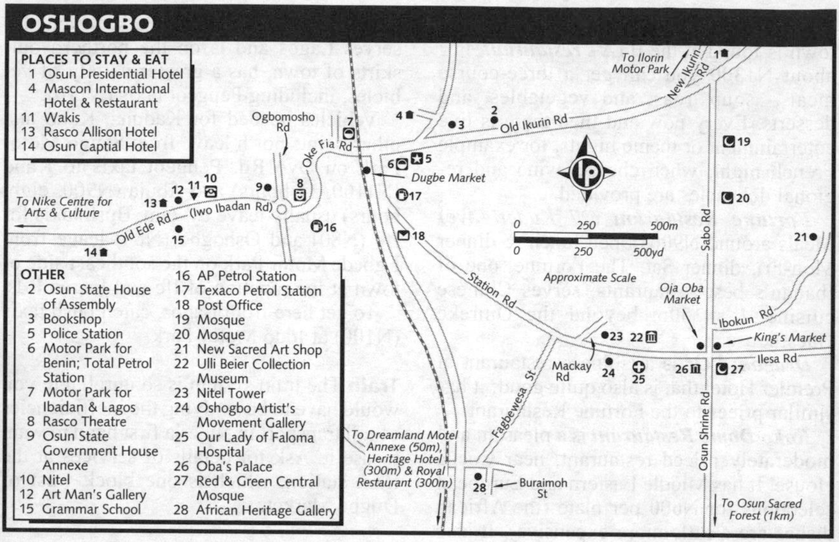
OSHOGBO
PLACES TO STAY & EAT
1 Osun Presidential Hotel
4 Mascon International Hotel & Restaurant
11 Wakis
13 Rasco Allison Hotel
14 Osun Captial Hotel
OTHER
2 Osun State House of Assembly
3 Bookshop
5 Police Station
6 Motor Park for Benin; Total Petrol Station
7 Motor Park for Ibadan & Lagos
8 Rasco Theatre
9 Osun State Government House Annexe
10 Nitel
12 Art Man's Gallery
15 Grammar School
16 AP Petrol Station
17 Texaco Petrol Station
18 Post Office
19 Mosque
20 Mosque
21 New Sacred Art Shop
22 Ulli Beier Collection Museum
23 Nitel Tower
24 Oshogbo Artist's Movement Gallery
25 Our Lady of Faloma Hospital
26 Oba's Palace
27 Red & Green Central Mosque
28 African Heritage Gallery
To Ilorin Motor Park
New Ikurin Rd
Old Ikurin Rd
Ogbomosho Rd
Oke Fia Rd
Dugbe Market
To Nike Centre for Arts & Culture
Old Ede Rd (Iwo Ibadan Rd)
Station Rd
Approximate Scale
0 250 500m
0 250 500yd
Oja Oba Market
Ibokun Rd
King's Market
Ilesa Rd
Sabo Rd
Osun Shrine Rd
Mackay Rd
Fagbewesa St
Buraimoh St
To Dreamland Motel Annexe (50m), Heritage Hotel (300m) & Royal Restaurant (300m)
To Osun Sacred Forest (1km)

movement that was started in the 1960s by a European couple, Ulli and Georgina Beier. Their students experimented with beads, wool, plastic strips and wood. To see some of the artists' work, you'll have to visit individual studios, as there is no central outlet for the sale of Oshogbo art (the Nike Centre for Arts & Culture is 1km out of town).

Two galleries stand out: the **Art Man's Gallery** *(Old Ede Rd)* and Jimoh Buraimoh's **African Heritage Gallery** *(1 Buraimoh St)*. There is also the small **Ulli Beier Collection Museum** *(Station Rd)*. The **New Sacred Art Shop** *(41A Ibokun Rd)* sells copies of Austrian sculptor Suzanne Wenger's *Sacred Groves of Oshogbo* as well as other pieces of art.

Be sure to wander through the **Oja Oba Market** across from the Oba's Palace. The market is packed with stalls selling juju material and a number of shrines to various gods. The richly painted building, decorated with intricate carvings and facing the present palace, is reputed to be the original Oba's palace in Oshogbo.

Places to Stay & Eat

This friendly and clean ***Osun Capital Hotel*** *(☎ 230396, Old Ede Rd)*, with singles with fan and shared bathroom for N350, is relatively cheap.

Rasco Allison Hotel *(☎ 233046, Old Ede Rd)* Singles N350. This place has an open bar, but the rooms are grimy.

Mascon International Hotel & Restaurant *(Just off Old Ikurin Rd)* Singles/doubles N300/480. Rooms at the Mascon International have fans and bathroom with buckets; the nightclub here is busy on weekends. The upstairs restaurant serves abysmal food and offers little choice.

Heritage Hotel *(☎ 234285, Okefia St)* Singles N900. The artist Jimoh Buraimoh's Heritage Hotel is 1km south of town. It has comfortable air-con singles with TV. The restaurant here serves suya.

Osun Presidential Hotel *(☎ 232399, Old Ikurin Rd)* Doubles N3000, plus N4000 deposit. The city's best hotel is the Osun Presidential. Rooms have air-con, TV and shower. It has a cinema (on weekends), a nightclub, and an overpriced restaurant.

You'll find many restaurants along Old Ede Rd; just look for the 'Food is Ready' signs. ***Wakis*** is on this strip. For a splurge go to ***Royal Restaurant*** *(Buraimoh St)* near Heritage Hotel, to the south of town.

Getting There & Around

Bush taxis leave throughout the day from the motor park on Oke Fia Rd near the town centre; typical fares are N80 to Ibadan, N175 to Lagos and N350 to Benin City.

The Sacred Forest

Since the 1950s, Austrian sculptor Suzanne Wenger has been working in the Sacred Forest outside Oshogbo to bring the Yoruba shrines back to life through her imaginative restorations.

Called Aduni Olosa, meaning 'Adored One', by the local inhabitants, Wenger is now so highly regarded that the local women have made her the priestess of two cults.

With the help of local artisans she has worked on restoring the old shrines while adding her own touches. The result is a forest of spectacular, monumental and truly unique shrines. While they are totally different in style from what is traditionally associated with African art, the inspiration is still Yoruba.

The principal shrine is that of the river goddess Oshuno, in a grove enclosed by an imaginatively designed wall. By the sacred river, near the Lya Mapa grove where huge new sculptures soar skywards, you can see a monumental and complex cement sculpture to Ifa, the divine Yoruba oracle. Another impressive sculpture, approximately 5m high, is the shrine to Onkoro, the mother goddess.

It's easy to get to Oshogbo from Lagos (Iddo Motor Park) or Ibadan (Egbede Motor Park).

For getting around Oshogbo, expect to pay about N30 for a taxi trip across town.

BENIN CITY

☎ 052 • pop 400,000

Until the British sacked it, Benin City was one of the great cities of West Africa, dating back to the 10th century AD. Human sacrifice was a part of Bini culture and was thought to appease the gods. When a British contingent arrived in 1897, a ceremony was held in an attempt to ward off the invaders. Upon entering the walled city, the conquering troops encountered the shocking sight of countless decapitated corpses. However, this didn't stop the British carting 2000 bronze statutes from the Oba's Palace back to Europe. The Western world was astounded by their quality and museums pounced on the work. The bronzes of Benin became one of the first styles of African art to win worldwide recognition.

Today Benin City, capital of Edo State, is a sprawling, undistinguished place. However, it has several interesting sights that locals will proudly show you, including the Okada's House opposite Bendal Edo Hotel. It is opulent, and has many interesting statues outside.

A good time to visit Benin City is December, when the seven-day Igue/Ewere Festival, featuring traditional dances, a mock battle and a procession to the palace, and the nine-day New Yams Festival take place around Edo State.

Orientation

Fortunately, you can find your way through the sprawl to most of the sights and services, as they are mostly near Ring Rd. This road circles King's Square, which has the National Museum at its centre. Akpakpava Rd runs northeast; Sapele and Sapoba Rds run southeast from Ring Rd. You will find plenty of places to stay, restaurants, shops and local transport along these routes.

Information

The official guides at the National Museum are great sources of information, and make up for the lack of an information office (a small tip is appreciated).

The post office is on Airport Rd next to the hospital.

The FBN is on Ring Rd.

National Museum

The museum *(admission N10; open 9am-6pm daily)*, built in 1973, is the city's major landmark, and is in the centre of town. The star attraction of the museum is the famous bronze work, produced mainly for the king's court. The pieces on display are good but not spectacular: the more notable pieces of art are on show in London. Photographs make up a sizeable part of the collection. Upstairs is an excellent Okokaybe dancer's costume and headdress, as well as masks, stools, doorways, terracotta, pottery and ivory carvings.

Warning

Benin City was off limits at the time of research due to violence that spilled over from nearby Warri. Although such problems flare up and fade away quickly, get an update on the situation in Lagos before heading out.

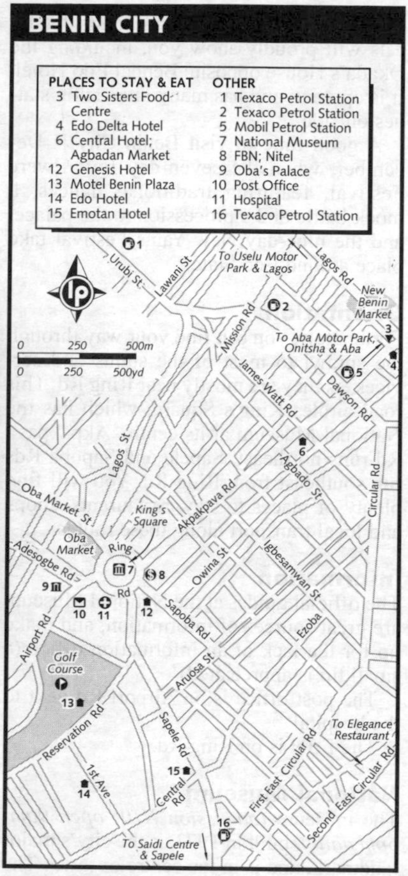
BENIN CITY
PLACES TO STAY & EAT
3 Two Sisters Food Centre
4 Edo Delta Hotel
6 Central Hotel; Agbadan Market
12 Genesis Hotel
13 Motel Benin Plaza
14 Edo Hotel
15 Emotan Hotel
OTHER
1 Texaco Petrol Station
2 Texaco Petrol Station
5 Mobil Petrol Station
7 National Museum
8 FBN; Nitel
9 Oba's Palace
10 Post Office
11 Hospital
16 Texaco Petrol Station
To Uselu Motor Park & Lagos
New Benin Market
To Aba Motor Park, Onitsha & Aba
Urubi St
Lawani St
Lagos Rd
Mission Rd
James Watt Rd
Dawson Rd
Lagos St
Agbado St
Circular Rd
Oba Market St
King's Square
Akpakpava Rd
Oba Market
Ring Rd
Adesogbe Rd
Owina St
Igbesamwan St
Sapoba Rd
Ezoba
Airport Rd
Golf Course
Aruosa St
Reservation Rd
Sapele Rd
To Elegance Restaurant
First East Circular Rd
Second East Circular Rd
1st Ave
Central Rd
To Saidi Centre & Sapele
0 250 500m
0 250 500yd

Oba's Palace

The mud-walled Oba's Palace, a block southwest of the museum, is quite spectacular. The palace contains sculptures, brass relics and other art depicting historical events during Benin City's heyday. It also has an impressive array of traditional crafts, historic bronzes, ivory and other works of art. You need the secretary's permission to visit, but he's a busy man. Moreover, you're supposed to request permission a week or so in advance, so few travellers actually manage to see the palace.

Places to Stay

Central Hotel *(☎ 200780, 76 Akpakpava Rd)* Singles/doubles with fan N350/480, doubles with air-con N550. This hotel is looking a bit rough around the edges, but it is friendly and has reasonable rooms. The rooms all have their own bathrooms (with buckets, of course), and the hotel has a restaurant and a bar (with live music).

Edo Delta Hotel *(128 Akpakpava Rd)* Singles/doubles N550/600, suites N850. The quiet and pleasant Edo Delta has rooms with fan and shared bathroom, as well as air-con suites with bathroom.

Genesis Hotel *(☎ 240066, 4 Sapoba Rd)* Singles/doubles N800/1100. For convenience, you can't beat the friendly Genesis Hotel, formerly Lixborr, just off King's Square. Rooms with air-con and bathroom are good value. It has a vibrant bar; the restaurant here is a bit pricey.

Edo Hotel *(☎ 200120, 1st Ave)* Singles/doubles with fan N850/1050. The best value is the old Edo, formerly Bendel Hotel, 1km southwest of the museum. It's set in extensive manicured grounds and has a lot of old colonial character.

Emotan Hotel *(☎ 200130, 1 Central Rd)* Rooms N2300. This well-maintained hotel just off Sapele Rd is the best buy in the 'slightly upmarket' category. The spacious rooms have colour TV and bathroom, and there is a restaurant.

Motel Benin Plaza *(☎ 201430, 1 Reservation Rd)* Singles/doubles N2500/2800, plus N4000 deposit. This place, near Emotan Hotel, has air-con rooms with TV.

Places to Eat

There are many ***street stalls*** along Akpakpava Rd, especially in the Agbadan Market next to Central Hotel, around Oba Market, and many stalls (including suya places) around New Benin Market on Lagos Rd.

Two Sisters Food Centre Meals around N150. This clean and friendly eatery is a great cheap place. It's opposite Edo Delta Hotel, and serves generous meals.

Elegance Restaurant *(Cnr Sapoba Rd & Murtala Mohammed Way)* is another excellent choice for cheap Nigerian dishes.

For European food, the best places are the ***restaurant*** at Emotan Hotel (with meals for N450) and the ***Saidi Centre*** *(Sapele Rd)*; the latter also serves Chinese food.

Getting There & Away

The motor park for Onitsha, Enugu and other points east is Aba Motor Park on Akpakpava Rd, several kilometres northeast of the museum. For Lagos (N300) and Ibadan (N250), the Uselu Motor Park is on Lagos Rd on the northwestern outskirts of town.

Large buses also serve these cities and are slightly cheaper than bush taxis. Ekene Dili Chukwu, one of the main companies, has offices at Mile-2 bus stop on Urubi St.

Getting Around

Around town, shared taxis will cost N30; motorcycle-taxis are N10 to N20, depending on the distance.

OKOMU SANCTUARY

Nature lovers wanting to see one of the few remaining areas of rainforest in Nigeria should head for this sanctuary *(NCF; ☎ 01-268 6163, 5 Moseley Rd, Ikoyi, Lagos)*, near Udo, 40 minutes by car northwest of Benin City. The NCF is the major force behind this important sanctuary, home to the endangered white-throated monkey and the elusive forest elephant, to say nothing of birds and butterflies. You can bird-watch from a tree house, a dizzying 65m above the ground, overlooking the lake. The reserve also has an educational centre.

The NCF has a ***dormitory*** at the educational centre with simple/plush rooms for N750/2200. There's better lodging at the African Timber & Plywood ***guesthouse***.

For permission to enter the sanctuary and to book accommodation, contact the NCF. To get here, you'll need your own transport or to take a taxi.

PORT HARCOURT

☎ 084 • pop 1 million

Built as a port for exporting coal from Enugu, Port Harcourt in Rivers State now has another *raison d'être*: oil. All around town you can see oil flares at night. Wealth has made Port Harcourt one of Nigeria's most expensive cities, but the fact that this wealth ends up in Abuja rather than the delta has also made it one of the country's most unpredictable and aggressive. It is continually plagued by power cuts and, enigmatically, fuel shortages.

New Market, on Bonny St (with its nearby fish market) are of interest, although beware of the many thieves.

On Azikwe Rd you'll find the train station, major banks, the post office and department stores such as Chanrais. Aggrey Rd in the old township is another commercial centre with food stalls and shops. The Rivers State Ministry of Tourism (☎ 334901) is up and functioning again at 35 Aba Rd. The Ideal Travel Agency in the Nigeria Airways building is a good source of information for trips to Brass and Bonny Islands in the Niger Delta (see The Niger Delta section, following).

Places to Stay

Port Harcourt's cheapest hotels are not cheap compared with hotels elsewhere in Nigeria, Lagos excepted.

Hotel Ferguson *(☎ 230505, 1B Elelenwo St)* Doubles/minisuites N3000/3750. The quiet, quirky Ferguson is one of the least-expensive and comfortable places you'll find in Port Harcourt, if you can put up with the antics of the chef. Forget eating or drinking here, but clean rooms with air-con, bathroom and TV provide a nice oasis.

Delta Hotel *(☎ 300190, 1-3 Harley St)* Doubles/mini-suites N2800/4000. The Delta is a good choice, and although it's a little removed from the interesting part of town, this makes it quiet and relaxing. The nicely maintained rooms have air-con, TV and telephone. It has a decent bar and restaurant.

Seanel International *(☎ 332141, 2 Okorodo St)* Singles/doubles N2500/3500. This place has small dark rooms. The singles have fans, and the doubles have air-con.

Cedar Palace Hotel *(☎ 300180, Harbour Rd)* Singles/doubles N2500/4500. This rundown hotel is in the central port area. Rooms have TV, fridge and shower. The restaurant serves basic meals; the popular bar attracts sailors.

Rachael Hotels Ltd *(☎ 334191, 4 Harbour Rd)* Doubles N3450. Close to the Cedar Palace is Rachael Hotels Ltd, which was inexplicably voted best hotel in Port Harcourt twice. It's since gone to seed, and has dusty halls and grimy rooms.

Presidential Hotel *(☎ 310400, Aba Rd)* Rooms from N11,000, plus N15,000 deposit. This is the city's top hotel and as the prices reflect, it's used to catering to the oil crowd. ADC Airlines, Chanchangi, Lufthansa and EAS Airlines have their offices here and you'll find it easy to change money. As a nonguest, you can also use the pool for N100, visit the town's best cinema or dine in the restaurants (see Places to Eat, following).

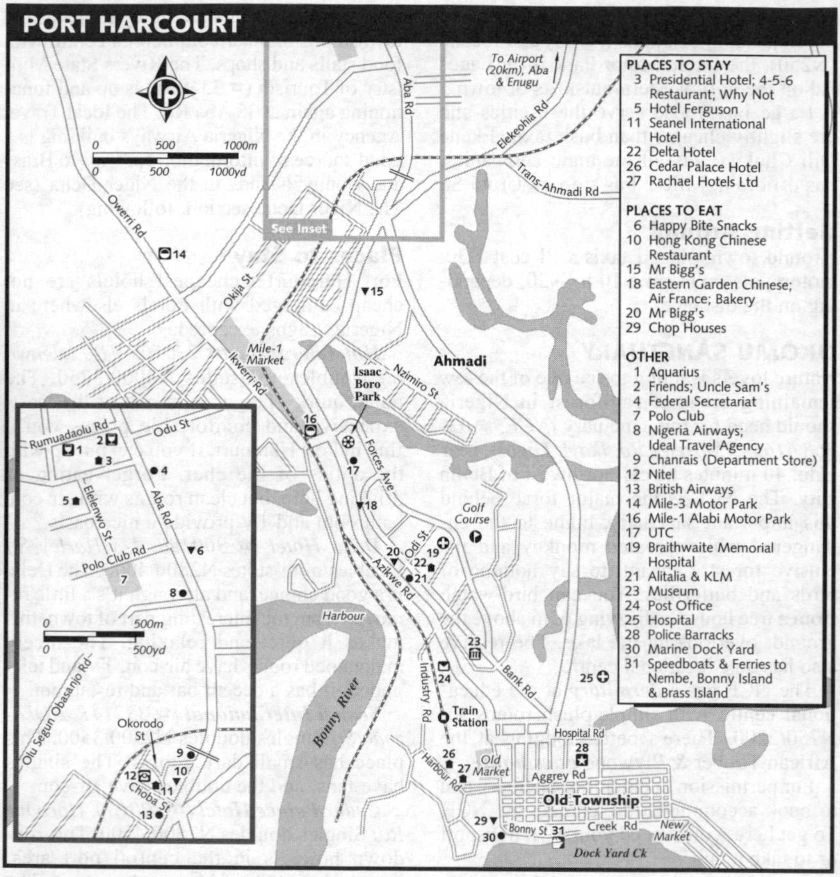
PORT HARCOURT
0
500
1000m
0
500
1000yd
To Airport (20km), Aba & Enugu
Aba Rd
Elekeohia Rd
Trans-Ahmadi Rd
See Inset
Owerri Rd
14
Okija St
15
Mile-1 Market
Ikwerri Rd
Isaac Boro Park
Nzimiro St
Ahmadi
16
17
Forces Ave
18
Golf Course
Odi St
19
20
22
21
Azikwe Rd
Harbour
Bonny River
Industry Rd
23
24
Bank Rd
25
Train Station
Hospital Rd
28
26
27
Old Market
Harbour Rd
Aggrey Rd
Old Township
29
30
Bonny St
31
Creek Rd
New Market
Dock Yard Ck
Rumuadaolu Rd
Odu St
1
2
3
4
5
Elelenwo St
Aba Rd
Polo Club Rd
6
7
8
0
500m
0
500yd
Olu Segun Obasanjo Rd
Okorodo St
9
10
12
11
Choba St
13
PLACES TO STAY
3 Presidential Hotel; 4-5-6 Restaurant; Why Not
5 Hotel Ferguson
11 Seanel International Hotel
22 Delta Hotel
26 Cedar Palace Hotel
27 Rachael Hotels Ltd
PLACES TO EAT
6 Happy Bite Snacks
10 Hong Kong Chinese Restaurant
15 Mr Bigg's
18 Eastern Garden Chinese; Air France; Bakery
20 Mr Bigg's
29 Chop Houses
OTHER
1 Aquarius
2 Friends; Uncle Sam's
4 Federal Secretariat
7 Polo Club
8 Nigeria Airways; Ideal Travel Agency
9 Chanrais (Department Store)
12 Nitel
13 British Airways
14 Mile-3 Motor Park
16 Mile-1 Alabi Motor Park
17 UTC
19 Braithwaite Memorial Hospital
21 Alitalia & KLM
23 Museum
24 Post Office
25 Hospital
28 Police Barracks
30 Marine Dock Yard
31 Speedboats & Ferries to Nembe, Bonny Island & Brass Island

Though it's not worth staying here, the bar is definitely worth a drink or two in the evening.

Places to Eat

For inexpensive chop, try any of the ***suya* stalls** scattered throughout the grid of the old township or the stalls at New Market. These stalls are all lit by lamps, and with the frequent power cuts in the port it is probably the best light you'll get. For predictable fast food, try ***Mr Bigg's*** just north of Chanrais supermarket on Azikwe Rd or ***Happy Bite Snacks*** on Aba Rd just south of the Federal Secretariat.

On Aba Rd there are some better restaurants with a wider range of cuisines and prices. For reasonable Chinese meals, try ***Hong Kong Chinese Restaurant*** on Aba Rd or ***Eastern Garden Chinese*** a block to the east of Aba Rd, south of Mile-1 Alabi Motor Park. There's also a ***bakery*** next door to the Eastern Garden that has excellent pastries and baked bread.

At Presidential Hotel, ***4-5-6 Restaurant*** serves passable but overpriced Chinese food (dishes from N1200) and ***Why Not*** has pizzas (N1200), good Lebanese dishes (N900) and European fare (N700). Remember to wear your long pants, or you may end up borrowing a pair from the cook.

Entertainment

Aquarius *(Rumuadaolu Rd)* Cover charge N100. This venue is one of the city's most popular nightclubs.

Friends Cover charge N100. Near Aquarius, and known to all taxi drivers, Friends is one of the hottest places in town, but ***Uncle Sam's***, entered from Friends, is even hotter (there's an additional N200 entry). Both these places are basically white male hang-outs with prostitutes galore.

The ***nightclub*** at Presidential Hotel is more comfortable for women.

Getting There & Away

Air Flying to and from Port Harcourt is a good alternative to taking buses and bush taxis, given the state of roads to nearby major cities, and the seemingly endless violence in Warri, between Lagos and Port Harcourt. The airport is 20km to the north on Elekeohia Rd. Almost all the domestic carriers have offices here.

Bus & Bush Taxi The main motor park for all destinations is on Owerri Rd at Mile-3. You'll probably arrive here. The smaller Mile-1 Abali Motor Park on Azikwe Rd is better for some destinations, including Aba (N100), Calabar (N350), Enugu (N200), Benin City (N350) and Lagos (N700). The best way to get here from Lagos is by overnight bus.

Boat Speedboats to the delta towns of Nembe, Bonny Island and Brass Island leave from the Bonny St Wharf (see Getting There & Away under Brass Island later in this chapter). The huge public ferries are cheaper but are dangerous; one went down a few years ago with the loss of at least 200 lives.

THE NIGER DELTA

The Niger Delta is Nigeria's most fascinating region, and anyone who perseveres with a visit to Nigeria, the toughest of destinations, should not miss it. However, extreme care should be taken as the delta is infamous for kidnappings. Foreigners are often presumed to be oil employees and, therefore, worth holding for ransom.

Those interested in forging into the hinterland can hire a car and driver at Presidential Hotel in Port Harcourt for the day for about N6000 and simply cruise around. Good destinations are Brass Island (see following), Kane in Ogoniland (two hours southeast of Port Harcourt), home of Ken Saro-Wiwa, or Akaraolu (45 minutes from Port Harcourt), a friendly fishing village suffering in the heat of an Italian natural-gas flare. Visiting small villages such as these make a trip to Nigeria worthwhile, as you can get a sense of the true difficulty of living in this oil-rich region. If you wish to spend the night, arrangements must be made with locals, as neither destination has restaurants or hotels.

Otherwise, you could hire a boat at the dock yard in Port Harcourt and get happily lost in this region of convoluted waterways, palm-fringed creeks, mangroves, palm oil distilleries and traditional fishing villages. Keep in mind that once you're on the water, extracting yourself from a difficult situation might not be easy.

Brass Island

This Nembe community is a paradise: it has a vehicle-free town centre, loads of places to buy fresh fish, comfy bars, and it offers tourists the chance to stay in the houses of villagers. However, it is hard to get to. Have all your immigration papers handy as the immigration officials will do anything to get a dash – don't give in!

Brass Island got its name from a misunderstanding. When the British arrived, eager to map this relatively unknown part of the world, they sought information from a lone woman. An officer gripped the woman by the shoulder and demanded 'Where are we?'. She retaliated with *'Barasi'* (meaning 'Leave me alone' in Nembe). The map makers gleefully jotted the location down as 'Brass'! The British traditions live on and you will see the village elders dressed in top hats and buttoned-up turn-of-the-century striped shirts and sporting walking sticks and ornamental umbrellas.

Once you get to Brass you have really arrived in remote Africa. It's reminiscent of Lamu in Kenya. Wander the streets, enjoy the food (periwinkles, scampi and lady fish), talk with the locals, watch future football champions battle it out barefoot on the dusty oval, sample good palm wine and enjoy the peaceful surroundings and 24-hour electricity.

Places to Stay & Eat There are two nice hotels in Brass, both in the southern part of town near the creek. One is known locally as ***Uncle Erasmus***. A bed in either will cost about N1200: the rooms have fans and windows with mosquito screens. Both have bars and restaurants.

You can also stay with locals, as we did. Ask at the wharf for ***Nana Begold*** – a stay at her home will be a highlight. The amenities are basic, but the food and hospitality are superb (N1500 would be fair for meals and bed).

There is a great ***bar*** near the creek. It has a rickety pool table, sumptuous African meals and cheap, cold beers.

Getting There & Away Brass Island can be reached from Port Harcourt or from Yenagoa, the capital of the newly created Bayelsa State (the former western section of Rivers). A speedboat from Yenagoa takes just over two hours to get to Brass (N250 to N500) and from Port Harcourt four hours (N500 to N600); local ferries cost N150 and N200, respectively. To get to Yenagoa from Port Harcourt take a bus from Mile-1 Alabi Motor Park (N100, two hours).

NIGERIA

CALABAR

☎ 087

Calabar is in the far southeast, and records twice as much rainfall as Lagos. Old colonial Calabar is popular with travellers passing through Nigeria, especially those headed for Cameroon, 25km away. High on a hill, Calabar commands a fine view of the Calabar River and the frenetic fish market at Hawkins Beach (busy on Thursday, Friday, Sunday and Monday).

Calabar is small by Nigerian standards, which makes it a liveable and likeable city, if you can overlook the Nigerian military personnel posted on every street corner defending against the constantly threatened police revolt.

If you don't feel like walking, you'll find that motorcycle-taxis are everywhere and are dirt cheap.

The beautiful old governor's residency on the hill overlooking the river has been converted into the city's **museum** *(admission N50; open 9am-6pm daily)*. It's well worth a visit. This fascinating and impressive collection covers the precolonial days, the slave-trade era, the palm-oil trade, the British invasion in the late 19th century and independence. It also has a great view of the river.

Places to Stay

Stardos Guesthouse *(7A O'Dwyer St)* The most inviting place to stay for cheap accommodation is the family-run Stardos. A furnished room with fan and bathroom with bucket shower will set you back N650 (N1000 with air-con).

Chalsma Hotel *(☎ 221942, 7 Otop Abasi St)* Singles/doubles with air-con from N1200/2500. This hotel is also a good choice in the budget range – some rooms have air-con and bathroom; there are also smaller rooms with fan that are a bit cheaper.

Ellinah Guest House *(☎ 223151, 20 Hawkins Rd)* Singles/doubles N400/600. This guesthouse has excellent-value meals, friendly staff and terrific views of the river, fish market and sunsets. The clean rooms contain TV and fridge are very reasonably priced. Make time to enjoy a pot of tea on the small terrace.

Nsisak Seaside Hotel *(45 Euo Edem St)* Rooms N600. The Nsisak Seaside Hotel is thoroughly rundown, but that's part of its appeal. Visitors staying in the threadbare rooms with their panoramic views will feel as if they're in the time of Francis Drake. The 3rd floor glassed-in bar is perfect for watching sunsets.

Metropolitan Hotel *(☎ 220913, Calabar Rd)* Doubles with TV, air-con & bathroom about N6500, plus N2500 deposit. The Metropolitan is the city's finest hotel; it's decidedly utilitarian but is comfortable.

Places to Eat

Mr Magik Restaurant is just off Inyang NTA Henshaw St. Mr and Mrs Magik will make you anything, but check the price before ordering. The Calabar soup with periwinkles and the local delicacy, *ekpang nkukwo ikpong* (cocoyam wrapped in cocoyam leaves; N100), are delicious. There is also pounded yam (N30) and pork kebabs (N120) – yum. Allow your hosts time to prepare the food.

Other places to eat include the ***chop houses*** on Calabar Rd across from the stadium; ***Glamour Restaurant*** *(77 Egerton St)*, where gari costs N100; the ***Maris Restaurant*** *(Chamley St)* for bush meat and plantain; and ***Freddy's Restaurant*** *(☎ 222821, 90 Atekong Dr)* for humous (N375), fish pepper soup (N300) and ice cream (N175).

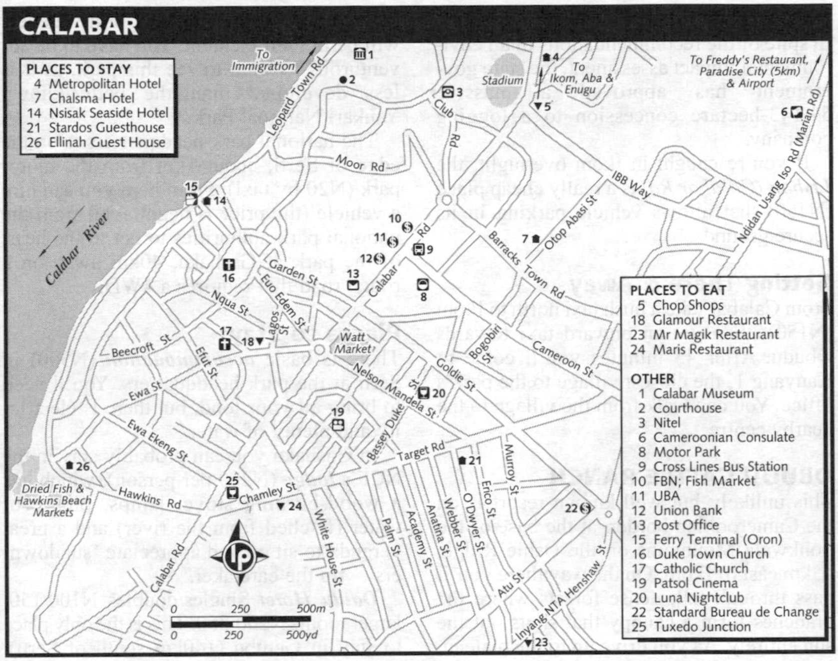
CALABAR
PLACES TO STAY
4 Metropolitan Hotel
7 Chalsma Hotel
14 Nsisak Seaside Hotel
21 Stardos Guesthouse
26 Ellinah Guest House
PLACES TO EAT
5 Chop Shops
18 Glamour Restaurant
23 Mr Magik Restaurant
24 Maris Restaurant
OTHER
1 Calabar Museum
2 Courthouse
3 Nitel
6 Cameroonian Consulate
8 Motor Park
9 Cross Lines Bus Station
10 FBN; Fish Market
11 UBA
12 Union Bank
13 Post Office
15 Ferry Terminal (Oron)
16 Duke Town Church
17 Catholic Church
19 Patsol Cinema
20 Luna Nightclub
22 Standard Bureau de Change
25 Tuxedo Junction
To Immigration
Leopard Town Rd
Stadium
To Ikom, Aba & Enugu
To Freddy's Restaurant, Paradise City (5km) & Airport
Ndidan Usang Iso Rd (Marian Rd)
Club Rd
Moor Rd
IBB Way
Otop Abasi St
Barracks Town Rd
Calabar River
Calabar Rd
Garden St
Euo Edem St
Nqua St
Lagos St
Watt Market
Beecroft St
Efut St
Ewa St
Ewa Ekeng St
Nelson Mandela St
Goldie St
Bogobiri St
Cameroon St
Bassey Duke St
Target Rd
Murroy St
Erico St
O'Dwyer St
Webber St
Anatina St
Academy St
Palm St
White House St
Chamley St
Hawkins Rd
Dried Fish & Hawkins Beach Markets
Atu St
Inyang NTA Henshaw St
0 250 500m
0 250 500yd

Entertainment

Luna Nightclub *(18 Nelson Mandela St)* has live music and also serves food.

Tuxedo Junction *(147 Calabar Rd)*, at the intersection with Chamley St, looks worn and out of energy, but it's still a popular place to head for if you like listening to music.

Paradise City is the most popular of the discos.

Getting There & Away

Nigeria Airways, Chanchangi and ADC Airlines have flights between Calabar and Lagos.

Bush taxis and minibuses leave from the motor park on Cameroon St. Cross Lines bus station is across the street and charges N500 for the four-hour ride to Port Harcourt, N700 to Lagos, N600 for the 12 hour ride to Abuja and N750 for the marathon ride to Kaduna; the condition of the buses is variable.

One way into Cameroon is north via Ikom and Mfum. Bush taxis to Mfum cost N50; from there you can walk into Cameroon.

AROUND CALABAR

A good day trip from Calabar is to the tranquil village of **Creek Town**, a short, relaxing trip up the river. You'll meet locals going about their business as you wander along the dusty roads. Look out for the incongruous colonial church.

CROSS RIVER NATIONAL PARK

This national park is north of Calabar and is set in a lush rainforest that contains waterfalls, birds and gorillas. You can hike in the park. Ask at the park office (3 Ebuta Crescent, Ette Agbor Layout, Calabar) for information and an introductory letter; it also has information on nearby Mbe Mountain National Park.

Cross River National Park is managed jointly by the World Wide Fund for Nature (WWF) and the NCF, which has a centre near Kanyang 1, north of Ikom on the road to Obudu. You can arrange for a guide there as well as get information on the **Mbe Mountain Conservation Project**, where the gorillas live.

The WWF has advised that the Ikrigon Forest Reserve, part of the Cross River

National Park, is under threat from logging. In spite of the recommendations of an environmental impact assessment, the state government has approved a massive 54,143-hectare concession to a logging company.

If you're caught in Ikom overnight, the ***Lisbon*** *(Calabar Rd)* is a really cheap place (N450) that allows vehicle parking in its secure grounds.

Getting There & Away

From Calabar take a bush taxi north to Ikom (N150), then get an onward taxi towards Obudu. After 45 minutes you'll come to Kanyang 1, the closest village to the park's office. You can walk from the village to the nearby centre.

NIGERIA

OBUDU CATTLE RANCH

This unlikely but well-known resort is on the Cameroonian border, at the base of the Sonkwala Mountains on the Oshie Ridge, 45km east of Ikom. On the way there you'll pass through tall, dense forests where the branches form a canopy that shuts out the sun entirely. As you drive up to the plateau, you'll see rolling mountain ranges.

Built during the 1950s by Scottish ranchers, this was at one time a well-functioning ranch-resort. These days it's rundown but it is slowly being renovated (with VSO's help).

Obudu Ranch Hotel has chalets, tennis courts and horses. The rooms are not cheap (around N2750); for reservations write to Obudu Cattle Ranch, PO Box 40, Obudu, Cross River State.

By vehicle the 110km drive east from Ogoja to the ranch via Obudu is straightforward and the road is sealed part of the way. Otherwise, take a motorcycle or bush taxi from Obudu, which is 44km north of the ranch.

GASHAKA GUMPTI NATIONAL PARK

Gashaka Gumpti *(admission N60)* is Nigeria's largest national park and has the country's highest mountain, **Chappal Wadi** (2418m). Within its large area is a plethora of rivers and the most diverse ecology of any Nigerian park, including guinea savanna, grasslands and pockets of mountain (or gallery) forest. Elephants, hippos, waterbucks, buffaloes, monkeys and big cats are all found here, and bird-watchers will be in their element. You have to be adventurous to want to see this park, as it is less developed than the better-known Yankari National Park.

The national park headquarters is on the edge of Serti, about 1km from the motor park (N20 by taxi). From here you can hire a vehicle (the price is negotiable) from the national park authorities to get to the heart of the park at Gashaka, 40km away on a rough road that requires a 4WD.

Places to Stay

There is basic ***accommodation*** (N300) in Serti at the park headquarters. You'll need to bring all your food, but there is electricity and plenty of water.

In Gashaka you can probably stay in the NCF's ***lodge*** (N200 per person), which has a wood-burning stove, lamps, plenty of water (fetched from the river) and a great veranda to sit on and appreciate 'sundowners' – tip the caretaker.

Daula Hotel Singles/doubles N100/150, larger rooms N200-350. This is the only place to stay in Gembu (140km south of Serti). There are rooms with shared bucket shower, and larger rooms with private bathroom.

Getting There & Away

Unless you have your own transport, you will have to juggle several bush taxis. To get to Serti from Jalingo or Wukari (N400), take the A4. To get to the park from Gembu, take a bush taxi on the road to Serti (N300).

The Centre

ABUJA

☎ 09

During the oil-boom days of the 1970s, the Nigerian government decided to construct a new capital in an undeveloped central area. Construction began in the early 1980s, which was the worst time possible, as oil revenues were beginning to slide. As a result, construction has proceeded at a snail's pace. The mosque (which is brilliantly lit at night), the law courts and the presidential guesthouse are finished, but the wide boulevards have relatively few vehicles and many lots are still vacant. During the monthly three-hour clean-up the town is as quiet as a morgue.

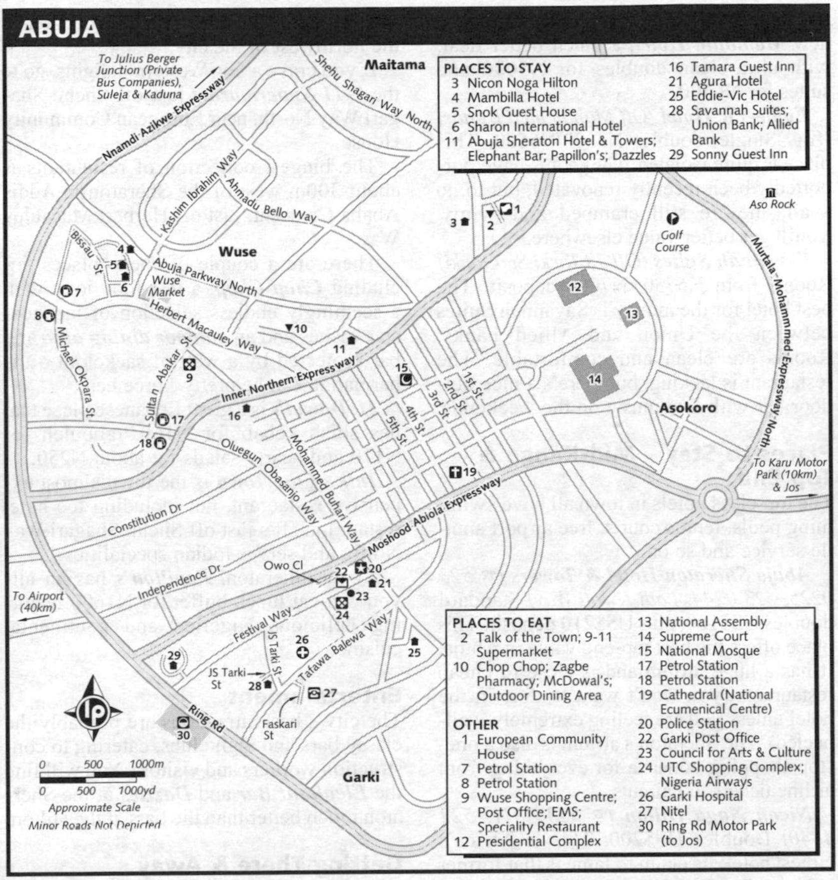
ABUJA
To Julius Berger Junction (Private Bus Companies), Suleja & Kaduna
Maitama
Shehu Shagari Way North
Nnamdi Azikwe Expressway
Kashim Ibrahim Way
Ahmadu Bello Way
Bissau St
Wuse
Abuja Parkway North
Wuse Market
Herbert Macauley Way
Michael Okpara St
Sultan Abakar St
Inner Northern Expressway
Oluegun Obasanjo Way
Mohammed Buhari Way
5th St
4th St
3rd St
2nd St
1st St
Constitution Dr
Independence Dr
Moshood Abiola Expressway
Owo Cl
To Airport (40km)
Festival Way
JS Tarki St
Tafawa Balewa Way
Ring Rd
Faskari St
Garki
Golf Course
Aso Rock
Murtala Mohammed Expressway North
Asokoro
To Karu Motor Park (10km) & Jos
Approximate Scale
Minor Roads Not Depicted
PLACES TO STAY
3 Nicon Noga Hilton
4 Mambilla Hotel
5 Snok Guest House
6 Sharon International Hotel
11 Abuja Sheraton Hotel & Towers; Elephant Bar; Papillon's; Dazzles
16 Tamara Guest Inn
21 Agura Hotel
25 Eddie-Vic Hotel
28 Savannah Suites; Union Bank; Allied Bank
29 Sonny Guest Inn
PLACES TO EAT
2 Talk of the Town; 9-11 Supermarket
10 Chop Chop; Zagbe Pharmacy; McDowal's; Outdoor Dining Area
OTHER
1 European Community House
7 Petrol Station
8 Petrol Station
9 Wuse Shopping Centre; Post Office; EMS; Speciality Restaurant
12 Presidential Complex
13 National Assembly
14 Supreme Court
15 National Mosque
17 Petrol Station
18 Petrol Station
19 Cathedral (National Ecumenical Centre)
20 Police Station
22 Garki Post Office
23 Council for Arts & Culture
24 UTC Shopping Complex; Nigeria Airways
26 Garki Hospital
27 Nitel
30 Ring Rd Motor Park (to Jos)

Abuja is only slowly becoming Nigeria's actual capital; ex-president Abacha moved his government here to a veritable fortress (he needed it!) on Aso Rock. While many official functions are now held in Abuja, which is the Federal Capital Territory (FCT), many ministries are still in Lagos.

One of Nigeria's more famous landmarks is **Zuma Rock**, only 55km from Abuja. This huge granite outcrop is approximately 300m high and 1km long. It's not exactly a spine-tingling sight, but it is somewhat impressive. To get there from Wuse market take a minibus to Suleja (about N75).

Information

The Abuja Sheraton Hotel and Nicon Noga Hilton have information desks. To make telephone calls, the Nitel office is on Faskari St in the Garki district. There's a post office and EMS parcel service in the Wuse Shopping Centre. Nigeria Airways has an office at the UTC shopping complex; the private airlines have desks at the Sheraton and the Hilton.

Places to Stay – Budget

There are not many 'cheap' hotels in Abuja. ***Sharon International Hotel*** *(220 Fort-lammy St)* off Bissau St and ***Tamara Guest Inn*** *(2059 Abidjan St)* have singles for about N1250, plus a deposit of N600, and doubles for N1500, plus a deposit of N750.

On Makeni St is ***Snok Guest House***, a bare-bones flophouse with nightmarish singles/doubles for N3000/3500. Across the street at 224 Cotonou Crescent is the brand new ***Mambilla Hotel***, a much better deal, with ultra-clean doubles for N5000 and suites for N6500.

Eddie-Vic Hotel *(Off Mohammed Buhari Way)* Singles/doubles N3500/N5500. This place is quite isolated. The rooms have purportedly been recently renovated, but to no avail; they're still cramped and grimy. You'll get better value elsewhere.

Savannah Suites *(Off JS Tarki St, Garki)* Rooms from N5750, N7000 deposit. The best hotel for the money is Savannah Suites between the Union and Allied banks. Rooms are clean and comfortable. The restaurant is lacking, but there's a nice outdoor bar with live music on the weekends.

NIGERIA

Places to Stay – Mid-Range & Top End

The top-class hotels in town all have swimming pools, tennis courts, free airport shuttle service and so on.

Abuja Sheraton Hotel & Towers *(☎ 523 0225, 523 0244, Ladi Kwali Way)* Standard doubles US$150, plus US$210 deposit. This place offers the best top-end value in Abuja. It has a huge atrium and is close to cheap restaurants (you won't want to dine in the hotel unless you are feeling extremely well-heeled). The Sheraton's atrium is also a one-stop shopping bonanza for everything from airline tickets to haircuts.

Nicon Noga Hilton *(☎ 523 4811, 523 4840)* Doubles US$200. This is Africa's largest hotel; its claim to fame is that former US president Bill Clinton stayed here on his two journeys to Nigeria during his time in office. The Hilton, like the Sheraton, has a resident rate that is considerably lower (N15,000 for the cheapest double room); if you can get a Nigerian to make your booking, you can pay in naira. As with the Sheraton, the Hilton is an oasis of Western spoils. All domestic airlines have offices here.

Agura Hotel *(☎ 523 1753, Festival Way)* Standard rooms N7500. The Agura offers the comforts of the bigger hotels for much less, and rooms are comfortable. It has a pool, tennis courts, airline offices, shops and an exchange bureau.

Places to Eat

Try one of the little ***chop houses*** around Wuse market or those outside the bus stations near the Julius Berger junction in the northwest of the city.

If you crave a few Western delights, go to the ***9-11 Supermarket*** just off Shehu Shagari Way North, near European Community House.

The biggest collection of restaurants is about 300m west of the Sheraton in Addis Ababa Crescent, just off Herbert Macauley Way.

There are a couple of cheap places, including ***Chop Chop***, a fast-food joint with a seemingly endless selection of inexpensive dishes and an ***outdoor dining area*** and bar protected by a wall of sackcloth – the harmattan can be pretty fierce here.

McDowal's is a great Lebanese place that has shish kebab for N160, tabouleh for N170 and hearty salads for about N250.

Talk of the Town is the town's most expensive restaurant, not including the hotel restaurants. It's just off Shehu Shagari Way North, and serves Indian specialities.

At the Sheraton, ***Papillon's*** has an all-you-can-eat lunch buffet for N1600 featuring delicious Nigerian and continental cuisine.

Entertainment

The city's best attractions are probably the classy bars and nightclubs, catering to construction workers and visitors. You will find the ***Elephant Bar*** and ***Dazzles*** at the Sheraton much better than the bars at the Hilton.

Getting There & Away

Nigeria Airways, ADC Airlines, Chanchangi, EAS Airlines, Skyline, Okada Air and Bellview Airlines have daily flights to and from Lagos; it costs N7000 one way. The airport is 40km west of town.

Bush taxis leave from the Karu Motor Park, 10km east of town on the Jos road. The major routes are to Kano (N400, five hours), Kaduna (N300, two hours), Jos (N400, three hours), Makurdi (N250, three hours), Onitsha (N500, four hours) and Lagos (N1000, 12 hours).

The private buses are much better than the bush taxis. Chisco and CN Okoli, both near the Julius Berger junction, charge about N2000 for an overnight trip ('night flight') to Lagos. The buses depart at 7pm and reach Lagos at about 5am or 6am the following morning.

JOS

☎ 073

Jos (the acronym for 'Jesus Our Saviour'), with a population of between one and two million, is one of the more popular places in Nigeria. The attractions here are the cooler climate and the unique Jos National Museum. At 1200m above sea level, the Jos Plateau is noticeably cooler than most other areas of the country; in fact at night it can get downright chilly, something few visitors expect. The stone-covered rolling hills also make it scenic. Ask a Nigerian – they'll lift their arms in the air and utter sweetly 'Jos!'.

Orientation & Information

The city has two main north-south drags. One is Bauchi Rd, along which you'll find the large, covered market, the train station and some commercial establishments; it becomes Murtala Mohammed Way in the south. Roughly 1km to the west is Gromwalk Rd, which becomes Gomwalk Rd further south. Beach Rd (known as 'The Beach') runs parallel to the now-defunct railway line.

The post office is in the city centre, while the pitiful Nitel office is on the outskirts of town on Yakubu Gowon Way, out near the old airport junction. Rayfield Travel Agency on Ahmadu Bello Way can make all travel bookings.

Jos National Museum

The highly recommended museum complex *(admission N10; open 8.30am-5.30pm daily)* is really four separate museums and a zoo.

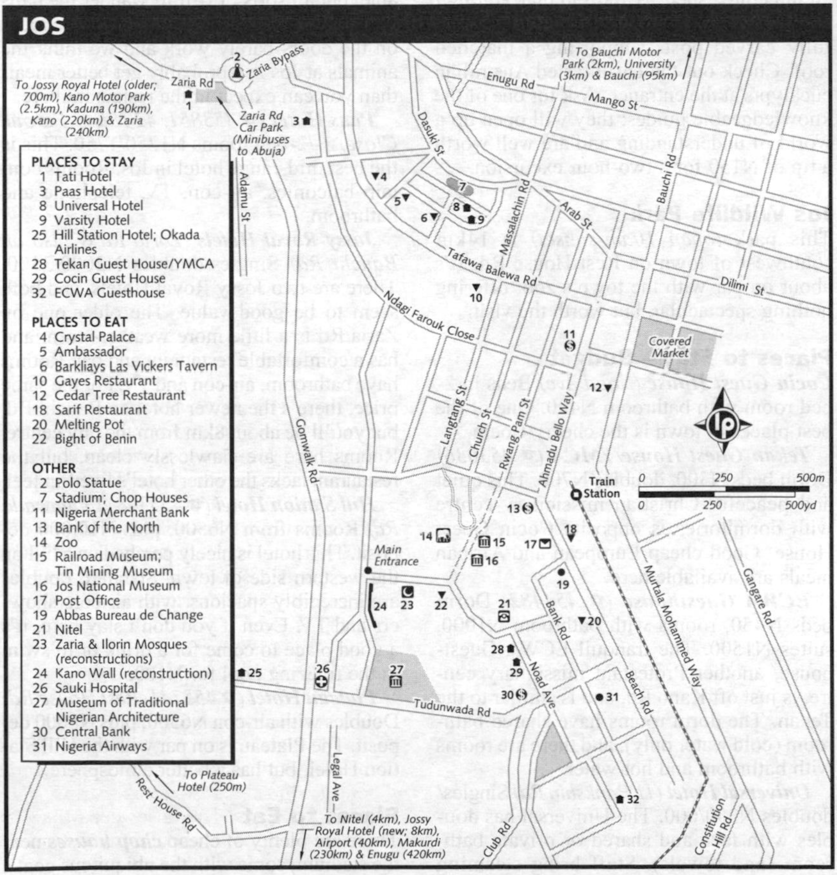
JOS
To Jossy Royal Hotel (older; 700m), Kano Motor Park (2.5km), Kaduna (190km), Kano (220km) & Zaria (240km)
Zaria Bypass
Zaria Rd
Zaria Rd Car Park (Minibuses to Abuja)
To Bauchi Motor Park (2km), University (3km) & Bauchi (95km)
Enugu Rd
Mango St
Dasuki St
Bauchi Rd
Adamu St
Massalachin Rd
Arab St
Tafawa Balewa Rd
Dilimi St
Ndagi Farouk Close
Covered Market
Langtang St
Church St
Rwang Pam St
Ahmadu Bello Way
Gomwalk Rd
Train Station
Main Entrance
Bank Rd
Murtala Mohammed Way
Gangare Rd
Noad Ave
Beach Rd
Tudunwada Rd
Legal Ave
Rest House Rd
Club Rd
Constitution Hill Rd
To Plateau Hotel (250m)
To Nitel (4km), Jossy Royal Hotel (new; 8km), Airport (40km), Makurdi (230km) & Enugu (420km)
0 250 500m
0 250 500yd
PLACES TO STAY
1 Tati Hotel
3 Paas Hotel
8 Universal Hotel
9 Varsity Hotel
25 Hill Station Hotel; Okada Airlines
28 Tekan Guest House/YMCA
29 Cocin Guest House
32 ECWA Guesthouse
PLACES TO EAT
4 Crystal Palace
5 Ambassador
6 Barkliays Las Vickers Tavern
10 Gayes Restaurant
12 Cedar Tree Restaurant
18 Sarif Restaurant
20 Melting Pot
22 Bight of Benin
OTHER
2 Polo Statue
7 Stadium; Chop Houses
11 Nigeria Merchant Bank
13 Bank of the North
14 Zoo
15 Railroad Museum; Tin Mining Museum
16 Jos National Museum
17 Post Office
19 Abbas Bureau de Change
21 Nitel
23 Zaria & Ilorin Mosques (reconstructions)
24 Kano Wall (reconstruction)
26 Sauki Hospital
27 Museum of Traditional Nigerian Architecture
30 Central Bank
31 Nigeria Airways

The Railroad Museum and the Tin Mining Museum are not very exciting. However, the pottery and much older terracotta collections (including Nok pottery from 500 BC) at the Jos National Museum are superb. And the intimate zoo, with its good selection of tigers, monkeys, baboons and birds of prey, is worth checking out for the N10 admission (separate from the admission to the pottery museum).

The Museum of Traditional Nigerian Architecture is also worth a visit. Spread out over 20 hectares are full-scale reproductions of buildings from each of Nigeria's major regions. You can see a reconstruction of the Kano wall (and go for a frightening walk along it), the old Zaria mosque with a Muslim museum inside, the Ilorin mosque, and examples of the major styles of village architecture, such as the circular *katanga* buildings of the Nupe people, with beautifully carved posts supporting a thatched roof. Check out the bat-infested Australian eucalypts at the entrance. Ask for one of the knowledgeable guides; they will open up a world of understanding and are well worth a tip of N150 for a two-hour excursion.

Jos Wildlife Park

This park *(open 10am-sunset)* is 14km southwest of town on Rest House Rd. It's about on par with the town's zoo; offering nothing spectacular, but worth the visit.

Places to Stay – Budget

***Cocin Guest House** (Noad Ave)* Beds in 2-bed room with bathroom N400. One of the best places in town is the cheery Cocin.

***Tekan Guest House/YMCA** (☎ 453036)* Dorm beds N300, doubles N700. This quiet and peaceful Christian missionary centre with dormitories is opposite Cocin Guest House. Good cheap European and African meals are available here.

***ECWA Guesthouse** (☎ 454482)* Dorm beds N450, rooms with bathroom N1000, suites N1500. The tranquil ECWA Guesthouse, another Protestant missionary centre, is just off Kano Rd, and is similar to the Tekan. The dorm rooms have shared bathroom (cold water only), and there are rooms with bathroom and hot water.

***Universal Hotel** (11 Pankshin Rd)* Singles/doubles N350/600. The Universal has doubles with fans and shared or private bathroom (and towels). Staff bring steaming buckets of hot water to your door in the morning!

***Varsity Hotel** (1 Nnamdi Azikiwe Ave: also known as Zik Ave)* Singles/doubles with bathroom N1000/1500. One block southeast of the Universal is the slightly more expensive Varsity, which has immaculate rooms; the hotel has a restaurant and a sedate bar.

Places to Stay – Mid-Range & Top End

***Tati Hotel** (☎ 455897, 452554, Cnr Zaria Rd & Zaria Bypass)* Rooms N2500 with bathroom, suites N4000, N1000 deposit. Only stay at the Tati if you've just broken both knees and are incapable of crawling to a taxi to take you elsewhere. Rooms are reasonable, but all sorts of riffraff wander the halls once staff flee for the night. Worse, the locks on the doors barely work and we think the animals at Jos zoo probably get better meals than you can expect in the restaurant here.

***Paas Hotel** (☎ 453851, 42 Ndagi Farouk Close)* 1-/2-bed rooms N1250/1750. This is the best mid-range hotel in Jos. Rooms contain balconies, air-con, TV, telephone and bathroom.

***Jossy Royal Hotels** (Zaria Rd & also on Bauchi Rd)* Singles/doubles N2000/3500. There are two Jossy Royal Hotels, and both seem to be good value. The older one on Zaria Rd is a little more weather-worn, and has a comfortable restaurant and bar. Rooms have bathroom, air-con and TV. For the same price, there's the newer hotel on Bauchi Rd, but you'll be about 8km from the city centre. Rooms here are flawlessly clean, but the restaurant lacks the other hotel's lived-in feel.

***Hill Station Hotel** (☎ 455398, Tudunwada Rd)* Rooms from N6500, plus N10,000 deposit. This hotel is nicely perched on a hill on the western side of town. Standard doubles are incredibly spacious, with air-con, showers and TV. Even if you don't stay here, it's a good place to come for a drink or to swim in the freezing pool for N100.

***Plateau Hotel** (☎ 455741, Rest House Rd)* Doubles with air-con N6500, plus N8000 deposit. The Plateau is on par with the Hill Station Hotel, but has a better atmosphere.

Places to Eat

There are plenty of cheap ***chop houses*** near the stadium, some with the ubiquitous goat's head soup. Within walking distance, on or close to Zik Ave, is the ***Ambassador, Crystal Palace*** (which has burgers and coffee), and ***Barkliays Las Vickers Tavern***. The more expensive ***Gayes Restaurant*** is also nearby; try local dishes such as *koko da kosat* (a custard-style corn mash; N60) or super tasty *fura da nano* (cow's milk with millet).

Another good Nigerian restaurant is ***Sarif*** *(Beach Rd)*; meals range in price from N250 to N500.

Fast-food addicts should head to ***Chicken George*** *(Bauchi Rd)*.

Bight of Benin is a wonderful place for lunch in the Jos Museum complex. It offers an interesting variety of reasonably priced Nigerian dishes, and you get to eat in a replica of a chief's house.

Melting Pot *(Beach Rd)* is also good for lunch, although it is a little more expensive than the Bight of Benin.

Cedar Tree Restaurant *(☎ 454890, Bauchi Rd)* is a Lebanese eatery, 5km south of the covered market opposite Tilley Gyado House. It is one of the best restaurants in town, and has humous (N200), falafel sandwiches (N150), kofta (N180) and a mixed grill (N300); a large Guinness costs N100.

Shahrazad *(Yakubu Gowon Way)* also serves excellent Lebanese food in the same price range as the Cedar Tree.

Entertainment

Azure Nightclub *(Langtang St)* is the best watering hole in the centre. It is a gathering place for the town's drug dealers, prostitutes and criminals, but they leave their professions behind when they are socialising.

The ever-popular ***Shahrazad*** (see Places to Eat) is also good for live music. It's one of the best nightclubs in town and often features local bands; it is popular with the surprisingly large expat community in Jos.

Getting There & Away

Air Nigeria Airways (☎ 452298) has numerous flights to Lagos (N5000), but virtually none to other cities. Its office is on Bank Rd. Okada Air has daily flights to Lagos; its office is in Hill Station Hotel. The airport is 40km south of town; the taxi trip costs N800.

Bus On long-distance routes, you can save a small amount by taking a large bus instead of a Peugeot taxi. Buses to Lagos cost from N700 to N800 and take about 12 hours; Plateau Express and Assisted Mass Transit leave from the sports stadium (on Tafawa Balewa Rd). Companies with buses that head east to Bauchi and Maiduguri, such as Yankari Express, and companies with buses heading south to Calabar, such as Cross Lines, operate next to the Bauchi Motor Park on Bauchi Rd, north of town.

Bush Taxi & Minibus Bush taxis and minibuses depart from the Bauchi Motor Park. Minibuses cost N250 to Abuja and Kano; the trip to either place can take up to four hours. A minibus to Kaduna costs N250. Bush taxis go to Kaduna (N300, 3½ hours), Kano (N400, six hours because of the road), Bauchi (N300, two hours), Enugu (N800, six hours) and Calabar (N1000, nine hours). Bush taxis and minibuses to Abuja (N300, 3½ hours) depart from the Zaria Rd Car Park.

Getting Around

For trips around town, expect to pay from N30 on a motorcycle-taxi and double that for a regular taxi.

KADUNA

☎ 062

In the early 20th century, the British intended Kaduna to be the seat of power in the north. Nonetheless, Kaduna has few points of historical interest.

The main street running north-south through the centre of town is the wide Ahmadu Bello Way, which becomes Junction Rd further south.

The British Council (☎ 236033) is on Yabuku Gowon Rd, near the post office and banks. The Nitel office, on the corner of Lafia and Kukawa Rds, is open 24 hours. The British deputy high commission (☎ 233 380) is at 2 Lamido Rd and the German consulate (☎ 223696) is on Ahmadu Bello Way.

The **museum** *(Ali Akilu Rd; admission N10; open 9am-6pm daily)*, at the northern end of the city on the road to Kano and across from the Emir's Palace, has masks, pottery, musical instruments, brasswork, woodcarvings and leather displays.

Places to Stay

Central Guest Inn *(182 Benue Rd)* Doubles N500. The noisy Central has doubles with a clean shared bathroom.

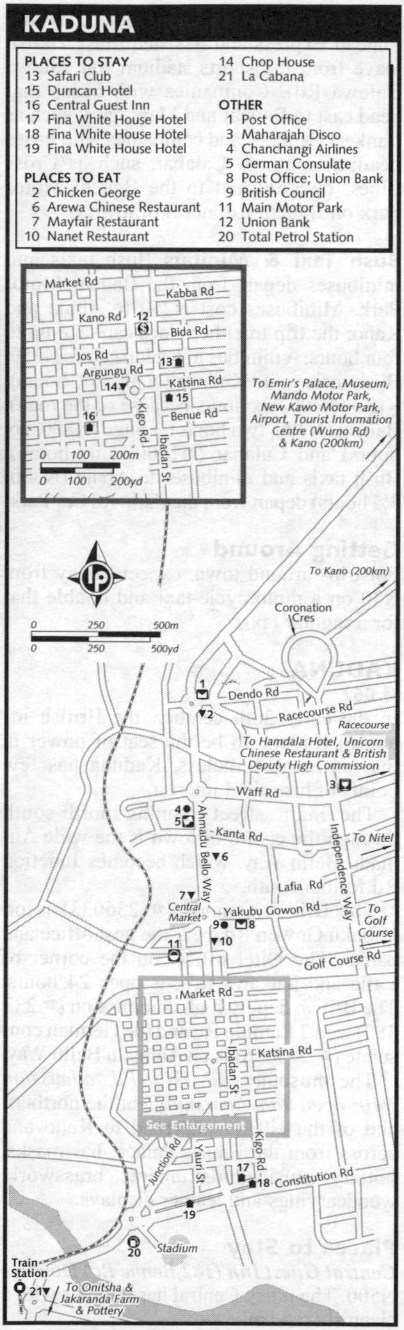
KADUNA
PLACES TO STAY
13 Safari Club
15 Durncan Hotel
16 Central Guest Inn
17 Fina White House Hotel
18 Fina White House Hotel
19 Fina White House Hotel
PLACES TO EAT
2 Chicken George
6 Arewa Chinese Restaurant
7 Mayfair Restaurant
10 Nanet Restaurant
14 Chop House
21 La Cabana
OTHER
1 Post Office
3 Maharajah Disco
4 Chanchangi Airlines
5 German Consulate
8 Post Office; Union Bank
9 British Council
11 Main Motor Park
12 Union Bank
20 Total Petrol Station
Market Rd
Kabba Rd
Kano Rd
Bida Rd
Jos Rd
Argungu Rd
Katsina Rd
Benue Rd
Kigo Rd
Ibadan St
To Emir's Palace, Museum, Mando Motor Park, New Kawo Motor Park, Airport, Tourist Information Centre (Wurno Rd) & Kano (200km)
0 100 200m
0 100 200yd
To Kano (200km)
Coronation Cres
0 250 500m
0 250 500yd
Dendo Rd
Racecourse Rd
Racecourse
To Hamdala Hotel, Unicorn Chinese Restaurant & British Deputy High Commission
Waff Rd
Ahmadu Bello Way
Kanta Rd
Independence Way
To Nitel
Lafia Rd
Central Market
Yakubu Gowon Rd
To Golf Course
Golf Course Rd
Market Rd
Katsina Rd
Ibadan St
See Enlargement
Junction Rd
Yauri St
Kigo Rd
Constitution Rd
Stadium
Train Station
To Onitsha & Jakaranda Farm & Pottery

Safari Club *(☎ 211838, 10 Argungu Rd)* Singles with fan N600. This is another cheap, lively place. The singles have clean bathrooms with bucket showers and there's a huge, active bar.

There are three ***Fina White House Hotels*** *(☎ 211852)*. The main one is at 23 Constitution Rd and has cramped doubles for N1500 with noisy air-con and bathroom. The management will farm you out to one of the better buildings if you ask – rooms with TV, air-con and bathroom cost from N2500.

Durncan Hotel *(Katsina Rd)* Rooms N6500/10,000 with fan/air-con. The grim Durncan has functional doubles with fan or air-con and TV.

Hamdala Hotel *(☎ 211005)* Rooms N4000, plus N3000 deposit. The Hamdala, a block to the east of the Durncan, is by far the best – some would say only – choice for accommodation in Kaduna. Rooms are very clean and comfortable and have TV, air-con and video. There are two buildings; rooms in the older motel complex are much cheaper and are just as comfortable.

Places to Eat

For non-African fare, a popular place is ***Chicken George*** *(Ahmadu Bello Way)*, a fast-food chain. For grilled chicken and beef, try the vendors opposite Durncan Hotel.

For cheap African food, the popular ***chop house*** *(Cnr Ahmadu Bello Way & Argungu Rd)* is unbeatable. The food is cooked in big, steamy pots and dished up by huge, sweaty women. It is open from lunch time until 9pm and a plate of food costs about N100.

The outdoor ***suya shack*** behind Hamdala Hotel serves delicious, made-to-order suya.

Nanet Restaurant *(Ahmadu Bello Way)* 3-course meal N1200-1500. Open 6.30am-10pm. This restaurant serves good Nigerian food in a middle-class setting (uniformed waiters and tablecloths).

Mayfair Restaurant is 100m north of Nanet Restaurant on the other side of the road. It is a good choice for a hearty English breakfast.

Arewa Chinese Restaurant *(☎ 212380, Ahmadu Bello Way)* Meals N500, buffet N1200. Open daily. For an excellent meal you can't beat this restaurant. It has an all-you-can-eat buffet every Sunday.

Unicorn Chinese Restaurant Meals around N700. Open daily. This restaurant at

Hamdala Hotel is quite good and has more than 120 choices. It's head and shoulders above the regular 1st-floor restaurant.

La Cabana *(Junction Rd)* Open nightly. For Lebanese and French food, try the fancy La Cabana, 2km south of the central market.

Entertainment

Central Guest Inn (see Places to Stay earlier) has a lively bar.

La Cabana (see Places to Eat earlier in this section) has a weekend nightclub, if you are looking for an upmarket place with dancing and drinking.

The ***nightclub*** at Hamdala Hotel is another good spot.

Maharajah Disco *(Cnr Independence Way & Waff Rd)* Cover charge N50. This remains the buzz place in town.

Getting There & Away

Air Nigeria Airways (☎ 210174) at 26 Ahmadu Bello Way and Chanchangi at Ahmadu Bello Way, have two daily flights to Lagos. Kabo Air (☎ 242248) also on Ahmadu Bello Way, 2km north of the central market, has flights to Lagos and other centres.

Bus & Bush Taxi The town's main motor park on Gombe Rd is across from the central market. For transport to Lagos go to the Mando Motor Park in the north on Ali Akilu Rd. The cheapest way to get to Lagos is on one of the overnight buses.

Bush taxis cost N400 for the 3½ hour trip to Jos and leave from the New Kawo Motor Park. Bush taxis to Zaria cost N200 and take one hour. To reach either Mando or Kawo Motor Parks, catch a minibus from the main motor park; the fare is N10.

BAUCHI

☎ 077

Bauchi city, capital of Bauchi State, is a convenient stop on your way to or from Yankari National Park. Muslim sharia law operates in Bauchi (see Society & Conduct earlier in this chapter); it is an unpretentious and not very exciting place. Those interested in politics may enjoy **Tafawa Balewa's Mausoleum** *(admission free; open 7am-6pm daily)*.

Places to Stay & Eat

De Kerker Lodge Rooms N650. This place, behind the stadium, is cheap, friendly and has ultra-basic rooms with fans. The communal toilet is dirty and water comes from the courtyard well.

Sogiji Hotel *(Maiduguri Rd)* Rooms with fan/air-con N800/1250. Rooms at the impersonal Sogiji have a large bed.

Zaranda Hotel *(☎ 435902, Jos Rd)* Rooms N5500, plus N1000 deposit. The Zaranda is several kilometres west of town. Rooms are very comfortable, and the hotel has a lively bar, an Internet centre and a booking office for Yankari National Park.

Horizontal Motel *(Jos Rd)* Rooms N1600. In town, the Horizontal, opposite Chicken George, has comfortable motel-style rooms.

Terry's Chinese Restaurant *(Maiduguri Bypass Rd)* Meal with beer around N400. This restaurant serves a good meal with cold beer.

Vital Inn is two blocks from De Kerker Lodge, and is the best watering hole in this mostly 'dry' town.

Getting There & Away

Bush taxis leave from Maiduguri Motor Park on Ningi Rd for Kano, while those for Jos depart from Jos Motor Park on Jos Rd. Transport to Yankari leaves from Minivan Motor Park. You can also hire a private car at Zaranda Hotel for the journey to Yankari National Park for N3000 if your negotiating skills are up to par.

YANKARI NATIONAL PARK

Open for wildlife viewing year-round, Yankari *(admission N100, photo permit N100)* is 225km east of Jos, and covers an area of 2244 sq km. It's a great, cheap place to visit. Around 600 elephants live here, making this one of the largest populations in any of West Africa's wildlife parks. Bushbucks and waterbucks are the most common animals, and are too numerous to count. The park is also home to buffaloes, hippopotamuses, lions, monkeys, warthogs, waterbucks, crocodiles and plenty of baboons. In fact, all you have to do to see baboons is show up; they'll eventually find their way to you.

Another great attraction of Yankari is the lake formed by the **Wikki Warm Springs**, near the park lodge. About 200m long and 10m wide, the springs are wonderful and scenic. The crystal-clear mineral water is a constant 31°C and, most importantly, is free

NIGERIA

of bilharzia. Baboons, and, occasionally, elephants, come down to the springs. Be careful if you forge out for an evening swim.

The best time to see animals is from late February to late April, before the rains, when the thirsty animals congregate at the Gaji River. Driving is permitted in the park, but most people take advantage of the park's two-hour tours at 7.30am and 3.30pm in specially converted trucks and buses. The tours are excellent value at N150 per person.

Places to Stay & Eat

***Wikki Warm Springs Hotel** (☎ 077-41174)* Camping N150 per person, bungalows with air-con & bathroom N1500. This hotel in the park is often full at weekends, so reservations are advisable. It has ageing circular bungalows that are in serious need of repair. Rates are reasonable. The restaurant, too, is well priced with meals for N250, but the food and service leave a lot to be desired. You can camp and get water from the lodge.

Getting There & Away

Minibuses for Yankari leave from Minivan Motor Park in Bauchi and charge N500. From the main gate wait for transport going into the park and cross your fingers; there is more traffic at the weekends (expect to pay N100 to get to the hotel). You can literally wait for days for a ride back to civilization if you don't arrange transport in advance.

The North

KANO

☎ 064

Dating back more than 1000 years, Kano is the oldest city in West Africa. For centuries it was one of the most active commercial centres in the region – a very important point at the crossroads of the trans-Saharan trading routes. Today, it is Nigeria's third-largest city (with a population of more than two million), the centre for the north and number one on most travellers' lists of places to see in Nigeria.

At the end of Ramadan (Sallah) and during Tabaski, 69 days later, Kano comes alive with a huge durbar. Hotel accommodation is hard to come by at these times. (See Public Holidays & Special Events earlier, for more details.)

Kano is a strict sharia place. Public smoking and drinking by Muslims is a serious violation of local laws. Although sharia doesn't technically pertain to non-Muslims, all visitors are expected to be on their best behaviour. Public drunkenness – or even the suspicion of it – is more than enough to land you in jail, possibly facing a painful punishment at the end of a cane.

One of Kano's attractions is the old city, although the newer section of town is lively, particularly north of Sabon Gari Market.

Air pollution in Kano has to be seen to be believed. In combination with the harmattan wind, it almost makes you choke.

Orientation

The centre of Kano is Sabon Gari Market. Just to the north is Sabon Gari itself, where most of the city's cheap hotels and restaurants are. The city's modern commercial centre is south of the market.

Major roads include E Bello Rd (not to be confused with Ahmadu Bello Way, 2km to the east) and Murtala Mohammed Way, running east-west along the southern side of the market.

The old city is about 1km to the southwest of the market, the boundary being the old city wall, which is now largely destroyed. Some of the gates in the wall, however, are still intact; the main gate is Kofar Mata, which leads to the central mosque and the Emir's palace. For a view over the entire city, climb Dala Hill north of Kurmi Market.

Information

There is an information office at the Kano State Tourist Camp (see Places to Stay later), a must for those interested in seeing Kano's sites. You can hire a tour guide here for a three-hour whistle stop of all the attractions for N1500. Niger has a consulate here.

Money There is a group of banks on and around Bank Rd. You can change money much faster at a bureau de change; one is on Bompai Rd across from Central Hotel. The fastest way to change money and get the best rate is with the black market dealers in shops at the front of Central Hotel (or others outside), but be careful.

Post & Communications The post office is at the eastern end of Post Office Rd.

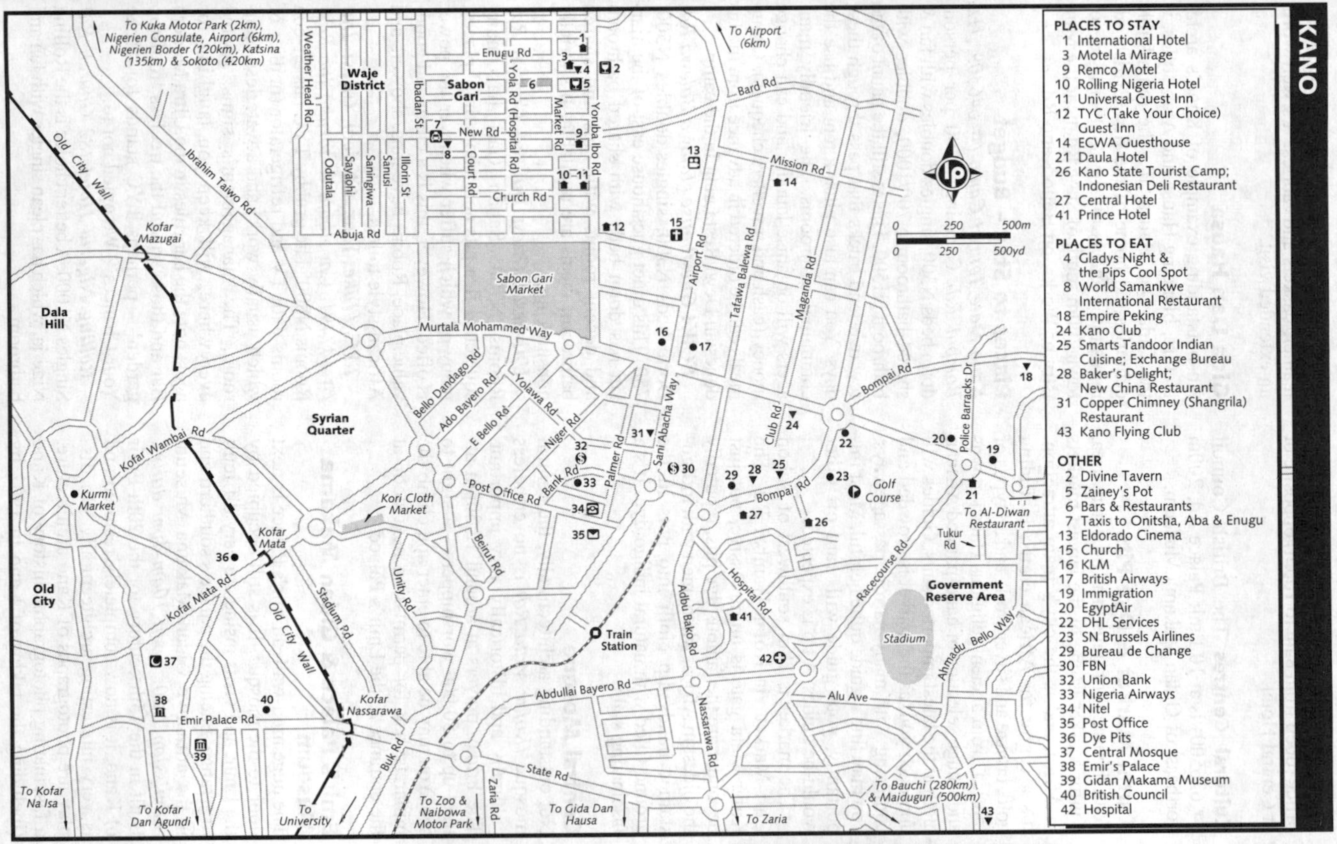
KANO
PLACES TO STAY
1 International Hotel
3 Motel la Mirage
9 Remco Motel
10 Rolling Nigeria Hotel
11 Universal Guest Inn
12 TYC (Take Your Choice) Guest Inn
14 ECWA Guesthouse
21 Daula Hotel
26 Kano State Tourist Camp; Indonesian Deli Restaurant
27 Central Hotel
41 Prince Hotel
PLACES TO EAT
4 Gladys Night & the Pips Cool Spot
8 World Samankwe International Restaurant
18 Empire Peking
24 Kano Club
25 Smarts Tandoor Indian Cuisine; Exchange Bureau
28 Baker's Delight; New China Restaurant
31 Copper Chimney (Shangrila) Restaurant
43 Kano Flying Club
OTHER
2 Divine Tavern
5 Zainey's Pot
6 Bars & Restaurants
7 Taxis to Onitsha, Aba & Enugu
13 Eldorado Cinema
15 Church
16 KLM
17 British Airways
19 Immigration
20 EgyptAir
22 DHL Services
23 SN Brussels Airlines
29 Bureau de Change
30 FBN
32 Union Bank
33 Nigeria Airways
34 Nitel
35 Post Office
36 Dye Pits
37 Central Mosque
38 Emir's Palace
39 Gidan Makama Museum
40 British Council
42 Hospital
0 250 500m
0 250 500yd
To Kuka Motor Park (2km), Nigerien Consulate, Airport (6km), Nigerien Border (120km), Katsina (135km) & Sokoto (420km)
To Airport (6km)
Waje District
Sabon Gari
Sabon Gari Market
Dala Hill
Syrian Quarter
Old City
Kurmi Market
Kori Cloth Market
Government Reserve Area
Stadium
Golf Course
Train Station
Old City Wall
Kofar Mazugai
Kofar Mata
Kofar Nassarawa
To Al-Diwan Restaurant
To Bauchi (280km) & Maiduguri (500km)
To Zaria
To Gida Dan Hausa
To Zoo & Naibowa Motor Park
To University
To Kofar Dan Agundi
To Kofar Na Isa
Murtala Mohammed Way
Sani Abacha Way
Ibrahim Taiwo Rd
Kofar Wambai Rd
Kofar Mata Rd
Emir Palace Rd
Stadium Rd
State Rd
Abdullai Bayero Rd
Nassarawa Rd
Hospital Rd
Racecourse Rd
Ahmadu Bello Way
Alu Ave
Bompai Rd
Club Rd
Police Barracks Dr
Tukur Rd
Airport Rd
Tafawa Balewa Rd
Maganda Rd
Mission Rd
Bard Rd
Enugu Rd
Yola Rd (Hospital Rd)
Market Rd
Yoruba Ibo Rd
New Rd
Court Rd
Church Rd
Abuja Rd
Ibadan St
Ilorin St
Sanusi
Saningiwa
Sayaohi
Odutala
Weather Head Rd
Bello Dandago Rd
Ado Bayero Rd
E Bello Rd
Yolawa Rd
Niger Rd
Palmer Rd
Bank Rd
Post Office Rd
Beirut Rd
Unity Rd
Buk Rd
Zaria Rd
Adbu Bako Rd

NIGERIA

International calls can be made at the Nitel office (open from 8am to 10pm) opposite or at Central Hotel.

Cultural Centres The British Council (☎ 626500) is at 10 Emir Palace Rd, 200m northeast of Gidan Makama Museum.

Kurmi Market & Dye Pits

With thousands of stalls in a 16-hectare area, Kurmi Market is one of the largest markets in Africa, and is the city's main attraction. It's a centre for African crafts, including gold, bronze and silver work, and all types of fabrics, from ancient religious Hausa gowns and a huge selection of hand-painted African cloth to the latest imported suits. Guides will approach you; as the market is crowded and confusing with many narrow passageways, you may find a guide quite helpful. Most importantly, your guide will ward off other would-be guides. A tip is expected.

The market is 2km southwest of Sabon Gari Market via Kofar Wambai Rd. The Kofar Mata gate is unimpressive, but just beyond it are the famous dye pits, reputedly the oldest in Africa, where men with indigo-stained hands dip cloth into pots in the ground filled with natural indigo dye. It's a fascinating sight.

Central Mosque

Not outstanding architecturally, the central mosque *(Kofar Mata Rd)* is nevertheless culturally and historically very important. The Friday prayers at around 12.30pm attract up to 50,000 worshippers – a sight to see. You may be able to enter and climb the minarets; ask for permission next door at the entrance to the Emir's Palace.

Emir's Palace & Gidan Makama Museum

The huge mud-walled Emir's Palace is next door to the mosque. It is still occupied by the Emir, and visits inside are very difficult to arrange. Facing the palace's southern end is the attractive Gidan Makama Museum *(admission N50; open 10am-4pm daily).* Built in the 15th century for the 20th Emir of Kano, it is now completely restored and is very interesting architecturally. On display are photographs of Kano architecture, a fascinating photographic history of Kano (including the taking of Kano in 1902 by the British) and various crafts, including leather, baskets and fabrics. It's well worth an extended visit.

Gida Dan Hausa

An outstanding example of Kano's architecture, blending Hausa and Arab styles, is the Gida Dan Hausa. It's the remarkable centuries-old home of the first British administrator and is on the southern side of town 200m south of State Rd, near the Ministry of Works, on Bello Kano Rd.

Places to Stay – Budget

Kano State Tourist Camp *(☎ 646309, 11A Bompai Rd)* Camping N300 per person, dorm beds N300, singles/doubles with fan & shared bathroom N700/1000, doubles with bathroom N1500. This is still the haunt of the few overland trucks that pass through these days. You can also pitch a tent and use the communal bathrooms. The friendly managers will organise laundry and can change money (cash and travellers cheques). Group meals can be ordered in advance from the Indonesian Dewi Restaurant in the camp.

ECWA Guesthouse *(Tafawa Balewa Rd)* Dorm beds N300, singles/doubles N500/750. This quiet guesthouse east of the market has dorm beds with shared bathroom and decent rooms with fans and shared bathroom; meals are available. It's strictly nonsmoking.

Universal Guest Inn *(86 Church Rd)* Rooms N700. Sabon Gari has many squelched flea pits and 'short time' places, many of which suffer whenever the power is offed. However, this is a clean and good-value place. Rooms have fans, showers and African-style toilets.

TYC (Take Your Choice) Guest Inn *(☎ 647491, Cnr Abuja & Yoruba Ibo Rds)* Rooms N800. The grubby TYC has air-con rooms with TV and refrigerator (neither of which usually work) and a waterless bathroom. The management's signs, posted everywhere, will keep you laughing for ages; note the bar rules in the Ultra Modern Bar and those around the treeless 'roof-top garden' – perhaps TYC stands for 'Take Your Chances'? We opted not to.

Rolling Nigeria Hotel *(82 Church Rd)* Singles N1000. A better choice is the Rolling Nigeria, which has clean singles with fan and bathroom.

Remco Motel *(☎ 628600, 61 New Rd)* Doubles N1500. The well-maintained Remco has very tidy doubles with air-con, TV (that works), fridge and bathroom with bucket showers. The restaurant serves good meals for about N200.

Places to Stay – Mid-Range & Top End

International Hotel *(30 Enugu Rd)* Singles/doubles N2500/3000, plus N1000 deposit. The International is quite a large place and looks like it's on its last legs. Rooms have air-con and TV, but are filthy and unkempt. The restaurant is decent and the hotel has a big bar (which can get noisy if there's a bachelor party in progress).

Motel La Mirage *(27 Enugu Rd)* Singles/doubles N2500/3500. La Mirage, across the street from the International, is a better choice for about the same rate. The rooms are small but good with air-con, fridge, TV and showers. There's an Internet café here.

Central Hotel *(☎ 625141, Bompai Rd)* Doubles/studio rooms for nonresidents N4500/5500, for residents N2500/3000, plus N5000/6000 deposit. The Central has noisy but spacious air-con rooms and studios and an erratic water supply. The rooms aren't worth the nonresident rate, but try asking for the resident rate: Even if it's obvious that you're not Nigerian, you'll probably get lucky. The central outdoor patio transforms into a lively bar at night, a sort of 'sharia-free' zone that attracts Muslims with vices on weekend nights. The nearby air-con bar is very popular with expats and overlanders who drift up from the tourist camp.

Daula Hotel *(☎ 628842, 152 Murtala Mohammed Way)* Singles/doubles N3000/4000. The Daula is better than the Central, and rooms have telephone, fridge and cable TV; it also has a pool.

Prince Hotel *(☎ 639402, Tamandu Close)* Rooms N6500, plus N3000 deposit. The Prince has luxurious rooms with fridge, TV and phone; it has an elegant restaurant with Euro-Afro cuisine for around N1000.

Places to Eat

Many of the cheap African restaurants close by 6pm or 7pm; hotel restaurants stay open later.

Opposite Central Hotel is an enclave of fast-food outlets and bakeries. Among them are ***Smarts Tandoor Royal Indian Cuisine***, which also has takeaway; a ***Baker's Delight***, which is much better than Central Hotel's restaurant for breakfast; and ***New China Restaurant***, which has good, inexpensive Chinese dishes for about N600.

Throughout Sabon Gari, especially at the eastern end of New Rd, there are plenty of cheap ***chop houses*** that serve great pepper soup, chicken pepper soup, goat's head soup (eyeballs and all), suya and gari. One good place is ***World Samankwe International Restaurant***, where for N80 you can stuff yourself. The 'best name' award for a chop house goes to ***Gladys Night & the Pips Cool Spot*** on Abeokuta Ave; the food isn't bad either.

Al-Diwan *(41D Hadejia Rd)* Meals N400-600, brunch N750. For excellent Lebanese, you can't beat Al-Diwan; it has a great Sunday brunch.

Empire Peking *(2 Bompai Rd)* Meals from N1000. This is one of the best, expensive restaurants in Kano.

Copper Chimney (Shangrila) Restaurant *(Cnr Sani Abacha Way & Yolawa Rd)* has good, reasonably priced Indian food, including soups, samosas and tandoori.

Kano Flying Club *(24 Magajin Rumfa Rd)* serves the cheapest European fare in town; you'll need to take out a temporary membership for N100.

Kano Club *(Cnr Bompai Rd & Murtala Mohammed Way)* has superb, cheap meals, but you have to be introduced by a member.

Entertainment

Bars Sabon Gari has heaps of bars; before cracking open your beer, though, it's good to check with a local to make sure you're not going to attract sharia police by doing so. Generally, it's OK to enjoy your drinks where they're sold to you, but taking them out of the bar is asking for trouble.

TYC (Take your Choice) Guest Inn (see Places to Stay earlier) has a ***roof-top garden*** with good views over the city, but that's about all. The ***Ultra Modern Bar*** downstairs will make you laugh – check out the bar rules written up on the walls.

The ***bars*** at Central Hotel are usually busy until the wee hours of the morning.

Nightclubs Sadly, sharia has caused the demise of almost all Kano's nightclubs, unless you count the bars at Central Hotel, which seems to have filled the void. Sharia or not, there will be no shortage of partiers and women of the night there most nights of the week. There's sometimes live music at the weekend.

Getting There & Away

Air International flights to/from Kano include the EgyptAir service to London via Cairo, KLM to Amsterdam and Sabena to Brussels. EgyptAir (☎ 630759) is on Murtala Mohammed Way, KLM (☎ 632632) is on Airport Rd just north of Murtala Mohammed Way and Sabena is on Bompai Rd (in the grounds of Central Hotel).

Nigeria Airways (☎ 623891), 3 Bank Rd, has two daily flights to Lagos, and Kabo Air, Skyline, Chanchangi and Okada Air go once a day. Okada Air has two flights a week to Yola.

The Kano international airport is 8km northwest of Sabon Gari Market. An airport tax of N200 applies to all domestic flights. A motorcycle-taxi ride to the airport from town will cost N100; a taxi is N300.

Bush Taxi & Minibus Kuka Motor Park, on the road to the airport on the western side of town, is the motor park for Sokoto and Katsina and also to Zinder and Maradi, both in Niger. Naibowa Motor Park, which serves points south (Zaria, Jos, Kaduna, Lagos etc), is on Zaria Rd on the southern outskirts of town. You can get minibuses and shared taxis for both motor parks from the Sabon Gari Market. A third motor park on Murtala Mohammed Way, east of Sabon Gari Market, serves points east, including Maiduguri. The trip from Zinder takes from six to eight hours by minibus (CFA3000).

Bush taxis to Sokoto (five hours) cost N500 and N250 to Katsina. To Zaria the two-hour ride costs N200. The three- to five-hour ride to Maradi in Niger costs N550.

From Naibowa Motor Park, Lagos is a 15-hour ride by bush taxi and costs N800. Bush taxis go to Benin City (N500, eight hours), Jos (N400, six hours), Maiduguri (N550, eight hours) and Kaduna (N200, 2½ hours).

Getting Around

In town, taxis and motorcycle-taxis are everywhere and cost from N50, depending on the length of your trip.

NIGERIA

Warning!

Due to a military blockade around the Katsina region in the wake of riots and the death of several police officers in the area, routes to Sokoto were off limits to travellers and the town couldn't be visited at the time of research.

AROUND KANO

About 200km east of Kano is the **Hadejia-Nguru Wetlands Conservation Project**. This area is a great place for the avid birdwatcher, as it is an important resting point for birds migrating to or from Europe, and is home to many indigenous water birds. The intrepid ornithologist interested in visiting this area should stop at the VSO office in Kano for further details. Ask for directions at the Kano State Tourist Camp.

SOKOTO

☎ 060

In the far northwestern corner of Nigeria, Sokoto is known for its Sultan's Palace and its market. The town became important in the early 19th century as the seat of the caliphate, which was established after Usman dan Fodio's Islamic jihad in 1807 that brought together the various Hausa city states. The present sultan, Maccido, effectively remains the head of Nigeria's Muslims today.

At the Sultan's Palace between 9pm and 11pm on Thursday, you can hear Hausa musicians outside playing to welcome in the Holy Day, Friday. The Shehu Mosque is nearby. At the end of Ramadan, long processions of musicians and elaborately dressed men on horseback make their way from the prayer ground to the Sultan's Palace.

The market, well known for its handmade leather goods, is held daily except Sunday; it's best on Friday.

Sokoto can be used as a base to visit the spectacular **Argungu Fishing & Cultural Festival** held every February, 100km to the southwest (for more details, see Public Holidays & Special Events earlier in this chapter).

Places to Stay & Eat

Catering Rest House *(☎ 232505)* Rooms N600. On the southern side of town, 200m from the post office, is the old government-run Catering Rest House. It's rundown and fairly dirty.

Ibro International Hotel *(☎ 232510, Abdullahi Fodio Rd)* Rooms N1100. For decent accommodation, try this hotel, near the intersection of the bypass road.

Shukura Hotel *(☎ 200019, Gusau Rd)* Doubles N2400. This hotel, south of the centre, has air-con doubles.

Shalom Restaurant *(Abdullahi Fodio Rd)* Meals from N100. The Shalom, close to Ibro International Hotel, has a wide range of cheap meals.

Getting There & Away

Nigeria Airways (☎ 232252) has flights three times weekly to Lagos; make sure your booking is secure.

Lots of bush taxis in Sokoto head for Kano, Zaria and Kaduna, Lagos and Illela–Birni N'Konni (the Nigerien border). They leave from the motor park facing the market on the northern side of town.

MAIDUGURI

☎ 076

Maiduguri is the booming capital of Borno State in the far northeastern corner of Nigeria. From March to May temperatures often reach 48°C. Very few travellers come here – usually just those on their way to or from northern Cameroon, when border crossings are possible.

Gomboru Market, or Monday Market, is in the heart of town just north of the Nepa Roundabout; Kamuri Market, or New Market, is on the eastern side of town, several blocks east of Kashim Ibrahim Rd and north of Customs Roundabout.

The city has a small museum worth seeing – it's on the eastern side of town off Bama Rd.

The train station is 250m north of Kashim Ibrahim Rd, but you won't see a moving train.

Places to Stay

The one-night cheap hotels are concentrated on the side streets off Kashim Ibrahim Rd; some of them rate the label 'accommodation'; others don't. Use them if you're really desperate.

Borno State Hotel *(☎ 233191, Italba Rd)* Singles with fan N350, air-con doubles N600. The Borno State is a good choice, and is set in leafy surroundings on Italba Rd off Shehu Lamisu Way.

Safari Hotel *(Italba Rd)* Doubles with bathroom & fan N450. If the Borno State is full, try Safari Hotel, 1km north on the same street. The decor is gloomy but it's friendly and good value.

Deribe Hotel *(☎ 232445)* Doubles with air-con about N3500, plus N7000 deposit. The city's top hotel is the Deribe, a block west of West End Roundabout and near Alliance Française.

Places to Eat & Drink

Not far from Safari Hotel are several ***street vendors*** and the ***New Villager Restaurant***, which has suya in the evening and spaghetti and beef for lunch. For other Nigerian chop in the heart of town, try the snack bar at ***UTC department store*** *(Kashim Ibrahim Rd)*, the ***Bosco Café*** between UTC and the post office, or ***Lalle Restaurant*** *(Post Office Roundabout)*. For fresh fish go to the collection of ***restaurants*** near Customs Roundabout.

The excellent ***Chinese Restaurant*** is between the train line and West End Roundabout; it has reasonable prices and is also a good place to come for a drink.

For cheap bars and dancing, head for the 'hotel' area north of Kashim Ibrahim Rd.

Getting There & Away

Nigeria Airways has flights from Maiduguri almost daily to Lagos and less frequently to Kano. The office is in the city centre, at 19 Hospital Rd, between the Banks and Post Office Roundabouts.

Bush taxis to Jos and Kano leave from Damboa Road Motor Park on the western edge of town, just off the airport road. For destinations north, east and south (including the Chadian and Cameroonian borders) go to Bama Motor Park on Bama Rd at the eastern side of town. A taxi to either motor park costs N100.

AROUND MAIDUGURI

Gwoza

Around 115km southeast of Maiduguri, Gwoza is in the western foothills of the scenic Mandara Mountains and is a good place for hiking. Although the area is extremely rocky, the people living here have terraced the hills and every available piece of earth is used to grow food.

You can sleep in Gwoza at the ***Government Rest House***.

Baga & Lake Chad

In recent years Lake Chad has receded northeastward across the border, which means that Nigeria is not nearly as good a vantage point for seeing the enormous lake as Chad or Cameroon. Given this, it is best to go when the water is at its highest, between December and February; Baga, 170km northeast of Maiduguri (and north of Dikwa), is the place to go. Be prepared, as immigration police are sure to hassle the hell out of you (because of incursions by Chadian rebels).

A 13km canal goes out to the Nigerian part of Lake Chad, and the bird-watching is excellent. Contact the Chad Basin Development Authority in Baga for permission to visit.

Minibuses and bush taxis leave from Baga Motor Park in Maiduguri. You can stay at ***Baga State Hotel*** or in rough ***huts*** in nearby Doro.

Senegal

More visitors come to Senegal than to any other country in West Africa. If you look at the social, cultural and physical diversity of the country it's easy to see why. The capital, Dakar, is a dynamic city with a breezy climate and cosmopolitan mix of Afro-French characteristics. Nearby is the historically and culturally fascinating Île de Gorée, and anyone even remotely interested in history will be impressed by the country's colonial capital, St-Louis. Senegal's coastline boasts long, sandy beaches both north and south of Dakar, and vast mazes of riverine waterways at the Siné Saloum Delta and through much of the subtropical Casamance region. There's a lot for wildlife enthusiasts too: Parc National du Niokolo-Koba is one of West Africa's major national parks, while Parc National aux Oiseaux du Djoudj and Parc National de la Langue de Barbarie are among the most important bird sanctuaries in the world. And then of course there's Senegal's greatest asset – its people.

Senegal at a Glance

Capital: Dakar
Population: 10.3 million
Area: 196,192 sq km
Head of State: President Abdoulaye Wade
Official language: French
Main local languages: Wolof, Mandinka/Malinké, Fula, Sérèr, Diola
Currency: West African CFA franc
Exchange rate: US$1 = CFA694
Time: GMT/UTC
Country telephone code: ☎ 221
Best time to go: November to February

MAURITANIA
ATLANTIC OCEAN
St-Louis p763
Dakar p746
Central Dakar p748
Île de Gorée p757
Cap Vert Peninsula p756
Thiès p761
Kaolack p774
Tambacounda p790
Petite Côte & Siné-Saloum Delta p770
Parc National du Niokolo-Koba p792
Ziguinchor p781
Casamance p778

Highlights

- Following in the footsteps of history in St-Louis
- Dancing with the locals as Youssou N'Dour plays up a storm in Dakar
- Dining on some of Africa's best food in Dakar
- Winding through the mangroves of the Siné-Saloum Delta in a pirogue
- Chilling out on the beautiful beaches of Casamance
- Swimming in secluded waterfalls in the hills of Bassari country

Facts about Senegal

HISTORY

Remains of organised societies from early in the 1st millennium AD have been discovered in several parts of Senegal, and the area was part of the great Islamic Sahel empires of Ghana (which flourished between the 8th and 11th centuries), Mali (13th to 15th centuries) and Songhaï (16th century). Smaller empires or kingdoms were also established during this period: Along the Senegal River, the Tuklur empire was established by the Tuklur people in the 9th to 10th centuries; and as Mali's power began to wane, the Wolof people established the empire of Jolof in the central region of today's Senegal. For more general details on the pre-European period, refer to History in the Facts about West Africa chapter.

European Arrival

The year 1443 marked medieval Europe's first direct contact with West Africa, when Portuguese explorers reached the mouth of the Senegal River. The following year they landed at Cap Vert, near present-day Dakar, and later settled on Île de Gorée – a vital base for ships trading along the coast.

Around 1600, the Dutch and the English entered the scene. For the next two centuries they fought with the French over the islands

SENEGAL

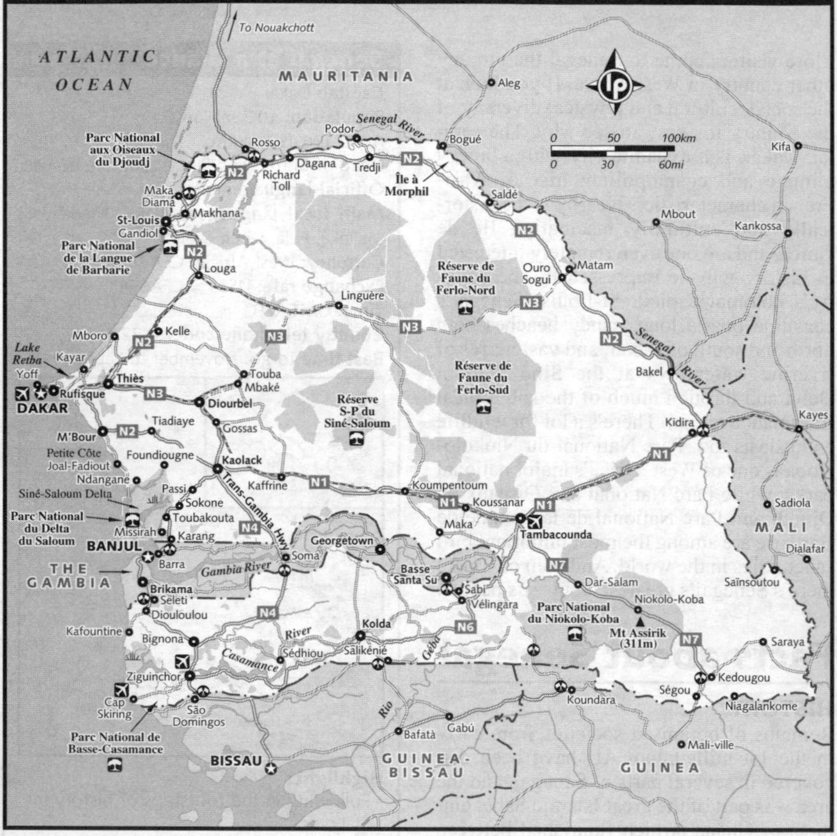
To Nouakchott
ATLANTIC OCEAN
MAURITANIA
Aleg
0 50 100km
0 30 60mi
Kifa
Parc National aux Oiseaux du Djoudj
Rosso
Podor
Senegal River
Bogué
Richard Toll
Dagana
Tredji
Île à Morphil
Maka Diama
St-Louis
Makhana
Gandiol
Saldé
Mbout
Kankossa
Parc National de la Langue de Barbarie
Louga
Réserve de Faune du Ferlo-Nord
Ouro Sogui
Matam
Linguère
Mboro
Kelle
Lake Retba
Kayar
Yoff
Thiès
Touba
Mbaké
Réserve de Faune du Ferlo-Sud
Bakel
Senegal River
Rufisque
DAKAR
Diourbel
Réserve S-P du Siné-Saloum
Kidira
Kayes
Tiadiaye
Gossas
M'Bour
Petite Côte
Joal-Fadiout
Foundiougne
Kaolack
Ndangane
Kaffrine
Koumpentoum
Siné-Saloum Delta
Passi
Sokone
Trans-Gambia Hwy
Koussanar
Sadiola
Parc National du Delta du Saloum
Toubakouta
Missirah
Maka
Tambacounda
MALI
BANJUL
Karang
Georgetown
Soma
Dialafar
THE GAMBIA
Barra
Gambia River
Basse Santa Su
Sabi
Saïnsoutou
Brikama
Séleti
Vélingara
Dar-Salam
Niokolo-Koba
Diouloulou
Parc National du Niokolo-Koba
Kafountine
Kolda
Mt Assirik (311m)
Bignona
River
Sédhiou
Salikénié
Géba
Saraya
Casamance
Ziguinchor
Kedougou
Cap Skiring
Koundara
Ségou
São Domingos
Niagalankome
Rio
Gabú
Bafatà
Parc National de Basse-Casamance
Mali-ville
BISSAU
GUINEA-BISSAU
GUINEA
N1
N2
N3
N4
N6
N7

of Gorée and St-Louis and for control of the lucrative trade in gold, ivory and, most importantly, slaves.

During the 18th century, St-Louis grew in size and importance, but after the slave trade was banned in 1815 the French were forced to look for new sources of wealth. Louis Faidherbe was appointed governor in 1845 and forced the local people around the Senegal River to grow groundnuts (peanuts) as a cash crop. With similar ruthlessness, over the next few decades French forces systematically moved inland, and Senegal became the gateway to the new territory of Afrique Occidentale Française (French West Africa).

Meanwhile, a marabout called Omar Tall had established an empire based around the town of Ségou in today's Mali. His soldiers spread west into Senegal where they clashed with the French forces moving inland. To protect the new colony from the north and east, Faidherbe established a chain of forts along the Senegal River (including Bakel, Matam and Podor), which can still be seen today. Faidherbe also established a settlement on the peninsula opposite Île de Gorée, which became Dakar.

The Marabouts

Omar Tall's forces were finally defeated by the French in 1864, but his missionary zeal inspired followers to continue the 'Marabout Wars', as they were called, for another three decades. By this time, the Wolof had embraced Islam and now fought fiercely against French expansionism. Soldiers of the Wolof

The Lions of Teranga

It wasn't supposed to happen like this. Senegal, a nation whose footballing history included forgetting to enter the 1990 World Cup qualifiers, had used the opening game of the 2002 World Cup in Japan and Korea to manufacture what has been described as 'the greatest football upset ever' by beating defending champions France 1-0. The irony was everywhere: the Lions of Teranga, as Senegal's football team is known, were made up almost exclusively of France-based players expertly marshalled by Bruno Metsu, a Michael Bolton lookalike Frenchman who calls Dakar home.

In Dakar, supporters who had simply hoped the team would not be embarrassed went mad. The victory over France was just the beginning. Players like El Hadji Diouf, Pape Bouba Diop, Ferdinand Coly, Khalilou Fadiga and Salif Diao became underdog heroes to much of the world as the Lions went on to draw 1-1 with Denmark before a nailbiting 3-3 draw with Uruguay took them to the second round.Two thrilling goals from Henri Camara, the latter an extra time golden goal, saw Senegal beat Sweden 2-1 and become only the second African team to reach the quarter finals in World Cup history. However it was there the dream ended when Turkey scored their own golden goal winner.

king Lat Dior repeatedly hindered French attempts to build a railway line between Dakar and St-Louis, neatly symbolising the conflict between the new and old orders. Another thorn in the French side was a marabout called Amadou Bamba (see the boxed text 'Bamba' later in this chapter). The last significant Wolof battle was in 1889 at Yang-Yang in northern Senegal (near present-day Linguère), where the army of Alboury Ndiaye was defeated by the French. Eventually, superior European firepower and a divided marabout-led army allowed the French to gain control of the whole region.

The Colonial Period

At the Berlin Conference of 1884–85, following the Scramble for Africa, the continent was divided between powerful European states. While Britain (with Germany and Portugal) got most of East and Southern Africa, the greater part of West Africa was allocated to France. At the end of the 19th century, French West Africa stretched from the Atlantic to present-day Niger.

In 1887, Africans living in the four largest towns in Senegal (Dakar, Gorée, St-Louis and Rufisque) were granted limited French citizenship, but compared with the British, the French did little to educate their colonial subjects. Only those needed to work for the French administration received secondary education in Dakar, which by this time had become the capital of French West Africa. (St-Louis remained the capital of Senegal-Mauritania.)

But in the early 20th century, things began to change. In 1914, Senegal elected its first African delegate, Blaise Diagne, to the French national assembly in Paris. After WWI, it became fashionable for politically conscious Senegalese to join French parties – particularly the increasingly powerful Socialists and Communists – and several Senegalese intellectuals went to France to study. One was Léopold Senghor, who became the first African secondary-school teacher in France. He began writing poetry and after WWII he helped found *Présence Africaine*, a magazine promoting the values of African culture.

Senghor was an astute politician, and shrewdly began building a personal power base that resulted in his election as Senegal's representative to the French national assembly. Meanwhile, the marabouts had become increasingly involved in politics, and through the 1950s Senghor made secret deals with leading figures, allowing them limited autonomy and control of the groundnut economy in return for their public support (ensuring safe votes from their followers in rural areas).

Independence

In the late 1950s, Senghor gained support from French Soudan (now Mali), Upper Volta (Burkina Faso) and Dahomey (Benin) to form the Mali Federation. But, like his earlier plans for a united French West Africa, this plan too failed when Upper Volta and Dahomey withdrew under pressure from France and Côte d'Ivoire. (Côte d'Ivoire's leader, Houphouët-Boigny, feared that within a federal union the richer territories, such as his own, would have to subsidise the poorer ones.) On 20 June 1960, Senegal and Mali became independent, while remaining within the French union, and Senghor became the first president. But two months later, the Senegal-Mali union broke up. Houphouët-Boigny had won the day, and French West Africa became nine separate republics.

Senegal's early independent years did not always run smoothly. In 1968, students rioted at the University of Dakar. Senghor sent in the military, but the situation was not resolved until workers and students were promised reforms.

The 1970s were less turbulent: Senghor held on to his position and remained a popular figure. In 1980, after 20 years as president, he did what no other African head of state had done before – he voluntarily stepped down. His hand-picked successor Abdou Diouf took over.

One of Diouf's first major moves was to help the president of Gambia, Dawda Jawara, who had been ousted in a coup. With help from Senegalese troops Jawara was restored, and this cooperation was formalised in the establishment of the Senegambia Confederation later in the same year.

In 1983 and 1988 Diouf's Parti Socialiste (PS) defeated a loose opposition, led by Abdoulaye Wade, in elections widely thought to be rigged. During the latter election Wade was arrested and charged with intent to subvert the government. He received a one-year suspended sentence and left for France.

By this time the Senegambia Confederation was in trouble, and in 1989 it was completely dissolved. But while Diouf was contending with this break-up and calls for political reform, he had two other major problems to deal with: a dispute with Mauritania and a campaign against separatists in the southern region of Casamance (see the Casamance section later in this chapter).

Wade returned from exile and stood again in the presidential election of 1993. Diouf won, but both Wade and his Parti Démocratique Sénégalais (PDS) had claimed a significant percentage of the vote. Unpopular austerity measures were introduced and a major devaluation of the CFA franc in early 1994 created further tensions.

Sopi (Change)

The PS won the 1998 parliamentary elections in another landslide and were again accused of rigging the result. But it was evident that the opposition was gaining momentum and a growing number of the electorate was dissatisfied. New election laws allowed the president a seven-year term, so Wade had to wait until 2000 to challenge Diouf once more.

By the time voting began in February 2000, Wade's *sopi* (Wolof for 'change') campaign had captured the imagination of the nation. Wade was elected and, in a sequence of events almost unheard of in Africa, Diouf accepted defeat and power was transferred peacefully. The people of Senegal were rightly proud of this affirmation of the strength of their democracy, and in January 2001 more than 90% voted for a new constitution allowing the formation of opposition parties, giving enhanced status to the prime minister and cutting the president's term from seven years back to five.

Following his election Wade had appointed another Diouf opponent, Moustapha Niasse, as prime minister, but it didn't take long for divisions to emerge between the two men and in March 2001 Niasse was sacked. His replacement was, in another first for Africa, a female judge, Madior Boye.

Despite the disharmony at the top, Wade's Sopi coalition, an alliance of 40 parties, won 89 of the 120 seats in the April 2001 parliamentary elections. After dominating parliament since 1960, the PS came third with just 10 seats. Ironically, sceptics believe that this huge electoral success could mean Wade, the long-suffering democrat, now has more seats than is healthy, making Senegalese politics in effect a one-party system all over again.

GEOGRAPHY

Senegal has an area of 196,192 sq km, similar in size to South Dakota in the USA; the Australian state of Victoria; and England and Scotland combined. The country is largely flat, with low foothills in the southeast. To the west, Senegal is fringed by the Atlantic Ocean coastline, some 600km in length, running roughly north-south and divided by the Cap Vert peninsula on which Dakar is built. Senegal's three major rivers flow east-west across the country into the Atlantic. In the north, the Senegal River forms the border with Mauritania. In southeastern Senegal, the Gambia River flows through Parc National du Niokolo-Koba before it crosses into

Gambia itself. South of Gambia is the Casamance River, which gives its name to the surrounding Casamance area.

CLIMATE

In northern and central Senegal the rainy season is July to September, while in Casamance it's June to early October. Rainfall ranges from an annual average of 300mm in the north to almost six times that amount in the south, with about 600mm in Dakar. The rainy season is also the hottest time of year, with temperatures around 30°C. November to March is dry and relatively cool, with temperatures around 24°C, but from December the skies are clouded by the dust of the harmattan.

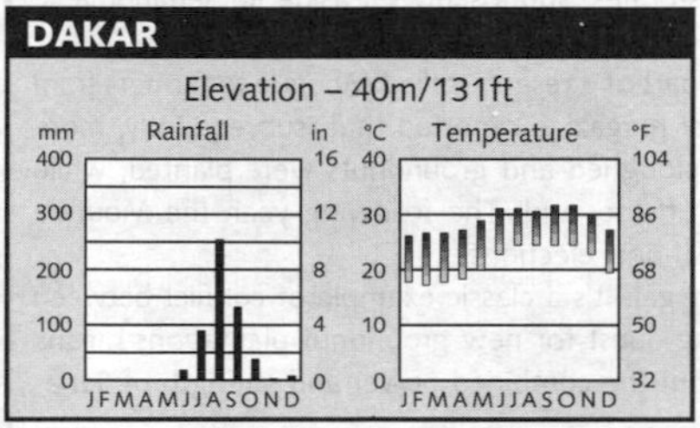
DAKAR
Elevation – 40m/131ft
Rainfall
Temperature
mm
in
°C
°F
400
300
200
100
0
16
12
8
4
0
40
30
20
10
0
104
86
68
50
32
JFMAMJJASOND
JFMAMJJASOND

ECOLOGY & ENVIRONMENT

In common with many West African countries, Senegal's most-pressing environmental issues include deforestation and soil erosion. These are linked to the ever-increasing demand for land for cultivation, both small-scale plots for subsistence farmers and larger commercial plantations. (See the boxed text 'Groundnuts' for a wider discussion of these issues.)

Meanwhile, off the coast of Senegal, overfishing to supply a growing local population and a lucrative export market means fish stocks are declining. The problem is exacerbated by unsustainable fishing methods such as the use of dynamite to stun shoals, although this way only about one-quarter of the fish killed can be 'caught' – the rest sink out of reach.

Even more cause for concern are the factory ships from Europe and East Asia that use vast nets to land huge catches. Most have negotiated fishing rights with the Senegalese government and provide a vital source of income for the country (although there are frequent reports of extra ships fishing illegally and of legal ships exceeding quotas), but for the local fishermen in their traditional boats, making a living from the sea becomes increasingly precarious.

FLORA

Senegal lies in the Sahel zone, with a natural vegetation of well-dispersed trees and low scrub. In the north, along the border with Mauritania, the landscape comes close to being desert, while the wetter Casamance region in the south is a fertile zone of forest and farmland.

FAUNA

Most of the birds occurring in Gambia can also be seen in Senegal (in fact Senegal has about 80 more species recorded), but the more widely dispersed nature of good bird-watching sites means Senegal has yet to become a major destination for ornithologists.

The coast and large estuaries of the rivers Senegal, Saloum and Casamance are notable staging points for waders, shore birds and vast flocks of European migrants, while avid bird-watchers can use the Cap Vert peninsula as a base from which to observe sea birds. Inland, the dry Sahel landscape supports several arid-savanna species that are hard to see elsewhere in Africa. Highly recommended is *A Field Guide to Birds of The Gambia & Senegal* by Clive Barlow & Tim Wacher.

Easily recognised mammal species in forested areas include baboons and three types of monkeys (vervet, patas and red colobus), while Parc National du Niokolo-Koba contains chimpanzee populations, their most northern outpost in West Africa. This park also has drier grassland areas where antelope species include cob, roan, waterbuck and Derby eland, and there's a chance of seeing hyenas and buffaloes, plus a few lonely hippopotamuses. The park has populations of lions, leopards and elephants, but you should count yourself very lucky indeed if you see either leopards or elephants. In wooded areas around the country you may also see oribis, duikers, warthogs and bush pigs.

NATIONAL PARKS

Senegal has six national parks: Parc National du Niokolo-Koba in southeast Senegal, the largest, with a wide range of habitat types

Groundnuts

For much of the 20th century the humble groundnut, or peanut, was pivotal in economic, social and religious life in Senegal. And while groundnuts are no longer the economic mainstay, their production still utilises about 40% of the country's arable land and employs one million people. Groundnuts grow like beans on low bushes, and are ideal for Senegal because they can survive in relatively dry areas. The harvested nuts are crushed to make oil, which is exported to Europe for use in food manufacture.

The main groundnut growing region is around the towns of Diourbel, Touba and Kaolack, and it's no coincidence that these are centres of the powerful Muslim brotherhoods whose marabouts (leaders) dominate much of Senegal's political and economic life. Many marabouts derive their wealth and power from the groundnut plantations on their land. This is particularly the case among the followers of the Mouride brotherhood, for whom work (on behalf of their marabout) is considered a great virtue.

Although groundnuts contribute to the economy, they also do damage. The plantations prevent local farmers from growing their own food and have a devastating effect on the environment. The crop absorbs nutrients, then at harvesting the whole plant – roots and all – is picked, leaving loose, dry soil exposed. The soil is soon exhausted or simply blown away, and new plantations have to be established. This reduces wildlife habitats and is a major issue in central Senegal as groundnut farmers expand into grazing reserves *(réserves sylvo-pastorales)* supposedly set aside for seminomadic people such as the Fula.

In 1991, the then president, Abdou Diouf, 'gave' part of a reserve called Mbegué to farmers from the Mouride brotherhood. The *New Internationalist* magazine reported that, subsequently, more than five million trees were cleared, the land was ploughed and groundnuts were planted, while 6000 Fula people and 100,000 cows were forced off the land. The following year, the Mouride leader urged his followers to support Diouf in the national elections.

Similar invasions have occurred elsewhere in Senegal. It's a classic example of conflict between farmers and nomads, but in this case the continuing quest for new groundnut plantations means the Fula are facing not just small-scale cultivators, but the combined power and strength of Senegal's political and religious establishment.

and associated wildlife; Parc National du Delta du Saloum, just north of Gambia, with mainly coastal lagoons, mangroves, sandy islands and a section of dry woodland; the Îles de la Madeleine, near Dakar; and, in northern Senegal, Parc National aux Oiseaux du Djoudj and Parc National de la Langue de Barbarie, both noted for their bird life. (Parc National de Basse-Casamance, an area of woodland and mangrove in the Casamance region, has been closed for years because of rebel activity.) Other protected areas include the Ferlo wildlife reserves in the north-central part of Senegal, and the Réserve de Bandia near the Petite Côte.

GOVERNMENT & POLITICS

Senegal is a republic, with the president and 120 members of the national assembly elected every five years. The political system is a multiparty democracy with a coalition called Sopi (Change), led by President Abdoulaye Wade's Parti Démocratique Sénégalais, currently in power. There are several opposition parties, the main ones being the Alliance of Forces of Progress (AFP) and the Parti Socialiste (PS), which ruled for 40 years until 2001. Although the country's human rights record is by no means unblemished, Senegal is still one of the least politically repressive countries in West Africa.

ECONOMY

Senegal's economy is based on agriculture, but that it employs 70% of the working population for just 19% of the gross national product is a reflection of the inefficiency that plagues the sector. Many of those people work in the production of groundnuts (see the boxed text 'Groundnuts'). Some diversification has been achieved, notably into cotton and rice, but production of subsistence crops such as millet is declining, and Senegal now imports about 35% of its food requirements. Fishing is a major activity on the coast, and fish account for a huge 27% of all foreign exchange earnings (US$2.8 billion).

As with many other developing countries, foreign debt remains a huge problem. Despite receiving debt relief to the tune of almost US$1 billion in recent years, Senegal still owes around US$3.5 billion to commercial banks and international bodies such as the World Bank. As Senegal becomes eligible for a variety of debt-relief initiatives, this total is expected to be significantly reduced. In the meantime, debt continues to absorb a large portion of the country's export earnings and, while trade figures remain negative, the loans cannot be cleared, and interest bills still need to be paid.

POPULATION & PEOPLE

The population of Senegal was estimated at 10.3 million in mid-2001, 45% of which was under 15 years old. Small families are not especially popular, with the average woman having five children. The dominant ethnic group is the Wolof (about 43% of the total), who live mostly in the central area, north and east of Dakar, and along the coast. The Sérèr (15%) also live in the central regions, while the Fula (23%), also called Fulani, Fulbe and Peul, live throughout northern and eastern Senegal, although they look on the Futa Toro region as their homeland. Other groups include the Tukulor (also spelt Toucouleur), inhabiting the north; the Mandinka, in the areas bordering Gambia; the Malinké in the northeast; and the Diola (also called Jola), found mainly in the Casamance. Minor groups include the Bassari and Bédik, who live in the remote southeastern part of Senegal, and the Lebu, who live almost exclusively in the town of Yoff outside Dakar.

Most Senegalese speak Wolof and about 90% are Muslim. Further homogeneity derives from the *cousinage* (or 'joking cousins') relationship that exists between different ethnic groups or clans, which allows very jocular and personal conversations even among strangers, and symbolises a deeper level of mutual support against outsiders.

ARTS

Arts & Craftwork

Senegal is not noted for its traditions of carving wooden masks and sculpture, but arts and crafts from many other parts of West Africa are available in Senegal, especially in the markets in Dakar.

Bukut: A Diola Masking Tradition

The Bukut is an initiation ceremony that takes place every 20 to 25 years and involves the gaining of knowledge and social status by young Diola men. Preparations for the Bukut start months in advance as the celebrations entail huge feasts involving the sacrifice of many cattle. It is during these preparations that mothers compose songs that are sung by the initiated during a ritual involving the passing of cloth called Buyeet. Each youth has his own song, which will not be sung again publicly until his death.

The initiates wear distinctive woven cane masks called Ejumbi, which have tubular eyes and are surmounted by a pair of massive cattle horns, when they return from the sacred forest. Not all initiates wear these masks, but those who do are believed to possess special powers of clairvoyance. The masks are created by the initiates with the assistance of tribal elders.

The Bukut represents Diola identity and is still considered a very important event. It has survived and adapted to Christianity and Islam.

John Graham

Fabrics of various styles and designs feature largely in Senegalese life, and travellers will find a wide range of clothes, wraps and wall-hangings available in markets. The tapestries of Thiès are famous and worth seeing, although they sell for thousands of dollars and are way beyond the budget of most travellers! (See the boxed text 'The Tapestries of Thiès' later in this chapter.)

Literature

Senegal's most influential writer is Léopold Senghor (1906–2001), the country's first president. He coined the term *negritude*, which emphasised indigenous ideas and culture, and his combined position as leading politician and leading literary figure made him unique in Africa.

Of the few Senegalese writers translated into English, probably the most famous is Sembène Ousmane. His classic *God's Bits of Wood* (1970) describes the struggles of striking railway workers in the late 1940s and the emergence of grassroots political consciousness in pre-independence Africa. His other books include *Black Docker*, based on his experiences in the port of Marseilles in the 1950s, and *Xala*, an attack on the privileged elite of Dakar.

A more recent Senegalese writer is Mariama Bâ, whose short but incisive novel *So Long a Letter* was first published in 1980 and won international acclaim. The common theme of ungainly transition between traditional and modern society is explored by a woman narrator whose much-loved husband takes a second wife.

Another woman writer is Aminata Sow-Fall; her 1986 novel *The Beggars Strike* is an ironic story highlighting the differences between rich and poor and questions the power of the political elite – a consistently popular theme in modern Senegalese literature.

Pop Music in Senegal

The father of modern Senegalese music is Ibra Kassé, who formed the Star Band de Dakar to play at his nightclub, The Miami, in the early 1960s. Through the 1970s, the music scene in Senegal, Mali and Guinea was dominated by large bands or 'orchestras'. The most famous of these, Orchestra Baobab, has recently reformed; several of their CDs are available internationally, and they have released numerous cassettes locally. Other great ensembles included Canari de Kaolack, the Royal Band, and Étoile de Dakar – whose mix of western Wolof drum rhythms and Western rock (known as *mbalax*) shot Youssou N'Dour to Stardom. He still plays regularly with his band Le Super Étoile at his Thiosanne nightclub in Dakar.

Touré Kunda (meaning 'Touré family' – the band was founded by four brothers) is very popular, as is the vocalist Thione Seck, formerly with Orchestra Baobab. The Latin influence is very strong in Senegal, and was best realised through the bold fusions of Africando. In contrast, Baaba Maal, a northern Fula, has stayed close to his musical roots.

Some other names to look out for include Ismael Lô, sometimes called the Senegalese Bob Dylan; and Idrissa Diop, who sings in Wolof and has performed before huge international audiences with his group Les Gaiendes (their music features percussion instruments of various kinds). The group Xalam developed a unique style combining African music, jazz, and rhythm and blues, and was one of the first West African bands to gain recognition in Europe. They no longer play live, but Xalam albums are still widely available. Others worth hearing are Le Super Cayor, Mansour Seck, Super Diamono and Étoile 2000.

SOCIETY & CONDUCT

Expect to shake a lot of hands during your visit, both when you enter and when you leave a gathering. This is usually a ritual reserved for men, but Western women are often afforded the status of honorary men so any extraneous shaking is unlikely to cause offence. If during your visit you are offered *attaya* (tea), realise that if you have one glass you are obliged to stay for the full three-glass ceremony.

In a traditional Wolof wedding, the grandmother and great aunts take the bride to the marriage chamber, lecture her and summon the husband to consummate the marriage. When this is done the older women exhibit the bloodstained sheet to the guests, after which the bride is smothered with gifts. (If you want to make a gift at any ceremony, a small amount of money is perfectly acceptable.)

At Christmas in St-Louis and Île de Gorée, crowds of people carry around large lanterns called *fanals* which are made in the shape of boats or houses, and are brightly painted with intricate decorations. This fascinating tradition originated during French colonial times, when wealthy inhabitants going to midnight mass would be led by slaves carrying lamps.

RELIGION

In Senegal about 90% of the population is Muslim, mainly the Wolof, Tukulor, Lebu, Fula and Mandinka people, while the Diola and Sérèr favour Christianity, although many people also follow traditional beliefs.

An all-pervading aspect of Islam in Senegal is the power of the marabouts and Islamic brotherhoods.

LANGUAGE

French is the official language and Wolof the principal African language. Other languages include Mandinka (and the closely related Malinké), Fula, Sérèr and Diola (not to be confused with Dioula, spoken in Côte d'Ivoire). English is spoken a little, in some tourist areas only. See the Language chapter for some useful expressions in French, Wolof, Mandinka/Malinké and Fula.

ANDREW BURKE

FRANCES LINZEE GORDON

ARIADNE VAN ZANDBERGEN

ARIADNE VAN ZANDBERGEN

West Africa's vast, open coastline plays an important role in the daily lives of many people. Fishing, shipping and recreation, in the form of the expanding tourist industry, all contribute to the local economy: pirogues on the beach at Bakau, Gambia (top); Ankobra Beach, Ghana (middle right); Porto Novo harbour, Cape Verde (bottom left); Sekondi-Takoradi port, Ghana (bottom right).

FRANCES LINZEE GORDON

ARIADNE VAN ZANDBERGEN

KIM WILDMAN

If you're tired of the baking West African desert or the uncomfortable steamy tropics, head for the coast and relax with the cooling sea breeze blowing in your face: the town of Paúl with its mountain backdrop, Santo Antão island, Cape Verde (top); Biriwa beach near Cape Coast, Ghana (bottom left); beach at Grand Popo, Benin (bottom right)

Marabouts & Brotherhoods

An understanding of Senegal's marabouts and the power of the Islamic brotherhoods *(confréries)* is fundamental to an understanding of Senegal itself. The subject involves religion, politics, economy, God and the state, and is remarkably complex.

Whereas orthodox Islam holds that every believer is directly in touch with Allah, the traditionally hierarchical societies of North and West Africa found it more natural to have religious leaders ascribed with divine power, providing a link between God and the common populace. These intermediaries became known as marabouts, and many are venerated by their disciples *(talibés)* as saints. The concept of brotherhoods – groups who follow the teachings of a particular marabout – was imported from Morocco. The leader of a brotherhood was known as a *cheik*, or *khalif*, and these terms are still used today.

Brotherhoods in Senegal include the Qadiriya, the Moroccan-based Tijaniya, and the Mouridiya, founded by a marabout called Amadou Bamba in the late 19th century and now the largest and most influential brotherhood, claiming over three million followers (see the boxed text 'Bamba' later in this chapter). One of Bamba's followers was Ibra Fall, who, with Bamba's blessing, founded the Baye Fall sect for whom labour replaced prayer as religious observance. Ibra's followers called him Lamp Fall, and Bamba excused them from prayer and fasting during Ramadan so long as they worked hard – yet another Senegalese spin on conventional Islam.

Today, you'll see images of Lamp Fall and Bamba painted on walls and buses all over Senegal. Bamba's 1907 return from exile is celebrated by the annual Magal pilgrimage to Touba, and it's significant that this, rather than any other Islamic holiday, is the major Mouride event.

The links between marabouts and politicians is a major feature of Senegalese life. When Abdou Diouf lost the support of the khalif of the Mourides in 2000, he also lost power. Soon afterwards, new president Abdoulaye Wade announced that Senegal's new international airport would be built outside Touba, the spiritual home of the Mourides – 194km from Dakar. However, sense seems to have prevailed and the plan has been scrapped.

Facts for the Visitor

SUGGESTED ITINERARIES

During a stay of just a week you could start in Dakar and spend two days visiting the frenetic markets and peaceful Île de Gorée, before heading north to St-Louis, from where you could visit the wildlife reserves of Parc National aux Oiseaux du Djoudj and Parc National de la Langue de Barbarie (allow one day each). Alternatively, you could head south to the beaches of the Petite Côte and the villages and mangroves of the Siné-Saloum Delta.

With three weeks you could do a circular tour, heading south to the Petite Côte, Siné-Saloum Delta and Kaolack before going east to Tambacounda. From Tamba you have options: You could return to Dakar through Gambia; come via the Senegal River route and St-Louis; or head south into the stunning Casamance region, to Ziguinchor and the beaches at Cap Skiring before returning north for your flight home. Yet another option would be to do the eastward leg through Gambia and the westward leg through Casamance, although this might be a rush in three weeks.

With five or six weeks, or even two months, you could do the same route in a much more relaxed manner, including detours off the circuit to the mosque at Touba, the Parc National du Niokolo-Koba and the little-visited but highly recommended Bassari country in the far southeast.

PLANNING

When to Go

The best time is mid-November to February when conditions are dry and relatively cool. From December to February is also the local 'trading season', when the harvest is completed and markets are busier. From March to May, the weather is dry but hotter, while June to October is the rainy season and also hot. Just before and after the rains conditions are humid with no storms to clear the air.

Maps

The locally produced *Carte du Sénégal* (at a scale of 1:912,000) is the best and cheapest available and includes an excellent street map of Dakar. Not quite as good but more widely available internationally is the *ITMB Senegal, Including Gambia* (1:800,000).

VISAS

Visas are not needed by citizens of the European Union (as it stands at the time of writing), Canada, Norway, South Africa, Japan, Israel, the USA and several other (mainly African) countries. Tourist visas for one to three months cost about US$15 to US$20. Australians and New Zealanders definitely *do* need a visa, despite what some Senegalese embassies (most notably the one in Bamako, Mali) have advised.

Visas for Onward Travel

In Senegal, you can get visas for the following nearby West African countries. All embassies are open weekday mornings; for visas it's best to go early. You usually need two photos. For embassy locations, see Embassies & Consulates following.

Burkina Faso Visas cost CFA13,000 and take two days. You need three photos.

Cape Verde Visas cost CFA21,200 and take 24 hours.

Gambia Visas cost CFA15,000 and they are issued within 24 hours.

Guinea Visas cost CFA20,000 and they are issued in 24 hours.

Guinea-Bissau Visas cost CFA10,000 for one month and are issued the same day if you arrive before noon. There is also an efficient consulate in Ziguinchor, where with CFA5000 and a photo you can get a visa in five minutes.

Mali Visas cost CFA7500 and take 48 hours.

Mauritania Visas cost CFA6000 to CFA9000, depending on nationality, and are issued on the spot by the consulate, which is around the side of the embassy, near the Independence Monument.

Togo Visas are issued by the French consulate for CFA40,000 in one day. You will need a letter from your embassy.

SENEGAL

EMBASSIES & CONSULATES

Senegalese Embassies & Consulates

In West Africa, Senegal has embassies in Burkina Faso, Cape Verde, Côte d'Ivoire, Gambia, Guinea, Guinea-Bissau and Mali. For details, see the Facts for the Visitor section of the relevant chapter. Elsewhere, Senegalese embassies and consulates include the following:

Belgium (☎ 02-673 00 97) 196 Av Franklin-Roosevelt, Brussels 1050
France (☎ 01 44 05 38 69) 22 rue Hamelin, 75016 Paris
Germany (☎ 0228-21 80 08) Argelanderstrasse 3, 53115 Bonn
UK (☎ 020-7938 4048) 39 Marloes Rd, London W8 6LA
USA (☎ 202-234 0540) 2112 Wyoming Ave NW, Washington, DC 20008

Embassies & Consulates in Senegal

Many embassies are in or near central Dakar, but there is a steady movement of the diplomatic corps towards the Point E and Mermoz areas, about 5km northwest of the centre.

Belgium (☎ 821 4027) Route de la Corniche-Est
Burkina Faso (☎ 827 9509) Lot 1, Liberty VI Extension; open 8am to 3pm Monday to Friday
Canada (☎ 823 9290) Blvd de la République
Cape Verde (☎ 821 3936) 3 Blvd el Haji Djily Mbaye; open 8.30am to 3pm Monday to Friday
Côte d'Ivoire (☎ 821 3473) 2 Av Albert Sarraut
France (☎ 839 5100) 1 Rue Assane Ndoye, near the Novotel
Gambia (☎ 821 7230 or 821 4476) 11 Rue de Thiong
Germany (☎ 823 2519) 20 Av Pasteur
Guinea (☎ 824 8606) Rue 7, Point E; open 9.30am to 2pm Monday to Friday
Guinea-Bissau (☎ 824 5922) Rue 6, Point E *Consulate in Ziguinchor:* (☎ 991 1046) Opposite the Hôtel le Flamboyant; open 8am to 2pm Monday to Friday
Mali (☎ 894 6950/9) 23 Corniche-Ouest, Fann; open 8am to 11am Monday to Friday
Mauritania (☎ 822 6238) Rue 37, Kolobane
Morocco (☎ 824 6927) Av Cheikh Anta Diop, Mermoz
The Netherlands (☎ 823 9483) 37 Rue Kléber
UK (☎ 823 7392) 20 Rue du Dr Guillet
USA (☎ 823 3496 or 823 3424) Av Jean XXIII

CUSTOMS

There are no limits on the amount of foreign currency tourists are allowed to bring into

Senegal, although CFA200,000 is the maximum amount of local currency foreigners can export.

MONEY

The unit of currency is the CFA franc.

country	unit		CFA
euro zone	€1	=	CFA656
UK	UK£1	=	CFA1024
USA	US$1	=	CFA694

Exchanging Money

Banks include Citibank; Compagnie Bancaire de l'Afrique Occidentale (CBAO); Banque Internationale pour le Commerce et l'Industrie Sénégalaise (BICIS), which is affiliated with and accepts cheques from BNP in France; and Société Générale de Banques du Sénégal (SGBS). There are branches in all main towns and at Dakar airport. If the airport branch is closed, you can change money at the airport bookshop, where commissions are lower.

There are plenty of ATMs in Dakar and a couple in Kaolack, St-Louis, Saly and Ziguinchor. SGBS and CBAO ATMs take Visa and MasterCard, but Bicis accepts only Visa cards. You can get a cash advance on your credit card, although some readers say this is more trouble than it's worth, if it's possible at all. In Dakar, the best place for a non-ATM credit card advance is the SGBS branch at the south end of Place de l'Indépendance.

Cashing travellers cheques in any major currency is easy in Dakar and St-Louis, but can be a protracted nightmare elsewhere. 'Western Union Money Transfer' signs seem to be breeding in Senegal, but the official agent for Western Union is CBAO.

POST & COMMUNICATIONS

Post

Senegal's postal service is relatively good. Sending a 10g letter to France/Europe/North America/Australasia costs CFA370/390/425/535, while a 2kg parcel costs CFA9600/10,600/12,100/20,100. The country's main poste restante is in Dakar, but avoid it unless you're desperate.

Telephone & Fax

There's a telecommunications revolution occurring in Senegal, with use of traditional and mobile phones soaring. Thousands of privately owned *télécentres* have popped up across the country providing a convenient and very efficient service. Alternatively, the government-operated Sonatel has four offices in Dakar and one in St-Louis, open from 9am to 11.30pm Monday to Saturday. Call prices have fallen recently but still aren't cheap. Local calls work out at about CFA50 per minute but this rises sharply if the call is long-distance or to a mobile number. International calls and faxes from either Sonatel or télécentres cost about the same at CFA600 per minute to Europe and CFA800 per minute to the USA, with a 20% reduction after 8pm and at weekends. Rates to Australia are higher.

Mobile (Cell) Phones Linking into one of the two local GSM phone networks is easy. SIM cards for either the Hello or Alize networks cost CFA25,000, with prepaid cards selling for around CFA5000, CFA10,000 or CFA50,000. Coverage is improving but there are many places where there is no service.

Email & Internet Access

In Dakar and all regional capitals there are Net bureaus, the general rule being that the more remote the town the slower and more expensive the service. In Dakar, Internet phone and video links are fairly common. An hour online costs from CFA500 to CFA1000.

DIGITAL RESOURCES

While most websites about Senegal are in French there are some that come with English options.

St-Louis city site Not all the links are in English, but details of transport, accommodation and cultural events usually are.
W www.saintlouisdusenegal.com/english

Au-Senegal Probably the best, most useful and most regularly updated site specifically for tourists.
W www.au-senegal.com

BBC News If there has been a major incident in Casamance, you'll read about it here. Just type 'Casamance' into the search box for the full archive.
W newssearch.bbc.co.uk

Senerap.com Some stories are in French, but you don't need to be a linguist to download MP3s of Dakar's latest rap and hip-hop hits.
W www.senerap.com

BOOKS

Senegalese literature is discussed under Arts in the Facts about Senegal section earlier in this chapter, and some general books that include coverage of Senegal are listed under Books in the Regional Facts for the Visitor chapter. One of the few locally produced guidebooks in English is *Gorée – The Island and the Historical Museum* (CFA3500).

NEWSPAPERS & MAGAZINES

Most newspapers and magazines are published in French, with a few in Wolof and other local languages. Senegal's main daily paper is *Le Soleil*, nominally independent but rarely too critical of the government.

RADIO & TV

The government radio stations broadcast in French, Wolof and other local languages. Government TV is all in French. Independent radio stations, also French-language, include Dakar FM and the lively Sud-FM. Independent TV is dominated by Canal + Horizons and French satellite stations, although some large hotels have sets tuned into CNN or BBC World. In Dakar it's possible to hear a BBC World Service relay on FM105.6.

PHOTOGRAPHY & VIDEO

You can photograph most things (providing the usual rules of politeness are observed), even the colourfully clad guards outside the presidential palace, although snapping military installations, airports or government buildings could still get you into trouble. Film is widely available, but you should bring your own slide film. For general information and advice, see Photography & Video in the Regional Facts for the Visitor chapter.

HEALTH

Malaria is a killer and exists year-round throughout the country. It is essential that you take appropriate precautions, especially if you're heading out of Dakar. Proof of yellow fever vaccination is mandatory if you are coming from an endemic area. For more information on these and other health matters, see Health in the Regional Facts for the Visitor chapter.

Water in Senegal's main cities and towns is generally clean and OK to drink, and even in some of the more remote places we had no trouble. Bottled water is also available in all but the smallest towns.

In Dakar you'll find the country's main hospitals as well as many private clinics and doctors. Around the country, most large towns have hospitals, doctors and clinics; if you need to find any of these, ask at a good hotel in the town.

WOMEN TRAVELLERS

Senegal does not pose any specific problems for women travellers. For general information and advice, see Women Travellers in the Regional Facts for the Visitor chapter.

DANGERS & ANNOYANCES

There are two main dangers you may encounter: the possibility of civil unrest in Casamance (see the boxed text 'To Go or Not to Go?' in the Casamance section of this chapter) and the possibility of being robbed in Dakar (see the boxed text 'Dangers in Dakar' in the Dakar section of this chapter).

BUSINESS HOURS

Businesses are open from 8am to noon and 2.30pm to 6pm Monday to Friday, and 8am to noon Saturday. Government offices keep the same hours. Most banks are open Monday to Friday, typically from 8.30am to 11.30am or noon, and 2.30pm to 4.30pm. Some banks open on Saturday until 11am.

PUBLIC HOLIDAYS & SPECIAL EVENTS

Public holidays include:

New Year's Day 1 January
Independence Day 4 April
Easter March/April
Labour Day 1 May
Assumption 15 August
All Saints Day 1 November
Christmas Day 25 December

Islamic holidays are also celebrated – for a table of dates, see Public Holidays & Special Events in the Regional Facts for the Visitor chapter. The major holidays are Independence Day (which coincides with the West African International Marathon in Dakar), the end of Ramadan (Koraté) and Tabaski.

Other festivals include the Grand Magal pilgrimage in Touba, 48 days after the Islamic new year; and the St-Louis International Jazz Festival, held every May. There's

SENEGAL

also the Paris-Dakar Rally, which ends at Lake Rose (near Dakar) in mid-January.

ACTIVITIES

One of the most popular activities among travellers are drumming courses. From Yoff and Malika, near Dakar, to Cap Skirring and Kafountine in the Casamance, drumming courses draw increasing numbers of tourists, often for weeks at a time.

Most major hotels have swimming pools that nonguests can use for a fee. Otherwise, Senegal's coast has many good beaches, although heavy undertows can make some dangerous. If sand is more your thing than sea, you might want to join a motorbike tour or learn the best way to pilot a 4WD through the Sahara sands. For details see the Organised Tours section in the Getting Around section later in this chapter.

At hotels on the coast, you can hire sailboards, or arrange water-skiing and several other motor-assisted sports. Dakar is also a base for diving and kayaking. Deep-sea sport fishing can be arranged in Dakar and other coastal centres. Depending on the season, ocean catches include barracuda, tuna, sailfish and blue marlin.

ACCOMMODATION

Senegal offers everything from top-class hotels and coastal resorts to dirty dosshouses. There is a good choice of *campements* (small and usually cheap establishments with basic rooms or bungalow, but seldom actual camping facilities) and simple hotels in the smaller towns and rural areas. All hotels charge a tourist tax of CFA600 per person, but it's not always included in the price.

Some hotels charge by the room, so it makes no difference to the price (apart from the tourist tax) if you are alone or sharing. In others, couples may be allowed to share a single. Breakfast usually costs extra.

The high season for hotel rates is usually from October to May. Other times may be cheaper, but some hotels close outside the high season.

FOOD

Senegal has some of the finest cuisine in West Africa – a very enjoyable feature of travel here. Common dishes include *mafé*, a groundnut-based stew, and *domodah*, the same stew with meat or vegetables added to it. Sometimes deep-orange palm oil is also added. *Tiéboudienne* (pronounced chey-bou-jen and also spelt 'thieboudjienne', and numerous other ways) is Senegal's national dish and consists of rice baked in a thick sauce of fish and vegetables. *Thieb khonkhe* (pronounced cheb-honk) is a similar dish which comes with a tomato paste. Especially popular at restaurants catering to tourists is *poulet yassa* – grilled chicken in onion and lemon sauce. Variations on the theme are *poisson yassa* (fish) and *viande yassa* (meat), or sometimes simply *yassa* – a bit of a lucky dip. Another equally variable favourite is *riz yollof*, also called *thieb yape*, which consists of vegetables and/or meat cooked in oil and tomatoes, served with rice.

DRINKS

Tea comes in two sorts: Western-style tea made with a tea bag, and local tea made with green leaves and served with loads of sugar in small glasses, called *attaya*. Coffee is almost exclusively instant Nescafé. Bottled soft drinks are widely available, usually for about CFA300.

Senegalese beer is good. Gazelle comes in 630ml bottles and costs between CFA500 and CFA1200. Flag is a stronger, more upmarket brew. A 330ml bottle costs CFA400 in the cheapest rural bar and CFA1500 or more in posh hotels (where they wouldn't dream of offering Gazelle). Flag is also available in larger bottles and on draught.

Getting There & Away

AIR

Senegal's main international airport is Dakar, served mainly by European, African and charter airlines. Airport tax is charged when you leave, but is usually included in your ticket price. If it is not included, the tax (levied at the airport) is US$20 or CFA10,000.

Europe & the USA

Airlines from Europe serving Senegal include Air France, Alitalia, TAP Air Portugal and Aeroflot. Fares on scheduled flights from London, via Europe, to Dakar start at about UK£450, rising by another UK£75 in

SENEGAL

the high season (October to May). Air France's daily flights between Paris and Dakar are €449 one way, €928 return. SN Brussels Airlines (the reincarnated Sabena) flies five times weekly between Brussels and Dakar, with return tickets starting at €550.

Alitalia flies twice or four times a week, depending on the season, between Milan and Dakar, while TAP Air Portugal has several flights a week from Lisbon. Lufthansa's charter partner, Condor, has one flight a week between Frankfurt and Dakar during the tourist season.

There are plenty of charter flights to Senegal with French and Belgian package-tour companies, all of them cheaper than the scheduled flights.

In Senegal, the best agency for charter flights is Nouvelles Frontières in Dakar (see Organised Tours in the main Getting Around section later in this chapter), with fares to Paris from around €380 one way.

From the USA you have to change planes in Europe.

Africa

Getting from Dakar to other parts of West Africa is relatively straightforward. But from Dakar to East, Central or Southern Africa is more difficult than it once was. Airline closures, particularly that of Air Afrique, and cutbacks mean it is now easier, cheaper and usually faster to go via Europe.

Within the region, Air Senegal International and Gambia International Airlines have at least one flight a day from Dakar to Banjul for CFA48,000 one way. Ghana Airways flies to Accra via Banjul on Sunday and Wednesday for CFA280,000/338,600 one way/return. Air Mali flies to Bamako on Monday and Friday for CFA83,800/154,800 one way/return. TACV Cabo Verde Airlines flies three times a week to Praia for CFA115,000/145,500 one way/return. On Tuesday Air Guinée flies from Dakar to Conakry via Banjul and Labe. The one-way/return fares to Conakry are about US$125/165.

Many travellers fly from Dakar to Casablanca (Morocco) to avoid the difficult overland section through Mauritania and Western Sahara. The usual one-way fare on Royal Air Maroc is US$530, and youth tickets are US$370.

LAND

Border Crossings

Senegal completely surrounds Gambia. There are three main border points of interest for travellers: at Karang, north of Barra on the main road to/from Kaolack and Dakar in central Senegal; Seleti, south of Brikama, on the main road to Ziguinchor in southern Senegal; and Sabi, south of Basse Santa Su (more commonly referred to as Basse) on the road to Vélingara. Other border crossing points include just south of Soma, and just north of Farafenni where the Trans-Gambia Hwy between north and south Senegal cuts through Gambia. There is also a series of dirt roads linking Kafountine and Brikama, though there's no border post on the Senegal side.

From Senegal to Guinea, the main crossing point is between Tambacounda and Labé. For Guinea-Bissau, the main crossing point is at São Domingos. Most travellers heading for Mali take the train, but the main road crossing point is at Kidira, between Tambacounda and Kayes.

The main border point between Senegal and Mauritania is at Rosso, but overlanders are increasingly crossing at Maka Diama, where the road along the top of the barrage (dam) links the countries just north of St-Louis.

Gambia

From Dakar there are buses to Barra (CFA3000 to CFA3500, six to nine hours), from where you get the ferry across the River Gambia to Banjul, or a bush taxi (known locally as a *taxi brousse* or *sept place*) to the border at Karang (CFA4500, six hours). From southern Senegal, bush taxis (Peugeots or minibuses) run regularly between Ziguinchor and the border town of Seleti (CFA2000, 1½ hours), where you change for Serekunda (CFA1000, one hour), and between Kafountine and Brikama (CFA1200, 1½ hours). It's also possible to travel between Tambacounda in eastern Senegal and Basse Santa Su in Gambia via Vélingara.

Guinea

Most traffic goes between Tambacounda and Labé in Guinea, usually via Koundara, and less often via Kedougou. For details, see Tambacounda and Kedougou later in this chapter.

Trains Between Senegal & Mali

The *Mistral International* (Senegalese) train departs Dakar on Wednesday at 10am. Tickets are sold on Mondays and Tuesdays from 8am to noon and 1pm to 5pm. The *Express International* (Malian) train departs Dakar on Saturday at 10am. Tickets are sold on Friday from 8am to noon and 1pm to 5pm. Times and fares for the *Express International* are shown in the following table. Times for the *Mistral International* are the same and fares about 15% more expensive.

destination	arrival time	1st class (CFA)	2nd class (CFA)	sleeper (CFA)
Bamako	3.20pm	34,250	25,100	51,390
Kayes	3.55am	19,800	14,515	33,320
Kidira	11.23am	17,050	12,495	n/a
Tambacounda	7.05pm	12,330	9035	n/a
Thiès	11.30am	6685	4900	n/a

Guinea-Bissau

Bush taxis run several times daily between Ziguinchor and Bissau (CFA4000, 147km) via São Domingos (the border) and Ingore. The road is in fairly good condition, but the ferries on the stretch between Ingore and Bissau can make the trip take anything from four to eight hours. Other options are to go from Tanaf to Farim or from Tambacounda via Vélingara to Gabú.

Mali

Bush Taxi Travellers have traditionally taken the train most, if not all, of the way from Dakar to Bamako. But a brand new highway, probably the best in the country, now links Tambacounda and the border at Kidira, making the bush-taxi option much more attractive. From Tambacounda to Kidira (three hours, 184km) a Peugeot taxi costs CFA4000, a minibus CFA2700, and the large express bus (operated as Transport Alzhar and owned by the Mouride Brotherhood, these buses are known throughout Senegal as the *car mouride*) CFA2300. In Kidira, you cross the road bridge to Diboli, from where bush taxis go to Kayes for CFA2500.

Train In theory, trains run between Dakar and Bamako twice a week in each direction and the trip takes about 35 hours. In practice this is crap – one train is often out of action; it's full of thieves; the trip usually takes 40 hours or longer; and it's not unusual to find broken tracks and derailments on the Mali side. In spite, or because, of these hardships, this trip will be one of the most memorable of your life, particularly the Mali leg.

You can get on or off at Tambacounda (eastern Senegal) or Kayes (western Mali), although between Kayes and Bamako the train is your only real option. Seats are numbered, although in 2nd class you should get to the train two hours before departure. The 1st-class seats are large and comfortable, while 2nd class is more crowded. Sleepers (couchettes) are basic but adequate. You can get cheap food at stations along the way, and the Mistral International (Senegalese) train has a restaurant car. In fact, the Mistral International is superior in almost every way to its Malian counterpart.

If there are no seats available, look out for touts on the platform selling unused tickets. You could also get your ticket in Tambacounda, although usually only 1st-class tickets are available.

At each border post you must walk to the immigration office. Even if your passport is taken by an officer on the train you still have to collect it yourself.

The Artful Dodger would be out of his depth on this train, and it wouldn't surprise if Fagin himself were the station master at Bamako. All you can do is be prepared: Be sure to carry a torch (flashlight); if you leave your seat, especially at night, ask a fellow passenger to watch your gear; and expect to become a target when the lights go out (often in the train and the station) as the train pulls into Kayes and Bamako. Good luck!

Car & Motorcycle The route from Tambacounda to Kayes is straightforward, but beyond here the road beside the railway is in very bad condition as far as Kita. The EU has promised to fix it, but at the present time the best route goes down to Diamou and then to Bafoulabe, from where a detour via Manatali takes you along decent dirt roads to Bamako.

Mauritania

Bush Taxi The main border point is at Rosso, where a ferry crosses the Senegal River. You can go direct to Rosso from Dakar in a Peugeot taxi (CFA4600, six hours), but most travellers stop off at St-Louis, from where a Peugeot taxi to Rosso (two hours) is CFA1540. You cross the river on the large ferry, which is free for passengers, or by pirogue (CFA650). From the Mauritanian immigration point it's 500m to the *gare routière* (bus station), from where bush taxis go to Nouakchott.

If border guards suggest you should offer them a *cadeaux* (a small gift or tip) to facilitate your passing, the answer is a polite 'no'. There are plenty of moneychangers, but don't change on the Senegal side as it's illegal to bring ouguiya into Mauritania.

Car & Motorcycle To avoid the notorious hassle at Rosso, drivers can cross the Senegal River at several ferries east of here, and at the Maka Diama, 97km southwest of Rosso and just north of St-Louis, although the track between Maka Diama and the main road on the Mauritanian side is very soft sand. The ferry here costs CFA5000/10,000 in winter/summer, and has a theoretical maximum weight of 2.8 tonnes per vehicle. There are border posts at both sides of the crossing.

SENEGAL

SEA

Pirogues go between the Siné-Saloum Delta and Banjul. For details see Getting There & Away under Palmarin & Djifer later in this chapter.

Getting Around

AIR

Air Senegal International has daily flights from Dakar to Ziguinchor for CFA44,000 one way. These go all the way to Cap Skirring twice a week for CFA59,500/110,500 one way/return. There's one flight a week to Tambacounda for CFA64,500 one way.

BUS, BUSH TAXI & MINIBUS

There are many and varied modes of public transport in Senegal. Vehicles can be grouped into two types: Express buses and bush taxis *(taxis brousse)*.

Express buses are the sort of large 50 to 60-seater buses you're probably used to seeing on suburban routes in cities the world over. Those in Senegal are not exactly luxurious, but apart from the Peugeot taxis they're generally the quickest way from A to B, and among the cheapest. In Senegal they're known as *grands cars* and even *très grands cars*, but the most common (and best understood) name is *car mouride*, acknowledging that all these are owned and operated by the leaders of the powerful Mouride brotherhood. To minimise confusion, we've referred to them as 'express buses' in this chapter.

Bush taxis are more complicated. This group includes several different vehicle types, most of which look fairly well-used, leave when full and stop regularly (the bigger the conveyance, the more often it stops). The fastest is the Peugeot taxi, which is most often known as a *sept place* (there are seven seats for seven passengers) but might also be called (confusingly) a *taxi brousse*. Peugeot taxis are usually comfortable, safe, and as fast as private vehicles once they're on their way.

Next quickest, but still pretty slow, is the minibus, typically a Nissan Urvan seating about 15 to 20 people and commonly known as a *petit car*.

Even slower are the ubiquitous white Mercedes buses that usually carry about 35 people and seem to stop every 200m. These can take twice as long as a Peugeot taxi but, thank God for small mercies, everyone gets a seat. In Dakar these are often called *N'Diaga N'Diaye* (pronounced njagga-njaye), but elsewhere this might not be understood. It's safer to ask for an *Alham* (shortened from Alhamdoulilahi, which means 'Thanks to God' and appears on the front of every such vehicle), or if this doesn't work a *grand car*, a term that seems to be interchangeable with the bigger express buses. In this chapter we've called them Alhams.

Finally there are the misleadingly named *cars rapides*, ancient French minibuses, usually painted orange and blue, which are battered, slow and crowded but generally very social. It's unlikely you'll find these on long-distance routes as they usually stick to urban routes.

Public transport fares are fixed by the government. As an example, some Peugeot-taxi destinations and fares from Dakar include Kaolack (CFA2200, three to four hours); St-Louis (CFA3100, four to five hours); and Ziguinchor (CFA6500, nine to ten hours). Minibuses are typically about 20% to 25% cheaper than Peugeot taxis, and buses about 30% to 35% cheaper.

TRAIN

Many visitors take the express train that runs between Dakar and Bamako (Mali), but few use this line to travel by train around Senegal itself, although you could use it between, say, Dakar and Tambacounda. For more details, see the entry under Mali in the Getting There & Away section earlier.

CAR

Most car-rental companies are based in Dakar – for more details see Getting Around under Dakar later in this chapter. Petrol costs about CFA450 per litre, diesel CFA350.

BOAT

The MS *Joola* is a large ferry that is supposed to run between Dakar and Ziguinchor via Île de Carabane. Sadly, it spent most of 2001 anchored in Dakar. Promises of its return 'next month' were issued regularly but at the time of writing it had failed to materialise. If it does sail again, you can expect the trip to take about 20 hours, and it will follow its old timetable, departing Dakar on Tuesday and Friday, Ziguinchor on Thursday and Sunday.

One-way fares from Dakar are the same to Carabane or Ziguinchor: CFA3500 in economy class; CFA6000 in 2nd class; CFA12,000 in a cabin with four beds; and CFA15,000 in a cabin with two beds. There are seats in economy class but no guaranteed places, while 2nd class has reservable reclining seats. To check the latest, call Sentram in Dakar (☎ 821 5852) or Ziguinchor (☎ 852 5443).

ORGANISED TOURS

If you're short of time you could get around the country on an organised tour. Most require a minimum of six to eight passengers, although there are some options for two or four.

Inter Tourisme (☎ 822 4529) 3 Allées Delmas, Dakar. Friendly and relatively cheap, Inter Tourisme offers one-day trips to Lake Rose for CFA25,000 per person, two-day trips to Siné-Saloum for CFA85,000 each for two people and five-day trips to Parc National du Niokolo-Koba and Bassari Country for CFA200,000 per person (a minimum of six).

Nouvelles Frontières (☎ 823 3434, fax 822 2817) 3 Blvd de la République, Dakar. The local office of the French international tour operator offers a wide range of excursions, and helps with hotel reservations.

Safari-Evasion (☎ 849 5252) 12 Av Albert Sarraut, Dakar. Safari-Evasion mainly arranges flights, but has a few tours to popular destinations, including four-day trips to St-Louis for CFA135,000 per person, and day trips to Lake Rose and Jaol Fadiout for about CFA25,000 per person.

Sahel Découverte (☎ 961 4263, ⓔ residenc@telecomplus.sn) Av Blaise Diagne, St-Louis. This company offers excursions with French-speaking tour leaders to Parc National de la Langue de Barbarie for CFA16,000 per person and to Parc National aux Oiseaux du Djoudj for CFA20,000, or a fascinating day trip into Mauritania for CFA40,000. Longer tours, including a desert tour, cost about CFA50,000 per day. All prices are based on a minimum of four people, but individuals can usually join groups.

Motor Dakar (ⓦ www.motordakar.com) If you've got a few spare euros and fancy a taste of the Paris-Dakar, this is for you. Multilingual Charly runs trips on Honda XR600 bikes, ranging from one-day desert riding classes (€225) to week-long raids up the coast (€1800). Bike, equipment, 4WD support, food and accommodation are included in the price.

Dakar

Some people say Dakar does not represent the 'real' Africa, but they're wrong. This city is the big, crowded, dirty, raw, chaotic, ambitious, in-your-face and utterly exciting face of the 'dark' continent, and for a glimpse of Africa's urban future, look no further than Dakar – this *is* as real as it gets. The cosmopolitan atmosphere, temperate climate, rocking range of bars and nightclubs, fascinating mix of African, French colonial and modern architecture and culture, and especially the range and quality of restaurants, make it well worth making Dakar's acquaintance.

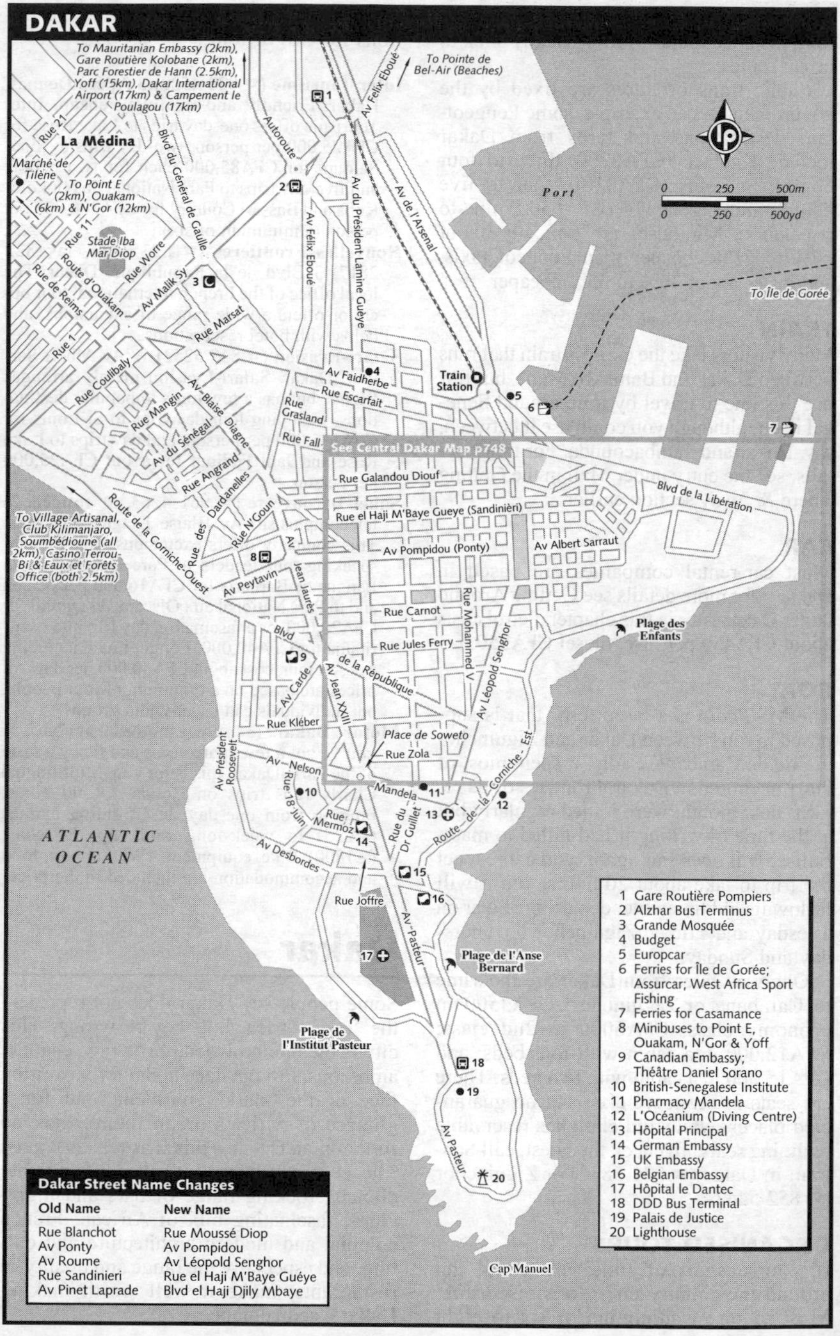
DAKAR
To Mauritanian Embassy (2km), Gare Routière Kolobane (2km), Parc Forestier de Hann (2.5km), Yoff (15km), Dakar International Airport (17km) & Campement le Poulagou (17km)
To Pointe de Bel-Air (Beaches)
La Médina
Marché de Tilène
To Point E (2km), Ouakam (6km) & N'Gor (12km)
Stade Iba Mar Diop
Rue 21
Rue 11
Rue 1
Route d'Ouakam
Rue de Reims
Rue Worre
Av Malik Sy
Rue Marsat
Blvd du Général de Gaulle
Autoroute
Av Félix Eboué
Av du Président Lamine Guèye
Av de l'Arsenal
Port
To Île de Gorée
Train Station
Av Faidherbe
Rue Escarfait
Rue Grasland
Rue Fall
Rue Coulibaly
Rue Mangin
Av Blaise Diagne
Av du Sénégal
Rue Angrand
Rue des Dardanelles
Rue N'Goun
See Central Dakar Map p748
Rue Galandou Diouf
Rue el Haji M'Baye Gueye (Sandinièri)
Blvd de la Libération
Av Pompidou (Ponty)
Av Albert Sarraut
To Village Artisanal, Club Kilimanjaro, Soumbédioune (all 2km), Casino Terrou-Bi & Eaux et Forêts Office (both 2.5km)
Route de la Corniche-Ouest
Av Peytavin
Av Jean Jaurès
Rue Carnot
Rue Mohammed V
Rue Jules Ferry
Blvd de la République
Av Léopold Senghor
Plage des Enfants
Av Carde
Av Jean XXIII
Rue Kléber
Place de Soweto
Rue Zola
Av Président Roosevelt
Av Nelson Mandela
Rue 18 Juin
Rue Mermoz
Rue du Dr Guillet
Route de la Corniche-Est
Av Desbordes
ATLANTIC OCEAN
Rue Joffre
Av Pasteur
Plage de l'Anse Bernard
Plage de l'Institut Pasteur
Cap Manuel
0 250 500m
0 250 500yd

1. Gare Routière Pompiers
2. Alzhar Bus Terminus
3. Grande Mosquée
4. Budget
5. Europcar
6. Ferries for Île de Gorée; Assurcar; West Africa Sport Fishing
7. Ferries for Casamance
8. Minibuses to Point E, Ouakam, N'Gor & Yoff
9. Canadian Embassy; Théâtre Daniel Sorano
10. British-Senegalese Institute
11. Pharmacy Mandela
12. L'Océanium (Diving Centre)
13. Hôpital Principal
14. German Embassy
15. UK Embassy
16. Belgian Embassy
17. Hôpital le Dantec
18. DDD Bus Terminal
19. Palais de Justice
20. Lighthouse

Dakar Street Name Changes

Old Name	New Name
Rue Blanchot	Rue Moussé Diop
Av Ponty	Av Pompidou
Av Roume	Av Léopold Senghor
Rue Sandinieri	Rue el Haji M'Baye Guéye
Av Pinet Laprade	Blvd el Haji Djily Mbaye

Dangers in Dakar

Dakar is notorious for muggings, scams and petty theft, frequently in broad daylight. The worst areas are the beaches around Dakar, in and around the markets, Av Pompidou and Place de l'Indépendance (especially outside the banks). Pickpockets operate wherever wealthy tourists can be surrounded by crowds, such as at the train station and on the Île de Gorée ferry.

Thieves often work in groups. One guy will touch your back, causing you to stop. A second tries to grab your wallet, while a third acts as a decoy. Watch out for 'traders' with only one item to sell. Beware too of people offering small gifts 'for friendship' – nothin' comes for nothin'.

Genuine street traders, of course, are not thieves. Some, however, may work with thieves to slow down potential targets. Either way, unless you genuinely want something, ignore them or try a firm but civil *'non merci'* (no thank you).

Despite these warnings, it's important to remember that only a tiny percentage of visitors are robbed, and a tourist being physically harmed is almost unheard of. Aggression is not a typical Senegalese trait. Most Senegalese are genuinely hospitable and wouldn't dream of hassling guests in their country.

The central area is easily explored on foot, and a variety of city buses run frequently to the suburbs. Also within reach are several good beaches, traditional fishing communities and some fascinating islands of historical and ecological interest.

Of course, Dakar won't be everyone's cup of tea. The noise, fumes and crowds can be bad, but what's most likely to wind you up is the unwanted attention you'll get from pestering traders (see the boxed text 'Dangers in Dakar'). If your courage fails, it's easy enough to spend time in parts of the city that tourists, and consequently the bad guys, don't frequent.

Orientation

The hub of Dakar is the Place de l'Indépendance, from which Av Léopold Senghor leads south in the direction of the Palais Présidentiel, Av Pompidou leads west to Marché Sandaga and Av Albert Sarraut leads east towards Marché Kermel. A good selection of shops, hotels, restaurants, cafés, bars and nightclubs are in this central area.

From the Palais Présidentiel, Blvd de la République extends west, past the cathedral. South of here are Place de Soweto, the IFAN Museum, the national theatre and several embassies.

From Marché Sandaga, Av Émile Badiane turns into Av Blaise Diagne and heads northwest to become Route d'Ouakam, passing through the suburbs of Point E, Mermoz and Ouakam, to finally reach Pointe des Almadies and N'Gor.

Information

Tourist Office A couple of free listings papers, *Dakar Tam Tam* and *l'Avis*, are available in hotels, restaurants and travel agencies and include phone numbers for these places plus embassies and hospitals.

Money On the west side of Place de l'Indépendance are Bicis, CBAO and Citibank, which all change money, while SGBS is at the southern end. CBAO has the quickest service, and Bicis is the next best. You can find a black market currency trader by just standing still for about 30 seconds outside one of these banks, but don't hand over your cash until you've carefully counted theirs.

Post & Telephone The main post office is on Blvd el Haji Djily Mbaye, near Marché Kermel. This is where you'll find the poste restante, but readers report this service is unreliable and holds letters for only 30 days.

For phone calls, Sonatel has an office on Blvd de la République (open from 7am to 11pm Monday to Saturday), and there are dozens of télécentres with similar rates.

Email & Internet Access There are a stack of Internet cafés in central Dakar, all of which charge between CFA500 and CFA1000 an hour. The fastest service is found at GSM Cybercafe (☎ 823 7326) on Av Pompidou, which is open from 8am to midnight daily. Just around the corner is NTIC (☎ 823 0980), 77 Rue Gomis, which charges only CFA500 an hour and is open 24/7. Another option is Cyber-Business Centre (☎ 823 3223, fax 826 9614), Av Léopold Senghor, which opens from 8am to midnight daily and has English-speaking staff. An hour will cost CFA1000.

SENEGAL

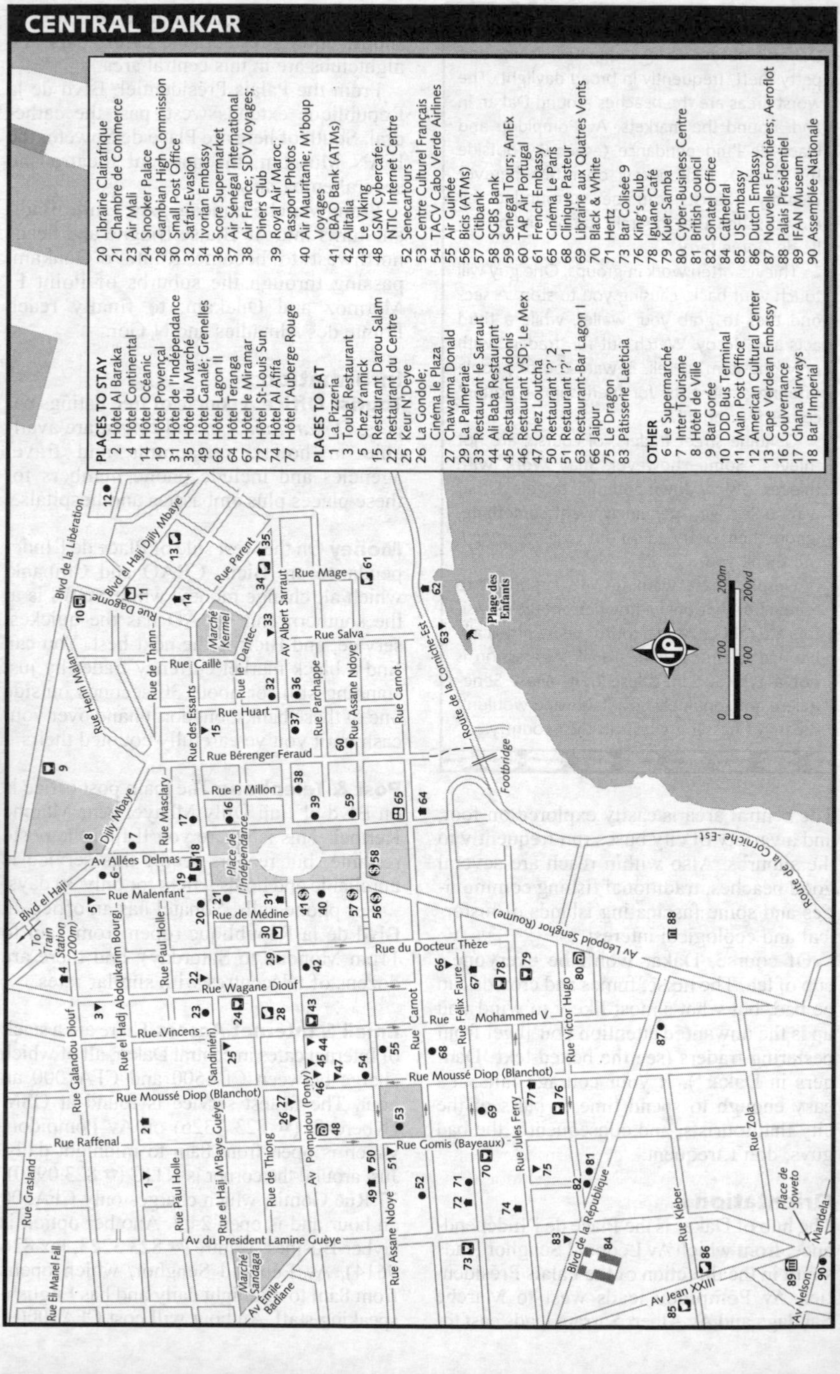
CENTRAL DAKAR
PLACES TO STAY
2 Hôtel Al Baraka
4 Hôtel Continental
14 Hôtel Océanic
19 Hôtel Provençal
31 Hôtel de l'Indépendance
35 Hôtel du Marché
44 Hôtel Ganalé; Grenelles
62 Hôtel Lagon II
64 Hôtel Teranga
67 Hôtel le Miramar
72 Hôtel St-Louis Sun
74 Hôtel Al Afifa
77 Hôtel l'Auberge Rouge
PLACES TO EAT
1 La Pizzeria
3 Touba Restaurant
5 Chez Yannick
15 Restaurant Darou Salam
22 Restaurant du Centre
25 Keur N'Deye
26 La Gondole; Cinéma le Plaza
27 Chawarma Donald
29 La Palmeraie
33 Restaurant le Sarraut
43 Ali Baba Restaurant
45 Restaurant Adonis
46 Restaurant VSD; Le Mex
47 Chez Loutcha
50 Restaurant '2' 2
51 Restaurant '2' 1
63 Restaurant-Bar Lagon I
66 Jaipur
75 Le Dragon
83 Pâtisserie Laeticia
OTHER
6 Le Supermarché
7 Inter Tourisme
8 Hôtel de Ville
9 Bar Gorée
10 DDD Bus Terminal
11 Main Post Office
12 American Cultural Center
13 Cape Verdean Embassy
16 Gouvernance
17 Ghana Airways
18 Bar l'Impérial
20 Librairie Clairafrique
21 Chambre de Commerce
23 Air Mali
24 Snooker Palace
28 Gambian High Commission
30 Small Post Office
32 Safari-Evasion
34 Ivorian Embassy
36 Score Supermarket
37 Air Sénégal International
38 Air France; SDV Voyages; Diners Club
39 Royal Air Maroc; Passport Photos
40 Air Mauritanie; M'boup Voyages
41 CBAO Bank (ATMs)
42 Alitalia
43 Le Viking
48 GSM Cybercafé; NTIC Internet Centre
52 Senecartours
53 Centre Culturel Français
54 TACV Cabo Verde Airlines
55 Air Guinée
56 Bicis (ATMs)
57 Citibank
58 SGBS Bank
59 Senegal Tours; AmEx
60 TAP Air Portugal
61 French Embassy
65 Cinéma Le Paris
68 Clinique Pasteur
69 Librairie aux Quatre Vents
70 Black & White
71 Hertz
73 Bar Colisée 9
76 King's Club
78 Iguane Café
79 Kuer Samba
80 Cyber-Business Centre
81 British Council
82 Sonatel Office
84 Cathedral
85 US Embassy
86 Dutch Embassy
87 Nouvelles Frontières; Aeroflot
88 Palais Présidentiel
89 IFAN Museum
90 Assemblée Nationale
Plage des Enfants
Footbridge
Route de la Corniche-Est
Av Léopold Senghor (Roume)
Marché Kermel
Place de l'Indépendance
Marché Sandaga
To Train Station (200m)
Place de Soweto
200m
200yd

Travel Agencies For flights to Europe or other parts of Africa, agencies include Senegal Tours (☎ 839 9900, fax 823 2644), 5 Place de l'Indépendance, which is also the American Express agent; SDV Voyages (☎ 839 0081, ⓔ dkrsdvagv@sdvsen.net), 51 Av Albert Sarraut, which is the Diners Club agent; and M'boup Voyages (☎ 821 8163, ⓔ mboup@telecomplus.sn), Place de l'Indépendance, where some staff speak English. For details of Dakar-based tour companies, see Organised Tours in the main Getting Around section earlier in this chapter.

Bookshops Librairie Clairafrique at the northwest corner of Place de l'Indépendance, and Librairie aux Quatres Vents (☎ 821 8083), Rue Félix Faure, have a wide range of books and magazines (although very little in English) and also sell maps. Both are open from 8.45am to 12.30pm and 3pm to 6.45pm Monday to Saturday. The second-hand bookstalls in the streets around the Marché Sandaga are also a good bet.

Cultural Centres The lively Centre Culturel Français (also called the Alliance Franco-Sénégalaise; ☎ 823 0320, ⓔ ccf@sentoo.sn), Rue Gomis, is the driving force behind much of the artistic and cultural endeavour in Dakar. It produces a regular guide to upcoming events and has a performance arena on site that hosts regular live events and films. The American Cultural Center (☎ 823 1185) is on Rue Abdoulaye Fadiga, near the main post office, while the British Council (☎ 822 2015) is on Blvd de la République and has a library.

Medical Services For major accidents, the Hôpital Principal (☎ 839 5050) is at the far southern end of Av Léopold Senghor, and Hôpital le Dantec (☎ 822 2420) is on Av Pasteur. Clinique Pasteur (☎ 821 2548) on Rue Carnot, west of Place de l'Indépendance, is the best place if you're after a malaria slide.

Dakar has many pharmacies. Those with 24-hour service include Pharmacy Mandela (☎ 821 2172) on Av Nelson Mandela near the Hôpital Principal.

Museum

IFAN Museum *(Institut Fondamental d'Afrique Noir; admission CFA2200; open 8am-12.30pm & 2pm-6.30pm daily)* is one of the best museums in West Africa. Displays show masks and traditional dress from the whole region (including Mali, Guinea-Bissau, Benin and Nigeria) and provide an excellent overview of styles, without bombarding you with so much that you can't take it all in. You can also see beautiful fabrics and carvings, drums, musical instruments and agricultural tools, though sadly not much from Senegal itself.

Markets

Marché Sandaga is very much aimed at locals, and you can buy just about anything here. The sheer choice of fabric stalls is a real attraction. Colourful cotton trousers and shirts are popular, but you can buy any cloth you fancy and have it made up into something by the local tailors according to your own design for around CFA2000.

The stalls in and around **Marché Kermel** east of Place de l'Indépendance on Rue le Dantec have more for tourists, with carvings, baskets, leatherwork and other souvenirs, as well as flowers and fruit. Unfortunately, both Marché Sandaga and Marché Kermel are plagued by hustlers, offering to be your 'guide'. If you can't ignore them, complain to a stallholder that it's putting you off buying. Alternatively, hire one to keep the others away.

Well worth a visit is **Marché de Tilène**, at the heart of La Médina, crowded with the sights and sounds of a traditional African market and relatively free of tourists (and thieves). You may need a guide as the original market hall is hard to find among the sprawl of tin-roofed shops and houses.

Other Attractions

The handsome white **Palais Présidentiel** is surrounded by sumptuous gardens and guards in colonial-style uniforms. Other interesting buildings from the same era include the **Gouvernance** *(Place de l'Indépendance)* and the **Chambre de Commerce** *(Place de l'Indépendance)*, the fine old **Hôtel de Ville** *(Town Hall; Av Allées Delmas)*, and the churchlike **train station**, a short distance further north.

Out of the city centre is the **Grande Mosquée**, built in 1964, with its landmark minaret. The surrounding area, called **La Médina**, while not picturesque, is a lively place contrasting sharply with the sophisticated city centre. Another reason to visit is that few tourists come here, so there's little hassle.

West of the centre, a visit to the fishing beach and market of **Soumbédioune** is good in the late afternoon when the fishing boats return. This is also a major centre of pirogue building, and behind the fish market you'll see carpenters turning planks and tree trunks into large ocean-going canoes.

Activities

Swimming About 1.5km northwest of downtown Dakar, near the ugly sculpture of the sitting man, there are two sandy beaches popular with locals. Keep a close eye on your gear here and be careful of the currents. N'Gor and Yoff also have beaches and Îles de la Madeleine has the best swimming spot for miles – see Cap Vert Peninsula later in this chapter.

Most top-end hotels have **pools** that are open to nonguests. Hôtel de l'Indépendance charges CFA3000 for its rooftop pool with a great view of Dakar (free if you have a meal). An Olympic-size pool was due to open in Point E at the time of publication and will be open to the public.

Diving & Kayaking The French-operated **L'Océanium** *(☎ 822 2441, ⓔ oceanium@arc.sn, Route de la Corniche-Est)* arranges a wide range of trips, with equipment. Courses include a complete beginner's introductory dive for CFA15,000. It also rents kayaks for CFA3000 an hour, or CFA5000 for half a day.

Fishing You can arrange deep-sea sport fishing at **West Africa Sport Fishing** *(☎ 823 2858, fax 823 4837)*, next to the Île de Gorée ferry port. During the fishing high season (May to October), a day out costs a mere CFA280,000. **Restaurant-Bar Lagon 1** *(☎ 821 5322)* also has a fishing centre and boasts several world record catches.

Places to Stay

A particularly aggressive breed of bed bugs seems to have advanced on Dakar and occupied strategic positions in the city's budget hotels. Our search for cheap, bug-free accommodation proved fruitless. Hopefully by the time you arrive they'll have moved on to Mali, or anywhere else! In downtown Dakar it's not advisable to wander around with a rucksack on while looking for lodgings. If you find a room anywhere within your price range, take it for one night and look for something cheaper the next day. Other budget options are listed under Cap Vert Peninsula later in this chapter.

Prices for budget hotels include tourist tax. At mid-range and top-end hotels, prices do not include tax, but all have rooms with private bathrooms, and restaurants serving breakfast and other meals.

Places to Stay – Budget

Hôtel du Marché *(☎ 821 5771, 3 Rue Parent)* Singles/doubles CFA8600/11,600. Near Marché Kermel, this place has big, basic fan rooms surrounding a peaceful, shady and pleasant courtyard.

Hôtel l'Auberge Rouge *(☎ 823 8661, Rue Moussé Diop)* Doubles CFA9500. This place gets mixed reviews. Some travellers describe it as peaceful; others complain of noisy comings and goings at night.

Hôtel Provençal *(☎/fax 822 1069, 17 Rue Malenfant)* Singles/doubles/triples from CFA9400/11,800/14,200. This is a popular place near Place de l'Indépendance. As with all cheapies, it is also a brothel, but it's fairly low-key. Rooms upstairs are quiet and airy and have fans.

Hôtel Continental *(☎ 822 1083, 10 Rue Galandou Diouf)* Singles/doubles CFA13,000/15,000. Probably the best choice in this bracket, this is a decent, well-organised hotel with a small local bar attached. Rooms have bathrooms and air-con and some contain a balcony.

Places to Stay – Mid-Range

Hôtel Océanic *(☎ 822 2044, ⓔ hotel-oceanic@sentoo.sn, 9 Rue de Thann)* Singles/doubles CFA21,600/25,800. Just north of Marché Kermel, this place is popular with travellers and good value (for Dakar), with spotless air-con rooms and a reasonably good restaurant attached.

Hôtel Al Baraka *(☎ 822 5532, fax 821 7541, 35 Rue el Hadj Abdoukarim Bourgi)* Singles/doubles CFA25,600/31,200. Spotlessly clean, modern rooms with air-con, TV, fridge and phone make the Baraka worth the money.

Hôtel Al Afifa *(☎ 823 8737, ⓔ gmbafifa@telecomplus.sn, 46 Rue Jules Ferry)* Singles/doubles CFA35,000/39,600. This place is ageing a little but retains some of its lustre.

SENEGAL

With a bar, restaurant and nightclub downstairs, you won't need to go too far for a drink.

Hôtel St-Louis Sun *(☎ 822 2570, Rue Félix Faure)* has pleasant air-con rooms around a green courtyard and arranges safe parking for cars. Singles/doubles/triples are CFA22,000/28,000/34,000.

Hôtel le Miramar *(☎ 849 2929, fax 823 3505, 25 Rue Félix Faure)* Singles/doubles CFA25,600/31,200. This busy place has colourful rooms with air-con, hot shower and TV, and rates include breakfast. Ask for a 6th-floor room.

Hôtel Ganalé *(☎ 821 5570, ⓔ hganale@sentoo.sn, 38 Rue Assane Ndoye)* Singles/doubles CFA25,000/30,000. The swish Hôtel Ganalé is the best value in this price range. The rooms, bar and restaurant are all pretty classy.

Places to Stay – Top End

Hôtel de l'Indépendance *(☎ 823 1019, ⓔ hotelhi@sentoo.sn, Place de l'Indépendance)* Singles/doubles CFA50,000/55,000. This is the most central of the top-end hotels and has great views, but they aren't really worth the money.

Hôtel Teranga *(☎ 823 1044, fax 823 5001, Place de l'Indépendance)* Rooms CFA95,000. This is Sofitel's recently renovated tour-group favourite. It's really very nice, but is a sea view worth CFA120,000 a night?

Hôtel Lagon II *(☎ 889 2525, ⓔ lagon@tpsnet.sn, Route de la Corniche-Est)* Singles/doubles CFA72,000/80,000. This place is so '70s you fully expect the Bee Gees to appear at the bar in sequined jump suits. But the rooms are still good, and the hotel, perched on stilts at the edge of the ocean, has grand views.

Places to Eat

Sick of rice and peanut sauce? Can't face another round of chicken yassa? Whether you've been in Africa a while or just arrived, you're going to love Dakar's rapidly maturing culinary scene. The French cuisine, a hangover from the colonial past, is a particular highlight, but there's more to Dakar than entrecote and *crème brûlée* (literally 'burnt cream'). Cape Verdean, Indian, Vietnamese, Thai, Lebanese, Italian, Korean and Mexican plus a remarkable array of seafood eateries are also available, and then there's the excellent African food…

Restaurants Highly recommended is ***Keur N'Deye*** *(☎ 821 4973, 68 Rue Vincens)* offering well-prepared Senegalese specialities and a good range of vegetarian dishes for around CFA15000. Most nights there will be a griot playing the kora, making it a great place to watch a performance at close quarters.

Chez Loutcha *(☎ 821 0302, 101 Rue Moussé Diop)* Meals CFA2500-3500. Open noon-3pm & 7pm-11pm Mon-Sat. The Cape Verdean and 'Euro-Africaine' cuisine is excellent and comes in enormous serves, and there's often a griot playing kora here as well. One well-travelled reader described Loutcha as 'among the best places I've eaten anywhere in the world'. Maybe. For the money, this should be your first stop.

Restaurant VSD *(Chez Georges; ☎ 821 0980, 91 Rue Mousse Diop)* Mains CFA3500. Open 7am-midnight daily. There's not much jazz at this intimate place any more, but the West African and international dishes are still good value.

Restaurant le Sarraut *(☎ 822 5523, Av Albert Sarraut) Menu du jour* CFA6500 Mon-Fri. Open 8am-midnight Mon-Sat. The adjoining bar gives Sarraut a vague air of rural France, and the food has been recommended.

Chez Yannick *(☎ 823 2197, Rue Malenfant)* Mains CFA5000. Open lunch & dinner daily. French food and a few miscellaneous international dishes are served in an airy outdoor setting.

La Pizzeria *(☎ 821 0926, 47 Rue el Hadj Abdoukarim Bourgi)* Pizzas & pasta from CFA3500. Open 7pm-late daily. La Pizzeria has excellent pizza and pasta, and a smooth fish soup for CFA2500.

Restaurant-Bar Lagon I *(☎ 821 5322, Route de la Corniche-Est)* Mains from CFA7000. Open noon-3pm & 7.30pm-11pm. Done out like an old-style cruise liner, complete with sails, rails and lifeboats, this place is classy and very expensive.

Le Dragon *(☎ 821 6676, 35 Rue Jules Ferry)* Mains CFA3000-5000. Open 6pm-11pm Mon-Sat. It's not the cheapest, but the Vietnamese food here is pretty good.

Jaipur *(☎ 823 3646, Rue Félix Faure)* Meals CFA4000. Open 7pm-11pm Mon-Sat.

This well-advertised Indian restaurant gets mixed reviews, but enough of them are good to make the curries and vegetarian baltis worth a try.

Le Mex *(☎ 823 6717, 91 Rue Moussé Diop)* Mains CFA3500. Open noon-2am daily. It's not quite El Paso, but the tapas (CFA500), *paninis* (filled breads; CFA1600) and other meals are a pleasant change. After 11pm the lights dim and the dancing begins.

Cafés & Patisseries Dakar has some excellent French-style patisseries and cafés, which are often called *salons de thé*, also selling ice cream, crepes, sandwiches and snacks.

Busy places along Av Pompidou include ***La Palmeraie*** *(☎ 821 1594)*, opposite Alitalia, and ***La Gondole*** *(☎ 821 8858)*, near the Cinéma le Plaza, which is famous for its ice cream. ***Pâtisserie Laeticia*** *(☎ 821 7548, Blvd de la République)* near the cathedral is calmer but service is poor. Most patisseries open for breakfast and close around 7.30pm, although some on Av Pompidou sell beer and stay open until late.

Fast Food & Cheap Eats All over Dakar are sandwich booths and coffee stalls. For something more substantial, along Rue Assane Ndoye you'll find women doling out ***rice and sauce*** for around CFA500, although most stop serving by mid-afternoon. Chawarmas are sold throughout the city for around CFA800. Favourites on Av Pompidou include ***Chawarma Donald***, where city workers queue three deep as Donald slices away in furnace-like heat; ***Ali Baba Restaurant*** *(☎ 822 5297)* which offers classier surroundings and a bigger range of Lebanese dishes; and ***Restaurant Adonis*** *(☎ 822 4086)*. Ali Baba and Adonis are open from 8am to 2am daily, while Donald's is more a daytime business.

The next four places serve good, cheap Senegalese food.

Touba Restaurant *(☎ 823 7646, 20 Rue Wagane Diouf)* Meals CFA600-1000. North of Av Pompidou, this place serves filling meals fast, and the mafé is top notch.

Restaurant du Centre *(☎ 822 0172, 7 Rue el Haji M'Baye Guéye)* Meals CFA1500-2000. Open 8am-midnight. Around the corner from Touba, this restaurant is a step up and there are far more dishes available on the menu. There's also a more upmarket version upstairs.

Restaurant Darou Salam *(Rue des Essarts)* Meals CFA800-1000. Open 8am-6pm. On the other side of the centre, this place serves filling African meals and is a popular lunch stop.

Restaurant '?' *(☎ 822 5072, Rue Assane Ndoye)* Meals CFA1500. Best value in this range are these two places (ask for 'Restaurant Point d'Interrogation'). Both are clean and friendly, open in the evening as well as all day, with filling and exceptionally flavoursome African dishes.

Self-Catering For imported items and food, try the ***Score Supermarket*** *(Av Albert Sarraut)* or ***Le Supermarché,*** three blocks north of Place de l'Indépendance, where the stock is more limited. Fruit and vegetable vendors sell their produce from outside Le Supermarché.

Entertainment

Bars On or near Av Pompidou there are a few bars including ***Le Viking*** *(Cnr Av Pompidou & Rue Mohammed V)*, open 10am to 3am daily, a European-style bar with sports on TV; and ***Snooker Palace*** *(☎ 822 9487, 44 Rue Wagane Diouf)*, where the tempo rises late at night. Much calmer are ***Bar l'Impérial*** *(☎ 822 2663)* at the north end of Place de l'Indépendance and ***Bar Colisée 9*** *(☎ 821 2217, Cnr Av du Président Lamine Guéye & Rue Félix Faure)* – both smart with small draught beers for around CFA800. There are several other watering holes on Rue Félix Faure.

Grenelles *(☎ 821 5570, 38 Rue Assane Ndoye)*, underneath Hotel Ganalé, is an imaginatively decorated place especially popular during the 6pm to 8pm happy hours, when two pints of Flag cost CFA1800.

Bar Gorée *(Blvd de la Libération)*, down near the Île de Gorée ferry terminal, is more African and entertaining. It has cheap beer, snacks and food, and music and dancing most evenings.

Music Venues, Nightclubs & Discos Dakar is one of the best cities in West Africa for live music and has several nightclubs where Senegalese bands perform at weekends – especially on Saturday night. Discos are usually held on Thursday, Friday and

Sunday. Most places have an entry fee of about CFA1000 to CFA2000 (although women often get in free) and up to CFA5000 if a band is playing. Sometimes the entry fee includes your first 'free' drink; otherwise beers are about CFA700 to CFA1500, depending on how smart the place is. Check the papers and listings magazines to see what's on. And don't expect the music to start before midnight – most places don't even start to fill up until about 11pm.

Thiossane *(☎ 824 6046, Sicap Rue 10)* World music fans should head for this hot and crowded club in the Medina, north of Marché Sandaga. It's owned by the legendary Youssou N'Dour and, when he's not touring, the man himself performs here most Friday and Saturday nights. Similarly popular with the Dakarois is ***Le Sahel*** *(☎ 821 2118, Centre Commercial sahm)* about 3km northwest of Marché Sandaga.

In central Dakar, fancy clubs and discos include ***King's Club*** *(32 Rue Victor Hugo)*, the New York–style ***Kuer Samba*** *(☎ 821 2296, Rue Jules Ferry)*, and opposite here the popular ***Iguane Café*** *(☎ 822 6553)*. For cheaper fun try ***Black & White*** *(☎ 821 5054, Rue Gomis)*, with entry and beer at more reasonable prices.

With an emphasis on local acoustic music, ***Planète Culture*** *(☎ 824 1655; Av Cheikh Anta Diop, Point E)* is a popular option a few kilometres north of the centre; it's open from 6pm to 3am Monday to Saturday. It's owned by local band Frères Guissé, which plays in the outdoor setting at least once a week.

Cinemas There are two cinemas worth checking out in Dakar. ***Cinéma Le Plaza*** *(☎ 823 8575, Av Pompidou)* and ***Cinéma Le Paris*** *(Rue Carnot)*, opposite the Hôtel Teranga, both show major releases and charge CFA1000 or CFA2000. Films in English are dubbed into French. The ***British-Senegalese Institute*** *(☎ 822 4023, Rue 18 Juin)* occasionally shows films in English.

Shopping

The Village Artisanal at Soumbédioune is the most popular place for souvenirs. You'll find a tremendous array of woodcarvings, metalwork, gold and silver jewellery, ivory, tablecloths, blankets, leather goods and clothing, but a lot of the stuff is churned out very quickly and you have to search hard for good-quality pieces.

For quality African art, head for Rue Mohammed V where several shops have masks, carvings and other objects from West Africa.

On the same street, shops sell Moroccan or Algerian-style carpets, leatherwork and pottery. Youths stroll the footpaths with boxes of music tapes for around CFA1500 and CDs for CFA5000. For a wider choice, check out the stalls in and around Marché Sandaga on Rue el Haji M'Baye Guéye.

Getting There & Away

Air Details of international flights to/from Dakar are given in the Getting There & Away section earlier in this chapter. Within Senegal, there are just Air Senegal International's services to Ziguinchor, Cap Skiring and Tambacounda – see the Getting Around section earlier.

For international flight inquiries, reconfirmations and reservations, airline offices in Dakar include the following:

Aeroflot (☎ 822 48 15) 3 Blvd de la République
Air France (☎ 829 77 77) 47 Av Albert Sarraut
Air Guinée (☎ 821 44 42) Av Pompidou
Air Mali (☎ 823 24 61) 14 Rue el Haji M'Baye Gueye, near Rue Vincens
Air Mauritanie (☎ 822 81 88) Place de l'Indépendance
Air Senegal International (☎ 823 56 29) 45 Av Albert Sarraut
Alitalia (☎ 823 38 74) 5 Av Pompidou
Ghana Airways (☎ 822 28 20) 21 Rue des Essarts, just off Place de l'Indépendance
Iberia (☎ 823 34 77) Place de l'Indépendance
Royal Air Maroc (☎ 843 47 52) Place de l'Indépendance
TACV Cabo Verde Airlines (☎ 821 39 68) 105 Rue Moussé Diop
TAP Air Portugal (☎ 821 00 65) Immeuble Faycal, just off Place de l'Indépendance
Tunis Air (☎ 823 14 35) 24 Av Léopold Senghor

Bus, Bush Taxi & Minibus Alhams, minibuses and Peugeot taxis for long-distance destinations leave from Gare Routière Pompiers, 3km north of Place de l'Indépendance. To get there from Marché Sandaga, take a *car rapide*, minibus or taxi for about CFA500. Some incoming transport may terminate at Gare Routière Kolobane, about 5km north of the centre on the other side of the autoroute. Some sample fares (in CFA) from Dakar are listed on the next page:

destination	Peugeot taxi	Alham	Express bus
Karang (Gambia)	4500	3500	3000
Kaolack	2600	1500	1250
Mbour	950	750	670
Richard Toll	4950	3880	3440
Rosso	4950	3880	3440
St-Louis	3100	2445	2150
Tambacounda	6800	5100	4400
Thiès	900	700	600
Dakar	6500	5000	4500

For an idea of journey times: From Dakar to St-Louis by Peugeot taxi takes about four hours, to Tambacounda about seven hours and to Ziguinchor from eight to 10 hours. Express buses take about half as long again, while the journey time in an Alham can be double. If you want to take a Peugeot taxi, walk past the Alhams (and the touts who will try to tell you all other transport has gone) to where the Peugeot taxis are lined up with signs indicating destinations. You don't need a guide.

For Tambacounda, Kaolack, Touba or St-Louis, the express buses *(cars mourides)* are fast, reliable and comfortable if you get a proper seat rather than a stool in the aisle. Fares are about 70% of Peugeot-taxi prices. Buses leave from a petrol station at an intersection on Av Malik Sy, near the Gare Routière Pompiers; go the day before you travel to reserve a seat and check departure times.

Train The train from Dakar goes to Bamako in Mali via several towns, including Thiès, Diourbel and Tambacounda. Passenger trains from Dakar to Kaolack no longer run, and they go to St-Louis only at holiday times.

Boat The MS *Joola* is meant to go from Dakar to Ziguinchor via Île de Carabane, but it was out of service for most of 2001. For more information see the main Getting Around section earlier in this chapter.

There's also a regular ferry service to Île de Gorée (CFA5000).

Getting Around

To/From the Airport The official taxi rate from the airport to central Dakar is CFA3000 (CFA3500 from midnight to 6am). The drivers will swear to Allah that the posted rates no longer apply, so bargaining is required.

A taxi from the airport to Yoff should be CFA1500, though you might have to wait to find a willing driver. From the city centre to the airport, it should be around CFA2500. You can get bus No 8, via Yoff, for CFA200.

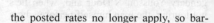

Airport Taxi Scams

Arriving at Dakar airport, be prepared for touts and hustlers offering their services. A common trick is for the tout to 'find' you a taxi (there's always loads at the rank to the right as you leave the terminal building) and then come with you into town. On the way he'll tell you whatever hotel you're heading for is full or burnt down, and you're welcome to stay at his place for a small fee. This may be a genuine earner or it may be a con. We've also heard of isolated incidents where touts and taxi drivers have colluded to rob passengers. The best way to deal with either case is to find your own taxi.

Bus Large and clean blue DDD (Dakar Dem Dikk, formerly Sotrac) buses serve the city centre and places around Dakar. They cost CFA140 for short rides and up to CFA200 for the longest rides. You get on at the back door and buy your ticket from the conductor's booth. For short trips in the city it's usually easier to use a car rapide or an Alham, but for longer trips to the towns and villages around Dakar the DDD buses are a good option. Some useful routes from central Dakar include No 5 to Guédiawaye, No 6 to Cambérene, No 7 to Ouakam, No 8 to Yoff and the airport, No 9 to Liberté VI, No 15 to Rufisque, and No 16 to Malika. The end of the road for many DDD buses is the bus terminus on Av Pasteur south of the city centre. However most of these buses stop around the junction near the Marche Sandaga. Note, however, that the recent history of these buses has been inconsistent, to put it mildly, so ask before you get on.

Following the DDD bus routes are privately owned buses, usually white 30-seater Mercedes Alhams, with fares usually CFA50 or CFA100 depending on the length of the trip. Destinations and routes are not marked, so you'll have to ask.

There are two main bus terminals for local buses. To get to destinations north of the city

SENEGAL

centre including N'Gor and Yoff, cars rapides and Alhams go from near Av Peytavin. For places east of Dakar, such as Rufisque, the main terminal is on Blvd de la Libération.

Car Rapide Dilapidated blue-and-yellow minibuses, known as cars rapides, are stuffed with people and cost about 25% less than other buses. Their destinations aren't marked, so you'll have to listen carefully to the destinations the young assistants yell out, or tell them your own destination.

Car The major self-drive car-rental agencies in Dakar include:

Avis (☎ 849 7757) Branches at the airport and Hotel Méridien Président
Budget (☎ 822 2513) Corner of Av du Président Lamine Guéye and Av Faidherbe, with agents at the airport and Hotel Méridien Président.
Europcar (☎ 822 0691) Corner of Blvd de la Libération and Allées Delmas
Hertz (☎ 822 2016) Branches at the airport and Hôtel Teranga

All the major agencies have similar rates. For the smallest models, they charge between CFA17,000 and CFA20,000 per day, as well as CFA160 to CFA190 per kilometre, around CFA4000 per day for insurance and 20% tax – it soon adds up.

Of the independent operators, Assurcar (☎ 823 7251, 638 4855) near the Gorée ferry pier is one of the cheapest and apparently fairly reliable. A Peugeot 205 is just CFA11,000 per day (CFA16,500 for a weekend), plus CFA110 per kilometre. Senecartours (☎ 822 4286, W www.senecartours.com), 64 Rue Carnot, is reliable, bigger and more expensive.

Taxi Taxis around Dakar are plentiful. Taxi drivers prefer to quote flat rates and even the locals have given up on the meter. For a short ride across the city centre, the fare should be around CFA300 to CFA400. From the Place de l'Indépendance to the Gare Routière Pompiers you'll probably pay CFA750. Late at night all rates are double.

CAP VERT PENINSULA

Île de Gorée

Île de Gorée, about 3km east of Dakar, is a wonderfully peaceful place, complete with colonial-style houses, narrow streets, trailing bougainvillea and a strong Mediterranean feel. With no cars (or fumes!), Gorée is a popular escape from Dakar, and the small beach is often busy at weekends. The only negatives about the island are the persistent offers of assistance you'll receive on arrival. You're not likely to get lost here, but guides can add to the enjoyment of your visit. Official guides at the *syndicat d'initiative* (tourist office; ☎ 822 9703) charge CFA2500 per person for a half-day tour, while freelancers charge whatever they can get away with! The syndicat d'initiative is open from 9am to 1pm and 2.30pm to 6pm daily.

The **IFAN Historical Museum** *(admission CFA200; open 10am-1pm & 2.30pm-6pm Tues-Sat)* at Fort d'Estrées on the northern end of the island has exhibits in French. Better is the **Musée de la Femme** *(admission CFA300; open 10am-5pm daily)* with displays on the role of Senegalese women in traditional and modern societies brought to life by the enthusiastic museum guide (CFA350). There is also the dull **Musée Maritime** and the more famous **Maison des Esclaves**. These two museums are open morning and afternoon, except Monday, and charge CFA300.

Le Castel is a rocky plateau with good views of the island and across to Dakar. It's covered with fortifications dating from different periods including two massive WWII guns, and its 64 subterranean rooms are now inhabited by a group of Baye Fall disciples (for more information on these, see the boxed text 'Marabouts & Brotherhoods' in the Facts about Senegal section).

Just behind the row of restaurants facing the jetty there's a small **tourist market** with crafts and materials, where the bargaining is far more relaxed than in Dakar.

Places to Stay & Eat The ***syndicat d'initiative*** *(☎ 822 9703, e s.i.goree@metissacana.sn)* has good rooms from CFA10,000. To find a room in a ***private home*** ask in the restaurants facing the ferry pier. Rates start at about CFA7500.

Auberge Keur Beer *(☎/fax 821 3801, e keurbeer@sentoo.sn)* Doubles from CFA23,000. Not far from the ferry pier, this stylish place has large rooms, friendly management and a good reputation.

Hostellerie du Chevalier de Boufflers *(☎ 822 5364, e goreeboufflers@ns.arc.sn)*

SENEGAL

CAP VERT PENINSULA

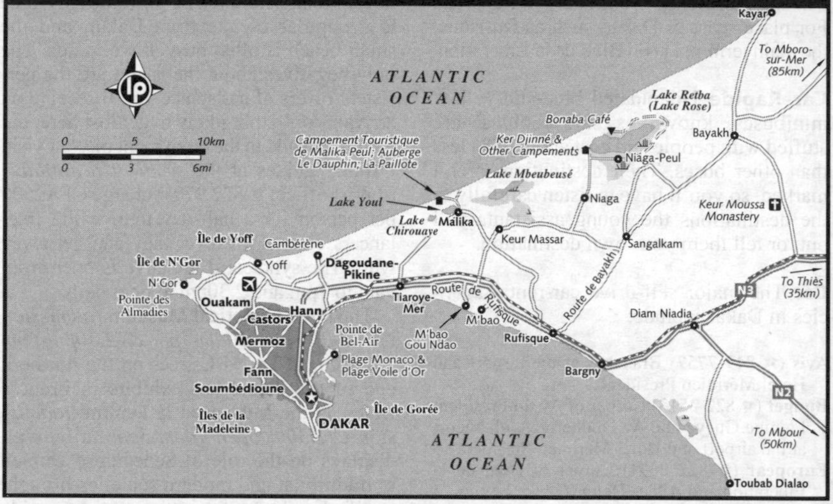
ATLANTIC OCEAN
0 5 10km
0 3 6mi
Kayar
To Mboro-sur-Mer (85km)
Lake Retba (Lake Rose)
Bonaba Café
Bayakh
Ker Djinné & Other Campements
Niaga-Peul
Campement Touristique de Malika Peul; Auberge Le Dauphin; La Paillote
Lake Mbeubeusé
Niaga
Lake Youl
Keur Moussa Monastery
Lake Chirouaye
Malika
Keur Massar
Sangalkam
Île de Yoff
Cambérène
Île de N'Gor
Yoff
Dagoudane-Pikine
N'Gor
Pointe des Almadies
Ouakam
Tiaroye-Mer
Route de Rufisque
Route de Bayakh
N3
To Thiès (35km)
Castors
Hann
M'bao
Diam Niadia
Mermoz
Pointe de Bel-Air
M'bao Gou Ndao
Rufisque
Plage Monaco & Plage Voile d'Or
Fann
Bargny
Soumbédioune
N2
Îles de la Madeleine
DAKAR
Île de Gorée
To Mbour (50km)
ATLANTIC OCEAN
Toubab Dialao

La Maison des Esclaves

Île de Gorée was a busy trading centre during the 18th and 19th centuries, and many merchants built houses where they lived or worked in the upper storey and stored their cargoes on the ground floor. The Maison des Esclaves (Slave House) is one of the last remaining 18th-century buildings of this type on Gorée. It was built in 1786 and renovated in 1990, with French assistance. With its famous doorway opening directly from the storeroom onto the sea, this building has enormous spiritual significance for some visitors, particularly African-Americans whose ancestors were slaves.

Walking around the dimly lit dungeons, particularly after a visit to the IFAN Historical Museum, you begin to imagine the horrors of incarceration. The curator will provide further gruesome details. In reality, however, despite the name, it's unlikely that the Maison des Esclaves was used to hold many captive slaves, apart from those who 'belonged' to the merchant and maybe a few for trading. In fact, some historians have pointed out that although the island was a vital trading centre and strategic port, and an important slave culture existed here, Gorée itself was never a major shipment point for slaves.

The practical obstacles of limited space and a lack of drinking water alone would have made transferring large numbers difficult. Of the 20 million slaves who were taken from Africa, only 300 per year may have gone through Gorée. Even then, the famous doorway would not have been used: a ship could not get near the dangerous rocks and the town had a perfectly good jetty a short distance away.

Additionally, records show that the original owners of the house were the mixed-race family of a French Navy surgeon, Jean Pépin, and not (as it is claimed) Dutch merchants – they were ejected from Gorée by the French in 1677.

The historians who refute Gorée's connections with slavery are anxious to avoid accusations of revisionism, and emphasise that many millions of slaves were taken from West Africa in the most appalling circumstances, and that the slave trade was undeniably cruel and inhumane. But they see the promotion of Gorée as a site of significance to the history of slavery as mere commercialism based on distortion, a cynical attempt to attract tourists who might otherwise go to Gambia's Jufureh or the slave forts of Ghana. Gorée's fabricated history boils down to an emotional manipulation by government officials and tour companies of people who come here as part of a genuine search for cultural roots.

Thanks to Chris de Wilde (specialist in 19th-century West African history) for his help with this section.

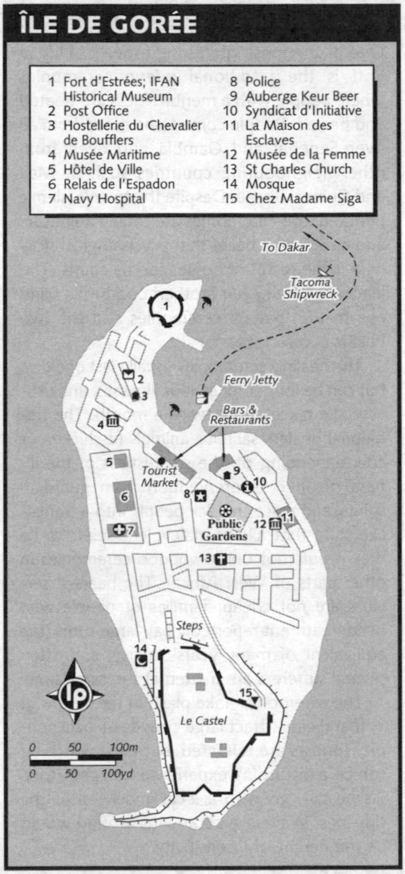
ÎLE DE GORÉE
1 Fort d'Estrées; IFAN Historical Museum
2 Post Office
3 Hostellerie du Chevalier de Boufflers
4 Musée Maritime
5 Hôtel de Ville
6 Relais de l'Espadon
7 Navy Hospital
8 Police
9 Auberge Keur Beer
10 Syndicat d'Initiative
11 La Maison des Esclaves
12 Musée de la Femme
13 St Charles Church
14 Mosque
15 Chez Madame Siga
To Dakar
Tacoma Shipwreck
Ferry Jetty
Bars & Restaurants
Tourist Market
Public Gardens
Steps
Le Castel
0 50 100m
0 50 100yd

Mains around CFA5000. This old place is best known as a restaurant. Its main courses may seem expensive, but you pay as much for the location and the shady terrace overlooking the harbour as for the food. Rooms are also available from CFA18,000.

Most other places to eat are in a rectangle facing the ferry jetty, with meals from around CFA2000. For cheaper fare seek out ***Chez Madame Siga***, a private house near the top of the ramp up to Le Castel. Tiéboudienne is CFA1000.

Getting There & Away A ferry runs roughly every one to two hours between 6am and 11pm from the port in Dakar to Île de Gorée. The trip across takes 20 minutes and costs CFA5000 return for foreigners.

Îles de la Madeleine

The Îles de la Madeleine are a national park about 4km off the mainland west of Dakar, consisting of a main island called Sarpan and two other islets. The islands are home to some interesting dwarf baobab trees, and the park is particularly noted as a good place to spot sea birds. A visit, combined with some swimming or snorkelling in the protected rock pool, is highly recommended.

There are absolutely no facilities for anything on the islands, and while the occasional keen bird-watcher has been known to camp overnight, most people and the park staff prefer visits limited to daylight hours.

To get there, go to the Eaux et Forêts department office on the Route de la Corniche-Ouest in Dakar, just north of the Casino Terrou-Bi. The office will take CFA1000 for entry to the park, and another CFA3000 per person for the 20-minute pirogue ride out there. You say when you want to return and the pirogue will come and pick you up. Quite simple really.

Pointe des Almadies

The Pointe des Almadies, Africa's westernmost point, is only 13km from central Dakar. The nearby Club Med has a boardwalk leading out to the point, but if you scramble over some black rocks you too can take the stroll west – just act as though you belong! The rest of the pointe is just a beach with shanty-like eateries and a line of ugly restaurants. In mitigation, the barbequed fish on the beach is great and the restaurants are popular at night – ***Le Récif des Almadies*** *(☎ 820 1160)*, open for lunch and dinner Thursday to Tuesday, has fish, French and Vietnamese dishes for less than CFA4000 and gets good reviews.

East of the point, the sheltered beach at **N'Gor** is good for swimming, and has a much better atmosphere, with a couple of increasingly popular 'surf camps' and a collection of shack-like restaurants where you can enjoy cheap seafood and a cold beer. ***Le Grand Bleu*** at the east end of the beach has friendly staff, excellent shrimp sandwiches for CFA1000 and grilled prawns for CFA3500. The much smarter ***La Brazzerade*** *(☎ 820 0364)* has a menu du jour for CFA7000 and a few pleasant but pricey rooms.

Other accommodation options in the village's maze of lanes include ***Waly's Surf***

Camp *(☎ 820 2757)*, which has basic rooms for CFA8000, and the infinitely better ***Surf Camp Colé*** *(☎ 820 2939)*, which has air-con doubles for CFA10,000. You'll need to seek directions to find these places.

The monolith on the headland to the east is ***Hotel N'Gor Diarama*** *(☎ 820 1005, fax 820 2723)*, with rooms at CFA40,000. Next door ***Club le Calao*** *(☎ 820 0540, fax 820 1180)* has comfortable thatched bungalows from CFA12,250 per person.

To reach N'Gor, you can take a No 8 bus from central Dakar to near the airport, and take a taxi from there for about CFA700, or take a N'Diaga N'Diaye along Av Cheikh Anta Diop.

Île de N'Gor A short boat ride (CFA500 return) north of N'Gor village is Île de N'Gor. It has two beaches and two restaurants, with meals from CFA2500, plus a couple of huts selling drinks and cheaper food. You can also hire simple sun shelters and water-sports equipment. Along from the main beach, ***Chez Carla*** *(☎ 820 1586)* serves excellent seafood dishes for around CFA3000 and has a few rooms from CFA15,000.

Yoff

A short distance east of N'Gor, but sharply contrasting in feel, is the town of Yoff. It may look like just another suburb but there's a vital sense of community here that marks it out from other places around Dakar. The town is self-administering, with no government officials, no official police force and next to no crime. The people are almost exclusively Lebu, a fiercely independent group, and nearly all are members of the Layen, smallest of the four Islamic brotherhoods. Their founder's mausoleum, topped with a green dome, is at the eastern end of town.

The main fishing beach is about 1km west, where large pirogues are launched into the rollers and women sell recent catches, still glistening, on the sand. Even if the waves weren't dangerously large, and even if the beach wasn't covered in the town's detritus, Yoff is no place for basking: Skimpy clothing is most inappropriate in this staunchly Muslim community. Forget about 'entertainment' too: There are no bars in Yoff, and drunkenness, even in private, is frowned upon. This is a place to wander around slowly and respectfully.

Yoff Healers

One of the most interesting aspects of life in Yoff is the traditional *ndeup* ceremonies where people with a mental illness are treated and healed. People come to be cured from all over Senegal and Gambia and even from other neighbouring countries such as Mali and Guinea-Bissau. Despite the town's Islamic heritage, the ceremonies are totally animistic, and based on a belief that psychological sickness is the result of possession by spirits. The leaders of the Leyen brotherhood turn a blind eye to the 'pagan' ceremonies and the two beliefs comfortably coexist.

The healing ceremonies usually last one day, but can be longer for serious illnesses, and usually take place about twice a month. The traditional healers sacrifice animals (a chicken or cow depending on the seriousness of the illness) to invoke intervention from guardian spirits, and place the sick people into a trance-like state that allows malevolent spirits to be drawn out (not unlike voodoo ceremonies in other parts of West Africa). The healers' services are not cheap; families of people who need treatment reportedly pay large sums (the equivalent of many years' salary), and often several sufferers are treated at the same time.

The ceremonies take place in the centre of Yoff and can attract large crowds of local people. Tourists are tolerated, but even watching can be a disturbing experience for spectators. It's best to go with a local and keep to the sidelines. Waving a zoom lens around would be the height of insensitivity.

There is an Internet bureau in the *mairie* (town hall) where an hour online costs CFA1000.

Places to Stay & Eat The long-standing ***Campement le Poulagou*** *(☎ 820 2347)* has rooms for CFA6000 per person. It has a fine balcony overlooking the busy beach from where the fishing boats are launched. If you phone in advance the owner will pick you up from the airport. Rates include breakfast.

Via Via *(☎/fax 820 5475, ⓔ viavia@sentoo.sn, Route des Cimetières)* Singles/doubles without bathroom CFA9000/16,000, quads CFA7500 per person. This place east of Yoff is the nearest Dakar has to a backpackers. The rooms are clean but the rates are a bit steep for what you get. The multilingual management can provide information about Senegal and arrange language or drumming courses.

Getting There & Away Yoff is near the airport, and easily reached from there by taxi. The fare is CFA1500 – don't be persuaded otherwise. From Dakar centre, a taxi to Yoff should cost around CFA2000. By public transport, take DDD bus No 8. Buses loop through Yoff centre, but to reach Campement le Poulagou or Via Via you have to get off on the main road and walk down small streets towards the beach. Both places are signposted.

Malika

About 20km from Dakar centre, and beyond the vast urban sprawl of Dagoudane-Pikine (now larger than Dakar itself), is the village of Malika – a great place to escape from the city and enjoy the beaches on the north side of the Cap Vert peninsula. ***Campement Touristique de Malika Peul*** *(☎ 658 4867)* has camp sites at CFA2000 per tent, and basic huts for CFA4000. There's a small bar-restaurant, and if you want drumming or kora lessons, a teacher can be arranged.

Two smaller places are east along the beach. ***Auberge le Dauphin*** *(☎ 643 5771)* has basic rooms for CFA7000 with breakfast; while ***La Paillote*** *(☎ 634 7828)* is probably a better bet with simple huts only metres from the water for CFA5000, plus CFA3000 per person for two meals.

From Dakar, take bus No 16 to Malika, and opposite the terminus follow a sandy track towards the ocean. After about a 15-minute walk, you pass a football field with a wall around it; take the left fork and it's another 10 minutes. Alternatively, a taxi from Dakar is CFA4500.

If you're driving, continue 6km beyond Tiaroye-Mer to a left turn signposted 'Sedima'. After 3km you reach a crossroads. The road straight ahead goes to Keur Massar and the road to the left goes to Malika.

Lake Retba

Lake Retba (also called Lake Rose) is about 10 times saltier than the ocean and famous for its pink hue when the sun is high – particularly in the dry season. If pink water and effortless floating aren't enough to entice you, the small-scale salt-collecting industry on the south side of the lake may be of more interest. Locals scrape salt from the shallow lake bed and load it into boats, before piling it onto the shore for sale. The lunch-time coachloads of tourists from Dakar can be disturbing – as can the crowds when the Paris-Dakar Rally finishes here in January – but normally morning and evening at Retba is very peaceful. You can also walk over the dunes to the ocean, though be careful not to leave anything of value on the beach or, if you drive, in your car.

Places to Stay & Eat Undoubtedly the best place to stay, and arguably the best place to eat, is ***Bonaba Café*** *(☎ 638 7538)*. Hidden away on the far side of the lake, this ultrarelaxed place is run by a friendly British couple. It has simple bungalows for CFA9000 (half board), and clean outdoor bathrooms. To get there, you can walk from the touristy area for 2km over the dunes, keeping the lake on your right; or take a pirogue from the salt village for CFA3000; or drive anticlockwise around the lake until you can't go any further.

At the touristy area most places cater for tour groups. The most pleasant option is ***Ker Djinné*** *(☎ 826 7141)* with rustic bungalows for CFA3000 per person.

Getting There & Away Take an Alham to Keur Massar (not to be confused with Keur Moussa, further to the east), then a local minibus to Niaga (CFA300). From here you'll probably have to walk the last 5km, which can be a real sweat. A round trip by taxi from Dakar will cost about CFA20,000.

Rufisque

Near Rufisque is ***Hippo Camp*** *(☎ 646 0541, ⓔ hippo-tours@gmx.de)*, which is ideal for overlanders. It's run by a German couple who have a reputation for knowing their way around the back roads of the region and is good for arranging spares, changing sump oil etc. The beach-front camp is well signposted, and camping space is CFA2500 while single/double rooms are CFA5000/7500.

Rufisque is on the main road out of Dakar and there's plenty of transport, including DDD bus No 15, plus frequent Alhams and cars rapides. The road is notorious for being congested and slow, so you might consider taking the local commuter train – there are several services each day.

Keur Moussa Monastery

The Benedictine monastery at Keur Moussa, about 50km from Dakar between Rufisque and Kayar, has a beautiful Sunday mass at 10am with music combining African instruments and Gregorian chants. Afterwards, the monks sell prayer books, CDs and cassettes of their music, and other items.

From Rufisque catch an Alham or minibus heading to Bayakh or Kayar. Ask the driver to drop you off at a junction 2km after the minibus turns off the main road, from where a dirt track leads east for 1.5km to the monastery – it's signposted and all the drivers know it. Getting a lift back to Dakar shouldn't be difficult as many people will be going that way after the mass.

Central & Northern Senegal

This section covers a vast area from the edge of the busy Cap Vert peninsula, just a short distance from Dakar, to the remote outer edges of northern Senegal on the border with Mauritania. It includes areas seldom visited by travellers, including the stunning Grande Côte and the inland rural heartland of Senegal. Places in this section are described roughly from the south to the north and east.

THIÈS

pop 262,500

Just 70km east of Dakar, Thiès is Senegal's second-largest city and a gateway to the central region. It feels small and relaxed, with a pleasant atmosphere, lots of shady trees and good restaurants. Thiès also has one major attraction: a famous tapestry factory.

Places to Stay

Hôtel-Bar Rex *(☎ 951 1081, 197 Rue Douaumont)* Rooms without/with air-con CFA7000/9600. Centrally located, this hotel has musty but otherwise clean rooms with bathroom. The staff is friendly and there's safe parking.

Hôtel Man-Gan de Thiès *(☎ 951 1526, Rue Amadou Sow)* Singles/doubles with bathroom CFA13,600/17,200. This hotel has a nice garden courtyard and clean doubles with air-con.

Hôtel du Rail *(☎ 951 2313)* Singles/doubles with bathroom CFA8900/9300. For a taste of the past, this old hotel, east of the town centre, has large tranquil air-con rooms.

Places to Eat

All the hotels do food. Otherwise, a stroll down Av Léopold Senghor will reveal the cheapie ***Restaurant International*** *(☎ 951 4269)*, the clean and tidy ***Restaurant les Vieilles Marmites*** *(☎ 951 4440)*, and the more expensive ***Restaurant le Kien-An***. North of the railway tracks are a ***bakery*** and a ***Jumbo supermarket***. On Av Général de Gaulle the ***Chez Rachid*** *(☎ 951 1878)* does good chawarma for CFA850 and is open from noon until midnight. Opposite and smarter is ***Restaurant le Cailcedrat*** *(☎ 951 1130)*, which serves beers, coffees, snacks for CFA750 and larger meals for CFA1500 to CFA4000.

Le Massa Massa *(☎ 952 1244)* Meals about CFA3000. Open lunch & dinner. Hidden away about 2km out of town, this French restaurant is a contender for best food, and value, in Senegal. The fish soup (CFA1800), lasagne (CFA2700), and steak in roquefort sauce (CFA4200) are all excellent. To get there, take a taxi (CFA400) along the road towards Dakar and look for the signs pointing right near the second Shell petrol station.

Entertainment

For a cheap drink with the locals, try ***Bar Sunukeur*** next to the cinema. For something more lively, the ***Queen Marina Nightclub*** plays a good mix of music and is open until 5am, with an admission charge of CFA1000.

Getting There & Away

Bush taxis and other transport leave from the gare routière on the southern outskirts. A private taxi between the town centre and the gare routière costs CFA325. Destinations and fares in a Peugeot taxi include Dakar (CFA900), Kaolack (CFA1600) and St-Louis (CFA2350).

GRANDE CÔTE

The Grande Côte starts where the Cap Vert peninsula merges with the mainland and continues north to St-Louis. It's one long,

THIÈS

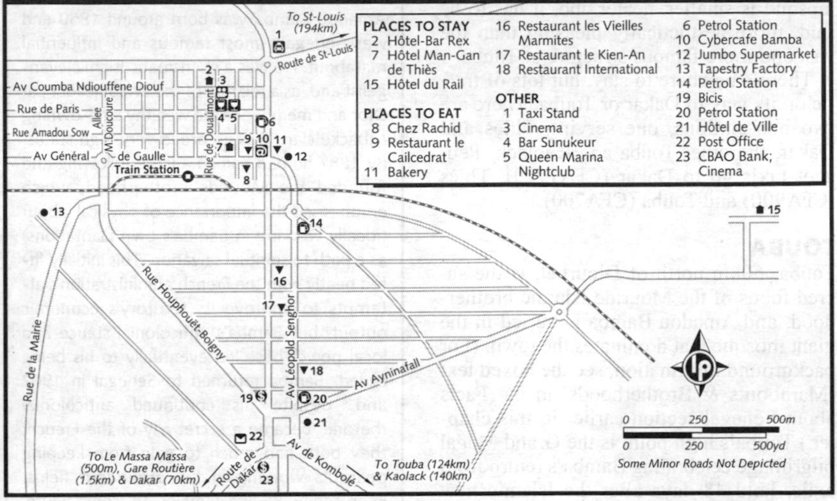
PLACES TO STAY
2 Hôtel-Bar Rex
7 Hôtel Man-Gan de Thiès
15 Hôtel du Rail
PLACES TO EAT
8 Chez Rachid
9 Restaurant le Cailcedrat
11 Bakery
16 Restaurant les Vieilles Marmites
17 Restaurant le Kien-An
18 Restaurant International
OTHER
1 Taxi Stand
3 Cinema
4 Bar Sunukeur
5 Queen Marina Nightclub
6 Petrol Station
10 Cybercafe Bamba
12 Jumbo Supermarket
13 Tapestry Factory
14 Petrol Station
19 Bicis
20 Petrol Station
21 Hôtel de Ville
22 Post Office
23 CBAO Bank; Cinema
To St-Louis (194km)
Route de St-Louis
Av Coumba Ndiouffene Diouf
Rue de Paris
Rue Amadou Sow
Av Général de Gaulle
Allee M. Doucoure
Rue de Douaumont
Train Station
Rue Houphouët-Boigny
Rue de la Mairie
Av Léopold Senghor
Av Ayninafall
Av de Kombolé
Route de Dakar
To Le Massa Massa (500m), Gare Routière (1.5km) & Dakar (70km)
To Touba (124km) & Kaolack (140km)
0 250 500m
0 250 500yd
Some Minor Roads Not Depicted

uninterrupted beach (at low tide it's possible to drive a car the whole way, and competitors in the final stage of the Paris-Dakar Rally do), but strong ocean winds and dangerous seas mean the Grande Côte has few settlements and fewer tourism facilities.

Mboro-sur-Mer is a fishing village off the beaten track and rarely reached by tourists, unlike **Kayar** (30km south), which is regularly included in tour itineraries. The only place to stay at Mboro-sur-Mer is the delightful ***Gîte de la Licorne*** *(☎ 955 7788)*, right on the beach. Single/double rooms cost CFA11,200/16,400 with breakfast. The gîte is usually closed from June to October so it's advisable to call ahead. Self-catering is possible.

Minibuses run from Thiès to Mboro town (CFA800), from where it's another 5km walk to Mboro-sur-Mer.

DIOURBEL

Diourbel is the former home of Amadou Bamba, the founding marabout of the

The Tapestries of Thiès

The factory of the Manufactures Sénégalaises des Arts Décoratifs (☎/fax 951 1131) was one of the many artistic endeavours inspired by President Senghor during the 1960s. Today, the factory is run as a cooperative, with designs for the tapestries chosen from paintings submitted by Senegalese artists.

Sizes of the tapestries vary but most are around 3m high by 2m wide. Preparing the design is a fascinating and elaborate process, taking many weeks. A large sketch of the painting is produced for the weavers to use as a pattern, but it is a reverse of the original because tapestries are made on the loom upside down.

All the weaving is done on manual looms, and two weavers complete about one square metre per month. Only eight tapestries are made from each design. Most find their way around the world as gifts from the government to foreign dignitaries; there's a huge tapestry hanging in Atlanta airport and another in Buckingham Palace. Others are for sale, but at CFA500,000 per square metre, most of us will be content to admire them in the exhibition room, which is open from 8am to 12.30pm and 3pm to 6.30pm Monday to Friday, and 8am to 12.30pm Saturday and Sunday. The admission fee is CFA1000. Individual visitors are not normally shown the workshops where the tapestries are actually made, but if you are genuinely interested, the exhibition supervisor might be able arrange for you to be shown around. If you phone ahead, your chances are better.

Mouride Islamic brotherhood. The main mosque is smaller, neater and, it has to be said, more aesthetically pleasing than the vast and more famous structure at Touba.

There's nowhere to stay, but lots of traffic on its way to Dakar or Touba. There are two bus stations, one serving Thiès and Dakar, the other Touba and Kaolack. Peugeot taxis go to Dakar (CFA1720), Thiès (CFA900) and Touba (CFA700).

TOUBA

Touba, 50km north of Diourbel, is the sacred focus of the Mouride Islamic brotherhood, and Amadou Bamba is buried in the giant mosque that dominates the town. (For background information, see the boxed text 'Marabouts & Brotherhoods' in the Facts about Senegal section earlier in this chapter.) Touba's high point is the Grand Magal pilgrimage celebrating Bamba's return from exile, held 48 days after the Islamic new year. At this time, about half a million Mourides flock into town, and every bus seat and hotel bed within a day's journey is occupied. Fridays are busy all year round.

Outside prayer times, guides are available to show you around the mosque and mausoleums, and it is inappropriate to enter without one. Some speak English. Fees should be agreed beforehand; about CFA1000 for an hour's tour is fair. The complex is still expanding to cater for the ever-growing crowds of followers, and the various stages of construction – from solid concrete columns to delicate hand-painted plaster reliefs – are interesting to observe.

No alcohol or cigarettes are allowed anywhere in Touba, and even hotels are seen as dens of iniquity. The nearest place to stay is at **Mbaké**, 10km to the south, which makes a good base for a day trip. The ***Campement Touristique le Baol*** *(☎ 976 5505)* has spartan rooms (perhaps to get pilgrims in an ascetic mood) in a homely setting. Singles/doubles cost CFA9500/12,700. The English-speaking staff can arrange guides for Touba.

To reach Touba from Dakar costs CFA3000 in a Peugeot taxi, CFA1500 in a car mouride and CFA1200 by minibus.

Bamba

Amadou Bamba was born around 1850 and was Senegal's most famous and influential marabout. He was a charismatic Islamic evangelist and, as a relation of the Wolof leader Lat Dior and member of the wealthy land-owning Mbacke clan, was accorded very high status. By 1887 he had gained a large following and founded the Mouride brotherhood, which emphasised the importance of physical labour (ideally working in Bamba's own plantations) as a path to spiritual salvation. This initially fitted neatly with the French administration's attempts to improve its territory's economic output, but Bamba's anticolonial stance and local power base led eventually to his being exiled. Bamba returned to Senegal in 1907 and, despite his continued anticolonial rhetoric, became a secret ally of the French; they both had much to gain from keeping peasants working in the groundnut fields. Even today, Bamba remains an iconic figure, and the convenient alliance between the brotherhoods and the government remains a major feature of modern Senegalese politics.

ST-LOUIS

pop 147,100

When you consider the enormous impact the French had on this continent it's fascinating to think that the place where it all began has barely changed for more than a century. Founded on a strategically important island in the Senegal River in 1659, St-Louis was the first French settlement in Africa. By the 1790s it had become a busy port and trading centre with a racially diverse population of 10,000. Most notable among the residents of St-Louis at this time were the *signares* – women of mixed race who temporarily 'married' European merchants based in the city, and thereby gained great wealth and privilege. They initiated the festival of decorated lanterns (fanals), which still occurs in St-Louis in the weeks around Christmas.

In the early 19th century, St-Louis became the capital of France's new African colonies. Dakar became the capital of French West Africa in 1904, but St-Louis remained the capital of Senegal (and Mauritania) until 1958, when everything was moved to Dakar.

St-Louis expanded slowly onto parts of the mainland (called Sor) and the Langue de Barbarie peninsula, but the face of the island itself barely changed throughout the 20th century. Ironically, this policy of neglect led unwittingly to the conservation of a range of

ST-LOUIS

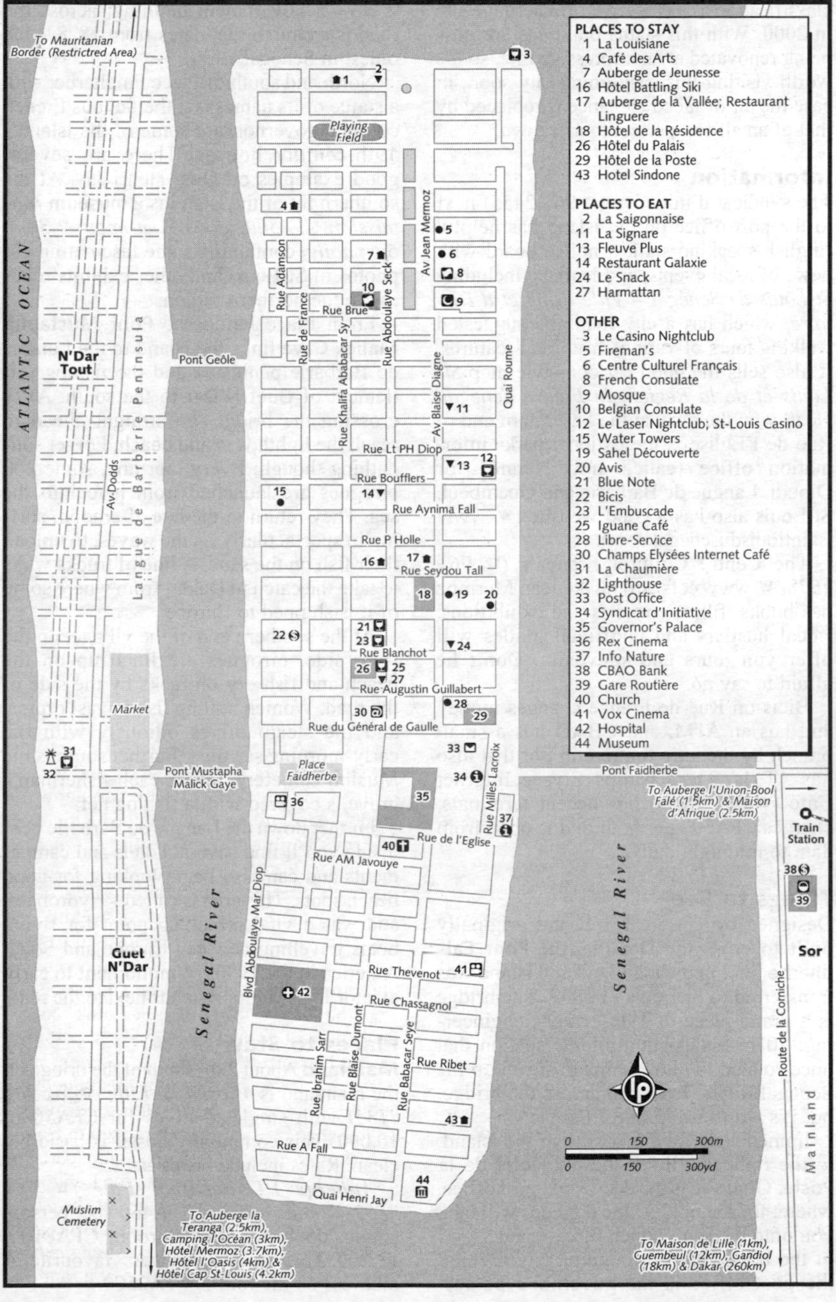
PLACES TO STAY
1 La Louisiane
4 Café des Arts
7 Auberge de Jeunesse
16 Hôtel Battling Siki
17 Auberge de la Vallée; Restaurant Linguere
18 Hôtel de la Résidence
26 Hôtel du Palais
29 Hôtel de la Poste
43 Hotel Sindone
PLACES TO EAT
2 La Saigonnaise
11 La Signare
13 Fleuve Plus
14 Restaurant Galaxie
24 Le Snack
27 Harmattan
OTHER
3 Le Casino Nightclub
5 Fireman's
6 Centre Culturel Français
8 French Consulate
9 Mosque
10 Belgian Consulate
12 Le Laser Nightclub; St-Louis Casino
15 Water Towers
19 Sahel Découverte
20 Avis
21 Blue Note
22 Bicis
23 L'Embuscade
25 Iguane Café
28 Libre-Service
30 Champs Elysées Internet Café
31 La Chaumière
32 Lighthouse
33 Post Office
34 Syndicat d'Initiative
35 Governor's Palace
36 Rex Cinema
37 Info Nature
38 CBAO Bank
39 Gare Routière
40 Church
41 Vox Cinema
42 Hospital
44 Museum
To Mauritanian Border (Restrictred Area)
ATLANTIC OCEAN
N'Dar Tout
Langue de Barbarie Peninsula
Av Dodds
Market
Pont Geôle
Playing Field
Rue Adamson
Rue de France
Rue Khalifa Ababacar Sy
Rue Abdoulaye Seck
Av Jean Mermoz
Av Blaise Diagne
Quai Roume
Rue Brue
Rue Lt PH Diop
Rue Boufflers
Rue Aynima Fall
Rue P Holle
Rue Seydou Tall
Rue Blanchot
Rue Augustin Guillabert
Rue du Général de Gaulle
Pont Mustapha Malick Gaye
Place Faidherbe
Pont Faidherbe
Rue Milles Lacroix
Rue de l'Eglise
Rue AM Javouye
To Auberge l'Union-Bool Falé (1.5km) & Maison d'Afrique (2.5km)
Train Station
Sor
Senegal River
Guet N'Dar
Blvd Abdoulaye Mar Diop
Rue Thevenot
Rue Chassagnol
Rue Ribet
Rue Ibrahim Sarr
Rue Blaise Dumont
Rue Babacar Seye
Rue A Fall
Quai Henri Jay
Route de la Corniche
Mainland
0 150 300m
0 150 300yd
Muslim Cemetery
To Auberge la Teranga (2.5km), Camping l'Océan (3km), Hôtel Mermoz (3.7km), Hôtel l'Oasis (4km) & Hôtel Cap St-Louis (4.2km)
To Maison de Lille (1km), Guembeul (12km), Gandiol (18km) & Dakar (260km)

classic architecture, and then to the island's classification as a Unesco world heritage site in 2000. With this status buildings are now being renovated at an impressive rate, so it's worth visiting this easy-going city soon, in case the air of faded elegance is replaced by that of an all-too-perfect tourist town.

Information

The syndicat d'initiative (☎ 961 2455) next to the post office on the island has helpful English-speaking staff, a notice board with news of local events, and leaflets, including *St-Louis de Sénégal – Ville d'Art et d'Histoire*, which has a city map and suggested walking tours of various historical features. It also sells the good cartoon-style map *St-Louis et de la Region du Fleuve Sénégal.* Nearby on the quay at the far eastern end of Rue de l'Eglise is the national parks information office (called Info Nature) for Djoudj, Langue de Barbarie and Guembeul. St-Louis also has a good website (W www.saintlouisdusenegal.com).

The Centre Culturel Français (☎ 961 1578, W www.ccfsl.sn) on Av Jean Mermoz has books, films, concerts and exhibitions. Local hustlers and unofficial guides will offer you tours and souvenirs. Don't be afraid to say no.

Bicis on Rue de France changes money and has an ATM, and CBAO has a small branch by the gare routière in Sor that also has ATMs. The Champs Elysée Internet Café (☎ 961 8029) has decent terminals, charges CFA500 per hour and is open from 8am to midnight daily.

Things to See

Designed by Gustav Eiffel and originally built to cross the Danube, the **Pont Faidherbe** linking the mainland and island was transferred to St-Louis in 1897. The bridge is a grand piece of 19th-century engineering: 507m long with a middle section that once rotated to allow ships to steam up the Senegal River. Taxis run across the bridge, but it's worth walking for the view.

Immediately after crossing to the island, to the right you'll see the old **Hôtel de la Poste**. Opposite is the deco-style post office, where, for a small fee, local guides will take you onto the roof, which offers good views of the bridge and surrounding city. Behind the post office is the **governor's palace**, which was a fort during the 18th century and is now a government building; across the road is a **church** that dates from 1828 – the oldest in Senegal.

North and south of Place Faidherbe, with a statue of its namesake, the famous French colonial governor, are some of the island's **19th-century houses**. There are several good examples on Quai Henri Jay. At the southern tip of the island is a **museum** *(admission CFA500; open 9am-noon & 3pm-6pm daily)* containing some fascinating old photos of St-Louis and other exhibits relating to the northern region.

From Place Faidherbe **Pont Mustapha Malick Gaye** links the island to the Langue de Barbarie peninsula and the fishing settlement of **Guet N'Dar** to the south. After crossing the bridge, go straight ahead to reach the lighthouse and **beach**. Forget sunbathing though: Every morning, some 200 pirogues are launched from here into the sea. They return in the late afternoon, surfing in spectacularly on the waves, to unload their fish on the sand. A line of trucks waits to take the catch to Dakar, from where some of it is shipped to Europe.

At the southern end of the village, on the river side, pirogues are lined up on the beach and fish dry on racks by the side of the road. Women boil up fish in vast drums, and the steam mixes odiously with the early-morning sea mist. Further south is the **Muslim cemetery**, where each fisherman's grave is covered with a fishing net.

Further down the Langue de Barbarie peninsula you'll find several hotels and campements and can also begin looking for good beach spots. This area is called l'Hydrobase, and was a vital refuelling point for flying boats travelling between Europe and South America in the 1930s. A **monument** to early aviator Jean Mermoz stands next to the road.

Places to Stay

Mainland About 2km south of the bridge on the mainland is ***Maison de Lille*** *(☎/fax 961 1135)* with singles/doubles for CFA5000/10,000. This community hostel is basic but clean. Rates include breakfast.

Auberge l'Union-Bool Falé *(☎ 961 3852)* Rooms with fan CFA4600 per person, singles/doubles with bathroom CFA8100/13,200. This is a shoestringers' favourite. A mattress on the roof is CFA2500.

SENEGAL

***Maison d'Afrique** (☎/fax 961 4500)* Singles/doubles CFA9600/12,600. In the same area as the auberge this place is clean and friendly and popular with locals – even Youssou N'dour stays here. A bathroom is an extra CFA2000. It's on the north side of Sor but is hard to find. Head for the village artisinal and start asking.

Island The pick of the budget options are the ***Auberge de Jeunesse** (☎ 961 2409, Rue Abdoulaye Seck)* and ***Auberge de la Vallée** (☎ 961 4722, Av Blaise Diagne)*. Both are clean, friendly and charge CFA5000 to CFA5500 per person, which is good value if you're in a double, but a bit steep for an eight-bed dorm. ***Café des Arts** (Rue de France)* is a small but colourfully decorated place near the north end of the island. The doubles cost CFA7000.

***La Louisiane** (☎ 961 4221, ⓔ louisiane@tpsnet.sn)* Singles/doubles with fan & bathroom CFA13,600/17,200. At the far north end of the island, this small and peaceful guesthouse offers great value and a stunning location. Even if you don't stay it's worth a visit for the mouthwatering local and European food at reasonable prices.

***Hôtel du Palais** (☎ 961 1772, Rue Blanchot)* Singles/doubles CFA15,000/17,600. The Palais has seen better days, but the huge upstairs rooms with balconies are reasonably good.

***Hôtel de la Résidence**(☎ 961 1259, ⓔ hotresid@sentoo.sn, Av Blaise Diagne)* Singles/doubles with bathroom CFA27,600/33,600. This place is ageing more gracefully, though the air-con rooms are a bit overpriced. The hotel bar is the centre of well-to-do St-Louis nightlife.

***Hôtel de la Poste** (☎ 961 1118, ⓔ htlposte@telecomplus.sn, Rue du Général de Gaulle)* Singles/doubles CFA27,000/33,500. The passengers on the flying boats used to stay here and you're still paying for this slice of history. The hotel's Safari Bar is full of colonial flashbacks, balding animal heads and all, but the rooms are disappointing.

***Hotel Sindone** (☎ 961 4245, ⓔ sindone@arc.sn, Quai Henri Jay)* Singles/doubles from CFA25,600/27,200. This stylish and airy hotel with a river view is top of the range.

Langue de Barbarie Places to stay within 4km of the centre are listed here. Options further away are in the Around St-Louis section following. Prices drop dramatically during the low season.

***Auberge la Teranga** (☎ 961 5050)* Singles/doubles CFA6400/8400. About 2.5km south of town, this simple but amiable place is aimed at backpackers. The rooftop restaurant does meals for CFA1500 to CFA2500.

***Camping l'Océan** (☎ 961 3118, fax 971 5784)* Camp sites CF1000 per person, singles/doubles with bathroom CFA11,200/15,200. Next along and probably the best value, this place is ideal for travellers with vehicles and/or tents. The rooms are clean with air-con an extra CFA5000. You can hire a tent for CFA1000.

***Hôtel Mermoz** (☎/fax 961 3668, ⓦ www.hotelmermoz.com)* Singles/doubles with fan CFA12,000/16,600. Further south, this place offers comfortable bungalows and a pool. Air-con is an extra CFA10,000.

***Hôtel l'Oasis** (☎/fax 961 4232, ⓔ nicooasissl@arc.sn)* Singles/doubles CFA11,200/17,000, with bathroom CFA15,700/23,600. Many travellers recommend this place, about 4km south of the centre, and the friendly, multilingual management. There are simple, good-quality huts (up to CFA33,500 for four people); or high-standard bungalows with bathroom – all with breakfast. Other meals start at CFA2500.

***Hotel Cap St-Louis** (☎ 961 3939, fax 961 3909)* Singles/doubles CFA10,400/14,800, with air-con and bathroom CFA21,900/28,300. Almost next door to Hôtel l'Oasis is this resort-style place with simple rooms and some air-con bungalows. Facilities include a swimming pool, strictly for guests, and a tennis court.

Places to Eat

More tourists means more money and, you guessed it, a growing number of cuisines and restaurants. The hotels also do food, some of it quite good.

In the city centre there are a couple of ***chawarma joints*** on Av Blaise Diagne. North of here, ***Restaurant Galaxie** (☎ 961 2468, Rue Abdoulaye Seck)*, ***Restaurant Linguere*** on the ground floor under Auberge de la Vallée, and ***Fleuve Plus*** on Rue Lt PH Diop all do good Senegalese food for around CFA1500 to CFA2000.

***Le Snack** (Av Blaise Diagne)* Pizzas CFA3500. Open lunch & dinner daily.

Locals say this place has the best pizzas, and the ice cream's not bad either.

Harmattan *(☎ 961 8253, Rue Augustin Guillabert)* Meals CFA3500. Open 10am-3pm & 6pm-midnight daily. On an international menu with a French bent, the brochettes (CFA2500) are excellent but the chawarma (CFA2500) a bit pricey. Harmattan also does cocktails for CFA2500.

La Saigonnaise *(☎ 961 6481)* Mains CFA3500. Open noon-midnight. At the north end of Rue Abdoulaye Seck, this Vietnamese place complements its great location (looking to Mauritania) with traditional Saigonnaise fare.

La Signare *(☎ 961 1932, Av Blaise Diagne)* Meals CFA7000. Open lunch & dinner Thur-Tues. Considered one of the top eateries in St-Louis, La Signare offers a menu du jour for CFA7000.

Self caterers will save money and have more fun shopping in the market just north of the bridge in Guet N'Dar. For European goods and French wine, head for the *libre-service* (A French-style minimarket) on Av Blaise Diagne.

St-Louis Jazz

Jazz is a big thing here, and it's not just the name shared with St Louis in Missouri, USA, where blues and jazz originated. Way back in the 1940s, jazz bands from St-Louis (Senegal) were playing in Paris and Europe. Worldwide interest was revived in the early 1990s with the introduction of the annual St-Louis International Jazz Festival, held every May, attracting performers and audiences from all over the world. Come if you're a jazz fan, but be prepared for full hotels and inflated rates. More information is available from the Centre Culturel Français (☎ 961 1578, e ccfsl@arc.sn).

Entertainment

Bars The ***Hôtel Battling Siki*** is named after Africa's only heavyweight boxing champion, which is appropriate as there's a good chance you'll see fists flying first-hand if you stop in for a drink. Instead, for a couple of quiet ones with the locals we recommend ***Fireman's***, just north of the French cultural centre, which has the cheapest beer around and, to quote one regular, 'the worst shitter in Senegal'.

Cleaner facilities and more-expensive drinks can be found in several bars just north of the centre. ***Blue Note*** *(Rue Abdoulaye Seck)* is a vaguely subversive scene with a mixed crowd. A couple of doors south, ***L'Embuscade*** *(☎ 961 7741)* has tap beer and tapas, while on the next block is ***Iguane Café*** *(☎ 961 52 12)*, a Cuban-themed bar.

Nightclubs For a taste of how Senegal's bright young things let their hair down, head to ***Le Laser*** *(☎ 961 53 98)*, part of the St-Louis Casino complex on the Quai Roume. There's a CFA2000 cover for tourists, which includes a drink, and it's closed on Monday and Tuesday. ***Le Casino Nightclub***, on a pontoon at the north end of the island, has nothing to do with the casino but gets lively on Friday and Saturday. In Guet N'Dar, ***La Chaumière*** is a bar and nightclub that's popular with both locals and tourists where you'll see more sweat and less make-up.

Getting There & Away

The gare routière is on the mainland 100m south of Pont Faidherbe (a taxi from here to the island costs CFA250). The fare to/from Dakar is CFA2150 by express bus, CFA2445 by Alham and CFA3100 by Peugeot taxi. To or from Richard Toll by Peugeot taxi costs CFA1540. A Peugeot taxi to Gandiol, from where boats to the Parc National de la Langue de Barbarie leave, costs CFA250.

Getting Around

Car & Bicycle Cars can be hired from the Avis agency at CFAO (☎ 961 1986), north of Hotel de la Poste on Quai Roume. Small cars cost CFA30,000 per day, including tax and 100km free. The agency is closed on Sunday. Several hotels and auberges hire out steel roadsters for about CFA2500 and mountain bikes ('VTTs' in French) for CFA5000 per day.

AROUND ST-LOUIS

Guembeul & Gandiol

About 12km south of St-Louis, **Réserve de Faune de Guembeul** *(admission CFA1000; open 7.30am-6.30pm daily)* is small, easy to reach and a good place to explore on foot. It protects endangered Sahel animals including dama gazelles, patas monkeys and sulcata tortoises, and 190 bird species have been spotted here.

The park is easy to reach by any bush taxi going between St-Louis and Gandiol, or by private taxi or rented bike. Guided walks cost CFA7000 for about three hours, less if you have more people.

Gandiol is a small village on the mainland about 18km south of St-Louis. From the lighthouse north of the village, ferries cross the estuary to the campements on the southern end of the Langue de Barbarie, and this is also the starting point for organised boat tours of the national park.

About 2km south of Gandiol are **Mouit** and the **national park office**. Nearby, on the edge of the river, the excellent ***Zebrabar*** *(☎ 638 1862, W www.regio-team.ch/zebrabar)* offers camping for CFA2000, single/double huts for CFA6000/9000 and bungalows for CFA12,000/15,000, and can set you up for boat rides or visits to the park.

A bush taxi runs a few times each day from St-Louis to Gandiol (CFA300). Sometimes this taxi continues to Mouit, otherwise you'll have to walk the last 2km from Gandiol to Mouit, or 2.5km to Zebrabar. A private taxi all the way from St-Louis to Zebrabar is CFA2500.

Parc National de la Langue de Barbarie

This national park *(admission CFA5000)* includes the far southern tip of the peninsula, some small islands, the estuary and a section of the mainland, and is home to numerous water birds – notably flamingos, pelicans, cormorants, herons and egrets. From November to April, these numbers are swelled by the arrival of migrants from Europe.

The usual (and best) way to experience the park is by boat, which will cruise slowly past the mud flats and islands where the birds feed and roost.

Places to Stay Both the following places provide meals, boat transfers and opportunities for fishing and sailboarding. Reservations are essential.

Campement Langue de Barbarie *(☎ 961 1118)* Singles/doubles CFA10,600/15,000. Run by Hôtel de la Poste, this smart place is in a wonderful position at the southern end of the peninsula, about 20km from St-Louis centre, and offers cottages for rent. Breakfast is CFA2000 and other meals cost CFA6000.

Campement Océan et Savane *(☎ 961 1260)* Half board CFA18,600 per person, full board CFA20,600 per person. Run by Hôtel de la Résidence, this place is good value and more relaxed, with accommodation in large Mauritanian-style tents.

Getting There & Away The usual approach is by boat from the mainland, normally from Gandiol or Mouit. Another option is to join an organised tour from St-Louis. For a list of tour operators, see Organised Tours in the main Getting Around section earlier in this chapter.

Parc National aux Oiseaux du Djoudj

This national park *(admission CFA2000 per person, plus CFA5000 per car; open 7am-dusk daily, 1 Nov-30 Apr)* is 60km north of St-Louis and is considered one of the premier places on earth to view birds migrating from Europe. The park incorporates a stretch of the Senegal River, with numerous channels, creeks, lakes, ponds, marshes, reedbeds and mud flats, plus surrounding areas of dry woodland. This range of habitats (and the park's status as one of the first places with permanent water south of the Sahara) means the park attracts numerous species, making it a sanctuary of global significance with Unesco world heritage and Ramsar status.

The park is most famous for its vast flocks of pelicans and flamingos. Even if you have no interest in ornithology, observing these comical birds at such close quarters is fascinating. Other easily recognisable species include spur-winged geese, purple herons, egrets, spoonbills, jacanas, cormorants and harriers. From November to April, various migrants arrive from Europe, especially waders. The sheer numbers that assemble here are staggering. Around three million individual birds pass through the park annually, and almost 400 separate species have been recorded.

There are a few mammals and reptiles in the park, most notably populations of warthogs and mongeese and a famously large python that lurks by the edge of the lake. Other mammals include jackals, hyenas, monkeys and gazelles.

To see the pelican colony, take the two-hour boat ride (CFA3000 per person). It is possible to visit out of season, but with few

Djoudj Tours

The tours offered by companies, hotels and guides in St-Louis all follow the same pattern, leaving at around 7am to reach the park by 8.30am. First they drive to the jetty for a two-hour boat ride through the creeks, the highlight of which is the enormous pelican colony. (The boats are owned by the hotel and the first trip goes at about 9am.) After lunch you drive to see flamingo flocks on the lake's edge.

Trying to do something 'unusual' will cause all sorts of confusion, and notwithstanding Djoudj's global status, there is no real set-up for ornithologists. Keen bird-watchers hoping to see a good range of species on an organised day trip from St-Louis are likely to find the visit quite frustrating. A better option might be to forget the local guides and hire your own taxi, or spend several days exploring the national park alone.

birds and no boat rides at this time, only keen birders should consider it.

Places to Stay Situated at the park's main entrance, ***Station Bioligique*** is a low-key camp with clean rooms (CFA6500 per person) that are mainly for research groups, but open to the public. Camping is allowed and decent meals cost CFA3500.

Hostellerie du Djoudj *(☎ 963 8702, fax 963 8703)* Singles/doubles CFA22,600/30,000. Also at the park entrance, this large place has comfortable rooms and a pool. You can charter a boat or 4WD for around CFA10,000 per hour, or hire mountain bikes. It's open from November to April.

Getting There & Away Most visitors reach the park on an organised tour (see Organised Tours in the main Getting Around section earlier in this chapter) or with a local guide. Some guides are members of a professional organisation; others are independent and charge about CFA4000 per person per day. On top of this you pay for transport (usually a taxi), park admission and boat rides. (Official guides have a permit that means the CFA5000 admission charge for cars is waived.)

Hiring a taxi from St-Louis costs around CFA7000 for four hours, or CFA20,000 for a day. It's very important to hire one in good mechanical condition, with a driver who knows the way. Make it clear beforehand what time you plan to return and never pay the whole fare in advance. Hiring a guide as well as the taxi and driver is optional.

If you're driving from St-Louis, take the paved highway towards Rosso for about 25km. Near Ross-Bethio you'll see a sign pointing to the park, which is about 25km further along dirt tracks.

SENEGAL RIVER ROUTE

The Senegal River marks the country's northern and eastern borders. In the 19th century, French colonial forces built a chain of forts – Dagana, Podor, Matam, Bakel and Kayes (in present-day Mali) – which later developed into major settlements and were linked by boats from St-Louis. Today, most of the traffic is on the main road that runs parallel to the river (but seldom close enough to see it). This good-quality road provides a rarely travelled route between St-Louis and Tambacounda, and between the national parks of Djoudj and Niokolo-Koba, but don't forget to fuel up at the main towns.

North of the river, the deserts of Mauritania mark the edge of the Sahara, and a journey along this road is as near to the desert as you can get in Senegal. The landscape is dry and the vegetation sparse. Sand drifts across the road, and the traditional *banco* (mud-brick) houses would blend almost completely into the background were it not for the Tukulor custom of decorating the outer walls in bold stripes of red, brown and yellow. To the south, the great Ferlo Plains stretch deep into central Senegal, with some parts set aside as wildlife reserves, although these dry areas are very hard to reach and have no tourist facilities.

Rosso-Senegal

This flyblown frontier town is some 100km northeast of St-Louis on the Senegal River. From here a ferry makes the crossing to Rosso-Mauritanie. The main street is full of hustlers, smugglers, moneychangers and minibus touts, and is certainly worth escaping quickly. If you do get stuck, the depressing ***Auberge du Walo***, 2km from the ferry, has rooms for CFA8000. Transport to St-Louis is CFA1550 by Peugeot taxi and CFA1070 by Alham. A local bush taxi to Richard Toll is CFA350.

Richard Toll was once a colonial town and is now the centre of Senegal's sugar industry. If you stay overnight here, an evening stroll to the crumbling **Château de Baron Roger** at the eastern end of town whiles away an hour or two. The attached overgrown ornamental park was laid out by one Claude Richard, hence the name Richard Toll, which means Richard's Garden.

Cheap places to stay seem nonexistent. ***Hôtel la Taouey*** *(☎ 963 3431)* on the river, north of the main street, has adequate but bare single/double rooms for CFA13,600/16,800. ***Gîte d'Étape*** *(☎ 963 3608)* occupies one of the most beautiful positions on the whole river, though the rooms, with air-con that's more con than air, are overpriced at CFA22,600/26,500.

On the main street are several eateries. ***Restaurant la Louis*** *(☎ 963 9467)* serves mafé, fish and rice (both CFA400) and cous cous with beef (CFA800), while ***Ker Mimichon*** does chicken meals for CFA1500.

Podor & Île à Morphil

Podor has a large fort and several old colonial buildings – but only history fans will get excited here. ***Gîte de Douwaya*** *(☎ 630 1751)* is opposite the gare routière and has rooms with bathroom for CFA8000. Buses stop at Treji (also spelt Tredji or Taredji) on the main road, and local bush taxis shuttle passengers the 20km to Podor for CFA375.

Podor is at the western end of Île à Morphil, which stretches for 100km between the main Senegal River and a parallel channel. A road runs along the island all the way to Saldé at its eastern end, where a ferry crosses over to Ngoui, near Pete. Travellers with wheels and plenty of time say this is an interesting route and the traditional villages of Guede and Alwar are particularly scenic.

Peugeot taxis run from Podor to St-Louis (CFA3100, four hours) and to Ouro Sogui (CFA4000, four to five hours). An Alham to Ouro Sogui costs CFA2000 but takes twice as long.

Matam & Ouro Sogui

Matam is something of a colonial relic 230km south-east of Podor, and is reached via a turn-off from Ouro Sogui. Over the years Matam has declined, while Ouro Sogui has grown into a lively trading centre and transport hub.

In Ouro Sogui, the best-value accommodation is the ***Auberge Sogui*** *(☎ 966 1198)* opposite the market, which has reasonable rooms without/with air-con for CFA5000/7500, though the shared bathrooms are grubby. Don't confuse this with ***Hôtel Auberge Sogui*** *(☎ 966 1536)*, a massive white monolith with air-con doubles for CFA15,500. Opposite is ***Hôtel Oasis*** which has an adjoining Internet bureau.

There are several cheap eateries on the same street, including ***Restaurant Teddoungal***, where beef and spaghetti costs CFA1000, and some good *dibieteries* (small stalls and shops selling grilled lamb and goat). Bicis and CBAO banks both have branches here.

Battered Peugeot taxis run to Dakar (CFA9250) and Bakel (CFA4000, two hours); Alhams cost CFA2600.

Bakel

Bakel is set among some rare rocky hills overlooking a bend in the river and is an interesting and picturesque place well worth a visit. The abandoned **Pavillon René Caillié** on a hill next to two large water tanks gives great views. The old **fort** is still in use and in good condition. Officially, it's closed to the public, but not many tourists come here and management seems happy to allow people to wander around. The large octagonal lookout tower at the southern edge of town and the nearby military cemetery are easily reached.

Hôtel Islam has spartan rooms without/with air-con for CFA3000/CFA10,000 per person. Downstairs there's a good local eatery with meals from CFA400.

On the waterfront is ***Bar-Resto Mbodick*** *(☎ 937 9031, 654 4623)*, the only watering hole in town that also does meals (CFA1500). The patron, Mamadou Loum, has information about boats going up and down the river.

At 4.30am, except on Fridays, an express bus leaves from the petrol station at the entrance to town for the border town of Kidira (CFA1000), and then on to Tambacounda (CFA3000, three to four hours). Other vehicles leave when they're full, which could take a while.

For the adventurous, motorised pirogues occasionally go between Matam, Bakel and Kayes, leaving Bakel from the 'port' near the Bar-Resto Mbodick.

Petite Côte

The Petite Côte is south of Dakar, stretching for about 70km between Rufisque and Joal-Fadiout. The southwest aspect, reliable weather conditions and clean sands make this Senegal's second-best beach area after Cap Skiring, and by far its most popular in terms of visitor numbers.

Beyond Rufisque, smaller roads turn off the main artery and lead down to a string of coastal villages that seem a million miles away from the madness of Dakar. For some reason few travellers stop in here, in sharp contrast to the package-tourist hell that is Saly-Portugal. So many tourists fly into Dakar and transit direct to Saly that a new international airport is being built southeast of Rufisque to serve them.

TOUBAB DIALAO

The fishing village of Toubab Dialao is about 10km from Bargny. Many travellers rave about ***Sobo-Bade*** *(☎/fax 836 0356, e sobo bade@sentoo.sn)*, built on a small cliff, surrounded by beautiful gardens and overlooking the beach and ocean. There is a range of rooms and prices, from simple four-bed rooms for CFA5000 per person, to double bungalows with bathroom and sea view for CFA17,000. Meals cost from CFA2500, with vegetarian choices and a *menu du jour* for CFA5500. Run by a Frenchman named Gérard, this place offers artistic workshops in dance, writing, percussion and sculpture.

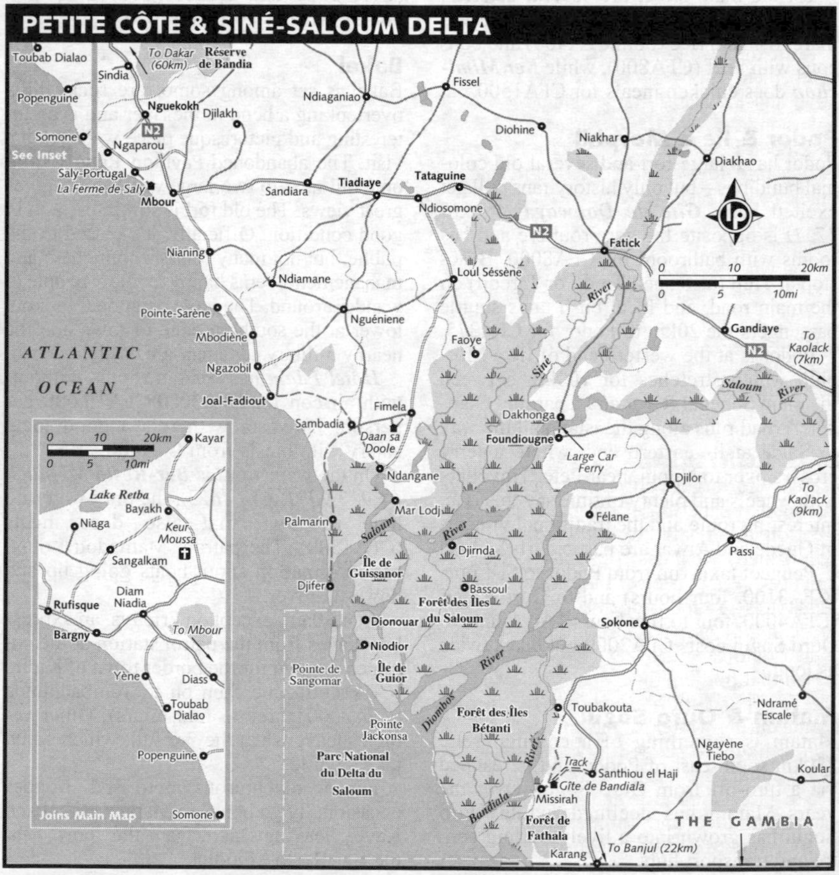
PETITE CÔTE & SINÉ-SALOUM DELTA
Toubab Dialao
Popenguine
Somone
See Inset
To Dakar (60km)
Réserve de Bandia
Sindia
Nguekokh
Djilakh
N2
Ngaparou
Saly-Portugal
La Ferme de Saly
Mbour
Sandiara
Tiadiaye
Tataguine
Ndiosomone
Ndiaganiao
Fissel
Diohine
Niakhar
Diakhao
Fatick
Nianing
Ndiamane
Loul Séssène
Pointe-Sarène
Nguéniene
Mbodiène
Ngazobil
Joal-Fadiout
ATLANTIC OCEAN
Faoye
Siné River
Gandiaye
To Kaolack (7km)
Saloum River
Fimela
Sambadia
Daan sa Doole
Dakhonga
Foundiougne
Large Car Ferry
Ndangane
Djilor
To Kaolack (9km)
Mar Lodj
Félane
Palmarin
Saloum River
Djirnda
Passi
Île de Guissanor
Bassoul
Djifer
Forêt des Îles du Saloum
Dionouar
Sokone
Niodior
Île de Guior
Pointe de Sangomar
River
Diombos
Toubakouta
Ndramé Escale
Forêt des Îles Bétanti
Pointe Jackonsa
Parc National du Delta du Saloum
Ngayène Tiebo
Track
Santhiou el Haji
Koular
Gîte de Bandiala
Missirah
Bandiala River
Forêt de Fathala
THE GAMBIA
Karang
To Banjul (22km)
0 10 20km
0 5 10mi
Kayar
Lake Retba
Bayakh
Niaga
Keur Moussa
Sangalkam
Diam Niadia
Rufisque
Bargny
To Mbour
Yène
Diass
Toubab Dialao
Popenguine
Somone
Joins Main Map

La Source Ndiambalane *(☎ 836 1703, ⓔ boulang@telecomplus.sn)* has similar rooms at similar prices, while ***Auberge La Mimosa*** *(☎/fax 826 7326)* has comfortable rooms and self-catering facilities, but no view and cheaper rates.

To get here from Dakar, take anything headed for Mbour and get off at the big junction where the roads to Thiès and Kaolack divide; local minibuses run from here to Toubab Dialao for CFA250. Alternatively, in Bargny, you may find something direct.

POPENGUINE

About 20 years ago Popenguine was *the* place for wealthy Dakarois to come. Then it stopped being trendy and became a really cool and unpretentious place to chill for a couple of days. One street back from the beach, ***Ker Cupaam*** *(☎/fax 956 4951)* is the pick of the accommodation options. It's a campement run by a local women's cooperative and has comfortable bungalows with bathroom for CFA10,000 including breakfast. Food is available here, but a better bet is ***L'écho-Côtier*** *(☎ 637 8772)*, a restaurant on the beach that has a large and varied menu and a *plat du jour* for CFA5000. For a cheaper meal, or an after-lunch drink, wander down the beach to the ***Chez Ginette*** *(☎ 957 7110)*, a rustic little bar where you can drink cheap beer while the waves lap at your feet. Ginette also has some basic rooms.

From Dakar, head for Mbour and get off at Sindia, from where infrequent bush taxis run to Popenguine for CFA200.

SALY-PORTUGAL

It's easy to forget you're in Africa in **Saly-Portugal**. It's the sort of coastal holiday destination found all throughout the world: palm-lined beaches, package tourists aplenty and a cluster of more than a dozen big hotels grouped together in a *domaine touristique* (tourist zone) with restaurants, banks, shops and a casino. The strip of beach that borders this zone is reserved for the European tourists who pack the domaine during winter, so the only Senegalese you're likely to see will be working in the service industry. However, Saly can be fun. There's lively nightlife and plenty of restaurants, both local and European.

Bicis and SGBS have branches near King Karaoke, both with ATMs. There are also two Internet centres: the extortionately priced Planet.Saly in the Centre Commercial; and an unnamed place that's better in every way in the village centre. It's worth picking up the free map of Saly-Portugal.

Places to Stay & Eat

A small selection of hotels is listed here, although most cater for groups and do not even have rates for individuals. If you phone before arrival, discounts may be available, but this is more easily done through a tour agency in Dakar; many offer special rates.

Les Cocotiers *(☎ 957 1491, ⓦ www.hotel-cocotiers.com)* Singles/doubles CFA22,500/27,000. This hotel is less fancy than most in Saly but it is right on the beach. Sadly, the hotel has blighted its view with a monstrous concrete pavilion out over the water.

Les Filaos *(☎ 957 1180, ⓔ nffilaos@sentoo.sn)* Half board CFA33,360 per person. This 110-room complex comes complete with *animateurs* to rev up the guests in case they get bored.

Savana Saly *(☎ 939 5800, ⓔ savana@telecomplus.sn)* Singles/doubles half board CFA45,000/55,000. This is one of the more luxurious places in Saly.

Auberge Khady *(☎/fax 957 2518)* Singles/doubles including bathroom & breakfast CFA14,400/21,600, bungalows CFA21,600/27,300. In the village of Saly-Niakhniakhale, just south of the big hotels, is this small and highly rated auberge, a vibrant place about 200m back from the sea. Rooms are simple but comfortable, and rates are about 25% lower out of season. Khady also has an excellent restaurant and a regular Friday night 'Senegalese Soiree'.

Ferme de Saly *(☎ 957 5006, 638 4790, ⓔ farmsaly@yahoo.fr)* Half board in huts with bathroom CFA15,000 per person, singles/doubles with breakfast CFA8000/14,000. About 2km south of the Auberge Khady, Ferme de Saly is far more in tune with its natural environs than anywhere else in Saly. This gîte is run by a jovial Frenchman who's been travelling for 30 years. Prices for half board drop to CFA12,000 from June to November.

You can eat wherever you choose to sleep, but if you get sick of buffet and fancy something Senegalese, try the ***Dibieterie Black & White*** *(☎ 551 2997)* in Saly-Niakhniakhale on the dirt road heading south.

Both the Auberge Khady and the Ferme de Saly arrange excursions and fishing trips, and the flashy places at Saly-Portugal offer water sports for nonguests. A taxi from Mbour is CFA1500.

MBOUR

About 80km south of Dakar, and 5km south of Saly, Mbour is a major fishing centre; the 200m-long market on the beach, plus all the surrounding marine-related commerce, is a site to behold. The market is a favourite for tour groups from Saly and thus attracts a motley crew of hustlers, though they're less persistent than their brethren in Dakar. As a major transport junction Mbour is a good jumping-off point for places along the coast.

Places to Stay & Eat

There are a few places to stay scattered around town, while the eating establishments are more central.

On the main square near the church is ***Les Citronniers*** *(☎ 957 2457)*, where rates for accommodation including breakfast are CFA12,000/20,000 for one/two people in simple four-bed rooms.

On the beach near here is Mbour's biggest hotel, the ***Centre Touristique Coco Beach*** *(☎ 957 1004)* where rooms with bathroom and air-con are good value at CFA15,000, and there's a pool. A few blocks south along the sandy street nearest the ocean is ***Le Bounty*** *(☎/fax 957 2951, e bounty@sentoo.sn)*, where there's a convivial atmosphere but room rates are a bit steep with singles/doubles at CFA15,000/20,000. A block back from the beach is ***Chez Charley***, which is essentially a few basic rooms with fan in a family compound for CFA10,000 with breakfast.

In the centre of town near the market, ***Café Luxembourg*** *(☎ 636 8839)* is a reliable option with meals for CFA2000 to CFA4000. Around the corner is a ***snack bar*** with chawarmas at CFA700. Just off Av Demba Diop, near the Total petrol station, is ***Kalom's Jakbah***, a popular local place with chawarma, dibieterie, mafé and other meals for CFA500 to CFA2000.

Getting There & Away

The trip between Mbour and Dakar costs CFA950 in a Peugeot taxi and CFA670 in an Alham. Minibuses south to Joal-Fadiout are CFA400.

NIANING

Nianing is 10km south of Mbour and boasts another line of hotels, although these are smaller and more pleasant than the Saly strip, and the village itself is much quieter than Mbour. ***Les Bourgain Villees*** *(☎ 957 5241)* is close to the beach, with rooms from CFA10,000; and ***Hôtel Le Ben'Tenier*** *(☎ 957 1420, e bentenier@telecomplus.sn)* is a friendly place with bungalows in a quiet garden for CFA10,600/16,000.

JOAL-FADIOUT

The twin villages of Joal and Fadiout have much to recommend them, for a day trip at the very least. Joal is on the mainland, while Fadiout covers a small island reached by a long wooden bridge. The island is composed entirely of clam shells that have accumulated over the centuries, and everything in the village is at least partly made of shells too. Fadiout is also one of those few remaining places completely free of cars, making a wander through the maze of laneways even more enjoyable.

The citizens of Joal and Fadiout are rightly proud of their religious tolerance. Christians and Muslims live in harmony here, with Fadiout's shrines to the Virgin Mary and large church complemented by an equally large mosque. A separate shell island is reached by another wooden bridge and is home to both Christian and Muslim cemeteries. Nearby is a group of curious basketlike granaries on stilts over the water. The idea is that even if the village burns down, at least the food for the rest of the year will be safe.

Places to Stay & Eat

The best cheap place to stay in Joal is ***Relais 114*** *(☎ 957 6178)*. It is operated by the friendly Mamadou Baldé, who is very proud of his performing pelicans and his English-speaking son. Basic clean rooms accommodate one to three people for CFA7500. Breakfast is CFA1500 and other tasty meals start at CFA2500. Near the bridge to Fadiout, ***Hôtel le Finio*** *(☎/fax 957 6112)* is more upmarket, but it lacks the Relais's soul. Single/double huts with bathroom and fan are CFA6500/ 12,000, twice that with air-con.

On Fadiout the only place to stay is the compact and relaxed ***Campement les Palétuviers*** *(☎/fax 957 6205)*. Very simple rooms are CFA4800 per person.

SENEGAL

Getting There & Away

A bush taxi to/from Mbour is CFA500. If you're heading on down the coast, from Joal to Palmarin costs CFA800. A Peugeot taxi goes direct to Dakar most mornings (without changing at Mbour) for CFA1500.

PALMARIN & DJIFER

The village of Palmarin (actually four villages in a group) is 20km south of Joal-Fadiout, where the beaches of the Petite Côte merge with the labyrinthine creeks of the Siné-Saloum Delta. The road here takes you through shimmering flatlands dotted with palm groves, traditional villages, shallow lagoons, mud flats and patches of salt marsh that attract huge flocks of wading birds.

The fishing village of Djifer is another 15km further south on the sandy Pointe de Sangomar peninsula jutting between the Atlantic Ocean and the mouth of the River Saloum. At the far end of the village is a huge fish market and port where many colourful fishing boats are drawn up on the beach. However, all those fish bones and a complete lack of sewerage services takes away from Djifer's charm.

Places to Stay & Eat

Near the village of Sessene, a part of Palmarin, ***Campement de Palmarin*** *(☎ 635 8789)* is on a sandy beach under the palms where weather-beaten bungalows cost CFA5000/8500 for singles/doubles. Behind the campement is a large lagoon – an excellent area to see wading birds.

Djifer has two campements. The smarter ***Campement Pointe de Sangomar*** *(☎ 835 6191 in Dakar)* is popular with groups of French hunters, and for facilities is still the best value. Half board costs CFA6000 per person in simple bungalows, and CFA13,000 in doubles with bathroom.

The quieter ***Campement la Mangrove*** *(☎ 956 4232)* is 2km north of Djifer; it offers basic huts for CFA5000 per person, and camping.

The campements provide food; or, there are several basic *gargottes* (cheap eateries). ***Café Ponti*** and ***Chez Marco*** both do good, big fisherman-sized helpings for CFA600.

Getting There & Away

Bush taxis go from Mbour and Joal-Fadiout to Palmarin and Djifer via Sambadia (also written Samba Dia). From Joal to Sambadia costs CFA400; from Sambadia to Palmarin or Djifer is CFA300.

Otherwise you could take a pirogue to or from Ndangane or Foundiougne (see the Siné-Saloum Delta section following). If you're heading to Gambia, cramped, uncomfortable and notoriously unsafe pirogues travel from Djifer to Banjul a few times per week for around CFA3000 per person. The trip takes about five hours, but may involve an overnight stop on a midway island. You have been warned! On arrival in Banjul go to the immigration office at the port and not the one in the city centre.

AROUND DJIFER

Places to visit near Djifer include the islands of **Guior** and **Guissanor**, on the other side of the River Saloum from the Pointe de Sangomar. This comes close to the heart of the Siné-Saloum Delta – beautiful, tranquil and almost completely devoid of tourist facilities. On Guior are the small fishing villages of **Niodior** and **Dionouar** and an upmarket lodge for anglers. The campements in Djifer run excursions to the islands from about CFA15,000 per boat for a half-day trip, or you can charter a pirogue yourself at the fishing beach for lower rates. A cheaper option is the public boat that runs between Djifer and Dionouar for CFA250 per person, but it only goes once a day in each direction, usually at about 1pm from Djifer.

Siné-Saloum Delta

South of the Petite Côte, between Kaolack and the Gambian border, the vast Siné-Saloum Delta is one of the most beautiful parts of Senegal. Formed where the Siné and Saloum Rivers meet the tidal waters of the Atlantic Ocean, it's an area of channels, lagoons, open forests, dunes and sand islands, and vast tracts of mangroves.

Part of the area is included in the Parc National du Delta du Saloum, which abounds with monkeys, and the range of habitats makes it particularly good for birding. Highly recommended is a trip by pirogue to see birds, including pelicans and flamingos, as well as traditional island fishing villages, or just to admire the fascinating scenery.

KAOLACK

Kaolack is a regional capital, the centre of Senegal's groundnut industry, and a handy gateway to the Siné-Saloum Delta. Although often regarded by travellers as little more than a junction town, it's a lively place and well worth visiting for a day or two.

Things to see include the large Moroccan-style **Grande Mosquée** north of the town centre – the pride of the Tidjaniya brotherhood – and what is reputed to be the second-largest covered **market** in Africa (after Marrakesh in Morocco). Despite these attractions few tourists come here, so there's little hassle. It's a great place to just wander around and soak up the atmosphere.

Banks with ATMs are CBAO and SGBS, and you can change money at Super-Service supermarket. Cadicom.sn Internet bureau has a good service for CFA1000 an hour.

Places to Stay

Hôtel Napoléon *(☎ 941 5191)* Doubles CFA9400. This is cheap but, being grotty and noisy, not cheap enough.

Etoile du Siné *(941 4458)* Rooms about CFA9500. Much better value is this friendly place on the main road to Tambacounda. The spotless rooms come with breakfast, and safe parking is available.

Mission Catholique *(☎ 941 2526)* Dorm beds CFA2000, singles CFA5000. This might be worth a try, but it's often full and there's no sharing.

Caritas *(☎ 941 2730)* Singles/doubles CFA10,000/15,000. Opposite the mission, this two-storey building with a green roof has modern rooms with bathroom and air-con.

Le Relais *(☎ 941 1000, e horizons@sentoo.sn)* Singles/doubles CFA22,200/27,200. South-west of town and right on the river, this place is the best in Kaolack. It's well managed and has a tempting pool and adjoining bar. Rooms have bathroom, air-con, TV, phone and there's even an Internet connection.

Places to Eat & Drink

For cheap eats there are several ***gargottes*** near the gares routières, and ***street food*** can be found around the market.

Chez Mariam *(☎ 941 4585)* Mains around CF2500. Open Mon-Sat. Northeast of the centre, Chez Mariam has chawarmas

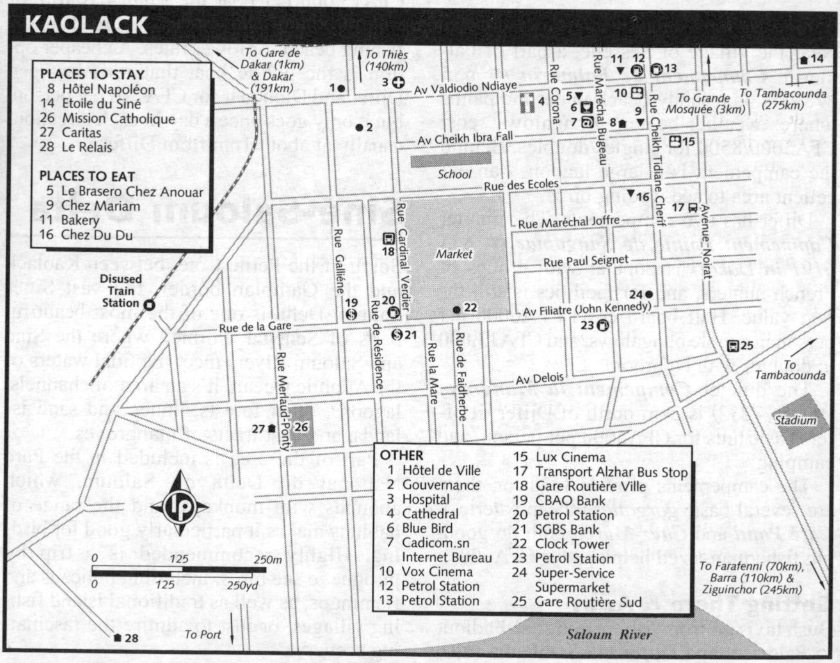
KAOLACK
PLACES TO STAY
8 Hôtel Napoléon
14 Etoile du Siné
26 Mission Catholique
27 Caritas
28 Le Relais
PLACES TO EAT
5 Le Brasero Chez Anouar
9 Chez Mariam
11 Bakery
16 Chez Du Du
OTHER
1 Hôtel de Ville
2 Gouvernance
3 Hospital
4 Cathedral
6 Blue Bird
7 Cadicom.sn Internet Bureau
10 Vox Cinema
12 Petrol Station
13 Petrol Station
15 Lux Cinema
17 Transport Alzhar Bus Stop
18 Gare Routière Ville
19 CBAO Bank
20 Petrol Station
21 SGBS Bank
22 Clock Tower
23 Petrol Station
24 Super-Service Supermarket
25 Gare Routière Sud
To Gare de Dakar (1km) & Dakar (191km)
To Thiès (140km)
Av Valdiodio Ndiaye
Av Cheikh Ibra Fall
School
Rue des Ecoles
Rue Maréchal Joffre
Rue Paul Seignet
Av Filiatre (John Kennedy)
Av Delois
Rue de la Gare
Rue Corona
Rue Maréchal Bugeau
Rue Cheikh Tidiane Cherif
Avenue Noirat
Rue Cardinal Verdier
Rue Galliéne
Rue de Résidence
Rue la Mare
Rue de Faidherbe
Rue Merlaud-Ponty
Market
Disused Train Station
To Grande Mosquée (3km)
To Tambacounda (275km)
To Tambacounda
Stadium
To Farafenni (70km), Barra (110km) & Ziguinchor (245km)
Saloum River
To Port
0 125 250m
0 125 250yd

and burgers for CFA500 to CFA1000 and other meals for a little more.

Chez Du Du (☎ *941 8767*) Mains CFA1500-2000. Open 9am-midnight daily. Best for quality and atmosphere, this place has chawarmas for around CFA700, pizzas for CFA3000, omelettes from CFA1000 and a huge choice of main meals. Beers are CFA600.

Le Brasero Chez Anouar (☎ *941 1608*) Meals about CFA3000. Open 7am-midnight daily. Good food and atmosphere make this one of the most popular places in Kaolack, especially for lunch. English-speaking Anouar is full of good advice.

Blue Bird (☎ *941 5350*) Open 8am-3am Mon-Sat, 6pm-2am Sun. For late-night entertainment, this is a favourite, with a bar and restaurant adjoining a good nightclub.

Getting There & Away

The town has three gare routières: Gare Routière de Dakar, on the northwestern side of town, for western or northern destinations; Gare Routière Sud, on the south-east side of the city centre, for Ziguinchor, Gambia and Tambacounda; and Gare Routière Ville for local bush taxis.

You can travel to or from Dakar by Peugeot taxi (CFA2600, three hours), minibus (CFA1500, five hours) or Alham (CFA1250, six hours). A Peugeot taxi to the Gambian border at Karang is CFA2000 (two hours); to Thiès is CFA1600. Transport Alzhar express buses running between Dakar and Tambacounda stop on Av Noirat.

NDANGANE & MAR LODJ

Ndangane (pronounced dan-gahn) is a village on the northern side of the delta that has grown in the past few years into a thriving tourist centre. From here you can get boats across the river to the village of Mar Lodj (also spelt Mar Lothie), a peaceful haven cut off by a branch of the River Saloum from the rest of the country. Several good campements make this a great place to slow down for a while.

The Business Centre le Sine, about 400m along the Fimela road, has Internet access from 8am to noon, and 4pm to 9pm.

Places to Stay & Eat

Ndangane Most of the accommodation and eating options are located around the end of the road to Fimela, which is also where most boat trips depart from. As you head back from the water you'll find ***Chez Mbake*** (☎ *936 3985, 669 3525*), a family-run place with five basic bungalows for CFA5000 per person. Opposite is ***Gîte Rural le Cormoran*** (☎*/fax 949 9316*), a smarter establishment with good, clean bungalows in a pleasant setting. Bed and breakfast costs CFA12,000/18,000 for singles/doubles.

As you keep going turn right along a dirt track for ***Les Anacardiers*** (☎ *949 9313*) which charges CFA7500 per person for good rooms with bathroom.

All the hotels do food. Other good options include ***Le Petit Paradis*** on the main drag, which serves cheap local dishes spiced up with inspiring conversation (in English) from the dignified and erudite owners.

Mar Lodj All the budget campements here charge CFA10,600/19,200 for bed and breakfast, less in the low season. Note that none have electricity yet. These include ***Mbine Diam*** (☎ *636 91 99*) with double huts in a shady garden; the small and relaxed ***Le Bazouk***; and the larger ***Limboko***. But the best value is ***Nouvelle Vague*** (☎ *936 3976, 634 0729*) with its 10 new bungalows, six of them overlooking the river. These guys, plus some of the other campements, will collect you from Ndangane for free if you call ahead. All these places organise boat trips or walks to the surrounding villages.

SENEGAL

Getting There & Away

Take any bus between Kaolack and Mbour, and get off at Ndiosomone, from where bush taxis shuttle back and forth to Ndangane. You can go direct from Dakar to Ndangane for CFA1500. From Mbour you can take bush taxis via Sambadia and Fimela.

To reach Mar Lodj from Ndangane there's an occasional public boat charging CFA250 one way. Otherwise, you have to charter. This should cost CFA4000 for the boat, but if there are more than four tourists the fare is CFA1000 each.

You can charter a pirogue between Ndangane and Djifer for about CFA15,000, or to Foundiougne for CFA25,000.

YAYEME

About 1.5km down a sandy track from Fimela is the tiny village of Yayeme. The only reason to go to Yayeme is to stay at ***Daan Sa Doole*** *(☎ 635 5274, e aloukum@hotmail.com)*. This ecologically friendly campement has been set up around a giant mango tree by a couple of multilingual young travellers. Right in the middle of the village, it's ideal for soaking up village life without hassle. Bungalows with bathroom are CFA9000 per person, while simpler rooms and *au naturel* showers and toilets are cheaper. Campers are also welcome. Call ahead between June and October.

From Fimela, just walk out along the road to Sambadia and take the left fork after 200m. Alternatively, call from Fimela or Sambadia for directions.

FOUNDIOUGNE

Once a French colonial outpost, the relaxed village of Foundiougne is easy to reach and a good place to arrange pirogue trips around the delta.

A string of campements runs west from the ferry pier. The first is ***Saloum Salaoum*** *(☎/fax 948 1269)*, a community-run place with a few rooms on the water for CFA15,000 for one to three people. Next are the two versions of ***Campement le Baobab***. The newer camp, also known as ***Chez Anne-Marie*** *(☎ 948 1262)*, has good-value single/double/triple rooms (and the baobab tree) costing CFA8000/14,000/18/000, including breakfast if you stay longer than one night. Opposite is ***Chez le Baobab No 1***, or Chez Ismaila *(☎/fax 948 1708)* with bungalows for CFA10,000. Other options include ***L'Indiana Club*** *(☎/fax 948 1213)* which has a pool, good food, and simple rooms with shared bathroom for CFA8,500 per person with breakfast; and ***Auberge les Bolongs*** *(☎/fax 948 1110, w www.lesbolongs.com)* where double huts cost CFA10,000.

All places to stay in Foundiougne arrange excursions from around CFA15,000 per half day and CFA25,000 per day for the boat (depending on petrol and the length of time required). Alternatively, negotiate a cheaper deal at the jetty.

Getting There & Away

A bush taxi from Kaolack to Foundiougne is CFA700. Otherwise, get anything between Kaolack and Karang on the Gambian border, and get off at Passi. From Passi to Foundiougne is CFA325.

From Dakar or Mbour, take anything heading for Kaolack, and get off at Fatick, then take a bush taxi to Dakhonga and catch a ferry across to Foundiougne for CFA100. Leaving Foundiougne, the first ferry at 7.30am connects with an Alham at Dakhonga, which goes all the way to Dakar for CFA1500.

To reach other parts of the delta by boat, you can charter a pirogue to Djifer or Ndangane for around CFA25,000. To Toubakouta is CFA30,000 and Missirah CFA35,000. Alternatively, ask about the public pirogue service from Foundiougne to Djifer via villages along the Saloum River, which is guaranteed to go on Tuesdays and occasionally runs on other days.

TOUBAKOUTA

About 70km southwest of Kaolack, Toubakouta is a good base for exploring the southern side of the delta. Birding is good in this area, but even if you're no fan of our feathered friends, you'll enjoy watching pelicans, flamingos, fish eagles, herons and egrets, especially when they roost at night at the *reposoir des oiseaux* (bird reserve) a short boat-ride away. In the town there is a Dutch-funded cybercafé called CyberLynda (☎ 936 9441), which charges CFA2250 and hour.

Hôtel les Palétuviers *(948 7776, w www.paletuviers.com)* Singles/doubles with breakfast CFA39,000/47,000, half board CFA42,000/55,000. This is one of the best-quality places on the whole delta, with around 50 double cottages in large grounds. All have air-con and private bathrooms and are furnished to a high standard. There's a wide choice of excursions, and tours by pirogue range from CFA8000 per person for an evening trip to CFA31,000 for an all-day tour to the mouth of the Saloum where dolphins are sometimes seen.

Cheaper lodgings can be found at ***Keur Youssou*** *(☎ 948 7728, 634 5905)* or ***Les Coquillages du Niombatto*** *(☎ 936 3441, e layoum@hotmail.com)*, both of which have clean, comfortable bungalows with bathroom for CFA12,500 including breakfast, and offer cheaper tours than the big hotels.

Peugeot taxis from Kaolack to Karang (CFA2000) will drop you off at Toubakouta, but you won't get any discount for getting off early. It's cheaper to go by minibus. The fare to/from Kaolack is CFA1000.

Mangroves

The mangrove is a tropical evergreen plant that grows on tidal mud flats and inlets all along the coast of West Africa. It plays a vital role for both the local populations and wildlife and has a fascinating reproductive system, perfectly adapted to its watery environment. It is one of very few plants that thrive in salt water, and this allows rapid colonisation of areas where no other plant would have a chance. In Senegal, the best place to see mangroves is the Siné-Saloum Delta, although they also grow in other river estuaries, and a long way upstream in the Gambia River.

Two types of mangrove can be seen and easily identified. The **red mangrove** (of which there are three species, although to the untrained eye they all look the same) is most prominent. It's easy to recognise by its leathery leaves and dense tangle of stilt-like buttress roots. The seeds germinate in the fruit while still hanging on the tree, growing a long stem called a 'radical'. When the fruit drops, the radical lodges in the mud and becomes a ready-made root for the new seedling.

The **white mangrove** is less common and is found mainly on ground that is only covered by particularly high tides. It does not have stilt roots. Its most recognisable characteristic is the breathing roots, with circular pores, that grow out of the mud from the base of the tree.

Mangrove trees catch silt, vegetation and other floating debris in their root systems. The mangrove's own falling leaves are added to the pile. As this mire becomes waterlogged and consolidated, it forms an ideal breeding ground for young mangroves. In this way, the mangrove actually creates new land. As the stands expand on the seaward side, the older growth on the landward side gradually gets further from the water. Eventually they die, leaving behind a rich soil perfect for cultivation.

The mangrove has many other uses. Oysters and shellfish cling to the roots as the tide comes in. When it retreats, they are left exposed and are easily gathered by local people. Mangroves are also fertile fishing grounds as fish like the darkness between the roots.

MISSIRAH

This small village south of Toubakouta is one of the nearest points to the **Parc National du Delta du Saloum** *(admission CFA2000)*. The vegetation includes tidal mud flats, mangrove swamps and the dry open woodland of the Forêt de Fathala, so there's a good range of birds and animals, including the plentiful but shy red colobus monkey. The park headquarters is 6km south of the village, and is where you pay the admission, though plans for an office in Missirah itself should have been realised by the time you read this.

About 2km east of Missirah is the ***Gîte de Bandiala*** *(☎ 948 77 35, ⓔ gitedubandiala@sentoo.sn)*. This place is peaceful, low-key and good value, making it a great base for exploring this part of the delta. Accommodation is in simple bungalows which are good value at CFA13,000/18,500 per person for half/full board. The friendly management can make suggestions for forest walks, and in the bar-restaurant are some useful bird charts with names in French and English. The gîte also has a water hole, where monkeys, warthogs and other animals come to drink. Tours by pirogue on the nearby creeks and lagoons cost CFA20,000 per boat for a half day. Fishing can also be arranged.

From Kaolack take any vehicle going along the main road towards Karang, get off at Santhiou el Haji (about 80km from Kaolack) and walk 8km west through the forest. Less strenuous would be to get off at Toubakouta and take a bush taxi for CFA300, or a taxi for CFA4000. A bush taxi leaves Missirah for Karang at about 7am every day, but you'll need to organise it the night before; it costs CFA500.

Casamance

Casamance is the part of Senegal south of Gambia, a beautiful region that differs culturally and geographically from the rest of the country. The majority of people who live here are non-Muslim Diola (Jola), while the Casamance River is a verdant labyrinth of creeks and lagoons that are dotted by small islands, palm groves, forest and mangroves. Cap Skiring is home to the finest beaches in the country, and Casamance has an excellent system of village-run *campements ruraux intégrés* (CRIs) that enable you to get a feel for traditional rural life. Sadly, these and many other tourist facilities have suffered during a long and violent separatist struggle.

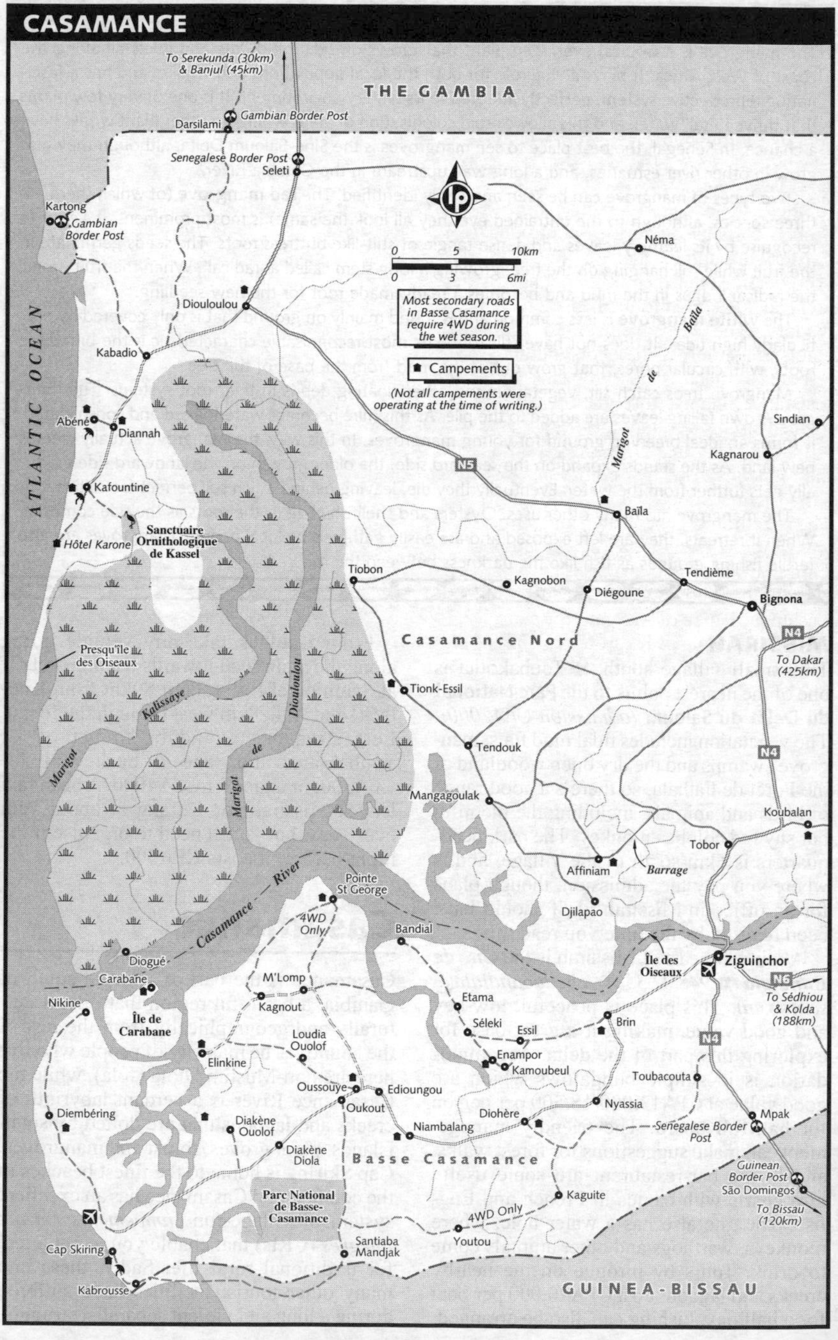
CASAMANCE
To Serekunda (30km) & Banjul (45km)
THE GAMBIA
Gambian Border Post
Darsilami
Senegalese Border Post
Seleti
Kartong
Gambian Border Post
0 5 10km
0 3 6mi
Néma
Diouloulou
Most secondary roads in Basse Casamance require 4WD during the wet season.
Kabadio
Campements
(Not all campements were operating at the time of writing.)
ATLANTIC OCEAN
Marigot de Baïla
Abéné
Diannah
Sindian
Kagnarou
N5
Kafountine
Baïla
Sanctuaire Ornithologique de Kassel
Hôtel Karone
Tiobon
Kagnobon
Diégoune
Tendième
Bignona
N4
Presqu'île des Oiseaux
Casamance Nord
To Dakar (425km)
Marigot de Kalissaye
Marigot de Diouloulou
Tionk-Essil
Tendouk
N4
Mangagoulak
Koubalan
Tobor
Affiniam
Barrage
Djilapao
Casamance River
Pointe St George
4WD Only
Bandial
Diogué
Île des Oiseaux
Ziguinchor
Carabane
M'Lomp
N6
Nikine
Kagnout
Etama
To Sédhiou & Kolda (188km)
Île de Carabane
Séleki
Brin
Loudia Ouolof
Essil
N4
Elinkine
Enampor
Kamoubeul
Toubacouta
Oussouye
Edioungou
Oukout
Nyassia
Diembéring
Diakène Ouolof
Niambalang
Diohère
Mpak
Senegalese Border Post
Diakène Diola
Basse Casamance
Guinean Border Post
São Domingos
Parc National de Basse-Casamance
Kaguite
To Bissau (120km)
4WD Only
Youtou
Cap Skiring
Santiaba Mandjak
Kabrousse
GUINEA-BISSAU

SENEGAL

The region divides into three main areas. Basse Casamance (Lower Casamance) is west of Ziguinchor and south of the river; Casamance Nord is north of the river; and Haute Casamance (Upper Casamance) is east of Ziguinchor.

History

In the 19th and early 20th centuries, the French colonial authorities controlled their territory through local chiefs. In Casamance, however, the Diola people do not have a hierarchical society and thus had no recognised leaders. The French installed Mandinka chiefs to administer the Diola, but they were resented as much as the Europeans, and Diola resistance against foreign interference remained strong well into the 1930s.

In 1943, the last Diola rebellion against the French was led by a traditional priestess called Aline Sitoe Diatta, from Kabrousse. The rebellion was put down and Aline Sitoe was imprisoned at the remote outpost of Timbuktu in neighbouring Mali, where she eventually died. She has been called the Casamance Joan of Arc, and for many years the Diola people of Kabrousse believed she would return and lead them to freedom.

The conflict that has plagued the region for the last 20 years originated from a pro-independence demonstration held in Ziguinchor in 1982, after which the leaders of the Mouvement des Forces Démocratique de la Casamance (MFDC) were arrested and jailed. Over the next few years the army clamped down with increasing severity, but this only galvanised the local people's anti-Dakar feelings and spurred the movement into taking more action.

In 1990, the MFDC went on the offensive and attacked military posts. The army responded by attacking MFDC bases in southern Casamance and over the border in Guinea-Bissau, which had been giving covert support to the rebels following a coastal territorial dispute with Senegal. As always, it was local civilians who came off worse, with both the Senegalese army and the MFDC accused of committing atrocities against people thought to be sympathetic to the opposite side.

As the '90s wore on, cease-fire agreements were signed and broken as periods of peace repeatedly ended in violence. In 1995, four French people touring Casamance disappeared. The Senegalese government blamed the MFDC, while Father Diamacoune Senghor, the MFDC's leader, accused the army of trying to turn international opinion against the rebels.

Peace talks continued but prospects for a lasting resolution were damaged when a group of hardliners broke away from the MFDC and resumed fighting following the government's refusal to consider independence for Casamance.

Meanwhile, Father Diamacoune urged his supporters to continue the search for reconciliation with the government. A new cease-fire was agreed in late 1997 but it did little to slow the mounting death toll, and during the following three years about 500 people were reported killed in ongoing fighting. His authority fading, Father Diamacoune unexpectedly signed a peace deal in March 2001. While the agreement provided for the release of prisoners, the return of refugees and the clearance of landmines, it fell short of the full autonomy many rebels sought. Divisions within the MFDC deepened; a bloody battle was fought between two opposing factions and many in Casamance had begun referring to some of the rebels as bandits, or common thieves. The power struggle at the top of the movement had still not been resolved in March 2002.

All this means any agreement on autonomy, and thus peace, seems as far away as ever, and the people of Casamance will have to live with a long-running, low-level conflict for some time yet.

ZIGUINCHOR

pop 206,000

Ziguinchor (pronounced zig-**an**-shor) is the main access point for travel in the Casamance region. As you come into town, the quiet and dusty streets don't look too promising, but soon the attractions begin to reveal themselves. The central area is quite compact and can easily be covered on foot. There's a pleasant, laid-back atmosphere, very little hassle and the best choice of places to stay and eat for all budgets in the whole country.

Information

The nearest Ziguinchor has to a tourist office is the bureau of the Campements Ruraux Intégrés (☎ 991 1375) at Centre Artisanal.

To Go or Not to Go?

It's the nature of news that you hear more about killing than about living, and in the case of Casamance good news is hard to find. This means the vast majority of Senegalese have little idea what is going on in Casamance, and you shouldn't rely on their judgement to come to a decision.

So how do you know whether it's safe or not? The simple answer is that with so many men with guns absolute safety cannot be guaranteed. But you can take some comfort in the fact that as of early 2002 the rebels were sticking to their policy of not targeting tourists. This doesn't mean civilians are not suffering; they are. But for most the suffering is greater for the lack of tourists and our dollars than any direct confrontation with separatist fighters.

While researching this book I was on a bush taxi stopped by rebels just after crossing the Gambian border at Darsilami. Three armed men in tattered fatigues welcomed me to 'Casamance' and said: 'Enjoy your visit, this is a wonderful place'. Whether these were the same men who three weeks earlier had murdered a priest and two bush-taxi drivers at a similar checkpoint, I will never know.

During the following two weeks I saw plenty of government soldiers while getting around most of the region, but had no trouble whatsoever. However, before each trip into rural Casamance I was sure to check on the latest security situation. In Ziguinchor you can ask at your hotel or the office of Campements Ruraux Intégrés (CRI), but a more grass-roots picture may be gleaned by talking to bush-taxi drivers: If they are reluctant to go you should be too. Another sensible tactic is to make sure you are not the first on the road in the morning or the last in the evening, and never drive at night. In Gambia, the bush-taxi drivers in Serekunda and Brikama usually have the latest information.

As a result of the unrest, some campements have closed or fallen into disrepair, but others remain impressively spic and span. If the situation improves more places are likely to reopen as tourists return.

Andrew Burke

Manager Adama Goudiaby can provide details on the campements or help with general queries. The people who run Hôtel le Flamboyant on Rue de France are also happy to share their knowledge with anybody stopping by for a drink or meal. Tour operators include Diatta Tour International (☎ 991 2781, fax 991 2981) on Rue du Général de Gaulle.

Money can be changed (very slowly) at the CBAO on Rue de France, or you could use SGBS's ATM on Rue Fargues.

There are post offices on Rue du Général de Gaulle and on Av Emile Badiane (formerly Rue du Dr Olivier) south of the Centre Artisanal, and several télécentres along Rue Javelier. You can send and receive email for CFA1000 an hour at Sud-Informatique (☎ 991 1573) or Web City (☎ 991 1044), both on Rue Javelier.

The Alliance Franco-Sénégalaise is on Av Lycée Guignabo, with exhibitions, courses and cultural events.

Things to See & Do

The lively **Marché St-Maur** *(Av Lycée Guignabo)*, 1km south of the centre, caters mainly for locals, selling fresh food and other items. Further south, vendors at the **Centre Artisanal** sell a wide variety of crafts from the area including woodcarvings and fabrics. This is also where the town's hustlers lurk. Back in town a wander along Rue du Général de Gaulle reveals an impressive range of French architecture.

Near the Rond-Point John-Paul II is **Africa Batik** *(☎ 991 2689)*, which offers batik-making courses for the bargain rate of CFA5000 a day, including materials.

Places to Stay – Budget

Auberge Kadiandou *(☎ 991 1071)* Singles/doubles with bathroom CFA5000/6000, rooms without bathroom CFA4000. This is a good-value cheapie, near the gare routière, with very clean rooms.

Hôtel le Bel Kady *(☎ 991 1122)* Singles/doubles CFA3500/4000. Just south of the market, this place has been popular for years, with friendly management, a good atmosphere and basic but decent rooms. Breakfast is CFA600, and local or Cape Verdean meals cost from CFA800 to CFA1500.

Campement N'Daary Kassoum *(☎ 991 1189, Rue de France)* Singles/doubles with

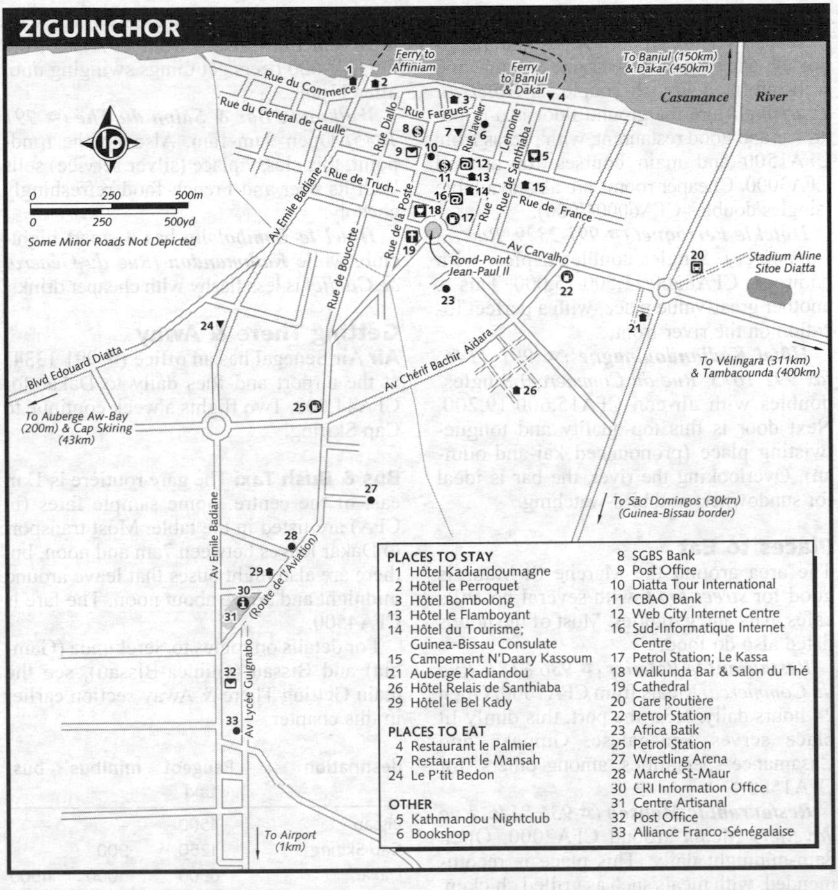
ZIGUINCHOR
Ferry to Affiniam
Ferry to Banjul & Dakar
To Banjul (150km) & Dakar (450km)
Casamance River
Rue du Commerce
Rue du Général de Gaulle
Rue Fargues
Rue Diallo
Rue Javelier
Lemoine
Rue de Santhiaba
Rue de Truch
Rue de France
Av Emile Badiane
Rue de la Poste
Rue de Boucotte
Rond-Point Jean-Paul II
Av Carvalho
Stadium Aline Sitoe Diatta
0 250 500m
0 250 500yd
Some Minor Roads Not Depicted
Blvd Edouard Diatta
Av Chérif Bachir Aidara
To Vélingara (311km) & Tambacounda (400km)
To Auberge Aw-Bay (200m) & Cap Skiring (43km)
To São Domingos (30km) (Guinea-Bissau border)
Av Emile Badiane
(Route de l'Aviation)
Av Lycée Guignabo
To Airport (1km)
PLACES TO STAY
1 Hôtel Kadiandoumagne
2 Hôtel le Perroquet
3 Hôtel Bombolong
13 Hôtel le Flamboyant
14 Hôtel du Tourisme; Guinea-Bissau Consulate
15 Campement N'Daary Kassoum
21 Auberge Kadiandou
26 Hôtel Relais de Santhiaba
29 Hôtel le Bel Kady
PLACES TO EAT
4 Restaurant le Palmier
7 Restaurant le Mansah
24 Le P'tit Bedon
OTHER
5 Kathmandou Nightclub
6 Bookshop
8 SGBS Bank
9 Post Office
10 Diatta Tour International
11 CBAO Bank
12 Web City Internet Centre
16 Sud-Informatique Internet Centre
17 Petrol Station; Le Kassa
18 Walkunda Bar & Salon du Thé
19 Cathedral
20 Gare Routière
22 Petrol Station
23 Africa Batik
25 Petrol Station
27 Wrestling Arena
28 Marché St-Maur
30 CRI Information Office
31 Centre Artisanal
32 Post Office
33 Alliance Franco-Sénégalaise

shower CFA4000/5000, doubles with bathroom CFA6000. Near the centre of town, this place could do with a lick of paint but is clean and functional enough.

Hôtel Relais de Santhiaba *(☎ 991 1199)* Singles/doubles without bathroom CFA4000/7000, with bathroom CFA6500/ 10,500. Off Av Cherif Bachir Aidara, this place is highly recommended. All rooms are very clean and breakfast is included in the price, but a fan costs an extra CFA1000 and air-con CFA2500. The ***restaurant*** serves good meals from CFA2400 to CFA3000, and pizzas from CFA1800. The hotel hires out bikes and arranges tours by bike and/or boat in the surrounding area.

Auberge Aw-Bay *(☎/fax 936 8076)* On the right as you head out of town toward Cap Skiring, this is a campement-style place with CRI rates (see the boxed text 'Village Campements' later in this chapter), clean rooms and friendly, well-informed management.

Places to Stay – Mid-Range & Top End

Le Bambolong *(☎ 938 8001, Rue Fargues)* Rooms CFA8000. Situated between the ferry jetty and port, this place has very nice rooms, but their proximity to the hotel's nightclub means disturbed sleep at weekends.

Hôtel le Flamboyant *(☎ 991 2223, ⓔ flamboyant@casamance.net, Rue de France)* Singles/doubles with bathroom CFA13,600/16,200. This classy place is possibly the best value in the country. The spotless rooms

SENEGAL

have air-con, fridge, phone and TV, and there's a swimming pool. Opposite le Flamboyant, and owned by the same amiable and well-informed French couple, is ***Hôtel du Tourisme***. Here the ground floor is a popular bar and good restaurant, with pizzas from CFA1500 and main courses for around CFA3000. Cheaper rooms are also available (singles/doubles CFA6000/7000).

Hôtel le Perroquet *(☎ 991 2329, Rue du Commerce)* Singles/doubles/triples with bathroom CFA8500/11,500/15,000. This is another great-value place, with a perfect location on the river front.

Hôtel Kadiandoumagne *(☎ 991 1146, fax 991 1675, Rue du Commerce)* Singles/doubles with air-con CFA15,600/19,200. Next door is this top-quality and tongue-twisting place (pronounced kaj-and-oum-an). Overlooking the river, the bar is ideal for sundowners and bird-watching.

Places to Eat

The area around the Marché St-Maur is good for ***street food***, with several no-frills cafés, bars and gargottes. Most of the hotels listed also do food.

Restaurant le Palmier *(☎ 936 8181, Rue du Commerce)* Meals from CFA1000. Open 24 hours daily. Near the port, this dimly lit place serves Senegalese, Guinean and Casamance specialities, among others, for CFA1500.

Restaurant le Mansah *(☎ 936 8146, Rue Javelier)* Meals around CFA2000. Open 8am-midnight daily. This place is recommended, with meals such as grilled chicken, tiéboudienne and prawn brochettes in *sauce piquante* (spicy sauce), all with chips and all at bargain prices.

Le P'tit Bedon *(☎ 991 2653, Av Emile Badiane)* Mains CFA4000. Open lunch & dinner. Le P'tit Bedon has probably the best menu in Ziguinchor, with a big selection of European and international dishes including beef stroganoff (CFA4500) and a number of good fish dishes – the *poisson veracruz* (CFA4000) is recommended.

Entertainment

Most of the hotels serve beers. Otherwise the rond-point is a good place to start.

Le Kassa *(☎ 936 8300)* Open 8am-2am daily. This is a popular local haunt and is surprisingly good considering it's attached to a petrol station. It's an eatery early, with local and Euro dishes from CFA1500, but the CFA600 beers get things swinging until after 11pm.

Walkunda Bar & Salon du Thé *(☎ 991 1845)* Open 9am-1am. Also on the rond-point, this classy place (silver service) sells both its beer and French food refreshingly cheaply.

Hôtel le Bombolong has a smart nightclub, while ***Kathmandou*** *(Rue du Général de Gaulle)* is less flashy with cheaper drinks.

Getting There & Away

Air Air Senegal has an office (☎ 991 1334) at the airport and flies daily to Dakar for CFA44,000. Two flights a week continue to Cap Skiring.

Bus & Bush Taxi The gare routière is 1km east of the centre. Some sample fares (in CFA) are listed in the table. Most transport to Dakar leaves between 7am and noon, but there are also night buses that leave around midnight and arrive about noon. The fare is CFA4500.

For details on routes to Serekunda (Gambia) and Bissau (Guinea-Bissau), see the main Getting There & Away section earlier in this chapter.

destination	Peugeot taxi	minibus	bus
Bissau	4500	–	–
Cap Skiring	1250	900	–
Dakar	6500	5000	4500
Elinkine	1250	750	–
Kafountine	2000	1500	1500
Kaolack	5000	3500	2500
Kolda	2850	2500	–
Oussouye	1000	750	–
Serekunda (Gambia)	3000	–	–
Soma	2500	2000	–
Tambacounda	6500	4500	–

Boat The MS *Joola* is supposed to run twice weekly between Dakar and Ziguinchor via Île de Carabane. It doesn't. For details see the Getting Around section earlier in this chapter, or call the port (☎ 991 2201).

Getting Around

Car The set-up for hiring cars in Ziguinchor is quite informal, but Diatta Tour Inter-

SENEGAL

national (see Information earlier) and most hotels will be able to help. Minor details such as insurance are sometimes a little hazy, but cars usually come with a driver, which cuts the hassle with paperwork and deposits. Expect to pay around CFA25,000 per day plus fuel. Another option is to hire a taxi; if you pay for fuel, the daily rate should be around CFA20,000.

Taxi The official rate for a taxi between Ziguinchor centre and the gare routière is CFA300. It's supposed to be the same for anywhere in town, but for longer rides you'll probably pay CFA500 to CFA750.

AROUND ZIGUINCHOR

A popular day trip is a pirogue ride to the villages of Affiniam and Djilapao on the north bank of the Casamance River.

Affiniam & Tionk Essil

Affiniam is a popular day trip destination from Ziguinchor. The main feature at Affiniam is actually the ***village campement*** which is a *case à impluvium* similar to the one at Enampor, but with a modern take on the traditional thatched roof – corrugated iron. Donatine, the delightful manager, charges standard CRI prices and it's worth staying long enough to have her show you around the surrounding area.

The public ferry from Ziguinchor runs several times a week. It stops at 'le port d'Affiniam' (about 1km from the campement) for one hour and then returns. The fare is CFA500. Alternatively, you can reach Affiniam by bike (if you're fit) or car: turn off the main road from Ziguinchor about 2km south of Bignona and cross the barrage (dam) to the northeast of Affiniam.

Tionk Essil (also spelt Thionck-Essyl) is about 20km north-west of Affiniam, in the transition zone between the mangrove swamps and sandy forests. This area is peaceful and beautiful, and there's a remarkably good community spirit among the villagers, but the village campement is closed to tourists.

Djilapao

Here you can visit some unusual two-storey mud-brick buildings *(cases étages)* and the house of a local artist which is decorated with murals, some rather risque. Most trips also go to the **Île des Oiseaux** where you can see pelicans, flamingos, kingfishers, storks, sunbirds and many other species of birds.

You can arrange pirogue rides at some of the hotels or at Restaurant le Mansah on Rue Javelier in Ziguinchor, where rates for day trips are around CFA15,000 per person including lunch. Local boatmen who loiter at the jetty near Hotel Kadiandoumagne charge around CFA25,000 per boat, but this is negotiable. Rates are also cheaper if you go for a shorter time. Once you've agreed on the trip duration, don't hand over the full payment until you get back.

A final option to consider is the public ferry – for details see Casamance Nord later in this chapter.

Village Campements

Among Casamance's attractions are its *campements ruraux intégrés* (CRIs) known to most locals as *campements du village* and to English speakers as village campements. They are humble lodgings built by villagers and run as cooperatives, with profits reinvested to build schools and health centres.

There are 10 CRI campements in Casamance, but the ongoing violence and the resulting prolonged downturn in tourism means only four are still open. The closed campements are in Diohère, Elinkine, Oussouye, Tionk Essil, Koubalan and Baïla. However, if peace is restored and tourism picks up, the campements will swiftly be knocked back into shape. In the meantime, rest assured that if you turn up and the campement is closed, accommodation will soon be found. When you arrive you'll probably find a campement built in the local style, with lighting by oil lamp, although most showers and toilets have running water. Prices at all CRIs are standardised: bed (with mosquito net) CFA3000, breakfast CFA1800, three-course lunch or dinner CFA2500, full board CFA9800, beer CFA750, soft drink CFA400 and mineral water CFA1000.

The CRI office is at the Centre Artisanal in Ziguinchor but its reservation system only works with at least a month's notice. As well as the CRIs, there are many privately owned campements with similar facilities and prices, although the profits go to the owner rather than to the village as a whole.

SENEGAL

BASSE CASAMANCE

Brin

Brin is on the road between Ziguinchor and Cap Skiring, where the track to Enampor branches off. At the heart of the village, ***Campement le Filao*** has bungalows in a lush garden and charges slightly lower than CRI prices. Brin is often overlooked, but it's in a nice area. You can walk in the surrounding forest or fields, or take pirogue rides.

On the road from Brin to Oussouye the village campements in **Diohère** and **Niambalang** were both closed when we passed.

Enampor

The campement here is a huge round mud house, called a *case à impluvium*, which is worth a visit even if you're not staying. Rainwater is funnelled into a large tank in the centre of the house through a hole in the roof (admitting a wonderful diffuse light). There are other such houses in Casamance, but this is a particularly good example. The manager will show you around for CFA100.

There's a daily Alham to Enampor from Ziguinchor in the afternoon (CFA400), returning in the morning.

Oussouye

Oussouye is between Ziguinchor and Cap Skiring, and is the main town in Basse Casamance. It's a sleepy place, although the market gets lively on some mornings.

For more activity, **Casamance VTT** (*☎/fax 993 1004, ⓔ casavtt@yahoo.fr, ⓦ casavtt.free.fr*) rents out mountain bikes for CFA7500 per day and organises cycling, hiking and pirogue tours from CFA9500 per day. At **Galerie Bahisen**, on the road towards Cap Skiring, local artists make well-finished works in wood, terracotta and other traditional materials to contemporary designs.

Places to Stay & Eat The ***village campement*** was closed when we passed, which was a pity as it's a beautiful example of local mud architecture. However, two other places are open, both on the same dirt road leading north from the rond pointe.

Auberge du Routard (*☎ 993 1025*) is a jovial place where women make batiks; basic, clean rooms are CFA3000, or CFA5500 for half board. A little further away is ***Campement Emanaye Oussouye*** (*☎ 933 1004, ⓔ emanaye@yahoo.fr*), a new place run by a former VTT guide with better-quality rooms than Routard. Singles/doubles with bathroom are CFA4500/60000, while half board is CFA7500 per person.

East of town, in the village of Edioungou (a centre for local pottery manufacture), the ***Campement des Bolongs*** (*☎ 993 1041*) is an ambitiously large place in a beautiful, tranquil setting overlooking a *bolong* (river). Singles/doubles with bathroom are CFA7000/10,000.

On the main street, ***Restaurant 2000***, ***Restaurant Sud*** and ***Chez Rachel*** all serve local meals for about CFA700, the last living up to its *service rapide* (quick service) slogan. The ***Télécentre et Buvette du Rond-Point*** is an ideal place for a quiet drink and any urgent phone calls you may need to make.

M'Lomp

On what is allegedly a tar road between Oussouye and Elinkine you'll pass through the village of M'Lomp, which has several two-storey **cases étages**, and some other houses with brightly decorated walls and pillars, all unique to this part of West Africa. The old lady who lives in the largest case étage near the main road will give you a tour for a small fee. In front of the largest case étage is an enormous fromager tree, at least 400 years old, and sacred in the village.

Decent food can be found at ***Le Pionnier***, just east of the junction, with local and European meals for CFA500 to CFA1000, and the big smiles free.

Pointe St George

Pointe St George lies to the north of M'Lomp on the Casamance River. The Hôtel Pointe St George remains closed, but a new ***village campement*** is operating. You'll need a 4WD to get here by road, or a pirogue from Ziguinchor will cost about CFA15,000.

Elinkine

Elinkine is a busy fishing village that is the jumping-off point for Île de Carabane. Sadly, all three campements here have closed. Fishermen from around West Africa come here to fish for shark, and the beach is now filthy.

Île de Carabane

Île de Carabane (sometimes spelt Karabane) is a really cool place to just hang out and not do too much. A beautifully peaceful island near the mouth of the Casamance River, it was an important settlement and trading station in early colonial times, but the French legacy is now largely in ruins. You can still see the ruined Breton-style church and the remains of a school, and along the beach is a cemetery with settlers' graves dating from the 1830s. The beach is good for swimming (you may see dolphins in the distance) and the island is also an excellent bird-watching site.

Places to Stay & Eat The following places are listed from east to west. All serve food, and to contact them by phone you must leave a message, as there is only one spot on the island where their mobile phones actually work.

Campement Barracuda *(☎ 659 6001, fax 936 9010)* Rooms CFA7500 with half board. Catering mainly for anglers, this place has a lively bar. Fishing excursions cost CFA20,000 to CFA35,000 per boat. Shorter trips for birding or visiting local villages cost around CFA8000.

Hôtel Carabane *(☎ 633 1782)* Singles/doubles CFA11,000/16,000. This delightful and well-maintained hotel is set in a lush and shady tropical garden. It was formerly a Catholic mission and the chapel is now the bar! The good-value rooms include breakfast, and the excellent three-course menu du jour is CFA4500. Reservations can be made through Diatta Tour International based in Ziguinchor.

Chez Helena *(☎ 654 1772, fax in Dakar 821 7305)* Rooms CFA4000, half/full board CFA6000/8000. Yes, you read right, this place is a bargain. It's run by the friendly, English-speaking Helena, and the rooms are more than comfortable.

Campement Badji Kunda Rooms CFA4000. This arty place is about 500m further along the beach. The owner is a sculptor and painter; his works (and those of other local artists) are on display and for sale here. Courses in local glass painting and pottery can be arranged.

Getting There & Away Île de Carabane is reached by pirogue from Elinkine. There is no regular service, although there's usually a boat at 3pm, returning at 9am the following day. Otherwise, you need to hang around on the waterfront until you see a boat leaving. The fare is CFA750 and the ride takes 30 minutes, or you can charter a boat for about CFA7500 each way.

From Carabane, Helena can organise a boat to take you to Cap Skiring for CFA19,200, or all the way to Kafountine or Ziguinchor for about CFA50,000. You can also get to Île de Carabane on MS *Joola* – when it's running. For details, see the Getting Around section earlier in this chapter.

CAP SKIRING

The beaches of Cap Skiring are some of the finest in West Africa, and it's no coincidence there are several resort-style hotels here. Like Saly and the Atlantic Coast in Gambia, Cap Skiring attracts plenty of European package tours, but there's more to it than that. The village is a lively place and there are plenty of cheaper campements appealing to independent travellers. If you want a few easy days of sun and sand, this is the place.

The village of Cap Skiring is 1km north of the junction where the main road from Ziguinchor joins the north-south coast road. It has shops, restaurants, bars and nightclubs, a market and a gare routière, but no Internet. Just outside the village you can't miss the high walls of the Club Med complex, or the *prison touristique* as it's known locally. Most other hotels and campements are south of Cap Skiring, along the coast road towards Kabrousse, 5km away.

Places to Stay

You'll find accommodation for all budgets in Cap Skiring, most of it overlooking the beach and offering all the associated facilities and activities you'd expect, though with differing quality and price. Half- and full-board deals are available everywhere, and in some of the bigger hotels are all that's available. Tours and day trips can be arranged. The list of accommodation is growing fast and not all options are listed here.

Places to Stay – Budget

Just south of the junction is a sandy track leading toward the beach, where you'll find the first three campements listed here.

Le Mussuwam *(☎/fax 993 5184)* Rooms without/with bathroom CFA3000/6000. This is a big place with lots of clean rooms. Air-con and hot water are extra.

Auberge de la Paix *(☎ 993 5145)* Rooms without/with bathroom CFA3000/6000 per person. This is a friendly place with a family feel (and family rooms are available). The renovated rooms with bathroom are best.

Campement Chez M'Ballo *(☎ 936 9102)* Rooms without/with bathroom CFA4000/7500. Similar in style and atmosphere to Auberge de la Paix, this campement is a good-value option.

Campement le Bakine *(☎ 641 5124)* Rooms/half board CFA3000/7000 per person. On the Ziguinchor road, near the junction, this creative campement has traditional cultural evenings in the bar-restaurant, which is open to all.

Auberge le Palmier *(☎ 993 5109)* Doubles with bathroom CFA10,000. In Cap Skiring village, the bar-restaurant serves meals from CFA5000 and seems popular with French travellers.

Places to Stay – Mid-Range & Top End

Hôtel la Paillote *(☎ 993 5151, ⓔ paillote@sentoo.sn)* Half board from CFA30,000 per person. This hotel is in a prime position and has bungalows set in lush tropical gardens. It's renowned for superb French food and a refined ambience.

Villa des Pêcheurs Aline Sitoe *(☎ 993 5253, ⓔ sitoe@arc.sn, ⓦ www.villadespecheurs.com)* On the same beachfront strip as the campements, this is a wonderful place with six comfortable rooms (all with bathroom) overlooking a tranquil stretch of beach. The managers speak some English and will go out of their way to ensure a smooth and enjoyable stay. Fishing trips can be arranged. For prices, contact the Hôtel le Flamboyant in Ziguinchor.

Hôtel les Hibiscus *(☎ 993 5136, ⓔ hibiscus@sentoo.sn)* Rooms CFA26,000 per person. Right on the border with Guinea-Bissau near Kabrousse is this small and tasteful hotel in lush gardens on the beach, where cool bungalows are decorated with stunning murals and include breakfast.

Also near Kabrousse are ***Le Royal Cap*** *(☎ 993 5119, fax 993 5127)* and ***Le Kabrousse*** *(☎ 993 5126)*, while 2km north of Cap Skiring is ***Le Savana Cap*** *(☎ 993 5152, 993 5192)*. These three ageing resorts are part of the Senegal Hotels group and all three were closed for renovation when we passed. If you arrive unaccompanied, half board will cost you from CFA40,000 to CFA60,000.

Places to Eat

All the hotels offer food and Cap Skiring village has several cheap eateries, with Senegalese dishes in the CFA500 to CFA1000 range. One local favourite is ***Mamans***, with plates for CFA500, while next door is ***Chez Lena Gourmandis*** *(☎ 936 9116)*, where you pay more for tablecloths and other such luxuries.

Also on the main street is ***Chez Delphine*** *(☎ 993 5276)*, the best pizza joint in town. Delphine opens at 5pm and once the last pizza is consumed she'll be found on the dance floor at Cap Skiring's hottest nightclub, ***Case Bambou***.

For self-caterers, the well-stocked ***Mini-Marché Chez Gnima*** is just south of the junction and opens from 7am to 1pm and 4pm to 8pm daily.

Getting There & Away

See the main Getting There & Away section earlier in this chapter for details of Air Senegal International flights to Dakar. Peugeot taxis (CFA1250) and Alhams (CFA900) run regularly throughout the day between Ziguinchor and Cap Skiring, although there's more traffic in the morning. You can't cross the border at Kabrousse.

Getting Around

Most hotels and campements have bicycles for hire and can arrange car hire or pirogue trips. Day trips start at around CFA15,000 for the boat. Alternatively, you can arrange (usually through your hotel or campement) for a boat to take you to Diakène Ouolof, Elinkine or Carabane.

AROUND CAP SKIRING

Diembéring

To escape the hustle and bustle of Cap Skiring, head for Diembéring, 9km to the north, whose authentic African feel is in marked contrast to its touristy neighbour. The quiet and hassle-free beach is about 1km from the village. The place to stay is ***Campement Asseb*** *(☎ 993 3106)*, a spacious and peaceful place near the big fromager tree at the entrance to town. It has rooms and meals at CRI rates.

SENEGAL

Diembéring can be reached by bicycle, although the road is sandy and hard work in the heat. A private taxi to/from Cap Skiring costs CFA5000 each way, or you can get the daily Alham from Ziguinchor, which passes through Cap Skiring around 5pm and returns early next morning.

Parc National de Basse Casamance

This national park has been closed for several years now. With no-one quite sure whether land mines have been laid in the area, it looks certain to remain closed for the foreseeable future.

CASAMANCE NORD

Bignona & Koubalan

Bignona is a crossroads town near the Trans-Gambia Hwy junction. The depressing ***Hôtel le Kellumack*** *(☎ 994 1011)* offers singles/doubles at CFA4000/5000, but the colonial-style ***Hôtel le Palmier*** *(☎ 994 1258)* is better, with rooms for CFA5000, or CFA7000 with hot water, and breakfast for CFA800.

Off the road between Ziguinchor and Bignona is Koubalan, where the village campement is closed until tourism picks up.

Diouloulou & Baïa

Dioloulou is about 20km south of the Gambian border, where the road to Kafountine branches off the main route between Serekunda and Ziguinchor. If you get stuck here, ***Relais Myriam*** *(☎ 936 9591)* has simple bungalows without/with bathroom for CFA2000/4000 per person, though the bathroom might disappoint as it's just a bucket shower.

There is a campement in the village of Baïa, between Bignona and Diouloulou, but it too was closed when we passed.

KAFOUNTINE & ABÉNÉ

Kafountine and Abéné are the hip face of tourism in Senegal. The two villages on the coast just south of Gambia have spawned more than 20 guesthouses, often the sort of places where the staff seem happy to drum the day away and everything is 'cool, mon'. The villages are separated from the rest of Casamance Nord by a large branch of the Casamance River called Marigot Diouloulou (*marigot* means 'creek'). This isolation has meant that, apart from one skirmish in March 2002, the area has largely avoided the conflict of the separatist movement, and looks more to the north than to the south: there's a relatively large proportion of Muslim Mandinka and Wolof mixed in with the Diola population, and people go to Brikama in Gambia for their shopping more often than they go to Ziguinchor.

The area has attracted artists from various parts of Senegal and Europe, and many of the campements arrange courses in drumming, dance and batik-making.

Kafountine

Kafountine is a large, spread-out village about 2km from the ocean, at the end of the tar road from Diouloulou. About 1.5km away on the coast is a large fish market and busy working beach. Fishing times depend on the tide, and it's fascinating to see the boats being launched or coming back after a long day at sea, surfing in on the rollers. Northward, a huge empty beach leads up the coast past Abéné towards the Gambian border.

Kafountine itself has the same disposition as most of the guesthouses – time is something these people are not short of. If you're arriving from Serrekunda in Gambia you'll probably feel as though you just shifted from fifth gear down to neutral. And that's not a bad thing.

Bird-Watching The creeks and lagoons around Kafountine are wonderful areas for watching birds, especially waders and shore birds. The most accessible place is the small pool near the Campement Sitokoto. A bit further away are several bolongs (rivers) and marigots (creeks) that are also rewarding. Certainly the most enjoyable viewing platform is the bar at Esperanto, where you can watch over the lake while imbibing a soothing sunset drink.

The Sanctuaire Ornithologique de la Pointe de Kalissaye is a group of sandy islands at the mouth of the Marigot Kalissaye, but they are usually covered in water. Most bird-watchers now head for the highly rated Sanctuaire Ornithologique de Kassel, which is about 5km southeast of Kafountine.

Another place is the Presqu'île des Oiseaux, a narrow spit of land between the ocean and a creek, noted for its huge populations of Caspian terns. It lies south of

SENEGAL

Hôtel le Karone; the hotel's management can arrange trips by 4WD vehicle.

Places to Stay & Eat Accommodation at Kafountine is very spread out and falls loosely into two areas: the northern strip, reached by turning right on the sandy road as it leads west from the village; and the southern strip, stretching along the main road south of Kafountine village. The following places are listed north to south, though this is not a complete list. Note that most phone and fax numbers are for telecentres in the village, so you'll have to leave a message.

Northern Strip The lodgings begin at the far north end of the beach, just inland from where a small point is punctated by the rusting remains of a wrecked freighter.

Esperanto *(☎/fax 936 9519, e antoeric@hotmail.com)* Bungalows CFA7500 per person. Esperanto is in a great location between the sea and a bird-filled bolong with attractively decorated rooms. Call ahead in September.

Le Fouta Djalon *(☎ 936 9494)* Rooms per person CFA9000, half board per person in bungalows CFA15,000. This place is smarter, with bungalows in wonderful gardens. The French management offers bike hire, birding and fishing trips as well.

Chez Yande *(☎/fax 936 9519, e kammerer_Gmbh@t-online.de)* Basic doubles CFA6000. This is a friendly campement, and English-speaking Yande is a wealth of information. The rooms are simple and the pool was empty when we passed, but with a few more people around this place would be a lot of fun.

Campement Diamoral *(Chez Espagnol)* Rooms CFA2500, full board per person CFA6000. This Catalan-Senegalese enterprise is about as cheap and uncomfortable as you get here, but its family atmosphere and optimistic attitude make up for the total lack of luxuries.

Kale Diang *(☎/fax 936 9519, e kalediang@hotmail.com)* Rooms CFA3200 per person. On a big plot of well-forested land, this Dutch-run establishment has comfortable rooms with simple bathrooms and an emphasis on traditional living. Food here is excellent: Breakfast is CFA1200, lunch CFA1800 and dinner CFA3200. Ask about pirogue excursions with Fela the rasta griot.

Le Bolonga *(☎ 994 8515)* Rooms CFA5000 per person, half board CFA10,000 per person. Another good-quality place, this one has fully functioning bathrooms and very good food.

Campement Sitokoto *(☎ 994 8512)* Just south of Bolonga this village-run place has rooms and meals at standard CRI prices. Rooms are basic but clean and the shared bathrooms have running water.

Southern Strip The southern strip begins where the main road reaches the coast.

A la Nature Restocases *(☎ 994 8524, e alanature@metissicana.sn)* Rooms B&B CFA4500 per person, half board CFA7500 per person. This is an elaborate, two-storey, beachfront venture with a rasta feel, lush garden, hammocks, drummers, basic bungalows and a solar-powered Internet connection.

On the beach to the north of here are a couple of cheap ***gargottes*** catering mainly for the local fishermen.

South of the fishing centre on the narrow spit of sand are neighbouring places that are both quite good. ***Le Saloulou*** *(☎/fax 994 8514, w www.saloulou.com)* has rooms for CFA8000 per person, while ***Le Bandoula Village*** *(☎ 994 85 11)* charges CFA12,000 per person. Both are well organised, offering tours of the surrounding bolongs and fishing trips.

Hôtel le Karone *(☎/fax 994 85 25, e karone@telecomplus.sn)* Half board CFA22,500 per person. About 2km further south is this upmarket hotel set in extensive gardens. There's a pool about 50m from the beach, and the thatched bungalows have air-con and hot showers.

Getting There & Away From Ziguinchor, bush taxis run directly to Kafountine. Or take any vehicle heading for Serekunda and change at Diouloulou, from where local bush taxis run to Kafountine for CFA500.

You can also get bush taxis to Kafountine from Serekunda or Brikama (Gambia), although direct traffic usually goes via the back roads and the sleepy Darsilami border rather than the main crossing at Seleti. Brikama to Kafountine is CFA1200. Another option is to cross the border just south of Kartung.

All bush taxis stop in the centre of Kafountine, from where shared taxis travel down the dirt road to the fishing beach, or you take a private taxi to your lodgings.

Getting Around Bicycles can be hired from a shop in the market, and from some of the campements. Rates are standardised at CFA2500 per day but the quality varies considerably, and rates may be negotiable.

Abéné

Abéné is 5km north of Kafountine, with a selection of places to stay in the village and on the beach, about 2km away. It's much quieter than Kafountine and harder to reach by local transport, so prepare for a few kilometres of hot walking.

Campement la Belle Danielle *(☎ 936 9542)* Rooms/half board CFA2500/6000 per person. Open Nov-June. This relaxed but well-organised place is in the heart of the village. Excursions are available and one of the friendly Konta brothers speaks good English. If you're coming from Kartong in Gambia, call ahead and the camp will send a Land Rover to collect you, and for a small fee will take your passport to Seleti to have it stamped.

The next two campements are all at the end of the road leading from the village to the beach.

Maison Sunjata *(☎/fax 994 8610, e info@senegambia.de)* Rooms/half board CFA7500/13,000 per person. Call ahead July-Oct. This small German-run place has clean, comfortable rooms. Try the delicious home-made (sugarless!) bisap (a red-coloured drink made from the hibiscus flower). Next door is the spacious Casamar, but it was closed when we visited and its future was unknown.

Campement le Kossey *(☎ 994 8609)* Rooms/half board CFA5000/10,000 per person. Along the beach is this more upmarket Italian-run place, where you'll find comfortable bungalows in a beautiful bougainvillea-laden garden.

Restaurant Chez Vero *(☎ 936 9514)* Dishes around CFA2000. Also near the beach, this place has decent meals and cold drinks.

Le Kalissai *(☎ 994 8600, e kalissai@sentoo.sn)* Singles/doubles CFA26,000/30,000. Take a right as you head towards the beach and 3km north is the vast, classy Kalissai, which has plush air-con bungalows in a shady palm grove and manicured gardens very close to the beach.

Unless you ask to be dropped at Abéné, most public transport between Diouloulou and Kafountine stops near a village called **Diannah**, 2km away. Near Diannah there are a couple of very basic campements – ask around in the village.

HAUTE CASAMANCE

Sédhiou & Kolda

East of Ziguinchor, Sédhiou and Kolda may be on your way to or from Tambacounda, or form part of a loop through this little-visited part of Casamance.

Sédhiou is on the north bank of the river. ***Hôtel la Palmeraie*** *(☎ 995 1102)* caters mostly for hunters and has comfortable air-con bungalows for CFA12,500/20,000. Local bush taxis go from Tanaf to Sandinier, from where a ferry crosses to Sédhiou. There are also bush taxis between Sédhiou and Bounkiling on the Trans-Gambia Hwy.

Kolda is a larger place with an easy atmosphere, friendly people and the cheapest beer in the country – ideal for experiencing typical southern Senegalese life. Everything centres on the three blocks opposite the post office. ***Hôtel Hobbe*** *(☎ 996 1170, e diahobbe@sentoo.sn)* is the best in town, with good rooms without/with air-con for CFA11,000/16,250, and it has an Internet bureau. ***Hôtel Moya*** *(☎ 996 1175)* is marginally cheaper, with uninspiring doubles without/with air-con for CFA10,800/13,800.

There's good ***street food*** near the market. Across the bridge and left is ***Badaala*** *(☎ 996 1012)*, a little taste of Dakar with decent food and cheap beer. ***Bamboo Bar*** opposite the Moya is also good for a drink.

A Peugeot taxi is CFA2500 to Tambacounda, and CFA2850 to Ziguinchor.

Eastern Senegal

Eastern Senegal is hot and flat, with a dry savanna landscape covered by bush and baobab trees. In the far south-east the plains give way to the rolling foothills of the Fouta Djalon in neighbouring Guinea. The region's main attraction has traditionally been Parc National du Niokolo-Koba – one of the largest parks in West Africa – where visitors have a reasonable chance of seeing large mammals. Not far behind is the town of Kedougou and surrounding Bassari country. Adventurous travellers are coming in rising numbers to the green hills, pristine waterfalls and traditional villages that make a striking contrast with the rest of the country.

TAMBACOUNDA

Tambacounda is a major crossroads town and the gateway to eastern Senegal. It has two main streets: Blvd Demba Diop, which runs east-west parallel to the train tracks, and Av Léopold Senghor, which runs north-south. The latter has shops, an Internet bureau and the SGBS bank, which changes money and gives cash advances on a Visa card. The main gare routière is at the southern end of town, west of Av Léopold Senghor. All taxi trips around town are CFA250.

Places to Stay

Chez Dessert *(☎ 981 1642, Av Léopold Senghor)* Rooms CFA3000 per person. A shoestringers' favourite for many years, this place has changed hands but still offers simple rooms, some very simple, and a small kitchen.

Hôtel Niji *(☎ 981 1259, e nijihotel@sentoo.sn)* Singles/doubles with bathroom CFA11,200/14,000. Just off Av Léopold Senghor, this place has fairly good fan rooms; air-con is an extra CFA4000.

Hôtel Asta Kébé *(☎ 981 1028, fax 981 1215)* Singles/doubles with air-con CFA16,000/21,000. This place is the best in town, but that's not saying much. However, it does have a swimming pool that nonguests can use for CFA1500, and fan rooms are cheaper.

Hôtel Keur Khoudia *(☎/fax 981 1102)* Singles/doubles with bathroom CFA11,700/16,000. West of the centre, this establishment offers decent bungalows with air-con and extremely lethargic management.

Places to Eat & Drink

There's a wide choice of ***gargottes*** and other cheap eateries at the main gare routière. You should be able to find something you like at ***Chez Eva***, ***Chez Asta*** or ***Chez Fatima***, all in a row on Blvd Demba Diop just west of the train station. They serve an interesting mix of local meals for CFA500 to CFA2000, and beer 24 hours.

Bar-Restaurant Chez Francis *(☎ 643 1231, Av Léopold Senghor)* is the most popular spot in town, with excellent steak and chips for CFA3000 and cheap, icy beer. ***La Hortencia***, near the station, does the best salads, while the ***Chez Kadeyssa*** does the best sandwiches. For drinking, ***Le Ninkinanka*** *(☎ 636 0046, Av Léopold Senghor)* is a cool choice, while the outlandishly large ***Complex Leggaal Pont*** *(☎ 981 7756)* gets more heated.

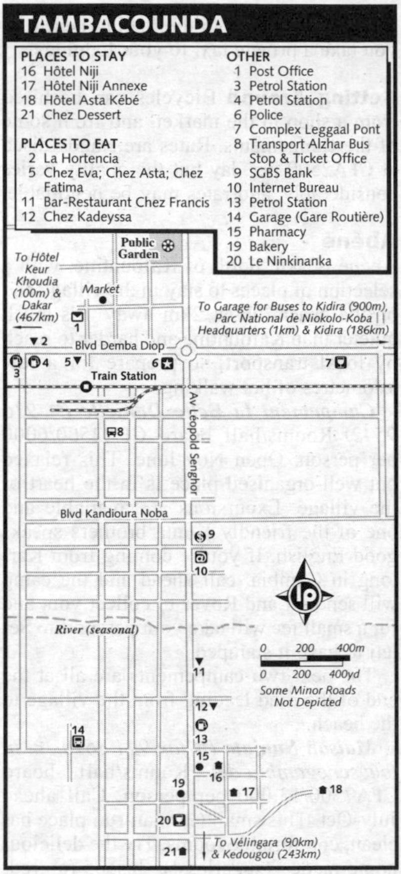
TAMBACOUNDA
PLACES TO STAY
16 Hôtel Niji
17 Hôtel Niji Annexe
18 Hôtel Asta Kébé
21 Chez Dessert
PLACES TO EAT
2 La Hortencia
5 Chez Eva; Chez Asta; Chez Fatima
11 Bar-Restaurant Chez Francis
12 Chez Kadeyssa
OTHER
1 Post Office
3 Petrol Station
4 Petrol Station
6 Police
7 Complex Leggaal Pont
8 Transport Alzhar Bus Stop & Ticket Office
9 SGBS Bank
10 Internet Bureau
13 Petrol Station
14 Garage (Gare Routière)
15 Pharmacy
19 Bakery
20 Le Ninkinanka
Public Garden
To Hôtel Keur Khoudia (100m) & Dakar (467km)
Market
To Garage for Buses to Kidira (900m), Parc National de Niokolo-Koba Headquarters (1km) & Kidira (186km)
Blvd Demba Diop
Train Station
Av Léopold Senghor
Blvd Kandioura Noba
River (seasonal)
0 200 400m
0 200 400yd
Some Minor Roads Not Depicted
To Vélingara (90km) & Kedougou (243km)

Getting There & Away

Bus & Bush Taxi From the main gare routière on the eastern side of town vehicles go to the Malian border at Kidira (CFA4000 by Peugeot taxi, CFA2700 by minibus). Vehicles to most other destinations go from the larger gare routière on the southern side of town (it swarms with touts, so watch

SENEGAL

your gear.) A minibus to Vélingara is CFA1000, from where you can cross into Gambia. To Dakar by Peugeot taxi is CFA6800, and by Alham CFA4400. The express bus (car mouride) leaves from outside the Transport Alzhar ticket office south of the train station at 4.30am daily for Dakar (CFA4000, eight hours) and Kaolack (CFA2500, five hours), but buy a ticket early the day before to get a good seat. The car mouride also goes to Kidira (CFA2000, three hours) and Kedougou (CFA2500, three hours). If you're heading for Guinea, most days a battered bush taxi goes to Koundara via Medina Gounas and Sambaïlo (where you may have to change); this rough, slow trip costs around CFA8000.

Train The express train between Dakar and Bamako (Mali) comes through Tambacounda twice a week in each direction. For more details see the main Getting There & Away section earlier in this chapter. Heading for Bamako it passes through Tambacounda on Wednesday and Saturday evening; the timetable says it departs at 7.05pm, but it's usually nearer 10pm, if you're lucky. Officially, a section of seating is reserved for passengers who board at Tambacounda. In reality, 2nd class is nearly always full, but 1st-class tickets are usually available. Fares from Tambacounda are CFA8060/10,095 (2nd/1st class) to Kayes and CFA14,165/19,320 to Bamako. Look out for touts selling unused tickets on the platform, but make sure your ticket relates to a real seat!

PARC NATIONAL DU NIOKOLO-KOBA

Niokolo-Koba is Senegal's major national park, a beautiful area of wilderness covering about 900,000 hectares, designated as a Unesco world heritage site and international biosphere reserve. The landscape is relatively flat, with plains that become marshy after rain, interspersed with hills – the highest is **Mt Assirik** (311m) in the southeast. The park is transected by the Gambia River and two tributaries – the Niokolo-Koba and the Koulountou. Vegetation includes dry savanna woodland and grassland, gallery forest, patches of bamboo and marshland.

Some 350 species of birds and about 80 species of mammal inhabit the park. African classics such as lions (about 500) and leopards are here, but are rarely seen (apart from the leopards in the enclosure near Simenti). Depending on who you believe, by early 2002 the number of elephants in the park was either none or about 15. However, this could change, as 11 elephants were airlifted into the park from Burkina Faso in May 2002 as part of a project aimed at repopulating the park. You do have a good chance of spotting waterbucks, bushbucks, kobs, duikers, baboons, monkeys (green and patas), warthogs, roan antelopes, giant Derby elands, hartebeests and possibly buffaloes. Chimpanzee troops are occasionally seen in the eastern and southern parts of the park. Hippos and three types of crocodiles – Nile, slender-snouted and dwarf – live in the rivers.

The park was neglected until the early 1990s, and poaching became a problem, but recent international funding for development as part of the Parc Transfrontalier Niokolo-Badiar transnational ecosystem (which includes areas in neighbouring Guinea) has improved the situation.

During the rains, and until late November, most park tracks are impassable without a 4WD. In December and January, conditions are pleasantly cool, but the best time for viewing wildlife is during the hot season in April and May, when the vegetation has withered and animals congregate at water holes.

A glossy visitor guide is available at the park entrance, with a park map and illustrations of some of the wildlife you could see. However, it's in French and costs CFA6000.

Information

Parc National du Niokolo-Koba is officially open from 15 December to 30 April, though you can visit any time. You enter the park at Dar Salam, where a locally run Biodiversity Centre is being built just inside the park gate. An hour further on is **Simenti**, which is the hub for most visitors; it's home to an uninspiring visitor information centre and the equally uninspiring Hôtel de Simenti. Many animals are concentrated around the Simenti area, although to see a wider selection you have to travel into the eastern sector of the park.

You must be in a vehicle to enter the park, and walking is not usually allowed unless you are accompanied by a park ranger. Even

SENEGAL

PARC NATIONAL DU NIOKOLO-KOBA

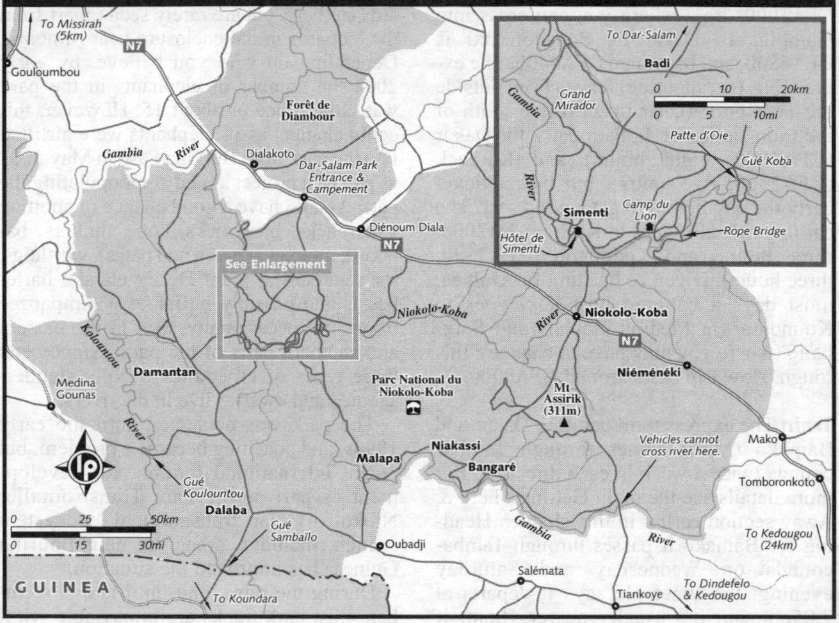
To Missirah (5km)
N7
Gouloumbou
Forêt de Diambour
Gambia River
Dialakoto
Dar-Salam Park Entrance & Campement
Diénoum Diala
N7
See Enlargement
Niokolo-Koba River
Niokolo-Koba
N7
Niéménéki
Koulountou River
Medina Gounas
Damantan
Parc National du Niokolo-Koba
Mt Assirik (311m)
Niakassi
Malapa
Bangaré
Vehicles cannot cross river here.
Mako
Tomboronkoto
Gué Koulountou
Dalaba
Gué Sambaïlo
Oubadji
Gambia River
To Kedougou (24km)
0 25 50km
0 15 30mi
GUINEA
To Koundara
Salémata
Tiankoye
To Dindefelo & Kedougou
To Dar-Salam
Badi
Grand Mirador
0 10 20km
0 5 10mi
Patte d'Oie
Gué Koba
Gambia River
Simenti
Camp du Lion
Hôtel de Simenti
Rope Bridge

in the dry season all tracks require 4WD vehicles, except between the park gate and Simenti and on some other tracks in the Simenti area.

The entrance fee is CFA2000 per person and CFA5000 per vehicle for 24 hours. Park-approved guides can be hired at the gate, in Simenti or in Tambacounda (they look for work around the popular tourist hotels and restaurants), for CFA6000 per day. They are good at showing you around, but lack of training means their knowledge of birds and animals is not the best, and only a couple speak any English.

Places to Stay & Eat

At the main park entrance, ***Dar-Salam Campement*** has clean bungalows with bathroom for CFA6600, and camping for CFA3000 per tent. Meals, like cross-cultural spaghetti with beef yassa (CFA3500), are also available. Inside the park camping is permitted, but this is very unusual and there are no facilities at all.

Most people stay at ***Hôtel de Simenti*** *(☎ 982 3650)*, a concrete monstrosity that would look more at home in an East London estate than it does in this pristine wilderness by the Gambia River. Ramshackle huts are CFA7000 (one or two people), single/double rooms with air-con CFA15,000/20,000, and full board CFA25,845/41,140. Otherwise breakfast is CFA2000, and filling meals are served for CFA5000. The hotel organises half-day drives for CFA6500 per person (minimum four people), and the visitor centre offers boat rides for CFA3500 per person, or walks in the bush with a ranger for about CFA3000. You can also walk to a nearby hide overlooking a water hole or grazing area (depending on the season), where you'll almost certainly see as many animals as you would from the back of a vehicle. If your visit is between mid-June and mid-December you'll need to book ahead if you want a room ready when you arrive.

Camp du Lion is a small campement 6km east of Simenti in a beautiful spot on the Gambia River. Very simple huts are available for CFA7000 and camp sites are CFA3000. Meals are CFA3500. This place is reachable in an ordinary car and there is a 4WD for excursions. You can also walk to the nearby Pointe de Vue, where hippos and other animals can be sighted drinking on the opposite bank of the river.

Getting There & Away

Whatever transport option you take, remember that morning and evening are the best times to see animals, so a one-day trip is hardly worth it. Note also that the best place to see chimpanzees is around Mt Assirik, but getting here from Simenti (4WD is essential) can take four hours, plus four hours back, which doesn't allow much time for viewing.

By public transport, take anything from Tambacounda heading towards Kedougou (you'll have to pay full fare: CFA2000 in a minibus, CFA3500 in a Peugeot taxi) and get off at the Dar-Salam entrance, where you can try hitching into the park. However, this seems to be a hit-and-miss endeavour.

Car Another option is to arrange car hire with guides in Tambacounda. This costs around CFA40,000 per day including fuel, driver and entry charge for the car. To this, add your own costs (accommodation, entry, guide etc). An all-inclusive two-day tour (car, fuel, driver, guide, entry for car and passengers, boat ride, food and accommodation at Camp du Lion) costs CFA120,000 for four people. Some hotels in Tambacounda have cars for hire, though this seems inconsistent.

Taxi Most travellers rent a Peugeot taxi in Tambacounda to at least reach the Simenti area (although to see more of the park, you need a 4WD). Rates begin at approximately CFA30,000 per day, with fuel. To this price add entrance fees (for you and the car), food and accommodation, plus a guide if you choose. The driver pays for his own food and accommodation, where necessary (the campement does not charge drivers).

If you don't want to launch headlong into haggling, ask the *chef du garage* (the manager, who has the respect of all the drivers) to help you find something suitable. Before sealing the deal, carefully check the taxi's condition, and if the rains have not long finished call at the main park headquarters in Tambacounda (☎ 981 1097) to ensure the track to Simenti is passable by 2WD.

BASSARI COUNTRY

The far southeast corner of Senegal is often called Bassari country after the local Bassari people, who are particularly noted for their traditional way of life and picturesque villages. The Bassari often feature on tour itineraries, but are just one of many tribes living in this area. Other groups include the Wolof, Bambara, Malinké, Fula and Bedik.

The landscape is hilly – a northern extension of neighbouring Guinea's Fouta Djalon region – and well vegetated, making it a pleasant contrast to the hot and dusty plains elsewhere in Senegal, and an increasingly popular destination for hiking, biking and motorcycling. Until recently you would have had a hard time explaining why you wanted to go walking in the bush to a remote waterfall or the top of a nearby hill. Now the guides find you.

Kedougou

Kedougou is the starting point for visits to Bassari country. It has lost some of its remote feel now that the tar road from Tambacounda links it to the rest of Senegal, but it's still a relaxed town, with an interesting mix of people and a busy market. Other facilities include a petrol station, several télécentres, Internet access for CFA3000 an hour at the Kedougou Multi-Service, and the blue-fronted Alimentation de Dioubo (☎ 985 1190) where English-speaking 'Darryl' is a mine of information on the local area and how best to get around. All these places are on or near the main street, which is also home to the gare routière.

Places to Stay & Eat All of these places arrange tours in the surrounding area or to Parc National du Niokolo-Koba. For lodgings, the ***Campement Diaw*** *(☎ 985 1124)* has good double huts for CFA6000/CFA12,000 without/with air-con, while the similarly priced ***Campement Moïse*** *(☎ 985 1139)* also has a 4WD for hire. The ***Relais de Kedougou*** *(☎ 985 1062, fax 985 1126)* is a more upmarket place in a picturesque riverside setting that attracts mostly hunters. It has double huts without/with air-con for CFA9000/16,000, and an equally attractive annexe called ***Hippo Lodge Safari*** about 4km out of town, where a bungalow with bathroom is just CFA6000.

All the accommodation places do food; otherwise there's a good choice of ***cheap eateries*** around the market and garage but not too much else.

Hiking & Biking to Guinea

We started from Dindefello at 7.30am on a Sunday by paying CFA500 for each bike to be carried to the top of the first hill, between Afia and Dande. From here we began biking for about 22km (mostly uphill) through crop fields, a few villages, and many creeks. The scenery was beautiful. Only going for the night, we bypassed the border control at Louga by keeping to the narrow trail – all the Senegalese know the way. The trail is also the shortest route to the village of Chiange, where we arrived after many punctures and gladly left our bikes in the chief's compound.

It was 3.30pm by now and we took a trail for about 13km up the mountainous Massif du Tamgué, all the way to Mali-ville. In places it's relatively steep, but from the plateau at the top the views were astounding. In the rainy season they say you can see all the way to the Gambia River and Kedougou. The path is easy to follow and runs across several plateaus and through several villages where there are always people around to help with directions. You can also see the Dame de Mali rock formation to the east of this trail. We eventually arrived at 9pm, having done the last couple of hours by torch (flashlight).

The best day to go is Sunday, when about 50 people take the path for the huge market in Mali-ville. You need to be in good shape. We weren't carrying heavy bags, but we did carry lots of water and we also filtered the water from creeks that we passed. If you're walking the entire trip you shouldn't have any problem sleeping in a village along the way.

Vonnie Moler

Getting There & Away Tambacounda to Kedougou is CFA2000 in a minibus, CFA2500 in the express bus that leaves at 5am except on Wednesday, and CFA3500 in a Peugeot taxi. The main road goes straight through Parc National du Niokolo-Koba, but park fees are not payable if you are just in transit. Minibuses occasionally go to the town of Mali (also called Mali-ville) in Guinea for CFA6000, from where a Peugeot taxi to Labé is CFA5000.

Readers report that it's also possible to combine biking and hiking from Dindifelo (38km from Kedougou) to Mali-ville in Guinea in a long day, or walk it in two days (see Lonely Planet's *The Gambia & Senegal* for full details). If you choose to do this, be sure to check it out in Kedougou before you set off. The campement in Dindifelo will be able to direct you to the start of the trail and if you go on a Sunday there will be plenty of locals to lead the way. It's best to stock up on bottled water and the like in Kedougou.

Around Kedougou

Kedougou makes an excellent base to explore the many traditional villages in the surrounding hills on foot, bicycle, motorbike, bush taxi or any combination of the above.

One of the nearest villages is **Bandafassi**, noted for its basket-makers. There's a shop selling cold drinks where you can refuel before hiking to the top of the nearby hill, which gives wonderful views. **Ibel** is a mainly Fula village 7km west of Bandafassi, and from here it's another 2km uphill to the Bedik village of **Iwol**, dominated by a huge and 'sacred' baobab tree. **Salémata**, 83km west of Kedougou by good dirt road, is in the heart of Bassari country. The surrounding hills – some more than 400m high – are beautiful. The best day to arrive is Tuesday, when the *lumo* (weekly market) is held.

Salémata has a small and friendly ***campement***, where double huts are CFA7500 and meals are around CFA3500. Steep prices, but you pay for the remote location. A good day walk from here is to **Etiolo**, a 15km return trip.

One of the most popular day trips from Kedougou is to the village of **Dindefelo**, 38km of bad road south of Kedougou. The lumo is on Sunday but there is at least one bus a day (CFA700) at other times. At the far end of the village is a Casamance-style ***village campement*** (☎ *658 8707)* charging CFA2500 per person in simple cement huts. From the campement you can hike 2km to Dindefelo's main attraction, a spectacular waterfall with a deep green pool at the bottom that's ideal for swimming. The campement will insist you take a guide to reach the waterfall, but it isn't really necessary. The campement charges CFA500 per person for visiting the waterfall, with the money going to the village fund.

SENEGAL

Sierra Leone

Warning

While life in many areas of Sierra Leone is rapidly returning to normal, the security, economic and political situations are still in a state of flux. Overland travel is especially dangerous, as armed bandits, former members of a variety of factions, and even some peacekeepers have been known to rob and extort money from travellers. Although Freetown is more secure than you would expect of the capital of a country that has suffered 10 years of war, it is still prone to spontaneous demonstrations, violent crime and political instability. Towns in the far east of the country, such as Koidu, Kailahun and Beudu, were still occupied by rebels at the time of writing and were off limits to travellers. Even if the situation improves, it will still be some time before these towns have anything to offer travellers.

Sierra Leone at a Glance

Capital: Freetown
Population: 5.1 million
Area: 72,325 sq km
Head of State: President Ahmed Tejan Kabbah
Official language: English
Main local languages: Krio, Mende, Temne
Currency: Leone
Exchange rate: US$1 = Le2035
Time: GMT/UTC
Country telephone code: ☎ 232
Best time to go: Mid-November to early May

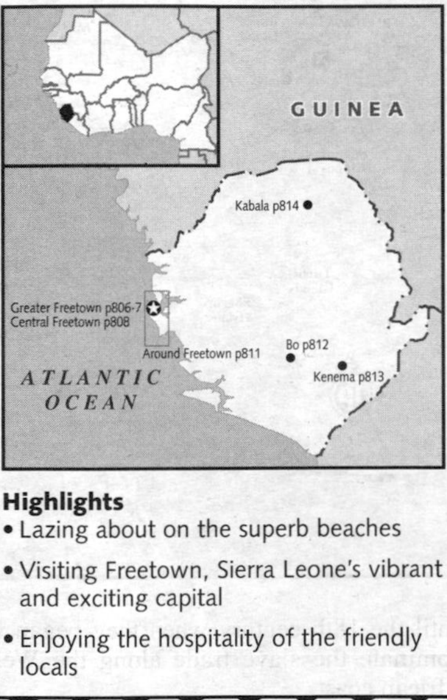

GUINEA
Kabala p814
Greater Freetown p806-7
Central Freetown p808
Around Freetown p811
Bo p812
Kenema p813
ATLANTIC
OCEAN

Highlights

- Lazing about on the superb beaches
- Visiting Freetown, Sierra Leone's vibrant and exciting capital
- Enjoying the hospitality of the friendly locals

After 10 years of almost constant warfare and uncertainty, much of Sierra Leone is now calm. The watershed event of 2002 was the destruction by the UN of more than 25,000 firearms, the symbolic end to the destabilisation brought about by the Revolutionary United Front (RUF) rebels that began in 1991. Despite these positive developments, Sierra Leone is still not a place for independent travellers. While the government controls major towns, rebel factions still maintain a presence in some areas in the east and north and the overall security situation remains tenuous.

Should the situation stabilise, Sierra Leone will be a terrific place to visit as it holds plenty of attractions, including beautiful beaches, lush and varied tropical landscapes, a dynamic culture and friendly people.

Facts about Sierra Leone

HISTORY

The region now called Sierra Leone was on the southern edge of the great Empire of Mali, which flourished between the 13th and 15th centuries (for more details on the early history of the region, see History in Facts about West Africa earlier in this book). Early inhabitants included the Temne, the Sherbro and the Limba, who were organised into independent chiefdoms. Mandingo/Malinké traders had also entered the region early on and integrated with indigenous peoples.

Contact with Europeans began in 1462 with the arrival of Portuguese navigators, who called the area Serra Lyoa (Lion Mountain), later modified to Sierra Leone. Around 120 years later, Sir Francis Drake stopped here during his voyage around the world. However, the British did not control the area

SIERRA LEONE

SIERRA LEONE
Kindia
Medina Oula
Outamba NP
Kilimi NP
Yana
GUINEA
CONAKRY
Forécariah
Kamakwie
Scarcies River
Little
Pamelap
Kambia
Pendembu
Fadugu
Rokel River
Bumbuna
Makeni
Port Loko
Magburaka
Pampana River
Lunsar
Sierra Leone River
Lungi
FREETOWN
Bunce Island
Masiaka
Mile 91
Waterloo
Songo
Kent
Banana Islands
Moyamba
Mano
Shenga
Bo
Tongo Field Diamond Centre
Sumbuya
Turtle Islands
Sherbro Island
Bonthe
Tumabum
Turners Peninsula
Pujehun
Lake Mape
Lake Mabesi
Sulima
Fairo
ATLANTIC OCEAN
0 25 50km
0 15 30mi
Faranah
Falaba
Gberia-Fotombu
GUINEA
Kabala
Koinadugu
Loma Mountains
Firawa
Kurubonla
Mt Bintumani (1945m)
Kissidougou
Kayima
Kono (Koidu-Sefadu)
Yengema
Masingbi
Guéckédou
To Voinjama
Koindu
Beudu
Kailahun
Mongeri
Sewa River
Boajibu
Pendembu
Kenema
Blama
Gola Hills
Moa River
Joru
Morro River
Bandajuma
Potoru
Tiwai Island WS
Mano River
Zimmi
Kongo
Mano River Bridge
Bo (Waterside)
Tubmonburg
LIBERIA
To Monrovia

until the 18th century when they began to dominate the slave trade along the West African coast.

The American War of Independence in the 1770s provided an opportunity for thousands of slaves to gain freedom by fighting for Britain. When the war ended, over 15,000 ex-slaves made their way to London, where they suffered unemployment and poverty. In 1787 a group of philanthropists purchased 52 sq km of land near Bunce Island in present-day Sierra Leone from a local chief for the purpose of founding a 'Province of Freedom' in Africa for the ex-slaves. This became Freetown. That same year, the first group of about 400 men and women (300 ex-slaves and 100 Europeans, mainly prostitutes) arrived.

Within three years, all but 48 settlers had deserted or had died of disease or in fights with the local inhabitants. But in 1792 the determined British philanthropists sent a second band of settlers, this time 1200 ex-slaves who had fled from the USA to Nova Scotia. Later, they sent 550 more from Jamaica. To the chagrin of the philanthropists, some settlers, both white and black, joined in the slave trade. In 1808 the British government took over the Freetown settlement and declared it a colony.

The Colonial Period

By the early 1800s, slavery had been abolished in Britain. Over the next 60 years, British warships plied the West African coast, trying to intercept slave ships destined for America. Freetown became the depot for thousands of 'recaptives' from all over West Africa as well as many migrants from the hinterland. By 1850, over 100 ethnic groups were represented in the colony. They lived in relative harmony, each group in a different section of town.

Like the previous settlers, the recaptives became successful traders and intermarried. All nonindigenous blacks became known collectively as Krios. British administrators favoured the Krios and appointed many to senior posts in the civil service.

Towards the end of the 19th century, the tide started to turn against the Krios, who were outnumbered 50 to one by indigenous people, and in 1924 the British administrators established a legislative council with elected representatives, to the advantage of the more numerous indigenous people. Many Krios, who continued to monopolise positions within the civil service, reacted by allying with the British. While other colonies clamoured for independence, they proclaimed loyalty to the Crown, and one group even petitioned against the granting of independence.

Independence

When independence was achieved in 1961, it seemed that Western-style democracy would work here. There were two parties of roughly equal strength, but they became divided along ethnic lines. The Sierra Leone People's Party (SLPP) was the party of the Mendes (the dominant ethnic group in southern Sierra Leone) and represented the tribal structure of the old colony. The All People's Congress (APC), formed by trade unionist Siaka Stevens, became identified with the Temnes of the north and voiced the dissatisfaction of the small modernising elite. The Krio community threw its support behind the SLPP, whose leader, Milton Margai, became the first prime minister.

Following Margai's death in 1964, his brother Albert took over and set about replacing the Krios in the bureaucracy with Mendes. The Krios took revenge in the 1967 elections by supporting the APC, which won a one-seat majority. A few hours after the results were announced, a Mende military officer led a coup, placing Siaka Stevens under house arrest. Two days later, fellow officers staged a second coup, vowing to end the corruption that was so widespread under the Margai brothers.

Stevens went into exile in Guinea and with a group of Sierra Leoneans began training in guerrilla warfare techniques for an invasion. This became unnecessary when a group of private soldiers mutinied and staged a third coup 13 months later – an African record for the number of coups in such a short period.

Stevens returned and formed a new government, but his first decade in office was turbulent. He declared a state of emergency, banned breakaway parties from the APC and put a number of SLPP members on trial for treason. Meanwhile, the economy continued to deteriorate. The iron-ore mine closed, diamond revenues dropped, living costs increased, students rioted, and Stevens again declared a state of emergency. The 1978 election campaign was almost a civil war between the major ethnic groups, and the death toll topped 100. Stevens won, and Sierra Leone became a one-party state.

Despite the one-party system, the 1982 elections were the most violent ever. Stevens was forced to give Mendes and Temnes equal representation in the cabinet, although this did not stop the deterioration of economic and social conditions. With virtually no support left, Stevens finally stepped down in 1985 at the age of 80, naming as his successor Major General Joseph Momoh, head of the army since 1970.

Under Momoh, the economy continued its downward spiral. By 1987 the inflation rate was one of the highest in Africa, budget deficits were astronomical, and smugglers continued to rob Sierra Leone of up to 90% of its diamond revenue.

Things worsened in late 1989 when civil war broke out in neighbouring Liberia. By early 1990, thousands of Liberian refugees had fled into Sierra Leone. The following year, fighting spilled across the border and the RUF, Sierra Leonean rebels who were opposed to Momoh, took over much of the eastern part of the country.

The Momoh government used the war in the east as an excuse to postpone elections but finally, in September 1991, a new constitution was adopted to allow for a multiparty system. Before an election date could be announced, though, a group of young military officers overthrew Momoh in April 1992. The National Provisional Ruling

Council (NPRC) was set up, and 27-year-old Captain Valentine Strasser was sworn in as head of state. Elections and a return to civilian rule were promised for 1995.

Soon, though, optimism began to fade. A major drain on resources was the continuing fighting in the east against the RUF, which expanded its control over the diamond-producing areas, robbing the government of a wealth of revenue. They were bolstered after the coup by supporters of the Momoh regime and by escaping rebels from Liberia. It soon became apparent that none of these groups was fighting for a political objective, but rather their goal was to control the diamond and gold fields. By late 1994 northern and eastern parts of the country had descended into near anarchy, with private armies led by local warlords, government soldiers, rebel soldiers and deserters from the Sierra Leonean and Liberian armies roaming the area at will and terrorising local communities.

In January 1996, Brigadier General Julius Maada Bio overthrew Strasser in a coup. Despite NPRC efforts at postponement, previously scheduled elections went ahead, and in March, Ahmed Tejan Kabbah – leader of the SLPP – was elected president. Kabbah's government continued peace talks with the RUF, which had been initiated by the previous military government, but his efforts bore little fruit.

On 25 May 1997, a group of junior military officers sympathetic to the RUF staged a coup in Freetown. President Kabbah fled to neighbouring Guinea, and a wave of looting, terror and brutality engulfed the capital. Guerrilla warfare spread throughout much of the country, perpetrated by the RUF and the occupying junta. By early 1998, there were few areas that had not been affected. Food and fuel supplies were scarce almost everywhere, and thousands of Sierra Leoneans had fled the country.

In February 1998, a Nigerian-led West African peacekeeping force (Ecomog), succeeded in ousting the junta leaders and in taking control of Freetown and many upcountry areas – although not before fleeing rebels had looted and destroyed much in their path. President Kabbah was reinstated in March, but the situation again refused to stabilise. On 6 January 1999, with nearly a quarter of the entire Nigerian military serving with Ecomog in Sierra Leone, the RUF staged its boldest assault yet on Freetown, code-named Operation No Living Thing. In the ensuing weeks, the city was virtually destroyed and over 6000 people killed before Ecomog again forced the rebels from the capital.

The bloody battle prompted the government to sign the controversial Lomé Peace Agreement with the RUF in the summer of 1999. Under the agreement, the RUF leader Foday Sankoh was to become the country's vice president and the cabinet minister in charge of the country's diamond production but he was arrested shortly after for supposedly plotting a coup. As part of the Lomé Peace Agreement, the UN deployed a peacekeeping mission, Unamsil, to Sierra Leone that has since become the largest and most expensive ever deployed by the world body. Unamsil's efforts to disarm the RUF ended in February, 2002, bringing another official end to the war. Elections held in May 2002 resulted in an 80% turnout of the 2.3 million registered voters and were deemed to have been Sierra Leone's most fair and trouble-free in decades. Kabbah was re-elected and the RUF's political party was soundly defeated, officially setting the stage for the country's best opportunity for lasting peace since the late 1960s.

While daily life in many areas is returning to normal, Sierra Leone still has a long way to go before the causes underlying the conflicts of the past decades can be addressed and a stable political situation arrived at.

GEOGRAPHY

The coastal zone, consisting of mangrove swamps, beaches and islands, is flat except for the 40km-long Freetown peninsula – one of the few places in West Africa where mountains rise near the sea. Inland is an undulating, forested and extensively cultivated plateau. In the northeast are the Loma Mountains; south of these are the twin towns of Koidu-Sefadu in Kono, the country's major diamond area.

Much of Sierra Leone's original forest cover has been destroyed by mining and detrimental agricultural practices; only about 5% remains today.

CLIMATE

Sierra Leone is one of West Africa's wettest countries, with an average annual rainfall of

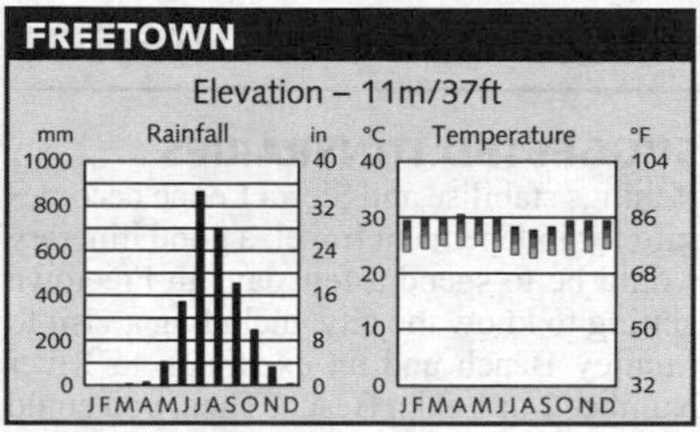
FREETOWN
Elevation – 11m/37ft
mm
Rainfall
in
°C
Temperature
°F
1000
800
600
400
200
0
40
32
24
16
8
0
40
30
20
10
0
104
86
68
50
32
JFMAMJJASOND
JFMAMJJASOND

over 3150mm. The rainy season stretches from mid-May to November, with July and August the wettest months. Humidity is particularly high in the coastal regions, although sea breezes afford some relief. The country's annual average temperature is 27°C; inland it gets much warmer. December and January are the coolest, driest months, but skies can be hazy from the harmattan (desert winds).

FLORA & FAUNA

Despite its small size, Sierra Leone is endowed with a broad range of vegetation zones, which are home to a variety of bird and animal species. The government has established several parks and reserves where wildlife can be protected, although due to the security situation most are now off limits to tourists and have suffered from a decade of neglect. One that is open is Outamba-Kilimi National Park in the northwest. During the war, however, much of Sierra Leone's native wildlife was displaced to calmer regions. A full accounting of the wildlife population has yet to take place. For more details contact the Conservation Society of Sierra Leone (☎ 229 716) at 4 Sanders St, Freetown.

GOVERNMENT & POLITICS

Sierra Leone is divided into 150 chiefdoms, each governed by a paramount chief and a council of elders. Paramount chiefs occupy 12 seats of Sierra Leone's 80-seat parliament, one from each of the country's national districts. At the time of writing, Unamsil was the de facto country administrator but the government was to start taking over its operations once the May 2002 elections had been certified.

ECONOMY

Sierra Leone – already one of the poorest countries in the world prior to the 1997 coup – is now even worse off. During the violent years since the coup, the country effectively ceased to function. Prices of goods skyrocketed, sustained by a vigorous black market that sprang up after the imposition of economic sanctions by the Economic Community of West African States (Ecowas). With the restoration of peace, goods are again coming freely into the country although supply to more remote areas – especially in the east – is erratic. Living conditions remain difficult, with an estimated 80% of the population living in poverty.

The country's economy is based on subsistence agriculture, although there is some hope that it will soon begin profiting from its vast reserves of diamonds, gold, rutile, oil and bauxite. Sierra Leone's principal crops are cassava and rice.

POPULATION & PEOPLE

Sierra Leone is one of the more densely populated countries in West Africa, home to an estimated 5 million people, although that figure is open to argument since so many people were killed or displaced in the fighting. There are over 15 indigenous ethnic groups. The two largest groups, the Temnes of the north and Mendes of the south, each comprise about one-third of the population. Other groups include the Limba and Koranko in the north, the Kissi in the east and the Sherbro in the southwest.

Krios, most of whom live in Freetown, constitute less than 2% of the population and are predominantly Christian. Many of the country's intellectuals and professionals are Krios. There are significant numbers of Mandingo/Malinké and Fula/Peul in the north and east, and a sizable Lebanese business community. For more information about the Fula and Malinké people, see the special section 'Peoples of the Region'.

ARTS

Sierra Leone is known for its fabrics, especially country cloth and *gara*. Country cloth is a coarse material woven from wild cotton into narrow strips that are joined to make blankets and clothing, then coloured indigo, green or brown using natural dyes. Gara is a thin cotton material, tie-dyed or batik-printed either with synthetic colours or natural dyes.

The Mendes produce the best-known masks. These are often used in initiation ceremonies of the women's *bundu* (secret societies).

Another traditional craft is the distinctive Temne basketry, made in the north of Sierra Leone. Look for it at the Basket Market on Wallace Johnson St or at the artisans' stalls along Lumley Beach Rd in Freetown.

RELIGION

About 40% of the population is Muslim, concentrated in the north and east. The remainder is Christian or adherents of traditional religions, which are still strong and which exert significant influence on the practice of Christianity.

LANGUAGE

There are more than a dozen tribal languages, the most common of which are Mende and Temne. English is the official language and Krio is the most widely spoken. See the Language chapter for a list of useful phrases in Krio.

Facts for the Visitor

SUGGESTED ITINERARIES

If things stabilise and Sierra Leone becomes safe for independent travel, a good itinerary would be to spend a few days in Freetown getting to know the city, including a visit to Lumley Beach and an excursion to River Number 2 or Lakka Beach. Then, you could head out to Bo and Kenema for a look at diamond mining before either heading back to Freetown or north to Kabala to go hiking and camping around Mt Bintumani and Outamba-Kilimi National Park.

PLANNING

The best time to visit is mid-November, after the rains and before dusty harmattan winds spoil the views.

The dated Shell map (1988) has the country on one side (1:396,000) and Freetown on the other. It's readily available on the

Diamond Mining in Sierra Leone

One of the many ironies of Sierra Leone is that while it's one of the poorest countries on earth – it comes in last on the UN Human Development Index – it is one of the best sources of wealth in the world. Hundreds of thousands of carats of diamonds wait under the jungle carpet to be mined, cut, polished and set into jewellery that will be worn by people the world over.

When the RUF began its war in 1991, its sole aim was to control the country's diamond mines. It used forced labour to extract the wealth, and the receptive government of Charles Taylor in Liberia and ask-no-questions Western diamond dealers to launder the gems and put them on the world market. These gems were then sold as talismans of love, honour and commitment. The money that the RUF reaped from this enterprise – estimated at between US$25 million and US$125 million per year – was used to buy weapons to continue their war. The RUF was a brutal and undisciplined force, who often resorted to the brutal tactic of amputating the limbs of innocent civilians in order to terrorise the population and ensure continued control over the diamond mines. It's estimated that over 75,000 people were killed during the war and another 20,000 were mutilated.

In 1999, nongovernmental organisations brought the issue of 'conflict diamonds' to international attention and introduced measures to combat the trade. Even then, however, Sierra Leonean diamonds were easily smuggled into legitimate buying channels, with some governments and diamond dealers choosing to continue to turn a blind eye. Diamonds are the most portable form of wealth known to man – 30g of gem-quality diamonds are equal in value to 18,000kg of iron ore – and smuggling them into another country to avoid either export taxes or their pedigree as 'conflict diamonds' barely slowed. In fact, it's believed that Osama bin Laden's Al-Qaeda terrorist network bought millions of dollars' worth of Sierra Leone diamonds prior to the 11 September 2001 terrorist attacks on the USA because they're easily resold into the world market and practically impossible to trace.

Since the end of the war in February 2002, many legitimate miners have gone back to work in places such as Kenema, Bo and Koidu. Even DiamondWorks, a large Canadian exploration company, has resumed operations in Kono district after a five-year hiatus. It's hoped that, with the help of the World Diamond Council, for the first time since independence, Sierra Leone will be able to harness the wealth of the diamond areas for the benefit of its citizens, who badly need medical, educational and career opportunities in the wake of one of the worst and most brutal wars of the 1990s.

DAVID ELSE

ARIADNE VAN ZANDBERGEN

ARIADNE VAN ZANDBERGEN

While deforestion is a major concern in West Africa, there are still many areas of the region that are lush and green, with flowing rivers and picturesque waterways: treading a fine line at Parc National du Niokolo-Koba, Senegal (top left); Wli (Agumatsa) Falls, the highest in West Africa, Ghana (top right); cruising along Lake Bosumtwi, Ghana (bottom)

ARIADNE VAN ZANDBERGEN

INGRID RODDIS

CARL DRURY

Whether you want to explore forests or rivers, there are plenty of places to escape the hustle and bustle of West Africa's cities and large towns. You never have to travel too far to get close to nature: Volta River estuary, Ghana (top); rubber-tree forest near Sekondi-Takoradi, Ghana (bottom left); Banfora's 'edge of greenery', one of Burkina Faso's highlights (bottom right).

street in Freetown (US$6). A good pocket-sized country map appears on the UN website (W www.un.org/Depts/dpko/); follow the links for Unamsil. A dated, but still useful, Freetown street map can be bought in most markets (US$3) or from vendors in front of Crown Bakery on Wilberforce St. Maps of Sierra Leone available outside Africa include one in the International Travel Map series (1997; 1:560,000) and one published by the Fachhochschule Karlsruhe (1994; 1:800,000).

VISAS & DOCUMENTS

Visas

All visitors need visas or entry permits, which are not available at the border. Visas are normally valid for 30 days and can be extended in Freetown at the Immigration Department offices (☎ 223034) on Rawdon St near the corner with Siaka Stevens St.

Before leaving Sierra Leone you will need to visit the same office to get a 'police clearance' (no cost). Clearances are issued between 8am and 6pm daily, usually with a minimum of hassle, but will only be granted within 48 hours of your departure. You'll need to show your passport and provide your departure date. The clearances can be used before the departure date given, but not afterwards.

Visas for Onward Travel If you're heading to Guinea, the Guinean embassy in Freetown issues visas within 72 hours for approximately US$45.

Vaccination Certificates

You'll need a certificate of vaccination for yellow fever and cholera to enter Sierra Leone.

EMBASSIES & CONSULATES

Sierra Leonean Embassies

Within West Africa, Sierra Leone has embassies, where you can get visas and entry permits, in Gambia, Guinea and Liberia, and, if they have reopened, also in Côte d'Ivoire, Nigeria and Senegal. For more details, see the Facts for the Visitor section of the relevant country chapter. In countries with no Sierra Leonean embassy, try the British diplomatic representation.

Elsewhere, Sierra Leone has the following embassies:

Belgium (☎ 02-771 0052) 410 Av de Terveuern, Brussels 1150
Germany (☎ 0228-35 20 01) Rheinallee 20, 53173 Bonn
UK (☎ 020-7636 6483) 33 Portland Place, London W1N 3AG
USA (☎ 202-939 9261) 1701 19th St NW, Washington, DC 20009

Embassies & Consulates in Sierra Leone

Diplomatic missions in Freetown include the following:

Germany (☎ 222511) Santanno House, 10 Howe St
Ghana (☎ 223461) 16 Percival St
Guinea (☎ 232584) Wilkinson Rd, 500m northwest of Congo Cross roundabout
Ireland (☎ 222017) 8 Rawdon St
Mali (☎ 231781) 40 Wilkinson Rd
Nigeria (☎ 224202) Nigeria House, Siaka Stevens St
UK (☎ 223961) 6 Spur Rd
USA (☎ 226481) 1 Walpole St

CUSTOMS

Importing or exporting more than US$5 in leones is illegal; you cannot convert excess leones back into foreign currency at the airport, but if you have enough (at least US$100 worth), you are able do this at some foreign-exchange (forex) bureaus.

Taking diamonds out of the country without an export licence is illegal.

MONEY

The unit of currency is the leone (Le). A unit of 100 leones is often referred to as a 'block'.

country	unit		leone
euro zone	€1	=	Le1983
UK	UK£1	=	Le3100
USA	US$1	=	Le2035
West African CFA	CFA100	=	Le302

If the leone continues to devalue, be prepared to lug around a lot of local cash. Note that US$100 bills get the best exchange rates.

Apart from the huge inflation occasioned by the war, prices have been fairly stable in real terms, and are expressed in US dollars throughout this chapter. Top-end hotels will require payment in hard currency.

There is a small black market, but exchange rates are usually better at the various banks and forex bureaus.

POST & COMMUNICATIONS

Post

The main post office in Freetown, on the corner of Siaka Stevens and Gloucester Sts, is open from 8am to 4.45pm Monday to Friday and 8am to 1pm on Saturday, but the postal service in Sierra Leone is useless for sending and receiving anything. If you must mail something, a better bet is the UN post office in Freetown, located at the Mammy Yoko Hotel in Aberdeen.

Telephone & Fax

International calls can be made at the post office (phonecard only), and at Sierra Leone External Telecommunications (SLET) behind the bus station (open 24 hours daily). A three-minute (minimum) call to the USA/UK/Australia costs about US$5/5/6. The telephone network within Freetown and to some upcountry towns is good. Phonecards for domestic and international calls are on sale all over Freetown and in the larger upcountry towns such as Bo and Kenema.

Celtel operates a very good mobile-phone network in Freetown and visitors can activate a temporary one-month GSM account for US$40. Contact the Celtel representative, who hangs out at the Mammy Yoko Hotel. The prefix for mobile telephone numbers is ☎ 036.

You can also send and receive faxes at SLET (fax 224439). Incoming faxes are held seemingly indefinitely, although there's no registration system.

Email & Internet Access

A number of Internet cafés have sprung up around Freetown, most notably one next door to Crown Bakery on Wilberforce St, but the connection speed is notoriously slow. America Online has two Freetown phone numbers for email access: ☎ 228850 and ☎ 293520.

DIGITAL RESOURCES

For a great source of up-to-the-minute news from a variety of local publications check out W www.allafrica.com. A useful website for travel around Sierra Leone, including transport availability and area closures, is W www.ipctravel.com, while the UN website W www.un.org/Depts/dpko (follow the Unamsil links) has information on security in Sierra Leone.

BOOKS

Fighting for the Rain Forest by Paul Richards is an analysis of issues underlying the country's ongoing political instability. *The Gullah* by Joseph Opala is a pamphlet published by the US Information Service; it includes fascinating information about the links between Sierra Leone and the Gullah people of southeastern USA. *Tales of the Forest* by Thomas Decker is a collection of local folk tales.

In a different category altogether is *The Heart of the Matter* by Graham Greene, a novel of colonial times, where Freetown becomes a setting for a tale of human weakness, waste and frustration.

FILMS

Amistad (1997) tells the story of Mende slaves, led by Sengbe Pieh, who in 1839 revolted to obtain their freedom while being shipped from one Cuban port to another. The Amistad case so fuelled anti-slavery feelings in the USA that it is considered one of the catalysts of the American Civil War and, later, Sierra Leone's drive for independence.

NEWSPAPERS, RADIO & TV

Eleven newspapers are distributed in Freetown; you can usually buy them together for US$3. Sierra Leone Broadcasting Corporation has the only TV station in the country; the news is broadcast at 8pm nightly. KISS-104 FM radio station has a good mix of local music, colourful commentary and news.

PHOTOGRAPHY & VIDEO

Photo permits are not required, but be cautious until the security situation stabilises; don't take snaps of government buildings, military sites, airports or harbours. For more general information on photography restrictions, see Photography & Video in the Regional Facts for the Visitor chapter.

HEALTH

You'll need proof of yellow fever and cholera vaccinations. Malaria risk exists year-round throughout the whole country, so get expert advice on appropriate precautions. See Health in the Regional Facts for the Visitor chapter for more details on this and other health matters.

The water is not safe to drink: it is best to boil, filter or otherwise purify it, or drink mineral water. Good pharmacies exist up and down Siaka Stevens St and on Congo Town Rd leading to Aberdeen.

WOMEN TRAVELLERS

Sierra Leone does not present any specific problems for women travellers. For general information, see Women Travellers in the Regional Facts for the Visitor chapter.

DANGERS & ANNOYANCES

Although Freetown and some upcountry towns are under the control of Unamsil troops, many areas, particularly the east, remain rebel territory despite a declaration of peace. Banditry and worse continue; before venturing out, get an update in Freetown.

In most areas there's a strictly enforced curfew from midnight to 6am (from 10pm in some upcountry towns). Much of Freetown has electricity in the evenings, although power cuts are common. Upcountry, electricity is either sporadic or nonexistent.

There are Unamsil and police checkpoints on many roads in Freetown, as well as the odd illegal RUF checkpoint on roads between some upcountry towns. Checkpoints on upcountry roads slow travel significantly and can be manned by extremely dangerous people. Travel on upcountry roads after dark is strongly discouraged.

If you're considering hiking on Freetown peninsula be aware of of land mines. Ask knowledgeable locals before setting off.

BUSINESS HOURS

Business hours are 8am to 5pm Monday to Saturday, although many places close at 1pm on Saturday. Government offices are open 8am to noon and 12.30pm to 3.45pm Monday to Friday and alternate Saturday mornings. Banking hours are from 8am to 5.30pm Monday to Thursday and 8am to 2pm Friday.

PUBLIC HOLIDAYS & SPECIAL EVENTS

Public holidays include:

New Year's Day 1 January
Easter March/April
Independence Day 27 April
Revolution Day 29 April
Christmas Day 25 December
Boxing Day 26 December

Sierra Leone also celebrates various Islamic holidays. For details about Islamic holidays, see Public Holidays & Special Events in the Regional Facts for the Visitor chapter.

If you're in Freetown on Easter Monday, visit Lumley Beach for National Kite-Flying Day. In major towns, the last Saturday of every month is Cleaning Day; on this day there's a virtual curfew until 10am while everyone supposedly cleans their yard or section of road, and fines of up to US$125 are levied on those found disobeying.

ACTIVITIES

The ocean is calm and warm and swimming is generally safe. Deep-sea fishing off the coast is considered among the best in the region. Once security stabilises, you can visit many excellent hiking areas, especially on Freetown peninsula and in the northeast mountains around Kabala, but caution should be exercised on the Freetown peninsula due to the danger of land mines.

ACCOMMODATION

With the deployment of Unamsil in late 1999, Sierra Leoneans set about repairing war damage to the capital and many hotels and guesthouses have reopened, with the notable exception of places in Makeni, which is a skeleton of its former self. Visitors will find no lack of places to stay in Freetown, though there are few budget options.

FOOD

Sierra Leone is known for its cuisine and every town has at least one chop bar (basic eating house) serving tasty, filling food. Rice is the staple and *plasas* (chopped potato leaves and pounded or ground cassava leaves cooked with palm oil and fish or beef) is the most common sauce. Other typical dishes are okra sauce, palm-oil stew, groundnut stew, pepper soup and, for special occasions, jollof rice. Street-food favourites include roasted groundnuts or corn, beef sticks, steamed yams, fried plantains or dough balls, and fried yams with fish sauce. Every town of any size also has a choice of Lebanese restaurants serving cheap and tasty food.

DRINKS

Star, the local beer, is reasonable, but the eternally recycled bottles don't do any favours for its carbonation. Gulder is usually a better alternative, and there never seems to be a shortage of Guinness, no matter how far off the beaten track you go. *Poyo* (palm wine) is light and fruity, but getting used to the smell and the life forms floating in your cup takes a while.

Getting There & Away

AIR

Freetown has two airports. Lungi is the main airport and all regional flights depart from here, with the exception of those operated by West Coast Airways. Hastings is a small airfield used for UN flights and domestic flights on West Coast Airways. Airport departure tax for regional flights is US$20 (payable in US dollars). There is no tax for flying within Sierra Leone on West Coast, but you may still be asked to pay by the touts who hang out at Hastings. Just ignore them.

Intercontinental flights into Sierra Leone have resumed. Ghana Airways, British Airways and Air France all fly daily into Accra, where passengers can continue to Freetown via Ghana Airways. As Ghana Airways seems to be operating with one foot in the grave, expect delays in Accra that can last for days. Only Sierra National Airlines flies direct to Freetown from London (US$895 return, twice weekly). Kevin McPhillips Travel (☎ 1293-822922 in the UK, 410-659 7776 in the USA) deals exclusively with trips to Sierra Leone. The boxed text summarises regional flights from Freetown; the prices quoted are approximate.

Regional Flights from Freetown

destination	no of flights per week	airline	one way/ return (US$)
Abidjan	4	Ghana Airways	250/395
Accra	4	Ghana Airways	267/400
Banjul	2	Bellview	200/325
Conakry	6	West Coast, Ghana Airways	70/140
Lagos	2	Bellview, Ghana Airways	350/550
Monrovia	2	Weasua, Ghana Airways	125/300

LAND & SEA

Border Crossings

There are open border crossings between Sierra Leone and Guinea at Pamelap, Medina Oula (also called Medina Dula) and Gberia-Fotombu. To/from Liberia, there are border crossings at Bo (Waterside) and Kongo.

Before setting out for any of these borders, make inquiries locally: many have been shut at various times due to the security situation.

Guinea

The main border crossing is at Pamelap. A daily SLRTC bus goes from Freetown to Pamelap (US$7), where you'll find bush taxis to Conakry (US$5). The direct bus service to Conakry from Freetown costs US$12. Bush taxis also run between Freetown and Conakry (US$15, 10 hours, 330km) direct or with a change of vehicle at Pamelap.

A ferry goes every couple of days to Freetown from Conakry's main port near the bus station. No advance reservations are necessary; inquire at the port for details.

It's possible to cross at Medina Oula (Medina Dula) between Makeni and Kindia, and between Kabala and Faranah, although there's little transport on this route; you'll probably have to hire a motorbike or a truck in Kabala to the border or on to Faranah.

The Koindu to Nongoa crossing is off limits to travellers. Despite the war being officially over, RUF units still fight with Liberian and Guinean forces in this region and the presence of a vehicle on the road leading to Koindu will attract artillery fire from Liberian rebels.

Liberia

The main route between Freetown and Monrovia is via Kenema, Zimmi and Bo (Waterside). The journey takes two days in the dry season (US$28, 650km). There is another route via Kongo (to the east of Zimmi), but the road is very rough and little transport is available.

Check in Freetown about the safety of these routes; when we were there, they were off limits due to Liberian rebel activity near Monrovia and Tubmanburg. The route via Koindu towards Voinjama is unsafe due to ongoing cross-border warfare between RUF and forces in Guinea and Liberia.

Getting Around

Air

West Coast Airways has flights between Freetown and Bo and Kenema (US$50) Monday to Saturday from Hastings Airfield.

Bus & Bush Taxi

SLRTC runs daily buses between Freetown and Pamelap (US$7, six hours), Bo (US$4, seven hours), Kenema (US$5, eight hours) and Kabala (US$5, eight hours).

Bush taxis and *poda-podas* (minibuses) run between Freetown and many upcountry towns, including Bo, Kenema, Makeni, Pamelap, Kambia and Kabala, though it's usually safer and more reliable to take the bus. They also link upcountry towns with each other and with surrounding villages.

Freetown

☎ 022

Though the evidence of the past decade's violence, in particular the scars from the extensive fighting during Operation No Living Thing, is everywhere in Freetown, the city's pep and optimism is often enough to remind visitors of what a vibrant and friendly place it once was – and hopefully will be again. The capital is hectic and energetic. It's crammed with war victims and refugees who have yet to return to their upcountry homes, but despite the brutality of the war, Freetown often seems safer and less threatening than other large West African cities.

Beautiful nearby beaches and stunning views of sea and mountains compensate for the chaos of downtown and for the city's all-too-frequent traffic jams.

Orientation

Central Freetown is set out on a grid pattern with Siaka Stevens St as the main thoroughfare, running northeast to southwest. Halfway along is the huge Cotton Tree, a good landmark with which to orient yourself. Within a few blocks of the tree are the post office, markets, banks and offices. Away from the central area, winding streets climb the surrounding hills. Mt Aureol and Leicester Peak overlook the city.

The main road to the east is Kissy Rd, although some shared taxis and poda-podas go along Fourah Bay Rd through the dock area. Going west, the main road follows Sanders St, Brookfields Rd and Main Motor Rd towards Aberdeen and Lumley.

At the northwestern tip of Freetown peninsula are Aberdeen village and Lumley Beach, the main areas visitors stay.

Information

Tourist Offices Neither the National Tourist Board (at the Cape Sierra hotel) nor the Ministry of Tourism and Culture (at Government Wharf) have maps or leaflets. IPC Travel (☎ 223551), on the corner of Rawdon and Siaka Stevens St, is a good source of information for travellers.

Money Credit cards and travellers cheques are worthless anywhere in Sierra Leone; bring cash in large-denomination bills for the best exchange rates. Main banks include Barclays on the corner of Siaka Stevens and Charlotte Sts, and Union Trust Bank on Howe St. There are forex bureaus on and around Siaka Stevens St and next to Angel's Delight Restaurant on Lumley Beach Rd in Aberdeen; all these give good rates.

Travel Agencies IPC Travel (☎ 223551), on the corner of Siaka Stevens and Rawdon Sts, is the best option for airline bookings and for group excursions (once the security situation stabilises).

Medical Services In the event of serious medical problems, travellers can appeal to Médecins Sans Frontières, which operates a camp for war wounded on Aberdeen Rd, about 500m west of Aberdeen Junction. Connaught Hospital is at the western end of Wallace Johnson St. For serious problems you'll need to go to Abidjan in Côte d'Ivoire.

Dangers & Annoyances Once the disarmament process began, many former combatants came to Freetown and it's not uncommon to find RUF soldiers on the beach or in the discos. Despite being 'disarmed',

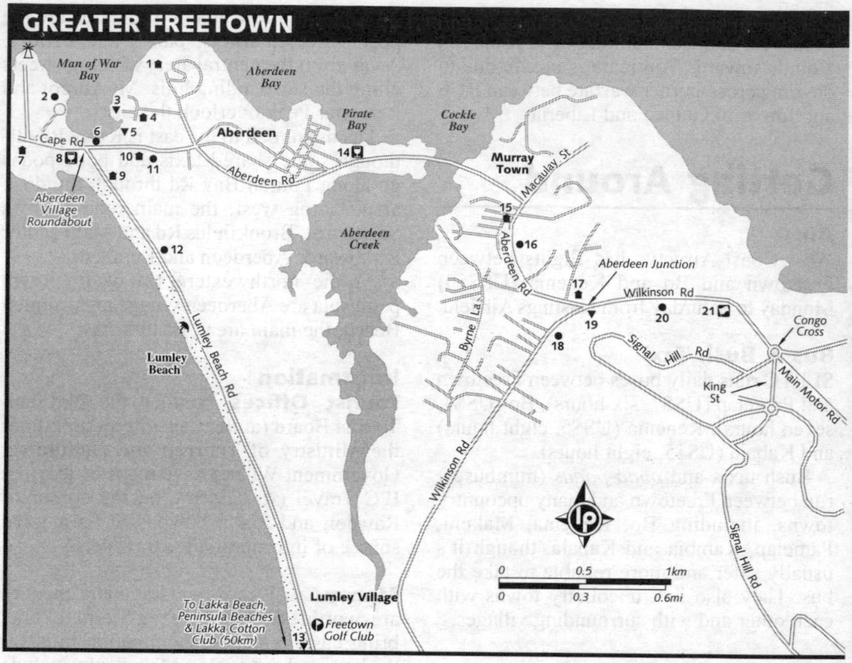
GREATER FREETOWN
Man of War Bay
Aberdeen Bay
Pirate Bay
Cockle Bay
Aberdeen
Cape Rd
Murray Town
Macaulay St
Aberdeen Rd
Aberdeen Village Roundabout
Aberdeen Creek
Aberdeen Junction
Wilkinson Rd
Congo Cross
Signal Hill Rd
Main Motor Rd
King St
Byrne La
Lumley Beach
Lumley Beach Rd
Wilkinson Rd
Signal Hill Rd
Lumley Village
To Lakka Beach, Peninsula Beaches & Lakka Cotton Club (50km)
Freetown Golf Club
0 0.5 1km
0 0.3 0.6mi

many still carry firearms. Violent crime is not generally a problem, but there have been a number of reports of armed robberies of expats living in private homes in Freetown. Con artists near the beaches try to sell 'diamonds', which are only shards of glass, to unsuspecting foreigners. Some even have ties to the police, who are always interested in arresting 'smugglers' who may be able to avoid jail time by offering a bribe. Most public areas including the main thoroughfares and gathering places are safe to walk, although take care after dark near the beaches.

Things to See & Do

Start your tour of Freetown by taking a walk down Siaka Stevens St. Halfway along is the 500-year-old **Cotton Tree**, the heart of town and the city's principal landmark. On Independence Ave, up the hill from the tree, is the **State House**, which is closed to the public. To the west of the Cotton Tree is the **National Museum**, which has a small but fascinating collection of tribal masks, juju trinkets and historical artefacts. To the east is a museum of another sort: the courthouse, which still bears signs of the damage caused by small arms and mortar fire during Operation No Living Thing.

Some of the old wood-framed **Krio houses** scattered throughout Freetown, particularly in the neighbourhood east of Siaka Stevens Stadium, are fascinating. Most date from the late 19th century and a few are even older.

The **Parliament** building is on Tower Hill, inland from the Paramount Hotel, although there's no public access to it. On Mt Aureol is **Fourah Bay College**, founded in 1827 by the Church Missionary Society and one of the oldest English-language universities in sub-Saharan Africa.

Magnificent views of the city and the bays can be had from **Hill Station**; take Pademba Rd south from the Cotton Tree and keep going uphill.

There are a number of rudimentary beer-shacks all along **Lumley Beach** offering sand volleyball, music and postcard views of the beach that are popular with UN and aid workers. The beach is rip-tide free and safe for swimming, although you may encounter a crab or two.

Although it's technically a members-only club, visitors can easily play a round of **golf**

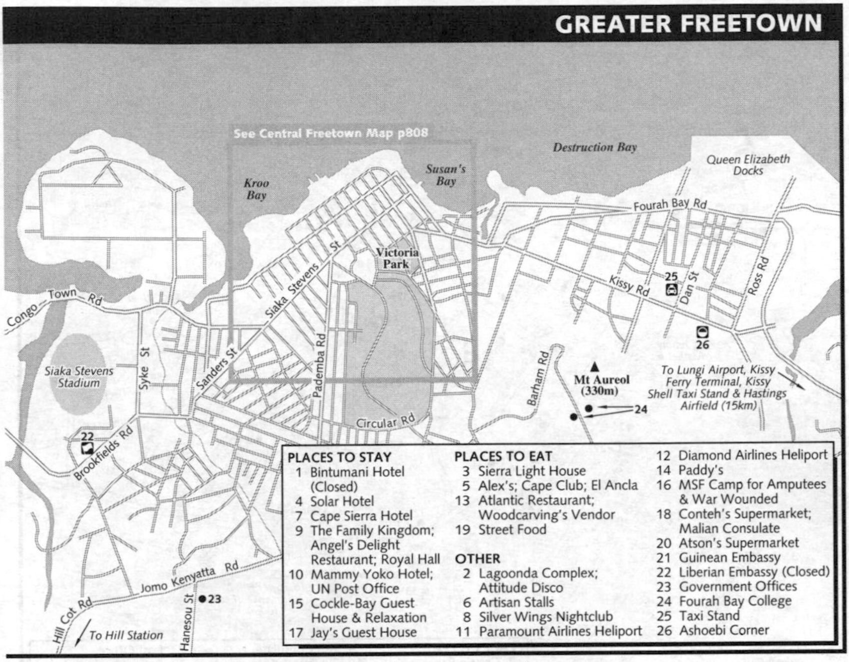
GREATER FREETOWN
See Central Freetown Map p808
Destruction Bay
Queen Elizabeth Docks
Kroo Bay
Susan's Bay
Fourah Bay Rd
Victoria Park
Siaka Stevens St
Kissy Rd
Dan St
Ross Rd
Congo Town Rd
Siaka Stevens Stadium
Syke St
Sanders St
Pademba Rd
Barham Rd
Mt Aureol (330m)
To Lungi Airport, Kissy Ferry Terminal, Kissy Shell Taxi Stand & Hastings Airfield (15km)
Circular Rd
Brookfields Rd
Jomo Kenyatta Rd
Hill Cot Rd
Hanesou St
To Hill Station
PLACES TO STAY
1 Bintumani Hotel (Closed)
4 Solar Hotel
7 Cape Sierra Hotel
9 The Family Kingdom; Angel's Delight Restaurant; Royal Hall
10 Mammy Yoko Hotel; UN Post Office
15 Cockle-Bay Guest House & Relaxation
17 Jay's Guest House
PLACES TO EAT
3 Sierra Light House
5 Alex's; Cape Club; El Ancla
13 Atlantic Restaurant; Woodcarving's Vendor
19 Street Food
OTHER
2 Lagoonda Complex; Attitude Disco
6 Artisan Stalls
8 Silver Wings Nightclub
11 Paramount Airlines Heliport
12 Diamond Airlines Heliport
14 Paddy's
16 MSF Camp for Amputees & War Wounded
18 Conteh's Supermarket; Malian Consulate
20 Atson's Supermarket
21 Guinean Embassy
22 Liberian Embassy (Closed)
23 Government Offices
24 Fourah Bay College
25 Taxi Stand
26 Ashoebi Corner

at the country's only course at Freetown Golf Club on Lumley Beach Rd, although only the truly desperate hacker will be satisfied. Wild animals, high tide and jungle obstacles make the course quite an adventure. Fees are US$5 and you can rent balls and clubs.

Places to Stay – Budget & Mid-Range

Jay's Guest House *(☎ 272470)* Rooms with fan/air-con US$40/55. This pleasant guesthouse opposite the petrol station at Aberdeen Junction has clean, comfortable rooms with bathroom. The staff here are very friendly and will help with meal arrangements. Transport, shared or private, is readily available at the taxi stand just outside the gate.

Cockle-Bay Guest House & Relaxation *(☎ 272789, 46A Cockle-Bay Rd)* Singles/doubles without bathroom US$15/20, doubles with bathroom US$40. This place, about 700m west of Aberdeen Junction, has basic rooms and can provide breakfast on request. The large double upstairs is the most comfortable and worth the extra rate.

Solar Hotel *(☎ 272531)* 2-person studios US$60, 2-person chalets US$80, 4-person cottages US$120. The Solar Hotel, 200m off Cape Rd and opposite the Mammy Yoko Hotel, is a bit run-down but is comfortable and overflowing with character. The Solar offers the best value for money. All rooms have air-con, kitchenettes and fridges. Meals at the restaurant start at about US$10. There is also a small swimming pool and a comfy open-air bar that's good for drinks at night.

Places to Stay – Top End

The hotels listed in this category are all situated in Aberdeen, at the western end of the peninsula.

Cape Sierra *(☎ 272272, Cape Rd)* Singles/doubles US$135/160. One of only two luxury hotels in operation (and the only one not occupied by Unamsil), Cape Sierra is at the northern end of Lumley Beach, overlooking an attractive stretch of sand. Air-con rooms are comfortable, but overpriced for what you get. Meals at the restaurant start at about US$11.

Mammy Yoko Hotel *(☎ 272444, Cape Rd)* Singles/doubles US$97/125. Mammy Yoko Hotel has reopened after the war only to be occupied by the UN, which uses the hotel's

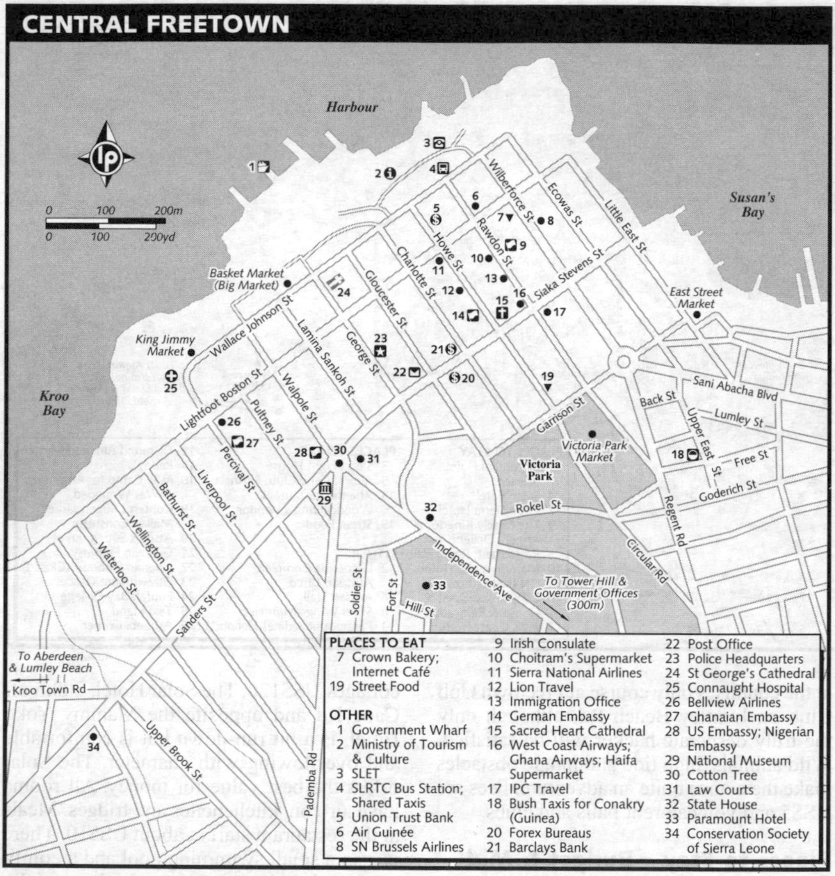
CENTRAL FREETOWN
Harbour
Susan's Bay
Kroo Bay
0 100 200m
0 100 200yd
Basket Market (Big Market)
King Jimmy Market
East Street Market
Victoria Park Market
Victoria Park
Wallace Johnson St
Lightfoot Boston St
Lamina Sankoh St
George St
Gloucester St
Charlotte St
Howe St
Rawdon St
Wilberforce St
Ecowas St
Little East St
Siaka Stevens St
Walpole St
Pultney St
Percival St
Liverpool St
Bathurst St
Wellington St
Waterloo St
Sanders St
Upper Brook St
Pademba Rd
Soldier St
Fort St
Hill St
Independence Ave
Garrison St
Rokel St
Circular Rd
Regent Rd
Upper East St
Back St
Sani Abacha Blvd
Lumley St
Free St
Goderich St
Kroo Town Rd
To Aberdeen & Lumley Beach
To Tower Hill & Government Offices (300m)
PLACES TO EAT
7 Crown Bakery; Internet Café
19 Street Food
OTHER
1 Government Wharf
2 Ministry of Tourism & Culture
3 SLET
4 SLRTC Bus Station; Shared Taxis
5 Union Trust Bank
6 Air Guinée
8 SN Brussels Airlines
9 Irish Consulate
10 Choitram's Supermarket
11 Sierra National Airlines
12 Lion Travel
13 Immigration Office
14 German Embassy
15 Sacred Heart Cathedral
16 West Coast Airways; Ghana Airways; Haifa Supermarket
17 IPC Travel
18 Bush Taxis for Conakry (Guinea)
20 Forex Bureaus
21 Barclays Bank
22 Post Office
23 Police Headquarters
24 St George's Cathedral
25 Connaught Hospital
26 Bellview Airlines
27 Ghanaian Embassy
28 US Embassy; Nigerian Embassy
29 National Museum
30 Cotton Tree
31 Law Courts
32 State House
33 Paramount Hotel
34 Conservation Society of Sierra Leone

upper floors as its Unamsil headquarters. The hotel still offers 20 comfortable 1st-floor rooms with air-con and cable TV to anyone who doesn't mind the constant hubbub of a UN mission. The hotel has a reasonably comfortable bar that offers a rudimentary breakfast and it plans to reopen its restaurant soon. Thanks to the UN, it also offers the best security of any hotel in Sierra Leone.

The Family Kingdom *(☎ 273133, 273136, Lumley Beach Rd)* 2-person studios US$70, guesthouse US$170 (sleeps 4). The most colourful and bizarre accommodation can be found at The Family Kingdom, a rambling compound of rooms, wildlife and playground equipment about 50m south of the corner of Lumley Beach and Cape Rds. All rooms have air-con, bathroom and TV. But the real attractions are inside the compound, which has enough playground equipment for several schools' worth of children, a wading pool, exercise gym and a dubious 'zoo'. The zoo is actually several cages housing aggressive and sick-looking mango monkeys, mongooses, rabbits, sea turtles and threadbare birds of prey. The complex has two restaurants, Royal Hall and Angel's Delight Restaurant (see Places to Eat).

Places to Eat

Street-food vendors, selling tasty fried pastries, dried meat and *suya* sticks (spiced beef or chicken on a kebab skewer) can be found throughout the city centre along Siaka Stevens St, along Lumley Beach Rd and at the Aberdeen village roundabout.

Crown Bakery *(☎ 222545, 6 Wilberforce St)* Mains from US$10. This bakery, near the corner of Lightfoot Boston St, is very popular and the food is delicious. Fried chicken starts at US$2; there are also sandwiches from US$2.50 and a selection of main dishes. The bakery goods are excellent.

Down the hill about 100m northwest of the Mammy Yoko Hotel are ***Alex's*** and ***Cape Club***, two popular and moderately priced bar/restaurants overlooking Man of War Bay. Both serve grills and fresh seafood for US$10 to US$20, and are good places for a drink. They're open from 11am daily (noon on Sunday).

Sierra Light House *(☎ 272110)* Fish & grills from US$5. Open from 7pm daily. The Sierra Light House is 100m past the Solar Hotel on the access road leading from Cape Rd. The food here is uninspired, but decent.

Angel's Delight Restaurant *(Lumley Beach Rd)* Meals from US$5-10. Open from 11am daily. Popular with the UN crowd for lunch and dinner, Angel's Delight, part of the Family Kingdom hotel complex, serves tasty Lebanese dishes, seafood and good pizzas.

Royal Hall *(Lumley Beach Rd)* Also at the Family Kingdom is this outdoor patio restaurant, serving basic sandwiches and burgers from US$3. It's a quiet place for lunch to escape the hubbub of the beach and often features live music and dance performances on weekend evenings.

Atlantic Restaurant Meals about US$10. This restaurant at the southern end of Lumley Beach has good fish dishes and a terrace, which is great for drinks at sunset.

For self-caterers, ***Choitram's Supermarket*** *(Rawdon St)* is well stocked, but expensive. ***Haifa Supermarket*** *(Cnr Rawdon & Siaka Stevens Sts)* is slightly cheaper. Two other good choices are ***Atson's*** and ***Conteh's***, both on Wilkinson Rd.

Entertainment

Most restaurants listed earlier are also bars.

Attitude Disco Cover charge US$7. This disco at the Lagoonda Complex near the Cape Sierra hotel in Aberdeen has good dancing on weekends. The complex also has a ***cinema*** on the ground floor, a quiet piano bar and a ***casino*** on the top floor. If you come here from the beach, though, be aware that a ban on short trousers at the complex is strictly enforced.

Silver Wings *(Cape Rd)* This place is between the Cape Sierra hotel and Aberdeen village roundabout. If you can fight your way through the prostitutes to the bar, you'll have earned yourself a drink. This lively, loud and colourful bar is popular on the weekends and is good for dancing.

Paddy's *(Cape Rd)* Sociology students will be fascinated with Paddy's on weekend nights; it attracts a baffling cross section of Freetown's population. Everyone from UN personnel to diamond smugglers to former RUF commanders bend their elbows in peace here and it is *the* destination on weekends, and often features live music as well. It's about 100m west of the Aberdeen bridge.

Alex's Sports Bar *(Off Cape Rd)* Within Alex's restaurant (see Places to Eat) is a comfortable bar with a wide-screen TV and a pool table.

Getting There & Away

Air Airlines with offices in Freetown include the following:

Bellview Airlines (☎ 227311) 31 Lightfoot Boston St
Ghana Airways (☎ 224871) 15 Siaka Stevens St
SN Brussels Airlines (☎ 226072) 14 Wilberforce St
West Coast Airways (☎ 227561) 18 Siaka Stevens St

Other airlines can be booked through IPC Travel (☎ 223551), on the corner of Siaka Stevens and Rawdon Sts.

Bus SLRTC buses leave in the mornings from the bus station (formerly the train station) on the corner of Rawdon and Wallace Johnson Sts. Buses are very crowded; you'll need to arrive an hour early to get a seat.

Bush Taxi & Minibus Bush taxis and poda-podas leave from various sites in Freetown (all in the centre or east of the centre), depending on their destination: the corner of Free and Upper East Sts for Conakry; Dan St for Bo and Kenema; Ashoebi Corner (2km east of centre on Kissy St) for Makeni and Kabala; and Kissy taxi stand (5km east of centre on Sani Abacha Blvd) also for Makeni and Kabala and other locations.

Getting Around

To/From the Airport Lungi airport (for regional and international flights) is about

25km north of central Freetown, on the other side of the river. You can cross the river in various ways, but the easiest and most hassle-free is to cross via old Russian helicopters operated by Paramount and Diamond Airlines. Both offer one-way service for US$20. Paramount will take you to the heliport 50m east of the Mammy Yoko Hotel on Cape Rd; Diamond will drop you further down Lumley Beach Rd, about 700m from Aberdeen village roundabout. Both airlines monitor arriving and departing commercial flights at Lungi and are generally reliable. Tickets to Freetown can be bought on arrival at Lungi airport from a number of helicopter service employees who stake out the baggage claim area, and return tickets to the airport are available at the heliports. Taxis stake out both heliports.

Hastings airfield (for domestic flights) is about 20km east of central Freetown (US$20 in a taxi). Allow at least 45 minutes to get there from downtown.

Shared Taxi & Poda-Podas Shared taxis in Freetown cost US$0.15 per ride; poda-podas cost US$0.10. To reach places near Lumley Beach, get a shared taxi from Siaka Stevens St to the Aberdeen village roundabout (just past the Mammy Yoko Hotel). The shared taxis then head down Lumley Beach Rd to Lumley village. At night taxis become increasingly hard to find – and more expensive – as curfew approaches (you cannot phone for one), and walking far after dark isn't advised.

Car Private cars with drivers can be hired at the Cape Sierra hotel. Expect to pay about US$150 per day with driver within Freetown, US$200 around the Freetown peninsula, and up to US$350 per day for 4WDs upcountry.

Taxi Freetown taxis don't have meters. A trip from Siaka Stevens St to the Lumley Beach area costs about US$2 if you bargain well. Longer hires in the city are about US$4 per hour.

AROUND FREETOWN

Be warned: land mines were planted in some areas of the **Freetown peninsula** during the 1997 and 1999 fighting. Make inquiries locally before venturing off main roads.

Bunce Island

Bunce (bun-see) Island is at the mouth of the Sierra Leone River, 18km east of Freetown. Its major attraction is the ruined fortress. First built in 1663 by the British as a trading base, it was levelled to the ground in 1702 by French warships. The ruins are of a second fort built soon after.

After the original British and French occupations, the fort was held by the Dutch, the Portuguese and the British (again). From 1750 to 1800, the island became notorious as one of the major collection points for slaves destined for Europe and the Americas. (The Gullah people of South Carolina are thought to have come from here.) Efforts are now being made to preserve its long-forgotten ruins.

Hiring a boat to get to Bunce is prohibitively expensive (US$150), and visitors are likely to be turned away at the shore once they arrive: RUF leader Fodoy Sankoh is currently being held there following several attempts by his supporters to get him out of the Freetown prison.

Beaches

Freetown lies at the northern end of a 40km-long mountainous peninsula with some of the best beaches in West Africa stretching along the western side of the peninsula. To reach the beaches by shared taxi from Freetown, stay in the vehicle past Aberdeen Junction to Lumley village, 4km further south, from where bush taxis and poda-podas run down the rutted dirt coastal road. Some tracks to the beaches aren't clear, so you may have to ask for directions.

South of Lumley village, 4km after Goderich village junction, is the turn-off for **Lakka Beach**. Lakka village is 2km further south, followed by **Hamilton Beach**.

Lakka Cotton Club *(Lakka Beach)* Doubles US$15. About an hour south of Aberdeen by shared taxi is the bucolic Lakka Cotton Club. Clean, comfortable beachfront apartments with bathroom and fan offer unparalleled views of the deserted white-sand cove. The resort has a clean pool, bar, restaurant and dilapidated tennis courts. Several small beach bars and restaurants are within an easy stroll. There is no phone, however, and it's far off the beaten track, so arrange return transport in advance. Also, be

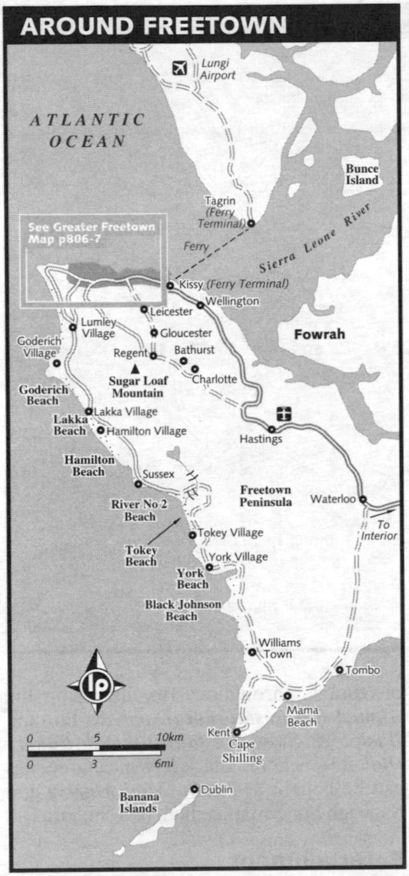
AROUND FREETOWN
Lungi Airport
ATLANTIC OCEAN
Bunce Island
Tagrin (Ferry Terminal)
See Greater Freetown Map p806-7
Ferry
Sierra Leone River
Kissy (Ferry Terminal)
Wellington
Leicester
Lumley Village
Goderich Village
Gloucester
Fowrah
Regent
Bathurst
Sugar Loaf Mountain
Charlotte
Goderich Beach
Lakka Village
Lakka Beach
Hamilton Village
Hastings
Hamilton Beach
Sussex
Freetown Peninsula
Waterloo
River No 2 Beach
To Interior
Tokey Village
Tokey Beach
York Village
York Beach
Black Johnson Beach
Williams Town
Tombo
Mama Beach
Kent
Cape Shilling
0 5 10km
0 3 6mi
Dublin
Banana Islands

aware that Lakka is the weekend destination for overworked aid workers and UN personnel; all-night parties are the norm.

The choicest beach of all is **River No 2**, halfway down the peninsula. Basic ***beach huts*** can be hired for US$3 per day; there's also a more expensive ***stone hut*** with simple beds and mosquito nets. Otherwise, you can pitch a tent. Arrangements can be made at IPC Travel on the corner of Rawdon and Siaka Stevens Sts in Freetown. Bring your own drinking water. Meals can be arranged with locals.

Attractive **Tokey Beach** is the cheapest place from which to hire a boat to the Banana Islands (see the following section). For a shorter boat trip, go up River No 2 to the waterfalls.

A few kilometres further south is York village, with **York Beach** nearby and **Black Johnson Beach** across the bay (5km by road). Some 20km further at the end of the peninsula is Kent village.

Banana Islands

Diving and snorkelling are superb off the Banana Islands, which are off the southeastern tip of the peninsula. The fishing is good too. In Dublin village, on the northern tip of the main island, there are the remains of a church, built in 1881, and a slave centre. Pay your respects to the chief before going off exploring and the locals will happily provide a tour guide. From June until the end of the rainy season, the seas are much too rough for excursions.

The best way to get to the Banana Islands is to hire a local fishing boat at Tokey Beach for US$50 (for the entire boat, including driver and food) if your negotiating skills are tuned up, which includes a lavish seafood meal upon your return. It's a three-hour round trip and you should allow at least an hour or more to explore the ruins in Dublin. You can also hire boats at Kent village at the southernmost tip of the peninsula and from Freetown.

The South & East

Southeastern Sierra Leone is humid, low-lying and forested. It also has the country's major diamond-mining areas, notably Tongo Field between Kenema and Koidu-Sefadu which, along with Koindu in the far-eastern tongue of the country, are also diamond-trading and smuggling centres. Areas such as Kailahun, Pendembu and Koindu east of Kenema are completely destroyed, clogged with refugees and still-active units of RUF and pro-government militias. Travel to these areas is not off limits, but it's definitely not advised. Many bridges leading to these areas were destroyed in the war and the only way in or out is via private 4WD or helicopter.

BO

☎ 032

Sierra Leone's second-largest city, Bo is a lively, pleasant town in the heart of Mende country. Although it suffered during the fighting between 1997 and 2001, with

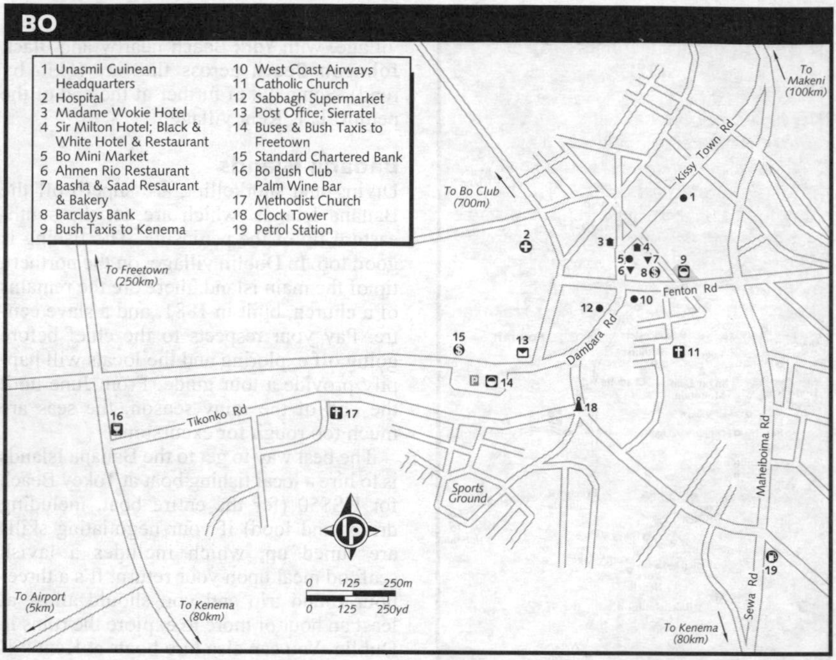
BO
1 Unasmil Guinean Headquarters
2 Hospital
3 Madame Wokie Hotel
4 Sir Milton Hotel; Black & White Hotel & Restaurant
5 Bo Mini Market
6 Ahmen Rio Restaurant
7 Basha & Saad Resaurant & Bakery
8 Barclays Bank
9 Bush Taxis to Kenema
10 West Coast Airways
11 Catholic Church
12 Sabbagh Supermarket
13 Post Office; Sierratel
14 Buses & Bush Taxis to Freetown
15 Standard Chartered Bank
16 Bo Bush Club Palm Wine Bar
17 Methodist Church
18 Clock Tower
19 Petrol Station
To Makeni (100km)
Kissy Town Rd
To Bo Club (700m)
Fenton Rd
Dambara Rd
To Freetown (250km)
Tikonko Rd
Sports Ground
Maheiboima Rd
Sewa Rd
To Airport (5km)
To Kenema (80km)
To Kenema (80km)
0 125 250m
0 125 250yd

almost all residents at least temporarily uprooted, it's now bustling again with diamond merchants, people from nongovernmental organisations (NGOs) and businessmen.

Places to Stay & Eat

Sir Milton Hotel Singles/doubles with bathroom US$15/20, doubles with air-con US$30. This centrally located hotel has clean rooms. The restaurant and outdoor patio serve very good groundnut stew and grills from US$2.

Madame Wokie Hotel Singles/doubles with bathroom US$15/20, rooms with air-con US$30. The Madame Wokie is the Sir Milton's slightly more run-down sister hotel across Dambara Rd. Rooms are basically the same, but there's no bar or restaurant.

Black & White Hotel & Restaurant Meals US$5. In spite of its name, the Black & White no longer offers accommodation, but the upstairs bar and restaurant have a commanding view of Bo's main intersection. The restaurant serves excellent groundnut stew and other local dishes.

Cheap and filling Lebanese and African food can be found at a number of small restaurants throughout Bo, including the ***Ahmed Rio Restaurant*** *(Dambara Rd)* and ***Basha & Saad Restaurant and Bakery*** *(Bojon St)* near the Black & White. Groceries can be bought at the ***Bo Mini Market*** and Sabbagh Supermarket, both on Dambara Rd.

Entertainment

At dusk in Bo, there's not much to do but camp out in your hotel bar and watch the passing crowds.

Black & White Hotel & Restaurant The breezy upstairs bar at the Black & White is a good place to relax in the afternoon and is a magnet for the town's singles on weekend nights.

Getting There & Away

West Coast Airways at 16 Fenton St flies between Freetown, Bo and Kenema (US$50) on Monday to Saturday, with a comfortable 15-seat prop plane. Bush taxis go regularly to Freetown (US$6, from Dambara Rd) and Kenema (US$2, from Fenton Rd). There's a daily SLRTC bus to Freetown (US$4, 6½ hours), departing about 7.30am from the bus and bush taxi stand on Dambara Rd. The buses always leave full; queues begin as early as 5am.

KENEMA

Kenema, once Sierra Leone's timber capital, is now its diamond capital while the diamond districts in Kono struggle with security and infrastructure issues. The main artery, Hangha Rd, is a crush of Lebanese diamond merchants and Sierra Leonean diggers and miners. Kenema is worth a visit to see diamond trading. On the northwest edge of town is **Kambui Hills Forest Reserve**, a large, woodland area and a good place for a walk.

Things to See & Do

It's enjoyable to stroll through Kenema's massive **markets** on Maxwell Khobe St and Hangha Rd. If you're interested, you can even buy a *shake-shake*, a circular mesh sieve that the diggers use to find diamonds in Kenema's many alluvial mines. Drop in on the friendly Lebanese **diamond merchants** and they may even let you eyeball the 'goods', raw stones that will eventually be turned into expensive jewellery sold around the world. It may be possible to visit a **mine** if you've got the stamina to endure the interrogation as to why you want to; inquire at the local office of the Minister of Mines and Natural Resources, which will be located in the administration block being built on Hangha Rd. Do not try to visit a mine without clearance.

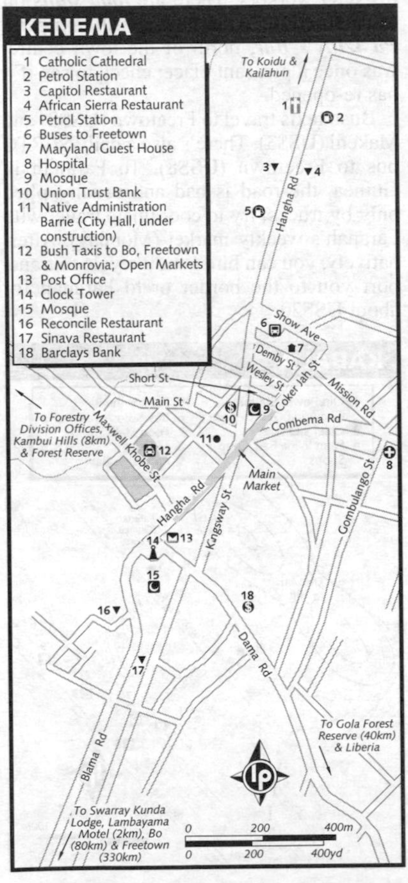
KENEMA
1 Catholic Cathedral
2 Petrol Station
3 Capitol Restaurant
4 African Sierra Restaurant
5 Petrol Station
6 Buses to Freetown
7 Maryland Guest House
8 Hospital
9 Mosque
10 Union Trust Bank
11 Native Administration Barrie (City Hall, under construction)
12 Bush Taxis to Bo, Freetown & Monrovia; Open Markets
13 Post Office
14 Clock Tower
15 Mosque
16 Reconcile Restaurant
17 Sinava Restaurant
18 Barclays Bank
To Koidu & Kailahun
Hangha Rd
Show Ave
Demby St
Wesley St
Coker Jah St
Mission Rd
Short St
Main St
Combema Rd
To Forestry Division Offices, Kambui Hills (8km) & Forest Reserve
Maxwell Khobe St
Main Market
Kingsway St
Gombulango St
Dama Rd
Blama Rd
To Gola Forest Reserve (40km) & Liberia
To Swarray Kunda Lodge, Lambayama Motel (2km), Bo (80km) & Freetown (330km)
0
200
400m
0
200
400yd

Places to Stay & Eat

Lodging options in Kenema are slim; the best bet is ***Lambayama Motel** (2 Aruna St)* about 2km east of the city centre, which has dirty singles for US$15. It also has a bar and a small, uncomfortable restaurant. The nearby ***Swarray Kunda Lodge*** is a similarly priced option, but has been the scene recently of at least one armed robbery and a number of 'fishing' incidents. This is a creative style of theft in which thieves use fishing poles to get beyond the bars on the windows to hook what they can. The only other option in town is the dismal ***Maryland Guest House** (Demby St)*, with hot, grimy singles for US$10. You'll need to look hard to find the entrance sawn out of the zinc corrugated sheeting.

Food options are better, but only slightly so. ***Sinava*** and ***Reconcile*** restaurants on Blama Rd are popular places for drinks and basic chicken-and-rice dishes for around US$5. ***The Capital Restaurant*** is a good restaurant on Hangha Rd with African and Lebanese dishes from US$10 and sandwiches from US$5. Across the street is the small and dilapidated ***African Sierra Restaurant***, which serves excellent African dishes. ***Street-food vendors*** are plentiful.

For drinks at night, your best bets are ***Reconcile*** or ***The Capital***.

Getting There & Away

West Coast Airways flies between Freetown, Bo and Kenema (US$50) Monday to Saturday, with a comfortable 15-seat propellor plane. SLRTC buses to Freetown (US$5) depart every morning from the bus station north of the centre. Bush taxis to Bo (US$2), Freetown, Monrovia in Liberia (about US$20) and most other destinations depart from the taxi park near the Maxwell Khobe St market. The hour-long ride to Bo is on a good tar road, the best in Sierra Leone. However, the ride south towards Monrovia is long and bumpy. Kenema to Fairo and the Mano River bridge (the Liberian border) is an all-day trip in the rainy season.

Travel around Kenema is best done on the back of a motorcycle for US$0.50.

The North

Northern Sierra Leone is the homeland of the Temne people. The landscape is higher and drier than in the southeast. Where they haven't been cultivated, the undulating hills are covered in light bush or savanna woodland, although ribbons of dense forest run along the major rivers. The hills become mountains in several places, with many peaks rising above 1500m. At the heart of the Loma Mountains in the northeast is Mt Bintumani (1945m).

MAKENI

☎ 052

Makeni, capital of the northern province, was once a busy town with a beautiful mosque; in the wake of the war, it's now a shadow of its former self, populated almost entirely by RUF political and military bosses. Though it still has a busy and well-stocked market in the town centre, there are no guesthouses and little for tourists to see and do. Despite the presence of Unamsil soldiers, the security situation is tenuous at best.

Bush taxis go daily to Freetown (US$5) and Kabala (US$3). The daily SLRTC bus to Freetown costs US$3.

OUTAMBA-KILIMI NATIONAL PARK

This national park (which is also called Kamakwie National Park or OKNP), near the border with Guinea, is a beautiful, peaceful place where you can experience some real West African wilderness. The park is easily reached by 4WD, or by public transport in the dry season. There are no roads inside the park, so visitors are encouraged to explore on foot or by canoe.

Getting there is a challenge given Makeni's barely functional circumstances. For further information, inquire in Freetown at IPC Travel.

KABALA

Kabala, the largest town in northern Sierra Leone, is at the end of the tar road and the last place of any size en route to Faranah, across the border in Guinea. It's quiet and friendly and well worth a visit. Local guides will be happy to lead you on a hike of the Gbawuria (**bow**-ree-ah) Hill, which overlooks the town and hosts a colourful all-night New Year's Eve celebration.

Gbawuria Guest House, on the western side of town, is the only place to stay. It has clean rooms for US$3, but it's usually full of NGO workers. There are ***food stalls*** on the main street north of the bush taxi park. ***Pa Willy's Bar***, north of the town centre, was once a pleasant place; check to see if it has re-opened.

Bush taxis travel to Freetown (US$8) and Makeni (US$3). There's also a daily SLRTC bus to Freetown (US$8). To Faranah in Guinea, the road is bad and usually plied only by trucks; try to coordinate travel with Faranah's weekly market (Monday). Alternatively, you can hire a motorcycle to transport you to the border or to Faranah for about US$20.

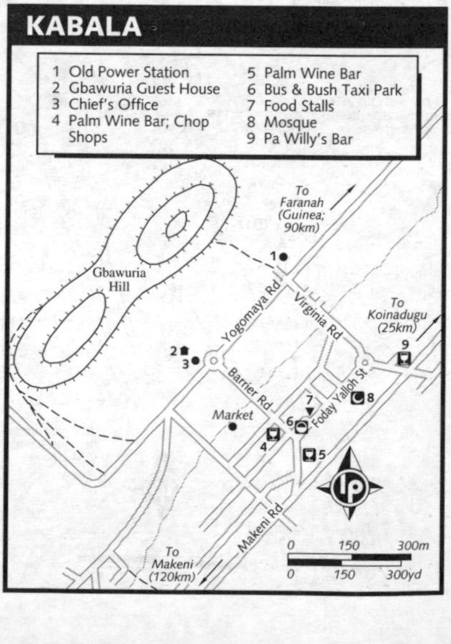
KABALA
1 Old Power Station
2 Gbawuria Guest House
3 Chief's Office
4 Palm Wine Bar; Chop Shops
5 Palm Wine Bar
6 Bus & Bush Taxi Park
7 Food Stalls
8 Mosque
9 Pa Willy's Bar
To Faranah (Guinea; 90km)
Gbawuria Hill
Yogomaya Rd
Virginia Rd
To Koinadugu (25km)
Barrier Rd
Market
Foday Yalloh St
Makeni Rd
To Makeni (120km)
0 150 300m
0 150 300yd

MT BINTUMANI

This mountain is situated at the centre of the Loma Mountains, 60km southeast of Kabala. In clear weather, views from the summit are excellent. The area around the mountain is the homeland of the Koranko people; some sections have been listed as a reserve, protecting the highland rainforest covering the lower slopes. The forest on the west side of the range is more impressive and in better condition.

There are several species of monkey and chimpanzee here. Above 1500m the forest gives way to grassland where you can spot baboons, wart hogs, duikers, porcupines and even buffaloes. In the rivers you may be lucky enough to see pygmy hippopotamuses and dwarf crocodiles, both very rare. The endangered rufous fishing-owl can also be seen in this area.

You can approach the mountain from Kabala via Koinadugu and Firawa, but it's more usual to approach from **Yifin** village (from where it's at least a four-day walk to and from the summit), east of the dirt road between Kabala and Bumbuna, or from **Kurubonla**, north of Kono (three days).

Take a guide (many paths are overgrown) and possibly porters, as you need to be self-sufficient with camping gear and food for at least five days. Buy all your food in Kabala (or Kono, if it has re-opened to travellers). Before setting out, get a briefing on the security situation in Freetown or Kabala.

Pay your respects to the chief in either Firawa, Yifin or Kurubonla (a gift of kola nuts or about US$1 is sufficient), and he'll help you find a guide and porters (about US$1 per day), and arrange accommodation with local people for around US$1.

Togo

For many years tiny Togo, a thin sliver of land wedged between Ghana, Burkina Faso and Benin, was one of West Africa's top travel destinations. Its deserted beaches, hiking, fascinating culture and friendly people made the country a traveller's paradise. The political turbulence in the early 1990s reduced the stream to a trickle, but in recent years the tide has been turning and slowly travellers are again being drawn by Togo's many charms.

Lomé, the capital, and the nearby beaches are the main attractions. On the coast at Aného you can observe life in a traditional fishing village or cross nearby Lake Togo in a canoe and visit Togoville, a fetish centre.

Upcountry, you'll pass through some beautiful hills and plateaus on your way to the northern national parks. The region around Kpalimé, near the Ghanaian border in the southwest, is scenic and known for its butterflies. The famous fortress-like mud-brick houses of the Tamberma people can be seen in the Kabyé region around Kara, a place that has withstood the onslaught of modernisation.

Togo at a Glance

Capital: Lomé
Population: 5 million
Area: 56,790 sq km
Head of State: President Gnassingbé Eyadéma
Official language: French
Main local languages: Ewe, Mina, Kabyé
Currency: West African CFA franc
Exchange rate: US$1 = CFA694
Time: GMT/UTC
Telephone country code: ☎ 228
Best time to go: Mid-July to mid-September

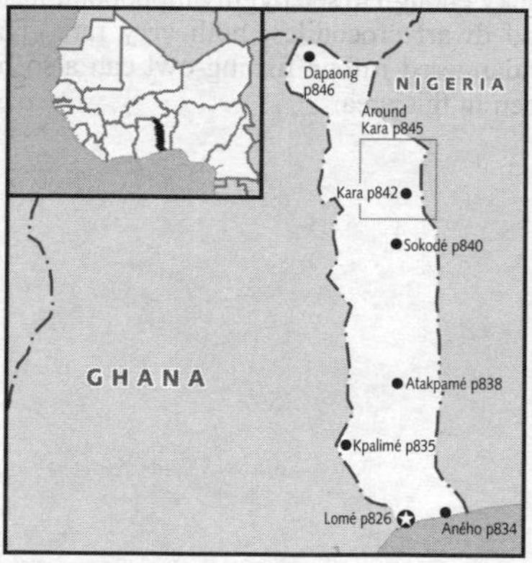
Dapaong p846
NIGERIA
Around Kara p845
Kara p842
Sokodé p840
GHANA
Atakpamé p838
Kpalimé p835
Lomé p826
Aného p834

Highlights

- Discovering the crumbling colonial charm of Aného, the former capital, set on a picturesque lagoon
- Hiking the beautiful hill country surrounding Kpalimé, well known for its butterflies
- Browsing through the bewildering collection of traditional medicines and fetishes on offer at the Marché des Fétiches in Lomé
- Enjoying Lake Togo's water sports, including windsurfing and water-skiing
- Having fun bargaining with Mama Benz, the smart wealthy women traders of Lomé's Grand Marché
- Gazing at the extraordinary tata compounds, built without tools, in the Tamberma Valley

Facts about Togo

HISTORY

The region that is now Togo was once at the edge of several empires, including the Dahomey and Akan-Ashanti, but never played a pivotal role in any. Various tribes moved into the country from all sides – the Ewe from Nigeria and Benin, and the Mina and Guin from Ghana – and settled along the coast.

With the establishment of a European presence in the 16th century, the zone created by this power vacuum was exploited as a conduit for the slave trade. The Mina benefited the most and became ruthless agents for the European slave-traders.

Colonial Period

With the abolition of slavery, by the mid-19th century, the Europeans turned their attention to trade in commodities – palm and coconut oil, cacao, coffee and cotton. The rivalry between Britain and France was

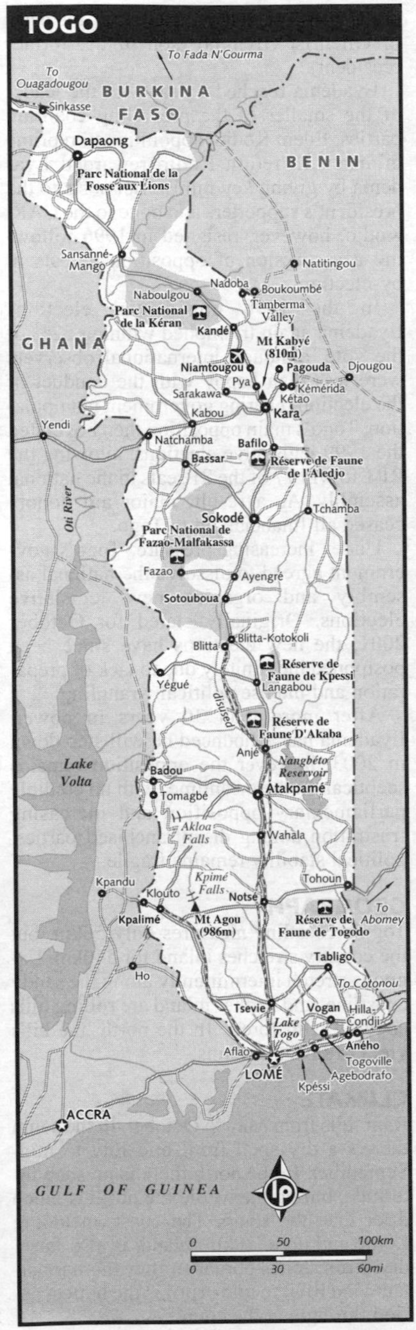
TOGO
To Fada N'Gourma
To Ouagadougou
BURKINA FASO
Sinkasse
Dapaong
BENIN
Parc National de la Fosse aux Lions
Sansanné-Mango
Natitingou
Nadoba
Boukoumbé
Naboulgou
Tamberma Valley
Parc National de la Kéran
Kandé
GHANA
Mt Kabyé (810m)
Niamtougou
Pagouda
Djougou
Pya
Kémérida
Sarakawa
Kétao
Kabou
Kara
Yendi
Natchamba
Bafilo
Bassar
Réserve de Faune de l'Aledjo
Oti River
Tchamba
Sokodé
Parc National de Fazao-Malfakassa
Fazao
Ayengré
Sotouboua
Blitta
Blitta-Kotokoli
Réserve de Faune de Kpessi
Yégué
Langabou
disused
Réserve de Faune D'Akaba
Anjé
Lake Volta
Nangbéto Reservoir
Badou
Tomagbé
Atakpamé
Akloa Falls
Wahala
Tohoun
Kpandu
Kpimé Falls
Klouto
Notsé
To Abomey
Kpalimé
Mt Agou (986m)
Réserve de Faune de Togodo
Tabligo
Ho
To Cotonou
Tsevie
Vogan
Hilla-Condji
Lake Togo
Aného
Aflao
LOMÉ
Togoville
Agbodrafo
Kpéssi
ACCRA
GULF OF GUINEA
0
50
100km
0
30
60mi

fierce. Germany, however, surprised them both by sending a ship to the coast of 'Togoland', as they called this area, in 1884. They signed a treaty in Togoville with local king, Mlapa, agreeing to 'protect' the inhabitants in return for German sovereignty.

Under the Germans, Togoland underwent considerable economic development before WWI. The Togolese, however, didn't appreciate the German's forced labour, direct taxes and 'pacification' campaigns, in which thousands of locals were killed, and so with the outbreak of WWI in 1914, they welcomed British forces with open arms. Encircled by British and French colonies, the Germans surrendered – the Allies' first victory in WWI.

After the war, Togoland was divided in two. Under the League of Nations mandate, France acquired the eastern two-thirds of the country and Britain the remainder, effectively dividing the populous Ewe.

Independence

After WWII, political groups on both sides of divided 'Togo' agitated for reunification. Following a 1956 plebiscite, hopes of reunification were dashed, when British Togoland was incorporated into the Gold Coast (current-day Ghana), which was on the brink of independence.

In 1956, French Togoland to the east became an autonomous republic. Then, in 1960, it gained full independence under the leadership of Sylvanus Olympio, who became the country's first president.

In 1963, Togo became the first African country to experience a military coup following independence. Olympio, a Ewe from the south, appeared to disregard the interests of northerners (whom he described as *petits nordiques*, or small northerners). When he refused to integrate into his army some 600 soldiers returning from the Algerian War, these predominantly Kabyé northerners rebelled. Olympio was killed at the gates of the US embassy as he sought refuge. He was replaced by Nicolas Grunitzky, who in turn was deposed in a bloodless coup headed by Étienne Eyadéma, a Kabyé from the north.

Eyadéma set out to unify the country's tribal groups, insisting on one trade union and one political party, the Rassemblement du Peuple Togolais (RPT). He established a cult of personality, surrounding himself with sycophantic staff and a chorus of cheering women in traditional dress.

On 24 January 1974, Eyadéma's private plane crashed near Sarakawa. Convinced that he had survived an assassination attempt, he became increasingly irrational and unpredictable.

Togo in the 1990s & Today

During 1990, France began pressuring Eyadéma to support a multiparty system. Eyadéma resisted and tried to portray African multiparty systems in a negative light by broadcasting scenes of strikes and violence in nearby countries on Togo's state-run TV station. In early 1991, prodemocracy forces started rioting and striking. Eyadéma responded by sending out his troops, who killed many of the protesters. In April 1991, 28 bodies were dragged out of Lomé-Bé Lagoon and dumped on the steps of the US embassy, indicating to the world the repressive nature of Eyadéma's dictatorship.

Finally bowing to international pressure Eyadéma agreed to a national conference in 1991 to decide the country's future. Delegates at the conference stripped Eyadéma of all his powers and installed an interim government, headed by Joseph Koffigoh, pending democratic elections. Months later, however, troops loyal to Eyadéma attacked Koffigoh's residence and detained him, leaving Eyadéma, once again, in full control of the government.

Once back in power, Eyadéma postponed the promised elections, prompting the trade unions to call a general strike in November 1992. The strike continued for months paralysing Togo's economy – banks and industries closed, exports lay stranded in deserted ports and tourism collapsed. In the ensuing violence some 250,000 southerners fled to neighbouring countries.

Eyadéma then won the August 1993 presidential elections in a contest boycotted by the opposition and denounced by international observers. In the following 1994 parliamentary elections, a coalition of two opposition parties, the Committee for Renewed Action (CAR) and The Union Togolaise Démocratique (UTD), won by a slim majority. The elections, however, were marred by the killing of three opposition members and were boycotted by the Union des Forces du Changement (UFC), the party of Gilchrist Olympio (son of the former president).

Eyadéma reached a deal with the leader of the smaller of the prevailing coalition parties, Edem Kodjo, appointing him prime minister. In return Kodjo rewarded Eyadéma by giving key ministerial posts to the president's supporters and none to the CAR. Kodjo, however, resigned in 1996 following a succession of opposition defeats in by-elections.

In the 1998 presidential elections Eyadéma again triumphed winning 52% of the vote, although international observers were less than happy with the conduct of the election. Fearing government manipulation, Togo's main opposition then boycotted the 1999 legislative elections, allowing the RPT to win 77 of the 81 seats in the national assembly. As a result, major aid donors ceased all financial aid to Togo.

Under increasing pressure, Togo's government agreed to dissolve the national assembly and organise new legislative elections. Originally slated for October 2001, the new elections have since been postponed indefinitely due to lack of preparation and intense political wrangling.

After more than 30 years in power, Eyadéma has announced he will step down in 2003, however the opposition remains sceptical. In the meantime, with no credible parliamentary opposition and increasing frustration among disenfranchised parties, political stability remains fragile.

GEOGRAPHY

Togo's coastline measures only 56km, but the country stretches inland for 540km. Lagoons stretch intermittently along the sandy coastline, and further inland are rolling hills covered with forest. In the north, the hills yield to savanna plains.

CLIMATE

Rain falls from May to October. In the south there's a dry spell from mid-July to mid-September. In the north there is no such interlude, but on the whole the north is much drier than the south. The coast, including Lomé and up to 10km inland, is also fairly dry. From mid-February (after the harmattan wind lifts) to mid-April is the hottest period throughout the country.

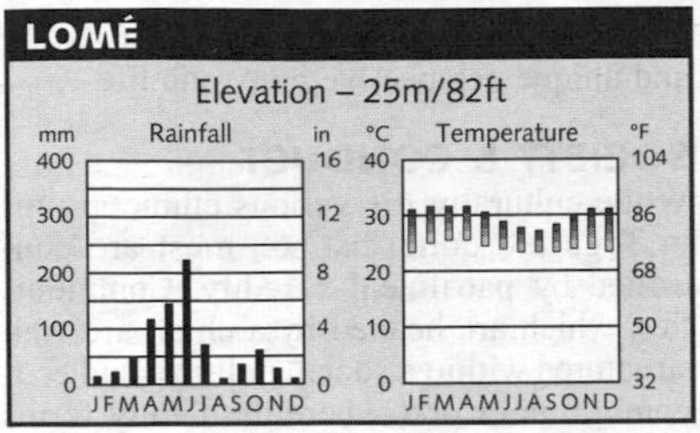
LOMÉ
Elevation – 25m/82ft
mm
Rainfall
in
°C
Temperature
°F
400
16
40
104
300
12
30
86
200
8
20
68
100
4
10
50
0
0
0
32
JFMAMJJASOND
JFMAMJJASOND

ECOLOGY & ENVIRONMENT

The pressure for land combined with lack of government commitment, scarce financial resources and entrenched but damaging traditional practices such as slash-and-burn agriculture, have taken a heavy toll on Togo's environment. In more recent times attempts have been made by forestry managers to involve local communities in the care of reafforested areas. In return for access to forests to retrieve fruits etc and some firewood, local farmers are asked to help in the prevention of forest fires – in the past they often deliberately lit fires to show their resentment at being denied access to protected areas.

The situation in Togo's national parks is particularly bad – very little wildlife remains and poaching and deforestation continue unhindered. The coastline is also in a precarious state. Since the construction of a second pier at Lomé's port, several beaches have disappeared. Pollution compounds the situation.

FLORA & FAUNA

Togo's two main wildlife reserves – Parc National de la Kéran and Parc National Fazao-Malfakassa – are disappointing as the larger mammals have largely been killed off. The Swiss Foundation Franz Weber is desperately trying to resurrect the latter park. Those mammals that remain, including buffaloes, antelopes and deer, are limited to the north while crocodiles and hippos are found in the rivers.

GOVERNMENT & POLITICS

Togo is technically a republic with a president elected by popular vote for a five-year term. However, you have to question how democratic a country is when the same president has clung to power for more than 30 years (see History earlier in this chapter for details). The next presidential elections are slated for 2003.

Togo's parliament is unicameral, consisting of the 81-seat national assembly whose members are elected for five-year terms. Executive power resides in the cabinet headed by the prime minister, who is appointed by the president.

ECONOMY

Togo's economy is reliant on agriculture, which contributes 42% of GDP and is the livelihood of 65% of the population. Collectively, cocoa, coffee, and cotton form 40% of exports. The industrial sector is dominated by phosphate mining, with Togo the world's fourth-largest producer.

The government's decade-long reform efforts stalled following the political unrest of 1992 to 1993. The modern sector collapsed, the tax base shrunk and GDP fell by 22% in just two years. But, it was the 50% devaluation of the CFA in 1994 that forced the government to launch renewed structural reforms.

After a brief period of modest growth, the Togolese economy was hit hard by a number of crises, which sent the country's economy spiralling again. Already weakened by the four-month energy crisis in 1998, the economy was further affected by the deteriorating social and political climate that followed the 1998 presidential elections and, most significantly, the withdrawal of financial assistance from major aid donors. This, combined with depressed commodity prices, hindered growth. However, in 1999, growth resumed and GDP increased by 3%.

During 2001 some of Togo's financial woes eased slightly with the signing of a multimillion dollar oil contract with the Togo Hunt Oil Company and China's cancellation of two-thirds of Togo's debt totalling some CFA18,800 million. Economic growth is predicted to continue.

POPULATION & PEOPLE

With about 40 ethnic groups and a population of some five million people, Togo has one of the more heterogeneous populations in Africa. The two largest groups are the Ewe and the Kabyé. The Kabyé (related to the Tamberma), who count President Eyadéma among their number, are concentrated in the north around Kara and in the centre.

The Ewe-related people are concentrated in the south, particularly on the cacao and coffee plantations in the southwest. They include the Anlo, Adja, Pla-Peda, Mina and Guin people. Although they call themselves Ewe, some of these groups, such as the Mina and the Guin, are not ethnic Ewe. The Guin are Ga people from Accra, while the Mina are Fanti people from the coast of Ghana. For more details on the Ewe, see the 'Peoples of West Africa' special section.

ARTS

Arts & Craftwork

The traditional arts and crafts of Togo are as varied as the people. In the remote northeast you'll find that ironwork, pottery and weaving predominates, while in the northwest decorative wood burning (the marking of wood or calabashes with intricate geometric designs) is common.

Batik and wax printing is popular throughout the country, but the most well-known textile is the Ewe kente cloth, which is usually less brilliantly coloured than the more famous Ashanti kente cloth.

Music & Dance

Music and dance plays an important part in the daily lives of the Togolese people. Dances revolve around traditional Togolese life incorporating themes such as hunting, fishing, warfare, harvesting and love.

As to be expected, there are diverse ranges of musical styles. While drums play a pivotal role in all festivities, in the south you'll find percussion instruments such as bells and gongs, in the central region you'll find *lithophones* (percussion instruments made of stone) and in the north flutes and a musical bow (an instrument played while holding an arrow).

Today, traditional music has fused with the contemporary sounds of West Africa, the Caribbean and South America to create a musical hybrid that includes highlife, reggae and soukous. Togo's most famous singing export was Bella Bellow, who dominated the local music scene until her death in 1973.

Literature

The country's best-known author is Tété-Michel Kpomassie, who was raised in a traditional Togolese family. Kpomassie's most famous book is *An African in Greenland*, an autobiography containing his fascinating and unique perspective on Arctic life.

SOCIETY & CONDUCT

While culturally the various ethnic groups in Togo are quite distinct, most are controlled by patrilineal heredity. Communities, which are headed by a chief, are well structured within a social, political and economic framework, where the family forms the heart and strong social-minded values are encouraged.

Customs, rites and superstitions play a large part in everyday life, with milestones such as births, puberty, marriage and death celebrated with fervour and associated with customary ceremonies (see boxed text 'Ewe & the Afterlife'). If you get the opportunity to attend one of these ceremonies, be respectful of local customs and be sure to dress conservatively.

Everyday conversations are often loud and animated, and minor disagreements can quickly escalate into heated arguments. But, disputes subside as quickly as they begin and within a matter of minutes adversaries are friends again. While these arguments are quite common it is totally unacceptable and ill-advised for visitors to emulate this behaviour.

The Togolese are proud and hospitable people, and readily welcome visitors into their homes. Be polite and do not flash your wealth. Also bear in mind that learning a few basic words will be hugely appreciated.

Ewe & the Afterlife

Togo's diverse cultural composition has given rise to a rich array of traditional practices. Many of the Ewe's funeral rites and conceptions of afterlife and death have a strong animist element.

According to the Ewe, once a person dies their *djoto* (reincarnated soul) will come back in the next child born into the same lineage, while their *luvo* (death soul) may linger with those still living, seeking attention and otherwise creating havoc. Funerals are one of the most important events in Ewe society and involve several nights of drumming and dancing, followed by a series of rituals to help free the soul of the deceased and influence its reincarnation.

RELIGION

Approximately 29% of Togolese are Christians, 12% are Muslims and the remaining 59% are animists.

LANGUAGE

French is the official language. The main African languages are Ewe, Mina and Kabyé, the language of the current president. For useful phrases in French, Ewe, Mina and Kabyé, see the Language chapter.

Facts for the Visitor

SUGGESTED ITINERARIES

Allow a week for exploring Lomé and surrounds, two weeks if you include Kpalimé and the central towns, and three weeks if you go to the far north for.

Within easy reach of Lomé, the Friday market in Vogan is particularly interesting; you can combine this trip with one to Aného, and spend a few days at Lake Togo. The area around Kpalimé, northeast of Lomé, is a great place to go hiking. From here, you could head for Atakpamé and the Akloa waterfalls outside Badou, then continue to Kara, a good area for cycling. The Tamberma Valley in the far north is home to the fascinating Tamberma people and well worth a visit. Also worth a short visit are Togo's two national parks: Fazao-Malfakassa in the central region and Kéran in the north.

PLANNING

The best time to visit is during the dry season (mid-July to mid-September in the south) when the roads are in good order. Unfortunately, this coincides with the dusty harmattan and is a rotten time for photographers.

The 1:500,000 *Carte Générale du Togo* (1991, L'Institut Géographique National) is the best and most recent country map available at bookshops in Lomé.

TOURIST OFFICES

The only tourist office is the Direction de la Promotion Touristique (☎ 221 43 13, 221 56 62) on Rue du Lac Togo in Lomé.

VISAS & DOCUMENTS

Visas

Visas are required for everyone except nationals of Economic Community of West African States (Ecowas) countries. Currently one-week extendable visas (CFA10,000) are issued at major border crossings with Ghana (Aflao/Lomé), Benin (Hilla-Condji) and Burkina Faso (Sinkasse). But it is essential to double-check this with a Togolese embassy or consulate (a French embassy or consulate in lieu), as the visa situation can change quite regularly.

Visa Extensions The *sûreté* (police station) in Lomé on Rue du Maréchal Joffre issues visa extensions within three days. They cost about CFA10,000 (depending on the length and type of visa) and four photos are required. The visa section is open from 7.30am to 11.30am and 2.30pm to 5.30pm Monday to Friday.

Visas for Onward Travel In Togo you can get visas for the following neighbouring West African countries:

Benin There is no Beninese embassy in Lomé, but temporary visas (CFA10,000) valid for two days are issued at the border on the Cotonou-Lomé road. These visas can be extended at the Direction Immigration/ Emigration in Cotonou for CFA12,000, and take three to four days to issue.

Burkina Faso & Côte d'Ivoire The French consulate in Lomé issues three-month visas for these countries. Visas cost CFA20,000, require two photos and take 48 hours to issue.

Ghana One-month visas cost CFA12,000 (less for Commonwealth citizens), require four photos and are issued within 48 hours.

Other Documents

Proof of yellow fever vaccination is required, but rarely checked at the border crossings. If you're driving, you need an International Driving Permit.

EMBASSIES & CONSULATES

Togolese Embassies & Consulates

In West Africa, Togo has embassies in Ghana and Nigeria. For details, see the Facts for the Visitor section of the relevant country chapter.

Outside West Africa, Togolese embassies and consulates include the following:

Belgium (☎ 02-770 17 91, 770 55 63) 264 Av de Tervueren, Brussels 1150
Canada (☎ 613-238 59 16) 12 Chemin Rouge Ottawa
France (☎ 01 43 80 12 13, fax 01 44 40 08 63) 8 Rue Alfred Roll, 75017 Paris
Germany (☎ 228-35 50 91) Beethovenstrasse 13 D, 5300 Bonn 2
USA (☎ 202-234 4212, fax 232 3190) 2208 Massachusetts Ave NW, Washington, DC 20008

Togo has embassies in Congo (Zaïre) and Gabon and consulates in Switzerland and Austria.

Embassies & Consulates in Togo

The following countries have diplomatic representation in Lomé:

France (☎ 221 25 71) *Embassy:* 51 Rue du Colonel de Roux, BP 337
Consulate: (☎ 221 25 76) Rue Bissaguet, BP 337; open 8am to 11.30am Monday to Friday
Germany (☎ 221 23 38) Blvd de la Marina (Route d'Aflao), BP 289
Ghana (☎ 221 31 94) 8 Rue Paulin Eklou, Tokoin; open 8am to 2pm Monday to Friday
Netherlands (☎ 221 08 59) Rue du Lac Togo
Nigeria (☎ 221 34 55) 311 Blvd du 13 Janvier
UK *Consulate:* (☎ 221 06 18, fax 226 49 89) Av de l'Amitié, Résidence du Bénin
USA (☎ 221 29 91, fax 221 79 52) Rue Vauban

CUSTOMS

There is no restriction on the importation of local currency. Declare any large sums of foreign currency you bring in because the export of foreign currency must not exceed the amount declared on arrival. You're not supposed to export more than CFA25,000.

Unlike many West African countries, exporting artwork requires no clearance from a museum.

MONEY

The unit of currency is the West African CFA franc.

country	unit		CFA
euro zone	€1	=	CFA656
UK	UK£1	=	CFA1024
USA	US$1	=	CFA694

Travellers cheques can be exchanged in Lomé and most major cities, but rates are about 3% to 5% lower than for cash. The main branch of Banque Togolaise pour le Commerce et l'Industrie (BTCI) in Lomé offers cash advances on Visa, but it is quicker to use its ATM (which accepts Visa only).

POST & COMMUNICATIONS

Post

Postcards and letters per 10g cost CFA400 to Europe and CFA450 to North America and Australasia. The poste restante at the main post office in Lomé is reliable.

Telephone & Fax

The international telephone service is good. International calls (and faxes) can be made from official telecom offices, or from the plethora of private telephone agencies in every town. The latter charge about CFA400 per minute to North America and Europe, and CFA500 to Australasia.

There are no telephone area codes in Togo.

Email & Internet Access

There are a growing number of Internet centres in Lomé – see Information in the Lomé section later this chapter for details.

DIGITAL RESOURCES

The best site is **W** www.republicoftogo.com, which has plenty of country information as well as news and travel links. *Togo Daily* is a useful English language newspaper online at **W** www.togodaily.com.

BOOKS

The Village of Waiting by George Packer is an interesting observation on life in Togo. It is one of the best books yet on the Peace Corps experience, covering a volunteer's two years in Lavié, and it's quite candid about the country's autocratic politics.

New Telephone Numbers

All telephone numbers changed from six-digit to seven-digit numbers in 2001. To save confusion, the first digit of the original telephone number has simply been repeated. Hence, numbers beginning with 2 are now preceded by 2 (eg 21 43 13 is now 221 43 13). Similarly, all numbers beginning with a 3, 4, 5, 6 and 7 are preceded by 3, 4, 5, 6 and 7 respectively. The exception is mobile (cell) phone numbers, which are all now preceded by 9.

NEWSPAPERS & MAGAZINES

The *Togo Presse* (in French, with some articles in Kabyé and Ewe) tends to take the official presidential line. Occasionally you may see opposition magazines. The cultural centres and big hotels may have week-old international newspapers and even older magazines.

PHOTOGRAPHY & VIDEO

Take care around the presidential palace, as travellers caught taking photos of it have been beaten by the police. For more information, see also Photography & Video in the Regional Facts for the Visitor chapter.

HEALTH

A yellow fever vaccination certificate is required of all travellers. Malaria risk exists year-round throughout the country, so take appropriate precautions. See Health in the Regional Facts for the Visitor chapter for more information on health matters.

WOMEN TRAVELLERS

In the predominantly Muslim northern towns of Sokodé, Bafilo and Kara, long dresses and sleeves are recommended. For more information, see Women Travellers in the Regional Facts for the Visitor chapter.

DANGERS & ANNOYANCES

Muggings and petty theft are rife in Lomé, especially along the beach and around the Grand Marché – see Information in the Lomé section later for details.

Police roadblocks in the countryside are common and tiresome, but generally harmless. Carry your passport with you.

BUSINESS HOURS

Business hours are from 8am to noon and 3pm to 6pm Monday to Friday, and 7.30am to 12.30pm Saturday. Government offices are open from 7am to noon and 2.30pm to 5.30pm Monday to Friday. Banking hours are generally from 7.30am to 11am and 2pm to 3pm Monday to Friday.

PUBLIC HOLIDAYS & SPECIAL EVENTS

Public holidays include:

New Year's Day 1 January
Meditation Day 13 January
Easter March/April
National Day 27 April
Labour Day 1 May
Day of the Martyrs 21 June
Christmas Day 25 December

See Public Holidays & Special Events in the Regional Facts for the Visitor chapter for a table of dates of Islamic holidays.

Special events include Evala, the wrestling festival in the Kabyé region around Kara, in July; the Dzawuwu-Za harvest festival in Klouto and the Ayiza harvest festival in Tsévié in August; and the Igname (yam) festival in Bassar in September. There are many others; contact the tourist office in Lomé for details.

ACTIVITIES

There are plenty of hiking opportunities in Togo, particularly in the Kpalimé region (see the boxed text 'Hiking in the Kpalimé Area' later in this chapter for details) and around the national parks.

For swimming, there are some good beaches near Lomé and at Aného, but the currents can be dangerous. Several of the top-end hotels have swimming pools and tennis courts. Water sports can be arranged at Lake Togo, and horse riding and whale watching can be organised in Lomé.

ACCOMMODATION

Accommodation in Togo is among the least expensive in West Africa. Decent singles/doubles cost about CFA3500/4500 (more in Lomé), while comfortable rooms with private bathroom and air-con cost about CFA9000/11,000. Prices include all taxes, and tariffs should be listed somewhere prominent in the hotel entrance.

Top-end hotels with swimming pools and other amenities can be found in Lomé, at Lake Togo and in Kara.

FOOD

The food in Togo is some of the best in West Africa and there are lots of places to try it, especially in Lomé. As in most of West Africa, meals are usually based on a starch staple accompanied by sauce. Sauces and starches come in many varieties (see the boxed text 'Togolese Tucker'). You'll find rice with groundnut (peanut) sauce *(riz sauce arachide)* at most places.

Togolese Tucker

Sauces

aglan – crab
arachide – groundnut (peanut)
aubergine – eggplant
épinards – spinach
gboma – spinach and seafood
lamounou déssi or *sauce de poisson* – fish
fufu – mashed yams
gari – a couscous-like grain made with manioc
monplé – a slightly sour pâte made with fermented corn
pâte or *acousmá* – a dough-like substance which can be made of millet, corn, plantains, manioc or yams

Staples

ablo – a slightly sweet pâte made with corn and sugar
djenkoumé – a red-coloured pâte made with palm oil, tomatoes and corn

Togolese Specialities

abobo – snails cooked like a brochette
egbo pinon – smoked goat
koklo mémé – grilled chicken with chilli sauce
koliko – fried yams, a popular street food

DRINKS

Togo also has its fair share of local brews. In the north, the preferred drink is *tchakpallo*, which is fermented millet with a frothy head, often found in the market areas. In the south, the most popular brews are palm wine and, to a lesser extent, *sodabe*, an unusually strong, clear-coloured alcohol distilled from palm wine, which will knock your socks off.

Getting There & Away

AIR

Togo's international airport is 7km northeast of the centre of Lomé. There is a CFA5000 departure tax.

Europe & the USA

Air France has three direct flights a week from Paris to Lomé (US$582/790 in low/high season). The fledgling Air Togo only operates one weekly flight between Lomé and Paris (CFA360,000 one way), despite advertising flights to London and Brussels. KLM-Royal Dutch Airlines periodically has good deals to/from Amsterdam for around US$1073 return, although normal fares are very expensive.

It may be cheaper to fly to Cotonou (Benin) or Accra (Ghana) and take a bush taxi from there.

From the USA, you'll have to take Air France from New York, and transfer in Dakar (Senegal), Abidjan (Côte d'Ivoire) or Ouadadougou (Burkina Faso), or go via Europe. Expect to pay around US$1279 return.

Africa

Air Burkina flies twice weekly from Lomé to Cotonou (US$32/35 one way/return) and thrice weekly to Ouagadougou (US$162/178). Air Gabon flies three times a week from Lomé to Abidjan (US$95/105), and Cameroon Airways offers a weekly service to Bamako (US$256/282).

From other parts of the continent, Kenya Airways flies once weekly between Nairobi and Lomé via Accra (US$827 return) and EgyptAir has a weekly flight between Lomé and Cairo via Accra (US$819 return).

LAND

Border Crossings

The main Benin border crossing at Hilla-Condji is relatively trouble free. It is open 24 hours daily, but temporary visas for Benin are only available from 8am to 6pm.

The main border crossing for Burkina Faso is at Sinkasse, north of Dapaong. Expect heavy searches at this border, which closes at 6.30pm.

The most popular border crossing to Ghana is via Aflao on the coastal road. It is currently open 6am to 10pm daily, however, the Togolese and Ghanaian governments are negotiating to have the border open 24 hours.

Benin

Bush taxis regularly ply the road between Lomé and Cotonou (CFA3000, three hours) via Hilla-Condji, while STIF (☎ 221 38 48) has buses (CFA3000) departing at 8.30am each day.

There are also border crossings at Tohoun (east of Notsé), Kémérida (northeast of Kara) and Nadoba (in the Tamberma Valley), but public transport in these areas is infrequent and Beninese visas are not readily available at these borders.

Burkina Faso

Minibuses and bush taxis for Ouagadougou depart daily from Gare d'Agbalepedo in northern Lomé (CFA15,000, 36 hours). Frequent police checkpoints on both sides makes this trip a nightmare, so it makes sense to do this trip in stages and stop over at Sokodé and/or Dapaong. Take a minibus from Dapaong to Bitou (CFA500), which is 40km from the border, then from there to Ouagadougou (CFA4000).

Ghana

From central Lomé it is only about 2km by foot, bush taxi or moto-taxi to the border. STIF buses run a daily service from Lomé to Accra (CFA4000) departing at 4pm.

Another frequently used border crossing is at Klouto (northwest of Kpalimé). A dearth of public transport and bad roads make the crossing more difficult – but not impossible – at Badou, Natchamba (accessible from Sokodé) and northwest of Dapaong at Sinkasse.

Getting Around

BUSH TAXI & MINIBUS

Togo has an extensive network of minibuses and bush taxis, and most vehicles are in reasonable condition. There are many police checkpoints, so travelling is often agonisingly slow. Passengers are charged a negotiable surcharge for luggage, which is based on size.

TRAIN

Togo no longer operates any passenger train services, although freight trains still run.

CAR & MOTORCYCLE

Most major roads in Togo are sealed and in fairly good condition. The one major exception is the stretch between Atakpamé and Wahala, which is badly potholed.

Lomé

pop 675,000

Before the country's political troubles in the 1990s, Lomé was the pearl of West Africa, boasting tranquil beaches, exotic markets and friendly people. The city still retains some charm, though, and is far nicer than other West African cities such as Cotonou (Benin) and Lagos (Nigeria). As well as the beaches, it has a lively nightlife, great restaurants and an intriguing fetish market.

Orientation

Orienting yourself is fairly easy in Lomé. Most places of interest are in, or just outside, the D-shaped central area defined by the coastal highway and the semicircular Blvd du 13 Janvier (often called Blvd Circulaire).

The heart of town is around the intersection of Rue de la Gare and Rue du Commerce, which becomes Rue du Lac Togo beyond the market area. The Grand Marché is a few blocks to the east of the intersection. About six blocks north of the market is Av du 24 Janvier, which runs east-west. Av Maman N'Danida (formerly Rue d'Amoutivé), which becomes Route d'Atakpamé, leads north from the centre out to the airport, university and, eventually, Atakpamé.

Maps The best map of Lomé is the *Lomé* city map (1998) available from most bookshops for CFA3000. Also worth picking up is the pocket-sized fold-up *Plan de Lomé* offered by the Direction de la Promotion Touristique for CFA1800.

The excellent *Guide Lomé* has a detailed street directory and is written in English and French. It costs CFA8000 and can be found at most bookshops.

Information

Tourist Offices Direction de la Promotion Touristique (☎ 221 43 13, 221 56 62) is next to the Star Librairie on Rue du Lac Togo and is open from 7am to noon and 2.30pm to 5pm Monday to Friday. While the staff are somewhat helpful, the free brochures they dole out are terribly outdated.

Money The major banks, including BIA-Togo, BTCI, UTB (Union Togolaise de Banque) and Ecobank, are conveniently

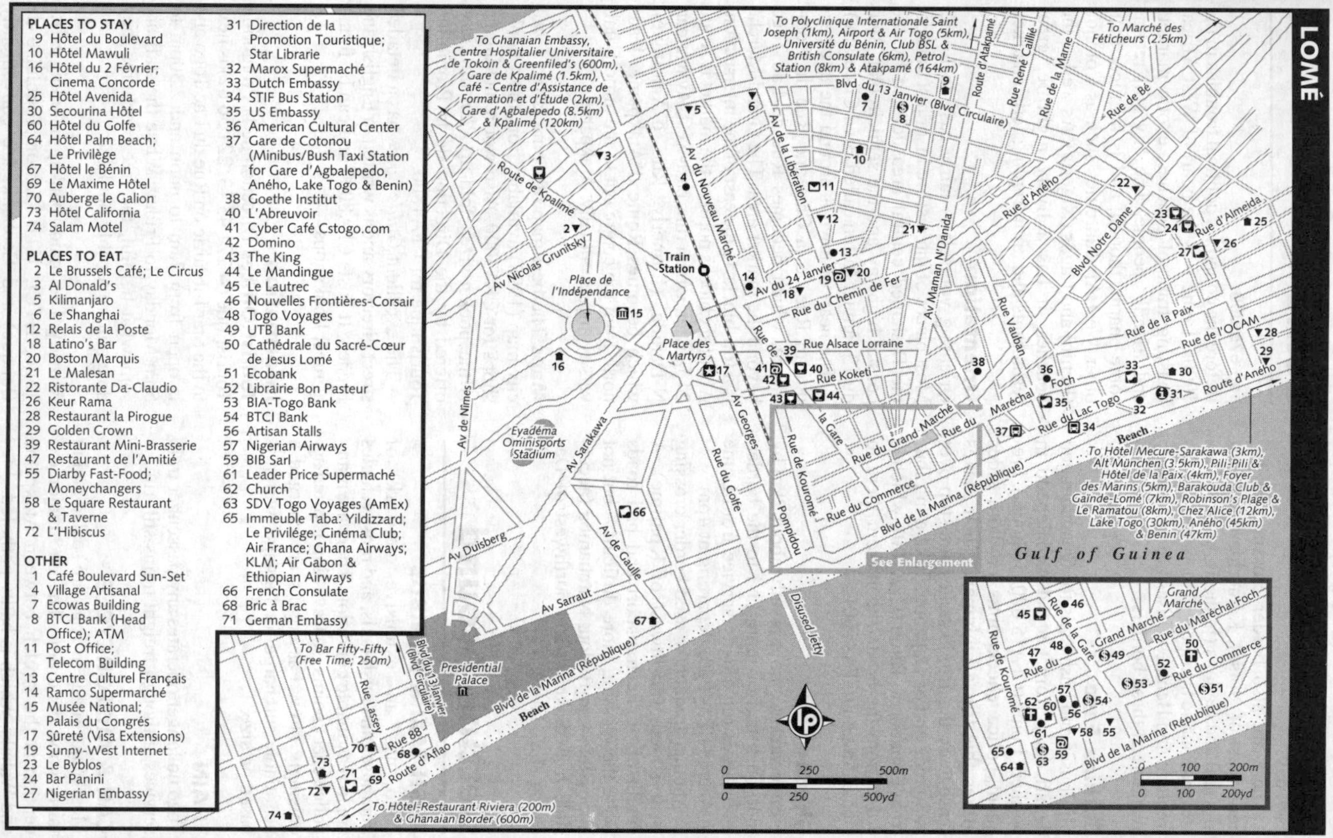
LOMÉ
PLACES TO STAY
9 Hôtel du Boulevard
10 Hôtel Mawuli
16 Hôtel du 2 Février; Cinema Concorde
25 Hôtel Avenida
30 Secourina Hôtel
60 Hôtel du Golfe
64 Hôtel Palm Beach; Le Privilège
67 Hôtel le Bénin
69 Le Maxime Hôtel
70 Auberge le Galion
73 Hôtel California
74 Salam Motel
PLACES TO EAT
2 Le Brussels Café; Le Circus
3 Al Donald's
5 Kilimanjaro
6 Le Shanghai
12 Relais de la Poste
18 Latino's Bar
20 Boston Marquis
21 Le Malesan
22 Ristorante Da-Claudio
26 Keur Rama
28 Restaurant la Pirogue
29 Golden Crown
39 Restaurant Mini-Brasserie
47 Restaurant de l'Amitié
55 Diarby Fast-Food; Moneychangers
58 Le Square Restaurant & Taverne
72 L'Hibiscus
OTHER
1 Café Boulevard Sun-Set
4 Village Artisanal
7 Ecowas Building
8 BTCI Bank (Head Office); ATM
11 Post Office; Telecom Building
13 Centre Culturel Français
14 Ramco Supermarché
15 Musée National; Palais du Congrés
17 Sûreté (Visa Extensions)
19 Sunny-West Internet
23 Le Byblos
24 Bar Panini
27 Nigerian Embassy
31 Direction de la Promotion Touristique; Star Librarie
32 Marox Supermaché
33 Dutch Embassy
34 STIF Bus Station
35 US Embassy
36 American Cultural Center
37 Gare de Cotonou (Minibus/Bush Taxi Station for Gare d'Agbalepedo, Aného, Lake Togo & Benin)
38 Goethe Institut
40 L'Abreuvoir
41 Cyber Café Cstogo.com
42 Domino
43 The King
44 Le Mandingue
45 Le Lautrec
46 Nouvelles Frontières-Corsair
48 Togo Voyages
49 UTB Bank
50 Cathédrale du Sacré-Cœur de Jesus Lomé
51 Ecobank
52 Librairie Bon Pasteur
53 BIA-Togo Bank
54 BTCI Bank
56 Artisan Stalls
57 Nigerian Airways
59 BIB Sarl
61 Leader Price Supermaché
62 Church
63 SDV Togo Voyages (AmEx)
65 Immeuble Taba: Yildizzard; Le Privilége; Cinéma Club; Air France; Ghana Airways; KLM; Air Gabon & Ethiopian Airways
66 French Consulate
68 Bric à Brac
71 German Embassy
To Ghanaian Embassy, Centre Hospitalier Universitaire de Tokoin & Greenfiled's (600m), Gare de Kpalimé (1.5km), Café - Centre d'Assistance de Formation et d'Étude (2km), Gare d'Agbalepedo (8.5km) & Kpalimé (120km)
To Polyclinique Internationale Saint Joseph (1km), Airport & Air Togo (5km), Université du Bénin, Club BSL & British Consulate (6km), Petrol Station (8km) & Atakpamé (164km)
To Marché des Féticheurs (2.5km)
To Hôtel Mecure-Sarakawa (3km), Alt München (3.5km), Pili-Pili & Hôtel de la Paix (4km), Foyer des Marins (5km), Barakouda Club & Gainde-Lomé (7km), Robinson's Plage & Le Ramatou (8km), Chez Alice (12km), Lake Togo (30km), Aného (45km) & Benin (47km)
To Bar Fifty-Fifty (Free Time; 250m)
To Hôtel-Restaurant Riviera (200m) & Ghanaian Border (600m)
Train Station
Place de l'Indépendance
Place des Martyrs
Eyadéma Ominisports Stadium
Presidential Palace
Grand Marché
Gulf of Guinea
Beach
Disused Jetty
See Enlargement
Blvd du 13 Janvier (Blvd Circulaire)
Route de Kpalimé
Av Nicolas Grunitsky
Av du Nouveau Marché
Av de la Libération
Av du 24 Janvier
Rue du Chemin de Fer
Av Maman N'Danida
Rue Alsace Lorraine
Rue Koketi
Rue Vauban
Rue d'Aného
Blvd Notre Dame
Rue d'Almeida
Rue de Bé
Rue de la Marne
Rue René Caillié
Route d'Atakpamé
Rue de la Paix
Rue de l'OCAM
Route d'Aného
Rue du Lac Togo
Rue du Maréchal Foch
Rue du Grand Marché
Rue de la Gare
Rue du Commerce
Rue de Kouromé
Pompidou
Blvd de la Marina (République)
Av Georges
Rue du Golfe
Av de Nîmes
Av Sarakawa
Av de Gaulle
Av Duisberg
Av Sarraut
Rue Lassey
Rue 88
Route d'Aflao
0 250 500m
0 250 500yd
0 100 200m
0 100 200yd

clustered in the centre, at or near the corner of Rue de la Gare and Rue du Commerce. All change cash and travellers cheques, but the BTCI's head office on Blvd du 13 Janvier is the best bet. It also has an ATM that accepts visa cards.

Moneychangers congregate near Chez Diarby restaurant on Rue du Commerce, but there is a good chance of being ripped off here. SDV Togo Voyages (☎ 221 26 11, fax 221 26 12) at 2 Rue du Commerce is the American Express representative.

Post & Communications The main post office, on Av de la Libération between Blvd du 13 Janvier and Av du 24 Janvier, has an efficient poste restante and is open 7am to 5pm Monday to Friday and 8am to noon Saturday.

The Telecom building is just behind the post office; open 7am to 6pm Monday to Friday, 8am to noon Saturday. Local and international calls can also be made from any of the multitude of private telephone agencies around the city.

There are numerous Internet cafés in Lomé. One of the most reliable is Cyber Café Cstogo.com (☎ 221 91 33, ⓔ cstogo@cstogo.com) opposite Restaurant Mini-Brasserie on Rue de la Gare (CFA500 per hour). Other good options include BIB Sarl (☎ 222 31 64) at 10 Rue du Commerce and Sunny-West Internet (☎ 221 74 29, ⓔ sunnyw@ifrance.com) at 42 Av du 24 Janvier.

CAFÉ – Centre d'Assistance de Formation et d'Étude (☎ 225 55 55, fax 225 66 66, ⓔ cafe@cafe.tg) on Route de Kpalimé is a reputable Internet service provider.

Travel Agencies & Tour Operators Lomé has no lack of travel agencies. Many offer excursions to the interior as well as side trips to Ghana and Benin. One of the best is SDV Togo Voyages (see Money earlier in this section). Other dependable agencies include Togo Voyages (☎ 221 12 77, fax 221 81 76) at 13 Rue du Grand Marché and Nouvelles Frontières-Corsair (☎ 221 08 03, fax 221 07 83) at 20 Rue de la Gare.

Bookshops The best bookshop is Librairie Bon Pasteur (☎ 221 36 28), a block west of the cathedral on Rue Aniko Palako. It is open from 8am to 12.15pm and 3pm and 6pm Monday to Friday. It sells maps and occasionally has English publications like the *International Herald Tribune* and *Time*.

Cultural Centres Centre Culturel Français (☎ 221 02 32, fax 221 34 42, ⓔ ccflome@togo-imet.com, Ⓦ www.ccf.tg.refer.org) at 19 Av du 24 Janvier offers regular films, concerts and exhibitions and has a good selection of books and up-to-date newspapers.

American Cultural Center (☎ 221 29 91, fax 221 77 94) is now located within the US embassy compound opposite the visa office on Rue du Maréchal Foch (entry is from Rue du Lac Togo).

Medical Services If you need a doctor or a dentist, contact an embassy for a list of recommended practitioners. For emergencies, try Polyclinique Internationale Saint Joseph (☎ 226 72 32) on Blvd de la Paix, or Centre Hospitalier Universitaire de Tokoin (☎ 221 25 01) on Route de Kpalimé.

Dangers & Annoyances There are lots of pickpockets around the Grand Marché and along Rue du Commerce, and muggings are frequent, some at knife-point. The worst thing you could do is walk along the beach alone at night. Indeed, walking anywhere around the city at night is dangerous – take a taxi. There are also a number of police roadblocks around the city at night that act as an unofficial revenue-collection exercise.

Place de l'Indépendance

The gilded bronze statue of President Eyadéma and the one of his mother were taken down in 1991 during the civil disturbances. To the square's east is Palais du Congrès, previously Eyadéma's RPT headquarters.

Musée National

The entrance to the museum *(☎ 221 68 09; admission CFA1000; open 8am-noon & 3pm-5.30pm Mon-Fri)* is at the back of the Palais du Congrès in Place de l'Indépendance. It houses historical artefacts, pottery, costumes, musical instruments, woodcarvings, traditional medicines, and 'thunder stones' (large rocks shaped like eggs) and cowrie shells, both formerly used as legal tender.

Marché des Féticheurs

The fetish market *(admission CFA5000 per person, plus CFA5000/10,000 per camera/*

video), 4km northeast of the centre in Akodessewa, has a remarkable supply of traditional medicines used by sorcerers, including skulls of monkeys and birds, porcupine skin, warthog teeth and all sizes of bones and skulls. It's also a great place to buy gris-gris charms, which are worn around the neck to ward off various evils. Although the market is an overpriced tourist trap, it's still worth a visit. To get there charter a taxi (CFA700) or jump on a moto-taxi (CFA500).

Activities

The surf in Lomé is very dangerous because of a strong undertow, and drownings are common – be careful. Many of the beaches are also used as the local toilet. The beaches east of Lomé are better and more secluded – see the Around Lomé section following.

The **swimming** pool at Hôtel Mecure-Sarakawa is Olympic size and admission costs CFA21,000 per month. Hôtel le Bénin and Foyer des Marins also have pools; both charge around CFA2000. The pool at Club BSL on Av de l'Amitié, 6km from the centre near the British consulate, is a great place to meet expats who'll happily give you the low down on Lomé. It costs CFA2500.

There are **tennis courts** at the large hotels and **horse riding** can be organised through Club Hippique (☎ 226 94 50), located near the airport, or through Hôtel Mecure-Sarakawa.

Gaïnde-Lomé (☎ 221 01 40, 904 20 10, ⓔ gained@netcom.tg), moored behind the fish market at the Rond-point du Port 7km east of the centre, operates **whale-watching** tours from early August to September as well as year-round **fishing** trips for CFA80,000/150,000 per half/full day (maximum of six people).

Places to Stay

The following entries are accommodation options within 5km of the centre of town. Other options (including camping) further from the centre are listed in the Around Lomé section.

Places to Stay – Budget

Hôtel du Boulevard *(☎ 221 15 91, 204 Blvd du 13 Janvier)* Rooms ÇFA3000-5000. The Boulevard is in a good location that's lively at night. It offers a large range of reasonably clean rooms.

Hôtel Mawuli *(☎ 222 12 75, 21 Rue Maoussas)* Singles/doubles with fan & shared bathroom CFA4000/5000, with air-con and bathroom CFA6500/7500. Near the central area, the Mawuli has surprisingly decent rooms. It's the pink building, two blocks south of the enormous Ecowas building.

Salam Motel *(☎ 222 25 34, Blvd de la Marina)* Rooms without/with fan CFA4000/5000, with air-con CFA7000. This ramshackled motel has clean cramped rooms with twin beds and a grubby shared bathroom. It attracts its share of lowlifes – lone travellers should be wary.

Hôtel California *(☎ 222 52 10, Rue 88)* Singles/doubles with fan CFA6500/7500, with air-con CFA10,500/11,500. This poorly signposted four-storey establishment behind the German embassy gets mixed reviews – the views and breezes are great, but the plumbing is unreliable and the restaurant rather unexciting.

Auberge le Galion *(☎ 222 00 30, ⓔ togogalion@yahoo.fr, 12 Rue des Camomilles)* Singles/doubles with fan CFA5000/6000, with air-con CFA10,000/12,000. If you don't mind paying a bit more, check out this excellent hotel. There's a lounge upstairs with relaxing armchairs and shelves full of books, and a bar downstairs, that is popular with locals and travellers. The rooms have clean bathrooms, but vary in standard – check a few out.

Places to Stay – Mid-Range

Foyer des Marins *(☎ 227 53 51, fax 227 77 62, Route d'Aného)* Rooms & apartments CFA10,000-20,000. This place is 5km east of the centre, just before the Rond-point du Port. Features include a pool, snack bar and bar. The only problem is that first priority is given to sailors, so call in advance.

Le Maxime Hôtel *(☎ 221 74 48, Route d'Aflao)* Rooms with bathroom & air-con CFA12,000. This long-standing place has a pleasant terrace.

Secourina Hôtel *(☎ 221 60 20, 63 Rue du Lac Togo)* Rooms with fan CFA8000, singles/doubles with air-con CFA11,000/12,000. The Secourina, a little closer to the centre, has quiet, comfortable rooms.

Hôtel-Restaurant Riviera *(☎ 221 42 26, fax 222 52 10, Route d'Aflao)* Rooms with air-con CFA12,000-18,000. This hotel is a good option for those wanting to stay close to the Ghanaian border. It also has a great Lebanese restaurant (see Places to Eat).

Hôtel Avenida *(☎ 221 46 72, fax 221 34 75, 30 Rue d'Almeida)* Rooms CFA13,500-15,000. The well-maintained Avenida, half a block east of Blvd du 13 Janvier near the Nigerian embassy, has good, clean rooms and a decent restaurant.

Hôtel du Golfe *(☎ 221 02 78, 221 65 45, fax 221 49 03, Rue du Commerce)* Singles with air-con CFA16,300-20,000, doubles with air-con CFA18,600-22,600. This hotel is possibly the best of the mid-range places. It's central, comfortable and reasonable value.

Places to Stay – Top End

Hôtel le Bénin *(☎ 221 24 85, fax 221 61 25, Blvd de la Marina)* Singles/doubles with city view CFA23,000/25,000, with sea view CFA26,000/28,000. Without doubt, the best value among all the top-end hotels is the independence-era Hôtel le Bénin, 500m west of the centre. It has clean, comfortable rooms.

Hôtel de la Paix *(☎ 221 52 97, fax 221 23 02, ⓔ hoteldelapaix@cafe.tg)* Rooms CFA25,000-35,000, suites/luxury suites CFA40,000/45,000. This declining hotel offers ocean nice views, a pool, a casino and a tennis court.

Hôtel Palm Beach *(☎ 221 85 11, fax 221 87 11, 1 Blvd de la Marina)* Rooms CFA50,000, suite/luxury suite CFA80,000/120,000. This well-located high-rise hotel features a pool, gym, cable TV and the up-market Le Privilège disco is nearby.

Hôtel Mecure-Sarakawa *(☎ 227 65 90, fax 227 71 80, ⓔ H2102@accor.hotels.com)* Rooms without/with ocean view CFA60,000/67,000, suite CFA75,000. The recently revamped Sarakawa, 3km east of the town centre on the road to Benin, is Lomé's top hotel. It has a wonderful Olympic-sized pool, horse riding, tennis court, and hairdresser.

Hôtel du 2 Février *(☎ 221 00 03, fax 221 62 66, ⓦ www.hotel2fevrier.com)* Rooms from CFA66,000, suite CFA90,000. Once Lomé's best hotel, the beleaguered Hôtel du 2 Février, west of Place de l'Indépendance, is devoid of guests unless there's a political party meeting or conference.

Places to Eat

Cafés & Snack Bars Just for fun try ***Al Donald's*** a cheeky rip-off of the American fast-food giant on Blvd du 13 Janvier.

For ice cream (CFA800-2000) the best place to go is ***Le Brussels Café*** *(☎ 221 46 63, 8 Av Nicolas Grunitsky)*. Its upstairs restaurant stocks Belgian beers.

Bar Fifty-Fifty *(Blvd du 13 Janvier)* Meals from CF850. Sometimes called 'Free Time', Bar Fifty-Fifty on the western side of the boulevard, is very popular and lively, but food is only served in the evenings.

Boston Marquis *(☎ 222 26 06, Av du 24 Janvier)* Meals CFA1000-1500. You can also get good, cheap food at this friendly restaurant opposite Centre Culturel Français.

Diarby Fast-Food *(☎ 221 75 11, Rue du Commerce)* Meals from CFA1000. Diarby Fast-Food serves a large variety of meals including burgers (from CFA1300), chicken and rice dishes (CFA2500) and sandwiches (from CFA1000), as well as a good choice of vegetarian dishes.

African Lomé has a good selection of African restaurants.

Restaurant de l'Amitié *(17 Rue du Grand Marché)* Meals from CFA1200. Open to 8pm. This popular little place offers huge servings of inexpensive Western, Guinean and Senegalese dishes as well as cheap beer.

Keur Rama *(☎ 221 54 62, Blvd du 13 Janvier)* Meals CFA2000-3000. Keur Rama, on the eastern side of town near the Nigerian embassy, offers Senegalese and Togolese cuisine. The house specialty is the delicious *chep boudjen* (fish cooked with cabbage, eggplant and carrots) for CFA2500.

Restaurant la Pirogue *(221 40 97, Cnr Blvd du 13 Janvier & Rue de l'OCAM)* Meals CFA2000-3000. This restaurant, several blocks south of Keur Rama, has similar prices, with French and Vietnamese dishes as well as a good African selection.

Kilimanjaro *(☎ 222 04 67, Blvd du 13 Janvier)* Mains CFA1900-6900. This one-time Ethiopian restaurant, just east of Av du Nouveau Marché, has recently been taken over by new management. Its tasty new menu consists of Algerian specialities such as *tajine* (a spicy lamb goulash; CFA4800) as well as a good mix of international dishes. Complementary tapas are provided and the service is exceptional.

Asian The best Chinese restaurants are on Blvd du 13 Janvier.

Golden Crown *(☎ 221 21 97)* Meals CFA2000-4000. At the eastern end of the boulevard, at the intersection with Route d'Aného ocean road, is this long-standing place. It offers good-quality food at moderate prices.

Le Shanghai *(☎ 222 26 28)* meals CFA2000-4000. Open Thur-Tues. Halfway along the boulevard is Le Shanghai, one of Lomé's best and most popular Chinese restaurants.

European There is an abundance of European restaurants in Lomé, most with a distinctly French flavour.

Ristorante Da-Claudio *(☎ 222 26 65, Blvd du 13 Janvier)* Pizzas CFA2000-4000, pasta CFA2000-3500. This restaurant, just north of the intersection with Blvd Notre Dame, is a great place to sample traditional Italian fare, and best of all, you have the choice between air-con dining inside and a relaxing terrace outside.

Relais de la Poste *(☎ 221 46 78, 6 Av de la Libération)* Mains around CFA2500. This charming relic has long been a mainstay of locals and expats alike. It has a convivial atmosphere and well-priced meals; a large plate of steak and chips costs CFA2500.

Auberge le Galion *(☎ 222 00 30, ⓔ togo galion@yahoo.fr, 12 Rue des Camomilles)* Mains CFA2300-3000. Le Galion offers decent meals in a quiet courtyard setting. The hearty *menu du jour* is CFA3800 and snack food is served all day.

Restaurant Mini-Brasserie *(☎ 221 32 34, 44 Rue de le Gare)* Mains CFA3000-6000. This enduring favourite is also a good spot to meet other travellers and have an ice-cold beer.

Le Maxime Hôtel *(☎ 221 74 48, Route d'Aflao)* Meals CFA2000-6000. A block away from le Galion, towards the beach, is the more expensive, but not as good, restaurant at this hotel.

Latino's Bar *(☎ 221 71 24, Av du 24 Janvier)* Meals CFA2500-4000. Latino's is an energetic restaurant-bar specialising in yummy Tex/Mex fare. House favourites include chili con carne, *bœuf à la mexicaine* (Mexican beef) and *poulet façon Latino's* (Latino's chicken).

Greenfield's *(☎ 222 21 55, Rue Akati)* Pizzas CFA2500-5000. With its bright, contemporary decor and fun menu Greenfield's, just off Route de Kpalimé near the Ghanaian embassy, has quickly become popular with Lomé's fashionable young set. There is a large outdoor dining area, a kid's playroom and even an open-air cinema (see Entertainment).

Pili-Pili *(☎ 222 31 68, Rue de l'Entente)* Meals from CFA3000. This place, on the eastern side of town behind Hôtel de la Paix, is an upmarket French restaurant, which also features African dishes.

Alt München *(☎ 227 63 21, Route d'Aného)* Meals from CFA3000. Open Thur-Tues. The seafood at this attractively decorated well-established place, just east of Hôtel Mercure-Sarakawa, is particularly good and the service is excellent.

L'Hibiscus *(☎ 222 74 99, 59 Rue de l'Ogou)* Mains around CFA4000. Open Mon-Sat. The new L'Hibiscus has fast become a local culinary favourite, so book ahead. The cuisine is southern French and the seafood is superb.

Le Square Restaurant & Taverne *(☎ 222 02 20, Rue du Commerce)* Meals CFA4000-7000. This small upmarket restaurant, between Hôtel du Golfe and Blvd de la Marina, is another good choice for fine French fare.

Barakouda Club *(☎ 246 47 46)* Mains around CFA4000. The Barakouda Club, with its pleasant outdoor terrace overlooking the harbour, is the ideal spot to sample the catch of the day.

Le Malesan *(☎ 221 80 74, 39 Av du 24 Janvier)* Entrees CFA5500-10,500, mains CFA6200-14,800. Le Malesan is definitely Lomé's most expensive splurge. The French cuisine is top-notch and the service impeccable, but a meal here will certainly leave a gaping hole in your pocket.

Lebanese Raved about locally, ***Hôtel-Restaurant Riviera*** *(☎ 221 42 26, Route d'Aflao)* offers well-priced authentic Lebanese meals for CFA2000 to CFA2500. Try the *Feuille de vignes* (stuffed vine leaves) for CFA1500.

Yildizzard *(☎ 221 2762, Av Georges Pompidou)* Meals from CFA3000. This place, on the 1st floor of the Immeuble Taba, behind Hôtel Palm Beach, is very popular with the Lebanese community; dishes are hearty.

Self-Catering The best supermarkets are the central ***Leader Price Supermarché,***

which sells a good variety of canned goods, and ***Ramco Supermarché*** on the corner of Av du 24 Janvier and Av du Nouveau Marché, which sells lots of American goods.

For meat products your best bet is the small ***Marox Supermarché*** on Rue du Lac Togo. Outside you'll find local vendors selling a wide array of fresh fruit and vegetables.

Entertainment

Bars A good place to soak up the local atmosphere is the highly animated bar at the ***Elf Station***, about 2km past the Université du Bénin on Route d'Atakpamé.

Bar Panini *(Blvd du 13 Janvier)* This is a great place to enjoy a beer and a late-night snack. There is often live music and it is generally packed.

Latino's Bar *(☎ 221 71 24, Av du 24 Janvier)* After the meals are cleared Latino's turns up the heat and becomes a sophisticated dance bar.

Café Boulevard Sun-Set *(Cnr Blvd du 13 Janvier & Route de Kpalimé)* With three distinct entertainment areas – an outdoor beer garden often hosting live music, the more intimate (and expensive) Sun-Set Club bar and the popular Millennium nightclub – Sun-Set caters to all tastes.

Nightclubs The European-oriented, disco-like nightclubs are expensive and have cover charges, typically CFA3000.

One of the hottest and best-known discos is ***L'Abreuvoir*** *(Rue de la Gare)* in the centre of town. Small beers are CFA2000, and there's a snack bar.

Just across the road is another popular bar/nightclub, ***Domino***, an infamous pick-up joint. (The area bounded by Restaurant Mini-Brasserie, Domino and L'Abreuvoir is known locally as the Bermuda Triangle – once you get inside you lose all bearings!)

Le Byblos *(Blvd du 13 Janvier)* Admission CFA3000-5000. Open from 10.30pm Wed-Sat. Just north of the Nigerian embassy is Le Byblos, a trendy nightclub that is a favourite haunt of rich young Togolese.

Le Circus *(☎ 221 46 63, 8 Av de Nicolas Grunitsky)* Admission CFA3500. Open Wed-Sun. North of Hôtel du 2 Février is Le Circus. It occasionally has live bands.

Other discos include ***The King*** at 4 Rue Koketi (admission CFA4000); and the glitzy ***Le Privilège*** at Hôtel Palm Beach (admission CFA4000), a barn-like place with expensive drinks that is popular with teenagers.

Music Venues ***Chez Alice*** *(☎ 227 91 72)* Admission for nonguests CFA4500. For live entertainment, head for Chez Alice, about 12km from the heart of Lomé on the coastal highway to Aného (take a bush taxi). Every Wednesday night, the Togolese dance group Sakra performs here. It's great fun and is always packed till the early hours of the morning.

Le Lautrec *(☎ 221 50 21, Rue de la Gare)* Currently the most popular jazz bar in Lomé, Le Lautrec has live music from Wednesday to Saturday. There is no cover charge but the price of drinks is high (CFA1500 for a local beer).

Le Mandingue *(☎ 222 76 48, Rue de la Gare)* This small bar-restaurant, not far from Le Lautrec, transforms into a smooth jazz club on weekends.

Cinemas The best cinemas are the air-conditioned ***Cinéma Concorde*** *(☎ 221 00 03)* at Hôtel du 2 Février, and ***Cinéma Club*** *(☎ 221 51 86)* behind Hôtel Palm Beach.

Greenfield's (see Places to Eat) runs an open-air cinema each Tuesday night at 7.30pm. Your CFA2500 entry fee includes a free drink and a minipizza.

Shopping

Arts & Craftwork The ***Grand Marché*** *(open to 4pm Mon-Sat)* has plenty of colourful cotton material, most of it wax cloth from Holland and cheaper African material. It's sold by the *pagne* (about 2m), the amount needed for a complete outfit. Don't be surprised if sellers sometimes refuse to sell less than this – it's not always easy to sell the rest.

For woodcarvings and brasswork, take a walk along Rue des Artisans, a short alley on the eastern side of Hôtel du Golfe, where there are many Senegalese and Malian traders. Their opening prices are usually extremely high, so come prepared for plenty of hard bargaining.

Bric à Brac *(☎ 221 02 45, ⓔ messie@bibway.com, 71 Blvd de la Marina)* For high-quality art, your best bet is Bric à Brac, a block east of Le Maxime Hôtel. The friendly owner has a showroom of good-quality West African pieces and her fixed prices are very reasonable.

Village Artisanal *(Av du Nouveau Marché)* This centre, between Av du 24 Janvier and Blvd du 13 Janvier, is an easygoing place to shop. You'll see Togolese artisans weaving cloth, carving statues, making baskets and lampshades, sewing leather shoes and constructing cane chairs and tables – all for sale at reasonable fixed prices.

Lomé is famous for leather sandals. They were originally all made at the Village Artisanal, but you can also buy them around the Grand Marché for about CFA3000.

Getting There & Away

Air The international airport (☎ 226 12 40) is 7km northwest of central Lomé. For details on flights to/from Lomé see the Getting There & Away section earlier this chapter.

For confirming flights or ticket sales the following airlines have offices in Lomé:

Air France (☎ 221 69 10) Immeuble Taba, Av Georges Pompidou
Air Gabon (☎ 221 05 73) Immeuble Taba, Av Georges Pompidou
Air Togo (☎ 226 22 11) Lomé international airport
Ethiopian Airways (☎ 221 70 74) Immeuble Taba, Av Georges Pompidou
Ghana Airways (☎ 221 56 92) Immeuble Taba, Av Georges Pompidou
KLM-Royal Dutch Airlines (☎ 221 6530) Immeuble Taba, Av Georges Pompidou
Nigeria Airways (☎ 221 32 54) Rue du Maréchal Foch

Bus, Bush Taxi & Minibus Bush taxis and minibuses travelling east to Aného (CFA600, one hour) and Cotonou (CFA3000, three hours) leave from Gare de Cotonou, about 200m west of the STIF bus station.

To Ghana it is best to catch a bush taxi or moto-taxi to the border and cross on foot. Buses for Accra leave from just across the Ghanaian border in Aflao.

Gare d'Agbalepedo, 10km north of central Lomé, serves all northern destinations. Services include: Atakpamé (CFA1700, three hours), Bassar (CFA3750), Dapaong (CFA5850, 14 hours), Kara (CFA3900, seven hours), Sokodé (CFA3400, six hours) and Ouagadougou (CFA15,000, 36 hours). There is also a daily STIF bus service from Lomé to Cotonou (CFA3000, three hours).

Minibuses to Kpalimé (CFA1000, three hours) leave from Gare de Kpalimé, 3km north of the centre on Route de Kpalimé.

Getting Around

To/From the Airport To the airport the taxi fare is about CFA1000 (but CFA1500 from the airport into the city).

Taxi & Moto-Taxi Taxis are abundant, even at night, and have no meters. Fares are CFA200 for a shared taxi (CFA300 after 6pm), more to the outlying areas, and CFA700 nonshared. A taxi by the hour should cost CFA2500 if you bargain well.

Moto-taxis (same as a *zemijdan* in Benin – a zippy little motor scooter) are also extremely popular (if a little scary) – the fare around town is around CFA150.

Car Elite Car (☎ 222 04 69, fax 222 05 00, e elitecar@togotel.net.tg) has a booth at the airport and at 215 Blvd du 13 Janvier, while Avis (☎ 221 05 82) has a booth at Hôtel Mecure-Sarakawa. In town, Avis is at 252 Blvd du 13 Janvier across the street from Elite Car. A Mitsubishi Colt with air-con costs around CFA20,000 per day plus petrol for travel not exceeding 150km.

AROUND LOMÉ

Beaches

East of Lomé, on or just off the highway to Lake Togo and Aného, are several popular beach resorts where you can camp or stay in bungalows. The first ones you come to, 9km from the centre, are Le Ramatou and Robinson's Plage. The well-marked turn-off is 1km east of the large roundabout at the port. A taxi from the Grand Marché in the centre of town costs around CFA1500.

Le Ramatou *(☎ 221 43 53, fax 222 02 72)* Camping per person CFA1000, bungalows with fan/air-con CFA6300/12,300. This beachfront place has big, plain bungalows with up to four single beds, all with mosquito nets. Erosion has caused some of the picnic and camping areas to have fallen into the sea, but swimming is still possible. Breakfast costs CFA1500 and the menu du jour is CFA5500.

Robinson's Plage *(☎ 947 0017)* Camping per person CFA1000, room with fan/air-con CFA8000/15,000. This popular spot, next door to Le Ramatou, is packed most

ARIADNE VAN ZANDBERGEN

FRANCES LINZEE GORDON

DAVID ELSE

DAVID ELSE

West Africa has few mountains and much of the region is flat or gently undulating plateau, but there are some exceptions: the village of Amani, in the Falaise de Bandiagara, Mali (top); Mandara Mountains, Cameroon (middle right); volcanic landscape on Mt Fogo, Cape Verde (bottom left); Fouta Djalon plateau, Guinea (bottom right)

DAVID ELSE

JOHN ELK III

PAUL DYMOND

It's impossible to escape the fact that most of northern West Africa is inhospitable desert. From Mauritania to Niger and beyond, the Sahara stretches like a blanket of sand: Tuareg men and their camels, Sahara desert, Mali (top); taking cover in a dust storm, near Timbuktu, Mali (middle); a seemingly endless sea of sand, near Chinguetti, Mauritania (bottom)

weekends. Its restaurant serves delicious, reasonably priced meals.

Chez Alice *(☎/fax 227 91 72, ⓔ chez alice@hotmail.com)* Camping CFA1000, bungalows CFA3500, rooms CFA4500-6000. This popular place is 4km further east in the small village of Avéposo. The accommodation is basic but clean and bathrooms are shared. There's live entertainment most nights (see Entertainment in the Lomé section). A bush taxi from Lomé is CFA200.

Lake Togo

This relatively shallow lake, part of the inland lagoon that stretches all the way from Lomé to Aného, is a popular weekend getaway for fans of water sports such as windsurfing and water-skiing.

Places to Stay & Eat There are two hotels on the southern side of the lake – both offering water sports.

L'Auberge du Lac *(☎ 227 09 10, 904 72 29)* Bungalows with bathroom & fan/air-con CFA7600/12,600. About 1km north of the village of Kpéssi and a few kilometres west of Agbodrafo, this auberge is beautifully situated among palm trees on an elevated knoll overlooking the lake. It has a restaurant and serene, spacious bungalows with two beds. Breakfast costs CFA1500.

Hôtel le Lac *(☎ 331 60 07, fax 331 60 19)* Singles/doubles with air-con CFA36,000/40,000. Several kilometres further east towards Aného is the top-notch Hôtel le Lac. Facilities include a good restaurant, a salt-water pool (CFA1000 for nonguests) and water-skiing (CFA4500). A three-course meal is CFA4000, and you can get snacks at the bar.

Getting There & Away From the Gare de Cotonou in Lomé, bush taxis and minibuses frequently travel along the coastal road to Aného, via Kpéssi and Agbodrafo.

Togoville

On Lake Togo's northern shore is Togoville, the historical centre of voodoo in Togo. It was from here that voodoo practitioners were taken as slaves to Haiti, now a major centre for voodoo. And it was here in 1884 that chief Mlapa III signed a peace treaty with the German explorer Nachtigal that gave the Germans rights over all of Togoland.

Today, the only attractions are the **chief's house**, the **church**, and the **artisanal**. The artisanal is between the village's main pier and the church, with its beautiful stained-glass windows, is nearby.

The chief's house, 100m west of the church, is an interesting modern structure called the Maison Royal. The only reason to come here is to meet the chief, Mlapa V Moyennant, who will gladly show you a room (the 'museum') that houses his throne as well as some interesting old photos of his grandfather. A *cadeau* (gift) is expected. The best time to visit is early on Saturday morning when he holds court *(fait la justice)* on the patio of his compound.

Alternatively, you could offer one of the local fishermen a small cadeau to take you with them on their daily fishing excursion, departing around 5.30am and returning around noon.

Places to Stay & Eat The surprisingly nice ***Hôtel Nachtigal*** *(☎ 333 70 76, in Lomé ☎ 221 8224, fax 221 6482)* 100m west of the market, has clean, pleasant rooms. There's also a tennis court and a large *paillote* (a covered outdoor terrace that usually has a restaurant and bar) where you can get breakfast (CFA2000) or a decent three-course meal (CFA3000). Rooms cost CFA6600/10,600 with fan/air-con.

Getting There & Away Getting here from Lomé is a bit of a hassle. By road catch a bush taxi to Aného (CFA600) then another from there to Togoville (CFA500). Otherwise, take a canoe from Agbodrafo, about 10km before Aného for CFA1500 return. If you hire a canoe to yourself (with a boatman), with hard bargaining expect to pay about CFA3000 return.

Vogan & Agoégan

The Friday **market** at Vogan is one of the largest and most colourful in Togo and should not be missed. It's a good place for practical items and there's an impressive selection of fetishes.

On Monday, there's also a vibrant **market** in Agoégan, on the intercoastal canal that divides Togo and Benin, about a 30-minute bush-taxi ride from Aného. Agoégan manages to remain pretty much untouched by outside influences.

The small ***Hôtel Medius*** *(☎ 333 10 00)*, not far from the market in Vogan, has clean rooms for CFA4300/7300 with fan/air-con and a bar-restaurant serving good-sized meals for around CFA1500.

The trip from Lomé takes one hour and costs about CFA1000 by bush taxi. If you're driving, go to Aného and take a left turn (north) to Vogan, circling around the lake. From Togoville, bush taxis (CFA500) to Vogan leave only on Friday morning.

The South

ANÉHO

pop 28,100

The colonial capital of Togo until 1920, Aného is 45km east of Lomé and 2km west of the Beninese border. Aného offers crumbling charm, but there is nothing much to do. Swimming at the beach is possible, but the currents can be dangerous.

At night, Aného comes alive with a surprising amount of activity for a small town. Along the streets you'll hear music and find vendors selling a variety of food.

Places to Stay

La Becca Hôtel *(☎ 331 05 15, Route de Togo-Bénin)* Rooms without/with fan CFA5000/6000. On the southern side of the bridge, this cheap and cheerful hotel is Aného's best budget option.

Hôtel de l'Oasis *(☎ 331 01 25, Route de Togo-Bénin)*, on the water's edge, 40m northeast of the bridge, is a popular place to stay. It has beautiful views and reasonable rooms, but they're usually fully booked on weekends. Rooms with fan/air-con will set you back CFA7800/9800.

Hôtel de l'Union *(☎ 31 00 69, fax 331 01 47, Route de Togo-Benin)* Singles/doubles CFA15,300/18,600. Hôtel de l'Union, located well away from the water at the southwestern entrance to town, has comfortable rooms.

Hôtel Night-Club *(☎/fax 331 03 04, Route de Togo-Benin)* Rooms with fan & shared bathroom CFA8300, with fan/air-con & bathroom CFA10,300/20,300. This new, upmarket hotel offers clean, modern rooms (a rare find in Togo), a magnificent sparkling swimming pool and a trendy nightclub.

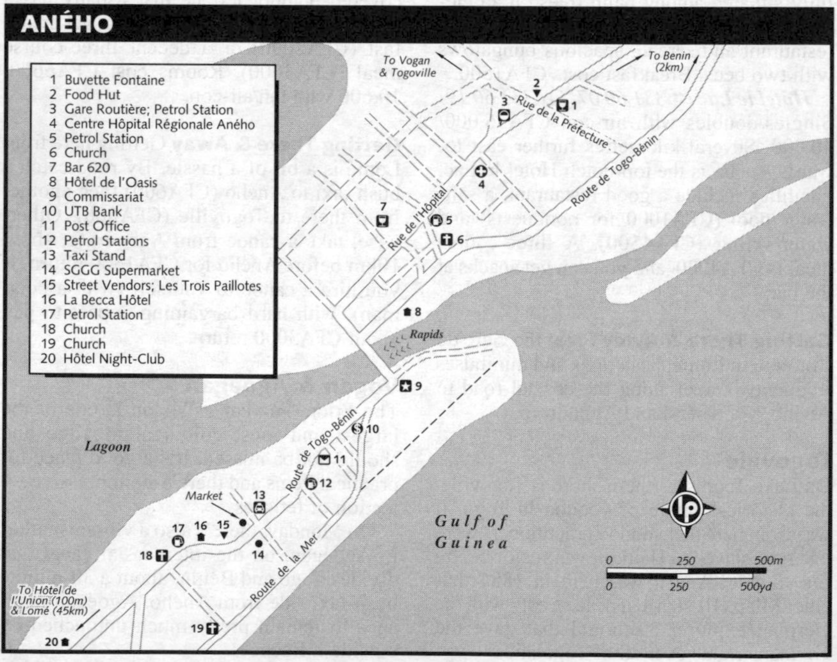
ANÉHO
1 Buvette Fontaine
2 Food Hut
3 Gare Routière; Petrol Station
4 Centre Hôpital Régionale Aného
5 Petrol Station
6 Church
7 Bar 620
8 Hôtel de l'Oasis
9 Commissariat
10 UTB Bank
11 Post Office
12 Petrol Stations
13 Taxi Stand
14 SGGG Supermarket
15 Street Vendors; Les Trois Paillotes
16 La Becca Hôtel
17 Petrol Station
18 Church
19 Church
20 Hôtel Night-Club
To Vogan & Togoville
To Benin (2km)
Rue de la Préfecture
Route de Togo-Bénin
Rue de l'Hôpital
Rapids
Lagoon
Market
Route de la Mer
Gulf of Guinea
To Hôtel de l'Union (100m) & Lomé (45km)
0 250 500m
0 250 500yd

Places to Eat

Opposite Buvette Fontaine, 200m east of the gare routière, there's a no-name ***food hut*** with cheap simple fare.

On the southwestern side of the bridge, there are ***street vendors*** in the market area across from SGGG supermarket. At night they sell omelettes, chicken, stews, brochettes, and pâte with sauce.

Apart from that the best dining option is the pleasant, but pricey restaurant at Hôtel de l'Oasis. The menu du jour here is CFA5200 and there is also a full à-la-carte menu (mains from CFA2000).

Entertainment

Les Trois Paillotes, next to the old market at the southwest end of town, is good for a drink in an outdoor setting.

Other bars include ***Buvette Fontaine***, near the gare routière, and ***Bar 620***, just off Rue de l'Hôpital in the northeast.

Hôtel Night-Club *(☎/fax 331 03 04)* Admission CFA3000. This is the best, and most expensive, place for dancing.

Getting There & Away

From the gare routière, at the northeastern end of town, bush taxis and minibuses head to Lomé (CFA600, one hour) as well as to the Beninese border and Cotonou.

KPALIMÉ

pop 48,300

Kpalimé (pah-lee-may), 120km northwest of Lomé, in the centre of the mountainous cacao and coffee region, is a good base for hiking (see the boxed text). It is noted for its mild climate, market and its Centre Artisanal (see Shopping later).

Nearby attractions include Klouto, home to a wonderful variety of butterflies and Mt Agou, Togo's highest peak at 986m. The magnificent **Kpimé Falls** *(admission CFA500)* about 15km northeast of Kpalimé, are usually a trickle, but it is an excellent spot for a swim. To visit the attractions charter a bush taxi.

Kpalimé is spread out, so covering it on foot takes time. There are four major tar roads leading out of town – northwest towards Klouto, northeast to Atakpamé, southwest to Ho (Ghana) and southeast to Lomé. The heart of the commercial district is around Rond-point Texaco.

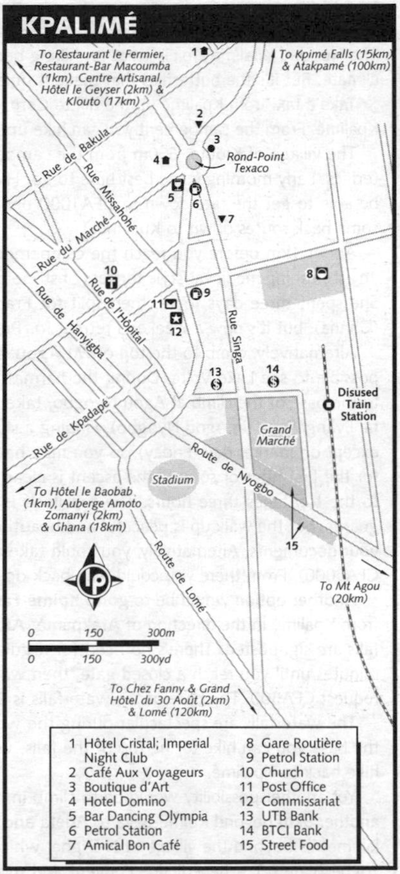
KPALIMÉ
To Restaurant le Fermier, Restaurant-Bar Macoumba (1km), Centre Artisanal, Hôtel le Geyser (2km) & Klouto (17km)
To Kpimé Falls (15km) & Atakpamé (100km)
Rond-Point Texaco
Rue de Bakula
Rue Missahohé
Rue du Marché
Rue de l'Hôpital
Rue de Hanyigba
Rue Singa
Rue de Kpadapé
Route de Nyogbo
Grand Marché
Stadium
Disused Train Station
To Hôtel le Baobab (1km), Auberge Amoto Zomanyi (2km) & Ghana (18km)
Route de Lomé
To Mt Agou (20km)
To Chez Fanny & Grand Hôtel du 30 Août (2km) & Lomé (120km)
0 150 300m
0 150 300yd
1 Hôtel Cristal; Imperial Night Club
2 Café Aux Voyageurs
3 Boutique d'Art
4 Hotel Domino
5 Bar Dancing Olympia
6 Petrol Station
7 Amical Bon Café
8 Gare Routière
9 Petrol Station
10 Church
11 Post Office
12 Commissariat
13 UTB Bank
14 BTCI Bank
15 Street Food

Places to Stay – Budget

Hôtel le Baobab *(Rue de Kpadapé)* Rooms CFA3500. This place, about 1km form the centre, offers cheap musty rooms with filthy shared toilets. Dinner is about CFA2000.

Auberge Amoto Zomanyi *(☎ 441 01 94, Rue de Kpadapé)* Singles/doubles with fan & shared bathroom CFA2500/3500. This friendly place is on the southwestern outskirts of town about 2km from the centre. It has clean, spacious rooms.

Hôtel Domino *(☎ 441 01 87)* Rooms without/with bathroom CFA3000/3500, with air-con CFA6000. The long-standing Domino, opposite Rond-point Texaco, is slightly better than the outside suggests. It has small, fairly grubby rooms with fan and shared bathroom. It also has rooms with

Hiking in the Kpalimé Area

The wooded Kpalimé area is great for hiking because of the thick vegetation, hilly terrain and cooler climate. But it's the butterflies that make it unique.

Take a taxi from Kpalimé up the hill to Campement de Klouto (670m), 12km to the northwest of Kpalimé. From the campement you can hike up **Mt Klouto** (741m) nearby and look over into Ghana.

The village of **Klouto**, 600m from the campement, is the starting point for hikes to see the butterflies. Early morning is the best time to go. Hire a guide in the village; with bargaining you should be able to get the rate down to CFA1000 per person. Afterwards, you could hike alone and take some back routes down to Kpalimé.

About 1km before you reach the campement you'll pass the paved turn-off for Château Viale, an astonishing medieval-style fortress of stone built by a Frenchman in 1944 as a retreat for his wife. She spent three days there, then split for France. On a clear day, there are views of Lake Volta (Ghana), but it's now a weekend retreat for President Eyadéma and is off limits to the public.

Alternatively, climb to the top of **Mt Agou** (986m), 20km southeast of Kpalimé, where it is also possible to see Lake Volta. During the harmattan season, though, views are disappointing. To get to the base of the climb at Agou Nyogbo, take a taxi from Lomé or Kpalimé and alight at the Hôpital Evangélique (in Agou Nyogbo). Finding a shared taxi (CFA500) headed to Agou can be difficult, except on market day (Friday), so you may have to charter one. In Agou, hire a guide to lead you for the first hour or so until the ascent is clear. After that just ask people along the way. The walk to the top takes three hours. The top itself is disappointing because of the antenna, fences and guards, but the walk up is peaceful and beautiful. Bring your passport as the guards may ask to see your documents. Alternatively, you could take a taxi all the way to the top of the mountain (about CFA5000). From there you could hike back down to the main Kpalimé/Lomé highway.

Another option would be to go to **Kpimé Falls**, north of Kpalimé. Take a taxi or a minibus north from Kpalimé in the direction of Atakpamé. After 9km you come to Kpimé-Séva, where the waterfalls are signposted. There's no need for a guide; just walk westward down the main track for 30 minutes until you reach a closed gate, then walk through a gap in it. The guardian at the gate will request CFA500. The base of the waterfalls is 200m or so from the gate.

The waterfalls are spectacular during the wet season, but almost dry the rest of the year. From the base you can hike to the top of the falls, where there's a lake and a panoramic view, and then hike back to Kpalimé.

Yet another possibility would be to climb in the **Danyi Plateau** area. To get there, continue north another 9km beyond Kpimé-Séva to Adéta and then turn left onto a tar road for the plateau. A few kilometres beyond the village of N'Digbé, which is on the plateau, is Abbaye de l'Ascension (e abzogbe@cafe.tg), a Benedictine convent and monastery, where you can overnight in a simple room with a shower (toilets are shared) for CFA5000. It is best to book ahead as the monastery is often full. There's also a small gift shop where you can purchase jars of honey and jams for around CFA800.

bathroom, and some with air-con. Pestering touts make this place an unattractive option.

Places to Stay – Mid-Range & Top End

Hôtel Cristal *(☎/fax 441 05 79, Rue de Bakula)* Rooms with fan CFA5300, singles/doubles with air-con CFA7800/8800. This large surprisingly modern hotel has 30 rooms and is clearly signposted from Rondpoint Texaco. The well-priced rooms are clean and neat and food is available. The hotel's nightclub is a popular spot on weekends, so it may get a little noisy.

Hôtel le Geyser *(☎ 441 04 67, e hotellegeyser@hotmail.com)* Rooms with fan/air-con CFA6300/10,300. The tranquil Hôtel le Geyser, 2km from the centre on the road to Klouto, is a pleasant place with a pool and an excellent restaurant (meals from CFA2700 to CFA3500).

Grand Hôtel du 30 Août *(☎ 441 00 95, fax 441 00 37, Route de Lomé)* Singles/doubles with air-con CFA10,300/12,600. This 30-year-old hotel, 2km south of town, has large, sparsely furnished rooms.

Chez Fanny *(☎/fax 441 00 91, Route de Lomé)* Rooms without/with air-con from

CFA7800/9800. Opposite Grand Hôtel du 30 Août is the quiet Chez Fanny. Once a private home, it has been turned into a small guesthouse and restaurant.

Places to Eat

The street ***stalls*** opposite the Grand Marché serve decent cheap food. Another good place for ***street food***, including delicious yam chips, is in the heart of town two blocks south of the Rond-point Texaco on Rue Singa.

Amical Bon Café *(Rue Singa)* serves good meals (including breakfast) from CFA1500, as does the reliable ***Café Aux Voyageurs***, just north of Rond-point Texaco.

Restaurant le Fermier Meals from CFA2500. Closed Mon. For excellent European food, try Restaurant le Fermier, on the northwestern outskirts of town.

Chez Fanny *(☎/fax 441 00 91, Route de Lomé)* Meals around CFA3000. This new restaurant is a popular place serving delicious French cuisine.

Restaurant-Bar Macoumba *(☎ 441 00 86)* Meals around CFA3000. For an upmarket restaurant serving Togolese fare, try the attractive open-air Macoumba, on the northern outskirts of town.

Entertainment

The best place for dancing is ***Bar Dancing Olympla***, on Rond-point Texaco.

Imperial Night Club, at Hôtel Cristal, is a popular disco that is liveliest at weekends. ***Bar Macoumba*** is another, but it's better for drinks than dancing.

Shopping

Kpalimé has a large, lively ***Grand Marché***. A good selection of Ghanaian kente cloth is sold here, but prices are higher here than in Kumasi.

Centre Artisanal *(☎ 441 00 77)* Open 7am-noon & 2.30pm-5.30pm Mon-Sat, 8.30am-1pm Sun & public holidays. The long-standing Centre Artisanal is about 2km north of the centre on the road to Klouto. Here you'll find a vast array of woodcarvings, including chiefs' chairs and tables carved out of solid blocks of wood, as well as pottery, macramé and batiks.

On the way up the hill to Klouto, you pass the ***Centre des Aveugles*** *(☎ 441 01 72)*, a centre for the blind, 4km from Kpalimé, which has a small gift shop where you can purchase crafts made by its residents.

The small ***Boutique d'Art*** on Rond-point Texaco also has an excellent selection of arts and craftwork (*djembe* drums, masks and statuettes).

Getting There & Away

The gare routière is in the heart of town, two blocks east of the petrol station on Rond-point Texaco. Regular services include Atakpamé (CFA1000, two hours), Kara (CFA4000, seven hours) and Lomé (CFA1300, three hours).

You can also get minibuses direct to Notsé (CFA1000), Tsévié (CFA1500), and to the Ghanaian border (CFA500), which closes at 6pm sharp, as well as direct to Ho in Ghana (CFA1200).

KLOUTO

The village of Klouto, 17km northwest of Kpalimé, is at the centre of the very scenic forested Kouma-Konda region. On the way, 7km from Kpalimé is the mineral-water spring, **Kamalo Falls**.

The big attraction in Klouto are to the masses of colourful butterflies in the surrounding forests – guided walks can be arranged at the Association Découverte Togo Profond (Adetop) and the Auberge des Papillons. See the boxed text 'Hiking in the Kpalimé Area' for more details.

Places to Stay & Eat

Auberge des Papillons *(☎ 441 00 31)* Doubles CFA2400. This friendly auberge is run by the inimitable M Prosper, the 'Butterfly Man'. It's fairly primitive, but clean. Cheap meals are available (eg, fufu with fish CFA2700).

Adetop *(☎/fax 441 02 08)* Dorm beds CFA3000. Another good place is the basic, but comfortable Adetop. Guided walks cost CFA5000 and the evening entertainment (singing, drumming and lessons on traditional medicine etc) is CFA7000. Breakfast is CFA800, and lunch or dinner will set you back CFA2000.

Campement de Klouto *(☎ 441 06 11)* Singles/doubles/triples CFA5000/7000/11,000. This 16-room facility, which was a German hospital before WWI, is an excellent spot for those seeking solitude. It's on top of a mountain, 12km northwest of Kpalimé, and a 30-minute walk from Klouto on the road to Ghana. It is quiet, shady and cool. The rooms are fairly large. Meals are around CFA4000 and breakfast is CFA1000.

Getting There & Away

To get from Kpalimé to Klouto, most people charter a taxi (about CFA4000 return). Taking a shared taxi is much cheaper, usually CFA300 from town to the police checkpoint. From there it's an easy walk to either the Campement de Klouto or Klouto village. To get back to Kpalimé, go to the checkpoint and wait for a shared taxi.

ATAKPAMÉ

pop 41,300

Once the favourite residence of the German colonial administrators, Atakpamé is in the heart of a mountainous area. The town is famous for its **stilt dancers**, and also its colourful Friday **market**.

The southern entrance to town is marked by a T-junction, the eastern leg of which bypasses the centre and continues on to Kara. The north-south leg is the highway from Lomé that continues into the centre of town.

Places to Stay

Auberge le Retour *(Rue de la Station de Lomé)* Rooms CFA2500. This poorly signed auberge, just off the highway opposite the Shell petrol station, has simple rooms with bucket shower and no fan. You'll have to bargain hard for a room as the original price we were quoted was a laughable CFA6000.

Foyer des Affaires Sociales *(☎ 440 06 53, Rue de la Station de Lomé)* Rooms with shared bathroom & fan/air-con CFA3000/4000. On the main highway, just north of the Shell petrol station, is this dormitory-like place. There is no restaurant, but its bare, clean rooms are a good deal.

Hôtel Miva *(☎ 440 04 37, Rue de la Station de Lomé)* Rooms with fan CFA3500. The homey Miva, 200m north of the junction to Kara and Lomé, is a much better place. It has small, decent rooms and clean, shared bathroom. Ask for a room at the back as it can be a little noisy.

Hôtel Relais des Plateaux *(☎ 440 11 05, Rue de la Station de Lomé)* Rooms with fan/air-con CFA5600/6600. The Relais des Plateaux, just south of the *commissariat*

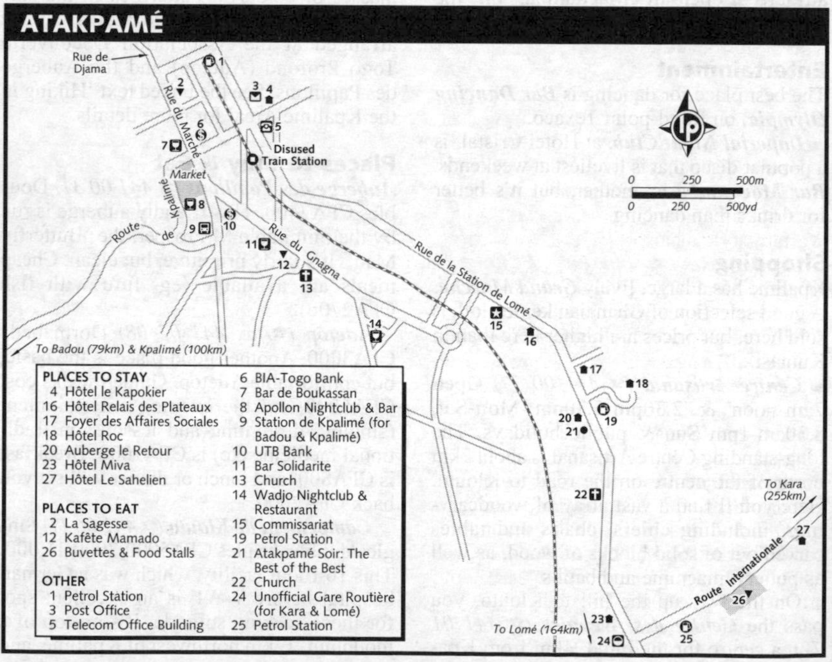
ATAKPAMÉ
Rue de Djama
Rue du Marché
Market
Kpalimé
Route de
Disused Train Station
Rue du Gnagna
Rue de la Station de Lomé
To Badou (79km) & Kpalimé (100km)
To Lomé (164km)
To Kara (255km)
Route Internationale
0 250 500m
0 250 500yd
PLACES TO STAY
4 Hôtel le Kapokier
16 Hôtel Relais des Plateaux
17 Foyer des Affaires Sociales
18 Hôtel Roc
20 Auberge le Retour
23 Hôtel Miva
27 Hôtel Le Sahelien
PLACES TO EAT
2 La Sagesse
12 Kafête Mamado
26 Buvettes & Food Stalls
OTHER
1 Petrol Station
3 Post Office
5 Telecom Office Building
6 BIA-Togo Bank
7 Bar de Boukassan
8 Apollon Nightclub & Bar
9 Station de Kpalimé (for Badou & Kpalimé)
10 UTB Bank
11 Bar Solidarite
13 Church
14 Wadjo Nightclub & Restaurant
15 Commissariat
19 Petrol Station
21 Atakpamé Soir: The Best of the Best
22 Church
24 Unofficial Gare Routière (for Kara & Lomé)
25 Petrol Station

(police station), has quiet, clean air-con rooms; but, those with fans are less enticing.

Hôtel le Kapokier *(☎ 440 02 84)* Rooms CFA6300. This hotel offers generous air-con rooms with bathroom (but shared toilet). Its restaurant is reasonably priced (mains around CFA1900) and has a pleasant outdoor setting. The hotel has no sign, so look for the large building overlooking the schoolyard, just up from the post office.

Hôtel Le Sahelien *(☎ 440 07 14, Route Internationale)* Rooms CFA8500. The new Hôtel Le Sahelien, on the main road to Kara, offers the best-value accommodation in Atakpamé. Its spacious, spotless rooms all have bathroom and colour TV. The rooftop bar and restaurant offer a breezy relaxed atmosphere. Meals range in price from CFA1000 to CFA4000.

On a hill off the main road, ***Hôtel Roc*** *(☎ 440 02 37, fax 440 00 33)* has good, clean rooms with excellent bathrooms, and most have balconies offering panoramic views of the city and surrounding hills. Singles/doubles/triples with air-con cost CFA11,000/13,000/14,500.

Places to Eat

Food stalls and cheap roadside ***buvettes***, where you can get delicious Togolese dishes, are dotted all over town.

The small ***Kafête Mamado*** is a great little omelette stand that also serves a good selection of tea and coffee.

Wadjo Mains CFA1000-3000. The upstairs restaurant at this popular nightspot (see Entertainment later) serves well-priced Western-style meals.

La Sagesse *(☎ 440 08 77, Rue du Marché)* Meals CFA1500-2300. The rustic La Sagesse, about 100m north of the market, is one of several inexpensive vibrant eateries offering local food along Rue du Marché. It serves surprisingly good food, with African dishes of your choice and desserts and salads.

Entertainment

Good places for beer include ***Apollon Nightclub & Bar*** just south of the market and down the hill and ***Bar Solidarité*** about 200m south of the market. Both serve cold brews from CFA400.

At night, the most popular places to dance the night away include ***Atakpamé Soir: The Best of the Best***, a bar-dancing joint just down from Auberge le Retour, and the plush ***Wadjo*** (admission CFA1000), just south of Rue du Gnagna.

Getting There & Away

Bush Taxi The road junction for Kara and Lomé, about 200m south of Hôtel Miva, serves as the unofficial terminal for all public transport to Lomé (CFA1700, three hours), Sokodé (CFA1900, 3½ hours) and Kara (CFA2200, five hours).

To get to Badou (CFA1000, 1½ hours) and Kpalimé (CFA1000, two hours), minibuses leave from Station de Kpalimé just south of the market.

BADOU

Badou, in the heart of the cacao area, is 88km west of Atakpamé. The major attraction is **Akloa Falls** (also spelt Akrowa) 11km southeast of town. Access to the falls is at **Tomagbé**, 9km to the south. There are minibuses from Badou to the waterfalls, but the walk from Badou to Tomagbé is pleasant. You have to pay CFA500 to the villagers at Tomagbé, which includes a guide if you want one.

The hike up the hill from Tomagbé to the waterfalls takes 40 minutes. It's a pleasant walk and not too strenuous, except in the wet season. The trip is worth it as the falls are beautiful and you can swim beneath them.

The place to stay is ***Hôtel Abuta*** *(☎ 443 00 16)*, which has doubles with air-con for CFA9500. Camping is permitted in the grounds for CFA1500 per person. Staff at the hotel will happily arrange a trip to the falls for you.

In Atakpamé, at Station de Kpalimé near the market, you can get a minibus to Badou (CFA1000, 1½ hours). Minibuses (CFA300) go from Badou to the waterfalls all day.

PARC NATIONAL DE FAZAO-MALFAKASSA

This 200,000-hectare national park is in the beautiful Malfakassa Mountains of central Togo, an area of thickly wooded savanna with plenty of waterfalls, cliffs and rocky hills.

The park, which was badly managed for a long time, has been taken over by the Swiss Fondation Franz Weber (e ffw@ffw.ch, w www.ffw.ch), which has concentrated its efforts on animal rehabilitation, the construction of trails and the provision of 4WD excursions. The hotel operates **wildlife drives** *(admission CFA18,000/13,000/9000/8000 for 1-2/3-4/6-7/10 people)* through the park. In a private vehicle it costs CFA10,000 per car plus CFA3000 per person. Although the park now boasts 60 elephants the chances of seeing much wildlife other than birds and monkeys are slim.

Adjoining Fazao is Malfakassa Zone de Chasse, an excellent area for hiking, and affording great views. If you want to hike, ask at Hôtel Parc Fazao for permission and bring plenty of water.

There are many good animal trails in Malfakassa; the best go along the mountain tops and south into the park. Orientation is easy even when you're hiking off trails due to the wide views from the mountain tops. In the wet season, walking up the slopes through the tall grass takes considerable effort.

Places to Stay & Eat

Hôtel Parc Fazao *(☎ 550 02 96, fax 550 01 75, ⓔ ffw.fazzo@rdd.tg)* Singles/doubles with air-con CFA16,000/20,000. Perched on a hill near Fazao village, and built like an African village, is the Parc Fazao, which has a restaurant. Rates are high, but include use of the pool and a guided tour of the village. Breakfast costs CFA2500 and the menu du jour is CFA4000. It is possible to ***camp*** in the park; ask at the hotel.

Getting There & Away

The marked turn-off for the Fazao section of the national park is in the village of Ayengré, 50km south of Sokodé on the main highway. You may have to wait a while for a ride to Hôtel Parc Fazao at Fazao. To get to the Malfakassa Zone de Chasse, catch a minibus from Sokodé towards Bassar and get off at the semi-abandoned village of Malfakassa in a pass near the highest point of these small mountains. From the village, hike south from the highway into the park.

The North

SOKODÉ

pop 120,400

Togo's second-largest city, Sokodé has no major sites, but is a pleasant place to spend a day or two. The town is spread out with shady trees everywhere, especially colourful flamboyants and mango trees. The heart of town is the T-junction just south of the market.

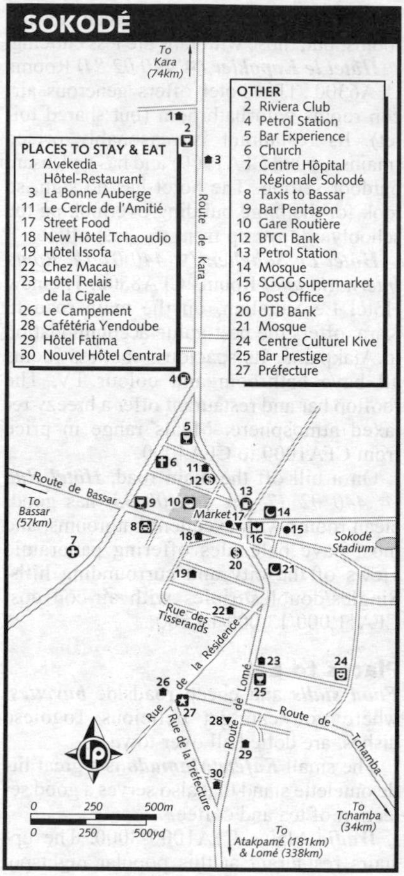
SOKODÉ
To Kara (74km)
PLACES TO STAY & EAT
1 Avekedia Hôtel-Restaurant
3 La Bonne Auberge
11 Le Cercle de l'Amitié
17 Street Food
18 New Hôtel Tchaoudjo
19 Hôtel Issofa
22 Chez Macau
23 Hôtel Relais de la Cigale
26 Le Campement
28 Cafétéria Yendoube
29 Hôtel Fatima
30 Nouvel Hôtel Central
OTHER
2 Riviera Club
4 Petrol Station
5 Bar Experience
6 Church
7 Centre Hôpital Régionale Sokodé
8 Taxis to Bassar
9 Bar Pentagon
10 Gare Routière
12 BTCI Bank
13 Petrol Station
14 Mosque
15 SGGG Supermarket
16 Post Office
20 UTB Bank
21 Mosque
24 Centre Culturel Kive
25 Bar Prestige
27 Préfecture
Route de Kara
Route de Bassar
To Bassar (57km)
Market
Sokodé Stadium
Rue des Tisserands
Rue de la Résidence
Rue de Lomé
Route de Lomé
Rue de la Préfecture
Route de Tchamba
To Tchamba (34km)
To Atakpamé (181km) & Lomé (338km)
0 250 500m
0 250 500yd

While Sokodé is a Muslim town many animist traditions survive. One of the more interesting ceremonies is Adossa, which takes place on the second day after the Prophet's birthday (for details on Islamic holidays see the Regional Facts for the Visitor chapter). During this spectacle, men engage in a series of violent dances after drinking a special potion that supposedly makes their skin impenetrable.

Places to Stay

Le Campement *(☎ 550 15 57, Rue de la Résidence)* Singles/doubles CFA2500/3500.

The tranquil Le Campement is up the hill from the *douane* (customs post) on the southern edge of town, a good walk from the centre. Its austere but spacious rooms have sheets, fan and bathroom.

Chez Macau *(☎ 550 11 98, Rue de la Résidence)* Rooms CFA3000. The rooms here are fetid, but the meals are cheap.

Hôtel Fatima Rooms CFA3300. Just off Route de Lomé you'll find the simple Hôtel Fatima. The rooms are passable – all have a shower, but the toilet is shared.

Hôtel Relais de la Cigale *(☎ 990 50 62, Route de Lomé)* Rooms CFA3500. Further north of Hôtel Fatima, on the main highway, the Relais de la Cigale has neat spartan rooms with fan and clean shared bathroom.

New Hôtel Tchaoudjo *(☎ 550 11 93, Route de Bassar)* Rooms with fan & shared bathroom CFA3500, with air-con CFA7000. Despite adding 'new' to its name the rooms are just as gloomy as they were when we last visited.

Hôtel Issofa *(☎ 550 09 89)* Rooms without/with bathroom CFA3500/4500, with air-con CFA8500. The Issofa is excellent value. The rooms are clean and comfortable and those with air-con are carpeted. Oddly the signs from the main street are spelt 'Essofa'.

La Bonne Auberge *(☎ 550 02 35, Route de Kara)* Rooms with bathroom & fan/air-con CFA3500/6500. About 2km north of the centre, this auberge has small clean rooms.

Avekedia Hôtel-Restaurant *(☎ 550 05 34, Off Route de Kara)* Rooms with fan CFA4500, singles/doubles with air-con CFA7500/9000. Just north of La Bonne Auberge is the recommended and very clean Avekedia, with a bar, restaurant and tidy rooms.

Le Cercle de l'Amitié *(☎ 550 09 06, Route de Kara)* Singles/doubles with fan CFA3800/5300, with air-con CFA7300/8800. This place is another bar-restaurant with rooms.

Nouvel Hôtel Central *(☎ 550 01 23, Route de Lomé)* Rooms CFA8500, bungalows CFA11,000. This large, quiet place is on shady grounds at the southern end of town. It has clean, spacious rooms and tiled bathrooms with hot water.

Places to Eat

For ***street food***, try the area around the central market.

A good place for cheap Togolese food is the friendly ***Cafétéria Yendoube*** on the southern side of town. A filling meal of couscous with tomato sauce is CFA600.

Hôtel Relais de la Cigale *(☎ 990 50 62, Route de Lomé)* Meals CFA1500-2500. This is one of the most attractive and relaxing hotel restaurants in town; it has an extensive menu.

Entertainment

Bar Prestige *(Route de Lomé)* This lively open-air place, on the main drag south of the central area, has loud African music and small draught beers for CFA150.

Riviera Club *(☎ 550 11 30, Route de Kara)* The highly animated Riviera Club is a hip dance club, drawing large crowds most weekends.

Bar Pentagon *(☎ 550 05 34, Route de Bassar)* If you're too hot to go dancing, head for Bar Pentagon, on the western side of town near the gare routière. In addition to loud music it has food, typically a plat du jour costs CFA800.

Other bars worth mentioning are the dependable ***Chez Macau*** *(Rue de la Résidence)*; and ***Bar Experience*** *(Route de Kara)* north of the BTCI Bank. Both also serve well-priced Togolese tucker (meals from CFA600).

Centre Culturel Kive *(☎ 550 09 68, Route de la Cigale)* Just beyond the Relais de la Cigale, the Centre Culturel Kive serves as an Internet centre (CFA500 per hour) and the local theatre (CFA100).

Getting There & Away

From the gare routière, which is situated one block west of the market on Route de Bassar, minibuses go regularly to Bassar (CFA800), Kara (CFA1000, one hour), Atakpamé (CFA1900, 2½ hours) and Lomé (CFA3400, six hours).

BASSAR

Renowned for its traditional hunters, Bassar is 57km northwest of Sokodé. It is also the site of the annual Igname (yam) festival in September, which involves lots of dancing, including fire dances.

The best place to stay is the dreary, state-run ***Hôtel de Bassar*** *(☎ 663 00 40)* with bungalows from CFA6000; it also has a disco and an unappetising restaurant.

There are lots of ***food stalls*** in and around the market, and a number of friendly bars.

Bassar can be easily reached by bush taxi from Sokodé (CFA800).

BAFILO

The predominantly Muslim town of Bafilo is in a very scenic setting just north of the Aledjo Fault, where the Route Internationale passes through an imposing break in the cliff, and is surrounded by a magnificent tract of forest.

Bafilo is a good place to stop for at least a day just to see **weavers** in action and to buy pagnes of cloth at very reasonable prices.

The small ***Hôtel Maza Esso*** *(Route de Kara)* is the only place to stay. It has a choice of rooms with fan (CFA3000) or air-con (CFA6000) and a ***restaurant-bar***.

KARA

pop 34,900

Laid out by the Germans on a spacious scale, Kara's a pleasant town and a good base for trips to the **Tamberma Valley** and the scenic **Mt Kabyé** (see Around Kara later this chapter).

Because President Eyadéma originally came from Pya, a Kabyé village about 20km to the north, he has pumped a lot of money into Kara, constructing a brewery, radio station and, most impressively, the party headquarters.

The Shell intersection on Route Internationale is where the tar road east to Benin and west to Ghana begin. The centre of town is about 500m to the west. That's where you'll find the big Tuesday **market**.

Kara has two good Internet centres: CIB-Net Cyber Espace (☎ 660 18 00, cib@cib-tg.net) on Rue de Chaminade, and Cyber Café Or@cle (☎ 660 04 98), just off Av Eyadéma opposite the market. Access costs around CFA400 per hour.

Places to Stay

West of the market towards Hôtel Kara are several cheap hotels. ***Hôtel Sapaw*** *(☎ 660 14 44)* charges CFA2800 for doubles with fan and clean bathroom; you can get food here as well. Just up from Hôtel Sapaw, ***Auberge Herzo*** *(☎ 660 02 98)* charges CFA2000 for spacious doubles with a fan and shared bathroom. Further north is the

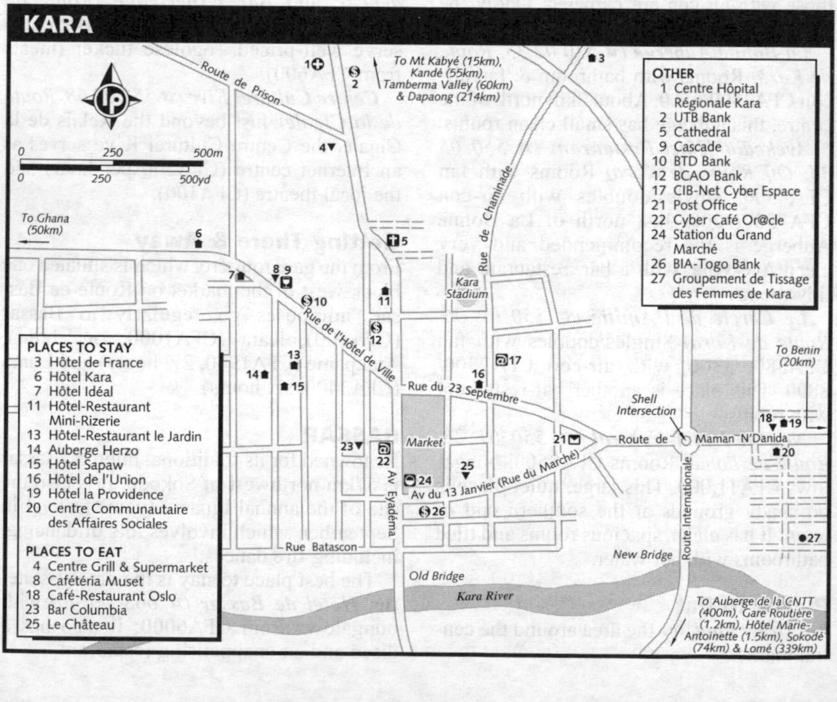
KARA
Route de Prison
To Mt Kabyé (15km), Kandé (55km), Tamberma Valley (60km) & Dapaong (214km)
0 250 500m
0 250 500yd
To Ghana (50km)
Rue de Chaminade
Kara Stadium
Rue de l'Hôtel de Ville
Rue du 23 Septembre
Market
Av Eyadéma
Av du 13 Janvier (Rue du Marché)
Rue Batascon
Old Bridge
Kara River
New Bridge
Route Internationale
Shell Intersection
Route de Maman N'Danida
To Benin (20km)
To Auberge de la CNTT (400m), Gare Routière (1.2km), Hôtel Marie-Antoinette (1.5km), Sokodé (74km) & Lomé (339km)
OTHER
1 Centre Hôpital Régionale Kara
2 UTB Bank
5 Cathedral
9 Cascade
10 BTD Bank
12 BCAO Bank
17 CIB-Net Cyber Espace
21 Post Office
22 Cyber Café Or@cle
24 Station du Grand Marché
26 BIA-Togo Bank
27 Groupement de Tissage des Femmes de Kara
PLACES TO STAY
3 Hôtel de France
6 Hôtel Kara
7 Hôtel Idéal
11 Hôtel-Restaurant Mini-Rizerie
13 Hôtel-Restaurant le Jardin
14 Auberge Herzo
15 Hôtel Sapaw
16 Hôtel de l'Union
19 Hôtel la Providence
20 Centre Communautaire des Affaires Sociales
PLACES TO EAT
4 Centre Grill & Supermarket
8 Cafétéria Muset
18 Café-Restaurant Oslo
23 Bar Columbia
25 Le Château

dreary ***Hôtel Idéal*** *(☎ 660 12 58, Rue de l'Hôtel de Ville)*, which charges CFA2500 for a large room with fan.

Auberge de la CNTT *(☎ 660 62 32, Route Internationale)* Rooms with fan/air-con CFA3800/6800. A notch up in price is the popular and well-maintained Auberge de la CNTT, on the south side of town.

Hôtel la Providence *(☎ 660 17 42)* Rooms with fan/air-con CFA5000/7000, bungalows with fan CFA3000. Another good budget choice is the Providence (previously called Hôtel Tombé) just off Route de Maman N'Dandia, with clean, spacious rooms.

Centre Communautaire des Affaires Sociales *(☎ 660 61 18, Route de Maman N'Danida)* Dorm beds CFA2000, rooms with fan/air-con CFA5500/7500, bungalows CFA10,000. This large, well-run centre has a bar-restaurant and is quite good value. Beds are in rooms with three bunk beds and fan. The shared bathrooms are clean.

Hôtel de France *(☎ 660 03 42, Off Rue de Chaminade)* Rooms with air-con & shower CFA7500-10,500. A good mid-range choice is Hôtel de France, with large, attractive rooms. There is also a great terrace area on the roof where you can watch the sun set over the town.

Hôtel-Restaurant Mini-Rizerie *(☎ 660 06 65, Av Eyadéma)* Rooms with fan/air-con CFA5600/7600. This place is close to the centre and there's a popular bar-restaurant.

Hôtel-Restaurant le Jardin *(☎ 660 01 34, Off Rue de l'Hôtel de Ville)* Rooms with air-con CFA8500. This delightful hotel has a pleasant garden and small but very attractive rooms, as well as Kara's top restaurant.

Hôtel Marie-Antoinette *(☎ 660 16 07, ⓔ hotel-marie-antoinette@gmx.net, ⓦ makara.multimania.com, Route Internationale)* Singles/doubles with fan CFA6500/7500, with air-con CFA9500/10,500. This new hotel, 1.5km from Kara, has cheery pink and blue bungalows and a pleasant restaurant.

Hôtel de l'Union *(☎ 660 14 88, Rue du 23 Septembre)* Rooms with air-con CFA12,300. This classy hotel offers clean, modern rooms.

Hôtel Kara *(☎ 660 05 17, fax 660 62 42, Rue de l'Hôtel de Ville)* Singles CFA18,800-22,100, doubles CFA25,300-29,100. This is the best and largest hotel in Kara. It has a pool, volleyball and tennis courts, shops, a nightclub and three classes of rooms.

Places to Eat

Kara has a number of cheap places serving superb Togolese food. One of the most popular eateries is ***Bar Columbia***, a small, open-air restaurant-bar, one block west of the market. The women pound away all morning on the corn and millet; by lunchtime it's difficult to find a seat. Their specialities are pâte and fufu.

Cafeteria Muset *(Rue de l'Hôtel de Ville)* Breakfast from CFA350, lunch/dinner CFA600/2500. Another good spot for cheap, filling meals is the friendly Cafeteria Muset, next to the Cascade bar.

Café-Restaurant Oslo Meals from CFA1200. Also worth a look is the Oslo, near Station de Tomdé, which serves decent well-priced meals.

Centre Grill Meals CFA1000-4500. Popular with expats, the Centre Grill has an extensive menu including Western favourites like pizzas, hotdogs and hamburgers, as well as traditional Togolese dishes.

Le Château *(☎ 660 60 40, Av du 13 Janvier)* Meals from CFA750. Open Tues-Sun. Le Château, an attractive bar-restaurant 50m east of the market, is a perennial favourite. It serves ice-cold beers for CFA250 and has a large menu with both African and European dishes. A large plate of fufu with *tomate boeys* (a tomato-based sauce) costs CFA950.

Hôtel-Restaurant Minl-Rlzerle (See Places to Stay) Breakfast CFA1400, lunch/dinner CFA1800/4000. Another winner is the long-standing Mini-Rizerie. It serves three-course French meals (CFA6500) and will also prepare Togolese food.

Hôtel-Restaurant le Jardin (See Places to Stay) Meals CFA1750-6500. The city's best restaurant is at this hotel. The menu is popular with locals and offers both French and Asian cuisine. The *crevettes au gingembre* (prawns with ginger; CFA1750) and the *riz cantonnais* (Cantonese rice; CFA1000) are particularly good.

Entertainment

One of the hottest African nightclubs in town is ***Bar la Détente*** near the market just off Av du 13 Janvier. Large Bière Béninoise here are CFA250 and draught beers are CFA150.

The lively open-air ***Cascade*** *(Rue de l'Hôtel Kara)* is another popular local haunt.

The best place to dance is the disco at ***Hôtel Kara***, but it's open on weekends only (CFA1000).

Shopping

Groupement de Tissage des Femmes de Kara, on the eastern side of town, sells high-quality African fabrics. From the Shell intersection, take the tar road east for 200m and just beyond Affaires Sociales turn right, heading south on a dirt road, and follow the signs.

Getting There & Away

From the main gare routière, about 2km south of the town centre, minibuses go regularly to Sokodé (CFA700, one hour), Dapaong (CFA2400) and Lomé (CFA3900, seven hours).

To get to the border with Ghana or Benin, get a minibus or bush taxi from Station du Grand Marché next to the market.

AROUND KARA

Sarakawa

Sarakawa, 23km to the northwest of Kara, is not worth a special visit, but if you are passing through, check out the huge monument commemorating the site where Eyadéma's plane crashed in 1974. The statue has Eyadéma pointing to the ground and saying, 'They almost killed me here'. To get here, take the Route Internationale north for about 10km, then the tar road west for 13km.

Mt Kabyé & Around

Mt Kabyé (810m) is roughly 15km north of Kara, in one of the most scenic areas in Togo. Heading from Kara, stop in **Landa**, a village 15km northeast of Kara where women make a variety of goods. Some 4km further east, on the main highway, is **Kétao**. The huge Wednesday market here is absolutely fascinating.

From here, head north for about 20km to **Pagouda**, where you may be able to hear traditional music (ask the chief).

The only place to stay is the derelict ***Hôtel de Pagouda***, which has gloomy air-con chalets for CFA5000. There is no restaurant here so you will need to bring your own supplies.

From Pagouda head west into an area renowned for its *forgerons* (blacksmiths) and on to **Pya**, Eyadéma's birthplace, on the Route Internationale, then south for about 14km back to Kara.

NIAMTOUGOU

This sleepy town, 28km north of Kara on Route Internationale, boasts an active Sunday **market**, where you'll find a good selection of baskets and ceramic bowls, and the great ***Codhni Artisanal Centre*** (☎ *665 00 30)* on the southern side of town. The centre has well made cloth (CFA3500) and dresses (CFA5500).

Motel de Niamtougou has spacious air-con singles/doubles for CFA4700/6300. It also has a bar and restaurant.

TAMBERMA VALLEY

The Tamberma Valley has a unique collection of fortified villages, founded in the 17th century by people who fled the slaving forays of the Abomey kings (see the boxed text 'Tamberma Compounds'). The valley

Tamberma Compounds

A typical Tamberma compound, called a *tata*, consists of a series of towers connected by a thick wall with only one doorway to the outside. In the past, the castle-like nature of these extraordinary structures helped ward off invasions by neighbouring tribes and, in the late 19th century, the Germans. Inside, there's a huge elevated terrace of clay-covered logs where the inhabitants cook, dry their millet and corn, and spend most of their leisure time.

Skilled builders, the Tamberma use no tools, and only use clay, wood and straw. The walls are banco, a mixture of unfired clay and straw, which is used as a binder. The towers, which are capped by picturesque conical roofs, are used for storing corn and millet. The other rooms are used for sleeping, bathing and, during the rainy season, cooking. The animals are kept under the terrace, protected from the rain.

Inside the compounds, there may be fetish animal skulls on the walls and ceilings and a tiny altar for sacrificing chickens. You may see a man and his son going off to hunt with bows and arrows. When the son gets old enough to start his own family, he shoots off an arrow and where it lands is where he'll construct his own tata.

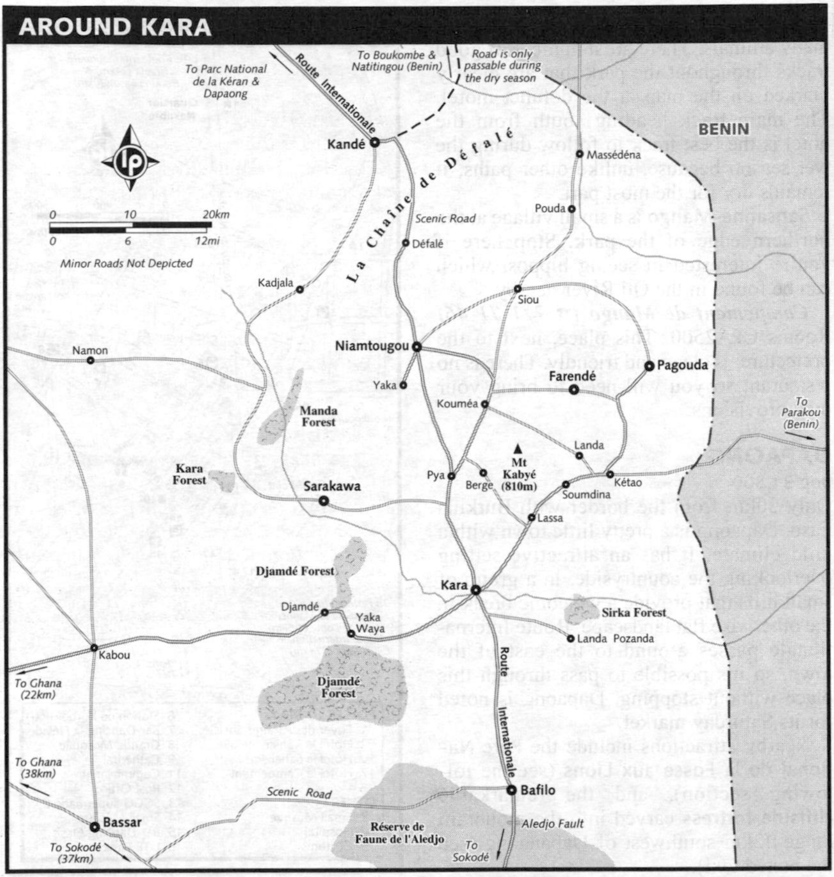
AROUND KARA
To Parc National de la Kéran & Dapaong
Route Internationale
To Boukombe & Natitingou (Benin)
Road is only passable during the dry season
BENIN
Kandé
La Chaîne de Défalé
Massédéna
Pouda
0 10 20km
0 6 12mi
Scenic Road
Défalé
Minor Roads Not Depicted
Kadjala
Siou
Namon
Niamtougou
Pagouda
Farendé
Yaka
Manda Forest
Kouméa
To Parakou (Benin)
Landa
Mt Kabyé (810m)
Kara Forest
Pya
Berge
Kétao
Sarakawa
Soumdina
Lassa
Djamdé Forest
Kara
Djamdé
Yaka Waya
Sirka Forest
Landa Pozanda
Kabou
Route Internationale
To Ghana (22km)
Djamdé Forest
To Ghana (38km)
Bafilo
Scenic Road
Bassar
Réserve de Faune de l'Aledjo
Aledjo Fault
To Sokodé (37km)
To Sokodé

is accessible from Kandé, 27km north of Niamtougou. If you ask around, you should be able to find one of the dirt tracks leading east for about 27km to one of the Tamberma villages near the Benin border.

In the heart of the village, not far from the central **market** is the small **Musée Tamberma** *(☎ 667 20 11; admission CFA500; open daily)*.

There is nowhere to stay in the villages, and only a rundown ***campement*** *(☎ 667 00 73)* in Kandé with beds from CFA2000. A better option is to stay overnight in Kara.

Getting There & Away

Bush taxis shuttle between Kandé and the fortified village of Nadoba on Wednesday (market day in Nadoba) and Friday (market day in Kandé). A chartered taxi for the day from Kara to visit a number of the villages costs about CFA15,000 (after much haggling). Alternatively, you could hike 20km east of Kandé to Warengo, then another 7km to Nadoba. Be sure to bring plenty of water.

PARC NATIONAL DE LA KÉRAN

During the dry season, a visit to what is left of this national park is recommended, which in recent years has been gobbled up by farmland. Heading north from Kandé towards Dapaong, look for a sign pointing to the park's entrance, about 2km from the road. The turn-off for Naboulgou, inside the park, is 32km north of Kandé. This is the site of the well marked, but now defunct, Motel de Naboulgou.

Unless you're very lucky, you won't see many animals. There are a number of good tracks throughout the park that are clearly marked on the map at the defunct motel. The main track heading south from the hotel is the best track to follow during the wet season because, unlike other paths, it remains dry for the most part.

Sansanné-Mango is a small village at the northern edge of the park. Stop here if you're interested in seeing hippos, which can be found in the Oti River nearby.

Campement de Mango *(☎ 771 71 46)* Rooms CFA2500. This place, next to the prefecture, is clean and friendly. There is no restaurant so you will need to bring your own provisions.

DAPAONG

pop 31,800

Only 30km from the border with Burkina Faso, Dapaong is a pretty little town with a mild climate. It has an attractive setting overlooking the countryside, in a group of small hills that provide a welcome break in the otherwise flat landscape. Route Internationale passes around to the east of the town, so it's possible to pass through this place without stopping. Dapaong is noted for its Saturday **market**.

Nearby attractions include the **Parc National de la Fosse aux Lions** (see the following section), and the remarkable **cliffside fortress** carved into the mountain range 42km southwest of Dapanaong (see the boxed text).

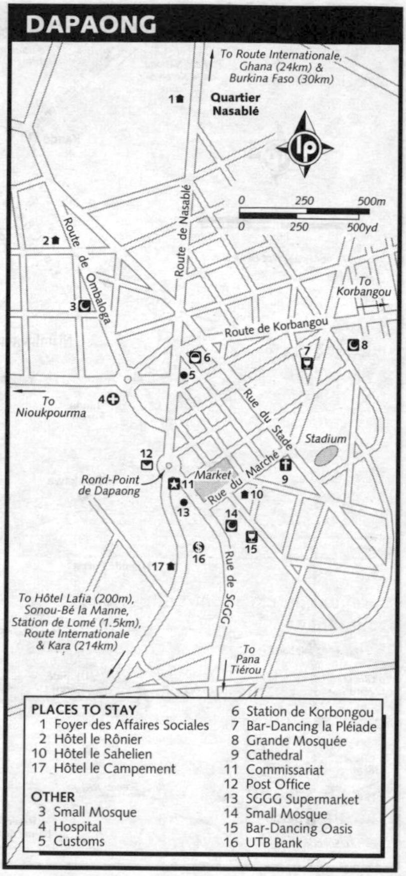
DAPAONG
To Route Internationale, Ghana (24km) & Burkina Faso (30km)
Quartier Nasablé
0 250 500m
0 250 500yd
Route de Nasablé
Route de Ombaloga
To Korbangou
Route de Korbangou
To Nioukpourma
Rue du Stade
Stadium
Rond-Point de Dapaong
Market
Rue du Marché
Rue de SGGG
To Hôtel Lafia (200m), Sonou-Bé la Manne, Station de Lomé (1.5km), Route Internationale & Kara (214km)
To Pana Tiérou
PLACES TO STAY
1 Foyer des Affaires Sociales
2 Hôtel le Rônier
10 Hôtel le Sahelien
17 Hôtel le Campement
OTHER
3 Small Mosque
4 Hospital
5 Customs
6 Station de Korbongou
7 Bar-Dancing la Pléiade
8 Grande Mosquée
9 Cathedral
11 Commissariat
12 Post Office
13 SGGG Supermarket
14 Small Mosque
15 Bar-Dancing Oasis
16 UTB Bank

Places to Stay & Eat

Foyer des Affaires Sociales *(☎ 770 80 29, Route de Nasablé)* Rooms without bathroom CFA1800, with fan/air-con CFA2200/3200. This is the cheapest place and it's on the main road heading north out of town. Its bare rooms have shared bathroom (with running water).

Hôtel Lafia Rooms with fan/air-con CFA3500/4500. On the opposite side of town on the main street leading to the centre is the Lafia, which is similar to Foyer des Affaires Sociales. It has clean rooms with shower, basin, and running water (toilets are shared).

Hôtel le Rônier Rooms with fan/air-con CFA2800/4500. This hotel, a few blocks northwest of the centre, has plain rooms with fan and shared bathroom, or rooms with air-con and bathroom, but there's no running water.

Hôtel le Sahelien *(☎ 770 81 84)* Rooms without/with bathroom CFA3000/4000, with air-con CFA6000. The Sahelien is in the heart of town and has large rooms. The hotel's best feature is its paillote restaurant.

Hôtel le Campement *(☎ 770 80 55)* Rooms with fan/air-con CFA8600/13,800. This hotel on the main road into town is a short walk up a hill from the centre. It's an attractive and relaxing place to stay. Its spacious rooms have decent bathrooms (toilets are shared) and, as an added bonus, have a free supply of condoms conveniently located on the nightstand beside the bed. There's also an active bar with ice-cold

Cliffside Fortress

Carved into the rocky cliffside in the remote mountain ranges 42km southwest of Dapaong is an amazing minifortress.

During the 19th century the Chokossi Empire, centred around Mango, established a feudal empire over much of northern Togo. The Moba people who lived on and around the plateau resented this and so built the cliffside dwellings as a secure location to retreat to whenever tax collectors or Chokossi soldiers appeared. Its precarious position, under the cliff's ledge, provided them with the perfect natural protection.

Thanks to German ingenuity it is possible to climb down to the long-since abandoned site via a fully protected steel ladder. Here you'll find a number of large conical clay containers, which were used to store food supplies, as well as the sleeping quarters and cooking areas used by the villagers as they waited out their foes.

To reach the escarpment, follow Route Internationale south of Dapaong for about 16km. Then turn left onto an unmarked dirt road. Follow this road 10km west to the village of Nano. Finding a shared taxi headed to Nano can be difficult, except on market day (Thursday), so you may have to charter one. In Nano you'll need to meet the local chief to obtain an official ticket (CFA2000) allowing you to visit the site. While you're here, hire a guide (around CFA2000) as the site is not signposted.

From Nano it is about another 16km up a rough dirt road (only passable by 4WD) to the top of the escarpment. Once at the top you must seek permission (again) from the chief of Nagou, the village nearest the site, who will expect to be paid (CFA1500).

If you plan to hike to the site be sure to bring plenty of water.

beers and an excellent but quite expensive restaurant.

Sonu-Bé la Manne Restaurant Rooms with fan/air-con CFA4600/6000. This place near Station de Lomé, about 2km out of the centre, has four spotless rooms with fan and bathroom.

In addition to eating at the hotels, good places to eat, drink and meet travellers include the spacious open-air ***Bar-Dancing la Pléiade*** and ***Bar-Dancing Oasis***.

Getting There & Away

Transport to the Burkina Faso border (CFA600) and Ouagadougou (CFA4000) depart regularly from Station de Korbongou, several blocks north of the market.

The main gare routière is Station de Lomé on Route Internationale, 2km south of the centre. From here you can get minibuses and bush taxis to Kara (CFA2400, four hours) and Lomé (CFA4500, 14 hours).

PARC NATIONAL DE LA FOSSE AUX LIONS

If you want to hike through some typical savanna woodland, the Fosse aux Lions might be of interest – but it's no longer a 'pit of lions'! It's 12km south of Dapaong, and Route Internationale runs straight through it, making access easy (take any bush taxi going along the highway). The entrance is signposted and there's no entrance fee. The Fosse is in a flat area at the base of a steep ridge. Hike up the cliffs for an excellent view of the surrounding countryside. Be sure to stock up on food and water in Dapaong as the water in the park is not safe to drink.

Language

Across West Africa, the region's myriad ethnic groups speak several hundred local languages, many subdivided into numerous distinct dialects. The people of Nigeria – West Africa's most populous country – speak at least 350 languages and dialects, while even tiny Guinea-Bissau (population just over one million) has around 20 languages.

Consequently, common languages are absolutely essential, and several are used. These may be the language of the largest group in a particular area or country. For example, Hausa has spread out from its northern Nigerian heartland to become widely understood as a trading language in the eastern parts of West Africa. Similarly, Dioula has become a common tongue in markets over much of the western part of the region. Also widespread are the former colonial languages of French, English and Portuguese. In some areas, the common tongue is a creole – a combination of native African and imported European languages.

Colonial Languages

FRENCH

Though we have used the polite verb form 'vous' in the following phrase list, the informal form 'tu' is used much more commonly in West Africa; you'll hear *s'il te plaît* more than *s'il vous plaît*, which may be considered impolite in France unless spoken between good friends. If in doubt in West Africa (when dealing with police, border officials or older people) it's always safer to use the polite 'vous' form. In this phrase list the polite form is used unless otherwise indicated – 'inf' for the informal, 'pol' for the polite.

Note that French uses masculine and feminine word forms; an adjective will agree in number and gender with the noun it modifies. Where two alternatives are given, in this guide we have indicated the masculine form with 'm', the feminine form with 'f'. Also note that where singular and plural forms of words are given, the singular is marked 'sg' and the plural, 'pl'.

Basics

I	*je*
you (sg)	*tu* (inf)/*vous* (pol)
he/she	*il/elle* (m/f)
we	*nous*
you (pl)	*vous*
they	*ils/elles* (m/f)

Don't Be Lost For Words in ...!

country	official language	principal African languages (in this guide)
Benin	French	Fon, Hausa, Yoruba
Burkina Faso	French	Dioula, Fon, Hausa, Moré, Senoufo
Cape Verde	Portuguese	Crioulo
Côte d'Ivoire	French	Dan (Yacouba), Dioula, Hausa, Senoufo
Gambia	English	Diola (Jola), Mandinka, Wolof
Ghana	English	Ewe, Ga, Hausa, Twi
Guinea	French	Fula (Futa Djalon), Malinké, Susu
Guinea-Bissau	Portuguese	Crioulo
Liberia	English	Dan (Yacouba)
Mali	French	Bambara, Malinké, Sangha dialect, Senoufo, Tamashek
Mauritania	Arabic (French still in common use)	Dioula, Fula (Fulfulde), Hassaniya, Wolof
Niger	French	Djerma, Fon, Hausa, Tamashek
Nigeria	English	Hausa, Igbo, Yoruba
Senegal	French	Crioulo, Diola, Fula (Fulfulde), Malinké, Mandinka, Wolof
Sierra Leone	English	Krio
Togo	French	Ewe, Fon, Kabyé, Mina

Hello/Good morning.	*Bonjour.*
Good evening.	*Bonsoir.*
Goodbye.	*Salut* or *A bientôt/ Au revoir.* (inf/pol)
Good night.	*Bonne nuit.*
How are you?	*Ça va/Comment allez-vous?* (inf/pol)
Fine, thanks.	*Bien, merci.*
Yes.	*Oui.*
No.	*Non.*
No, thank you.	*Non, merci.*
Please.	*S'il vous plaît.*
Thank you.	*Merci.*
You're welcome.	*De rien/ Je vous en prie.*
Excuse me.	*Excusez-moi/Pardon.*
What's your name?	*Comment vous appelez-vous?*
My name is ...	*Je m'appelle ...*

Language Difficulties

Do you speak English?	*Parlez-vous anglais?*
I understand.	*Je comprends.*
I don't understand.	*Je ne comprends pas.*

Getting Around

I want to go to ...	*Je veux aller à ...*
What's the fare to ...?	*Combien coûte le billet pour ...?*
When does (the) ... leave/arrive?	*À quelle heure part/ arrive ...?*
bus	*le bus*
train	*le train*
boat	*le bateau*
Where is (the) ...?	*Où est ...?*
airport	*l'aéroport*
bus station/ bush taxi park	*la gare routière*
ferry terminal	*la gare maritime*
ticket office	*la billeterie*
train station	*la gare*
I'd like a ... ticket.	*Je voudrais un billet ...*
one-way	*aller simple*
return	*aller retour*
first class	*première classe*
second class	*deuxième classe*
Which bus goes to ...?	*Quel bus part pour ...?*
Does this bus go to ...?	*Ce bus-là va-t-il à ...?*

Signs – French

Entrée	**Entrance**
Sortie	**Exit**
Chambres Libres	**Rooms Available**
Complet	**No Vacancies**
Renseignements	**Information**
Ouvert/Fermé	**Open/Closed**
Interdit	**Prohibited**
(Commissariat de) Police	**Police Station**
Toilettes/WC	**Toilets**
Hommes	**Men**
Femmes	**Women**

How many buses per day go to ...?	*Il y a combien de bus chaque jour pour ...?*
Stop here, please.	*Arrêtez ici, s'il vous plaît.*
Wait!	*Attendez!*
May I sit here?	*Puis-je m'asseoir ici?*
first	*premier*
next	*prochain*
last	*dernier*
the ticket	*le billet*
the timetable	*l'horaire*
crowded	*beaucoup de monde*
daily	*chaque jour*
early	*tôt*
late	*tard*
on time	*à l'heure*
quickly	*vite*
slowly	*lentement*
the address	*l'adresse*
the city	*la ville*
the number	*le numéro*
the street	*la rue*
village	*le village*
Where can I rent a ...?	*Où est-ce que je peux louer ...?*
bicycle	*un vélo*
car	*une voiture*

Directions

How far is ...?	*À combien de kilomètres est ...?*
Where (is ...)?	*Où (est ...)?*
Go straight ahead.	*Continuez tout droit.*
Turn left.	*Tournez à gauche.*
Turn right.	*Tournez à droite.*

near	*proche*
far	*loin*
here/there	*ici/là*
next to	*à côté de*
opposite	*en face*
behind	*derrière*
north	*nord*
south	*sud*
east	*est*
west	*ouest*

Around Town

For other common French terms which may prove useful as you move 'around town' see the Glossary following this chapter.

a bank	*une banque*
the beach	*la plage*
the ... embassy	*l'ambassade de ...*
the market	*le marché*
a pharmacy	*une pharmacie*
the post office	*la poste*
a public telephone	*une cabine téléphonique*
a restaurant	*un restaurant*

I want to change ...	*Je voudrais changer ...*
(cash) money	*de l'argent*
travellers cheques	*des chèques de voyage*

What time does it open/close?	*Quelle est l' heure de ouverture/fermeture?*

Accommodation

Where is ...?	*Où est ...?*
the campground	*le camping*
the hotel	*l'hôtel*

Do you have any rooms available?	*Avez-vous des chambres libres?*

I'd like a ... room.	*Je cherche une chambre ...*
single	*à un lit*
double	*double*

Can I see the room?	*Puis-je voir la chambre?*
How much is it per night?	*Quel est le prix par nuit?*
How much is it per person?	*Quel est le prix par personne?*
That's too much for me.	*C'est trop cher pour moi.*
Do you have a cheaper room?	*Avez-vous une chambre moins chère?*
This is fine.	*Ça va bien.*

air-conditioning	*climatisation*
a bed	*un lit*
a blanket	*une couverture*
full/no vacancies	*complet*
hot water	*eau chaude*
a key	*une clef/clé*
a sheet	*un drap*
a shower	*une douche*
the toilet	*les toilettes*

Shopping

I'm looking for the market?	*Je cherche le marché?*
Where can I buy ...?	*Où est-ce que je peux acheter ...?*
Do you have ...?	*Avez-vous ...?*
(How much/many do you want?)	*(Vous en désirez combien?)*
That's enough.	*Ça suffit.*
I'd like (three).	*J'en voudrais (trois).*
How much is it?	*Ça coûte combien?*
How much for (two)?	*Combien ça fait pour (deux)?*

batteries	*des piles*
coffee	*du café*
gas cylinder	*une bonbonne de gas*
matches	*des alumettes*
newspaper	*un journal*
stamps	*des timbres*
toothpaste	*du dentifrice*
washing powder	*de la lessive*

big/small	*grand/petit*
more/less	*plus/moins*
open/closed	*ouvert/fermé*

Health

I need a doctor.	*J'ai besoin d'un médecin.*
Where is the hospital?	*Où est l'hôpital?*
I feel dizzy.	*J'ai des vertiges.*
I feel nauseaous.	*J'ai des nausées.*
I'm pregnant.	*Je suis enceinte.*

I'm ...	*Je suis ...*
diabetic	*diabétique*
epileptic	*épileptique*
asthmatic	*asthmatique*
allergic to antibiotics	*allergique aux antibiotiques*

Emergencies – French

Help!	*Au secours!*
Call the police!	*Appelez la police!*
Call a doctor!	*Appelez un médecin!*
I've been robbed.	*On m'a volé.*
Go away!	*Allez-vous-en!*
I'm lost.	*Je me suis égaré(e).*

aspirin	*l'aspirine*
condoms	*des préservatifs*
diarrhoea	*la diarrhée*
medicine	*le médicament*
sanitary napkins	*des serviettes hygiéniques*
tampons	*des tampons hygiéniques*

Time, Days & Numbers

What time is it?	*Quelle heure est-il?*
It's (two) o'clock.	*Il est (deux) heures.*
It's quarter past six.	*Il est six heures et quart.*
It's quarter to seven.	*Il est sept heures moins le quart.*
At what time?	*À quelle heure?*
When?	*Quand?*

now	*maintenant*
after	*après*
today	*aujourd'hui*
tomorrow	*demain*
yesterday	*hier*
(in the) morning	*(du) matin*
(in the) afternoon	*(de l') après-midi*
(in the) evening	*(du) soir*
day	*jour*
night	*nuit*
week/month/year	*semaine/mois/an*

Monday	*lundi*
Tuesday	*mardi*
Wednesday	*mercredi*
Thursday	*jeudi*
Friday	*vendredi*
Saturday	*samedi*
Sunday	*dimanche*

January	*janvier*
February	*février*
March	*mars*
April	*avril*
May	*mai*
June	*juin*
July	*juillet*
August	*août*
September	*septembre*
October	*octobre*
November	*novembre*
December	*décembre*

0	*zéro*
1	*un*
2	*deux*
3	*trois*
4	*quatre*
5	*cinq*
6	*six*
7	*sept*
8	*huit*
9	*neuf*
10	*dix*
11	*onze*
12	*douze*
13	*treize*
14	*quatorze*
15	*quinze*
16	*seize*
17	*dix-sept*
18	*dix-huit*
19	*dix-neuf*
20	*vingt*
21	*vingt-et-un*
22	*vingt-deux*
30	*trente*
40	*quarante*
50	*cinquante*
60	*soixante*
70	*soixante-dix*
80	*quatre-vingts*
90	*quatre-vingt-dix*
100	*cent*
101	*cent un*
125	*cent vingt-cinq*
200	*deux cents*
300	*trois cents*
1000	*mille*

one million	*un million*

PORTUGUESE

Like French, Portuguese is a Romance language (ie, one closely derived from Latin). In West Africa it's the official language in Cape Verde and Guinea-Bissau.

Note that Portuguese uses masculine and feminine word endings, usually '-o' and '-a' respectively – to say 'thank you', a man will therefore say *obrigado*, a woman, *obrigada*.

Greetings & Civilities

Hello.	*Bom dia/Olá/Chao.*
Good morning.	*Bom dia.*
Good evening.	*Boa tarde.*
Goodbye.	*Adeus/Chao.*
See you later.	*Até logo.*
How are you?	*Como está?*
I'm fine, thanks.	*Bem, obrigado/a.*(m/f)
Yes/No.	*Sim/Não.*
Maybe.	*Talvez.*
Please.	*Se faz favor/por favor.*
Thank you.	*Obrigado/a.*
Excuse me.	*Desculpe/Com licença.*
Sorry/Forgive me.	*Desculpe.*
What's your name?	*Como se chama?*
My name is ...	*Chamo-me ...*

Language Difficulties

Do you speak English?	*Fala inglès?*
I understand.	*Percebo/Entendo.*
I don't understand.	*Não percebo/entendo.*

Getting Around

I want to go to ...	*Quero ir a ...*
How long does it take?	*Quanto tempo leva isso?*
What time does the ... leave/arrive?	*A que horas parte/chega o ...?*
bus	*autocarro*
train	*combóio*
boat	*barco*
next	*próximo*
first	*primeiro*
last	*último*
timetable	*horário*
Where is the ...?	*Onde é a ...?*
airport	*aeroporto*
bus stop	*paragem de autocarro*
train station	*estação ferroviária*
I'd like a ...ticket.	*Queria um bilhete ...*
one way	*simples/de ida*
return	*de ida e volta.*
1st class	*primeira classe*
2nd class	*segunda classe*
I'd like to hire ...	*Queria alugar ...*
a car	*um carro*
a bicycle	*uma bicicleta*
How do I get to ...?	*Como vou para ...?*
Is it near/far?	*É perto/longe?*
Go straight ahead.	*Siga sempre a direito.*
Turn left.	*Vire á esquerda.*
Turn right.	*Vire á direita.*

Signs – Portuguese

Entrada	**Entrance**
Saída	**Exit**
Entrada Grátis	**Free Admission**
Informações	**Information**
Aberto	**Open**
Encerrado (or Fechado)	**Closed**
O Posto Da Polícia	**Police Station**
Proíbido	**Prohibited**
Empurre/Puxe	**Push/Pull**
Quartos Livres	**Rooms Available**
Lavabos/WC	**Toilets**
h, Homens	**Men**
s, Senhoras	**Women**

Accommodation

I'm looking for ...	*Procuro ...*
a guesthouse	*uma pensão*
a hotel	*uma hotel*
a youth hostel	*uma pousada de juventude*
a bed	*uma cama*
a cheap room	*um quarto barato*
a single room	*um quarto individual*
a double room (with twin beds)	*um quarto de casal (duplo)*
Do you have any rooms available?	*Tem quartos livres?*
How much is it per night/per person?	*Quanto é por noite/por pessoa?*
Is breakfast included?	*O pequeno almoço está incluído?*
Can I see the room?	*Posso ver o quarto?*
Where is the toilet?	*Onde ficam os lavabos (as casas de banho)?*
It is very dirty/noisy/expensive.	*É muito sujo/ruidoso/caro.*

Health

I'm sick.	*Estou doente.*
I need a doctor.	*Preciso um médico.*
Where is a hospital/medical clinic?	*Onde é um hospital/um centro de saúde?*

Emergencies – Portuguese

Help!	*Socorro!*
Call the police!	*Chame a polícia!*
Call a doctor!	*Chame um médico!*
I've been robbed.	*Fui roubado/a.*
Go away!	*Deixe-me em paz!*
I'm lost.	*Estou perdido/a.*

I'm ...	*Sou ...*
diabetic	*diabético/a*
epileptic	*epiléptico/a*
asthmatic	*asmático/a*
allergic to antibiotics	*alérgico/a a antibióticos*

aspirin	*aspirina*
condoms	*preservativo*
diarrhoea	*diarreia*
dizzy	*vertiginoso*
medicine	*remédio/medicamento*
nausea	*náusea*
sanitary napkins	*pensos higiénicos*
tampons	*tampões*

Time, Dates & Numbers

What time is it?	*Que horas são?*
When?	*Quando?*
today	*hoje*
tonight	*hoje á noite*
tomorrow	*amanhã*
yesterday	*ontem*
morning/afternoon	*manhã/tarde*

Monday	*segunda-feira*
Tuesday	*terça-feira*
Wednesday	*quarta-feira*
Thursday	*quinta-feira*
Friday	*sexta-feira*
Saturday	*sábado*
Sunday	*domingo*

1	*um/uma*
2	*dois/duas*
3	*três*
4	*quatro*
5	*cinco*
6	*seis*
7	*sete*
8	*oito*
9	*nove*
10	*dez*
100	*cem*
1000	*mil*
one million	*um milhão*

African Languages

BAMBARA & DIOULA

Differences between Bambara and Dioula (also known as Jula) are relatively minor and the two languages share much of their vocabulary, eg, 'Goodbye' in Bambara is *kan-bay*, in Dioula it is *an-bay*.

Bambara (called *bamanakan* in Bambara) is the predominant indigenous language of Mali, while Dioula is widely spoken as a first language in Côte d'Ivoire and Burkina Faso. Dioula is one of West Africa's major lingua francas (a common language used for communication between groups with different mother tongues) so the words and phrases included following can be used not only in Burkina Faso, Côte d'Ivoire and Mali but also in southeastern Mauritania (Néma and south), eastern Senegal, and parts of Gambia. In addition there are also distinct similarities between Bambara/Dioula and the Mandinka of northern Gambia and parts of southern Senegal, and most Senoufo speakers in southern Mali (Sikasso region), southwestern Burkina Faso, and northern Côte d'Ivoire (Korhogo region) can speak Bambara/Dioula. It's not hard to see that some knowledge of it will prove very useful in this part of West Africa!

Bambara and Dioula are normally written using a phonetic alphabet; in this guide we've mostly used letters common to English. Some specific pronunciations you'll need to be aware of are:

a	as in 'far'
e	as in 'bet'; the combination **eh** is pronounced somewhere between 'ey' and the 'e' in 'bet'
i	as in 'marine'
o	as in 'hot'
u	between the 'u' in 'pull' and the 'oo' in 'boot'
g	always hard, as in 'get'
j	as in 'jet'
ñ	as in the 'ni' in 'onion'
ng	as the 'ng' in 'sing' – indicates that the preceding vowel is nasal
r	almost a 'd' sound

In the following phrase lists variation in vocabulary is indicated by (B) for Bambara and (D) for Dioula.

Greetings

The response to any of the following greetings (beginning with *i-ni-* ...) is *n-ba* (for men) and *n-seh* (for women).

Hello.	*i-ni-**cheh***
Hello. (to someone working)	*i-ni-**baa**-rah* (literally, to you and your work)
Good morning.	*i-ni-**soh**-goh-mah* (sunrise to midday)
Good afternoon.	*i-ni-**ti**-leh* (12 noon to 3 pm)
Good evening.	*i-ni-**wu**-lah* (3 pm to sunset)
Good night.	*i-ni-**suh*** (sunset to sunrise)
Goodbye.	***kan**-beng* (B) ***an**-beng* (D)

Note In this guide bold letters indicate where the stress falls within a word.

Please.	*S'il vous plaît.* (French)
Thank you.	*i-ni-**cheh**/ **bah**-si-tay* (lit: no problem)
Sorry/Pardon.	***ha**-keh-toh*
Yes.	***ah**-woh*
No.	***ah**-yee* (B)/***uh**-uh* (D)
How are you?	*i-kah-kéné*
I'm fine.	*tuh-**roh**-teh*
And you?	*eh-dung?*
Can you help me please?	***ha**-keh-toh, i-**bay**-say-kah **nn** deh-meh wa?*

What's Spoken Where?

INDIGENOUS LANGUAGE	Benin	Burkina Faso	Cape Verde	Côte d'Ivoire	Gambia	Ghana	Guinea	Guinea-Bissau	Liberia	Mali	Mauritania	Niger	Nigeria	Senegal	Sierra Leone	Togo
	COUNTRIES (WHERE SPOKEN)															
Bambara/Dioula	–	■	–	■	–	–	–	–	–	■	■	–	–	–	–	–
Crioulo	–	–	■	–	–	–	–	■	–	–	–	–	–	■	–	–
Dan (Yacouba)	–	–	–	■	–	–	–	–	■	–	–	–	–	–	–	–
Diola (Jola)	–	–	–	–	■	–	–	–	–	–	–	–	–	■	–	–
Djerma (Zarma)	–	–	–	–	–	–	–	–	–	–	–	■	–	–	–	–
Ewe	–	–	–	–	–	■	–	–	–	–	–	–	–	–	–	■
Fon (Fongbe)	■	■	–	–	–	–	–	–	–	–	–	■	–	–	–	■
Fula (Pulaar)	–	–	–	–	–	–	■	–	–	–	–	–	–	■	–	–
Ga (Adangme)	–	–	–	–	–	■	–	–	–	–	–	–	–	–	–	–
Hassaniya	–	–	–	–	–	–	–	–	–	–	■	–	–	–	–	–
Hausa	■	■	–	■	–	■	–	–	–	–	–	■	■	–	–	–
Igbo	–	–	–	–	–	–	–	–	–	–	–	–	■	–	–	–
Kabyé	–	–	–	–	–	–	–	–	–	–	–	–	–	–	–	■
Krio	–	–	–	–	–	–	–	–	–	–	–	–	–	–	■	–
Malinké	–	–	–	–	–	–	■	–	–	■	–	–	–	■	–	–
Mandinka	–	–	–	–	■	–	–	–	–	–	–	–	–	■	–	–
Mina	–	–	–	–	–	–	–	–	–	–	–	–	–	–	–	■
Moré	–	■	–	–	–	–	–	–	–	–	–	–	–	–	–	–
Sangha dialect	–	–	–	–	–	–	–	–	–	■	–	–	–	–	–	–
Senoufo	–	■	–	■	–	–	–	–	–	■	–	–	–	–	–	–
Susu	–	–	–	–	–	–	■	–	–	–	–	–	–	–	–	–
Tamashek	–	–	–	–	–	–	–	–	–	■	–	■	–	–	–	–
Twi	–	–	–	–	–	■	–	–	–	–	–	–	–	–	–	–
Wolof	–	–	–	–	■	–	–	–	–	–	■	–	–	■	–	–
Yoruba	■	–	–	–	–	–	–	–	–	–	–	–	■	–	–	–

Do you speak English?	*i-beh-say-kah* ***ahng**-gih-lih-**kahng*** *meng wa?*
Do you speak French?	*i-beh-seh-kah* *tu-**bah**-bu-**kan*** *meng wa?*
I only speak English.	*nn-beh-seh-kah* ***ahng**-gih-lih-**kahng*** *meng doh-rohn*
I speak a little French.	*nn-beh-seh-kah* *tu-**bah**-bu-**kan*** *meng **doh**-nee*
I understand.	*nn-y'**ah**-fah-mu*
I don't understand.	*nn-**m'ah**-fah-mu*
What's your (first) name?	*i-toh-goh?*
My name is ...	***nn**-toh-goh ...*
Where are you from?	***i**-beh-boh-**ming**?*
I'm from ...	***nn**-beh-boh ...*
Where is ...?	*... beh-**ming**?*
Is it far?	***ah**-kah-**jang**-wah?*
straight ahead	***ah**-beh-tih-**leng***
left	***nu**-man-boh-loh-feh* (lit: nose-picking hand)
right	***ki**-ni-boh-loh-feh* (lit: rice-eating hand)
How much is this?	***ni**-ñeh-**joh**-li-yeh?*
That's too much.	*ah-**kah**-geh-**leng** – **bah**-ri-kah!* (lit: lower the price)
Leave me alone!	***boh**'i-sah!*

1	***keh**-leng*
2	*fih-**lah*** (or *flah)*
3	***sahb**-bah*
4	***nah**-ni*
5	***du**-ru*
6	***woh**-roh*
7	***woh**-lon-flah*
8	***shay**-ging*
9	***koh**-nohng-tahng*
10	***tahng***
11	***tahng**-ni-kay-len*
12	***tahng**-ni-**flah***
13	***tahng**-ni-**sah**-bah*
14	***tahng**-ni-**nah**-ni*
15	***tahng**-ni-**doo**-ru*
16	***tahng**-ni-**woh**-roh*
17	***tahng**-ni-**woh**-lon-flah*
18	***tahng**-ni-**shay**-ging*
19	***tahng**-ni **koh**-nohn-**tahng***
20	*mu-**gang***
30	***bi**-sahb-bah*
31	***bi**-sahb-bah-ni-**keh**-leng*
40	***bi**-nah-ni*
50	***bi**-du-ru*
60	***bi**-woh-roh*
70	***bi**-woh-lon-fla*
80	***bi**-shay-ging*
90	***bie**-koh-nohn-tahng*
100	***keh**-meh*
1000	***wah***
5000	***wah**-du-ru*
one million	*wah-wah* or *millar*

With thanks to Andy Rebold.

CRIOULO

Crioulo is a Portuguese-based creole spoken (with more or less mutual intelligibility) in the Cape Verde islands, Guinea-Bissau (where it's the lingua franca and 'market language') and parts of Senegal and Gambia. Nearly half the Crioulo speakers of Cape Verde are literate in Portuguese but since independence in 1975 Crioulo has become increasingly dominant; upwards of 70% of the country's population speak Crioulo. Even allowing for regional differences the phrases listed below should be understood in both Cape Verde and Guinea-Bissau.

Good morning.	*bom-**dee**-ah*
Good evening.	*bow-ah **no**-tay*
Goodbye.	***nah**-buy*
How are you?	*ou-**kor**-poh ees-tah-**bon**?*
I'm fine.	*tah-**bon***
Please.	*puhr-fah-**bohr***
Thank you.	*ob-ree-**gah**-doh*
How much is it?	*kahl eh **preh**-suh*

1	*ahn*
2	*dohs*
3	*trehs*
4	***kwah**-tuh*
5	***sin**-kuh*
6	***say**-ehs*
7	***seh**-tee*
8	***oy**-tuh*
9	***noh**-vee*
10	*dehs*
11	***ohn**-zee*
12	***doh**-zee*
13	***treh**-zee*
14	*kah-**toh**-zee*
15	***kihn**-zee*
16	*dee-zah-**say**-ehs*

17	*dee-zah-**seh**-tee*
18	*dee-**zoy**-tuh*
19	*dee-zah-**noh**-vee*
20	***vin**-tee*
30	***trin**-tah*
100	*sehn*
1000	*meel*

DAN (YACOUBA)

Dan (also known as 'Yacouba') is one of the principal African languages spoken in Côte d'Ivoire (in and around Man). There are also a significant number of Dan speakers in Liberia (where it's referred to as 'Gio'). There are a couple of major dialects and more than 20 sub-dialects; as a result most communication between different language groups in the region is carried out in Dioula (see the Bambara/Dioula section in this guide for a comprehensive list of Dioula words and phrases).

Good morning.	*un-**zhoo**-bah-boh* (man)
Good morning.	***nah**-bah-boh* (woman)
Good evening.	*un-**zhoo**-attoir* (man)
Good evening.	***nah**-attoir* (woman)
How are you?	*bwee-**ahr**-way*
Thank you.	***bah**-lee-kah*

DIOLA (JOLA)

The Diola people inhabit the Casamance region of Senegal, and also the southwestern parts of Gambia, where their name is spelt Jola. Their language is Diola, also known as Jola, which should not be confused with the Dioula/Jula spoken widely in other parts of West Africa. Diola society is segmented and very flexible, so several dialects have developed which may not be mutually intelligible between different groups even though the area inhabited by the Diola is relatively small.

Hello/Welcome.	*kah-sou-mai-kep*
Greetings. (reply)	*kah-sou-mai-kep*
Goodbye.	*ou-kah-to-rrah*

DIOULA (JULA)

Refer to the Bambara/Dioula section earlier in this language guide.

DJERMA (ZARMA)

After Hausa, Djerma (pronounced *jer-mah*, also known as Zarma) is Niger's most common African language (people with Djerma as their first language make up around a quarter of the country's population). It's spoken mostly in the western regions including around Niamey, and it is one of the official national languages used for radio broadcasts.

Good morning.	*mah-teen-keh-**nee***
Good evening.	*mah-teen-**hee**-ree*
How are you?	***bar**-kah?*
Thank you.	*foh-foh*
Goodbye.	*kah-**lah** ton-ton*

EWE

Ewe (pronounced *ev-vay*) is the major indigenous language of southern Togo. It is also an official language of instruction in primary and secondary schools in Ghana where it's spoken mainly in the east of the country; you'll find that Twi (the language of the Ashanti and the Fanti) is the more universally spoken language of Ghana. There are also several closely related languages and dialects of Ewe spoken in Benin.

Good morning/ evening.	*nee-**lye**-nee-ah*
	***mee**-lay* (response)
What's your name?	*n-koh-**woh**-day?*
My name is ...	*nk-nee-**n**-yay ...*
How are you?	*nee-**foh**-ah?*
I'm fine.	***mee**-foh*
Thank you.	*mou-**doh**, ack-pay-**now***
Goodbye.	*mee-**ah doh**-goh*

FON (FONGBE)

Fon (called Fongbe in the language itself) belongs to the Kwa group of the Gbe language family, *gbe* being the Fon word for 'language'. It is another of the major lingua francas of West Africa, spoken for the most part in Nigeria and Benin, but also used widely in Côte d'Ivoire, Burkina Faso, Niger and Togo. While Fon is subject to clear dialectal variation depending on region, you should find that the list of words and phrases below will be universally understood.

The Fon language is written using the IPA (International Phonetic Alphabet); for the sake of simplicity we've used a pronunciation system which uses letters common to English. Fon is a tone language (ie, intended meaning is dependent upon changes in pitch within the normal range of a speaker's voice) with a standard system of five tones; in this guide we have simplified things by using only two written accents for tones (acute accent, eg, **á**, for a high tone, grave accent, eg, **à**, for a low tone) – an unmarked vowel has a mid-tone.

Pronounce letters as you would in English, keeping the following points in mind:

a as in 'far'
e as in 'met'
i as in 'marine'
o either as in 'hot' or as in 'for'
u as in 'put'
g as in 'go'
h silent
hng indicates that the preceding vowel is nasalised, eg, the 'ing' sound in 'sing'
ñ as the 'ni' in 'onion'

Hello.	*ò-kù*
Goodbye.	*é-dà-bòh*
Please.	*kèhng-kéhng-lèhng*
Thank you.	*àh-wàh-nu*
You're welcome.	*é-sù-kpéh-ah*
Sorry/Pardon.	*kèhng-kéhng-lèhng*
Yes.	*ehng*
No.	*éh-woh*
How are you?	*neh-àh-dèh-gbòhng?*
I'm fine.	*ùhn-dòh-gàhng-jí*
And you?	*hweh-loh?*
Can you help me please?	*kèhng-kéhng-lèhng-dá-lòh-mì?*

Do you speak ...?	*àh-sèh ... àh?*
English	*glèhng-síhng-gbè*
French	*flàng-sé-gbè*

I only speak English.	*glèhng-síhng-gbè kéh-déh-wèh-ùn-sèh*
I speak a little French.	*ùn-sèh flàng-sé-gbè kpèh-dèh*
I understand.	*ùn-mòh-nu-jéh-mèh*
I don't understand.	*ùn-mòh-nu-jéh-mèh-ah*
What's your name?	*neh-àh-nòh-ñí?*
My name is ...	*ùn-nòh-ñí ...*
Where are you from?	*tòh-téh-mèh-nùh-wéh-ñí-wèh?*
I'm from ...	*... nùh-wéh-ñí-mì*
Where is ...?	*fi-téh-wéh ...?*
Is it far?	*eh-lihng-wéh-ah?*
straight ahead	*treh-leh-leh*
left	*àh-myòh*
right	*àh-dì-sí*
How much is this?	*nà-bí-wèh-ñí-éh-lòh?*
That's too much.	*éh-vá-khìh-díhng*
Leave me alone!	*joh-mí-dóh!*

1	*òh-deh*
2	*òh-wèh*
3	*à-tòhng*
4	*eh-nèh*
5	*à-tóhng*
6	*à-yì-zéhng*
7	*teh-weh*
8	*ta-toh*
9	*téhng-nèh*
10	*woh*
11	*woh-dòh-kpóh*
12	*weh-wèh*
13	*wah-tòhng*
14	*weh-nèh*
15	*à-fòh-tòhn*
16	*à-fòh-tòhng-nù-kúhng-dòh-póh*
17	*à-fòh-tóhng-nu-kúhng-wèh*
18	*à-fòh-tóhng-nu-kúhng-à-tòhng*
19	*à-fòh-tóhng-nu-kúhng-èh-neh*
20	*kòh*
30	*gbàhng*
40	*kàhng-déh*
50	*kàhng-déh-woh*
60	*kàhng-déh-koh*
70	*kàhng-déh-gbàhng*
80	*kàhng-wèh*
90	*kàhng-wèh-woh*
100	*kàhng-wèh-kòh*
1000	*à-fàh-tóhng*

one million	*mì-yóhng-dòh-kpóh*

With thanks to Aimé Avolonto.

FULA (PULAAR)

Fula, also known as Pulaar, is one of the languages of the Fula people found across West Africa, from northern Senegal to Sudan in the east, and as far south as Ghana and Nigeria. The Fula are known as Peul in Senegal (they are also called Fulani and Fulbe).

There are two main languages in the Fulani group:

- Fulfulde, spoken mainly in northern and southern Senegal (includes the dialects known as Tukulor and Fulakunda).
- Futa Fula (also known as Futa Djalon), the main indigenous language of Guinea, also spoken in eastern Senegal.

It's worth noting that these far-flung languages have many regional dialects which aren't always mutually intelligible between different groups.

Fulfulde

The following words and phrases should be understood through most parts of Senegal. Note that **ng** should be pronounced as one sound (like the 'ng' in 'sing'); practise isolating this sound and using it at the beginning of a word. The letter **ñ** represents the 'ni' sound in 'onion'.

Hello.	*no ngoolu daa* (sg)
	no ngoolu dong (pl)
Goodbye.	*ñalleen e jamm*
	(lit: Have a good day)
	mbaaleen e jamm
	(lit: Have a good night)
Please.	*njaafodaa*
Thank you.	*a jaaraama* (sg)
	on jaaraama (pl)
You're welcome.	*enen ndendidum*
Sorry/Pardon.	*yaafo* or *achanam hakke*
Yes.	*eey*
No.	*alaa*
How are you?	*no mbaddaa?*
I'm fine.	*mbe de sellee*
... and you?	*... an nene?*
Can you help me please?	*ada waawi wallude mi, njaafodaa?*
Do you speak English/French?	*ada faama engale/faranse?*
I only speak English.	*ko engale tan kaala mi*
I speak a little French.	*mi nani faranse seeda*
I understand.	*mi faami*
I don't understand.	*mi faamaani*
What's your name?	*no mbiyeteedaa?*
My name is ...	*ko ... mbiyetee mi*
Where are you from?	*to njeyedaa?*
I'm from ...	*ko ... njeyaa mi*
Where is ...?	*hoto woni?*
Is it far?	*no woddi?*
straight ahead	*ko yeesu*
left	*nano bang-ge*
right	*nano ñaamo*
How much is this?	*dum no foti jarata?*
That's too much.	*e ne tiidi no feewu*
Leave me alone!	*accam!* or *oppam mi deeja!*

1	*go-o*
2	*didi*
3	*tati*
4	*nayi*
5	*joyi*
6	*jeego*
7	*jeedidi*
8	*jeetati*
9	*jeenayi*
10	*sappo*
11	*sappoygoo*
12	*sappoydidi*
13	*sappoytati*
20	*noogaas*
30	*chappantati*
100	*temedere*
1000	*wujenere*
one million	*miliyong goo*

With thanks to Fallou Ngom.

Futa Fula (Futa Djalon)

This variety of Fula known as Futa Fula or Futa Djalon is predominant in the Futa Djalon region of Guinea. It is named after the people who speak it, and is distinct from the variety known as Fulfulde which is spoken in northern and southern Senegal.

Good morning/ Good evening.	*on-**jaa**-rah-mah*
How are you?	*ta-nah-lah-**ton**?*
I'm fine.	*ta-nah-**oh**-alah*
Where is ...?	*koh-hon-toh woh-nee?*
Thank you.	*on-**jaa**-rah-mah*
Goodbye.	*on-ount-tou-mah*

GA & ADANGME

Ga (and its very close relative Adangme) is one of the major indigenous languages spoken in Ghana, mostly around Accra.

Good morning/ Good evening.	*meeng-gah-bou*
How are you?	*tey-yoh-tain?*
I'm fine.	*ee-oh-joh-bahn*
What's your name?	*toh-cho-boh-tain?*
My name is ...	*ah-cho-mee ...*
Thank you.	*oh-yeh-rah-**don***
Goodbye.	*bye-bye*

HASSANIYA

Hassaniya is a Berber-Arabic dialect which is spoken by Moors of Mauritania. It's also the official language of Mauritania.

Good morning.	*sa-**la**-mah ah-**lay**-koum*
Good evening.	*mah-sah el-**hair***
How are you?	*ish-**tah**-ree?*
Thank you.	***shuh**-krahn*
Goodbye.	*mah-sa-**lahm***

HAUSA

Hausa is spoken and understood in a vast area of West Africa and beyond. Dialectal variation is not extreme in Hausa so the phrases included in this language guide will be universally understood, and will prove useful in Benin, Burkina Faso, Côte d'Ivoire, Niger, Nigeria and northern Ghana (where it is the principal language of trade).

Hausa is a tone language (where pitch variation in a speaker's voice is directly related to intended meaning) with three basic tones assigned to vowels: low, high and rising-falling. Standard written Hausa isn't marked for tones – our pronunciation guide for the words and phrases included below doesn't show them either. Your best bet is to learn with your ears by noting the inflection of African speakers.

The consonants **b**, **d** and **k** have 'glottalised' equivalents where air is exhaled forcefully from the larynx (the voice box); these glottal consonants are represented in this guide by **B**, **D** and **K** respectively.

The difference between short and long vowels is also overlooked in standard written Hausa; to help with pronunciation long vowels are represented in this guide by double vowels, eg, *aa'aa* (no).

Hello. (greeting)	*sannu*
Hello. (response)	*yauwaa sannu*
Good morning.	*eenaa kwanaa*
Good morning. (response)	*lapeeyaloh*
Good evening.	*eenaa eenee*
Good evening. (response)	*lapeeyaloh*
Goodbye.	*sai wani lookachi*
Please.	*don allaah*
Thank you.	*naa goodee*
Don't mention it/ It's nothing.	*baa koomi*
Sorry, pardon.	*yi haKurii, ban ji ba*
Yes.	*ii*
No.	*aa'aa*
How are you?	*inaa gajiyaa?*
I'm fine.	*baa gajiyaa*
And you?	*kai fa?*
What's your name?	*yaayaa suunanka?*
My name is …	*suunaanaa ...*
Where are you from?	*daga inaa ka fitoo?*
I'm from …	*naa fitoo daga ...*
Can you help me please?	*don allaah, koo zaa ka taimakee ni?*
Do you speak English/French?	*kanaa jin ingiliishii/ faransancii?*
I speak only English.	*inaa jin ingiliishii kawai*
I speak a little French.	*inaa jin faransancii kaDan*
I understand.	*naa gaanee*
I don't understand.	*ban gaanee ba*
Where is …?	*inaa ...?*
Is it far …?	*da niisaa ...?*
straight ahead	*miiKee sambal*
left	*hagu*
right	*daama*
How much is this?	*nawa nee wannan?*
That's too much.	*akwai tsaadaa ga wannan*
Leave me alone!	*tafi can!*

1	*d'aya*
2	*biyu*
3	*uku*
4	*hud'u*
5	*biyar*
6	*shida*
7	*bakwai*
8	*takwas*
9	*tara*
10	*gooma*
11	*gooma shaa d'aya*
12	*gooma shaa biyu*
13	*gooma shaa uku*
14	*goma shaa hud'u*
15	*goma shaa biyar*
16	*gooma shaa shida*
17	*gooma shaa bakwai*
18	*gooma shaa takwas*
19	*gooma shaa tara*
20	*ashirin*
30	*talaatin*
40	*arba'in*
50	*hamsin*
60	*sittin*
70	*saba'in*
80	*tamaanin*
90	*casa'in*
100	*d'arii*
1000	*dubuu*
one million	*miliyan d'aya*

With thanks to Dr Malami Buba.

IGBO (IBO)

Igbo, also known as Ibo, is the predominant indigenous language of Nigeria's southeast, where it is afforded the status of official language; it's used in the media and in government, and is the main lingua franca of the region. There are over 30 dialects of Igbo, each with varying degrees of mutual intelligibility.

Good morning.	*ee-**bow**-lah-chee*
Good evening.	*nah-**no**-nah*
How are you?	*ee-**may**-nah ahn-**ghan**?*
Thank you.	*ee-**may**-nah*
Goodbye.	*kay-**may**-see-ah*

KABYÉ

After Ewé, Kabyé is Togo's most common African language, predominant in the Kara region. One Kabyé word you'll always hear is *yovo* (white person).

Good morning	*un-lah-**wah**-lay.*
How are you?	*be-jah-un-sema*
I'm fine.	*ah-**lah**-fia*
Thank you.	*un-lah-**bah**-lay*
Goodbye.	*be-**lah**-bee-tasi*

KRIO

Krio is Sierra Leone's most common non-colonial language. Its major ingredient is English, but its sound system and grammar have been enriched by various West African languages. Because Krio was imported by different slave groups, there are strong differences between the Krio spoken in various regions, so strong in fact that some people find it easier to understand the Krio of Nigeria than the Krio spoken in other parts of Sierra Leone.

Hello.	***kou**-shay*
Hi mate.	*eh bo*
How are you?	*how-dee boh-dee?*
I'm fine.	***boh**-dee fine/no bad* (more common)
Thank God.	*ah tel god tenk-kee*
Thank you.	***tenk**-kee*
Please.	***dou**-yah (ah-beg)* (added for emphasis)
Goodbye.	*we go see back*
How much?	*ow mus?*
food	*chop*
Sierra Leone	*salone*

MALINKÉ

Malinké is spoken in the region around the borders between Senegal, Mali and Guinea. It's one of Senegal's six national languages. While it's very similar in some respects to the Mandinka spoken in Gambia and Senegal (they share much of their vocabulary), the two are classed as separate languages.

Good morning.	*nee-soh-mah*
Good evening.	*nee-woo-lah*
How are you?	*tan-ahs-teh?*
Thank you.	*nee-kay*
Goodbye.	*m-bah-ra-wa*

MANDINKA

Mandinka is the language of the Mandinka people found largely in central and northern Gambia, and in parts of southern Senegal. The people and their language are also called Mandingo and they're closely related to other Mande-speaking groups such as the Bambara of Mali, where they originate. Mandinka is classed as one of Senegal's national languages.

In this guide, **ng** should be pronounced as the 'ng' in 'sing' and **ñ** represents the 'ni' sound in 'onion'.

Hello.	*i/al be ñaading* (sg/pl)
Good bye.	*fo tuma doo*
Please.	*dukare*
Thank you.	*i/al ning bara* (sg/pl)
You're welcome.	*mbee le dentaala/ wo teng fengti* (lit: It's nothing)
Sorry/Pardon.	*hakko tuñe*
Yes.	*haa*
No.	*hani*
How are you?	*i/al be kayrato?* (sg/pl)
I'm fine.	*tana tenna* (lit: I'm out of trouble) *kayra dorong* (lit: peace only)
And you?	*ite fanang?*
What's your name?	*i too dung?*
My name is ...	*ntoo mu ... leti*
Where are you from?	*i/al bota munto?* (sg/pl)
I'm from ...	*mbota ...*
Can you help me please?	*i/al seng maakoy noo, dukare?* (sg/pl)
Do you speak English/French?	*ye angkale/faranse kango moyle?*

I speak only English.	*nga angkale kango damma le moy*
I speak a little French.	*nga faranse kango domonding le moy*
I understand.	*ngaa kalamuta le/ ngaa fahaam le*
I don't understand.	*mmaa kalamuta/ mmaa fahaam*
Where is ...?	*... be munto?*
Is it far?	*faa jamfata?*
Go straight ahead.	*sila tiling jan kilingo*
left	*maraa*
right	*bulu baa*
How much is this?	*ñing mu jelu leti?*
That's too much.	*a daa koleyaata baake*
Leave me alone!	*mbula!*

1	*kiling*
2	*fula*
3	*saba*
4	*naani*
5	*luulu*
6	*wooro*
7	*woorowula*
8	*sey*
9	*kononto*
10	*tang*
11	*tang ning kiling*
12	*tang ning fula*
13	*tang ning saba*
20	*muwaa*
30	*tang saba*
100	*keme*
1000	*wili kiling*
one million	*milyong kiling*

With thanks to Fallou Ngom.

MINA (GENGBE)

Mina (also known as Gengbe) is the language of trade in southern Togo, especially along the coast. It belongs to the Gbe (*gbe* meaning 'language') subgroup of the vast Kwa language family. Other Gbe languages of Togo include Ajagbe, Fongbe, Maxigbe and Wacigbe.

Good morning.	***soh**-bay-doh*
(reply)	*dosso*
How are you?	*oh-**foin**?*

Note In this guide bold letters indicate where the stress falls within a word.

Arabic Islamic Greetings

Traditional Arabic Islamic greetings are very common in Muslim West Africa – they're easy to learn and will be very much appreciated.

Greetings.	*salaam aleikum* (peace be with you)
Greetings to you too.	*aleikum asalaam* (and peace be with you)

I'm fine.	*aaaa* ('a' as in 'bat')
Thank you.	***ack**-pay*
Goodbye.	***soh**-day-loh*

MORÉ

Moré (the language of the Mossi) is spoken by more than half the population of Burkina Faso – with over 4½ million speakers it's the country's principal indigenous language.

Good morning.	***yee**-bay-roh*
Good evening.	*nay-**zah**-bree*
How are you?	*lah-**fee**-bay-may?*
I'm fine.	*lah-**fee**-bay-lah*
Thank you.	*un-**pus**-dah **bar**-kah*
Goodbye.	*when-ah-**tah**-say*

SANGHA DIALECT

Sangha is one of the main dialects (from around 48 others!) spoken by the Dogon people who inhabit the Bandiagara Escarpment in central Mali. Dialectal variation can be so marked that mutual intelligibility between the many Dogon groups is not always assured.

Good morning.	*ah-**gah**-poh*
Good evening.	*dee-**gah**-poh*
How are you?	*ou **say**-yoh?*
I'm fine.	***say**-oh*
Thank you.	*bee-ray-**poh***
Goodbye.	*ee-eyeh-**ee way**-dang*
Safe journey!	*day-gay-day-**yah***

SENOUFO

The Senoufo words and phrases listed following will prove useful if you're travelling through southern Mali, southwestern Burkina Faso and northern Côte d'Ivoire.

Senoufo pronunciation can be a very difficult prospect for foreigners, and with no official written form the task of matching the sounds of the language with letters on a page presents quite a challenge. The pronunciation system used in this guide provides rough approximations only. Try to pick up the sounds and inflections of the language by listening to fluent Senoufo speakers.

- **a** as in 'far'
- **e** as in 'bet'; the combination **eh** is pronounced somewhere between 'ey' and the 'e' in 'bet'
- **é** as the 'ay' in 'bay'
- **i** as in 'marine'
- **o** as in 'hot'
- **u** between the 'u' in 'pull' and the 'oo' in 'boot'
- **g** always hard, as in 'get'
- **ñ** as in the 'ni' in 'onion'
- **ng** as the 'ng' in 'sing' – indicates that the preceding vowel is nasal

Hello.	*kéné*
Goodbye.	***wu**-ñeh-té-reh*
Thank you.	***fah**-nah*
Sorry/Pardon.	*yah-**hé**-yah*
Yes.	*huh* or ***mi**-loh-goh*
No.	***mé**-tyeh*
How are you?	*mah-choh-**loh**-goh-lah?*
I'm fine.	*min-bé-**gé**-bah-mén*
And you?	***mohn**-dohn?*
What's your name?	***mehn-mah**-mi-**ihn**-yeh?*
My name is ...	*mehn-**mihn**-yeh ...*
Do you speak ...?	*mun-nah ... chi-**yé**-ré-**lu**-gu-lah?*
English	***ahn**-gih-lih-**kan***
French	*tu-**bah**-bu-**kan***
I only speak English.	***min**-nah **ahn**-gih-lih-**kan** chi-**yé**-reh-yeh-ké-né*
I speak a little French.	***min**-nah tu-**bah**-bu-**kan** chi-**yé**-reh **tyeh**-rih-**yeh***
Can you help me please?	*nah-**pu**-gu?*
I understand.	***mihn**-i-**tyeng*** or *mah-loh-**goh***
I don't understand.	***mihn**-nay-**chi**-mehn*
Where are you from?	*shi-moh-**nah** yih-rih-**ré**?*
I'm from ...	***mihn**-na-**yih**-rih ...*
Where is ...?	*shi-**ohng**-yeh ...?*

Note In this guide bold letters indicate where the stress falls within a word.

Is it far?	*kah-lé-**li**-lah?*
left	*kah-**mohn***
right	***kin**-yih-kah-**nih**-gi-heh-**yeh**-ré*
How much is this?	*jur-gi-**nah-deh**-leh?*
That's too much.	*kah-lah-**rah**-wah-ah, **deh**!*
Leave me alone!	***yi**-ri-wah!* or *meh-**yah**-bah!*

Numbers

Numbers in Senoufo can be a very complicated affair. For example, the number 'one hundred' translates literally as 'two-times-five-times-two-times-four-plus-two-times-ten' – use the numbers in the Bambara/Dioula section earlier in this guide and you'll have no trouble being understood.

With thanks to Andy Rebold.

SUSU

Susu is Guinea's third–most common indigenous language. It's spoken mainly in the south around Conakry.

Good morning.	*tay-nah mah-ree*
Good evening.	*tay-nah mah-fay-yen*
How are you?	*oh-**ree** toh-nah-moh?*
Thank you.	*ee-noh-wah-lee*
Goodbye.	*une-**gay**-say-gay*

TAMASHEK

Tamashek (spelt variously 'Tamasheq', 'Tamachek', 'Tamajeq' and more!) is the language of the Tuareg. There are two main dialects: Eastern (spoken in western Niger and eastern Mali) and Western (spoken in western Niger, the Gao region of Mali, and northern Nigeria).

How do you do?	*met-al-ee-khah* (pol) *oh-yeek* (inf)
I'm fine.	*eel-kharass*
How's the heat?	*min-ee-twixeh* (a traditional greeting)
Good/Fine.	*ee-zott*
How much?	*min-ee-kit?*
Thank you.	*tan-oo-mert*
Goodbye.	*harr-sad*

TWI

Twi (pronounced 'chwee'), the language of the Ashanti, is the most widely spoken African language in Ghana, where it is the official language of education and literature. Along with Fanti it belongs to the large Akan language family. Most of the dialects within this group are mutually intelligible.

Hello.	*ah-**kwah**-bah*
Hello. (in reply)	*yaah*
Good morning.	*mah-**cheeng***
Good evening.	***mah**-joh*
How are you?	***ay**-tah-sein?*
I'm fine.	***ay**-yah*
Please.	*meh-**pah**-woh-cheh-oh*
Thank you.	*may-**dah**-say*
Yes.	*aahn*
No.	*dah-beh*
Do you speak English?	*woh-teh **broh**-foh ahn-nah*
I don't understand.	*uhm-**tah** seh*
I'd like ...	*meh-**pay** ...*
Are you going to (Accra)?	*yah-coh (accra)?*
Let's go.	***yen**-coh*
Safe journey.	*nan-tee yee-yay*
Goodbye.	*mah-**krow***

1	*bee-**ah**-koh*
2	*ah-bee-**ehng***
3	*ah-bee-**eh**-sah*
4	*ah-**nahng***
5	*ah-**nuhm***
6	*ah-**see**-yah*
7	*ah-**sohng***
8	*ah-**woh**-tweh*
9	*ah-**kruhng***
10	*duh*
11	*duh-bee-**ah**-koh*
20	***ah**-dwoh-nuh*
100	*oh-**hah***
1000	*ah-**pehm***

WOLOF

Wolof (spelt Ouolof in French) is the language of the Wolof people, who are found in Senegal, particularly in the central area north and east of Dakar, along the coast, and in the western regions of Gambia. The Wolof spoken in Gambia is slightly different to the Wolof spoken in Senegal; the Gambian Wolof people living on the north bank of the Gambia River speak the Senegalese variety. Wolof is used as a common language in many parts of Senegal and Gambia, often instead of either French or English, and some smaller groups complain about the increasing 'Wolofisation' of their culture.

For some traditional Arabic Islamic greetings which are used in Muslim West Africa, see the boxed text 'Arabic Islamic Greetings' earlier in this guide.

Most consonants are pronounced as they are in English; when doubled they are pronounced with greater emphasis. Some vowels have accented variants.

a	as in 'at'
à	as in 'far'
e	as in 'bet'
é	as in 'whey'
ë	as the 'u' in 'but'
i	as in 'it'
o	as in 'hot'
ó	as in 'so'
u	as in 'put'
g	as in 'go'
ñ	as the 'ni' in 'onion'
ng	as in 'sing'; practise making this sound at the beginning of a word
r	always rolled
s	as in 'so', not as in 'as'
w	as in 'we'
x	as the 'ch' in Scottish loch

Hello.	*Na nga def.* (sg) *Na ngeen def.* (pl)
Good morning.	*Jàmm nga fanaane.*
Good afternoon.	*Jàmm nga yendoo.*
Goodnight.	*Fanaanal jàmm.*
Goodbye.	*Ba beneen.*
Please.	*Su la nexee.*
Thank you.	*Jërëjëf.*
You're welcome.	*Agsil/agsileen ak jàmm.* (sg/pl)
Sorry/Pardon.	*Baal ma.*
Yes.	*Waaw.*
No.	*Déedéet.*
How are you?	*Jàmm nga/ngeen am?* (sg/pl) (lit: Have you peace?)
I'm fine.	*Jàmm rekk.*
And you?	*Yow nag?*
How is your family?	*Naka waa kër ga?*

What's your first name?	*Naka nga/ngeen tudd?* (sg/pl)
What's your last name?	*Naka nga sant?*
My name is ...	*Maa ngi tudd ...*
Where do you live?	*Fan nga dëkk?*
Where are you from?	*Fan nga/ngeen jòge?* (sg/pl)
I'm from ...	*Maa ngi jòge ...*
Do you speak English/French?	*Dégg nga.Angale/ Faranse?* (sg/pl)
I speak only English.	*Angale rekk laa dégg.*
I speak a little French.	*Dégg naa tuuti Faranse.*
I don't speak Wolof/French.	*Màn dégguma Wolof/ Faranse.*
I understand.	*Dégg naa.*
I don't undestand.	*Dégguma.*
I'd like ...	*Dama bëggoon ...*
Where is ...?	*Fan la ...?*
Is it far?	*Sore na?*
straight ahead	*cha kanam*
left	*cammooñ*
right	*ndeyjoor*
Get in!	*Dugghal waay!*
How much is this?	*Lii ñaata?*
It's too much.	*Seer na torob.*
Leave me alone!	*May ma jàmm!*

Monday	*altine*
Tuesday	*talaata*
Wednesday	*àllarba*
Thursday	*alxames*
Friday	*àjjuma*
Saturday	*gaawu*
Sunday	*dibéer*

0	*tus*
1	*benn*
2	*ñaar*
3	*ñett*
4	*ñeent*
5	*juróom*
6	*juróom-benn*
7	*juróom- ñaar*
8	*juróom- ñett*
9	*juróom- ñeent*
10	*fukk*
11	*fukk-ak-benn*
12	*fukk-ak- ñaar*
13	*fukk-ak- ñett*
14	*fukk-ak-ñeent*
15	*fukk-ak-juróom*
16	*fukk-ak-juróom benn* (lit: ten-and-five one)
17	*fukk-ak-juróom ñaar*
18	*fukk-ak-juróom ñett*
19	*fukk-ak-juróom ñeent*
20	*ñaar-fukk* (lit: two-ten)
30	*fanweer*
40	*ñeent-fukk* (lit: four-ten)
50	*juróom-fukk* (lit: five-ten)
60	*juróom-benn-fukk* (lit: five-one-ten)
70	*juróom-ñaar-fukk* (lit: five two-ten)
80	*juróom-ñett-fukk*
90	*juróom-ñeent-fukk*
100	*téeméer*
1000	*junne*
one million	*tamñareet*

With thanks to Mamadou Cissé.

YORUBA

Yoruba belongs to the Kwa group of the Ede language family (*ede* is the Yoruba word for 'language'). Along with Fon it is one of the main lingua francas in much of the eastern part of West Africa but it is principally spoken as a first language in Benin and Nigeria. As with the majority of indigenous West African languages, Yoruba is subject to a degree of dialectal variation, not surprising given the broad geographical area its speakers are found in; fortunately, the majority of these variants are mutually intelligible.

Yoruba is normally written using the IPA (International Phonetic Alphabet). It is a tone language, ie, changes in voice-pitch are important in giving words their intended meaning. To give a comprehensive description of the five-tone Yoruba vowel system would require more space than we have available here. For simplicity we have used an acute accent (eg, **á**) to represent a high tone, a grave accent (eg, **à**) to represent a low tone; unmarked vowels take a mid-tone.

The pronunciations we give for the words and phrases below are rough approximations only. Pronounce letters as you would in English, keeping the following points in mind:

a	as in 'far'
e	as in 'met'
i	as in 'marine'
o	as in 'hot'; as in 'or'
u	as in 'put'
g	as in 'go'
h	not pronounced
hng	indicates that the preceding vowel is nasalised, eg, the 'ing' in 'sing'

Hello.	*báh-oh*
Goodbye.	*óh-dà-bòh*
Please.	*eh-dá-kuhn*
Thank you.	*eh-sheh-wuh*
You're welcome.	*eh-woh-lèh*
Sorry/Pardon.	*eh-dá-kuhn*
Yes.	*eh*
No.	*èh-ré-woh*
How are you?	*shéh-wà-dá-dah?*
I'm fine.	*àh-dúh-kpéh*
And you?	*èh-nyi-na-nkóh?*
What's your name?	*bá-woh-leh-má-jéh?*
My name is ...	*moh-máh-jéh ...*
Where are you from?	*à-ráh-iboh-loh-jéh?*
I'm from ...	*à-ráh ... ni mi*

Can you help me please?	*eh-dá-kuhn eh-ràhng-mi-lóh-wóh?*
Do you speak English?	*sheh-gbóh geh-sì?*
Do you speak French?	*sheh-gbóh frahng-séh?*
I only speak English.	*geh-sì ni-kahng nì-moh-gbóh*
I speak a little French.	*moh-gbóh frahng-séh dí-èh*
I understand.	*óh-yéh-mi-sí*
I don't understand.	*kòh-yéh-mi-sí*

Where is ...?	*iboh nih ...?*
Is it far?	*oh jin-ni*
straight ahead	*troh-loh-loh*
left	*òh-túhng*
right	*òh-sìhng*
How much is this?	*é-loh-lèh-yi?*
That's too much.	*ó-wáhng-jùh*
Leave me alone!	*fi-mí-nlèh!*

1	*eh-ní*
2	*èh-ji*
3	*eh-tah*
4	*eh-rihng*
5	*à-rúng*
6	*èh-fàh*
7	*èh-jeh*
8	*èh-joh*
9	*eh-sahng*
10	*eh-wah*
11	*móh-kàhng-lah*
12	*mé-ji-lah*
13	*méh-tà-lah*
14	*méh-ri-lah*
15	*má-rùhng-lah*
16	*méh-rihng-dóh-gúhng*
17	*méh-tá-dóh-gúhng*
18	*méh-jì-dóh-gúhng*
19	*òh-kahng-dóh-gúhng*
20	*òh-gúhng*
30	*méh-wah-lé-lóh-gbòhng*
40	*òh-gbòhng*
50	*méh-wàh-lé-lóh-gbòhng*
60	*òh-góhng-lé-lóh-gbòhng*
70	*òh-gúhng-méh-wa-lé-lóh-gbòhng*
80	*òh-gbòhng-méh-jì*
90	*méh-wah-lé-lòh-gbohng-mé-jì*
100	*òh-gúhng-lé-lóh-gbong-mé-jì*
one million	*mi-lì-yohng kahng*

With thanks to Aimé Avolonto.

Glossary

The following is a list of words and acronyms used in this book that you are likely to come across in West Africa. The glossary has been subdivided into the following broad categories:

Food & Drinks

afra – grilled meat, or grilled-meat stall
agouti – see *grasscutter*
akoumé – see *pâte*
aloco – fried bananas with onions and chilli
arachide – see *groundnut*
attiéké – grated *cassava*

benchi – black bench peas with palm oil and fish
bisap – purple drink made from water and hibiscus leaves
brochette – cubes of meat or fish grilled on a stick
buvette – small bar or drinks stall

caféman – man serving coffee (usually Nescafé), sometimes tea, and French bread with various fillings; found in Francophone countries mainly, usually only in the morning
cane rat – see *grasscutter*
capitaine – Nile perch (fish)
carte – menu
cassava – a common starch staple derived from the root of the cassava plant, usually ground to a powder and eaten as an accompaniment like rice or couscous; the leaves are eaten as a green vegetable; also called *gari* or *manioc*
chakalow – millet beer
chawarma – a popular snack of grilled meat in bread, served with salad and sesame sauce; originally from Lebanon, it's now found in towns and cities all over West Africa
chop – meal, usually local style
chop shop – a basic local-style eating house or restaurant (English-speaking countries); also called a *rice bar*
cocoyam – starch-yielding food plant, also called taro
couscous – semolina or millet grains, served as an accompaniment to *sauce*

dibieterie – grilled-meat stall
domodah – groundnut-based stew with meat or vegetables

épinard – spinach

felafel – Lebanese-style deep-fried balls of ground chickpeas and herbs, often served with chickpea paste in sandwiches
feuille sauce – sauce made from greens (usually *manioc* leaves)
foufou – see *fufu*
foutou – sticky yam or plantain paste similar to *fufu*; a staple in Côte d'Ivoire
frites – hot potato chips or french fries
fufu – a staple along the southern coast of West Africa made with fermented *cassava*, *yams*, *plantain* or *manioc* which is cooked and puréed; sometimes spelt 'foufou'

gargotte – simple basic eating house or stall in Senegal, parts of Mali and Gambia; also spelt 'gargote' or 'gargot'
gari – powdered *cassava*
gari jollof – *gari* with rice and tomatoes; see also *jollof rice*
gombo – okra or lady's fingers
grasscutter – a rodent of the porcupine family, known as *agouti* in Francophone countries; sometimes called *cane rat*, it's popular in stews
groundnut – peanut; sometimes called 'arachide'

haricot verte – green bean

igname – see *yam*

jaxatu – bitter flavouring
jollof rice – common dish throughout the region consisting of rice and vegetables with meat or fish; called 'riz yollof' in Francophone countries

kedjenou – Côte d'Ivoire's national dish; slowly simmered chicken or fish with peppers and tomatoes

kinkiliba – leaf that is sometimes used in coffee, giving it a woody tang
kojo – millet beer
koutoukou – a clear, strong alcohol homemade in Côte d'Ivoire

mafé – groundnut-based stew; also spelt 'mafay'
Maggi – brand name for a ubiquitous flavouring used in soups, stews etc throughout the region
manioc – see *cassava*
maquis – rustic open-air restaurant originating in Côte d'Ivoire, primarily serving braised fish and grilled chicken with *attiéké*, and traditionally open only at night
menu du jour – meal of the day, usually at a special price; often shortened to 'menu'

palaver sauce – there are regional variations, but this sauce is usually made from spinach or other leaves plus meat/fish; also spelt 'palava'
palm wine – a milky-white low-strength brew collected by tapping palm trees
patate – sweet potato
pâte – starch staple, often made from millet, corn ('pâte de maïs'), *plantains*, *manioc* or *yams*, eaten as an accompaniment to sauce; also called 'akoumé'
pito – local brew in northern Ghana
plantain – a large green banana, which has to be cooked before eating
plasas – pounded potato or *cassava* leaves cooked with palm oil and fish or beer
plat du jour – the dish of the day, usually offered at a special price
poisson – fish
pomme de terre – potato
poulet – chicken
poulet yassa – grilled chicken in onion and lemon sauce; a Senegalese dish that is found in many countries throughout the region; similarly you get 'poisson yassa' (fish), 'viande yassa' (meat) and just 'yassa'
pression – draught beer

rice bar – see *chop shop*
riz – rice
riz sauce – very common basic meal (rice with sauce)
riz yollof – see *jollof rice*
rôtisserie – food stall selling roast meat

salon de thé – literally 'tearoom'; café
sauce – basis of meals throughout the region; usually made from whatever is available and eaten with an accompanying starch staple like rice or *fufu*
snack – in Francophone Africa this means a place where you can get light meals and sandwiches, not the food itself; you'll often see signs saying 'Bar – Snack', meaning you can get a beer or coffee too
sodabe – a spirit made in Togo
spot – simple bar
sucrerie – soft drink (literally 'sweet thing')
suya – *Hausa* word for *brochette*

tiéboudienne – Senegal's national dish, rice baked in thick sauce of fish and vegetables; also spelt 'thieboudjenne'
tô – millet or sorghum-based *pâte*
tomate – tomato

viande – meat

yam – edible starchy root; sometimes called 'igname'
yassa – see *poulet yassa*
yollof rice – see *jollof rice*

Getting Around

autogare – see *gare routière*
autoroute – major road or highway

bâché – covered pick-up ('ute') used as a basic bush taxi (from the French word for tarpaulin)
brake – see *Peugeot taxi*
bush taxi – along with buses, this is the most common form of public transport in West Africa; there are three main types of bush taxi in West Africa: *Peugeot taxi*, minibus and pick-up *(bâché)*

car – large bus, see also *petit car*
cinq-cent-quatre – see *Peugeot taxi*
compteur – meter in taxi
couchette – sleeping berth on a train
car rapide – minibus, usually used in cities; often decrepit, may be fast or very slow
courrier postale – postal van; sometimes the only means of public transport between towns in rural areas

déplacement – a taxi or boat that you 'charter' for yourself
dournis – minibus

essence – petrol (gas) for car
fula-fula – converted truck or pick-up; rural public transport

garage – bush taxi and bus park
gare lagunaire – lagoon ferry terminal
gare maritime – ferry terminal
gare routière – bus and bush-taxi station, also called 'gare voiture' or 'autogare'
gare voiture – see *gare routière*
gasoil – diesel fuel
goudron – tar (road)

IDP – International Driving Permit

occasion – a lift or place in a car or bus (often shortened to 'occas')

line – fixed-route shared taxi
lorry park – see *motor park*

mobylette – moped
motor park – bus and bush-taxi park (English-speaking countries); also called 'lorry park'

péage – toll
petit car – minibus
pétrole – kerosene
Peugeot taxi – one of the main types of bush taxi; also called 'brake', 'cinq-cent-quatre', 'Peugeot 504' or *sept-place*
pinasse – large *pirogue*, usually used on rivers, for hauling people and cargo
pirogue – traditional canoe, either a small dugout or large, narrow sea-going wooden fishing boat
piste – track or dirt road
poda-poda – minibus

quatre-quatre – 4WD or 4x4, a four wheel drive vehicle

sept-place – *Peugeot taxi* seven-seater (usually carrying up to 12 people)

taxi brousse – bush taxi
taxi-course – shared taxi (in cities)
town trip – private hire (taxi)
tro-tro – a minibus or pick-up

woro-woro – minibus

zemidjan – motorcycle-taxi

Terms for Cape Verde & Guinea-Bissau

aluguer – for hire (sign in minibus)
arroz de marisco – seafood and rice

banco – bank
barco – large boat

cachupa – the Cape Verdean national dish; a tasty stew of several kinds of beans plus corn and various kinds of meat, often sausage or bacon
caju – cashew nut
caldo – soup
caldo de peixe – fish soup
caña – home-brew rum
canoa – motor-canoe
casa de pasto – no-frills restaurant
cascata – waterfall
Ceris – a bottled beer
cidade – city
coladeiras – old-style music; romantic, typically sentimental upbeat love songs
correios – post office

estrada – street

fado – haunting melancholy blues-style Portuguese music
funaná – distinctive fast-paced music with a Latin rhythm that's great for dancing; usually features players on the accordion and tapping with metal

gelado – ice cream

horário – timetable

ilha – island

jardim – garden

kandonga – truck or pick-up

lagoa – lagoon
largo – small square
livraria – bookshop

macaco – monkey; a popular meat dish in upcountry Guinea-Bissau
mercado – market

mornas – old-style music; mournful and sad, similar to the Portuguese *fado* style from whence they may have originated
museu – museum

papelaria – newsagency
paragem – bus and bush-taxi park
pastel com diablo dentro – literally 'pastry with the devil inside'; a mix of fresh tuna, onions and tomatoes wrapped in a pastry made from boiled potatoes and corn flour, deep fried and served hot
pastelaria – pastry and cake shop
pensão – hotel or guesthouse
platô – plateau
pousada – guesthouse
pousada municipal – town guesthouse
praça – park or square
praia – beach

residencial – guesthouse
ribeiro – stream
rua – street

toca-toca – small minibus in Bissau

verde – green
vinhos verde – semisparkling Portuguese white wine

Miscellaneous

abusua – clan or organisation of the Akan
adinkra – hand-made printed cloth from Ghana worn primarily by the *Ashanti* on solemn occasions
Afrique Occidentale Française – see *French West Africa*
Afro-beat – a fusion of African music, jazz and soul originated and popularised by Fela Kuti of Nigeria; along with *juju* it's the most popular music in Nigeria
Akan – a major group of peoples along the south coast of West Africa; includes the *Ashanti* and *Fanti* peoples
akuaba – *Ashanti* carved figure
animism – the base of virtually all traditional religions in Africa; the belief that there is a spirit in all natural things and the worship of those spirits, particularly human spirits (those of ancestors) which are thought to continue after death and have the power to bestow protection
asantehene – the king or supreme ruler of the *Ashanti* people
Ashanti – the largest tribal group in Ghana, concentrated around Kumasi
aso adire – a broad term for dyed cloth, a common handicraft found in many markets in Nigeria
auberge – in France it's a hostel, but in West Africa it's used (occasionally) to mean any small hotel

balafon – xylophone
Bambara – Mali's major ethnic group found in the centre and south and famous for its art, especially wooden carvings
banco – clay or mud used for building
bar-dancing – term widely used throughout the region for a bar which also has music (sometimes live) and dancing in the evening
barrage – dam across river, or roadblock
bic – disposable ball-point pen ('Biro')
bidon – large bottle, container or jerry can
bidonville – shantytown
board – see *pension*
bogolan cloth – often simply called *mud cloth*, this is cotton cloth with designs painted on using various types of mud for colour; made by the *Bambara* people of Mali but is found throughout the region
boîte – small nightclub (literally 'box')
bolong – literally 'river' in Mandinka, but when used in English context it means creek or small river
bombax tree – see *fromager tree*
boubou – the common name for the elaborate robe-like outfit worn by men and women; also called 'grand boubou'
BP – Boîte Postale (PO Box)
Bundu – Krio word for 'secret society'; used in Liberia and in certain parts of Sierra Leone and Côte d'Ivoire; includes the Poro society for men and the Sande for women

cadeau – gift, tip, bribe or a handout
carnet – document required if you are bringing a car into most of the countries of the region
carrefour – literally 'crossroads', but also used to mean meeting place
carrefour des jeunes – youth centre
campement – loosely translated as 'hostel', 'inn' or 'lodge', or even 'motel', but it is not a camping ground (ie, a place for tents); traditionally, campements offered simple accommodation but many today have quality and prices on a par with mid-range hotels

case – hut
case de passage – very basic place to sleep (often near bus stations) with a bed or mat on the floor and little else, and nearly always doubling as a brothel; also called 'chambre de passage' or 'maison de passage'
cases étages – two-storey mud houses
CFA – the principal currency of the region; used in Benin, Burkina Faso, Côte d'Ivoire, Guinea-Bissau, Mali, Niger, Senegal and Togo
chambre – room
chambre de passage – see *case de passage*
chambre ventilé – room with a fan
charms – see *fetish*
chasée submersible – see *pont submersible*
chèche – light cotton cloth in white or indigo blue that *Tuareg* men wear to cover their head and face
chiwara – a headpiece carved in the form of an antelope and used in ritualistic dances by the Bambara
climatisée – air-conditioned; often shortened to 'clim'
commissariat – police station
cotton tree – see *fromager tree*
CRI – Campements Rurals Integrés; system of village-run campements in the Casamance region of Senegal
croix d'Agadez – Tuareg talisman that protects its wearer from the 'evil eye'

Dahomey – pre-independence name of Benin
dash – bribe or tip (noun); also used as a verb, 'You dash me something...'
demi-pension – half board (dinner, bed and breakfast)
djembe – type of drum
Dogon – people found in Mali, east of Mopti; famous for their cliff dwellings, cosmology and arts
durbar – ceremony or celebration, usually involving a cavalry parade, found, for example, in the Muslim northern Nigerian states

Ecomog – *Ecowas* Monitoring Group; a military force made up of soldiers from the member armies of *Ecowas*
Ecowas – Economic Community of West African States
Eid al-Fitr – feast to celebrate the end of *Ramadan*
Eid al-Kabir – see *Tabaski*
Empire of Ghana – no geographic connection with the present-day country of Ghana; one of the great *Sahel* empires that flourished in the 8th to 11th centuries AD and covered much of present-day Mali and parts of Senegal
Empire of Mali – Islamic *Sahel* empire that was at its peak in the 14th century, covering the region between present-day Senegal and Niger; its capital was at Koumbi Saleh in southern Mauritania
en suite – a French term used in Britain to mean a hotel room with private bathroom attached; also used in some Anglophone countries in West Africa (although not in French-speaking countries!)

fanals – large lanterns; also the processions during which the lanterns are carried through the streets
fanicos – laundry men
Fanti – part of the Akan group of people based along the coast in southwest Ghana and Côte d'Ivoire; traditionally fishing people and farmers
fast food – European or American style snacks (eg, hot dogs, hamburgers) not necessarily served quickly
fête – festival
fêtes des masques – ceremony with masks
fetish – sacred objects in traditional religions, sometimes called 'charms'
fiche – form (to complete)
Foulbé – see *Fula*
French West Africa – area of West and Central Africa acquired by France at the Berlin Conference in 1884–85 which divided Africa up between the European powers; 'Afrique Occidentale Française' in French
fromager tree – found throughout West Africa and also known as the 'bombax tree', 'kapok tree' or 'cotton tree', it is recognisable by its yellowish bark, large pod-like fruit and exposed roots
Fula – a people spread widely through West Africa, mostly nomadic cattle herders; also known as 'Fulani', 'Peul' or 'Foulbé'

gara – thin cotton material
GDP – gross domestic product
gendarmerie – police station/post
girba – water bag
gîte – in France, this mean a small hotel or holiday cottage with self-catering facilities;

in West Africa it is occasionally used interchangeably with *auberge* and *campement*
GNP – gross national product
Gold Coast – pre-independence name for modern state of Ghana
Grain Coast – old name for Liberia
grand boubou – see *boubou*
griot – traditional musician or minstrel (praise singer) who also acts as historian for a village, clan or tribe or family going back for many centuries; the term is actually French in origin (it is pronounced 'gree-oh') and is probably a corruption of the *Wolof* 'gewel' or Tukulor 'gawlo'; the *Mandinka* word is 'jali'
grisgris – a charm or amulet worn to ward off evil (pronounced 'gree-gree', also written 'grigri' or 'grisgri')
gué – ford or low causeway across river

harmattan – wind from the north which carries dust from the desert, causing skies to become hazy throughout West Africa from December to March
Hausa – people originally from northern Nigeria and southern Niger, mostly farmers and traders
highlife – a style of music, originating in Ghana, combining West African and Western influences
hôtel de ville – town hall

ibeji – *Yoruba* carved twin figures
Igbo – one of the three major people groups in Nigeria, concentrated predominantly in the southeast
IGN – Institute Géographique National; the French IGN produces maps of most West African countries; several West African countries have their own IGN institution, although maps are not always available
IMF – International Monetary Fund
immeuble – large building, for example, office block
impluvium – large round traditional house with roof constructed to collect rain water in central tank or bowl
insha'allah – God willing, ie, hopefully (Arabic, but used by Muslims in Africa)

jali – see *griot*
juju – see *voodoo*
juju – the music style characterised by tight vocal harmonies and sophisticated guitar work, backed by traditional drums and percussion; it is very popular in southern Nigeria, most notably with the *Yoruba*

kandab – a large belt used to climb trees to collect palm wine
kapok tree – see *fromager tree*
kente cloth – probably the most expensive material in West Africa; made with finely woven cotton, and sometimes silk, by Ghana's *Ashanti* people
Kingdom of Benin – no relation to the present-day country, this was one of the great West African kingdoms (13th to 19th centuries); based in Nigeria around Benin City and famous for its bronzes
kola nuts – extremely bitter nuts sold everywhere on the streets and known for their mildly hallucinogenic and caffeine-like effects; they are offered as gifts at weddings and other ceremonies
kora – harp-like musical instrument with over 20 strings
Koran – see *Quran*
kwotenai kanye – earrings

Lobi – people based in southwest Burkina Faso and northern Côte d'Ivoire, famous for their figurative sculpture and compounds known as *soukala*
lumo – weekly market, usually in border areas
luttes – traditional wrestling matches
lycée – secondary school

mairie – town hall; mayor's office
maison de passage – see *case de passage*
malafa – crinkly voile material worn as a veil by women in Mauritania
Malinké – Guinea's major ethnic group, the people are also found in southern Mali, northwestern Côte d'Ivoire and eastern Senegal; closely related to the *Bambara* and famous for having one of the great West African empires; also related to the *Mandinka*
Mandinka – people group based in central and northern Gambia and Senegal; also the name of their language, which is closely related to Malinké; both Malinké and Mandinka are part of the wider Manding group.
marabout – Muslim holy man
marigot – creek
Maurs – see *Moors*
mestizos – people of mixed European and African decent

Moors – also called 'Maurs'; the predominant nomadic people of Mauritania, now also well known as merchants and found scattered over French-speaking West Africa
Moro-Naba – the king of the *Mossi* people
Mossi – the people who occupy the central area of Burkina Faso and comprise about half the population of Burkina Faso as well as the bulk of Côte d'Ivoire's migrant labour force
Mourides – the most powerful of the Islamic brotherhoods in Senegal
mud-cloth – see *bogolan cloth*

nomalies – sandstone ancestor figures

OAU – Organisation of African Unity
oba – a *Yoruba* chief or ruler
orchestra – in West Africa, this means a group playing popular music

pagne – a length of colourful cloth worn around the waist as a skirt
paillote – a thatched sun shelter (usually on a beach or around an open-air bar-restaurant)
palava – meeting place
paletuviers – mangroves
patron – owner, boss
peintures rupestres – rock paintings
pension – simple hotel or hostel, or 'board'; see also *demi-pension*
pension complet – full board (lunch, dinner, bed and breakfast)
pension simple – bed and breakfast
Peul – see *Fula*
pont submersible – a bridge or causeway across a river which is covered when the water is high
posuban – ensemble of statues representing a proverb or event in *Fanti* culture
préfecture – police headquarters
PTT – post (and often telephone) office in Francophone countries

Quran – Islamic holy book, also written 'Koran'

Ramadan – Muslim month of fasting
Ramsar – an international convention primarily concerned with the conservation of wetland habitats and associated wildlife

Sahel – dry savanna area south of the Sahara desert; most of Senegal, Gambia, Mali, Burkina Faso and Niger
Samory Touré – Guinean hero who led the fight against the French colonialists in the late 19th century
Scramble for Africa – term used for the land-grabbing frenzy in the 1880s by the European powers in which France, Britain and Germany laid claim to various parts of the continent
serviette – towel (in bathroom)
serviette de table – table napkin, serviette
serviette hygiénique – sanitary pad (feminine pad, feminine towel)
sharia – Muslim law
shukublai – distinctive baskets that are traditionally made by Temne women in Sierra Leone
Songhaï – ethnic group located primarily in northeastern Mali and western Niger along the Niger River
soukala – a castle-like housing compound of the Lobi tribe found in the Bouna area of southern Burkina Faso
spirale antimostique – mosquito coil
syndicat d'initiative – tourist information office

Tabaski – Eid al-Kabir; also known as the Great Feast, this is the most important celebration throughout West Africa
taguelmoust – shawl or scarf worn as headgear by *Tuareg* men
tama – hand-held drum
tampon – stamp (eg, in passport)
tampon hygiénique – tampon; see also *serviette hygiénique*
tampon periodique – see *tampon hygiénique*
tata somba – a castle-like house of the Betamaribé tribe who live in northwestern Benin
télécentre – privately run telecommunications centres
togu-na – traditional *Dogon* shelter where men sit and socialise
totem – used in traditional religions, similar to a fetish
toubab – white person; term used primarily in Gambia, Senegal, Mali and some other *Sahel* countries
Tuareg – nomadic descendants of the North African Berbers; found all over the Sahara, especially in Mali, Niger and southern Algeria

ventilé – see *chambre ventilé*

voodoo – the worship of spirits with supernatural powers widely practised in southern Benin and Togo; also called 'juju'

wassoulou – singing style made famous by Mali's Oumou Sangaré

WHO – World Health Organization

Wolof – Senegal's major ethnic group; also found in Gambia

Yoruba – a major ethnic group concentrated in southwestern Nigeria

Thanks

Many thanks to the following travellers who used the *West Africa* guidebook and wrote to us with helpful hints, useful advice and interesting anecdotes about travelling in West Africa.

Ole Aanerod, Gomez Adekunle, Sabine Agena, Jamie Anderson, Ruben Andersson, Pierre-Marie Andre, Yiannis Andredakis, Antonio Antiochia, Sarah Armstrong, Unai Arribas, Jacob Attito, Jorg Ausfelt, Hans-Jochen Baethge, Kamran Baig, Jerry Baker, Monica Baker, Kareen Bar-Akiva, Shiriin Barakzai, Kriss Barker, Frank Barresi, Andrew Bartram, Bernard Baxter, Angus Beare, Salah Benacer, Lucy Bentham, Kim Berman, Michel Bla, Lex Van Boeckel, Jose Boehm, Filip Bogaert, Barbara Bohl, Mies Bono Mas, Dr Stuart Borthwick, Piero Boschi, Jane Boughton, Arie Bouman, Leigh Bowden, Rachel Boyd, Eric Boyajian, Steve Brooks, Anna Brown, Matt Brown, Jean-Baptiste Bruderer, Ingmar Bruin, Steve Bryant, S Calder, Antonello Calvi, Paul S Cariker, Sarah Castle, Greg Clarke, Brad Clinehens, April Coetzee, Bryant Collins, Ross Connell, Andrew Connor, Erika Connor, Graeme Counsel, Steve Crerar, Christian Crolla, Cora Dankers, Kimee Davidson, Franco Del Monaco, Joanna Depledge, Andre DeSimone, Emily Donovan, Sephane Doppagne, Kathy Duarte, Rossana Dudziak, Birgit Dufour, Hamish Duncan, Maria-Louise Dungworth, Nelly Dupuis, Beda Durschei, Matt Ebiner, Edit Eliasson, Samuel Enilo, Karen Espley, K Etchells, Jannie Faas, Franziska & Ruth Faeh, Brian Fagan, Caryll Fagan, Jack Fellinga, Ferdinand Fellinger, Suzanne Ferrie, DG Finley, D Flynn, Agner Fog, Elisabeth Furst, Michael Gallagher, Vitoria Gasteiz, Ev Gerson, Bob Gibbons, Christopher Gilbert, I Goedbloed, Bart Googens, Franz-Josef Gottschalk, Sascha Grabow, Fred Grant, Tony Grooms, Guy Hagan, Sally Hagen, Stephen Haines, Ali Hammoud, David Hapgood, Hette Harder, Jennifer Hawkins, Martin Hess, Art Hilado, Shonah Hill, Michelle & Alan Hinde, John Hindson, Ralph Holmes, Lee-Anne Horwood, Keiran Houghton, Jocelyn James, Rogier Jaspers, Annelies Jensen, VB Jensen, BJ Johnson, Eric Johnson, Margaret Johnson, Wendy & Howard Jones, Wendy Kerselaers, Marcel Koudstaal, Wilza Kouwer, Blaz Krhin, Kielke Krikke, Greg Lane, Brigid Laughlin, Pászthory László, Michael Lees, Willem & Joany Lisman, Oili Liutu, Fiona Lovatt Davis, Christophe Lucet, Erich Ludwig, Kirsten Lund Larsen, Carrie Lyle, Peter Lyon, Joseph Machnica, Diana Maestre, Andrew Manos, Chloe Marshall, Amy H Martin, Seamus Martin, Pat McFeely, Elizabeth McGrath, Jonathan McKallip, Sallyanne McKern, R N McLean, Duncan McNair, Moises Mendoza, Lydia Mickunas, Marilyn Middleton, Markella Mikkelsen, Ram Mohan, Ilse Monsted, Mike Moore, Carolina Moreira, Paul Morley, Pam Newton, Graham Norton, Camilla Opoku, Michael Padua, Christopher Palmer, Christian Pannatier, Les Parkes, Scott Pegg, Anthony Penney, Mary-Lou Penrith, Andrea Petic, Claudia Alice Pinkas, Catherine Potter, Deborah Pownall, Nick Pretzlick, Sian Pritchard-Jones, Marie Pueyo, Jacob Quarcoo, Thomas Rau, Sara Richelson, Caroline Robert-Esteban, Andrea Rogge, Irene Saletan, Sian Salter, Stefan Samuelsson, Elie Schecter, Michael Scheiwein, Lisa Schipper, Stefan Scibor, Jan Severing, Min & Brian Shu, Anthea Sims Wallace, Billy Skoric, Mark Stadel, Manuela Stahl, Urs Steiger, Laura Steinberger, Eduard Stomp, Pamela De Stratford, Jean-Francois Tackoen, Line Tangen, Jay E Taylor, Mark ter Heegde, Kimberley Thornton, Elanor Tipple, Bruce Toman, Carol Tompkins, Jaume Tort, Michael Turner, Juha Vakkuri, Marc Valliant, An van Assche, Jelle van de Veire, Kim van den Berg, Angelique van der Made, Sylvia van der Oord, Erwin van Engelen, Sidney Vanton, Annemarie Visser, Sophie Warning, Dominik Weiss, James Wilson, Ron Wilson, Manfred Wolfensberger, David Wottergren, Mark Wright, Tajudean O Yaqub, Nicolien Zuijdgeest

LONELY PLANET

You already know that Lonely Planet produces more than this one guidebook, but you might not be aware of the other products we have on this region. Here is a selection of titles that you may want to check out as well:

French phrasebook
ISBN 0 86442 450 7
US$5.95 • UK£3.99

Portuguese phrasebook
ISBN 0 86442 589 9
US$7.95 • UK£4.50

Africa on a shoestring
ISBN 0 86442 663 1
US$29.99 • UK£17.99

Read This First: Africa
ISBN 1 86450 066 2
US$14.95 • UK£8.99

Travel Photography
ISBN 1 86450 207 X
US$16.99 • UK£9.99

The Gambia & Senegal
ISBN 1 74059 137 2
US$19.99 • UK£12.99

Healthy Travel Africa
ISBN 1 86450 050 6
US$5.95 • UK£3.99

Available wherever books are sold

FRENCH
PHRASEBOOK
WITH TWO-WAY DICTIONARY

PORTUGUESE
PHRASEBOOK
WITH TWO-WAY DICTIONARY

AFRICA
ON A SHOESTRING

lonely planet
Read This First:
AFRICA

TRAVEL PHOTOGRAPHY

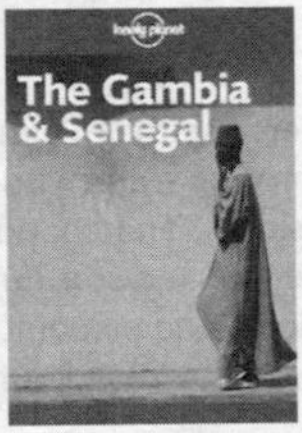
lonely planet
The Gambia
& Senegal

lonely planet
healthy travel
Africa

LONELY PLANET

ON THE ROAD

Malawi

Travel Guides explore cities, regions and countries, and supply information on transport, restaurants and accommodation, covering all budgets. They come with reliable, easy-to-use maps, practical advice, cultural and historical facts and a rundown on attractions both on and off the beaten track. There are over 200 titles in this classic series, covering nearly every country in the world.

Lonely Planet Upgrades extend the shelf life of existing travel guides by detailing any changes that may affect travel in a region since a book has been published. Upgrades can be downloaded for free from **www.lonelyplanet.com/upgrades**

AFRICA
ON A SHOESTRING

For travellers with more time than money, **Shoestring** guides offer dependable, first-hand information with hundreds of detailed maps, plus insider tips for stretching money as far as possible. Covering entire continents in most cases, the six-volume shoestring guides are known around the world as 'backpackers bibles'.

LONDON

For the discerning short-term visitor, **Condensed** guides highlight the best a destination has to offer in a full-colour, pocket-sized format designed for quick access. They include everything from top sights and walking tours to opinionated reviews of where to eat, stay, shop and have fun.

CitySync lets travellers use their Palm™ or Visor™ hand-held computers to guide them through a city with handy tips on transport, history, cultural life, major sights, and shopping and entertainment options. It can also quickly search and sort hundreds of reviews of hotels, restaurants and attractions, and pinpoint their location on scrollable street maps. CitySync can be downloaded from **www.citysync.com**

Barcelona

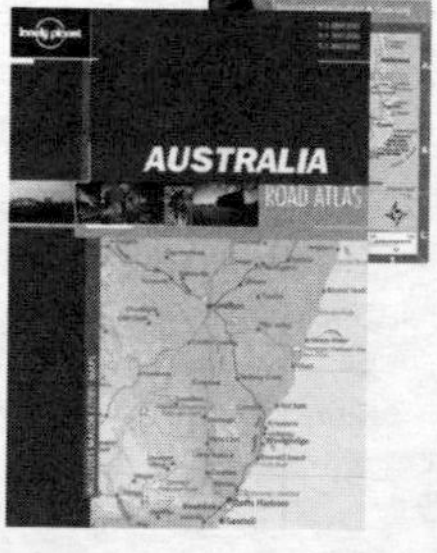
AUSTRALIA
ROAD ATLAS

MAPS & ATLASES

Lonely Planet's **City Maps** feature downtown and metropolitan maps, as well as transit routes and walking tours. The maps come complete with an index of streets, a listing of sights and a plastic coat for extra durability.

Road Atlases are an essential navigation tool for serious travellers. Cross-referenced with the guidebooks, they also feature distance and climate charts and a complete site index.

ESSENTIALS

Read This First books help new travellers to hit the road with confidence. These invaluable predeparture guides give step-by-step advice on preparing for a trip, budgeting, arranging a visa, planning an itinerary and staying safe while still getting off the beaten track.

Read This First:
EUROPE
healthy travel
Africa
VIETNAMESE
PHRASEBOOK
TRAVEL PHOTOGRAPHY
Travel
Journal

Healthy Travel pocket guides offer a regional rundown on disease hot spots and practical advice on predeparture health measures, staying well on the road and what to do in emergencies. The guides come with a user-friendly design and helpful diagrams and tables.

Lonely Planet's **Phrasebooks** cover the essential words and phrases travellers need when they're strangers in a strange land. They come in a pocket-sized format with colour tabs for quick reference, extensive vocabulary lists, easy-to-follow pronunciation keys and two-way dictionaries.

Miffed by blurry photos of the Taj Mahal? Tired of the classic 'top of the head cut off' shot? **Travel Photography: A Guide to Taking Better Pictures** will help you turn ordinary holiday snaps into striking images and give you the know-how to capture every scene, from frenetic festivals to peaceful beach sunrises.

Lonely Planet's **Travel Journal** is a lightweight but sturdy travel diary for jotting down all those on-the-road observations and significant travel moments. It comes with a handy time-zone wheel, a world map and useful travel information.

Lonely Planet's eKno is an all-in-one communication service developed especially for travellers. It offers low-cost international calls and free email and voicemail so that you can keep in touch while on the road. Check it out on **www.ekno.lonelyplanet.com**

FOOD & RESTAURANT GUIDES

Lonely Planet's **Out to Eat** guides recommend the brightest and best places to eat and drink in top international cities. These gourmet companions are arranged by neighbourhood, packed with dependable maps, garnished with scene-setting photos and served with quirky features.

out to eat
sydney
2001
World Food
ITALY

For people who live to eat, drink and travel, **World Food** guides explore the culinary culture of each country. Entertaining and adventurous, each guide is packed with detail on staples and specialities, regional cuisine and local markets, as well as sumptuous recipes, comprehensive culinary dictionaries and lavish photos good enough to eat.

LONELY PLANET

OUTDOOR GUIDES

For those who believe the best way to see the world is on foot, Lonely Planet's **Walking Guides** detail everything from family strolls to difficult treks, with 'when to go and how to do it' advice supplemented by reliable maps and essential travel information.

lonely planet
Hiking in the
USA
CYCLING
AUSTRALIA
WATCHING WILDLIFE
SOUTHERN AFRICA
Diving & Snorkeling
Hawaii

Cycling Guides map a destination's best bike tours, long and short, in day-by-day detail. They contain all the information a cyclist needs, including advice on bike maintenance, places to eat and stay, innovative maps with detailed cues to the rides, and elevation charts.

The **Watching Wildlife** series is perfect for travellers who want authoritative information but don't want to tote a heavy field guide. Packed with advice on where, when and how to view a region's wildlife, each title features photos of over 300 species and contains engaging comments on the local flora and fauna.

With underwater colour photos throughout, **Pisces Books** explore the world's best diving and snorkelling areas. Each book contains listings of diving services and dive resorts, detailed information on depth, visibility and difficulty of dives, and a roundup of the marine life you're likely to see through your mask.

LONELY PLANET

LONELY PLANET . . .
UNPACKED
Chasing Rickshaws
ALASKA
lonely planet

OFF THE ROAD

Journeys, the travel literature series written by renowned travel authors, capture the spirit of a place or illuminate a culture with a journalist's attention to detail and a novelist's flair for words. These are tales to soak up while you're actually on the road or dip into as an at-home armchair indulgence.

The range of lavishly illustrated **Pictorial** books is just the ticket for both travellers and dreamers. Off-beat tales and vivid photographs bring the adventure of travel to your doorstep long before the journey begins and long after it is over.

Lonely Planet **Videos** encourage the same independent, tough-minded approach as the guidebooks. Currently airing throughout the world, this award-winning series features innovative footage and an original soundtrack.

Yes, we know, work is tough, so do a little bit of deskside dreaming with the spiral-bound Lonely Planet **Diary** or a Lonely Planet **Wall Calendar**, filled with great photos from around the world.

TRAVELLERS NETWORK

Lonely Planet Online. Lonely Planet's award-winning Web site has insider information on hundreds of destinations, from Amsterdam to Zimbabwe, complete with interactive maps and relevant links. The site also offers the latest travel news, recent reports from travellers on the road, guidebook upgrades, a travel links site, an online book-buying option and a lively travellers bulletin board. It can be viewed at **www.lonelyplanet.com** or AOL keyword: lp.

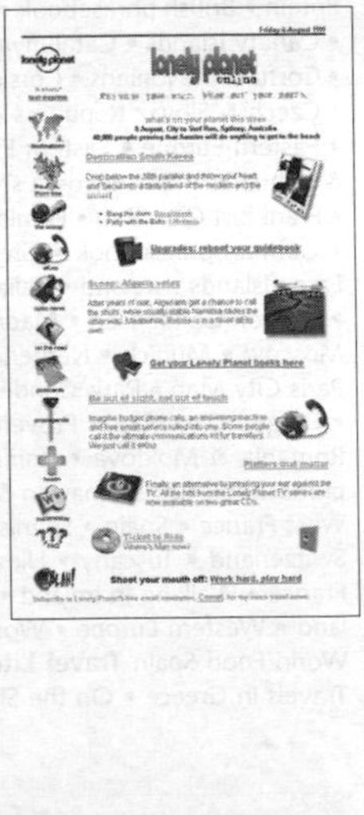
lonely planet online
Upgrades: reboot your guidebook
Get your Lonely Planet books here
Shoot your mouth off: Work hard, play hard

Planet Talk is a quarterly print newsletter, full of gossip, advice, anecdotes and author articles. It provides an antidote to the being-at-home blues and lets you plan and dream for the next trip. Contact the nearest Lonely Planet office for your free copy.

Comet, the free Lonely Planet newsletter, comes via email once a month. It's loaded with travel news, advice, dispatches from authors, travel competitions and letters from readers. To subscribe, click on the Comet subscription link on the front page of the Web site.

LONELY PLANET

Mail Order

Lonely Planet products are distributed worldwide. They are also available by mail order from Lonely Planet, so if you have difficulty finding a title please write to us. North and South American residents should write to 150 Linden St, Oakland, CA 94607, USA; European and African residents should write to 10a Spring Place, London NW5 3BH, UK; and residents of other countries to Locked Bag 1, Footscray, Victoria 3011, Australia.

INDIAN SUBCONTINENT & THE INDIAN OCEAN Bangladesh • Bengali phrasebook • Bhutan • Delhi • Goa • Healthy Travel Asia & India • Hindi & Urdu phrasebook • India • India & Bangladesh City Map • Indian Himalaya • Karakoram Highway • Kathmandu City Map • Kerala • Madagascar • Maldives • Mauritius, Réunion & Seychelles • Mumbai (Bombay) • Nepal • Nepali phrasebook • North India • Pakistan • Rajasthan • Read This First: Asia & India • South India • Sri Lanka • Sri Lanka phrasebook • Tibet • Tibetan phrasebook • Trekking in the Indian Himalaya • Trekking in the Karakoram & Hindukush • Trekking in the Nepal Himalaya • World Food India **Travel Literature:** The Age of Kali: Indian Travels and Encounters • Hello Goodnight: A Life of Goa • In Rajasthan • Maverick in Madagascar • A Season in Heaven: True Tales from the Road to Kathmandu • Shopping for Buddhas • A Short Walk in the Hindu Kush • Slowly Down the Ganges

MIDDLE EAST & CENTRAL ASIA Bahrain, Kuwait & Qatar • Central Asia • Central Asia phrasebook • Dubai • Farsi (Persian) phrasebook • Hebrew phrasebook • Iran • Israel & the Palestinian Territories • Istanbul • Istanbul City Map • Istanbul to Cairo • Istanbul to Kathmandu • Jerusalem • Jerusalem City Map • Jordan • Lebanon • Middle East • Oman & the United Arab Emirates • Syria • Turkey • Turkish phrasebook • World Food Turkey • Yemen **Travel Literature:** Black on Black: Iran Revisited • Breaking Ranks: Turbulent Travels in the Promised Land • The Gates of Damascus • Kingdom of the Film Stars: Journey into Jordan

NORTH AMERICA Alaska • Boston • Boston City Map • Boston Condensed • British Columbia • California & Nevada • California Condensed • Canada • Chicago • Chicago City Map • Chicago Condensed • Florida • Georgia & the Carolinas • Great Lakes • Hawaii • Hiking in Alaska • Hiking in the USA • Honolulu & Oahu City Map • Las Vegas • Los Angeles • Los Angeles City Map • Louisiana & the Deep South • Miami • Miami City Map • Montreal • New England • New Orleans • New Orleans City Map • New York City • New York City City Map • New York City Condensed • New York, New Jersey & Pennsylvania • Oahu • Out to Eat – San Francisco • Pacific Northwest • Rocky Mountains • San Diego & Tijuana • San Francisco • San Francisco City Map • Seattle • Seattle City Map • Southwest • Texas • Toronto • USA • USA phrasebook • Vancouver • Vancouver City Map • Virginia & the Capital Region • Washington, DC • Washington, DC City Map • World Food New Orleans **Travel Literature**: Caught Inside: A Surfer's Year on the California Coast • Drive Thru America

NORTH-EAST ASIA Beijing • Beijing City Map • Cantonese phrasebook • China • Hiking in Japan • Hong Kong & Macau • Hong Kong City Map • Hong Kong Condensed • Japan • Japanese phrasebook • Korea • Korean phrasebook • Kyoto • Mandarin phrasebook • Mongolia • Mongolian phrasebook • Seoul • Shanghai • South-West China • Taiwan • Tokyo • Tokyo Condensed • World Food Hong Kong • World Food Japan **Travel Literature:** In Xanadu: A Quest • Lost Japan

SOUTH AMERICA Argentina, Uruguay & Paraguay • Bolivia • Brazil • Brazilian phrasebook • Buenos Aires • Buenos Aires City Map • Chile & Easter Island • Colombia • Ecuador & the Galapagos Islands • Healthy Travel Central & South America • Latin American Spanish phrasebook • Peru • Quechua phrasebook • Read This First: Central & South America • Rio de Janeiro • Rio de Janeiro City Map • Santiago de Chile • South America on a shoestring • Trekking in the Patagonian Andes • Venezuela **Travel Literature**: Full Circle: A South American Journey

SOUTH-EAST ASIA Bali & Lombok • Bangkok • Bangkok City Map • Burmese phrasebook • Cambodia • Cycling Vietnam, Laos & Cambodia • East Timor phrasebook • Hanoi • Healthy Travel Asia & India • Hill Tribes phrasebook • Ho Chi Minh City (Saigon) • Indonesia • Indonesian phrasebook • Indonesia's Eastern Islands • Java • Lao phrasebook • Laos • Malay phrasebook • Malaysia, Singapore & Brunei • Myanmar (Burma) • Philippines • Pilipino (Tagalog) phrasebook • Read This First: Asia & India • Singapore • Singapore City Map • South-East Asia on a shoestring • South-East Asia phrasebook • Thailand • Thailand's Islands & Beaches • Thailand, Vietnam, Laos & Cambodia Road Atlas • Thai phrasebook • Vietnam • Vietnamese phrasebook • World Food Indonesia • World Food Thailand • World Food Vietnam

ALSO AVAILABLE: Antarctica • The Arctic • The Blue Man: Tales of Travel, Love and Coffee • Brief Encounters: Stories of Love, Sex & Travel • Buddhist Stupas in Asia: The Shape of Perfection • Chasing Rickshaws • The Last Grain Race • Lonely Planet ... On the Edge: Adventurous Escapades from Around the World • Lonely Planet Unpacked • Lonely Planet Unpacked Again • Not the Only Planet: Science Fiction Travel Stories • Ports of Call: A Journey by Sea • Sacred India • Travel Photography: A Guide to Taking Better Pictures • Travel with Children • Tuvalu: Portrait of an Island Nation

Index

Abbreviations

B – Benin
BF – Burkina Faso
C – Cameroon
CV – Cape Verde
CI – Côte d'Ivoire
FR – Forest Reserve
G – Gambia
GHA – Ghana
GUI – Guinea
GB – Guinea-Bissau
L – Liberia
M – Mali
MAU – Mauritania
N – Niger
NIG – Nigeria
NP – National Park
NR – Nature Reserve
PN – Parc National
S – Senegal
SL – Sierra Leone
T – Togo

Text

Bold indicates maps.

Bold indicates maps.

D

Bold indicates maps.

Bold indicates maps.

Bold indicates maps.

Boxed Text

MAP LEGEND

CITY ROUTES
Freeway
Freeway
Highway
Primary Road
Road
Secondary Road
Street
Street
Lane
Lane
On/Off Ramp
Unsealed Road
One-Way Street
Pedestrian Street
Footbridge
REGIONAL ROUTES
Tollway; Freeway
Primary Road
Secondary Road
Minor Road
BOUNDARIES
International
State
Disputed
Fortified Wall
HYDROGRAPHY
River; Creek
Lake
Spring; Rapids
Waterfalls
TRANSPORT ROUTES & STATIONS
Train
Underground Train
Ferry
Walking Trail
Path
Pier or Jetty
AREA FEATURES
Building
Park; Gardens
Market
Sports Ground
Beach
Cemetery
Campus
Plaza
POPULATION SYMBOLS
CAPITAL
National Capital
CAPITAL
State Capital
CITY
City
Town
Town
Village
Village
Urban Area
MAP SYMBOLS
Place to Stay
Place to Eat
Point of Interest
Airfield; Airport
Bank
Bird Sanctuary
Border Crossing
Bus Stop/Terminal
Camping Area
Castle
Cinema
Church
Embassy/Consulate
Ferry Terminal
Golf Course
Hospital
Internet Cafe
Lighthouse
Lookout
Monument
Mosque
Museum
National Park
Petrol Station
Police Station
Post Office
Pub or Bar
Ruins
Shopping Centre
Stately Home
Taxi Rank
Telephone
Theatre
Tomb
Tourist Information
Transport
Trekking Hut
Volcano
Zoo

Note: not all symbols displayed above appear in this book

LONELY PLANET OFFICES

Australia
Locked Bag 1, Footscray, Victoria 3011
☎ 03 8379 8000 fax 03 8379 8111
email: talk2us@lonelyplanet.com.au

USA
150 Linden St, Oakland, CA 94607
☎ 510 893 8555 TOLL FREE: 800 275 8555
fax 510 893 8572
email: info@lonelyplanet.com

UK
10a Spring Place, London NW5 3BH
☎ 020 7428 4800 fax 020 7428 4828
email: go@lonelyplanet.co.uk

France
1 rue du Dahomey, 75011 Paris
☎ 01 55 25 33 00 fax 01 55 25 33 01
email: bip@lonelyplanet.fr
www.lonelyplanet.fr

World Wide Web: www.lonelyplanet.com *or* AOL keyword: lp
Lonely Planet Images: lpi@lonelyplanet.com.au